Tiller's Guide to
INDIAN COUNTRY

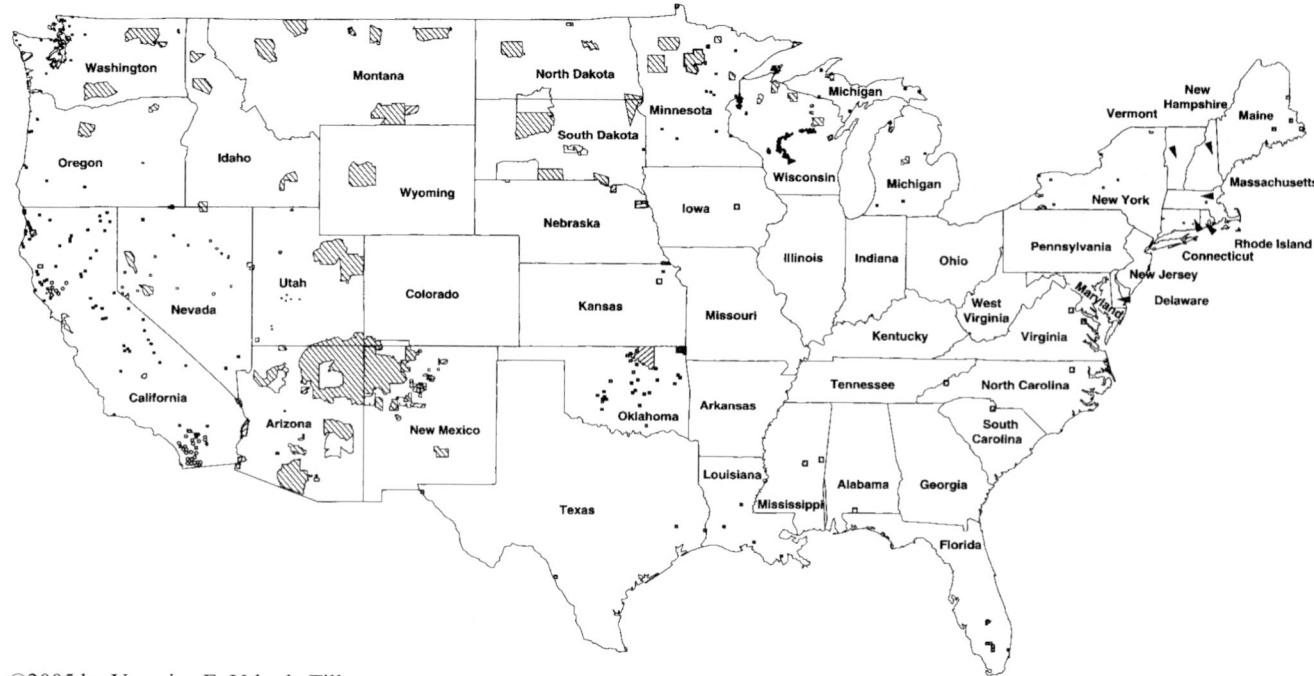

Library of Congress Cataloging-in-Publication Data

Tiller, Veronica E. Velarde.
 Tiller's guide to Indian country : economic profiles of American
Indian reservations / edited and compiled by Veronica E. Velarde Tiller.—
2005 ed.
    p. cm.
 "Featuring Honoring Nations from Harvard University's Project on
American Indian Economic Development."
 Includes bibliographical references and index.
 ISBN-13: 978-1-885931-04-7 (alk. paper)
 1. Indian reservations—Economic aspects—United States—Directories.
2. Indians of North America—Economic conditions—Directories. 3.
Indian business enterprises—United States—Directories. 4. Honoring
Contributions in the Governance of American Indian Nations (Program) I.
Title: Guide to Indian country. II. Title: Economic profiles of American
Indian reservations. III. Malcolm Wiener Center for Social Policy.
Harvard Project on American Indian Economic Development. IV. Title.

 E93.T55 2005
 970.004'97—dc22

2005012917

Book Layout and Cover Design by Mary M. Velarde

Tiller's Guide to
INDIAN COUNTRY

ECONOMIC PROFILES OF
AMERICAN INDIAN RESERVATIONS

Edited and Compiled by
VERONICA E. VELARDE TILLER

Featuring Honoring Nations from Harvard University's Project on
American Indian Economic Development

BowArrow
PUBLISHING COMPANY

BowArrow Publishing Company
Albuquerque, New Mexico USA

DANIEL K. INOUYE
UNITED STATES SENATOR
HAWAII

**PREFACE
TO THE 2005 EDITION OF
TILLER'S GUIDE TO INDIAN COUNTRY:
ECONOMIC PROFILES OF AMERICAN INDIAN RESERVATIONS
BY
SENATOR DANIEL K. INOUYE
FORMER CHAIRMAN, VICE CHAIRMAN AND CURRENT MEMBER
U.S. SENATE COMMITTEE ON INDIAN AFFAIRS**

Over the course of my twenty-eight years of service on the U.S. Senate Committee on Indian Affairs, I have had the opportunity to come to know Indian country and the vast array of languages, cultures, and history that are unique to each tribe and community of Native peoples.

As history informs us, the tribes whose homelands lay in what is now the eastern, northeastern and southeastern United States were forcibly removed from those areas to make way for the immigrants who came to America's shores and decided to settle on lands that subsequently came under the control of the original thirteen colonies. Later, as non-Indian settlement expanded westward, Native people were again relocated to regions west of the Mississippi River.

Torn from their traditional homelands, separated from their subsistence lifestyles, forced onto lands that were not hospitable to the agrarian way of life that the American government sought to have the indigenous people take up, forbidden to speak their native languages or practice their historic traditions and culture, Native people and the communities to which they were removed suffered the devastating consequences of dire economic circumstances. Those circumstances, and the inability to control or remedy them, brought about a pervasive despair that continued as generation after generation of American Indians and Alaska Natives were born into poverty or isolated in the most remote areas of our country.

Government policies designed to address the conditions of the indigenous, native people of the United States ranged from soliciting American Indians to join forces with the revolutionary troops, recognizing the pre-existing sovereignty of the Indian nations and entering into treaties with them, wars aimed at exterminating the Native people, forced relocation that resulted in America's own diaspora, reorganization and Federal recognition of tribal governments, termination of that Federally-recognized status, and finally, self-determination and self-governance. It is this most recent government policy that has enabled Native people to regain control over their lives, their economies, and their futures.

Throughout this tortuous history, the economic conditions of Native people and their communities have been largely hidden from America's awareness and in their place, stereotypes have thrived in the darkness of ignorance. Today, tribal governments are actively employing every conceivable means of revitalizing their economies, and this *Guide to Indian Country* is a valuable tool that will continue, as it has in the past, to dispel myths and to inform those who desire to work with Native people and their governments to achieve the economic renaissance that is the birth right of this nation's First Americans.

Aloha,

DANIEL K. INOUYE
United States Senator

Washington, D.C.
April 28, 2005

In 1996, Tiller Research Inc.(TRI) was proud to produce Tiller's Guide to Indian Country (TGIC). The first of its type, our reference guide brought current, pertinent information about state and federally recognized Indian reservations to the bookshelves. It offered readers up-to-date and first-hand information about tribal nations, and gave Indian people a voice in the telling of their own histories. TGIC brought to the field a comprehensive guide to the economic status of reservations in this nation, providing data collected directly from tribes as well as from available resources.

In gathering information for the 1996 edition, I realized that historical and anthropological information about tribal nations in the United States abounded, as did sterile statistical data. There was nothing, however, that presented tribes as living cultures, as vibrant economies, and as enduring communities that have persisted and sometimes prospered and flourished right alongside mainstream American society. The significance of our work became clear. With TGIC, we were not only compiling a thorough and accurate reference work, but we were adding life to the sterile statistics compiled by government. We were presenting an alternative image to the American stereotype of Indian reservations. We were showing how often tribes actually underpin local and regional economies. We were also presenting a factual portrait of tribal life in late 20th Century America.

In all regions of the country, tribes were involved in an astonishing range of economic activities. From the Menominee Tribe's forest products in Wisconsin to the information technology investments by the Confederated Salish and Kootenai Tribes of Montana, ancient cultures are providing both goods and services to 21st Century America. In Mississippi's delta region, the Mississippi Choctaw Tribe anchors the economy of an entire region. We believe that Tiller's Guide to Indian Country remains the only publication to focus on the economic viability as well as the cultural vitality of tribal nations and communities throughout modern America.

We began on January 16, 2004, to collect information for this edition of TGIC, hoping as we did with the first edition to rely heavily on the tribes themselves for information and to check the accuracy of information from public sources. Through questionnaires, we heard from tribal governments, planning offices, economic development offices, public relations officers, chief executive officers (chairmen, governors, presidents, and chiefs), tribal administrators, and environmental protection coordinators. Through personal visits, e-mail, telephone conferences, faxes, and regular post, a blizzard of data and information flew back and forth. Agencies such as the U.S. Environmental Protection Agency, the Indian Health Service, and the Bureau of Indian Affairs cooperated with information provided through➡

ACKNOWLEDGEMENTS

Without the support of a dedicated and hard-working team of writers, researchers, editors, proofreaders, a graphic designer, an indexer, and the Tiller Research project staff, this 2005 edition of Tiller's Guide would not have been completed. With an endeavor of this nature it is near impossible to thank everyone who contributed but there are various individuals who should be acknowledged.The main writers for Alaska were Edward C. McClure, Thomas Sanchez, and Tammy Moon. For the Lower 48 states, the primary writers were Andrea Hernandez Holm and Tammy Moon. Our special thanks and recognition go to Edward McClure and Andrea Holm, both first-class writers, for their keen analytical skills, and research and writing abilities. Tammy Moon, another excellent writer is also to be commended. Other contributing writers were Janet Fowler, Deborah Perlow, Suzy Baldwin, Joana Stancil, Brian Ramirez, and Stacey Moreton. Brian Ramirez was our lead internet researcher, working both on Alaska and the Lower 48 states. Assisting with the internet research were Nathan Fawcett and Derrick Lente. The technical editors for Tiller's Guide were Gary C. Cooper for Alaska and Shirley Coe for the Lower 48 states. Our proofreaders were Rebecca Hunter, Cheryl Slosberg, Florence Plecki and Janice St. Germain. All the graphics, including the cover design and page layout, were the work of Mary M. Velarde, who is especially acknowledged for her creativity, innovation, and untiring efforts in getting the guide to press. Providing us with indexing service was Francine Cronshaw of East Mountain Editing Services of Tijeras, New Mexico. TRI staff members who assisted with the management of this project were Stephanie D. Lucero, Annette Mckee, Stacey A. Moreton, Jennifer A. Smith, Courtney S. Folden, Cynthia Mauck, Vicki Finnegan, Stacey Velarde Sanchez, and Patricia Stappenbeck. A very special thank you goes to Roberta Serafin for her support and encouragement every step of the way.

Tiller Research had a team of field researchers visiting Indian reservations, rancherias, and communities to collect data in various states and regions: Blair Lynn Velarde (southern California), Liana Staci Hesler (Oklahoma), Rita Yazzie (reservations near Phoenix, Arizona), and Derrick Lente (four New Mexico Pueblos). Visiting the tribes of Colorado, Oregon, Idaho, Montana, Nevada, eastern Washington, and northern Utah were Everett Serafin, Roberta Serafin and Reba June Serafin. A special thanks goes to Roberta Serafin for her assistance with the trips to North and South Dakota; to Blair Lynn Velarde for the visits to the tribes of Kansas, Nebraska, western South Dakota, Minnesota and Wisconsin; to Reba June Serafin for her visits with the Florida tribes; to Christina V. Harrison for the trips to northern California and northern Arizona; and to Mary Velarde for her visits to Maine tribes.

Tiller's Guide to Indian Country would not be a premiere reference guide without the cooperation, kindness, and hospitality of the people of Indian Country. We cannot thank them enough for their input. There are two lists, the first, The Special Tribal Reviewers/Contributors, acknowledges those individuals who made a special effort by reviewing our draft profiles and ➡

their web sites regarding federal programs and services to tribes. We were delighted to learn the extent to which these federal agencies themselves now turn to Tiller's Guide for authoritative information regarding their client communities. Long-time activists such as Comanche LaDonna Harris have succeeded admirably in demanding that Indian communities that were largely bypassed by the industrial revolution not be ignored by the information revolution. Most tribes, we discovered, now have their own web sites, as do a number of their individual tribal programs and enterprises. We also found a good deal of our own information from the 1996 edition on tribes' own websites. The internet was a key resource in developing this edition of Tiller's Guide to Indian Country. Where possible, we have provided links in this edition to individual tribal web sites for additional information.

In addition to the research and inquiries conducted from our offices, we also dispatched a small army of field researchers, made up almost exclusively of my sisters and nieces, to visit more than 220 reservations and Indian communities in the "Lower 48" states. From treaty fishing "grounds" at the very mouth of the Klamath River in Oregon to the bottom of the Grand Canyon; from the Las Vegas-style Indian casinos of San Diego County to the tribal bison herds on the high plains of Montana and the Dakotas; and from the Florida Everglades to

the island chain of the Penobscot River in Maine, we "kicked the tires" of Indian country USA for this 2005 edition of Tiller's Guide.

We were confronted at every stop with evidence of an explosion of tribal economic activity in the past decade. The burgeoning gaming industry is the most publicized, and it has been remarkable. From the Florida Seminole Tribe's opening of a high stakes bingo hall in 1979, Indian gaming has grown to an $18 billion per year industry. Federal law requires formal agreements with surrounding states for the most sophisticated gaming operations, and for the most part these are negotiated successfully. Those disputes that do arise have all been resolved peacefully, although some have been the cause of serious consternation. When agents of the State of Arizona seized gaming machines on the Fort McDowell Reservation in Arizona, tribal members formed a human chain around the facility to prevent exit of either agents or machines without running over a tribal member. When the federal government seized tribal bank accounts of the Santee-Sioux of Nebraska for allegedly illegal gaming operations, the Mdewankton Sioux of Minnesota provided their Santee relatives with a $5 million grant to continue tribal operations until the dispute was resolved. In 2005, more than 225 tribes operate gaming facilities that generate revenues to improve tribal infrastructure, expand human services, ➡

ACKNOWLEDGEMENTS

even rewriting sections of profiles. They are tribal employees who care about their jobs, tribes, and people and want the general public to have accurate information about their tribes. Many of these individuals also hosted TRI staff while visiting their reservations and communities. They all made a valuable contribution to this guide. The second list, Tribal Personnel and Individuals, acknowledges tribal employees from various departments (executive, economic development, public relations, tribal administration, cultural preservation, libraries, environmental protection, and business corporations, to name a few) and individuals who provided Tiller Research with information about their tribes. These individuals contributed to the review of final draft profiles, or provided general assistance throughout the process. Many of the personnel and individuals assisted us by guiding us during our visits to their reservations, taking their valuable time to meet with us while we were there, giving us special and discounted rates, sending us in the right direction and to the right people on our quest to gather information, and showing us great kindness.

We also wish to acknowledge the State of Alaska, Department of Commerce, Community and Economic Development, Division of Community Advocacy, for all the wonderful information on the Alaskan Native Villages and communities available on their web site. Various Bureau of Indian Affairs Regional Offices throughout the United States provided us with their land acreage reports and we thank them for their information. A special thanks goes to Trib Choudary of the Navajo Nation Eco-

nomic Development Department for his 2000 census data of all 562 federally recognized tribes. Providing us a useful listing for the educational statistics from the U.S. Census was Anita Choudary. Michael A. Corfman of Casino City Press of Newton, Massachusetts, allowed us access to his database, from which we received the latest information on Indian gaming statistics. We are also grateful to Imre Sutton for his leads to helpful and knowledgeable individuals in California. A sincere thanks to Amy Besaw, Andrew Lee, Jr., Shelly D. Coulter, Miriam Jorgensen, and Joseph P. Kalt of the Harvard Project on American Indian Economic Development at Harvard's Kennedy School of Government, Cambridge, Massachusetts for allowing us to include the Honoring Contributions in the Governance of American Indian Nations (popularly known as Honoring Nations) from 1999 to 2003 in Tiller's Guide. Senator Daniel K. Inouye of Hawaii, who has served for 28 years as the chairman and vice chairman of the U.S. Senate Committee on Indian Affairs has my deep appreciation for contributing to Tiller's Guide with his preface.

Tiller's Guide is well illustrated with photographs. Taking the photographs in 2004 for Tiller Research were Everett Serafin, Reba June Serafin, Christina V. Harrison, Mary Velarde, Alyssa Davies, Derrick Lente, Liana Staci Hesler, and Blaine Lynn Velarde. Several photographs taken by Emily Tiller Frederiks for the 1996 edition were also included. Individuals who loaned us photographs were Lt. Governor Leon Roybal of San Ildelfonso Pueblo, New Mexico; Louis Weller of Weller Archi-

tects of Albuquerque, New Mexico; Larry Olsen of LA Olson & Associates of Billings, Montana; Mike Holleyman of Holleyman Associates of Oklahoma City, Oklahoma; Joanna Murray of the Cheyenne River Sioux Tribe, Eagle Butte, South Dakota; and Darren Wright of Gay Head, Massachusetts. The Quinault Beach Resort of the Quinault Indian Nation of Washington, the National Park Service, and the Louisiana Office of Tourism also allowed us to use their photographs and we thank them. Other people who supported us and greatly deserve our appreciation are my husband, David C. Harrison, Patricia Zell, Former Democratic Staff Director/Chief Counsel, U.S. Senate Committee on Indian Affairs, and Edward J. Cadena, Deputy Director of the U.S. Small Business Administration from the New Mexico District, Albuquerque.

Veronica E. Velarde Tiller, Ph.D.
(Jicarilla Apache)
Editor & Compiler
Tiller Research, Inc.
Albuquerque, New Mexico ■

develop educational programs, expand land holdings, and support local charities, public school systems, law enforcement agencies, emergency services, and health care facilities among others.

Gaming in Indian country has generated its stereotype as false as any of those that preceded it, that all Indian tribes and individuals are now awash in gaming dollars. Not all tribes even have gaming operations, and a number of them have declined offer after offer to join the parade of gaming tribes. Many of these tribes still depend on the more traditional enterprises such as agriculture, mining, manufacturing, information and technology, arts and crafts, forestry, fisheries, communications, and tourism and recreation. The Lac Courte Oreilles Tribe owns and operates one of the first Indian-owned radio stations in the country. The Oneida Nation of Wisconsin owns and operates successful agricultural enterprises, as do a number of tribes in the Southwest. The Osage Tribe of Oklahoma has produced oil and gas from its 1.4 million-acre estate in Oklahoma for a century. The Mescalero Apache Tribe in New Mexico operates three popular recreation and ski resorts. A number of tribes operate various enterprises on tribally owned industrial parks. And others boast business centers, office complexes, and commercial shopping malls on tribal lands.

Natural resources continue to provide the backbone of many tribal economies. With an annual allowable cut of more than one billion board feet on a sustained yield basis, forestry promises to sustain some tribal economies for generations to come. Hundreds of millions of tons of low-sulfur sub-bituminous coal underlie thousands of acres of Western reservation lands. Oil and gas resources continue to flow from Indian lands, even as much of the industry shifts its efforts to offshore and foreign prospects. Rights to precious water throughout the major river basins of the West are seen as increasingly valuable, not only for agriculture but also for municipal and industrial use. More and more tribes are concentrating on instream flow requirements to maintain fisheries, wildlife habitat, and environmental values. Tribes are increasingly taking control of these valuable resources from the federal agencies that have traditionally managed them. In Arizona, the Ak-Chin Indian Community has persevered to see implementation of the nearly thirty-year-old Ak-Chin Water Settlement Act of 1978. The Southern Ute Tribe stood virtually alone for as long to see ground broken on the Animas-La Plata Project, perhaps the last major water development project for the Bureau of Reclamation. In the northwest, tribes have secured water to preserve their treaty-protected fishing rights to anadromous fisheries. Many tribes are investing proceeds from their ➡

SPECIAL TRIBAL REVIEWERS/CONTRIBUTORS: (Listed by state and reservation name)

CALIFORNIA Lee Acebedo, Bill Mesa, Darlene Suarez (Jamul) Stan Anderson (Tuolumne) Carol Bill (Cold Springs) Diana Chihuahua, (Torres Martinez), Franklin A. Dancy, (Morongo) John Elliot (Manzanita), Juana Majel-Dixon (Pauma), Will Micklin, (Ewaiiaayp), Jerry Paresa (San Manuel); COLORADO Edwina Silas, Troy Ralstin, (Ute Mountain Ute) Edna Frost, Chuck Farago, Jim Formea, (Southern Ute); MAINE Alberta Downing, Melvin Francis, Sr., (Pleasant Point), Russell Dennis, (Aroostock) Don Levasseur, (Houlton Maliseet), Roger Ritter, Robert Tyler, (Indian River Township) Craig Sanborn, Tim Walton, (Penobscot); MASSACHUSETTS Beverly Wright (Wampanoag Tribe of Gay Head); MICHIGAN George Beck (Lac Vieux Desert), William Mrdeza (Saginaw), Sue Spriver, Reneé Robinson (Sault Ste. Marie), Glenn Zaring, Jonnie J. Sam II, Bill Brooks, (Little River Band); MINNESOTA Reneé Gale, Victoria White (Leech Lake); MONTANA Theresa Aragon (Crow), Caroline Brown, (Fort Belknap), Bob Gauthier (Flathead), Joe Gervais, (Blackfeet); NEBRASKA Rick Thomas (Santee Sioux); NEW MEXICO Bernadine Garcia (Acoma), Sharon Hausam (Sandia) , Andrew Othole (Zuni), Thora Padilla (Mescalero Apache), Kenneth Pin (Santo Domingo), Governor Tom Talache, Jr. (Nambé); NEVADA Anita Collins (Walker River), Chuck Rosenow, (Reno-Sparks); OKLAHOMA Margaret Anquoe (Cheyenne-Arapahoe), Ron Barnett (Thlopthlocco Creek), Guy Munroe and Ron Feazle (Kaw Nation), Carla Norman (Seminole), Tony Salazar (Kickapoo), Tamara Summerfield (Quapaw), Pam Wall (Creek Nation) Jennifer Smith; OREGON Kevin Craig (Coquille), Kim Rogers (Grand Ronde), Michael Rondeau (Cow Creek), Francis Somday (Coos Bay); SOUTH CAROLINA Gilbert Blue (Catawba); SOUTH DAKOTA Sam Allen (Santee Sioux), Denelle High Elk, Deanna Lebeau, Narcisse Rousseau (Cheyenne River Sioux), Ben Janis, Scott Jones, Toni Rouillard Wells (Lower Brule), Angie Johnson (Sisseton-Wahpeton), Myrna Leader Charge (Rosebud); TEXAS Sylvia Garcia, Carlos Hisa, (Ysleta de Sur Pueblo) Sharon Miller (Alabama-Coushatta) Margie Salazar (Kickapoo); UTAH Armand Accuttroop, (Uintah-Ouray) Bruce Perry (Northwestern Band); WASHINGTON Ken Stocks, Paul Wilson (Kalispel), David Ernst, John Otterson (Spokane) Linda Cawyer, Annette Nesse (Jamestown S'Klallam), Natalie Charley, Rich Wells, Max Stocks, (Quinault), Leonard Forsman (Suquamish), Larry Goodrow (Skokomish), Joan Koenig (Squaxin Island), Casey Stevens (Stillaguamish), Tracie Stevens (Tulalip), Curt Wolters (Lummi); WISCONSIN Richard Ackley, Jr. (Mole Lake), Richard Hartmann (St. Croix), Wayne Lindemans (Red Cliff), Denise Palmer, (Stockbridge-Munsee), Bobbi Webster (Oneida).

Tribal Personnel and Individuals: (Listed by state and reservation name)

ALABAMA Sandra Hiebert (Poarch Creek); ARIZONA Collette Altaha (Fort Apache), Trib Choudary (Navajo Nation), Helema Andrews (Salt River Pima-Maricopa), Carl Antone (Gila River), Sabrina Campbell (Tohono O'odham), Marilyn Celestine, Jerry C. Holland, Walt Nader, Richard Carons (Tonto Apache), Michele Crank (Fort McDowell), Jack Ehrhart (Hualapai), Brian Golding, Sr. (Fort Yuma), Evelyn James (San Juan), Lynnia Key (San Carlos), Lincoln Manataja, Linda Mahone, (Havasupai), Gary Goforth, Nora McDowell (Fort Mojave), Chris Moss (Yavapai-Prescott), Letticia Baltazar, Luci Ponticelli (Pascua Yaqui), Fred Shupla, Royce M. Jenkins, (Hopi), Bartholomew Smith (Ak-Chin), Ted Smith, Sr., (Camp Verde), Paul Soto (Cocopah), Greg Sprawls, Cindy Homer, Veronica Murdock, Herman Lasson, Orlando Short, Sr., (Colorado River), Gary Tom (Kaibab); CALIFORNIA Todd G. Hooks (Agua Caliente), Eileen Anthony (Chemehuevi), Wanda Balderama, Don Ray, Valeria Stanley, (Hopland), Steve Baldy (Big Lagoon), Leslie Keig (Alturas) Michelle Berditschevsky and Brandy Gemmill (Big Bend, Likely, Lookout, Montgomery Creek), Dino Beltran (Lower Lake), Loren Bommelyn, Dorothy Perry (Smith River), Angie Bill, Thelma Bradford, Karen Flores (Cortina), Reyna Beasley (Viejas), Debra Breidenbach-Sterling, Karen Kupcha (Augustine), Lavina Brooks, Peggy O'Neil, Arnie Nova, Willard Carlson (Yurok), Raymond Brown, Cheryl Steele, Sandy Thomas (Elem), Terry Brown, Mark Macarro, Jody de la Torre (Pechanga), Pam Baumgartner, Silvia Burley (Valley Miwok Tribe, California), Raymond Torres (Torres Martinez), Judy Cleveland (Big Valley), Anthony Collins, Georgia Tucker (Sycuan), Brian Connolly (Campo), Nancy Conrad, David Martinez (Cabazon), Lorraine Dalamino, Andrew Moro (Pala), Louise Davis (Redding), Becky Day (Tuolumne), Michel DeMers (North Fork), Butch Denny (Santa Rosa), Mike Despain (Greenville), Richard Drake (Fort Independence), Evelyn Duro, (Los Coyotes) Doug Elmets (Rumsey), Doug Elmets (United Auburn), Trina Fitzgerral (Sherwood Valley), Kathy Frazier (Enterprise), Tilda Green (San Pasqual), Wanda Green, Ray Martel, Terri Camarena (Elk Valley), Manuel Hamilton (Ramona), Rich Hoffman (Jackson), Michael Holman (Potter Valley), Jaclyn Traversie, Danny Jordan, Will Hostler, (Hoopa Valley), Loren Joseph (Lone Pine), Leslie Keig (Montgomery Creek), Joe Kennedy (Timbisha Shoshone), Lavon Kent (Quartz Valley), Bruce Klein (Bishop), Ron Knight, Don Rich (Pinoleville), Diana L. Kosar (Robinson), Irvin Lent (Big Pine), Cheryl Bettega, Ronald Lincoln. Sr. (Round Valley), Tom Linton (Morongo), David Lockart (Chico), Latisha Miller, Leslie Loshe

economic activities to expand their land base and to reacquire ancestral homelands. More and more tribes are diversifying their economies in order to maintain sacred sites and regions of incomparable beauty in their natural states.

In addition to economic growth in Indian country, we have also witnessed over the last several years the recognition and restoration of a number of tribal nations to federal status, such as the Ione Miwok Band in California (1994), Lower Lake Rancheria Koi Nation (2000) the Cowlitz Indian Tribe of Washington (2002) and the Match-E-Be-Nash-She-Wish commonly known as the Gun Lake Tribe (1998). It is important to note that even today, there remain numerous tribal communities across the country with no federal recognition. Some, like the Independent or Traditional Seminole of Florida, seem to have no interest in gaining state or federal recognition, while still others continue to fight for it.

The economic relationship between tribal nations and non-Indian communities and governments in general has changed dramatically as well in the last decade. In a number of instances, tribes have become the largest employers in the communities, counties, and regions in which they are located. During the late 1990s in Connecticut, the Mohegan tribe and the Mashantucket

Pequot tribes combined offered nearly 16,000 jobs to the general public, exceeding the number of jobs lost in federal defense cuts in the state. The Mashantucket Pequot is the single largest private employer in that state and its casino alone provides over 11,000 employment opportunities. Direct employment opportunities are not the only contributions that tribes make to local economies. Particularly among tribes with casinos and gaming enterprises, tribal monies support improvements to the local infrastructure (road, sewer, water, and waste disposal system), emergency services, and businesses and enterprises. Tribes also contribute substantial funds to educational programs, health facilities, and non-profit organizations. And tribes are also quick to assist others when possible-during aftermath of the terrorist attacks in New York city on September 11, 2001, the Mashantucket Pequot tribe utilized its high-speed ferry system, Fox Navigation, to evacuate victims from and to transport medical personnel to the Twin Towers. Tribes from across the nation, both large and small, offered millions of dollars in assistance to the recovery and rescue efforts. And in 2002, the St. Regis Mohawk Tribe hosted the largest event ever held at its casino, a recognition ceremony in honor of the 800 tribal members of the International Association of Bridge, Structural, Ornamental and Reinforcement Iron Union, many of whom worked tirelessly at Ground Zero. ➡

Tribal Personnel and Individuals: (Listed by state and reservation name) [continued]

(Paskenta), James Mackay (Susanville), Vickey Macias (Cloverdale), Scott McCrea (Mesa Grande), Nancy McDarment, John Nash (Tule River), Melba Burress (Berry Creek), Elizabeth Elgin DeRouen, Lailia DeRouen (Dry Creek), Sean Minder (Bridgeport), Virgil Moorehead (Big Lagoon), Renee Brown, Shannon Morganson (Colusa), Rhonda Morningstar Pope (Buena Vista), Barbara Murphy (Redding), Jeff Murray (Shingle Springs), Tracy Nelson (La Jolla), Greg Nesty (Trinidad), Elizabeth Hansen, Mary Nevarez, Judy Fisch (Redwood Valley), Ted Ochoa (Coyote Valley), Rebecca Osuna, Melissa Castro (Inaja-Cosmit), Gwendolyn Parada, James Hill (La Posta), Rick Poe (Manchester Point), Virginia Sutter (Manchester Point), Lloyd Powell (Cedarville), LaMar Price, Brandie Taylor, (Santa Ysabel) Arla Ramsey (Blue Lake), Lisa Rathbun (Guidiville), Carol Reeves (Rohnerville), Lorell Ross (Graton), Michael Russell (Table Mountain), Jerome Salgado, Sr., (Cahuilla), Tootie Sam (Fort Bidwell), Joseph Saulque (Benton Paiute), Tammy Peevler, Rob Shaffer (Rincon), Cheryl Seidner, Maura Eastman (Table Bluff), Robert Selgado, Sr., Vicki Varres (Soboba), Jose Simon, Pamela Reyes-Gutierrez (Middletown), David Smith (Santa Ynez), Eliza Swearinger (Grindstone Indian), Brandie Taylor (Santa Ysabel), Cristy Taylor, Merle Stevenson, Debra Sanders, (Laytonville), Robert Stone, Guy Taylor (Mooretown), Leanna Thomas (Twenty-Nine Palms), Sue Thomas, Cheryl Hinton (Barona), Sandi Tripp, Sara Spence (Karuk), Iris Picton, David Tomas (Upper Lake), Donald Valenzuela (Resighini), Juan Mancias, Rose Mary Want (Scotts Valley); CONNECTICUT Arthur Henick (Mashantucket Pequot), Chuck Bunnell, Kevin Meisner, Dale White, Melissa Zobel (Mohegan); FLORIDA Wanda Bowers, Sally Tommy, Sandy Selner (Seminole), IOWA Alison Davenport (Sac and Fox); IDAHO Francis Devereaux, Charles Morris, (Coeur d'Alene), Rosemary A. Devinney, Jon Norstog, Darrel Shay (Fort Hall), Cassandra Kipp (Nez Perce), Patty Perry (Kootenai); KANSAS Louis DeRoin, Joana Comer, Leon Campbell, (Iowa), Christopher W. Dunn, H. Jason Auvil, (Kickapoo), Nancy Keller, Gina Kneib, Don Bucky Pilcher (Sac and Fox), Latane N. Donelin, Jon Bursaw, Ryan Dyer, Verna Simon (Prairie Band Potawatomi); LOUISIANA Earl Barbry, Jr. (Tunica-Biloxi), Jason Emery, Kim Walden (Chitimacha), Phyllis Nicols (Coushatta), Walter Nope (Jena Band); MASSACHUSETTS Victoria Wright, Darren Wright, (Gay Head); MAINE Rosa McNally, Norma Jean Saulis, John Ouedellett, Jerolyn Ireland, (Aroostook); MICHIGAN Kathy Adair (Bay Mills), Dave Anthony, Ken Meshigaud (Hannahville), Dan Green (Pine Creek), Kim Klopstein (L'Anse), Michelle Lacount, Su Lantz (Little Traverse Bay Bands), John Miller (Pokagon), Sandra Raphael (Grand Traverse), Bill Brooks, Mark Dougher, Jay Sam, (Little River), Andrew Sprague (Match-E-Be-Nash-She-Wish), Crista Payment, (Sault Ste. Marie); MINNESOTA Mitch Corbine (Mille Lacs), Stephanie Fox, Diane Ralston (Prairie Island), Gary Fuller, Roger Head (Red Lake), Jason Hollinday, Dennis Peterson, Margaret Robideaux (Fond du Lac), Su Lantz (Upper Sioux Community), Ann Larson, Dawn Pendleton (Lower Sioux), Tessa Lehto (Shakopee), Dana Logan (Grand Portage), Mike Triplett (White Earth); MISSISSIPPI Kevin Edwards (Choctaw); MONTANA Shawn Real Bird, Noel Two Leggins, (Crow), Larry Morsette, Jr., Marva Stump (Rocky Boy), C. John Healy, Sr., Carol Stiffarm, (Fort Belknap), Joe Little Coyote, Geri Small, (Northern Cheyenne), Dennis Fitzpatrick, Ed Wagner, Debora Juarez (Blackfeet), Rodney Miller, Jim Rued, Don Ewert, Lee Abbott (Fort Peck); NEBRASKA Janet Bass, John Blackhawk, Virgil Free, Louie Houghton, Joi Long (Winnebago), John Fremont, Tony Provost (Omaha), Caroll Kitchi, Chris Weber (Ponca), James Trudell (Santee Sioux); NEVADA Greg Holley, Bernice Lalo, Donna Hill, (Battle Mountain), Garrett Furuichi, Val Nevers (Carson), Maria Barry, Herman Atkins, Lindsey Manning (Duck Valley), Lisa Ann George, Virginia Sanchez, Carrie Sligar (Duckwater), Gloria Two Eagles, Fermina Stevens (Elko), Christine Stones (Ely), Larry Curly, Robert Valpert (Fallon), Karen Cruthcher (Fort McDermitt), Gloria Hernandez, Alfreda Mitre (Las Vegas), Monty George, Harry Summerfield, Glen Wason (Lovelock), Phil Swain (Moapa), David Koch, John Van Etten, Tim Wadsworth (Pyramid Lake), Lorayn London, (South Fork), Garrett Furuichi, (Stewart) Robyn Berdette, Julie Crutcher (Summit Lake), Elwood Mose, Ursula Powers, (Te-Moak Tribe), Anita Collins, Richard Whitefeather (Walker River), Kristi Begay (Wells Band), Linda Ayer, Tom Watson (Winnemucca), Garrett Furuichi (Woodfords), Wayne Garcia, Duane Masters, (Yerington), Dennis Bill, Lisa Kagel (Yomba); NEW MEXICO Herman Agoya, Earl Salazar (San Juan), Clee Melvin (Cochiti), Rob Ariwite (Laguna), John Armijo, Timothy Armijo, Marlene Gachupin (Jemez), Everett Serafin, Alberta Velarde (Jicarilla Apache), Laura Benavidez, Paul Rainberg (Nambé), William Christian, Melissa Gipson, Elmer Torres, Leon T. Roybal (San Ildefonso), Charles Dorame, Carol Woods (Tesuque), Michael Eriacho, Jerry Pino, Sr. (Ramah), Lori Vincente, Denise Garandonegro (Alamo), Tina Romero, Millie Weller (Taos), Ava Hanna (Zuni), Valentina Herrera (San Felipe), Nora Morris (To'Hajiilee), Daniel Moya, George Rivera (Pojoaque), Peter Pino, Stanley Pino, Tammy Pino (Zia) Brian Ramirez, Calvin Tafoya (Santa Clara), Lorraine Snake (Picuris), Nathan Tsosie (Santa Ana), Phil Tsosie (Isleta); NEW YORK Mark Emery (Oneida), Darwin Hills (Tonawanda), William Papineau, Sheree Bonaparte, (St. Regis Mohawk), Millie Fox, Karla Nephew, Gina Paradis, Carol Thompson, Natalie Hemlock, Martin Seneca, Jr. (Seneca/Allegany and Cattaraugus), Alma Patterson, Kenneth Patterson (Tuscarora), Irving Powless (Onondaga), Anita Thompson, Sharon LeRoy (Cayuga); NORTH CAROLINA Sarah Crow (Eastern Cherokee); NORTH DAKOTA John Allery (Turtle Mountain), Charlie Murphy (Standing Rock) Glenda Embry, Marion Spotted Bear (Fort Berthold), Kenny Graywater (Spirit Lake), Angie Johnson (Sisseton-Wahpeton Sioux), OKLAHOMA: Lionel Ahdunko, Pam Baumgartner (Caddo), Judy Allen, Gary Whitedeer (Choctaw), Deborah Bailey (Sac and Fox), Ron Barnett

The growing economic stability among tribal nations is also allowing tribes to provide assistance to one another. The Mohegan Tribal Nation in Connecticut has achieved such financial success through its enterprises that in 1997, it returned $2.2 million to the U.S. Department of Housing and Urban Development. It has since returned its allotted federal funds so that they may be redistributed to tribes with greater economic need. The Mdewankton Sioux Tribe of Minnesota has donated more than $100 million to less fortunate tribes throughout the country. A number of tribal nations have formed economic partnerships, political alliances, and commissions such as the Northwoods Niiji Enterprise Community, Inc. (NNEC), Four Fires LLC, and the Eight Northern Indian Pueblos Council. These organizations promote economic growth; ensure representation at the city, state, and federal level; and support cultural retention and preservation.

The twin explosions of economic activity and information on the superhighway in Indian country have forced difficult editorial decisions in this edition. In the Lower 48, we left the information highway and hit the real highway from coast to coast and border to border. The sheer size of Alaska and the absence of real highways to many villages prohibited that approach. We did establish contacts in as many villages as possible, as well as with Alaska Native organizations and corporations. The scope and magnitude of economic activity among Alaska Natives convinced us to deal separately in this edition with the Alaska Native Corporations, with new categories and subsections in an attempt to capture the amazing entrepreneurial spirit that has emerged among them. It is difficult to convey the apparent dichotomy presented by an Inupiat Village President directing the terms of a multi-million dollar acquisition from his position in a walrus-hide whaling boat in the Arctic Ocean. I call it an apparent dichotomy because it is unfathomable to most of us. He simply calls it a day in his life, tending to both his corporate and his traditional responsibilities.

We have been honored by the courtesy, professionalism, hospitality, and friendship extended to us by the many people we have encountered, and we thank them for their kindnesses. We appreciate the recognition of our efforts to provide our readers with comprehensive, accurate, and appropriate information about America's tribal nations. It is our hope that we our readers, both our past and new readers, will have a better understanding of Indian Country with this new edition of *Tiller's Guide*. ∎

Tribal Personnel and Individuals: (Listed by state and reservation name) [continued]

(Thlopthlocco Creek), Chief Bearskin, Ellis Enyart (Wyandotte), Kenneth Blanchard, Jean Kovacs, Anna Dereberry Livingston (Absentee Shawnee), Aaron Brummett (Eastern Shawnee), Michael Burgess, Vicki Canfield, Laura Harris, Joene Schonch (Comanche), Carter Camp (Ponca), Vickie Canfield (Citizen Potawatomi Nation), Juana Chaddlesone (Wichita Agency), Michael Darrow, Steve Buckner, Timothy Harjo (Fort Sill), Rhonda Dixon (Ottawa), Betty Durkee, Thomas Fredericks, Guy Munroe (Kaw), Bill Fife (Alabama-Quassarte) Robyn Elliott, Brad Fortner (Chickasaw), John Froman (Peoria), Michelle Garcia, Diane Jobe (Iowa), Michael Gawhega (Otoe-Missouria), Bobby Jay (Apache), Julia Lookout, Carrie Rogers, Anthony Whitehorn (Osage), Carl Martin (Tonkawa), Diane Moppin, Tarpie Yargee (Alabama Quassarte), Julie Moss, Laverna Stapleton (United Keetoowah), Julie Olds (Miami), Martha Perez, Martha Koomsa-Perez, (Kiowa), Jim Rementer (Delaware), Sandy Selner (Seminole), Dennis Sisco (Seneca-Cayuga), Chadwick Smith, Felcia Wing, Melissa Young (Cherokee Nation), Jennifer Smith (Muscogee Creek), Julia Syitakf (Cheyenne-Arapaho), Lindsey Teter (Pawnee), Patricia Trolinger (Modoc) Jeff Whekins (Delaware); **OREGON** Pam Lynn Barlow, Sherri Groh (Siletz), Michael Clements, Ray Rangela, Lavonne Rotz, Sal Sahme (Warm Springs), Teresa Crane, Joan Deroko, Bill Tovey (Umatilla), Howard Crombie, Pat Davis, (Coos Bay), Kenton Dick, (Burns Paiute), Barbara Kirk, Loren Schonchin (Klamath), Keith Hatch (Celilo Village), Mark Healy (Coquille), Kim Rogers (Grand Ronde), Sheri Shaffer (Cow Creek); **RHODE ISLAND** Eric Wilcox (Narragansett); **SOUTH CAROLINA** Gilbert Blue (Catawba); **SOUTH DAKOTA** Fabian Betone, Denelle High Elk, Edward Raventon, Narcisse Rousseau, Emily Smith (Cheyenne River Sioux), Duane Big Eagle, Frank Lawrence, Quintin Mghee (Crow Creek), Micheal Jandreau (Lower Brule), Vonnie Bush (Pine Ridge), Philmon Two Eagles, Charles Columbe, Robert Moore, Steve Emery (Rosebud), Elliott Halsey (Yankton), Judith H. Petersen, Thomas R. Allen, (Flandreau Santee Sioux); **TEXAS** Arturo Sinclair; **UTAH**, Robert Colorow, Maxine Natchee (Uintah and Ouray), Chrissandra Murphy, Paul Tsosie (Goshute), Beverly Slack (Skull Valley), Laura Tom (Paiute); **WASHINGTON** Ryland Bowechop, Bud Denney (Makah), Henry Cagey (Lummi), Teri Johnson-Davis, Jerry Meninick, Kevin Shendo (Yakama), Dennis Crawford (Quileute), Nancy DeCouteau, Gloria Green, Jason Joseph, David Shaw (Sauk-Suiattle), Phil Dorn, Sally Kass, Barrett Schmanska (Port Gamble), John Halliday (Muckleshoot), Jeff Hertz (Nooksack), Cynthia Iyall (Nisqually), Rick Landers (Samish), Lennea Magnus (Chehalis), John Miller (Lower Elwha), Carolee Morris (Cowlitz), Ray Mullen (Snoqualmie), Charlene Nelson (Shoalwater Bay), Charles O'Hara, Allen Rozema (Swinomish), Gary Passmore (Colville), Harry Pateus (Upper Skagit), Victoria Pavel (Skokomish), Francis Cullooyah, Thomas Sawyer, Alice Ignace (Aunt Alice) (Kalispel), Donna Scott (Hoh), Bill Veliz, John Weymer, Judy Wright (Puyallup), Crystal Thompson (Quinault); **WISCONSIN** Brian Kowalkowski, John Chapman, Michael Chapman, Carrie Grignon, Renee Mahkimetas, Jeremy Weso, Allen W. Quinney (Menominee), Emerson Coy, Leanna Coy, Gloria Cobb, Brian Gauthier (Lac du Flambeau), Gus Frank (Forest County Potawatomi), Colene Frye (St. Croix), Larry Garvin, Tracy L. Littlejohn, Paul Rosheim, Stewart J. Miller (Ho-Chunk), Kevin Hasterballer, Luann Wiggins, Sue Erickson, (Bad River), Jill Martin, (Stockbridge-Munsee), Ray DePerry, (Red Cliff), Pam Rebitzke, Toni Phillite, Thomas Vanzile, (Mole Lake), Paul Dianah Ton (Lac Courte Oreilles), John Brueninger, Bobbi Webster (Oneida); **WYOMING** Richard Brannan, Mike La Jeunesse (Wind River).

TABLE OF CONTENTS	Page		Page		Page
ALABAMA		Deering	94	Kodiak	148
Poarch Creek Reservation	1	Dillingham	94	Kokhanok	148
		Diomede	95	Koliganek	149
ALASKA		Dot Lake	96	Kongiganak	149
Introduction	3	Douglas	96	Kotlik	150
Adak	41	Dutch Harbor	96	Kotzebue	152
Afognak	42	Eagle	97	Koyuk	154
Agdaagux	42	Eek	98	Koyukuk	155
Akhiok	43	Egegik	99	Kwethluk	156
Akiachak	45	Eklutna	100	Kwigillingok	158
Akiak	46	Ekuk	100	Kwinhagak	159
Akutan	47	Ekwok	101	Larsen Bay	161
Alakanuk	48	Elim	102	Lesnoi	162
Alatna	49	Emmonak	103	Levelock	162
Aleknagik	49	English Bay	103	Lime Village	164
Algaaciq	51	Evansville	104	Louden Village	164
Allakaket	52	Eyak	105	Lower Kalskag	165
Ambler	53	False Pass	106	Manley Hot Springs	166
Anaktuvuk Pass	54	Fort Yukon	107	Manokotak	167
Anchorage and Fairbanks	55	Gakona	108	Marshall	169
Andreafsky	56	Galena	109	Mary's Igloo	170
Angoon	56	Honoring Nations Honoree 2002	110	McGrath	170
Aniak	57	Gambell	112	Mekoryuk	172
Annette Island Reserve	58	Georgetown	113	Mentasta	173
Anvik	59	Golovin	113	Metlakatla	174
Arctic Village	59	Goodnews Bay	114	Minto	175
Asa'carsarmiut	60	Grayling	115	Mountain Village	176
Atka	61	Gulkana	116	Naknek	177
Atkasook	62	Haines	116	Nanwalek	179
Atmautluak	62	Hamilton	116	Napaimute	180
Atqasuk	63	Healy Lake	117	Napakiak	180
Barrow	64	Holikachuk	117	Napaskiak	181
Beaver	65	Holy Cross	117	Nelson Lagoon	183
Belkofski	66	Hoonah	118	Nenana	184
Bethel	66	Hooper Bay	119	New Allakaket	186
Bill Moore's Slough	66	Hughes	120	New Koliganek	187
Birch Creek	66	Huslia	121	New Stuyahok	188
Brevig Mission	67	Hydaburg	122	Newhalen	189
Buckland	68	Igiugig	123	Newtok	190
Cantwell	69	Iliamna	124	Nightmute	191
Chalkyitsik	70	Inalik	125	Nikolai	193
Chanega	71	Iqurmuit	125	Nikolski	194
Cheesh-Na	72	Ivanoff Bay	127	Ninilchik	195
Chefornak	73	Juneau	127	Noatak	197
Chenega, Chenega Bay	73	Kaguyak	127	Nome	198
Chevak	74	Kake	128	Nondalton	200
Chickaloon	75	Honoring Nations Honoree 2003	129	Nooiksut	201
Honoring Nations Honoree 2002	76	Kaktovik	131	Noorvik	201
Chignik	78	Kalskag	132	Northway Village	203
Chignik Lagoon	79	Kaltag	133	Nuiqsut	204
Chignik Lake	80	Kanatak	134	Nulato	206
Chilkat	81	Karluk	134	Nunakauyarmiut	207
Chilkoot	82	Kasaan	135	Nunam Iqua	208
Honoring Nations Honoree 2002	83	Kasigluk	136	Nunapitchuk	209
Chinik	85	Kenai, Kenaitze	127	Ohgsenakale	210
Chistochina	85	Ketchikan	137	Ohogamiut	210
Chitina	86	Kiana	139	Old Harbor	210
Chuathbaluk	87	King Cove	140	Orutsararmiut	212
Chuloonawick	88	King Island	140	Oscarville	213
Circle	88	King Salmon	140	Ouzinkie	214
Clark's Point	89	Kipnuk	142	Paimiut	216
Copper Center	90	Kivalina	143	Pauloff Harbor	216
Cordova	90	Klawock	144	Pedro Bay	216
Council	90	Klukwan	145	Perryville	217
Craig	90	Kluti-Kaah	145	Petersburg	219
Crooked Creek	91	Knik	146	Pilot Point	219
Curyung	92	Kobuk	147	Pilot Station	221

Pitka's Point	222
Platinum	223
Point Hope	224
Point Lay	226
Port Graham	227
Port Heiden	229
Port Lions	231
Portage Creek	233
Pribilof Islands	234
Qagan Tayagungin	237
Qawalangin	238
Quinhagak	239
Rampart	239
Red Devil	240
Ruby	242
Russian Mission	242
Saint George	242
Saint Mary's	242
Saint Michael	243
Saint Paul	244
Salamatoff	244
Sand Point	245
Savoonga	245
Saxman	247
Scammon Bay	248
Selawik	249
Seldovia Village	250
Shageluk	251
Shaktoolik	252
Sheldon's Point	252
Shishmaref	253
Shoonaq'	254
Shungnak	255
Sitka	256
Skagway	256
Sleetmute	257
Solomon	258
South Naknek	258
Stebbins	259
Stevens Village	260
Stony River	261
Takotna	262
Tanacross	263
Tanana	264
Tatitlek	265
Tazlina	266
Telida	267
Teller	268
Tetlin	269
Togiak	270
Toksook Bay	271
Tuluksak	271
Tuntutuliak	272
Tununak	273
Twin Hills	274
Tyonek	275
Ugashik	276
Umkumiute	277
Unalakleet	277
Unalaska	278
Unga	278
Upper Kalskag	278
Venetie	278
Wainwright	280
Wales	281
White Mountain	282

Woody Island	283
Wrangell	283
Yakutat	284

ARIZONA

Ak-Chin Reservation	287
Camp Verde Yavapai-Apache Reservation	288
Cocopah Indian Reservation	292
Colorado River Indian Tribes Reservation	294
Fort Apache Indian Reservation	298
Honoring Nations Honoree 2000	301
Fort McDowell Yavapai Nation	303
Fort Mojave Reservation	304
Fort Yuma-Quechan Tribe Reservation	305
Gila River Reservation	306
Honoring Nations Honoree 2002	309
Havasupai Reservation	314
Hopi Reservation	316
Honoring Nations Honoree 2000	320
Hualapai Indian Reservation	322
Kaibab Paiute Indian Reservation	324
Navajo Nation	326
Honoring Nations Honoree 1999	334
Honoring Nations Honoree 1999	335
Honoring Nations Honoree 2000	336
Honoring Nations Honoree 2002	339
Pascua Yaqui Reservation	342
Salt River Pima-Maricopa Indian Community	344
San Carlos Apache Reservation	347
Honoring Nations Honoree 2000	350
San Juan Southern Paiute Council	351
Tohono O'odham Reservation	352
Tonto Apache Reservation	354
Yavapai-Prescott Reservation	356
Zuni Pueblo (see NM)	357

CALIFORNIA

Introduction	359
Agua Caliente Indian Reservation	363
Alturas Rancheria	365
Augustine Reservation	365
Barona Band of Mission Indians Reservation	366
Benton Paiute Reservation	369
Berry Creek Rancheria of Maidu Indians	370
Big Bend Rancheria	371
Big Lagoon Rancheria	371
Big Pine Reservation	373
Big Sandy Rancheria Band of Western Mono Indians	374
Big Valley Rancheria	376
Bishop Reservation	378
Blue Lake Rancheria	380
Bridgeport Reservation	382
Buena Vista Rancheria	383
Cabazon Reservation	384
Cahuilla Reservation	386
California Valley Miwok Tribe	387
Campo Reservation	388
Capitan Grande Reservation	390
Cedarville Rancheria	390
Chemehuevi Reservation	391
Chicken Ranch Rancheria	393
Chico Rancheria	394
Cloverdale Rancheria of Pomo Indians	395
Cold Springs Rancheria	396

Colorado River Tribe (see AZ)	
Cachil DeHe Band of Wintun Indians of the Colusa Indian Community	397
Cortina Indian Rancheria	398
Coyote Valley Band of Pomo Indians Reservation	400
Honoring Nations Honoree 2002	402
Cuyapaipe Reservation (see Ewiiaapaayp, CA)	
Dry Creek Rancheria	403
Elem Indian Colony	404
Elk Valley Rancheria	406
Enterprise Rancheria	408
Ewiiaapaayp Indian Reservation	409
Fort Bidwell Reservation	410
Fort Independence Paiute Reservation	411
Fort Mojave Reservation	412
Fort Yuma (see AZ)	
Graton Rancheria	415
Greenville Rancheria	416
Grindstone Indian Rancheria	417
Guidiville Rancheria	418
Hoopa Valley Reservation	419
Hopland Reservation	422
Inaja-Cosmit Reservation	424
Ione Band of Miwok Indians	425
Jackson Rancheria	426
Jamul Indian Village	427
Karuk	428
La Jolla Reservation	430
La Posta Reservation	431
Laytonville Rancheria	432
Likely Rancheria	434
Lone Pine Reservation	434
Lookout Rancheria	435
Los Coyotes Reservation	436
Lower Lake Rancheria	437
Manchester Point Arena Rancheria	438
Manzanita Reservation	439
Mesa Grande Reservation	440
Middletown Rancheria	441
Montgomery Creek Rancheria	442
Mooretown Rancheria	443
Morongo Reservation	444
North Fork Rancheria of Mono Indians	446
Pala Reservation	447
Paskenta Band of Nomlaki Indians Rancheria	448
Pauma and Yuima Reservation	449
Pechanga Reservation	450
Picayune Rancheria	452
Pinoleville Rancheria	453
Pit River Tribes	454
Potter Valley Rancheria	455
Quartz Valley Indian Community	456
Ramona Reservation	457
Redding Rancheria	458
Redwood Valley Rancheria	459
Resighini Rancheria	460
Rincon Reservation	461
Roaring Creek Rancheria	463
Robinson Rancheria	463
Bear River Band of the Rohnerville Rancheria	465
Round Valley Indian Reservation	466
Rumsey Indian Rancheria	468
San Manuel Reservation	470

San Pasqual Reservation ... 472
Santa Rosa Rancheria ... 473
Santa Rosa Reservation ... 474
Santa Ynez Reservation ... 475
Santa Ysabel Reservation ... 477
Scotts Valley Band of Pomo Indians
   of the Sugar Bowl Rancheria ... 478
Sheep Ranch Rancheria
   (see California Valley Miwok Tribe)
Sherwood Valley Rancheria ... 479
Shingle Springs Rancheria ... 481
Smith River Rancheria ... 482
Soboba Band of Luiseño Indians ... 484
Sulpher Bank *(see Elem Indian Reservation)*
Susanville Indian Rancheria ... 485
Sycuan Rancheria ... 487
Table Bluff Reservation ... 489
Table Mountain Rancheria ... 490
Timbisha Shoshone Reservation ... 491
Torres Martinez Reservation ... 492
Trinidad Rancheria ... 493
Tule River Reservation ... 495
Tuolumne Rancheria ... 496
Twenty-Nine Palms Reservation ... 498
United Auburn Indian Community ... 498
Upper Lake Rancheria ... 500
Viejas Reservation ... 501
   Honoring Nations Honoree 2002 ... 504
Washoe Reservation *(see NV)*
X-L Ranch Reservation ... 506
Yurok Reservation ... 506

COLORADO
Southern Ute Reservation ... 509
Ute Mountain Ute Reservation ... 512

CONNECTICUT
Mashantucket Pequot Reservation ... 517
Mohegan Indian Reservation ... 519

FLORIDA
Introduction ... 523
Big Cypress Reservation ... 526
Brighton Reservation ... 527
Fort Pierce Reservation ... 528
Hollywood Reservation ... 528
Immokalee Reservation ... 529
Miccosukee Reservation ... 530
Poarch Creek Reservation
   (see Poarch Creek Reservation, AL)
Tampa Reservation ... 531

IDAHO
Coeur d'Alene Reservation ... 533
Duck Valley Reservation
   (see Duck Valley, NV)
   Honoring Nations Honoree 1999 ... 537
Fort Hall Reservation ... 538
Kootenai Reservation ... 542
Nez Perce Reservation ... 544
   Honoring Nations Honoree 1999 ... 547

IOWA
Sac & Fox Reservation ... 549

KANSAS
Iowa Reservation ... 551
Kickapoo Reservation ... 552
Prairie Band Potawatomi Reservation ... 554
Sac and Fox Reservation ... 557

LOUSIANA
Chitimacha Reservation ... 559
Coushatta Reservation ... 561
Jena Band of Choctaw Reservation ... 562
Tunica-Biloxi Reservation ... 563

MAINE
Passamaquoddy Tribe
   of Maine Introduction ... 565
Aroostook Band of Micmac Indians ... 566
Houlton Maliseet Reservation ... 569
Indian Township Reservation ... 571
Penobscot Reservation ... 572
Pleasant Point Reservation ... 575

MASSACHUSETTS
Gay Head Reservation ... 577

MICHIGAN
Bay Mills Chippewa Reservation ... 581
Grand Traverse Reservation ... 583
   Honoring Nations Honoree 1999 ... 585
   Honoring Nations Honoree 2000 ... 585
Hannahville Reservation ... 586
Pine Creek ... 588
Isabella Reservation ... 590
Lac Vieux Desert Reservation ... 592
L'anse Reservation (Keweenaw Bay) ... 593
Little River Band of Ottawa Indians ... 595
Little Traverse Bay Bands Reservation ... 597
Match-E-Be-Nash-She-Wish ... 599
Pokagon Band of Potawatomi Indians ... 600
Sault Ste. Marie Reservation ... 602

MINNESOTA
Bois Forte Reservation ... 605
Fond du Lac Reservation ... 607
   Honoring Nations Honoree 1999 ... 609
   Honoring Nations Honoree 2000 ... 610
Grand Portage Reservation ... 611
Leech Lake Reservation ... 613
Lower Sioux Reservation ... 617
Mille Lacs Reservation ... 619
   Honoring Nations Honoree 1999 ... 623
   Honoring Nations Honoree 2000 ... 624
Prairie Island Community ... 625
Red Lake Band Reservation ... 627
Shakopee Reservation (Prior Lake) ... 630
Upper Sioux Reservation ... 632
White Earth Reservation ... 635
   Honoring Nations Honoree 2000 ... 639

MISSISSIPPI
Choctaw Reservation ... 643
   Honoring Nations Honoree 1999 ... 644
   Honoring Nations Honoree 2003 ... 645
   Honoring Nations Honoree 2003 ... 647

MONTANA
Blackfeet Reservation ... 649
Crow Reservation ... 653
Flathead Reservation ... 655
   Honoring Nations Honoree 2003 ... 659
Fort Belknap Reservation 661
Fort Peck Reservation ... 664
Northern Cheyenne Reservation ... 667
Rocky Boy's Reservation ... 670

NEBRASKA
Iowa Reservation *(see Iowa Reservation, KS)*
Omaha Reservation ... 673
Pine Ridge Reservation
   (see Pine Ridge, SD)
Ponca Tribe of Nebraska ... 675
Sac and Fox Reservation
   (see Sac and Fox, KS)
Santee Sioux Nation ... 676
Winnebago Nebraska Reservation ... 677
   Honoring Nations Honoree 2000 ... 681

NEVADA
Battle Mountain Reservation ... 683
Carson Colony ... 684
Dresslerville Colony ... 685
Duck Valley Reservation ... 686
Duckwater Reservation ... 689
Elko Colony ... 690
Ely Shoshone Reservation ... 691
Fallon Colony and Reservation 692
Fort McDermitt Reservation ... 694
Goshute Pauite Tribe of Utah
   and Nevada *(see Goshute, UT)*
Las Vegas Colony and Reservation ... 696
Lovelock Colony ... 697
Moapa River Reservation ... 698
Pyramid Lake Reservation ... 700
Reno-Sparks Colony ... 702
South Fork Reservation ... 704
Stewart Indian Colony ... 705
Summit Lake Reservation ... 705
Te-Moak Tribe of Western Shoshone ... 706
Walker River Reservation ... 707
Washoe Reservation ... 709
Wells Band Colony ... 711
Winnemucca Colony ... 712
Woodfords Colony ... 713
Yerington Colony and Reservation ... 714
Yomba Colony ... 715

NEW MEXICO
Acoma Pueblo ... 717
Alamo Reservation ... 719
Cañoncito Reservation
   (see To'Hajiilee Reservation)
Cochiti Pueblo ... 720
Isleta Pueblo ... 722
Jemez Pueblo ... 724
Jicarilla Apache Reservation ... 727
   Honoring Nations Honoree 1999 ... 733
Laguna Pueblo ... 734
Mescalero Apache Reservation ... 736
Nambé Pueblo ... 738
Navajo Reservation *(see Navajo, AZ)*

Picuris Pueblo   741
Pojoaque Pueblo   743
    Honoring Nations Honoree 2000   745
Ramah Pueblo   746
San Felipe Pueblo   748
San Ildefonso Pueblo   750
San Juan Pueblo   752
Sandia Pueblo   753
    Honoring Nations Honoree 1999   756
Santa Ana Pueblo   756
Santa Clara Pueblo   759
Santo Domingo Pueblo   761
Taos Pueblo   762
Tesuque Pueblo   764
To'Hajiilee Reservation
    (formerly Cañoncito Navajo)   766
Ute Mountain Reservation
    (see Ute Mountain, CO)
Zia Pueblo   767
Zuni Pueblo   769
    Honoring Nations Honoree 2002   771
    Honoring Nations Honoree 2003   773

NEW YORK
Seneca Nation Introduction   775
Allegany Reservation   777
Cattaraugus Reservation   778
Cayuga Nation   779
Oil Springs Reservation   780
Oneida Reservation   780
Onondaga Reservation   782
St. Regis Mohawk Reservation   784
Tonawanda Reservation   787
Tuscarora Nation   788

NORTH CAROLINA
Eastern Band of Cherokee
    Indians Reservation   789
Honoring Nations Honoree 1999   790

NORTH DAKOTA
Fort Berthold Indian Reservation   793
Lake Traverse Reservation
    (see Lake Traverse, SD)
Spirit Lake (formerly Devil's Lake
    Sioux Reservation)   796
Standing Rock Reservation
    (see Standing Rock, SD)
Turtle Mountain Reservation
    and Trenton Indian Service Area   799

OKLAHOMA
Absentee-Shawnee Tribe   803
Alabama-Quassarte Tribal Town   804
Apache Tribe of Oklahoma   806
Caddo Tribe   807
Cherokee Nation   808
    Honoring Nations Honoree 2002   813
    Honoring Nations Honoree 2003   815
Cheyenne-Arapaho Reservation   816
Chickasaw Nation   818
    Honoring Nations Honoree 2003   822
Choctaw Nation of Oklahoma   824
Citizen Band Potawatomi   828
Comanche Tribe of Oklahoma   831
Creek (Muskogee) Nation   834

Delaware Reservation   837
Eastern Shawnee Reservation   838
Fort Sill Apache Tribe   840
Iowa Reservation   842
Kaw Tribe of Oklahoma   847
Kickapoo Tribe of Oklahoma   850
Kiowa Indian Tribe of Oklahoma   851
Miami Tribe of Oklahoma   852
Modoc Tribe of Oklahoma   853
Osage Reservation   854
Otoe-Missouri Reservation   858
Ottawa Tribe   859
Pawnee Tribe   861
Peoria Tribe of Oklahoma   863
Ponca Reservation   865
Quapaw Tribe of Oklahoma   866
Sac and Fox Reservation   868
Seminole Tribe of Oklahoma   869
Seneca-Cayuga Tribe of Oklahoma   871
Thlopthlocco Tribal Town   872
Tonkawa Tribe of Oklahoma   874
United Keetoowah Band of Cherokee   875
Western Delaware   877
Wichita Tribe   878
Wyandotte Reservation   880

OREGON
Burns Paiute Reservation   883
Celilo Village   884
Confederated Tribes of Coos,
    Lower Umpqua, and Siuslaw Indians 885
Coquille Indian Tribal Community   887
    Honoring Nations Honoree 2002   890
Cow Creek   892
Fort McDermitt (see Fort McDermitt, NV)
Grand Ronde Reservation   893
    Honoring Nations Honoree 2002   897
Klamath Reservation   898
Siletz Reservation   901
Umatilla Reservation   904
Warm Springs Reservation   907

RHODE ISLAND
Narrangansett Reservation   911

SOUTH CAROLINA
Catawba Reservation   913

SOUTH DAKOTA
Cheyenne River Sioux Reservation   915
    Honoring Nations Honoree 1999   919
Crow Creek Sioux Reservation   920
Flandreau Santee Sioux Reservation   922
Lake Traverse Reservation   924
Lower Brule Reservation   926
Pine Ridge Reservation   931
Rosebud Reservation   934
    Honoring Nations Honoree 1999   936
Standing Rock Reservation   937
Yankton Reservation   940

TEXAS
Alabama-Coushatta Reservation   943
Kickapoo Reservation   945
Tigua (see Ysleta del Sur Pueblo, TX)
Ysleta del Sur Pueblo (formerly Tigua) 947

UTAH
Goshute Reservation   949
Navajo Reservation (see Navajo, AZ)
Paiute Reservation (Shivwits, Cedar City,
    and Kanosh Reservations)   951
Skull Valley Reservation   952
Uintah & Ouray Reservation   954
Ute Mountain (see Ute Mountain, CO)
Washakie Indian Reservation
    (Northwestern Band of Shoshoni)   957

WASHINGTON
Chehalis Reservation   959
Colville Reservation   961
Cowlitz   964
Hoh Reservation   965
Jamestown Reservation   966
Kalispel Reservation   969
Lower Elwha Reservation   971
Lummi Reservation   973
    Honoring Nations Honoree 2002   976
Makah Reservation   978
Muckleshoot Indian Reservation   981
Nisqually Reservation   983
Nooksack Reservation   984
Port Gamble Reservation   985
Port Madison Reservation   987
Puyallup Reservation   989
    Honoring Nations Honoree 1999   992
Quileute Reservation   993
Quinault Reservation   996
Samish Indian Tribe   1000
Sauk-Suiattle Reservation   1001
Shoalwater Bay Reservation   1002
Skokomish Reservation   1003
Snoqualmie Tribe   1005
Spokane Reservation   1008
Squaxin Island Reservation   1011
Stillaguamish Reservation   1013
Swinomish Reservation   1015
    Honoring Nations Honoree 2000   1018
Tulalip Reservation   1020
    Honoring Nations Honoree 2003   1023
Upper Skagit Reservation   1024
Yakama Reservation   1026
    Honoring Nations Honoree 2002   1029

WISCONSIN
Bad River Reservation   1031
Forest County Potawatomi Reservation   1033
Ho-Chunk Reservation   1035
Lac Courte Oreilles Ojibwa Reservation 1038
    Honoring Nations Honoree 2003   1040
Lac du Flambeau Reservation   1042
Menominee Reservation   1046
    Honoring Nations Honoree 2003   1049
Mole Lake Reservation   1051
Oneida Reservation   1053
Red Cliff Reservation   1057
St. Croix Chippewa Reservation   1059
Stockbridge-Munsee Reservation   1062

WYOMING
Wind River Reservation   1065

MAPS

Alaska	40
Arizona	286
California	358
Florida	522
Idaho	532
Iowa	548
Michigan	580
Nebraska	672
New Mexico	716
North Dakota	792
Oklahoma	802
Oregon	882

PHOTOGRAPHS

AL-FrtPage,	1
Courtesy of National Park Service	
AL-FrtPg	3
AK-FrtPg, duplicate photo	41
TRI-AZ-frontpage-001	287
TRI-AZ-1143 Yavapai-Apache Bldg.	290
TRI-AZ-1153 Cliff Castle Casino	290
TRI-AZ-1155 Native Visions Office	290
TRI-AZ-1148 Yavapai Veteran Memorial	291
TRI-AZ-1159 Road to Tribal headquarters	291
TRI-AZ-1 Sunrise at Blue Water Casino	296
TRI-AZ-2 Blue Water Casino Hotel	296
TRI-AZ-7 Colo. River Bldg. Materials	296
TRI-AZ-10 Blue Water Casino	296
TRI-AZ-0014 CRIT headquarters	296
TRI-AZ-0022 Marina, Blue Water Casino	296
TRI-AZ-0023 Marina, Blue Water Casino	296
TRI-AZ-5 CRIT Farmlands	297
TRI-AZ-6 CRIT Farmlands	297
TRI-AZ-9 Colo. River Sand & Rock Co.	297
TRI-AZ-0013 Private hay field	297
TRI-AZ-1071 CRIT Sand & Rock Co.	297
TRI-AZ-1072 CRIT Sand & Rock Co.	297
TRI-AZ-1093 Ahkhav Preserve	297
TRI-AZ-1263 Canadian truck at FATCO	300
TRI-AZ-1252 Fort Apache Timber Co.	300
TRI-AZ-1186 Hon-Dah Casino & Resort	300
TRI-AZ-1184 Hon-Dah Sport	300
TRI-AZ-1210 Traditional Apache camp	300
TRI-AZ-1246 Fort Apache Timber Co.	300
TRI-AZ-1239 Fort Apache Timber Co.	300
TRI-AZ-046 Havasupai community	315
TRI-AZ-044 Helicopter at Havasupai	315
TRI-AZ-055 Havasupai Lodge	315
TRI-AZ-051 C. Harrison & helicopter	315
TRI-AZ-078 Mule train	315
TRI-AZ-081 Mule train	315
TRI-AZ-084 Sign on rim of canyon	315
TRI-AZ-058 Home at Havasupai	316
TRI-AZ-060 Towering cliffs	316
TRI-AZ-064 Navajo Falls	316
TRI-AZ-028 Open range on Route 66	323
TRI-AZ-030 Clinic at Hualapai	323
TRI-AZ-001 Hualapai Lodge	323
TRI-AZ-002 Hualapai Lodge	323
TRI-AZ-NJ-001 Navajo Museum	330
TRI-AZ-008 Navajo Council Chambers	330
TRI-AZ-009 Karigan Office Complex	330
TRI-AZ-026 View, Navajo Reservation	331
TRI-AZ-019 View, Navajo Reservation	331
TRI-AZ-004 Hogan at Navajo Museum	331

TRI-AZ-1165 Tribal Admin. bldg.	355
TRI-AZ-1175 Casino sign at Fort Apache	355
TRI-AZ-1180 The Mazatzai Casino	355
TRI-CA-FRONTPAGE-2A	359
TRI-CA-001 Heritage Plaza	364
TRI-CA-002 Sign, Agua Caliente Casino	364
TRI-CA-002-B Tribal Museum	368
TRI-CA-003 Tribal Office	368
TRI-CA-005 Scene near Big Valley	377
TRI-CA-006 Sign Konocti Vista Casino	377
TRI-CA-007 Blue Lake Alpine Casino	381
TRI-CA-008 Blue Lake's Transit Bus	381
TRI-CA-009 Blue Lake Tribal Building	381
TRI-CA-005-Cz Cabazon Cultural Museum	385
TRI-CA-006-Clla Cahuilla Tribal Office	386
TRI-CA-007-Clla Cahuilla Creek Casino	386
TRI-CA-008-Cp Campo Tribal Office	389
TRI-CA-017 Cortina Rancheria Sign	398
TRI-CA-018 Cortina's Tribal Office	399
TRI-CA-019 Coyote Valley Police Dept.	401
TRI-CA-020 Coyote Valley Logo on truck	401
TRI-CA-021 Elk Valley Casino	407
TRI-CA-022 Tribal Office Building	407
TRI-CA-009-E Administration Building	410
TRI-CA-010-E So. Indian Health Clinic	410
TRI-CA-027 Welcome sign to Hoopa	421
TRI-CA-028 Hoopa River	421
TRI-CA-029 Hoopa Tribal Bldg.	421
TRI-CA-030 Hoopa Valley Fire Department	421
TRI-CA-031 Hopland School	423
TRI-CA-032 Hopland Tribal Offices	423
TRI-CA-033 Hopland Tribal Police Car	423
TRI-CA-011-J Jamul Tribal Office	428
TRI-CA-012-J Jamul Fire Station	428
TRI-CA-013-LJ LaJolla Trading Post	431
TRI-CA-014-LJ La Jolla Race Track	431
TRI-CA-016-LC Los Coyotes Sign	437
TRI-CA-041 Middletown Tribal Building	441
TRI-CA-042 Twin Pine Casino	441
TRI-CA-017-R Sign for Anza Valley Center	457
TRI-CA-046 Resighini Tribal Office	461
TRI-CA-019-R Rincon Casino and Resort	462
TRI-CA-R-020-R Harrah's in Valley Center	462
TRI-CA-050 Sign for Robinson Rancheria	464
TRI-CA-051 Expansion of Robinson Casino	464
TRI-CA-052 View of Clear Lake	464
TRI-CA-053 Loleta Union Elem. School	466
TRI-CA-054 Loleta Family Fun Day	466
TRI-CA-055 Sign at Tribal Complex	467
TRI-CA-056 Round Valley Health Clinic	467
TRI-CA-057 Parking at Casino Hotel	469
TRI-CA-058 Cache Creek Mini Mart	469
TRI-CA-059 Rumsey Tribal Building	469
TRI-CA-060 Vineyards at Casino	469
TRI-CA-SY-022 Sign for Health Center	477
TRI-CA-SY-023 Youth Complex	477
TRI-CA-063 Table Bluff Office Bldg.	489
TRI-CA-064 Sign for Table Bluff	489
TRI-CA-065 Northern Coast Inn	494
TRI-CA-066 Pacific Ocean Highway	494
TRI-CA-067 Pier at Seascape Restaurant	494
TRI-CA-068 Cher-AE Heights Casino	494
TRI-CA-29Pm-026 29 Palms Casino	498
TRI-CA-29Pm-025 29 Palms logo	498
TRI-CA-Vj-030 Viejas Outlet Mall	503
TRI-CA-Vj-029 Viejas Outlet Center sign	503

TRI-CA-075 Sign at Weitchpec	508
TRI-CA-076 Riverview at Weitchpec	508
TRI-CA-077 Yurok Tribal Office	508
TRI-CA-078 Klamath River	508
TRI-CO-FRONTPAGE, Courtesy	509
of National Park Service	
TRI-CO-7 Leonard C. Burch Bldg.	511
TRI-CO-9 Inside Burch Tribal Bldg.	511
TRI-CO-11 Tribal Council Chambers	511
TRI-CO-13 Vietnam Memorial	511
TRI-CO-1A Tribal Office Complex	514
TRI-CO-6 Ute Mountain Casino	514
TRI-CO-12A Child Development Ctr.	514
TRI-CO-18A Chief Ignacio Justice Ctr.	514
TRI-CO-23A Ute Mtn. Travel Center	514
TRI-CT-FRONTPAGE	517
TRI-CT-14B Sculpture Foxwoods	518
TRI-CT-21A Foxwoods Resort Casino	518
TRI-CT-22B Pequot Museum	518
TRI-CT-23A Pequot Museum	518
TRI-CT-24A Police & Fire Dept.	518
TRI-CT-12A Foxwoods Casino	518
TRI-CT-11A Sculpture, Mohegan Sun	520
TRI-CT-14A Mohegan Sun Casino	520
TRI-CT-20A Sign, Mohegan Casino	520
TRI-CT-22A Mohegan Sun Casino	520
TRI-FL-FRONTPAGE	523
TRI-ID-FRONTPAGE	533
TRI-ID-002 Tribal Building Complex	535
TRI-ID-003 Display in front of Trading Post	535
TRI-ID-004 Wellness Center	535
TRI-ID-005 Casino Hotel	535
TRI-ID-006 Sign at Coeur D'Alene	535
TRI-ID-010 Shoshone Bannock Sch.	541
TRI-ID-011 Day Care Building	541
TRI-ID-012 Playground at Day Care	541
TRI-ID-014 Rodeo Grounds	541
TRI-ID-013 Trading Post 15	541
TRI-ID-015 Shoshone Bannock Casino	541
TRI-ID-016 Limestone Compound	546
TRI-ID-009 Nez Perce logo	546
TRI-ID-008 Appaloosa Stallion	546
TRI-ID-007 PI-NEE-WAUS Center	546
TRI-ID-006 Housing Authority Sign	546
TRI-IA-FrontPage	549
TRI-KS-Frontpage	551
TRI-KS-051 Signs to White-Cloud	552
TRI-KS-052 Iowa Tribe sign	552
TRI-KS-041 Kickapoo Truck Plaza	553
TRI-KS-043 Gaming Comm. office	553
TRI-KS-046 Kickapoo Health Center	553
TRI-KS-048 Kickapoo Headstart Bus	553
TRI-KS-024 Prairie Band Casino	555
TRI-KS-032 Prairie Band Casino	555
TRI-LA-FrtPg2, Copyright LA	559
Office of Tourism	
TRI-ME-FRONTPG	565
TRI-ME-1741 View of Aroostook	567
TRI-ME-1743 Tribal offices	567
TRI-ME-1745 Tribal Administrator	567
TRI-ME-1749 Daycare classroom	567
TRI-ME-1753 Penobscot Hall	567
TRI-ME-1765 Aroostook Tribal bldg.	567
TRI-ME-1763 Canoe at museum	568
TRI-ME-1766 Micmac Health Dept.	568
TRI-ME-1767 Micmac Health Clinic	568

TRI-ME-1769 Clinic exercise room	568	MS-FrtPg, Courtesy of National Park Service	641	TRI-NV-018 Mercedes-Benz dealership	703
TRI-ME-1795 View of Micmac Clinic	568	MT-Frontpg	649	TRI-NV-020 South Fork Hay field	704
TRI-ME-1804 Maliseet office sign	569	TRI-MT-001 Welcome sign	650	TRI-NV-021 So. Fork Admin. Bldg.	704
TRI-ME-1858 River on reservation	569	TRI-MT-002 Native Am. National Bk	650	TRI-NV-022 Cattle on Colony lands	704
TRI-ME-1809 Maliseet Tribal office	570	TRI-MT-003 View of College	650	TRI-NV-023 Sign for Taxation Dept.	708
TRI-ME-1826 Maliseet Health Clinic	570	TRI-MT-004 Siyeh Development, Inc.	650	TRI-NV-024 Agai Dicutta Senior Ctr.	708
TRI-ME-1829 Maliseet Housing office	570	TRI-MT-005 Blackfeet Heritage Center	650	TRI-NV-025 Taxation Dept. Bldg.	708
TRI-ME-1844 Old school bus	570	TRI-MT-006 Tepees at fairgrounds	650	TRI-NV-026Walker River School	708
TRI-ME-1989 Indian Township Bldg.	571	TRI-MT-007 Sign for Tribal Building	654	TRI-NV-027 Sign for Washoe Hdqtrs.	710
TRI-ME-1990 Indian Township sign	571	TRI-MT-008 Veterans Memorial Park	654	TRI-NV-035 View of reservation	710
TRI-ME-2031 Daycare Center	571	TRI-MT-009 Apsaalooke Visitors Ctr.	654	TRI-NV-035 Wells Colony Housing	712
TRI-ME-2041 Indian Township Clinic	571	TRI-MT-010 Little Big Horn Casino	654	TRI-NV-029 Winnemucca Smoke Shop	712
TRI-ME-2043 Forest Department office	571	TRI-MT-011 Ihkasahpua Seven Stars	654	TRI-NV-030 Sign tribal enterprises	714
TRI-ME-2002 Creative Apparel workers	572	TRI-MT-012 Welcome sign at Flathead	657	TRI-NV-032 Sign Arrowhead Market	714
TRI-ME-2007 Assembling apparel	572	TRI-MT-013 Salish Kootenai College	657	TRI-NV-033 Arrowhead Market	714
TRI-ME-2020 Creative Apparel's bldg.	572	TRI-MT-014 Metal Statue of Eagle	657	TRI-NV-034 Alfalfa fields	714
TRI-ME-1867 Penobscot Tribal bldg.	574	TRI-MT-016 Dome of tribal bldg.	657	TRI-NM-Frtpg	717
TRI-ME-1893 Penobscot Police dept.	574	TRI-MT-017 Old Tribal Office Complex	657	TRI-NM-Co-001 Marina, Cochiti Lake	721
TRI-ME-1895 Penobscot fire truck	574	TRI-MT-018 View of Flathead Lake	658	TRI-NM-Co-004 Cochiti Golf Course	721
TRI-ME-1896 Tribal Court sign	574	TRI-MT-020 Hydroelectric power plant	658	TRI-NM-Is-001 View of Isleta Lakes	723
TRI-ME-1921 Water system construction	574	TRI-MT-021 Kerr Dam & MT Power Co.	658	TRI-NM-Is-002 Isleta Church	723
TRI-ME-1935 Canoe crafting art studio	574	TRI-MT-023 Welcome, Ft. Belknap	662	TRI-NM-Jz-016 Scenic view on Highway 25	725
TRI-ME-1943 Penobscot canoe	574	TRI-MT-024 Meat Packing Co.	662	TRI-NM-Jz-009 Outside Indian Oven	725
TRI-ME-1945 Passamaquoddy Tribal bldg.	575	TRI-MT-025 KGBA 88.1 FM	662	TRI-NM-Jz-003 Walatowa Visitor Center	725
TRI-ME-1949 Totem pole	575	TRI-MT-026 Kwik Stop	662	TRI-NM-Jz-005 Mural at Walatowa Center	725
TRI-ME-1956 School	575	TRI-MT-027 Seal inside Council	662	TRI-NM-Jz-013 Wood cutting equipment	725
TRI-ME-1985 Gas station and gift shop	575	TRI-MT-028 Ft. Belknap College	662	TRI-NM-Jz-010 Walatowa Woodlands Yard	725
TRI-ME-1975 Wapanahki Museum	575	TRI-MT-029 Ft. Peck Museum	665	TRI-NM-Jz-018 Future airport site	726
TRI-ME-1971 Pleasant Point Health Clinic	576	TRI-MT-030 Adm. & College Bldgs.	665	TRI-NM-Jz-015 Metal Building	726
TRI-ME-1981 Oceanview of reservation	576	TRI-MT-031 Buildings on Hilltop	665	TRI-NM-jan-026 Ishoteen Jud. Complex	728
TRI-ME-1982 Boys & Girls club sign	576	TRI-MT-032 West Electronics, Inc.	665	TRI-NM-jan-023 Dulce Fire Dept.	728
TRI-ME-1965 Tribal court chambers	576	TRI-MT-033 West Electronics, Inc.	665	TRI-NM-jan-029 Dulce School Bldg.	728
TRI-MA-FrtPg	577	TRI-MT-034 A & S Industries, Inc.	665	TRI-NM-jan-028 Senior Citizen Building	728
TRI-MA-0448 Wampanoag Tribal bldg.	578	TRI-MT-043 Lame Deer High School	668	TRI-NM-jan-025 Jicarilla Student Residence	729
TRI-MA-0450 Housing & playground	578	TRI-MT-036 Law Enforcement Ctr.	668	TRI-NM-jan-027 Ishoteen Jud. Complex	729
TRI-MA-0451 Tribal housing	578	TRI-MT-037 Law Enforcement Ctr.	668	TRI-NM-jan-031 Jicarilla Supermarket	729
TRI-MA-0452 Tribal housing	578	TRI-MT-038 No. Cheyenne Health Ctr.	668	TRI-NM-jan-033 Best Western-Jicarilla Inn	729
TRI-MI-FrtPg, Courtesy	581	TRI-MT-039 Sign Rocky Boy	671	TRI-NM-jan-035 Dulce Elementary School	731
of National Park Service		TRI-MT-040 Chippewa Operations	671	TRI-NM-jan-036 Sign Dulce Elem. Sch.	731
MN-FrtPg2	605	TRI-MT-041 Rocky Boy College	671	TRI-NM-jan-038 Health Care Facility	731
TRI-MN-FL-130 Black Bear Casino	609	TRI-MT-042 Rocky Boy Utility Bldg.	671	TRI-NM-jan-024 Sign Student Residence	731
TRI-MN-FL-129 Black Bear Casino	609	NE-FrtPg3	673	TRI-NM-jan-042 Dulce Athletic Complex	732
TRI-MN-LL-003 No. Lights Casino	616	TRI-NE-SSx-004 Ohiya Casino	677	TRI-NM-jan-049 Apache Nugget Casino	732
TRI-MN-LL-002 Leech Lake Casino	616	TRI-NE-SSx-081 Pony Express sign	677	TRI-NM-jan-041 Jicarilla Child Dev. Ctr.	732
TRI-MN-LL-001 Busn. Corp. Leech Lk.	616	TRI-NE-SSx-075 Tribal Court office	677	TRI-NM-jan-051 Gas Well	732
TRI-MN-LSx-244 Sign, Lower Sioux	618	TRI-NE-SSx-080 Pony Express gas station	677	TRI-NM-jan-003 Buffalos at Chama Ranch	732
TRI-MN-LSx-243 Lower Sioux Comm.	618	TRI-NE-001 Winnebago Veterans Hdqtrs.	680	TRI-NM-jan-004 Buffalos at Chama Ranch	732
TRI-MN-LSx-247 Water Tower with logo	618	TRI-NE-002 Winnebago Headstart	680	TRI-NM-Lg-003 Route 66 Travel center	735
TRI-MN-LSx-246 Car window view	618	TRI-NE-003 Winnebago Health Bldg.	680	TRI-NM-Lg-014 Route 66 Casino	735
TRI-MN-ML-116 Grand Casino sign	622	TRI-NE-004 View of Winnebago Sch.	680	TRI-NM-Lg-005 Travel Center	735
TRI-MN-ML-121 Mille Lacs Museum	622	TRI-NE-005 Sign for Police Dept.	680	TRI-NM-Mes-005 Lake view of golf course	737
TRI-MN-ML-113 Grand Market	622	TRI-NV-Frontpage	683	TRI-NM-Mes-007 Inn of the Mountain Gods	737
TRI-MN-ML-124 Woodlands Nat'l Bk.	622	TRI-NV-001 Battle Mtn. Smoke Shop	684	TRI-NM-Mes-006 Golf ball with logo	737
TRI-MN-PI-001 Treasure Is. Casino	627	TRI-NV-002 Carson Youth Center	685	TRI-NM-Nb-002 Nambe Falls Rec. Area	739
TRI-MN-PI-002 Treasure Is. Casino	627	TRI-NV-005 Elko Band Adm. Bldg.	690	TRI-NM-Nb-003 Nambe sign	739
TRI-MN-RL-001 Reservation boundary	628	TRI-NV-006 Elko Smoke Shop	690	TRI-NM-Nb-004 Nambe Lake	740
TRI-MN-RL-002 Red Lake Supermarket	628	TRI-NV-007 Sign for Fallon Bldg.	693	TRI-NM-Nb-001 View of Nambe Lake	740
TRI-MN-RL-003 Red Lake Fisheries	629	TRI-NV-008 Vew of Fallon Headstart	693	TRI-NM-Poj-003 Poeh Museum	744
TRI-MN-RL-004 Tree Nursery	629	TRI-NV-009 Sign for Lovelock Offices	698	TRI-NM-Poj-004 Sign for the Poeh Center	744
TRI-MN-USx-006 Prairie Edge Casino	633	TRI-NV-010 Lovelock Rec. Center	698	TRI-NM-Poj-001 Gold Dust Restaurant	744
TRI-MN-USx-005 Prairie Edge Casino	633	TRI-NV-012 Numana Hatchery	701	TRI-NM-Poj-006 Pojoaque Supermarket	744
TRI-MN-USx-007 Statue of buffalo hunter	634	TRI-NV-013 Mural, Hatchery	701	TRI-NM-Poj-005 Cities of Gold Hotel view	744
TRI-MN-USx-008 Statue of buffalo hunter	634	TRI-NV-014 Tanks at Hatchery	701	TRI-NM-SFpe-001 Speedway near Casino	749
TRI-MN-WE-97 Shooting Star Casino	636	TRI-NV-015 Pyramid Lake Museum	701	TRI-NM-SFpe-003 Hollywood Speedway	749
TRI-MN-WE-99 Shooting Star Casino	636	TRI-NV-016 View of Pyramid Rock	701	TRI-NM-Si-076 Historic Marker	751
TRI-MN-WE-98 Shooting Star Casino	636	TRI-NV-017 Reno Smoke Shop	703	TRI-NM-Si-079 View of Black Mesa	751

TRI-NM-Si-073 Village houses & shops   751
TRI-NM-Si-080 Village at San Ildefonso   751
TRI-NM-Si-082 San Ildefonso Church   751
TRI-NM-Si-077 Kiva at San Ildefonso   751
TRI-NM-San-002 Hayfield scene   754
TRI-NM-San-003 Sandia Lakes   754
TRI-NM-San-004 Bien Mur Ind. Market   754
TRI-NM-San-005 Hotel construction   754
TRI-NM-Sa-007 Prairie Star Restaurant   758
TRI-NM-Sa-008 Entrance to Prairie Star   758
TRI-NM-Sa-004 Prairie Star Restaurant   758
TRI-NM-Sa-001 Santa Ana Golf Course   758
TRI-NM-Sa-005 Prairie Star at sunset   758
TRI-NM-Zia-001 Irrigated Cornfield   768
TRI-NY-FrtPg-082   775
TRI-NY-Oda-175 Oneida Office   782
TRI-NY-Oda-176 Oneida's SavOn   782
TRI-NY-Oda-177 Shako-wi-Cult. Ctr.   782
TRI-NY-Ono-173 Tsha'tton'nonyen'dak   783
TRI-NY-Ono-174 Sports Arena   783
TRI-NY-Moh-178 Site of Old Bingo   786
TRI-NY-Moh-179 View of Tribal Office   786
NC-FrtPg, Courtesy   789
    of National Park Service
TRI-ND-FrtPg   793
TRI-OK-FrtPg-2   803
TRI-OK-001 Tribal Police & trailer   808
TRI-OK-002 Hasinai Center   808
TRI-OK-003 Health Ctr., Tahlequah   810
TRI-OK-004 Children's Village   810
TRI-OK-005 Ga Du Gi Health Ctr.   810
TRI-OK-006 Early Childhood Unit   810
TRI-OK-007 Early Childhood Unit   810
TRI-OK-008 Bedre Choc. Factory   820
TRI-OK-009 Bedre Choc. Factory   820
TRI-OK-009a Jones Academy Dormitory   826
TRI-OK-011Firelake Conv. Store   830
TRI-OK-013 Cubs Den Day Care   841
TRI-OK-014 Cubs Den Day Care   841
TRI-OK-020 Wellness/Fitness Ctr.   844
TRI-OK-022 Voc. Rehabilitation Ctr.   844
TRI-OK-023 Multi-Purpose Bldg.   844
TRI-OK-029 Pow Wow Grounds   844
TRI-OK-038 Dept. of Transp.   851
TRI-OK-039 Wellness Center   859
TRI-OK-040 Trueman Learning Ctr.   859
TRI-OK-042 Pawnee Health Center   862
TRI-OK-043 Construction, Family Ctr.   862
TRI-OK-045 Safety Ctr. & Tribal Police   865
TRI-OK-046 Valdez Soc. Services Ctr.   865
TRI-OK-057 O-Gah-Pah school bus   867
TRI-OK-058 Quapaw Admin. Bldg.   867
TRI-OK-048 Wellness Center, Stroud   869
TRI-OK-049 Ind. Health Serv. Stroud   869
TRI-OK-050 Food Distribution   870
TRI-OK-051 Dialysis Center   870
TRI-OK-052 Emblem on water tower   873
TRI-OK-055 Casino & Conv. store   880
TRI-OK-056 Bearskin Healthcare Ctr.   880

TRI-OR-FrtPg   883
TRI-OR-001 Mill Casino & Hotel   889
TRI-OR-002 Mill Casino Hotel sign   889
TRI-OR-003 Cow Creek Offices sign   892
TRI-OR-004 Health and Wellness Center sign   894
TRI-OR-005 Welcome sign   894
TRI-OR-015 Gas station/convenience store   894
TRI-OR-006 Health and Wellness Center   894
TRI-OR-003B Educational Facility sign   895
TRI-OR-010 Veterans Memorial   895
TRI-OR-012 Spirit Mountain Casino   895
TRI-OR-011 Seal of Klamath Tribes   899
TRI-OR-012 Klamath Tribal Bldg.   899
TRI-OR-013 Mural in Tribal Bldg.   899
TRI-OR-014 Kla-Mo-Ya Casino   899
TRI-OR-015 Siletz Tribal Building   902
TRI-OR-016 Siletz Gas & Mini Mart   902
TRI-OR-018 Tepees at Pow-Wow   902
TRI-OR-019 Siletz Busn. Corp.   902
TRI-OR-017 Tenas Illahee Center   903
TRI-OR-020 Chinook Winds   903
TRI-OR-022 Umatilla Conv. Store   905
TRI-OR-025 Grain Pile & Shaft   905
TRI-OR-026 Wildhorse Resort   905
TRI-OR-024 Grain Pile & Shaft   906
TRI-OR-028 Wildhorse Golf Course   906
TRI-OR-028a Sign for Warm Spgs.   909
TRI-OR-029 Wm Spgs. Power Entrps.   909
TRI-OR-030 Wm Spgs. Forest Prod.   909
TRI-OR-033 Wm Spgs. Dam   909
TRI-RI-FrtPg, Courtesy   911
    of National Park Service
SC-FrontPg-1   913
SD-FrtPg-2   915
TRI-SD-cr-001 Cheyenne River Bldg.   917
TRI-SD-cr-002 Meat packing plant   917
TRI-SD-cc-003 Welcome sign   921
TRI-SD-cc-005 Lone Star Casino and Hotel   921
TRI-SD-LT-001 Sisseton-Sioux   925
    Wahpeton College
TRI-SD-lb-009 View, Missouri River   928
TRI-SD-lb-006a Community Center   928
TRI-SD-lb-007 Lower Brule Bldg.   928
TRI-SD-lb-008 Johnston Cultural Center   928
TRI-SD-lb-012 GSI Grain Silos   930
TRI-SD-lb-002b Game Dept.   930
TRI-SD-lb-014 Zimmatic Irrig. Equipment   930
TRI-SD-lb-015 Gravel Pit   930
TRI-SD-pr-009 Oglala historical marker   932
TRI-SD-pr-010 Big Crow Recreation Ctr.   932
TRI-SD-rd-013 Rosebud Casino   935
TRI-SD-rd-017 Rosebud Tribal Court   935
TRI-SD-rd-015 Rosebud Reservation   935
TRI-SD-rd-016 Rosebud Dam Sign   935
TRI-SD-sr-015 Standing Rock Service Ctr.   938
TRI-SD-sr-016 Prairie Knights Casino   938
TRI-SD-sr-017 Tesoro Gas Station   938
TRI-SD-sr-018 Sitting Bull   938
TRI-SD-yk-001 Sign, Yankton Sioux   942

TRI-SD-yk-002 Campus at Marty   942
TRI-SD-yk-004 School at Yankton   942
TRI-TX-Frontpage, Courtesy   943
    of National Park Service
TRI-UT-FrontPg   949
TRI-UT-001 Sign, Unitah-Ouray   955
TRI-UT-002 Ute Super Market   955
TRI-UT-003 Ute Gas Station   955
TRI-UT-004 Ute Manufacturing Co.   955
TRI-UT-005 Cattle Pen   955
TRI-WA-001 Kalispel Indian Res. sign   970
TRI-WA-002 Pow Wow facilities   970
TRI-WA-003 Buffalo herd   970
TRI-WA-004 Northern Quest Casino   971
TRI-WA-001a Quinault Indian Nation   999
    Resort and Casino
TRI-WA-002b Quinault Indian Nation   999
    Resort and Casino
TRI-WI-FrtPg   1031
TRI-WI-001 Bad River Bingo   1032
TRI-WI-004 Chief Blackbird Ctr.   1032
TRI-WI-FC-005 Sign forTribal Center   1034
TRI-WI-FC-006 Forest Cty. Wellness Ctr.   1034
TRI-WI-hc-007 Wa Ehi Hoci Court Bldg.   1037
TRI-WI-hc-008 Wa Ehi Hoci Court Ctr.   1037
TRI-WI-007 LCO Casino Lodge   1039
TRI-WI-011 LCO Quick Stop   1039
TRI-WI-012 LCO Comm. Ctr.   1039
TRI-WI-010 Fed. Credit Union   1039
TRI-WI-009 Welcome to LCO sign   1039
TRI-WI-LdF-167 Smoke Shop   1045
TRI-WI-LdF-171 Ojibwe Museum   1045
TRI-WI-LdF-172 Family Resource Ctr.   1045
TRI-WI-LdF-168 Recreation Van   1045
TRI-WI-Mn-021 Amphitheater   1048
TRI-WI-Mn-007 MTE   1048
TRI-WI-Mn-024 Wolf River   1048
TRI-WI-Mn-008 MTE   1048
TRI-WI-Mn-006 MTE   1048
TRI-WI-ML-124 Mole Lake sign   1053
TRI-WI-ML-123 Mole Lake Motel   1053
TRI-WI-Oda-127 Oneida Farms   1055
TRI-WI-Oda-126 Tribal Bldg.   1055
TRI-WI-Oda-125 Oneida Farms   1055
TRI-WI-026 Red Cliff Marina   1058
TRI-WI-028 Stockbridge Office   1063
TRI-WI-032 Little Star Store   1063
TRI-WI-031 Munsee Museum   1063
TRI-WI-030 Munsee Museum   1063
TRI-WI-033 North Star Casino   1063
TRI-WY-FrtPg, Courtesy   1065
    of National Park Service
TRI-WA-005 Spokane Reservation sign   1009
TRI-WA-006 Two Rivers Casino and Resort   1009
TRI-WA-007 Spokane Tribal Adm. Bldg.   1009
TRI-WA-008 Two Rivers Casino and Resort   1009
TRI-WA-009 Yakama Cultural Center sign   1028
TRI-WA-010 Yakama Cultural Center   1029
TRI-WA-011 Yakama Veterans Memorial   1029

This reference guide profiles by state the economy of every federally recognized Indian reservation in the United States. Wherever possible, this Guide has relied upon information provided by the Indian tribes regarding their land holdings; their culture and history; and their infrastructure and economic enterprises. This work is an update of the 1996 edition of Tiller's Guide to Indian Country. That work is the single most consulted and authoritative source of information on the Indian tribes of the contiguous 48 states and Alaska. This guide includes a few tribes who have not (as of 2004) established a tribal land base.

CONTACT INFORMATION
The format used here lists on the outside column on the first line of each profile the name of the reservation (where one exists). The second line provides the status of the reservation. The third line identifies the name of the tribal group(s) occupying the reservation. The third line identifies the county or counties in which the reservations are located. The next section has the tribe's address, telephone numbers and dedicated lines for facsimile transmission or reception, followed by the tribe's official web site and or web site that provides information about the tribe. The user is cautioned to verify these numbers periodically.

DEMOGRAPHIC INFORMATION
The next set of data displayed pertains to the extent of Indian land holdings on the reservation, and demographic information regarding the tribe(s) on the reservation. The information regarding land holdings was taken from either the U.S. Bureau of Indian Affairs statistics, or from the tribes themselves. The demographic data were taken mostly from the 2000 Decennial Report of the United States Bureau of the Census or from Labor Force Reports of the U.S. Bureau of Indian Affairs, except where a Tribe offered more current or more accurate information. The figures can vary and this guide provides the information and makes no claims to its absolute accuracy.

LOCATION AND LAND STATUS
The section on Location and Land Status situates each reservation geographically within the State. This section also describes such anomalies as non-contiguous reservation tracts and recently acquired lands, which may or may not (in 2004) have acquired reservation status. If all the land tenures described do not add up to the total reservation area, it is not necessarily a mistake. Tribes throughout the length and breadth of the country are disputing their jurisdictional areas, their off-reservation treaty-protected areas, and even ownership of large tracts of land. For instance, surveying errors of the 19th Century are still being corrected by the Congress and the courts of the United States in the late 20th Century. Thus, the brief history of the reservation lands in this section intimates no opinion regarding the ultimate resolution of such disputes, but describes the generally accepted view of the extent of Indian land holdings associated with each reservation. For states such as Alaska and California with peculiarly complex histories, supplemental information is provided as an aid to the user.

CULTURE AND HISTORY
Great efforts were made to enable Tribes to provide their own information regarding these aspects of their Tribal profiles. This section includes information on broad ethnohistories, historic linguistic groupings, and historic geographic ranges of the Tribe(s) occupying the present reservation. Here, too, special introductions on Alaska, California, Flordia, Maine, and New York have been included to avoid repetition of large numbers of similar histories.

GOVERNMENT
This section describes briefly the method by which the Tribe(s) of each reservation presently govern themselves, and their territories. Many Tribes provided far more detailed information than could be accommodated in a brief profile. For this edition, more detailed information on tribal departments have been added, as well as information on tribal business corporations.

ECONOMY
The economy of each reservation is described briefly, including information regarding agricultural and livestock, forestry, fisheries, gaming, construction, mining, industrial parks, manufacturing, services and retail, and tourism and recreational activity. New categories including finance/banking, insurance, media and communications, real estate and commercial development, and telecommunications, were added to accommodate economic sectors that were either not part of tribal economies or have become viable part of tribal economies since the 1996 edition was issued.

INFRASTRUCTURE AND COMMUNITY FACILITIES
These sections describe transportation, utility, and delivery services available to each reservation. Community facilities, including tribal governmental facilities, public meeting, recreational, and housing facilities are included. The sections on education and health were also given more attention in this edition.

MAPS
There are only 7 State maps included in this volume. Each of the tribes in the Lower 48 states have locator maps that point out the location within the state where they are located.

HONORING NATIONS
A special feature of this guide is the Honoring Contributions in the Governance of American Indian Nations (popularly known as Honoring Nations). This national awards program identifies, celebrates, and shares outstanding examples of tribal governance. Administered by the Harvard Project on American Indian Economic Development at Harvard's Kennedy School of Government, the program spotlights and awards tribal government programs and initiatives that are especially effective in addressing critical concerns and challenges facing the more than 560 Indian nations and their citizens. The Honorees from 1999 to 2003 were included to provide the reader with a wider perspective on Indian tribes, their government and its programs.

Photo Courtesy of National Park Service

Poarch Creek

LOCATION AND LAND STATUS

The Poarch Band of Creek Indians of Alabama Reservation is located in southwestern Alabama. Reservation lands are located approximately 56 miles northeast of Mobile.

The Tribe, the only federally recognized tribe in Alabama, obtained recognition April 12, 1985 with 228.47 acres of land in Escambia County, Alabama. The tribe also has holdings in other counties in Alabama and Florida.

CLIMATE

There is no climate data recorded for Atmore, Alabama; however, the reservation lands are less than 30 miles from Mobile. The year-round average daily high temperature in Mobile is 77°F, with the highest ever recorded, 104°F. The year-round average daily low temperature is 57°F, with the lowest on record being 3°F. The area receives approximately 66 inches of precipitation annually, with less than 1 inch falling as snow.

CULTURE AND HISTORY

The Creek Nation originally occupied a territory covering nearly all of Georgia and Alabama at least since the 1700s. The modern-day Poarch Band is a segment of the original Creek Nation. They have avoided removal for nearly 150 years.

The War of 1812 divided the Creek Nation into two factions, one which supported the new United States government and another that didn't. Upon the victory of the friendly Creek party and their Federal allies, the Creek Nation entered into a treaty. They reluctantly ceded huge amounts of land to the U.S. including the present site of the Poarch Band of Creek Indians reservation. Those Creeks who actively fought along side the U.S. were rewarded with a land grant of one square mile.

Many Creeks remained in their homeland in southwestern Alabama after the Creek Removal of 1836, some with their own land allotments. The town of Poarch served as a focal point for the Indian community and as a result, the Poarch Band remained cohesive and kept its identity through many decades without federal recognition and in spite of overt discrimination and segregation. From the 1940s through the 1970s, volunteer political actions accomplished very broad legal and moral gains for the Poarch Creek Band. These actions ultimately led to its present status as a federally recognized Indian tribe with a steadily building tribal economy.

The Poarch Creek Band of Indians established the Creek Indian Arts Council to work in conjunction with their tribal council to record, preserve, and display the rich history, religion, culture and art of the tribe.

GOVERNMENT

A constitution and bylaws were adopted in 1985 pursuant to the Indian Reorganization Act of 1934. Tribal government consists of three branches: Legislative, Executive and Judicial. The Legislative Branch of Tribal Government is governed by a nine-member Tribal Council that meets regularly. One third of the members are elected each year.

The Executive Branch is responsible for overall management of daily tribal government activities and oversees contracts, grants, and budgets. Departments of the Executive Branch include Tribal Administration, Federal Accounting, Education, Social and Human Services, Health Department, Community Relations, Public Safety, Public Works, Tribal Enrollment/Cultural Archives, Tribal Development and Land, Economic Development, Tribal Court, and Planning. The Tribal Council delegates most of its executive authority to the Tribal Administrator. The Tribal Social and Human Services Department works to enhance wellbeing, stability, and unity of families and children. Programs include: child welfare and emergency food, housing, energy assistance, and childcare. The Cultural Archives Office oversees elections, cultural programs, and maintains a Tribal enrollment database.

The Judicial Branch consists of a full-time law enforcement staff and tribal court system established in 1987 consisting of the Supreme Court and Court of Appeals. The Tribal Supreme Court enforces the following codes and ordinances: criminal, civil probate, traffic, juvenile, domestic relations, estates, game and fish, personnel and ethics, housing, gaming and elections. The Tribal Court exercises jurisdiction over Indians in all misdemeanor criminal offenses, traffic matters, and civil and juvenile cases. In 1997 the Tribe received a U.S. Department of Justice grant to enact a Drug Court on the Reservation. This program has been extremely helpful to tribal members. It provides immediate and direct treatment for drug offenders, which includes a twelve-month, four-phase approach to substance abuse. The Poarch Creek Indian Drug Court has been named a mentor court by the National Association of Drug Court Professionals.

The Poarch Creek Tribal Police provides 24 hour police and dispatch coverage within a 17 mile radius of the reservation. Their responsibilities include traffic patrol, residential and commercial building patrol, and safety programs. In 2004, the department has four police officers, two corporals, and one chief of police. Tribal Police Officers are cross-deputized with the county.

The tribe is a member of the United South and Eastern Tribes (USET). Under PL-638, the tribe contracts with the Bureau of

Poarch Creek Reservation
Federal reservation
Creek
Escambia County, Alabama

Poarch Band of Creek Indians
5811 Jack Springs Rd.
Atmore, AL 36502
334-368-9136
334-368-1026
poarchcreekindians-nsn.gov

Total area
(Tribal source, 2004)
228.47 acres

Federal trust lands
(Tribal source, 2004)
157.64 acres

Tribally owned lands
(Tribal source, 2004)
2,459.506 acres

Population *2000 census*
156

Tribal enrollment
(BIA labor report, 2001)
2,228

Total labor force *2000 census*
1,669

High school graduate or higher
27.6%

Unemployment rate *2000 census*
2%

Per capita income *2000 census*
$6,231

Poarch Creek

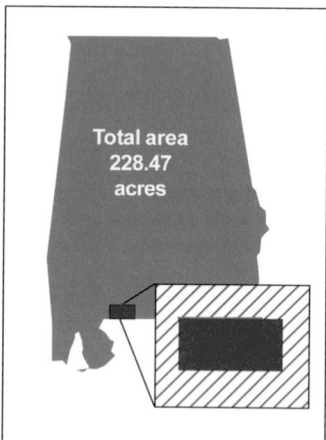

Total area
228.47
acres

ENVIRONMENTAL CONCERNS

Gravel mining operations are up-stream from tribal lands. These businesses create problems in that water on tribal property may become polluted and damage the naturally occurring plant and animals, which depend on these waterways. Tribal members also use these waterways for recreational purposes such as fishing and swimming. The Tribal Development and Land Department is in the process of collecting water samples in these areas, analyzing the data, and reporting the outcomes to EPA.

The tribe had made an effort in the past to be more environmentally friendly by beginning a recycling campaign. The initial effort did not work well, so the tribe now has a baler and storage facility that enable them to be more successful at recycling. The goal is to enlist the support of tribal employees as well as tribal members living on the reservation. Community meetings, advertising campaigns in the tribe's newsletter, and child education are several ways the tribe is working to make a difference.

Indian Affairs to administer key programs or services to band members living in five counties in Alabama and Florida.

BUSINESS CORPORATION

Creek Indian Enterprises (CIE) is the economic development arm for the Band. CIE, managed by a five member Board of Directors, is responsible for the management and operation of all tribal commercial properties and subsidiary enterprises as well as planning for future economic development endeavors. Since its creation in January of 1988, the tribe has embarked upon many business ventures including a ten-acre industrial park, which includes lease properties and an incubator facility that accommodates Community Recovery Services (CRS), specializing in disaster recovery. As well as a small business incubator that currently supports Wilderness Wisdom, a cultural education business owned and operated by a Tribal member. In 2004, enterprises included Best Western Hotel and Restaurant, Muskogee Metalworks Manufacturing Company, Perdido River Farms, Magnolia Branch Wildlife Reserve, Premier Family Eyecare, Poarch Road Service Center, Tallapoosa Entertainment Center, and Riverside Entertainment.

ECONOMY

Tribal government, via its programs, services and the Creek Indian Enterprises, is the major contributor to the band's thriving economy. Agriculture, livestock, manufacturing, and gaming are among the many industries found on the reservation.

Government as Employer. The tribal government employs approximately 180 people.

Agriculture and Livestock. Perdido River Farms is approximately 1,800 acres of tribal land used for agriculture, aquaculture and the grazing of 500 cattle and 30 sheep. A pecan orchard occupies 178 acres and there is a 12-acre catfish farm. Crops include wheat, corn, cotton, and soybeans. Most of the cropland is leased to area farmers.

Gaming. The tribe owns three Class II gaming enterprises. In 1985 the tribe opened the Creek Bingo Palace in Atmore, featuring 200 slot machines and a 1,200-seat bingo hall. It is within one-mile of their 88-room Best Western Hotel. The Riverside Entertainment Center in Wetumpka has 200 slots and a 215-seat bingo hall. The Tallapossa Entertainment Center in Montgomery, Alabama is a 14,000 square foot facility that has 694 slot machines. About 25 percent of Wetumka Bingo profits are put into an endowment fund with the purpose of supporting the Arts Council.

Industrial Parks. The tribe owns and operates a ten-acre industrial park located on Highway 21.

Manufacturing. Manufacturing is an important part of the tribal economy. The tribe owns and operates Muskogee Metalworks (MMW). This enterprise is a SBA 8 (a) and HUB Zone certified. MMW has been in operation since 1989 primarily designing and manufacturing metal fabricated hardware. In 2001, the product line was expanded to include electronic assemblies and electro-mechanical production. In April of 2001, MMW entered into a Joint Venture (JV) agreement with Manufacturing Technology, Inc. (MTI) of Ft. Walton Beach, Florida. Through the JV, MTI and MMW were able to secure a five year, $47 million dollar contract with the U.S. Army's PEO-STRI.

Real Estate/Commercial Development. The Tribe is committed to providing tribal members with safe and affordable housing through a variety of means including a mutual help ownership program, a tribally owned and operated low income rental housing program, and Tribally Assisted Home Ownership Program (TAHO). In 2004, the low-income rental-housing program had assisted 30 senior citizens and 76 single families. Eighty housing units were completed by 1989.

Services and Retail. In 1985 the tribe purchased the Best Western Hotel located on I-65 in Atmore, Alabama. The hotel has 88 rooms and full meeting and conference facilities. Adjacent to the hotel is the Creek Family Restaurant. Located within the Creek Bingo Palace complex is the Creek Smoke Shop and the Palace Printing Company. Calvin McGee Cultural Center, named after a former Chief of the Poarch Creek Indians, opened in 1997, home to a candy making shop, gift shop, museum, and classroom. Premier Eye Care, Tallapoosa Entertainment Center, and Riverside Entertainment are other retail establishments.

Media and Communications. The Poarch Band of Creek Indians produces a monthly publication called the *Poarch Creek News.*

Tourism and Recreation. The Calvin McGee Cultural Center is open to the public, and with its museum and classroom provide for a combination of learning, culture, history, and fun. The Cultural Center opened in 1997. The center is a refurbished version of the Poarch Creek Indian Consolidated School that existed from 1946 through 19 70. The Creek Indian Arts Council, established to work in consultation with the tribal council on cultural, artistic, and historical matters, sponsor corporative planning, research, and public education programs at the center. Animal enthusiasts will enjoy the Wildlife Reserve located at Magnolia Branch. The annual Thanksgiving Day Pow-Wow is recognized as one of the top tourist attractions in the Southeast.

INFRASTRUCTURE

The reservation is located 56 miles northeast of Mobile on State Highway 21 just six miles south of U.S. Interstate 80. Atmore, the principal town of the reservation, is at the junction of U.S. Highway 31 and State Highway 21.

Water Supply. Utilities, including water, wastewater systems, and solid waste collection services are provided by the Poarch Creek Indian Public Works.

COMMUNITY FACILITIES AND SERVICES

The tribe owns several administrative office complexes, a gym with classrooms, Tribal Police Department, a senior center and a fire station. The Poarch Volunteer Fire Department has 28 Certified Volunteer Fire Fighters from the community.

Education. The Poarch Band of Creek Indian's Education Department is dedicated to further developing and improving the basic education of tribal members. The Education Department administers various education, employment, and training programs to ensure these goals.

The Johnson O'Malley program, funded by the BIA, provides after school tutoring for tribal youth and high school students, cultural presentations at local schools within the five county service areas, and vocational/academic counseling for eligible high school students. There is a state run Even Start program (for four year olds) located on the reservation. It is a joint partnership in which the Tribe contributes several forms of assistance. The State of Alabama bears the financial end of the program.

Health Care. The Tribe's health department consists of health administration and health department clinics. The health administration department assists with third-party billing, receipts, contracting services, and maintaining agreements with outside providers. While the clinics provide basic medical services, pharmaceutical services, dental services, public health nursing services in clinics and homes, and care for acute and chronic illnesses. They also provide WIC and nutrition services. Services not covered at the clinic are referred out to medical or dental professionals in the Mobile, Alabama or Pensacola, Florida areas. The medical clinics employ 25 people and the dental clinic employs 4 people.

Alaska has about one-sixth of the land area of the United States, but only 626,932 (0.22 percent) of its people. Its terrain and climate vary from difficult to frighteningly dangerous. In 2000, 119,241 Alaskans (19 percent) identified themselves as Native, alone or in combination with another race or ethnicity.

Alaska Natives are more diverse in culture and heritage than all the Indians of the "Lower 48" combined. Some encountered non-Natives for the first time as recently as the early twentieth century. There are elders alive today who remember growing up in a world without metal. Some Alaska Natives live traditionally. Some have completely assimilated into the culture of the non-Natives. Most live-comfortably or not-between the two. Irrespective of the degree to which they have adopted non-Native technology and culture, the Natives of Alaska wish to retain and preserve their unique heritage, a heritage shaped by the challenging environments in which they live.

WHAT MAKES ALASKA DIFFERENT?

The economic circumstances of Alaska Natives are different from those of the Indians of the Lower 48.

First, in 1971, the Alaska Native Claims Settlement Act (ANCSA) created an entirely different relationship among the Alaskan Natives, the federal and state governments, and the land. A parallel network of for-profit corporations, owned by Natives but not tied to Native entities in any official sense, were granted degrees of conventional Anglo-American ownership rights in about one-ninth the territory of the state. Rights to traditional uses (for example, subsistence) of other land continue, but they are determined by state law (or federal agency regulations on federal land), not federal statutes or treaties. With one exception, none of the Native entities has independent jurisdiction over ANCSA corporate lands.

Second, there are more than 200 BIA-recognized Alaskan Native entities, many of which are very, very small. Several Lower 48 tribes have more members than the total number of Alaskan Natives. Many Native entities have most of their members living away from their traditional lands. Sixteen have *no* members remaining in their ancestral villages *(see pages 37).*

Third, the geographical dispersion and physical isolation of most Alaskan Native entities are striking. Most villages cannot be reached at all by land, except perhaps in the winter. They are dependent on air transportation for timely movement of people and freight. The nearest village may be 50 miles away or more. The nearest lawyer or banker may be several hundred miles away-by air.

Fourth, there is incredible variety in government, government contractor, and other organizational relationships. Most villages have a BIA-recognized Native entity, a municipal government, an ANCSA village corporation, an ANCSA regional Native corporation, a regional Native health organization, and a regional Native housing organization. Some have more, such as a borough government, a supratribal Native organization, area service organizations such as utilities, and specific resource management organizations. Sometimes a Native entity will cover more than one community, and sometimes a community will have more than one Native entity within its borders. Some village corporations have merged together, and some have merged into their regional Native corporations. Many villages lie entirely within federal or state lands such as national parks and wildlife refuges, and are subject to those regulations. Add the social and cultural effects of the small village populations, and one finds that each Native Alaskan community is unique.

HISTORICAL BACKGROUND

The first humans in the Americas were Siberian hunters, ancestors of most of the present-day Native Americans, who followed Ice Age mammals into Alaska over the Bering Land Bridge. Genetic evidence suggests that several waves of migrants came across the land bridge. When the ice receded, the sea level rose until Alaska and Siberia were again separated by the Bering Sea. The earliest artifacts yet found in Alaska date from about 12,000 years ago, toward the end of the Ice Age.

The forerunners of the Inupiat culture apparently came about 6,000 years ago. Their culture developed in Western Alaska and spread south and west into the Aleutian Islands and east across the Arctic to Greenland about 4,000 years ago. The Arctic Small Tool tradition, starting in Siberia, was the technological base. From Alaska's southern, western, and northern coasts around to Greenland, the Inupiat and the cultures descended from them-the *Alutiiq, Aleuts,* and *Yup'ik*-fished and hunted sea mammals such as whales, walruses, and seals. Some groups depended on caribou hunting. Despite these differences, the Inupiat were fairly uniform culturally, because about 1,000 years ago the whaling-oriented Thule culture, with its innovations of dog teams and kayaks, spread from Alaska to Greenland.

The origins of the Indians of Alaska are less clear. There was an early divergence between the *Athabascan* people of the Interior and the *Eyak, Tlingit,* and *Haida* peoples of the southeast coastal region. The Athabascans developed a migrating hunting culture, widely dispersed across the Interior's difficult terrain and bitter climate. The Indians of the southeast created a settled culture based on the abundant aquatic and timber resources and mild climate of the coastline, similar to other cultures of the Pacific Northwest coast.

One should not assume that pre-contact Alaska was peaceful or unchanging. Both oral traditions and artifacts indicate frequent wars both within and among the major ethnic groups, over hunting grounds, key terrain and trade routes, and political dominance. However, there was substantial trade and other peaceful interaction as well. For example, there are stories about young Athabascan men from the Interior traveling west as far as Siberia to trade for coral jewelry to be used as gifts to prospective brides. In spite of the dispersion of the Alaskan Natives, their pre-contact history was as complex as that of the Lower 48.

The European discovery of Alaska occurred as the result of a Russian expedition led by the Danish-born Vitus Bering in 1741. Until that time it was not known whether North America and Siberia were separate continents. As a result of that expedition, the Czar not only learned of a new land to the east but also of its natural richness. The expedition brought back a number of sea-otter furs, which became the motivation for private expeditions funded by Siberian merchants. For the next 43 years, Russians founded no settlements in Alaska, but numerous bands of fur collectors enslaved Aleut hunters in the quest for the furs, eventually as far as the coast of northern California. The outrageous treatment of Native hunters eventually awoke some concern on the part of the Russian crown, which became interested in converting these new subjects to the Russian Orthodox religion.

In 1784, a Russian settlement was established on Kodiak Island, to the south of the Alaska Peninsula. This led to the granting of a commercial and governing monopoly to the Russian American Company which was to last from 1799 until the sale of Alaska to the United States in 1867. In 1800, a fort was established near the present-day location of Sitka, in Tlingit territory in southeast Alaska; this became the capital of Russian America. Until the cession of Alaska to the United States, the fur trade continued to be of first importance to Russia, but missionaries were also active, especially on Kodiak Island in Southeast Alaska and in the Yukon-Kuskokwim Delta among the Yup'ik. In both of these endeavors, the Russians were more like the Spanish than the British in their official attitude toward the Native inhabitants as sources of labor and tribute. They did not establish sizable colonies, nor did they have any interest in Native lands for such purposes.

When the United States purchased Alaska from Russia in 1867, the rights of Alaska Natives were not of great concern to the officials involved in the enormous transaction. The Treaty of Cession of 1867 states that "... the Uncivilized tribes will be subject to such laws and regulations as the United States may, from time to time, adopt in regard to aboriginal tribes in that country." In 1884, after 17 years of intensive exploitation by U.S. interests and rule from Washington by executive decree, Congress passed the Alaska Organic Act, in effect making Alaska a territory of the United States. This act extended the laws of Oregon to Alaska and prepared the way for the promulgation of local laws. Included in the act was the provision that "Indians or other persons in said district shall not be disturbed in the possession of any lands actually in their use or occupation or now claimed by them but the terms under which such persons may acquire title to such lands is reserved for future legislation by Congress." This reserve clause was, in practice, ignored when it came to making land available for canneries, mines, homes, and other purposes of the non-Native immigrants.

Until the end of the nineteenth century, Alaska Natives were affected by the American presence to the extent that their lands were attractive to the newcomers. While this was also true in the Lower 48, the sheer size and difficult logistics of Alaska protected many Native peoples from the onslaught of outsiders. In the early 1900s, however, federal policy shifted to a more consciously assimilationist stance with respect to Native Americans, and Alaska slowly came to be included in this shift. Nevertheless, only a few reservations were ever established in the state, and the new direction was seen mainly in the building of BIA schools.

Alaska was admitted as a state in 1959. In the Alaska Statehood Act, a fundamental contradiction arose in that the act prohibited the acquisition by any party of lands that "may be held by any Indians, Eskimos, or Aleuts ..." but at the same time it gave the state the right to lands that were "vacant, unappropriated and unreserved ..." There was no such land of any value, since Native peoples occupied or customarily used all productive lands in the state.

GEOGRAPHY AND CLIMATE

The physical geography of Alaska ranges from Arctic tundra to jagged mountains to archipelagos. At 663,267 square miles, it is 2.3 times the size of Texas-larger than most of the earth's countries. Working counter-clockwise from the north, Alaska can be conveniently divided into five areas. From the Canadian border, along the Arctic Ocean and the Chukchi Sea, to the Bering Straits and Norton Sound, the far north includes the vast plain of the North Slope, the mountains of the Brooks Range, the northwest coastal plain, and the rocky Seward Peninsula, reaching out to Russia. Most of this region is north of the Arctic Circle. East and south of Norton Bay, through the Bering Sea to the North Pacific, the southwest includes the vast, wet delta of the Yukon and Kuskokwim rivers, the arc of the Alaskan Peninsula and Aleutian Islands, and, to the south of the Alaskan Peninsula, the Kodiak Islands. This area is dominated by water, ocean, lakes, and rivers. The south central area, home to more than half of Alaska's people, runs from Cook Inlet, the Kenai Peninsula, Prince William Sound, and the Copper River catchment area, to the Canadian border, taking in an area that is fertile, temperate, and accessible. The southeast "panhandle" is a forested network of islands and fjords, temperate and wet. The interior, consisting of the catchment area of the Yukon River and its tributaries and the Alaska Range to its south, is almost half the land area of the state, with broad valleys punctuated by glacier-swept hills. The combination of difficult terrain and a more difficult climate makes movement a challenge throughout the state, and agriculture largely impossible outside the south central area. However, the mountains hold extensive deposits of metal ores and minerals.

The human geography of Alaska is at once highly concentrated and widely dispersed. The total population of Alaska in 2000 was 626,932; the Native population was 119,241 (19 percent). More than 60 percent of Alaska's population lives in or near Anchorage, on the south central coast, including almost a third of the Native population. Economically, Anchorage dominates Alaska. With a quarter of a million people and 22 percent of all Alaskan Natives, Anchorage is almost 10 times more populous than the next largest city, Fairbanks. Fairbanks dominates the interior of Alaska. Juneau, the third largest city and state capitol, and Sitka, the fourth-largest city, are in the more densely populated southeastern panhandle. Around the periphery, the cities of Barrow (North Slope), Kotzebue (northwest), Nome (Seward Peninsula), Bethel and Dillingham (southwest), Kodiak (Kodiak Island in the south), Valdez and Cordoba (south central) are much smaller, a few thousand people, yet serve as economic and administrative hubs for their respective regions. Beyond these concentrations, both Native and non-Native people are dispersed into hundreds of small, isolated, and widely separated villages. Areas as large as Texas may have as few as 10,000 inhabitants. It is important to keep in mind that many Native Alaskans, often members of distant Native entities, live and work in the major metropolitan areas.

The climate in Alaska ranges from cool to very, very cold, with precipitation ranging from soggy along the southern coast to Arctic desert in the interior and northern slope. Some areas of the interior see swings of more than 100°F from summer highs to winter lows. In the maritime south, from the Aleutians to the southeastern panhandle, seasonal differences may be as little as 30°F. The interaction between weather and transportation is very important. Frozen rivers and seas block water access as much as eight months of the year, but permit surface travel using everything from snowshoes and dog sleds to large snowmachines. *(What's a "snowmachine"? See page 39.)* Sometimes even more conventional motor vehicles can use ice roads on frozen rivers. With the year-round dependence on air travel for movement of people and cargo, bad flying weather will isolate a community.

INFRASTRUCTURE AND PUBLIC SERVICES

The primary influences on the infrastructure and provision of public services in Alaska are the dispersion of its people and its climate.

Transportation. The climate and the physical dispersion of the Native communities make transportation both difficult and expensive. Most communities do not have road or rail access to a major metropolitan area or even to other nearby communities. They are dependent on aircraft for most movement of people and goods. In one community, children fly across a broad river to school every day. "Bush pilots" are a state icon. Most communities have water access for at least part of the year. For communities away from the sea, major rivers such as the Yukon, the Kuskokwim, and the Copper are navigable for some distance inland. Most communities get deliveries of bulk cargo by barge once or twice a year, and use small boats for local travel. For those communities without water, road, or rail access, delivery of bulk cargo is very difficult. Road and rail access are limited to the mainland, with connections among the major metropolitan areas and routes parallel to the Alaska Pipeline from the southern coast to the North Slope. Road and rail traffic from the southeastern panhandle to the rest of the state must pass through Canada.

Energy. All Alaskan communities are electrified, and all Native Alaskans have access to electric power in their homes and work places. Outside the few metropolitan areas, there are few interconnected electric power grids. Most rural communities must generate their electricity locally, and most do so by means of diesel-engine-driven generators. A few have access to hydroelectric, wind, or solar power. The cost differential is subsidized by the state. When combined with the general dependence on fuel oil for heat, the diesel power plants create a heavy demand for bulk oil. Most communities have substantial bulk oil storage capacity. Distribution is a major concern. Communities with water access get their oil by barge in the summer. Except for those few communities with road or rail access to one of the major ports, communities without water access get their oil by snowmachine in the winter.

Telecommunications. All Native Alaskans have access to telephone service in their homes and work places. Smaller communities usually have a central satellite link to which local subscribers are connected by wire. Internet access varies widely. However, every school in Alaska has state-funded Internet access. Many communities have cable television systems using satellite links. Individual satellite service is generally available but becomes more difficult as one moves north. Most communities can receive one or more broadcast AM radio stations. The state-funded Alaska Rural Communications Service (ARCS) has television broadcast repeaters in most communities that are out of range of the major metropolitan areas. Programming is an eclectic mix of public and commercial. Alaskans by necessity make use of an extensive teleconferencing system operated by state or local government.

Education. Education is overseen by the state, but the schools are operated by school districts, which may be organized by a municipality or region. All boroughs and first-class cities operate their own school districts, as do a few second-class cities. In addition to city and borough school districts, there are 19 regional school districts, each of which supervises at least some schools in Native communities. Schools in smaller communities are not your stereotypical one-room schoolhouse, even if the number of grades served exceeds the number of students. After a successful civil rights lawsuit, the state was forced to provide equal educational opportunities to the Native villages. The state seems to have taken this to heart, and most villages have modern school buildings, excellent student-teacher ratios, and extensive books and supplies. Every school has Internet access, and most have computer labs. The school library is usually the community's public library, and sometimes the school is the community's largest employer. Most of the regional ANCSA corporations and regional nonprofit organizations and many of the village corporations have extensive scholarship and skill training programs. Throughout Alaska-even in non-Native communities-there is a profound interest in preserving Alaska's Native heritage by teaching it in the schools. In some communities, most or all instruction is in the Native language through third or fourth grade, then shifting to English but continuing to include the local Native culture in the curriculum.

Water and waste systems. Water and waste disposal systems are locally operated and range from hauling water from the washeteria and honeybuckets to the sewage lagoon-and sometimes even outhouses-to extensive municipal piped water and sewer systems. *(What's a "washeteria" or a "honeybucket"? See page 39.)* Often a community will have a mix of systems.

Health care. Health care, funded by the Indian Health Service but provided by regional or local Native health organizations, ranges from full hospital care in the larger centers, such as Barrow and Bethel, to village health clinics staffed by itinerant professionals and minimally trained "health assistants," sometimes several hours by plane from the nearest full-time professionally staffed clinic.

Public safety. Alaska state troopers have jurisdiction throughout the state, and in many areas are the only law enforcement officers available. Larger municipalities may have city or borough police departments. One unique institution is the state Village Public Safety Officer (VPSO) program. As of August 2004, 54 villages had assigned VPSOs. These officers are trained by the state and carry state credentials but are employed by regional nonprofit organizations. They are trained in both law enforcement and emergency response, with a focus on operating in the Native village environment. Their level of training is not as high as the state troopers or the police in the major cities, but it equals or exceeds most local police in smaller communities. Their jurisdiction is limited to local ordinances and minor offenses.

GOVERNMENT RELATIONS

This peculiar history has led to the unique set of circumstances present in Alaska today, especially with regard to the relations of Native American organizations with the federal government and among themselves. Except for the federal reservation at Metlakatla on Annette Island in the southeast, there are no Indian reservations in the state. Instead, there are over 200 village corporations and 13 regional corporations, for-profit entities created by the 1971 federal Alaska Native Claims Settlement Act. The village corporations own the surrounding lands that in the Lower 48 would usually be reservation lands, while the regional corporations also own land, and the mineral rights to all Native-owned lands. They manage the monies paid by the federal government for aboriginal lands taken by the government. Land in the state is also owned by the federal government, the state government, non-Native cities and towns, and individuals.

In addition to the governing bodies of the village corporations, the villages also typically have "traditional" village councils, led by a chief or president, or Indian Reorganization Act councils. Both types of bodies function as official representatives of the village to the bureaucratic outside world, historically the Bureau of Indian Affairs. Many of them are cities (first- or second-class), incorporated under the laws of the state of Alaska, with a city council and a mayor, city school system, utilities, etc. Finally, it should be noted that some funds for community projects are administered by the 12 nonprofit corporations that are the descendants of the largely tribal groups formed to press for the land settlement in the 1960s, and which were the political ancestors of the regional corporations.

Federal

With the implementation of the Alaska Native Claims Settlement Act and the contracting-out of most BIA and Indian Health Service functions to Native organizations, the relationship between the federal government and Native Alaskan communities has veered further from the pattern seen in the Lower 48. Many functions performed directly by federal agencies in the Lower 48 are funded by those agencies but performed by either Native nonprofits, Native entities, or by ANCSA corporations. The BIA continues to provide grant aid to the Native entities, particularly for infrastructure, as does the Department of Energy. Housing and Urban Development provides grant aid for housing and related infrastructure. The Department of Transportation and the Army Corps of Engineers build and upgrade the airfields vital to many communities' contact with the rest of the world, harbor facilities, and flood and erosion control structures. They also provide disaster response. These activities are in many ways handled in a manner more similar to non-Indian communities than to reservations in the Lower 48.

Legislative favor has also heavily influenced relations between the federal government and Alaska Natives. A critical aspect of this relationship is the preference accorded the ANCSA corporations for government contracting. Not only are the ANCSA corporations accorded a preference-if their bid is similar to a non-preferential contractor's bid, the ANCSA corporation gets the contract-but federal agencies may award substantial contracts to ANCSA corporations on a noncompetitive basis. Another example of such favor was the unique right of ANCSA corporations to sell their net operating losses to other corporations for cash, which provided much needed cash infusions to many corporations that had been initially mismanaged.

Another area of interaction between the federal government and Alaskan Natives concerns the use of federal lands. Many Native communities are physically located within National Parks, National Forests, or other federal reserves. Many Natives retain rights to use particular federal lands for traditional activities, especially subsistence. This places Natives under federal jurisdiction when on federal land, subject to agency regulations and law enforcement. Subject to some specific statutory rights granted Alaskan Natives, the agencies that manage federal lands have broad powers within their own statutory authority to regulate the use of those lands by Alaskan Natives.

State

With the exception of the Annette Island Reserve, there are no self-governing Indian reservations in Alaska. Functions performed by the BIA or reservation governments in the Lower 48 are, for the most part, performed by the state and its subunits. These include planning and zoning, education, regulation, law, and the administration of justice. Planning and zoning are the responsibilities of municipalities (boroughs, Home Rule cities, and first class cities) or, within the Unorganized Borough (see "Municipalities" below), the state itself.

Education is the responsibility of municipalities or state-operated regional school districts, and is funded and regulated by the state. See the discussion under "Infrastructure" above.

The state is very supportive of local Native desires concerning cultural preservation.

Economic, environmental, and other regulatory matters are handled by the state government, although some have been delegated to municipalities by state law.

The law, both civil and criminal, is state law. State statutes grant Native entities in the Unorganized Borough and incorporated municipalities the power to pass local ordinances, including the regulation of alcoholic beverages. This means that, for example, state family law is used to decide marital and parent-child issues such as divorce and adoption.

Administration of justice is a matter of state law. The state troopers have state-wide jurisdiction (other than on Annette Island). Many municipalities have their own police departments, but Native entities (with a few exceptions) do not. Village public safety officers have state-granted authority. The state court system handles all major civil and criminal cases. The state has granted Native entities the authority to create tribal courts and other dispute-resolution systems, with jurisdiction only over local and internal tribal matters.

Municipalities

Alaska is the only state in which the land is not organized into political subdivisions equivalent to counties in the other states. Most of the state consists of the "Unorganized Borough"-everything outside a municipality. In order to secure maximum self-government for the people of the state in line with the state constitution, numerous city and borough governments have been created to provide essential public services.

Cities and boroughs are municipalities incorporated to perform both regulatory (police, zoning, animal control, etc.) and proprietary (water, sewer, airport, etc.) functions. There are three types of boroughs and three types of cities, along with "unified" municipalities-merged city-borough governments with the powers of boroughs.

Boroughs. Boroughs are formed to provide services to people residing in a large geographic area including two or more communities. They are somewhat similar to counties. Including the three unified municipalities, there are 16 organized boroughs in Alaska, covering about 39 percent of the state. Approximately 86 percent of the state's population lives in an organized borough or unified municipality. There are three classes of boroughs that differ in how they may acquire additional powers, as well as in other administrative details. The governing structure of a borough consists of an assembly (a legislative body of 5 to 16 members), a school board, a planning commission, and a mayor. Bor-

oughs range in size from the tiny Bristol Bay Borough (1,300 people in three communities and 850 square miles of territory) and the City and Borough of Yakutat (700 people, 9,250 square miles) to the vast North Slope Borough (10,000 people on 95,000 square miles-larger than 39 states-running from Canada to the Chukchi Sea) and the Municipality of Anchorage (260,000 people on 2,000 square miles).

Cities. Alaska has 12 Home Rule cities, 21 first-class cities, and 112 second-class cities. Almost all have Native entities associated with them, and most of the smaller ones are largely populated by Natives. Metlakatla, in the federal reservation on Annette Island, is recognized by the state as a city for legal purposes. Home Rule cities have their own schools and planning and zoning services, even if they are located within a borough. First-class cities must have at least 400 people, the mayor is directly elected by the voters and is not a member of the city council, and, if the city is in the Unorganized Borough, it provides its own schools and planning and zoning services. Second-class cities may be organized with as few as 25 registered voters. The mayor is elected by and from the city council, and they rely on the school districts and planning and zoning services of the borough or region in which they are located. Cities range in size from the Home Rule city of Fairbanks, with more than 32,000 people, to the second-class city of Kupreanof, with 24 people.

More important than the municipality's limited self-government and ability to provide necessary services is its power to tax. Municipalities can levy both property and sales taxes, limited depending on the type of municipality. North Slope Borough was very frankly organized to provide its mostly Inupiat residents the ability to tax the property and equipment used in Arctic oil production. With this revenue, the borough has been able to provide extensive public services throughout the North Slope, services well beyond what its residents could afford on their own.

Unincorporated Communities

Unlike in the Lower 48, where they fall under county government, the state recognizes many unincorporated communities. The territory of such a community is termed a *townsite.* Most are predominantly Native Alaskan, so the state grants the Native entities authority to regulate their members through ordinances and tribal dispute-resolution systems. In one area-alcoholic beverages-they have the authority to regulate non-Natives, although they must rely on state law enforcement and courts to enforce such rules on non-Natives. Such communities appear on maps and in state databases as distinct entities, and are recognized as statistical areas by the U.S. Census Bureau.

In Alaska, a *townsite* refers to a community that has received a subdivisional survey under the federal laws that enabled residents to petition for the withdrawal and survey of public land in a community, after which qualified or vested individuals were deeded lots and the remainder was held in trust for future occupants. Townsites are private or local-government property. Incorporation is irrelevant to townsite presence or absence. Most unrestricted townsite lots are owned by city governments, Native entities, or private individuals. Restricted townsite lots are owned by individual Natives and administered by regional nonprofit organizations or Native entities under contract from the BIA.

THE CULTURES

At a first approximation, Alaska Natives can be divided into Indians and Inupiat. However, the term *Inupiat* ("real people") is ambiguous. It can refer to all of the Inuit-related peoples of Alaska, but this ignores the vast cultural differences between the Inupiat of the North Slope and Bering Sea and related cultures: The Aleuts, of the Aleutian Islands; the Alutiiq, of South Central Alaska; the Yup'ik of the southwestern part of the state; and the Siberian Yupik of St. Lawrence Island. Unless the context demands otherwise, this Guide uses the term "Inupiat" to refer to the branch of the North American Inuit culture living on the North Slope of Alaska and along the coast of the Bering Sea, and "Inupiat-related" to refer to all these together.

When it comes to "Indians," there are the numerous Athabascan peoples of the Interior (related linguistically to the Navajos and Apaches of the Southwest United States and traditionally highly mobile hunters and gatherers); the northern representatives of the Northwest Coast cultures, the Tlingits, Haidas, and (extinct) Eyaks (distantly related linguistically to the Athabascans and to Na-Dene peoples of the American Southwest-Navaho and Apache); and the Tsimshians (linguistically related to the Penutian tribes of California, Oregon, Washington, and British Columbia).

It is important to understand that, due to geographical isolation, the cultural differences between and even within these groups can be as great as those between the Chinese and the Bantu. However, trade among the various peoples has led to significant transfer of vocabulary, technologies, and other aspects of culture. Furthermore, the influence of Russian and Western European/American cultures varies from village to village. As a result, many aspects of culture can vary within the major cultural units and even between one village and the next.

Aleut *(Unangan)*

The Aleuts *(AL-ee-yutes)* or *Unangan* live on the Alaska Peninsula, the Aleutian Islands, and the Pribilof Islands in the Bering Sea. Their language, divided into distinct eastern and western dialects, is related to the Inupiat languages. Before contact with the West, they made their living from the sea, taking fish, shellfish, and sea mammals. They were the people most heavily affected by Russian incursions in the mid-eighteenth century. Russian fur collectors and their armed crews enslaved groups of Aleut hunters and forced them to leave their families to hunt fur-bearing sea mammals, primarily sea-otters, from the swift kayaks called *baidarkas*. Prior to contact, the Unangan population was probably around 20,000. Hardship and disease reduced these numbers to fewer than 5,000. Today there are about 4,000 Unangan people. When the worst period of exploitation ended, after the sea otter fur trade collapsed, the Aleuts were left with a heritage of Russian names, the Russian Orthodox religion, and a Cyrillic system for writing their language.

Alutiiq

The *Alutiiq* live around Prince William Sound and on Kodiak Island. The language of the Alutiiq is *Sugpiaq*, which is related to the Inupiat languages. Like the Aleuts, before contact with the West they made their living from the sea, taking fish, shellfish, and sea mammals. The Alutiiq were heavily affected by Russian incursions in the mid-eighteenth century. Even their name for themselves-Alutiiq-is derived from the Russian word for the peoples of coastal Alaska. Prior to contact, the Alutiiq population was probably around 20,000. Hardship and disease reduced these numbers to fewer than 5,000, and today the population remains at that level. They retain a heritage of Russian names and the Russian Orthodox religion. There are two distinct subcultures within the Alutiiq:

The *Koniag* residents of Kodiak Island and the nearby mainland, before the heavy-handed influence of the Russians, were a warlike and adventuresome people. They remain sea people, with a life-style centered on subsistence on the ocean.

The *Chugash* culture, now reduced to five villages on the mainland around Prince William Sound, was always heavily influenced by the adjacent Athabascan, Eyak, Tlingit, and Aleut cultures. Its members were aggressive and highly skilled sea mammal hunters, but are now some of the most "Americanized" Native peoples.

Athabascan Indian

There are 11 Athabascan-speaking groups in Alaska: The *Ahtna* of the Copper River Basin; the *Dena'ina* of Cook Inlet (also spelled "Tanaina"); the *Deg Xinag* (or *Deg Het'an*) of the middle Yukon River (formerly known as

Ingalik-the names *Ingalik* and *Ingalit* formerly used are unacceptable to its members); the *Holikachuk* of the middle Yukon and Innoko rivers; the *Upper Kuskokwim* Athabascans; the *Koyukon* of the Yukon and Koyukuk rivers; the *Tanana* of the Yukon and lower Tanana rivers; the *Tanacross* of the middle Tanana River; the *Upper Tanana* Athabascans; the *Gwich'in* of the northeast Interior; and the *Hän* on the Yukon where it crosses into Canada. They are linguistically related to the Athabascans of the American Northwest, the Navajo, and the Apache. Culturally they are very different. They occupy vast areas of the interior of the state, stretching from Cook Inlet in the south to above the Arctic Circle in the north, and from the Canadian border in the east almost to the Bering Sea in the west. While there are cultural differences among the different groups, their languages are closely related, and all share a subsistence-based way of life. In addition, all but those people living along the lower Yukon River (and therefore heavily influenced by Inupiat-related cultures) are matrilineal; descent is determined through the mother, and tribal members belong to the clan of their mother, which in turn belongs to one of two divisions of Athabascan society called *moieties*. Tribal ceremonies such as the potlatch and stick dance, both associated with funerals, continue to be an important part of Athabascan life. There are approximately 13,700 Athabascan people living in Alaska today. Other than the Dena'ina, who are located in the Anchorage area, most of these peoples still live in their traditional villages, using them as bases for wide-ranging subsistence activities.

Inupiat

The *nupiat* live mainly in the northern coastal areas of the state, from Unalakleet on the west coast (Norton Sound) north to Barrow and east to the Canadian border. They are part of the *Inuit* people who occupy the Arctic coast of North America east to Greenland. In Northern Alaska, the small Inupiat settlements were traditionally made up of extended families. On the North Slope, the economies of the villages were focused on hunting the bowhead whale and other marine mammals, as well as on fishing and gathering during the summer months. These activities are still important today. One exception is the village of Anaktuvuk Pass, in the Brooks Range, which has historically depended on caribou for its survival. Today there are approximately 12,000 Inupiat people in Alaska.

Linguistic distinctions are important among the Inupiat. Within *Inupiaq* there are two major dialect groups, each with two dialects. North Alaskan Inupiaq includes the North Slope or *Tareumiut* ("people of the sea") dialect (spoken along the Arctic coast as far south as Kivalina) and the *Malimiut* dialect (spoken south of Kivalina in and around

Kotzebue, along the Kobuk River, and at the head of Norton Sound, especially in Koyuk and Unalakleet). The *Nunamiut* ("people of the land") dialect, found primarily at Anaktuvuk Pass, is transitional between the North Slope and Malimiut dialects. The other major dialect group is Seward Peninsula Inupiaq, found on the Seward Peninsula and in the area of Norton Sound. This group includes the Bering Strait dialect (spoken on King Island and the Diomedes and in the coastal villages north and west of Nome) and the *Qawiaraq* or *Kauweramiut* dialect (spoken in Teller near the original place named Qawiaraq and in the villages west and south of Nome as far as Unalakleet). People within the dialect groups can understand each other with some degree of confidence, but there are such vocabulary differences between the two groups that understanding is difficult.

Siberian Yupik
The residents of the two villages on Saint Lawrence Island, whose western tip is only about 50 miles from Siberia, speak the Siberian Yupik language, which is closely related to Yup'ik and Sugpiaq. Traditionally they had ties of kinship and trade with the Siberian mainland. Until the late nineteenth century, they had little contact with the rest of Alaska. With the fall of the Iron Curtain, they are finally able once more to communicate with and visit their relatives in Siberia. Like other Inupiat-related peoples, the people of Saint Lawrence Island have traditionally hunted sea mammals, fished, and gathered berries and other plant resources. Many people continue to follow a subsistence life-style and continue many of their traditional customs. Their language is probably the strongest Native language in Alaska today, with almost all the children learning it from their parents. There are about 1,100 Siberian Yupik in Alaska today.

Southeast Alaskan Indian
The Indians of the Alaska "panhandle" live in an archipelago of heavily forested islands and the coastal area of the mainland, with deep fjords interspersed with glaciers. The *Tlingit* Indians are the most numerous of the southeast peoples, with a population of approximately 20,000; there are about 1,800 *Haida* Indian people; and there are about 2,400 *Tsimshian* Indians. All three peoples belong to the Northwest Coast culture area, characterized by the use of clan houses with elaborately carved crests and house posts with carvings of important clan animals ("totem poles") and the institution of the potlatch, complex public ceremonies in which vast amounts of goods were given away or destroyed. The *Eyak* of Prince William Sound, now extinct as a people, were similar in culture to the Alaskan Athabascan groups, although the Eyak language was only distantly related to the Athabascan languages. For centuries, Eyak

traders connected the Southeastern Indians, the Athabascans of the Interior, and the Alutiiq to their west. The Tsimshian of Metlakatla, while from the Northwest Coast culture, are linguistically distinct. They were a Christian settlement founded by immigrants from Canada in the mid-nineteenth century. Today all southeast Indians depend on fishing and logging for their economic survival. Although very westernized, some of the traditional ways of life are still practiced.

Yup'ik *(Central and other)*
The *Yup'ik* ("real people") live in the southwestern area of the state, along the Bering Sea coast and inland along the rivers of the Yukon-Kuskokwim Delta, between Bristol Bay in the south and Norton Sound in the north. Note the apostrophe in their name. This denotes a "hard *p*" sound. Their language is one of four Inupiat-derived languages spoken in the state, and it is the language with the most speakers, around 13,000 out of a total population of approximately 18,000. Traditionally, the Yup'ik people have lived in villages, with seasonal camps for harvesting fish, berries, and other subsistence resources. Many people continue to follow these patterns today, although wage labor has become more important. The Yup'ik culture is more consistent than other Native cultures, although there are dialects spoken in more isolated locations: *Unaliq*, along Norton Sound south of Unalakleet; *Cup'ik* in Hooper Bay and Chevak; *Cup'ig* on Nunivak Island; and a separate Yup'ik dialect in Egegik. With a few exceptions, the Yup'ik were the last Native people to come into serious contact with non-Natives.

ALASKA NATIVE CLAIMS SETTLEMENT ACT OF 1971
The Alaska Native Claims Settlement Act of 1971 (ANCSA), together with subsequent related legislation, created a unique land ownership and financial regime for the Natives of Alaska.

HISTORY
As in the rest of the country, the Bureau of Indian Affairs was responsible for any interactions between Native peoples and the federal government, beginning with the establishment of Alaska as a "district," or territory, in 1884; but there was no reservation system accompanying the appropriation of Native land and resources. By the 1960s, however, pressure increased on Congress to acknowledge Alaska Native ownership of the land prior to European settlement, to guarantee a land base to Native communities, and to compensate them for land taken in the past. While motivated in part by sentiments of justice and fairness, this change is more probably the result of huge discoveries of oil on the North Slope, in Inupiat territory, and the concomitant desire to clarify questions of landownership prior to exploitation of the new resource.

The outcome of all these concerns was the Alaska Native Claims Settlement Act of 1971, usually referred to as the ANCSA or the "Settlement Act."

The ANCSA completely changed the relationship between Alaska Natives and the federal government. Where before there was an unspecified number of "tribes," for the monetary compensation and land-claims purposes of the act there were only corporations (except for the Annette Island Reserve, the only remaining reservation in the state). The transition to this modern business form has been a profound change.

Under the act, the approximately 80,000 Alaska Natives received fee-simple title to 40 million acres of land through more than 200 village and 12 (later 13) regional corporations, in which they became stockholders. Compensation for claims extinguished was set at $962.5 million, to be paid over a number of years, also through the corporations. Through the ANCSA, Alaska Natives obtained title to more land than was held in trust for all other Native Americans, and compensation for lands given up was nearly four times the amount all Indian tribes had won from the Indian Claims Commission over its 25 years of operation.

Of the 40 million acres awarded in the settlement, 22 million were for selection by village corporations; the number of acres to which a village was entitled was determined by enrollment. For example, a village with an enrollment of 25 to 99 people was entitled to select three townships (108 square miles, or 69,120 acres), while one with an enrollment of 100 to 199 received four. A village with over 600 people enrolled received seven townships (very few villages are this large). Today, most of the village corporations have completed all the steps in the selection and documentation process and received title to most selected land.

Village corporations own only the surface estate of lands they have selected. The rights to the subsurface estate (minerals) belong to the regional corporations. In addition, 16 million acres of land, with all associated rights, were selected by the regional corporations on the basis of land area within their regions, rather than population.

The remaining 2 million acres of awarded land were set aside for grants of title to special Native corporations organized in the non-Native cities of Sitka, Kenai, Kodiak, and Juneau, which had been historic Native places *(see page 36)* and to other groups and individuals in special situations, as well as for cemeteries and historic sites.

Payments from the federal Alaska Native Fund were made only to regional corporations, which in turn retained part of the funds and paid out part to individual Natives and village corporations. The amount of money each regional corporation received was based on its proportion of the total number of enrolled Natives.

In all of this complex process, the state-law business corporation, whether village or regional, was the vehicle of settlement. Since this form of organization was foreign to most of the Native population, a lengthy process of stockholder education followed the passage of the bill and still goes on today.

Several problems have arisen with the ANCSA. First have been the complex processes and bureaucratic procedures built into the act. For instance, lengthy lawsuits resulted from a need to clarify which revenues were required to be shared among the regional corporations and which could be kept by the corporations generating them. Second was concern over the provision of the act stating that as of 1991, shares of the corporations could be sold on the open market, with no provisions as to Native ethnicity, and the related provision that Natives born after the passage of the ANCSA were not eligible to own stocks or receive dividends except by inheritance. This concern was addressed by the U.S. Congress in 1987, giving the corporations the right to extend the original restrictions on owning stock, to continue protecting undeveloped land, and to vote on whether to issue stock to "new Natives," i.e., those born after December 18, 1971.

The final problem was the assumption in the original act that through the agency of the financial resources and the new corporate structures it created, Alaska Native village life would be transformed into a variant of mainstream American culture and economy. This has not happened; Alaska Natives remain as committed as ever to their subsistence way of life. This orientation has caused several conflicts with the state of Alaska, with partial resolutions. In the end, however, any satisfactory resolution must involve some consideration of the traditional leadership structures of the villages-the chiefs, presidents, and councils that the ANCSA failed to mention at all.

Whereas it is clear that the act was an attempt to settle a chaotic and unjust set of circumstances, the choice of corporations as the vehicle of the settlement and the underlying assumption that the traditional ways of life in the villages would soon be supplanted have proven to be problematic in themselves. There is some sentiment among Native peoples, in fact, that land ownership should be transferred from the corporations to the traditional tribal governments.

VILLAGE CORPORATIONS

The ANCSA village corporations have become important to the economies of Native Alaskan communities. Some have become large international operating enterprises or investment managers. Others remain focused on business within their communities. Many have been able to exploit corporate lands for timber or development. Their relationships with other community organizations-municipal governments and Native entities-vary from tightly integrated to competitive. Some are substantial employers in their communities. While the subsurface rights associated with village corporation land belong to their respective regional corporations, the regional corporations must obtain the consent of the village corporations before undertaking any activities on that land.

Some village corporations have merged together to gain the advantages of economies of scale, for example, the 14 village corporations that merged to form the Kuskokwim Corporation. Others have merged into their regional corporations to reduce overhead, for example, into Ahtna, Koniag, and NANA. When ANCSA corporations merge, the consent authority of the village corporation for subsurface activities within the boundaries of the Native village is delegated to another entity in the Native village composed of the Native residents.

NONPARTICIPANTS

Several Native entities are either partial or total nonparticipants in the ANCSA process. The reservation at Metlakatla on Annette Island was not included in the process at all. The ANCSA provided that the village corporations associated with those Native entities that already had reserves could choose to obtain title, both surface and subsurface, to those lands, in lieu of the land and money to which they would be entitled under the act. The village corporations for Arctic Village, Elim, Gambell, Savoonga, Tetlin, and Venetie elected this option. The village corporations for Gambell and Savoonga jointly own most of Saint Lawrence Island. Venetie and Arctic Village not only took title to their existing reserves, but conveyed these lands to their Native entity and dissolved their village corporations, refusing to participate in the ANCSA process any further. Note that Doyon, Limited, their regional Native corporation, continues to provide benefits to the members of the Native Village of Venetie.

REGIONAL CORPORATIONS

The thirteen regional Native corporations are important economic entities in the lives of Alaskan Natives. Twelve of the regional corporations were formed on the basis of Native associations that had existed previously and largely followed traditional ethnic lines. The thirteenth was established in Seattle for Natives who live outside of Alaska and who preferred not to enroll in one of the others. The number of village corporations associated with each regional corporation varies from a low of 5 for Chugach Alaska Corporation to a high of 51 for Calista Corporation. Each is among the largest corporations in Alaska, however measured.

Ahtna, Incorporated (Ahtna)

Introduction
Ahtna is one of the thirteen regional corporations established under ANCSA. In 1980, seven of the eight village corporations within its region merged with Ahtna, and Ahtna assumed the management of all former village corporation lands. Ahtna also possesses the subsurface estate of Chitina Native Corporation lands. This split estate requires Ahtna to obtain permission from Chitina Native Corporation before developing any subsurface resource on Chitina lands.

Entitlement
Ahtna owns approximately 1,528,000 acres of land that had been conveyed by December 31, 1997, from an entitlement of 1,770,000 acres under ANCSA. Ahtna received $13 million in the deal. Ahtna, Incorporated, owns 609,472 acres in fee simple title within the boundaries of the Wrangell-St. Elias National Park and Preserve. Ahtna holds title to 3,000 acres within Denali, with approximately 25,000 acres under selection. Within Wrangell-St. Elias, Ahtna has approximately 600,000 acres conveyed, with an equal amount in selections.

Within the Ahtna region, lands have been classified under ANCSA to accomplish the settlement process. The eight villages within Ahtna were allocated 714,240 acres of land surrounding the villages. Based on population, the villages are entitled to this acreage. Additionally, Ahtna, Inc. received close to 45,000 acres in bonus selections to be distributed among the eight villages based upon their historic use and subsistence needs. Ahtna, Incorporated also owns 609,472 acres in fee simple title within the boundaries of the Wrangell-St. Elias National Park and Preserve.

Corporate governance
In 1980, Ahtna merged with seven of its eight village corporations, leading to a 13-member board to oversee the corporation's future direction. The shareholders of the former village corporations maintain shareholder committees known as Successor Village Organizations (SVOs). Each SVO reserves the right to withhold consent, if reasonable, to any type of new development within former village lands. Ahtna has approximately 1,200 shareholders, of which the majority reside in the Copper River region.

Ahtna, Incorporated

P.O. Box 649
Glennallen, AK 99588
907-822-3476
907-822-3495 Fax
ahtna-inc.com

Organization

*Ahtna Construction and
    Primary Products
    Corporation (AC&PPC)*

*Ahtna Development
    Corporation (ADC)*

*Ahtna Enterprises
    Corporation (AEC)*

*Ahtna Government Services
    Corporation (AGSC)*

*Ahtna Technical Services
    Incorporated (ATSI)*

*Wire-Communications
    and Electrical, Inc.*

Organization

Ahtna employs 375 people in its corporate office, joint ventures, and subsidiaries. There are 55 additional employees in shareholder employment. Ahtna has six operating subsidiaries and two joint ventures. Subsidiaries are involved in construction, pipeline maintenance, facilities maintenance, administrative and janitorial services, electrical contracting, fiber-optic telecommunication, forestry, and gravel sales. First tier and major second tier subsidiaries include:

Ahtna Construction and Primary Products Corporation (AC&PPC), located in Glennallen, Alaska, was organized in 1974 as a wholly owned subsidiary of Ahtna, Incorporated. AC&PPC received its 8(a) certification in March 2000 and Hubzone status in October 2001. The company is certified in oil spill response, along with performing major projects for Alyeska Pipeline Service Company for the past 20 years. Other lines of business include general highway construction, building construction, electrical and mechanical services, rock crushing, and the sale of processed materials.

Ahtna Development Corporation (ADC) is a wholly owned subsidiary. ADC received its 8(a) certification in 1994. ADC's core businesses are operations and maintenance (O&M), specializing in facilities management, information technology, records management, help desk, and imaging.

Ahtna Enterprises Corporation (AEC) is a wholly owned 8(a) subsidiary specializing in governmental contracting. Core business operations include demolition, fuels reduction (National Fire Plan), vertical construction, civil work, and environmental cleanup.

Ahtna Government Services Corporation (AGSC) was founded in January 1999. AGSC received its 8(a) certification in 1999. AGSC is a full-service governmental contractor with government-approved pricing and accounting systems. Ahtna Government Services Corporation's three major market sectors are environmental engineering and demolition, general contracting, and professional services. AGSC provides these services worldwide. AGSC is concentrating on construction and base-maintenance operations to develop relationships to open doors to the professional service aspect of privatization.

Ahtna Technical Services Incorporated (ATSI) was formed in October 1999. ATSI received its 8(a) certification in 2001. With a work backlog of $5 million per year till 2007, ATSI has achieved a national contract presence in facility operations and maintenance (O&M), and shared services. ATSI is currently marketing its services as a preferred technical service provider.

Wire-Communications and Electrical, Inc., established in 1968, specializes in all aspects of communication and electrical projects. They are presently performing work for local, state, and federal government agencies. They also perform work for

military installations and private-sector businesses. Wire-Communications currently sells video conferencing equipment (to include tele-medicine and distance learning), key telephone systems, voice mail systems, and PBXs. Wire-Communications, received its 8(a) certification in 1999 and works closely with the GSA under a 10-million-dollar Indefinite Delivery/Indefinite Quality (ID/IQ) contract.

Village Corporations

Ahtna represents eight villages, with only one remaining village corporation :

Cantwell	Yedatene Na Corporation (merged into Ahtna in 1980)
Chistochina	Cheesh-Na, Incorporation (merged into Ahtna in 1980)
Gakona	Gakona Corporation (merged into Ahtna in 1980)
Gulkana	Sta-Keh Corporation (merged into Ahtna in 1980)
Kluti-Kaah (Copper Center)	Kluti-Kaah Corporation (merged into Ahtna in 1980)
Mentasta	Mentasta, Incorporation (merged into Ahtna in 1980)
Tazlina	Tazlina, Incorporation (merged into Ahtna in 1980)
Chitina	Chitina Native Corporation (chose not to merge with Ahtna)

Income Operations

Although tourism fuels the economy in the Copper River Valley, 90 percent of Ahtna's business is outside the state.

Natural-resource holdings include surface estate, subsurface, and timber. The surface estate (excluding timber and including gravel) and management responsibility for the surface estate would reside in a unit of the parent company named the land department. The subsurface estate (excluding gravel) and management responsibilities for those assets were given to Ahtna Minerals Company, Inc. (AMC). Timber assets and management responsibility for those assets were transferred to subsidiary Ahtna Forest Products Inc.

Ahtna also owns janitorial services for military hospitals in Alaska and a 50-person Immigration and Naturalization Service facility in Batavia, New York. Ahtna has contract services in Germany and Korea, and Ahtna Government Services maintains offices in San Francisco, Los Angeles, Fresno, Sacramento, and Honolulu. Another subsidiary, Ahtna Enterprises built a $3-million visitors' center at Denali National Park and Preserve near Healy.

Ahtna's nearly 1.8 million acres in the Copper River and Cantwell/Broad Pass areas of east-central Alaska includes or is adjacent to the original Kennicott copper deposits, the Valdez Creek and Nabesna gold mines, and the Healy coal fields. Ahtna's lands contain gold, copper, base metals, platinum and tungsten mineralization, coal deposits, and indications of oil and gas. During the 1970s

Ahtna completed a grassroots exploration and mineral inventory program, which identified several promising mineral prospects for further exploration. Reports from this effort are available, as are core and assay data from subsequent exploration. BLM released reports about the mineral potential of some Ahtna land selections that are within or border national park lands.

Ahtna plans to expand its tourism-related business to take advantage of its location relative to and holdings in Denali and Wrangell-St. Elias National Parks.

Results
Revenue for Ahtna, Incorporated, in 2000 was $62,028,126, thanks to government contracts and job opportunities beyond Alaska.

The Aleut Corporation (TAC)

Introduction
The Aleut Corporation (TAC) is the ANCSA regional corporation for the western end of the Alaska Peninsula and the Aleutian, Shumagin, and Pribilof Islands of Alaska. It is a for-profit corporation organized in 1972 under the laws of the State of Alaska, with certain restrictions imposed by federal law. It has evolved from a commercial fishing business into a multisector concern, with its focus on government contracting. It has 3,249 shareholders, gross revenues of $49.1 million in FY2003, and assets (as of March 31, 2003) of $48.5 million. Based on gross revenue, TAC was ranked as the 12th largest Alaskan corporation by *Alaska Business Monthly* in 2002. TAC's headquarters is officially in Anchorage. There are 13 ANCSA village corporations in the TAC area.

Entitlement
Under the ANCSA, TAC was entitled to 66,000 acres of selected land in its geographic area, $19,504,000, and the subsurface rights to 1,572,000 acres. The lands selected by the corporation included areas on the Alaska Peninsula and the Aleutian, Shumagin, and Pribilof islands. Its original selection strategy was to acquire aggregate sources and other natural resources of commercial value, of which there were few. It also acquired the village site of Attu and numerous historical and cemetery sites throughout the Aleut Region. Through an exchange with the U.S. government, the corporation acquired the closed military facility on Adak Island, which, historically, was an early Aleut community. Adak is at the center of TAC's strategy for providing jobs and an economic base within its corporate area.

History
The Aleut Corporation is one of the 13 regional Native Alaskan corporations established under the ANCSA. As the Aleut culture is based on fishing, for 20 years the corporation focused on commercial fishing and related business. It was not profitable. In the early 1990s, TAC took advantage of its minority ownership to move into government contracting, where it was much more successful. One of TAC's early contracts was as caretaker of the dormant navy base at Adak, which had been an Aleut village before World War II. At the same time, TAC began to approach the U.S. government about taking over Adak permanently. This became the central goal of the corporation and was completed in 2004.

The Naval Facilities Engineering Command, in its "Adak Island Update: Adak Land Transfer Fact Sheet," states the following:

> The most noteworthy feature of the land exchange agreement is the conveyance of 47,271 acres of the former Naval Air Facility (NAF) Adak property to TAC, in exchange for TAC's relinquishment of a similar acreage of prioritized, valid ANCSA surface and subsurface property. TAC will acquire the downtown area of Adak, where the former NAF was located and which includes the airfield; port facilities; utilities infrastructure; and light industrial, administration, commercial, recreational, and residential areas. The facilities and improvements located on the northern portion of Adak Island are valued at approximately $1.5 billion. This real estate and the associated facilities will be used as the core of the future economy for Adak Island.

A further benefit of acquiring and developing Adak has been its selection by the Department of Defense as the base for the new mid-course radar system, a $900-million investment. While the development of Adak has been a financial burden on the corporation, it appears to be an investment that is paying off. Adak became a second class city in 2001, making it the southernmost city in Alaska. TAC intends to develop Adak as a support center for international fishing fleets, U.S. government activities (environmental cleanup and another radar site), ocean research, and tourism.

Corporate governance
Under the terms of the ANCSA, Alaskan Natives enrolled in one of the 11 BIA-recognized villages in the region and certain other Alaskan Natives were enrolled in the corporation. Each received 100 shares of the corporation's stock. This stock may not be transferred or encumbered except in certain specific circumstances involving gifts, court action, or death. Even then the stock carries voting rights only if the shareholder is an eligible Alaskan Native or descendant of a Native. As of March 31, 2003, the corporation had 3,249 shareholders. The shareholders elect a nine-member board of directors charged with the operation of the corporation. Three of the members of the board of directors are also officers of the corporation, and a fourth is a former president. Three of the directors live in Unalaska, three in Anchorage, and one in Seattle.

The Aleut Corporation (TAC)
4000 Old Seward Highway
Suite 300
Anchorage, AK 99503
907-561-4300
907-563-4328 Fax
aleutcorp.com

Organization

Aleut Enterprise Corporation
Akima Corporation.
Ki LLC
SMI International Corporation
TekStar, Inc.
Alaska Trust Company
Aleut Real Estate

The Aleut Corporation (TAC)

Organization
TAC is organized in a network of subsidiaries and joint ventures. There are seven "first tier" subsidiaries.

Aleut Enterprise Corporation. Development of Adak includes property leasing, port services, fixed-base aircraft services, fuel sales, vehicle rental, and a fuel terminal facility in Cold Bay.

Akima Corporation. Akima is a joint venture with NANA Development Corporation in the federal government operations and maintenance contracting business with special emphasis in the southeast region of the Lower 48. It is only 20 percent owned by TAC.

Ki LLC. Ki LLS is a Joint venture with NANA Development Corporation in the federal government operations and maintenance contracting business with special emphasis in research, development, test and evaluation, and communications. It is only 25 percent owned by TAC.

SMI International Corporation. SML has federal government logistics, communications, and base operations and maintenance (O&M) contracts in nine states and four overseas locations.

TekStar, Inc. TekStar performs federal government O&M contracts.

Alaska Trust Company. Alaska trust provides specialized trust services to take advantage of Alaska's liberal trust laws. It is 73 percent owned by TAC and is the only such corporation in Alaska.

Aleut Real Estate. This firm engages in commercial real estate activities.

Village Corporations
TAC represents 13 village corporations:

Akutan	Akutan Corporation
Atka	Atxam Corporation
Belkofski	Belkofski Corporation
Nikolski	Chaluka Corporation
False Pass	Isanotski Corporation
King Cove	King Cove Corporation
Nelson Lagoon	Nelson Lagoon Corp.
Unalaska	Ounalaska Corporation
St. George	St.George Tanaq Corp.
Pauloff Harbor	Sanak Corporation
Sand Point	Shumagin Corporation
St. Paul	Tanadgusix Corporation
Unga	Unga Corporation

Relationships
Among the other regional corporations, TAC has several joint ventures with NANA involving government contracting. Six of the villages are from the Aleutians East Borough, the mayor of which was a director of the corporation as of 2003-04.

Income Operations
External
Government contracting. This category includes federal government logistics, communications, base operations and maintenance (O&M) contracts in nine states and four overseas locations, and two joint ventures with NANA. Revenues from contracting have been dropping steadily as TAC's subsidiaries "graduate" from the 8(a) minority ownership preference program. TAC must now compete with the major base-support contractors. Gross revenues were $34,745,000 in FY2003.

Software. Gross revenues were $3,085,000 in FY2003. This subsidiary was sold in 2004.

Real estate rental. This category includes the development of Adak and commercial real estate in Anchorage, Alaska, and Colorado Springs, Colorado. Other real estate investments are located in Valdez, Alaska, Portland, Oregon, and elsewhere in Alaska. Gross revenues were $2,683,000 in FY2003.

Fuel sales (port and aircraft services). Adak is the major marine refueling station for this region of the North Pacific. The island's underground tank farm has a storage capacity for over 22 million gallons of marine diesel, gasoline and jet fuel. Gross revenues were $5,520,000 in FY2003.

Trust services. See Organization above.

Internal
Adak development. As of FY2003, this had not generated revenues outside the contracting, real estate rental, and fuel sales categories above. Plans are described under History above. It is important to note that this is not just an investment but is intended to provide jobs, housing, and other facilities for shareholders within the TAC area.

Gravel and rock sales. This category generated $268,000 in sales in FY2003.

Section 7(i) revenue sharing from the other Alaskan Native regional corporations in FY2003 totaled $975,000.

TAC maintains an investment pool called the Permanent Fund. Profits from the portfolio are reinvested in the fund. At the end of FY2003, the fund was valued at $5,380,000.

Other Operations
TAC made contributions in FY2003 to charitable and not-for-profit organizations that benefit company shareholders and their descendants in the amount of $266,000, up from $214,000 in the prior year. The development of Adak should have a profound effect on employment, housing, and the availability of other amenities within the TAC area.

Results
For the fiscal year ending March 31, 2003, TAC reported consolidated net income of $2,807,000, compared to $2,233,000 in the prior year. However, gross revenues dropped substantially from FY2001 to FY2002, and then again from FY2002 to FY2003. TAC appears to be putting all its eggs into the Adak basket as its contracting subsidiaries "graduate" from federal minority ownership preference programs.

Arctic Slope Regional Corporation (ASRC)

Introduction

Arctic Slope Regional Corporation (ASRC) is the ANCSA regional corporation for the northern coast of Alaska. It is a for-profit corporation organized in 1971 under the laws of the State of Alaska, with certain restrictions imposed by federal law. Its geographic area is coextensive with North Slope Borough, with which it maintains a close and interesting relationship, described under History below. It has evolved into a diversified services, extraction, and manufacturing concern, with its focus on the petroleum industry. It is the third-largest corporation in Alaska, with annual revenues hovering around $1 billion. ASRC is on the Forbes 500 list of leading privately held companies, and according to *Alaska Business Monthly* magazine, is the number-one revenue-producing Alaskan-owned company. It is also Alaska's largest private employer, with more than 6,500 employees worldwide including about 3,500 in Alaska. ASRC's headquarters is officially in Barrow, but many of its corporate administrative functions are located in Anchorage.

Entitlement

Under the ANCSA, ASRC was entitled to 5.1 million acres of selected land in its geographic area, $22.5 million, and the subsurface rights to the land granted to the eight village corporations located within its geographic area (see Organization below). ASRC explicitly sought land with high resource potential. It now owns approximately five million acres of land with either known or probable oil, gas, coal, and mineral deposits. Because of the existence of vast petroleum reserves in ASRC's geographic area, its ANCSA entitlements are both more restricted and more valuable than those of the other 12 ANCSA regional corporations.

History

Passage of the ANCSA during the period when the exploitation of petroleum under Alaska's North Slope was beginning to take off created an economic opportunity not to be missed. ASRC was quick to take advantage of it. Its goals were clear: Gain title to the lands with the greatest resource potential, then find, extract, and market those resources. These goals were to be met without compromising the traditional value for subsistence that the land holds for Native Alaskans. This has involved entering into agreements with federal and state governments, lawsuits against those governments, and Congressional intervention in the Alaska National Interest Lands Conservation Act (ANILCA). It has exploited the existence of many pre-ANCSA Native allotments in the National Petroleum Reserve-Alaska (NPR-A) to bargain for favorable land exchanges with the federal government.

One of the critical externalities contributing to the success of ASRC was the simultaneous and coterminious creation of North Slope Borough. The creation of North Slope Borough as a self-rule political subunit of the State of Alaska was pushed through the state legislature by the same people who were instrumental in the passage of the federal ANCSA and in the initial organization of ASRC. The Prudhoe Bay oil fields were on land that was not available for selection by ASRC. The organization of North Slope Borough created a political entity with property taxation authority over the assets employed by the oil industry in exploiting the fields. By keeping property tax rates at an acceptable level, North Slope Borough enabled the people of the area to tap into the huge wealth being extracted while keeping the support and cooperation of the oil industry.

ASRC got off to a slow start, losing money 5 out of its first 10 years in business. It entered into partnerships with more experienced firms to improve its intellectual capital. It made substantial revenues in the 1990s selling exploration rights, but the economic slowdown around the turn of the century stopped that process. Being well-capitalized, ASRC exploited the downturn to improve its property holdings. Low levels of activity in Alaska's oil and gas industry hurt the revenues of subsidiary ASRC Energy Services, which contributes about half of the ASRC's revenues. However, revenues from construction and government contracting activities outside Alaska have been growing. As a minority-owned firm, ASRC gets preferential treatment for federal contracts. Diversifying out of Alaska and out of energy production and services, it is making itself less vulnerable to local business conditions and the instability of the petroleum industry.

To aid its evolution from oil field service provider and landowner to independent oil and gas producer in its own right, in 2003 ASRC entered into a "mentoring" agreement with major North Slope producer BP Exploration (Alaska) Inc., Alaska's largest investor and one of the biggest oil and gas companies in the world. The agreement "establishes a framework for sharing data and technical knowledge" between the two companies. ASRC intends to enhance its existing exploration, development, and operating capabilities. It also gains access to land and resources it was precluded from selecting under the ANCSA.

Corporate governance

Under the terms of the ANCSA, Alaskan Natives enrolled in one of the eight BIA-recognized villages in the ASRC region were enrolled in the Corporation. Each received 100 shares of the corporation's stock. This stock may not be transferred or encumbered except in certain specific circumstances involving gifts, court action, or death. Even then the stock carries voting rights only if the shareholder is an eligible Alaskan Native or descendant of a Native. The corporation has five classes of stock as of December 31, 2002:

Class A 1,000,000 shares authorized, 353,700 outstanding. Originally issued to shareholders enrolled in a village corporation.

Arctic Slope Regional Corporation (ASRC)
Barrow Office
P.O. Box 129
Barrow, Alaska 99723
907-852-8633
907-852-5733 Fax

Anchorage Office
3900 C Street, Suite 801
Anchorage, AK 99503-5963
907-339-6000
907-339-6028 Fax
asrc.com

Arctic Slope Regional Corporation (ASRC)

Village Corporations

ASRC represents eight villages on the North Slope of Alaska (from west to east along the coast):

Point Hope
    Tigara Corporation

Point Lay
    Cully Corporation

Wainwright
    Olgoonik Corporation

Atqasuk
    Atqasuk Corporation

Barrow
    Ukpeagvik Inupiat Corporation

Nuiqsut
    Kuukpik Corporation

Kaktovik
    Kaktovik Inupiat Corporation and (inland to the south)

Anaktuvuk Pass
    Nunamiut Corporation

Class B 500,000 shares authorized, 19,900 outstanding. Originally issued to shareholders eligible but not enrolled in a village corporation.

Class C 1,000,000 shares authorized, 480,400 outstanding. Issued to Alaskan Natives born after December 18, 1971, to an eligible parent. Not inheritable.

Class D 300,000 shares authorized, 41,400 outstanding. Issued to non-Natives born to an eligible Alaskan Native parent. Not inheritable.

Class E 10,000 shares authorized, 700 outstanding. Issued to Alaska Natives who were eligible for enrollment at the time Class A shares were issued but who were not enrolled.

All five classes are fully and equally participating. The shareholders elect a 15-member board of directors charged with the operation of the corporation. It appears that five of the directors are from Barrow, one from each of the other seven villages, and three at-large. Including the chairman (who is a vice-president), eight of the directors are officers of the corporation. One of the non-officer directors represents Barrow; the other six represent other villages. Four of the Barrow representatives and all three at-large directors are officers.

Organization

ASRC is organized in a network of subsidiaries and joint ventures. There are 17 first tier subsidiaries, including the consolidated headquarters support organization. To some extent ASRC competes with itself in a number of areas, having both union and "merit" subsidiaries.

ASRC Energy Services provides engineering, construction, project management, maintenance, and operations, specializing in energy and industrial projects. It has operations in Canada, Great Britain, Russia, and along the U.S. Gulf Coast. This company generated revenues of $373.1 million in 2002, 38 percent of total ASRC revenues. It was formerly known as Natchiq. ASRC Energy Services built the 25-mile Kenai-Kachemak Pipeline (KKPL), a new 12-inch pipeline built in 2003 to carry gas from new discoveries near Ninilchik, on the Kenai Peninsula, to the Enstar Natural Gas Co. system. The KKPL pipeline is now being extended further south on the peninsula by ASRC. ASRC will probably be involved in the construction of the Alaska part of a new gas pipeline from the North Slope to the U.S. Midwest, and may have an ownership interest in it. ASRC Energy Services includes more than 20 subsidiaries organized into three business units:

(1) Operations and Maintenance (formerly known as APC Natchiq and Natchiq Sakhalin Ltd.), is primarily focused in Alaska and Russia. Natchiq Sakhalin, LLC, supplies oil and gas project services in Russia's Far East. It was created in 1998 as a joint venture with Russia's Dalectromontazh to develop Sakhalin region oil and gas projects, combining Western technologies and Arctic experience with 50 percent Russian ownership for effective Russian project management. ASRC Energy Services Inspection, Inc., supplies inspection services and engineering support for a variety of industries.

(2) Pipeline, Power, and Communications is focused on the pipeline and power transmission industry in Alaska and the Lower 48. Houston Contracting Company, Ltd., is one of the oldest union pipeline construction companies in the United States. It was purchased by ASRC in 1985. Houston/Nana, partly owned by Nana Corp., another ANCSA regional corporation, maintains the Trans-Alaska Pipeline System and the Valdez Marine Terminal. Global Power and Communications, LLC, is a union electrical contractor that builds power transmission lines, fiber optic communications systems, and power distribution and commercial electrical installations.

(3) Engineering and Technology (Omega Natchiq, Tri-Ocean Natchiq, and E&P Technology) is focused on Gulf Coast fabrication, domestic and international engineering, drilling support, well completion, and exploration and production management, with projects in Russia, India, Colombia, and North America.

Arctic Slope Compliance Technologies
ASRC Constructors, Inc.

Petro Star Inc. was organized in 1984 to produce light fuels for homes and businesses in Alaska. Petro Star built a refinery along the Trans-Alaska Pipeline near Fairbanks and acquired a number of fuel distribution companies in northern and interior Alaska. In 1991, Petro Star expanded into the lubricants market with the purchase of Alaska Lube and Fuel, now known as Petro Star Lubricants. In 1993, Petro Star Valdez Refinery began continuous operations. In 1994, with continuous and stable operations, Petro Star began servicing military and commercial aviation clients in Anchorage, now the refinery's largest business sector. A year later the company acquired Valdez Petroleum Terminal. Petro Star began serving customers in western Alaska with the purchase of Kodiak Oil Sales in 1997 and North Pacific Fuel in 1998. Petro Star operates a fully integrated petroleum refining, distribution, and marketing network that serves the Alaska market. Its refineries in Valdez and North Pole support a distribution and marketing system for residential, commercial, institutional, and military customers. These refineries produce jet, heating, and diesel fuels from crude oil drawn from the Trans-Alaska Pipeline.

ASRC Federal is a major defense contractor, headquartered in Greenbelt, Maryland.

ASRC Aerospace Corporation operates through three principal business segments, Engineering Services, Information Systems/Information Management, and Engineering Products. Each is comprised of multiple operating units engaged primarily in U.S. government contracts. Fifteen major contracts provided a base of 700+ personnel in 2002. Core competencies include systems engineering and operations, information management, hardware maintenance and operations, hardware electronics, software engineering, and spaceport and range research and technology.

Arctic Slope World Services (ASWS) was formed by ASRC in 1997 when it, in effect, merged two of its contracting subsidiaries. It has annual revenues of $90 million and 481 employees with operating locations in various states, Greenland, and England. ASWS provides radar, electrical, and communications system operations and maintenance, utilities and facilities operations and maintenance, base operations support, aviation support, security, and environmental, safety, and quality-control management.

ASRC Communications is a technical services and information technology company offering a variety of analytical, computer technology, and other types of support for government and commercial customers. Services include developing, modifying, and testing software for military applications, creating Web sites that control and provide access to databases, operating and maintaining computer networks and help desks, installing network and communication cabling, test and evaluation planning and executing for military systems, developing intelligence doctrine and testing intelligence-gathering devices for the army, and operating warehouses and maintaining government computer facilities.

FSSI is a 17-year-old company that was previously an independent government contractor specializing in logistics and transportation. Recently, all contracts were fulfilled and the company was being allowed to expire. Having an excellent record of past performance, ASRC purchased it in 2000, making it a 100 percent Alaskan Native American-owned company. It has offices in Virginia and Alabama, as well as in Anchorage. Contracting experience includes operations and maintenance for facilities, power and heating plants, and water and wastewater systems; solid waste services, hazardous waste management, and environmental services; real property management, housing management and maintenance, and roads and grounds maintenance; transportation, supply, warehousing, and fuels management; airfield management and defueling/refueling operations; quality control, administration, and publications; and contract administration, finance, human resources, and labor relations.

ASRC Airfield and Range Services

ASRC Management Services

ASCG, Inc., in an architectural and engineering services subsidiary founded in 1981. ASCG holds the distinction of being the first start-up subsidiary of ASRC, rather than resulting from a merger or an acquisition. It was ranked 133rd among the nation's Top 500 Design Firms and 82nd among the Top 100 Pure Design Firms by *Engineering*

News Record (ENR). It was selected to design and build the first Indian casino in the scenic Columbia River Gorge of Oregon. This is a large and controversial project carrying an estimated $100 million price tag, less than an hour's drive from Portland and owned by the Confederated Tribes of the Warm Springs.

Arctic Slope Technical Services, Inc., provides program management services, construction management, surveying, architecture, engineering, and other technical services to a broad clientele. It is based in New Mexico.

Puget Plastics Corporation manufactures custom injection-molded plastic parts, precision fabricated metal products and electronic assemblies and subassemblies for clients in the computer, electronics, aerospace, automotive, and consumer products industries.

Top of the World owns a hotel and a restaurant in Barrow and conducts tours of the North Slope area and the Alaskan Interior.

Alaska Growth Capital is a development financing bank that targets higher-risk commercial and industrial developments with a special emphasis in rural Alaska. Services include: construction lending, lines of credit, permanent working capital, equipment, and leasehold improvements; SBA, USDA, and BIA loan guarantee programs; and commercial real estate.

SKW Eskimos, Inc., is a commercial, industrial, earthwork, paving, and oil field service construction company which has operated throughout the state of Alaska since 1974.

Income Operations
Nearly two-thirds of ASRC's revenues come from oil; construction, environmental services, and government services provide about a quarter, with engineering, manufacturing, and other projects making up the rest. See "Organization" above.

External
Contracting. See ASRC Energy Services, Arctic Slope Compliance Technologies, Arctic Slope World Services, and ASRC Management Services

Defense contracting. See ASRC Federal, ASRC Aerospace Corporation, Arctic Slope World Services, ASRC Communications, FSSI, ASRC Airfield and Range Services, and ASRC Management Services.

Engineering and consulting. See ASRC Energy Services; Arctic Slope Compliance Technologies; ASRC Management Services; ASCG, Inc.; and Arctic Slope Technical Services, Inc.

Manufacturing. See ASRC Energy Services and Puget Plastics Corporation.

Petroleum refining and marketing. See ASRC Energy Services and Petro Star Inc.

Arctic Slope Regional Corporation (ASRC)

Organization

ASRC Energy Services

Arctic Slope Compliance Technologies

ASRC Constructors, Inc.

Petro Star Inc.

ASRC Aerospace Corporation

Arctic Slope World Services (ASWS)

ASRC Communications

FSSI

ASRC Airfield and Range Services

ASRC Management Services

ASCG, Inc.

Arctic Slope Technical Services, Inc.

Puget Plastics Corporation

Top of the World

Alaska Growth Capital

SKW Eskimos, Inc.

Arctic Slope Regional Corporation (ASRC)

Construction. See ASRC Energy Services; ASRC Constructors, Inc.; and SKW Eskimos, Inc.

Internal

Exploitation (petroleum, coal, minerals, metals) The Land Department of ASRC headquarters is responsible for the exploitation of ASRC holdings. In 1996, the Alpine oil field was discovered in the Colville River Delta near Nuiqsut. Half of it is under ASRC and Kuukpik Corporation lands. This deposit has estimated recoverable reserves of more than 350 million barrels. Production began in November 2000 with an estimated 60,000 barrels to 80,000 barrels pumped daily. Alpine is the fifth largest discovery on the North Slope. Discovery of the Fiord oil field, a 50-million-barrel satellite field to the north, and the Nanuq oil field, a 40-million-barrel satellite field to the south, increases the potential of finding such satellite accumulations in the area. ASRC and Kaktovik Inupiat Corporation own 92,000 subsurface and surface acres respectively in the coastal plain of the 19.8-million-acre Arctic National Wildlife Refuge. The acreage surrounds the Village of Kaktovik, the only settlement in the refuge. This has placed ASRC, supporting exploitation of the refuge, in opposition to many other Native Alaskan communities. ASRC has land entitlements in northwest Alaska that have excellent potential to host world-class zinc-lead-silver sulfide deposits. The Red Dog Mine, the world's largest lead/zinc mine, lies just outside ASRC lands. An estimated four trillion tons of high-quality bituminous coal, one-ninth of the world's known coal reserves and one-third of U.S. reserves, lie under the North Slope. ASRC holds title to extensive deposits of gravel, a key ingredient for oil field, pipeline, and industrial development in Arctic Alaska.

Travel, tourism and related services. See Top of the World.

Petroleum industry services (including pipelines and construction). See ASRC Energy Services; Arctic Slope Compliance Technologies; and ASRC Constructors, Inc.

Petroleum refining and marketing. See Petro Star Inc. Petro Star was responsible for 27 percent of ASRC revenues for FY2002.

Construction (other than petroleum industry). See SKW Eskimos, Inc.

Communications. ASRC owns Barrow Cable Television and ASRC Wireless Services, Inc. A bid to control Alaska's wireless telephone industry failed when the U.S. Supreme Court held that the Federal Communications Commission had erred in re-auctioning licenses owned by a bankrupt telecom company.

Retail and services. See Petro Star Inc.

Financial. See Alaska Growth Capital.

Other Operations

Development. ASRC's regional development efforts center around training programs for shareholders in oil-industry skills and college and vocational school scholarships in oil-industry-related vocations for shareholders. See the Arctic Slope Land and Resources Scholarship, below.

Cultural. In addition to financial support of various Inupiat organizations and institutions, ASRC helped create Inupiat House at the University of Alaska Fairbanks to help shareholders adjust to college life.

Educational. The Arctic Education Foundation, operated by ASRC, promotes, develops, implements, sponsors, and operates programs of assistance for "worthy and needy Inupiat Natives of the Arctic Slope Region of Alaska, or descendants of such persons, so as to aid them in the furtherance of their education or vocational training." The Land Department of ASRC offers a scholarship program to provide financial support to selected ASRC shareholders who wish to earn a college degree in natural resource development, for tuition and certain other expenses in full-time four-year degree programs in geology, petroleum engineering, or mineral engineering. In addition to financial support, ASRC mentors the scholarship recipients and assists in providing degree-related summer employment within ASRC or the Alaska mining and petroleum industries.

Environmental. ASRC lands have unique recreational values and offer spectacular wilderness experiences. Portions of ASRC lands are adjacent to or within national parks, reserves, and wildlife refuges. ASRC has entered into agreements that protect critical habitats and wildlife and has adopted appropriate operating procedures and restrictions in crucial habitat and scenic areas. ASRC has contributed lands to the National Park System and has granted conservation easements on nearly 52,000 acres of its lands within the Gates of the Arctic National Park and Preserve.

Results

From ASRC's 2002 annual report:

In 2002, the Company reported revenue of $974 million, an 8.3 percent decline from the previous year. As you'll see from reading this report, other key indicators of financial performance were also down, some considerably. Net income for the year was $16.8 million, a 45.6 percent drop from the year before. However, the Company's financial strength was sufficient to support distribution of $9.2 million in dividends, an increase of 7.8 percent over 2001. The Board of Directors and management are keenly aware of the importance of higher dividends to our shareholders, even as our shareholder population increases with the birth and enrollment of new children. The number of shares outstanding rose 2.4 percent in 2002.

Since inception, the Company has distributed more than $146 million in shareholder dividends and Elders' Trust distributions, over 30 percent of which have been distributed in the last five years.

The Company's financial performance (dividends plus growth in shareholders' equity) compares favorably to the S&P 500 Index with dividends-a standard benchmark of the biggest corporations in the country. This comparison holds true for performance over 1-, 3-, 5-, 10- and 20-year horizons.

Our focus on improving cash flow has paid off. At the end of 2002, we had more than $83 million in cash, despite a reduction of more than $38 million in our debt over the past two years. Healthy cash flow and less debt give us a stronger balance sheet, which in turn provides the Company greater ability to finance future growth. Only with future growth can the Company pay larger dividends to an ever-increasing number of shareholders.

However, not all shareholders are happy with these results. In early 2004, dissident shareholders organized a petition drive to call a special meeting of the shareholders and demand increased dividend payouts and more transparency and accountability in corporate decision-making and operations. The dissidents want management to explain how $1 billion in revenues becomes dividends of around $500 per shareholder. This is the first shareholder revolt in ASRC history.

Arctic Slope Regional Corporation (ASRC)

Bering Straits Native Corporation (BSNC)

Introduction
Bering Straits Native Corporation (BSNC) is the ANCSA regional corporation for the Bering Straits/Seward Peninsula/Norton Sound region of western Alaska. It is a for-profit corporation organized June 23, 1972, under the laws of the State of Alaska, with certain restrictions imposed by federal law. Its geographic area is the same as the Nome Census Area, in the Unorganized Borough. It has evolved into a diversified business concern, with its focus on investments, real estate development, auto and equipment rentals, mining services, quarry stone and services, construction and environmental services, and electrical contracting. Recent gold discoveries may shift that focus. BSNC has some 6,200 shareholders. It had revenues for 2002 over $10 million, although it posted a $556,000 net loss. BSNC's headquarters is in Nome.

Entitlement
Under the ANCSA, BSNC was entitled to 127,759 acres of selected land in its geographic area, $38 million, and the subsurface rights to the land granted to 17 of the village corporations located within its geographic area (see Organization below). As of March 31, 2002, BSNC had received interim conveyance or patent to 67,054 acres of land (surface and subsurface rights) and 1,987,301 acres of subsurface rights to the village corporation land.

History
Organized in 1972 under the ANCSA, BSNC had a rocky beginning. Its area did not have the convenient timber, oil, or gas resources of other regional corporations, and lack of experience led to poor investments with its cash distribution. Among other disasters, the corporation's construction company underbid a dock project by millions of dollars, and the corporation ran out of money for a hotel it started to build in Fairbanks. Its finances got tangled with those of the village corporations, and there were allegations of mismanagement of investment funds. BSNC repaid $14 million and conveyed subsurface rights to 900,000 acres to village corporations. It filed for Chapter 11 bankruptcy in 1986, and was reduced almost to a shell.

Clever federal legislation saved BSNC. When the sale of net operating losses was ended in 1986, Alaska's congressional delegation successfully exempted the ANCSA corporations. By 1989, the corporation was solvent, mostly through the sale of its earlier losses. The revived corporation turned to cautious investments. It has moved into government contracting, starting with environmental cleanup and electrical construction both in Alaska and in the Lower 48. In 1995, BSNC established a $1 million permanent fund to provide for future dividends to shareholders. In May 1999 Bering Straits Development opened the Aurora Inn in Nome, which was being doubled in size as of 2004.

This area was once the center of Alaskan gold mining, but the easily accessible gold was quickly depleted. However, improvements in extraction technology in recent years have made some deposits again viable, and BSNC is profiting from the leasing of exploration and exploitation rights. A substantial gold field has been discovered at Rock Creek near Nome that may yield up to one million ounces. The mining company anticipates an early 2005 decision on whether or not to develop.

Corporate governance
Under the terms of the ANCSA, Alaskan Natives enrolled in one of the 17 BIA-recognized villages in the Bering Straits/Seward Peninsula/Norton Sound region as of December 18, 1971, were enrolled in the corporation. There were originally 6,333 shareholders, each receiving 100 shares of the corporation's stock. The shareholders elect a 15-member board of directors charged with the operation of the corporation. It appears that most of the directors are not officers or employees of the corporation.

Bering Straits Native Corporation (BSNC)
P.O. Box 1008
Nome, AK 99762
907-443-5252
907-443-2985
beringstraits.com

**Bering Straits Native
Corporation (BSNC)**

Organization

*Bering Straits Development
Company*

Stampede Ventures

Golden Glacier Inc.

Sound Quarry, Inc.

Eagle Electric, LLC

Inuit Services, Inc.

Cape Nome Products

Organization

The headquarters structure for BSNC includes departments for Administration (stockholder and staff relations); Finance/Controller (accounting and daily operations); Land Department (manages all land assets); and the Bering Straits Foundation (shareholder "welfare of spirit through education and cultural preservation"). BSNC is organized in a network of subsidiaries and joint ventures. There are seven "first tier" subsidiaries.

Bering Straits Development Company (real estate holdings and hotel)

Stampede Ventures (automobile rental)

Golden Glacier Inc. (gold mining operations)

Sound Quarry, Inc. (hard rock subsurface sales)

Eagle Electric, LLC, (electrical construction service; also in North Carolina) and Eagle Eye Electric LLC (Las Vegas, Nevada)

Inuit Services, Inc. (seeking federal contracts)

Cape Nome Products (granite products)

Village Corporations

BSNC represents 20 villages on the Bering Straits/ Seward Peninsula/Norton Sound region:

Brevig Mission	Brevig Mission Native Corporation
Council	Council Native Corp.
Elim (See note)	Elim Native Corp.
Golovin	Golovin Native Corp.
Koyuk	Koyuk Native Corp.
King Island	King Island Native Corporation
Diomede	Diomede Native Corp.
Mary's Igloo	Mary's Igloo Native Corporation
Savoonga (See Note)	Savoonga Native Corp.
Shaktoolik	Shaktoolik Native Corp.
Shishmaref	Shishmaref Native Corp.
Gambell (See note)	Sivuqaq Incorporated
Nome	Sitnasuak Native Corp.
Solomon	Solomon Native Corp.
St. Michael	St. Michael Native Corp.
Stebbins	Stebbins Native Corp.
Teller	Teller Native Corp.
Unalakleet	Unalakleet Native Corp.
Wales	Wales Native Corp.
White Mountain	White Mountain Native Corporation

Note that three villages located within the BSNC area, Elim, Savoonga, and Gambell (*q.v.*), elected to retain title to their preexisting reserved lands, rather than select lands through the ANCSA process and therefore the subsurface rights to their land does not belong to BSNC.

Relationships

BSNC has exploration and development arrangements with Novagold that have located several potential gold fields in the Nome area.

Income Operations

External

Investments in securities provided 29 percent of 2000 revenue.

Rentals from real estate investments provided 27 percent of 2000 revenue. Bering Straits Development Co. is BSNC's largest subsidiary, with assets of $8.66 million. Among other real estate investments, it owns and operates a 200-space mobile home park in Valdez.

Federal contracts provided 36 percent of 2000 revenue, and this sector is growing. Inuit Services' specialty is environmental cleanup. It has contracts to clean up old military sites in the Seward Peninsula area, among others.

Construction, particularly electrical subcontracting, in Alaska, Nevada, and North Carolina also contributes to income.

Internal

Rental from real estate investments includes a hangar in Unalakleet, rental units in Nome, and Nome's Old Federal Building.

Tourism and travel operation include the Aurora Inn in Nome, owned and operated by Bering Straits Development Company.

Automobile rental operations include Stampede Ventures.

Mining and related industries include gold mining and mine services, rock mining and sales, and granite products.

Other Operations

BSNC is helping build quality housing for teachers in the villages, hoping that this will mean lower teacher turnover and better education. The Bering Straits Foundation provides scholarships for shareholders and supports a program that brings doctors into communities to work with elders. BSNC is also active in repatriation of Native artifacts and remains from the Smithsonian and in other Native advocacy issues. Subsidiary Inuit Services, Inc., has provided material, equipment, supervision, architectural, mechanical, and electrical installation services for rebuilding in the villages after disasters.

Results

BSNC returned to solvency in the 1990s, showing a profit for 10 years before dropping into the red in 2001 and 2002. It remains one of the smallest and poorest of the regional Native corporations, but the discovery of exploitable gold fields may change this status dramatically.

Bristol Bay Native Corporation (BBNC)

Introduction

Bristol Bay Native Corporation (BBNC) is the ANCSA regional corporation for the area surrounding Bristol Bay in southwest Alaska, an area about the size of Ohio. It is a for-profit corporation organized June 13, 1972, under the laws of the State of Alaska, with certain restrictions imposed by federal law. Its geographic area is coextensive with the Dillingham Census District and the small Bristol Bay Borough. It has its focus on investments, petroleum sales, and contract services. BBNC had 7,067 shareholders (6,948 voting) as of March 31, 2003. Total revenues for fiscal year 2002 were $187.4 million. BBNC's headquarters is officially in Dillingham, but most of its corporate administrative functions are located in Anchorage.

An important and unusual aspect of the relationship between BBNC and the Bristol Bay area is the lack of involvement of BBNC in the dominant area industry, fishing. Many of the village corporations are actively involved in the fishing industry, and most of the directors of the corporation are or have been commercial fishermen. It appears that the role of BBNC is to provide economic diversification to a region that is, perhaps, overly dependent on fishing.

Entitlement

Under the ANCSA, BBNC was entitled to 2.9 million acres of selected land in its geographic area, $32,694,953, and the subsurface rights to the land granted to the village corporations located within its geographic area (see Organization below). As of 2003, it had received interim conveyance to 2,728,000 acres of subsurface estate with patent to 1,661,000 of this and interim conveyance to 75,000 acres of surface and subsurface estate with patent to 62,000 acres.

History

BBNC began with its cash award and no major natural resources. It entered a variety of industries with, at best, mixed results. The corporation narrowed its scope of diversification in the mid-1990s, reinforcing its more successful endeavors in environmental services and government contracting. However, it maintained a portfolio of marketable securities that now constitutes half of its assets (not including its land holdings). This portfolio has served as a buffer against losses incurred by operating companies. BBNC has maintained a fairly high level of dividends, dipping into the investment portfolio when necessary and making large distributions when major assets are sold. As of 2003, it had distributed over $45 million in dividends since its organization. The corporation's goals have been to support its shareholders steadily, even at the cost of lower rates of return. It supported the area fishing industry by opposing petroleum exploitation in the Bristol Bay basin. However, with steady loss of employment in the fishing industry, BBNC has begun supporting exploration and exploitation as a source of jobs for its shareholders.

Corporate governance

Under the terms of the ANCSA, Alaskan Natives enrolled in one of the 29 BIA-recognized villages or otherwise connected with the corporation's area were enrolled in the corporation. Each received 100 shares of the corporation's stock. This stock may not be transferred or encumbered except in certain specific circumstances involving gifts, court action, or death. Even then the stock carries voting rights only if the shareholder is an eligible Alaskan Native or descendant of a Native. BBNC had 7,067 shareholders (6,948 voting) as of March 31, 2003. The shareholders elect an 11-member board of directors charged with the operation of the corporation. Of the directors, only the chairman of the board appears on the list of officers and staff members, as president and CEO, as of 2003.

Organization

BBNC is organized in a network of subsidiaries and joint ventures. It makes a conscious effort to enter industries and acquire going concerns that will provide job opportunities for its shareholders. There are six "first tier" subsidiaries:

Bristol Environmental and Engineering Services Corporation was organized in 1994. It provides environmental, civil engineering, and construction management services.

CCI, Inc. provides oil field services, including removal of hazardous wastes, environmental surveys, and specialty coatings. A majority interest was purchased in 1998; it became wholly owned in 2001.

PetroCard Systems, Inc. (84 percent). Offers cardlock and mobile fleet fueling in Washington State. A majority interest was purchased in 1997.

SpecPro, Inc., provides environmental, information management, and engineering and technical services, mostly on federal contracts. A majority interest was purchased in 1998; it became wholly owned in 2001. It includes Vista International Operations, purchased in 2001.

BBkp, Inc., architects specializing in health care, housing, hospitality industry, and military base reuse studies, was organized in 1996.

Kakivik Asset Management, LLC (67 percent), performs nondestructive testing and inspection for the petroleum and construction industries. BBNC bought out one of the founding partners in 2001 to obtain majority control.

Village Corporations

BBNC works with 25 village corporations in 32 villages in Southwest Alaska around Bristol Bay and in the Dillingham area:

Kokhanok, Newhalen, Port Heiden, South Naknek, and Ugashik

Alaska Peninsula Corporation

Bristol Bay Native Corporation (BBNC)
P.O. Box 3310
Dillingham, AK 99576
907-443-5252
bbnc.net

Bristol Bay Native Corporation (BBNC)

Organization

Bristol Environmental & Engineering Services Corporation

CCI, Inc.

PetroCard Systems, Inc.

SpecPro, Inc.

BBkp, Inc.

Kakivik Asset Management, LLC

Aleknagik	Aleknagik Natives Ltd.
Ivanof Bay	Bay View Incorporated
Egegik	Becharof Corporation
Chignik Lagoon	Chignik Lagoon Native Corporation
Chignik Lake	Chignik River Ltd.
Dillingham, Ekuk, and Portage Creek	Choggiung Ltd
Ekwok	Ekwok Natives Ltd.
Chignik	Far West Incorporated
Igiugig	Igiugig Native Corp.
Iliamna	Iliamna Natives Ltd.
Nondalton	Kijik Corp.
Koliganek	Koliganek Natives Ltd.
Levelock	Levelock Natives Ltd.
Manakotak	Manokotak Natives Ltd.
Perryville	Oceanside Native Corp.
Knugank (Note1)	Olsonville Inc.
Naknek	Paug-Vik Inc.
Pedro Bay	Pedro Bay Native Corp.
Pilot Point	Pilot Point Native Corp.
Clarks Point	Saguyak Inc.
New Stuyahok	Stuyahok Ltd.
Port Alsworth (Note 2)	Tanalian Inc.
Togiak	Togiak Natives Ltd.
Twin Hills	Twin Hills Native Corp.
King Salmon	(Note 3)

Note 1. Not federally recognized; Olsonville Inc. is not an ANCSA corporation.

Note 2. Not federally recognized; Tanalian Incorporated is not an ANCSA corporation. The State of Alaska shows the village to be located in the Cook Inlet Region Incorporated area.

Note 3. The Village of King Salmon was not included in the ANCSA and does not have a village corporation.

The BBNC leadership works closely with the village corporations and the individual shareholders in the villages, holding town meetings in the villages frequently and providing local instruction to shareholders on the legal and other aspects of the corporation's form and operations. BBNC appears to have excellent working relationships with the village corporations.

Relationships

With neither significant timber or subsurface resources nor major political units within its area, BBNC appears to have no major business, political, or support relationships.

Income Operations

BBNC does not distinguish between income operations within and without its corporate area and is not exploiting its land.

Investments in marketable securities. The portfolio loss in FY2003 was more than five times the net earnings of all the operational elements totaled. This is a "paper" loss, as these securities have not been sold and may appreciate in the future. The portfolio is doing significantly better than all the major securities indices.

Environmental and remediation services. Bristol Environmental and Engineering Services Corporation, SpecPro, and CCI all provide services in this area. SpecPro focuses on government contracts, which are growing. CCI works with the petroleum industry. Bristol Environmental is primarily a consulting firm for both the private and public sectors.

Oil field services. BBNC moved into this area with its purchase of CCI, but declining North Slope oil production has cut revenues while overhead has increased as a percentage of revenues, leading to net revenue decreasing steadily and a loss in 2003.

Fleet fueling in Washington State. Slightly more than half of 2003 operating company net earnings came from PetroCard sales, although earnings dropped for three consecutive years. BBNC attributes this drop to the economic slump in the Pacific Northwest. Gallons sold actually increased from 2002 to 2003, but this was due to new sales locations, new customers, and probably aggressive pricing.

Information technology services. Spec Pro provides IT services to federal government agencies, including the Defense Department, Drug Enforcement Agency, Department of Energy, Environmental Protection Agency, U.S. Army Corps of Engineers, U.S. Forest Service, and Department of Agriculture. SpecPro has been able to retain existing contracts and win new ones.

Architecture and associated services. Provided by BBkp, this is a small part of BBNC from a revenue perspective but appears to be important from a "public service" standpoint, as these services are primarily for health care facilities, public housing, and other public facilities in Alaska.

Corrosion inspection services. Kakovik performs nondestructive (e.g., radiological) inspection of pipelines and other materials. Kakivik inspects the Alyeska Pipeline and has expanded to support other customers in Alaska. Earnings increased 400 percent from 2002 to 2003, and constituted almost 30 percent of BBNC operating companies' 2003 net earnings.

Engineering support services. These services are provided by SpecPro (federal contracts) and Bristol Environmental and Engineering Services Corporation (public and private sector).

Other Operations

BBNC provides corporate, shareholder, and office services to village corporations within its area. Through its BBNC Education Foundation, the Corporation provides scholarships and management training for shareholders.

Results

BBNC prides itself on steady, predictable returns to its shareholders. Since its organization, it has paid out almost half-again more in dividends than its initial cash entitlement and still has grown to around $143 million in value, *not including its land.*

Its securities portfolio suffered losses soon after 2000, but only one-third of the loss of the broader market. Furthermore, these losses are unrealized-BBNC did not sell these securities-and with the recovery of the markets can anticipate a return to profitability. Its operations in the private sector have tracked the economy overall, while government contracting and inspection services have continued to grow. In spite of the economic downturn of the years immediately following 2000, BBNC has been able to increase dividends for 13 consecutive years through 2004.

Bristol Bay Native
Corporation (BBNC)

Calista Corporation (Calista)

Introduction
Calista Corporation (Calista-pronounced "cha-LIS-ta") is the ANCSA regional corporation for much of the Kuskokwim River drainage, the lower Yukon, and the coastline stretching from the northern edge of Bristol Bay to the southern edge of Norton Sound, largely roadless and one of the poorest areas in Alaska. Calista is a for-profit corporation organized June 12, 1972, under the laws of the State of Alaska, with certain restrictions imposed by federal law. It is the second-largest of the 13 regional corporations. Its geographic area is roughly coextensive with the Bethel Census Area. There are no boroughs within its area. It has evolved into a multisector concern, with its focus on exploitation of the mineral content of its land. Calista's headquarters is in Anchorage, but some administrative functions are located in Bethel. In the Yup'ik language, the name Calista is formed from cali which means "work" and ista which means "someone who or something which does: worker."

Entitlement
Under the ANCSA, Calista was entitled to 238,000 acres of selected land in its geographic area, $80.1 million, and the subsurface rights to the approximately 6.2 million acres of land granted to the 46 village corporations located within its geographic area (see below). Calista made regional selections in areas of high mineral potential. It owned approximately 4.9 million acres of land as of 2002. In 2001, Calista sold some of its land to the federal government, the former Calista land becoming part of the Yukon Delta National Wildlife Refuge. Congress agreed to pay more than $39 million for 218,000 acres of wetlands, valued by federal appraisers as being worth $5 million. Subsistence hunting and fishing rights, as well as wildlife habitat and conservation values, were preserved in the sale.

History
With more than 13,300 original shareholders, Calista Corporation is the second largest in terms of enrollment of the 13 regional corporations formed under the ANCSA. Its area is home to some of the strongest traditional cultures in the state. It started badly, spending almost all of its cash entitlement on real estate and operational investments that proved disappointing. For example, it lost about $20 million building the Sheraton Anchorage Hotel during boom years and selling it during the bust. It lost millions building a resort near Willow in anticipation of a state government move that never occurred. In its first 30 years, Calista shareholders received dividends only twice, for a total of about $50 per 100 shares. By 1990, Calista's assets dwindled from the $80.1 million ANCSA entitlement to $6.4 million. Through 1990, Calista had real losses of nearly $117 million, even after the sale of net operating losses averted an even larger deficit by bringing in $18 million. In the 1990s, it diversified into services with unique demands, title companies and newspapers, and in subsidiaries that support oil and mining, including oil field services, equipment leasing, and mining camp operations. In 1996, Calista joined a cooperative venture with 18 other ANCSA corporations, including several village corporations, to purchase products and fuel in bulk and lower retail costs for residents. Western Alaska Village Enterprises filed for Chapter 11 bankruptcy in 2000. By 2000, Calista had grown to $62 million in total assets, including the $39 million from the land sale to the federal government, with revenues consistently exceeding $10 million and positive net profits. The current corporate strategy is to exploit its land holdings, primarily through mineral and, possibly, petroleum extraction. The corporate area has known deposits of gold, silver, mercury, and platinum, including North America's largest platinum placer deposit and one of the world's largest gold deposits. The terrain is consistent with petroleum deposits. Calista has also established an investment fund of marketable securities similar to that maintained by most other regional corporations to maintain liquidity for dividends, scholarships, and other goals.

Corporate governance
Under the terms of the ANCSA, Alaskan Natives enrolled in one of the 56 BIA-recognized villages or otherwise connected with the Calista area were enrolled in the corporation. Each of the original 13,303 shareholders received 100 shares of the corporation's stock. This stock may not be transferred or encumbered except in certain specific circumstances involving gifts, court action, or death. Even then the stock carries voting rights only if the shareholder is an eligible Alaskan Native or descendant of a Native. The total number of shareholders has fluctuated as a result of transfers through inheritance and gifting of shares, but the total number of shares outstanding remains the same. As of 2002, the corporation had 12,472 shareholders. The shareholders elect an 11-member board of directors charged with the operation of the corporation. Calista's board of directors is passive and directs policy by motion and resolution. With the exception of the CEO, none of the directors is an officer of the corporation. Day-to-day management is conducted by the administration team working in cooperation with external affairs, human resources, legal affairs, shareholder services, finance and accounting, and the land and natural resources

Calista Corporation (Calista)
601 W. 5th Ave., Suite 200
Anchorage, AK 99501-2225
907-279-5516
907-272-5060 Fax
calistacorp.com

Calista Corporation (Calista)

Organization

Tunista Inc.

Tunista Properties Inc.

Yulista Management Services Inc.

Chiulista Camp Services, Inc.

Ookichista Drilling Services, Inc.

Ilikista Ventures, Inc.

departments. More than 50 percent of the members of the corporate staff are Calista shareholders.

Organization

Calista is organized in a network of subsidiaries and joint ventures. There are six "first tier" subsidiaries.

Tunista Inc., provides construction, renovations, design-build, operations and maintenance of base housing, facility management, fire detection and smoke alarms, and information technology consulting, mostly via federal and Alaska government contracting.

Tunista Properties Inc. manages the non-ANCSA properties of Calista, construction, build-to-suit, and property management.

Yulista Management Services Inc. provides professional and technical services, including metrology, precision measurement equipment laboratory (PMEL) services, rapid prototyping, science and engineering, facility operations and maintenance, and administrative support services, for the federal government. It has undertaken a joint venture with Maryland-based Science and Engineering Services Inc. on a $1.1 billion contract for technical support at the Army's Huntsville, Alabama, missile development center. Yulita has experience in municipal planning, economic and natural resource studies, natural gas well operations, and remote-site logistics and transportation.

Chiulista Camp Services, Inc., provides remote camp facility leasing, management, and services. It has contracts in Anchorage and at Donlin Creek, Prudhoe Bay, and other remote Alaska mining and petroleum production sites. It provides exploration and remote camp temporary personnel such as heavy equipment operators and mechanics, construction trades, geotechs, diamond core drillers and helpers, survey personnel, and the like. It was started in 1996 at Donlin Creek.

Ookichista Drilling Services, Inc., provides petroleum and exploration drilling equipment, personnel, and construction. It has a joint venture with Nordic Well Servicing, Inc., to provide workover, completion, and coil tubing services on the North Slope, Prudhoe Bay, and Kuparuk. The joint venture is called Nordic-Calista Well Services, Inc.

Ilikista Ventures, Inc., is a holding company for Calista's minority ownership of title companies in Anchorage, Fairbanks, Juneau, and Kenai and its majority ownership of Alaska Newspapers, Inc. (nine papers including the *Anchorage Chronicle*).

Village Corporations

Calista represents 56 villages in the Yukon-Kuskokwim River Delta, the Kuskokwim Mountains, Nunivak Island, and the Bering Sea coast from the mouth of the Yukon River south to Cape Newenham, and 46 ANCSA village corporations.

Akiachak	Akiachak Limited
Alakanuk	Alakanuk Native Corp.
Platinum	Arviq Incorporated
Scammon Bay	Askinuk Corporation
Atmautluak	Atmautluak Limited
Mountain Village	Azachorok Inc.
Bethel	Bethel Native Corp.
Chefornak	Chefarnrmute Inc.
Chevak	Chevak Company Corp.
Nightmute, Umkumiute	Chinuruk Inc.
Chuloonawick	Chuloonawick Corp.
Emmonak	Emmonak Corp.
Eek	Iqfijouaq Company
Kasigluk	Kasigluk Inc.
Akiak	Kokarmuit Corp.
Bill Moore's Slough	Kongniglkilnomuit Yuita Corp.
Kotlik	Kotlik Yupik Corp.
Kipnuk	Kugkaktlik Limited
Goodnews Bay	Kuitsarek Inc.
Aniak, Chuathbaluk, Crooked Creek, Georgetown, Lower Kalskag, Napamiute, RedDevil, Sleetmute, Stony River, and Upper Kalskag	Kuskokwim Corp.
Kwethluk	Kwethluk Inc.
Kwigillingok	Kwik Incorporated
Lime Village	Lime Village Company
Marshall	Maserculiq Inc.
Napakiak	Napakiak Corporation
Napaskiak	Napaskiak Corporation
Newtok	Newtok Corporation
Mekoryuk	Nima Corporation
Andreafsky	Nerkilikmute Native Corporation
Toksook Bay	Nunakauyak Yupik Corporation
Hamilton	Nunapiglluraq Corp.
Nunapitchuk	Nunapitchuk, Limited
Ohogamiut	Ohog Incorporated
Oscarville	Oscarville Native Corp.
Paimiut	Paimiut Corporation
Pilot Station	Pilot Station Inc.
Pitka's Point	Pitka's Point Native Corporation
Quinhagak	Qanirtuuq, Inc.
Kongiganak	Qemirtalek Coast Corp.
Russian Mission	Russian Mission Native Corporation
St. Mary's	St. Mary's Native Corp.
Hooper Bay	Sea Lion Corporation
Nunam Iqua	Swan Lake Corporation
Tuluksak	Tulkisarmute, Inc.
Tuntutuliak	Tuntutuliak Land Ltd.
Tununak	Tununrmiut Rinit Corp.

Relationships

Calista has a mixed relationship with its village corporations, some of which faced bankruptcy because of failed joint investments. Calista has competed with the area development nonprofit for federal housing funds, which has created ill-feeling towards the corporation. It has close working relationships with Placer Dome and NovaGold Resources, the past and present developers of the Donlin Creek gold deposits.

Income operations
Internal [sic: External]

External

Government contracting, including construction, base operations, and technical services. See Tunista Inc., Tunista Properties Inc., and Yulista Management Services Inc., above.

Oil drilling services. See Ookichista Drilling Services, Inc., above.

Remote camp leasing and services. See Chiulista Camp Services, Inc., above.

Investment real estate. Properties include a four-building, multistory business complex in Bethel; U.S. post offices in Kotlik, Chefornak, Nunapitchuk, and Nulato; three multistory office warehouses in Anchorage; an eight-plex apartment complex in Bethel; a remote historical gold mining camp that is used today as an outdoor retreat; and a large number of parcels of undeveloped land in the Matanuska-Susitna Valley and Kenai Peninsula.

Publishing and printing. Businesses include nine newspapers across the state and a full-service printing operation in Anchorage.

Land title services.

Internal

Donlin Creek. Resources now are estimated at 22.9 million ounces of gold, making Donlin Creek the 22nd-largest gold deposit in the world. Much of this is Calista property. This is powder embedded in rock, not placer deposits, so extraction will be expensive. As of 2001, Placer Dome and NovaGold had invested more than $13 million in development, and further expenses for transportation and power will be high. But at present and projected gold prices, this remains a hugely profitable deposit.

Placer gold and platinum. Calista leases land for small-scale placer gold production and one of the largest placer platinum production operations in North America.

Construction materials. Sand, gravel, and quarry rock are of growing importance. The primary limitation is transportation.

Other Operations
The Akilista Fund receives 10 percent of 7(i) receipts and net profits from operations to build a long-term investment portfolio, provide financial assistance to the Calista Scholarship Fund, and, eventually, to become a source of shareholder dividends and other shareholder programs. Ten percent of Calista's annual Akilista Fund contribution is donated to the Calista Scholarship Fund. Calista takes a strong advocacy role to maintain its shareholders' subsistence way of life and is a strong proponent for education funding and the construction of schools in rural areas.

Results and projections
Calista pulled in $28.9 million in revenues in 2002, with a $1.2-million profit, a 70 percent revenue boost over 2001. However, its 7(i) receipts from natural resource exploitation from other regional corporations were more than twice its revenues from exploitation of its own land. Calista anticipates growth in government contracting but places its primary hopes on Donlin Creek for gold revenues and as a catalyst for economic development generally.

Calista Corporation (Calista)

Chugach Alaska Corporation (CAC)

Introduction
Chugach Alaska Corporation (CAC) is the ANCSA regional corporation for the Prince William Sound area of Alaska. It is a for-profit corporation organized June 23, 1972, under the laws of the State of Alaska, with certain restrictions imposed by federal law. Its region is located in the Unorganized Borough, near the cities of Valdez and Cordova. It specializes in government contracting. As of 2004, it had around 2,000 shareholders and 5,082 employees (815 in Alaska, 107 shareholders, descendants, and spouses). Revenues for 2003 exceeded a half-billion dollars. CAC's headquarters is located in Anchorage. In 2003, CAC ranked fifth in *Alaska Business Monthly's* "Top 49ers" a ranking of the top Alaskan owned and operated businesses.

Entitlement
Under the ANCSA, CAC was entitled to 928,000 acres of selected land in its geographic area, $23.5 million, and the subsurface rights to the land granted to the five village corporations located within its geographic area (see below). As of 2003, it owned approximately 94 percent of its land entitlement. CAC selected lands that have potential for economic development including commercial timber, minerals, and potential for tourism, and lands of cultural and historical importance to the Chugach people.

History
Under ANCSA, CAC received $11.5 million and was promised 930,000 acres. Conveyance of the lands was delayed, and the corporation received another $12 million in 1982 to make up for lost opportunities because of the delays. CAC's region is rich in fish and timber, and that almost proved to be its downfall. The corporation invested in canneries, but a salmon glut and a botulism scare knocked the bottom out of the market. The recession of the 1980s made its timber resources not worth the cost of building roads to them. Then the *Exxon Valdez* oil spill devastated its fisheries, tourism, and shareholder land base.

CAC was able to recapitalize by realizing $54 million from the sale of its net operating losses to corporations needing tax writeoffs. By 1989, the corporation was out of the red. But by 1991, CAC was

Chugach Alaska
Corporation (CAC)
560 E. 34th Avenue, Suite 200
Anchorage, AK 99503-4196
907-563-8866
907-563-8402 Fax
chugach-ak.com

Chugach Alaska Corporation (CAC)

Village Corporations

CAC represents five villages on Prince William Sound:

Chenega Bay
Chenega Corporation

Nanwalek
English Bay Corporation

Eyak (in Cordova)
Eyak Corporation

Port Graham
Port Graham Corporation

Tatitlek
Tatitlek Corporation

Only 488 Alaskan Natives are shown in the 2000 census as living in these villages.

back some $30 million in debt and filed for Chapter 11 bankruptcy. With nothing left locally to exploit, CAC took advantage of its status as a disadvantaged, minority-owned business to obtain priority for government contracts. It was the first of the ANCSA corporations to take advantage of the SBA 8(a) program. It was amazingly successful. By June 2000, CAC was able to make the final payment due its creditors under its bankruptcy agreement, with 2000 revenues of $219.8 million, of which $217.5 million resulted from government contracts. By 2003, annual revenues had reached more than a half-billion dollars, and three of CAC's subsidiaries successfully had made the transition to the competitive market from the SBA 8(a) program.

Among CAC's contracts are two worth $170 million apiece for base operations at MacDill Air Force Base in Tampa, Florida, and Kirtland Air Force Base in Albuquerque, New Mexico. The approval of these bids motivated a lawsuit by the American Federation of Government Employees, which claims the sole-source contracting is unfair, but the army, air force, and navy have commended CAC for exemplary performance in providing efficient and cost-effective facilities operations and maintenance services. As of 2004, CAC had operations in 17 states and at U.S. bases in Canada, Turkey, Spain, Korea, Japan, Guam, Wake Island, and other South Pacific sites. Contracts include monitoring seismic activity in support of the International Nuclear Test Ban Treaty, environmental and hazardous-materials training and monitoring in Korea, and its primary business of base operations. In 2002, CAC teamed with Bechtel and Lockheed Martin to win a contract for missile defense support services on Kwajalein Atoll in the Pacific that potentially is worth billions of dollars in revenues. As of 2004, CAC was also competing for defense contracts for construction and humanitarian affairs in Iraq.

Corporate governance

Under the terms of the ANCSA, Alaskan Natives enrolled in one of the five BIA-recognized villages or otherwise connected with CAC's region were enrolled in the corporation. Each received 100 shares of the corporation's stock. This stock may not be transferred or encumbered except in certain specific circumstances involving gifts, court action, or death. Even then, the stock carries voting rights only if the shareholder is an eligible Alaskan Native or descendant of a Native. As of the end of 2003, the corporation had more than 2,000 shareholders (1,900 voting). The shareholders elect a nine-member board of directors charged with the operation of the corporation. The board, all of whom are Alaska Natives, selects the president. As of 2004, the directors include the corporate secretary and the corporate treasurer; three more directors serve as secretary/treasurers of subsidiaries.

Organization

CAC is organized in a network of subsidiaries and joint ventures. There are six "first tier" subsidiaries

Chugach Support Services Inc. provides military base operations and maintenance, construction

management, and facilities operation. It also provides operations, training, management, and maintenance services for the U.S. Department of Labor Job Corps Program.

Chugach Development Corporation Inc. provides facilities operations, management, maintenance services, as well as management information systems, information technology, and environmental services, primarily from the U.S. armed forces; it also manages what is generally considered to be the best-trained and -equipped open water- spill response group in the world.

Chugach Management Services Inc. provides base operations and maintenance, construction management, facilities operation, and environmental services; performs cadastral surveying, design, and construction of commercial facilities; and specializes in rapid response to construction requirements.

Chugach Systems Integration, LLC, provides information technology consultation and clerical support services.

Chugach Telecommunications and Computers Inc. provides computer and communication systems integration and telecommunication consultation and services.

Chugach Mckinley, Inc., is a construction firm.

Relationships

As the most successful 8(a) federal contractor, CAC is sought out by large service corporations as a prospective partner. CAC appears to have close relationships with the Alaska state government and the nonprofit organizations supporting Native Alaskans within its region. The commissioner of the State Department of Economic and Community Development is a CAC director, as are the executive director of the Alaska Native Coalition on Employment and Training, the president of the Native Village of Eyak Traditional Council, the president of the Tatitlek Village IRA Council (and former Chairman of the North Pacific Rim Housing Authority), the former president of the Chugach Heritage Foundation, and a staff member of the Alaska Housing Finance Corporation and director of the Port Graham Corporation.

Income Operations

External

Base operating services include military facilities operation and maintenance.

Construction services include design and construction of commercial and governmental facilities; maintenance, repair, and minor construction projects; and Department of Defense Job Order Contracting (pre-negotiated quick-response construction contracts).

Education services include operations, training, management, and maintenance services for the Department of Labor Job Corps Program in Alaska, New Mexico, and Florida.

Environmental services regulatory compliance, employee training, site assessments, and investigations and remediation.

Information technology services include systems implementation, information system projects, management information systems outsourcing, supporting technology services, facilities management, and professional consulting.

Telecommunications operations include communication systems and integration of computer and communication systems.

Internal

In 2003, internal operations accounted for less than 1/20th of one percent of CAC's revenues. The coastal portions of the region support mixed Sitka spruce and Western hemlock forests, but access is prohibitively expensive at current market prices. Historically, the Chugach region was one of the foremost mining regions in Alaska. CAC owns known mineralized subsurface rights across its region, but little action is being taken to exploit these properties. The first producing oil wells in Alaska were located in the CAC region. CAC holds title to over 10,100 acres of oil and gas estate and preferential exchange rights to an additional 55,375 acres, but it is undertaking very limited exploration. CAC holds title to extensive hard rock and gravel deposits in many key locations in South Central Alaska. CAC has provided aggregate for highway construction and maintenance and dam construction, and rip-rap (large rocks for waterfront stabilization) for riverbank stabilization, mostly within its region. With most of the land in its region owned by the federal and state governments and reserved as national forest, national park, and state wilderness, CAC has unique tourism opportunities, including glaciers and Prince William Sound. However, as of 2004 tourism had not yet recovered from the *Exxon Valdez* oil spill.

Other Operations

CAC provides scholarships, internships, and apprenticeships for shareholders, their descendents, and their spouses. In addition, it is the primary sponsor of the Chugach Heritage Foundation (cultural preservation) and Chugachmiut (health services provider). As the only centralized organization within its region, CAC also supports the Chugach Regional Resources Commission (business development) and the North Pacific Rim Housing Authority.

Results

Preliminary 2003 operating results showed revenues exceeding one-half billion dollars and net income of $29 million. As of spring 2004, assets totaled approximately $149 million. From 2002 to 2003, earnings from operations more than doubled, gross revenue increased over 50 percent, net income almost doubled, and assets increased by 41 percent while liabilities increased by only 34 percent. For 2003, CAC declared shareholder dividends totaling $24 per share, the largest in its history, and a special elders' dividend of $500 for each original shareholder over age 65. Barring a change in the federal government's policy of outsourcing support activities for the armed forces, continued growth is likely.

Chugach Alaska Corporation (CAC)

Cook Inlet Region, Incorporated (CIRI)

Introduction

Cook Inlet Region, Incorporated, (CIRI) is the ANCSA regional corporation for the Cook Inlet of southwest Alaska. It is a for-profit corporation organized June 8, 1972, under the laws of the State of Alaska, with certain restrictions imposed by federal law. Its geographic area includes the City of Anchorage, Matanuska-Susitna Borough, parts of Kenai Peninsula Borough, and a small part of Lake and Peninsula Borough. It has evolved into an investor rather than an operating concern, and has become the most successful of the regional corporations in terms of net profits. It has approximately 7,000 shareholders but fewer than 75 employees. Because CIRI tends to buy and sell large investments, annual revenues vary dramatically from year to year. CIRI's headquarters is in Anchorage. CIRI is unusual in that very few of its shareholders live in the seven ANCSA villages in its region. It is even more unusual in that it is the federally designated tribal authority for South Central Alaska (all other regions have separate tribal councils). This means that CIRI is the primary recipient of federal aid to Native Alaskans and supports the nonprofit organizations that provide health, housing, and other services to Native Alaskans in its region.

Entitlement

Under the ANCSA, CIRI was entitled to 2.4 million acres of selected land in its geographic area, $34 million, and the subsurface rights to the land granted to the seven village corporations located within its region (see below). However, most of the land within its region was owned by the federal government or private landowners, and was not available for distribution. In compensation, CIRI received rights to federal lands nationwide that the government was selling. Within Alaska, it now owns approximately 632,600 acres of surface estate and 1,543,500 acres of subsurface estate. Its selections within its region were made carefully with regard to petroleum potential, tourism, and development potential.

History

From its inception, CIRI approached the goal of taking care of Alaskan Natives in its region with a strategy different from the other regional corporations. CIRI's leadership was able to withstand shareholder pressure for dividends and jobs and orient its investments towards its bottom line. By making profitable investments, it would create wealth for its shareholders, and the social problems of its shareholders would be ameliorated. It

Cook Inlet Region, Incorporated (CIRI)
P.O. Box 93330
Anchorage, AK 99509-3330
907-274-8638
ciri.com

Cook Inlet Region, Incorporated (CIRI)

Organization

CIRI Alaska Tourism Corporation

CIRI Telecommunications

Peak Oilfield Service Company

Alaska Interstate Construction LLC

followed a long-term strategy of paying 35 percent of its profits in dividends and reinvesting the other 65 percent. In the 1980s it used its rights in federal lands to buy many investment properties. It was not invested in tourism or fishing when the *Exxon Valdez* oil spill occurred, so it suffered less than others. By 1990, it had distributed more than its original capitalization to its shareholders in dividends and yet continued to grow. Through the 1990s, CIRI invested heavily in telecommunications and Lower 48 real estate and successfully timed disposal of many of those investments.

CIRI's biggest success story exemplifies its business strategy. In the mid-1990s, CIRI entered a series of auctions for wireless-spectrum licenses in which the Federal Communications Commission provided set-asides and credits to help small-business entrepreneurs to share in the booming wireless market. CIRI was awarded a set of licenses in spite of its size through a special FCC exemption allowing a tribal entity to treat its telecommunications investments separately from other revenue, thus enabling CIRI to qualify as a small business. CIRI partnered with Western Wireless in this process, and then part of Western Wireless became VoiceStream. CIRI traded some of its licenses to VoiceStream in exchange for stock. Then, in 1999, Deutsche Telekom agreed to buy VoiceStream, paying $90 each for shares that cost CIRI about $14 each. CIRI was able to pay out extraordinary dividends totaling $650 per share in 2000 without diluting its shareholders' equity. For the typical CIRI shareholder, this was a $65,000 payment.

CIRI has become so successful that it no longer qualifies for the special tax incentives for Native corporations. Its income is taxable, and its dividends (with some exceptions) are taxable to its shareholders. This has led to a change in investment strategy, as income-producing real property became less attractive. CIRI had held many of those properties for 10, 20, or 30 years and could foresee little further appreciation. From 1999 through 2004, CIRI disposed of much of its passive real estate holdings while investing in active real estate investments such as resorts.

Corporate governance

Under the terms of the ANCSA, Alaskan Natives who were enrolled in one of the seven BIA-recognized villages or were otherwise connected with CIRI's area were enrolled in the corporation. Each received 100 shares of the corporation's stock. This stock may not be transferred or encumbered except in certain specific circumstances involving gifts, court action, or death. Even then the stock carries voting rights only if the shareholder is an eligible Alaskan Native or descendant of a Native. As of 2003, CIRI had 7,200 shareholders. The shareholders elect a 15-member board of directors charged with the operation of the corporation. As of June 7, 2003, none of CIRI's officers was a director. It should be noted that although there are strong minorities of directors and shareholders opposed to the management's reinvestment strategy, the board as a whole has consistently supported management's recommendations on major investments.

Organization

Unlike most ANCSA regional corporations, CIRI is organized primarily as an investment firm. It does have several operating subsidiaries, but these account for only a small part of its revenues.

CIRI Alaska Tourism Corporation operates tour packages, cruises, lodging, transportation, an RV park, sightseeing, and adventure activities; it purchased Kenai Fjords Tours and Prince William Sound Cruises and Tours in 1997, and the Seward Windsong Lodge in 1999; it opened the Talkeetna Lodge in 1999. CIRI sold Prince William Sound Cruises and Tours in 2002 when the events of September 11 reduced tourism to the Valdez area.

CIRI Telecommunications has a majority investment in Cook Inlet/T-Mobile USA PCS.

Peak Oilfield Service Company provides oilfield services in Alaska.

Alaska Interstate Construction LLC, provides general construction in Alaska.

Village Corporations

CIRI represents seven ANCSA villages on Cook Inlet and immediately inland:

Chickaloon	Chickaloon-Moose Creek Native Assoc. Inc.
Eklutna	Eklutna Inc.
Knik	Knikatnu Inc.
Ninilchik	Ninilchik Native Association Inc.
Salamatof	Salamatof Native Association Inc.
Seldovia	Seldovia Native Association Inc.
Tyonek	Tyonek Native Corporation

The following five Native corporations also work with CIRI, but are not ANCSA corporations or villages:

Susitna	Alexander Creek Inc.
Anchorage	Caswell Native Association
Susitna	Gold Creek-Susitna NCI
Y [sic]	Montana Creek Native Association
Anchorage	Point Possession Inc.

Relationships

As a major investor, CIRI has established ongoing relationships with Deutsche TeleKom (wireless communications), Woodbine Development Corp. (resorts in Nevada and Arizona), and adjacent regional corporation Doyon (tourism), among others. It also has a close and effective relationship with the Alaska congressional delegation and state government.

Income operations

External

Construction services include general construction in Alaska.

Oilfield support includes operations in Alaska.

Tourism operations include tour packages, cruises, lodging, transportation, sightseeing, and adventure activities.

Telecommunications operations include personal communications services (PCS) in New Orleans, Philadelphia, Las Vegas, south Texas, and other major markets in the U.S. The corporation is a founding investor in Alaska Communications System. CIRI is an active participant in PCS through its remaining ventures with Deutsche Telekom AG, although at a significantly reduced level.

Major investments include destination resort hotels and casinos in Nevada and Arizona. In 2003, CIRI became the first Alaska Native corporation to be licensed to own and operate a casino in Nevada. CIRI owns 9.75 percent of a potential natural gas pipeline from the North Slope through Canada to the Lower 48, in partnership with MidAmerican Energy Holding Co. (largely owned by Berkshire Hathaway Corporation) and Pacific Star Energy (an umbrella group of 12 Native corporations).

Real estate holdings outside Alaska are focused on multitenant office/warehouse and business parks located in Washington, New Mexico, Arizona, Florida, and Hawaii. In Alaska, the company's income property portfolio consists primarily of commercial office space. CIRI is the largest private landowner in South Central Alaska. The company develops real estate projects throughout the United States, including in 2003-04 a 100-acre commercial business park in San Antonio, Texas, and a 285,000-square-foot warehouse in Miami, Florida.

Internal
Tourism operations are in development. Some of CIRI's properties offer spectacular views and ready access to major recreation areas, and the corporation is developing those locations as tourist destinations.

Petroleum operations include royalty interests in the Kenai gas field, and other producing fields; other lands are subject to various leasing and exploration arrangements. CIRI's natural resources strategy is to be an active landowner, with occasional participation in working interests but most often royalty interests only. In 2003, Aurora Gas LLC began gas production from Lone Creek well no. 1, where it leases the subsurface estate from CIRI. CIRI also expects Aurora to drill another well to the north of the existing well, also on CIRI lands.

CIRI has other oil and gas leases on the Kenai Peninsula with Marathon Oil Company and Unocal. In 2001, Marathon Oil Company began natural gas production from the Wolf Lake Field, located within the Kenai National Wildlife Refuge; CIRI owns the subsurface mineral rights and will receive royalties.

Timber tracts total 22,672 hectares on the Kenai Peninsula; most of CIRI's timber has been killed by the spruce bark beetle infestation.

Other Operations
CIRI is unique in that it is the federally designated tribal authority for South Central Alaska. Under that umbrella, the corporation helps operate nonprofit service providers such as Alaska's People, Southcentral Foundation, Cook Inlet Tribal Council, and Cook Inlet Housing Authority, among others, which deliver Native social, health, and housing services. Alaska's People is a nonprofit job referral and placement agency that helps find jobs for more than 1,500 Alaska Natives a year. The Southcentral Foundation concentrates on the health and well-being of the Alaska Native population in the CIRI region, operating 65 different programs in 2000. The CIRI Foundation provides scholarships, grants, and fellowships to shareholders. The Cook Inlet Housing Authority uses federal, state, and corporation funds for affordable housing for Native Alaskans in the CIRI region. For example, the housing authority's Safe and Healthy Home Program provides weatherization, handicap accessibility, and emergency repairs for Alaska Natives and American Indian elders and disabled living in the Cook Inlet region. The Cook Inlet Tribal Council provides social and medical services to the region's Native Alaskan population. CIRI also plays a prominent role in developing cultural institutions that benefit Natives throughout the state. These include the Alaska Native Heritage Center, a statewide cultural preservation and educational institution; Koahnic Broadcast Corp., operator of the nation's first urban Native public radio station; and the Alaska Native Justice Center, which works on behalf of Alaska Natives in the state and federal justice systems.

Results
From 1980 through the third quarter of 2003, CIRI paid out more than $801 million in dividends and other distributions to its shareholders, $468 million from 2000 through 2002 alone. Shareholders' equity held steady at $660 million from 2001 through 2003 in spite of the economic slowdown. In 2003 it ranked second among *Alaska Business Monthly's* "Top 49 Businesses."

Doyon, Limited (Doyon)
1 Doyon Place, Suite 300
Fairbanks, AK 99701
907-459-2000 or
1-888-478-4755
907-459-2060 Fax
doyon.com

Organization

Doyon Tourism, Inc., (DTI)
Doyon Drilling, Inc., (DDI)

Doyon Development Corporation

Doyon Government Services (DGS)

Doyon Universal Services J.V. (DUS)

Doyon Properties, Inc.

Doyon, Limited (Doyon)

Introduction

Doyon, Limited, (Doyon) is the ANCSA regional corporation for the Alaskan interior. It is a for-profit corporation organized June 23, 1972, under the laws of the State of Alaska, with certain restrictions imposed by federal law. Its geographic area is the largest of the regional corporations, mostly in the Unorganized Borough and Fairbanks-North Star Borough, from the Canadian border almost to Norton Sound, an area the size of France. It is primarily invested in operating subsidiaries and its land entitlement. It has more than 14,000 shareholders. Approximately 25 percent of shareholders live in the Lower 48 and 11 percent in Anchorage. Doyon's corporate offices are in Fairbanks. As of 2004, it had more than 1,100 employees.

Entitlement

With the land entitlement of 12.5 million acres, Doyon is the largest private landowner in Alaska and is one of the largest private landowners in North America. At least three-quarters of the entitlement has been conveyed.

History

Voting shares of stock were originally issued to 9,061 Alaska Natives who had a tie to the region. In March 1992, shareholders approved giving stock to Native children born between 1971 and 1992, missed enrollees, and elders who were age 65 by December 1992. The same issue was to be placed before the shareholders in 2006.

Corporate governance

Doyon is managed by a 13-member board of directors. Directors are elected to staggered three-year terms by the shareholders. Interim vacancies are filled by the board. As of late 2004, none of the directors were officers or employees of the corporation. One director, who had served as the corporate secretary while a director, resigned in 2004 to take a full-time position with the corporation. Day-to-day management is performed by a President/CEO.

Organization

In addition to several subsidiaries, Doyon is engaged in several joint ventures, one with ARAMARK to provide services at Denali National Park. First tier subsidiaries include the following:

Doyon Tourism, Inc., (DTI) was formed as part of Doyon's strategic plan to expand its tourism business. DTI is comprised of the Kantishna Roadhouse, Denali River Cabins, and Kantishna Wilderness Trails.

Doyon Drilling, Inc., (DDI) was formed in 1982 as a joint venture between Doyon, Limited and Nugget Alaska Inc. In 1993, Doyon purchased Nugget Alaska's interest, becoming the sole owner of DDI. DDI operates on the North Slope of Alaska with five rigs designed to drill oil wells in Northern Alaska

conditions. The rigs are some of the most technologically advanced land drilling rigs in the world.

Doyon Development Corporation was organized in 2004 to hold SBA 8(a) subsidiaries and oversee related investments, such as Doyon's 30 percent ownership of Angeles Composite Technology, Inc., in Port Angeles, Washington.

Doyon Government Services (DGS) is a holding company which oversees and coordinates the operations of five limited liability corporations: Doyon Logistics, Doyon Project Services, Doyon Security Services, Doyon Environmental & Engineering, and Doyon Composites Manufacturing. The mission of DGS is to develop business in the federal arena by marketing existing Doyon capabilities through the Small Business Administration 8(a) program.

Doyon Universal Services J.V. (DUS) is a joint venture between Doyon and Universal Services Alaska, LLC. The company provides catering, security, facility maintenance, and other remote site support services to oil and gas, construction, and mining facilities throughout Alaska. It also provides services to clients in Anchorage and Fairbanks.

Doyon Properties, Inc., manages existing Doyon real estate assets and develops and markets other real estate related services.

Village Corporations

Doyon represents 27 communities with 22 village corporations:

Eagle Village	Hungwitchin Corp.
Evansville	Evansville Inc.
Fort Yukon	Gwitchyaa Zhee Corp.
Galena	Gana-A' Yoo Ltd.
Grayling	Hee-Yea-Lingde Corp.
Healy Lake	Mendas Cha-ag Native Corp.
Holy Cross	Deloycheet Inc.
Hughes	K'oyitl'ots'ina Corp.
Huslia	K'oyitl'ots'ina Corp.
Kaltag	Gana-A' Yoo Ltd.
Koyukuk	Gana-A' Yoo Ltd.
Manley Hot Springs	Bean Ridge Corp.
McGrath	MTNT Ltd.
Minto	Seth-De-Ya-Ah Corp.
Nenana	Toghotthele Corp.
New Allakaket	[none]
Nikolai	MTNT Ltd.
Northway Village	Northway Natives Inc.
Nulato	Gana-A' Yoo Ltd.
Rampart	Baan-O-Yeel Kon Corp.
Ruby	Dineega Corp.
Shageluk	Zho-Tse Inc.
Stevens Village	Dinyea Corp.
Takotna	MTNT Ltd.
Tanacross	Tanacross Inc.
Tanana	Tozitna Ltd.
Telida	MTNT Ltd.

Relationships

Doyon is closely associated with the Tanana Chiefs Conference, the regional nonprofit corporation.

Income Operations

External
See above under "Organization."

Internal
Doyon's Lands and Natural Resources Department manages its ANCSA lands, focusing on "balanced" natural resource development. It appears that as of 2004 Doyon is still exploring its lands for opportunities.

Other Operations

The Doyon Foundation promotes the health, education, social and economic development, and well-being of Alaska Natives through basic educational grants and competitive academic achievement scholarships, a natural resources program, internships, professional development workshops,
high school career and college fairs, leadership programs, and cultural preservation projects.

Doyon has focused on increasing shareholder employment. From 2002 through mid-2004, the overall number of employees increased by 3.5 percent and the number of shareholder employees by 32 percent. As of 2004, about one-third of its employees were shareholders.

Results

Revenues totaled $47,654,726 in the year 2000. Almost half came from Doyon Drilling, almost a third from investment income, less than 10 percent each from real estate and tourism, and smaller amounts from natural resources and joint ventures. In 2004, the board of directors declared a distribution of $3.11 per share, totaling $4.2 million constituting 50 percent of its average net profits for the previous five years. This is its twentieth dividend, with nearly $84-million paid since Doyon's organization.

Doyon, Limited (Doyon)

Koniag, Incorporated (Koniag)

Introduction

Koniag, Inc. (Koniag) is the ANCSA regional corporation for Kodiak Island. It is a for-profit corporation organized June 23, 1972, under the laws of the State of Alaska, with certain restrictions imposed by federal law. Its geographic area generally coincides with Kodiak Island Borough. It has evolved into a diversified investment concern, with about one-quarter of its assets in investment securities, one-third in real estate, and one-third in operating companies. It has approximately 3,400 shareholders and had revenues of $109 million in the year ending March 31, 2004. Koniag has corporate offices in Anchorage and Kodiak.

Entitlement

Under the ANCSA, Koniag was entitled to 800,000 acres of selected land in its geographic area, $23 million, and the subsurface rights to the land granted to the original nine village corporations located within its geographic area (see below). As much of the nearby and desirable land was unavailable for selection, Koniag was able to select subsurface rights to land on the Alaska Peninsula across from Kodiak. Some of those lands were later exchanged for mature timberland on Afognak Island. As of 2004, it owned 161,664 acres of surface estate and 773,687 acres of subsurface estate.

History

In the early 1970s, an investment strategy based on natural resources made sense. Between 1972 and 1980, Koniag invested in fisheries support and processing and oil and gas exploration. The corporation also invested in real estate, construction, transportation, and several local Kodiak businesses. In the early 1980s, Kodiak fishing collapsed. Stocks had plummeted, and the crowning blow was a botulism death from canned salmon in February 1982. Even before the collapse of fishing, Koniag had never made a profit. Koniag lost money steadily and by 1983, the corporation's accumulated debt had reached more than $11 million. Koniag had lost money every year and was very close to bankruptcy. The downward spiral continued into 1984, when Koniag's accumulated losses climbed to $23 million, equal to the amount Koniag had received under ANCSA. The problems were aggravated by contentious and costly litigation involving the merger of several village corporations into Koniag. The merger litigation dragged on until 1984, when it was finally settled. In 1985, a new board and management cut staff and salaries, instituted procedures to improve accountability, and began to liquidate assets that were not generating income. Koniag slowly began to revive. After a loss of $4.8 million in 1984, the corporation recorded its first profit, $1 million, in 1985. By 1989, Koniag had its fifth consecutive year of profits, bolstered by the sale of net operating losses. That year also saw the first timber operations of Afognak Joint Venture among Koniag and several village corporations. Koniag's guiding principles were controlled growth and cautious and conservative investments. In 1994, 10 years after losing all of the capital received under ANCSA, Koniag had restored the full $23 million and declared its first dividend.

Corporate governance

Under the terms of the ANCSA, Alaskan Natives enrolled in one of the 10 BIA-recognized Native entities in or otherwise connected with Koniag's region were enrolled in the corporation. Each received 100 shares of the corporation's stock. This stock may not be transferred or encumbered except in certain specific circumstances involving gifts, court action, or death. Even then the stock carries voting rights only if the shareholder is an eligible Alaskan Native or descendant of a Native. As of March 31, 2004, Koniag had approximately

Koniag, Incorporated (Koniag)

Anchorage office:
4300 B St., Suite 407
Anchorage, AK 99503
907-561-2668 or
800-327-7649
907-562-5258 Fax

Kodiak office:
202 Center Ave., Suite 201
Kodiak, AK 99615
907-486-2530 or
800-658-3818
907-486-3325 Fax
koniag.com

Koniag, Incorporated (Koniag)

Organization

Sonneville International Corporation (SIC)

Permanent Way Corporation (PWC)

Koniag Development Corporation (KDC)

Koniag Services, Inc.

Frontier Systems Integrator, LLC

Washington Management Group, Inc., (WMG)

XMCO, Inc.,

Integrated Concepts and Research Corporation (ICRC)

Clarus Technologies

Karluk Wilderness Adventures (KWA)

Angeles Composite Technologies, Inc.,

Professional Computing Resources, Inc. (PCR)

3,400 shareholders. The shareholders elect an eight-member board of directors charged with the operation of the corporation. As of March 31, 2004, only one member of the board (the president) appeared to be an officer of the corporation.

Organization

Koniag is organized in a network of wholly and partially owned subsidiaries. Not including real estate investments, Koniag has only three first tier subsidiaries. However, one of those-Koniag Development Corporation-owns most of Koniag's operational subsidiaries. First tier and major second tier subsidiaries include:

Sonneville International Corporation (SIC) and the Permanent Way Corporation (PWC), based in Alexandria, Virginia, serve railroad-building clients throughout the world with innovative low-vibration track technology. PWC manufactures and installs the specialized track systems for domestic customers, SIC for foreign customers.

Koniag Development Corporation (KDC) is a holding company. New investments are often acquired in the name of KDC. It has been a legal entity with its own board of directors, but no employees. That is changing, as more of Koniag's new and existing subsidiaries are placed under the KDC umbrella. Eventually, KDC will operate as Koniag's business arm and manage most of the business operations and real estate holdings.

Koniag Services, Inc., is a wholly owned subsidiary of Koniag Development Corporation and certified under the Small Business Administration's §8(a) program for small disadvantaged businesses. It is headquartered in Anchorage.

Frontier Systems Integrator, LLC, specializes in telecommunications consulting, project development, project management, and security services. Its core expertise is in wireless and emergency communications. KDC owns 80 percent of this company. Frontier is certified as a small disadvantaged business under the SBA's §8(a) program.

Washington Management Group, Inc., (WMG) was acquired Koniag Development Corporation very early in 2002. WMG offers consulting services to companies seeking to sell their commercial products and services to the federal government. The process for listing a product or service on the General Services Administration's Multiple Award Schedule program, or other government procurement programs, can be extremely difficult and expensive for a company to achieve using in-house resources. WMG guides its clients through the entire process, including negotiation of pricing, establishing terms and conditions, and other important services. WMG is located in Washington DC with clients that include Fortune 500 companies.

XMCO, Inc., is another subsidiary. Koniag Development Corporation currently holds a 95 percent interest in XMCO, Inc., which it acquired in 2001. Based near Detroit, Michigan, XMCO provides ser-

vices to several branches of the U.S. Department of Defense, as well as a number of commercial customers. XMCO offers services in program management support, systems integration, and logistics support, which includes writing technical manuals, providing maintenance engineering services, and developing training courses.

Integrated Concepts and Research Corporation (ICRC) is another partially owned KDC subsidiary. KDC owns a 60 percent interest in ICRC which is certified by the U.S. Small Business Administration as a disadvantaged, minority owned business under §8(a) of the Small Business Act. ICRC is a diversified engineering and technical services company that serves federal agencies as well as commercial customers in three core areas: information technology, aerospace services, and advanced vehicle technologies.

Clarus Technologies is based in Bellingham, Washington, and manufactures a number of highly innovative products related to the reprocessing of fluids. Koniag Development Corporation purchased a 90 percent interest in Clarus Technologies in 2001. Clarus Technologies is an engineering and manufacturing company focused on improving existing fluid reprocessing technologies and creating innovative solutions to new challenges within the industry. Clarus has been certified as a small disadvantaged business under the Small Business Administration's §8(a) program and recently added environmental services to its lines of business.

Karluk Wilderness Adventures (KWA) is a wholly owned subsidiary of Koniag Development Corporation. The KWA program is collaboratively designed in cooperation with Koniag, the community of Larsen Bay, the Kodiak National Wildlife Refuge, the Alaska Department of Fish and Game, and MUM Alaska. KWA manages fishing and wildlife resources of the Karluk River to provide a "high quality Alaskan outdoor experience."

Angeles Composite Technologies, Inc., is a composites manufacturing company. In July 2003, Koniag Development Corporation closed on the purchase of a majority interest. KDC owns 60 percent of Angeles Composite Technologies, Inc. (ACTI), of Port Angeles, Washington. ACTI was recently certified as a small disadvantaged business under the SBA's §8(a) program. The company manufactures composites parts for the aerospace industry. ACTI has been in business about seven years. Its major clients are Boeing and Bombardier Aerospace, a Canadian company. As of 2004, Koniag intended to sell half its interest.

Professional Computing Resources, Inc. (PCR), founded in 1982, is based in Grand Rapids, Michigan. PCR designs and builds cutting-edge telecommunications and data management software. PCR supplies multifunction telemanagement software to the telecom industry. PCR intends to expand its market share into the government sector, specifically, the U.S. Department of Defense. Koniag acquired PCR in April 2004.

Village Corporations

Koniag represents eight villages and the City of Kodiak on Kodiak Island, with seven village corporations:

Afognak	Afognak Native Corporation (now Port Lions)
Akhiok	Akhiok-Kaguyak, Inc.
Kaguyak	Akhiok-Kaguyak, Inc. (zero population)
Karluk	(Karluk Native Corporation-merged into Koniag, Inc.)
Larsen Bay	(Anton Larsen, Inc.-merged into Koniag, Inc.)
Old Harbor	Old Harbor Native Corp.
Ouzinkie	Ouzinkie Native Corporation
Port Lions	Afognak Native Corporation
Shoonaq'	Natives of Kodiak, Inc. (City of Kodiak)
Woody Island	Lesnoi, Inc.(zero population)

There are six "unlisted" corporations associated with Koniag:

Ayakulik Inc. (abandoned village of Ayakulik)
Bell's Flats Natives Inc.(abandoned village of Bell's Flats)
Litnik Inc.(abandoned village of Litnik)
Shuyak Inc. (abandoned village on Shuyak Island)
Uganik Natives Inc. (abandoned village of Uganik)
Uyak Inc. (abandoned village of Uyak)

These are villages that were denied ANCSA status and which are not recognized by the BIA.

Income Operations

As of 2004, Koniag's assets were allocated as follows: investment securities 26 percent, operating companies 35 percent (see the discussion under Organization above), real estate 36 percent, and other 3 percent. Koniag's investment real estate includes office buildings, warehouses, apartment buildings, and a hotel. Properties are located in Alaska, Washington State, Utah, New Mexico, and Arizona. Koniag's ownership interest in these properties ranges from 10 percent to 100 percent. In its fiscal year ending in 2004, approximately 93 percent of Koniag's revenue was derived from prime contracts or subcontracts with the U.S. Government.

Other Operations

Koniag Education Foundation promotes the education of Alaska Natives from the Koniag region through scholarships and grants. Koniag also makes significant donations to other Alaska Native organizations, including the Alaska Native Heritage Center, the Alutiiq Museum and Archaeological Repository, the Alaska Native Justice Center, Koahnic Broadcast Corporation, and the Alaska Federation of Natives.

Results

In 2004, after two poor years, Koniag had net income of $1.7 million on revenues of $109 million. This was the first year revenues exceeded $100 million.

Koniag, Incorporated (Koniag)

NANA Regional Corporation, Inc. (NANA)

Introduction

NANA Regional Corporation, Inc., (NANA) is located in northwest Alaska; its boundaries are also those of the Northwest Arctic Borough. The NANA region spans 38,000 square miles, most of which is above the Arctic Circle. As of 2002, it had 10,120 shareholders, the majority of whom live in the NANA region. NANA has a number of diversified subsidiaries, accounting for 2,000 jobs and $80 million in payroll in Alaska in 1998 and revenues totaling $176,233,497 in the year 2000.

Entitlement

Under the ANCSA, NANA and the village corporations merged into it were entitled to cash totaling approximately $44 million, land, including the surface and subsurface estate, of 2,055,616 acres, and title to subsurface estate rights only on 187,716-acres. As of 2003, it had received interim conveyance or patent to 1,508,646-acres of surface estate and 1,379,329 acres of subsurface estate.

History

NANA is one of 12 regional Native corporations created in Alaska by the ANCSA. NANA's predecessor, the Northwest Arctic Native Association, played a key part in the effort to secure passage of the claims act.

Corporate governance

As of 2003, NANA had the following classes of common stock outstanding:

Class A common stock to those Natives who enrolled in the NANA Region as residents of one of its villages;

Class B common stock to those Natives who are enrolled in the NANA Region but elected not to be registered as residents of any of its villages;

Class C common stock to those Natives who were eligible to, but did not, enroll in the NANA Region in 1971, and also did not enroll under ANCSA;

Class D common stock to Natives born after 1971 who meet certain eligibility requirements. In January 1991, the shareholders of NANA authorized the issuance of Class D common stock to Natives born after 1971 who met certain eligibility requirements. They are eligible to receive 50 or 100 shares of Class D common stock based on their parental original enrollment. Class D common stock carries certain restrictions.

NANA Regional Corporation, Inc. (NANA)
P.O. Box 49
Kotzebue, AK 99752
907-442-3301
907-442-2866 Fax
nana.com

NANA Regional
Corporation, Inc. (NANA)

Organization

Akima Corporation (Akima)
TKC Communications, LLC
Ki, LLC
NANA Services, LLC
NANA Pacific, LLC

*NANA Management
    Services LLC*

NANA Colt Engineering, LLC
DOWL, LLC
NANA Oilfield Services, Inc.
Maniilaq, Ltd.
NANA Lynden Logistics, LLC
NANA Dynatec Drilling, LLC
NANA/VECO
Houston/NANA, LLC
Kotzebue Properties
Nullagvik Hotel, Inc.
Tour Arctic Corporation

The board of directors of NANA includes two directors from each of the communities (only one from Kotzebue), two at-large directors, and one ex-officio elder director. As of 2004, none of the directors was an officer of the corporation.

Organization
NANA is organized in a network of subsidiaries and joint ventures. NANA Development Corporation serves as the business arm of NANA, overseeing operations and providing centralized administrative support. As of 2003, other first tier and major second tier subsidiaries included:

Contracted government services. NANA owns a controlling interest in five government service providers:

Akima Corporation (Akima) located in Anchorage and Charlotte, North Carolina. Akima is owned 80 percent by NANA and 20 percent by The Aleut Corporation. It is a service contractor to the U.S. Government, providing a wide range of functions, primarily base operations support, for the air force, navy, army, NOAA, NIOSH, and two classified facilities. Other services support telecommunication, transportation and vehicle maintenance, and laboratory and other research facility operations.

TKC Communications, LLC, is located in Anchorage, with significant operations in Fairfax, Virginia.

Ki, LLC, is located in Colorado Springs, Colorado.

NANA Services, LLC, is located in Seattle, Washington.

NANA Pacific, LLC, located in Anchorage, provides design-build technical services to the Pacific Rim, employing more than 4,000 professionals in more than 30 industries throughout the region in 2001.

Hospitality and tourism, in-state. This segment consists of four Marriott hotels located in Alaska but outside the NANA region. In Anchorage, NANA owns a 60 percent interest in the Courtyard, the SpringHill Suites, and the Residence Inn. NANA's 40 percent business partner is SODEXHO Marriott Management, Inc. In addition, NANA owns a minority interest in the SpringHill Suites in Fairbanks. All of NANA's hotels are managed by NANA Management Services, LLC.

Professional and management services.

NANA Management Services, LLC, is owned 51 percent by NANA Development Corporation and 49 percent by SODEXHO Management, Inc. It provides integrated services, such as facilities management, including food services at both remote and urban facilities; housekeeping, janitorial, transportation, and reception and reservations services; health, safety, and security services; corporate services; and training systems. Its subsidiaries include NMS Employee Leasing, NANA Training Systems, Purcell Services, and WorkSafe, Inc.

NANA Colt Engineering, LLC, provides a broad range of engineering capabilities to Alaska's petroleum, mining, government, and utility industries.

DOWL, LLC, employs approximately 140 persons and provides civil engineering and related services, such as land surveying and geotechnical and environmental engineering services, primarily to rural Alaska. It designs roadways, highways, and trail systems; water, sewer, and storm drain systems; and performs complete facility site planning and design, from conceptual stages, through engineering study phases and design drawings. It then provides assistance to owners during construction. DOWL is headquartered in Anchorage, maintains a field laboratory in Kodiak, and has branch offices in Redmond, Washington, and Tucson, Arizona.

Oilfield and mining support.

NANA Oilfield Services, Inc., located in Deadhorse, Alaska, operates a petroleum-product distributorship and an equipment-rental service at Deadhorse, on the North Slope.

Maniilaq, Ltd., trains and maintains first-responder crews for emergency oil-spill response in the Valdez-Prince William Sound area.

NANA has ownership interests in several firms providing contract support to the oil field and mining industries. These companies include:

NANA Lynden Logistics, LLC, which provides trucking and other transportation services;

NANA Dynatec Drilling, LLC, which has contracts for exploratory drilling for mining operations in Alaska;

NANA/VECO Joint Venture which has been engaged in construction activities; and

Houston/NANA, LLC, which provides equipment maintenance and warehouse services to the operator of the Trans-Alaska Pipeline.

Real estate
Kotzebue Properties manages NANA's investments in residential, commercial, and undeveloped real estate in the Kotzebue area.

Hospitality and tourism, in-region
Nullagvik Hotel, Inc., is a 70-room hotel in Kotzebue.

Tour Arctic Corporation operates ground tours in Kotzebue and Kiana.

Village Corporations
NANA represents 11 communities: Ambler, Buckland, Deering, Kiana, Kivalina, Kobuk, Kotzebue, Noatak, Noorvik, Selawik, and Shungnak. All the village corporations except Kikiktagruk Inupiat Corp. (Kotzebue)

were merged into NANA. When ANCSA corporations merge, the consent authority of the village corporation for subsurface activities within the boundaries of the Native village is delegated to another entity in the Native village composed of the Native residents. As a condition of NANA's merger with the village corporations, the Native entities in each village were given this consent authority.

Relationships
The Northwest Arctic Leadership Team includes the governing bodies of NANA, Maniilaq Association (the regional nonprofit), Northwest Arctic Borough, and Northwest Arctic Borough School District, which work together to address critical issues in the region.

Income Operations
External]
See Organization above.

Internal
The Red Dog Mine, operated by Teck Cominco on NANA land, is the largest zinc producer in the world. It is NANA's showpiece, with 51 percent of the mine's jobs held by NANA shareholders. Discovered in 1953, the Red Dog is located in the DeLong Mountains of Alaska's Brooks Range, approximately 90 miles north of Kotzebue and 55 miles from the Chukchi Sea. NANA earns royalties from

zinc and lead production at the mine, most of which are shared with other Native corporations. Other natural resource income comes from gravel sales, land leases, and minor holdings in the Endicott and Sag Delta oil fields.

NANA owns and operates the Nullagvik Hotel in Kotzebue and owns Tour Arctic Corporation, which operates tours in Kotzebue and Kiana.

Other Operations
NANA operates the Aqqaluk Trust. In 2003, NANA contributed $500,000 to the Aqqaluk Trust for scholarships and an additional $1.1 million for other social and cultural programs. Earnings from NANA's business activities are used, in part, for investments in social and cultural programs of importance to shareholders. Expenditures are made at the direction of the board and reflect the guidance of the applicable committees of the board. Expenditures were also made to support other organizations involved in Alaska Native issues of concern to NANA shareholders and the NANA Region.

Results
As of the fiscal year ending in 2003, NANA's revenues had reached $263 million, with profits of $2.1 million. Assets reached $174 million, and shareholders' equity increased to $42.57 per share. NANA declared a $1.50 per share dividend for fiscal year 2003.

NANA Regional
Corporation, Inc. (NANA)

Sealaska Corporation (Sealaska)

Introduction
Sealaska Corporation (Sealaska) is southeast Alaska's regional Native for-profit corporation formed under the 1971 Alaska Native Claims Settlement Act (ANCSA). It was established for the area covered by the Alaskan operations of the Tlingit-Haida Central Council. Sealaska Corporation has become the third-largest Alaska-owned, Alaska-based corporation, and it is the largest private landowner in Southeast Alaska. Timber is the corporation's primary source of income, with its investment portfolio providing additional revenue. As of 2002, it had about 17,200 shareholders.

Entitlement
ANCSA land conveyed to Sealaska totaled 289,800 acres. Sealaska also received $93-million under ANCSA. Sealaska's monetary share was the highest among the corporations because it had the largest number of shareholders. Sealaska owns 3.5 billion board feet of merchantable timber located on 290,000 acres of surface estate and 600,000-acres of subsurface estate, all in Southeast Alaska.

History
From its web site: "Sealaska became one of 13 for-profit regional corporations in Alaska to receive land and capital to serve our shareholders in southeast Alaska. We received our first land conveyances in 1979. For the past 30 years Sealaska has diversified through many businesses and be-

come a leading exporter and one of the strongest economic and political forces in Alaska."

Corporate governance
Sealaska has six officers and a seven-member board of directors. The Sealaska board of directors is comprised of a diverse group of Southeast Alaska Natives. Sealaska is owned by Tlingit, Haida, and Tsimshian shareholders whose ancestry is rooted in Southeast Alaska. Sealaska has the most shareholders of any Alaska Native corporation. Almost half of the shareholders live in the region, 10 percent live in other areas of the state, and the remainder live outside Alaska.

Organization
Subsidiaries include the following:

Sealaska Timber Corporation dominates the operations, revenues, and profits of Sealaska. It grows, harvests, and markets Sitka spruce, Alaska red and yellow cedar, and Western hemlock on and from Sealaska's 290,000 acres in the Tongass National Forest, mostly shipping round logs to Asia.

Synergy Systems, Inc., is a certified SBA §8(a) company located in Redmond, Washington. It is one of the largest prototype and limited-run manufacturing facilities in the Northwest and is a Microsoft premier vendor.

Sealaska Corporation
(Sealaska)
One Sealaska Plaza
Ste. 400
Juneau, AK 99801-1276
  907-586-1512
  907-586-2304 Fax
  sealaska.com

Organization

Sealaska Timber Corporation
Synergy Systems, Inc.
TriQuest Precision Plastics
Alaska Coastal Aggregate

Sealaska Corporation (Sealaska)

TriQuest Precision Plastics is a joint venture between Sealaska and Nypro, Inc., 80 percent-owned by the former and operated by the latter. It is located in Guadalajara, Mexico, and does precision injection molding.

Alaska Coastal Aggregate is an SBA §8(a) company that manages and markets Sealaska's sand, rock, and gravel resources.

Village Corporations

Sealaska represents 10 communities and the urban tribes of Juneau and Sitka, with 12 village corporations:

Saxman	Cape Fox Corporation
Juneau	Goldbelt, Incorporated
Hydaburg	Haida Corporation
Hoonah	Huna Totem Corporation
Kake	Kake Tribal Corporation
Kasaan	Kavilco, Incorporated
Klawock	Klawock Heenya Corporation
Klukwan	Klukwan, Incorporated
Angoon	Kootznoowoo, Incorporated
Craig	Shaan-Seet, Incorporated
Sitka	Shee Atiká, Incorporated
Yakutat	Yak-Tat Kwaan, Incorporated

Relationships

Sealaska is closely tied to the Central Council of the Tlingit and Haida, the regional nonprofit corporation and a significant political force.

Income Operations

External

In addition to the operations of the subsidiaries described above, Sealaska has a broad investment portfolio called the Permanent Fund, including key investments in Indian gaming in Southern California and in Native American National Bank, based in Browning, Montana, the first nationwide American Indian bank focusing on investments in American Indian enterprises. In 2003, Sealaska Corporation announced a financing agreement with Aviarc Corporation. Aviarc will build a market share for its Internet-enabled trade document management software for importers, exporters, brokers, and logistics providers.

Internal

In addition to the timber industry, its primary focus since its organization, Sealaska generates revenue from mining and marketing construction materials like rock, sand, and gravel. Contracting with the federal government to survey lands, leasing logging roads to third parties, pursuing land exchanges with state, federal, and private entities, and exploring technologies to turn wood waste into fuel-grade ethanol also generate revenue.

Other Operations

The Sealaska Heritage Institute provides scholarships for southeast Alaskan Natives, hosts biennial festivals, produces publications, supports heritage and language programming, maintains tribal archives, and advocates for language and culture issues.

Results

For the year ending December 31, 2002, Sealaska had earnings of $40.0 million on revenues of $169.5 million with almost no debt. The book value of Sealaska stock was $91.19 per share (*not* including the value of land, timber, and natural resources).

The 13th Regional Corporation (13th)

The 13th Regional Corporation (13th)
1156 Industry Drive
Seattle, Washington 98188
206-575-6229
206-575-6283 Fax
the13thregion.com

Introduction

The region of the 13th Regional Corporation encompasses all places except Alaska. Its shareholders live in every state, and some live outside of the country as far as Australia. After several false starts and significant mismanagement, it now specializes in SBA §8(a) contracting.

Entitlement

The 13th Regional Corporation received $52 million, its per-capita share of the cash distributed to the Alaska Native Claims Settlement Act (ANCSA) regional Native corporations, of which half was required to be distributed to its shareholders. It was not entitled to any land.

History

The 13th Regional Corporation was formed under Alaska Law as a private for-profit entity on December 19, 1975. The 13th Regional Corporation was the last of the regional corporations formed by Alaska Natives as a result of ANCSA. Many nonresident Alaska Natives wanted a corporation located outside of Alaska. BIA objected because not enough Alaska Natives were interested in joining it. However, after litigation, many nonresident Alaska Natives were given the choice of joining the corporation where they had lived in Alaska or joining the 13th Regional Corporation. Some were assigned to the 13th by the BIA. All corporations formed under ANCSA, except the 13th, were entitled to select land in Alaska for transfer to corporate ownership. The 13th does not receive money from other regional Native corporations through ANCSA's profit-sharing provisions. Early investments of the corporation included a fishing fleet; real estate in Seattle; and land in Cold Bay, Alaska. The corporation created numerous subsidiaries in the course of pursuing business opportunities. It lost millions of dollars and underwent several major changes in management and board membership.

Corporate governance

The 13th Regional Corporation began with 4,537 shareholders and as of 2003 had 5,500 shareholders. Its board of directors includes a chairman, president, senior vice president, vice president, secretary, treasurer, and three directors.

Organization

Subsidiaries include the following:

Alindeska Environmental Services, LLC, is a §8(a) environmental services firm specializing in federal government work.

Alindeska Electrical Contractors, LLC, in Poulsbo, Washington, is a §8(a) industrial electrical contractor specializing in federal government work.

North Star Industrial Contractors, LLC, also in Pousbo, Washington, is a §8(a) industrial construction contractor specializing in federal government work.

Examplar Technology and Communications (formerly Alindeska Technology LLC), in Seattle, Washington, is a §8(a) information technology consultant specializing in identifying, securing, building, integrating, and deploying information services in the areas of content management and personal file management.

M Kennedy Company is a §8(a) construction firm specializing in federal government work. It was started in 1979 as a sole proprietorship and incorporated in 1992. The 13th Regional Corporation purchased 51 percent ownership in late 1997 to enable it to meet the qualifications for SBA 8(a) status. Its corporate offices are in Lakewood, Washington.

Northwest Business Services Group, LLC, owns the franchises for and operates the UPS Stores in Oregon, Montana, and western Washington. It is §8(a) certified and as of 2002 was entering the information technology marketplace.

Income Operations

See the discussion of subsidiaries under Organization above.

Other Operations

The 13th Regional Heritage Foundation administers a scholarship program designed to recognize and provide financial support to Native Alaskan students with demonstrated scholastic ability who are seeking higher education in the traditional university, local community college, or vocational studies. The 13th Regional Corporation continues to litigate and lobby for a land entitlement like that awarded to the other ANCSA regional corporations.

The 13th Regional Corporation (13th)

Organization

Alindeska Environmental Services, LLC

Alindeska Electrical Contractors, LLC

North Star Industrial Contractors, LLC

Examplar Technology and Communications

M Kennedy Company

Northwest Business Services Group, LLC

OTHER NATIVE ECONOMIC ENTITIES

Regional nonprofit corporations. Most of the regions that define the areas of responsibility for the ANCSA regional corporations also have regional nonprofit Native corporations, which may or may not be closely tied to the ANCSA regional corporation. Actually, these corporations pre-date the ANCSA regional corporations, and the nonprofits' boundaries were used to determine the ANCSA corporation boundaries. In addition to having provided key grass-roots support for the passage of the ANCSA, these organizations may provide Native health services (and sometimes non-Native health services as well) and training for Native job-seekers and perform regional development, housing, and cultural preservation functions.

Indian Health Service contractors. Unlike the Lower 48, the Indian Health Service (IHS) provides no direct medical services in Alaska. It contracts with various regional and local organizations to provide health care to eligible people. The boundaries of the regional health care contractors roughly match those of the regional Native corporations, with some significant exceptions. In addition to clinics in each community, the contractors operate subregional clinics and regional hospitals with progressively higher levels of medical care. Many also provide services to non-Natives on a contract basis.

Regional development organizations. Many areas have Native economic development organizations as well as general economic development organizations.

Regional housing organizations. The HUD contractor for Indian housing may be the same regional nonprofit as the IHS contractor or may be a separate organization.

Special purpose organizations (service, regulatory). Several of the major service and regulatory organizations in Alaska are closely tied to the Native community, including the Alaska Village Electric Cooperative (AVEC) and organizations involved in the promotion and regulation of fishing.

COMMUNITIES

Census versus tribal dispersion; inclusion of non-Native residents. The population and employment figures given for a community reflect only those members of the Native entity who reside at that physical location, together with non-Natives who reside there. Many Alaska Natives live and work in the metropolitan areas-Anchorage, Fairbanks, Juneau, etc.-or in other communities or in the Lower 48. Sixteen "villages" have no residents at all, yet are federally recognized Native entities. Natives and non-Natives are not distinguished at this level of analysis.

Sample data in small communities. Census data is gathered by two different means. Basic data on population-the original reason for the census-is "enumerated", that is, each person is counted individually. Data on housing, employment, and other issues is gathered by sample; people are randomly selected to receive the "long form" census report. Although the Census Bureau used samples larger than the national one-in-seven average for rural Alaskan communities, the information remains statistically suspect.

Name confusion. Depending on whom you are reading, a community may have several different names. The incorporated city or state-recognized community name-the name that appears on road maps-may be different from the operant word in the name of the federally recognized Native entity. This Guide is organized by the latter. In some cases, the name may have changed over time, but the older name may still be used by many sources. In some cases, the residents use a name different from the federally recognized name or the state recognized name. Some names are very similar, such as Napakiak and Napaskiak.

Old information. Even in such wonderful resources as the Alaska State Department of Community and Regional Affairs Community Database, information varies widely in currency. Generally, the date of latest information for Alaska in this Guide is the summer of 2004, but some information is older, and it is difficult to distinguish old from new.

TWO RECOGNIZED SUPRATRIBAL ORGANIZATIONS

The *Inupiat Community of the Arctic Slope* (ICAS) was organized in 1971 to represent the interests of the Inupiat residents of North Slope Borough. Inupiat were concerned that the North Slope Borough government was a creature of the state and did not represent Inupiat interests and also that the ANCSA village corporations and the Arctic Slope Regional Corporation could eventually fall under the influence or control of non-Natives and would not, in fact, represent Inupiat interests. Mostly a political organization, the ICAS is an IRA regional Native government. It did receive some direct BIA funding for welfare assistance programs and health services in the late 1970s, but local spending irregularities eventually led to a loss of federal funding. The ICAS retains the political potential as a legal structure for establishing an Inupiat government on the North Slope should the federal government grant jurisdictional sovereignty to Native Alaskans.

The *Central Council of the Tlingit and Haida Indian Tribes* (Central Council) predates the ANCSA. It represents the interests of the Tlingit, Haida, and Tsimshian Indians of the southeast panhandle of Alaska, including communities not recognized under the ANCSA or by the Bureau of Indian Affairs. It also represents Tlingit communities outside Alaska, both in Canada and in the Lower 48. In addition to political action, it is involved in vocational education and economic development and is itself a federally recognized Native entity.

URBAN TRIBES

The ANCSA, §14(h)(3), provides that the Native Alaskans living in four specific cities-Juneau, Kenai, Kodiak, and Sitka-have a land entitlement of 23,040 acres each near their respective municipalities. These cities include BIA-recognized tribes. Except for the fact that these tribes have no specific location within their respective cities, they and their "urban corporations" are the same as other Alaskan tribes and Native corporations. Under the Alaska Native Claims Settlement Act Amendments of 1976, the urban corporation for each of these four cities was granted $250,000.

As these tribes are embedded in urban areas and have no residential territory of their own, it is unnecessary to describe them in detail. The following table identifies these urban tribes:

BIA-recognized Native entity	City	Location and demographics	ANCSA corporation
Douglas Indian Association P.O. Box 240541 Douglas, AK 99824 907-364-2916 907-364-2917 Fax Tlingit	City & Borough of Juneau 155 South Seward Street Juneau, AK 99801 907-586-5240 907-586-5385 Fax juneau.org	On the mainland of Southeast Alaska, opposite Douglas Island, 900 air miles northwest of Seattle and 577 air miles southeast of Anchorage. Total population: 30,711 AIAN population: 3,496 (16.6%)	Goldbelt, Incorporated 9097 Glacier Hwy. #200 Juneau, AK 99801 907-790-4990 907-790-4999 fAX goldbelt.com
Kenaitze Indian Tribe (IRA) P.O. Box 988 Kenai, AK 99611-0988 907-283-3633 907-283-3052 Fax Dena"ina Athabascan	City of Kenai 210 Fidalgo Ave., St. 200 Kenai, AK 99611 907-283-7535 907-283-3014 Fax kenai.ak.us	On the western coast of the Kenai Peninsula, fronting Cook Inlet, 65 air miles and 155 highway miles southwest of Anchorage. Total population: 6,942 AIAN population: 842 (12.1%)	Kenai Natives Association, Inc. 215 Fidalgo Ave. #101 Kenai, AK 99611-7776 907-283-4851 907-283-4854 Fax Entitlement conveyed: 22,368 acres
Shoonaq' Tribe of Kodiak 312 W Marine Way Kodiak, AK 99615 907-486-4449 907-486-3361 Fax Alutiiq	City of Kodiak 710 Mill Bay Road Room 220 Kodiak, AK 99615 907-486-8636 907-486-8633 Fax city.kodiak.ak.us	Near the eastern tip of Kodiak Island in the Gulf of Alaska, 252 air miles south of Anchorage and a 4-hour flight from Seattle Total population: 6,334 AIAN population: 829 (13.1%)	Natives of Kodiak, Inc. 215 Mission Rd. #201 Kodiak, AK 99615 907-486-3606 907-486-2745 Fax
Sitka Tribe of Alaska (IRA) 456 Katlain Street Sitka, AK 99835-7505 907-747-3207 907-747-4915 sitkatribe.org Tlingit; Haida; Aleut; Tsimsian	City & Borough of Sitka 100 Lincoln Street Sitka, AK 99835 907-747-3294 907-747-7403 Fax cityofsitka.com	On the west coast of Baranof Island fronting the Pacific Ocean, on Sitka Sound, 95 air miles southwest of Juneau. Total population: 8,835 AIAN population: 2,178 (24.7%)	Shee Atiká, Incorporated 315 Lincoln St. #300 Sitka, AK 99835 907-747-3534 907-747-5727 Fax sheeatika.com

ZERO POPULATION: VILLAGES WITH NO NATIVE ALASKANS

As of the 2000 census, there are 16 historic Native Alaskan villages that no longer have any Native Alaskan residents. However, all are BIA-recognized Native entities, and all but one have associated ANCSA entitlements. The following table identifies, locates, and describes the entities associated with these villages:

Village	Location	ANCSA entitlement	BIA-recognized entity (Traditional unless IRA is specified)	ANCSA village corporation
Belkofski (Unangan)	Eastern end of the Alaska Peninsula, 12 miles southeast of King Cove. Most members live in King Cove.	77,188 acres	Native Village of Belkofski P.O. Box 57 King Cove, AK 99612 907-497-2673 907-497-2304 Fax	Belkofski Corporation P.O. Box 46 Belkofski, AK 99612
Bill Moore's Slough (Yup'ik)	On the left bank of Apoon Pass, southwest of Kotlik, in the Yukon Delta. Most members live in Kotlik.	69,120 acres	Village of Bill Moore's Slough P.O. Box 20288 Kotlik, AK 99620 907-899-4232 907-899-4461 Fax	Kongnikilnomuit Yuita Corp. P.O. Box 20037 Kotlik, AK 99620 Phone: 907-899-4232 Fax: 907-899-4461 Fax
Chulloonawick (Yup'ik)	On the North bank of Kwikpak pass in the Yukon-Kuskokwim Delta. Most members live in Emmonak.	69,120 acres	Chuloonawick Native Village P.O. Box 245 Emmonak, AK 99581 907-949-1345 907-949-1384 Fax	Chuloonawick Corporation 301 Calista Court, Suite A Anchorage, AK 99508 907-562-7008
Council (Inupiat)	At the terminus of the Nome/Council road, 60 miles northeast of Nome. It lies on left bank of the Niukluk River. Most members live in Nome.	84,378 acres	Native Village of Council P.O. Box 2050 Nome, AK 99762, 907-443-7649 907-443-5965 Fax	Council Native Corporation P.O. Box 1183 Nome, AK 99762 907-443-5554
Ekuk (Yup'ik)	On the east coast of Nushagak Bay, 17 miles south of Dillingham. Most members live near Dillingham.	76,800 acres	Native Village of Ekuk P.O. Box 530 Dillingham, AK 99576 907-842-3842 907-842-3843 Fax	Choggiung, Limited P.O. Box 330 Dillingham AK 99576 907-842-5218 907-842-5462 Fax
Hamilton (Yup'ik)	On the right bank of Apoon Pass, southwest of Kotlik, in the Yukon Delta. Most members live in Kotlik.	69,120 acres	Native Village of Hamilton P.O. Box 20248 Kotlik, AK 99620 907-899-4252 907-899-4202 Fax	Nunapiglluraq Corporation P.O. Box 20249 Hamilton, AK 99620 907-899-4027
Kaguyak (Alutiiq)	At the head of Kaguyak Bay, on the southeast coast of Kodiak Island. Members live in Old Harbor	90,880 acres	Kaguyak Village P.O. Box 5078 Akhiok, AK 99615 907-836-2231 907-836-2232 Fax	Akhiok-Kaguyak, Inc. 1400 W. Benson Blvd. Anchorage, AK 99503 907-258-0604 907-258-0608 Fax
Kanatak (Alutiiq)	On the south coast of the Alaska Peninsula, west of Kodiak Island, at the foot of Mount Becharof on Portage Bay.	None(abandoned since the 1950s)	Native Village of Kanatak (IRA council) MSC 177 P.O. Box 875910 Wasilla, AK 99654-9717 907-357-7174 907-376-7203 Fax	None
King Island (Inupiat)	40 miles west of Cape Douglas in the Bering Sea, south of Wales. Members live in Nome.	120,960 acres	King Island Native Community (IRA council) P.O. Box 992 Nome, AK 99762 907-443-5494 907-443-3620 Fax	King Island Native Corp. P.O. Box 992 Nome, AK 99762 907-443-5494 907-443-3620 Fax
Lesnoi (Alutiiq)	In Chiniak Bay, 2.6 miles east of Kodiak. Also called Woody Island. Most members live in Kodiak.	161,276 acres	Lesnoi Village P.O. Box 9009 Kodiak, AK 99615 888-414-2821 907-486-2738 Fax woodyisland.com	Leisnoi, Inc. 711 H Street Anchorage, AK 99501 907-562-1126 907-562-1128 Fax

ZERO POPULATION: VILLAGES WITH NO NATIVE ALASKANS (continued)

Village	Location	ANCSA entitlement	BIA-recognized entity (Traditional unless IRA is specified)	ANCSA village corporation
Mary's Igloo (Inupiat)	On the northwest bank of the Kuzitrin River, on the Seward Peninsula, northeast of Nome. Most members live in Teller.	104,320 acres	Native Village of Mary"s Igloo P.O. Box 630 Teller, AK 99778 907-642-3731 907-642-2189 Fax	Mary"s Igloo Native Corp. P.O. Box 590 Teller, AK 99778 907-642-3731 907-642-2189 Fax
Napaimute (Inupiat)	On the north bank of the Kuskokwim River, 28 miles east of Aniak in the Kilbuck-Kuskokwim Mountains. Most members live in Aniak.	69,120 acres	Native Village of Napaimute P.O. Box 1301 Bethel, AK 99559 907-471-2325 907-471-2325 Fax	The Kuskokwim Corporation 4300 B Street, Suite 207 Anchorage, AK 99503 907-243-2944 907-243-2984 Fax kuskokwim.com
Ohogamiut (Yup'ik)	On the Yukon River, 22 miles southeast of Marshall, in the Yukon-Kuskokwim Delta. Most members live in Marshall.	69,120 acres	Village of Ohogamiut P.O. Box 49 Marshall, AK 99585 907-679-6517 907-679-6516 Fax	Ohog Incorporated General Delivery Marshall, AK 99585
Paimiut (Yup'ik)	On Kokechik Bay, on the east bank of the Lithkealik River. Most members live in Hooper Bay.	69,120 acres	Native Village of Paimiut P.O. Box 100193 Anchorage, AK 99510 907-561-9878 907-563-5398 Fax	Paimiut Corporation General Delivery Piamiut, AK 99604 907-527-4915
Pauloff Harbor (Alutiiq)	On the northern coast of Sanak Island, 50 miles southeast of False Pass. Most members live in Sand Point.	77,248 acres	Pauloff Harbor Village P.O. Box 97 Sand Point, AK 99661 907-383-6075 907-383-6094 Fax	Sanak Corporation P.O. Box 194 Sand Point, AK 99661 907-383-6075 907-383-6074 Fax
Unga (Alutiiq)	On the southeast coast of Unga Island, in the Shumagin Islands of the Aleutian Chain. Most members live in Sand Point.	77,188 acres	Native Village of Unga P.O. Box 508 Sand Point, AK 99661 907-383-5215 907-383-5553 Fax	Unga Corporation P.O. Box 130 Sand Point, AK 99661 907-383-5215 907-383-5215 Fax

UNRECOGNIZED BUT IMPORTANT

Anchorage and Fairbanks are the two largest urban centers in Alaska, and have large Native populations. Unlike the "urban tribe" cities, neither has a BIA-recognized Native entity. Nonetheless, they have significant economic impact. Adak is a new Native community, created by a regional Native corporation to provide an economic base for the Aleutian Islands.

Anchorage

In addition to being by far the largest population center in Alaska, Anchorage is the center of commerce for the state. Almost 27,000 Anchorage residents reported being all or part Alaska Native or Indian in the 2000 census. Most of the ANCSA regional corporations have either their headquarters or their main commercial office in Anchorage, as do many village corporations and subsidiaries. The Alaska Federation of Natives, primarily representing the interests of the regional Native corporations, the Alaska Inter-Tribal Council, representing the interests of the Native tribes and villages, the Alaska Native Heritage Center, the leading Native cultural center, the Alaska Native Tribal Health Consortium, and its Alaska Native Medical Center are statewide organizations with their respective headquarters in Anchorage. CIRI, the regional Native corporation, Cook Inlet Tribal Council, Inc., the regional Native nonprofit providing services other than health care; and the Southcentral Foundation, the regional Native health care provider, have their headquarters in Anchorage. Approximately one-third of CIRI's shareholders, many of whom are *not* members of recognized Native entities, live in Anchorage. For Native Alaskans in Anchorage, the regional organizations perform many of the functions of a village or tribal council.

Fairbanks

More than half of the Native population of the Alaskan Interior-two-thirds of the state's land area-lives in the Fairbanks area. More than 8,000 Fairbanks North Star Borough residents reported being all or part Alaska Native or Indian in the 2000 census. Most are members of recognized Native entities. Both Doyon, Limited, the ANCSA regional Native corporation, and Tanana Chiefs Conference, the regional Native nonprofit and health care provider, have their headquarters in Fairbanks. The Fairbanks Native Association serves many of the functions of a village or tribal council, including behavioral health, education, employment, and community services, for the Native residents of the Fairbanks area. It is the Public Law 93-638 tribal government contractor for Fairbanks and Fairbanks North Star Borough.

Fairbanks Native Association
201 First Avenue #200
Fairbanks, AK 99701
907-452-1648
907-456-4148 Fax
fairbanksnative.org

Adak

Adak is a large and well-developed air and sea port, about halfway along the great circle route from Japan to Washington State. The Aleut Corporation-the Native Alaskan regional corporation for the Alaskan Peninsula and the Aleutian Islands-exchanged much of its ANCSA land entitlement for the former Naval Air Station on Adak Island in 2004. On March 17, 2004, 47,271 acres were conveyed to The Aleut Corporation. There is no BIA-recognized Native entity, but it is reasonable to anticipate that its growing Native population will be recognized in the future. Aleut Enterprise Corporation, a subsidiary of the Aleut Corporation, serves some of the same functions as an ANCSA village corporation. A profile like those of recognized Native entities can be found beginning on page 41.

FREQUENTLY ASKED QUESTIONS

What on Earth is a "washeteria"? The washeteria is a key source of potable water in a village and offers shower facilities, washers, and dryers critical to personal hygiene, especially during the long winter season.

What is a "honeybucket"? A honeybucket is a device for providing an indoor toilet when no connection to a sewer or septic tank is available. When full, it must be taken to the local sewage treatment facility and emptied. It is similar to the black-water tank in a recreational vehicle or commercial aircraft.

What is a "snowmachine"? According to the Alaska Division of Motor Vehicles, a snowmachine "is a vehicle propelled by mechanical power, supported in part by skis, belts, cleats, or low pressure tires and primarily designed to travel over ice and snow." It is an Alaskan expression for vehicles ranging from a one-person sporting snowmobile to the large, track-laying Tucker Sno-Cat®.

Who or what is "AVEC"? AVEC is the abbreviation for the "Alaska Village Electrical Cooperative, Inc.," a rural electrical cooperative formed by 51 Alaskan communities, serving about 20,000 people.

What are "anadromous fish"? Fish, such as a salmon, that live part of their lives in fresh water and part of their lives at sea.

What is the "SBA §8(a) program"? The federal Small Business Administration's §8(a) Small Business Development Program is named for a section of the Small Business Act. It was created to help small disadvantaged businesses compete in the American economy by giving them preferential access the federal procurement contracts. Under certain circumstances, the government can offer a §8(a) business a sole-source contract on a no-bid basis. Alaskan Native §8(a) corporations have a further advantage, in that there is no limit on the value of contracts they are awarded.

Why is the term "Eskimo" not used in Tiller's Guide? "Eskimo" is considered an offensive term by most Inupiat and Inupiat-related Natives.

THE COMMUNITIES

The entries for the individual villages that follow differ in several ways from reservation entries in the rest of the directory.

Contact information is given for village corporations and city governments, as well as the Native entity itself.

One major area of difference is the acreage figures given for land belonging to the village. The number, "Area of entitlement under ANCSA," represents the land area the village

corporation has received or will receive. As of 2004, most of this land had been conveyed to the corporations or other arrangements (such as exchanges) made. In addition, cities have jurisdiction over their land, and unincorporated communities with townsites *(see page 6)* have identified territories and boundaries. This community land is not included in the ANCSA figure but is usually set out in the Physical Description.

Two population figures are listed. The first is from the 2000 census, the second the state Demographer's estimate for 2003.

Because rural communities in Alaska are rarely located in proximity to any larger city or town, employment information reported in the 2000 U.S. Census for these communities probably reflects economic activities in the villages themselves to a much greater extent than it does for communities outside Alaska. For that reason, we have included these figures in the entries here, but not for reservations in the contiguous states.

You will frequently see mention of "fishing permits" in the discussion of a community's economy. Fishing permits are issued by the Alaska State Commercial Fishing Entry Commission, established in 1973 to monitor and regulate fishery stocks in state waters and commercial access to them. Anyone involved in commercial fishing in state waters must have one of these permits, which are issued for specific species and fishing methods. They are given preferentially to those who depend on fishing for their livelihood; most are issued to residents of rural communities. They are an indication of the extent of commercial fishing in a village, but may not be used when catches are poor.

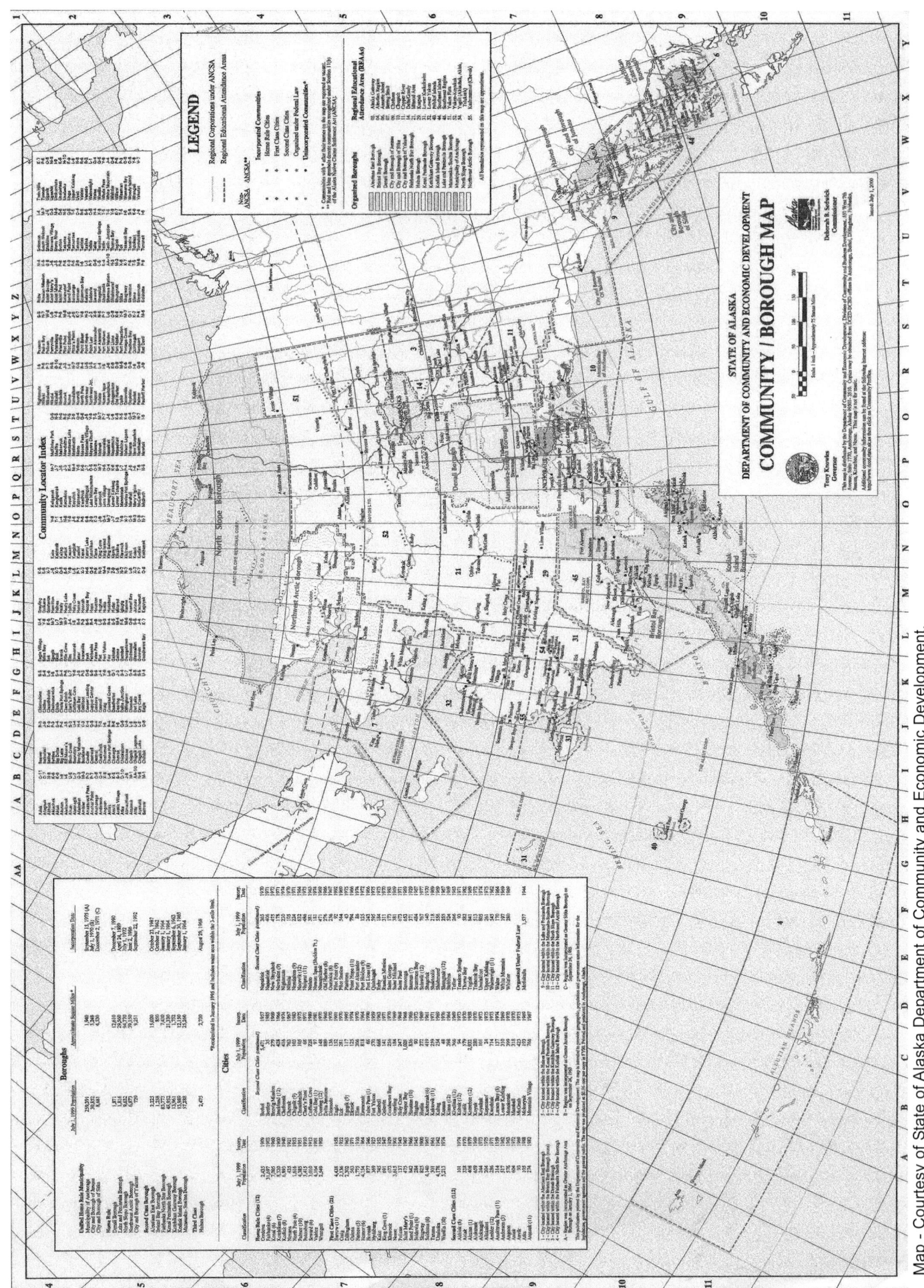

Map - Courtesy of State of Alaska Department of Community and Economic Development.

A dak

LOCATION

Adak is the northern two-fifths of Adak Island in the Aleutian Island Chain. It lies 1,300 miles southwest of Anchorage and 350 miles west of Unalaska/Dutch Harbor. Adak is the southern-most community in Alaska, on the latitude of Vancouver Island in Canada. It lies on the great circle navigation route, halfway between Seattle and Japan, and 1,400 miles from Magadan in Eastern Russia.

PHYSICAL DESCRIPTION

Adak includes 122.4 square miles of land and 4.9 square miles of water. The balance of the 280-square-mile island remains part of the National Maritime National Wildlife Refuge. The island is a wind swept volcano reaching 3,924 feet (Mt. Moffett), with little vegetation.

CLIMATE

Adak lies in the maritime climate zone, characterized by persistently overcast skies, high winds, and frequent cyclonic storms. Winter squalls produce wind gusts in excess of 100 knots. During the summer, there is extensive fog. Average temperatures range from 20°F to 60°F, but wind chill can be severe. Total precipitation is 64 inches annually, with an average accumulated snowfall of 100 inches, primarily in the mountains.

CULTURE AND HISTORY

Adak Island, historically occupied by Unanga Aleuts, was abandoned in the early 1800s as the hunters followed the Russian fur trade eastward and famine set in. However, the Aleuts continued to actively hunt and fish around the island over the years, until World War II broke out. Adak army installations allowed U.S. forces to mount a successful offensive against the Japanese-held Aleutian islands of Kiska and Attu. After the War, Adak was developed as a naval air station, playing an important role during the Cold War as a submarine surveillance center.

Large earthquakes rocked the Island in 1957, 1964, and 1977. At its peak, the station housed 6,000 sailors, navy civilians, and their families. The station had outstanding facilities, including an $18-million hospital built in 1990. Beginning in 1994, missions and people were transferred out. The station officially closed in 1997.

One of the first government contracts won by the Aleut Corporation was as caretaker of the dormant base. The Aleut Corporation acquired the base under a land transfer agreement completed in 2004. About 30 families with children relocated to Adak in September 1998, most of them Aleut Corporation shareholders, and a school was reopened. The community incorporated as a second-class city in April 2001.

GOVERNMENT

Adak is a second-class city with a mayor and city council in the unorganized borough. As many of the residents are employees of Aleut Enterprise Corporation, other subsidiaries of the Aleut Corporation, or the city government itself, the city is responsive to the development goals of the Aleut Corporation.

ECONOMY

With its complete military base infrastructure (modern airport, ice-free deep-water port, major fuel storage capabilities, and 30,000 acres of land available for lease or sale), the Aleut Corporation is developing and marketing Adak as a convenient and ready central locaion for government environmental cleanup, defense activities and commercial fishing fleets, ocean research, tourism activities in the North Pacific and Bering Sea. Adak is already the major marine refueling station for this region of the North Pacific, with gross revenues of $5,520,000 in fiscal year 2003.

Fisheries. Adak is in the middle of one of the world's richest fishing regions. The Adak Fishing Development Council operates a seafood processing and cold storage plant, processing cod, crab, halibut, and other bottom fish. Norquest-Adak Seafood processes Pacific cod, pollock, mackerel, halibut, albacore, and brown king crab. Four residents hold commercial fishing permits, primarily for groundfish.

Government as employer. While the exact number of residents employed by the city, state, and federal governments is changing, it is not clear whether the proportion of government employees will increase or decrease over time. Adak is being marketed as a convenient location for U.S. government activities in the North Pacific and as of 2004 had landed the primary support base for the sea-based, X-band radar, part of the Ground-Based Midcourse Defense (*GMD*) System, and a $900 million investment.

Tourism and recreation. Aleut Enterprise Corporation owns the Hotel Adak and one of the two car rental firms. Attractions include marine mammals, caribou hunting, fishing, hiking, and the World War II military installation facilities.

INFRASTRUCTURE

As a former naval air station, Adak has the complete infrastructure for a community of 6,000 people. The city government operates the water, sewage, landfill, diesel power generation, and electrical distribution systems.

Transportation. Adak's location and existing facilities make it useful as an air and maritime hub at the north end of the North Pacific.

[A-dack]

Ethnicity: Aleut

Municipality

City of Adak
P.O. Box 2011
Adak, AK 99546
  907-592-4513
  907-592-4262 Fax

Subsidiary of ANCSA regional corporation

Aleut Enterprise Corporation
840 K Street, Suite 202
Anchorage, AK 99501
  907-562-5444
  907-562-8208 Fax

2003 Population
state demographer estimate
150

Population *census 2000*
316

Percent Native *census 2000*
37.3%

NOTE

Adak is not a typical Native Alaskan community. The Aleut Corporation–the Native Alaskan regional corporation for the Alaskan Peninsula and the Aleutian Islands–exchanged much of its ANCSA land entitlement for the former naval air station on Adak Island in 2004. On March 17, 2004, 47,271 acres were conveyed to the Aleut Corporation. There is no BIA recognized tribal council. Aleut Enterprise Corpora-tion, a subsidiary of the Aleut Corporation, serves some of the same functions as an ANCSA village corporation. Much of the information in this profile is subject to rapid change as the city is developed.

Adak

Air. Adak Airport was built as a complete military airfield with two 7,800-foot asphalt-paved runways, paved taxiways and aircraft parking, over 70,000 square feet of maintenance hangar space, IFR navigation and full instrument landing, control tower and terminal building, fully equipped crash and fire station, ground support equipment, and fuel handling and storage. Alaska Airlines, Pen Air, and Evergreen International operate scheduled passenger and cargo service from Anchorage and Cold Bay. Flight time to Anchorage is three hours.

Water. Sweeper Cove is a harbor well protected by a 1,050-foot breakwater and with water deep enough for most Pacific ships. The Port of Adak maintains over 330 linear feet of deep-draft moorage at three cargo and petroleum piers. Fuel transfer takes place at the Sweeper Cove fuel dock. Fuel transfer operations are supported by numerous pipelines, booster pumps, and specialized equipment assisting petroleum transfers to and from the adjacent underground tank farm. The city has requested funds to greatly expand the Sweeper Cove small-boat harbor, including new breakwaters, a 315-foot dock, and new moorage floats.

Land. There are approximately 16 miles of paved roads and other gravel and dirt roads.

Water and waste systems. All homes and facilities are connected to city water and sewer. Water is obtained from Lake Bonnie Rose, Lake De Marie, and Nurses Creek, stored in seven water tanks throughout the community, and piped to facilities and housing units. There is a piped sewer system, and the wastewater treatment system discharges through a marine outfall line to Kuluk Bay. There is a permitted landfill with balefill.

Fuel storage. The Aleut Corporation has an underground tank farm with a capacity exceeding 22 million gallons of marine diesel, gasoline, and jet fuel.

Telecommunications. Local telephone service is provided by ACS of the Northland, long distance by AT&T Alascom and GCI. Internet service is provided by Core Communications, cable service by Adak Cablevision. No commercial radio stations broadcast to Adak, but an ARCS repeater broadcasts public television.

COMMUNITY FACILITIES AND SERVICES
Education. Adak School covers grades K—12, with 18 students and 3 teachers in 2003. It is operated by the Aleutian Region School District, a state Regional Educational Attendance Area.

Health care. The Adak Medical Center is owned and operated by Eastern Aleutian Tribes. It is a qualified Emergency Care Center and provides family practice and referral, lab, pharmacy, and public health services. It is supplemented by the Adak Volunteer Fire Department and EMS.

Public safety. Law enforcement is performed by city public safety, state troopers in King Salmon, and Unalaska Public Safety. Emergency response is provided by the Adak Volunteer Fire Department and EMS.

Afognak
See Port Lions

Agdaagux

Also known as King Cove

Ethnicity: Unangan

Municipality
City of King Cove
P.O. Box 37
King Cove, AK 99612-0037
907-497-2340
907-497-2594 Fax

Native entity
Agdaagux Tribe of King Cove
P.O. Box 249
King Cove, AK 99612
907-497-2648
907-497-2803 Fax

ANCSA village corporation
King Cove Corporation
P.O. Box 38
King Cove, AK 99612
907-497-2312
907-497-2444 Fax

Area of entitlement under ANCSA
	128,646 acres
Total labor force	657
High school graduate or higher	74.2%
Bachelor's degree or higher	4.2%
Unemployment rate	6.4%
Per capita income *(1999)*	$17,791
Population *2000 census*	792
2003 population	737
state demographer estimate	
Percent Native *2000 census*	47.9%

LOCATION
Agdaagux (King Cove) is a small Pacific seaport near the extreme western tip of the Alaska Peninsula, 625 miles southwest of Anchorage. Nearby communities include Cold Bay and False Pass.

PHYSICAL DESCRIPTION
The community is on a sand spit and adjacent uplands, which are located at the north end of a natural bay, nestled between high mountain ridges. The community is surrounded by steep slopes that are deeply incised by numerous small streams.

CLIMATE
Agdaagux has a maritime climate, with mild winters and cool summers. Winter temperatures average between 20°F and 30°F, while summer temperatures range between 30°F and 60°F. Average annual precipitation is 33 inches, including 52 inches of snow. Wind speed averages 15 knots. King Cove Harbor is ice-free year-round.

CULTURE AND HISTORY
In addition to Unangan Aleut fishermen and their families, early settlers of Agdaagux were Scandinavians and other Europeans. In 1911, Pacific American Fisheries built a salmon cannery at the present-day site of the village. Houses, roads, and other facilities grew around the cannery.

GOVERNMENT
King Cove, the second-largest community in the Aleutians East Borough, was incorporated in 1947 as a first-class city. The city uses the manager form of administration, together with a mayor and city council. It has an office in Anchorage at 3380 C Street, Suite 205, Anchorage, AK 99503; (907) 274-7555, Fax (907) 276-7569.

The native members of the community are represented by the BIA-recognized Agdaagux Tribe of King Cove, a traditional village council headed by a president.

VILLAGE CORPORATION
King Cove Corporation is the ANCSA village corporation. Shareholders also hold shares in the Aleut Corporation, the regional Native corporation.

ECONOMY
Agdaagux's economy depends almost completely on the year-round commercial-fishing and seafood-processing industries. Income is supplemented by subsistence activities. Salmon, caribou, geese, and ptarmigan are food sources.

Fisheries. Sixty-two residents hold commercial fishing permits, chiefly for salmon. The Peter Pan Seafoods facility is one of the largest cannery operations in Alaska. Up to 500 nonresidents are brought in seasonally to work in the cannery.

Government as employer. Of the 450 employed residents, 76 work for the city, state, or federal government.

Services and retail. There are 38 businesses in the community, including a marine repair business, a fiberglass repair business, a bakery, a baby shop, a guide service, restaurants, taxi services, contractors, and child care services.

Tourism and recreation. Agdaagux is known for its spectacular scenery, providing opportunities for photography, birding, hiking, wildlife viewing, and scenic walking. Pavlov Volcano can be seen from within the community, and Belkofski Bay and Leonard's Harbor are primary areas for hunting bear, caribou, and geese. Visitors also enjoy fishing for salmon, halibut, cod, and Dungeness crab near the village. Tours are provided of one of the largest seafood-processing operations in the nation. Visitor attractions also include the hydroelectric facility. Wilderness guide charter services are available. Accommodations include apartments and an inn.

Transportation. Two taxi companies and two car/truck rental businesses operate in the city.

INFRASTRUCTURE
Transportation. Agdaagux is accessible only by air and sea. The state provides a 3,360- by 115-foot gravel runway. The airport lies in a valley between two volcanic peaks where gale force crosswinds are common. As of 2004, the U.S. Army Corps of Engineers has approved a road to Cold Bay through the Izembek National Wildlife Refuge, to access that community's airport. The Corps of Engineers also approved a hovercraft-landing pad. The state ferry operates bimonthly between May and October. The ferry and marine cargo services use one of three docks owned by Peter Pan Seafoods. The city provides a deep water dock. The North Harbor, which is ice-free year-round, provides moorage for 90 boats. As of 2003, the Corps of Engineers and Aleutians East Borough were building a new harbor and breakwater. Upon completion, the city will operate the new Babe Newman Harbor, which will provide additional moorage for 60-foot to 150-foot fishing vessels.

Electricity. Community electricity is provided by a hydroelectric power plant located at Delta Creek, backed by a 2,700-kilowatt diesel plant. The system is owned by the Borough and operated by the City of King Cove. Peter Pan Seafoods, one of the largest cannery operations in Alaska, provides its own electricity.

Fuel storage (gallons). Peter Pan Seafoods (522,515); City Electric (127,800); Aleutians East Schools (5,300); King Cove Corp. (5,000); Gould & Sons (2,800).

Water and waste systems. Ram Creek supplies water with a sheetpile dam, which stores about 980,000 gallons of unfiltered water. There is also a well field at Delta Creek and a newer storage tank. A piped water system serves all residents, and a piped sewage collection system connects all homes and facilities to central septic tanks. Two lift stations and tanks provide primary (20,000 gallons) and secondary treatment (84,000 gallons) of waste, with discharge through an outfall line. All households are plumbed. The city provides garbage collection biweekly and aluminum is recycled. The landfill is nearing capacity.

Telecommunications. In-state phone service is provided by Interior Telephone Co./TelAlaska, long distance phone service by AT&T Alascom or Interior Telephone. Internet service is provided by Arctic Net/TelAlaska Inc. or GCI. One FM radio station broadcasts from Agdaagux, and residents can receive AM broadcasts from Nome, Dillingham, Bethel, Anchorage, and Sand Point. King Cove Corporation provides cable television service. The Alaska Rural Communications Service and the King Cove School each broadcast one television channel from local repeaters.

COMMUNITY FACILITIES AND SERVICES
The city operates the electrical, water, and waste disposal systems and operates one of the community's two harbors and the community center, which has a gym.

Education. King Cove School is in the Aleutians East Borough School District. The school has 105 students and 12 teachers. The School library serves as the community's public library.

Health care. King Cove Medical Clinic is operated by Eastern Aleutian Tribes, Inc. The clinic is a qualified emergency care center. Auxiliary health care is provided by King Cove Volunteer Fire and Rescue. Higher levels of medical care are available at the Bristol Bay Area Health Corporation hospital in Dillingham, about 384 miles away.

Public safety. Law enforcement is provided by the city police department, a state village public safety officer, backed by state troopers in Dillingham. Emergency response is provided by the King Cove Volunteer Fire and Rescue.

Agdaagux
Also known as King Cove

Akhiok

Total area of entitlement under ANCSA

164,460 acres

Akhiok and Kaguyak
Conveyed through 2003

150,535.67 acres

Akhiok and Kaguyak

Total labor force	30
High school graduate or higher	14
Bachelor's degree or higher	3
Unemployment rate	14.3%
Per capita income *(1999)*	$8,472
Current population	51
2003 state demographer estimate	
Population *2000 census*	80
Percent Native *2000 census*	93.8%

LOCATION
Akhiok is located on the southern tip of Kodiak Island at Alitak Bay, 340 air miles southwest of Anchorage.

PHYSICAL DESCRIPTION
The City of Akhiok encompasses 7.9 square miles of land and 2.5 square miles of water. Akhiok is situated in a small cove at the tip of a peninsula in Alitak Bay. The gently rolling terrain surrounding the village consists mostly of moist tundra with tall grasses and some low-growing alder and dwarf birch. The village is surrounded by the Kodiak National Wildlife Refuge. The geology of the surrounding area consists of Quaternary deposits. There is a shrimp fishing area immediately offshore, and a salmon fishing area nearby to

Akhiok

[AH-key-ock]
Ethnicity: Alutiiq

Municipality
City of Akhiok
1400 W. Benson Blvd.
Anchorage, AK 99503-3676
907-836-2323
907-836-2209 Fax

**Village council;
BIA recognized
traditional council**

Native entity
Native Village of Akhiok
P.O. Box 5050
Akhiok, AK 99615-5050
907-836-2229
907-836-2345 Fax

ANCSA village corporation
Akhiok-Kaguyak, Inc.
1400 W. Benson Blvd. #350
Anchorage, AK 99503
907-258-0604
907-258-0608 Fax
akhiokpp@carcom.com

Akhiok

the southeast. The city is in a sea otter area and near a harbor seal area. There are no high-density areas of large terrestrial mammals nearby.

Kodiak Island and surrounding areas experience frequent earthquakes with magnitudes of under 6.0 on the Richter scale. Since 1899, 82 earthquakes of Richter magnitude 6.0 or greater have been recorded in the Cook Inlet area, and 26 of these were actually triggered within the area. The 1964 Alaska earthquake and resultant tsunami provide a relatively recent example of the very real threat posed by earthquake activity near the City of Akhiok and in the Kodiak region. Although Akhiok survived the earthquake and tsunami undamaged, long-term damage to waterfront facilities occurred as a result of tectonic subsidence. The amount of subsidence caused by the 1964 earthquake was estimated at 2 to 2.5 feet, causing flooding and inundation of low-lying coastal areas.

Wildland fires have occurred in the Akhiok region in the past and have threatened populated areas. Several active volcanoes that can affect the region are located along the Kenai and Alaska Peninsulas and Katmai Coast. These volcanoes are mildly explosive and have been active for some time, as indicated by numerous buried ash layers in surrounding soils. In 1912 the Kodiak region was blanketed in volcanic ash from the Katmai/Novarupta eruption on the Katmai Coast. That volcano blew an estimated six cubic miles (more than 33,000 million tons) into the air from vents in the Valley of Ten Thousand Smokes.

CLIMATE
Marine conditions typically prevail. Summers are cool, wet, and windy. Severe storms are common in winter, but freezing weather is rare. Annual precipitation is 35 inches. Temperatures range from 25ºF to 54ºF. Weather extremes such as high winds, large hail, and heavy rainfall threaten the area. Winds in excess of 50 miles per hour occur occasionally, and wind gusts may reach speeds of 90 miles per hour or more. Freezing rain, occasional heavy snowfall, and high winds are the dominant winter weather hazards that affect the area.

CULTURE AND HISTORY
Russians in the early 1900s occupied the original village of Kashukugniut as a sea-otter-hunting colony. In 1880 the name Akhiok appeared in the census. In 1881 residents relocated to the present site at Alitak Bay. Akhiok is an Alutiiq village that relies on fishing and subsistence harvesting of ducks, seal, deer, rabbit, and bear.

GOVERNMENT
The village was incorporated as a second-class city in 1972, with a mayor and city council. Akhiok has an advisory school board and a planning commission. A traditional tribal council is recognized by the Bureau of Indian Affairs, and the Native Village of Akhiok is a federally recognized tribe.

VILLAGE CORPORATION
Akhiok-Kaguyak was formed by the merger of the corporations of Akhiok and Kaguyak. Shareholders in the village corporation are also shareholders in Koniag Incorporated, the regional Native corporation *(see Alaska introduction)*.

ECONOMY
Akhiok relies on fishing and subsistence activities, including harvesting salmon, crab, shrimp, clams, ducks, seal, deer, rabbit, and bear. Public-sector employment and seasonal work generate cash flow in the community. Five commercial fishing permits are active. A cabins/outfitting store is the only registered business. The community expects to develop a fish smokery and cold-storage facility. In 2003, Akhiok shareholders individually received $200,000 from liquidation of a $36 million trust fund provided in the *Exxon Valdez oil* spill settlement.

Government as employer. Eighteen residents work in city, borough, state, or federal government.

INFRASTRUCTURE
Transportation. The city is accessible only by air and water. Air access to Akhiok is always weather-dependent. The state provides a 3,320- by 60-foot gravel runway. Island Air Service offers regular passenger flights; scheduled and charter flights also are available from the City of Kodiak. A seaplane base is located at Moser Bay. Barge services are sporadic. A breakwater and boat launch is ready for use, but the existing dock is a temporary structure. Small boats may be beached or anchored in Akhiok Bay. The road system in Akhiok is limited to gravel roads and paths. There are some vehicles and ATVs in the community.

Electricity. The city provides electricity.

Water and waste systems. Water, drawn from a dam and reservoir on a small stream, is treated and stored. A piped gravity water and sewer system serves all 25 homes in Akhiok. Residents boil their drinking water but plans for a new water source are expected. During especially cold winters, Akhiok has had freeze out problems with the water supply. The City of Akhiok provides refuse disposal. A new landfill site is under development.

Telecommunications. Local telephone service is available through Pacific Telecommunications, while long distance service is provided by Alascom. One television channel is provided by the Rural Alaska Television Network. Many residents have CB radios, and some have VHF marine radios, although these cannot reach Kodiak. There are telephones in most homes, and seven long-distance trunks serve the community. Telephone service in Akhiok is dependent upon electrical supply. Without electricity, the phones would cease working after one or two days of running on battery power. There is a VHF base and antenna at the clinic, along with several handhelds. With no single side band (SSB) radios on hand, a power failure would leave Akhiok without communications with Kodiak City.

COMMUNITY FACILITIES AND SERVICES
Education. Akhiok School is in the Kodiak Island Borough School District, and has 16 students and 2 teachers. The school library serves as the city library.

Health care is provided by the Akhiok Health Clinic, owned by the city and leased to the U.S. Public Health Service. The Clinic is administered by the Kodiak Area Native Association. The clinic is staffed by a Community Health Practitioner and two Community Health Aides and can handle initial medical response to almost any kind of emergency. The village public safety officer is EMT certified. There are no doctors or registered nurses in Akhiok; therefore, most health care is provided by EMT- or ETT-trained personnel who are supported by doctors from the Kodiak Area Native Association. The Akhiok Village Response Team offers auxiliary health care. Further medical care requires a flight to Kodiak or Anchorage.

Public safety. Law enforcement and emergency response resources are limited in Akhiok. The village public safety officer has primary responsibility, backed by state troopers in Kodiak.

Total area of entitlement under ANCSA
115,200 acres

Total labor force	200
High school graduate or higher	86
Bachelor's degree or higher	21
Unemployment rate	25.5%
Per capita income *(1999)*	$8,321
Current Population	633
2003 state demographer estimate	
Population *2000 census*	585
Percent Native *2000 census*	96.4%

LOCATION
Akiachak is on the west bank of the Kuskokwim River, 18 miles northeast of Bethel, on the Yukon-Kuskokwim Delta.

PHYSICAL DESCRIPTION
The area encompasses 6.8 square miles of land and 0.1 square mile of water.

CLIMATE
Annual precipitation is 16 inches, with yearly snowfall of 50 inches. Summer temperatures vary from 42°F to 62°F; winter temperatures range from -2°F to 19°F.

CULTURE AND HISTORY
Akiachak is a Yup'ik Eskimo village with a fishing and subsistence lifestyle. Early Yup'ik Eskimos used the area as a seasonal subsistence site. Called "Akiakchagamiut" in the 1890 census, the village then had a population of 43.

GOVERNMENT
The Akiachak Native Community is a federally recognized tribe with an IRA tribal council. Akiachak incorporated as a second-class city in 1974, but the city government was repealed in 1987, ending all city administration. It is in the Unorganized Borough.

VILLAGE CORPORATION
Shareholders in the village corporation are also shareholders in Calista Regional Native Corporation *(see Alaska introduction)*.

ECONOMY
Education and public services offer year-round employment. Residents also rely on seasonal work, such as commercial fishing, construction, and Bureau of Land Management firefighting. Bristol Bay offers villagers some work at its canneries. A fish processing facility and freezer are planned. Subsistence activities provide most food sources. Sparse fish returns in recent years have significantly hurt the community. Seventy residents hold commercial fishing permits (salmon, herring roe, or both). Private businesses include a video rental store, grocery, technical consulting service, air transportation service, real estate office, and merchandise store.

Government as employer. Of 149 employed residents, 126 work in local, state, or federal governments.

INFRASTRUCTURE
Transportation. The state provides a 1,649- by 40-foot gravel airstrip. Public seaplane facilities provide scheduled and chartered services year-round. Relocation of the airport is planned. Snow machines, boats, and all-terrain vehicles are available. Artic Circle Air Service, Aviation, and Hageland Aviation offer passenger flight service. A trail is open to Bethel in winter. Barges transport bulk fuel and supplies during the summer.

Electricity. The Akiachak Native Community Electric, operated by Akiachak, Limited, provides electricity to the community from a 570-kilowatt diesel generator.

Fuel. Akiachak, Limited, has a fuel storage and sales facility at the village.

Water and waste systems. Currently, a piped system serves 12 facilities, the school, and teachers' housing. Most residents haul water from the washeteria. More than two dozen households have honeybuckets hauled by the city; others tow their own honeybuckets or use septic tanks. Construction of a piped water and gravity sewer system is in progress. A new well, water tank, and water treatment plant are in operation. The new lagoon is open and accessible by road. Construction to plumb and connect more than 60 homes on the west side will continue through 2005. The purchase of an incinerator will allow waste heat use for public buildings.

Telecommunications. Local and long distance telephone services are provided by United Utilities. One AM and one FM radio station broadcast to the area. Cable access is provided by the village, and the Rural Alaska Television Network and one commercial television station broadcast to the area.

COMMUNITY FACILITIES AND SERVICES
Education. Akiachak School is in the Yupiit School District. The school has 186 students and 12 teachers. The school library serves as the village library.

Health care services are provided by Akiachak Health Clinic under lease to the U.S. Public Health Service and administered by the Yukon-Kuskokwim Health Corporation.

Public safety. Law enforcement is provided by the village police department, a state village public safety officer (VPSO), and state troopers in Bethel. Emergency response is provided by the state VPSO and the village volunteer fire department.

[ACK-ee-uh-chuck]
Ethnicity: Yup'ik

Native entity
Akiachak Native Community
P.O. Box 70
Akiachak, AK 99551
907-825-4626
907-825-4029 Fax

ANCSA village corporation
Akiachak, Limited
P.O. Box 51010
Akiachak, AK 99551-0010
907-825-4328
907-825-4115 Fax

A kiak

[ACK-ee-ack]
Ethnicity: Yup'ik

Municipality
City of Akiak
P.O. Box 187
Akiak, AK 99552
  907-765-7411
  907-765-7512 Fax

Native entity
Akiak Native Community
P.O. Box 52165
Akiak, AK 99552
  907-765-7112
  907-765-7512 Fax

ANCSA village corporation
Kokarmuit Corporation
P.O. Box 215
Akiak, AK 99552
  907-765-7228
  907-765-7619 Fax

Total area of entitlement under ANCSA	
	115,200 acres
Total labor force	91
High school graduate or higher	55
Bachelor's degree or higher	10
Unemployment rate	16.5%
Per capita income *(1999)*	8,326
2003 population	337
state demographer estimate	
Population *2000 census*	309
Percent Native *2000 census*	95.1%

LOCATION
Akiak is on the west bank of the Kuskokwim River, 42 air miles northeast of Bethel, in the Yukon-Kuskokwim Delta.

CLIMATE
Annual precipitation is 16 inches, with yearly snowfall of 50 inches. Summer temperatures range from 42°F to 62°F; winter temperatures vary from -2°F to 19°F.

PHYSICAL DESCRIPTION
The City of Akiak includes 1.97 square miles of land and 1.09 square miles of water. Much of the city appears to be subject to flooding and is built below the Corps of Engineers recommended building elevation. Flooding occurred in 1920, 1964, 1968, 1978, and 1988. On the tundra there are no trees, but there are mosses, lichens, and dwarf woody plants. The tundra has continuous grass cover except along streams. Trees line the rivers and creeks: cottonwood, black spruce, and birch.

CULTURE AND HISTORY
Akiak is a Yup'ik word meaning "the other side." The name stems from its location as the point where area Inupiat crossed the Kuskokwim River into the Yukon River basin in winter. A post office was established in 1916. A U.S. Public Health Service hospital opened in the 1920s. This is a Yup'ik village with a fishing and subsistence tradition.

GOVERNMENT
Akiak was incorporated as a second-class city in 1970, with a mayor and city council. The village has an advisory school board and a planning commission.

VILLAGE CORPORATION
The Akiak Native Community is a federally recognized traditional tribal council. Shareholders in the village corporation are also shareholders in Calista Regional Native Corporation *(see Alaska introduction)*.

ECONOMY
City, school, and public services offer year-round employment. Commercial fishing and Bureau of Land Management firefighting provide seasonal income. Development of tourism and a fish processing plant are in the community's plans. Akiak residents rely on subsistence and fishing activities, but sparse fish returns in recent years have significantly hurt the community.

Fisheries. Twenty-seven residents hold commercial fishing permits (salmon drifts, net fisheries).

Government as employer. Of the 76 employed residents, 51 work in city, state, or federal government.

Services and retail. A food service holds the only active business license.

INFRASTRUCTURE
Transportation. The airport has a gravel runway, which gives access to chartered or private air year-round. Arctic Circle Air Service, Grant Aviation, and Hageland Aviation offer passenger flight service. Snow machines, all-terrain vehicles, and skiffs are used widely for local transportation. Docking facilities are not available. During the winter, residents use trucks, cars, and snowmachines to travel on the river ice. During the summer, residents use boats and the hovercraft to travel on the river. Food and other supplies come into Akiak by plane or hovercraft from Bethel or Anchorage. Fuel and building materials are brought to Akiak by barge. Approximately one-half mile of gravel road forms a square around the center of the village, legs reaching out to connect the gas station, the landfill, and the airport.

Electricity is provided by the city, operating a diesel plant with a capacity of 383-kilowatts.

Fuel storage (gallons). Kokarmiut Corp. (316,000); Yupiit Schools (70,250); City Electric (26,000); Army National Guard (5,500).

Water and waste systems. A new well, water treatment plant, and storage tank are now operating. The school and clinic connect directly to the water plant. More than a dozen homes have wells, septic systems, and plumbing. Sewage disposal is by septic tanks, honeybuckets, or privies, but major improvements are underway. A piped water and gravity sewer system is under construction for 70 homes that are without water and sewer service. Most residents go to the washeteria for laundry and bathing. The city provides septic pumping services.

Telecommunications. Local telephone service is provided by United Utilities while long distance service is provided by AT&T Alascom or United Utilities. Cable is provided by GCI Cable. One television channel is provided by the Rural Alaska Television Network, while an additional channel can be received from Bethel. One AM and one FM radio station broadcast to the area. GCI provides Internet service at the school only.

COMMUNITY FACILITIES AND SERVICES
Education. Arlicaq School is in the Yupiit School District. The school has 9 teachers and 99 students in grades K—12. The school is the local public library.

Health care. Edith Kawagley Memorial Clinic is available. The clinic is undergoing expansion and renovation.

Public safety. Law enforcement is provided by a state village public safety officer, the city police department, and state troopers in Bethel. Emergency response is provided by the Akiak volunteer fire department.

Total area of entitlement under ANCSA	
	102,917 acres
Total labor force	602
High school graduate or higher	279
Bachelor's degree or higher	0
Unemployment rate	83.9%
Per capita income *(1999)*	$12,258
2003 population	787
state demographer estimate	
Population *2000 census*	713
Percent Native *2000 census*	16.4%

LOCATION

Akutan is located on Akutan Island in the eastern Aleutians, the largest of the Krenitzin Islands of the Fox Island group. Akutan is 35 miles east of Unalaska, and 766 air miles southwest of Anchorage.

PHYSICAL DESCRIPTION

Akutan Island is an active volcano. Mount Akutan, 4,244 feet high, erupted at least 8 times in the twentieth century, most recently in 1992. There was also an earthquake in 1996. The city is located on the north shore of Akutan Harbor, near the eastern end of the island. The city encompasses 14.0 square miles of land and 4.9 square miles of water. The area around the city is essentially treeless. Arctic-alpine species of vegetation are concentrated between the sea and about 1,000 feet, above which very little grows. At the lower elevations, the land is covered by a mat of vegetation consisting of about 500 species of vascular plants, bryophytes, and lichens. The sea around the island is rich in animal and plant life to a depth of about 60 feet, and the island is in the middle of a major king crab fishing area. The island is home to seagoing waterfowl and marine mammals.

CLIMATE

A maritime climate zone prevails with mild winters and cool summers. Temperatures range from 22°F to 55°F. Annual precipitation averages 28 inches. High winds and storms are common in winter; fog in summer.

CULTURE AND HISTORY

Akutan's origins go back to 1878 as a fur storage and a trading port. A Russian Orthodox church and a school opened in the same year. In 1912 the Pacific Whaling Company built a whale processing station across the bay from Akutan. During World War II, the U.S. government relocated Akutan residents to the Ketchikan area. The village was reestablished in 1944. Akutan is the site of a traditional Unangan village. The majority of residents are transient fish processing workers who live in group quarters.

GOVERNMENT

Akutan was incorporated as a second-class city in 1979, with a mayor and city council. The village has an advisory school board and planning commission. It is located in the Aleutians East Borough. The traditional Akutan Tribal Council serves as tribal government for the Alaska Native members of the community; typically the five-member council oversees issues affecting the tribe, such as health care or social services. Akutan is the only remaining Aleut village with a traditional chief.

VILLAGE CORPORATION

Shareholders in the village corporation are also shareholders in Aleut Regional Native Corporation *(see Alaska introduction)*.

ECONOMY

Akutan's cash-based economy relies on commercial fish processing. Subsistence foods include seal, salmon, herring, halibut, clams, wild cattle, and game birds. Many residents are seasonally employed. Seven residents hold commercial fishing permits (salmon, herring, halibut, clams). Akutan Corporation operates a small hotel and a bed-and-breakfast. Other businesses include a news publisher, café, retail store, grocery, bar, diving service, and check-cashing service.

Fish processing. Trident Seafoods runs a large processing plant west of the city. Deep Sea Fisheries also has a permanent processing vessel in the bay. Trident Seafoods is one of the largest fish processing plants in Alaska.

Government as employer. Of the 97 employed residents, 31 work in local, state, or federal government.

INFRASTRUCTURE

Transportation. Akutan is accessible only by boat and amphibious aircraft. A dock and a small-boat mooring basin are available. Plans are underway to develop a large boat harbor. The state ferry travels from Kodiak in spring and autumn. Cargo is transported weekly by freighter from Seattle. The city owns a landing craft. Akutan has no airstrip, but a seaplane base is available. Daily air service comes from nearby Unalaska. High waves, however, may limit accessibility during winter months.

Electricity is provided by the city, operating a hydroelectric plant with diesel backup and total capacity of 380-kilowatts.

Fuel storage (gallons). Trident Seafoods (1,786,590); city (72,400); Aleutians East Schools (1,100).

Water and waste systems. Water drawn from a stream and dam is treated and piped into homes. Two new water catchment dams, a 125,000-gallon water storage tank, and a treatment plant are in the funding process. Sewage is piped to a community septic tank, and refuse is collected regularly. A new landfill site and incinerator are in service.

Telecommunications. Cable television service is available from the city, and there is a telephone system operated by Pacific Telecommunications; long distance service is provided by AT&T Alascom or GCI. GCI also provides Internet service. The Alaska Rural Communications Service public television network appears to be available.

COMMUNITY FACILITIES AND SERVICES

Education. Akutan School is in the Aleutians East Borough District. The school has 16 students and 2 teachers in grades K—12. The student body is 94 percent Native Alaskan. The city operates a public library. Together, the city and the traditional council operate a small museum. The St. Alexander Nevsky Russian Orthodox Church is a newly reconstructed historic site.

Health care. Anesia Kudrin Memorial Clinic, currently under renovation, is available. Akutan First Responders provides auxiliary health care. Both medical operations offer flights to Unalaska and Anchorage.

Public safety. Law enforcement is provided by a state village police officer (VPSO), and the city police department, backed up by state troopers in Dillingham. Emergency response is provided by the state VPSO and the city volunteer fire department.

[ACK-oo-tan]
Ethnicity: Aleut

Municipality
City of Akutan
P.O. Box 109
Akutan, AK 99553
  907-698-2228
  907-698-2202 Fax

Native entity
Native Village of Akutan
P.O. Box 89
Akutan, AK 99553-0089
  907-698-2300
  907-698-2301 Fax

ANCSA village corporation
Akutan Corporation
P.O. Box 8
Akutan, AK 99553
  907-698-2206
  907-698-2207 Fax

Alakanuk

[ah-LUCK-uh-nuck]
Ethnicity: Yup'ik

Municipality
City of Alakanuk
P.O. Box 167
Alakanuk, AK 99554
907-238-3313
907-238-3620 Fax

Native entity
Alakanuk Traditional Council
P.O. Box 149
Alakanuk, AK 99554
907-238-3419
907-238-3429 Fax

ANCSA village corporation
Alakanuk Native Corporation
P.O. Box 148
Alakanuk, AK 99554
907-238-3117
907-238-3120 Fax

Total area of entitlement under ANCSA	138,240 acres
Total labor force	177
High school graduate or higher	111
Bachelor's degree or higher	19
Unemployment rate	21.5%
Per capita income *(1999)*	$6,884
2003 population	666
2003 state demographer estimate	
Population *2000 census*	652
Percent Native *2000 census*	97.9%

LOCATION
Alakanuk is located at the east entrance, mostly on the south and east side, of Alakanuk Pass, the major southern channel of the Yukon River, 15 miles from the Bering Sea. It is part of the Yukon Delta National Wildlife Refuge. It lies 8 miles southwest of Emmonak and approximately 162 air miles northwest of Bethel.

PHYSICAL DESCRIPTION
The area encompasses 32.4 square miles of land and 8.7 square miles of water. The flood of record (1952) reached 12.8 feet above mean sea level; the village is 8 feet above sea level. It is the longest village on the lower Yukon-the development stretches over a three-mile area along the pass. Approximately 25 homes along the bank are being threatened by erosion.

CLIMATE
Annual snowfall averages 60 inches; yearly precipitation is 19 inches. Temperatures range from-25°F to 79°F. Strong winds prevail in autumn and winter.

CULTURE AND HISTORY
Alakanuk is a Yup'ik word meaning "wrong way," applied here to a village on a confusing network of watercourses. The village was first officially reported in 1899. A Yup'ik shaman named Anguksuar and his family were the first settlers. A post office opened in 1946. Two years later, the school was relocated to nearby St. Mary's. Commercial fishing and a subsistence lifestyle characterize the culture. Many residents travel to Emmonak to shop and attend social events and basketball tournaments.

GOVERNMENT
Alakanuk incorporated as a second-class city in 1969, with a mayor and city council. The city has an advisory school board and planning commission. A traditional tribal council also is recognized.

VILLAGE CORPORATION
Shareholders in the village corporation are also shareholders in Calista Regional Native Corporation *(see Alaska introduction)*.

ECONOMY
Alakanuk has a seasonal economy hinged on fishing and subsistence. Seventy-six residents hold commercial fishing permits (salmon, beluga, whale). Many residents have gill net permits, and set net fishermen sell their salmon to Seattle fish buyers. Salmon, beluga whale, seal, moose, and rabbit provide food. Sparse fish returns in recent years have significantly hurt the community. A number of residents still trap. Government employment and retail businesses provide limited year-round employment. Alakanuk Native Corporation operates a store. Other private businesses include a store and warehouse, café, home furnishing store, commercial fishing, taxi service, grocery store, a gunsmith, and a small hamburger stand with takeout service.

Government as employer. Of 139 employed residents, 101 work in city, state, or federal government.

NFRASTRUCTURE
Transportation. The state operates a 2,200- by 55-foot gravel airstrip. An airport relocation project is underway. Grant Aviation, Hageland Aviation, and Tanana Air Service offer scheduled flight services. Travelers on the Yukon River and Bering Sea can get to Alakanuk by barge and riverboat. There are no roads connecting Alakanuk with other communities, but ice roads are open for winter travel. Snowmachines and boats are used in local transportation.

Electricity is provided by Alaska Village Electric Cooperative in cooperation with the city. They operate a diesel plant with a capacity of 850-kilowatts.

Fuel storage (gallons). Lower Yukon Schools (132,000); Alakanuk Native Corporation (124,000); AVEC (117,029); city water plant (40,000); city (4,000).

Water and waste systems. The city operates a piped water and sewer system to nearly all of the homes. Residents dump their honeybuckets in a sewage lagoon. Water, drawn from the Alakanuk Slough, is treated and stored in a tank and piped to most residences. A new pipe system serves more than 80 homes, the school, and teachers' housing. New facilities include a water treatment plant, a heated 300,000-gallon water storage tank, a vacuum sewage plant, a sewage lagoon, arctic piping, and household plumbing. A new subdivision is currently underway, and nine homes will be connected to the piped utilities. DEC funding will connect 20 homes with piped service. Ten homes have been moved from the erosion zone on the river bank and are ready for service. Ten other homes are on a waiting list. The city has completed a feasibility study for an area across the river. Funding is being sought for the expansion.

Telecommunications. Local and long distance phone service and Internet service are provided by United Utilities. An Alaska Rural Communications System repeater broadcasts to the area, as do two AM radio stations. The city provides cable service.

COMMUNITY FACILITIES AND SERVICES
Education. Alakanuk School is in the Lower Yukon School District. The school has 217 students in grades K—12 and 14 teachers. The school library also serves the community.

Health care is provided by the Alakanuk Health Clinic, owned by the city and leased to the U.S. Public Health Service. The clinic is administered by Yukon Kuskokwim Health. The Pearl E. Johnson Subregional Clinic is available in Emmonak, and Bethel Hospital in Bethel.

Public safety. Law enforcement is provided by the city police department, backed by state troopers in Nome and Bethel. Emergency response is provided by the Alakanuk Volunteer Fire Department.

Total area of entitlement under ANCSA
                                       69,120 acres
Total labor force   14
High school graduate or higher   8
Bachelor's degree or higher   4
Unemployment rate   14.3%
Per capita income *(1999)* $14,109
2003 population   21
     state demographer estimate
Population *2000 census*   35
Percent Native *2000 census*   97.1%

LOCATION
Alatna is on the north bank of the Koyukuk river, southwest of its junction with the Alatna River, approximately 190 air miles northwest of Fairbanks and 57 miles upriver from Hughes. Alatna lies just west of the municipal boundaries of the City of Allakaket.

PHYSICAL DESCRIPTION
The area encompasses 36.5 square miles of land. All buildings are now on high ground after the flood of 1994. The Alatna River is a designated National Wild and Scenic River.

CLIMATE
A continental climate with extreme temperatures prevails. Average highs of 70°F in July to average lows of below 0°F in January. Extended periods of -40°F are common. Annual precipitation is 13 inches; yearly snowfall is 72 inches.

CULTURE AND HISTORY
Koyukon Athabascans and Kobuk, Selawik, and Nunamiut Eskimos originally inhabited the area. The Koyukon followed the seasons as they hunted game and fish. Various bands established a shared settlement after 1851. Athabascans and Eskimos used the traditional vicinity of Alatna as a trading center. St. John's-in-the-Wilderness Episcopal Mission was founded in 1906 on the Koyukuk River. A post office was established in the mid-1920s. In 1938, the community was called Allakaket, while the name Alatna was accepted by an Eskimo community across the river. In 1975, the community incorporated. In 1994, flood waters toppled nearly all of the community's public and residential buildings. When the community rebuilt near the old city, Alatna was no longer within the incorporated community limits. Descendents of Kobuk Eskimos dominate the village's population. The residents rely on subsistence activities.

GOVERNMENT
The village is not incorporated, and is located in the Unorganized Borough. Alatna Village is a federally recognized traditional council.

VILLAGE CORPORATION
K'oyittl'ots'ina, Limited, is the village corporation for A'atna, A'akaket, Hughes, and Huslia. It's the fifth largest village corporation. Shareholders in the village corporation are also shareholders in Doyon regional Native corporation *(see Alaska introduction)*.

ECONOMY
The economy is seasonal and subsistence-based. Salmon, whitefish, moose, bear, small game, and berries are the most important food sources. Trapping or traditional Native handicrafts provide some income. Construction and Bureau of Land Management offer summer employment.

Government as employer. There are 12 employed residents, 6 of whom work in village, state, or federal government.

INFRASTRUCTURE
Transportation. Winter trails connect to Hughes, Bettles, and Tanana, but otherwise there are no roads to other villages. River transportation is available during the summer. The state provides a 3,500-foot lighted runway year-round. Shallow water prohibits barge service.

Electricity. Alatna shares an Alaska Power and Telephone electrical intertie with Allakaket.

Water and waste systems. Villagers tow water and use honeybuckets or outhouses. Residences are without plumbing, but major improvements are forthcoming. Completed facilities include a water source, water treatment plant, washeteria, and sewage lagoon. Alatna residents go to Allakaket for washeteria and landfill services.

Telecommunications. Local telephone service is provided by Bettles Telephone Company, a subsidiary of Alaska Power and Telephone. Long distance service is provided by AT&T Alascom.

COMMUNITY FACILITIES AND SERVICES
Education. Alatna students attend school in Allakaket.

Health care. The small Alatna Health Clinic is available. Other medical facilities are in Allakaket.

Public safety. Public safety services are provided by the state village public safety officer in Allakaket, backed by state troopers in Bethel.

[uh-LAT-na]
Ethnicity: Kobuk Inupiat

Native entity
Alatna Village
P.O. Box 70
Alatna, AK 99720
   907-968-2304
   907-968-2305 Fax

ANCSA village corporation
K'oyitl'ots'ina, Limited
1603 College Road
Fairbanks, AK 99709
   907-452-8119
   907-452-8148 Fax

Aleknagik   Aleknagik

Total area of entitlement under ANCSA
                                      118,340 acres
Total labor force   88
High school graduate or higher   41
Bachelor's degree or higher   14
Unemployment rate   21.6%
Per capita income *(1999)* $10,973
Current population   235
     2003 state demographer est.
Population *2000 census*   221
Percent Native *2000 census*   84.6%

LOCATION
Aleknagik is situated on the north and south shores of Lake Aleknagik, at the head of Wood River on the southeast end of the lake, 16 miles northwest of Dillingham.

PHYSICAL DESCRIPTION
The city encompasses 11.6 square miles of land and 7.2 square miles of water and is dispersed thinly throughout this area. It is partially surrounded on the west, east, and north by the Ahklun Mountains. The topography in the immediate area consists of glacially rounded mountains and hills with elongated, glacially carved lakes. The geology is largely glacial

[uh-LECK-nuh-gik]
Ethnicity: Yup'ik
Municipality
   City of Aleknagik
   P.O. Box 33
   Aleknagik, AK 99555-0033
      907-842-5953
      907-842-2107 Fax

Native entity
   Aleknagik Traditional Council
   P.O. Box 115
   Aleknagik, AK 99555
      907-842-2080
      907-842-2081 Fax

ANCSA village corporation
   Aleknagik Natives Limited
   P.O. Box 1630
   Dillingham, AK 99576-1630
      907-842-2385
      907-842-1662 Fax

Aleknagik

moraine and drift, with volcanic intrusives to the northeast and alluvial deposits to the southeast (down the Wood River). Vegetation is upland spruce-hardwood forest and bottomland spruce-poplar forest. Lake Aleknagik is a medium-density waterfowl area, and the lake and Wood River are major anadromous fish locations, with feeding concentrations of bears common.

CLIMATE

Aleknagik is in a transitional climate zone with a maritime influence. Average summer temperatures vary from 30°F to 66°F; average winter temperatures range from 4°F to 30°F. Annual precipitation can top 35 inches, including 93 inches of snow. Fog and low clouds are common during the midsummer months.

CULTURE AND HISTORY

Aleknagik means "wrong way home," explained by the erroneous direction taken by Natives returning home along the Nushagak River. Heavy fog caused Natives to follow the Wood River, winding up at Aleknagik Lake instead of the village. In 1929, the census listed 55 residents in the Wood River Village to the south. In the late 1940s, a Seventh-Day Adventist mission and school were established on the north shore. During the 1950s, a Moravian church and a Russian Orthodox church were built in Aleknagik. More than 35 families resided along the lake at the time. In 1959, a summer road linked the south shore to Dillingham. The road was upgraded in the late 1980s for year-round access. Aleknagik is a traditional Yup'ik Eskimo community, with historical influences from the Seventh-Day Adventists, Russian Orthodox, and Moravians.

GOVERNMENT

Aleknagik was incorporated as a second-class city in 1973, with a mayor and city council. It is located in the Unorganized Borough. The traditional tribal council also is recognized.

VILLAGE CORPORATION

Shareholders in the village corporation Aleknagik Natives Limited, are also shareholders in Bristol Bay regional Native corporation *(see Alaska introduction)*.

ECONOMY

Commercial and subsistence activities are prevalent in summer on the Bristol Bay coast. Trapping also provides income. Fish, game, and berries are subsistence food sources. Salmon, freshwater fish, moose, and caribou, are harvested. Dismal fish returns in recent years have hurt the community.

Fisheries. Thirty-three residents hold commercial fishing permits for salmon or freshwater fish or both.

Government as employer. Of the 69 employed residents, 33 work for the city, state, or federal governments.

Services and retail. Businesses include a fishing store, bed-and-breakfast, marina retail, a private barge landing and warehouse, and an outfitters store. The facility most visible to the public is the salmon and environmental research station of the Fisheries Research Institute of the University of Washington, School of Aquatic and Fishery Sciences. The Seventh-Day Adventist Church operates a mission school northeast of the city.

INFRASTRUCTURE

Transportation. Aleknagik is the only community in the region with a road to Dillingham. The city has a new airport with a 2,070 by 90 foot gravel airstrip on the north shore. Scheduled flights are available from Dillingham. Residents use skiffs to get to town on the south shore. Floatplanes use Moody's Aleknagik Seaplane Base on the north shore. The private Tripod Airport, with a gravel airstrip located southeast of Aleknagik, and the Seventh-Day Adventist's Mission School Airport, with a gravel and dirt airstrip located northeast of the city, are available. On the north shore of Aleknagik Lake are a 100-foot dock, breakwater, barge landing, boat launch ramp, and boat lift. Skiffs, all-terrain vehicles, and snowmachines are other modes of transportation in season.

Electricity. Nushagak Electric Cooperative in Dillingham provides electricity to Aleknagik.

Water and waste systems. Nearly 50 homes have indoor plumbing, and most households use individual wells. A dozen homes do not have water or sewer service. Water hauling from the community center and the use of a spring-water catchment system are other sources. Sewage disposal comes from septic tanks, leechate fields, and public sewage lagoons. Eleven shared residential effluent pumps in the north shore discharge into a piped system. Three landfills are open.

Telecommunications. Local telephone service is available through Nushagak Telephone Cooperative; long distance service is provided by Alascom or GCI. One television channel is available through the Rural Alaska Television Network. Internet service is available through GCI or Nushagak Telephone.

COMMUNITY FACILITIES AND SERVICES

In addition to a community hall and city council offices, there are three churches in Aleknagik: Moravian, Russian Orthodox, and Seventh-Day Adventist.

Education. Aleknagik School is in the Southwest Regional School District. The school has 33 students and 5 teachers. The school library serves as the community library.

Health care. The North Shore and South Shore Health Clinics are available. The Aleknagik First Responders Group provides auxiliary health care. Kanakanak Hospital in Dillingham is 25 miles by road.

Public safety. Law enforcement is provided by a state village public safety officer and the state troopers in Dillingham. In addition to the Aleknagik First Responders Group, emergency response is provided by the Aleknagik Volunteer Fire Department and a city ambulance.

Total area of entitlement under ANCSA
(Does not include Andreafsky)   115,200 acres
Total labor force   247
High school graduate or higher   34.2%
Bachelor's degree or higher   15.2%
Unemployment rate   11.3%
Per capita income *(1999)* $15,837
Population *2000 census*   500
2003 population   585
     2003 state demographer estimate
Percent Native *2000 census*   87.6%

LOCATION
Algaaciq (Saint Mary's) is located on the north bank of the Andreafsky River 5 miles from its confluence with the Yukon River, 3.5 miles northeast of Pitka's Point, in the Yukon-Kuskokwim Delta of southwest Alaska. It is 450 miles west-northwest of Anchorage.

PHYSICAL DESCRIPTION
Algaaciq (Saint Mary's) covers 44.0 square miles of land and 6.3 square miles of water. It is located on Southwestern Alaska's coastal plain, an area of broad, flat delta covered with numerous rivers, streams, lakes, sloughs, and ponds. The delta area was created over the course of time by the Yukon and Kuskokwim rivers. Vegetation in and around Algaaciq (Saint Mary's) is spruce-poplar forest in the bottomland, spruce-hardwood forest in the uplands, areas of high brush, moist tundra, wet tundra, and alpine tundra/barren ground.

CLIMATE
The climate is continental and there is a significant maritime influence. Winter temperatures may be as low as -44°F, while summer temperatures may reach 83°F. Annual precipitation measures 16 inches, including 60 inches of snowfall. The Yukon River is free of ice from June through October.

CULTURE AND HISTORY
Algaaciq (Saint Mary's) is a Yup'ik community, with a culture centered on fishing and subsistence activities. The histories of the two adjacent communities of Algaaciq and Andreafsky are intertwined. Andreafsky was established in 1899 by the Northern Commercial Company as a supply depot and winter headquarters. The village was named for the Andrea family, which settled there and built a Russian Orthodox church. In 1903, Jesuit missionaries established a mission and school 90 miles downriver from Andreafsky. By 1915, there were 70 full-time students. The slough surrounding the mission became severely silted, and in 1948 the decision was made to move to higher ground. Materials salvaged from a gold-rush-era hotel were used to construct the new mission and several homes in Andreafsky. In 1949 more building materials were salvaged from Galena Air Force Station and transported to Algaaciq to build a new school. During the 1950s, Yup'ik families moved into the area. The area surrounding the mission incorporated as the City of Saint Mary's in 1967, while Andreafsky remained unincorporated. In 1980, the residents of Andreafsky voted for annexation to the city. The mission school was closed in 1987.

GOVERNMENT
Saint Mary's was incorporated as a first-class city in 1967, with a city manager, mayor, and city council. It is located in the Unorganized Borough *(see Alaska introduction)*. The Yup'ik villages of Algaaciq and Andreafsky are within the City of Saint Mary's. The Algaaciq Native Village is a BIA-recognized traditional council headed by a president. It is also known as Algaaciq Tribal Government. Andreafsky has its own village council.

VILLAGE CORPORATION
Saint Mary's Native Corporation is the ANCSA village corporation for Algaaciq. Shareholders in the village corporation also hold shares in Calista Corporation regional Native corporation *(see Alaska introduction)*. Andreafsky has its own village corporation.

INFRASTRUCTURE
Transportation. Saint Mary's is primarily accessible by air and water. It is served by barge, large commercial vessels, and aircraft. The airfield is state-owned and has two airstrips: a 6,003- by 150-foot gravel runway and a 1,900- by 60-foot crosswind strip. The airfield has jet capability, but such service was discontinued in 1990. Saint Mary's is connected to Andreafsky, Pitka's Point, and Mountain Village via a 22-mile road. The road is not maintained year round, but can be traveled by snowmachines in the winter. The dock on the Andreafsky River is the only deep-water dock in the area.

Electricity. Alaska Village Electric Cooperative (AVEC) provides electricity generation and distribution to all residents from a diesel powerplant.

Fuel storage (gallons). Yukon Fuel Company (615,000 gallons); Alaska Village Electric Cooperative (AVEC) (217,200); Alaska Department of Transportation (98,000); city schools (72,500); Saint Mary's Mission and Airstrip (20,500); Alaska Court System (10,000); PenAir (9,300); Northern Air Cargo (6,400); six others (15,000). Bulk fuel is available for purchase by residents. Seventy percent of homes are heated by oil.

Water and waste systems. The majority of the city's buildings 120 homes and facilities have complete plumbing and sewer, although an estimated 15 residences haul water and use honeybuckets. A 1.7-million-gallon sewage lagoon provides sewage treatment. Domestic water originates in the Alstrom Creek Reservoir and is treated before being distributed throughout the community. Waste heat from the electric plant powers the water system.

Telecommunications. Telephone and cable service are available to all homes and private and public facilities. Local telephone service is provided by United Utilities, while long distance service is provided by AT&T Alascom or United Utilities. One television channel is offered by the Alaska Rural Communications System and cable television is available through Frontier Cable. Three AM radio stations serve the area. One television channel is rebroadcast locally. The Internet service provided by GCI is available only at the school.

ECONOMY
The economy of Saint Mary's is subject to seasonal fluctuations. Employment peaks during the summer fishing season. Cash income is supplemented by subsistence activities. Salmon, moose, bear, and waterfowl are harvested.

Fisheries. Commercial salmon fishing is an important seasonal source of income for city residents and the Alaska State Commercial Fisheries Entry Commission reports that 65 residents hold commercial fishing permits. Cold storage at the dock is available.

Also known as Saint Mary's

Ethnicity: Yup'ik

Municipality
City of Saint Mary's
P.O. Box 209
Saint Mary's, AK 99658
 907-438-2515
 907-438-2719 Fax

Native entity
Algaaciq Native Village
P.O. Box 48
Saint Mary's, AK 99658
 907-438-2932
 907-438-2227Fax

ANCSA village corporation
Saint Mary's Native
Corporation
P.O. Box 149
Saint Mary's, AK 99658
 907-438-2961
 907-438-2315 Fax

NOTE
Algaaciq (Saint Mary's) is a unique community in that it has two recognized Native Alaskan entities with separate ANCSA corporations, each with its own entitlements and authority. Andreafsky is within the city limits of Saint Mary's, but is recognized by the State of Alaska as a separate "community" within Saint Mary's. This profile applies to Andreafsky unless otherwise stated. Information unique to Andreafsky will be found in the Andreafsky profile.

Algaaciq

Also known as Saint Mary's

Government as employer. The city, state, and federal governments employ 100 people, or 40.5% of the workforce.

Services and retail. Saint Mary's has two general stores, Alaska Commercial Company and Yukon Traders.

Tourism and recreation. The Andreafsky River is a National Wild River. From Saint Mary's one may boat upriver to enjoy the pristine scenery, wildlife (including bears, foxes, beavers, eagles, falcons, owls, and geese), and vegetation. There is a gift store in the village and a bed-and-breakfast business.

COMMUNITY FACILITIES AND SERVICES
Community facilities include a regional post office and a community hall. As of 2003, a new training and conferencing center was under contract. A washeteria is located nearby in Pitka's Point. The city provides waste collection and disposal, and water supply.

Education. Saint Mary's School District operates 1 school, Saint Mary's School, with 14 teachers and 170 students in grades K—12. The school library serves as the community public library.

Health care. Health care is provided by the John Afcan Memorial Subregional Clinic, owned and operated by the Yukon-Kuskokwim Health Corporation.

Public safety. Law enforcement is provided by the city police department, backed by state troopers posted in the city. Emergency response is provided by the city volunteer fire department, which has a fire truck and an ambulance.

ENVIRONMENTAL CONCERNS
Saint Mary's is located within the Yukon Delta National Wildlife Refuge, 22 million acres of nesting habitat for millions of waterfowl including emperor geese, ducks, and other shorebirds, and home to a wide variety of mammal species such as brown and black bear, caribou, moose, wolf, and muskox.

The Alaska National Interest Lands Conservation Act of 1980 classified the Andreafsky River as a National Wild River. Preserving this wild character is made easier by the lack of accessibility, although from Saint Mary's visitors may boat upriver to enjoy the pristine scenery, wildlife (including bears, foxes, beavers, eagles, falcons, owls, and geese), and vegetation.

llakaket

See also Altna and New Allakalet

[al-uh-KACK-ut]
Ethnicity: Koyukon
           Athabascan

Municipality
  City of Allakaket
  P.O. Box 30
  Allakaket, AK 99720
    907-968-2423
    907-968-2233 Fax

Native entity
  Allakaket Village
  P.O. Box 50
  Allakaket, AK 99720
    907-968-2237
    907-968-2233 Fax

ANCSA village corporation
for Alatna, Allakaket, Hughes, Huslia; the fifth largest village corporation
  K'oyitl'ots'ina, Limited
  1603 College Road
  Fairbanks, AK 99709
    907-452-8119
    907-452-8148 Fax

Total area of entitlement under ANCSA	
	92,160 acres
Total labor force	59
High school graduate or higher	29
Bachelor's degree or higher	7
Unemployment rate	39.0%
Per capita income *(1999)*	$9,484
2003 population	102
2003 state demographer estimate	
Population *2000 census*	133
Percent Native *2000 census*	97.0%

LOCATION
Allakaket is on the south bank of the Koyukuk River, southwest of its junction with the Alatna River, approximately 190 air miles northwest of Fairbanks and 57 miles upriver from Hughes. The village of Alatna is located directly across the river. It is on the western edge of the Kanuti National Wildlife Refuge.

PHYSICAL DESCRIPTION
The area encompasses 3.6 square miles of land and 0.7 square mile of water.

CLIMATE
This is a cold, continental climate with extreme temperature differences. The average high temperature in midsummer is 70°F; the average low in winter drops below 0°F. Annual precipitation is 13 inches; yearly snowfall is 72 inches.

CULTURE AND HISTORY
Koyukon Athabascans and Kobuk, Selawik, and Nunamiut Inupiat originally inhabited the area. The Koyukon followed the seasons as they hunted game and fish. Various bands established shared settlements after 1851. Athabascans and Inupiat used the traditional vicinity of Alatna as a trading center. St. John's-in-the-Wilderness Episcopal Mission was founded in 1906 on the Koyukuk River. A post office was established in the mid-1920s. In 1938, the community was called Allakaket while the name Alatna was accepted by the Inupiat community

across the river. In 1975 the community incorporated, including both Allakaket and Alatna. In 1994 flood waters toppled nearly all of the community's public and residential buildings. The community rebuilt near the old city, but some new houses and public buildings now lie outside of the incorporated city boundaries. New Allakaket and Alatna are outside the city limits. The city is mainly an Athabascan community. Kobuk Eskimos live in Alatna. Visitors go to the area villages for traditional festivities. Subsistence activities are the mainstay of the culture.

GOVERNMENT
Allakaket was incorporated as a second-class city in 1975, with a mayor and city council. The village has an advisory school board and planning commission. It is located in the Unorganized Borough. Allakaket Village is a federally recognized village.

VILLAGE CORPORATION
K'oyitl'ina, Limited, is the village corporation for Alatna, Allakaket, Hughes, and Huslia. It is the fifth largest village corporation. Shareholders in the village corporation are also shareholders in Doyon, Limited, regional Native corporation *(see Alaska introduction).*

ECONOMY
Subsistence is central to the economy. Salmon, whitefish, moose, bear, small game, and berries are the most important food sources. Caribou are taken when available. The city, school, tribe, and village corporation store are the primary employers. There are some part-time cash jobs. Construction and the Bureau of Land Management firefighting provide summer jobs.

Services and retail. Trapping and native handicraft merchandising also provide some income to residents. Private businesses include two grocery stores, a maintenance service, retail store/mercantile, and a women's advocacy organization.

Government as employer. Of the 28 employed residents, 13 work in city, state, or federal government.

INFRASTRUCTURE
Transportation. Connection from Allakaket to Hughes, Bettles, and Tanana comes from winter trails, since there is no road link. Shallow water precludes commercial barge access. A state-owned 4,000-foot long by 100-foot wide gravel runway is open year-round. A $6 million airport improvement is in progress. The FAA created Class E airspace upward from 700 foot and 1,200 foot above the surface, so that aircraft can execute new Standard Instrument Approach Procedures and a new Textual Departure Procedure. Passenger flights are available from Arctic Circle Air Service, Frontier Flying Service, Larry's Flying Service, Servant Air, Tanana Air Service, Warbelow's Air Ventures, and Wright Air Service.

Electricity is provided by the Alaska Power and Telephone Company, which operates a 380-killowatt capacity diesel plant.

Fuel storage (gallons). City (12,000); Yukon/Koyukuk Schools (11,000); Brice Construction (10,000); Allakatna Co-op Store (9,252).

Water and waste systems. Allakaket now has a new washeteria, well, treatment plant, 100,000-gallon water storage tank, sewage lagoon, and force main. The lagoon is connected to the washeteria and school. Residents tow treated water and haul honeybuckets or use pit privies. Infrastructure improvements to provide a flush/haul system are in progress. A new landfill and access road are currently being built.

Telecommunications. Local telephone service is provided by Bettles Telephone Co., a subsidiary of Alaska Power and Telephone. Long distance service is available from AT&T Alascom. One television channel is provided by the Alaska Rural Communications Service. The school has Internet access through GCI.

COMMUNITY FACILITIES AND SERVICES
The Koyukuk River flood in 1994 destroyed or badly damaged most public facilities.

Education. Allakaket School is in the Yukon/Koyukuk district. The school has 52 students and 4 teachers. The school library serves as the community library.

Health care is provided by the Allakaket Health Clinic, which is also available to the residents of Alatna; it is owned by the city and leased to the U.S. Public Health Service. The clinic is administered by the Tanana Chiefs Conference.

Public safety. Both law enforcement and emergency response are provided by the state village public safety officer.

Allakaket
See Also Altna and New Allakalet

Ambler

Ambler

Total area of entitlement under ANCSA	
	92,160 acres
Total labor force	104
High school graduate or higher	20
Bachelor's degree or higher	23
Unemployment rate	27.9%
Per capita income *(1999)*	$13,712
2003 population	291
2003 state demographer estimate	
Population *2000 census*	309
Percent Native *2000 census*	86.7%

LOCATION
Ambler is located on the north bank of the Kobuk River, near the confluence of the Ambler and the Kobuk rivers. It lies 45 miles north of the Arctic Circle. It is 138 miles northeast of Kotzebue, 30 miles northwest of Kobuk, and 30 miles downriver from Shungnak.

PHYSICAL DESCRIPTION
The area encompasses 9.5 square miles of land and 1.3 square miles of water. Flood hazard exists in Ambler. Just downstream, the Kobuk Valley National Park encompasses 1.7 million acres. It is the site of the Great Kobuk Sand Dunes—25 square miles of shifting sand where the temperatures can exceed 90°F in the summer, the world's largest active dune flat in the Arctic latitudes.

CLIMATE
Ambler is in the continental climate zone where temperatures average -10°F to 15°F in winter, and 40°F to 65°F in summer. Record temperatures have dipped to -65°F and risen to 92F°. Annual snowfall is 80 inches and yearly precipitation averages 16 inches.

CULTURE AND HISTORY
Ambler is named for James M. Ambler, U.S. Navy surgeon on the USS Jeannette, who died in the early 1880s in the Lena River Delta while on an Arctic expedition. When Natives from Shungnak and Kobuk migrated upstream for subsistence advantages in 1958, Ambler became a permanent settlement. Kowagniut Inupiat today continues a traditional subsistence lifestyle.

GOVERNMENT
Ambler was incorporated as a second-class city in 1971, with a mayor and city council. The village has an advisory school board and a planning commission. Ambler is located in the Northwest Arctic Borough, which has authority over education, taxation, planning, and zoning. The Ambler Traditional Council is a federally recognized tribe in the community.

REGIONAL CORPORATION
All village corporations in the NANA area merged into the regional corporation. The NANA Regional Corporation and the borough share the same boundaries.

ECONOMY
School, city, clinic, and local stores are the sources of cash employment. Basket making is the principal commercial craft activity in Ambler. Birch-bark baskets made in Ambler are sold throughout Alaska. Some mining is active. Subsistence is a major part of the local economy. Fish and game are essential food sources. Chum salmon and caribou are the most important food sources. Freshwater fish, moose, bear, and berries are also harvested. Gift shops sell baskets, fur pelts, jade, quartz, bone, and ivory carvings. A lapidary facility for artisans has been proposed.

Also known as Ivisaappaat

Ethnicity: Kowagniut Inupiat

Municipality
City of Ambler
P.O. Box 9
Ambler, AK 99786
907-445-2122
907-445-2174 Fax

Native entity
Ambler Traditional Council
P.O. Box 47
Ambler, AK 99786
907-445-2238
907-445-2181 Fax

ANCSA regional corporation
NANA Regional Corporation, Inc.
P.O. Box 49
Kotzebue, Alaska 99752
907-442-3301
907-442-2866 Fax
website: nana.com

Ambler

Also known as Ivisaappaat

Fisheries. Five residents hold commercial fishing permits (chum salmon, freshwater fish).

Government as employer. Of the 75 employed residents, 43 work in city, borough, state, or federal government.

Services and retail. Private businesses include a radio/television repair shop, air service, electronic service, aviation maintenance, retail clothing, and general stores.

INFRASTRUCTURE

Transportation. Barge, plane, small boat, and snowmachine are the chief means of transportation. There are no roads outside of Ambler. The state provides a 3,000- by 60-foot lighted gravel airstrip with a gravel crosswind airstrip. Bering Air, Hageland Aviation, Tanana Air Service, and Warbelow's Air Ventures offer scheduled passenger flights. Daily scheduled services are available outbound from Kotzebue, and charter flights are provided by air taxis. Major improvements have been completed on the airstrip. In summer, Crowley Marine Services transports fuel and supplies by barge. Boats provide travel between villages and for subsistence activities. Residents travel by snowmachines and all-terrain vehicles in winter.

Electricity is provided by a 744-killowatt diesel plant operated by Alaska Village Electric Cooperative (AVEC).

Fuel storage (gallons). Village Council (238,100); AVEC (100,800); Northwest Arctic Schools (29,000); Nunamiut Aviation Fuel (12,000); Ambler Air Service (2,153).

Water and waste systems. The central source of water comes from a 167-foot well near the Kobuk River. Water is piped to most houses after being treated and stored in a 210,000-gallon tank. A standby well is located at the water treatment plant. Arctic pipes collect sewage, which flows to a facultative lagoon via two lift stations. The sewage is discharged to a natural watershed before it is released into the Kobuk River. A piped water and sewer system serves more than 50 residences. More than a dozen other homes and offices are expected to be connected when project funds are granted. A new water treatment plant, washeteria, and sewage lagoon recently received funding. There is no landfill access.

Telecommunications. Local telephone service is provided by OTZ Telephone Cooperative, while long distance service is provided by AT&T Alascom, GCI, or OTZ Telephone. Internet service is provided by GCI. One AM radio station broadcasts to Ambler. Cable television service is provided by the city, and one television channel is provided by the Alaska Rural Communications Service.

COMMUNITY FACILITIES AND SERVICES

Education. Ambler School is in the Northwest Arctic School District. The school has 90 students and 9 teachers. The school library serves as the community library.

Health care is provided by the Ambler Health Clinic, owned by the city and leased to the U.S.

Public Health Service. It is operated by Maniilaq Association.

Public safety. Law enforcement is provided by the state village public safety officer (VPSO), backed by state troopers in Kotzebue. Emergency response is provided by the VPSO and the Ambler Volunteer Fire Department.

naktuvuk Pass

[an-ack-TOO-vick]
Ethnicity: Nunamiut

Municipality
City of Anaktuvuk Pass
P.O. Box 21030
Anaktuvuk Pass, AK 99721
907-661-3612
907-661-3613 Fax

Native entity
Village of Anaktuvuk Pass
P.O. Box 21065
Anaktuvuk Pass, AK 99721
907-661-2535
907-661-2536 Fax

ANCSA village corporation
Nunamiut Corporation
P.O. Box 21009
Anaktuvuk Pass, AK 99721
907-661-3220
907-661-3025 Fax

Total area of entitlement under ANCSA	92,160 acres
Total labor force	150
High school graduate or higher	76
Bachelor's degree or higher	18
Unemployment rate	33.3%
Per capita income *(1999)*	$15,283
2003 population	319
state demographer estimate	
Population *2000 census*	282
Percent Native *2000 census*	88.3%

LOCATION
Anaktuvuk Pass is located on the divide between the Anaktuvuk and John rivers in the central Brooks Range. It lies about 250 miles northwest of Fairbanks and about the same distance southeast of Barrow. The community is located within the gates of the Arctic National Park and Preserve.

PHYSICAL DESCRIPTION
The City of Anaktuvuk Pass encompasses 4.8 square miles of land and 0.1 square mile of water. It sits at 2,200 feet elevation and is treeless. Much of the land is subject to occasional flooding, is poorly drained, and has a high permafrost table.

CLIMATE
High elevation keeps summers cool with an average temperature of 50ºF. January temperature averages -14ºF.

Extreme temperatures have reached records of -56ºF and 91ºF. Annual precipitation averages 11 inches, with yearly snowfall of 63 inches.

CULTURE AND HISTORY
Anaktuvuk ("the place of caribou droppings") Pass is the last remaining settlement of the Nunamiut (inland northern Inupiat). Culture changes in response to Western civilization and the dearth of caribou in the mid-1920s forced the Nunamiut to leave the Brooks Range. In 1938, many coastal Nunamiuts returned to the mountains at Killik River and Chandler Lake. In 1949 Chandler Lake families migrated to Anaktuvuk Pass. The Killik River group also moved to Anaktuvuk Pass, and Nunamiuts from other areas later joined the growing settlement. A Presbyterian church opened in 1966. Villagers live a more sedentary lifestyle than their nomadic predecessors. The Nunamiut residents rely on subsistence activities. Anaktuvuk Pass is the only non-coastal community in the North Slope borough, and its Nunamiut people the only people in the Borough dependent on caribou rather than fish and marine mammals or employment in the petroleum industry.

GOVERNMENT
Anaktuvuk Pass was incorporated as a second-class city in 1959, with a mayor and city council. The village has an advisory school board and planning commission. The Village of Anaktuvuk Pass is a federally recognized tribe and traditional tribal council. The council is also known as the Nasragmiut Tribal Council

VILLAGE CORPORATION

Shareholders in the village corporation are also shareholders in Arctic Slope Regional Corporation (see Alaska introduction).

ECONOMY

The physical isolation of Anaktuvuk Pass has deterred communal economic and employment opportunities. Caribou is the primary source of meat. Other subsistence foods include trout, grayling, moose, sheep, brown bear, ptarmigan, and water fowl. Some villagers hunt, trap, sell skins, guide hunters, or design skin masks and clothing for income. Others find seasonal work in surrounding communities. Private businesses include a construction company, hotel, and general store owned by the village corporation, and a gift store, pizza parlor, and child care center.

Government as employer. Of the 100 employed residents, 69 work in city, borough, state, or federal government.

INFRASTRUCTURE

Transportation. North Slope Borough operates a 4,800-foot gravel airstrip for year-round flight access. A $3.4-million airport improvement project has been completed. Arctic Circle Air Service, Evert Air Alaska, Frontier Flying Service, Larry's Flying Service, Tanana Air Service, Warbelow's Air Ventures, and Wright Air Service offer scheduled flight service. Anaktuvuk Pass is not accessible by road. In winter, "cat-trains" move cargo from the Trans-Alaska pipeline haul road. Snow machines and all-terrain vehicles provide local travel.

Electricity is provided by the borough, which operates a diesel power plant with a capacity of 1,315-kilowatts.

Fuel distribution. The village corporation sells propane fuel and gasoline.

Water and waste systems. Anaktuvuk Pass provides two major wells, including a treated watering point at Nunamiut School. Tankers deliver water to holding tanks for household use. Nearly all residents have kitchen running water; others tow water for themselves. Honeybuckets are hauled. A $17-million project will soon provide piped water and sewer and household plumbing. Flush toilets and showers for all residences are in the planning. A new landfill was expected to open in 2004.

Telecommunications. Local telephone service is provided by the Arctic Slope Telephone Association Co-op. Long distance service is provided by AT&T Alascom, GCI, or Arctic Slope Telephone. Internet service is provided by GCI. One FM radio station is located in Anaktuvuk Pass. Cable television service is available through the village corporation, and two broadcast channels are provided by the Rural Alaska Television Network.

COMMUNITY FACILITIES AND SERVICES

North Slope Borough supplies all utilities.

Education. Nunamiut School is in the North Slope Borough District. The school has 94 students in grades K—12 and 10 teachers. The school library serves as the community library. The Simon Paneak Memorial museum focuses on the early natural, geological, and cultural history of the area. The museum also displays Nunamiut clothing, household goods, and hunting implements used around the time of the first contact with Europeans.

Health care. The Anaktuvuk Pass Health Clinic, staffed by community health aides, is open during the day and is available 24 hours a day in case of emergency; it is owned by the North Slope Borough and leased to the U.S. Public Health Service. It is administered by the North Slope Regional Health Corporation. The Anaktuyuk Pass Volunteer Fire Department provides auxiliary health care.

Public safety. Law enforcement is provided by the North Slope Borough Police Department; emergency response by the borough and the Anaktuvuk Pass Volunteer Fire Department.

Anchorage & Fairbanks

Anchorage & Fairbanks

Anchorage and Fairbanks are the two largest urban centers in Alaska and have large Native populations. Unlike the "urban tribe" cities, neither has a BIA-recognized Native entity. Nonetheless, they have significant economic impact.

ANCHORAGE

In addition to being by far the largest population center in Alaska, Anchorage is the center of commerce for the state. Almost 27,000 Anchorage residents reported being all or part Alaska Native or Indian in the 2000 census. Most of the ANCSA regional Native corporations have either their headquarters or their main commercial offices in Anchorage, as do many village corporations and subsidiaries. The Alaska Federation of Natives, primarily representing the interests of the regional Native corporations, the Alaska Inter-Tribal Council, representing the interests of the Native tribes and villages, the Alaska Native Heritage Center, the leading Native cultural center, and the Alaska Native Tribal Health Consortium and its Alaska Native Medical Center, are statewide organizations with their respective headquarters in Anchorage. CIRI, the regional Native corporation, Cook Inlet Tribal Council, the regional Native nonprofit providing services other than health care, and the Southcentral Foundation, the regional Native health care provider, all have their headquarters in Anchorage. Approximately one-third of CIRI's shareholders, many of whom are not members of recognized Native entities, live in Anchorage. For Native Alaskans in Anchorage, the regional organizations perform many of the functions of a village or tribal council.

FAIRBANKS

More than half of the Native population of the Alaskan interior– two thirds of the state's land area–live in the Fairbanks area. More than 8,000 Fairbanks North Star Borough residents reported being all or part Alaska Native or Indian in the 2000 census. Most are members of recognized Native entities. Both Doyon, Limited, the ANCSA regional Native corporation, and Tanana Chiefs Conference, the regional Native nonprofit and health care provider, have their headquarters in Fairbanks. The Fairbanks Native Association serves many of the functions of a village or tribal council, including behavioral health, education, employment, and community services for the Native residents of the Fairbanks area. It is the Public Law 93-638 tribal government contractor for Fairbanks and Fairbanks North Star Borough.

Fairbanks Native Association
201 First Avenue #200
Fairbanks, AK 99701
907-452-1648
907-456-4148 Fax
fairbanksnative.org

A ndreafsky

[an-dree-AFF-ski]
Ethnicity: Yup'ik

Municipality
(Located within the City of Saint Mary's. See Algaaciq.)

Native entity
Yupiit of Andreafski
P.O. Box 88
Saint Mary's, AK 99658
   907-438-2312
   907-438-2512 Fax

ANCSA village corporation
Nerkilikmute Native
   Corporation
P.O. Box 87
Saint Mary's, AK 99658
   907-438-2332
   907-438-2919 Fax

NOTE
Andreafsky is located within the city limits of the City of Saint Mary's, which also includes another BIA-recognized Native entity, Algaaciq Native Village. Except as indicated in this profile, all information in the profile for Saint Mary's applies to Andreafsky.

Total area of entitlement under ANCSA	
	69,120 acres
Total labor force	67
High school graduate or higher	24.4%
Bachelor's degree or higher	10.3%
Unemployment rate	14.9%
Per capita income *(1999)*	$12,161
Population *2000 census*	127
2003 population	149
state demographer estimate	
Percent Native *2000 census*	90.6%

LOCATION
Andreafsky is located within the city limits of the City of Saint Mary's, on the north bank of the Andreafsky River, 3.5 miles northeast of where the Andreafsky River joins the Yukon River at Pitka's Point in the Yukon-Kuskokwim Delta. It constitutes the western half of the city.

CULTURE AND HISTORY
Andreafsky is primarily a Yup'ik village with a commercial fishing and subsistence lifestyle. Historically the Yup'ik people were very mobile, traveling with the migration of game, fish, and plants. The ancient settlements and seasonal camps contained small populations, with numerous settlements throughout the region consisting of extended families or small groups of families.

By 1899 the village was a supply depot and winter quarters for the Northern Commercial Company's riverboat fleet. The village was originally called "Clear River," but was named for the Andrea family who settled here. The family built a Russian Orthodox Church. A Roman Catholic mission was estab-

lished nearby in 1949, and a number of Yup'ik families moved to the area in the 1950s. The area adjacent to the mission became the incorporated City of Saint Mary's in 1967, although Andreafsky chose to remain independent. In 1980, residents of Andreafsky voted for annexation to the city. Before it joined the city, Andreafsky had its own community hall, fuel storage, three stores, and support for floatplanes.

GOVERNMENT
Yupit of Andreafski is the BIA-recognized traditional council for the Native population of Andreafsky.

VILLAGE CORPORATION
The ANCSA village corporation is Nerkilikmute Native Corporation. Its shareholders are also shareholders in the regional Native corporation, Calista Corporation.

ECONOMY
Subsistence activities include catching salmon at family fish camps, gathering berries, and hunting moose, bear, and game birds. Some residents trap.

Fisheries. Most residents fish commercially and sell their catches to commercial fish buyers in the Saint Mary's area.

Government as employer. Governments at the city, state, and federal levels employ 22 residents.

INFRASTRUCTURE
Transportation. Local roads provide access to Saint Mary's, Pitka's Point, Mountain Village, and the St. Mary's airport. River-going vessels have easy access during the ice-free summer months. Two major barge lines serve the village.

A ngoon

[an-GOON]
Ethnicity: Kootznoowoo
           Tlingit

City of Angoon
P.O. Box 189
Angoon, AK 99820
   907-788-3653
   907-788-3821 Fax

Native entity
Angoon Community
   Association
P.O. Box 188
Angoon, AK 99820
   907-788-3411
   907-788-3412 Fax

ANCSA village corporation
Kootznoowoo, Incorporated
8585 Old Dairy Road #201
Juneau, AK 99801
   907-790-2992
   907-790-2995 Fax
   kootznoowoo.com

Total area of entitlement under ANCSA	
23,040 acres (under §16(b))	
Total labor force	226
High school graduate or higher	119
Bachelor's degree or higher	37
Unemployment rate	12.8%
Per capita income *(1999)*	$11,357
Population *2000 census*	572
2003 population	505
state demographer estimate	
Percent Native *2000 census*	86.4%

LOCATION
This Tlingit community is the only permanent settlement on Admiralty Island, located on the southwest coast at Kootznahoo Inlet adjacent to Mitchell Bay. Angoon is 55 miles southwest of Juneau and 41 miles northeast of Sitka. It is surrounded on land by the Admiralty Island National Monument, with 955,000 acres of wilderness in southeast Alaska's Tongass National Forest.

PHYSICAL DESCRIPTION
The area encompasses 22.5 square miles of land and 16.1 square miles of water. Most of Admiralty Island is spruce-hemlock rainforest with small areas of muskeg. Above the timberline the forest gradually changes to alpine-tundra with rock

outcrops and permanent to semipermanent ice fields. Admiralty Island has high densities of Alaskan brown bear. Mitchell Bay hosts marine mammals such as harbor seals and porpoises, sea lions, and occasionally humpback whales. Many waterfowl and seabirds overwinter and many of the nearby tributary streams have strong runs of salmon in the late summer and fall.

CLIMATE
Maritime climate prevails, with cool summers and mild winters. Summer temperatures range from 45°F to 61°F; winter temperatures vary from 25°F to 39°F. Extreme temperatures have reached records of -6°F and 77°F. Annual precipitation is 43 inches, with yearly snowfall of 63 inches.

CULTURE AND HISTORY
Angoon, translated from Tlingit, means "Town on the Portage" or "Isthmus Town." This Kootznoowoo Tlingit community is the only permanent settlement on Admiralty Island. Kootznoowoo means literally "Brown Bear Fort" or "Fortress of the Bears," referring to Admiralty Island, which hosts the largest population of brown bears in the world. The word is vocalized in Tlingit with sounds that do not occur in English or other European languages. Fur trading dominated the community's economy in the mid-1800s. In the late 1870s, the Northwest Trading Company opened a trading post and

whaling station on nearby Killisnoo Island and hired villagers as whale hunters. Whaling, a BIA school, and a Russian Orthodox church brought in scores of Tlingits to Killisnoo. In 1882 a whaling vessel accident killed a Tlingit shaman and villagers demanded payment of 200 blankets to the man's family. The Northwest Trading Co. sought assistance from the U.S. Navy at Sitka. The navy cutter USS Corwin subsequently destroyed the village. Six Native children perished. (In 1973, a $90,000 out-of-court settlement was awarded to Angoon from the federal government for the assault.) Whaling did not last long after the early 1900s, and many Tlingits found work in Killisnoo. In 1928 many Tlingits returned to Angoon after Killisnoo was razed by fire. This is a Tlingit community that relies on commercial fishing and a subsistence way of life. The Angoon Community is a federally recognized tribe.

GOVERNMENT

Angoon was incorporated as a second-class city in 1963, with a mayor and city council. The village has an advisory school board and a planning commission. A traditional tribal council, the Angoon Community Association also is recognized.

VILLAGE CORPORATION

Shareholders in the village corporation, Kootznoowoo, Incorporated, are also shareholders in Sealaska regional Native corporation (see Alaska introduction).

ECONOMY

Commercial fishing and a subsistence lifestyle fuel the economy, despite low salmon prices. Local resources include deer, salmon, bear, halibut, shellfish, geese, seaweed, and berries. State and federal grants have brought in a shellfish farm. The Chatham School District is the main employer, although some logging jobs are offered on nearby Prince of Wales Island.

Fisheries. Fifty-six residents hold commercial fishing permits (salmon, halibut, shellfish).

Government as employer. Of the 197 employed residents, 87 work in local, state, or federal government.

Services and retail. Businesses include day-care centers, lodges, a tree thinning company, a trading company, telecommunications and education services, a card and crafts shop, automotive repair, and an arts workshop. Tourism is not a priority.

INFRASTRUCTURE

Transportation. Floatplane and boat are the only accessible means of transportation into Angoon. A state-owned seaplane base on Kootznahoo Inlet offers scheduled and charter floatplane services. A draft dock, a boat harbor with 45 berths, and a state ferry terminal are available in Angoon. Barge and ferry bring in freight. The streets are graveled and narrow, and there are few amenities for visitors. A unique feature of Admiralty Island is the Cross-Island Canoe Route which connects Mole Harbor in Seymour Canal to Angoon. The route passes through as many as eight lakes connected by maintained portage trails dating back to the l930's.

Electricity. Three diesel-fueled generators in Angoon, with a total capacity of 1,260-killowatts, are operated by the Tlingit-Haida Regional Electric Authority.

Water and waste systems. Water from Tillinghast Lake reservoir is treated and piped into the community. Development of a water source at Favorite Bay Creek has been funded. A project is in its early stages for three miles of waterline to the new Tillinghast Lake Water Treatment Plant. Nearly all of Angoon's homes have a piped system and completed plumbing. A secondary treatment plant moves piped sewage to an ocean outfall. The plant recently opened a new 500,000-gallon water tank. Refuse is hauled by the city to a nearby landfill.

Telecommunications. Local telephone service is provided by ACS of the Northland or Pacific Telecommunications. Long distance service is available through Alascom. The Internet service provider is ACS Internet. One FM radio station, one commercial television station, and Alaska Rural Communications Service broadcast to Angoon, and the city operates a cable television system.

COMMUNITY FACILITIES AND SERVICES

Education. Angoon School is in the Chatham School District. The school has 125 students and 11 teachers. The school library serves as the community library.

Health care is provided by the Angoon Health Clinic, owned by the city and leased to the U.S. Public Health Service. It is administered by the Southeast Alaska Regional Health Corporation. In case of emergency, the first responder is the Angoon Emergency Response Team.

Public safety is provided by the Angoon Public Safety Department. Emergency response is provided by the city public safety department and the Angoon Volunteer Fire Department.

A niak   Aniak

Total area of entitlement under ANCSA	
	115,200 acres
Total labor force	267
High school graduate or higher	114
Bachelor's degree or higher	66
Unemployment rate	13.1%
Per capita income *(1999)*	$16,550
Population *2000 census*	572
Current population	551
2003 state demographer estimate	
Percent Native *2000 census*	73.3%

LOCATION

Aniak is located on the south bank of the Kuskokwim River at the head of Aniak Slough, 59 miles southwest of Russian Mission in the Yukon-Kuskokwim Delta. It lies 92 air miles northeast of Bethel and 317 miles west of Anchorage.

PHYSICAL DESCRIPTION

Aniak covers 5.75 square miles, more or less, and is located on low ground along the Kuskokwim River. Most of the city is within a 100-year flood zone. There is a mineralized area to the east, and a petroleum basin to the west-southwest of the city. The vegetation is bottomland spruce-poplar forest. This part of the Kuskokwim River basin and up Aniak Slough are moose wintering areas. The area is a medium-density waterfowl range and a major waterfowl migration route. Aniak is near the western edge of the general caribou range.

CLIMATE

Weather conditions are maritime in the summer and continental in winter. Temperatures range from -55°F to 87°F. Average annual precipitation is 19 inches, with yearly snowfall of 60 inches.

[ANN-ee-ack]
Ethnicity: Yup'ik, Tanaina Athabascan

Municipality
City of Aniak
P.O. Box 189
Aniak, AK 99557
907-675-4481
907-675-4486 Fax

Native entity
Aniak Traditional Council
P.O. Box 176
Aniak, AK 99557
907-675-4349
907-675-4456 Fax

ANCSA village corporation
The Kuskokwim Corporation
4300 B Street, Suite 207
Anchorage, AK 99503
907-243-2944
907-243-2984 Fax

Aniak

Annette Island
Reserve

See Metlaktla

CULTURE AND HISTORY

Aniak is a Yup'ik Eskimo word meaning "the place where it comes out," referring to Aniak Slough, which played an important role in the placer gold rush of 1900-1901. A store and post office opened in 1914 and, within a short time, the native community was established. Gold was discovered near Aniak in 1932. A territorial school opened in 1936, and construction of an airfield began three years later. Aniak's population is primarily Yup'ik Eskimos and Tanaina Athabascans. Many residents travel to fish camps each year.

GOVERNMENT

The city was incorporated in 1972, with a mayor and city council. The city has an advisory school board and a planning commission. The Aniak Traditional Council is the federally recognized traditional tribal council.

VILLAGE CORPORATION

The Kuskokwin Corporation was formed by the merger of the village corporation of Aniak, Chuathbaluk, Crooked Creek, Georgetown, Lower Kalskag, Napaimute, Red Devil, Sleetmute, Stony River, and Upper Kalskag. Shareholders in the village corporation also hold shares in Calista Regional Native Corporation *(see Alaska introduction)*.

ECONOMY

Government, transportation, and retail services are the core sources of Aniak's economy. Part-time income is generated from subsistence activities and some commercial fishing.

Fisheries. Fourteen residents hold commercial fishing permits for salmon. Salmon, moose, bear, birds, berries, and home gardening provide food. Poor fish returns in recent years have hurt the community. The School District, Kuskokwim Native Association, Bush-Tell, and the Aniak Subregional Clinic provide year-round work.

Government as employer. Of 232 employed residents, 100 work in local, state, or federal government.

Services and retail. Private businesses include the power company, fishing guides, air transportation, maintenance services, propane sales, general merchandise shops, restaurants, grocery stores, real estate office, construction companies, audiology service, day-care centers, and lodges.

INFRASTRUCTURE

Transportation. There is no year-round overland access to Aniak. Within the city there are a number of cleared and graded streets, paving unknown. The state-owned airport has a 6,000-foot-long asphalt runway, lighted, and equipped for instrument approaches. Several carriers and charter operators provide scheduled flights. Floatplanes can land on Aniak Slough. Barges transport fuel oil and gasoline in summer, while air services bring in general supplies year-round. There is a winter trail to Kalskag; snowmachines are used on winter trails and the frozen river.

Electricity is provided by Aniak Power and Light, a private operator running a diesel plant with a 1,160-kilowatt capacity.

Fuel storage (gallons). Moffit Contracting (682,000); Aniak Power and Light (195,000); Kuspuk Schools (142,100); Ryan Air (72,230); Steve Hill (21,000); Alaska Commercial (15,200); Bush-Tell (6,000); Arctic Transportation (4,000); Alaska Department of Transportation (3,800); Hageland Aviation (1,900); city maintenance shop (1,500).

Water and waste systems. More than 150 homes are plumbed and have individual wells. The village has a central well, and there are additional wells at Auntie Marie Nicoli School and the Joe Parent Vocational Education Center. More than 20 households haul their own water. A central piped sewage system is available to most households; however, the system does not serve the school, the clinic, or the Napat subdivision across Aniak Slough. The system has four lift stations, and wastewater is treated in a lagoon. Individual septic tanks are in some residences, but drainfield problems have forced some residents to use pit privies. The city provides septic pumping services. Funding has been granted to replace failing drainfield systems by expanding the piped sewer to serve the remainder of the city and the school.

Telecommunications. Local telephone and Internet service are provided by Bush-Tell. Long distance service is available through Alascom. Cable television service is not available. One television channel is broadcast from the Rural Alaska Television Network. One local radio station broadcasts both AM and FM.

COMMUNITY FACILITIES AND SERVICES

Education. Aniak School (grades 6—12) and Auntie Mary Nicoli Elementary (pre-elementary to 5th grade) are in the Kuspuk School District. Aniak School has 73 students and 8 teachers; and Auntie Mary School has 81 students and 6 teachers. The city has a public library.

Health care is provided by the Clara Morgan Subregional Clinic. KNA Community Counseling Center provides consumer and psychiatric services. The Aniak Volunteer Fire Department is an auxiliary health care unit.

Public safety. Law enforcement is provided by state troopers, who have an office in the city. Emergency response is provided by the city volunteer fire department.

Total area of entitlement under ANCSA
92,223 acres

Total labor force	40
High school graduate or higher	36
Bachelor's degree or higher	2
Unemployment rate	27.5%
Per capita income *(1999)*	$8,081
2003 population	108
state demographer estimate	
Population *2000 census*	104
Percent Native *2000 census*	90.4%

LOCATION
Anvik is located in Interior Alaska on the Anvik River, west of the Yukon River, 34 miles north of Holy Cross.

PHYSICAL DESCRIPTION
The city encompasses 9.5 square miles of land and 2.4 square miles of water. Flood hazard exists, and some of the city is located below the flood level of 100.15 feet. The Iditerod Trail passes through Anvik. It is located in a low-occurrence petroleum basin.

CLIMATE
Weather conditions have a continental influence. Temperatures range from -60°F to 87°F. Annual precipitation is 21 inches; yearly snowfall averages 110 inches.

CULTURE AND HISTORY
This is an Athabascan tribe. Originally the village was on the other side of the river, at an area called "the point." When an Episcopal mission and school opened in 1887, Natives crossed the river. The settlement opened a post office in 1897. Outbreaks of the flu hit the mission in the early 1900s and again in the late 1920s, leaving many children orphaned. In the 1920s sternwheelers towed supplies to Anvik. Some villagers found contract work cutting wood for the sternwheelers' fuel. Traders also bought furs and fish from resident sellers. A plane on skis arrived in the community in the early 1930s. The local Athabascan Indians pursue a subsistence lifestyle and home gardening activities.

GOVERNMENT
Anvik was incorporated as a second-class city in 1972, with a mayor and city council. The village has an advisory school board and a planning commission. The Anvik Tribal Council is a federally recognized tribe.

VILLAGE CORPORATION
Shareholders in the village corporation, Inglasik, Incorporated, are also shareholders in Doyon, Limited, regional Native corporation *(see Alaska introduction)*.

ECONOMY
Anvik has a seasonal economy, but the main employer is the Anvik Tribal Council. Villagers depend on subsistence activities. The city helps fish processors with fresh water. Many residents trap, while others sell handicrafts and produce from their home gardens.

Fisheries. Fourteen residents hold commercial fishing permits.

Government as employer. Of the 29 employed residents, 16 work in city, state, or federal government.

Services and retail. Private businesses include two grocery stores and two guide outfits.

INFRASTRUCTURE
Transportation. Barge and floatplanes enter the village in summer via the Anvik River, west of the Yukon. Additional dock and harbor facilities are on the city's wish list. The state-owned gravel airstrip is 2,910- by 75-feet, open year round. Three-wheelers, snowmachines, and dog teams can access three miles of area roads.

Electricity. Alaska Village Electric Cooperative (AVEC) provides electricity from a 332-kilowatt diesel plant.

Fuel storage (gallons). AVEC (52,972); Ingalik Incorporated (29,490); Iditarod Schools (21,126); Anvik Commercial Co. (16,555); Chase Ent. Store (10,520); city (6,500).

Water and waste systems. Individual water wells, piped sewage disposal, and full plumbing are in most homes. Thirteen homes need plumbing, sixteen need a septic tank, and four need new water wells. Funds have been requested for those homes. The washeteria has treated well water. Blackwell School is connected to the city's water system and has its own drainfield.

Telecommunications. Local telephone service is available from Bush-Tell; long distance service is provided by AT&T Alascom. Two AM radio stations broadcast to the area. One channel of television is available from the Alaska Rural Communications Service. Internet service is available only at Blackwell School through GCI.

COMMUNITY FACILITIES AND SERVICES
Education. Blackwell School is in the Iditarod Area School District. The school has 23 students and 3 teachers. The school library serves as the community library. The local historical society has a small museum with artifacts from the area's Athabascan, Russian, and Alaskan history.

Health care is provided by the Anvik Health Clinic, owned by the village corporation and leased by the U.S. Public Health Service. It is administered by the Yukon-Kuskokwim Health Corporation. Clara Morgan Subregional Clinic in Aniak and the Bethel Hospital are also available.

Public safety. Law enforcement is provided by the state village public safety officer, backed by state troopers in Aniak. Emergency response is provided by the state VPSO and the Anvik Volunteer Fire Department.

[AN-vick]
Ethnicity: Ingalik Athabascan

City of Anvik
P.O. Box 50
Anvik, AK 99558
  907-663-6328
  907-663-6321 Fax

Native entity
Anvik Tribal Council
P.O. Box 10
Anvik, AK 99558
  907-663-6322
  907-663-6357 Fax

ANCSA village corporation
Ingalik, Incorporated
General Delivery
Anvik, AK 99558
  907-663-6396
  907-663-6355 Fax

Arctic Village
See Venetie

Asa'carsarmiut

Also known as Mountain Village

Ethnicity: Yup'ik

Municipality
City of Mountain Village
P.O. Box 32085
Mountain Village, AK
          99632-0085
907-591-2929
907-591-2920 Fax

Native entity
Asa'carsarmiut Tribe
P.O. Box 32007
Mountain Village, AK 99632
907-591-2814
907-591-2811 Fax

ANCSA village corporation
Azachorok Incorporated
P.O. Box 213
Mountain Village, AK 99632
907-591-2527
907-591-2127 Fax

Total area of entitlement under ANCSA	
	138,240 acres
Total labor force	260
High school graduate or higher	41.3%
Bachelor's degree or higher	10.3%
Unemployment rate	30.8%
Per capita income *(1999)*	$9,653
Population *2000 census*	755
2003 population	750
state demographer estimate	
Percent Native *2000 census*	93.5%

LOCATION
Mountain Village is located within the Yukon Delta Wildlife Refuge on the north bank of the lower Yukon River near the western coast of Alaska. It lies approximately 20 miles west of Saint Mary's and 470 miles northwest of Anchorage. It sits at the base of Azachorok Mountain, a 500-foot monolith encountered by all who travel the Yukon River.

PHYSICAL DESCRIPTION
The area encompasses 4.3 square miles of land.

CLIMATE
The climate in Mountain Village is continental, but has strong maritime influences from its proximity to the Pacific Ocean. Temperatures range from average lows of -44°F in the winter to average highs of 80°F in the summer months. Annual precipitation averages 16 inches, with snowfall averaging 44 inches per year. High winds and low visibility are common during winter. The Lower Yukon is frozen over from October to mid-June. At this latitude, the region experiences approximately 20 hours of daylight per 24-hour period in June, declining to less than 4.5 hours in December.

CULTURE AND HISTORY
Asa'carsarmiut, formerly Mountain Village, is a primarily Yup'ik community with traditional subsistence practices in place; the people harvest salmon, moose, and waterfowl. Commercial fishing and fish processing provide income for several residents and some trap for both personal and business reasons. There are no cultural events open to the public. Mountain Village was only a summer fish camp until the opening of the first general store and a missionary school in 1908, which prompted nearby villagers to migrate. A post office was established in 1923, followed by a salmon saltery in 1956 and a cannery in 1964. All three have since closed, but the city was incorporated in 1967 and was selected as headquarters for the Lower Yukon School District in 1976.

GOVERNMENT
The City of Mountain Village is a second-class city, incorporated in 1967, located in the Unorganized Borough. It uses the city manager form of government for day-to-day operations, together with a seven-member city council including the mayor. A 3percent sales tax is collected. The Asa'carsarmiut Tribe, also known as the Asa'carsarmiut Tribal Council and formerly known as the Native Village of Mountain Village, is a BIA-recognized Native entity with a traditional village council headed by a president.

VILLAGE CORPORATION
Azachorok Incorporated is the ANCSA village corporation. Shareholders in the village corporation are also shareholders in Calista Corporation, the regional Native corporation.

INFRASTRUCTURE
Transportation. A summer road links Mountain Village to Pitka's Point, Andreafsky, and Saint Mary's, and in summer it is accessible by riverboat or barge. For year-round travel and commerce the residents rely upon Hageland Aviation and Tanana Air Service. The State of Alaska owns and maintains the 2,520- by 60-foot gravel airstrip. Floatplanes land on the Yukon River. Snowmobiles and skiffs are used for local transportation, although there are three taxicab firms. In 2001 the Department of Transportation funded the design of a runway rehabilitation project with all improvements slated to be completed in 2004. The project will resurface and extend the length of the runway and expand the safety area, rehabilitate the airport apron, and resurface the taxiway.

Electricity. Electricity is provided by the Alaska Village Electrical Cooperative (AVEC) from a 1,858-kilowatt diesel plant.

Fuel storage (gallons). Azachorok (224,650); Lower Yukon Schools (206,040); AVEC (196,149); city (23,020); Army National Guard (2,000); Hageland Aviation (1,495).

Water and waste systems. Water is derived from a well and is treated. Mountain Village operates a piped water and sewer system that serves 200 households and facilities. A system expansion for the east side, including household plumbing for 18 units, was recently completed. A new landfill is now available.

Telecommunications. Local telephone service is provided by United Utilities, long distance service by AT&T Alascom or United Utilities. AM radio stations from Nome, Bethel, Kotzebue, Dillingham, Anchorage, and elsewhere broadcast to the Asa'carsarmiut area. Two television channels are broadcast from local repeaters, one from the Alaska Rural Communications Service and one from the village corporation.

ECONOMY
Mountain Village has a seasonal economy based on fishing and subsistence; several villagers hold commercial fishing licenses. Some residents trap for additional income. Others have found employment since 1997 via the Traditional Arts and Crafts Entrepreneurship Project funded by the Alaska Department of Community and Economic Development. These residents make handcrafted items marketed in the Mountain Village Native Store. The area's economy is limited by the availability of transportation. A summer road links Asa'carsarmiut to Pitka's Point, Andreafsky, and Saint Mary's, but the community is primarily accessible only by air or water. In 2002 the Alaska Department of a Community and Economic Development funded the development plan which may result in future economic improvements. Out of 180 residents employed, 136 are employed in education, health and social services, or public administration.

Fisheries. Several villagers hold commercial fishing licenses.

Government as employer. Of 180 employed residents, 124 work for the city, state, or federal government.

Manufacturing. The Traditional Arts and Crafts Entrepreneurship Project, funded by the Alaska Department of Community and Economic Development, assists residents who make handcrafted items marketed in the Mountain Village Native Store.

Services and retail. The village corporation operates a general store and bulk fuel sales. A second general store is operated by the tribal council. The city also has two gift shops and two video stores.

Tourism and recreation. The city and the village corporation have rental units. Mountain Village lies within the Yukon Delta National Wildlife Refuge and is within 100 miles of the Innoko National Wildlife Refuge.

COMMUNITY FACILITIES AND SERVICES
The city has a city/community hall and a teen center and operates the water and waste disposal system.

Education. The Lower Yukon School District operates the Ignatius Beans School, serving 257 students in grades K—12 with 18 teachers. The school library serves as the community's public library.

Health care. Health care for the community is provided by the Mountain Village Health Clinic, operated by the Yukon-Kuskokwim Health Corporation. Renovations to this facility were made in 1997-98. It is backed by the John Afcan Memorial Subregional Clinic in nearby Saint Mary's. Residents have access to a full range of medical care in Bethel, approximately 157 miles distant at the Yukon Kuskokwim Delta Regional Hospital, or in Nome, approximately 194 miles away, at the Norton Sound Regional Hospital.

Public safety. Law enforcement is provided by a state village public safety officer (VPSO), backed by state troopers in Saint Mary's. Emergency response is provided by the VPSO and the city volunteer fire department.

ENVIRONMENTAL CONCERNS
The eastern end of the city along the Yukon River suffers from active erosion.

Asa'carsarmiut
Also known as Mountain Village

Atka

Atka

Total area of entitlement under ANCSA
102,917 acres

Total labor force	56
High school graduate or higher	23
Bachelor's degree or higher	2
Unemployment rate	0.0%
Per capita income *(1999)*	$17,080
2003 population	95
state demographer estimate	
Population *2000 census*	92
Percent Native *2000 census*	91.3%

LOCATION
Atka is located on Atka Island, 1,200 air miles southwest from Anchorage, 350 miles west of Unalaska, and 90 miles east of Adak.

PHYSICAL DESCRIPTION
At 410 square miles, Atka Island is the twenty-first largest island in the United States. The City of Atka encompasses 8.7 square miles of land and 27.4 square miles of water. Until the incorporation of Adak, it was the westernmost community in the United States. It lies within the Aleutian National Wildlife Refuge. In addition to the reindeer introduced onto the island of Atka in 1914, foxes, seals, and sea lions are seen. Atka is far from the major fishing areas of the southeastern Bering Sea, but it is in the middle of major king crab and black cod fishing grounds and near major ocean salmon fishing grounds. Vegetation is Arctic/alpine. Below 1,000 feet the surface is covered by a blanket of about 500 species of vascular plants, bryophytes, and mosses. Above 1,000 feet, plant life is very sparse. At the north end of Atka Island, 13 miles north of the city, is the active Korovin volcano, which most recently erupted in 1998. Atka is subject to earthquakes, generally mild with little or no damage. In 2003 there was a magnitude 5.3 earthquake centered less than two miles from Atka. At its current location, flood hazard is low, although high-water incidents are not unknown.

CLIMATE
Atka lies in a maritime climate zone. Winter temperatures range from 20ºF to 40ºF degrees; summer varies from 40ºF to 60ºF. Annual precipitation averages 60 inches; yearly snowfall is 61 inches. Calm, foggy weather prevails in summer, harsh storms in winter.

CULTURE AND HISTORY
Unangas have occupied the island for at least 2,000 years, speaking the western dialect, known since the Russian era as "Aleuts." Archaeological evidence suggests human occupation going back to prehistoric times. Atka became an important trade site and harbor for Russians in the mid-1700s. In the 1860s the site became a settlement. In the 1920s fox farming kept Atka solvent. During World War II the people of Atka were evacuated to the Ketchikan area, and the village was burned by the U.S. to prevent advancing Japanese forces from using it in an invasion. After the war, Atkans returned to the community, along with Aleuts from Attu, who had been Japanese prisoners. Although a traditional Unangan settlement, the Aleut language is spoken in only 25 percent of homes. Much of village life centers on the St. Nicholas Russian Orthodox Church. The people depend on a subsistence lifestyle.

GOVERNMENT
Atka was incorporated as a second-class city in 1988, with a mayor and seven city councilors. It is located in the Unorganized Borough. The Native Village of Atka is a federally recognized tribe.

VILLAGE CORPORATION
Shareholders in the ATXAM village corporation are also shareholders in Aleut Regional Native Corporation (*see Alaska introduction*).

ECONOMY
Wages earned from the halibut fishery and subsistence living fuel the economy. A halibut and black cod processing plant (Atka Pride Seafoods) operates seasonally for the local fleet. A number of offshore fish processors carry out crew changes through Atka. Year-round income opportunities in the village are limited to education- and government-related work. A reindeer herd of over 2,500 head provides a source of meat.

Fisheries. Nine residents hold commercial fishing permits.

Government as employer. Of 56 employed residents, 17 work in city, state, or federal government jobs.

Services and retail. Other businesses include two grocery stores and a small hotel near the new dock (see Transportation, below). The hotel and dock services are provided by

[AT-ka]
Ethnicity: Unangan (Aleut)

Municipality
City of Atka
P.O. Box 47070
Atka, AK 99547
907-839-2233
907-839-2234 Fax

City Administrator Office
P.O. Box 765
Unalaska, AK, 99685

Native entity
Native Village of Atka IRA
P.O. Box 47030
Atka, AK 99547-0030
907-839-2229
907-839-2269 Fax

ANCSA village corporation
Atxam Corporation
P.O. Box 47001
Atka, AK 99547
907-839-2237
907-839-2234 Fax

Atka

APICDA Joint Ventures, a for-profit subsidiary of the Aleutian Pribilof Island Community Development Association.

Tourism and recreation. The Village Council operates a four-room bed-and-breakfast (with gambling) and a snack bar.

INFRASTRUCTURE
Transportation. The state provides a 3,287- by 84-foot lighted asphalt runway. Unalaska offers scheduled air services, and planes can be chartered from Cold Bay or Unalaska. Coastal Transportation provides freight service in late spring to early autumn. The city completed a commercial dock in 1997. The dock is capable of hosting the vast majority of harvesting vessels operating in the Bering Sea/Aleutian Island fisheries. The facility has a mean lower low water (MLLW) controlling depth of 18 feet at the pier face. While the dock is 100 feet long, mooring buoys at each end allow it to safely service much longer vessels.

Electricity. Andreanof Electric provides electricity through a 125-kilowatt diesel plant. Hydroelectric potential at Chuniisax Creek has been under development for a long time (it is referred to on the 1978 Community Map and was still under comment in 2003). Construction was expected to begin in 2003.

Fuel storage (gallons). Atka Native Store (67,300); Andreanof Electric (43,700); Atka Fisherman's Association (39,300). A proposed bulk fuel upgrade project was approved by the National Marine Fisheries Service, Department of Commerce, in January 2004.

Water and waste systems. Water drawn from a stream and wooden reservoir dam is stored in two 30,000-gallon water tanks before distribution. Piped water and sewer system and plumbing are available to all homes. Sewage is connected to a central septic system; garbage collections are in service. Wastewater flows untreated through outfall lines into Nazan Bay. As of 2004, funds to increase water capacity, replace the water treatment system, change connections, and treat the sewage outfall, have been requested.

Telecommunications. Local telephone service is provided by Pacific Telecommunications; long distance service is provided by AT&T Alascom. Internet service is provided by GCI. Cable television service is provided by the village corporation, and the Alaska Rural Communications System broadcasts to the area.

COMMUNITY FACILITIES AND SERVICES
Education. The Yakov E. Netsvetov School in Atka is in the Aleutian Region School District. The School has 19 students in grades K—12 and 2 teachers. The school maintains a display of local artifacts. The school library serves as the community library.

Health care is provided by the Atka Health Clinic, owned by the city and leased by the U.S. Public Health Service. The clinic is administered by the Aleutian/Pribilof Island Association. An Indian Health Service doctor, dentist, and optometrist visit the community yearly and a state public-health nurse visits the village twice during the year. There is a limited pharmacy available. The nearest full-service clinic is in Unalaska, and the closest hospital is in Anchorage.

Public safety. Law enforcement is provided by a state village public safety officer (VPSO), backed by state troopers in Dillingham. Emergency response is provided by the VPSO and the Atka Volunteer Fire Department.

Atkasook

See Atqasuk

Atmautluak

Alternative spelling Amauthluak

[aht-MOUTH-luck]
Ethnicity: Yup'ik

Native entity
Atmautluak Traditional
    Council
P.O. Box 6568
Atmautluak, AK 99559
    907-553-5610
    907-553-5216 Fax

ANCSA village corporation
Atmautluak Limited
P.O. Box 6548
Atmautluak, AK 99559
    907-553-5428
    907-553-5420 Fax

Total area of entitlement under ANCSA	
	92,160 acres
Total labor force	120
High school graduate or higher	64
Bachelor's degree or higher	12
Unemployment rate	10.8%
Per capita income *(1999)*	$8,501
2003 population	279
state demographer estimate	
Population *2000 census*	294
Percent Native *2000 census*	95.9%

LOCATION
Atmautluak lies on the west bank of the Pitmiktakik River in the Yukon-Kuskokwim Delta, 20 miles northwest of Bethel.

PHYSICAL DESCRIPTION
Atmautluak encompasses 0.6 square mile of land and 2.7 square miles of water. The village is built above the 100-year flood elevation. The land around the village is very flat with small willow bushes along creeks and sloughs. The village is in a drier area, but there is a lake in the center of the village. There are boardwalks throughout the well-traveled areas of the village.

CLIMATE
Annual precipitation is 16 inches, with yearly snowfall of 50 inches. Summer temperatures range from 42ºF to 62ºF; winter temperatures vary from -2ºF to 19ºF.

CULTURE AND HISTORY
Although Yup'ik have lived in the region for thousands of years, Atmautluak was settled in the 1960s. The area's high ground, which reduces flooding, and its abundant subsistence resources attracted settlers. This is a traditional Yup'ik village with a subsistence and fishing lifestyle.

GOVERNMENT
Atmautluak is unincorporated and located in the Unorganized Borough. It was incorporated in 1976 but reverted years later to the present traditional village council government. The Atmautluak Traditional Council is a federally recognized tribe.

VILLAGE CORPORATION
Shareholders in the Atqasuk village corporation also hold shares in Calista Corporation regional Native corporation.

ECONOMY
The school, retail businesses, and the village government generate cash income to supplement the subsistence lifestyle.

Fisheries. Thirty-one residents hold commercial fishing permits. Dismal fish returns in 2000-03 significantly hurt the community.

Government as employer. Of the 107 employed residents, 74 work for the village, state, or federal government.

Services and retail. Businesses include a grocery store, mercantile, air transportation support services, and two day-care centers.

INFRASTRUCTURE
Transportation. The state provides a 2,000- by 25-foot gravel airstrip year-round for chartered or private planes. As of 2003, runway, taxiway, and apron improvements are in progress. Skiffs are used for travel in summer while snowmachines, all-terrain vehicles, and dog sleds are used in winter. Bethel is about one and a half hours by boat or about 25 to 30 minutes by snowmachine in the winter. A winter trail is open to nearby Nunapitchuk.

Electricity is provided by Atmautluak Joint Utilities by means of a 395-kilowatt diesel plant.

Fuel storage (gallons). Village corporation/Lower Kuskokwin School District (179,250); Lower Kuskokwim Schools (4,000).

Water and waste systems. Villagers haul treated well water and also draw from the Pitmiktakik River. Residents tow honeybuckets to sewage bunkers. Household plumbing is not available. A washeteria is open, new as of 2003. The school is connected to the city water plant and to the washeteria's septic system.

Telecommunications. Local telephone service is available through United Utilities, while long distance service is provided by AT&T Alascom or United Utilities. Internet service is provided by Unicom/United Utilities and by GCI at the school. One AM and one FM radio station broadcast to the area, together with one commercial television station and the Alaska Rural Communications System. The village council provides cable service.

COMMUNITY FACILITIES AND SERVICES
Education. The Joann A. Alexie Memorial School is in the Lower Kuskokwim School District. The school has 81 students in grades K—12 and six teachers. The school library serves as the community library.

Health care is provided by the Atmautluak Health Clinic, owned by the village and leased to the U.S. Public Health Service. The clinic is operated by the Yukon-Kuskokwim Health Corporation.

Public safety. Law enforcement is provided by a state village public safety officer (VPSO), backed by state troopers in Bethel. Emergency response is provided by the VPSO and the Atmautluak Volunteer Fire Department.

Atmautluak

Atqasuk

Atqasuk

Total area of entitlement under ANCSA	
	69,120 acres
Total labor force	70
High school graduate or higher	36
Bachelor's degree or higher	4
Unemployment rate	5.7%
Per capita income (1999)	$14,732
2003 population	247
state demographer estimate	
Population *2000 census*	228
Percent Native *2000 census*	94.3%

LOCATION
Atqasuk is located between the Meade River and Ikmakrak Lake, 60 miles south of Barrow.

PHYSICAL DESCRIPTION
The area encompasses 38.9 square miles of land and 3.5 square miles of water. When the community was reestablished in 1977, it was placed high enough above the Meade River to avoid flooding. The terrain is flat and treeless.

CLIMATE
Arctic weather conditions prevail. Daily minimum temperature falls below freezing most of the year. Temperature extremes range from winter lows of -56°F to summer highs of 78°F. Yearly precipitation is five inches, with annual snowfall of 22 inches.

CULTURE AND HISTORY
Inupiat have traditionally hunted and fished the area. *Atqasuk* means "the place to dig the rock that burns." During World War II, government and private facilities in Barrow used bituminous coal mined in Atqasuk. By 1970 the village was unpopulated. Then in 1977 the community was reestablished by former residents of Barrow. This is a traditional Inupiat village. Subsistence activities are important to the people's lifestyle.

GOVERNMENT
In the North Slope Borough, Atqasuk was incorporated in 1982 with a mayor and city council. The city has an advisory board and a planning commission. Atqasuk Village is the federally recognized tribe.

VILLAGE CORPORATION
Shareholders in the Atqasuk village corporation are also shareholders in the Arctic Slope regional Native corporation *(see Alaska introduction).*

ECONOMY
Education and government services are the primary sources of full-time employment. Subsistence activities are essential to the economy. Villagers also generate cash income from trapping and by selling furs. The Barrow Arctic Science Consortium operates the Atqasuk Research Center for the National Science Foundation.

Government as employer. Of the 66 employed residents, 49 work for the city, borough, state, or federal government.

Services and retail. Private businesses include a hotel and restaurant, a grocery and merchandise store, a gasoline station owned by the village corporation, construction companies, a taxi service, and a specialty food store.

INFRASTRUCTURE
Transportation. Air travel is the only means of year-round access. Land transportation offers only seasonal passage. The Edward Burnell Sr. Memorial Airport is a North Slope Borough operation, with a 4,370- by 110-foot gravel runway that will accommodate C-130 transport aircraft. In winter, "cat-trains" transport freight overland from Barrow. Snowmachines, all-terrain vehicles, and boats are used for local travel. As of 2003, a docking facility on the Meade River is in the city's plans.

Also known as Atkasook

[AT-kuh-suck]
Ethnicity: Inupiat

Municipality
City of Atqasuk
P.O. Box 91119
Atqasuk, AK 99791
　907-633-6811
　907-633-6812 Fax

Native entity
Atqasuk Village
P.O. Box 91109
Atqasuk, AK 99791
　907-633-2575
　907-633-2576 Fax

ANCSA village corporation
Atqasuk Corporation
P.O. Box 91120
Atqasuk, AK 99791
　907-633-6414
　907-633-6213 Fax

Atqasuk

Electricity is provided by North Slope Borough by means of a 1,015-kilowatt diesel plant.

Fuel storage (gallons). Atqasuk Corporation/North Slope Borough (NSB) Fuel (580,000); NSB Power/Water (87,500); NSB Services (10,000); NSB School (10,000); NSB Fire (7,000); NSB Clinic (6,700); NSB Heavy Equipment (5,000); Atqasuk Corporation Store (2,000); city hall/community center (2,000); NSB Police (1,100).

Water and waste systems. The Atqasuk Corporation supplies village water, sewer, and refuse disposal. The North Slope Borough provides the washeteria and landfill. Water, drawn from Imakrak Lake, is treated and available at a watering point. Delivery to household water tanks is available. Most homes have tanks that provide kitchen running water. Running water and flush systems are in most homes, the school, and village facilities. Trucks haul honeybucket bunkers to the sewage lagoon. As of 2004, a piped water and sewer system, including household plumbing, flush toilets, and showers, was being engineered by the North Slope Borough.

Telecommunications. Local telephone service is provided by the Arctic Slope Telephone Association Co-operative, long distance service by AT&T Alascom, GCI, or Arctic Slope Telephone. Internet service is available from GCI or ASTAC. One AM radio station broadcasts to the area. The Alaska Rural Communications System broadcasts television to the area, and cable service is available from the City of Atqasuk.

COMMUNITY FACILITIES AND SERVICES

Education. Meade River School is in the North Slope Borough School District. The school has 92 students in grades K—12 and nine teachers. The School library is also the community library.

Health care is provided by the Atqasuk Health Clinic, owned by the North Slope Borough and leased to the U.S. Public Health Service. The clinic is operated by the North Slope Regional Health Corporation. The nearest hospital is Samuel Simmonds Memorial Hospital in Barrow.

Public safety. Law enforcement is provided by the North Slope Borough Police Department. Emergency response is provided by the Atqasuk Volunteer Fire Department.

Barrow

Also known as Ukpeagvik

[BARE-row]
Ethnicity: Inupait

Municipality
City of Barrow
P.O. Box 629
Barrow, AK 99723
907-852-5211
907-852-5871 Fax

Native entity
Native Village of Barrow
P.O. Box 1130
Barrow, AK 99723
907-852-4411
907-852-8844 Fax

ANCSA village corporation
Ukpeagvik Inupiat
Corporation
P.O. Box 890
Barrow, AK 99723
907-852-4460
907-852-4459 Fax
ukpik.com

Total area of entitlement under ANCSA	
	215,810 acres
Total labor force	2,276
High school graduate or higher	782
Bachelor's degree or higher	512
Unemployment rate	12.7 %
Per capita income (1999)	$22,902
Current population	4,417
state demographer estimate	
Population *2000 census*	4,581
Percent Native *2000 census*	64.0 %

LOCATION
Barrow, the northernmost community in North America, is located on the Chukchi Sea coast, 10 miles south of Point Barrow from which it takes its name. It lies 725 air miles from Anchorage.

PHYSICAL DESCRIPTION
The area encompasses 18.4 square miles of land and 2.9 square miles of water (Esatkoak and Tasigarook Lagoons). The Browertown district of the city lies northeast of central Barrow along the Chukchi Sea coast, across the two lagoons. The UIC-NARL research facility (until 1980 the Naval Arctic Research Laboratory or NARL), including Ilisagvik College, lies about 4 miles northeast of central Barrow, along the coast. Most of the city is subject to flooding from storm surges, although the last known flood event was in 1970. In 1963, a storm surge caused a water-level rise of approximately 10 feet above normal sea level, with a wave height of 16.4 feet. Floodwaters extended approximately three-quarters of a mile behind the Naval Arctic Research Laboratory.

CLIMATE
Barrow has an arctic climate. Annual precipitation is 5 inches, with yearly snowfall of 20 inches. Temperatures range from -56°F in winter to 78°F in summer. There is no sunset from May 10 through August 2, and no sunrise from November 18 through January 24. For 324 days of the year, the low temperature falls below freezing.

CULTURE AND HISTORY
Archaeological sites suggest human occupation in the area from AD 500 to AD 900. Inupiat villagers traditionally rely on subsistence marine mammal hunting, fishing, and inland hunting. Barrow was named in honor of Sir John Barrow, second secretary of the British Admiralty and promoter of Arctic exploration. A Presbyterian church opened in 1899, and a post office was established two years later. In 1946 exploration of the Naval Petroleum Reserve Number 4 started (now National Petroleum Reserve in Alaska, NPR-A). The Naval Arctic Research Laboratory was built near Barrow. When the navy moved out in 1980, the laboratory was acquired by the village corporation, which has developed it as a research base and community college. Barrow's development has been helped by the formation of the North Slope Borough, the Arctic Slope Regional Corporation, the Prudhoe Bay oil fields, and the Trans-Alaska Pipeline. Inupiat make up the majority of residents. Cultural activities include marine mammal hunts and other subsistence practices.

GOVERNMENT
The largest community in and seat of government for North Slope Borough, Barrow was incorporated as a first-class city in 1958, with a mayor and city council. The city has an advisory school board and a planning commission. The Native Village of Barrow is a federally recognized tribe.

VILLAGE CORPORATION
Shareholders in Barrow's UKpeagvik Inupiat village corporation are also shareholders in the Arctic Slope Regional Corporation *(see Alaska introduction).*

ECONOMY
The North Slope Borough is the city's chief employer. Oil field operations are supported by numerous businesses. State and federal agencies are important employers, while cash income is generated by arts and crafts. Tourists are attracted to the midnight sun. Some residents continue to rely on subsistence food sources, such as whale, seal, polar bear, caribou, and fish.

Fisheries. Seven residents hold commercial fishing permits.

Services and retail. There are 167 active business licenses in Barrow.

Government as employer. Of the 1,986 employed residents, 1,176 work for the city, borough, state, or federal government.

INFRASTRUCTURE

Transportation. Year-round passage to Barrow depends on scheduled jet services. The state-owned Wiley Post-Will Rogers Memorial Airport serves as the regional transportation center for the borough. The renovated airport has a 6,500-by 150-foot asphalt runway. Marine and land transportation provide seasonal entry to the city. As of 2003, funds had been requested for a small harbor. The borough operates a local bus service, and there are five taxicab and two car-rental companies. Accommodations are available at three hotels, two inns, and one bed-and-breakfast.

Electricity. Electricity is provided by the Barrow Utilities and Electric Cooperative from its 20,300-killowatt natural-gas-fired Barrow Power Plant.

Fuel storage (gallons). Airport (240,000); Eskimos Inc./Barrow Airport (27,000).

Water and waste systems. Water drawn from a dam on Isatkoak Lagoon is stored in a tank. Piped water is available to most residences, but nearly 50 percent of the residents use honeybuckets for sewage disposal. As of 2003, funds had been requested to connect piped water to remaining houses and to build a second water reservoir.

Telecommunications. The local telephone system is operated by the Arctic Slope Telephone Association Cooperative. Long distance service is provided by AT&T Alascom, GCI, or Arctic Slope Telephone. Both GCI and Arctic Slope Telephone provide Internet service. One AM and two FM radio stations

broadcast from Barrow. In addition to cable service provided by ASRC Communications, the Alaska Rural Communications System broadcasts two television channels from Barrow.

COMMUNITY FACILITIES AND SERVICES

Barrow Utilities and Electric Cooperative operates the water and sewage treatment plants and electric power and distributes piped natural gas for indoor heating. The North Slope Borough is responsible for other utilities, including refuse collection.

Education. Ilisagvik College is a community college offering both vocational and academic courses, with around 700 students, mostly part-time, and 13 full-time faculty. It is located on the campus of the old Naval Arctic Research Laboratory. The North Slope Borough School District operates Barrow High School, grades 9—12, with 325 students and 28 staff; Eben Hopson Middle School, grades 6—8, with 286 students and 26 staff; and Ipalook Elementary School, preschool through 5th grade, with 591 students and 43 staff. The Tuzzy Consortium Library serves as the public library for Barrow and supports the other North Slope Borough libraries. The Inupiat Heritage Center, located at Ilisagvik College, has a variety of exhibits, collections, educational outreach, performances and activities, meeting rooms, and reference materials on Inupiat culture and history.

Health care. Samuel Simmonds Memorial Hospital and North Slope Borough Clinic are available. The clinic's search and rescue provides critical-care air ambulance service. Borough volunteer fire department/EMS/search and rescue/medevac provide auxiliary health care.

Public safety. Law enforcement is provided by the Borough police department, backed by a state trooper post in the city. Emergency response is provided by the Barrow Volunteer Fire Department and the borough ambulance service. The state superior court judge for the North Slope area of the Second Judicial District sits in Barrow.

Beaver

Total area of entitlement under ANCSA	
	136,725 acres
Total labor force	86
High school graduate or higher	66.2%
Bachelor's degree or higher	-
Unemployment rate	17.91%
Per capita income *(2000)*	$8,441
Population *2000 census*	84
Percent Native *2000 census*	95.2%

LOCATION

Beaver is located on the north bank of the Yukon River, approximately 60 miles southwest of Fort Yukon and 110 miles north of Fairbanks. Beaver is located in the Fairbanks Recording District. The area encompasses 20.5 square miles of land and 1.1 square miles of water.

CLIMATE

A continental subarctic climate prevails in the area. July temperatures vary from 65ºF to 72ºF, while January temperatures may fall to -60ºF. Extreme temperatures have been recorded at 90ºF in summer to -70ºF in winter. Yearly precipitation averages close to 7 inches; annual snowfall is 43 inches.

CULTURE AND HISTORY

Beaver was founded as the Yukon River terminus for miners amid gold discoveries in the Chandalar region in 1907. At that time, the Alaska Road Commission opened a trail from Beaver to Caro on the Chandalar River. By 1910 there was a store in Beaver, and a few freight companies operated on the trail, commonly known as Government Road. In 1911 when the gold rush fizzled, a group of Eskimos arrived and worked in the trading post. A post office opened in 1913, and a second trading post opened seven years later. A school opened in 1928; two years later an airstrip was built. In 1974 residents became shareholders in a store set up as a cooperative by the village council. The population of Beaver is predominantly mixed Athabascan Indian and Yup'ik Eskimo. Subsistence activities are an important source of food. The Beaver Village Council is a federally recognized tribe in the community.

GOVERNMENT

The village is unincorporated. A traditional tribal council is recognized. Shareholders in its village corporation are also shareholders in the Doyon, Limited, Regional Native Corporation *(see Alaska introduction).*

Ethnicity: Kutchin (Gwich'in), Eskimo

ANCSA village corporation
Beaver Kwit'chin Corporation
P.O. Box 73602
Fairbanks, AK 99707
907-456-2464

Beaver

Belkofski

See Zero AIAN Population

Bethel

See Orutsaramuit

Bill Moore's Slough

See Zero AIAN Population

ECONOMY

This is a subsistence-driven community. Moose, salmon, freshwater fish, bear, and waterfowl supply meat. Popular activities include berry picking and gardening. Meager fish returns in recent years have significantly impacted the community. The school, post office, clinic, and village council are the primary employers. Bureau of Land Management fire fighting, construction jobs, trapping, handicrafts, and firewood sales generate seasonal income.

Construction. Construction employs five residents.

Government as employer. Of the 55 employed residents, 29 work for the local, state, or federal government.

Services and retail. Businesses include a utilities electric company, tour guides, video rental, and a co-op.

INFRASTRUCTURE

Transportation. Eighteen capital projects, funded by grants, are active in Beaver. The state provides a 3,954- by 75-foot lighted, gravel airstrip. Air cargo and barges bring in fuel, store goods, and supplies in the summer. Residents use trucks, all-terrain vehicles, snowmachines, and dog teams for local and seasonal travel.

Water and waste systems. A new well and pumphouse are open for treated-water pickup. Residents rely on honeybuckets for home sewage disposal; a village-operated vehicle hauls waste. The washeteria is open for bathing and laundry. The washeteria and school use individual septic systems. Renovation has been completed on the water tank, water treatment system, and washeteria. Plans are in progress for a piped water and sewer system. A new landfill is now open.

Electricity. Beaver Joint Utilities provides electricity.

Telecommunications. In-state phone service is provided by United Utilities; long distance service is provided by Alascom and United Utilities. Internet service is provided only for the school by GCI. One television channel is available through the Rural Alaska Television Network. Two AM radio stations are available. Teleconferencing is available from Alaska Teleconferencing Network.

COMMUNITY FACILITIES AND SERVICES

Facilities include a community hall named the Beaver Council House.

Education. Beaver School is in the Yukon Flats School District. The school has 21 students and one teacher.

Health care. Health care is provided by the Beaver Health Clinic, owned by the village and leased to the U.S. Public Health Service. The clinic is administered by the Tanana Chiefs Conference.

Birch Creek

Also known as Dendu Gwich'in Tribe

ANCSA village corporation
Tihteet' all, Inc.
General Delivery
Birch Creek Village
Via Fort Yukon, AK 99740
907-221-9113

Total area of entitlement under ANCSA	132,602 acres
Total labor force	18
High school graduate or higher	84.6%
Bachelor's degree or higher	-
Unemployment rate	0%
Per capita income *(2000)*	$5,952
Population *(2000)*	28
Percent Native *(2000)*	100%

LOCATION

The village is located along Birch Creek, approximately 26 miles southwest of Fort Yukon. Birch Creek is located in the Fairbanks Recording District. The area encompasses 6.1 square miles of land and 0.3 square mile of water.

CLIMATE

A continental subarctic climate, marked by seasonal extreme temperatures, prevails. Winters are severe and long; summers are warm and brief. July temperatures vary from 65ºF to 72ºF, while the average low temperature in January dips below zero. Extended periods of -50ºF to -60ºF are common in winter. Annual precipitation is about 6.5 inches; yearly snowfall is 43.4 inches.

CULTURE AND HISTORY

The Dendu Gwich'in traditionally lived in most of the Yukon Flats south of the Yukon River, including parts of the Crazy and White Mountains. Birch Creek was first reported in 1862 by a clergyman who visited a camp established to provide fish for the Hudson's Bay Company in Fort Yukon. Birch Creek Jimmy founded Birch Creek in 1898. The great chief built a cabin at the site of the Hudson's Bay fish camp. Later, family members joined him. In the early 1900s the group moved upstream to the site of the present village. In the early 1950s a school opened and this influenced villagers to adopt a less nomadic lifestyle. In 1973, the village opened its first airstrip. The Dendu Gwich'in Tribal Council is a federally recognized tribe in the community. Local Dendu Gwich'in Athabascans practice subsistence activities.

GOVERNMENT

The village is unincorporated. A traditional tribal council is recognized.

VILLAGE CORPORATION

Shareholders in the village corporation are also shareholders in the Doyon Regional Native Corporation *(see Alaska introduction)*.

ECONOMY

The village depends on subsistence activities. Wage income opportunities are limited. Bureau of Land Management firefighting, construction, the school, and the village tribal council provide some jobs. Promoting tourism and expanding merchant opportunities are village planning priorities.

Government as employer. Two employed residents of Birch Creek work for the local government.

Services and retail. One business license is registered to a finance/insurance company.

INFRASTRUCTURE

Fifteen capital projects, funded by grants, are active in Birch Creek.

Transportation. A state-owned 4,000- by 75-foot lighted gravel airstrip is open. Construction is in progress for a new cross-wind airstrip. Skiffs, snowmachines, all-terrain vehicles, and motorbikes provide travel to hunting, fishing, and recreation destinations. Barge service is not available. A 26-mile trail to Ft. Yukon is open in winter.

Water and waste systems. Water, drawn from Birch Creek and a slant well, is treated and stored in an 80,000-gallon tank. Villagers tow water from the water plant. Residents dispose honeybuckets in the sewage lagoon; other villagers use outhouses. Residences are not plumbed. A new water intake, water treatment improvements, washeteria renovation, and sewage lagoon are completed projects. The water tank and foundation need repair and funds have been requested. A new landfill is needed.

Electricity. Birch Creek Village Electric provides electricity.

Telecommunications. Local telephone service is provided by United Utilities; long distance service is provided by Alascom. Cable television is available, and one channel is offered by the Rural Alaska Television Network. Three radio stations are available to residents. Teleconferencing is available from Alaska Teleconferencing Network.

COMMUNITY FACILITIES
The tribe operates the washeteria and provides electricity.

Education. There are no state-operated schools in Birch Creek.

Health care. Birch Creek Clinic is available.

Brevig Mission

Total area of entitlement under ANCSA	
	113,920 acres
Total labor force	153
High school graduate or higher	78.3%
Bachelor's degree or higher	13%
Unemployment rate	2.4%
Per capita income *(2000)*	$7,278
Population *2000 census*	276
Percent Native *2000 census*	92%

LOCATION
Brevig Mission is located at the mouth of Shelman Creek on Port Clarence, 5 miles northwest of Teller and 65 miles northwest of Nome. Brevig Mission is located in the Cape Nome Recording District. The area encompasses 2.6 square miles of land and 0.1 square mile of water.

CLIMATE
When the Bering Sea freezes, the area experiences maritime climate with continental influences. Summer temperatures average 44°F to 57°F; winter temperatures average -9°F to 8°F. Annual precipitation is 11.5 inches, with yearly snowfall of 50 inches.

CULTURE AND HISTORY
The nomadic Kauwerak Eskimos hunted and fished in the area.They traded furs with Siberia, Little Diomede, and King Island, and formed friendly associations with Wales and Little Diomede. In the late 1800s, the U.S. government opened "Teller Reindeer Station." The village became known as "Teller Mission" after a Lutheran Mission was built at the present townsite in 1900. The government provided the mission with 100 reindeer on a five-year loan. Reindeer were important to the economy of the village for several years until the industry significantly diminished in the early 1970s. In 1963 the Brevig Mission post office opened. Brevig Mission is predominantly Inupiat Eskimo with a subsistence lifestyle. The Native Village of Brevig Mission is a federally recognized tribe in the community.

GOVERNMENT
Brevig Mission was incorporated as a second-class city in 1969, with a mayor and six city councillors. The city also has an advisory school board.

VILLAGE CORPORATION
Shareholders in Breviag Mission Native corporation are also shareholders in the Bering Straits Regional Native Corporation *(see Alaska introduction).*

ECONOMY
The city and school district are the primary employers. Arts and crafts sales generate some income. Sparse job openings, high unemployment, and limited work in mining and construction plague Brevig Mission. Villagers subsist on fish, game, and sea mammals.

Government as employer. Of the 80 employed residents, 65 work for the local, state, or federal government.

Services and retail. There are seven current business licenses in Brevig Mission. Businesses a include grocery store, bingo parlor, concession stand, washeteria, and general store.

Tourism and recreation. Visitor attractions include a 100-year-old church, local dog musher, and both July Fourth and Christmas activities. Cultural events include the Thanksgiving Potlatch and the Christmas Potlatch and Games.

Transportation. Four airline services are available to residents. Nine residents are employed in production, transportation, or material moving industries.

INFRASTRUCTURE
Nine capital projects, funded by grants, are active in Brevig Mission.

Transportation. Brevig Mission is accessible year-round by air and sea. In winter, passage is over ice or land. A cargo ship makes an annual stop. The state provides a 3,000- by 100-foot gravel airstrip. A 2,110- by 75-foot gravel crosswind strip also is available. Nome offers regular air and charter services. Teller also offers charter service. The village is five miles from Brevig Mission and can be reached by road. The state also maintains a 72-mile gravel road between Teller and Nome during the summer. A dock on Port Clarence is in the planning stages.

Electricity. Alaska Village Electric Cooperative (AVEC) provides electricity.

Water and waste systems. An $8.5 million piped water and sewer system and new landfill is almost complete. Water, supplied by two underground wells near Shelmon Creek, is treated and stored in a 100,000-gallon tank at the washeteria. The city provides piped water to the school. Some villagers haul water to home storage tanks by snowmachines or all-terrain vehicles. Ten residents tow honeybuckets to bunkers, which the city dumps into a sewage lagoon. The landfill is open.

[BREH-vig]
Ethnicity: Kauwerak Eskimos

ANCSA village corporation
  Brevig Mission Native
    Corporation
  P.O. Box 85024
  Brevig Mission, AK 99785
  907-642-4091

Brevig Mission

Telecommunications. Long distance service is provided by Alascom. Cable television is available, and one channel is offered by the Rural Alaska Television Network. Two radio stations are available in the community. Internet service and teleconferencing are both available.

COMMUNITY FACILITIES
Area facilities include a teen center and community hall.

Education. Brevig Mission School is in the Bering Straits School District. The school has 101 students and 9 teachers.

Health care. Health care is provided by the Brevig Mission Health Clinic, owned by the village and leased to the U.S. Public Health Service; it is administered by the Norton Sound Health Corporation.

Buckland

[BUCK-lund]
Ethnicity: Inupiat Eskimo

ANCSA village corporation
NANA Corporation
P.O. Box 49
4706 Harding Drive
Kotzebue, AK 99752
907-442-3301

Total area of entitlement under ANCSA	92,160 acres
Total labor force	220
High school graduate or higher	71.8%
Bachelor's degree or higher	11.5%
Unemployment rate	3.8%
Per capita income *(2000)*	$9,624
Population *2000 census*	406
Percent Native *2000 census*	96.7%

LOCATION
Buckland is located on the west bank of the Buckland River, about 75 miles southeast of Kotzebue. Buckland is located in the Cape Nome Recording District.

PHYSICAL DESCRIPTION
The area encompasses 1.2 square miles of land and 0.2 square mile of water.

CLIMATE
The village is in the transitional climate zone, which produces cool summers (mid-80s) and cold winters (-60ºF). Annual precipitation 9 inches, and yearly snowfall is 40 inches. Flying in winter is hampered by crosswinds.

CULTURE AND HISTORY
Villagers have moved many times along the river to Elephant Point, Old Buckland, and New Site. There is archaeological evidence of prehistoric occupation in the Elephant Point area. The Inupiat Eskimos rely on reindeer, beluga whale, and seal for subsistence. Buckland is an Inupiat Eskimo village with a subsistence lifestyle. The Native Village of Buckland is a federally recognized tribe in the community.

GOVERNMENT
Buckland is part of the Northwest Arctic Borough *(see Alaska introduction).* It was incorporated as a second-class city in 1966 with a mayor and seven city councillors. The city has an advisory school board. A planning commission is under the Northwest Artic Borough. A traditional tribal council also is recognized. It also has an Indian Reorganization Act village council headed by a president.

VILLAGE CORPORATION
Its village corporation has merged with the regional Native corporation, NANA; residents are shareholders in both.

ECONOMY
The school, city, health clinic, and stores are primary employers. Some mining exists. Villagers rely on a subsistence lifestyle for most food sources. More than 2,000 reindeer are managed and workers are compensated in meat. A Native-food-products and crafts-manufacturing facility is being planned to produce reindeer sausage, berry products, Labrador tea, and ivory and wood carvings.

Construction. Approximately 12 residents are employed in construction.

Fisheries. One resident holds a commercial fishing permit.

Government as employer. Of the 94 employed residents, 54 work for the local, state, or federal government.

Services and retail. Businesses include a clothing store, gun shop, variety store, and gasoline/oil sales.

INFRASTRUCTURE
Twenty-one capital projects, funded by grants, are active in Buckland.

Transportation. No roads extend outside the village, but planes, small boats, barges, and snowmachines have passage into Buckland. A state-owned 3,200- by 75-foot gravel airstrip serves scheduled and chartered flights. Fuel is brought in by Crowley Marine barges, and various lighterage companies deliver cargo and supplies in summer.

Electricity. The city provides electricity.

Water and waste systems. Water drawn from the Buckland River is treated at the washeteria and stored in a 100,000-gallon tank. Water is individually hauled or truck delivered to some residential tanks. The village pumps flush/haul waste tanks or haul honeybuckets to the sewage lagoon. Only 8 homes and the school have plumbing, while 74 homes are not plumbed. Improvements are underway on a new water treatment plant and at the sewage lagoon. Residents dispose of refuse in dumpsters, which are hauled to the landfill. Of 70 housing units in the village, 69 are occupied; all are heated with oil.

Telecommunications. Local telephone service is provided by OTZ Telephone Company while long distance service is available through Alascom. The city provides cable television service, and one channel is available through the Rural Alaska Television Network. One radio station is available in the community. Internet service is provided by GCI, Teleconferencing is available from Alaska Teleconferencing Network.

COMMUNITY FACILITIES
Facilities include a community building.

Education. Buckland School is in the Northwest Arctic School District. The school has 170 students and 13 teachers.

Health care. Health care is provided by the Buckland Health Clinic, owned by the city and leased to the U.S. Public Health Service; it is administered by Maniilaq Association.

Total area of entitlement under ANCSA	
	69,120 acres
Total labor force	200
High school graduate or higher	85%
Bachelor's degree or higher	17.2%
Unemployment rate	11%
Per capita income *(2000)*	$22,615
Population *2000 census*	222
Percent Native *2000 census*	27%

LOCATION

Cantwell is located on the George Parks Highway at the west end of the Denali Highway, 211 miles north of Anchorage and 28 miles south of Denali (Mount McKinley) Park. Part of the community is located on the Alaska Railroad. The areas known as Kantishna and Carlo Creek are located nearby. Cantwell is located in the Nenana Recording District. The area encompasses 118.3 square miles of land and 0.5 square mile of water.

CLIMATE

The climate is continental, with long, cold winters and mild summers. Annual precipitation is 15 inches, with yearly snowfall of 78 inches. Extreme temperatures have been recorded at -54°F in winter and 89°F in summer.

CULTURE AND HISTORY

The Cantwell River used to be called the Nenana River. Nomadic Indians, who hunted, fished, and trapped in interior Alaska, were the earliest settlers in the Cantwell area. The village itself began as a flag stop on the Alaska Railroad. Natives in the Cantwell area are primarily Athabascan Indians. The Native Village of Cantwell is a federally recognized tribe in the community.

GOVERNMENT

The village is unincorporated. A traditional tribal council is recognized.

VILLAGE CORPORATION

Shareholders in its village corporation are also shareholders in the Ahtna, regional Native corporation *(see Alaska introduction)*.

ECONOMY

Highway tourism and transportation fuel the village's economy. Construction jobs also provide part-time and seasonal wages. Subsistence hunting, fishing, trapping, and gathering are essential to most Natives.

Construction. Approximately 16 residents are employed in construction.

Fisheries. One resident holds a commercial fishing permit.

Government as employer. Of the 121 employed residents, 43 work for the local, state, or federal government.

Manufacturing. Two residents are employed in manufacturing.

Services and retail. There are more than 40 registered business licenses. Companies include a trading post, outfitter store, construction business, snow removal service, leather goods store, hammock store, food stores, propane sales, and restaurants. Retail trade employs 15 residents.

Tourism and recreation. Fishing adventures, fly-fishing guides, sightseeing, and flying services are all available in Cantwell. Several lodges are available, including a bed-and-breakfast, two RV parks, and cabins. The arts, entertainment, recreation, and accommodation/food service industries collectively employ 24 workers.

INFRASTRUCTURE

Six capital projects, funded by grants, are active in Cantwell.

Transportation. Cantwell is accessible by road, rail, and air. In summer, the George Parks Highway connects to Fairbanks and Anchorage, and the Denali Highway links Denali Park with the Richardson Highway. Two privately owned airstrips are available. Cantwell Heights Property Owners operate a 2,080- by 70-foot gravel airstrip. A privately owned helipad is available at the Igloo. Train service is provided by the Alaska Railroad.

Electricity. Golden Valley Electric Association provides electricity.

Water and waste systems. Individual water wells and septic systems are available at the school and in most homes. Plumbing is in more than half of the residences. Garbage is deposited in a Borough transfer station, then dumped at the regional landfill near Anderson.

Telecommunications. Local telephone service is provided by the Matanuska Telephone Association, while long distance service is available through Alascom. One television channel is available through the Rural Alaska Television Network. Six radio stations are available in the community. Internet service and teleconferencing are both available.

COMMUNITY FACILITIES

Facilities include a community hall, and both public and school libraries.

Education. Cantwell School is in the Denali Borough Schools. The school has 23 students and 4 teachers.

Health care. Health care is provided by the Cantwell Health Clinic, owned by the village and leased to the U.S. Public Health Service; the clinic is administered by the Copper River Native Association.

Ethnicity: Ahtna Athabascan

ANCSA village corporation
Ahtna, Inc.
P.O. Box 649
Glenallen, AK 99588
  907-822-3476

Chalkyitsik

[chall-KEET-sick]
Ethnicity: Kutchin *(Gwich'in)*
Athabascan

ANCSA village corporation
Chalkyitsik Native Corporation
P.O. Box 53
Chalkyitsik, AK 99788
   907-662-2563

Total area of entitlement under ANCSA	
	91,790 acres
Total labor force	47
High school graduate or higher	30.2%
Bachelor's degree or higher	4.7%
Unemployment rate	0%
Per capita income *(2000)*	$11,509
Population *2000 census*	83
Percent Native *2000 census*	95.2%

LOCATION
Chalkyitsik is located on the Black River about 50 miles east of Fort Yukon. Chalkyitsik is located in the Fairbanks Recording District. The area encompasses 8.7 square miles of land and 0.3 square mile of water.

CLIMATE
Climate is continental Arctic, dominated by extreme seasonal temperatures. Winters are long and severe; summers are warm and brief. July temperatures vary from 65°F to 72°F, while the average low temperature in January dips well below zero. Extended periods of -50°F to -60°F are typical. Extreme temperatures have been recorded from -71°F in winter to 97°F in summer. Annual precipitation is 6.5 inches; yearly snowfall is 43.4 inches.

CULTURE AND HISTORY
Chalkyitsik means "fish hooking place," where the Gwich'in traditionally have gathered for seasonal fishing. Archaeological excavations suggest occupancy of the region to around 10,000 BC. Early Natives lived nomadic lives, moving to headwaters at the Black River from autumn to spring, and then moving downriver in summer to fish. Early explorers called the inhabitants Black River Gwich'in Natives. In the early 1900s, the Black River band settled in Salmon Village, about 70 miles upriver from the present site. In the late 1930s, a boat headed for Salmon Village was forced to unload at Chalkyitsik because of low water. The site became a seasonal fishing camp with a small number of cabins; a school was built, and the Black River people began a settlement there. By 1969 Chalkyitsik had more than 25 houses, a store, a community hall, and two churches. Chalkyitsik is a traditional Gwich'in Athabascan village, with a subsistence lifestyle. Big game and fish provide stable food sources. The Chalkyitsik Village Council is a federally recognized tribe in the community.

GOVERNMENT
Chalkyitsik is an unincorporated village. A traditional tribal council is recognized.

VILLAGE CORPORATION
Shareholders in its village corporation are also shareholders in the Doyon, Limited, Regional Native Corporation *(see Alaska introduction)*.

ECONOMY
The school district, village council, clinic, and government agencies offer limited part-time employment. Bureau of Land Management fire fighting, making sleds and snowshoes, trapping, and handicrafts provide seasonal work. The village economy relies on subsistence activities.

Government as employer. Of the 17 employed, 6 work for the local, state, or federal government.

Services and retail. Businesses include an air transportation service and two grocery/variety stores.

INFRASTRUCTURE
Twenty-two capital projects, funded by grants, are active in Chalkyitsik.

Transportation. Entry is primarily by air. The state provides a 4,000- by 90-foot gravel runway. All-terrain vehicles, snowmachines, and skiffs are used for fishing, hunting, and recreation. No roads connect Chalkyitsik with other communities. In winter a riverboat trail is open to Fort Yukon. Barge service is no longer available.

Water and waste systems. Water drawn from a well under the Black River is treated and stored in a 100,000-gallon tank. The village provides water to the school (although a study was recently completed to bring a piped water and sewer system to the school). Residents tow water from the new water treatment plant/washeteria/clinic building and use honeybuckets or outhouses for sewage disposal. Homes are not plumbed. A second water well has been funded. A piped water and sewer system to ten Westside homes is being reviewed. A landfill relocation study also is in progress.

Electricity Chalkyitsik Village Energy Systems provides electricity.

Telecommunications. Local telephone service is provided by United Utilities, Inc., while long distance service is available through Alascom. Cable television service is available in addition to one channel through the Rural Alaska Television Network. Two radio stations are available in the community. Internet service is provided by GCI. Teleconferencing is available from Alaska Teleconferencing Network.

COMMUNITY FACILITIES AND SERVICES
An elder nutrition program is provided for senior citizens. Facilities also include a recreation hall and community center.

Education. Tsuk Taih School is in the Yukon Flats School District. The school has 21 students.

Health care. Health care is provided by the Chalkyitsik Health Clinic, which is owned by the village and leased to the U.S. Public Health Service. The clinic is administered by the Tanana Chiefs Conference.

Total area of entitlement under ANCSA
                                        76,093 acres
(see discussion of the Habitat Lands Transaction, below)

Total labor force	27
High school graduate or higher	22
Bachelor's degree or higher	6
Unemployment rate	14.8%
Per capita income *(1999)*	$13,382
2003 population	99
state demographer estimate	
Population *2000 census*	86
Percent Native *2000 census*	77.9%

LOCATION
Chanega is located on Crab Bay on Evans Island, 42 miles southeast of Whittier, on Prince William Sound. It is 104 miles southeast of Anchorage.

PHYSICAL DESCRIPTION
Chanega Bay sits 100 feet above the waters of Crab Bay. The area encompasses 28.8 square miles of land and 0.3 square mile of water. In its present location, there has been no reported flooding.

CLIMATE
Winter temperatures vary from 17°F to 28°F; summer temperatures range 49°F to 63°F. Yearly precipitation is 66 inches, including annual snowfall of 80 inches.

CULTURE AND HISTORY
Chanega (meaning "along the side") is a very old village on Prince William Sound. The original Chanega Village was the oldest continuously inhabited place on Prince William Sound, located on the southern tip of Chanega Island. Chanega is remembered in oral traditions. According to legend, it was near Chanega that Raven first brought light to the world. The people of Chanega were known as great sea mammal hunters-they were "soaked in grease," people said in other parts of Prince William Sound. In the early days, the leadership of important chiefs helped the village to become rich through trade and to survive in times of war. In 1786 the English captain Nathaniel Portlock met Chanega's Chief Taatucktellingnuke when he traveled to Portlock's ship in a large skin boat *angyaq* that held 25 men, women, and children. Portlock wrote that the people of Chanega were fond of fish, wild celery, and, especially, herring eggs on seaweed, a treat that was enjoyed by the people of Prince William Sound until the *Exxon Valdez* oil spill contaminated both. It is also known that Vitus Bering stayed off the shores of Chanega Island during his travels, and when Lord Baranof was attempting to develop trade around Prince William Sound, he married Anna of Chanega.

On Good Friday, March 24, 1964, the original Chanega Village site on Chenega Island was completely destroyed by a tsunami resulting from Alaska's great 1964 earthquake. One-third of all Chanega residents died, constituting the earthquake's single largest death site. Residents who escaped went to live at Tatitlek, Cordova, and Anchorage. In 1984, the village was reestablished as "Chenega Bay" on Evans Island. In the mid-1980s, the village was rebuilt.

Then, on Good Friday, March 27, 1989, nearly 25 years to the day following the 1964 disaster, the oil tanker *Exxon Valdez* hit a reef off nearby Bligh Island, spilling millions of gallons of oil into Prince William Sound. The new Village of Chanega found itself awash with oil covering its beaches, and then inundated with cleanup activities and associated personnel. The people of Chanega are still feeling the devastation created by the *Exxon Valdez* oil spill. The community lived a subsistence lifestyle that was nearly destroyed by the oil spill.

Chanega's beautiful Russian Orthodox church, completed in 1999, is featured prominently at the heart of the village, just as the Russian Orthodox religion, introduced at the time of the arrival of Russian fur traders, remains at the center of many residents' lives today.

GOVERNMENT
The village is unincorporated and lies in the Unorganized Borough. The IRA tribal council is recognized by the federal government and serves as the governing body for the community.

VILLAGE CORPORATION
Most of Chanega Corporation's operations focus on government contracting, including facilities operations and maintenance, environmental remediation, power management, construction, electrical assembly, metal/composite fabrication, logistics and material management, security, information technology services, training, military operations, and base operations. It owns 51 percent of a joint venture providing information technology services to the Geospatial-Intelligence Agency. The Corporation also owns two major hotels in Anchorage.

In 1974 Chanega Corporation had 69 original shareholders, each with 100 shares. As of 2003 these 6,900 shares were owned by 136 shareholders, many of whom do not live in Chanega. Shareholders in Chanega Corporation are also shareholders in Chugach Alaska Corporation *(see Alaska introduction)*.

Habitat lands transaction. From 1974 to 1997, Chanega Corporation's main asset was approximately 79,000 acres of land acquired as part of its ANCSA entitlement. In 1997 the corporation sold surface title or conservation easements to more than 59,000 acres to the U.S. Forest Service and the State of Alaska for $34 million, which quickly altered the corporation's primary asset base from land to cash. Within the area sold it retained nine development sites, the original Chanega village site, and all shareholder homesites. It also retained around 20,000 unencumbered acres. The corporation then placed $14 million of the proceeds in a trust to provide shareholders with dividends in perpetuity. This trust, valued at nearly $20 million in 2003, had distributed nearly $4 million through 2003.

ECONOMY
Commercial fishing and subsistence activities are the primary sources of support. Sport fishing, hunting, and ecotourism opportunities, and the nearby Chanega Glacier attract tourists. Limited cash employment opportunities have led to significant loss of population. Chanega Bay Hotel, and the Jumping Salmon Lodge, cater to visitors.

Fisheries. Commercial fishing is one of the community's primary sources of support. A small oyster farm supplements the economy. Three residents hold commercial fishing permits.

Also known as Chenega Bay, Chenega *(local preference)*; **Caniqaq in Alutiiq**

[chuh-NEE-guh]
Ethnicity: Alutiiq

Native entity
Native Village of Chanega
P.O. Box 8079
Chenega Bay, AK 99574-9999
   907-573-5132
   907-573-5120 Fax

Also known as the Chanega IRA Council

ANCSA village corporation
Chanega Corporation
4000 Old Seward Highway
Suite 101
Anchorage, AK 99503
   907-277-5706
   907-277-5700 Fax
   chenega.com

Chanega

Also known as Chenega Bay,
Chenega (local preference)

Government as employer. Of the 23 employed residents, 20 work for the village council or for the state or federal government.

INFRASTRUCTURE

Telecommunications. All homes and public and private buildings have telephone service. Internet service is available at the school only. There is cable television service and an Alaska Rural Communications System repeater broadcasts one television channel. Local telephone service is provided by United Utilities, Inc., while long distance service is available through AT&T Alascom or United Utilities. One AM radio station broadcasts to the Chanega area.

Electricity generation and distribution. Electricity is generated at a 217-killowatt diesel plant. All homes and public and private buildings have electricity.

Fuel storage (gallons). Village council (60,000); Chugach Schools (12,000).

Water and waste systems. There is piped distribution to all households provided by a surface water collection system with a dam, treatment, and storage capacity of 50,000 gallons. Villagers have regular boil-water warnings. Although sewage is piped to a 20,000-gallon community septic tank, some residents use individual septic tanks. Refuse collection is ongoing. An oil and hazardous waste recycling center is now open.

Transportation. As one of the centers of the response to the *Exxon Valdez* oil spill, Chanega has an extensive, modern infrastructure including an oil-spill-response/ferry dock, which is used by the Alyeska Pipeline Service Company to store oil-spill-response equipment and by the State of Alaska Marine Highway system as a regularly scheduled ferry stop. A small boat harbor and dock are open. The "New Chanega" airport has a 3,000- by 75-foot gravel runway, and a floatplane landing area is available. Scheduled and chartered flights are available from Cordova, Valdez, Anchorage, and Seward.

COMMUNITY FACILITIES AND SERVICES

Community facilities include an office building, community hall, school, two teachers' houses, a church, and a community store. The village council provides electricity generation and distribution, fuel storage, waste collection and disposal, and water supply.

Education. Chanega School is in the Chugach School District. The school has 11 students and 3 staff members. Chanega School Library serves as the village's public library.

Health care. Health care is provided by the Chanega Health Clinic, owned by the village council and leased to the U.S. Public Health Service. The clinic is operated by the Chugachmiut Regional Health Corporation. In 2003 Chugachmiut won a federal contract to build a new clinic.

Public safety. Law enforcement is provided by state troopers in Valdez. Emergency response is provided by EMS-trained residents associated with the clinic.

ENVIRONMENTAL CONCERNS

The *Exxon Valdez* oil spill destroyed many of the subsistence opportunities available to the residents of Chanega and crippled the commercial fishing industry on Prince William Sound. Even after 15 years, many food sources remain contaminated.

Cheesh-Na

Also known as Chistochina

[chis-toe-CHEE-nuh]
Ethnicity: Ahtna Athabascan

ANCSA corporation
Ahtna, Incorporated
P.O. Box 649
Glennallen, AK 99588
907-822-3476

Total area of entitlement under ANCSA	
	69,120 acres
Total labor force	83
High school graduate or higher	54%
Bachelor's degree or higher	10%
Unemployment rate	41.2%
Per capita income *(2000)*	$12,362
Population *2000 census*	75
Percent Native *2000 census*	76%

LOCATION
Chistochina is located at mile 32.7 on the Tok Cutoff to the Glenn Highway, 42 miles northeast of Glennallen. Chistochina is located in the Chitina Recording District.

PHYSICAL DESCRIPTION
The area encompasses 359.4 square miles of land and 0.4 square mile of water. Sinona Creek, Bolder Creek, Chistochina River, and Copper River surround the village.

CLIMATE
The climate in Chistochina is continental, with typical long, cold winters and warm summers. Yearly snowfall averages 61 inches, with annual precipitation of 13 inches. Temperatures have reached extremes of -62°F to 91°F.

CULTURE AND HISTORY
Chistochina began as an Ahtna fish camp and a stopover place for traders and trappers. The village access road later became part of the Valdez-Eagle Trail constructed by miners during the gold rush to the Eagle area in 1897. Gold was mined along the upper Chistochina River and its runoff creeks. Chistochina Lodge was built as a roadhouse for prospectors. The trail was used for the construction of U.S. Army Signal Corps telegraph lines from Valdez to Eagle between 1901 and 1904. The area was settled by homesteaders, although it has remained the most traditional of all the region's communities. Subsistence is a crucial component of the lifestyle. The Chistochina Village Council is a federally recognized tribe in the community.

GOVERNMENT
Chistochina is unincorporated and is located in the Unorganized Borough (*see Alaska introduction*). The Native community is governed by a traditional council headed by a president.

VILLAGE CORPORATION
Shareholders in the village corporation are also shareholders in Ahtna, Inc., regional Native corporation (*see Alaska introduction*).

ECONOMY
Subsistence hunting, fishing, trapping, and gathering are the basis of the village's economy. Most cash employment is seasonal.

Construction. Six residents are employed in construction.

Government as employer. Of the 30 employed residents, 24 work for the local, state, or federal government.

Services and retail. The Sinona Creek Campground is available to the community.

INFRASTRUCTURE
Eight capital projects, funded by grants, are active in Chistochina. Chistochina is accessible year-round by the Glenn and Richardson Highways. Small planes may land at a state-owned 2,060- by 90-foot airstrip.

Water and waste systems. Almost half of residents have individual wells; others haul treated water from the community center. A few villagers use individual septic tanks, but the majority have outhouses or pit privies. About 40 percent of homes are fully plumbed. The landfill is in relocation. A washeteria and a new landfill are needed in the village. Alaska Power Company provides electricity. Local telephone service is provided by the Copper Valley Telephone Co-op (Glennallen exchange), while long distance service is available through Alascom. Cable television service is available, as is one channel through the Rural Alaska Television Network and one radio station. Teleconferencing is available through the Glennallen legislative information office. Internet service is also available.

COMMUNITY FACILITIES AND SERVICES
Area facilities include a recreation building, community hall, and library with a computer lab.

Education. Chistochina School is in the Copper River School District. The school has nine students and one teacher.

Health care. Health care is provided by the Chistochina Health Clinic, owned by the village corporation and leased to the U.S. Public Health Service. The clinic is administered by the Mount Sanford Tribal Council. Area hospitals or health clinics include Cross Road Medical Center in Glennallen. The Regional Health Corp. provides community-based services. The community health aide serves the elderly and homebound clients, provides health education, and conducts dog-shot clinics. The CHA provides staffing at the clinic, contract health care, and dental services. Copper River EMS Council and Cross Road Medical Center in Glennallen provide auxiliary health care.

Cheesh-Na
Also known as Chistochina

Chefornak

Chefornak

Total area of entitlement under ANCSA	
	92,160 acres
Total labor force	202
High school graduate or higher	60.2%
Bachelor's degree or higher	5.6%
Unemployment rate	11.9%
Per capita income *(2000)*	$8,474
Population *2000 census*	394
Percent Native *2000 census*	98%

LOCATION
Chefornak is located on the south bank of the Kinia River, at its junction with the Keguk River, in the Yukon-Kuskokwim Delta. The village lies within the Clarence Rhode National Wildlife Refuge, established for migratory waterfowl protection. Chefornak is 98 air miles southwest of Bethel and 490 miles southwest of Anchorage. Chefornak is located in the Bethel Recording District. The area encompasses 5.7 square miles of land and 0.8 square mile of water.

CLIMATE
Chefornak is in a marine climate, with annual precipitation of 22 inches and yearly snowfall of 43 inches. Summer temperatures range from 41°F to 57°F; winter temperatures vary from 6°F to 24°F.

CULTURE AND HISTORY
Yup'ik Eskimos have historically lived in the area. Alexie Amagiqchik arrived from a Bering Sea village in the early 1950s and opened a store at the site. Others from the original village succeeded Amagiqchik and settled in Chefornak. As traditional Yup'ik Eskimo villagers, Chefornak residents follow a subsistence lifestyle that includes commercial fishing. The Village of Chefornak is a federally recognized tribe in the community.

GOVERNMENT
Chefornak was incorporated as a second-class city in 1974, with a mayor and six city councillors. The city has an advisory school board. A traditional tribal council also is recognized.

VILLAGE CORPORATION
Shareholders in the village corporation are also shareholders in Calista Regional Native Corporation *(see Alaska introduction).*

ECONOMY
Government employment offers the only year-round employment. Otherwise, job opportunities are seasonal in Chefornak. Subsistence activities, particularly trapping, bring supplemental income. In the spring, sea mammals are harvested; in summer, herring are caught along with whitefish and waterfowl; and in fall several fish species are taken, including pike, tomcod, and smelt. Chefornak is interested in developing its fisheries, products by establishing a fish-processing operation for herring, flounder, cod, and whitefish. A mink and fox farm is also a possibility. The village would like to develop a market for traditional cultural activities of the area, including arts and crafts.

Construction. Four residents are employed in construction.

Fisheries. Commercial fishing permits for herring roe and salmon fisheries are held by 27 residents. Halibut and salmon are processed in Chefornak. The village operates a fish freezer for commercial and subsistence catches. The 1992 Community Development Quota program increased the pollack groundfish quota for small communities such as Chefornak.

Government as employer. Of the 118 employed residents, 74 work for the local, state, or federal government.

Manufacturing. One resident is employed in manufacturing.

Services and retail. Businesses include a light plant, day-care service, mining company, general merchandise store, and utility company.

Transportation. Six airline services are available in Chefornak.

[chuh-FORE-nuck]
also Chefarnok

Ethnicity: Yup'ik Eskimo

ANCSA village corporation
Chefarnrmute Inc.
110 Airport Way
Chefornak, AK 99561
    907-867-8115
    907-867-8895 Fax
chefarnmuteinc.com

Chenega,
Chenega Bay
See Chanega

Chefornak

Chenega,
Chenega Bay

See Chanega

INFRASTRUCTURE
Thirteen capital projects, funded by grants, are active in Chefornak.

Transportation. The state provides a 2,500- by 35-foot gravel airstrip for year-round chartered and private air access. A seaplane base is available, and a new airport will soon be under construction. Fishing boats and skiffs are used for local transportation. Snowmachines provide winter transportation. Trails are available in winter to Kipnuk and Kasigluk.

Electricity. Naterkaq Light Plant provides electricity.

(Water and waste systems). Village water is accessible from 12 wells and a new water treatment plant. The school well is unusable. Villagers haul from different watering points. Plumbing is available to only six households; 50 residences use honeybuckets; and two dozen homes use a hauling service. Infrastructure improvements and a new washeteria are in progress. A piped water system is in its early stages of planning.

Telecommunications. Local telephone service is provided by United Utilities, while long distance service is available through Alascom. Cable television service is available, along with one broadcast television station. One radio station is available in the community. Internet service is provided only to the school by GCI. Teleconferencing is available from Alaska Teleconferencing Network.

COMMUNITY FACILITIES AND SERVICES
Village facilities include a community hall.

Education. Chaputnguak School is in the Lower Kuskokwim School District. The school has 147 students and eight teachers.

Health care. Health care is Provided by the Chefornak Health Clinic, owned by the village and leased to the U.S. Public Health Service. The clinic is administered by the Yukon-Kuskokwim Health Corporation.

hevak

Also known as Kashunamiut

[CHEE-vack]
Ethnicity: Yup'ik Eskimo

ANCSA Corporation
Chevak Company
  Corporation
P.O. Box 236
Chevak, AK 99653
  907-858-7920
  907-858-7311 Fax

Total area of entitlement under ANCSA	
	138,240 acres
Total labor force	404
High school graduate or higher	74.9%
Bachelor's degree or higher	10.5%
Unemployment rate	15.1%
Per capita income *(2000)*	$7,550
Population *2000 census*	765
Percent Native *2000 census*	95.9%

LOCATION
Chevak is located on the north bank of the Niglikfak River, 17 miles east of Hooper Bay in the Yukon-Kuskokwim Delta. Chevak is located in the Bethel Recording District. The area encompasses 1.1 square miles of land and 0.1 square mile of water.

CLIMATE
Chevak has a maritime climate of heavy winds and rain. Temperatures vary from -25°F in winter to 79°F in summer. Annual snowfall is 60 inches. Freeze-up begins at the end of October; break-up occurs in June.

CULTURE AND HISTORY
Chevak also is called New Chevak because prior to 1950 villagers lived in another village called Chevak. Flooding caused from high storm tides forced residents of Old Chevak, on the north bank of the Keoklevik River, to abandon the village. The U.S. Coast and Geodetic Survey reported the new site of Chevak in 1948. A post office opened in 1951. Chevak is a Yup'ik Eskimo village. Commercial fishing and subsistence activities are essential to the village culture. The Chevak Tribal Council (also known as Kashunamiut) is a federally recognized tribe in the community.

GOVERNMENT
Chevak was incorporated as a second-class city in 1967 with a mayor and city council. A traditional tribal council also is recognized.

VILLAGE CORPORATION
The Chevak village corporation operates a satellite TV service. Shareholders in the Chevak Company are also share-holders in Calista regional Native corporation *(see Alaska introduction).*

ECONOMY
Bureau of Land Management and construction projects provide summer jobs. Summer employment in Chevak fuels the economy until winter months bring a lapse in full-time work. Subsistence activities and handicraft merchandising supplement incomes. Ten residents are employed in construction.

Fisheries. Eighteen residents hold commercial fishing permits. Salmon, seal, walrus, clams, and waterfowl are harvested. The 1992 Community Development Quota program encouraged commercial fishing opportunities by increasing the pollack groundfish quota for small communities such as Chevak.

Government as employer. Of the 231 employed residents, 115 work for the local, state, or federal government.

Services and retail. Chevak residents hold 13 current business licenses. Businesses include a gift shop, repair shop, grill, general merchandise stores, and the traditional council. Thirty-six residents work in retail trade. Education, health, and social services employ 98 residents, and public administration employs 38.

Tourism and recreation. There are a video-tape rental business and a recreation center run by the traditional village council and the village corporation. The arts, entertainment, recreation, and accommodation/food service industries collectively employ 17 residents. Visitor attractions include bird watching and the Clarence Rhodes National Wildlife Refuge. Cultural events include Cultural Heritage Week, Winter Carnival, and Tundrafest.

INFRASTRUCTURE
Seventeen capital projects, funded by grants, are active in Chevak.

Transportation. Six airline companies provide service in the Chevak area. Although the state provides a 2,610- by 40-foot gravel airstrip, heavy winds and rain can preclude air passage. Relocation of the airport is in progress. Chevak Lake and the Ninglikfak River are available for floatplane landings. Docking facilities are not available. A barge landing is open for cargo off-loading. In summer, skiffs are used for local travel on the river; in winter, snowmachines are used. Trails in winter are open to Scammon Bay, Hooper Bay, and Newtok.

Electricity. Alaska Village Electric Cooperative (AVEC) provides electricity.

Water and waste systems. Piped water and sewer systems to the school and 170 households are nearly completed. A new landfill, a washeteria renovation, a new watering point, a water treatment plant, a 150,000-gallon water storage tank, a sewage lagoon, and a vacuum sewer plant are now in service. Construction of water and sewer mains and household connections are in progress. Nearly 90 homes have been connected. Other households rely on water hauling and the use of privies. Rain catchment systems are in some homes.

Telecommunications. Local telephone service is provided by United Utilities, while long distance service is available through Alascom. Cable television service is available, as is one channel through the Rural Alaska Television Network. Internet service is available for the school only. One radio station is available to the community. Teleconferencing is available from Alaska Teleconferencing Network.

COMMUNITY FACILITIES AND SERVICES
Facilities include a youth center, community hall and a school/community library.

Education. Chevak School is in the Kashunamiut School District. The school has 349 students and 25 teachers.

Health care. Health care is provided by the Chevak Health Clinic, owned by the city and leased to the U.S. Public Health Service. The clinic is administered by the Yukon-Kuskokwim Health Corporation.

Chevak
Also known as Kashunamiut

Chickaloon

Chickaloon

Total area of entitlement under ANCSA	65,400 acres
Total labor force	226
High school graduate or higher	88.4%
Bachelor's degree or higher	19%
Unemployment rate	24.2%
Per capita income *(2000)*	$14,755
Population *2000 census*	16,918
Percent Native *2000 census*	9.2%

LOCATION
Chickaloon begins at milepost 72 on the Glenn Highway, 26 miles northeast of Palmer in the Talkeetna Mountains. It is a 90-minute drive from Anchorage. The Chickaloon and Kings rivers drain into the Matanuska River. Chickaloon is located in the Palmer Recording District.

PHYSICAL DESCRIPTION
The area encompasses 79.4 square miles of land and 0.8 square mile of water.

CLIMATE
Winter temperatures vary from -3ºF to 39ºF and summer temperatures range from 40ºF to 69ºF. Yearly precipitation is 16.5 inches, including an annual snowfall of 69 inches.

CULTURE AND HISTORY
Dena'ina Athabascan and Ahtna Indians have inhabited the area for centuries. During the Russian fur-trading era, Ahtna transported pelts from the Dena'ina along the Matanuska River to Copper Fort in the east. The Chickaloon River was named after Chief Chiklu. Chickaloon was a government townsite; in 1916 it became the terminus of the Matanuska Branch of the Alaska Railroad. The Chickaloon Bridge opened in 1917. Sutton, at the Wishbone Hill Naval Coal Reserve, Chickaloon Mine, Coal Creek, and Carbon Creek were coal mining sites until 1925 when coal mining dwindled. By the end of the 1930s, Chickaloon was a dying village. In 1958 Chickaloon was opened to homesteaders after the naval reserve land reverted to public domain. The Chickaloon Native Village and the Chickaloon Community Council are the core of the community. Athabascan and non-Native villagers rely strongly on subsistence activities. The Chickaloon Village is a federally recognized tribe in the community.

GOVERNMENT
Chickaloon is unincorporated. A traditional tribal council is recognized.

VILLAGE CORPORATION
Shareholders in the village corporation are also shareholders in Cook Inlet Regional Native corporation *(see Alaska introduction).*

ECONOMY
A motel/lodge, gas station, store, and post office are the primary employers. Some villagers commute to the Palmer/Wasilla area for work.

Construction. There are a custom carpentry business and a woodwork shop in the village. Approximately 15 residents are employed in construction.

Government as employer. Of the 116 employed residents, 42 work for the local, state, or federal government.

Services and retail. There are 35 current businesses licenses in Chickaloon. Businesses include a horse ranch, gunsmith, novelties store, trading post, soap and supply, construction, water transportation, and retail trade. Six residents work in retail trade; 6 in education, health and social services; and 29 residents in public administration.

Tourism and recreation. Four lodges are available to tourists, including one bed-and-breakfast. Several businesses offer guides and wilderness adventures. The arts, entertainment, recreation, and accommodation/food service industries collectively employ 22 residents. Visitor attractions include King Mountain State Recreation Site, Bonnie Lake State Recreation Site, and Long Lake State Recreation Site.

INFRASTRUCTURE
Seven capital projects, funded by grants, are active in Chickaloon.

Transportation. A statewide highway system provides passage to Chickaloon. Goods are received from the Palmer/Wasilla area or Anchorage. Private airstrips are in the region.

[CHICK-uh-loon]
Ethnicity: Tanaina *(Dena'ina)*
Athabascan

ANCSA village cooperative
Chickaloon-Moose Creek
Native Association, Inc.
Star Route 3, Box 8342
Palmer, AK 99645
907-746-2548

Chickaloon

Water and waste systems. Individual water wells and septic tank systems are available to 75 percent of the residences. Most houses are plumbed. A borough refuse transfer station is near Sutton.

Electricity. Matanuska Electric Association provides electricity.

Telecommunications. Local telephone service is provided by Matanuska Telephone Association. Long-distance service is available through Alascom. Four television stations are available to residents, as well as most Anchorage radio stations. Internet service is provided by MTA Online.

COMMUNITY FACILITIES AND SERVICES
Education. There are no schools in the community. The Ya Ne Dah Ah "Ancient Teachings" School, a traditional-language elementary school, is in nearby Moose Creek. Also see profile for Ya Ne Dah Ah School.

Health care. Valley Hospital in Palmer and Anchorage hospitals are available. Sutton EMS offers auxiliary health care.

Honoring Nations Honoree 2002

Text in its entirety from: The Harvard Project On American Indian Economic Development

John F. Kennedy School of Government Harvard University

Honoring Nations Honoree 2002
Ya Ne Dah Ah School

Dedicated to providing community youth with the skills necessary for functioning in a modern world while maintaining Native knowledge and practices, the Ya Ne Dah Ah School is Alaska's only tribally owned and operated full-time primary school and day care facility. Located in a two-room schoolhouse and supported entirely by private donations and tribal funding, the School's twenty students are taught—and excel in—the conventional topics of science, math, English, and social studies. In addition, the students learn Ahtna Athabascan history, language, music, and art—topics and skills that the Village of Chickaloon values and that community members help the School to teach.

While many of Alaska's 227 federally recognized tribes confront challenges related to isolation and distance from sustainable economic activity, Chickaloon Village's challenges stem from its proximity to mainstream society. An Ahtna Athabascan Indian community in the Matanuska Valley of Alaska, Chickaloon Village and its 250 tribal members are only sixty miles northeast of Anchorage, and thus, they have been under particularly intense pressures of acculturation. Once the stewards of vast landholdings, they have become a minority in their own homeland. There are not many Native speakers left, many cultural practices have become endangered, and worse, some have been lost. Chickaloon youth have been beset with problems characteristic of urban areas. And unlike what is found throughout much of Indian Country, where a growing number of tribes are exercising their sovereignty to successfully overcome chronic socioeconomic problems, Native leaders in Alaska face the unwelcome reality that Alaskan borough, city, and state governments possess jurisdiction over education and other essential tribal government functions. For example, although the Alaska State Legislature receives federal funding for Indian education, most monies are funneled into the state system.

The education of Native youth in the Alaskan public school system has long been a topic of deep concern to tribal leaders and Native parents at Chickaloon and elsewhere. Such concern is warranted: Native students in Alaska's public schools suffer from much lower rates of educational attainment drop out at much higher rates than their non-Native peers at both the state and national levels. Indeed, there is a longstanding distrust among Natives of "conventional" classroom methods and even of the public schools' educational intentions themselves—distrust that is fueled by the fact that most Alaskan public schools lack Native-relevant curricula despite large Native student populations.

Concerned about the quality of education that their students were receiving in the public school system, coupled with a desire to curb the decline of Ahtna Athabascan cultural practices, the Chickaloon Village decided to take matters into their own hands in 1992. In a path-breaking exercise of sovereignty, the Village established the Ya Ne Dah Ah, or "Ancient Teachings," School—the first and only full-time, year-round, tribally owned and operated day care and elementary school in Alaska. Founded and staffed by tribal members who had seen the positive impact of tribally run schools in other Native communities outside of Alaska, the Ya Ne Dah Ah School acknowledges the crisis in Alaskan indigenous education and confronts it at a local level. The School provides its students with an education that integrates Athabascan heritage and mainstream education. In particular, its curriculum effectively melds traditional teachings with modern non-Native subjects, creating a learning environment in which Native students can identify with and feel connected to their culture and community while learning to understand and function productively in the non-Native world. Like many other tribal schools, Ya Ne Dah Ah is committed to providing students with an education that instills respect for human dignity, diversity, and self-determination.

The Ya Ne Dah Ah School educates the majority of elementary school-aged children in Chickaloon Village. Currently, twenty children attend Ya Ne Dah Ah, most of whom are tribal members, though several students are tribal government employees' children and other non-tribal community members. This year, the children attending the Ya Ne Dah Ah School are between the ages of one and twelve and in grades six and below. The School is growing with the children, so next year it also will offer a seventh grade curriculum. Ultimately, the Chickaloon Village government hopes to expand the Ya Ne Dah Ah School's facilities and student population, creating a multicultural education system that will serve all Village members from birth through adulthood (adult-education courses and even a tribal college have been discussed). The School's past success speaks highly of its capacity to realize these dreams. Ten years ago, the School began with a part-time, volunteer teacher; today, it employs a full-time, certified teacher.

These expansions of the Chickaloon Village school's budget, student population, services, and academic activities stand in stark contrast to neighboring public schools. Indeed, many Natives are returning to the area so that their children can attend the Ya Ne Dah Ah School, and now, the very existence of a waiting list is a telling measure of the School's success. The students' academic records are another important draw. Unlike most other schools that serve Alaska Native populations, Ya Ne Dah Ah students remain in school—dropouts are not a problem. Furthermore, they score higher on standardized tests than their national counterparts. The Chickaloon Village School Board keeps a close eye on these results. It reviews the Ya Ne Dah Ah School's progress on an annual basis, charts individual students' achievements according to federally and state approved assessment methods, and communicates findings to parents and to the Tribal Council in regular progress reports.

The Ya Ne Dah Ah School's success is the result of several distinctive factors. First, it is an essential government function that is integrated into Chickaloon Village and local Ahtna Athabascan life. An Alaska Daily News article reported that, "Nothing the tribe does is as important as running its school. Polls of tribe members place education and cultural preservation as the top priority." While parental participation is nearly 100 percent-parents volunteer to help with School events, provide all School transportation needs, and even teach in the School—other adult community members contribute to facility maintenance and education efforts as well. The School has inspired an admirable commitment among its faculty. The cultural teacher and day care teacher are returning to the local university to receive more formal education training. Tribal offices are also actively involved in the School's curriculum. For instance, Chickaloon's Health Department provides health education; its Community Oriented Policing Services program offers safety classes; and the Department of the Environment teaches map making and assists with science classes. In addition to the support of parents, community members, and the tribal council, the Ya Ne Dah Ah School depends upon the support of surrounding schools and other Native villages. Area public schools provide services such as access to a swimming pool and library on a weekly basis. Members of other Athabascan villages, such as Arctic Village and Copper Center, visit regularly and even teach the Chickaloon children traditional songs and dances of the Athabascan people.

In the absence of federal and state support, this extensive community involvement has been crucial to the School's survival. Indeed, a second factor in the Ya Ne Dah Ah School's success has been its ability to accomplish so much with so few financial resources. Ya Ne Dah Ah School's $150,000 annual budget—none of which comes from state or federal sources because the Village is unwilling to rescind aspects of its sovereignty—does not afford the School many amenities that non-Native schools enjoy. The School operates in a donated two-room schoolhouse without running water; its day care facility is housed in a small separate building. The School relies on private sources of funding by working closely with private foundations and CIRI (the Native regional corporation), ultimately gaining 98 percent of its annual budget from these sources. The Tribe supplies the remaining 2 percent of funding through bake sales, pow-wow proceeds, and individual donations. In other words, private contributions, volunteer labor, and an education board that manages to do a great deal with scarce funds have made it possible for the Ya Ne Dah Ah School to function on a shoestring budget.

A third factor in the Ya Ne Dah Ah School's success has been its determination to promote Athabascan culture in its curriculum. As noted, "Ya Ne Dah Ah" means "Ancient Teachings," and the School has become a center for the maintenance and dissemination of Athabascan cultural practices. Although there are fewer than fifty fluent Ahtna Athabascan speakers in the world and most of them are over fifty years old, the students in the Ya Ne Dah Ah School are now learning the language. They study Ahtna Athabascan not just in "language"

classes, but also through their work in math, culture, social studies, and art. The Ya Ne Dah Ah School also is piloting culturally specific units such as Songs & Dance, Potlatches, Fish Traps & Wheels, Birch Bark Basket Making, and Yenida'a Stories, all of which feature reading materials, hands-on activities, and multimedia videos. And there is evidence that these investments are paying off. The first graduate of the Ya Ne Dah Ah School is now the instructor of the Ya Ne Dah Ah School youth dance and drum group as well as an Ahtna language teacher; one of the only young people in all of Alaska to speak the traditional Ahtna language, he is a source of pride for the entire Nation. Last year, Ya Ne Dah Ah School students welcomed tribal leaders from across the US to a three-day environmental health conference in Anchorage with an hour-long performance of traditional drumming and dancing. Further, the culturally relevant teachings of the Ya Ne Dah Ah School are giving rise to responsible and informed tribal citizens whose respect for Ahtna Athabascan traditions and culture are enabling them to create even more effective and appropriate Village governance.

A final demonstration of the Ya Ne Dah Ah School's success is its ability to merge cultural teachings with mainstream curriculum and to share that learning. Relying on both traditional and contemporary methods of teaching, the Ya Ne Dah Ah staff offer instruction in the Ahtna Athabascan language, respect for the environment, traditional values, ethics, Athabascan cultural practices, math, social studies, science, and language arts. Not surprisingly, the Ya Ne Dah Ah School has become a catalyst for curriculum development. The Chickaloon Village's Department of Education supports a Curriculum Development Project that creates high-tech, multimedia Ahtna Athabascan cultural heritage curricula found nowhere else in Alaska. These curricular units are fully integrated into the Ya Ne Dah Ah School and have recently been integrated into the neighboring Matanuska-Susitna Borough School District that serves over five thousand students. These units are targeted for statewide and national distribution in the next two years.

The Ya Ne Dah Ah School exemplifies a commitment to perpetuating Native sovereignty in an environment sometimes unsympathetic to that stance. By reclaiming its own educational process and successfully merging cultural and modern curricula, the School has exceeded state and national standards while reinvigorating the traditional life of the Village. With its solid academic foundation, its substantial local support, its partnerships with private foundations, and its evidence of success, the Ya Ne Dah Ah School serves as a model for Indian nations.

Lessons
Indian nations and Native villages that are deeply committed to self-determination are persistent in their efforts to overcome political, financial, and institutional obstacles to self-governance. A "can-do" attitude is a prerequisite for tribal success.

Tribal schools can combine traditional teachings and Native culture with mainstream curriculum by involving elders and other community leaders in students' education, teaching math and science through "real life" applications, and offering Native language, music, art, and history classes. The pursuit of culturally sensitive teaching need not inhibit a school's ability to produce students who excel by standard measures of academic achievement.

Schools that encourage parents, family members, and community leaders to become involved in their children's education help ensure student success. Community involvement also gives schools access to a broader range of resources and teaching tools.

Chickaloon

**Honoring Nations
Honoree 2002**

**Text in its entirety from:
The Harvard Project On
American Indian Economic
Development**

**John F. Kennedy School
of Government
Harvard University**

Chignik

Also known as Chignik Bay

[CHIG-nick]
Ethnicity: Alutiiq Aleut

ANCSA village corporation
Far West, Incorporated
P.O. Box 3572
Kodiak, AK 99615
907-846-5900

Total area of entitlement under ANCSA	
	119,086 acres
Total labor force	65
High school graduate or higher	74.1%
Bachelor's degree or higher	13%
Unemployment rate	35.2%
Per capita income *(2000)*	$16,166
Population *2000 census*	79
Percent Native *2000 census*	60.8%

LOCATION
The City of Chignik is located on Anchorage Bay on the south shore of the Alaska Peninsula. It lies 450 miles southwest of Anchorage and 260 miles southwest of Kodiak. Chignik is located in the Aleutian Islands Recording District.

PHYSICAL DESCRIPTION
The area encompasses 11.7 square miles of land and 4.2 square miles of water.

CLIMATE
The village has a maritime climate dominated by warm, rainy winters and cool summers. Cloud cover and heavy winds prevail in winter. Summer temperatures vary from 39°F to 60°F; winter temperatures average 20°F degrees. Annual precipitation is 127 inches; yearly snowfall is 58 inches.

CULTURE AND HISTORY
Originally "Kalwak" was located at the site until it was destroyed in the late 1700s during the Russian fur boom. In the late 1800s *Chignik,* meaning "big wind," became a fishing village and cannery. Workers and supplies were transported between Chignik and San Francisco by sailing ship, and Chinese crews from San Francisco traveled to Chignik after winter to work for the cannery. A post office opened in 1901. Coal mining was active at that time. Currently two of the historical canneries are in operation. Alutiiq live in the village. Residents rely on subsistence harvesting of fish and caribou. The Chignik Bay Village Council is a federally recognized tribe in the community.

GOVERNMENT
The village was incorporated as a second-class city in 1983, with a mayor and city council. The seven members of the Chignik City Council are elected to three-year staggered terms. The mayor is elected by membership of the City Council. The traditional Chignik Bay Village Council, headed by a president, also has seven members.

VILLAGE CORPORATION
Shareholders in the Far West village corporation also hold shares in Bristol Bay Native Corporation *(see Alaska introduction).*

ECONOMY
Commercial fishing and subsistence activities fuel the cash economy. Chignik has 2 fish-processing plants, and an average of 700 people come to the village each summer to work in the plants or to fish. Villagers rely on subsistence foods, including salmon, trout, crab, clams, caribou, and moose.

Construction. Two residents are employed in construction.

Fisheries. Sixteen residents hold commercial fishing permits. Two privately owned companies operate fish-processing plants in Chignik. Salmon, herring roe, halibut, cod and crab are all processed in Chignik. During the summer, 600 to 800 people come to Chignik to fish or work in the processing plants.

Government as employer. Of the 35 employed residents, 27 work for the local, state, or federal government.

Services and retail. Chignik holds 14 current business licenses. Businesses include a bakery, real estate office, community hall, thrift shop, welding and repair shop, laundry, guide services, lodges, and restaurants. Retail trade employs four residents. Education, health & social service industries employ 14 residents.

Tourism and recreation. The mixed Aleut-Scandinavian history of the area and the two seafood-processing facilities, built in the late 1800s, are visitor attractions. Hunting (moose, brown bear, caribou, and ducks) is popular, as is halibut fishing. Sightseeing and photography of wildlife, birds, and the landscape are also popular attractions.

INFRASTRUCTURE
Seventeen capital projects, funded by grants, are active in Chignik.

Transportation. Chignik is accessible by air and sea. The state operates a 2,600- by 60-foot gravel runway and a seaplane base. King Salmon and Port Heiden have scheduled flights. Chignik Fisheries owns a 1,630-foot gravel airstrip. Barge services are available weekly from late spring through early fall and monthly during the rest of the year. The state ferry operates bimonthly from Kodiak between May and October. A 600-foot privately owned dock and a boat haul-out are available. A breakwater, 110-slip small-boat harbor, and public dock are under development. All-terrain vehicles and skiffs provide local travel. Roads are being discussed to run between Chignik, Chignik Lagoon, Chignik Lake, and the city landfill.

Electricity. The feasibility of hydroelectric generation at Indian Lake is being studied. Chignik Electric provides electricity.

Water and waste systems. Indian Creek provides water from a dam and a reservoir. The school and all households are connected to treated and piped-in water. A backup water supply comes from a well. A 200,000-gallon water contact tank and a filtration system to bring the water into compliance are in the funding stages. In 45 households, piped sewage is collected in community septic tanks, and wastewater is discharged by ocean outfall lines. Other residences use individual septic tanks. All homes are plumbed. A new landfill and access road are now open.

Telecommunications. Local telephone service is provided by Pacific Telecommunications, while long distance service is available through Alascom. Cable television service is also available, as is one channel through the Rural Alaska Television Network. Internet service is provided by GCI, and teleconferencing is available from Alaska Teleconferencing Network.

COMMUNITY FACILITIES AND SERVICES
Area facilities include a community hall.

Education. Chignik Bay School is in the Lake and Peninsula School District. The school has 14 students and 2 teachers.

Health care. The one-bed Chignik Bay Subregional Clinic is staffed by two community health aides and a physician's assistant. The clinic has lab, x-ray, and pharmacy services available. The nearest hospitals are located in Kodiak and Anchorage. The clinic is administered by the Bristol Bay Area Health Corporation.

Total area of entitlement under ANCSA
95,466 acres

Total labor force	76
High school graduate or higher	70%
Bachelor's degree or higher	12%
Unemployment rate	0%
Per capita income *(2000)*	$28,940
Population *2000 census*	103
Percent Native *2000 census*	82.5%

LOCATION
Chignik Lagoon is located on the south shore of the Alaska Peninsula, 450 miles southwest of Anchorage. It lies 180 air miles south of King Salmon, 8.5 miles west of Chignik and 16 miles east of Chignik Lake. Chignik Lagoon is located in the Aleutian Islands Recording District.

PHYSICAL DESCRIPTION
The area encompasses 13.1 square miles of land.

CLIMATE
The community is in a maritime climate, with cool summers and warm, wet winters. Heavy cloud cover and harsh winds prevail in winter. Summer temperatures vary from 39ºF to 60ºF; winter temperatures range from 21ºF to 36ºF. Annual precipitation is 127 inches; yearly snowfall is 58 inches.

CULTURE AND HISTORY
The village was established close to Chignik. The lagoon residents have always depended on various sea mammals for their food supply. The sea otter population was eradicated during the Russian fur boom in the late 1700s. Disease and warfare also added to the woes of the Native population, but fishing, in later years, helped the village to prosper. The Koniag people who live in the village are descendants of both Koniags and Aleuts. Chignik Lagoon is a traditional Koniag village that has an influx of fishermen in the summer. The population rises by 200 during the fishing season. The Chignik Lagoon Village Council is a federally recognized tribe in the community.

GOVERNMENT
The village is unincorporated. A traditional tribal council is recognized.

VILLAGE CORPORATION
Shareholders in the village corporation are also shareholders in Bristol Bay regional Native corporation *(see Alaska introduction)*.

ECONOMY
The village council, electric plant, and school offer full-time work. Fishing fuels the economy of Chignik Lagoon. The area is a regional fishing center and the success of the salmon fleet is essential to the community. Two onshore processors are in Chignik. Subsistence activities are vital to the village's food sources.

Construction. Approximately 11 residents are employed in construction. A lumber saw and mill plant is currently in operation.

Fisheries. Twenty-nine residents hold commercial fishing permits. Two onshore processors operate out of nearby Chignik.

Government as employer. Of the 40 employed residents, 19 work for the local, state, or federal government.

Services and retail. Chignik Lagoon holds 14 current business licenses. Businesses include a day care, country store, bed-and-breakfast, technical service, power utility company, the village council, fishing guides, and airway services.

INFRASTRUCTURE
Five capital projects, funded by grants, are active in Chignik Lagoon.

Transportation. Air and sea are the main transportation passages into the village. No roads are available to other communities, but there are plans to build roads to link Chignik, Chignik Lagoon, Chignik Lake, and the landfill. The state provides a 1,600- by 60-foot gravel airstrip and a public small-boat harbor and seaplane base. Nearby King Salmon offers scheduled and charter flights. Supplies on cargo ship come yearly into Chignik Lagoon. Residents use all-terrain vehicles and skiffs for local travel. Boat haul-outs are available.

Electricity. Chignik Lagoon Power Utility provides electricity.

Water and waste systems. An infiltration gallery from a surface source is available. The piped water system is available to most residences, although a few households have individual wells. Plumbing, using individual septic tanks, has been completed in the majority of households. Construction is in progress for new wells, a pumphouse and waterline to the storage tank, a new sewage system, sewage treatment plant, ocean outfall, and landfill. A new incinerator is available at the landfill.

Telecommunications. Local telephone service is provided by Pacific Telecommunications, while long distance service is available through Alascom. One television channel is available through the Rural Alaska Television Network. One radio station is available to the community. Internet service is provided by GCI. Teleconferencing is available from Alaska Teleconferencing Network.

COMMUNITY FACILITIES AND SERVICES
Facilities include a subsistence building and an IRA office.

Education. Chignik Lagoon School is in the Lake and Peninsula School District. The school has 22 students and 4 teachers.

Health care. Health care is provided by the Chignik Lagoon Health Clinic, owned by the village and leased to the U.S. Public Health Service; the clinic is administered by Bristol Bay Area Health Corporation.

[CHIG-nick]
Ethnicity: Koniag Aleut

ANCSA village corporation
Chignik Lagoon Native
Corporation
P.O. Box 3084
Kodiak, AK 99615
907-840-2268

Chignik Lake

[CHIG-nick]
Ethnicity: Alutiiq Aleuts

ANCSA village corporation
Chignik River Limited
General Delivery
Chignik Lake, AK 99548
907-845-2228

Total area of entitlement under ANCSA
99,961 acres

Total labor force	84
High school graduate or higher	57.1%
Bachelor's degree or higher	8.6%
Unemployment rate	8.6%
Per capita income *(2000)*	$13,843
Population *2000 census*	145
Percent Native *2000 census*	87.6%

LOCATION

Chignik Lake is located on the south side of the Alaska Peninsula next to the body of water of the same name. It lies 13 miles from Chignik, 265 miles southwest of Kodiak, and 474 miles southwest of Anchorage. Chignik Lake is located in the Aleutian Islands Recording District.

PHYSICAL DESCRIPTION

The area encompasses 12.3 square miles of land and 9.6 square miles of water.

CLIMATE

Cool summers and warm, rainy winters characterize the maritime climate of Chignik Lake. Summer temperatures vary from 39°F to 60°F; winter temperatures range from 21°F to 50°F. Extreme temperatures from -12° to 76° have been recorded. Annual precipitation averages 127 inches; yearly snowfall is 58 inches.

CULTURE AND HISTORY

The present population takes its roots from the Alutiiq near Illnik and the old village of Kanatag near Becharof Lake. The community was settled in 1903 with a single family residence. In 1950 a school was built and many people from nearby villages moved to Chignik Lake. Chignik Lake is predominantly an Alutiiq fishing community. The Chignik Lake Traditional Council is a federally recognized tribe in the community

GOVERNMENT

Chignik Lake is not an incorporated municipality but is part of the Lake and Peninsula Borough *(see Alaska introduction)*. Local government functions are carried out by the five-member Chignik Lake Traditional village Council. The president is elected to a three-year term of office, and the vice-president and secretary-treasurer serve two-year terms; the other two members are elected to a one-year term.

VILLAGE CORPORATION

Shareholders in the Chignik River village corporation are also shareholders in Bristol Bay Native Corporation *(see Alaska introduction)*.

ECONOMY

Fishing and subsistence hunting are vital to the village's economy. Success of the salmon-fishing fleet is important to the community. Neighboring Chignik offers some Chignik Lake villagers summer work in commercial fishing or work at the community's fish processors.

Fisheries. Eight residents hold commercial fishing permits.

Government as employer. Approximately 27 residents work for the local, state, or federal government.

Services and retail. Chignik Lake holds nine current business licenses. Businesses include a hardware store, bookkeeping company, welding-repair shop, hotel, and guide services. Retail trade employs 2 people; education, health & social services employs 11 residents; and public administration employs 16 residents.

INFRASTRUCTURE

Seven capital projects, funded by grants, are active in Chignik Lake.

Transportation. Chignik Lake is primarily accessible by air. The state provides a 2,800- by 60-foot gravel airstrip. Seaplanes may land at Chignik Lagoon. Regularly scheduled and charter flights are available. In summer, goods are lightered weekly to Chignik Lake by way of Chignik Lagoon and transported over land; in winter the loads arrive monthly. The state ferry provides service to Chignik Lagoon four times annually. Harbors, docks, barge passages, or boat haul-outs are not available. All-terrain vehicles and skiffs are used for local travel. Building roads to link Chignik, Chignik Lagoon, Chignik Lake, and the city landfill is being studied.

Electricity. Chignik Lake Electric Utility generates power during the summer months; in winter, electricity is purchased from the school district.

Water and waste systems. All 32 homes have treated, piped well water, which is stored in a wood stave tank. Twenty-two households are plumbed, and the school has a well. Fifteen HUD houses are connected to a central sewer system with a waste pump and lagoon. Other homes use individual septic systems. A water and sewer master plan has been funded. A new landfill is open.

Telecommunications. Local telephone service is provided by Pacific Telecommunications, while long distance service is available through Alascom. One television channel is available through the Rural Alaska Television Network and one FM radio station is available. Teleconferencing is available from Alaska Teleconferencing Network.

COMMUNITY FACILITIES AND SERVICES

Area facilities include a council building.

Education. Chignik Lake School is in the Lake & Peninsula School District. The school has 38 students and 4 teachers.

Health care. Health care is provided by Chignik Lake Health Clinic, staffed by two community health aides and administered by the Bristol Bay Area Health Corporation. No x-ray, laboratory, or pharmacy facilities are available. An Indian Health Service doctor and a State of Alaska public health nurse see patients in Chignik Lake twice yearly. A dentist and optometrist visit annually. The closest full-service hospital is located in Kodiak, 250 miles to the northeast.

Total area of entitlement under ANCSA	
	23,040 acres
Total labor force	95
High school graduate or higher	64.1%
Bachelor's degree or higher	7.8%
Unemployment rate	44.8%
Per capita income *(2000)*	$11,612
Population *2000 census*	139
Percent Native *2000 census*	88.5%

LOCATION
Klukwan is located beside the Chilkat River, about 22 miles north of Haines, in Southeast Alaska.

CLIMATE
Klukwan has a maritime climate, characterized by cool summers and mild winters. Average summer temperatures range from 42°F to 66°F; winter temperatures range from 4°F to 31°F. The village receives much less precipitation than is typical for Southeast Alaska.

CULTURE AND HISTORY
Klukwan is a traditional Tlingit village. This Chilkat Indian Village is known for its mountain-goat-hair blankets and woven artwork of cedar bark. The village lies on the Chilkat Pass, a gold-trading route to the interior, which was heavily traveled by prospectors. The area hosts the largest concentration of bald eagles in the world at the Chilkat Bald Eagle Reserve. There is a federally recognized tribe in the community—the Chilkat Indian Village of Klukwan. Fishing, logging, and subsistence activities support the community. Residents subsist on salmon and eulachon from the Chilkat River.

GOVERNMENT
Klukwan is unincorporated under Alaska law and is located in the Unorganized Borough *(see Alaska introduction)*. It is governed by an Indian Reorganization Act Council, headed by a president.

VILLAGE CORPORATION
Shareholders in the village corporation also hold shares in Sealaska Corporation regional Native corporation *(see Alaska introduction)*. Headquartered in Juneau, Kluckwan, Inc., is the ANCSA village corporation for the village of Chilkat. It is a holding company owning an entitlement of 23,000 acres of forested land in Southeast Alaska's rain forest, diversified financial investments, and subsidiary companies operating throughout Alaska and Northwest Washington in heavy civil construction, explosive products and drilling accessories, manufacturing specialty plywood products, mining services, tourism, marine services, and managed timber regeneration. Since 1986, Chilkat has annually made the (Alaska Business Monthly) top 49 list of successful companies.

ECONOMY
Commercial fishing, logging, and subsistence activities support the community. Commercial fishing is the main source of income for Klukwan residents. Logging on village-corporation lands on the island provides seasonal jobs. Subsistence activities provide a major supplement to cash income. Salmon, halibut, shellfish, deer, mountain sheep, bear, and berries are harvested in season. Several residents participate in blanket weaving, jewelry making, and moccasin sewing. A cultural heritage center and museum to attract tourism, featuring Tlingit artifacts and a bald eagle observatory, is part of the community's economic vision.

Construction. Seven residents are employed in construction.

Government as employer. Of the 32 employed residents, 10 work for the local, state, or federal government.

Services and retail. There are no active business licenses in the community. Education, health, and social service professions employ 12 residents; public administration, 6; and financial and related businesses, 3.

INFRASTRUCTURE
Transportation. Klukwan is accessible from the Haines Highway, which is connected to the Alcan Highway through Canada. Residents rely on the scheduled air flights, harbor, dock, barge, ferry, and trucking services of Haines.

Water and waste systems. Water drawn from a groundwater infiltration gallery is stored in a 126,000-gallon tank. Approximately 90 percent of homes are connected to the piped water and sewer system and are fully plumbed. Due to seasonal water shortages and boil-water notices, the village is seeking funding for a new water source and a 200,000-gallon water tank with chlorine treatment. Expansion or relocation of the landfill is being considered. A recycling center is available. Eight capital projects, funded by grants, are active in Klukwan.

Electricity is provided by Tlingit-Haida Regional Electrical Authority.

Telecommunications. In-state phone service is provided by Alaska Telephone Company/AP&T; long distance phone by AT&T Alascom. Internet service is provided by ICE Communications. Alaska Rural Communications Services provides television access. One radio station is on the air. There is no cable provider.

COMMUNITY FACILITIES
Local facilities include the Village Council/ANS Hall and the Chilkat Museum.

Education. Klukwan School is in the Chatham Schools District. The school has 41 students and 3 teachers.

Health care. Local hospitals or health clinics include Klukwan Health Center. Auxiliary health care is provided by Klukwan EMS.

Also known as Klukwan
(preferred spelling over Kluckwan)

[CHILL-cat]
Ethnicity: Tlingit

ANCSA village cooperative
Klukwan, Incorporated
P.O. Box 209
Haines, AK 99827
  907-766-2211
  907-789-3525 Fax
klukwan.com

Chilkoot

[CHILL-koot]
Also known as Haines

Ethnicity: Tlingit

Native entity
Chilkoot Indian Association
P.O. Box 490
Haines, AK 99827-0490
907-766-2323
907-766-2365 Fax

Total area of entitlement under ANCSA	
	not reported
Interim conveyance *(1994)*	892 acres
Total labor force	1,381
High school graduate or higher	87.8%
Bachelor's degree or higher	20%
Unemployment rate	13.6%
Per capita income *(2000)*	$22,505
Population *2000 census*	1,811
Percent Native *2000 census*	18.5%

LOCATION

Haines is located on a narrow peninsula extending into Lynn Canal, between Chilkoot and Chilkat inlets, 65 miles north of Juneau. It lies just south of the border with the Canadian province of British Columbia.

CLIMATE

Haines has a maritime climate characterized by cool summers and mild winters. Average summer temperatures range from 46°F to 66°F; winter temperatures range from 23°F to 36°F.

CULTURE AND HISTORY

The Haines area was called *Dtehshuh*, meaning "end of trail," by the Chilkat Indians. In 1881, S. Young Hall, a Presbyterian minister, received permission from the Chilkat Indians to build the Willard Mission and School. The mission was renamed Haines in 1884 in honor of F. Haines, who chaired the committee that had raised funds for the mission's construction. Four canneries had been constructed in the area by the turn of the century. During the Klondike gold rush, Haines grew as a mining supply center, since the Dalton Trail from Chilkat Inlet to Whitehorse offered an easier route to the Yukon for prospectors. Gold was also discovered in this area in 1899 in the Porcupine District. The first permanent U.S. military installation, Fort William H. Seward, was constructed in Haines in 1904. Historically in Chilkat Indian territory, Haines is now predominantly a non-Native community. The Native population of Haines primarily lives in Chilkoot, a Tlingit village within the city boundary. Haines is home to the world's largest congregation of bald eagles, who feed from the hot-spring-fed rivers. The Chilkat Bald Eagle Reserve is a major attraction in southeast Alaska. The Chilkoot Indian Association of Haines is a federally recognized tribe in the community.

GOVERNMENT

In 1910 Haines was incorporated as a first-class city with a mayor and a city council. The community is located in the Haines Borough *(see Alaska introduction)*. Shareholders in the village corporation also hold shares in the Sealaska regional Native corporation *(see Alaska introduction)*.

ECONOMY

Commercial fishing, timber, government, tourism, and transportation are the primary employers. Seasonal employment also brings in income. Tourism and the visitors Haines draws from its road connection to the state ferry are vital. In 2001, Royal Caribbean Cruise Lines ceased serving Haines as a port of call. More than 45,000 cruise ship passengers visit annually. The Chilkat Bald Eagle Preserve draws visitors from around the world.

Construction. Several construction companies are located in Haines. Other businesses include masonry, carpentry, welding, and excavating. Approximately 92 residents are employed in construction.

Fisheries and forestry. Several lumber companies and a logging company are located in Haines. Approximately 128 area residents hold commercial fishing permits. Farming, fishing, and forestry industries employ 25 residents.

Government as employer. Of the 772 employed residents, 180 work for the local, state, or federal government.

Manufacturing. There are two boat-building and repair business, several woodworking companies, and a textile business. Approximately 19 residents are employed in manufacturing.

Mining. One mine is in operation, employing three residents. Coeur-Alaska has plans to develop the Kensington Mine, providing jobs for Haines residents. Rubicon Minerals Corporation bought a 99-year lease in 1998 on 340 claims in the district. Most of their activity to date has been prospecting. Mining and hunting industries employ 21 residents.

Services and retail. Services are extensive in the Haines area. Approximately 345 businesses are in the community, including travel agencies, real estate agencies, retail stores, geological services, Web design, aquarium and pet supply, stable and saddlery, appliance service, art studios, bakery and café, newspaper publisher, and a brewing company. Retail trade employs 96 residents; wholesale trade 7; education, health, and social services, 125; financial and related businesses, 28; professional, scientific, administrative, and waste management, 52; public administration, 53; and information services employs 20 residents.

Tourism and recreation. At least 21 lodging facilities are available in the Haines area. Lodging facilities include a hotel, four motels, seven bed-and-breakfasts, a camp and international hostel, hitch-up RV park, camper park, and several campgrounds. The Chilkat Bald Eagle Preserve, located 18 miles from Haines, attracts more than 4,000 bald eagles from October to January. Visitor attractions include Sheldon Museum and Cultural Center, Chilkat Center for the Arts, Alaska Indian Arts Center, Chilkat Center of the Performing Arts, Totem Village, Fort W.H. Seward, and a gold rush town created for the movie "White Fang." Other attractions include the local scenery, hiking, camping, fishing, cross-country skiing, snowmobiling, dog sledding, and a golf links and driving range. Haines is known for its strawberries; in 1909, the Alaskan hybrid "Burbank" was a prizewinner in Seattle. The annual strawberry festival developed into the Southeast Alaska State Fair, which attracts thousands of visitors each year. Other events include the Alcan 200 Road Rally, Actfest Theater Festival, Bald Eagle Run, Mayfest, Haines Craft Beer and Home Brew Festival, King Salmon Derby, Annual Alaska Mardi Gras, Kluane to Chilkat Bike Relay, Summer Solstice Celebration, Fourth of July/Independence Day Celebration, Mt. Riley Run, Haines Rodeo, Bald Eagle Music Festival, and the Alaska Bald Eagle Festival. Restaurant fare ranges from sushi to Mexican food. Other services include mountain, nature, fishing, river and lake tours, a day spa, therapeutic massage, outfitters, and craft shops. Arts, entertainment, recreation, accommodation, and food service industries employ 108 residents.

Transportation. Three airline companies, two taxi cab companies, and a water-passenger transportation service operate in the Haines area. Transportation, warehousing, and utility industries employ 54 residents.

INFRASTRUCTURE

Thirty-two capital projects, funded by grants, are active in Haines.

Transportation. Haines is a major trans-shipment point because of its deep-water port and dock. The city has year-round road access to Canada and interior Alaska on the Haines and Alaska Highways. It is a northern terminus of the Alaska Marine Highway (ferry) System, a cruise ship port of call, and a hub for transportation to and from southeast Alaska. The state provides a 4,000- by 100-foot paved runway, with daily scheduled flights to Juneau by small aircraft. A state-owned seaplane base, 2 small-boat harbors with a total of 240 moorage slips, a state ferry terminal, and a cruise ship dock also are available. Freight arrives by ship, barge, plane, and truck.

Electricity. Alaska Power Company provides electricity.

Water and waste systems. Water drawn from Lilly Lake and Piedad Springs is treated and stored in a 500,000-gallon tank. Sewage is collected by a piped system and receives primary treatment before discharge through two ocean outfalls. Almost all households are fully plumbed. A few homes use wells and septic tanks. Haines Sanitation collects refuse and owns the landfill. Recycling and hazardous-waste disposal programs are provided by the city.

Telecommunications. Local telephone service is provided by GTE Alaska, while long distance service is available through Alascom. Internet service is provided by GCI, ICE Communications, and SEAKnet. Teleconferencing is available through Alaska Teleconferencing Network and the Sitka Legislative Information Office. Cable television service is available, and Rural Alaska Television Network provides television access. Two radio stations are available to residents.

COMMUNITY FACILITIES AND SERVICES

Local area facilities include the Borough/Chilkat Center for the Arts, Borough/Sheldon Museum & Cultural Center, Haines Senior Center, senior housing, and both public and school libraries. A landfill is available.

Education. There are three schools in the community under the Borough of Haines. The schools have a combined student enrollment of 319 students with 24 teachers.

Health care. Health-care facilities include Haines Medical Clinic and Haines Public Health Center. The clinic is a qualified emergency care center and is owned and operated by Lynn Canal Medical Corporation. Lynn Canal Human Resources and Counseling Center also is available. Auxiliary health care is provided by Haines Volunteer Fire Department/EMS.

Chilkoot
Also known as Haines

Honoring Nations Honoree 2002

Nation Building Among the Chikoot Tlingit

Excluded by the Alaska Native Claims Settlement Act in 1971, the Chilkoot Tlingit's political presence was reduced to a mailbox and storage room in the basement of a meeting hall in Haines, Alaska. Embracing the concept of self-determination, the Chilkoot Indian Association has been engaged in a process of nation building since 1990. The Tribe is rewriting its constitution, developing institutional capacity, rebuilding a land base, forging government-to-government relationships with surrounding jurisdictions, and improving services for its citizens.

Following the purchase of Alaska by the United States in 1867, the Chilkoot Tlingit slowly became a minority population with limited influence in local and regional affairs. Slightly less than half of the Tribe's 480 citizens live in the Haines, Alaska area where they represent between 10 and 15 percent of the total population. Although the Chilkoot Tlingit were formally recognized under the Indian Reorganization Act (IRA) of 1934, the passage of the Alaska Native Claims Settlement Act of 1971 left them a landless community because the population of the community was predominantly non-Indian. Lacking both a land base and status as an incorporated Native village, assets that other southeast Alaskan Native villages had used to build economic and political strength, the tribal government of the Chilkoot Tlingit—the Chilkoot Indian Association—languished. Although periodic efforts to reinvigorate the Tribe and its culture occurred throughout the 1970s, these efforts foundered. Tension between non-Natives and Natives, or worse, Non-Natives' dismissal of Native issues and needs, did not help. Local schools rebuffed the Tribe's attempts to include any Tlingit culture, language, or history studies in their curricula. Often, the only attention the larger non-Native population paid to the Chilkoot Tlingit involved the use of their songs and dances to attract tourism. With a political organization diminished to the point of solely managing internal ceremonial affairs and a summer fish camp, the Chilkoot Tlingit had become, in many senses, an invisible population.

Frustrated by this powerlessness, in 1990 the Chilkoot Tlingit decided to take matters into their own hands and turn their aspirations for practical sovereignty into reality. Their goal was both simple and profound: they were going to build an Indian nation by developing institutions that would advance the Tribe politically, socially, economically, and culturally. Embracing the ideology of self-determination and inspired by other tribes' success, the Chilkoot Indian Association used $30,000 in revenues from the sale of a tribal building to begin its work. The first task was to reactivate the dormant tribal government and reestablish basic governing institutions.

Rekindling the Chilkoot Indian Association set into motion a process of nation building that has intensified over the past decade. Today, the Chilkoot Indian Association consists of an active six-member tribal council and a president. Council members are elected to two-year, staggered terms and the tribal council appoints a president who serves a one-year term. The president hires staff to develop and manage six governmental departments that oversee tribal accounting, environmental protection, education, real estate, Native American Housing Assistance and Self-Determination Act (NAHASDA) funds, and grants from the Administration for Native Americans (ANA). Additionally, the Chilkoot Indian Association has developed a strategic plan to continue to refine its governmental institutions. With input from clan leaders, elders, and tribal citizens who help ensure the legitimacy and cultural appropriateness of the evolving governing institutions, the Tribe is actively involved in reforming its tribal constitution, governmental structure, codes, policies, and operations.

Having started with a single basement office in the Alaskan Native Brotherhood/Alaskan Native Sisterhood Hall and a pile of unopened mail from the 1970s, the Chilkoot Indian Association is now a revitalized government around which the tribal community has coalesced. Although it started with a deficit of $1,500 in 1989, the Tribe now administers an annual budget

Honoring Nations Honoree 2002

Text in its entirety from: **The Harvard Project On American Indian Economic Development**

John F. Kennedy School of Government Harvard University

Chilkoot

**Honoring Nations
Honoree 2002**

Text in its entirety from:
**The Harvard Project On
American Indian Economic
Development**

**John F. Kennedy School
of Government
Harvard University**

of $750,000, which funds programs in education, health, housing, land, and economic development. Initially a landless political entity, the Chilkoot Indian Association successfully negotiated for the return of 73 acres that the Presbyterian Church had acquired from local clans. Additionally, the Tribe persuaded the Haines borough government to convey 70 acres of sensitive cultural lands, and the Tribe is now utilizing its status as a government to rehabilitate, with the intention of reclaiming, tribal lands expropriated by the Department of Defense. Once a volunteer effort, the tribal government now has a staff of 38 full and part-time employees. Consistent with the Tribe's insistence that it be treated as a sovereign government—and backed up by proven governmental success—the Chilkoot Indian Association has gained recognition from multiple entities including the city, borough, state, and federal governments. The Tribe also regularly partners with these governments on projects that enhance the well being of tribal citizens and the surrounding communities.

The Chilkoot Indian Association's nation-building efforts have led to many successes. Four are illustrative of its effective problem-solving abilities. First, as recently as the late 1990s, the local medical clinic was operating in substandard facilities, reliant on obsolete technology, and on the verge of closing due to financial instability. When clinic doctors approached the Chilkoot Indian Association seeking assistance, the tribal council worked with the Southeast Alaska Regional Health Consortium to bring the clinic under the consortium's operations. By quickly bringing financial stability and improved services to its Native and non-Native client base, the Chilkoot Indian Association ensured its community access to state-of-the-art health care.

Second, the Chilkoot Indian Association brought necessary funding and expertise to the Haines community's solid waste management problem. To achieve this, it partnered with the Central Council of Tlingit and Haida Indians. The Chilkoot's Environmental Protection Agency (EPA) director succeeded in upgrading the community's recycling efforts, installing a transfer station, and bringing together Indian and non-Indian parties to create a process for developing a more effective community-wide solid waste management plan. Although the Chilkoot Tlingit previously had no say in such issues, their efforts not only addressed the problems of solid waste management, but also raised the Tribe's visibility within the community as a government that can get things done.

Third, the Tribe sought its own NAHASDA grant, and through this effort, has been able to improve both the access to and the quality of the stock of housing for its tribal citizens. For example, the Tribe uses NAHASDA funds to assist tribal citizens in undertaking necessary housing renovations and home improvements. It also uses NAHASDA funds to provide housing assistance grants for its college students, wherever they pursue their post-secondary education. That the Tribe itself administers these funds is significant: Up until the 1990s, all Native programs were administered outside the community and the limited services and programs that were available were often inaccessible, slow to be provided, or did not meet local needs.

Finally, through a Memorandum of Understanding with the US Army, the Chilkoot Indian Association is partnering with the Bethel Native Corporation to demolish an inactive tank farm located on ancestral tribal lands. The Tribe received funding to undertake contamination testing and has to date removed four buildings containing significant hazardous waste. Not only has this effort created eight employment opportunities for tribal citizens, but it also has allowed the Tribe to consider development options that would follow the completion of demolition and remediation (if it is able to get the land deeded back to the Tribe).

Significantly, the rebuilding of the Chilkoot Tlingit's political presence has resulted in a cultural resurgence. For decades, ceremonies were infrequent, ancient traditions were being forgotten, and cultural pride was waning. Yet the process of nation building, through its focus on empowerment and self-determination, has reversed these trends. Tribal citizens are now proud to identify themselves as the area's aboriginal people and have reinstated their historic relationship with the land, the sea, and the larger Tlingit community. This pride has practical consequences. For example, the Chilkoot Indian Association is working with the local school system to institute Tlingit history, culture, and language into its curriculum. The greatest measure of the Tribe's success at reinstilling cultural values and of the recognition and respect now afforded Tlingit Indians came during the 2000 high school graduation, when the entire audience, Native and non-Native alike, stood and sang a Chilkoot song that has been adopted as the Tlingit's national anthem. In short, the Chilkoot Indian Association recognizes that political development can and should coincide with cultural investment.

The Chilkoot Indian Association has solidified its status as a tribe—a status that it has earned by building capable institutions of self-governance and by becoming known as a government that can get things done. The Tribe has leveraged its limited financial resources through collaborative efforts and partnerships with local schools, the library, health clinic, utilities, and the US Army to provide services to its tribal citizens. Additionally, the Tribe works collaboratively with the regional Native corporation and surrounding Native villages, village corporations, and First Nations of Canada. The Chilkoot Indian Association also participates in the National Congress of American Indians, the Alaska Intertribal Conference, and the Alaska Federation of Natives. The Tribe's president was appointed a seat on the State Tribal Relations Committee that drafted the Alaska State Millennium Agreement in which the State of Alaska officially recognized the continued existence of sovereign tribal governments within its borders. Indeed, the Chilkoot Tlingit have demonstrated the effectiveness of building such relationships—they have mutual benefits and can produce results that a small tribe cannot achieve alone.

Whether taking control of programs that have long been administered outside the community, acquiring a land base, engaging in government-to-government relationships, or working with citizens to create a vision for the Tribe that is dramatically different than that held in the past, the Chilkoot Indian Association is exercising its sovereignty in exciting and important ways. Further, the Chilkoot Tlingit prove that assertions of sovereignty, supported by capable institutions of government, assist in successful tribal nation-building. This is a tribe that is not only here to stay, but will continue to grow stronger long into the future.

Lessons
Indian nations' social, economic, and political goals are nearly impossible to pursue in the absence of core institutions of self-government. Effective self-governance often requires tribes to build or reform tribal institutions—constitutions, political structures, policies, and procedures—so that they can make full use of natural, human, and financial resources.

Leveraging partnerships with other governments and organizations may be especially important for small and/or rural tribes. Such partnerships allow tribes to access funding and expertise that might not otherwise be available to them.

The only way for Indian nations to gain non-Indian citizens' and governments' respect is to earn it. Tribes that are able to solve compelling problems and administer programs and services well are more likely to cultivate widespread support for their nation-building efforts.

Total area of entitlement under ANCSA	
	99,860 acres
Total labor force	84
High school graduate or higher	80.3%
Bachelor's degree or higher	18.3%
Unemployment rate	3.5%
Per capita income *(2000)*	$13,281
Population *2000 census*	144
Percent Native *2000 census*	92.4%

LOCATION
Golovin is located on a point of land by Golovin Bay on the Seward Peninsula, 70 miles east of Nome.

CLIMATE
Marine climatic influences prevail during the summer, when the sea is ice free. Summer temperatures range from 40°F to 60°F; winter temperatures range from -21°F to 19°F. Average annual precipitation is 10 inches, including 38 inches of snowfall.

CULTURE AND HISTORY
Golovin was named for a captain of the Russian Navy. The Eskimo village of Chinik, located at the present site of Golovin, was originally settled by the Kauweramiut Eskimos who later mixed with the Unaligmiut Eskimos. After gold was discovered at Council, Golovin became a supply point for the Council goldfields. In 1887 the Mission Covenant of Sweden established a church and school at the site. Reindeer herding was an integral part of the missions in the area in the early twentieth century. Golovin is an Inupiat Eskimo village with a fishing, herding, and subsistence lifestyle. The Chinik Eskimo Community is a federally recognized tribe in the community

GOVERNMENT
Golovin was incorporated as a second-class city under Alaska law in 1971, with a city council and a mayor. The community is located in the Unorganized Borough *(see Alaska introduction)*. There is also a traditional village council headed by a president; the village in this context is referred to as Chinik. Shareholders in the village corporation also hold shares in the Bering Straits regional Native corporation *(see Alaska introduction)*.

ECONOMY
Golovin's economy is based on subsistence activities, reindeer herding, fish processing, and commercial fishing. Fish, beluga whale, moose, and reindeer are the main subsistence species utilized.

Construction. Four residents are employed in construction.

Fisheries. Fourteen residents hold commercial fishing permits, mostly in beluga and whale.

Government as employer. Of the 55 employed residents, 37 work for the local, state, or federal government.

Services and retail. Nine businesses are in the community, including the Golovin Native Corporation, a utility company, cable television, and the City of Golovin. The village corporation operates a lumber and building-materials business. Retail trade employs 9 residents; education, health, and social services, 22; public administration, 9 professional, and scientific, administrative, and waste management employs 2 residents.

Tourism and recreation. Visitor attractions include the Nome-Golovin Snowmachine Race, which is held in March. Lodging consists of one business that rents rooms.

Transportation. Four airline companies service Golovin. Transportation, warehousing, and utility industries employ six residents.

INFRASTRUCTURE
Twenty-seven capital projects, funded by grants, are active in Golovin.

Transportation. There are no roads outside the city so Golovin is limited to air and sea access. Scheduled and chartered flights are available from Nome. The airport was recently relocated, and a new state-owned airport with a 4,000- by 75-foot gravel runway is available. There is no dock; supplies are lightered from Nome and off-loaded on the beach. A cargo ship brings supplies once a year to Nome. A feasibility study for a small-boat harbor has been requested by the city.

Electricity. Golovin Power Utilities provides electricity.

Water and waste systems. Development of a community-wide piped water and sewer system is in progress. Water pumped from Chinik Creek is treated and stored in three large tanks. Approximately half of households are plumbed. Twenty-eight homes currently have water delivered by truck, 27 haul their own water, and 13 collect rain water during the summer. Ten households with septic tanks have drainfield failures. Funds are available for a new 1.2-million-gallon water tank and washeteria.

Telecommunications. Local telephone service is provided by Mukluk Telephone Company, while long distance and Internet services are available through Alascom. Internet service is also provided by GCI and Mukluk Telephone. Teleconferencing is available through Alaska Teleconferencing Network. Golovin Native Corporation provides cable television service, and Rural Alaska Television Network provides television access. Two radio stations are available to residents.

COMMUNITY FACILITIES AND SERVICES
Local facilities include a community hall. Twenty-five households use honeybuckets and 21 homes use pit privies. A new landfill is under construction.

Education. There is one school in the community, under the Bering Strait School District, with 50 students and 6 teachers.

Health care. Health care is provided by the Golovin Health Clinic, owned by the city and leased to the U.S. Public Health Service. The clinic is administered by the Norton Sound Health Corporation.

Also known as Golovin

[GOLL-uh-vin]
Ethnicity: Inupiat Eskimo

Native entity
Golovin Native Corporation
P.O. Box 62099
Golovin, AK 99762
  907-779-3251
  907-779-3261 Fax

Chistochina
See Cheesh-Na

[CHIT-nuh or CHIH-tee-nuh]
Ethnicity; Ahtna Athabascan

ANCSA village corporation
Chitina Native Corporation
P.O. Box 3
Chitina, AK 99566
907-823-2223

Total area of entitlement under ANCSA
	115,200 acres
Total labor force	104
High school graduate or higher	85.7%
Bachelor's degree or higher	11.4%
Unemployment rate	32.7%
Per capita income *(2000)*	$10,835
Population *2000 census*	106
Percent Native *2000 census*	55.7%

LOCATION
Chitina is located on the west bank of the Copper River at its confluence with the Chitina River, at mile 34 of the Edgerton Highway, 53 miles southeast of Copper Center. It lies outside the western boundary of the Wrangell-St. Elias National Park and Preserve, 66 miles southeast of Glennallen. Chitina is located in the Chitina Recording District.

PHYSICAL DESCRIPTION
The area encompasses 84.6 square miles of land and 11.1 square miles of water.

CLIMATE
The climate in Chitina is continental, with typical long, cold winters and warm summers. Yearly snowfall averages 52 inches, with annual precipitation of 12 inches. Temperature extremes have been recorded from -58°F to 91°F.

CULTURE AND HISTORY
Athabascan Indians have evidently occupied this region for the last 5,000 to 7,000 years. Chitina was historically a large Native village whose population was slowly decimated by the influx of outside people, disease, and conflicts. Rich copper deposits were discovered at the turn of the century along the northern flanks of the Chitina River Valley, bringing a rush of prospectors and homesteaders to the area. The Copper River and Northwestern Railway enabled Chitina to develop into a thriving community by 1914. It had a general store, clothing store, meat market, stables, a tinsmith, five hotels, rooming houses, a pool hall, bars, restaurants, dance halls, and a movie theater. Almost all of Chitina was owned by Otto Adrian Nelson, a surveying engineer for the Kennecott Mines. He supplied electric power to all structures with a unique hydroelectric system. After the mines closed in 1938, Chitina became a ghost town, with only the Natives and a few non-Natives staying on. In 1963 the Nelson estate was purchased by "Mudhole" Smith, a pioneer bush pilot, who sold off the townsite and buildings. Currently the community has a mixed population of Ahtna Indians and non-Natives. Most residents are involved in subsistence activities year-round. During the summer, subsistence dip-netting for salmon on the Copper River attracts a large number of Alaskans from Anchorage and other areas of the state. The Chitina Traditional Indian Village is a federally recognized tribe in the community.

GOVERNMENT
Chitina is unincorporated and is part of the Unorganized Borough *(see Alaska introduction)*. The native residents of Chitina are governed by a traditional village council headed by a president.

VILLAGE CORPORATION
Chitina Native Corporation operates guided fishing trips, cabins, and a bed-and-breakfast. It is working to develop a full service RV park near the Chitina airport. Chitina Electric Company is working with the Alaska Energy Authority to research the possibility of repairing the existing hydroelectric power plant. Although Chitina Native Corporation chose not to join the other seven village corporations in merging with the Ahtna, Inc. regional Native corporation in 1980, Ahtna possesses the subsurface estate of Chitina Native Corporation lands. This split level estate requires Ahtna to obtain permission from Chitina Native Corporation before developing any subsurface resource on Chitina lands. Shareholders in the village corporation also hold shares in Ahtna, Inc. regional Native corporation *(see Alaska introduction)*.

ECONOMY
The village council, the village corporation, and the National Park Service are the primary sources of employment. Many villagers are self-employed or work in retail establishments. Fishermen, tourists, and campers provide summer cash income in fish guiding and other services. Many villagers participate in year-round subsistence activities.

Construction. Five residents are employed in construction.

Fisheries. Two residents hold commercial salmon fishing permits.

Government as employer. Of the 39 employed residents, 11 work for the local, state, or federal government.

Services and retail. Chitina holds 31 current business licenses. Businesses include a gift shop, café, trading post, photography, outfitters, and technical services. Retail trade employs 10 residents; public administration employs 8 residents; and education, health and social services employs 3 residents.

Tourism and recreation. There is a fishing camp in the village, as well as several other guide services. There are also several restaurants and a stable that offers horseback riding. Other attractions include Wrangell-St. Elias National Park Service Ranger Station, hiking, fishing, rafting, swimming, mountain biking, berry picking, and hunting. Winter activities include cross-country skiing, skijoring, ice fishing, dog mushing, and viewing the northern lights. Lodging includes several cabins and a motel.

INFRASTRUCTURE
Sixteen capital projects, funded by grants, are active in Chitina.

Transportation. The Edgerton Highway and Richardson Highway link Chitina with the rest of the state road system. The state owns Chitina Airport, with a 2,850- by 75-foot gravel airstrip, five miles north of the village along the Edgerton Highway. One airline service provides seasonal service. A shuttle bus is also available.

Electricity. Chitina Electric provides electricity.

Water and waste systems. Villagers tow water from a well at the fire hall or have individual wells. Some residents use stream water in the summer. Outhouses and individual septic systems provide sewage disposal. Less than 20 percent of homes are completely plumbed. Copper Basin Sanitation offers refuse collection. A piped water and sewer system is part of a feasibility study. The community needs a refuse transfer facility and has partial funding to buy an incinerator. The area serves a heavy influx of summer tourists. The Department of Transportation is building a visitor wayside with parking and an RV dump station.

Telecommunications. Local telephone service is provided by the Copper Valley Telephone Co-op; long distance service is available through Alascom. Cable television service is available, as is one channel through the Rural Alaska Television Network. Teleconferencing is available through the Glennallen legislative information office.

COMMUNITY FACILITIES AND SERVICES
Facilities include a community hall. A youth center, museum, and library are under construction.

Education. There are no state-operated schools located in Chitina.

Health care. Health care is provided by the Chitina Health Clinic, owned by the village and leased to the U.S. Public Health Service. The clinic is administered by the Copper River Native Association. Health facilities also include Copper Center Clinic and Cross Road Medical Center in Glennallen. Copper River EMS Council, Copper Center Clinic, and Cross Road Medical Center in Glennallen provide auxiliary health care.

Chuathbaluk

Total area of entitlement under ANCSA
                                  92,160 acres
Total labor force   90
High school graduate or higher   88.6%
Bachelor's degree or higher   12.9%
Unemployment rate   5.4%
Per capita income *(2000)* $10,100
Population *2000 census*   119
Percent Native *2000 census*   94.1%

LOCATION
Chuathbaluk is located on the north bank of the Kuskokwim River, 11 miles upriver from Aniak in the Kilbuk-Kuskokwim Mountains. It is 87 air miles northeast of Bethel and 310 miles west of Anchorage. Chuathbaluk is located in the Kuskokwim Recording District.

PHYSICAL DESCRIPTION
The area encompasses 3.5 square miles of land and 1.8 square miles of water.

CLIMATE
A continental climate prevails in Chuathbaluk. Yearly snowfall averages 85 inches, with an annual precipitation of 17 inches. Temperatures range from -55°F to 87°F. Heavy winds can cause flight delays in the fall.

CULTURE AND HISTORY
The population of Chuathbaluk is made up mostly of Yup'ik Eskimos, but with some Ingalik (Athabascan) Indians as well. In the early and mid-1800s, Ingalik Indians resided in summer camps at the site of what is now Chuathbaluk. By 1833 natives had established a settlement in the area, which came to be known variously as Chukbak, Saint Sergius Mission, Kuskokwim Russian Mission, and Little Russian Mission. The village's present name derives from the Yup'ik Eskimo word "curapalek," meaning "hills where the big blueberries grow." The area's rich natural resources and abundant wildlife were mainstays for the local Native population and for Russian and American fur traders and merchants. In the mid-1800s to early 1900s, Russian and American settlers occupied a site 10 miles east of the village. This site, known as the Kolmakov Redoubt, was included in the National Register of Historic Places in 1972. The Russian Orthodox Church established a missionary presence in the community in 1891.

By 1894 Saint Sergius Mission had been constructed, and residents of Kukuktuk, 20 miles downriver, moved to the site.

Much of the village population was lost to an influenza epidemic in 1900, and by 1929 the site was deserted, although Russian Orthodox Church members from surrounding areas continued to hold services at the mission. In 1954 the Sam Phillips family from Crow Village resettled at the abandoned mission site, joined later by others from nearby communities. The church was rebuilt in the late 1950s, and a state school opened in the 1960s. The Chuathbaluk Traditional Council is a federally recognized tribe in the community.

GOVERNMENT
Chuathbaluk was incorporated as a second-class city in 1975. It is governed by a seven-member city council, from which the mayor is elected. A city manager, who reports directly to the council, manages day-to-day operations. Municipal powers govern the community's streets and sidewalks, police protection, and community centers and extend to the city-owned landfill, fuel, heavy equipment rental, and laundromat operations. An advisory school board has been formed. Chuathbaluk's Native population is represented by a seven-member traditional council and by the Kuskokwim Native Association, which receives direction from the council. As the official tribal governing body of the village, the traditional council is eligible to administer various federal programs and grants. The council has sponsored training programs on land administration and tribal governmental skills. It is currently involved in economic development efforts (tourism, crafts, roads), social development, and suicide-prevention programs.

VILLAGE CORPORATION
The Kuskokwim Corporation was formed in 1977 when 10 ANCSA village corporations located along the middle region of the Kuskokwim River merged. The villages were Lower Kalskag, Upper Kalskag, Aniak, Chauthbaluk, Napaimute, Crooked Creek, Red Devil, Georgetown, Sleetmute, and Stony River. The corporation invests in stocks, bonds, and real estate. It also owns interests in operating businesses, including a telecommunications bandwidth and service provider. In addition, the corporation has entered a surface lease agreement for the development of one of the largest undeveloped gold resources in the world, Donlin Creek, located on land to which Kuskokwim has retained the rights. The corporation's subsidiaries include an SBA certified 8(a) small business that provides engineering, remediation, and construction services throughout Alaska and the lower 48 states. Shareholders in the merged village corporation are also shareholders in Calista Corporation regional Native corporation *(see Alaska introduction)*.

**[CHUATH-bah-luck]
formerly Russian Mission**

**Ethnicity: Yup'ik Eskimo,
Ingalik Athabascan**

ANCSA village corporation
Kuskokwim Corporation
4300 B Street, Suite 207
Anchorage, AK 99503
    907-276-2101
    800-478-2171
    kuskokwim.com

Chuathbaluk

ECONOMY

Most residents in Chuathbaluk make their living from subsistence hunting, fishing, and gathering activities. During the summer, residents fish for king, silver, and chum salmon, trout, dolly varden, pike, grayling, and char. Commonly hunted animals are waterfowl, rabbit, porcupine, moose, and black bear. Blueberries, salmon berries, blackberries, currants, raspberries, and cranberries are harvested in the summer and fall. Summer seasonal employment includes firefighting for the Bureau of Land Management, work at the sawmill, and commercial fishing. Some year-round employment is provided by public services, including the health clinic, city and tribal governments, the school district, and the post office. Artisans produce handicrafts such as beadwork, fur garments, mukluks (fur boots), parkas, and ulus (Eskimo women's knives). Residents have been instrumental in the establishment of the Interior Rivers Arts and Crafts Cooperative in Aniak. The community has also sponsored the establishment of a sports-fishing service.

Fisheries. One resident holds a commercial salmon fishing permit.

Government as employer. Of the 53 employed residents, 32 work for the local, state, or federal government.

Services and retail. Chuathbaluk enterprises hold seven current business licenses. Businesses include a gas station, a boat builder, a trading post, and grocery stores. Retail trade employs 3 residents; education, health and social services employ 20 residents; and public administration employs 7.

Transportation. Three airline services are available in Chuathbaluk. Approximately 13 residents are employed in transportation, warehousing, or utility industries.

INFRASTRUCTURE

Fourteen capital projects, funded by grants, are active in Chuathbuluk.

Transportation. The Kuskokwim River serves as the major carrier for supply barges from Aniak and Bethel, skiffs, and floatplanes. A 1,560- by 45-foot state-owned gravel airstrip is just north of the village, with scheduled air service. In winter, ski planes land on the frozen river and vehicles are driven on the ice road to nearby communities.

Electricity. The Middle Kuskokwim Electric Co-op provides power from Chuathbaluk to Stony River.

Water and waste systems. Water is pumped from a 105-foot well into a storage tank, then treated and hauled from this point by residents. A washeteria is open. The school has its own watering point, and some residences have individual wells. Full plumbing is not available. Honeybuckets and privies are used by most residents for waste disposal; some households have septic tanks. The school and clinic and many residences have a septic tank/leachfield system. Clay and silt have damaged the septic systems. A water and sewer master plan has been completed. Repairs to the pump house, water treatment, washeteria, school sewage lagoon, and other components are in progress after funding. Refuse is collected regularly.

Telecommunications. Local telephone service is provided by United Utilities, while long distance service is available through Alascom. Cable television service is available, as well as one channel through the Rural Alaska Television Network.

COMMUNITY FACILITIES

Education. Crow Village Sam School in Chuathbaluk belongs to the Kuspuk School District. The school has 37 students and four teachers.

Health care. Health care is provided by the Chuathbaluk Health Clinic, owned by the city and leased to the U.S. Public Health Service. It is administered by the Yukon Kuskokwim Health Corporation. The nearest hospital is located in Bethel. Clara Morgan Subregional Clinic also is available.

Chuloonawick

See Zero AIAN Population

ircle

Ethnicity: Kutchin *Gwich'in* Athabascan

ANCSA village corporation
Danzhit Hanlaii Corporation
General Delivery
Circle, AK 99733
907-773-1280

Total area of entitlement under ANCSA	115,982 acres
Total labor force	50
High school graduate or higher	52.5%
Bachelor's degree or higher	-
Unemployment rate	24%
Per capita income *(2000)*	$6,426
Population *2000 census*	100
Percent Native *2000 census*	85%

LOCATION

Circle is located on the south bank of the Yukon River at the edge of the Yukon Flats, 160 miles northeast of Fairbanks. It is at the eastern end of the Steese Highway. Circle is located in the Fairbanks Recording District.

PHYSICAL DESCRIPTION

The area encompasses 107.7 square miles of land and 0.5 square mile of water.

CLIMATE

Circle has a continental subarctic climate, with typical seasonal extremes in temperature. Winters are long and harsh, summers warm and brief. Summer temperatures range from 65°F to 72°F; winter temperatures vary from -71°F to 0°F. Annual rainfall averages 6.5 inches; yearly snowfall is 43.4 inches.

CULTURE AND HISTORY

Circle was a supply point for goods shipped up the Yukon River and then overland to the mining camps. The present population of Circle is predominantly Kutchin Athabascans, who practice a subsistence lifestyle. Circle Native Community is a federally recognized tribe in the community.

GOVERNMENT

Circle is unincorporated and is located in the Unorganized Borough *(see Alaska introduction)*. It is governed by a village council headed by a chief and organized under the Indian Reorganization Act of 1934.

VILLAGE CORPORATION

Shareholders in the Danzhit Hanlaii village corporation are also shareholders of Doyon, Limited, regional Native corporation *(see Alaska introduction)*.

ECONOMY

Government-related employers are the primary sources of employment. Almost all residents are involved in subsistence. Salmon, freshwater fish, moose, and bear are the major sources of meat. Income also is supplemented by trapping and handicrafts.

Fisheries. Two residents hold commercial fishing permits for salmon, freshwater fish.

Government as employer. Of the 19 employed residents, 17 work for the local, state, or federal government.

Services and retail. Businesses include telecommunications, utilities, and grocery stores.

Tourism and recreation. Recreation attracts visitors to Circle seasonally. Circle Hot Springs was closed in October 2002. Some persons live in the community only during summer months. A 25-room hotel is under construction.

INFRASTRUCTURE
Sixteen capital projects, funded by grants, are active in Circle. A feasibility study and master plan is underway to examine infrastructure alternatives.

Transportation. The Steese Highway provides passage from Circle to Fairbanks. Barges deliver goods by the Yukon River in summer. All-terrain vehicles, snowmobiles, and dog sleds are used for recreation and subsistence activities. A new state-owned 3,000- by 60-foot, lighted gravel airstrip is open. Floatplanes land on the river.

Electricity. Circle Electric Inc. provides electricity.

Water and waste systems. Villagers haul treated well water from the washeteria/fire station or the school. Outhouses and honeybuckets are used for sewage disposal. Plumbing facilities are not available. The landfill is open.

Telecommunications. Local telephone service is provided by Circle Telephone, while long distance service is available through Alascom. One channel of television is offered by the Rural Alaska Television Network. Three radio stations are available to residents. Internet service is provided for the school only. Teleconferencing is available through the Alaska Teleconferencing Network.

COMMUNITY FACILITIES AND SERVICES
Area features include a community center, museum, and library.

Education. Circle School is in the Yukon Flats School District. The school has 24 students and 3 teachers.

Health care. The Circle Health Clinic, owned by the village and leased to the U.S. Public Health Service, is administered by the Tanana Chiefs Conference. Available hospitals or health clinics also include Fairbanks hospitals. Central Rescue Squad offers auxiliary health care.

Clark's Point

Total area of entitlement under ANCSA
110,948 acres

Total labor force	59
High school graduate or higher	76.5%
Bachelor's degree or higher	3.9%
Unemployment rate	10.7%
Per capita income *(2000)*	$10,989
Population *2000 census*	75
Percent Native *2000 census*	92%

LOCATION
Clark's Point is located on a spit on the northeastern shore of Nushagak Bay, 15 miles from Dillingham and 337 miles southwest of Anchorage. Clark's Point is located in the Bristol Bay Recording District.

PHYSICAL DESCRIPTION
The area encompasses 3.1 square miles of land and 0.9 square mile of water.

CLIMATE
Clark's Point is located in a climatic transition zone. The primary influence is maritime, although the Arctic climate also impacts the region. Summer temperatures range from 37°F to 66°F; winter temperatures vary from 4°F to 30°F. Yearly precipitation is 20 to 26 inches, including annual snowfall of 82 inches. Fog and low clouds are common during winter months.

CULTURE AND HISTORY
Clark's Point was settled in the late 1800s, when a salmon saltery was established there by John W. Clark. The point originally had an Eskimo name, "Saguyak," but there is no evidence of a settlement at the site prior to the establishment of the saltery. The community was founded on the fishing operations of white settlers, although presently its population is predominantly Eskimo and Aleut.

GOVERNMENT
Clark's Point was incorporated as a second-class city in 1971 and is located in the Unorganized Borough *(see Alaska introduction)*. It has a seven-member city council that meets every other month. The mayor is elected by and from the membership of the city council to a one-year term.

VILLAGE CORPORATION
Clark's Point Village Council is a federally recognized tribe in the community. Shareholders in the village corporation are also shareholders in Bristol Bay Native Corporation *(see Alaska introduction)*.

ECONOMY
Commercial fishing fuels the economy in Clark's Point. Trident Seafoods operates an onshore facility. All residents depend on subsistence to some extent and commute if necessary. Salmon, smelt, moose, bear, rabbit, ptarmigan, duck, and goose are harvested. Exchange relationships exist with other nearby communities.

Fisheries. Sixteen residents hold commercial salmon fishing permits.

Government as employer. Of the 25 employed residents, 14 work for the local, state, or federal government.

Manufacturing. Five residents are employed in manufacturing.

Services and retail. Clark's Point has no active businesses. Education, health and social services industries employ seven residents; transportation, warehousing and utilities two; and public administration employs eight residents.

Transportation. Two airlines provide service to Clark's Point.

Ethnicity: Yup'ik Eskimo, Alutiiq Aleut

ANCSA village corporation
Saguyak Incorporated
P.O. Box 4
Clark's Point, AK 99569
907-236-1244

Clark's Point

Copper Center
See Kluti Kaah

Cordova
See Eyak

Council
See Zero AIAN Population

INFRASTRUCTURE
Seven capital projects, funded by grants, are active in Clark's Point.

Transportation. Air transport is the primary passage into Clark's Point. Dillingham offers regular and charter flights. There is a state-owned 2,600- by 70-foot gravel runway, and floatplanes land on Nushagak River. Freight is brought by barge to Dillingham and then flown or lightered to the community. The only boat moorage is an undeveloped spit dock owned by the city; boats land on the beach. Trident Seafoods owns a private dock for fish processing. All-terrain vehicles and snowmachines are used for local travel.

Electricity. Trident Seafoods supplies its own power, and the school has back-up generators. The City of Clark's Point provides electricity.

Water and waste systems. Spring-fed wells provide water to the village. The water is treated with chlorine and fluoride. Nearly 80 percent of households are connected to the piped water system; the remainder use individual wells. A piped gravity sewage system is available to 40 percent of homes and the school. Residents below the bluff rely on septic tanks or pit privies. More than 20 residences have piped water and sewer. The clinic and city offices use honeybuckets.

Telecommunications. Local telephone service is provided by the Nushagak Telephone Co-op, while long distance service is available through Alascom. Cable television service is available, as well as one channel through the Rural Alaska Television Network and two radio stations. Internet service is available.

COMMUNITY FACILITIES AND SERVICES
Education. Clarks Point School is in the Southwest Region School District. The school has 17 students and 2 teachers.

Health care. Health care is provided by the Clark's Point Health Clinic. It is administered by the Bristol Bay Area Health Corporation. Auxiliary health care is provided by Clark's Point First Responders.

Craig

Ethnicity: Tlingit, Haida

ANCSA village corporation
Shaan Seet Inc.
P.O. Box 690
Craig, AK 99921
907-826-3251
shaanseet.com

Total area of entitlement under ANCSA	
	23,040 acres
Total labor force	1,023
High school graduate or higher	89%
Bachelor's degree or higher	17.4%
Unemployment rate	9%
Per capita income *(2000)*	$20,176
Population *2000 census*	1,397
Percent Native *2000 census*	36%

LOCATION
Craig is located on a small island off the west coast of Prince of Wales Island and is connected by a short causeway. It is 31 road miles west of Hollis. It lies 56 air miles northwest of Ketchikan, 750 air miles north of Seattle, and 220 miles south of Juneau. Craig is located in the Ketchikan Recording District.

PHYSICAL DESCRIPTION
The area encompasses 6.7 square miles of land and 2.7 square miles of water.

CLIMATE
Prince of Wales Island is dominated by a cool, moist, maritime climate. Summer temperatures range from 49°F to 63°F; winter temperatures range from 32°F to 42°F. Yearly precipitation is 120 inches, with annual snowfall of 40 inches. Gales are common in fall and winter.

CULTURE AND HISTORY
Historically, the Tlingit and Haida Indians have utilized the area around Craig for its rich resources. A salmon saltery and cold-storage plant were built in 1911; a cannery was built in the area in 1912. A sawmill, school, post office, and a number of years of excellent pink-salmon runs contributed to the growth of the community through the late 1930s. In 1972 a large sawmill was built six miles from Craig, near Klawock, which provided year-round jobs and helped to stabilize the economy. Today Craig is primarily a non-Native fishing community with influences from its Tlingit-Haida culture and history. The Craig Community Association is a federally recognized tribe in the community.

GOVERNMENT
Craig is a first-class city, incorporated in 1922, with a mayor and city council, and is located in the Unorganized Borough (*see Alaska introduction*). It also has a traditional village council, organized under the Indian Reorganization Act of 1934 and headed by a president.

VILLAGE CORPORATION
Shaan-Seet, Inc. (SSI), incorporated in 1973, is located in Craig, within the territory of Sealaska Corporation, which owns the subsurface rights to SSI lands. The primary business of Shaan-Seet are timber and timber-related operations including contract logging, heavy equipment operations, leasing and heavy construction, lodging and charter fishing operations, and commercial and residential property management. In 1980 Congress enacted the Alaska National Interest Lands Conservation Act (ANILCA) as an amendment to ANCSA. One section of ANILCA authorized village corporations to distribute lands to their shareholders for home sites. The first village corporation to attempt the home site lottery, SSI distributed 317 lots to the original Shaan-Seet shareholders in 1984. The Margaret Hamilton Demmert Scholarship Fund, established in 1984, has funded many shareholders in vocational and college-accredited courses. There are currently 532 shareholders of Shaan-Seet, Inc. Shaan-Seet shareholders also hold shares in Sealaska regional Native corporation (*see Alaska introduction*).

ECONOMY
The fishing industry, logging support, and sawmill operations fuel the economy. A fish-buying station and a cold-storage plant are in the community. Craig has grown as a service and transportation center for the Prince of Wales Island communities. Shan-Seet Village Corporation Timber Operations, the Viking Lumber Company, government, and commercial services also are big sources of employment. Deer, salmon, halibut, shrimp, and crab are harvested for recreational or subsistence purposes.

Construction. There are three construction businesses in Craig in addition to a welding, fabrication business and a bobcat service. Fifty-seven residents are employed in construction.

Fisheries and forestry. Two-hundred residents hold commercial fishing permits for salmon, halibut, shrimp, and crab. A fish-buying station and a cold-storage plant are located in Craig, as well as logging support. Approximately 121 residents are employed in farming, fishing, or forestry industries.

Government as employer. Of the 719 employed residents, 166 work for the local, state, or federal government.

Manufacturing. There are a sawmill and a wood-products plant in the city as well as a boat repair business. There is also a pottery manufacturing company. Approximately 34 residents are employed in manufacturing.

Services and retail. Services are extensive in Craig, catering not only to residents but also to customers in numerous surrounding villages. There are several child-care services, two schools of music, and stores selling everything from electrical appliances to general merchandise to sporting goods. There are also numerous repair services in Craig for everything from household goods to boats and automobiles. Retail trade employs 90 residents; wholesale trade another 18; financial and related businesses 11; public administration 37; and education, health, and social services 127.

Tourism and recreation. There are several restaurants, a video store, café, and bookstore. Eight businesses provide lodging for visitors, which include two RV parks and one bed-and-breakfast. Sea tours, sportfishing, coastal adventures, and more than nine charter services are available in Craig. Visitor attractions include the village totem pole, fishing, diving, and hiking. Cultural events include a fishing derby, Christmas bazaar, and various entertainment events. Arts, entertainment, recreation, accommodation, and food service industries collectively employ 65 residents.

Transportation. There are three taxi companies, three car rental companies, and a trucking service company. Four airline companies provide service to Craig. Transportation, warehousing, and utility industries employ 41 residents.

INFRASTRUCTURE
Nineteen capital projects, funded by grants, are active in Craig.

Transportation. Nearby Klawock Airport offers scheduled air transportation to Ketchikan. Craig maintains a state-owned seaplane base at Klawock Inlet and a U.S. Coast Guard heliport. The state ferry serves Hollis and transports passengers,

cargo, and vehicles to the island. There are two small-boat harbors at North Cove and South Cove. A small transient float and dock are in the downtown area, and a boat launch ramp is at North Cove. The J.T. Brown Marine Industrial Center is in progress on False Island on the north side of Crab Bay. The facility will include a dock and boat launch. Freight arrives by cargo plane, barge, and ferry in Hollis. A paved road links Hollis, Craig, Klawock, and the airport.

Electricity. Alaska Power and Telephone Co., based in Skagway, owns and operates diesel power systems in Hydaburg and Craig and a hydroelectric facility at Black Bear Lake, which provides electricity to many Island communities. Alaska Power Company provides electricity.

Water and waste systems. All residences are fully plumbed. Water, supplied by a dam on North Fork Lake, is treated and stored in a tank before being piped to homes. A new water tank is needed. Sewage is collected by a piped gravity system and receives primary treatment before discharge into Bucareli Bay. Refuse is dumped at the Klawock landfill. The city also participates in annual hazardous-waste collection events. A new regional landfill is needed.

Telecommunications. Local telephone service is provided by National Utilities, while long distance service is available through Alascom. Craig Cable TV, Inc. provides cable television service, and one channel is offered by the Rural Alaska Television Network. Three radio stations as well as Internet service and teleconferencing are available to residents.

COMMUNITY FACILITIES
Facilities include a youth center, city hall, city swimming pool, and both school and public libraries.

Education. There are four schools in the community under Craig City Schools. Their combined number of students is 860, with 35 teachers.

Health care. Health resources include Seaview Medical Center, Craig Health Center, and a public health nurse. The clinic is a qualified Emergency Care Center. Craig EMS and Prince of Wales Island Area EMS provide auxiliary health care.

Crooked Creek

Total area of entitlement under ANCSA
92,160 acres

Total labor force	90
High school graduate or higher	55.7%
Bachelor's degree or higher	2.9%
Unemployment rate	42%
Per capita income *(2000)*	$6,495
Population *2000 census*	137
Percent Native *2000 census*	93.4%

LOCATION
Crooked Creek is located on the north bank of the Kuskokwim River at its junction with Crooked Creek. It lies in the Kilbuk-Kuskokwim Mountains 50 miles northeast of Aniak, 141 miles northeast of Bethel and 275 miles west of Anchorage. Crooked Creek is located in the Fairbanks Recording District.

PHYSICAL DESCRIPTION
The area encompasses 101.1 square miles of land and 7.4 square miles of water.

CLIMATE
A continental climate prevails, with annual snowfall of 85 inches and yearly precipitation of 17 inches. Temperatures range from -59°F to 94°F. High winds often deter flights in the fall and winter.

CULTURE AND HISTORY
Historically this site was used as a summer camp for residents of Kwigiumpainukamuit. In 1890 a permanent settlement was established as a way station for the Flat and Iditarod gold-mining camps, providing easy access to the Kuskokwim River. In 1914 a roadhouse was established upriver from the creek mouth, in what became known as the "upper village" of Crooked Creek. A post office was opened in 1927, and a school was built in 1928. The "lower village" of Crooked Creek was settled by Yup'ik Eskimos and Ingalik Indians. By the 1940s there were a Russian Orthodox church (St. Nicholas Chapel) and several homes. The upper and lower halves of the village still remain today. The Native Village of Crooked Creek is a federally recognized tribe in the community.

Ethnicity: Yup'ik Eskimo, Ingalik Athabascan

ANCSA village corporation
Kuskokwim Corporation
4300 B Street, Suite 207
Anchorage, AK 99503
907-243-2944
800-478-2171

Crooked Creek

GOVERNMENT

Crooked Creek is an unincorporated community within the Unorganized Borough *(see Alaska introduction)*. The Native population is represented by a five-member traditional council, headed by a president.

VILLAGE CORPORATION

The Kuskokwim Corporation was formed in 1977 when 10 ANCSA village corporations located along the middle region of the Kuskokwim River merged. The villages were Lower Kasklag, Upper Kalskag, Aniak, Chuathbaluk, Napaimute, Crooked Creek, Red Devil, Geogetown, Sleetmute, and Stony River. The corporation invests in stocks, bonds, and real estate. It also owns interests in operating businesses, including a telecommunications bandwidth and service provider. In addition, the corporation has entered a subsurface lease agreement for the development of one of the largest undeveloped gold resources in the world, Donlin Creek, located on land to which Kuskokwim has retained surface rights. The corporation's subsidiaries include an SBA certified 8(a) small business that provides engineering, remediation, and construction services to the lower 48 states. Shareholders in the merged village corporation are also shareholders in Calista Corporation regional Native corporation *(see Alaska introduction.)*

ECONOMY

Subsistence activities are the mainstay of the village's economy. Salmon, moose, caribou, and water fowl are staples of the diet. The school and store offers a few year-round positions. Some villagers trap and sell pelts. The Calista Corp., Kuskokwim Corp., and Placer Dome U.S. have signed an exploration and mining lease for Donlin Creek, north of Crooked Creek. Placer Dome has a 70 percent interest and will invest $30 million to conduct a feasibility study and develop a working gold mine by 2007, producing an estimated 600,000 ounces a year.

Fisheries and forestry. Four residents are employed in farming, fishing, or forestry professions.

Government as employer. Of the 29 employed residents, 19 work for the local, state, or federal government.

Services and retail. Businesses include a quilt store, fishing lodge, trading post, and transportation services.

INFRASTRUCTURE

Twenty-one capital projects, funded by grants, are active in Crooked Creek.

Transportation. The Kuskokwim River is the local highway. The frozen river becomes a winter ice road. All-terrain vehicles and snow machines are used for area travel. Skiffs and barges provide cargo in summer. A state-owned and-operated 1,997- by 60-foot gravel airstrip is open southwest of the village. The airport and the upper/lower villages are connected by a suspension bridge over Crooked Creek.

Electricity. Electricity is provided by Middle Kuskokwim Electric Cooperative.

Water and waste systems. All homes lack plumbing; residents haul water and honeybuckets. A new well provides treated water, and a new washeteria has been completed. The school, store, and three homes have individual wells, septic tanks, and plumbing. The school septic drainfield is failing. The community needs a new water tank and landfill with access road.

Telecommunications. Local telephone service is provided by Bush-Tell, while long distance service is available through Alascom. One television channel is offered by the Rural Alaska Television Network. Internet service is available only for the school.

COMMUNITY FACILITIES

Facilities include a community center.

Education. There is one school located in the community with 49 students and 4 teachers.

Health care. Health-care facilities include Crooked Creek Health Clinic and Clara Morgan Subregional Clinic. The village health clinic is owned by the village corporation and leased to the U.S. Public Health Service; it is operated by the Yukon-Kuskokwim Health Corporation. Hospital services are provided by the Yukon-Kuskokwim Delta Regional Hospital in Bethel.

uryung

Also known as Dillingham and Kanakanak

Ethnicity: Yup'ik Eskimo, Alutiiq Aleut, Athabascan Indian

ANCSA village corporation
Choggiung Limited
104 Main St.
Dillingham, AK 99576
907-842-5218

Total area of entitlement under ANCSA

	175,506 acres
Total labor force	1,702
High school graduate or higher	83.5%
Bachelor's degree or higher	21.9%
Unemployment rate	7.1%
Per capita income *(2000)*	$21,537
Population *2000 census*	2,466
Percent Native *2000 census*	60.9%

LOCATION

Dillingham is located at the extreme northern end of Nushagak Bay in northern Bristol Bay, at the confluence of the Wood and Nushagak rivers. It lies 327 miles southwest of Anchorage, and is a 6 hour flight from Seattle. Dillingham is located in the Bristol Bay Recording District.

PHYSICAL DESCRIPTION

The area encompasses 33.6 square miles of land and 2.1 square miles of water.

CLIMATE

The primary climatic influence is maritime; however, the Arctic climate of the interior also affects the Bristol Bay coast. Average summer temperatures range from 37°F to 66°F; average winter temperatures range from 4°F to 30°F. Yearly precipitation is 26 inches, with annual snowfall of 65 inches. Heavy fog is common in July and August. Winds of up to 60 to 70 mph blow between December and March.

CULTURE AND HISTORY

Historically the area around Dillingham was inhabited by Eskimos and Athabascans and became a fur-trade center when Russians erected the Alexandrovsky Post there in 1818. The community was known as Nushagak by 1837, when a Russian Orthodox mission was established. In 1884 the first salmon cannery in the Bristol Bay region was built there; 10 more were constructed within the next 17 years. The post office was named after U.S. Senator Paul Dillingham in 1904, and the town site now known as Dillingham was first surveyed in 1947. Traditionally a Native area with Russian influences, Dillingham is now a highly mixed population of non-Natives,

Eskimos, Aleuts, and Indians. The outstanding commercial-fishing opportunities in the Bristol Bay area are the focus of the local culture. The Curyung Native Village Council is a federally recognized tribe in the community.

GOVERNMENT

Dillingham was incorporated as a first-class city in 1963, with a mayor and city council; it is located in the Unorganized Borough (see Alaska introduction). The six city council members are elected to three-year, staggered terms of office; the mayor is elected to a three-year term by Dillingham voters. It also has a traditional village council headed by a chief.

VILLAGE CORPORATION

Choggiung, Limited, was founded under the 1971 Alaska Native Claims Settlement Act. Choggiung owns most of the land in the area and permits are required to use any private lands. Shareholders in the village corporation are also shareholders in Bristol Bay Native Corporation (see Alaska introduction).

ECONOMY

Dillingham is the economic, transportation, and public-service center for western Bristol Bay. Commercial fishing, fish processing, cold storage, and support of the fishing industry are the primary activities. Icicle, Peter Pan, Trident, and Unisea operate fish-processing plants in the city. The population doubles in spring and summer. Seasonal work is stabilized by the city's role as the regional center for government and services. Several villagers rely on subsistence activities, and trapping of beaver, otter, mink, lynx, and fox provide cash income. Salmon, grayling, pike, moose, bear, caribou, and berries are harvested.

Construction. There are two construction companies, a sand and gravel business, and a welding and machine shop in Dillingham. Approximately 53 residents are employed in construction.

Fisheries and forestry. Commercial fishing permits are held by 277 residents salmon. Approximately 60 residents are employed in farming, fishing, and forestry industries.

Government as employer. Of the 1,154 employed residents, 436 work for the local, state, or federal government.

Manufacturing. There are a clothing and textile manufacturer, a woodworking company, and three boat-building and repair businesses in Dillingham. There is also a fabrication business in the village. Approximately 22 residents are employed in manufacturing.

Services and retail. There are 217 current business licenses in Dillingham, catering not only to this community but also to customers in numerous surrounding villages. There are nine childcare services, several outfitters, and stores selling everything from electrical appliances to general merchandise to sporting goods. There are also numerous repair services, a moving and storage company, a bookkeeping and consulting business, and a taxidermist. Retail trade employs 115 residents; wholesale trade 10; financial and related businesses 38; education, health, and social services 422; and public administration 115.

Tourism and recreation. There are several restaurants, a bookstore, marine and fish supply, video rental, and five lodging businesses. Fishing adventures, air adventures, and charter services are available. Visitor attractions include Wood-Tikchik State Park, Katmai National Park, Peter Pan Cannery Tour, Samuel K. Fox Museum, historic buildings, and viewing walrus at Round Island. Sport fishing, kayaking, camping, and hunting are also available. Cultural events include Blessing of the Feet, No-See-Um Festival, Beaver Round-Up Festival, and a Christmas bazaar. Arts, entertainment, recreation, and accommodations/food service industries collectively employ 37 residents.

Transportation. There are four taxi companies, one rental car company, three trucking and courier services, a water-freight transportation company, and six airline businesses in Dillingham. Transportation, warehousing, and utility industries employ 115 residents.

INFRASTRUCTURE

Twenty-four capital projects, funded by grants, are active in Dillingham.

Transportation. Dillingham can be reached by air and sea. The state provides an airport with a 6,404- by 150-foot paved runway and flight service station. Regular jet flights are available from Anchorage. A seaplane base, owned by the Bureau of Land Management, is available three miles west at Shannon's Pond. Kanakanak Hospital provides a heliport. A city-operated small-boat harbor is available along with a dock, barge landing, boat launch, and boat haul-out facilities. It is a tidal harbor and only for seasonal use. Two barge lines make scheduled trips from Seattle. A 23-mile gravel road to Aleknagik is open.

Electricity. Nushagak Electric owns and operates a diesel plant in Dillingham which also supplies power to Aleknagik. Nushugak Electric Cooperative provides electricity.

Water and waste systems. The majority of houses are fully plumbed. Dillingham's water, drawn from three deep wells, is treated, stored in tanks (1.3 million gallons) and distributed. The city's piped water system serves approximately 40 percent of homes; the other 60 percent of households use individual wells. The core townsite is served by a piped sewage system. Waste is treated in a sewage lagoon, even though the majority of residents have septic systems. Funding is needed for the city to extend piped water to the old airstrip and Kenny Wren Road and expand sewer service to the northeast. Dillingham Refuse provides refuse collection services. The senior center collects aluminum for recycling, and NAPA recycles used batteries. The chamber of commerce coordinates recycling of several materials, including fishing web. A new landfill has been constructed.

Telecommunications. Local telephone service is provided by the Nushagak Telephone Co-op, while long distance service is available through Alascom. Both Internet and teleconferencing services are available. Cable television service is available, and one channel is offered by the Rural Alaska Television Network. Three radio stations are available to the community.

COMMUNITY FACILITIES AND SERVICES

Facilities include a youth center, community hall, city hall, senior center, senior apartments, both city and school libraries, and the Samuel K. Fox Museum.

Education. The Dillingham City School District operates two schools in the community, attended by 526 students and taught by 40 teachers.

Health care. Health-care facilities clinics include Kanakanak Hospital/PHS, Dillingham Medical Clinic, Dillingham Health Center. The hospital is a qualified acute care facility. Also available: IHS Jake's Place (crisis, respite, lodging, health care); BBAHC Our House (emergencies, crisis, respite, lodging, health care); and BBAHC Community Mental Health Center. Auxiliary health care is provided by Dillingham Volunteer Fire and Rescue Squad and BBAHC Medevac.

Curyung

Also known as Dillingham and Kanakanak

Deering

Ethnicity: Inupiat Eskimo

ANCSA village corporation
NANA Corporation
P.O. Box 49
4706 Harding Drive
Kotzebue, AK 99752
  907-442-3301

Total area of entitlement under ANCSA	
	92,800 acres
Total labor force	91
High school graduate or higher	64.4%
Bachelor's degree or higher	9.6%
Unemployment rate	17%
Per capita income *(2000)*	$11,000
Population *2000 census*	136
Percent Native *2000 census*	94.1%

LOCATION

Deering is located on Kotzebue Sound at the mouth of the Inmachuk River, 57 miles southwest of Kotzebue. It is built on a flat sand-and-gravel spit 300 feet wide and a half-mile long. Deering is located in the Cape Nome Recording District. The area encompasses 5.1 square miles of land and 0.1 square mile of water.

CLIMATE

Deering is located in the transitional climate zone, with typical long, cold winters and cool summers. The average low temperature in January is -18°F; the average high in July is 63°F. Temperature extremes have been recorded from -60°F to 85°F. Yearly precipitation is 9 inches, with annual snowfall of 36 inches.

CULTURE AND HISTORY

The village was established in 1901 as a supply station for interior gold mining near the historic Malimiut Eskimo village of Inmachukmiut. The present name was taken from the schooner *Abbey Deering*. Today the population of the village is primarily Inupiat Eskimo. The Native Village of Deering is a federally recognized tribe in the community.

GOVERNMENT

Deering was incorporated in 1970 as a second-class city under Alaska, with a mayor and city council; it is located in the Northwest Arctic Borough *(see Alaska introduction)*. It also has a village council, organized under the Indian Reorganization Act of 1934, headed by a president.

VILLAGE CORPORATION

Shareholders in the village corporation are also shareholders in NANA regional Native corporation *(see Alaska introduction)*.

ECONOMY

Deering's economy is primarily based on the subsistence activities of the residents. The Karnun-Moto reindeer herd of 1,400 animals provides some local employment. A number of residents earn their income from handicrafts and trapping, while the school, city, retail shops, the nonprofit Native corporation Manilaaq, and an airline provide the only year-round employment. Some mining occurs in the Seward Peninsula's interior. The village wants to develop eco-tourism, including a 38-mile road to Inmachuk Springs for tourists.

Fisheries. Three residents hold commercial fishing permits for pink salmon, tomcod, herring.

Government as employer. Of the 44 employed residents, 29 work for the local, state, or federal government.

Services and retail. Businesses include a video-rental store, child care center, gift shop, and retail stores.

INFRASTRUCTURE

Sixteen capital projects, funded by grants, are active in Deering.

Transportation. Deering is accessible year-round by plane. A new state-owned 2,600- by 50-foot gravel airstrip, with a 2,080- by 60-foot gravel crosswind strip, enables flights by several Kotzebue air services. Crowley Marine Services barges fuel and goods from Kotzebue each summer. Small boats, ATVs, and snowmachines are used for local travel. Winter trails are available to Candle and Buckland.

Electricity. Ipnatchiaq Electric Company provides electricity.

Water and waste systems. Water, drawn from the Inmachuk River, is treated and pumped to a 400,000-gallon insulated storage tank. Water is delivered to residential tanks or hauled from the watering point. A water haul and vacuum sewer system are being improved. A new washeteria and water treatment plant are expected to open soon. The village would like to purchase an incinerator with waste heat recovery to reduce the volume of refuse.

Telecommunications. Local telephone service is provided by OTZ Telephone Company, while long distance service is provided by Alascom. The city of Deering provides a cable television service, and one television channel is offered by the Rural Alaska Television Network. One radio station is available to the community. Internet service is provided by GCI, and teleconferencing is provided by the Alaska Teleconferencing Network

COMMUNITY FACILITIES AND SERVICES

Facilities include a community building and both school and city libraries.

Education. Deering School is in the Northwest Arctic School District. The school has 44 students and 4 teachers.

Health care. Health care is provided by the Deering Health Clinic, owned by the city and leased to the U.S. Public Health Service. The clinic is operated by Manilaaq Association.

Dillingham

See Curying

Total area of entitlement under ANCSA	
	105,600 acres
Total labor force	88
High school graduate or higher	55.9%
Bachelor's degree or higher	11.8%
Unemployment rate	2.2%
Per capita income *(2000)*	$9,944
Population *2000 census*	146
Percent Native *2000 census*	93.8%

LOCATION
Diomede is located on the west coast of Little Diomede Island in the Bering Straits, 135 miles northwest of Nome. It is only 2.5 miles from Big Diomede Island, Russia, and the international boundary lies between the two islands. Diomede is located in the Cape Nome Recording District.

PHYSICAL DESCRIPTION
The area encompasses 2.8 square miles of land.

CLIMATE
Summer temperatures average 40°F to 50°F; winter temperatures average from -10°F to 6°F. Yearly precipitation is 10 inches, with annual snowfall of 30 inches. During summer months, cloudy skies and fog prevail. Winds blow consistently from the north, averaging 15 knots with gusts to 60 or 80 mph.

CULTURE AND HISTORY
Diomede is a traditional Eskimo village with a culture centered on subsistence activities. Sea mammals, polar bears, cod, crab, and birds are all important subsistence resources. Mainland Eskimos traditionally travel to Diomede Island to hunt polar bears. Historically, Diomede residents hunted on both sea and ice and traded with Natives in both Asia and Alaska. They were closely related to families living on Big Diomede Island. When the Soviet Union sealed its borders, Big Diomede Island became a military base and all Native residents were moved to the mainland of Siberia. The Native Village of Diomede (also know as Inalik) is a federally recognized tribe in the community.

GOVERNMENT
Diomede was incorporated under Alaska law as a second-class city in 1970, with a mayor and city council; it is located in the Unorganized Borough *(see Alaska introduction)*. It also has an Indian Reorganization Act village council, headed by a president.

VILLAGE CORPORATION
Shareholders in the Diomede village corporation also hold shares in the regional Bering Straits Native Corporation *(see Alaska introduction)*.

ECONOMY
Residents of Diomede rely almost entirely on subsistence activities for their livelihoods. Fish, crab, walrus, seal, beluga whales, and polar bear are important subsistence resources. Employment is limited to jobs with the city and school; seasonal mining, construction, and commercial-fishing work has declined in recent years. Ivory carving provides supplemental income for a number of village residents; the city acts as a wholesale agent for the carvings.

Construction. Two residents are employed in construction.

Fisheries and forestry. Farming, fishing, or forestry accounts for one resident's employment.

Government as employer. Of the 45 employed residents, 35 work for the local, state, or federal government.

Services and retail. Businesses include the washeteria, city council, Native village council, electronic shop, grocery stores, and a real estate agent.

INFRASTRUCTURE
Seventeen capital projects, funded by grants, are active in Diomede.

Transportation. Constant winds from the north hamper accessibility. The state provides a heliport for weekly mail delivery. Steep slopes and rocky terrain prohibit the use of an airstrip, so skiplanes land on an ice strip in winter. Floatplane pilots are reluctant to land on the rough, often foggy, open sea in summer. Regular flights are scheduled from Nome when weather allows. There is a breakwater and small-boat harbor. Skin boats are still a popular method of sea travel. It is 28 miles to Wales. Cargo barges are limited by sea or ice conditions but usually make yearly stops. Lighterage services from Nome are available.

Electricity. Diomede Joint Utilities provides electricity.

Water and waste systems. Water drawn from a mountain spring is treated and stored in a 434,000-gallon tank, and families haul water from this point. The tank is filled for winter use, but the water supply typically runs out around March. The washeteria is then closed, and residents are required to melt snow and ice for drinking water. The village needs funding for a 600,000-gallon steel tank and to improve the water catchment system. The school has requested funding for a 500,000-gallon water storage tank to alleviate demands on the city water supply and serve as a community backup. Privies and honeybuckets are used. A septic system and seepage pit serves the washeteria and clinic. The Public Health Services has limited waste-disposal methods due to soil condition, ground-cover limitations, and steep terrain. Refuse is disposed on the pack ice in winter; combustibles are burned. Funding has been requested for refuse collection and the purchase of an incinerator.

Telecommunications. Local telephone service is provided by the Mukluk Telephone Company, while long distance service is provided by Alascom. One television channel is offered by the Rural Alaska Television Network. Two radio stations are available to residents. Teleconferencing is available from the Alaska Teleconferencing Network.

COMMUNITY FACILITIES AND SERVICES
Education. Diomede School is in the Bering Strait School District. The school has 39 students and 6 teachers.

Health care. Health care is provided by the Little Diomede Health Clinic, owned by the city and leased to the U.S. Public Health Service; it is administered by the Norton Sound Health Corporation. Emergencies are handled by the Diomede Volunteer Fire Department First Responders.

Also known as Inalik

[DIE-oh-meed]
Ethnicity: Inupiat Eskimo

Municipality
City of Diomede
P.O. Box 7039
Little Dieomede, AK 99762
907- 686-3071
907-686-2192 Fax

Native entity
Native Village of Diomede
P.O. Box 7079
Little Diomede, AK 99762
907- 686-2175
907- 686-2203 Fax

ANCSA village corporation
Diomede Native Corporation
P.O. Box 7040
Little Diomede, AK 99762
907- 686-3221
907- 686-3222 Fax

Ethnicity: Tanacross
           Athabascan

ANCSA village corporation
Dot Lake Native Corporation
P.O. Box 275
Dot Lake, AK 99737
   907- 882-2695

Total area of entitlement under ANCSA	
	69,120 acres
Total labor force	31
High school graduate or higher	68.4%
Bachelor's degree or higher	-
Unemployment rate	0%
Per capita income *(2000)*	$7,476
Population *2000 census*	38
Percent Native *2000 census*	73.7%

LOCATION
The Native Village of Dot Lake is located off of the Alaska Highway, 50 miles northwest of Tok, and 155 road miles southeast of Fairbanks. The village lies south of the Tanana River. The area is divided into two separate communities: the Native Village of Dot Lake and Dot Lake, the highway community. Dot Lake Village is located in the Fairbanks Recording District.

PHYSICAL DESCRIPTION
The area encompasses 3.6 square miles of land.

CLIMATE
Dot Lake Village is located in the continental climatic zone, with cold winters and warm summers. In winter, ice fog and smoke conditions are common. Average low in winter is -22°F; during summers, the average high is 65°F. Extreme temperatures have been recorded from -75°F to 90°F. Yearly precipitation is 9 inches, with annual snowfall of 27 inches.

CULTURE AND HISTORY
Archaeological evidence at nearby Healy Lake suggests more than 10,000 years of human occupation. Dot Lake was once a seasonal hunting camp for Athabascans from George Lake and Tanacross. An Indian freight trail ran north to the Yukon River, through Northway, Tetlin, Tanacross, and Dot Lake. During construction of the Alaska Highway in the mid-1940s, a work camp occupied Dot Lake's present location. Several local Natives worked on the road project. Dot Lake Village was settled by a single family in 1946. In the next four years other families moved permanently to Dot Lake from George Lake, Sam Lake, and the Tanacross area, obtaining home sites or Native allotments. Some of the old work camp structures were converted into homes. In 1971 seven new homes were constructed along the lake. The Dot Lake Native Corporation developed a shareholder's subdivision, consisting of 53 one-acre lots. In 1994 and 1996 nine additional Indian Housing Authority homes were built. The Native Village of Dot Lake is a traditional Upper Tanana Athabascan village.

GOVERNMENT
Dot Lake is unincorporated and is located in the Unorganized Borough *(see Alaska introduction)*. It is governed by a traditional village council, headed by a president. Shareholders in the Dot Lake village corporation also hold shares in Doyon, Limited regional Native corporation *(see Alaska introduction)*.

ECONOMY
Employment in the area is limited to the village council, Tanana Chiefs Conference, and the school. Villagers sell parkas, moccasins, beadwork, and other handicrafts. In the summer the Bureau of Land Management hires fire-fighting crews. Subsistence activities are vital to the community. Moose, ducks, geese, ptarmigan, porcupines, caribou, whitefish, and other freshwater fish are important resources. Salmon are primarily caught in the Copper River area.

Fisheries. One resident holds a commercial salmon fishing permit.

Government as employer. Of eight employed residents, none work for the local, state, or federal government.

Services and retail. Currently there are no active business licenses in Dot Lake Village.

INFRASTRUCTURE
Five capital projects, funded by grants, are active in Dot Lake Village.

Transportation. Dot Lake is not accessible by water. The village lies along the Alaska Highway, and trucks and buses bring in supplies. Scheduled bus services to Fairbanks and Delta Junction are available. Delta Junction and Tok are the closest public airstrips. A privately owned strip in Dot Lake was converted to a helicopter landing pad. Snowmachines and all-terrain vehicles provide local travel. Some villagers use riverboats for fishing and hunting.

Electricity. A line extension from Tok provides electricity to Dot Lake Village. The landfill is not open to the public, pending an upgrade.

Water and waste systems. Dot Lake Utility provides a piped water system to eight homes. A new utility building consists of a well, washeteria, showers, water storage, community septic system, and an underground utilidor with a circulating heat loop providing home heating. Individual wells and septic tanks are in 11 households and the school. A piped water or septic system serves all but two houses.

Telecommunications. Local telephone service is provided by the National Utilities, while long distance service is provided by Alascom. One channel of television can be received from Fairbanks, and one channel is offered by the Rural Alaska Television Network. One radio station is available to residents. Internet service is provided for the school only. Teleconferencing is available from the Alaska Teleconferencing Network or through the Tok legislative information office.

COMMUNITY FACILITIES AND SERVICES
Education. There are no schools in Dot Lake Village. Students go to classes in neighboring Dot Lake.

Health care. Health care is provided by the Dot Lake Health Clinic, owned by the village and leased to the U.S. Public Health Service; it is administered by the Tanana Chiefs Conference. Emergencies are handled by the McComb Plateau Emergency Medical Service Association.

Douglas
See Urban Tribe Section

Dutch Harbor
See Qawalangin

Total area of entitlement under ANCSA	
	92,160 acres
Total labor force	96
High school graduate or higher	81.4%
Bachelor's degree or higher	-
Unemployment rate	14.3%
Per capita income *(2000)*	$20,221
Population *2000 census*	77
Percent Native *2000 census*	39%

LOCATION

The City of Eagle and Eagle Village are located on the Taylor Highway, six miles west of the Alaska-Canadian border. Eagle is on the left bank of the Yukon River at the mouth of Mission Creek. The Yukon-Charley Rivers National Preserve is northwest of the area. Eagle is located in the Fairbanks Recording District.

PHYSICAL DESCRIPTION

The area encompasses 1.0 square mile of land.

CLIMATE

Interior Alaska experiences seasonal temperature extremes. January temperatures range from -22ºF to -2ºF, but can drop as low as -60ºF; July temperatures vary from 50ºF to 72ºF. Yearly precipitation is 11.3 inches. Ice fog occurs during long cold spells.

CULTURE AND HISTORY

The area has been the historical home of the Kutchin (Gwich'in) Indians. A log-house trading station called Belle Isle was established at the site around 1874 and operated intermittently until its development as a mining camp in 1889. The community was then named Eagle City, after the nesting eagles on nearby Eagle Bluff. A U.S. Army camp was built there in 1899, and a year later Fort Egbert was built; it was abandoned in 1911. The Valdez-Eagle telegraph line was completed in 1930. Most Eagle residents are Non-native; however, nearby Eagle Village is home to over 30 Natives. Subsistence activities are a major part of the lifestyle.

GOVERNMENT

Eagle was incorporated under Alaska law as a second-class city in 1901, with a mayor and city council; it is located in the Unorganized Borough (see Alaska introduction). It also has a village council organized under the Indian Reorganization Act of 1934, headed by a first chief.

VILLAGE CORPORATION

Shareholders in the village corporation also hold shares in Doyon, Limited, regional Native corporation *(see Alaska introduction)*.

ECONOMY

Retail businesses, mining, and seasonal employment such as Bureau of Land Management fire fighting provide the majority of employment opportunities in the area. Year-round positions are limited, and subsistence activities are of major importance.

Fisheries and farming. Farming, fishing, or forestry accounts for one resident's employment.

Government as employer. Of the 48 employed residents, 21 work for the local, state, or federal government.

Mining. There is a placer-mining operation in the village.

Services and retail. There are 25 current business licenses in Eagle. Businesses include a trading company, grocery store, drywall and acoustical business, and a realty company. Retail trade employs 3 residents; education, health, and social services 13; and public administration 8 residents.

Tourism and recreation. Three lodging facilities are available, including a bed-and-breakfast and a campground. Services include canoe rentals, café, gift shop, and craft shop. Visitor attractions include two national landmarks: Judge Wickersham's Courthouse and the Customs House. Float trips are available in the Yukon-Charley Rivers National Preserve, and visitors ride the *Yukon Queen* riverboat from Dawson to Eagle. Other attractions include the Eagle historic walking tour, biking or hiking American Summit, and Fort Egbert/Redmen Hall. Cultural events include a spring carnival, the Percy DeWolfe sled dog race, and the Yukon Quest sled dog race. Arts, entertainment, recreation, and accommodations/food services collectively employ five residents.

Transportation. Four airline companies service Eagle. Transportation, warehousing, and utility industries employ three residents.

INFRASTRUCTURE

Eleven capital projects, funded by grants, are active in Eagle.

Transportation. Eagle has passage to the state road system and to Canada only during summer months by way of the Taylor and Top of the World highways. The state provides a 3,600- by 75-foot gravel airstrip. Flights originate from Fairbanks and Tok, and floatplanes land on the Yukon River. A public boat landing is open.

Electricity. Alaska Power Company provides electricity.

Water and waste systems. The vast majority of villagers haul water from the community well. The school uses its own well and septic system. About 21 occupied homes have full plumbing with individual wells and septic tanks. Outhouses are used by other households. The landfill in Eagle Village is open. A permitted seepage disposal site is available.

Telecommunications. Local telephone service is provided by the Nushagak Telephone Co-op, while long distance service is available from Alascom. Teleconferencing is available from the Alaska Teleconferencing Network or through the Tok legislative information office. One television channel is offered by the Rural Alaska Television Network. Internet service is available.

COMMUNITY FACILITIES AND SERVICES

Local facilities include the Eagle Historical Society Museums, and both public and school libraries.

Education. Eagle Community School is in the Alaska Gateway School District. The school has 20 students and 2 teachers.

Health care. Health care is provided by the Eagle Health Clinic, owned by the village and leased to the U.S. Public Health Service; the clinic is administered by the Tanana Chiefs Conference. Ambulance service is provided by Eagle Emergency Medical Service.

Ethnicity: Kutchin *Gwich'in*
Athabascan

ANCSA village corporation
Hungwitchin Corporation
2004 Sandvik Rd., Apt. 208
Fairbanks, AK 99709
907-479-2619

E_{ek}

Ethnicity: Yup'ik Eskimo

Iqfijouaq Company
P.O. Box 49
Eek, AK 99578
    907-536-5211

Total area of entitlement under ANCSA	
	115,200 acres
Total labor force	159
High school graduate or higher	64.2%
Bachelor's degree or higher	5.8%
Unemployment rate	17.9%
Per capita income *(2000)*	$8,957
Population *2000 census*	280
Percent Native *2000 census*	96.8%

LOCATION
Eek lies on the south bank of the Eek River, 12 miles east of the mouth of the Kuskokwim River. It is 35 air miles south of Bethel in the Yukon-Kuskokwim Delta and 420 miles west of Anchorage. Eek is located in the Bethel Recording District.

PHYSICAL DESCRIPTION
The area encompasses 0.9 square mile of land and 0.1 square mile of water.

CLIMATE
Eek is located in a marine climate. Annual precipitation is 22 inches, with yearly snowfall of 43 inches. Summer temperatures range from 41ºF to 57ºF; winter temperatures vary from 6ºF to 24ºF.

CULTURE AND HISTORY
The area has historically been the home of Yup'ik Eskimos and is still a traditional Eskimo village. It was founded by residents of an older village that was affected by erosion. A post office was established in 1949. About half of the families move to fish camps each summer; those who stay participate in the commercial fishery. The Eek Traditional Council is a federally recognized tribe in the community.

GOVERNMENT
In 1970 Eek was incorporated as a second-class city, with a mayor and city council; it is located in the Unorganized Borough *(see Alaska introduction)*. Eek also has a traditional village council, headed by a president.

VILLAGE CORPORATION
Shareholders in the Iqfijouaq village corporation are also shareholders in Calista regional Native corporation *(see Alaska introduction)*.

ECONOMY
Eek's economy is a mix of subsistence and cash activities. Commercial fishing, fish processing, and construction provide summer employment. All families participate in either commercial or subsistence fishing.

Construction. Two residents are employed in construction.

Fisheries. Forty-four residents hold commercial fishing permits. The 1992 Community Development Quota program increased the pollack groundfish quota for small communities like Eek.

Government as employer. Of the 55 employed residents, 34 work for the local, state, or federal government.

Services and retail. There are seven current business licenses for Eek. Businesses include trading posts, a grocery store, day care center, and air transportation service. Retail trade employs 2 residents; education, health and social services 22; public administration 7; and arts, entertainment, recreation, and accommodations/food service industries collectively employ 14 residents.

Transportation. Six airline companies service Eek.

INFRASTRUCTURE
Fourteen capital projects, funded by grants, are active in Eek.

Transportation. The state provides a 1,420- by 35-foot gravel airstrip for chartered and private air access. The airport will be relocated in the future. The Eek River provides a seaplane base. Fishing boats, skiffs, and snowmachines are used for local travel. A one-mile gravel road is open in the village. Winter trails are marked to Quinhagak, Eek Island, and the Kwethluk River. Barges deliver fuel and supplies in summer.

Electricity. Alaska Village Electric Cooperative (AVEC) provides electricity.

Water and waste systems. Water drawn from the Eek River is treated and stored in a tank at the washeteria. Some residences have tanks that provide running water to the kitchen, but houses do not have additional plumbing. Rain catchment systems and ice melt are also used for drinking water. Honeybuckets are disposed of in a sewage lagoon. Infrastructure improvements are underway. Funding has been granted for a new water intake, water treatment plant, 100,000-gallon water tank, washeteria, sewage lagoon, and vehicles for honeybucket and refuse hauling. A new landfill is needed.

Telecommunications. Local telephone service is provided by United Utilities, while long distance service is available through Alascom. Teleconferencing is available from the Alaska Teleconferencing Network. Internet service is provided by GCI for the school only. Cable television service is available, and one channel is offered by the Rural Alaska Television Network. Two radio stations are available to the community.

COMMUNITY FACILITIES AND SERVICES
Education. There is one school located in the community, attended by 76 students and taught by 7 teachers.

Health care. Health care is provided by the Eek Health Clinic, owned by the village and leased to the U.S. Public Health Service; the clinic is administered by the Yukon-Kuskokwim Health Corporation.

 gegik

Total area of entitlement under ANCSA
94,470 acres

Total labor force	80
High school graduate or higher	54.7%
Bachelor's degree or higher	-
Unemployment rate	27.6%
Per capita income *(2000)*	$16,352
Population *2000 census*	116
Percent Native *2000 census*	76.7%

LOCATION

Egegik is located on the south bank of the Egegik River on the Alaska Peninsula, 100 miles southwest of Dillingham and 326 air miles southwest of Anchorage. Egegik is located in the Kvichak Recording District.

PHYSICAL DESCRIPTION

The area encompasses 32.8 square miles of land and 101.2 square miles of water.

CLIMATE

Egegik's predominantly maritime climate brings cool, humid, and windy weather. Summer temperatures vary from 44°F to 65°F; winter temperatures range from -24°F to 40°F. Yearly precipitation is 20 to 26 inches, with annual snowfall of 45 inches.

CULTURE AND HISTORY

The Egegik River is one of the most productive salmon rivers in Bristol Bay; during the commercial-fishing season, the population swells to over 3,500. Across the river is the settlement of Coffee Point, the site of a salmon-processing plant and individual fish camps. The name of the village is derived from the Yup'ik Eskimo word *igagik*, meaning "neck." Settlement of the Bristol Bay region first occurred over 6,000 years ago; Yup'ik Eskimos and Athabascan Indians jointly occupied the area. Egegik is also on the traditional border between Yup'ik Eskimo territory to the north and Alutiiq Aleut territory to the south. The village was first reported as a fish camp in 1876 and later developed around a salmon saltery established in 1895. During the influenza outbreaks that began in 1918, Natives from other villages moved to Egegik in an attempt to isolate themselves from the disease. Today subsistence is still a basic part of the lifestyle of most residents. The Egegik Village Council is a federally recognized tribe in the community.

GOVERNMENT

Egegik is one of the unincorporated communities in the Lake and Peninsula Borough *(see Alaska introduction)*. The local governing body is the Egegik Village Council, a seven-member traditional council that meets monthly, headed by a president. Council members serve three-year staggered terms.

VILLAGE CORPORATION

Shareholders in the Becharot village corporation also hold shares in Bristol Bay Native Corporation *(see Alaska introduction)*.

ECONOMY

Approximately 1,000 to 2,000 fishermen and cannery workers converge on the village during the commercial fishing season. Subsistence harvest, commercial fishing, and fish processing are the mainstays of the economy. Five onshore processors are located on the Egegik River, three on the north shore and two on the south shore. Numerous floating processors participate in the Egegik fishery. Subsistence hunting and fishing activities are an important part of the lifestyle and local diet. Seal, beluga, salmon, trout, smelt, grayling, clams, moose, bear, caribou, porcupine, waterfowl, and ptarmigan are all subsistence resources.

Fisheries. There are two canneries and freezer facilities in the village. A seafood-processing plant is in operation in nearby Coffee Point. Forty-five residents hold commercial fishing permits seal, beluga, salmon, trout, smelt, grayling, clams. Four residents are employed in farming, fishing, or forestry industries.

Government as employer. Of the 21 employed residents, 14 work for the local, state, or federal government.

Services and retail. There are seven active business licenses in Egegik. Businesses include a trading post, grocery store, day care center, and cafés. Wholesale trade employs three residents; education, health and social services six; and public administration six residents.

Tourism and recreation. One lodge and one hotel provide lodging facilities. Visitor attractions include the Becharof National Wildlife Refuge. Cultural events include a winter fest.

Transportation. An airport shuttle service is available. Transportation, warehousing, and utility industries employ five residents.

INFRASTRUCTURE

Twelve capital projects, funded by grants, are active in Egegik.

Transportation. The community is accessible by air and water. The city provides a 5,600- by 100-foot lighted gravel runway with crosswind airstrip, two miles northwest of Egegik. Scheduled and charter flights are available. The Bartletts also maintain a private 2,800-foot airstrip across from Coffee Point. A new public dock is open, and the boat harbor holds 150 vessels. A boat haul-out is available. Two privately owned docks and marine storage are available. Anchorage and Seattle provide barge services to the village. Skiffs, all-terrain vehicles, and snowmachines are used for local travel.

Electricity. Egegik Light and Power Company provides electricity.

Water and waste systems. Two wells supply Egegik's water, which is treated with fluoride. Four tanks have a total water storage capacity of 122,500 gallons. Half of all residences are plumbed. Eleven homes, the school, clinic, and city offices, are connected to a piped water and sewer system. Thirteen other homes are connected only to the piped sewage system. Nineteen villagers use honeybuckets, 10 residents use septic tanks or seepage pits, and sewage pumping services are available. Funds are available to expand piped water and sewer to 17 households. Canneries draw water from School Lake and Grandma's Lake. A new landfill with a batch oxidation incinerator is available.

Telecommunications. Local telephone service is provided by Pacific Telecommunications, while long distance service is available from Alascom. Teleconferencing is available from the Alaska Teleconferencing Network or through the Dillingham legislative information office. Internet service is provided for the school only. One television channel is offered by the Rural Alaska Television Network. One radio station is available to the community.

EE-guh-gick
Ethnicity: Yup'ik Eskimo,
Alutiiq Aleut

ANCSA village corporation
Becharof Corporation
1577 C Street Plaza, #124
Anchorage, AK 99501
907-263-9820
907-274-3721 Fax

Egegik

COMMUNITY FACILITIES AND SERVICES
Facilities include a recreation center, community center, city hall, and both public and school libraries.

Education. Egegik School is in the Lake and Peninsula School District. The school has 12 students and 1 teacher.

Health care. Health care is provided by the Egegik Health Clinic, owned by the village and leased to the U.S. Public Health Service; the clinic is administered by the Bristol Bay Area Health Corporation and staffed by two full-time community health aides. An Indian Health Service doctor and dentist visit at least twice a year; an optometrist visits every other year. Patients travel to the Kanakanak Hospital in Dillingham or to Anchorage for nonroutine care.

Eklutna

Also see Anchorage

[ee-KLOOT-nuh]
Ethnicity: Tanaina *(Dena'ina)*
Athabascan

ANCSA village corporation
Eklutna, Incorporated
16515 Centerfield Drive
Suite 201
Eagle River, AK 99577
907-696-2828
907-696-2845 Fax

Total area of entitlement under ANCSA	
	124,727 acres
Total labor force	291
High school graduate or higher	90.1%
Bachelor's degree or higher	36.4%
Unemployment rate	5.8%
Per capita income *(2000)*	$29,375
Population *2000 census*	394
Percent Native *2000 census*	13.2%

LOCATION
Eklutna is located at the head of the Knik Arm of Cook Inlet, at the mouth of the Eklutna River, 25 miles northeast of Anchorage. It is within the boundaries of the Municipality of Anchorage. Eklutna is located in the Anchorage Recording District.

PHYSICAL DESCRIPTION
The area encompasses 12.4 square miles of land and 5.7 square miles of water.

CLIMATE
The average temperatures in January vary from 6ºF to 14ºF; in July, 47ºF to 67ºF. Yearly precipitation is 16.5 inches.

CULTURE AND HISTORY
The Eklutna area was the site of many Athabascan Indian villages as long as 800 years ago. Today's residents are descendants of the Tanaina tribe. Russian Orthodox missionaries arrived in the 1840s, and a railroad station was built in 1918. Brightly-colored "spirit houses" in the Russian style now lend character to Eklutna. The Russian Orthodox religion is still prevalent. Eklutna Cemetery, dating back to 1650, became a historical park in the 1980s and consists of a small museum and gift shop, prayer chapels, two Russian Orthodox churches, and the cemetery that is still used today. More than 100 brightly-colored "spirit houses" are on the burial ground, a custom that combines Athabascan and Russian Orthodox practices. The Native Village of Eklutna is a federally recognized tribe in the community.

GOVERNMENT
Eklutna is an unincorporated community within the municipality of Anchorage *(see Alaska introduction).* It also has a traditional village council headed by a president.

VILLAGE CORPORATION
Incorporated in 1971 under ANCSA, Eklutna Incorporated has played a vital role in the economic landscape of the Anchorage area. Eklutna is the largest private landowner in Anchorage, with significant holdings in Mat-Su Valley, owning or entitled to receive more than 90,000 acres of land from Eagle River to Palmer. Today, the corporation represents more than 150 shareholders and manages a variety of investments, including shopping centers, office buildings, and residential developments. Visitors who want to access Eklutna Incorporated land need either an individual permit or a corporate permit. Shareholders in the village corporation also hold shares in Cook Inlet regional Native corporation *(see Alaska introduction.)*

ECONOMY
The majority of non-Native residents are employed in Anchorage, with incomes averaging $31,679 per capita, according to the 2000 U.S. Census. Eklutna's Danaina residents, however, have significantly lower incomes-averaging $19,494 per capita.

Construction. Six residents are employed in construction.

Government as employer. Of the 203 employed residents, 91 work for the local, state, or federal government.

Manufacturing. Five residents are employed in manufacturing.

Services and retail. There are no active business licenses in the village.

INFRASTRUCTURE
Four capital projects, funded by grants, are active in Eklutna.

Transportation. The village lies on the highway between Anchorage and Palmer, with ready access to a variety of transportation services in those communities. Two privately owned airstrips are located in the area as well as the Alaska Railroad system.

Electricity. Chugach Electric Association purchases power from the federally owned Eklutna Hydro Facility. Matanuska Electric Association provides electricity.

Water and waste systems. Most of the residences are fully plumbed, with a community well water system and individual septic tanks. Waste Management collects refuse for disposal in the municipal regional landfill.

Telecommunications. Local telephone service is available through the Matanuska Telephone Association; long distance and Internet services are provided by Alascom and GCI. Teleconferencing is available from the Alaska Teleconferencing Network. Three television stations can be received from Anchorage, as well as all Anchorage radio stations.

COMMUNITY FACILITIES AND SERVICES
Facilities include a community hall that was constructed in 1962.

Education. There are no state-operated schools located in the community.

Health care. Health-care facilities include Eklutna EMS/Health Clinic, Eagle River private clinics, and Anchorage hospitals. Auxiliary health care is provided by Chugiak Volunteer Fire and Rescue, Eagle River private clinics, and Anchorage hospitals.

Ekuk

See Zero Population Section

Total area of entitlement under ANCSA	
	93,682 acres
Total labor force	63
High school graduate or higher	64.7%
Bachelor's degree or higher	5.9%
Unemployment rate	20%
Per capita income *(2000)*	$11,079
Population *2000 census*	130
Percent Native *2000 census*	93.8%

LOCATION
Ekwok is located along the Nushagak River, 43 miles northeast of Dillingham and 285 miles southwest of Anchorage. The local terrain is hilly and characterized by spruce and birch forests.

CLIMATE
Ekwok's climatic transition zone—with a maritime influence—is modified by the continental climate of interior Alaska. Cloudy skies, mild temperatures, heavy precipitation, and periods of strong surface winds are common. Summer temperatures range from lows of 37°F to highs of 77°F. Winter temperatures average lows of 30°F and highs of 40°F.

CULTURE AND HISTORY
Ekwok is the oldest continuously occupied Yup'ik Eskimo village on the river. It was originally settled during the early 1900s, when settlers came to the area to fish and harvest the abundant supply of wood. The settlement was first used as a fish camp and base for berry picking. The name means "beginning of higher ground." The village was said to be the largest settlement along the river by 1923. In 1930 the Bureau of Indian affairs established a school in Ekwok. Mail service began in 1930 with the opening of a post office that served the entire river for a time. Service was extremely irregular; residents depended on infrequent deliveries from Dillingham by dogsled. In 1941 Ekwok officially opened a post office. The village continued to grow slowly, drawing residents from coastal communities in the region. Many of the earliest homes in Ekwok were located in a low, flat area near the riverbank. When the village suffered from the effects of severe flooding in the early 1960s, the villagers relocated to higher ground at Ekwok's current location. The Southwest Region Education Attendance Area took over the school from the BIA in 1971, and in 1980 a high school was built. The Yup'ik Eskimo village continues its fishing and subsistence lifestyle. The Ekwok Village Council is a federally recognized tribe in the community.

GOVERNMENT
Ekwok was incorporated as a second-class city in 1974, with a mayor and city council. The community is located in the Unorganized Borough *(see Alaska introduction)*. The village has a traditional tribal council headed by a president. Holders of shares in the village corporation are also shareholders in the Bristol Bay regional Native corporation *(see Alaska introduction)*.

ECONOMY
The main source of income in Ekwok is the salmon-fishing industry. A few residents trap for furs. The entire population depends on subsistence activities for various food sources. With fresh produce hard to come by, many residents grow gardens in the summer. The village corporation owns a fishing lodge, and gravel is mined near the community.

Fisheries. Six residents hold commercial fishing permits.

Government as employer. Of the 28 employed residents, 21 work for the local, state, or federal government.

Mining. There is a gravel mine near the village.

Services and retail. There are eight businesses in the community, including a lodge, kennel, grocery store, retail shops, and fishing guide services. Education, health, and social services employ 11 residents; public administration employs 8 residents.

Tourism and recreation. The village corporation owns a fishing lodge, located two miles downriver. Fishing guides and two lodges are available. Visitor attractions include sightseeing, sport fishing, bird watching, and hunting. Arts, entertainment, recreation, accommodations, and food service industries collectively employ two residents.

Transportation. Two airlines service Ekwok. Transportation, warehousing, and utility industries collectively employ five residents.

INFRASTRUCTURE
Eleven capital projects, funded by grants, are active in Ekwok.

Transportation. Air transport is most frequently used to reach Ekwok. Regular and charter flights are available from Dillingham. The state provides a 2,720- by 75-foot gravel runway. Floatplanes land on the Nushagak River. Cargo is brought by barge during ice-free months from Dillingham. There are no docking facilities, but a barge off-loading area exists. Skiffs, all-terrain vehicles, and snowmachines are used for local travel to other villages.

Electricity. Electricity is provided by Ekwok Electric.

Water and waste systems. Individual wells provide water for the majority of the community. Twenty HUD homes have individual wells and a piped septic system. The city operates a piped sewage system with sewage lift station that connects to 16 additional residences. The remaining homes use septic systems or a flush/haul system; a sewage pumper is available. Nearly 42 homes have complete plumbing. Refuse collection services are available.

Telecommunications. Local telephone service is available through the Bristol Bay Telephone Co-op, Inc., while long distance service is provided by Alascom. Internet service is provided by GCI, and teleconferencing is available through Alaska Teleconferencing Network. Rural Alaska Television Network provides television access. Two radio stations are available to residents.

COMMUNITY FACILITIES AND SERVICES
Facilities include a city hall/community center, and a village council building. Senior citizens receive in-home assistance and care. The community needs a washeteria with a water source and treatment system.

Education. The William "Sonny" Nelson School in Ekwok is part of the Southwest Region Regional Education Attendance Area. The school has 26 students and 3 teachers. The school district operates a Yup'ik Eskimo culture program. The school has a display of artifacts. Vocational programs are offered by the Bristol Bay Native Association.

Health care. Health care is provided by the Ekwok Health Clinic, owned by the village and leased to the U.S. Public Health Service. The clinic is administered by the Bristol Bay Area Health Corporation. Auxiliary health care is provided by Ekwok Fire and EMS and Ekwok First Responders.

[ECK-wock]
Ethnicity: Yup'ik Eskimo

Native entity
Ekwok Natives Limited
P.O. Box 42
Ekwok, AK 99580
907-464-3317
907-464-3305 Fax

Elim

[EE-lim]
Ethnicity: Inupiat Eskimo

ANCSA village corporation
Elim Native Corporation
P.O. Box 39010
Elim, AK 99739
907-890-3741
907-890-3091 Fax

Total area of entitlement under ANCSA	
	297,982 acres
Total labor force	222
High school graduate or higher	77.4%
Bachelor's degree or higher	7.5%
Unemployment rate	26%
Per capita income *(2000)*	$10,300
Population *2000 census*	313
Percent Native *2000 census*	94.9%

LOCATION
Elim is located on the northwest shore of Norton Bay on the Seward Peninsula, 96 miles east of Nome and 460 miles northwest of Anchorage.

CLIMATE
Elim has a subarctic climate, with maritime influences when Norton Sound is ice free. Summers are cool and moist; winters are cold and dry. Summer temperatures range from lows of 46°F to highs of 62°F; winter temperatures range from lows of -8°F to highs of 8°F. Average annual precipitation is 19 inches, including about 80 inches of snow.

CULTURE AND HISTORY
This settlement was formerly the Malimiut (Inupiat) Eskimo village of Nuviakchak. The area was a federal reindeer reserve, established in 1911, but reservation status was eliminated by the Alaska Native Claims Settlement Act *(see Alaska introduction)*. The village corporation now owns the former reservation. The Covenant Mission church and school opened in 1914, which attracted more people to the village. The Iditarod dogsled race from Anchorage to Nome passes through the village. Elim today is an Inupiat Eskimo village with a fishing and subsistence lifestyle. The Native Village of Elim is a federally recognized tribe in the community.

GOVERNMENT
Elim is a second-class city, incorporated in 1970, with a mayor and city council, located in the Unorganized Borough (see Alaska introduction). The community also has a village council, organized under the Indian Reorganization Act of 1934 and headed by a president. Shareholders in the village corporation also hold shares in the Bering Straits regional Native corporation *(see Alaska introduction)*.

ECONOMY
The Elim economy is based on subsistence activities. Year-round cash employment is offered only by the city and the school. Unemployment is high, and seasonal part-time employment in nearby Nome has declined recently, due to a depressed gold market. Residents rely on fish, seal, beluga whale, reindeer, moose, and the produce from summer gardens to supplement cash earnings.

Fisheries. Thirty-nine residents hold commercial fishing permits. The village would like to develop a fish-processing plant.

Government as employer. Of the 91 employed residents, 63 work for the local, state, or federal government.

Manufacturing. Two residents are employed in manufacturing.

Services and retail. There are six businesses in the community, including a taxi service, Elim Native Store, grocery stores, and two day-care centers. Retail trade employs 2 residents; education, health and social services employs 49; information services 2; and public administration employs 22 residents.

Tourism and recreation. The Elim carnival is a visitor attraction. Arts, entertainment, recreation, accommodations, and food service industries employ four residents.

Transportation. Four airline companies service Elim. Transportation, warehousing, and utility industries employ two residents.

INFRASTRUCTURE
Seventeen capital projects, funded by grants, are active in Elim.

Transportation. Elim is reached primarily by air and water. The state provides a 3,000- by 60-foot gravel runway. Elim Native Corp. also owns a private 4,700-foot paved airstrip with a 1,390-foot crosswind runway at Moses Point. The village does not have a dock, so supplies must be lightered to shore by a company operating from Nome. Plans are underway to develop a harbor and dock; an access road is under construction. Freight is brought into Nome yearly by cargo ship.

Electricity. Electric power is provided by the Alaska Village Electric Cooperative, generating power by burning oil.

Water and waste systems. Water is drawn from a well and is treated. BIA and HUD housing, and water and sewer systems built by PHS in the mid-1970s, have provided residents with piped water and sewer, indoor water heaters, and plumbing, including in-home washers and dryers. Wastes flow to a sewage treatment plant with ocean outfall. The landfill is not open to residents. The city needs a new water source, since water shortages occur, and to replace cracked PVC pipes.

Telecommunications. Local telephone service is available through the Mukluk Telephone Company; long distance service is provided by Alascom. Internet service is available through Arctic.Net/TelAlaska Inc. and GCI. Teleconferencing is provided by Alaska Teleconferencing Network. Cable television service is available, and Rural Alaska Television Network provides television access. Two radio stations are available to residents.

COMMUNITY FACILITIES AND SERVICES
Local facilities include a city building and both public and school libraries.

Education. The Aniguiin School in Elim is in the Bering Straits School District. The school has 96 students and 9 teachers.

Health care. Health care is provided by the Elim Health Clinic, owned by the city and leased to the U.S. Public Health Service. The clinic is administered by the Norton Sound Health Corporation.

Total area of entitlement under ANCSA
                                     138,240 acres
Total labor force   448
High school graduate or higher   71.3%
Bachelor's degree or higher   4.5%
Unemployment rate   23.1%
Per capita income (2000) $9,069
Population 2000 census   767
Percent Native 2000 census   93.9%

LOCATION
Emmonak is located at the mouth of the Yukon River, on the north bank of Kwiguk Pass, in the Yukon-Kuskokwim Delta, 175 miles northwest of Bethel.

CLIMATE
Emmonak lies in the maritime climate zone. Temperatures range from winter lows of -25°F to summer highs of 79°F. Average annual precipitation is 19 inches, including snowfall of from 50 to 60 inches. The growing season is 100 days long.

CULTURE AND HISTORY
Emmonak is a Yup'ik Eskimo village involved in commercial fishing and fish processing, as well as subsistence activities. The original settlement was 1.4 miles south of its present location; residents were forced to move because of flooding. Residents of Chuloonawick, a nearby fishing camp, also live in Emmonak. The Emmonak Village is a federally recognized tribe in the community.

GOVERNMENT
Emmonak was incorporated as a second-class city in 1964 and is located in the Unorganized Borough (see Alaska introduction). The community also has a traditional village council headed by a president. Shareholders in the village corporation also hold shares in the Calista Corporation regional Native corporation (see Alaska introduction).

ECONOMY
Emmonak has a seasonal economy with most activity occurring during the summer. The city is becoming a center for commercial fishing, fish purchasing, and fish processing on the lower Yukon River. Subsistence activities and trapping are important economic activities for most village residents during the fall and winter. Yukon Delta Fish Marketing Co-op and the Bering Sea Fisheries process and export salmon from Emmonak. Subsistence activities, trapping, and public assistance support income. The majority of the community travels to fish camps during the summer months to dry salmon for winter use. Moose, beluga whale, seal, and waterfowl also are utilized.

Construction. Approximately 21 residents are employed in construction.

Fisheries. Approximately 101 residents hold commercial fishing permits.

Government as employer. Of the 217 employed residents, 123 work for the local, state, or federal government.

Manufacturing. Six residents are employed in manufacturing.

Mining. Mining and hunting industries employ seven residents.

Services and retail. There are 13 businesses in the community, including a women's shelter, restaurants, realty offices, taxi service, equipment supply and repair, and a fish marketing co-op. Retail trade employs 32 residents; information services, 2; financial and related businesses, 6; education, health, and social services, 76; and public administration employs 37 residents.

Tourism and recreation. Visitor attractions include kayaking the Yukon Delta National Wildlife Refuge, bird watching, camping, fishing, and nature photography. A hotel and a bed-and-breakfast are available. Emmonak has a pool hall and a gift shop. Arts, entertainment, recreation, accommodations, and food services employ five residents.

Transportation. Three airline companies service Emmonak. One taxi is available. Transportation, warehousing, and utility industries employ 19 residents.

INFRASTRUCTURE
Seventeen capital projects, funded by grants, are active in Emmonak.

Transportation. Emmonak relies on air and water transportation. The state provides a 4,400- by 75-foot gravel airstrip. There are no connecting roads to outside villages, but there are winter trails to Kotlik, Alakanuk, and Sheldon Point for snowmachine travel. Skiffs and all-terrain vehicles are used during the summer for local transportation.

Electricity. Electricity is available to residents from the Alaska Village Electric Cooperative, generating power by burning oil.

Water and waste systems. Water, drawn from the Yukon River, is treated. Piped water and sewer services have recently been expanded to the west side where more than 160 homes, businesses, and the school are now served with an above-ground circulating water system and vacuum sewage system. Water storage capacity has been doubled to serve the system expansion. The landfill must be relocated.

Telecommunications. Local telephone service is provided by United Utilities, while long distance service is available through Alascom. Internet service is provided by Unicom/United Utilities. Teleconferencing is available through Alaska Teleconferencing. Cable television service is available and Rural Alaska Television Network provides television access. Two radio stations are available to residents.

COMMUNITY FACILITIES AND SERVICES
Local facilities include a city teen center and a community center. A new washeteria is under construction.

Education. Emmonak School is in the Lower Yukon School District. The school has 229 students and 17 teachers.

Health care. Health care is provided by the Emmonak Health Clinic, owned by the city and leased to the U.S. Public Health Service. The clinic is administered by the Yukon-Kuskokwim Health Corporation. Pearl E. Johnson Subregional Clinic also is available.

[ee-MAHN-nuck]
Ethnicity: Yup'ik Eskimo

ANCSA village corporation
Emmonak Corporation
P.O. Box 49
Emmonak, AK 99581
    907-949-1411
    907-949-1412 Fax

English Bay
See Nanwalek

Evansville

Ethnicity: Nunamiut Eskimo,
Kokyukon
Athabascan

ANCSA village corporation
Evansville, Incorporated
122 First Ave., Suite 2028
Fairbanks, AK 99701-4871
907-451-8008
907-451-7695 Fax

Total area of entitlement under ANCSA
69,120 acres
Total labor force 30
High school graduate or higher 85.2%
Bachelor's degree or higher 11.1%
Unemployment rate 0%
Per capita income *(2000)* $15,745
Population *2000 census* 71
Percent Native *2000 census* 35.2%

LOCATION
Evansville is located 180 air miles and 250 road miles northwest of Fairbanks, adjacent to Bettles.

CLIMATE
The area experiences a continental climate with extreme temperature differences. Winter lows may reach -40°F or below, while summer temperatures may be as high as 70°F. Average annual precipitation is 13.4 inches, including 77 inches of snowfall.

CULTURE AND HISTORY
Nrmarniut Eskimos and Koyukon Athabascan Indians have lived as neighbors and kin in the area for generations. The village was named for Wilford Evans, Sr., who owned a trading post and river-barge business in Allakaket. He opened a sawmill and built the Bettles Lodge and General Store. The population of Evansville is a mixture of Athabascans and Inupiat Eskimos. The Evansville Tribal Council is a federally recognized tribe in the community.

GOVERNMENT
Evansville is unincorporated and is located in the Unorganized Borough *(see Alaska introduction)*. The village is governed by a traditional council headed by a chief. Shareholders in the village corporation are also shareholders in the Doyon Limited regional Native corporation *(see Alaska introduction)*.

ECONOMY
Evansville's economy is linked to air transportation, visitor services, and government, as well as its proximity to the city of Bettles. Ninety percent of the heads of household are employed, most full-time. Government agencies provide employment in the Kanuti Refuge and Gates of the Arctic National Park.The community is accessible by road in winter, which significantly reduces the cost of goods and supplies. The FAA, National Park Service, school, and city provide year-round employment. During the summer a BLM fire-fighting station and guides for the Brooks Range offer seasonal employment. Subsistence activities are important to the Native residents; however, subsistence use by the non-Natives is substantially lower. Salmon, moose, bear, caribou, and sheep are utilized.

Urban hunters, who drive up the Dalton Highway, also compete for local game. The tribe provides a tribal office and operates a clinic.

Construction. Five residents are employed in construction.

Government as employer. Of the 25 employed residents, 8 work for the local, state, or federal government.

Services and retail. Businesses in the community include management and technical services and a general contractor. Education, health, and social service industries employ six residents; public administration, two; and professional, scientific, administrative, and waste management employ nine residents.

Tourism and recreation. There are tourist facilities in nearby Bettles.

INFRASTRUCTURE
Seven capital projects, funded by grants, are active in Evansville.

Transportation. The Hickel Trail, a 30-mile winter road, periodically gives access to the Dalton Highway, which leads to Fairbanks. The Koyukuk River is used in the summer, but no commercial barge is available. A state-owned airport in Bettles is classified as a transport center, with a flight service station and a float pond. Trucks, cars, snowmachines, and all-terrain vehicles are used for local travel.

Electricity. Electricity is provided by Alaska Power Company.

Water and waste systems. Individual water wells, septic tanks, and complete plumbing are available only to about half of the households. Funds were recently provided to install individual systems for several homes that are without indoor plumbing. A new landfill in Evansville is operated by the City of Bettles.

Telecommunications. Local telephone service is provided by National Utilities, while long distance service is available through Alascom. Rural Alaska Television Network provides television access.

COMMUNITY FACILITIES AND SERVICES
There are no state operated schools located in the community. A community center is under construction.

Health care. Health care is provided by the Frank Tobuk, Sr., Health Clinic, owned by the village and leased to the U.S. Public Health Service. The clinic is administered by the Tanana Chiefs Conference.

Total area of entitlement under ANCSA	
	148,730 acres
Total labor force	78
High school graduate or higher	33
Bachelor's degree or higher	10
Unemployment rate	10.3%
Per capita income *(1999)*	$18,241
2003 population	144
state demographer estimate	
Population *2000 census*	168
Percent Native *2000 census*	8.3%

LOCATION
Eyak is located on the Copper River Highway within the Cordova city limits, 5.5 miles southeast of central Cordova on the Malaspina Coastal Plain. Cordova is located at the southeastern end of Prince William Sound in the Gulf of Alaska, on Orca Inlet at the base of Eyak Mountain.

PHYSICAL DESCRIPTION
Eyak covers 13.5 square miles of land at the east end of Eyak Lake in the City of Cordova. High water is an ongoing problem, although the last major flood was in 1995, caused by rainfall.

CLIMATE
Eyak's climate has a primarily maritime influence. Winter temperatures range from lows of 17°F to highs of 28°F; summer temperatures range from 49°F to 63°F. Average annual precipitation is 66 inches, including 80 inches of snowfall.

CULTURE AND HISTORY
Old stories say the Eyak people moved from the interior of Alaska down the Copper River to the mouth of the Copper River Delta. They lived off the rich salmon runs and abundant wildlife of the delta. The Eyak were always a relatively small group, and the neighboring Tlingit, Chugachigmuit, and Alutiiq continuously pressured them, raiding their fishing grounds and more peacefully assimilating the Eyak through intermarriage. The Eyak intermediated trade among the Tlingit to the east, the Athabascan Ahtna to the north along the Copper River, and the Chugachigmuit to the west.

The Eyak got along better with the Tlingits than any of the other surrounding cultures due to the close relationship between the languages. The Eyak have a separate language, which is a branch of the Athabaskan-Eyak-Tlingit language family of the Na-Dene group. Eyak was spoken in the nineteenth century from Yakutat along the south-central Alaska coast to Eyak at the Copper River delta, but by the twentieth century it survived only at Eyak. Note that the Eyak culture and language, while related to and often miscategorized as such, are not Athabascan. In many respects, the Eyak culture is closer to that of the Chugachigmuit and Tlingit.

The Russians who first traded in Alaska recognized the Eyak as a distinct culture with its own territory. By the 1880s, however, Tlingit expansion had reduced the Eyak to about 200 people on the Copper River Delta. At that point Americans arrived. The Americans opened canneries, and competed with the Eyak for Copper River salmon, slowly taking over their jobs and their food. Between disease and poverty, the Eyak as a separate people almost disappeared. The last tribal member to fluently speak Eyak was born in 1920.

During the twentieth century, many people came to Cordova from Chugachigmuit settlements on Prince William Sound, including the village of Nuchek (abandoned in 1929-30), and more recently Tatitlek and Chanega *(c.f.)*. The effects of the Good Friday earthquake of 1964 and the *Exxon Valdez* oil spill of 1989 accelerated this trend. When the Alaska Native Claims Settlement Act (ANCSA) was passed in 1971, it did not include a Native village in the Cordova area. Area Native Alaskans petitioned and lobbied for the creation of an ANCSA village corporation and succeeded. Eyak Corporation was incorporated in 1973 representing 326 original shareholders, the majority of whom were of Alutiiq descent. The physical location has become largely a non-Native community, but the few remaining Eyak and the other Native Alaskans in Cordova are working together to protect traditional Eyak lands along the Copper River Delta and to revive Eyak cultural traditions.

GOVERNMENT
Eyak is part of the City of Cordova, a home rule city located in the Unorganized Borough *(see Alaska introduction)*. The community was annexed to the city in 1993. It has a federally recognized traditional village council, the Native Village of Eyak. The Native Village is identified by the Bureau of Indian Affairs as the Native entity for Cordova, and appears to have the support of the city government.

VILLAGE CORPORATION
The Eyak Corporation functions as the village corporation for Cordova and is one of five village corporations located within the Chugach region. From 1978 it was the largest private landowner in the Cordova area. In 1995 the Corporation sold timber rights to 2,052 acres to the Federal government for $3.45 million. In 1997, as part of the *Exxon Valdez* settlement, the Corporation sold 75,425 acres (surface rights, conservation easements, or timber easements) to the federal and state governments for $45.1 million. As of early 2004, Eyak Corporation had 391 shareholders. Its shareholders also hold shares in the Chugach Alaska Corporation regional Native corporation *(see Alaska introduction)*.

ECONOMY
The economy of Eyak is integrated into the economy of Cordova. Commercial fishing, fish processing, logging, and retail businesses in Cordova provide employment.

Fisheries. While Eyak has no fishing industry of its own, commercial fishing and fish processing in Cordova provide employment for many residents.

Government as employer. Of the 70 employed residents, 15 work for the city, state, or federal government.

INFRASTRUCTURE
Transportation. Cordova can be reached only by air or water. It is linked directly to the North Pacific Ocean shipping lanes through the Gulf of Alaska. It receives year-round barge services and State Ferry service. The Merle K. "Mudhole" Smith Airport is state-owned and-operated, with a 7,499- by 150-foot asphalt runway and a 1,875- by 30-foot gravel crosswind runway. The state-owned and city-operated Cordova Municipal Airport has a 1,800- by 60-foot gravel runway. Daily scheduled jet flights and air taxis are available. Floatplanes land at the Lake Eyak seaplane base or the boat harbor. Harbor facilities include a breakwater, dock, a small-boat harbor with 850 berths, boat launch, boat haul-out, a ferry terminal, and

Also known as Cordova

[EE-yak]
Ethnicity: Alutiiq; Eyak

Municipality
City of Cordova
P.O. Box 1210
Cordova, AK 99574
907-424-6200
907-424-6000 Fax
cityofcordova.net

Native entity
Native Village of Eyak
P.O. Box 1388
Cordova, AK 99574-1388
907-424-7738
907-424-7739 Fax

ANCSA village corporation
Eyak Corporation
P.O. Box 340
Cordova, AK 99574-0340
907-424-7161
907-424-5161 Fax

Eyak

Also known as Cordova

marine repair services. A 48-mile gravel road provides access to the Copper River Delta to the east. Plans for a highway up the Copper River to connect with the statewide road system are controversial. The Merle K. "Mudhole" Smith Airport is state-operated. Other transportation services, including operation of the state-owned Cordova Municipal Airport, are provided by the city or by private firms.

Electricity. Electricity is provided by Cordova Electric Cooperative, from both diesel and hydroelectric power plants. One of the diesel plants is in Eyak. All homes and buildings in Eyak, both private and public, have electricity.

Fuel storage and distribution is available in and from Cordova.

Water and waste systems. Almost 90 percent of homes are fully plumbed and use individual wells. Cordova is requesting funds to extend its piped water system to Eyak Lake and River residences along the Copper River Highway. Many area homes are subject to high water, which increases the risk of well water contamination. Most homes use individual septic systems. Refuse is disposed of in a Class 2 landfill.

Telecommunications. All homes and buildings, both private and public, have access to telephone and cable service. One AM radio station broadcasts from Cordova, and residents can receive others from Valdez, Anchorage, and Glennallen. Two FM radio stations broadcast from Cordova. The Alaska Rural Communications System broadcasts two television stations locally. Local telephone service is provided by the Cordova Telephone Co-op, while long distance service is available from AT&T Alascom or GCI. GCI also provides local cable service.

COMMUNITY FACILITIES AND SERVICES

Other than the Ilanka Health Center and the Ilanka Cultural Center and Museum, there are no public facilities in Eyak. The City of Cordova provides waste collection and disposal, water supply, a youth recreation center, law enforcement, and emergency response. The Cordova Public Library serves the community.

Education. Children attend the two Cordova city schools, Cordova Junior/Senior High School (grades 7–12) and Mount Eccles Elementary (grades preschool through 6). The Cordova Public Library serves the community. The Ilanka Cultural Center and Museum, operated by the village council, has historical and contemporary exhibits of the Native peoples and cultures of the Copper River and Prince William Sound area.

Health care. Health-care is provided by the Ilanka Health Center, owned and operated by the Native Village of Eyak, and serving both Native and non-Native patients. It is backed by the Cordova Community Medical Center, a qualified acute care and long-term care facility operated by the City of Cordova.

False Pass

Ethnicity: Unangan Aleut

Isanotski Corporation
101 Isanotski Drive
False Pass, AK 99583
907-548-2217
907-548-2317 Fax

Total area of entitlement under ANCSA	77,188 acres
Total labor force	55
High school graduate or higher	65.2%
Bachelor's degree or higher	17.4%
Unemployment rate	0%
Per capita income *(2000)*	$21,465
Population *2000 census*	64
(village information)	69
Percent Native *2000 census*	65.6%

LOCATION

False Pass is located nearly 650 miles southwest of Anchorage. It is on the eastern shore of Unimak Island, adjacent to Isanotski Strait, which separates the Alaska Peninsula from Unimak Island. The strait is a direct and well-used access from the Pacific Ocean and Gulf of Alaska to the fishing grounds of the Bering Sea and Bristol Bay.

CLIMATE

False Pass has a maritime climate, with mild winters and cool summers. Winter lows average 11°F, with highs averaging 40°F; summer temperatures range from 32°F to 55°F. The village is situated on the Pacific west-to-east storm track, causing the prevailing southeast winds to be constant and often strong. Snowfall averages 56 inches, with total annual precipitation of 33 inches.

CULTURE AND HISTORY

The English name of the village derives from the fact that the Bering Sea side of the strait is extremely shallow. The Aleut name of the community is *Isanax,* translated as "the pass." False Pass was settled in the early 1900s by the homesteader William Gardner. In 1917 a cannery was relocated from Morzhovoi Bay to the present-day location of False Pass. The cannery expanded, and additional people from nearby areas such as Morzhovoi, Sanak Island, and Ikatan moved to the village. In the early 1960s, an airstrip and school opened in the village. The community is primarily Unangan. Fishing, fish processing, and subsistence activities are the mainstays of the lifestyle. The False Pass Tribal Council is a federally recognized tribe in the community.

GOVERNMENT

False Pass was incorporated as a second-class city in 1990, with a mayor and city council. False Pass is one of six communities in the Aleutians East Borough *(see Alaska introduction)*. The village has a traditional tribal council, headed by a president.

VILLAGE CORPORATION

Isanotski Corporation was formed under ANCSA in 1971. The corporation currently has approximately 70 shareholders, most of Aleut origin. The corporation's land endowment stretches from the Gulf of Alaska to the Bering Sea on both sides of Isanotski Strait. Businesses include storage facilities for fishing gear and boats. Shareholders in the village corporation also hold shares in the Aleut Corporation regional Native corporation *(see Alaska introduction)*.

ECONOMY

The local economy is based on the commercial salmon, halibut, herring, and cod fisheries. False Pass is also an important refueling stop for fishing fleets en route to Bristol Bay and the Bering Sea. Bering Pacific and Peter Pan Seafoods process the commercial catch. Cash income is supplemented by subsistence hunting and fishing. Salmon, halibut, geese, caribou, seals, and wild cattle on Sanak Island are utilized.

Construction. Two residents are employed in construction.

Fisheries and forestry. Eleven residents hold commercial fishing permits. Farming, fishing, and forestry industries employ 10 residents.

Government as employer. Of the 41 employed residents, three full-time and three part-time employees work for the local, state, or federal government.

Manufacturing. Two residents are employed in manufacturing.

Services and retail. The community holds three business licenses, including one by the City of False Pass. Retail trade employs two residents; education, health, and social services, nine; public administration, six; and professional, scientific, administrative, and waste management employ three residents.

Tourism and recreation. Visitor attractions include scenic viewing, bear watching, hunting, and fishing. Lodging is available in the summer only. Arts, entertainment, recreation, accommodations, and food service industries employ three residents.

Transportation. Transportation, warehousing, and utility industries employ six residents.

INFRASTRUCTURE
Five capital projects, funded by grants, are active in False Pass.

Transportation. Boats and aircraft provide the only means of transportation into False Pass. The state provides a 2,100- by 80-foot gravel airstrip and a seaplane base. Mail and passenger flights are available during the week. There is no boat harbor, but a dock and a boat ramp are available. A boat haul-out and a storage facility are being built. The Corps of Engineers is designing a $13 million small-boat harbor. Cargo barges are available from Seattle. The state ferry operates once a month between May and October from Kodiak.

Electricity. Electricity is provided by False Pass Electric Association.

Water and waste systems. Water, drawn from a nearby spring and reservoir is treated and stored in a 65,000-gallon tank. A piped water system is available to most households. Residents use individual septic tanks for sewage disposal, and the city operates a septic sludge tanker and sludge disposal site. All homes are fully plumbed. Wastewater from seafood processing flows directly into an outfall line. Water system improvements were recently funded, including an enlarged dam and a second 65,000-gallon water tank. The city provides refuse service during the week.

Telecommunications. Local telephone service is provided by Pacific Telecommunications; long distance service is available from Alascom. Internet service is provided by GCI. Teleconferencing is available from Alaska Teleconferencing Network. Cable television service is available, and Rural Alaska Television Network provides television access. One radio station is available to residents.

COMMUNITY FACILITIES AND SRVICES
Local area facilities include a youth center, city office, and both public and school libraries.

Education. The False Pass School is operated by the Aleutians East Borough School District. The school has 12 students and 2 teachers.

Health care. Health care is provided by the False Pass Health Clinic, owned by the city and leased to the U.S. Public Health Service. It is administered by the Eastern Aleutian Tribe. Auxiliary health care is provided by False Pass First Responders.

Fort Yukon

Total area of entitlement under ANCSA	
	214,479 acres
Total labor force	449
High school graduate or higher	69.2%
Bachelor's degree or higher	13.1%
Unemployment rate	18%
Per capita income *(2000)*	$13,360
Population *2000 census*	595
Percent Native *2000 census*	88.7%

LOCATION
Fort Yukon is located on the north bank of the Yukon River, at its junction with the Porcupine River, about 145 miles northeast of Fairbanks.

CLIMATE
Fort Yukon's climate is one of extremes. The winters are long and harsh, and the summers are warm but short. After freeze-up, the plateau is a source of cold, continental Arctic air. Winter low temperatures range from -76°F to 0°F; summer high temperatures range from 65°F to 80°F or above. Annual precipitation averages 6.6 inches, with 43.4 inches of yearly snowfall.

CULTURE AND HISTORY
Most Fort Yukon residents are descendants of the Yukon Flats, Chandalar River, Birch Creek, Black River, and Porcupine River Gwich'in Athabascan tribes. The village was founded in 1847 by Alexander Murray as a Canadian outpost in Russian territory. It soon became an important trade center for the Kutchin Indians. A post office was established in 1898. Subsistence is an important component of the local culture. The Native Village of Fort Yukon is a federally recognized tribe in the community.

GOVERNMENT
Fort Yukon was incorporated as a second-class city in 1959 and is located in the Unorganized Borough *(see Alaska introduction)*. It also has a village council, headed by a first chief, constituted in accordance with the Indian Reorganization Act of 1934.

VILLAGE CORPORATION
The village corporation, Gwitchyaa Zhee Corporation, provides electricity through Gwitchyaa Zhee Utility Company. Shareholders in the village corporation also hold shares in Doyon, Limited, regional Native corporation whose assets of 12.5 million acres make Doyon the largest private land owner in North America *(see Alaska introduction)*.

ECONOMY
City, state, and federal agencies and the village corporation are the primary employers in Fort Yukon. Residents also rely on subsistence activities. The school district is the largest employer. The BLM operates an emergency fire fighting base at the airport. The U.S. Air Force operates a White Alice Radar Station in Fort Yukon. Trapping and Native handicrafts also provide income. Residents rely on subsistence foods.

**Ethnicity: Kutchin (Gwich'in)
Athabascan**

Gwitchyaa Zhee Corporation
P.O. Box 329
Ft. Yukon, AK 99740
   907-662-3056
   907-662-2646 Fax

Fort Yukon

Salmon, whitefish, moose, bear, caribou, and waterfowl provide most meat sources.

Construction. Eight residents are employed in construction.

Fisheries. One resident holds a commercial fishing permit. Farming, fishing, and forestry industries employ six residents.

Government as employer. Of the 237 employed residents, 150 work for the local, state, or federal government.

Mining. Mining and hunting employ four residents.

Services and retail. There are 31 businesses in the community, including a general store, day care, fur cooperative, utility shop, fuel company, outpost, public broadcasting company, and the City of Fort Yukon. Retail trade employs 16 residents; public administration, 89; education, health, and social services, 75; financial and related businesses 2; information services, 2; and professional, scientific, administrative, and waste management employ 5 residents.

Tourism and recreation. At least five lodging accommodations are available, including a hotel, lodge, and a number of bed-and-breakfast facilities. Fort Yukon experiences spectacular northern lights. Fort Yukon is located eight miles north of the Arctic Circle. Sightseeing air tours are available. Other visitor attractions include the Yukon Flats National Wildlife Refuge, the largest Athabascan village in the interior, the most northern point of the Yukon River, an Athabascan beaded altar cloth in the St. Stephens Episcopal Church, a three-story log cabin, and a replica of a Hudson Bay Company fort. Services include a deli, café, and tour service. Arts, entertainment, recreation, accommodations, and food services employ three residents.

Transportation. Eight airline companies service Fort Yukon. Transportation, warehousing, and utility industries employ 13 residents.

INFRASTRUCTURE

Twenty-four capital projects, funded by grants, are active in Fort Yukon.

Transportation. Fort Yukon is accessible by air in winter and by barge and boat during the summer. Heavy cargo is brought in by barge from the end of May through mid-September. A barge off-loading area is available, but no dock. Skiffs and riverboats are used for recreation, hunting, fishing and other subsistence activities. The state provides a 5,810- by 150-foot lighted gravel airstrip. Hospital Lake, adjacent to the airport, is used by floatplanes. There are 17 miles of local roads for cars and trucks. The city transit bus system provides local transportation. In winter snowmachines and dog sleds are used on area trails or the frozen river.

Electricity. Electricity is provided by Gwitchyaa Zhee Utilities.

Water and waste systems. Water drawn from two wells is treated and stored in a 110,000-gallon tank. A combination of piped water, water delivery, and individual wells serve households. A flush/haul system, septic tanks, honeybuckets, and outhouses are used for sewage disposal. Half of all residences are plumbed. A piped water system and household septic tanks are available. The city has funds to repair the piped water system and to build a piped gravity sewer system to serve 250 residences and businesses.

Telecommunications. Local telephone service is provided by Interior Telephone Company, while long distance service is available through Alascom. Internet service is available by GCI for the school only. Cable television service is available, and Rural Alaska Television Network provides television access. Two radio stations are available to residents. Teleconferencing is available through Alaska Teleconferencing Network and the Tok Legislative Information Office.

COMMUNITY FACILITIES AND SERVICES

Facilities include Youth R Us, senior services, a library, a community center gym, and recent construction of a tribal hall.

Education. Fort Yukon School is in the Yukon Flats School District. The school has 116 students and 12 teachers. Yukon Flats Correspondence School has six students.

Health care. Health care is provided by the Yukon Flats Health Center, owned and run by the city of Fort Yukon. The health center is administered by the Tanana Chiefs. Auxiliary health care is provided by Fort Yukon EMS and Rescue Squad.

akona

[guh-KOH-nuh]
Ethnicity: Ahtna Athabascan

ANCSA village corporation
Ahtna, Inc.
P.O. Box 649
Glennallen, AK 99588
907-822-3476
907-822-3495 Fax

Total area of entitlement under ANCSA
74,715 acres

Total labor force	155
High school graduate or higher	89.4%
Bachelor's degree or higher	27.3%
Unemployment rate	14.9%
Per capita income *(2000)*	$18,143
Population *2000 census*	84
Percent Native *2000 census*	20.2%

LOCATION

Gakona is located at the confluence of the Copper and Gakona rivers, 15 miles northeast of Glennallen. The community lies at Mile 2 on the Tok Cutoff to the Glenn Highway, just east of the Richardson Highway.

CLIMATE

Gakona is located in the continental climate zone. Temperatures range from winter lows of -62°F to summer highs of 91°F. Snowfall averages 61 inches, with an annual precipitation of 13 inches.

CULTURE AND HISTORY

Gakona is a non-Native community although the surrounding Copper River area is populated by Ahtna Indians. Athabascan Indians have lived in the Copper River basin for thousands of years. Gakona traditionally served as a wood and fish camp and later became a permanent village. In 1904, Doyle's Roadhouse was constructed at the junction of the Valdez-Eagle and Valdez-Fairbanks trails and became a stopping point for travelers. There was also a stagecoach station and blacksmith shop. All these buildings are still standing. Gakona Lodge was built in 1929 and is on the National Register of Historical Places. The lodge contains many relics of the gold-rush era. The community has a commercial district, a non-Native residential area, and an Athabascan village. The Native Village of Gakona is a federally recognized tribe in the community.

GOVERNMENT

Gakona is unincorporated and is located in the Unorganized Borough (see Alaska introduction). The community has a traditional village council, headed by a president.

VILLAGE CORPORATION

Shareholders in the village corporation also hold shares in Ahtna regional Native corporation (see Alaska introduction).

ECONOMY

Gakona depends upon local businesses and seasonal tourist travel. Summers provide employment opportunities for local fishing and hunting guides, rafting operations, and outfitters. There is a motel, restaurant, bar, newspaper print shop, sawmill, and dogsled builder in Gakona. Some residents rely on subsistence activities and trapping. Recording equipment for the High Frequency Active Auroral Research Program (HAARP) is near Gakona.

Construction. Nine residents are employed in construction. There is a welding service in Gakona.

Fisheries and forestry. Three residents hold commercial fishing permits. Farming, fishing, and forestry industries employ two residents.

Government as employer. Of the 63 employed residents, 24 work for the local, state, or federal government.

Manufacturing. Three residents are employed in manufacturing. There is a sawmill, newspaper, and print shop and a dogsled maker in Gakona.

Services and retail. Services are extensive in Gakona, catering mainly to tourists. There are 73 businesses in the community, including a day care, kennel, mineral surveyor, trading post, construction outfits, and the Cheesh Na Tribal Council. Retail trade employs 8 residents; education, health, and social services, 14; professional, scientific, administrative, and waste management, 6; financial and related businesses, 2; and public administration employs 5 residents.

Tourism and recreation. Visitor attractions include fishing, rafting, and jet boats. Events in June include an antique car show and a half-way to New Year's Eve party. At least eight lodging services are available including an RV park, campground, bed-and-breakfast, and lodge. Other services include ranch and fishing guides, guide and flying service, glacier guide service, fishing and camping club, restaurants, handicrafts, stained glass studio, outfitters, and therapeutic massage. Arts, entertainment, recreation, accommodations, and food services employ eight residents.

Transportation. Transportation, warehousing, and utility facilities employ five residents. A trucking company is located in Gakona.

INFRASTRUCTURE

Six capital projects, funded by grants, are active in Gakona.

Electricity. Electricity is provided by Copper Valley Electric Association.

Water and waste systems. Individual wells and septic systems and complete plumbing are in all households. The school uses its own well water system. Funds have been requested to build a new water well and a storage tank for a HUD housing complex. Copper Basin Sanitation provides refuse collection services.

Telecommunications. Local telephone and Internet service is provided by the Copper Valley Telephone Co-op, while long distance service is available through Alascom. Teleconferencing is available through the Glennallen legislative information office. Cable television service is available, and Rural Alaska Television Network provides television access. Two radio stations are available to residents.

COMMUNITY FACILITIES AND SERVICES

Residents have requested funds for a new community hall.

Education. Gakona School has 17 students and 1 teacher, kindergarten through sixth grade.

Health care. Gakona Health Clinic is available, as is Cross Road Medical Center in Glennallen. Auxiliary health care is provided by Copper River EMS, Gulkana Clinic, and Cross Road Medical Center in Glennallen.

Galena

Total area of entitlement under ANCSA	115,200 acres
Total labor force	495
High school graduate or higher	81.3%
Bachelor's degree or higher	28.6%
Unemployment rate	8.7%
Per capita income (2000)	$22,143
Population 2000 census	675
Percent Native 2000 census	67.4%

LOCATION

Galena is located on the north bank of the Yukon River, 45 miles east of Nulato and 270 air miles west of Fairbanks.

CLIMATE

Galena experiences a cold, continental climate with extreme temperature differences. Temperatures range from -40°F or below in the winter to 70°F and above in the summer. Average precipitation is 12.7 inches, including 60 inches of annual snowfall.

CULTURE AND HISTORY

Galena was established near an old fish-camp site in 1917 as a supply point for the area's lead-ore mines. In 1920 Koyukon Athabascans living upriver began moving to Galena to sell wood to steamboats and to haul freight for the mines. The establishment of the Galena and Campion Air Force bases in the 1950s brought more growth and change to Galena. Many of Galena's residents are descendants of Louden. Subsistence food sources include salmon, whitefish, moose, and berries. The Louden Tribal Council is a federally recognized tribe in the community.

GOVERNMENT

Galena was incorporated as a first-class city in 1971, with a city manager, mayor, and city council. The village is located in the Unorganized Borough (see Alaska introduction). There is also a traditional village council, headed by a chief. Shareholders in the village corporation also hold shares in the Doyon Limited regional Native corporation (see Alaska introduction).

Also known as Louden Village

[guh-LEE-nuh]
Ethnicity: Koyukon Athabascan

ANCSA village corporation
Gana-A' Yoo, Limited
3000 A Street #417
Anchorage, AK 99503
  907-569-9599
  907-569-9699 Fax

Galena

Also known as Louden Village

ECONOMY

Galena serves as the transportation, government, and commercial center for the western interior. Federal, state, city, school, and village government jobs dominate, but Galena has other jobs in air transportation and retail businesses. Construction work and Bureau of Land Management fire fighting provide seasonal employment. Low market prices have shut down the Illinois Creek gold mine, 50 miles southwest of Galena.

Construction. Approximately 30 residents are employed in construction.

Fisheries. Thirty-one residents hold commercial fishing permit, mostly in salmon and whitefish. Farming, fishing, and forestry industries employ three residents.

Government as employer. Of the 334 employed residents, 227 work for the local, state, or federal government.

Manufacturing. A blacksmith business is located in Galena. Three residents are employed in manufacturing.

Services and retail. Services are extensive in Galena, catering not only to this community but also to customers in numerous surrounding villages. There are 36 businesses in the community, including construction, gun shop, arctic cat sales and service, electric company, heating company, a development corporation, a security company, and a wireless business. Retail trade employs 20 residents; education, health, and social services, 148; public administration, 53; information services 7; and professional, scientific, administrative, and waste management professions employ 7 residents.

Tourism and recreation. Galena holds popular traditional festivals like the Yukon Jamboree, the Kiyu Bonfire, and the Winter Carnival. Four lodging facilities are available, including two bed-and-breakfasts. Several guide and tour services are available. Arts, entertainment, recreation, accommodations, and food service industries employ 29 residents.

Transportation. Seven airline companies and one car rental company service Galena. A transportation service is located in Galena. Transportation, warehousing, and utility industries employ 14 residents.

INFRASTRUCTURE

Twenty-nine capital projects, funded by grants, are active in Galena.

Transportation. Galena serves as a regional transport center for surrounding villages. The state-owned Edward G. Pitka Sr. Airport provides the only year-round access. There is a paved, lighted 7,254- by 150-foot runway and a 2,786- by 80-foot gravel ski strip next to the main runway. Cargo barges access Galena through the rivers from mid-May through mid-October. A boat launch was recently completed. Pickups, cars, snowmachines, skiffs, and all-terrain vehicles are used for local travel. Frozen rivers in winter are used for travel to Ruby, Koyukuk, Kaltag, and Nulato. A frozen trail in winter is available to Huslia.

Electricity. The City of Galena provides electricity.

Water and waste systems. Water is drawn from wells and treated. Twenty-eight residences and the school are connected to a piped water and sewer system. More than 110 households now use a flush/haul system. Construction of a new well, water treatment system, and storage tank are underway. Additional homes are being added to the piped water system. The city provides refuse collection and landfill use. Improvements are needed.

Telecommunications. Local telephone service is provided by Interior Telephone Company and the U.S. Air Force, while long distance service is available through Alascom. Internet service is provided by Arctic.Net/TelAlaska and for the school only by GCI. Teleconferencing is available from Alaska Teleconferencing Network and the Tok legislative information office. Rural Alaska Television Network provides television access. One radio station is available to residents.

COMMUNITY FACILITIES AND SERVICES

Local facilities include a community hall, public and school libraries, and a village council that hosts youth activities. Senior citizen services are available, which include an elder's lunch program. Construction of a washeteria is in progress. Twenty households use honeybuckets, and others have individual septic tanks. A landfill is available.

Education. There are four city schools in Galena under the Galena City School District. The schools collectively have 3,889 students and 63 teachers.

Health care. Health-care facilities clinics include Galena Health Center and the Galena Public Health Office. The clinic is a qualified emergency care center. X-ray, laboratory, dental, dental X-ray, and darkroom are available. The clinic is owned by the city and leased to the U.S. Public Health Service. It is administered by the Tanana Chiefs Conference.

Honoring Nations Honoree 2002

Yukaana Development Corporation, Louden Tribal Council

The Louden Tribal Council created the Yukaana Development Corporation (YDC) in 1997 to address the concerns of environmental degradation and environmental justice, and to improve Yukaana citizens' training and employment opportunities. The first tribally owned corporation in the State of Alaska, YDC led a successful effort to clean the contamination caused by a local military base, and has provided training and employment opportunities to over 100 tribal and community members in this rural region.

The traditional homeland of the Louden Tribe is in the interior region of Alaska, near the hub village of Galena, which lies 270 air miles west of Fairbanks. Most of the Tribe's 575 members live in or near Galena, and like many other Alaska Natives, they rely upon subsistence fishing, hunting and gathering. These activities occur primarily within the three national wildlife refuges surrounding Galena.

Galena is also home to the United States Air Force Galena Air Station, which was established in 1940 as part of the military's Aircraft Lend Lease Program. While the relationship between the Louden Tribe and the Air Force has been largely positive from a government-to-government standpoint, the build up and operations of the Galena Air Force Station have severely damaged the environment. Throughout the base's active lifespan, the Air Force has dumped 55-gallon drums that were used to transport petroleum products on adjoining tribal and tribal subsistence land. Periodic flooding of the Yukon River has scattered tens of thousands of these drums in the wetlands downriver from Galena. For example, in 1945, a major flood deposited an estimated 250,000 drums in sloughs behind the village, along stream banks and throughout adjoining wooded areas. Clearly, the drums have caused surface pollution—they remain highly visible from the air. Worse, petroleum contaminants have seeped out of the drums and into the underlying watershed. Millions of gallons of fuel float atop the village's aquifer.

Unfortunately, until the early 1990s, there was little the Louden Tribe could do. Like many other rural Alaska villages, the Tribe historically has faced high rates of unemployment, has been allowed little control over its limited resources, and has depended heavily on the state and federal governments for transfer payments. Among other deficiencies, the tribal government had insufficient financial and human resources to conduct environmental studies.

In 1992 tribal leaders initiated a series of community planning sessions intended to give the Tribal Council greater strategic direction and, ultimately, to strengthen the Tribe's governmental capacity. Almost immediately, consensus was reached on the Tribe's mission: "To Govern Ourselves." Moreover, both the community and the tribal government embraced a theme that would guide their actions from then on: "Neel ghul neets niiy," which translates to "We Work Together, We Help Each Other."

In correspondence with this renewed commitment to self-governance and cooperation, tribal members voiced a number of community goals. These included new job opportunities, improved health and well being, and a clean environment. Community members were particularly concerned about environmental contamination in Galena. Despite the military's claim that its presence had not affected human health, community members asserted that the Air Force Station had damaged the health of their homeland and compromised their hunting, fishing and subsistence resources.

In 1994-95, with grant funding, the Tribe undertook a series of studies to assess the environment. An independent environmental engineering firm found significant contamination of heavy metals, pesticides and petroleum-based products, and it recommended that as many as 64 sites receive further environmental assessment. The new data convinced the Tribe that it must take action.

The Tribe considered two options—engage in costly litigation against the U.S. military, or work cooperatively with it to remedy the situation. Consistent with "Neel ghul neets niiy," the Tribe chose the latter, and in 1996 brought together 27 state and federal agencies in a public meeting to demonstrate the Tribe's willingness to cooperate, government-to-government basis, in environmental remediation. Drum removal was the community's top priority.

While the Air Force was committed to the project, the Louden Tribe encountered several practical obstacles. First, tribal and community members were untrained in environmental remediation, making it impossible for them to participate, much less lead an environmental clean up until they obtained proper certification. Second, there were no environmental remediation businesses in or near Galena. Up to this point, contractors from outside the region would come to Galena, bring their own trained employees, do the work and leave. In fact, local hire was only about 20 percent on any contracted project.

To address the first problem, the Tribe decided that it would build its pool of qualified labor by collaborating with the Environmental Protection Agency, the Alaska Department of Environmental Conservation, laborers' and operators' unions

and others to train community members. Then the Tribe took the lead in establishing a regional job bank for Galena and five surrounding villages. All six villages joined in the Koyukon Labor Agreement, which stipulates that any company seeking to hire laborers for a project in the region (any project, not just an environmental clean-up project) must first submit a call for local hires.

In 1997, having developed a pool of qualified labor, the Tribe was ready to address the second problem, the lack of a local environmental remediation business. To do so, the Council made a move that was unprecedented in Alaska—it created the Yukaana Development Corporation (YDC) as a for-profit tribal corporation, chartered under State of Alaska Laws. The Louden Tribal Council realized, creatively, that YDC could be both an economic development strategy and a means for addressing its citizens' environmental degradation, environmental justice and self-determination concerns.

To help assure YDC's success, the tribal government has insulated YDC from internal and external (government-to-government) political issues. In particular, it created a seven-member corporate Board of Directors, whose members operate under conflict of interest rules. The tribal government is then able to concentrate on political concerns (such as its relationship with the USAF), and YDC's Directors are able to focus on economic development, profit generation, training and employment. All dividends from YDC are to be assigned back to the Tribe to expand programs and services for the tribal community's benefit.

The Louden Tribal Council has enjoyed many successes since YDC's incorporation. Indeed, this operation represents many firsts. Not only is YDC the first tribally owned enterprise in Alaska, but it works under the first memorandum of agreement between a tribe and the USAF, and Louden is the first tribe to be approved to provide environmental remediation services to a semi-active military base in Alaska.

As an environmental remediation business, YDC is meeting critical needs. In November 1997, Yukaana employees were able to respond to a large oil spill in a bay 1,200 miles away within 12 hours, an effort that earned the Louden Tribe a citation from the State of Alaska. Shortly thereafter, Arctic Slope Construction, Inc. (ASCI) subcontracted YDC to stage and compact 38,000 barrels (contaminated and uncontaminated) for removal. In 1999, YDC was the major subcontractor on a $2.7 million project to clean a 10-mile radius surrounding the Galena Air Force Station, and the company successfully removed 12,000 55-gallon drums and 3,200 barrels of tar products from the area. Today, YDC continues to provide environmental remediation and demolition services for the Air Force through its partnerships with the Bethel Native Corporation International and ASCI (the latter has been an ongoing mentor to YDC in the managerial and technical aspects of environmental remediation contracts). While there is much to be done before the Louden Tribe will consider the area environmentally clean, YDC's achievements already have given them great success in self-governance. The Corporation increases the Tribe's control over matters, environmental or otherwise, that concern its people.

YDC has increased training and employment opportunities in a region where such opportunities are highly seasonal and very scarce. Depending on the remediation needs stipulated in its contracts, YDC works with its partners—the laborers' and operators' unions, the EPA and others—to organize workforce training. As a result, more than 120 community members (representing one-fifth of the tribal membership) have received certification in handling hazardous material and,

Galena

Honoring Nations Honoree 2002

Text in its entirety from: The Harvard Project On American Indian Economic Development

John F. Kennedy School of Government Harvard University

Galena

of these, 36 are additionally qualified for asbestos abatement and lead-based paint removal. It is through such collaboration and training that the Corporation has been able to gain the necessary technical expertise to continue to expand its portfolio of services and offer new employment opportunities. Local hire on contracted projects now exceeds 80 percent.

Moreover, while tribal members expressed an interest in remediation from the start, YDC's development and growth have further galvanized the community. Members and non-members alike acknowledge the benefits that YDC has brought—a sense of shared pride, renewed commitment to community action, and perhaps most importantly, the notion of "Neel ghul neets niiy."

This initiative is easily replicable among the more than 200 federally recognized tribes in the Alaska. Already, YDC is assisting the Naknek, a village in the Bristol Bay region, to establish a for-profit tribal corporation with 8(a) minority contractor status. Further, there are more than 600 military sites in Alaska (most abandoned, most contaminated) that present significant demand for environmental remediation services. To be sure, the Louden Tribe is already laying the groundwork for replication. They are working with the U.S. Fish and Wildlife Service and Galena City Schools to develop and deliver curriculum to Native students about environmental protection.

The Louden Tribe's creation of Yukaana Development Corporation is an impressive contribution to good governance. The Tribe, in pursuit of self-determination, has created a self-sustaining and growing for-profit institution that offers employment opportunities in a region where such opportunities are scarce. It has taken positive steps towards achieving a healthier eco-system by dramatically reducing the contamination that has long plagued its traditional hunting and fishing areas. And importantly, it has created an ownership structure in an environment where such structures are difficult to develop. The initiative sets an important example for Indian nations throughout Alaska and the lower-48 states as well.

Lessons
In many cases, community goals cannot be met unless a tribe first pursues self-governance. An important opportunity for tribes in Alaska may be the formation of tribally owned corporations that meet the specific needs of the community.

Tribes that seek opportunities to engage in cooperative government-to-government relationships with U.S. agencies and departments can realize long-term benefits across a variety of areas. They may also bolster their ability to exercise their sovereignty.

Partnerships with nonprofit organizations, governmental agencies and other outside entities can give tribes access to goods and services that they don't possess internally, and assist tribal governments in accomplishing their goals and objectives.

Gambell

Also know as Sivuqaq

Ethnicity: Siberian Eskimo

Municipality
Sivuqaq Incorporated
P.O. Box 101
Gambell, AK 99742
  907-985-5826
  907-985-5426 Fax

Total area of entitlement under ANCSA
                  1,135,950 acres

Total labor force	386
High school graduate or higher	60.9%
Bachelor's degree or higher	8.3%
Unemployment rate	19.5%
Per capita income (2000)	$8,764
Population 2000 census	649
Percent Native 2000 census	95.8%

LOCATION AND LAND STATUS
Gambell is located on the northwest cape of St. Lawrence Island, 200 miles southwest of Nome, in the Bering Sea. It is 36 miles from the Chukotsk Peninsula in Siberia. In 1891 President Theodore Roosevelt declared the entire island a reindeer reserve; this status carried with it the claim to the island on the part of the residents of the villages of Gambell and Savoonga, the only villages on the island. With the passage of the 1971 Alaska Native Claims Settlement Act, the islanders elected to accept the former reserve lands as their part of the settlement. While this made them ineligible for some of the provisions of the act, it also resulted in a land base that is much larger than that otherwise provided for in ANCSA.

CLIMATE
Gambell has a maritime climate, with continental influences in the winter. Average summer temperatures range from 34°F to 48°F, while average winter temperatures range from -2°F to 10°F. Extreme winds with relatively mild temperatures are typical for St. Lawrence Island.

CULTURE AND HISTORY
St. Lawrence Island has been inhabited for as long as 10,000 years. There was little contact with the outside world, other than with related groups in Siberia, until European traders began to frequent the area. In the eighteenth and nineteenth

centuries, more than 4,000 people inhabited the island, in 35 villages. In 1891 President Roosevelt established the island as a reindeer reserve. The isolation of Gambell has helped to maintain the traditional Siberian Yupik Eskimo culture, language, and subsistence lifestyle based on marine mammals. Walrus-hide boats are still used for hunting. The Native Village of Gambell is a federally recognized tribe in the community.

GOVERNMENT
Gambell was incorporated as a second-class city in 1963, with a city council and a mayor. The city is located in the Unorganized Borough (see Alaska introduction). It also has an Indian Reorganization Act (1934) council,. The clinic is a qualified emergency care center headed by a chief. Shareholders in the village corporation also hold shares in the Bering Straits regional Native corporation (see Alaska introduction).

ECONOMY
The economy is largely subsistence harvests from the sea-seal, walrus, fish, and beluga whale. Foxes are trapped for supplemental cash income. Some reindeer roam free on the island, but most harvesting occurs out of the other village on the island, Savoonga. The sale of ivory carving and archaeological artifacts are other sources of income. Many tourists are attracted to the community's abundant seabird colonies.

Government as employer. Of the 124 employed residents, 76 work for the local, state, or federal government.

Services and retail. There are 12 businesses, including a construction business, a deli, day-care centers, and a Yupik translation project. Retail trade employs 10 residents; education, health and social services, 52; public administration, 27; information services, 3; and professional, scientific, administrative, and waste management professions employ 2 residents.

Tourism and recreation. One lodge is available in Gambell. Services include movie rentals and recreational services. Visitor attractions include the Saint Lawrence Island original ivory co-op, bird watching, and cultural tours. Arts, entertainment, recreation, accommodations, and food service industries employ 11 residents.

Transportation. There is an airport maintenance business. Three airline companies service Gambell. Transportation, warehousing, and utility industries employ 17 residents.

INFRASTRUCTURE
Thirteen capital projects, funded by grants, are active in Gambell.

Transportation. Gambell's isolated location on an island with no seaport depends on air transport. The state-owned airport, under major improvements, provides a 4,500-foot long by 96-foot wide asphalt runway. Regular flights from Nome and charters from Unalakleet are available. Lighterage services bring freight from Kotzebue and Shishmaref.

Electricity. Alaska Village Electric Cooperative (AVEC) provides electricity.

Water and waste systems. Water drawn from wells and Troutman Lake is treated and stored in three storage tanks. More than 115 homes have piped water and sewer system. Approximately 37 homes in the original townsite still haul water and honeybuckets. A new water source is needed. The landfill is closed. The city wants to develop a new site.

Telecommunications. Local telephone service is provided by United Utilities, while long distance service is available through Alascom. Internet service is provided by GCI for the school only. Teleconferencing is available through Alaska Teleconferencing Network. Rural Alaska Television Network provides television access. Two radio stations are available to residents.

COMMUNITY FACILITIES AND SERVICES
Area facilities include a teen center and a village council. The schools and washeteria have individual water wells and septic tank systems.

Education. Gambell School is in the Bering Strait School District. The school has 176 students and 16 teachers.

Health care. Bessie A. Kaningok Health Clinic is available. The clinic is a qualified emergency care center.

Gambell
Also known as Sivuqaq

Georgetown

Total area of entitlement under ANCSA	69,120 acres
Population *2000 census*	3
Percent Native *2000 census*	100%

LOCATION
Georgetown is located on the north bank of the upper Kuskokwim River, in the Kilbuck-Kuskokwim Mountains. It is east of the mouth of the George River, 16 miles northwest of Red Devil.

CLIMATE
Georgetown has a continental climate, with temperatures ranging between -59°F in the winter and as high as 94°F in the summer. Precipitation amounts to 17 inches annually, including yearly snowfall of 80 inches.

CULTURE AND HISTORY
Gold was found along the George River near Georgetown in 1909. This mining settlement and the river were named for three traders: George Hoffman, George Fredericks, and George Morgan. Georgetown is currently used as a seasonal fish camp. There are no year-round residents, and wage employment is not available. Georgetown residents are Yup'ik Eskimos and Tanaina Athabascans, and depend upon a subsistence lifestyle. The Native Village of Georgetown is a federally recognized tribe in the community.

GOVERNMENT
The village is unincorporated and is located in the Unorganized Borough *(see Alaska introduction)*. There is a village council, headed by a president.

VILLAGE COROPRATION
The Kuskokwim Corporation was formed in 1977 when 10 ANCSA village corporations located along the middle region of the Kuskokwim River merged. The villages were Lower Kalskag, Upper Kalskag, Aniak, Chuathbaluk, Napaimute, Crooked Creek, Red Devil, Georgetown, Sleetmute, and Stony River. The corporation invests in stocks, bonds, and real estate. It also owns interests in operating businesses, including a telecommunications bandwidth and service provider. In addition, the corporation has entered a surface lease agreement for the development of one of the largest undeveloped gold resources in the world, Donlin Creek, located on land to which Kuskokwim has retained surface rights. The corporation's subsidiaries include an SBA certified 8(a) small business that provides engineering, remediation, and construction services throughout Alaska and the lower 48 states. Shareholders in the merged village corporation are also shareholders in Calista Corporation regional Native corporation *(see Alaska introduction)*.

ECONOMY
Georgetown serves as a seasonal fish camp. There is no cash economy.

Services and retail. There are two businesses: a fishing guide charter and a construction company.

Government as employer. None.

INFRASTRUCTURE
The Kuskokwim River serves as the major transportation link to other villages. Barges serve villages upriver and Georgetown. In the winter transportation is primarily by snowmachine and aircraft. There is no central electric system in Georgetown. Two of the four existing homes have wells. Outhouses are used for sewage. Individual generators provide electricity.

COMMUNITY FACILITIES
There are no public facilities in Georgetown.

Education. There are no state operated schools located in the community.

Health care. Clara Morgan Subregional Clinic is available in Anik.

Georgetown

Ethnicity: Yup´ik Eskimo

ANCSA village corporation
Kuskokwim Corporation
P.O. Box 104460
Anchorage, AK 99610
  907-276-2101

Golovin
See Chinik

113

Goodnews Bay

Ethnicity: Yup´ik Eskimo

ANCSA village corporation
Kuitsarak, Incorporated
P.O. Box 150
Goodnews Bay, AK 99589
  907-967-8428
  907-967-8226 Fax

Total area of entitlement under ANCSA	
	115,200 acres
Total labor force	150
High school graduate or higher	55.6%
Bachelor's degree or higher	4.3%
Unemployment rate	13.2%
Per capita income *(2000)*	$6,851
Population *2000 census*	230
Percent Native *2000 census*	93.9%

LOCATION

Goodnews Bay is located on the north shore of Goodnews Bay, at the mouth of Goodnews River. It is 116 air miles south of Bethel, 110 miles northwest of Dillingham, and 400 miles west of Anchorage. The setting is characterized by scenery of great beauty, composed of mountains, rivers leading up from the bay, lakes and ponds, and a variety of trees and brush.

CLIMATE

Goodnews Bay is in a transitional climatic zone, exhibiting characteristics of both a marine and continental climate. Summer temperatures range from 41°F to 57°F; winter temperatures vary from 6°F to 24°F. Average annual precipitation is 22 inches, including 43 inches of yearly snowfall.

CULTURE AND HISTORY

This is a traditional Yup'ik Eskimo village, practicing subsistence, trapping, and fishing lifestyles. In the Yup'ik language, residents call the village *Mumtraq*. The village was moved to its present location due to constant flooding and storms at the old site; shortly thereafter, in the 1930s, a government school and post office were built. A high school was built in 1979. The Native Village of Goodnews is a federally recognized tribe in the community.

GOVERNMENT

In 1970 Goodnews Bay incorporated as a second-class city, with a mayor and city council. The community is located in the Unorganized Borough *(see Alaska introduction)*. It also has a traditional village council, headed by a president.

VIILAGE CORPORATION

Kuitsarak, Inc., is the village corporation for Goodnews Bay. The Native village and Kuitsarak are currently putting together the needed legal procedures and documents to reconvey land from the corporation to the village for local governing needs. Kuitsarak represents its shareholders in ANCSA land claims matters and is instrumental in assuring the success of the water and sewer and other developments for the community in giving right-of-way and easements. Both entities have a close working relationship. Shareholders in the village corporation also hold shares in the Calista Corporation Regional Native Corporation *(see Alaska introduction)*.

ECONOMY

The city, school, local businesses, and commercial fishing provide the majority of the income. Subsistence activities supplement many incomes. Many residents engage in trapping. Salmon, seal, walrus, birds, berries, moose, and bear are an integral part of the lifestyle.

Construction. One resident is employed in construction.

Fisheries. Forty-one residents hold commercial fishing permits for salmon and herring roe fisheries. The 1992 Community Development Quota Program increased the pollack ground fish quota for small communities, benefiting the village.

Government as employer. Of the 59 employed residents, 49 work for the local, state, or federal government.

Services and retail. There are nine businesses in the community, including a trading post, cable television company, grocery stores, rental business, and a real estate office. Retail trade employs 10 residents; public administration, 14; and education, health, and social service professions employ 17 residents.

Tourism and recreation. Visitor attractions include a scenic viewpoint, and Schouten's private collection of local artifacts. Cultural events include the Qigcik conference. Lodging consists of one bed-and-breakfast. Arts, entertainment, recreation, accommodations, and food service industries employ six residents.

Transportation. Four airline companies service Goodnews Bay. Transportation, warehousing, and utility industries employ 11 residents.

INFRASTRUCTURE

Twelve capital projects, funded by grants, are active in Goodnews Bay.

Transportation. A state-owned 2,835- by 80-foot gravel airstrip is available year-round for chartered or private planes. Docking facilities are not available, although locals use boats and skiffs during the summer months. Snowmachines are the primary means of travel in the winter. Winter trails are marked along the Coastal Trail (60.3 miles) and the Arolik Trail (60.1 miles) Barges deliver fuel and other supplies in the summer.

Water and waste systems. Currently, treated well water is hauled from the new watering point. Homes are not plumbed. A piped circulating water/vacuum sewer system and plumbing for 77 homes are under construction. The school has requested funds to be connected to the city sewage lagoon.

Electricity. Alaska Village Electric Corporation (AVEC) provides electricity.

Telecommunications. Local telephone service is provided by United Utilities. Long distance service is available through Alascom. Internet service is provided for the school by GCI. Cable television service is available and Rural Alaska Television Network provides television access. One radio station is available to residents.

COMMUNITY FACILITIES

Local area facilities include the Goodnews Bay Community Hall and a Village Council. Honeybuckets are hauled by the city.

Education. Rocky Mountain High School in the community is in the Lower Kuskokwim School District. The school has 66 students and 5 teachers.

Health care. Health care is provided by the Goodnews Bay Health Clinic, owned by the city and leased to the U.S. Public Health Service. Auxiliary health care is provided by Goodnews Bay First Responder Group.

rayling

Total area of entitlement under ANCSA
92,160 acres
Total labor force 105
High school graduate or higher 67.5%
Bachelor's degree or higher 9.6%
Unemployment rate 20%
Per capita income *(2000)* $7,049
Population *2000 census* 194
Percent Native *2000 census* 91.8%

LOCATION
Grayling is located in interior Alaska on the west bank of the Yukon River, east of the Nulato Hills, 18 air miles north of Anvik.

CLIMATE
Grayling's climate is continental. Temperatures range from winter lows of -60°F to summer highs of 87°F. Snowfall averages 110 inches, with 21 inches of total precipitation per year.

CULTURE AND HISTORY
In 1900 the *Nunivak*, a U.S. Revenue steamer, stopped for fuel in Grayling and reported 75 inhabitants. The village was later abandoned until 1962, when residents of Holikachuk moved to the site. The population of Grayling is comprised of Holikachuk and Ingalik *Athabascan* Indians. Subsistence activities are an important aspect of the village culture. Every other year, Grayling is a checkpoint on the annual 1,159-mile Iditarod dogsled race from Anchorage to Nome. The Organized Village of Grayling is a federally recognized tribe in the community.

GOVERNMENT
Grayling was incorporated as a second-class city in 1969, with a mayor and city council. The community is located in the Unorganized Borough *(see Alaska introduction)*. It also has a village council, organized under the Indian Reorganization Act of 1934 and headed by a president. Shareholders in the village corporation also hold shares in the Doyon regional Native corporation *(see Alaska introduction)*.

ECONOMY
Grayling's economy is heavily dependent on subsistence activities. Cash employment is generated primarily in seasonal work during the summer. Subsistence activities include fishing, hunting, trapping, gathering, and gardening. Salmon, moose, black bear, small game, and waterfowl are utilized.

Fisheries. Nine residents hold commercial fishing permits, mostly in salmon.

Government as employer. Of the 52 employed residents, 17 work for the local, state, or federal government.

Mining. Mining and hunting industries employ two residents.

Services and retail. There are seven businesses in the community, including the City of Grayling, lodging, a fuel business, and video rentals. Retail trade employs seven residents; education, health, and social services, 22; and public administration employs six residents.

Tourism and recreation. The annual 1,049 mile Iditarod sled dog race includes Grayling as a checkpoint every other year. One bed-and-breakfast is available. Arts, entertainment, recreation, accommodations, and food services employ six residents.

Transportation. Three airline companies service Grayling. Transportation, warehousing, and utility industries employ six residents.

INFRASTRUCTURE
Twenty-six capital projects, funded by grants, are active in Grayling.

Transportation. No roads connect Grayling with other communities. In the summer, access to Grayling is by air, riverboat, or barge. The state owns and operates a 2,315- by 60-foot gravel runway. Skiffs are used for transportation up and down the river in summer.

Water and waste systems. Water, drawn from an infiltration gallery at Grayling Creek, is treated, stored, and piped throughout the community. All but three homes are connected to the piped water and sewer system. Grayling has recently upgraded the water treatment and plumbed 20 homes.

Electricity. Alaska Village Electric Cooperative (AVEC) provides electricity.

Telecommunications. Local telephone service is provided by Bush-Tell, while long distance service is available through Alascom. Internet service is provided for the school by GCI. Teleconferencing is available through Alaska Teleconferencing Network. Rural Alaska Television Network provides television access. Two radio stations are available to residents.

COMMUNITY FACILITIES
Local facilities include a teen center, the Hee Yea Lingde Corporation building, and a village council. A new landfill site has been funded.

Education. David-Louis Memorial School in the community is in the Iditarod Area Regional Educational Attendance Area. The school has 52 students and 6 teachers.

Health care. Health care is provided by the Grayling Health Clinic, owned by the city and leased to the U.S. Public Health Service. The clinic is administered by the Yukon Kuskokwim Health Corporation. Clara Morgan Subregional Clinic also is available in Anik.

Also know as Holikachuk

[GRAY-leeng]
Ethnicity: Holikachuk, Ingalik Athabascan

Hee-Yea-Lingde Corporation
P.O. Box 9
Grayling, AK 99590
  907-453-5133
  907-453-5133 Fax

Gulkana

[gull-KANN-uh]
Ethnicity: Ahtna Athabascan

ANCSA regional corporation
Ahtna, Incorporated
P.O. Box 649
Glennallen, AK 99588
907-822-3476
907-822-3495 Fax

Total area of entitlement under ANCSA	
	92,160 acres
Total labor force	61
High school graduate or higher	83.5%
Bachelor's degree or higher	26.2%
Unemployment rate	38.9%
Per capita income *(2000)*	$13,548
Population *2000 census*	164
Percent Native *2000 census*	46.3%

LOCATION
Gulkana is located on the east bank of the Gulkana River at its confluence with the Copper River. The community lies at mile 127 of the Richardson Highway, 14 miles north of Glennallen and on the edge of the Wrangell-St. Elias National Park and Preserve.

CLIMATE
Gulkana is in a continental climate zone, characterized by long, cold winters and short, warm summers. Temperatures range from winter lows of -65°F to occasional summer highs of 91°F. Average annual precipitation is 11 inches, including 47 inches of yearly snowfall.

CULTURE AND HISTORY
Gulkana is an Athabascan village. Subsistence activities supplement incomes. Gulkana was originally established in 1903 as a telegraph station and was called Kulkana, after the nearby river. The Gulkana Roadhouse was built in the early 1900s by C. L. Hoyt, a fur dealer who ran it until 1916. A store and a post office were also located nearby. The original settlement was located across the river from the present site; the first house was built in the new location in the early 1950s. Eventually all the villagers moved their homes. The Gulkana Village Council is a federally recognized tribe in the community.

GOVERNMENT
Gulkana is unincorporated under Alaska law and is located in the Unorganized Borough *(see Alaska introduction)*. Native residents are represented by a traditional village council, headed by a president.

VILLAGE CORPORATION
In 1980 the Gulkana village corporation, Sta-Keh, along with six other Ahtna village corporations merged with the existing Alaska Native regional corporation, Ahtna, Inc., *(see Alaska introduction)*. Ahtna assumed the management of all former village corporation lands. The total land area managed is 1.77 million acres. The primary assets managed are surface estate (including gravel), subsurface minerals, and timber. Management is in "accordance with cultural and traditional uses and values, land protection, acquisition, conservation development strategies, and principles of culturally appropriate stewardship."

ECONOMY
Residents of Gulkana rely to a great extent on subsistence activities to supplement their incomes. Employment is limited, as there are no businesses in the community. Employment is limited to the village council and seasonal construction, although the Wrangell-St. Elias National Park and Preserve provides some federal employment.

Government as employer. Of the 22 employed residents, 14 work for the local, state, or federal government.

Services and retail. No business licenses are registered in Gulkana. Retail trade employs 4 residents; education, health, and social services, 4, public administration, 12; and arts, entertainment, recreation, accommodation, and food service industries employ 2 residents.

INFRASTRUCTURE
Fourteen capital projects, funded by grants, are active in Gulkana.

Transportation. The Richardson Highway passes close by the community and is maintained year-round. A state-owned 5,000- by 100-foot asphalt runway is available at the Gulkana Airport.

Water and waste systems. Water drawn from a well is treated and stored in a 100,000-gallon tank. A new infiltration gallery on the Gulkana River is under constructions and water treatment improvements are in progress. Most homes have a piped water and sewer system. A community septic tank treats wastewater. Individual wells and septic tanks are also used by a number of residences. A master plan is underway to examine connection of all homes to a new system. Permafrost and high water tables are problematic in this region. Copper Basin Sanitation provides refuse collection and uses the landfill at Glennallen.

Electricity. Copper Valley Electric Association provides electricity.

Telecommunications. Local telephone and Internet service are provided by the Copper Valley Telephone Co-op (Glennallen exchange), while long distance service is provided by Alascom. One radio station is available to residents.

COMMUNITY FACILITIES
A laundromat and a washeteria are needed in the community.

Education. There are no state-operated schools located in the community.

Health care. Health care is provided by the Gulkana Health Clinic, owned by the village and leased to the U.S. Public Health Service. The clinic is administered by the Copper River Native Association.

Haines
See Chilkoot

Hamilton
See Zero Population Section

Healy Lake

Total area of entitlement under ANCSA
69,120 acres

Total labor force	43
High school graduate or higher	80%
Bachelor's degree or higher	16.7%
Unemployment rate	17.9%
Per capita income *(2000)*	$18,128
Population *2000 census*	37
Percent Native *2000 census*	73%

LOCATION
The community of Healy Lake is on the shore of the five-mile long Healy Lake, which lies in the course of the Healy River, 29 miles east of Delta Junction.

CLIMATE
Healy Lake lies within the continental climate zone, with cold winters and warm summers. Average temperatures range from -32°F in the winter to 72°F in the summer.

CULTURE AND HISTORY
The community is located in the traditional territory of the Tanacross Athabascan Indian people. The culture remains tied to the land and to the subsistence activities connected with it. The village name was first reported in 1914 by the U.S. Geological Survey. The Healy Lake Village Council is a federally recognized tribe in the community.

GOVERNMENT
Healy Lake is unincorporated and is located in the Unorganized Borough *(see Alaska introduction)*.

VILLAGE CORPORATOIN
Shareholders in the village corporation are also shareholders in the Doyon regional Native corporation *(see Alaska introduction)*.

ECONOMY
Most residents of Healy Lake rely on subsistence activities for there are few year-round jobs. Some private sector and government employment is available. Recreational use of the lake in the summer attracts Fairbanks residents.

Government as employer. Of the 23 employed residents, 12 work for the local, state, or federal government.

Manufacturing. Two residents are employed in manufacturing.

Mining. Mining and hunting industries employ two residents.

Services and retail. No business licenses are registered for Healy Lake. Education, health, and social services employs six residents; public administration, eight; professional, scientific, administrative, and waste management industries, two; and arts, entertainment, recreation, accommodation, and food service industries employ three residents.

INFRASTRUCTURE
Eight capital projects, funded by grants, are active in Healy Lake.

Transportation. The Tanana River provides boat access to Healy Lake at Big Delta. There is no direct road access. During the winter, residents fly into the community by skiplane or drive in by ice road.

Water and waste systems. Healy Lake has a new water treatment plant and watering point. Full plumbing is available to only 4 of the 11 year-round households in Healy Lake. An alternative waste disposal site is being studied.

Electricity. Alaska Power Company provides electricity.

Telecommunications. Local telephone service is provided by National Utilities, while long distance service is available through Alascom. Internet service is provided, for the school only, by GCI. One television channel can be received from Fairbanks, and Rural Alaska Television Network provides television access.

COMMUNITY FACILITIES
Area facilities include a village/community hall. Healy Lake has a new washeteria.

Education. There are no state-operated schools located in the community.

Health care. Healy Lake Clinic is available.

Also known as Healy Fork

[HEE-lee]
Ethnicity: Tanacross Athabascan

Mendas Cha-ag Native Corporation
457 Cindy Drive
Fairbanks, AK 99701
907-452-3094

Holikachuk
See Grayling

Holy Cross

Total area of entitlement under ANCSA
138,727 acres

Total labor force	165
High school graduate or higher	83.6%
Bachelor's degree or higher	7.5%
Unemployment rate	28.2%
Per capita income *(2000)*	$8,542
Population *2000 census*	227
Percent Native *2000 census*	96.5%

LOCATION
Holy Cross is located in interior Alaska, on the west bank of Ghost Creek Slough, off the Yukon River, 420 miles southwest of Fairbanks.

CLIMATE
The climate of Holy Cross is continental, with long, harsh winters and brief, warm summers. Temperatures can range from winter lows of -62°F to summer highs of 93°F. Snowfall averages 79 inches, with 19 inches of total precipitation per year.

CULTURE AND HISTORY
In the 1880s, a mission and a school were established by the Rev. Aloysius Robert, who came to Alaska across the Chilkoot Trail. Ingalik (Athabascan) Indians then migrated to Holy Cross to establish the village. Holy Cross is an Ingalik Indian village. Residents rely on subsistence and fishing-related activities. Holy Cross Village is a federally recognized tribe in the community.

Ethnicity: Ingalik Athabascan

ANCSA village corporation
Deloycheet, Incorporated
P.O. Box 228
Holy Cross, AK 99602
907-476-7177
907-476-7176 Fax

Holy Cross

GOVERNMENT

In 1968 Holy Cross was incorporated as a second-class city, with a mayor and city council. The community is located in the Unorganized Borough (see Alaska introduction). Holy Cross also has a traditional council, headed by a chief.

VILLAGE CORPORATION

Shareholders in the village corporation are also shareholders in the Doyon regional Native corporation (see Alaska introduction).

ECONOMY

Holy Cross has a seasonal economy, with its peak during the summer commercial-fishing season. Approximately 50 full-time positions are available in the community, in addition to summer construction projects. Subsistence hunting, fishing, trapping, and gardening supplement cash income.

Construction. Six residents are employed in construction.

Fisheries. Nine residents hold commercial fishing permits.

Government as employer. Of the 56 employed residents, 37 work for the local, state, or federal government.

Services and retail. Seven businesses are in the community, including Holy Cross Tribal Store, airport maintenance, and a grocery store. Retail trade employs one resident; public administration, 6; and education, health, and social services employs 25 residents.

Tourism and recreation. Services include a hotel/lodge and a number of wilderness adventure tours. Events include the Agricultural Fair, Spring Carnival, Spring Clean-Up, Memorial Day; and Easter.

Transportation. Four airline companies service Holy Cross. Transportation, warehousing, and utility industries employ nine residents.

INFRASTRUCTURE

Eleven capital projects, funded by grants, are active in Holy Cross.

Transportation. Holy Cross relies on air and boat transportation. The state provides a 4,000- by 100-foot gravel airstrip. Barge service is available in summer. Residents use boats for fishing, subsistence, and recreation. Three-wheelers, motor bikes, snowmachines, and dog teams are used on local roads.

Water and waste systems. Water, drawn from a deep well, is treated. A new backup well, new pump house and water treatment facility are now available. More than 70 households and the school are connected to the piped water and sewer system, including plumbed kitchens. Some residents tow water from the washeteria and use honeybuckets or outhouses. A master plan is underway to examine and engineer expansion of the system.

Electricity. Alaska Village Electric Cooperative (AVEC) provides electricity.

Telecommunication. Local telephone service is provided by Bush-Tell, Inc., while long distance service is available through Alascom. Internet service is provided for the school by GCI. Teleconferencing is available through Alaska Teleconferencing Network. Rural Alaska Television Network provides television access. Four radio stations are available to residents.

COMMUNITY FACILITIES

Area facilities include Holy Cross Community Hall, Village Council and both public and school libraries. Senior citizen services include an Elder Nutrition Program.
The village washeteria is available. Honeybuckets are used by residents. Landfill improvements are needed.

Education. Holy Cross School is in the Iditarod Area Regional Education Attendance Area. The school has 57 students and four teachers.

Health care. Health care is provided by the Holy Cross Health Clinic, owned by the city and leased to the U.S. Public Health Service. The clinic is administered by the Yukon-Kuskokwim Health Corporation. Theresa Demientieff Health Clinic and Clara Morgan Subregional Clinic also are available.

Hoonah

[HOO-nah]
Ethnicity: Tlingit

ANCSA village corporation
Huna Totem Corporation
9301 Glacier Hwy. Suite A-103
Juneau, AK 99801
907-789-1773
907-789-1896 Fax

Total area of entitlement under ANCSA	
	23,040 acres
Total labor force	656
High school graduate or higher	80.5%
Bachelor's degree or higher	15.4%
Unemployment rate	20.5%
Per capita income *(2000)*	$16,097
Population *2000 census*	860
Percent Native *2000 census*	69.4%

LOCATION

Hoonah is located on the northeast shore of Chichagof Island, 40 air miles west of Juneau.

CLIMATE

Hoonah's maritime climate is characterized by cool summers and mild winters. The airport is closed 20 to 30 days a year, due to poor weather. Foggy periods prevail in the fall. Summer temperatures range from 52°F to 63°F; winter temperatures vary from 26°F to 39°F.

CULTURE AND HISTORY

Hoonah is the largest Tlingit village in Alaska and is the principal village for the Huna, a Tlingit tribe that relocated from the Glacier Bay-Icy Strait area. In 1880 the Northwest Trading Company built the first store in Hoonah. In 1881 the Presbyterian Home Mission and school were built. In 1912 a large cannery was established north of town. In 1944 a fire destroyed much of the city and many priceless Tlingit cultural objects. The federal government assisted in rebuilding the community. Commercial fishing and logging help support the community, but most residents maintain a subsistence lifestyle. The Hoonah Indian Association is a federally recognized tribe in the community.

GOVERNMENT

Hoonah was incorporated in 1946 as a first-class city, with a mayor and city council. The community is located in the Unorganized Borough (see Alaska introduction). Hoonah also has a village council, organized under the Indian Reorganization Act of 1934 headed by a president.

VILLAGE CORPORATION

Huna Totem Corporation, incorporated in 1973, is owned by approximately 1200 Alaska Native shareholders whose aboriginal ties are to the Village of Hoonah. Under ANCSA, Human Totem received a cash distribution, as well as 20,040 acres of land. Huna Totem is one of the more successful Native village corporations in Alaska. Its revenues derives from passive investments in stocks and bonds and from active operations in tourism, money management, commercial real estate, and banking. These latter enterprises include businesses in Nevada and California as well as Alaska. Shareholders in Huna Totem Corporation are also shareholders in the Sealaska regional Native corporation (see Alaska introduction).

ECONOMY
Fishing and local government are mainstays of the economy. Salmon, halibut, shellfish, deer, waterfowl, and berries are harvested. The city and school district are the main public sector employers. The Hoonah Cold Storage Plant provides some work. Major private employers are Whitestone Logging and Southeast Stevedoring, a sort yard and timber transfer facility.

Construction. There are several construction businesses, two building supply companies, and a lumber and milling business. Ten residents are employed in construction.

Fisheries and forestry. Approximately 117 residents hold commercial fishing permits, chiefly in salmon, halibut, and shellfish. A cold storage facility is located in Hoonah. A lumber and milling business, a sawmill, and a logging company operate in Hoonah. The Sealaska Corporation and the Huna Totem Corporation (the village corporation) own the land on which the logging takes place. Farming, fishing, and forestry industries employ 45 residents.

Government as employer. Of the 317 employed residents, 103 work for the local, state, or federal government.

Manufacturing. Approximately 36 residents are employed in manufacturing.

Mining. Mining and hunting industries employ 30 residents.

Services and retail. There are 83 businesses in the community, including business management services, education consultant, graphics shop, woodworks, child-care center, cafés, cleaning services, and retail stores. Retail trade employs 20 residents; wholesale trade, 2; education, health, and social services, 74; financial and related businesses, 6; public administration, 29; and professional, scientific, administrative, and waste management professions employ 6 residents.

Tourism and recreation. Eight lodging facilities are available, including a number of bed-and-breakfast facilities. Services include sports and deep-sea charters, touring and guiding services, marine storage facility, outfitters, a tackle company, bike repair, and health massage. Visitor attractions include the Hoonah Heritage Center, a packing company, totem poles, a museum, and a canoe at the school. Wilderness activities include whale watching. ANB/ANS and the Hoonah Indian Association sponsor some cultural events. Other attractions include Glacier Bay sightseeing, sport fishing, and bicycle tours. Arts, entertainment, recreation, accommodation, and food service industries employ 15 residents.

Transportation. Three airline companies and one taxicab company service Hoonah. Transportation, warehousing, and utility industries employ 42 residents.

INFRASTRUCTURE
Twenty-two capital projects, funded by grants, are active in Hoonah.

Transportation. Hoonah relies on air transportation for small freight and passengers. The state provides an airport with a 2,997- by 75-foot asphalt runway and a seaplane base. A state ferry terminal and a harbor/dock area are available. Barges and planes bring in freight. Northwest Chichagof Island provides an extensive logging road system.

Water and waste systems. Water, drawn from Shotter, Dalton, and Spud creeks, is treated, and piped to all residences and facilities. A new water treatment facility is operating. Piped sewage is processed in a sewage treatment plant. Nearly all homes are fully plumbed. The city provides garbage collection services.

Electricity. The Tlingit-Haida Regional Electric Authority operates three diesel-fueled generators in Hoonah and also provides electricity.

Telecommunications. Local telephone service is provided by Pacific Communications Inc., while long distance service is available through Alascom. Internet service is provided by Hoonah.Net. Teleconferencing is available through Alaska Teleconferencing Network and the Sitka Legislative Information Office. Rural Alaska Television Network provides television access. Cable is provided by the Tlingit and Haida Central Council. One radio station is available to residents.

COMMUNITY FACILITIES
Local facilities include a city youth center, the ANB/ANS hall, city hall, a senior center, senior housing, the Hoonah Indian Association, and both public and school libraries.

Education. Hoonah Elementary School and Hoonah Middle/High School are operated by the city of Hoonah. The two schools have a combined student enrollment of 194.

Health care. Hoonah Medical Clinic is available. The clinic is a qualified emergency care center. Auxiliary health care is provided by Hoonah Volunteer EMS.

Hooper Bay

Hooper Bay

Total area of entitlement under ANCSA	
	161,280 acres
Total labor force	593
High school graduate or higher	72%
Bachelor's degree or higher	8.2%
Unemployment rate	37.3%
Per capita income (2000)	$7,841
Population 2000 census	1,014
Percent Native 2000 census	95.8%

LOCATION
Hooper Bay is located 20 miles south of Cape Romanof, 25 miles south of Scarnmon Bay, in the Yukon-Kuskokwim Delta.

CLIMATE
Mean annual snowfall is 75 inches, with yearly precipitation of 16 inches. Temperatures range between winter lows of -25°F and summer highs of 79°F.

CULTURE AND HISTORY
The village is separated into two sections: a heavily built-up townsite located on gently rolling hills and a newer section in the lowlands. "Askinuk" is the early Eskimo name for Hooper Bay. The present-day Eskimo name, "Naparagamiut," means "stake-village people." Hooper Bay is a traditional Yup'ik Eskimo community, with a heavy emphasis on subsistence activities. Members of the Village of Paimiut also live in Hooper

Also known as Naparyarmiut

[HOO-pur]
Ethnicity: Yup´ik Eskimo

ANCSA village corporation
Paimiut Corporation
General Delivery
Hooper Bay, AK 99604

119

Hooper Bay

Also known as Naparyarmiut

Bay. The Native Village of Hooper Bay is a federally recognized tribe in the community.

GOVERNMENT

Hooper Bay was incorporated in 1966 as a second-class city, with a mayor and city council. The community is in the Unorganized Borough *(see Alaska introduction)*. Hooper Bay also has a traditional village council, headed by a president.

VILLAGE CORPORATION

Shareholders in the village corporation are also shareholders in the Calista Corporation regional Native corporation *(see Alaska introduction)*.

ECONOMY

Commercial fishing and subsistence activities fuel the economy. Most employment is seasonal, with peak economic activity in the summer and little income-producing activity in winter. Salmon, walrus, beluga whale and waterfowl are harvested. Coastal Villages Seafood processes halibut and salmon in Hooper Bay. Bureau of Land Management firefighting offers summer work. Grass baskets and ivory handicrafts generate some income. The Naparyarmiut Arts and Crafts Cooperative is under development.

Fisheries. Forty-seven residents hold commercial fishing permits, chiefly in salmon. The 1992 Community Development Quota Program increased the Pollack ground fish quota for small communities like Hooper Bay.

Government as employer. Of the 202 employed residents, 107 work for the local, state, or federal government.

Manufacturing. Five residents are employed in manufacturing.

Services and retail. There are eleven businesses in the community, including a grocery store owned by the Naparyarmiut Ayagyugait, a flight school, automotive repair, lock and key shop, day care, and a newspaper publisher. Retail trade employs 20 residents; education, health, and social services, 102; public administration, 37; finance and related businesses, 7, and information services employs 2 residents.

Tourism and recreation. Accommodations include one lodge. Arts, entertainment, recreation, accommodation, and food service industries employ 11 residents.

Transportation. Seven airline companies service Hooper Bay.

Transportation, warehousing, and utility industries employ eight residents.

INFRASTRUCTURE

Twenty capital projects, funded by grants, are active in Hooper Bay.

Transportation. Residents rely on air and water transportation. The state provides a 3,300- by 75-foot paved runway. Shipments of fuel and other bulk supplies are brought in during the summer by barge lines. A commercial fishing dock is under construction. Skiffs are used in summer for local travel. Winter trails are open to Scammon Bay, Chevak, and Paimiut.

Water and waste systems. Residents tow treated water from the washeteria or other watering points. Three new wells are in operation, three miles northeast of town. The school has its own water system. Homes are not plumbed. The city is undergoing major improvements for a piped water and vacuum sewer system. Access roads and construction pads are now open. The landfill includes a new sewage lagoon, with a combined area of 20 acres.

Electricity. Alaska Village Electric Cooperative (AVEC) provides electricity.

Telecommunications. Local telephone service is provided by United Utilities, while long distance service is available through Alascom. Teleconferencing is available through Alaska Teleconferencing Network. Rural Alaska Television Network provides television access. Cable services are provided by Frontier Cable. Three radio stations are available to residents.

COMMUNITY FACILITIES

A new water treatment/washeteria facility is under construction. Honeybuckets are dumped at collection points. The landfill has been expanded. Local facilities also include the Brown Council Building. Funds have been requested for a youth center.

Education. Hooper Bay School is in the Lower Yukon Regional Education Attendance Area. The school has 393 students and 26 teachers.

Health care. Health care is provided by the Hooper Bay Health Clinic, owned by the city and leased to the U.S. Public Health Service. The clinic is administered by the Yukon-Kuskokwim Health Corporation. Pearl E. Johnson Subregional Clinic also is available.

Hughes

Also known as
Hut'odleekkaakk'et

[HEWZ]
Ethnicity: Koyukon,
            Athabascan,
            Kobuk, Selawik,
            Nunamiut Eskimo

K'oyitl'ots'ina, Ltd.
1603 College Rd.
Fairbanks, AK 99707
  907-452-8119
  907-452-8148 Fax

Total area of entitlement under ANCSA
                              69,120 acres

Total labor force	50
High school graduate or higher	68.2%
Bachelor's degree or higher	9.1%
Unemployment rate	14.3%
Per capita income *(2000)*	$10,194
Population *2000 census*	78
Percent Native *2000 census*	79.5%

LOCATION

Hughes is located on the east bank of the Koyukuk River, about 115 air miles northeast of Galena and 210 air miles northwest of Fairbanks.

CLIMATE

The area experiences a cold, continental climate, with extreme temperature differences. Temperatures range from 40°F or below in the winter to 70°F and above in the summer. Average annual precipitation is 12.7 inches, including 30 inches

of yearly snowfall.

CULTURE AND HISTORY

Historically Hughes was a trading center of the Native peoples of the region-Koyukon Athabascan Indians and Kobuk, Selawik, and Nunamiut Eskimos. In 1910 it was named after New York Governor Charles Hughes. It served as a riverboat landing and supply port for the Indian River goldfields until 1915, when the local mining industry declined. Traditional ways of life persist, and subsistence activities remain the central focus of village culture. Hughes is a Koyukon Athabascan village. Hughes Village (also known as Hut'odleekkaakk'et Tribe) is a federally recognized tribe is the community.

GOVERNMENT

In 1973 Hughes was incorporated as a second-class city, with a mayor and city council. The community is located in the Unorganized Borough *(see Alaska introduction)*. It also has a traditional village council, headed by a chief.

VILLAGE CORPORATION

Shareholders in the village corporation are also shareholders in the Doyon regional Native corporation (see Alaska introduction).

ECONOMY

Subsistence is the focus of the local economy. Salmon, freshwater fish, moose, black bear, rabbits, waterfowl, and berries are utilized. Caribou are also sought when available. The city, school, tribal clinic, and store provide part-time work. Bureau of Land Management emergency firefighting, construction work, skin sewing, beadwork, sled building, and trapping provide seasonal income.

Government as employer. Of the 18 employed residents, 16 work for the local, state, or federal government.

Manufacturing. Two residents are employed in manufacturing.

Services and retail. There are four businesses in the community, including a garden supply store, a fishing guide service, general store, and a power/light company. Education, health, and social service professions employ 11 residents.

Tourism and recreation. Potlatches and dog races attract visitors from surrounding villages. A guide service is available.

Transportation. Transportation, warehousing, and utility industries employ five residents.

INFRASTRUCTURE

Twenty-one capital projects, funded by grants, are active in Hughes.

Transportation. River transportation is very important to Hughes, although barge service is not reliable because of shallow water. Air transportation brings in most fuel and heavy freight. The state provides a lighted, gravel 3,400- by 100-foot runway. Snowmachines, all-terrain vehicles, and skiffs are used for local travel. The frozen river serves as an ice road during winter, allowing residents to visit area villages.

Water and waste systems. Thirty outhouses were built in 1984 to replace the frozen septic tank systems. Many Hughes residents haul treated water from the central watering point. Eleven houses, the school, teacher's apartments, clinic, and city and tribe offices have piped water. Septic tanks are connected in community facilities. But full plumbing is not available so most residents use honeybuckets and outhouses. Sanitation improvements are under a feasibility study. The city uses an incinerator to reduce the volume of refuse and participates in a recycling program. Preliminary work has begun on a new landfill site, new sewage lagoon, and water treatment improvements.

Electricity. Hughes Power & Light provides electricity.

Telecommunications. Local telephone service is provided by Pacific Telecommunications, while long distance service is available through Alascom. Internet service is provided for the school only by GCI. Teleconferencing is available through Alaska Teleconferencing Network. Rural Alaska Television Network provides television access. One radio station is available to residents.

COMMUNITY FACILITIES

Local facilities include a community hall and a community library. An Elder Nutrition Program services the community's senior citizens. The Village Council sponsors a youth center. A new site for the landfill has begun.

Education. Johnny Oldman School in the community is operated by the Koyukuk Regional Education Attendance Area. The school has 17 students and 1 teacher.

Health care. Health care is provided by the Hughes Health Clinic, owned by the city and leased to the U.S. Public Health Service. The clinic is administered by the Tanana Chiefs Conference.

Hughes

Also known as
Hut'odleekkaakk'et

Huslia

Total area of entitlement under ANCSA	
	69,120 acres
Total labor force	188
High school graduate or higher	69.4%
Bachelor's degree or higher	9%
Unemployment rate	18.3%
Per capita income *(2000)*	$10,983
Population *2000 census*	293
Percent Native *2000 census*	95.2%

LOCATION

Huslia is located on the north bank of the Koyukuk River, about 170 river miles northwest of Galena and 290 air miles west of Fairbanks.

CLIMATE

Huslia has a cold, continental climate, with extreme temperature differences. Temperatures range from -40°F or below in the winter to over 70°F in the summer. Average precipitation is 13 inches, including 70 inches of yearly snowfall.

CULTURE AND HISTORY

Traditionally, this has been a Koyukon Athabascan area, whose people maintained strong trading ties with the Kobuk River Eskimos. In 1843 Russian explorers made contact with Athabascans approximately 50 miles downriver from the current town site. Outside missionary activity increased after 1870. The Cutoff Trading Post was established in the 1920s, about four miles away from the current village. Huslia is an Athabascan village, and most residents are related by birth or marriage. The Huslia Village is a federally recognized tribe in the community.

GOVERNMENT

In 1969 Huslia was incorporated as a second-class city, with a mayor and city council. The community is located in the Unorganized Borough (see Alaska introduction). The village also has a traditional village council, headed by a chief.

VILLAGE CORPORATION

Shareholders in the village corporation are also shareholders in the Doyon regional Native corporation (see Alaska introduction).

ECONOMY

Subsistence is vital to the local economy. Most cash opportunities are in part-time positions or self-employment. The city and school provide most full-time employment. During the summer months, Bureau of Land Management emergency firefighting and area construction jobs supplement other cash income. Salmon, whitefish, moose, bear, caribou, small game, waterfowl, and berries provide most food sources.

Huslia

[HOOS-lee-uh]
Ethnicity: Koyukon
Athabascan

K'oyitl'ots'ina, Ltd.
1603 College Rd.
Fairbanks, AK 99709
907-452-8119
907-452-8148 Fax

121

Huslia

Construction. Approximately 13 residents are employed in construction.

Fisheries. Two residents hold commercial fishing permits, chiefly salmon and whitefish.

Government as employer. Of the 94 employed residents, 44 work for the local, state, or federal government.

Mining. Mining and hunting industries employ four residents.

Services and retail. There are 10 businesses in the community, including a retail store, bakery, the Huslia City Council, two general stores, and a gas and oil company. Retail trade employs 8 residents; education, health, and social services, 33; public administration, 14; and professional, scientific, administrative, and waste management professions employ 6 residents.

Tourism and recreation. Services include a bed-and-breakfast and a river guide service. The Head Start Program has cultural artifacts on display. Arts, entertainment, recreation, accommodation, and food service industries employ three residents.

Transportation. Seven airline companies service Huslia. Transportation, warehousing, and utility industries employ three residents.

INFRASTRUCTURE
Transportation. River transportation is used extensively in the summer. Cargo arrives by barge twice each year. Huslia is accessible by air year-round. The state provides a 4,000- by 75-foot lighted gravel airstrip. Plans are in progress for relocation of the airport. A new airstrip site is open. Snowmachines, all-terrain vehicles, and skiffs are used for local travel. Huslia has a network of winter trails, and the frozen river is used to get to area villages.

Water and waste systems. Piped water and sewer is available in Huslia. Water, drawn from a well, is treated. Approved funds will provide indoor plumbing and connect 25 new HUD homes and 11 others to the piped water and sewer system. Funds have been requested to replace the water storage tank, water treatment building, washeteria and landfill. A new site for the landfill is being planned.

Electricity. Alaska Village Electric Cooperative (AVEC) provides electricity.

Telecommunications. Local telephone service is provided by Pacific Telecommunications, while long distance service is available through Alascom. Internet service is provided for the school by GCI. Teleconferencing is available through Alaska Teleconferencing Network. Rural Alaska Television Network provides television access. One radio station is available to residents. Eighteen capital projects, funded by grants, are active in Huslia.

COMMUNITY FACILITIES
Funds have been requested to replace the washeteria and landfill. Local facilities include the Huslia Community Hall and the Elders Center.

Education. A Head Start Program is available to the community's children. Johnny Huntington School in Huslia is operated by the Yukon-Koyukuk Regional Education Attendance Area. The school has 68 students and 7 teachers.

Health care. Health care is provided by the Huslia Health Clinic. The clinic is owned by the city and leased to the U.S. Public Health Service. It is administered by the Tanana Chiefs Conference.

Hydaburg

[HIGH-duh-burg]
Ethnicity: Haida

Haida Corporation
P.O. Box 89
Hydaburg, AK 99922
   907-285-3721
   907-285-3944 Fax

Total area of entitlement under ANCSA
                                        25,245 acres
Total labor force   267
High school graduate or higher   76.8%
Bachelor's degree or higher   12.5%
Unemployment rate   31.3%
Per capita income *(2000)* $11,401
Population *2000 census*   382
Percent Native *2000 census*   89.5%

LOCATION
Hydaburg is located on the southwest coast of Prince of Wales Island, 45 air miles northwest of Ketchikan.

CLIMATE
Prince of Wales Island is dominated by a cool, moist, maritime climate. Average summer temperatures vary from 46°F to 70°F; winter temperatures range from 32°F to 42°F.

CULTURE AND HISTORY
Hydaburg is the largest Haida village in Alaska. Haida Indians originally migrated to Prince of Wales Island, a predominantly Tlingit area, from Graham Island in Canada. After combining three villages, the present site was chosen as the Hydaburg Indian Reservation in 1912. The new village established a trading company, store, and sawmill. However, the villagers were never comfortable with the arrangement, and at their request in 1926, the land was restored to its former status as a part of the Tongass National Forest. The townsite was established on 189 acres of the land reserved for that use. The first fish-processing plant opened in the village in 1927, and three other canneries operated there through the 1930s. Residents maintain a subsistence and commercial-fishing lifestyle. The Hydaburg Cooperative Association is a federally recognized tribe in the community.

GOVERNMENT
In 1927 Hydaburg was incorporated under Alaska law as a first-class city, with a mayor and city council. The community is located in the Unorganized Borough *(see Alaska introduction)*. When the Indian Reorganization Act (IRA) was amended in 1936 to include Alaska Natives, Hydaburg became the first village to form an IRA council, still operating and headed by a president.

VILLAGE CORPORATION
Haida Corporation, the ANCSA village corporation for Hydaburg, had 550 original shareholders when the corporation came into existence in 1972. Today it has over 730 shareholders. Haida Corporation has extensive land and timber holdings in Southeast Alaska, primarily on Prince of Wales Island. It also holds the Federal Energy Regulatory Commission (FERC) license for construction of a 5-megawatt hydroelectric generating facility on Reynolds Creek on Prince of Wales Island. Shareholders in the village corporation are also shareholders in the Sealaska Regional Native Corporation *(see Alaska introduction)*.

ECONOMY

Fishing and timber are the mainstay of Hydaburg. Subsistence food sources include deer, salmon, halibut, shrimp, and crab. The Haida Corporation owns a substantial timber holding, although it has long suspended logging because of a decline in the timber market. The corporation's log storage facility and sort yard are leased to Sealaska Corporation. There residents work for Southeast Stevedoring in shipping and loading timber. The city, school, Haida Corporation and SEARCH are other leading employers. The community is interested in developing a fish-processing facility, a U.S. Forest Service Visitor Center, specialty woodworking, and a mini-mall/retail center.

Construction. Approximately 11 residents are employed in construction.

Fisheries and forestry. Thirty-nine residents hold commercial fishing permits, chiefly for salmon, halibut, shrimp, and crab. Farming, fishing, and forestry employ three residents.

Government as employer. Of the 90 employed residents, 54 work for the local, state, or federal government.

Mining. Mining and hunting industries employ two residents.

Services and retail. There are 10 businesses in the community, including a logging company, towing, oil delivery, cable television, a sandwich shop, and an artistry and inspiration business. Retail trade employs 8 residents; education, health, and social services, 40; finance and related businesses, 3; public administration, 7; and professional, scientific, administrative, and waste management employ 4 residents.

Tourism and recreation. One boarding house and a bed-and-breakfast are available for lodging. Recreational charters and a diving and recreation business are also available. Visitor attractions include the Haida Cultural Center Museum and totem park. Arts, entertainment, recreation, accommodation, and food service industries employ two residents.

Transportation. One airline company services Hydaburg. Transportation, warehousing, and utility industries employ seven residents.

INFRASTRUCTURE

Eleven capital projects, funded by grants, are active in Hydaburg.

Transportation. The state provides a seaplane base in Hydaburg, with an FAA-designated approach. Scheduled flights from Hydaburg connect in Ketchikan. An emergency heliport is also available. The city owns a dock and small-boat harbor. A breakwater and a boat launch are needed. A road leads to Craig, Klawock and Hollis, where the state ferry docks. Weekly barges from Seattle deliver goods; cargo also arrives on the ferry and is trucked to Hydaburg.

Water and waste systems. The Hydaburg River provides water, which is treated and piped throughout the city. Piped gravity sewage is treated at a secondary treatment plant. Nearly all households are plumbed. Funds have been requested to build a new dam to increase the water supply. The city is looking into improving waste disposal.

Electricity. Alaska Power & Telephone Co. provides diesel power systems in Hydaburg and Craig, which provide electricity to many Island communities. Alaska Power Company provides electricity to Hydaburg.

Telecommunications. Local telephone service is provided by National Utilities, while long distance service is available through Alascom. Internet service is provided by Alaska Power & Telephone Company. Teleconferencing is available through Alaska Teleconferencing Network and the Sitka Legislative Information Office. Cable service is provided by Hydaburg Cable TV. Rural Alaska Television Network provides television access. One radio station is available to residents.

COMMUNITY FACILITIES

Local facilities include the Hydaburg Municipal Building, the ANB Hall; and a City Day-Care/Youth Center.

Education. Hydaburg Elementary School and Hydaburg Junior/Senior School are operated by the Hydaburg City School District. The schools have a combined student enrollment of 96 students, with a total of 10 teachers.

Health care. Hydaburg Health Clinic is available. Auxiliary health care is provided by Hydaburg EMS and by Prince of Wales Island Area EMS.

Igiugig

Total area of entitlement under ANCSA	69,623 acres
Total labor force	9
High school graduate or higher	11
Bachelor's degree or higher	0
Unemployment rate	0%
(see ECONOMY, below)	
Per capita income *(1999)*	$13,172
Current Population	50
2003 state demographer estimate	
Population *2000 census*	53
Percent Native *2000 census*	83%

LOCATION

Igiugig is located on the south shore of the Kvichak River, at the outlet to Iliamna Lake (the largest in Alaska), 50 miles southwest of Iliamna and 50 miles northeast of King Salmon.

CLIMATE

Igiugig lies within a transitional climatic zone. Average summer temperatures range from 42°F to 62°F; average winter temperatures range from 6°F to 30°F. The record high was 91°F and the record low -47°F. Total precipitation in the area averages 26.2 inches annually, including an average snowfall of 64.3 inches.

CULTURE AND HISTORY

The Kiatagmiut (Yup'ik) Eskimos originally lived in Kaskanak on the right bank of the Kvichak River, about seven miles from the outlet of Iliamna Lake. At the turn of the century, these people moved upriver to the present site of Igiugig, which had long been used as a fish camp by the people of the region. Today about one-third of the village's population can trace their roots to the village of Branch on the Branch River; residents of that village moved to Igiugig as it began to develop. Igiugig began as a fishing village; commercial and subsistence fishing continue to sustain the community. Historically an Eskimo village, it is now composed of a population that is 80 percent Alutiiq Aleut, who depend upon commercial fishing and a subsistence lifestyle. Sport fishing attracts visitors during summer months.

[ig-ee-UH-gig]
Ethnicity: Yup'ik; Alutiiq Aleut

Native entity
Igiugig Village Council
P.O. Box 4008
Igiugig, AK 99613
907-533-3211
907-533-3217 Fax
igiugig.com

ANCSA village corporation
Igiugig Native Corporation
P.O. Box 4009
Igiugig, AK 99613-4009
907-533-8001
907-533-3217 Fax
igiugig.com

Igiugig

GOVERNMENT
Igiugig is unincorporated and is located in the Lake and Peninsula Borough (see Alaska introduction). The Igiugig Village Council is a federally recognized tribe and has a five-member traditional council, headed by a president.

VILLAGE CORPORATION
Shareholders in the Igiugig village corporation also hold shares in the Bristol Bay regional Native corporation (see Alaska introduction).

ECONOMY
Salmon fishing is the mainstay of Igiugig's economy. During the red-salmon season, almost everyone leaves the village to fish in Bristol Bay. Many residents travel to Naknek each summer to fish or work in the canneries. Subsistence is also an important contributor to residents' livelihoods. Salmon, trout, whitefish, moose, caribou, and rabbit are eaten. Some trapping occurs. Note that although the unemployment rate in 2000 census was zero, fully 55% of the adults were not in the work force.

Fisheries. Five residents hold commercial fishing permits.

Services and retail. There are 10 businesses in the community, including an electric company, auto repair shop, air transportation company, boarding house, gun shop, and contractor companies.

Government as employer. Of the nine employed residents, seven work for the village, borough, state, or federal governments.

INFRASTRUCTURE
Transportation. Igiugig is accessible primarily by water and air. Charter flights are available from Iliamna and King Salmon. The state provides a 3,000-foot by 75-foot gravel runway. A small public dock is open. Barges deliver goods from Naknek or Dillingham in the autumn. Igiugig Corporation operates a barge system on Lake Iliamna.

Electricity is provided by the Igiugig Electric Company, owned by the village council, operating a 120-kilowatt diesel plant.

Water and waste systems. Water is drawn from the Kvichak River. Twelve homes are connected to a piped water and sewer system; two additional homes are connected to sewer only. The school operates its own system. A new landfill and access road are under development.

Telecommunications. Local telephone service is provided by Bristol Bay Telephone Cooperative, while long distance service is available through Alascom. The Rural Alaska Television Network provides television access. Internet access is available at the school.

COMMUNITY FACILITIES AND SERVICES
Education. Igiugig School is in the Lake and Peninsula School District. The school has 14 students and two teachers. The school library serves as the village library.

Health care is provided by the Igiugig Health Clinic, owned by the village council and leased to the U.S. Public Health Service. The clinic is administered by the Bristol Bay Area Health Corporation. Auxiliary health care is provided by Igiugig Village Response Team.

Public safety. There are no local law enforcement or fire fighting capabilities.

Iliamna

Also known as Nilavena

[ill-ee-AM-nuh]
Ethnicity: Tanaina Athabascan; Yup'ik; Alutiiq

Native entity
Iliamna Village Council
also known as
Nilavena Tribal Council
P.O. Box 286
Iliamna, AK 99606
907-571-1246
907-571-1256 Fax
arctic.net

ANCSA village corporation
Iliamna Natives Limited
P.O. Box 245
Iliamna, AK 99606
907-571-1246
907-571-1256 Fax

Total area of entitlement under ANCSA	73,059 acres
One hundred seven acres has been conveyed to a land trust for the village.	
Total labor force	63
High school graduate or higher	20
Bachelor's degree or higher	22
Unemployment rate	0%
Per capita income (1999)	$19,741
Current population	92
2003 state demographer estimate	
Population *2000 census*	102
Percent Native *2000 census*	57.8%

LOCATION
Iliamna is located on the northwest side of Iliamna Lake, near the Lake Clark National Park and Preserve, 225 miles southwest of Anchorage. The nearest neighboring communities are Nondalton, Port Alsworth, Pedro Bay, and Kokhanok.

CLIMATE
Iliamna lies within a transitional climate zone, with warm summers and cold winters. January temperatures average 20°F, and the average for July is 65°F. Average annual precipitation is 26 inches, with yearly snowfall of 64 inches. Prevailing winds are from the east.

CULTURE AND HISTORY
The community of Iliamna was founded in 1800 by Athabascan Indians who came to the area to trap, hunt, and fish. At present, the Native population consists of Tanaina (Athabascan) Indians, Yup'ik Eskimos, and Alutiiq Aleuts. The name Iliamna is derived from an Athabascan word meaning "big ice" or "big lake." Prior to 1935, "Old Iliamna" was located near the mouth of the Iliamna River. Around 1935 the Indian village moved to its present location, approximately 40 miles from the old site. Much of Iliamna's current size and character can be attributed to the development of fishing and hunting lodges; the first opened in the 1930s, a second in the 1950s, and several others in the 1970s and 1980s. Iliamna Lake offers exceptional sport fishing for 13 species of Alaska game fish, including rainbow trout that grow to more than 30 inches in length.

GOVERNMENT
Iliamna is unincorporated and is located in the Lake and Peninsula Borough (see Alaska introduction). The Iliamna Village Council, also know as Nilavena Tribal Council, is a federally recognized tribe. The village is governed by a five-member traditional village council, headed by a president.

VILLAGE CORPORATION
Shareholders in the village corporation are also shareholders in the Bristol Bay regional Native corporation (see Alaska introduction).

ECONOMY
Iliamna's economy is based on the commercial salmon fishery in Bristol Bay and on tourism. Most natives and an increasing number of non-Natives depend to a varying extent on subsistence hunting and fishing as well. Subsistence species including salmon, trout, grayling, moose, caribou, bear, seal, porcupine, and rabbit. Northern Dynasty Minerals is ex-

ploring the gold, copper, and molybdenum potential of the Pebble Deposit, 15 miles from Iliamna.

Fisheries. Seventeen residents hold commercial fishing permits.

Services and retail. There are 39 businesses in the community, including a bed-and-breakfast, cottage, video rental store, guide service, air services, taxi company, and company management services.

Government as employer. Of the 63 employed residents, 29 work for the village, borough, state, or federal governments.

INFRASTRUCTURE

Transportation. Iliamna is primarily accessible by air and water. An 8-mile gravel road links Iliamna to Newhalen, and a 22-mile road from Iliamna to Nondalton is under construction. The state provides two gravel airstrips located between Iliamna and Newhalen. One measures 5,080- by 100-feet, the other 4,800- by 150-feet. Additional facilities include: floatplane facilities at Slop Lake, East Bay, and Pike Lake; a private airstrip at Iliamna Roadhouse; and private floatplane access at Summit Lake. Barge services are available via the Kvichak River. A breakwater, boat harbor, and dock are available.

Electricity is provided by the I-N-N Electric Cooperative, which operates the recently completed Tazimina Hydroelectric Project with diesel backup. (It also serves Newhalen and Nondalton.)

Water and waste systems. Iliamna residents use individual water wells and septic systems. Most of the homes (85 percent) are fully plumbed. A well provides water to the community building, village office, and washeteria. Septic pumping services are provided by the village. Residents transport refuse to the landfill.

Telecommunications. Local telephone service is provided by Interior Telephone Company, while long distance service is available through AT&T Alascom, GCI, or Interior Telephone. The Rural Alaska Television Network provides television access; there is no cable service. Three AM radio stations broadcast to the Iliamna area. Internet service is provided by GCI.

COMMUNITY FACILITIES AND SERVICES

Education. There are no schools located in the village. Students from Iliamna attend school in Newhalen, under the Lake and Peninsula Borough School District.

Health care is provided by the Iliamna Health Clinic, privately owned and leased to the U.S. Public Health Service. The clinic is administered by the Bristol Bay Area Health Corporation. Emergency medical services are provided by the Iliamna/Newhalen Rescue Squad.

Public safety. Law enforcement is provided by Alaska state troopers. The village has a volunteer fire department. Rescue services are provided by the Iliamna/Newhalen Rescue Squad.

Iliamna
Also known as Nilavena

Inalik
See Diomede

qurmuit

Iqurmuit

Total area of entitlement under ANCSA	
	92,160 acres
Total labor force	106
High school graduate or higher	30
Bachelor's degree or higher	13
Unemployment rate	21.7%
Per capita income (1999)	$8,358
2003 population	310
state demographer estimate	
Population 2000 census	296
Percent Native 2000 census	93.9%

LOCATION

Russian Mission is located in the Yukon-Kuskokwim Delta in southwest Alaska, on the west bank of the Yukon River, 25 miles southeast of Marshall and 100 river miles upriver from Saint Mary's. It is 72 air miles from Bethel and 376 miles west of Anchorage. It is located in the Yukon Delta National Wildlife Refuge.

PHYSICAL DESCRIPTION

The City contains 5.7 square miles of land and 0.5 square mile of water. Russian Mission is on southwestern Alaska's coastal plain, an area of broad, flat delta covered with numerous rivers, streams, lakes, sloughs, and ponds. Surrounded by spruce, alder, and willow trees, the community sits nestled on a hill side overlooking the Yukon River and tundra flats to its south. Russian Mission is located within the Yukon Delta National Wildlife Refuge, 22 million acres of nesting habitat for millions of waterfowl including emperor geese, ducks, and other shorebirds, and home to a wide variety of mammal species such as brown and black bears, caribou, moose, wolves, and musk ox. Salmon, moose, black bear, porcupine, rabbit, and waterfowl are abundant in the area around Russian Mission. The Area Use Map of 2001 shows extensive berry picking areas on the shores of nearby Nunvotchuk Lake.

CLIMATE

Russian Mission is located in a continental climate zone with a significant maritime influence. Winter temperatures may be as low as -54ºF, while summer temperatures may reach 86ºF. Annual precipitation is 16 inches, including snowfall of 60 inches. Heavy north winds often limit air access in the fall and winter. The Lower Yukon is free of ice from mid-June through October.

CULTURE AND HISTORY

Russian Mission is a Yup'ik community, with a subsistence-oriented culture. The harvesting of salmon, moose, black bear, porcupine, rabbit, waterfowl, and berries are part of the way of life for the Yup'ik. The village was established in 1837 as a fur trading post for the Russian American Company. In 1842 the Russian explorer Alexseev Zagoskin noted the presence of an Inupiat village at the same location, called Ikogmiut, meaning "people of the point." In 1857 Jacob Natzuetov, a Russian-Aleut priest, established the first Russian Orthodox mission for interior Alaska at the site. It was renamed from Pokrovskaya Mission to Russian Mission in 1900. Russian Mission's population levels have fluctuated significantly over the past 100 years. In 1880 there were 143 residents. Population grew to 350 persons by 1902 and then dropped sharply. In 1960, Russian Mission had 102 residents. The population increased more than 40 percent between 1960 and 1970; it increased another 68 percent between 1970 and 1990. Russian Mission still carries its rich Russian traditions. The people are friendly and will gladly offer a tour of the Russian Orthodox church, where one may see many icons that were transported from Russia in the 1800s. A highlight of the year is (Slaviq), or Russian Orthodox Christmas.

GOVERNMENT

Russian Mission was incorporated as a second-class city in 1970, with a seven-member city council including the mayor. It is located in the unorganized borough *(see Alaska intro-*

**Also known as
Russian Mission**

Ethnicity: Yup'ik

Municipality
City of Russian Mission
P.O. Box 49
Russian Mission, AK 99657
  907-584-5111
  907-584-5476 Fax

Native entity
Iqurmuit Traditional Council
P.O. Box 9
Russian Mission, AK 99657
  907-584-5511
  907-584-5593 Fax

ANCSA village corporation
Russian Mission Native
  Corporation
P.O. Box 48
Russian Mission, AK 99657
  907-584-5885
  907-584-5311 Fax

Iqurmuit

Also known as Russian Mission

duction). The Iqurmuit Traditional Council of five members is recognized by the BIA.

ECONOMY

Employment opportunities are provided by local public services and commercial fishing. Seasonal employment includes U.S. Bureau of Land Management firefighting and construction. Some income is also earned from trapping. Subsistence activities (harvesting of salmon, moose, black bear, porcupine, rabbit, and waterfowl, and berry picking) provide an important supplement to cash income. There are also several stores and a day care center.

VILLAGE CORPORATION

The Russian Mission Native Corporation (formerly the Native Village of Russian Mission; also known as the Russian Mission Traditional Council) has 122 shareholders. Its major business is selling oil and gas in the village. There are five members on its board. The corporation owns one store in the city. Shareholders in the corporation also hold shares in Calista Corporation regional native corporation (see Alaska introduction).

Fisheries. The Alaska State Commercial Fisheries Entry Commission reported 11 fishing permits issued to Russian Mission residents in 2002. They covered halibut, Dungeness crab, and salmon gillnet fisheries.

Manufacturing. There is a wood-products business in the city.

Mining. There is a mining enterprise in the city.

Services and retail. There are four general stores in Russian Mission.

Transportation. The transportation industry employs five residents of Russian Mission.

Government as employer. The city government employs six people, the state government employs 25, and the federal government employs an additional three.

INFRASTRUCTURE

Electricity. Electricity is available to all residents from Alaska Village Electric Cooperative's (AVEC) 541-kilowatt diesel plant.

Fuel storage (gallons). Bulk fuel is available for purchase by residents. Storage: Village Corp. (63,219); AVEC (58,830); Lower Yukon Schools (29,830); Native Store (10,775); City Water (7,930); City (4,600).

Telecommunications. Telephone service is available to all residents. Local telephone service is provided by United Utilities, while long distance service is available through AT&T. The school has Internet service. One television channel is rebroadcast locally by the Alaska Rural Communications System. Three AM radio stations, KICY-AM, KYUK-AM, and KNOM-AM, serve the area.

Transportation. The location of Russian Mission on the Yukon River allows water access by barge and small boats. During the summer months, commercial barge lines deliver fuel and other bulk supplies. Although no roads connect Russian Mission to other communities, the river provides surface access after freeze-up in the winter. Russian Mission has a 2,700-foot gravel airstrip, owned and maintained by the State of Alaska and served by five air transportation companies. Construction on a new runway began in 2000. There are daily scheduled flights. Heavy north winds often limit air access in the fall and winter, however, and the airstrip is sometimes flooded in the spring.

Water and waste systems. The city provides piped treated water to community residents from a community well. There is a piped-sewage service that serves the majority of the community's homes, as well as a honeybucket dump.

COMMUNITY FACILITIES AND SERVICES

The city provides fuel storage, waste collection and disposal, and water supply. The city also operates a washeteria. The Iqurmuit Traditional Council owns the Russian Mission Native Store.

Education. The Russian Mission School serves students from kindergarten through high school. It is operated by the Lower Yukon School District. The school has an innovative curriculum. It combines standard classroom teaching of basic studies with hands-on experiential outdoor Yup'ik activities. In the fall, the students gillnet salmon, pick berries, and hunt moose. Trapping beavers and setting nets under the ice for whitefish are winter activities. The goal is to make the students proficient in subsistence skills by the eighth grade. The Lower Yukon School District is expanding the program to other schools in the district. The city operates a public library.

Health care. Provided by the Russian Mission Health Clinic (renovated in 1994), owned by the city and leased to the U.S. Public Health Service. It is backed up by the Clara Morgan Sub-Regional Clinic in Aniak. Both are operated by the Yukon-Kuskokwim Health Corporation.

Public safety. Law enforcement is provided by the state village public safety officer (VPSO) and the city police department, backed by state troopers in Saint Mary's. Emergency response is provided by the VPSO and the city volunteer fire department.

Total area of entitlement under ANCSA
81,502 acres

Total labor force	16
High school graduate or higher	7
Bachelor's degree or higher	0
Unemployment rate	0%
Per capita income (1999)	$21,983
Current population	3
2003 state demographer estimate	
Population 2000 census	22
Percent Native 2000 census	95.5%

LOCATION
Ivanof Bay is located at the head of Ivanof Bay, near Perryville, on the northeast end of the Kupreanof Peninsula, 350 miles southwest of Anchorage. Neighboring communities are Chignik, Chignik Lake, and Chignik Lagoon.

CLIMATE
Ivanof Bay has a maritime climate, characterized by cool summers, relatively warm winters, and rainy weather. Precipitation averages 125 inches annually, including 58 inches of snow. The average temperature in January is 15°F; the average for July is 70°F.

CULTURE AND HISTORY
The village occupies the site of a former salmon cannery that operated from the 1930s to the early 1950s. In 1965 several families moved from Perryville because they believed the water quality to be better and food resources more abundant. Ivanof Bay maintains traditional Aleut cultural activities. Residents practice a subsistence lifestyle during the winter, while in the summer most residents leave the community to work in the commercial salmon industry in the Chignik area.

GOVERNMENT
Ivanof Bay is unincorporated and is part of the Lake and Peninsula Borough (see Alaska introduction). The Ivanof Bay Village Council is a federally recognized tribe with a five-member traditional council, headed by a president, that provides local government services to the residents of the community.

VILLAGE CORPORATION
Shareholders in the Bay View village corporation also hold shares in the Bristol Bay regional Native corporation (see Alaska introduction).

ECONOMY
The local economy is based on the commercial salmon-fishing industry in the summer, with residents participating in subsistence activities during the winter. Many trap in the winter.

The people depend upon subsistence hunting and fishing, and use salmon, trout, crab, clams, moose, caribou, bear, porcupine, and seals.

Fisheries. Two residents hold commercial fishing permits for salmon and halibut.

Government as employer. Of the 16 employed residents, 15 work for the local, borough, state, or federal governments.

INFRASTRUCTURE
Transportation. Bay View Incorporated owns a private 1,500-foot gravel airstrip, and Ivanof Bay is accessible by floatplane. There are monthly flights from King Salmon in the winter and biweekly flights in the summer, weather permitting. Bulk cargo goods are barged to Chignik Bay. There is no public dock or harbor. All-terrain vehicles and skiffs are the chief means of local travel.

Electricity is provided by the village council, which operates a diesel plant.

Water and waste systems. Water, drawn from a well and nearby stream, is stored in a 20,000-gallon tank. A well is available to the school. All facilities and homes have access to the community water system. Sewage is handled by individual septic tanks. A sludge disposal site was recently completed. Villagers haul their own refuse. A new landfill is being developed.

Telecommunications. Local telephone service is provided by Pacific Telecommunications, while long distance service is available through Alascom. The Rural Alaska Television Network provides television access. Cable service is not available. Two AM radio stations broadcast to the Ivanof Bay area. Internet access is available only at the school. In-state phone service is available from ACS of the Northland.

COMMUNITY FACILITIES AND SERVICES
Education. The school at Ivanof Bay is part of the Lake and Peninsula Borough School District and offers instruction from kindergarten through high school. The school library also serves as the village library.

Health care is provided by the Ivanof Bay Health Clinic, owned by the village and leased to the U.S. Public Health Service. The clinic is administered by the Bristol Bay Area Health Corporation. Auxiliary health care is provided by Ivanof Bay First Responders.

Public safety. There is no local law enforcement. Fire and rescue services are provided by Ivanof Bay First Responders.

[EYE-van-off BAY]
Ethnicity: Alutiiq Aleut

Native entity
Ivanof Bay Village Council
P.O. Box 500
Perryville, AK 99648-0500
907-669-2219
907-669-2219 Fax

ANCSA village corporation
Bay View Incorporated
P.O. Box 233407
Anchorage, AK 99523-3407
907-561-6493
907-345-9017 Fax

Juneau
See Urban Tribes under Douglas

Kaguyak
See Zero Population Section

Kake

[CAKE]
Ethnicity: Tlingit

Municipality
City of Kake
P.O. Box 500
Kake, AK 99830
    907-785-3804
    907-785-4815 Fax

Native entity
Organized Village of Kake
P.O. Box 316
Kake, AK 99830-0316
    907-785-6471
    907-785-4902 Fax

ANCSA village corporation
Kake Tribal Corporation
P.O. Box 263
Kake, AK 99830
    907-785-3221
    907-785-6407 Fax

Juneau Office
2211 N. Jordan Ave.
Juneau, AK, 99801
    907-790-2214
    907-790-2264 Fax

Total area of entitlement under ANCSA	23,040 acres
Retained land under §16(b)	
Total labor force	330
High school graduate or higher	189
Bachelor's degree or higher	46
Unemployment rate	24.8%
Per capita income *(1999)*	$17,411
Current population	682
2003 state demographer estimate	
Population *2000 census*	710
Percent Native *2000 census*	74.6%

LOCATION
Kake is located on the northwest coast of Kupreanof Island, along Kaku Strait, 38 air miles northwest of Petersburg.

CLIMATE
Kake has a maritime climate, characterized by cool summers, mild winters, and fairly heavy precipitation. Average summer temperatures range from 44°F to 62°F; winter temperatures range from 26°F to 43°F.

CULTURE AND HISTORY
Kake is a Tlingit village with a fishing, logging, and subsistence lifestyle. Troubles with white settlers in the middle of the nineteenth century led to the so-called Kake War. During successive conflicts with the U.S. Navy, three Kake villages were destroyed. The Kakes did not rebuild for many years but finally settled at their present site in the late 1800s. In 1891, a government school and store were built. A Society of Friends mission also was established. In 1912 the first cannery was built near the village; it was purchased by the village in the 1940s. In the late 1940s, timber harvesting and processing began at a local sawmill. Traditional customs are still observed in Kake. The world's largest totem pole was commissioned by the village and carved by Chilkats in 1967 for Alaska's centennial. The 132-foot totem pole now stands on a bluff overlooking the town.

GOVERNMENT
Kake was incorporated as a first-class city in 1952, with a mayor and city council. The community is located in the Unorganized Borough *(see Alaska introduction)*. The Organized Village of Kake is a federally recognized tribe in the community, with a traditional village council presided over by a president. Shareholders in the Kake village corporation also hold shares in the Sealaska regional Native corporation *(see Alaska introduction)*.

ECONOMY
The largest employers are the city and school district. Fishing and seafood processing contribute considerably to the economy.

Fisheries. Salmon, halibut, shellfish, deer, bear, waterfowl, and berries are important food sources. The non-profit Gunnuk Creek Hatchery has assisted in sustaining the salmon fishery. Kake Foods produces smoked and dried salmon and halibut. Sixty-seven residents hold commercial fishing permits.

Forestry. Turn Mountain Timber, a joint venture between Whitestone Logging and Kake Tribal Corporation, employs residents in logging village corporation lands. Southeast Stevedoring, a Sealaska contractor, also provides employment at the log sort yard and transfer facility at Point McCarny.

Government as employer. Of the 248 employed residents, 79 work for the city, state, or federal governments.

Services and retail. There are 28 businesses in Kake, including Kake Tribal Fuel, Kake Tribal Logging and Timber Company, a day care center, grocery store, tree service, lodges, inns, and a stationery and gift store.

INFRASTRUCTURE
Transportation. Kake can be reached by air and sea.

Air. Scheduled floatplane and air taxi flights are available from Petersburg, Juneau, Sitka, and Wrangell. The state provides a 4,000- by 100-foot lighted paved runway, and a seaplane base at the city dock.

Water. State ferry and barge services are available. A small boat harbor, boat launch, deep-water dock, and state ferry terminal also are available. A breakwater is currently being built.

Land. There are more than 120 miles of logging roads in the Kake vicinity but no connections to other communities on Kupreanof Island.

Electricity is provided by the Tlingit-Haida Regional Electrical Authority, a state agency, which operates a 2,230-kilowatt diesel plant.

Water and waste systems. Water pumped from a dam at Gunnuck Creek is treated and stored in a tank and piped throughout the community. In July 2000 the dam failed, and makeshift systems of pumps now supply city water. A piped sewer system and primary treatment plant is provided by the city. Almost all residences are fully plumbed. The city provides refuse collection, recycling, and hazardous waste disposal.

Telecommunications. Local telephone service is provided by Pacific Telecommunications, while long distance service is available through Alascom. The city provides cable television service. The Rural Alaska Television Network provides television access. Internet service is provided by SEAKnet and GCI (at the schools only).

COMMUNITY FACILITIES AND SERVICES
Education. Kake Elementary School has 65 students and nine teachers. Kake High School has 88 students and seven teachers. The schools are operated by the Kake City School District. There is a city public library.

Health care is provided by the Kake Health Center, owned by the city and leased to the U.S. Public Health Service. The health center is administered by the Southeast Alaska Regional Health Corporation. Auxiliary health care is provided by Kake EMS.

Public safety. The city police department provides local law enforcement, and Kake EMS provides rescue services.

**Honoring Nations
Honoree 2002**

**Text in its entirety from:
The Harvard Project On
American Indian Economic
Development**

**John F. Kennedy School
of Government
Harvard University**

In 1999, in an effort to curb youth alcohol abuse, tribal members of the Organized Village of Kake (federally recognized Tribe of Kake, Alaska) established the Healing Heart Council and Circle Peacemaking, a reconciliation and sentencing process embedded in Tlingit traditions. Working in seamless conjunction with Alaska's state court system, Circle Peacemaking intervenes in the pernicious cycle by which underage drinking becomes an entrenched pattern of adult alcoholism. Today, the program not only enforces underage drinking sentences in an environment where such accountability had been rare, but also restores the Tlingit culture and heals the Kake community.

For generations, the Tlingit people of Kake, Alaska, have witnessed their youth population's descent into patterns of underage drinking and substance abuse. Over time, these illegal behaviors have grown more damaging—prodded onward by intensifying patterns of "self-medication" for depression, anxiety, and other stresses associated with poverty. The result was an emerging adult population mired in alcoholism.

Alcohol abuse is not only a chronic problem in Kake, but also throughout Alaskan tribal villages and Indian Country, where it contributes to numerous social ills. A 1998 report of the National Institute on Alcohol Abuse and Alcoholism linked alcohol abuse to "child abuse, accidental death, assaults, rape, and suicide" and ranked Alaska among the five states that had the "highest annual rates" of these ills. The report also observed that approximately 67 percent of Alaska Native deaths between 1990 and 1993 were alcohol related. More generally, alcohol abuse has been identified as a factor in half of the top ten leading causes of death among American Indians and Alaska Natives.

The Organized Village of Kake had long recognized the devastating toll of rampant alcoholism. Unfortunately, one of the means of combating the problem—the justice system-appeared unavailable to Kake's Native citizens. The Alaska State justice system had not successfully addressed these issues in Alaska Native communities for decades. A primary problem was that its resources were stretched thin. The juvenile probation officer assigned to Kake lived on another island that was accessible only by ferryboat or plane. Responding to felony offenses consumed most of his time; therefore, he could pay only limited attention to the seemingly less serious misdemeanors of Kake's youth. Unfortunately, without the consequences that good probation monitoring could provide, the minor infractions of village youth tended to grow into entrenched adult behavior.

By the late 1990s, Kake residents realized that without breaking this cycle, the Village's future looked bleak. Despite the confined jurisdictional space in which they operated (the state of Alaska has authority over most aspects of criminal justice in Native Alaska), they also realized that they could craft a solution that relied on local human and cultural resources. Looking to the philosophy of peacemaking and the process of "circle sentencing," Kake village volunteers organized the Healing Heart Council and Circle Peacemaking in 1999. This reconciliation and sentencing process is embedded in Tlingit tradition and works in conjunction with the Alaska State court system.

Circle Peacemaking begins when a Kake juvenile enters a guilty plea with the state court. Then, the state judge, with the concurrence of the prosecutor, the public defender, and the offender, may turn the juvenile's case over to the Healing Heart Council for sentencing. The Council initiates Circle Peacemaking by bringing together a group of village volunteers to formally sentence the young offender(s). Through the close attention, encouragement, and admonishment of this circle of volunteer justices, the juvenile's misdemeanors have a lower probability of leading to more serious adult substance abuse and crime. Circle Peacemaking heals the offender by addressing the underlying causes of the offending behavior and restores the rupture in community life by repairing the relationship between the offender and victim.

More specifically, Circle Peacemaking involves the participation of individuals and groups who rarely come together under western systems of justice—the offender, the victim, families, friends, church representatives, police, substance abuse counselors, and concerned or affected community members. Participants, who may number from six to sixty, sit in a circle while a Keeper of the Circle facilitates the discussion. Discussions always begin and end with a prayer, and negative comments are strictly forbidden. Circle discussions are kept entirely confidential, and the Keeper encourages participants to speak from their hearts. The meetings typically last two to four hours, but they can only end when forgiveness and healing are apparent and consensus is reached about the offender's sentence. This sentence then becomes public.

But Circle Peacemaking does not conclude with sentencing. The circle participants are themselves responsible for ensuring that offenders adhere to their sentences. A typical sentence for underage alcohol consumption might include a curfew, community service, or a formal apology. It might also require that the offender meet with elders or others who have worked through comparable experiences. Frequently, a sentence requires the offender's participation in other support circles. Importantly, the circle participants play a key role in assessing whether the offenders compliance is satisfactory. It is not uncommon for them to call for additional circles. Noncompliant offenders must return to the Alaska State court for sentencing.

Since its inception, the dedication of volunteers and judicious use of its minimal annual budget—a few thousand dollars in most years-have enabled Circle Peacemaking to expand its jurisdiction from underage alcohol consumption cases to include broader community needs. Today, the Healing Heart Council offers not only sentencing circles for juvenile offenders, but also sentencing circles for adult offenders who request Circle Peacemaking, healing circles for victims, intervention circles for individuals who seem to be losing control of their lives, celebration circles for offenders who have completed their sentencing requirements, and critical incident circles for individuals involved in an accident or crime who require immediate counseling. Additionally, the Healing Heart Council offers annual Circle Peacemaking Workshops that attracts an average of 24 participants from Kake and other villages who are interested in learning how the Alaska State court system and Circle Peacemaking complement each other.

Kake

Honoring Nations Honoree 2002

Text in its entirety from:
The Harvard Project On American Indian Economic Development

John F. Kennedy School of Government Harvard University

This interest is itself evidence of Circle Peacemaking's success in Kake. Only two offenders out of the eighty sentenced during the program's first four years rejected a circle's outcome and returned to state court for sentencing. All of the twenty-four juveniles who were assigned to circle sentencing for underage drinking successfully completed the terms of their sentences. Circle Peacemaking also reports very low levels of recidivism. Sixty-eight adults participated in circles without repeating their offenses or violating other laws during their probation periods. At the time of writing, approximately thirty village residents are enrolled in substance abuse recovery programs. Circle Peacemaking veterans are moving on with their lives in other ways as well. Several have gone on to trade schools to complete their education; several are enrolled in universities. One adult veteran of a circle is now a juvenile justice associate and working on an alcohol abuse counseling certificate. These successes are reflected in a positive trend in the circles themselves. Over four years, the number of mandated sentencing circles decreased and the number of volunteer support circles increased—initiated by individuals who have not yet committed offenses and are determined to avoid doing so. Unsurprisingly, Kake now sponsors well-attended sobriety marches, and Village residents have begun to comment on the perceptible difference in their community. It is a community in which the intergenerational pattern of substance abuse is being broken, and where youth and adults alike face brighter, healthier futures.

Significantly, Kake Circle Peacemaking's successes are occurring where the Alaska State court system repeatedly failed. Over four years, Circle Peacemaking has experienced a 97.5 percent success rate in sentences fulfillment compared to the Alaskan court system's 22 percent success rate. The State of Alaska's Judicial Board recognized Kake Circle Peacemaking for its effectiveness as a judicial process and selected it from among 250 applications to win the Spirit of United Youth Courts of Alaska. The Chief Justice of Alaska visited Kake to investigate Circle Peacemaking. Impressed with the Healing Heart Council's achievements, he mentioned Circle Peacemaking in his State of the Judiciary address. Kake has also sent representatives of Circle Peacemaking to communities throughout Alaska. Haines, Sitka, and the Juvenile Justice Center in Anchorage are now using Circle Peacemaking to address juvenile crime with positive results.

The success of the Healing Heart Council and Circle Peacemaking in curbing underage drinking is only the beginning of a number of remarkable successes. Three of these deserve special mention. First, Circle Peacemaking offers healing for both the offender for whom the circle is called and for the entire community. In large part, this is because community-mindedness is the foundation for Circle Peacemaking. Even though the state court process tends to be impersonal, involve few reciprocal commitments, offer limited oversight, and provide a small amount of opportunities for rehabilitation, the circle process complements it by fulfilling the specific judicial needs of Kake. Community members personally commit to the offender and, through these multiple, ongoing relationships, gradually rebuild the offender's commitment to the community. By placing offenders within a circle of caring individuals who have committed themselves to offer only constructive commentary, peacemaking circles break patterns of retributive justice that distances the offender from the community. Participants regularly remark that the process affects every member of the circle. This has been particularly apparent during sentencing circles for underage drinkers, in which both youth and their parents found the encouragement and support to end their substance abuse.

Second, as it succeeds in healing the community, Circle Peacemaking promotes the health of Kake's Tlingit culture. As noted, the Healing Heart Council and Circle Peacemaking have strong traditional roots. The Council practices a form of community justice reminiscent of the Deer People, an almost-forgotten group of traditional Tlingit peacemakers who healed, restored, and prevented escalating harms within their villages by consulting with all who were affected by the actions of an offender. Contact and colonialism eroded these practices-practices that the Healing Heart Council's founders, once they determined a course of action, were eager to revive. To do so, they invited Canada's Yukon Territory Tlingit Circle Peacemaking facilitators to Kake to study the peacemaking circles of the Carcross Tlingits. Now, Circle Peacemaking perpetuates Tlingit culture in Kake. In the circle, participants pass a diamond willow talking stick to order the discussion. The willow's brown, diamond-shaped marks represent the eyes of elders who watch to see if their community members aid one another through their comments. Circle participants are particularly encouraged to share traditional stories and pass on the knowledge borne of their own experiences. The Healing Heart Council reports that youth who have participated in Circle Peacemaking feel a renewed interest in their culture. Kake Circle Peacemaking grooms the future leaders of its community by discouraging the illicit use of alcohol and drugs among its youth. In demonstrating the power of Tlingit cultural practices to address modern problems, Circle Peacemaking ensures that those leaders will lead in accordance with Tlingit cultural values.

Third, it is significant to note that Kake Circle Peacemaking is succeeding because of, and not in spite of, all of its cultural realities. Skeptics of Circle Peacemaking challenged the ability of an isolated, small, and socially interconnected village to establish a successful sentencing process. In Circle Peacemaking, however, these realities lie at the heart of the circles' successes. Circle Peacemaking is not an impersonal, but a deeply personal justice system that depends upon and promotes the interconnectedness of a compact and culturally whole village. The successes of Kake Circle Peacemaking rely on the village's determination to understand and utilize its most salient characteristics as strengths.

This has, of course, been especially significant considering the neglect and even outright hostility that the Alaska state government so frequently displays toward Alaskan tribes. It should be noted, in conclusion, that notwithstanding targeted state efforts to reduce tribal decision-making power, Kake has instituted a system of justice that increases tribal sovereignty. It has done so in a manner that commands the respect of the state judicial system while honoring its own community traditions. Although peacemaking courts are spreading throughout Indian Country, their influence in Alaska has been limited. Other than Kake, the Metlakatla Tribe is the only tribe in Alaska that takes on criminal cases beyond its Indian Child Welfare load. In Alaska, the barriers to constructing tribal courts capable of entering into full faith and comity agreements with the state courts or of raising sentencing controversies to the level of federal court review, as tribal peacemaker courts have done elsewhere, are significant. Still, Kake Circle Peacemaking has, to the great benefit of its village, expertly assumed a state court function that was otherwise executed ineffectively. The Organized Village of Kake intends to make Circle Peacemaking a permanent fixture of self-governance by enshrining it in their constitution. Circle Peacemaking's success and the village's determination to ensure its perpetuation stand as significant triumphs in the development of a robust tribal judicial system. These are remarkable and desperately needed achievements in Alaska.

Total area of entitlement under ANCSA
                    92,160 acres

Total labor force	138
High school graduate or higher	54
Bachelor's degree or higher	26
Unemployment rate	15.2%
Per capita income *(1999)*	$22,031
Current population	295
2003 state demographer estimate	
Population *2000 census*	293
Percent Native *2000 census*	84%

LOCATION
Kaktovik is on Barter Island, 90 miles west of the Canadian border and 310 miles southeast of Barrow. The village is on the northern edge of the 20.3 million-acre Arctic National Wildlife Refuge.

CLIMATE
The climate of Kaktovik is Arctic. Temperatures range from -56°F in the winter to highs of 78°F in the summer. Precipitation is light, at 5 inches per year, with yearly snowfall averaging 20 inches.

CULTURE AND HISTORY
Until the late nineteenth century, the island was a major trade center for the Inupiat and was especially important as a bartering place for Natives from Alaska and Canada. The ruins of Old Kaktovik can be seen from the road into the village from the airport. Due to Kaktovik's isolation, the village has maintained its Inupiat Eskimo traditions. Subsistence is highly dependent upon caribou.

GOVERNMENT
Kaktovik was incorporated as a second-class city in 1971, with a mayor and city council. The community is located in the North Slope Borough *(see Alaska introduction)*. The village also has a traditional council, headed by a president.

VILLAGE CORPORATION
The Native Village of Kaktovik is a federally recognized tribe. Shareholders in the Kaktovik Inupiat village corporation also hold shares in the Arctic Slope regional Native corporation *(see Alaska introduction)*.

ECONOMY
Economic opportunities in Kaktovik are limited due to the community's isolation, and unemployment is high. More than half of the working residents of the village are employed by the North Slope Borough, and another 15 percent work for the school district. About one-quarter of the work force is employed in the private sector, primarily by Native corporations and their affiliates. As is true for other communities in the region, subsistence hunting and fishing play a major role in Kaktovik's economy. Residents hunt in nearby areas for Dall sheep, moose, caribou, and fox. The community also produces arts and crafts for sale, such as etched baleen, carved ivory, and masks. Part-time seasonal jobs, such as construction projects, also provide income.

Government as employer. Of the 117 employed residents, 81 work for the city, borough, state, or federal governments.

Services and retail. There are 16 businesses in the community, including a lumber and timber enterprise, a gasoline station, outfitting store, hotel, plumbing services, electric company, and lodging.

INFRASTRUCTURE
Transportation. Year-round access to Kaktovik is only by air travel. The U.S. Air Force owns Barter Island Airport, which is operated by the North Slope Borough. Seasonal access to Kaktovik is provided by marine and land transportation. Funding has been requested to build a dock and boat ramp.

Electricity is provided by North Slope Borough, which operates a 1,380-kilowatt diesel plant in Kaktovik.

Water and waste systems. Water drawn from a surface source is treated and stored in a 680,000-gallon water tank. Trucks deliver water to home holding tanks; approximately 80 percent of homes have running water in the kitchen. Honeybuckets are used for sewage disposal, and hauling is provided by the borough. A piped system with flush toilets, showers, and plumbing for all households has received preliminary funding.

Telecommunications. Local telephone service is provided by the Arctic Slope Telephone Cooperative, while long distance service is available through Alascon, GCI, or Arctic Slope Telephone. Cable television service is available from the city government. The Rural Alaska Television Network provides television access, and one AM radio station (KBRW) broadcasts to the Kaktovik area. Internet services are provided by GCI and ASTAC.

COMMUNITY FACILITIES AND SERVICES
The North Slope Borough provides all utilities in Kaktovik.

Education. The Harold Kaveolook School in Kaktovik has 85 students and ten teachers. The school library also serves as the city library.

Health care is provided by the Kaktovik Health Clinic, owned by the North Slope Borough and leased to the U.S. Public Health Service. Auxiliary health care is provided by Kaktovik Volunteer Fire Department.

Public safety. Law enforcement is provided by the North Slope Borough Department of Public Safety. Fire and rescue are provided by the Kaktovik Volunteer Fire Department.

Includes Barter Island

[kack-TOH-vick]
Ethnicity: Inupiat

Municipality
City of Kaktovik
P.O. Box 27
Kaktovik, AK 99747
  907-640-6313
  907-640-6314 Fax
kaktovik.com

Native entity
Native Village of Kaktovik
P.O. Box 130
Kaktovik, AK 99747
  907-640-2042
  907-640-2044 Fax

ANCSA village corporation
Kaktovik Inupiat Corporation
P.O. Box 73
Kaktovik, AK 99747
  907-640-6120
  907-640-6720 Fax

Also known as Upper Kalskag

[KAL-skag]
Ethnicity: Yup'ik

Municipality
City of Upper Kalskag
P.O. Box 80
Upper Kalskag, AK 99607
  907-471-2220
  907-471-2237 Fax

Native entity
Village of Kalskag
P.O. Box 50
Kalskag, AK 99607
  907-471-2207
  907-471-2207 Fax

ANCSA village corporation
The Kuskokwim Corporation
4300 B Street, Suite 207
Anchorage, AK 99503
  907-243-2944
  907-243-2984 Fax
  kuskokwim.com

Total area of entitlement under ANCSA	92,160 acres
Total labor force	91
High school graduate or higher	35.1%
Bachelor's degree or higher	13.5%
Unemployment rate	12.1%
Per capita income *(1999)*	$7,859
Population *2000 census*	230
2003 population	231
state demographer estimate	
Percent Native *2000 census*	90.4%

LOCATION
Kalskag (Upper Kalskag) is located on the north bank of the Kuskokwim River, two miles upriver from Lower Kalskag. It lies 30 miles west of Aniak, 99 miles northeast of Bethel and 348 miles west of Anchorage.

PHYSICAL DESCRIPTION
The area encompasses 3.8 sq. miles of land and 0.4 sq. mile of water. The surrounding area is dominated by flat, virtually treeless tundra, dotted with meltwater ponds called "potholes," and veined by smaller rivers, creeks and sloughs, making year-round roads virtually impossible. Significant flooding occurred as recently as 1964 and 1984.

CLIMATE
Despite maritime influences from the Bering Sea, the climate of Kalskag is semi-Arctic; annual precipitation averages 19 inches, including 60 inches of snowfall. Midwinter temperatures dip as low as -55°F with a year-round average low of 19.7°F. Summertime highs reach 87°F, but the year-round average high is 36.8°F. The Kuskokwim River is frozen over from October until mid-June. The area receives approximately 19 hours of sunlight in June, declining to 13 hours by September.

CULTURE AND HISTORY
Kalskag is a Yup'ik village which was strongly influenced by the Roman Catholic Church. In 1898, Nicholas Kameroff, Sr. and Olinga (Avakumoff) Kameroff and their eight children first settled the community. The village was a fish camp known as "Kessiglik." Around 1900, residents of "Kalthagamute" began to move to the village. In 1930, the BIA established a government school, and by 1932, residents of neighboring communities relocated to Kalskag. In 1940, Paul Kameroff, Sr. established a general store, post office, coffee shop, and a barging company. At this time, the community owned and worked a herd of 2,100 reindeer. During the 1930s, Russian Orthodox practitioners in the village relocated to establish Lower Kalskag, three miles to the southwest. The villagers who remained were primarily Roman Catholic practitioners. The city was incorporated in 1975. Still living on their traditional homelands, villagers harvest over 700 pounds of fish and sea mammals, moose, black bear, caribou, porcupine, waterfowl and other birds, greens, and berries per year, in a harsh semi-Arctic environment where hunger is an ever-present danger. Although it is a largely cash-poor economy, the people have enjoyed a productive subsistence lifestyle. Central Alaskan Yup'ik lies geographically and linguistically between Alutiiq and Siberian Yupik. The use of the apostrophe in Central Alaskan Yup'ik, as opposed to Siberian Yupik, denotes a long *p*. The word *Yup'ik* represents not only the language but also the name for the people themselves (*yuk* "person" plus *pik* "real"). Villagers have adopted the use of the English language (primarily for business), while carefully protecting use of the Native language. Now only semi-nomadic, the people of Kalskag retreat to fish camps only during the summer.

GOVERNMENT
Kalskag was incorporated as Upper Kalskag in 1975, a second-class city located in the Unorganized Borough. The city is governed by a seven-member city council, including the mayor. The Village of Kalskag is a BIA-recognized Native entity with a traditional council.

VILLAGE CORPORATION
The ANCSA village corporation is the Kuskokwim Corporation, formed in 1977 by the merger of 10 village corporations along the middle Kuskokwim River. In addition to over 950,000 acres of surface rights, it owns a substantial securities portfolio, investments in three apartment complexes in Fairbanks, a hotel in Fairbanks, a Hispanic broadcasting network, a telecommunication bandwidth and service provider, an engineering, remediation, and construction services firm, and a casino opportunity near Denver, Colorado. It owns the surface rights to the Donlin Creek property, one of the world's largest undeveloped gold deposits. In 2003, it was beginning to pursue §8(a) federal contracting opportunities and establish partnerships and mentor-protégé relationships with established contractors. Shareholders in the Kuskokwim Corporation are also shareholders in Calista Corporation, the regional Native corporation.

ECONOMY
Most cash income in Kalskag is derived from employment at the school, city, or clinic. Some residents trap or work as Bureau of Land Management fire fighters. Subsistence activities provide most food sources. Salmon, moose, rabbit, and waterfowl are the primary resources. A few residents maintain gardens. Fifty-nine of 80 employed residents work in education, health and social services, or public administration.

Fisheries. Three residents hold commercial fishing permits.

Government as employer. Fifty-three of 80 employed residents work for the city, state, or federal government.

Services and retail. There is one general store in Kalskag, and the stores of Lower Kalskag are easily accessible.

Tourism and recreation. The city is located within the Yukon Delta National Wildlife Refuge and within 100 miles of the Innoko National Wildlife Refuge. Austere accommodations for visitors are available at the school, clinic, and city office.

INFRASTRUCTURE
Transportation. A state-maintained 4.2-mile gravel road connects Kalskag and Lower Kalskag. The Kuskokwim River affords easy access by skiff in summer and snowmachine in winter. Barges deliver cargo and bulk fuel during the summer. The state-owned 3,200- by 75-foot gravel airstrip is shared by Kalskag and Lower Kalskag. Five air services serve the airstrip. Daily scheduled air services deliver passengers, mail and other cargo year-round. Winter trails exist to Russian Mission (25 miles) and Aniak (15 miles).

Electricity. The Alaska Village Electrical Cooperative (AVEC) provides electricity from Lower Kaskag.

Fuel storage (gallons). Kuspuk Schools (49,200); Morgan Fuel Service (36,800); Kalskag Store/Twin City Fuel (36,200); city (2,500); Ausdahl Mercantile (1,980).

Water and waste systems. Nearly all homes, the school and the store have individual wells with potable water and indoor plumbing. The city's piped gravity sewage system with lift stations, force main, and lagoon now serves over 60 households and facilities. However, some residents still use outhouses. The city operates a Class 3 landfill for both itself and Lower Kalskag.

Telecommunications. Local telephone service is provided by Bush-Tell, long distance service by AT&T Alascom. Internet service is available at the School from GCI. More than ten AM radio stations from Bethel, Nome, Dillingham, Anchorage, and other locations broadcast to the area. Alaska Rural Communications System repeaters in Kalskag broadcast two television channels to the area.

COMMUNITY FACILITIES AND SERVICES
The city operates the waste disposal system and has a multipurpose facility and city office.

Education. The Joseph S. and Olinga Gregory Elementary School is operated by the Kuspuk School District and serves sixteen students from Kalskag and Lower Kalskag in grades 5 and 6 with two teachers. Students in grades K-4 attend Zackar Levi Elementary School in Lower Kalskag. Students in grades 7-12 attend George Morgan Junior/Senior High School, located between the cities of Upper and Lower Kalskag. The school libraries serve as the community public libraries.

Health care. The Catherine Alexie Health Clinic is operated by the Yukon-Kuskokwim Health Corporation. Higher levels of medical care are available at the Clara Morgan Sub-Regional Clinic in Aniak and the Yukon Kuskokwim Delta Regional Hospital in Bethel.

Public safety. Law enforcement is provided by state troopers in Aniak. Emergency response is provided by the city volunteer fire department.

Kalskag
Also known as Upper Kalskag

Kaltag

Kaltag

Total area of entitlement under ANCSA	
	115,200 acres
Total labor force	159
High school graduate or higher	73.1%
Bachelor's degree or higher	10.1%
Unemployment rate	29.9%
Per capita income *(1999)*	$9,361
Population *2000 census*	230
2003 population	229
state demographer estimate	
Percent Native *2000 census*	87%

LOCATION
Kaltag is located on the west bank of the Yukon River, 75 miles west of Galena and 335 miles west of Fairbanks.

PHYSICAL DESCRIPTION
The City has 23.3 square miles of land and 4.1 square miles of water. It is situated on a 35-foot bluff at the base of the Nulato Hills, west of the Innoko National Wildlife Refuge.

CLIMATE
The area experiences a cold, continental climate, with extreme temperature differences. Temperatures range from -40°F and below in the winter to well above 70°F in the summer. Average annual precipitation is 16 inches, including 74 inches of snowfall.

CULTURE AND HISTORY
Kaltag was established in the early 1900s, when residents of three nearby villages moved to the site. Before that time it was used as a cemetery. The village was named by the Russians for the Yukon Indian name Kaltaga. Steamboat traffic related to gold prospecting peaked in 1900. Most of the village residents are Koyukon Athabascans. The Stick Dance Festival draws visitors to Kaltag from many neighboring villages. This one-week festival of potlatches is sponsored by relatives of a recently deceased person, in appreciation of those who helped during their time of mourning.

GOVERNMENT
Kaltag was incorporated in 1969 as a Second-Class City, with a mayor and city council. It is located in the Unorganized Borough. It also has a BIA-recognized traditional council, the Village of Kaltag, headed by a first chief.

VILLAGE CORPORATION
Gana-A' Yoo, Ltd., is the consolidated successor to the four merged ANCSA village corporations of Kaltag, Galena, Koyukuk, and Nulato. The company provides rental services in Galena, Kaltag, Koyukuk, and Nulato and is a member of a consortium of Native companies investing in a Fairbanks hotel project now under development. Shareholders in the corporation also own shares in Doyon, Limited, the regional Native corporation.

ECONOMY
Subsistence is an important part of the local economy. Salmon, whitefish, moose, bear, waterfowl, and berries are harvested. The village, school, BLM firefighting, commercial fishing, and fish processing provide most cash jobs.

Fisheries. Eighteen residents hold commercial fishing permits, chiefly for salmon and whitefish.

Government as employer. Of the 69 employed residents, 42 work for the local, state, or federal government.

Services and retail. Businesses in the community include an outfitters store, a general contractor, and two grocery stores.

Tourism and recreation. Visitor attractions include the Iditarod Trail, Kaiyuh Flats, Nulato Hills, and riverfront scenery. Cultural events include the Stick Dance (held in alternating years with Nulato), the blanket toss, wash tub dance, spring carnival, and the Lady Wildcats Annual Basketball Tournament.

INFRASTRUCTURE
Transportation. The state operates a 3,900- by 100-foot lighted gravel airstrip, providing Kaltag with year-round air service (weather permitting). Seven airline companies service Kaltag. Barges deliver heavy cargo three times a year. Snowmachines, all-terrain vehicles, and riverboats provide local transportation. In winter, the frozen river, local trails, and the 90-mile Old Mail Trail to Unalakleet are used for woodcutting and trap lines.

Electricity. The Alaska Village Electrical Cooperative (AVEC) provides electricity from a 573-kilowatt diesel plant.

Fuel storage (gallons). Kaltag Cooperative Industries (108,000); AVEC (91,000); Yukon-Koyukuk Schools (33,200); city (19,300);

[CALL-tag]
Ethnicity: Koyukon Athabascan

Municipality
City of Kaltag
P.O. Box 9
Kaltag, AK 99748
    907-534-2301
    907-534-2236 Fax

Native entity
Village of Kaltag
P.O. Box 129
Kaltag, AK 99748
    907-534-2224
    907-534-2299 Fax

ANCSA village corporation
Gana-A' Yoo, Limited
P.O. Box 38
Galena, AK 99741
    907-656-1609
    907-656-1609 Fax
    khotol.com

Kaltag

Kanatak

See Zero Population Section

Catholic church (9,000); Army National Guard (3,000); Alaska DOT/ Airport (1,000).

Water and waste systems. Piped water and sewer are available. A circulating water and gravity sewage system is used. Water, drawn from a well, is treated. Most residences are fully plumbed.

Telecommunications. In-state telephone service is provided by ACS of the Northland, long distance service by AT&T Alascom. GCI provides Internet access at the School. Residents can receive AM radio broadcasts from Nome, Galena, McGrath, Anchorage, and other points. The Alaska Rural Communications Service and the village each broadcast a channel of television from local repeaters.

COMMUNITY FACILITIES AND SERVICES
The city operates the water and waste disposal systems, the washeteria, and the Takathlee Tondin Kuskino community hall. There is a youth center operated by the Tanana Chiefs Conference.

Education. Kaltag School is operated by the Yukon-Koyukuk School District. There are 56 students and six teachers. The school library serves as the community public library.

Health care. The Kaltag Health Clinic is operated by the Tanana Chiefs Conference. Emergency service is provided by volunteers and a health aide. Auxiliary health care is provided by Kaltag Rescue. Higher-level medical care is provided by the Chief Andrew Isaac Health Center of the Tanana Chiefs Conference, in Fairbanks Memorial Hospital, Fairbanks.

Public safety. Law enforcement is provided by state troopers in Galena. Emergency response is provided by the city volunteer fire department and Kaltag Rescue.

Karluk

[CAR-luck]
Ethnicity: Alutiiq

Native entity
Native Village of Karluk
P.O. Box 22
Karluk, AK 99608
907-241-2218
907-241-2345 Fax

ANCSA regional corporation
Koniag, Incorporated
202 Center Ave., Suite 201
Kodiak, AK 99615
907-486-2530
800-658-3818
907-486-3325 Fax

Total area of entitlement under ANCSA	92,160 acres
Total labor force	11
High school graduate or higher	9
Bachelor's degree or higher	0
Unemployment rate	0.0%
Per capita income *(1999)*	$13,736
2003 population	24
state demographer estimate	
Population *2000 census*	27
Percent Native *2000 census*	96.3%

LOCATION
Karluk is located on the northwest side of Kodiak Island, on Shelikof Strait. The City of Kodiak is 88 air miles to the northeast, and Anchorage is 301 miles away, also to the northeast.

PHYSICAL DESCRIPTION
Karluk encompasses 47 square miles of land and 21 square miles of water. The terrain of the area is characterized by low-lying mountains, laced with rivers and streams. In the summer months, the mountains are a deep emerald green. The Karluk River runs through the community and features all five species of salmon. Karluk is built on Tertiary and Cretaceous granitic rock. Moist and wet tundra vegetation types predominate. Minor mudslides have been observed in the hill area near town but these do not currently threaten populated areas. Significant coastal erosion has occurred in several places, primarily adjacent to and at the mouth of the lagoon. Past episodes of erosion following severe weather caused the community to be relocated further inland from the mouth of the lagoon. The Karluk spit is a dynamic feature constantly changing due to the forces of erosion. Although the town has been relocated, coastal erosion still has the potential to limit residential and commercial development as well as threaten municipal buildings and roads in a few places. In particular, the hillside road leading down to the lagoon from the airstrip is eroding. Kodiak Island and the nearby mainland experience frequent earthquakes with magnitudes less than 6.0 on the Richter scale. Since 1899, 82 earthquakes of Richter magnitude 6.0 or greater have been recorded in the Cook Inlet area, and 26 of these were actually triggered within the area. The 1964 Alaska earthquake and resultant tsunami provide a relatively recent example of the very real threat posed by earthquake activity near Karluk and in the Kodiak region. Although Karluk survived the earthquake and tsunami with no significant damage, the earthquake's affects were felt in the community, followed by low, quiet sea level rises which did not cause any measurable shoreline flooding. The amount of subsidence caused by the 1964 earthquake is estimated at 1.5 feet, causing tides to run slightly earlier in the area. However, the subsidence caused no significant adverse effects. Although Karluk is surrounded primarily by low-lying brush rather than forested areas, fires have occurred in the Karluk region in the past and could threaten the local population. In 1912 the Kodiak region was blanketed in volcanic ash from the Katmai/ Novarupta eruption on the Katmai Coast.

CLIMATE
Karluk's maritime climate is characterized by mild winters and cool summers, with fairly heavy precipitation. Prevailing wind directions vary, with wind speeds between five and twenty miles per hour. Temperatures in January range between 0°F and 35°F; the range in July is between 40°F and 70°F. Average annual precipitation varies between 25 and 35 inches. There are no regular occurrences of severe weather such as typhoons or tornadoes; however, weather extremes such as high winds, large hail, storm surge, or heavy rainfall threaten the area. Winds in excess of 50 miles per hour occur occasionally, and wind gusts may reach speeds of 90 miles per hour or more. Freezing rain, occasional heavy snowfall, and high winds are the dominant winter weather hazards that affect the area. Periods of extreme cold occur on a less frequent basis.

CULTURE AND HISTORY
Karluk is the Alutiiq word for "fish," which is appropriate considering that it boasts of having the greatest salmon stream in the world. It is an Alutiiq village with a fishing and subsistence lifestyle. Archaeological evidence indicates that Karluk has been inhabited for more than 7,000 years. There are 36 registered archaeological sites in the area. In 1786 Russians established a trading post, constructing a village on both sides of the Karluk River in the area of the Karluk Lagoon. Many tanneries, salteries, and canneries were subsequently established in the area. In the early 1900s, additional canneries were constructed by the Alaska Packers Association, but these were closed in the late 1930s due to overharvesting. In 1978 storms and high winds forced the entire community to move and reestablish itself upriver, approximately three-quarters of a mile away from the old site.

GOVERNMENT
Karluk is an unincorporated village within the Kodiak Island Borough *(see Alaska introduction)*. The village is governed by a seven-member Indian Reorganization Act tribal council, headed by a president. Council members are elected for three-year staggered terms.

REGIONAL CORPORATION

Qualified residents hold shares in the regional Native corporation, Koniag, Incorporated *(see Alaska introduction)*. The ANCSA village corporation merged into Koniag in 1980.

ECONOMY

Commercial salmon fishing and salmon processing are the primary sources of livelihood in the village. However, the salmon markets fluctuate dramatically from year to year, and the Kodiak Salmon Packers, cannery in nearby Larsen Bay did not operate during the 2002 season. The majority of the population depend on and actively participate in subsistence hunting and fishing activities. Salmon, trout, ducks, seals, and deer are harvested. Private businesses in the community include two campgrounds and fishing guide services.

Government as employer. Of the eleven employed residents, nine work for the council or for the borough, state, or federal governments.

INFRASTRUCTURE

Transportation. Karluk has no overland access roads; visitors must travel there by air or water. Several local commercial air carriers service Karluk, with daily mail flights scheduled and charter flights available from Kodiak. Air access to Karluk is always weather-dependent. The state provides a 2,000- by 50-foot gravel airstrip. There is no aviation fuel available. There is a seaplane base at Karluk Lake, and floatplanes may also land in the lagoon, weather and tide permitting. There is no regular commercial ferry service to Karluk. Barge service is offered bimonthly from Kodiak, and goods are lightered to shore by skiff. The road system in Karluk is limited to gravel roads and paths. There are a few functioning vehicles and several ATVs in the community. Accommodations are available at the Karluk Lodge.

Electricity. Alutiiq Power Company, owned by the Village Council, provides electricity from a 175-kilowatt capacity diesel plant. Many homes also have generators, but there is no community-wide backup power system.

Fuel storage (gallons). Village council (50,000). Home heating fuel shortages have occurred in the past.

Water and waste systems. Piped water and community septic systems are available. Water drawn from a creek is treated and stored in a 50,000-gallon tank. All residences are fully plumbed. No refuse collection service is available; the landfill is a temporary, non-permitted site.

Telecommunications. In-state phone service is provided by ACS of the Northland, long distance service by AT&T Alascom. There is one FM radio station that broadcasts to the area. The Alaska Rural Communications Service provides television access. Many residents have CB radios, and some have VHF marine radios, although these cannot reach Kodiak and sometimes cannot reach Larsen Bay, the community closest to Karluk. There are telephones in most homes; however, telephone service is dependent upon electricity, and Karluk has no reliable backup electrical power generation. There are no single side band (SSB) radios in the community. Therefore, in a major emergency where telephone service and electric power are down, Karluk would be unable to communicate with Kodiak.

COMMUNITY FACILITIES AND SERVICES

Education. The school was closed during the 1999/2000 year and again for the 2002/2003 year due to low enrollment (fewer than 10 students).

Health care. The Karluk Clinic, operated by the Kodiak Area Native Association, provides basic health care and emergency medical services to the community. There are no doctors or registered nurses in Karluk; therefore, most health care is provided by Community Health Aides who are supported by doctors from the Kodiak Area Native Association. Karluk does not have an ambulance. The clinic is stocked with medical equipment and supplies and can handle initial medical responses to most emergencies.

Public safety. The village public safety officer position was vacant as of 2004, and there is no fire department. Therefore, all law enforcement and emergency response services are provided from outside the community, through the state troopers in Kodiak and Kodiak City and borough emergency services.

K asaan

Total area of entitlement under ANCSA	
	23,040 acres
Total labor force	34
High school graduate or higher	70.0%
Bachelor's degree or higher	6.7%
Unemployment rate	20.0%
Per capita income *(1999)*	$19,744
Population *2000 census*	39
2003 population	55
state demographer estimate	
Percent Native *2000 census*	48.7%

LOCATION

Kasaan is situated on the east side of Prince of Wales Island, on Kasaan Bay, 30 miles northwest of Ketchikan.

PHYSICAL DESCRIPTION

The area encompasses 5.3 square miles of land and 0.9 square mile of water.

CLIMATE

The area is dominated by a maritime climate, with relatively warm winters, cool summers, and a fair amount of precipitation. Average summer temperatures range between 46°F and 70°F; winter temperatures range between 32°F and 42°F.

CULTURE AND HISTORY

Originally Tlingit territory, Kasaan gets its name from the Tlingit word meaning "pretty town." Haidas migrated north from the Queen Charlotte Islands in the early 1700s to the island and established the village known as "Old Kasaan." In 1898 the Copper Queen mine, camp, sawmill, post office, and store were built on Kasaan Bay, and the Haida people were relocated to this new village. In 1902, the first salmon cannery was constructed in the village. The cannery burned in 1907, 1910, and again in 1911, but it was rebuilt each season and operated sporadically until 1953. During this time, Kasaan had a school, three stores, a Presbyterian church, and other businesses. Chief Sonihat built the Quail House, a traditional longhouse, which became the focus of the new Kasaan Totem Park, established during the 1930s. Many of the totems left from the old village site were moved to the park. The area has many historic Native sites. Kasaan was traditionally a Haida village, but the population has become mixed, now including Haida, Aleut, and other Alaskan Native descendants. Subsistence activities provide a major supplement to villagers' incomes.

[kuh-SANN]
Ethnicity: Haida

Municipality
City of Kasaan
P.O. Box KXA
Kasaan, AK 99950
907-542-2212
907-542-2223 Fax

Native entity
Organized Village of Kasaan
P.O. Box 26-Kasaan
Ketchikan, AK 99950-0340
907-542-2230
907-542-2223 Fax

ANCSA village corporation
Kavilco, Incorporated
One Copper Crescent Drive
P.O. Box KXA-Kasaan
Kasaan, AK 99950-0340
907-542-2214
907-542-2215 Fax
kavilco.com

Kasaan

GOVERNMENT
Kasaan was incorporated in 1976 as a second-class city, with a mayor and city council. It is located in the Unorganized Borough. It also has an Indian Reorganization Act village council, the Organized Village of Kasaan, headed by a president. Note that as of 2004, the same individual appears as the mayor of the city and the president/administrator of the village.

VILLAGE CORPORATION
Kavilco Incorporated is the community's ANCSA village corporation. When it was organized, Kavilco was the smallest village corporation in Southeast Alaska, having only 120 shareholders. Kavilco received its land patent from the United States on December 5, 1979, making it the first village corporation in Southeastern Alaska to receive all of its land entitlement under ANCSA. In 1987, 194 acres of Kavilco's real property were distributed to the shareholders in the form of individual lots of 1.4 acres in size, more or less, and the timber rights on the remaining 22,861 acres were sold. However, Kavilco retained all other rights to the surface estate of the real property. On November 1, 1989, Kavilco began operating as a self-managed, closed-end management investment company, registered with the Securities and Exchange Commission under the Investment Company Act of 1940. The contract for timber rights expired at the end of 2001, so Kavilco again has control over all surface rights to its land. In addition to the field office in Kasaan, Kavilco has a business office in Seattle. Shareholders in the village corporation also hold shares in Sealaska Corporation, the regional Native corporation.

ECONOMY
Commercial fishing is the primary income-producer in Kasaan. The village native corporation, Kavilco Corporation, provides a significant income for its shareholders from the sale of timber rights and investments. Most residents participate in subsistence or recreational activities for food sources, harvesting deer, salmon, halibut, shrimp, and crab.

Fisheries. One resident holds a commercial fishing permit for salmon, halibut, shrimp, and crab.

Government as employer. Of the 16 employed residents, 11 work for the city, state, or federal government.

Forestry. Kasaan has two logging service companies.

Services and retail. Businesses include a finance company and a publishing company.

Tourism and recreation. Attractions include the Kasaan Boardwalk, the Totem Park/Clan House and Cemeteries, and the Totem Park Trail. A fishing guide service is available.

INFRASTRUCTURE
Transportation. Kasaan can be accessed by floatplane and boat, and by land from elsewhere on Prince of Wales Island. A seaplane base accommodates charter flights and air freight services from Ketchikan. A dock at the old cannery site and a small-boat harbor are available. Cargo planes and barges bring in freight. The community has requested funds to develop a breakwater, deep-sea port, and industrial park at Tolstoi Bay. Kasaan is connected by a gravel road to the Prince of Wales Island road system and by road to Thorne Bay.

Electricity. The Inside Passage Electric Co-operative (formerly the Tlingit-Haida Regional Electric Authority) provides electricity from a 246-kilowatt diesel plant.

Fuel storage (gallons). City Bulk Fuel (10,208).

Water and waste systems. Water, drawn from a water infiltration gallery at Linkum Creek, is treated and piped to all residences in the core area. Homes use individual septic tanks, and 95 percent of households are fully plumbed. The city provides refuse collection services each week. The city uses the Thorne Bay landfill.

Telecommunications. In-state phone services are provided by ACS of the Northland, and long distance service by AT&T Alascom. There is one AM and one FM radio station.

COMMUNITY FACILITIES AND SERVICES
The city operates the water and waste systems. Other community facilities include the Kasaan Community Hall and the Kasaan People's Wellness Library.

Education. Kasaan School is operated by the Southeast Island School District. The school has 12 students, one teacher, and the school library is the community's public library.

Health care. Provided by the Kasaan Health Center, operated by the South East Alaska Regional Health Corporation. Auxiliary health care is provided by Kasaan EMS.

Public safety. Law enforcement is provided by state troopers in Ketchikan. Emergency response is provided by Kasaan EMS.

Kasigluk

[ka-SEE-ga-luck or KAH-si-gluhk]
Ethnicity: Yup'ik

Native entity
Native Village of Kasigluk
P.O. Box 19
Kasigluk, AK 99609
907-477-6405
907-477-6212 Fax

ANCSA village corporation
Kasigluk Incorporated
P.O. Box 39
Kasigluk, AK 99609
907-477-6113
907-477-6026 Fax

Total area of entitlement under ANCSA	
	115,200 acres
Total labor force	310
High school graduate or higher	64.8%
Bachelor's degree or higher	6.6%
Unemployment rate	21.3%
Per capita income *(1999)*	$7,194
Population *2000 census*	543
2003 population	529
state demographer estimate	
Percent Native *2000 census*	96.7%

LOCATION
Kasigluk is located approximately 26 miles northwest of Bethel. The community is actually made up of Old and New Kasigluk, surrounded by the Johnson River and a network of lakes. It is adjacent to and west of Nunapitchuk. In some sources, Kasigluk or Nunapitchuk is also known as Akolmiut. In the 1970 census, Kasigluk and the nearby villages of Atmautluak and Nunapitchuk were enumerated as "Akolmiut."

PHYSICAL DESCRIPTION
The area encompasses 12.2 square miles of land and 1.1 square miles of water.

CLIMATE
The climate is largely maritime, with some continental influences in the winter. Summer temperatures range from 42°F to 62°F; winter temperatures range between -2°F and 19°F. Annual precipitation averages 16 inches, including yearly snowfall of 50 inches.

CULTURE AND HISTORY
Kasigluk is a Yup'ik village, maintaining strong cultural traditions. In the 1940 U.S. census, it was listed as an Eskimo village, one of the "Tundra Villages," with a population of 66. A post office was established in 1962. The Kasigluk community practices a fishing and subsistence lifestyle.

GOVERNMENT

The community is governed by the Native Village of Kasigluk, a BIA-recognized traditional council. In 1982, Kasigluk incorporated as a second-class city in the Unincorporated Borough. However, in 1986, the city council resigned and the city was dissolved in 1996.

VILLAGE CORPORATION

Kasigluk Incorporated is the ANCSA village corporation. Its shareholders also hold shares in Calista Corporation, the regional Native corporation.

ECONOMY

As with other villages in the region, Kasigluk's economic base is a mix of subsistence and cash-generating activities. Employment opportunities are available through local government, the school district, and commercial fishing.

Fisheries. Forty-six residents hold commercial fishing permits, chiefly for salmon set net and herring roe.

Government as employer. Of the 144 employed residents, 101 work for the village, state, or federal government.

Services and retail. There are two general stores in the community.

Transportation. There are a taxicab company and an air transport services firm in Kasigluk.

INFRASTRUCTURE

Transportation. The state operates a 3,000- by 60-foot gravel airstrip for chartered and private air transportation year-round. Four airline companies service Kasigluk. Residents use skiffs to get to Bethel and other area villages during the summer. Winter travel is by snowmachine. In winter, a trail is open to Chefornak. There are no docking facilities, but barges from Bethel deliver fuel and supplies in summer.

Electricity. The Alaska Village Electrical Cooperative (AVEC) provides electricity from a 499-kilowatt diesel plant.

Fuel storage (gallons). Kasigluk Incorporated (136,500); Lower Kuskokwim Schools (116,750); village council (16,500); Army National Guard (2,000).

Water and waste systems. Treated well water is hauled from the washeteria, and individual wells are also available. The Akula Heights subdivision uses the school well. Honeybuckets are hauled to sewage bunkers. Household plumbing is not available. Major infrastructure improvements have been funded for two new wells, water treatment, a 100,000-gallon storage tank, a new washeteria, and a new sewage lagoon.

Telecommunications. In-state phone service is provided by United Utilities, long distance by AT&T Alascom. Internet service is provided by Unicom, with GCI providing Internet access to the schools. The village provides cable television service. Residents can receive AM radio broadcasts from Bethel, Nome, Dillingham, Anchorage, and other locations and television station KYUK from Bethel. The Alaska Rural Communications Service broadcasts two television channels from a local repeater.

COMMUNITY FACILITIES AND SERVICES

The village operates the limited water and waste disposal systems, the cable television system, the washeteria, and the community hall.

Education. There are two schools in Kasigluk operated by the Lower Kuskokwim School District, Akiuk School (also called Akiuk Memorial School) and Akula Elitnaurvik School. The two schools have combined student enrollment of 168 and 14 teachers, and both serve students in grades K-12. The school libraries serve as the community public libraries.

Health care. The Kasigluk Health Clinic is operated by the Yukon-Kuskokwim Health Corporation. The Yukon Kuskokwim Delta Regional Hospital is located in nearby Bethel.

Public safety. Law enforcement is provided by the village police department, backed by state troopers in Bethel. Emergency response is provided by the Akolmiut Volunteer Fire Department.

Kenai and Kenaitze

See Urban Tribes under Kenaitze

Ketchikan

Alaska Native Claims Settlement Act (ANCSA) Land Status
The community of Ketchikan is recognized by BIA as an "Alaska Native Village" entity; however, the community was not included in the ANCSA settlement. Consequently, there is no ANCSA information for Ketchikan.

Total labor force	6,092
High school graduate or higher	88.6%
Bachelor's degree or higher	21.4%
Unemployment rate	8.2%
Per capita income *(1999)*	$22,484
Population *2000 census*	7,922
2002 population	8,002
state demographer estimate	
Percent Native *2000 census*	22.70%

LOCATION

Ketchikan is located on the southwestern coast of Revillagigedo Island, opposite Gravina Island, near the southern boundary of Alaska. It is about 680 miles north of Seattle and 235 miles south of Juneau. The 2.2 million-acre Misty Fiords National Monument is 22 air miles east of Ketchikan. It is the first Alaska port of call for northbound cruise ships and state ferries.

CLIMATE

A maritime climate zone prevails in the area. Warm winters, cool summers, and heavy precipitation are characteristic of the climate. Summer temperatures vary from 51°F to 65°F; winter temperatures range from 29°F to 39°F. Ketchikan averages 162 inches of precipitation annually, including 32 inches of yearly snowfall.

CULTURE AND HISTORY

Tongass and Cape Fox Tlingits have used Ketchikan Creek as a fish camp, which they called *"kitschk-hin,"* meaning creek of the "thundering wings of an eagle." The numerous fish and timber resources brought non-Natives to Ketchikan. In 1885, Mike Martin bought 160 acres from Chief Kyan, which later became the township. One year later, the first cannery opened near the mouth of Ketchikan Creek. Four additional canneries opened in 1912. A post office opened in Ketchikan in 1892. A few years later, nearby gold and copper discoveries briefly brought activity to Ketchikan as a mining supply center. In 1936 seven canneries opened, producing 1.5 million cases of salmon. The need for lumber for new construction and pack-

[KETCH-ih-kan]
Ethnicity: Tlingit

Municipality
City of Ketchikan
334 Front Street
Ketchikan, AK 99901
907-225-3111
907-225-5075 Fax
city.ketchikan.ak.us

Village Corporation
Ketchikan Indian Corporation
2960 Tongass Avenue
Ketchikan, AK 99901
907-225-5158
907-247-5158 Fax
kictribe.org

Ketchikan

ing boxes led to the Ketchikan Spruce Mills, which operated from 1903 until the early 1970s. Ketchikan became a supply center for area logging during World War II when spruce was in high demand. In 1954, a pulp mill was built at Ward Cove near Ketchikan. Its operation sparked community growth. The pulp mill shut down in 1997, after its long-term contract with the U.S. Forest Service for timber was canceled. Ketchikan is a diverse community, but most Native residents are Tlingit. Totem Bight State Historical Park, Saxman Native Village, and the Totem Heritage Center Museum present the largest collection of totem poles in the world. There is a federally recognized tribe in the community-the Ketchikan Indian Corporation.

GOVERNMENT
Ketchikan was incorporated as a home rule city in 1900. The community has a mayor, a six-member city council, and a planning commission under the Ketchikan Gateway Borough.

VILLAGE CORPORATION
Shareholders in the village corporation also hold shares in Sealaska regional Native corporation.

ECONOMY
Ketchikan is an industrial center and a major port of entry in Southeast Alaska, with a diverse economy. A large fishing fleet, fish processing, tourism, and timber fuel the economy. Several processing and cold-storage facilities support the fishing industry. The state-operated Deer Mountain Hatchery produces more than 450,000 king, coho, steelhead, and rainbow trout each year. Cruise ships bring over 650,000 visitors, and another 50,000 independent travelers visit Ketchikan annually. A visitors' center and retail space for 20 tourism operators is made available by the Ketchikan Visitors Association.

Construction. Approximately 276 residents are employed in construction. Services include: roofing, painting, masonry, drywall, insulation, flooring, plumbing, and heating. General contractors and electrical contractors are also available.

Fisheries. Approximately 401 area residents hold commercial fishing permits. Farming, fishing, and forestry industries employ 85 residents.

Government as employer. Of the 3,974 employed residents, 982 work for the local, state, or federal government.

Manufacturing. Approximately 219 residents are employed in manufacturing. Several manufacturing companies are located in Ketchikan. Products manufactured include: specialty foods and beverage, footwear, furniture, kitchen cabinets, wood products, and apparel. Businesses also include ship and boat building, metalworking, cement, and concrete product manufacturing, and a textile product mill.

Mining and hunting. Approximately 85 residents are employed in mining and hunting industries. Nine mining businesses are registered in Ketchikan. They specialize in metal ore mining, nonmetallic mineral mining and quarrying, and mining support services.

Services and retail. Businesses in Ketchikan are numerous and include specialty shops, galleries, jewelry and fur shops, lodging, restaurants, adventure tours, retail stores, arts-and-crafts shops, bookstores, woodworking, realty offices, sea tours, and a Web-design business. Retail trade employs 427 residents; wholesale trade, 85; financial and related business, 229; professional, scientific, administrative and waste management, 238; education, health and social services, 731; information services, 93; and public administration industries, 393.

Tourism and recreation. Accommodations are extensive, and include a lodge, hotel, motel, youth hostel (summer only), bed-and-breakfast, and an RV park. Visitor attractions include Misty

Fiords National Monument and Wilderness, Totem Bight State Historical Park, Saxman Totem Park and Carving Center, Totem Heritage Center Museum, SEAVIC, Tongass Historical Museum, and the Creek Street Historic District & Dolly's House. Fishing charters and camping are also available. Events include the Festival of the North, Celebration of the Sea, Fourth of July/Timber Carnival, King of Kings Salmon Derby, Little League Salmon Derby, Blueberry Arts Festival, Winter Arts Faire, and the Festival of Lights. Arts, entertainment, recreation, accommodations, and food service industries employ 414 residents.

Transportation. Seven airline companies, four taxi companies, and three rental car agencies service Ketchikan. Transportation, warehousing, and utility industries employ 430 residents.

INFRASTRUCTURE
There are 91 capital projects, funded by grants, active in Ketchikan.

Transportation. Three northbound and three southbound departures are available daily for regularly-scheduled jet services. The state provides Ketchikan International Airport on nearby Gravina Island. The airport has a paved, lighted 7,500-by 150-foot asphalt runway. Ketchikan also provides air taxi services to surrounding communities. Tongass Narrows, Peninsula Point, Ketchikan Harbor, and Murphy's are nearby floatplane landing facilities. Ketchikan is the first port of call in Alaska for cruise ships and Alaska Marine Highway vessels. Harbor and docking facilities include a breakwater, a deep draft dock, five small-boat harbors, a dry dock and ship repair yard, a boat launch, and a state ferry terminal. The privately owned shipyard is available to the Alaska Ferry and offshore fish processors for repair work. The Inter-Island Ferry Authority in Craig is coordinating funding to develop year-round ferry service between Ketchikan and Hollis.

Electricity. Ketchikan Public Utilities provides electricity. Ketchikan Public Utilities purchases power from the state-owned Swan Lake Hydro Facility and owns three hydroelectric plants—Ketchikan, Beaver Falls, and Silvis—and two diesel-fueled plants. Approximately $2.5 million in funds will cover costs to design and build a 57-mile power transmission intertie between Swan Lake and Tyee Lake hydroelectric projects.

Fuel storage (gallons). White Pass Alaska (6,902,100); Andrews Oil (920,500); Ketchikan Utilities (230,000); Boyer Alaska Barge Lines (150,000); Island Fuels Inc./Petro Alaska (60,000); E.C. Phillips & Son (9,100); Ward Cove Packing (7,000); and Salmon Falls Marine.

Water and waste systems. Water, drawn from a dam on Ketchikan Lake, is chlorinated, stored, and piped to homes within Ketchikan's boundaries. The borough operates a water treatment facility at Mountain Point, south of the city. Rain catchment systems are used in a few residences. The city owns a central sewage collection system with primary treatment. A new borough sewage treatment plant is located at Mountain Point. Nearly all homes are fully plumbed.

Telecommunications. In-state phone service is provided by Ketchikan Public Utilities; long distance service by GCI and ACS Long Distance. Internet service is provided by ACS Internet and AT&T WorldNet. Teleconferencing is through Alaska Teleconferencing Network and the City of Ketchikan Legislative Information Office. There are four radio stations in the community. Alaska Rural Communications Service provides television access (KUBD, KTOO). Cable provider is GCI Cable.

COMMUNITY FACILITIES AND SERVICES
Local facilities include the Ted Ferry Civic Center, American Legion Hall, Tongass Historical Museum, Centennial Museum, a university, a movie theater, and the Valley Park Pool. The

city has upgraded the Deer Mountain landfill with an incinerator, balefill system, recycling and resource re-use, and household hazardous waste collection events. The city also ships baled refuse out of Alaska.

Education. There are 11 schools in the community with a combined enrollment of 2,352 students and 140 teachers. The schools are under the Ketchikan Gateway School District.

Health care. Local hospitals or health clinics include Ketchikan General Hospital, Ketchikan Tribal Health Clinic, Gateway Center for Human Services, and U.S. Coast Guard (USCG)

Ketchikan Dispensary. The hospital is a qualified acute care facility and Medevac service. The USCG facility provides emergency support only and is a qualified emergency care center. Long-term care is provided by Ketchikan Pioneers' Home and by Island View Manor. Gateway Center for Human Services provides specialized care. Ketchikan is classified as small city and is found in EMS Region 3A in the Southeast Region. Emergency services have limited highway, marine, airport, seaport, and heliport access. Emergency service is provided by 911 and volunteers. Auxiliary health care is provided by Ketchikan Fire Department, South Tongass Fire/EMS Division, and the Pond Reef Volunteer Fire/EMS.

iana

Total area of entitlement under ANCSA	
	115,200 acres
Total labor force	203
High school graduate or higher	77.6%
Bachelor's degree or higher	13.3%
Unemployment rate	11.6%
Per capita income *(1999)*	$11,534
Population *2000 census*	388
2003 population	408
state demographer estimate	
Percent Native *2000 census*	92.8%

LOCATION
Kiana is located on the north bank of the Kobuk River, 57 air miles east of Kotzebue.

PHYSICAL DESCRIPTION
The city covers 0.2 square mile of land.

CLIMATE
Kiana is in a transitional climate zone, characterized by long, cold winters and cool summers. Temperatures range from winter lows of -54°F to summer highs above 80°F. Snowfall averages 60 inches per year, with total average precipitation of 16 inches.

CULTURE AND HISTORY
Kiana means "place where three rivers meet." It has long been the central village of the Kobuk River Kowagmiut Inupiat. In 1909, it became a supply center for the Squirrel River placer mine. Kiana is a traditional Inupiat village, practicing a subsistence lifestyle.

GOVERNMENT
Kiana was incorporated in 1964 as a second-class city, with a mayor and city council. It is located in the Northwest Arctic Borough. It also has a BIA-recognized traditional village council, the Native Village of Kiana, headed by a president. The council is also the Public Law 93-638 tribal government contractor.

VILLAGE/REGIONAL CORPORATION
The ANCSA village corporation for Kiana merged into NANA Regional Corporation, which now serves as both the village and regional Native corporations for the community.

ECONOMY
Kiana's economy relies on traditional subsistence activities, augmented by a cash economy. Chum salmon, freshwater fish, moose, caribou, waterfowl, and berries are harvested. The school, city, and Maniilaq Association provide the majority of year-round employment. The Red Dog Mine also offers area employment. Kiana is one of the more modern villages

in the borough. Seasonal employment includes work on river barges, Bureau of Land Management firefighting, and jade mining. There is local interest in building a whitefish and turbot processing plant. Kiana also wants to develop eco-tourism, primarily guided river trips to the Great Kobuk Sand Dunes.

Fisheries. Two residents hold commercial fishing permits, chiefly for salmon, chum, and freshwater fish.

Government as employer. Of the 99 employed residents, 52 work for the city, state, or federal government.

Services and retail. Businesses in the community include a sled shop, a retail store, an auto repair service, equipment rental and leasing, a snowmachine retail store, and two trading posts.

Tourism and recreation. River charter and guide services and one lodge are available.

INFRASTRUCTURE
Transportation. Transportation relies on plane, small boat, and snowmachine. The state provides the Bob Baker Memorial Airport, which has a 3,400- by 100-foot lighted gravel runway. Six airline companies service Kiana. Daily scheduled flights and charter flights are available. Crowley Marine Services barges fuel and supplies in summer, and local store owners provide boats to transport supplies upriver. Boats, all-terrain vehicles, and snowmachines are used extensively for local travel. Trucks also are available. A road extends along the river to Kobuk Camp, and a network of old trading trails is open.

Electricity. The Alaska Village Electrical Cooperative (AVEC) provides electricity from a 1,163-kilowatt diesel plant.

Fuel storage (gallons). AVEC (120,300); Northwest Arctic Schools (107,700); city (94,300); Kiana Trading Post (51,400); Blankenship Trading Post (7,100); Alaska Department of Transportation (2,900); city firehouse (2,200).

Water and waste systems. A 200,000-gallon steel tank is intermittently filled from two wells near the Kobuk River. Water is chlorinated before distribution through underground water mains. More than 70 households have piped water and sewer. These services also are available to the clinic, school, and community hall. A six-inch underground gravity sewer system drains to a lift station and is pumped through a buried force main to the sewage treatment lagoon northeast of the village. Nineteen households haul water and use honeybuckets or septic tanks.

[kai-ANN-uh]
Ethnicity: Kowagmiut Inupiat

Municipality
City of Kiana
P.O. Box 150
Kiana, AK 99749
   907-475-2136
   907-475-2174 Fax

Native entity
Native Village of Kiana
P.O. Box 69
Kiana, AK 99749
   907-475-2109
   907-475-2180 Fax

ANCSA village/regional corporation
NANA Regional Corporation
P.O. Box 49
Kotzebue, AK 99752
   907-442-3301
nana.com

Kiana

King Cove
See Agdaagux

King Island
See Zero Population Section

King Salmon

Also known as Sovonoski

Ethnicity: Alutiiq; Athabascan; Inupiat

Native entity
King Salmon Tribe
P.O. Box 68
King Salmon, AK 99613-0068
907-246-3449
907-246-3553 Fax

Total labor force	271
High school graduate or higher	90
Bachelor's degree or higher	79
Unemployment rate	8.9%
Per capita income *(1999)*	$26,755
2003 population	385
state demographer estimate	
Population *2000 census*	442
Percent Native *2000 census*	30.1%

LOCATION
King Salmon is located on the north bank of the Naknek River on the Alaska Peninsula, about 15 miles upriver from Naknek and about 10 miles downriver from Naknek Lake in the Katmai National Monument. It is 284 miles southwest of Anchorage.

PHYSICAL DESCRIPTION
The area encompasses 169.6 square miles of land and 1.4 square miles of water, including the former King Salmon Air Force Base. The terrain is flat and wet, moist tundra, but there has been no known flooding. It is only 59 feet above sea level. In addition to normal moist tundra flora and fauna, it is a waterfowl use area and a moose intensive use area. There are bald eagle and raptor nesting areas to the immediate southeast. Minerals are limited to sand and gravel deposits along the rivers and major streams, but there is a high likelihood of oil or gas deposits.

CLIMATE
The climate is mainly maritime, characterized by cool, humid, and windy weather. Average summer temperatures range from 42°F to 63°F; average winter temperatures range from 29°F to 44°F. Extremes from -46°F to 88°F have been recorded. Total precipitation is 20 inches annually, including 45 inches of snowfall. Fog is common during summer months.

CULTURE AND HISTORY
The Native population is a mixture of Alutiiq, Athabascans, and Yup'ik Inupiat. Present-day tribal members are descendents of groups that were forced to relocate from several places, including the village of Sovonoski, due to the 1912 eruption of Mount Katmai on the east coast of the Alaskan Peninsula. In the 1930s, an air navigation silo was built at King Salmon, and, at the beginning of World War II, an Air Force base. In 1949, the U.S. Army Corps of Engineers completed a road from the base and village to Naknek near the coast. Government offices, such as the National Park Service, Fish and Game, and the Weather Bureau, moved in for the convenience of the air base. The King Salmon Inn opened in 1956. In 1962 the State created the Bristol Bay Borough, the first and smallest borough in Alaska, which included the

Kiana (continued)

Telecommunications. In-state phone service is provided by OTZ Telephone Co-op, long distance phone service by AT&T Alascom, GCI, or OTZ Telephone. Internet service is provided by GCI. The city and the Alaska Rural Communications Service each broadcast a television channel from local repeaters. The city also provides cable television service. Residents can receive AM radio broadcasts from Kotzebue, Nome, Anchorage, and other sources.

COMMUNITY FACILITIES AND SERVICES
The city operates the water, sewer, and cable systems, the fire hall, and city offices. The village council has a building and serves as the local member of the AVEC electrical cooperative.

Education. Kiana School is operated by the Northwest Arctic School District. The school has 124 students and 12 teachers. The school library serves as the community's public library.

Health care. The Kiana Health Clinic is operated by the Maniilaq Association. Higher-level medical care is available at the Manilaq Health Center in Kotzebue.

Public safety. Law enforcement is provided by a village police officer, backed by state troopers in Kotzebue. Emergency response is provided by the city volunteer fire department.

King Salmon (continued)

unincorporated communities of Naknek, South Naknek, and King Salmon. In 1993, the air force base went into state-owned caretaker status. It continues to support military activities as a forward deployment location for all the armed services, and hosts U.S. Coast Guard law enforcement and search-and-rescue missions. The borough and the state also make use of facilities on base. Although King Salmon was not included in the ANCSA, the King Salmon Tribe became a federally recognized entity as of December 29, 2000. While Native Alaskan residents have retained some parts of their cultures, they have generally assimilated into the majority culture.

GOVERNMENT
King Salmon is an unincorporated village in Bristol Bay Borough. Bristol Bay Borough was incorporated as the state's first borough in 1962, and remains the state's smallest in population. The borough functions as the official governing body for Naknek, South Naknek, and King Salmon, and provides most common municipal services. The main borough offices are located in Naknek, although the public safety departments are located in King Salmon.

VILLAGE CORPORATION
Organized after the ANCSA, King Salmon has no village corporation. However, it appears that many residents are shareholders in Bristol Bay Native Corporation, the regional ANCSA corporation.

ECONOMY
Government jobs, transportation, fishing-related employment, and tourism are the mainstays of the King Salmon economy. It is the transportation hub for the Bristol Bay and Lake and Peninsula areas. As such, many area-wide enterprises are located in King Salmon even though they may not serve the community at all. For example, the Lake and Peninsula School District headquarters is in King Salmon, although the community is served by the Bristol Bay Borough Schools. Similarly, the Lake and Peninsula Business Development Center provides support to businesses in the Lake and Peninsula Borough.

Construction. An electrical contractor, a well-drilling contractor, and a greenhouse are located in King Salmon.

Fisheries. Fishing-related business, including commercial fishing, processing, and transportation, comprise the largest business sector in King Salmon. Thirty-six residents hold commercial fishing permits, and there are two fish wholesalers. The Bristol Bay red-salmon fishery is the largest in the world, and as King Salmon is the major air transportation point for Bristol Bay, it is the hub for fresh salmon. This part of King Salmon's economy has been hurt by some poor seasons, such as in the early 1970s, 1982, and 1997, and the decline in salmon prices in recent years.

Government as employer. Of 247 employed residents, 86 work for borough, state, or federal governments. Several government contractors are also located in King Salmon. Although the air force base has been turned over to the state, its military capabilities are maintained by the Alaska Air National Guard. It continues to serve as a standby base and forward deployment station, so military units are frequently on station.

Manufacturing. Alaskan Metal Fish makes steel models of Alaska game fish. Organized after the ANCSA, King Salmon has no village corporation. However, it appears that many residents are shareholders in Bristol Bay Native Corporation, the regional ANCSA corporation.

Services and retail. As the transportation hub for the area, King Salmon has services in greater numbers than its population would suggest. Many are tourist- or transportation-oriented (see below). Services for both the local population and visitors include six telecommunications firms, four food services, two auto repair firms, two other repair services, two physical therapy practices, a speech therapy practice, a beauty salon, a day care service, a home furnishings store, a florist, and Patterson Sanitation and Refuse Service. Service contractors include one landscape care contractor and two building-cleaning services. Professional services include four photographic and art studios, two government consultants, an investment firm, a medical transcription service, and a service that assists communities and organizations in getting grant money.

Tourism and recreation. Fishing for all five species of salmon and rainbow trout is one of this area's top attractions. King Salmon is also a primary departure point for the Katmai National Park and Preserve, which includes the McNeil River State Game Sanctuary, Brooks Camp, and the Valley of Ten Thousand Smokes. Many businesses in King Salmon are tourist-oriented, including at least ten hotels, lodges, inns, and cabin rentals (most of which also offer guide services and tours); at least twelve fishing, tour, and wilderness guide services; two specialty seafood stores; a tackle shop; two gift shops; and a boat rental firm.

Transportation. Air services employ a large portion of the community, as King Salmon Airport, formerly the air force base, is the major air transportation hub for the region. This makes it the summer hub for wilderness and fishing adventures in the area. Alaska Air and Penn Air have scheduled flights to King Salmon. There are three charter air firms, three air transportation support firms, and a fuel wholesaler. Other transportation-related businesses include two inland water transportation companies, a freight trucking company, and a warehousing and storage firm.

INFRASTRUCTURE
Transportation. King Salmon is the air transportation hub for Bristol Bay. Formerly an air force base, the state-owned airport has an 8,500-foot paved, lighted runway, a 4,000-foot asphalt and gravel crosswind runway, and a Federal Aviation Administration air traffic control tower. There are scheduled jet flights and charter services to and from Anchorage. A 4,000-foot stretch of the Naknek River is designated for floatplanes. A seaplane base is also located at Lake Brooks, within the Katmai National Park to the east. Four docks are available on the Naknek River, three government and one public dock owned by the Bristol Bay Borough. Cargo goods are delivered to Naknek by barge and trucked upriver to King Salmon via the 15-mile connecting road. During winter, an ice road across the Naknek River provides access to South Naknek;

otherwise access to South Naknek is by air or water. Vehicles are the primary means of local transportation; boats are used during summer.

Electricity is provided by the Naknek Electric Association, a Rural Electrical Association Cooperative, using diesel generators in Naknek. All homes and other facilities have access to electricity. Even after being drawn down, the King Salmon Airport remains the Co-op's single largest user.

Water and waste systems. Approximately 80 percent of homes have individual wells and are fully plumbed. Most of these wells are shallow and range from 30 to 40 feet. FAA housing, located on the east side, and the airport are served by their own well systems. The borough operates a piped sewage system that serves most residents. The former air force base has an independent piped sewage system and lagoon. Some residents use individual septic tanks. The Borough operates a landfill, incinerator, and balefill, located between King Salmon and Naknek for use by both communities. Garbage collection is contracted to a private firm, Peterson Sanitation.

Telecommunications. All homes and private and public buildings have access to telephone and Internet service. Residents can receive one FM radio station from Naknek and several AM stations from Dillingham, Anchorage, McGrath, Nome, Bethel, and Homer. In addition to cable service available to all residents, an Alaska Rural Communications Service repeater broadcasts two television stations.

COMMUNITY FACILITIES AND SERVICES
Community facilities include the King Salmon Visitor's Center, a community hall (the Comserfac Building), and the Kvimarvik Swimming Pool (in Naknek), all maintained by the borough. The village council provides fuel storage and water supply.

Telecommunications. Bristol Bay Telephone Cooperative, located in King Salmon, provides local telephone and cable service, long distance telephone service (along with AT&T Alascom and GCI), and Internet service (along with GCI). Law enforcement is provided by the borough police department, which operates out of King Salmon Airport, backed by a state trooper post also at the airport. The borough police department has a chief, two officers, and six dispatchers. In addition to law enforcement, it assists other law enforcement agencies and court personnel with administrative support, and provides the public with full-time motor vehicle services, functioning as a local department of motor vehicles office. The police department conducts all search-and-rescue missions within the Bristol Bay Borough area. Emergency response is provided by Bristol Bay Borough Emergency Services, including a volunteer fire battalion and Emergency Medical Services squad in King Salmon. Most of the King Salmon fire equipment is located in the airport fire station. The EMS squad has an ambulance and can provided basic life support services.

Education. There are no primary or secondary schools located in King Salmon. Students in grades K-12 are bused to Naknek, 15 miles away, to attend school. The public library for King Salmon is the Martin Monsen Regional Library in Naknek.

The Southwest Alaska Vocational Center was established in 2002. It provides ongoing skill development and retraining services in several areas of potential reemployment for local residents, including skills in the construction trades, energy development, heavy equipment operation, computer hardware, commercial hardware, commercial operators' licenses, refrigeration, and welding. The center provides vocational training that will facilitate entry into oil and gas industry jobs.

King Salmon
Also known as Sovonoski

King Salmon

Also known as Sovonoski

It is operated by the Bristol Bay Housing Authority, which leased a 26,000-square-foot building from the U.S. Air Force and renovated it. Educational spaces include classrooms, shops, instructor offices, and support spaces. Residential areas include dormitory rooms for 32 students and a three-bedroom caretaker apartment.

Health care. The King Salmon Health Clinic is owned by the village council and operated by the Bristol Bay Area Health Corporation, which also operates the Camai Clinic in Naknek and a hospital in Dillingham for more serious matters.

ENVIRONMENTAL CONCERNS

King Salmon Air Force Base left behind a legacy of environmental threats, most of which have been remediated although monitoring continues throughout. Soil and groundwater are contaminated by petroleum and trichloroethene. Petroleum releases and spills from former underground storage tanks have harmed soil and groundwater. Petroleum-contaminated groundwater from a former tank farm seeped into the wetlands near the Naknek River. Petroleum and trichloroethene contamination from the former fire training areas has harmed Red Fox Creek. Buried drums and dumped items could harm King Salmon Creek and the adjacent wetlands. Buried drums, dumped items, and petroleum contaminants may harm the adjacent wetlands. People may be exposed to pollutants through vapor inhalation, direct contact with the skin, or accidental ingestion of contaminated soil or water at these sites. No private or public drinking water wells have been harmed by these contaminated sites.

Kipnuk

[KIP-nuck]
Ethnicity: Yup'ik

Native entity
Native Village of Kipnuk
P.O. Box 57
Kipnuk, AK 99614-0071
907-896-5427
907-896-5022 Fax

ANCSA village corporation
Kugkaktlik Limited
P.O. Box 36
Kipnuk, AK 99614
907-896-5414
907-896-5140 Fax

Total area of entitlement under ANCSA	
	115,200 acres
Total labor force	431
High school graduate or higher	60.7%
Bachelor's degree or higher	5.8%
Unemployment rate	34%
Per capita income *(1999)*	$8,589
Population *2000 census*	644
2003 population	649
state demographer estimate	
Percent Native *2000 census*	98%

LOCATION

Kipnuk is located approximately 85 air miles southwest of Bethel, along the west bank of the Kugkaktlik River, within the Yukon-Kuskokwim Delta. The built-up area is approximately four miles inland from the Bering Sea coast, but the village limits extend to the seacoast and the river.

PHYSICAL DESCRIPTION

The area encompasses 19.4 square miles of land and 0.2 square mile of water. The area is very flat and low, and a severe coastal storm or high water on the river may flood the community. There was some flooding in 2000.

CLIMATE

The community is in the marine climate zone, characterized by relatively mild winters and cool summers, with a fair amount of precipitation. Winter temperatures range between 6°F and 24°F; summer temperatures range from 41°F to 57°F. Annual precipitation averages 22 inches, including 43 inches of yearly snowfall.

CULTURE AND HISTORY

Kipnuk is a traditional Yup'ik community, maintaining a subsistence lifestyle. Yup'ik have inhabited the region for thousands of years. According to early BIA records, the village was established around 1922. Commercial fishing is an important income source.

GOVERNMENT

Kipnuk is unincorporated and is located in the Unorganized Borough. It is governed by the Native Village of Kipnuk, a BIA-recognized traditional village council headed by a president.

VILLAGE CORPORATION

Kugkaktlik Limited is the ANCSA village corporation; shareholders also hold shares in Calista Corporation, the regional Native corporation.

ECONOMY

Residents of Kipnuk rely on seasonal employment opportunities in commercial fishing and construction. Other employment is provided by local and state government. Subsistence activities, including hunting, fishing, and gathering, are a major part of the economy. Coastal Villages Seafood, processes halibut and salmon in Kipnuk. Income is also obtained by trapping. The community is considering the establishment of an arts and crafts marketing cooperative.

Fisheries. Ninety-seven residents hold commercial fishing permits.

Government as employer. Of the 170 employed residents, 121 work for the local, state, or federal government.

Services and retail. Businesses in the community include child care services, a trading company, a gas station, a grocery store, a movie rental store, and a general mercantile store.

INFRASTRUCTURE

Transportation. The state provides a 2,120- by 35-foot gravel airstrip, with regularly scheduled air taxi service. Six airline companies service Kipnuk. Charter services and a seaplane base also are available. Boats and skiffs are used by residents for local travel in summer. Snowmachines are used in winter. Winter trails are open to Tuntutuliak, Chefornak, and Kwigillingok. Docking facilities are in the community's construction plans. Barges deliver cargo from Bethel.

Electricity. Electricity is provided by Kipnuk Light Plant, an arm of the village council, from a 650-kilowatt diesel plant.

Fuel storage (gallons). Kugkaktlik (324,500); village power plant (151,300); Lower Kuskokwim Schools (70,200); Kashatok Brothers Store (13,800).

Water and waste systems. A 210,000-gallon water storage tank is filled from a reservoir on a nearby lake. Residents haul treated water from several watering points. Honeybuckets are hauled by the village to a sewage lagoon. Homes are not plumbed. As of 2003, construction had begun to improve infrastructure, including a new reservoir pump house, a water treatment plant, and a sewage lagoon. The village council provides refuse collection service and operates the Class 3 landfill.

Telecommunications. In-state phone service is provided by United Utilities, long distance phone service by AT&T Alascom or United Utilities. Internet service is provided at the school by GCI. The community can receive AM radio broadcasts from Bethel, Nome, Dillingham, Anchorage, and other points. The village and the Alaska Rural Communications Service each provide one broadcast television channel from local repeaters. Frontier Cable provides cable television service.

COMMUNITY FACILITIES AND SERVICES

The village operates the electric power system, the water and waste systems, one television repeater, and the Kanganak Community Hall.

Education. Chief Paul Memorial School is operated by the Lower Kuskokwim Regional School District. The school has 213 students and 15 teachers. The school library serves as

the community's public library.

Health care. The Kipnuk Clinic is operated by the Yukon-Kuskokwim Health Corporation. Emergency service is provided by a health aide. Higher levels of health care are available at the subregional clinic in Toksook Bay and the Yukon Kuskokwim Delta Regional Hospital in Bethel.

Public safety. Law enforcement is provided by a state village public safety officer (VPSO), backed by state troopers in Bethel. Emergency response is provided by the village volunteer fire department.

K ivalina

Total area of entitlement under ANCSA
92,160 acres

Total labor force	235
High school graduate or higher	59.7%
Bachelor's degree or higher	6.5%
Unemployment rate	25.5%
Per capita income *(1999)*	$8,360
Population *2000 census*	377
2003 population	388
state demographer estimate	
Percent Native *2000 census*	96.6%

LOCATION

Kivalina is located at the tip of an eight-mile barrier reef between the Chuckchi Sea and the Kivalina River. It lies 80 air miles northwest of Kotzebue.

PHYSICAL DESCRIPTION

The city covers 1.9 square miles of land and 2.0 square miles of water.

CLIMATE

Kivalina lies in a transitional climate zone, characterized by long, cold winters and cool summers. Temperatures range from winter lows of -54°F to summer highs of over 80°F. Snowfall averages 50 inches, with 10 inches of yearly precipitation. The Chukchi Sea is ice free and open to boat traffic from mid-June to the first of November.

CULTURE AND HISTORY

Kivalina is a traditional Inupiat village. It has long been a stopping-off place for seasonal travelers between Arctic coastal areas and Kotzebue Sound communities. It is the only village in the region where people hunt the bowhead whale. Subsistence activities provide most food sources.

GOVERNMENT

Kivalina was incorporated in 1969 as a second-class city, with a mayor and city council. It is located in the Northwest Arctic Borough. It also has a village council organized under the Indian Reorganization Act, the Native Village of Kivalina, headed by a president.

VILLAGE/REGIONAL CORPORATION

The ANCSA village corporation for Kivalina merged into NANA Regional Corporation, which now serves as both the village and regional Native corporations for the community.

ECONOMY

Kivalina's economy depends on subsistence practices. Seal, walrus, whale, salmon, whitefish, and caribou are used. Year-round employment is provided by the school, city, Maniilaq

Association, village council, airlines, and local stores. The Red Dog Mine also offers work to residents.

Fisheries. Six residents hold commercial fishing permits, chiefly for salmon.

Government as employer. Of the 82 employed residents, 45 work for the city, state, or federal government.

Manufacturing. Native carvings and jewelry are produced from ivory and caribou hooves. The community is interested in developing an arts and crafts center that could be readily moved to the new city site.

Services and retail. There are five businesses in the community: a clothing store, two general merchandise stores, and two retail shops.

INFRASTRUCTURE

Note that the community has plans to relocate to a new site, 7.5 miles away. Much of the infrastructure will change if and when this move is completed.

Transportation. Plane and barge are the major means of transportation into the community. The state provides a 3,000-foot long by 60-foot wide gravel airstrip that serves daily flights from Kotzebue. Six airline companies service Kivalina. Crowley Marine Services barges goods from Kotzebue during July and August. Small boats, all-terrain vehicles, and snowmachines are used for local travel. Two main hunting trails follow the Kivalina and Wulik Rivers.

Electricity. The Alaska Village Electrical Cooperative (AVEC) provides electricity from a 1,040-kilowatt diesel plant.

Fuel storage (gallons). Native Store (135,800); AVEC (98,800); Northwest Arctic Schools (49,600); Army National Guard (10,000); city washeteria (7,800); Alaska Department of Transportation (2,700).

Water and waste systems. Water, drawn from the Wulik River by way of a three-mile surface transmission line, is stored in a 700,000-gallon raw water tank. It is then treated and stored in a 500,000-gallon steel tank. Water is hauled by residents from this tank. One-third of residents have tanks that provide kitchen running water, but homes are not fully plumbed. The school and clinic have individual water and sewer systems. Residents haul their own honeybuckets to bunkers. A new landfill and honeybucket disposal site recently opened.

Telecommunications. In-state phone service is provided by OTZ Telephone Co-op, long distance phone service by AT&T

[kiv-uh-LEE-nuh]
Ethnicity: Kowagmiut Inupiat

Municipality
City of Kivalina
P.O. Box 50079
Kivalina, AK 99750
907-645-2137
907-645-2175 Fax

Native entity
Native Village of Kivalina
P.O. Box 50051
Kivalina, AK 99750
907-645-2153
907-645-2193 Fax

ANCSA village/regional corporation
NANA Regional Corporation
P.O. Box 49
Kotzebue, AK 99752
907-442-3301
nana.com

Kivalina

Alascom, GCI, or OTZ Telephone. Internet service is provided by GCI. The city and the Alaska Rural Communications Service each broadcast a television channel from local repeaters. The city also provides cable television service. Residents can receive AM radio broadcasts from Nome, Kotzebue, Anchorage, Bethel, and other sources.

COMMUNITY FACILITIES AND SERVICES
The city operates the water and waste disposal systems, the cable system, the washeteria, and the fire hall, and is the local member of the AVEC electrical cooperative.

Education. McQueen School is operated by the Northwest Arctic Borough. The school has 127 students and eight teachers. The school library serves as the community's public library.

Health care. The Kivalina Health Clinic is operated by the Maniilaq Association. Higher-level medical care is available at the Manilaq Health Center in Kotzebue.

Public safety. Law enforcement is provided by state troopers in Kotzebue. Emergency response is provided by the city volunteer fire department.

Klawock

[kla-WOCK]
Ethnicity: Tlingit

Municipality
City of Klawock
P.O. Box 469
Klawock, AK 99925
907-755-2261
907-755-2403 Fax
cityofklawock.com

Native entity
Klawock Cooperative
Association
P.O. Box 430
Klawock, AK 99925
907-755-2265
907-755-8800 Fax

ANCSA village corporation
Klawock Heenya Corporation
P.O. Box 129
Klawock, AK 99925
907-755-2270
907-755-2966 Fax
klawockheenya.com

Total area of entitlement under ANCSA	23,040 acres
Total labor force	616
High school graduate or higher	80.8%
Bachelor's degree or higher	8.5%
Unemployment rate	15.7%
Per capita income *(1999)*	$14,621
Population *2000 census*	854
2003 population	851
state demographer estimate	
Percent Native *2000 census*	58.1%

LOCATION
Klawock is located on the west coast of Prince of Wales Island, across from Klawock Island, in Southeast Alaska. It is 7 miles north of Craig and 56 air miles west of Ketchikan, closer to Seattle than to Anchorage.

PHYSICAL DESCRIPTION
The city encompasses 0.6 square mile of land and 0.3 square mile of water.

CLIMATE
Klawock is dominated by a cool maritime climate. Average temperatures in the summer range from 46°F to 70°F; average winter temperatures range from 32°F to 42°F. Gale winds are common in fall and winter months.

CULTURE AND HISTORY
Early inhabitants of Klawock came from Tukekan, a Tlingit winter village to the north. The history of Klawock is closely tied to the fishing industry. A trading post and salmon saltery were established in 1868, and the first cannery in Alaska was built in 1878. The subsequent canneries established in the area were operated by Chinese laborers. A hatchery for red salmon operated at Klawock Lake between 1887 and 1917. In 1934, "Hawock" received federal funds for cannery operations, on the condition that the village be liquor-free. In 1971, the Alaska Timber Corporation built a sawmill. Soon afterward, the Klawock Hennya Corporation, the Shaan Seet Corporation of Craig, and Sealaska Timber Corporation expanded area facilities with a log-sort yard outside of Klawock and a dock on Klawock Island. The island has been greatly influenced by logging operations. The community takes great pride in its totem park, which displays 21 restored original and replica totem poles from the old village. Most residents pursue a subsistence lifestyle.

GOVERNMENT
Klawock was incorporated in 1929 as a first-class city, with a mayor and city council; it is located in the Unorganized Borough. It also has a BIA-recognized Native entity, the Klawock Cooperative Association, organized under the Indian Reorganization Act and headed by a president. The association

was originally formed in 1934 as a nonprofit organization to own and operate the cannery. There is a five and one-half percent sales tax in Klawock, of which one-half percent goes directly to education. There is no property tax in the city.

VILLAGE CORPORATION
Klawock Heenya Corporation is the community's ANCSA village corporation. Its enterprises include commercial and residential real estate and a gasoline station. Shareholders in the village corporation also hold shares in Sealaska Corporation, the regional Native corporation.

ECONOMY
The economy has been dependent on fishing and cannery operations in the past, then on the timber industry. Sealaska's logging operations, through a contract with Shaan Seet, provides work in logging and ship-loading in the Klawock and Craig area. However, the timber industry is in decline as of 2004. The state operates a fish hatchery on Klawock Lake that contributes to the local salmon population. City and school district jobs contribute significantly to employment. Subsistence foods include deer, salmon, halibut, shrimp, and crab.

Construction. Businesses include construction surveying, contractors, custom siding, and concrete specialties.

Fisheries. Forty-seven residents hold commercial fishing permits, chiefly for salmon, halibut, shrimp, and crab.

Government as employer. Of the 372 employed residents, 57 work for the city, state, or federal government.

Manufacturing. Klawock has a custom boat and repair business and a custom-made-kayak company.

Services and retail. There are numerous businesses in the community, including research and development, technology services, a sports rental store, a computer store, inns and diners, a realty office, a gunsmith, and construction contractors.

Tourism and recreation. Visitor attractions include the Klawock Totem Park, which features original and replica totems; Prince of Whales Fish Hatchery, the second oldest fish hatchery in Alaska; and the Clan House. Recreational activities include fishing, and hunting for bear and deer. Events include the Seafest Celebration and Fishing Derby and the Native Cultural Fair. Lodging accommodations include two lodges, two inns, cabins, and an RV park. Wilderness guides and charters are available.

Transportation. Three taxi companies and a trucking company operate out of Klawock.

INFRASTRUCTURE
Transportation. Klawock relies on air transportation from Ketchikan for access to the mainland. However, it is linked by the Prince of Wales Island road system to other communities.

The only airstrip on Prince of Wales Island is located here, with a 5,000 by 100-foot paved runway. The state operates a seaplane base on the Klawock River. Ferry transportation is available to nearby Hollis. Klawock has a small-boat harbor and boat launch ramp. At Klawock Island, a deep-draft dock is available, which is primarily used for loading timber. Freight arrives by cargo plane, barge, and truck.

Electricity. The Inside Passage Electric Co-operative (formerly the Tlingit-Haida Regional Electric Authority) purchases electricity from Alaska Power & Telephone over the Craig/Klawock intertie. It also owns four standby diesel generators in Klawock.

Fuel storage (gallons). Klawock Island Fuels (120,000); Viking Lumber Co. (19,984); Inside Passage Electric Co-operative (1,000).

Water and waste systems. Nearly all homes are fully plumbed. Water drawn from a dam on Half Mile Creek is treated, stored in a tank, and piped throughout Klawock. Most homes have piped sewage collection, which receives secondary treatment. Refuse collection, provided by the city, is hauled to a permitted landfill shared with Craig and other island residents.

Telecommunications. In-state phone service is provided by ACS of the Northland; long distance phone service by AT&T Alascom. Internet service is provided by Alaska Power & Telephone Company. The public library offers free Internet access. One FM radio station broadcasts from Klawock, and residents can receive FM broadcasts from Craig and AM broadcasts from Petersburg, Ketchikan, Juneau, Seattle, and Portland. The Alaska Rural Communications Service broadcasts two television channels from repeaters in Klawock and two from Craig.

COMMUNITY FACILITIES AND SERVICES
The city operates the water and waste disposal systems, refuse collection, trailer court, boat harbor, liquor store, boat ramp, schools, and library.

Education. The City of Klawock (Klawock City School District) operates two collocated schools, one with grades K-6 and a second with grades 7-12. Enrollment averages 200 yearly. The Klawock Public Library serves the community.

Health care. The Alicia Roberts Medical Center is operated by the South East Alaska Regional Health Cooperative. It is a qualified Emergency Care Center. Auxiliary health care is provided by the Klawock Volunteer Fire/EMS and the Prince of Wales Island Area EMS. For higher levels of health care, medical centers in Wrangell and Petersburg and the Ketchikan General Hospital are all within 100 miles of Klawock.

Public safety. Law enforcement is provided by the city police department and a local state trooper post. Emergency response is provided by the Klawock Volunteer Fire/EMS and the Prince of Wales Island Area EMS.

Kluti-Kaah

Total area of entitlement under ANCSA	
	115,200 acres
Total labor force	237
High school graduate or higher	90.6%
Bachelor's degree or higher	19.5%
Unemployment rate	26.8%
Per capita income *(1999)*	$15,152
Population *2000 census*	492
Percent Native *2000 census*	40.2%

LOCATION
Copper Center is located along the Richardson Highway between mileposts 100 and 105. It is on the west bank of the Copper River at the confluence of the Klutina River. It lies just west of the Wrangell-St. Elias National Park. Copper Center is located in the Chitina Recording District.

PHYSICAL DESCRIPTION
The area encompasses 13.7 square miles of land.

CLIMATE
Copper Center is located in the continental climate zone, with typical long, cold winters and warm summers. Temperature extremes have dropped to -74°F and risen to 96°F. Yearly precipitation is 9 inches, with annual snowfall of 39 inches.

CULTURE AND HISTORY
Athabascan people have occupied the Copper River basin for the past 5,000 to 7,000 years. They had fish camps at every bend in the river and villages at several points. Copper Center was a large village at one time, and in the last decade of the 19th century became a "tent city" for miners looking for a shortcut to the Klondike. In 1896 Ringwald Blix built a roadhouse that was highly regarded for its outstanding services. It was located on the Fairbanks-Valdez Trail and therefore became the principal supply center for the miners in the Nelchina-Sustina region. In 1932 the original roadhouse was destroyed in order to build the Copper Center Lodge. This lodge is now on the National Register of Historic Places and is considered the jewel of Alaskan roadhouses. The first church in the Copper River region, the Chapel on the Hill, was built here in 1942 by Vince Joy and U.S. Army volunteers stationed in the area. Over the years, Mr. Joy built other churches and a Bible college in the area. The Native Village of Kluti-Kaah is a federally recognized tribe in the community.

GOVERNMENT
The village is unincorporated and is located in the Unorganized Borough *(see Alaska introduction)*. It is governed by a traditional council, headed by a president.

VILLAGE CORPORATION
The Kluti-Kaah corporation merged with Ahtna Inc., regional Native corporation *(see Alaska introduction)*. In 1980, seven of the eight Ahtna Village Corporations—Chistochina (Cheesh-Na), Incorporated, Cantwell (Yedatene Na Corporation), Gakona (Gakona Corporation), Gulkana (Sta-Keh Corporation), Kluti-Kaah (Kluti-Kaah Corporation), Mentasta (Mentats, Incorporated, and Tazlina (Tazlina, Incorporated)—merged with existing Alaska Native regional corporation, Ahtna, Inc. Ahtna assumed the management of all former village corporation lands. The total land area managed is 1.77 million acres. The primary assets managed are surface estate (including gravel), subsurface minerals, and timber Management is "in accordance with cultural and traditional uses and values, land protection, acquisition, conservative development strategies, and principles of culturally appropriate stewardship."

ECONOMY
The economy of Copper Center is based on local services and businesses, the National Park offices, and tourism. Many native residents also depend on subsistence hunting, fishing, trapping, and gathering.

Also known as Copper Center

Ethnicity: Ahtna Athabascan

ANCSA village/regional corporation
AHTNA, Inc.
P.O. Box 649
Glenallen, AK 99588
907-822-3476

Kluti-Kaah

Also known as Copper Center

Construction. Five residents are employed in construction.

Fisheries. Eight residents hold commercial salmon fishing permits.

Government as employer. Of the 90 employed residents, 28 work for the local, state, or federal government.

Manufacturing. Three residents are employed in manufacturing.

Services and retail. Approximately 142 businesses are located in Copper Center. Businesses include a book store, plumbing service, realty, gift shop, day care, dog kennel, and country store. A business center is also available for office services and Web design. Retail trade employs 6 residents; wholesale trade, 5; education, health and social services 20; public administration 10; and finance, insurance, real estate, rental and leasing employs 7 residents.

Tourism and recreation. Guided tours, riverboat services, adventure charters, and aviation tours are all available in Copper Center. Lodging is available in a campground, RV park, bed-and-breakfast, and a lodge. Three riverboat charter services operate from Copper Center. An art gallery is located in the village as well as a candle shop, pottery shop, and quilt shop. Several restaurants, an espresso shop, and video rental are also available. Visitor attractions include The National Park Service's Wrangell-St. Elias Visitor Center and the George I. Ashby Memorial Museum. Arts, entertainment, recreation, accommodations, and food services employ 13 residents.

Transportation. Three riverboat charter services operate from Copper Center.

INFRASTRUCTURE
Nine capital projects, funded by grants, are active in Copper Center.

Transportation. Copper Center lies on the Richardson Highway. A state-owned 2,200 by 55-foot gravel airstrip provides for chartered flights and general aviation.

Electricity. Copper Valley Electric Association provides electric power which it purchases from the state-owned Solomon Gulch Hydro Facility.

Water and waste systems. Most residents rely on individual water wells and septic tanks. Others haul treated well water from a site operated by Copper Center Safe Water. A private Glennallen company delivers water to home storage tanks. The well at Kluti-Kaah Memorial Hall is contaminated and on boil-water notice. The school operates its own well-water system. Most households are fully plumbed.

Telecommunications. Internet service and local telephone service are provided by the Copper Valley Telephone Co-op, while long distance service is available through Alascom. Teleconferencing is available through the Alaska Teleconferencing Network. One television channel is offered by the Rural Alaska Television Network, and residents are also able to receive a channel from Glennallen. One radio station is available to residents.

COMMUNITY FACILITIES AND SERVICES
Area facilities include the Kluti-Kaah community hall, George I. Ashby Memorial Museum, and a library located in Kenny Lake. A renovated or new washeteria is needed in the community. Copper Basin Sanitation provides refuse collection. A landfill and incinerator are available.

Education. Copper Center School is in the Copper River School District. The school has 52 students and five teachers.

Health care. Provided by the Copper Center Health Clinic, owned by the village and leased to the U.S. Public Health Service. It is administered by the Copper River Native Association. Available hospitals or health clinics also include Cross Road Medical Center in Glennallen and Copper River Native Association (health care, transportation, cultural activities). Auxiliary health care is provided by Copper River EMS Council, and Cross Road Medical Center in Glennallen.

Knik

Also known as Knik-Fairview

[kuh-NICK]
Ethnicity: Tanaina Athabascan

Village council
Knik Tribal Council
P.O. Box 877885
Wasilla, AK 99687
907-376-9028

ANCSA village corporation
Knikatnu, Incorporated
P.O. Box 872130
Wasilla, AK 99687-2130
907-376-2845
907-376-2847 Fax

Total area of entitlement under ANCSA	
	56,497 acres
Total labor force	5,014
High school graduate or higher	88.6%
Bachelor's degree or higher	15.5%
Unemployment rate	13.5%
Per capita income *(1999)*	$20,895
Population *2000 census*	7,049
2002 population	8,488
state demographer estimate	
Percent Native *2000 census*	8.70%

LOCATION
Knik-Fairview is on the northwest bank of the Knik Arm of Cook Inlet, 37 road miles northwest of Anchorage in the Mat-Su Borough.

CLIMATE
The average temperatures in January vary from -28°F to 39°F; in July, 44°F to 83°F. Annual precipitation is 16.5 inches, including 48 inches of yearly snowfall.

CULTURE AND HISTORY
Knik is a Dena'ina (Tanaina) Athabascan Indian name meaning "fire," which originally applied to several villages at the head of Cook Inlet. A Russian Orthodox mission was built in

Knik in the mid-1830s. The primary village was listed as "Kinik" in the 1880 U.S. census. During the 1880s, George Palmer's Store thrived off of the local fur trade. Gold found in interior Alaska in 1908 brought prospectors and supplies to Knik. Construction of the Iditarod Trail brought mail from Knik to Nome and shipments of gold by dog team to meet the boat at Knik. By1914 the town had 500 people during the summer and 1,000 during the winter. When the Alaska Railroad bypassed Knik in 1915, residents relocated to Anchorage and Wasilla. Camp 13 of the Matanuska Colony, with six farms, was established along Fairview Road in 1935. World War II and Korean War veterans also homesteaded the land. In the 1960s many of the historic docks and the commercial district were destroyed when Knik-Goose Bay Road was built. Low housing costs, the semirural lifestyle, and a tolerable commute to Anchorage have contributed to the growth in the Mat-Su Valley. Knik is a checkpoint for the Iditarod Sled Dog Race and is called the "Dog Mushing Center of the World."

GOVERNMENT
This is an unincorporated community, originally called Knik. The Mat-Su Borough changed the name to Knik-Fairview and expanded the boundaries in preparation for the 2000 census. The Mat-Su communities in 2000 were brought in alignment with the community councils and the borough's upgraded 911 emergency-response regions. The community has become

relatively large, with over 2,600 homes, although there is a federally recognized tribe in the community-the Knik Tribal Council.

ECONOMY
Agriculture and gravel extraction occur locally. Most residents are employed in Palmer, Wasilla, or Anchorage in a variety of retail, services, city, borough, state, or federal government positions.

Construction. Approximately 372 residents are employed in construction.

Fisheries. Farming, fishing, and forestry industries employ 28 residents.

Government as employer. Of the 2,789 employed residents, 503 work for the local, state, or federal government.

Manufacturing. Approximately 57 residents are employed in manufacturing.

Mining and hunting. Mining and hunting industries employ 142 residents.

Services and retail. Area businesses include retail stores, construction companies, public administration offices, food services and lodging, and education/health/social service agencies. Many services are extensive in the Palmer-Wasilla area, including wholesale and retail trade companies. Retail trade employs 333 residents; wholesale trade, 68; information services, 114; financial and related businesses, 137; professional, scientific, administrative, and waste management, 173; education, health, and social services, 584; and public administration, 152.

Tourism and recreation. Accommodations include a lodge and campground. Visitor attractions include the Knik Museum and Mushers' Hall of Fame, Athabascan graveyard, and Settlers Bay Golf Course. Arts, entertainment, recreation, accommodations, and food service industries employ 195 residents.

Transportation. Transportation, warehousing, and utility industries employ 207 residents.

INFRASTRUCTURE
Transportation. The area is linked to Anchorage, the remainder of the state, and Canada by the George Parks Highway, Glenn Highway, and other local roads. The Alaska Railroad serves the Fairbanks-to-Seward route. Scheduled commuter and air-taxi services are available at the Wasilla and Palmer airports. Floatplanes land at Wasilla Lake, Jacobsen Lake, and Lake Lucille. There are 10 additional private airstrips in the area. Commercial jet flights are available at the Anchorage International Airport.

Electricity. Matanuska Electric Association provides electricity.

Fuel. Piped natural gas for heating is available to most households.

Water and waste systems. Individual water wells, septic systems, and full plumbing are in most homes.

Telecommunications. In-state phone service is provided by Matanuska Telephone Association; long distance service by AT&T Alascom and GCI. Alaska Rural Communications Service provides television access. There are three radio stations in the community. GCI Cable TV provides cable.

COMMUNITY FACILITIES AND SERVICES
The borough landfill in Palmer is used, and private refuse collection is available.

Education. Goose Bay Elementary School has 407 students and 27 teachers; Snowshoe Elementary School has 387 students and 21 teachers. Both schools are in the Matanuska-Susitna School District. High-school students who live in Knik-Fairview are bused to nearby Wasilla.

Health care. Valley Hospital in nearby Palmer and hospitals in Anchorage are available for health care.

Knik
Also known as Knik-Fairview

Kobuk

Kobuk

Total area of entitlement under ANCSA
	69,120 acres
Total labor force	65
High school graduate or higher	63.8%
Bachelor's degree or higher	8.5%
Unemployment rate	0.0%
Per capita income *(1999)*	$9,845
Population *2000 census*	109
2003 population	125
state demographer estimate	
Percent Native *2000 census*	93.6%

LOCATION
Kobuk is located on the south bank of the Kobuk River, about 7 miles northeast of Shungnak and 128 air miles northeast of Kotzebue.

PHYSICAL DESCRIPTION
The City has 16.1 square miles of land and 0.7 square mile of water.

CLIMATE
Kobuk lies in the continental climate zone, characterized by long, cold winters and relatively warm summers. Temperatures can range from winter lows of -68°F to highs of 90°F in the summer. Snowfall averages 56 inches, with total annual precipitation of 17 inches.

CULTURE AND HISTORY
Kobuk is the smallest village in the Northwest Arctic Borough. It was founded in 1899 as a supply point for mining activities in the Cosmos Hills to the north and was then called Shungnak. Due to river erosion, most Shungnak residents moved 10 miles downstream to a new site. Those who remained at the old village renamed it Kobuk. It is an Inupiat village, practicing a traditional subsistence life-style.

GOVERNMENT
Kobuk was incorporated in 1973 as a second-class city, with a mayor and city council. It is located in the Northwest Arctic Borough. The Native Village of Kobuk is the federally recognized Native entity, a traditional village council headed by a president.

VILLAGE/REGIONAL CORPORATION
The ANCSA village corporation for Kobuk merged into NANA Regional Corporation, which now serves as both the village and regional Native corporations for the community.

ECONOMY
The economy of Kobuk is subsistence-oriented. Cash em-

[KOH-buck]
Ethnicity: Inupiat

Municipality
City of Kobuk
P.O. Box 20
Kobuk, AK 99751
907-948-2217
907-948-2228 Fax

Native entity
Native Village of Kobuk
P.O. Box 51039
Kobuk, AK 99751
907-948-2203
907-948-2123 Fax

ANCSA village/regional corporation
NANA Regional Corporation
P.O. Box 49
Kotzebue, AK 99752
907-442-3301
nana.com

Kobuk

ployment is limited to the school, city, and clinic. Seasonal construction and U.S. Bureau of Land Management firefighting provide some income as well. Whitefish, caribou, and moose provide the majority of meat sources.

Government as employer. Of the 29 employed residents, 23 work for the city, state, or federal government.

Services and retail. Businesses in the community include a gas station, retail stores, air transportation services, and hunting guide services.

INFRASTRUCTURE

Transportation. Kobuk's major means of transportation are barge, plane, small boat, and snowmachine. The state provides a 2,518- by 58-foot lighted gravel airstrip, which serves scheduled air carriers. Four airline companies service Kobuk. Floatplanes land on the Kobuk River. Crowley Marine Services barges fuel and supplies in spring and autumn. There is a barge off-loading area. Boats, all-terrain vehicles, and snowmachines provide local transportation. Many trails are available along the river for year-round intervillage travel and subsistence activities. There is a road open to Shungnak.

Electricity. Kobuk Valley Electric Co-operative purchases power from the Alaska Village Electrical Cooperative over the Kobuk-Shungnak intertie.

Fuel storage (gallons). City (16,900); Northwest Arctic Schools (11,700); Kobuk Store (8,700).

Water and waste systems. A piped water and sewer system, including household plumbing, serves the community. A 30-foot well provides water, which is treated and stored by the washeteria. Waste is disposed of at Dall Creek. Individuals haul their own trash to a Class 3 landfill.

Telecommunications. In-state phone service is provided by OTZ Telephone Co-op, long distance phone service by AT&T Alascom, GCI, or OTZ. Internet service is provided by GCI. Alaska Rural Communications Service provides television access from a local repeater. Residents can receive one radio station.

COMMUNITY FACILITIES AND SERVICES

The city operates the water and waste systems, the landfill, and the washeteria, and has a city public safety building. There is also a community building.

Education. Kobuk School has 42 students, three teachers, and is operated by the Northwest Arctic School District. High School students attend school in nearby Shungnak. The school library serves as the community's public library.

Health care. Local health care is provided by the Kobuk Health Clinic, operated by the Maniilaq Association.

Public safety. Law enforcement is provided by a state village public safety officer (VPSO), supported by state troopers in Kotzebue. Emergency response is provided by the city volunteer fire department.

Kodiak

See Urban Tribes under Shoonaq'

Kokhanok

[KOCK-hone-ack]
Ethnicity: Alutiiq

Native entity
Kokhanok Village
P.O. Box 1007
Kokhanok, AK 99606-1007
907-282-2202
907-282-2264 Fax

ANCSA village corporation
Alaska Peninsula Corporation
P.O. Box 334
King Salmon, AK 99613
907-274-2433
907-274-8694 Fax

Total area of entitlement under ANCSA	
	101,827 acres
Total labor force	121
High school graduate or higher	77.6%
Bachelor's degree or higher	11.8%
Unemployment rate	11.4%
Per capita income *(1999)*	$7,732
Population *2000 census*	174
2003 population	182
state demographer estimate	
Percent Native *2000 census*	90.8%

LOCATION
Kokhanok is located on the southern shore of Iliamna Lake, 200 miles southwest of Anchorage, on the Alaska Peninsula.

PHYSICAL DESCRIPTION
The area encompasses 21.3 square miles of land and 0.1 square mile of water. It is a moose intensive-use area, there is bald eagle nesting nearby, and there are waterfowl throughout the area. Vegetation is upland spruce-hardwood forest. The village lies in a high-occurrence mineralized area, on the border of a copper-silver-gold-molybdenum metal province and within a moderate-occurrence oil and gas province.

CLIMATE
Kokhanok lies in a transitional climate zone, with a maritime climate prevailing during most of the year. Average summer temperatures range from 40°F to 64°F; winter temperatures range from 3°F to 30°F. The record high is 84°F; the record low, -47°F. Precipitation averages 32 inches annually, including 89 inches of snowfall. Wind storms and ice fog are common during winter.

CULTURE AND HISTORY
This fishing village was first listed in the U.S. census in 1890.

The village has a mixed Native population, primarily Alutiiq, but with Yup'ik and Athabascan Indians as well. Subsistence activities are the focal point of the culture. In the summer, a few families move to a fish camp three miles from the village, near the mouth of the Gibraltar River. Some people go to Naknek to fish for red salmon in June and July.

GOVERNMENT
Kokhanok is unincorporated and is located in the Unorganized Borough. It is governed by a federally recognized traditional village council, headed by a president.

VILLAGE CORPORATION
Alaska Peninsula Corporation serves as the ANCSA village corporation for Kokhanok. It is the merged village corporations of Kokhanok, Newhalen, Port Heiden, South Naknek, and Ugashik. Shareholders in the village corporation also hold shares in Bristol Bay Native Corporation.

ECONOMY
The school is the largest employer in Kokhanok. Subsistence hunting and fishing near the community supplement the cash economy. Some residents go to the Bristol Bay area each summer to fish. People heavily rely on subsistence activities; many families have a summer fish camp near the Gibraltar River. Salmon, trout, grayling, moose, bear, rabbit, porcupine, and seal are gathered. Twenty-six residents are employed in education, health, and social services.

Fisheries. Eight persons currently hold commercial fishing permits, chiefly for salmon and trout.

Government as employer. Of the 39 employed residents, 33 work for the local, state, or federal government.

Services and retail. Kokhanok has an outfitter's store, a general store, a grocery store, and a retail shop.

Tourism and recreation. One bed-and-breakfast facility is available for lodging. The Kokhanok Carnival is a big visitor attraction. Katmai National Park and Preserve is several miles south of the village.

INFRASTRUCTURE

Transportation. Kokhanok is accessible by air and water. The state provides a 2,920 by 60-foot gravel airstrip and a seaplane base, which serve scheduled and charter air services from Anchorage, Iliamna, and King Salmon. Supplies delivered by barge by way of the Kvichak River must be lightered to shore. Docking facilities are not available. The community wants to develop a boat harbor and launch ramp. Skiffs, all-terrain vehicles, and trucks provide local travel.

Electricity. Kokhanok Village generates power during the summer, using a 375-kilowatt diesel plant. In winter, the village purchases electricity from the school district.

Fuel storage (gallons). Village (58,900); Roehl's Enterprises; (3,800); Lake and Peninsula Schools (3,600).

Water and waste systems. Thirty-five residences have a piped water and sewer system. Others haul water and use honeybuckets, septic tanks, or outhouses. The school operates its own well and water treatment facility.

Telecommunications. Local phone service is provided by ACS of the Northland; long distance phone service by AT&T Alascom. Internet service is provided for the school by GCI. Alaska Rural Communications Service provides television access. Three radio stations can be received.

COMMUNITY FACILITIES AND SERVICES
The village provides electricity, water and sewer, and fuel oil, and maintains a community hall.

Education. Kokhanok School is in the Lake and Peninsula School District. The school has 46 students, five teachers, and the school library serves as the public library.

Health care. Provided by the Kokhanok Clinic, operated by the Bristol Bay Area Health Corporation. Auxiliary health care is provided by the Kokhanok First Responders.

Public safety. Law enforcement is provided by a state village public safety officer (VPSO), backed by state troopers in McGrath. Emergency response is provided by the village volunteer fire department and the Kokhanok First Responders.

Kokhanok

Koliganek
See New Koliganek

Kongiganak

Kongiganak

Total area of entitlement under ANCSA	
	115,200 acres
Total labor force	143
High school graduate or higher	45.2%
Bachelor's degree or higher	4.3%
Unemployment rate	3.5%
Per capita income _(1999)_	$9,881
Population _2000 census_	359
2003 population	401
state demographer estimate	
Percent Native _2000 census_	97.2%

[kahn-GIG-uh-nuk]
Ethnicity: Yup'ik

Native entity
Native Village of Kongiganak
P.O. Box 5069
Kongiganak, AK 99559
907-557-5226
907-557-5224 Fax

ANCSA village corporation
Qemirtalek Coast Corporation
P.O. Box 5070
Kongiganak, AK 99559
907-557-5529
907-557-5711 Fax

LOCATION
Kongiganak is located on the west shore of Kuskokwim Bay, west of the mouth of the Kuskokwim River, above the Kongnignanohk River. It lies 11 miles east-northeast of Kwigillingok, 90 miles southwest of Bethel, and 451 miles west of Anchorage.

PHYSICAL DESCRIPTION
The village covers 1.7 square miles of land and 0.2 square mile of water. Most of the village is located nine or ten feet above the estimated 100-year flood level. It is located 5.5 miles upstream of the mouth of the Kongnignanohk River but is still susceptible to coastal storms. The terrain around the village is flat, wet tundra, with very few trees.

CLIMATE
Kongiganak is located in a marine climate. Precipitation averages 22 inches, with 43 inches of snowfall, annually. Average daily summer temperatures range from 41°F to 57°F, average daily winter temperatures from 6°F to 24°F.

CULTURE AND HISTORY
Kongiganak is a traditional Yup'ik Eskimo village with a fishing and subsistence lifestyle and culture. Children grow up speaking Yup'ik as their first language—classes through the third grade are taught in Yup'ik. The crime rate at Kongiganak is extremely low and the people of the community are honest and friendly. There is a 9 p.m. curfew for all school age children. The Moravian church is a very active part of the community. Until the 1940s, the absence of commercial resources made the area unattractive to non-Natives. Today's elders were born into a world very much like that of their ancestors, especially in their reliance on subsistence hunting and fishing. Despite the changes of the last forty years, many traditions continue, especially dancing and elaborate community gift-giving. The area historically has been occupied by Yup'ik. The village was permanently settled in the late 1960s by former residents of Kwigillingok _q.v.,_ who were seeking higher ground to escape periodic flooding.

GOVERNMENT
Kongiganak is unincorporated, and is located in the Unorganized Borough. It is governed by the Native Village of Kongiganak, a BIA-recognized traditional council.

VILLAGE CORPORATION
Qemirtalek Coast Corporation is the ANCSA village corporation for Kongiganak. It operates a general store and gas station in the village and holds minority interests in a number of Calista Corporation's enterprises, including Alaska Newspapers. Shareholders in Qemirtaliek Coast Corporation are also shareholders in Calista Corporation, the ANCSA regional Native corporation.

ECONOMY
Approximately half of the employment in Kongiganak is at the school, the remainder with village services, stores, and commercial fishing. Education, health and social services, or public administration employ 72 of 138 employed residents. Poor catches and reduced salmon prices in recent years have hurt the economy. Subsistence activities and some trapping are important supplements.

Fisheries. While 20 residents hold commercial fishing permits, in 2002 only 8 residents actually engaged in commercial fishing. Poor returns and reduced salmon prices in recent years have affected the economy. The (gross) earnings from fishing in 2002—all from salmon—totaled only $41,259.

149

Kongiganak

Government as employer. The village, state, or federal government employ 85 of 138 employed residents.

Manufacturing. One local firm manufactures textile products.

Services and retail. There are two small general stores, one operated by the village corporation. The corporation store is bigger than the other and has a gas station. The village council operates a Native craft supply store. Other retail stores include a video store, a marine store (boat, motor, and snowmobile parts and other hardware), and a gun store. At least one person provides child care services.

INFRASTRUCTURE

Transportation. There are no roads in or to Kongiganak. Boardwalks serve as walkways within the village. Most travel to and from the village is done by aircraft, four-wheel-drive vehicle, boat, or snowmobile. There are winter trails to Kwigillingok and Tuntutuliak, the next villages along the coast in each direction. One end of the state-owned 1,885- by 35-foot gravel airstrip, significantly improved in the mid-1990s, is located in the middle of the village. Further improvements, including runway rehabilitation and extension and construction of a terminal building, are planned for the middle to late years of the first decade of the twenty-first century. Servicing airlines include Arctic Circle Air Service, Era Aviation, Grant Aviation, Hageland Aviation, Inland Aviation Services, and Yute Air. There are no docking facilities. Barges deliver cargo once or twice each summer.

Electricity. Electricity is provided by Puvurnaq Power Company, a private operator, from a 300-kilowatt diesel plant. As of 2003, upgrades to the power system were in progress.

Fuel storage (gallons): Qemirtalek Coast Corporation (86,800); Puvurnaq Power (76,500); Lower Kuskokwim Schools (71,600); village corporation (51,900); A&L Variety Shop (8,900); Moravian church (3,000); Army National Guard (1,900). Fuel storage improvements exceeding $4 million in cost were completed in the first decade of the twenty-first century.

Water and waste systems. Treated surface water is hauled to homes and other users from the washeteria, which is operated by the village council. Some residents use rain catchment during the summer and ice melt in the winter. Homes are not plumbed. From 1999 through 2003, $3 million in improvements were made to the water system, including building a new washeteria, converting the old washeteria into a water treatment plant, and water source and storage improvements. The village council hauls honeybuckets from disposal bunkers to a pre-treatment plant at the sewage lagoon. Homes are not plumbed. The village council also operates a landfill. The sewer plant was renovated in 1999, and improvements to the sewage lagoon to counter flooding were made in 2002.

Telecommunications. Local telephone service is provided by United Utilities, long distance service by AT&T Alascom or United Utilities. Internet service is available at the school from GCI. Thirteen AM radio stations broadcast to the area from Bethel, Nome, Dillingham, Anchorage, and elsewhere. The Alaska Rural Communications System broadcasts two television channels from a repeater in Kongiganak, and Qemirtalek Coast Corporation provides limited cable service.

COMMUNITY FACILITIES AND SERVICES

The village council has a community hall and office and operates the water supply and waste disposal systems and a Native craft supply store. Law enforcement is provided by a state village public safety officer (VPSO), backed by state troopers in Bethel. Emergency response is provided by the VPSO and the volunteer fire department.

Education. The Dick R. Kiunya Memorial School, operated by the Lower Kuskokwim School District, serves 110 students in grades K-12 with 8 teachers. It has a Web site. The community and the school district asked for $13 million in improvements to the school beginning in fiscal year 2005. The school library serves as the community's public library.

Health care. Local health care is provided by the Lillian E. Jimmy Memorial Health Clinic operated by the Yukon-Kuskokwim Heath Corporation. It was built in the mid-1990s. The nearest hospital is the Yukon-Kuskokwim Delta Regional Hospital, about 90 miles away in Bethel.

otlik

[KAWT-lick]
Ethnicity: Yup'ik

Municipality
City of Kotlik
P.O. Box 20268
Kotlik, AK 99620-0268
907-899-4313
907-899-4826 Fax

Native entity
Village of Kotlik
P.O. Box 20210
Kotlik, AK 99620
907-899-4326
907-899-4790 Fax

ANCSA village corporation
Kotlik Yupik Corporation
P.O. Box 20207
Kotlik, AK 99620
907-899-4014
907-899-4528 Fax

Total area of entitlement under ANCSA	115,200 acres
Total labor force	197
High school graduate or higher	40.5%
Bachelor's degree or higher	6.9%
Unemployment rate	24.4%
Per capita income *(1999)*	$7,707
Population *2000 census*	591
2003 population	609
state demographer estimate	
Percent Native *2000 census*	96.1%

LOCATION

Kotlik is located on the east bank of Kotlik Slough, 35 miles northeast of Emmonak in the Yukon-Kuskokwim Delta. It lies 165 air miles northwest of Bethel, and 460 miles from Anchorage.

PHYSICAL DESCRIPTION

The city covers 3.8 square miles of land and 0.8 square mile of water, in treeless, marshy tundra where the Yukon River Delta flows into Norton Sound. Most of the city is located on the mainland, but substantial parts are located on two islands separated from the rest of the city by waterways 250 to 400 feet wide. Flooding was about four feet deep during the 1974 "flood of record." A waterline mark was left on the city hall 24 inches above ground level and on the water storage tank 23 inches above ground level. Water in the community was about two feet deep during the most recent flood in 1987.

CLIMATE

The climate of Kotlik is subarctic. Temperatures range between -50°F and 87°F. There is an annual average of 16 inches of precipitation, including 60 inches of snowfall. High winds and poor visibility are common during fall and winter. Norton Sound and the Yukon River are icefree from mid-June through October.

CULTURE AND HISTORY

Kotlik is a Yup'ik village with a traditional fishing, trapping, and subsistence lifestyle. The first language of many residents is the Norton Sound dialect of Central Alaskan Yup'ik, which lies geographically and linguistically between Alutiiq and Siberian Yupik. (The use of the apostrophe in Central Alaskan Yup'ik, as opposed to Siberian Yupik, denotes a long *p*.) The word *Yup'ik* represents not only the language but also the name for the people themselves (*yuk* "person" plus *pik* "real"). Kotlik gets its name from the Yup'ik word for pants, because the Yukon River parts here like legs on a pair of trousers. The city has a Roman Catholic church and an Assembly of God church. A typical subsistence hunting and fishing cycle includes fishing for herring in the spring, then moving to a summer fish camp for fish to dry for the winter, perhaps with whaling in good weather, followed by seal hunting in the early fall.

The community grew rapidly during the mid-1960s when the BIA built a school and residents of the nearby villages of Channiliut, Hamilton, Bill Moore's Slough, and Pastolaik (now summer fish camps) relocated there. Both Hamilton *q.v.* and Bill Moore's Slough *q.v.* remain BIA-recognized Native entities, although all their members live in Kotlik or elsewhere. Due to its location with easy access by large riverboats and barges, Kotlik became one of the larger ports and commercial centers of the lower Yukon River. Many residents are descendants of Russian traders that settled in the area surrounding Saint Michael after 1867. The city incorporated in 1970.

GOVERNMENT
Kotlik incorporated in 1970 as a second-class city. It has a five-member city council, including the mayor and vice mayor, with a city manager to run day-to-day operations. The city levies a sales tax of 3 percent. The Village of Kotlik, also referred to as the Kotlik Traditional Council, is the BIA-recognized Native entity for Kotlik.

VILLAGE CORPORATION
Kotlik Yupik Corporation is the ANCSA village corporation. It sells bulk and retail petroleum, manages property, and leases commercial and industrial equipment. As of 2003 it was building a salmon freezer plant, for which it had already secured a building site, two tenders, and other equipment. It is estimated that this plant would provide 30 to 40 jobs for a further capital investment of $500,000. Shareholders in the village corporation are also shareholders in Calista Corporation, the regional Native corporation.

ECONOMY
Kotlik has a seasonal economy. Fishing and fish processing are the primary income generators. Residents hold 79 commercial fishing permits. The community is interested in developing a seafood processing facility and an arts and crafts project. Kotlik's residents rely heavily on subsistence foods, and many families have fish camps on the Yukon River. Salmon, moose, beluga whale, and seal are harvested. Income is also derived from trapping. Almost 60 percent of the work force works in educational, health and social services, or public administration.

Fisheries. In 2003, 83 Kotlik residents held commercial fishing permits and 81 engaged in commercial fishing, with a total gross income of $254,113. Most fished for salmon, some for herring, and a few for crab. As of 2003, the village corporation was building a salmon freezer plant, for which it had already secured a building site, two tenders, and other equipment. It is estimated that this plant would provide 30 to 40 jobs for a further capital investment of $500,000.

Government as employer. The city, state, and federal governments employ 76 Kotlik residents.

Mining. The community has identified a gravel site 15 miles from the city that has potential for oil and gas development.

Services and retail. There are two stores with basic supplies, fairly well stocked. The village corporation sells bulk and retail petroleum, manages property, and leases commercial and industrial equipment. A child care service, a building cleaning service, and a restaurant round out the retail sector.

Tourism and recreation. Accommodations include the City Lodge and the School. Visitor attractions include berry picking, fishing, ice fishing, seal hunting, and plant collecting. The late winter community potlatch also attracts visitors.

INFRASTRUCTURE
Transportation. There is no road access to Kotlik, although it is easily accessible by barge. The river is used by the fifty or so commercial and private boats owned by residents. Primary day-to-day access is by air, using the state-owned 4,422-foot long by 100-foot wide gravel airstrip. Grant Aviation, Hageland Aviation, Tanana Air Service, and Yute Air serve Kotlik. The airport was greatly improved in the 1990s at a cost exceeding $11.5 million. The Corps of Engineers built $2.5 million in river navigation improvements beginning in 2002, and the city would like to have a dock facility and barge landing site built. As of 2003, access within Kotlik was provided by boardwalks. The city has asked for conventional road access linking major facilities, the airport, and the landfill. Design work began in 1998. With the identification of a source of gravel 15 miles away, the last practical barrier to construction is gone.

Electricity. The city, through Kotlik Electric Services, provides electricity from an 825-kilowatt diesel plant. The powerhouse was upgraded at a total cost exceeding $3 million shortly after 2000.

Fuel storage (gallons). Kotlik Yupik Corporation (220,000); Kotlik Electric Services (50,000); Lower Yukon Schools (48,955); city (18,100); Alaska Commercial Store (15,000). A new bulk fuel facility was built shortly after 2000 at a cost exceeding $3 million.

Water and waste systems. The city provides piped water to the homes and other users on the mainland. Those on the islands were not yet served as of 2002, and were required to haul treated water across the Kotlik Slough from the washeteria, collect rainwater, or melt ice. The city wishes to connect these isolated customers to its piped water system. Construction of a 212,000-gallon water storage tank began in 2001. The water treatment plant, which gets its water from surface water sources, was upgraded in 1999. The city operates a piped vacuum sewer system for the homes and other users on the mainland. Those on the islands were not yet served as of 2002, and were required to haul honeybuckets to containers. Some still use outhouses. As of 2003, the city was considering an incinerator and recycling to reduce solid waste, as it is difficult to trench and bury waste in the wet tundra.

Telecommunications. Local telephone service is provided by United Utilities, long distance service by AT&T Alascom or United Utilities. The city provides cable television service. Thirteen AM radio stations from Nome, Bethel, Dillingham, Anchorage, and other locations broadcast to the area. The Alaska Rural Communications Service broadcasts two television channels from a repeater located in Kotlik.

COMMUNITY FACILITIES AND SERVICES
The city has a community hall, renovated in 1999, and a teen center. It has asked for funding for a community complex and gymnasium. The city operates the landfill, water and sewer systems, washeteria, electric utility, and cable television system. Law enforcement is provided by the city police officer, backed by state troopers in St. Mary's. Emergency response is provided by the city volunteer fire department. The school gymnasium is available for community use.

Education. The Lower Yukon School District operates the Kotlik School, serving 204 students in K-12 grade with 14 teachers. A new school building was completed in time for the 2004-05 school year, at a total cost exceeding $19 million. While the school has a strong academic reputation, many

Kotlik

experienced teachers retired soon after 2000. The school library serves as the community's public library.

Health care. The Kotlik Clinic, operated by the Yukon Kuskokwim Health Corporation, is supported by the Pearl E. Johnson Sub-Regional Clinic in nearby Emmonak. Local emergency service is provided by a health aide. As of 2002, the clinic was reported to need expansion and new equipment. The clinic is further supported by the Yukon Kuskokwim

Delta Regional Hospital in Bethel, but the Norton Sound Regional Hospital in Nome is actually 45 miles closer.

ENVIRONMENTAL CONCERNS

Kotlik's primary environmental concern is riverbank erosion, mainly as a result of waves generated by boat wakes and by winds. A concrete revetment built by the state in the 1980s is failing. In 2003, the Corps of Engineers budgeted $2.5 million for erosion control for Kotlik.

Kotzebue

[KAWT-zuh-byoo]
Ethnicity: Inupiat

Municipality
City of Kotzebue
P.O. Box 46
Kotzebue, AK 99752
907-442-3401
907-442-3742 Fax
kotzpdweb.tripod.com

Native entity
Native Village of Kotzebue
P.O. Box 296
Kotzebue, AK 99752
907-442-3467
907-442-2162 Fax

ANCSA village corporation
Kikiktagruk Inupiat Corp.
P.O. Box 1050
Kotzebue, AK 99752
907-442-3165
907-442-2165 Fax
kicorp.org

Total area of entitlement under ANCSA	
	164,364 acres
Total labor force	1,391
High school graduate or higher	32.4%
Bachelor's degree or higher	17.9%
Unemployment rate	9.8%
Per capita income *(1999)*	$18,289
Population *2000 census*	3,082
2003 population	3,076
state demographer estimate	
Percent Native *2000 census*	76.7%

LOCATION

Kotzebue is on the Baldwin Peninsula in Kotzebue Sound, on a three-mile-long spit which ranges in width from 1,100 to 3,600 feet. It is located near the discharges of the Kobuk, Noatak and Ssezawick Rivers, 549 air miles northwest of Anchorage and 26 miles above the Arctic Circle.

PHYSICAL DESCRIPTION

The City has 27.0 square miles of land and 1.7 square miles of water. A coastal storm in 1990 likely represents the 100-year flood event, and floodwaters did not reach the first floor of any major building.

CLIMATE

Kotzebue is located in the transitional climate zone, which is characterized by long, cold winters and cool summers. The average low temperature during January is -12ºF; the average high during July is 58ºF. Temperature extremes have been measured from -52ºF to 85ºF. Annual snowfall averages 40 inches, with total precipitation of 9 inches per year. Kotzebue Sound is ice free from early July until early October.

CULTURE AND HISTORY

The residents of Kotzebue are primarily Inupiat, and subsistence activities are an integral part of the lifestyle. The Inupiaq name is Kikiktagruk, which means "a place that is shaped like a long island" or "almost an island." Inupiat residents speak the Malimiut dialect of Inupiaq. The name "Inupiaq," meaning "real or genuine person" (*inuk* "person" plus -*piaq* "real, genuine"), is often spelled "Iñupiaq" in the Malimiut dialect. It can refer to a person of this group ("He is an Inupiaq") and can also be used as an adjective ("She is an Inupiaq woman"). "Inupiat" refers to the people collectively (for example, "the Inupiat of the Kobuk River"). This site has been occupied by Inupiat for at least 600 years, and was the hub of ancient Arctic trading routes long before European contact, due to its coastal location near a number of rivers. The German Lt. Otto Von Kotzebue "discovered" Kotzebue Sound in 1818 for Russia. The community was named after the Kotzebue Sound in 1899 when a post office was established. Since the turn of the twentieth century, expansion of economic activities and services in the area has enabled Kotzebue to develop rela-

tively rapidly. The city was incorporated in 1958. An air force base and White Alice Communications System station were later established nearby.

GOVERNMENT

The City of Kotzebue was incorporated in 1958, and uses the city manager form of government. It levies sales, accommodations, and liquor taxes of 6 percent. The Native Village of Kotzebue, also known as the Kotzebue IRA Council, is a BIA-recognized Native entity and IRA tribal council and is a Public Law 93-638 tribal government contractor.

VILLAGE CORPORATION

Kikiktagruk Inupiat Corporation (KIC) is the ANCSA village corporation, the only village corporation in the NANA Regional Corporation area not merged into NANA. As of 2003, there were 1,953 KIC shareholders, who are also shareholders in NANA. KIC offers construction services, energy sales, vehicle and heavy equipment rentals, facilities leasing and management, property maintenance, hardware, automotive supplies, lumber, light-duty and recreational vehicle repair, and architectural and engineering, commercial, and interior design services in Northwest Alaska and elsewhere. KIC's subsidiaries have HUB Zone and women-owned business enterprise status, and the development subsidiary is also a §8(a) firm. As of 2003, KIC was aggressively moving into information technology services and minority business enterprises contracts. It was profitable in the fiscal year ending in 2003 for the first time in many years.

ECONOMY

Kotzebue is the service and transportation center for all villages in the northwest region. It has a healthy cash economy, a growing private sector, and a stable public sector. Due to its location at the confluence of three river drainages, Kotzebue is the transfer point between ocean and inland shipping. It is also the air transport center for the region. Activities related to oil and minerals exploration and development have contributed to the economy. The majority of income is directly or indirectly related to government employment, such as the school district, Maniilaq Association, the city, and the borough. In 2000, education, health and social services, and public administration employed 618 of 1,255 employed residents. The Cominco Alaska Red Dog Mine is a significant regional employer. Most residents rely on subsistence to supplement income.

Communications and information services. Kotzebue boasts the OTZ Telephone Cooperative and an information services/software development firm.

Construction. There are three construction firms in Kotzebue.

Fisheries. Historically, commercial fishing for chum salmon provided some seasonal employment. However, in 2003 only 2 of 133 commercial fishing permits were used, and in 2002 only 3 of 131. In 2004, the state Department of Commerce, Community, and Economic Development funded an economic development project in an attempt to restore the industry. *Government as employer.* The city, borough, state, and federal governments employ 474 residents.

Services and retail. This sector is robust, with 22 retail stores, 28 real estate leasing firms, 14 counseling and consulting firms, 6 building services firms, 2 family services firms, 26 day care providers, 2 photo studios, 2 caterers, 8 automotive repair firms, 2 hairdressers, and 2 dog breeders.

Tourism and recreation. Accommodations are available at Bayside Inn and Restaurant, Lagoon B&B, Nullagvik Hotel and Restaurant, and Sue's B&B. There are five sit-down restaurants and five-limited service restaurants, three tour guide firms, and a waterway sightseeing firm. Special events include an April snowmachine race and three major sled dog races.

Transportation. Kotzebue has one scheduled and two charter airlines, five aviation services firms, a warehousing firm, at least three taxicab firms, and an inland water transportation firm.

INFRASTRUCTURE
Transportation. Air is the primary means of transportation year-round. The state-owned Ralph Wien Memorial Airport supports daily jet service to Anchorage and several air taxis to the region's villages. It has a 5,900- by 150-foot main paved runway and 3,800- by 100-foot crosswind gravel runway. As of 2003, over $21 million in improvements were underway, including a new operations building, fencing for the entire airport, rehabilitation and expansion of the parking apron, and elimination of approach obstacles. A further $11 million in improvements are planned. Nine airlines offer service to Kotzebue. A seaplane base is also operated by the state. The shipping season lasts 100 days, from early July to early October, when the sound is ice free. Due to river sediments deposited by the Noatak River 4 miles above Kotzebue, the harbor is shallow. As of 2003, the Corps of Engineers had partially completed $5 million in improvements. Still, deep draft vessels must anchor 15 miles out, and cargo is lightered to shore. As of 2003, the feasibility of developing a deep water port was being examined. There are 26 miles of local gravel roads, used by cars, trucks, and motorcycles during the summer. Snowmachines are preferred in winter for local transportation. There are at least three taxicab firms in the city. There is an integrated ground transportation system for shipping ore concentrates from the Red Dog Mine to dedicated port facilities in Kotzebue, built in the 1990s at a cost of $337 million.

Electricity. Electricity is provided by the Kotzebue Electric Association, a rural electrical cooperative, which relies on diesel, wind, and natural gas plants with a total capacity of 20,390 kilowatts. Kotzebue uses ten 50-kilowatt wind turbines to supplement electricity.

Fuel storage (gallons). Crowley Marine Services Tank Farm (6,200,000), Airport/Bering Air (20,000), Air National Guard (17,000).

Water and waste systems. Water is supplied by the 150-million-gallon Vortac Reservoir, located one and a half miles from the city. Water is treated and stored in a 1.5-million-gallon tank. Funds have been appropriated to construct a second 1.5-million-gallon tank. Water is heated with a waste-heat recovery system at the electric plant, and distributed in circulating mains. Piped sewage is treated in a 32-acre zero-discharge lagoon west of the airport; significant improvements were funded in 2003. As of 2002, around 80 percent of homes were fully plumbed, and 521 homes were served by the city sys-

tem, with two further service extensions funded in 2002. The 30-year-old PVC water and sewer mains are currently undergoing replacement at a cost exceeding $7 million. The city operates a Class 2 landfill with balefill.

Telecommunications. Local telephone service is provided by OTZ Telephone Co-op, long distance service by AT&T Alascom, GCI, or OTZ Telephone. ACS Internet, GCI, and OTZ Telephone Cooperative provide Internet service, and GCI Cable, operates a cable television system. One AM radio station, KOTZ, broadcasts from Kotzebue, and stations from Nome, Bethel, Anchorage, Barrow, and elsewhere broadcast to the area. Two channels of broadcast television service can be received from Alaska Rural Communications Service repeaters located in Kotzebue.

COMMUNITY FACILITIES AND SERVICES
Community facilities include City Hall, the city entertainment center, recreation center, and the Boys and Girls Club. The state superior court for Northwest Alaska is located in Kotzebue. The city operates the water and waste disposal systems, and provides law enforcement through the city police department, which is backed by a state trooper post in the city. Emergency response is provided by the Kotzebue Volunteer Fire Department, Maniilaq Air Ambulance, and NANA Search and Rescue. Maniilaq provides significant services for seniors, including the Senior Cultural Center, a transit service, and a residential facility. An unusual aspect of community services in Kotzebue is housing for the Native population. Since 1989, the federal Department of Housing and Urban Development has granted more than $45 million to the Native Village of Kotzebue and NANA Regional Corporation for housing.

Education. Northwest Arctic School District operates an elementary school (grades K—6, 32 teachers serving 420 students) and a middle/high school (grades 7—12, 27 teachers serving 401 students). It also operates a district-wide correspondence school program, in grades K-12, for isolated students. As of 2003, significant improvements to both schools were funded and in the design stage, $8 million for Nelson Elementary and $16 million for Kotzebue High. The University of Alaska Fairbanks has its Chukchi Campus in Kotzebue. Most students of Chukchi Campus do not live in Kotzebue. Rather, students "attend" classes from the villages where they live, via satellite-assisted audio conference, with fax machines and electronic mail sending written assignments between instructor and students, who live in communities scattered across rural Alaska. Chukchi both "imports" and "exports" postsecondary education throughout rural Alaska, offering certificates, two- and four-year degrees in many academic disciplines including teacher certification, rural development, health, social work, computers, and other fields. The campus is also the location for the Chukchi Consortium Library, which serves as the public library in Kotzebue. The NANA Museum of the Arctic has collections of artifacts portraying Inupiat culture and Arctic wildlife, Inupiat storytelling, and other Inupiat cultural performances.

Health care. The Maniilaq Health Center is the regional hospital for Northwest Arctic Borough, and is operated by the Maniilaq Association, the regional health corporation and Public Law 93-638 tribal government contractor. The hospital is a qualified Acute Care facility. Maniilaq also provides long-term care in the community.

ENVIRONMENTAL CONCERNS
Coastal erosion, while not severe, threatens the shoreline of the city.

K oyuk

[KOY-yuck]
**Ethnicity: Unalit Yup'ik and
Malemiut Inupiat**

Municipality
City of Koyuk
P.O. Box 53029
Koyuk, AK 99753
   907-963-3441
   907-963-3442 Fax

Native entity
Native Village of Koyuk
P.O. Box 53030
Koyuk, AK 99753
   907-963-3651
   907-963-2353 Fax

ANCSA village corporation
Koyuk Native Corporation
P.O. Box 50
Koyuk, AK 99753
   907-963-2424
   907-963-3552 Fax

Total area of entitlement under ANCSA	
	92,160 acres
Total labor force	107
High school graduate or higher	53.1%
Bachelor's degree or higher	1.4%
Unemployment rate	34.6%
Per capita income *(1999)*	$8,736
Population *2000 census*	297
2003 population	340
state demographer estimate	
Percent Native *2000 census*	94.3%

LOCATION
Koyuk is located on the Koyuk River at its mouth, at the northeastern end of Norton Bay on the Seward Peninsula. It is 132 miles east of Nome and 75 miles north of Unalakleet.

PHYSICAL DESCRIPTION
The city encompasses 4.7 square miles of land. It is surrounded on 3 sides by hills covered by spruce trees; the south side looks out over the Koyuk River, tundra, and Norton Bay. Major floods occurred in 1913, 1963, and 1974. The most recent flood was in 1993. Flooding is bad when the wind comes off Norton Bay, due to the shallow depth of the bay.

CLIMATE
Koyuk has a subarctic climate with a maritime influence. The typical summer high temperature ranges from 46°F to 62°F, the winter low temperature from -8°F to 8°F. Annual precipitation is 19 inches, including 40 inches of snowfall. Extremes from a low of -49°F to a high of 87°F have been recorded. Norton Bay is usually ice free from May to October.

CULTURE AND HISTORY
Koyuk is a traditional Malemiut Inupiat and Unalit Yup'ik village that speaks the Malimiut dialect of Inupiaq. Residents maintain a subsistence lifestyle. A site just to the south of Koyuk has traces of early man that are 6,000 to 8,000 years old. Lt. Zagoskin of the Russian Navy noted the village of "Kuynkhak-miut" in 1842-44. The Western Union Telegraph Expedition of 1865 found the village of "Konyukmute." Around 1900, the present site began to be populated because supplies could easily be lightered to shore. Two boom towns grew up nearby around 1914: Dime Landing and Haycock. In addition to gold, coal was mined a mile upriver to supply steam ships and for export to Nome. The first school began in the church in 1915; the U.S. government built a school in 1928. The city was incorporated in 1970. Koyuk has a Covenant church.

GOVERNMENT
Koyuk is a second-class city, incorporated in 1970, and located in the Unorganized Borough. The city is governed by a seven-member council that includes the mayor, vice mayor, secretary, and treasurer. It imposes a 2 percent sales tax. The Native Village of Koyuk is a BIA-recognized IRA tribal council.

VILLAGE CORPORATION
The ANCSA village corporation is the Koyuk Native Corporation, the shareholders of which are also shareholders in the regional Native corporation, Bering Straits Native Corporation. Koyuk Native Corporation is engaged in fuel sales and operates a food store.

ECONOMY
The Koyuk economy is based on subsistence, supplemented by limited part-time and temporary jobs. Unemployment is high. Some income is derived from reindeer herding. The main sources of meat are fish, reindeer, seal, beluga whale, and moose. Government, education, health, and social services employ more than half of employed residents.

Fisheries. There is a small amount of commercial fishing, primarily for herring. Thirteen residents hold commercial fishing permits.

Government as employer. There are 47 Koyuk residents employed by the city, state, or federal governments.

Services and retail. There are two stores that carry food, ammunition, and other essentials, a video store, a hunting and trapping supply and repair store, and four daycare operators.

Transportation. One business is registered in Koyuk as providing scheduled air transportation.

INFRASTRUCTURE
Transportation. The only regular access to Koyuk is by air, plus boats in summer and snowmachines in winter. Regular flight service from Nome and Unalakleet is available, the number of flights depending on the weather. There are no roads connecting Koyuk with other villages, although an 18-mile road to Six Mile Point is under construction. There is a state-owned 3,000- by 60-foot gravel runway, which was improved in the early 1990s. Supplies arrive in Nome and are lightered to shore. There is no dock in the village, although the city has requested funds for a small-boat harbor feasibility study.

Electricity. Electricity is provided by the Alaska Village Electrical Co-operative (AVEC), of which the city is a member, from a 771-kilowatt diesel plant. The generator was replaced in 1993.

Fuel storage (gallons). Koyuk Native Corporation (98,800); AVEC (71,250); Bering Straits Schools (65,500); City (16,000); Alaska Department of Transportation/Airport (3,000).

Water and waste systems. A piped water system serving most of the city's residents has been completed. A central watering point also exists. Funds have been requested to construct a new water plant. Water is chlorinated before delivery. A piped sewer system serving most of the city's residents has been completed. The school has requested funding to connect to the new sewer system. Some residents use honeybuckets or outhouses. The landfill was renovated in 2002.

Telecommunications. In-state telephone service is provided by Mukluk Telephone/TelAlaska, long distance service by AT&T Alascom, GCI, or Mukluk Telephone. GCI provides Internet services. Several AM radio stations broadcast to Koyuk from Nome and elsewhere. There are two locally broadcast television channels, from the Alaska Rural Communications Service and the city, and the city provides cable service.

COMMUNITY FACILITIES AND SERVICES
The city has a community hall and operates the water, sewer, and cable systems, the washeteria, refuse collection, and the landfill.

Education. The Koyuk-Malemute School serves 119 students in grades preschool through 12, with 10 teachers. It is operated by the Bering Straits School District. The School building was replaced in 2002. The city operates a public library.

Health care. Local health care is provided by the Koyuk Village Clinic, operated by Norton Sound Health Corporation. Emergency service is provided by a health aide. The nearest hospital is the Norton Sound Regional Hospital in Nome. In 2003, funding was approved for a new clinic.

Public safety. Law enforcement is provided by a state village public safety officer (VPSO) (position vacant as of August 2004), backed by state troopers in Nome. Emergency response is provided by the VPSO and the Koyuk Volunteer Fire Department. A fire equipment and storage facility was built in 2000, and equipment and training were upgraded in 2003.

Koyukuk

Total area of entitlement under ANCSA	
	91,900 acres
Total labor force	52
High school graduate or higher	43.9%
Bachelor's degree or higher	10.5%
Unemployment rate	23.1%
Per capita income *(1999)*	$11,341
Population *2000 census*	101
2003 population	111
state demographer estimate	
Percent Native *2000 census*	91.1%

LOCATION

Koyukuk is located on the Yukon River near the mouth of the Koyukuk River, 30 miles west of Galena and 290 air miles west of Fairbanks. It is adjacent to the Koyukuk National Wildlife Refuge and the Innoko National Wildlife Refuge.

PHYSICAL DESCRIPTION

The area encompasses 6.2 square miles of land and 0.1 square miles of water. The community has experienced severe flooding from both the Yukon and Koyukuk Rivers, and residents want to relocate. The Yukon River flood of 1963 rose to more than eight feet over much of the village.

CLIMATE

The area experiences a cold, continental climate with extreme temperature differences. The average daily high temperature during July is in the low 70s; the average daily low temperature during January ranges from below zero to 10°F. Sustained temperatures of -40°F are common during winter. Extreme temperatures have been measured from -64°F to 92°F. Average annual precipitation is 13 inches, with 60 inches of snowfall. The rivers are ice free from mid-May through mid-October.

CULTURE AND HISTORY

The Koyukon Athabascans traditionally had spring, summer, fall, and winter camps, and moved as the wild game migrated. Because of its prominent location at the confluence of the Koyukuk and Yukon Rivers, Athabaskan people have gathered at Koyukuk for hundreds of years. The Koyukon name for the village is *Meneelghaadze T'oh* (literally "the village at the base of Meneelghaadze bluff"). Friendships and trading between the Koyukon and Inupiat of the Kobuk area has occurred for generations. Residents are primarily Koyukon Athabascans with a subsistence lifestyle. Koyukuk is known for its hospitality, and has a tradition of many musicians, singers and songwriters. A smallpox epidemic, the first of several major epidemics, struck the Koyukon River valley in 1839. A military telegraph line was constructed along the north side of the Yukon around 1867, and Koyukuk became the site of a telegraph station. A trading post opened around 1880, just before the gold rush of 1884-85. The population of Koyukuk at this time was approximately 150. Missionary activity was intense along the Yukon, and a Roman Catholic mission and school opened downriver in Nulato in 1887. A measles epidemic and food shortages during 1900 tragically reduced the Native population by one-third. Gold seekers left the Yukon after 1906, but other mining activity, such as the Galena lead mines, began operating in 1919. The first school was constructed in 1939. After the school was built, families began to live at Koyukuk year-round. The city was incorporated in 1973. During 1987 and 1988 the village's old generator building was converted into the new Saint Patrick's Church (Roman Catholic). It replaced an earlier church that had been built between 1958 and 1962.

GOVERNMENT

The City of Koyukuk incorporated in 1973 as a second-class city. It is located in the Unorganized Borough. It has a seven-member city council, including the mayor who conducts day-to-day operations. The Koyukuk Native Village, also known as the Koyukuk Tribal Council, is a BIA-recognized traditional council, led by a first chief.

VILLAGE CORPORATION

Gana-A'Yoo Limited is the ANCSA village corporation for Koyukuk, Galena, Nulato and Kaltag. It was formed in 1978 by the consolidation of the four individual village corporations of those villages. A nine-member board of directors, elected from more than 1,150 shareholders, directs the management team responsible for day-to-day operations. It has two subsidiaries and a joint venture with over 300 employees nationwide and revenues in 2002 of over $4.6 million. Subsidiary Khotol Services Corporation is a §8(a) firm specializing in federal defense contracting. Yistletaw Properties, owns a minority interest in a hotel in Fairbanks. A joint venture with a subsidiary of the Compass Group, the largest foodservice company in the world, provides food service, catering, housekeeping, operations, and maintenance to remote camps in the interior of Alaska. Shareholders of Gana-A'Yoo Limited are also shareholders of Doyon, Limited, the regional Native corporation.

ECONOMY

Governments, the Native village, the clinic, the school, and the store provide the only year-round employment. Fire fighting, construction work, and other seasonal jobs often conflict with subsistence opportunities. Trapping and beadwork supplement incomes. Subsistence foods include salmon, whitefish, moose, waterfowl, and berries. Of the 40 employed residents, 21 work in education, health and social services, or public administration.

Fisheries. One resident holds a commercial salmon-fishing permit, but it was not used in 2003.

Government as employer. Twenty-nine of 40 employed residents work for the city, state, or federal government.

Services and retail. The city has one general store and one recreational rental shop.

Tourism and recreation. Accommodations for visitors are available at the school.

INFRASTRUCTURE

Transportation. The state-owned 2,645- by 60-foot lighted gravel runway provides year-round transportation. Evert Air Alaska, Frontier Flying Service, Larry's Flying Service, Ser-

Also known as
Meneelghaadze T'oh

[KOY-yuh-kuck]
Ethnicity: Koyukon Athabascan

Municipality
City of Koyukuk
P.O. Box 49
Koyukuk, AK 99754
907-927-2214
907-927-2215 Fax

Native entity
Koyukuk Native Village
P.O. Box 109
Koyukuk, AK 99754
907-927-2253
907-927-2220 Fax

ANCSA village corporation
Gana-A'Yoo Limited
3000 A Street, Suite 417
Anchorage, AK 99503
907-569-9599
907-569-9699 Fax
khotol.com

Koyukuk

Also known as
Meneelghaadze T'oh

vant Air, and Tanana Air Service serve Koyukuk. The runway was resurfaced in the early 1990s, and as of 2003 contracts had been let for $11 million in improvements. The river is heavily traveled when ice free, from mid-May through mid-October. Cargo is delivered by barge about four times each summer. Numerous local trails and winter trails to Chance and Nulato are used by residents. Snowmachines, all-terrain vehicles, and riverboats are used for local transportation.

Electricity. The city provides electricity from a 245-kilowatt diesel plant. Just under $2 million in improvements to the plant and distribution system were funded in 2003.

Fuel storage (gallons). City lease from Yukon Koyukuk School District (63,800); city fuel depot (20,400); Yukon Koyukuk Schools (10,800); Army National Guard (3,000); Alaska Department of Transportation (1,000).

Water and waste systems. The city provides treated well water at the washeteria. As of 2003, a water haul system was planned. Households are not plumbed, and residents use honeybuckets. As of May of 2003, seven households were on a new city-operated flush/haul system. The city operates a Class 3 landfill built in 1999-2001. As of 2003, the city planned to expand the flush/haul system to all homes.

Telecommunications. Local telephone service is provided by ACS of the Northland, long distance service by AT&T Alascom.

GCI provides Internet service at the school. At least one AM radio station broadcasts to the area, and one television channel is broadcast from an Alaska Rural Communication System repeater in the village.

COMMUNITY FACILITIES AND SERVICES
The city operates the washeteria and provides electricity, water and waste services, and fuel sales. The city office building serves as the community hall. In 2003, the city had proposed building a multipurpose building.

Education. Yukon-Koyukuk School District operates the Ella B. Vernetti School, serving 22 students in preschool through tenth grade with three teachers. The city operates a public library.

Health care. The Koyukuk Health Clinic is operated by the Tanana Chiefs Conference. Emergency service is provided by volunteers and a health aide. The Clinic is supported by a subregional clinic in Galena and the Chief Andrew Isaac Health Center located within Fairbanks Memorial Hospital.

Public safety. Law enforcement is provided by state troopers in Galena. Emergency services are provided by the city volunteer fire and EMS department.

ENVIRONMENTAL CONCERNS
The community has experienced severe flooding from both the Yukon and Koyukuk rivers, and residents want to relocate.

Kwethluk

[KWEETH-luk]
Ethnicity: Yup'ik

Municipality
City of Kwethluk
P.O. Box 50
Kwethluk, AK 99621
907-757-6022
907-757-6497 Fax

Native entity
Organized Village of Kwethluk
P.O. Box 129
Kwethluk, AK 99621-0129
907-757-6714
907-757-6328 Fax

ANCSA village corporation
Kwethluk Incorporated
P.O. Box 110
Kwethluk, AK 99621
907-757-6613
907-757-6212 Fax

Total area of entitlement under ANCSA
	138,240 acres
Total labor force	207
High school graduate or higher	43.8%
Bachelor's degree or higher	3.7%
Unemployment rate	15.5%
Per capita income *(1999)*	$6,503
Population *2000 census*	713
2003 population	730
state demographer estimate	
Percent Native *2000 census*	94.8%

LOCATION
This is a Yup'ik community located 12 air miles east of Bethel on the Kwethluk River at its junction with the Kuskokwim. The village is the second largest along the Lower Kuskokwim River, following Bethel. Travel time to Bethel is 30 minutes by boat in the summer and fall, 45 minutes by snow machine in the winter.

PHYSICAL DESCRIPTION
The city encompasses 10.3 square miles of land and 1.7 square miles of water-a rectangle four miles east-west by three miles north-south. The built-up area is centered about one and one-half miles east of the west boundary and one-half mile south of the north boundary, running east to west along the shore of the river. The terrain is flat, wet tundra. Flooding occurs from both ice-jams and high runoff levels annually, but rarely reaches any buildings. A flood in 1989 reached the school, and the 1972 flood may have been two feet higher.

CLIMATE
Kwethluk's annual precipitation averages 16 inches, including snowfall of 50 inches. Daily average temperatures in summer run from 42°F to 62°F, in winter from -2°F to 19°F. Extremes have been recorded from -46°F to 86°F. The Kuskokwim River is typically icefree from June through October.

CULTURE AND HISTORY
Kwethluk is a Yup'ik community that practices a subsistence lifestyle. Subsistence activities play a central role in the lifestyle; salmon, moose, and caribou are the staples of the diet. The Native language, Central Alaskan Yup'ik, lies geographically and linguistically between Alutiiq and Siberian Yupik. (The use of the apostrophe in Central Alaskan Yup'ik, as opposed to Siberian Yupik, denotes a long *p*.) The word (*Yup'ik* represents not only the language but also the name for the people themselves (*yuk* "person" plus *pik* "real".) For most of the residents, Yup'ik is their first language. The name Kwethluk is derived from *kwikli*, meaning "river."

Archaeological evidence from a nearby site indicates that the area has been occupied since prehistoric times. In the late 1800s, families from four villages on the Kwethluk River joined others living at the site. A measles epidemic struck in the late 1890s. The Moravian church built a chapel in 1896, followed by a Russian Orthodox church in 1912. Discovery of gold in nearby creeks in 1909 attracted prospectors to the area, but the finds proved disappointing, and most of the prospectors were gone by 1911. One placer deposit, discovered on the upper Kwethluk River was worked until World War II. A Moravian orphanage was established three miles upriver, and a BIA school was built in 1924. By 1939, the villagers owned 31,000 reindeer, used for food and skins. A tuberculosis epidemic at this time again reduced the population. A post office was established in 1947, and a Native-owned store opened in 1948. An airstrip was cleared in 1956. Snow machines replaced dog teams in the 1960s as the principal form of winter transportation. The city incorporated in 1975.

GOVERNMENT
Kwethluk incorporated in 1975. It is governed by a seven-member city council, including the mayor, with a city manager to run day-to-day operations. The city levies a 5 percent local sales tax. The Organized Village of Kwethluk is a BIA-recog-

nized IRA council, and also serves as the Public Law 93-638 tribal government contractor.

VILLAGE CORPORATION
Kwethluk Incorporated is the ANCSA village corporation. A subsidiary provides electricity for the village. Its shareholders are also shareholders in Calista Corporation, the regional Native corporation.

ECONOMY
The largest employers are the school district, village corporation, store, and health clinic. Seal meat and seal oil are obtained in trade with coastal relatives and neighbors. Most families travel to fish camps each summer. More than 70 percent of employed residents work in educational, health, social services, or public administration.

Fisheries. In 2003, 53 residents held commercial fishing permits, but only 31 used them. Gross earnings in 2002 from salmon alone were $12,852, in 2003, $37,176. Subsistence fishing is much more important. A 1986 study found that during the summer, nearly 50 percent of Kwethluk households moved to 52 different fish camps, and many other households helped in fish camps as fishermen or processors. Most fish camps were operating by mid-June, and by mid-July most Chinook salmon fishing was completed. Most of the fish camps are located within eight river miles of the village, and include cabins, fish and net drying racks, and steam baths. Fish camps are used consistently by the same families, some for more than fifty years, although relocation may be required by changes in the river. The fishing areas are near the fish camps on the Kuskokwim and Kwethluk rivers and Kuskokuak Slough.

Government as employer. The city, state, or federal governments employ 95 residents.

Services and retail. Kwethluk boasts three general stores, a video store, a limited-service restaurant, and a religious bookstore.

Transportation. One taxicab company operates in the community, and two shipping agents support the airport.

Tourism and recreation. Accommodations are available at the School and the IRA Council Office Building.

INFRASTRUCTURE
Transportation. Local travel is by snowmachine, all-terrain vehicle, or skiff. The river becomes an ice road in the winter, and winter trails are marked to Eek, Three Step Mountain, and Columbia Creek. A single gravel road runs the east-west length of the village. In the late 1990s and the first decade of the twenty-first century, access roads to the landfill, clinic, and airport were built. Year-around access is by air, using a state-owned 1,750- by 35-foot gravel airstrip or a seaplane base. Arctic Circle Air Service, Grant Aviation, and Hageland Aviation serve Kwethluk. A new airport was under construction in the early and middle years of the fist decade of the twenty-first century. Barge services deliver cargo during the summer. There are no docking facilities.

Electricity. Electricity is provided by Kuiggluum Kallugvia, a subsidiary of the village corporation, from a 707-kilowatt diesel plant.

Fuel storage (gallons). Kwethluk Incorporated (89,707); Lower Kuskokwim Schools (71,790); city (17,000); Kuiggluum Kallugvia (25,000); Army National Guard (5,250).

Water and waste system. The joint City-Village Kwethluk Utilities Commission operates the water supply system. Residents haul water for household use. None of the homes had complete plumbing before about 2004. The school and teachers' housing have their own systems. The washeteria and water treatment plant were rehabilitated in the late 1990s, and a new water treatment plant was under construction in 2002 as part of a new $16 million piped water and sewer system serving the entire community.

The joint City-Village Kwethluk Utilities Commission operates the waste disposal systems. None of the homes had complete plumbing before almost 2004. The School and teachers' housing have their own systems. Until they are connected to the new $16 million piped water and sewer system, residents use outhouses or honeybuckets emptied into sewage container disposal bins which are then hauled to the sewage lagoon. The Commission also operates a Class 3 landfill.

Telecommunications. Local telephone service is provided by United Utilities, long distance service by AT&T Alascom or United Utilities. United Utilities also makes Internet service available through Unicom. GCI provides Internet service to the school. Thirteen AM radio stations broadcast to the Kwethluk area. KYUK-TV, Native public television, broadcasts to Kwethluk from Bethel, and the Alaska Rural Communications System broadcasts two channels from a repeater located in Kwethluk.

COMMUNITY FACILITIES AND SERVICES
In addition to the Council Office Building, which serves as a community hall, there is a public safety building and a community learning and activity center. Preliminary work on a new community center is complete, and a multipurpose building has been proposed. The city and village have formed a joint Kwethluk Utilities Commission to provide water supply, waste disposal, and washeteria services. The city provides a manager for the airport. Law enforcement is performed by the state village public safety officer (VPSO) and the city police department, backed by state troopers in Bethel. Emergency response is provided by the VPSO and the city volunteer fire department.

Education. The Lower Kuskokwim School District operates Ket'achik Aap'alluk Memorial School, serving 220 students in grades K—12 with 15 teachers. The school has its own Web site. Students are taught in Yup'ik through third grade. The state has proposed a $16 million renovation and addition to the school building for fiscal year 2005. The school library serves as the community's public library.

Health care. The Sarah S. Nicholai Memorial Health Clinic, operated by Yukon Kuskokwim Health Corporation, was built in the 1990s. Emergency service is provided by a health aide. The nearest hospital is Yukon Kuskokwim Delta Regional Hospital in Bethel.

Kwigillingok

[kwih-GILL-in-gawk]
Ethnicity: Yup'ik

Native entity
Native Village of Kwigillingok
P.O. Box 49
Kwigillingok, AK 99622-0049
907-588-8626
907-588-8429 Fax

ANCSA village corporation
Kwik Incorporated
P.O. Box 50
Kwigillingok, AK 99622
907-588-8112
907-588-8313 Fax

Total area of entitlement under ANCSA	115,194 acres
Total labor force	109
High school graduate or higher	46.7%
Bachelor's degree or higher	5.3%
Unemployment rate	28.4%
Per capita income *(1999)*	$7,577
Population *2000 census*	338
2003 population	343
state demographer estimate	
Percent Native *2000 census*	97.9%

LOCATION
Kwigillingok is on the western shore of Kuskokwim Bay near the mouth of the Kuskokwim River. It lies 77 miles southwest of Bethel and 388 miles west of Anchorage. Kipnuk, 60.5 miles away, is the next village on the coast to the west; Kongiganak, 19.5 miles away, is the next village on the coast to the east.

PHYSICAL DESCRIPTION
Kwigillingok encompasses 20.2 square miles of land and 0.1 square mile of water. It lies on rolling, wet tundra. The terrain underneath and around the village is flat—there are no mountains, hills, or trees. It is stretched out from east to west. There are boardwalks through the village that were floated by high water during a major coastal storm in 1979. The fuel storage area was also flooded. Koniganak, the nearest village, can be seen with the naked eye on clear days. The road from the airport to the post office is the only one in the village, and it is part gravel, part mud. There are about a hundred houses in Kwigillingok, most unique in design and painted different colors.

CLIMATE
Kwigillingok is located in a marine climate. Annual precipitation averages 22 inches, with 43 inches of snowfall. Average daily summer temperatures range from 41°F to 57°F, average daily winter temperatures from 6°F to 24°F.

CULTURE AND HISTORY
Kwigillingok is a traditional Yup'ik village, practicing a commercial fishing and subsistence lifestyle. The first language of most residents is Central Alaskan Yup'ik, which lies geographically and linguistically between Alutiiq and Siberian Yupik. The use of the apostrophe in Central Alaskan Yup'ik, as opposed to Siberian Yupik, denotes a long *p*. The word *Yup'ik* represents not only the language but also the name for the people themselves (*yuk* "person" plus *pik* "real"). The area has long been occupied by the Yup'ik. A Moravian church was established around 1920.

GOVERNMENT
Kwigillingok is unincorporated and located in the Unorganized Borough. It is governed by the Native Village of Kwigillingok, a BIA-recognized IRA council.

VILLAGE CORPORATION
Kwik Incorporated is the ANCSA village corporation. It operates a general store and a gas station and provides cable television service to the village. Shareholders in the village corporation are also shareholders in Calista Corporation, the regional Native corporation.

INFRASTRUCTURE
Electricity. Electricity is provided by Kwig Power Company, owned by the village council, from a 500-kilowatt diesel plant.

The distribution system was upgraded in 1995-96 and the plant itself in 2002-03.

Fuel storage (gallons). Kwik Incorporated (166,900); Lower Kuskokwim Schools (112,500); Army National Guard (4,300); village council (3,000).

Water and waste systems. Water is currently derived from snow melt held in a reservoir, filtered and chlorinated in a new (2002) treatment plant, and hauled to residents. This community water system is operated by the village council. The school operates its own surface water treatment facility. Most homes are not plumbed. Actions are underway to develop a piped water supply system. Honeybuckets are disposed of by residents in pits maintained by the village council, although preliminary actions were funded in 2003 for a flush/haul system. The school shares a sewage lagoon with the washeteria. The village council also operates a Class 3 landfill established in 1999.

Transportation. Except for the gravel road between the airport and the post office, there are no roads in or to Kwigillingok. Boardwalks serve as walkways within the village. Most travel to and from the village is done by aircraft, four-wheel-drive vehicle, boat, or snowmobile. There are winter trails to Kongiganak and Kipnuk, the next villages along the coast in each direction. The state-owned 2,510- by 60-foot gravel airstrip and a seaplane base are available, and significant improvements were planned in 2004. Servicing airlines include Arctic Circle Air Service, Era Aviation, Grant Aviation, Hageland Aviation, Inland Aviation Services, and Yute Air. There are no docking facilities, although a number of residents have fishing boats or skiffs for travel to Bethel and area villages. Snowmachines and all-terrain vehicles are used in winter.

Telecommunications. Local telephone service is provided by United Utilities, long distance service by AT&T Alascom or United Utilities. Internet service is available at the School from GCI. Thirteen AM radio stations broadcast to the area from Bethel, Nome, Dillingham, Anchorage, and elsewhere. The Alaska Rural Communications System broadcasts two television channels from a repeater in Kwigillingok, and Kwik Incorporated provides cable service.

ECONOMY
Most employment in Kwigillingok is with the school, village government, stores, or commercial fishing. Income is supplemented by subsistence activities. A regional arts and crafts cooperative markets local handicrafts; the village would like to expand this program. Educational, health, and social services, and public administration employ almost 60 percent of the work force.

Fisheries. While 22 residents held commercial fishing permits (mostly for salmon) in 2003, only four actually engaged in commercial fishing, with gross earnings of $24,691.

Government as employer. Sixty residents work for the village, state, or federal government.

Manufacturing. Cottage industry handicrafts are supported by a regional arts and crafts marketing program.

Services and retail. Two general stores, one owned by the village corporation and the other privately owned, are fairly well stocked. The village corporation store also has a gas station. There are two other retailers and a firm offering educational services.

Transportation. One commercial warehouse supports the airfield.

COMMUNITY FACILITIES AND SERVICES
The village has a community hall and operates the utility systems except for cable television, which is provided by the village corporation, and other telecommunications services

Education. The Lower Kuskokwim School District operates the Kwigillingok School, serving 110 students in grades K-12 with eight teachers. The school has its own Web site ("under construction" as of September 2004). The school is located on one end of the village, so students and staff living at the other end have a long commute. The village and the school district have asked for more than $12 million in improvements beginning in 2005. The school library serves as the community's public library.

Health care. The Yukon Kuskokwim Health Corporation operates the Kwigillingok Health Clinic. Emergency service is provided by a health aide. The nearest hospital is the Yukon Kuskokwim Delta Regional Hospital in Bethel.

Public safety. Law enforcement services are provided by a state village public safety officer (VPSO) and a village police department, backed by state troopers in Bethel. Emergency response is provided by the state VPSO and the village volunteer fire department.

Kwigillingok

Kwinhagak

Kwinhagak

Total area of entitlement under ANCSA	
	115,030 acres
Total labor force	150
High school graduate or higher	40.4%
Bachelor's degree or higher	4.1%
Unemployment rate	15.3%
Per capita income *(1999)*	$8,127
Population *2000 census*	555
2003 population	579
state demographer estimate	
Percent Native *2000 census*	97.3%

LOCATION
Kwinhagak is on the Kanektok *(Qanirtuuq)* River, less than a mile from the east shore of Kuskokwim Bay. It is 71 miles south-southwest of Bethel, a community of 5,000 which serves as the air transportation hub for the region, and 400 miles west of Anchorage. It is 39 miles from Goodnews Bay, the next coastal community to the south, and 39 miles from Eek, the next coastal community to the north.

PHYSICAL DESCRIPTION
The village includes 4.7 square miles of land and 0.6 square mile of water. Spring ice breakup generally does not cause flooding, but the Kanektok River rises significantly three to four weeks after spring breakup, due to snow melt in the mountains. This rise may flood the airport road.

CLIMATE
Quinhagak is located in a marine climate. Annual precipitation averages 22 inches, with 43 inches of snowfall. Summer average daily temperatures range from 41°F to 57°F, and winter average daily temperatures range from 6°F to 24°F. However, extremes have been measured from -34°F to 82°F.

CULTURE AND HISTORY
The population of the community is primarily Yup'ik Eskimo. The Yup'ik name is *Kuinerraq*, meaning "new river channel." Kwinhagak is a long-established village dating back to AD 1,000. It was the first village on the lower Kuskokwim to have continuing contact with Europeans. The village appeared on a map in 1826. After the purchase of Alaska by the United States in 1867, the Alaska Commercial Company sent annual supply ships to Kwinhagak with goods for Kuskokwim River trading posts. In 1904 a mission store opened, followed by a post office in 1905 and a school in 1909. In 1915 the Kuskokwim River was charted, so goods were barged directly upriver to Bethel. In 1928 the first electric plant opened; the first mail plane arrived in 1934. The city was incorporated in

1975. A Moravian mission was built in 1893, and its church remains the only religious facility in the community. Many if not most of the people in the community are members of this church.

GOVERNMENT
The City of Quinhagak was incorporated as a second-class city in 1975 and is located in the Unorganized Borough. The Native Village of Kwinhagak is the federally recognized Native entity, organized under the IRA. Its charter, constitution, and bylaws were approved by the BIA in 1948. At the time this profile was written, the same person was president of the village council and chairman of Qanirtuuq, Incorporated, the ANCSA village corporation. The city appears to be relatively unimportant, as municipal services are provided by the village under an agreement with the city.

Tribal court. The Kwinhagak Tribal Court was formed several years ago to help address alcohol as the number one problem in the village. The court consists of a chief justice and an alternate justice, along with three elders and two alternate elders, all elected at a general village meeting. The chief justice presides and administers the court. The first chief justice had been the state magistrate at Kwinhagak for eight years until the magistrate position was discontinued. The court handled 281 cases in 1997 (including 114 curfew, 104 alcohol, 13 minor consuming alcohol, 12 disturbing the peace, 9 civil, and 29 other cases), and 112 cases in 1998. The court has jurisdiction over violations of village (tribal) ordinances and civil matters arising under village ordinances. The court screens the cases and refers appropriate cases to state courts or youth services. At a hearing, the offender, the police officer, and the judges talk about what happened, and the Court imposes an appropriate penalty—warning, community service, fine, jail time. In an unusual case, the court imposed banishment on a village member who persisted in bringing alcohol to the community. Each time he did so, the community had more domestic violence and accidents. After a year of exile, his family asked that he be allowed to return. This was allowed on condition of further community service, and he has not been in trouble since.

VILLAGE CORPORATION
The ANCSA village corporation is Qanirtuuq, Incorporated. In addition to owning the larger general store and the hardware store, it owns Kanektok River Safaris, a sportfishing guide service on the Kanektok River. Shareholders in Qanirtuuq, Incorporated, are also shareholders in Calista Corporation, the regional Native corporation.

Also known as Quinhagak

[KWI-nuh-gak or QUINN-uh-hawk] Ethnicity: Yup'ik

Municipality
City of Quinhagak
P.O. Box 90
Quinhagak, AK 99655
  907-556-8202
  907-556-8166 Fax

Native entity
Native Village of Kwinhagak
P.O. Box 149
Quinhagak, AK 99655
  907-556-8165
  907-556-8166 Fax

ANCSA village corporation
Qanirtuuq, Incorporated
P.O. Box 69
Quinhagak, AK 99655
  907-556-8289
  907-556-8814 Fax

Kwinhagak

Also known as Quinhagak

Ownership of the land along the nearby Arolik River, a prized sport fishing venue, is in dispute between state and federal land managers. The Bureau of Land Management determined that portions of the Arolik River were non-navigable and conveyed the shorelands to Quanirtuuq, Incorporated, as part of its ANCSA entitlement. However, the State of Alaska asserts that the river is navigable, and therefore it received title to the river under the Alaska Statehood Act of 1958 and title to submerged lands under the U.S. Submerged Lands Act of 1953. The State of Alaska asserts that those shorelands that BLM conveyed to Quanirtuuq were not in federal ownership and not under BLM authority to convey. The question most likely will be decided by the courts. Quanirtuuq is actively enforcing its claim against those who touch land along the river without village permission.

ECONOMY

Most employment is with the school, various levels of government, and commercial fishing. Income is also earned from trapping, basket weaving, skin sewing, and ivory carving. Subsistence remains an important part of the livelihood; seal and salmon are staples of the diet.

Fisheries. Between 80 and 100 residents hold commercial fishing permits for salmon net and herring roe fisheries. The commercial fishermen have organized themselves to improve market conditions and stabilize prices.

The Village owns a fish processing facility for halibut and salmon, operated by Coastal Villages Seafoods, a subsidiary of the Coastal Villages Region Fund. The plant was built in 1992 with federal and state grants. By 2000 production had reached more than 400,000 pounds, producing high-quality headed and gutted and filleted fish, and paying relatively high prices to local fishermen. Fish are flown in wetlock boxes to Bethel and then on to Anchorage and the Lower 48. During the 2000 season the plant employed about 40 people, including workers from other villages in the area. Since 2000 the operator has made substantial investments in equipment and employee facilities to expand production. The plant benefits from the high quality of fish caught in ocean bright condition nearby and consistent fishery openings over the season. The cost of flying out the processed fish is a continuing problem.

Government as employer. Government at various levels together constitutes the largest employer in Quinhagak. These include the school, the city and the village, the village and regional ANCSA corporations, and state and federal units.

Services and retail. There are several other businesses operating in Kwinhagak, some privately owned and some owned by the village or the ANCSA village corporation. Privately owned businesses include a general store, a fishing guide and tour service owned by the village corporation, and a video store. The village corporation operates a general store and a hardware store. Many people rely on telephone, mail, and Internet ordering for much of their shopping.

Tourism and recreation. Tourism is not yet important to the local economy, but it is growing. Fishing (salmon, rainbow trout, and char) and river float trips are the main visitor attractions. Efforts have been made to promote sportfishing guide service Kanektok River Safaris, (a subsidiary of Quanirtuuq, Inc.). Together with subsidiaries of two other ANCSA corporations, Kanektok River Safaris, is developing the recreational potential of the Arolik River, a prized sport fishing venue, which runs within six kilometers of Kwinhagak. As for visitor accommodations, two rooms above the water treatment plant are available through the village office at $75 per night.

INFRASTRUCTURE

Transportation. Kwinhagak is not accessible by road or rail, relying on air transportation for passenger, mail, and cargo service. Fish are exported by air, although a harbor and dock were recently completed and barges deliver heavy goods at least twice a year. Floatplanes land on the Kanektok River, but most air traffic uses the Quinhagak Airport. The existing 2,600- by 60-foot gravel airstrip is subject to flooding and undermining by erosion. A new airstrip, when complete, will be long enough to permit direct flights to Anchorage. As of 2004, the airport had no aircraft servicing capabilities. Airline services are provided by Arctic Circle Air Service, Era Aviation, Grant Aviation, Hageland Aviation, Inland Aviation Services, and Yute Air. Boats, all-terrain vehicles, snow machines, and some automobiles are used for local transportation. Winter trails are marked to Eek (39 miles) and Goodnews Bay (39 miles). Recent government-funded capital projects include relocation of the airport, winter trail marking, harbor pre-construction, and four miles of local road improvements

Electricity. Electricity is provided by Alaska Village Electrical Co-operative (AVEC), a Rural Electric Association co-op of which the city is a member. It runs a 633-kilowatt diesel plant.

Fuel storage (gallons). Qanirtuuq Store (145,200); AVEC (104,300); village (43,700); Lower Kuskokwim Schools (42,200); city (12,900); A&C Market (9,600); Army National Guard (4,500); Moravian church (3,700).

Water and waste supply. Water is derived from a well near the Kanektok River. The water treatment plant, storage tank, and waterline were relocated in 1997 as part of a new flush/haul system for the community. The school and washeteria are connected directly to the water plant. Many households still haul water. Many households still use honeybuckets or septic tanks, and funds have been requested to expand the flush/haul system. Recent government-funded capital projects include sanitation improvements.

Telecommunications. Local telephone service is provided by United Utilities, long distance by AT&T Alascom or United Utilities. GCI provides Internet service to the school. Television service is available by satellite (Dish Network), and an Alaska Rural Communications System repeater located in the village broadcasts two channels. Thirteen AM radio stations from Bethel, Nome, Dillingham, Anchorage, and other locations broadcast to the area.

COMMUNITY FACILITIES AND SERVICES

All services are provided by the Native Village of Kwinhagak, under agreement with the city. An old BIA building has been renovated as a new washeteria and health clinic. Recent government-funded capital projects include sanitation improvements, small business development assistance, a youth center and multipurpose facility (mental health counseling, elder services office, health education and youth activities program area, a community resources room, and kitchen), relocation of the airport, winter trail marking, housing administration, operating and construction (HUD Indian Housing Block Grant funding), harbor pre-construction, Headstart building, the fish processing plant, four miles of local road improvements, and the washeteria and health clinic. Law enforcement is provided by tribal police. The nearest state troopers are in Bethel. Emergency response is provided by the Quinhagak EMS Quick Response Team.

Education. Kwinhagak has one school covering grades K-12, Kuinerrmiut Elitnaurviat, operated by the Lower Kuskokwim School District, with approximately 150 students and 12 teachers. The school provides a bilingual education program, with only one hour each day of instruction in English and the balance in Yup'ik in grades K-4, with the proportions reversed in grades 5-12. Traditional Yup'ik literature and skills are taught in standards-based instruction, often by tribal elders. The school has a computer center with Internet access and its own Web site. It also has a pool and provides the public library for the community.

Health care. The village, under an agreement with the Yukon-Kuskokwim Health Corporation, operates the Quinhagak Clinic, which is backed up by the Quinhagak EMS Quick Response Team. The nearest hospital is the Yukon Kuskokwim Delta Regional Hospital in Bethel.

Larsen Bay

Total area of entitlement under ANCSA
115,200 acres

Total labor force	39
High school graduate or higher	22
Bachelor's degree or higher	9
Unemployment rate	10.3%
Per capita income (1999)	$16,227
2003 population	96
state demographer estimate	
Population 2000 census	115
Percent Native 2000 census	79.1%

LOCATION
The City of Larsen Bay is located on Larsen Bay on the northwest coast of Kodiak Island. It is 60 miles southwest of the City of Kodiak and 283 miles southwest of Anchorage. The village is located where Larsen Bay joins Uyak Bay.

PHYSICAL DESCRIPTION
The area encompasses 5.4 square miles of land and 2.2 square miles of water. It is built on Cretaceous and Upper Jurassic rock, almost on top of a major fault line. Moist or wet tundra vegetation types predominate. Harbor seals enjoy Larsen and Uyak Bays. Larsen Bay is on Seldovia tides, with a maximum tidal range of approximately 14.9 feet. There has been no known flooding in the city itself. Minor mudslides have been observed in the hill area near the hydroelectric plant but do not threaten populated areas. Significant coastal erosion has occurred in several places in Larsen Bay, primarily along the shoreline adjacent to the town. The erosion has the potential to harm residential and commercial development as well as municipal buildings and roads in a few places. Larsen Bay's water supply is fed from deeper in the interior of the island, where thawing snow in the mountains provides a fairly reliable water source. However, water supply to many local homes may be blocked by extremely cold weather, when water pipes may freeze. The most serious threat posed by drought in Larsen Bay is the disruption of hydroelectric power. However, the city also has a backup diesel generator to help such a situation. Kodiak Island and surrounding areas experience frequent earthquakes with magnitudes of under 6.0 on the Richter scale. Since 1899, 82 earthquakes of Richter magnitude 6.0 or greater have been recorded in the area, and 26 of these were actually triggered within the area. The 1964 Alaska earthquake and resultant tsunami provide a recent example of the threat posed by earthquake activity near the city. Although Larsen Bay survived the earthquake and tsunami undamaged, long-term damage to waterfront facilities occurred as a result of tectonic subsidence. The amount of subsidence caused by the 1964 earthquake has been estimated at two to four feet, causing flooding and inundation of low-lying coastal areas. Although the forest lands in the area are small compared to other parts of Alaska, fires have occurred in Larsen Bay and have threatened populated areas. In 1912, the Kodiak region was blanketed in volcanic ash from the Katmai/Novarupta eruption on the Katmai Coast.

CLIMATE
The climate of the Kodiak Islands is dominated by a strong marine influence. There is little or no freezing weather, moderate precipitation, and frequent cloud cover and fog. Severe storms are common from December through February. Annual precipitation is 23 inches. Temperatures remain within a narrow range, from 32ºF to 62ºF. There are no regular occurrences of severe weather such as typhoons or tornadoes in Larsen Bay; however, weather extremes such as high winds, large hail, and heavy rainfall threaten the area. Winds in excess of 50 miles per hour occur occasionally, and wind gusts may reach speeds of 90 miles per hour or more. Freezing rain, occasional heavy snowfall, and high winds are the dominant winter weather hazards that affect the area. Periods of extreme cold occur on a less frequent basis.

CULTURE AND HISTORY
Larsen Bay is a traditional Alutiiq settlement practicing a commercial fishing and subsistence lifestyle. The area is thought to have been inhabited for at least 2,000 years. Hundreds of artifacts have been uncovered in the area. Russian fur traders frequented the island in the mid-1700s. The bay was named for Peter Larsen, an Unga Island furrier, hunter, and guide. In the early 1800s, there was a tannery in nearby Uyak Bay. Alaska Packers Association built a cannery in the village in 1911 which is still in operation.

GOVERNMENT
Larsen Bay was incorporated as a second-class city in 1974. It is located in the Kodiak Island Borough. It has a mayor and city council. The Native Village of Larsen Bay is a federally recognized traditional council. It is also a Public Law 93-638 tribal government contractor.

VILLAGE CORPORATION
In 1980 the village corporation, Anton Larsen, Inc., merged into the Koniag regional Native corporation (*see Alaska introduction*).

ECONOMY
The economy of Larsen Bay is primarily based on fishing, commerce, subsistence, and sport. Seventeen residents hold commercial fishing permits. In the summer months when the Kodiak Salmon Packers cannery is operating, an additional 200 to 300 people live and work at the cannery. However, the salmon markets fluctuate dramatically from year to year, and the cannery did not operate during the 2002 season. There are very few year-round employment positions other than government service. A large majority of the population depends on subsistence activities. Salmon, halibut, seal, sea lion, clams, crab, and deer are caught. Most private businesses support tourism, including lodging (six), outfitting (two), and guide services (five), all of which are seasonal. Larsen Bay has one small grocery store operated by Kodiak Salmon Packers. Store hours vary, and it is only open during the summer months when the cannery is active. There are no restaurants, but there is a dining facility at the cannery to feed workers when the cannery is active.

[LAR-sun]
Ethnicity: Alutiiq

Municipality
City of Larsen Bay
P.O. Box 8
Larsen Bay, AK 99624-0008
907-847-2211
907-847-2239 Fax

Native entity
Native Village of Larsen Bay
P.O. Box 35
Larsen Bay, AK 99624
907-847-2207
907-847-2270 Fax

ANCSA regional corporation
Koniag, Incorporated
202 Center Ave., Suite 201
Kodiak, AK 99615
907-486-2530
800-658-3818
907-486-3325 Fax

Larsen Bay

Lesoni
See Zero Population Section

See Zero Population Section

Government as employer. Twenty-one residents are employed by the city, borough, state, or federal government.

INFRASTRUCTURE

Transportation. Larsen Bay is accessible by air and by water. Access to Larsen Bay is always weather dependent. Regular Island Air Service and charter flights are available from Kodiak. There is a state-owned, lighted 2,700- by 75-foot gravel airstrip and a seaplane base. There is no regular commercial ferry service to Larsen Bay. There are private docking facilities available at the cannery able to accommodate fairly large vessels, with a dock approximately 1000 feet long. A new breakwater and boat harbor were completed in the fall of 2002. A cargo barge arrives every six weeks from Seattle. The road system in Larsen Bay is limited to gravel roads and paths. There are some vehicles (fewer than 50) and also 40-60 ATVs in the community.

Electricity is provided by the city-run Larsen Bay Utility Company by means of a state-owned hydroelectric plant with a 475-kilowatt capacity diesel backup. There is also backup electrical generation capacity at the school.

Fuel storage (gallons). Kodiak Salmon Packers (128,900); City (75,400).

Water and waste systems. Water and sewer services are provided by the city. Water is supplied by two groundwater sources—a gravity feed from the Trout Creek hydroelectric plant and a backup well—and stored in a 200,000-gallon steel tank. A water supply line is connected to the hydroelectric plant and used to reduce utility expenses to both the service plant and the customers. All 40 homes are connected to the piped water system. During especially cold winters, Larsen Bay has had freezing problems with the water supply. A community septic tank with outfall line serves approximately half of the homes, and the rest are on individual septic systems. Weekly refuse collection service is provided.

Telecommunications. Local telephone service is provided by ACS of the Northland, long distance by AT&T Alascom. There are telephones in most homes, and thirteen long distance trunks serve the community. Telephone service in Larsen Bay is dependent upon electrical supply. Without electricity, the phones would cease working after one or two days of running on battery power. Starband provides Internet service. One FM radio station broadcasts to the Larsen Bay area, and the Alaska Rural Communications Service provides television. As of 2003, the community did not have cable access. Many residents have CB radios, and some have VHF marine radios, although these cannot reach Kodiak. There is a single side band (SSB) radio at the clinic, but as of 1999 it was not reliable. Therefore, in a major emergency where telephone service and electric power are down, Larsen Bay would be unable to communicate with Kodiak.

COMMUNITY FACILITIES AND SERVICES

Education. The Larsen Bay School has 25 students in grades K-12, and three teachers. It is operated by the Kodiak Island Borough Schools. While the school has a library, there is no public library in the community.

Health care. The Larsen Bay Clinic is owned by the village council and operated by the Kodiak Area Native Association. It provides basic health care and emergency medical services to the community. There are no doctors or registered nurses in Larsen Bay, so most health care is provided by EMT- or ETT-trained personnel supported by doctors from the Kodiak Area Native Association. Seriously injured or ill patients are evacuated to a hospital in Kodiak or Anchorage. Larsen Bay does not have an ambulance but the community would like to get one. The clinic is stocked with a diverse collection of medical equipment and supplies and can handle initial medical response to almost any kind of emergency.

Public safety. Law enforcement is provided by the village public safety officer in residence, backed by state troopers in Kodiak. Emergency response is provided by the Larsen Bay Volunteer Fire Department. Larsen Bay has a fire truck with a 1,000-gallon capacity. The fire truck also has a siren, which is presently the only means for alert and warning in the community.

Levelock

[LEEV-lock]
Ethnicity: Yup'ik, Unangan, Athabascan

Native entity
Levelock Village
P.O. Box 70
Levelock, AK 99625
  907-287-3030
  907-287-3032 Fax

ANCSA village corporation
Levelock Natives Limited
P.O. Box 109
Levelock, AK 99625
  907-287-3040
  907-287-3022 Fax

Total area of entitlement under ANCSA
	96,771 acres
Total labor force	34
High school graduate or higher	25
Bachelor's degree or higher	3
Unemployment rate	0.0%
Per capita income *(1999)*	$12,199
2003 population	71
state demographer estimate	
Population *2000 census*	122
Percent Native *2000 census*	95.1%

LOCATION
Levelock is situated on the west bank of the Kvichak River, 35 miles northwest of King Salmon, in the Bristol Bay region of Southwest Alaska. Anchorage is 278 air miles to the northeast, and Dillingham is 56 miles to the west.

CLIMATE
The climate in Levelock is strongly influenced by its proximity to the Bering Sea and summertime easterly winds. Fog and low-lying coastal clouds are common in the summer, when temperatures average between 30°F and 66°F. In the winter, weather patterns are chiefly affected by continental patterns bringing cold temperatures on northerly winds; temperatures in the winter average between 4°F and 30°F, keeping the Kvichak River frozen over from November until June. The area receives approximately 26 inches of precipitation every year, a figure which includes an average 70 inches of snow. The region experiences approximately 19 hours of daylight in June, declining to 13 by September. Daylight hours in winter do not go below 8 hours.

PHYSICAL DESCRIPTION
Encompassing 14.5 square miles of land, the terrain surrounding the village consists of flat tundra with some small spruce and birch trees. The geology of the area around Levelock is glacial moraine and drift. The vegetation is moist tundra. The village is on the boundary between high-(to the south) and medium-(to the north) density waterfowl areas, and the Kvichak River is a major anadromous fish stream.

CULTURE AND HISTORY
Levelock is a village of Yup'ik, Unangan, and Athabascan peoples, whose commercial fishing and subsistence activities are the focus of the community. The people harvest salmon, trout, moose, caribou, and berries and share communally with one another for the benefit of all. Native languages are used.

Early Russian explorers reported the existence of a village named Kvichak at the present-day location of Levelock. Like other nineteenth century native villages, in 1837 the population was reduced to half its number by the smallpox epidemic that swept through what we now refer to as the Bristol Bay region of Alaska. By the 1890 census, the village was mentioned again, but no measure of population was taken at that time. The population was further reduced by the measles epidemic of 1900 but still existed (although renamed "Levelock's Mission") as of 1908, when a survey of Russian missions was made. The 1918-1919 worldwide flu epidemic found its way to Levelock, but still the village rebounded and rebuilt. By 1925, a fish cannery had begun operating in Levelock, and although it burned in 1930, a second cannery was built within three years. Many of the village homes were converted to fuel oil heat, and by 1930 the first school was built. A post office was established in 1939, and yet another cannery was in operation by the 1950s.

The people of Levelock depended on snow shoes and then snowmobiles for transportation until the 1990s, when many village improvements, including year-round roads, a 110-foot unloading dock at the beach area of the Kvichak River, and an airstrip, were added. Now bulk goods can be delivered by air transport and river barge. Economic development initiatives since 1997 have permitted the village to add additional village amenities, upgrade village facilities and infrastructure, build new housing, and improve village streets and access roads.

GOVERNMENT
The five-member traditional Levelock Village Council serves as the local government. The council is also recognized by the Bureau of Indian Affairs as the local tribal governing body.

VILLAGE CORPORATION
Levelock Natives Limited is the ANCSA village corporation. Its shareholders are also shareholders in Bristol Bay Native Corporation.

ECONOMY
Commercial fishing remains the economic focus of village life outside subsistence activities.

Fisheries. In the 2000 census, 15 residents held commercial fishing permits, but most residents travel to Naknek to fish or work in the canneries during the summer season. There is a 2 percent raw fish tax. Consideration for development of a fish-processing plant at Levelock was initiated in 2003 when a feasibility study was funded by the Alaska Department of Community and Economic Development.

Government as employer. The borough, state, and federal governments employed 25 people in Levelock in the 2000 census.

Manufacturing. The manufacture and marketing of traditional apparel continues.

Services and retail. Businesses include Auvie's Video Rental, G.T. Repair, Gram's House, and the N and B Variety Store.

Tourism and recreation. Major tourist attractions in a hundred-mile radius of Levelock include: Yukon Delta National Wildlife Refuge, Lake Clark National Park and Preserve, Katmai National Park and Preserve, Becharof National Wildlife Refuge, Kodiak Island National Wildlife Refuge, Aniakchak National Monument and Preserve, and Alaska Peninsula National Wildlife Refuge. A 6 percent accommodations tax is collected from guests staying at Levelock Natives Limited Lodging and five other area facilities.

INFRASTRUCTURE
Transportation. Levelock is most easily accessible by air and water, especially in winter. However, with completion of the Williamsport Pile Bay Road, commerce among communities has increased. The Bureau of Indian Affairs funded upgrading and improving village streets in 2002 and in that same year there were two other roads under construction, the Igiugug Road and the Levelock-Aleknagik Road. The construction projects themselves improved the local economy by increasing job possibilities for those not engaged in commercial fishing. River barges carry bulk goods on the Kvichak River, using the 110-foot unloading dock in the beach area at Levelock to unload.

Electricity. The Village Council operates the Levelock Electric Cooperative, generating power from a 360-kilowatt diesel plant.

Fuel storage (gallons). The Village Council provides a bulk-fuel service. Storage: Village Council (156,800 gallons); Lake and Peninsula Schools (31,500).

Telecommunications. Local telephone service is provided by the Bristol Bay Telephone Cooperative, and long distance services by AT&T Alascom, GCI, or Bristol Bay Telephone. One FM radio station and one AM radio station broadcast to the area. The village provides a cable television service, and one channel is broadcast locally by the Alaska Rural Communications System. Internet services are provided by GCI.

Water and waste systems. Residents use individual and community wells and a surface source for water. Individual septic tanks are the primary means of sewage disposal for the community. The village council provides refuse collection services between May and September and septic pumping.

COMMUNITY FACILITIES AND SERVICES
Community facilities include a washeteria operated by the village council, a recreation center, and a multipurpose center. The village council provides electricity generation and distribution, bulk fuel, refuse collection services between May and September, and septic pumping.

Education. The Levelock School is operated by the Lake and Peninsula Borough School District, with 2 teachers and 17 students in preschool through twelfth grade. The school library serves as the community's public library.

Health care. The Levelock Health Clinic provides health care. It is owned by the village council, leased to the U.S. Public Health Service, and operated by the Bristol Bay Area Health Corporation. Medical flights to the Kanakanak Hospital in Dillingham, the closest full-service medical facility, are available. Auxiliary health care is provided by Levelock First Responders.

Public safety. Law enforcement is provided by a state village public safety officer (VPSO), backed by state troopers in King Salmon. Emergency response is provided by the VPSO, the Levelock Volunteer Fire Department, and the Levelock First Responders.

Lime Village

Ethnicity: Dena'ina
Athabascan

Native entity
Lime Village
Box LVD
McGrath, AK 99627-0052
907-524-3701
907-524-3701 Fax

ANCSA village corporation
Lime Village Company
P.O. Box LVD-Lime Village
McGrath, AK 99627
907-526-5228
907-526-5235 Fax

Louden Village

See Galena

Total area of entitlement under ANCSA
69,120 acres
2003 population   43
    state demographer estimate
(Note: Data from the 2000 census is incomplete for Lime Village.)

LOCATION
Lime Village is an isolated community located on the south bank of the Stony River, 50 miles southeast of its junction with the Kuskokwim River. The village is 185 air miles west of Anchorage and 111 miles south of McGrath.

PHYSICAL DESCRIPTION
The total area encompasses 80.3 square miles of land and 2.2 square miles of water at approximately 500 feet above sea level. The community is located on a bluff 30 to 50 feet above the river. Sand and gravel are available along the river, which is also a major anadromous fishery stream. Caribou and moose are present throughout the area. The village itself is in a bottomland spruce-poplar forest, with upland spruce-hardwood forest to the north and south. Flooding was unknown until the 2002 spring thaw, when river ice left the channel and pushed the washeteria off its foundation.

CLIMATE
The continental climate in Lime Village allows for temperature fluctuations ranging between -47°F and 82°F. Precipitation, much of which falls as snow, averages 22 inches annually. The Kuskokwim and Stony Rivers are frozen over from late October to mid-June. At this latitude, the region experiences just over 19 hours of daylight in June, declining to almost 5.5 in December.

CULTURE AND HISTORY
Lime Village is a Dena'ina Athabascan community practicing a subsistence lifestyle. The people are dependent upon nature to provide them with salmon, moose, bear, caribou, waterfowl, and berries. Named for the nearby limestone hills, the area now known as Lime Village was first used as a summer fish camp by people from nearby Lake Clark. The earliest recorded permanent settlement of Lime Village occurred in 1907, when Paul, Evan, and Zacar Constantinoff became year-round residents. A Russian Orthodox chapel, built in honor of Saints Constantine and Helen, was built in 1960, and a school in 1974.

GOVERNMENT
Lime Village, also known as Lime Village Traditional Council, is governed by a seven-member traditional council, headed by a president and recognized by the Bureau of Indian Affairs.

VILLAGE CORPORATION
Lime Village Company is the ANCSA village corporation. Shareholders in the village corporation are also shareholders in Calista Corporation, the regional Native corporation *(see Alaska introduction)*.

ECONOMY
Some residents find seasonal work with the Bureau of Land Management as firefighters and others run traplines, but most income comes from public assistance programs.

Transportation. One private firm supports the airfield.

Tourism and recreation. Major tourist attractions in a hundred-mile radius of Lime Village include: Denali National Park and Preserve, Lake Clark National Park and Preserve, Yukon Delta National Wildlife Refuge, Katmai National Park and Preserve, Kenai National Wildlife Refuge, Chugach National Forest, and Kenai Fjords National Park.

INFRASTRUCTURE
Transportation. Lime Village is dependent on small riverboats and airplanes for transportation until the Stony River freezes over. Then dog teams and snowmachines contribute to ground travel and commerce. The Stony River is too shallow to permit large barges to land and resupply the village, so villagers depend on the state-maintained airstrip, although it is in need of expansion to accommodate larger planes and small jets. A master plan was funded in 2000 by the Federal Aviation Administration and may result in the needed improvements. The airfield is served by Tanana Air Service. The Alaska Department of Community and Economic Development funded a project to upgrade existing roads in Lime Village in 1998.

Electricity. Electricity is provided by the Lime Village Power System, in place since March 1998. It uses an ecologically friendly experimental hybrid photovoltaic-battery-diesel power plant to reduce consumption of natural resources while continuing to provide for expanding village demands for electricity.

Fuel storage (gallons): Iditarod Area Schools (8,000); village council (7,200); electric utility (3,000); United Utilities (1,000). A consolidated bulk fuel storage facility was constructed in 2002.

Water and waste systems. A sanitation master plan, funded by the Alaska Native Tribal Health Consortium, was completed prior to construction of the new village washeteria in 2002 and may result in needed improvements. However, as of 2004, domestic sewage was disposed of primarily in pit privies, and 22 homes in the village were not fully plumbed. The school and teacher's housing are connected to individual wells and septic systems.

Telecommunications. Local telephone service is provided by United Utilities, long distance service by United Utilities or AT&T Alascom. GCI provides Internet service at the school. A local Alaska Rural Communications Service repeater broadcasts one television channel, and one AM radio station in McGrath broadcasts to the Lime Village area.

COMMUNITY FACILITIES AND SERVICES
The village has a community building and operates the washeteria rebuilt in 2002-04. Law enforcement is provided by state troopers in McGrath, emergency response by the village volunteer fire department.

Education. Iditarod Area School District operates the Lime Village School, serving 15 students in grades K-12 with two teachers. Improvements to and expansion of the school were planned for 2004.

Health care. The Lime Village Health Clinic, operated by Yukon Kuskokwim Heath Corporation, provides medical services for community members. It is a one-room residence in need of replacement. Staff at the clinic must haul water and use a pail toilet. Emergency service is provided by a health aide. The clinic is supported by the Clara Morgan Subregional Clinic in Aniak and the Yukon Kuskokwim Delta Regional Hospital in Bethel.

Total area of entitlement under ANCSA
	90,880 acres
Total labor force	167
High school graduate or higher	41.2%
Bachelor's degree or higher	10.5%
Unemployment rate	42.1%
Per capita income (1999)	$7,654
Population 2000 census	267
2003 population	267
state demographer estimate	
Percent Native 2000 census	95.5%

LOCATION
Lower Kalskag is located on the north bank of the Kuskokwim River, just downriver from Kalskag (Upper Kalskag), within the boundaries of the Yukon Delta National Wildlife Refuge. The city is 26 river miles west of Aniak, 89 miles northeast of Bethel, and 350 air miles west of Anchorage.

PHYSICAL DESCRIPTION
The community encompasses 1.3 square miles of Kuskokwim Delta lowlands and 0.4 square mile of Kuskokwim River water at an elevation of less than 300 feet above sea level. The surrounding area is dominated by flat, virtually treeless tundra, dotted with meltwater ponds called "potholes," and veined by smaller rivers, creeks and sloughs, making year-round roads virtually impossible.

CLIMATE
Despite maritime influences from the Bering Sea, the climate of Lower Kalskag is semi-Arctic; annual precipitation averages 19 inches, including 60 inches of snowfall. Mid-winter temperatures dip as low as -55°F with a year-round average low of 19.7°F. Summertime highs reach 87°F, but the year-round average high is 36.8°F. The Kuskokwim River is frozen over from October until mid-June. The area receives approximately 19 hours of sunlight in June, declining to 13 hours by September.

CULTURE AND HISTORY
Still living on their traditional homelands, villagers harvest over 700 pounds of fish and sea mammals, moose, black bear, caribou, porcupine, waterfowl and other birds, greens, and berries per year, in a harsh semi-Arctic environment where hunger is an ever-present danger. Although it is a largely cash-poor economy, the people have enjoyed a productive subsistence lifestyle. Many community members participate in the Marshall Dog Sled Races, held in March, and there are traditional dances and fiddle dances attended by many people from among 52 neighboring Yup'ik, Inupiat, and Alutiiq villages. Central Alaskan Yup'ik lies geographically and linguistically between Alutiiq and Siberian Yupik. The use of the apostrophe in Central Alaskan Yup'ik, as opposed to Siberian Yupik, denotes a long *p*. The word *Yup'ik* represents not only the language but also the name for the people themselves (*yuk* "person" plus *pik* "real."). Villagers have adopted the use of the English language (primarily for business), while carefully protecting use of the Native language. Now only semi-nomadic, the people of Lower Kalskag retreat to fish camps only during the summer. Prior to 1930, the site was used as a fish camp for families of Kalskag, a separate community three miles to the northeast. In 1930, Russian Orthodox residents of Kalskag, a predominantly Roman Catholic village, began to establish themselves in Lower Kalskag because of religious differences, making it a year-round settlement for the first time. These settlers built the Russian Orthodox Chapel of St. Seraphim in 1940, a school in 1959, a post office in 1962, a saw-mill in 1965, followed by a power plant in 1969, the same year the city of Lower Kalskag was incorporated as a second-class city. A new building for the church was added in the late 1970s.

GOVERNMENT
Located in the Unorganized Borough, Lower Kalskag was incorporated as a second-class city in 1969. The Village of Lower Kalskag is a BIA-recognized Native entity, governed by a traditional village council headed by a president.

VILLAGE CORPORATION
The ANCSA village corporation is The Kuskokwim Corporation, formed in 1977 by the merger of ten village corporations along the middle Kuskokwim River. In addition to over 950,000 acres of surface rights, it owns a substantial securities portfolio, investments in three apartment complexes in Fairbanks, a hotel in Fairbanks, a Hispanic broadcasting network, a telecommunication bandwidth and service provider, an engineering, remediation, and construction services firm, and a casino opportunity near Denver, Colorado. It owns the surface rights to the Donlin Creek property, one of the world's largest undeveloped gold deposits. In 2003, it began to pursue §8(a) federal contracting opportunities and establish partnerships and mentor-protégé relationships with established contractors. Shareholders in the Kuskokwim Corporation are also shareholders in Calista Corporation, the regional Native corporation.

ECONOMY
Lower Kalskag's economy continues to be subsistence-based. Seasonally, residents engage in commercial fishing or work for the Bureau of Land Management as fire fighters.

Government as employer. Thirty-six of 51 employed residents work for the city, state, or federal government.

Services and retail. The city has two general stores, a tobacco store, a bulk fuel dealer, and two video stores.

Tourism and recreation. The city is located within the Yukon Delta National Wildlife Refuge and within 100 miles of the Innoko National Wildlife Refuge.

INFRASTRUCTURE
Transportation. Winter trails exist to Russian Mission (40 miles) and Aniak (26 miles); residents use snowmobiles and airplanes in the winter to travel to these farther locations. A 4.2-mile gravel road connecting Lower Kalskag with Kalskag is maintained by the State of Alaska. Because of its location on the Kuskokwim River (second largest in Alaska), commercial barge lines are able to deliver fuel and other bulk supplies in the summer; during the winter months, residents are limited to snowmobiles or air travel for personal and business transportation. The river affords easy access by skiff in summer and snowmachine in winter. There is a 3,200-foot gravel airstrip maintained by Alaska's Department of Transportation, serving both Kalskags. Passengers and air freight arrive year-round via scheduled daily flights by Frontier Flying Service, Grant Aviation, Hageland Aviation, Inland Aviation Services, and Tanana Air Service.

Electricity. The Alaska Village Electrical Cooperative (AVEC), of which the city is a member, generates electricity from an 835-kilowatt diesel plant.

Fuel storage (gallons): AVEC (103,500); Twin Cities (74,770); Kuspuk Schools (16,000).

Water and waste systems. Water is drawn from a community well. The school, clinic, and over 40 percent of homes use

[KAL-skag]
Ethnicity: Yup'ik

Municipality
City of Lower Kalskag
P.O. Box 69
Lower Kalskag, AK 99626
  907-471-2228
  907-471-2228 Fax

Native entity
Village of Lower Kalskag
P.O. Box 27
Lower Kalskag, AK 99626
  907-471-2379
  907-471-2378 Fax

ANCSA village corporation
The Kuskokwim Corporation
4300 B Street, Suite 207
Anchorage, AK 99503
  907-243-2944
  907-243-2984 Fax
  kuskokwim.com

Lower Kalskag

individual septic tanks and have complete plumbing. A 10,000-gallon community septic tank allows for piped sewage collection to part of the city and funds have been requested to connect the 20 remaining homes using septic tanks to the system to prevent effluent ponding. A Class 3 landfill is operated by the City of Upper Kalskag for both Kalskag and Lower Kalskag.

Telecommunications. Local telephone service is provided by Bush-Tell, long distance service by AT&T Alascom. Internet service is available at the school from GCI. More than ten AM radio stations from Bethel, Nome, Dillingham, Anchorage, and other locations broadcast to the area. Alaska Rural Communications System repeaters in Kalskag (Upper Kalskag) broadcast two television channels to the area.

COMMUNITY FACILITIES AND SERVICES
The city operates the piped water and sewer systems.

Education. The Kuspuk School District operates the Zackar Levi Elementary School, serving students in grades K-4, in Lower Kalskag. Students in grades 5 and 6 attend the Joseph and Olinga Gregory Elementary School in Kalskag, while students in grades 7 through 12 attend George Morgan Junior/Senior High School, located between the cities of Upper and Lower Kalskag. The school libraries serve as the community public libraries.

Health care. The Lower Kalskag Health Clinic, built in 1998, is operated by Yukon Kuskokwim Health Corporation. Indian Community Development Block Grant Program monies were accessed in 1999 to provide a larger facility with a kitchen for itinerant health care specialists. It is backed by the Clara Morgan Subregional Clinic in Aniak and the Yukon Kuskokwim Delta Regional Hospital in Bethel.

Public safety. Law enforcement is provided by state troopers in Aniak.

Manley Hot Springs

Ethnicity: Koyukon
Athabascan

Native entity
Manley Hot Springs Village
P.O. Box 105
Manley Hot Springs, AK 99756
907-672-3177
907-672-3200 Fax

ANCSA village corporation
Bean Ridge Corporation
P.O. Box 110
Manley Hot Springs, AK 99756
907-672-3331
907-672-3232 Fax

Total area of entitlement under ANCSA	68,528 acres
Total labor force	40
High school graduate or higher	80.0%
Bachelor's degree or higher	26.7%
Unemployment rate	6.7%
Per capita income *(1999)*	$21,751
Population *2000 census*	72
2003 population	73
state demographer estimate	
Percent Native *2000 census*	23.6%

LOCATION
Located at the end of Elliott Highway (Highway 2), Manley Hot Springs is about 5 miles north of the Tanana River on Hot Springs Slough and 160 road miles west of Fairbanks.

PHYSICAL DESCRIPTION
The Village encompasses 54.3 square miles of land, mostly low, rolling hills and swampy river valleys, approximately 320 feet above sea level. The Tanana River, swollen with spring run-off in an area of already low lands and swampy sloughs, has subjected Manley Hot Springs to several floods throughout its history. The worst in recent memory occurred in May of 1956. Other floods in 1961, 1962, and 1982 were also devastating to the area.

CLIMATE
Interior Alaska (generally) has an unpredictable, generally cold, continental climate, with dramatic thunderstorms including hail and lightning and rapid temperature swings. Manley Hot Springs is no exception. Daily summer high temperatures average in the upper 50s with occasional highs to 93°F and recurring (although infrequent) summertime snows. Winter lows range between -21°F and -6, with recorded extremes to -70°F. Annually, the area receives 15 inches of precipitation; snowfalls of 59.3 inches are a part of that, causing periodic spring flooding. Most of interior Alaska experiences 21 hours of daylight in June, declining to just over three hours by mid-December.

CULTURE AND HISTORY
Manley Hot Springs is located in traditional Koyukon Athabascan territory. Athabascan Indians have inhabited the interior regions of Alaska for thousands of years, following a traditional nomadic hunting-and-gathering way of life. Koyukon occupies the largest territory of any Alaskan Athabascan language. It is spoken in three dialects—Upper, Central, and Lower—in 11 villages along the Koyukuk and middle Yukon

rivers. The total current population is about 2,300, of whom about 300 speak the language. Manley Hot Springs is largely non-Native—only 17 of the residents reported themselves as Native in the 2000 census. However, the Native people celebrate their heritage with boat races, Athabascan ceremonies in July, and a spring carnival. Many participate in the Stanley Dayo Championship Sprint Dog Race in March.

In 1902, a mining prospector by the name of John Karshner claimed a 278-acre homestead near Baker Creek that included hot springs, started a vegetable farm, and thus first settled the area then referred to as Baker's Hot Springs. The area became a resupply point for nearby miners. The next year, Sam's Rooms and Meals, now called the Manley Roadhouse, opened to better serve the suddenly burgeoning community. Farming, poultry, and livestock operations were successful enough to not only supply the needs of the growing community, but to export to other areas as well. The community's namesake, Frank Manley, built the four-story Hot Springs Hotel in 1907. The 45-room luxury hotel offered guests an array of services, such as a barber shop, hot baths, a billiard room, a bowling alley, and an Olympic-size indoor swimming pool with water heated by the natural hot springs. Summer guests typically arrived by steamer on the Tanana River. Winter trips took two days from Fairbanks by overland stage. The community—then known as Hot Springs—prospered because of the mining and the early tourism industry, boasting an Alaska Commercial Company store, a newspaper, a bakery, clothiers, and other businesses. By 1910, the population was estimated to be more than 500. In 1913 tragedy struck and the entire resort community burned to the ground. Very few stayed to rebuild, so that by 1920, when the mining industry was declining, only 29 residents remained in Hot Springs, which was renamed Manley Hot Springs in 1957. A school was opened in 1958, and in 1959 completion of Elliott Highway (Highway 2) gave Manley Hot Springs a summer land link to Fairbanks. The State of Alaska began maintaining the road for year-round use in 1982. In 1985 another resort hotel was opened, but it closed in 1997.

GOVERNMENT
Manley Hot Springs is an unincorporated village in the Unorganized Borough. The Native residents are governed by a BIA-recognized traditional council headed by a president.

VILLAGE CORPORATION
The ANCSA village corporation is the Bean Ridge Corporation. Its shareholders are also shareholders in Doyon, Limited, the regional Native corporation. Bean Ridge has an al-

ternate address of P.O. Box 72220, Fairbanks, AK 99707.

ECONOMY

Many area residents garden their own fresh produce; for meat they hunt moose and fish for salmon. Bulk goods and fuel are delivered to Manley Hot Springs via truck on the Elliott Highway or Tanana River barge in summer and by Tanana Air Service year-round. Because of the mining industry and the resort hotel and other tourist-targeted businesses, Manley Hot Springs enjoys a diversified local economy with a full array of grocery and other retail stores. Many people have more than one kind of income in addition to their subsistence activities, and a barter system thrives among local residents.

Fisheries. Nine residents hold commercial fishing permits.

Government as employer. Of the 36 residents employed, 22 work for either the state or federal government.

Tourism and recreation. Major tourist attractions within a hundred-mile radius include Yukon Flats National Wildlife Refuge, Kanuti National Wildlife Refuge, Koyokuk National Wildlife Refuge, Nowitna National Wildlife Refuge, and Denali National Park and Preserve. Local visitor attractions include fishing charters, fish camps, gold mine tours, and sled-dog tours. Accommodations include a public campground, the Manley Roadhouse, and a bed-and-breakfast. There are two wilderness charter services, and Native guides offer tourists charter fishing trips and camps.

INFRASTRUCTURE

Transportation. The Elliott Highway (Highway 2) provides a direct land link from the Tanana River Landing three miles southwest of the village, through Manley Hot Springs, to Fairbanks. Goods and fuel are typically delivered by truck. There are also the Manley Hot Springs-Tofty Road and the North Slough Front Road. The Tanana River landing is used to launch fishing boats, and river barge services are sometimes provided during summer months, but there is no docking facility at the landing due to severe erosion. The state-owned 2,875- by 30-foot gravel runway is available year-

round. In 2003 lights were added at the airport, and the runway was extended and relocated, allowing larger planes and small jets to land. Construction was slated to be finished in 2005. Scheduled service is provided three days each week by Tanana Air Service.

Electricity. Electricity is provided by the privately owned Manley Utility Company, generating power from a 480-kilowatt diesel plant.

Water and waste systems. Water is provided for residents of Manley Hot Springs at a central location in the village by the Manley Community Association. Individual wells are also used. Outhouses and septic tanks are the primary means of sewage disposal. The landfill operated by the Community Association is at mile 158 Elliott Highway.

Telecommunications. Local telephone service is provided by United Utilities, and long distance service by United Utilities or AT&T Alascom. GCI provides Internet service at the school. Radio stations from Fairbanks and some other locations can be received. Cable television service is available. One television channel is broadcast locally by the Alaska Rural Communications System; one channel can be received from Fairbanks and one from North Pole.

COMMUNITY FACILITIES AND SERVICES

The landfill operated by the Manley Community Association, is at mile 158 Elliott Highway. A clinic/washeteria is located one mile east of town, operated by the Manley Village Council. There are a multipurpose community activities building and a tribal hall. Law enforcement is provided by state troopers in Fairbanks. Emergency response is provided by a local volunteer fire department.

Education. Gladys Dart School, serving 15 students in preschool through twelfth grade with two teachers, is operated by the Yukon-Koyukuk School District. The school library serves as the community's public library.

Health care. The Manley Hot Springs Health Clinic is operated by the Tanana Chiefs Conference. Emergency service is provided by volunteers and a health aide.

M anokotak

Total area of entitlement under ANCSA
125,620 acres

Total labor force	104
High school graduate or higher	56
Bachelor's degree or higher	19
Unemployment rate	13.5%
Per capita income *(1999)*	$9,294
2003 population	405
state demographer estimate	
Population *2000 census*	399
Percent Native *2000 census*	94.7%

LOCATION

Manokotak is located 25 miles southwest of Dillingham on the Igushik River. The city lies just north of a spit of land between the Kulukak Bay on the west and the Nushagak Bay (part of the Bering Sea) on the east. Manokotak is located within the Togiak National Wildlife Refuge and in close proximity to Wood-Tikchik State Park.

PHYSICAL DESCRIPTION

Manokotak encompasses 36.4 square miles of low lands and 0.9 square mile of water, at 30 feet above sea level. It is a six-

mile by six-mile (36 section) square. A lone hill just outside the populated area rises to the elevation of 850 feet above sea level. The geology of the area is coastal interlayered alluvial and marine sediments. The vegetation is wet tundra. The Igushik River is a major anadromous fish stream, and the area south of the city is a medium-density waterfowl area.

CLIMATE

Because of its proximity to the coastline of Alaska, the city is subject to high winds and dense low-lying fog periodically through the year. The primary climatic patterns are maritime, although the area is listed as a transition zone because of dramatic Arctic continental influences. Summertime temperatures average between 40ºF and 70ºF. In the winter temperatures average between 4ºF and 30ºF. Precipitation ranges from 20 to 26 inches annually, with 87 inches of snowfall per year. The Igushik River is frozen over from mid-November throughout May of each year. At this latitude, the region experiences approximately 18 hours of daylight per 24 hour period in June, declining to 6.5 hours in December.

CULTURE AND HISTORY

A consolidated Yup'ik village, Manokotak maintains primarily

[man-noh-KOH-tuck]
Ethnicity: Yup'ik

Municipality
City of Manokotak
P.O. Box 170
Manokotak, AK 99628-0170
907-289-1027
907-289-1082 Fax

Native entity
Manokotak Village
P.O. Box 169
Manokotak, AK 99628
907-289-2067
907-289-1235 Fax

ANCSA village corporation
Manokotak Natives Limited
P.O. Box 149
Manokotak, AK 99628-0149
907-289-1062
907-289-1007 Fax

Manokotak

a hunting, fishing, and trapping subsistence lifestyle, dependent upon the harvest of herring, salmon, trout, berries, waterfowl, sea lions, and beluga whales. The merger of two separate villages, Igushik and Tuklung, in 1946-47 created a permanent settlement known as Manokotak, one of the newer villages in the Bristol Bay region. Additional Native people migrated from Kulukak, Togiak, and Aleknagik to join the community, retreating back to fish camps at Igushik and Ekuk only in the summer. Many were attracted to the area by a fur industry dependent on trapping small game such as fox, beaver, mink, and otter, but it has declined since the 1960s. A post office was established in 1960 and the city was incorporated in 1970.

GOVERNMENT
Manokotak is a second-class city with an eight-member city council, including a mayor, president, vice president, and secretary. The Native population of the village is represented by a BIA-recognized traditional village council, headed by a president.

VILLAGE CORPORATION
Manokotak Natives Limited is the ANCSA village corporation. Subsidiaries provide local electricity and fuel storage. Shareholders in the village corporation are also shareholders in the regional Bristol Bay Native Corporation.

ECONOMY
Manokotak is accessible only by air and water, limiting the amount of commerce and industry available to local residents. Most are engaged in the commercial fishing industry; 96 residents hold commercial fishing permits for salmon and herring. Many residents continue trapping fox, beaver, mink, and otter. Barter and communal sharing among Yup'ik villages is common, and Manokotak has traditional sharing relationships with Togiak and Twin Hills.

Fisheries. During the fishing season, 95 percent of the residents leave Manokotak to participate in the fishery in Togiak Bay.

Government as employer. As of the 2000 census, 73 people work for the city, state, or federal government.

Manufacturing. Residents make and sell items such as ivory carvings, baskets, and masks.

Services and retail. Retail services include day care centers and The Co-op, a discount general store.

Tourism and recreation. Manokotak is located within Togiak National Wildlife Refuge, where visitors can go hiking and camping. It is close to Wood-Tikchik State Park and within 100 miles of the Yukon Delta National Wildlife Refuge, the Katmai National Park and Preserve, and the Becharof National Wildlife Refuge. Visitors can view and purchase locally made arts and crafts.

Transportation. Local transportation firms include a taxicab company and transportation and charter companies.

INFRASTRUCTURE
Transportation. Manokotak has four named roads: Manokotak Heights Road, Manokotak Airport Road, Salmon Road, and the Weary River Road. This last road leads from the village down to a barge landing at Weary River. Construction began on a 6.5-mile road to a barge landing area on the Snake River in 1998. The Manokotak Trail to Dillingham is used by snowmachines during winter to haul fuel. Other winter trails

are used by ATVs and snowmobiles. The state-owned airport located just north of the village has a 2,720- by 60-foot lighted gravel airstrip and a 5,000-foot designated seaplane base, with regular and charter flights available to and from Dillingham. Some cargo delivery occurs on the Igushik River, but because of its tight meandering loops, river distance is much longer than when covered in air miles and therefore water transportation is not a preferred mode of transportation. There are no docks on the Igushik River either, and the mud beach is sometimes a quagmire of impassable muck.

Electricity. Electricity is provided by Manokotak Power Company, a subsidiary of the village corporation, from a 1,784-kilowatt diesel plant.

Fuel storage (gallons). Manokotak Natives Limited (91,100); Southwest Region Schools (45,000); Manokotak Power Company (21,400); Moravian church (2,700); Army National Guard (1,500); Manukutaag Trading Co. (1,450).

Water and waste systems. Water is drawn from two community wells, treated, then stored in a 150,000-gallon water storage tank, owned and maintained by the city. A piped water system, constructed in 1972, serves 68 households and the school with complete plumbing. Some housing units have their own wells, as does Manokotak Heights, a subdivision located 4 miles south of the main village. Water shortages have occurred, so in 2004 a feasibility study was underway to examine water improvements. A piped sewer system serves 68 households and the school. Manokotak Heights has its own treatment plant. A landfill is operated by the city. In 2004, a feasibility study was underway to examine sewer and landfill improvements.

Telecommunications. Local telephone service is provided by the Nushagak Telephone Co-op, Inc., long distance service by AT&T Alascom, GCI, or Nushagak Telephone. Internet service is provided by GCI. Four AM radio stations broadcast to the area. Cable television service is provided by the Manokotak Cable Company, and one channel is broadcast locally by the Alaskan Rural Communications Service.

COMMUNITY FACILITIES AND SERVICES
Community facilities include a washeteria and the village council-operated Youth Center. The city provides waste disposal and water supply. The village corporation provides electricity generation and distribution and fuel storage.

Education. The Manokotak School has 142 students in grades K-12, taught by seventeen teachers. It is operated by the Southwest Region School District. The school library serves as the community public library.

Health care. The Manokotak Health Clinic, located along with city and village council offices in an old warehouse, is owned by the village council, leased to the U. S. Public Health Service, and operated by the Bristol Bay Area Health Corporation. The clinic experiences water-freezing problems. The village plans to construct a new clinic and multipurpose facility. Emergency care is provided by the Manokotak First Responders. The nearest full-service medical facility is the hospital in Dillingham.

Public safety. Law enforcement is provided by a state village public safety officer (VPSO), backed by state troopers in Dillingham. Emergency response is provided by the VPSO, the city volunteer fire department, and the Manokotak First Responders.

Total area of entitlement under ANCSA
115,200 acres

Total labor force	135
High school graduate or higher	41.7%
Bachelor's degree or higher	6.1%
Unemployment rate	11.9%
Per capita income *(1999)*	$9,597
Population *2000 census*	349
2003 population	368
state demographer estimate	
Percent Native *2000 census*	97.7%

LOCATION

Marshall is in southwest Alaska, north of Arbor Island, on the north bank of the Yukon River between the villages of Pilot Station and Russian Mission in the Yukon-Kuskokwim Delta lowlands, at less than 200 feet above sea level. It is near Poltes Slough on the northeastern boundary of the Yukon Delta National Wildlife Refuge. Marshall is approximately 80 air miles to the north of Bethel, 60 air miles east of Mountain Village, and 140 miles upriver from the mouth of the Yukon on the Bering Sea.

PHYSICAL DESCRIPTION

The village encompasses 4.7 square miles of land. It is located on the north side of a high bank of the river which is referred to as Fortuna Ledge. This ledge affords Marshall protection from flooding in the spring. However, the nature of the mountain and valley country to the east, the pattern of the winter winds, and the felling of most of the taller spruce trees early in its history make it a very breezy community to live in during the winter. Marshall is surrounded by tundra and taiga (subarctic forest) on a gentle slope leading up to the flanks of Pilcher Mountain, named after a miner who used to live in the area. The geology is variable, although most of it is a green to dark gray sedimentary rock in various stages of metamorphosis. Embraced by a series of low, partially timbered mountains on its east side, across from the village to its west lies the flat tundra, which consists of a maze of sloughs, sandbars, and green meadows. The most southerly point of the 1800-mile-long Yukon River is located approximately 20 miles east of Marshall at Devil's elbow.

CLIMATE

Marshall is most heavily influenced by maritime climatic patterns, characterized by relatively warm winters and cool summers, with heavy winds in the fall and winter. The growing season lasts approximately 100 days. Winter low temperatures reach -54°F, and summer temperatures as high as 86°F. The Lower Yukon is frozen over from October through mid-June. At this latitude there are approximately 19 hours of daylight per 24-hour period in June, declining to approximately 5.5 in December. Precipitation at Russian Mission, a village 20 miles directly east of Marshall at approximately the same elevation, averages 20 inches annually, with approximately 71 inches of snowfall each year.

CULTURE AND HISTORY

Marshall is a traditional Yup'ik village, depending on subsistence and fishing-related activities to support most residents. The majority of the community is made up of people from the abandoned villages of Ohagamiut and Takshak with many also coming from present day Pilot Station and Russian Mission. Central Alaskan Yup'ik lies linguistically between Alutiiq and Siberian Yupik. The use of the apostrophe in Central Alaskan Yup'ik, as opposed to Siberian Yupik, denotes a long *p*.

The word *Yup'ik* represents not only the language but also the name for the people themselves (*yuk* "person" plus *pik* "real"). An expedition came upon a village called "Uglovaia" at this site in 1880. Gold was discovered in 1913, and the white settlement at this location was originally called Fortuna Ledge. It was a placer-mining camp, named for the first child born there, Fortuna Hunter. The camp was conveniently located for riverboat landings on a channel of the Yukon River, enabling easy resupply and early tourism. A post office was established in 1915, and the population grew to over 1,000. Later the village was named for Thomas Riley Marshall, vice president of the United States under Woodrow Wilson from 1913-21. The community became known as "Marshall's Landing." When the village incorporated in 1970, it was officially named Fortuna Ledge, but as it continued to be referred to as Marshall by local residents, the name was officially changed (again) to Marshall in 1984.

GOVERNMENT

The City of Marshall was incorporated as a second-class city in 1970. It has a mayor and a seven-member city council. The city has a manager to handle day-to-day operations. The Native people have a BIA-recognized traditional village council with seven members, the Native Village of Marshall. For some time, the traditional council president was also the mayor, and the city manager was also a member of the traditional council. There is a four percent sales tax.

VILLAGE CORPORATION

The ANCSA village corporation for Marshall is Maserculiq ("red fish," meaning salmon) Incorporated, the 125 shareholders of which are also shareholders in Calista Corporation, the regional Native corporation. Maserculiq owns Marshall Enterprises (general store and gas station), Maserculiq Fish Processing Plant, which sells most of its fish to the Japanese under the "Yukon King" brand name, and Fair View Manor Apartments in Homer.

ECONOMY

Marshall has a seasonal subsistence economy with fishing, fish processing, and BLM fire fighting positions available every summer. Villagers harvest salmon, moose, waterfowl, bears, and berries. Trapping small game and manufacturing handicrafts supplement incomes, and many are dependent on government transfer payments.

Fisheries. Thirty-nine residents hold commercial fishing permits, and others work in the Yukon River salmon-fishing industry in season. The Maserculiq Fish Processing Plant, which sells most of its fish in Japan under the "Yukon King" brand name, buys salmon from some 3,000 fishermen along the lower Yukon River.

Government as employer. Sixty-five of 110 employed residents work for the city, state, or federal government.

Services and retail. There are three general stores in the community: Hunter Sales and Rooming, the Fortuna Ledge Co-Op Store, and the MasInc. store. Other businesses include several child daycare services, a taxicab company, retail stores, and charter transportation companies.

Tourism and recreation. Marshall lies right at the edge of the Yukon Delta National Wildlife Refuge, and is within 100 miles of the Innoko National Wildlife Refuge. The annual Marshall dog races, a weeklong event in late winter, brings competi-

Ethnicity: Yup'ik

Municipality
City of Marshall
P.O. Box 9
Marshall, AK 99585
907-679-6215
907-679-6220 Fax

Native entity
Native Village of Marshall
P.O. Box 110
Marshall, AK 99585
907-679-6302
907-679-6187 Fax

ANCSA village corporation
Maserculiq Incorporated
P.O. Box 90
Marshall, AK 99585
907-679-6512
907-679-6740 Fax
yukonking.com

Marshall

Mary's Igloo

See Zero Population Section

tors and spectators from all over Alaska.

INFRASTRUCTURE

Transportation. There are no roads connecting to Marshall, so access is primarily by air or, when the river is ice free, by boat or barge. Many residents have boats. There are winter trails for all-terrain-vehicles, dog teams and snowmachines. There is a state-owned gravel airstrip, 3,201 by 100 feet, served by Arctic Circle Air Service, Grant Aviation, Hageland Aviation, and Inland Aviation Services. In 2003 the airport was upgraded, the airstrip was relocated, an access road was re-habilitated, and snow removal equipment was purchased and stored at the terminal. Fall and winter winds limit air access. Within Marshall, there are about five miles of road between the village and the airport. There is also a network of winter trails between Marshall and Pilot Station and between Marshall and Russian Mission.

Electricity. Electricity is provided to residents by the Alaska Village Electric Cooperative (AVEC), of which the city is a member, from a 655-kilowatt diesel plant.

Fuel storage (gallons). Maserculiq Inc. (110,000); AVEC (76,560); Lower Yukon Schools (46,000); Hunter Store (17,000); city (14,200); Maserculiq Fish Processing Plant (10,000).

Water and waste systems. The city provides water from five wells, and operates a piped water and sewer system serving 70 percent of the city's homes. The other homes must haul water and use honeybuckets. Funds have been requested to

expand the piped systems to the remaining unserved homes and the fish processing plant. The city operates a Class 3 landfill and refuse collection.

Telecommunications. Local telephone service is provided by United Utilities, long distance service by United Utilities or AT&T Alascom. Several AM radio stations from Bethel, Nome, and elsewhere broadcast to the area, and the Alaska Rural Communications Service broadcasts two television channels from repeaters located in Marshall.

COMMUNITY FACILITIES AND SERVICES

The city has a multiuse community center, a teen/youth center, and a public safety building, and operates the water and waste disposal systems.

Education. Marshall School serves 118 children K-12, with 8 teachers. It is operated by the Lower Yukon School District. The school library serves as the community's public library.

Health care. Theresa Elia Memorial Health Clinic is operated by the Yukon-Kuskokwim Health Corporation. It is backed by the John Afcan Memorial Subregional Clinic in St. Mary's and the Yukon Kuskokwim Delta Regional Hospital in Bethel. Emergency service is provided by a health aide.

Public safety. Law enforcement is provided by a state village public safety officer (VPSO) and two village police officers, backed by state troopers in St. Mary's. Emergency response is provided by the VPSO and the city volunteer fire department.

McGrath

Ethnicity: Upper Kuskokwim Athabascn

Municipality
City of McGrath
P.O. Box 30
McGrath, AK 99627
907-524-3825
907-524-3536 Fax
mcgrathalaska.net

Native entity
McGrath Native Village
P.O. Box 134
McGrath, AK 99627
907-524-3024
907-524-3899 Fax

ANCSA village corporation
MTNT Limited
P.O. Box 309
McGrath, AK 99627
907-524-3391
907-524-3701 Fax
mcgrathalaska.net

Total area of entitlement under ANCSA	
	91,880 acres
Total labor force	230
High school graduate or higher	35.3%
Bachelor's degree or higher	15.1%
Unemployment rate	8.4%
Per capita income *(1999)*	$21,553
Population *2000 census*	401
2003 population	415
state demographer estimate	
Percent Native *2000 census*	54.6%

LOCATION
McGrath is in interior Alaska, 221 miles northwest of Anchorage and 259 miles southwest of Fairbanks.

PHYSICAL DESCRIPTION
McGrath is adjacent to the Kuskokwim River directly south of its confluence with the Takotna River. The area encompasses 48.9 square miles of land and 5.7 square miles of water, at an elevation of 344 feet above sea level.

CLIMATE
The McGrath area has a cold, continental climate, with a slight maritime influence during summer. Summer temperatures average between from 62°F and 80°F. Winter temperatures vary from -64°F to 0°F. Precipitation is light, with average annual snowfalls of 86 inches and average rainfalls totaling only 4 to 10 inches. The Kuskokwim River is frozen over from October through June. At this latitude, the region experiences just over 19 hours of daylight in a 24-hour period in June, declining to 5.5 in December.

CULTURE AND HISTORY
Despite its economic successes, subsistence activities remain an important part of daily life for the local Athabascan and Yup'ik peoples, who comprise more than half of the population of McGrath. About 10 families in town have dog teams which they enter into the Iditarod, the Kuskokwim 300, and Mail Trail 200 sled dog races. Other cultural events include the annual Shoppers Fair, Fourth of July festivities, seasonal hunts, and native celebrations. The Tochiak Historical Society Museum houses artifacts that explain the community's cultural heritage to visitors. McGrath was originally a seasonal Upper Kuskokwim Athabascan site used as a meeting and trading place for Big River, Nikolai, Telida, and Lake Minchumina residents, with Old Town McGrath located across the river from where it is today. In 1904, Abraham Appel established a trading post at the old site and by 1906-07 it was a bustling regional mining supply center for gold mining in the Innoko District and Ganes Creek. A town was established in 1907 and named for Peter McGrath, a local U.S. Marshal. In 1909, the Alaska Commercial Company opened a store and from 1911 to 1920, hundreds of people mushed their way on the Iditarod Trail on their way to the Ophir gold districts, contributing to McGrath's role as a supply center. But the mining industry suffered sharp declines after 1925, and when a major flood devastated the area in 1933, several residents moved to the south bank of the Kuskokwim to start over. Eventual natural changes in the course of the river rendered the new location useless as a river stopping point. Nonetheless, in 1937 the Alaska Commercial Company re-opened a store at the new location, and by 1940 an airstrip had been cleared, the FAA had installed an entire communications complex, and a school was built. As part of the Lend-Lease Program between

the U.S. and Russia, McGrath became an important re-fueling stop for airplanes flying over Alaska during World War II. A boarding school was built in 1964, attracting high school students from neighboring villages. The City of McGrath was incorporated in 1975. Upper Kuskokwim Athabascan is spoken in the villages of Nikolai, Telida, and McGrath in the Upper Kuskokwim River drainage. Of a total population of about 160 people, about 40 still speak the language.

GOVERNMENT
The City of McGrath is a second-class city in the Unorganized Borough, with a mayor and city council. The BIA-recognized Native Village of McGrath has a traditional village council, presided over by a first chief.

VILLAGE CORPORATION
MTNT Limited is the ANCSA village corporation for McGrath, Takotna, Nikolai, and Telida. As McGrath has three times the population of the other three villages combined, it tends to dominate the corporation. Shareholders in MTNT are also shareholders in Doyon, Limited, the regional Native corporation.

ECONOMY
McGrath is the regional center on the upper Kuskokwim for education, transportation, and mining exploration. It benefits by its fortunate position as the northernmost point on the Kuskokwim River accessible by large riverboats and by its position along the Iditarod Trail, making it a hub for interior Alaska. McGrath enjoys a widely diverse cash economy, with over 45 businesses of all types licensed. The median household income is one of the best in Alaska at $43,056. Nevertheless, many families rely on subsistence activities to supplement their incomes: salmon, bear, rabbits, moose, caribou, and berries are harvested. Others tend gardens and trap small game. The Nixon Fork gold mine, northeast of McGrath, ceased operations when gold prices declined.

Government as employer. Ninety-nine of 206 employed residents work for the city, state or federal government.

Manufacturing. McGrath has a boat builder and a manufacturing plant supporting construction.

Services and retail. McGrath has lodging, photography shops, restaurants, day-care providers, wilderness charter firms, outfitters, air transport and airline services, and a videotape rental store.

INFRASTRUCTURE
Transportation. There are no road connections to McGrath. Winter trails are marked to Nikolai (50 miles) and Takotna (20 miles); they are used by trucks, all-terrain vehicles and snowmobiles. There are two miles of paved streets within the city limits. Residents rely on year-round air services, such as Penn Air and Tanana Air Service, and on barge services (during summer months) for cargo delivery. There is no dock on the Kuskokwim River at McGrath; however, there is a single boat-launch ramp. The state-owned airport facilities were undergoing improvements in 2002, including construction of an apron, and an extension, widening, and strengthening of the crosswind runway. The 5,435- by 150-foot main airstrip is asphalt. There is a seaplane base on the Kuskokwim River.

Electricity. McGrath Light & Power, a subsidiary of MTNT, provides electricity to McGrath from a 2,685-kilowatt diesel plant in McGrath.

Fuel storage (gallons). MTNT Ltd. Electric (223,400); B.J. Magnuson Fuel (193,500); Don Harris (80,000); Federal Aviation Administration (55,300); city (48,600); Alaska Department of Transportation (21,700); McGuire's Tavern (20,200); AK DNR Airport (20,000); AK DNR Camp (10,300); KSKO Radio (10,000); AK Fish & Game (7,200); Alaska State Troopers (3,000); US Fish & Wildlife (2,500); Village Camai Center (2,000); Catholic Church (1,200); Alaska Commercial Co. Store (1,100).

Water and waste systems. Individual wells and septic tanks are used by the majority of residents. Limited city piped water and sewage systems serve approximately 34 homes. Complete plumbing facilities are found in 145 households. Funds have been requested to expand the piped sewer system to the 144 houses and businesses currently using septic tanks. A private firm, McGrath Trash & Refuse, collects refuse for disposal at the City landfill, a Class 3 facility. In 2003, a new permanent surface water intake structure was under construction.

Telecommunications. Local telephone service is provided by United KUC, long distance by AT&T Alascom. Internet services are provided by McGrath Light & Power, and at McGrath School by GCI. Residents can receive one AM public radio station from McGrath, KSKO, and other AM stations from Anchorage, Galena, Dillingham, and other locations. McGrath Broadcasting Co. provides cable TV services to the area. Three television channels are broadcast from local repeaters, two from the Alaska Rural Communications System and one from the Iditarod Area School District.

COMMUNITY FACILITIES AND SERVICES
McGrath is the center for public services for the surrounding interior communities. In addition to the services provided by MTNT, the headquarters of the Iditarod Area School District is located here. The city operates the water and sewer systems, the washeteria, and the landfill.

Public safety. Law enforcement is provided by a state village public safety officer (VPSO position vacant as of August 2004) and a state trooper post in the city. Emergency response is provided by the VPSO, the city volunteer fire and rescue, and the Kuskokwim Valley Rescue Squad.

Education. McGrath School, operated by the Iditarod Area School District, serves 86 children in grades K-12. The district's Distance Learning-Correspondence Center, serving 95 remote students in grades K-12, is also located in McGrath. The Tochiak Historical Society Museum maintains a collection of artifacts. The city supports a community public library.

Health care. The McGrath Health Center, a qualified Emergency Care Center, is operated by the Tanana Chiefs Conference (TCC). The Center serves as a sub-regional clinic for the area, and is supported by Fairbanks Memorial Hospital and the TCC's Chief Andrew Isaac Health Center located there. Specialized care is available from the Four Rivers Counseling Center.

Mekoryuk

[ma-KOR-ee-yuck]
Ethnicity: Nuniwarmiut Cup'ig

Municipality
City of Mekoryuk
P.O. Box 29
Mekoryuk, AK 99630
907-827-8314
907-827-8626 Fax

Native entity
Native Village of Mekoryuk
P.O. Box 66
Mekoryuk, AK 99630
907-827-8828
907-827-8133 Fax

ANCSA village corporation
NIMA Corporation
P.O. Box 52
Mekoryuk, AK 99630
907-827-8636
907-827-8639 Fax

Total area of entitlement under ANCSA
                              115,200 acres
Total labor force   96
High school graduate or higher   63.9%
Bachelor's degree or higher   1.7%
Unemployment rate   13.3%
Per capita income *(1999)* $11,957
Population *2000 census*   210
2003 population   205
  state demographer estimate
Percent Native *2000 census*   96.7%

LOCATION
Mekoryuk is the only village on Nunivak Island. It is located at the mouth of Shoal Bay on the north shore of the island in the east Bering Sea, 30 miles off the coast of mainland Alaska and the Yukon-Kuskokwim Delta. Mekoryuk is 149 air miles west of Bethel and 553 miles west of Anchorage.

PHYSICAL DESCRIPTION
Mekoryuk covers 7.4 square miles of land and 0.1 square mile of water, at an elevation of 50 feet above sea level. Nunivak Island, including Mekoryuk, is a National Wildlife Refuge. The island is 45 miles wide by 65 miles long.

CLIMATE
Nunivak Island's climate is strongly influenced by the surrounding Bering Sea. Fog and stormy weather are common. The area receives approximately 15 inches of precipitation annually; annual snowfall averages 57 inches. Summer temperatures range between 34°F and 54°F; winter temperatures range between 3°F to 20°F. Winter extremes of -48°F have been recorded; summer highs to 76°F. At this latitude, the area experiences approximately 19 hours of daylight per 24-hour period in June, declining to 5.5 in December.

CULTURE AND HISTORY
Nunivak Island is in the traditional territory of the Nuniwarmiut Cup'it, a Yup'ik people. Cup'ig (pronounced "CHUP-pik") is the name used for both the language and individuals (the plural is Cup'it) in the Nunivak dialect of Central Alaskan Yup'ik.

Nunivak Island has been inhabited for 2,000 years. The first European contact was made in 1821 by the Russian-American Company, which recorded 400 people living in 16 villages on the Island. A summer camp was noted at the current site of Mekoryuk (Mikuryarmiut) in 1874, and in 1891 a Russian found 702 Natives occupying 9 villages on the island including permanent residents at the current city site. An epidemic in 1900 nearly wiped out the population; however, leaving only four surviving families. In the 1930s the Evangelical Covenant Church was built by a Native missionary at the present village site, followed by a Bureau of Indian Affairs (BIA) school in 1939, which brought people from other areas of the island.

A Russian-Native trader introduced reindeer to the island for commercial purposes in 1920; the operation was purchased by the Bureau of Indian Affairs in the 1940s, a slaughterhouse was added in 1945. The business is now run by the village council. Some reindeer were crossed with caribou imported to the island from Denali Park, resulting in larger animals, but the herds were more difficult to manage. Musk-oxen were also imported. A herd of 34 were brought to the island from Greenland in 1934 in an effort to save the species from extinction. This effort has proven successful; calves from this herd have been introduced into other areas of Alaska. As of

2003 there were approximately 4,000 reindeer and about 550 musk-oxen on the island, with no predators.

Through the 1940s, the traditional practice was for women to live in semi-subterranean sod houses while the men stayed at one or more kasigi, communal houses. Christian missionaries banned Native religious practices. The decades between 1940 and 1960 brought many "modern" changes to the Island. The first post office on the Island was built in 1941 and an airstrip in 1957. A unit of the Alaska Territorial (now National) Guard was formed, and men from the island went to Fort Richardson near Anchorage for training. By this time the City of Mekoryuk had consolidated many of the traditional villages, and was the only permanent community on the island; it was incorporated in 1969. Other island families that had moved to Bethel to be near the high school returned annually for late-spring fishing and sea mammal hunting, and a high school was built in Mekoryuk in 1978 to accommodate these families.

GOVERNMENT
Mekoryuk was incorporated as a second-class city in 1969, with a mayor and city council, and is located in the Unorganized Borough. The Native Village of Mekoryuk is a BIA-recognized Indian Reorganization Act village council, headed by a president.

VILLAGE CORPORATION
NIMA Corporation is the city's ANCSA village corporation. Its subsidiaries are NIMA Store Inc. (general store in Mekoryuk), NICEA LLC (Nunivak Island Cultural Education and Adventures—alternative education, wildlife viewing, and outdoor adventure activities such as hiking, backpacking, and kayaking), and NHR LLC (Nuniwarmiut Home Renovators, Anchorage). NIMA's shareholders also hold shares in Calista Corporation, the regional Native corporation.

ECONOMY
The residents maintain reindeer and musk-oxen herds, and practice a subsistence lifestyle dependent upon the harvest of sea mammals, hunting, fishing, gathering, and gardening. Families retreat to fish camps for two to four weeks annually to catch and dry fish for winter use. Salmon, reindeer, seal meat, and oil are important dietary staples. Trapping is carried out both for commercial and personal purposes. Many residents offer guide services to tourists interested in hunting, fishing, and wildlife viewing and photography on the island. Employment by the school, city, village corporation, and (seasonally) commercial fishing dominate the local economy.

Fisheries. Fifty-five residents hold commercial fishing permits, primarily for halibut and herring roe. Coastal Villages Seafood, owned by the village council, processes halibut and salmon.

Government as employer. Fifty of 77 employed residents work for either the city, state or federal government.

Manufacturing. Bering Sea Reindeer Products Company is operated by the village council. Residents engage in Native craft activities, such as knitting qiviut (musk ox woolen underwear).

Services and retail. Local firms include a home supply store, arts and Native craft outlets, a grocery store, wilderness guide services, and a video rental shop.

Tourism and recreation. Many residents offer guide services to tourists interested in hunting, fishing, and wildlife viewing and photography on the island. Accommodations include three bed-and-breakfasts.

INFRASTRUCTURE

Transportation. Mekoryuk relies heavily on air transportation for passenger, mail, and cargo service. A 3,270-foot runway, served by Arctic Circle Air Service and Era Aviation, allows year-round access-weather permitting. Barges from Bethel deliver goods once or twice each summer. There are no roads on Nunivak Island; boats, snowmobiles, and all-terrain-vehicles are used for local travel. A breakwater protects the city shoreline from Bering Sea waves. Construction of port facilities began in 2003, with completion projected for 2006.

Electricity. Electricity is provided by the Alaska Village Electrical Cooperative (AVEC), of which the city is a member, from a 577-kilowatt diesel plant.

Fuel storage (gallons). NIMA Corp. (95,130); Lower Kuskokwim Schools (90,400); AVEC (84,900); city (34,700); Bering Sea Reindeer Products (15,900); Army National Guard (3,000).

Water and waste systems. Water for the community is drawn from a community well, is filtered, chlorinated and stored in a tank prior to distribution. Some residents haul water from surface sources. A flush/haul system currently serves about 90 percent of homes and funding has been acquired to complete service to the remaining homes which use honeybuckets. The school has its own well. In 2002 the state funded the design and construction of a 5,100-foot force main and two pump stations to hook up the washeteria and the school to the sewage lagoon. A Class 3 landfill is operated by the city.

Telecommunications. Local telephone service is provided by United Utilities, long distance services by United Utilities or AT&T Alascom. GCI provides Internet service to the school. The city has operated a cable television system since 1997. Residents can receive AM radio from stations in Nome, Bethel, Anchorage, Kotzebue, and other locations. The city and the Alaska Rural Communications System each broadcast one television channel from local repeaters.

COMMUNITY FACILITIES AND SERVICES

The city hall serves as the community hall and operates the water, waste disposal, and cable television systems.

Education. Nuniwarmiut School serves students in grades K-12, and is operated by the Lower Kuskokwim School District. The school is beginning a Cup'ig language immersion program for grades K-3. The school library serves as the community's public library.

Health care. The Mekoryuk Health Clinic is operated by the Yukon-Kuskokwim Health Corporation and supported by the Yukon Kuskokwim Delta Regional Hospital in Bethel. The Norton Sound Regional Hospital in Nome is a few miles closer.

Public safety. Law enforcement is provided by a state village public safety officer (VPSO; position vacant as of August, 2004), backed by state troopers in Bethel. Emergency response is provided by the VPSO (if available) and the city volunteer fire department.

M entasta

Total area of entitlement under ANCSA	
	69,120 acres
Total labor force	42
High school graduate or higher	28
Bachelor's degree or higher	9
Unemployment rate	33.3%
Per capita income *(1999)*	$11,108
2003 population	143
state demographer estimate	
Population *2000 census*	143
Percent Native *2000 census*	71.1%

LOCATION

The village of Mentasta Lake is located west of Mentasta Lake, 6 miles off the Tok-Slana Cutoff of the Glenn Highway on the west side of Mentasta Pass, 38 miles southwest of Tok Junction and 100 miles west of the Canadian border.

PHYSICAL DESCRIPTION

The area encompasses 303.1 square miles of land and 2.0 square miles of water, at elevations between 201 and 500 feet above sea level. It is located in the Slana River valley and is surrounded by mountains reaching above 6,000 feet. Extensive sand and gravel deposits are good foundation material for road construction and often free of permafrost. The village lies within 100 miles of the Kluane Wildlife Sanctuary in Yukon Territory, Canada, the Tetlin National Wildlife Refuge, the Wrangell-St. Elias National Park and Preserve, and the Yukon-Charely Rivers National Preserve. The village lies directly above the Denali Fault, which ruptured in 2002 causing a magnitude 7.9 earthquake.

CLIMATE

Mentasta Lake is located in the continental climate zone. Temperatures range from winter lows of -57°F to occasional summer highs of 93°F. Average snowfall is 69 inches, with 16 inches total precipitation per year. At this latitude, the region experiences approximately 20 hours of daylight per 24-hour period in June, declining to less than five hours of daylight in December.

CULTURE AND HISTORY

According to local Native oral traditions, the Ahtna Athabascan people have occupied this area of central Alaska for more than 40,000 years. They have been in the area for at least thousands of years. Evidence of early village settlements has been located at various sites around the lake. The area was rich in wildlife (sheep, mountain goat, moose, fox, beaver, porcupine, salmon, trout) and supported the peoples' subsistence activities richly, a tradition which continues today. The area around Mentasta Lake is reportedly the best-known route of Native migration across the Alaska Range. The U.S. Army Signal Corps established a telegraph station at Mentasta Pass in 1902. The Lake is currently home to many families from Nabesna, Suslota, Slana, and other villages within the area.

GOVERNMENT

The village of Mentasta Lake is an unincorporated entity located in the Unorganized Borough of Alaska. It is governed by a traditional village council, headed by a first chief.

VILLAGE CORPORATION

In 1980 the original ANCSA village corporation, Mentasta,

Also known as Mentasta Lake

[men-TASS-tuh]
Ethnicity: Ahtna Athabascan

Native entity
Mentasta Traditional Council
P.O. Box 6019
Mentasta Lake, AK 99780
  907-291-2319
  907-291-2305 Fax

ANCSA regional corporation
Ahtna, Incorporated
P.O. Box 649
Glennallen, AK 99588
  907-822-3476
  907-822-3495 Fax

Mentasta

Also known as Mentasta Lake

Incorporated, was merged into Ahtna, Incorporated, the regional Native corporation. Ahtna assumed the management of the former village corporation lands. The former village corporation became a shareholder committee known as the Successor Village Organization, which has the right to veto any type of new development within former village lands.

ECONOMY

Subsistence hunting, fishing, trapping, and gathering make up much of Mentasta Lake's economy. Cash employment is limited to a construction business, which is seasonal, and the Mentasta Lodge, which also runs an adjoining café and adjacent laundromat. In 1998, the Alaska Department of Community and Economic Development funded an overall economic development plan for the community, which may result in additional economic initiatives. In the year 2000, the median household income was $17,344, far below other native villages of similar size in the same region of Alaska.

Government as employer. The 2000 census indicates 28 residents are government workers, either state or federal.

Tourism and recreation. The Mentasta Lodge, with its cafe and laudromat, is on the Tok Cutoff of the Glenn Highway, about 10 miles from the village. The village lies within 100 miles of the Kluane Wildlife Sanctuary in Yukon Territory, Canada; the Tetlin National Wildlife Refuge, the Wrangell-St. Elias National Park and Preserve, and the Yukon-Charely Rivers National Preserve.

INFRASTRUCTURE

Transportation. Mentasta Lake has a six-mile road connection to the Tok Cutoff of the Glem Highway, which provides road access to the urban areas of the state and, through Canada, to the lower 48 states as well. There is also a small airstrip located near Mentasta Lodge.

Electricity. Electricity is provided by the Alaska Power & Telephone Company from a 217-kilowatt diesel plant.

Water and waste systems. Almost half of homes have individual wells and are fully plumbed. Water is provided at a central point in the village, drawn from a community well. Treated well water is available from the washeteria. Almost half of homes have septic tanks and are fully plumbed. Outhouses are used by the remaining residents. A piped community sewage and septic field system is funded and slated to be installed in 2004. A Class 3 landfill is owned and operated by the Village Council; however, it was listed as inactive during the 2000 Census.

Telecommunications. Local telephone service is provided by the Copper Valley Telephone Cooperative, long distance service from AT&T Alascom. Internet service, available only at the school, is provided by GCI. Radio station KCAM-AM broadcasts to the area. One television channel is broadcast locally from an Alaska Rural Communications System repeater.

COMMUNITY FACILITIES AND SERVICES

The village council provides waste collection and disposal, water supply, a washeteria, and a multipurpose facility housing a youth/recreation center and the public library.

Education. The Mentasta Lake School serves 36 students in grades K-12, has 3 teachers, and is operated by the Alaska Gateway School District.

Health care. The newly-constructed Mentasta Lake Health Clinic is owned by the village, leased to the U.S. Public Health Service, and administered by the Mt. Sanford Tribal Consortium. For emergencies, there is a Mentasta Rescue Squad, operating since 1999.

Public safety. Law enforcement is provided by State Troopers in Tok. Emergency response is provided by the Mentasta Rescue Squad.

Metlakatla

Also known as
Annette Island Reserve

[MET-luh-KAT-luh]
Ethnicity: Tsimshian

Native entity
Metlakatla Indian Community
P.O. Box 8
Metlakatla, AK 99926
907-886-4441
907-886-7997 Fax

NOTE

Metlakatla is located in and controls the Annette Island Reserve, the only federal Indian reservation in Alaska. It did not participate in the ANCSA, has no village corporation, nor are its members shareholders in the regional Native corporation.

Total labor force	664
High school graduate or higher	44.9%
Bachelor's degree or higher	10.5%
Unemployment rate	20.2%
Per capita income *(1999)*	$16,176
Population *2000 census*	1,447
2003 population	1,398
state demographer estimate	
Percent Native *2000 census*	89.2%

LOCATION

Annette Island is located on the Clarence Strait opposite Ketchikan near the southern end of the Alaskan panhandle. Metlakatla is located at Port Chester on the west coast of Annette Island, 15 miles south of Ketchikan. By air, it is 3.5 hours from Anchorage and 1.5 hours from Seattle.

PHYSICAL DESCRIPTION

The reservation encompasses 130.2 square miles of land and 83.8 square miles of water.

CLIMATE

Metlakatla is in the maritime climate zone. Weather conditions produce warm winters and cool summers. Average yearly snowfall is 61 inches. Average annual precipitation is 115 inches but more than 200 inches of annual rainfall has been recorded. Average summer temperatures range from 36°F to 52°F; average winter temperatures vary from 28°F to 42°F.

CULTURE AND HISTORY

Metlakatla means "saltwater channel passage." Canadian Tsimshians who migrated from Prince Rupert, British Columbia, in 1887, founded Metlakatla. The Reverend William Duncan of the Anglican Church, who worked with the tribe in the 1850s, had requested land from President Grover Cleveland for the Tsimshians. A local search committee selected the island. By 1890 the island had more than 800 residents. In 1891 the U.S. Congress declared Annette Island a federal Indian reservation. The Natives built homes, a church, school, sawmill, cannery, and a hydroelectric plant. During World War II, the U.S. Army built an air base a few miles away, and the U.S. Coast Guard maintained a base on the island until the mid-1970s. The Annette Island Reserve is the only federal reservation for indigenous peoples in Alaska. The community is traditionally Tsimshian.

GOVERNMENT

Congress declared Annette Island a federal Indian reservation in 1891. The community is organized under the Indian Reorganization Act, is governed by a council of 12 elected members, and is under the jurisdiction of the Portland Area Office of the Bureau of Indian Affairs. The 86,000-acre island

and surrounding 3,000 feet of coastal waters are exempt from state jurisdiction. The community regulates commercial fishing in the waters, and also operates its own tribal court system, including a Tribal Juvenile Court and Tribal Appellate Court. The community did not participate in the Alaska Native Claims Settlement Act, has no "village corporation," and its members are not shareholders in the regional Native corporation. State records show that Metlakatla was incorporated in 1944, but it is treated by the state government as a unique political entity.

ECONOMY

Fishing, fish processing, wood-products industries, and services maintain the Annette Island Reserve's economy. No local or state taxes are charged because the community is a federal Indian reservation. Metlakatla Indian Community is the largest employer on the reservation, operating the hatchery and all local services. The community has its eye on developing tourism.

Fisheries. A salmon hatchery on Tamgas Creek releases five salmon species. The community owns the Annette Island Packing Co., a cold-storage center. Forty-nine residents hold commercial fishing permits (salmon, halibut, cod, seaweed, clams).

Government as employer. Of 501 employed residents, 286 work in local, state, or federal government.

Services and retail. Businesses include child care centers, gas services, gift shops, construction companies, fishing guides, and household services.

INFRASTRUCTURE

Transportation. Metlakatla is accessible by air and water. The Annette Island Airport has a 7,500-foot asphalt runway and a 5,700-foot gravel crosswind runway. State-owned and community-owned seaplane bases are at Port Chester. Ketchikan offers scheduled floatplane service. Port facilities include a dock with a barge ramp, two small boat harbors, and two marine ways. Major improvements are in progress at Tamgas Harbor. Improvements to the ferry facilities are under construction. Barges deliver freight. A $40 million road project will connect a part of Annette Island and Ketchikan. The 14.7-mile Waldon Point Road should be available in 2007.

Electricity. Metlakatla Power and Light provides electricity and owns the Purple Lake and Chester Lake Hydroelectric facilities, and the Centennial Diesel Plant. Total capacity is 8,242 kilowatts.

Fuel storage (gallons). Metlakatla Power and Light (410,000); Annette Island Gas Service (79,948); Annette Island Packing (33,000); Annette Island Schools (10,000); William Duncan Church (1,000); community hall (1,000); Mini Mart (1,000).

Water and waste systems. Water is drawn from a dam on Chester Lake to a 200,000-gallon water tank in the main community. Untreated water from Yellow Hill Lake also serves Annette and the airport. A piped gravity sewage system in the main community provides primary treatment in an aerated lagoon with discharge through an ocean outfall. Nearly 500 homes and the school are plumbed and on the system. Individual septic tanks serve the Annette and airport area. Old sewer mains at 100 homes will be replaced.

Telecommunications. Local telephone service is provided by GTE Alaska or Alaska Telephone Company/AT&T, while long distance service is available through Alascom. The Internet service provider is Metlakatla.Net. One FM and one AM radio station broadcasts to the area, as do one commercial television channel and the Rural Alaska Television Network. The community provides a cable service.

COMMUNITY FACILITIES AND SERVICES

Education. The three schools on the reservation are under the Annette Island School District. Metlakatla High School has 97 students and 11 teachers; Leask Middle School has 49 students and 6 teachers; and Richard Johnson Elementary has 149 students and 14 teachers. The community supports the Duncan Cottage museum and the Centennial Public Library.

Health care. Annette Island Family Medical Center is available. The Volunteer Fire/EMS/Ambulance service provides auxiliary health care.

Public safety. Law enforcement is provided by the Metlakatla Police Department, emergency response by the Metlakatla Volunteer Fire/EMS/Ambulance Service.

M into

Total area of entitlement under ANCSA	
	115,200 acres
Total labor force	71
High school graduate or higher	31.5%
Bachelor's degree or higher	3.2%
Unemployment rate	16.2%
Per capita income *(1999)*	$9,639
Population *2000 census*	258
2003 population	234
state demographer estimate	
Percent Native *2000 census*	92.2%

LOCATION

Minto is conveniently located on an 11-mile spur road off of Elliott Highway (Highway 2) in interior Alaska.

PHYSICAL DESCRIPTION

Minto occupies 135.1 square miles of land and 3.6 square miles of water on the west bank of the Tolovana River at an elevation of between 50 and 22 feet above sea level.

CLIMATE

Minto has a cold, continental climate, with extreme temperature differences. Temperatures range from -50°F in the winter, with regular, extended periods of -40°F, to 70°F or higher in the summer. Average annual precipitation is 12 inches, with 50 inches of snowfall. High winds are typical in the winter; therefore, wind-chill factors are dramatic. At this latitude, the region experiences almost 22 hours of daylight per 24-hour period in June, declining to less than 4 hours in December.

CULTURE AND HISTORY

The residents of Minto are primarily Tanana Athabascans who maintain subsistence hunting and fishing traditions. Several families have seasonal fishing and hunting camps and trapping areas on the Tanana River and Goldstream Creek, where

[MIN-toe]
Ethnicity: Tanana Athabascan

Native entity
Native Village of Minto
P.O. Box 58026
Minto, AK 99758
   907-798-7112
   907-798-7627 Fax

ANCSA village corporation
Seth-De-Ya-Ah Corporation
P.O. Box 56
Minto, AK 99758
   907-798-7181
   907-798-7556 Fax

Minto

Mountain Village

See Asa'carsarmiut

salmon, whitefish, moose, bear, small game, waterfowl, and berries are used. Minto is in the westernmost portion of traditional Tanana Athabascan territory. During the late 1800s, the Minto Band traveled throughout the area, trading furs for manufactured goods and food items. It first became a permanent settlement when members of this band built cabins on the banks of the Tanana River and stayed year-round. Others, from Nenana, Toklat, Crossjacket, and Chena, pitched tents there during the summer fishing season. Gold was discovered north of Fairbanks in 1902, bringing many new people into the area, and the Bureau of Indian Affairs opened a school in 1937. In 1969 the village was relocated to its present site, an old fall and winter camp 40 miles north of the original village site, to escape frequent river flooding and stream bank erosion. New housing and a new school were completed by 1971. Tanana Athabascan is now spoken only at Nenana and Minto. The Athabascan population of those two villages is about 380, of whom about 30, the youngest approaching age 60, speak the language.

GOVERNMENT
Minto is an unincorporated village located in the Unorganized Borough. The BIA-recognized Native Village of Minto is governed by an Indian Reorganization Act council, headed by a president.

VILLAGE CORPORATION
Seth-De-Ya-Ah Corporation is the ANCSA village corporation, with an alternative address of P.O. Box 849, Fairbanks, AK 99707. Shareholders in the village corporation are also shareholders in Doyon, Limited, the regional Native corporation.

ECONOMY
Subsistence is an important part of the local economy, with several families maintaining seasonal fishing and hunting camps and trapping areas on the Tanana River and Gold Stream Creek. Some residents have taken year-round jobs working at the Minto School, the village-operated Lake View Lodge, the Health Clinic, the village council, or the area development corporation. Some work for the Bureau of Land Management as fire fighters each summer; others are employed by the Tolovana Construction Company, and Northfork Store and Fuel.

Government as employer. Twenty-one of 42 employed residents work for the state or federal government.

Manufacturing. Minto has an Arts and Crafts Center, at which residents make traditional birch-bark baskets and beaded skin and fur items.

Tourism and recreation. Lodging is provided by the village-operated Lake View Lodge, a popular destination, especially for duck hunters. Minto is within 100 miles of the following:

Gates of the Arctic National Park and Preserve, Kanuti National Wildlife Refuge, Yukon Flats National Wildlife Refuge, Yukon-Charley Rivers National Preserve, Koyukuk National Wildlife Refuge, Nowitna National Wildlife Refuge, and Denali National Park and Preserve.

INFRASTRUCTURE
Transportation. Trucks, cars, snowmobiles and all-terrain vehicles are used. The Tolovana River allows boat access to the Tanana and Nenana rivers, but no barge service is available because both rivers are too shallow; however, riverboats are used for transportation, recreation, and subsistence hunting and fishing. The state owns and operates a 2,000- by 65-foot gravel airstrip outside of the village. Design for new airport facilities was begun in 2003. These plans call for the removal of trees and other obstructions, the construction of an apron, a taxiway and a new runway, with completion slated for 2005. Arctic Circle Air Service and Tanana Air Service deliver goods and passengers to Minto.

Electricity. Electricity is available from the Alaska Village Electrical Cooperative (AVEC), from a 558-kilowatt diesel plant.

Fuel storage (gallons). AVEC (42,000); Yukon-Koyukuk Schools (15,000).

Water and waste systems. The water system at Minto is operated by the village council and by individual homeowners. Water is drawn from two community wells, treated, then distributed in a heated circulating water line. Fifty-two homes are connected to the water and sewer system and have complete plumbing.

Telecommunications. Local telephone service is provided by United Utilities, and long distance services by AT&T Alascom or United Utilities. Internet service is available at the school from GCI. AM radio stations can be received from Nenana, North Pole, Anchorage, and Fairbanks. Two television channels are broadcast by the Alaska Rural Communications Service in Minto, and the village owns a third television repeater.

COMMUNITY FACILITIES AND SERVICES
The village operates the water and sewer systems, a washeteria for the community, the community hall, and the village youth center. Services for seniors are offered at the community hall by the village council.

Education. Minto School, operated by the Yukon-Koyukuk School District, serves students in pre-kindergarten through 12th grade.

Health care. The Minto Health Clinic, operated by the Tanana Chiefs Conference (TCC), offers medical services to the community. It is supported by Fairbanks Memorial Hospital and the TCC's Chief Andrew Isaac Health Center.

Total area of entitlement under ANCSA
128,109 acres

Total labor force	320
High school graduate or higher	141
Bachelor's degree or higher	78
Unemployment rate	9.4%
Per capita income *(1999)*	$21,182
Population *2000 census*	678
2003 population	614
state demographer estimate	
Percent Native *2000 census*	47.1%

LOCATION

Naknek is located on the north bank of the Naknek River, at the northeastern end of Bristol Bay. The village is about 15 miles downriver from King Salmon, at the base of the Alaska Peninsula, and approximately 297 miles southwest of Anchorage.

PHYSICAL DESCRIPTION

The area encompasses 84.2 square miles of land, mostly lowlands and slough, and 0.7 square mile of water, at an elevation of less than 50 feet above sea level. It is an area rich with wildlife, including many species of birds, caribou, and brown bear. The vegetation is mostly moist tundra, becoming wet tundra to the east. There are sand and gravel deposits along the major streams and the Naknek River. The village lies within a high-occurrence gas and oil province. The Naknek River is a major anadromous fish habitat. The entire area is a waterfowl use area. Beluga whales feed offshore, and the gray whale spring migration passes nearby.

CLIMATE

The climate is maritime, strongly influenced by its proximity to Bristol Bay, with a lot of cool, windy days or humidity and fog. Continental climate influences cause periodic rapid fluctuations. Summer temperatures average between 42°F and 63°F, with extremes to 88°F. Winter temperatures average between 29°F and 44°F, with extremes of -46°F. Total precipitation is 20 inches annually, including 45 inches of snow. At this latitude, the area experiences approximately 18 hours of daylight in a 24-hour period in June, declining to just over 6 hours in December.

CULTURE AND HISTORY

The Naknek region, abounding in lakes and rivers, was first settled over 6,000 years ago, with hunting camps along the Naknek River that date to 4,000 or 5,000 years ago. The early history of the lower Naknek River is not clear, but by the first recorded European encounter with the village in 1821, it was an Aglurmiut Yup'ik community. In 1821, Russian Capt. Lt. Vasiliev noted the existence of the original Eskimo village of "Naugeik," but it was later given the spelling "Naknek" by Captain Tebenkov of the Imperial Russian Navy. The Russians built a fort near the village and fur trappers capitalized on the wide variety of common small game, including beaver and fox, for some time prior to the U.S. purchase of Alaska. Salmon-processing techniques were developed shortly after the Civil War, and by 1883 the first salmon cannery was opened in Bristol Bay. The Homestead Act, in 1863, cleared the way for canneries to acquire land for their plants; eleven more were in operation by 1900. Aglurmiut, Alutiiq, and Athabascan families in the area moved to Naknek for cannery jobs. The Act also opened land to settlement by other individuals and institutions. The parcel owned by the Russian Orthodox church on the north bank of the river was the first land transaction recorded in Naknek. Squatters built shelters on the church property and were eventually sold individual plots in what became the center of Naknek. A U.S. post office was established in 1907, and since then, Naknek has developed into a multicultural center of commerce centered on the commercial fishing industry.

Naknek is now a community with a mixed population of non-Natives, Yup'ik, Alutiiq, and Athabascan Indians with a subsistence lifestyle. Cultural events include traditional dancing, a "Fishtival" the last week of July, and berry-picking throughout July and August. In 2003, residents were designing a planned Naknek-King Salmon Alutiiq Cultural Center. The Alaska Department of Community and Economic Development funded the creation of the Bristol Bay Salmon Camp at Naknek in 2003, an annual summer aquatic science academy for rural middle- and high-school students in the Bristol Bay region. Supplemental enrichment activities take place throughout the school year to reinforce each student's cultural understanding. Because of its proximity to Katmai National Park, the village is heavily influenced by growing tourism.

GOVERNMENT

Naknek is an unincorporated village in Bristol Bay Borough, which serves as its civil government, unlike most boroughs in Alaska. Bristol Bay Borough is the oldest (1962) and smallest borough in Alaska. The Native Alaskan community in Naknek is governed by a traditional village council, headed by a president.

VILLAGE CORPORATION

Paug-Vik Incorporated, Limited, is the ANCSA village corporation for Naknek. Shareholders in the village corporation also hold shares in Bristol Bay Native Corporation.

ECONOMY

The economy of Naknek is dependent upon a seasonal commercial red-salmon fishing and fish-processing industry. Median household income in 1999 was $53,393, one of the highest in Alaska. In 1997, the Alaska Department of Community and Economic Development funded the development of an overall economic development plan, with stated regional priorities: construction of a fishermen's dock, a freight dock, and an industrial park.

Construction. There is a general building contractor in the village, as well as several renovation businesses and a cabinet shop.

Fisheries. Naknek serves as a service center for the huge red-salmon fishery in Bristol Bay, with thousands of people from neighboring areas coming in during every fishing season to help catch and process millions of pounds of salmon. The fish is trucked over the Naknek-King Salmon road to jets waiting to transport it to distribution centers throughout the L1ower 48 states. Trident Seafoods, North Pacific Processors, Ocean Beauty, and other fish processors operate facilities in Naknek.

Government as employer. Naknek is the seat of the Bristol Bay Borough government. A total of 101 residents of Naknek worked for either the borough, state, or federal government as of the 2000 census.

Manufacturing. There is a boat-building and repair business in the village. In 2001 a feasibility study was conducted to determine the viability of a seafood processing plant.

[NACK-neck]
**Ethnicity: Aglurmiut Yup'ik;
Alutiiq; Athabascan**

Governing body
Bristol Bay Borough
P.O. Box 189
Naknek, AK 99633
907-246-4224
907-246-6633 Fax
theborough.com

The Borough functions as the chief governing body for the communities of Naknek, South Naknek, and King Salmon.

Native entity
Naknek Native Village
P.O. Box 106
Naknek, AK 99633-0106
907-246-4210
907-246-3563 Fax

ANCSA village corporation
Paug-Vik Incorporated, Limited
P.O. Box 61
Naknek, AK 99633
907-246-4277
907-246-4419 Fax

Naknek

Services and retail. As Naknek is the center of the Bristol Bay Borough and a regional hub, services are extensive, ranging from stores selling general merchandise, food, clothing, and liquor to apartment management, auto repair, other repair services, lodging and restaurants, day-care centers, and tour operators.

Tourism and recreation. Naknek is within 30 miles of the Katmai National Park and Preserve and the Becharof National Wildlife Refuge. It is also within 100 miles of the Kodiak National Wildlife Refuge on Kodiak Island. The Cottonwood Lodge, Naknek Hotel, the D&D Restaurant, and some bed-and-breakfasts are available for tourists. A number of residents provide guided wilderness, fishing, and backcountry tours.

INFRASTRUCTURE

Transportation. Primarily accessible by air and sea, Naknek does connect to the Alaska Peninsula Highway via a 15.5-mile road to King Salmon, improved in 1997. In the year 2000, 3.5 miles of bike and pedestrian trails were constructed in Naknek, connecting the downtown area to the Donna G. Subdivision and Mile Marker 4 of the Alaska Peninsula Highway. In 2002, the Pederson Point Road was extended and 2nd Avenue was reconstructed, and in 2003, a potential Bristol Bay-Naknek to South Naknek Road was under consideration.

The Tibbetts Airport has a lighted 1,700- by 60-foot gravel runway. The state-owned Naknek Airport, located one mile north of Naknek, has a 1,950- by 50-foot lighted gravel runway and a 2,000-foot floatplane base. In 2002, runways were extended and other airport improvements were made at these facilities, with an airport master plan study under development, slated for completion in 2005. Jet service is available at King Salmon and there are several charter air services serving the local airports. Bristol Bay Borough operates the cargo dock at Naknek, called the Port of Bristol Bay, with 800 feet of berthing space, a concrete surface, and cranes.

Electricity. Electricity is available to residents from the Naknek Electric Association, a rural electric co-operative, from a 12,257-kilowatt diesel plant. In 1998, AEA funded a hydroelectric/tidal power feasibility study, to assess the possibility of hydro-generated power, using Kvichak Bay tidal energy to generate electricity.

Fuel storage (gallons). Naknek Electric Association (1,660,000); Bristol Bay Borough (48,500); Trident Seafoods (31,000); Nelbro Packing Co. (24,200); Southwestern AK Construction (6,000); Paug-Vik Inc. (5,200); Peninsula Auto (4,000); Naknek Engine Sales and Service (2,500).

Water and waste systems. The Borough provides piped water from a community well, and some homes, the schools, and HUD housing have individual wells. Almost all homes are fully plumbed; extensive rehabilitation has been underway since 1999, including the replacement of septic tanks with the installed piped system for all houses in the Airplane Lake subdivision. The sewer lines were also extended from the Donna G. Subdivision eastward along the Alaska Peninsula Highway, a distance of approximately 12,800 feet. Also included in the project is preliminary field/design work for the Nornak Lake subdivision sewer extension. Some of this work was still underway in 2003. Bristol Bay Borough operates a Class 2 landfill. Refuse is collected by private contractor, Patterson Sanitation Company. In 2002, landfill improvements were undertaken and were still in progress in 2004.

Telecommunications. Local telephone service is provided by the Bristol Bay Telephone Cooperative, long distance service by GCI or Bristol Bay Telephone. Cable service is offered by Bristol Bay Telephone and Internet services by Bristol Bay Telephone or GCI. One television channel is broadcast locally by the Alaska Rural Communications Service, and one AM radio station and one FM radio station broadcast to the area.

COMMUNITY FACILITIES AND SERVICES

Community facilities include a multi-use community center, built in 1998, which includes the medical clinic. The borough operates a public swimming pool and gym, the public library, and the landfill, and provides sewage collection and disposal and water supply. In 2002, the community completed a feasibility study for construction of the Bristol Bay-Alutiiq Cultural Center.

Education. The Bristol Bay Borough School District operates Bristol Bay High School, serving 114 students in grades 7-12 with 11 teachers, and Naknek Elementary School, serving 109 students in preschool through sixth grade with 8 teachers.

Health care. The newly-constructed Camai Community Health Center, a qualified Emergency Care Center, is owned by the borough and the village council, leased to the U.S. Public Health Service, and operated by the Bristol Bay Area Health Corporation. Emergency care is also provided by Bristol Bay Borough Emergency Services. Ambulance services are provided by the Bristol Bay Volunteer Rescue Squad. There is long-term residential care for elders available at the Southwest Elders Home.

Public safety. Law enforcement is provided by the borough police department, backed by state troopers in King Salmon. Emergency response is provided by Bristol Bay Borough Emergency Services.

Total area of entitlement under ANCSA	
76,400 acres	
Total labor force	79
High school graduate or higher	35
Bachelor's degree or higher	5
Unemployment rate	5.1%
Per capita income *(1999)*	$10,577
Population *2000 census*	177
2003 population	214
state demographer estimate	
Percent Native *2000 census*	93.2%

LOCATION
Nanwalek, called English Bay until 1991, is located at the southern tip of the Kenai Peninsula, 10 air miles southwest of Seldovia and 2 trail miles west of Port Graham.

PHYSICAL DESCRIPTION
Nanwalek is a coastal village encompassing 8.5 square miles of land.

CLIMATE
Due to its location at the tip end of a peninsula, Nanwalek is almost surrounded by water and therefore has a maritime climate. Winter temperatures average between 14°F and 27°F; summer temperatures range from 45°F to 60°F, with average annual precipitation of 24 inches; snowfalls rarely accumulate more than 4 feet. Daylight hours in June average nineteen hours; December has an average of 5.5 daylight hours in a 24-hour period.

CULTURE AND HISTORY
Nanwalek is a traditional Alutiiq village whose people have lived near the shores of English Bay on the Cook Inlet for thousands of years. A Russian trading post built in 1785 at the site attracted many Alutiiq families from villages near Prince William Sound, from Yalik, and from other settlements on the Kenai Peninsula because of the fur trade centered there. They stayed in the area and worked as marine mammal hunters, coal miners, trappers, and commercial fishermen. A Russian Orthodox church was built in the community in 1870 and re-placed by a new structure in 1930. This building has now been designated a National Historic Landmark. The villagers by local consensus changed the name in 1991 from English Bay to Nanwalek, "place by lagoon," an Alutiiq name that reflects its Native roots.

Although traditionally the people called themselves Sugpiaq (-*suk* "person" plus -*piaq* "real"), the name Alutiiq was adopted from a Russian plural form of *Aleut*, which Russian invaders applied to the Native people they encountered from Attu to Kodiak. Many of the residents as of 2004 are of mixed Russian and Alutiiq lineage, with a strong, traditional subsistence culture. Despite employment income from local canneries and other sources, many families continue to rely on the harvest of various species of fish, seals and sea creatures, plants, and many other wild foods throughout the year. The villagers speak Sugtestun, the Chugash dialect of Alutiiq, similar to Yup'ik. They maintain strong cultural traditions including the celebration of Núwikútaq, which welcomes in the New Year, and other Native ceremonies. Use of the Sugtestun language is maintained through language programs at the school, supported by efforts by the village council. Traditional crafts, such as the construction of sea kayaks, are cultivated by local artisans.

GOVERNMENT
Nanwalek is an unincorporated village in the Kenai Peninsula Borough. It has an IRA village council, headed by a president.

VILLAGE CORPORATION
English Bay Corporation is the ANCSA village corporation for Nanwalek. In 1997, the Corporation sold surface title to 32,537 acres of land within the Kenai Fjords National Park and the Alaska Maritime National Wildlife Refuge to the Federal government for $15.37 million. Certain access rights for subsistence activities were reserved. The Corporation has committed $500,000 from its proceeds to establish a special cultural conservation fund to survey, protect, curate, and interpret archaeological sites and cultural artifacts which are associated with the lands acquired. Shareholders also hold shares in Chugach Alaska Corporation regional Native corporation. The local address for the English Bay Corporation is P.O. Box 8058, Nanwalek, AK, 99603-6658.

ECONOMY
The economy of Nanwalek is primarily subsistence-based. Nanwalek's economy is limited by the lack of year-round road access. The school and summer employment at the cannery in Port Graham provide some residents with cash income. Nanwalek is within 50 miles of the Kenai National Wildlife Refuge and the Kenai Fjords National Park and within 100 miles of Chugach State Park, all of which attract tourists. The median household income in the year 1999 was $42,500, one of the highest in the State of Alaska.

Fisheries. Seven residents hold commercial fishing permits. In addition to seasonal fishing, the community is working on a project to reestablish the local sockeye salmon run, which has been very low in recent years.

Government as employer. As of the 2000 census, 21 Nanwalek residents worked for the borough, state, or federal governments.

Manufacturing. Two craftsmen are employed in the construction of native sea kayaks.

Services and retail. Private services available in Nanwalek include two day-care facilities and a grocery store.

Tourism and recreation. The Nicholas Bed and Breakfast and Dog Fish Bay Sportsman's Lodge are available to visitors.

INFRASTRUCTURE
Transportation. There are 9 local-only community streets and a trail connecting Nanwalek to Port Graham, the nearest village. There is an airstrip just outside the village, owned and maintained by the State of Alaska and served by Homer Air. It has a single gravel runway, 1,850- by 50-foot. Nanwalek's economy is limited by the lack of year-round road access. Boats are the primary means of local transportation for all residents, although many use aircraft for longer distance travel. The state ferry provides service to nearby Seldovia.

Electricity. Electricity is available to all homes and public and private buildings, generated at diesel and hydroelectric plants and provided by the Homer Electric Association.

Water and waste systems. There is piped water in the village, drawn from a surface stream; the water is filtered prior to distribution. In 1999-00, the U.S. Department of Agriculture and

Also known as English Bay

[nan-WAH-leck]
**Ethnicity: Chugachigmuit
Alutiiq**

Native entity
Native Village of Nanwalek
P.O. Box 8028
Nanwalek, AK 99603
  907-281-2274
  907-281-2252 Fax

ANCSA village corporation
English Bay Corporation
1637 Stanton Ave.
Anchorage, AK 99508
  907-281-2208
  907-281-2220 Fax

Nanwalek

Also known as English Bay

Napaimute

See Zero Population Section

the Alaska Native Tribal Health Consortium funded water system upgrades, including the development of a new surface water source and intake, transmission line, reservoir, filtration modifications, and the installation of an insulated steel water storage tank to increase pressure for new homes. In 2003, a completely new water treatment plant and transmission line to five additional homes was funded. There is also a piped-sewage system, utilizing a community septic system serving all homes in the village. Most homes are completely plumbed, but some home-owners in Nanwalek own and maintain outhouses. There is a Class 3 landfill.

Telecommunications. Telephone service is available to all homes and public and private buildings. Local telephone service is provided by ACS of the Northland, and long distance services are available through AT&T Alascom. One FM and three AM radio stations broadcast to the Nanwalek area. One television channel is broadcast locally by the Alaska Rural Communications System.

COMMUNITY FACILITIES AND SERVICES
Community facilities include the community building, housing the Nanwalek Clinic among other offices and services. The village council provides waste collection and disposal (except for the landfill operated by the Kenai Peninsula Borough) and water supply.

Education. Nanwalek School serves children in grades K-12. There are 76 students and 6 staff. It is operated by the Kenai Peninsula Schools.

Health care. Health care is provided by the Nanwalek Clinic, owned by the village council and leased to the U.S. Public Health Service; it is operated by the Chugachmiut Regional Health Corporation. It was relocated to a newly constructed Community Building in 2001. Emergency services are provided by the Nanwalek First Responders.

Public safety. Law enforcement is provided by state troopers in Homer. Emergency response is provided by the Nanwalek First Responders.

Napakiak

[nuh-PAH-key-ack]
Ethnicity: Yup'ik

Municipality
City of Napakiak
P.O. Box 34009
Napakiak, AK 99634
907-589-2611
907-589-2612 Fax

Native entity
Native Village of Napakiak
P.O. Box 34069
Napakiak, AK 99634
907-589-2135
907-589-2136 Fax

ANCSA village corporation
Napakiak Corporation
P.O. Box 34030
Napakiak, AK 99634
907-589-2227
907-589-2412 Fax

Total area of entitlement under ANCSA

	115,200 acres
Total labor force	130
High school graduate or higher	37.2%
Bachelor's degree or higher	1.8%
Unemployment rate	13.1%
Per capita income *(1999)*	$7,319
Population *2000 census*	353
2003 population	380
state demographer estimate	
Percent Native *2000 census*	96.6%

LOCATION
Napakiak is on the north bank of the Kuskokwim River at Johnson's Slough (also called the Johnson River), near an area of the river called Kuskokwim Bay, at an elevation of less than 50 feet above sea level. It is 15 miles southwest of Bethel and 407 miles west of Anchorage. Napakiak is located entirely within the Yukon Delta National Wildlife Refuge.

PHYSICAL DESCRIPTION
The city encompasses 4.7 square miles of land and 0.3 square mile of water. It is on an island between Johnson's Slough and the Kuskokwim River. The village is split, with newer housing is at one end, the airstrip in the middle, and the older end. Prior to 1997 the island village experienced flooding and erosion of the sandbar at Johnson's Slough on which the community was built, precipitating a move of all public facilities and homes to a site located on a bluff across the Slough.

CLIMATE
The climate of Napakiak is strongly influenced by storms and weather patterns in the Bering Sea, as well as by inland continental weather. Summer temperatures range from 42°F to 62°F, with extremes of 86°F recorded. Winter temperatures vary between -2°F and 19°F with extremes to -46°F. Average annual precipitation is 16 inches, including 50 inches of snowfall. The Kuskokwim River is frozen over from October through mid-June. At this latitude, the region experiences approximately 19 hours of daylight in a 24-hour period in June, declining to 5 1/2 in December.

CULTURE AND HISTORY
Napakiak residents, primarily Yup'ik who have lived in this region for a thousand years, maintain a culture centered on fishing and other subsistence activities. The village was first reported in 1878, downriver from its present site. It is mentioned in 1884 by Moravian church explorers, whose report suggests that the new village location was occupied by that year. By 1910, the village had 166 residents. Moravian church missionaries constructed a church in the village between 1926 and 1929. A Bureau of Indian Affairs (BIA) school opened in 1939, and in 1946 a Native-owned store operated by the Village Cooperative opened. These were followed by a post office in 1951, a National Guard Armory in 1960, and the first airstrip in 1973, shortly after incorporation in 1970.

GOVERNMENT
The City of Napakiak was incorporated as a second-class city in 1970. The Native Village of Napakiak is a BIA-recognized Indian Reorganization Act council, headed by a president.

VILLAGE CORPORATION
Napakiak Corporation is the community's ANCSA village corporation. Shareholders also hold shares in Calista Corporation, the regional Native corporation.

ECONOMY
Residents of Napakiak practice a largely subsistence lifestyle, with dietary dependence on moose, bear, seals, salmon, and waterfowl. Napakiak is accessible only by air and water, somewhat limiting economic opportunity. However, there are sources of income for residents, including the school, local, state, and federal governments, and seasonal commercial fishing, construction, and trapping.

Fisheries. Many residents hold commercial fishing licenses, primarily for herring roe and salmon net-fishing.

Government as employer. Sixty-nine of 101 employed residents work in the city, state, or federal government.

Services and retail. Local businesses include a native craft store, a video rental shop, two daycare centers, and two general stores.

Tourism and recreation. The village operates a tourist lodging. Napakiak is located entirely within the Yukon Delta National Wildlife Refuge and lies within 150 miles of the Innoko National Wildlife Refuge.

Transportation. A marina and a taxicab company operate in Napakiak.

INFRASTRUCTURE

Transportation. Napakiak is accessible only by air and water, somewhat limiting economic opportunity. However, in winter the river becomes a frozen road, connecting Napakiak to Bethel. During the relocation of the community, the city has been constructing roads to access the new sewage lagoon, resurfacing others, and improving access to the river barge landing area. There are, however, no year-round roads connecting Napakiak with other villages. As of 2004 a winter trail ran to Bethel, but the community was interested in construction of a nine-mile year-round road to Bethel. A state-owned 3,269- by 60-foot gravel runway and a seaplane landing area are served by Arctic Circle Air Service, Grant Aviation, and Hageland Aviation. The Kuskokwim River, a major thoroughfare for this region, is a primary means of travel and transportation for goods. River barges from Bethel deliver goods during the summer, and in the winter the river becomes a frozen road to many area villages, used by dog sleds, snowmobiles, and on travelers foot. There is a dock haul-out and harbor on the Kuskokwim, with a riverside boardwalk.

Electricity. Electricity is purchased and transmitted by overhead lines from Bethel Utilities and distributed locally by the privately operated Napakiak Ircinraq Power Company. There is also a local 300-kilowatt diesel plant.

Fuel storage (gallons). Lower Kuskokwim Schools (76,156); Napakiak Corporation (70,200); Marina (3,200); Jung's Trading Post (1,530).

Water and waste systems. The city owns and operates a piped water system with multiple watering points; water is both filtered and chlorinated prior to distribution. The city also operates the washeteria. Beginning in 1997, the water and sewage systems were overhauled during the move of the entire village to higher ground, to be completed in 2004. The project included the improvement of home plumbing fixtures, revitalization of the community well and the water treatment plant, a sewage lagoon and a pumper. New haul vehicles, system infrastructure, and computer software were purchased. Innovative haul units were installed in houses, the washeteria was refurbished, and dumpsite improvements were made. All housing is to be installed on the new system when complete. In 2002 work on a new Class 3 landfill site began.

Telecommunications. Local telephone service is provided by United Utilities, long distance service by AT&T Alascom. Internet service is provided by Unicom/United Utilities, and by GCI at the school. Napakiak Corporation operates the community's cable television system. Residents can receive AM radio transmissions from Bethel, Nome, Dillingham, Anchorage, and other locations, as well as one FM station from Bethel. One local television channel broadcasts from Bethel to the Napakiak area, as do two Alaska Rural Communications Service repeaters in Bethel.

COMMUNITY FACILITIES AND SERVICES

The city operates the water and waste disposal systems and the washeteria, and has a public safety building. As of 2003 the village council was building a community hall.

Education. The William N. Miller Memorial School, operated by the Lower Kuskokwim School District, serves children in grades K-12th. The school library serves as the community's public library.

Health care. Health care is provided by the Napakiak Health Clinic operated by the Yukon-Kuskokwim Health Corporation, and supported by the Yukon Kuskokwim Delta Regional Hospital in nearby Bethel.

Public safety. Law enforcement is provided by a state Village Public Safety Officer (VPSO), backed by State Troopers in Bethel. Emergency response is provided by the city volunteer fire department.

Napaskiak

Total area of entitlement under ANCSA	
	115,200 acres
Total labor force	136
High school graduate or higher	45%
Bachelor's degree or higher	4.8%
Unemployment rate	1.5%
Per capita income *(1999)*	$8,162
Population *2000 census*	390
2003 population	419
state demographer estimate	
Percent Native *2000 census*	98.2%

LOCATION

Napaskiak is located on the southeast bank of the Kuskokwim River, along the Napaskiak Slough in the Yukon Delta National Wildlife Refuge. Napaskiak is seven miles southeast (downstream) of Bethel, seven river miles upstream from Napakiak, and approximately 400 air miles due west of Anchorage.

PHYSICAL DESCRIPTION

The city area encompasses 3.5 square miles of land and 0.4 square mile of water at an elevation of less than 165 feet above sea level. The surrounding area is characterized by flat, virtually treeless tundra, dotted with numerous meltwater ponds called "potholes" and veined by smaller rivers, creeks, and sloughs. During the winter months, the river often freezes to a depth of more than six feet.

CLIMATE

The climate in Napaskiak is not only strongly influenced by storms and weather patterns originating in the Bering Sea, but by inland continental weather systems as well, especially in winter. Average summer daily temperatures range from 42°F to 62°F; average winter daily temperatures vary from -2°F to 19°F. Average annual precipitation is 16 inches, including at least 50 inches of snowfall. At this latitude, the region experiences approximately 19 hours of daylight in a 24-hour period in June, declining to 5.5 in December.

CULTURE AND HISTORY

Historically, this region of Alaska has been occupied by Yup'ik practicing a subsistence lifestyle dependent upon the harvest of bear, moose, caribou, waterfowl and fish, especially salmon. All the Pacific Ocean species of salmon have spawning beds on the various tributaries of the Kuskokwim River. All except pink salmon are fished by the men of the community using gill nets. The women prepare these fish in a variety of ways

[nuh-PASS-key-ack]
Ethnicity: Yup'ik

Municipality
City of Napaskiak
P.O. Box 6078
Napaskiak, AK 99559-6078
907-737-7432
907-737-7989 Fax

Native entity
Native Village of Napaskiak
P.O. Box 6009
Napaskiak, AK 99559
907-737-7364
907-737-7039 Fax

ANCSA village corporation
Napaskiak, Incorporated
P.O. Box 6069
Napaskiak, AK 99559
907-737-7413
907-737-7128 Fax

Napaskiak

using all of the fish except the entrails and gills. King salmon, chum salmon, and red salmon are dried on outdoor fish drying racks after having been split and sliced to promote thorough drying. After the fish are dried, they are taken to the family smoke house where they are smoked using green balsam poplar (cottonwood). A variety of furbearers and birds are abundant in their seasons and are taken to supplement the salmon harvested in the summer. Beaver, muskrat, snowshoe hare, mink, and otter are harvested both for their meat and for their skins. Ptarmigan, locally referred to as "tundra chicken," are hunted in March when they forsake a solitary lifestyle and begin to gather in large flocks. Ducks, geese, sandhill cranes, common snipe, and other waterfowl are also harvested in their season. In September, the men travel upriver by boat to hunt moose and caribou. Caribou have returned to the near vicinity of Napaskiak for the first time since the building of the Alaska railway earlier in the twentieth century. From mid-July through September, the tundra provides a bountiful harvest of wild berries. A community at this location was first reported by the U.S. Coast and Geodetic Survey in 1867, then, in the 1880 U.S. census, a population of 196 people was reported. By 1890 the numbers had dropped to 97 and were as low as 67 in 1939. The city was incorporated in 1971.

GOVERNMENT
Napaskiak was incorporated as a second-class city in 1971, with a mayor and city council; it is located in the Unorganized Borough. The Native Village of Napaskiak is a BIA-recognized traditional village council, headed by a president.

VILLAGE CORPORATION
Napaskiak, Incorporated, is the ANCSA village corporation. Shareholders also hold shares in Calista Corporation, the regional Native corporation.

ECONOMY
The economy of Napaskiak is very much subsistence based, but there are sources of income for residents.

Fisheries. Some residents hold commercial fishing licenses, primarily for salmon drift netting.

Government as employer. Seventy-four of 132 employed residents of Napaskiak work for the city, state, or federal government.

Services and retail. There are a gas station and a retail store in the village.

Tourism and recreation. Visitor attractions include dog mushing events, including the annual sled dog competition. Accommodations are available at the school or the city office overnight room.

INFRASTRUCTURE
Transportation. Napaskiak is accessible by air and water; it is connected to other villages only by winter trails-there are no year-round roads into the community. A state-owned 3,400-foot gravel airstrip and seaplane base west of the village provides year-round chartered and general-aviation flights. The airstrip is served by Arctic Circle Air Service, Grant Aviation, and Hageland Aviation. The Kuskokwim River is a major transportation route 10 months of the year. For about a month during freeze up and another month during breakup, the river is unsafe. From late May through mid-October, outboard skiffs are used for family and work transportation. Families rely on their boats for subsistence activities, to travel to Bethel and other nearby villages, and to haul lumber for house construction and 55-gallon drums of gasoline and stove oil. River barges deliver goods in the summer months. Snowmobiles and all-terrain vehicles are used in the winter months, and during the winter months taxicabs operate on the river providing another commercial travel option.

Electricity. Electricity is provided by Napaskiak Electric Utility from a 355-kilowatt diesel plant.

Fuel storage (gallons). City Electric (43,200); Lower Kuskokwim Schools (42,000); Army National Guard (1,500); Napaskiak Inc. (1,500)

Water and waste systems. The city draws water from a central watering point and community wells. The village council, in a memorandum of understanding with the city, treats, filters, and chlorinates the water. The city operates a village sewer system that includes a sewage pumper and lagoon. Since 1998 major improvements in the water and sewage systems throughout the community have been made every year, including the addition of 30 homes onto the system in 2002. There are many residents utilizing honeybucket pits and outhouses. The city operates a Class 3 landfill.

Telecommunications. Local telephone service by United Utilities, long distance by United Utilities or AT&T Alascom. Internet service is provided by Unicom/United Utilities and, at the school, by GCI. Residents can receive AM radio transmissions from Bethel, Nome, Dillingham, Anchorage, and other locations, as well as one FM station from Bethel. One local television channel broadcasts from Bethel to the Napaskiak area, as do two Alaska Rural Communications Service repeaters in Bethel.

COMMUNITY FACILITIES AND SERVICES
The city and village council jointly operate the water system, and the city operates the waste disposal systems. There is a city office building and a community building.

Education. The Z. John Williams Memorial School, which serves children in grades K-12, is operated by the Lower Kuskokwim School District. It is to be renovated in 2005. The school library serves as the community's public library.

Health care. The Yago Clark Memorial Health Clinic, finished in 2002, is operated by the Yukon-Kuskokwim Health Corporation and is backed up by the Yukon Kuskokwim Delta Regional Hospital in nearby Bethel.

Public safety. Law enforcement is provided by a state village public safety officer (VPSO), backed by state troopers in Bethel. Emergency response is provided by the VPSO and the city volunteer fire department.

Total area of entitlement under ANCSA
76,983 acres

Total labor force	39
High school graduate or higher	17
Bachelor's degree or higher	4
Unemployment rate	28.6%
Per capita income *(1999)*	$27,596
Population *2000 census*	83
2003 population	64
state demographer estimate	
Percent Native *2000 census*	81.9%

LOCATION

The village of Nelson Lagoon is situated on a tiny strip of land jutting out into the Bering Sea, just off the northern coast of the Alaska Peninsula. It is 80 miles northwest of Cold Bay and 580 miles southwest of Anchorage.

PHYSICAL DESCRIPTION

The narrow sand spit on which the village is built separates Nelson Lagoon, the body of water for which the community is named, from Bristol Bay. The entire village area encompasses 135.3 square miles of land and 61.4 square miles of water, at an elevation of less than 165 feet above sea level. The community enjoys scenic views of the active Pavlof Volcano and other mountains of the Alaska Peninsula. While Nelson Lagoon is near potential oil and gas deposits, the only mineral resource nearby is coal fields about 25 miles to southwest that have never been commercially exploited.

The village is located in a prime biological area with a diverse population of land, aquatic, coastal and marine birds, land and marine mammals, and fresh- and saltwater fish. The in-shore area consists of intertidal mud and sand flats which, together with sand dunes, barrier islands, and upland heath and salt meadows, provide a mix of coastal habitats. Within the lagoon area, the wildlife is concentrated near the village. The protected waters host most of the bird species of the Alaska Peninsula, supporting several hundred thousand waterfowl and shorebirds during spring migration and more than a million during fall migration and winter. It is also a prime salmon and marine mammal area, with the nearby stream and lake systems supporting major sockeye populations, among others, together with seals, sea otters, and gray whales. Land vegetation includes a beach strand zone with beach ryegrass and sandwort, and a lowland zone with wet tundra vegetation and dwarf willows. Marine vegetation includes extensive beds of eelgrass in the tidal marshes and algae in tidal sloughs. The tidal flats support clams, small crustaceans, and worms.

CLIMATE

Almost surrounded by the cold waters of the Bering Sea, Nelson Lagoon has a maritime climate with frequent, dramatic weather changes and constant prevailing winds of 20 to 25 miles per hour. Nelson Lagoon enjoys relatively mild winters and cool summers, with temperatures averaging between 25°F to 45°F in the winter and between 45°F and 60°F in the summer, although extremes from -15°F to 75°F have been recorded. Total annual precipitation averages 32 inches, with annual snowfalls of 56 to 61 inches. At this latitude, the region experiences approximately 17.5 hours of daylight in a 24-hour period in June, declining to slightly less than 7 hours of daylight in December.

CULTURE AND HISTORY

Named for Edward William Nelson, an explorer in the Yukon Delta region between 1877 and 1920, Nelson Lagoon was founded in the early 1900s as a summer fish camp by settlers of Alutiiq and Scandinavian descent. A salmon saltery began operations in 1906, which attracted Scandinavian commercial fishermen, but it closed in 1917. The community never really started gaining in population until 1965, when a school was built and the village became occupied year-round. A dock, boat ramp, harbormaster's office and warehouse were completed in the mid- to late-1990s.

The subsistence-based Alutiiq culture of Nelson Lagoon is centered on commercial fishing and hunting and other subsistence activities, with the abundance of the Lagoon and nearby Bear River providing adequate resources for the entire village. The residents enjoy a strong sense of loyalty to one another and community pride with a firm desire to maintain their life-ways with slow, monitored, well-managed growth and economic development. Residents participate in community-wide potlucks, traditional potlatches, basketball and volleyball leagues, and an annual Christmas pageant and routinely sponsor school fundraising events.

GOVERNMENT

Nelson Lagoon is unincorporated and is located in the Aleutians East Borough. It is governed by a traditional village council, headed by a president.

VILLAGE CORPORATION

Nelson Lagoon Corporation is the ANCSA village corporation. Its shareholders also hold shares in the Aleut Corporation, the regional Native Alaskan corporation.

ECONOMY

Although there has been some tourism in the region, Nelson Lagoon residents have historically depended largely upon salmon gillnet-fishing as their source of income. In 2002, 24 residents held commercial fishing permits. Subsistence activities and some trapping of small game, both for personal and commercial use, supplements the income of many families.

Construction. A construction company is licensed to do business in Nelson Lagoon.

Fisheries. Nelson Lagoon residents have historically depended largely upon salmon gillnet-fishing as their source of income. In 2002, 24 residents held commercial fishing permits. Plans include a small seafood- and salmon-processing and cold storage facility.

Government as employer. In the 2000 census, nine Nelson Lagoon residents worked for the borough, state, or federal government.

Services and retail. Businesses licensed in Nelson Lagoon include a fuel company, a general merchandise store, a daycare center, and an accounting firm.

Tourism and recreation. Nelson Lagoon is within 30 miles of the Alaska Peninsula National Wildlife Refuge, within 60 miles of the Aniakchak National Monument and Preserve, and within approximately 100 miles of the Becharof National Wildlife Refuge. There is lodging available at either the Tides Inn and Café or the Bering Inn. There are two gift shops in the village and a videotape rental business.

Transportation. A trucking company is licensed to do business in Nelson Lagoon.

Ethnicity: Alutiiq

Native entity
Native Village of Nelson Lagoon
P.O. Box 13
Nelson Lagoon, AK 99571
907-989-2204
907-989-2233 Fax

ANCSA village corporation
Nelson Lagoon Corporation
General Delivery
Nelson Lagoon, AK 99571
907-989-2204
907-989-2233 Fax

Nelson Lagoon

INFRASTRUCTURE

Transportation. Nelson Lagoon is accessible only by air and sea; there are no year-round roads connecting it with regional villages. A state-owned 4,000- by 75 wide gravel runway permits regularly scheduled flights and residents rely upon the airport for personal and business travel, although a dock, boat ramp, harbormaster's office, and warehouse were completed in the mid- to late-1990s, permitting larger sea-going craft to utilize the Lagoon's protected waters for commercial purposes. Some inbound freight is landed 30 miles away at Port Moller. In 2003, the village regraded and resurfaced the gravel access road between the airport and North Main Street in Nelson Lagoon, a total distance of about 1½ miles. A Trail Plan was developed for the community, which included adding street lights in the village and reconstructing the road leading from the village to the landfill. With assistance from the Department of Community and Economic Development, the Aleutians East Borough funded construction of a boat ramp and dock, a small-boat harbor, and other marine improvements such as the dredging of the main river channel and the addition of buoys. In 2004, equipment for a travel lift pier was to be purchased. Snow removal equipment, a grader, and fire trucks were purchased and stationed at the airport, and a new terminal building was to be constructed in 2003.

Electricity. Electricity is provided by the Nelson Lagoon Electric Cooperative, which generates power at a 312-kilowatt diesel plant.

Fuel storage (gallons). Bulk fuel is available for purchase by residents. Nelson Lagoon Fuel Enterprise (140,000); Harold Thompson (3,000); Aleutians East Schools (1,500).

Water and waste systems. The water supply for the community is provided by a freshwater lake about 10 miles from Nelson Lagoon; there are no community wells. The village council operates a piped water system that treats, filters, and chlorinates the water prior to delivery, with a 600,000-gallon water storage tank that provides a sufficient quantity for community needs with no periods of shortfall. This distribution system and storage tank underwent major repairs in 1998, and all homes are connected; however, some residents also use individual wells. Water system improvements continued throughout 2000-2003 with the construction of a water treatment plant. Individual septic systems are used. There are no garbage collection services, but a landfill is available.

Telecommunications. Local telephone service is provided by ACS of the Northland, long distance service by AT&T Alascom or GCI. Internet services are provided by GCI. One television channel is offered by the Alaska Rural Communications System, and one radio station broadcasts to the area.

COMMUNITY FACILITIES AND SERVICES
The village council provides the water supply and operates the landfill and a washeteria. A community hall and multipurpose building was scheduled to be completed in 2003.

Education. The Nelson Lagoon School, which serves eleven students in grades K-12, is operated by the Aleutians East School District. It has two teachers. The school's multipurpose room serves as the community gymnasium.

Health care. Health care is provided by the Nelson Lagoon Health Clinic. The facility is owned by the village, leased to the U.S. Public Health Service, and operated by the Eastern Aleutian Tribe. Nelson Lagoon First Responders are available to respond to emergencies.

Public safety. Law enforcement is provided by a state village public safety officer (VPSO), backed by state troopers in King Salmon. Emergency response is provided by the VPSO and the Nelson Lagoon First Responders.

ENVIRONMENTAL CONCERNS
In 2003, the Department of Community and Economic Development funded the Nelson Lagoon Coastal Protection Project to protect and restore the natural features of the Nelson Lagoon shoreline while developing a model for erosion control that may be effective for other coastal communities throughout Alaska.

Nenana

[nuh-NAN-uh]
Ethnicity: Tanana Athabascan

Municipality
City of Nenana
P.O. Box 70
Nenana, AK 99760
  907-832-5441
  907-832-5503 Fax
  fairbanks-alaska.com

Native entity
Nenana Native Association
P.O. Box 356
Nenana, AK 99760
  907-832-5461
  907-832-1077 Fax

ANCSA village corporation
Toghotthele Corporation
P.O. Box 249
Nenana, AK 99760
  907-832-5461
  907-832-1077 Fax

Total area of entitlement under ANCSA	
	138,240 acres
Total labor force	223
High school graduate or higher	31.1%
Bachelor's degree or higher	9.9%
Unemployment rate	14.9%
Per capita income *(1999)*	$17,334
Population *2000 census*	402
2003 population	441
state demographer estimate	
Percent Native *2000 census*	47.3%

LOCATION
Nenana is in interior Alaska, just off the George Parks Highway (Highway 3) and at Mile Marker 412 of the Alaska Railroad. It is 40 air miles southwest of Fairbanks, or 55 miles by road, and 304 road miles northeast of Anchorage.

PHYSICAL DESCRIPTION
The city lies on the south bank of the Tanana River just east of the mouth of the Nenana River. The area encompasses 6.0 square miles of land and 0.1 square mile of water at 350 feet above sea level. In 1967 the community was devastated by one of the largest floods ever recorded in the valley.

CLIMATE
Nenana has a cold, continental climate, with slight maritime influences, creating potentially extreme temperature fluctuations. The daily minimum winter temperatures are well below zero, commonly reaching lows of -50°F with extremes of -69°F, while average daily summertime highs range between 65°F to 70°F, with extremes above 80°F. The highest temperature ever recorded was 98°F. Average annual precipitation is 11 inches, including 49 inches of snowfall. The Tanana River is frozen over from mid-October to mid-May. At this latitude, the region experiences well over 21 hours of daylight in a 24-hour period in June, declining to over 3.5 hours in December.

CULTURE AND HISTORY
Nenana is in the westernmost portion of traditional Tanana Athabascan territory. The present population of Nenana is diverse, a mixture of Athabascans, Inupiat, Yup'ik, Alutiiq, and non-Natives. The majority of these residents maintain a culture centered on subsistence activities. The community now called Nenana was first known as Tortella, the transliteration of a Native word *toghotthele*, meaning "mountain that parallels the river." Long accustomed to trade with Europeans, the Tanana people made trading journeys to the village where Russian traders bartered for durable and manufactured goods.

Gold was discovered in Fairbanks in 1902 and brought increased trading activity and settlement with it. To resupply river travelers and miners, a trading post and road house was established in 1903, and an Episcopal mission was built upriver in 1905. A post office opened in 1908. Native children from other communities attended school in Nenana, and by 1915 construction projects, including work on the Alaska Railroad, doubled Nenana's population. In 1917, surveyors for the Alaska Railroad and local residents created a fun tradition of guessing the date and time of the ice break-up on the Tanana River. That event became the Nenana Ice Classic, a now popular annual competition. The community incorporated in 1921, and a railroad depot was completed in 1923, just after President Warren Harding drove the final (golden) spike at the north end of the 700-foot steel bridge over the Tanana River to celebrate completion and the official opening of the railroad. Nenana's 5,000 people had transportation to Fairbanks and Seward. Many of the newly-arrived were quick to leave following completion of the railroad. Population during the 1930 census was only 291, and the community fell into an economic slump. It wasn't until the construction of an Air Force base in Clear, Alaska, in 1961, 21 miles southwest of Nenana, that new vitality was breathed into the local economy when many civilian contractors found homes in Nenana and commuted daily to the base. This resulted in a year-round road south to Clear, and to the north, vehicles were ferried across the Tanana River until construction of a bridge opened easier travel to Fairbanks. In 1967 the community was devastated by one of the largest floods ever recorded in the valley. The George Parks Highway was completed in 1971, providing a shorter, more direct route to Anchorage. Nenana, home to several Iditarod sled dog race competitors and former champions, celebrates its cultural history. Residents have opened the Nenana Native Cultural Center (2003) and the Alaska Railroad Depot Historical Museum at the site of the original railroad depot. There is also a Visitor Center and the Golden Railroad Spike Historic Park and Walking Path. In 1999, an Athabascan Heritage Park was completed. Annually, the residents hold several events: Nenana Ice Classic (March-April), Nenana Tripod Weekend (March), Nenana River Daze (June), Fourth of July Celebration, and the Nenana Whitewater Festival in July. Tanana Athabascan is now spoken only at Nenana and Minto. The Athabascan population of those two villages is about 380, of whom about 30, the youngest approaching age 60, speak the language.

GOVERNMENT
Nenana was incorporated as a home-rule city in 1921, with a mayor and city council. It is located in the Unorganized Borough. The BIA-recognized Nenana Native Association has a traditional village council, headed by a chief.

VILLAGE CORPORATION
Toghotthele Corporation is Nenana's ANCSA village corporation. Shareholders also hold shares in Doyon, Limited, the regional Native corporation.

ECONOMY
Nenana has a strong seasonal private-sector economy, serving as a rail-to-river transportation hub for the interior region of Alaska. The majority of Native households rely on subsistence foods, such as salmon, moose, caribou (by permit), bear, waterfowl, and berries, but the traditional subsistence lifestyle of the residents is now supplemented by occasional, seasonal, or full-time employment.

Construction. There is a general building contractor employing 14 residents in the construction fields.

Agriculture. A few residents are employed in agriculture on a farm located just outside town.

Fisheries. Many residents hold commercial fishing permits. There is a salmon-baking and-smoking operation that employs a few residents in season.

Government as employer. Sixty-nine of 170 employed residents work for the city, state, or federal government, including those who work for the school district and state highway maintenance.

Manufacturing. There are wood-product manufacturing businesses and a bed manufacturer in the city.

Services and retail. There is good retail presence including fuel supply, two handyman/repair services, general merchandise stores, a lumber store, several retail stores, a number of computer services, four auto-repair shops, and business and management services.

Tourism and recreation. Nenana lies within 100 miles of the following: Yukon Flats National Wildlife Refuge, Kanuti National Wildlife Refuge, Nowitna National Wildlife Refuge. It is less than 60 miles north of the northern border of the Denali National Park and Preserve. Residents have opened the Nenana Native Cultural Center (2003) and the Alaska Railroad Depot Historical Museum at the site of the original railroad depot. There is also a visitor center, the Golden Railroad Spike Historic Park and Walking Path, and the Athabascan Heritage Park. Annually, residents hold several events: Nenana Ice Classic (March-April), Nenana Tripod Weekend (March), Nenana River Daze (June), Fourth of July Celebration, and the Nenana Whitewater Festival in July. Lodging of various types is available to tourists and area visitors to these events, including the Tripod Motel and the Roughwoods Inn. There is also the Nenana Valley RV Park and Campground, a number of restaurants, several bars, and fishing camps.

Transportation. Yutana Barge Lines is the major private employer in Nenana, supplying villages along the Tanana and Yukon Rivers each summer with cargo and fuel. Other transportation-related firms include barge maintenance and repair services, a school bus repair shop, a trucking company, and several water freight-transportation companies.

INFRASTRUCTURE
Transportation. Nenana has excellent air, river, road, and railroad access. The George Parks Highway links Nenana, Fairbanks, and Anchorage together with the rest of the state and through Canada with the lower 48 states. Beginning in 1997, several road stabilization and rehabilitation projects were undertaken, including the repair of the Nenana River bridge supports on Parks Highway in 1998, city street repair (chip and seal) in 1999, with ongoing improvements continuing into 2000-01. These streets were to be resurfaced in 2004. The road connecting to the cemetery was resurfaced in 2003. The city is constructing a system of bike trails and has additional repairs planned for the Tanana River Bridge on the Alaska Highway slated for completion during 2004. A series of scenic waysides along the Parks Highway to Fairbanks were being constructed in 2004. The City of Nenana maintains the airport and floatplane base located just south of the city. The municipal airport features a 5,000- by 100-foot asphalt, lighted runway, in addition to a 2,520- by 80-foot turf air strip. The airport provides air taxi service to Fairbanks, and the Alaska Railroad provides daily freight service. There is also a floatplane-skiplane landing area. The Nenana Port Authority operates cargo loading and unloading facilities, including a dock, bulkhead, and warehouse. Taxis are available.

Electricity. Electricity is available to residents from the Golden Valley Electric Association from a diesel plant.

Nenana

Fuel storage (gallons). Yutana Barge Lines (600,000); Nenana Heating Service (84,000); Federal Aviation Administration (16,000).

Water and waste systems. The city provides piped water with water drawn from a central location and two community wells. Some residents also have individual wells. Most (215) of the homes in the city are connected to the piped water and sewer system; the school is also connected. The city operates a piped sewer system including lift station, pumper, and a secondary treatment plant. Some individual homes use septic systems and outhouses. A washeteria is operated by the privately owned Nenana Inn. Refuse is collected by a private firm, and hauled to the newly-constructed Denali Borough Regional Landfill, located south of Anderson, and in 2003, a solid waste transfer station was to have been constructed.

Telecommunications. Local telephone service is provided by ACS of the Northland, long distance services by AT&T Alascom. Internet services are provided by MTA Online, and, at the school, by GCI. One AM radio station, KIAM, broadcasts from Nenana, and residents can receive other AM stations from North Pole, Anchorage, and Fairbanks. The University of Alaska broadcasts public radio from an FM repeater in Nenana. There are three television broadcast repeaters, from the Alaska Rural Communications Service, the University of Alaska, and the city.

COMMUNITY FACILITIES AND SERVICES

The city operates the water and sewer systems, and two community centers—the Coghill Civic Center and the George Hall Community Center. Services for senior citizens are available at the Nenana Tortella Council on Aging and the Marge Anderson Senior Citizen Center.

Education. Nenana City Public School serves children in grades K-12, with expanded facilities that house a vocational education program. There were plans to build a student living center in 2004. These facilities are managed by Nenana City School District, but there is also the CyberLynx Correspondence School operated by the Yukon-Koyukuk School District. The city operates a public library.

Health care. Health care is provided by the Nenana Native Clinic, operated by the Tanana Chiefs Council (TCC). Other medical services are available from the Nenana Volunteer Fire/EMS in emergency situations, and from Fairbanks Memorial Hospital and the TCC's Chief Andrew Isaac Health Center located there. In 2001, the city added facilities to treat alcohol and other substance addictions with the construction of Railbelt Mental Health, which also serves Healy area residents.

Public safety. There is a volunteer fire department to serve the community, and law enforcement is provided by the city police department, backed by a state troopers post in the city.

New Allakaket

See also Allakaket

[al-uh-KACK-ut]
Ethnicity: Koyukon Athabascan

Allakaket Village
P.O. Box 50
Allakaket, AK 99720
907-968-2237
907-968-2233 Fax

ANCSA village corporation
for Alatna, Allakaket, Hughes, and Huslia; most residents of New Allakaket are shareholders.

K'oyitl'ots'ina, Limited
1603 College Road
Fairbanks, AK 99709
907-452-8119
907-452-8148 Fax

Total area of entitlement under ANCSA

	None
Total labor force	8
Unemployment rate	8.5%
Per capita income *(1999)*	$5,578
2003 population state demographer estimate	38
Population *2000 census*	36
Percent Native *2000 census*	100%

LOCATION
New Allakaket is on the south bank of the Koyukuk River, adjacent to and south of the City of Allakaket. It lies approximately 190 air miles northwest of Fairbanks and 57 miles upriver from Hughes.

PHYSICAL DESCRIPTION
The area encompasses 2.2 square miles of land and 0.5 square mile of water.

CLIMATE
This is a cold, continental climate with extreme temperature differences. The average high temperature in midsummer is 70°F; the average low in winter drops below zero. Annual precipitation is 13 inches; yearly snowfall is 72 inches.

CULTURE AND HISTORY
After the destruction of Allakaket in 1994, the community rebuilt near the old city, but some new houses and public buildings now lie outside of the incorporated city boundaries. New Allakaket is outside the city limits. Visitors go to the area villages for traditional festivities. Subsistence activities are the mainstay of the culture.

GOVERNMENT
New Allakaket is unincorporated and is located in the Unorganized Borough. Most residents are members of Allakaket Village, a federally recognized tribe.

VILLAGE CORPORATION
Shareholders in the K'oyitl'ot'sina village corporation are also shareholders in Doyon, Limited, regional Native corporation (see Alaska introduction).

ECONOMY
See Allakaket.

COMMUNITY FACILITIES AND SERVICES
There are no community facilities or services in New Allakaket except as provided to the City of Allakaket. See Allakaket.

Total area of entitlement under ANCSA
96,070 acres

Total labor force	109
High school graduate or higher	76.8%
Bachelor's degree or higher	11.6%
Unemployment rate	13.2%
Per capita income *(1999)*	$13,242
Population *2000 census*	182
2003 population	200
state demographer estimate	
Percent Native *2000 census*	87.4%

LOCATION

Koliganek is located on the west bank of the Nushagak River, 65 miles northeast of Cape Dillingham.

PHYSICAL DESCRIPTION

The area encompasses 12.5 square miles of land and 0.1 square mile of water.

CLIMATE

Koliganek is in a climatic transition zone. The primary influence is maritime, although continental climate also affects the weather, especially in the winter. Average summer temperatures range from 37°F to 66°F; winter temperatures range from 4°F to 30°F.

CULTURE AND HISTORY

Koliganek is a Yup'ik village, first listed in the 1880 census as "Kalignak." Since that time, the village has moved four miles downstream from the original site. The village shows cultural influences both from its Yup'ik heritage and from the Russian Orthodox religion. Subsistence activities are an important part of the lifestyle.

GOVERNMENT

Koliganek is unincorporated and is located in the Unorganized Borough. It is governed by the federally recognized New Koliganek Village Council, a traditional village council headed by a president.

VILLAGE CORPORATION

Koliganek Natives Limited is the ANCSA village corporation. Shareholders in the village corporation also hold shares in Bristol Bay Native Corporation, the regional Native corporation.

ECONOMY

The school and village organizations provide most year-round employment; education, health, social services, and public administration employ 39 of the 66 employed residents. Some commercial fishing also occurs. Many residents trap. Subsistence activities are an important part of the economy.

Fisheries. Eighteen residents hold commercial fishing permits, chiefly for salmon.

Government as employer. Of the 66 employed residents, 55 work for the local, state, or federal government.

Services and retail. There are 17 businesses in the community, including Koliganek co-op store, day care centers, a video-rental store, lodges, a variety store, and a fishing guide service.

Tourism and recreation. Sport adventures and fishing guides are available. Three lodges and one bed-and-breakfast offer lodging.

INFRASTRUCTURE

Transportation. The state operates a 3,000- by 75-foot runway. Boats and all-terrain vehicles are used in the summer; snow machines in the winter. There are no docking facilities; goods are lightered from Dillingham.

Electricity. The Village Council provides electricity from a 100-kilowatt diesel plant and purchases power from the school district.

Fuel storage (gallons). Electric Utility (60,000); Southwest Region Schools (60,000); village council (20,000).

Water and waste systems. Koliganek has operated a piped system for many years. Water, drawn from a central well, is treated. More than 30 homes and facilities are connected to the piped water and a community septic tank. Eight homes have individual wells and septic systems. Fifteen households haul water and honeybuckets.

Telecommunications. In-state phone service is provided by Bristol Bay Telephone Co-op; long distance phone service by AT&T Alascom, GCI, or Bristol Bay Telephone. Internet service is provided by GCI. Alaska Rural Communications Service provides television access. At least two radio stations can be received in the community.

COMMUNITY FACILITIES AND SERVICES

The village council operates the water, waste disposal, and electricity systems, fuel oil sales, and the Village Council Building.

Education. Koliganek School is operated by the Southwest Region School District. The school has 79 students and seven teachers. Its library serves as the community's public library.

Health care. Local health care is provided by the Koliganek Health Clinic, operated by the Bristol Bay Area Health Corporation. Emergency service is provided by a health aide. Auxiliary health care is provided by Koliganek First Responders and the VPSO. Higher levels of care are available in Dillingham, 65 miles away.

Public safety. Law enforcement is provided by a state village public safety officer (VPSO) backed by state troopers in Dillingham. Emergency response is provided by the village volunteer fire department and the Koliganek First Responders.

[koh-LIG-uh-neck]
Ethnicity: Yup'ik

Native entity
New Koliganek Village Council
P.O. Box 5057
Koliganek, AK 99576-5057
  907-596-3434
  907-596-3462 Fax

ANCSA village corporation
Koliganek Natives Limited
P.O. Box 5023
Koliganek, AK 99576
  907-596-3434
  907-596-3462 Fax

New Stuyahok

[new STEW-yuh-hawk]
Ethnicity: Yup'ik

Municipality
City of New Stuyahok
P.O. Box 10
New Stuyahok, AK 99636
907-693-3171
907-693-3176 Fax

Native entity
New Stuyahok Traditional
Council
P.O. Box 49
New Stuyahok, AK 99636
907-693-3173
907-693-3179 Fax

ANCSA village corporation
Stuyahok Limited
P.O. Box 50
New Stuyahok, AK 99636
907-693-3122
907-693-3148 Fax

Total area of entitlement under ANCSA	
	118,952 acres
Total labor force	159
High school graduate or higher	119
Bachelor's degree or higher	25
Unemployment rate	17%
Per capita income *(1999)*	$7,931
Population	493
Percent Native	96.0%

LOCATION

New Stuyahok is in extreme southwest Alaska, along the Nushagak River, about 12 miles upriver from Ekwok and 52 miles northeast of Dillingham.

PHYSICAL DESCRIPTION

New Stuyahok lies at an elevation of less than 100 feet above sea level. The entire city area encompasses 32.6 square miles of land and 2.0 square miles of water.

CLIMATE

New Stuyahok is located in a climatic transition zone. The primary influence is maritime; however, because of the inland location of the village, an interior continental climate significantly modifies local weather. The area is characterized by cloudy skies, mild temperatures, moderately heavy precipitation, and strong surface winds. Average summer temperatures range from 37°F to 66°F; winter temperatures vary from 4°F to 30°F. Annual precipitation ranges from 20 to 35 inches. Most of the precipitation occurs in August and September, with fogs and low clouds common. Outside of storm activity, New Stuyahok is among the windiest and most turbulent of upper Bristol Bay villages. High northeast winds generated from pressure centers offshore in Bristol Bay can average 25 to 35 miles per hour and can continue for days or weeks at a time. Stronger winds are not uncommon. The Nushagak River is frozen over from mid-November to June. At this latitude, the region experiences over 18 hours of daylight during June, declining to 6 hours in December.

CULTURE AND HISTORY

Stuyahok is a southern Yup'ik Eskimo word meaning "going-down-the-river place." New Stuyahok's present location is the third site that villagers can remember, having moved downriver to the Mulchatna area from the "Old Village" in 1918. The Yup'ik Eskimo community has strong Russian Orthodox influences. During the 1920s and 1930s, the village of Stuyahok was engaged in herding reindeer for the U.S. government, but by 1942 the herd had dwindled, the village had been subjected to flooding, and the site was too far inland to receive barge service. So, in order to have better access to the Bristol Bay salmon fishery as well as a more convenient location for the development of barge service, the community of Stuyahok moved downriver to the present location in 1942. The first school in New Stuyahok was a log structure built in 1961. A post office and an airstrip were added in the 1960s, and after years of slow, steady growth, a sudden 40 percent increase in population happened throughout the 1970s. Increases are most likely attributable to the presence of the school, post office, improved medical care, and increased accessibility. Residents celebrate their cultural heritage each year during the New Stuyahok Beaver Festival.

GOVERNMENT

New Stuyahok, located in the Unorganized Borough, was incorporated as a second-class city in 1972 with a mayor and a city council, has a traditional council, headed by a president.

VILLAGE CORPORATIOIN

Shareholders in the village corporation also hold shares in Bristol Bay Native Corporation, a regional Native Alaskan corporation.

ECONOMY

New Stuyahok is primarily reached only by air which limits economic opportunity. The primary economic base is the commercial salmon-fishing industry. However, there are a total of 17 businesses licensed in New Stuyahok, including numerous child care services and a general store. Durable and manufactured goods are delivered most often by air transport. The Department of Community and Economic Development funded the construction of a new multi-office building in 1998. A city survey of the townsite was completed in the year 2000 and in 2004, the city is completing aerial mapping of the area.

Government as employer. The city, state, and federal governments employ 88 residents.

Subsistence. New Stuyahok residents practice a fishing and subsistence lifestyle with salmon, moose, caribou, rabbit, ptarmigan, duck, and geese making up a large part of the daily diet. These necessities are often traded between communities; the barter system thriving in an area where small-game trapping supplements both personal and commercial income for most residents.

INFRASTRCUTURE

Transportation. New Stuyahok is accessible by air and water. There are no year-round roads into the city. There are some city streets, and these were upgraded in 1999. Guest accommodations are available at the clinic, in the city office building, and at the school.

Air. Durable and manufactured goods are delivered most often by air transport. The state owned and operated a gravel airstrip, but it was located on a hilltop where windy conditions often precluded landing. In 1998, the Federal Aviation Administration funded the Stuyahok Airport Master Plan Study, which resulted in the relocation of the entire facility to a more suitable location. The city acquired land, constructed a new 3,200-foot runway and safety area, added a parking area and taxiway, including sufficient lighting, built a year-round access road and a building in which to house new snow removal equipment. The airport is served by Arctic Circle Air Service and Grant Aviation.

Water. Nushagak River barges deliver bulk goods during the summer months. The Department of Community and Economic Development funded the construction of a boat dock and storage ramp on the Nushagak River in 1998.

Electricity is provided by the Alaska Village Electric Cooperative (AVEC), generating power by burning oil.

Water and waste systems. The City of New Stuyahok provides piped water drawn from multiple watering points and two community wells. The water is chlorinated prior to delivery. The majority of the homes and public facilities are connected to the system and have complete plumbing. Some residents use individual wells; they maintain outhouses and utilize honeybuckets or septic tanks. The city also provides piped-sewage service including lift station and sewage lagoon and a honeybucket dump. The Alaska Native Tribal Health Consortium funded a water quality and corrosion study in 1998 which led to water and sewage system improvements, such as the construction of the main and auxiliary percolation lagoons, installation of a new sewer main in 2002-03, and development of a utility master plan. The city operates a Class 3 landfill and collects refuse from homes in the city.

Telecommunications. Local telephone service is available through the Bristol Bay Telephone Cooperative, with long distance services now widely available since deregulation. Internet services are available from GCI. One TV channel is offered by the Rural Alaska Television Network.

COMMUNITY FACILITIES AND SERVICES
Education. Chief Ivan Blunka School, operated by the Southwest Region School District, serves all children grades K-12.

Health care is available through the New Stuyahok Health Clinic, owned by the village, leased to the U.S. Public Health Service and operated by the Bristol Bay Area Health Corporation. The facility was expanded and renovated in 1997. Emergency services are available to the community by the New Stuyahok First Responders.

Public safety. The city's law enforcement needs are met by the state village public safety officer (VPSO) and by troopers stationed in Dillingham; the city has its own public safety building which also houses the volunteer fire department and EMS unit. The Alaska Department of Community and Economic Development funded "Project Code Red" which purchased vehicles and equipment for the New Stuyahok First Responder, with assistance from the United States Department of Agriculture's Rural Development Program.

Newhalen

Total area of entitlement under ANCSA
   404,764 acres (Alaska Peninsula)

Total labor force	48
High school graduate or higher	31
Bachelor's degree or higher	8
Unemployment rate	31.3%
Per capita income *(1999)*	$9,448
Population *2000 census*	160
Current population	167
state demographer estimate	
Percent Native *2000 census*	91.3%

LOCATION
Newhalen is a second-class city in the Lake and Peninsula Borough, 320 miles southwest of Anchorage, and 5 miles south of the town of Iliamna, at the base of the Alaska Peninsula.

PHYSICAL DESCRIPTION
Newhalen is situated at the mouth of the Newhalen River on the north shore of a large inland lake, Iliamna, at an elevation of less than 165 feet above sea level. It covers 6.1 square miles of land and 2.3 square miles of water.

CLIMATE
The village is located in a transitional climate zone, with average summertime temperatures ranging between 42°F and 62°F. The record high is 91°F. Winter temperatures vary between 6°F and 30°F, with a record low of -47°F. Total precipitation near Newhalen averages 26 inches annually including average snowfalls totaling 64 inches. At this latitude, the region experiences over 18.5 hours of daylight in a 24-hour period in June, declining to 6 hours in December.

CULTURE AND HISTORY
Newhalen is an Anglicized version of the original name, Noughelin. It has traditionally been a southern Yup'ik Eskimo village, and now includes Eskimos, non-Natives, Aleuts, and Athabascan Indians. Most practice a subsistence lifestyle. The 1890 U.S. census listed the Eskimo name of "Noghelinghmiut," meaning "people of Noughelin," at this location, with a population of 16. The village was originally established in the 1800s as a fishing camp and hunting/trapping area; now, during summer months, most residents leave Newhalen for fish camps on the Nushagak River and other areas of Bristol Bay.

GOVERNMENT
Newhalen, incorporated as a second-class city in 1971, has a mayor, city council, and a traditional council with a president.

VILLAGE CORPORATION
The Alaska Peninsula corporation was formed from the merged village corporations of Kokhanok, Newhalen, Port Heiden, South Naknek, and Ugashik. Shareholders in the village corporation also hold shares in Bristol Bay Native Corporation.

ECONOMY
Residents depend on subsistence hunting and fishing near the community to supplement their incomes. They harvest salmon, trout, grayling, moose, caribou, rabbit, porcupine, and seals. Many also now have seasonal incomes derived from commercial salmon fishing, a mainstay of Newhalen's economy, even though most of the actual fishing and related industry occurs in Bristol Bay. Thousands of sport fishermen converge into the area every summer for the trophy trout in Iliamna Lake. There are, therefore, a number of businesses in the area to accommodate tourists, including four that provide lodging. There are two taxi companies and plans to add a community store in 2003.

Government as employer. Nineteen residents are employed by the city, borough, state or federal governments.

Tourism and recreation. Newhalen is within 60 miles of the Lake Clark National Park and Preserve and the Katmai National Park and Preserve. It is within 100 miles of the Becharof National Wildlife Refuge. Thousands visit each summer to fish the rapids of Newhalen River and to fish for trout in Iliamna Lake. Others come to watch and photograph bears and to enjoy the scenic views. The city hosts the Iliamna/Newhalen Dog Races each year and the Lake Iliamna Shoot Out.

INFRASTRUCTURE
Transportation. There is only one year-round gravel road into Newhalen, which somewhat limits commercial activity; it connects the city with Iliamna and provides access to the airport. However, durable and manufactured goods are delivered via air transport. There are two state-owned gravel airstrips, one 5,080- by 100-foot the other 4,800- by 150-foot. Scheduled and charter air services are available from King Salmon. A local priority is the construction of a road between Iliamna and Nondalton, with a bridge over the Newhalen River. In the summer months, barges operating on the Kvichak River deliver bulk goods, and some goods and boats are transported over-

Ethnicity: Yup'ik; Aleut; Athabascan

Municipality
City of Newhalen
P.O. Box 165
Newhalen, AK 99606
  907-571-1226
  907-571-1540 Fax
arctic.net

Native entity
Newhalen Tribal Council
P.O. Box 207
Newhalen, AK 99606
  907-571-1720
  907-571-1537 Fax
arctic.net

ANCSA village corporation
Alaska Peninsula Corporation
800 Cordova Street #102
Anchorage, AK 99501
  907-274-2433
  907-274-8694 Fax

Newhalen

land from Iliamnna Bay on Cook Inlet to Pile Bay on Iliamnna Lake, then across the lake to Newhalen.

Electricity. The Iliarnna Newhalen Power Company, operated by the I-N-N Electric Cooperative, owns a diesel plant in Newhalen and 50 miles of distribution line to connect the three communities of Iliamna, Newhalen, and Nondalton. The Tazimina Hydroelectric Project has recently been completed, providing alternative sources of power for the three towns, as well.

Water and waste systems. The City of Newhalen operates a piped water system, serving all 51 homes with water drawn from a community well; the water is filtered prior to distribution. Residents also make use of individual wells and surface water sources. The city operates a piped sewer system including pumper and lagoon, and there are community and individual septic tanks used. Some homes own and maintain outhouses. Beginning in 2001 and continuing throughout 2004, these systems are undergoing dramatic improvement, including restoration of the sewage lagoon, improvements to both the well and pump houses in 2002, and a water and sewer feasibility study in 2004 to assess the improvements. The Alaska Department of Community and Economic Development funded rehabilitation of the local landfill in 1999. It is operating in 2004 as a Class 3 facility. The school recycles aluminum and newspapers.

Telecommunications. Local telephone service is provided by the Interior Telephone Company/TelAlaska, and long distance services are now widely available since deregulation. Internet services are provided by GCI. One television channel is offered by the Rural Alaska Television Network.

COMMUNITY FACILITIES AND SERVICES
The City of Newhalen operates a community center at City Hall, with regular bingo games operated by the village council. Youth services and teen activities are offered at the recreation center, built in 2000. In 1998, a play deck was constructed at Aquivik (City) Park.

Education. Newhalen School, which serves students in grades K-12, is operated by the Lake and Peninsula School District. In 1997, the school was outfitted with electric boilers that use surplus energy from Tazimina Hydroelectric Project, an innovative cost-and energy-savings strategy. The school library serves as the city library.

Health care. Provided by the Newhalen Health Clinic, owned by the village, leased to the U.S. Public Health Service and operated by Bristol Bay Area Health Corporation (BBAHC). Emergency services are provided by the Iliamna/Newhalen Rescue Squad.

Public safety. Law enforcement services are provided by the Alaska state troopers stationed in McGrath. Fire and rescue services are provided by the Iliamna/Newhalen Rescue Squad.

Newtok

[NOO-tock]
Ethnicity: Yup'ik

Native entity
Newtok Village
P.O. Box 5545
Newtok, AK 99559
907-237-2314
907-237-2428 Fax

ANCSA village corporation
Newtok Corporation
P.O. Box 5528
Newtok, AK 99559
907-237-2512
907-237-2227 Fax

Total area of entitlement under ANCSA	92,160 acres
Total labor force	134
High school graduate or higher	45.4%
Bachelor's degree or higher	2.0%
Unemployment rate	15.6%
Per capita income *(1999)*	$9,514
Population *2000 census*	321
2003 population	329
state demographer estimate	
Percent Native *2000 census*	96.9%

LOCATION
Newtok is in extreme Southwest Coastal Alaska. It is 94 miles northwest of Bethel, on the Ninglick River, north of Nelson Island, in the Yukon-Kuskokwim Delta region.

PHYSICAL DESCRIPTION
The village area encompasses 1.0 square miles of land and 0.1 square mile of water, approximately 20 miles inland from the Bering Sea.

CLIMATE
Newtok is located in the marine climate zone, characterized by moderate temperatures and frequent precipitation. Summer average daily temperatures vary between 42°F and 59°F; in the winter, between 2°F and 19°F. Average annual precipitation is 17 inches per year, including an average snowfall of 22 inches. At this latitude, the region experiences approximately 19 hours of daylight in June, declining to 5.5 in December.

CULTURE AND HISTORY
The people of Newtok, a traditional Yup'ik village, share a strong cultural heritage with the communities of Tununak, Nightmute, Toksook Bay, and Chefornak on nearby Nelson Island. Together the five villages make up the *Qualuyaarmiut,* or "dipnet people," whose ancestors have lived on the Bering Sea coast for at least 2,000 years. Being relatively isolated, the village had only intermittent outside contact until the 1920s. Around 1949 the village was relocated from Old Kealavik, ten miles away, to its present location on higher ground. A school was built in 1958, although many high school students traveled to Bethel, St. Mary's, Sitka, or Anchorage to complete their education. This was often their first exposure to life outside the village; they returned with command of the English language and modern American culture. Tuberculosis was a major health problem, resulting in many residents being sent to Seattle, Washington, and Mt. Edgecombe in Southeast Alaska, for treatment. As recently as the 1960s, villagers traveled before spring ice breakup by dogsled to their traditional summer fishing camp *Nilikhrguk,* on the north coast of Nelson Island, where they lived in tents all summer long. After the herring run, men traveled to the Bristol Bay area to work in the canneries. The 1970s saw the abandonment of the last *qasegiq,* the traditional men's community house. Housing projects were built, and a high school was constructed in Newtok in the 1980s. The village was incorporated as a city in 1976, but the city was dissolved in 1993. In 2002-03, plans were underway to relocate to a new site called *Taqikcaq,* approximately 5 miles away on Nelson Island. In 2003 Congress authorized an exchange of lands between the U.S. Fish and Wildlife Service and the Newtok Corporation. Newtok maintains an active subsistence lifestyle with a relatively high degree of traditional practice and cultural customs, more so perhaps than in other parts of Alaska due to its isolation.

GOVERNMENT
An unincorporated village in the Unorganized Borough, Newtok is governed by a traditional village council headed by a president.

VILLAGE CORPORATION
Newtok Corporation is the ANCSA village corporation. Its shareholders also hold shares in Calista Corporation, the regional Native corporation.

ECONOMY

Employment opportunities in Newtok are primarily in commercial fishing, the school, government offices, the health clinic, and other village services. Subsistence activities and trapping supplement cash income for most residents. There are a general store and three retail food stores, a video store, and a day-care provider.

Fisheries. Twenty-seven residents hold commercial fishing permits.

Government as employer. Sixty-one of 101 employed residents work for either the state or federal government.

Tourism and recreation. Newtok lies within the Yukon Delta Wildlife Refuge.

INFRASTRUCTURE

Transportation. Except in the winter, Newtok can be reached only by air and water. A State-owned 2,202- by 35-foot gravel airstrip provides charter and private air access year-round (weather permitting) with services by Arctic Circle Air, Era Aviation, Hageland Aviation, Inland Aviation, and Yute Air. A seaplane base is also available. In 2004-05 the village was conducting an airport master plan study to determine the feasibility of building a new airport facility. The Bureau of Indian Affairs funded an initiative in 2002 to mark the winter trails leading into the village from Chevak (50 miles), and from Tununak, Toksook Bay, Nightmute, and Manaryarapiaq (33.8 miles). River barges deliver cargo during the summer months.

Electricity. Electricity is provided by the Ungusraq Power Company, owned and operated by the Village Council, from a 265-kilowatt diesel plant. The power system underwent major renovation and upgrade in 2000-02.

Fuel storage (gallons). Lower Kuskokwim Schools (121,070); Newtok Corporation (55,955); Newtok Corporation Store (52,200); Tom's Store (4,125); Agayuvik Holy Family Church (3,000); Army National Guard (2,500).

Water and waste systems. There are community wells, a surface water source and a central watering point in Newtok. The village council operates the water system and the washeteria. In 2002, a water storage tank was installed for the community and the water treatment plant was renovated. Other than a few houses with plumbing installed under a flush/haul demonstration project, homeowners utilize a honeybucket dump. The village council operates a Class 3 landfill.

Telecommunications. Local telephone service is provided by United Utilities, long distance services by AT&T Alascom or United Utilities. GCI provides Internet service at the School. The village can receive AM radio broadcasts from Nome and Bethel. An Alaska Rural Communications System repeater broadcasts two television channels.

COMMUNITY FACILITIES AND SERVICES

The village council operates Quyurrvik Hall, a community center which was expanded and renovated in the year 2000 with funding obtained from the Department of Community and Economic Development. Emergency response is provided by the village volunteer fire department.

Education. Ayaprun School which serves children in grades K-12, and is operated by the Lower Kuskokwim School District. The school library serves as the community's public library.

Health care. Health care is provided by the Newtok Health Clinic, operated by the Yukon-Kuskokwim Health Corporation. It is supported by the sub-regional clinic in Toksook Bay and the Yukon Kuskokwim Delta Regional Hospital, about 192 miles away in Bethel.

ENVIRONMENTAL CONCERNS

The present village site is experiencing severe erosion along the banks of the Ninglick River. The average annual erosion rate is 90 feet per year, and it is expected that the land under Newtok will erode by 2011. In an exchange with the federal government, the people of Newtok will relocate their village across the Ninglick River to an upland area in the Yukon Delta National Wildlife Refuge on Nelson Island. Newtok Corporation will give up approximately 11,105 acres on the mainland and relinquish selection rights to approximately 996 acres on Baird Inlet Island, both locations being important wildlife habitat. In exchange, Newtok Corporation will receive title to approximately 10,943 acres of surface and subsurface estate on the northern shore of Nelson Island adjacent to lands already owned by the corporation.

Nightmute

Total area of entitlement under ANCSA	
	69,120 acres
Total labor force	106
High school graduate or higher	45.3%
Bachelor's degree or higher	8.5%
Unemployment rate	10.8%
Per capita income *(1999)*	$9,396
Population *2000 census*	208
2003 population	228
state demographer estimate	
Percent Native *2000 census*	94.7%

LOCATION

Nightmute is located approximately 100 miles west of Bethel, on Nelson Island, in the Yukon-Kuskokwim Delta region of extreme Southwest Alaska. It is about 18 miles upriver from Toksook Bay.

PHYSICAL DESCRIPTION

The city lies at an elevation of less than 165 feet above sea level. Its area encompasses 97.0 square miles of land and 4.6 square miles of water.

CLIMATE

Nightmute is located in the marine climate zone, with relatively warm winters and cool summers. Summer daily average temperatures range between 41°F and 57°F; winter temperatures vary from 6°F to 25°F. Precipitation averages 22 inches, including 43 inches of snowfall annually. At this latitude, the region experiences approximately 19 hours of daylight in a 24 hour period in June, declining to just over 5.5 hours in December.

CULTURE AND HISTORY

The area around Nightmute was relatively isolated from outside contact until the twentieth century and has kept its traditions and traditional Yup'ik culture intact, regularly practicing potlatch and participating in Eskimo dances. Nightmute's people share a cultural heritage with the nearby Nelson Island communities of Newtok, Tununak, and Toksook Bay, and

Ethnicity: Yup'ik

Municipality
City of Nightmute
P.O. Box 90010
Nightmute, AK 99690
907-647-6426
907-647-6427 Fax

Native entity
Native Village of Nightmute
P.O. Box 90021
Nightmute, AK 99690
907-647-6213

ANCSA village corporation
Chinuruk, Incorporated
P.O. Box 90009
Nightmute, AK 99690
907-647-6115
907-647-6126 Fax

Nightmute

the village of Chefornak. The people from these five villages are known as the Quluyaarmiut, or "dipnet people," whose ancestors have lived on the Bering Sea coast for the past 2,000 years. In 1964 many residents moved to Toksook Bay for economic reasons. Nightmute was incorporated in 1974.

GOVERNMENT
Nightmute was incorporated as a second-class city in 1974, in the Unorganized Borough. It has a mayor and city council. The Native Village of Nightmute, also called the Nightmute Traditional Council, is a BIA-recognized Native entity headed by a president.

VILLAGE CORPORATION
Chinuruk, Incorporated, is the ANCSA village corporation. It is the merged corporations of Nightmute and Umkumiut. Its shareholders also hold shares in Calista Corporation, the regional Native corporation.

ECONOMY
The economy of Nightmute in the twenty-first century is a mixture of traditional subsistence practices and income-generating employment in several village or private initiatives, government offices, and retail.

Fisheries. Thirty-one residents hold commercial fishing permits, primarily for herring roe and salmon drift-net fishing.

Government as employer. Of 89 employed residents, 46 work for the city, state, or federal government.

Services and retail. The city has a general store, two video stores, and a pool hall. Nightmute Enterprises provides an outlet for locally-handcrafted traditional artistic items.

Tourism and recreation. Nightmute lies within the Yukon Delta National Wildlife Refuge. Guest accommodations are available at the city building and at the school.

INFRASTRUCTURE
Transportation. The community is accessible by air and water only. A state-owned 1,650- by 45-foot gravel airstrip is used by chartered and private aircraft. A seaplane landing area is also available. Available airline services include: Arctic Circle Air Service, Era Aviation, Grant Aviation, Hageland Aviation, Inland Aviation Services, Inc., and Yute Air. Airport facilities were to be upgraded in 2004, including an extension of the existing runway and rehabilitation of the apron and taxiway, construction of a storage building for snow removal equipment and acquisition of that equipment, and the construction of a runway safety area. There are no river docking facilities, although many residents use fishing boats or skiffs for local travel. Cargo and supplies must be lightered up the Tuqsuk River. Winter trails are marked from Nightmute to Toksook Bay (20 miles), Cak'caaq (25 miles), and Baird Inlet (50 miles).

Snowmobiles and all-terrain vehicles are used during the winter months.

Electricity. Electricity is provided by the Alaska Village Electric Cooperative (AVEC) from a 348-kilowatt diesel plant AVEC acquired the Nightmute Power Company in 1998.

Fuel storage (gallons). AVEC (89,900); Chinurak Store (40,400 gals.); Lower Kuskokwim Schools (27,500); Army National Guard (3,000); Our Lady of Perpetual Help Catholic Church (1,650).

Water and waste systems. Available for residents of Nightmute there are community wells and a central watering point, drawn from a surface source. The city operates the sewage system which includes a pumper and lagoon. As of 2003, 29 homes were installed on the water and sewer systems. Also in 2003, aerial mapping of the sewage lagoon was completed and a study undertaken to determine the feasibility of building a washeteria. The city operates a Class 3 landfill.

Telecommunications. Local telephone service is provided by United Utilities, long distance service by United Utilities or AT&T Alascom. The area can receive AM radio stations from Bethel, Nome, Dillingham, and some more distant locations. There are two television channels broadcast from a local Alaska Rural Communications Service repeater. Internet service from GCI is available at the school.

COMMUNITY FACILITIES AND SERVICES
The city operates a combined city/community hall for its residents.

Education. Nightmute School, which serves students in pre-school and grades K-12, is operated by the Lower Kuskokwim School District. Renovations, including a new addition to the school building, were planned for 2005. The school library serves as the community's public library.

Health care. Health care is provided by the Nightmute Health Clinic, operated by the Yukon-Kuskokwim Health Corporation. Emergency service is provided by a health aide. The Clinic moved to a new building in the year 2001. It is supported by a new sub-regional clinic in nearby Toksook Bay and the Yukon Kuskokwim Delta Regional Hospital about 204 miles away in Bethel.

Public safety. Law enforcement is provided by a city police officer, backed by state troopers in Bethel. Emergency response is provided by the city volunteer fire department and a city ambulance.

ENVIRONMENTAL CONCERNS
The shores of Nelson Island are under increasing threat of erosion damage.

Total area of entitlement under ANCSA
69,120 acres

Total labor force	29
High school graduate or higher	50.0%
Unemployment rate	18.3%
Per capita income *(1999)*	$11,029
Population *2000 census*	100
2003 population	127
state demographer estimate	
Percent Native *2000 census*	81.0%

LOCATION

Nikolai is on the south fork of the Kuskokwim River, 46 miles east of McGrath.

PHYSICAL DESCRIPTION

The city encompasses 4.5 square miles of land and 0.3 square mile of water at an average elevation of approximately 1,500 feet above sea level.

CLIMATE

Nikolai has a cold, continental climate, with a slight maritime influence, especially during the summer. Summer temperatures range between 42°F and 80°F; winter temperatures vary from -62°F to 0°F. Precipitation is light, averaging only 16 inches per year, including an average snowfall of 56 inches. The Kuskokwim River is frozen over October through June. It this latitude, the region experiences approximately 21 hours of daylight in June, declining to approximately 4 hours in December.

CULTURE AND HISTORY

Nikolai is historically an Upper Kuskokwim Athabascan village centered on subsistence activities. It became the site of a trading post and roadhouse during the gold rush of the late nineteenth century. Situated on the Rainy Pass Trail, it connected the Ophir mining district to Cook Inlet and had a population of six in 1899. It later became a winter trail station along the Nenana-McGrath Trail, used until 1926. By 1927 the St. Nicholas Orthodox Church was constructed. In 1948, a private school was established, and in 1949 a post office opened. The community was first opened to year-round accessibility in 1962, when residents cleared an airstrip. The city was incorporated in 1970. The present site was established around 1918 and serves as a checkpoint during the Iditarod dogsled race from Anchorage to Nome, held annually in March. Upper Kuskokwim Athabascan is spoken in the villages of Nikolai, Telida, and McGrath in the Upper Kuskokwim River drainage. Of a total population of about 160 people, about 40 still speak the language.

GOVERNMENT

Nikolai was incorporated as a second-class city in 1970, with a mayor and city council. It is located in the Unorganized Borough. Nikolai Village, also known as Nikolai Edzeno' Village Council, is a BIA-recognized Native entity with a traditional council headed by a first chief.

VILLAGE CORPORATION

MTNT Limited is the ANCSA village corporation for McGrath, Takotna, Nikolai, and Telida. As the "N" in MTNT, Nikolai is the second-largest participating village although it has less than one-quarter the population of McGrath. Shareholders in MTNT are also shareholders in Doyon, Limited, the regional Native corporation.

ECONOMY

Access to Nikolai is by air or water only, and the economy depends to a large extent on seasonal cash jobs and year-round subsistence activities. Residents harvest salmon, bear, moose, caribou, and rabbits. Some tend gardens during the short growing season and some depend upon trapping (both for commercial and personal purposes) and production and sales of Native handicrafts. Village employment peaks during the summer months, when construction gets underway. Governments provide all year-round employment opportunities in the village.

Government as employer. All 18 of the employed residents work for the city, state, or federal government.

Services and retail. There are several businesses located in Nikolai, including two stores, two restaurants, and a publisher.

Tourism and recreation. There are hunting-guide services available to tourists and the city operates a lodge. Nikolai is within 60 miles of Denali National Park and Preserve and the Nowitna National Wildlife Refuge. It is approximately 100 miles from the eastern border of the Innoko National Wildlife Refuge and 100 miles north of the northern border of the Lake Clark National Park and Preserve.

INFRASTRUCTURE

Transportation. A state-owned 4,003- by 75-foot gravel airstrip is served by Tanana Air Service. Barges on the Kuskokwim River supply fuel and heavy equipment during the summer months. All-terrain vehicles and snowmobiles are used during the winter for local travel and commerce. A winter trail is marked to McGrath (50 miles).

Electricity. Electricity is available to residents via the Nikolai Light and Power Company, now part of McGrath Light and Power, from a 110-kilowatt diesel plant.

Fuel storage (gallons). City (72,200); Iditarod Schools (15,300).

Water and waste systems. Residents use individual wells. The city provides a piped-sewage service for 33 homes; the remaining 15 homes use septic tanks. The city operates a Class-3 landfill.

Telecommunications. Local and long distance telephone services are provided by United Utilities. The City of Nikolai provides a cable television service and Internet service is provided at the School by GCI. The Alaska Rural Communications Service broadcasts television from a local repeater.

COMMUNITY FACILITIES AND SERVICES

The City of Nikolai operates the sewer, landfill, and cable television systems, and a recreation center.

Education. Top of the Kuskokwim School, which serves schoolchildren in grades 8-12, is operated by the Iditarod Area School District. The city has a public library.

Health care. Health care is provided by the Nikolai Health Clinic operated by the Tanana Chiefs Conference (TCC), supported by the TCC's sub-regional clinic in McGrath and Fairbanks Memorial Hospital and the TCC's Chief Andrew Isaac Health Center located there.

Public safety. Law enforcement is provided by state troopers in McGrath, emergency response by local volunteers.

[NICK-oh-lie]
Ethnicity: Upper Kuskokwim Athabascan

Municipality
City of Nikolai
P.O. Box 9145
Nikolai, AK 99691-0045
907-293-2113
907-293-2115 Fax

Native entity
Nikolai Village
P.O. Box 9105
Nikolai, AK 99691
907-293-2311
907-293-2481 Fax

ANCSA village corporation
MTNT Limited
P.O. Box 309
McGrath, AK 99627
907-524-3391
907-524-3701 Fax
mcgrathalaska.net

Nikolski

[nih-COAL-skee]
Ethnicity: Unangan (Aleut)

Native entity
Native Village of Nikolski
P.O. Box 105
Nikolski, AK 99638
    907-576-2225
    907-576-2205 Fax

ANCSA village corporation
Chaluka Corporation
General Delivery
Nikolski, AK 99638
    907-576-2216

Total area of entitlement under ANCSA	77,188 acres
Total labor force	22
High school graduate or higher	11
Bachelor's degree or higher	6
Unemployment rate	0.0%
Per capita income (1999)	$14,083
Population 2000 census	39
Current population	41
state demographer estimate	
Percent Native 2000 census	69.2%

LOCATION

Nikolski is located in the Unorganized Borough, on Nikolski Bay near the southwest point of Umnak Island in the Fox Islands, one of the southernmost islands in the Aleutian chain. It lies 116 air miles west of Unalaska and 900 air miles from Anchorage.

PHYSICAL DESCRIPTION

The village area encompasses 132.1 square miles of land and 0.7 square mile of water at an elevation of 127 feet above sea level. The village is located in a biologically prime, diverse, and productive area, which has contributed to its long history of habitation. Most of the nearby islands are part of the Aleutian National Wildlife Refuge. The sea in front of the village has dense mats of attached algae, which in turn support a wide variety of marine animals, including birds and mammals. Sea otters, harbor seals, sea lions, and whales are concentrated in the area. The village is adjacent to the rich fishing grounds of the Bering Sea and the Alaska/Aleutian shelf, and is within a prime king crab area. There are no large predators on Umnak Island, and the island is home to many ptarmigan, foxes, rabbits, songbirds, eagles, and waterfowl. Vegetation around the village is primarily arctic/alpine plant types, mostly as a thick mat of vascular plants and mosses. Nearby Mount Vsevidef and the Okmok Caldera at the northeast end of the island are both volcanoes active in the second half of the twentieth century.

CLIMATE

Nikolski lies in a maritime climate zone characterized by mild, wet, windy winters and cool, foggy summer days. Temperatures range from winter lows of 11°F to summer highs of 65°F. Total annual precipitation averages 21 inches, including an average snowfall of 41 inches. At this latitude, the region experiences approximately 18 hours of daylight in June, declining to approximately 8 hours in December.

CULTURE AND HISTORY

Nikolski is a traditional Unangan community, reputedly the oldest continuously-occupied community in the world. The nearby Chaluka archaeological site indicates that people have lived continuously in the Nikolski area for approximately 8,500 years. In 1834, the village was the site of a sea otter hunting camp. In 1920, a boom in fox-farming occurred in Nikolski. During World War II, when the Japanese attacked Unalaska and seized Attu and Kiska Islands in the Aleutians, residents were evacuated to the Ketchikan area. A sheep ranch that began in 1926 still operates as part of the Aleutian Livestock Company. Today, the Unangan language is spoken in most homes. Subsistence activities, including the harvest of salmon, seals, halibut and waterfowl, sheep-and-cattle raising, and commercial fishing, sustain the community and form the nucleus of village culture.

GOVERNMENT

Nikolski is unincorporated and is located in the Unorganized Borough. It is governed by an Indian Reorganization Act council, headed by a president.

VILLAGE CORPORATION

Chaluka Corporation is the village corporation for Nikolski. Shareholders in the village corporation also hold shares in the Aleut Corporation, the regional Native corporation.

ECONOMY

Most residents support themselves by working outside the village at crab canneries and on fish/seafood processing ships. The Aleutian Livestock Company runs between 4,000 and 7,000 sheep, 300 head of cattle, and 30 horses on Umnak Island. Subsistence activities provide a substantial supplement to villagers' incomes. The village has expressed an interest in enticing former residents to return to Nikolski by developing a value-added fish processing plant and a sport fishing lodge. Toward this end, a sport-fishing charter boat was recently purchased by the Aleutian Pribilof Island Community Development Association (APICDA).

Government as employer. In the 2000 census, fifteen residents were employed by either the State or Federal government.

Tourism and recreation. Guests of residents and tourists who visit to take advantage of prime hunting and fishing on the islands or tour the old village sites stay in the Ugludax Lodge, built in 2003, and at a mobile home owned by the Chaluka Corporation.

INFRASTRUCTURE

Transportation. Nikolski is accessible by air and water. There are no roads leading into the community; however, they do have a main street within the community, constructed in 2003. The village has access to a 3,500-foot unlighted gravel runway, which supports passenger, mail, and cargo service. The facility is owned by the United States Air Force and served by Penn Air, but access is sometimes limited by strong winds in the winter and dense fog in the summer. A new access road to the airport was built and new airfield maintenance and navigational equipment purchased in 2003.

There is no landing or port facility for ships in the village. The federal government vessel *Northstar* stops once or twice a year. Barges deliver cargo and passengers which must be lightered three miles to the beach.

Electricity. Electricity is provided by the Umnak Power Company, owned and operated by the village council, from a 185-kilowatt diesel plant. In 2003, the entire rural power system was upgraded.

Fuel storage and distribution. Beginning in 1997, upgrades to the bulk fuel tank farm have been implemented, increasing total fuel oil capacity significantly. Storage (gallons): Umnak Power Company (29,000); Nikolski Native Store (24,900); Chaluka Corporation Ranch (6,300); Aleutian Region Schools (6,000).

Water and waste systems. The village council operates a piped water system and chlorinates the water prior to distribution. All homes are fully plumbed. Beginning in 1999, equipment upgrades and system rehabilitation to the water system are in process. Residents use individual septic tanks and outhouses for sewage disposal; the council provides septic pumping services. All homes are fully plumbed. A new access road to the disposal area was built in 2003, and beginning in 1999, equipment upgrades and system rehabilitation to the sewer system are in process.

Telecommunications. Local telephone service is provided by ACS of the Northland, long distance services by AT&T Alascom. The Nikolski IRA Council provides cable television service to the community. Internet services are provided by GCI.

COMMUNITY FACILITIES AND SERVICES

In 2003, a new community center, the IRA Council Building, was built in Nikolski with funding acquired through the Alaska Department of Community and Economic Development. The village council provides cable television, electricity generation and distribution, fuel storage, waste collection and disposal, and water supply.

Education. The Nikolski School, which serves fifteen students in grades K-12 with one teacher, is operated by the Aleutian Region School District. A multipurpose room was added to the building in 2001.

Health care. Health care is provided by the Nikolski Health Clinic, owned by the village and leased to the U.S. Public Health Service. It is operated by the Aleutian Pribilof Island Association.

Public safety. Law enforcement is provided by state troopers in Dutch Harbor.

Ninilchik

Total area of entitlement under ANCSA
	168,702 acres
Total labor force	356
Unemployment rate	18.0%
Per capita income *(1999)*	$18,463
Population *2000 census*	777
Current population	777
state demographer estimate	
Percent Native *2000 census*	16.6%

LOCATION
Ninilchik is an unincorporated village entity on the west coast of the Kenai Peninsula, on the Sterling Highway (Highway 1), 38 miles southwest of the city of Kenai in south-central Alaska. The recognized village boundaries run from Soldatna in the north to Homer in the south.

PHYSICAL DESCRIPTION
The area encompasses 207.6 square miles of land and 0.1 square mile of water at an elevation of less than 165 feet above sea level. The view from the village to the west, across Cook Inlet, takes in Mount Augustine to the southwest and Mount Iliamna, 10,198-foot-high Mount Redoubt, and Mount Spur to the west-northwest. The area is tectonically active. In 1912 the eruption of nearby Mount Katmai covered the village in a thick layer of ash, the 1964 Alaskan earthquake shook the area, and in 1990 a major eruption of Mount Redoubt again brought ashes to Ninilchik.

CLIMATE
Ninilchik lies in the maritime climate zone, with relatively mild winters and cool, wet summers. Summer temperatures range between 45°F and 60°F; winter temperatures between 14°F and 27°F. Average annual precipitation is 24 inches. At this latitude, the region experiences approximately 19 hours of daylight in a 24-hour period in June, declining to just over 5.5 hours by December.

CULTURE AND HISTORY
The entire Kenai Peninsula was historically fur-farming and fishing territory for Dena'ina Indians. The Village of "Niqnilchint," as it was originally called, was settled by Russian Company employees during the 1820s and 1830s, many of whom married into the Dena'ina Indian community and made homes in this, their "lodge by the river," in rustic Russian-style log homes on the banks of the Ninilchik River. In 1847, Grigorii and Mavra Kvasnikoff moved their large family from Kodiak to Ninilchik. Mr. Kvasnikoff was a Russian Orthodox missionary from the Moscow area. Mrs. Kvasnikoff was an Alutiiq from Kodiak. Many of the current Native residents are descendants of the Kvasnikoffs. In 1896, a Russian village school was built, and in 1901, the Russian Orthodox church was constructed and dedicated. The Russian Orthodox influence remains strong to this day. The first American teacher arrived in 1911. A large fish cannery began operating in 1949, and the next year the Sterling Highway reached Ninilchik (although it was not paved until 1967), bringing people from many neighboring Native villages drawn by the prospect of economic prosperity.

The greatest cultural change occurred in the 1940s, as non-Native homesteaders moved into Ninilchik in substantial numbers, to the point where it is now less than 20 percent Native. The traditional Native village remains a major part of the community, however. The village is actively involved in local issues and is a leading advocate for the senior center, and the non-Native community works cooperatively with the village on many local issues. Although it is no longer considered a rural community by Alaska's Department of Community and Economic Development, Ninilchik remains an agricultural settlement.

GOVERNMENT
Ninilchik is unincorporated and located in the Kenai Peninsula Borough. The village is governed by a traditional village council, headed by a president and chairman. A vice president, secretary-treasurer, and two directors sit on the council; elections are held annually. An elders council meets quarterly and provides input, guidance, and direction to the Ninilchik Traditional Council. These elders are appointed by the Traditional Council and are respected and honored for their contribution to the success of the tribal organization because of their knowledge of and history with the tribe.

Ninilchik has a tribal court system with judges elected annually; there are two trial judges, an elder judge, and two alternative judges. A presiding appeals judge presides over any case accepted for appellate review, and a second appeals judge is appointed by the traditional council. The presiding judge and the judge appointed by the council jointly select a third judge. Traditionally, the council resolved problems by seeking consensus among the people involved. Council mem-

[nuh-NIL-chick]
Ethnicity: Dena'ina
Athabascan, Alutiiq

Native entity
Ninilchik Village
P.O. Box 39070
Ninilchik, AK 99639
907-567-3313
907-567-3308 Fax
ninilchiktribe-nsn.gov

ANCSA village corporation
Ninilchik Native
Association, Inc.
701 West 41st Ave. #201
Anchorage, AK 99503-6604
907-562-8654
907-344-8634 Fax
nnai.net

Ninilchik

bers and respected village elders met with and counseled people behaving improperly and compelled behavior changes. The traditional council continues use of these informal methods in situations where deemed appropriate, notwithstanding the tribal court. The village is governed by the Constitution of the Ninilchik Tribe. There are ordinances in place governing the conduct of elections, enrollment requirements, the judiciary, domestic violence crimes, and a consultation ordinance, designed to establish a clear process for documenting the nature and results of consultations between the village and federal, state, nonprofit, and other agencies and organizations.

VILLAGE CORPORATION

Ninilchik Native Association, Inc., (NNAI) is owned by approximately 310 shareholders as of 2004. The corporation's shares are divided into two classes, essentially distinguishing between Native and non-Native shareholders. The approximately 270 Native shareholders receive dividends and hold voting rights. The 30-plus non-Native shareholders, most of whom received shares thorough inheritance from Native shareholders, are entitled to dividends but do not have voting rights.

NNAI is managed by a nine member Board of Directors. For its first few decades, NNAI earned income through timber and land sales. More recently, it has diversified. Alaska Resource Development, LLC, is the holding company for NNAI business development which has three lines of business as of 2004.

Resource Development Company is a Ninilchik-based construction company focused on providing shareholder job opportunities while taking advantage of gas field activity in the central Kenai Peninsula, performing road maintenance, construction and upgrading, land clearing, gravel screening and sales along with gas company support services and providing yard space for other gas field support services.

Frontier Organic Company uses fish waste and timber waste to compost into a soil supplement product. Frontier Organic anticipates expanding into other waste management businesses.

White Mountain Construction is a Small Business Administration-approved 8(a) company targeting Department of Defense base maintenance activities.

Shareholders in the village corporation also hold shares in Cook Inlet Regional Corporation.

ECONOMY

While Ninilchik's main industries are fishing and tourism, the subsistence base of its economy continues. Residents harvest razor clams, salmon, halibut, berries, small game, and river trout to supplement their household incomes. Other industries of importance are timber harvests from lands belonging to the village corporation and the area's agricultural enterprises. Ninilchik River and Cook Inlet sport fishing encouraged the development of many seasonal tourist-related services. Many residents find employment in oil and gas processing, sawmills, commercial fishing, retail businesses, and tourism-related services. In the 2000 census, the median household income was $36,250.

Agriculture and forestry. Ninilchik is one of the few areas in the state that supports agriculture, and the harvesting of timber on village corporation lands remains an important source of income.

Construction. See the discussion of Resource Development Company, above.

Fisheries. Commercial fishing is an important source of income for some residents—49 hold commercial fishing permits. A fish cannery, Deep Creek Custom Packing, is a major private employer in the area. Fishing for king salmon on Deep Creek and the Ninilchik River lures thousands of sport fishermen to Ninilchik in May and June. In 2003, the village expanded the harbor area and improved the dock and constructed a fish-waste disposal system.

Government as employer. In the 2000 census, 55 residents of Ninilchik worked for the borough, state, or federal governments.

Tourism and recreation. Many popular events and festivals draw tourists into Ninilchik every year, and a number of residents are employed in tourism-related businesses in the greater Kenai area. The village is within 40 miles of Kenai National Wildlife Refuge, the Kenai Fjords National Park, and Lake Clark National Park and Preserve, just across Cook Inlet. It is within 100 miles of Katmai National Park and Preserve. Ninilchik Beach Campground is a popular place for razor clamming, with a day-use parking area and more than 100 undeveloped camp sites. Accommodations are available at eighteen lodges, bed-and-breakfasts, and recreational vehicle camps. There is an automated teller machine (ATM) at the general store.

INFRASTRUCTURE

Transportation. Ninilchik is accessible by air, sea, and land. The Sterling Highway (Highway 1) provides access to Anchorage and other Alaskan communities and beyond that, through Canada, to the Lower 48. There are many year-round roads in the community, and in 2003, the community was accessing funding to install street lighting along Sterling Highway and to replace the Ninilchik River Bridge leading to the Village with a two-lane bridge. Also in 2003, villagers constructed a safe pedestrian and bicycle pathway along the Sterling Highway. Intersection improvements are planned for the Sterling Highway-Ninilchik Intersection in 2004. At Caribou Hills, an area along the Ninilchik River experiencing increased stream-bank erosion damage because of heavy traffic by ATVs and snowmobiles, one large bridge and four small bridges were built over drainages in order to protect the watershed.

A state-owned 2,400- by 60-foot dirt and gravel airstrip is available Homer, 40 miles south on the Sterling Highway, also offers an airport, harbor and docking facilities, and state ferry access. Ninilchik's harbor was constructed in the early 1970s. Boats can launch from Ninilchik or Deep Creek beaches.

Electricity. Electricity is provided by the Homer Electric Association.

Water and waste systems. Most homes use individual water wells or have water delivered. The village council operates a central watering point, with filtered and chlorinated water. Two-thirds of all residences have individual septic systems and full plumbing; others use privies. Refuse is collected by the borough. Marathon Oil operates a refuse transfer facility at Ninilchik.

Telecommunications. Local telephone service is provided by ACS of the Northland, long distance services by ACS or GCI. Internet services are provided by Core Communications or Peninsula Internet. There is public Internet access at the senior center. Five television stations and 10 radio stations broadcast to the Ninilchik area.

COMMUNITY FACILITIES AND SERVICES

Community facilities include the senior center and a public library, operated by the village, which also provides a central watering point and a plethora of social services for community members. Services include financial assistance for adult vocational training, higher education, youth participation in organized sports activities, general and burial, and child care; child welfare services and referrals; and the educational fishery program, designed to teach young people and new members the ways of the ancestors in subsistence fishing habits and skills.

Education. The Ninilchik School, which serves 186 students in grades K-12 with 13 teachers, is operated by the Kenai Peninsula School District.

Health care. Health care is provided by the Ninilchik Health Clinic, owned and operated by the village. The clinic supplies services in the following categories: community health/aides, midlevel nursing services, OB/GYN services, pharmacy, X-ray and lab, eye clinics and dental care, alcohol abuse prevention services, and diabetes screening and prevention. Emergencies are handled by the Ninilchik Emergency Services and there are two full-service hospitals nearby, the South Peninsula Hospital in Homer and the Central Peninsula Hospital in Soldotna.

Public safety. Law enforcement is provided by the state troopers post in Ninilchik. Emergency response is provided by Ninilchik Emergency Services.

ENVIRONMENTAL CONCERNS
The village operates a comprehensive environmental program, monitoring natural resources and potential hazardous sites. Staff members work cooperatively with regional EPA enforcement staff, ADEC, and designated spill response members having jurisdiction within tribal boundaries on issues involving suspected or real spills, and hazardous or toxic sites. Watershed data and water quality staff work to develop watershed protection guidelines and regulatory ordinances, adopt water quality monitoring programs, school educational programs, inventory all water and wastewater sites and respective use volumes, inventory contaminated sites, and compile historical knowledge of significant environmental changes or hazards in the region.

N oatak

Total area of entitlement under ANCSA	
	115,200 acres
Total labor force	142
High school graduate or higher	101
Bachelor's degree or higher	21
Unemployment rate	25.4%
Per capita income *(1999)*	$9,659
Population *2000 census*	428
Current population	469
state demographer estimate	
Percent Native *2000 census*	96.0%

LOCATION
Noatak is an unincorporated village located on the west bank of the Noatak River, 55 miles north of Kotzebue and 70 miles north of the Arctic Circle, in the Northwest Arctic Borough.

PHYSICAL DESCRIPTION
Noatak is an isolated community, the only settlement on the entire 396-mile length of the Noatak River, surrounded by the Brook Range and Noatak National Preserve on the east and Cape Krustenstern to the west. The village area encompasses 11.6 square miles of land and 0.7 square mile of water, at an elevation of 30 feet above sea level. Beyond the village proper, it is an area virtually untouched by humans; grizzly bears, wolves, moose, fox, and other wildlife vastly outnumber humans.

The Noatak River, the longest river in any national park, drains the largest protected, pristine watershed in the United States. From its source in the higher elevations of the Brooks Range, the river flows west through a narrow valley and passes briefly through the northwestern most boreal forest on the continent before slowing down as it widens and passes through a wide flood plain. The river, like the village, is bounded on all sides by the snowcapped peaks of the Brooks Range, and 330 miles of its length have been federally designated as "wild and scenic" and, therefore, protected, with strict rules governing its use and enjoyment. Eventually, it empties into Kotzebue Sound, the tidewaters of the Chukchi Sea.

Area lakes endure heavy camping traffic each summer. At the put-in and take-out points, erosion damage is evident, as it is along the banks of the Noatak also. Under particular threat are Twelvemile Slough, Portage Lake, Nelson Walker Lake, Pingo Lake, and Lake Matcharak, where vegetation around the lakes has been destroyed, already detracting from the area's wild character and visual beauty. The Noatak drainage basin is protected as a biosphere reserve, an internationally recognized United Nations scientific program, wherein the area's ecological and genetic components are monitored to establish baseline data for measuring changes in other ecosystems worldwide. The area is home to huge herds of caribou, Dall sheep, several species of raptors, grizzly bears, shaggy musk oxen, foxes, and wolves.

CLIMATE
Noatak is located on the border between a transitional climatic zone and a continental zone. Its climate is characterized by long, cold winters and mild, warm summers. Winter temperatures average between -21°F to 15°F; in the summer, they range between 40°F to 60°F, with recorded extremes of -59°F and 75°F. Total average annual precipitation is 10-13 inches, with 48 inches of snowfall. The Noatak River is frozen over from late September or early October until late May or early June. At its extreme northern latitude, the region experiences up to 24-hours of daylight in June, declining to approximately 1 hour of daylight in December.

CULTURE AND HISTORY
The population of Noatak is almost completely Inupiat Eskimo. It was established as a fishing and hunting camp in the nineteenth century. The rich resources of this region enabled the camp to develop into a permanent settlement. The 1880 U.S. census listed the site as Noatagamiut, an Inupiat word meaning "inland river people." Subsistence activities are the central focus of the culture, and most families travel to fish camps during the summer.

GOVERNMENT
Noatak is unincorporated and is located in the Northwest Arctic Borough. It is governed by an Indian Reorganization Act council, headed by a president.

VILLAGE/REGIONAL CORPORATION
The Noatak village corporation merged into ANCSA regional Native corporation *(see Alaska introduction).*

[NO-uh-tack]
Ethnicity: Inupiat

Native entity
Native Village of Noatak
P.O. Box 89
Noatak, AK 99761
 907-485-2173
 907-485-2137 Fax

ANCSA regional corporation
NANA Regional Corporation
P.O. Box 49
Kotzebue, AK 99752
 907-442-3301
 907-442-2866 Fax
nana.com

Noatak

ECONOMY

Noatak's economy is principally based on subsistence, although cash employment is available. The school district and the nonprofit Native corporation, Maniilaq, are the primary employers. During the summer, many residents travel to seasonal fish camps at Sheshalik and Kotzebue, where the men work as commercial fishermen and the women participate in subsistence fisheries, harvesting chum salmon and whitefish. Some residents take seasonal jobs as fire fighters, and several residents hold commercial fishing permits. There are eleven businesses licensed in Noatak, including three stores, a gift shop, a videotape rental business, and two snack stores.

Government as employer. Sixty-three residents work for the village, borough, state, or federal governments.

Tourism and recreation. Tourists visit Alaska's far north to paddle the Noatak River. Classified as a national wild and scenic river, the Noatak is the longest of all federally designated rivers. It is available for float-trips by inflatable canoe and kayak, sightseeing, wildlife viewing opportunities, and photography. Tourists hike the pristine wilderness areas surrounding the village. Noatak lies within 20 miles of the Noatak National Preserve on the east and Cape Krustenstern to the west, abutting Kotzebue Sound. It is also within 100 miles of Selawik National Wildlife Refuge, Kobuk Valley National Park, and the Bering Land Bridge National Preserve.

INFRASTRUCTRURE

Transportation. Noatak is primarily reached by air. The state-owned lighted gravel runway is 4,000- by 60-feet, served by five regional cargo, mail, and passenger air services: Bering Air, Grant Aviation, Hageland Aviation, Servant Air, and Tanana Air Service. There are no roads linking the village to other parts of the state. However, there are historic Noatak River trails that are still in use today for travel and commerce between villages and for subsistence activities. A barge service delivers fuel and supplies during the summer via the Noatak. Small boats, all-terrain vehicles, and snowmobiles are used extensively for local transportation. In 2002, a feasibility study was initiated to determine the economic advisability of building a harbor on the Noatak River at Noatak.

Electricity is provided by the Alaska Village Electric Cooperative (AVEC). Power is generated by burning fuel oil.

Fuel. Several businesses in Noatak own bulk fuel tanks, and in 1997 the village council constructed a fill line running from the airport directly to its tank farm. Additional upgrades to the tank farm and facilities are planned.

Water and waste systems. The village council operates a piped, circulating water system with water pulled from the Noatak River serving 77 homes, the school, and businesses in Noatak. There is a community well that sometimes runs dry, but no individual wells, since groundwater wells have been largely unsuccessful in the area. The water is chlorinated prior to distribution. Beginning in 1999 various improvements and upgrades to the local water and sewer systems were begun, including an investigation of groundwater resources and a design for new wells and innovative waste heat alternatives. In that year, the village also constructed an emergency sewer lift station and made other emergency sewer system renovations, but they were not sufficient to prevent a failure of the sewage system during the winter of 2001. So, in 2002, the Sanitation Master Plan was updated to address the issue of low water production. New wells were drilled and an existing one upgraded; well transmission lines were extended, wellheads were installed, and additional heat tape and insulation were added around all existing lines. The village council operates a Class 3 landfill for the community.

Telecommunications. Local telephone service is available through the OTZ Telephone Co-op, and long distance services are now widely available since deregulation. The village council operates a local cable television company. Internet services are provided by GCI.

COMMUNITY FACILITIES AND SERVICES

Education. Napaaqtugmiut School, which serves students in grades K-12, is operated by the Northwest Arctic School District.

Health care is provided by the Noatak Health Clinic, owned by the village, leased to the U.S. Public Health Service, and operated by the Maniilaq Association, a Native nonprofit corporation. Although the clinic facility was expanded and renovated in 1994, the village wants a new clinic.

Public safety. The village operates a volunteer fire department.

N ome

Ethnicity: Inupiat

Municipality
City of Nome
P.O. Box 281
Nome, AK 99762
907-443-6663
907-443-5349 Fax

Native entity
Nome Eskimo Community
P.O. Box 1090
Nome, AK 99762
907-443-2246
907-443-3539 Fax

ANCSA village corporation
Sitnasuak Native Corporation
P.O. Box 905
Nome, AK 99762
907-443-2632
907-443-3063 Fax

Total area of entitlement under ANCSA	
	242,606 acres
Total labor force	1,733
High school graduate or higher	592
Bachelor's degree or higher	429
Unemployment rate	10.9%
Per capita income *(1999)*	$23,402
Population *2000 census*	3,505
Current population	3,448
State Demographer estimate	
Percent Native *2000 census*	58.7%

LOCATION

Nome is a first-class city in the Unorganized Borough, located 539 air miles northwest of Anchorage, on the south shore of the Seward Peninsula, facing Norton Sound on the Bering Sea. Nome is 102 miles south of the Arctic Circle and 161 miles east of Russia.

PHYSICAL DESCRIPTION

The city area encompasses 12.5 square miles of land and 9.1 square miles of water, at an average elevation of 13 feet above sea level.

CLIMATE

Nome's climate has both subarctic and maritime influences. January temperatures range between -3°F and 11°F; July temperatures typically range between 44°F and 65°F. Average annual precipitation totals 18 inches, including 56 inches of snowfall. At this latitude, the region experiences almost 22 hours of daylight in a 24-hour period in June, declining to just over 3.5 hours in December.

CULTURE AND HISTORY

Historically, Malimiut, Kauweramiut, and Unalikmiut Inupiat Eskimos have occupied the Seward Peninsula, with a well-developed culture adapted to the environment. Around 1870 or 1880, the caribou population declined on the peninsula, and the local people changed their way of life in response to the loss of this major source of food. The discovery of gold at nearby Council in 1898 and on the sandy beaches of Norton Sound in 1900 brought thousands of prospectors to Nome and created a seemingly-overnight boom town of 20,000 prospectors, gamblers, claim jumpers, saloon keepers, and prostitutes. By 1900, a narrow-gauge railroad and telephone line from Nome to Anvil Creek had been built. The city was incorporated in 1901. By 1902, when the more easily accessed claims had been exhausted, large mining companies took over mining operations and the individual miners trickled out of Nome. A worldwide outbreak of influenza in 1918, the Great Depression, and World War II, all negatively affected the area's population as well. Then in 1934, a disastrous fire destroyed more of the city's buildings and many homes. Today, the population of Nome is a diverse community of Inupiat Eskimos, former villagers from King Island, and non-Natives.

GOVERNMENT
Nome was incorporated as a first-class city in 1901; it is located in the Unorganized Borough. It also has an Indian Reorganization Act council, headed by a president. A state superior court is located in Nome.

VILLAGE CORPORATION
Shareholders in the village corporation also hold shares in Bering Straits Native Corporation.

ECONOMY
Nome serves as the economic hub of the Bering Straits-Seward Peninsula region. The median household income is $59,402 (2000 census), the highest in Alaska. Government services provide the majority of employment opportunities, while retail services, transportation, mining, medical services, and other businesses also provide year-round income. Subsistence activities remain of great importance to most Nome residents. There are five general building-contractors in the city, a heavy-construction company, a number of handyman services, several clothing-manufacturing businesses in the village, as well as businesses producing hides and jewelry. There are four business involved in gravel-and-sand extraction. There are four taxi services, a school-bus business, two trucking companies, several scheduled air-transportation services, an air-cargo service, and several charter air-transportation services. Sixty residents hold commercial fishing permits. The Sitnasuak Native Corporation has opened an economic development office in Nome with several on-going projects and planned initiatives that will improve the economic opportunities even further for Native residents and others.

Government as employer. City, state, and federal governments employ 456 Nome residents. Several regional state and federal offices and facilities, such as the Anvil Mountain Correctional Center, employ substantial numbers of Nome residents.

Mining. NovaGold Resource Inc., operates a mine at Rock Creek, 7 miles north of Nome, and plans to be producing by 2006. Some small gold mines continue to provide some employment.

INFRASTRUCTRUE
Transportation. Historically, Nome has been accessible only by air and water.

Air. The Nome Airport has two paved runways. One is 6,001 feet long and 150 feet wide, and the other is 5,576- by 150-feet. An $8.5 million airport improvement project, beginning in 1997 and continuing throughout 2005, will correct many deficiencies when complete. New taxiways and aprons were designed and constructed; improvements to the safety area, including the removal of obstructions and rehabilitation of the runways have already been completed (2001-03). Planned

for 2004 and 2005 is the acquisition of additional land for airport construction, an update to the existing Airport Master Plan, the purchase of snow removal equipment and the construction of the building to house the new machinery. Scheduled jet flights are available, as well as charter and helicopter services.

Water. The Bering-seaward side of the city is protected by a 3,350-foot-long seawall composed of granite boulders trucked in from Cape Nome. This breakwater, built in 2002, protects a small boat harbor and sand storage building constructed in 1997-98, a harbormaster's office built in 2001, a port and berthing facilities that can accommodate vessels up to 18 feet of draft, and the city itself from the pounding of the Bering Sea's frigid surf. The harbor was dredged in 2000, and other harbor improvements have been in process throughout 2002 and 2003. Lighterage services distribute cargo to area communities.

Land. Three firms offer car rentals. Beginning in 1997, the City of Nome began a series of improvements to local streets, including the installation of tourist signage and resurfacing. In 2001, the project expanded to include the construction of a new road from Nome to Council. The Bureau of Indian Affairs funded the construction of a road to Fort Davis. Work was begun on a road from Nome to Teller in 2003. In 2004, work began to replace eight miles of the Glacier Creek Road, which allows access to the Rock Creek Mine.

Electricity is provided by the city-operated Nome Joint Utility Systems, generating power by burning oil. The power grid has also been undergoing major renovation since 2000, with the installation of additional lines, the extension and/or rehabilitation of others, and upgrade of a diesel generator to 4400-kilowatt. Renovations include a retrofit of the diesel generator to use exhaust and jacket cooling water as the heat source for a Kalina Bottom Cycle system that produces 500- to 700-kilowatts. There is also a project, underway since 2001, to assess and develop wind resources as a source of alternative energy. A wind project development agreement has been made with the City of Nome to monitor three sites and determine the feasibility of incorporating wind-generated energy into a proposed new power plant, with construction slated to begin in 2004.

Water and waste systems. A newly renovated piped water system is operated by the Nome Joint Utility System; the city also provides trucked delivery of water, with water drawn from community wells. The water is chlorinated at the Snake River Power Plant, heated, and then pumped to residences. In 1997, repair and renovation of the water and sewer systems began, and parts of the entire system have been either repaired or replaced altogether, including the replacement of the worn, wooden utilidor. New lines were extended to additional homes throughout Nome, and many old lines have been replaced; many have been abandoned. The city operates a piped sewage system including a lagoon; there are homeowners who utilize septic systems. Refuse collection services are provided by a contractor, which hauls it to a new Class 2 landfill.

Telecommunications. Local telephone service is available from GTE Alaska, while long distance services are now widely available via a number of carriers since deregulation. Cable television is made available by GCI Cable, which also provides Internet services along with Nome.net.

COMMUNITY FACILITIES AND SERVICES
The city operates a community center where services for senior citizens are offered, and a city hall building where the everyday functions of city government and administration are housed. There is a youth recreation facility; that building has

Nome

NOTE

Nome is not considered a Native Alaskan place for most federal and state purposes, although it has a substantial native Alaskan population and an ANCSA "village" corporation.

Nome

been undergoing renovations yearly since 1997. New programs and services for youth have been made available, and the building was expanded in the year 2000. The City Hall Building was expanded in 2002.

Education. There are three schools in Nome operated by the City. Anvil Science Academy serves students in grades 5-8 only. Nome Elementary serves students in preschool and kindergarten through grade 6. The Nome-Belz Jr./Sr. High School, which serves students in grades 7-12, has been undergoing mechanical and electrical upgrades (1999 and 2003); the gymnasium was renovated and an addition added in 2003. The City of Nome operates a public library.

Health care is provided by the Norton Sound Regional Hospital, a private medical facility; it is a qualified acute-care facility.

Medevac service is administered by the city and Norton Sound Health Corporation. Emergency services are provided by the Nome Volunteer Ambulance Service and the Norton Sound Health Corporation Medevac. The clinic was renovated in 1994. Long term care is available at the Quyaana Care Center. In 2003, a new hospital was under design. Specialized services are available at the Norton Sound Community Mental Health Center, at Turning Point-Saquigvik, a transitional living facility, and at the XYZ Senior Center.

Public safety. Law enforcement services are provided by the city police department and a state trooper post. The Nome Youth Facility, a detention center for adjudicated youth, was built in 2002. Fire services are provided to the city by the Nome Volunteer Fire Department, which operates and houses the Nome Volunteer Ambulance Department.

Nondalton

[non-DOLL-tun]
Ethnicity: Tanaina
       Athabascan; Iliamna

Municipality
City of Nondalton
P.O. Box 089
Nondalton, AK 99640
   907-294-2235
   907-294-2235 Fax

Native entity
Nondalton Tribal Council
P.O. Box 49
Nondalton, AK 99640
   907-294-2220
   907-294-2234 Fax

ANCSA village corporation
Kijik Corporation
4155 Tudor Centre Dr. #104
Anchorage, AK 99508
   907-561-4487
   907-562-4945 Fax

Total area of entitlement under ANCSA	
	126,410 acres
Total labor force	75
High school graduate or higher	49
Bachelor's degree or higher	10
Unemployment rate	37.3%
Per capita income (1999)	$8,411
Population 2000 census	221
Current population	217
state demographer estimate	
Percent Native 2000 census	90.0%

LOCATION
Nondalton is a second-class city located on the west shore of Six Mile Lake, in the Lake and Peninsula Borough of Alaska. The city lies between Lake Clark and Iliamna Lake, 190 miles southwest of Anchorage.

PHYSICAL DESCRIPTION
The City of Nondalton encompasses 8.4 square miles of land and 0.4 square mile of water. Although the surrounding local terrain is mountainous, Nondalton sits at an elevation of less than 165 feet above sea level. Lakes in this region of Alaska are the spawning habitat for many of Bristol Bay's salmon. Waters from Upper and Lower Tazimina Lakes flow into the Tazimina River, pass over a 70-foot falls, and tumble into Six Mile Lake, located just below Lake Clark. The Newhalen River connects Lake Clark and Six Mile Lake with Iliamna Lake.

CLIMATE
Nondalton lies in a transitional climate zone, with warm summers and cold winters. Rainfall averages 26 inches annually, including 64-70 inches of snowfall. Prevailing winter winds are northerly, and during the summer months easterly winds are common. Summertime temperatures range between 42°F and 62°F, and winter temperatures range between 6°F and 30°F, with recorded extremes of 91°F and -47°F. At this latitude, the region experiences approximately 18.5 hours of daylight in a 24-hour period in June, declining to 6 in December.

CULTURE AND HISTORY
Nondalton is a Tanaina (Dena'ina) Indian village with a subsistence-centered culture. Salmon canneries opened in the Bristol Bay area in late 1884, and by the early 1900s, some Dena'ina were obtaining cash income from this industry. The name was first recorded in 1909 by the United States Geological Survey when they found the village located on the north shore of Six Mile Lake. The spread of infectious diseases in

surrounding villages such as Kijik (now a National Historic Landmark), around 1909, and a desire to be closer to the trading posts and salmon canneries of Bristol Bay, brought scores of new people to Old Nondalton. By 1940, the depletion of wood in surrounding areas and encroaching mud flats near the lake's shores forced the village to move to its present location. Other migrations led some villagers to neighboring Lime Village and a network of kinship and trade relations remains an important cultural link between the residents of Lime Village and Nondalton to this day. The city was incorporated in 1971.

GOVERNMENT
Nondalton was incorporated as a second-class city in 1971, with a mayor and city council. It also has a traditional village council, headed by a president.

VILLAGE CORPORATION
Shareholders in the Kijik village corporation, formerly Nondalton Native Corporation, also hold shares in Bristol Bay Native Corporation.

ECONOMY
Commercial fishing remains an important source of income in Nondalton; most residents leave the village for this purpose during the summer months; 14 residents hold commercial fishing permits. Another source of cash income is gold and copper mining in the area and seasonal fire-fighting jobs are available with the U.S. Bureau of Land Management. The community also relies on subsistence hunting and fishing to supplement cash incomes: salmon, trout, grayling, moose, caribou, bear, Dall sheep, rabbit, and porcupine are harvested. There are seven businesses currently licensed in Nondalton, including a bed-and-breakfast, a hunting guide service, and a fishing lodge.

Government as employer. Thirty-three Nondalton residents work for either the city, borough, state, or federal governments.

Tourism and recreation. Tourists enjoy several annual Six Mile Lake cultural events and school-sponsored activities. There is a restaurant in the village, as well as a fishing camp and a fishing and hunting guide service to accommodate guests interested in plying the salmon- and trout-rich waters of the Tazimina River or any other of the region's many pristine lakes and rivers. Six Mile Lake borders the Lake Clark National Park and Preserve, and Nondalton lies within 100 miles of the Katmai National Park and Preserve.

INFRASTRUCTURE
Transportation. Nondalton is primarily accessible by air and water.

Air. The State of Alaska owns and maintains a 2,800- by 75-foot gravel runway; there is no crosswind runway or tower service. There is scheduled air service from Iliamna, and charter flights are available from King Salmon via Iliamna Air Taxi. In 2003, there were plans to resurface the airport's runway, purchase snow removal equipment for the airport and build a building to house it.

Water. Bulk goods are received in Iliamna then taken by a cat-trail to Fish Camp, located across from Nondalton on the east side of the lake, where they are then ferried by skiff or barge to the west side. Limited and costly barge service is available for the delivery of goods, but there are no docking facilities.

Land. A proposed project among several local communities to improve upon an existing 22-mile pioneer (rough-cut) road between Nondalton and Iliamna was scheduled to begin construction in 2003. This project includes the construction of a bridge over the Newhalen River. In 2002, the Bureau of Indian Affairs funded improvements to all 25 miles of local roads in Nondalton.

Electricity. The I-N-N Electric Cooperative owns a diesel plant in Newhalen and 50 miles of distribution line to connect Iliamna, Newhalen, and Nondalton. The Tazimina Hydroelectric Project has recently been completed and powers the three communities.

Water and waste systems. The City of Nondalton provides piped water from a community well and a surface source; the water is chlorinated prior to distribution. Due to drastically increased demand in the 1990s, the city undertook massive rehabilitation and expansion of existing water capacity beginning with an engineering study funded in 1999 by the Alaska Native Tribal Health Consortium. That water source

evaluation led to the development of an Emergency Water Distribution and Sanitation Master Plan the same year, and in 2002 improvements to the well and pump housing were underway. There are plans for the drilling of test wells, pilot testing to determine quantity and quality of any discovered water, and a leak survey to be completed at those new well sites in 2004. The city provides piped-sewage service, including lift station and lagoon. Refuse collection is not provided; however, a new 60-acre Class 3 landfill was constructed near the city in 1997, with an incinerator and incinerator building and proper facility fencing. The new Iliamna-Nondalton road, when completed, will allow access to this facility.

Telecommunications. Local telephone service is provided by Pacific Telecommunications, and long distance services are now widely available since deregulation. One television channel is offered by the Rural Alaska Television Network and Internet services are available from GCI.

COMMUNITY FACILITIES AND SERVICES
The City of Nondalton operates a community center and public park.

Education. The Nondalton School, which serves students in grades K-12, is operated by the Lake and Peninsula School District. It also houses services for senior citizens. It was renovated in 1997, with new electric boilers outfitted to utilize surplus energy from Tazimina Hydroelectric Project installed in series with the existing oil-fired boilers.

Health care is provided by the Nondalton Health Clinic, owned by the city, leased to the U.S. Public Health Service, and operated by the Bristol Bay Area Health Corporation. Emergency response is provided by the Nondalton First Responders.

Public safety. Nondalton is served by a city police force and by Alaska state troopers stationed in McGrath, over 150 miles distant. The City of Nondalton maintains a volunteer fire department and supports operations of the Nondalton First Responders.

Nooiksut
See Nuiqsut

Noorvik

Total area of entitlement under ANCSA	
	138,240 acres
Total labor force	225
High school graduate or higher	151
Bachelor's degree or higher	24
Unemployment rate	10.1%
Per capita income *(1999)*	$12,020
Population *2000 census*	634
Current population	649
state demographer estimate	
Percent Native *2000 census*	95.0%

LOCATION
Noorvik is a second-class city located on the right bank of the Nazaruk Channel of the Kobuk River, 33 air miles northwest of Selawik and 45 air miles east of Kotzebue, in the Northwest Arctic Borough of Alaska. It is located downriver from the 1.7-million-acre Kobuk Valley National Park, and lies entirely within the Selawik National Wildlife Refuge in extreme northwestern Alaska.

PHYSICAL DESCRIPTION
Noorvik encompasses 1.0 square mile of land and 0.4 square mile of water, at an elevation of less than 165 feet above sea level.

CLIMATE
Noorvik is located in a transitional climate zone, characterized by long, cold winters and cool summers. Temperatures range between -10°F to 15°F in the winter and between 40°F to 65°F during summer months. Extremes of -54°F and 87°F have been recorded. Snowfall averages 60 inches, with average annual precipitation totaling 16 inches per year. The Kobuk River is frozen over from mid-October to early June. At this latitude, the region experiences up to 24 hours of daylight during mid-June, declining to 1.5 hours by December.

CULTURE AND HISTORY
Noorvik is primarily an Inupiat Eskimo community, with a subsistence culture. The village was established by Kowagmiut (Inupiat) Eskimo fishermen and hunters from Deering and Oksik, a few miles upriver, in the early 1900s. The name *Noorvik* means "a place that is moved to." A post office was

[NOR-vick]
Ethnicity: Kowagmiut Inupiat

Municipality
City of Noorvik
P.O. Box 146
Noorvik, AK 99763
    907-636-2100
    907-636-2135 Fax

Native entity
Noorvik Native Community
P.O. Box 209
Noorvik, AK 99763
    907-636-2144
    907-636-2284 Fax

Noorvik

established in 1937, and the city government was incorporated in 1964.

GOVERNMENT

Noorvik was incorporated as a second-class city in 1964, with a mayor and city council. It also has an Indian Reorganization Act council, headed by a president which is also the Public Law 93-638 tribal government contractor.

VILLAGE/REGIONAL CORPORATION

The village corporation was merged into NANA regional Native corporation *(see Alaska introduction)*.

ECONOMY

As of 2004, a thriving commercial economy exists in Noorvik with many residents employed in one of the many business initiatives of the NANA Regional Corporation. Other income-producing employment is found with the school district, the nonprofit Native corporation, the health clinic, and some retail stores. Some seasonal employment is available at the Red Dog Mine, in firefighting for the U.S. Bureau of Land Management, or in the commercial fishing industry in Kotzebue. Subsistence activities also contribute to many residents' household resources, including caribou, fish, moose, waterfowl, and berries. The median household income in the 2000 census is $51,964, one of the highest in Alaska. Private businesses include several retail stores and an aircraft salvage firm, among others.

Government as employer. Eighty-six residents of Noorvik work for the city, borough, state, or federal governments.

INFRASTRUCTURE

Transportation. Noorvik is accessible only by air and water; there are no roads linking the village to other areas of Alaska. The major means of transportation are plane, boat, barge, all-terrain vehicle, and snowmobile.

Air. The State of Alaska owns and maintains the Bob Curtis Memorial Airport at Noorvik. The facility, which was moved and upgraded throughout the years 1998-2003, features a 4,000- by 100-foot lighted gravel runway and a 2,600-foot gravel crosswind runway. The $5-million-dollar airport is now the second largest in the borough. Several regional air taxis provide service to Kotzebue and surrounding cities: Bering Air, Cape Smythe Air, Grant Aviation, Hageland Aviation, Servant Air, and Tanana Air Service.

Water. A lighterage company, Crowley Marine Services, barges fuel and supplies to the village during the summer months.

Land. Locally, a gravel road leads from Hotham Peak to the local landfill and there was a DCED project in 1999 to upgrade all local roads with new drainage/culvert systems to prevent soil erosion. Additional work was completed in 2002.

Electricity is provided by the Alaska Village Electric Cooperative (AVEC), generating power by burning oil. This co-op is operated jointly with the city. The residents of Noorvik have expressed an interest in generating electricity through the use of wind energy, and in 2002 a wind-monitoring tower was installed.

Water and waste systems. The city operates a piped water system with water drawn from multiple surface watering points; the water is filtered and chlorinated. Groundwater wells have proven unsuccessful. Beginning in 1997, water system upgrades have been in process, including the addition of 15 houses to the system and construction of a new water/sewer connection for the school. Outdated plumbing fixtures were replaced in 106 homes in 1997. In 2000, a water main and house plumbing were extended to provide water and sewer service to 16 houses, with work continuing on additional laterals to even more homes throughout 2002. Noorvik funded the construction of a new honeybucket dump station (lagoon) and Class 3 landfill in 2002, and closed the old site. The community is studying alternate collection and disposal methods as part of an update to its Sanitation Facilities Master Plan in 2003. The city operates a piped sewage system which includes a lift station and lagoon.

Telecommunications. Local telephone service is provided by the OTZ Telephone Company, and long distance services are now widely available since deregulation. The city provides cable television service in the village, and Internet services are provided by GCI.

COMMUNITY FACILITIES AND SERVICES

Funds have been requested to construct a multipurpose facility, including a new washeteria, a recreation center, a Head Start and day care center, a restaurant, a Native crafts production facility, and a food processing plant.

Education. Noorvik Elementary School and Aqqaluk High School serve students in grades K-12. They are both governed by the Northwest Arctic School District, operated by the Borough. Activities outside of school are provided by a youth group and by programs offered at the recreation center, built in 1997. There are libraries at both schools.

Health care. Health care is provided by the Noorvik Health Clinic, constructed in 1998. The facility is owned and operated by the U.S. Public Health Service and administered by Maniilaq Association.

Public safety. Law enforcement is provided by the city police department, housed at the city public safety building built in 2003, the state's village public safety officers, and state troopers in Kotzebue. Fire protection is provided by a volunteer fire department.

Total area of entitlement under ANCSA

	115,200 acres
Total labor force	74
High school graduate or higher	42.4%
Unemployment rate	18.9%
Per capita income *(1999)*	$10,300
Population *2000 census*	107
2003 population	95
state demographer estimate	
Percent Native *2000 census*	95.3%

LOCATION
Northway Village is located in the interior of Alaska, 50 miles southeast of Tok, on a 9-mile spur road off the Alaska Highway (Highway 2). The village sits between Nabesna River and Skate Lake, 42 miles west of the border with Yukon Territory of Canada.

PHYSICAL DESCRIPTION
Northway Village lies within the Tetlin National Wildlife Refuge, composed of the broad basins of the Chisana and Nabesna rivers, extensive marshy sloughs, and lakes. Flowing northward from their glacier origins in the Wrangell Mountains, these rivers join north of the village to form the Tanana River. The village area encompasses approximately 2.6 square miles of land and 0.1 square mile of water at an elevation of approximately 1,716 feet.

CLIMATE
Northway is in the continental climate zone, with long, cold winters and relatively short, warm summers. Temperatures range from average winter lows of -27°F to average summer highs of 69°F, with extremes of -72°F and 91°F recorded. Average precipitation is 10 inches per year, including approximately 30 inches of snowfall annually. At this latitude, the region experiences 19-20 hours of daylight in a 24-hour period in June, declining to an average of 5 hours in mid-December.

CULTURE AND HISTORY
The area around Northway has traditionally been Upper Tanana (Athabascan) Indian territory. Seminomadic Athabascan Indians have lived in the interior of Alaska for thousands of years practicing a subsistence lifestyle. Periodic trips to trading posts along the Yukon River brought them into first contact with white traders in the late 1880s. White traders first entered the areas of Scottie and Gardiner Creeks and the Chisana, Nabesna, and Tanana Rivers as early as 1912, and by the 1920s, the traders had established trading posts in those areas as well. Road construction crews of the Alaska Highway and those that built the Northway Airfield, established as a link in the Northwest Staging Route during World War II, brought a permanent non-Native population to the area. A post office was established in 1941, and in 1942 the name of the village was changed to Northway to honor the village chief, T'aiy Ta', who had adopted the name from a riverboat captain who traveled the Tanana and Nabesna Rivers in the early 1900s. Chief Walter Northway was thought to be 117 years old at the time of his death in 1993. Cultural traditions such as dancing, crafts, hunting, and trapping continue today. Upper Tanana Athabascan is spoken mainly in Northway, Tetlin, and Tok, but has a small population also across the border in Canada. The Alaskan population is about 300, of whom perhaps 105 speak the language.

GOVERNMENT
Northway Village is unincorporated and is located in the Unorganized Borough. It is governed by a traditional village council, headed by a president. Naabia Niign Ltd. is the commercial subsidiary of the village.

VILLAGE CORPORATION
Northway Natives, Incorporated, is the ANCSA village corporation. Its shareholders also hold shares in Doyon, Limited, the regional Native corporation.

ECONOMY
Doyon, Limited, the regional Native corporation, has played a key role in the development of employment opportunities for the communities of Northway, although subsistence activities continue to be an important part of the economy. Moose, rabbit, ptarmigan, ducks, geese, whitefish, and berries are harvested, and some families travel to the Copper River during salmon runs. In Northway Village, most full-time wage employment is available through government facilities or services for the airport, where an FAA flight service station and a U.S. Customs office are located. There is some seasonal income derived from fire fighting for the U.S. Bureau of Land Management and from summer construction jobs. Locally hand crafted tribal arts and crafts, such as birch-bark baskets, moccasins, mukluks, mittens, hats, and beadwork accessories are marketed at Naabia Niign Arts and Crafts, a gift shop in Northway made possible by the regional corporation.

Government as employer. Sixteen of 30 employed Northway Village residents work for either the state or federal government.

Services and retail. There are no businesses located in the village, but the Northway community as a whole has a variety of retail services, including a taxidermy service, grocery stores, snowplowing and waste-removal services, a liquor store, and a coin-operated laundry.

Tourism and recreation. Fishing the Tanana River is a favorite draw into the Northway communities' area, as is the entirety of the Tetlin National Wildlife Refuge. Fish native to this interior area are the pike and grayling; some area lakes are stocked with rainbow trout and lake trout. Three-hundred thousand sandhill cranes fly into the Tetlin National Wildlife Refuge each autumn. The Fish and Wildlife Service reports that 114 nesting and 68 migrating species use this area each season, among them trumpeter swans, ospreys, bald eagles, and other raptors. Mammal species found in the refuge include black and brown bears, moose, wolves, snowshoe hares, and lynx. Caribou prowl the areas close to the highway in winter. The airport and Highway 2 make access easy, accommodations available for tourists and guests of residents include the Naabia Niign Campground, operated by the village, and a motel at the airport. In the refuge, there are campgrounds at Deadman Lake and Lakeview Campground and two public-use cabins, one at Wellesley Lake and another at Jatahmund Lake, although these require airplane or snowmobile travel. The refuge features a system of well-marked trails leading deep into pristine wilderness areas for pedestrian and ATV or snowmobile travel, and hiking within the Refuge is unrestricted, although foot traffic is often impeded by extremely dense vegetation and grass tussocks in sloughs. Walking is

Ethnicity: Upper Tanana Athabascan

Native entity
Northway Village
P.O. Box 516
Northway, AK 99764
907-778-2311
907-778-2220 Fax

ANCSA village corporation
Northway Natives, Incorporated
P.O. Box 401
Northway, AK 99764
907-778-2298
907-778-2266 Fax

NOTE
Northway consists of three separate settlements: Northway Junction, at milepost 1264; Northway, at the airport; and Northway Village, 2 miles north of the airport. The information in this profile refers to Northway Village, the BIA-recognized Native entity. Although the other two communities have substantial Native populations, they are not recognized as Native communities by the BIA or for the ANCSA. It is important to recognize that the three communities are economically and socially integrated for many purposes, but are administratively separate.

easier in the higher altitudes of the foothills of the Nutzotin and Mentasta Mountains. For those who prefer travel by truck and car, pullouts along the Alaska Highway are great spots for photography and wildlife viewing, and there are additional accommodations available in Tok, at lodges in Wrangell-St. Elias National Park, and along the Glenn Highway Cutoff southwest of Tok. The visitor center at Tetlin National Wildlife Refuge is open daily between Memorial Day and Labor Day. It is located at mile 1229, seven miles from the border with Canada.

INFRASTRUCTURE
Transportation. Northway Village is connected to the Alaska Highway (Highway 2) by an unpaved road. A WWII-era highway, the Alaska Highway runs northwest from Northway to Tok, or southeast toward its origin in Dawson Creek, British Columbia, Canada, thus connecting tiny Northway with Southern Alaska. From Northway, scheduled buses and trucking services are available for passengers and cargo. In 1999, this stretch of Highway 2 was relevelled and resurfaced. The state operates the airport at Northway, which features a 3,304- by 100-foot gravel-dirt runway. Regular and charter flights to Fairbanks are provided by 40 Mile Air.

Electricity. Electricity is provided by the privately owned Alaska Power Company from a diesel plant.

Water and waste systems. Residents haul their water from a central watering point operated by the village. A flush/haul system was finished in May 2003. Residents haul their own honeybuckets. Refuse collection is provided by Naabia Niign, then hauled to Northway's Class 3 landfill.

Telecommunications. Local telephone service is provided by ACS of the Northland, long distance service by AT&T Alascom. Internet service is available from GCI at the school in Northway. Broadcast television service is provided by the Alaska Rural Communications Service.

COMMUNITY FACILITIES AND SERVICES
The Northway Village council, directly or through its Naabia Niign subsidiary, operates the local washeteria, water supply, and waste disposal systems. There is a community center in the village.

Education. Children attend the Walter Northway School in Northway, and there is a public library in Northway.

Health care. Health care is provided by the Northway Health Clinic in Northway Village, operated by the Tanana Chiefs Conference. A new building for the clinic was finished in May 2003. Emergency services are provided by Northway First Responder Service.

Public safety. Law enforcement is provided by state troopers stationed in Northway. Emergency response is provided by Northway First Responder Service.

Nuiqsut

[new-WICK-sit]
variant spelling: Nooiksut

Ethnicity: Inupiat

Municipality
City of Nuiqsut
P.O. Box 148
Nuiqsut, AK 99789
907-480-6727
907-480-6928 Fax

Native entity
Native Village of Nuiqsut
P.O. Box 169
Nuiqsut, AK 99789
907-480-3010
907-480-3009 Fax

ANCSA village corporation
Kuukpik Corporation
P.O. Box 187
Nuiqsut, AK 99789
907-480-6220
907-480-6126 Fax

Total area of entitlement under ANCSA	
	137,881 acres
Total labor force	193
High school graduate or higher	86
Bachelor's degree or higher	15
Unemployment rate	8.8%
Per capita income *(1999)*	$14,876
Population *2000 census*	433
Current population	416
2003 state demographer estimate	
Percent Native *2000 census*	89.1%

LOCATION
Nuiqsut is located about 35 miles from the Beaufort Sea coast and 154 miles southeast of Barrow, on the extreme North Slope of Arctic Alaska. It sits on the west bank of the Nechelik Channel of the Colville River.

PHYSICAL DESCRIPTION
The city encompasses 9.2 square miles of land at an elevation of less than 165 feet above sea level. Nuiqsut is an isolated community at the center of a vast tundra, dominated by grass and sedge vegetation. It is a permafrost region characterized by low-banked meandering streams, an occasional pingo (ice-cored hill), wet, marshy sloughs, and shallow freshwater lakes covering as much as 50-75 percent of its total surface area. Dense stands of willow trees, 8 to 10 feet high, appear occasionally, and frost cracks, polygonal ground, and cottongrass tussocks are common features of the terrain. Frozen for most of the year, the Colville River floods each spring as ice on its uppermost reaches melts. Subsurface coal, oil, and natural gas are found throughout the river basin. Nuiqsut lies 50 miles downriver from the site of a $20-million environmental cleanup of PCBs and other toxins that leached into the Colville River. The U.S. Army Corps of Engineers began work in 2000 at the site of the former Umiat Air Station, a remote military installation south of Prudhoe Bay. Built during World War II, the post was once a refueling stop for military planes bound for Distant Early Warning sites on the continent's northernmost edge. It was also the site of extensive oil exploration. The site was listed as one of the highest cleanup priorities and remains a lingering source of environmental concern for all residents living within the watershed of the Colville River. Since Nuiqsut was relocated in 1973, there has been no known flooding. The airport has been relocated and is no longer subject to flooding. The Colville River basin is well-known for a plethora of birds and other wildlife species. Nesting raptors, Arctic peregrine falcons, golden eagles, and rough-legged hawks are a few of the winged creatures seldom seen elsewhere in such numbers. The river also provides an important year-round habitat for brown bears, wolves, and moose, and produces a significant number of dinosaur fossils.

CLIMATE
Nuiqsut's climate is Arctic. Temperatures range from winter lows of -56°F to summer highs of 78°F, with low temperatures below 32°F on 297 days per year. The mean daily temperature during the winter is -20°F. Precipitation is light, averaging only 5 inches, including annual snowfall of 20 inches, qualifying it as a "cold desert" climate. Because of its extreme polar latitude, the sun is up at Nuiqsut from May 15 until July 28, with a full 24 hours of daylight during much of June. The sun is down from November 25 throughout January 18, with no daylight for much of December.

CULTURE AND HISTORY
For over 8,000 years, the Colville Delta has been a gathering and trading place for the Inupiat and has always offered good hunting and fishing. Rivers teem with whitefish, burbot, arctic

char, grayling, and an occasional salmon; spotted seals, which penetrate inland in search of these fish, are also harvested, and lake trout abound in the region's thaw and mountain lakes. Bowhead whales, caribou, a periodic moose, wolves, grizzly bear, wolverine, and fox are also taken. Today, Nuiqsut is an Inupiat village with a culture continuing to focus on traditional subsistence activities. An older Village of Nuiqsut (Itqilippaa) was abandoned in the late 1940s because there was no school. In 1973, with belongings packed on sleds hauled by tractors and snowmobiles, 27 families from Barrow arrived at the present location. They lived in a tent village for a year and a half before permanent housing could be built, using snow/ice blocks to help insulate tent walls in the winter months. The Arctic Slope Regional Corporation funded the construction of the village in 1974, including a school and housing, and the city was incorporated as a second-class city in 1975.

GOVERNMENT
Nuiqsut was incorporated as a second-class city in 1975, with a mayor and city council. It is located in the North Slope Borough. It also has a traditional village council, headed by the mayor.

VILLAGE CORPORATION
Shareholders in the Kuukpic village corporation also hold shares in the Arctic Slope regional Native corporation *(see Alaska introduction)*.

ECONOMY
Like that of most all North Slope villages, Nuiqsut's economy is based primarily on subsistence hunting and fishing. However, nearly one-third of the work force is employed in the private sector, mostly by the Kuukpik Corporation (the ANCSA village corporation) and the construction industry that has evolved from projects initiated by the Arctic Slope Regional Corporation. Many residents are employed by the borough. Most of the businesses in the city are part of Kuukpik Corporation, including a hardware store, a general store, the fuel pump station, a surface transportation firm, and an air cargo service. Other private businesses include a construction services firm and a lubricants distributor. Most transient traffic occurs as a result of the oil industry. Workers in several sectors of this industry fly from village to village on their way to the oil fields. In this way, Nuiqsut, although isolated, is connected to Anaktuvuk Pass, Bettles, Fort Yukon, and Prudhoe Bay, as well as Anchorage and villages in Interior Western Alaska. Some tourism is stimulated by the Colville River. However, weather extremes hold this to a minimum. The village is about 100 miles from the northern border of the Arctic National Wildlife Refuge.

Government as employer. Ninety-one residents work for either the city, borough, state or federal government.

INFRASTRUCTURE
Transportation. Air travel provides the only year-round access to the city. A 4,343- by 90-foot gravel airstrip, located eight trail miles south of the city, is owned and operated by the North Slope Borough. It is served by scheduled and charter flights from Barrow and Fairbanks, by Cape Smythe Air, Frontier Flying Service, Hageland Aviation Services, and Kuupik Northern Air Cargo (freight only). Freight arrives by air year-round. The airport facility was improved with an extended safety area in the year 2000. In summer months only, there is marine access to Nuiqsut from Barrow via the Beaufort Sea

(Arctic Ocean), and overland access via a series of rough-cut trails connecting villages to oil fields, made by the petroleum industry. One local road, the Colville River Road, was constructed with assistance from the Bureau of Indian Affairs during 1997; the grades were leveled and drainage added in 1998. The city also has a public transit system. Nuiqsut residents have access to the Dalton Highway four months out of the year. It is the most northern town in Alaska with road access. Lodging is available at the Kuukpik Hotel, a subsidiary of the village corporation, which also operates a restaurant.

Electricity is available to residents through the North Slope Borough Power Company, generating power from a 3,745-kilowatt diesel plant.

Fuel. Piped natural gas is available to residents from the Alpine oil field, substantially decreasing the cost of running the diesel electric generator and of heating homes and other facilities. Storage (gallons): North Slope Borough (NSB) Fuel Station (468,000); NSB Electric (160,000); NSB Municipal (32,000); city (10,000); NSB Fire/Rescue (8,000); NSB Clinic (6,500); NSB Schools (2,750); NSB old Public Safety (2,000); Kuukpik Presbyterian Church (2,000); NSB Police (1,100); Assembly of God (1,100).

Water and waste systems. The North Slope Borough provides a piped water system with water drawn from a freshwater lake, then treated and chlorinated prior to distribution. There is also a central watering point within the community, and the borough provides a trucked water delivery service as well. Permafrost prevents the use of individual or community wells. The borough operates the community washeteria. The borough also operates a piped sewer system including pumper, lift station, and lagoon, and operates a honeybucket haul service for those residents continuing use of honeybuckets and outhouses. Many residents have septic systems, and there is a community septic tank for public buildings. The borough collects refuse throughout the community.

Telecommunications. Local telephone service is provided by the Arctic Slope Telephone Association Cooperative, and long distance services by AT&T Alascom, GCI, or Arctic Slope Telephone. Internet service is provided by GCI. One AM radio station broadcasts from Nuiqsut. The city provides cable television service, and the Alaska Rural Communications System broadcasts one channel from Nuiqsut.

COMMUNITY FACILITIES AND SERVICES
Education. Nuiqsut Trapper School, which serves students in pre-school and in grades K-12, is administered by the North Slope Borough School District. It serves 143 students with 17 teachers. The Trapper School Community Library serves both the school and the city and is a member of the Tuzzy Library Consortium.

Health care. The Nuiqsut Health Clinic, owned by the North Slope Borough, is leased to the U.S. Public Health Service and administered by the North Slope Regional Health Corporation. Samuel Simmonds Memorial Hospital in Barrow is the nearest hospital. Emergencies are handled by the Nuiqsut Volunteer Fire Department, which owns an ambulance.

Public safety. Law enforcement is provided by the North Slope Borough Police Department. Emergency response is provided by the Nuiqsut Volunteer Fire Department and Rescue Squad.

Nulato

Municipality
City of Nulato
P.O. Box 65009
Nulato, AK 99765
907-898-2205
907-898-2203 Fax

Native entity
Nulato Village
P.O. Box 65409
Nulato, AK 99765-0049
907-898-2339
907-898-2207 Fax

ANCSA village corporation
Gana-A'Yoo, Limited
3000 A Street #417
Anchorage, AK 99503
907-569-9599
907-569-9699 Fax

.

Total area of entitlement under ANCSA	
	114,586 acres
Total labor force	126
High school graduate or higher	55.0%
Bachelor's degree or higher	6.5%
Unemployment rate	24.4%
Per capita income *(1999)*	$8,966
Population *2000 census*	336
2003 population	342
state demographer estimate	
Percent Native *2000 census*	94.0%

LOCATION
In far West Central Alaska, Nulato is 35 miles west of Galena and 310 air miles west of Fairbanks.

PHYSICAL DESCRIPTION
Nulato sits on the west bank of the Yukon River in the Nulato Hills. The city encompasses 42.7 square miles of land and 2.0 square miles of water, at an elevation of less than 165 feet above sea level.

CLIMATE
Nulato is located in the continental climate zone, with weather characterized by extreme temperature differences, long cold winters, and warm, short summers. Average daily highs in July are in the lower 70s; the average daily lows in January are well below 0°F with several consecutive days of -40°F common each winter. Extremes of 90°F in the summer and -55°F in the winter have been recorded. Average annual precipitation is approximately 16 inches, including an average annual snowfall of 74 inches. The Yukon River is frozen over from mid-October through mid-May. At this latitude, the region experiences over 21 hours of daylight in a 24-hour period in June, declining to less than 4 in December.

CULTURE AND HISTORY
Nulato residents are predominantly Koyukon Athabascans, with a culture focused on trapping and subsistence activities, migrating among spring, summer, fall, and winter camps, following wild game. Subsistence foods are a major portion of the diet, and many families travel to fish camps each summer. Salmon, moose, bear, small game, and berries are eaten. Koyukon occupies the largest territory of any Alaskan Athabascan language. It is spoken in three dialects—Upper, Central, and Lower—in 11 villages along the Koyukuk and middle Yukon rivers. The total current population is about 2,300, of whom about 300 speak the language. Nulato was traditionally the site for trading between Koyukon Athabascans and Inupiat from the Kobuk area. Western contact increased rapidly after a Russian explorer established a fur trading post in 1839. The Western Union Telegraph Company explored the area around 1867. Many natives moved to the area after a Roman Catholic mission and school were built there in 1887, but epidemics claimed hundreds of lives after the onset of the Yukon-Koyukuk gold rush of 1884. Food shortages and a measles epidemic claimed up to one-third of all village residents during 1900 alone. A post office opened at Nulato in 1897. Gold seekers left the Yukon after 1906. Nulato incorporated as a second-class city in 1963, and soon thereafter a clinic, a water supply system, a new school, and telephone and television services were developed. In 1981, large-scale housing development began at a new townsite on the Nulato Hills north of the city, about two miles from the old townsite.

GOVERNMENT
Nulato was incorporated as a second-class city in 1963, with a mayor and city council; it is located in the Unorganized Borough. It also has a BIA-recognized traditional village council, Nulato Village, also known as the Nulato Tribal Council.

VILLAGE CORPORATION
Gana-A'Yoo Limited is the ANCSA village corporation for Nulato, Koyukuk, Galena, and Kaltag. It was formed in 1978 by the consolidation of the four individual village corporations. A nine-member board of directors, elected from more than 1,150 shareholders, directs the management team responsible for day-to-day operations. It has two subsidiaries and a joint venture with over 300 employees nationwide and revenues in 2002 of over $4.6 million. Subsidiary Khotol Services Corporation is a §8(a) firm specializing in federal defense contracting. Yistletaw Properties owns a minority interest in a hotel in Fairbanks. A joint venture with a subsidiary of the Compass Group, the largest food service company in the world, provides food service, catering, housekeeping, operations, and maintenance to remote camps in the interior of Alaska. Shareholders of Gana-A'Yoo Limited are also shareholders of Doyon, Limited, the regional Native corporation.

ECONOMY
A few Nulato residents work in projects initiated by either the regional Native corporation or in the village Native corporation. In the summer, some residents find employment in U.S. Bureau of Land Management emergency fire-fighting positions, commercial fishing, and fish processing plants. Trapping is the village's largest private-sector income-producer during winter.

Government as employer. Forty-four of 74 employed residents work for either the city, state or federal governments.

Services and retail. Nulato has three general stores, a sewing shop, and a maintenance and snow removal service.

Tourism and recreation. Wildlife viewing and photography opportunities and fishing the Nulato River are favorite regional attractions for tourists. Many guests of family members also come to the village to participate in local patriotic and cultural celebrations: Spring Carnival, Memorial Day, Fourth of July, Fifth of August Races, potlatches, and the stick dance. Guests and tourists may stay at the school, the city office building, the Bunkhouse, or Fred's House (a motel). Only the Yukon separates Nulato from the Innoko National Wildlife Refuge. Nulato is also 25 miles south of the southern border of the Koyukuk National Wildlife Refuge and lies within 100 miles of the Nowitna National Wildlife Refuge.

INFRASTRUCTURE
Transportation. The city is primarily accessible by water and air. The Yukon River is the primary access mode in summer and winter. Barges deliver cargo during summer months, but there is no dock or loading facility. The river becomes an ice road during winter for vehicles and snowmachines. Cars, trucks, snowmobiles, all-terrain vehicles, and skiffs are used by residents on the ice and surrounding areas. Nulato is accessible by air year-round, using the village airport, a state-owned 4,000- by 100-foot lighted airstrip. It is served by Arctic Circle Air Service, Evert Air Alaska, Frontier Flying Service, Larry's Flying Service, Servant Air, Tanana Air Service

and Warbelow's Air Ventures. Numerous trails are used by residents, especially in the winter, for trapping and woodcutting. There is one main road within the city.

Electricity. Electricity is available to residents from the Alaska Village Electrical Cooperative (AVEC), operating an 897-kilowatt diesel plant.

Fuel storage (gallons). City Fuel Depot (116,900); AVEC (114,800); Yukon Koyukuk Schools (88,700); City Old Town Water (45,500); H&H Enterprises (12,600); City New Town Washeteria (5,800); Mountain General Store (9,500); Army National Guard (6,000); city office (1,500).

Water and waste systems. A piped water and sewer system, including lift station and lagoon, serves 53 homes in the Nulato new (upper) subdivision or town site, complete with bathroom and kitchen plumbing installations. There is a washeteria in the lower town site, and 45 homes in the lower town site were added to the new piped water and sewer system shortly after 2000. Water is drawn from a community well. As of 2003, a new Class 3 landfill was under construction.

Telecommunications. Local telephone service is provided by ACS of the Northland, long distance services by AT&T Alascom. Internet services are provided at the school by GCI. In addition to public radio broadcast from nearby Galena,

Nulato can receive AM radio stations from McGrath, Nome, Anchorage, and other locations. Two television channels are broadcast from local repeaters, one by the Alaska Rural Communications Service, the other by the village.

COMMUNITY FACILITIES AND SERVICES
The city operates the water and waste disposal systems and has an office building. The village council features a community hall/activity center for adults and a separate facility for youth.

Education. The Andrew K. Demoski School, which serves students in preschool and in grades K-12, is operated by the Yukon/Koyukuk School District. The facility was slated to receive a new roof in 2005. The school library serves as the community's public library.

Health care. The Nulato Health Clinic is operated by the Tanana Chiefs Conference. Emergency service is provided by volunteers and a health aide. The clinic is supported by a subregional clinic in Galena and the Chief Andrew Isaac Health Center located within Fairbanks Memorial Hospital.

Public safety. Law enforcement services are provided by a state village public safety officer (VPSO-position vacant as of August 2004), backed by state troopers stationed in Galena. There is a volunteer fire department and EMS housed at the city fire hall.

Nunakauyarmiut

Nunakauyarmiut

Total area of entitlement under ANCSA	
	115,200 acres
Total labor force	323
High school graduate or higher	59%
Bachelor's degree or higher	9.2%
Unemployment rate	15.3%
Per capita income *(1999)*	$8,761
Population *2000 census*	532
Percent Native *2000 census*	97.6%

LOCATION
Toksook Bay is one of three communities located on Nelson Island, approximately 150 miles northwest of Bethel in Southwest Alaska. The community is situated in the Kangirlbar Bay, across from Nunivak Island. Its closest neighbor is the village of Tummak, about 6.5 miles to the northwest.

CLIMATE
Toksook Bay is located in the maritime climate zone, with relatively warm winters and cool summers. Precipitation averages 22 inches, with 43 inches of snowfall annually. Summer temperatures range from 41°F to 57°F; winter temperatures vary from 6°F to 24°F.

CULTURE AND HISTORY
Toksook Bay is a traditional Yup'ik Eskimo community, with a culture centered on subsistence activities. The Nelson Island area has been utilized by Yup'ik Eskimos for thousands of years, but the village was first established in 1964, when a number of families living in Nightmute moved to the location. There is a federally recognized tribe in the community—the Nunakauyak Traditional Council (also know as the Nunakauyak Tribe).

GOVERNMENT
Toksook Bay was incorporated under Alaska law as a second-class city in 1972, with a mayor and city council; it is located in the Unorganized Borough *(see Alaska introduction)*. The village also has a traditional council headed by a president.

VILLAGE CORPORATION
Shareholders in the village corporation are also shareholders in Calista Regional Native Corporation *(see Alaska introduction)*.

ECONOMY
Toksook Bay residents rely on a combination of cash-generating and subsistence activities for their livelihood. Commercial fishing, the school, city and the tribal council are the primary income producers. Subsistence activities, including hunting, fishing, and berry picking, are a major part of village life. Coastal Villages Seafood processes halibut and salmon in Toksook.

Construction. Two residents are employed in construction.

Fisheries. Ninety-three residents hold commercial fishing permits for herring roe and salmon net fisheries. Farming, fishing, and forestry industries employ four residents.

Government as employer. Of the 184 employed residents, 114 work for the local, state, or federal government.

Hunting and Mining. Three residents are employed in hunting and mining industries.

Manufacturing. Four residents are employed in manufacturing.

Services and retail. There are seven businesses in the community, including the Nunakauiak Yupik Corporation, a general merchandise store, and the Qaluyaat Herring Fishermen's

Also known as Toksook Bay

[TOOK-sook or TUCK-sook] and Nunakauy

Ethnicity: Yup'ik Eskimo

Municipality
City of Toksook Bay
P.O. Box 37008
Toksook Bay, AK 99637
  907-427-7613
  907-427-7811 Fax
  toksookbayalaska.com

Native entity
Nunakauyak Traditional
  Council
P.O. Box 37048
Toksook Bay, AK 99637
  907-427-7114
  907-427-7714 Fax

ANCSA village corporation
Nunakauiak Yupik Corporation
P.O. Box 37068
Toksook Bay, AK 99637
  907-427-7929
  907-427-7326 Fax

Nunakauyarmiut

Association. Retail trade employs 32 residents; education, health, and social services, 72; and public administration, 35.

Tourism and recreation. Limited guest accommodations are provided by Nunakauiak Yupik Corporation. Two video-rental businesses are located in Toksook Bay. Arts, entertainment, recreation, accommodations, and food service industries employ 10 residents.

Transportation. Six airline companies service Toksook Bay. Transportation, warehousing, and utility industries employ nine residents.

INFRASTRUCTURE
Twenty capital projects, funded by grants, are active in Toksook Bay.

Transportation. The state provides a 1,788-foot long by 55-foot wide gravel airstrip for year-round scheduled and chartered service. Major airport improvements are near completion. Fishing boats, skiffs, snow machines, and all-terrain vehicles provide local transportation. In winter trails with markers are available to Nightmute, Tununak, Newtok, and Chefornak. Docking facilities are not available but boat haul-out services are. Barges deliver goods in summer.

Electricity. Alaska Village Electric Cooperative (AVEC) provides electricity.

Fuel storage (gallons). AVEC (147,475); Nunakauiak Yupik Corp. (120,020); Lower Kuskokwim Schools (34,460); City (26,000); and the Army National Guard (5,000).

Water and waste systems. Water drawn from a well and infiltration gallery is treated and stored in a 212,000-gallon tank, then piped throughout the community. Most occupied homes are fully plumbed. However, several households must depend on hauled water.

Telecommunications. In-state phone service is provided by United Utilities; long distance service by AT&T Alascom and United Utilities. Internet service is provided by GCI. Teleconferencing is available through Alaska Teleconferencing Network. There are three radio stations in the community. Alaska Rural Communications Service provides television access. Most homes have a satellite dish.

COMMUNITY FACILITIES AND SERVICES
Local facilities include a city hall and a multipurpose facility. Some home-care is provided to seniors by YKHC. Most residences have a gravity piped sewer system. The city provides refuse collection service and maintains the landfill. The traditional council operates the washeteria. Several households must depend on honeybuckets.

Education. Nelson Island Area School, in the Lower Kuskokwim School District, has 191 students and 14 teachers.

Health care. Health resources include Toksook Bay Health Clinic. Toksook Bay is classified as an isolated village; it is found in EMS Region 7A in the Yukon/Kuskokwim Region. Emergency services have coastal and air access. Emergency service is provided by a health aide. Auxiliary health care is provided by YKHC Sub-Regional Clinic.

Nunam Iqua

Formerly Sheldon Point

[NOO-nam ICK-wa]
Ethnicity: Yup'ik Eskimo

ANCSA village corporation
Swan Lake Corporation
P.O. Box 25
Sheldon Point, AK 99666
907-498-4227
907-498-4242 Fax

Total area of entitlement under ANCSA	
	92,160 acres
Total labor force	85
High school graduate or higher	54%
Bachelor's degree or higher	9.5%
Unemployment rate	40.7%
Per capita income *(2000)*	$6,725
Population *2000 census*	164
Percent Native *2000 census*	93.9%

LOCATION
Nunam Iqua is on a south fork of the Yukon River, about 9 miles south of Alakanuk and 18 miles southwest of Emmonak on the Yukon-Kuskokwim Delta. The community is 500 miles northwest of Anchorage.

CLIMATE
The climate has a maritime influence, averaging 60 inches of annual snowfall and 18 inches of yearly precipitation. Temperatures range from -25°F to 78°F. Strong winds in the fall and winter often restrict accessibility. The Bering Sea is ice free during the summer months.

CULTURE AND HISTORY
Nunam Iqua was historically the site of summer fish camps near the Black River. In Yup'ik, *Nunam Iqua* means "end of the tundra." In the late 1930s and early 1940s, a man by the name of Sheldon owned and operated a fish saltery at the site. Later the saltery was run by Northern Commercial Company. The census recorded 43 residents in the village in 1950. The City of Sheldon Point was formed in 1974; however, in 1999 residents voted to change the city's name to the City of Nunam Iqua. This Yup'ik Eskimo village depends on commer-

cial fishing and subsistence activities. There is a federally recognized tribe in the community—the Native Village of Sheldon Point. An annual potlatch is held in the village every March.

GOVERNMENT
Before taking its new name of Nunam Iqua, Sheldon Point was incorporated as a second-class city in 1974, with a mayor and a city council. It has a traditional village council, headed by a president.

VILLAGE CORPORATION
Shareholders in the village corporation also hold shares in Calista regional Native corporation (*see Alaska introduction*).

ECONOMY
Commercial fishing is the economic core of Nunam Iqua. Government organizations and the private sector offer a few year-round jobs. Subsistence activities and trapping supplement income. Salmon, beluga whale, seal, moose, and waterfowl are harvested.

Fisheries. Twenty-four residents hold commercial fishing permits, chiefly for salmon.

Government as employer. Of the 35 employed residents, 23 work for the local, state, or federal government.

Services and retail. There are five businesses in the community: the Nunam Iqua Electric Company, the City of Nunam Iqua, the Nunam Iqua Tribal Council, and two trading posts. Retail trade employs nine residents; education, health, and social services, nine; public administration, nine, and information services, three.

Transportation. One airline company services Nunam Iqua. Transportation, warehousing, and utility industries employ three residents.

INFRASTRUCTURE
Eighteen capital projects, funded by grants, are active in Nunam Iqua.

Transportation. Nunam Iqua has easy access by boat and barge. The state provides a 3,015- by 60-foot gravel airstrip. Kwemeluk Pass and Swan Lake offer floatplane landing sites. In winter, snowmachines are the primary means of local transportation.

Electricity. Nunam Iqua Electric Company provides electricity.

Water and waste systems. Residents haul treated well water from a new storage tank. Water delivery also is an option. Honeybuckets are disposed into bunkers, and hauled to a waste site by the city. A community septic tank is available; some households have plumbing. A comprehensive master plan has been completed for a piped system. Funds are now available for major improvements. There is a temporary refuse site; the community needs a new landfill.

Telecommunications. In-state and long distance phone service is provided by United Utilities. Internet service is provided by Unicom/United Utilities. Teleconferencing is available through Alaska Teleconferencing Network. Swan Lake Corporation is the cable provider. There are two radio stations in the community.

COMMUNITY FACILITIES AND SERVICES
Local area facilities include a community hall, city museum, and both school and public libraries.

Education. Nunam Iqua (Sheldon Point) School, in the Lower Yukon School District, has 76 students and six teachers.

Health care. Local health clinics include Sheldon Point Health Clinic and Pearl E. Johnson Subregional Clinic. Nunam Iqua/Sheldon Point is classified as an isolated village and is found in EMS Region 7A in the Yukon/Kuskokwim Region. Emergency services have coastal, seaport, and air access. A health aide provides emergency care.

N unapitchuk

Total area of entitlement under ANCSA	
	199,304 acres
Tribal enrollment *(February, 2004)*	634
Total labor force	163
High school graduate or higher	42.0%
Bachelor's degree or higher	9.5%
Unemployment rate	10.3%
Per capita income *(1999)*	$8,364
Population *2000 census*	466
2003 population	498
state demographer estimate	
Percent Native *2000 census*	95.9%

LOCATION
Nunapitchuk is located approximately 23 miles northwest of Bethel on the west bank of the Johnson River in the Kuskokwim Delta of southwestern Alaska.

PHYSICAL DESCRIPTION
The village area encompasses 7.9 square miles of land and 0.7 square mile of water at an elevation of less than 165 feet above sea level, within the Yukon Delta Wildlife Refuge. The surrounding area is dominated by flat, virtually treeless tundra, dotted with meltwater ponds called "potholes" and veined by smaller rivers, creeks, and sloughs.

CLIMATE
Nunapitchuk's climate is primarily maritime with some continental influences, especially in the winter. Average summer temperatures range between a low of 42°F and a high of 62°F. Average winter temperatures vary between a low of -2°F and a high of 19°F. The area averages 16 inches of precipitation, including an annual average of 50 inches of snowfall. At this latitude, the region experiences approximately 19 hours of daylight in a 24-hour period in June, declining to approximately 5.5 by mid-December.

CULTURE AND HISTORY
Nunapitchuk is a Yup'ik village, first listed in the 1940 U.S. census with a population of 121, whose members share a largely subsistence-oriented culture. The community was incorporated as a second-class city in 1969, and in the 1970 census, Nunapitchuk and the nearby villages of Atmautluak and Kasigluk were enumerated as "Akolmiut."

GOVERNMENT
Nunapitchuk was incorporated as a second-class city in 1969, with a mayor and city council; it is located in the Unorganized Borough. It also has a BIA-recognized Indian Reorganization Act council, the Native Village of Nunapitchuk, headed by a president.

VILLAGE CORPORATION
Nunapitchuk, Limited, is the ANCSA village corporation. Its shareholders also hold shares in Calista Corporation, the regional Native corporation.

ECONOMY
The residents of Nunapitchuk rely on a combination of cash income and subsistence activities for their livelihoods. Employment opportunities are mainly with government agencies and commercial fishing. Other residents work on projects initiated by the regional Native corporation, Calista Corporation.

Fisheries. Commercial salmon net-fishing is important to the village's economy. In the mid-1990s, the village purchased a fish processing barge to locate on the river.

Government as employer. One hundred and four of 135 employed residents work for either the city, state, or federal government.

Services and retail. The city has two general stores, a movie theater, a video arcade, a sporting goods store, a video rental shop, a limited-service restaurant, and a child-care provider.

Tourism and recreation. Visitors may stay at the IRA Council Building and at the school.

INFRASTRUCTURE
Transportation. Access to Nunapitchuk is primarily by air and water. A state-owned 2,500- by 120-foot gravel airstrip located

[noo-nah-PIT-chuck]
Ethnicity: Yup'ik

Municipality
City of Nunapitchuk
P.O. Box 190
Nunapitchuk, AK 99641
907-527-5327
907-527-5011 Fax

Native entity
Native Village of Nunapitchuk
P.O. Box 130
Nunapitchuk, AK 99641
907-527-5705
907-527-5711 Fax

ANCSA village corporation
Nunapitchuk, Limited
P.O. Box 129
Nunapitchuk, AK 99641-0129
907-527-5717
907-527-5229 Fax

Nunapitchuk

Ohgsenakale

See Portage Creek

Ohogamiut

See Zero Population Section

on the east side of the Johnson River provides year-round chartered passenger and cargo service. The airport is served by Arctic Circle Air, Grant Aviation, Hageland Aviation, and Inland Aviation Services. In 2003, the Department of Transportation funded the design for airport reconstruction and relocation, with construction to start in 2004. A dock, small-boat harbor, and seaplane landing area are available on the Johnson River. Many residents keep fishing boats or skiffs, which they use for travel in summer. Snowmobiles, all-terrain vehicles, and dogsleds are used for travel on the frozen river during winter. Winter trails are marked to Atmautluak (7 miles) and Akula Heights (2.5 miles).

Electricity. Electricity is available to residents from the Alaska Village Electric Cooperative (AVEC), of which the city is a member, generating power from a 1,858-kilowatt diesel plant.

Fuel storage (gallons). Alaska Village Electric Cooperative (AVEC) (158,250); Village Corp. (111,000); Lower Kuskokwim Schools (84,750); city (15,750).

Water and waste systems. The City of Nunapitchuk provides water from a central tap; water is drawn from a community well. The city also offers water-truck delivery of water and operates a washeteria in the community. From 1997, continuing throughout 2003, the entire system was upgraded and renovated. Flush tank/haul systems were installed to almost all the homes in the village. Eight-foot-wide boardwalks were built to accommodate all-terrain vehicle traffic for movement of a honeybucket haul system. Two new sewage lagoons and a new lagoon access road were built. The city collects refuse and hauls it to its Class 3 landfill.

Telecommunications. Local telephone service is provided by United Utilities, long distance services by AT&T Alascom or United Utilities. Cable television is offered by Icuicaraq Cable (owned by the village corporation) and Internet service by Unicom/United Utilities and, at the school, by GCI. Residents can receive AM radio broadcasts from Bethel, Nome, Dillingham, Anchorage, and other locations. One television station in Bethel and two channels from Alaska Rural Communications System repeaters in nearby Kasigluk can be received in Nunapitchuk.

COMMUNITY FACILITIES AND SERVICES
The city operates the water and waste disposal systems, a community building, and a recreation center. The village corporation operates the cable television system. The village council has a building.

Education. The Anna Tobeluk Memorial School serves 159 students in grades K-12 and is operated by the Lower Kuskokwim School District. The school library serves as the community's public library.

Health care. Health care is provided by the Nunapitchuk Health Clinic, operated by the Yukon-Kuskokwim Health Corporation, supported by the Yukon Kuskokwim Delta Regional Hospital about 41 miles away in Bethel.

Public safety. Law enforcement is provided by a state village public safety officer (VPSO) and city police, backed by state troopers in Bethel. Emergency response is provided by the VPSO and the city volunteer fire department.

Old Harbor

Ethnicity: Alutiiq

Municipality
City of Old Harbor
P.O. Box 109
Old Harbor, AK 99643
  907-286-2203
  907-286-2278 Fax

Native entity
Village of Old Harbor
P.O. Box 62
Old Harbor, AK 99643
  907-286-2215
  907-286-2277 Fax

ANCSA village corporation
Old Harbor Native Corporation
P.O. Box 71
Old Harbor, AK 99643
  907-286-2286
  907-286-2287 Fax

Total area of entitlement under ANCSA
  115,200 acres

Total labor force	74
High school graduate or higher	79
Bachelor's degree or higher	6
Unemployment rate	23.0%
Per capita income *(1999)*	$14,265
Population *2000 census*	237
Current population	211
state demographer estimate	
Percent Native *2000 census*	85.7%

LOCATION
Old Harbor sits on the southeast coast of Kodiak Island, facing Sitkalidak Strait, separated from the Gulf of Alaska by Sitkalidak Island. It is 70 miles southwest of Kodiak and 322 miles southwest of Anchorage.

PHYSICAL DESCRIPTION
The city encompasses 21.0 square miles of land and 6.2 square miles of water. Kodiak Island has unique geography. With green, snow-tipped mountains giving way to deep, forested fjords, it is known as Alaska's Emerald Isle, so reminiscent of Ireland or Norway's green. The lush vegetation and diverse ecosystems of the area abound with wildlife of countless species, the most famous being the Kodiak brown bears. Old Harbor is built on Tertiary and Cretaceous granitic rock. The vegetation in the area consists of alpine tundra types. The shoreline is a harbor seal area, and there are nearby marine bird colonies. There has been no flooding reported since fill was placed in the old village center. Small landslides have occurred in the hill area adjacent to the city. These threaten the road as well as several businesses and commu-

nity buildings. Erosion is occurring along the road at the head of the bay but does not threaten any residential areas or businesses. Old Harbor's water supply is fed from deeper in the interior of the island, where thawing snow in the mountains provides a fairly reliable water source. The water is collected, treated, and then piped to local residences. Water shortages are rare; however, water supply to many local homes may be stopped by extremely cold weather when water pipes may freeze. Old Harbor is in the process of switching to hydroelectric power. Once the power supply has changed, the most serious threat posed by a drought will be the disruption of hydroelectric power. Kodiak Island and surrounding areas experience frequent earthquakes with magnitudes of under 6.0 on the Richter scale. Since 1899, 82 earthquakes of Richter magnitude 6.0 or greater have been recorded in the area, and 26 of these were actually triggered within the area. The 1964 Alaska earthquake and resultant tsunami provide a relatively recent example of the very real threat posed by earthquake activity. The amount of subsidence caused by the 1964 earthquake was estimated at 2 to 2.5 feet, causing flooding and inundation of low-lying coastal areas. Although most of the forest and brush areas around Old Harbor are relatively small compared to other areas in Alaska, fires have occurred here the past and have threatened populated areas. In 1912, the Kodiak region was blanketed in volcanic ash from the Katmai/Novarupta eruption on the Katmai Coast.

CLIMATE
The climate of Old Harbor is maritime, with moderate winters and cool summers, frequent cloud cover and fog year-round. Severe storms are most likely from December through February. Average annual precipitation is 60 inches. Prevailing winds are southerly, between 15 and 20 knots, and temperatures

range from winter lows in the 20s to summer highs of 60°F. At this latitude, the region experiences just over 18 hours of daylight in a 24-hour period mid-June, declining to 6.5 hours by mid-December. There are no regular occurrences of severe weather such as typhoons or tornadoes in Old Harbor; however, weather extremes such as high winds, large hail, and heavy rainfall do threaten the area. Winds in excess of 50 miles per hour occur occasionally, and wind gusts may reach speeds of 90 miles per hour or more. Freezing rain, occasional heavy snowfall, and high winds are the dominant winter weather hazards that affect the area. Periods of extreme cold occur on a less frequent basis.

CULTURE AND HISTORY

Old Harbor is a traditional Koniag Alutiiq village with a subsistence-centered culture. Old Harbor was settled more than 5,000 years ago. The community is the site of the first Russian colony in Alaska. Grigori Shelikov, the founder of the Russian-American colonies, entered the harbor on the southeast coast of Kodiak Island in 1784. The first colony was devastated by a tsunami, and the people relocated to the northeast coast and did not return until 1884. In 1964, the Good Friday earthquake and resulting tsunami destroyed the community; only two homes and the church remained standing. The community has since been rebuilt in the same location. Village residents continue a traditional Alutiiq culture.

GOVERNMENT

Old Harbor is located in the Kodiak Island Borough. It was incorporated as a second-class city in 1966, with a city manager, mayor, and city council.

VILLAGE CORPORATION

The community also has a seven-member tribal council, headed by a president, to represent the Alaska Native residents of the community. Shareholders in the village corporation are also shareholders in Koniag, Incorporated, the regional Native corporation. Residents of Kaguyak (q.v.) live in Old Harbor.

ECONOMY

Old Harbor's economy is centered around commercial salmon fishing. Most residents depend to some extent on subsistence activities to supplement their incomes. Salmon, halibut, crab, deer, seal, rabbit, and bear are harvested. However, tourism is a growing part of the economy, and there are two timber companies located in Old Harbor. As of 2003, the city had plans to construct a smoked salmon plant.

Government as employer. As of the 2000 census, there were a total of 25 residents of Old Harbor working for the city, borough, state, or federal governments.

Services and retail. Besides timber interests, there are a number of other private businesses, many of them stimulated by the economic presence of Koniag, Incorporated, the regional Native corporation. There are two grocery stores, two lodges, a general merchandise store, and a sporting goods store. There are child-care services, a bakery, and an equipment leasing firm, among others.

Tourism and recreation. Famous for the huge and numerous Kodiak brown bears and world-class sport fishing, Kodiak Island has become a popular tourist destination due to its proximity to the Alaskan mainland, its relatively easy accessibility, and its moderate climate. The island bustles with activities and cultural events appealing to locals and tourists alike. Photography of the brown bears is a huge draw to the Island, as is the abundance of succulent seafood. Sport-fishermen and hikers enjoy the island in droves. Old Harbor has three hunting-and-fishing charters, a restaurant, and accommodations

at the Bay View Bed and Breakfast and the Sitkalidak Lodge. Old Harbor is in the Kodiak National Wildlife Refuge and is less than 60 miles from the Chugach National Forest. By air, it is less than 100 miles from the Becharof National Wildlife Refuge and the Katmai National Park and Preserve.

INFRASTRUCTURE

Transportation. Old Harbor is accessible only by air and water, and access is weather dependent. The State of Alaska owns and operates a newly extended, 2,750- by 60-foot runway and a seaplane base, with regular and charter flights available from Kodiak. There is no flight tower service, nor is there a crosswind runway. The facility is served by Island Air Service. There is no aviation fuel available. In 2001, the village constructed a small-boat harbor, featuring a 150-foot dock and moorings for 55 boats. The facilities also include a boat haul-out, marine storage, and an unloading area on the beach. Seattle-based and local barge services are available. The city had plans to expand the facility in 2004. The city maintains two miles of gravel road within the community. These were reconstructed and improved in 1999. Residents have roughly 75-100 vehicles and 40-60 ATVs.

Electricity is provided by the city. In 2000, it built a 380-kilowatt hydroelectric project on Lagoon Creek to replace diesel generation of electric power and reduce consumption of heating fuel. There are several portable generators that could be used as a backup power sources in an emergency.

Fuel. Old Harbor has had problems with fuel shortages in the past. However, as of 2003 the city was in the process of replacing the city tank farm, and with the construction of this new tank farm, fuel shortages should become less of a problem. The city had plans to build a propane facility in 2004.

Water and waste systems. The city provides water from a dammed creek and infiltration gallery. The water is filtered and chlorinated prior to distribution in a piped water system. In 2003, several improvements were made to the water treatment plant and other facilities. Piped-sewage service is also available, operated by the city. All homes and public buildings are connected to the water and sewer systems and have complete plumbing. Refuse collection services are available. The city also operates a landfill.

Telecommunications. Local telephone service is provided by ACS of the Northland and long distance service by AT&T Alascom. One FM public radio station broadcasts from Old Harbor, and residents can receive a number of AM stations from Kodiak City and the mainland. The city and the Alaska Rural Communications System broadcast television stations from Old Harbor. Cable television service is available. Many residents have CB radios, and some have VHF marine radios, although these cannot reach Kodiak from Old Harbor. There are telephones in most homes. Telephone service in Old Harbor is dependent upon electrical supply. Without electricity, the phones cease working after one or two days of running on battery power.

COMMUNITY FACILITIES AND SERVICES

Education. Old Harbor School, which serves students in kindergarten through 12th grade, is operated by the Kodiak Island Borough School District. In 2003, Koniag, Incorporated, the regional native association, aided improvements to the city pre-school, purchased new equipment, and updated the facility. The Old Harbor Library is operated by the city.

Health care is provided by the Old Harbor Clinic, owned by the City, leased to the U.S. Public Health Service, and operated by the Kodiak Area Native Association. There are no doctors or registered nurses in Old Harbor; therefore, most

Old Harbor

health care is provided by EMT or ETT trained residents who are supported by doctors from the Kodiak Area Native Association. Seriously injured or ill patients are evacuated to a hospital in Kodiak or Anchorage. The Old Harbor Clinic provides basic health care and emergency medical services to the community. Old Harbor has a working ambulance outfitted with first aid and emergency medical equipment, including oxygen and a defibrillator. The clinic is stocked with a diverse collection of medical equipment and supplies and can handle the initial medical response to almost any kind of emergency.

Orutsararmuit

Also known as Bethel

Ethnicity: Yup'ik Eskimo

Municipality
City of Bethel
P.O. Box 1388
Bethel, AK 99559
907-543-2047
907-543-4171 Fax
cityofbethel.org

Native entity
Association of Village Council Presidents
P.O. Box 219
Bethel, AK 99559
907-543-3521
907-543-3369 Fax

ANCSA Village Corporation
Bethel Native Corporation
P.O. Box 719
Bethel, AK 99559
907-543-2124
907-543-2897 Fax
bnc-alaska.com

Total area of entitlement under ANCSA	161,280 acres
Total labor force	3,697
High school graduate or higher	84.2%
Bachelor's degree or higher	22.7%
Unemployment rate	8.95%
Per capita income (1999)	$20,267
Population 2000 census	5,471
Percent Native 2000 census	68%

LOCATION
Bethel is located at the mouth of the Kuskokwim River, 40 miles inland from the Bering Sea. It is located in the Bethel Recording District. The area encompasses 43.8 square miles of land and 5.1 square miles of water.

PHYSICAL DESCRIPTION
The headquarters for the Yukon Delta National Wildlife Refuge are located in Bethel. The Yukon and Kuskolwim rivers flow through the refuge, part of which is in the Tundra. More than half of the refuge is below 100 feet in elevation and is a flat, broad delta with rivers, streams, lakes, and ponds. Next to this area of wetlands and tundra are 2.5 million acres of forest and shrub habitat with mountains exceeding 4,000 feet in elevation. Two large islands—the Nelson and Nunivak—are located in the refuge. The refuge is an important shorebird nesting area. Birds from the Atlantic Ocean and the east coast of Asia nest or stop to rest and feed in the refuge.

CLIMATE
Annual precipitation averages 16 inches, with yearly snowfall of 50 inches. Summer temperatures range from 42ºF to 62ºF; winter temperatures average -2ºF to 19ºF.

CULTURE AND HISTORY
Yup'ik Eskimos first called the village Mumtrekhlogamute, meaning "Smokehouse People." The 1880 census recorded 41 people in Bethel, then an Alaska Commercial Company Trading Post. In 1884, the Moravian Church opened a mission. Villagers moved to the current location after erosion problems beset them. A post office was established in 1905. Bethel's trading, transportation, and distribution opportunities brought in numerous Natives from nearby villages. The practices and language of the traditional Yup'ik Eskimo prevail in the area. Villagers rely on subsistence activities and commercial fishing.

GOVERNMENT
Bethel was incorporated as a second-class city in 1957, with a mayor and city council. The city has an advisory school board and a planning commission. The Orutsararmuit Native Council is a federally recognized tribe in the community. Federal and state agencies have established regional offices in Bethel.

VILLAGE CORPORATION
Bethel Native Corporation (BNC) is the sixth largest Alaska Native Claims Settlement Act (ANCSA) village corporation. BNC and its subsidiaries provide engineering, construction, real estate development, and security services to government agencies and private industry. The companies are 8(a) HUBZone firms and are GSA approved contractors specializing in projects in remote locations. Services include environmental remediation system construction, engineering, design, procurement, installation, construction management, commissioning and performance testing, land development, surveying, civil/structural design and construction, electrical subcontracting, power plant/process design and construction, and enhanced environmental design. Shareholders in BNC are also shareholders in the Calista regional Native corporation *(see Alaska introduction)*.

ECONOMY
Bethel provides food, fuel, transportation, medical care, and other services for 56 villages in the Yukon-Kuskokwim Delta. Commercial fishing also is an important source of income. Sparse fish returns in recent years have significantly impacted the community.

Construction. Approximately 125 residents are employed in construction.

Fisheries. Two hundred residents hold commercial fishing permits, chiefly for salmon and herring roe net fisheries. Eleven residents are employed in farming, fishing, and forestry industries.

Government as employer. Of the 2,459 employed residents, 922 work for the local, state, or federal government.

Manufacturing. Six residents are employed in manufacturing.

Services and retail. Services are extensive in Bethel, catering not only to this town of more than 5,000 people but also to customers in numerous surrounding villages. There are 6 child-care services, 23 rental companies, and 8 construction companies. Stores sell everything from electrical appliances to general merchandise to pottery. There also are numerous repair services in Bethel, offering household goods and service to boats and aircraft. Engineering and technology services also are available in the community. Retail trade employs 192 residents; wholesale trade another 16; financial and related businesses, 71; transportation, warehousing, and utilities, 341; education, health, and social services, 986; public administration, 333; and information services, 38. More than 300 business licenses are registered in the village.

Transportation. There are at least five taxi companies, three rental car companies, three water-freight transportation companies, a water passenger-transportation service, and ten air-transportation businesses. Approximately 286 residents are employed in production, transportation, or material-moving industries.

Tourism and recreation. There are several restaurants. Nine businesses provide lodging for visitors, and several companies provide wilderness charter services. There is a bowling alley, boat shop, and marine. Services include massage therapy and yoga instruction. The arts, entertainment, recreation, and accommodation/food service industries employ a combined total of 100 workers. Visitor attractions include the Yupik Cultural Center, Bethel Visitors Center, and the U.S. Fish and Wildlife headquarters. Cultural events include the Camai Dance Festival, Mink Festival, two-dog sled races, and the Kuskokwim Ice Classic.

INFRASTRUCTURE
Fifty-nine capital projects, funded by grants, are active in Bethel.

Transportation. The state runs Bethel Airport, a regional transportation center served by several passenger airlines, cargo carriers, and air-taxi services. The airport offers a 6,398- by 150-foot asphalt runway and a 1,850- by 75-foot gravel crosswind runway. A $7 million renovation and expansion project is earmarked for the airport. Hangar Lake and H Marker Lake are nearby floatplane bases. The Port of Bethel is the northernmost medium-draft port in the United States. A small-boat harbor, dry land storage, and transient moorage on the seawall are available. River travel is open in the summer; in winter, the river is used as a 150-mile ice road to surrounding communities. Deliveries of goods to the Kuskokwim villages are made possible by barge service in Bethel. Sixteen miles of local roads are open, including winter trails to Napakiak and Akiachak.

Electricity. Bethel Utilities Corporation provides electricity.

Fuel storage (gallons). Yukon Fuel Co. (9.4 million); Crowley Marine (5.6 million); Airport (120,500); Bethel Utilities Corp. (51,000); U.S. Federal Aviation Administration (44,000).

Water and waste systems. Central piped water and sewer systems are available to some households. Water is delivered to and sewage is hauled by truck from 75 percent of Bethel's residences. Individual wells and septic tanks are connected to numerous facilities. Use of honeybuckets is not permitted for health reasons. Extensions of the piped systems to the city subdivision and Old Town are in progress. Water treatment plant improvements have been completed in Bethel Heights. A project to connect more than 100 houses to a piped system is in the early funding stage.

Telecommunications. Local telephone service is provided by GTE Alaska, while long distance service is available through Alascom. Prime Cable of Alaska provides cable television service, and one channel is offered by the Rural Alaska Television Network. Two AM radio stations are available in the community. Internet service and teleconferencing are both available.

COMMUNITY FACILITIES AND SERVICES
Local area facilities include a city youth center, community hall, senior center, VFW hall, museum, and library.

Education. Approximately 1,328 students attend six schools in the community. The schools are under the Lower Kuskokwim School District.

Health care. Health care is provided by the Yukon-Kuskokwim Delta Regional Hospital, owned and run by the U.S. Public Health Service; the hospital is a qualified acute-care facility. It is administered by the Yukon-Kuskokwim Health Corporation.

ENVIRONMENTAL CONCERNS
A fuel tank at the Bureau of Indian Affairs Administrative Site near Bethel spilled 106,000 gallons of diesel fuel in 1993. The spill was the result of a broken pipe and was discovered in April of that year. The impact area was approximately 27 acres of seasonal stream and tundra area. A cleanup was performed.

Oscarville

Total area of entitlement under ANCSA
	69,120 acres
Total labor force	13
High school graduate or higher	25%
Unemployment rate	0.0%
Per capita income *(1999)*	$5,824
Population *2000 census*	61
Percent Native *2000 census*	100%

LOCATION
Oscarville is located six miles southwest of Bethel, in the Kuskokwim Delta of Southwest Alaska. It is situated on the north bank of the Kuskokwim River, across from Napaskiak.

PHYSICAL DESCRIPTION
Oscarville is on the north bank of the Kuskokwim River at an elevation of less than 165 feet above sea level. The village area encompasses 1.5 square miles of land and 0.1 square mile of water. The terrain is flat, almost treeless tundra dotted with meltwater ponds called "potholes" and veined by smaller rivers, creeks, and sloughs.

CLIMATE
The weather in Oscarville is strongly influenced by storms and patterns in the Bering Sea, as well as by continental weather patterns. Average precipitation is 16 inches, including falls of 50 inches per year. Daily summer temperatures average between 42°F and 62°F, winter temperatures from -2°F to 19°F. The Kuskokwim River is frozen over from October through mid-June. At this latitude, the region experiences approximately 19 hours of daylight in a 24 hour period in June, declining to approximately 5.5 hours by mid-December.

CULTURE AND HISTORY
The year-round residents of Oscarville are primarily Yup'ik, with a culture focused on subsistence activities and commercial fishing. In 1908, Oscar Samuelson and his wife, a Yup'ik from the Nushagak (Dillingham) region, moved from Napaskiak across the river and opened a trading post. Over the years native families settled nearby, and the site became known as Oscarville. By 1955, there were 13 homes and 2 warehouses in the village. A village school was built by the BIA in 1964. The Samuelson family continued to operate the store until 1975, when it was sold. It was closed in the early 1980s.

GOVERNMENT
Oscarville is unincorporated and is located in the Unorganized Borough. It is governed by Oscarville Traditional Village, a BIA-recognized Native entity, also called the Oscarville Tribal Council or the Native Village of Kuiggayagaq.

Ethnicity: Yup'ik

Native entity
Oscarville Traditional Village
P.O. Box 6129
Napaskiak, AK 99559
907-737-7099
907-737-7428 Fax

ANCSA village corporation
Oscarville Native Corporation
P.O. Box 1554
Oscarville, AK 99559

Oscarville

VILLAGE CORPORATION
Oscarville Native Corporation is the ANCSA village corporation. From its ANCSA land entitlement, it has conveyed land for a community hall to the village. Shareholders in the village corporation are also shareholders in Calista Corporation, the regional Native corporation.

ECONOMY
The economy of Oscarville is based upon commercial fishing and employment within the local and state governments, primarily the Qugcuun Memorial School and the Oscarville Health Clinic. Most residents rely on subsistence fishing, hunting, and trapping to supply food. Salmon, waterfowl, moose, bear, and seals are hunted. Trapping and handicrafts provide some income. Residents rely on neighboring communities Napaskiak and Bethel for most services, such as the post office and airstrip. One resident holds a commercial permit for the salmon net fishery. Of the 13 employed residents, 11 work in education, health services, or social services.

Government as employer. Of 13 employed residents of Oscarville, 8 work for either the state or federal government.

Tourism and recreation. Oscarville is located within the Yukon Delta National Wildlife Refuge. Tourists and guests of residents are lodged at the village school.

INFRASTRUCTURE
Transportation. Oscarville can be reached by boat during the summer or snowmobile during the winter months. The community has no airport; however, residents use the airport facilities across the river at Napaskiak, and rely on it for passenger, mail, and cargo services. Residents use skiffs to get back and forth between villages. Barge services deliver goods once a year. The Kuskokwim River is an important means of transportation in summer, and in the winter it is used as an ice road. However, during breakup and freeze-up, the community experiences periodic, albeit temporary, isolation.

Electricity. Electricity is imported from the Bethel Utilities Corporation.

Fuel storage (gallons). Lower Kuskokwim Schools (27,976); village council (20,000).

Water and waste systems. Water is drawn from a community well and made available to residents at the village washeteria, owned and maintained by the village council. A few homes have individual systems that collect and use rainwater, and approximately 25 percent of homes have running water to the kitchen, but no homes in the community have complete plumbing. Residents use outhouses and honeybuckets; sewage is disposed of by hauling it to a lagoon outside town. The school has its own well and sewage lagoon. The village has made application for funding to upgrade all water and sewage facilities, including an increase in water storage capacity, renovation of the washeteria, installation of plumbing in all homes, and conversion to a flush/haul system. The village council operates a Class 3 landfill.

Telecommunications. Local telephone service is provided by United Utilities, long distance service by AT&T Alascom. Residents can receive AM radio transmissions from Bethel, Nome, Dillingham, Anchorage, and other locations, as well as one FM station from Bethel. One local television channel broadcasts from Bethel to the area, as do two Alaska Rural Communications Service repeaters in Bethel.

COMMUNITY FACILITIES AND SERVICES
The village council operates the washeteria, the central water point, the sewage lagoon, and the landfill.

Education. Qugcuun Memorial School, which serves 22 children in grades K-12, is operated by the Lower Kuskokwim School District. There is a library at the school, which serves as the community's public library. The school building is slated for major renovations in 2005.

Health care. The Oscarville Health Clinic is operated by the Yukon Kuskokwim Health Corporation and backed by the Yukon Kuskokwim Delta Regional Hospital in nearby Bethel. The clinic hauls water and uses a pail toilet and is in need of a facilities upgrade.

Public safety. Law enforcement is provided by state troopers in Bethel.

Ouzinkie

[ooh-ZINK-ee]
Ethnicity: Alutiiq

Municipality
City of Ouzinkie
P.O. Box 109
Ouzinkie, AK 99644-0109
907-680-2257
907-680-2223 Fax

Native entity
Ouzinkie Tribal Council
P.O. Box 130
Ouzinkie, AK 99644
907-680-2259
907-680-2214 Fax

ANCSA village corporation
Ouzinkie Native Corporation
P.O. Box 89
Ouzinkie, AK 99644
907-680-2208
907-680-2268 Fax

Total area of entitlement under ANCSA	151,052 acres
Total labor force	86
High school graduate or higher	57
Bachelor's degree or higher	14
Unemployment rate	11.6%
Per capita income *(1999)*	$19,324
Population *2000 census*	225
Current population	170
2003 state demographer estimate	
Percent Native *2000 census*	87.6%

LOCATION
Ouzinkie is located on the southwest shore of Spruce Island, which lies off the northeast end of Kodiak Island, in the Gulf of Alaska. The City of Kodiak is 10 air miles south of the village, and Anchorage is 247 air miles to the northeast.

PHYSICAL DESCRIPTION
The city encompasses 6.0 square miles of land and 1.7 square miles of water at an elevation of 20 feet above sea level.

Spruce Island derives its name from an abundance of tall spruce trees found there. Low-lying areas throughout the island are often swampy. Ouzinkie has a maximum tidal range of 9.1 feet. Significant coastal erosion has occurred in several places, primarily along the shoreline in the harbor area. The erosion does not threaten residential and commercial development. However, as of 2001 there was a boardwalk in this area in danger of collapsing. The city actively attempts to refortify these eroding coastal areas. Kodiak Island and surrounding areas experience frequent earthquakes with magnitudes of under 6.0 on the Richter scale. Since 1899, 82 earthquakes of Richter magnitude 6.0 or greater have been recorded in the area, and 26 of these were actually triggered within the area. The 1964 Alaska earthquake and resultant tsunami provide an example of the threat posed by earthquake activity. Ouzinkie homes and businesses suffered significant structural damage from the earthquake and tsunami, and long-term damage to waterfront facilities occurred as a result of tectonic subsidence. The amount of subsidence caused by the 1964 earthquake was estimated at as much as 5 feet, causing flooding of low-lying coastal areas.

CLIMATE

The climate of Ouzinkie is primarily maritime, with moderate precipitation, little or no actual freezing weather, but with cool temperatures, and frequent periods of foggy, cloudy weather. Annual rainfall averages 60 inches, with an average of 87 inches of snowfall between December and April. There are no regular occurrences of severe weather such as typhoons or tornadoes. However, weather extremes such as high winds, large hail, or heavy rainfall threaten the area. Winds in excess of 50 miles per hour occur occasionally, and wind gusts may reach speeds of 90 miles per hour or more. Freezing rain, occasional heavy snowfall, and high winds are the dominant winter weather hazards. Prevailing winds are from the southeast, averaging 20 miles per hour. Temperatures range from winter lows of 32°F to summer highs of 62°F. At this latitude, the region experiences approximately 18 hours of daylight in a 24-hour period at mid-June, declining to 6.5 hours by mid-December.

CULTURE AND HISTORY

Ouzinkie is mostly Alutiiq, with the majority being lifelong residents. There are many historical Russian influences in the culture. The village was founded in the early 1800s by the Russian American Company as a retirement community, deriving its name either from the Russian word *uzenkiy* meaning "village of Russians and Creoles" or from the Russian word *ooska* meaning "narrow." Ouzinkie was the home of St. Herman of Alaska, the first canonized Russian Orthodox saint in North America. In 1898 the present Russian Orthodox church was built, and, by 1927, a post office had been established. In 1964, the Good Friday earthquake and resulting tsunami destroyed the Ouzinkie Packing Company cannery, a major economic force in the community. Following the disaster, the city's store and dock were rebuilt, but not the cannery. The city government was incorporated in 1967. In the late 1960s, the Ouzinkie Seafoods cannery was built. It burned down in 1976, and as of 2004, no canneries operate in the city.

GOVERNMENT

Ouzinkie was incorporated as a second-class city in 1967, with a mayor and city council; it is located in the Kodiak Islands Borough. The Ouzinkie Tribal Council, headed by a president, is a federally recognized tribe. In 2001, the president of the tribal council was also the vice mayor of the city.

VILLAGE CORPORATION

Shareholders in the village corporation are also shareholders in Koniag, Incorporated, the regional Alaska Native corporation *(see Alaska introduction)*.

ECONOMY

The economy of Ouzinkie relies primarily on commercial salmon fishing. Approximately 25 residents hold commercial fishing permits. Ouzinkie Native Corporation and Koniag, Incorporated, the regional Native corporation, have supported economic development. Almost all residents supplement their income (and diets) with subsistence activities for various food sources. Salmon, crab, halibut, shrimp, clams, ducks, deer, and rabbit are harvested. In the 2000 census, the median household income was $52,500, one of the highest in Alaska.

Government as employer. Forty-six residents of Ouzinkie work for the city, borough, state, or federal government.

Services and retail. There is a fish-buying business, a privately owned bed-and-breakfast, and three charter-boat services. Log Cabin (lodging) and the Qudiyuq Arts and Crafts manu-facturing and outlet are operated by the village corporation. There are a grocery store, a catalog mail-order business, and a veterinarian. Other services include a fuel and supply dealer and a general-repair business.

Tourism and recreation. The history of the Russian Orthodox church brings many tourists into the village. Once there, they can book charter halibut-fishing excursions, go on long nature walks, enjoy whale watching, or experience true wilderness adventures. Tourists and guests of residents may stay at the apartment building operated by the city, at the apartments maintained by the village corporation, or at the privately operated Bay View Bed and Breakfast. There is a gift shop operated by the tribal council. Ouzinkie is within 40 miles of the northern boundary of Kodiak National Wildlife Refuge.

INFRASTRUCTURE

Transportation. The village is accessible by air and water, but access is always weather dependent. The State of Alaska's 2,500-foot gravel runway is maintained by the city, as is a floatplane base where planes can land and pull up to the beach at Ouzinkie Harbor. Three scheduled flights arrive daily, and there are charter services available from Kodiak, all by Island Air Services. The airport has been under ongoing expansion and renovations since 2001. The runway was extended and widened, and there were plans to move the entire facility in 2004. Ouzinkie Harbor also features docking facilities for barges delivering cargo from Seattle and Kodiak. The village completed construction of a breakwater, expanded harbor, and dock in 2003. The road system in Ouzinkie is limited to a few miles of gravel roads and paths. There are approximately 40-60 ATVs and some other vehicles (fewer than 50 in 2001).

Electricity is available to residents from the city using hydroelectric power from a dam on Mahoona Lake at Katmai Creek, backed by an 885-kilowatt diesel generator. Production capacity has been under improvement since 1997 with the purchase and installation of new generators.

Fuel storage (gallons). Ouzinkie Native Corporation Fuel Facility (71,600); Kodiak Island Schools (5,200); city (1,400).

Water and waste systems. The city provides piped water to its residents from a dam on Mahoona Lake and Katmai Creek; the water is both filtered and chlorinated prior to distribution. The city water and sewer systems have been undergoing consistent rehabilitation and expansion since 1999. As of 2004, the system serves 80 homes and commercial facilities with a piped sewage system, central septic treatment system and sludge disposal site. Refuse is collected by the city and hauled to a landfill completed in 1997.

Telecommunications. Local telephone service is provided by ACS of the Northland and long distance services by AT&T Alascom. One AM radio station from Kodiak and a number of AM stations on the mainland broadcast to the Ouzinkie area. The Alaska Rural Communications System broadcasts two television channels in the area, and another public channel and a commercial channel from Kodiak can be received. Cable television services are offered by Island Cable TV. Many residents have CB radios, and some have VHF marine radios, most of which can reach Kodiak. There are telephones in most homes. There are single side band (SSB) radios on several of the fishing boats in the harbor, and the Ouzinkie Clinic has a dedicated SSB radio. In a major emergency where telephone service and electric power are down, Ouzinkie would rely on VHF radio to communicate with Kodiak.

Ouzinkie

Paimiut

See Zero Population Section

Pauloff Harbor

See Zero Population Section

COMMUNITY FACILITIES AND SERVICES

Education. Ouzinkie School serves 50 students in grades 2-12 with six teachers and is operated by Kodiak Island Borough School District. Kodiak Community College offers various courses in Ouzinkie throughout the year, and the Ouzinkie Native Corporation offers educational scholarships to all shareholders. The Ouzinkie Tribal Council Media Center is the city's public library.

Health care. The Ouzinkie Clinic, owned by the city and leased to the U.S. Public Health Service, is administered by the Kodiak Area Native Association. The Ouzinkie Clinic provides basic health care and emergency medical services to the community. Ouzinkie has a small ambulance for emergency trans-

port. The clinic is stocked with a diverse collection of medical equipment and supplies and can handle initial medical response to almost any kind of emergency. A doctor from the Indian Health Service visits Ouzinkie monthly. The nearest hospital is Providence Kodiak Island Medical Center, about 13 miles away in Kodiak. As of 2004, a new clinic was under construction.

Public safety. Law enforcement is provided by the village public safety officer (VPSO), backed by state troopers stationed in Kodiak. Emergency response is provided by the VPSO, the Ouzinkie Volunteer Fire Department and, offshore, by the United States Coast Guard. As of 2001, the VPSO was also the fire chief.

Pedro Bay

[PAY-droh]
Ethnicity: Dena'ina
                    Athabascan

Village council
Pedro Bay Village
P.O. Box 47020
Pedro Bay, AK 99647-0020
    907-850-2225
    907-850-2221 Fax
    pedrobay.com

ANCSA village corporation
Pedro Bay Native Corporation
P.O. Box 47015
Pedro Bay, AK 99647-0015
    907-850-2323
    907-850-2221 Fax

Total area of entitlement under ANCSA

	97,002 acres
Total labor force	27
High school graduate or higher	35.5%
Bachelor's degree or higher	19.4%
Unemployment rate	0.0%
Per capita income *(1999)*	$18,420
Population *2000 census*	50
Current population	45
state demographer estimate	
Percent Native *2000 census*	64.0%

LOCATION
Pedro Bay is 176 miles southwest of Anchorage, on the northeast end of Iliamna Lake and 24 miles from lower Cook Inlet.

PHYSICAL DESCRIPTION
The village area, encompassing 17.3 square miles of land and 1.6 square miles of water, is located in a heavily wooded area of the Alaska Peninsula, an area dense with birch, cottonwood, alder, willow, and white spruce trees, at an elevation of less than 165 feet above sea level.

CLIMATE
Pedro Bay lies in a transitional climate zone with strong maritime influences. The climate is characterized by warm summers and cold winters with an average annual rainfall of 26 inches and 64 inches of snow each year. Prevailing winds are from the east at 10 miles per hour. January low temperatures range between -5°F and 20°F; July high temperatures vary between 60°F and 70°F. At this latitude, the region experiences approximately 18.75 hours of daylight in any 24-hour period of June, declining to 6 hours in December.

CULTURE AND HISTORY
Pedro Bay is a Dena'ina Indian village with a culture centered on subsistence activities in a region of Alaska historically occupied by the Dena'ina people. The community was named for a man known as "Old Pedro," who lived in the area in the early 1900s, and a post office was established in 1936. Since 1980 the population of the village has more than doubled as more and more of the tribal members return to live in the area.

GOVERNMENT
The community of Pedro Bay is unincorporated and is located in the Lake and Peninsula Borough. Pedro Bay Village, the

BIA-recognized Native entity, is governed by a traditional village council headed by a president.

VILLAGE CORPORATION
Pedro Bay Native Corporation is the ANCSA village corporation. Shareholders in the village corporation also hold shares in Bristol Bay Native Corporation.

ECONOMY
The economy of Pedro Bay is based primarily on the commercial drift-net salmon fishery with some increasing emphasis on tourism. Most residents travel to Bristol Bay each summer to fish for salmon, and subsistence practices supplement most villagers' incomes; salmon, trout, moose, bear, rabbit, and seal are harvested. There is one ranch in the village. In 2004 a barge landing site on Iliamna Lake was to be completed at Pedro Bay, a valuable addition to the local economy as a shipping point and site to offload fuel and other supplies. This will considerably lower the cost of many goods for Pedro Bay and other villages lying along the newly constructed road from Williamsport-Pile Bay to the lake.

Fisheries. The local economy of Pedro Bay is based primarily on the commercial drift-net salmon fishery with some increasing emphasis on tourism. Most residents travel to Bristol Bay each summer to fish for salmon.

Government as employer. The 2000 census counted 16 residents working for the borough, state, or federal governments.

Services and retail. Businesses in Pedro Bay include a general store, a sewing and piece-goods store, a store where Native arts and crafts are marketed operated by Pedro Bay Native Corporation, a daycare center, three field outfitters, a repair service, and at least two guide services.

Tourism and recreation. Tourists are drawn to the Village of Pedro Bay by the recreational opportunities to be found on Iliamna Lake and the region's rivers. Kayaking vacations include wildlife-viewing, whale-watching, fishing, camping, hiking, walking, and wilderness adventures for all levels of ability. There are lodges, fishing guide services, and outfitters to serve visitors. The area is served by the Iliamna Air Taxi. Pedro Bay lies within 20 miles of the Lake Clark National Park and Preserve and 60 miles from Katmai National Park and Preserve. It lies just across Cook Inlet (within 100 miles) from the Kenai National Wildlife Refuge.

INFRASTRUCTURE

Transportation. Pedro Bay is accessible only by water and air, with local roads leading to the landfill (built 1998) and to Barney's Bay. These roads were improved in 1999 and a new bridge built. Beginning in 2001, with plans for building a new barge landing site, a road from Williamsport-Pile Bay to Pedro Bay extending all the way to Iliamna Lake was built, allowing other villages better access to the lake and increasing traffic through Pedro Bay from the other areas. In 2003 the bridge over Rushing Creek was replaced. The new barge landing site was slated for completion in 2004.

There is regular flight service from Iliamna, and charter services are available from King Salmon at the state-owned 3,000-foot gravel airstrip. The facility has no crosswind runway or tower, but in 2002-03, the facility was undergoing major improvements that may correct the deficits.

Barge service is available to Naknek, and a lighterage (barge) service transports cargo from Naknek via the Kvichak River to Iliamna Lake during the summer months. Goods are also sent by barge from Homer to Iliamna Bay on the Cook Inlet side and portaged over a 14-mile road to Pile Bay, 10 miles to the east. Individuals may also charter barges from Pile Bay or from Homer.

Electricity. Pedro Bay Village provides electricity from a 212-kilowatt diesel plant. In 1997 there were improvements to the electric distribution system, including the replacement of transformers and extensions to the underground cables, which expanded service to several additional homes. INN Electric has asked for funding to construct an intertie to Pedro Bay from the Tazimina Hydroelectric Plant.

Fuel storage (gallons). Bulk fuel is available for purchase by residents. Storage (gallons): village council (29,500); Lake and Peninsula Schools (28,200).

Water and waste systems. Residents obtain water from individual wells and from Iliamna Lake. In 2002, the Lake and Peninsula Borough was improving the water system for Pedro Bay. The school and the clinic have their own water systems. Most year-round homes have septic systems and are fully plumbed. The school and the clinic have their own septic systems. The village council provides honeybucket-hauling and septic-pumping services and maintains a six-acre Class 3 solid waste landfill and transfer facility built in 2001. Aluminum recycling is organized by the school.

Telecommunications. Local telephone service is provided by ACS of the Northland; long distance services by AT&T Alascom. One television channel is offered by the Alaska Rural Communications Service. Internet services are available from GCI at the school only. Three AM radio stations broadcast to the area.

COMMUNITY FACILITIES AND SERVICES

Community facilities include the multipurpose Nilavena Community Building and a washeteria operated by the village council, which also provides electrical generation and distribution, fuel sales and storage, honeybucket-hauling and septic-pumping services, and the landfill and transfer facility. Aluminum recycling is organized by the school.

Education. Dena'ina School, which serves students in grades K-12, is operated by the Lake and Peninsula School District. In 2003 the school was to be moved to a new location and completely renovated. It serves 14 students with two teachers. The school library serves as the community public library.

Health care. Health care is provided by the newly-constructed Pedro Bay Health Clinic, owned by the village, leased to the U.S. Public Health Service, and administered by the Bristol Bay Area Health Corporation. Emergencies are handled by the Pedro Bay First Responders.

Public safety. Law enforcement is provided by state troopers in Iliamna. Emergency response is provided by the Pedro Bay First Responders.

Perryville

Perryville

Total area of entitlement under ANCSA	
	93,022 acres
Total labor force	36
High school graduate or higher	20
Bachelor's degree or higher	2
Unemployment rate	11.1%
Per capita income *(1999)*	$20,935
Population *2000 census*	107
Current population	106
state demographer estimate	
Percent Native *2000 census*	98.1%

LOCATION

Perryville is located on the Pacific (south) side of the Alaska Peninsula, near Ivanof Bay, Chignik, Chignik Lake, and Chignik Lagoon, in the Lake and Peninsula Borough. The community is approximately 268 miles from King Salmon, 275 miles southwest of Kodiak, and about 500 miles southwest of Anchorage.

PHYSICAL DESCRIPTION

The village area encompasses 9.2 square miles of land and 0.1 square mile of water at an elevation of less than 165 feet above sea level, in the Alaska Peninsula National Wildlife Refuge. The area is a waterfowl and bald eagle intensive-use area, and both walrus and sea lions use nearby beaches. The gray whale spring migration passes just offshore. Several nearby streams support anadromous fish. The vegetation is high brush. It lies within a moderate-occurrence oil and gas province, and within a metal (gold, silver, copper, lead, zinc) province. To the north is an area of potential geothermal energy, including an active volcano about 20 miles north.

CLIMATE

Perryville has a maritime climate with cool summers, relatively warm winters, and wet, rainy weather during the fall and summer. Low clouds, rain squalls, fog, and snow showers frequently limit visibility. Average summer temperatures range between 39°F and 60°F, winter temperatures average 21°F to 50°F, with extremes from 80°F in the summer to winter lows of -35°F. Average annual precipitation is 127 inches, including 58 inches of snow. Storms with winds as high as 100 miles per hour have been experienced. At this latitude, the region experiences approximately 17.5 hours of daylight in a 24-hour period in mid-June, declining to just over 7 hours by mid-December.

Ethnicity: Alutiiq

Native entity
Native Village of Perryville
P.O. Box 101
Perryville, AK 99648-0101
    907-853-2203
    907-853-2230 Fax

ANCSA village corporation
Oceanside Native Corporation
P.O. Box 84
Perryville, AK 99648
    907-853-2300
    907-853-2301 Fax

Perryville

Perryville, founded in 1912 as a refuge for Alutiiq people driven away from Douglas, Katmai, and other villages by the eruption of Mt. Katmai, maintains its culture with a focus on subsistence activities. On founding their village, the refugees built a school and a Russian Orthodox church where they placed icons taken from the churches in their old villages. The community was named for Captain Perry of the ship that transported people from the Katmai area southward, first to Ivanof Bay and then to the new village location. The village was originally called "Perry," then "ville" was added to conform to the post office name, established in 1930. Many Perryville residents worked at the canneries in Chignik for at least part of the year. In the 1960s, about 40 people left Perryville to settle a new village at Ivanof Bay.

GOVERNMENT
Perryville, located in the Lake and Peninsula Borough, is unincorporated. It is governed by an Indian Reorganization Act village council, presided over by a president.

VILLAGE CORPORATION
Oceanside Native Corporation is the ANCSA village corporation. Shareholders in the village corporation also hold shares in Bristol Bay regional Native corporation *(see Alaska introduction)*.

ECONOMY
A large portion of the cash in the community is derived from commercial fishing, with the economic well-being of the village closely linked to the red salmon run. A majority leave Perryville every summer to fish in Chignik or Chignik Lagoon. Some residents trap during the winter, and all rely heavily on subsistence activities to supplement their income. Salmon, trout, marine fish, crab, clams, moose, caribou, bear, porcupine, and seal are harvested. By far, most of those who work year-round are employed in education, health, and social services. Completion of the harbor and barge-landing site at Perryville will significantly lower the costs of goods.

Fisheries. Fishing is extremely important for the economy of the village. Until Perryville's harbor is completed in 2005, the fishing boats are kept in the villages of Chignik and Chignik Lagoon. In 2003, Alaska's Department of Community and Economic Development funded coho salmon restoration for subsistence runs in the Kametolook River, a project undertaken by the Bristol Bay Native Association and the Perryville Chignik Subsistence Workgroup on behalf of the entire community.

Government as employer. In the 2000 census, there were 27 residents of Perryville employed by the borough, state, or federal government.

Services and retail. There are a variety store, a general store, and a retail food store in the village, as well as a toy shop and a building-rental business. A total of eleven businesses are currently licensed in the community, including two day-care facilities and a bed-and-breakfast.

Tourism and recreation. Perryville lies within the Alaska Peninsula National Wildlife Refuge and is within 100 miles of the Aniakchak National Monument and Preserve.

INFRASTRUCTURE
Transportation. Perryville is accessible only by air and sea; however, there are some local roads. In 1999, the Tsunami Shelter road was graded and new drains added, and a new road was built to the bulk-fuel tank farm. Work began on a road running from Perryville to Ivanof Bay in 2003. Regular and charter flight services are available from King Salmon. There is a 2,500- by 50-foot gravel runway and seaplane base almost on the beach, owned by the State of Alaska, with scheduled and charter flights. The runway was scheduled for rehabilitation in 2005. Cargo barges arrive each spring from Seattle and Anchorage, delivering fuel and other supplies. There are two public docks, completed in 2003; construction of a harbor and barge-landing site was slated for completion by April 2005.

Electricity. Electricity is provided by the village council from a 475-kilowatt diesel plant.

Fuel storage (gallons). Bulk fuel is available for purchase by residents. Village Council (72,500); Lake and Peninsula Schools (21,900).

Water and waste systems. The village council operates a piped water system. The water is filtered and chlorinated prior to distribution. The water source is a 60,000-gallon timber dam gravity system on a nearby stream. Water is stored in a new 50,000-gallon tank, serving 30 homes and the school. Some residents maintain individual wells. Water facilities were upgraded in 1998-99, including construction of a raw-water infiltration gallery and the water storage tank. Residents use individual septic tanks, as well as a community septic system in public buildings. The landfill is recorded as inactive.

Telecommunications. Local telephone service is provided by ACS of the Northland, long distance by AT&T Alascom or GCI. Two AM radio stations broadcast to the area. One television channel is broadcast locally by the Alaska Rural Communications System and Internet service is provided by GCI.

COMMUNITY FACILITIES AND SERVICES
The village council provides electricity generation and distribution, fuel storage, limited waste collection and disposal, and water supply. In 1998, the village built a community office building.

Education. Perryville School, which serves 34 students in grades K-12 with three teachers, is operated by the Lake and Peninsula School District. There is a library at the school, which serves as the community public library.

Health care. Health care is provided by the Perryville Health Clinic, owned by the village, leased to the U.S. Public Health Service, and administered by the Bristol Bay Area Health Corporation.

Public safety. Law enforcement is provided to citizens in Perryville by Alaska state troopers stationed in King Salmon. Emergency response is provided by the Perryville First Responders.

Petersburg

Population *2000 census*	3,224
2003 population	3,060
state demographer estimate	
Percent Native *2000 census*	12.0%

NOTE

Petersburg is primarily a non-Native community. While the Petersburg Indian Association is a BIA-recognized Native entity, less than one-eighth of the population of the City of Petersburg is Native Alaskan. Except for basic orientation information, this profile discusses only those aspects of Petersburg that are unique to its Native residents.

LOCATION

Petersburg is located on the northwest end of Mitkof Island, where the Wrangell Narrows meets Frederick Sound. It lies midway between Juneau and Ketchikan, about 120 miles from either community.

PHYSICAL DESCRIPTION

The city covers 43.9 square miles of land and 2.2 square miles of water.

CLIMATE

Petersburg's climate is characterized by mild winters, cool summers, and year-round rainfall. Summer high temperatures range from 40°F to 56°F. Winter low temperatures range from 27°F to 43°F. Annual precipitation averages 106.3 inches, including 97 inches of snow.

CULTURE AND HISTORY

The community maintains a mixture of Tlingit and Scandinavian culture. Tlingit Indians from Kake used the north end of Mitkof Island as a summer fish camp. Some reportedly began living year-round at the site. Petersburg was named after Peter Buschmann, a Norwegian immigrant and a pioneer in the cannery business, who arrived in the late 1890s. Petersburg has developed into one of Alaska's major fishing communities.

GOVERNMENT

Petersburg Indian Association is a BIA-recognized Native entity and IRA tribal council. The community is also known by its Tlingit name, Seet Kah.

VILLAGE CORPORATION

While Petersburg has no ANCSA village corporation, its members are at-large shareholders in Sealaska Corporation, the regional Native corporation. Legislation has been introduced in Congress to provide ANCSA village corporations for five "panhandle" Native entities, including Petersburg, that did not get them under the ANCSA, but it has not yet been passed into law.

COMMUNITY FACILITIES AND SERVICES

Health care. Village members are eligible for medical care from the Southeast Alaska Regional Health Consortium (SEARHC), a nonprofit organization that provides health care services to Alaska Natives and American Indians residing in the region. SEARHC contracts for care locally. Hospital-level care is available at SEARHC-operated Mt. Edgecumbe Hospital in Sitka.

Also known as Seet Kah

Ethnicity: Tlingit

Municipality
City of Petersburg
P.O. Box 329
Petersburg, AK 99833
907-772-4519
907-772-3759 Fax
ci.petersburg.ak.us

Native entity
Petersburg Indian Association
IRA
P.O. Box 1418
Petersburg, AK 99833
907-772-3636
907-772-3637 Fax

Pilot Point

Total area of entitlement under ANCSA	
	98,937 acres
Total labor force	52
High school graduate or higher	84.1%
Bachelor's degree or higher	0.0%
Unemployment rate	7.7%
Per capita income *(1999)*	$12,627
Population *2000 census*	100
Current population	70
state demographer estimate	
Percent Native *2000 census*	86.0%

LOCATION

Pilot Point is located on the north shore of the Alaska Peninsula. It lies 84 air miles south of King Salmon and 368 air miles southwest of Anchorage.

PHYSICAL DESCRIPTION

The city encompasses 25.4 square miles of land and 115.1 square miles of water at the eastern edge of Ugashik Bay, at an elevation of less than 165 feet above sea level.

CLIMATE

Pilot Point's maritime climate is characterized by cool, humid, windy weather. Average summer temperatures range from 41°F to 60°F; winter temperatures range from 20°F to 37°F. Precipitation averages 19 inches per year, with 38 inches of snowfall. At this latitude, the region experiences over 18 hours of daylight in a 24-hour period in mid-June, declining to 6.5 hours by mid-December.

CULTURE AND HISTORY

There is a history of ethnic diversity in Pilot Point. At present, the community primarily consists of Natives of Alutiiq ancestry, with a culture focused on fishing and subsistence activities. In 1889 the village was called "Pilot Station" and was a community of Alutiiq and Yup'ik who had gathered there because of a fish-salting plant. The first cannery was built in 1891, and three additional plants were built over the next four years, bringing many more people of various nationalities to work in the canneries and as riverboat pilots. Reindeer-herding experiments at Ugashik helped to repopulate the area after the devastating 1918 flu epidemic, although the effort eventually failed. A Russian Orthodox church and a Seventh-Day Adventist church were built in the village and a post office was established in 1933, at which time the name was changed to Pilot Point. The deterioration of the harbor forced the last cannery to close in 1958. Pilot Point incorporated as a city in 1992.

GOVERNMENT

Pilot Point incorporated in 1992 as a second-class city, with a mayor and city council, in the Lake and Peninsula Borough.

Ethnicity: Alutiiq

Municipality
City of Pilot Point
P.O. Box 470
Pilot Point, AK 99649
907-797-2205
907-797-2211 Fax

Village council
Native Village of Pilot Point
P.O. Box 449
Pilot Point, AK 99649
907-797-2208
907-797-2258 Fax

ANCSA village corporation
Pilot Point Native Corporation
P.O. Box 487
Pilot Point, AK 99649
907-797-2206
907-797-2228 Fax

Pilot Point

The "Native Village of Pilot Point" is a traditional village council, headed by a president.

VILLAGE CORPORATION
Pilot Point Native Corporation is the ANCSA village corporation. Shareholders also hold shares in Bristol Bay Native Corporation, the ANCSA regional Native corporation *(see Alaska Introduction)*.

ECONOMY
The residents of Pilot Point depend largely on commercial salmon fishing for the majority of their cash income. Subsistence activities supplement diets and income; salmon, caribou, moose, geese, and porcupine are harvested, and trapping is a source of income in the winter. By far, more residents work in commercial fishing or hold jobs in the schools or clinic—17 people work in education, health and the social services.

Fisheries. The residents of Pilot Point depend largely on commercial salmon fishing for the majority of their cash income.

Government as employer. In the 2000 census, there were 32 residents of Pilot Point working for the city, borough, state, or federal government.

Services and retail. There is a general store in the village and there are several other retail stores, several repair services, and an investment firm.

Tourism and recreation. Tourists and guests of residents stay at the Caribou Lookout Lodge, Kramer's, or Ace's Tundra Loon Club. Pilot Point lies within 20 miles of the Becharof National Wildlife Refuge and the Alaska Peninsula National Wildlife Refuge, within 60 miles of the Aniakchak National Monument and Preserve, and within 100 miles of the Katmai National Park and Preserve.

INFRASTRUCTURE
Transportation. Pilot Point is accessible only by air and water. There are two gravel runways, and two air-taxi services provide regular flights six days a week out of King Salmon as part of the mail service. The airport was relocated in 1999 and in 2003 a building was built to house the newly-acquired snow removal equipment. There were plans for additional improvements in 2004.

Barge service is available from Seattle in the spring and fall and can be chartered from Naknek. A dock is available in the natural harbor formed by Dago Creek. In 1998, the bulkhead was upgraded, and in 2003, it was to be expanded to accommodate barge and freight offloading.

Some local roads were resurfaced in 1998, and in the year 2000, the Alaska Department of Community and Economic Development funded a feasibility study for the design of additional roads. The Ugashik River Road was completed in 2002, then graded, and proper drainage was added. In 2003, a road from Pilot Point to Egegik was under construction and repairs were made to the road going to the landfill. Residents depend upon all-terrain vehicles, snowmobiles, skiffs, and trucks.

Electricity. The city operates a 350-kilowatt diesel plant. Since 2001, the community has been participating in an engineering study to monitor wind strength. Plans were to install a wind turbine during the summer of 2002 to supplement traditionally-produced electricity.

Fuel storage (gallons). Bulk fuel is available for purchase by residents. City (128,900); Lake and Peninsula Schools (7,000).

Water and waste systems. Water in Pilot Point is provided by individual wells and a community well. The school also has its own system. The city operates a piped-sewage system including a lift station and sewage lagoon. Pilot Point participated in a sanitation facilities study in 1998 to determine what improvements might be made to correct failing septic systems, to drill new wells, and to relocate the landfill. Work began in 2000, including the installation of lines to the Dago Creek lift station and lagoon and construction of the new landfill and an access road to it. Rehabilitation of existing septic systems continued throughout 2002 and 2003. The city operates a Class 3 landfill.

Telecommunications. Local telephone service is provided by ACS of the Northland, long distance services by AT&T Alascom or GCI. One channel of television is rebroadcast locally by the Alaska Rural Communications Service. Internet service is available from GCI or, at the school only, by Bristol Bay Telephone Cooperative. One AM radio station broadcasts to the area.

COMMUNITY FACILITIES AND SERVICES
Community facilities include a washeteria and a community hall which houses all city offices. Plans were underway in 2003 for the construction of a new multipurpose building.

The city provides electricity generation and distribution, fuel storage, and waste disposal.

Education. Pilot Point School serves 25 children in grades K-12. It is operated by the Lake and Peninsula School District with three teachers. The school library serves as the community public library.

Health care. Health care is provided by the Pilot Point Health Clinic, operated by the Bristol Bay Area Health Corporation. In 2002, the city made much-needed building repairs and renovations to the clinic building.

Public safety. Law enforcement is provided by state troopers stationed in King Salmon and by a village public safety officer. The latter position was vacant as of August 2004. Emergency response is provided by Pilot Point First Responders.

Total area of entitlement under ANCSA	
	114,994 acres
Total labor force	165
High school graduate or higher	29.4%
Bachelor's degree or higher	7.0%
Unemployment rate	16.9%
Per capita income *(1999)*	$7,311
Population *2000 census*	550
2003 population	564
state demographer estimate	
Percent Native *2000 census*	97.6%

LOCATION
Pilot Station is located on the northwest bank of the Yukon River, 11 miles east of St. Mary's and 26 miles west of Marshall, in the Yukon River delta.

PHYSICAL DESCRIPTION
The village area encompasses 1.7 square miles of land and 0.6 square mile of water at an elevation of less than 165 feet above sea level. One of the more beautiful villages on the Yukon Delta, Pilot Station is situated on a hillside overlooking the Yukon River. Most of the housing is surrounded by large spruce trees.

CLIMATE
The climate of Pilot Station is more maritime than continental, with relatively mild winters and cool, wet summers. Temperature extremes can range from winter lows of -44°F to summer highs of 83°F. Precipitation totals approximately 16 inches annually, including snowfalls of 60 inches or more. The lower Yukon River is frozen over from late October until mid-June.

CULTURE AND HISTORY
Pilot Station is a traditional Yup'ik village. The ruins of Kurgpallermuit, an ancient village now a designated historic site, are located nearby. Oral tradition holds that it was occupied during the bow and arrow wars between the Yukon and Coastal Natives. A Russian Orthodox church, one of the oldest permanent structures in the region, was built in the early 1900s. Local riverboat pilots who used the village as a station checkpoint were responsible for the name change to *Pilot Station*; it was first officially recorded this way in 1916 by the United States Geological Survey and was incorporated under that name as a second-class city in 1969. The community is occupied primarily by Yup'ik people largely dependent upon a fishing and subsistence lifestyle.

GOVERNMENT
The City of Pilot Station was incorporated as a second-class city in 1969. It is located in the Unorganized Borough. The city has a mayor, a city administrator (manager), a city clerk, and a city council. The city assesses a 4 percent sales tax. It also has a traditional village council, the Pilot Station Traditional Village, headed by a president.

VILLAGE CORPORATION
Pilot Station Incorporated is the ANCSA village corporation. It has a real estate venture with the Pitka's Point village corporation. Together, they own two condominiums that are rented out in Anchorage, with one in the Mountain View area, and the other in the Lake Otis Area. The corporation also operates the Pilot Station Native Store and another store in the village. Shareholders in the village corporation also hold shares in Calista Corporation, the regional Native corporation.

ECONOMY
Most of the employment in the city is with the school or in city and state governments, although there are now eight businesses licensed in the community. Calista Corporation, the regional Native corporation, was instrumental in the development of the Pilot Station Native Store, an outlet for handcrafted arts and crafts. However, commercial fishing remains a primary part of the private-sector cash economy, and trapping and subsistence activities supplement most residents' income. Salmon, moose, bear, porcupine, and waterfowl are harvested.

Government as employer. Seventy-six of 112 employed residents of Pilot Station work for either the city, state or federal governments.

Services and retail. The city has two general stores, two video stores, a limited-service restaurant, a clothing store, a computer store, and a daycare provider. The village has three stores. The Pilot Station Native Store is the largest general store, supplying villagers with most basic food items, some clothing and a limited hardware selection.

Tourism and recreation. Pilot Station lies within the Yukon Delta National Wildlife Refuge.

Transportation. The city has a taxicab company.

INFRASTRUCTURE
Transportation. Pilot Station is accessible by air and water only; it has no road connections with other communities. A state-owned 2,541- by 55-foot gravel airstrip is served by Grant Aviation, Hageland Aviation, and Tanana Air Service, bringing cargo, passengers, and mail. Heavy winds of up to 50 miles per hour during fall and winter limit air access. The village is easily accessible by river vessels in the summer months. During the summer, boats are used for commercial and subsistence fishing and for travel to nearby locations. Barges deliver fuel and other bulk supplies. Snow machines and dogsleds are the most common means of transportation during the six months of winter.

Electricity. Electricity is available to residents from the Alaska Village Electric Cooperative (AVEC), generating power from a 942-kilowatt diesel plant.

Fuel storage (gallons). Village corporation/city (102,800); AVEC (96,340); Lower Yukon Schools (47,725); city (5,260); Native Store (5,000).

Water and waste systems. The city operates a piped water and sewer system, which has been consistently upgraded and rehabilitated since 1997 when a new water treatment plant was finished and a new 200,000-gallon storage tank added. There have been additional service connections to homes, a new pump for the well, a new lift station, a new lagoon, and new water mains added throughout the city in a multiphase, multiyear total water/sewage system overhaul. Over half of all homes in the community are on the city system. The water is drawn from a community well. The school operates its own water system. The city operates a Class 3 landfill.

Telecommunications. Local telephone service is provided by United Utilities, and long distance services by United Utilities or AT&T Alascom. The city can receive three AM radio stations from Bethel and Nome. The city operates the

Ethnicity: Yup'ik

Municipality
City of Pilot Station
P.O. Box 5040
Pilot Station, AK 99650
   907-549-3211
   907-549-3014 Fax
   lysd.gcisa.net

Native entity
Pilot Station Traditional Village
P.O. Box 5119
Pilot Station, AK 99650
   907-549-3373
   907-549-3301 Fax

ANCSA village corporation
Pilot Station Incorporated
P.O. Box 5059
Pilot Station, AK 99650
   907-549-3512

Pilot Station

Tutalgarmiut Yuraviat cable television service and a one-channel television broadcast repeater. The Alaska Rural Communications System operates a second television repeater. The village health clinic is equipped with a shortwave radio and is used for backup communication with the Regional Hospital in Bethel when the telephones are out. VHF and CB radios are also used extensively for local communications.

COMMUNITY FACILITIES AND SERVICES
The city operates the water and waste disposal systems, the cable television system, and regular bingo games in the lower level of the city hall, which serves as the community hall.

Education. The Pilot Station School, in a new building built since 1998, serves students in grades K-12. It is operated by the Lower Yukon School District. The city has a public library.

Health care. Health care is provided by the Pilot Station Health Clinic, known locally as the Nastasia Evan Memorial Clinic and operated by the Yukon-Kuskokwim Health Corporation. It is supported by the John Afcan Memorial Sub-Regional Clinic in St. Mary's and the Yukon Kuskokwim Delta Regional Hospital in Bethel. Because of the flood hazard at its old site, a new facility was built shortly after 2000. Emergency service is provided by a health aide.

Public safety. Law enforcement services are provided by a village public safety officer (VPSO) and the city police department (a chief and two officers), backed by Alaska state troopers stationed in St. Mary's. Emergency response is provided by the VPSO and the city volunteer fire department.

ENVIRONMENTAL CONCERNS
Floods in 1985 and 1989 flowed over the top of the river bank, flooding the city. Newer residential areas and the new clinic are on a hillside above the 100-year flood line, but most of the city remains in the floodplain.

Pitka's Point

[PIT-kas]
Ethnicity: Yup'ik

Native entity
Native Village of Pitka's Point
P.O. Box 127
Saint Mary's, AK 99658
   907-438-2833
   907-438-2569 Fax

ANCSA village corporation
Pitka's Point Native
   Corporation
P.O. Box 289
Saint Mary's, AK 99658
   907-438-2953
   907-438-2276 Fax

Total area of entitlement under ANCSA	68,665 acres
Total labor force	44
High school graduate or higher	28.4%
Bachelor's degree or higher	6.0%
Unemployment rate	13.8%
Per capita income *(1999)*	$10,488
Population *2000 census*	125
2003 population *state demographer estimate*	107
Percent Native *2000 census*	93.6%

LOCATION
Pitka's Point is located near the junction of the Yukon and Andreafsky rivers, five miles northwest of St. Mary's, three miles from the St. Mary's airport.

PHYSICAL DESCRIPTION
The village area encompasses 1.5 square miles of land, at an elevation of less than 165 feet above sea level. The surrounding area is dominated by flat wetlands dotted with meltwater ponds called "potholes" and veined by smaller rivers, creeks and sloughs.

CLIMATE
The climate of Pitka's Point is affected by maritime and continental influences with temperatures ranging from lows of -44°F in the winter months to extreme summer highs of 83°F. Annual precipitation is 16 inches, including 60 inches of snowfall. At this latitude, the region experiences just over 20 hours of daylight in a 24 hour period in mid-June, declining to 4.75 hours by mid-December.

CULTURE AND HISTORY
Pitka's Point is a Yup'ik village originally called "Nigiklik" by the first settlers, a Yup'ik word meaning "to the north." The United States Geological Survey first reported the village location in 1898. The village was later renamed for a trader who opened a general store, a branch of the Northern Commercial Company.

GOVERNMENT
Pitka's Point is unincorporated and is located in the Unorganized Borough. It is governed by the Native Village of Pitka's Point, a BIA-recognized traditional village council headed by a president.

VILLAGE CORPORATION
Pitka's Point Native Corporation is the ANCSA village corporation. It has a real estate venture with the Pilot Station village corporation. Together, they own two condominiums that are rented out in Anchorage, with one in the Mountain View area and the other in the Lake Otis Area. Shareholders in the village corporation also hold shares in Calista Corporation, the regional Native corporation.

ECONOMY
The economy of Pitka's Point is dependent upon the summer fishing season, supplemented with some year-round cash enterprises and subsistence activities. Salmon, moose, bear, and waterfowl are harvested. Most supplies are brought in through Saint Mary's.

Fisheries. Two residents hold commercial fishing permits.

Government as employer. Of 33 employed residents, 19 work for the state or federal government.

Tourism and recreation. Pitka's Point lies within the Yukon Delta National Wildlife Refuge.

INFRASTRUCTURE
Transportation. Pitka's Point is primarily accessible by air and water via the Yukon River. Every family in Pitka's Point owns a skiff. There is one 17.7-mile road connecting the village with the St. Mary's airport and Mountain Village, giving residents access to the transportation facilities at St. Mary's, where both regular and charter flights are available. Residents rely on snowmobiles for local winter transportation, using the frozen Yukon River as a winter trail. A system of wooden boardwalks throughout the community facilitates foot traffic.

Electricity. Electricity is provided by the Alaska Village Electric Cooperative plant in St. Mary's.

Fuel storage (gallons). Lower Yukon Schools (22,320); village corporation (15,000).

Water and waste systems. There is a central watering point in the village, drawing water from a community well and a small stream with an infiltration gallery. There is a honeybucket dump in the village, and a community septic system, including lagoon, is used for sewage disposal at all public facilities.

There are a washeteria and sauna, renovated in 2000. Moving toward a piped water and sewer system for all homes in the community, the water and sewage infrastructure has been under consistent improvement since completion of the Facilities Master Plan in 2002. The village council operates a Class 3 landfill, with refuse collection services available.

Telecommunications. Local telephone service is provided by United Utilities on the St. Mary's exchange. Long distance service is available from AT&T Alascom. Three AM radio stations can be received at Pitka's Point. One television channel is broadcast from an Alaska Rural Communications System repeater.

COMMUNITY FACILITIES AND SERVICES
The village council operates the water and waste disposal systems, the washeteria, the sauna, and a community hall.

Education. Pitka's Point School serves students in grades K-12 and is operated by the Lower Yukon School District. The school library serves as the community's public library. There were renovations planned for the school in 2005.

Health care. Health care is provided by the Pitka's Point Health Clinic, operated by the Yukon-Kuskokwim Health Corporation. It is supported by the John Afcan Memorial Sub-Regional Clinic in nearby St. Mary's and the Yukon Kuskokwim Delta Regional Hospital in Bethel. Emergency service is provided by a health aide.

Public safety. Law enforcement services are provided by state troopers in St. Mary's, emergency response by the village volunteer fire department.

Platinum

Total area of entitlement under ANCSA	
	69,120 acres
Total labor force	33
High school graduate or higher	29.3%
Bachelor's degree or higher	0.0%
Unemployment rate	20%
Per capita income *(1999)*	$7,632
Population *2000 census*	41
2003 population	40
state demographer estimate	
Percent Native *2000 census*	92.7%

LOCATION
Platinum is located 123 miles southwest of Bethel, below Red Mountain on the southern shore of Goodnews Bay. The village of Goodnews Bay lies approximately 11 miles away, across the bay.

PHYSICAL DESCRIPTION
Platinum is located on the Bering Sea coast, encompassing 44.6 square miles of land and 0.1 square mile of water at an elevation of less than 165 feet above sea level.

CLIMATE
Platinum is located in a transitional climate zone, exhibiting primarily marine climatic influences. Summer high temperatures range between 53°F and 57°F; winter highs average from 6°F to 9°F. Extremes have been recorded from -34°F to 82°F. Average annual precipitation is 22 inches, including 43 inches of snowfall. At this latitude, the region experiences approximately 18.5 hours of daylight in a 24-hour period in June, declining to 6 hours by mid-December.

CULTURE AND HISTORY
Platinum is a Yup'ik village, located about 10 miles away from the only platinum mine in the United States, near a traditional village site called Arviq. A Yup'ik man, Walter Smith, discovered traces of platinum in the area in 1926. Between 1927 and 1934, several small placer mines operated on creeks in the area. Approximately 3,000 troy ounces of platinum were mined during that time period, valued at $48 per ounce. In 1935 a post office was opened. In October 1936, three miners hit the big strike when drilling a hole through beach gravel. The miners traveled to the Lower 48 for heavy equipment, where word soon spread about the "white gold" discovery. The stampede was on, with prospectors arriving daily by boat and plane. Individual claims were bought out by two companies, the larger of which eventually acquired title to over 150 claims. In 1937 one of the two companies built a large dredge at the site, and the mine developed into an extensive complex, with office buildings, bunkhouses, a recreation hall, shops, and a cafeteria. By 1975 545,000 ounces of platinum had been removed. Estimates of the platinum reserves are over 500,000 ounces. The mine closed in 1990. Because the community was founded as a commercial center, and has always seen an influx of outsiders, local traditions have not been retained as much as in other villages. Platinum is one of the few Native villages in the region in which the first language of the children is English.

GOVERNMENT
Platinum was incorporated as a second-class city in 1975, with a mayor and a city council. It is located in the Unorganized Borough. Platinum Traditional Village is a BIA-recognized council, headed by a president.

VILLAGE CORPORATION
Arviq, Incorporated, is the ANCSA village corporation. Its shareholders also hold shares in Calista Corporation, the regional Native corporation.

ECONOMY
Platinum derives its economic base more from cash than subsistence activities, an anomaly among the villages of the region. Commercial fishing is the largest private employer in the community, primarily herring-roe and salmon net-fishing. Other employment is found with the school, the mining company, and government agencies. Platinum is a major supplier of gravel to area villages. Nevertheless, subsistence remains an important part of the residents' lifestyle. Seal, salmon, waterfowl, other small game, and berries are harvested in season. Seagrass is gathered for traditional basket weaving.

Government as employer. The city, state, or federal government employs 20 of 24 employed residents.

Services and retail. Businesses in Platinum include a vehicle dealership and a trading post which serves as an outlet for Native crafts.

Tourism and recreation. Tourists and guests of residents may stay at the Platinum Commercial Company Hotel. A tour of the platinum mine is a tourist attraction. Platinum lies within 100 miles of the southern border of the Yukon Delta National Wildlife Refuge.

Ethnicity: Yup'ik

Municipality
City of Platinum
P.O. Box 47
Platinum, AK 99651-0047
907-979-8114
907-979-8210 Fax

Native entity
Platinum Traditional Village
P.O. Box 8
Platinum, AK 99647
907-979-8177
907-979-8178 Fax

ANCSA village corporation
Arviq, Incorporated
P.O. Box 9
Platinum, AK 99651
907-979-8113
907-979-8229 Fax

Platinum

INFRASTRUCTURE

Transportation. Platinum is accessible by air and water. The community relies heavily on air transportation for passengers, mail, and cargo service. There are two gravel airstrips, originally constructed for the mine operation, which are served by Arctic Circle Air Service, Era Aviation, and Yute Air. One is state-owned, at 3,304 by 60 feet with a 1,924- by 40-foot cross-wind runway. The second, 2,000 by 75 feet, is owned by the Platinum Mine. A seaplane base is also available. Barge services are available during the spring and fall, and boats are used heavily during the summer months for fishing, hunting, visiting, and wood gathering. Bulk goods are delivered twice a year. During the winter, residents rely on snowmobiles and all-terrain vehicles for local transportation and subsistence activities.

Electricity. Electricity is available to residents from the City of Platinum which generates power at a 75-kilowatt diesel plant.

Fuel storage (gallons). Arviq Inc. (67,100); Lower Kuskokwim Schools (7,000); city power plant (5,600).

Water and waste systems. The City of Platinum maintains the water system; it was originally built and owned by the mining company. Water is available at several points in the village, drawn from a community well and a surface source. Some individuals maintain wells as well. Residents own and maintain outhouses, and there are some homes with septic systems; sewage is disposed of in a honeybucket dump. The city operates a landfill and collects refuse.

Telecommunications. Local telephone service is available from United Utilities Inc. and long distances services from United Utilities or AT&T Alascom. GCI provides Internet service to the school. The village council operates the cable television system, and the Alaska Rural Communications System broadcasts one television channel from a local repeater. Residents can receive at least one AM radio station from Bethel. In nearby Goodnews Bay, several AM radio stations can be received from Bethel, Dillingham, Nome, Anchorage, and other locations.

COMMUNITY FACILITIES AND SERVICES

The city operates the electrical, water, and waste disposal systems. The village council operates the cable television system. Emergency response is provided by the city volunteer fire department.

Education. Arviq School serves students in grades K-12. It is operated by the Lower Kuskokwim School District. The school library serves as the community public library.

Health care. Health care is provided by the Platinum Health Clinic, operated by the Bristol Bay Area Health Corporation. It is supported a sub-regional clinic in Togiak and by Kanakanak Hospital in Dillingham, although the Yukon Kuskokwim Delta Regional Hospital in Bethel is significantly closer. Emergency service is provided by a health aide.

Point Hope

Ethnicity: Tikeraqmuit Inupiat

Municipality
City of Point Hope
P.O. Box 169
Point Hope, AK 99766
907-368-2537
907-368-2835 Fax

Native entity
Native Village of Point Hope
P.O. Box 109
Point Hope, AK 99766
907-368-2330
907-368-2332 Fax

ANCSA village corporation
Tikigaq Corporation
P.O. Box 9
Point Hope, AK 99766
907-368-2235
907-368-2668 fax

NOTE
In March, 2003, the population was reported at 805 and the labor force at 356.

Total area of entitlement under ANCSA
	138,240 acres
Total labor force	322
High school graduate or higher	145
Bachelor's degree or higher	47
Unemployment rate	25.5%
Per capita income *(1999)*	$16,641
Population *2000 census*	757
Current population	725
state demographer estimate	
Percent Native *2000 census*	90.6%

LOCATION
Point Hope is located in the North Slope Borough near the end of a triangular spit that juts 15 miles into the Chukchi Sea, about 330 miles southwest of Barrow, on the North Slope of Alaska. It is the westernmost village in the North Slope Borough. Point Lay is the next village to the east in the North Slope Borough, but Shishmaref to the south is 125 miles closer.

PHYSICAL DESCRIPTION
The peninsula on which the village is located, Point Hope or Tikerq Peninsula (or Promontory), forms the westernmost extension of the northwest Alaska coast. The village area encompasses 6.3 square miles of land and 0.1 square mile of water at an elevation of 40 feet above sea level. Point Hope lies within 100 miles of the northern border of the Cape Krusenstern National Monument and approximately 100 miles of the westernmost border of the Noatak National Preserve. There has been no flooding at the new town site. In the 1970s, the community moved 2 miles to the east from the original location, which was subject to flooding. At the old village site, flooding was in low areas and depressions, mostly caused by hydrostatic pressure from offshore waves forcing ground wa-

ter to rise. Wave run-up from a 1991 storm reached an elevation of about 10 to 11 feet at the north end of the runway. The Chukchi Sea surrounds the Point Hope Promontory on three sides. Up to five miles from the shore, the water reaches depths of no more than 60 feet. The shoreline consists of cliffs and beach ridges. The cliffs, which rise from 3 to 1,000 feet, are paralleled by sand and gravel beaches. Sediments deposited by the Ipewik and Kukpuk branches of the Kuukpak River form the beach ridges that extend into the sea in a triangular shape. Area mountains reach elevations of 1,000-2,000 feet-the Lisburne Hills to the north and the Kemegrak Hills to the south of the village. Sea ice can be present from October to early July. Point Hope is located 90 miles north of the latitudinal tree line and 40 miles north of the last alder shrubs.

CLIMATE
Point Hope is located in the Arctic climate zone with temperatures ranging from winter lows of -49°F to summer highs of 78°F. Precipitation is light, only 10 inches annually, with average snowfalls totaling 36 inches. The Chukchi Sea is ice free from late June until mid-September. At this extreme northern latitude the sun is up for almost 80 days from mid-May until late July or early August and for approximately 60 days, from mid-November until mid-January.

CULTURE AND HISTORY
The Point Hope Peninsula is one of the longest continually inhabited areas in North America. Some of the earliest residents came to hunt bowhead whales over 2,000 years ago, after crossing the Siberian land bridge. Visitors to the area can see the remains of Old Tigara Village, a prehistoric site with the remains of sod houses. There is an even earlier site with about 800 house pits, known as Ipiutak, which was occu

pied from around 500 BC to AD 100. Ipiutak and the surrounding archaeological district are on the National Register of Historic Places. In addition to the prehistoric village sites, there are old burial grounds in the area, including a cemetery marked by large whalebones standing on end.

The Tikeraqmuit Inupiat people historically exercised dominion over a vast region extending from the Utukok to Kivalin Rivers and to areas far inland. Commercial whaling activities brought westerners, many of whom hired local villagers. By the late 1880s, shore-based whaling stations such as Jabbertown had been established, but these disappeared with the demise of commercial whaling in the early 1900s. Point Hope's government was incorporated in 1966 and in the early 1970s the village was moved to the present location because of erosion and periodic storm flooding from the Chukchi Sea. Today, Point Hope is a culturally intact Tikeraqmuit Inupiat village with a culture and economy based largely on marine subsistence activities.

GOVERNMENT
Point Hope was incorporated as a second-class city in 1966, with a mayor and city council. It is located in the North Slope Borough of Alaska. It also has an Indian Reorganization Act village council, headed by a president.

VILLAGE CORPORATION
Shareholders in the village corporation also hold shares in the Arctic Slope regional Native corporation, active in the oil industry *(see Alaska introduction)*. Tikigaq Corporation has five U.S. Small Business Administration 8(a) certified subsidiary companies: Aglaq Construction Enterprises, Agviq Environmental Services LLC, Tikigaq Engineering Services, Naniq Systems, and Tikigaq Technology Services.

ECONOMY
Point Hope is the second-largest city on the North Slope, with an economy largely based on subsistence hunting and fishing. The North Slope Borough employs more than 40 percent of the working population, and the school district employs another 28 percent. Close to one-fourth of the labor force works in the private sector. The median household income surveyed in the 2000 census was $63,125, the highest in Alaska. The Arctic Slope Regional Corporation is largely responsible for the high levels of economic development initiatives and construction projects in the area. Residents produce a wide array of arts and crafts, including carved ivory, Eskimo clothing and parkas, baleen, baskets, whalebone masks, caribou-skin masks, etched baleen, Eskimo parkas, ivory-tipped harpoons, and bird spears. These are marketed through the Chukchi Sea Trading Company, a Native arts and crafts cooperative.

Government as employer. City, borough, state or federal governments employ 152 Point Hope residents.

Services and retail. Private businesses include a grocery store, a general store, a vehicle dealership, a dog kennel, a child-care service, a bookkeeping service, and a restaurant. The peninsula offers good access to marine mammals, and ice conditions allow easy boat launchings in the spring whaling season. Seals, bowhead whales, beluga whales, caribou, polar bears, birds, fish, and berries are harvested.

INFRASTRUCTURE
Transportation. Air travel is Point Hope's only year-round means of access. There is a state-owned 4,000- by 75 foot paved airstrip served by Bering Air, Cape Smythe Air Ser-

vice, Grant Aviation, Hageland Aviation, Servant Air, and Tanana Air Service. In 2000, snow removal equipment was purchased and permanently housed at the airport. The city is accessible by boat during the summer months, and barge services bring bulk goods at that time. During the winter, land transportation by means of all-terrain vehicles and snowmobiles is also possible. Point Hope also has a public transportation system using buses. As of 2003 there were plans to pave approximately five miles of existing streets in conjunction with underground utility improvements which would involve excavation of about half the street system in 2004. Lodging is offered to guests of residents and tourists at the Whaler's Inn.

Electricity is provided by the Borough, which generates power at a 2,925-kilowatt diesel plant.

Fuel storage (gallons). NSB/Tikigag Corporation Fuel Station (1,237,000); NSB Municipal (10,000); NSB Fire (7,000); Alaska National Guard (5,000); NSB Maintenance (5,000); NSB Schools (4,000); NSB Sewage Plant (2,500); NSB Power Plant (2,000).

Water and waste systems. Water is obtained from a lake six miles to the east and is filtered, chlorinated, and stored in a tank prior to distribution. Desiring a water/sewer system with household plumbing, flush toilets, and showers, the community began an ambitious upgrade of water and sewer facilities in 1999, continuing through 2002. The borough maintains a washeteria and operates a landfill.

Telecommunications. Local telephone service is provided by the Arctic Slope Telephone Association Cooperative, and long distance services are available from AT&T Alascom, GCI, and Arctic Slope Telephone. Internet services are provided by GCI. One AM radio station serves the area, and one FM radio station broadcasts from Point Hope. Cable television is available from the City of Point Hope, and the Alaska Rural Communications System broadcasts television to the area.

COMMUNITY FACILITIES AND SERVICES
North Slope Borough (NSB) provides all utilities in Point Hope. In 2003, there were plans to open a community recreation center and a visitor center at Point Hope.

Education. The new village was almost literally built around the Tikigaq School, which offers classes from preschool through 12th grade and adult basic-education classes. It has 261 students and 26 teachers. As of March 2003, the principal of the school reported that it had 293 students. It is a member of the North Slope Borough School District, operated by the borough. The city maintains a community library.

Health care is provided by the Point Hope Health Clinic, owned by the North Slope Borough, leased to the U.S. Public Health Service and operated by the North Slope Regional Health Corporation. While the clinic is supported by the hospital in Barrow, the hospitals in Nome, Kotzebue, and Bethel are actually closer. Any treatment requiring a physician must be provided at Kotzebue, 180 air miles away. Major health care is provided in Anchorage at the Alaska Native Medical Center.

Public safety. Law enforcement is provided by the North Slope Borough Police Department. The city operates a volunteer fire department, which also has emergency rescue services and equipment.

Point Lay

Ethnicity: Inupiat

Native entity
Native Village of Point Lay
P.O. Box 59
Point Lay, AK 99759
907-833-2775
907-833-2576 Fax

ANCSA village corporation
Cully Corporation Inc.
P.O. Box 59089
Point Lay, AK 99759
907-833-2705
907-833-2715 Fax

Total area of entitlement under ANCSA	
	90,009 acres
Total labor force	100
High school graduate or higher	43
Bachelor's degree or higher	7
Unemployment rate	4.0%
Per capita income *(1999)*	$18,003
Population *2000 census*	247
Current population	265
state demographer estimate	
Percent Native *2000 census*	88.3%

LOCATION

Point Lay is an unincorporated village located in the North Slope Borough south of the Kokolik River mouth, about 182 miles west-southwest of Barrow. The next community to the west along the coastline is Point Hope, 135 miles west-south-west. The next community to the east along the coastline is Wainwright, 93 miles east-northeast.

PHYSICAL DESCRIPTION

The area encompasses 30.5 square miles of land and 4.0 square miles of water. In spite of its Inupiat name, the area around Point Lay is flat tundra.

CLIMATE

The climate is Arctic. Temperatures range from -55°F to 78°F. Precipitation is light, averaging 6.9 inches annually, with snow-fall of 21 inches. The Chukchi Sea is ice free from late June until September.

CULTURE AND HISTORY

The Inupiat name for the village, Kali (also spelled Culi or Cully), means "mound". Point Lay is one of the more recently established Inupiaq villages on the Arctic coast, and has historically been occupied year round by a small group of one or two families. They were joined in 1929-30 by several more families from Point Hope. The deeply indented shoreline has prevented effective bowhead whaling, but the village participates in beluga whaling. In 1974, the village moved from the old site on a gravel barrier island just offshore. The old village site is now used as a summer hunting camp. Some residents of Barrow and Wainwright relocated to the village in the mid-1970s. Due to seasonal flooding from the Kokolik River, in the late 1970s the village relocated again to a site near the Air Force Distant Early Warning station to the south. Homes were relocated to the new townsite. Point Lay is a traditional Inupiat Eskimo village, with a dependence subsistence activities. For recreation, residents enjoy snowmobiling, hunting, fishing, and trapping. There are two churches (Point Lay Baptist, St. Alban's Episcopal). There are a number of regionally recognized artists, craftsmen, and dancers.

GOVERNMENT

Unlike the other seven communities in North Slope Borough, Point Lay is not incorporated. The Borough is responsible for almost all government functions and services. North Slope Borough has employees at Point Lay, including the clinic staff, elections registrar, fire department, municipal services, police department, teleconference center, village liaison, washeteria, and wildlife management. The Native Village of Point Lay is the BIA-recognized IRA village council. The council has a mayor, a vice-mayor, a secretary/treasurer, and four members. Cully Corporation is the ANCSA village corporation.

VILLAGE CORPORATION

Cully Corporation has a chairman, a president/CEO, vice president, corporate secretary, treasurer, assistant treasurer, and two additional directors. The Anchorage office address is: 3820 Lake Otis Parkway, Suite #111, Anchorage, AK 99508; Phone: 907-569-2705; Fax: 907-569-2715. Shareholders in the village corporation also hold shares in Artic Slope regional Native corporation *(see Alaska introduction)*.

ECONOMY

Point Lay's economy is primarily based on subsistence hunting, fishing, and whaling. Economic opportunities in Point Lay are influenced by the fact that it is relatively isolated and is the smallest village in the region. Most year-round employment opportunities are with the borough government. Most private employment is with Cully Corporation and Arctic Slope Regional Corporation. A construction company (Beluga Construction) and a bush air carrier (Cape Smythe) have offices in Point Lay. Subsistence activities provide food; seals, walrus, beluga, caribou, and fish are staples of the diet.

Government as employer. Village, borough, state, and federal governments employ 64 Point Lay residents.

INFRASTRUCTURE

Transportation. A public 3,519- by 80-foot gravel airstrip, owned by the U.S. Air Force, provides Point Lay's only year-round access. The FAA is funding extensive improvements planned for fiscal year 2005, including extending the runway and rehabilitating the runway lighting, for a total of $12,480,000. Service to Point Lay is available by scheduled airline flights and charters from Barrow. Sea access is available in the summer, and large freight is delivered by barge. Land access is dependent on cold, dry weather. Local road improvements were funded in 2002 and 2004 for a total of $1,550,000.

Electricity. The North Slope Borough provides public electricity from a 985-kilowatt diesel generator.

Fuel storage (gallons). Bulk fuel storage totals 586,000 gallons, all at borough facilities. Available fuel includes propane, diesel, and regular gasoline.

Water and waste systems. Water and sewage are provided by the North Slope Borough. Water is delivered from a fresh-water lagoon at a minimal cost. Households have water delivered to home tanks, which allows running water for the kitchen. The borough provides free trash and sewage pick-up services including honeybucket hauling. A piped water and sewer system is currently in the planning stages for Point Lay, including household plumbing, flush toilets and showers.

Telecommunications. Local telephone service is provided by the Arctic Slope Telephone Association Cooperative, long distance service by Arctic Slope Telephone and GCI, which is also the Internet service provider. Television is available by cable provided by the village and by an ARCS repeater. One AM radio station broadcasts to Point Lay.

COMMUNITY FACILITIES AND SERVICES

Public facilities include a cultural center, post office, police station, washeteria, and a fire station equipped with fire engines and an ambulance. The village council owns the store that sells groceries and clothing.

Education. Point Lay's Kali School provides education from preschool through grade 12, as well as adult basic education. It has 89 students and 10 teachers and is operated by the North Slope Borough Schools. It shares its library with the community.

Health care. A health clinic, staffed by community health aides, is open each day and is available 24 hours a day for emergencies. The nearest hospital is in Barrow. Fire, rescue, and auxiliary health care is provided by Point Lay Volunteer Fire Department.

Public safety. Law enforcement and emergency response are provided by North Slope Borough.

Port Graham

Total area of entitlement under ANCSA

	111,642 acres
Total labor force	76
High school graduate or higher	2
Bachelor's degree or higher	0
Unemployment rate	22.4%
Per capita income *(1999)*	$13,666
Current population	165
state demographer estimate	
Population *2000 census*	171
Percent Native *2000 census*	88.3%

LOCATION

The village of Port Graham is located at the southern end of the Kenai Peninsula on the shore of Graham Bay, an arm of Cook Inlet. It is adjacent to and east of Nanwalek, 7.5 air miles southwest of Seldovia, 28 air miles south of Homer, and about 180 air miles southwest of Anchorage.

PHYSICAL DESCRIPTION

Port Graham encompasses 5.9 square miles of land. The land is very gravelly and stony glacial till. Because of mild temperatures and heavy snowfall, soils seldom freeze. Steep slopes and poor drainage limit development potential in most of this area. In some areas, soils support stands of commercial timber, but logging is limited in most places due to rough terrain. Groundwater potential is severely limited by bedrock at or near the surface on slopes and by saltwater intrusion and high water table in some of the low-lying areas. Shallow alluvial fans support a few domestic wells, but community and industrial systems rely primarily on surface water. The Kenai Fjords National Park is entirely within Kenai Peninsula Borough and contains 76,000 acres belonging to Port Graham Corporation, English Bay Corporation, and Chugach Alaska, (the ANCSA corporations for Port Graham, Nanwalek, and the Prince William Sound region, respectively). This land has the potential to be developed for minerals, resorts, recreation residences, mariculture sites, fish camps, and other development uses, subject to Park Service regulations.

According to the Native Allotment Act of 1906, Alaska Natives could apply for up to 160 acres of land. This Act precedes and is separate from ANCSA and was suspended in 1971 after the passage of ANCSA. There are 72 allotments located on the tip of the peninsula with a total of 9,345 acres, primarily concentrated around the villages of Seldovia, English Bay, and Port Graham. These allotments, in most cases, have direct access to the coast and have economic potential, primarily timber.

CLIMATE

Winter temperatures range from 14°F to 27°F, summer temperatures from 45°F to 65°F. Average annual precipitation is 24 inches. Late spring and early fall frosts and moderate summer temperatures limit the total number of growing degree-days. During June, daylight increases to 19 hours.

CULTURE AND HISTORY

The Village of Port Graham is a traditional Chugash community and the native people of Port Graham call themselves *Sugpiaq,* meaning "real people." The Chugash cultural heritage is a six-thousand-year combination of Yupik Eskimo, Alutiiq, and several Indian groups (Athabascan, Tlingit) cultures. The language is primarily Alutiiq. The ancestors of the people of Port Graham came from villages on the south side of the Kenai Peninsula, along Prince William Sound. Port Graham's Alutiiq name, Paluwik, was also the name of one of the most important prehistoric village sites in Prince William Sound until the 1700s. The culture is strongly based on the traditional language, a subsistence lifestyle, cultural traditions, and self-government. The Native culture has been preserved and perpetuated through the handing down from generation to generation of the subsistence lifestyle including fishing, hunting, and berry picking, surviving both Russian and American impacts.

By 1909, Port Graham was the site of a cannery and wharf. With some interruptions, there has been a cannery or salmon processing plant there ever since. Port Graham is almost adjacent to Nanwalek. Although there are numerous familial connections between Port Graham and Nanwalek, the villages have very different characters. One historic difference is that Port Graham has a long-standing connection with commerce. Port Graham is the only remote village in the region to have two stores.

GOVERNMENT

Port Graham is an unincorporated village located in Kenai Peninsula Borough. It is governed by the Port Graham Village Council, a traditional council and federally recognized Indian tribe. The village council is a five-member council, comprised of the first chief, second chief, secretary, treasurer, and a member. The council operates a wide variety of social, cultural, community development, and economic development programs. More than half of the land within the village consists of pre-ANCSA Native Allotments managed by the federal Bureau of Land Management.

VILLAGE CORPORATION

Shareholders in Port Graham Corporation, the ANCSA village corporation, are also shareholders in Chugash Alaska Corporation, the regional Native corporation.

ECONOMY

Port Graham is an isolated community accessible only by air or water. Its economy is based on fish processing, subsistence activities, logging, government services, and some private business activities. Conventional employment is primarily with the local school, the village council, the health clinic and commercial fishing. The regional ANCSA corporation, Chugach Alaska Corporation, appears to have a growing economic role in the community. Port Graham has a lumber store, aviation services, two general stores, and a fishing boat charter

Also known as Paluwik

Ethnicity: Chugash

Native entity
Port Graham Village Council
P.O. Box 5510
Port Graham, AK 99603
  907-284-2227
  907-284-2222 Fax

ANCSA village corporation
Port Graham Corporation
P.O. Box 5569
Port Graham, AK 99603
  907-284-2212
  907-284-2219 Fax

Port Graham

Also known as Paluwik

agency. Port Graham Corporation provides retail gasoline and bulk petroleum. Port Graham Corporation operates a washeteria. Accommodations for travelers include two bed-and-breakfasts. Tourism and recreation are not significant contributors to the economy of Port Graham.

Fish processing. A new $4.5 million fish cannery opened on June 19, 1999, the former plant and salmon hatchery having been destroyed by fire in 1998. Village members organized funding to rebuild the facilities because insurance covered only part of the loss. The cannery provides seasonal employment for 70 Port Graham and Nanwalek residents. The hatchery, a village council project, was rebuilt in a separate but adjacent building during the summer of 1999. Red salmon fry are raised for area lakes, and pink salmon are raised for the cannery. The major pink salmon-producing stream in this portion of the Kenai Peninsula Borough is the Graham, with escapement estimates ranging from 5,000 to 40,000 annually. Significant further investments in fish canning, processing, and the hatchery are contemplated.

Forestry. Timber is largely Sitka spruce with some mountain hemlock. The yield averages 20 to 25 thousand board feet per acre on the better sites. The majority of commercial forest stands have reached maturity and are losing volume to decay and insects.

Government as employer. Village, borough, state, and federal governments employ 20 workers.

Subsistence is traditionally and currently the predominant use of wild resources around Port Graham. Wild resources comprise a major proportion of the daily diets of village members, and play a significant role in the cultural and social structure of the community. A 1987 study found that Port Graham residents harvested 227.4 pounds of wild resources per person. Wild resources are shared widely among friends and relatives, and are important in passing knowledge between generations. Federal subsistence regulations vary over time. Subsistence food includes salmon and other cold-water fish, clams and other shellfish, octopus, crab, land and sea otter, harbor seal, sea lion, goat, moose, black bear, deer, grouse, duck, geese and other birds, eggs, salmonberry and other berries, goose tongue, and seaweed. The subsistence salmon fishing season in the Port Graham area extends from May 10 to September 30. The subsistence halibut fishing season occurs between February 1 and December 31. Shellfish and other marine invertebrates are harvested year-round. The expanding sea otter population has severely depleted the invertebrate species used for subsistence.

INFRASTRUCTURE
Transportation. Port Graham is accessible by air and water, and by land from Nanwalek only.

Air. A State-owned 1,975- by 45-foot dirt/gravel unattended VFR airstrip runs through the middle of Port Graham. Homer Air provides scheduled and air taxi services. Limited aircraft services are available. Delayed for several years due to land ownership issues, the Port Graham Airport Master Plan is expected to be implemented after FY 2006. The plan includes moving the airport up-valley to a more suitable site, with a 3,300-foot runway, at a cost exceeding $4 million.

Water. Port Graham offers substantial docking facilities, including the cannery dock, with a 110-foot face and mooring dolphins 40 feet off each end. It provides limited fish and cargo off-loading, fuel delivery, boat fueling, and moorage space for commercial fishing vessels. The largest boat typically to use the dock is a Petro Marine fuel barge 200 feet long. A floating skiff dock is currently tied alongside the cannery dock and is used by smaller boats. There is also a log transfer dock consisting of an earth-filled bulkhead with a 150-foot face. It was designed to have mooring anchors and buoys 150 feet off each end to handle log barges up to 400 feet long. The water depth at mean low water is 22 feet. Larger local fishing and workboats anchor in the bay but are not protected. Several other fishing boats are pulled out of the water. The village council is pursuing funds to build a breakwater for protected anchorage and a protected area for the floating skiff dock. There is a gravel beach ramp at an old Windy Bay log transfer facility site, and it is suitable for launching trailered small boats.

The Alaska Marine Highway (state ferry system) is evaluating the possibility of adding another vessel, which would allow the expansion of service to Port Graham. The village would like to be served by the state ferry system and have water transportation for its fish products. The community of Port Graham is very much in favor of a regular ferry connection to Homer and Seldovia.

Land. The trafficability of the four-mile trail from Nanwalek is unknown, but Nanwalek is otherwise accessible only by air and water as well. Port Graham has road access to Windy Bay on the south side of the Kenai Peninsula, trafficability unknown. The road serves as the primary route to resource development and subsistence use areas. Current conditions do not provide for the general use of the road. The village has asked that BIA fund improvement of this road for potential landfill and airport development, and for use as a tsunami evacuation road, at a cost of $2.5 million. There are no taxis or car rentals available.

Electricity. Electricity is provided by the Homer Electric Association, a Rural Electrical Association co-op, using hydroelectric and natural gas. The electrical supply is unreliable, with the marine electrical cable at the end of its useful life, aging electrical generators, and the recent retirement of the Seldovia-based repairman. Longer and more frequent electrical power outages are anticipated. With a 2.5-hour battery life on the phone system, residents may find themselves without access to 911 or other emergency services before power is restored.

Fuel storage (gallons). Port Graham Corporation owns a consolidated bulk fuel facility with a total tank capacity of 91,200 gallons.

Water and waste systems. The village council operates the water and sewage systems. Water from a small stream nearby is treated and stored in a 150,000-gallon tank built in 2000. Port Graham has a piped water system. Sewage is disposed in a community septic tank. A sludge lagoon was recently completed. This system serves 66 homes and facilities; almost 90 percent of households are fully plumbed. The community has requested funds for a new 150,000-gallon water storage tank to provide better treatment and pressure, and to connect its Duncan Heights Subdivision to the system. The Seldovia River has been identified as a future source of water, with the possibility of power generation from pumping water over the ridge to Port Graham and taking advantage of the drop to produce power. A large landfill (over four acres) is operated by the Port Graham Corporation under contract to the borough. Hazmat is periodically transported to Homer.

Telecommunications. Local telephone service is provided by ACS of the Northland, long distance service by AT&T Alascom. Wireless telephone access is poor. Local television service includes an ARCS repeater and PBS station KAKM. Three AM and one FM radio station broadcast to Port Graham. There is no cable provider, but satellite dish service is available.

COMMUNITY FACILITIES AND SERVICES

Public services and facilities are operated by a variety of organizations, including the village council, the borough, the regional Native Alaskan health organization, and Port Graham Corporation. Public buildings include the community center, which houses social services, tribal offices, and language and environmental programs; a fire hall/emergency services center multi-use facility; and elder supportive housing/assisted living. The school library is also the community library.

Education. Port Graham School provides education in grades K-10, with 32 students and three teachers. It is operated by the Kenai Peninsula Borough School District. The citizens of Port Graham place a great deal of emphasis on students getting a good education. "Our children must learn to adapt to both the village culture and the culture outside of the village." The school includes a small gym, three regular classrooms, a library, a science lab, and a computer lab with twelve computers for student use connected to the Internet via a two-way satellite connection.

Health care. Local health care is provided by the Port Graham Health Clinic, operated by Chugachmiut, the regional Native Alaskan health care organization. Higher levels of care are available by flight to Homer. Emergency care is provided by Port Graham EMS/Ambulance.

Public safety. There is no local law enforcement; state troopers are available in Homer. Rescue and fire response are provided by Port Graham EMS/Ambulance, a volunteer organization.

Port Graham
Also known as Paluwik

Port Heiden

Port Heiden

Total area of entitlement under ANCSA
69,120 acres

Total labor force	48
High school graduate or higher	21
Bachelor's degree or higher	7
Unemployment rate	16.7%
Per capita income *(1999)*	$20,532
Population *2000 census*	119
2003 population	87
state demographer estimate	
Percent Native *2000 census*	78.2%

LOCATION
Port Heiden is a spread-out fishing community at the mouth of the Meshik River on the north side of the Alaska Peninsula. It is 425 miles southwest of Anchorage and 8 miles away from the Aniakchak National Preserve and Monument.

PHYSICAL DESCRIPTION
It covers 50.7 square miles of land and 0.7 square mile of water. The terrain around the community is tundra and swamp. There has been no flooding at the city's new location.

CLIMATE
Port Heiden has a maritime climate, with cool, breezy summers, relatively warm winters, and rain. Snowfall averages 58 inches per year. January temperatures average 25 degrees, and July temperatures average 50 degrees. The climate is characterized by frequent and rapid weather changes, influenced by low-pressure cells over the Aleutians and highs over the mainland. The sun is above the horizon about 6 hours a day in December and 20 hours in June, and in midsummer darkness never really takes over the night.

CULTURE AND HISTORY
Port Heiden is located near the site of the old village of Meshik. Influenza epidemics during the early 1900s forced the residents of Meshik to relocate to other villages. During World War II, Fort Morrow was built nearby, and 5,000 soldiers were stationed there. The fort was abandoned after the war, but some area residents chose to stay. The army left behind a long airstrip and more than 60 miles of improved dirt roads. A school was established in the early 1950s, which attracted people from surrounding villages. Port Heiden incorporated in 1972. The community recently relocated inland five miles because storm waves had eroded much of the old town site and threatened to destroy community buildings. It is reported that the well-known black sand beaches of Port Heiden are eroding rapidly.

Port Heiden is a traditional Alutiiq community, with a commercial fishing and subsistence lifestyle. They are maritime people obtaining most of their food and livelihood from the sea. Historically, sea mammal hunters traveled long distances in their skin covered *qayaq.* Although traditionally the people called themselves *Sugpiaq* (*-suk* "person" plus *-piaq* "real"), the name *Alutiiq* was adopted from a Russian plural form of *Aleut,* which Russian invaders applied to the Native people they encountered from Attu to Kodiak. The Alutiiq language is closely related to Central Alaskan Yup'ik. The Old Russian imprint is strong, in the influence of the Orthodox church, Russian words in the vocabulary, and other cultural influences.

GOVERNMENT
Port Heiden is a second-class city located in the Lake & Peninsula Borough. The Native Village of Port Heiden is a Federally recognized tribe. The city government consists of a mayor and seven-member council. Day-to-day responsibilities are handled by an administrator and clerk. The Bristol Bay Native Association, a regional organization linking the area's traditional councils, provides the village public safety officer, a nutrition site manager, and a chore worker to Port Heiden.

VILLAGE CORPORATION
Kokhanok, Newhalen, Port Heiden, South Naknek, and Ugashik merged their respective ANCSA corporations into the Alaska Peninsula Corporation. The Alaska Peninsula Corporation does not seem to be a major contributor to Port Heiden's economy. Shareholders in Alaska Peninsula Corporation are also shareholders in Bristol Bay Native Corporation, the regional Native corporation.

ECONOMY
Most of Port Heiden's residents make their living salmon fishing near the Meshik River. Beyond commercial fishing, subsistence fishing and hunting of marine mammals provide a substantial part of the local diet, along with game, birds, plants, and berries. Tourism is not a large part of Port Heiden's economy, but the Alaska Peninsula National Wildlife Refuge and the Aniakchak National Monument and Preserve are nearby and attract visitors.

Fisheries. Most of Port Heiden's residents make their living salmon fishing. Twenty-one salmon fishing vessels are owned by residents, and seventeen residents hold commercial fishing permits. Subsistence fishing is also important to the com-

Also known as Meshik

[HIGH-dun]
Ethnicity: Koniagmiut Alutiiq

Municipality
City of Port Heiden
P.O. Box 49050
Port Heiden, AK 99549
    907-837-2209
    907-837-2248 Fax

Native entity
Native Village of Port Heiden
P.O. Box 49007
Port Heiden, AK 99549
    907-837-2296
    907-837-2297 Fax

ANCSA village corporation
Alaska Peninsula Corporation
800 Cordova Street #102
Anchorage, AK 99501
    907-274-2433
    907-274-8694 Fax

Port Heiden

Also known as Meshik

munity. There appears to be discussion about setting up a seafood cooperative.

Government as employer. As of the 2000 census, there were six government workers at all levels (city, borough, state, federal).

Services and retail. Private services in Port Heiden include four lodgings, a gift shop, a retail store, a photo studio or lab, a car rental agency, a guide service, and an airport services firm.

Transportation. Port Heiden hosts scheduled air service, air taxi service, and charter boats to the Alaska Peninsula National Wildlife Refuge and the Aniakchak National Monument and Preserve. Regular air transportation services are provided by Arctic Circle Air Service, Reeve Aleutian Airways, and Peninsula Airways.

INFRASTRUCTURE

Transportation. Access to Port Heiden is by air or water. It can be reached in winter, in good weather, by snowmobile. This may change dramatically if a proposed roads from Port Heiden to Ugashik is funded, at an estimated cost of $119,847,000, or a proposed road to Chignik Lagoon is built. Port Heiden, Chignik Lagoon, and the Bristol Bay Native Corporation support the latter.

When Fort Morrow was abandoned at the end of World War II, the army left 60 miles of improved dirt roads. The state upgraded some roads in the mid-1990s. BIA has scheduled further road construction in 2004. Local travel is by automobile, ATVs (called "hondas" by local residents), and snowmachine. There are no taxis, but there is a car rental company.

Port Heiden has a natural boat harbor, but there is no dock. Marine facilities include a boat haul-out with inside storage space for fur boats and outside space for 20 vessels, an unloading area on the beach, and additional storage facilities. Cargo from Seattle is delivered twice yearly by a BIA-chartered barge, and is lightered to and offloaded on the beach.

The airport, located near the old World War II military base, serves as the area's transportation hub. Passengers frequently change planes there when going to the communities on the south (Pacific) side of the Alaska Peninsula. The state-owned airport consists of an unattended, lighted gravel runway, 5,000 feet long by 100 feet wide, that can accommodate up to Boeing 737 aircraft. The runway is soft when wet and during the spring thaw. The only services provided are cargo handling. Traffic is at a rate of 3,500 operations per year. In 2003 the FAA funded rehabilitation of the runway and construction of runway safety areas for a total cost of $4,444,000. The resurfac-

ing of the runway was scheduled for completion in October, 2003. BIA funded upgrading the airport road in 2001, and the Alaska Department of Transportation has funded various improvements including fencing, a rescue and firefighting building, and equipment.

Electricity. The city provides electricity from a 375-kilowatt diesel generator, installed in 1993. There is also a wind energy project in Port Heiden.

Fuel storage. Bulk fuel tank capacity exceeds a half-million gallons.

Water and waste systems. Individual wells are used by most homes. The school operates its own well. Of 37 occupied households 31 are fully plumbed. Individual septic tank systems are used by most homes. The school operates its own treatment system. The city provides septic pumping services and collects refuse three times a week. The landfill is located 6.5 miles northeast of the community. A feasibility study for community sanitation improvements was funded in 2003, as were four new wells and six new septic fields.

Telecommunications. All homes, private, and public buildings have access to telephone service. One AM radio station broadcasts to the area. Local telephone service is provided by ACS of the Northland, long distance and Internet service by GCI.

COMMUNITY FACILITIES AND SERVICES

The relocation of Port Heiden from the coast required new public facilities. The new community center houses the clinic, the city office, a recreational center, a kitchen, and rooms for guests. Another multipurpose public building has been proposed. The city has an airport manager and provides electricity, bulk fuel storage, and refuse collection. Law enforcement is provided by a village public safety officer, backed by state troopers in Dillingham. Emergency response is provided by the Port Heiden Rescue Squad.

Education. Meshik School, operated by Lake and Peninsula Borough, provides education in grades K-12 to between 32 and 38 students. There are three teachers and eight staff members, four classrooms, a computer lab, a library, a small gymnasium, and a kitchen. The gym and the library are the only such facilities in the community, and the school library serves as the community's public library.

Health care. Health care is provided by the Port Heiden Health Clinic, operated by the Bristol Bay AHC, backed by the rescue squad. The new multipurpose building includes upgraded space for the clinic.

Total area of entitlement under ANCSA
    239,008 acres (including Afognak)
Total labor force   95
High school graduate or higher   59
Bachelor's degree or higher   34
Unemployment rate   4.2%
Per capita income *(1999)* $17,492
Population *2000 census*   256
2003 population   251
    state demographer estimate
Percent Native *2000 census*   63.7%

LOCATION
Port Lions is a coastal community of around 250 people located on both sides of Settler Cove, on the north coast of Kodiak Island, 247 air miles southwest of Anchorage and 34 miles northwest of Kodiak City.

PHYSICAL DESCRIPTION
The area encompasses 6.3 square miles of land and 3.7 square miles of water. Settler Cove is well-sheltered, and the community is located in a transition zone between a spruce forest to the north and high brush and grasses to the south. Port Lions is built on Tertiary and Cretaceous granitic rock, surrounded by Cretaceous and Upper Jurassic rocks. There are marine bird colonies and deer high-density areas nearby. Significant coastal erosion has occurred in several places in Port Lions, primarily along roadways, where heavy rains have washed out roads. Erosion may limit residential and commercial development as well as damage municipal buildings in a few places. Kodiak Island and the nearby mainland experience frequent earthquakes with magnitudes below 6.0 on the Richter scale. Since 1899, 82 earthquakes of Richter magnitude 6.0 or greater have been recorded in the area, and 26 of these were actually triggered within the area. The 1964 Alaska earthquake and resultant tsunami provide a relatively recent example of the very real threat posed by earthquake activity. The earthquake and tsunami destroyed the village of Afognak, causing those residents to relocate and rebuild Port Lions at its present location. Port Lions is still vulnerable to the possible effects of an earthquake and resultant tsunami, and many residents still remember the 1964 event. It has been reported that during extreme high tides and correct wind conditions, the resulting storm surge may overtop Kizhuyak Drive, but no flooding had been reported as of 2002. Although most of the forest areas in the Port Lions region are relatively small when compared to other areas in Alaska, it is among the more forested areas in the Kodiak region. Fires have occurred in Port Lions the past and have threatened populated areas. In 1912, the Kodiak region was blanketed in volcanic ash from the Katmai/Novarupta eruption on the Katmai Coast.

CLIMATE
The climate is dominated by a strong marine influence. There is frequent cloud cover and fog, moderate precipitation, and little or no freezing weather. Temperatures remain within a narrow range, from 20°F to 60°F. Severe storms are common in the winter. Average annual precipitation is 54 inches, including 75 inches of snow. There are no regular occurrences of severe weather such as typhoons or tornadoes; however weather extremes such as high winds, large hail, or heavy rainfall threaten the area. Winds in excess of 50 miles per hour occur occasionally, and wind gusts may reach speeds of 90 miles per hour or more. Freezing rain, occasional heavy snowfall, and high winds are the dominant winter weather hazards that affect the area. Periods of extreme cold occur on a less frequent basis.

CULTURE AND HISTORY
In 1964, the Alutiiq village of Afognak was destroyed by a tsunami. The former residents founded Port Lions, named in honor of the Lions Clubs for their financial support in rebuilding. Port Lions was incorporated as a second-class city in 1966. Afognak was a federally recognized Native village, and the Port Lions Traditional Tribal Council was recognized as well. The former has been merged into the latter. Similarly, Afognak and Port Lions each had its own ANCSA village corporation, each of which had its own land entitlements. They have merged into the Afognak Native Corporation. The majority of the population are Alutiiq. The Native language is now spoken fluently by fewer than 30 Alutiiq people. Efforts are being made to preserve and revive the Alutiiq culture. Most residents lead a commercial fishing and subsistence lifestyle. Popular recreational activities are hunting, biking, fishing, and four-wheeling.

GOVERNMENT
Port Lions is incorporated as a second-class city, located in Kodiak Island Borough. The mayor of the city, the president of the tribal council, and the president of the village corporation are different people, and the organizations have different office locations and contact information.

The Port Lions Traditional Tribal Council, formed by the merger of the Afognak and Port Lions councils, is the BIA-recognized tribe and village council.

VILLAGE CORPORATION
The ANCSA village corporation is Afognak Native Corporation, formed by the merger of the village corporations of Afognak and Port Lions in 1977. Afognak Native Corporation was formed in 1977 through the merger of Port Lions Native Corporation and Natives of Afognak, Inc., two original ANCSA corporations. The shareholders of both corporations are all descendants of residents of old Afognak Village on Afognak Island. The corporation cuts spruce on Afognak Island. Subsidiary Alaska Timber Marketing provides marketing and shipping services for timber products from the State of Alaska. This company's primary responsibility is to export 25 million board feet of Alaska Sitka Spruce annually from Afognak Island. In its own name, through Afognak Joint Venture (of which Afognak Native Corporation owns 45 percent), and together with the other village corporations from Kodiak Island, Afognak Native Corporation controls timber rights or owns outright most of Afognak Island. In November 1998, the Afognak Joint Venture sold surface title to about 41,350 acres of land on northern Afognak Island to the state and federal governments, retaining timber rights to some 2,213 acres for 15 years. The price was $74 million.

Afognak Native Corporation provides management services to the joint venture, and has become one of the most successful providers of contract services to the federal government through its subsidiary, Alutiiq, LLC. Alutiiq began by capturing the base operating support contract at Kirtland Air Force Base, New Mexico. Alutiiq now has over 2300 employees providing contract services in 14 states and 5 countries, with annualized revenues of approximately $150 million. Afognak Native Corporation also develops local tourism-based indus-

Ethnicity: Alutiiq

Municipality
City of Port Lions
P.O. Box 110
Port Lions, AK 99550
    907-454-2332
    907-454-2420 Fax

Native entity
Port Lions Traditional Tribal
    Council
P.O. Box 69
Port Lions, AK 99550
    907-454-2234
    907-454-2434 Fax

ANCSA village corporation
Merged corporations of Afognak and Port Lions
    Afognak Native Corporation
    215 Mission Road #212
    Kodiak, AK 99615
        907-486-6014
        907-486-2514 Fax

Port Lions

tries, such as subsidiary Kodiak Sports and Tour, which offers sport fishing, water taxi service, wildlife viewing, boat charters, and serves as a tour-booking service for the area. "Port Lions ... offers the amenities of larger destinations such as full-service hunting and fishing lodges, the beauty of waterfalls tucked away in spruce-filled coves, beach combing, and sea kayaking through the still, blue waters of Kizkuyak Bay."

ECONOMY

Since its founding, the economy of Port Lions has been based primarily on commercial fishing, fish processing, logging, and tourism. Twenty-four residents hold commercial fishing permits, and all of the residents depend to some extent on subsistence food sources such as salmon, crab, halibut, shrimp, clams, duck, seal, deer, and rabbit. However, the Afognak Native Corporation has become a major factor in the economic well-being of the community. *(See VILLAGE CORPORATION above.)*

Most private businesses in Port Lions are travel-and-tourism related, including five lodging and food and seven boat charters and fishing and hunting guides. Others include a commercial fishing vessel, a fuel oil dealer, two field outfitters, and two general stores. In season, floating processors operate at the city dock. However, there are no cannery or cold storage facilities that would attract more fishing ventures. As of 2003, the city, the tribal council, and the village corporation have proposed building a seafood processing plant (cannery and cold storage) on the old Wakefield cannery site. It is near the city dock and the infrastructure associated with the cannery remains.

Government as employer. As of 2000 census, there were 57 government workers at all levels (city, borough, state, and federal).

INFRASTRUCTURE

Transportation. Port Lions is accessible by air and water. The state ferry operates bimonthly from Homer and Kodiak city between April and October. Barge service is available from Seattle. The City dock and harbor provide 82 boat slips. The city dock and harbor, including a new breakwater and water main, were built in 1992-96. In 2003, the Army Corps of Engineers provided $5 million for further harbor construction, with the design work due in August 2006. Improvements including extending the breakwater, a dry dock, cold storage, and a warehouse have been proposed.

Regular and charter flights are available from Kodiak and elsewhere into the existing Port Lions Airport or by seaplane to the city dock. Air access to Port Lions is always weather-dependent. There are approximately eight scheduled flights daily from Anchorage to Kodiak city, and approximately six scheduled flights daily from Kodiak city to Port Lions. The main airlines for this route are Peninsula Airlines and Island Air Service. Flight time from Kodiak to Port Lions is about ten (10) minutes, and the cost approximately $60 round trip. (Note that the Anchorage-Kodiak flight costs around $250 round trip.) Once you get to Port Lions, however, there are no taxis or rental cars. Accommodations are available. The Port Lions Airport is an unattended state-owned 2,200- by 75-foot gravel airstrip. No aircraft services are available. It is well-used, with some 5,300 flight operations per year. The Federal Aviation Administration has funded a master plan study of Port Lions' airport requirements, and plans to fund construction of a new airport for $8 million.

Electricity is provided by the Kodiak Electric Association, a Rural Electric Association cooperative utility. Kodiak Electric operates and purchases power from the state-owned Terror Lake Hydroelectric Facility and operates a diesel-powered plant in Port Lions.

Fuel. Bulk fuel oil is provided by Kizhuyak Oil Sales, which owns a 90,600-gallon tank with the Village Council. Kodiak Electric also has a 1,100-gallon fuel tank.

Water and waste systems. The present community water and sewer system was built in 1992-93. More than 100 residences are connected and 95 percent of these have complete plumbing. Further improvements were made in 2003, and improvements to the water treatment plant have been requested. The Branchwater Creek Reservoir provides water, which is treated and stored in a 125,000-gallon tank. After years of repairs, the reservoir dam was replaced in 1999-00. The sewer system includes a community septic tank and sewage lift station. A new two-acre landfill site has been established. The city operates the water and sanitation systems.

Telecommunications. Local telephone service is provided by Interior Telephone (subsidiary of TelAlaska); long distance by AT&T Alascom or Interior Telephone. Television service is transmitted by satellite (Dish Network), cable (Eyecom Cable, Inc.—subsidiary of TelAlaska) and Alaska Rural Communications Service repeater. One FM public radio station broadcasts from Port Lions, and residents can receive several AM stations from Kodiak, Anchorage, and Homer. Many residents have CB radios, and some have VHF marine radios, although these cannot reach Kodiak. There are telephones in most homes. Telephone service in Port Lions is dependent upon electrical supply. Without electricity, the phones would cease working after one or two days of running on battery power. There is a single side band (SSB) radio at the clinic, but it does not function reliably; the Harbormaster has another.

COMMUNITY FACILITIES AND SERVICES

Education. The Port Lions School is operated by the Kodiak Island Borough School District. It has 48 students in grades K—12, with six teachers. Afognak Native Corporation provides financial support to students for higher education, vocational education, and other career enhancement. The Jessie Wakefield Memorial Library's collection includes 10,000 books and periodicals, 180 audio items, and 390 video items for circulation, plus Internet terminals for use by the public. Considering it serves a population of around 250 people, it is an interesting reflection on the community that patrons make 4,000 visits each year, and check out materials 7,500 times.

Health care. Health care is provided locally by the Port Lions Clinic, which is operated by the Kodiak Area Native Association. The Port Lions Clinic provides basic health care and emergency medical services. Providence Kodiak Island Medical Center in Kodiak City provides emergency room and advanced medical treatment. Port Lions has an ambulance and a clinic van, but as of 1999 the ambulance was in need of repair. The clinic is stocked with a diverse collection of medical equipment and supplies and can handle initial medical response to almost any kind of emergency.

Public safety. Law enforcement is provided by the village public safety officer (VPSO), backed by the state troopers in Kodiak City. Fire and rescue are provided by Port Lions Fire Department. The VPSO is the fire chief.

Total area of entitlement under ANCSA
130,673 acres

Current Population 61
State Demographer estimate
Population *2000 census* 36
Percent Native *2000 census* 81.6%

LOCATION
Portage Creek is located at the mouth of Portage Creek, a tributary of the Nushagak River, 29 air miles southeast of Dillingham.

PHYSICAL DESCRIPTION
Portage Creek covers 13.1 square miles of land. The surrounding terrain for a distance of about five miles is flat grasslands with stands of cottonwood and spruce, with moist tundra outside the immediate vicinity of the creek. Beyond that radius, the trees give way to numerous lakes of all sizes. The geology in the immediate area of the community is coastal interlayered alluvial and marine sediments surrounded by glacial moraine and drift. The Nushagak River and Portage Creek are both major anadromous fish streams, thus attractive to bears, and the area is a medium density waterfowl area.

CLIMATE
Portage Creek is located in a climatic transition zone. The primary influence is maritime, although a continental climate affects the weather. Average summer temperatures range from 30°F to 66°F; winter temperatures range from well below zero to 30°F. Annual precipitation ranges from 20 to 35 inches. Fog and low clouds are common during the summer. The Nushagak River is ice-free from June through mid-November.

CULTURE AND HISTORY
This site was used for generations by the Yup'ik Eskimos as an overnight summer camp. Portage Creek was so named because it was used to portage boats from the Nushagak River to the Kvichak River, so travelers could avoid the open waters of Bristol Bay and the long trip around Etolin Point. The village was permanently settled in 1961 by some families from Koliganek and other villages up the Nushagak River. A Bureau of Indian Affairs school was established in 1963. By 1965, eleven families lived in the settlement. The 1980 census listed 48 residents, although the Bristol Bay Native Association estimated a population of 80 in that year. Through the mid-1980s Portage Creek was an active community, but the population subsequently declined. As the children from the original families graduated from the eighth grade, families moved to Dillingham and New Stuyahok where better school facilities were available. The village is a popular recreational fishing and camping site from May through July and a hunting location for Yup'ik residents of the area.

GOVERNMENT
Portage Creek is not incorporated and is located in the Unorganized Borough. Government is by the Portage Creek Village Council, a traditional council recognized by the BIA as the Ohgsenakale Tribe. There is also a community non-profit organization, the Portage Creek Association, which may be the same as the Ohgsenakale Association formed when Portage Creek's ANCSA village corporation merged with that of Dillingham.

VILLAGE CORPORATION
Portage Creek's ANCSA village corporation, Ohgsenakale, merged with Dillingham's village corporation, Choggiung, Limited. Members of Portage Creek's former village corporation formed the Ohgsenakale Association to provide land management guidelines to Choggiung, Limited.

ECONOMY
The residents of Portage Creek primarily depend on subsistence fishing and hunting and hosting recreational sport fishermen and hunters. A guide service operates year-round. A general store and lodge operates during the summer months. The Nushagak River is claimed to be the most productive king salmon river in the world and also hosts rainbow, grayling, and pike. The area is prime country for hunting moose, caribou, duck, and geese. Relating to subsistence activities, the residents have an exchange (barter) arrangement with several villages closer to the sea. Since 1999 the residents have been eligible to take part in Alaska's Community Development Quota program, which gives rural coastal villages a share of the Bering Sea commercial fishing harvests.

Government as employer. There are no government employees in Portage Creek.

INFRASTRUCTURE
Transportation. Travel in and out of Portage Creek is by air, by boat, or in the winter by snowmobile. There are no improved roads in or to Portage Creek, although in 1998 the state funded trail improvements. The Portage Creek Airport is owned by the State of Alaska and is maintained during the summer months. It has two runways; the longest is a gravel runway extending 1,920 feet. The airport is at an elevation of 137 feet and is located within a mile of the village. Seaplanes may land on the Nushagak River. Cargo goods are lightered to the beach, as there are no docking facilities.

Electricity. Electrical power is provided by individual generators, and there are no natural gas suppliers.

Water and waste systems. Water is obtained by local haul from the Nushagak River. Sewage is removed by honey buckets.

Telecommunications. Local telephone service is provided by the Nushagak Telephone Co-op, long distance by AT&T Alascom. Internet service is provided by GCI at the Portage Creek School. Satellite (dish) telecom services are available. One television station and two radio stations transmit to the Portage Creek area.

COMMUNITY FACILITIES AND SERVICES
Education. The Portage Creek School, grades K-8, had 14 students and two teachers as of 2002.

Health care. Portage Creek has no local health care facilities; the nearest health care facility is in Dillingham.

Also known as Ohgsenakale

Ethnicity: Yup'ik

Native entity
Portage Creek Village Council
P.O. Box PCA
Portage Creek, AK 99576
907-842-1299
907-842-1299 Fax

ANCSA village corporation
Choggiung, Limited
P.O. Box 330
Dillingham, AK 99576
907-842-5218
907-842-5462 Fax

Community non-profit; appropriate village entity
Portage Creek Association
c/o Choggiung
Portage Creek, AK 99576
907-842-5218
907-842-5462 Fax

Pribilof Islands

[PRI-bill-off]
Ethnicity: Unangan

Municipalities
City of Saint George
P.O. Box 929
Saint George Island, AK 99591
907-859-2263
907-859-2212 Fax

City of Saint Paul
P.O. Box 901
Saint Paul Island, AK 99660
907-546-2331
907-546-3199 Fax

Native entity
Pribilof Islands Aleut Commu-
nities of Saint Paul and Saint
George Islands
P.O. Box 940
Saint George Island, AK 99591
907-859-2205
907-859-2242 Fax

ANCSA village corporations
Saint George Tanaq
Corporation
2600 Denali Street, Suite 300
Anchorage, AK 99503
907-272-9886
907-272-9855 Fax
stgeorgetanaq.com

Tanadgusix Corporation
P.O. Box 88
Saint Paul Island, AK 99660
907-546-2312
907-546-2366 Fax
beringsea.com

NOTE
"Pribilof Islands Aleut Communities of Saint Paul and Saint George Islands" is a single Alaskan Native entity with two cities, Saint George and Saint Paul. They are also separate census areas. Therefore, this profile is organized differently from others in this Guide.

	St. George	St. Paul	Total
Total area of entitlement under ANCSA	129,082	154,413	283,495
Total labor force	79	298	377
High school graduate or higher	26.2%	25.0%	25.3%
Bachelor's degree or higher	8.1%	7.2%	7.4%
Unemployment rate	3.8%	13.4%	11.4%
Per capita income (1999)	$21,131	$18,408	$18,998
Population [(2000 census)]	149	539	688
Current population	152	532	684
2003 state demographer estimate			
Percent Native [(2000 census)]	92.1%	86.5%	87.7%

LOCATION
The five Pribilof Islands are located at the southern edge of the Bering Sea shelf in the south-central Bering Sea, 300 miles west of the Alaska mainland and 250 miles north of the Aleutian Islands. The City of Saint George is located on Saint George Island, the second largest of the islands, situated on a small bay on the northeastern shore of the island. The City of Saint Paul is located on Saint Paul Island, the largest of the five islands, on the southern tip of the island. The islands of Saint George and Saint Paul are 47 miles apart, to the north and south respectively. They are 800 miles southwest of Anchorage and 250 to 300 miles northwest of Dutch Harbor.

PHYSICAL DESCRIPTION
The Pribilof Islands were formed about 2.2 million years ago by the eruption of basaltic lava onto the southern edge of the Bering Sea shelf. Fossil remains (including mammoths) on the islands date back to the Pleistocene Epoch. The islands are vegetated with lush grass, dwarf willows (the only native trees), lichen, mosses, and flowering plants. The Pribilof Islands are in the most diverse biological region in the Northern Hemisphere. The islands provide nesting and breeding grounds for thousands of migratory marine mammals and birds. More than 2.5 million seabirds (more than 210 species) nest along the cliffs of the northern coast of Saint George Island. It is the largest seabird colony in the Northern Hemisphere and includes species such as puffins, murres, auklets, and kittiwakes. Two-thirds of the world's population of fur seals-1.3 to 1.4 million-migrate to the Pribilofs to breed and rear their young. The Bering Sea is inhabited by halibut and many marine invertebrates. The nearly extinct and now protected northern right whale has been seen near the island. The uplands are home to songbirds, blue foxes, lemmings, and a small herd of reindeer (introduced in 1911) on Saint George.

Saint George Island is 11 miles long by two miles wide, with steep sea cliffs (up to 1,012 feet) and a surface terrain that has been smoothed by glaciers; the former volcanic cones are now rounded hills. The City of Saint George is situated on a small bay on the northeastern shore of the island, while the new port at Zapadni Bay is on the southwestern shore. The remainder of the island is undeveloped. The City of Saint George includes 34.8 square miles of land and 147.6 square miles of water.

Saint Paul Island was formed about 1.2 million years ago and future eruptions of lava are expected. The island has sea cliffs, sandy beaches, and well-shaped cinder cones. Rush Hill (665 feet above sea level) is Saint Paul Island's highest point. The Island's land area is 44 square miles. The City of Saint Paul is located on the southern tip of the island, on a hilly area overlooking coastal flatlands. The city includes 40.3 square miles of land and 255.2 square miles of water.

CLIMATE
The Arctic maritime climate of the Pribilofs is controlled by the cold waters of the Bering Sea. The weather is generally cloudy and foggy in the summer, with high humidity. Prevailing winds are northerly during winter months and southerly during the summer. Gale-force winds may occur between October and April. Severe winter storms, with wind and icy conditions, may occur between November and March. Mean winter temperatures range between 20ºF and 30ºF, while summer temperatures vary between 40ºF and 50ºF. The average annual precipitation on Saint George is 23 inches, including average snowfall of 57 inches, while the average annual precipitation on the more southern Saint Paul is 25 inches, including snowfall of 56 inches. The Bering Sea ice pack rarely extends to the Pribilof Islands.

CULTURE AND HISTORY
The Pribilof Islands are predominantly an Unangan (Aleut) community, with small Inupiat and Indian populations. The Russian Orthodox church plays a strong role in community cohesiveness. Villagers harvest fur seals for subsistence purposes, but commercial fur-seal harvesting ended in 1973 on Saint George, in 1983 elsewhere in the Pribilofs. Ownership of fur-seal pelts is now prohibited, except for subsistence purposes. Halibut, reindeer, marine invertebrates, plants, and berries also contribute to the subsistence economy.

The Pribilof Islands were discovered in 1786 by Russian fur traders searching for the famed northern fur-seal breeding grounds. In 1788 the Russian American Company enslaved and relocated Unangans from Siberia, Atka, and Unalaska to the Islands to hunt fur seals; their descendants live on the islands today. Between 1870 and 1910, the U.S. government leased the Pribilof Islands to private companies, which provided housing, food, and medical care to the Unangans in exchange for work in the fur-seal plant. In 1910 the U.S. Bureau of Fisheries took control of the islands, but poverty conditions ensued due to overharvesting of the seals. During World War II, residents were moved to southeast Alaska, as part of the area-wide evacuation.

In 1979, the Pribilof Unangans received $8.5 million in partial compensation for the unfair and unjust treatment to which they were subjected under federal administration between 1870 and 1946. After formally ending the commercial seal harvest and federal oversight in 1983, the U.S. government provided $8 million and $12 million respectively to help develop and diversify the economies of Saint George and Saint Paul. This left residents to develop an economy based on commercial fishing, which lasted until the Opilio Crab Disaster (see Environmental Concerns, below) in 2000, when tourism joined commercial fishing as the community's main economic forces.

GOVERNMENT

Saint George and Saint Paul were each incorporated as second-class cities in 1983, each with a mayor and city council, located in the Unorganized Borough. Together, they have the BIA-recognized Pribilof Islands Aleut Communities of Saint Paul and Saint George Islands, a traditional village council headed by a president. Note that this Native entity is often called the "Saint George Tribal Council" on Saint George and the "Saint Paul Tribal Council" on Saint Paul. There is a United States Coast Guard LORAN (Long Range Aids to Navigation) Station on Saint Paul Island.

VILLAGE CORPORATION

The Pribilof Islands are unique in that a single BIA-recognized Native entity has two ANCSA village corporations, one for each city. Shareholders also hold shares in The Aleut Corporation regional Native corporation.

Saint George Tanaq Corporation is the ANCSA village corporation for Saint George. The corporation's Web site states the following: "The company has real estate holdings of 128,646 acres located on Saint George Island, Umnak Island, Unalaska Island, and on the Alaska Peninsula. Of importance, the company's primary operational focus is real property development, management, and leasing; commercial construction related to environmental remediation and general contracting; investment management; ranching; and hotel and tourism management." Subsidiary Saint George Delta Fuel offers retail fuel service for the port facilities.

Tanadgusix (Unangan, meaning "our land") Corporation (often seen as "TDX Corporation") is the ANCSA village corporation for Saint Paul. Its Web site states the following:

Employing 110, TDX is a diversified company and an active developer and investor in the fish processing, hotel, shipping, commercial real estate, tourism, environmental engineering industries and energy development and services. Although TDX has equity investments in Seattle and Portland hotels, the majority of its business activity has been focused on the Alaskan market. To further diversify the Corporation, TDX has been working in the Government sector environmental and power projects at various military installations throughout the United States.

Through the sweeping Alaska Native land claim settlements of the 1970s, TDX controls significant real estate holdings on Saint Paul Island as well as in the Aleutians . . . TDX owns over 95 percent of the primarily open land [on Saint Paul Island] . . . TDX is an equity investor in Saint Paul's fish processing industries, and owns a variety of the island's commercial real estate properties and warehousing facilities. TDX also owns the local hotel, the cable television franchise, SaintPaul's wildlife and Eco-tour operation and Alaska's largest wind diesel hybrid power system.

TDX owns and operates investments off the Island, including the Anchorage Westcoast International Inn, the Seattle Paramount Hotel and the Portland Paramount Hotel. TDX also owns and operates the Sand Point Electric Company and the Sand Point Fuel Company servicing the community of Sand Point.

ECONOMY

The federally controlled fur-seal industry dominated the economy of Saint George until 1973, of Saint Paul until 1983. Commercial fishing and tourism, in addition to subsistence activities, are important contributions to the economy of the islands. Although subsistence has not historically been the focus of the local culture, today halibut and seal are shared and exchanged with relatives living in other communities. Reindeer, marine invertebrates, plants, and berries are also central to the subsistence economy. Federal disaster funding from the Opilio Crab Disaster (see Environmental Concerns, below) helped the Pribilofs' economy develop in new directions. In Saint George, funding was provided for building repairs and restoration, the Saint George Tanaq Tourism Project, tourism marketing, construction of a new fire hall, repairs to the health clinic, the Saint George Fisherman Association Generator Project, a harbor upgrade, and the Saint George Hotel renovation. In Saint Paul, it supported water system improvements, a tribal government and business development center, a restaurant, economic diversification, a Bering Sea Fishermen's Association project, and government housing diversification. Environmental restoration work has also supported the residents since funding for the cleanup began in the 1990s.

Government as employer. The city, state, and federal governments employ 166 people, almost half the working population.

Fisheries. Commercial fishing employs many residents of Saint George and Saint Paul. The communities serve as the major ports within the central Bering Sea for international and domestic fleets. In 1990 the City of Saint George opened its new harbor at Zapadni Bay, and the Saint Paul port opened to provide support services to the Bering Sea fishing fleet. Development of the latter continues. There are 43 residents of the Pribilof Islands who hold commercial fishing licenses. Two seafood processors operate in Saint George and two in Saint Paul, and several offshore processors are serviced out of Saint Paul. The Saint George Aquiculture Association is promoting salmon and shellfish programs.

Manufacturing. There is a boat-building business in Saint Paul.

Services and retail. Each city has several retail stores and repair shops. Saint George also has a hardware store, a lumber yard, a child care service, and a marine supply service.

Tourism and recreation. Tourism is a growing industry in the Pribilof Islands. Federal disaster funding from the Opilio Crab Disaster (see Environmental Concerns, below) in 2000 helped Saint George develop its tourism sector. Saint George has a hotel and a gift shop catering to tourists, a restaurant, and a video rental business. Tourist attractions include the historic Saint George Russian Orthodox Church, the fur-seal rookeries, and extensive bird habitat areas in the cliffs on the island (see Physical Description, above). The renovated Saint George Hotel, designated a National Historic Landmark, was originally built by the Federal government to house visiting officials and can accommodate up to 18 visitors. On Saint Paul, bird watching (more than 210 species of nesting sea birds) and visiting fur-seal rookeries lure nearly 700 tourists per year to the island. Lodging is available at the King Eider Hotel and there is a restaurant.

Pribilof Islands

INFRASTRUCTURE
Saint George

Transportation. Saint George is accessible only by air and water. There are two airstrips: one city-owned, and a newly-constructed state-owned airport with a 5,000- by 150-foot gravel runway. Regularly scheduled flights to Saint Paul and the mainland are offered by two air transportation companies. Cargo services from Anchorage to Saint George are also available. Most freight and supplies are delivered by ship from Anchorage on a monthly or bimonthly schedule; cargo from Seattle arrives five or six times a year. There are three docks in the community one of which is operated by the village corporation. The inner harbor and dock in Zapadni Bay, five miles from the city have been completed. There is a taxi service in the village.

Electricity. The city, through its Saint George Municipal Electric Utility, provides electricity from a 605-kilowatt diesel plant.

Fuel storage distribution. Saint George Delta Fuel, a subsidiary of Saint George Tanaq Corporation, offers retail fuel service for the port facilities. These include: Marine diesel, unleaded gasoline, heating fuel oil, Jet A aviation fuel, lubricants and package products. Storage (gallons): Saint George Delta Fuel Company (1,066,200); Saint George Tanaq Corporation (5,200); City (4,000); Peninsula Airways (2,000); Pribilof Island Schools (1,000).

Water and waste systems. The city provides piped water to 97 percent of the homes, drawing from several community wells. Funding has been requested to upgrade and replace aging water system components. Even though there is a piped-sewage system, a few residents (9 percent) use individual septic tanks. Refuse collection and disposal are provided by the city although plans have been made to close the current landfill and develop a new landfill.

Telecommunications. Local telephone service is provided by ACS of the Northland, while long distance service is available through AT&T Alascom. The village council provides Internet and cable television service. One television channel is broadcast locally from an Alaska Rural Communications Service repeater. Radio stations KUHB-FM and KNOM-AM serve the area.

Saint Paul:

Transportation. Saint Paul is accessible by air and water. The State of Alaska owns the local airport, which has a 6,500- by 150-foot gravel runway and is undergoing improvements. The airport is serviced by two air transportation companies and there are regularly scheduled flights. Most supplies and freight arrive in Saint Paul by ship at the harbor, which has a 700-foot dock. As of 2003, a small-boat harbor was under construction by the Corps of Engineers.

Electricity. Electricity is provided by the city-owned Saint Paul Municipal Electric Utility from a 3,680-kilowatt diesel plant. As of 2003, a new power plant was under construction, and a small demonstration wind turbine provided power to the village office and a greenhouse.

Fuel storage (gallons). Bulk fuel is available for purchase by residents. City (1,854,600); TDX Corporation (1,573,200); U.S. Coast Guard (300,800); Trident Seafoods (12,300); City Electric (12,100); Reeve Aleutian Airways (10,200); Pribilof Island Schools (3,000); Pribilof Island Processors (1,900).

Water and waste systems. The city provides treated piped water to residents from community wells and a community septic system for sewage disposal. All 167 houses and other buildings are fully plumbed. The city has refuse collection and supports a recycling program. A landfill, incinerator, sludge,

and oil disposal site is available in addition to three other land-fills.

Telecommunications. Local telephone service is provided by ACS of the Northland, while long distance service is available through AT&T Alascom. TDX Corporation, the ANCSA village corporation, provides Internet and cable television service. One television channel is broadcast locally from an Alaska Rural Communications Service repeater. Radio station KUHB-FM provides service to the area.

COMMUNITY FACILITIES AND SERVICES
The City of Saint George operates a community center and a public safety building, and provides electricity generation and distribution, fuel storage, waste collection and disposal, and water supply. The City of Saint Paul operates an auditorium. A recreation center for young people is managed by TDX Corporation. The city provides electricity generation and distribution, fuel storage, waste collection and disposal, and water supply.

Education. The Pribilof Islands School District operates schools in both cities: The Saint George School, with 2 teachers and 22 students in kindergarten through grade 12, and the Saint Paul School, with 10 teachers and 112 students in grades K-12. Other educational opportunities include the Saint George Aquiculture Association, which offers on-the-job training and academic programs in hatchery management, and university courses for credit offered by the University of Alaska Distance Education program. Both cities have public libraries.

Health care. Each city has a clinic operated by the Aleutian Pribilof Islands Association. Both clinics were upgraded in 2002 with federal funding from the Opilio Crab Disaster.

Public safety. Law enforcement is provided to Saint George by a state village public safety officer, backed by state troopers in Dillingham. Emergency response is provided by the Saint George Emergency Medical Service/First Responders. In Saint Paul law enforcement is provided by the city police department, emergency response by the Saint Paul Emergency Medical Service Rescue Squad.

ENVIRONMENTAL CONCERNS
Population declines in more than 17 species of marine mammals, fish, and seabirds have been linked to the decades of intensive fishing in the Bering Sea surrounding the Pribilof Islands. Under the Marine Mammal Protection Act, fur seals are now listed as a depleted species. Commercial hunting was stopped on Saint George in 1973 and throughout the region in 1983.

In 2000, the Pribilofs were declared part of a federal disaster area due to an economic crisis brought on by a crash in the population of the opilio crab (a very desirable and profitable shellfish). The Alaska Department of Fish and Game cut the 2000 opilio-crab-harvesting quota to 28.5 million pounds (only 14 percent of the 1999 harvest) after fishery surveys showed a disturbing decline in crab numbers.

As of 2004, the National Oceanic and Atmospheric Administration (NOAA) was completing a federal hazardous-waste cleanup on the two islands. Cleanup of waste left by various U.S. agencies includes removal of leaky fuel tanks, debris, abandoned cars and trucks, oil barrels, and asbestos-tainted buildings. Since the mid-1990s, NOAA spent over $50 million on the restoration work using environmental firms launched by the local village corporations.

Qagan Tayagungin

Total area of entitlement under ANCSA
154,376 acres

Total labor force	617
High school graduate or higher	368
Bachelor's degree or higher	46
Unemployment rate	30.8%
Per capita income *(1999)*	$21,954
Population *2000 census*	952
2003 population	947
state demographer estimate	
Percent Native *2000 census*	44.2%

LOCATION
Sand Point is located by Humboldt Harbor on Popof Island, on the Pacific side of the Alaska Peninsula, 570 miles southwest of Anchorage.

PHYSICAL DESCRIPTION
Sand Point is on Popof Island, one of the rugged volcanic islands that make up the Aleutian chain curving off mainland Alaska toward the southwest. The island is of volcanic origin with terrain smoothed by a Pleistocene ice cap. The coastline is convoluted and the terrain hilly and rugged. Sand Point includes 7.8 square miles of land and 21.1 square miles of water. There is fishing for Pacific cod, salmon, Dolly Varden, trout, halibut, king crab, Tanner crab, shrimp, and sablefish. There is hunting for moose, ptarmigan, bear, and caribou. Gull eggs may be collected during the spring nesting season, and beachcombers collect ribbon kelp, butter clams, sea urchins, and chitons. Salmonberries, mossberries, and blueberries can be found in late July and August.

CLIMATE
Sand Point lies in the maritime climate zone. Temperatures range from winter lows of -9°F to summer highs of 76°F. Snowfall averages 52 inches, with total annual precipitation of 33 inches.

CULTURE AND HISTORY
Sand Point is a mixed community with a large Unangan population. The city is self-sufficient with an emphasis on commercial fishing. Cultural events in the community include a Fourth of July celebration, Cultural Camp, and Christmas Community Potluck. The village corporation's motto is "Remembering the past anticipating the future." Sand Point was founded in 1898 as a trading post and cod-fishing base by a San Francisco fishing company. Local Aleuts and Scandinavian fishermen settled the community, which served as a repair and supply center for gold miners in the early 1900s. Beginning in the 1930s, fishing and fish processing became the primary economic activity. St. Nicholas Chapel, a Russian Orthodox church built in 1933, is listed on the National Register of Historic Places. A halibut-processing plant was constructed in 1946.

GOVERNMENT
Sand Point was incorporated as a first-class city in 1966, with a mayor and city council; it is located in the Aleutians East Borough *(see Alaska introduction)*. The offices of the Aleutians East Borough are located in Sand Point. Sand Point also has a traditional village council, headed by a president.

VILLAGE CORPORATION
Shumagin Corporation is the ANCSA village corporation. Shareholders also hold shares in the Aleut Corporation, the regional Native corporation *(see Alaska introduction)*.

ECONOMY
Sand Point serves as base for the largest fishing fleet in the Aleutian chain. Commercial fishing is the mainstay of the local economy, but a number of other cash-employment opportunities are available, and residents rely on subsistence activities as well to supplement their incomes.

Construction. There is a construction business in the village, as well as a number of handyman services. The construction industry and related businesses employ 39 city residents.

Fisheries. There are three major seafood-processing enterprises in the city, which attract a large, transient population available for seasonal cannery work. One of the seafood-processing companies has a major bottomfish and salmon plant in the city, as well as providing fuel and other services to community residents. The second company owns a storage and transfer station in the city. In 1991 a third seafood-processing company moored a floating processor near the city dock for Pacific cod processing. According to the Alaska Commercial Fisheries Entry Commission, 117 residents hold commercial fishing permits.

Government as employer. The city, borough, state, and federal governments employ 68 people.

Manufacturing. There are several boat-building and repair businesses in the city. Manufacturing employs 193 residents.

Services and retail. There are several general stores, a hardware store, a variety store, an automotive-supply store, a toy store, and a number of other retail stores. In addition there are a bookkeeping service, a machine shop, and several child care services in the village. Information services employ 5 city residents; retail trade 12; finance and related businesses 8; professional and scientific services 2; education, health, and social services 44; and other services 21.

Tourism and recreation. There are several restaurants in the village, a bed and breakfast, an outfitter, a videotape rental business, and several charter fishing businesses. Tourist attractions include the historic Russian Orthodox church, a fish hatchery, the Sand Point Boat Harbor, buffalo hunting, caribou hunting, hiking trails, bird watching, and whale watching. Delores Stokes, a native of Sand Point and an employee of the school, describes the village: "We have pizza, Chinese food, a café by the harbor." In many ways, Sand Point is like many small towns in the United States.

Transportation. In addition to the infrastructure operators, there are a taxi service and several car rental companies in the city. The transportation industry employs 21 village residents.

INFRASTRUCTURE
Transportation. Sand Point has a new airport served by three air transportation companies, with a 4,000-foot runway, and a 25-acre boat harbor with four docks, 134 boat slips, and a 150-ton lift. Scheduled air, ship, and barge services supply the community. The port ranks fourth in Alaska for the number of embarking passengers. Direct flights to Anchorage are available. The state ferry operates bimonthly from May through October.

Electricity. Electricity is available to residents from the Sand Point Electric Company (owned and operated by TDX Corporation, the ANCSA village corporation for Saint Paul), gener-

Also known as Sand Point

Ethnicity: Unangan (Aleut)

Municipality
City of Sand Point
P.O. Box 249
Sand Point, AK 99661
907-383-2696
907-383-2698 Fax

Native entity
Qagan Tayagungin Tribe
of Sand Point Village
P.O. Box 447
Sand Point, AK 99661-0447
907-383-5616
907-383-5814 Fax

ANCSA village corporation
Shumagin Corporation
P.O. Box 189
Sand Point, AK 99661
907-383-3525
907-383-5356 Fax

Qagan Tayagungin

Also known as Sand Point

ating power from a 2,800-kilowatt diesel power plant. TDX also owns and operates the Sand Point Electric Company.

Fuel storage and distribution. Bulk fuel is available for purchase by residents. The Sand Point Fuel Company is owned and operated by TDX Corporation, the ANCSA village corporation for Saint Paul. Storage (gallons): Trident Seafoods (642,000); Sand Point Electric (40,000); Aleutian Commercial (2,350); Reeve Aleutian Airways (1,500); Shumagin Distributors (1,000); city (1,000); Peter Pan Seafoods (1,000).

Water and waste systems. The city provides its residents with piped water from a surface source. The city provides a piped sewage-disposal service and a landfill service for refuse.

Telecommunications. Local telephone service is provided by the Interior Telephone Company/TelAlaska; long distance service is available through AT&T Alascom or GCI. Internet service is provided by Arctic.Net/TelAlaska, or GCI. Wireless Internet service is available at Humbolt Harbor and is provided by Shumagin Corporation. One channel of television is offered by the Alaska Rural Communications Service. Satellite television is available. Radio station KSDP-AM serves the area.

COMMUNITY FACILITIES AND SERVICES

Community facilities include a community center and city hall. The city provides waste collection and disposal and water supply.

Education. The Sand Point School, kindergarten through grade twelve, is operated by the Aleutians East School District. The school has 112 students, 14 teachers, 2 education aides, 3 maintenance personnel, one librarian, and a Web site that includes postings of students' work. The city operates a public library.

Health care. Health care is provided by the Sand Point Community Health Center, owned by the village corporation and leased to the U.S. Public Health Service. It is operated by Eastern Aleutian Tribes, Inc. Emergencies are handled by Sand Point Emergency Medical Services.

Public safety. Law enforcement is provided by the city police department, emergency response by Sand Point Emergency Medical Services.

Qawalangin

Also known as Dutch Harbor/Unalaska

Ethnicity: Unangan Aleut
Municipality
City of Unalaska
P.O. Box 610
Unalaska, AK 99685-0610
907-581-1251
ci.unalaska.ak.us

Native entity
Qawalangin Tribal Council
P.O. Box 334
Unalaska, AK 99685
907-581-2920
907-581-3644 Fax

ANCSA village corporation
Ounalaska Corporation
P.O. Box 149
Unalaska, AK 99685
907-581-1276
907-581-1496 Fax
ounalashka.com

Total area of entitlement under ANCSA 115,200 acres

Total labor force	3,720
High school graduate or higher	78.1%
Bachelor's degree or higher	11.2%
Unemployment rate	13.4%
Per capita income *(1999)*	$24,676
Population *2000 census*	4,283
Percent Native *2000 census*	9.3%

LOCATION
Unalaska is located at Dutch Harbor on Unalaska Island in the Aleutian island chain. It lies 800 miles from Anchorage and 1,700 miles northwest of Seattle. The great circle shipping route from major West Coast ports to the Pacific Rim nations passes within 50 miles of the town.

CLIMATE
Unalaska is located in a maritime climate zone, with relatively warm, wet winters and cool, moist summers. January temperatures range from 25°F to 35°F; July temperatures vary from 43°F to 53°F. Average annual precipitation is 58 inches. Mean wind speed is 17 miles per hour.

CULTURE AND HISTORY
Unalaska began as an Aleut village influenced by early Russian explorers and the fur-seal industry. The community is now primarily non-Native, although it is culturally diverse, due to its large-scale fish-processing activities. Subsistence activities remain central to the culture of the Aleut community, and many long-term non-Native residents also depend to a large extent on subsistence resources. Dutch Harbor provides natural protection for fishing vessels, and the rich resources of the area have allowed Unalaska to develop rapidly. The name Dutch Harbor is often applied both to the harbor itself and to the portion of the city on Amanak Island, which at one time was a separate community (now it is within the corporate boundaries of Unalaska). In 1787 several hunters were enslaved and relocated by the Russian American Company to the Pribilof Islands to work in the fur seal harvest. In 1820 the Russian Orthodox Church of the Holy Ascension was built. The first priest of Unalaska, Ivan Veniaminov, composed the first Aleut writing

system with local assistance and translated scripture into Aleut. Since Aleuts were not forced to give up their language or culture by the Russian Orthodox priests, the church remained strong in the community. Between 1880 and 1925, the Methodist Church operated a school, a clinic, and the Jesse Lee Home for orphans. During the World War II Aleutian campaign, the Russian Orthodox church was nearly destroyed by evacuating army troops. There is a federally recognized tribe in the community—the Qawalangin Tribe of Unalaska.

GOVERNMENT
Unalaska was incorporated as a first-class city in 1942, with a mayor, city manager, and council; it is located in the Unorganized Borough *(see Alaska introduction)*. Alaska Native residents are represented by a traditional village council headed by a president.

VILLAGE CORPORATION
Shareholders in the Ounalaska village corporation also hold shares in Aleut Corporation Regional Native Corporation *(see Alaska introduction)*.

ECONOMY
Unalaska's strong economy is based on commercial fishing, fish processing, and fleet services, such as fuel, repairs, maintenance, trade, and transportation. The community enjoys a strategic position in a rich fishing area that is also ideal for transshipment of cargo among Pacific Rim trading partners. The Great Circle shipping route from major West Coast ports to the Pacific Rim passes within 50 miles of Unalaska, and Dutch Harbor provides a natural protection for fishing vessels. Although local employment is boosted by onshore and offshore processors, nonresident workers are usually brought in during the peak season. Westward Seafoods, Unisea, Alyeska, Icicle, Trident, and Royal Aleutian Seafoods process the commercial catch. Unalaska has a budding tourist industry and a new convention and visitors' bureau.

Construction. Construction employs 135 residents.

Fisheries. Fifty residents hold commercial fishing permits. Farming, fishing, and forestry industries employ 360 residents.

Government as employer. Of the 2,681 employed residents, 346 work for the local, state, or federal government.

Hunting and mining. Employs 60 residents in the hunting and mining industries.

Manufacturing. Employs 985 residents.

Services and retail. There are 85 businesses in the community, including automotive repair, gift store, snow-plowing services, construction, building supply company, computer system design services, ironworks shop, restaurants, and a real estate office. Retail trade employs 108 residents; wholesale trade, 171; education, health, and social services, 154; public administration, 175; financial and related businesses, 41; professional, scientific, administrative, and waste management industries, 51; and information services, 42.

Tourism and recreation. Accommodations include three inns. Services include charter and tour services and a restaurant. Visitor attractions include chartered sport halibut fishing, tours of Unangan archeological sites (Ounalashka Corp.), the Russian Orthodox Church of the Holy Ascension, Museum of the Aleutians, and the Aleutian World War II National Park. Arts, entertainment, recreation, accommodations, and food service industries employ 145 residents.

Transportation. Two airline companies, five taxi companies, and two vehicle rental companies service Unalaska. Transportation, warehousing, and utility industries employ 196 residents.

INFRASTRUCTURE
Seventy-two capital projects, funded by grants, are active in Unalaska.

Transportation. The state provides a 3,900- by 100-foot paved runway for daily scheduled flights. A seaplane base also is available. The state ferry operates bimonthly from Kodiak from spring through summer. The city operates three of the ten major docks in Unalaska. A refurbished World War II sub dock offers ship repair services. The International Port of Dutch Harbor serves fishing vessels and shipping, with 5,200 feet of moorage and 1,232 feet of floating dock. The small-boat harbor provides more than 238 moorage slips. The Corps of Engineers plans to make harbor improvements and to develop a second small-boat harbor in South Channel Iliuliuk Bay, called the "Little South America." A $9-million construction project to add a 500-foot extension to the Marine Center dock is in progress.

Electricity. Unalaska Electric Utility provides electricity. All onshore processors generate their own electrical power.

Fuel storage. Delta Western; North Pacific; Offshore Systems.

Water and waste systems. A new water reservoir is now available at Icy Creek. Water is also supplied by a dam at Pyramid Creek and Unalaska Creek and is chlorinated and stored in a tank. Funding is sought to build a two-million-gallon backup storage tank above Ballyhoo Road. The city's piped water system serves all homes and onshore fish processors. Piped sewage receives primary treatment before discharge into Unalaska Bay. Most homes have plumbing; a few households use septic tanks or privies.

Telecommunications. In-state phone service is provided by Interior Telephone Company/TelAlaska, long distance service by AT&T Alascom, GCI, Interior Telephone/TelAlaska, and Alaska Wireless Communications. Internet service is provided by Arctic.Net/TelAlaska and GCI. Teleconferencing is available through Alaska Teleconferencing Network and the Dillingham Legislative Information Office. There are two radio stations in the community. Alaska Rural Communications Service, KIAL, and K081W-LPTV provide television access. The cable provider is Eyecom/TelAlaska.

COMMUNITY FACILITIES AND SERVICES
Local facilities include the Unalaska Community Center, Unalaska City Hall, and the Museum of the Aleutians, which features both Native heritage and military. Unalaska has both public and school libraries, and the Unalaska Senior Citizens, Inc./Father Ishmail Gromoff Senior Center. The city has a new Class 1 lined six-acre landfill and baler; recycling and hazardous waste disposal is available.

Education. Two schools in the community are under the Unalaska City Schools. The two schools have a combined enrollment of 390 students with 29 teachers.

Health care. Health resources include Iliuliuk Family and Health Services and Oonalaska Wellness Center (A/PIA). The clinic is a qualified emergency care center. Unalaska is classified as an isolated town/subregional center and is found in EMS Region 2H in the Aleutian/Pribilof Region. Emergency services have limited highway, limited marine, and airport access. Emergency service is provided by 911 telephone service, volunteers, and a health aide. Unalaska Volunteer Fire/EMS and Unalaska Search and Rescue Divers provide auxiliary health care.

Qawalangin
Also known as
Dutch Harbor/Unalaska

Quinhagak
See Kwinhagak

Rampart

Rampart

Total area of entitlement under ANCSA	
	92,160 acres
Total labor force	22
High school graduate or higher	9
Bachelor's degree or higher	0%
Unemployment rate	31.8%
Per capita income *(1999)*	$12,438
Current Population	21
state demographer estimate	
Population *2000 census*	45
Percent Native *2000 census*	91.1%

LOCATION
Rampart is located on the south bank of the Yukon River, approximately 75 miles upstream from its junction with the Tanana River, 100 miles northwest of Fairbanks.

PHYSICAL DESCRIPTION
The name Rampart refers to the range of low mountains through which the Yukon River passes. The surrounding area includes a wetland basin underlain by permafrost and mixed forests of spruce, birch, and aspen. It is just southwest of the 9-million-acre Yukon Flats National Wildlife Refuge (established in 1980), an area of international significance to migratory waterfowl such as ducks and a permanent residence for 13 species of birds and many mammals (e.g., moose, beaver, lynx, marten, mink, river otter, wolf, grizzly bear, and Dall sheep).

CLIMATE
Rampart's climate is characterized by daily and seasonal extremes, as is characteristic of the continental subarctic climate. The Rampart winters are long and harsh; the summers are short and warm. Daily minimum temperatures between

Ethnicity: Koyukon Athabascan

Native entity
Rampart Village Council
P.O. Box 67029
Rampart, AK 99767
907-358-3312
907-358-3115 Fax

ANCSA village corporation
Baan O Yeel Kon Corporation
P.O. Box 74558
Fairbanks, AK 99708
907-456-6259
907-456-4486 Fax

Rampart

November and March are usually below 0°F. Extended periods of -50°F to -60°F are common. Summer high temperatures run 65°F to 72°F with a record high of 97°F. Total annual precipitation averages 6.5 inches, with 43.4 inches of snowfall. The Yukon River is ice free from the late May through mid-September.

CULTURE AND HISTORY
The population of Rampart is predominantly Koyukon Athabascan Indian, with a subsistence-oriented culture. Rampart City was established in 1897 as a supply point for gold miners working south of the Yukon. A gold rush in 1898 to areas near Rampart expanded the local population to as high as 10,000 people. During this period, Rampart's economy boomed with hotels, saloons, a hospital, a newspaper, and many merchants. The boom ended as new gold deposits were found near Nome and Fairbanks, and miners and merchants moved on, leaving only a small Native community. From 1900 to 1925, the University of Alaska managed an agricultural research station near Rampart and by 1920 had more than 90 acres under cultivation. The research focused on grain and legume breeding and test plots of vegetables, strawberries, flowers, and field crops.

GOVERNMENT
Rampart is unincorporated and is located in the Unorganized Borough (see Alaska introduction). It is governed by a traditional village council, headed by a chief.

VILLAGE CORPORATION
Baan O Yeel Kon Corporation is the ANCSA village corporation. Shareholders in the village corporation also hold shares in Doyon, Limited, the regional Native corporation (see Alaska introduction).

ECONOMY
The economy of Rampart is heavily dependent on subsistence activities. Salmon, whitefish, moose, caribou, waterfowl, and small game provide meat. Vegetable gardening and the picking of wild berries also supplement the villagers' diet. Cash employment opportunities are part-time or seasonal and are mainly available at the store, clinic, village council, and in commercial fishing and fire fighting. A salmon cannery was established in the 1940s, and a sawmill and logging operation was built in the 1950s, but neither are in operation today. Residents continue to work in nearby gold mines. There are a snowplowing and waste-removal service, a general store, and a food store in the village.

Fisheries. Commercial fishing is an important seasonal addition to the village economy. A commercial fishing season with specific salmon fishing periods is announced for each summer. There are four commercial fishing permit holders in Rampart. Sport fishing of king salmon is also available in the Yukon River near Rampart.

Government as employer. The federal and state governments employ six residents.

INFRASTRUCTURE
Transportation. Air transportation is the only year-round means of access. The state-owned 3,500 -by 75 foot lighted gravel airstrip was originally constructed in 1939 by the Alaska Road Commission, and improvements were made in 1990. Boats, all-terrain vehicles, snowmachines, and motorbikes are used for subsistence and recreation in and around the village. A 30-mile trail, used only in winter, runs from the Elliott Highway north to Rampart. Freight and fuel are shipped to Rampart by barge during the summer.

Electricity. Electricity is provided by the Village of Rampart, generating power by burning diesel.

Water and waste systems. Treated water, drawn from a community well, is available for hauling from a 35,000-gallon water tank installed in 1996. Residents use outhouses for sewage disposal and there is also a sewer lift station and sewage lagoon. In 1999 a study was conducted to determine the feasibility of piped water and a sewer system. Currently, homes are not plumbed. Upgrades and relocation of the landfill are being studied.

Telecommunications. Local telephone service is provided by United Utilities, while long distance service is available through Alascom. One television channel is offered by the Rural Alaska Television Network and three AM radio stations service the area.

COMMUNITY FACILITIES AND SERVICES
Education. There is no school in the village itself. The village school was closed in 1999 due to falling enrollment. Consequently, a number of families have moved from the village.

Health care. Health care is provided by the Rampart Health Clinic, owned by the village.

Public safety. There is a volunteer fire brigade.

Red Devil

Ethnicity: Yup'ik; Deg Xinag and Dena'ina Athabascan

Native entity
Village of Red Devil
P.O. Box 61
Red Devil, AK 99656
907-447-3223
907-447-3224 Fax

ANCSA village corporation
The Kuskokwim Corporation
4300 B Street, Suite 207
Anchorage, AK 99503
907-243-2944
907-243-2984 Fax

Total area of entitlement under ANCSA 69,120 acres	
Total labor force	11
High school graduate or higher	15
Bachelor's degree or higher	0
Unemployment rate	36.4%
Per capita income (1999)	$5,516
Population 2000 census	48
Current population	41
state demographer estimate	
Percent Native 2000 census	52.1%

LOCATION
Red Devil is located on both banks of the Kuskokwim River, at the mouth of Red Devil Creek. It lies 75 miles northeast of Aniak, 161 miles northeast of Bethel, and 250 miles west of Anchorage, in southwest Alaska.

PHYSICAL DESCRIPTION
Red Devil includes 2.2 square miles of water and 24.2 square miles of land. It is on the banks of the Kuskokwim River surrounded by the Kilbuck-Kuskokwim Mountains. Valley regions are vegetated with spruce and poplar forest, upland areas are forested with spruce and hardwoods, and patches of alpine tundra are nearby. The area is known for its mercury, antimony, and gold deposits.

Red Devil has experienced severe flooding of the Kuskokwim River. In May 2002 nineteen residents were airlifted to safety by the National Guard. Spring flooding is likely to occur when increasing temperatures cause river ice to break up and collect in ice dams that block normal river flow causing flooding of low-lying areas.

Lightning-generated wildfire is also a potential threat to the community, as it was in July 1997 when the 480,000-acre Inowak fire came within five miles of Red Devil and other neighboring communities. Wildfires near communities are fought both by ground crews and by airdrops of fire retardants, but fires are often left to burn out in the sparsely populated areas of Southwestern Alaska.

CLIMATE

Red Devil is located in the continental climate zone, with harsh winters and warm, short summers. Temperatures range from winter lows of -58°F or below and summer highs of 90°F. Annual snowfall averages 85 inches, with total precipitation of 20 inches. High winds often cause flight delays in the fall and winter. From mid-June through October, the Kuskokwim River is ice free.

CULTURE AND HISTORY

Residents of Red Devil share a subsistence-oriented culture. Salmon, bear, moose, caribou, rabbit, waterfowl, and berries are harvested in season. Half the population of the village is primarily of mixed Yup'ik and Athabascan descent, while half of the residents are non-Native. Red Devil was named after a mercury mine established in 1921 by Hans Halverson. The mercury deposits were discovered in the nearby Kilbuck-Kuskokwim Mountains. The mine produced 2.7 million pounds of mercury between 1921 and 1971, when the mine closed due to depletion. A post office was established in 1957 and a state school opened in 1958. After the closure of the mine and the subsequent loss of jobs, the population dropped from 152 persons in 1960 to 48 persons in 2000.

GOVERNMENT

Red Devil is unincorporated and is located in the Unorganized Borough (see Alaska introduction). It is governed by a traditional village council, headed by a president.

VILLAGE CORPORATION

The Kuskokwim Corporation is the merged ANCSA village corporations of Lower Kalskag, Upper Kalskag, Aniak, Chuathbaluk, Napaimute, Crooked Creek, Red Devil, Georgetown, Sleetmute, and Stony River. Assets include marketable securities ($8.3 million at December 31, 2001), interests in three apartment complexes and a hotel in Fairbanks, the privatization of Air Force housing in Anchorage, and a telecommunication bandwidth and service provider. It has leased its surface rights in the Donlin Creek mining property to developer Nova Gold. Shareholders in the Kuskokwim village corporation also hold shares in Calista Corporation, the regional native corporation *(see Alaska introduction)*.

ECONOMY

There are few employment opportunities in Red Devil since the closing of the mine. Residents primarily rely on subsistence fishing, hunting, and gathering for their livelihoods. Some local businesses and the school provide periodic employment. Summer work is sometimes available in U.S. Bureau of Land Management firefighting or in commercial fishing. Local private businesses include a charter air service, an aviation support services, a gasoline station and grocery store, a lodge, and a textile products wholesaler.

Government as employer. No residents work for the state or federal governments.

INFRASTRUCTURE

Transportation. The village is accessible only by air and water. A 4,800-foot gravel runway, owned and maintained by the state of Alaska, provides year-round air access. Regular weekday air service is provided from Aniak, in addition to charter flights. The Kuskokwim River provides water access during the summer, as well as surface access after the river freezes in the winter. Bulk supplies and fuel oil are delivered by barge during the summer months. Snowmachines provide transportation to neighboring villages in the winter. Accommodations are available at the Airport Board and Room and the Red Devil Lodge.

Electricity. Electricity is provided by the Middle Kuskokwim Electric Cooperative from a diesel power plant.

Fuel storage(gallons). Bulk fuel for heating is available for purchase by residents. Storage (gallons): Middle Kuskokwim Electric (42,500); Mid Kusko Marine (23,500); Red Devil Lodge (22,800); Kuspuk Schools (17,900).

Water and waste systems. Water is available from individual wells and from the nearby river. Few houses are fully plumbed. Sewage is disposed of in individual septic tanks and residential outhouses. A new site for the landfill is required.

Telecommunications. All homes and other facilities have access to telephone service. Satellite television is available using a larger-than-standard satellite dish. One television channel is broadcast locally by the Rural Alaska Communications Service. Local telephone service is provided by Bush-Tel, while long distance service is available through AT&T Alascom.

COMMUNITY FACILITIES AND SERVICES

Education. The village school, George Willis School, serves students from kindergarten through high school. The school is operated by the Kuspuk Regional Education Attendance Area and employs two teachers.

Health care. Health care is provided locally by the Red Devil Clinic, owned by the village council and operated by the Yukon-Kuskokwim Health Corporation (YKHC). The village clinic is backed by the nearby Sleetmute Health Clinic, the Clara Morgan Sub-Regional Clinic in Aniak, and the Yukon-Kuskokwim Delta Regional Hospital in Bethel, also operated by YKHC.

Public safety. Law enforcement is provided by state troopers in Aniak, emergency response by the Red Devil volunteer fire department.

ENVIRONMENTAL CONCERNS

Due to the mercury mining from 1921 to 1971 at the Red Devil Mine in the mountains surrounding the village, in 1999 the U.S. Bureau of Land Management conducted waste identification and removal actions. The Alaska Department of Environmental Conservation is reviewing the mercury levels in soil and tailings near the mine and water of the Red Devil Creek and the Kuskokwim River, both of which flow through the village of Red Devil.

Red Devil

Community nonprofit corporation
Red Devil People & Community, Inc.
P.O. Box 88
Red Devil, AK 99656
907-447-3203
907-447-3203 Fax

Ethnicity: Koyukon Athabascan

Municipality
City of Ruby
P.O. Box 90
Ruby, AK 99768
    907-468-4401
    907-468-4443 Fax

Native entity
Native Village of Ruby
P.O. Box 210
Ruby, AK 99768
    907-468-4479
    907-468-4474 Fax

ANCSA village corporation
Dineega Corporation
P.O. Box 28
Ruby, AK 99768
    907-468-4405
    907-468-4403 Fax

Russian Mission

See Iqurmuit

Saint George

See Pribilof Islands

St. Mary's

See Algaaciq

Total area of entitlement under ANCSA	
	115,200 acres
Total labor force	72
High school graduate or higher	41
Bachelor's degree or higher	7
Unemployment rate	23.6%
Per capita income *(1999)*	$9,544
Population *2000 census*	188
Population	169
state demographer estimate	
Percent Native *2000 census*	86.2%

LOCATION
Ruby is located on the south bank of the Yukon River, about 50 miles east of Galena and 230 miles west of Fairbanks, in the interior of the state. The village is near the Nowitna National Wildlife Refuge.

PHYSICAL DESCRIPTION
The city area includes 7.6 square miles of land. Ruby and the nearby Nowitna National Wildlife Refuge are in a lowland basin with numerous wetlands surrounded by alpine tundra. The area is characterized by mature white spruce forests and pristine wildlife and waterfowl habitat.

CLIMATE
Ruby has a cold, continental climate, with extreme temperature differences between summer and winter. Winter daily low temperatures average 10°F to below zero with periods of -40°F common occurrences. Summer high temperatures are generally in the low 70s and may reach 90°F. Average precipitation is 17 inches, including 66 inches of snowfall annually. The Yukon River is free of ice from mid-May to mid-October.

CULTURE AND HISTORY
Ruby's residents are Koyukon Athabascans of the Nowitna-Koyukuk band, a formerly nomadic group who traditionally followed game with the changing seasons. Traditional culture and subsistence pursuits remain an integral part of village life. In the gold rush of the late 19th century, Ruby served as a supply point for prospectors. It was named after the red stones (mistakenly thought to be rubies) found on the riverbank there. Gold strikes in 1907 and 1911 attracted hundreds of prospectors to the area. At the height of the mining days, over 1,000 miners lived in and near Ruby. The largest gold nugget ever found in Alaska was unearthed near Ruby in 1998. The nugget weighs 294.1 troy ounces (about 20 pounds). At the March 2004 gold price, its value is approximately $116,000. Long Creek Mine is still maintained as a historical attraction for tourists. The city was first incorporated in 1913 and initially governed by miners. The community decreased in population rapidly at the end of the gold rush, and by 1939 only 139 residents remained. World War II closed the remaining mines, and non-Native residents moved out. In 1973, Ruby was incorporated as a second-class city.

GOVERNMENT
Ruby was incorporated as a second-class city in 1973, with a mayor and city council. It is located in the Unorganized Borough (see Alaska introduction). It also has a traditional village council, headed by a president.

VILLAGE CORPORATION
Dineega Corporation is the ANCSA village corporation. Share-

holders also hold shares in Doyon, Limited, the regional native corporation (see Alaska introduction).

ECONOMY
Most employment is provided by the city, school, tribal council, village corporation, and the health clinic. Ruby also has a number of small family-operated businesses. Summer fire fighting for the Bureau of Land Management, native handicrafts, and winter trapping are also sources of cash income. As of 2003, there were plans to purchase and renovate a sawmill and mill shed. Subsistence activities are an important part of the local economy; salmon, whitefish, moose, bear, ptarmigan, waterfowl, and berries are harvested.

Fisheries. Eight residents hold commercial fishing permits.

Government as employer. City, state, and federal governments employ 26 residents of the village.

Services and retail. There are several general stores in the village, as well as a fuel-oil dealer.

Tourism and recreation. The area around Ruby is popular with visitors for hunting and fishing. The aurora borealis is clearly visible from this region. There is a bed-and-breakfast catering to tourists, as well as a hunting and fishing guide service. Visitors also enjoy the historic Long Creek Gold Mine and the village serves as an Iditarod Trail Sled Dog Race checkpoint in March of even-numbered years. The nearby Nowitna National Wildlife Refuge is 2.1 million acres of lowland forests, wetlands, and alpine tundra. This large roadless area is summer home to more than 120 bird species and breeding habitat for trumpeter swans, white-fronted geese, canvasback ducks, cranes, and other migratory species. Mammals in the refuge include both black and grizzly bears, moose, wolves, lynx, marten, and wolverine. Fish are abundant in the streams, rivers, and lakes. Species include king and chum salmon, northern pike, sheefish, burbot, whitefish, sucker, and arctic grayling. A view back in time to the Pleistocene can be found in the extensive fossil beds of the seven-mile long Palisades bluff area of the Refuge.

INFRASTRUCTURE
Transportation. Ruby is accessible by air and water transportation only. Ruby's state-owned runway is served by five air transportation companies. A barge service makes about four trips to deliver bulk goods each year, but there is no dock or freight facility in the village. Float planes land in the Yukon River in the summer. Trucks, boats, ATVs, and snowmachines provide local transportation depending on the season. Trails and roads to the old mines provide access for hunting, berry picking, and fuel-wood cutting.

Electricity. Electricity is provided by the city, generating power from a 600-kilowatt diesel plant.

Fuel storage (gallons). Dineega Fuel Co. (194,800); Yukon Koyukuk Schools (65,610); city (12,000); Alaska Department of Transportation (4,000).

Water and waste systems. The city provides water at a central location, drawn from a community well drilled in 1993. Residents use individual septic tanks and outhouses for sewage disposal. A new landfill was constructed in 1993 for disposal of refuse.

Telecommunications. Local telephone service is provided by Yukon Telephone Company, while long distance service is available through AT&T Alascom. Internet access is available at the school through GCI. One television channel is provided by the Alaska Rural Communications System. Satellite television is available. Radio stations KIAM-FM and KIYU-AM serve the area.

COMMUNITY FACILITIES AND SERVICES
Community facilities include a washeteria, recreation hall, library, and public campground, operated by the city. The city provides water and electricity, and operates the landfill.

Education. The Merreline A. Kangas School has four teachers and 43 students in preschool through twelfth grade. It is operated by the Yukon/Koyukuk School District.

Health care. The Ruby Health Clinic was rebuilt in 1997 and is owned by the city. The clinic is leased to the U.S. Public Health Service and operated by the Tanana Chiefs Conference.

Public safety. Law enforcement is provided by state troopers in nearby Galena. Emergency response is provided by the city volunteer fire department, which has rescue and ambulance capabilities, and the Ruby Rescue Squad.

Saint Michael

Total area of entitlement under ANCSA	
	125,440 acres
Total labor force	113
High school graduate or higher	78
Bachelor's degree or higher	17
Unemployment rate	21.2%
Per capita income *(1999)*	$10,692
Population *2000 census*	368
2003 Population	413
state demographer estimate	
Percent Native *2000 census*	93.2%

LOCATION
Saint Michael is located on the east coast of Saint Michael Island in Norton Sound, 48 miles southwest of Unalakleet and 125 miles southeast of Nome, on the west coast of the state. The island is located in the Yukon-Kuskokwim Delta region.

PHYSICAL DESCRIPTION
The city includes 21.8 square miles of land and 6.3 square miles of water. The area around Saint Michael is a flat, treeless grassland that is home to many nesting seabirds. The Bering Sea is extremely shallow, and Saint Michael is the deep-water bay that is closest to the Yukon River. The bay is protected from the open sea.

CLIMATE
Saint Michael is located in the subarctic climate zone, with some maritime influence during the summer and continental influence during the winter. Summer temperatures range from 40°F to 60°F; winter temperatures vary from -4°F to 16°F. Average annual precipitation is 12 inches, including snowfall of 38 inches. Summer weather is often rainy and foggy. Norton Sound is free of ice from June to November.

CULTURE AND HISTORY
Saint Michael has a largely Yup'ik (Norton Sound) Inupiat population with strong historical Russian influences. Seal, moose, caribou, fish, beluga whale, and berries are harvested by the villagers. Redoubt Saint Michael was built by the Russian American Company in 1833 as a fortified trading post; it was the northernmost Russian settlement in Alaska. A Native village was to the northeast of the trading post. When the United States purchased Alaska in 1867, most Russians left the area, and in 1897 Fort Saint Michael was established as a U.S. Army post. During the gold rush of 1897, Saint Michael became a major pathway to the mining areas up the Yukon River as well as an important trading post for the Inupiat. The local population grew to an estimated 10,000. The consolidation of people from surrounding villages heightened after the measles epidemic of 1900, and the influenza epidemic of 1918 wiped out many small settlements. Saint Michael continued to be an important shipping depot until the building of the Alaska Railroad in 1923. The population of the village decreased to the 2000 census population of 368 people. Remnants of earlier machinery and boom times remain on the beaches. The city was incorporated in 1969.

GOVERNMENT
Saint Michael was incorporated as a second-class city in 1969, with a mayor and city council; it is located in the Unorganized Borough *(see Alaska introduction)*. It also has an Indian Reorganization Act village council, headed by a president.

VILLAGE CORPORATION
St. Michael Native Corporation is the ANCSA village corporation. Shareholders also hold shares in Bering Straits Native Corporation, the regional Native corporation *(see Alaska introduction)*.

ECONOMY
Saint Michael's economy is based on subsistence food harvests, supplemented by part-time wage earning. Seal, beluga whale, moose, caribou, fish, and berries are important staples. Most cash-income positions are found in city government, the village council, the village corporation, the school, and local stores. Local carvers and other artisans sell Native artwork. In 1993, the Stebbins/St. Michael Reindeer Corral project was completed for a herd on nearby Stuart Island.

Fisheries. Commercial fishing of herring is an important seasonal source of income for some village residents. Many residents participate in the commercial herring fishery during the summer months. Six residents hold commercial fishing permits. The Saint Michael area is a rich herring fishery of commercial importance with a 2003 allowable harvest of 5,062 tons.

Government as employer. The city, state, and federal governments employ 44 people.

Services and retail. The St. Michael Native Store sells groceries.

Tourism and recreation. Several fishing and tour guides are based in Saint Michael, as is a business offering dog sledding excursions. There are areas of the island for bird watching and local villagers who are willing to provide boat and hiking outings for bird and marine mammal watching.

Ethnicity: Yup'ik

Municipality
City of Saint Michael
P.O. Box 59070
Saint Michael, AK 99659
907-923-3222
907-923-2284 Fax

Native entity
Also know as St. Michael IRA Council

Native Village of Saint Michael
P.O. Box 59050
Saint Michael, AK 99659
907-923-2304
907-923-2406 Fax

ANCSA village corporation
Saint Michael Native Corporation
P.O. Box 59049
Saint Michael, AK 99659
907-923-3143
907-923-3142 Fax

Saint Michael

Saint Paul

See Pribilof Islands

INFRASTRUCTURE

Transportation. Saint Michael is accessible by air and sea only. The airport has a 4,000- by 75-foot gravel airstrip that is owned by the state. Regular and charter flights are available from Nome and Unalakleet, and the airport is served by three air transportation companies. A seaplane base is also available. The city has a good natural harbor, but no dock. Barge service is provided on a frequent basis from Nome, and Saint Michael receives at least one annual shipment of bulk cargo by barge. There is a 10.5-mile road to Stebbins. The village school provides some sleeping accommodations.

Electricity. All residents have access to electricity, which is provided from a 771-kilowatt diesel plant. Electricity is provided by the Alaska Village Electric Cooperative.

Fuel storage (gallons). Bulk fuel is available for purchase by residents.Bering Strait School District (80,500); AVEC (76,000); Alaska Commercial Co. (32,000); city (14,000); Army National Guard (10,000); Alaska Department of Transportation (3,000); Yutana Barge Line (unknown).

Water and waste systems. The city provides treated water from Clear Lake at a central 1.2-million-gallon tank. As of 2003, a new system was being constructed to provide household plumbing. Forty-four homes were already connected on this system and 37 additional homes were soon to be connected. Homes not currently on the community water system haul water from the central water tank. There is a community septic system for sewage disposal with a piped gravity-and-vacuum sewer system under construction. As of 2003, 44 homes had sewer service on this new system and 37 additional homes were soon to be connected. Homes not currently on the community sewer system haul use a honeybucket-hauling service.

Telecommunications. All residents have access to telephone service. Local telephone service is provided by the Mukluk Telephone Company/TelAlaska, while long distance service is available through AT&T Alascom, GCI, or Mukluk Telephone. Internet is available through GCI. One television channel is broadcast locally by an Alaska Rural Communications System repeater. Satellite television is available. Radio stations KICY-AM and KNOM-AM serve the area.

COMMUNITY FACILITIES AND SERVICES

Community facilities include a community center, with child and elderly day care and the youth recreation center are in the works. The city provides waste collection and disposal and water supply.

Education. Anthony A. Andrews School serves 143 students in preschool through twelfth grade. It is operated by the Bering Strait School District and has twelve teachers. The school library serves as the community public library.

Health care. Health care is provided by the Katherine L. Kobuk Memorial Health Clinic (remodeled in 2003), owned by the city and operated by the Norton Sound Health Corporation.

Public safety. Law enforcement is provided by the state village public safety officer (VPSO), backed by state troopers in Nome. Emergency response is provided by the VPSO and the city volunteer fire department.

Salamatof

Ethnicity: Tanaina Athabascan

Native entity
Village of Salamatof
P.O. Box 2682
Kenai, AK 99611
907-283-7864
907-283-6470 Fax

ANCSA village corporation
Salamatof Native Association, Inc.
P.O. Box 2682
Kenai, AK 99611-2682
907-283-7864
907-283-6470 Fax

Total area of entitlement under ANCSA
	109,571 acres
Total labor force	269
High school graduate or higher	227
Bachelor's degree or higher	56
Unemployment rate	15.2%
Per capita income *(1999)*	$16,306
Population *2000 census*	954
Current population	902
state demographer estimate	
Percent Native *2000 census*	22.3%

LOCATION
Salamatof is located on the Kenai Peninsula, on the east shore of Cook Inlet, at the mouth of Salamatof Creek, 5.5 miles northwest of the city of Kenai.

PHYSICAL DESCRIPTION
Salamatof includes 8.1 square miles of land and 0.1 square mile of water. The area bordering Cook Inlet is a lowland forest composed of spruce and birch. The area is heavily dotted with lakes. Upper Cook Inlet has abundant salmon resources including chinook, sockeye, coho, pink, and chum. Nearby lowlands, lakes, and other areas of the peninsula are included in the Kenai National Wildlife Refuge.

CLIMATE
Salamatof is located in the maritime climate zone. January temperatures range from 4ºF to 22ºF; July temperatures vary from 46ºF to 61ºF. The average annual precipitation is 20 inches.

CULTURE AND HISTORY
Salamatof is a Tanaina Indian village, first reported in 1911 by the U.S. Geological Survey. While the Kenai Peninsula is now largely non-Native, the community retains much of its traditional culture.

GOVERNMENT
Salamatof is unincorporated under Alaska law and is located in the Kenai Peninsula Borough *(see Alaska Introduction)*. Alaska Native residents are governed by a traditional village council, headed by a president.

VILLAGE CORPORATION
Shareholders in the village corporation, Salamatof Native Association, also hold shares in Cook Inlet Regional Corporation *(see Alaska Introduction)*.

ECONOMY
Economic opportunities in the region are diverse. Residents are able to find employment in oil and gas processing, the timber industry, commercial and sport fishing, government, retail business, and tourism-related services.

Fisheries. Commercial fishing is a source of income for village residents, although the Alaska Commercial Fisheries Entry Commission reports that there are no commercial fishing permit holders in Salamatof.

Government as employer. Village, borough, state, and federal governments employ 32 people.

Services and retail. Services are extensive on the Kenai Peninsula. There are hotels and restaurants to serve those visiting the area.

Tourism and recreation. The village itself is attempting to develop a lake resort area. Tourism, especially combined with fishing and hunting, is a growing industry on the Kenai Peninsula. The nearby Kenai National Wildlife Refuge is known as a "little Alaska," as it includes areas of all habitat types found in Alaska. It attracts more than half a million visitors per year.

INFRASTRUCTURE
Transportation. The Sterling Highway provides access to Anchorage and other communities in the state and beyond. The city of Kenai offers an airport and docking facilities. Floatplanes are able to land on Arness Lake and the Lower Salamatof Creek. There is local taxi service, and rental cars are available in the area.

Electricity. Electricity is provided by the Homer Electric Association, generating power by burning natural gas and utilizing hydroelectric generation.

Fuel storage and distribution. Over 70 percent of housing units are heated with natural gas, while the rest are heated with wood, propane, oil, and electric heat.

Water and waste systems. The Kenai Peninsula Borough provides approximately half of the households in the village with piped water; the rest obtain their water from individual wells. Refuse is disposed of at a transfer site in nearby Kenai.

Telecommunications. Local telephone service is provided by ACS of Northland, while long distance service is available through AT&T Alascom. Internet service is provided by ACS, Arctic.net, and TelAlaska. Several television channels are available from Anchorage with GCI Cable, providing cable television service. Radio stations KWHQ-FM, KPEN-FM, KWVV-FM, KDLL-FM, and KZXX-AM service the area.

COMMUNITY FACILITIES AND SERVICES
Education. There are no schools in Salamatof. Children attend nearby schools operated by the Kenai Peninsula Borough.

Health care. Health care is provided by the Central Peninsula Hospital in nearby Soldotna. The regional health corporation is Chugachmiut.

Salamatof

Sand Point
See Qagan Tayagungin

Savoonga

Savoonga

*Total area of entitlement under ANCSA
1,135,843 acres

Total labor force	265
High school graduate or higher	162
Bachelor's degree or higher	14
Unemployment rate	37.4%
Per capita income *(1999)*	$7,725
Population *2000 census*	643
2003 Population	704
state demographer estimate	
Percent Native *2000 census*	95.5%

Total area of entitlement under ANCSA Savoonga chose to accept fee title (jointly with Gambell) to its former Reserve lands, 1,135,843 acres, in lieu of an ANCSA entitlement.

LOCATION
Savoonga is located on the northern coast of St. Lawrence Island in the Bering Sea, 164 miles west of Nome and 39 miles southeast of Gambell.

PHYSICAL DESCRIPTION
St. Lawrence Island, at 1,983 square miles, is the fifth largest island in the United States and is so near to Russia that the mountains of Siberia are visible on a clear day. The city is situated with the Bering Sea to the north and Atuk Mountain (elevation 2,207 feet) to the south, and includes 6.1 square miles of land. The island is vegetated with lush grass, dwarf willows (the only native trees), lichen, mosses, and flowering plants.

CLIMATE
Savoonga has a subarctic maritime climate, with some continental influences in the winter. Summer temperatures range from 40°F to 51°F and winter temperatures vary from -7°F to 11°F. Average precipitation is 10 inches annually, including 58 inches of snowfall. The island is subject to prevailing winds of around 18 miles per hour. The Bering Sea is frozen from mid-November to late May.

CULTURE AND HISTORY
Savoonga is a traditional St. Lawrence Yup'ik Inupiat village with a subsistence lifestyle based on whale and walrus hunting. Savoonga is known as the "Walrus Capital of the World." Whale, seal, walrus, and reindeer comprise 80 percent of islanders' diets. Most residents are bilingual with Siberian Yup'ik being their first language.

St. Lawrence Island has been inhabited for several thousand years, and the Island had a population of about 4,000 by the 19th century. Residents had little contact with the rest of the world until European traders began to frequent the area. A tragic famine occurred on the island in 1880, reducing the population to an estimated 500. In 1891 President Theodore Roosevelt declared the entire island a reindeer reserve; this status carried with it the claim to the island on the part of the residents of the villages of Gambell and Savoonga, the only villages on the island. In 1900 a herd of reindeer was moved to the island, and by 1917 the herd had grown quite large, so the community was moved to its present location where grazing lands are better.

On passage of the 1971 Alaska Native Claims Settlement Act, the islanders elected to accept the former reserve lands as their part of the settlement. While this made them ineligible for some of the provisions of the act, it also resulted in a land base-1,135,843 acres is held jointly with Gambell-that is much larger than that otherwise provided for in the ANCSA. Also, they hold both surface and subsurface rights.

GOVERNMENT
Savoonga was incorporated as a second-class city in 1969, with a mayor and city council; it is located in the Unorganized Borough *(see Alaska introduction)*. Native Village of Savoonga is an Indian Reorganization Act village council, headed by a president.

VILLAGE CORPORATION
The ANCSA village corporation, Savoonga Native Corporation, jointly with the village corporation for Gambell, holds fee

[suh-VOON-guh]
Ethnicity: Siberian Yup'ik

Municipality
City of Savoonga
P.O. Box 40
Savoonga, AK 99769
907-984-6614
907-984-6411 Fax

Native entity
Native Village of Savoonga
P.O. Box 120
Savoonga, AK 99769
907-984-6414
907-984-6027 Fax

ANCSA village corporation
Savoonga Native Corporation
P.O. Box 160
Savoonga, AK 99769
907-984-6613

245

Savoonga

title to the former Reserve lands. Shareholders hold shares in the Bering Straits Native Corporation, the regional native corporation (see Alaska introduction).

ECONOMY

The economy of Savoonga is largely based on the subsistence hunting of walrus, seal, fish, and beluga whales, with some cash income. Reindeer harvests occur, but the herd is not managed. Fox trapping is a secondary source of income. Nearly all households (98 percent) harvest birds (geese, ducks, loons, gulls, cormorants, murres, auklets) and bird eggs (murres) as part of their subsistence lifestyle. Islanders are known for their outstanding ivory carvings, and there is some tourism from bird-watchers.

Fisheries. One resident has a commercial fishing license and fishing employs two residents. A small fish processing facility was completed in the mid-1990s.

Government as employer. The city, state, and federal governments employ 138 people.

Services and retail. There is a general store in the village and several grocery stores. Retail trade employs 19 village residents, finance and related businesses 2, and professional services other than health and education 4. The Savoonga Native Store carries food and basic necessities.

Tourism and recreation. There are several gift stores in the village, a lodge for visitors, and a videotape rental service. Tourists come to St. Lawrence Island for the bird watching (migratory birds such as geese and ducks and seabirds such as loons, murres, puffins) and marine mammal watching (whales, seals, and walruses). The Savoonga Walrus Festival is held each May. Accommodations include the Alanga Lodge and Alowa's Lodge.

INFRASTRUCTURE

Transportation. Because of iced-in conditions during the winter and the lack of a seaport, the village is dependent on air transport. Regular air service is available from Nome and Unalakleet from Bering Air, Grant Aviation, and Hageland Aviation. The state-owned airstrip (4,402 feet by 100 feet) was recently improved. There is no dock, so bulk supplies must be lightered from Kotzebue to Savoonga and offloaded on the beach. Residents use boats in the summer to travel to Gambell. The transportation industry employs seven persons.

Electricity. Electricity is available to all residents from a 1,246-kilowatt diesel plant.

Fuel storage and distribution. Bulk fuel is available for purchase by residents. Storage (gallons): Village Store (279,000); Bering Straits Schools (149,500); Alaska Village Electric Cooperative (136,200); city (28,500); Alaska Department of Transportation (9,500); National Guard (7,500); Presbyterian church (5,900).

Water and waste systems. Water is available at the city-operated washeteria, drawn from a community well and stored in a 100,000-gallon tank. Piped water service is available to 45 homes; the remaining homes haul water from the washeteria. Sewer service is available to 45 homes; the remaining homes use honeybuckets.

Telecommunications. Telephone and cable services are available to all residents. The school has Internet access provided by GCI. Local telephone service is provided by United Utilities, while long distance service is available through AT&T Alascom or United Utilities. Cable television service is available from Frontier Cable. Radio stations KICY-AM and KNOM-AM serve the area, and one television station is broadcast locally from an Alaska Rural Communications Service repeater.

COMMUNITY FACILITIES AND SERVICES

The City of Savoonga (through its nonprofit Savoonga Joint Utilities) provides water and waste disposal. Fuel oil is provided by the village store. Electricity is provided by the Alaska Village Electric Cooperative.

Education. Hogarth Kingeekuk Senior Memorial High School has 200 students in grades K-12, with 17 teachers. It is operated by Bering Strait School District. The school library serves as the city's public library.

Health care. Health care is provided by the newly built Savoonga Clinic, owned by the City. It is operated by the Norton Sound Health Corporation.

Public safety. Law enforcement is provided by the city police officer, backed by state troopers in Nome. Emergency response is provided by the Savoonga First Responders/Rescue Team and the volunteer fire department.

ENVIRONMENTAL CONCERNS

The St. Lawrence Island is home and breeding ground for numerous bird species: emperor geese, snow geese, northern pintails, mallards, eiders, loons, gulls, murres, auklets, puffins. Spectacled eiders (listed as threatened in 1993 under the Endangered Species Act) migrate across the island. The Bering Sea is rich with marine life: walrus, seals, bowhead whales, beluga whales, halibut, crabs, marine plants, and seaweed.

There is concern about cancer-causing PCBs leaking from transformers and dumped barrels in an abandoned military base in the Northeast Cape area. Low levels of PCBs have been found in blood samples of villagers. PCBs are accumulated in local fish that are consumed in the traditional subsistence diet of the villagers. The Northeast Cape-White Alice Tram and Debris Removal project is being conducted by the U.S. Army Corps of Engineers and includes the removal of tram towers, wires, cables, and other debris. Total cost of the project is expected to exceed $19 million.

Total area of entitlement under ANCSA
23,040 acres

Total labor force	234
High school graduate or higher	97
Bachelor's degree or higher	23
Unemployment rate	22.2%
Per capita income (1999)	$15,642
Population [(2000 census)]	431
2003 population	425
(state demographer estimate)	
Percent Native [(2000 census)]	70.1%

LOCATION
Saxman is located on the west side of Revillagigedo Island, three miles south of Ketchikan, on the South Tongass Highway.

PHYSICAL DESCRIPTION
Saxman is located on a protected harbor in the Tongass Narrows. It includes 1.0 square mile of land. Revillagigedo Island, where Saxman is located, is the fifth largest island in the U.S. and includes a part of the Tongass National Forest. The Tongass National Forest is the largest U.S. National Forest at 17 million acres, including five million acres of wilderness, rugged shorelines, islands, and two National Monuments. The area is a part of the coastal rainforest of southeastern Alaska. The area is heavily forested (western hemlock, sitka spruce, western red cedar, yellow cedar, mountain hemlock, and shore pine) and supports a wide range of birds and mammals: swans, cranes, hummingbirds, deer, wolves, porcupines, and bear. Many sport fish also live in this area: salmon, cutthroat trout, steelhead trout, and Dolly Varden.

CLIMATE
Saxman lies in the maritime climate zone noted for its warm winters, cool summers, and heavy precipitation. Average summer temperatures range from 46ºF to 59ºF and average winter temperatures range from 29ºF to 48ºF. The record high temperature is 97ºF; the record low is -4ºF. Precipitation averages 163 inches per year, including 69 inches of snow.

CULTURE AND HISTORY
Saxman is a Tlingit community. Most residents maintain a culture centered on subsistence activities. A new totem-pole-carving center fosters traditional skills and provides tourism opportunities. In 1886 a Presbyterian teacher named Samuel Saxman and a Tlingit village elder were lost at sea while searching for a new community site at which to establish a church and a BIA school. Tongass and Cape Fox Tlingit from area villages chose the site of Saxman for the school and church in 1894. The economy was based on fishing and cutting lumber for local use. In the 1930s many totem poles and ceremonial artifacts were retrieved by the Civilian Conservation Corps from the ancestral villages at Tongass, Cat, Pemock Islands, and Cape Fox, and restored and placed in Saxman as part of a U.S. Forest Service program.

GOVERNMENT
Saxman was incorporated as a second-class city in 1930, with a mayor and city council; it is located in the Ketchikan Gateway Borough (see Alaska introduction). It also has an Indian Reorganization Act council, headed by a president.

VILLAGE CORPORATION
The Cape Fox Corporation is the ANCSA village corporation for both Saxman and nearby Ketchikan. Shareholders in the village corporation also hold shares in Sealaska Corporation regional Native corporation (see Alaska introduction).

ECONOMY
Most employment opportunities are in nearby Ketchikan, at the pulp mill, on the state ferry, in fish processing, and in government. The city provides some employment at the Saxman Seaport, and the Cape Fox Corporation offers both year-round and seasonal tourist-related employment. The Saxman Totem Park was recently expanded to become a cultural center, including a tribal house, a totem-carving shed, and a hall for traditional Tlingit dance exhibitions. Harvested deer, salmon, and halibut significantly contribute to the local diet.

Construction. The construction industry employs 19 residents of Saxman.

Fisheries. Commercial fishing is an important source of self-employment; one resident holds a commercial fishing permit.

Government as employer. Government employs 36 people.

Manufacturing. Manufacturing employs seven residents.

Services and retail. As Saxman is very close to the larger city of Ketchikan, most services are located there.

Tourism and recreation. Tourism is an important source of income for village residents, especially in connection with the totem park. Arts, entertainment and related fields employ 17 persons. Visitor attractions include the Saxman Village Tour, Saxman Totem Park, Saxman Tribal House, and the Edwin C. DeWitt Carving Center. The Saxman Native Totem Park was created in the late 1930s when the Civilian Conservation Corps and the U.S. Forest Service teamed up to retrieve and restore 24 totem poles from throughout the region and placed them in Saxman. This is the largest collection of original totem poles in the United States. A replica of a traditional clan house, built entirely of western red cedar, is open to the public. Theatrical productions depict the oral history of the Tlingit and include songs and dances.

Transportation. Saxman Seaport offers dock and commercial barge off-loading facilities and a rail-barge terminal (built in 1967) that serves as the area's major cargo container terminal. The transportation industry employs 13 Saxman residents.

INFRASTRUCTURE
Transportation. Saxman and the much larger city of Ketchikan are connected by the South Tongass Highway. Scheduled jet and air-taxi services are available in Ketchikan. The community relies on Ketchikan for its boat-moorage and ferry services. Saxman Seaport offers dock and commercial barge off loading facilities and a rail-barge terminal (built in 1967) that serves as the area's major cargo container terminal.

Electricity. Electricity is available to residents from Ketchikan Public Utilities *(see the profile for Ketchikan).*

Water and waste systems. The City of Saxman provides piped water to residents, as well as water at a central location, drawn from a surface source and stored in a 128,000-gallon tank. The city also provides a piped sewage-disposal service, utilizing a new sewage treatment plant. A private company collects refuse which is disposed of at the nearby Ketchikan landfill.

Telecommunications.. Local telephone service is provided by Ketchikan Public Utilities, while long distance service is avail-

Ethnicity: Tlingit

Municipality
City of Saxman
Route 2, Box 1 - Saxman
Ketchikan, AK 99901
907-225-4166
907-225-6450 Fax

Native entity
Organized Village of Saxman
Route 2, Box 2
Saxman, AK 99901
907-247-2502
907-247-2504 Fax

ANCSA village corporation
Ketchikan and Saxman
Cape Fox Corporation
P.O. Box 8558
Ketchikan, AK 99901
907-225-5163
907-225-3137 Fax

Saxman

able through AT&T Alascom, GCI, or ACS Long Distance. Internet service is available from Ketchikan Public Utilities. Cable television is available from GCI Cable. Residents can receive the public television station in Juneau, KTOO, from a repeater in Ketchikan, one local Ketchikan television station, and two television channels from Alaska Rural Communications Service repeaters.

COMMUNITY FACILITIES AND SERVICES
Community facilities include the community hall (which has a gymnasium), the Cape Fox Heritage Building, the Beaver Tribal House, and senior housing. The city provides water and sewer.

Education. The community children attend schools in Ketchikan operated by the Ketchikan Gateway Schools.

Health care. Health care is provided by the Ketchikan General Hospital, three miles from Saxman.

Public safety. Law enforcement is provided by state troopers in Ketchikan. Emergency response is provided by the city fire department, supported by borough fire halls.

Scammon Bay

[SKAMM-in]
Ethnicity: Yup'ik Eskimo

ANCSA village corporation
Askinuk Corporation
P.O. Box 89
Scammon Bay, AK 99662
  907-558-5411
  907-558-5412 Fax

Total area of entitlement under ANCSA	92,160 acres
Total labor force	248
High school graduate or higher	69.9%
Bachelor's degree or higher	12.2%
Unemployment rate	12.8%
Per capita income *(2000)*	$7,719
Population *2000 census*	465
Percent Native *2000 census*	97.4%

LOCATION
Scammon Bay is located to the north of the Askinuk Mountains in the Yukon-Kuskokwim Delta of southwest Alaska on the south bank on the Kun River, one mile from the Bering Sea.

CLIMATE
Scammon Bay is located in the maritime climate zone, characterized by relatively warm winters, cool summers, and fairly heavy precipitation. Temperatures range from winter lows of -25°F to summer highs of 79°F. Annual precipitation is 14 inches, including 65 inches of yearly snowfall. Easterly winds during the winter cause severe wind-chill factors.

CULTURE AND HISTORY
Scammon Bay is a Yup'ik Eskimo community with a culture centered on fishing and subsistence activities. The community is known in Eskimo as Mariak, and its residents are called Mariagamiut. The English name was adopted to honor Captain Charles Scammon, who served as the marine chief of the Western Union Telegraph Expedition from 1856 to 1867. Most residents travel to the Black River each summer for fish camp, 50 miles to the north. There is a federally recognized tribe located in the community-the Scammon Bay Traditional Council.

GOVERNMENT
Scarnmon Bay was incorporated as a second-class city in 1967, with a mayor and city council; it is located in the Unorganized Borough (see Alaska introduction). It also has a traditional village council, headed by a president.

VILLAGE CORPORATION
Askinuk Corporation is the ANCSA village corporation of Scammon Bay. Its shareholders consist of several hundred Native Alaskans residing in the village as of December 1971 and their descendents. It operates a store and fuel depot in the village and has also received the surface rights to certain trust lands utilized for subsistence. To establish low prices for its general store merchandise, Askinuk joined the Alaska Native Industries Cooperative Association (ANICA), whose members are generally Native village corporations. Shareholders in Askinuk village corporation are also shareholders in Calista regional Native corporation *(see Alaska introduction)*.

ECONOMY
Employment in Scammon Bay centers on the commercial fishing industry, U.S. Bureau of Land Management emergency firefighting, and various handicrafts and construction projects. Subsistence activities involve harvesting fish, beluga whales, walrus, seals, birds, and berries.

Fisheries. Forty-nine residents hold commercial fishing permits, chiefly for salmon. The 1992 Community Development Quota Program increased the Pollack ground fish quota for small communities such as Scammon Bay.

Government as employer. Of the 109 employed residents, 66 work for the local, state, or federal government.

Services and retail. There are 12 businesses in the community, including a mercantile store, real estate office, fishing guide, air transportation maintenance service, city utilities, café, and two grocery stores. Retail trade employs 23 residents; education, health, and social services, 54; public administration, 11; and information services, 3.

Tourism and recreation. Local events include sled dog races, snowmachine lap race, Eskimo dancing, and basketball tournaments. Services include a video rental store and a hunting/ supply business.

Transportation. Six airline companies service Scammon Bay. Transportation, warehousing, and utility industries employ 10 residents.

INFRASTRUCTURE
Seventeen capital projects, funded by grants, are active in Scammon Bay.

Transportation. Scammon Bay is accessible by air and water. The state provides a 3,000- by 75-foot gravel airstrip, and the city owns a seaplane base on the Kun River. Bulk supplies are delivered in summer by barges. In winter, trails are open to Hooper Bay and Chevak. Residents use snowmachines and skiffs for local transportation.

Electricity. Alaska Village Electric Cooperative (AVEC) provides electricity. Development of a small hydroelectric plant is being looked into by AVEC and the city.

Water and waste systems. Water drawn from an infiltration gallery on a small stream south of the city is treated and stored in a 100,000-gallon tank. Ninety-two of 99 homes and the school are fully plumbed and are connected to a piped water and sewer system. A few residents use honeybuckets. There is no washeteria. A new landfill and access road are now open.

Telecommunications. In-state phone service is provided by United Utilities, long distance service by AT&T Alascom and

United Utilities. Teleconferencing is available through Alaska Teleconferencing Network. Alaska Rural Communications Service provides television access. There are two radio stations in the community. The City of Scammon Bay is the cable provider.

COMMUNITY SERVICES AND FACILITIES
Local facilities include Yower Hall.

Education. Scammon Bay School is in the Lower Yukon School District. The school has 175 students and 12 teachers.

Health care. Local health resources include Scammon Bay Health Clinic and the Pearl E. Johnson Subregional Clinic. Scammon Bay is classified as an isolated village and is found in EMS Region 7A in the Yukon/Kuskokwim Region. Emergency services have coastal, seaport, and air access. A health aide provides emergency care.

Selawik

Selawik

Total area of entitlement under ANCSA	138,240 acres
Total labor force	446
High school graduate or higher	57.8%
Bachelor's degree or higher	5.6%
Unemployment rate	34.3%
Per capita income *(2000)*	$8,170
Population *2000 census*	772
Percent Native *2000 census*	95.3%

LOCATION
Selawik is located at the mouth of the Selawik River where it empties into Selawik Lake, about 70 miles southeast of Kotzebue and just north of the Seward Peninsula. It lies 670 miles northwest of Anchorage. Selawik is near the Selawik National Wildlife Refuge, a key breeding and resting spot for migratory waterfowl.

CLIMATE
Selawik has a transitional climate zone, characterized by long, cold winters and cool summers. Temperatures range from winter lows of -50°F to occasional summer highs of 83°F. Snowfall averages 40 inches, and average total precipitation is 10 inches yearly.

CULTURE AND HISTORY
Selawik is an Inupiat Eskimo community, with an active culture centering on traditional subsistence activities. Occasionally, bartered seal and beluga whale supplement the diet, which ordinarily centers on ducks, ptarmigan, roots, greens, and berries, as well as fish and land mammals. *Selawik* is an Inupiat Eskimo name for a species of fish. The village was first reported in the 1840s as "Chllvik" by Lieutenant O.A. Zagoskin of the Imperial Russian Navy. Ivan Petrof counted 100 "Selawigamute" people in his 1880 census. Around 1908, the site had a small wooden schoolhouse and church. The village has continued to grow and has expanded across the Selawik River onto three banks, linked by bridges. There is a federally recognized tribe located in the community-the Native Village of Selawik.

GOVERNMENT
Selawik was incorporated as a second-class city in 1977, with a mayor and city council; it is located in the Northwest Arctic Borough (see Alaska introduction). It also has an Indian Reorganization Act council, headed by a president.

VILLAGE CORPORATION
Shareholders in the village corporation also hold shares in NANA Regional Native Corporation (see Alaska introduction).

ECONOMY
Inhabitants of Selawik subsist mainly on whitefish, sheefish, caribou, moose, ducks, ptarmigan, and berries. Bartered seal and beluga whale sometimes supplement the diet. The school, the city, the IRA, Maniilaq, and three grocery stores are the primary employers. Handicrafts are made and sold within and outside the community. The Red Dog Mine, Bureau of Land Management emergency firefighting, and lighterage operations offer seasonal work.

Construction. Two residents are employed in construction.

Fisheries. Three residents hold commercial fishing permits, chiefly for salmon.

Government as employer. Of the 130 employed residents, 69 work for the local, state, or federal government.

Mining. Mining and hunting industries employ eight residents.

Services and retail. There are 11 businesses in the community, including cafés, grocery store, airport maintenance, day care services, and Selawik water utility. Retail trade employs 14 residents; wholesale trade, 2; education, health, and social services, 40; public administration, 19; financial and related businesses, 3; and information services, 2.

Tourism and recreation. Local events include Spring Inupiaq Cultural Week, Memorial Singsparation, Fourth of July, Fall Inupiaq Cultural Week, Thanksgiving Feast, Thanksgiving City League Basketball Tournament, and a Christmas Program and Feast. Accommodations include a camp area. Businesses include a video and gift store, and the Selawik racing association.

Transportation. Ten airline companies service Selawik. Transportation, warehousing, and utility industries employs 24 residents.

INFRASTRUCTURE
Sixteen capital projects, funded by grants, are active in Selawik.

Transportation. Selawik is accessible by plane and barge. The city provides Roland Norton Memorial Airport, which has a 3,000- by 70-foot gravel runway. The state provides a 3,000- by 60-foot gravel airstrip with a 2,670- by 60-foot crosswind strip. Scheduled flights are available to Kotzebue and area communities. Docking facilities and a barge landing area are available. Crowley Marine Services ships freight during the summer upriver from Kotzebue. Boardwalks have been built within the village. Residents use boats, all-terrain vehicles, and snowmachines for local transportation.

Electricity. Alaska Village Electric Cooperative (AVEC) provides electricity.

Water and waste systems. A circulating water and vacuum sewer system are now operating. A central treatment facility can pump up to 8,000 gallons of water daily from the Selawik River. Fifty-three homes in the West II area and 20 new HUD

[SELL-uh-wick]
Ethnicity: Inupiat Eskimo

NANA Regional Corporation
P.O. Box 49
4706 Harding Drive
Kotzebue, AK 99752
907-442-3301

Selawik

homes are plumbed and connected. About 30 homes on the island and near the airport are now connected. A new permitted landfill is needed.

Telecommunications. In-state phone service is provided by OTZ Telephone Co-op, long distance service by AT&T Alascom, GCI, and OTZ Telephone. Internet service is provided by GCI. Teleconferencing is available through Alaska Teleconferencing Network and the Kotzebue Legislative Information Office. Alaska Rural Communications Service provides television access. There is one radio station in the community. The City of Selawik is the cable provider.

COMMUNITY FACILITIES AND SERVICES
Local facilities include a community building, city office/multi-purpose facility, and both school and city libraries.

Education. School is in the Northwest Arctic School District. The school has 266 students and teachers.

Health care. Selawik Health Clinic provides health care in the community. Selawik is classified as an isolated village and is found in EMS Region 4A in the Maniilaq Association Region. Emergency services have lake and air access. Volunteers and a health aide provide emergency care. Selawik Area Volunteer Emergency Rescue provides auxiliary health care.

Seldovia Village

[sell-DOAV-ee-uh]:
Also Known as Seldovia

Ethnicity: Den'aina
Athabascan; Sugpiaq Eskimo
(Alutiiq)

Local Contacts and Regional/State Organizations with Local Offices
There are no local organizations or contacts for this community.

Note
[Alaska Native Claims Settlement Act (ANCSA) Land Status] Seldovia Village was not included in ANCSA and it is not federally recognized as a Native village. Consequently, there is no ANCSA information for Seldovia Village.

Total labor force	97
Unemployment rate	10.5%
Per capita income *(1999)*	$21,396
Population *2000 census*	144
2003 Population	138
state demographer estimate	
Percent Native *2000 census*	40.3%

LOCATION
Seldovia Village is northeast of the City of Seldovia, across from Homer on the south shore of Kachemak Bay, a 15-minute flight. Flight time to Anchorage is 45 minutes.

CLIMATE
Winter temperatures in Seldovia vary from 12°F to 21°F; summer temperatures range from 48°F to 65°F. Yearly precipitation is 34.5 inches.

CULTURE AND HISTORY
Seldovia Village is northeast of Seldovia. Native residents are mixed Dena'ina Indian and Sugpiaq Eskimo (also known as Alutiiq). The name Seldovia comes from the Russian word *Seldevoy*, meaning "herring bay." Between 1869 and 1882 a trading post was located in the village. A post office opened in 1898. The village developed around commercial fishing and fish processing. About 40 percent of Seldovia Village residents are Native. Approximately 97 of the 159 homes in this area are vacant and used only seasonally. Commercial fishing and subsistence are an integral part of the local culture.

GOVERNMENT
Seldovia Village is unincorporated. There are no city or borough officials in this community.

ECONOMY
Nearby Seldovia City is a commercial fishing center.

Construction. Ten residents are employed in construction.

Fisheries. Farming, fishing, and forestry industries employ six residents.

Hunting and mining. Hunting and/or mining industries employ four residents.

Manufacturing. Employs two residents.

Services and retail. There are no business licenses established in the community. Retail trade employs seven residents; education, health and social services, six; and public administration, three.

Transportation. Transportation, warehousing, and utility industries employ four residents.

INFRASTRUCTURE
No capital projects are active in Seldovia Village.

Electricity. Homer Electric Association provides electricity.

Water and waste systems. Individual wells and on-site septic tanks serve households outside the City of Seldovia.

Transportation. Jakolof Bay road links Seldovia Village to Seldovia. Villagers use the airport, seaplane base, and harbor at Seldovia. The state ferry system connects the City of Seldovia to Homer. The Kachemak Bay Ferry and Mako Water Taxi also are available for passenger commutes to Homer.

Telecommunications. There is no in-state phone service, long distance service, television or cable access in the community.

COMMUNITY FACILITIES AND SERVICES
Education. Students attend school in Seldovia.

Health care. Seldovia Medical Clinic provides health care to the village. The Seldovia Volunteer Fire and Rescue provides auxiliary health care to Seldovia Village.

Total area of entitlement under ANCSA
92,160 acres

Total labor force   76
High school graduate or higher   73.8%
Bachelor's degree or higher   9.2%
Unemployment rate   27.4%
Per capita income *(2000)* $7,587
Population *2000 census*   129
Percent Native *2000 census*   96.9%

LOCATION
Shageluk is located in the interior of Alaska, on the east bank of the Innoko River, approximately 20 miles east of Anvik and 34 miles northeast of Holy Cross.

CLIMATE
Shageluk is located in the continental climate zone, characterized by long, cold winters and short, warm summers. Summer temperatures range from 42°F to over 80°F; winter temperatures vary from -62°F to 0°F. Average annual snowfall is 110 inches, and total precipitation averages 21 inches per year.

CULTURE AND HISTORY
Shageluk is a Deg Hit'an Athabascan community that relies on subsistence activities. It was first reported in 1850. Residents of Shageluk moved in the mid-1960s from a flood-prone location to a higher site, two miles east on the Innoko River. Every other year, the village is a checkpoint for the Iditarod Dogsled Race from Anchorage to Nome. There is a federally recognized tribe in the community-the Shageluk Native Village.

GOVERNMENT
Shageluk was incorporated as a second-class city in 1970, with a mayor and city council; it is located in the Unorganized Borough (see Alaska introduction). It is governed by an Indian Reorganization Act council, headed by a chief.

VILLAGE CORPORATION
The village corporation, Zho-Tse, was named after Shageluk's hill. Shareholders in the Zho-Tse village corporation also hold shares in Doyon, Limited regional Native corporation (see Alaska introduction).

ECONOMY
The city and the school are the primary employers. Construction projects during the summer offers seasonal employment. Residents depend upon subsistence activities. Trapping and gardening also are sources of income. Salmon, moose, bear, small game, and waterfowl provide food sources. A new store in the village is now open.

Fisheries. One resident holds a commercial fishing permit.

Government as employer. Of the 45 employed residents, 31 work for the local, state, or federal government.

Services and retail. There are four businesses in the community: air transportation support, public administration offices, a café, and a gasoline station. Retail trade employs 1 resident; education, health, and social services, 20; and public administration, 18.

Transportation. Four airline companies service Shageluk. Transportation, warehousing, and utility industries employ six residents.

INFRASTRUCTURE
Thirteen capital projects, funded by grants, are active in Shageluk.

Transportation. Access to Shageluk is by air or water. The state provides a 3,400- by 60-foot gravel airstrip. A seaplane base also is available. Major airport improvements are in progress. All-terrain vehicles, snowmobiles, and dog sleds are used for local transportation. Every other year Shageluk is a check point for the Iditarod dog sled race.

Electricity. Alaska Village Electric Cooperative (AVEC) provides electricity.

Water and waste systems. Residents haul treated well water and dispose of honeybuckets in pit privies or bunkers. The washeteria is available for bathing, laundry, and water. City water is made available to the school and the washeteria. Homes are not fully plumbed. HUD houses use pit privies. A sanitation master plan has been completed; the design and engineering of a community system need funding.

Telecommunications. In-state phone service is provided by Bush-Tell, long distance service by AT&T Alascom. Internet service is provided for the school by GCI. Teleconferencing is available through Alaska Teleconferencing Network. Alaska Rural Communications Service provides television access. There are two radio stations in the community. The City of Shageluk is the cable provider.

COMMUNITY FACILITIES AND SERVICES
Local facilities include a city building and teen center.

Education. Innoko River School is in the Iditarod Area School District. The school has 35 students and four teachers.

Health care. Local health clinics include Shageluk Health Clinic and Clara Morgan Subregional Clinic. Shageluk is classified as an isolated village and is found in EMS Region 7A in the Yukon/Kuskokwim Region. Emergency services have river, seaport, and air access. A health aide provides emergency care.

[SHAG-uh-look]
Ethnicity: Ingalik Athabascan

ANCSA village corporation
Zho-Tse, Incorporated
P.O. Box 108
Shageluk, AK 99665
907-473-8229

Shaktoolik

[shock-TOO-lick]
Ethnicity: Inpuiat Eskimo

ANCSA village corporation
Shaktoolik Native Corporation
P.O. Box 46
Shaktoolik, AK 99771
  907-955-3241
  907-955-3242
  907-955-3243 Fax

Total area of entitlement under ANCSA
          121,280 acres

Total labor force	57
High school graduate or higher	78.6%
Bachelor's degree or higher	7.7%
Unemployment rate	27.7%
Per capita income *(2000)*	$10,491
Population *2000 census*	230
Percent Native *2000 census*	94.8%

LOCATION
Shaktoolik is located on the east shore of Norton Sound, 125 miles east of Nome and just south of the Seward Peninsula.

CLIMATE
Shaktoolik is in the subarctic climate zone, with maritime influences when Norton Sound is ice free; freezing causes more influence from the continental climate. Summer temperatures range from 47°F to 62°F; winter temperatures vary from -4°F to 11°F. Average annual precipitation is 14 inches, including 43 inches of snowfall.

CULTURE AND HISTORY
Shaktoolik is a Malimiut Eskimo village, with a culture centered on fishing and subsistence activities. It was the first and southernmost Malimiut Eskimo settlement on Norton Sound, occupied as early as 1839. The village was originally located at the mouth of the Shaktoolik River and has since moved four times to its present, more sheltered, location. Twelve miles northeast is Iyatayet, a site that is between 6,000 and 8,000 years old. Reindeer herds were managed in the Shaktoolik area around 1905. Subsistence resources include seal, beluga whale, caribou, reindeer, moose, and fish. There is a federally recognized tribe in the community-the Native Village of Shaktoolik.

GOVERNMENT
Shaktoolik was incorporated as a second-class city in 1969, with a mayor and city council; it is located in the Unorganized Borough (see Alaska introduction). It also has an Indian Reorganization Act council, headed by a president.

VILLAGE CORPORATION
Shareholders in the village corporation also hold shares in Bering Straits Regional Native Corporation *(see Alaska introduction)*.

ECONOMY
Subsistence, supplemented by part-time wage earnings, is the core of Shaktoolik's economy. A village priority is the development of a new fish processing facility. Reindeer herding provides both income and meat. Fish, crab, moose, beluga whale, caribou, seal, rabbit, geese, cranes, ducks, ptarmigan, berries, greens, and roots also are primary food sources.

Fisheries. Thirty-three residents hold commercial fishing permits, chiefly for salmon and crab. Farming, fishing and or forestry industries employ two residents.

Government as employer. Of the 68 employed residents, 41 work for the local, state, or federal government.

Services and retail. There are five businesses in the community: two grocery stores, two day care centers, and a bed-and-breakfast. Retail trade employs 12 residents; education, health, and social services, 26; and public administration, 15.

Tourism and recreation. A bed-and-breakfast is available for lodging.

Transportation. Four airline companies service Shaktoolik. Transportation, warehousing, and utility industries employ 10 residents.

INFRASTRUCTURE
Eight capital projects, funded by grants, are active in Shaktoolik.

Transportation. Shaktoolik is primarily accessible by air and sea. The state provides a 4,000- by 75-foot gravel airstrip. The Alex Sookiayak Memorial Airstrip allows for regular service from Nome. All-terrain vehicles, motorbikes, trucks, and boats are used in summer; in winter, travel is by snowmachine and dog team. Cargo is barged to Nome, and then lightered to shore. There are no docking facilities in Shaktoolik.

Electricity. Alaska Village Electric Cooperative (AVEC) provides electricity.

Water and waste systems. Water is pumped from the nearby Togoomenik River to the pump house. There it is treated and stored in an 848,000-gallon insulated tank near the washeteria. Most residences are connected to a piped water and sewage collection system. Three-fourths of households have full plumbing and kitchen facilities. The school is connected to city water, and has received funds to develop a sewage treatment system to serve the community. The city provides an incinerator for disposal of refuse. The landfill is not permitted and needs to be relocated.

Telecommunications. In-state phone service is provided by Mukluk Telephone Company/TelAlaska, long distance service by AT&T Alascom, GCI, and Mukluk Telephone. Internet service is provided by GCI. Teleconferencing is available through Alaska Teleconferencing Network. Alaska Rural Communications Service provides television access. There are two radio stations in the community. The Shaktoolik Native Corporation is the cable provider.

COMMUNITY FACILITIES AND SERVICES
Local area facilities include a community building, city office, and teen center. An Elder Meal Program is available to senior citizens.

Education. Shaktoolik School is in the Bering Straits School District. The school has 57 students and eight teachers.

Health care. Shaktoolik Health Clinic provides health care to the community. Shaktoolik is classified as an isolated village and is found in EMS Region 5A in the Norton Sound Region. Emergency services have coastal and air access. A health aide provides emergency service.

Sheldon's Point
See Nunam Iqua

Total area of entitlement under ANCSA	
	124,280 acres
Total labor force	207
High school graduate or higher	48.0%
Bachelor's degree or higher	8.9%
Unemployment rate	16.4%
Per capita income *(1999)*	$10,487
Population *2000 census*	562
2003 population	594
state demographer estimate	
Percent Native *2000 census*	94.5%

LOCATION

Shishmaref is located on Sarichef Island, between Shishmaref Inlet and the Chukchi Sea, just north of Bering Strait. Shishmaref is 5 miles from the mainland, 126 miles north of Nome and 100 miles southwest of Kotzebue. The village is surrounded by the 2.6 million-acre Bering Land Bridge National Reserve. It is part of the Beringian National Heritage Park, endorsed by Presidents Bush and Gorbachev in 1990.

PHYSICAL DESCRIPTION

The city covers 2.8 square miles of land and 4.5 square miles of water only a few miles south of the Arctic Circle. It is on a sand spit only a few feet above the ocean. The land on the mainland, which is about five miles away, is flat tundra for many miles. Winter storms can cause significant flooding, with major floods in 1973 and 1989. During October 1997, a severe storm eroded over 30 feet of the north shore, requiring 14 homes and the National Guard Armory to be relocated. Five additional homes were relocated in 2002. Storms continue to erode the north (Chukchi Sea) shoreline three to five feet per year.

CLIMATE

The area experiences a transitional climate between the frozen Arctic and the continental interior. Summers can be foggy, with daily average temperatures ranging from 47°F to 54°F; winter daily average temperatures run from -12°F to 2°F. Average annual precipitation is about 8 inches, including 33 inches of snow. The Chukchi Sea is frozen from mid-November through mid-June.

CULTURE AND HISTORY

Shishmaref is a traditional Inupiat village with a fishing and subsistence lifestyle. Despite the rapid changes of the twentieth century, its people still obtain a good deal of their physical and spiritual sustenance from their traditional lands and waters. The town has a large Lutheran church.

Traditionally, people of this region traded and hunted with each other and neighboring groups, often traveling across Bering Strait to Siberia to trade with residents there. Sea mammal hunting (walrus, seals, and whales), fishing (salmon, arctic char, whitefish, herring, halibut, crabs), hunting (caribou and small mammals), and trapping characterized people's activities before the twentieth century. The original Inupiat name for the island was "Kigiktaq." Sporadic, though sometimes intense, contact between the local people and European and American traders, explorers, and whalers began in the late eighteenth century and continued into the nineteenth century. In 1816, Lt. Otto Von Kotzebue named the inlet "Shishmarev" after a member of his crew. Excavations at "Keekiktuk" by archaeologists around 1821 provided evidence of Inupiat habitation from several centuries before. Just before the gold rush, Sheldon Jackson introduced domesticated reindeer to the

region as a means of supplementing people's food and economic resources. When gold was discovered in Nome in 1898, the area soon attracted many American and European businessmen, miners, and traders. By 1900 the village had become a supply center for gold mining activities and was named after the inlet. A post office was established in 1901. Two devastating epidemics in 1901 and 1918 halved the population. The city government was incorporated in 1969. During October 1997, a severe storm eroded over 30 feet of the north shore, requiring 14 homes and the National Guard Armory to be relocated. Five additional homes were relocated in 2002. With no end in sight to the erosion, in July 2002 residents voted to relocate the community, but as of 2004 relocation had not yet been funded.

GOVERNMENT

Shishmaref is a second-class city located in the Unorganized Borough. The Native Village of Shishmaref is a BIA-recognized IRA council.

VILLAGE CORPORATION

The ANCSA village corporation is Shishmaref Native Corporation, which identifies itself as a civic organization. As of 2003, a conflict was holding up the process of reconveying §14(c)(3) land to the city. It may be that the proposed relocation to the mainland is also delaying such matters. Shareholders in the village corporation are also shareholders in the regional Native corporation, Bering Straits Native Corporation *(see Alaska introduction)*.

ECONOMY

The Shishmaref economy is based on subsistence supplemented by part-time wage earnings. Year-round jobs are limited. Villagers rely on fish, walrus, seal, polar bear, rabbit, and other subsistence foods. Public administration and educational, health, and social services employ almost half the work force.

Government as employer. The city, state, and federal government employ 117 residents.

Livestock raising. Two reindeer herds are managed from Shishmaref. Reindeer skins are tanned locally, and meat is available at the village store.

Manufacturing. Shishmaref has a strong Inupiat arts and crafts tradition. The Melvin Olanna Friendship Center and Carving Shop, a cultural center and carving facility, was recently completed for local artisans. The Tannery, operated by the village council, tans deer skins and sells local "cottage industry" leather products.

Services and retail. Shishmaref has two general stores, the Shishmaref Native Store operated by the village corporation, and the privately owned Nayokpuk General Store. The former stocks food and beverages, some clothing, fuel, firearms, and ammunition. There are two video rental shops, a snack bar, and two shops selling Native arts and crafts in addition to the Tannery and the Melvin Olanna Friendship Center and Carving Shop.

Tourism and recreation. Accommodations are limited. Nayokpuk General Store has a trailer for rent, the Lutheran church has visitor facilities, rooms may be rented in private homes, or visitors may be accommodated on the school floor. Attractions include the Tannery, the Melvin Olanna Friendship Center and Carving Shop, the two general stores, and

[SHISH-muh-reff]
Ethnicity: Inupiat

Municipality
City of Shishmaref
P.O. Box 83
Shishmaref, AK 99772
  907-649-3781
  907-649-2131 Fax

Native entity
Native Village of Shishmaref
P.O. Box 72110
Shishmaref, AK 99772
  907-649-3821
  907-649-2104 Fax

ANCSA village corporation
Shishmaref Native Corporation
P.O. Box 72151
Shishmaref, AK 99772
  907-649-3751
  907-649-3731 Fax

Shishmaref

Shoonaq'

See Urban Tribes

Also known as Kodiak

the Shishmaref Dog Mushers Association. The Shishmaref Carnival in April features dog races, basketball tournaments, and other competitions.

Transportation. One local firm provides support for air and water transportation.

INFRASTRUCTURE

Transportation. Primary access to Shishmaref is by air, with the number of daily flights dependent on the weather. A state-owned 5,000- by 70-foot paved runway was built in the early 1990s, with improvements in the late 1990s. Scheduled, charter, and freight services are available from Nome from Baker Aviation, Bering Air, Grant Aviation, and Hageland Aviation. Most residents own boats for trips to the mainland. In 2002, the U.S. Army Corps of Engineers funded improvements for navigation in the Bering Strait.

Electricity. Electricity is provided by the Alaska Village Electrical Co-operative (AVEC), of which the city is a member, from a 971-kilowatt diesel plant.

Fuel storage (gallons). IRA Store (130,200); Alaska Village Electric Cooperative (AVEC) (122,200); city (87,200); Nayokpuk Trading Post (82,600); Bering Straits Schools (54,200); National Guard (9,700); city water (8,200); Lutheran church (6,900); U.S. Fish and Wildlife (3,100).

Water and waste systems. The city obtains water from a surface source, treats it in a recently upgraded plant, chlorinates it, and stores it in a tank built in the mid-1990s. Improvements to the water system were underway as of 2002, including a piped delivery system and household plumbing. Homes not yet connected have water delivered by truck from a central watering point. Residents use outhouses and honeybuckets, the latter hauled by the city. As of 2002, improvements were underway including a new flush/haul system and household plumbing. The public buildings are connected to a sewage lagoon. A new landfill and access road were completed in the late 1990s.

Telecommunications. Local telephone service is provided by Mukluk Telephone Co./TelAlaska, long distance service by AT&T Alascom, GCI, or Mukluk Telephone. GCI and Nome.net provide Internet services. At least thirteen AM radio stations broadcast to the area from Nome, Kotzebue, Bethel, Anchorage, and other locations. The Alaska Rural Communications Service broadcasts two television channels locally, and Shishmaref Village Corporation provides cable services.

COMMUNITY FACILITIES AND SERVICES

The washeteria, operated by the city, was renovated in 2003. Other community facilities include the city sports center, and the council-operated Melvin Olanna Friendship Center which serves as a youth center and community hall. The city operates the water and waste disposal systems.

Education. Shishmaref School serves 173 students in grades preschool through twelve, with 16 teachers. It is operated by the Bering Straits School District. The school is also part of the STEP/STAR learning system, which provides students access to additional course offerings via satellite. The school's roof was replaced in 2002 at a cost of more than $8 million. The Nellie Weyiouanna Ilisaavik Library is operated by the city. In addition to their other functions, the council-operated Shishmaref Tannery and Melvin Olanna Carving Center serve as teaching centers for elders to teach traditional skills to the children of the community.

Health care. Health care is provided by the Katherine Miksruaq Olanna Health Clinic, operated by Norton Sound Health Corporation and renovated in 2002-03. Emergency service is provided by a health aide. The nearest hospital is Norton Sound Regional Hospital in Nome, about 136 miles away. The city volunteer fire department/emergency services also provides health care.

Public safety. Law enforcement is provided by a state village public safety officer (VPSO)(position vacant as of August 2004), backed by state troopers in Nome. Emergency response is provided by the VPSO and the city volunteer fire department/emergency services.

ENVIRONMENTAL CONCERNS

Shishmaref is washing away at a rate of three to five feet per year on the north (Chukchi Sea) side of the village. There is controversy over the cause between those who blame global warming, those who maintain that a current moving across the shore is stripping the sand away, and those who hold storm surges responsible. Whatever the cause or causes, preventive measures have failed. In 2000, the BIA funded preliminary work on relocation, and in 2002 the community voted to relocate to the mainland. This means abandoning homes and territory that the people have used for generations. However, the cost has been estimated at greater than $100 million, and federal emergency funds are not available for this kind of gradual destruction. One likely site for a new village is a barge-accessible spot known as West Nunatak, on the mainland about seven miles to the southwest of the present village location.

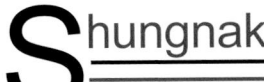
Total area of entitlement under ANCSA
92,160 acres

Total labor force	109
High school graduate or higher	51.5%
Bachelor's degree or higher	9.0%
Unemployment rate	27.5%
Per capita income *(1999)*	$10,377
Population *2000 census*	256
2003 population	264
state demographer estimate	
Percent Native *2000 census*	94.5%

LOCATION
Shungnak is located on the west bank of the Kobuk River about 150 miles east of Kotzebue. The original settlement was 10 miles further upstream at Kobuk.

PHYSICAL DESCRIPTION
The city covers 8.4 square miles of land and 1.3 square miles of water. Except for a few storage buildings and two or three houses, the city is located on a bluff above the Kobuk River. A flood in 1985 came within two inches of the door threshold of one of those houses. A flood in 1937 was probably higher, but still nowhere near the height of the bluff.

CLIMATE
The community is located in the transitional climate zone. Average daily winter temperatures run from -10°F to 15°F. Average daily summer temperatures range from 40°F to 65°F. Temperature extremes have been recorded from -60°F to 90°F. Snowfall averages 80 inches, with an average annual total precipitation of 16 inches. The Kobuk River is navigable from the end of May to mid-October.

CULTURE AND HISTORY
Shungnak is a traditional Inupiat village with a subsistence lifestyle. Inupiat residents speak the Malimiut dialect of Inupiaq. The name "Inupiaq," meaning "real or genuine person" (-*inuk* "person" plus -*piaq* "real, genuine"), is often spelled "Iñupiaq" in the Malimiut dialect. It can refer to a person of this group ("He is an Inupiaq") and can also be used as an adjective ("She is an Inupiaq woman"). "Inupiat" refers to the people collectively (for example, "the Inupiat of the Kobuk River").

Founded in 1899 as a supply point for mining activities in the Cosmos Hills, the village was forced to move in the 1920s because of river erosion and flooding. The old site, 10 miles upstream, was renamed Kobuk by those who remained there. The new village was named "Kochuk," but later reverted to the original name of the old village, Shungnak. This name is derived from the Inupiaq word *issingnak*, which means "jade", found throughout the surrounding hills.

GOVERNMENT
The city government was incorporated in 1967, and is one of the 12 communities in the Northwest Arctic Borough. It has a seven-member council, including the mayor, who is responsible for day-to-day operations. It levies a sales tax of 2 percent. The Native Village of Shungnak is a BIA-recognized Native entity and IRA tribal council.

VILLAGE CORPORATION
Shungnak, along with all of the other communities in the Northwest Arctic Borough except Kotzebue, merged its ANCSA village corporation into NANA Regional Corporation, the ANCSA regional Native corporation *(see Alaska introduction)*.

ECONOMY
Shungnak subsists mainly on fishing, seasonal employment, hunting, and trapping. Subsistence food sources include sheefish, whitefish, caribou, moose, ducks, and berries. More than half of employed residents work in education, health and social services, or public administration. The federal Bureau of Land Management provides seasonal employment in fire fighting, hiring over 30 residents each year. Shungnak also has a strong arts-and-crafts industry. Residents make and sell finely-crafted baskets, masks, mukluks, parkas, hats, and mittens. The community wants to develop a visitor center, mini-mall, post office, and clinic complex.

Government as employer. Of employed residents, 42 work for the city, borough, state, or federal government.

Manufacturing. Shungnak has a strong arts-and-crafts industry. Residents make and sell finely-crafted baskets, masks, mukluks, parkas, hats, and mittens.

Services and retail. Shungnak has two general stores and two day-care providers.

Tourism and recreation. Accomodations include Shungnak Lodge and Commack's Lodge.

INFRASTRUCTURE
Transportation. Shungnak is accessible by plane, barge or small boat. The state-owned lighted gravel runway is 4,000 feet long by 60 feet wide, and has scheduled regional air services. Servicing lines include Bering Air, Hageland Aviation, Servant Air, Tanana Air Service, and Warbelow's Air Venture. Major airport improvements were made in the late 1990s. Fuel and supplies are barged in each summer. Small boats, all-terrain vehicles, snowmachines, and dog sleds are used for local travel and subsistence activities. Trails along the river are still used for inter-village travel.

Electricity. Electricity is provided by the Alaska Village Electrical Cooperative (AVEC), of which the city is a member, from a 1,248-kilowatt diesel plant.

Fuel storage (gallons). AVEC (122,400); IRA Store (74,300); Northwest Arctic Schools (41,700); city (16,400); Commack Lodge (8,100); Army National Guard (6,900); Alaska Department of Trsnportation (2,800).

Water and waste systems. A 200,000-gallon steel storage tank is intermittently filled from the Kobuk River. Construction began on a new storage tank and water treatment plant in 2003. Piped water and sewer are provided to 53 homes (those at the top of the bluff), the clinic, school, and community building. Shungnak has a 6-inch buried gravity sewage main, which drains into a small diked lake one-half mile northwest of the city. The few houses at the foot of the bluff haul water and use outhouses. The city also operates a Class 3 landfill.

Telecommunications. Local telephone service is provided by OTZ Telephone Co-op, long distance service by AT&T Alascom, GCI, or OTZ Telephone. GCI provides Internet service, and the city operates a cable television system. One FM radio station (K204AS, 88.7 FM, a repeater for KOTZ in Kotzebue) broadcasts from Shungnak. AM radio stations from Galena, Anchorage, Nome, Barrow, Kotzebue, and elsewhere broadcast to the area. Two channels of broadcast television service can be received from repeaters located in Shungnak, one from the Alaska Rural Communications Service and one owned by the city.

[SHUNG-nack]
Ethnicity: Inupiat

Municipality
City of Shungnak
P.O. Box 59
Shungnak, AK 99773
907-437-2161
907-437-2176 Fax

Native entity
Native Village of Shungnak
IRA
P.O. Box 64
Shungnak, AK 99773
907-437-2163
907-437-2183 Fax

ANCSA village corporation
NANA Regional Corporation
P.O. Box 49
Kotzebue, AK 99752
907-442-3301
907-442-2866 Fax
nana.com

Sitka
See Urban Tribes

Shungnak

Sitka
See Urban Tribes

COMMUNITY FACILITIES AND SERVICES
The city has a public safety building and a recreation center, and in 2003 was proposing to build a multipurpose community/cultural/recreation center. The village has an office which serves as a community hall. The city operates the water and waste disposal systems, the cable system, and a one-channel broadcast television repeater. The village operates a general store and provides bulk fuel sales.

Education. The Northwest Arctic School District operates the Shungnak School, serving 75 students in grades K-12 with eight teachers. The school library serves as the community library.

Health care. Maniilaq Health Corporation, the regional non-profit health services provider, operates the new (2002-03) Shungnak Clinic. Emergency service is provided by volunteers and a health aide. It is supported by the Maniilaq Health Center in Kotzebue.

Public safety. Law enforcement is provided by state troopers in Kotzebue, emergency response by the city volunteer fire department.

Skagway

Ethnicity: Tlingit

Municipality
City of Skagway
P.O. Box 415
Skagway, AK 99840
907-983-2297
907-983-2151 Fax
skagway.org

Native entity
Skagway Village
P.O. Box 1157
Skagway, AK 99840
907-983-4068
907-983-3068
skagwaytraditional.org

NOTE
Skagway is a non-Native tourist community. While Skagway Village is a BIA-recognized Native entity, only about one-twentieth of the population of the City of Skagway is Native Alaskan. Except for basic orientation information, this profile discusses only those aspects of Skagway that are unique to its Native residents.

Population *2000 census*	862
2003 population	845
state demographer estimate	
Percent Native *2000 census*	5.1%

LOCATION
Skagway is located 90 miles northeast of Juneau at the northernmost end of Lynn Canal, at the head of Taiya Inlet. It lies 108 road miles south of Whitehorse, just west of the Canadian border at British Columbia.

PHYSICAL DESCRIPTION
The area encompasses 452.4 square miles of land and 11.9 square miles of water.

CLIMATE
Skagway experiences a maritime climate with cool summers and mild winters. Summer high temperatures range from 45°F to 67°F. Winter low temperatures range from 18°F to 37°F. Skagway receives less rain than is typical of Southeast Alaska, averaging 26 inches of precipitation per year, including 39 inches of snow.

CULTURE AND HISTORY
Skagway is predominantly a tourist community, with historic Tlingit influences. The Tlingit name for the area was *Skagua*, meaning "the place where the north wind blows," or *Shgagwéi*, "wind off the mountain." It was a subsistence area for the *Lkóot* (Chilkoot) band of Tlingit from the area northeast of Haines and the area around Klukwan and the focus of important Tlingit trade routes to the interior. The Tlingit have always been a commercial people and used these routes to trade items like fish and seal oils, seafood, and shells to the *Gunanaa* (Interior Tribes) in exchange for moose hides and meat and valuable minerals like copper.

Skagway was not permanently settled until Captain William Moore and Skookum Jim, a Tlingit from the Yukon Territory, discovered the White Pass route into interior Canada in 1887, and later that year Captain Moore and his son Bernard staked a claim and built a cabin on the waterfront. Ten years later, gold was discovered in the Klondike, and Skagway was the beginning of the easiest route north to the gold fields. In the first year of the gold rush, the population reached 20,000. Skagway became the first incorporated city in Alaska in 1900. Its population at that time was 3,117, making it the second-largest settlement in Alaska. The Native population was high during the early twentieth century, but disease and racism cut the population by eighty to ninety-five percent by mid-century.

GOVERNMENT
Skagway Village is a BIA-recognized Native entity and traditional tribal council. It is also known locally as the Skaqua Traditional Council or Skagway Traditional Council.

VILLAGE CORPORATION
While Skagway has no ANCSA village corporation of its own, its members are at-large shareholders in Sealaska Corporation, the regional Native corporation, and may be shareholders in another village corporation (for example, Goldbelt in Juneau or Klukwan, Inc.). Legislation has been introduced in Congress to provide ANCSA village corporations for five "panhandle" Native entities, including Skagway, that did not get them under the ANCSA, but it has not yet been passed into law.

COMMUNITY FACILITIES AND SERVICES
The village is building a tribal community center. As of May 2004 it had an estimated completion date in September or October.

Health care. Village members are eligible for medical care from the SouthEast Alaska Regional Health Consortium (SEARHC), a nonprofit organization that provides health care services to Alaska Natives and American Indians residing in the region. SEARHC contracts for care locally, or residents may travel to the SEARHC subregional clinic in Haines. Hospital-level care is available at SEARHC-operated Mount Edgecumbe Hospital in Sitka.

Total area of entitlement under ANCSA
92,160 acres

Total labor force	29
High school graduate or higher	50.0%
Bachelor's degree or higher	12.0%
Unemployment rate	27.6%
Per capita income *(1999)*	$8,150
Population *2000 census*	100
2003 population	72
state demographer estimate	
Percent Native *2000 census*	89.0%

LOCATION
Sleetmute is located on the east bank of the Kuskokwim River, 1.5 miles north of its junction with the Holitna River. It lies 79 miles east of Aniak, 166 miles northeast of Bethel, and 243 miles west of Anchorage.

PHYSICAL DESCRIPTION
The area encompasses 99.5 square miles of land and 5.8 square miles of water. In 1964, the entire community, including the airstrip, was flooded to a depth of five feet. A 1971 flood reached a level approximately two feet lower. The 100-year flood level is estimated to be one to two feet higher than the 1964 flood.

CLIMATE
The climate in Sleetmute is continental with temperatures ranging from -58°F to 90°F. Average annual precipitation is 22 inches, including 85 inches of snow. High winds often cause flight delays in the fall and winter. The Kuskokwim River is ice free from mid-June through October.

CULTURE AND HISTORY
Sleetmute is a Deg Xinag Athabascan village, and subsistence activities contribute substantially to local diets. Of a total population of about 275 Deg Xinag people in several villages, about 40 speak the language, which is well documented. Sleetmute was founded by Deg Xinag Athabascans. The name means "whetstone people," referring to slate deposits found nearby. Frederick Bishop started a trading post at Sleetmute in 1906. A school opened in 1921, followed by a post office in 1923. A Russian Orthodox church, The Saints Peter and Paul Mission, was built in 1931.

GOVERNMENT
Sleetmute is an unincorporated village located in the Unorganized Borough. It is governed by the Village of Sleetmute, a BIA-recognized Native entity, also known as the Sleetmute Traditional Council.

VILLAGE CORPORATION
The ANCSA village corporation is the Kuskokwim Corporation, formed in 1977 by the merger of ten village corporations along the middle Kuskokwim River. In addition to over 950,000 acres of surface rights, it owns a substantial securities portfolio, investments in three apartment complexes in Fairbanks, a hotel in Fairbanks, a Hispanic broadcasting network, a telecommunication bandwidth and service provider, an engineering, remediation, and construction services firm, and a casino opportunity near Denver, Colorado. It owns the surface rights to the Donlin Creek property, one of the world's largest undeveloped gold deposits. In 2003, it was beginning to pursue §8(a) federal contracting opportunities and establish partnerships and mentor-protégé relationships with established contractors. Shareholders in the Kuskokwim Corporation are also shareholders in Calista Corporation, the regional Native corporation.

ECONOMY
Most cash income in Sleetmute is derived seasonally from Bureau of Land Management fire fighting, trapping, or from cannery work in other communities. The school is the primary employer. Most foods are derived from subsistence fishing, hunting, and gathering. Salmon, moose, bear, porcupine, rabbit, waterfowl, and berries are harvested in season.

Fisheries. One resident holds a commercial fishing permit, but as of 2003 it has not been used since 1995. Many residents travel to fish camps during the summer.

Government as employer. Ten residents work for the village, state, or federal government.

Manufacturing. There is a woodworking shop in the village.

Services and retail. Sleetmute has two general stores, one with a gas station, and a bulk petroleum dealer.

Tourism and recreation. Accommodations are available at the Two Rivers, and there is an "outdoor recreation resort" and guide service.

INFRASTRUCTURE
Transportation. The Kuskokwim River provides barge and boat transportation in the summer, and snowmachines are used on the frozen river in the winter. The 3,100- by 60-foot gravel airstrip is owned and maintained by the state. Scheduled weekday service is provided, with Hageland Aviation, Inland Aviation Services, and Tanana Air Service providing service to Sleetmute. As of 2003, the Federal Aviation Administration had planned to rehabilitate the airstrip beginning in 2005 at an estimated cost of $4 million. As of 2003, the Bureau of Indian Affairs had funded construction of village streets at an estimated cost of $2.5 million.

Electricity. Electricity is provided by the Middle Kuskokwim Electric Cooperative from a 140-kilowatt diesel plant.

Fuel storage (gallons). Kuspuk Schools (33,100); village council/fuel depot (28,600); Middle Kuskokwim Electric Cooperative (17,600); Hill Enterprises (7,500); Crescent Lake Lodge (5,000).

Water and waste systems. A central well with treated water and several individual wells are used in the community. Water is pumped by hand to fill gravity storage tanks at each house. Privies, honeybuckets, and seepage pits are used by 27 homes. Eleven homes and the school use individual systems and are completely plumbed. Significant further upgrades, including the installation of piped water and sewer systems, were in preliminary stages in 2004. There is a Class 3 landfill southeast of the airstrip.

Telecommunications. Local telephone service is provided by Bush-Tell, long distance service by AT&T Alascom. Internet service is provided to the school by GCI. The Alaska Rural Communications Service has a television broadcast repeater in the community.

COMMUNITY FACILITIES AND SERVICES
In 2001 a fire destroyed the building with the laundromat, clinic,

[SLEET-myoot]
Ethnicity: Deg Xinag
Athabascan

Native entity
Village of Sleetmute
P.O. Box 34
Sleetmute, AK 99668
907-449-4213
907-449-4203 Fax

ANCSA village corporation
The Kuskokwim Corporation
4300 B Street, Suite 207
Anchorage, AK 99503
907-243-2944
907-243-2984 Fax
kuskokwim.com

Sleetmute

offices and meeting hall, and satellite dish. A new washeteria and a core services facility were under construction as of 2003. The central well and waste disposal systems are operated by the village.

Education. The Kuspuk School District operates the Jack Egnaty Sr. School, serving 25 students in grades K-12 with two teachers. The school library serves as the community's public library.

Health care. As of 2003, a new Sleetmute Clinic was under construction, the previous clinic having been destroyed by fire in 2001. It is operated by the Yukon-Kuskokwim Health Corporation and backed by the Clara Morgan Sub-Regional Clinic in Aniak. Emergency service is provided by a health aide.

Public safety. Law enforcement is provided by a state village public safety officer (VPSO) (position vacant as of August 2004), backed by state troopers in Aniak. Emergency response is provided by the village volunteer fire department.

Solomon

Ethnicity: Inupiat Eskimo

Solomon Native Corporation
P.O. Box 243
Nome, AK 99762
  907-443-7526
  907-443-7527 Fax

Total area of entitlement under ANCSA
                                    69,120 acres
Population *2000 census*   4
Percent Native *2000 census*   75%

LOCATION
Solomon is located 30 miles east of Nome, on the Norton Sound coast of the Seward Peninsula.

CLIMATE
Solomon is predominately in the maritime climate zone, with strong continental influences. Summers are short, wet, and mild; winters are cold and windy. Temperatures range between winter lows of -30°F and summer highs of 56°F.

CULTURE AND HISTORY
Solomon was originally settled by Inupiat Eskimos of the Fish River Tribe. It became a mining camp at the height of the Nome gold rush. Only one family lives at the site year-round; it is a subsistence-use area for Nome residents. There is a federally recognized tribe in the community-the Native Village of Solomon.

GOVERNMENT
Solomon is unincorporated and is located in the Unorganized Borough *(see Alaska introduction)*. It is governed by a traditional village council, headed by a president.

VILLAGE CORPORATION
Shareholders in the village corporation also hold shares in Bering Straits Regional Native Corporation *(see Alaska introduction)*.

ECONOMY
Solomon residents depend almost entirely upon subsistence hunting and fishing for their livelihood. There are limited summer jobs in the area and in Nome. Some gold mining still occurs.

Government as employer. No residents employed in government.

Services and retail. There are no businesses in the community.

INFRASTRUCTURE
Four capital projects, funded by grants, are active in Solomon.

Transportation. Solomon is located along the Nome/Council Road. The Solomon Village Corporation owns a 1,150- by 35-foot dirt and gravel airstrip. Charter flights are available from Nome. Snowmachines and dogsleds are used in winter for transportation.

Water and waste systems. Residents haul water from Manilla Creek, Jerusalem Creek, or Solomon River. Honeybuckets are used by villagers.

Electricity. Solomon Gulch Hydro provides electricity.

Telecommunications. In-state phone service is provided by Mukluk Telephone Co./TelAlaska; long distance service by AT&T Alascom.

COMMUNITY FACILITIES AND SERVICES
No public facilities or schools are available in Solomon.

Health care. Local hospitals or health clinics include Norton Sound Regional Hospital in Nome. Norton Sound Regional Hospital in Nome provides auxiliary health care.

South Naknek

Also known as Qinuyang

[NACK-neck]
Ethnicity: Alutiiq Aleut

Alaska Peninsula Corporation
800 Cordova Street #102
Anchorage, AK 99501
  907-274-2433
  907-274-8694 Fax

Total area of entitlement under ANCSA
                                    92,160 acres
Total labor force   112
High school graduate or higher   81.9%
Bachelor's degree or higher   8.5%
Unemployment rate   24.1%
Per capita income *(2000)* $13,019
Population *2000 census*   137
Percent Native *2000 census*   83.9%

LOCATION
South Naknek is on the south bank of the Naknek River, across the river from Naknek on the Alaska Peninsula, 297 miles southwest of Anchorage.

CLIMATE
South Naknek has a predominantly maritime climate, characterized by cool, humid, and windy weather. Occasional continental climatic influences cause temperature extremes. Average summer temperatures range from 42°F to 63°F; winter temperatures range from 4°F to 29°F. Annual precipitation averages 20 inches, including yearly snowfall of 45 inches.

CULTURE AND HISTORY
South Naknek is a traditional Aleut village, with a subsistence-oriented culture. A Native village known as Qinuyana was once located on the site where the village developed. South Naknek was settled early in the twentieth century, as a result of salmon-cannery development on the south shore of the Naknek River. People began to settle on the riverfront, and soon South

Naknek began to grow (although few parcels of land were actually privately owned). Many of the villagers came to South Naknek from the villages of New and Old Savonoski. South Naknek was one of the many villages along the Bristol Bay Coast visited by reindeer herders. Fresh reindeer meat provided a welcome variation in residents' diet. There is a federally recognized tribe in the community—the South Naknek Village Council.

GOVERNMENT
South Naknek is unincorporated under Alaska law and is located in the Bristol Bay Borough *(see Alaska introduction)*. It is governed by a traditional village council, headed by a president.

VILLAGE CORPORATION
Shareholders in the village corporation also hold shares in Bristol Bay Regional Native Corporation *(see Alaska introduction)*.

ECONOMY
Commercial fishing and salmon processing are the mainstays of South Naknek's economy. Other than seasonal fishing and related jobs, most employment is in public services. A few people trap, and most residents depend on subsistence hunting and fishing to supplement their incomes. Trident Seafoods operates in South Naknek. Salmon, trout, caribou, rabbit, porcupine, and seal are utilized.

Construction. Four residents are employed in construction.

Fisheries. Forty-three residents hold commercial fishing permits, chiefly for salmon. Farming, fishing, and forestry employ two residents.

Government as employer. Of the 44 employed residents, 28 work for the local, state, or federal government.
Manufacturing. There are two boat-building businesses in the village. Four residents are employed in manufacturing.

Services and retail. There are 11 businesses in the community, including an automotive repair and maintenance business, a day care center, a lodge, an electronics and appliance store, and the Native Village of South Naknek. Education, health, and social services employ 14 residents; financial and related businesses, 3; and public administration, 11.

Transportation. Two transportation companies are located in South Naknek (one is primarily a school bus transportation company). Transportation, warehousing, and/or utility industries employ two residents.

INFRASTRUCTURE
Eight capital projects, funded by grants, are active in South Naknek.

Transportation. South Naknek is accessible by air or sea. The state provides lighted, gravel runways. One is 2,260- by 60-feet; the other is 3,310- by 60- feet. The PAF Cannery airport is within three miles of South Naknek. The airport has a 750- by 30- foot dirt strip and a 650- by 75- foot crosswind strip. Scheduled and charter flight services are available. Floatplanes use a 3,000-foot designated stretch of the Naknek River. The frozen river in winter can be used as an ice road to Naknek and King Salmon. An unmaintained road to New Savonoski is open. The borough provides a mid- and high-tide cargo dock at South Naknek with 200-foot of berth space for barges. For local travel, residents use trucks, cars, all-terrain vehicles, snowmachines, and boats.

Water and waste systems. Most of the residents depend on individual water wells and septic systems, while others use a piped water and sewer system. Thirty houses are now connected to a piped water and sewer system. Two permitted landfills are open; one is run by the borough, the other by Peter Pan Seafoods.

Electricity. Power lines cross the Naknek River east of Naknek and connect to South Naknek. Naknek Electric Association provides electricity.

Telecommunications. In-state phone service is provided by Bristol Bay Telephone Co-op, long distance service by GCI and AT&T. Internet service is provided by Bristol Bay Telephone Cooperative and GCI. Alaska Rural Communications Service provides television access. There are two radio stations in the community. Cable service is not provided.

COMMUNITY FACILITIES AND SERVICES
Local facilities include a community hall and the library.

Education. South Naknek Elementary School is in the Bristol Bay Borough School District. The school has 13 students and one teacher. Students from sixth grade through high school are flown to Naknek daily to attend school.

Health care. Local hospitals or health clinics include South Naknek Health Clinic and Camai Medical Center. South Naknek is classified as an isolated village and is found in EMS Region 2I in the Bristol Bay Region. Emergency services have limited highway, coastal, air, and river access. Volunteers and a health aide provide emergency service. Bristol Bay Borough Emergency Services and Camai Medical Center provide auxiliary health care.

Stebbins

Total area of entitlement under ANCSA	
	124,800 acres
Total labor force	339
High school graduate or higher	62.6%
Bachelor's degree or higher	12.2%
Unemployment rate	22.6%
Per capita income *(2000)*	$8,249
Population *2000 census*	547
Percent Native *2000 census*	94.7%

LOCATION
Stebbins is located on the northwest coast of St. Michael Island, 120 miles southeast of Nome in Norton Sound. The village of St. Michael is 15 miles away to the southeast.

CLIMATE
Stebbins is located in the subarctic maritime climate zone, with continental influences during the winter. Average summer temperatures range from 40°F to 60°F; winter temperatures vary from -4°F to 16°F.

CULTURE AND HISTORY
Stebbins is a Yup'ik Eskimo village, with a subsistence-oriented culture; the Native name for the village is *Tapreq*. The Eskimo village of Atroik was reported on this site in 1898. Fort St. Michael was built by the Russian-American Company at nearby St. Michael. There is a federally recognized tribe in the community-the Stebbins Community Association.

Ethnicity: Yup'ik Eskimo

Stebbins Native Corporation
P.O. Box 71110
Stebbins, AK 99671
907-934-3074
907-934-2399 Fax

Stebbins

GOVERNMENT

Stebbins was incorporated as a second-class city in 1969, with a mayor and city council. It is located in the Unorganized Borough *(see Alaska introduction)*. It also has an Indian Reorganization Act village council, headed by a president.

VILLAGE CORPORATION

Shareholders in the village corporation also hold shares in Bering Straits Regional Native Corporation *(see Alaska introduction)*.

ECONOMY

The economy of Stebbins is based on subsistence activities, supplemented by part-time wage earnings. The city government and schools provide the only full-time positions in the village. Reindeer herding was important in the past, and there is still an unmanaged herd on nearby Stewart Island. The commercial herring fishery has become increasingly important, including fishing on the lower Yukon River. Residents depend on fish, seal, reindeer, and beluga whale to supplement their incomes. Summer gardens provide vegetables.

Fisheries. Eighteen residents hold commercial fishing permits.

Government as employer. Of the 161 employed residents, 125 work for the local, state, or federal government.

Manufacturing. Two residents are employed in manufacturing.

Services and retail. There are 10 businesses in the community, including a general store, day care center, rock products company, trading post, and the Stebbins Native Store. Retail trade employs 18 residents; financial and related businesses, 2; education, health, and social services, 84; and public administration, 30.

Tourism and recreation. Cultural events include a three-day Potlatch and Yupik Cultural Week. Arts, entertainment, recreation, accommodations, and food service industries employ seven residents. There is a video rental store in the village.

Transportation. Four airline companies service Stebbins. Transportation, warehousing, and utility industries employ six residents.

INFRASTRUCTURE

Nine capital projects, funded by grants, are active in Stebbins.

Transportation. Stebbins is accessible by air and sea. The state provides a 3,000- by 60-foot gravel runway. Regular flights, charters, and freight services are available at Bethel. Supplies are brought in annually by a cargo ship. Dock facilities are not available; lighterage of goods to shore is provided out of Nome. Snowmachines are used for overland travel in the winter.

Electricity. Alaska Village Electric Cooperative (AVEC) provides electricity.

Water and waste systems. Major improvements are under construction to enable a piped water and vacuum sewer system, with household plumbing. Residents haul water and deposit honeybuckets in bunkers. Water, drawn in summer from Big Clear Creek, is treated and stored in a 1,000,000-gallon steel water tank. Watering points are available in the village during summer, distributed from the tank by plastic pipelines. A reservoir at Clear Lake and a new water storage tank will soon alleviate winter water shortages. The landfill is not permitted. The city collects refuse from central bins.

Telecommunications. In-state phone service is provided by Mukluk Telephone/TelAlaska, long distance service by AT&T Alascom, GCI, and Mukluk Telephone. Internet service is provided by GCI. Teleconferencing is available through Alaska Teleconferencing Network. Alaska Rural Communications Service provides television access. There are two radio stations in the community. The city is the cable provider.

COMMUNITY FACILITIES AND SERVICES

Local area facilities include a city community hall, a teen center, and housing facilities for senior citizens.

Education. Tukurngailnguq School is in the Bering Straits School District. The school has 201 students and 18 teachers.

Health care. Local hospitals or health clinics include Stebbins Health Clinic. The clinic is a qualified emergency care center. Stebbins is classified as an isolated village and is found in EMS Region 5A in the Norton Sound Region. Emergency services have coastal and air access. A health aide provides emergency service.

Stevens Village

Ethnicity: Koyukon Athabascan

ANCSA village corporation
Dinyea Corporation
P.O. Box 71372
Fairbanks, AK 99707
907-474-8224
907-474-8224 Fax

Total area of entitlement under ANCSA

	111,727 acres
Total labor force	62
Unemployment rate	38.9%
Per capita income *(2000)*	$7,113
Population *2000 census*	87
Percent Native *2000 census*	95.4%

LOCATION

Stevens Village is located on the north bank of the Yukon River, 17 miles upstream of the Dalton Highway bridge crossing and 90 miles northwest of Fairbanks.

CLIMATE

Stevens Village is located in the subarctic climate zone, characterized by seasonal extremes of temperature. Winters are long and harsh; summers are warm and short. Summer temperatures range from 65°F to 80°F or above; winter temperatures range from as low as -71°F to 0°F. Annual precipitation averages 6.5 inches, including 43 inches of snowfall.

CULTURE AND HISTORY

The Native population is predominantly Koyukon Indian, with a culture centered on subsistence activities. Founded by three Athabascan Indian brothers, the village was named for Old Steven, when he was elected chief. During the gold rush in the nineteenth century, residents cut wood for mining operations and for fueling steamboats traveling the Yukon River. There is a federally recognized tribe in the community-the Stevens Village IRA Council.

GOVERNMENT

Stevens Village is unincorporated and is located in the Unorganized Borough *(see Alaska introduction)*. It is governed by an Indian Reorganization Act village council, headed by a first chief.

VILLAGE CORPORATION

Shareholders in the village corporation also hold shares in Doyon Regional Native Corporation *(see Alaska introduction)*.

ECONOMY

The economy of Stevens Village is heavily dependent upon subsistence activities, although there is some seasonal and part-time employment from the school, clinic, village council, and Bureau of Land Management firefighting. Stevens Village is heavily dependent upon subsistence activities. Salmon, whitefish, moose, bear, waterfowl, and small game are the primary food sources, along with berries and garden vegetables.

Fisheries. Three residents hold commercial fishing permits, chiefly for salmon and whitefish.

Government as employer. Of the 22 employed residents, 12 work for the local, state, or federal government.

Services and retail. There are two businesses in the community: a grocery store and an air transportation support company. Education, health, and social service industries employ nine residents and public administration employs eight residents.

Tourism and recreation. The village corporation owns a tour company, Yukon River Tours, which offers summer river trips and overnight stays at a traditional fish camp. The tour teaches visitors about the Koyukon Athabascans' culture and history and the villagers' present way of life.

Transportation. Two airline companies service Stevens Village. Transportation, warehousing, and utility industries employ four residents.

INFRASTRUCTURE

Twenty-seven capital projects, funded by grants, are active in Stevens Village.

Transportation. The state provides an airstrip for access to Stevens Village. The new airport has a 2,120- by 60-foot lighted gravel runway. Barge delivery of fuel arrives three times each summer; goods are off-loaded at the barge landing. Skiffs, all-terrain vehicles, snowmachines, and dog teams are used for recreation and subsistence fishing and hunting.

Electricity. Stevens Village Energy Systems provides electricity.

Water and waste systems. Treated river water is hauled from a central tap; some residences use surface sources. Residents use honeybuckets and outhouses for sewage disposal. Household plumbing is not available. A sanitation master plan is in progress. Improvements are underway at the washeteria. A new landfill site and access road are being developed.

Telecommunications. In-state phone service is provided by United Utilities, long distance service by AT&T Alascom and United Utilities. Internet service is provided by GCI for the school only. Teleconferencing is available through Alaska Teleconferencing Network. Alaska Rural Communications Service provides television access. There are two radio stations in the community. There is no cable provider.

COMMUNITY FACILITIES AND SERVICES

Local facilities include a multi-purpose community hall.

Education. Stevens Village School is in the Yukon Flats School District. The school has 21 students and two teachers.

Health care. Local health clinics include Stevens Village Health Clinic. Stevens Village is classified as a highway village and is found in EMS Region 1C in the Interior Region. Emergency services have limited highway, river, and air access. A health aide provides emergency service.

Stony River

Total area of entitlement under ANCSA	69,120 acres
Total labor force	49
High school graduate or higher	33.3%
Bachelor's degree or higher	?
Unemployment rate	38.1%
Per capita income *(2000)*	$5,469
Population *2000 census*	61
Percent Native *2000 census*	85.2%

LOCATION

Stony River is located on the north bank of the Kuskokwim River, two miles from its junction with the Stony River, in southwest Alaska. The village is 99 miles east of Aniak, 185 miles northeast of Bethel, and 225 miles west of Anchorage.

CLIMATE

Stony River's climate is continental, characterized by seasonal extremes of temperature. Winter temperatures can range as low as -58°F, while summer highs may reach 90°F. Total precipitation averages 22 inches per year, including 85 inches of yearly snowfall. High winds often cause flight delays in the fall and winter.

CULTURE AND HISTORY

Stony River, also known as Moose Village and Moose Creek, originated as a trading post and riverboat landing to supply mining operations in the north. The first trading post opened in 1930, and a post office was established in 1935; both of these facilities were used by Eskimos and Indians living in the area. By the early 1960s, several families had established year-round residency, and a school was opened. The majority of the current population is Yup'ik Eskimo, Ingalik Indian, and Tanaina (Dena'ina) Indian. There is a federally recognized tribe in the community—the Village of Stony River.

GOVERNMENT

Stony River is unincorporated and is located in the Unorganized Borough (*see Alaska introduction*). It is governed by a traditional village council, headed by a president.

VILLAGE CORPORATION

The Kuskokwim Corporation was formed in 1977 when 10 ANCSA village corporations located along the middle region of the Kuskokwim River merged. The villages were Lower Kalskag, Upper Kalskag, Aniak, Chauthbaluk, Napaimute, Croked Creek, Red Devil, Georgetown, Sleetmute, and Stony River. The corporation invests in stocks, bonds, and real estate. It also owns interests in operating businesses, including a telecommunications bandwidth and service provider. In addition, the corporation has retained surface rights. The corporation's subsidiaries include an SBA certified 8(a) small business that provides engineering, remediation, construction services throughout Alaska and the lower 48 states. Shareholders in the village corporation also hold shares in Calista Regional Native Corporation (*see Alaska introduction*).

Ethnicity: Yup'ik Eskimo

ANCSA village corporation
Kuskokwim Corporation
P.O. Box 104460
Anchorage, AK 99610
907-276-2101
907-276-8728 Fax

Stony River

ECONOMY

Residents of Stony River rely primarily on subsistence fishing, hunting, and gathering activities for their livelihoods. Fish commonly utilized include salmon, whitefish, turbot, grayling, and trout. Game animals include moose, caribou, bear, waterfowl, ptarmigan, rabbit, and porcupine. Berries are gathered in the fall. Summer seasonal employment is sometimes available through firefighting for the U.S. Bureau of Land Management.

Construction. Two residents are employed in construction.

Government as employer. Of the 13 employed residents, 2 work for the local, state, or federal government.

Service and retail. There are three businesses in the community: an air transportation support service, a boarding house, and a petroleum products company. Education, health, and social service industries employ seven residents.

Transportation. Two airline companies service Stony River. Transportation, warehousing, and utility industries employ four residents.

INFRASTRUCTURE

Ten capital projects, funded by grants, are active in Stony River.

Transportation. Stony River is accessible by riverboat in summer and snowmachines in winter. Cargo and bulk fuel are delivered by barge. The state provides a 2,601- by 45-foot gravel/dirt airstrip. Mail and other cargo are delivered by weekday air services.

Electricity. The Middle Kuskokwim Electric Co-op provides power from Chuathbaluk to Stony River.

Water and waste systems. Water is drawn from individual wells, although the clinic; the school, and washeteria have their own wells. Septic tanks and some outhouses are used for sewage disposal. Household plumbing is not available so residents rely on the washeteria for laundry and for bathing. Feasibility and engineering of a piped water system is complete now, including individual septic tanks for all homes. Funds are needed to build a community system. The school uses a septic tank/drainfield system. A landfill near the school is open.

Telecommunications. In-state phone service is provided by Bush-Tell, long distance service by AT&T Alascom. Internet service is provided by GCI for the school only. Teleconferencing is available through Alaska Teleconferencing Network. Alaska Rural Communications Service provides television access. There is one radio station in the community. There is no cable provider.

COMMUNITY FACILITIES AND SERVCIES

Local facilities include the Stony River Community Hall.

Education. Gusty Michael School is in the Kuspuk School District. The school has 17 students and two teachers.

Health care. Local health clinics include Stony River Health Clinic and Clara Morgan Subregional Clinic. Stony River is classified as an isolated village and is found in EMS Region 7A in the Yukon/Kuskokwim Region. Emergency services provide a health aide and have river and air access.

Takotna

[tuh-KOTT-nuh]
Ethnicity: Ingalik Athabascan

Native entity
Village council
Takotna Village
P.O. Box TVC
Takotna, AK 99675-9999
907-298-2212
907-298-2314 Fax

ANCSA village corporation
MTNT Limited
P.O. Box 309
McGrath, AK 99627
907-524-3391
907-524-3701 Fax

Total area of entitlement under ANCSA	
	69,120 acres
Total labor force	29
High school graduate or higher	76%
Bachelor's degree or higher	16%
Unemployment rate	0%
Per capita income *(2000)*	$13,143
Population *2000 census*	50
Percent Native *2000 census*	85.2%

LOCATION

Takotna is located in the interior of Alaska, on the north bank of the Takotna River, in a broad, scenic river valley. The community is 17 air miles west of McGrath, 250 miles southwest of Fairbanks, and 250 miles northwest of Anchorage in the Kilbuck-Kuskokwim Mountains.

CLIMATE

Takotna has a cold, continental climate, with some maritime influences during the summer. Summer temperatures average 41°F to 80°F; winter temperatures range from -42°F to 0°F.

CULTURE AND HISTORY

Takotna is predominantly a non-Native community, but about 45 percent of the population is Ingalik Indian, with a subsistence-oriented culture. Gold discoveries in the upper Innoko region led to the founding of Takotna, which primarily served as a mining-supply center for the region. There is a federally recognized tribe in the community—the Takotna Village.

GOVERNMENT

Takotna is unincorporated and is located in the Unorganized Borough *(see Alaska introduction)*. The village has a traditional council, headed by a chief, which represents the Alaska Native members of the community. Shareholders in its village corporation are also shareholders of Doyon Regional Native Corporation *(see Alaska introduction)*.

ECONOMY

Takotna has a combined cash and subsistence economy. Employment is primarily through the school district, post office, clinic, local businesses, and some seasonal construction. Approximately 80 percent of residents are involved in subsistence activities. Moose and salmon are the primary meat sources. Gardening in summer is common among the residents.

Construction. One resident is employed in construction.

Government as employer. Of the 12 employed residents, 9 work for the local, state, or federal government.

Services and retail. There are four businesses in the community, including a postal delivery service, general freight company, cash-and-carry store, and the Takotna Community Association. Information services employ two residents; and education, health, and social services employ nine residents.

Tourism and recreation. The community is a checkpoint for the Iditarod sled dog race.

Transportation. One airline company services Takotna.

INFRASTRUCTURE

Ten capital projects, funded by grants, are active in Takona.

Transportation. Access to Takotna is by air or water. The state provides a 1,717-foot by 65-foot gravel airstrip and a 3,800-foot gravel runway at nearby Tatalina Air Force Station. Sterling Landing, 24 miles southeast of Takotna, provides off-loading of cargo. Tatalina AFS, Sterling Landing, and existing mines are linked by 80 miles of roads. In winter a trail is open to nearby McGrath.

Electricity. Takotna Community Association Utilities provides electricity.

Fuel storage (gallons). Takotna Community Association (173,400).

Water and waste systems. Residents haul treated water from the washeteriaand from the Takotna Waterworks. Full plumbing is not available although approximately 20 percent of houses have storage tanks with running water for the kitchen. Individual wells and septic tanks are used in community buildings. Honeybuckets and outhouses are used for sewage disposal. A feasibility study for water and sewer improvements is complete, but funds are needed for construction. There are no restrooms or running water facilities at the high school.

Telecommunications. In-state phone service is provided by United Utilities; long distance service by AT&T Alascom and United Utilities. Internet service is provided for the school only by GCI. Teleconferencing is available through Alaska Teleconferencing Network. Alaska Rural Communications Service provides television access. There is one radio station in the community but no cable provider.

COMMUNITY FACILITIES AND SERVICES

Local facilities include a community hall, a community library, and a washeteria.

Education. Takotna School is in the Iditarod Area School District. The school has 21 students and two teachers.

Health care. Local health resources include Takotna Health Clinic. Takotna is classified as an isolated village and is found in EMS Region 1C in the Interior Region. Emergency services have limited highway, river, and air access. A health aide and volunteers provide emergency service. Takotna EMS provides auxiliary health care.

Tanacross

Total area of entitlement under ANCSA	
	92,160 acres
Total labor force	115
High school graduate or higher	60.4%
Bachelor's degree or higher	4.4%
Unemployment rate	57.1%
Per capita income *(2000)*	$9,429
Population *2000 census*	140
Percent Native *2000 census*	90%

LOCATION

Tanacross is located on the banks of the Tanana River, 12 miles northwest of Tok, in the east-central interior of Alaska.

CLIMATE

Tanacross lies within the continental climatic zone, with long, cold winters and short, warm summers. In the winter, cold air settles in the valley, and ice fog is common. Average temperatures range from -22°F in the winter to 65°F in the summer.

CULTURE AND HISTORY

Tanacross is a traditional Tanacross Athabascan village, with a subsistence-oriented culture. The village was formed when residents moved from Mansfield Village to what was originally called Tanana Crossing; the name was then shortened to Tanacross. During World War II, the military developed an airfield at Tanacross, which functioned as an emergency deployment post. There is a federally recognized tribe in the community-the Native Village of Tanacross.

GOVERNMENT

Tanacross is unincorporated and is located in the Unorganized Borough *(see Alaska introduction).*

VILLAGE CORPORATION

In addition to acreage surrounding Tanacross that is important for subsistence, the village corporation also has extensive holdings with highway frontage in Tok and where the highways from Anchorage and Fairbanks join together at Tok Junction. Most shareholders in Tanacross, Inc., live in the village, but a growing number live elsewhere. Shareholders in the Tanacross village corporation are also hold shares in Doyon, Limited, regional Native corporation.

ECONOMY

The tribe provides employment at the washeteria and clinic. The tribe has formed two profit-making corporations-Orh Htaad Global Services and Dihthaad Construction-to employ its members. Some residents are able to work during the summer as emergency firefighters for the Bureau of Land Management; other residents make handicrafts to sell or engage in trapping. The entire community depends on subsistence activities for food. Whitefish, moose, porcupine, rabbit, ptarmigan, ducks, and geese are utilized. Caribou is hunted by lottery permit. Nearby Copper River draws salmon fishermen each summer.

Government as employer. Of the 24 employed residents, 9 work for the local, state, or federal government.

Services and retail. There are two businesses in the community: a general contractor and the Tanacross Village Council grocery store. Education, health, and social service industries employ 12 residents; public administration employs 3 residents.

Transportation. Transportation, warehousing, and utility industries employ two residents.

INFRASTRUCTURE

Fifteen capital projects, funded by grants, are active in Tanacross.

Transportation. Tanacross is a mile north of the Alaska Highway. Cars, trucks, and snowmachines are used for local travel. Tok offers regular air and bus services. A 5,100-foot paved runway, owned by the U.S. Bureau of Land Management, is located one mile south of Tanacross. However, it is not maintained in winter.

[TAN-uh-cross]
Ethnicity: Tanacross Athabascan

ANCSA village corporation
Tanacross, Incorporated
P.O. Box 76029
Tanacross, AK 99776
907-883-4130
907-258-4129 Fax

Tanacross

Electricity. Alaska Power Company provides electricity.

Water and waste systems. Piped service is available in Tanacross. Water is treated, stored in a 25,000-gallon tank, and piped to most households. Some residents have individual wells. Half of Tanacross households have piped sewage and septic systems; individual septic tanks also are used. Funds have been requested to replace seven failing individual septic tanks with a piped central septic system. The landfill is not permitted.

Telecommunications. In-state phone service is provided by Alaska Telephone Company/AT&T; long distance service by AT&T Alascom. Internet service is provided by GCI for the school only. Teleconferencing is available through the Tok Legislative Information Office.

COMMUNITY FACILITIES
Facilities include a community hall and the Athabascan Cultural Center and Museum.

Education. Tanacross School is in the Alaska Gateway School District. The school has 10 students and 1 teacher.

Health care. Local health clinics include Tanacross Health Clinic. Tanacross is classified as an isolated village and is found in EMS Region 3A in the Southeast Region. Emergency services have highway and air access. A health aide provides emergency service.

Tanana

[TAN-uh-naw]
Ethnicity: Koyukon
            Athabascan

ANCSA village corporation
Tozitna, Limited
P.O. Box 77129
Tanana, AK 99777
907-366-7255
907-366-7122 Fax

Total area of entitlement under ANCSA
                                138,240 acres
Total labor force   210
High school graduate or higher   77.5%
Bachelor's degree or higher   8.4%
Unemployment rate   23.7%
Per capita income *(2000)* $12,077
Population *2000 census*   308
Percent Native *2000 census*   81.5%

LOCATION
Tanana is located in interior Alaska, two miles west of the junction of the Tanana and Yukon rivers and 130 miles west of Fairbanks.

CLIMATE
Tanana has a cold, continental climate, with slight maritime influences during the summer months. Temperatures range from -50°F or below in the winter to 70°F and above in the summer. Average precipitation is 13 inches, including 50 inches of yearly snowfall.

CULTURE AND HISTORY
Tanana is primarily a Koyukon Athabscan village, where traditional ways of life persist; subsistence activities, potlatches, dances, and foot races are all part of the local culture. The village was a traditional trading settlement for area Koyukon and Tanana Indians, long before European contact. Between 1887 and 1900, the St. James Mission built an elaborate school and hospital complex, an important source of services and social change on both rivers. In 1898, Fort Gibbon was founded at Tanana to maintain the telegraph line. The community's location is still well suited to its role as a trading hub. There is a federally recognized tribe in the community-the Native Village of Tanana.

GOVERNMENT
Tanana was incorporated as a first-class city in 1961, with a mayor and city council, and is located in the Unorganized Borough *(see Alaska introduction)*. The village also has an Indian Reorganization Act village council, headed by a president.

VILLAGE CORPORATION
Shareholders in its village corporation also hold shares in Doyon regional Native corporation *(see Alaska introduction)*.

ECONOMY
Two-thirds of the full-time jobs in Tanana are with the city, school district or Native council. There are a number of positions with local businesses and services. BLM firefighting, trapping, construction work, and commercial fishing are important seasonal cash sources. Subsistence foods include salmon, whitefish, moose, bear, ptarmigan, waterfowl, and berries.

Construction. Three residents are employed in construction.

Fisheries. Seventeen residents hold commercial fishing permits, chiefly for salmon and whitefish. Farming, fishing and forestry industries employ seven residents.

Government as employer. Of the 100 employed residents, 67 work for the local, state, or federal government.

Services and retail. There are 16 businesses in the community, including a pet care company, grocery store, real estate office, freight transportation company, and the Tanana Gas Company. Retail trade employs 12 residents; education, health, and social services, 42; public administration, 23; and professional, scientific, administrative, and/or waste management industries, 7.

Tourism and recreation. Visitor attractions include Tanana and Yukon Rivers, Nuchalawoyya, and various recreational opportunities. Events include the Nuchalawoyya Festival, held every other year; potlatches; Indian dancing; canoe racing; and the Yukon River Championship Dog Races in spring. Two bed-and-breakfast facilities are available for lodging. Tanana has a video rental business.

Transportation. Seven airline companies service Tanana. Transportation, warehousing, and utility industries employ seven residents.

INFRASTRUCTURE
Eighteen capital projects, funded by grants, are active in Tanana.

Transportation. Tanana is accessible only by air and river transportation. More than 30 city-maintained local roads are available. The city provides a dock on the river; staging and storage is available for off-loading of barged goods. The state provides the Ralph M. Calhoun Memorial Airport, which has a 4,400- by 150-foot lighted gravel runway. Floatplanes land on the Yukon River. Residents use cars, trucks, snowmachines, all-terrain vehicles, and riverboats for local transportation.

Electricity. Tanana Power Company provides electricity.

Water and waste systems. Too'gha, Inc., a non-profit utility board, operates water and sewer utilities. Water is drawn from three wells near the Yukon River. Four watering points are available. Nearly all residents haul their own water from the washeteria and use privies and honeybuckets. A piped water and sewer system serves the Tanana Hospital, clinic, Regional Elders Residence, and the tribal council building. A new washeteria and water treatment plant are now open. Construction is in progress to install pipes in 40 downtown homes. The landfill uses an incinerator and provides recycling services.

Telecommunications. In-state phone service is provided by Yukon Telephone, long distance service by AT&T Alascom. Internet service is provided by Supervisions Cable ISP and by GCI for the school only. Teleconferencing is available through Alaska Teleconferencing Network. Alaska Rural Communications Service provides television access. There is one radio station in the community. Supervisions Cable TV provides cable service.

COMMUNITY FACILITIES
Local facilities include the Tanana Tribal Council, a library and residential facility for senior citizens.

Education. Two schools-Maudrey J. Sommer and Yukon River Academy Correspondence-are under the Tanana City Schools. The schools have a combined enrollment of 80 students with eight teachers.

Health care. Local hospitals or health clinics include Tanana Health Center. The clinic is a qualified emergency care center with X-ray and pharmacy services. Tanana is classified as an isolated town/Sub-Regional Center and is found in EMS Region 1C in the Interior Region. Emergency services have limited highway, river, and airport access. Emergency service is handled by 911 telephone service, a health aide, volunteers and provides auxiliary health care.

Tatitlek

Total area of entitlement under ANCSA:
137,246 acres

Total labor force	38
High school graduate or higher	37
Bachelor's degree or higher	2
Unemployment rate	7.9%
Per capita income *(1999)*	$13,015
Population *2000 census*	107
Current population	111
state demographer estimate	
Percent Native *2000 census*	85.0%

LOCATION
Tatitlek is located on the northeast shore of Tatitlek Narrows, on Prince William Sound. It lies 30 miles east of Valdez, near Bligh Island, and 30 miles northwest of Cordova.

PHYSICAL DESCRIPTION
The area encompasses 7.3 square miles of land. There has been no known flooding.

CLIMATE
Tatitlek is located in the maritime climate zone. Winter temperatures range from 17°F to 28°F; summer temperatures vary from 49°F to 63°F. Average annual precipitation includes 28 inches of rain and 150 inches of yearly snowfall.

CULTURE AND HISTORY
Tatitlek is a coastal Alutiiq village, with a fishing and subsistence-based culture. The name means "windy place" in Alutiiq. It nestles between mountains and sea among spruce and hemlock trees along the northeast shore of Tatitlek Narrows. The blue dome of the Russian Orthodox church graces the horizon near the waterfront. Like many Alutiiq villages, its has moved several times. Beginning in the nineteenth century, its residents began trading furs for European goods. First, hunters traded sea otter pelts with the Russians at Nuchek and, by the 1890s, with American traders at the Alaska Commercial Company store at Tatitlek. Many new people came to the region in the early 1900s as prospectors passed through the village on their way to mines on the Copper River. The present spelling was published in 1910 by the U.S. Geological Survey, which indicated that the village originally stood at the head of Gladhaugh Bay before it was moved to its present site. A copper mine opened at nearby Ellamar in 1898, and a cannery at Ellamar (1940 to 1954) provided jobs for people from Tatitlek. In 1989, the *Exxon Valdez* ran aground not far from Tatitlek and spilled millions of gallons of crude oil into the waters of Prince William Sound. Even though currents carried the oil away from the village, the harvest of subsistence species decreased that year by 89 percent.

Today, many Tatitlek families participate in commercial fishing for salmon and halibut. All through the year they also hunt, fish, and gather plants and beach foods for their own use. Seals, salmon, and herring are some of the most important wild foods. Each spring, Tatitlek puts on a heritage festival for students from Alaska schools. Students spend a week learning traditional crafts and activities.

GOVERNMENT
Tatitlek is unincorporated and is located in the Unorganized Borough (see Alaska introduction). It has an Indian Reorganization Act village council, the Native Village of Tatitlek, headed by a president and federally recognized. The council serves as the governing body for the community.

VILLAGE CORPORATION
In June and October 1998, Tatitlek Corporation transferred to the state and federal governments surface title to 32,284 acres of land and conservation easements on 37,530 acres. The total acreage protected is 69,814. Two of the parcels acquired, Bligh Island and Two Moon Bay, were the third- and fourth-highest ranked parcels in Prince William Sound. The acquisition includes timber-only conservation easements on the north shore of Port Fidalgo and on land at Sunny Bay. The Trustee Council contributed $24.7 million to this acquisition, and the federal government contributed an additional $10 million from the federal restitution fund, for a total purchase price of $34.7 million. Shareholders in the village corporation are also shareholders in Chugach Alaska Corporation *(see Alaska introduction).*

ECONOMY
Commercial fishing, fish processing, and oyster farming are the primary sources of employment in Tatitlek. Subsistence activities provide the majority of food items for residents. A coho salmon hatchery at Boulder Bay is nearing completion for subsistence use. As of 2003, construction of a fish and game processing facility is in progress. A community store is now open.

Fisheries. Commercial fishing, fish processing, and oyster farming are the primary sources of employment in Tatitlek. Four residents hold commercial fishing permits. A coho salmon hatchery at nearby Boulder Bay is nearing completion for subsistence use.

Tátitláq in Alutiiq

**[tuh-TIT-leck]
Ethnicity: Chugachigmuit
Alutiiq**

Native entity
Native Village of Tatitlek
P.O. Box 171
Tatitlek, AK 99677
  907-325-2311
  907-325-2298 Fax

ANCSA village corporation
Tatitlek Corporation
P.O. Box 650
Cordova, AK 99574-0650
  907-424-3777
  907-424-3773 Fax

Tatitlek

Government as employer. Of the 35 employed residents, 14 work for the village, state, or federal government.

Manufacturing. One firm manufactures apparel accessories, leather goods, and similar products

Services and retail. One firm provides commercial equipment maintenance. In-state phone service is provided by Copper Valley Telephone Cooperative, long distance service by AT&T Alascom. GCI Cable is the cable provider, and GCI provides Internet service at the school. Air charters are available in Valdez and Cordova.

INFRASTRUCTURE

Transportation. Boats are the chief means of local travel. The Corps of Engineers is considering a breakwater and small-boat harbor. The state provides a 3,700- by 150-foot lighted gravel airstrip and a seaplane landing area.

Electricity. Electricity is generated from a 411-kilowatt diesel plant. All homes and private, and public buildings have access to electricity.

Fuel storage (gallons). Chugach Schools (20,000); village council (12,000); Alaska Department of Transportation (3,000).

Water and waste systems. Water drawn from a dam is treated and stored in a 170,000-gallon tank. Thirty-four houses have access to a piped water system. Funds are available to expand water storage capacity and treatment. Thirty-four houses have access to a piped sewer system. The community septic tank discharges through an ocean outfall. Funds are avail-

able to improve the solid waste operation. An oil and hazardous waste recycling center also is available to residents.

Telecommunications. All homes and private and public buildings have access to telephone and cable television service. Two AM radio stations broadcast to the area, and an Alaska Rural Communications System repeater broadcasts one television channel. Internet service is only available at the school.

COMMUNITY FACILITIES AND SERVICES

The village council provides electricity generation and distribution, fuel storage, waste collection and disposal, and water supply. The school library serves as the community public library.

Education. Tatitlek Community School is in the Chugach School District. The school has 32 students in grades preschool through 12 and three teachers, with a total staff of seven.

Health care. Local health care is provided by the Tatitlek Health Clinic, owned by the village council and operated by Chugachmiut Regional Health Corporation. Tatitlek EMS offers auxiliary health care. Emergency services have coastal, air, seaport, and helicopter access.

Public safety. Law enforcement is provided by state troopers in Valdez, emergency response by Tatitlek EMS.

ENVIRONMENTAL CONCERNS

While Tatitlek was fortunate that currents carried the oil from the *Exxon Valdez* away from the village, the destruction and possible contamination of subsistence species remains a concern.

Tazlina

[taz-LEE-nuh]
Ethnicity: Ahtna Athabascan

Native entity
Village council
Tazlina Village Council
P.O. Box 87
Glennallen, AK 99588
907-822-4375
907-822-5865 Fax

ANCSA village corporation
Ahtna, Incorporated
P.O. Box 649
Glenallen, AK 99588
907-822-3476

The Association of Tazlina Residents - community nonprofit
P.O. Box 532
Glennallen, AK 99588
907-822-8311

Total area of entitlement under ANCSA

	92,160 acres
Total labor force	107
High school graduate or higher	85.6%
Bachelor's degree or higher	11.2%
Unemployment rate	12.8%
Per capita income *(1999)*	$23,992
Population *2000 census*	339
Percent Native *2000 census*	25.7%

LOCATION
Tazlina is located five miles south of Glennallen on the Richardson Highway, approximately 150 miles northeast of Anchorage.

CLIMATE
Tazlina is located in the continental climate zone. Temperatures range from -74°F during the winter to occasional summer highs of 97°F. Snowfall averages 39 inches, with total annual precipitation of 8 inches.

CULTURE AND HISTORY
Historically, the village was used as a fish camp by Ahtna Indians moving up and down the Copper River and its tributaries. Today the village is mostly non-Native, with some residents depending on subsistence fishing and hunting. During the pipeline era, Tazlina developed around the old Copper Valley School, built to board students from all over the state. The school closed in 1971 when local high schools were constructed in remote areas and boarding schools were discontinued. There is a federally recognized tribe in the community—the Native Village of Tazlina. Two organizations represent Tazlina: the Athabascan village council and The Association of Tazlina Residents.

GOVERNMENT
Tazlina is unincorporated under Alaska law and is located in the Unorganized Borough *(see Alaska introduction)*. The village has a traditional council, headed by a president, which represents the Alaska Native members of the community.

VILLAGE CORPORATION
Shareholders in the village corporation are also shareholders in Ahtna Inc. regional Native corporation. *(See Alaska introduction)*.

ECONOMY
The economy in Tazlina is based on local businesses, employment in state and federal government, tourism, and subsistence fishing and hunting. The Prince William Sound Community College, Division of Forestry, State Highway Maintenance Station, Division of State Parks, and Division of Communications are in the area.

Construction. Ten residents are employed in construction.

Government as employer. Of the 70 employed residents, 15 work for the local, state, or federal government.

Services and retail. Local businesses include a combined grocery, liquor, hardware, gas, and sporting goods store, a wholesale bread distributor, a freight service, and an RV park. Retail trade employs 15 residents; education, health and social services 6; financial and related businesses 5; public administration; and information services one.

Tourism and recreation. Arts, entertainment, recreation, accommodations, and food service industries employ 10 residents.

Transportation. Transportation, warehousing, and utility industries employ four residents.

Tazlina

INFRASTRUCTURE

Five capital projects, funded by grants, are active in Tazlina.

Transportation. Tazlina is located on the Richardson Highway. Air travel is not popular because it is costly and often more time-consuming than road-travel but guides and subsistence hunters prefer using planes. The state provides a 900- by 42-foot gravel airstrip. There is a seaplane facility at Smokey Lake.

Electricity. Copper Valley Electric Association provides electricity.

Water and waste systems. Full plumbing is available to all occupied homes. The majority of residents have individual wells and septic systems. Others haul well water from the Copper Center Safewater well, or have water delivered by truck from Glennallen.

Telecommunications. In-state phone service is provided by Copper Valley Telephone Cooperative, long distance service by AT&T Alascom and GCI. Internet service is provided by Copper Valley Telephone Cooperative. Alaska Rural Communications Service provides television access. There is no radio station or cable provider in the community.

COMMUNITY FACILITIES AND SERVICES

Local facilities include a community building and a hockey rink. A watering point and an RV dump station are high in the needs of the community. Copper Basin Sanitation from Glennallen collects refuse.

Education. There are no schools directly in the community.

Health care. Tazlina is classified as an isolated village and is found in EMS Region 2E in the Copper River Region. Emergency services have highway, air, seaport, and satellite access. Volunteers provide emergency service. Copper Center Clinic and Cross Road Medical Center in Glennallen are available for auxiliary health care.

Telida

Telida

Total area of entitlement under ANCSA	
	69,120 acres
Total labor force	0
High school graduate or higher	60.2%
Bachelor's degree or higher	6.8%
Unemployment rate	0%
Per capita income *(1999)*	$0
Population *2000 census*	3
Percent Native *2000 census*	100%

LOCATION

Telida is located in the interior of the state, on the south side of the Swift Fork of the Kuskokwim River, about 50 miles northeast of Medfra and 175 miles northwest of Anchorage.

CLIMATE

The area experiences a cold, continental climate, with slight maritime influences during the summer. Summer temperatures average from 42°F to 80°F; winter temperatures vary from -60°F to 0°F.

CULTURE AND HISTORY

Telida is an Upper Kuskokwim Athabascan village with a culture centered on subsistence activities. Athabascan Indian folklore indicates that Telida's residents are descended from two sisters, survivors of a Yukon Indian attack, who fled from the McKinley area to Telida Lake and discovered whitefish at its outlet. There is a federally recognized tribe in the community—the Telida Village.

GOVERNMENT

Telida is unincorporated and is located in the Unorganized Borough *(see Alaska introduction)*. It is governed by a traditional council headed by a chief.

VILLAGE CORPORATION

Shareholders in the MTNT village corporation are also shareholders in Doyon, Ltd. regional Native corporation *(see Alaska introduction)*.

ECONOMY

Telida's economy is heavily dependent on subsistence activities. Employment is primarily with the school and the village administration and in seasonal summer jobs. Trapping, handicrafts, and gardening generate some income for residents.

Government as employer. None of the residents work for the local, state, or federal government.

Services and retail. There are no registered business licenses in the community.

INFRASTRUCTURE

Four capital projects, funded by grants, are active in Telida.

Transportation. Access to Telida is primarily by air, and a 1,900-by 40-foot turf/dirt airstrip is available. Small boats enter into Telida with little trouble but large boats are thwarted by downriver snags and sticks. Road access is limited to a winter trail that connects the village with Nikolai. Snowmobiles, motorbikes, and all-terrain vehicles provide local transportation.

Electricity. Telida Village Utility provides electricity.

Fuel storage (gallons). Iditarod Area Schools (5,000).

Water and waste systems. Water is hauled from the school watering point or the river. There is no household plumbing in the community. Outhouses are used for sewage disposal. Traditional steam baths are available.

Telecommunications. In-state phone service is provided by United Utilities, long distance service by AT&T Alascom. Alaska Rural Communications Service provides television access. There is one radio station in the community. Teleconferencing is available through Alaska Teleconferencing Network. There is no cable provider.

COMMUNITY FACILITIES AND SERVICES

Education. There are no schools in the community.

Health care. Telida Health Clinic provides health care to the community.

[tuh-LYE-duh]
Ethnicity: Upper Kuskokwim Athabascan

Native entity
Village council
Telida Village
P.O. Box 32
McGrath, AK 99627
  907-524-3550
  907-524-3163 Fax

ANCSA village corporation
MTNT Limited
P.O. Box 309
McGrath, AK 99627
  907-524-3391
  907-524-3701 Fax

Teller

Ethnicity: Inupiat Eskimo

Municipality
City of Teller
P.O. Box 548
Teller, AK 99778
907-642-3401
907-642-2051 Fax

Native entity
Native Village of Teller
P.O. Box 567
Teller, AK 99778
907-642-3381
907-642-2072 Fax

ANCSA village corporation
Teller Native Corporation
P.O. Box 590
Teller, AK 99778
907-642-4011
907-642-2181 Fax

Total area of entitlement under ANCSA	132,800 acres
Total labor force	163
High school graduate or higher	60.2%
Bachelor's degree or higher	6.8%
Unemployment rate	14.7%
Per capita income *(1999)*	$8,618
Population *2000 census*	268
Percent Native *2000 census*	92.5%

LOCATION
Teller is located on the Seward Peninsula, on a spit between Port Clarence and Grantley Harbor, 72 miles northwest of Nome.

CLIMATE
The climate in Teller is maritime when ice-free, changing to a continental climate after freeze-up. Average summer temperatures range from 44°F to 57°F; winter temperatures range from -9°F to 8°F. Average annual precipitation is 11.5 inches, including 50 inches of snowfall.

CULTURE AND HISTORY
Teller is a traditional Inupiat Eskimo village with a culture centered on subsistence activities. Many current residents are originally from Mary's Igloo. The village became a permanent settlement in 1900 after the Blue Stone placer discovery 15 miles to the south. During the boom years Teller had a population of about 5,000 and was a major regional native trading center. Seals, beluga whales, fish, reindeer, and other local resources are utilized. There is a federally recognized tribe in the community-the Native Village of Teller.

GOVERNMENT
Teller was incorporated in 1963 as a second-class city with a mayor and city council; it is located in the Unorganized Borough *(see Alaska introduction)*. There is also a traditional village council, headed by a president.

VILLAGE CORPORATION
Shareholders in the village corporation are also shareholders in Bering Straits regional Native corporation *(see Alaska introduction)*.

ECONOMY
The Teller economy is based on subsistence food harvests derived from seals, beluga whale, fish, reindeer, and other local resources supplemented by part-time wage earnings. Some fox are trapped, and reindeer herding has been practiced since Teller's founding. There is a herd of over 1,000 reindeer in the area, and the annual roundup provides meat and some cash income for residents. More than one-third of village households produce and sell crafts or artwork. Some residents trap fox.

Construction. One resident is employed in construction.

Government as employer. Of the 58 employed residents, 34 work for the local, state, or federal government.

Services and retail. There are six businesses in the community, including a cab service, bus transportation, general merchandise and clothing stores, and a gas station. Retail trade employs 13 residents; education, health, and social services, 29; finance and related businesses, 2; professional, scientific, administrative, and waste management, 5; and public administration, 2.

Tourism and recreation. Two bed-and-breakfast facilities are available.

Transportation. Four airline companies, two taxi companies, and one car rental business service Teller. Transportation, warehousing, and utility industries employ two residents.

INFRASTRUCTURE
Fourteen capital projects, funded by grants, are active in Teller.

Transportation. Teller has a road link to Nome (72 miles) during the summer months via a gravel road. Teller is accessible by sea and air. The state provides a 3,000-foot long by 60-foot wide gravel runway with regular flight service from Nome. Dock facilities are not available; goods are lightered from Nome and off-loaded on the beach. Port Clarence, a natural harbor, is being considered for a deep water port.

Electricity. Teller Power Company provides electricity.

Fuel storage (gallons). Teller Commercial Co. (218,900); Village Corp. Fuel (129,800); Bering Straits School (71,200); Lutheran Church (6,100); Native Corporation Store (3,500); Alaska Department of Transportation (3,300); Army National Guard (2,300); Teller Power (1,900); city clinic (1,000).

Water and waste systems. Water is hauled in summer by city truck from the Gold Run River and delivered to home storage tanks. All-terrain vehicles and snowmachines are used by some residents to haul water. In winter treated water is delivered from a large storage tank at the washeteria. Some residents melt ice. Preliminary work has started on a piped water and sewer system but is suspended pending the development of a new water source.

Telecommunications. In-state phone service is provided by Mukluk Telephone Co./TelAlaska, long distance service by AT&T Alascom, GCI, and Mukluk Telephone. Internet service is provided by GCI and Nome.net. Teleconferencing is available through Alaska Teleconferencing Network. Alaska Rural Communications Service provides television access. Two radio stations are in the community. There is no cable provider.

COMMUNITY FACILITIES AND SERVICES
Local facilities include a community hall. A teen center is under construction. The school operates its own sewer system. More than 40 residents use honeybuckets, which are hauled by the city. Septic tanks are in a few homes and facilities. Construction of a new landfill is in progress. The community participates in hazardous waste collection.

Education. James C. Isabell School is in the Bering Straits School District. The school has 76 students and eight teachers.

Health care. Teller Health Clinic provides health care to the community. Teller is classified as an isolated village and is found in EMS Region 5A in the Norton Sound Region. Emergency services have limited highway, coastal, and air access. A health aide provides emergency care.

Total area of entitlement under ANCSA
743,159 acres

Total labor force	70
High school graduate or higher	45.5%
Bachelor's degree or higher	3.6%
Unemployment rate	46.9%
Per capita income (1999)	$7,371
Population [(2000 census)]	124
Percent Native [(2000 census)]	92.7%

LOCATION AND LAND STATUS

Tetlin is located along the Tetlin River between Tetlin Lake and the Tanana River, 12 miles southeast of Tok, 75 miles from the Canadian border in the interior of the state.

With the passage of the Alaska Native Claims Settlement Act in 1971, residents elected to retain the land previously set aside for the Tetlin Indian Reserve. By the provisions of section 19(b) of ANCSA, "...Village Corporation shall not be eligible for any other land selections under this Act or to any distribution of Regional Corporation funds pursuant to section seven, and the enrolled residents of the Village Corporation shall not be eligible to receive Regional Corporation stock." While this has meant that Tetlin does not take part in a number of provisions of that act, it has maintained a larger land base than would have been the case under ANCSA.

CLIMATE

Tetlin lies within the continental climatic zone, with long, cold winters and short, warm summers. Average temperatures range from winter lows of -33°F to summer highs of 72°F.

CULTURE AND HISTORY

Tetlin is an Upper Tanana Indian community. Partly due to their isolation, residents have been able to maintain their traditional Athabascan culture, centered on subsistence activities. Athabascan Indians have historically lived in this area, moving among several seasonal hunting and fishing camps. There is a federally recognized tribe in the community-the Native Village of Tetlin.

GOVERNMENT

The community of Tetlin is unincorporated and is located in the Unorganized Borough *(see Alaska introduction)*. The village is governed by a traditional council headed by a chief.

VILLAGE CORPORATION

Tetlin has no village corporation, and residents do not hold shares in any regional native corporation *(see Alaska introduction)*.

ECONOMY

The school, tribe, clinic, store, and post office are primary employers. Many residents engage in trapping or make and sell handicrafts. Fire fighting for the Bureau of Land Manage-ment offers summer work when required. Nearly all families participate in yearly subsistence activities. Whitefish, moose, ducks, geese, spruce hens, rabbits, berries, and roots are harvested.

Construction. Two residents are employed in construction.

Government as employer. Of the 17 employed residents, 8 work for the local, state, or federal government.

Services and retail. There are no business licenses registered in the community. Education, health, and social service professions employ five residents, and public administration employs one resident.

Transportation. One airline company services Tetlin. Transportation, warehousing, and utility industries employ three residents.

INFRASTRUCTURE

Nine capital projects, funded by grants, are active in Tetlin.

Transportation. Tetlin is accessible by road. Cars, trucks, skiffs, and snowmachines are used by many residents for hunting, fishing, and hauling wood. The village provides a 1,700-foot turf airstrip. Scheduled and charter flights are available from Tok.

Electricity. Alaska Power Company provides electricity.

Fuel storage (gallons). Village Corp. (120,000); village council (45,000).

Water and waste systems. All residents haul treated well water from the school or washeteria, and use honeybuckets or outhouses. Construction of a flush/haul system is in progress, including the plumbing of 42 households.

Telecommunications. In-state phone service is provided by Alaska Telephone Company/AP&T; long distance service by AT&T Alascom. Internet service is provided to the school by CGI. Teleconferencing is available through Alaska Teleconferencing Network and the Tok Legislative Information Office. Alaska Rural Communications Service provides television access. There is no radio station or cable service in the community.

COMMUNITY FACILITIES AND SERVICES

Local facilities include a community hall. The landfill is not permitted.

Education. Tetlin School is in the Alaska Gateway School District. The school has 28 students and two teachers.

Health care. Tetlin Health Clinic provides health care to the community. Tetlin is classified as an isolated village and is found in EMS Region 1C in the Interior Region. Emergency services have air access. A health aide and volunteers provide emergency service.

[TET-linn]
Ethnicity: Upper Tanana Athabascan

Native entity
Tetlin Tribal Council
P.O. Box TTL
Tetlin, AK 99779
907-324-2130
907-324-2131 Fax

Togiak

[TOAG-ee-ack]
Ethnicity: Yup'ik Eskimo

Municipality
City of Togiak
P.O. Box 190
Togiak, AK 99678
907-493-5820
907-493-5932 Fax

Native entity
Togiak Traditional Council
P.O. Box 310
Togiak, AK 99678-0310
907-493-5004
907-493-5005 Fax

ANCSA village corporation
Togiak Natives Corporation
P.O. Box 150
Togiak, AK 99678
907-493-5520
907-493-5554 Fax

Total area of entitlement under ANCSA	156,637 acres
Total labor force	519
High school graduate or higher	67.1%
Bachelor's degree or higher	7%
Unemployment rate	26.8%
Per capita income (1999)	$9,676
Population 2000 census	809
Percent Native 2000 census	92.7%

LOCATION

The village of Togiak is located at the head of Togiak Bay two miles west of the Togiak River, on Bristol Bay in Southwest Alaska. The community lies 67 miles west of Dillingham and only a few miles from the village of Twin Hills.

CLIMATE

Togiak is located in a climatic transition zone. The primary influence is maritime; however, the continental climate of interior Alaska also affects the Bristol Bay coastal region. The area is characterized by cloudy skies, mild temperatures, and moderately heavy precipitation. The area also is often affected by strong surface winds. Average summer temperatures range from 37°F to 66°F; winter temperatures range from 4°F to 30°F. Annual precipitation ranges from 20 to 26 inches, with most of the precipitation occurring in the summer months when low clouds and rain can reduce visibility.

CULTURE AND HISTORY

Togiak is a traditional Yup'ik Eskimo village with a subsistence-oriented culture. A number of residents of the Yukon-Kuskokwim region migrated south to the Togiak area after a devastating influenza epidemic in 1918-19; many Togiak residents, therefore, have ancestral ties to the Yukon-Kuskokwim region, as do people in the nearby village of Twin Hills. Togiak was previously located on the opposite shore from the present-day site, but heavy winter snowfalls make wood gathering difficult at Old Togiak, so residents gradually settled at a new site on the opposite shore. After the Bureau of Indian Affairs school was closed in 1938, no teacher came to the village until 1950, when a school was established in the old church. Togiak maintains a fairly stable year-round population without the seasonal fluctuations commonly associated with Bristol Bay villages. Commercial and subsistence fishing are available in the waters near the village, so residents do not set up summer fish camps elsewhere. There is a federally recognized tribe in the community—the Togiak Traditional Council.

GOVERNMENT

Togiak was incorporated as a second-class city in 1969, with a mayor and city council; it is located in the Unorganized Borough (see Alaska introduction). There also is a traditional village council, headed by a president.

VILLAGE CORPORATION

Shareholders in the village corporation also hold shares in Bristol Bay Regional Native Association (see Alaska introduction).

ECONOMY

Togiak's economic base is primarily commercial salmon, herring fishing, and herring roe-on-kelp fisheries. A few residents trap, and many harvest herring roe-on-kelp. The community relies heavily on subsistence activities, often covering long distances for food sources. Seal, sea lion, whale, and walrus are among the major species harvested. Fishermen use flat-bottom boats for the shallow waters of Togiak Bay. An on-shore fish processor and several floating processing facilities are near Togiak.

Construction. Five residents are employed in construction.

Fisheries. Approximately 244 residents hold commercial fishing permits. Farming, fishing, and forestry industries employ four residents.

Government as employer. Of the 173 employed residents, 99 work for the local, state, or federal government.

Services and retail. There are 19 businesses in the community, including Togiak Natives Limited, Nanguciulnguq Arts Center, a lumber supply company, private airplane service, public airplane service, bus transportation, and real estate offices. Retail trade employs 18 residents; education, health, and social services, 63; public administration, 38; and financial and related businesses, 3.

Tourism and recreation. Accommodations include one inn and one lodge. Arts, entertainment, recreation, accommodations, and food service industries employ 12 residents.

Transportation. Two airline companies service Togiak. Transportation, warehousing, and utility industries employ 14 residents.

INFRASTRUCTURE

Seventeen capital projects, funded by grants, are active in Togiak.

Transportation. The state provides a 4,400-foot long by 98-foot wide lighted gravel airstrip with a 1,200-foot long by 49-foot wide crosswind airstrip. Scheduled and chartered flights are available from Dillingham. Freight is transported to Togiak by air or barge and lightered to shore. Docking facilities are not available. Skiffs, cars, all-terrain vehicles, and snowmachines are used for local travel.

Electricity. Alaska Village Electric Corporation (AVEC) provides electricity.

Fuel storage (gallons). City (239,900); AVEC (135,700); Southwest Region Schools (59,400); Alaska Commercial Co. Store (2,000); Army National Guard (2,000); Moravian church (1,900); Togiak Lumber (1,700); Village Council (1,000); and BBNA Head Start Building (1,000).

Water and waste systems. Water drawn from a well is treated and stored in a 500,000-gallon tank. About 125 residences are connected to a piped water and sewer system; the remaining homes have new individual wells and septic tanks. In all, 210 homes are completely plumbed; 14 are not. The water system is close to 30 years old and shows signs of broken or corroded pipes, valves, and service connections.

Telecommunications. In-state phone service is provided by United Utilities Inc; long distance service by AT&T Alascom, GCI, United, and Nushagak. Internet service is provided by GCI. Teleconferencing is through Alaska Teleconferencing Network and the Dillingham Legislative Information Office. There is one radio station in the community. Alaska Rural Communications Service provides television access. The cable provider is Frontier Cable.

COMMUNITY FACILITIES AND SERVICES

Facilities include the Nangucuilnguq Arts & Crafts Center, and the Traditional Council Senior Center. More than 35 new HUD housing units were recently completed in the Togiak Heights Subdivision, with a sewage system. A new landfill is now available.

Education. Togiak School is in the Southwest Region School District. The school has 229 students and 17 teachers.

Health care. Local health resources include Togiak Sub-Regional Clinic. The clinic is a qualified emergency care center. Togiak is classified as an isolated town/sub-regional center; it is found in EMS Region 2I in the Bristol Bay Region. Emergency Services have coastal and air access. Emergency service is provided by volunteers and a health aide. Auxiliary health care is provided by Togiak First Responders Group.

Togiak

Toksook Bay

See Nunakauyarmiut

Tuluksak

Tuluksak

Total area of entitlement under ANCSA
92,160 acres
High school graduate or higher 65.6%
Bachelor's degree or higher 8%
Per capita income *(1999)* $7,132
Population *2000 census* 428
Percent Native *2000 census* 94.2%

LOCATION

Tuluksak is approximately 35 miles northeast of Bethel, in Southwest Alaska. The community is located on the south bank of the Tuluksak River at its junction with the Kuskokwim River.

CLIMATE

Tuluksak is located in a zone of mixed continental and maritime climatic influences. Precipitation averages 16 inches per year, including snowfall of 15 inches. Summer temperatures range from 42°F to 62°F; winter temperatures vary from -2°F to 19°F.

CULTURE AND HISTORY

Tuluksak is a traditional Eskimo village with a culture centered on subsistence activities. The name is derived from a Yup'ik term meaning "related to loon." The 1880 census listed the village population as 150. There is a federally recognized tribe in the community-the Tuluksak Native Community. Cultural events include the Camai Festival and the AFN Convention.

GOVERNMENT

Tuluksak was incorporated as a second-class city in 1970 and is located in the Unorganized Borough *(see Alaska introduction)*. However, the community has abandoned its city government in favor of a more traditional village government, a council organized under the Indian Reorganization Act.

VILLAGE CORPORATION

Shareholders in the Tulkisarmute village corporation are also shareholders in Calista Regional Native Corporation *(see Alaska introduction)*.

ECONOMY

The school, village government, and services are the chief employers. Subsistence activities are an important sector of the village economy and include hunting, fishing, and gathering. A village store was recently completed.

Fisheries. Twenty-nine residents hold commercial fishing permits.

Government as employer. Of the 126 employed residents, 118 work for the local, state, or federal government.

Services and retail. There are three businesses in the community, including an air transportation maintenance company, grocery store, and recreation facility. Retail trade employs 15 residents; education, health, and social services, 80; and public administration, 21.

Transportation. Three airline companies service Tuluksak. Transportation, warehousing, and utility industries employ six residents.

INFRASTRUCTURE

Thirteen capital projects, funded by grants, are active in Tuluksak

Transportation. The state provides a 2,461- by 30-foot gravel airstrip year-round. Docking facilities are not available, but cargo barges deliver in the summer. Fishing boats, skiffs, snowmachines, and all-terrain vehicles provide local transportation.

Electricity. Traditional Power Utility provides electricity.

Fuel storage (gallons). Yupiit Schools (122,811); Tulkisarmute Inc. (50,000); village council (25,000); Army National Guard (6,500).

Water and waste systems. Residents haul treated well water. One watering point with storage capacity of less than 7,000 gallons serves the community, washeteria, clinic, and school. Homes are not plumbed. Funding has been granted for water treatment, water storage, and sewage lagoon improvements.

Telecommunications. In-state phone service is provided by United Utilities, long distance service by AT&T Alascom and United Utilities. Internet service is provided for the school by GCI. Teleconferencing is available through Alaska Teleconferencing Network. There are two radio stations in the community. There are no television stations in Tuluksak; however, some residents have satellite dishes.

COMMUNITY FACILITIES AND SERVICES

Local facilities include the old city building, and both public and school libraries. The washeteria was rehabilitated eight years ago, but water shortages are limiting its use. Honeybucket collection service and a central honeybucket disposal facility are available.

Education. Tuluksak School is in the Yupiit School District. The school has 140 students and 12 teachers.

Health care. Health resources include Tuluksak Health Clinic. Tuluksak, classified as an isolated village, is found in EMS Region 7A in the Yukon/Kuskokwim Region. Emergency services have river and air access. A health aide provides emergency service.

[too-LOOK-sack]
Ethnicity: Yup'ik Eskimo

Native entity
Village council
Tuluksak Native Community
P.O. Box 95
Tuluksak, AK 99679-0095
907-695-6420
907-695-6932 Fax

ANCSA village corporation]
Tulkisarmute, Incorporated
P.O. Box 95
Tuluksak, AK 99679
907-695-6420
907-693-6932 Fax

Tuntutuliak

[tun-too-TOO-lee-ack]:
abbr. Tunt
Ethnicity: Yup'ik Eskimo

Native entity
Tuntutuliak Traditional Council
P.O. Box 8086
Tuntutuliak, AK 99680
907-256-2128
907-256-2080 Fax

ANCSA village corporation
Tuntutuliak Land Limited
P.O. Box 8106
Tuntutuliak, AK 99680
907-256-2315
907-256-2441 Fax

Total area of entitlement under ANCSA	
	115,200 acres
Total labor force	177
High school graduate or higher	62.9%
Bachelor's degree or higher	5.7%
Unemployment rate	14.7%
Per capita income *(1999)*	$7,918
Population *2000 census*	370
Percent Native *2000 census*	98.9%

LOCATION
Tuntutuliak is located 40 miles southwest of Bethel in Southwest Alaska. The community is situated on the Kinak River about 3 miles from its meeting with the Kuskokwim River and about 40 miles from the Bering Sea coast.

CLIMATE
Tuntutuliak has a maritime climate with relatively warm winters and cool summers. Summer temperatures range from 42°F to 62°F; winter temperatures vary from -2°F to 19°F.

CULTURE AND HISTORY
Tuntutuliak is a traditional Eskimo village; Yup'ik is the first language of the majority of residents. The name of the village means "place of many reindeer." The village was originally situated four miles east of its present location and was called Kinak. Kinak was visited in 1879 by E. W. Nelson, a Smithsonian naturalist, who reported a population of about 175. In 1908, a Moravian minister moved to the village. There were 130 people living there at the time. The villagers expressed interest in a school to the minister, who recommended to the Bureau of Education that one be built; a government school was built in 1909. Due to problems with acquiring teachers, however, the school was closed in 1917 and the building was moved to the village of Eek. It is thought that some villagers may have moved to Eek so their children could attend school. In 1923 the first Moravian chapel was built, and in the late 1920s a trader named John Johnson began operating a store and trading post in the village. In 1945 Kinak residents decided to move to higher ground since the river had shifted away from the village. Residents moved the village to its present site, renamed Tuntutuliak. The Bureau of Indian Affairs built a school in 1957 after villagers petitioned the government. In 1960 the first post office opened. There is a federally recognized tribe located in the community-the Tuntutuliak Traditional Council.

GOVERNMENT
Tuntutuliak is unincorporated and is located in the Unorganized Borough *(see Alaska introduction)*. It is governed by a traditional village council, headed by a president.

VILLAGE CORPORATION
Shareholders in the Tuntutuliak village corporation are also shareholders in Calista regional Native corporation *(see Alaska introduction)*.

ECONOMY
The school, services, commercial fishing, and fish processing are the primary income providers. Cash is also generated by trapping, basket weaving, skin-sewn products, and other native handicrafts. Subsistence foods are a majority of the diet, and about half of the community's families go to fish camp each summer.

Construction. The construction industry employs 16 residents.

Fisheries. Fifty-one residents hold commercial fishing permits for salmon net and herring roe fisheries.

Government as employer. Of the 99 employed residents, 44 work for the local, state, or federal government.

Manufacturing. One resident is employed in manufacturing. *Services and retail.* There are nine businesses in the community, including the washeteria, trading post, electrical service, welding shop, air transportation maintenance service, retail store, and interior design services. Retail trade employs 17 residents; education, health, and social services, 39; and public administration, 9.

Transportation. Six airline companies service Tuntutuliak. Transportation, warehousing, and utility industries employ 10 residents.

INFRASTRUCTURE
Fourteen capital projects, funded by grants, are active in Tuntutuliak.

Transportation. Tuntutuliak depends heavily on air transportation for passengers, mail, and cargo service. The state provides a 1,772- by 28-foot gravel runway. A public seaplane base is available on the Qinaq River. Plans to relocate the airport are in progress. Goods are delivered by barge services six times a year. Boats and snowmachines provide local transportation. In winter, trails are marked to Kipnuk, Toundra, and Kongiganak.

Electricity. The Tuntutuliak Community Service Association provides electricity.

Fuel storage (gallons). Village Council (86,900); Lower Kuskokwim Schools (74,400); Qinarmiut Corp. (71,700).

Water and waste systems. Functioning household plumbing is not available.

Telecommunications. In-state phone service is provided by United Utilities, long distance service by AT&T Alascom and United Utilities. Internet service is provided for the school by GCI. Teleconferencing is available through Alaska Teleconferencing Network. There are two radio stations in the community. Alaska Rural Communications Service and KYUK provide television access; the cable provider is Quinarmiut Cablevision (village corporation).

COMMUNITY FACILITIES AND SERVICES
Local facilities include the Tuntutuliak Community Hall. The Tuntutuliak Community Service Association, a nonprofit arm of the village council, operates the utilities. A new landfill, sewage lagoon, and a four-mile sanitation boardwalk are now open. The school has its own well and sewage lagoon, but improvements are needed. A flush/haul system is under construction, including household plumbing. Honeybuckets are used by residents.

Education. Lewis Angapak Memorial School is in the Lower Kuskokwim School District. The school has 103 students and eight teachers.

Health care. Health resources include Kathleen Daniel Memorial Hospital. Tuntutuliak is classified as an isolated village and is found in EMS Region 7A in the Yukon/Kuskokwim Region. Emergency services have coastal and air access. A health aide provides emergency service.

Total area of entitlement under ANCSA
	115,200 acres
Total labor force	176
High school graduate or higher	65.8%
Bachelor's degree or higher	3.4%
Unemployment rate	19.8%
Per capita income *(1999)*	$7,653
Population *2000 census*	325
Percent Native *2000 census*	96.9%

LOCATION
Tununak is located 115 miles northwest of Bethel in Southwest Alaska, situated in a small bay on the northwest coast of Nelson Island.

CLIMATE
Tununak is located in the marine climate zone with relatively warm winters and cool summers. Summer temperatures can range from 42°F to 59°F; winter temperatures vary from 20F to 19°F. Average annual precipitation is 17 inches, including snowfall of 22 inches.

CULTURE AND HISTORY
Tununak is a traditional Eskimo village with a culture centered on subsistence activities. The first detailed outside exploration of the area was made in the winter of 1878-79 by E. W. Nelson, a Smithsonian naturalist. His records indicate that six people were living in Tununak at that time. In 1889 the Jesuits sent a missionary to the village, and a small chapel was built along with a school. However, by 1892 the school had closed because of the difficulties associated with the migratory nature of the people and their close ties with their own traditions. In 1925 a government school was built in Tununak, and a general store was opened four years later. Residents continued to retain their traditional customs and life-styles; as late as 1936 some people continued to live in the semi-subterranean Native sod homes indigenous to the area. In 1934, the Jesuit mission was reopened by Father Deshout. The 1950s brought the greatest life-style changes to the Nelson Islanders. Many villagers experienced their first sustained exposure to outsiders through their involvement with the Alaska Territorial Guard, working in fish canneries, and seeking health care treatment. By the 1970s, snowmobiles were replacing dogsled teams, and more contemporary housing supplanted Native architecture in spite of its environmental superiority. There is a federally recognized tribe in the community-the Native Village of Tununak.

GOVERNMENT
Tununak was incorporated as a second-class city in 1975 and is located in the Unorganized Borough *(see Alaska introduction)*. However, the city government subsequently resigned, and all governmental functions are performed by the village Indian Reorganization Act council, headed by a president.

VILLAGE CORPORATION
Shareholders in the Tununrmiut Rinit village corporation also hold shares in Calista Regional Native Corporation *(see Alaska introduction)*.

ECONOMY
The school district, village corporation, stores, and commercial fishing are the primary employers. Trapping and native crafts also generate cash. Subsistence activities are an important contributor to villagers' diets. Seal meat, seal oil, and herring are the staples of the diet. Beluga whale and walrus also are hunted. A lottery to hunt musk ox on Nelson or Nunivak Islands is available to residents. Coastal Villages Seafood processes halibut and salmon in Tununak.

Construction. Five residents are employed in construction.

Fisheries. Fifty-three residents hold commercial fishing permits.

Government as employer. Of the 85 employed residents, 59 work for the local, state, or federal government.

Services and retail. There are five businesses in the community, including airport maintenance, the Tununak Traditional Council, a telecommunications company, and two professional/technical companies. Retail trade employs 18 residents; education, health, and social services, 35; public administration, 10; and information services, one.

Transportation. Six airline companies service Tununak. Transportation, warehousing, and utility industries employ nine residents.

INFRASTRUCTURE
Twelve capital projects, funded by grants, are active in Tununak.

Transportation. Tununak relies heavily on air transportation for passengers, mail, and cargo service. The state provides a 2,010- by 40-foot gravel airstrip. Goods are delivered by barge two to four times in summer, and goods are lightered to shore. Boats, snowmachines, and all-terrain vehicles are used extensively for local transportation.

Electricity. Alaska Village Electric Cooperative (AVEC) provides electricity.

Fuel storage (gallons). Tununrmiut Rinit Corp. Store (120,400); AVEC (79,800); Lower Kuskokwim Schools (70,300); Tununak Elders Council (15,600); and the Army National Guard (6,300).

Water and waste systems. Water is drawn from Muskox Creek. A flush/haul system has been installed in 18 homes. Most residents currently haul water from six watering points. The school provides its own piped water system, and sewage discharges to the village drainfield.

Telecommunications. In-state phone service is provided by United Utilities, long distance service by AT&T Alascom and United Utilities. Internet service is provided for the school by GCI. Teleconferencing is available through Alaska Teleconferencing Network. There are three radio stations in the community. Alaska Rural Communications Service provides television access; the cable provider is Frontier Cable.

COMMUNITY FACILITIES AND SERVICES
Local facilities include an IRA building. There are 13 honeybucket hoppers along the length of the village, serving more than 65 households. The community depends on the washeteria for laundry and bathing. Improvements are needed at the landfill and washeteria.

Education. Paul T. Albert Memorial, the community's school, is in the Lower Kuskokwim School District. The school has 110 students and 8 teachers.

Health care. Health resources include Tununak Health Clinic. Tununak is classified as an isolated village and is found in EMS Region 7A in the Yukon/Kuskokwim Region. Emergency services have coastal and air access. A health aide provides emergency service.

**[too-NOO-nuck]; var. Tananak
Ethnicity: Yup'ik Eskimo**

Native entity
BIA-Recognized IRA Council, but does not represent village
  Village council
  Tununak IRA Council
    P.O. Box 77
    Tununak, AK 99681
    907-652-6527
    907-652-6011 Fax

Tununak Traditional Council
P.O. Box 97
Tununak, AK 99681
  907-652-6312
  907-652-6912 Fax

ANCSA village corporation
Tununrmiut Rinit Corporation
P.O. Box 89
Tununak, AK 99681
  907-652-6311
  907-652-6315 Fax

NOTE
Village council. Not recognized by BIA but is Traditional Council elected to represent village. Formerly Tununak Traditional Elders Council.

Twin Hills

Ethnicity: Yup'ik Eskimo

Native entity
Twin Hills Village Council
P.O. Box TWA
Twin Hills, AK 99576-8996
907-525-4821
907-525-4822 Fax

ANCSA village corporation
Twin Hills Native Corporation
P.O. Box TWA
Twin Hills, AK 99576-8996
907-525-4327
907-525-4820 Fax

Total area of entitlement under ANCSA
69,950 acres
Total labor force 30
High school graduate or higher 56.7%
Bachelor's degree or higher 20%
Unemployment rate 0%
Per capita income *(1999)* $16,856
Population *2000 census* 69
Percent Native *2000 census* 94.2%

LOCATION
Twin Hills is located near the mouth of the Twin Hills River, a tributary of the Togiak River, on Bristol Bay in southwest Alaska, 386 miles southwest of Anchorage. The village of Togiak is located only a few miles away.

CLIMATE
Twin Hills is in a climatic transition zone. The primary influence is maritime, but the continental climate of interior Alaska also affects the Bristol Bay coastal region. Average summer temperatures range from 37°F to 66°F; average winter temperatures vary from 4°F to 30°F. Average annual precipitation ranges from 20 to 26 inches, with most of the precipitation occurring in summer months.

CULTURE AND HISTORY
Twin Hills is a traditional Eskimo village with a culture centered on subsistence activities. The village was established in 1965, following severe flooding in the upper Togiak Bay area. Like the residents of nearby Togiak, the people of Twin Hills have strong cultural ties to the Yukon-Kuskokwim region because many of their ancestors migrated south to the Togiak area following a devastating influenza epidemic in 1918-19. The school was built in 1972, and a post office was established in 1977. There is a federally recognized tribe in the community-the Twin Hills Village Council.

GOVERNMENT
Twin Hills is unincorporated and is located in the Unorganized Borough *(see Alaska introduction)*. The village is governed by a five-person traditional village council, whose officers are elected to two-year terms and whose members are elected to one-year terms.

VILLAGE CORPORATION
Shareholders in the Twin Hills village corporation are also shareholders in Bristol Bay Native Corporation *(see Alaska introduction)*.

ECONOMY
Steady income is from limited village council and post office employment. Fishermen use special flat-bottomed boats for the shallow waters of Togiak Bay. Togiak Fisheries and other cash buyers generate a market for fishermen. The community relies on subsistence activities for food sources. Seal, sea lion, walrus, whale, salmon, clams, geese, and ducks are harvested. Twin Hills, Togiak, and Manokotak engage in an exchange relationship. Seal oil is exchanged for blackfish. Handicrafts also generate supplemental income.

Fisheries. Fifteen residents hold commercial fishing permits (salmon, herring, herring roe on kelp, or sac roe).

Government as employer. Of the 15 employed residents, 9 work for the local, state, or federal government.

Manufacturing. Three residents are employed in manufacturing.

Services and retail. There is one business in the community: a snow-removal service. Education, health, and social service professions employ 10 residents; public administration employs 2 residents.

Transportation. Two airline companies service Twin Hills.

INFRASTRUCTURE
Ten capital projects, funded by grants, are active in Twin Hills.

Transportation. Twin Hills is primarily accessible by air and water. Dillingham provides regular and charter flights. The state provides a 3,000- by 60-foot lighted gravel runway on a ridge east of the village. Most cargo deliveries are by air. Docking facilities are not available. There is a boat landing; bulk goods must be lightered to shore. Cars, all-terrain vehicles, and snowmachines provide local transportation. Residents drive along the beach to get to the Togiak Fisheries cannery.

Electricity. Twin Hills Village Council provides electricity.

Fuel storage (gallons). Togiak Fisheries Inc. (127,500); Southwest Region Schools (31,300); Village Council (29,400).

Water and waste systems. Piped water and sewer systems have been installed in Twin Hills. Water drawn using a submersible pump is treated and stored in a 60,000-gallon steel tank. More than 20 occupied households have piped services and full plumbing. Seven new HUD housing units have individual wells and septic tanks. The school operates its own system. Water and sewer improvements are currently being studied.

Telecommunications. In-state phone service is provided by United Utilities Inc., long distance service by GCI and United Utilities. Internet is provided by GCI. Teleconferencing is available through Alaska Teleconferencing Network. Alaska Rural Communications Service provides television access. No radio stations or cable provider in the community.

COMMUNITY FACILITIES AND SERVICES
Local facilities include a recreation center and a village council building. A coin-operated washeteria is available. The gravity sewage system feeds to a nearby disposal lagoon. Seven new HUD housing units have individual wells and septic tanks. Landfill improvements are currently being studied.

Education. Twin Hills School is in the Southwest Region School District. The school has 13 students and two teachers.

Health care. Health resources include Twin Hills Health Clinic. Twin Hills is classified as an isolated village and is found in EMS Region 2I in the Bristol Bay Region. Emergency services have limited air and river access. Emergency service is provided by a health aide. Twin Hills First Responder Group provides auxiliary health care.

Total area of entitlement under ANCSA

	193,515 acres
Total labor force	144
High school graduate or higher	70.7%
Bachelor's degree or higher	4.9%
Unemployment rate	27.3%
Per capita income *(1999)*	$11,261
Population *2000 census*	193
Percent Native *2000 census*	95.3%

LOCATION
Tyonek lies on the northwest shore of Cook Inlet, 43 miles southwest of Anchorage.

CLIMATE
The climate in Tyonek is maritime, with relatively mild winters and cool summers. Temperatures range from winter lows of -27°F to occasional summer highs of 91°F. Average annual precipitation is 23 inches.

CULTURE AND HISTORY
Tyonek is a Tanaina (Dena'ina) Indian village with a subsistence-oriented culture. It was first reported in 1880 as Toyonok, which means "little chief." The village has also been called Beluga and Moquawkie. There is a federally recognized tribe in the community- the Native Village of Tyonek.

GOVERNMENT
Tyonek is unincorporated under Alaska law and is located in the Kenai Peninsula Borough *(see Alaska introduction)*. The village is governed by an Indian Reorganization Act village council.

VILLAGE CORPORATION
Shareholders in the Tyonek village corporation also hold shares in Cook Inlet Regional Native Corporation *(see Alaska introduction)*.

ECONOMY
Tyonek's economy is based on limited local employment, supplemented by subsistence activities. Tourism is a growing source of income for the community, especially with the development of fishing-and-hunting guide services. Subsistence activities provide salmon, moose, beluga whale, and waterfowl. Tyonek offers recreational fishing-and hunting-guide services. Some residents trap in winter. The North Foreland Port Facility at Tyonek is the preferred site for export of Beluga coal.

Construction. The construction industry employs 11 residents.

Fisheries. Twenty residents hold commercial fishing permits.

Government as employer. Of the 64 employed residents, 30 work for the local, state, or federal government.

Services and retail. There are eight businesses in the community, including an oilfield contractor, day care service, general store, ice cream shop, cigarette shop, and the Native Village of Tyonek. Education, health, and social service professions employ 17 residents; public administration, 14.

Tourism and recreation. One village guest house is available. Arts, entertainment, recreation, accommodations, and food service industries employ eight residents.

Transportation. Transportation, warehousing, and utility industries employ five residents.

INFRASTRUCTURE
Eight capital projects, funded by grants, are active in Tyonek.

Transportation. There is no road access to Tyonek. Permission is required to land at the 3,000- by 90-foot gravel airstrip, which is owned by the Village of Tyonek. Regularly-scheduled flights are available. The state provides a 4,003-foot gravel airstrip at Nikolai Creek, and a 2,400-foot gravel airstrip, owned by Arco Alaska, is in Beluga. A road links Tyonek to nearby Beluga. Barges deliver heavy goods to Tyonek.

Electricity. Chugach Electric Association provides electricity.

Fuel storage (gallons). Village council (4,000).

Water and waste systems. A piped water and sewer system serves approximately 90 homes and facilities. Water, drawn from Second Lake, is treated and stored in a 175,000-gallon tank. Back-up water supplies are available from a lake near the airport. The community wants to develop a groundwater source.

Telecommunications. In-state phone service is provided by Matanuska Telephone Association, long distance service by AT&T Alascom. Teleconferencing is available through Alaska Teleconferencing Network. Two local radio stations and two television stations are in the community. There is no cable provider.

COMMUNITY FACILITIES AND SERVICES
Local facilities include a community hall, a youth recreation center, and a library that services the school and community. A small coin-operated washeteria, with one washer and dryer, is available.

Education. Tebughna School is in the Kenai Peninsula School District. The school has 43 students and four teachers.

Health care. Health resources include Tyonek Health Clinic (Indian Creek Health Dept.). Tyonek is classified as an isolated village and is found in EMS Region 2J in the Kenai Peninsula Region. Emergency services have highway, coastal, and air access. Emergency service is provided by volunteers and a health aide. Tyonek Volunteer Rescue Squad provides auxiliary health care.

[tie-OH-neck]
Ethnicity: Tanaina (Dena'ina)
Athabascan

Native entity
Native Village of Tyonek
P.O. Box 82009
Tyonek, AK 99682-2009
  907-583-2201
  907-583-2442 Fax

ANCSA village corporation
Tyonek Native Corporation
1689 C Street, Suite 219
Anchorage, AK 99501-5131
  907-272-0707
  907-274-7125 Fax

Ugashik

[yoo-GASH-ick]
Ethnicity: Alutiiq Aleut

Native entity
Ugashik Traditional Village
    Council
206 E. Fireweed Lane
Suite 204
Anchorage, AK 99503
    907-338-7611
    907-338-7659 Fax

ANCSA village corporation
Alaska Peninsula Corporation
P.O. Box 334
King Salmon, AK 99613

Total area of entitlement under ANCSA	
	69,120 acres
Total labor force	10
High school graduate or higher	60%
Bachelor's degree or higher	-
Unemployment rate	-
Per capita income *(1999)*	$12,530
Population *2000 census*	11
Percent Native *2000 census*	81.8%

LOCATION
Ugashik is located on the northwest coast of the Alaska Peninsula, on the east bank of the Ugashik River, 16 miles upriver from Ugashik Bay and about 350 miles southwest of Anchorage.

CLIMATE
Ugashik's maritime climate is characterized by cool, humid, and windy weather. Average summer temperatures range from 41°F to 60°F; winter temperatures vary from 12°F to 37°F. Total precipitation is 19 inches annually, including an average snowfall of 38 inches.

CULTURE AND HISTORY
Ugashik is a traditional Aleut site; however, few people live in the village year-round. Most descendants of former residents of the village now live in nearby Pilot Point, on the coast. Fishing and subsistence activities remain important parts of the local culture. The Russian Ivan Petrof recorded the Eskimo village of Oogeshik at this site in 1880. It was one of the largest villages in the region, until the influenza epidemic of 1919 decimated the population and the local cannery temporarily closed. The village has remained small since that time, although canneries have been maintained in the area up to the present. A post office was maintained intermittently from 1932 to 1963. There is a federally recognized tribe in the community—the Ugashik Traditional Council. Tribal members live throughout Alaska, California, and Washington.

GOVERNMENT
Ugashik is unincorporated and is located in the Lake and Peninsula Borough *(see Alaska introduction)*. It is governed by a traditional village council headed by a president.

VILLAGE CORPORATION
Shareholders in the Alaska Peninsula village corporation also hold shares in Bristol Bay Native Corporation *(see Alaska introduction)*.

ECONOMY
Commercial fishing is the basis of Ugashik's economy. Residents also depend on subsistence hunting and fishing; commercial fisherman often keep some of the fish they catch for their own use. Subsistence activities provide food sources, including salmon, trout, grayling, moose, caribou, and bear.

Construction. One resident is employed in construction.

Fisheries. Four residents hold a commercial fishing permit (salmon, trout, grayling).

Government as employer. Of the four employed residents, all four work for the local, state, or federal government.

Services and retail. There are two businesses in the community: an automotive equipment rental company and a grant-making enterprise. Public administration employs three residents.

INFRASTRUCTURE
Twelve capital projects, funded by grants, are active in Ugashik.

Transportation. Ugashik is accessible by air and water. The Bureau of Land Management provides a 5,280-foot gravel airstrip at Ugashik Bay, 12 miles from Ugashik. There is a 3,200-foot gravel airstrip in the village. The state provides a 3,000- by 60-foot gravel runway. A new barge landing is now open. Barged freight is brought in from Naknek. Funds are needed to rebuild the community dock. Skiffs and all-terrain vehicles provide local transportation.

Electricity. Individual generators provide electricity. Ugashik has no public electric services. A central electric system and bulk fuel storage facility are needed.

Fuel storage (gallons). Briggs Way Cannery (17,000).

Water and waste systems. Ugashik has no public water or sewer services. Ten new wells are now available, including service lines and plumbing. All homes have individual wells. Septic systems are still used by some residents.

Telecommunications. In-state phone service is provided by ACS Radio Telephone, long distance service by ACS Radio Telephone. Internet service is provided by Starband. There is one radio station in the community. Alaska Rural Communications Service provides television access. There is no cable provider, but satellite dish programming is available.

COMMUNITY FACILITIES AND SERVICES
A sewage pumper is available. A landfill is needed.

Education. There are no schools in Ugashik.

Health care. No services are available in the community.

Umkumiute

Total area of entitlement under ANCSA
69,120 acres

LOCATION
Umkumiute is located on Nelson Island, in the Yukon-Kuskokwim Delta of southwest Alaska, adjacent to Toksook Bay.

CLIMATE
The island experiences a marine climate. Summer temperatures range from 41°F to 57°F; winter temperatures vary from 6°F to 24°F. Precipitation averages 22 inches, including 43 inches of snowfall annually.

CULTURE AND HISTORY
Umkumiute is an Eskimo summer fish camp; at present there are no year-round residents. As a seasonal fish camp, it provides subsistence food items for area residents. The resources of this area have been used by Yup'ik Eskimos for thousands of years.

GOVERNMENT
Umkumiute is unincorporated and is located in the Unorganized Borough (see Alaska introduction). It has a traditional village council, headed by a president.

VILLAGE CORPORATION
Shareholders in the Chinuruk village corporation also hold shares in Calista regional Native corporation (see Alaska introduction).

ECONOMY
Umkumiute has no economy, but it is an important site for subsistence resources that supplement the incomes of residents of Nelson Island communities. As a seasonal-use fish camp, Umkumiute provides subsistence food items for area residents.

INFRASTRUCTURE
Two capital projects, funded by grants, are active in Umkumiute.

Transportation. The Toksook Bay airstrip provides access to the island. Boats or skiffs are used for local transportation.

[OOM-kuh-myoot]; var. **Umkumiut**
Ethnicity: Yup'ik Eskimo

Native entity
Umkumiut Tribal Council
P.O. Box 90062
Nightmute, AK 99690
907-647-6145
907-647-6112 Fax

ANCSA village corporation
Chinuruk, Incorporated
General Delivery
Nightmute, AK 99680

Unalakleet

Total area of entitlement under ANCSA
180,374 acres

Total labor force	502
High school graduate or higher	82.7%
Bachelor's degree or higher	18%
Unemployment rate	14.6%
Per capita income (1999)	$15,845
Population 2000 census	747
Percent Native 2000 census	87.7%

LOCATION
Unalakleet is located on Norton Sound at the mouth of the Unalakleet River, 148 miles southeast of Nome and 395 miles northwest of Anchorage.

CLIMATE
Unalakleet has a subarctic climate with considerable maritime influences. Winters are cold and dry, while summers are cool and moist. Average summer temperatures range from 47°F to 62°F; winter temperatures range from -4°F to 11°F. Precipitation averages 14 inches annually, including 41 inches of snowfall.

CULTURE AND HISTORY
Unalakleet has a history of diverse cultures and flourishing trade activity; it lies on the border between the Inupiat and Yup'ik Eskimo areas of the state. Archaeologists have dated house remains along the beach ridge to approximately 2,000 years ago. Unalakleet is the terminus for the Kaltag Portage, an important winter travel route connecting to the Yukon River. Indians on the upper river were considered "professional" traders, who had a monopoly on the Indian-Eskimo trade across the Kaltag Portage. The Russian American Company built a post there in the 1830s. In 1901, the U.S. Army Signal Corps built over 605 miles of telegraph line from St. Michael to Unalakleet, over the portage to Kaltag and Fort Gibbon. There is a federally recognized tribe in the community-the Native Village of Unalakleet. Fish, seal, caribou, moose, and bear are utilized.

GOVERNMENT
Unalakleet was incorporated under Alaska law as a second-class city in 1974, with a mayor and city council; it is located in the Unorganized Borough (see Alaska introduction). It also has an Indian Reorganization Act village council headed by a president.

VILLAGE CORPORATION
Shareholders in the Unalakleet village corporation also hold shares in Bering Straits Regional Native Corporation (see Alaska introduction).

ECONOMY
Unalakleet's economy is the most active and diverse in Norton Sound and takes place alongside a traditional Eskimo subsistence lifestyle. Employment in government organizations and village schools is relatively plentiful in Unalakleet. A herd of musk oxen is maintained near the village, and the underwool (qiviut) is hand-knit by village residents. Both commercial fishing for herring and herring roe and subsistence activities are major components of Unalakleet's economy. Norton Sound Economic Development Council operates a fish processing plant. Tourism is becoming increasingly important; there is world-class silver fishing in the area.

Construction. Ten residents are employed in construction.

Fisheries. Approximately 109 residents hold commercial fishing permits.

Government as employer. Of the 258 employed residents, 161 work for the local, state, or federal government.

[YOO-nuh-luh-kleet]
Ethnicity: Inupiat Eskimo

Municipality
City of Unalakleet
P.O. Box 28
Unalakleet, AK 99684
907-624-3531
907-624-3130 Fax

Native entity
Native Village of Unalakleet
P.O. Box 270
Unalakleet, AK 99684
907-624-3622
907-624-3402 Fax

ANCSA village corporation
Unalakleet Native Corporation
P.O. Box 100
Unalakleet, AK 99684
907-624-3411
907-624-3833 Fax

Unalakleet

Unalaska

See Qawalangin

Unga

See Zero Population Section

Upper Kalskag

See Kalskag

Manufacturing. Five residents are employed in manufacturing.

Services and retail. There are 29 businesses in the community, including an engine repair shop, hardware store, boat storage, construction company, and aviation services. Retail trade employs 23 residents; education, health, and social service, 127; public administration, 33; financial and related businesses, 11; and information services, 5.

Tourism and recreation. Accommodations include one lodge and one inn. Services include guide services, two cafés, a video mart, a fur and fabric shop, and a shop specializing in yarn art, sewing, and hand crafts. Visitor attractions include sport fishing for silvers. Arts, entertainment, recreation, accommodations, and food service industries employ nine residents.

Transportation. Six airline companies and one trucking company service Unalakleet. Transportation, warehousing, and utility industries employ 31 residents.

INFRASTRUCTURE
Sixteen capital projects, funded by grants, are active in Unalakleet.

Transportation. The state provides a 6,004-foot long by 150-foot gravel runway and a gravel strip that is 2,000 feet long and 80 feet wide. There are regular flights to Anchorage. Cargo is lightered from Nome; a dock is available. All-terrain vehicles, snowmachines, and dogsleds in winter provide local transportation.

Electricity. Matanuska Electric Association owns and operates the electrical system in Unalakleet through the Unalakleet Valley Electric Cooperative. Unalakleet Valley Electric Cooperative provides electricity.

Fuel storage (gallons). Alaska Village Electric Cooperative (AVEC) (358,000); West Coast Aviation (336,700); Native

Corp. (261,900); Bering Straits Schools (94,000); City Water (66,300); Alaska Department of Transportation (48,300); Alaska Commercial Company (24,300); Ryan Air (17,000); Peninsula Air (1,900); Covenant Church (1,500).

Water and waste systems. Water drawn from an infiltration gallery on Powers Creek is treated and stored in a million-gallon steel tank. The water source is insufficient during extremely cold weather, and a feasibility study is in progress. More than 190 households are connected to the piped water and sewer system and have full plumbing. Only two households haul water and use honeybuckets.

Telecommunications. In-state phone service is provided by United KUC, long distance service by AT&T Alascom and GCI. Internet service is provided by GCI and Nome.net. Teleconferencing is available through Alaska Teleconferencing Network and the Nome Legislative Information Office. There is one radio station in the community. Alaska Rural Communications Service provides television access; cable provider is Frontier Cable.

COMMUNITY FACILITIES AND SERVICES
Local facilities include the Unalakleet Ticasuk Library and a city office. Residents haul refuse to the baler facility for transfer to the landfill. Refuse collection is available for commercial customers.

Education. Unalakleet School is in the Bering Straits School District. The school has 210 students and 19 teachers.

Health care. Health resources include Euksavik Clinic. The clinic is a qualified emergency care center. Unalakleet is classified as an isolated town/Sub-Regional Center and is found in EMS Region 5A in the Norton Sound Region. Emergency services have river and air access. Volunteers and a health aide provide emergency services.

Venetie

[VEEN-uh-tie]
Ethnicity: Gwich'in Athabascan

Native entity
Native Village of Venetie Tribal
Government
P.O. Box 81080
Venetie, AK 99781
907-849-8212
907-849-8097 Fax

	Venetie	Arctic Village	Total
Total labor force	69	56	125
High school graduate or higher	55.1%	37.5%	47.2%
Bachelor's degree or higher	5.8%	35.7%	19.2%
Unemployment rate	36.2%	16.1%	27.2%
Per capita income *(1999)*	$7,314	$10,761	$8,882
Population *2000 census*	199	166	365
Current population state demographer estimate	202	152	354
Percent Native *2000 census*	96.5%	92.1%	94.5%

LOCATION
Venetie is located on the north side of the Chandalar River, 45 miles northwest of Fort Yukon and 150 miles north of Fairbanks, in the interior of the state. Arctic Village is on the east fork of the Chandalar River, 100 miles north of Fort Yukon and 290 miles north of Fairbanks, near the northern border of the Venetie Indian Reservation, on the southern boundary of the Arctic National Wildlife Refuge.

PHYSICAL DESCRIPTION
Venetie encompasses 20.8 square miles of land. The area is heavily wooded boreal forest. The community was relocated in the late 1970s and is now above the floodplain of the Chandalar River. The sewage lagoon flooded in May 1998 due to heavy rainfall and rapid snowmelt. Arctic Village encompasses 61.7 square miles of land and 8.1 square miles of water. It is wooded and rolling to mountainous beyond the flood plain of the Chandalar River. The school, washeteria, water plant, water tank, sewage lagoon, and at least two houses in Arctic Village are below the building elevation level recommended by the U.S. Army Corps of Engineers.

CLIMATE
Winter low temperatures vary between -71°F and 0°F, and extended periods of -50°F to -60°F are common. Summer high temperatures range from 65°F to 72°F. Precipitation averages 6.5 inches, including snowfall of 43 inches, and 9 inches in Arctic Village with a yearly snowfall of 53 inches.

CULTURE AND HISTORY

Until the 1950s, the Neets'aii Gwich'in ("residents of the north side") traditionally hunted fish and game in the seasonal camps and settlements of Arctic Village, Christian, Venetie, and Sheenjak. Archaeological evidence suggests that the Arctic Village area existed as a community as early as 4500 BC. In the early 1900s, settlers began to give the village permanency. The population largely comprises descendants of Neets'aii Gwich'in and, to a lesser extent, Gwichyaa Dihii Gwich'in Indians. The founder of Venetie, "Old Robert," chose it as a settlement location because of its plentiful fish and game. In 1943, the Venetie Indian Reservation was established by area villagers to protect the land for subsistence use. Natives of the region traditionally spent only the coldest winter months in cabins, while camping for the remainder of the year in subsistence food-gathering pursuits. Subsistence activities remain an important part of the local culture. In 1971, the Alaska Native Claims Settlement Act (ANCSA) was passed and Venetie and Arctic Village opted for title to the 1.8 million acres of land in the former reservation. Residents continue to pursue a seasonal subsistence lifestyle. Both communities were settled by the formerly nomadic Gwich'in because their forests and rivers provided timber for fuel and shelter, furred animals, and abundant fish. More important, this area is winter range for varying populations of the vast Porcupine caribou herd. Drifting across the mountains from their summer breeding grounds in the Arctic Refuge on the coast of the Beaufort Sea, the caribou move south and east into the Porcupine River drainage and Canada's Yukon Territory, where most of the animals overwinter. Each Gwich'in family needs 8 to 12 animals to provide sufficient dried meat and hides to feed and clothe themselves through the winter.

GOVERNMENT

Venetie and Arctic Village are unincorporated and are located in the Unorganized Borough. Together they are governed by a BIA-recognized Indian Reorganization Act village council, the Native Village of Venetie Tribal Government, headed by a first chief. Venetie has no village corporation, and residents do not hold shares in any regional Native corporation. The Tribal Government owns the former reservation lands outright. It was in the *Venetie* Case [*Alaska v. Native Village of Venetie Tribal Government*, 522 U.S. 520 (1998)] that the United States Supreme Court determined that, under the ANCSA, neither the former reservation land conveyed to the Venetie and Arctic Village tribes nor the land conveyed to the Native Alaskan corporations were "Indian Country" in the sense of jurisdiction for taxation or law enforcement purposes.

INFRASTRUCTURE

Venetie

Electricity. Venetie Village Electric, an arm of the village council, provides electricity by means of a 430-kilowatt diesel plant. The Stanley Frank Washeteria and Water Treatment Plant uses a small solar power system to generate some electricity.

Fuel storage (gallons). Yukon Flats Schools (48,900); Village Council Electric (13,000); village council (2,000).

Water and waste systems. Water, drawn from a well near the Chandalar River, is treated and stored in a tank. Residents haul water and honeybuckets. As of 2004, only eight homes have functioning plumbing. A flush/haul system is under construction in Venetie; as of 2002, four homes were served.

Transportation. Access to Venetie is almost exclusively by air. The Venetie Tribal Council owns and operates the 4,100-by 65-foot dirt and gravel airstrip. The Chandalar River provides access by boat during the summer months. There is no

barge service because of shallow water. Motorbikes, all-terrain vehicles, snowmobiles, and dog teams provide local transportation.

Telecommunications. Local phone service is provided by United Utilities, long distance service by AT&T Alascom or United Utilities. Internet service is available at the schools through GCI. Alaska Rural Communications Service provides one channel of television from a local repeater, and the village provides another. AM radio stations can be received in Venetie from Fort Yukon, Fairbanks, Anchorage, and other sources.

Arctic Village

Electricity. Arctic Village Electric Company, an arm of the Village Council, provides electricity from a 90-kilowatt diesel plant. A small solar power system powers the washeteria.

Fuel storage (gallons). Yukon Flats Schools (31,000); Village Electric (12,000); village office (5,455); U.S. Fish and Wildlife (4,105); Village Fuel Sales (2,100).

Water and waste systems. Water, drawn from the Chandalar River, is treated and hauled from the washeteria, the only facility with running water. Household plumbing is nonexistent. Water is available to two large school tanks directly from village sources. Water is hauled to the clinic, which uses a pail toilet. Villagers use outhouses or haul their honeybuckets. Alternatives for water safety, washeteria upgrades, and a new landfill (away from the airport) were being studied as of 2003.

Transportation. Air transportation is the only year-round passage to the community. Ice fog is a common problem for air services in winter. The tribal government provides a 4,500-by 75-foot gravel airstrip. All-terrain vehicles and snowmachines support local travel. Some dog teams are used. There are accommodations available at the Community Lodge (five rooms).

Telecommunications. Local phone service is provided by United Utilities, long distance service by AT&T Alascom or United Utilities. Internet service is available at the schools through GCI. Alaska Rural Communications Service provides television access from a local repeater. The terrain precludes any broadcasting to Arctic Village.

ECONOMY

Venetie (including Arctic Village) is heavily dependent on subsistence activities. Caribou, moose, sheep, bear, porcupine, rabbit, and ptarmigan are hunted. Freshwater fish, waterfowl, and berries are harvested. Construction, Bureau of Land Management firefighting, guiding, and wildlife surveying for the U.S. Fish and Wildlife Service offer seasonal work. Individual income also is generated by trapping and by selling firewood. Most cash employment is through the schools, clinics, post offices, stores, and village council. The Alaska National Guard has used Venetie as a cold-weather-survival training-school location. The Bureau of Land Management seasonally employs fire fighters from the village. Development of a lumber mill in Venetie and tourism promotion are current interests of the community. Another community interest is to build cabins from local logs to house visitors, and developing arts and crafts activities, cultural activities, and a museum.

Government as employer. Of the 91 employed residents, 62 work for the village, state, or federal government.

Services and retail. There is a general store in Venetie and two grocery stores in Arctic Village.

Venetie

NOTE

Venetie is a single Alaskan Native entity with two communities, Venetie and Arctic Village. They are also separate census areas. Therefore, this profile is organized differently from others in this Guide.

ANCSA NOTE

Venetie and Arctic Village opted for title to the 1.8 million acres of land in the former reservation, which the members of those tribes now own as tenants in common through the Native Village of Venetie Tribal Government. There is no village corporation, and residents are not shareholders of the regional Native corporation, although the Native Village of Venetie is in the Doyon, Limited, region. In 1943 the Venetie Indian Reservation was established at 1.8 million acres; it included Arctic Village. When the Alaska Native Claims Settlement Act was passed in 1971, Arctic Village and Venetie elected to keep their reserve status. By the provisions of section 19(b) of ANCSA, "the Village Corporation shall not be eligible for any other land selections under this Act or to any distribution of Regional Corporation funds pursuant to section 7, and the enrolled residents of the Village Corporation shall not be eligible to receive Regional Corporation stock."

Venetie

COMMUNITY FACILITIES AND SERVICES

The tribe operates the water supply systems, sewage disposal systems, electrical systems, fuel sales, and the washeterias in the two communities.

Education. John Fredson School in Venetie and the Arctic Village School are operated by the Yukon Flats School District. The former has 44 students and 5 teachers, the latter 52 students and 7 teachers. In both communities, the school library serves as the community library.

Health care. The Myra Roberts Clinic in Venetie and the Arctic Village Health Clinic are operated by the Tanana Chiefs Conference. A health aide provides emergency care. Higher levels of care are available by flight to Fort Yukon, about 87 miles away, and Fairbanks, about 178 miles away.

Public safety. Law enforcement is provided by the state troopers in Fairbanks, emergency response by community volunteer fire departments.

Wainwright

Ethnicity: Inupiat

Municipality
City of Wainwright
P.O. Box 9
Wainwright, AK 99782
907-763-2815
907-763-2811 Fax

Native entity
Village of Wainwright
P.O. Box 143
Wainwright, AK 99782
907-763-2535
907-763-2536 Fax

ANCSA village corporation
Olgoonik Corporation
P.O. Box 29
Wainwright, AK 99782
907-763-2614
907-763-2926 Fax
olgoonik.com

Total area of entitlement under ANCSA	170,870 acres
Total labor force	261
High school graduate or higher	137
Bachelor's degree or higher	31
Unemployment rate	21.8%
Per capita income *(1999)*	$16,709
Population *2000 census*	546
Current population *state demographer estimate*	553
Percent Native *2000 census*	93.0%

LOCATION

Wainwright is located on the coast of the Chukchi Sea of the North Slope of Alaska, three miles northeast of the Kuk River estuary and about 72 air miles southwest of Barrow. Distinguish the City of Wainwright from Fort Wainwright, a U.S. Army post near Fairbanks.

CLIMATE

Wainwright's climate is Arctic. Temperatures range from winter lows of -56°F to occasional summer highs of 80°F. Precipitation is light, averaging five inches annually, including yearly snowfall of 12 inches.

PHYSICAL DESCRIPTION

The city covers 17.6 square miles of land and 24.9 square miles of water. The Chukchi Sea is ice free from mid-July through September. Wainwright was flooded in October of 1963, August of 1970, and the fall of 1986. The storm in 1963 was reported as a surge of four feet caused by strong winds from the south, with the waves reaching the top of the bluff. The storm in 1970 was reported to have a surge of 1.5 feet caused by 30-knot winds from the west, which were sustained for 48 hours. The storm in 1986 was caused by 75 mile per hour winds, but no flooding was reported. It is not known which storm was the worst. Now there is very little chance of flooding because of the community's elevation, although there is high potential for beach erosion.

CULTURE AND HISTORY

Wainwright is a traditional Inupiat village, with a culture centered on a subsistence lifestyle. The area around Wainwright has historically been well populated. A map of 1853 reports the Native name of the village to be Olrona. The lagoon was named in 1826 by the captain of a U.S. naval vessel for one of his crew members, Lieutenant John Wainwright. The present village site was chosen by the captain of a ship delivering school construction materials in 1904 because sea-ice conditions were favorable for landing. The ancestors of the Inupiat in the village were the Utukamiut ("people of the Utukok River") and Kukmiut ("people of the Kuk River"). In the spring, the community gathers for Nalukataq, the feast after a successful whaling season. At this festival and on other occasions, Eskimo dances are performed by the villagers. Other activities include boating, snowmobiling, and smelt fishing in the spring.

GOVERNMENT

Wainwright was incorporated as a second-class city in 1962, with a mayor and city council; it is located in the North Slope Borough *(see Alaska introduction)*. There is a federally recognized tribe, the Village of Wainwright, with a traditional council headed by a president.

VILLAGE CORPORATION

Shareholders in the Olgoonik village corporation also hold shares in Arctic Slope Regional Native Corporation *(see Alaska introduction)*.

ECONOMY

Economic opportunities in Wainwright are influenced by its proximity to Barrow and by the fact that it is one of the older, more established villages. The private sector is larger in Wainwright than most other villages; approximately 55 percent of the work force is employed by private businesses, mostly the village and regional corporations. The borough employs close to 29 percent of the work force, and the school district employs another 11.7 percent. Wainwright's subsistence hunting is based primarily on whales and caribou. Bowhead and beluga whale, seal, walrus, polar bear, birds, and fish are harvested. The sale of local Inupiat arts and crafts, including carved ivory figurines and jewelry, baleen boats, whale bone carvings, clocks, knitted caps and gloves, supplements income. Olgoonik Corporation, pronounced *ol-OON-ick*, Wainwright's village corporation, runs the Native store and sells groceries, clothing, first-aid supplies, hardware, camera film, and sporting goods. Fuel available includes marine gasoline, diesel, propane, unleaded, regular, and supreme. Other private businesses include another store, taxi services, and the Olgoonik Hotel and Restaurant. SKW/Eskimos, a subsidiary of Arctic Slope Regional Corporation, and Kuk Construction, a subsidiary of Olgoonik Corporation, have operations in the City.

Government as employer. A total of 151 city residents work for the city, borough, state, or federal government.

INFRASTRUCTURE

Transportation. Air travel is the only year-round access to Wainwright. The North Slope Borough provides a 4,494- by 90-foot gravel airstrip, serviced by scheduled and chartered flights from Barrow. Marine access is available in the summer, and a popular mode of transportation during winter months is by snowmachine. Freight arrives by cargo plane and barge. Local taxicab and car rental services are available, and accommodations are available at the Olgoonik Hotel.

Electricity is provided by a 1,950-kilowatt diesel plant operated by North Slope Borough.

Fuel storage (gallons). North Slope Borough (NSB) Schools/ Olgoonik Corporation Fuel Station (908,000); NSB Power (500,000); Olgoonik Corporation (50,000); NSB Schools (10,000); NSB Water (10,000); NSB Fire (7,500); NSB Clinic (6,000); city (2,400); Olgoonik Hotel and Restaurant (1,500); NSB Sewage (1,500); SKW/Eskimos (1,000).

Water and waste systems. Water, drawn from nearby Merekruak Lake, is treated and stored in tanks. From the tanks, trucks haul water and deliver to the community's homes. Honeybuckets are used for sewage disposal, and the borough provides hauling services. Most of the households have running water in the kitchen. As of 2003, a flush haul system with holding tanks, plumbing, flush toilets, and showers, was in the development stage.

Telecommunications. In-state phone service is provided by Arctic Slope Telephone Association Co-operative, long distance service by AT&T Alascom, GCI, or Arctic Slope Telephone. GCI provides Internet services. AM radio stations from Barrow, Nome, and Kotzebue can be received in the area. The Alaska Rural Communications System broadcasts two television stations locally, and cable television service is available.

COMMUNITY FACILITIES AND SERVICES
The North Slope Borough provides all utilities in Wainwright.

Education. Alak School is in the North Slope Borough School District. The school has 149 students in pre-kindergarten through grade 12 and 17 teachers. The Alak School Library serves as the community library.

Health care. Wainwright Health Clinic provides health care to the community. Emergency services have coastal and air access. The Wainwright Volunteer Fire Department is available for auxiliary health care. The nearest hospital is Samuel Simmonds Memorial Hospital in Barrow, about 74 miles away by air.

Public safety. Law enforcement is provided by the North Slope Borough Police Department, backed by state troopers in Barrow. Emergency response is provided by the Wainwright Volunteer Fire Department.

Wales

Total area of entitlement under ANCSA
108,800 acres
Total labor force	105
High school graduate or higher	79.2%
Bachelor's degree or higher	18.1%
Unemployment rate	18.9%
Per capita income *(1999)*	$14,877
Population *2000 census*	152
Percent Native *2000 census*	90.1%

LOCATION
Wales is located on Cape Prince of Wales, at the western tip of the Seward Peninsula, 111 miles northwest of Nome.

CLIMATE
The climate of Wales is primarily maritime when the Bering Strait is ice free, usually from June to November. After freeze-up, there is an abrupt change to a cold, continental climate. Average summer temperatures range from 40°F to 50°F; winter temperatures vary from -10°F to 6°F. Average annual precipitation is 10 inches, including 35 inches of yearly snowfall. Frequent fog, wind, and blizzards limit access to the community.

CULTURE AND HISTORY
Wales is an Inupiat Eskimo village, with a strong, traditional whaling culture. Ancient songs, dances, and customs are still practiced. In the summer Little Diomede residents travel to the village in large, traditional skin boats. Before the influenza epidemic of 1918, it was the region's largest and most prosperous village, with more than 500 residents. A burial mound of the Birnirk Culture, almost 1,500 years old, was discovered near Wales and is now a national landmark. In 1827, the Russian navy reported the Eskimo villages of Eidamoo near the coast and King-a-ghe, farther inland. In 1890, the American Missionary Association established a mission here, and in 1894, a reindeer station was organized. There is a federally recognized tribe in the community-the Native Village of Wales (also known as Kingigin).

GOVERNMENT
Wales was incorporated under Alaska law as a second-class city in 1964, with a mayor and city council; it is located in the Unorganized Borough *(see Alaska introduction).* It also has an Indian Reorganization Act village council headed by a president.

VILLAGE CORPORATION
Shareholders in the village corporation also hold shares in Bering Straits regional Native corporation *(see Alaska introduction).*

ECONOMY
The economy of Wales is based on subsistence hunting and fishing, trapping, traditional arts and crafts, and some mining. A private reindeer herd is managed out of the village, and local residents are employed to assist in the harvest. Whales, walrus, polar bear, moose, salmon, and other fish are utilized.

Construction. One resident is employed in construction.

Government as employer. Of the 60 employed residents, 36 work for the local, state, or federal government.

Services and retail. There are ten businesses in the community, including gasoline stations, grocery stores, and Wales Native Corporation businesses, such as a general store, real estate, automotive repair, performing arts, and cable network access. Retail trade employs 2 residents; education, health, and social services, 34; and public administration, 6.

Tourism and recreation. The Native Corporation provides lodging accommodations.

Transportation. Four airline companies service Wales. Transportation, warehousing, and utility industries employ six residents.

INFRASTRUCTURE
Sixteen capital projects, funded by grants, are active in Wales.

Also known as Kingigin

Ethnicity: Inupiat Eskimo

Municipality
City of Wales
P.O. Box 489
Wales, AK 99783
907-664-3501
907-664-3671 Fax

Native entity
Native Village of Wales
P.O. Box 549
Wales, AK 99783
907-664-3062
907-664-2200 Fax

ANCSA village corporation
Wales Native Corporation
P.O. Box 529
Wales, AK 99783
907-664-3641
907-664-3641 Fax

Wales

Also known as Kingigin

Transportation. Wales is accessed by air and sea only. The state provides a 4,000- by 75-foot gravel airstrip. The winter ice on the straits is often used by planes. Scheduled and charter flights are available. A barge delivers cargo that is lightered a half mile to shore. Skin boats are used for sea travel, and snowmobiles are popular in winter. A new 6.5-mile road to Tin City is now open.

Electricity. Alaska Village Electric Cooperative (AVEC) provides electricity.

Fuel storage (gallons). Native Store (102,200); U.S. Navy (97,600); Native Corp. (97,500); AVEC (51,100); Bering Straits Schools (43,500); City Water (7,900); City Office (3,500); Army National Guard (2,900).

Water and waste systems. Two new groundwater wells have been drilled. The community needs a pumphouse and watering point enclosure. Water is drawn from Gilbert Creek in summer. Residents haul treated water from a 500,000-gallon storage tank at the washeteria. A few residents use untreated water from Village Creek and a few households have plumbing. Piped water is available at the school, clinic, and city building. One septic system serves the school and a second septic system serves the teacher's housing, the clinic, and city building.

Telecommunications. In-state phone service is provided by Mukluk Telephone Company/TelAlaska, long distance service by AT&T Alascom, GCI, and Mukluk Telephone. Internet service is provided by AT&T Alascom, GCI, and Mukluk Telephone. Teleconferencing is available through Alaska Teleconferencing Network. Alaska Rural Communications Service provides television access. There are two radio stations in the community. Wales Native Corporation is the cable provider.

COMMUNITY FACILITIES AND SERVICES
Local facilities include the Wales Community Building and a school/city library. Almost all residents use honeybuckets, and a honeybucket haul system is in place. The landfill is not permitted.

Education. Wales-Kingikmiut School is in the Bering Straits School District. The school has 46 students and seven teachers.

Health care. Wales Health Clinic provides health care to the community. Wales is classified as an isolated village and is found in EMS Region 5A in the Norton Sound Region. Emergency services have coastal and air access. A health aide provides emergency care.

White Mountain

Ethnicity: Inupiat Eskimo

Municipality
City of White Mountain
P.O. Box 130
White Mountain, AK 99784
907-638-3411
907-638-3421 Fax

Native entity
Native Village of White
Mountain
P.O. Box 84082
White Mountain, AK 99784
907-638-3651
907-638-3652 Fax

ANCSA village corporation
White Mountain Native Corp
P.O. Box 81
White Mountain, AK 99784
907-638-3651
907-638-3652 Fax

Total area of entitlement under ANCSA	128,846 acres
Total labor force	129
High school graduate or higher	67.3%
Bachelor's degree or higher	11.2%
Unemployment rate	18.8%
Per capita income *(1999)*	$10,034
Population *2000 census*	203
Percent Native *2000 census*	86.2%

LOCATION
White Mountain is located on the west bank of the Fish River, on the Seward Peninsula, 63 miles east of Nome.

CLIMATE
White Mountain has a transitional climate, with less extreme seasonal and daily temperatures than other area communities. Continental influences prevail in the ice-bound winter months. Average summer temperatures range from 41°F to 61°F; winter temperatures vary from -7°F to 15°F. Annual precipitation is 15 inches, including 58 inches of yearly snowfall.

CULTURE AND HISTORY
White Mountain is an Eskimo village with historical influences from the gold rush. The entire population depends on subsistence hunting and fishing, and most spend the summer months at fish camps. The Eskimo fish camp of Nutchirviq was located at the site of the present village. The bountiful fish in both the Fish and Inukluk rivers supported the area's Native population. White Mountain grew after the influx of prospectors from the gold rush of 1900. The first structure was a warehouse built by the miner Charles Lane to store supplies for his claim in the Council District. It was also the site of a government-subsidized orphanage, which became an industrial school in 1926. There is a federally recognized tribe in the community—the Native Village of White Mountain.

GOVERNMENT
White Mountain was incorporated under Alaska law as a second-class city in 1969, with a mayor and city council; it is located in the Unorganized Borough *(see Alaska introduction)*. It also has an Indian Reorganization Act village council headed by a president.

VILLAGE CORPORATION
Shareholders in the village corporation also hold shares in Bering Straits regional Native corporation *(see Alaska introduction)*.

ECONOMY
The community relies on subsistence hunting and fishing, and most spend the summer at fish camps. Salmon, other fish, beluga whale, seal, moose, reindeer, caribou, and brown bear are utilized. The school, Native store, post office, city, IRA, and airline agents are the primary employers. Construction outside White Mountain and fire fighting provide seasonal employment. Ivory and bone carvings generate some income. One resident operates a reindeer farm.

Fisheries. Four residents hold commercial fishing permits.

Government as employer. Of the 39 employed residents, 30 work for the local, state, or federal government.

Services and retail. There are five businesses in the community, including a day care center, adventure company, and the White Mountain Volunteer Fire Department. Retail trade employs 2 residents; education, health, and social services, 29; and public administration, 5.

Tourism and recreation. One bed-and-breakfast, which includes a café, is available for lodging. Visitor attractions include year-round subsistence and sport fishing.

Transportation. Four airline companies service White Mountain. Transportation, warehousing, and utility industries employ three residents.

INFRASTRUCTURE
Twenty-one capital projects, funded by grants, are active in White Mountain.

Transportation. There are no roads into White Mountain; access is by air and sea. The state provides a 3,000-foot gravel runway. Regularly scheduled flights are available from Nome. Supplies to White Mountain are lightered from Nome and offloaded on the beach. Docks are not available, and a cargo barge has no passage to White Mountain. The community is looking into either a road to Golovin to permit fuel deliveries or the construction of a docking facility for barges.

Electricity. White Mountain Utilities provides electricity.

Fuel storage (gallons). Bering Straits Schools/city (131,600); Native Store (43,500); Tom Gray Reindeer Farm (4,900); AK DOT (3,000); Corp. Lodge (2,000).

Water and waste supply. Water drawn from a well near the Fish River is treated. Nearly 50 houses and facilities are connected to the piped water and sewer system. The school, which operates its own water and sewer system, is seeking connection to the city system.

Telecommunications. In-state phone service is provided by Mukluk Telephone Company/TelAlaska, long distance service by AT&T Alascom, GCI, and Mukluk Telephone. Internet service is provided by GCI and Nome.net. Teleconferencing is available through Alaska Teleconferencing Network. Alaska Rural Communications Service provides television access. There are two radio stations in the community. The City of White Mountain provides cable access.

COMMUNITY FACILITIES AND SERVICES
Local facilities include the Village Council/Community Building. A nutrition program is available to elders. Fifteen HUD homes are under development, and a master plan is in progress to look into system expansion alternatives. Funding is pending to relocate the landfill; the current site is not permitted. Eighteen households haul honeybuckets.

Education. White Mountain School is in the Bering Straits School District. The school has 59 students and seven teachers.

Health care. White Mountain Health Clinic provides health care to the community. White Mountain is classified as an isolated village and is found in EMS Region 5A in the Norton Sound Region. Emergency services have river and air access. A health aide provides emergency care.

White Mountain

Woody Island
See Zero Population under Lesnoi

Wrangell

Population *2000 census*	2,308
2003 population	2,113
state demographer estimate	
Percent Native *2000 census*	23.8%

NOTE
Wrangell is, primarily, a non-Native community. While the Wrangell Cooperative Association is a BIA-recognized Native entity, less than one-quarter of the population of the City of Wrangell is Native Alaskan. Except for basic orientation information, this profile discusses only those aspects of Wrangell that are unique to its Native residents.

LOCATION
The City of Wrangell is located on the northwest tip of Wrangell Island, 155 miles south of Juneau and 89 miles northwest of Ketchikan. It is near the mouth of the Stikine River, a historic trade route to the Canadian Interior.

PHYSICAL DESCRIPTION
The city covers 45.3 square miles of land and 25.6 square miles of water.

CLIMATE
Wrangell is in the maritime climatic zone, with cool summers, mild winters, and year-round rainfall. Summer high temperatures range from 42°F to 64°F. Winter low temperatures range from 21°F to 44°F. Average annual precipitation is 82 inches, including 64 inches of snowfall. Fog is common from September through December.

CULTURE AND HISTORY
Wrangell is primarily a non-Native community with a mixture of Tlingit, Russian, British and American historical influences. Logging and fishing have long supported the community.

Wrangell is one of the oldest non-Native settlements in Alaska. In 1811, the Russians began fur trading with area Tlingits. The island was named for Ferdinand Von Wrangel, manager of the Russian-American Company around 1830. The Tlingits claimed their own ancient trade rights to the Stikine River and protested when the Hudson Bay Company began to use their trade routes. But two epidemics of smallpox, in 1836 and 1840, reduced the Tlingit population by half. In 1868 a U.S. military post called Fort Wrangell was established, named for the Island. The City was incorporated in 1903. By 1916 fishing and forest products had become the primary industries.

GOVERNMENT
Wrangell Cooperative Association is a BIA-recognized Native entity and IRA tribal council. The community is also known by its Tlingit name, *Kaachxana-aakw.*

VILLAGE CORPORATION
While Wrangell has no ANCSA village corporation, its members are at-large shareholders in Sealaska Corporation, the regional Native corporation. Legislation has been introduced in Congress to provide ANCSA village corporations for five "panhandle" Native entities, including Wrangell, that did not get them under the ANCSA, but it has not yet been passed into law.

COMMUNITY FACILITIES AND SERVICES
Health care. Association members are eligible for medical care from the SouthEast Alaska Regional Health Consortium (SEARHC), a nonprofit organization that provides health care services to Alaska Natives and American Indians residing in the region. SEARHC contracts for care locally. Hospital-level care is available at SEARHC-operated Mt. Edgecumbe Hospital in Sitka.

Also known as
Koachxana-aalow

Ethnicity: Tlingit

Municipality
City of Wrangell
P.O. Box 531
Wrangell, AK 99929
907-874-2381
907-874-3952 Fax
wrangell.com

Native entity
Wrangell Cooperative Association
P.O. Box 868
Wrangell, AK 99929
907-874-3481
907-874-2982 Fax

Yakutat

City and Borough

[ACK-uh-tat]
Ethnicity: Tlingit

Municipality
City & Borough of Yakutat
P.O. Box 160
Yakutat, AK 99689
    907-784-3323
    907-784-3281 Fax

Native entity
Yakutat Tlingit Tribe
P.O. Box 418
Yakutat, AK 99689
    907-784-3238
    907-784-3595 Fax

ANCSA village corporation
Yak-Tat Kwaan, Incorporated
P.O. Box 416
Yakutat, AK 99689
    907-784-3335
    907-784-3622 Fax

Total area of entitlement under ANCSA	23,040 acres
Total labor force	613
High school graduate or higher	87.9%
Bachelor's degree or higher	21.8%
Unemployment rate	7.8%
Per capita income *(1999)*	$22,579
Population *2000 census*	680
Percent Native *2000 census*	55.1%

LOCATION
Yakutat is an isolated community in the lowlands along the Gulf of Alaska, 212 miles northwest of Juneau and 225 miles east of Cordova, at the mouth of Yakutat Bay.

CLIMATE
Yakutat has a maritime climate characterized by relatively mild, often rainy weather. Average winter temperatures range from 17°F to 39°F; summer temperatures vary from 42°F to 60°F. Yakutat receives some of the heaviest precipitation in the state.

CULTURE AND HISTORY
Yakutat has a diverse cultural history. The original settlers are believed to have been Eyak people from the Copper River area, who were conquered by the Tlingits. The area maintains its traditional Tlingit culture, with influences from the original Eyaks, as well as from Russian, English, and American traders and miners. Fishing and subsistence activities remain an important part of the culture. The village name derives from a Tlingit word meaning "the place where the canoes." The Russian American Company built a fort in Yakutat in 1805. Because they would not allow the local Tlingits access to their traditional fisheries, a war party attacked and destroyed the post. In 1884 the Alaska Commercial Company opened a store in Yakutat. By 1886 beaches in the area were being mined for gold. In 1889 the Swedish Free Mission church had opened a school and sawmill in the area. A cannery, sawmill, store, and railroad were constructed beginning in 1903; most residents moved to the current site of Yakutat to be closer to this cannery, which operated through 1970. During World War II a large aviation garrison and paved runway were constructed. Troops were withdrawn after the war, but the runway is still in use. There is a federally recognized tribe in the community-the Yakutat Tlingit Tribe.

GOVERNMENT
Yakutat was incorporated as a home-rule borough in 1992, with a mayor, city manager, and council; it is located in the Borough of Yakutat *(see Alaska introduction)*. Yakutat also has a traditional village council headed by a president.

VILLAGE CORPORATION
Shareholders in the Yak-Tat Kwaan village corporation also hold shares in Sealaska regional Native corporation *(see Alaska introduction)*.

ECONOMY
Yakutat's economy is dependent on hunting, fishing, fish processing, and government. North Pacific Processors is the primary private employer. Saltwater and freshwater fishing in the Situk River are considered choice recreational fishing opportunities. Salmon, trout, shellfish, deer, moose, bear, and goats are harvested.

Construction. Approximately 32 residents are employed in construction.

Fisheries. Approximately 162 residents hold commercial fishing permits. Fishing, farming, and forestry industries employ 103 residents.

Government as employer. Of the 440 employed residents, 102 work for the local, state, or federal government.

Hunting and mining. Approximately 33 residents are employed in hunting and mining industries.

Manufacturing. Approximately 25 residents are employed in manufacturing.

Services and retail. There are 120 businesses in the community, including a day care, trading company, flower shop, investment company, general store, welding services, construction business, photography business, hardware store, and lumber company. Retail trade employs 21 residents; education, health, and social services, 62; public administration, 30; financial and related businesses, 9; and information services, 5.

Tourism and recreation. Accommodations include five lodges, one inn and four bed-and-breakfast facilities. Visitor attractions include the glaciers, wildlife, camping, hunting, fishing, and hiking. Services include several guide, adventure, and charter businesses, marine tours, outfitters, a bead and gift shop, and a massage business. Arts, entertainment, recreation, accommodations, and food service industries employ 43 residents.

Transportation. Two airline companies, a taxi company, and a car rental business service Yakutat. Transportation, warehousing, and utility industries employ 64 residents.

INFRASTRUCTURE
Nineteen capital projects, funded by grants, are active in Yakutat.

Transportation. Scheduled jet flights, air taxis, and floatplanes have access to Yakutat. The state provides two jet-certified runways; one 6,475- by 150-foot (concrete); the other 7,745- by 150-foot (asphalt). The airport is three miles southeast of the community; a seaplane base is one mile northwest. Five airstrips in the area are operated by the U.S. Forest Service, and the National Park Service operates one airstrip at East Alsek River. The borough operates the state-owned boat harbor and the dock at Ocean Cape. The only sheltered deepwater port in the Gulf of Alaska is Monti Bay. Goods are delivered by barges each month in the winter, and more often in summer. The new state ferry *Kennicott* serves Yakutat during the summer.

Electricity. Yakutat Power provides electricity, using four diesel-fueled generators.

Fuel storage (gallons). Delta Western (6,468,000); Alaska Department of Transportation (14,800); Sitka Sound Seafoods (12,200).

Water and waste systems. Water, drawn from four wells, is treated and piped to more than 190 homes and to the schools. Piped sewage receives primary treatment; a secondary treatment facility will soon be in operation.

Telecommunications. In-state phone service is provided by ACS of the Northland, long distance service by AT&T Alascom. Internet service is provided by ACS Internet. Teleconferencing is available through Alaska Teleconferencing Network and the Sitka Legislative Information Office. Alaska Rural Communications Service provides television access. There is one radio station in the community. There is no cable provider in Yakutat.

COMMUNITY FACILITIES AND SERVICES

Local facilities include the Community Hall/ANB Hall and the Yakutat City Hall. Senior services include the Southeast Nutrition Program. Refuse is collected by a private company while the borough operates the landfill.

Education. Yakutat School is in the Yakutat City School District. The school has 145 students and 17 teachers.

Health care. Yakutat Community Health Center provides health care to the community. Yakutat is classified as a large town/regional center and is found in EMS Region 3A in the Southeast Region. Emergency services have limited highway, limited marine, coastal, airport, and seaport access. Volunteers and a health aide provide emergency care. The Yakutat Volunteer EMS/Rescue is available for auxiliary health care.

ARIZONA

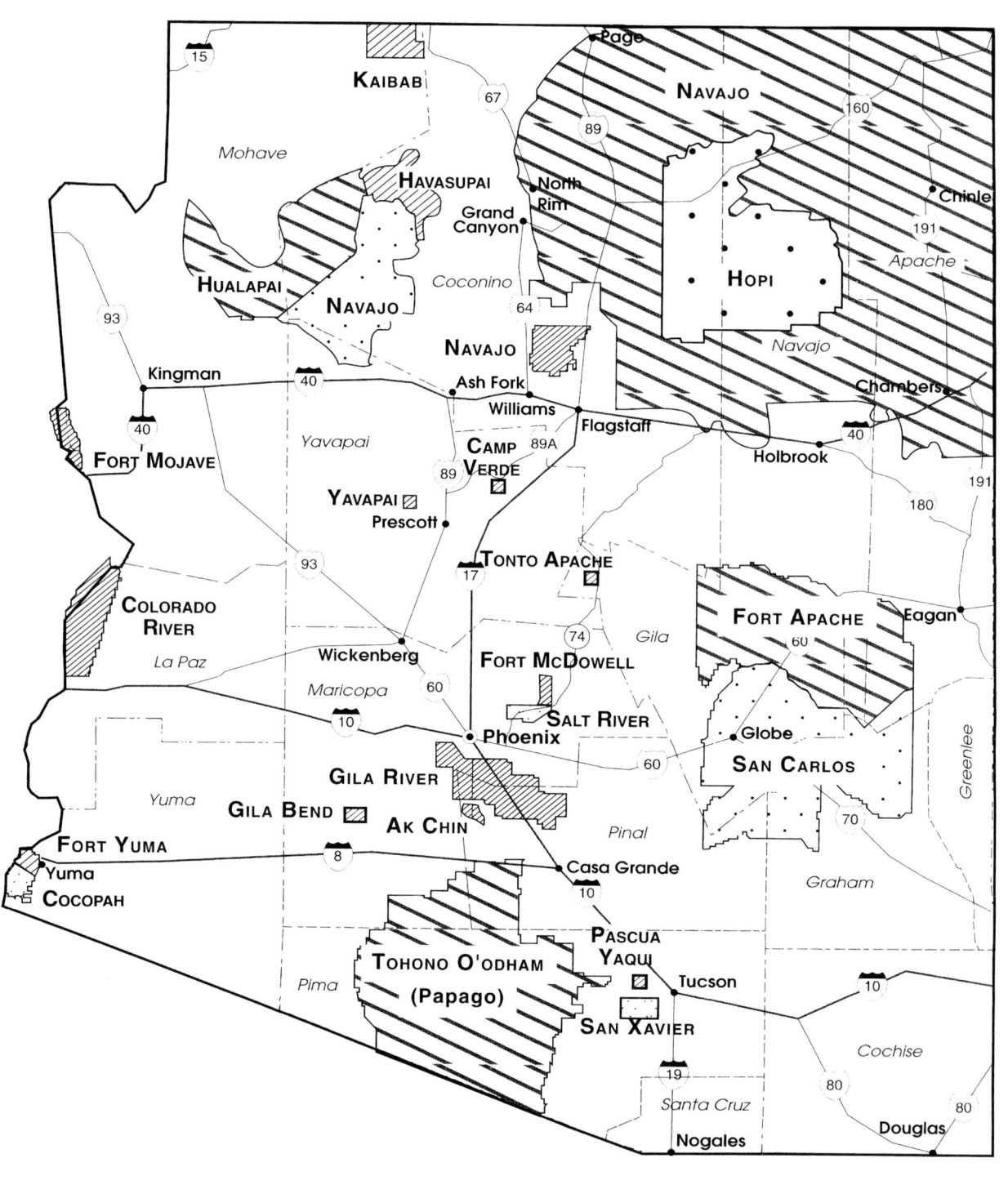

Map from Tiller's Guide to Indian Country (1996 edition)

k-Chin

LOCATION AND LAND STATUS

The Ak-Chin Indian Community is located 36 miles south of Phoenix in the northwestern corner of Pinal County within the Santa Cruz Valley of south-central Arizona. The Community borders the city of Maricopa and is at an elevation of approximately 1,200 feet above sea level in the Sonoran Desert. It is 43 miles northwest of the Casa Grande National Monument.

The Ak-Chin Indian Reservation was established by an Executive Order issued by President Taft on May 28, 1912, with 47,600 acres, but it was reduced to 21,840 acres by an Executive Order on September 2, 1912, when the president rescinded his original order.

PHYSICAL DESCRIPTION

Reservation lands are primarily high desert with irrigated lands for farming. There are no rivers with year-round flow located on reservation lands, and there are only three washes.

CLIMATE

The climate is typical of the desert regions of the southwestern states, with very warm and dry temperatures for most of the year. The average temperature is 69°F. with summer highs sometimes exceeding 110°F. Winter temperatures are mild, averaging approximately 54°F. and rarely dipping below 30°F. The area receives less than 10 inches of precipitation annually.

CULTURE AND HISTORY

In 1874, a small band of Tohono O'odham people migrated from the Tohono O'odham Nation to the present-day site of the Ak-Chin Indian Community to farm at the end of Vekol Wash. In later years, members of the Gila River Pimas assisted with the harvest. The two tribes came together and formed the Ak-Chin Indian Community. They speak Uto-Aztecan languages that are closely related to each other; other languages of the family are spoken from California south into central Mexico and beyond. The Tohono O'odhams were agriculturalists who moved frequently to find new water sources. Their traditional territory extended from Ak-Chin to Sonora, Mexico. One of the most significant events in the tribe's recent history has been its successful fight with the U.S. Department of the Interior, seeking full implementation of the Ak-Chin Water Settlement Act, passed on July 28, 1978. The act was finalized in 1982 by the passage of Public Law 98-530, giving the Ak-Chin Indian Community the means to fulfill the tribe's goal of self-sufficiency.

GOVERNMENT

The reservation's governing body is the Ak-Chin Indian Community Council, as provided under the Articles of Association, approved December 1961. The tribal government is organized under provisions of the Indian Reorganization Act of 1934. The council is comprised of a chairman, a vice-chairman, an ap-

pointed secretary-treasurer, and three members. The active boards and commissions are the farm board, and the education, housing, gaming, industrial park, and planning and zoning committees. Government departments include fire, EPA and public works, tribal court, police, parks and recreation, and maintenance. The tribe maintains its own police department, tribal court, and detention center.

ECONOMY

The Ak-Chin economy is based on agriculture, gaming, and an industrial park.

Agriculture and Livestock. The tribal council established the Ak-Chin Community Farms Enterprise in 1962. Cotton and alfalfa are the principal harvest crops of the Ak-Chin Farms. The farms began turning a profit in the first three years, which prompted the tribe to embark upon its successful fight with the U.S. Department of the Interior, wherein the tribe sought full implementation of the Ak-Chin Water Settlement Act. This law provided for the delivery of 75,000 acre-feet of permanent water. Under this Act the tribe entered into an agreement with Del Webb Corporation allowing Del Webb the option to lease water from the Ak-Chin Reservation for development of its properties.

Gaming. Harrah's Ak-Chin Casino Resort, located on Highway 347 south of Maricopa, features video and electronic slot machines, blackjack, poker, bingo, live entertainment, and a dance floor. Three restaurants and a lounge offer fine and casual dining. The complex features a 5,000-square-foot ballroom, conference rooms, a gift shop, several dining venues, and valet parking. The hotel offers 146 suites, a fitness center, and a swim-up bar in the outdoor pool. In 2004, the casino donated a 2004 Chevy Silverado food delivery van to the Pinal-Gila Area Agency to deliver food to homebound residents in the region. The donation was made possible through Harrah's Employees Reaching Out (HERO), an employee-based volunteer group.

Industrial Parks. A 109-acre industrial park, constructed in 1971, is located at the southeast corner of the reservation, adjacent to the Maricopa-Casa Grande Highway and the Southern Pacific Railroad. It has its own domestic water well and sewage-treatment system. It is suitable for light industry and agriculture-related industry.

Services and Retail. A non-tribally owned convenience store is located on the reservation. The Vekol Commissary has been in operation for over 30 years. It offers fuel services, groceries, a deli, a pizzeria, and a fresh meats department. The business employs a number of tribal members and also provides a venue for local vendors to display their goods.

Ak-Chin Reservation
Federal reservation
Pima and Tohono O'odham
Pinal County, Arizona

Ak-Chin Indian Community
42507 W. Peters & Nall Road
Maricopa, AZ 85239
520-568-1000
520-568-4566 Fax

Total area *(BIA, 2004)*
21,840 acres

Tribally owned lands *(BIA, 2004)*
21,840 acres

Tribal enrollment
(Tribal source, 2004)
743

Total labor force
2000 census
255

High school graduate
2000 census
46.7%

Bachelor's degree
2000 census
2.2%

Unemployment rate
(Tribal source, 2004)
5.3%

Unemployment rate
2000 census
9.80%

Per capita income
$8,418

Ak-Chin

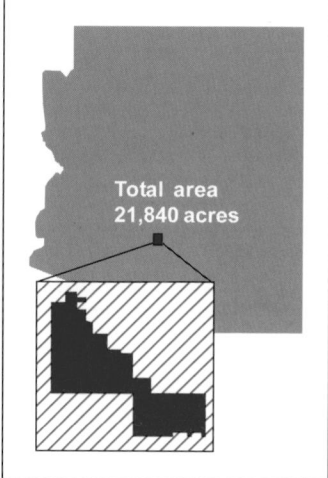

Total area
21,840 acres

Media and Communications. The tribe produces the *Ak-Chin O'odham Runner*, a newspaper published twice monthly.

Tourism and Recreation. The Ak-Chin Him-Dak ("Way of Life") Eco-Museum and Archives is located on the reservation. The Ak-Chin Him-Dak Eco-Museum is unique, in that it is not restricted to a building with professional curators but is comprised of the land and tribal members. The museum exhibits contemporary basketry, photos, and artifacts of tribal farming, and a Veteran's memorial. It also features a garden area and a traditional adobe home. The museum hosts an annual Thanksgiving dinner for tribal elders and an annual Native American Day celebration.

Casa Grande Ruins National Monument is located 43 miles to the southeast near Coolidge, Arizona. Other sites of interest in the area include the Butterfield Stage Trail. The annual O'odham Tash Days are held in the nearby city of Casa Grande. The event draws thousands of visitors to the area. It features a rodeo, a carnival, a powwow, a parade, vendors, and exhibits. Other special events include the Him-Dak Anniversary Celebration on the second Saturday in April, a picnic and fireworks on the Fourth of July, Indian Recognition Day on the last Saturday in September, and the St. Francis Church Feast.

INFRASTRUCTURE
The reservation is intersected by the Maricopa Highway (State Route 238) running north-south. Interstate 10 is accessible approximately 16 miles north of the community, and Highway 84 is about 10 miles south. The tribe has improved a number of roads on the reservation in recent years.

Housing. The tribe has completed a number of new housing areas on the reservation, including roads and utility systems. A few traditional adobe homes still stand, though few continue to be used as residences. Newer structures are quickly replacing them.

Electricity. Arizona Public Service provides electric power.

Water Supply. The tribe provides its own water and sewage service, which was completed in 2004. The tribe maintains a wastewater treatment center served by one lagoon.

Transportation. Commercial train service is available in the city of Maricopa. Bus services are available in Casa Grande, about 35 miles from Ak-Chin. Commercial air service is available in Phoenix.

COMMUNITY FACILITIES AND SERVICES
The tribe maintains a newly constructed recreation center that features a pool with water slides, an indoor gym, outdoor basketball courts, and a weight room. A community center houses a preschool program and community meeting rooms. The tribe also offers an elders' center, an elders' housing project, St. Francis of Assisi Church, and a community cemetery. The Milton Antone Memorial Park features a playground, ramadas, barbeque areas, and athletic fields. Community groups include the Youth Council, AmerInd Club, and the Ak-Chin Veteran's Group. The Veteran's Group hosts an annual celebration that features athletic events, a walk, and social activities.

Education. The nearest schools are Maricopa Elementary School and Maricopa Public High School, less than five miles from the community. The tribe offers a preschool program and a GED program. Colleges, community colleges, and postsecondary programs are available in the Phoenix metro area and in Casa Grande.

Health Care. The U.S. Public Health Service provides a small clinic on the reservation. Major medical services are offered at Sacaton's Hohokam Medical Center. Phoenix Indian Medical Center in Phoenix also provides medical care for Ak-Chin tribal members. Medical care is also available in Casa Grande, about 35 miles east of the community. The tribe's Diabetes Prevention Team hosts an annual Diabetes Awareness and Prevention Day. A renal care facility is located on the reservation.

Camp Verde

Camp Verde Yavapai-Apache Reservation
Federal reservation
Yavapai and Apache
Yavapai County, Arizona

Camp Verde Reservation
Yavapai-Apache Nation
2400 West Datsi Street
P.O. Box 1188
Camp Verde, AZ 86322
928-567-3649
928-567-3994 Fax
yavapai-apache.org

LOCATION AND LAND STATUS
The Camp Verde Indian Reservation is composed of five separate parcels, with tribal headquarters located in Middle Verde, the largest of these. Camp Verde is located roughly 75 - 90 miles north of Phoenix in the upper Verde Valley of central Arizona.

The Yavapai-Apache Camp Verde Reservation was established by an Executive Order of President Ulysses S. Grant on November 9, 1871. The reservation contained 640 acres in Yavapai County. The reservation was closed in 1875, and its residents were moved against their will to the San Carlos Apache Reservation to the south, where they were forced to remain for 25 years. In 1900, as more and more of the people "drifted home" to their original territory, they resettled the areas now occupied. The reservation was reestablished in 1909, and additional lands were acquired in 1915, 1917, 1967, and 1974, accounting for the separate parcels that now comprise the reservation. In May 2004, the tribe was awaiting Bureau of Indian Affairs (BIA) approval of trust status for 1,200 acres of tribal land. A water rights legal battle has delayed a final decision.

PHYSICAL DESCRIPTION
The terrain is characterized by rolling hills and terraces suitable for irrigated agriculture or grazing, with lush green expanses of riparian corridor along the Verde River banks and intermittent streams. The village of Camp Verde sits at an elevation of approximately 3,180 feet above sea level.

CLIMATE
The entire Verde River valley enjoys an arid Upper Sonoran climate and vegetation. The average year-round temperature is 61°F. Summertime highs peak above 100°F, often in July and August, while winter lows seldom drop below 25°F and average 42°F. The area receives approximately 13 inches of precipitation each year, with approximately 2.5 inches falling as snow.

CULTURE AND HISTORY
The Yavapai (Wipukyipai) and Apache (Dil zhéé) peoples have lived in central Arizona for centuries. The Yavapai are one of 15 bands of Native people who make up the Pai-speaking Yuman language group. Historically, several extended Yavapai families camped together during times of the year when resources could be gathered, grown, or hunted efficiently by a local band. Sometimes smaller family groups moved to new harvest areas on their own, but up to ten families would camp and travel together. Yavapais lived in caves or built rock shelters with partial windbreaks of stone and mud plaster at the opening, in pole-frame huts thatched with strong grass fibers, or in larger, mud-covered houses. Open-faced shades, or ramadas, were used during hot

summer months. The people used bows and arrows to hunt deer, pronghorn antelope, and mountain sheep. Tobacco grew wild in the area and was harvested for trade, and the two groups cultivated corn, squash, and beans. Nuts, seeds, berries, and fruits were also harvested.

The Yavapais utilized both war chiefs and civic leaders. A civic leader was usually an older man and a former war chief. He advised people when and where to hunt and gather food and was often a persuasive orator who gave public lectures each morning about good behavior. Advisory chiefs continued to encourage people with these morning speeches through the 1930s, even in mining camps.

Sturdy, lightweight basketry was the most important kind of container traditionally used by the Yavapais. The women also manufactured burden baskets and tightly coiled baskets used for carrying, storing, winnowing, roasting, and for carrying water. Baskets were a trade specialty used in bartering with neighboring tribes such as the Navajos. The sale of baskets to tourists later became a primary source of revenue.

Until the early 1860s, when gold was discovered in central Arizona, the Yavapais had little contact with whites. During the seventeenth and eighteenth centuries, Yavapai people occasionally visited Spanish missions to the south, and Anglo-Americans made several expeditions into the Yavapai homelands in the early nineteenth century. Facing increased encroachment onto their game and agricultural lands, and under attack themselves, the Yavapais began fighting back. In 1865, about 2,000 Yavapais agreed to settle on the Colorado River Reservation; however, it was not large enough to sustain them and the other tribes now sharing it. Attempts were made to settle the Yavapais next to Camp McDowell, a military outpost located in the lower Verde Valley, but the people left after a short trial period, partially because they were in danger from white soldiers and Pima Indian scouts. At one time, a reservation was promised them near Camp Reno, in the Tonto Basin near Mount Oral. Although they found it acceptable, the reservation was never established. On November 9, 1871, a Presidential Executive Order established the Rio Verde Reservation in the Middle Verde Valley.

On December 21, 1871, General George Crook ordered all "roving Apaches" to move to the reservation or be considered hostile. In enforcing this order, the U.S. Army killed a large band of Yavapais in the Salt River Canyon. This attack, which occurred on December 27, 1872, has come to be known as the Massacre at Skeleton Cave. By 1873, most Yavapais had been brought to the Rio Verde Reservation near Camp Verde. They excavated an irrigation ditch and produced several successful harvests. However, a group of Tucson contractors pressed the government to move these people to the San Carlos Reservation. Relocation came in the form of a forced midwinter march of over 180 miles in 1875. Some escaped and others remained behind within their familiar home ranges, farming and working for white settlers.

At San Carlos, the Yavapais were separated from the Apaches, although relations between the two peoples were peaceful and there was some intermarriage. In the 1880s and 90s, Indian agents at San Carlos allowed many Yavapais to return to their homelands, which made their lands at San Carlos available for lease to white interests. Most Yavapais returned to the Verde Valley and worked on farms and ranches. Some found employment in mines, at smelters, or on road construction. Most settled at the abandoned military post at Fort Verde, so that by 1907, the Bureau of Indian Affairs (BIA) established a day school there. In 1910, 40 acres of land with water rights were set aside for those returning; only 18 of those acres were suitable for farming.

In 1912, due to the number of Yavapais working in copper mines and at the smelter in Clarkdale, about 18 miles northwest of Camp Verde, the BIA opened a day school there as well. In 1914 and 1916, an additional 448 acres with water rights, more suitable for farming, were set aside for the Yavapais 8 miles west of Camp Verde, at Middle Verde. Mine closures in the 1930s and 40s greatly affected Yavapai workers, and more people returned to the reservations to expand farming and cattle-ranching activities. In 1969 a parcel of 60 acres near Clarkdale was designated as reservation land for Yavapai people living there. The U.S. Department of Housing and Urban Development provided financial assistance for the construction of new homes.

In the early twentieth century, when the reservation was reestablished, both Yavapai and Apache peoples settled on the land, and their histories are now highly intertwined. Today, the Nation is comprised of descendants from both the Yavapai and Dil'zhéé Apache peoples. The two tribes have adopted some aspects of one another's culture, but they have led largely separate lives in the Verde Valley-Prescott area. The lands, which are regarded as "the beginnings of their heritage and the sustainers of their lives," are sacred to all tribal members. The heritage of each tribe and their spiritual ties to the land remain strong. Social dances, overseen by medicine men, go all night for several days.

The word Dil'zhéé translates roughly to "we hunt." The Dil'zhéé Apache people, long referred to as the Tonto Apaches, are reclaiming use of their traditional name. A website devoted to the continuation and preservation of Dil'zhéé culture through the use of oral history, language, and content, focuses on the four communities of the Yavapai-Apache Nation: Middle Verde, Camp Verde, Rimrock, and Clarkdale, Arizona; it states, "Verde Valley Apaches are not Tonto Apaches nor should they be called Tonto."

GOVERNMENT
The governing body for the tribe is an Indian Reorganization Act nine-member community council, consisting of a chairman, a vice-chairman, and seven members, each serving staggered terms of four years.

The tribes, organized under the Indian Reorganization Act of 1934, have a constitution and bylaws that were approved in 1937. They have both judicial and combination legislative and executive branches of government. The separate Indian communities of Camp Verde, Middle Verde, and Clarkdale combine to elect one council. In 1992, their name was formally changed to the Yavapai-Apache Nation.

The Camp Verde Yavapai-Apache Nation, under PL-638, contracts with the BIA to administer key programs and services. A complete list of tribal offices is as follows: administration, Apache Culture, BIA Police, community services, alcohol and substance abuse, higher education, social services, roads and maintenance, waste works, day care, economic development, enrollment, finance, fire station, housing, judicial, recreation, Clarkdale Recreation, Middle Verde, seniors, and tribal police. In 2004, the administration was developing a security patrol for deployment in the housing department's neighborhoods.

The eight-member Yavapai-Apache Gaming Management Negotiating Team was created by council resolution in 1999. This resolution was reaffirmed and amended in May 2003, "to evaluate and negotiate gaming management proposals and contracts." In 2004, the tribal council approved a judicial code, and a stated goal of the Nation was to develop a more clearly defined law and order code. Drafts of the criminal code, the criminal rules of procedure, and the juvenile code were completed in 2003 and were to be approved by the tribal council in 2004.

Camp Verde Yavapai-Apache

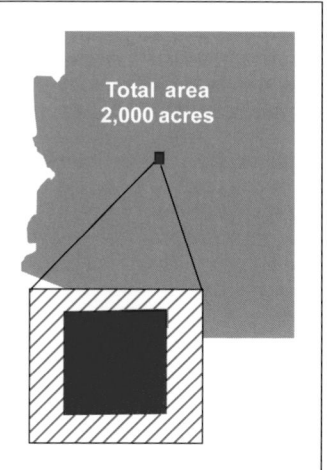

Total area
2,000 acres

Total area *(Tribal source, 2004)*
2,000 acres

Tribally owned lands *(BIA, 2004)*
1,866.56 acres

Population *2000 census*
743

Tribal enrollment
(Tribal source, 2004)
2,000

Total labor force
2000 census
237

Total labor force
(AZ Dept. of Economic Security)
235

High school graduate or higher
2000 census
54.5%

Bachelor's degree or higher
2000 census
8.2%

Unemployment rate
2000 census
12.66%

Unemployment rate
(AZ Dept. of Economic Security)
7.7%

Per capita income
$8,347

Camp Verde Yavapai-Apache

The tribe is a member of the Indian Development District of Arizona. With revenues flowing from the success of a casino, the Nation has focused on improving social services, education, acquiring more land for housing and economic development projects, and the development of heritage tourism.

Government as Employer. The Yavapai-Apache Nation has become the primary public employer on the reservation and throughout the entire Verde Valley.

Economic Development Projects. The tribe constructed a shopping center and now operates a convenience mart, a service station, and a recreational vehicle park. They keep a tribal cattle herd on 180 acres of leased lands, and farming and sand and gravel mining employ several tribal members. Two smoke shops opened in 1982.

The tribe also owns and operates Cliff Castle Lodge Motel and Casino, located just off the interstate, attracting tourists off the I-17 conduit, as well as residents from the Navajo and Hopi Indian reservations.

Small businesses, owned and operated by tribal members, are being initiated as a result of assistance from the small business development program sponsored by the tribal economic development department. Upon completion of educational workshops, would-be entrepreneurs qualify for access to small business financing.

In February 2004, following a thorough financial review of tribal government and businesses, the chairman of the tribe implemented policies designed to reduce overspending in tribal government, in all enterprises, and at the casino.

TRI-AZ-1143

TRI-AZ-1143 Entrance to the Yavapai-Apache Tribal Building

TRI-AZ-1153 Cliff Castle Casino entrance with the Yavapai-Apache Nation Police Station at Camp Verde in the foreground

TRI-AZ-1155 Native Visions Tourism office, which offers heritage and scenic van tours, horseback riding, and authentic Yavapai-Apache tribal and southwestern arts and crafts

TRI-AZ-1153

TRI-AZ-1155

In a May 31, 2004, Report to the Yavapai-Apache Nation's Tribal Members, the chairman stated that a per capita payment system had been approved by the tribal council and that administrative staff were developing a five-year casino revenue implementation plan wherein 10 percent of all casino revenues would go directly to tribal members annually. Payouts from the 10 percent are to be initiated in 2005. An additional 5 percent would go into the per capita investment account maintained by the tribal government.

In May 2004, tribal goals were to enhance: (1) economic development, fiscal planning, and economic drivers; (2) public safety, educational programming, and social and health planning; (3) community infrastructure development, and (4) governmental structure and the overall mission.

Action steps toward attaining the first goal include increasing effort in creating tribal jobs, increasing productivity in existing enterprises, and separating initiatives from departmental status into independently operated enterprises functioning under business standards. Y-A Sand and Rock, Yavapai-Apache Construction, and tourism, are the first three businesses being moved

from departmental status to stand-alone businesses in order to create a profit-yielding environment. Partnerships with outside (off-reservation) businesses are being developed as well. The newly formed Enterprise Development Corporation is overseeing these steps.

Built as a long-term investment, in 2004, the tribe created the White Hills Corporation which owns and operates the Sonic/ Mobil convenience mart on leased land in Camp Verde, Arizona. Proceeds from the enterprise go toward loan repayment and the purchase of the property on which it sits. The Nation, via the land and water department and the attorney general's office, is developing commercial codes and zoning ordinances that facilitate the development of new businesses on tribal land.

Agriculture and Livestock. The tribe leases 180 acres of reservation land to non-Indians for farming, which generates an annual income; 180 acres are leased for irrigated agriculture; and there are beef and dairy cattle on another 180 acres of reservation rangelands. The herds, poultry, and irrigated crops of hay, grain, and fruit provide income for tribal members.

Tribal lands that have been mined for sand and rock, then been reclaimed, are subsequently utilized for planting.

Gaming. The tribe opened the 12,000-square-foot Cliff Castle Casino in May 1995 on 72 acres adjacent to Montezuma Castle National Monument. The business moved into a new 110,000-square-foot intergenerational entertainment, lodging and conference facility at the end of 1999, and it has become a major private employer for the reservation with over 300 employees in the year 2000. The casino complex features 540 slot machines, a separate poker room, Storytellers Gourmet Steakhouse, a 20-lane bowling center, family dining, four bars, a malt shop, and a play area for children. Live entertainment at the facility includes comedians, bands, dancing, karaoke, televised sporting events, and an open-air venue, the Stargazer Pavilion, where concerts, powwows, professional wrestling, and bike rallies are held. A free shuttle runs from Cottonwood to the casino on the first and third Tuesdays of each month.

Revenues generated by gaming have enabled the Nation to: (1) raise the entire community's standard of living; (2) supply additional social services to the elderly; (3) provide educational opportunities for all ages; (4) serve as the foundation for growing the Nation's land base; (5) foster long-term economic development; and (6) fund tribal programs to nurture and support traditional customs and values.

Revenues generated by gaming have also permitted the development of initiatives for other tribes. The first contract, with the Tuolumne Band of Me-Wuk Indians of central California, proved successful, so in 2003, the Yavapai-Apache Nation negotiated a multimillion dollar contract to construct a casino for the La Posta Indian Band near San Diego, California. Under California rules, by limiting the size of their casino to 350 slot machines, the La

Posta Band was eligible for statewide revenue-sharing funds from other tribes. Thus, the Yavapai-Apache Nation provides capital as a cosigner on loans, but the Nation will not operate the casino when it opens. Under the terms of the contract, the Yavapai-Apache Nation receives a percentage of the profits for a specified number of years.

The Nation received a Leadership Award from the National Indian Gaming Association at the annual conference in Albuquerque, New Mexico, on April 5, 2004, for their work in helping other Indian tribes with the construction of casinos.

Construction. The tribe participates in SIKU-NYA, a joint-venture construction company with the Alaska-based UICC. This joint venture won the contract to remodel the tribe's Cliff Castle Casino, and it built the LaPosta Indian Band's Casino in California throughout 2003 and 2004. A major road reconstruction project got underway in Middle Verde in April 2004.

Mining. The tribe owns a sand and gravel mining operation.

Manufacturing. The Nation owns 30 percent interest in Drake Cement, a Peruvian-based cement manufacturing plant owned by ARPL. The tribe is working with owners to build a sister-operation in Drake, Arizona. Construction of the plant is to begin in 2005.

Tourism and Recreation. The Yavapai-Apache Visitor Activity Complex, built and operated by the tribe near the Montezuma Castle National Monument, is located beside interstate I-17 and includes an Information Center, a U.S. Park Service office, arts and crafts shops, a convenience market, and a service station. The tribe also owns an RV park, a lodge with 82 rooms, a convention center with a capacity for 400, a private campground, and a meeting facility with seating for 200. There is a restaurant at the Cliff Castle Lodge and Casino, along with bowling lanes, a swimming pool, a Jacuzzi, guided tours of the reservation, and Native Visions stables, which offers horseback riding tours. Within the casino, the Dragonfly Lounge features Native-American musicians and songwriters.

The reservation lies within the Coconino National Forest. The Prescott National Forest lies to the east and the Kaibab National Forest to the north. Tonto National Forest is also nearby. Fort Verde State Park, where four of the original adobe buildings stand open to the public, is located nearby in the town of Camp Verde. The park's museum contains early military artifacts, Indian relics, and implements used by the earliest Verde Valley settlers.

Three area national monuments-Montezuma Castle, Montezuma Well, and Tuzigoot-prehistoric Indian cliff dwellings, and pueblos, are within 25 miles of the reservation. In February the tribe celebrates Commemoration Day; in September, Indian Day; and the Verde Powwow is held at Cliff Castle July 12 through 14.

The tribes operate the Yavapai-Apache Nation's tourism office called Native Visions Tourism, offering heritage and scenic van tours, horseback riding, and authentic Yavapai-Apache tribal and southwest arts and crafts.

Media and Communications. Gah'nahvah/Ya Ti', a free biweekly newspaper, is available on the reservation; radio stations are received from both Sedona and Cottonwood; and a number of television stations are received from Phoenix, Flagstaff, and Prescott.

INFRASTRUCTURE
Transportation. Camp Verde is located on State Highway 279, which connects with I-17, the major north-south highway for the area. A major road reconstruction project got underway in Middle Verde in April 2004. Bus and truck services are available in Camp Verde, five miles away. Camp Verde residents have access to the nearby Cottonwood Airport, which has two runways; one paved and one unpaved. There is also a paved strip in Montezuma Heights. An international airport is available at Phoenix. Numerous commercial air and train companies operate out of Flagstaff, 50 miles north of the reservation.

Electricity. Electricity is provided by the Arizona Public Service Company, and natural gas by Southern Union Gas Service.

Water Supply. The reservation has its own water system, installed by the U.S. Public Health Service, which was being rehabilitated in 2004. The tribe also operates the Middle Verde Indian Sewer System, but many individuals maintain septic tanks for sewage disposal.

Telecommunications. Telephone services are offered by Qwest, but there are no local Internet service providers, or any cable television and cable Internet providers.

Housing. In 2004, the Yavapai-Apache Tribal Housing Department was involved in rehabilitating 36 low-rent housing units on the reservation and building new low-income tax credit housing units for tribal members in the community of Middle Verde. This includes the addition of 12 duplex units and two laundromats, one in Middle Verde and another in Clarkdale.

The Nation's housing priority is not only to provide safe housing for a backlist of enrolled tribal members, but to do so with an eye toward landscape and the larger ecological environment, so that a sense of true tribal community is fostered. Before additional tribal housing can be built, however, additional acreage must be placed into trust. *(See Location and Land Status, above.)*

TRI-AZ-1159

COMMUNITY FACILITIES AND SERVICES
The new Yavapai-Apache Cultural Center houses the offices of Yavapai and Dil zhéé Apache Cultural Preservation, as well as language programs for both Yavapais and Apaches, a traditional basket-weaving class, and the tribal art and artifact collections. Throughout 2003 and 2004, tribal administration conducted meetings with tribal elders to establish the Yavapai Elder's Cultural Advisory Committee under the overall direction of the culture department. This group will define cultural priorities for the Nation and offer counsel to the administration and council regarding heritage- and language-preservation issues. A new community center boasts a weight room and gymnasium with hardwood floors. There is a public library on the reservation as well, and a heritage park features lighted baseball fields, basketball courts, volleyball courts, and a snack bar. Boys and Girls Clubs meet at the newly constructed Teen Center, which opened in January 2004. The center has computers available for use by young people. There are summer bowling leagues for young people.

TRI-AZ-1148

TRI-AZ-1148 Yavapai-Apache Veterans Memorial

TRI-AZ-1159 Intersection of I-17 and the road leading to tribal headquarters, with the Cliff Castle Casino in the background

Camp Verde Yavapai-Apache

A grant for construction of a senior center in Clarkdale has been acquired, but in May 2004, construction had not yet begun. The housing department built playgrounds near housing units in Clarkdale and Camp Verde.

Public Safety. The reservation is served by three police officers provided by the BIA and has a 12-person fire department. A police substation was opened in Middle Verde within the fire station complex. Additional law enforcement office space is available in the Clarkdale Community Building.

Education. Both Cottonwood and Camp Verde have Head Start programs for reservation preschoolers, operating in their own building. Elementary and high school students attend local public schools and college courses are available from Yavapai College.

Health Care. There is a private hospital in Cottonwood and a U.S. Public Health Service hospital in Camp Verde. Prescott and Phoenix both have larger hospitals. Public-health nursing services are provided through a contract arrangement with the Yavapai County Health Department. Three community health representatives are employed by the tribe and act as liaisons with the Public Health Service staff. Contract hospital and medi-

cal services are authorized through local physicians and clinics in Camp Verde, Clarkdale, Cottonwood, Prescott, and Sedona.

In 2004, the Nation was working with the Indian Health Service to expand services from three days per week to four at the Yavapai-Apache Health Center. Alcohol and substance abuse services and programs in behavioral health are available, as well as nutrition classes and dental care. The Inter-Tribal Council of Arizona operates a women's, infants and children's nutrition program at the food bank in Middle Verde.

ENVIRONMENTAL CONCERNS

In 2004, the tribe's land water board and council were developing an overall land and water use plan. Air quality is also an issue of concern for the nation.

Because of its checkerboard nature, the reservation lands comprising the Camp Verde Yavapai-Apache Reservation have separate environmental challenges. Middle Verde is located in a flood plain. An arroyo dissects the Clarkdale community. In the community of Camp Verde, there is very limited land space due to encroachment by private development. Rimrock, also, is physically limited in size and, subsequently, in available natural resources.

Cocopah

Cocopah Indian Reservation
Federal reservation
Cocopah
Yuma County, Arizona

Cocopah Tribe
County 15 and Avenue G
Somerton, AZ 85350
928-627-2102
928-627-3173 Fax
cocopah.com

LOCATION AND LAND STATUS

The Cocopah Reservation is located in extreme southwestern Arizona, near the town of Somerton, approximately 13 miles south of Yuma, 15 miles north of San Luis, Mexico, and 180 miles east of San Diego. There are three parcels, known as East Cocopah, West Cocopah, and North Cocopah; all lie completely within Yuma County. Tribal administration is located in Somerton, in the West Cocopah parcel. The region is one of low-lying desert with the Colorado River bordering North Cocopah. Privately owned farms surround the reservation.

The reservation was established by Executive Order on September 27, 1917, by President Woodrow Wilson. This order established the West and East Reservations with approximately 1,772 acres. On April 18, 1985, President Ronald Reagan signed the Cocopah Land Acquisition Bill, HR 730, which increased the reservation by nearly 4,237 acres, including a North Reservation of 600 acres.

CLIMATE

Less than 300 feet above sea level, the area near Somerton, Arizona, including the Cocopah Indian Reservation, has an extremely hot, dry climate typical of the Sonoran Desert. The year-round temperature averages 74ºF. with summertime highs frequently exceeding 110ºF. Winter lows seldom go below 40ºF. The area averages slightly less than three inches of precipitation per year.

CULTURE AND HISTORY

The Cocopah Indians are one of the Yuman tribes with a language belonging to the Hokan family which is spoken by peoples from southern Oregon south into Mexico. Around 1760, the Yuma, Maricopa, and Cocopah Indians formed one tribe, known as the Coco-Maricopa Tribe, living around the Gulf of California, near the mouth of the Colorado River. Sometime after that, they migrated northward and settled along the Colorado River. The Yumas were traditionally expert farmers of the flatlands of the Colorado River. Historically the Cocopahs lived in rectangular structures supported by a four-post frame with connecting beams

or by two posts supporting a longitudinal beam, with walls made of sticks covered with arrow weed and earth, and having an earthen hearth.

Prior to 1900, mesquite was probably the most important wild plant food used by the Cocopahs. Wood rats, raccoons, and beavers were also important sources of food. Fish are no longer an important part of the diet because of dwindling access to the river.

Leadership of the people was and is determined by ability and experience; figures of importance were believed to derive their powers from dreams. The ability to speak well and to serve as a consultant and advisor to the people bears even more weight today. Funeral orators, singers, and, until the 1950s, healing shamans, were traditional figures of importance in Cocopah society. The most elaborate social and ritual events are those associated with their traditions concerning death and the dead.

The ancestors of the Cocopahs may have been among the first Native Americans in the Southwest to encounter Europeans. Hernando de Alarcón made contact with the river people in 1540, and in that same year Melchior Diaz visited the river people and wrote of semisubterranean houses covered with straw and of long structures that could shelter 100 people at a time. The Cocopahs established well-worn foot trails into what is now California, east along the Gila River and southward to the Sierra de Juarez. Seasonally many Cocopah families traveled for extended stays in the high country to visit PaiPai or Kumeyaay friends and family, using horses for travel when available.

George R. Derby and Major Samuel P. Heintzelman visited the Cocopahs below Fort Yuma in the 1850s. Cocopah weapons, food, and agriculture were virtually unchanged from those mentioned by Alarcon 300 years earlier. The 1850s saw the beginning of more intensive contact and communication between the Cocopahs and the non-Indian people who now settled along the lower Colorado River valley. The first written mention of Cocopahs living near Yuma was by Jacobo Blanco in 1873 when they were occupying land between Fort Yuma and the mouth of the Colorado River. In the last half of the nineteenth century, the Cocopahs became very active in the river trade, supplying steamboats on the Colorado with wood for fuel. They became well-known for their skill as river pilots and navigators. When ethnologist W. J. McGee visited the Cocopahs in 1900, he wrote that they were divided into seven groups, each one identified by its leader.

In the early 1900s, four politically autonomous bands of Cocopahs lived in dispersed rancherias throughout the Colorado River delta. Many members of the Hwanyak band established themselves permanently near Somerton by 1910. In 1917, government decree gave the American Cocopahs legal title to three small areas of land as a reservation, under the jurisdiction of the Yuma Agency of the BIA. In 1961, the Cocopahs in Arizona began to organize to improve housing, introduce electricity, and complete their first tribal building. They revised their constitution in 1968 with advice from the Navajo Nation. Ceremonial buildings were constructed on both the East and West Reservations; the octagonal tribal building was completed in 1976. In the 1970s the Cocopahs focused their attention on education by introducing a Head Start program, followed by an individualized Indian instruction program. In 1976, they instituted special tutoring at the high school level in a learning center on the East Reservation. Also in the 1970s, the Cocopahs began reviving traditional beadwork and clothing, in addition to developing their ability in the fine arts. A new importance was placed on traditions, and young people began learning songs and legends from their elders. At the same time, they were becoming better adapted to living and working alongside their non-Indian neighbors.

Perhaps the most dramatic change for the Cocopahs has been that after hundreds, perhaps thousands, of years of being river people who traveled the waterways on tule rafts, most no longer live near or depend upon the river. Dams and diversions have reduced the Colorado River to almost no flow in the lower delta regions, and only a meager amount flows in the section that cuts through one small piece of American Cocopah land. That section has been put to use by the U.S. government for agricultural drainage. These changes have necessarily altered the cultural significance traditionally placed upon the river.

GOVERNMENT
The Cocopahs are governed by a popularly elected tribal council, consisting of a chairman, a vice-chairman, and three members, with a tribal constitution approved under the Indian Reorganization Act of 1934. The tribe has entered into a PL-638 self-determination contract with the U.S. government to administer programs and services that might otherwise have been administered by the federal government.

ECONOMY
Although the Cocopahs' economy is largely dependent upon agriculture and the leasing of farmlands, tourism and gaming are also valuable sources of revenue and employment.

Agriculture and Livestock. Despite declining flows of the Colorado River over Cocopah lands, agriculture is very important to the reservation economy, with 2,400 acres of irrigated, tillable acreage. Much of the land is farmed through leases to non-Indians, yielding significant annual incomes to tribal members. With the acquisition of 4,000 additional acres in 1985, the tribe initiated several new economic development enterprises, creating job opportunities designed to achieve tribal self-sufficiency.

Gaming. The Cocopah Bingo Hall, located in Somerton along Highway 95 in the East Cocopah Reservation, opened as a joint venture with private developers in 1987. The facility, expanded in 1994, is now operating under a gaming compact with the State

of Arizona. The facility boasts 475 electronic games, slot machines, bingo tables, and a souvenir gift shops featuring T-shirts, jackets, caps, totes, key chains, coffee mugs, and a large selection of genuine Native American crafts and one-of-a-kind gifts.

Services and Retail. The tribe has a convenience store, a gas station, and a smoke shop.

Tourism and Recreation. The Cocopah Bend Recreational Vehicle Resort, 4 miles from downtown Yuma and 10 miles from San Luis, Mexico, features full hookups, on-site management, and a full-time activity director. Amenities at the resort include an 18-hole golf course, a heated, Olympic-size swimming pool, a spa and weight room, tennis courts, a woodworking shop, a community building, and a dance hall.

The Cocopah Tribe opened a tribal museum and tribal cultural center in October 1996. The community's traditional tribal dance grounds are used for tribal social events such as dances, hand games, and annual festivities. Nearby attractions include the California dunes and Yuma historic district. Regional golf courses and night sports add variety to the entertainment possibilities while in the area. Tourists enjoy shopping in San Luis, Mexico, a port-of-entry community, and they can fish, water ski, and swim at lakes along the Colorado River. There are numerous motel and other lodging facilities in Yuma and San Luis.

Visitors can attend any of several special tribal events, such as the Cocopah Annual Miss Cocopah Pageant held in February. In April they can help celebrate Land Acquisition Day or participate in the annual Easter Egg Hunt. A community celebration is held every year during the Fourth of July, and the people hold annual Sports Day events. In November, there is a Veterans Day Parade and Powwow and a community Thanksgiving dinner, followed by the Children's Christmas Party in December. There are also regularly scheduled festival days and a street fair.

Scenic train excursions from Yuma to the West Cocopah Reservation are provided in cooperation with the Yuma Valley Live Steamers where an early 1800s Cocopah Indian Village has been re-created, Cocopah elders prepare authentic Cocopah jewelry and fry bread, made available to guests of the ride and to museum visitors. Nontribal attractions include the California dunes, fishing, water skiing, swimming at lakes along the Colorado River.

INFRASTRUCTURE
The reservation is easily accessed from Interstate 8, which passes near Yuma, and from Arizona State Highway 95, which crosses the reservation. The nearest commercial transportation by air, bus, train, and truck is also in Yuma, 17 miles away. The Yuma International Airport has a 13,300-foot lighted runway.

Electricity. Provided by Arizona Public Service Company.

Fuel. Southwest Gas Company supplies natural gas.

Water Supply. There is a community water system, installed by the U.S. Public Health Service, but many residents continue to use water wells. Residents use individual septic tanks for sewage disposal. In 1987, the tribe entered into an agreement with Yuma County to operate a landfill.

COMMUNITY FACILITIES AND SERVICES
There are many community facilities on the reservation, including cry houses for funerals, baseball and softball fields, a basketball court and playground, an elderly training center, a vocational training center, a drop-in center, an elderly residential home, an east reservation park, and a drug-treatment center. There is also a community building and a powwow grounds on the North Cocopah Reservation.

Cocopah

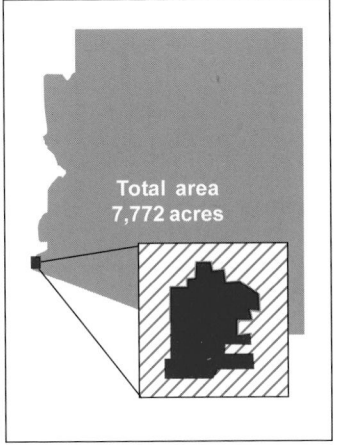

Total area
7,772 acres

Total area *(BIA, 2000)*
6,226.30 acres

Total area *(Tribal source, 2004)*
7,772 acres

Population *2000 census*
1,025

Tribal enrollment
519

Total labor force
(Tribal source, 2004)
268

Total labor force
2000 census
184

High school graduate or higher
2000 census
67.2%

Bachelor's degree or higher
2000 census
16.3%

Unemployment rate
2000 census
15.22%

Per capita income
2000 census
$12,094

Cocopah

Public Safety. Police protection is offered by the tribe under a contract with the BIA, while tribal volunteers provide fire protection.

Education. Cocopah students attend elementary school in Yuma and Somerton, then middle school and high school in Yuma. There is a Head Start program operating in its own building.

Health Care. The Fort Yuma Indian Hospital in Winterhaven, California, approximately 20 miles away on the Fort Yuma Reservation, has 19 beds. The Fort Yuma Service Unit provides community health nursing, project sanitation engineering, environmental health technicians, medical health services, community health education, and a dental health program.

olorado River

Colorado River Indian Tribes Reservation
Federal reservation
Chemehuevi, Hopi, Mohave, and Navajo
La Paz County, Arizona; San Bernardino and Riverside counties, California

Colorado River Indian Tribes
Reservation
Route 1, Box 23-B
Parker, AZ 85344
928-669-9211
928-669-1216 Fax
itcaonline.com

LOCATION AND LAND STATUS

The Colorado River Indian Reservation Tribe (CRIT) was established on March 3, 1865. Reservation lands include almost 270,000 acres along both sides of the Colorado River between Parker, Arizona, and Blythe, California. The largest portion of land, consisting of 225,996 acres, is located in La Paz County, Arizona, and 42,696 acres are in San Bernardino and Riverside counties, California.

PHYSICAL DESCRIPTION

Most of the territory is characterized as low, arid desert land; however, the 45-mile corridor adjacent to the Colorado River is rich, loamy, fertile river-bottom land. Parker, Arizona, sits at 425 feet above sea level; the median elevation for the reservation is 413 feet.

CLIMATE

The climate for most of the entire region encompassing the CRIT reservation is that of extremely hot, dry desert. The year-round temperature averages 70ºF, with summertime highs averaging well above 100ºF, and winter lows seldom dropping below 35ºF. The highest recorded temperature at Parker, Arizona is 127ºF, while the lowest ever recorded is 9ºF. The area receives approximately five inches precipitation per year.

CULTURE AND HISTORY

The CRIT Reservation is home to four tribes. The original inhabitants were the Mohaves and the Chemehuevis, who have farmed on the lower Colorado River since recorded history. They were later joined by relocated Navajos and Hopis after World War II. The Chemehuevis traditionally lived between the Mohaves and the Quechans, who lived farther to the south.

Major traditional crops were corn, melons, pumpkins, native beans, roots, and mesquite beans. *(See Hopi and Navajo Nation entries for more information.)* The Colorado River peoples lived in scattered groups, in homes made of brush placed between upright mesquite logs or in houses made of mud and wood, and they traveled the river in reed rafts.

The Mohaves welcomed initial Spanish explorers, then changed their position when a new life-style was imposed on them. The first Spaniard known to have contacted Mohaves was Juan de Oñate, who met them near the junction of the Colorado and Bill Williams rivers in 1604. Later, Father Francisco Garces arrived in the Mohave Valley in 1776 and estimated the population to be 3,000 souls. However, no missions or Spanish settlements were established in Mohave territory, and the people maintained their independence until the advent of the Americans. The Mohaves obtained wheat and horses from the Quechans. They probably also obtained some horses from raids on Spanish mission communities in California. During the 1820s, the first Anglo-American trappers and fur traders came to Mohave country. Some white American parties passing through in subsequent years had

trouble with the Mohaves, such as the Lorenzo Sitgreaves Expedition, which the Mohaves attacked in 1851. In 1857, the Quechan-Mohave allies suffered a great defeat at the hands of an alliance of Pima and Maricopa warriors. In 1858, the Mohaves attacked a wagon train bound for California, leading to the establishment of Fort Mohave in the Mohave Valley. In 1859, the resistance of the Mohaves ended after they lost a battle with U.S. forces.

The reservation was formed in 1865. In an effort to "civilize" and educate the Indians of the CRIT, the U.S. government opened the first boarding school in the area, at the northern end of the reservation, adjacent to the town of Parker, in 1879. The first Presbyterian Church was organized on March 15, 1914.

The development of a reliable irrigation system has played an important role in the history of the CRIT. In 1867, Congress appropriated funds to develop the Grant-Dent Canal, named after President Ulysses S. Grant and Superintendent of Indian Affairs George W. Dent. Although it was built to divert river water to irrigate crops on the reservation, a reliable irrigation supply was not developed until the early twentieth century. It was the intent of the U.S. government to teach Mohaves and Chemehuevis modern farming techniques.

The Allotment Act of April 21, 1904, brought legal allotments to the Colorado River Reservation members, beginning with 5 acres and changing to 10 acres per member in 1911. This process remained in effect until 1940, when the tribal council adopted a land code, making it possible for tribal members with allotments to exchange them for 40-acre assignments. In 1945, the CRIT passed a change in the assignment program to increase the size of the farm unit from 40 to 80 acres, the same year that the Navajos and Hopis were relocated from their homes in northeastern Arizona to the CRIT reservation. Present day tribal members may lease their lands, and many have developed home sites on their allotted or assigned lands. Soon after the powers of the tribal council were established, the department of the interior and the war relocation authority made an agreement to place a Japanese internment camp on Colorado River Indian lands. The Poston Relocation Center, which was one of ten wartime camps established to house some 20,000 internees, opened May 8, 1942, and closed November 28, 1945. Accepting the decision meant not losing land permanently to the war department. Compensation came in the form of improvements to the land and development of irrigation facilities.

After World War II, the U.S. government developed a theory of a surplus Indian population, such that where the land base was considered insufficient to support the total number of tribal members, the "surplus" would be moved off the land. In the case of the Colorado River Reservation, people from the Navajo and Hopi reservations were offered farms on the reservation; the

294

tracts included both traditional Mohave and Chemehuevi lands and some that were previously developed under the war relocation authority. In 1952 tribal members voted to rescind Ordinance No. 5 which reserved a portion of the reservation for colonization, but the action was ignored by the department of the interior. On April 30, 1964, Congress finally recognized "beneficial ownership" of the reservation by the CRIT, thereby repealing the ordinance. In the latter half of the twentieth century, the CRIT continued to assert their right to protect their traditional lands. In 1963, a water-rights case, *Arizona v. California*, established the extent of state and Indian water rights in favor of the CRIT and four other tribes along the Colorado River, setting the stage for ever-increasing economic development in the area.

GOVERNMENT

On August 13, 1937, voting members of the CRIT approved the Indian Reorganization Act of 1934 and adopted a constitution and bylaws for governing the tribes. Jay Gould, a Mohave, was elected as the first tribal chairman on September 18, 1937. They are governed by a tribal chairman, a vice-chairman, a secretary, a treasurer, and five members, serving four-year terms. There are currently 28 departments within the tribal administration. There is also a committee system to assist the council with special needs; committee members are appointed by the council for two- or four-year terms. There are ten permanent committees, five boards, and one commission. The tribes, under PL-638, contract with the BIA to administer key programs and services.

ECONOMY

The reservation economy, once centered only on agriculture, recreation, government, and light industry, has burgeoned since the grand opening of the Blue Water Casino in 1999. There are many varied businesses and commercial leases and an ever-increasing number of tribal enterprises on the reservation, including supplemental revenue-building operations such as mineral leases, loan fees, water revenues, administrative charges, rentals, mining fees, court fines, fish-and-game permits, and sales of businesses.

Economic Development Projects. The tribes are members of the Indian Development District of Arizona.

Agriculture and Livestock. Agricultural production is a primary economic activity for CRIT members. Approximately 84,500 acres of fertile farmlands adjacent to the river allow irrigated production of cotton, alfalfa, wheat, feed grains, lettuce, tomatoes, peanuts, and melons. Another 50,500 acres are available for agricultural development. There is a cotton mill on the reservation that has entered into a joint venture with an Australian company.

Gaming. The Blue Water Casino originally opened in 1995. A new casino building and a 200-room hotel were built in early 1999, offering a Las Vegas-style gaming atmosphere with 460 slot machines, bingo, keno, and poker tables. Fine dining, a snack bar, and two cocktail lounges are available, along with 200 rooms, luxury suites with a view of the river, an indoor water park with four swimming pools and a three-story water slide, a children's pool, a Jacuzzi, live entertainment at a 5,000-seat outdoor amphitheater, and a 165-slip private marina. Miniature golf, an Olympic-style exercise center, and various retail shops are also on-site. The resort features over 8,000 square feet of conference space with six meeting rooms and banquet and catering services. There are plans for a four-screen theater to be built at the site.

Construction. There is one construction company owned and operated on the reservation by a tribal member.

Industrial Parks. Light industry is expanding in the Colorado River Tribes Industrial Park, a fully improved 140-acre industrial complex with rail and highway access, paved streets, and complete utilities. First created in 1970, the industrial park is located 50 miles south of Interstate 40 and 50 miles north of Interstate 10, making it very accessible. In 1992, a 10-acre recycling plant opened that cleans approximately 3.5 million pounds of activated carbon per year, and employs several tribal members. There is one plastics manufacturer located in the park.

Mining and Manufacturing. Colorado River Sand and Rock, a tribally owned and operated company, supplies ready-mixed concrete, asphalt, sand, and gravel to the Arizona Department of Transportation, California Department of Transportation, and to contractors and homeowners in Parker, Quartzsite, Blythe, and surrounding areas. Purchased in 1997 in support of the tribal construction industry, it was so successful that the tribe opened a second off-reservation facility in 2000 in Ehrenberg, Arizona. The company also mines sand and gravel on the reservation. It employs 19.

Real Estate/Commercial Development. CRIT has a real estate office that oversees leasing, management, and acquisition and disposal of residential and commercial lands. The town of Parker is checkerboarded with Indian allotments, reservation lands, and non-Indian land leases for residential and business purposes. CRIT has been leasing its lands since 1904 as a way to develop its raw agricultural lands. Some of the business leases to non-Indians are Big River Realty, Big River Inn, Dumas Bar, and Big River Family Park and Clubhouse. This leasing policy has led to the development of Indian lands. Many housing developments have occurred, including the pending planned community of Big River Development, one of many non-Indian companies working with CRIT.

Services and Retail. Tribally owned companies on the reservation include a marina sales and service company, a construction company, a tire center, a farm machinery sales and service dealership, a convenience store, a radio station, smoke shops, and arts and crafts enterprises. The tribes own the Moovalya Plaza Shopping Center, CRIT-ACCO, and CRIT Farms, and it operates Colorado River Building Materials. The tribes built a multiscreen movie theater next to the casino and resort.

Tourism and Recreation. The Blue Water Marine Park, constructed by the tribes, is located on the reservation. There is an established tourism and recreation industry, with marinas, lodging facilities, food-and-beverage establishments, a videotape rental store, beaches, mobile-home parks, and cabanas. Recreational-development leases are available. Ahakhav Preserve, located near the tribal administration complex, consists of about 250 acres of aquatic habitat, a landscaped picnic area, and a nature trail planted with native mesquite, cottonwood and willow. The preserve offers environmental and nature study programs for tribal youth, and families enjoy fishing and bird watching, canoeing, hiking, swimming, camping, and family and tribal events. Special events at the reservation include National Indian Days and the Miss Indian Arizona Pageant in September, an All-Indian Rodeo and Christmas Program in December, and the CRIT beauty pageants in July. There are annual celebrations on the Fourth of July, yearly Thanksgiving dinners for the entire community, and an entire calendar of other community events throughout the year, such as water-sports competitions and boat races.

The Colorado River is the greatest recreational and most scenic attraction at the reservation and in the surrounding region. Reservoirs (Lakes Moovalya and Havasu), formed behind Headgate and Parker Dams, provide facilities for swimmers,

Colorado River

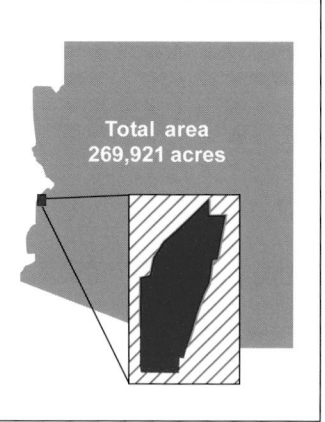

**Total area
269,921 acres**

Total area
269,920.52 acres *(BIA, 2004)*
225,998.29 acres *(AZ)*
43,922.23 acres *(CA)*

Total area *(Tribal source, 2004)*
269,921 acres

Allotted lands *(AZ)* *(BIA, 2004)*
5,873.24 acres

Population *2000 census*
7,466

Tribal enrollment
(Tribal source)
3,595

Total labor force
2000 census
3,779

High school graduate or higher
2000 census
64.3%

Bachelor's degree or higher
2000 census
8.9%

Unemployment rate
2000 census
9.61%

Colorado River

TRI-AZ-0014

TRI-AZ-10

TRI-AZ-1

TRI-AZ-7 .

TRI-AZ-2

TRI-AZ-0022

TRI-AZ-0023

TRI-AZ-1 Sunrise on the marina at the Blue Water Casino

TRI-AZ-0014 Sign at Colorado River tribal headquarters

TRI-AZ-10 Entrance to the Blue Water Casino

TRI-AZ-7 Colorado River Building Materials in Parker, Arizona

TRI-AZ-2 Blue Water Casino Hotel

TRI-AZ-0022 The 165-slip marina with boat launch at the Blue Water Casino

TRI-AZ-0023 Marina at Blue Water Casino

boaters, and water skiers along 90 miles of shoreline. Historic sites at or near the reservation include the tribally maintained Old Mohave Presbyterian Mission, located 18 miles south of Parker. The Poston Memorial Monument and Kiosk, dedicated to those who were incarcerated at Poston during World War II, is located in nearby Poston, Arizona. River fishing for trout, striped bass, catfish, crappie, and bluegill is excellent. Dove, quail, waterfowl, rabbit, and predator hunting is excellent. Reservation hunting and fishing permits are required. Camping permits are also available.

Lodging for tourists and guests of residents is available at the Blue Water Resort and Casino, where every room has a view of the Colorado River. A 165-slip marina with a boat launch is available at the resort, and sandy beaches for swimming line the river at water's edge. Activity Island features a miniature golf course, a video arcade, and the 18-hole Emerald Golf Course. There is a gift shop on the premises, as well as a new five screen movie theater.

INFRASTRUCTURE
The reservation is adjacent to Interstate 10, which runs along its southern border. There are train, bus, and truck services available in the town of Parker on the reservation. Commercial air service is available 60 miles away in Blythe, California, and nearby at the regional Avi Suquilla Airport facility, where there is

a 4,782-foot lighted, paved runway, UNICOM radio, and fuel. It is conveniently located adjacent to Interstate 95.

Electricity. Arizona Public Service Company supplies electricity to Parker and other parts of the reservation. The BIA/CRIT power distribution system, known as the Headgate Rock Hydroelectric Power Plant, also provides electricity to the reservation and surrounding area. It was rehabilitated in the late 1990s to integrate 19,500 kilowatts of hydroelectric power into the power system, since the tribes have senior water rights to 717,000 acre-feet of the Colorado River, which is almost one-third of the allotment for the entire state of Arizona. Income from sales of electricity by CRIT Utilities and increased conservation by power customers is repaying plant construction costs. The tribe is currently working on an agreement with the Bureau of Indian Affairs and the Bureau of Reclamation to take over this power plant in 2005.

Fuel. Southwest Gas Corporation provides natural gas.

Water Supply. The utility provider is CRIT Regional Water System which is tribally owned and operated.

COMMUNITY FACILITIES AND SERVICES
There is a cultural research library-museum-archive open to the public, located in the tribal administrative center, two gymnasi-

TRI-AZ-9

TRI-AZ-1071

TRI-AZ-1072

TRI-AZ-5

TRI-AZ-6

TRI-AZ-0013

TRI-AZ-1093

ums, two parks, two baseball diamonds, fairgrounds, a community center, a senior park, rodeo grounds, a marina with a trailer park, beaches, cabanas, and a picnic area on the reservation. There is also a senior citizen center.

Public Safety. CRIT has its own police force and utilizes a volunteer fire department.

Education. All students, except for a few boarding-school students, attend public schools in the area. A number of students attend off-reservation institutions of higher education. There are plans to build two new schools at Parker and La Pera.

Health Care. There is a 20-bed hospital in Parker, operated by the Indian Health Service, which features a laboratory and full x-ray and emergency room facilities. CRIT provides outpatient mental health services, a community health representative, and outpatient and residential alcohol services to Indian people on the reservation. There are additional hospitals in Yuma, Arizona, 125 miles south of Parker.

ENVIRONMENTAL CONCERNS
The CRIT Environmental Protection Office is charged with the protection and preservation of the reservation's air quality, land base, and water quality. It manages various programs that focus on such issues as pesticide management, solid waste disposal, water quality from non-point sources (wetlands restoration), air quality, and hazardous materials disposal.

TRI-AZ-9 & TRI-AZ-1071 Colorado River Sand and Rock Company

TRI-AZ-1072 Colorado River Sand and Rock Company sign

TRI-AZ-5 & TRI-AZ-6 CRIT farmlands consisting of approximately 84,000 acres of irrigated crops

TRI-AZ-0013 A Colorado River tribal member's private hay field

TRI-AZ-1093 Part of the 250-plus acre Ahakhav Preserve

Fort Apache

Fort Apache Indian Reservation
Federal reservation
White Mountain Apache
Navajo, Apache, and Gila
counties, Arizona

White Mountain Apache Tribe
PO Box 1150
Whiteriver, AZ 85941
928-338-4346
928-338-4778 Fax
wmat.nsn.us

Total area
1,684,225.73 acres (BIA, 2004)
505,722.77 acres (Apache County)
650,341.96 acres (Navajo County)
528,161.00 acres (Gila County)

Population 2000 census
12,429

Tribal enrollment (BIA, 2001)
12,900

Tribal enrollment
(Tribal source, 2004)
13,556

Total labor force 2000 census
3,696

High school graduate or higher
2000 census
54.3%

Bachelor's degree or higher
2000 census
6.3%

Unemployment rate
2000 census
22.46%

LOCATION AND LAND STATUS

Located in east-central Arizona, Fort Apache Indian Reservation consists of desert foothills, canyon beds, and forested mountains where elevations exceed 11,000 feet. The reservation is approximately 75 miles long and 45 miles wide. The White River community serves as the business center for the tribe and is the location of the BIA agency. Residential communities are located at McNary, North Fork, Seven Mile, East Fork, Canyon Day, Cedar Creek, Carrizo, Forestdale, and Cibecue.

The joint White Mountain-San Carlos Apache Reservation was established by an Executive Order on November 9, 1871, and supplemented by an Executive Order on December 14, 1872. It was set aside on lands surrounding Fort Apache, a military outpost initially known as Camp Ord, designed to protect white settlers in the Arizona Territory.

PHYSICAL DESCRIPTION

Whiteriver, Arizona, the tribal headquarters, sits at an elevation of 5,280 feet above sea level.

CLIMATE

The average year-round high temperature is 71°F. The average low temperature is 38°F. The area receives just over 18 inches of precipitation annually, almost all of it (17.9 inches) falling as winter snow.

CULTURE AND HISTORY

The White Mountain Apaches, considered the eastern-most group of the western Apache peoples, traditionally lived in an area bounded by the Pinaleño Mountains to the south and the White Mountains to the north. The evidence is unclear as to what motivated these Athabascan-speaking people to relocate to this region from the plains of Texas and New Mexico where they had settled, probably in the early 1500s, after leaving Canada or Alaska. The new geographic location and their contact with other area populations brought about linguistic, social, and cultural changes that set them apart from other Apache peoples. At the time of the Anglo-American occupation of Arizona, the White Mountain Apaches represented the largest division of the Western Apache people, with an estimated 1,400 to 1,500 people.

While they are primarily a nomadic people, the Western Apaches probably learned agricultural techniques from either the Navajos or the western Pueblos and built small farming settlements. Traditionally, the advent of spring signaled the time when people moved to their farms, where they cultivated limited quantities of corn, beans, and squash. When the first shoots of their crops appeared, they split into gathering groups of women and hunting groups of men, leaving the group's elders and children to tend the crops. The introduction of the horse greatly increased the range of the Western Apaches, allowing them to establish an intricate network of trade and raiding routes. This lifestyle continued, except for a brief time during the Spanish colonial period, until their forced relocation to reservations.

In reaction to Apache raids and attacks on Spanish settlements beginning in the mid-eighteenth century, the Spanish government unsuccessfully attempted to control and to defeat them by military means. By 1786, it had become clear that the Spanish goal of extermination was unrealistic. In response, the Spanish Viceroy Bernardo de Galvez conceived of a new "Indian policy," designed to placate the Western Apaches by settling them in villages near the Spanish military encampments, offering them supplies and, most significantly, offering them alcohol. The Spanish hoped this policy would convince the Western Apaches to remain peaceful, and, through an addiction to alcohol, would create a dependency upon the Spanish. For nearly 25 years this policy worked with moderate success, yet the Mexican War of Independence, ending in 1821, prevented its continuation. When the Mexican government, beset with serious financial problems, could no longer subsidize the Apaches, the people left to regroup in their traditional territories. By 1831, the Western Apaches had resumed their intensive raiding activities, throwing the Mexican state of Sonora into intense disarray. From then until the Anglo-Americans assumed control of Arizona in 1853, the Spanish population of Sonora declined dramatically.

After the ratification of the Gadsden Purchase in 1853, Anglo settlers and prospectors began to intrude upon the domain of the Western Apaches. At first the people were wary but peaceful, but when it became clear that the new settlers sought to control the Apaches and usurp their territory, the people responded with open hostility. This resulted in a dramatic 40-year war of epic proportions, ending with the irreversible defeat of the Western Apaches and their relocation to reservations.

By 1870, it was becoming increasingly clear that the Territory of Arizona lacked the military means to exterminate the Apaches and that the Apaches, in turn, needed some protection from the genocidal practices of the local populace. On May 16, 1870, an Army post was erected at the confluence of the east and north forks of the White River in order to house the White Mountain Apaches. Fort Apache, now listed on the National Historic Register, was the most isolated of the U. S. Army installations. Following the Camp Grant Massacre in 1871, during which a mob of enraged citizens from Tucson, together with a group of Papago Indians, slaughtered more than 75 Western Apache women and children, the federal government implemented a new "peace policy" in Arizona, calling for the collection of all Apaches on reservations. As part of this policy, indigenous peoples were settled on their own territories, provided with protection, and encouraged to make a living through agriculture and the raising of livestock.

While a large tract of land was marked off around Fort Apache for the Cibecues and the northern bands of the White Mountain Division, in 1874 the department of the interior embarked upon a "removal campaign" designed to concentrate all the Western Apaches, Chiricahuas, and the Yavapais on the San Carlos Apache Reservation. These peoples actively resisted, and many Apache and others escaped the confines of the reservation. During this unrest, the U.S. Army under General Crook led a group of White Mountain Apaches deep into Sonora's Sierra Madre Mountains, where they entered into negotiations with Geronimo that ultimately resulted in his surrender and the surrender of nearly 400 Chiricahua Apaches. With peace restored in 1884, several groups of Apaches, including Geronimo and a small band of dissident Chiricahuas, were returned to Fort Apache. Here, under strict military supervision, they worked to construct irrigation dams and to plant crops. While suffering devastating cultural losses, the Western Apaches were at least able to adapt to reservation life without further loss of life.

After the turn of the twentieth century, Fort Apache residents began working in the wage economy to supplement their subsistence needs. In 1907, over 80 men were employed by the U.S. Cavalry to cut hay for horses stabled at Fort Apache, while others worked as cowboys for Anglo cattle ranchers who leased reservation grazing land. By 1918, the population had risen to

2,456, and the federal government issued 400 cattle to Apaches so they could start their own livestock business.

By 1931, there were approximately 20,000 head of cattle on the Fort Apache Reservation. Economic opportunities were further expanded during the early 1920s with the establishment of a lumbering operation which has since become a major industry, processing over 50 million board feet annually. In 1954, the White Mountain Apache Tribe, by this time a legally constituted body governed by an elected tribal council, responded to the outdoor interests of an increasing number of tourists by creating a lucrative recreation enterprise.

In 1985, a fire in the sole surviving barracks at Old Fort Apache, a building being used as the tribe's cultural center, resulted in the loss of many tribal artifacts and irreplaceable collections of art. Fearful of the same thing happening to the remaining buildings at Old Fort Apache, the tribe developed a master plan for Fort Apache Historic Park, sought funding from the World Monuments Fund and established the Fort Apache Heritage Foundation to seek donations and work in partnership with the National Endowment for the Humanities and the National Park Service to rehabilitate the buildings. By 2000, nine of the Park's 26 buildings had been restored. The Fort Apache Historic Park, now a source of Apache pride, includes the former military cemetery, "Geronimo's Cave," and the fourteenth-century reconstructed Kinishba Ruins National Monument. *(See Tourism and Recreation, below.)*

GOVERNMENT
The White Mountain Apache Tribal Council was established under the provisions of the Indian Reorganization Act of June 18, 1934, adopting a constitution in August 1938. This constitution was amended in 1958 and 1993. The elected council includes a chairperson, who presides over all tribal council meetings and exercises authority delegated by law, ordinance, or tribal council; a vice-chairperson; and nine members at large elected from four districts, each serving four-year terms.

The tribe, under PL-638, contracts with the BIA to administer key programs and services.

The tribe has a legal office which acts in an advisory and ministerial rather than a judicial capacity, under the general supervision of the tribal attorney or the tribe's general counsel. The office falls under the daily supervision of the tribal chairman with duties similar to that of the attorney general of the federal or state government. The legal department advises the chief executives and departmental heads regarding questions of law touching upon their official duties. The tribal attorney, acting under the direction of the chairman or by tribal council resolution, is responsible for instituting, conducting, and maintaining all suits and legal proceedings deemed necessary for the enforcement of tribal laws and the preservation of order, tribal rights, and resources.

Tribal government has made a plethora of social services available to community members, including: the Job Training Partnership Act, WIC, weatherization, a safety department, food distribution, and elderly services.

ECONOMY
Apache Enterprises operates the 127-room Hon Dah Hotel, Restaurant, and RV Park; Apache Service Station; Corrizo Food Store; Cedar Creek Food Store, Seven-Mile Food Store; and many other businesses on the reservation.

Economic Development Projects. With the plentiful resources and scenic beauty of its land, the White Mountain Apache Tribe has gained a national reputation for its network of enterprises, including Fort Apache Timber Company, a finger-jointing and edge-gluing plant that uses the sawmill's low-grade lumber, and a lumber and hardware retail center in Hon Dah. Another major employer is the wildlife and outdoor recreation division of the tourism office, which capitalizes on tribal control of 800 miles of streams and 2,300 acres of reservoirs to provide a wide variety of fishing and camping experiences. This office also organizes waterfowl and big-game hunts, issuing permits seasonally. There is one bank on the reservation.

Agriculture and Livestock. Reservation rangeland supports a 15,000-head tribal herd, primarily consisting of purebred whiteface cattle, generating up to 50 or more full-time jobs. As support for the cattle industry, the tribe runs a feedlot, a hay-and-grain store, and a 900-acre irrigated farm that produces alfalfa for feed.

Forestry. The reservation's 800,000-acre forest of ponderosa pine, spruce, and fir trees generates approximately 320 Apache jobs in the timber and timber-management fields, producing an annual allowable cut of 76 million board feet for FATCO, the Fort Apache Timber Company. The company operates two small sawmills, a large mill, and a planning mill with dry kilns, netting over $5 million annually in stumpage revenue for the tribe's operating budget. With the development of a remanufacturing facility, the tribal forest industry also produces a number of standard and special-order wood products, such as: (1) edge-glued and ripped-dimension lumber; (2) block-board core panels for solid-core doors and furniture; (3) profile step-glued parts for window, door, and cabinet components; (4) truck flying and decking; (5) specialty items such as turning squares, spindles, columns, posts, stair treads, stadium seats, church pews, and veneer-laminated products; (6) dimensions lumber; (7) nonstructural lumber; (8) finger-joint studs; and (9) special-order production items.

Gaming. The tribe operates the Sunrise Park Resort, a ski resort, and the Hon-Dah Casino (Hon-Dah means "welcome") is located just around the corner from the ski resort. The Hon-Dah Casino and Resort is a 15,000-square-foot facility offering slot machines and table games, live entertainment and lodging for hundreds of guests.

Fisheries. The tribe owns and manages Alchesay Fish Hatchery.

Construction. The White Mountain Apache Housing Authority was the only Indian housing authority in Arizona to get a HUD-sponsored ROSS grant in 2003. ROSS (Resident Opportunities and Self-Sufficiency) grants allow tribal public housing residents to start homebuyer education and resident services programs. Each program received $350,000 in funding to develop a GED scholarship program, create neighborhood associations, a construction apprentice program, conduct annual job fairs, implement a financial education program, and develop savings accounts for residents of the expanding Apache Dawn housing project. The Hon-Dah Home Center employs a number of tribal members.

Manufacturing. The McDonnell-Douglas Company contracts with the Apache Aerospace Company to produce prefabricated materials and other accessories for Apache Helicopter. Another tribally owned company, Apache Materials, produces earth-friendly construction materials.

Industrial Parks. There are two industrial parks with full utilities available.

Services and Retail. Apache Enterprises operates several convenience markets, grocery stores, and gas stations, including Hon Dah Restaurant, Apache Service Station, Corrizo Food Store, Cedar Creek Food Store, and Seven Mile Food Store.

Fort Apache

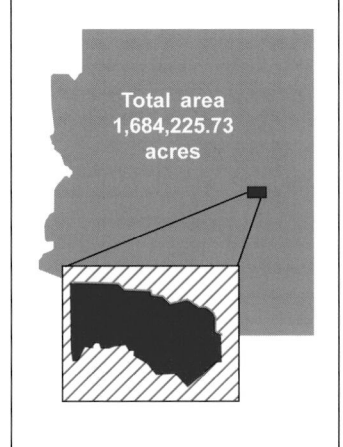

Total area
1,684,225.73
acres

ENVIRONMENTAL CONCERNS
The persistent threat and almost-annual reality of wildfires has plagued all residents of Arizona in the years since 2001. The 1.6 million acres of pristine land that make up the Fort Apache Reservation lie within 25 miles of the western edge of the Apache-Sitgreaves National Forest and 25 miles slightly north and west of Tonto National Forest, placing the reservation squarely in the danger zone during fire season. A photograph of Hurricane Lake, only one portion of this vast tribal wilderness area, is available at www.162.42.237.6/wmatod/index.htm.

The area of Arizona that includes the Fort Apache Reservation is a breeding ground for the Mexican wolf, listed as an endangered species since 1976. On November 15, 2002, an alpha female of the lupine pack was found dead of unnatural causes near Maverick Mountain on the White Mountain Apache Reservation. The suspicious circumstances surrounding the death are being investigated.

Fort Apache

TRI-AZ-1186

TRI-AZ-1184

TRI-AZ-1210

TRI-AZ-1263

TRI-AZ-1252

TRI-AZ-1246

TRI-AZ-1239

TRI-AZ-1186 The Hon-Dah Casino and Resort

TRI-AZ-1184 Hon-Dah Ski and Outdoor Sport

TRI-AZ-1210 A traditional Apache camp near the White Mountain Apache Cultural Center at White River

TRI-AZ-1263 A Canadian truck picking up lumber from FATCO

TRI-AZ-1252, TRI-AZ-1246 & TRI-AZ-1239 The Fort Apache Timber Company (FATCO), which has two sawmills, a large mill, and a planning mill with dry kilns.

Media and Communications. A biweekly newspaper, *The Apache Scout*, is published on the reservation.

Tourism and Recreation. White Mountain Apache Tribe Wildlife and Outdoor Division activities include a hunting program, a rent-by-the-lake program, river running, and canyoneering. Fishing, hunting, backcountry safaris and tours, and other outdoor adventures are a huge draw for tourists. Hawley Lake Cabins and Resort is available in McNary, Arizona, within walking distance of Hawley Lake and Earl Park Lake.

Because the area is so rich in natural resources, there are innumerable wildlife viewing opportunities along 500 miles of cold streams and 30 artificial lakes, which offer year-round trout fishing, ice fishing during the winter months, as well as a number of tribally operated campgrounds. Sunrise Park Ski Resort, the largest in Arizona, offers downhill skiing with 65 runs for skiers at all levels of proficiency, a separate snowboarding area, and cross-country ski trails. The resort features a unique children's "ski-wee" area.

The Sunrise Park Lodge is a 100-room hotel offering fine dining, an indoor pool and whirlpool, a lounge, and a game room. A pool, spa, and sauna are available, and during the summer months, a marina is open for boat rentals. Mountain biking, swimming, horseback riding, music festivals, rock climbing, rappelling, canyoneering, and wilderness hikes are also very popular activities on the reservation. White-water rafting, canoeing, and kayaking are possible on the Salt River, which originates on reservation lands. Guided tours are offered between February

and June. The Hon-Dah RV Park, next to the casino, has 198 camp sites, a recreation room and covered picnic pavilion, handicap-accessible restrooms and showers and full utility hookups.

Many visitors enjoy historical and cultural sites at the 288-acre Old Fort Apache Park, the Kinishba archaeological ruins, petroglyph sites, Geronimo's Cave, the Heritage Museum, and regional festivals such as Hon-Dah's Powwow in the Pines, Mountain Frontier Days, the White Mountain Native American Arts and Crafts Festival, the annual Bluegrass Festival, and the Fall Festival.

Old Fort Apache, listed on the National Register of Historic Places, is now owned by the White Mountain Apache Tribe. Old Fort Apache is recognized for its association with Geronimo and Cochise, famous leaders from the various Apache bands who were pursued by soldiers from Fort Apache. Located at the foot of the White Mountains, the fort serves as the focal point for the protection, celebration, and revitalization of the tribe's culture and history; it is the only former U.S. military base under the interpretive control of an Indian tribe. Established in 1969 on the grounds of Old Fort Apache, the White Mountain Apache Cultural Center (Nohwiké Bágowa, or "House of Our Footprints") serves as a repository for the tribe's cultural heritage through the preservation of oral histories, archival materials, and objects of cultural, historical and artistic significance. Using exhibits and educational programs, the center fosters an appreciation for the history and cultural traditions of the White Mountain Apache people. The center developed an artist-in-residence program in 1999 to provide opportunities for local artists to develop their skill and show their work to the public. Also on the grounds at Old Fort Apache is the Theodore Roosevelt School. Originally built as a BIA school, it operates today as a boarding and day school serving approximately 100 Native American students.

Special tribal events also attract many tourists onto the reservation: In April, there is the Canyon Day Open Show, and in May, there is the Junior Rodeo and the Headstart Rodeo and Parade. The Sunrise Dance Ceremonies begin in May and continue throughout September each year. The Old Timers Junior Rodeo is held in August, followed by the Tribal Fair and Rodeo in September.

INFRASTRUCTURE
U.S. Highways 60, 73, and 260 cross the Fort Apache Indian Reservation. A commercial air shuttle to Phoenix operates from an airport 10 miles from the reservation at Show Low, Arizona. There is a 6,270-foot paved and lighted runway and UNICOM radio access at the Whiteriver Airport.

Electricity. Electricity is provided by the Navopache Electric Cooperative.

Fuel. Propane gas comes from Doxol.

Water Supply. Water is available via community systems operated by the tribal utility authority. The Whiteriver Regional System handles sewage disposal.

Telecommunications. GTE West provides telephone service. The tribe operates a radio station and five cable-television channels. The tribe has its own fire and police departments.

COMMUNITY FACILITIES AND SERVICES
There are three community centers, a rodeo and fairgrounds, an indoor swimming pool, Old Fort Apache and the Cultural Center, a library, and three gymnasiums available to Fort Apache residents.

Education. In Whiteriver, there are two public elementary schools, one junior high school, and a high school, along with a branch of Northland Pioneer College. There are also three BIA schools and a Lutheran mission school. (Please see Economy and Tourism, and Recreation for additional details.)

Health Care. The Indian Health Service operates a 50-bed hospital at Whiteriver, providing a full range of inpatient, outpatient, and community health care. Emergency air evacuations to the larger facilities in Phoenix are available by contracted helicopter service. There are a number of various mental health and substance abuse treatment options available on the reservation, and there is an outpatient and emergency care clinic in Cibecue, as well as an EMS unit.

Fort Apache

Honoring Nations Honoree 2000

Wildlife and Outdoor Recreation Program White Mountain Apache Tribe (Whiteriver, AZ)

The White Mountain Apache Wildlife and Outdoor Recreation Program performs all wildlife conservation/management activities for the Tribe and operates a self-sustaining business enterprise based on the Tribe's thriving recreation and tourism industry. The Program's effective management techniques have allowed the White Mountain Apache to gain control over their wildlife and recreation resources and to manage these resources in accordance with Apache values.

Located on 1.6 million acres of resource-rich land, the Fort Apache Reservation is known for its scenic high elevation lakes and over 500 miles of cold streams, pristine lands and thriving wildlife, making it a popular outdoor destination area for visitors throughout Arizona and the southwestern United States. Until the early 1980s, however, the tribe had minimal management control over its abundant natural and wildlife resources. Although the Tribe had long possessed a fame and fish department, the Arizona Game and Fish Department regulated all non-member hunting activities on tribal lands. The Tribe had little input into the State's process of establishing non-member hunting seasons or setting harvest levels for reservation wildlife. By the 1970s, tribal managers had grown increasingly concerned that the State's liberal issuance of big game hunting permits at below-market prices was irresponsible from a conservation standpoint. Further, the Tribe was missing out on a potentially lucrative source of income.

Seeking to expand its jurisdictional control over its resources, the Tribe filed a lawsuit against the State of Arizona in the late 1970s. The issue ultimately found its way to the U.S. Supreme Court: in 1982, in a related case, *Mescalero Apache Tribe v. State of New Mexico*, the Court recognized tribes' sovereign authority over the management of tribal fish and wildlife resources. This decision paved the way for the White Mountain Apache Tribe to institute its own management practices and to develop innovative, culturally appropriate recreation-based businesses. Building on its success in fisheries management (a program contracted from the BIA some years earlier), the Tribe established its wildlife management program through another 638 contract with the BIA and focused on the development of various big- and small-game hunting programs.

Since assuming management control, the tribe has developed one of the most respected resource management divisions in Indian Country and worldwide. With a full-time staff of 40 and a seasonal staff of 70, comprised almost entirely of tribal members, the wildlife and outdoor recreation division (W&ORD) is the umbrella for a spectrum of conservation and enterprise functions. The W&ORD houses several departments aimed at conservation: a law enforcement department with 12 certified tribal game rangers, and a fish and wildlife department employing tribal biologists and technicians who, among other activities, manage a sensitive-species program. The W&ORD also oversees two profit-generating tribal enterprises: the outdoor recreation department which sells permits for recreation activities, and the trophy hunting program which is anchored by the tribe's world-renowned elk hunting program, and also includes hunts for pronghorn antelope, bighorn sheep, bear, mountain lion and turkey.
The W&ORD has been successful in both preserving the reservation's wildlife population and creating sustainable revenue streams for the tribe--functions that the tribe has shown can be complementary despite the commonly held belief that they are diametrically opposed.

For example, the division's strategy of pursuing conservative harvest levels and strict monitoring practices, which are articulated in the tribe's self-designed game and fish dode, has resulted in an extremely healthy wildlife population. In fact, the tribe has produced more Boone and Crockett record-book elk than

Honoring Nations
Honoree 2000

Text in its entirety from:
The Harvard Project On
American Indian Economic
Development

John F. Kennedy School
of Government
Harvard University

Fort Apache

**Honoring Nations
Honoree 2000**

Text in its entirety from:
**The Harvard Project On
American Indian Economic
Development**

**John F. Kennedy School
of Government
Harvard University**

any other individual land management area in the world. Indeed, the W&ORD's mantra of "quality over quantity" is paying off: trophy bull elk packages command a price of $14,500, and in a special sealed-bid auction conducted by the tribe in 2000, one trophy bull elk hunt sold for a record $38,000. Critically, the W&ORD is constantly searching for ways to link its successful conservation efforts with new profit-generating activities to meet the ever-evolving demand for outdoor recreation services and to enhance the funding base for conservation and resource management programs. Taking the success of its trophy elk hunt sales to the next level, the W&ORD has established outfitted fishing expeditions, a rent-a-lake program and guided canyoneering, camping, hiking, and white water rafting trips. In short, self-governance over resource management has given the W&ORD freedom to innovate in its enterprise development. The tribe now generates over $600,000 annually in profits from its W&ORD enterprises.

There are other hallmarks of the W&ORD's success. The division's sound biological strategy has not only enabled the tribe to generate profits once unimaginable under state management, but it has given the tribe the necessary expertise to take on sensitive plant and animal management--a balanced approach that distinguishes it from most wildlife management programs in Indian Country. An example is the tribe's work in recovering the native Apache Trout. The U.S. Fish and Wildlife Service (USFWS) acknowledges that the tribe's biological expertise and active local participation have been the primary reasons why this once-endangered species has been upgraded to threatened status and is well on its way to being completely de-listed. By combining strong will, good management and technical know-how, the tribe has avoided the costly and time-consuming litigation that has plagued other tribes' involvement in recovery efforts. In fact, state and federal agencies have asked the tribe to lend its expertise to partnerships for the recovery of a variety of threatened species, including the Mexican spotted owl and the Mexican gray wolf.

Several key factors underlie the W&ORD's sustained success in resource management. First, the tribe is fully dedicated to managing its own resources rather than relying on outsiders. Since the legal win in the Supreme Court in the 1980s, the tribe has consistently sought to further expand and exercise its jurisdictional sovereignty. In the mid-1990s, the tribe's relationship with the USFWS became strained by a series of proposed species listings and critical habitat designations involving tribal lands. Compelled to defend its own management capabilities, the tribe went toe-to-toe with the USFWS. After lengthy negotiations, the two entities signed a path-breaking "Statement of Relationship" which

recognizes the tribe's sound institutional capacity and allows the tribe to carry out its own management and protections for the threatened and endangered species on the reservation. This example provides an important lesson for all Indian nations: Not only must tribes be willing to expand and defend their sovereignty, but their sovereignty must be backed by capable institutions.

Second, the W&ORD understands that community support is directly tied to the effectiveness of its work. The division actively seeks elder involvement, largely through an elders advisory board, which has led to the tribe's list of sensitive species being even broader than those of the state or federal government. Another example is the W&ORD's approach to managing tribal citizens' hunting. In the late 1980s, the W&ORD established a separate harvest system for tribal citizens, which provides subsidized game tags, sets aside hunting areas on the reservation, and designates special seasons for big game hunting. Moreover, tribal member hunting fees support the W&ORD's conservation fund which in turn supports hunter education, a "report a poacher" program, and a college scholarship program for tribal members pursuing degrees in fields related to natural resource management. Clearly, these efforts to reach out to citizens and to embrace their ideas, needs and cultural connections to natural resources, not only improve program management, but also citizens' acceptance of W&ORD's activities, and help ensure program success.

The wildlife and outdoor recreation division's many achievements are a tremendous source of pride for citizens of the White Mountain Apache Tribe. By combining a strong will for self-management of the tribe's abundant natural resources with an unwavering pursuit of excellence in outdoor enterprise development, the White Mountain Apache Tribe has laid the foundation for the sustained use of the outdoors for generations to come.

Lessons:
· Profitability and conservation are not mutually exclusive and, in fact, can be mutually beneficial. For example, the profitability of tourism and outdoor recreation enterprises can be directly tied to the tribe's competency in natural resource management and conservation.

· Strong institutional capacity enables tribes to exert their jurisdictional sovereignty more effectively and may even lead to new opportunities for the exercise of sovereignty.

· Tribal codes, regulations and policies gain acceptance and effectiveness when they reflect community values.

Fort McDowell

LOCATION AND LAND STATUS

The Fort McDowell Yavapai Nation is located in central Arizona, about 45 miles northeast of Phoenix.

PHYSICAL DESCRIPTION

Fort McDowell, Arizona, sits at an elevation of over 1,200 feet above sea level. Most of the land lies at an elevation of about 1,350 feet and varies from tree-lined river bottoms to rolling hills covered with cacti. The Verde River flows north to south throughout the nation, dissecting the Sonoran Desert with a rich riparian corridor of green. Thirty miles east of the nation, the Four Peaks rise to more than 7,000 feet.

CLIMATE

The average year-round temperature is a comfortable 69ºF, with summer highs above 100ºF and winter lows never dropping below the 30s. The area receives less than eight inches of precipitation annually, with no snowfall during the winter months.

CULTURE AND HISTORY

Residents of Fort McDowell are descended from bands of Apache, Mojave, and Yavapai people who were assigned to the Fort McDowell Military Reservation at the end of the Indian wars during the second half of the nineteenth century. The current 40-square-mile nation represents only a small part of the traditional lands of these nomadic peoples; their aboriginal homelands once included all of the Mogollon Rim country and the greater part of the state of Arizona. They hunted meat and gathered food in the desert lowlands and surrounding highlands.

Soon after the nation was established, local non-Indians attempted to have the residents removed and relocated to the Salt River Pima-Maricopa Indian Nation. Although the attempt failed, lack of federal funds to construct facilities to protect irrigation structures forced many Yavapai residents to seek wage labor or to raise cattle. The nation was created by an Executive Order on September 15, 1903, for the Kwevikopaya (Southeastern Yavapai) who lived in the Matazal-Four Peaks and Superstition Mountain region. It was one of the most important outposts in the Southwest during the Apache Wars of 1865 through 1891.

The Fort McDowell Yavapai Nation claims the famous historical personage of Dr. Carlos Montezuma, a Yavapai man stolen by Pima Indians and sold to an Italian photographer who took him to Chicago to be educated. In 1889, Dr. Montezuma, or Wassaja, was one of the first Native Americans to receive a degree in medicine. Late in his life, he fought for Native American rights and led the struggle to regain the Yavapai-Apache homeland, becoming one of the first known advocates for human rights.

In November 1981, community members voted against the sale of their land to the federal government for construction of the Orme Dam, which was to be built at the confluence of the Verde and Salt rivers near the southern border of the Nation. The project would have flooded the entire nation area and forced residents from their ancestral homelands. The tribal victory was an important historical landmark in reaffirming tribal sovereignty. A tribal fair and rodeo are held annually in mid-November to commemorate the event.

During the early 1990s, several casinos, including the one in Fort McDowell, were in operation in Arizona while numerous tribes waited to sign gaming compacts with the Arizona state government in accordance with the 1988 Indian Gaming Regulatory Act. The governor, however, was opposed to Indian gaming and called upon the U.S. Attorney General's office for support. One morning in mid-May, federal agents raided five Indian casinos, including the Fort McDowell facility, and seized all gaming machines. A three-week standoff between tribal members and government officials persuaded Arizona's governor to sign the gaming contract, and the day of the raid is now commemorated as Tribal Sovereignty Day on May 12.

GOVERNMENT

Fort McDowell is governed by a popularly elected tribal council consisting of a president, vice-president, treasurer, non-voting secretary, and two tribal members, each serving a four-year term. Terms are staggered. There is also a planning commission, a citizens' advisory committee, and a housing authority. In January 2000 the tribe held its first election under a new constitution passed on October 19, 1999. Under the new constitution, the staggered council positions carry four-year terms. The tribe has 14 governmental departments including administration and finance, community and economic development, environmental protection, education, health, social services, law enforcement, and tribal court. There is a community health representative program with three community health representatives at Fort McDowell. Social service programs include two tribal social workers, a social service aide, and a court liaison worker.

The Fort McDowell Tribal Police Department has 23 sworn officers and six civilian employees, and it uses a community-based policing approach to law enforcement services on the nation. In accordance with the community-based approach, officers conduct presentations at schools, hold community meetings, visit and coordinate events at the elder center, and are involved with young people working with the Fort McDowell Youth Council, in addition to other more traditional law enforcement services and practices.

The tribal judiciary branch is separate from the tribal court as mandated by the tribal constitution. The tribal court system consists of a chief judge, an associate judge, a bailiff, a court administrator, several court clerks, a probation officer, and a juvenile officer. This branch also houses the prosecutor's office.

ECONOMY

The nation's economy is closely tied to the surrounding urban communities of Rio Verde, Fountain Hills, Mesa, Scottsdale, and Phoenix. Sources of tribal revenue include leasing land and water to businesses, public institutions and municipalities in the area. The nation also owns a number of successful enterprises that contribute to its economic status. Fort McDowell Yavapai Nation is able to support local economies by providing employment opportunities through its businesses and its sizeable donations to local organizations and groups. The tribe has also donated millions of dollars to each of Arizona's state universities.

Economic Development Projects. Current projects under development by the tribe include a resort and conference center and an RV park. Facilities are expected to be completed in 2005. The Fort McDowell Resort and Conference Center has been slated as a Radisson four-star facility. It will offer 247 rooms, a restaurant, a swimming pool, two Jacuzzis, a fitness center, a water play area, an 18,000-square-foot grand ballroom, and a total of 23,000 square feet of meeting space. The Asah Bweh Oou-O RV Park will offer 150 full-service hookup sites, recreational trails, and free shuttle service to the casino and resort. It will also include a clubhouse that offers a hospitality room, laundry facilities, bathrooms, showers, a swimming pool, and a spa.

Fort McDowell Yavapai Nation
Federal reservation
Mohave, Apache, Yavapai
Maricopa County, Arizona

Fort McDowell Yavapai Nation
P.O. Box 17779
Fountain Hills, AZ 85269
480-837-5121
480-816-7138
480-816-0294 Fax
480-837-7038 Fax
fortmcdowell.org

Total area (BIA, 2004)
22,586.11 acres

Tribally owned lands (BIA, 2004)
22,586.11 acres

Population 2000 census
824

Tribal enrollment (BIA, 2001)
939

Total labor force
2000 census
217

High school graduate or higher
2000 census
67.6%

Bachelor's degree or higher
2000 census
4.6%

Unemployment rate
2000 census
15.67%

Per capita income
$19,293

Fort McDowell

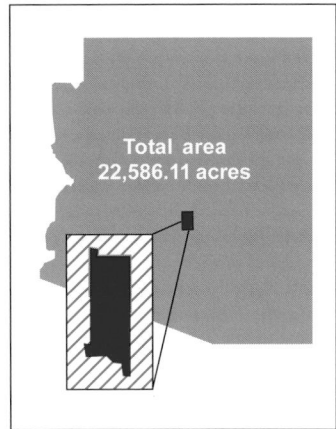

Total area
22,586.11 acres

Fort Mojave

See California

Variables affecting the development of the community at Fort McDowell include water resources (the Verde River bisects the nation) and the development of the nearby Phoenix metropolitan area.

Agriculture and Livestock. The 2,000-acre tribal farm and nursery is a large employer on the nation. In 1990, the tribe forged a water settlement with the federal government ensuring the tribe 36,000 acre-feet of water annually, half from the Central Arizona Project and half from the Verde River. As part of the settlement, a $13 million low-interest loan from the Bureau of Reclamation was used to expand the farming operation from 700 to 2,000 acres. The tribe planted 50,000 pecan trees and 30,000 citrus trees, including orange, lemon, tangelo, and grapefruit trees. In addition to the pecan and citrus groves, the tribe grows 600 acres of alfalfa. Crops are watered via a computerized watering system that conserves millions of gallons of water in comparison to traditional methods. The farm uses only about a quarter of its secured water rights.

Gaming. The Fort McDowell Casino was constructed in 1984. Since then, it has been expanded to its current size of nearly 150,000-square-feet and employs 950 people. It features 700 slot machines, live keno, high-stakes bingo, pari-mutuel waging, a card room, and several restaurants. The bingo hall has been rated one of the top 10 bingo halls in the country.

Adjacent to the casino is a 72-par, 7,225-yard professional golf course, We-Ko-Pa (We-Ko-Pa means "Four Peaks Mountain"). It was completed in December 2001 and offers a 21,000-square-foot clubhouse, a pro shop, a full-service restaurant, a bar, and private conference rooms. The facilities are located near the city of Fountain Hills, at the east edge of Scottsdale, Arizona. The tribe utilizes the marketability of this region to maximize profit for the tribes.

Mining. Fort McDowell Yavapai Materials is a tribally owned and operated sand and gravel operation. The company was the first tribally owned enterprise, established over 20 years ago. It operates pit quarries and ready-mix plants on and off tribal lands. The company maintains its own quality-control lab and provides material for both commercial and residential projects. Recent company projects have included the warning track at the Bank One Ball Park in downtown Phoenix, the Peoria Sports Complex, the Tucson Sports Complex, and the We-Ko-Pa Golf Course. The company has also supplied materials to the City of Las Vegas, Nevada. Fort McDowell Landscape Supply provides work for a number of nation residents.

Services and Retail. The tribe owns and operates Ba'Ja Gas Station and Store, located on the Beeline Highway. The facility offers gas services and a convenience store.

Tourism and Recreation. Tourists are drawn to the area because of the dramatic landscape and views of surrounding mountain ranges--including the Four Peaks, McDowell Mountains, Red Mountains, and the Superstitions--and the rolling lowlands. The casino is another major attraction, bringing many regional residents back to the nation on a regular basis. The golf course and luxury lodging appeal to many visitors. For those seeking a wilder western experience, Fort McDowell Adventures offers guided trails, hayrides, overnight camping trips, cowboy games, old time photos, cattle drives, private rodeos, and an Old West-themed banquet area. Facilities on the site include La Puesta del Sol and The Ranch. La Puesta is a ramada that can hold up to 1,000 guests for dining and dancing. The Ranch is an open-air venue that has a capacity of 400 people.

The community celebrates Orme Dam Recognition Day (also referred to as Victory Day) in November and Sovereignty Day each May.

The nearby Phoenix metropolitan area offers a variety of activities ranging from theater productions and professional sports to major cultural events.

INFRASTRUCTURE
Arizona State Highway 87 runs through the nation from east to west.

Electricity. Electricity is available from the Salt River Project, and natural gas is available from Fountain Hills L.P. Gas Company.

Water Supply. The water system, installed by the U.S. Public Health Service, is operated by the Fort McDowell Water Company. There is no community sewer system; residents utilize individually maintained septic systems. Refuse is collected by the Ft. McDowell Public Works Department.

Transportation. Commercial transportation by air, truck, train, and bus is available in Phoenix, 45 miles from the nation. Air transport facilities are located at Falcon Field in Mesa, at the Scottsdale Airpark, and at Phoenix Sky Harbor International Airport.

Telecommunications. Telephone services are offered by Qwest throughout the state of Arizona.

COMMUNITY FACILITIES AND SERVICES
Community facilities include a full-service recreation center, a softball field, and a library.

Education. The 'Hmañ 'shawa Elementary School is a private school funded entirely by the Fort McDowell Yavapai Nation to serve the educational needs of the tribe's youngsters. It offers culturally relevant lessons while weaving native language into the regular curriculum.

Health Care. The Wassaja Memorial Health Center serves all community residents and any American Indian not covered elsewhere, providing both inpatient and outpatient care. A community health nurse also spends one day a week in the community. Other health services include health education and consultation in social services, environmental health, and nutrition. There are limited health services available in the home. These are case management services for discharge planning from hospitals or skilled nursing facilities. Nonemergency transportation to and from medical appointments is available for those who have no other means of transportation. One day per week, the health center conducts a diabetes clinic, and there are medical specialties offered at the facility on a rotating basis, including optometry and podiatry. Other programs include the family service administration, which offers alcohol and substance abuse programs and manages the Indian child welfare programs.

ENVIRONMENTAL CONCERNS
Water supply is perhaps the most pressing concern on tribal lands. Access to irrigation water has been an issue of great political strife for tribes in Arizona. Congress approved the Central Arizona Project (CAP) in 1968, for the construction of a dam at the confluence of the Salt and Verde rivers. The dam, to be named Orme Dam, would have flooded more than half the nation, including most of the tribal farm. The tribes fought the project for 10 years, and they were eventually successful.

The tribe leases 4,300 acre-feet of water to Phoenix, and it plans to lease more of its CAP allocation to other communities. The Arizona tribes have also insisted that the Verde River keep enough water to sustain wildlife habitat for bald eagles and other riparian-dependent species.

LOCATION AND LAND STATUS

The Fort Yuma-Quechan Tribe Reservation, consisting of 43,958 acres, is located in Imperial County, California, and in Yuma County, Arizona. Reservation lands lie along both sides of the Colorado River, so the federal reservation actually borders Arizona, California, Baja California, and Mexico. The Quechan Tribe received a private gift of a 320-acre parcel of land in fee-simple status, located near Dateland, Arizona. The tribe also owns several other fee-simple parcels near the southwestern boundary of the reservation, within the Winterhaven Township and within the city of Yuma.

The Fort Yuma-Quechan Tribe Reservation is an irrigated agricultural community consisting of low-lying desert land bordered by the Colorado River on the east, with mesas and mountains to the west. San Diego, California, is 180 miles to the west, and Phoenix, Arizona, is 180 miles to the east.

The Fort Yuma-Quechan Tribe Reservation was established by an Executive Order on January 9, 1884, which was preceded by an Order of Intent dated July 6, 1883. The northwestern portion of the reservation was restored by Notice of Secretarial Determination dated January 30, 1981.

CLIMATE

Yuma sits at an elevation of 207 feet above sea level. The average year-round temperature is 76°F, with highs averaging 88°F and lows averaging 64°F. The highest temperature ever recorded for Yuma is 124°F, and the lowest temperature ever recorded is 31°F. The area receives just over four inches of precipitation annually with no reported snowfalls.

CULTURE AND HISTORY

The Yumas, who today prefer to be called the Quechans, a Hokan-speaking people, have occupied the lands on the banks of the Colorado River since recorded time. They lived in large mud-covered log houses or in straw-roofed underground grass huts to escape the desert heat. The houses were not in villages but were scattered about the bottomlands of the Colorado River Valley.

The Quechans took advantage of the Colorado River's annual flooding in their farming practices, raising maize, wheat, beans, cantaloupes, watermelons, calabashes, and some cotton and tobacco. Wild seeds, fish, and game supplemented the Quechans' farm produce. The Quechan people traveled great distances to visit other people, to trade, and to carry on warfare. They ranged as far as Sonora, Needles, and the Pacific Coast in their travels.

Friendly relations existed between the Quechan Nation and the Spanish Empire until the 1780s. In late 1780, the Spanish selected Conception, what is now Fort Yuma, as a site for one of two pueblos in the Quechans' homeland. By 1781, when the pueblo was beginning to take form, Quechan-settler relations began to deteriorate, due in great part to the loss and destruction of land and crops. The Quechans revolted against the occupation of their lands. With help from allies, primarily the Mojaves, the Quechans launched an assault on the year-old Spanish mission and fort, regaining their independence and maintaining it until the Anglo-American invasion around 1850. The Fort Yuma-Quechan Tribe reservation was established in 1884 at the site of the old Spanish pueblo. Originally constructed in 1789, the mission building has been refurbished by the tribe and is now used for important tribal functions.

GOVERNMENT

Exercising its inherent power, the tribe adopted a constitution on December 18, 1936, following the process outlined in the Indian Reorganization Act of 1934. The constitution was amended on November 18, 1974, and again on May 21, 1997. The tribal council consists of a president, a vice president, and five members-at-large. The president and vice president serve four-year terms, and the council members serve two-year terms.

The tribe, under PL-638, contracts with the BIA to administer key programs and services.

ECONOMY

Once centered almost exclusively on agriculture, the reservation's economy is now more diverse, including gaming, tourism, and small tribal enterprises.

In 1999 the Quechan Tribe identified its economic development priorities in a report, "A Nation with a Future." It emphasized taking advantage of its location along Interstate 8, with the possible development of a shopping mall, and of its international border location near Tijuana and San Luis, with the development of a port of entry. On-reservation development plans include a mini-mall that will provide retail services, continued expansion of its RV parks, a tire-recycling facility, and assumption of ownership of quarrying and road maintenance services.

Several key entities within the tribal structure deal with business and economic development: the Quechan Economic Development Administration, the tribal council, and the Quechan Economic Development Administration Committee. The economic development administration issues business permits and helps initiate the business development process. The council approves leases, reviews business proposals, enters into agreements, and levies and collects taxes. The economic development administration committee creates the tribe's overall economic development plans.

Government as Employer. Approximately 200 tribal members are employed by the tribe through various programs, enterprises, and administrative offices.

Economic Development Projects. In addition to the services offered by the Paradise Casino, the tribe owns various service enterprises: the Pipa Market, a small grocery store on the reservation, and Hub Liquors, a small convenience store in the Winterhaven township, as well as several RV parks and a parking lot near the U.S.-Mexico border just outside the port of entry into Algodones, Baja California, Mexico. This lot's capacity is 5,000 vehicles per day during peak season.

Agriculture and Livestock. There are 700 acres of tribal and allotted lands under cultivation on the reservation, most of it irrigated under lease and farmed by the lessee, generating considerable income for the tribe's members.

Gaming. Gaming began in 1974 with a 300-seat bingo hall. By Tribal Resolution 42-94, the Quechan Tribe authorized reservation gaming and developed the Paradise Casino on reservation lands in Arizona. The Paradise Casino opened for business on August 5, 1996. In 2000, the tribe developed additional gaming space on reservation lands in California, adjacent to the existing Paradise Casino. This Class II and III casino boasts 750 slots and gaming tables, restaurants, bars, and live entertainment. The casino spurred much of the economic growth for the reservation, and construction industries now employ a number of community members.

**Fort Yuma-Quechan Tribe
    Reservation
Federal reservation**
Quechan
**Quechan Imperial County,
California, and Yuma County,
Arizona**

Fort Yuma-Quechan Tribe
P.O. Box 1899
Yuma, AZ 85366
    760-572-0213
    760-572-2102 Fax
    indianaffairs.state.az.us

Total area
43,960.84 acres *(BIA, 2004)*
42,059.38 acres *(CA)*
1,901.46 acres *(AZ)*

Allotted lands
8,124.00 acres *(CA)*

Population *2000 census*
2,376

Tribal enrollment *(BIA, 2001)*
2,668

Total Labor Force *2000 census*
731

High school graduate or higher
2000 census
58.3%

Bachelor's degree or higher
2000 census
2.7%

Unemployment rate *2000 census*
19.70%

Per capita income
$8,402

Fort Yuma

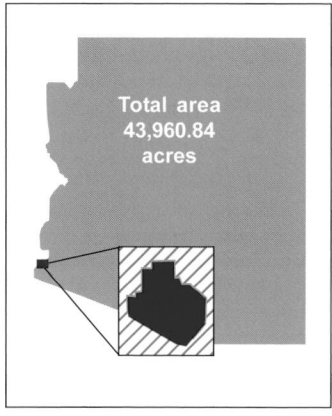

Total area
43,960.84
acres

Tourism and Recreation. The tribe operates four trailer and RV parks to serve "snowbirds" who escape to the area from colder climates every year from November through March. Other nearby attractions include the California dunes, Yuma's historic areas, golf courses, night spots, and shopping at San Luis, a port-of-entry community for Mexico. Fishing, water skiing, and swimming at lakes along the Colorado River are seasonally available. The tribe's fish and game department issues fishing licenses. The Fort Yuma Quechan Museum displays cultural artifacts and photographs of the tribe and has a gift shop attached to it where tourists can buy authentic handmade Native arts and crafts.

INFRASTRUCTURE
The southern region of the reservation is bisected by Interstate 8, providing ready access to San Diego, California. Interstate 8 connects with Interstate 10 to the east in Arizona, which runs northwest to Phoenix and southeast to Tucson. The reservation is also bisected by the Union Pacific Railroad.

Electricity. The Imperial Irrigation District provides electrcity.

Fuel. Natural gas is supplied by Ferrellgas of Yuma.

Water Supply. The Quechan Utility Company provides water and refuse collection services to reservation households.

COMMUNITY FACILITIES AND SERVICES
The tribe's community center has an Olympic-size swimming pool and a softball field. The tribe is currently developing a new education complex, a campus where a variety of education-related tribal programs will be located, including Head Start, Johnson-O'Malley, higher education, adult job training, and daycare facilities.

Housing. According to the U.S. Census, there are 977 housing units on the Quechan Reservation. Since that year the Quechan Housing Authority added 45 new mutual-help and low-rental homes.

Education. Students from the reservation attend elementary, middle, and high schools within the San Pasqual Valley Unified School District, in Winterhaven, California.

Health Care. The Indian Health Service's Fort Yuma Service Unit is located on the reservation, providing hospital and field services. The 127-bed hospital is JCAHO-accredited. It has an outpatient clinic that can support approximately 25,000 out-patient visits per year. Surgical and other medical emergencies requiring intensive medical attention are referred to Yuma Regional Medical Center or the Phoenix Indian Medical Center. Community health nursing, project engineering sanitation services, mental health education, and a dental health program are available at the service unit on the reservation.

G ila River

Gila River Reservation
Federal reservation
Pima and Maricopa
Pinal and Maricopa counties,
Arizona

Gila River Pima-Maricopa
Indian Community
P.O. Box 97
Sacaton, AZ 85247

520-562-6000
520-562-6010 Fax
gric.nsn.us

LOCATION AND LAND STATUS
The 373,000+ acres (approx. 600 square miles) that comprise the Gila River Indian Community are located in south-central Arizona, south of Phoenix. Gently sloping hills, freestanding buttes, and mountain ranges, make up the surrounding terrain bordering the southern Phoenix suburbs of Tempe, Mesa, Gilbert, Coolidge, and Casa Grande. The reservation's desert topography varies in elevation from 935 to 1,450 feet, with irrigated properties between 1,000 and 1,500 feet above sea level. The Gila River Indian Reservation was established by Executive Order on February 28, 1859, and by executive orders between 1876 and 1915 in Maricopa and Pinal counties.

PHYSICAL DESCRIPTION
Although the reservation topography varies greatly, the elevation at Sacaton, the tribal headquarters, is 1,170 feet above sea level.

CLIMATE
High temperatures at Sacaton average almost 86ºF. Low temperatures average a moderate 53ºF. The area receives almost eight inches of precipitation annually.

CULTURE AND HISTORY
The Pimas are believed to have descended from a prehistoric people called Hohokam who lived in southern Arizona prior to 8000 BC. The once-thriving Hohokams developed extensive irrigation systems for their crops throughout the Gila and Salt River valleys, but they were reduced to small villages by the late 1600s, the time of European contact.

The Pimas identify themselves as Akimel O'odham, "people of the river," in recognition of the Gila River's life-giving presence in their territorial homeland. The migratory Maricopas, or Pee Posh ("the people"), arrived from the southern Colorado River area and became allies with the agricultural Akimel O'odhams, who taught them irrigation practices and farming.

The Maricopas also relied on water from the Gila River for agriculture. In the nineteenth century, when settlers diverted the entire flow of the Gila River for their own lands, the Pima and Maricopa Indians confederated to fight the encroachment. By 1859, a reservation was established by an act of Congress. From their earliest interactions, the two tribes agreed that they would follow their own traditions, but they would be governed by a single tribal council. Thus it remains today. Since the late 1990s, agricultural, industrial, and recreational economic development projects have allowed the tribes to move from federal dependence to increasing self-reliance and prosperity.

GOVERNMENT
The Gila River Indian Community (GRIC) Council, consisting of a governor, a lieutenant governor, and 17 elected council members, serve three-year terms of office. The community voted on and adopted a constitution and bylaws in 1939, under the Indian Reorganization Act of June 15, 1934. The Sacaton tribal headquarters serves residents throughout the seven community districts.

The tribes, under PL-638, contract with the BIA to administer key programs and services. The tribes have their own judicial system housed inside a justice complex. They have a chief judge, two associate judges, two children's court judges, and a judge pro-tempore. In 2001,local city fire departments provided the community fire protection with a total of 68 fire fighters, divided among three stations. The BIA Police Department has 57 officers at two police stations, and there are 76 licensed, professional emergency medical staff stationed at three locations.

A goal of the GRIC leadership is to guide the community's economic development, and to use revenues to provide effective community service programs. The tribal economic development department is charged with providing adequate resources to accomplish this mission. Hailed as a model for Indian Country, the GRIC Economic Development Department has innovated development strategies that not only have increased the tribe's economic viability, but have positively impacted the greater Phoenix metropolitan area's economic health as well.

To strengthen the role young people have within the community, a youth council has been established as well as partnerships with programs such as The Close Up Foundation. The goal is to involve middle and high school students in the tribal governmental process, and to encourage personal growth and build effective student leaders. The public relations office oversees the marketing of all tribal amenities, and the department of environmental quality ensures ongoing, ecologically sound conservation and preservation policies. The natural resources committee reviews all land-use actions, and the office of real estate services-real property executes administrative duties associated with land acquisition and trust status. A grants coordinator is a member of the tribal operations staff.

ECONOMY
Agriculture continues to play an important economic role for the Gila River Indian Community. Increasing revenues from casinos and other enterprises have permitted the tribe to diversify and reinvest in the community to provide for many social programs, recreational facilities, and cultural projects.

Government as Employer. In 2004, it was estimated that as many as 2,000 people work for the tribal government, via its various enterprises, programs, and services.

Economic Development Projects. The tribe owns several enterprises, including: Gila River Gaming Enterprises, Lone Butte Industrial Corporation (in Chandler, Arizona), Gila River Health Care Corporation, Gila River Farms, Gila River Arts and Crafts Center, Gila River Telecommunications, Gila River Displays, and the Whirlwind Golf Club. There are also some privately owned tribal initiatives operating in the area, including: the Firebird International Raceway and Prismsoft, an information technology provider operating in Glendale, Arizona. Other major employers in the area include: Honeywell, John Deere, Pimalco (Alcoa), and United Metro (Kiewit). Current information regarding the community's economic development initiatives is available from the Gila River Indian Community Economic Development Department.

The community's 25-year master development plan projected the development of 48,000 acres of reservation land with sports complexes, industry, office buildings, a cargo airport with related warehousing and light industry, agriculture, and a floodway-greenbelt corridor. These goals were almost all realized in 2004. So notable are the tribe's accomplishments, *The Washington Post* has published stories about the casino, resort, restaurants, and its golf courses being the largest in the greater Phoenix area in terms of geography and membership.

Agriculture and Livestock. Agriculture continues to play an important economic role for the Gila River reservation. Even schoolchildren are introduced to the importance of agriculture in everyday life.

The tribe established Gila River Farms and a farm board to oversee operations in 1968. GRIC owns and operates a chemical fertilizer plant, a cotton gin, and grain storage facilities. Crops grown on the community's 15,000 acres include cotton, wheat, millet, alfalfa, barley, melons, pistachios, citrus, and vegetables. Olives, hand-picked for worldwide distribution, are grown on 500 acres. Independent farms lease and cultivate 22,000 acres of similar crops on the reservation for a total value in excess of $25 million.

Gaming. The Gila River Indian Community signed a gaming compact with the State of Arizona in 1993. Wild Horse Pass, Vee Quiva, and Lone Butte are the three gaming facilities that comprise the Gila River casinos.

Named for the herds of wild horses that still roam the buttes and mesas surrounding the greater Phoenix metropolitan area, Wild Horse Pass Casino is Arizona's largest casino (197,410 square feet). It is located just off I-10 on Maricopa Road, south of Chandler. It features 750 slot machines, a 50-table live poker room, keno, 30 blackjack tables, craps, a 1,500-seat bingo hall, as well as a restaurant with a buffet, two delis, and a gift shop.

West of Phoenix, Vee Quiva Casino, a 69,000-square-foot facility, features nearly 500 slot machines (both classic reel machines and video), video keno, 10 poker tables, 6 blackjack tables, a 500-seat bingo hall, and the Santa Cruz Restaurant. There is also a small deli in the complex and a gift shop. "Vee Quiva" are O'odham and Pee Posh words meaning "Mountain West."

Lone Butte Casino, the community's newest gaming facility, is a 30,000-square-foot facility, featuring live-dealer blackjack, 450 classic reel and video slots, video keno, and video poker. Together these casinos employ nearly 2,000 people, 60 percent of whom are tribal members. Revenues are returned to the community for programs that benefit community members, while stimulating the economy of the entire Phoenix area.

Fisheries. The GRIC owns and operates Pisces Aquaculture, a fish farm. Twenty acres are devoted to breeding ponds where catfish, bass, tilapia, shrimp, and koi are raised for domestic and foreign markets.

Construction. In 1969, GRIC was the only Indian tribe to be awarded a grant to participate in the HUD Model Cities program. Recent construction projects completed include the elderly-nutrition building and a new youth home. The juvenile detention center, children's court, tribal ranger program, irrigation rehabilitation program, and contracts and grants office are additional programs in operation. Thirty HUD housing units were built in the late 1990s. With economic initiatives taking center stage, the reservation's construction industry is burgeoning in the new millennium.

Industrial Parks. The community currently operates three industrial parks that are home to 36 local and national companies, with more than 1,477 acres available for light or heavy industries or agribusinesses.

Lone Butte Industrial Park, a totally community-owned enterprise, is managed and operated by the Lone Butte Industrial Development Corporation. The park, nationally acclaimed as one of the most successful industrial parks in the United States, consists of 720 acres which are subdivided into lots ranging in size from 5 to 40 acres. The community council appoints its board of directors. Located northeast of the Maricopa Road and I-10 interchange, freight can be shipped and delivered by truck or rail. In 2004, the park was approximately 65 percent developed, with 45 tenants who employed approximately 2,500 people.

San Tan Industrial Park is located on State Highway 87, south of Chandler, Arizona. It, too, is operated by a board of directors appointed by the community council. San Tan, with over 150 acres of developable land, is easily accessed via I-10 and the greater Phoenix area.

Blackwater Industrial Park is located at the far eastern end of the community, two miles north of Highway 87 near Coolidge, Arizona. This park has over 260 acres available for business development with access to the Union Pacific Railroad.

Wild Horse Pass Business Park is a 500-acre build-to-suit business community located adjacent to I-10 and the Phoenix Sky Harbor International Airport. Featuring ready-for-development infrastructure and redundant fiber optics, all utilities are available to prospective entrepreneurs. Various financial incentives are offered to potential business owners. In 2004 the list of tenants

Gila River

Total area *(BIA, 2004)*
371,822.63 acres
88,637.78 acres *(Maricopa county)*
283,184.85 acres *(Pinal county)*

Tribally owned lands *(BIA, 2004)*
274,319.48 acres

Allotted lands *(BIA, 2004)*
97,500.17 acres

Government site *(BIA, 2004)*
2.98 acres

Population *2000 census*
11,257

Population *(Tribal source, 2002)*
14,000

Tribal enrollment *(BIA, 2001)*
20,479

Total labor force
2000 census
3,247

High school graduate or higher
2000 census
52.4%

Bachelor's degree or higher
2000 census
1.6%

Unemployment rate
2000 census
23.87%

Per capita income
$6,133

Gila River

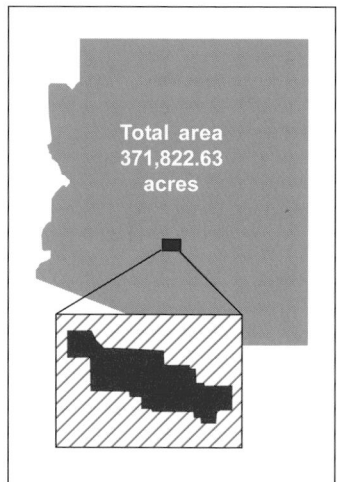

Total area 371,822.63 acres

included: Honeywell, John Deere, Home Depot, El Paso Natural Gas, and Ferrell Gas. The Wild Horse Pass Development Authority has offices in Chandler, Arizona.

Services and Retail. The community owns and operates many businesses on the reservation, including: Casa Blanca Market, Komatke Market, Sacaton Supply, Sacaton Gas Station, and Casa Blanca RV Park. There is one bank.

Kai (Pima for "seed") Restaurant, which opened in October 2002 at the Sheraton Wild Horse Pass Resort and Spa, is an upscale restaurant that serves contemporary cuisine utilizing traditional Native crops and other reservation-grown ingredients. Tribal farmers provide many products used in the recipes, including: citrus fruits such as mineolas, tangelos, tangerines, and Valencia oranges; olives and olive oil; and herbs, squash blossoms, greens, and other vegetables grown in the Gila Crossing Community School (a pre-K-8 school) garden in Laveen, Arizona. Local hunters provide venison and other meat.

The Blackwater Development Corporation leases land to store used tires hauled in from a six-county area. They are stored until taken to industrial recyclers.

Media and Communications. The community has a monthly newspaper, *The Gila River Indian News*, and access to radio and television broadcasts from Phoenix and Tucson.

Tourism and Recreation. With a relatively new tourism department (established in 2004), the Gila River Indian Community is a driving force behind the tourism industry for the Phoenix metropolitan area. The Gila River Arts and Crafts Center, located adjacent to I-10, sells one of Arizona's finest selections of Southwest Indian arts and crafts, pottery, and jewelry. A museum, coffee shop, and restaurant are available, including the Gila Heritage Park, a theme park operated by the Gila River Indian Lands. Self-guided tours walk visitors through displays of traditional Pima, Maricopa, Papago, and Apache homes. There are annual events such as the tribal fair, Mul-Chu-Tha, with its parade, an Indian rodeo, arts and crafts, Indian dances, and food in February, and the St. John's Indian Mission Festival, which attract tourists and residents alike. The first week in October, the Russell Moore Music Festival honors community member Russell "Big Chief" Moore, a musician who was popular during the country's big band era. The 440-acre Firebird Lake marina complex was developed in 1972. In 1983, the tribal government and the Marina Corporation subleased the entire Firebird Lake marina complex to a group known as the Firebird International RacePark, featuring an outdoor amphitheater, Compton Terrace. The raceway offers year-round speedboat and drag strip racing, and the Bondurant Professional School of Driving. Three 18-hole championship golf courses at The Whirlwind Golf Club (two are managed by Troon Golf) highlight the local landscape, with saguaros, palo verde, mesquite, and cottonwood trees throughout the grounds. Each hole of the course is represented by a different "whirlwind," a classic basket-weaving design. The courses are home to PGA's Buy.com Golf Tournament which brings in thousands of golf fans from around the globe every year. As companion to the tribe's 500-room Sheraton Wild Horse Pass Resort and Spa, the golf courses complement other luxury amenities, such as the 17,500-square-foot Aji Spa, the rustic 300-acre Koli Equestrian Center, and the 8,500-square-foot clubhouse. Each room at Wild Horse Pass Resort is culturally themed. Internal terraces overlook a three-story cascading waterfall; outside, there are three pools with waterfalls, and bridges and a river walk connect guests to restaurants, a poolside bar and grill, and scenic vistas beyond resort boundaries.

The Casa Grande Ruins National Monument, a four-story pueblo built by the Hohokam Indians in the thirteenth century, is just a few miles south and west of the reservation. The Gila River Indian Arts and Crafts Center and Heritage Museum, located along I-10 at the Casa Grande exit, has a fine selection of Southwest Indian arts and crafts. The center, which GRIC incorporated in 1970, features a restaurant and coffee shop that serve authentic Indian food. The family-oriented educational experience includes self-guided tours and options for groups by prior arrangement. Basket- and pottery-making demonstrations, Indian dance groups, and meeting rooms for business, parties, weddings, and other social events are also available.

The HuHuGam Heritage Center, a nonprofit cultural resource center housing archaeological findings, artifact collections, and museum exhibitions, opened in 2004. The center is an architectural masterpiece featuring an ethnobotanical garden, multipurpose rooms, community kitchen, historical and legal libraries and archives, a viewing courtyard, and a ball court/amphitheater in the ancient tradition.

INFRASTRUCTURE

Transportation. Memorial Airfield, a tribally owned commercial and private aircraft facility, is located in the community's north central land-use area. The U.S. Department of War built the 1,350-acre airfield during World War II as an auxiliary airfield to Williams Air Force Base. The U.S. Air Force returned the airfield to the tribe and allotted landowners in 1964. Florence, Casa Grande, Coolidge, and Chandler airports and the Phoenix Sky Harbor International Airport are close to the reservation. The Federal Aviation Administration provided funding to the community to develop an airport master plan.

Interstate 10 runs north-south through the reservation, intersecting with Phoenix to the north and with Interstate 8 approximately 20 miles south.

Electricity. Electricity is provided on the reservation (and statewide) by Arizona Public Service. Electricity is also available from the Salt River Project and the San Carlos Irrigation Project. Natural gas is provided by Southwest Gas Corporation.

Water Supply. Water and sewer services are provided by the GRIC Department of Public Works.

Telecommunications. Gila River Telecommunications, a state-of-the-art telephone and telecommunications service, provides telephone, Internet, high-speed data capabilities, and wireless technologies. In 2003, Gila River Telecommunications was presented with the 2003 National Technologies Award for Outstanding Leadership and Achievement for Native Businesses. The National Indian Business Association presented the award at the 11th Annual Conference and Trade Show in Crystal City, Virginia.

Housing. The University of Arizona's School of Architecture teamed up with the Gila District 6 Housing Committee to teach building methods that hold to traditional cultural preferences. The resulting rammed-earth structures feature low initial construction costs and low lifelong maintenance and operating costs. They are in high demand on the reservation. In 2004, the tribes were considering the possibility of acquiring additional lands for housing.

COMMUNITY FACILITIES AND SERVICES

Eight community centers, one museum, two youth shelters, five gymnasiums, and eight parks are available in the Gila River Indian Community.

Finished in July 2001, Keli Akimel ("Old Man River") recreation center features baseball fields, a sand volleyball court, a playground for children, and a small skateboard facility. The facility was constructed in partnership with the Phoenix Suns, who invested $1.4 million. The community also created two Boys & Girls Clubs in 2001, becoming the first tribe in Arizona to promote the health, leadership, and education of its young people in this way. The Sacaton Club is home to an Intel Computer Clubhouse that provides safe and educational after-school activities with adult mentors. The club facility includes a gym, a kitchen, and conference rooms. Valley National Bank has a local office.

Public Safety. The Gila River Fire Department had grown from a single volunteer unit in 1993, to a wide-ranging life safety agency operating with nearly 80 fire fighters at three stations. The fire department provides fire prevention education, emergency medical care and rescue services, and hazardous materials management. GRIC created the first Native American Fire Fighters Apprenticeship Program in the United States, preparing Indian young people for careers in firefighting services.

The Gila River Police Department has over 100 sworn police officers and civilian employees providing law enforcement services to a 600-square-mile area. It supports a citizen police academy, a program that introduces community youth to various units such as the special response team, K-9 Unit, investigations, and D.A.R.E. programs.

Education. A Head Start program and six elementary/junior high schools serve schoolchildren on the reservation. The Gila Crossing Community School, formerly a BIA school, became a grant-funded school operated by the community in 1995. Located approximately four miles from the town of Laveen, Arizona, the facility serves students in preschool through sixth grades. The school

received a state charter in 2002. Nearly $6 million annually goes to aid high school students entering college, vocational schools, or certificated programs.

Health Care. Health care is provided by Indian Health Services, Sacaton Service Unit, Phoenix Service Unit, and the community's health services branch. HuHuKam Memorial Hospital, managed by a tribal corporation in Sacaton, provides 20 beds for inpatient care, and for outpatient services such as diabetes prevention education and treatment, high blood pressure screenings and exercise, and support programs for the elderly. An 81-bed nursing home is available. Another outpatient clinic and dental services are available at the Phoenix medical center. There is an active cancer survivors group at the reservation.

ENVIRONMENTAL CONCERNS
A hazardous waste dump consisting of over 11,000 tons of tires were piled three stories high on Gila River Reservation land leased to tire recycling companies for temporary storage. In August 1998, an arsonist set the huge piles on fire, resulting in the evacuation of area homes. Black smoke smoldered from the mounds for months afterward while the tribe negotiated with tire recyclers who had been remiss in hauling them away, and with Maricopa County officials and officials from five other counties who used the dump-site, over responsibility for cleanup. Airborne contamination was obvious and visible; soil contamination of petroleum-based by-products was suspected.

Honoring Nations Honoree 2002

Akimel O'odham/Pee-Posh Youth Council Gila River Indian Community

Chartered under the laws of the Gila River Indian Community, the Akimel O'odham/Pee-Posh Youth Council gives youth a formal voice in tribal governance and prepares the next generation of leadership. Comprised of twenty young leaders between the ages of fourteen and twenty-one, who are elected by their peers to serve two-year terms, the Youth Council advises the Tribal Government on a diverse range of issues including youth delinquency, substance abuse, and teen pregnancy. In addition, the Youth Council engages tribal youth in a variety of initiatives that enhance understanding of and participation in tribal public service.

Of the nearly 16,985 tribal citizens in the Gila River Indian Community, half are under the age of eighteen. Like Indian youth elsewhere, Gila River youth are challenged by a host of problems. Gang violence, drug and alcohol abuse, and teen pregnancy are particularly acute on the 372,000-acre reservation, which borders the cities of Tempe, Phoenix, Mesa, and Chandler. Until the late 1980s, however, Gila River youth had little or no say in crafting policy responses to these and other matters affecting their population. In fact, many youth were disillusioned with or simply didn't understand their tribal government. This was the result, in part, of the government's own attitude about youth and their role in the Community. As one leader acknowledged, "the tribal government has always focused on the elders, but youth and their issues were historically overlooked."

Frustrated by their lack of power and influence in Community affairs, several Gila River youth organized the Akimel O'odham/Pee-Posh Youth Council (Youth Council) in 1987. Formed as a small, grassroots organization, the Youth Council sought to establish a voice for youth within the tribal government and to increase the level of communication and respect between adults and youth. Organizers quickly discovered, however, that the successful pursuit of these goals would require the tribal

government's involvement. Consequently, they began soliciting the support of tribal leaders, educators, and government officials. It was an effort that paid off quickly: In October 1988, the Youth Council was officially chartered under the laws of the Gila River Indian Community. The youth were granted a formal voice in tribal government.

Today, the Youth Council consists of twenty representatives between the ages of fourteen and twenty-one. Two youth represent each of the Community's seven districts and six youth represent the Gila River Indian Community at large. To become a member of the Youth Council, interested individuals must complete a rigorous and competitive nomination, application, and election process. Youth Council members serve two-year terms, which are staggered to help ensure continuity in leadership and membership. To enhance their effectiveness as representatives of the Gila River Indian Community, Youth Council members undergo substantial leadership training in public speaking, writing, teambuilding, self-esteem development, parliamentary procedures, and conflict resolution. Youth Council members also abide by a strict, self-defined and self-administered code of ethics that is intended to hold members to standards commensurate with the leadership positions that they occupy.

As elected representatives who serve the interest of their peers, Youth Council members possess significant public service responsibilities. They communicate regularly with other youths to identify and understand the myriad of issues, concerns, and challenges that children, teens, and young adults encounter. They formulate policy stances and debate them with their fellow Youth Council members at regularly scheduled meetings, and they present their ideas and policy solutions to the Community's elected leadership and other tribal government officials. In addition to these responsibilities, Youth Council members are expected to organize and participate in Community activities and

Honoring Nations Honoree 2002

Text in its entirety from: The Harvard Project On American Indian Economic Development

John F. Kennedy School of Government Harvard University

Gila River

309

Gila River

Honoring Nations Honoree 1999

Text in its entirety from:
The Harvard Project On American Indian Economic Development

John F. Kennedy School of Government
Harvard University

events. For instance, the Youth Council provides technical assistance to other youth organizations on the reservation, and its members regularly volunteer at school and social events. Moreover, members of the Youth Council participate in local, state, regional, and national conferences and seminars as presenters, moderators, and panelists on issues pertaining to youth and youth/adult relationships. Although these responsibilities are extremely time-consuming, Youth Council members embrace them with a profound sense of duty and appreciation.

Perhaps not surprisingly, the Youth Council has a long list of accomplishments spanning its fourteen years of existence. The sheer number of participants and beneficiaries is impressive. Since the Council's creation, more than three hundred youths have served on the Youth Council itself, while more than eight thousand youth and Community members have been involved in its program activities. The Youth Council has coordinated fifteen leadership conferences, conducted a series of youth leadership development seminars, represented youth in dozens of conferences, and provided substantive input on a wide range of issues to tribal decision makers.

A number of examples highlight the depth and breadth of the Youth Council's achievements. In 1993, the Youth Council spearheaded Kids Voting, a program that prepares youth for an active civic life by allowing them to "vote" on tribal election days. Remarkably, tribal leaders credit a 7 percent increase in adult voter turnout to the program, which, by design, locates the mock polls next to the real polls and, thus, encourages greater adult voting. In 1996, the Youth Council also spearheaded the development of the first Boys and Girls Club serving a Native American community in Arizona, a particularly important achievement given the high rates of delinquency on the reservation and among American Indians in Arizona generally. In 1998, the Youth Council was awarded a grant from the Close Up Foundation to develop a program that annually brings together hundreds of Native youth to explore citizens' rights and responsibilities for tribal government. In 2001, the Youth Council's continuing advocacy for a teen court met with success when the Judicial Branch of the Gila River Indian Community received a grant from the US Department of Justice to establish a teen court aimed at reducing, controlling, and preventing crime among Gila River Indian youth.

Importantly, the Akimel O'odham/Pee-Posh Youth Council is producing and grooming leaders. A testament to the quality training they receive, Youth Council members have been elected to serve on numerous national boards and commissions including, among others, the National Congress of American Indians Youth Commission, the US Department of Transportation's National Organizations for Youth Safety, and the Millennium Young People's Congress. Members have testified before Committees in the US Senate and US House of Representatives, met with policymakers to lobby on issues of importance, and attended White House functions. The fact that approximately 90 percent of former Youth Council members return to the Community to work and live after receiving their education is a powerful reminder of how important it is to involve youth in civic life. Former Youth Council members have assumed leadership positions with the Gila River Indian Community Tribal Council, Gila River Boys and Girls Clubs, Gila River Health Care Corporation, and Gila River Gaming Enterprises. In preparing youth for future roles as participants, leaders, and citizens of tribal government, the Youth Council has identified an effective way to bring about positive, permanent change within the Gila River Indian Community.

The accomplishments of the Akimel O'odham/Pee-Posh Youth Council have earned them widespread admiration and respect on and off-reservation. Three factors appear to be powerful indicators of the Youth Council's success. The first is the Community's recognition that youth can and should play a critical role in tribal governance. By encouraging and fostering youth participation in tribal government, the Youth Council has made use of a valuable and previously untapped resource. For many, the Youth Council provides compelling proof that youth can be articulate and persuasive spokespeople by informing tribal, state, and national leaders about issues affecting them, by providing guidance and feedback in policy formation, and finally, by encouraging community members to learn how they can hold elected leaders and governments accountable. The future of Indian nations to be self-governing depends upon knowledgeable, motivated, and skilled youth to assume leadership positions.

A second factor that bolsters the Youth Council's effectiveness is the seriousness with which its members and the tribal government take the Youth Council's responsibilities. In fact, the tribal government treats the Youth Council like any other tribal government program or department. Last year, for example, the Gila River Indian Community Tribal Council directed the Youth Council to justify its budget in great detail. While members of the Youth Council were frustrated that they had to spend so much time defending activities that they felt should be beyond question or reproach, they also knew that they were being held accountable as a legitimate governing institution. Similarly, members of the Youth Council take their roles and responsibilities as Community leaders seriously. Members commit to a code of ethics that strictly forbids substance use, gang participation, and inappropriate behavior (including inappropriate dress). Although violations are rare, members who break these standards are sanctioned swiftly and sternly by their peers. The code of ethics also is reinforced by a shared demand for excellence: by setting the bar high for their own participation, the Youth Council proves to its members and others that they can live exemplary lives. Adults in the Community have taken notice. The Akimel O'odham/Pee-Posh Youth Council's code of ethics already is being replicated within the Gila River Indian Community tribal government.

A third factor that undergirds the Youth Council's success is its commitment to investing in itself. These investments take many forms. For one, the Youth Council's robust, well-documented, and periodically updated by-laws show that it pays attention to its own governance. Among these by-laws are staggered election terms (only a few positions come up for election each year), an organizational attribute that many tribal governments throughout Indian Country do not enjoy. Training in culturally appropriate forms of governance is another investment the Youth Council makes. While elements of this "cultural match" are obvious-the Youth Council president calls meetings to order with a gavel made of cactus, as did historical Akimel O'odham and Pee-Posh leaders-other elements run deeper. The Youth Council's structure itself is significant: the Council's representation by district reflects the fact that district allegiances are noticeably strong in the Community. These innovations are hallmarks of good governance.

The youthfulness of Native America is one of its most striking facts. The median age of the American Indian population is twenty-two and the youth population is growing faster than any other segment of Indian society. Investments in youth development are essential. Appropriately, tribal efforts towards youth development frequently focus on at-risk youth. Such efforts, however, should not eclipse the need for tribes to invest in youth who exhibit leadership potential. Indian nations cannot afford to lose the interest of their youth, especially if they are to be successful in sustaining self-determination. Although the Akimel O'odham/Pee-Posh Youth Council was formed, in large part, to offer youth a voice in addressing at-risk youth issues, the program is geared toward empowering and training future leaders. As tribes consider how to build the next generation of leaders, the Akimel O'odham/Pee-Posh Youth Council offers an excellent model of a youth development program that recognizes and facilitates the significant role youth may play in nation building.

Lessons

Statements about the importance of tribal youth should be backed by concrete investments in their development. For example, tribal leaders can facilitate the establishment of youth councils; fund, host, and participate in youth activities and events; and encourage youth to participate in national organizations. These and other investments inspire youth to make a positive difference in the community and build up the pool of future leaders.

With appropriate training and organizational support, youth can make meaningful contributions to tribal governance. They can offer input into the issues affecting their peers, provide guidance and feedback in policy formation, and serve as effective spokespeople for the tribe.

Like tribal governments, tribal youth councils require good organization. By-laws, staggered terms, a code of ethics, election rules, and clear processes for decision making are institutional ingredients for success.

Honoring Nations Honoree 2003

Assuring Self-Determination Through an Effective Law Enforcement Program Gila River Police Department Sacaton, AZ

Honoring Nations
Honoree 2003

Text in its entirety from:
The Harvard Project On
American Indian Economic
Development

John F. Kennedy School
of Government
Harvard University

Recognizing that effective law enforcement is both an essential governmental function and an important expression of sovereignty, the Gila River Indian Community assumed responsibility for its own policing in the late 1990s. Since taking over management from the Bureau of Indian Affairs (BIA), the Gila River Police Department dramatically strengthened its capacity to enforce laws and enhanced public safety-improvements that are especially important because of the Community's proximity to a major metropolitan center. With its cadre of highly trained officers, the Gila River Police Department exemplifies the kind of efficiency and responsiveness gains possible under tribal control.

During the last decade, national studies revealed disturbing trends in criminal activity within American Indian communities. These communities are plagued by unusually high and climbing crime rates. In the late 1990s, for example, the Bureau of Justice Statistics reported that American Indians sustained a rate of violent victimization double that of African Americans and roughly two and a half times that experienced by Caucasians. Studies also reported that the most prevalent crime in Indian Country-aggravated assault-occurred at twice the rate experienced in the US generally.

Regrettably, the prevalence of crime in Indian communities did not translate to enhanced law enforcement. Indian Country is commonly under-policed; in fact, a 1997 report to the Attorney General and Secretary of the Interior represented law enforcement in Indian County as "inadequate." According to this report, the typical Indian community has only 1.3 officers for every thousand citizens. At the same time, Indian Country also struggles with jurisdictional complications. Policing is often compromised because tribal officers are not certified to respond to certain criminal incidents, including crimes committed by non-Indians on Indian lands. These inadequacies result in even more daunting statistics. In 1999, the Bureau of Justice Statistics reported that nearly 70 percent of violent victimization experienced by Indians was not committed by Indians. Studies also noted that American Indians were more likely than any other population subgroup to sustain a serious injury during a violent incident.

The Gila River Indian Community was not immune to these trends in criminal activity. In 1995, the Community discovered that dangerous crimes occurred at the rate of one crime for every forty-two individuals, and crimes of all sorts occurred at the rate of three crimes for every eight individuals. The BIA designated the Gila River Indian Community a crime "red zone" by the late 1990s.

The Community struggled against several of the factors that make policing Indian Country such a complicated matter. For one, the Community's 370,000 acre reservation is located within miles of Phoenix and is split by the I-10 corridor. As a result, the Community deals with crimes (and frequency of crimes) most rural communities rarely confront. During the 1990s, the Community's BIA law enforcement detachment was too small to patrol such a large area. Moreover, because BIA officers worked out of a central office-as opposed to establishing "beats" that divided up the large reservation-they found it difficult to respond to calls and arrive on-scene in a reasonable amount of time. Adding to these difficulties, BIA officers held only federal certification, leaving them unauthorized to police criminal activity among non-Indians. In the absence of a Memorandum of Agreement with state officers to assist the Community in handling such incidents, these non-Indian crimes were regularly ignored. Community citizens felt increasingly helpless.

Convinced that something must be done to improve safety for its citizens and the quality and responsiveness of its police services, the Gila River Indian Community decided to take over law enforcement on their reservation. So in 1998, under a PL 93-638 contract with the BIA, the Community established the Gila River Police Department (GRPD).

With full support from the Community's tribal government, the GRPD immediately and systematically began to address the limitations against which the BIA struggled. When the Community took over management in 1998, for example, the law enforcement responsibilities were shouldered by a mere fifteen officers. After an aggressive effort to increase staffing, today, the Department maintains an organization of ninety-two employees, seventy-one of whom are sworn police officers. The GRPD also initiated a structural solution to the challenge of patrolling such a large area. Rather than working from a central office, the GRPD regularly patrol beats, allowing them to respond more quickly to incidents. Under BIA management, emergency calls often took an hour or more to respond to and routine calls could take as long as a day. Now, on average, GRPD officers respond to emergency calls within nine minutes and to routine calls within thirteen minutes. The Community also invested in E911 service so that cellular 911 calls from the reservation are sent directly to their dispatch rather than being routed through Arizona's 911 system. GRPD response times are faster than most Arizona police departments.

Gila River

Honoring Nations Honoree 2003

Text in its entirety from:
The Harvard Project On American Indian Economic Development

John F. Kennedy School of Government Harvard University

The GRPD also addresses the jurisdictional challenges that constrain so many tribal and BIA police forces. In order to protect both Community citizens and the thousands of non-Indians who visit the reservation for business or recreation, the GRPD ensures that every one of its officers meets or exceeds the training and certification requirements of police officers throughout the state of Arizona. Officers hold triple certification: they work with the Gila River Law Enforcement Commission to achieve tribal officer status, with the state of Arizona to gain state peace officer certification, and with the BIA to become federally certified officers. GRPD officers are legally authorized and qualified to handle virtually every criminal incident that occurs in the Community.

Not surprisingly, the Gila River Police Department is succeeding in its law enforcement mandate. Currently, the GRPD is in the accreditation process from the Commission on Accreditation for Law Enforcement Agencies, a national organization that determines through a rigorous, on-site assessment whether individual departments meet the standards of the nation's finest policing agencies. As a testament to its effectiveness, the GRPD is exceeding the standards of surrounding communities. Statistics in 2002 showed an 8 percent decrease in criminal activities such as homicide, rape, burglary, motor vehicle theft, and armed assault from 2001. This decrease is a significant achievement at a time when many neighboring communities, including Phoenix, have seen a rise in such crimes. These successes have earned the GRPD widespread respect not only from outsiders, but most importantly, from the Community citizens themselves.

Understandably, the Gila River Indian Community makes significant demands upon the Department. The Community understands that no nation is truly sovereign unless it possesses the ability to establish and enforce its own laws. By establishing its own law enforcement agency, the Community exercises its sovereignty and in doing so, makes the reservation a safer place to live, work, and visit. Critically, the GRPD constantly strives to improve itself. While it already possesses far superior tools for law enforcement than available under BIA management, the

GRPD continues to solicit Community input on how to improve its services. Such attention to continuous quality improvement helps to solidify GRPD's effectiveness as an institution of self-governance. The tribal government requires, as well, that the GRPD stay at the cutting edge of law enforcement. The GRPD embraces this challenge and consistently complements its conventional police operations with community services. These services include community-based policing, neighborhood block watch programs, a citizen police academy, and a citizens-in-policing volunteer program. All of these programs foster better relationships between officers and Community citizens. Some programs also actively involve citizens in the crime prevention process. The GRPD believes that citizens who are familiar with the Department and its services help the Department to better serve the Community. These citizens share information with others and help to create a more knowledgeable and safety-conscious community.

Finally, it is important to the Community that the GRPD be motivated by Community values. The GRPD works actively to incorporate Akimel O'odham and Pee-Posh values into its policing work. It does this, in part, by encouraging Community citizens to consider careers within the Department. Today, 41 percent of GRPD police officer are Native, 22 percent of the sworn compliment are from the Community. In order to develop a pool of future officers from Community citizens, the GRPD established the Police Explorer Program, which provides opportunities for youth to participate in law enforcement activities and generate interest in law enforcement careers. Similarly, the Police Cadet Program hires high school students to perform part-time work within the Department. Such programs help the GRPD to positively influence youth and encourage their commitment to serving the Community through law enforcement.

As the Gila River Police Department consistently meets and exceeds the Community's expectations, it justifies the Community's push to assume management of their own law enforcement. The GRPD demonstrates that such an endeavor is an investment in Community safety, values, and sovereignty.

Honoring Nations Honoree 2003

Gila River Telecommunications, Incorporated Chandler, AZ

In 1988, the Gila River Indian Community decided that it could no longer tolerate inadequate telecommunications services. Because the regional provider was unable to offer services at a reasonable cost or within an acceptable time frame, the Community developed and launched its own company, Gila River Telecommunications, Incorporated. Now a recognized leader in Indian Country telecommunications, this tribal company has more than doubled telephone access among Community residents and facilitated the Community's dramatic economic growth by providing state-of-the-art telecommunications services to businesses on reservation lands.

In the late 1980s, fewer than one of four homes in the Gila River Indian Community had telephone service. Regrettably, this dearth of service did not distinguish the Community from many other Indian tribes. At the time, federal reports suggested that although telephone service had an overall penetration rate of 94.9 percent nationally, the rate was as low as 47 percent on tribal lands. The Gila River Indian Community, like many other Indian nations, was convinced that something had to be done to bring

telecommunications to its citizens. Conversations with the regional telecommunications provider were discouraging: the tribal government was told that installing basic telephone service for a single customer within the reservation's boundaries could cost as much as $20,000. Repeated attempts to obtain services at reasonable rates were met only with frustration.

These telecommunications deficits raised two serious concerns at Gila River. First, many reservation residents lacked the basic services necessary for handling emergency situations. Without telephones, Community residents confronted long delays in gaining assistance in critical circumstances. Second, the Community recognized that the vibrancy of its economy depended upon improved telecommunications services. Although rurally located, the Gila River Indian Community occupies prime lands bordering metropolitan Phoenix, Arizona, and contains approximately fifteen miles of Interstate 10, the primary corridor between Phoenix and Tucson. The economic development that the Community intended to pursue was possible only if it could supply sophisticated telecommunications services to both tribal and non-tribal businesses seeking to locate on the reservation.

Frustrated by the costly alternatives, the Gila River Indian Community decided to tackle the problem itself. In 1988, the Community's tribal government established Gila River Telecommunications, Incorporated (GRTI) with the goal of providing reasonably priced telephone service to over fifteen thousand reservation residents.

The challenges GRTI confronted were significant. A joint venture with a rural telephone holding company allowed the Community to obtain loans from a federal entity, the Rural Utilities Service, and from the private sector to purchase facilities previously held by the regional provider. However, most of this equipment and technology was antiquated. Non-digital switches and decaying copper cable-primary causes of poor existing service-led to frequent outages during heavy storms. Using a $17.2 million Rural Utilities Service loan, GRTI improved and expanded the network's capacity. It installed eight digital switches, replaced 342 miles of copper cable, ran 117 miles of fiber-optic cable, added two wireless transmission towers, and ran wires to previously underserved locations.

Today, GRTI offers service to thousands of customers across the reservation. It has successfully borne the costs of constructing and modernizing its facilities in order to realize its mission to provide "quality state-of-the-art service with affordable and profitable pricing to ensure customer and employee satisfaction," as it continues "to seek opportunities to meet the growing needs of the Gila River Indian Community." Having served 650 customers in 1989, it now serves 3,717. Although the Community does not yet meet the national average for residential telephone service penetration, GRTI works tirelessly to increase availability for its customer base. GRTI has also achieved impressive non-residential service penetration, providing telecommunication services to most tribal government offices and to the vast majority of businesses located within the reservation boundaries. As hoped, GRTI's telecommunications infrastructure has helped these ventures thrive. The tribal government's recently developed justice complex and Hohokam Heritage Center, tribal businesses such as the 500-room Wild Horse Pass Resort and Spa and the Firebird International Raceway, and non-tribal businesses such as the Bondurant School of High Performance Driving and the tenants of the Community's three industrial parks all rely on GRTI services. Overall, GRTI's growth rate in residential and business line access averages 10-12 percent annually, while the telecommunication industry's national average is only 4 percent.

Throughout this remarkable expansion, GRTI has been able not only to offer affordable rates, but also to expand service offerings to meet the needs of customers who require state-of-the-art telecommunications technology. In addition to basic telephone services, GRTI offers business phone systems, public pay phones, enhanced 911 service, and dial-up and DSL internet service. When the Federal Communications Commission (FCC) opened a lottery accepting bids for cellular service along the Interstate 10 corridor, GRTI submitted a bid and won. GRTI then partnered with AllTel, a company subsequently purchased by Verizon. This partnership continues to generate substantial revenue for the tribally owned company. GRTI hopes to offer web design and web hosting services in the near future.

Moreover, GRTI is competitive in the marketplace. The company has been profitable for years, and has survived and flourished in the face of competition. The company's 2002 Annual Report shows revenues of $7.1 million, expenses of $6.1 million for a $975,000 operating budget, and a non-operating income of $4 million for a net profit of $4.1 million. As a company, GRTI is valued at $32.8 million. All of this has been achieved in spite of the fact that GRTI is not the reservation's sole telecommunications provider. Indeed, GRTI's managers tend to view competi-

tion as an advantage that builds the company's potential for strong future growth. GRTI's competition for Community business with non-Indian companies has increased its technological sophistication, promoted excellence in operations and services, and positioned GRTI to begin offering services off the reservation.

GRTI's accomplishments are all the more impressive for having been realized within a socially responsible company. GRTI is committed to the well-being of the Gila River Indian Community and demonstrates this commitment through a variety of programs and services. For example, GRTI's Fresh Start Program serves Community members whose telephone service has been disconnected because of unpaid bills. Through the program, GRTI has reestablished service for over two hundred customers who have agreed to make modest monthly payments on unpaid balances. GRTI also promotes the federal Enhanced Lifeline and Link-Up Programs among Community customers. With over nine hundred enrolled Community members, the Lifeline Program provides low-income customers with various monthly service discounts while the Link-Up Program offers such customers a discount of one half their initial installation fees. Rural Telecommunications celebrated GRTI for its promotion of these federal programs within the Community. Finally, GRTI publishes a monthly newsletter announcing new programs, products, services, and sales, and sponsors events such as Diabetes Awareness Day that not only promote the health of the Community but offer residents the opportunity to meet company staff and ask questions about GRTI services.

GRTI is similarly committed to its employees. Sixty-six percent of GRTI employees, including key staff members and managers, are American Indians. GRTI considers them to be its "strongest asset," and invests substantially in their training. To this end, GRTI has developed a relationship with nearby South Mountain Community College to provide employees with training as they earn credits toward a degree. The company also provides internal cross-training to every employee, thus ensuring employees' continuing professional development through the acquisition of new skills while guaranteeing that the company's diverse skill needs can be met by more than one individual. Recognizing the importance of attracting future employees from within the Community, GRTI offers scholarships to qualified eighth graders and high school graduates and sponsors two high school juniors for the Foundation for Rural Service Youth Tour. During this four-day program, Community students travel to Washington, DC to learn firsthand about the telecommunications industry and relevant legislative processes.

Gila River Telecommunications, Inc. is a socially minded, strategically managed company that succeeds in offering its customers sophisticated telecommunications services at reasonable rates. A leader in the tribal telecommunications industry, GRTI is recognized and respected for its trailblazing efforts. GRTI has consulted with many tribes, was praised by the American Indian Report as one of the most successful tribally owned telecommunications companies in the nation, and, at the invitation of the Senate Committee on Indian Affairs in 2003, presented valuable testimony on the status of telecommunications in Indian Country. GRTI has not recommended that every tribe follow its lead. Much has changed since 1988. FCC policies and incentives have shifted, allowing other tribes to take advantage of existing telecommunications infrastructures more easily. But the remarkable successes of the GRTI, born of a bold vision, endure. Confronted with a serious challenge, the Gila River Indian Community organized a cutting edge company that remains an industry leader.

Gila River

**Honoring Nations
Honoree 2003**

Text in its entirety from:
The Harvard Project On
American Indian Economic
Development

John F. Kennedy School
of Government
Harvard University

Havasupai

Havasupai Reservation
Federal reservation
Havasupai
Coconino County, Arizona

Havasupai Tribe
P.O. Box 10
Supai, AZ 86435
928-448-2731
928-448-2551 Fax
havasupaitribe.com

Total area *(BIA, 2004)*
188,077.38 acres

Tribally-owned *(BIA, 2004)*
188,077.38 acres

Population *2000 census*
503

Tribal enrollment *(BIA, 2001)*
674

Total labor force *2000 census*
95

High school graduate or higher
2000 census
53.3%

Bachelor's degree or higher
2000 census
7.5%

Unemployment rate
2000 census
14.74%

Per capita income
$7,422

LOCATION AND LAND STATUS

The Havasupai Reservation lies on the northwestern edge of the Coconino Plateau in Havasu Canyon, southwest of Grand Canyon National Park and northeast of the Kaibab National Forest. It is located 60 miles north of Highway 66, almost in the center of the Grand Canyon National Park, and it can be reached solely by helicopter, on horseback or by foot trails. Thus, the reservation enjoys the only mule-train postal delivery in the United States. The nearest community is Peach Springs, 64 miles southwest from Hualapai Hilltop.

The reservation was established in 1880 and substantially enlarged in 1974, when Congress established a 160,000-acre reservation and designated 95,300 additional acres within the Grand Canyon National Park as a traditional-use area for the Havasupai people.

PHYSICAL DESCRIPTION

The reservation has been called "the Shangri-La of the Desert" because of its lush green riparian areas along the Colorado River and its isolation from the busy-ness of the rest of the world. Blue-green water falls dramatically over the lip of the canyon in several places, creating breathtaking, cascading natural beauty renowned the world over. Atop the Coconino Plateau, noteworthy gorges and geographic features, such as The Great Thumb, Long Mesa, and Tenderfoot Mesa, converge at the south end of the reservation. Topography on the plateau varies from rolling, gentle slopes, to escarpments of Kaibab limestone, a contributor to the greenish-blue tint of the famous falls on Havasu Creek, which runs through the village. The elevation at Supai, the tribal headquarters, is 3,210 feet above sea level. The elevation at Hualapai Hilltop is 5,200 feet.

CLIMATE

Year-round high temperatures average 77°F. Year-round low temperatures average 46°F. The average annual precipitation is only 2.1 inches; snowfall is rare.

CULTURE AND HISTORY

The Havasupais are a Yuman-speaking tribe, related by language to peoples occupying land in present-day southern Oregon, south into central Mexico. They call themselves the Havasuw 'Baaja ("People of the blue-green water"), and they are probably direct descendants of the Cohonina people who inhabited the plateau region south of the Grand Canyon around 600 AD. Centuries later, between 1050 and 1200 AD, the Havasupais left the Coconino Plateau for the safety and rich agricultural lands of Cataract Creek Canyon below, and after 1300 AD they lived in both areas.

In winter, the Havasupais hunted plentiful antelope, deer, mountain sheep, and rabbits living on the Coconino Plateau. The plateau also afforded many edible plants, pinon nuts, wild teas, mescal, and wild grasses, which the Havasupais gathered. During the months between April and September, the Havasupais harvested corn, beans, and squash in the canyon, irrigating their crops and storing food for the winter, duties shared by the entire family.

Nuclear and extended families were the basis of Havasupai social and political organization, performing all tasks needed to survive and acting as an independent economic unit. However, prior to the establishment of the reservation, some groupings of different families joined together in regional bands. Children were raised by mothers, grandmothers, and siblings. Each family eco-nomic unit was on the same level as others; there were no social classes or ranking. Prestige was accorded to an individual based upon individual merit, skill, industriousness, or other admired characteristics. Individual preferences guided the choice of a marriage partner, which was then approved by parents.

Havasupai houses reflected their lifestyle and the variation in seasons. Winter homes were well insulated, while summer homes had thatched walls and dirt-covered roofs, and were used only for sleeping. Shades built with an open-post frame and thatched roofs were especially welcoming on hot days.

The availability of animals and fauna on the Coconino Plateau were crucial to the health and existence of the Havasupais, who traded with the Mojaves, Navajos, Hopis, and Hualapais, exchanging buckskins, agricultural goods, and basketry for horses, pottery, cotton goods, jewelry, and buffalo hides. In later years, as whites began to migrate westward, the natural habitat was destroyed by cattle, mining activities, and general misuse. The encroachment of miners and cattle ranchers into Havasupai territory led to the establishment of the 518-acre reservation at the bottom of the canyon in 1880, and the tribe's economic viability was threatened as over 90 percent of their aboriginal lands were lost. From 1880 to 1939, the tribe's economic independence was completely destroyed.

Jobs became available with the BIA, with the National Park Service, and with ranchers who grazed their cattle on public or private lands. The BIA estimated that there were 80 head of cattle and 600 head of horses in 1937. The tribe also established a small herd of cattle and grazed it on lands leased from the government. The revenues from tribal cattle ranching exceeded the value of farming activities by the 1920s. By the 1940s, the tribe's seasonal migration from the canyon to the plateau had ceased, and the Havasupais cultivated more land in the canyon to offset the loss of plateau grazing and hunting lands.

In 1955, the BIA closed a local day school, setting the economy back, as it was a primary source of employment for the reservation's residents. Goods at the tribal store in the canyon were too expensive to purchase, and once again, many Havasupais relied on their private gardens for food and income. The economy improved in the 1960s due to the influx of thousands of tourists. In 1971, a land-claim struggle, partially financed by the income generated from Grand Canyon tourism, culminated in the Congressional Act of 1974 that expanded the reservation's land base; in 1975, Congress reallocated 185,000 acres of original hunting grounds back to the tribe.

The Havasupai Tribal Council became involved in another land battle along the southern and eastern boundaries of the reservation, where uranium deposits had been found. Their case was heard by the U.S. Supreme Court on the basis that the mining at Red Butte violated a Havasupai sacred site, but unfortunately the high court did not agree with the claim. These two battles have been a unifying political force leading to increased tribal participation in political issues and helping to break down the high level of mistrust between the majority of tribal members, the BIA, and the council.

The native language, Havasupai, never completely abandoned as a spoken language, has been a written language for about 20 years.

TRI-AZ-046

TRI-AZ-044

Havasupai

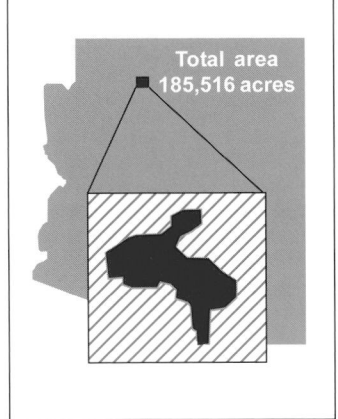
Total area
185,516 acres

TRI-AZ-055

TRI-AZ-051

TRI-AZ-084

TRI-AZ-078

TRI-AZ-081

GOVERNMENT

The tribe is governed by the seven-member Havasupai Tribal Council. The tribe, under PL-638, contracts with the BIA to administer key programs and services.

ECONOMY

The economy of the Havasupai Reservation depends largely on a combination of tourism and agriculture; therefore, the largest employer on the reservation today is the tribe itself, via its various enterprises.

Agriculture and Livestock. The reservation enjoys a long growing season and an abundant water supply; over 50 percent of the reservation is classified as range or grazing land. The tribal cattle herd generates significant tribal and personal income. Fields within the reservation are still cultivated by families or individual members with land assignments.

Economic Development Projects. The tribe operates a café, a grocery store, a museum and cultural center, and an art and silkscreen studio. The tribal Havasupai Trading Company operates a general store in the canyon.

Construction. Largely because of increased tourism, the construction industry is a growing source of income for residents.

Tourism and Recreation. The Havasupai Tribal Arts Enterprise and Tourist Enterprise employ tribal members working in the tourist industry. A tribal museum is located in the tribal arts enterprise building. Today, although visitation is limited to prevent overcrowding and damage to the delicate canyon ecosystem, more than 30,000 tourists visit the reservation to hike or ride horseback and stay at the Havasupai Lodge or the tribe's campgrounds. Annually, tourism accounts for over half of tribal income. Visitors purchase Havasupai gifts and souvenirs, in addition to paying for food and lodging.

The trail to the bottom of the canyon is 8.7 miles long and may be hiked, or traveled with the aid of rented horses and mules. It is important to limit the number of visitors to such a fragile environment. Advance reservations and a fee are required before a hike is made. Reservations at the tribal lodge should be made months in advance.

The famous blue-green water draws thousands to remote places in the canyon where four waterfalls beckon with thundering sound and unique mineral-tinted colors. Navajo Falls, located one and one-half miles from the village, is named for a Supai chief. The 100-foot Havasu Falls is another half mile downriver. Mooney Falls is the highest, most dramatic waterfall, tumbling over 200 feet to the canyon floor. Beaver Falls, farthest away from the village, is the least known. Strenuous hiking is required to visit the falls. There are good foot trails but some are very steep and slippery. There are also several caves to explore.

TRI-AZ-046 The Havasupai community as viewed from helicopter

TRI-AZ-044 By helicopter is one of three ways to get to the Havasupai community and tribal headquarters (the other two being by mule or on foot)

TRI-AZ-055 Havasupai Lodge, located in the community area at the bottom of the canyon

TRI-AZ-051 Christina Harrison, TRI field assistant, leaving the helicopter at the community lands

TRI-AZ-078 & TRI-AZ-081 Mule train bringing in supplies and mail

TRI-AZ-084 Sign on a mesa at the rim of the canyon

Havasupai

TRI-AZ-064

TRI-AZ-064 Navajo Falls-one of the famous blue-green waterfalls at Havasupai

TRI-AZ-060 Towering cliffs surrounding the community at the bottom of the canyon

TRI-AZ-058 Residential home at the bottom of the canyon at Havasupai

TRI-AZ-060

TRI-AZ-058

The tribe operates three primitive campgrounds (without flush toilet facilities) throughout the canyon. Amenities include fresh spring water, eco-friendly composting toilets, and picnic tables. Campfires are not permitted and trash must be packed out. Bathing in the creek is permitted only with biodegradable soaps and shampoos.

In January, the Havasupais celebrate Land Day. A Peach Festival is held the second weekend of August annually, and it includes a rodeo, traditional dancing, and pageantry. A community health fair is also held annually, and every autumn the tribe celebrates the Grandmother Canyon Gathering.

INFRASTRUCTURE
Helicopter service is available to and from the reservation on Fridays and Sundays. There are no external roads into the reservation. Several horse trails and foot trails lead from the reservation to inner recesses of the canyon and up to the rim of the Coconino Plateau. Mail is delivered by pack mule train, the only U.S. postal delivery service of its type in existence.

Electricity. Electricity is available through the Mohave Electric Cooperative, administered by the BIA.

Water Supply. Water and sewer services are provided by Havasupai Tribe Utilities.

COMMUNITY FACILITIES AND SERVICES
There is a broad range of community facilities, including a community center and tribal offices, a library, a senior-citizen center, a school multipurpose room, a community playing field, a basketball court, rodeo grounds, a museum and cultural center, and an art and silkscreen studio. There is a post office in the village and one church.

Public Safety. There is a volunteer fire department, and BIA provides the community with law enforcement protection on contract with the tribe.

Education. There is a Head Start program for preschool students, and Havasupai Elementary provides education to students in grades K-8. Beyond that, students must leave the reservation to attend boarding schools.

Health Care. Health care is provided by a U.S. Public Health Service clinic in the community, staffed by a physician's assistant. One full-time doctor is available for outpatient and emergency care. There are additional services in the nearby town of Peach Springs.

Hopi

Hopi Reservation
Federal reservation
Hopi, Coconino and Navajo
counties, Arizona

Hopi Reservation
  Cultural Preservation Office
P.O. Box 123
Kykotsmovi, AZ 86039
  928-734-3000
  928-734-2435 Fax
  hopi.nsn.us

LOCATION AND LAND STATUS
The Hopi Reservation is located in the high deserts of northeastern Arizona, approximately 65 miles north of Interstate 40. It is bounded on all sides by the Navajo Indian Reservation. The tribal headquarters are located in Kykotsmovi, Arizona, while the BIA agency serving the reservation is located in Keams Canyon, approximately 21 miles east of the headquarters.

By an Executive Order on December 16, 1882, the Hopi Tribe was granted approximately 2.6 million acres of land; however, they never enjoyed complete use of this allocated region. At the time of the original order, about 300 Navajos lived within the region's boundaries, and over the years, as the Navajos settled closer and closer to Hopi villages, conflicting claims were pursued in court. In 1936, as part of a stock-reduction plan to address overgrazing, the BIA divided the Hopi and Navajo reservations into 18 land-management and grazing districts, which left the Hopis with exclusive rights to only about one-fifth of the original allocation (District Six). Legal maneuvering over land rights

has continued up to the present time. In 1962, the U.S. Supreme Court ruled that, except for District Six, the two tribes had equal rights to the land. The Navajo-Hopi Land Act Settlement, passed by Congress in 1974, led to the partitioning of the land. Subsequent rulings, including that by the U.S. District Court of Arizona in 1992, continued the process of repartitioning the original allocations. As of 1994, original Hopi holdings have been reduced by more than a million acres.

The Hopi villages sit atop either First Mesa, Second Mesa, or Third Mesa, situated on or below rocky promontories extending southwest from Black Mesa. They overlook five drainages, or washes: Jeddito, Polacca, Oraibi, Dinnebito, and Moenkopi. The villages of Hanoki (Hano or Tewa), Sitsomovi (Sichomovi), and Waalpi (Walpi) sit atop First Mesa, about 11 miles west of Keams Canyon, and the community of Polacca sits below. First Mesa villages are world-renowned for their hand-coiled, white pottery. Second Mesa is home to three villages: Musungnuvi

(Mishongnovi), Supawlavi (Shipaulovi), and Songoopavi (Shongopovi). The population on Third Mesa is centered in the communities of Orayvi (Oraibi), Kiqotsmovi (Kykotsmovi), Hoatvela (Hotevilla), and Paaqavi (Bacavi). Munqapi (Moencopi) is also considered a Third Mesa village. Every village is separate and autonomous.

PHYSICAL DESCRIPTION
The northern part of this 4,000-square-mile reservation is composed of steep mesa and valley terrain, ranging from 4,700 to 7,800 feet in elevation. The southern part is characterized by wide, rolling valleys and semidesert grasslands and scrub. Mesa tops are often dotted with piñon and juniper woodlands, where deer, antelope, bobcats, badgers, coyotes, rabbits, and reptiles roam abundantly. Most of the reservation is open land used for grazing and livestock production.

CLIMATE
Temperatures have been recorded for Keams Canyon, 21 miles distant, where the average year-round high temperature is 66°F. The average year-round low temperature is 34.5°F. The semi-arid area receives just over 10 inches of precipitation annually, and 10 inches of snowfall.

CULTURE AND HISTORY
The exact origin of the Hopi people is unknown, but the Hopi people refer to their ancestors as Hisatsinom (People of Long Ago), although archaeologists refer to them as Anasazi or San Juan basket makers. By whatever name, these Native people had learned to make pottery and had developed elaborate pit houses by 500 AD. By 700 AD they were cultivating corn, beans, and cotton and settling in small settlements in a region stretching from the Grand Canyon to Toko'navi (Navajo Mountain), toward the Lukachukai Mountains near the New Mexico/Arizona border, and south to the Mogollon Rim. Small masonry villages were built between 900 and 1100 AD, but a severe, long-lasting drought forced the abandonment of 36 of the 47 mesa-top villages. Following the drought, the 11 remaining villages grew in size, and three more were developed. Thus, the modern-day Hopis have lived in the Black Mesa region of the Colorado Plateau for nearly a thousand years. The Hopi village of Old Oraibi was built at least as early as 1550, and it is considered to be one of the oldest continuously occupied cities in the United States. The Spanish visited the Hopi region several times between 1540 and the Pueblo Revolt in 1680. During the revolt, the Hopis moved many of their villages to mesa tops for defensive purposes and sheltered refugees from other pueblos. Although the Hopis adopted the use of horses, burros, domesticated sheep, and cattle from the Spanish, and new fruits and vegetables were introduced into their diet, the Spanish made no effort to control the Hopis, and they remained isolated, maintaining their own sovereignty through much of the twentieth century. At present, the Hopis live in 13 villages on three fingerlike mesas projecting south from Black Mesa and to the west along Moencopi Wash. They call their homeland Tutsqua.

Contact with whites was sporadic prior to 1848, increasing during the 1850s and 1860s as U.S. government surveyors, investigators, missionaries, and BIA employees streamed into the area. The first Hopi Indian agent was appointed in 1870, followed in 1874 by the establishment of the Hopi Indian Agency in Keams Canyon. In 1882 President Chester Arthur established the Hopi Reservation through an executive order, with 2.5 million acres. A policy of forced assimilation followed, and attempts to eradicate remaining vestiges of Hopi culture and religion accompanied legalized efforts to take their land through the allotment system. Tension between those who accepted white ways and those who resisted culminated in a split in the village of Oraibi in 1906. The Indian Reorganization Act of 1934 codified the U. S. government's obligations to protect the rights of all Native Americans, and soon thereafter the Hopis formed a tribal council to establish a single representative body with which the federal government could do business.

Hopi material culture has included a wide variety of ceramics, basketry, textiles, silver work, religious objects (including kachina dolls), and implements relating to agriculture and hunting. The Hopis continue to produce traditional textiles for trade or sale on the burgeoning Native American arts market.

The twentieth century was one of rapid cultural change for the Hopi people. In 1910, the federal government attempted to allot Hopi lands, but it succeeded only at Moenkopi before abandoning the effort. Between 1894 and 1912, schools were established near the Hopi villages, and in 1913 a government hospital was opened at Keams Canyon. The service of many Hopis in the two world wars established important contacts with the outside world. In 1950, Congress passed the Navajo-Hopi Act, and $90 million was spent to improve the reservation's infrastructure. In 1961 the secretary of the interior authorized the tribal council to lease Hopi lands; in 1966, the council allowed Peabody Coal Company to begin leasing 25,000 acres of reservation land for strip mining, which began on Black Mesa in 1970. Farming decreased noticeably during the 1960s and 1970s, while the population grew to over 7,300 by 1990. In 1970 the Hopi Cultural Center opened, as part of an effort to create more employment on the reservation. By 1980 the reservation's economy had begun to shift decisively from one based on subsistence agriculture and sheepherding to one based on wage labor. Jobs exist primarily at area coal mines, in the service industry, or connected to the tourist trade, including the production of crafts such as kachina dolls and traditional pottery. There are world-renowned silversmiths and potters among the Hopis, many of whom use centuries-old methods and clays gathered from below the Hopi mesas decorated with traditional Hopi symbolism, including eagles, parrots, roadrunners, migration patterns, pueblo style villages, rain and clouds, lightning, waves, and corn.

Central to their cultural heritage, the Hopis carefully guard tribal traditional knowledge, passed on via the interactive method of storytelling. In this way, lessons about the origin of all people (the Emergence Story) are passed on while providing lessons for how to live today. Although each story is entertaining, it is also educational, with messages passed along on many levels. Each clan of Hopi people guards its own understanding of the Emergence, respecting the privacy of each separate clan to maintain specific sacred oral traditions. Together, the Hopis practice a variety of annual dances and ceremonies serving religious and community needs; among them, the Kachina Dance, Snake Dance, and Flute Ceremony. The Hopis celebrate the summer solstice and hold seasonal ceremonies that seek to improve individual and tribal harmony with nature and with the caretaker of the earth, Maasaw. Other ceremonies seek to enhance prospects for good health and a long, happy life. Corn is central to the Hopi belief system, with rituals symbolizing humility, cooperation, respect, and stewardship of the earth. Using Katsinam, spirit messengers who send messages and teach appropriate behavior, the Hopis hold annual sings and dances to honor the presence of the Katsinam in their midst. There are between 250 and 500 Katsinam, representing various beings found throughout nature, from animals to clouds. In July, the last dance of the season serves to send the Katsinam back to their spiritual home, at the San Francisco peaks, Kisiau and Waynemai. Katsina (kachina) carvings, painted wooden figurines symbolizing the various Katsinam, are called Tihu by the Hopis. Tihu are given to young people at various critical phases of spiritual development in order to learn about the particular Katsinam it represents and the physical and spiritual energies it embodies. There is significant controversy among the people about the commercial sale of such religious figures.

Hopi

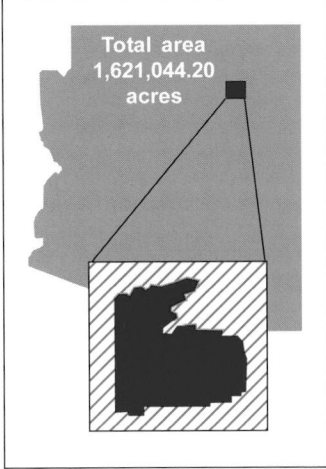

Total area 1,621,044.20 acres

Total area (BIA, 2004)
1,621,044.26 acres

Tribally owned lands (BIA, 2004)
1,621,044.26 acres
1,065,164 (Navajo county)
55,880.20 (Coconino county)

Population 2000 census
6,946

Tribal enrollment
(Tribal source, 2004)
12,053

Total labor force 2000 census
2,280

High school graduate or higher
2000 census
67.1%

Bachelor's degree or higher
2000 census
10.1%

Unemployment rate
2000 census
18.03%

Per capita income
$9,600

Hopi

The Hopi language is of the Uto-Aztecan language family, which includes those of indigenous peoples living from Idaho and northeastern California and Nevada south into central Mexico. Most of those who speak the language today consider the language to have three distinct, but mutually intelligible dialects, affiliated with each of the three mesas on which the Hopis live: First Mesa, Second Mesa, and Third Mesa. To preserve fluency in the Native language, tribal government has developed Hopi language programs and encouraged its use in schools.

GOVERNMENT

The Hopi Tribal Council was established under the Indian Reorganization Act of 1934, and the first tribal constitution was adopted December 19, 1936. The council, largely inactive for the next 15 years, was reconstituted in 1950 and finally given federal recognition in 1955. Today the council is composed of a chairman and vice-president, each serving four years, and council members serving two years. Council members come from four different districts: First Mesa, Second Mesa, Third Mesa, and the Moenkopi District. The council meets quarterly, on the first day of December, March, June, and September.

While the tribal council represents Hopi people in external matters, the 12 Hopi villages remain quasi-independent. Only one village has adopted a constitution and established a western form of government, with the remaining 11 villages varying in the degree to which they adhere to the traditional Hopi form of governance. Oraibi remains strictly traditional. Some villages have blended traditional practice with western governing policies by maintaining a village chief or leader (Kikmongwi), but also having representation on the tribal council. The council office is in Kykotsmovi. Like the U.S. government, Hopi government has an executive branch, a legislative branch, and a judicial system with many teams and departments to provide services and to oversee various functions of daily life on the reservation. The tribe, under PL-638, contracts with the BIA to administer key programs and services. The more traditional style of Hopi government is based on the divine plan of life laid out by Maasau, the Guardian of the Fourth World. In this mode of governing, each village is a complete and independent entity, wherein the village leader is also the head of all religious and nonreligious authority. The Kikmongwi controls all village and clan lands, with community consensus keeping individual authority in check. A council of hereditary clan leaders acts as advisors to the kikmongwi, interpreting religious and cultural teachings and influencing ceremonial events and the personal behavior of each clan member.

ECONOMY

The Hopi economy is based upon a diverse mixture of artistic and handcrafted endeavors that depend upon the tourism market, the cattle industry, and coal mining. The largest employers on the Hopi Reservation are the Hopi Tribal Government, schools, and Indian Health Service. Private and informal sector economic activities account for over 54 percent of employment, and they include service stations, restaurants, tourism, arts and crafts, livestock production, and construction. A growing number of Hopis go onto higher education and professional careers away from the reservation. The impact of modern education and economics has strained the traditional Hopi way of life. A man with a full-time job has little time left over to tend to his fields or take part in the yearlong religious ceremonies. Yet the fields remain and ceremonies continue.

Government as Employer. Federally funded programs of the BIA, Indian Health Service, and the Hopi Tribal Government provide approximately 46 percent of all employment among tribal members.

Economic Development Projects. The tribe has a number of ongoing projects, including construction of housing located near coal-mining operations; full development of the recently revamped Hopi Industrial Park; renovation of the Hopi Cultural Center Museum, conference room, and four craft shops; commercial development of a 30-acre tract of land at First Mesa; and construction of a small shopping mall at Bacavi Village and a motel-restaurant complex at Moenkopi Village. Private sector service stations, motels, restaurants, arts and crafts shops, and other services account for about 54 percent of all employment on the reservation. Other economic activities include cattle production, tourism, coal mining royalties, and construction. Fine Hopi overlay jewelry, hand-woven baskets, pottery, and hand-carved kachina dolls are sold to tourists.

Agriculture and Livestock. Archaeological records show that agriculture was introduced to the Southwest from Meso-america as early as 1500 BCE. Farming and gardening are acts of faith for the Hopis and essential elements of Hopi culture that serve as a religious focus as well as an economic activity. While not as vital as they once were, gardening, small-scale farms, and cattle and sheep ranches still have a significant economic impact on the reservation. Centuries-old agricultural methods include dry farming in the washes or valleys between the mesas and gardening below each village on extensive gravity-fed irrigated terraces running along the mesa walls. Winter snows and summer monsoon rains make dry farming possible. Terrace irrigation is possible because of the perennial springs at each village. Community members employ a combination of modern and traditional implements, such as tractors, discs, hoes, and digging sticks. Cutworms, coyotes, rabbits, crows, ravens, flood, drought, and the arid climate itself make farming a high-risk venture. Being a matriarchal society, farm and garden plots belong to the women of each clan. Corn, squash, melons, beans, and fruit trees are cultivated.

Construction. A considerable number of tribal members are employed within the construction industry on the reservation, either under the auspices of private developers or by the tribal government, through BIA and government grants.

Industrial Parks. The tribe operates a 200-acre industrial park in Winslow, Arizona, with complete utilities and recently expanded housing opportunities nearby.

Manufacturing. The production of Hopi kachina dolls, hand-built pottery, hand-woven baskets, and overlay jewelry provide a source of revenue for the reservation.

Mining. Since June 6, 1966, Peabody Western Coal Company has operated the Black Mesa Mine on lands leased by the Hopis. The entire mine complex, consisting of two separate but adjacent operations, the Black Mesa Mine and the Kayenta Mine, is located in the northeastern corner of Arizona, approximately 125 miles northeast of Flagstaff. The Black Mesa Preparation Plant, operated by Black Mesa Pipeline, is also located at the site. The complex covers approximately 62,753 acres of Hopi and Navajo tribal lands, of which 6,137 acres are Hopi surface ownership. The two mines produce in excess of 12 million tons of sub-bituminous coal annually, employing 750 American Indians, or 90 percent of the total available workforce. Royalties, water payments, and taxes from coal mining provide approximately 80 percent of the Hopi tribe's general operating budget. The extracted coal fuels power plants in Page, Arizona, and Laughlin, Nevada, which provide electricity for 3.5 million families.

Under federal law, the National Environmental Policy Act (NEPA) requires that a federal agency contemplating a major federal action consider the environmental impacts of that action. Thus, an Environmental Impact Statement (EIS) was completed for the Black Mesa and Kayenta mines in June 1990. Topics covered in the EIS included hydrology, climate, air quality, soils and vegetation, cultural resources, and socioeconomic impacts.

Tourism and Recreation. The Hopi villages are historic and constitute primary tourist attractions in their own right. The oldest of these is Old Oraibi Village, built around 1150. Walpi is another noted village, with high-rise buildings and breathtaking backdrops, especially at sunset. Villages are open daily, and most social dances remain open to non-Indian guests. The Hopis are well known for their beautifully crafted basketry, polychrome pottery, carved kachina figures, and jewelry, which are sold at various locations throughout the reservation. They have a rich variety of dances and ceremonies serving their religious and community needs; they are held throughout the year and attract many visitors. The best known are the Kachina Dance, the Snake Dance, and the Flute Ceremony. The Hopis also celebrate the summer solstice, hold a rodeo, and celebrate other festivals during the year.

There are approximately 15 privately owned arts-and-crafts stores on the reservation. The Hopi Cultural Center on Second Mesa and the Hopi Silvercraft Cooperative Guild are two of the reservation's main cultural attractions. The Honani Gallery, Dawa's, and Monongya Gallery are also available on the reservation. The topography surrounding Hopiland offers outdoor lovers beautiful desert landscape vistas with high mesas and buttes.

The Hopi Reservation has a cultural center and museum and the Veterans Memorial Center. Three gas stations, one laundromat, and arts-and-crafts shops are found on the reservation, many owned by tribal members. The Hopi Cultural Center Motel, atop Second Mesa, provides lodging for guests of residents and tourists. Near it are a restaurant, a museum, and a camping area. Other accommodations can be secured in Tuba City, Winslow, and Flagstaff, from 50 to 100 miles away.

INFRASTRUCTURE
Arizona State Highway 264 runs east-west through the heart of the reservation. Interstate 40 passes east-west due south of the reservation, from which State Highway 77 cuts north directly to the reservation. U.S. 89 from Flagstaff intersects Highway 264, as does U.S. 160, on the north side of the reservation.

The Turquoise Trail Highway connects Hopi villages to the Black Mesa and Kayenta mine complex, The Black Mesa and Lake Powell Railroad, an isolated 78-mile single transient, connects the mines and the Navajo Generating Station power plant near Page, Arizona. It operates nearly 24 hours a day. Polacca Airport, two miles west of the village of Polacca, has a 4,200-foot paved lighted runway; other air services are available in Holbrook, Winslow, and Flagstaff. Holbrook, about 75 miles from the reservation, has commercial train and bus service.

Electricity. The Arizona Public Service Company provides electricity to the reservation.

Fuel. Amerigas, Ikard Newsom, and Ferrell Gas provide propane services.

Water Supply. There are four subsurface aquifers on Black Mesa. Wells tapping the N-aquifer are the sole source of drinking water for Hopi villages. Water for livestock and wildlife comes from springs, stock ponds, and wells tapping shallower aquifers. The U.S. Public Health Service and the Navajo Tribal Utility Authority provide water and sewage service.

Telecommunications. Universal Telephone and Navajo Communication supply telephone service.

COMMUNITY FACILITIES AND SERVICES
The reservation has both a weekly and a biweekly newspaper. Residents can receive television and radio broadcasts from Flagstaff, Tuba City, Winslow, and Holbrook.

Education. There are six elementary schools, a junior high school, and a high school located on the reservation. There is a boarding school in Keams Canyon, and Northland Pioneer Community College serves 17 communities within Navajo County. Northern Arizona University offers community college and university courses via satellite and television. The Hopi Tribal Grants and Scholarship Program established a $10 million education endowment fund in 2001 and provides tuition assistance to approximately 450 students attending regionally accredited colleges and universities annually, while the Hopi Adult Vocational Training Program annually funds about 45 students pursuing vocational and technical training.

Health Care. The Hopi Health Care Center at Polacca and a full-service hospital in Tuba City provide health care, offering everything from emergency care to optometry and dental services. U.S. Indian Health Service contracts to furnish the tribe with mental health services, alcoholism rehabilitation, substance-abuse programs, and administrative support services.

ENVIRONMENTAL CONCERNS
Some Hopis, environmentalists, and archaeologists fear that the Hopis living on and near Black Mesa are facing forced relocation, environmental devastation, destruction of historic artifacts, and potential cultural extinction because of multinational corporations such as Peabody Western Coal Company, which pumps 4,000 acre-feet of water a year from the N-aquifer underlying the reservation. (An acre-foot equals approximately 325,000 gallons.) A controversial resolution passed by the Hopi Tribal Council in March 2002 created collaboration with Reliant Energy of Houston, Texas, to build a 1,200-megawatt coal-fired electricity generating station on Black Mesa, a project that would require at least 2,500 acre-feet of groundwater a year to operate. Tribal members in many communities opposed development of the plant, and demonstrations at tribal council headquarters ensued. On May 23, 2002, the tribal council announced a reversal of its decision and rescinded its resolution of partnership with the company after unfavorable news reports about Reliant Energy and Reliant Resources' alleged unfair business practices during California's energy crisis.

In other areas of the reservation, hundreds of sinkholes have opened up; one series runs along a fault line dissecting the length of Tonizhoni Valley, or "Beautiful Water." Hopi ranchers first noticed the holes in the late 1980s. Some holes are described as cracks in the earth's surface, approximately 30 feet deep, that weren't always present. Tribal elders, who document the drying up of seeps and springs once depended upon for fresh water, insist the holes are a new phenomenon. The holes are especially prevalent near Big Mountain, Tonizhoni Valley, Oraibi Wash, and Dinebito Wash-communities, or washes that are located in the Black Mesa area. All fall within the one-time joint use area near the Hopi Reservation. Hydrologists consulted by the Black Mesa Trust, a grassroots organization formed in 2001 by a group of concerned Hopis to research the depletion of the N-aquifer, say the holes are a serious sign of aquifer collapse. Such damage, if aquifer collapse is indeed found to be the cause of the sinkholes, is irreversible.

Cleanup and reclamation of the 400 surface acres per year that the mines' operations disturb continued into 2004. Bulldozers push dirt and rocks back into the mine pit and contour the land back to its approximate original shape. Tractors then till the slopes to prevent erosion and drill-plant more than 20 pounds of seeds per acre. The Surface Mining Control and Reclamation Act of 1977 stipulated stricter reclamation requirements, including the use of native seeds. The seed mix used at Black Mesa Mine contains 85 percent medicinally useful and/or culturally important native plants, such as green Mormon tea, banana leaf yucca, four-wing saltbush, cliff rose, gambel oak, fringed sage, Indian rice grass, needle-and-thread grass and piñon pine. This costs the company $2,000 per acre to plant. Acres replanted with rangeland grasses, such as blue grama grass, galleta grass, alkali sacaton grass and four-wing saltbush, are more economical.

After exploring viable alternatives to the Mohave plant's power-generating capabilities, which is now fueled by coal from Black Mesa and Kayenta Mines, then transported to Laughlin, Nevada, as slurry with water from the N-aquifer, the Navajo Nation Council voted to order Peabody Energy to halt pumping water from the Navajo N-aquifer, effective December 31, 2005. The order is credited to the council's inter-government relations committee, which introduced a resolution.

Honoring Nations Honoree 2000

Text in its entirety from:
The Harvard Project On American Indian Economic Development

John F. Kennedy School of Government Harvard University

Honoring Nations Honoree 2000

Two Plus Two Plus Two Program Hopi Junior/Senior High School

The Two Plus Two Plus Two college transition program is a partnership between Hopi Jr./Sr. High School, Northland Pioneer College and Northern Arizona University that enrolls senior high school students in classes offering concurrent college level credits. Upon graduation, students can earn up to 30 transferable credits to any accredited state college or university. The Program is helping Hopi students attain advanced educational degrees and, in doing so, is empowering them with technological and academic skills that they can bring back to the rural reservation.

By the late twentieth century, the increasing influence of Western society and, in particular, the transition to a wage-based economy, posed a serious threat to the time-honored traditions and heritage of Hopi society. Many Hopi citizens confronted the difficult choice of either staying geographically and culturally connected to their traditional way of life or relocating somewhere off-reservation where opportunities for education and employment were more plentiful. Even when technical and well-paying jobs were created on the reservation, they were often filled by outsiders who better met the positions' high educational and experience qualifications. While it was not universally the case, a pattern had developed in which promising Hopi students either graduated from college and did not return to the reservation, or dropped out of college and returned to the reservation with undeveloped skills. In sum, necessary educational choices and their resultant employment patterns chipped away at the fabric of Hopi culture. A critical case in point was the opening of a new Hopi health care center. The facility offered many new positions for doctors, nurses and other healthcare professionals, but most of these jobs were eventually filled by non-Hopi applicants. Indeed, the health center's staffing pattern was clear proof that more needed to be done to ensure that Hopi youth received top-notch educational and professional training, and applied that training in the community. When Hopi tribal leaders, school administrators and staff met to discuss possible programmatic solutions, they expressed several key goals: expanding opportunities for Hopi high school students to attend post-secondary schools, easing students' transition from high school to college, helping students maintain close ties to their Native culture, and making it possible for young Hopi professionals to secure positions within the Hopi community. Fortunately, with their exceptional Hopi Junior/Senior High School - which the Nation took over from BIA management in 1995 - the Hopi were institutionally capable of satisfying these goals. Perhaps more importantly, the group recognized that all of the goals could be achieved at once, through a program it developed and named Two-Plus-Two-Plus-Two.

Launched in 1997, Two-Plus-Two-Plus-Two is a college transition program that involves two years of high school, two years of post-secondary education leading to an Associate degree, and two additional years of college leading to a Bachelor degree. Organizationally, it is an alliance between Hopi Junior/Senior High School (HJSHS), Northland Pioneer College (NPC, an Arizona community college) and Northern Arizona University (NAU). Operationally, Two-Plus-Two-Plus-Two is a concurrent credit program, which means that students who are enrolled in the Program earn college credits toward an Associate or Bachelor degree while taking qualified classes at HJSHS. Credit-conferring classes are taught on-site by HJSHS faculty certified to teach at the community college level and by NPC faculty and also off-site via interactive educational television. Credits earned are transferable to any accredited state college or university.

As noted, the Program's ultimate goal is to increase the number of skilled Hopi professionals on the reservation. To reach it, Two-Plus-Two-Plus-Two takes a creative approach to the preliminary problem - keeping families together at home while simultaneously enabling youth to seek post-secondary credit that helps pave the way toward a college degree. While they are still in the familiar, supportive and traditional atmosphere of the Hopi Reservation, Two-Plus-Two-Plus-Two familiarizes students with the demands of college-level curricula through direct experience, thus increasing their skills, confidence and chances of educational success. With its focus on science and math, the Program's curriculum is appropriate to the Hopi community's needs and is economically meaningful. And, through collaboration with existing programs, such as NAU's Upward Bound program and Educational Talent Search and the University of Arizona's Health Careers Pathway Program, Two-Plus-Two-Plus-Two is able to provide Hopi students with top-notch career development services and guidance. Thus, the Program fosters a link between home and higher education that could be the difference between leaving the reservation forever or returning to vital reservation-based jobs and the Hopi way of life.

The distance learning component of the Two-Plus-Two-Plus-Two Program deserves special attention, as it is not simply a group of high school students watching a pre-taped university lecture. The Program has incorporated the latest interactive technology, including T-100 Internet capability and an advanced interactive satellite teleconference system, so that students can participate in real time with off-site classes. Remarkably, they can even raise their hands and be called on by off-site professors! Other evidence of the effective implementation of the distance learning model is that HJSHS faculty are able to teach cooperatively with the faculty of NPC and NAU. For example, while the Two-Plus-Two-Plus-Two Program's "pre-med" chemistry class is taught primarily over interactive television by a NAU professor, the HJSHS chemistry teacher conducts labs and offers tutorials.

The Program is young, but there are early indications that Two-Plus-Two-Plus-Two is successful. Since the Program's creation, there has been a growing demand for math and science courses at Hopi Junior/Senior High School, and students are clearly being prepared to excel in even the most rigorous college environments. For example, approximately 50 percent of the NAU students enrolled in the pre-med chemistry class mentioned above drop out, but in the 1999-2000 academic year, all eight of the Hopi high school students taking the class completed it successfully. In fact, a HJSHS student earned the highest grade in the class overall. Also since the inception of Two-Plus-Two-Plus-Two, a substantially increased number of Hopi Junior/Senior High School students have enrolled in college. A full 45 percent of the 2001 graduating class will attend two- or four-year institutions of higher education, with three-quarters of those accruing concurrent credit through the Two-Plus-Two-Plus-Two Program. Indeed, interest in higher education has increased so much that both NAU and NPC have made physical investments at Hopi - NAU built a distance learning center at HJSHS, and NPC built a branch building on the HJSHS campus, where it offers nursing training courses. Finally, while no firm data are yet available, it appears that increasing numbers of Hopi students are staying in college. As the Program's first graduates move toward graduation from college and university, even more conclusive indicators of the Program's success will become evident, in reservation return rates, for example, and changing staffing patterns at employment centers like the new health care facility at First Mesa.

Perhaps the most important reason for the Two-Plus-Two-Plus-Two Program's success is its institutional base at Hopi Junior/Senior High School. Once a BIA-controlled school, at which low student achievement, outdated curricula, poorly maintained facilities, and high teacher and staff turnover were the norm, HJSHS has been a fully tribally controlled school since 1995. (The school operates as a P.L. 100-297 Federal Grant School.) Recognizing the major problems caused by a lack of self-governance over education, tribal members and the tribal government worked together to achieve this autonomy and strengthen the Hopi educational system - an investment of effort that has reaped tremendous awards. Student achievement has risen, facilities have been improved dramatically and teacher turnover is low as compared not only to tribal, but also to state-funded public schools. In addition to community and government support, a significant contributing factor in this remarkable turnaround is the school's capable and goal-oriented local School Board. The five-member Board insists on hiring the best teachers, administrators and staff, and they have created a rewarding environment that promotes employee retention and innovation. In sum, because Hopi Junior/Senior High School is a strong institution - it competes with the best schools found anywhere - it is capable of initiating, supervising and following through on bold plans for change, such as the Two-Plus-Two-Plus-Two-Program.

A specific example of this point is the financial stability that HJSHS enjoys, which helps ensure the sustainability of Two-Plus-Two-Plus-Two. Under BIA management, the high school operated with budget deficits; since the Hopi Nation assumed control, the school has maintained fiscal health, without any significant increases in federal funding. This financial security means that HJSHS is able to pay tuition and fees for university courses that the Two-Plus-Two-Plus-Two Program participants enroll in, which is a substantial incentive both to participate in the Program and to stay in college.

The Two-Plus-Two-Plus-Two Program is remarkable for its ambitious and creative approach to addressing specific educational challenges at the Hopi Nation. When faced with a real educational, demographic and economic crisis, tribal leaders were intent on not giving in to the forces that made it difficult for young tribal members to seek higher education and, if they did so, to be comfortable returning to the reservation. Instead, Hopi's leaders made a commitment to enrich, strengthen and encourage Hopi youth to fulfill their educational aspirations, with the understanding that investing in their children's education was also an investment in the Nation's economy, social development and ability to self-govern. They created a program that encourages and prepares greater numbers of Hopi high school students to pursue college, while also making it possible for those students to spend less time away from home. The Two-Plus-Two-Plus-Two Program already has been a major contributing force behind the positive change in secondary and post-secondary achievement among Hopi youth. By all indications, the Program also will accomplish its most lofty goal: inspiring students to attain educational excellence while remaining active participants in their culture.

Lessons:
· Tribes that assert control over their educational systems have the independence and flexibility to create innovative programs that are appropriate for meeting their communities' cultural and economic needs.

· When faced with low student achievement and high post-secondary drop out rates, tribes can increase student success by creating college transition programs. Local institutions of higher education can be effective partners in supporting and preparing Native high school students.

· Interactive distance learning can increase students' access to technically advanced subjects and even allow them to remain on the reservation while obtaining college credit.

Hopi

**Honoring Nations
Honoree 2000**

**Text in its entirety from:
The Harvard Project On
American Indian Economic
Development**

**John F. Kennedy School
of Government
Harvard University**

Hualapai

Hualapai Indian Reservation
Federal reservation
Hualapai
Mohave, Coconino, and
Yavapai counties, Arizona

Hualapai Indian Reservation
P.O. Box 179
928-769-2216
928-769-2343 Fax
grandcanyonresort.com

Total area *(BIA, 2004)*
992,462.95 acres

Tribally-owned lands *(BIA, 2004)*
992,462.95 acres
578,180 acres *(Coconino county)*
412,982.95 acres *(Mohave county)*
1,300 acres *(Yavapai county)*

Population *2000 census*
1,353

Tribal enrollment
(Tribal source, 2004)
1,947

Total labor force *2000 census*
391

High school graduate or higher
(Tribal source, 2004)
23.4%

High school graduate or higher
2000 census
63.4%

Bachelor's degree or higher
2000 census
5.3%

Unemployment rate
(Tribal source, 2004)
40%

Unemployment rate *2000 census*
18.16%

Per capita income
$8,147

LOCATION AND LAND STATUS

The Hualapai Reservation is almost a million acres (992,463) of rugged rangelands and forest in an area of northwestern Arizona neighboring the Grand Canyon. The Hualapai tribal headquarters are located in the community of Peach Springs.

President Chester Arthur established the reservation by an Executive Order on January 4, 1883, creating an area that initially totaled 500,000 acres. In June 1911, 60 acres in the Big Sandy were added by an Executive Order. In May 1943, the Secretary of the Interior ordered odd sections previously owned by the Santa Fe Railroad to be added to the reservation. The Santa Fe Railroad deeded 6,440.68 acres in Clay Springs to the reservation in 1947. In the last seven years the tribe has acquired several more parcels of land. The tribe received a donation of 203.1 acres of land in Truckee, California, which is under fee status. The tribe also purchased two parcels of land in Arizona including 118 acres near Truxton and the 112-acre Hunt Ranch located on the western boundary of the reservation. The tribe is considering designating these two parcels as fee status rather than federal trust.

PHYSICAL DESCRIPTION

Elevations range from 2,000 to 7,000 feet above sea level, with terrain ranging from barren, grassy plains and plateaus to densely wooded regions.

CLIMATE

Temperatures range from 21°F in January to 91°F in July. Annual rainfall is 10 to 11 inches, and average snowfall is 16 to 17 inches. Precipitation ranges from 10 to 25 inches per year. Diverse geography accounts for the amount of precipitation, with the higher pine-clad elevations receiving from 15 to 20 inches annually.

CULTURE AND HISTORY

The Hualapai Indians (Hwal'bay means "people of the tall pine") are descendants of a group known archaeologically as the Cerbat, and together with the Havasupai and the Yavapai, they comprise the Upland Yuman language group of the Pai branch of the Yuman linguistic family. The Hualapais and the Havasupais have occupied northwest central Arizona for thousands of years, with aboriginal territory spanning over five million acres along the middle corridor of the Colorado River and Grand Canyon area. The people refer to this region as Hakataya or "the backbone of the river." The tribes subsisted primarily through hunting wild game, collecting cactus fruit, gathering roots, seeds, and berries, and cultivating gardens. Early physical remains of the Pai have been found along the Willow Beach banks near the Hoover Dam dating back as early as A.D. 600. Today, a common creation myth among the Pai peoples binds them spiritually to Spirit Mountain, or "Wikahme," along the Colorado River near Bullhead City, Arizona.

Significant numbers of white fur trappers and prospectors began entering Hualapai territory during the 1820s and dramatically increased by the late 1840s, provoking occasional attacks by the Hualapais, but mostly they were accommodated. In fact, the Hualapais soon became a cheap, reliable source of labor for the prospectors. When, in 1874, the U.S. Army forcefully removed the tribe to the Colorado River Reservation, many Hualapais died along the way. One year later most escaped the encampment and fled back to the traditional homeland. A few others fled south; thus the Paipai in Mexico are considered brothers and sisters. The miners supported the Hualapais' return two years

later from the encampment. For the miners, establishment of the reservation meant a continued source of cheap labor; for the area ranchers, the reservation's acreage freed up the majority of the tribe's ancestral lands for grazing.

During the Depression, many Hualapais were employed on the reservation through New Deal programs like the Civilian Conservation Corps. After the Corps was terminated, a number of tribal members took up cattle raising. Colorado River rafting tours began during the 1980s, providing some much-needed economic diversification.

Social and ceremonial gatherings such as powwows, festivals, and holidays remain integral parts of community life. In such settings, the Hualapai language is still extensively used, and in this way it remains a fundamental part of contemporary Hualapai culture.

GOVERNMENT

The tribe is organized under the 1934 Indian Reorganization Act. In 1938 the tribe adopted a new constitution and bylaws and established tribal membership. An elected nine-member council was devised, and the Peach Springs settlement was designated as the tribal headquarters. Tribal council members serve staggered four-year terms. In June 1970, the tribe ratified a new constitution, a document that received input from all interested tribal members during the preceding two-year period. It was amended again in 1991.

The tribe, under PL-638, contracts with the BIA to administer key programs and services. The tribal court, designated as a separate governmental entity, receives administrative and financial support from the offices and departments of the Hualapai tribe. Tribal programs include several in health, forestry, and natural resources.

BUSINESS CORPORATION

The Grand Canyon Resort Corporation (GCR), a committee of tribal and nontribal members, guides tribal business decisions. This corporation oversees tribal tourism-related endeavors.

ECONOMY

The tribal economy is based on tourism, river rafting, hunting expeditions, individual cattle ranching, and traditional and modern folk arts.

Government as Employer. The tribal government employs significant numbers of tribal members either directly (through administration and services) or indirectly (through tribally owned businesses). In the 2000 census, tribal or federal government employed 193 people on the Hualapai Reservation.

Economic Development Projects. The GCR corporation's initiatives include tourism at Grand Canyon West; Hualapai River Runners, which offers one- and two-day guided river trips; the Hualapai Lodge; River Running Restaurant; and Hualapai Wildlife conservation, which sells big-game hunting permits for Rocky Mountain bighorn sheep, trophy elk, antelope, deer, and mountain lion.

The economic, social, and governmental progress made possible by these enterprises has resulted in many community improvements, such as the construction of 200 new homes, the paving and curbing of 14 miles of streets, the installation of 300 streetlights, and improvements to the water and sewer system to provide an infrastructure for future growth.

TRI-AZ-028

TRI-AZ-001

TRI-AZ-002

TRI-AZ-030

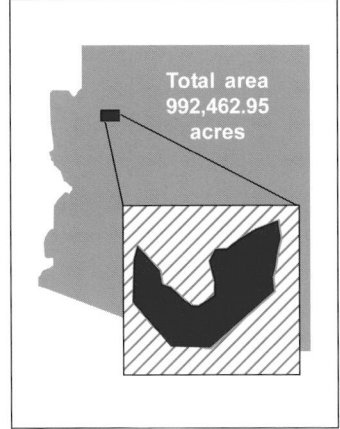

Total area
992,462.95
acres

The tribal department of planning and economic development is working on a master development plan modeled on the concept of the world banking system used by other countries. This is the first of its kind being developed in Indian Country. They are also looking at renewable energy for the tribe, whether it is solar or wind. The tribe has already received a $2-million grant for solar energy at Grand Canyon West.

Agriculture and Livestock. Cattle ranching serves as one of the primary sources of income for the Hualapai tribe.

Peach Springs, the tribal capital located 50 miles east of Kingman on Historic Route 66, owes its name to peach trees growing at springs nearby.

Tourism and Recreation. The tribe's biggest income is the tourism at Grand Canyon West, with helicopter, hummer, and ATV tours. The tribe operates a Colorado rafting enterprise that only increases in popularity; hence, the rafting operation now figures prominently in the tribe's economic picture.

Peach Springs has the only road leading into the Grand Canyon, the 21-mile scenic Diamond Creek Road. The tribe maintains the road, which is only passable in dry weather, and issues sightseeing permits for its use. Historic Route 66 also passes through Peach Springs. A rustic campground near the Colorado River is available, and there are picnic tables for day use only. Hiking on the Hualapai Reservation is also permitted. Hualapai Folk Arts features traditional tribal and modern art for sale.

The 60-room Hualapai Lodge offers amenities to tourists desiring a more comfortable stay in the area. As an alternative to the more highly developed (and congested) areas, Grand Canyon West, a tribal settlement perched 3,600 feet above the Colorado River on the canyon's rim, hosts more than 30,000 guests per month. It attracts tourists interested in big-game hunting for bighorn sheep, elk, antelope, and mountain lions, or in fly-fishing and river running. The facility is located near the Grand Wash Cliffs at the edge of the Colorado Plateau and the end of the Grand Canyon. Nontribally operated lodging is available in the nearby communities of Truxton (9 miles west), Grand Canyon Caverns (12 miles east), Seligman (38 miles west), and Kingman (50 miles west).

Just east of Peach Springs, Grand Canyon Caverns offer guided tours through multiple subterranean chambers. Lake Mead National Recreation Area lies to the west of the reservation.

Tourists are welcome to visit during several tribal events. In April the tribe holds a memorial run for those who were force-marched to La Paz in southern Arizona. In May, Route 66 Days draws many classic car buffs and others to Peach Springs. In June, tribe members hold the Sobriety Festival. In July, they celebrate their annual youth powwow. In August, they elect Miss Hualapai. Indian Day, in October, is a cultural highlight of the year.

INFRASTRUCTURE
U.S. Route 66 passes through the reservation in an east-west direction. Interstate 40 passes directly south of the reservation, also in an east-west direction. The nearest commercial airport is located in Kingman, about 50 miles away, but the reservation also has access to two 5,000-foot landing strips, one just 7 miles east of Peach Springs and the other at Grand Canyon West. Peach Springs lies along the main line of the Santa Fe Railroad and along Route 66. Diamond Creek Road, the only road into the Grand Canyon, begins at Peach Springs as well.

Recent successful economic endeavors have permitted several improvements to reservation infrastructure, including the construction of more than 300 new homes, improvements to the tribally owned and operated community water and sewer systems, and the paving of over 14 miles of town streets.

Electricity. Electricity is provided on the reservation by Mohave Electric Cooperative.

Telecommunications. Telephone services are available from Frontier Communications.

COMMUNITY FACILITIES AND SERVICES
The tribe maintains a tribal community center and an office complex in Peach Springs. Other limited facilities, include a general store, a post office, a service station, a senior citizens center, a gift shop, a gymnasium, a rodeo arena, ball fields, and a laundromat. The Hualapai Lodge, built in 1997, has a restaurant and gift shop. A family resource and training center, a multipur-

TRI-AZ-028 Open range country on Route 66, which leads to the Hualapai community and tribal headquarters

TRI-AZ-001 Hualapai Lodge

TRI-AZ-002 The 60-room Hualapai Lodge

TRI-AZ-030 The Indian Health Clinic at Hualapai

Hualapai

pose building-EMS, youth center, and a new cultural center have been or are being built using U.S. Department of Housing and Urban Development funding.

Public Safety. The 12-member Hualapai Tribal Police Department began operations in July 2002, with a community-oriented policing philosophy. The BIA provides the department with dispatch and detention services. So that tribal police can enforce tribal, state, and applicable federal laws against both Indians and non-Indians, sworn members of the department are required to meet Arizona peace officers' standards and training requirements, as well as BIA training and certification requirements. BIA also provides fire protection in cooperation with the local volunteer fire department. Construction will begin on a new juvenile center in 2005.

Education. Students travel about 40 miles to attend high school at a BIA boarding school or attend public schools in Peach Springs. Peach Springs School, serving students in grades K-12, has a student body of 300, and it is served by 48 faculty and auxiliary staff. The Hualapai Head Start Program serves preschool children three to five years of age. School buses from Seligman High School, Kingman High School, and Peach Springs Elementary School transport students to each school from Peach Springs. Mohave Community College offers classes on the reservation.

Four churches are located on the reservation, including the Hualapai Bible Mission, a Latter-Day Saints church, a Foursquare church, and an Episcopal church.

Health Care. Health care is provided by the Indian Health Service Clinic in Peach Springs. There are three medical doctors, four registered nurses, and two public health nurses on staff. Dental services are also available. Full-service medical facilities are available in Kingman. The Hualapai tribe supplies emergency and ambulance service through the Public Law 93-638 process with the Indian Health Service. Completion of a new clinic was finished in 2003, and a new dialysis center was completed in 1998.

ENVIRONMENTAL CONCERNS
A solar grant was provided by the U.S. Department of Agriculture (USDA) for Grand Canyon West to provide solar-energy electricity.

Kaibab Paiute

Kaibab Paiute
Indian Reservation
Federal reservation
Paiute
Coconino and Mohave
counties, Arizona

Kaibab-Paiute Reservation
HC 65 Box 2
Fredonia, AZ 86022
928-643-7245
928-643-7260 Fax
itcaonline.com

LOCATION AND LAND STATUS
Established by Executive Orders of June 11, 1913, and July 17, 1917, the Kaibab-Paiute Reservation consists of five villages: Kaibab, Juniper, Redhills, Steamboat, and Six-Mile. It is located in northwestern Arizona in the Kaibab Plateau Basin, just across the Utah-Arizona border from Zion National Park, 50 miles northwest of the Grand Canyon. The reservation is accessible by highway from Utah and by backcountry roads from the Kaibab Plateau. Fredonia is the tribal headquarters.

PHYSICAL DESCRIPTION
The semiarid region is surrounded by red rock country, with rolling grasslands dotted with naturally occurring springs supporting high desert vegetation. Piñon and juniper grow readily in the surrounding high country. Elevations on the reservation vary between 4,400 feet above sea level in the south along the Coconino and Mohave county lines, to 7,910 feet at Fredonia.

CLIMATE
The average year-round high temperature in Fredonia is almost 58°F. The average low temperature is 31°F. The area receives approximately 21 inches of precipitation annually, with 105 inches falling as snow.

CULTURE AND HISTORY
The Kaibab-Paiute band belongs to the larger Southern Paiute Nation, which has historically occupied the region that is now southern Utah, northern Arizona, and the Great Basin of southeastern Nevada. Their language belongs to the Numic branch of the Uto-Aztecan linguistic family. Ancestral Kaibab-Paiutes gathered grass seeds, hunted animals, and raised crops near the springs for which Pipe Spring National Monument is named for at least 1,000 years. Mormon immigrants brought cattle to the area in the 1860s, and by 1872 a fortified ranch house, which came to be called Winsor Castle, was built over the main spring, and a large cattle ranching operation was established. The isolated outpost served as a way station for people traveling across the Arizona Strip, that part of Arizona separated from the rest of the state by the Grand Canyon. The Paiutes stayed in the area, and by 1907 the Kaibab-Paiute Indian Reservation was established.

Pipe Spring and the ranch remained in private hands. In 1923, the U.S. government purchased the ranch and established it as a national monument.

By the beginning of the twentieth century, when the Southern Paiutes had lost most of their ancestral territory to the incoming Mormons, California and Nevada ranchers and the Navajos, their hunting, gathering, and farming activities became ever more restricted. They found income as laborers on area farms and ranches, as domestic workers, and by selling Native arts and crafts.

Historically the Paiutes have received minimal government attention and support in terms of educational, health, and economic needs. Between 1900 and 1940, a number of government-run schools were established at Las Vegas, Nevada, and other communities; the longest-lasting one operated for 30 years at Kaibab. When local schools were not available, Paiute children were often sent away to government boarding schools. During this time, the Paiutes suffered tragically high losses due to epidemic tuberculosis, frequent pneumonia, whooping cough, influenza, and outbreaks of measles. Not until the 1930s did the Paiute birth rate begin to exceed their death rate. Most of the Southern Paiute tribes were formally organized under the Indian Reorganization Act of 1934, which was intended to give Indian tribes increased autonomy.

Well into the middle of the twentieth century, most Paiutes were consigned to the ranks of underemployed, unskilled rural labor, due to discrimination, inadequate educational opportunities, and the lack of an adequate resource base. In the 1960s, however, their fortunes finally began to improve somewhat. In 1965, the U.S. Indian Claims Commission awarded them over $7 million in compensation for aboriginal lands illegally taken from them. Kaibab was one of the bands that allocated a large portion of its award fund to economic and social development, which would in turn provide continuing income to the tribe and employment to its members. In 2004 almost one-half of all enrolled tribal members lived off-reservation.

GOVERNMENT

The Kaibab-Paiute tribal government consists of a chairman, a vice-chairman, a secretary, a treasurer, and three council members, each serving a three-year term. The present constitution was adopted on June 7, 1987, and was approved by the Secretary of the Interior on July 14, 1987.

The tribe, under PL-638, contracts with the BIA to administer key programs and services, with the following tribal departments available for community members: administration; housing; community health; tobacco prevention; diabetes prevention; Title III, VI, and XX programs; behavioral health; environmental department; water resource department; Southern Paiute Consortium and Cultural Resources; volunteer language program; wildlife fisheries and parks; maintenance and operations; roads; library, education, and enrollment department; BIA Law Enforcement; and courts.

ECONOMY

While farming and ranching have remained the economic mainstays of this remote region, tourism and recreation are on the rise, as well as other more controversial industries such as hazardous-waste disposal. In 1991, the Kaibab turned down a project that would have built the largest hazardous-waste incinerator in the West on their reservation.

Government as Employer. Tribal government is a major employer on the reservation.

Economic Development Projects. Most businesses on the reservation are owned and operated by the tribe, including a visitor's center at Pipe Spring National Monument, Red Cliffs Mobil, a convenience store and gas station, and an RV park and campground. Numerous land-and road-use leases also provide revenue.

The tribe built the Paiute Tribal Museum of Culture and History at Pipe Spring National Monument, an attraction that draws over 50,000 visitors a year. They are also planning a campaign to produce small-business development along Arizona Highway 389.

The tribe sought and won a grant from the U.S. Department of Agriculture for rural economic development. With the funding, the tribe plans to become a regional provider of high-speed Internet access across northwestern Arizona and southwestern Utah.

Agriculture and Livestock. The tribal agricultural program includes a tribal orchard, consisting of 1,300 fruit trees, and an agricultural irrigation system, which supports a large-scale, 250-acre farm enterprise that supplies alfalfa to area livestock owners. Many tribal members also maintain gardens on the reservation.

Gaming. A casino that the Kaibab-Paiutes built and operated along Arizona Highway 389, north of the Grand Canyon, was not successful, and it closed in September 1996, after only two years of operation.

Tourism and Recreation. In a unique partnership with the National Park Service initiated in 1998, the tribe owns and operates a tourism complex at Pipe Spring National Monument. The joint venture museum features the Zion Natural History Association Bookstore, a snack bar, and a visitor center with a gift shop. (The Pipe Spring National Monument is located entirely within the reservation boundary.) A nearby attraction, the old Mormon Fort at Pipe Spring, was built in 1870. The facility features a reenactment of Anglo settler life in the Old West. The tribe also maintains a 48-unit campground and RV park, with showers and tent sites. During Labor Day weekend, the Kaibabs sponsor a Paiute cultural fair and a Kaibab-Paiute Heritage Day Celebration.

The reservation is surrounded by historic sites and geological wonders. Steamboat Rock is on the reservation, and the North Rim of the Grand Canyon is only a few hours' drive. Cedar Breaks National Monument, Coral Pink Sand Dunes, Utah State Park, Kaibab National Forest, Lake Powell, Kanab Creek, Glen Canyon, and Lake Mead National Recreation Area are also within easy driving distance.

INFRASTRUCTURE

Arizona State Highway 389, the main route for tourist traffic between Las Vegas and Lake Powell, passes east-west directly through the reservation. U.S. 89, a major north-south route, skirts the eastern border. Commercial bus and truck lines serve Fredonia, a mile east of the reservation, while airline and train services are available at Cedar City and St. George, Utah, each about 80 miles distant. Community members have access to a 5,300-foot paved, lighted runway in Kanab, Utah, 20 miles north.

Electricity. Electricity is provided to the reservation by Garkane Power Association.

Fuel. Natural gas is supplied by Petrolane, of Kanab, Utah, and by the Utah Gas Service.

Water Supply. Water is provided by the tribal department of public works and by the town of Fredonia water department.

Telecommunications. Telephone service is made available statewide by South Central Communications.

COMMUNITY FACILITIES AND SERVICES

The tribe maintains a multipurpose building for recreational activities, a gymnasium, tribal administration, a senior citizens building, law enforcement, and judicial services.

Education. Reservation students in kindergarten through the third grade attend school in Moccasin, Arizona, while students in fourth through the twelfth grades are bused to Fredonia.

Health Care. Most medical and dental needs are provided by contract care at Indian Health Service (IHS) clinics in Kanab, Utah, and by IHS hospitals in Keams Canyon and Phoenix. The tribe also contracts with IHS for transportation to these facilities.

Kaibab Paiute

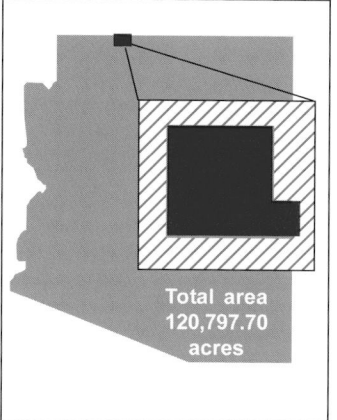

Total area
120,797.70
acres

Total area *(BIA, 2004)*
120,797.70 acres

Tribally-owned lands *(BIA, 2004)*
120,797.70 acres
13,300.11 acres *(Coconino county)*
107,497.59 acres *(Mohave county)*

Population *2000 census*
196

Tribal enrollment
(Tribal source, 2004)
270

Total labor force *2000 census*
109

High school graduate or higher
2000 census
83%

Bachelor's degree or higher
2000 census
7.1%

Unemployment rate
2000 census
9.17%

Per capita income
$7,951

Types of Lands	Arizona	New Mexico	Utah	Total Land
Navajo Nation Trust	10,158,784.82	2,795,418.26	1,223,933.96	14,178,137.04
Navajo Nation Fee	585,169.98	357,000.00	424.90	942,594.88
Individual Indian Allotment	81,963.81	671,043.50	9,741.80	762,749.11
State Lands Lease	256,905.79	126,760.10		383,665.89
BLM Leases		150,002.23		150,002.23
U.S. Forest Service Permit	174,000.00			174,000.00
Government E.O. PLO & School Tract		91,838.99	5.99	91,844.98
New Lands	345,032.00			345,032.00
Total Lands	11,601,856.40	4,192,063.08	1,234,106.65	17,028,026.13
The Navajo Nation has:	17,028,026.13 acres of land or 26,606.29 sections square miles of land or 739.06 townships of Navajo Nation lands and lease lands.			
Source: Title Section ONLA, Lands Department, Division of Natural Resources.				

LOCATION AND LAND STATUS

The Navajo Nation, comprised of 26,606 square miles, is the largest Indian reservation in the United States, both in terms of land base and tribal enrollment. The land base, comparable in size to the state of West Virginia, is located in northeast Arizona, northwest New Mexico, and southeast Utah. Window Rock, Arizona, in the southeast corner of the reservation, is the capital of the Navajo Nation. The Navajo Tribe is the only Arizona tribe not served by the Bureau of Indian Affairs' Phoenix Area Office; because of its size, the tribe has its own area office, located in Gallup, New Mexico.

The original Navajo Reservation, established pursuant to a treaty concluded on June 1, 1868, and ratified by Congress on July 25, 1868, contained 3,414,528 acres, only about 10 percent of the land the Navajos earlier owned and used. The original reservation was expanded by Executive Orders in 1878, 1880, 1882, 1884, 1900, 1901, 1905, 1907, and 1908. In 1911, lands in New Mexico were restored to the public domain. Minor revisions to the Navajo Reservation's size were made in 1912, 1913, 1914, 1915, and 1917. Executive Orders in 1917 and 1918 again expanded the reservation. In 1930 and 1931, the reservation was expanded by Congressional Acts. In 1933, Congress added 552,000 acres in Utah to the reservation, and in 1934 provided for some smaller additions. Minor changes were made to the size of the reservation in 1948, 1949, and 1958. Court decisions in 1962, 1963, and 1977 reallocated some areas of the Navajo Reservation to the Hopis.

In addition to the main Navajo Reservation, there are three satellite areas of Navajo land located in New Mexico. The Cañoncito Reservation, the present boundaries of which were established in 1960, contains 57,863 acres of trust land. The Alamo Reservation, established in 1964, contains 62,000 acres. The Ramah Reservation, established in 1931, contains 91,456 acres. Today, the total acreage of the Navajo Reservation, including the main reservation, trust lands of the Eastern Navajo, and the satellite lands of Cañoncito, Alamo, and Ramah, is 16,224,896 acres.

PHYSICAL DESCRIPTION

The landscape varies from arid deserts to alpine forests, with elevations varying from 5,500 feet to more than 10,500 feet. The elevation at Window Rock, the Navajo Nation's capitol, is 6,760 feet above sea level. Wind, water, and volcanic activity have shaped the spectacular canyons, mesas, mountains, and deserts of the Navajo Nation over millions of years. The effects of these natural forces can be seen in scenic wonders located within the Navajo Reservation, including Canyon de Chelly, Monument Valley, Shiprock, Grandfalls, the Chuska Mountains, the Rainbow Bridge, and the Painted Desert.

CLIMATE

The average year-round high temperature is 64°F. The average year-round low temperature is 32° F. The area receives almost 12 inches of precipitation annually, with 30 inches of snowfall.

CULTURE AND HISTORY

The Navajos (Ni'hookaa Diyan Diné, or "Holy Earth People" or "Lords of the Earth") have been in the Southwest since at least the year 1300 AD after migrating southward from western Canada over 1,000 years ago. During the 1600s, Navajos acquired horses and sheep from the Spaniards, along with the knowledge of working with metal and wool.

The Navajos resisted Spanish domination during the late eighteenth and nineteenth centuries, also fighting against Anglo colonization after 1846, when the Americans took over the southwestern territory once owned by Mexico. Fighting continued throughout the 1850s until 1864, when the Navajos were rounded up and forced onto the infamous "Long Walk" to Fort Sumner, New Mexico, where they were taught a sedentary, agricultural lifestyle. However, by 1868 the experiment was recognized as a failure, and a new treaty established the Navajo Reservation, allowing the people to return to a portion of their land. There they practiced a mixed subsistence economy of agriculture and herding. The discovery of oil and gas on the reservation in 1921, and the later discovery of uranium, provided the stimulus for modern economic development. Today, the people call themselves Diné, meaning "The People." They call their traditional homelands Dinetah.

Dinetah, the Navajo homeland, is defined by four sacred mountains which represent the four cardinal directions. Mount Blanca (Tsisnaasjini' or "Dawn or White Shell Mountain") is the eastern reference point, near Alamosa, Colorado. It is the tallest mountain in the Colorado Sangre de Cristo range. In the south, Mount Taylor (Tsoodzil, or "Blue Bead Mountain" or "Turquoise Mountain") rises high and majestic, north of Laguna, New Mexico. The San Francisco Peaks (Doko'oosliid, or " Abalone Shell Mountain") define the westernmost edge of Dinetah, near Flagstaff, Arizona. Mount Hesperus (Dibe Nitsaa or "Big Mountain Sheep") is the sacred mountain of the north, located in the La Plata range of the Rocky Mountains in Colorado.

The Navajo people are most closely related by language and culture to the Apache peoples of the Southwest; their language also shows a relationship to the Athabascan peoples of Alaska and Canada. Navajo religion shares many elements with the religions of nearby Pueblo peoples, and it was the Tewa Indians who first called them "Navahu," which means "the large area of cultivated land."

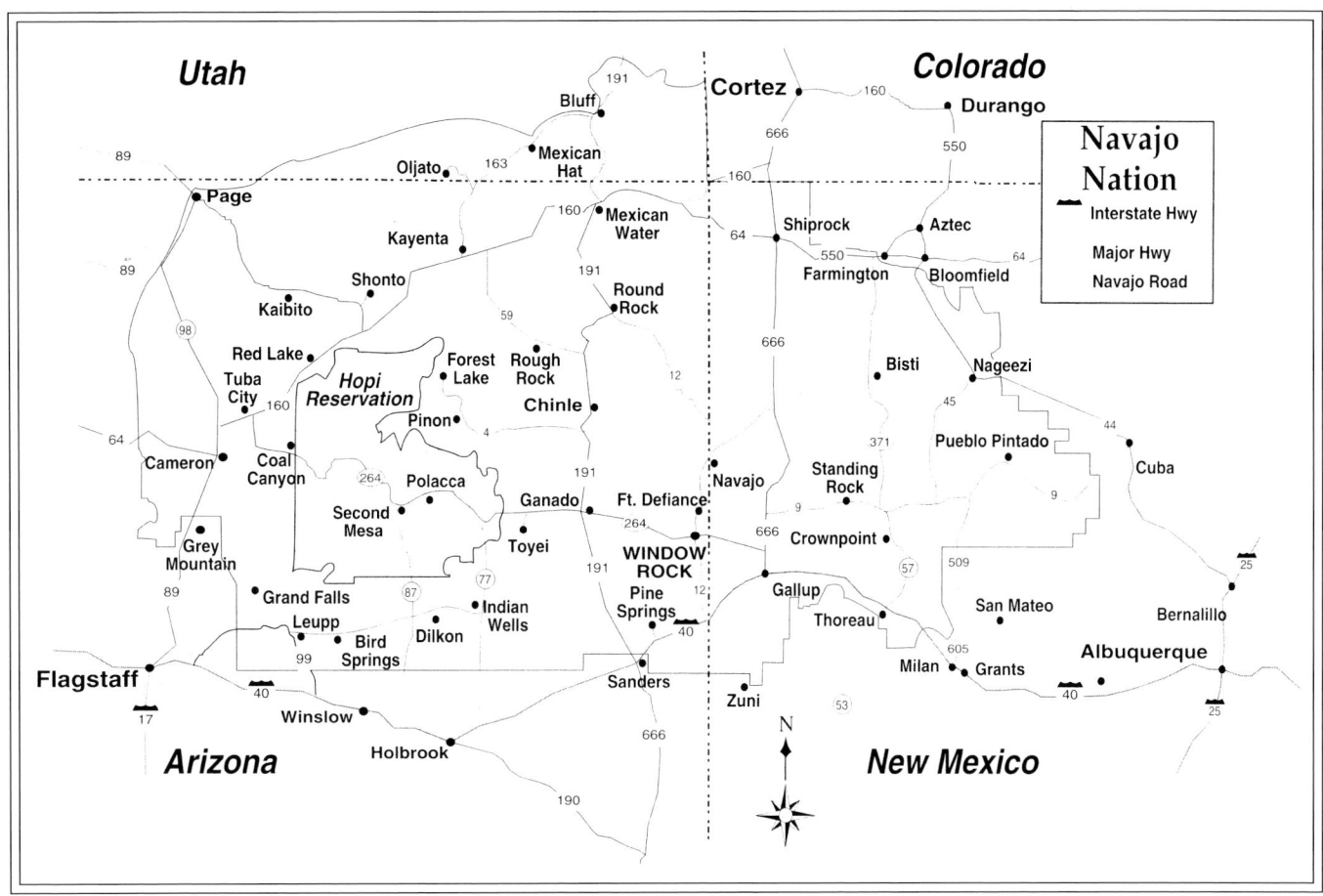

The extended kin group, made up of two or more families centered on a mother and her daughters, is an important unit of Navajo social organization. It is a cooperative unit of responsible leadership, bound together by ties of marriage and close family relationships. Women hold an important social position in the tribe. Religion and language are still at the core of Navajo culture. Ceremonial sand paintings are used in healing rituals for many types of physical, emotional, and social imbalances. About 80 percent of the Navajo people still speak their language, although the elderly are disturbed that fewer children attempt to practice and maintain it. During World War II, the Navajo language was used as a code to confuse the enemy. These "code talkers," although shrouded in secrecy at the time, have become heroes to the American people, thanks to a movie extolling their courage under fire. It was the only code never broken during World War II.

According to census 2000 data, 168,000 enrolled tribal members are living on the nation's tribal lands. The rest of the population is made up of nonmembers who live and work on the reservation. Another 80,000 Navajos reside in or near the bordering towns: Farmington, Gallup, and Grants, New Mexico; Page, Flagstaff, Winslow, and Holbroook, Arizona; and Cortez, Colorado, and Blanding, Utah. Others live in small towns and metropolitan areas throughout the United States.

GOVERNMENT
The Navajo Tribal Council was first formally recognized by the federal government in 1923. The Navajo Tribe rejected the Indian Reorganization Act of 1934 (IRA) and is, therefore, not organized under that Act. Between 1936 and 1938, the Navajos attempted a constitutional government; it was refused by the Secretary of the Interior who cited factionalism among the tribal members as a reason for denial. The BIA issued federal regulations, "Rules for the Governance of the Navajo Tribal Council," in 1938, and democratic elections to the Navajo Nation Council have been held every four years since then. The rules, as amended in December 1989, are the basis for all tribal operations. The Navajo Nation, under PL-638, contracts with the BIA to administer key programs and services.

The nation is headed by a council consisting of 88 members which represents the 110 local government subdivisions (chapters) that make up the Navajo Nation. Twelve standing committees conduct business between quarterly full council sessions. Representation is also included from Alamo, Cañoncito, and Ramah reservations in New Mexico. Each of the 110 chapters also has an elected president, vice-president, secretary-treasurer, and a grazing committee member, serving four-year terms. All programs and projects are processed through the appropriate standing committee before submission to the Navajo Nation Council.

The Navajo Nation has a three-branch government, similar to that of the United States. The Navajo Nation Bill of Rights is similar in structure, as well, to that of the federal government. The executive branch is headed by a tribal president, chosen by popular election every four years. During the same election year, the 88 council delegates are elected. Every two years, the council elects a "speaker" who presides over all council sessions, in addition to administratively overseeing the legislative branch. The judicial branch, created April 1, 1959, is headed by a chief justice who is nominated by the president and confirmed by the council. The judicial branch consists of a supreme court, seven district courts, seven family courts, and traditional peacemaker courts. Peacemaker courts are alternatives to typical courtroom settings, in that these courts use traditional Navajo laws and procedures in mediation to resolve disputes. The Navajo Nation Code, a comprehensive set of written rules and laws, is enforced by the Navajo Nation Courts, which dispose of over 90,000 cases per year. Courtrooms are open only to those attorneys who are members of the Navajo Nation Bar Association.

In 1974, the Navajo Nation established the Navajo Nation Tax Commission to, in part, levy and collect taxes. Although the commission does not levy franchise, income, personal property, or unemployment taxes, it does levy the following taxes on the Navajo Nation:

i. Possessory Interest Tax (PIT): This is a tax on the taxable value of a possessory interest granted by the Navajo Nation. A possessory interest is the right to be on Navajo land performing a particular activity. The most common forms of possessory interests are oil and gas leases, coal leases, rights-of-way, and business site leases. The Office of the Navajo Tax Commission uses common appraisal methods to place a market value on the possessory

Navajo

Navajo Nation
Federal reservation
Apache, Coconino, and Navajo
counties, Arizona; Bernalillo,
Cibola, McKinley, Rio Arriba,
Sandoval, San Juan, and
Socorro counties, New Mexico;
and San Juan County, Utah

Navajo Nation
P.O. Drawer 9000
Window Rock, AZ 86515
928-871-6352
928-871-4025 Fax
indianaffairs.state.az.us

Total land area
(see page 326)

Population
180,462

Labor Force
51,363

High school graduate or higher
55.9%

Bachelor's degree or higher
7.3%

Unemployment rate
25.05%

Per capita income
$7,269.00

interest. Then, the tax rate of 3 percent is applied to the taxable value. Possessory interests with a taxable value of less than $100,000 are not taxed.

The PIT is assessed annually on August 1, with one-half of the payment due November 1 and the remainder due the following May 1.

ii. Business Activity Tax (BAT): This is a tax on the net source gains (gross receipts less deductions) from the sale of Navajo goods or services, with the legal incidence of the tax on the party receiving the gross receipts. The net source gains are taxed at a rate of 5 percent.

iii. Oil and Gas Severance Tax (SEV): This is a tax on the removal of oil and/or gas from any lands located within the jurisdictional territory of the Navajo Nation, regardless of ownership of such lands. The tax rate is 4 percent.

The SEV is a self-reporting tax, with monthly returns due 45 days after the end of the month.

iv. Hotel Occupancy Tax (HOT): This is a tax on the amount paid for the rental of a room in a hotel, motel, or bed and breakfast. The tax rate is 8 percent.

v. Tobacco Products Tax and Licensing Act (TOB): This is a tax on the sale of tobacco products within the Navajo Nation by a distributor or retailer. The tax rate is 40¢ per pack of cigarettes.

vi. Fuel Excise Tax (FET): The Navajo Nation Fuel Excise Tax became effective on October 1, 1999. This tax, with a rate of 18¢ per gallon, is administered in a manner similar to state gasoline taxes.

vii. Sales Tax: This tax went into effect on April 1, 2002; it replaced the Business Activity Tax for Construction. The tax rate is 3 percent of gross receipts. It is very similar to state gross receipts taxes. The tax is imposed on all sales of goods or services within the Navajo Nation.

ECONOMY

The Navajo Nation is so vast and its chapters so diverse that there is no one way to characterize the nation's economic base as a whole, and to give a thorough accounting of each chapter is beyond the scope of this text. (There are a total of 800 employers in Navajoland, including various BIA and governmental sectors.) Within each chapter, however, there are principal economic activities, a few of which are summarized here.

In Chinle, most jobs are in the public sector, in the Chinle Unified School District, or in chapter and nation government offices; however, there are a growing number of commercial industries. Tseyi Shopping Center, a 65,000-square-foot retail center, is occupied by retail, medical, and government services, with plans for expansion that include adding a major department store, more shops and offices. Chinle anticipates an increase in tourism, so the plans are to add motels, campgrounds, and cultural facilities.

Peabody Coal Company owns and operates the Kayenta and Black Mesa mines and a central warehouse in the Kayenta District, so it has become a primary employer for the region. There is also a thriving commercial sector where many Navajos work in the service industries in support of mine activity and a burgeoning tourism market. Mojave Power Plant, the principal buyer of Black Mesa coal, is scheduled to shut down its operation in 2005. This will have a severely adverse impact on the economy of the Kayenta area.

Leupp is experiencing dramatic growth in high-tech industries. Tooh Dineh Industries manufactures computer peripherals for the information, communication, and transportation fields. There is an industrial park for light industry and office space. As in other chapters, Leupp anticipates increased tourism and is planning to add hotels and other accommodations.

Major employers in Many Farms include the nation, the BIA, the IHS, other governmental offices and some commercial services centered on tourism. Attractions in the area include Window Rock, the Painted Desert, Petrified Forest National Monument, Monument Valley, and the Hopi Indian Reservation. The chapter has plans to add motels, campgrounds, and cultural facilities.

Although there is very little economic activity now, New Land anticipates an increase in tourism, especially along the I-40 corridor bisecting their area. The Santa Fe Railway runs parallel to the interstate and creates access to transportation for light industry and other commercial ventures. The nation's Hospitality Enterprises built a travel center at Navajo, within the New Land chapter, with future plans for a motel, an RV park, and restaurants.

An economic powerhouse, the Window Rock/Fort Defiance area is a commercial and administrative hub for the entire nation. As the capital, it receives the most commercial traffic and is the center of administrative and governmental decision making. The 78,000 square foot Window Rock Shopping Center is already open for business, as is the 50,950 square foot St. Michael's Center.

Government as Employer. According to a survey conducted by the division of economic development, the various governments-federal, state, county, municipal, or the Navajo Nation-employed over 8,500 people in 2001, with a total salary and benefits of over $216 million. Those employed by the tribe receive generous employee benefits including life insurance, health coverage that includes Native healers, short-term disability compensation, vision care, dental benefits, and reductions in the cost of prescriptions.

Economic Development Projects. The Navajo Nation's Division of Economic Development (DED) is one of 12 divisions of the executive branch. Within DED, a support services department identifies sources of financing, conducts overall business planning and manages the Navajo Business and Industrial Fund, the small business lending program, and the micro-enterprise loan program. The project development department is designed to promote and develop major economic opportunities for the nation in three priority areas: industrial development, tourism development, and commercial development. The business regulatory department oversees all of these activities, including business licensing and small business development.

Designated in 1989 as an Arizona Enterprise Zone, the northwest corner of the reservation (Apache and Navajo counties) is eligible to receive private investment incentives. These include state income and property tax credits for any business operating there. The Omnibus Budget Reconciliation Act of 1993 also extended certain federal tax incentives to potential private businesses, including accelerated depreciation on capital assets, and credit against income liability based on the number of employees. In order to attract investors, the nation does not tax corporate income, inventories, personal income, unemployment, or property. The Navajo Preference in Employment Act was enacted to give Navajo workers hiring preference in all employment and training opportunities on the reservation. There is a prevailing wage rate for non-federally financed construction projects.

Wells Fargo, the only financial institution represented on the reservation, operates four branches, but had historically refused to cash Social Security checks for seniors, forcing them off the reservation for those banking services. In the early years of the twenty-first century, Wells Fargo agreed to cash Social Security checks. The bank also extended its hours of operation by two hours each day to better serve the nation's communities. The nation hopes to attract additional financial institutions to the reservation, where 81,000 Navajo are employed and in need of banking services close to home. One such institution, Bank of America, has announced a $750 billion investment in community development over the next 10 years in ethnically and culturally diverse markets. The tribe itself has two financial institutions, the personal and home loan program and the business and industrial fund, to aid individuals and small businesses, respectively.

Over $2 million in economic development money was awarded to Arizona tribes in January 2004. Over $1.4 million of the windfall results from the federal appropriations process. Another $700,000 comes directly from the Department of Housing and Urban Development. The Navajo Nation received $415,000 of these monies to update law enforcement crime-prevention technologies and to make improvements to Navajo Mountain Road. The Tuba City Department of Law will get $20,000 for a new intoxilyzer, a machine that measures blood alcohol content via respiration.

Navajo Nation Shopping Centers, Inc., once a part of the Navajo Nation's Division of Economic Development, is a Navajo-owned corporation that has given rise to 10 shopping centers in the following locations: Window Rock, Tuba City, Kayenta, Shiprock, Crownpoint, St. Michael's, Navajo Pine, and Pinehill. The Piñon Shopping Center was completed in 1993 and the Dilkon Shopping Center was completed in 2002. Headquartered in Window Rock, this corporation boasted $92,733,342 in gross sales for 2002, employing 1,080 people in various tenant businesses.

In the Navajo Nation's 2002 -2003 Comprehensive Economic Development Strategy, the tribe spelled out economic development priorities for the immediate and intermediate future. One goal is to increase the number of industrial plants located on nation lands, including the following: 1) a latex glove manufacturing plant, 2) a sewing factory, 3) a facility to manufacture military-issue biochemical decontamination kits, 4) a water bottling plant, and 5) a housing plant manufacturing facility. The nation is a participating member of the Indian Tribal Economic Alliance and is working in cooperation with nine other member tribes to develop information technologies that digitize information for publication on the World Wide Web. They also plan to further develop other tourism potential (see Tourism and Recreation, below).

To facilitate these economic initiatives, the nation recognizes its need to engage in additional commercial and real estate development, revise business site lease regulations, implement a local governance act which would permit chapter-level governments to formulate their own land-use plans, etc-and to increase financing opportunities in order to stimulate additional growth in the number of small business enterprises. It is believed that by doing so, the Nation will stem the flow of capital into neighboring border towns.

In order to guarantee cohesiveness among the various parts of these measures, the tribe is engaged in comprehensive land-use planning. As of December 2003, land-use planning was complete for 67 of the 110 chapters.

Forestry. There are approximately 700,000 acres of pine-fir forest and 4.5 million acres of piñon-juniper lands in the Navajo Nation. The annual sustained-yield cut is presently 35 million board feet per year. Total forestry employment is approximately 1,000 people, generating an estimated annual economic output of about $87 million. Revenues to the tribal government from timber sales and the activity of the Navajo Forest Industries amount to about $1.5 million prior to 2000.

The Navajo Forestry Department sold 22.4 million board feet of timber and forested 456 acres in fiscal year 1993. The department also gave out 256,772 permits for post-and-pole cutting and 4,509 permits for Christmas-tree cutting. The department also has a cooperative agreement with the U.S. Forestry Service to provide tribal employees with work experience within the U.S. Forestry Service. Under this agreement, 30 tribal employees were hired for regular forest-management jobs and 131 for fire fighter jobs. These employees were assigned to the Dixie National Forest in Utah. Approximately 135 miles of primary haul and seconda (spur) haul roads were finalized for improvement and maintenance, and 14 miles of new construction have been planned.

Navajo Forest Products Industries (NFPI) used to be the largest purchaser of timber from the Navajo forest. Because of cutting restrictions imposed on NFPI, the plant had to close its operations on July 25, 1994.

Gaming. In November 2003, New Mexico's Governor Bill Richardson signed a gambling compact between the state and the Navajo Nation for a casino to be built by the To'hajiilee Chapter 25 miles west of Albuquerque. The compact is similar to that signed by 11 other tribes in New Mexico since 2001. In 2003, construction had not yet begun, but the tribe plans to offer a gaming facility to include 700-800 slot machines and other tourist-attractive businesses such as a truck stop, a hotel, a restaurant, and sports and recreation facilities. After long debate and two separate tribal votes in defeat of gaming, one in 1994 and another in 1997, the tribe finally consented to the facility at To'hajiilee, but declared that it would be the only casino site in the entire Navajo Nation, a sort of pilot project. Under the compact, which expires in 2015, the tribe agrees to pay the State of New Mexico a percentage of slot machine proceeds.

Construction. Over 2,000 people are involved in the construction industry, employed by over 100 enterprises; the Navajo Engineering and Construction Authority oversee this. By its nature, however, construction provides only temporary employment to the Navajo people. Construction activities are geared toward the development of much-needed housing for the Navajo people, community development projects, and various shopping centers. Annual revenues have averaged $45 million since 2000, with total annual payrolls exceeding $10 million.

Manufacturing. Eight employers on the Navajo Nation fall under the category of manufacturing according to the U.S. Standard Industrial Classification code. However, only three of them can be categorized as manufacturing firms in the true sense of the word. These are: Raytheon Missile Systems Company, located in the NAPI facility in Shiprock: Mechtronics of Arizona in Fort Defiance; and Tooh Dineh Industries in Leupp. Hughes Missile Systems owned the first two long ago; they have changed their ownership and names (particularly the one in Fort Defiance) a number of times. All manufacturing firms together employed a total of 302 individuals in 2003. Only a few years back, the three firms had close to 300 employees each.

Cabinets Southwest, located at the Church Rock Industrial Site, is limited in expansion potential because of timber availability on Navajo lands.

Industrial Parks. The Navajo Nation's Industrial Development Unit operates within the project development department of the economic development division to manage industrial sites on the reservation.

Navajo

TRI-AZ-009

TRI-AZ-001

TRI-AZ-008

TRI-AZ-001 The Navajo Nation Museum at Window Rock, Arizona

TRI-AZ-008 The Navajo Nation's Council Chambers at Window Rock

TRI-AZ-009 The Karigan Professional Office Complex, designed by Louis Weller Architects of Albuquerque, New Mexico

There are seven locations in the Navajo Nation with industrial parks.

(1) The Shiprock, New Mexico, industrial park covers 50 acres, with a 54,538-square-foot industrial building available. About 15 percent of it is developed. The Navajo Wool Marketing Industry occupies another 3,000-square-foot building.

(2) The undeveloped Shush Be Toh, New Mexico, industrial park covers 320 acres of land located in close proximity to Interstate 40 and the Atchison, Topeka, and Santa Fe Railroad.

(3) The Church Rock, New Mexico, industrial park has 75 acres of land. Land uses within the site include a sewage lagoon serving the Church Rock community, a 72,500-square-foot industrial building, and four vacant buildings.

(4) The 50-acre Fort Defiance, Arizona, industrial park is located in the southeast corner of the Navajo Reservation, six miles north of Window Rock. The site is home to Packard Hughes's Interconnect wiring facility, the Navajo Housing Authority, Tru Value Lumber and Blaze Construction Company. All utilities are available.

(5) The Chinle industrial park, located in the center of Chinle, Arizona, contains a total of 30 acres, with 18 acres available. The site is home to the Coca Cola Bottling Company (Wometco Coca Cola), the Navajo Wool Marketing Program, Plateau Materials, Midway Resale Outlet, a car dealership, the Navajo Nation Resource, and maintenance departments.

(6) The Leupp, Arizona, industrial park has 100 acres of semi-developed land, with one 5,696-square-foot multipurpose light-industrial building, utilized by the Leupp Chapter, Coconino County Solid Waste, and the Navajo Nation Water Development offices.

(7) The Navajo Agricultural Products Industry (NAPI) industrial park in Ojo Amarillo, New Mexico, covers a 300-acre site and currently contains several NAPI-related agribusinesses.

A major electronics-assembly plant owned by a division of Hughes Missile Systems is also located on the premises. This facility is housed in a 30,000-square-foot building within the park. The company employs approximately 140 Navajo workers for assembly tasks at the NAPI facility. The "Navajo Pride" label appears on several NAPI-grown products including potatoes, onions, and alfalfa pellets. The Navajo Nation has approximately 6,000 active livestock-grazing permits, involving almost 400,000 head of cattle, horses, sheep, and goats on over 13.5 million acres. NAPI itself runs over 17,000 head of cattle. In addition to the seven industrial sites listed above, a 30,000-square-foot industrial facility completed in 1991 in New Lands, Arizona, is managed by the Office of Navajo and Hopi Indian Relocation.

Transportation. The Navajo Transit System, in operation since 1980, is the sole public transportation system represented on the Navajo Nation. In 2003, the system utilized 23 buses and 3 vans, offering local fixed-route service and chartered interstate transportation to 20 states and Washington, D.C. There are 10 Bluebird Luxury Tour coaches available for the chartered trips.

Media and Communications. The Navajo Nation is served by two weekly newspapers, *The Navajo Times* and the *Navajo-Hopi Observer*. The nation also owns and operates two Native American radio stations. KTNN AM 660, originating in Window Rock, is The Voice of the Navajo Nation, broadcasting 50,000 watts, 24 hours a day in both Navajo and English, with nighttime signals reaching the entire western United States and northwest Mexico. KWRK 96.1 FM is a 100,000-watt stereo station serving the Four Corners and Gallup areas. Several other stations are received on various areas of the reservation. Three Albuquerque TV channels and cable TV service are available.

The Nation's newspaper, *The Navajo Times*, had a weekly world readership of over 100,000 people in 2003, making it the largest Native-American owned weekly newspaper in the world. Its website is also busy, with approximately 7,500 hits per day.

Mining. Mining is one of the largest sectors of the Navajo economy. The Pittsburg & Midway Coal Mining Company's McKinley Mine (a surface mine) is located near Blackhat, New Mexico, on 15,000 acres of leased tribal land. It began operations in 1962, and in the twenty-first century, it has a production capacity of 6.5 -7.5 million tons annually.

Approximately 1,500 tribal members are involved in the overall mining industry, or 4.6 percent of the total employment on the Navajo Nation in 2003. Mining is the single largest source of revenue to the tribal government. Coal mining, plus oil and natural gas extraction, generate more than $75 million annually through royalties. In 1991, the nation drafted a specific energy policy, motivated by the discrepancy between its rich energy resources and the lack of electricity and gas services in many Navajo homes. The policy outlined a plan to give the nation control over its energy resources, resulting in the creation of the Navajo Oil and Gas Company, incorporated in 1997. The company has its own refinery, using oil produced on Navajo lands, and it purchased gathering pipelines from Giant Industries in 2002. Wholesale and retail operations flowing from this energy resource generated an immediate profitable return, and the nation is in the process of acquiring large additional tracts of land holding sizeable reserves of oil. The company was building a headquarters office site at the Karigan industrial development in 2003.

It is a sad fact that Peabody Coal Company may close its operations in 2005 and Pittsburg & Midway may close in 2008. Closure of these two mining operations will severely impact the Navajo Nation's economy, both in terms of revenue to the Navajo Government and of high-paying jobs for the Navajo people.

(For information regarding the Peabody Energy's Arizona Mines, partially located on Navajo tribal lands, see Environmental Initiatives/Concerns, below.)

Tourism and Recreation. The Navajo Nation created a parks and recreation department in 1958, charged with the responsibility of overseeing the special land uses of its many vast landscapes and of protecting its land for the benefit of future generations. It is one of the oldest programs in the Navajo Nation government, enforcing all laws, regulations, and policies governing Navajo Nation parks, monuments, and recreation areas.

The Navajo Nation Tourist Development Initiative works to strengthen an ever-increasing Arizona tourism market on the reservation, developing the Navajo Tourism Master Plan. The nation's goal is to tap into a larger percentage of this highly lucrative industry on behalf of its people.

With an estimated annual visitation of over 2.5 million people, Navajo Nation tribal parks and recreation areas are becoming an important source of income for service businesses on the reservation. Archaeological and historic sites abound throughout this enormous reservation, with sweeping vistas ranging from spectacular rock formations to isolated canyons. There are 15 tribal parks and national monuments in Navajoland.

Recreational possibilities include hiking, running, cycling, racing, boating, softball, basketball, trophy fishing in over a dozen lakes and ponds, and camping. Lake Powell alone boasts 2,000 miles of shoreline for such activities. In 1999, the tribe opened a day-use boat ramp on Lake Powell, having a picnic area and restrooms, with plans to expand the facility into a larger, more extensive marina, the Antelope Point Marina.

Small and big game hunting permits (mostly deer and turkey) are available from September through December from the Navajo Fish and Wildlife Department.

Filmmakers have shot on location at Canyon de Chelly National Park, Monument Valley, Tribal Park, the Little Colorado River, and Rainbow Bridge National Monument, exposing vast numbers of people to the area's scenic wonders. The most highly visited sites include: Chaco Culture National Historical Park, Navajo National Monument Valley, Window Rock, Four Corners Monument, Petrified Forest National Park, and the Bisti Badlands. Monument Valley, one of the most highly photographed spots on earth, showcases wind- and time-carved sandstone masterpieces towering over the desert floor at heights of between 400 and 1,000 feet. Various angles often produce dramatic lighting surrounding the pinnacles for landscape photography at its finest. At the visitor center, the world-famous Mitten Buttes, Antelope Canyon (Tse bighanilini, or "the place where water runs through rocks"), and Merrick Butte are visible. Narrated guided tours of the valley in open-air jeeps offer an easy way to see portions of the vast topography not otherwise available to tourists. Landmarks like Ear of the Wind can only be accessed via these guided tours.

A 36-acre lake located in Bowl Canyon, the Asaayi (pronounced Ah-sy-yeh) Lake Recreation Area, is the tribally operated gateway to the Chuska Mountain. It is one of the nation's major attractions, providing outdoor adventures to individuals and groups of all sizes. Hiking, fishing, picnicking, canoeing, camping, cabins with bunk beds, showers, restrooms, and outdoor facilities are available. The area is open from April until October, weather permitting.

There are also a large number of annual fairs, festivals, and rodeos held at various locations on the reservation, including powwows, traditional songs and dances, and native food com-

petitions. The "World's Largest American Indian Fair," the five-day Navajo Nation Fair, attracts tourists from around the world each September to Window Rock, Arizona. One of the event's highlights is the All-Indian Rodeo in which more than 900 Indian cowboys and cowgirls from eight different Indian rodeo associations compete. The event also features horse racing, bull riding, an intertribal powwow, arts and crafts exhibits, the Miss Navajo Nation competition, an Indian fry bread contest, a cute baby contest, concerts, country and western dances, song and dance competitions, agricultural and livestock exhibits, food booths, carnival rides, and a parade. In October, the Shiprock Navajo Fair is the most traditional of all the nation's fairs. Specific information is available from the Navajoland Tourism Department in Window Rock.

The Navajos are world-renown for their silverwork and rug weaving. Tribal artisans and craftspeople use a variety of materials for their finished products, such as gold, raw coral, black onyx, turquoise, homegrown wools, and hand-spun yarns. They are perhaps best known for their distinctive squash blossom necklaces, one of their most traditional jewelry pieces, and rugs with difficult and complex designs, such as the two-faced, pictorial, sand painting, and raised outlook. Saddle blankets, another popular style of rug, usually aren't as large nor as difficult to make as the others, and are, therefore, slightly more affordable for the average collector.

TRI-AZ-026

TRI-AZ-019

TRI-AZ-004

TRI-AZ-026 & TRI-AZ-019 Scenic view of the Navajo reservation

TRI-AZ-004 This hogan is located on the grounds of the Navajo Nation Museum and Library at Window Rock, Arizona

Navajo

In 1974, the Navajo Nation established the Navajo Nation Tax Commission to, in part, levy and collect taxes. Although the commission does not levy franchise, income, personal property, or unemployment taxes, it does levy the following taxes on the Navajo Nation:

i. Possessory Interest Tax (PIT): This is a tax on the taxable value of a possessory interest granted by the Navajo Nation. A possessory interest is the right to be on Navajo land performing a particular activity. The most common forms of possessory interests are oil and gas leases, coal leases, rights-of-way, and business site leases. The Office of the Navajo Tax Commission uses common appraisal methods to place a market value on the possessory interest. Then, the tax rate of 3 percent is applied to the taxable value. Possessory interests with a taxable value of less than $100,000 are not taxed.

The PIT is assessed annually on August 1, with one-half of the payment due November 1 and the remainder due the following May 1.

ii. Business Activity Tax (BAT): This is a tax on the net source gains (gross receipts less deductions) from the sale of Navajo goods or services, with the legal incidence of the tax on the party receiving the gross receipts. The net source gains are taxed at a rate of 5 percent.

Basket weaving, although seemingly less important as a Navajo art form in the modern art world, has a major symbolic significance among the people because it represents an individual's mental well-being. Each part of a basket has special significance in Navajo mythology: the core of the basket represents the emergence of the Holy People into the present (fourth) world, followed by a black layer of triangles representing the four sacred mountains. This area surrounding the core represents the earth, and beyond that a red design represents the clouds and darkness of the sky. The black triangular designs on the outside of the basket represent Holy People, including Yellow Corn and Dawn. Finally, the basket's outer edge represents relationship to others.

Sand paintings are also popular among visitors to Navajoland. Believed to have originated with the Holy People who lived in the underworld, sand paintings are primarily ceremonial in nature; however, as long as the Holy People are not depicted, commercial sand painting is permissible. Tourists typically enjoy sand-painted nameplates, containers, vases, etc., spin-offs of the true art form.

The Navajo Nation Zoo and Botanical Park is the only tribal zoo in America. Located near Window Rock, the Nation boasts that the animals housed at this facility are living in truly natural habitats, surrounded by vegetation and rock forms familiar to their native territories. Most of the 30 species represented at the facility come from elsewhere in Navajoland; they are animals and birds that have been injured or orphaned and are therefore unable to safely return to the wilds. Greenery at the park is native open dwarf forest, characterized by piñon pines, juniper, and grassland. Four-winged shadscale and Siberian elms provide shade for the wildlife.

A tourism brochure and map, developed by the tribe, lists five visitor centers and 13 Navajo Nation lodgers in convenient locations throughout the reservation. Working in close cooperation with tourism development initiatives, the Navajo Arts and Crafts Enterprise works to improve the quality of workmanship and to assist tribal artisans in marketing their works. The Enterprise guarantees buyers that each piece manufactured by its members is authentically handcrafted, a unique feature that encourages the burgeoning art-based tourism sector of the economy.

INFRASTRUCTURE
Transportation. U.S. Highway 89 crosses the western part of the reservation running north-south; U.S. 666 runs north-south in the eastern part of the reservation; U.S. 160 crosses the northern part of the reservation from east to west; and Interstate 40 runs along the southern boundary of the reservation. In addition, there are a number of state and tribal roads connecting Navajo communities. Altogether there are more than 2,000 miles of paved roads on the reservation. Motor freight carriers serve all major reservation communities. Window Rock Airport, at Window Rock, Arizona, has a 7,000-foot lighted runway and provides charter service. Chinle Airport has a 4,800-foot unpaved landing strip. Other communities within the Navajo Nation, including Tuba City, Arizona, have unpaved landing strips. The nearest commercial airline and train services are at Gallup and Farmington, New Mexico, and Flagstaff, Winslow, Grand Canyon, and Page, Arizona.

Utilities. The Navajo Tribal Utility Authority is the major supplier of electricity, natural gas, water, and sewer services on the reservation. In a few areas, Arizona Public Service supplies electricity, and bottled gas is marketed by private companies. Dine Power Authority (DPA), a Navajo Nation enterprise, in partnership with Western Area Power Administration (Western), a power-marketing agent of the Department of Energy, has proposed the construction of the Navajo Transmission Project (NTP), a 500-kilovolt transmission line to deliver power from northwest New Mexico across northern Arizona to southern Nevada. According to DPA and Western, NTP will provide an economical source of transmission capacity that would reduce heavy loads in the region. In addition, the NTP would meet a portion of the electrical load growth projected in the area, while providing additional sources of revenues for the nation and increasing employment opportunities on the reservation.

Telecommunications. Telephone services are available from the Navajo Communications Company, doing business as the Frontier Company in 2003. It was 100 percent digital in 2003, providing Internet and wireless technologies to nation residents. It is the largest provider of cable TV service on the reservation as well, with 4,000 subscribers.

Housing. The Navajo Housing Authority first received funding and support from the 1937 Housing Act which permitted implementation of mutual help, public rentals, homeownership and Section 8, and voucher programs. Under Section 184, the Act funded loan-guarantee programs as well.

In 1996, passage of the Native American Housing Assistance and Self-Determination Act made the construction of sustainable communities a reality, with appropriations amounting to an average of $91 million annually between 1998 and 2002.

COMMUNITY FACILITIES AND SERVICES
Public Safety. Law enforcement is provided throughout the reservation by the Navajo Nation Police Department. Local communities maintain community centers.

Education. Educational facilities include 57 state-supported public schools, 13 community-contracted schools, 47 BIA schools, and a few private mission schools. There are 123 Head Start programs dotting the Navajo Nation. Higher education can be obtained at the Northland Pioneer College and at the Crownpoint Institute of Technology. The former Navajo Community College, now known as Diné College, is located at Tsaile, Arizona. The 15,000-square-foot Karigan Child Care Center, completed in September 2001, is located on 113 acres purchased from privately held Karigan Estates. It can serve up to 170 children.

Diné College, chartered by the nation in 1968, is a four-year accredited, multi-campus postsecondary public institution, integrating key cultural principles throughout various courses of study. It was the first college established by Native Americans for Native Americans, setting a precedent for future tribal development of educational facilities. The school was first fully accredited by the North Central Association (NCA) Commission on Institutions of Higher Education in 1976. The college is governed by an eight-member board of regents confirmed by the Government Services Committee of the Navajo Nation Tribal Council. In a unique collaborative partnership with Arizona State University, Diné College bestowed its first baccalaureate degrees under the Diné Teacher Education Program in 1998. In 1999, the State of Arizona amended the tax codes to allow distribution of transaction-privilege tax revenues collected on the Navajo Nation to Diné College. This amendment ensures that the school receives $1.75 million annually for 10 years for its maintenance, renewal, and capital expenditures. With the increased revenues, Diné College plans to build new buildings at all of its Arizona campuses. Beyond the main campus at Tsaile, ("place where the stream flows into the canyon"), Arizona, there are satellite locations in Window Rock, Chinle, Ganado, Kayenta, and Tuba City, Arizona, and in Shiprock and Crownpoint, New Mexico. General education programs are offered at all campuses.

In Farmington, the Navajo Preparatory School (NPS) serves over 200 Navajo and other Native American high school students. Four new dormitory buildings increased capacity at the school to 300 in the early years of the twenty-first century. The facility boasts that over 90 percent of NPS graduates enroll (and most graduate) from colleges or technical programs throughout the United States. The school features a low faculty-to-student ratio, culturally diverse staffing, summer enrichment programs, and a plethora of quality after-school activities. In 2004, many of the buildings on the campus were are in need of rehabilitation.

Health Care. The Navajo Area Indian Health Service (NAIHS) delivers comprehensive health services to all American Indians in parts of the states of Arizona, New Mexico, Colorado, and Utah. These services include inpatient, outpatient, and community programs in six hospitals, seven clinics or health centers (some of which include emergency care), and 15 part-time health stations. The six hospitals range in size from the 32-bed Crownpoint, New Mexico, facility to the Gallup Indian Medical Center in Gallup, New Mexico, with 99 beds. The Navajo Tribe itself operates the Navajo Division of Health, created in 1977 and headquartered in Window Rock, Arizona. This agency oversees quality and guarantees that culturally acceptable health care is available and accessible to all Native Americans. The Navajo Nation also provides health-related and educational services in the areas of nutrition, aging, substance abuse, community health representative (outreach), and emergency medical services (ambulance). The NAIHS is one of 12 regional administrative units of the Indian Health Service, an agency of the U.S. Public Health Service Department of Human Health Services.

There are 12 health care centers in the region: Chinle Comprehensive Health Care Facility, Crownpoint Health Care Facility, Dizlth-Na-O-Dith-Hle, Fort Defiance Indian Hospital, Gallup Indian Medical Center, Inscription House Health Center, Kayenta Health Center, Shiprock-Northern Navajo Medical Center, Tohatchi Health Care Center, Tsaile Health Center; Tuba City Indian Medical Center, and the Winslow Health Center.

A unique feature of the NAIHS is that all staff are trained to provide cross-cultural medicine, so cultural taboos among various populations of Native Americans are avoided, and subtleties in intertribal and interpersonal relationships are honored. Care is provided in a cultural context so that correct remedies may be pursued.

ENVIRONMENTAL CONCERNS
The Navajo Environmental Protection Agency, founded in 1972, was charged with the responsibility of protecting the people and their environment from contaminants and of ensuring compliance with and enforcement of all applicable environmental laws.

The Navajo Nation participated in a collaborative project with the U.S. Departments of Agriculture and Environmental Protection Region 9, which closed former logging roads on the reservation and reinforced highly eroded upstream drainage areas negatively impacting Asaayi Lake. The Asaayi Lake Project, which placed waterbars, check dams, low water crossings and other mitigation controls on former logging roads and closed them to all future traffic, was approximately 50 percent complete in 2002. To further reduce high sediment content in the lake, more work was done in 2003. The nation graded slopes, installed additional check dams, and revegetated damaged areas.

The nation focused on non-point source pollution along the Pueblo Colorado Wash. The Ganado/Indian Wells Stream Bank Stabilization Project was initiated to remove potentially hazardous household and commercial wastes, such as paint, paint thinner, vehicles, motor oil, and coolants, from along the stream's banks. Sixteen hundred feet of fencing was installed to keep out livestock and cars; soil and slope stabilization measures were installed; and turf reinforcement mats were established. Native vegetation was then planted, including grasses and 400 willow and cottonwood trees. Educational outreach was a key part of the project to prevent future degradation.

A $7.65 million Congressional energy and water appropriation earmarked for Arizona received presidential approval in November 2003, clearing the way for the Navajo Nation to secure $4 million for its projects. Designated the Energy and Water Development Appropriations Act, H.R. 2754, the legislation funded a broad range of initiatives designed to mitigate drought damage and increase access to electricity throughout the state of Arizona and, specifically, on the reservation. Three million of the Nation's $4 million appropriation will fund the Navajo Electrification Demonstration Project, a program that serves the Arizona portion of the Navajo Nation, as well as the White Mountain Apache and San Carlos Apache reservations.

With the funding, the nation is developing and extending renewable power technologies--such as fuel cells, solar photovoltaics, solar thermal systems, and wind technologies--to rural communities in a geographic service area larger than the state of Illinois. The remaining $1 million will fund drought assistance programs on the reservation, ensuring that water systems serving primary communities throughout the nation receive adequate water resources for irrigation and drinking purposes.

The State of New Mexico, the Navajo Nation, and the federal government potentially settled a 30-year water-rights battle in December 2003. Ending the suit initiated in New Mexico state courts in 1975, the tribe agreed to a 322,000 acre-feet annual share of San Juan River water, with the caveat that they were to claim no additional amounts of water in the future. In exchange, the nation receives approximately $900 million earmarked for public works projects, such as agricultural irrigation systems and drinking water pipelines to communities on the eastern side of the reservation. Final settlement is contingent upon tribal council approval, congressional passage of an appropriation, and approval by officials in the state of New Mexico and the Interstate Stream Commission. A bill in the New Mexico legislature was to have been introduced during spring 2004.

The Four Corners Power Plant, located on tribal land, is one of the largest coal-fired power generating stations in the United States. It has been in operation since 1963. The station burns an average of 28,000 tons of low-sulfur coal daily to generate up to 2,040 megawatts of electricity, sufficient to power over 300,000 homes. Morgan Lake, a manmade body of water located nearby, supplies all the cooling water for the plant. Arizona Public Service, which owns three units, operates the entire plant, utilizing a wet venture scrubber system to control both sulfur dioxide and particulate emissions. Other units are owned by other power entities in adjoining states. The Navajo Generating Station, a coal-fired steam electric generating plant near Page, Arizona, has been operating since 1968. With a net output of 2,250 megawatts, the plant uses approximately eight million tons of coal per year from Peabody Western Coal's Kayenta Mine and 30,000 acre-feet of water drawn from Lake Powell annually. Both the mining activity and the water levels on Navajo and Hopi lands are topics of major environmental concern.

Environmentalists and archaeologists fear that the Hopis living on and near Black Mesa, which lies completely surrounded by the Navajo Nation, are facing forced relocation, environmental devastation, destruction of historic artifacts, and potential cultural extinction because of multinational corporations such as Peabody Western Coal Company which pumps 4,000 acre-feet of water a year from the N-aquifer underlying the reservation. (An acre-foot equals approximately 325,000 gallons.) In areas of the reservation, hundreds of sinkholes have opened up, first noticed by Hopi ranchers in the late 1980s.

Some holes are described as cracks in the earth's surface, approximately 30 feet deep, that weren't always present. Tribal elders, who document the drying up of seeps and springs once depended upon for fresh water, insist the holes are a new phe-

iii. Oil and Gas Severance Tax (SEV): This is a tax on the removal of oil and/or gas from any lands located within the jurisdictional territory of the Navajo Nation, regardless of ownership of such lands. The tax rate is 4 percent.

The SEV is a self-reporting tax, with monthly returns due 45 days after the end of the month.

iv. Hotel Occupancy Tax (HOT): This is a tax on the amount paid for the rental of a room in a hotel, motel, or bed and breakfast. The tax rate is 8 percent.

v. Tobacco Products Tax and Licensing Act (TOB): This is a tax on the sale of tobacco products within the Navajo Nation by a distributor or retailer. The tax rate is 40¢ per pack of cigarettes.

vi. Fuel Excise Tax (FET): The Navajo Nation Fuel Excise Tax became effective on October 1, 1999. This tax, with a rate of 18¢ per gallon, is administered in a manner similar to state gasoline taxes.

vii. Sales Tax: This tax went into effect on April 1, 2002; it replaced the Business Activity Tax for Construction. The tax rate is 3 percent of gross receipts. It is very similar to state gross receipts taxes. The tax is imposed on all sales of goods or services within the Navajo Nation.

nomenon. The holes, especially prevalent near communities or washes located near Black Mesa, are a serious sign of aquifer collapse. Such damage, if aquifer collapse is indeed found to be the cause of the sinkholes, is irreversible.

Cleanup and reclamation of the 400 surface acres per year that the mining operations disturb continued into 2004. Bulldozers push dirt and rocks back into the mine pit and contour the land back to its approximate original shape. Tractors till the slopes to prevent erosion and drill-plant more than 20 pounds of seeds per acre. The

Surface Mining Control and Reclamation Act of 1977 stipulated stricter reclamation requirements, including the use of native seeds. The seed mix used at Black Mesa Mine contains 85 percent medicinally useful and/or culturally important native plants such as green Mormon tea, banana leaf yucca, four-wing saltbush, cliff rose, Gambel oak, fringed sage, Indian rice grass, needle-and-thread grass, and piñon pine. This costs the company $2,000 per acre to plant. Acres replanted with rangeland grasses, such as blue grama grass, galleta grass, alkali sacaton grass, and four-wing saltbush are more economical.

Honoring Nations Honoree 1999

Text in its entirety from:
The Harvard Project On American Indian Economic Development

John F. Kennedy School of Government Harvard University

Honoring Nations Honoree 1999

Navajo Studies Department Rough Rock Community School

By the early 1960s, residents of Rough Rock, Arizona, a town on the Navajo Reservation, had become deeply concerned about their children's lack of knowledge of Navajo ways. Community members felt strongly that a primary cause of the problem was the "foreign" educational system imposed upon its children. Not only did the U.S. government and state institutions-that is, non-Indians-control Navajo education, but in their hands, education was a means of assimilating American Indian children into mainstream society, removing all traces of Native culture and language. In earlier generations, children had at least received a cultural education at home. But the progressive impact of non-Indian schools meant that fewer and fewer families were able or inclined to teach Navajo traditions.

Thus, in 1966, in an effort to prevent the educational system from further eroding Navajo culture, Rough Rock became the first Native community in the United States to assume control of a Bureau of Indian Affairs (BIA) school. By contracting with the BIA to take over school management, local educators gained authority to create a culturally appropriate educational system based on Navajo ways of thinking, learning, and teaching. Through their efforts, the high school soon offered a unique pedagogy, one that combined western educational models with Navajo traditions.

In the mid-1990s, however, school administrators determined that the School could-and should-teach Navajo knowledge in a more intentional way. As a result, they created the Rough Rock Community School's Navajo Studies Department, which consolidates and augments the School's Navajo culture and language programs. Through the Department's efforts, the School now offers 23 Navajo Studies courses, teaching topics as diverse as

conversational Navajo, Navajo philosophy, and contemporary issues facing the Navajo Nation.

The success of the Navajo Studies program is evident in several ways. For example, the Nation's Tribal Council has recognized Rough Rock as the only Navajo Studies school on the Reservation. In response to demand, the School has both grown in size and opened enrollment to students from any of the Navajo Nation's 110 chapters. In other words, Rough Rock has effectively become a magnet school for training in Navajo Studies. The Department is also developing a comprehensive Navajo Studies curriculum to be used by other reservation schools. Its availability will help combat the persistent, reservation-wide loss of cultural knowledge-despite high language retention among the Nation's general population, 80 percent of students entering reservation Head Start programs do not speak Navajo.

Clearly, the Rough Rock Community School has had an important impact on the Navajo Nation. First through the integration of western and Navajo teaching approaches, and later through the development of the Navajo Studies curriculum, the School has helped to ensure the survival of Navajo ways. But of equal importance is the impact that Rough Rock has had on all Native Nations. As the first school to be controlled entirely by a local Indian community, Rough Rock paved the way for over 200 more contract schools, which allow Indian students from all tribes to attain a western education and, at the same time, learn about their own history, traditions, and language. And, because the U.S. Congress' 1975 legislation providing for tribal self-determination in all federally funded Indian programs was motivated by the need for self-determination in Indian education, local control at Rough Rock was a critical part of a larger-and transforming-movement in Indian Country.

Honoring Nations Honoree 1999

New Law and Old Law Together Judicial Branch

For hundreds of years, the Navajo lived under a traditional justice system composed of both Navajo common law and consensus-oriented judicial procedures.

The aim of the justice system was simple: to restore harmony. But beginning in 1892, with the forced introduction of the Bureau of Indian Affairs' Courts of Indian Offenses, this harmony began to rupture. The break was made complete with the Navajo Nation's

wholesale adoption of a western court system in 1959. Over the next 25 years, the Nation wrestled with the alienating and disempowering effects of laws and procedures inconsistent with their culture and history. Tribal members who were used to resolving their own disputes were made dependent on modern institutions, including western-style police and judiciaries. Self-reliance and community participation withered.

By the early 1980s, members of the Judicial Branch recognized that, in order for the court system to regain its legitimacy and effectiveness, it needed reform. In 1981, the Chief Justice of the Navajo Supreme Court began reintegrating traditional Navajo law into the Nation's court system, a policy which received official support with the Navajo Tribal Council's passage of the Judicial Reform Act four years later. In 1982, the Judicial Branch created the Navajo Peacemaking Division, a forum for community-led, consensus-based dispute resolution. The goal of the Peacemaking Division is not to replace the previously established court system but to provide an alternative to it for certain types of disputes. Resolution techniques are drawn from the Navajo philosophy of K'e, which values responsibility, respect, and harmony in relationships. Instead of a single judge adjudicating guilt or innocence and imposing a sentence, Navajo peacemaking is characterized by a participatory process in which the affected parties work with a community leader to resolve their own problems.

Today, Navajo common and statutory laws are the "laws of preferences" in the Nation's Supreme Court, seven district courts, and five family courts, and 250 Peacemakers in the Nation's 110 districts successfully help to resolve a wide variety of individual, business and property disputes. This unique integration of Navajo and Western law occurs on a daily basis. For instance, bar membership rules require formal training in Navajo common law as a condition to practicing in Navajo Nation courts. The courts actively use this common law to decide cases, although legal opinions are published in English. In many instances, disputants can choose to resolve their differences in either a Western-style or traditional forum.

The strength of the Judicial Branch's mixed legal system is buttressed by its independence from other branches of government. On many reservations, the tribal council and executive leaders control the judiciary through discretionary hiring and firing practices and reversals of judicial decisions. The Navajo Nation has taken numerous steps to avoid these pitfalls. For example, the hiring process balances legislative and executive branch influence, as the Navajo Tribal Council's Judiciary Committee creates a list prospective judges, an appointee of the Tribal President selects nominees, and the full Council confirms appointments. More importantly, the Judicial Branch has full and binding judicial review over actions of the Nation's legislative and executive branches--including the power to overturn legislation, prevent indiscriminate terminations, and enforce the separation of powers between all three branches of government.

The Judicial Branch's success has had a positive impact on tribal and non-tribal courts across the country. Judges from the Navajo Nation meet regularly with their counterparts in surrounding state courts, which now refer cases to both divisions of the Navajo court system. Indian and non-Indian courts refer to opinions published by the Navajo Nation courts and rely on the Navajo Peacemaker Division as a model for alternative dispute resolution. And, since 1992, the Navajo Nation Supreme Court has held over a dozen sessions in off-reservation venues, a practice that enables law students, legal scholars, and the public to witness and gain a better understanding of the Navajo's unique system of justice.

The Navajo Nation Judicial Branch's innovative legal system is independent, fair, responsive, and consistent with the Nation's culture and traditions. Perhaps the Branch's most important contribution to governance, however, is its ongoing exercise of de facto sovereignty. By establishing and enforcing Navajo laws in Navajo ways, the court system-which handles over 9,000 cases per year-exemplifies the Navajo Nation's commitment to self-government and self-determination.

Navajo

**Honoring Nations
Honoree 1999**

**Text in its entirety from:
The Harvard Project On
American Indian Economic
Development**

**John F. Kennedy School
of Government
Harvard University**

Honoring Nations Honoree 1999

Tax Initiative Economic Development Kayenta Township Commission

The town of Kayenta is located in the north-central region of the Navajo Nation. As the gateway to scenic Monument Valley and other important Southwestern Native sites, the area attracts thousands of visitors each year. Yet despite its prime location, the Navajo community in Kayenta has long been unable to act upon the promise of tourism-related development: Non-Navajos own more than half of the businesses in the area, and the Indian unemployment rate hovers near 50 percent.

As early as 1970, community members recognized that many of their economic problems could be attributed to a lack of local control over administrative powers that, used strategically, could promote appropriate development. These powers were held by the Navajo Nation central government, which is headquartered about 150 miles away in Window Rock, Arizona. The central government was responsible for all decisions involving infrastructure development, land use and zoning, housing, business development, taxation, bond issues, public safety, and even recreation-an odd distribution of responsibilities that can be traced directly to federal involvement in Indian affairs. These programs either are presently or were historically managed by the Bureau of Indian Affairs, and it has been easier for the Bureau to centralize these functions than to work at the grass roots. Shifting responsibility back to the community level would give the citizens of Kayenta the resources to provide services and create policy that could improve community infrastructure, attract business, and, ultimately, provide jobs and income. It was with these goals in mind that initial planning for the Township began in the early 1980s.

By 1985, advocates from Kayenta had persuaded the Navajo Nation Council to create a pilot township program at Kayenta, authorize funding, and approve the program's use of 3,606 acres of Navajo trust land. A number of local residents held grazing rights to this land, however, so it was a year later, when five individuals who were convinced of the wisdom of the township plan agreed to relinquish their rights that the road was finally clear for legal creation of the Township. After this high-water mark, planning continued at a deliberate pace. In 1990, the Township Pilot Project hired a planner to investigate taxation options, and in 1996 the Navajo Nation passed a resolution establishing the Kayenta Retail Sales Tax Project. In March 1997 Township residents elected the first five-member Kayenta Township Commission, and shortly thereafter, the Commission began to develop a system of municipal codes, levied a 2.5 percent retail sales tax, and hired a Town Manager. Today, the Commission oversees a variety of development endeavors that address the socio-economic needs of the Township's 5,000 residents.

The government structure of the Township is modeled after other municipal governments. The five popularly elected members of the Township Commission serve four-year staggered terms and are responsible for setting goals and establishing Township ordinances. The Town Manager is responsible for implementing and

Navajo Nation

Honoring Nations Honoree 1999

Text in its entirety from:
The Harvard Project On
American Indian Economic
Development

John F. Kennedy School
of Government
Harvard University

enforcing these ordinances (especially the tax ordinance) and for identifying funding for community projects. Six full-time staff members assist the Township Commission and Town Manager. The relationship between the Township and the local Navajo Chapter government is similar to that of a city and a county government and is defined by a memorandum of agreement. As in a county-city relationship, the Kayenta Chapter has some authority within "city limits," but the Township exercises no powers outside its boundaries.

Today, Kayenta Township's numerous successes demonstrate how local empowerment and governance can foster self-determined, self-sustaining economic development that addresses community-specific needs.

For example, town leaders were eager to streamline the business development process, particularly the involved procedure for securing a business site lease. Prior to 1996, business land leases required a recommendation by the local chapter, tribal administrative review and recommendation, approval by the Tribal Council's Economic Development Committee, the signature of the Navajo Nation President, and finally, review and approval from the BIA Area Office. But with the establishment of Kayenta Township, the Commission gained the authority to lease Township land. Now, business site leases within the Township only require approval from the Township Commission, along with the Navajo Nation President's signature and BIA approval as trustee-a radical change that has worked to attract new businesses. In 1999 at least five businesses were in the leasing process.

A second key success concerns revenue, and the possibilities that local revenues create. The Township's authority over land leases has kept lease income in local coffers, and the retail sales tax has enabled the Commission to tap a previously untapped-and significant-revenue source. (Between June 15, 1997 to December 31, 1998, the tax raised $670,834.) This income is invested directly in local infrastructure projects and used to leverage external investment from the bond market, commercial banks, and private investors. Besides creating jobs, the Commission's current list of projects demonstrates the Township's commitment to improving local residents' quality of life. These projects include: construction of a solid waste transfer station and closure of an existing dump; construction of a women's shelter; construction of a housing development; surveying, zoning, and lease negotiation for private home construction; surveying and planning for a 34 acre recreational complex; fundraising for a public safety complex; and fundraising to improve the community's water supply.

The Kayenta Township was created on the premise that local challenges require local solutions. The Township embodies the Navajo Nation's desire for increased local governmental autonomy, most recently articulated in the 1998 Local Governance Act, which gave chapters new governmental opportunities and authority. The Township is rapidly taking control of its future, from developing laws and ordinances that were once absent, to creating a revenue stream independent of Window Rock's appropriations. As the only self-sufficient "township" located on an Indian reservation in the United States, the Kayenta Township is an important model of self-governance.

Honoring Nations Honoree 2000

Navajo Child Special Advocacy Project Division of Social Services

Responding to a rash of child sexual abuse cases in Arizona and a federally legislated opportunity to craft tribal solutions, the Navajo Child Special Advocacy Program was launched in 1990 to provide Western and Navajo therapy to children who have been sexually abused. With five offices on the reservation, the Program administers sand, art and play therapy, energy psychology and trauma reduction counseling, and provides services and referrals for traditional Navajo therapy. They also conduct forensic interviews. By effectively addressing a pressing but rarely discussed social problem, the Program is helping to create a safe environment that nurtures children and families' physical, mental and spiritual well being.

In spite of the vital importance of protecting and promoting children's physical, emotional and mental well being, research shows that, in the United States as a whole, as many as one out of every four children is or will be a victim of sexual abuse. The effects of such abuse are devastating. Victims experience tremendous pain, confusion, shame and a feeling of hopelessness, and not only they but their families struggle to cope with the horror and stigma of the experience. The problems are particularly pronounced in Indian Country, where sexual abuse occurs at rates about three times the national average. Indian nations must also deal with more prevalent occurrences of the problems with which child sexual abuse is correlated, including alcoholism, substance abuse, poverty and isolation. Sadly, child abuse is often intergenerational, typically perpetrated by someone the victim knows and trusts (such as a relative, family friend or caretaker). As a societal taboo, the abuse goes vastly underreported. Too many governments - both Native and non-Native - are poorly equipped to address child sexual abuse when it occurs, and even fewer possess the necessary institutional capacity to break the cycle of abuse.

Although the "silent problem" of child sexual abuse has long existed on Indian reservations in the Southwest, the Navajo Nation, like many other tribes, did not commit much energy or many resources to addressing it until the mid-1980s. At that time, the issue gained regional and national attention when a federal government-employed teacher on the nearby Hopi Reservation was convicted for molesting dozens of Native children. This shocking incident brought the problem into public discourse and exposed the tribes' and federal government's inadequacies in providing treatment for victims and their families. For the Navajo Nation, the incident prompted self-assessment of its social services. The discoveries were disturbing. Child victims and their families had few resources to turn to for help; the social and legal services that did exist were disorganized and unstructured; treatment was fragmented; and criminal investigations were handled inconsistently and often inappropriately. For the federal government, the incident at Hopi caused lawmakers to realize that little assistance had been provided by either the Bureau of Indian Affairs (BIA) or the Indian Health Service (IHS) to help Indian nations develop and deliver adequate child protection services for their citizens. Unfortunately, it took a crisis to force tribal and federal policy makers into action.

Both the federal government and the Navajo Nation acted swiftly. Senators John McCain and Dennis DeConcini, among others, introduced federal legislation that created strict rules for reporting sexual abuse within federal agencies working on Indian reservations, and provided tribes with resources needed for establishing child protection services. Seizing the opportunity to address this sensitive issue within their homeland, the Navajo Nation created an ad hoc committee to develop a child sexual abuse program within its Division of Social Services and to seek federal funding made available under the new legislation. The Navajo Nation was one of three Indian nations to subsequently receive federal funds, and in October 1990 the Navajo Child Sexual Abuse Program was born (it was later renamed to Navajo Child Special Advocacy Program).

The Navajo Child Special Advocacy Program (NCSAP) seeks to provide comprehensive outpatient therapeutic services to children between the ages of 3 and 17 who have been traumatized by sexual abuse. The Program's philosophy is that all children of the Navajo Nation are entitled to a safe, healthy and loving environment, which nurtures and protects their emotional, mental, physical and spiritual well being. In order to serve the large, geographically diffuse population, the NCSAP has five offices spread across the Navajo Reservation and employs five clinical supervisory social workers, seven Masters-level therapists and five traditional counselors - all of whom are Navajo. It offers Western-based clinical treatment and therapeutic services, including sand, art and play therapy, energy psychology, and trauma reduction counseling, as well as Navajo-based treatment and services, including indigenous diagnosis and counseling and referrals to medicine persons and traditional healers. Additionally, NCSAP conducts forensic interviews of child victims, which are used by criminal investigators for legal proceedings against the perpetrators. To ensure coordination between treatment, criminal investigation and prosecution, NCSAP works closely with a multidisciplinary team comprised of representatives from the various tribal, state and federal programs and agencies that play a role in preventing and responding to child sexual abuse. Finally, NCSAP regularly engages in community outreach and education in an effort to inform the Navajo citizenry of its services and to raise awareness about the problem of child sexual abuse.

NCSAP's very existence is an outstanding accomplishment. Recognizing that effective self-governance requires tribes to confront even the most highly stigmatized and difficult social problems, the Navajo Nation acted upon its solemn responsibility to foster the existence of a safe and healthy environment for its most vulnerable citizens - its children. The Navajo Nation accepted the challenge of responding to an issue that many communities would rather keep secret. Indeed, good governance mandates that Indian nations be responsive to compelling social problems that threaten the welfare of their citizens.

While the creation of a tribal child sexual abuse program is laudable, so too is the Navajo Nation's commitment to developing and maintaining a first-rate program. Four aspects of NCSAP deserve particular attention.

First, through meticulous data collection and management, NCSAP and its partner agencies have been able to gain a better understanding of the scope and patterns of child sexual abuse. For example, NCSAP discovered that in 1999 alone, 861 sex abuse cases were substantiated and almost 7,000 reports of abuse and neglect were reported. They also learned that 88 percent of child abuse cases involve children under the age of five and that 85 percent of parents are victims of childhood sexual abuse. As upsetting as these figures are, NCSAP understands that data collection, coupled with detailed internal performance tracking, enables it to measure progress and structure services to best meet institutional objectives.

Second, the NCSAP has tailored itself to meet the specific needs of the Navajo people, demonstrating that culture is an important consideration in service provision. As noted, one of NCSAP's most unique characteristics is its combination of Western and Indigenous therapeutic approaches, an integration that ensures cultural relevancy and, likely, strengthens sexual abuse treatment. More comprehensively, the philosophy of K'e (whose central tenants are responsibility, respect and harmony in relationships) runs throughout all of NCSAP's activities. For example, traditional counselors provide education on the Navajo clan system, parenting, child development and other Navajo traditional beliefs and practices, and they provide referrals to medicine persons who can perform ceremonies and prescribe herbal medicines. Also, NCSAP brings services directly to its clients and serves entire families. Interaction between NCSAP staff often occurs in the Navajo language, takes place in a home/hogan setting where the victim or family is most comfortable, and includes non-offending members of the family, a practice which reflects NCSAP's understanding that the family plays a key role in a child's healing process and in restoring K'e.

Third, NCSAP has developed an effective forensic interview process that has enhanced the ability of tribal, state and federal authorities to prosecute sex offenders. Because sexually abused children sometimes do not show physical signs of abuse, forensic interviews are one of the most important components of a child sex abuse investigation; in fact, legal prosecution often hinges upon the details obtained in the interview process. Despite their importance, there was no formal protocol for conducting forensic interviews prior to NCSAP's creation. Interviews were often conducted by non-qualified individuals (such as school personnel), and cases were lost. Worse, because of overlapping jurisdictional lines and a multitude of legal authorities, a child might have suffered the additional trauma of being interviewed multiple times by multiple individuals. Today, all cases of sexual abuse follow a standardized procedure: Child Protective Services assigns a primary social worker to a case, and the social worker contacts a qualified forensic interviewer to conduct and video/audio tape the interview. The tape is then forwarded to the appropriate legal authority (tribe, state, federal government) for prosecution. Since NCSAP took on the role of forensic investigator and instituted a coordinated set of procedures, the process not only has become more focused on the care of the victim, but conviction rates have also increased.

Finally, NCSAP has accomplished the almost insurmountable task of coordinating the efforts of separate agencies by forming a core discipline group to address child sexual abuse. Members of the group include criminal investigators, prosecutors, social workers, therapists, IHS physicians and mental health staff, BIA school authorities and professionals in other Navajo government departments. The multidisciplinary group meets monthly. In addition to these efforts, NCSAP is actively involved in several intertribal child sexual abuse alliances, in order to develop and share best practices. This multidisciplinary approach improves efficiency in service provision by eliminating process redundancy, clarifies the roles of the numerous agencies involved in addressing child sexual abuse (which are articulated in detail in a protocol manual), and is allowing NCSAP and the Navajo Division of Social Services to assume greater control of processes that were once managed exclusively by the BIA and the FBI.

The Navajo Child Special Advocacy Program is confronting and dealing with an extremely difficult, yet common, social problem in Native America. NCSAP's exemplary work provides much-needed treatment for Navajo society's most at-risk individuals and families, demonstrating that it is indeed possible to treat children with the protection, dignity and respect they deserve. It is a worthwhile example for other governments, Indian and non-Indian, to follow.

Navajo Nation

**Honoring Nations
Honoree 2000**

Text in its entirety from:
The Harvard Project On
American Indian Economic
Development

John F. Kennedy School
of Government
Harvard University

Lessons:

· Good governance mandates that Indian nations be responsive to compelling social problems, and often, the response requires coordination between tribal and federal agencies. Creating multidisciplinary teams, developing detailed protocols and working closely with other tribal and non-tribal agencies are several ways to craft effective institutional responses.

· Successful programmatic intervention begins with extensive data collection and information management. Maintaining clear records and detailed data enables tribal programs to track progress and tailor services to best meet community needs.

· Matching social services to community needs may require the integration of Western and indigenous practices. For example, Western therapy can be integrated with traditional approaches to healing.

Honoring Nations Honoree 2000

Archaeology Department - Training Programs - Window Rock, Flagstaff AZ & Farmington, NM

Honoring Nations Honoree 2000

Text in its entirety from:
The Harvard Project On American Indian Economic Development

John F. Kennedy School of Government Harvard University

Motivated by the idea that Navajos should decide how their culture is preserved and protected, the Navajo Nation Archaeology Department partnered with nearby universities to create two Training Programs for Navajo students interested in careers in cultural preservation. The Programs combine academic training with field experience and are successfully expanding the pool of Navajo professionals qualified to work in key tribal cultural resource positions. In doing so, the Programs meet important community needs and add new perspectives to the fields of anthropology and archaeology.

In an effort to exert greater control over its cultural resources, the Navajo Nation created the Navajo Nation Archaeology Department (NNAD) in 1977. The Department, which oversees the largest American Indian cultural resource management program in U.S., facilitates historic preservation on the more than 16 million acres of Navajo lands. Its three offices annually conduct hundreds of archaeological survey and excavation projects to ensure that proposed development does not damage significant historical, archaeological or traditional cultural places.

Since its inception, the NNAD has played an important role in strengthening the Navajo Nation's cultural self-determination. By the late 1980s, however, the NNAD's leadership recognized a disturbing trend - only half of the NNAD's employees were Navajo, and among senior staff, less than 10 percent were Navajo. Worse yet, virtually no Navajo anthropologists or archaeologists were emerging through the university pipeline. Indeed, cultural preservation at Navajo and throughout Indian Country has been almost exclusively the domain of the Western scientific community, leaving Native peoples with little say over how their rich cultures are interpreted, recorded and transmitted. The NNAD knew that unless it took action, these important opportunities to interpret and protect Navajo history, identity and culture might slip further out of Navajo hands.

In thinking about how to increase the representation of Navajo citizens in cultural preservation positions, the NNAD made several strategic decisions. First, it decided that simply employing more Navajos in the NNAD - or advancing those already within the Department - would be unfeasible since few possessed the requisite academic credentials and training. Instead, the NNAD decided to focus on increasing the supply of qualified Navajos, a task that would take time but would have long-term benefits. Second, the NNAD decided that it must actively participate in the education and training of the next generation of Navajo anthropologists and archaeologists. Since several nearby universities had mandates to work with local communities, and there were Navajo students majoring in anthropology and archaeology at these universities, the NNAD saw the desirability of institutional cooperation. By creating training programs at these institutions, the NNAD made it possible for Native students not only to take the necessary coursework but also to acquire the culturally specific tools and approaches that would make their work on Navajo lands most effective.

In 1988, the NNAD established its first Training Program in cooperation with Northern Arizona University (NAU) in Flagstaff, Arizona. In 1993, it established another program at the NNAD-Farmington office in cooperation with Ft. Lewis College in Durango, Colorado. Navajo students who are enrolled full-time at either institution and who are majoring in Anthropology or Indigenous Studies are eligible for part-time employment or internships with

their school's respective NNAD Training Program. The Programs give practical work experience to Navajo undergraduate and graduate students through rigorous field and laboratory training. In the field, students acquire basic archeological inventory and excavation skills. Laboratory work includes artifact processing and analysis, basic computer skills and report preparation. The students also take field trips to important sites and attend lectures about a variety of topics, including the Native American Graves Protection and Repatriation Act, and federal and tribal law. In all aspects of the Programs, NNAD encourages students to draw upon indigenous knowledge that has been historically, and unfortunately, devalued by Western-trained scientists.

The Training Programs have been successful on many fronts. First, the Programs are building a pool of qualified Navajo professionals who are prepared to take key tribal positions in cultural resource management. By providing one-on-one training, creating a supportive learning environment, and engaging students in community service, the Programs help insure degree completion. Navajo students participating in the Training Program at NAU are nearly four times as likely to complete their degree as their American Indian classmates across all majors. The combination of personalized academic training with practical application also gives the Programs' students a competitive advantage vis-à-vis other students (Native or non-Native) on the Navajo or open job market. Already, the Programs' graduates have taken positions in the Navajo Nation's Archaeology Department, Housing Authority, Historic Preservation Department and the Department of Natural Resources.

Second, the Programs meet important community needs. As part of their training, students contribute substantively to the NNAD's work. In 2000, students worked with NNAD archaeologists on Navajo Nation-contracted projects for the Bureau of Land Management, the State of Utah and Peabody Western Coal Company. The NNAD Training Programs also possess a student-based contracting service whereby Navajo citizens can hire students at subsidized cost to identify and map any historic, prehistoric, or traditional and culturally important places on land being considered for development. This service ensures that development will not disrupt or destroy sensitive or sacred sites. Another way the Programs give back to the community is through outreach and education. Students attend high school career days to encourage other Navajos to consider careers in cultural preservation, make presentations to youth groups, and produce educational materials (for example, an interactive CD-ROM that documents vandalism of traditional cultural places) to teach others about cultural resource management and good stewardship practices. In response to the high volume of inquiries about the Programs, one student is even developing a "How To" manual that will assist other tribes in developing similar training programs.

Third, the NNAD Training Programs are bringing fresh new perspectives and approaches to the fields of anthropology and archaeology. One of the most innovative features of the Training Programs is that the students' training is not limited to a Western academic approach. Rather, the Programs embrace oral history and indigenous knowledge as valid anthropological approaches - and indeed believe they are essential for understanding and interpreting Navajo culture. Students are encouraged to draw upon the wisdom of their elders for their classes and in their fieldwork, to employ culturally appropriate techniques for handling (or in some cases, not handling) sacred objects, and to develop a better understanding of themselves and their culture. They are also encouraged to educate fellow students, teachers and others about how Navajo-controlled archaeology and anthropology play an essential role in preserving and enhancing Navajo history, values, practices and holy places for future generations. Students attest that their distinctly Navajo approach to cultural preservation is not always immediately welcomed by Western-trained scholars and students. At the same time, they feel that others are slowly coming to appreciate that Navajo approaches are as valid as they are different. For example, an ancient pot that had been discovered and analyzed by non-Navajo archaeologists was re-analyzed by a team from NNAD, who discovered that the prevailing interpretation of the pot's inscriptions was incorrect. The pattern did not represent a snake, but instead a traditional corn planting and harvesting method! In effect, the NNAD Training Programs are creating a cadre of well-qualified professionals who are not just archaeologists or anthropologists, but who are Navajo archaeologists and Navajo anthropologists. One can expect that this cadre will continue to challenge the status quo in ways that enhance these disciplines and fields of study.

At the core of this governance contribution is the idea that Navajos ought to be in a position to decide how their culture is to be protected and preserved. The NNAD's efforts to empower the Navajo people to control their cultural future on their own terms and with their own set of highly qualified professionals exemplifies a genuine commitment to self-determination.

Lessons:

· Assuming greater management control over cultural resources and increasing tribal stewardship of these resources are important objectives. Tribal governments should empower their citizens with the skills necessary to lead these efforts.

· Tribally supported training programs are an effective means for increasing the supply of qualified Native professionals across many different fields. Tribes and educational institutions can develop partnerships in which students can combine academic training with practical, on-reservation fieldwork.

· Indian nations need not rely on outsiders to analyze, interpret and transmit their unique cultures. There is tremendous value in creating Native approaches to scholarship and building the corpus of indigenous knowledge.

Navajo Nation

**Honoring Nations
Honoree 2000**

Text in its entirety from:
The Harvard Project On
American Indian Economic
Development

John F. Kennedy School
of Government
Harvard University

Honoring Nations Honoree 2002

Government Reform, Diné Appropriate Government, Local Governance Projects
The Office of Navajo Government Development (Window Rock, Arizona)

Recognizing the demand for a government that would respond to the unique needs of the Diné people, the Navajo Nation created the Commission on Navajo Government Development and its administrative arm, the Office of Navajo Government Development, in 1989. With the sole responsibility of undertaking government reform, the Commission and Office have educated the Navajo population on governmental issues and increased local participation in governance and the government reform process. These organizations are unique-and uniquely successful-in institutionalizing the process for undertaking on-going government reform in Indian Country.

With a population of approximately 225,000, the Navajo Nation is the largest Indian nation in the United States. It spans 17.5 million acres and stretches across northwest New Mexico, northeast Arizona, and southeast Utah. Traditionally, Navajo political decision making took place at a local level with bands of ten to forty families comprising political units. In the early 1920s, however, outside oil interests-eager to tap the Navajo Nation's potential energy riches-urged the US Department of the Interior to authorize the establishment of a centralized Navajo Tribal Council for the purpose of approving oil leases. In 1923, the Interior Department created the Navajo Tribal Council, the first body in Navajo history organized to act on behalf of the entire Nation. In 1989, the Nation endured a nationally publicized standoff between Council members supporting and opposing the Council's all-powerful chairman. In the aftermath of the turmoil and through a series of amendments to Title 2 of its Governing Code, the Nation reorganized its government into three branches and renamed the "Navajo Tribal Council" the "Navajo Nation Council." These amendments were viewed as a temporary measure intended to take place concurrently with a reform effort to reexamine the basic governing structure of the Nation. However, this reform did not take place, nor did the Navajo people have the opportunity to ratify the Title 2 amendments at a referendum. Because the Navajo people never consented to the establishment of the Council as the governing body in 1923 and did not

have the opportunity to ratify the Title 2 amendments in 1989, there has long been a broad desire among the Navajo people to reform their government.

While additional reform was not forthcoming in 1989, the Navajo Nation Council did create the means for it by establishing the Commission on Navajo Government Development and its administrative arm, the Office of Navajo Government Development. The Commission and Office are the only permanent government entities in Indian Country specifically charged with developing and helping to implement government reform on an on-going basis. The Commission on Navajo Government Development, which by statute, includes representatives from the five Navajo agencies (political subdivisions of the Nation), the three central government branches (the executive, legislative, and judicial branches), the Women's Commission, and Diné College, as well as a medicine man and a graduate school student, is designed to solicit and address Navajo attitudes towards government and government reform. All of the representatives are nominated by their respective entities and then confirmed by the Navajo Nation Council to serve a term of two years, with the exception of the medicine man and the five agency representatives, who serve terms of four years. The Office of Navajo Government Development, staffed by lawyers and policy professionals, is designed to implement the recommendations and advice of the Commission. Working with the Navajo people, the Commission and Office review and evaluate existing Navajo Nation government institutions and develop recommendations for government reforms for consideration and adoption by the Nation. Much of the Commission and Office's work is driven by grassroots outreach and information gathering efforts. To date, the groups' work has included reforms in executive branch policy, a review of the Navajo Nation Council's organization and procedure, a review of aspects of the Local Governance Act, and a Nation-wide convention and referendum on further changes to the Nation's Code. The comprehensiveness of this approach is unique in Indian Country.

Navajo Nation

Honoring Nations
Honoree 2002

Text in its entirety from:
The Harvard Project On
American Indian Economic
Development

John F. Kennedy School
of Government
Harvard University

Notably, the Commission and Office have been successful in working with the Navajo people to develop culturally appropriate government reforms. The Commission and Office were significantly involved in conceptualizing and drafting the Local Governance Act (LGA) of 1998, which devolves powers from the central Navajo Nation Council to local government units, the 110 chapters. The LGA allows chapters that are governance-certified by the Navajo Nation Council to acquire, sell, and lease property and issue property-use permits; enter into contracts for the provision of goods and services; enter into intergovernmental agreements with federal, state, and tribal entities; and adopt ordinances relating to land use planning, taxing, alternative governance models, and zoning. The Commission and Office's determination to return power to local government units as the Navajo people desired means not only that they worked for the passage of the LGA, but that they have assisted chapters in obtaining governance certification. Recognizing that many chapters had applied for certification but that several years after the Act's passage only a few had gained full LGA status, the Commission and Office sought and obtained grant funds to initiate the Land Use Planning component of the Act. The Land Use Planning Project allows chapters to hire Navajo consultants to develop land use plans, which will move them closer to governance certification. A majority of the plans will be complete by the end of fiscal year 2002.

While working with local chapters to implement the LGA, the Commission and Office discovered pervasive discontent with the Nation's central government, especially the Navajo Nation Council. Determined to transform this discontent into proposed amendments for central governmental reform, the Commission and Office initiated the Government Reform Project. Throughout 2001, the Commission and Office conducted a series of regional summits in order to solicit the input of the Navajo people on governmental reform. These summits were crucial in clarifying Navajo citizens' demands for a government consistent with their culture and tradition. In 2002, the Commission and Office organized this input into proposed amendments to the Navajo Nation Code and organized a convention to vote on the proposed amendments. Having formalized a process by which to elect convention delegates, the Commission and Office held the Statutory Reform Convention in May 2002. Delegates from 109 of the 110 chapters attended the Convention and approved twenty-nine proposed amendments. If adopted by the Navajo Nation Council, the amendments will result in a more effective and culturally appropriate Navajo government.

Two strategies have enabled the Commission on Navajo Government Development and the Office of Navajo Government Development to work towards a more culturally appropriate form of Navajo government that is free from federally imposed structures and regulations. First, the Commission and Office have actively involved the Navajo people in government reform. The Commission and Office continually work to educate the Navajo citizenry about the history, structure, and purpose of their government. They have published a highly readable and readily available brochure on tribal governance, Handbook on Navajo Nation Government, as well as a report, Engaging the Navajo People in the Process of Government Reform, which details the strengths and weaknesses of the existing Navajo government and recommends strategies for individual involvement in the reform effort. The Commission and Office also have gone to great lengths to hear the voice of the people on government reform.

Their Government Reform Project began with a series of public hearings, workshops, and agency summits designed to solicit the opinions of Navajo citizens. While a reform effort rarely reaches all people, the Government Reform Project's public hearings have set a very high standard, and the Commission and Office continue to meet regularly with schools, youth and elder groups, business leaders, veterans, and current US military personnel. To close the circle of communication and outreach, the Commission and Office keep citizens informed of progress on the Government Reform Project through the regular publication of newspaper-like updates on summit and convention issues and findings.

Second, the Commission and Office have established a helpful web of working relationships within the Navajo Nation government. The Commission and Office maintain strong ties to the Navajo Nation Executive Branch, the Navajo Nation Council, the five regional agencies, and the 110 local chapters. These relationships highlight the Commission and Office's unique model of leveraging the legal authority and funding of a government to turn grassroots citizens' concerns into government reforms. Critically, while the Office is technically a part of the legislative branch, the Commission and Office's careful attention to their relationship with the Navajo Nation Council has increased their ability to independently promote government reform. For example, in 2001, the Navajo Nation Council asked the Commission and Office to review the Council's organization. The resulting report led to many proposals to improve Council efficiency, and convinced many delegates of the Commission and Office's non-political agenda. Although the Commission and Office might benefit from even greater independence, their skill in maintaining working relationships with the government institutions on which they depend results in deliberate, productive reform that makes the Navajo government increasingly responsive to the Navajo people.

While many Indian Nations are making great strides in government reform by means of constitutional change, the Commission on Navajo Government Development and the Office of Navajo Government Development exemplify an innovative and different means of reform-a permanent government institution to work on fundamental, grassroots-driven governmental change. The comprehensiveness of this approach to producing a culturally appropriate form of government is unique in Indian Country.

Lessons

Replacing imposed governing structures with tribally designed institutions is a difficult and long-term undertaking. Creating an office or commission that focuses solely on improving government performance can be an excellent way for Indian nations to motivate, inform, and manage constitutional and governmental reform.

Like other nations, Indian nations are challenged to create or reform governing institutions to match their unique political cultures. Tribal traditions are resources that tribal governments can tap in their efforts to develop institutions of self-government - ones that are both legitimate and able to advance a tribe's strategic goals.

Public hearings, workshops, and summits can be useful means of soliciting citizens' input and opinions about necessary governmental reforms. Providing regular updates to the tribal citizenry - via mailings, radio, television, etc. - can also sustain public support for reform efforts.

Corrections Project Department of Behavioral Health Services Window Rock, AZ

In 1983, the Navajo Nation Corrections Project emerged as the only tribally funded program in the country to provide American Indian inmates in tribal, state, and federal prisons access to traditional religious ceremonial practices. A pioneer in the realm of prisoner advocacy, the Navajo Nation Corrections Project not only promotes Native inmates' dignity and recovery through access to culturally appropriate religious rites, but also wages a passionate defense of a basic human and civil right already guaranteed to non-Native inmates: the free practice of their religions.

Like other Indian nations, the Navajo Nation confronts the difficult reality that many of its citizens are incarcerated in tribal, state, and federal prisons. In 1996, the US Department of Justice's publication "American Indians and Crime" reported that the number of American Indians per capita confined in state and federal prisons was 38 percent above the national average. The rate of confinement in local jails is estimated to be even higher-nearly four times the national average. On any day in 1996, sixty thousand American Indians were under correctional care, custody, or control.

Religious freedom, a right granted to prisoners throughout the US, has not been sufficiently realized for American Indian prisoners. Native inmates across the country are denied these religious freedoms because of ignorance, cultural bias, or outright malfeasance by prison officials. As a result, thousands of Native prisoners serve lengthy terms without access to their religious rites and practices, such as sweat lodges, talking circles, pipe ceremonies, Native American Church prayer services, and counseling sessions-practices that could be a meaningful part of rehabilitation. Supporters of Native inmates' religious freedom assert that correctional facilities that ban sweat lodges, talking circles, and possession of religious items lose much of their rehabilitative power. Inmates without the ability to exercise their religious freedom, especially those recovering from substance abuse, may be more prone to recidivism.

The Constitution guarantees religious freedom to all Americans and it is reiterated on behalf of American Indians in the Native American Religious Freedom Act of 1978. For years, however, state and federal prisons have abused or neglected these guarantees. In 1993, federal legislation that included provisions to address the religious rights of Native prisoners, the Native American Free Exercise of Religious Freedom Act, was introduced to Congress. Regrettably, it was not passed and reintroduction has not occurred. Still, even if this federal legislation is adopted, the provisions of the act will extend only to federal-not to state-prisons. State prison reforms will require attention on a state-by-state basis. While such federal and state legislative reforms proceed slowly, thousands of Native inmates remain confined without a freedom that is theoretically guaranteed to them.

In 1983, determined to address this persistent problem, the Navajo Nation created the Navajo Nation Corrections Project to advocate for religious freedom. Housed within the Navajo Nation's Department of Behavior Services, the federally-funded Corrections Project is sustained by volunteer efforts. The staff, including a director/spiritual leader and two traditional religious practitioners, is dedicated to three core activities: they offer religious services to Native inmates for the purpose of rehabilitation and recovery; introduce federal and state legislation on the issue of American Indian inmate religious freedom; and assist in the enforcement of existing laws pertaining to Native prisoners' religious rights.

Over twenty years, the Navajo Nation Corrections Project has touched the lives of thousands of Native inmates in tribal, state, and federal prisons. The Corrections Project's staff travels weekly to prisons throughout the country to offer Native inmates counseling and religious services. Since 1983, they have visited forty-six federal corrections facilities and seventy-three state facilities located in dozens of states, from California to Pennsylvania and from North Dakota to Texas. The staff regularly visits the correctional facilities located on the Navajo reservation, as well. In 2002 alone, Corrections Project staff visited thirty prisons and provided counseling and ceremonial services to 2,176 clients. During these visits, Corrections Project staff offered ninety sweat lodge ceremonies, ten pipe ceremonies, twelve talking circles, four Native American Church prayer services for the families of inmates, ninety group counseling sessions, and twenty-five individual family counseling sessions. In addition to providing such religious services through their own efforts, the Corrections Project advocates for additional personnel within prisons. In 2002, for example, the Project successfully negotiated for the appointment of a full-time chaplain in the New Mexico Corrections Department, a position subsequently filled by a Navajo spiritual leader. The Corrections Project staff reports marked improvement in Native inmates' behavior and firmly believe that their success in bringing religious ceremonies and counseling to prison facilities will better equip individuals to reenter society.

The Corrections Project has also been instrumental in formulating and passing state and federal legislation that guarantees inmates' rights to practice their religions. Among the Corrections Project's main goals is to develop legislation that can be applied uniformly across states. The Corrections Project authored, or co-authored, legislation in New Mexico (1983, 1996), Arizona (1984), Colorado (1992), and Utah (1995). These four states developed legal protections for American Indian inmates to freely exercise their spiritual and religious beliefs without fear of retaliation or discrimination in state facilities. The legislation affords Native inmates access to traditional spiritual leaders, religious items and materials, and sites of worship such as sweat lodges, talking circles, and individual outdoor prayer spaces. Moreover, Native inmates are not forced to cut their hair if it conflicts with their traditional religious beliefs or practices.

In addition to providing direct services and drafting or advocating for legislation that protects Natives' religious rights, the Corrections Project also concentrates on enforcement. Many state prisons ignore or deny Native inmates' requests to practice their religion despite legislative guarantees. The Corrections Project staff vigilantly reminds officials of the law. On several occasions, when reminders were not acted upon, the Corrections Project reported the violations to the Civil Rights division of the US Department of Justice. The Corrections Project has also testified before the US Senate Committee on Indian Affairs hearings on the proposed Native American Free Exercise of Religion Act in 1992 and again in 1994. As a direct result of these hearings, several state and federal prisons began to implement policies that allowed Native inmates access to religious practices.

The Navajo Nation Corrections Project's successes are due to several effective and interconnected strategies. First, the Corrections Project refuses to accept prison officials' cultural ignorance or bias as the grounds for denying Native inmates their constitutional and human right to practice their religion. Unfortunately, the precedent for denying American Indians the free practice of their religions on just such a basis is already well established. Beginning in the early nineteenth century and continuing

Honoring Nations Honoree 2003

Text in its entirety from:
The Harvard Project On
American Indian Economic
Development

John F. Kennedy School
of Government
Harvard University

Navajo Nation

**Honoring Nations
Honoree 2003**

Text in its entirety from:
**The Harvard Project On
American Indian Economic
Development**

**John F. Kennedy School
of Government
Harvard University**

as late as 1978, the US government outlawed countless Native religious ceremonies and practices on the basis of ignorance and fear while it steadily destroyed religious items and materials in an effort to assimilate Native peoples into the dominant society. The Corrections Project insists that prejudice should not serve as a justification for systematically or arbitrarily denying Native inmates their religious rights-and, as a result, their right to a recovery.

Second, the Navajo Nation Corrections Project possesses an unwavering commitment to raising awareness about Native inmates' rights to religious freedom among prison officials and state, national, and international government officials and agencies. In conjunction with the Native American Rights Fund, the Corrections Project initiated a discussion about Native inmates' religious rights with the Association of State Correctional Administrators. In 2002, the Corrections Project passed a resolution at the annual convention of the National Congress of American Indians declaring the protection of American Indians' civil rights a national priority and calling upon President George W. Bush and Attorney General John Ashcroft to enhance legal protections for Native inmates' free exercise of religion. The Project also initiated a discussion with the Civil Rights Division of the US Justice Department regarding a formal investigation of the violation of Native inmates' rights to the free exercise of religion. Similarly, the Corrections Project has been aggressive in its determination to educate international audiences regarding the abuse of Native inmates' civil rights in US prisons. The Project raised this concern over the abuse of Native inmates' religious rights before the United Nations Commission on Human Rights in Geneva, Switzerland, and again as part of the UN Regional PrepCom for the Americas in Santiago, Chile in 2000. In 2001, it presented this concern at the UN World Conference Against Racism in Durban, South Africa.

Third, the Navajo Nation Corrections Project strives to protect the civil rights of all American Indians. The staff provides religious services not only for Navajo inmates, but for all Native inmates, and also defends all Natives' basic rights. The Corrections Project enhanced its leverage by collaborating with organizations on the local, regional, national, and international levels-including various departments and projects within the Navajo Nation, the Navajo Medicine Men Association, the Oglala Sioux Tribe, the Minnesota Council on Crime and Justice, the Sun Dancers, the Native American Rights Fund, the American Indian Movement, the Native American Church of North America, the National Congress of American Indians, and the International Indian Treaty Council. The Navajo Nation Corrections Project's determination to turn the sobering scale of incarcerated Native inmates' rights should stand as an inspiration to all Indian nations confronting serious challenges.

Already, several nations have turned to the Navajo Nation Corrections Project for guidance in serving the religious needs of their own incarcerated populations. With an inordinately high percentage of Native Americans held in local, state, and federal prisons, the need for other tribes to join with the Navajo Nation Corrections Project in the defense of Native inmates' rights is pressing. As Indian nations across the country learn from the Correction Project's determination to address the dual concerns of rehabilitating the Native inmate population while defending their basic civil and human rights, the leverage in enforcing existing law and shaping critical public policy will only grow. Through its own efforts, the Navajo Nation Corrections Project has already altered the experience of the individual Native inmate-offering access to religious services while defending constitutional rights guaranteed to Native and non-Native inmates alike.

Pascua Yaqui

**Pascua Yaqui Reservation
Federal reservation
Pascua Yaqui
Pima County, Arizona**

Pascua Yaqui Tribe
7474 South Camino de Oeste
Tucson, AZ 85746
520-883-5000
520-883-5014 Fax
pascuayaqui-nsn.gov

LOCATION AND LAND STATUS
The Pascua Yaqui Reservation is located in southern Arizona, 15 miles southwest of Tucson. Situated near Picture Rocks, Old Tucson, and Saguaro National Monument, the reservation is bounded by state, private, and federal lands. In 1952, the original 40-acre Pascua Village was annexed by the City of Tucson, where some Yaquis continue to live. In 1964, Congressman Morris K. Udall introduced a bill in Congress for the transfer of 202 acres of desert land southwest of Tucson to the Yaquis, who were looking for a home where they could retain their tribal identity. The bill was approved in August 1964, and the Pascua Yaqui Association, a nonprofit Arizona corporation, was formed to receive the deed for the land from the U.S. Bureau of Land Management.

The reservation, referred to as New Pascua, was formally established on September 18, 1978, when President Jimmy Carter signed Senate Bill 1633, which extended federal benefits to the Pascua Yaqui Indians in Arizona. In 1982 the reservation acquired an additional 690 acres. The following are Pascua communities in the Tucson area: New Pascua, Old Pascua, Barrio Libre, and Marana. Outside of Tucson are other communities: Penjamo in Scottsdale, Guadalupe in Tempe, and High Town in Chandler.

CLIMATE
Tucson sits at an elevation of 2,584 feet above sea level. The arid Sonoran Desert climate is characterized by year-round average high temperatures in the 80s, with high temperatures often reaching over 100°F in summer months. The highest temperature ever recorded was 117°F. The year-round average low temperature is 55°F. The lowest temperature ever recorded was 16°F. The area receives approximately 12 inches of precipitation annually, with less than 2 inches of that falling as snowfall each year.

CULTURE AND HISTORY
The traditional territory of the Yaqui people was along the Yaqui River in southern Sonora, Mexico. Descendants of the ancient Toltecs, the Yaquis speak a Cahitan language of the Uto-Aztecan language family; peoples speaking other languages of the family are found from northeastern California south into central Mexico.

By 552 AD, Yaquis were living in small family clusters along the Yaqui River (Yoem Vatwe), north to the Gila River, where they practiced a hunting and gathering subsistence lifestyle. They also cultivated corn, beans, and squash on small family plots. The people were traders, traveling widely throughout what is now the south-central United States and northern Mexico, exchanging foods, furs, shells, salt, and other goods with the Shoshones, the Comanches, the Pueblos, the Pimas, the Aztecs, and the Toltecs. They sometimes settled among these other Native groups. By 1414, the Yaquis were organized into autonomous, yet unified, culturally distinct groups.

The Yaquis first encountered the whites in 1533, when a Spanish military expedition searching for slaves passed through their area. The Spanish on this occasion were defeated, but many Yaquis died. Between 1608 and 1610 the Spanish repeatedly attacked. The Yaquis raised a fighting force of 7,000 and successfully withstood the attacks. They welcomed Jesuit priests into their communities to build missions and build the economy, which led to the development of eight sacred towns or "pueblos" around the mission churches: La Navidad del Senor de Vikam, Santa Rosa de Vahkom, La Asuncion de Nuestra Senora de Rahum, Espiritu Santo (Ko'okoim), Santa Barbara de Wiivisim, San Ignacio de Torim, San Miguel de Veenem, and La Santisima Trinidad de Potam.

When silver was discovered in the Yaqui River Valley in 1684, the Spanish began making incursions once again. In 1740, the Yaquis allied with the Mayo tribe to force the Spanish out, and for the next 190 years, they engaged the Spanish, and then the Mexicans after Mexico won independence from Spain. Juan Banderas, a notable Yaqui leader, tried to unite the Mayo, Opata, and Pima tribes to force Mexicans out of Indian Country. He was caught in 1833 and executed.

Mexican troops occupied many Yaqui pueblos and deported them to work as slaves in Yucatan, Oaxaca, Vera Cruz, Mexico City, and Guadalajara. Some were shipped as far as Bolivia, the islands of the Caribbean, and northward into the United States. In 1868, 600 Yaqui men, women, and children were captured near Vahkom Pueblo by Mexican state and federal troops. They were disarmed, and 450 of them were locked in a church. During the night, the church was shelled, and 120 of the people inside the church were killed. Still more lost their lives due to smallpox; by 1887, only 4,000 Yaquis remained in the Rio Yaqui area.

The Yaquis suffered severe persecution under the reign of Mexican President Porfirio Diaz (1884 - 91), as they fought to preserve their rich agricultural land. The majority were ultimately forced to abandon their communities. Individually and in small groups, many Yaquis crossed into Arizona as political refugees, eventually settling in small villages in southern Arizona. Gradually they spread out, settling north of Tucson in a village they named Pascua Village, and in Guadalupe, which is close to Tempe and Scottsdale, in the Phoenix metropolitan area. In 1897, a peace treaty was signed at Ortiz, Sonora, Mexico, between the Yaquis and the Mexican government, but battles and the deportation of Yaquis continued for two more years. Old Pascua Village was established in 1903. Many more Yaquis moved there to escape the violence of the 1910-1920 Mexican Revolution; by 1920, there were probably more than 2,000 Yaquis in Arizona. While originally treated as aliens, most are now U.S. citizens. The people who remained in Mexico returned to their villages after the Mexican Revolution, where President Lazaro Cordenas established the Yaqui Indigenous Community in 1938.

The autonomous Yaqui villages in Arizona became larger, and by 1952, they were surrounded by urban communities. In 1964, with the aid of Congressman Morris K. Udall, the Pascua Yaquis received 202 acres of desert land to call their own. At first, the State of Arizona was largely uncooperative; officials maintained that these poverty-stricken people should be shipped back to Mexico. The founding of New Pascua and much of its development was due to the vision and constant effort of tribal member Anselmo Valencia, who for many years served as head of the Pascua Yaqui Easter Ceremonial Society, called the Kohtumbrem.

Historically involved in the cultivation of crops, the Yaqui people worked as agricultural laborers, primarily picking cotton, until 1948, when mechanized picking made their jobs obsolete in Arizona. Since the 1960s, the Yaqui Tribe has provided job training, particularly in the construction industry, in an attempt to combat high unemployment rates. Those Yaquis who moved to the new land, now the Pascua Yaqui Indian Reservation, waged a long and difficult battle to secure federal recognition for their tribe, and on September 18, 1978, they were successful.

The Yaqui people continually strive to preserve aspects of their traditional culture, while seeking economic independence through employment in non-Native community and economic development on the reservation. Yaqui scholars have developed a writing system to help teach the language to nonspeakers, and many children participate in bilingual programs in the school system. Approximately 25,000 Yaquis currently live in the eight towns established by Jesuits in the seventeenth century in Mexico.

GOVERNMENT
The tribe is organized under the terms of the Indian Reorganization Act of 1934. The Pascua Yaqui Reservation is governed by a seven-member elected tribal council which includes a chairperson, a vice-chairperson, and a secretary. The tribal constitution was ratified by the tribe on January 26, 1988, and was approved by the Secretary of the Interior on February 18, 1988. Biweekly council meetings are usually held on Thursday evenings, and a community meeting is held on the third Saturday of each month at council chambers in Tucson. The tribe, under PL-638, contracts with the BIA to administer key programs and services.

ECONOMY
The government, gaming, and tourism contribute to the Pascua Yaqui's economy. The tribe is looking to further develop its economy through small commercial manufacturing leases. The reservation is located within an enterprise zone. The tribe offers various incentives and tax credits, to potential businesses wanting to locate on the reservation. Some of the incentives include accelerated rates of depreciation on capitalized buildings and equipment, pollution control tax credits, research and development tax credits and enterprise zone tax credits. Various qualifying businesses can also tap into Arizona's Job Training Fund. Businesses considering the reservation as a place of business are offered exemptions of personal and real property taxes.

Government as Employer. Tribal government, via various economic development projects under direct management of tribal leadership, is the single largest employer on the reservation.

Gaming. On January 12, 1992, the tribe enacted Ordinance No. 92-12 to authorize gaming on its reservation. It opened a 9,000-square-foot bingo hall that same year. Two years later, on March 10, 1994, the Casino of the Sun opened its doors to business. Open since October 10, 2001, the Casino del Sol has become the most lucrative tribal enterprise to date. Casino del Sol is a 75,000-square-foot facility featuring 507 slots, 20 table games, 12 poker tables, 600 bingo seats, seven restaurants and the Anselmo Valencia Tori Amphitheater, a 4,400-seat, open-air concert venue, southern Arizona's largest. The amphitheater offers 6 corporate boxes, 1,600 theater seats and 2,800 lawn seats. The casino employs 442 people, and remains under the direct management of tribal leadership. Revenues generated by the tribe's gaming enterprises provide funds for education, housing, health care, public safety, and other essential social services for tribal members.

Industrial Parks. One 40-acre industrial park is located on the reservation. As of 2004, no utilities were available at this site, and the lands are still vacant.

Manufacturing. The Pascua Yaqui Adobe Company is a tribally owned and operated producer of cement-stabilized, pressed, natural adobe brick. The tribe is developing other plans for small commercial manufacturing leases on the reservation.

Services and Retail. The tribe owns and operates a landscape nursery business, a AAA Pet Lodge for travelers, a smoke shop and a Chevron station.

Pascua Yaqui

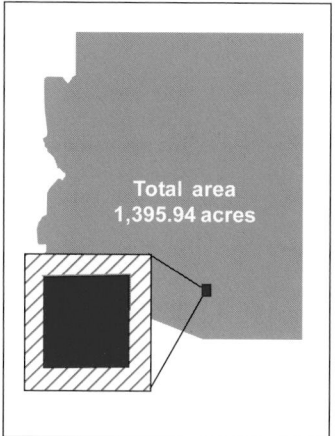

Total area
1,395.94 acres

Total area *(BIA, 2004)*
1,395.94 acres

Tribally-owned lands *(BIA, 2004)*
1,395.94 acres

Population *2000 census*
3,315

Tribal enrollment
(Tribal source, 2004)
3,002

Total labor force *2000 census*
1,085

High school graduate or higher
2000 census
41.3%

Bachelor's degree or higher
2000 census
1.9%

Unemployment rate
2000 census
18.16%

Per capita income
$5,921

343

Pascua Yaqui

Tourism and Recreation. The Pascua Yaqui Reservation is situated in the midst of a number of scenic drives and recreational opportunities. Skiing is available an hour from the reservation at Mt. Lemmon, and Saguaro National Monument is located a few miles to the north. Other nearby tourist attractions include the San Xavier del Bac Mission on the nearby Tohono O'odham Indian Reservation, Old Tucson Studios, the Arizona-Sonora Desert Museum, and Kitt Peak National Observatory. The nearby Santa Catalina, Tucson, and Rincon mountains provide hiking and camping opportunities.

In addition to Casino del Sol, the tribe sponsors the Yaqui Easter ceremonies, a traditional Native American festival dating back to the seventeenth century. An important annual event, the celebration combines both Catholic liturgy and a ceremony that dramatizes the crucifixion of Jesus. Tribal Recognition Day is celebrated annually on September 18.

In November 1999, the tribe celebrated the first Harvest Festival just before Thanksgiving, a now-annual event in which students and townspeople display and sell handmade arts and crafts items made from the fruits of the community's organic garden. Soap, bird feeders, wreaths, ornaments, corn husk dolls, seed balls, painted gourds, and chile ristras can be purchased, as well as baked goods and traditional foods. The event features live entertainment and is open to the public.

INFRASTRUCTURE
Both Interstate 10 and 19 pass close to the reservation. Tucson International Airport is 15 miles from the reservation.

Electricity. Trico Electric Corporation provides electricity to the reservation.

Fuel. The reservation uses natural gas supplied by Southwest Gas.

Water Supply. Water is provided by the City of Tucson.

Transportation. A wide variety of commercial transportation and freight services are available in nearby Tucson.

Media and Communications. The community publishes a monthly newspaper, the *Pascua Pueblo News*, and receives radio and television broadcasts from Tucson.

COMMUNITY FACILITIES AND SERVICES
The Pascua Yaqui Tribe maintains several community facilities, including the tribal offices, a senior center and greenhouse, library, park, community center, recreation center, and an education center. The tribe used U.S. Housing and Urban Development community block grants to remodel a fire station and purchase a fire engine, in addition to constructing the senior citizens' center and a recreation park.

In 2000 the tribe constructed a semipermanent traditional Yaqui shade ramada, to provide shade and to shelter the outdoor classroom near the community garden planted in 1997. The community also has planted a 600-square-foot pollinator garden to provide rest and sustenance for migratory bird populations flying over seasonally. The gardens provide a hands-on, outdoor science classroom for students.

An Explorer Post on the reservation offers youth an opportunity to learn and practice the values most highly prized by the community: ethical leadership, responsibility, commitment to others, and enjoying life to the maximum while learning about career opportunities. The program serves youth ages 14-21.

Education. Kindergarten through high school students attend Tucson public schools. A 10,838-square-foot pre-school opened in September 2002, with the capacity to serve 138 youngsters. Programs incorporate the teaching of the Yaqui Culture.

Health Care. The reservation has one health clinic and two hospitals operating via PL-638 contracts with the U.S. Indian Health Service. The facilities are within a 15-minute drive in Tucson, and they feature a community health representative program, a recreation program, and a field nurse. Clinic and hospital care is contracted with Rio Clinic and the University of Arizona Hospital, both in Tucson.

There is also one provider of alternative health care on the reservation, Yaqui Healer's House. The facility features an alternative medicine program, a community health nurse, the community health representative, a diabetes program, an HIV/AIDS prevention program, a managed care office, a mental health program, a WIC program, and the GAMBRO Dialysis Center. Transportation is available to any community member in need. The Yaqui Healer's House also offers an alcohol and substance abuse program and a youth wellness program. The center sponsors a Boy's and Girl's Club at the location.

Salt River

Salt River Pima-Maricopa Indian Community
Federal reservation
Maricopa, Pima
Maricopa County, Arizona

Salt River Pima-Maricopa
Indian Community
10005 East Osborn Road
Scottsdale, AZ 85256
480-850-8000
480-850-8014 Fax
srpmic-nsn.gov

LOCATION AND LAND STATUS
The Salt River Pima-Maricopa Indian Community (SRPMIC) is located east of Phoenix in south-central Arizona, adjacent to the cities of Scottsdale, Tempe, Mesa, and Fountain Hills, and it shares a border with the Fort McDowell Indian Nation. The SRPMIC lies in the transitional area between the Sonoran Desert and the Mexican highlands. The Salt River flows along the southern border of the reservation, and the Arizona Canal transverses it. The Granite Reef Dam and Aqueduct are located along the southern boundary of the community. Red Mountain, located on the eastern boundary, can be seen throughout the community.

An Executive Order on June 14, 1879, established the reservation and held 46,627 acres in trust, of which 25,229 acres were divided into twenty-, ten-, and five-acre allotments. The original number of allotments in 1911 was 943; by the mid-1980s, the number had increased to more than 2,300. During the same period, at least 150 of the allotments were in severe heirship status, which means that each of them was divided among 20 to 200 individual landowners with varying fractional interest. To respond to this problem, Congress passed the Land Consolidation Act of 1982, at the request of the community. The community maintains 19,000 acres as a natural preserve.

Elevations range between 1,170 feet in the lowlands to the peak of Red Mountain at 2,830 feet. Rolling lands are found in the southwestern portion of the reservation. The western region lies within an alluvial basin with fertile agricultural lands.

CLIMATE
The year-round average high temperature in Scottsdale is 86°F. The year-round average low is 53.5°F. The area receives just over nine inches of precipitation annually.

CULTURE AND HISTORY

The Salt River Pima-Maricopa Indian Community (SRPMIC) is comprised of two distinct tribes: the Akimel Au-Authm ("river people"), or Pima, and the Xalychidom Piipaash ("people who live toward the water"), or Maricopa. The Pimas speak a Uto-Aztecan language related to the languages of peoples from the Great Basin of California and Nevada to central Mexico. The Maricopas speak a dialect of the Yuman branch of the Hokan language family, similar to that spoken by peoples from southern Oregon to southern Mexico. They share cultural values.

Both the Maricopas and Pimas have traditionally been river-basin desert farmers in the area, providing protection for one another against invasion by Yuman and Apache tribes; thus, their histories are intertwined. The Pimas believe they descend from the ancient Hoo-hoogam, or Hohokam ("those who have gone"), who lived in the river valleys of Arizona as early as 300 BC, creating an elaborate irrigation system to farm the arid desert land. Remnants of those ancient canals can still be found, although they are now modernized. The Maricopas, living in small bands along the Lower Colorado and Gila rivers, were less sedentary than the Pimas. They were driven toward the Pima settlements by shortages of water and the pressure of warfare with other tribes.

The earliest mention of the Pimas was made by the Spaniard Marcos de Nize in 1589. Padre Eusebio Francisco Kino, a Jesuit, made several trips into the Gila River area between 1694 and 1699. He is believed to have introduced wheat to the area. Even before the arrival of the Spanish, the Pimas and Maricopas had an impressive agricultural economy, benefiting both from year-round irrigation systems using water from the Gila River and from the cultivation of drought-resistant corn. The result was more food to store away in case of drought and more food and cotton for trade. While the Pimas often traded with other tribes, during dry years when the nearby and closely related Tohono O'odham had little to trade, the Pimas served as employers of Tohono O'odham people who moved to their territory to cultivate the crops.

Agricultural production increased after the Pimas received wheat from the Spanish; it was planted in the fall and harvested in the spring, so it did not conflict with planting and harvesting corn. Wheat was valued highly by the Spanish and later by other European immigrants. It proved to be a profitable trade item for the tribe, providing members with a source of currency. Increasing production and trading success led to more cooperation and to more economic specialization, with men concentrating on farming and women on producing crafts for trade. Pima people are known for watertight, intricately woven basketry. Maricopa women specialized in pottery, typically made of red clay. Both art forms are now on display at the Community's Hoo-hoogam Ki Museum. Robust long-distance runners, they served as trusted scouts for the U.S. Cavalry, and they continue to serve in the armed forces today.

By the mid-1800s, the Spanish had designated the Pimas as a nation, with a governor and an active tribal council. The Pimas passed into American jurisdiction after the Mexican-American War, when much of the Southwest was ceded to the United States. In 1856, some Pimas and Maricopas joined the U.S. Army in one of its first combined military operations, in this case against the Apaches.

Approximately 60,000 gold seekers passed through Pima villages en route to the California gold fields between 1848 and 1854. The influx of these outsiders caused a great increase in demand for Pima wheat, leading to a boom economy and an enormous expansion of production.

The decline of the Pima economy began in earnest at the end of the Civil War when immigrants began settling in the area that would become the city of Phoenix. They constructed a dam on the Gila River upriver from the Pima and Maricopa villages and began irrigating their fields, often letting the water go to waste rather than leading the canals back to the river. This competition led a number of Pimas to move south to a new location on the Salt River. On June 14, 1879, this new settlement was recognized and established as the Salt River Indian Reservation.

Throughout much of the twentieth century, Pima and Maricopa residents of the reservation have continued to farm, relying on irrigation techniques developed over centuries of experience in a desert environment. They increasingly became involved in the economy of the surrounding urban areas, especially following the great population growth of the Phoenix metropolitan area after World War II, but they have retained strong spiritual connections to their core beliefs.

To assist in the preservation of the O'odham (Pima) and Piipaash (Maricopa) languages, the tribes initiated the O'odham-Piipaash Language Program, which conducts accredited community-wide language classes, provides translation assistance to individuals and staff members in all tribal offices, uses immersion teams to provide a natural context for language participation, and has planned to weave language use into curricula instruction in all pre-kindergarten classes, elementary, middle, and high school coursework, and in adult basic education classes. This program collects language recordings and other cultural information from tribal elders for use by future generations.

GOVERNMENT

The Salt River Pima-Maricopa Indian Community was created by Executive Order of President Rutherford B. Hayes on June 14, 1879. The tribe's official governing body is the Salt River Pima-Maricopa Indian Community Council which is composed of a president and vice-president elected at large for four-year terms, and seven popularly elected members. Members are elected from one of two electoral districts for four-year terms.

The SRPMIC entered into a self-governance compact with the BIA to administer key programs and services. The tribal government, authorized by the constitution approved under the Indian Reorganization Act of 1934, is divided into major departments that oversee the following programs and services on behalf of the community: administration, office of the general counsel, treasury, gaming regulatory office, self-governance, community development, economic development, engineering and construction, education, human resources, community relations, congressional and legislative affairs, cultural and environmental resources protection, finance, fire, health and human services, community court, public works, transportation, recreation, museum, purchasing, and learning center. The tribal finance department provides a full range of financial services to all community members. Engineering and construction services conducts GIS mapping, oversees water resources, completes surveys, issues building permits, oversees compliance with tribal building codes, and oversees all phases of building design and construction for the community.

The Salt River Police Department had 71 commissioned officers and 27 civilian staff members in 2003. All officers enforce tribal and state laws, and they receive a special law enforcement officer commission through the BIA that allows them to investigate federal crimes, as well.

An archaeological and cultural resources program was initiated in 1995 as part of cultural and environmental services, a division

Salt River

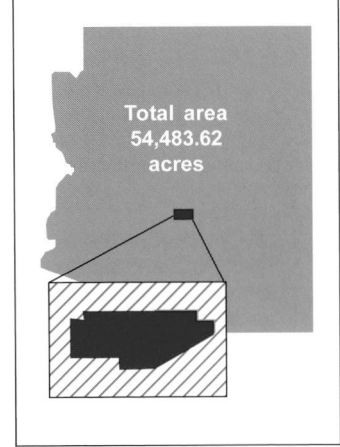

Total area
54,483.62
acres

Total area *(BIA, 2004)*
54,483.62 acres

Tribally-owned lands *(BIA, 2004)*
30,078.93 acres

Allotted lands *(BIA, 2004)*
24,404.69 acres

Population *2000 census*
6,405

Population *(Tribal source, 2004)*
7,000+

Tribal enrollment *(BIA, 2001)*
7,371

Total labor force
2000 census
2,041

High school graduate or higher
2000 census
64.4%

Bachelor's degree or higher
2000 census
4.9%

Unemployment rate
2000 census
9.46%

Per capita income
$9,592

Salt River

ENVIRONMENTAL CONCERNS

The tribes maintain a cultural and environmental services division within the community development department. The cultural and environmental services division operates environmental programs, among them an air quality program whose primary objectives are to: regularly determine the status of air quality at the community (as affected by its proximity to the Greater Phoenix Metropolitan Area), conduct regulatory and enforcement inspections, implement the tribal (air quality) implementation plan, and monitor ambient air quality on an ongoing basis. In cooperation with the U.S. Environmental Protection Agency (USEPA), all federal Clean Air Act guidelines are enforced. The tribe is working with the USEPA to develop a network of air quality monitoring stations at various locations within the reservation boundaries. In 2004 the community was classified as "nonattainment" for: (1) particulate matter, (2) carbon monoxide emissions, and (3) ozone formation as a result of air pollutants.

of the community development program. The cultural resources program ensures that archaeological and historical sites scattered throughout the community are identified, protected, and preserved in accordance with traditional cultural values. The program also oversees repatriation efforts flowing from discoveries made off-reservation. Such resources are protected by a tribal antiquities ordinance and the Native American Graves Protection and Repatriation Act. The tribe's historic preservation office regulates this compliance process.

ECONOMY

The economy of the Salt River Pima-Maricopa Indian Community is diversified, with commercial and agricultural enterprises. The tribe leases property to a number of businesses including several large national retailers, and it owns seven enterprises. It also imposes sales and tobacco taxes.

Agriculture and Livestock. Approximately 13,000 acres are under cultivation in cotton, melons, potatoes, onions, broccoli, and carrots. Approximately 240 wild horses graze on lands located west of Beeline Highway. The tribes have built a holding facility which is used during the adoption process and when monitoring the health of the horses. Nineteen thousand acres are maintained as a natural preserve.

Gaming. Under the Arizona Gaming Compact, the Salt River Pima-Maricopa Indian Community is allowed two gaming facilities.

Casino Arizona at McKellips is located east of the 101 Pima Freeway at McKellips. Casino Arizona at Talking Stick is located off the 101 Pima Freeway on Indian Bend.

The casinos hold 1,500 ticket-pay multidenominational slot machines, including 80 high-limit slots, live blackjack, 50 poker tables, and live fast-action keno. There's also a mahogany paneled high-stakes poker room. The Starz Sportsbar offers video poker slots and numerous televisions for viewing sporting events.

Casino Arizona at McKellips offers four new restaurants including a unique buffet, four lounges that include a piano bar and a live entertainment showroom, a gift shop, complimentary valet parking, and free shuttle service.

Casino Arizona at Talking Stick offers three lounges including the Blue Coyote Sports Bar, Wandering Horse Lounge, and Signals Lounge.

Construction. A construction company leases space from the tribe. All construction occurring on the Salt River Pima-Maricopa Indian Community lands must use community-owned sand, gravel, and cement companies.

Manufacturing and Mining. Two of the community's enterprises, Phoenix Cement and Salt River Sand and Rock, have merged businesses to create the Salt River Materials Group, which utilizes resources from the reservation for production. Newly purchased technologies employed at the facility are expected to increase output from approximately 700,000 tons in 2002 to approximately 1.2 million tons annually. Phoenix executive and managerial staffs have completed a five-year plan to direct future operations.

There are five sand-and-gravel mining wash-plant operations on the reservation, operated by the tribally owned Salt River Materials Group, formerly Salt River Sand and Rock. In January 2003, the company acquired 285 additional acres near Gila Bend for future mining of aggregates. A property previously used as a cattle feedlot is also being restored for the company's potential future use.

Real Estate/Commercial Development. The SRPMIC has concentrated its commercial development along the western bound-

ary of the community, alongside the 101 Pima Freeway. A 140-acre retail center, The Pavilions, is the nation's largest commercial development on Indian land. Tenants include Target, Home Depot, Best Buy, Ross, Marshalls, United Artists, Cost Plus Imports, Circuit City, and Toys 'R' Us. Located elsewhere on community land, Wal-Mart altered its architectural and exterior design to blend more closely with community aesthetics.

Other commercial properties exist along the Pima and McDowell commercial corridors. These properties are easily accessed by the 101 Pima Freeway, 202 Red Mountain Freeway, I-10 and I-17 freeways, and SR 87 Highway. Major public employers include the Pavilions, BIA, the tribal government via its various programs and initiatives, and Scottsdale Community College. The 26-acre Chaparral Business Center, completed prior to 2002, has tenants such as Fender Guitar Corporation and Salt River Devco Asset Management's second office, the Property Development Division. Western International University opened offices there in January 2002. The Chaparral Business Center has enjoyed 100 percent occupancy since the offices of Casino Arizona Training and Development Center opened there.

Services and Retail. The tribe owns seven business enterprises: Cypress Golf Course; Talking Stick Golf Club; Salt River Landfill; Saddleback Communications; Salt River Devco; Red Mountain Trap and Skeet; and Salt River Materials Group, formerly Salt River Sand and Rock and Phoenix Cement Company. The community also operates two gaming facilities and leases property to more than 20 businesses. Smaller businesses include a drive-in movie theater, convenience stores, and a nursery.

Tourism and Recreation. The Salt River Pima-Maricopa Indian Community is adjacent to Scottsdale and to the greater metropolitan area of Phoenix with all of its recreational outlets. Before leaving the community, one may want to play a round of golf on one of the community's two golf courses.

Cypress Golf Course consists of two nine-hole courses-- the Long Nine for the conditioned golfer, and the Short Nine for the beginner and those who want to gain on their short game. There is also 500 square feet of retail discount golf merchandise including the latest in golf equipment.

Talking Stick Golf Club is a 36-hole, signature golf course open to the public. It is owned by the Salt River Pima-Maricopa Indian Community and located on community land. The course was designed by architect Bill Coore and two-time Masters Champion Ben Crenshaw. The course is leased to and operated by Troon Golf, and was designed to cater to the high-end consumer. It is home to the Golf Digest Instructional School, under the direction of Tim Mahoney. Student golfers have access to video equipment, nearly 100 hitting stations, and a 170-yard practice hold adjacent to the range. On the premises are a clubhouse, golf shop, restaurant, and locker room.

There are water sports and other outdoor recreation activities at Saguaro, Canyon, Apache, and Roosevelt lakes to the east. Regularly scheduled live entertainment, including comedy acts and musicians, can be found at Showstoppers Live in the Casino Arizona at the McKellips location, off the 101 Pima Freeway. Red Mountain Trap and Skeet, which hosts annual national trap-shooting competitions, has been featured on the cover of *Trap & Field Magazine*, read by outdoor enthusiasts across the nation.

The community's cultural museum, the Hoo-hoogam Ki (meaning, "House of those who have gone"), allows visitors to learn tribal history and view baskets, pottery, artifacts, and photographs. An outdoor dining area at the museum features Indian fry bread and other cultural foods.

Visitors may also attend many of the tribe's annual events which include: the New Year's Eve Chicken Scratch Dance; New Year's Basketball Invitational; A'al Tash Rodeo Days, the Valentine Classic Basketball Tournament, the Fall Carnival, the Red Mountain Eagle Powwow in November, and the Junior Miss and Miss Salt River pageants in March. In 2004, the tribe celebrated 125 years as an established community with a Celebration Day on June 12.

INFRASTRUCTURE
State Highway 87 intersects the southern portion of the reservation. The Pima Freeway and the Red Mountain Freeway also offer access to the reservation. Commercial airline and bus services are located in Phoenix. Nearby Scottsdale Municipal Airport and Falcon Field in Mesa also offer air transportation. Many overnight and freight services deliver to the reservation. The Central Arizona Project canal and aqueduct run through the reservation. Southern Pacific and Santa Fe Railroads service the greater Phoenix metropolitan area.

Transportation. Because the community is not linked to Phoenix's metropolitan mass transit system, transportation service is provided by Salt River Transit.

Water Supply. There are two sources of water for the reservation--individual wells and water from the City of Phoenix. The community's public works department manages its domestic water and wastewater systems; septic tanks are used for sewage disposal. The community operates the Salt River Landfill which also recycles materials at the River Recycling Materials Recovery Facility. In FY 2002, MRF was awarded the Governor's Spirit of Success Award by the Arizona Department of Commerce. An educational video produced by the enterprise received a Communicator Award, and the Maricopa Association of Governments awarded the facility a Desert Peaks Award in honor of their recycling innovations.

Electricity. Electricity is provided by the Salt River Project, and natural gas is provided by Southwest Gas Corporation which also makes propane available.

Telecommunications. Telephone services are available from the community's Saddleback Telecommunications. Saddleback also installs business and industrial phone systems throughout the community. Throughout 2002, the community renovated essential services and installed fiber and copper cable, adding electronic equipment to enhance service capabilities. In 2003, broadband Internet capacity was being upgraded with digital subscriber line (DSL) technologies.

COMMUNITY FACILITIES AND SERVICES
Community facilities include: five parks, two swimming pools, a library, a museum, five ball diamonds, three recreation centers, a new high school, one movie theater, and one drive-in theater. Golf courses include Cypress, an 18-hole course, Pavilion Lakes, and Talking Stick Golf Club featuring two 18-hole courses. The community has its own fire department and law enforcement. Each entity has a main station and two substations, one in the Lehi District and one off the 101 Pima Freeway at Indian Bend.

Health Care. Health services are provided by the U.S. Public Health Service, which operates the community health center and dialysis treatment center. Inpatient care and a full range of medical specialties are available at Indian Medical Center in Phoenix.

With funding assistance supplemented by the U. S. Department of Homeland Security, the Tribal Emergency Response Commission has prepared an emergency planning booklet with tips and strategies for survival in the event of a major terrorist event or other catastrophe.

San Carlos Apache

LOCATION AND LAND STATUS
The San Carlos Apache Reservation includes approximately 2,896 square miles of south-central Arizona, and is located 20 miles east of the town of Globe and about 100 miles west of the metropolitan Phoenix area. The town of San Carlos, off State Highway 70, is the population center and location of the tribal headquarters.

An Executive Order on November 9, 1871, established a joint White Mountain-San Carlos Indian Reservation. The two tribal entities were partitioned into separate reservations along the Salt River by an Act of Congress on June 17, 1897. The San Carlos Reservation lands were increased by an Executive Order on December 14, 1972.

PHYSICAL DESCRIPTION
Renowned for its natural beauty, this immense reservation ranges from low plains and rolling desert hills dotted with saguaro cacti, to piñon pine-forested, high-mountain terrain. The elevation at San Carlos, the tribal headquarters, is 6,040 feet.

CLIMATE
Due to the large land mass and varying topography, the potential for different weather systems on the reservation is great. The average year-round high temperature at San Carlos is a moderate 68°F. The average year-round low temperature is 37°F. The area receives almost 19 inches of precipitation annually, with approximately 12 inches of that falling as snow.

CULTURE AND HISTORY
World-renowned basket weavers, the San Carlos Apaches are a branch of the Athabascan peoples who migrated to the Southwest from the interior of Alaska and Canada, probably about the tenth century. Athabascan languages are still spoken by peoples in the north as well as by a few small groups in northern California. Today the tribe is composed of members from many different Apache bands such as the Aravaipas, Chiricahuas, Coyoteros, Mimbrenos, Mogollons, Pinalenos, San Carlos's, and Tontos. It is the seventh largest reservation in the nation in terms of population and the largest in land mass.

The reservation and tribe were named for their location near the intersection of the San Carlos and Gila Rivers, where the U.S. Army had established a military fort. Although greatly feared by Anglo settlers in the area during the mid-nineteenth century, the Apaches were ultimately forced from their land and onto the reservation, which was established in 1871. It was to this lonely outpost that the great Chief Cochise was taken after his surrender in 1873, and it was from this location that Geronimo led his escaping followers to freedom. After the discovery of copper and silver in the Miami and Clifton-Morenci areas, the U.S. government took back large areas of the reservation five different times by 1902. The repossessed land was eventually given back in 1972.

San Carlos Apache Reservation
Federal reservation
San Carlos Apache
Gila, Graham, and Pinal counties, Arizona

San Carlos Apache Tribe
P.O. Box "0"
San Carlos, AZ 85550
928-475-2361
928-475-2567 Fax
itcaonline.com

San Carlos Apache

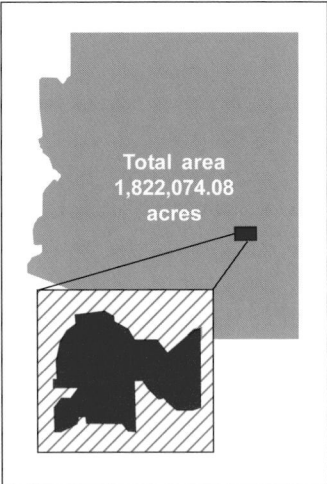

Total area
1,822,074.08
acres

Total area *(BIA, 2004)*
1,822,074.08 acres
622,274.00 acres *(Gila county)*
138,289.99 acres *(Pinal county)*
799.96 acres *(Allotted lands)*
1,060,710.13 acres *(Graham county)*

Population *2000 census*
9,385

Tribal enrollment
(Tribal source, 2004)
8,921

Total labor force *2000 census*
2,679

High school graduate or higher
2000 census
57.6%

Bachelor's degree or higher
2000 census
2.8%

Unemployment rate
2000 census
35.42%

Unemployment rate
(Tribal Source)
35.42%

Per capita income
$5,200

GOVERNMENT

The tribal government, formed as a result of the Indian Reorganization Act of 1934, is governed by an elected conucil representing four districts that operate under a written charter (ratified in 1955) and a constitution (adopted in 1936, revised in 1954, and amended in 1984). The council has a chairman, vice-chairman, secretary, and nine elected district representatives, each representing one of four districts. All serve staggered four-year terms. The Bylas District elects three council members, while Gilson Wash, Peridot, and Seven Mile districts elect two members each.

The tribe, under PL-638, contracts with the BIA to administer key programs and services, such as the tribal court system which includes tribal judges and the San Carlos Tribal Police Department, to enforce ordinances. Additional tribal departments manage the community's economic, educational, legal, health, and cultural affairs.

ECONOMY

Gaming, forestry, tourism, mining, and agriculture sustain the local economy in a blend of tradition and industry. Most enterprises on the reservation are operated by the tribe which subsequently employs most working members of the tribe, approximately 500 people in 2004.

Major private employers on the reservation are the Apache Gold Casino (employing more than 400 people), Apache Timber Products, Bashas, Noline's Country Store, and the San Carlos Lake Development Corporation. Primary public employers include the BIA (employing over 100 people), the Indian Health Services (employing over 150), Rice School District, and the San Carlos Apache Tribe. Many Apaches work off the reservation in neighboring Globe, Ft. Thomas, and Safford, Arizona. As home to one of the largest group of Southwest forest fire fighters, the San Carlos Apache Reservation deploys over 1,000 trained men and women during periods of national emergency.

Government as Employer. The federal government employs tribal members in the delivery of health, education, and economic services. Tribal enterprises and the tribal government employ many more tribal members. The San Carlos Unified School District also provides employment.

Economic Development Projects. Toward the end of the 1990s, the tribe was awarded community and economic development grants, which were used for projects such as the Peridot Shopping Center. Since all land and natural resources on the reservation are tribally owned, they are controlled by the tribal council. The San Carlos Telecommunications Utility has been developed and is owned by the tribe.

Agriculture and Livestock. The tribe's cattle ranching operations are its third-largest source of income, generating over $1 million in annual livestock sales. Five tribal cattle associations (each with its own board of directors) manage the industry for the reservation, raising commercial Hereford cattle as well as tribally owned herds whose revenues contribute to the tribal budget. In addition to cattle, one association raises working ranch horses to sell on contract to other tribal nations or individuals.

The tribe considers the redevelopment of agriculture a high priority. Reservation farms have generated profit from crops such as alfalfa and jojoba beans. With assistance from the BIA, the tribe revamped its extensive irrigation facilities by installing new pipelines and irrigation pumps, and by reconditioning ditches. An agricultural development committee oversees the future of the reservation's agricultural lands.

Forestry. Much reservation land is canopied by ponderosa pine, alligator juniper, oak, and piñon pine, approximately one-third of which are carefully managed to secure sustainable production of forest products. This saw timber is harvested under strict controls so as to maintain a tree canopy of many age classes. Located at Cutter, Arizona, the San Carlos Apache Timber Products Company owns and operates a sawmill. The facility includes a planer and a dry kiln for the production of finished products.

Gaming. The tribe owns and operates the Apache Gold Casino and the 146-room Best Western Apache Gold Hotel, employing approximately 450 tribal members and non-members from adjacent communities. Opened in November 1996, the 60,000-square-foot casino features 500 slot machines, a 1,000-seat bingo room, 6 poker tables, keno, and Race Book. The resort complex includes 5,000 square feet of convention space, a cabaret with nightly live entertainment, a gift shop, a 60-space RV park with showers, a swimming pool, phones and satellite TV, a convenience store, two restaurants, and an 18-hole championship golf course, Apache Stronghold. Capitalizing on the land's natural beauty while preserving the people's cultural heritage is a hallmark of the facility where 14 archaeological sites have been meticulously protected.

The Apache Gold Resort complex includes the Pavilion, a newly constructed state-of-the-art covered-roof multipurpose arena where rodeos, car shows, horse shows, concerts, and pow-wows are held.

Mining. Deposits in Arizona are the major source in the United States of the semi-precious gemstone peridot. Peridot is found only in the Red Sea, in Myanmar (formerly Burma), and in the state of Arizona. The yellow- to olive-green gem is highly prized for the manufacture of birthstones and other jewelry. It is estimated that 80 percent to 95 percent of the world's supply of peridot is mined on basalt-lined Peridot Mesa at the reservation, making it the single largest productive peridot mine in the world. The gems are recovered after washing out into gullies and canyons, or they are drilled and blasted out of the host stone, basalt. Although rare, stones as large as 15 and 22 carats have been cut from San Carlos peridot. They are manufactured by tribal members for the tourist market.

Peridot can be mined only by specific individuals and families from the San Carlos Apache Reservation. Once sold primarily in lots of uncut material, in 2004 many individuals were contracting for cutting services and marketing the cut stones.

Industrial Parks. The San Carlos Industrial Park, conveniently located on U.S Highway 70 at Cutter, adjacent to the Globe-San Carlos Regional Airport, was in the design phase in 2004. A spur line of the Southern Pacific Railroad serves the park, and the town of Globe, seven miles west of Cutter, is the connecting point for U.S. Highway 70, U.S. Highway 77, and Arizona State Highway 60.

Tourism and Recreation. The primary recreational attractions to the reservation are its diverse natural landscapes, which range from the Sonoran Desert to mixed-conifer forests. The tribe encourages visitor enjoyment of these areas; fees for hunting, fishing, camping, and recreation are a major source of tribal revenue. Hunting for big and small game (such as elk, bighorn sheep, antelope, javelina, wild turkeys, and migratory birds) is available year-round. Visitors also enjoy whitewater rafting, kayaking, and canoeing in the Salt River Canyon. In addition, the reservation offers thousands of miles of charted hiking and camping.

There are over 200 small ponds (called tanks) and many lakes and streams, offering year-round warm-water and cold-water fisheries (by tribal permit). San Carlos Lake, formed by the construction of Coolidge Dam on the Gila River, has 158 miles of shoreline, and stores 19,500 acres of water; it is the largest body of water in Arizona. While considered one of the premier large-mouth bass lakes in the Southwest, San Carlos Lake is also full of catfish, crappie, and sunfish. Another excellent warm-water fishery is Talkalai Lake, named after the famous Apache chief. It is stocked with trout, bass, channel catfish, crappie, and bluegill.

San Carlos Lake Development Corporation, a tribal entity, has significantly improved lakeside campgrounds by remodeling the ramadas and installing a concrete boat ramp at Soda Canyon. There are also a remodeled store and tackle shop, a boat storage facility, and a RV- and mobile-home park. On many summer weekends, traditional Apache ceremonies take place, and visitors are allowed to observe portions of some rituals. The casino sponsors a powwow each year in February, and in March the tribe holds an Indian Festival. In April, the Mt. Turnbull Rodeo continues a decades-long tradition, and in June, the San Carlos Apache celebrate their Independence Day on the 18th. The annual All-Indian Rodeo and Fair is held in November.

U.S. Highway 60, a direct route between Globe and Show Low, Arizona in the north, cuts through the Salt River Canyon, commonly called the Mini Grand Canyon. During spring melt-off in the higher elevations, this river runs fast and deep; white-water rafting, kayaking, and canoeing are popular sports. The reservation is within 50 miles of the southeast border of Tonto National Forest and within 25 miles of the following designated wilderness areas: Superstition, Salt River Canyon, and Four Peaks, all of which increase tourist traffic to the reservation. Other popular fishing destinations are Point of Pines Lake, a high mountain lake; Seneca Lake, just north of Globe; and the Black River and Salt River recreation areas, at the reservation's northern border.

The tribe opened a cultural center on September 12, 1995, in Peridot, Arizona. A special exhibit, Window on Apache Culture, describes the Apache's spiritual beginnings and ceremony, such as the Changing Woman Ceremony. Cultural education and demonstrations are available for schools and other groups.

The tribally owned RV park, Apache Gold, is located just east of Globe, with 60 sites for weary travelers and year-round amenities, such as satellite TV, a swimming pool, laundry facilities, handicap-accessible restrooms, showers, 24-hour security, an on-site manager, phones, and gasoline at the convenience store.

INFRASTRUCTURE
U.S. Highway 70, a primary scenic route between Phoenix, Arizona and Lordsburg, New Mexico, bisects the reservation, passing through the San Carlos Industrial Park at Cutter and the town of San Carlos. In addition, U.S. 60, the direct route between Show Low and Globe, cuts through Salt River Canyon on the reservation. Overnight truck delivery is available to metropolitan Phoenix, Tucson, El Paso, Albuquerque, Las Vegas, Nogales, and Sonora; second-day service is available to Los Angeles and San Diego. Passenger and freight bus services are available daily from Globe and Miami, Arizona. Residents have access to the local airstrip in San Carlos, which has a lighted and paved 7,000-foot runway, and to Globe Airport, 18 miles to the west, which has a 4,750-foot lighted and paved runway and a UNICOM navigation system.

Electricity. Electricity is available on the reservation from Arizona Public Service Company, Graham County Utilities, or the San Carlos Irrigation Project.

Fuel. Southwest Gas Corporation provides natural gas.

Telecommunications. Telephone and high-speed Internet services are provided by the tribally owned and operated San Carlos Apache Telecommunications Utility. The reservation receives numerous radio stations from Globe, Safford, Tucson, and Phoenix. Apache Cablevision, now owned by the San Carlos Telecommunications Utility, offers basic cable television service to San Carlos and Peridot.

COMMUNITY FACILITIES AND SERVICES
The San Carlos Apache Tribe community facilities include a library, a rodeo arena, six ball fields, two convenience stores, a supermarket, a gas station, and a coin-operated laundromat.

Education. The San Carlos Unified School District offers education from K-12. Tuition assistance for college bound students is available through the tribe's education department, and the adult education program offers post high school opportunities geared towards trade skills for students seeking training and employment programs. Adult education and GED preparation is also provided through the education department.

Health Care. There is a 32-bed U.S. Public Health Service hospital, with seven doctors and two staff dentists. The facility includes an emergency room, a laboratory, X-ray services, social and psychological services, and inpatient and outpatient care.

ENVIRONMENTAL CONCERNS
Illegal dumping was unheard of on the reservation prior to 1998 when three open dump sites were available to all community members; however, once the new landfill opened and curbside pickup was made available, 14 illegal dump sites developed, ranging in size from one-half to six acres. Those residents who resisted paying the service fee for curbside pickup were responsible.

To combat the illegal dumping and offer alternatives to curbside pickup, the tribe built two transfer stations with white goods drop-off zones at convenient locations. The Mt. Turnbull Sanitation Service marketed the facilities with flyers listing the transfer stations' rates and a list of acceptable items, and then it offered a trial period of operation only two days per month.

The existing illegal dump sites remained a cause of concern for the San Carlos Apache EPA staff, who feared they might contaminate groundwater supplies, so they obtained a federal EPA General Assistance Program (GAP) grant for solid waste implementation to clean up the sites over a two-year period. In partnership with the BIA and the IHS, the tribe collected all unwanted and abandoned cars and white goods, hauling them to a landfill or scrap metal yard. The tribe used money from the sales of the scrap metal to cover the costs of removing items such as automobiles and refrigerators that contained hazardous chemicals.

Enforcement is a critical component of the tribe's solid waste plan. Tribal EPA staff work closely with tribal police and game department rangers to enforce the illegal dumping ordinance. The tribe also capitalizes on marketing opportunities via newspaper articles and public-access cable TV to advertise the "No Dumping" message, and it has hung signs warning illegal dumpers of potential consequences.

Honoring Nations Honoree 2000

Elders Cultural Advisory Council Forest Resources

Formed by Tribal resolution in 1993, the San Carlos Elders Cultural Advisory Council advises the Tribal Council on matters of culture, conducts consultations with off-reservation entities regarding cultural matters and administers the cultural preservation activities of the Tribe. As a source of traditional wisdom, the Elders Council plays an active role in the Tribe's governance by providing insight on diverse issues, including resource management, leadership responsibilities, environmental issues, cultural practices and repatriation.

Traditional Apache culture is based on an intimate spiritual connection with and knowledge of the natural world. The elders believe that such connection and knowledge are necessary to respect one's self, other humans and all living things. Having spent most of their lives outdoors and being taught by the wisdom of their elders, they embrace and encourage self-reliance and discourage dependence on others. For today's elders, to be Apache is to be able to think for one's self, to know the rich history of their peoples, to speak the Native tongue, to participate in ceremonies, and to act responsibly and respectfully towards other humans and the natural world.

The fast-paced world of automobiles, fast food, video games and television has taken its toll on traditional Apache culture. Of course, all cultures change over time. But from the viewpoint of the San Carlos Apache elders, the changes in their community have been particularly worrisome. The youth no longer eat the traditional foods that once kept Apache fit and strong, and obesity runs rampant among the more than 10,000 Indians who call the San Carlos Reservation home. Traditional knowledge about plants and animals is being lost as the young spend much of their time indoors watching television or playing video games. Dependence on federal government goods and services has become an acceptable way to live. Interest in the ancient traditions and ceremonies is slowly being replaced by interest in activities and values associated with the dominant non-Indian culture. In short, despite a long and rich history of tribal strength and pride, the elders are upset about what the Apache people are becoming.

Furthermore, the elders at San Carlos are concerned about questions of governance. As the keepers of traditional knowledge and history, the elders remember - or have been told about - a time when leaders emerged because of their abilities, wisdom, achievements and public-minded character. They recall a time when important decisions were made with "one community mind" and in the best long-term interest of the nation - when political corruption simply was not tolerated. Indeed, the well-documented recent political history of the San Carlos Apache is nothing the elders can be proud of. Throughout the 1990s, San Carlos suffered from debilitating political instability, which has manifested in protests, takeovers, and demonstrations. Financial mismanagement has led to large governmental deficits, and the government is recognized more for its turmoil than for its ability to provide essential governmental services. Governmental ineffectiveness has left the reservation with a weak economy and poor social conditions that are akin to those found in many third-world countries.

In the midst of such cultural, political and economic difficulties lies a kernel of hope and inspiration - the San Carlos Elders Cultural Advisory Council (ECAC). Formed in November 1993 by Tribal Council resolution, the all-volunteer ECAC was established to advise the Tribal Council on cultural matters, to carry out consultations with off-reservation entities on culturally related matters,

and to execute various projects related to cultural preservation. It is comprised of elders from the reservation's four districts and meets every two to four months.

While much of the Council's initial work was concentrated on ethnobotany (and, particularly, on recording the names, uses and appropriate treatment of culturally important plant life), today it engages in a much broader range of activities. The ECAC regularly gives its traditional views to the Tribal Council and other decision makers on a wide variety of matters. The ECAC has provided guidance on tribal environmental policies, including Mexican spotted owl surveys and reservation-based mining; on cultural policies such as the inappropriate use of depictions of the Gaan (Mountain Spirits); and on guidelines for non-tribal researchers. It carries out cultural consultations with off-reservation entities, especially federal and state agencies that administer lands in traditional Apache areas, and advises the Bureau of Indian Affairs on the location of graves and sacred sites that should not be disturbed by tree harvesting. The ECAC also helps administer and oversee cultural preservation activities. For example, it is involved in activities related to the Native American Graves Protection and Repatriation Act (NAGPRA) and the Western Apache Place Names Project, and it helps collect traditional information on the natural world to be used in reservation school curriculum.

In engaging in these many comment and consultation processes, the ECAC has achieved important successes. When the elders felt that tribal citizens were being disrespectful and wasteful in how they cut and disposed of shade material used for camps in the Sunrise Dances, they published an instructive article in the Apache Mocassin on the proper collection, use and disposal procedures. The elders have also provided traditional guidance on penal approaches, on the appropriate way for the Tribe to develop a funeral home, and on the appropriateness of a motorcross race sponsored by the Tribe's casino. Much of this advice has been followed. When the Tonto National Forest imposed permit fees for tribal citizens gathering acorns in traditional hunting areas, the ECAC worked with the Tribal Council to get a tribal resolution passed, confronted the U.S. Forest Service and succeeded in changing the policy.

Moreover, the ECAC has been remarkably successful in its NAGPRA and cultural preservation work. The ECAC took the initiative to form a Western Apache coalition, comprised of the five Western Apache tribes, in order to deal with NAGPRA-related issues in a coordinated fashion. Not only has this coalition strengthened the tribes' claims - to date, over 70 objects have been repatriated to San Carlos alone - but it has helped tribes throughout Indian Country by establishing precedents in justifications of claims. The coalition was also instrumental in convincing the U.S. National Forest Service to give the San Francisco Peaks (a mountain held sacred to the Apaches) special protection and helped to place Mt. Graham, another sacred mountain, on the National Register of Historic Places.

In all of its activities, the ECAC consults its membership - who range in age from mid-40s to late-90s - and, as necessary, other elders respected for their wisdom and knowledge of Apache language, culture and outdoor living skills. While the ECAC operates strictly by consensus, the administrative functions are conducted by a coordinator and a facilitator who jointly organize the meetings, visit home-bound elders or medicine people, and transcribe conversations into letters, memoranda and articles. To ensure its long-term sustainability, the ECAC retains younger elders within its membership, who are mentored by older members. Both to smooth this administrative process and to create a record of its decisions, the ECAC oftentimes expresses its views or provides guidance in the form of letters, which are sent to department heads or the elected tribal leadership.

Compelled by their belief that the traditional Apache way of life is the most responsible, beautiful and proper way for Apaches to live, the ECAC has also become an important, and much needed, check on government. The ECAC is deeply committed to making the tribal government more responsible and accountable by giving the traditional perspective an institutionalized and formal voice that the politicians cannot avoid. Although their views are not always welcome, the ECAC members feel strongly that leaders need the guidance of their elders to properly and wisely carry out their tremendous responsibilities to the people and to the land.

Several examples demonstrate the ECAC's interventions in support of improved governance. When the Tribal Council decided to renew a contract with a company that was buying springwater from a sacred spring on the reservation without community consent, the ECAC vigorously reprimanded the Tribal Council. In 1999, when the Tribe's financial mismanagement became especially bad, the ECAC met and wrote a letter to the Tribal Council reminding them of the proper ways leaders ought to behave. At the same time, the elders agreed that ECAC would set an example of self-reliance by foregoing tribal monies in favor of operating as a self-sustaining volunteer entity. Commenting on Apache leadership, the elders believe:

The values of self-reliance, respect and deep connection to nature are central to traditional Apache life, and are underlying themes in all ECAC activities, consultations and messages. These qualities, along with a great traditional knowledge help make a whole, successful person. A person with these qualities will be a good leader. The ECAC tries to bring these qualities and tradi-

tional knowledge to their own leaders in order for them to more effectively care for the people and their land.

The ECAC stands out on a number of dimensions. As an all-volunteer group, the program operates with minimal funding, it is replicable any place a dedicated elder could be recruited as coordinator, and it is a significant contribution at a reservation that suffers from dire political problems. Around Indian Country, elders are consulted for NAGPRA repatriations, for guidance in tribal policy, for assistance in cultural revitalization, and for wisdom in family life. In many instances, however, these efforts are ad hoc and yield only a small portion of the benefit that arises from paying consistent attention to elders' vision and values. The ECAC at San Carlos, in contrast, is a refreshing and instructive example of how elders can play a critical role in advancing the social, economic, political and spiritual health of an Indian nation. The knowledge they possess is essential to the long-term health of the Apache people and the environment, and the perspectives they bring to questions of governance are invaluable. The ECAC serves as a conscience for the San Carlos Apache Tribe by tapping, discussing and then articulating its members' understanding of Apache values. The Elders Cultural Advisory Council is a keeper and carrier of traditional Apache wisdom whose actions and advice will benefit the Tribe for generations to come.

Lessons:

· As keepers of traditional wisdom, elders can and should play an active role in tribal governmental affairs, including cultural matters, leadership responsibilities and language preservation.

· One way to utilize the knowledge of elders is to formally recognize a council of elders that is empowered to make recommendations, provide guidance and advise tribal decision makers.

· In some cases, elders groups from different reservations or Indian nations should work together in order to maximize effectiveness when dealing with other governments (both tribal and non-tribal).

San Carlos Apache

Honoring Nations Honoree 2000

Text in its entirety from: The Harvard Project On American Indian Economic Development

John F. Kennedy School of Government Harvard University

San Juan

San Juan

LOCATION AND LAND STATUS
Federally recognized in 1989, the San Juan Southern Paiute Tribe is the newest federally recognized Indian nation in the state of Arizona. As of 2000, the San Juan Southern Paiute Tribe did not have a land base, but it is negotiating with the Navajo Nation to secure land in the Rough Rock to Willow and Hidden Springs region, as well as in the Navajo Mountain area. They are also negotiating a lease agreement with the Navajo Nation to lease farming land in the Paiute Farms region.

Most members live in two separate communities, one near Willow Springs and the other near Paiute Canyon and Navajo Mountain. They live within the Navajo Nation and on nine other reservations throughout Arizona, Utah, and Nevada. Tuba City, the tribal headquarters site, is located approximately 1 mile east of US 89, 8 miles north of the junction of U.S.160, and 35 miles north of Flagstaff. Navajo Mountain is a sacred site to the San Juan Southern Paiutes.

CLIMATE
The tribe lives in various locations throughout the Southwest, thus making a summation of climate conditions impossible for all but tribal headquarters at Tuba City, Arizona. Tuba City's elevation is 4,940 feet. Year-round daily high temperatures average 70.1°F. Year-round daily low temperatures average almost 39°F.

The area receives an annual average of 6.6 inches of rain and 7 inches of snow.

CULTURE AND HISTORY
The Southern Paiutes have lived in northern Arizona and southern Utah for hundreds of years, where they subsisted as hunter-gatherers. Many now live in southern Nevada as well. They speak a language belonging to the Numic branch of the Uto-Aztecan language family, which is related to languages spoken by peoples ranging from the Great Basin to central Mexico.

Paiute boys and men were taken by the Spanish and sold as slaves to work the mines of central Mexico. Thus disenfranchised, the Southern Paiutes lost their land base, and by the 1800s they had become laborers and craftsmen, scattered among other Indian tribes.

The San Juan Southern Paiutes share a common heritage with the Southern Paiutes of northern Arizona, Utah, Nevada, and California, while maintaining their unique Native language. They live in various communities located within the Navajo Reservation, primarily in Willow Springs, near Tuba City, and at Navajo Mountain on the Arizona and Utah border with California.

San Juan Southern Paiute Council
Federally recognized tribe
Southern Paiute and Navajo
Coconino County, Arizona

San Juan Southern Paiute Council
Southern Paiute Field Station
P.O. Box 2663
Tuba City, AZ 86045
928-283-4583
928-283-5535 Fax
itcaonline.com

San Juan

Tribal enrollment
(BIA labor report, 2001)
254

Tribal enrollment *(Tribal source)*
265

Total labor force
(BIA labor report, 2001)
66

Unemployment rate
(BIA labor report, 2001)
82%

The San Juan Southern Paiutes have a rich artistic tradition, especially in weaving. The San Juan Southern Paiute Yingup Weavers Association, a tribal organization, has been recognized for excellence by the National Endowment for the Arts.

GOVERNMENT
The San Juan Southern Paiute Council (Shuupara`api), under PL-638, contracts with the BIA to administer key programs and services. The council is chaired by a president, a vice-president, and five additional members, and they meet regularly. The San Juan Southern Paiutes adopted a tribal constitution in 1996.

ECONOMY
The tribal economy is largely dependent upon livestock and subsistence crop farming. Tribal artisans are known for hand-woven traditional baskets crafted with ancient techniques passed down from generation to generation.

Economic Development Projects. The tribe's foremost economic development priority is to obtain a land base for housing and businesses. In 2000 the San Juan Southern Paiute Council initiated steps toward establishing an overall economic development plan. The tribe is negotiating land purchases with the Navajo Nation.

Tourism and Recreation. The Annual San Juan Southern Paiute Powwow is held the second weekend of June in Hidden Springs, Arizona. The second week of August they hold a Family Reunion.

COMMUNITY FACILITIES AND SERVICES
Education. Students from the reservation attend Tuba City district schools.

Health Care. An IHS hospital is located in Tuba City.

Tohono O'odham

Tohono O'odham Reservation (formerly Papago Indian Reservation)
Federal reservation
Tohono O'odham (Papago)
Pima, Pinal, Maricopa, Cochise, Yuma counties, Arizona

Tohono O'odham Nation
P.O. Box 837
Sells, AZ 85634
520-383-2028
520-383-3379 Fax
itcaonline.com

LOCATION AND LAND STATUS
The Tohono O'odham Nation, formerly known as the Papago Indian Reservation, is located in south-central Arizona, adjacent to the Mexican border. It is comprised of four specific, noncontiguous parcels: Tohono O'odham, formerly known as the Papago Indian Reservation, established in 1916; Sells, established in 1917; Gila Bend, established in 1882; and San Xavier del Bac, close to Tucson, established in 1874. There is also a 20-acre Village of Florence on the outskirts of the city of Florence. The total acreage of the reservation is comparable to the state of Connecticut, stretching along 75 miles of the U.S. border with Mexico, and northward for over 90 miles through the Sonoran Desert. On January 14, 1916, the Papago Indian Reservation was established. Sells, commonly called the Main Reservation, was established by Executive Order in 1917. San Xavier del Bac Reservation, with more than 71,000 acres, was registered as a National Historic Landmark. In 1882, 10,377 acres were set aside by Executive Order for the Gila Bend Reservation. The town of Sells is the tribal headquarters. Approximately 1,000 tribal members are Mexican nationals, of whom approximately 500 live in the United States without documents.

PHYSICAL DESCRIPTION
The elevation at Sells, the tribal headquarters, is 1,830 feet above sea level. Topography ranges between wide desert valleys, plains, and mountains reaching nearly 8,000 feet. Two very high mountains, Baboquivari Peak (7,730 feet. above sea level) and Kitt Peak (6,785 feet) are considered sacred by the Tohono O'odhams. The famous Kitt Peak National Observatory sits atop Kitt Peak.

CLIMATE
The year-round average high temperature is 85°F, and the year-round average low is 59°F. The area receives approximately nine inches of precipitation annually, with less than one inch of that falling as snow.

CULTURE AND HISTORY
Members of the Tohono O'odham Nation are primarily Pima and Papago Indians. Their languages are closely related to the Uto-Aztecan language family. Peoples speaking other languages of this family are found from the Great Basin south into central Mexico. Expert irrigation farmers, both the Pimas and the Papagos have lived a seminomadic lifestyle in many parts of the desert Southwest, including parts of northern Mexico. They cultivate foods for everyday living and herbs for traditional remedies or for ceremonial and social purposes. Some became cattle ranchers after the Spanish introduced cattle to the area.

Beginning around 1821, Papago lands and water sources were encroached upon by immigrant farmers, ranchers, and miners; the Papagos resisted. Nineteen years later, the Papagos were fighting against Mexicans, a struggle that lasted for three years, at the end of which they negotiated a surrender. The Gadsden Purchase, closely following the Treaty of Guadalupe Hidalgo ending the Mexican-American War in 1848, added an international boundary through traditional Tohono O'odham lands. By 1898, however, many of the remaining Papagos had left Mexico as a result of local hostility and greater job opportunities in Arizona. One source of income for tribal members was the sale of wood and farm produce; some people also worked on immigrant ranches and in mines. During the Great Depression, a division of the Civilian Corps for Indians was also a source of income for many on the reservation.

In the early decades of the twentieth century, the federal government policy of sending Indian children to boarding schools meant that Pima and Papago children were removed from their families for long periods. The formation of the Papago Indian Good Government League, however, led to the provision of land for day schools in the Arizona communities of Sells, San Miguel, Cocklebur, and Gila Bend in 1911. Four of the schools were completed by 1916.

Tohono O'odham culture remains very much alive in the new millennium, as seen in the tribal rituals, tourist activities, and the traditional band music known as "chicken scratch." The language thrives as well, both in private homes and in public schools. After a lengthy legal process, in 1976 the tribe was awarded $26 million for land and mineral claims against the federal government, adding to the tribe's ability to develop economic opportunities on the reservation.

GOVERNMENT
The Tohono O'odham Nation, under PL-638, contracts with the Bureau of Indian Affairs (BIA) to administer key programs and services. They are governed by the Tohono O'odham Legisla-

tive Council. There are 11 political districts, each of which elects two members to the council, and a local government that maintains ties with the council. The council functions as the legislative branch and is headed by a chairman, vice-chairman, and a secretary.

The Tohono O'odham Justice Center is a separate branch. The center sits across from the main tribal headquarters. There are four courtrooms, office space including the judges' offices, and a lobby/reception area. Some judges are tribal members, while others serve on a rotating basis from the Tucson area, as the nation is part of Pima County.

Main departments under the executive office are the general support service, planning department, economic development department, thepartment of public safety, department of membership services, department of education, and department of human services.

ECONOMY
The economy of the nation is driven in the twenty-first century by private business and industry. Because of gaming revenues, the nation has become the fifteenth largest employer in Pima County, with more than 2,400 people on tribal payrolls; more than 80 percent are Tohono O'odhams. Agriculture, construction, retail tourism, and the utilities sector also rank very high in terms of employment and income for community members; and opportunities are expected to continue growing as the tribe implements additional development plans.

Government as Employer. Tribal, federal, and state agencies are the largest employers on the reservation. Public employers include the BIA, Indian Oasis Elementary School, and the Tohono O'odham Indian Nation.

Economic Development Projects. Tribal enterprises include the Desert Diamond Casino, Desert Diamond II Casino, and the Golden Ha:san Casino. Major private employers on the reservation include Anita's Construction, Bashas', Sells Shell Gas Station, Tohono Video and Rent-a-Flick, Turquoise Turtle, Coyote Convenience Store, Solano's Construction, Benny Burgers, and the Tohono O'odham Café.

Agriculture and Livestock. The economy of the Tohono O'odham Reservation is no longer exclusively agriculturally based, even though the nation operates four farms totaling 10,000 acres on which they raise cotton, hay, and broccoli. Agriculture is, however, a major sector of the economy. From 1917 to 1960, Papagos provided much of the labor in the fields of Arizona's staple crop, cotton. Cattle ranching and related activities form a major economic sector, second only to land leasing and income from mining.

Today, there are two kinds of cattle operations on the reservation: joint ventures and family subsistence ranching. Large operations involving multiple owners often consist of more than 1,000 head of cattle, while family herds usually contain 10 to 20 head.

Gaming. Gaming was first authorized on August 11, 1993, and the tribe opened a bingo casino in San Xavier, near Tucson. Later that same year, the Desert Diamond Casino opened near the Tucson International Airport with 808 slot machines, live blackjack, poker, a large bingo center, keno, and a snack bar and cafeteria. The facility was expanded to 48,000 square feet in 1995. A second, smaller casino, Golden Ha:san, opened in 1999 in the town of Why, Arizona, with 100 slot machines. In 2000 the tribe opened a third casino, Desert Diamond II, which is south of Tucson on I-19 in the San Xavier District. It offers an entertainment venue with meeting and banquet space for business, organizational, and social events. Gaming employed over 2,400 people

in 2004, making it the thirteenth largest employer in the area.

Industrial Parks. The San Xavier Industrial Park, equipped with full utilities, is owned and operated by the Tohono O'odham Nation and is located seven miles southeast of Tucson, adjacent to the Southern Pacific Railroad and the Tucson International Airport. Twenty-three acres of the park lie within the Tucson foreign-trade zone. Tenants include Caterpillar, a manufacturer of heavy equipment, and the Desert Diamond Casino. The Tohono O'odham Nation is the first Indian nation to be located in a foreign-trade zone, where quotas and duties are suspended while goods remain in the zone.

Land Leasing. Most land leases are for agricultural and industrial purposes, producing the single largest source of money for many in the Tohono O'odham economy. However, some income is also derived from the lease of land to the Kitt Peak National Observatory. On the San Xavier Reservation, most of the leased land is allotted; revenues, therefore, go directly to individuals.

Mining. Copper mines owned by the tribe are one of the major income producers on the reservation. Mining leases in the Sif Oidak District, along with royalties, have generated millions of dollars for the tribe. There are also three major ongoing joint-venture mining and chemical operations.

Media and Communications. There is a biweekly newspaper published on the reservation, *The Papago Runner.* In 2000 the Nation built a radio station that broadcasts O'odham waila music and a variety of contemporary music. It also built a cultural museum.

Tourism and Recreation. Activities of interest to tourists center on gaming, the All-Indian Papago Tribal Fair and Rodeo, and the Kitt Peak National Observatory, located 56 miles southwest of Tucson. The observatory has 22 optical telescopes and 2 radio telescopes, and it offers guided tours. Camping and picnic areas are available.

In the Hickiwan District in the Santa Rosa Valley, the Ventana Cave archaeological site is open to the public. Casa Grande National Monument is also nearby, a ruin of the Hohokam people, who are believed to be the ancestors of the Tohono O'odhams.

Nicknamed "The White Dove of the Desert," the internationally recognized Mission de San Xavier del Bac, founded in 1700, is the most famous landmark on the San Xavier parcel. Still used by the Tohono O'odhams, it is one of the best preserved and most beautiful examples of Mission architecture in the Southwest. It has been designated a National Historic Landmark. An Indian arts and crafts market is located nearby as well as the sacred Baboquivari Mountain Park, which has picnic facilities. The Tohono O'odhams believe this mountain, which is located in the Baboquivari District, is the home of I'itoi, the Papago Creator. Annually, during the first weekend in February, the nation holds a rodeo that draws many tourists to the area.

INFRASTRUCTURE
The San Xavier Reservation is accessible by Interstate 19, south of Tucson. The rest of the reservation can be reached by Arizona State Highway 86 which connects to Interstate 19. State Highway 85, which runs north-south in the western part of the reservation, connects to Interstate 8 just north of the reservation. Interstate 10 passes to the north of the reservation on the east side. In Tucson, freight services are available on the Southern Pacific Railroad and from more than 32 truck freight companies. Two airports are used frequently, one in Sells which has a 6,000-foot runway, and one in Tucson. The Tucson International Airport is 60 miles northeast of the main reservation and provides a full range of private and commercial flights.

Tohono O'odham

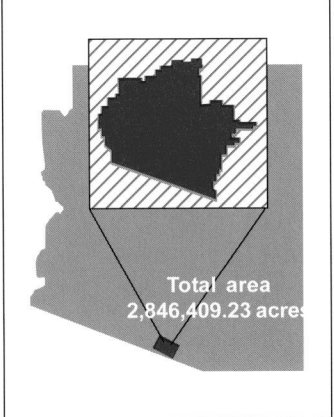

Total area
2,846,409.23 acres

Total area *(BIA, 2004)*
2,846,409.23 acres

Tribally-owned lands
2,805,126.07 acres

Individually owned lands
41,003.26 acres

Government lands
280.00 acres

Population *2000 census*
10,483

Tribal enrollment *(BIA, 2001)*
25,588

Tribal enrollment
(Tribal source, 2004)
24,000

Total labor force *2000 census*
2,947

High school graduate or higher
2000 census
62.1%

Bachelor's degree or higher
2000 census
5.4%

Unemployment rate
2000 census
23.96%

Per capita income
$6,998

353

Tohono O'odham

Utilities. The Tohono O'odham Utility Authority provides electricity, telephone, water, and sewer services to homes and businesses. Water can also be obtained through the Central Arizona Project. Arizona Paging, out of Sierra Vista, offers pager service.

COMMUNITY FACILITIES AND SERVICES
Currently, per initiatives in 1997, five recreations centers are being built in the following districts: Sells, San Xavier, Pisinemo, Hickiwan and Menagers Dam. The estimated completion date is April 2005.

There is a rodeo arena, a baseball and basketball facility, and a tribal office complex.

Public Safety. The Nation funds its own fire department and relies upon the BIA for police protection.

Education. Education is provided by seven preschools, seven elementary schools, four junior high schools, and three high schools. In addition, there is a BIA boarding school, and a day and boarding school for the disabled. The Tohono O'odham Community College was established as a two-year college and now partners with the Career Center to provide all levels of postsecondary education. Pima Community College and the University of Arizona are nearby.

Health Care. Health care is provided at the 40-bed U.S. Indian Health Service hospital in Sells and by four outpatient clinics located in Santa Rosa Village, San Xavier, San Lucy, and Pisinemo. There is also a 60-bed nursing home, the Archie Hendricks Nursing Home, built by the tribe. A clinic is located on the westside of the Nation, south of State Highway 86. There are plans to build a dialysis center.

Tonto Apache

Tonto Apache Reservation
Federal reservation
Tonto Apache Tribe

Tonto Apache Tribe
#30 T.A.R.
Payson, AZ 85541
928-474-5000
928-474-9125 Fax
itcaonline.com

Total area *(Tribal source, 2004)*
129 acres

Total area *(BIA, 2004)*
85acres

Other *(CO) (Tribal source, 2004)*
44 acres

Tribally owned lands
85 acres

Population *2000 census*
132

Tribal enrollment
(Tribal source, 2004)
123

Total labor force
2000 census
50

High school graduate or higher
2000 census
76.3%

Unemployment rate
2000 census
6.00%

Per capita income
$11,258

LOCATION AND LAND STATUS
The Tonto Apache Reservation is located on Highway 87 in central Arizona, 94 miles northeast of Phoenix and 94 miles southeast of Flagstaff, within the town limits of Payson, Arizona. The reservation was originally named Te-go-suk, or "Place of the yellow water."

Public Land Order 5422, on May 31, 1974, set aside 85 acres of National Forest land to be held in trust by the U.S. government as an Indian reservation for the use and benefit of the Payson Community of Tonto Apache Indians. The tribe has purchased 270 acres via an exchange process with the Forest Service. This acreage in not yet in trust. A 44-acre parcel of land located in Salida, Colorado, near scenic Poncho Pass was purchased in 2001. In the summer of 2004 this site was used for a summer cultural and recreational camp for Tonto Apache youth. Plans are to acquire an additional 300 acres.

CLIMATE
The elevation at Payson, the tribal headquarters, is 4,850 feet above sea level. The average year-round high temperature is 71°F. The average year-round low temperature is 35°F. The area receives approximately 21 inches of rain annually and 21 inches of snowfall.

CULTURE AND HISTORY
The Tonto Apaches are of the Western Apache peoples, speaking an Athabascan language related to Navajo in the Southwest, as well as to languages spoken by a few groups in northern California and indigenous peoples in the interior of Alaska and Canada. They once occupied a vast territory extending south from Flagstaff and Winslow to the Mogollon Rim and into the Tonto Basin. Their domain also included the land from the Sierra Ancha range west to the Mazatzal Mountains and the Verde Valley.

Historically, the Tonto Apaches were seminomadic, migrating from winter camps in the Tonto Basin to summer camps in the high country. They cultivated garden plots along streams in the valleys, gathered wild plants, and hunted game for their subsistence. After gold was discovered in Black Mountain in 1868, white prospectors and settlers encroached upon their lands. They actively resisted the intrusions until their forced surrender in the late 1870s at Camp Verde. The Rio Verde Reserve, near Camp Verde, was established in 1871 for the Tonto and Yavapai Indians; but it was dissolved in 1875 when 1,400 Tonto and Yavapai Apaches were forcibly marched, through snowy mountains, to the San Carlos Apache Reservation. Twenty years later, many returned to the Payson area, and they have continuously occupied areas on the East Verde near Sycamore and Webber Creek near Gisela in the Tonto National Forest before it was established in 1905. During the 1960s the tribe began a campaign for federal recognition. On October 6, 1972, the Tonto Apaches were reestablished as a federally recognized tribe under PL 92-470. Two years later on May 31,1974 they were given their current 85-acre reservation.

Members of the Tonto Apache tribe are well-known in the art world for their outstanding beadwork and basketry.

GOVERNMENT
The tribal council, composed of a chairperson, vice-chairperson, and three other members, provides legislative authority and policy direction for all tribal programs. The chairman serves a four-year term, and the council members serve a two-year term. The tribe has seven departments: health and welfare, recreation, finance, personnel, contracts and grants, procurement, and maintenance. The tribe also has its own judicial system consisting of one judge, a court clerk, and an administrator. A tribal police department was established in 2002, and today there are seven officers and one chief of police; all are Bureau of Indian Affairs (BIA) certified.

The Tonto Apache Reservation, under PL-638, contracts with the BIA to administer key programs and services, such as social services, the tribal court, roads, utilities, and law enforcement. The tribe funds its own higher education and vocational scholarships. Tribal government employs about 75 people, both Indian and non-Indian, who have excellent employee benefits including medical insurance that covers medical and dental care, a prescription co-pay plan for the non-Indian employee, and a 401(K) plan. This insurance is self-funded by the tribe and its various enterprises.

ECONOMY
Good highway frontage is permitting a great degree of additional economic development. The primary public employer is the tribe, via its many initiatives, including a casino and lodge.

Government as Employer. The tribal government employs 83 reservation residents.

Gaming. In 1993 the Tonto Apache Tribe entered into a gaming compact with the State of Arizona. Through a joint venture with British American bingo, the Tonto Apaches opened their first class III gaming facility, the Mazatzal Casino, in October 1993 in a modular building with 90 slot machines and a small snack bar. Less than a year later, on September 3, 1994, the expanded Mazatzal Casino opened, a 12,000-square-foot facility featuring 380 slot machines, a poker room, a 300-seat bingo hall, a restaurant, a sports lounge, the Dream Catcher Gift Shop, and an arcade. Still another expansion took place on April 27, 1995. Plans are in the making to build a 210,000-square-foot casino with 375 machines and conference facilities for 500 people. The Mazatzal Casino is one of the major employers in the region with over 300 employees, the majority of whom are non-Indians.

Casino revenues generate much needed financial support to tribal members for health, education, and better living conditions. Additionally, the tribe has donated several thousand dollars to various local nonprofit charities in Payson, Arizona as well as to the school district.

Services and Retail. The tribe owns the Mobile Market, which opened July 4, 1998 and is located on the reservation. It is a full service convenience market with six gas pumps and tax-free cigarettes. The tribe also owns the Marble Slab Creamery icecream parlor located on Main Street in Payson, and the 47-room Paysonglo Lodge in Payson (both purchased in 2001). The lodge has a heated swimming pool and offers a casino stay-and-play package for casino customers.

Tourism and Recreation. Ideally situated to take advantage of the high volume of tourism in and around the Payson area, the Tonto Apache Reservation adjoins the Tonto National Forest, an area rich with outdoor recreation opportunities, including hunting, camping, and winter sports such as, skiing, cross-country snowshoe racing, and snowmobiling. The reservation is just minutes away from the scenic Mogollon Rim, a steep escarpment dividing Arizona's northern plateau region from the lower desert areas in south-central Arizona. Other local attractions include a fish hatchery; Tonto Natural Bridge, the largest travertine bridge in the world; Zane Grey's historic cabin; and Strawberry Schoolhouse, the oldest standing schoolhouse in Arizona.

The community of Payson hosts over 40 annual arts and entertainment events, such as a rodeo, a Fiddler's Contest and Bluegrass Festival, a chili cook-off, the Logger's Sawdust Festival, an art festival in October, November's Swiss Village, and the Town Hall Christmas Lighting in December.

INFRASTRUCTURE
Arizona State Highway 87 passes through Payson and continues northeast 90 miles to Winslow, Arizona, and southwest 94 miles to Phoenix. Arizona State Highway 260 stretches southward from Payson to the New Mexico line.

Electricity. Electricity is available through Arizona Public Service Company.

Fuel. Natural gas is provided by various local dealerships.

Water Supply. The tribe provides water to the reservation through a recently completed expanded water system. Sewage disposal and treatment is provided by the Northern Gila County Sanitary District.

Transportation. The Payson airport, located 2 miles north of the center of town, has a single lighted 5,000-foot runway. The nearest commercial and passenger carriers are in Phoenix at Sky Harbor International Airport. Other transportation services available in Payson include bus and truck-freight services.

Telecommunications. Local telephone service is offered by Qwest. There is one local radio station, plus a number of others from the Phoenix and Flagstaff areas, with reception in Payson, along with cable television service.

COMMUNITY FACILITIES AND SERVICES
The community consists of approximately 27 houses, paved streets, and underground utilities. In 2003, the tribal offices moved into a new two-story tribal governmental complex with a daycare center. A new recreation center, which will have a swimming pool, library, computer room, and youth activity center, was scheduled for completion in January 2005. There is a city fire department in Payson. Law enforcement services are provided by the BIA and the Payson police department.

Education. Education is available to students from preschool through high school in the Payson Unified School District. Preschool is also available through the tribe's Head Start program. Every household has a wireless computer system with Internet access. Pima Community College is located in Payson, and Eastern Arizona College currently has a satellite learning facility there. Payson's newspaper, the *Payson Roundup*, is published twice weekly.

Health Care. Contracted medical services are available at the Payson Regional Medical Center. The tribe has a CHR unit for the community. The tribe has a self-funded medical coverage plan for its members and employees.

Tonto Apache

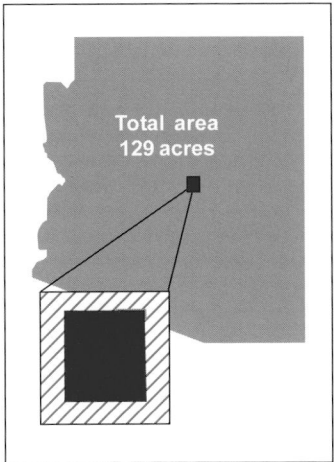

Total area
129 acres

TRI-AZ-1165 Entrance to the tribal administration building

TRI-AZ-1180 The Mazatzal Casino, which features 380 slot machines, poker room, bingo hall, restaurant, sports lounge, gift shop, and arcade

TRI-AZ-1175 Hotel and casino sign at Fort Apache

TRI-AZ-1165

TRI-AZ-1180

TRI-AZ-1175

Yavapai-Prescott

Yavapai-Prescott Reservation
Federal reservation
Yavapai
Yavapai County, Arizona

Yavapai-Prescott Reservation
530 East Merritt
Prescott, AZ 86301
928-445-8790
928-778-9445 Fax
ypit.com

Total area *(BIA, 2004)*
1,402.80 acres

Tribally owned lands *(BIA, 2004)*
1,402.80 acres

Population *2000 census*
182

Tribal enrollment *(BIA, 2001)*
159

Total labor force *2000 census*
69

High school graduate or higher
2000 census
78.6%

Bachelor's degree or higher
2000 census
6.0%

Unemployment rate
2000 census
2.9%

Per capita income
$14,217

LOCATION AND LAND STATUS

The Yavapai-Prescott Indian Reservation is located in central Arizona, within the northern boundaries of the city of Prescott. The reservation was established by an Act of Congress on June 7, 1935, which provided for 75 acres for the Yavapai-Prescott Community Association and by an Act on May 18, 1956, which set aside 1,320 acres.

PHYSICAL DESCRIPTION

At an elevation of about 5,040 feet, the reservation is surrounded by pine-forested mountains. The mean elevation is 5,042 feet above sea level.

CLIMATE

The average year-round high temperature is a moderate 70°F, with the highest recorded temperature being 103°F. The average year-round low temperature is 40º F. The lowest temperature ever recorded was -5°F. The area receives just over 12 inches of rain annually and averages 17 inches of snowfall.

CULTURE AND HISTORY

The Yavapais speak a Yuman dialect of the Hokan language family, similar to that spoken by the Havasupais and Hualapais in Arizona, and by peoples living in areas from northern California to southern Mexico.

Traditionally the Yavapais were hunter-gatherers, basket makers and small-scale farmers, inhabiting some 15,000 square miles of what is now Arizona. After the Civil War, when gold was discovered in the middle of Yavapai territory and settlers began to encroach, frontier military posts were established to force the Yavapais onto reservations. This policy culminated in 1872, when the massacre of Yavapais at Skeleton Cave broke Yavapai resistance, and they were forced onto a reservation at Camp Verde, not far from the present reservation. They stayed there until 1875 when they were moved to the San Carlos Apache Reservation where they stayed until the turn of the century. They were then divided and sent to three different reservations: the Fort McDowell Reservation, the Camp Verde Reservation, and the Yavapai-Prescott Reservation. On the grounds of the former Fort Whipple Military Reserve, the first reservation established exclusively for Yavapai was a mere 75 acres. Despite the addition of 1,320 acres in 1956, some Yavapais remain at the Fort McDowell and Camp Verde reservations.

Many aspects of traditional Yavapai culture may still be seen today; especially noteworthy are their pottery and woven baskets. Another aspect of present-day Yavapai culture is the continuing practice of their traditional religion.

GOVERNMENT

The Yavapai-Prescott tribe, under PL-638, contracts with the BIA to administer key programs and services. They are governed by a board of directors consisting of a president, vice-president, and three members. The board members serve two-year terms, and meet the second Friday of each month. The tribe operates under Articles of Association Bylaws, approved in 1962.

The tribe has planning, zoning, environmental, and real estate departments to provide assistance to current and prospective entrepreneurs, and an environmental action committee to manage environmental initiatives and oversee mitigation projects on the reservation.

ECONOMY

The tribe is a member of the Indian Development District of Arizona, an organization whose purpose is to promote the economic and social development of the reservations in the state. Tribal enterprises have branched into retail businesses, gaming, and commercial real estate development. Major public employers on the reservation include Bucky's Casino, Yavapai's Casino and the tribal government via its many initiatives.

Government as employer. The tribe is the fourth largest employer on the reservation.

Agriculture and Livestock. While no farming is presently engaged in on the reservation, tribal members still graze a few personally owned livestock.

Gaming. The tribe operates two casinos. Bucky's Casino, a 24,000-square-foot gaming facility located at the Prescott Resort and Conference Center, offers 300 slot machines and 6 poker tables. The hotel offers luxurious accommodations, live entertainment, a sports lounge, a swimming pool, tennis and racquetball courts, a weight training room, a whirlpool, a sauna, and massage. There are abundant golf courses in the area. The resort is in the center of a region filled with entertainment and recreational activities. Across from the hotel's entrance are additional gaming facilities at the Yavapai Casino and at the Cantina, as well as a service station, a convenience store, and the tribe's shopping center. The resort complex includes casual and gourmet dining and 10,099-square-feet of convention space.

At Yavapai Casino and at the Cantina are another 175 slot machines, blackjack, and bingo. The Gold Rush Express shuttle service makes daily runs from Phoenix, free of charge to casino patrons. In May 2003, the tribe renewed its gaming compact with the State of Arizona to continue gaming operations for another 23 years.

Real Estate/Commercial Development. Frontier Village, a shopping center the tribe built along Highway 69 in Prescott, houses 60 retail establishments such as Office Max, Burger King, Outback Steakhouse, Blockbuster Video, Target, Home Depot, Red Lobster, Taco Bell, Subway, and a smokeshop. These establishments employ over 2,500 people, many from the tribe. There are four banks.

Industrial Parks. The 12-acre Sundog Business Park, located on Highway 89 in Prescott, was one of the tribe's first business ventures. It features 26 industrial pads and tenants, such as Champions, MCK, EZ Transmix Company, Precision Marble, Prescott Steel and Supply, and Sundog Mini Storage. The tribe can accommodate a range of business developments.

Tourism and Recreation. In 2004 the tribe hosted the "Gathering of the Pai's." The three Yavapai groups take turns hosting the annual Ba'ja Days cultural events.

Not all of the reservation has been developed or is even open to development, so the pristine natural beauty of the landscape and surrounding geographic features, such as Thumb Butte and Granite Mountain, offer scenic vistas at every turn. Prescott National Forest, over 1.2 million acres of wilderness, is accessible via the Scenic Highway from Prescott. Hiking, fishing, bird watching, and hunting are popular draws to the area's many lakes: Lynx, Willow, Granite Basin, Watson, and Goldwater. The area is also popular as a winter ski destination.

Although not on the reservation, Sharlot Hall Museum and Smoki Museum in Prescott have pioneer exhibits and Indian artifacts from the Old West, recreating aspects of Southwest Indian culture.

INFRASTRUCTURE

An airport, Ernest A. Love Field, serves Prescott and all surrounding communities, with regular daily flights of both commercial and private aircraft.

The reservation is accessible by two major highways, U.S. 69 which runs east-west, and U.S. 89 which runs north-south. Commercial and charter air services are available at Prescott Municipal Airport, six miles north of the reservation. Bus and truck-freight services are also available in Prescott.

The Yavapai-Prescott Indian Tribe maintains the water and sewer systems for the reservation. Arizona Public Service Company provides electricity, and Southern Union Gas Company supplies natural gas. Telephone services are provided by Qwest.

COMMUNITY FACILITIES AND SERVICES

Public Safety. Under a cooperative agreement with the City of Prescott, the tribe's police department is staffed by both its own officers and some city officers, providing cross-jurisdictional police protection on the reservation. There are eight officers on the force. A similar agreement, made in 2001 for fire protection, is provided through payment of tribe fees to Prescott's fire department.

The tribe operates its own youth programs which supplement the classes students attend in Prescott public schools, which serve reservation students from preschool through high school. Prescott College, a private four-year college, and a community college are located in Prescott.

The tribe has built the Yavapai-Prescott Indian Tribe Community Gathering Center, expanded the tribal office complex, and added a library and tennis and basketball courts.

Health Care. There are two hospitals in the area, the Yavapai Regional Medical Center and the Whipple Veterans Administration Hospital; both facilities offer acute and long-term care. The Yavapai County Health Department provides public-health nursing services, and comprehensive medical care is available at the Phoenix Indian Medical Center. Other health services are offered in Prescott.

ENVIRONMENTAL CONCERNS

A former wood treatment and processing plant located on what are now reservation lands was designated a CERCLA (Comprehensive Environmental Response Compensation and Liability Act) site in 1992. Cleanup work began in 1996.

Paving parking lots at development sites has created soil erosion damage in surrounding areas, as rain that usually seeps into the soil is diverted into streams and channels, decreasing plant productivity and thereby increasing erosional damage.

The tribe is working to write a fire management plan for the reservation. The plan will take into consideration the regional urban landscape as well as the tribe's own biological, geological, and cultural resources. Interested members participate in the Wildland/Urban Interface project (WUI) which was developed to reduce the dangers of wildfires by encouraging the creation of defensible space around every home.

The tribe's environmental action committee is monitoring the Granite Creek Riparian Wetland Restoration Project, an attempt to restore cottonwoods, ashes, willows, grasses, and shrubs along the banks that were damaged beyond all natural repair by herds of cattle and sheep grazing the creek's flood plain for decades. In the late 1800s, gold mining further damaged the area, as did gravel mining which was conducted well into the 1890s, disrupting the creek's natural flow and ultimately displacing the channel altogether. Industrial debris has been removed, and an irrigation system was installed. New trees are now growing and being monitored for height, width, canopy cover, and overall health.

Yavapai-Prescott

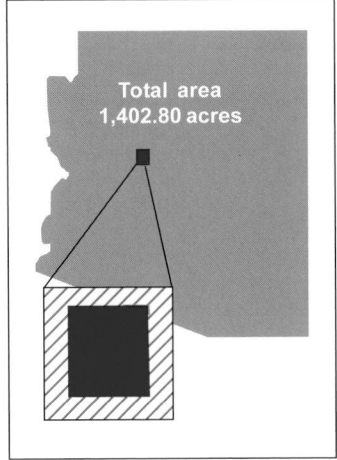

Total area
1,402.80 acres

Zuni
Reservation
See New Mexico

CALIFORNIA

Map from Tiller's Guide to Indian Country (1996 edition)

A- BIG VALLEY
B- COLUSA
C- CORTINA
D- MIDDLETOWN
E- ROBINSON
F- RUMSEY
G- SULPHUR BANK
H- UPPER LAKE

1- AUGUSTINE
2- BARONA
3- CABAZONE
4- CAHUILLA
5- CAMPO (SYCAMORE VALLEY)
6- CAPTAIN GRANDE
7- CUYAPAIPE
8- JAMUL INDIAN VILLAGE
9- INAJA-COSMIT
10- LA JOLLA
11- LA POSTA
12- MANZANITA

13- MESA GRANDE
14- PAUMA & YUIMA
15- PECHANGA
16- RAMONA
17- RINCON
18- SAN PASQUAL
19- SANTA ROSA
20- SOBOBA
21- SAN YSABEL
22- SYCUAN
23- VIEJA

CALIFORNIA
INTRODUCTION

In 2000 California had the second-largest Native American population of any state, second only to Alaska. While most are native California Indians, many have come from other states to seek employment in the metropolitan areas of the state, one of the ten largest economies in the world. The California peoples increasingly live in urban areas as well, but there are over 100 reservations, many of them in remote rural areas. In addition to the groups recognized by the federal government, with rights to government services and sovereign status, there are currently approximately 40 groups attempting to gain federal recognition.

Prior to the coming of the Europeans, the peoples of California lived in all areas of the state, making use of the varied resources found there. Any land that could support human life was utilized; there was no empty land. The contrast between the land area used by Native Americans before the eighteenth century and the minuscule land base they now possess is striking.

The history of California Indians falls into three more or less distinct periods: the period before contact with Europeans (until the middle of the sixteenth century), the Spanish/Mexican period (1769-1846), and the American period.

THE PRECONTACT PERIOD
While we do not know much about these early residents of the state, over the thousands of years their descendants have lived there they developed very different ways of life, attuned to the land and resources of California's distinct climatic and ecological zones. In the cool, moist northwestern comer of the state, people were dependent on salmon and acorns in the river valleys, and on shellfish, ocean fish, and acorns along the coast. In the temperate central coastal areas, large sea fish and sea mammals were important sources of food. The peoples of the inland lakes and valleys, were dependent on freshwater fish and waterfowl, as well as some acorns. The peoples of the foothills and mountains, with larger settlements depended on acorns and other plant foods, as well as some game. East of the Sierra Nevada range the people were hunters and gatherers as well as desert farmers.

By the time Europeans came onto the scene, California was home to numerous "tribelets," groupings of several villages, whose members spoke dozens of languages from seven major language families. In very few other places in the world was there such a diversity of cultures and high population densities; in most areas of the state, this came about without the development of agriculture.

It would be difficult to overstate the importance of acorns as a staple food source for most early people in California; even those peoples in the northern part of the state who depended on salmon also used acorns. After being ground and treated to remove the toxic tannic acid, the acorns were usually made into a kind of soup or gruel, often called "acorn mush." The abundance of oaks and the great variety of other vegetable and animal foods made it possible for permanent and semi-permanent villages to flourish; a development that usually implies the start of agriculture.

Housing ranged from temporary, simple structures in the desert south to more elaborate cedar-plank houses in the north. While pottery was not used, basketry had reached heights of artistic and utilitarian development, even being used as cooking vessels by means of hot stones placed in water. Many of the groups living in the rich acorn and salmon regions developed extensive material cultures, with elaborately decorated objects representing prosperity and personal wealth. Government of the tribelets was generally carried out by a council of elders.

Relations among the groups appear to have been generally peaceful, with well-developed trading networks between coastal and inland peoples, as well as between the northern and southern parts of the state.

THE SPANISH/MEXICAN PERIOD
Although the Spanish had explored and claimed the coast of what they called "Alta California" as early as 1542, it was not until 1769 that they actually established a permanent presence there. During the two centuries between these dates, Spanish, English, Russian, and French ships visited California, either exploring or stopping for provisions on the way to other destinations. When the Spanish finally decided to send a colonizing expedition northward, under Gaspar de Portola, it was because they felt the need to guard against territorial incursions from the Russians and the English; although the desire to win converts to the Christian faith was also an important motive.

In establishing their chain of missions along the California coast, the Spanish employed a combination of armed force and religious persuasion, with force predominating. The missions were built by forced Indian labor, and the new converts were encouraged to settle at the mission sites in much larger communities than was their custom. When people proved reluctant to change their way of life, soldiers were used to forcibly move them to the missions, where they were kept in sex-segregated quarters and prevented from leaving. In addition to the cultural disruption brought about by these conditions, the introduction of European diseases to a previously unexposed population caused the deaths of over two-thirds of the estimated 1769 population of 300,000 by 1832. As the labor force declined because of deaths and desertions, Spanish soldiers ranged farther afield to secure new "converts." And the diseases spread to more distant communities ahead of the Europeans.

In 1834, under independent Mexican rule, the missions were "secularized," and their Indian residents were released from the virtual slavery in which they had lived. At that time it is estimated that somewhat more than 100,000 Native Americans lived in the state, most of them following their traditional way of life in dispersed villages.

The Spanish made no treaties with any Indian peoples, since by their right of discovery the land was theirs to use as they saw fit; they did recognize Indian title to the lands taken for the missions, but use and occupancy was at the discretion of the conquerors. When the missions were dissolved, the lands were distributed to their Indian residents, although much of this land was later seized by Mexican ranchers. Under the Mexican government, 1821-1846, large land grants were made to non-Indians, with the tacit understanding that the Indians living on them would be available as a labor force for the grantees.

THE AMERICAN PERIOD
Mexico lost California to the United States as one of the provisions of the Treaty of Guadalupe Hidalgo, which ended the Mexican-American War in 1848. That same year, gold was discovered at Sutter's Fort, prompting a huge influx of Americans seeking their fortunes. Individual whites often killed Indians occupying or frequenting promising mining sites. Indians did not always passively tolerate the barbaric incursions of these

newcomers, but when they mounted any organized resistance, the U.S. military retaliated in force. Adding to the immense disruption of this period was the spread of diseases to tribes who had been too remote from the missions to have been affected before this time.

In 1851-1852 a federal treaty commission was sent westward to deal with the "Indian problem" and actually entered into 18 treaties, setting aside reservations totaling some 8.5 million acres. However, because of protests from immigrants that these reservations included too much prime mining and farming land, the treaties were never ratified (and were in fact kept secret until 1905). Instead reservations were set up for the "subsistence and protection" of the California Indians, none of them containing more than 25,000 acres, with the idea of removing all Indian peoples from lands considered valuable by the newcomers. By 1867 there were four such reservations-Hoopa Valley, Round Valley, Smith River, and Tule River-and approximately 400,000 American immigrants. By 1906, 35 reservations had been established, mostly with the goal of clearing land for the immigrants. In addition, a few rancherias (the Spanish term for a small Indian settlement) had been recognized, usually involving a single community of one cultural group. The total area of the reservations setup in the nineteenth century was less than 500,000 acres.

By the turn of the century, the total Indian population of the state is estimated to have been around 16,500; of this number, 11,800 were considered "landless." To address this situation, the U.S. Congress authorized an investigation of the prevailing conditions, and in1906, after the revelation of the 1851-1852 treaties that were never ratified, public reaction supported the passage of the first appropriations. A series of appropriations for monies to be used to purchase land for landless Indians were renewed almost annually until 1934. In 1934 the Indian Reorganization Act intended to give Native American groups more autonomy, included a mechanism for the acquisition of land for Indians.

Between 1906 and 1934, 54 rancherias and one "Indian village" were established, in addition to eight "reservations." The former followed the pattern of setting aside a small area of land around a settlement, while the latter now either represented lands bought for Indians previously without land or lands traditionally inhabited and used by groups east of the Sierra divide. These eastern reservations fit the pattern of reservations elsewhere in the West, while the rancherias are a particular California institution.

To round out the cycle of land expropriation and later reservation, in the mid-1950s Congress passed PL 83-280 (67 Stat. 588), terminating federal supervision and control over selected tribes, in the interest of "emancipating" them from their "dependent" status on the federal government. This action affected some 40 California rancherias; they lost the right to certain federal programs, and their land no longer had the protection that federal status provides. By the mid-1960s, how-ever, the policy was recognized as a failure. In the 1980s a class-action suit was filed by Tillie Hardwick, a Pomo Indian from Pinoleville Rancheria, with the aim of "un-terminating" the terminated communities. In 1983 the suit was won, resulting in the restoration of federal recognition to 17 rancherias. Even today, however, a number of California rancherias are still waiting for the reversal of their termination.

The heritage of the foreign invasions is still evident. The "mission Indians" are the descendants of people forced by the Spanish into the mission system, in the coastal areas of the southern two-thirds of the state. Many of the reservations begun in the nineteenth century are still in existence, the majority of them including descendants of different tribal and linguistic groups, removed from their lands by the U.S. military. And many of the modern rancherias and eastern reservations are the modern descendants of villages or traditional areas too remote or on land considered of too little value to cause the Americans to evict their residents. Other rancherias have developed from small communities formed on the outskirts of American settlements by Indians fleeing from or avoiding removal to the reservations. In all of these situations, the question of land ownership is extremely complex, involving several layers of expropriation and illegal seizure; we have done our best to clarify the situation. In recent years California Indian groups have been actively pursuing land issues, both separately and in connection with campaigns for federal recognition. In light of the history of the state, it is inspiring that California's Native American people can still keep their traditions alive and work for a positive future.

THE CULTURES

California groups are so diverse that it is possible here to give only the barest outline of the location of traditional lands, language affiliations, means of subsistence, and present-day location. It should also be kept in mind that members of all cultural groups now live in urban areas of the state, sometimes far removed from their ancestral lands. This situation is a major reason for the discrepancy between the numbers of people belonging to each cultural group discussed below and the total number of Indians in California. People living off the reservations over several generations may become "lost" to their ancestral culture group.

CAHTO
The traditional lands of the Cahto were the southernmost of those inhabited by the Athabascan groups clustered in the northwestern corner of the state. Their language relates them distantly to the Athabascan peoples of the interior of Alaska and northern Canada, as well as to the Navajos and Apaches of the southwest. They lived in the hills and oak savannahs of the coast range, where a variety of vegetable sources, primarily acorns, formed the staple foods. Present-day Cahto people live on the Laytonville Rancheria.

CAHUILLA
The Cahuilla homeland lies in inland southern California; they traditionally spoke a language belonging to the Takic branch of the Uto-Aztecan language family, a family that covers much of the southwest and extends into central Mexico. The groups or "tribelets" of this people made their living partly in the foothill and mountain regions (where they depended on a variety of vegetable staples, especially acorns), and partly in the desert lands to the east of the Sierra divide (where they depended largely on piñon nuts and mesquite beans as staple foods). Today Cahuilla people live on the Agua Caliente, Augustine, Cabazon, Cahuilla, Los Coyotes, Morongo, Ramona, Santa Rosa, Soboba, and Torres Martinez reservations.

CHEMEHUEVI
The Chemehuevi are the southernmost group of the Southern Paiutes; they are closely related to the Southern Paiutes of Southern Nevada. They traditionally spoke a language from the Southern Numic branch of the Uto-Aztecan language family. They made their living either by desert hunting and gathering (depending on piñon nuts or mesquite beans as a staple food), or by desert farming along the Colorado River in the Chemehuevi Valley. Currently, Chemehuevi people live primarily on the Chemehuevi Reservation, but they are also represented on the Agua Caliente, Cabazon, Colorado River Indian Tribes, and Morongo reservations.

CHILULA
The Chilula are one of the Athabascan peoples of the extreme northwestern corner of the state. They are distantly related by language to the Athabascan peoples. Some Chilula "tribelets" traditionally made a living by gathering a variety of vegetable foods, primarily acorns, in the foothills; others depended on the semiannual king salmon runs along the main streams and certain tributaries of the large rivers in the area. Chilula people today live primarily on the Hoopa Reservation.

CHUMASH
The Chumash people originally occupied lands in southern California in present-day Ventura, Santa Barbara, and San Luis Obispo counties. They traditionally spoke one of five closely related Hokan languages, related in turn to many others in northern California and to the south and east, into Mexico and the Great Basin. Many of the Chumash groups made their living by sea hunting and fishing, taking large sea fish and sea mammals (on land), as well as utilizing shellfish resources along the coast and on the Channel Islands. The development of sea-going canoes made this way of life possible. Island groups practiced the classic California pattern of dependence on acorns and other gathered vegetable staples, as well as small game. Today Chumash people live on the Santa Ynez Indian Reservation and in such towns as Santa Barbara and Ventura, in addition to the larger southern California cities.

CUPENO
The Cupefio people traditionally occupied lands some 50 miles inland and 50 miles north of the current Mexican border, in the foothills of the Coast

Range. They traditionally spoke a Takic language of the Uto-Aztecan language family. It is closely related to the Cahuilla language. The Cupetio people made their living by depending on vegetable staples, mainly acorns, in addition to hunting, mostly for small game; their settlements tended to be fairly permanent, with some seasonal movement. At the present, Cupefio people live on the Pala and Morongo reservations.

HUPA

The Hupa people traditionally occupied lands in the far northwestern comer of the state. Their language belongs to the Athabascan language family. Their way of life was based on the semiannual king salmon runs that still occur on the Trinity River, which flows through the center of the Hoopa Valley Reservation. In addition, they made use of vegetable foods, especially acorns. Both these resources remain important as ceremonial foods. Today Hupa people live on the Hoopa Valley Reservation, in the heart of their traditional territory.

KARUK

The traditional lands of the Karuk people were located in far northwestern California, inland along the middle section of the Klamath River. Their language is one of the Hokan language family. Traditionally they made a living by depending on the salmon runs that occurred twice a year, in addition to gathering vegetable foods. Today Karuk people live in the Orleans district in Humboldt County, the Happy Camp district, the Yreka district, and the Forks of the Salmon region in Siskiyou County.

KAWAIISU

The Kawaiisu people still live in their traditional core area in Kern County, in the foothills between the Mohave Desert and the San Joaquh Valley. Their language belongs to the Southern Numic branch of the Uto-Aztecan language family. There is evidence that the Kawaiisu have lived in this same area for more than 2,000 years, where they depended primarily on acorns and other vegetable staples, as well as small-game hunting. Their villages were semi-permanent, with some seasonal movement. Some people of Kawaiisu descent live on the Tule River Reservation.

KITANEMUK

The Kitanemuk people traditionally lived in southern California near present-day Bakersfield, in Kern County. Through the nineteenth century, they lived in the Tejon Ranch Indian community. This community never became a reservation. Their language belongs to the Uto-Aztecan family. Their way of life was the classic California foothills pattern, based on acorns and other vegetable staples, with small-game hunting also of importance; they lived in semi-permanent villages. Today a number of people of Kitanemuk descent live on the Tule River Reservation, as well as on private land near their homeland.

KUMEYAAY (DIEGUEÑO)

Traditionally the lands of the Kumeyaay extended from 50 to 75 miles both north and south of the present Mexican border, as well as from the California coast almost to the Colorado River. Traditionally they spoke a Hokan language of the Yuman branch. They made their living in areas stretching from the coast up into the southern Coast Range and on east into the desert, depending on marine resources, vegetable foods such as acorns, and dry farming. In the eighteenth century, there were some 50 bands of Kumeyaay; today they live on the Barona, Campo, Cuyapaipe, Inaja-Cosmit, La Posta, Manzanita, Mesa Grander Pala, San Pascual, Santa Ysabel, Sycuan, and Viejas reservations, as well as in the Jamul Indian Village.

LUISEÑO-JUANENO

Traditionally the Luisefio-Juaneiro people occupied approximately 50 miles of the southern California coastline, north of present-day San Diego and south of Los Angeles, north of the lands of the Kumeyaay, extending inland for about 30 miles. Their language belongs to the Takic branch of the Uto-Aztecan language. They traditionally made their living by utilizing marine resources on the coast and by gathering vegetable foods in the foothills of the Coast Range to the east; there their villages tended to be semi-permanent, with some seasonal movement. Currently Luiseiio-Juanefio people live on the La Jolla, Pala, Pechanga, Paurna-Yuima, Rincon, and Soboba reservations.

MAIDU

The traditional lands of the Maiduan peoples were in the north-central part of the state. The three closely related peoples usually called Maidu were the Maidu of Plumas and Lassen counties, the Konkow of Butte and Yuba counties, and the Nisenan of Yuba, Nevada, Placer, Sacramento, and El Dorado counties. Their languages are of the Penutian family, which includes a large group of central and northern California languages. Their traditional way of life ranged from the valley ecological type, dependent on mixed resources of fish and vegetables (mainly tule and acorns), to the foothills ecological type, the classic California way of life dependent mainly on acorns and some small game. Today Maiduan people live on the Auburn, Berry Creek, Chico, Enterprise, Greenville, Mooretown, and Susanville rancherias, as well as the Round Valley Reservation.

MATTOLE

The Mattole people occupied a homeland in the northwestern comer of the state, close to the present-day border with Oregon; their lands included a stretch of coastline and some inland river valleys. Their traditional language is an Athabascan language. They made their living by fishing and gathering along the coast and depending on king salmon and other resources along the major rivers of their territories. At present, their descendants are represented only on the Rohnerville Rancheria.

MIWOK

There are three main Miwok groups-the Coast Miwok, the Lake Miwok, and the Sierra Mewuk, with homelands in north-central California. The Coast Miwok lived along the Pacific Coast from present-day Sausalito to Duncan's Point, including Bodega Bay, Tomales Bay, and San Pablo Bay inland to the area near Sonoma. The Lake Miwok lands were located to the east and south of Clear Lake, and the Sierra Mewuk lands were located in the Sierra Nevada foothills of the central part of the state. These groups spoke Hokan languages. The coast people depended on tideland gathering of fish and shellfish, with secondary use of acorns and game; the lake people used fish, waterfowl, and other lake foods, as well as acorns and game; and the Sierra people depended on king salmon in the major river valleys, with increasing use of acorns and game in the foothills. The Lake Miwok people live today on the Middletown Rancheria. Many Sierra Mewuk people still live on their traditional lands, either on the Jackson, Shingle Springs, and Tuolumne rancherias and the California Valley Miwok, Buena Vista, and Chicken Ranch rancherias (which have little or no trust lands), or in surrounding areas.

MOJAVE (MOHAVE)

Traditionally the Mojave people occupied lands along the Colorado River from the area of present-day Hoover Dam downriver beyond the city of Blythe (approximately 200 miles), as well as a vast inland region to the west. Their language belongs to the Yuman branch of the Hokan family, so that the Mojave are related linguistically to peoples from northern California, south into Mexico, and east into the Great Basin and beyond. They made their living as desert farmers, using the floodwaters of the Colorado, and depended on fishing, hunting, and trapping, as well the mesquite bean. Today Mojave people live on or near the Fort Mojave Reservation, located along the Colorado River in the states of California, Arizona, and Nevada; another several thousand live on the Colorado River Reservation.

MONO, WESTERN (MONACHE)

The traditional territory of the Western Mono people was the south-central Sierra Nevada foothills. Their language belongs to the Uto-Aztecan language family, related to Paiute and to languages extending eastward into the Great Basin and the southwest. Their main food resource was acorns, while they depended to a lesser extent on other vegetable foods and game. Today they live on the Big Sandy, Cold Springs, and North Fork rancherias, as well as in the town of Dunlap.

PAIUTE

There are three main groupings of Paiute people: the Northern Paiute, Owens Valley Paiute, and Southern Paiute. Only the first two groups lived in what is now California; they traditionally occupied the eastern slope of the Sierra Nevada, from the northern border with Oregon south to Owens Valley. Their languages are Uto-Aztecan. Traditionally they made their living by hunting and gathering, with some irrigating of areas supporting plants with edible seeds and roots. Today Northern Paiute people live in the Bridgeport Colony, on the Cedarville Rancheria, and the Fort Bidwell Reservation, while Owens Valley Paiutes live on the Benton, Bishop, Big Pine, Lone Pine, and Fort Independence reservations.

PIT RIVER (ACHUMAWI, ATSUGEWI)

The 11 bands of the Pit River Tribe have traditionally occupied lands along the Pit River and its tributaries, in the far northeastern part of the state. Their languages, Achumawi and Atsugewi, are closely related Hokan languages. Traditionally their way of life depended on fish and other river resources, as well as on acorns and other vegetable foods growing in the river valleys. Today the 1,350 or so tribal members live on the Alturas, Big Bend, Likely Lookout, Montgomery Creek, Redding, Roaring Creek, and Susanville rancherias, as well as on the Pit River and Round Valley.

POMO

The Pomo people, traditionally speaking seven related but mutually unintelligible languages, still live in their ancestral lands in northwestern California. Their languages belong to the Hokan family. Along the coast they made their living by gathering shellfish and fishing, relying secondarily on acorns and game; along major rivers they were able to depend on king salmon. Today Pomo people live on or near the Big Valley, Cloverdale, Dry Creek, Grindstone, Guidiville, Hopland, Lytton, Manchester/Point Arena, Middletown, Pinoleville, Potter Valley, Redwood Valley, Robinson, Scotts Valley, Sherwood Valley, Stewarts Point, and Upper Lake rancherias, the Coyote Valley, and Round Valley reservations, and the Elem Indian Colony.

SERRANO

The Serrano people traditionally lived in much of the Mojave Desert and the San Bernardino Mountains, in southern California. Their language belongs to the Takic branch of the Uto-Aztecan language family. They made their living by hunting and gathering in the desert areas and by relying on acorns and game in the foothill regions, where the settlements were more permanent. Today Serrano people live on the San Manuel Reservation, on or near the Morongo Reservation, or on or near the Soboba Reservation.

SHASTA

The Shasta people traditionally lived in the northernmost part of California and southern Oregon. Their language belongs to the Hokan family. Traditionally they made their living by depending on the semiannual king salmon runs along the major rivers of their territory, using acorns and game only secondarily. Today the Shasta people in California live on the Quartz Valley Reservation.

SHOSHONE

The traditional lands of the Shoshone people in California are located in the east-central area to the east of the Sierra Nevada, including Owens Valley and the lands south of it. The Shoshone language is, closely related to Paiute and belongs to the Uto-Aztecan family. Traditionally the Shoshone people made a living by desert hunting and gathering; they lived in particular areas in small, extended-family groups. Today the Shoshone people in California live mainly on the Big Pine, Bishop, Timbi-Sha, and Lone Pine reservations.

TOLOWA

The Tolowa have traditionally lived in the coastal redwood forest area of the northwestern most corner of the state, extending into southern Oregon. Their language belongs to the Athabascan language family. They traditionally made their living by depending on salmon, using other marine and land resources to a lesser extent. Today the Tolowa people live primarily on the Elk Valley and Smith River rancherias.

TUBATULABAL

The traditional lands of the Tubatulabal people are located in the Kern River Valley in the southern Sierra Nevada, extending from the sources of the north and south forks of the river, near Mt. Whitney, to about 40 miles below the junction of the two. Their language belongs to the Uto-Aztecan language family but is very different from neighboring languages of this type. They traditionally made their living by relying on acorns (and pine nuts in some areas) as their staple, with other vegetable foods and game playing a smaller role. Today some Tubatulabal people still live in the Kern River Valley-and are currently seeking federal recognition; more live outside the area, a number of them on the Tule River Reservation.

WAILAKI

The traditional lands of the Wailaki people are located in the northwestern corner of the state, 50 miles or so inland from the Pacific Coast, mainly in the foothills of the Coast Range. Their language belongs to the Athabascan language family. Their traditional way of life combined the use of acorns as the principal staple with other vegetable foods and game and, along the main rivers, with salmon. At the present time, many of the Wailaki people live on the Round Valley Reservation; in 1991 a group was formed to seek separate federal recognition of the tribe, apart from the Round Valley organization

WAPPO

The Wappo people traditionally lived in a mountainous area of northern California, including the Russian River valleys and part of the Napa Valley. Their language, together with Yuki, forms a branch of the Penutian family, which includes a large group of central and northern California languages. Their traditional way of life was based on the resources of Clear Lake in areas adjacent to that body of water and partly on acorn gathering as a main staple, with other vegetable foods and game of secondary importance. Today a small number of Wappo people continue to live in theiir traditional territory; they have no reservation lands.

WASHOE

The traditional lands of the Washoe people covered an area of more than 4,000 square miles centered on Lake Tahoe, on the present California-Nevada border. The Washoe language is a Hokan language. Their way of life was based on desert hunting and gathering, with frequent seasonal movement of bands based on extended families. Today Washoe people live in the Woodfords Indian Colony in Alpine County; others live on the Susanville Rancheria and on private lands in the area.

WHIIKUT

The ancestral lands of the Whilkut people are located in the northwestern corner of the state, near those of other Athabascan peoples. The Whilkut language was related to the other California Athabascan languages. Traditionally the Whilkut people based their way of life on salmon in the major rivers of their territory, and using acorns as their main staple in the areas away from the rivers. Today their descendants live principally on the Hoopa Valley Reservation and share Hupa and other local tribal ancestry.

WINTUN

There are three divisions of the Winti people: the Wintu, Nornlaki, and Patwin. Their traditional lands are located in the greater Sacramento Valley with the Sacramento River a major feature of all the regions, from the Wintu mountain rivers in the north, through the Nomlaki plains, to the marshes, valleys, and hills of the Patwin. Their languages are of the Penutian family. In some areas, they were able to depend on the semiannual runs of king salmon up major rivers; in some the resources were more mixed, with both fish and land resources being of about equal weight; and in others, the pattern of dependence on acorns with secondary use of other vegetable foods and game prevailed. Today people of Wintun descent live on the Colusa, Cortina, Grindstone Creek, Redding, and Rumsey rancherias, as well as the Round Valley Reservation.

WIYOT

The traditional lands of the Wiyot people are located on the far northwest coast of California, along the shores of Humboldt Bay and the mouths of the Mad and Eel rivers. Their language belongs to the Algonquin language family. Their way of life was based on coastal-tideland gathering of shellfish and other marine resources, in addition to fishing; land resources were used to a much lesser extent. Today people of Wiyot descent mostly live in non-Indian communities in northern California, while a lesser number live on the Blue Lake, Rohnerville, and Table Bluff rancherias.

YANA

Traditionally the Yana people occupied lands adjacent to and extending to the southwest of Mt. Lassen, in the northern part of the state. Their language belongs to the Hokan language family. There are no speakers of yana today. Their traditional way of life depended on acorns as the main staple, with other vegetable foods and game playing a smaller role in their subsistence. Today some people of Yana descent live on the Redding Rancheria.

YOKUTS

Traditionally Yokutsan speakers occupied the San Joaquin Valley and foothills in the central part of the state. Their languages are of the Penutian family. Along the major rivers, king salmon provided the major staple; in valleys with lesser tributaries, a mixed resource base of fish, vegetable foods, and game was available; and in the foothills, acorns were the principal food source, with other vegetable foods and game playing a secondary role. Today the Yokuts people live in two federally unrecognized tribes as well as on the Pacific, Santa Rosa, and Table Mountain rancherias and the Tule River Reservation.

YUKI

The ancestral lands of the Yuki people are located in northwestern California, just south of the area historically occupied by Athabascan speakers. Their language, together with Wappo, forms one branch of the Penutian family, which includes a large group of central and northern California languages. Along the coast, people traditionally depended on fish and shellfish, with land resources of secondary importance; along the major rivers, king salmon formed the main staple food resource, with acorns and game of lesser prominence; and in the foothills of the Coast Range, acorns formed the most important staple, followed by other vegetable foods and game. Today most of the Yuki people live on the Round Valley Reservation, in addition to descendants of more mixed heritage.

YUROK

The Yurok people traditionally lived along the lower Klamath River and on the Pacific Coast near its mouth, in the far northwestern corner of the state. Their language belongs to the Algonquin family. Their traditional way of life varied from that of coastal-tideland gathering along the coast, in which fish and shellfish were of prime importance, to reliance on salmon along the major rivers in the area, with vegetable foods and game playing a lesser role in the diet. Today the Yurok people live mainly on the Yurok Reservation (formally the Hoopa Valley Extension) and the Big Lagoon, Blue Lake, Elk Valley Resighini, Smith River, and Tsurai (Trinidad) rancherias, as well as in nearby non-reservation areas.

Agua Caliente

LOCATION AND LAND STATUS
The Agua Caliente Indian Reservation is located 100 miles southeast of Los Angeles, in and around Palm Springs. The reservation is primarily comprised of allotted lands, which were originally found in a checkerboard pattern, covering every other square mile in the city. Today approxi-mately 6,700 acres of the 23,173.12-acre reservation lie within the city limits. The Agua Caliente Band is the city's largest single landowner. However, tribally owned lands are limited to Indian Canyon, the two cemeteries, and the Hot Springs area where the tribally owned Spa Hotel and tribal offices were built.

The reservation was originally established in 1876, consisting of 1.5 acres set aside for the tribe by President Grant. On September 9, 1887, the General Allotment Act granted the tribe an additional 31,500 acres. The Mission Indian Relief Act passed by Congress in 1891 authorized allotments from the acreage, comprising the reservation at Palm Springs, California. However, more than 50 years passed before the secretary of the interior approved the allotment selections. The Equalization Act of September 21, 1959, finalized the individual Indian allotments and set aside the tribal reserves of Palm, Andreas, Murray, and Tahquitz canyons.

PHYSICAL DESCRIPTION
The Cahuilla tribal lands are picturesque with chaotic, rocky gorges, sheer cliffs, and small canyons that have Washington filifera palm trees. The Tahquitz Canyon Falls drops 60 feet to granite floors of canyon wilderness that has often been used in movies. Palm, Andreas, and Murray canyons' spectacular sights have been preserved for hiking and equestrian trails.

CULTURE AND HISTORY
The Agua Caliente Band of Cahuilla Indians is composed of several small groups who in the 1870s were living in the area of present-day Palm Springs. Commander Jose Maria Estudillo wrote the first recorded history of the tribe in 1822, when the Mexicans were seeking a route from Sonora, Mexico, to California. The Cahuilla Indians named the area "Se-Khi" for boiling water, and the Mexicans named it Agua Caliente for hot water. The tribe established complex communities in the Palm, Murray, Andreas, Tahquitz, and Chino canyons, with an average of 100 to 200 inhabitants per village. Several villages together made up a larger political and territorial unit, often called a tribelet. Each tribelet was divided into lineages which consisted of both nuclear and extended families. Cahuilla society as a whole was divided into two groups, or moieties. With abundant water supply, plant, and animal life, the Cahuilla Indians thrived. They grew crops of melons, squash, beans, and corn, gathered plants and seeds for food, medicines, and basket weaving, and hunted animals.

Cahuilla ceremonial life was rich and varied, and the people had a reputation for integrity, peace, and independence. Their diet consisted of piñon nuts, acorns, mesquite beans, and the dates of native palms, in addition to rabbits, squirrels, deer, mountain sheep, and quail. Agaves were eaten, but they also provided fiber for making nets, slings, sandals, and other items.

The Cahuillas were isolated from the active centers of Spanish colonization and travel, and they were thus spared many of the abuses and diseases due to Spanish and Mexican immigration. This relative peace ended in the 1860s, when many tribal members died from measles, smallpox, dietary changes, and harassment by whites.

Today, remnants of the Cahuilla society such as rock art, house pits, foundations, food preparation areas, irrigation ditches, dams, reservoirs, and ancient trails can still be seen in the canyons, providing a testament to the rich culture and perseverance of the Cahuilla Tribe.

GOVERNMENT
The Agua Caliente Band of Cahuilla Indians adopted its constitution and bylaws in 1957, and amended both in 1966. The tribe's constitution and bylaws outline the two-tiered democratic tribal government structure: the tribal membership and the elected tribal council. The tribal council consists of five council members: a chairman, a vice-chairman, a secretary/treasurer, and two members. The chairman, vice-chairman, and secretary/treasurer serve two-year terms. Members serve a one-year term.

The tribal government is designed to: oversee tribal activities; protect and preserve tribal property, such as wildlife and natural resources; repair and maintain facilities; cultivate tribal arts and culture; and work with local, community, and other governments to foster harmonious relationships. The Agua Caliente Band of Cahuilla Indians is a PL-638 tribe. Tribal departments include a tribal council, tribal administration, tribal operations, tribal planning, tribal family services, and tribal construction.

Agua Caliente Indian Reservation
Federal reservation
Cahuilla
Riverside County, California

Agua Caliente Band
of Cahuilla Indians
600 East Tahquitz Canyon Way
Palm Springs, CA 92262
760-325-3400
760-325-0593 Fax
aquacaliente.org

Total area *(BIA realty, 2003)*
22,677.43 acres

Total area *(Tribal source, 2004)*
23,173.12 acres

Tribally owned
(BIA realty, 2003)
3,258.54 acres

Individually owned
(BIA realty, 2003)
19,418.89 acres

Population *2000 census*
21,358

Tribal enrollment
(BIA labor report, 2001)
415

Total labor force
2000 census
8,695

Agua Caliente

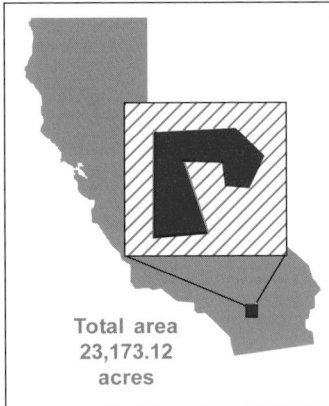

Total area
23,173.12
acres

High school graduate or higher
2000 census
88.6%

Bachelor's degree or higher
2000 census
29.4%

Unemployment rate
2000 census
5.7%

Per capita income
2000 census
$32,059

BUSIINESS CORPORATION

Formed in 1989, the Agua Caliente Development Authority, an economic development subsidiary, consists of tribal and community members, and it is designed to increase tribal assets. It has initiated a joint venture development with a private entity to develop commercial and housing projects on tribal land.

ECONOMY

Congressional authorization for the long-term leasing of trust lands in 1959 allowed the tribe and tribal members to lease their land, thereby increasing their income and economic self-reliance. Development was slightly clouded during the late 1960s when the tribal council filed a lawsuit on behalf of the tribe against Riverside County. Despite the fact that the court ruled against the tribe, finding that the county could levy a possessor interest tax on developers of trust land, leasing still remains a valuable contributor to the tribe's economy. Gaming, tourism, and retail are also large contributors to tribal economy.

Economic Development Projects. The tribe plans to build a cultural museum in Tahquitz Canyon. The site has been selected and design work completed. Construction is expected to begin in late 2005.

Gaming. The tribe owns two gaming facilities. The Agua Caliente Casino, located on Bob Hope Drive in Rancho Mirage, has 1,140 slots/VLTs, 48 table games, 10 poker tables, 700 bingo seats, six restaurants, two entertainment venues, and 2,650 parking spaces with a total 45,000 square feet. The casino employs 1,200 employees.

The second gaming facility owned by the Agua Caliente Tribe is the Spa Hotel, which has been upgraded to a casino. The Spa Resort Casino features 1,000 slots/VLTs, 30 table games, 230 hotel rooms, seven restaurants, and an entertainment venue, with a total 20,000 square feet. Spa amenities include a wide variety of spa services and treatments, including Swedish massage, aromatherapy, shiatsu, sports massage, European facials, and stone therapy, each with a professional massage therapist, an esthetician, or a spa technician.

Tourism and Recreation. The present site of the Spa Hotel and Mineral Springs was an ancient gathering place for Cahuilla Indians. The hot springs were traditionally used for curative purposes and bathing. Public bathhouses have been in operation since 1870. Since the initial purchase, the Spa has been upgraded to a Spa Resort Casino, The Spa Hotel, located in downtown Palm Springs, was purchased by the tribe in September 1992, and it is an internationally renowned resort offering tennis, golf, swimming, hot mineral baths, conference facilities, and spa treatments. Tribal lands also include Tahquitz, Andreas, Murray, and Palm canyons, which are located to the southwest

of Palm Springs; they are the network of canyons known as Indian Canyons. Listed on the National Register of Historic Places, they offer a vast network of hiking and equestrian trails and are home to the greatest concentration of wild desert palm trees in the world. There are several streams fed by spring runoff from Mount San Jacinto. Shaded picnic facilities are provided, although fires and camping are not allowed. The trading post sells refreshments, art, books, jewelry, baskets, and other items. The park is operated by the tribe, and in conjunction with the trading post, it provides a major source of tribal revenue.

INFRASTRUCTURE

Palm Springs is easily accessible from Interstate 10. There is a municipal airport serving both freight and passenger flights, and bus and truck services are available.

Electricity. Southern California Edison provides electricity.

Fuel. Southern California Edison supplies gas to this area.

Water Supply. The tribe is served by City Desert Water Agency.

Media and Communications. The Agua Caliente Tribe has its own news publication called *ASWET.*

COMMUNITY FACILITIES AND SERVICES

The tribe maintains a tribal administration building and a youth center.

Education. Tribal members attend area schools and colleges. There is an educational computer center on the reservation.

Health Care. Tribal health care is provided by the Riverside/San Bernardino County Health Care clinics. The clinics include the Agua Caliente Outreach Office in Palm Springs. The clinic provides outreach and chemical dependency programs. The Cahuilla/ Santa Rosa Outreach Office is located on Contreras Road in Anza, and it offers medical, mental health, chemical dependency, and outreach services. The Pechanga Health Care Center is located on Pechanga Road in Temecula, and it offers medical, mental health, chemical dependency, outreach, and senior nutrition programs with Meals on Wheels. Local private physicians, dentists, and other services not met by the clinics are available in Palm Springs.

ENVIRONMENTAL CONCERNS

The Cahuilla Tribe seeks to protect and preserve the natural vegetation, wildlife (in particular the big horn sheep) and Cahuilla cultural heritage found in their ancestral lands known as the Indian Canyons. The tribe has drafted, and is seeking, federal approval of a multi-species habitat conservation plan. The tribe was a founder of the Santa Rosa and San Jacinto Mountains National Monument.

TRI-CA-001 Heritage Plaza, an Agua Caliente – Tribal Development, Environmental Department

TRI-CA-002 Sign for the Agua Caliente Casino Entrance

TRI-CA-001

TRI-CA-002

Total area *(BIA realty, 2003)*	20 acres
Tribally owned *(BIA realty, 2003)*	20 acres
Population *(Tribal source)*	11
Tribal enrollment	9
Total labor force *(BIA labor report, 2001)*	8
Total labor force *(Tribal source)*	10
Total labor force **2000 census**	2
Unemployment rate	30%
(BIA labor report, 2001)	
Unemployment rate **2000 census**	0%
High school graduate or higher	40%
2000 census	
Bachelor's degree or higher	0%
2000 census	
Per capita income **2000 census**	$12,695
Per capita income *(Tribe,2004)*	$8,500

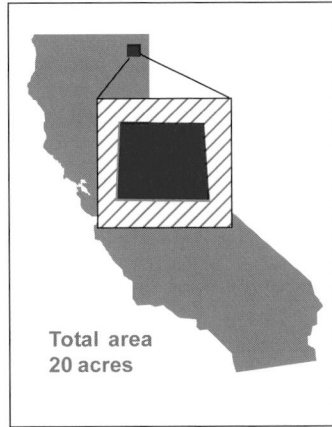

Total area
20 acres

Alturas Rancheria
Federal reservation
Pit River (Achomawi)
Modoc County, California

Alturas Rancheria
P.O. Box 340
Alturas, CA 96101
530-233-5571
530-233-4165 Fax

(See Pit River Tribe for further information on the following subjects: Culture and History, Government, and Community Facilities and Services)

LOCATION AND LAND STATUS
The Alturas Rancheria is located in Modoc County, California.

CULTURE AND HISTORY
Members of the Alturas Rancheria belong to the Pit River Tribe. The Pit River Tribe is comprised of 11 bands. Tribal members traditionally occupied lands along the Pit River and its tributaries.

ECONOMY
Gaming. The Alturas Casino is located in Alturas, California. It features 86 slots/VLTs, 2 table games, and 60 bingo seats. The 5,000-square-foot facility also features one restaurant.

ugustine

LOCATION AND LAND STATUS
The Augustine Reservation, belonging to the Augustine Band of Cahuilla Mission Indians, comprises most of a one-square- mile tract of land located in southern California.

CULTURE AND HISTORY
The Augustine Band of Cahuilla Mission Indians is comprised of the members of a single family. Members are descendants of the Cahuilla Tribe.

Members of the Cahuilla Tribe reside throughout southern California, primarily in the Mojave and Sonoran deserts. Traditional divisions of the Cahuilla Tribe were the Cahuilla, Mountain Cahuilla, and Desert Cahuilla groups. Tribal members gathered mesquite beans and pine nuts; farmed corn, squash, and beans; and did some hunting for subsistence. The Cahuilla people lived primarily in villages located near natural game habitats and plant sources.

No Cahuilla band in southern California accepted the provisions of the Indian Reorganization Act of 1934. However, the bands continue to assert tribal sovereignty and have remained active in the assertion of their autonomy as nations. During the 1940s and 50s, Cahuilla bands filed Indian Claims Commission cases in pursuit of tribal lands seized by the government or non-tribal entities. They also sought retribution for the loss of water rights.

Members of the Cahuilla bands reside primarily on nine reservations, in some cases with Chemehuevi (Southern Paiute), Cupeno, and Serrano peoples.

Cahuilla artisans are renowned for their basketry. The art of basket weaving was particularly strong among the Cahuillas during the 1920s and 30s. Though the practice has diminished since then, a revival of this art form has occurred in recent years.

GOVERNMENT
Over the past five years, the legal work has been done to create a complete government, and the tribal leadership is now developing the infrastructure required for the tribe to become an independent, successful community. A casino, which the tribe developed on the reservation, provided the necessary income to create this government and to put their ambitious economic development program into place.

ECONOMY
The Augustine Reservation used the casino revenue to get their economy up and running. They are now ready to begin the second phase of their plan and diversify their economic development project by delving into different areas such as retail, agriculture, housing, and an alternative energy system, which will end the tribe's dependence on fossil fuels. As of 2004, 400 people are employed in the casino, the gaming commission, or the tribal government.

Gaming. The band owns the Augustine Casino near Coachella, California. The casino offers 700 slots/VLTs, 2 poker tables, and 8 table games. The 32,000-square-foot facility features the Café 24 and employs 350 people.

Augustine Reservation
Federal reservation
Riverside County, California

Augustine Band of Cahuilla
Mission Indians
84-001 Avenue 54
Coachella, CA 92236

P.O. Box 846
Coachella, CA 92236
760-369-7171
760-369-7161 Fax

Total area *(BIA realty, 2003)*
502.29 acres

Tribally owned lands
(BIA realty, 2003)
341.8 acres

Individually owned
(BIA realty, 2003)
160.49 acres

Tribal enrollment
(BIA labor report, 2001)
8

Augustine

Total labor force
(BIA labor report, 2001)
1

Total labor force *2000 census*
0

Unemployment rate
(BIA labor report, 2001)
0%

Unemployment rate
2000 census
0%

The Augustine Casino is accessible from I-10 and Highway 111. Travelers can take the Jefferson, Jackson, or Monroe exit, continue south to Avenue 54, then east to Van Buren.

Tourism and Recreation. The tribal casino serves as the primary tourist attraction owned and operated by the tribe.

INFRASTRUCTURE
Interstate 10, one of the two most traveled east-west routes in the country, is located a few miles north of the reservation. Route 86 South runs a similar distance to the northeast. The reservation is well served by arterial streets on each of its principal boundaries. The reservation is nearly adjacent to the Desert Resorts Regional Airport.

Transportation. All commercial transportation facilities are available at Indio, seven miles from the reservation.

ENVIRONMENTAL CONCERNS
The tribe is concerned about the negative impact the surrounding communities are having on the reservation. The natural aquifers the reservation depends on for water are being depleted faster than they are being replenished. Attempts have been made to bring in water from other sources, but this has just caused further problems by introducing contaminants.

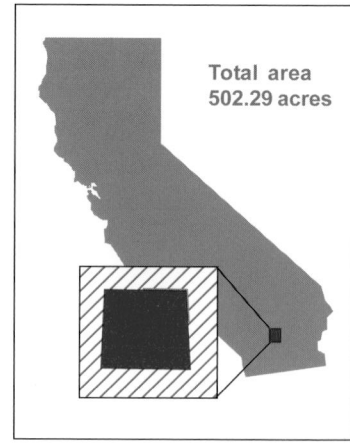

Total area
502.29 acres

These surrounding communities have also had a negative impact on the reservation through increased air pollution, sewage, and general resource consumption. All of these factors have contributed to a continually lower quality of life on the reservation that the tribe would like to combat.

Barona

Barona Band of Mission Indians Reservation
Federal reservation
'Iipay-Tipai/Kumeyaay (Diegueño)
San Diego County, California

Barona Band of Mission Indians
1095 Barona Road
Lakeside, CA 92040
619-443-6612
619-443-0681 Fax
baronatribe.org

LOCATION AND LAND STATUS
Located in the mountain foothills of San Diego County, approximately 30 miles east of San Diego, the Barona Reservation spans 5,900 acres of flat and rocky terrain. The reservation was created in 1931 upon 5,900 acres purchased by the federal government for Kumeyaay tribal members residing on the Capitan Grande Indian Reservation.

On December 27, 1875, an Executive Order established the Capitan Grande Reservation on 15,573 acres. Kumeyaay tribal members resided at the Los Conejos and El Capitan communities within the reservation boundaries. In 1932 the City of San Diego proposed the creation of a dam on tribal lands and received congressional permission to forcibly relocate the Kumeyaay residents. The El Capitan Reservoir was completed in 1935 to feed the San Diego River, and was located on the Capitan Grande Indian Reservation; the reservoir was removed from tribal ownership, and water rights were awarded by the City of San Diego. Residents were forced to relocate to lands they purchased with money they received as compensation for the loss of inundated lands.

Originally named Cañada de San Vicente y Mesa del Padre Barona, the parcel purchased by the Barona group was a former ranch situated in traditional Kumeyaay/Diegueño homelands. The group resettled there in 1932, bringing the remains of their ancestors from the Capitan Grande site.

The Capitan Grande Reservation remains jointly patented to the Viejas and Barona Bands of the Kumeyaay Tribe, though no tribal members reside there. The Barona Band plans to purchase additional lands in order to increase its land base.

PHYSICAL DESCPRITION
The Barona Reservation is zoned for residential, commercial, agricultural, recreational, and public services areas within its boundaries. Although small, the reservation is scattered and includes several ranches, much cleared land, some small farms, and clusters of comfortable homes.

CLIMATE
The climate is moderate; temperatures range from summer highs of 103°F to winter lows of 20°F. Rainfall averages about six inches per year.

CULTURE AND HISTORY
The residents of the Barona Reservation, located in traditional Kumeyaay/Diegueño territory, are descendants of the Hokan-speaking peoples, an ancient language group found throughout California and on into southern Mexico. They are one of 12 bands of the Kumeyaay/Diegueño Tribe. Other bands include the Viejas, Campos, Cuyapaipes, Inaja-Cosmits, Jamuls, La Postas, Manzanitas, Mesa Grandes, San Pasquals, Santa Ysabels, and Sycuans. The coastal country and the Salton Sea margins contain archaeological evidence suggesting that they are some of the oldest known Indian-inhabited areas in the United States; middens, or refuse heaps, have been found that date back some 20,000 years.

The Spanish did widespread missionary work in the southern portion of the state where the Coastal Hokans held extensive territory. Due in large part to the Catholic Church's policy of assimilation, much of the cultural history of this tribe was lost. Against great odds, the people living close to the Diegueño Mission maintained some of this cultural heritage. Currently living on the Barona Reservation are members of the Ipai Tribe, formerly residing east of La Jolla, and members of the Tipai Tribe, formerly residing in the San Diego area.

The Barona Band originally resided on Capitan Grande Indian Reservation northwest of Alpine, California. The reservation was created in 1875 within the traditional Kumeyaay homelands. The reserved area encompassed 18,000 acres and was the largest in the county at the time. In 1931 the City of San Diego received approval from the U.S. Congress to forcibly remove the tribe from 2,800 acres in order to create a flood plain by damming the San Diego River. The tribe was compensated with $400,000. Using these funds, tribal members living in Los Conejos bought a parcel of land to create the Barona Reservation, and members living in Los Conejos moved on to a 1,600-acre parcel of land to create the Viejas Reservation. The dam was consequently developed, and El Capitan Dam constitutes a 1,574-acre reservoir, the largest in the county, and a 190-square-mile watershed. In total, over 15,000 acres were lost to the tribe in the creation of the dam. Furthermore, the tribes were not permitted to retain any water rights to the area.

While the Viejas and Barona Bands continue to share a joint-trust patent for the Capitan Grande Reservation, no tribal members reside there. Descendants of the former Capitan Grande communities now constitute the Viejas Band and the Barona Band.

GOVERNMENT

The Barona Reservation is currently governed by a seven-member elected tribal council, including a chairman and vice-chairman. Members of the council serve four years. The tribal council conducts all business for the band, including those activities related to planning and economic development. Decisions on land or other tribal resources are referred to the general council, composed of all the tribe's voting members.

Historically the Kumeyaay people have been politically active in their support for the authority of their tribal leadership. By the late 1800s, many Kumeyaay leaders were forced underground, in response to a BIA order forcing tribal leaders to unequivocally obey local agents. In response, Kumeyaay leaders created organizations that opposed the BIA. These organizations have remained strong, often blocking BIA policies judged detrimental by tribal members.

Tribal government departments include the Indian Child Welfare Act Committee, Barona Library, childcare center, Head Start, charter school, culture, recreation and community services, fire, and tribal digital village.

ECONOMY

In 1984 the gaming industry began to transform this once impoverished community into the thriving economic success it is today. While gaming is by far the most important factor in the tribe's economic self-reliance, tribal government, tourism, recreation, and retail continue to provide revenue and employment opportunities for tribal members.

Government as Employer. BIA funds provide part-time salaries for the tribal office staff, teachers in the Head Start programs, and workers involved in the reservation's senior nutrition program.

Economic Development Projects. Recent economic improvements include renovations to the community center with full emergency services, a $3.3 million wastewater treatment plant, and $2.5 million in road construction.

Agriculture and Livestock. A fire in 2003 destroyed much of the forested land and the tribal livestock enterprise.

Gaming. The U.S. Supreme Court ruled in 1982 that high-stakes bingo was legal in California. In April 1983, the Barona Tribe opened the first Native American owned high-stakes bingo hall in the state. Since its opening, the hall has opened and closed a number of times. The addition of a card room in 1991 and an off-track betting parlor in 1992 bolstered the bingo hall's revenue. The tribe opened the Barona Big Top Casino in 1994. It is the first themed casino to be located on Native American lands, as

well as the first facility to offer a Las Vegas-style buffet. In 1999 the tribe introduced the first pull-tab machines in San Diego County at their facility. In 2000 the tribe's gaming facility was ranked as the seventh-largest tribally owned casino in the nation by *Gaming and Wagering Magazine.*

In December 2002, the Barona Tribe opened the Barona Valley Ranch Resort and Casino. The 300,000-square-foot casino has 2,000 slots/VLTs, 54 table games, 10 poker tables, and 600 bingo seats. The resort offers a 120,000-square-foot convention center, 397 hotel rooms, six restaurants, and a spa. The facilities also include a fitness center and a lakefront wedding chapel. The enterprise employs approximately 2,900 people.

Revenues from gaming have hugely increased the economic and overall well-being of the Barona Tribe. Gaming revenues made possible the tribe's state-of-the-art fire station, a 24-hour emergency crew, a daycare center, the tribal museum, the community center, new housing units, a scholarship program, and full health care coverage for tribal members, including nontribal spouses and children. The tribe is also a substantial contributor to San Diego charities. Revenues from the tribe's successful gaming industry are shared with tribal members in the form of annual per-capita payments.

Construction. The tribe operates a senior home improvement program. It renovates the homes of tribal elders. Improvements to homes are intended to bring them up to acceptable living standards and include upgraded septic systems, handicapped accessibility, and roofing repairs. The tribe has also financed the construction of 12 homes for tribal families with children.

Services and Retail. Service and retail businesses on the reservation include: The Tradin' Post, a convenience store, and a videotape rental business. The tribe owns Barona Station, a $600,000 gas station. It employs 18 individuals.

Media and Communications. The tribe publishes a weekly newspaper, the *Barona News,* and the *Barona Spirits Speak,* the newsletter of the Barona Cultural Center and Museum.

Tourism and Recreation. The Barona Cultural Center and Museum opened in 2000. It is the only museum in the county dedicated to the area's indigenous populations. The museum is professionally staffed with a director, curator, assistant curator, collections manager, senior archivist and an education coordinator; the only one of its kind on an Indian reservation in San Diego county. The museum features artifacts, dioramas, and exhibits that are a testament to the tribe's presence in the region for more than 10,000 years. Programs include guided tours, demonstrations, and presentations. The museum's staff includes several adult and school-aged tribal volunteers who serve as docent guides for tours. The museum's classes and exhibits are focused on actively involving tribal members in the preservation of the tribe's heritage. Traditional classes are offered exclusively to tribal members and include basket weaving, pottery, stories, and the construction of a Kumeyaay style house, called an 'ewaa. Internet access is available to allow students the opportunity to communicate with Indians in other communities. The museum has formed partnerships with the Barona Head Start Program and childcare center, and has created an annual Thanksgiving event with the Barona Indian School.

It has partnerships with most of the museums, universities and colleges in the San Diego area. It is also a community partner with the National Museum of the American Indian and the Smithsonian in Washington, DC. The museum serves thousands of San Diego school children and their teachers with tours, outreaches, and other programming throughout the year. The museum is working in conjunction with the University of California

Barona

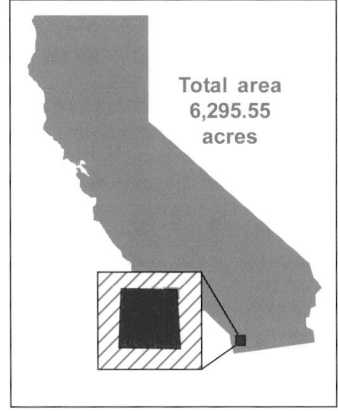

Total area
6,295.55
acres

Total area *(BIA realty, 2003)*
6,295.55 acres

Total area *(Tribal source, 2004)*
5,900 acres

Tribally owned *(BIA realty, 2003)*
6,295.55 acres

Population *2000 census*
536

Tribal enrollment
(BIA labor report, 2001)
362

Total labor force
2000 census
131
Total labor force
(BIA labor report, 2001)

266
High school graduate or higher
2000 census
70.9%

Bachelor's degree or higher
2000 census
4%

Unemployment rate
2000 census
5.3%

Unemployment rate
(BIA labor report, 2001)
80%

Per capita income *2000 census*
$32,313

Barona

and Hewlett-Packard to create a tribal digital village to include Barona and 16 other reservations in San Diego County.

The tribe opened the Barona Creek Golf Club in 2001. It is an 18-hole championship golf course rated the fourth-best facility in California by *Golfweek*. The course is located adjacent to the casino complex.

The Barona Reservation leases land for two recreational facilities, the Ultra-Light Park and the Mini-Motorcycle Park. The tribe leases an acre of land for the Ultra-Light Park, which is a motorized-glider sport facility. The six acres for the Mini-Motorcycle Park are leased to a private corporation which pays the tribe per event. The tribe also owns a motor speedway used for auto racing.

The tribe celebrates the Barona Band of Mission Indian history in the museum, and with annual activities including a tribal softball tournament, community celebrations and events, and an annual powwow.

INFRASTRUCTURE

Wildcat Canyon Road is the reservation's main road. It enters the reservation in the southwest portion and exits the reservation at San Vicente Road on the reservation's northwest corner. The road is maintained by the County of San Diego. The tribe and the BIA maintain all other roads. The closest state roads are Highway 67 which runs north from Riverside west of the reservation, and Highway 78 which intersects Highway 67 at Pomona to the north of the reservation. The tribe has completed $2.5 million in road construction and infrastructure on the reservation.

Electricity. San Diego Gas and Electric Company provides electricity to the reservation.

Fuel. San Diego Gas and Electric provides fuel.

Water Supply. Water is stored in an 850,000-gallon tank for use by the community and enterprises on the reservation. Sewage is disposed of by means of individual septic tanks.

Transportation. Commercial airline and train services are available at San Diego, 31 miles west of the reservation. Bus service can be obtained in El Cajon, 17 miles south; and freight services are available in Ramona, 12 miles south of the reservation. The casino operates a fleet of buses.

COMMUNITY FACILITIES AND SERVICES

Completion of the $2 million renovations at the Barona Community Center included the development of a tribal meeting hall, a senior activity center, an exercise and weight room, the Barona Museum, and the gaming commission office. Facilities include a gymnasium, tennis courts, an Olympic-size pool, and a ballfield. In addition, the reservation has a number of community ballfields and a gymnasium.

The Barona reservation is also home to a picturesque Mission-style church designed in 1932 by noted San Diego architect Irving Gill. A 15-foot tall sculpture honoring Barona's war veterans is located on the grounds.

Public Safety. The Barona Volunteer Fire Department and regional rural fire district provide fire protection.

Education. Tribal youth attend Charter Elementary School at the tribe's charter school, Barona Indian School. The school facility includes a tutoring and computer center, a library, a Head Start program, and high school classrooms. The program offers a curriculum that meets state academic standards while providing instruction in Kumeyaay/Diegueño cultural elements. Scholarships are available through the tribe to eligible tribal members seeking a post-secondary education. The tribe also offers language and arts programs to tribal members.

Health Care. The Barona Tribe provides 100 percent medical, dental, and vision insurance coverage for all members through the Southern Indian Health Council. Tribal members can visit the Campo Medical/Dental Clinic in Campo, California, for their medical and dental needs. La Posta Outreach Substance Abuse Center provides outpatient substance abuse counseling and treatment sources; and the youth regional treatment center provides medically monitored inpatient youth substance abuse treatment. The emergency services department handles the reservation's paramedic services.

ENVIROMENTAL CONCERNS

The environmental devastation that resulted from the 2003 wildfires has created a number of concerns for the tribe. In addition to destroying its livestock, the fires destroyed much of the tribe's forests. The effects on the land include water contamination, air pollution, soil erosion, and plant and wildlife loss. The destruction of topsoil and ground cover has also created the problem of flooding, leading to further soil erosion and contamination.

TRI-CA-002B The Barona Cultural Center and Museum

TRI-CA-003 Tribal Office

TRI-CA-br002

TRI-CA-br003

LOCATION AND LAND STATUS

Benton Reservation occupies 160 acres on the eastern slope of the Sierra Nevada Range in central California. It is located north of the Owens Valley, about 60 miles due east of Yosemite National Park, and about 10 miles from the Nevada border along Highway 6. The reservation was established by an Executive Order on July 22, 1915. The tribe purchased an additional 2.5 acres using HUD Grant Funds on August 24, 1984.

CULTURE AND HISTORY

The people of the Benton Reservation belong to the Owens Valley Band of Paiute Indians. The Benton Reservation is actually located north of Owens Valley and is the smallest of the area reservations. Benton's small land base prohibited traditional Paiute subsistence patterns of hunting local game and collecting native plants. Moreover, the federal government's land choice was not conducive to serious farming or ranching. Hence, from 1915, the residents subsisted on small-scale farming and gardening, along with menial employment at area ranches and towns. (*For additional cultural information, see California introduction.*)

In 1937 the City of Los Angeles (through an act of Congress) was empowered to exchange the Owens Valley Reservation lands for 1,391 acres it had previously owned; its motivations here involved Mono Lake Basin water rights. Los Angeles' domination of the region spelled the end of the local farming and ranching economy. By the 1970s and 80s, tourism had become a mainstay of the valley's economy. Aside from tourism, some tribal members work in area mines and as service providers through the tribal government, the county, or the state. While Benton is typically grouped with the other four valley reservations, it is not party to the Owens Valley Paiute-Shoshone Board of Trustees; hence, its isolation from the other four Paiute reservations remains more than merely geographic.

GOVERNMENT

The tribe is organized under the 1934 Indian Reorganization Act. Its constitution and bylaws were approved on February 27, 1976, and were amended on February 27, 1979. The reservation is governed by the Utu Utu Gwaitu Tribal Council. The council is comprised of five members elected to staggered two-year terms by the general council. Officials include a chairperson, vice-chairperson, and a secretary/treasurer. The tribal council meets monthly, while the general council meets annually on the last Saturday in May. This is a PL-638 self-governing tribe. The tribal government provides basic administrative services of the tribe as well as some scholarship and housing programs. Departments of the tribal government are health and social services, which serve as the tribe's main source of employment. An arbitration council is currently in the works.

ECONOMY

The region surrounding the reservation has traditionally supported ranching and limited agriculture, a little mining and, in more recent times, primarily tourism. At present, the very limited population of the reservation presents perhaps the biggest challenge to the tribe's economic development.

Government as Employer. Tribal government employs three people.

Services and Retail. The tribe owns the Benton Station, which includes a café and general store and is located on the reservation. In addition, the tribe owns a trailer park with six spaces and five rental units, and the Superior Saddletree Company, which constructs saddletrees, an item used in the manufacture of saddles.

Tourism and Recreation. The reservation's beautifully scenic location serves as its prime resource for economic development. It is located less than 60 miles east of Yosemite National Park (one of the most visited U.S. parks), about 40 miles from Mono Lake, and is adjacent to the high peaks of the Sierra Nevadas. The tribe maintains an RV park that has commercial trailer spaces and cabins. The tribe hopes to continue to capitalize on its scenic location and expand its tourism market.

INFRASTRUCTURE

The reservation is accessible by U.S. Highways 6 and 120. The nearest commercial air service is at Bishop, about 35 miles to the south. Commercial truck lines provide service to the reservation.

Electricity. Southern California Edison furnishes the reservation with electric power.

Fuel. Tribal members use bottled, tank, and LP gas as sources of fuel.

Water Supply. Water service is provided by the tribe's community system. Sewage service is handled by septic tanks.

Transportation. Dial-a-Ride provides shuttle service into Bishop twice a week. Freight, FedEx, UPS, and USPS service the reservation.

Telecommunications. Verizon provides telephone service to the reservation. Approximately 53 percent of households have telephone service.

COMMUNITY FACILITIES AND SERVICES

The tribe has a community center and a community health representative building.

Education. Tribal members attend area schools and colleges, including Edna Beaman Elementary school (five miles away) and Bishop Community College (40 miles away).

Health Care. Benton Paiute Reservation is serviced by the Toiyabe Indian Health Project located in Bishop. Three clinics are in the network of providers: Bishop Clinic, located in Bishop; Camp Antelope Clinic, located in Coleville; and Lone Pine Clinic, located in Lone Pine. All three clinics offer ambulatory, rural primary care.

Benton Paiute Reservation
Federal reservation
Paiute
Mono County, California

Tribal Council
Utu Utu Gwaitu Paiute
567 Yellow Jacket Rd.
Benton, CA 93512
760-933-2321
760-933-2412 Fax

Total area (BIA realty, 2003)
160 acres

Tribally owned lands
(BIA realty, 2003)
160 acres

Population 2000 census
50

Total labor force 2000 census
17

High school graduate or higher
2000 census
62.5%

Bachelors degree or higher
2000 census
0%

Unemployment rate
2000 census
23.5%

Per capita income 2000 census
$4,885

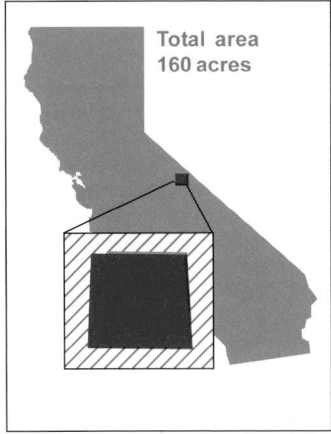

Total area
160 acres

Berry Creek

Berry Creek Rancheria of Maidu Indians
Federal reservation
Maidu
Butte County, California

Tyme Maidu Tribe
Berry Creek Rancheria
of Maidu Indians
5 Tyme Way
Oroville, CA 95966
530-534-3859
530-534-1151 Fax

Total area *(BIA realty, 2003)*
65.04 acres

Tribally owned lands
(BIA realty, 2003)
65.04 acres

Population
574

Tribal enrollment
574

Total labor force
2000 census
35

High school graduate or higher
2000 census
100%

Bachelor's degree or higher
2000 census
12.8%

Unemployment rate
2000 census
34.3%

LOCATION AND LAND STATUS

The reservation lies within Berry Creek Canyon and at the base of the Sierra Nevada in north-central California, near the town of Oroville. Sacramento is 75 miles away.

On March 1, 1916, the U.S. government purchased 32 acres from the Central Pacific Railway Company for the tribe, which was formerly known as the Dick Harry Band of Indians. In 1987 the tribe purchased a separate parcel of 33 acres, which is the site of the community. The new land was granted trust status pursuant to the Indian Land Consolidation Act of 1983.

PHYSICAL DESCRIPTION

The Feather River is within a mile of the reservation, and the forested lands support wildlife including deer, mountain lions, and bears.

CULTURE AND HISTORY

Members of the Berry Creek Rancheria belong to the Tyme Maidu group of Native peoples. Traditionally, the Maidus resided throughout the drainages of the American and Feather rivers. The traditional Maidu language of the tribe belongs to the California branch of the Penutian language family, including languages spoken by peoples from southern Alaska to the southeastern region of the United States to the Yucatan Peninsula. A number of tribal members speak the language today.

Sitto Cemetery and Bald Rock Dome are of major cultural significance to the tribe.

GOVERNMENT

The tribal Articles of Association were approved in 1977 and were amended in 1980 and 1983. The general council consists of four members who serve four-year staggered terms. Officials include a chairperson, vice-chairperson, a secretary, and a treasurer.

The tribal cultural committee is charged with safeguarding artifacts and sacred sites whenever they are jeopardized by timber harvests, construction, or excavation.

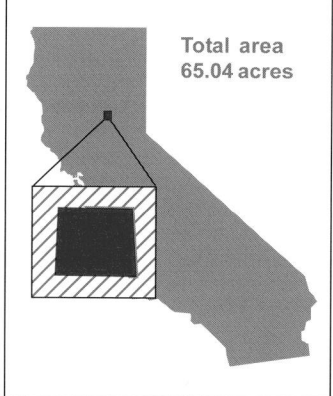

Total area
65.04 acres

ECONOMY

The tribe's gaming operations generate a major source of revenue for the tribe, and the tribe now has a bowling alley that the major bowling leagues use throughout the year. Butte County as a whole and the nearby town of Oroville are less developed than the more distant city of Chico. Many men work in the forestry industry, while some of the women are seasonally employed in canneries. More and more women are pursuing higher education.

Government as Employer. In 1995 the tribe employed 5 people. As of 2004 the tribe had 19 tribal office employees.

Gaming. The tribe owns the Gold Country Casino. It offers 900 slots/VLTS, 16 table games, 4 poker tables, and 300 bingo seats. The 60,000-square-foot facility includes a full-service restaurant, gift shop, and an entertainment venue. The game floor is regularly updated to provide guests with the most current and popular gaming machines. The showroom seats 1,000 guests and is a smoke-free entertainment facility. The casino currently employees over 400.

By January 2005, a six-story, 234,000-square-foot hotel will be completed at the casino complex. The hotel will offer 87 guest rooms, conference facilities, a buffet, piano bar, and a gift shop. A steakhouse with outdoor dining facilities will occupy the sixth floor. Other features include a two-story waterfall, a lounge area on the game floor, and interior decorations centered around the art of Maidu basketry.

Tourism and Recreation. While the reservation does not operate or host tourist activities, the nearby Oroville Lake Recreational Facility offers fishing and camping, and Chico State University hosts a powwow in September.

INFRASTRUCTURE

The reservation is accessible by California State Highway 162, connecting to Highway 70, a major artery, at Oroville. Part of the reservation is also adjacent to Highway 142.

Electricity. The Pacific Gas and Electric Company provides gas and electric services.

Water Supply. Water is provided to the community through the Oroville irrigation district. The Lake Oroville Area Public Utility District provides sewer services.

Transportation. A private airport is located in Oroville; a commuter airport is located in Chico; and an international airport is located in Sacramento. Bus service is available in Oroville, as well as several freight-delivery services.

COMMUNITY FACILITIES AND SERVICES

The tribe owns a 6,000-square-foot community center that includes a large multipurpose room, kitchen, and a playground. Tribal offices are also located there. Medical and educational services are available in the Town of Oroville.

Health Care. Tribal members may receive medical services at the Feather River Tribal Health Clinic in Oroville.

# Big Bend

(See Pit River Tribe for further information on the following subjects: Culture and History, Government, Economy, and Community Facilities and Services)

Total area *(BIA realty, 2003)*   40 acres

LOCATION AND LAND STATUS
The 40-acre Big Bend Rancheria lies along the Pit River, a tributary of the Sacramento River, in north-central California, 58 miles from the city of Redding and approximately 20 miles from tribal headquarters in Burney.

Big Bend Rancheria was established by the Executive Order of July 28, 1916. The formerly independent rancheria became part of the greater Pit River Tribe's land base after their federal recognition in 1976.

PHYSICAL DESCRIPTION
The rancheria is located on the edge of the spectacular Shasta-Trinity National Forest.

ECONOMY
The Pit River Tribe's economy is largely dependent upon gaming and tribal government. Tourism and recreation provide off-reservation revenue and employment opportunities.

Government as Employer. Federal and state jobs serve as an important source of employment for Shasta County residents, with jobs located primarily in Redding.

Agriculture and Livestock. While there is currently no agricultural production on the rancheria, strawberries, which are exported to southern Europe, are a principal crop in Shasta County.

Forestry. Because of the vast timber resources found in Shasta County, jobs created though lumber and wood-products businesses employ a substantial number of area residents, including tribal members.

Gaming. The Pit River Tribe owns the Pit River Casino in Burney, California. The 8,600-square-foot casino offers patrons 108 slots and video lottery tables, 3 table games, and a bingo area that seats 70. The casino has one restaurant.

Tourism and Recreation. Since the Shasta-Trinity National Forest covers much of the county, tourism accounts for a substantial amount of the area's revenues. The region's plentiful hunting and fishing opportunities are an important tourist attraction. The Sacramento River joins a network of rivers and streams to feed Shasta Lake in the Whiskeytown-Shasta-Trinity National Recreational Area, where many types of fish abound. Other popular sites include Lassen Volcanic National Park, Lava Beds National Monument, and Burney Falls State Park.

INFRASTRUCTURE
California State Highway 299 runs 10 miles south of the rancheria, connecting by a branch road. Redding, the area's commercial center, lies 58 miles from the rancheria.

Electricity. The Pacific Gas and Electric Company serves the area's electricity needs.

Water Supply. The rancheria has well water. Sewage disposal is by means of septic tanks, installed by the United States Public Health Service.

Transportation. The nearest air service is available in Redding, at the Redding Municipal Airport; truck, rail, and bus services are also available in the city.

Big Bend Rancheria
Pit River (Achomawi)
Shasta County, California

Pit River Tribal Council
37014 Main Street
Burney, CA 96013
530-335-5421
530-335-3140 Fax

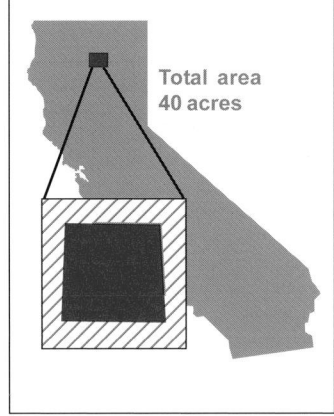

Total area
40 acres

Big Lagoon

LOCATION AND LAND STATUS
The Big Lagoon Rancheria is located in northern California on Highway 101, approximately 70 miles south of the Oregon border. The Big Lagoon Rancheria was established by an Executive Order of July 1918 on a parcel of nine acres. An additional 11 acres contiguous to the rancheria was purchased in 1985. This parcel was granted trust status in 1994. The tribe has also purchased lands within 20 miles of the Big Lagoon Rancheria.

CULTURE AND HISTORY
Members of the Big Lagoon Rancheria are descended from the Tolowa and Yurok Tribes of northern California. The ancestral lands of the Tolowas were in the coastal redwood forests of the northwestern regions of present-day California. The indigenous language of the Tolowas belongs to the Athabascan family. Traditional sustenance of the tribe was primarily salmon. The ancestral lands of the Yuroks were also in the northwestern regions of California. They resided primarily along the Lower Klamath River and on the Pacific Coast near the mouth of the river. Tribal members relied primarily on fish and shellfish for sustenance.

Spanish explorers arrived in California in the late 1500s. During the time of Spanish, and later Mexican, dominance in the territory, lands were seized from the Native populations and held in trust for the crown. The indigenous people were displaced, enslaved, and often murdered. Americans arrived in California in the mid-1800s, and they initiated a war with Mexico for rights to the California regions. The Spanish Mexicans were defeated, and in 1848 the Treaty of Guadalupe ended the Mexican-American War.

Upon the discovery of gold in northern California, Euro-Americans began arriving in the state in droves. In 1850 the California territory became a state and passed the Act for the Government and Protection of Indians. This act mandated the regulation of Indian affairs to the state, permitted Euro-Americans the right to assume custody of Native children, prohibited the use of Native testimony against a Euro-American charged with a crime, and permitted unemployed Native peoples to be arrested and hired out, a form of state-sanctioned indentured servitude. The state further protected prospectors and settlers as they encroached upon tribal territories and seized water sources in the area.

Big Lagoon Rancheria
Federal reservation
Yurok and Tolawa
Humboldt County, California

Big Lagoon Rancheria
P.O. Box 3060
Trinidad, CA 95570
707-826-2079
707-826-0495 Fax

Big Lagoon

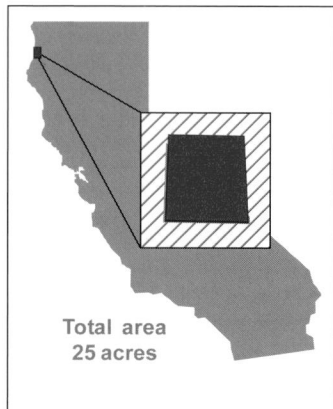

Total area
25 acres

Total area *(BIA realty, 2003)*
25 acres

Tribally owned *(BIA realty, 2003)*
25 acres

Population *2000 census*
24

Tribal enrollment
(BIA labor report, 2001)
18

Total labor force
(BIA labor report, 2001)
13

Total labor force
2000 census
5

High school graduate or higher
2000 census
42.9%

Unemployment rate
(BIA labor report, 2001)
69%

Unemployment rate
2000 census
100%

Per capita income
2000 census
$2,252

Between 1851 and 1853, Indian commissioners negotiated 18 treaties between the government and multiple Native groups. The agreements were to reserve over 7.5 million acres for various tribes across the state, but the senate did not ratify these Barbour Treaties. The tribes were not informed of this decision until the twentieth century and proceeded to live in agreement with the mandates outlined by the treaties. They ceded millions of acres of land to the government and confined themselves to the reservations designated by the Barbour Treaties.

Local, state, and federal agencies condoned the effort to commit genocide against the Native people of California. Indigenous people were openly murdered, attacked, and enslaved. The atrocities committed against the indigenous groups so outraged the Mexican government that officials crossed the U.S.-Mexico border to conduct investigations, and they threatened to bring arms against the citizens of California if the violence did not cease. The intervention on their behalf and their ability to isolate themselves in the mountainous regions of the state enabled some tribes to escape total decimation. However, from an estimated population of over 150,000 in 1845, by 1855 the Native population was reduced to less than 50,000. By 1900, less than 16,000 indigenous people remained.

The Big Lagoon Rancheria was targeted for termination by the federal government in 1968. It was not terminated, and has maintained its status as a federally recognized tribe. The rancheria continues to increase its land base and expand its operations.

GOVERNMENT
Big Lagoon Rancheria is governed by a business council. The Big Lagoon Rancheria Business Council is responsible for governing the people, resources, land, and waters of the tribe in accordance with the tribal constitution. The business council is elected by the tribe's general council. The general council retains the authority of: initiative, referendum, and recall; to sell or relinquish tribal lands; to sell or relinquish tribal hunting or fishing rights; to terminate the Big Lagoon Rancheria; to grant or relinquish tribal jurisdiction; to revoke, terminate, or diminish tribal rights as provided by federal law; and to waive the tribe's immunity from lawsuits.

The general council consists of all tribal members over the age of 18. Tribal members are identified by three provisions. First, persons identified on the Plan of Distribution of 1968; second, persons of lineal descent from those persons identified on the Plan of Distribution of 1968 and who possess one-eighth degree or more of Indian blood; and third, persons who possess one-eighth degree or more of Indian blood who have been adopted by an ordinance of the business council in accordance with federal law. The tribe is governed under the constitution of the Big Lagoon Rancheria as amended in 1985.

The Big Lagoon Rancheria contracts a number of BIA programs and services, including higher education, roads, aid to tribal government, social services, community fire, and Indian child welfare. The tribe manages HUD funding for various housing services on the rancheria. In addition, the tribe has charted the Two Feathers Native American Family Services, an organization that develops and delivers social services to tribal members and Native Americans residing in the county. There is no tribal court. The tribe uses state and federal courts.

ECONOMY
One of the tribe's enterprises is in the tourism industry, which contributes to the tribal economy. The tribe owns a hotel that maintains 16 employees. The hotel is located in the historic town of Arcata, a seaside town that draws an ample amount of visitors.

The tribe is in the planning and development phases of constructing a state-of-the art health fitness facility on tribal fee property located in the nearby town of McKinleyville, California. The grand opening for the health fitness facility is projected for December 2005.

Government as Employer. The tribal administration consists of five full-time and two part-time employees.

Gaming. In 1996, the tribe began the development of a gaming operation. The development has since ceased as a result of statewide issues and concerns revolving around Indian gaming. The ongoing problems in the state over Indian gaming issues forced the tribe to seek legal action in order to secure a gaming compact. The Big Lagoon Rancheria is currently involved in court-ordered negotiations with the State of California. The parties are now negotiating terms for a class III gaming operation.

Real Estate/Commercial Development. In 1985, the tribe purchased 11 acres, and this parcel was accepted into trust status in 1994, thereby increasing the tribe's land base from the original 9 acres. The rancheria is now home to eight housing units, a recently refurbished community water facility, and an upgraded roads system. The tribe intends to add further housing in 2005.

The tribe has purchased a 5-acre parcel of lands, and a 16-acre parcel of lands—both located within half a mile of the rancheria. In 2004, the tribe also purchased a 2-acre parcel about 20 miles from the rancheria. The tribe intends to open a health fitness center on the site in December of 2005.

Tourism and Recreation. The tribe owns the historic Hotel Arcata located in Arcata, California. Established in 1915, the hotel is located along the northern seacoast and offers guests the opportunity to experience the wonder of the redwood forests. The hotel amenities include the Tomo Japanese Restaurant, the Natural Selection gift shop, and the Panache beauty salon. There is a banquet room with a capacity of 85 individuals. The hotel is located in the historic plaza and provides easy access to local shopping, sightseeing, and hiking. The tribal hotel maintains 16 employees.

COMMUNITY FACILITIES AND SERVICES
Two Feathers Native American Family Services is a tribally chartered entity responsible for providing various social services. Two Feathers provides services not only to tribal members and their families, but also to other Native American families within Humboldt County. Programs include Indian child welfare, domestic violence prevention, counseling, and other Native cultural activities.

Education. Tribal youth attend local California elementary and high schools.

Health Care. Tribal members may receive medical services through United Indian Health Services. There are clinics located in Crescent City, Fortuna, Smith River, Klamath, Arcata, and Hoopa, California.

ENVIRONMENTAL CONCERNS
The tribe recently established the tribal environmental program. The tribal environmental program will be responsible for coordinating the development of tribal environmental policies, ordinances, programs, and assessments.

LOCATION AND LAND STATUS
The Big Pine Reservation is located at the eastern base of the Sierra Nevada, 18 miles from the town of Bishop, California. The reservation spans 279 acres of high desert valley along plunging mountainsides. Elevations range from 3,700 feet to 4,200 feet above sea level. The reservation is accessed by U. S. Highway 395 in Big Pine, on both sides of Bartell Road, east of the highway. Big Pine sits at the eastern base of the Sierra Nevada in the high desert of Owens Valley. Rectangular parcels dot the eastern side of Big Pine, many built under the auspices of the Owens Valley Indian Housing Authority.

An Executive Order on March 11, 1912, set apart lands for the Bishop Colony and Big Pine Colony reservations. An act of Congress on April 20, 1937, authorized the secretary of interior to exchange Indian lands and water rights for land owned by the City of Los Angeles in Inyo and Mono counties. Completed in 1939, the exchange resulted in the trade of 3,000 acres of trust property for 1,500 acres of level valley. Title to the land is held in trust, under the authority of the Bureau of Indian Affairs. In 1996, the tribe was in water rights litigation with the City of Los Angeles.

CULTURE AND HISTORY
Members of the Big Pine Band of Owens Valley are descendants of the Owen Valley Pauite and Panamint Shoshone tribes. The Shoshone language spoken by tribal members is related to the larger Uto-Aztecan language group. Uto-Aztecan languages are spoken by peoples from the Great Basin to central Mexico. Originally controlling a vast territory along the Owens River, today Owens Valley Paiutes occupy four tracts in only a small fraction of that area.

Traditionally the Paiutes practiced hunting and gathering for subsistence, with some production of wild seed and root crops. By employing an innovative irrigation system composed of an extensive network of ditches, the Paiutes were able to channel water to various places in the valley. Unfortunately the small size of the parcels set aside for reservations prevented the continuation of either type of economic activity. Out of necessity, the residents turned to small-scale farming and participation in the wage economy, working for local ranchers and farmers.

The Paiutes, including those of Big Pine, were not settled on reservations until after 1900. In 1902 a portion of what had been Camp or Fort Independence, a military post, was officially set aside for use by local Indians.

The greatest impact on the livelihood of the Owens Valley Paiutes occurred after the 1937 congressional act that ceded all previously owned Indian land to the City of Los Angeles, in exchange for 1,391 acres of city-owned property. This transfer ultimately ended the ranching and farming economies that Big Pine residents had depended on for wage labor. Since most of the land in the Owens Valley is owned by the City of Los Angeles, land there has become a valuable and scarce resource. The Big Pine Reservation hopes to capitalize on the value of that resource through leasing and the development of its industrial park.

While the use of the Paiute language has been decreasing,, Big Pine members are actively working to reintroduce many traditional language and cultural skills. Tribal members still practice traditional rituals such as the Cry Dance for the deceased and the Sweat House Ceremony.

GOVERNMENT
The Big Pine Reservation operates under the Trust Agreement of April 1, 1939, and the Assignment Ordinance of April 1962. The tribe has a constitution and is governed by an elected five-member tribal council. Council members include a chairperson, vice-chairperson, secretary, treasurer, and a member-at-large. The members serve two-year terms.

The Owens Valley Paiute-Shoshone Board of Trustees includes a contributing member from the Big Pine Reservation. The board considers issues that impact all the indigenous people in the valley and oversees the running of the Paiute-Shoshone Health Clinic and Cultural Center located on the Bishop Reservation.

BUSINESS CORPORATION
In January 1989, the tribal council chartered the Big Pine Paiute-Shoshone Economic Development Corporation. Its primary goal is the expansion and development of the Big Pine Tribal Council Industrial Park.

ECONOMY
The tribal economy is largely sustained by the leasing of tribal lands. The tribe has its own sales-tax ordinance and pays approximately one-quarter of a million dollars per year to the State of California in the form of fuel taxes.

Government as Employer. The tribal council employs 14 people, 10 of whom are tribal members. Five members work for the state or federal government.

Agriculture and Livestock. Agricultural production takes place on 27 percent of reservation land, or 75 acres. Farmland has been utilized primarily for growing alfalfa or grain hay, along with some small-scale corn cultivation for personal use.

Gaming. The tribe operated a small casino at one time. During the Proposition 1A controversy, however, the casino was closed.

Industrial Parks. The Big Pine Tribal Council Industrial Park is located on 24.5 acres of land on the south end of the reservation, with direct access from Interstate 395. A frozen-foods business is leasing land in the park, and in 1996 two businesses were in the process of locating to the park. These businesses were expected to reduce reservation unemployment by 30 percent, by creating 30 to 45 new jobs.

Real Estate/Commercial Development. The reservation leases land to an auto-salvage yard and operates a park for 30 mobile homes.

Services and Retail. The service sector functions as the area's largest source of employment. There is a home-based pottery business on the reservation, a landscaper, a plumber, and a building contractor, as well as a number of other small businesses in the area. There is a reservation-based trucking company and a truck stop on the reservation.

Big Pine Reservation
Federal reservation
Owens Valley Paiute-Shoshone
Inyo County, California

Big Pine Tribe of Owens
   Valley
Paiute-Shoshone Indians
P.O. Box 700
Big Pine, CA 93513
760-938-2003
760-938-2942 Fax

Total area
279 acres

Population *2000 census*
462

Tribal enrollment
(BIA labor report, 2001)
398

Tribal members in area
403

Total labor force
(BIA labor report, 2001)
297

High school graduate or higher
77.4%

Bachelor's degree or higher
4.1%

Unemployment rate
(BIA labor report, 2001)
61%

Unemployment rate
(2000 census)
16.13%

Per capita income *2000 census*
$11,763

Big Pine

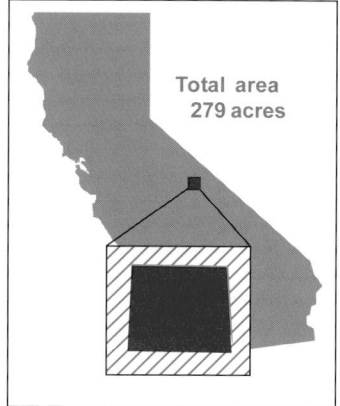

Total area
279 acres

The tribe manages two hotels. The Big Pine Motel offers units with kitchens and facilities feature outdoor barbeque areas. The Glacier Lodge in Big Pine Canyon offers cabins, RV parking, and meals.

Tourism and Recreation. The tribe manages a small herd of horses that are used for backpacking expeditions in the Sierras.

INFRASTRUCTURE
U.S. Highway 395 cuts through the reservation, running north and south. California Highway 168 runs east-west from Big Pine to the state of Nevada where it intersects with U.S. 95.

Electricity. The Los Angeles Department of Water and Power provides electricity to the reservation.

Water Supply. Water is supplied by two wells and a reservoir on the reservation; water and sewage-disposal services are provided by Big Pine Tribal Utilities.

Fuel. Propane gas can be purchased from local dealers in Bishop.

Transportation. The town of Big Pine, which lies a mile outside the reservation, has bus and truck services. The nearest railroad access is 150 miles away, in Mojave. There is an airport at Bishop, 18 miles from the reservation. While Bishop's airport can accommodate jet aircraft, it offers no commercial service; the nearest commercial carriers use the Mammoth Lakes Airport,

approximately 50 miles from the reservation. Several freight carriers are based in the town of Bishop.

COMMUNITY FACILITIES AND SERVICES
There is a 2,200-square-foot tribal office building, built in 1982 through a U.S. Housing and Urban Development block grant. In 1996 there was a 1,500-square-foot building that houses medical and dental care on the reservation; the latter provides after-school tutoring for 25 to 30 students. In 1996 the tribe set aside land in the southeast portion of the reservation for a recreational park for the Save the Children youth program.

Education. Reservation children are educated in public schools in the adjacent community, and tribal members also use these school buildings for recreational purposes; they may also travel to the Bishop Reservation to use the Owens Valley Board of Trustees' Community Facility Building. The tribe maintains the Big Pine Indian Education Center.

A library is located within the tribe's K-12 school. It houses an expansive collection of books and offers computers for community members' use. Internet access is available at the computer lab. The tribe intends to pursue grants and funds to help staff the library.

Health Care. Health care is available through the Toiyabe Health Clinic. Clinics are available in Bishop, Coleville, and Lone Pine. Medical and mental health services are also available at the Northern Inyo Hospital in Bishop and at the county mental hospital in Big Pine.

Big Sandy

**Big Sandy Rancheria Band
of Western Mono Indians
Federal reservation
Western Mono (Monache)
Fresno County, California**

Big Sandy Rancheria Band
of Mono Indians
P.O. Box 337
Auberry, CA 93602
559-855-4003
559-855-4129 Fax

Total area *(BIA realty 2003)*
128.83 acres

Tribally owned *(BIA realty 2003)*
75.56 acres

**Tribal enrollment
331**

Total labor force
(BIA labor report, 2001)
163

Total labor force
2000 census
50

LOCATION AND LAND STATUS
Big Sandy Rancheria lies on the western edge of the Sierra National Forest. The closest town is Auberry, California while Fresno, the nearest urban area, is only 40 miles to the southwest. Shaver Lake, within the Sierra National Forest, is only 15 miles from Big Sandy. A small reservation, Big Sandy is partially located on a flood plain, which hinders the community's ability to expand. Big Sandy, along with two other rancherias, was established by the federal government as lands for the Western Mono people in 1909. Big Sandy's federal status was initially rescinded during the 1950s, yet pursuant to the decision in *Big Sandy Band v. Watt* in the 1980s, both community and individually owned lands were accepted into federal trust.

PHYSICAL DESCRIPTION
The rancheria is situated in a north-to-northwest trending valley that is formed by the northwestern slopes of Bald Mountain. The valley is drained by Backbone Creek and its three tributaries. The elevation ranges from 2,580 to 2,880 feet above sea level. The terrain is characterized by wild grasses, poison oak, and oak and manzanita groves.

CULTURE AND HISTORY
The Western Mono Indians who live on the Big Sandy Rancheria are descendants of people who traditionally spoke a Shoshonean language, a large language group within the family of Uto-Aztecan languages spoken in the Great Basin, in parts of California, by the Comanches, and by the Aztecs in Mexico. Economic pressures and government policies contributed to the Western Mono leaving their traditional homes in the Central Sierra Nevada of California and moving into more developed areas during the early 1900s.

The Western Mono people were considered legally landless until pressure from the Northern California Indian Association, a Protestant activist group, pressured the federal government to create three small rancherias for them in 1909. On Big Sandy Rancheria, the American Home Baptist Mission Society established churches and schools at an early date. A number of individuals were also able to acquire land through the allotment process.

The California Rancheria Act of 1958 authorized the termination of rancheria trust lands, including those held in trust for the Big Sandy Rancheria. Termination included the redistribution of tribal lands as well as termination of federal recognition. It resulted in the termination of government-to-government relations between the tribe and the United States government.

The tribe's federal status was restored by the U.S. District Court in the 1983 case *Big Sandy v. Watt*. However, during the time that the Big Sandy Tribe was unrecognized, it was denied access to federal programs that could have assisted the tribe in strengthening its government, building a sustainable economy, and enhancing the services it could provide to tribal members. Consequently, the extensive period between termination and restoration adversely affected the economic and social development of the Big Sandy Band.

The small size of the rancheria has always represented its biggest challenge in terms of economic development. Prior to World War I, rancheria members worked as loggers, ropers, sheep shearers, and general ranch hands. Women usually worked in the service industry as domestics or as aides in health care.

During the summer logging season, families of loggers returned to their mountain homes where they continued their traditional gathering practices. Urban pull factors, such as better jobs and educational opportunities, dramatically decreased the community's population after World War II.

The Big Sandy Rancheria, along with the Wobonuch Rancheria, are the joint recipients of a National Park Service grant designed to help preserve the groups' heritage and culture. (*See California's introduction for additional cultural information.*)

GOVERNMENT
The rancheria is governed by a five-member tribal council, including a chairperson, a vice-chair, secretary, treasurer, and a member-at-large. All members serve for two years. The tribal council also functions as the committee for economic development.

ECONOMY
Agriculture and Livestock. Although agriculture serves as Fresno County's number one industry, the size of the Big Sandy Rancheria precludes much agricultural activity.

Gaming. The Big Sandy Tribe operates the Mono Wind Casino. Located in Auberry, California, the casino offers 329 slots/VLTs and 2 table games. The 10,000-square-foot facility includes 2 restaurants. The casino employs 150 individuals.

In partnership with Caesars Entertainment in Las Vegas, the tribe is developing a $200-million gaming facility. The intended development will occupy a 40-acre parcel northeast of Friant, about 15 miles from the Mono Wind Casino. The casino will be located on tribal lands located approximately 10 acres northeast of Fresno. The facility will include a 75,000-square-foot gaming area, 2,000 slots, and 20 game tables. The complex will feature a hotel with over 200 guest rooms. An initial agreement for the development and management of the facility has been signed by Caesars and the Big Sandy Band.

Prior to the development of the project, a number of approvals must be secured. The agreement reached between the parties requires the approval of the National Indian Gaming Commission. The tribe is also required to amend its current gaming compact with the State of California, or negotiate a new one.

Tourism and Recreation. The Big Sandy Rancheria's primary natural attraction is its proximity to the Sierra National Forest's many hiking and camping amenities. The band intends to develop economic options to capitalize on the fact that its land abuts

these resources. The tribe is currently exploring options for expanding its role in the local ecotourist market. The tribe would like to purchase land along State Highway 168 to build a motel, a museum, and a crafts store. The tribe is also considering less capital-intensive ways of entering the tourism market.

INFRASTRUCTURE
The closest state road to the Big Sandy Rancheria is California State Highway 168, running south of the community, which serves as a direct link into both Fresno and the Sierra National Forest. The U.S. Forest Service is considering designating Highway 168 a scenic byway.

Water Supply. Domestic and commercial water is provided to residencies of the Big Sandy Reservation by eight privately-owned wells, five community wells, and one open well. The tribe uses a semiautomatic chlorine system to treat the water supply. In order to preserve the quality of water, the tribe works to lessen the presence of coliform leachate in the groundwater. Wastewater on the rancheria is handled by individual septic systems and fields, though this has created problems during run-off periods. In 1997 the tribe recognized the need for updates and expressed the desire to develop a wastewater treatment system that could better serve the needs of the rancheria.

COMMUNITY FACILITIES AND SERVICES
The community's tribal hall contains health facilities and a public library.

Health Care. Health care is available to tribal members through Central Valley Indian Health. Available services include medical, mental health, dental, nutrition, WIC, outreach, podiatry, and substance abuse programs. Centers are located in Fresno and King counties.

ENVIRONMENTAL CONCERNS
The tribe has identified four primary issues of environmental concern on the rancheria. The quality of groundwater is a critical concern as it serves as the primary source of domestic water. The state of the community wastewater facilities is another concern. The majority of individually-owned septic systems are outdated and a number of problems arise in the use of drainage fields during run-off season. The tribe has identified the need to develop a solid waste management program as well. The tribe is also concerned with the presence of lead paint in school equipment and intends to replace or repair items as needed.

Big Sandy

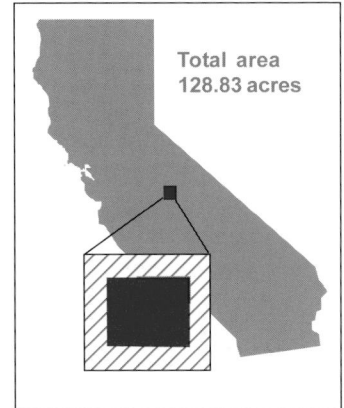

Total area
128.83 acres

High school graduate or higher
2000 census
77.2%

Unemployment rate
(BIA labor report, 2001)
55%

Unemployment rate
2000 census
16.2%

Per capita income
2000 census
$8,119

Big Valley

Big Valley Rancheria
Federal reservation
Pomo
Lake County, California

Big Valley Rancheria
2726 Mission Rancheria Road
Lakeport, CA 95453
707-263-3924
707-263-3977 Fax
bigvalleyrancheria.com

Total area (BIA realty 2003)
99.52 acres

Total area (Tribal source, 2004)
171 acres

Tribally owned lands
84.73 acres

Individually owned lands
14.79 acres

Population 2000 census
225

Tribal enrollment
696

Total labor force 2000 census
55

High school graduate or higher
2000 census
37.5%

Bachelor's degree or
higher 2000 census
0%

Unemployment rate
2000 census
10.9%

Per capita income
2000 census
$4,192

LOCATION AND LAND STATUS

The Big Valley Rancheria is home to a band of Pomo Indians. The original rancheria was comprised of 126 acres. The tribe bought an additional 40 acres to build housing for tribal members and another 5 acres on which they built a recreation center. The rancheria, situated along the southern shores of Clear Lake, the largest fresh water lake in California, is approximately 125 miles north and west of Sacramento and almost 70 miles due north of Santa Rosa.

PHYSICAL DESCRIPTION

Lakeport, California, sits at an elevation of 1,380 feet above sea level, surrounded by the rolling hills of California's Wine Country. Mt. Konocti is a prominent geographic feature in the area, visible against the horizon from all parts of the rancheria.

CLIMATE

The daily year-round average high temperature is 72ºF, with the highest temperature ever recorded being 110ºF. The daily year-round average low temperature is 41ºF. The lowest temperature on record is 14ºF. The area receives approximately 28.4 inches of precipitation annually.

CULTURE AND HISTORY

The Big Valley Band of Pomo Indians descend from the Xa-Ben-Na-Po Pomo Indians who have inhabited the region surrounding Clear Lake for over 11,800 years. They were one of various bands of Pomos who used this area for a subsistence lifestyle dependent upon the rich lands and waters of what is now Lake County, California. The people speak the Eastern Pomo language.

A 72-square-mile reservation, encompassing Mt. Konocti and a long stretch of waterfront property along the southern shores of Clear Lake, was first set aside by treaty in 1851. That same year Congress passed the Land Claims Act of 1851, mandating that claims to all lands in California be presented within two years of the date of the act. So, when an Executive Session of the U.S. Senate refused to ratify the 1851 treaty and 17 other California treaties, and filed them under an injunction of secrecy (not subsequently lifted for 53 years), the Indians didn't know they still needed to present their claims and were left landless, without treaty-protected legal title to their lands.

Many years later, the various bands near Clear Lake were given small parcels of land called rancherias. The one now known as the Big Valley Rancheria originally had been established as a Catholic mission in 1877. The U.S. Department of the Interior purchased the land in 1914, and in 1936 the tribe was federally recognized under the Indian Reorganization Act.

In 1963 the tribal government was terminated under the California Rancheria Act of 1959 and was not subsequently reestablished until 1983. During the intervening 20 years, almost half of the original rancheria land had been sold to non-Indians. The tribe began the process of reclaiming rights of self-determination in 1983 by reforming tribal government via the 1936 Constitution. They also began buying back the lands.

In 1994, the tribe built the Konocti Vista Casino in defiance of local, federal, and state officials, and it quickly became one of the larger employers in Lake County. In 1999 alone, the casino contributed more than 2.8 million payroll dollars to the local economy. The tribe participates in the Greater Lakeport Chamber of Commerce and co-sponsors local bass tournaments, Sum-

mer Concerts in the Park, and other community events. In 1999, they adopted a master land use plan to guide future economic and natural resource development of the rancheria. The mission, as stated in the master land use plan, is "to provide economic self-sufficiency, improve self-esteem, promote quality future development, provide for and maintain a government for the community, protect the environment and enrich tribal life by preserving, documenting, and teaching the Pomo culture for future generations." Also in 1999, the tribe formed a housing authority to build safe, affordable housing for tribal members on rancheria land. In 2001, construction started on a 40-acre walled and gated community with its own community center. Language classes and field trips ensure that future generations of Pomos continue to learn the Native language and understand the historical context of their cultural survival.

GOVERNMENT

The Big Valley Band of Pomo Indians is a PL-638 self-governing tribe with a constitution and bylaws approved on January 15, 1936, under the Indian Reorganization Act of 1934. These documents were amended in 1940, and at this time they are working on adopting a new constitution. The tribal council has formed gaming and culture committees to oversee programs and services on behalf of all tribal members.

ECONOMY

The tribe has been working toward a diversified economy, but it is largely dependent upon the Konocti Vista Casino located near Clear Lake, a tourist destination, for revenue. The tribe operates an RV campground and a smoke shop adjacent to the casino.

Gaming. In operation since 1994, Konocti Vista Casino features both reel and video slot machines, video poker machines, video poker, and table games.

Tourism and Recreation. The Konocti Vista Casino was being expanded in 2004 to include an 80-room resort hotel and an RV campground with full amenities. A photo of the Konocti Vista Resort Hotel is available at www.kvcasino.com/kvc7/Hotel/hotel.htm. There is a marina at the site, conference facilities and meetings rooms, and a swimming pool. A golf course is located nearby. The Ku-HuGui Café is located inside the hotel.

Annually, the rancheria hosts the three-day cultural celebration known as the Big Valley Tule Boat Workshop and Race, drawing several tribes from surrounding areas to compete. "Tule," the name applied to certain varieties of bulrushes native to California, are harvested on the rancheria, fashioned into boats under the guidance of Pomo elders, then launched in competition with one another. The event is held during summer solstice. The rancheria is within 25 miles of Clear Lake State Park, and Mendocino National Forest is on the opposite shore of Clear Lake, easily accessible via highways 29 and 20.

INFRASTRUCTURE

Electricity. Electricity is provided by Pacific Gas and Electric Company.

Water Supply. The tribe owns and operates a wastewater treatment plant.

Telecommunications. Telephone services are offered by Pacific Bell.

Big Valley

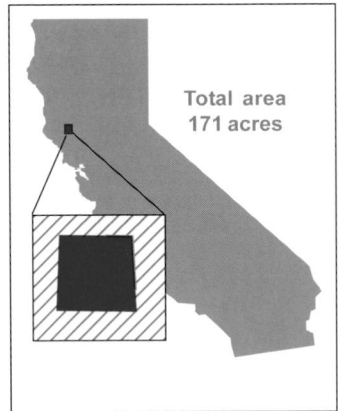

Total area
171 acres

COMMUNITY FACILITIES AND SERVICES

Big Valley community center and gymnasium have been completed since 2001. The facility has a weight room, kitchen facilities, gymnasium, restrooms, and shower rooms. Photos of this facility are available at www.big-valley.net/news/gym_done.htm. The tribe airs a radio program called, "The Big Valley Messenger," produced by the Big Valley Culture Committee.

Education. School-age children at the rancheria attend public schools in Lakeport, California.

Health Care. Health care is available via the Indian Health Service facility in Lakeport.

ENVIRONMENTAL CONCERNS

Big Valley Rancheria has an environmental protection department that oversees protection of the ecosystem around Clear Lake, the largest freshwater lake in California. Also probably the oldest freshwater lake in North America, Clear Lake supports a diverse aquatic abundance of algae, zooplankton, and insects, which in turn support a variety of fish, birds, and mammals. Land uses around the lake during the past century have resulted in nutrient load and subsequent algal blooms. Open-pit mining of mercury nearby, and the backfilling of waste rock into the water, have resulted in the elevation of inorganic mercury levels to 1,000 times the naturally occurring levels, thereby causing the bioaccumulation of the organic form of mercury, methylmercury. Fish from the lake can be eaten in limited quantities.

Past use of the insecticide DDT continues to negatively affect Clear Lake and may still impact the functioning of the area's wildlife. An exotic plant species, hydrilla, could impede navigation in the lake's shallower waters; and the herbicide used to combat hydrilla is also of concern. The agricultural application of pesticides throughout the watershed, especially on pear orchards immediately adjacent to the rancheria, is also of concern. Solid waste management is a high priority, and the tribe has made dumpsters available for household trash. Lead based paint and indoor air quality in older housing are issues of concern.

A quality assurance program plan is being revised to meet U.S. EPA standards, and an environmental survey of all tribally owned lands and waters has been completed and will be included in the new work plan. In cooperation with the local conservation district, the tribe works with the Natural Resource Conservation Service to coordinate efforts with property owners in developing a pollution prevention program under U.S. EPA's Clean Water Act, Section 106 Program.

The Rancheria Environmental Department staff is working on several environmental ordinances and a general statement of intent to protect the environment and the cultural resources within rancheria boundaries. The environmental departments of six tribes located near the lake have formed a group called the Hinthil Environmental Resource Consortium and they are working in concert to produce a Lake County Cultural Protection Ordinance. This collaborative group acts in a government-to-government capacity with county, state, and federal governments. These departments utilize GIS/GPS data to track water quality in the lake, and they are working together to develop an educational brochure for use in Lake County schools on the biological habitat of local wetland areas. The brochure will highlight traditional uses of wetland plants and beneficial effects of sustainable practices.

The Big Valley Environmental Protection Office was instrumental in developing a solid waste transfer station and recycling center. Recycling programs were initiated in all tribal governmental offices for aluminum, plastics, and glass. They also initiated a program using tribal youth to pick up litter three times per year. The tribe is developing a pesticide-sampling analysis plan to monitor for pesticide drift from area farmer, and it is reviewing all groundwater and well data for pesticide residue. With its emphasis on cultural resource protection, this office also sponsors the Tule Boat Workshop and Race.

TRI-CA-005

TRI-CA-006

TRI-CA-005 Sign for Big Valley's Konocti Vista Casino

TRI-CA-006 Typical northern California scene near Big Valley Rancheria

Bishop

Bishop Reservation
Federal reservation
Paiute-Shoshone
Inyo County, California

Paiute-Shoshone Indians
of the Bishop
Community of the Bishop
Colony
P.O. Box 548
Bishop, CA 93514
760--873-3584
760-873-4143 Fax
paiute.com

Total area *(BIA realty, 2003)*
875 acres

Tribally owned *(BIA realty, 2003)*
875 acres

Population *2000 census*
1,441

Tribal enrollment
1,408

Total labor force *2000 census*
653

Total labor force
(Tribal source, 2004)
508

High school graduate or higher
2000 census
70.7%

Bachelor's degree or higher
2000 census
5.2%

Unemployment rate
2000 census
10.57%

Unemployment rate
(Tribal source, 2004)
39.6%

Per capita income
2000 census
$10,188

LOCATION AND LAND STATUS

The Bishop Reservation is located in Owens Valley of Inyo County, California. It is situated at the eastern base of the Sierra Nevada mountain range.

An Executive Order on March 11, 1912, set apart 67,000 acres of land for the Bishop Colony and Big Pine Colony reservations. An act on April 20, 1937, authorized the secretary of the interior to exchange these lands and the water rights to bodies of water located within the lands for an area owned by the City of Los Angeles in Inyo and Mono counties. The BIA traded the lands for 875 acres that constitute the present-day Bishop Reservation. Title to the land is held in trust, and the BIA exercises authority.

PHYSICAL DESCRIPTION

Composed of dry valleys and green mountains, the reservation averages 4,400 feet in elevation. Most of the land is irrigated for agricultural production and used for home sites. Inyo County contains both the highest and lowest points of elevation in the continental United States. Mt. Whitney reaches more than 14,496 feet above sea level, while Badwater in Death Valley is 282 feet below sea level.

CULTURE AND HISTORY

Members of the Bishop Reservation are descended from the Northern Paiute and Shoshone tribes of California. Owens Valley, where the present-day reservation is located, was the southernmost permanent home of the Paiutes prior to European contact. Archeological findings include petroglyphs, obsidian chips, and house rings that indicate a Native population residing in the area at least 3,000 years ago. The Shoshonean-speaking Bishop Reservation Paiutes are linguistically related to the greater Uto-Aztecan language group. Originally controlling a vast territory along the Owens River, today the Owens Valley Paiutes occupy only a small fraction of that area.

Spanish explorers arrived in California in the late 1500s. During the time of Spanish, and later Mexican, dominance in the territory, lands were seized from the Native populations and held in trust for the crown. The indigenous people were displaced, enslaved, and often murdered. Americans arrived in California in the mid-1800s, and they initiated a war with Mexico for rights to the California regions. The Spanish Mexicans were defeated, and in 1848 the Treaty of Guadalupe ended the Mexican-American War.

Americans began to establish settlements in the Owens Valley in the mid-1800s. They used the lands primarily for cattle ranching. Tensions between the ranchers and the Paiutes were punctuated by regular skirmishes between the two. In 1862, in the Battle of the Ditch, or Battle of Bishop Creek, some 500 Paiutes engaged in battle with a group of citizen militia.

Upon the discovery of gold in northern California, Euro-Americans began arriving in the state in droves. In 1850, the California territory became a state and passed the Act for the Government and Protection of Indians. This act mandated the regulation of Indian affairs to the state, permitted Euro-Americans the right to assume custody of Native children, prohibited the use of Native testimony against a Euro-American charged with a crime, and permitted unemployed Native peoples to be arrested and hired out, a form of state-sanctioned indentured servitude. The state further protected prospectors and settlers as they encroached upon tribal territories and seized water sources in the area.

Between 1851 and 1853, Indian commissioners negotiated 18 treaties between the government and multiple Native groups. The agreements were to reserve over 7.5 million acres for various tribes across the state, but the senate did not ratify these Barbour Treaties. The tribes were not informed of this decision until the twentieth century and proceeded to live in agreement with the mandates outlined by the treaties. They ceded millions of acres of land to the government and confined themselves to the reservations designated by the Barbour Treaties.

Local, state, and federal agencies condoned the effort of to commit genocide against the Native people of California. Indigenous people were openly murdered, attacked, and enslaved. The atrocities committed against the indigenous groups so outraged the Mexican government that officials crossed the U.S.-Mexico border to conduct investigations, and they threatened to bring arms against the citizens of California if the violence did not cease. The intervention on their behalf and their ability to isolate themselves in the mountainous regions of the state enabled some tribes to escape total decimation. However, from an estimated population of over 150,000 in 1845, the Native population was reduced to 16,000 by 1905.

Now living on four small tracts of reserved lands, the Paiutes, including those of Bishop, were not settled on reservations until after the turn of the century. The greatest impact on the livelihood of the Owens Valley inhabitants occurred after a 1937 Congressional Act ceded all previously owned Indian land to the City of Los Angeles in exchange for 875 acres of city-owned land. This transfer ultimately ended the ranching and farming economies that the Bishop residents had depended upon as a source of employment. Currently the majority of tribal income stems from land leasing.

Bishop residents are actively attempting to revive Native language skills and other cultural activities. The Bishop Reservation, along with Big Pine, annually hosts a powwow to celebrate their rich cultural heritage.

GOVERNMENT

The tribe is organized under the Trust Agreement of April 1939 and the Assignment Ordinance of April 1962. The reservation is governed by an elected five-member council. Council officials include a chairperson, vice-chairperson, a secretary, and a treasurer. Tribal officials serve two-year staggered terms. The Owens Valley Paiute-Shoshone Board of Trustees is responsible for administering programs that affect all of the valley's Native Americans. The Board is composed of representatives from Bishop, Big Pine, and Lone Pine reservations.

The tribe maintains a judicial system. It has a tribal court and police department. Other governmental departments include education, environment, elders center, TERO, maintenance, and administration.

BUSINESS CORPORATION

The tribe has established the Bishop Paiute Development Corporation. The corporation is responsible for the development of economic projects for the tribe. It employs four people.

The Bishop Paiute Gaming Corporation is a California-chartered entity owned and operated by the Bishop Paiute tribe. The corporation operates and manages the Paiute Palace Casino.

ECONOMY

The tribal economy is largely supported by the tribe's casino and its involvement in leasing tribal lands.

Government as Employer. The tribe employs over 100 people in its various departments, programs, and business entities.

Economic Development Projects. Economic development on the Bishop Reservation is overseen by the Bishop Paiute Development Corporation. Their projects have included the further development of the industrial park. The tribe is also developing an RV park along Highway 95.

The tribe has completed construction of a 50,000-square-foot office building on the reservation. It houses the Department of the Interior, Bureau of Land Management, Department of Agriculture, and Inyo National Forest staffs. The development of this type of office complex on a reservation is perhaps one of the first of its kind in the nation.

Agriculture and Livestock. Within Bishop Reservation, over 100 acres of land are used for agricultural purposes. There are approximately 240 head of cattle and 100 head of horses grazed on the reservation.

Gaming. The Paiute Palace Casino is owned and operated by the tribe's chartered business corporation. The casino offers 300 slots/VLTs, 7 table games, and one restaurant. Future additions will include video poker and an Omaha Hi table. The casino opened in October 1995 at a temporary site and reopened in 1996 at its existing site. The casino is one of the largest Native American-employing casinos in the state of California with over 85 percent of its employees identifying as Native American. Further expansions of the casino are in the planning stages. Renovations will include additions to the gaming facilities and the construction of a resort.

Construction. The Bishop Community Development Division develops and constructs housing on the reservation with crews comprised of tribal members. It currently employs 28 tribal members.

Industrial Parks. Within Bishop Reservation, along its Highway 168 boundary, the tribe has designated 72 acres for a commercial and industrial park. Currently the park houses a recreational vehicle storage area and a mini-storage facility. Forty-nine acres are available for leasing. The park currently does not have access to sewage disposal and water facilities; the tribe has applied for assistance from the U.S. Department of Commerce Economic Development Administration for infrastructural development.

Services and Retail. The Paiute Place Gas Station is located north of the City of Bishop along Highway 395. It employs 22 individuals. Facilities include a convenience store, and firewood and ice sales. The station sells gas at reduced prices and, as a result, is extremely successful in the region.

The Bishop Reservation has a 42-unit mini-storage enterprise located within the commercial and industrial park. All units are currently filled. The net income garnered from this facility has exceeded $20,000 per year for a number of years.

Tourism and Recreation. The Owens Valley Paiute and Shoshone Cultural Center and Museum offers educational displays regarding the history of the Paiute and Shoshone tribes in Owens Valley.

Owens Valley is home to numerous outdoor attractions, including Bishop Creek Canyon, South Lake, Buttermilk Country, North Lake, Rock Creek Canyon, Ancient Bristlecone Pine Forest, and the Mount Whitney State Fish Hatchery. There are several RV parks, resorts, and hotel accommodations available to visitors throughout the valley.

The region surrounding the Bishop Reservation boasts a number of petroglyphs. The creators of these works were ancestors of the Paiute tribal members. The petroglyphs are accessible to tourists through the Maturango Museum, or by individual exploration. Many of the sites are at least 8,000 years old.

INFRASTRUCTURE

Highway 395 runs north-south near the reservation, and Highway 6 runs east-west intersecting the town of Bishop. State Highway 168, also known as West Line Street, passes through the reservation.

Electricity. Electricity is provided by Southern California Edison.

Water Supply. Residents use well water from two large reservoirs that are connected to a regional wastewater sewage treatment plant.

Transportation. Air transportation, bus service via Greyhound, and trucking are all available in the adjacent town of Bishop. While Bishop's airport does not provide commercial service, it can accommodate jet air traffic. There are plans to enlarge the Bishop airport to include commercial air service for the Eastern Sierras.

COMMUNITY FACILITIES AND SERVICES

Community events are held in the Owens Valley Indian Education Center and the Owens Valley Paiute-Shoshone Indian Cultural Center. A daycare center and a food supply center, which are housed in an historic tribal office, are located on the reservation. The tribe operates the Owens Valley Career Development Center which provides vocational training and support to community members

Education. Tribal youth attend public school in the nearby town of Bishop. Cerrocoso Community College is also located there. The tribe offers a Head Start program. It employs a staff of 16. The tribe's education department provides a youth sports program.

Health Care. The Toiyabe Indian Health Project provides health services to members of the Paiute, Shoshone, and Washoe tribes. The organization is a coalition of representatives from each tribe and community working to provide quality services to their members. Clinics are located in Bishop, Lone Pine, and Camp Antelope. The project employs over 100 individuals. The tribe also operates a dialysis center. The Northern Inyo Hospital is in nearby Bishop.

ENVIRONMENTAL CONCERNS

The tribe's environmental department provides programs and services to address issues of environmental concern on the reservation. Identified priorities include air pollution, water quality, fire safety, and vegetation management. The department employs a staff of six.

Bishop

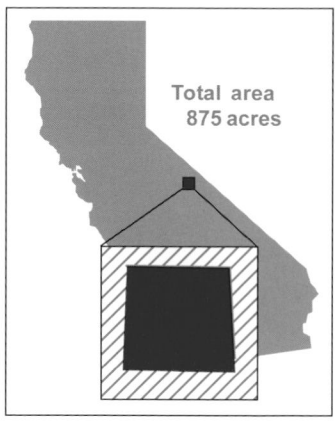

Total area
875 acres

Blue Lake

Blue Lake Rancheria
Federal reservation
Wiyot, Yurok, and Hupa
Humboldt County, California

Blue Lake Rancheria
P.O. Box 428
Blue Lake, CA 95525
707-668-5101
707-668-4272 Fax
allianceofcatribes.org

Total area *(BIA realty, 2003)*
19.4 acres

Total area *(Tribal source, 2004)*
76 acres

Total area *(Tribe source, 2002)*
19.40 acres

Tribally owned land
(BIA realty, 2003)
10 acres

Tribally owned land
(Tribal source, 2004)
10 acres

Non-trust lands
(Tribal source, 2004)
43 acres

Individually owned
(BIA realty, 2003)
9.4 acres

Population *2000 census*
78

Tribal enrollment
(BIA labor report, 2001)
48

Tribal enrollment
(Tribal source, 2004)
51

LOCATION AND LAND STATUS

Blue Lake Rancheria consists of 31 acres in the city of Blue Lake, California, 12 miles north of Eureka and 5 miles east of Arcata, in Humboldt County. The property gained federal trust status on December 15, 1983. The rancheria's land size has increased since 1996 with the purchase of 45 acres. Of this amount, 40 acres is used for a mobile home park, 2 acres for low-income housing, and as of 2004, 3 acres remained undeveloped. These 45 acres are not yet held in trust.

Ownership of trust lands terminated under PL 85-671 on August 18, 1958, was returned to the tribe in 1983, as a result of the *Tillie Hardwick v. United States* decision. They regained Rancheria Road, which had been deeded to Humboldt County; however, two parcels previously deeded to the City of Blue Lake by the BIA have not been reacquired. Separate parcels of Wiyot land are located at Rohnerville and Table Bluff.

CLIMATE

Climate data has not been recorded for Blue Lake, California. However, data is available for the community of Arcata, located approximately five miles due west of the reservation. Year-round daily high temperatures at Arcata average 57°F. The highest temperature ever recorded was 85°F. Year-round daily low temperatures average 47°F, with the lowest ever recorded being 26°F. The maritime climate is influenced by Pacific weather patterns and averages almost 42 inches of precipitation annually. The elevation at Blue Lake is less than 500 feet above sea level.

CULTURE AND HISTORY

The Blue Lake Rancheria is located within the traditional territory of the Wiyot people, who, like the Yuroks, traditionally lived along the Eel and Mad rivers in northern California, ranging into neighboring forests and prairies, areas that now include the cities of Eureka and Arcata, California. Inland areas were heavily forested with ancient redwood trees from which they fashioned long log canoes. There were dunes and tidal marshes along the Pacific shoreline where they gathered clams and acorns. Duluwat Island, now called Indian Island, about one and a half miles offshore in Humboldt Bay, was a ceremonial center for at least 20 small Wiyot communities. These Native peoples speak an Algonquian language similar to that of the Great Lakes and northern plains Ojibwe people.

The Wiyots were not heavily influenced by the Spanish, whose mission building stopped at the San Francisco Bay area. However, the Wiyots were not only forced out of their traditional territory, but were killed in large numbers by later Euro-American settlers during the 1850s following the American victory in the Mexican War. Miners, farmers, and ranchers poured into California and settled near the town now known as Eureka.

On February 25, 1860, the Wiyots experienced a tragedy that devastated their numbers and has remained a pervasive part of their cultural heritage and identity. As they slept on Indian Island this fateful morning, large numbers of Native people were massacred by Eureka citizens wielding axes, knives, and bludgeons. Tribal healers and leaders (mostly women) were there to conduct annual World Renewal ceremonies. Two other village sites, on the Eel River and on the South Spit, were also raided. Over 100 people were killed in a single night. Survivors were corralled at Fort Humboldt and then taken to a prison camp at Round Valley. By 1860, only an estimated 200 people remained. By 1910, fewer than 100 full-blood Wiyot people lived in Wiyot territory due to the ravages of disease, slavery, death marches, and massacres.

Contemporary Wiyots remember and honor those who died during the massacre, with an annual candlelight vigil in Eureka, reminding area residents of the need for participation by Wiyot Indians in the development and management of the Humboldt Bay area.

GOVERNMENT

The tribe is organized under an IRA Constitution approved by the secretary of the interior on March 22, 1989. Resident members of the rancheria, ages 18 or over, make up the general council, which serves as the governing body. The five-member business council, elected by the general council for two-year terms, includes a chairperson, a vice-chairperson, and a secretary/treasurer. Their actions are subject to review by the general council.

The tribal government operates essential services and programs, such as a court for tribal workers pertaining to occupational injuries. They participate in a consortium dealing with family matters, but they have not yet developed a tribal court system (although there were plans for one in 2004). Currently, the tribal council settles all disputes. Under PL-280, law enforcement is provided to the tribe by Humboldt County.

BUSINESS CORPORATION

In 1988 the business council formed the five-member Charter Development Corporation, which manages the tribe's economic activities and acts as the planning committee for the office of economic development.

ECONOMY

The Blue Lake Rancheria engages in agriculture, gaming, construction both on and off of the rancheria, and various other enterprises, including an employment agency. The tribe plans to further its economic success and diversity by investing in off-reservation companies.

Economic Development Projects. In 2004 the tribe was planning to purchase additional land to construct a television station. They were also working with the City of Blue Lake to obtain a foreign trade zone designation for the community airstrip and industrial park. In the future, the tribe would like to add a golf course, country club, and sports complex to include indoor and outdoor swimming pools, soccer, football, and baseball fields.

The tribe is interested in further economic diversification with the opening of call centers, a radio station, general retail stores (such as convenience markets, delis, banks, and photo-development kiosks), an RV park and campground, and a medical complex.

Agriculture and Livestock. A seedling conifer nursery established in 1988 failed to turn a profit, and the rancheria chose instead to focus on vegetable and flower cultivation. The success of this venture has resulted in expansion of the facilities and increased vegetable harvest. The operations, concentrating on vegetables, flowers, and herbs, employ over 35 people.

Gaming. The tribally owned Blue Lake Casino opened for business in June 1993, featuring 500 slot machines, 16 table games, 5 poker tables, and 500 bingo seats. Four restaurants are located on the premises. The casino employs approximately 220 people. The rancheria has formed its own gaming commission to oversee the development of these facilities and ensure compliance with State of California rules and regulations.

Revenues from the casino have funded expansions in all tribal departments and provided for increases in programs and services, including a scholarship fund for nontribal community students. A specified percentage of the proceeds generated by casino operations are donated to regional not-for-profit entities, such as the St. Joseph Hospital Foundation, Little League baseball teams, the League of Women voters, City of Eureka recreation programs, and the American Cancer Society.

Construction. The Blue Lake Housing Authority, which has been in operation for over 30 years, has grown into a diversified construction company seeking contracts throughout the region. The tribe also owns and operates a remodeling company in Sacramento, California.

Industrial Parks. An industrial park is located in the nearby City of Blue Lake; this enterprise has been a tremendous economic boon for the city.

Services and Retail. In addition to various small retail services on the reservation and in the casino, the tribe owns part interest in a computer company in Maine, and it owns and operates Mainstay Staffing, a temporary employment agency headquartered at the rancheria. Mainstay Staffing refers employees to tribal enterprises and other companies throughout California. Mainstay Staffing provides employment opportunities for over 16,000 people.

Tourism and Recreation. Mad River offers excellent fishing in the vicinity of the Rancheria. There is a state-owned fish hatchery in the city of Blue Lake. Blue Lake is also the historical home of the Arcata and Mad River Railhouse and the site of the Dell'Arte School of Physical Theater, which is known for its "commedia" style of acting. The tribe has plans to develop a Cultural Heritage Preservation Park and Interpretive Center for the Mad River Valley, which would incorporate stream and watershed protection activities and a museum dedicated to regional Native tribes.

INFRASTRUCTURE
Highway 299, three-tenths of a mile from the rancheria, connects with U.S. 101, providing access to other routes north and east of Humboldt County. The nearest airport is nine miles away and the nearest bus service is two miles away. The Northwest Pacific Railway runs through the city of Blue Lake.

Electricity. Electricity is provided by Pacific Gas and Electric Company.

Fuel. Gas service is also provided by Pacific Gas and Electric Company.

Water Supply. Water and sewage are provided to the rancheria by the City of Blue Lake.

Telecommunications. Access to high-speed Internet services is provided by Cox Cable Company.

Transportation. The tribe operates the Blue Lake Transit System and Rancheria Dial-a-Ride program, a public transportation system on contract with local town governments. The buses also act as the shuttle service for the casino.

COMMUNITY FACILITIES AND SERVICES
The Blue Lake Rancheria's new community center was dedicated in May 1994. This building houses the tribal government's administrative programs and tribal activities. The Sylvia Daniels Memorial Library is located inside the tribal office building. The Rancheria's Dial-a-Ride program provides low-cost transportation services to the elderly and disabled. Blue Lake Elderly Services provides home-delivered meals and other nutrition services. The Blue Lake Grange Community Commodities Program provides fresh vegetables from the greenhouse gardens. A food program, which caters to schools and other off-reservation institutions throughout the region, serves meals at two grammar schools for children under 18 twice a day. This program also caters 28,600 frozen meals, 3,900 individual hot meals, and 2,800 congregate hot meals to over 135 elderly citizens throughout Humboldt and Trinity counties in California.

Public Safety. Law enforcement services are provided by the Humboldt County Sheriff's Department and a police substation in Blue Lake. The tribe pays the salaries of two officers at the substation. A volunteer fire department at Blue Lake serves the rancheria.

Education. Tribal schoolchildren attend public schools at either Blue Lake Elementary or Arcata High School. Humboldt State University is located in nearby Arcata.

Blue Lake

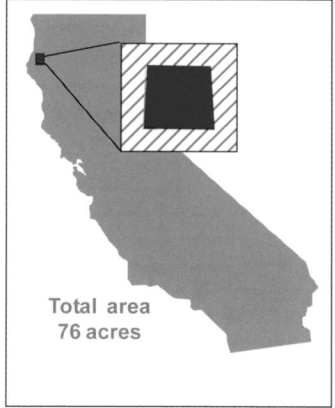

Total area
76 acres

TRI-CA-009

TRI-CA-007

TRI-CA-008

Total labor force *2000 census*
44

Total labor force
(BIA labor report, 2001)
43

High school graduate or higher
2000 census
51.6%

Bachelor's degree or higher
2000 census
8.1%

Unemployment rate
2000 census
11.36%

Per capita income
2000 census
$13,859

TRI-CA-009 Blue Lake Tribal Building

TRI-CA-007 Blue Lake Rancheria's Alpine Casino

TRI-CA-008 Blue Lake's Transit System Bus near Tribal Building

Blue Lake

Health Care. The tribe has planned to develop an elderly assisted-living facility and daycare center. The tribe distributes educational materials to the public regarding diabetes prevention, breast cancer, prostate cancer, drug and alcohol abuse prevention, and the prevention of child abuse.

Housing. Although expanded to include other construction projects, the tribal housing authority provides low-to-moderate income housing for Native and non-Native people. The housing authority purchased land to develop the Blue Lake Mobile Home Park, and other properties are being considered for additional tribal housing.

ENVIRONMENTAL CONCERNS

The tribe used trees from a seedling conifer tree nursery that failed to make a profit for the Native Redwood Forest Rehabilitation Project, a program of the Intertribal Sinkyon Wilderness Park Project in which the tribe actively participates. The Wiyot Tribe is a member of the Native Park Council. The tribal EPA office has entered into a consortium with other interested entities to study the Mad River. The rancheria is associated with, or a member of CalTrans Adopt-a-Highway Program and Wildflower Restoration Project, Keep America Beautiful, Northern California Champion Community Partners, and the Strategic Partnership Coalition of Coastal Governments. The tribe plans to develop a community-wide recycling program and solid waste management plan, with weekly curbside pickup and a community compost bin.

Bridgeport

Bridgeport Reservation
Federal reservation
Paiute
Mono County, California

Bridgeport Paiute Indian
Colony
P.O. Box 37
Bridgeport, CA 93517
760-932-7083
760-932-7846 Fax

Total area *(BIA realty, 2003)*		40 acres
Tribally owned *(BIA realty, 2003)*		40 acres
Tribal members in area		91
Tribal enrollment *(BIA labor report, 2001)*		113
Total labor force *2000 census*		30
Total labor force *(BIA labor report, 2001)*		36
High school graduate or higher		75%
2000 census		
Bachelor's degree or higher		0%
2000 census		
Unemployment rate *2000 census*		20%
Unemployment rate		25%
(BIA labor report, 2001)		
Per capita income *2000 census*		$11,781

LOCATION AND LAND STATUS

The Bridgeport Colony spans 40 acres of undeveloped land adjacent to the community of Bridgeport in Mono County, California, close to the Nevada border. The reservation is bounded by the Bodie Hills on the east, alluvial fans on the north and south, by the Bridgeport Reservoir to the west, and the community of Bridgeport to the southwest. The Bridgeport Colony was established by Executive Order on October 18, 1974.

PHYSICAL DESCRIPTION

The average elevation of Bridgeport is about 6,500 feet.

CULTURE AND HISTORY

Residents of the Bridgeport Colony are members of the Northern Paiute people, who traditionally occupied a large area paralleling the eastern slopes of the Sierra Nevada and Cascade ranges from roughly Mono Lake in California to John Day River in Oregon. The northern Paiutes living around Mono Lake traditionally subsisted by hunting regional game, gathering native plants, and fishing in area streams and lakes.

Paiute peoples originally inhabited parts of California, Oregon, Nevada, Utah, and Arizona. All these culturally related people spoke a language belonging to the Numic branch of the Uto-Aztecan language family, other languages of which are spoken by peoples from the Great Basin into central Mexico.

After gold was discovered in the Sierra Nevada in the middle of the 1800s, Paiute people were forced out of their traditional territories. This contact sometimes resulted in warfare as the Paiutes attempted to defend their ancestral territory. By the start of the twentieth century, less than five percent of the original area remained in Indian control. An executive order established the first Paiute reservations at Pyramid and Walker lakes in western Nevada in 1874. Many Paiute groups did not go to these reservations, refusing to abandon their traditional lands.

The Bridgeport Paiutes have lived on the land adjacent to the Town of Bridgeport for well over a century. They were employed in service jobs in the town and also worked as ranch hands. By the middle of the 1930s, many of the northern Paiutes had apparently assimilated into the Euro-American culture.

Bridgeport tribal land was threatened in 1968 when a contractor, wishing to build a subdivision, produced a title for the land. Evidently, the land patent had been issued illegally to a non-Indian in 1914. This patent disbursement contradicted the Desert Land Act, which prohibited issuing patents to land on which the occupants have always resided.

Through their own lobbying efforts, the Bridgeport Paiutes acquired 40 acres of Bureau of Land Management land less than a mile from their camp in 1974. President Ford signed the Cranston-Tunny Bill, which put this land into trust for the Bridgeport Paiute. A few members retain their Paiute language skills, and many practice other traditional art forms. Bridgeport Paiute elders cook traditional foods, such as acorn or pine-nut soup and biscuits. In addition, many residents make traditional baskets, do bead work, and make arrowheads. (*See California introduction for additional cultural information.*)

GOVERNMENT

The Bridgeport Reservation is governed by a general council composed of all tribal members 18 years or older. Thirty percent of the tribe represent a quorum. The council is presided over by an elected chairperson, vice-chairperson, and secretary-treasurer. The tribe's constitution, adopted under the Indian Reorganization Act of 1934, was approved by the Commissioner of Indian Affairs on July 21, 1976.

ECONOMY

The tribe is exploring means to enter the tourism industry in order to bolster the tribal economy.

Government as Employer. A primary source of tribal employment stems from county and state highway department and U.S. Forest Service jobs.

Manufacturing. The tribe is considering many labor-intensive subcontracted manufacturing projects. The on-site training common to this type of work would be very beneficial to the tribal members.

Tourism and Recreation. Because of the numerous recreational attractions in Mono County, such as Mammoth Lakes and the June Lake Loop, the tribe is primarily focusing its economic development toward this market. Unfortunately many visitors, who come primarily from the Los Angeles area, miss the eastern portion of the state where Bridgeport is located. However, the area has the potential to expand its tourist market base, with ice skating, boating, fishing, camping, hunting, and a ranger station already located in the town of Bridgeport.

INFRASTRUCTURE
Highway 395 runs north-south within a mile of the reservation. This artery links scenic and recreational attractions in Mono County with the cities of Los Angeles and Reno. Access to California's Central Valley from Mono County is provided by California routes 120 (by way of Tioga Pass), 108 (Sonora Pass), and 89 (Monitor Pass). These roads are open during the summer months.

Water Supply. The Bridgeport Public Utility system supplies water to the reservation; the reservation has its own sewage system.

Transportation. A bus terminal is located in the Town of Bridgeport, as are freight services. Commercial air service is available at the Mammoth Lake Airport, and a general-aviation airport is located in Bridgeport. Rental cars may be obtained at the Mammoth Lake Airport.

Telecommunications. Telephone service is provided by Continental Telephone Company of California.

COMMUNITY FACILITIES AND SERVICES
The colony received over $100,000 in Indian Housing Block Grant funds to meet housing needs of the tribe.

Education. Elementary school children attend school in Bridgeport, while high school students must travel to Coleville, about 35 miles away.

Health Care. Tribal members may receive health services through Toiyabe Indian Health Project, Inc. Clinics are located in Bishop, Lone Pine, and Camp Antelope. Services include comprehensive medical and dental, health education, optometry, community health, and family service programs. In addition, Northern Inyo Hospital in Bishop, the Mono General Hospital in Bridgeport, and a small hospital in Mammoth Lake serve the community, as does Mono County Mental Health Department.

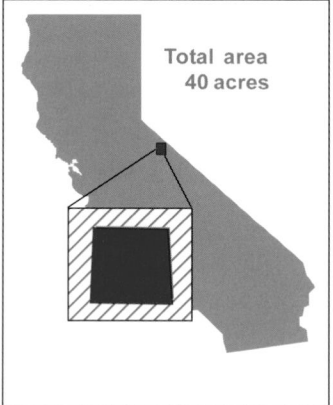

Total area
40 acres

Buena Vista

LOCATION AND LAND STATUS
Buena Vista Rancheria of Me-Wuk Indians is a small federally recognized reservation located near the community of Buena Vista, in north central California. The rancheria is located approximately 40 miles south and east of Sacramento.

CLIMATE
No climate information has been recorded for Buena Vista, California; however, there is data for Independence, California, which lies 35 miles due east. The year-round daily average high-temperature at Independence is 71°F. The year-round average daily low temperature is 42°F. The area receives approximately six inches of precipitation annually.

CULTURE AND HISTORY
Archaeological remains of several ancient Me-Wuk roundhouses show centuries of occupation and ritual use of rancheria land.

The 1905-1906 Special Census of Non-reservation Indians of California listed only 9 full-blooded members of the Me-Wuk Indians. By 1915, there were 20 more members listed; however, most were listed as residents of the Ione Rancheria, located several miles north of the original Buena Vista Rancheria lands. The Buena Vista Rancheria of Me-Wuks was disbanded in 1958. Its members, who numbered only two at that time, were given land in compensation.

The Buena Vista Rancheria was restored to federal recognition in 1984, as the result of a settlement involving various California tribes whose recognition was terminated by Congress between 1958 and 1962. The Bureau of Indian Affairs has determined that Buena Vista Rancheria membership belongs only to those who received rancheria land in the 1950s, their dependents, or their lineal descendants, creating dissent among competing factions within the tiny band.

GOVERNMENT
The Buena Vista Rancheria was restored to federal recognition in 1984.

Gaming. One of the women claiming tribal leadership has proposed development of a $100 million, 200,000-square-foot casino complex, to be constructed on rancheria land. This band member sought and obtained a compact with the State of California in 1998, which would permit gaming under the Indian Gaming Regulatory Act. The other woman claiming tribal leadership has staunchly opposed the casino's construction, and has fought its development in the court system. In 2004, the California legislature and the governor signed the compacts, clearing the way. The compact faces final review by the Bureau of Indian Affairs.

When completed, the complex will feature 1,800 slot machines, blackjack tables, four restaurants, a 1,200-seat theater, a 250-seat cabaret theater and a 2,000-car garage. The State of California, under terms of the compact, would receive approximately 15 percent of the proceeds, rising to 25 percent if revenues reach or exceed certain limits.

Buena Vista Rancheria
Federal Reservation
Miwok (Me-Wuk)
Amador County, California

Buena Vista Rancheria
of Me-Wuk Indians
#6 Glynnis Falls Ct.
Sacramento, CA 95831
209-274-6512
209-274-6514 Fax

Total area
(BIA realty, 2003)
0 acres

Tribal enrollment
(BIA labor report, 2001)
12

Total labor force
(BIA labor report, 2001)
6

Unemployment rate
(BIA labor report, 2001)
17%

Cabazon

Cabazon Reservation
Federal reservation
Cahuilla
Riverside County, California

Cabazon Band of Mission
Indians
84-245 Indio Springs Parkway
Indio, CA 92203
760-342-2593
760-347-7880 Fax
cabazonindians.com

Total area *(BIA realty, 2003)*
1,376.16 acres

Total area *(Tribal source, 2004)*
1,706 acres

Tribally owned *(BIA realty, 2003)*
948.81 acres

Individually owned
(BIA realty, 2003)
427.35 acres

Population *2000 census*
806

Tribal enrollment
(BIA labor report, 2001)
30

Total labor force *2000 census*
366

High school graduate or higher
2000 census
32.6%

Bachelor's degree or higher
2000 census
3.5%

Unemployment rate *2000 census*
36.6%

Per capita income
2000 census
$7,734

LOCATION AND LAND STATUS

The Cabazon Reservation spans 1,706 acres in southern California. It is located seven miles from the agricultural community of Indio, 18 miles from Palm Springs, and is adjacent to the city of Coachella to the south. It is approximately 130 miles east of Los Angeles.

An Executive Order on May 15, 1876, established this reservation, and an Executive Order on May 3, 1877, restored a section to the public domain. In 1895 the area was increased by the return of some of the land removed by the 1877 order, under authority of the Act for the Relief of Mission Indians (26 Stat. 712-714 c.65) of January 12,1891.

PHYSICAL DESCRIPTION

The Cabazon Reservation is located in the flat, dry lands of an urban environment in southern California.

CLIMATE

The region's average temperature ranges from 31ºF to 107ºF between winter and summer. Annual rainfall is approximately 2.8 inches.

CULTURE AND HISTORY

Members of the Cabazon Band of Mission Indians belong to the Cahuilla Tribe. The Cahuilla Tribe is comprised of two moieties and approximately 12 patrilineal clans. Other Cahuilla bands in southern California include the Agua Caliente Band of Cahuilla Indians, the Augustine Band of Mission Indians, the Cahuilla Band of Mission Indians, the Ramona Band of Mission Indians, the Morongo Band of Mission Indians, the Santa Rosa Band of Mission Indians, Los Coyotes Indians, and the Torres Martinez Band of Desert Cahuillas. The Cabazon Band takes its name directly from Chief Cabazon, the leader of the Desert Cahuillas during the mid-1830s.

The Cahuillas have resided in southern California for at least 2,500 years. They traditionally located their villages in areas where native plants and wild game were abundant. The Cahuilla language belongs to the Uto-Aztecan language family which includes languages spoken by peoples from the Great Basin south to central Mexico. Linguistic evidence suggests that by 1000 BC, the Cahuillas became a separate linguistic, and somewhat culturally independent, tribe.

The Cahuilla people encountered Euro-Americans in the late 1700s when the Spanish began to settle in southern California. The arrival of foreign illnesses in the mid-1800s greatly reduced the Cahuilla population. In addition, the arrival of the Southern Pacific Railroad initiated widespread encroachment upon tribal lands, and the Cahuillas were forced to relocate from their traditional territories. The Cabazon Band was living near Indio in 1876 when an Executive Order established the Cabazon Reservation there. The reservation originally included three parcels of land totaling 2,400 acres. The railroad claimed 700 acres to create a railroad system and for interstate right-of-way.

None of the several Cahuilla reservations located in southern California accepted the terms of the Indian Reorganization Act of 1934, which was intended to grant more autonomy to Indian tribes and required the development of tribal constitutions. The Cahuillas remained politically active throughout the twentieth century, filing Indian Claims Commission cases during the 1940s and 1950s for traditional lands taken by non-Indians and the government and suing the government for damages resulting from the loss of water rights.

GOVERNMENT

The general council, composed of all adult tribal members over the age of 18, governs the Cabazon Reservation. Officers, including a chairperson, two vice-chairpersons, a secretary-treasurer, and a liaison to the general council, are elected for four-year terms. All business matters are overseen by the business committee, which reports to the general council. The general council meets four times annually; the business committee meets weekly. The tribe is organized under Articles of Association approved on April 13, 1965, and is a PL-638 tribe.

The Cabazon Band has a tribal council, tribal court, development department, public affairs department, gaming commission, public safety department, fire department, and a law enforcement department. In 2003, the tribe launched the East Valley Tourist Development Authority which is headed by an appointed board of directors made up of notable business, legal, and government (retired) officials.

The tribe maintains a public safety department which houses the police department and the fire department. The police department employs 26 police officers and staff. Police officers are federally certified and have additional training through the Department of the Interior. The fire department has a battalion chief and six fire apparatus engineers. The department services the reservation, as well as local towns and communities in Riverside County.

ECONOMY

The tribe is supported in large part by revenue earned from the Cabazon gaming operations. While gaming plays an important role in the Cabazon Band of Mission Indians' economic self-reliance, the key to the tribes past, present, and future economic success is economic diversity. The tribe owns and operates numerous businesses in various industries, each contributing to the tribe's economic status and its ability to establish the financial sovereignty it seeks.

Economic Development Projects. The tribe is in the process of constructing hotel facilities on the reservation. The tribe is also in the development stages of a shopping center on non-reservation land contiguous to the reservation, in addition to a second hotel, a golf course, time-shares and condominiums, and a housing development on its land in Coachella.

Agriculture. Agriculture and agribusiness have played an important role in the overall economic development of Coachella Valley, but while grapes are grown on the reservation, little other agricultural development has occurred.

Gaming. The tribe owns and operates the Fantasy Springs Resort Hotel and Casino in Indio. The casino offers over 1,956 gaming machines, blackjack and poker tables, and off-track horse race betting. The Fantasy Springs Casino underwent a 70,000-square-foot expansion in 2003. Expanded facilities feature two new restaurants, an entertainment lounge, enlarged gaming areas, 6,000 square feet of meeting rooms, a gift shop, and a box office. Facilities include a 750-seat Bingo Palace with smoking and nonsmoking areas, a Bingo Snack Bar, and its own beverage stations and restrooms. Fantasy Springs Resort Casino, which opened a hotel and convention center in December 2004, employs 1,200 people as of February 2005, and it is one of the largest employers in the Coachella Valley. The new hotel and convention center boast five restaurants: the Sunset View Lounge, the Bistro, the Buffet, the Fantasy Grille, and the Springs Bar and Players Steak House.

In addition to supporting the tribe's general budget, revenues from the tribe's gaming operations are donated to local charities and groups fighting for sovereign rights. Some of the organizations that the tribe has contributed to include the ABC Recovery Center, AIDS Assistance program, American Diabetes Association, American Lung Association, California State University, City of Indio Police Department K-9 Unit, Coachella Valley Special Olympics, Family YMCA of the Desert, Mizell Senior Center, Toys for Tots, United Cerebral Palsy, and United Way.

Industrial Parks. The Cabazon Resource Recovery Park occupies 640 acres on the reservation. The park is designated to serve as a home for ecologically sensitive industries working toward increased efficiency and environmentally sound business. The park currently houses Colmac Energy, a privately owned biomass waste energy facility, and First Nations Recovery, a crumb rubber recycling facility. The tribe added a soils reclamation business to the park in 2004. Proposed projects for the park include metals reclamation, biomass gasification, and soils and fertilizer production.

Manufacturing. The tribe owns First Nations Recovery, a recycling company that collects and transports recyclable tires. It has the capability to reproduce materials as crumb rubber for asphalt and molding applications. First Nations Recovery received the Project Achievement Award of 1999 and the Clean Cities Outstanding Private Sector Award of 2000. One of its most successful projects has been recycling recalled Firestone tires, ensuring that the damaged materials do not re-enter the consumer market. The company's largest project so far has involved recycling 965,000 pounds of asphalt for an Arizona highway.

Real Estate/Commercial Development. Painted Canyon Estates is a gated community in Coachella on the Cabazon Reservation. It is one of the first housing developments to be built on tribal lands in California under provisions of the HUD 184 Indian Home Loan Guarantee Program.

Services and Retail. The tribe offers the Cabazon United States Export Assistance Center. The organization offers new-to-export and new-to-market counseling services to businesses with export potential. Services include the development of business client-based activities and travel and tourism information distribution. The center was created in collaboration with the U.S. Department of Commerce. It is the first to be established on the reservation of a self-governing nation.

Fantasy Lanes Family Bowling Center is a tribal enterprise located on the reservation. The bowling center offers 40 lanes, laser-tag and bumper bowling, a video arcade, a lounge, and a pro shop. There is also a supervised play area for children.

Media and Communications. The Cabazon Tribe operates *The Talking Stick*, a television program broadcast nightly on PAX TV and rebroadcast on the Time Warner cable channel. The program provides educational and informational stories relevant to the reservation community and surrounding area. The tribe is a partner in the Coachella Valley Printing Group. The company oversees the production of printed material for tribal government and business entities. It also offers graphics design, scanning, printing, and archiving services to the public. The tribe has merged its in-house printing business with Coachella Valley Printing. It is located in a 15,000-square-foot production building near the reservation.

The tribe produces *The Cabazon Circle*, a monthly newsletter, as well as quarterly special editions that go out to the local public. It also maintains a tribal website and produces tribal informational videos.

Tourism and Recreation. The mild winter climate has lured many tourists and retirees to Coachella Valley. Seasonal residency has increased dramatically over the past few years. Therefore, the tribe is interested in expanding its participation in the tourism and recreation sectors.

The Cabazon Nation also owns the Cabazon Cultural Museum. It features historical exhibits and displays, and offers classes on Cahuilla culture and history. Classes are conducted through the University of California at Riverside. Building expansions are planned to begin in 2005. Each November, the Cabazon Band of Mission Indians hosts the Indio Powwow to honor, preserve, and introduce others to Native-American culture. Through their semiannual powwows and newly completed Cabazon Cultural Museum, the tribe hopes to continue fostering a sense of community among Native Americans, as well as to provide others with the opportunity to celebrate and embrace the richness of their culture.

INFRASTRUCTURE

Commercial transportation facilities are available at Indio, seven miles from the reservation. The reservation's nearest major artery is Interstate 10, which borders the reservation. U.S. Highway 60 runs three-tenths of a mile south of the reservation, and it is intersected by many other major roadways. The Southern Pacific Railroad crosses its southwestern corner.

Electricity. The Imperial Irrigation District supplies electricity to the reservation.

Fuel. Southern California Gas Company provides residents with natural gas.

Water Supply. The City Desert Water System provides water and sewer services on the reservation.

Transportation. The casino offers shuttle services for clients. Palm Springs Airport offers commercial services. Private flights can go through Bermuda Dunes Airport or Thermal Airport.

COMMUNITY FACILITIES AND SERVICES

The tribe provides employment training and opportunities for tribal members in all tribally owned and operated businesses.

Education. Tribal members either attend private local schools, schools in the Desert Sands Unified Schools District, or Coachella Unified School District, depending on where they live. The Cabazon Tribe offers education grants and financial assistance to eligible tribal members.

Health Care. The tribe pays for all medical, dental, and vision costs for tribal members through the tribe's health insurance.

TRI-CA-cz005

Cabazon

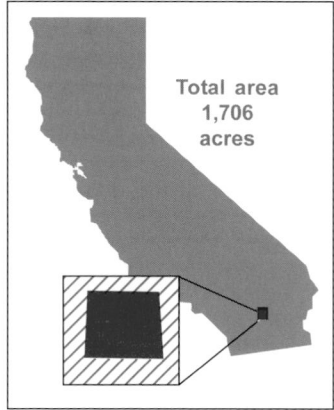

Total area
1,706
acres

ENVIRONMENTAL CONCERNS

The Cabazons strive to maintain and develop environmentally sound industries that preserve, recycle, and/or transform waste streams. Water quality and air pollution are concerns to the tribe. The tribe has a continuous involvement in government activities connected with saving the Salton Sea.

Cahuilla

Cahuilla Reservation
Federal reservation
Cahuilla
Riverside County, California

Cahuilla Band of Indians
P.O. Box 391760
Anza, CA 92539-1760
951-763-5549
951-763-2808 Fax
cahuilla.com

Total area (BIA realty, 2003)
18,884.26 acres

Tribally owned lands
(BIA realty, 2003)
2,611 acres

Population 2000 census
154

Tribal enrollment
(BIA labor report, 2001)
297

Total labor force 2000 census
59

Total labor force
(BIA labor report, 2001)
114

High school graduate or higher
2000 census
76.9%

Bachelor's degree or higher
2000 census
3.3%

Unemployment rate
2000 census
5.1%

Unemployment rate
(BIA labor report, 2001)
11%

Per capita income
2000 census
$9,401

TRI-CA-006Clla Cahuilla Tribal Office

TRI-CA-007Clla Cahuilla Creek Casino on
Highway 371

LOCATION AND LAND STATUS
The Cahuilla Reservation lies in the Peninsular Range of southern California, 48 miles southwest of Palm Springs. The reservation was established by Executive Order on December 27, 1875. The acreage was increased on March 14, 1877, and was reduced two months later. The land base increased again with additions on April 14, 1926, and March 4, 1931, bringing the reservation to its present total area of 18,884 acres. All land is held in trust. Only 2,000 acres belong to the tribe in common; the remainder is allotted to individual members of the Cahuilla Band.

The present-day reservation is located within the ancestral lands of the tribe on the site of an ancient community called Paui.

PHYSICAL DESCRIPTION
Cahuilla Reservation terrain contains giant boulders, rolling hills, dry wash beds, and desert brush. It is located between Mt. Palomar and San Jacinto, at 4,000 feet above sea level.

CLIMATE
Weather on the reservation is cool and dry. The average rainfall is between 14 and 15 inches per year.

CULTURE AND HISTORY
Members of the Cahuilla tribe have long resided in the area of southern California where the present reservation exists. The language of the Cahuilla people belongs to the Takic branch of the Uto-Aztecan greater linguistic family. Elder reservation residents continue to speak their ancestral language. Some forms of traditional music, such as Bird Songs and Peon Songs, remain important and are performed regularly on social occasions.

The Cahuilla tribes were assigned to reservations during the mid-1800s. The Cahuilla Reservation was created by an Executive Order in 1875. The Cahuillas were able to maintain their traditional subsistence patterns of hunting native game and gathering piñon nuts and mesquite beans.

During the first part of the twentieth century, the Cahuillas derived their income from wage labor, farming, and raising stock on reservation lands. In the early years of the twentieth century, Cahuilla reservations retrieved some of the land that had been returned to the public domain by the 1891 Act for the Relief of Mission Indians. None of the Cahuilla reservations participated in the Indian Reorganization Act of 1934. Cahuilla reservations joined other southern California Indian groups in the Indian Claims Commission cases of the 1940s and 1950s, and some have sued the government for determination of damages in respect to the loss of water rights. For tribal leaders, tribal autonomy remains a priority today.

In April 2004, the State of California demanded that California tribes renegotiate their gaming compacts to provide an additional $500 million collectively to the state. The state has compacts with 61 tribes, each for 20 years, but they are renegotiable after three years of existence. The response from many California tribes has been an unwillingness to renegotiate at this time.

GOVERNMENT
Members age 21 or older make up the tribe's general council, and they elect a tribal council every two years. Tribal council officers include a chairperson, vice-chairperson, a tribal administrator, and two council members. The tribal council also serves as the Overall Economic Development Committee. Additional committees are formed around issue-specific concerns such as personnel, economic development (Cahuilla Economic Ad Hoc Committee/C.E.A.), housing (All Mission Indian Housing Authority/A.M.I.H.A.), health (Riverside-San Bernardino County Indian Health), and education (Title V). The standing committees (Tribal Council, C.E.A.), building, housing improvement projects, and personnel) function within established policies and procedures. The tribe is organized under a non-IRA constitution which was revised in 1983. It is a PL-638 Tribe.

ECONOMY
Cahuilla Creek Casino is one of the tribe's major sources of income. The economy is also sustained by leasing tribal lands.

The on-reservation population of Cahuilla Reservation is small. As land ownership is under the control of individual tribal members, it is difficult for the tribe as a whole to undertake any profitable enterprise. The scarcity of water, as well, limits development.

Government as Employer. The Administration for Native Americans supplies grants for tribal employees.

Economic Development Projects. The tribe has been considering a number of commercial ventures including the development of a convenience store, shopping mall, and a resort/spa complex. Before the tribe can undertake these projects, it must address the immediate needs of the reservation community and establish policies to regulate the environmental impact of development.

As much of the reservation land is individually controlled, individual tribal members have development plans for their assignments. On one such assignment, a tribal member is developing housing tracts with a golf course in association with a private

TRI-CA-006-Clla

TRI-CA-007-Clla

outside investor. Another tribal member is conducting feasibility studies for the development of a hotel with a mini-mall. This project is also being explored with an outside joint investor.

Agriculture and Livestock. Most reservation land is leased for grazing. There is some agricultural cultivation in the valley along Cahuilla Creek.

Gaming. The tribe owns and operates Cahuilla Creek Casino on Highway 371 in Anza. The casino offers 180 slots/VLTs, three table games, and thee restaurants. It also offers live entertainment. It is open 24 hours a day, seven days a week.

Mining. A sand, gravel, and cement plant is located on the reservation.

Tourism and Recreation. The reservation hosts an annual cultural festival.

INFRASTRUCTURE
State Route 371 is the primary access route to the reservation. The reservation itself has about 16 miles of dirt road under BIA jurisdiction, none of which is in good condition. I-15 runs about 25 miles west of the reservation.

Electricity. Southern California Edison supplies electricity to the reservation.

Fuel. Bottled gas is available.

Water Supply. Homes in Cahuilla have individual septic systems; the Indian Health Service regulates these systems. The tribe does not have a community water system. Individual homes use separate wells, although recent droughts have made these wells insufficient to supply the community's needs. Solid waste disposal is handled at Riverside County transfer stations.

Transportation. The Town of Hemet, 38 miles away, has the nearest train, bus, truck, and commercial air service.

COMMUNITY FACILITIES AND SERVICES
Community facilities on the reservation include a tribal hall, which houses tribal administration services. The tribe provides culture retention classes. It also has a local chapter of the anti-substance abuse program M.A.D.D. The tribe hopes to develop a library on the reservation.

Health Care. Services are available at the Indian Health Center and at the hospital in Hemet.

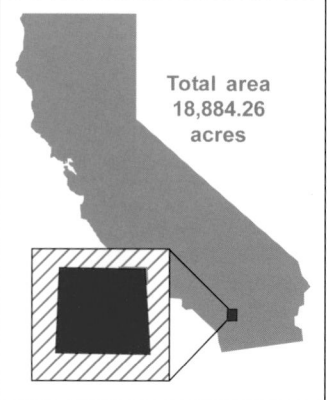

Total area
18,884.26
acres

California Valley

Total area *(BIA realty, 2003)*	0.92 acres
Individually owned	0.92 acres
(BIA realty, 2003)	

CULTURE AND HISTORY
Members of the California Valley Miwok Tribe belong to the Northern Sierra group of the Miwok Tribe. The Miwoks traditionally occupied territories in north-central California. The tribe was previously known as the Sheep Ranch Band of Me-Wuk Indians of California; they officially changed their name on June 7, 2001.

Traditional Miwok culture was irrevocably altered upon the arrival of European explorers and, later, Euro-American settlers. Tribal populations were devastated by the introduction of European diseases, the enforced incarceration of indigenous people on reservations, and the further usurpation of tribal lands by settlers.

Although the Miwok Tribe supported and assisted the United States during the Mexican-American War, the U.S. Senate failed to ratify a number of treaties between the tribe and the federal government. These treaties would have established several reserved parcels for the tribe. Without the federal government's protection, Miwok tribal members were subjected to indentured slavery and outright extermination. As a result of the genocidal tactics, the Miwok were forced to endure, the communities were destroyed or dispersed, and the tribal population greatly reduced.

Many of the Miwok Bands were terminated as federally recognized nations between 1934 and 1972, losing their tribal assets and land base. Most of the groups have regained status, though the Nevada City, Strawberry Valley, and Wilton bands remain unrecognized. In spite of the overwhelming attempts to first eliminate and later assimilate indigenous people, many Miwok tribal members have maintained cultural traditions. Tribal members continue to uphold traditional spiritual beliefs and celebrate cultural events; and although there is no all-inclusive organization, the Miwok bands have continued to work together to preserve the Miwok culture and promote the needs of the Miwok people. The Northern Sierra Mewuk Language Program has been created to assist in preserving the indigenous language, and the Mariposa-Amador-Tuolomne-Calaveras Indian Health Board has been established to provide health programs to Miwok tribal members.

The tribe is currently seeking a land base in its aboriginal territory, which includes Alameda, Alpine, Amador, Calaveras, Contra Costa, El Dorado, Fresno, Madea, Mariposa, Merced, Sacramento, San Joaquin, Solano, Stanislaus, and Tuolumne.

GOVERNMENT
The tribe adopted a constitution on March 6, 2000. The governing body is a tribal council that consists of a chairperson, a vice-chairperson, and a secretary. Each are elected to six-year terms. There are also a tribal consultant, a bookkeeper, an Indian artisan representative, and two tribal attorneys.

California Valley Miwok Tribe
Formerly known as Sheep
Ranch
Federal reservation
Me-Wuk
Calaveras County, California

California Valley Miwok Tribe
10601 Escondido Place
Stockton, CA 95212
209-931-4567
209-931-4833 Fax
californiavalleymiwoktribe-
nsn.com

Campo

Campo Reservation
Federal reservation
Kumeyaay
San Diego County, California

Campo Band of Kumeyaay
36190 Church Rd., Suite 1
Campo, CA 91906
619-478-9046
619-478-5818 Fax
campo-kumeyaay.org

Total area *(BIA realty, 2003)*
15,480.28 acres

Tribally owned *(BIA realty, 2003)*
15,480.28 acres

Population *2000 census*
351

Tribal enrollment
(BIA labor report, 2001)
294

Total labor force *2000 census*
95

Total labor force
(BIA labor report, 2001)
175

High school graduate or higher
2000 census
59.1%

Bachelor's degree or higher
2000 census
7.4%

Unemployment rate
2000 census
13.7%

Unemployment rate
(BIA labor report, 2001)
45%

Per capita income
2000 census
$6,805

LOCATION AND LAND STATUS

The Campo Indian Reservation is located in southeastern San Diego County atop the Laguna Mountains. The reservation was established on 710 acres on February 10, 1893, following an Executive Order on January 12,1891. Eighty acres were added on February 2,1907, and 13,610 acres were added on December 14, 1911. Later additions brought the reservation to its current size. All land on Campo is tribal-owned land; there are presently no allotments or assignments.

PHYSICAL DESCRIPTION

The Campo Reservation is located in undeveloped regions of San Diego County. It is located at the headwaters of Campo Creek, La Posta Creek, Miller Creek, and Canada Verde, and in the headwaters of the Tule Creek as well. It is situated approximately 45 miles inland from the Pacific coast. The reservation contains 31 miles of streams, 80 acres of wetlands, and 10 lakes.

CLIMATE

Campo, California, receives an annual average precipitation of 14 inches, and an average snowfall of 0.5 inch. The annual average temperature reaches 76°F.

CULTURE AND HISTORY

The Campo people are part of the Kumeyaay Indian Tribe, whose historic territory reached from northern San Diego County to the Salton Sea and 50 miles into Baja California. The Kumeyaays first encountered Spanish explorers in 1542. Over the next 200 years, the Spanish continued to arrive along the Pacific coast and venture inland. Contact between the Spanish and the Kumeyaays was violent, but the Kumeyaays managed to escape capture or confinement numerous times. In 1769 a mission was established in San Diego, and the Kumeyaays began a series of attacks on the Franciscans and Spaniards living there. The Spanish were not defeated, and the mission eventually drew Kumeyaay converts. 1n 1779 a fort was established above the Kumeyaay village at Cosoy. Small skirmishes continued to flare up between the Kumeyaays and the settlers, and in 1774 the mission was moved six miles north to Mission Valley in order decrease tensions between the tribe and the Spanish. In 1775 the Kumeyaays waged war against the Spanish and attacked the mission. The battle resulted in the destruction of the mission and the deaths of all residents. Spanish and Mexican soldiers eventually managed to achieve dominance in the coastal area of San Diego County, but the interior was under the direct control of the Kumeyaay people until after the Mexican-American War.

Americans arrived in the San Diego area in the 1840s. The Kumeyaay tribes offered their assistance to the American military in the efforts to overthrow Spanish-Mexican forces. The Spanish Mexicans were defeated, and in 1848 the Treaty of Guadalupe ended the Mexican-American War. Upon the discovery of gold in northern California, Euro-Americans began arriving in the state in droves. In 1850 the California territory became a state and passed the Act for the Government and Protection of Indians. This act mandated the regulation of Indian affairs to the state, permitted Euro-Americans the right to assume custody of Native children, prohibited the use of Native testimony against a Euro-American charged with a crime, and permitted unemployed Native peoples to be arrested and hired out, a form of state-sanctioned indentured servitude. The state further protected prospectors and settlers as they encroached upon tribal territories and seized water sources in the area.

In January 1852, the Treaty of Santa Ysabel was negotiated between the government and the Ipai and Tipai Kumeyaay bands.

The treaty was one of 18 that would be negotiated between the government and multiple Native groups between 1851 and 1853. The agreements were to reserve 7.5 million acres for various tribes across the state, but the senate did not ratify the treaties. The Kumeyaays and other affected tribes were left vulnerable to forcible evictions and dislocation from remaining lands. Local, state, and federal agencies condoned the effort to commit genocide against the Native people of California. Indigenous people were openly murdered, attacked, and enslaved. The atrocities committed against the indigenous groups so outraged the Mexican government that officials crossed the U.S.-Mexico border to conduct investigations, and they threatened to bring arms against the citizens of California if the violence did not cease. The intervention on their behalf and their ability to isolate themselves in the mountainous regions of the state enabled some tribes to escape total decimation. However, from an estimated population of over 150,000 in 1845, the Native population was reduced to less than 50,000 by 1855. The Kumeyaay tribes were fortunate in the relatively small number of losses they experienced until smallpox swept through the region in the 1860s, but the population of the clans was reduced from 2,000 in 1850 to 200 by 1890. By 1900, less than 16,000 indigenous people remained in the area.

Although reduced in size and suffering from the loss of access to traditional water supplies and lands, the Kumeyaays continued to engage in conflict with the Americans throughout the latter half of the nineteenth century. In 1875 the Kumeyaay clans were excluded from an Executive Order that created reservations throughout San Diego. By 1890 the clans had become scattered and were suffering from the continuing attacks by Americans, diseases, and starvation. In 1891, Congress passed the Act for the Relief of the Mission Indians in the State of California. A reservation was created for the mountain clans of the Kumeyaay Tribe, and in 1893 the Campo Indian Reservation was established.

As a result of the government's failure to ratify the treaty of 1850, many Kumeyaay bands refused to acknowledge the authority of the federal government. Some Kumeyaays continued to live off-reservation in mountain areas until the expansion of Campo in 1911. Tensions grew until 1929 when an altercation between tribal members and BIA police resulted in several deaths at Campo. Campo people continued to maintain their independence whenever possible, refusing to participate in the Indian Reorganization Act of 1934. With the passage of PL-280 in 1950, the BIA closed its Campo offices. Tribal members responded by burning all BIA structures on the reservation. In 1975 the Campo people established a constitution to formalize governmental operations.

GOVERNMENT

The tribe is organized under a non-IRA Constitution that established a legislative branch, an executive branch, and a judicial branch. The seven-member elected executive committee includes a chairperson, vice-chairperson, secretary, and treasurer. Officers serve four-year terms. The executive committee serves as the overall economic development plan committee as well. The judicial branch represents the tribe in matters involving the BIA, the federal and state courts, and the tribal environmental court.

BUSINESS CORPORATION

Muht-Hei, the tribal development corporation, was established in 1989 and manages the tribe's economic interests. Projects have included a commercial municipal solid-waste facility, a recycling facility sand mine, concrete mixing and transit, and a biweekly newspaper. Proposed projects include a manufacturing plant and a wind-powered electrical generating plant.

ECONOMY

Muht-Hei, the tribe's development corporation, serves as an important source of tribal income and employment, as do the tribe's governmental departments, programs, and enterprises. Job growth in San Diego County between 1986 and 1990, according to the California Employment Development Department, was strongest in the services sector, followed by retail and wholesale trade, and government. The tribe hopes to capitalize on the heavy traffic along Interstate 8 for its development efforts.

Government as Employer. The Campo tribal government employs many tribal members in the fire department, Campo Environmental Protection Agency, education, public works, administrative services, in the preschool, housing authority, and other departments.

Agriculture and Livestock. In 1995 the tribe voted to discontinue the use of tribal lands for commercial grazing. Although the tribe has suffered a loss of revenue, it has successfully begun the restoration of tribal wetlands. The Campo Environmental Protection Agency owns and operates a tree nursery. Trees are available for resale, and saplings are used to reforest tribal lands.

Forestry. The tribe manages a nursery that produces seedlings. It supplies oak, willow, cottonwood, cypress, and pine saplings for tribal reforestation programs. The trees are also available for residential landscaping. The tribe manages an orchard of eucalyptus trees to be used for firewood by reservation residents.

Gaming. The Campo Band owns the Golden Acorn Casino and Travel Center. It offers over 750 Vegas-style slot machines, video poker, video keno, and progressives. There are also blackjack and poker tables. Facilities include three restaurants and a bar. The casino employs 400 individuals.

Construction. The Muhtay Construction Company employs tribal members for construction projects on the reservation. The Campo Indian Housing Authority, which oversees the building of new homes on the reservation, was established in 1993.

Mining. The Campo Material Company supplies sand and other building material to the construction industry. The reservation serves as one of only a few sources of high-grade plaster sand in the area. In 1996 the company sought minority status from the state of California and San Diego County.

Industrial Parks. Construction of the Muht-Hei Waste Management Facility, a jointly owned landfill spanning 400 acres began in 1994.

Retail Services. Adjacent to the hotel is the travel center which includes a full convenience store. It also offers amenities for professional truck drivers, including a lounge, Internet access, laundry facilities, and private showers.

Media and Communications. The tribal newspaper, *East County Register*, employs three people and provides a forum for discussion of policy issues with the larger community.

INFRASTRUCTURE

Interstate 8 and U.S. 80 traverse the reservation to the north, and U.S. 94, to the south.

Electricity. San Diego Gas and Electric Company provides electricity to residents.

Fuel. Propane gas is purchased from private vendors.

Water Supply. Individual wells supply water to the community, while septic tanks handle most of the sewage.

Telecommunications. Telephone service is provided by Pacific Bell Telephone Company Air Touch, and U.S. West Cellular.

Transportation. The San Diego-Imperial Valley Railroad runs from San Diego east to Imperial Valley, passing four-tenths of a mile east of the reservation. San Diego International Airport, located 66 miles away, provides commercial area service. The reservation is served by various shipping companies, including Federal Express and UPS. The reservation's public transport van connects with the San Diego Transit Authority and operates six days a week transporting tribal members to the urban San Diego area. The reservation's casino also operates a bus system.

COMMUNITY FACILITIES AND SERVICES

A tribal administration building, located on the south end of the reservation, houses the community center, satellite health services center, and tribal offices. In addition, the reservation has a fire department.

Education. The tribe operates Head Start programs on the Barona, Campo, La Jolla, and Santa Ysabel reservations. Each site serves up to 20 children and families and employs five individuals. The tribe offers preschool programs, tutoring services, adult education classes, and scholarships to its members.

Health Care. Tribal members receive health care services at the Southern Indian Health Clinic. The main IHS health clinic, is in Alpine, 30 miles away.

ENVIRONMENTAL CONCERNS

The tribe created the Campo Environmental Protection Agency in 1990. One of the tribe's primary concerns is water quality because the tribal lakes provide the only source of game fish and are the reservation's main water resource. A 1998 Report indicated that the tribe had successfully restored Campo Creek. EPA's Indian Environmental General Assistance program, has developed a network of cooperation between indigenous nations in both the U.S. and Mexico to address environmental issues.

In 1995 the tribe's solid-waste regulatory program received approval from the EPA, the first tribal program to be recognized in the nation. The tribe continues to meet or exceed state regulations of waste management. It has also received national recognition for its wetlands restoration project on Diabold Creek.

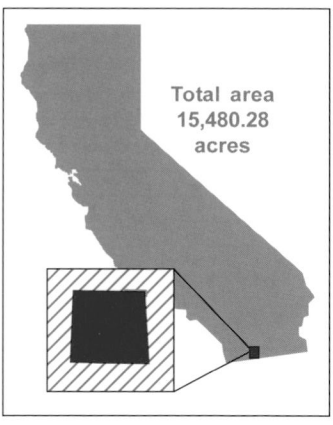

Total area
15,480.28
acres

TRI-CA-008-Cp Campo Tribal Office

Capitan Grande

Capitan Grande Reservation
Federal reservation
Kumeyaay (Diegueño)
San Diego County, California

Viejas Band of Kumeyaay
Indians, Barona Band
of Mission Indians
Capitan Grande Reservation
kumeyaay.com

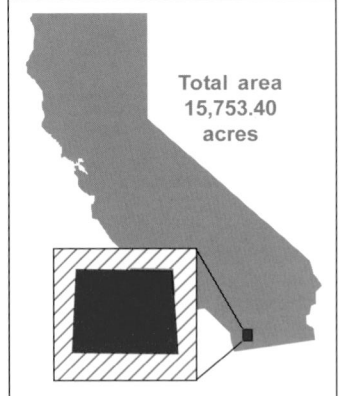

Total area
15,753.40
acres

Total area *(BIA realty, 2003)*   15,753.40 acres
Tribally owned   15,753.40 acres
(BIA realty, 2003)

(Please see Barona Reservation and Viejas Reservation for further information.)

LOCATION AND LAND STATUS

Located in the mountain foothills of San Diego County, approximately 30 miles east of San Diego, the Capitan Grande Reservation spans 15,753.4 acres. The Capitan Grande Reservation was established by an Executive Order on December 27, 1875, and an Executive Order on May 3, 1877, both of which restored portions to public domain. An additional Executive Order on June 19, 1883, set apart certain lands for the reservation. The reserved area encompassed 18,000 acres and was the largest in the county at the time.

In 1932 the City of San Diego received approval from the U.S. Congress to forcibly remove the residing Kumeyaay bands from 2,800 acres in order to facilitate the creation of a flood plain from the damming of the San Diego River. The tribe was compensated with $400,000. Using these funds, tribal members living in the village of El Capitan bought a parcel of land to create the Barona Reservation, and members living in the village of Los Conejos moved onto a 1,600-acre parcel of land to create the Viejas Reservation. The dam was consequently developed, and El Capitan Dam constitutes a 1,574-acre reservoir, the largest in the county, and a 190-square-mile watershed. In total, the tribe lost over 15,000 acres to the dam's creation. Furthermore, the tribe was not permitted to retain any water rights to the area.

While the Viejas and Barona bands continue to share a joint-trust patent for the Capitan Grande Reservation, no tribal members reside there. Descendants of the former Capitan Grande communities now constitute the Viejas Band and the Barona Band.

CULTURE AND HISTORY

The Capitan Grande Reservation was created in 1875 by Executive Order. The reservation was established on lands located near the Capitan Grande Canyon, approximately 35 miles east of San Diego. At one time, the San Diego River coursed through the canyon. Farming was the traditional means of sustenance for indigenous groups residing in the region. Original residents of the Capitan Grande Indian Reservation belonged to Kumeyaay communities at the villages of El Capitan and Los Conejos.

Capitan Grande Reservation, which was established in 1891, included portions of ancestral land of the Los Conejos Band. In 1853 the federal government allowed other Indians from Mission San Diego to relocate to Capitan Grande. Throughout the nineteenth century, various Kumeyaay groups were moved to the reservation. As the non-Indian population in the surrounding areas grew, demand for water increased. San Diego built Lake Cuyamaca, laying its flume through the Capitan Grande Reservation. The dam drew upon most of the San Diego River waters that the Kumeyaays used. They were left with only a small share from the city's flume, resulting in crop losses on Indian farms.

The city later decided to dam the river and create El Capitan Reservoir, commandeering all the water. Though the Kumeyaays protested, Congress granted the city permission to purchase the heart of the Capitan Grande Reservation upon which the Kumeyaays had built their homes. The dam was constructed, and tribal lands were flooded. Tribal members were forced to relocate. The city compensated the tribe for the loss of lands, and residents from El Capitan used the funds to purchase the Cañada de San Vicente y Mesa del Padre Barona Ranch, and they organized as the Barona Band of Mission Indians. Residents from Los Conejos moved to the former Baron Long Ranch and organized as the Viejas Band of Kumeyaay Indians. Capitan Grande Indian Reservation remains in joint-trust for the Barona and Viejas bands.

Cedarville

Cedarville Rancheria
Federal reservation
Paiute
Modoc County, California

Cedarville Rancheria of
Northern Paiute Indians
200 South Howard Street
Alturas, CA 96101
530-233-3969
530-233-4776 Fax
citlink.net

LOCATION AND LAND STATUS

The Cedarville Rancheria lies on the eastern slope of the Warner Mountain Range in the uppermost northeastern corner of California, about 50 miles from the Nevada border off State Highways 299 and 447. The Warner Mountains border the valley to the west and the Hays Canyon Range lies to the east in Nevada. The rancheria is located in Cedarville but the rancheria headquarters are in Alturas, the Modoc County seat.

The rancheria lands were gifted to people of Cedarville who petitioned for federal recognition. There are about seven families who live on the rancheria.

CLIMATE

The average elevation is 4,700 feet. Average precipitation varies from 12 to 16 inches, with average accumulated snow depth of 18 inches or less in winter months. Mean temperatures range from 71°F in summer to 30°F in the winter months.

CULTURE AND HISTORY

The residents of the Cedarville Rancheria belong to the Northern Paiute Tribe of the western Great Basin. The Northern Paiutes originally occupied a vast range along the eastern slopes of the Sierra Nevada and Cascade ranges from Mono Lake, California, to John Day River, Oregon. For subsistence, the Paiute traditionally depended upon the region's ample resources of game and native plants.

By the beginning of the twentieth century, Euro-American encroachment eroded the Paiute territory to less than five percent of its original size. The Native Americans of this region actively resisted these incursions on their traditional territories. Various skirmishes culminated in the Modoc War, 1872-1873, when a group of about 70 dissident Modoc Native people and their families held off several hundred U.S. soldiers for a number of months in the Lava Beds area of northern California, west of Surprise Valley.

In 1864 the settlers of Surprise Valley appealed to the military for protection. Also, John Bidwell, Brigadier General of the California Militia, a prominent landholder, agriculturalist, and entrepreneur, appealed for protection of commerce along the roads in and out of Surprise Valley. In response, Fort Bidwell became one of a network of military posts established in the California-Nevada-Oregon Border Triangle area beginning in 1857. Until the end of the "frontier" period, Fort Bidwell was used for controlling the Native populations.

When Fort Bidwell was turned into a BIA boarding school in 1898, many Paiute people camped near the school until officials determined that the presence of parents and relatives near the children was detrimental to the latter's becoming "civilized." These camps were forcibly evacuated around 1904.

Passage of the Dawes Act of 1887 provided for individual, rather than tribal, ownership of former Paiute lands. Between 1893 and 1897, 165 allotments were made to members of the Surprise Valley Paiute group in the vicinity of Cedarville and Fort Bidwell. Today the reservation contains many valuable archeological and historical sites, such as the ruins of the original fort.

GOVERNMENT
Members aged 18 or older make up the tribe's community council and elect the community council every three years. The community council elects an executive committee consisting of a chairman, a secretary, and a treasurer. The rancheria's constitution and bylaws were organized under the Indian Reorganization Act of 1934. Additional committees are formed around issue-specific concerns such as personnel and economic development. The rancheria has an environmental protection office.

Government as Employer. The rancheria employs eight people: five in administration, two in maintenance, and one as the custodian.

Economic Development Projects. The rancheria has several economic development projects underway. One is the development of tourism. Surprise Valley is considered a gateway to the nearby Modoc National Forest and the South Warner Wilderness area with abundant recreational opportunities such as fishing, hunting, biking, hiking, scenic driving, horseback riding and packing trips. Everyone traveling to the recreational areas has to come through Cedarville. Rancheria members want to take advantage of the location by creating a tourist center consisting of a gas station, a gift shop featuring Paiute art work, basketry, and other Native crafts, and a smoke shop.

Services and Retail. In November 2004, the rancheria opened for business a 17-unit rental storage facility.

INFRASTRUCTURE
State Highways 299 and 447 are the primary access routes to the rancheria.

Electricity. Pacific Power supplies electricity to the rancheria.

Fuel. Bethel's Propane sells fuel to the community.

Water Supply. The community water is supplied by the Cedarville Water Department.

COMMUNITY FACILITIES AND SERVICES
There is a community center on the rancheria that has a meeting room, an administrative office, kitchen, and library. A park and playground are nearby. All community meetings and activities take place here, such as the annual elders' dinners and the summer preschool program. The community also has a garden and arboretum where trees are planted in honor of past community members.

Education . Children from the rancheria attend public schools in Cedarville.

Health Care. The Modoc Indian Health facility in Alturas serves this community.

ENVIRONMENTAL CONCERNS
Water quality and watershed protection to prevent landslides and erosion are of great concern to the tribe. The EPA office strives to encourage the community to be a "Green Community" by sponsoring a Beautification Day and observing Arbor Day by planting trees in areas such as the mountainsides.

Cedarville

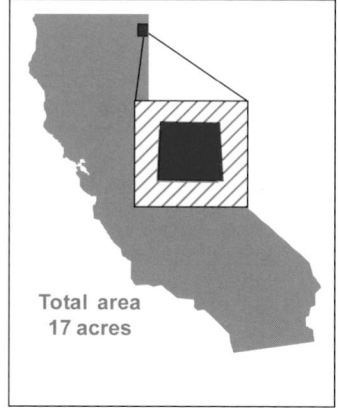

Total area
17 acres

Total area *(BIA realty, 2003)*
17 acres

Tribally owned *(BIA realty, 2003)*
17 acres

Tribal Enrollment
29

Total labor force
2000 census
8

High school graduate or higher
2000 census
26.7%

Bachelor's degree or higher
2000 census
0%

Unemployment rate *2000 census*
0%

Chemehuevi

Chemehuevi

Total area *(BIA realty, 2003)*	30,653 acres
Tribally owned	30,653.87 acres
(BIA, Realty, 2003)	
Population	325
Tribal enrollment *(BIA labor report, 2001)*	708
Total labor force *2000 census*	141
High school graduate or higher	61.9%
2000 census	
Bachelor's degree or higher	1.8%
2000 census	
Unemployment rate *2000 census*	8.5%
Per capita income	$13,130

LOCATION AND LAND STATUS
The Chemehuevi Reservation is located on the shores of Lake Havasu, in southeastern California on the Arizona border; 25 miles of the reservation boundary run along the shores of the lake, and 27 acres are located on prime lakefront property. The Chemehuevi Reservation was established by an Executive Order in 1970.

PHYSICAL DESCRIPTION
The reservation is divided into two distinct parts. The northern section is mostly flat mesa land, gently sloping from the Chemehuevi Mountains to the lake, with no deep washes. The southern section is filled with winding canyons, picturesque cliffs, and deep bays and coves.

CULTURE AND HISTORY
The Chemehuevi people are considered to be the most southern group of the Southern Paiute Indians, who are linguistically related to the greater Uto-Aztecan language family which includes languages spoken by peoples from the Great Basin south into central Mexico. For subsistence, the Chemehuevis traditionally gathered seeds and, after the coming of the Spanish, planted wheat along the Colorado River.

The Nuwu (the people), or Chemehuevis (Those that play with fish), have always resided in the Mojave Desert. Traditional homelands included the mountains and canyons of the Mojave Desert, as well as the shoreline of the Colorado River. The

Chemehuevi Reservation
Federal reservation
Chemehuevi
San Bernardino County,
California

Chemehuevi Indian Tribe
P.O. Box 1976
Havasu Lake, CA 92363
760-858-4301
760-858-5400 Fax
chemehuevi.net

Chemehuevi

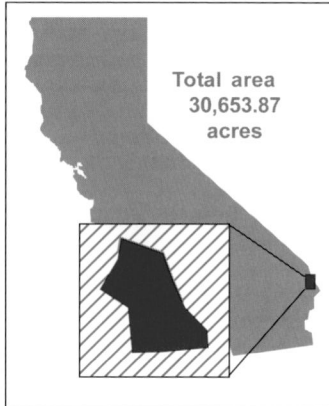

Total area
30,653.87
acres

Chemehuevis are a division of the Southern Paiute Tribe, and members of the Great Basin cultural region.

While originally occupying a territory that extended from the Tehachapi Mountains to the Colorado River and from southern Nevada to the vicinity of Parker, Arizona, the Chemehuevis became quite dispersed after 1900, as non-Indians moved onto their traditional lands. The Chemehuevis lived at that time on Cottonwood Island, along Beaver Lake, in the Needles region, and in the Chemehuevi Valley. Because the Chemehuevi Tribe was not organized then, the federal government considered them to be illegally occupying government property along the Colorado River. Those residing along the river in the Chemehuevi Valley were ultimately forced to move when their lands were flooded for the California Parker Dam project in 1930. Many of the farm families living in this region scattered throughout the United States; some sought wage employment, while others settled on the nearby Colorado River Reservation.

In 1951 the Chemehuevi Business Committee joined other Southern Paiute people in an Indian Claims Commission case. Eventually the Chemehuevis were awarded $82,000 to compensate for the land used by the Metropolitan Water District. This money was not disbursed until the 1960s, after a congressional Special Committee on Chemehuevi Affairs decided which of the contesting parties should receive the compensation. In 1970 the tribe was officially recognized, and the Chemehuevi Indian Reservation was set aside the following year.

The Chemehuevi culture has a rich legacy of storytelling, song, and dance. Significant events such as historical annual migration patterns and the seasonal movements of animals are featured in many tribal songs. The Chemehuevi Salt Song is of particular importance as it celebrates the cycles of life and death and distinguishes the tribe from other indigenous groups in the region. Chemehuevi artisans are known world wide for their coil baskets woven of willow and devil's claw. Unfortunately, the art is in danger of extinction as cultural knowledge wanes among tribal members.

GOVERNMENT

The reservation is governed by a nine-member elected tribal council, with a constitution and bylaws drawn up under the Indian Reorganization Act of 1934. The council includes a chairperson, a vice-chairperson, and a secretary-treasurer. Tribal officers serve for three-year terms. In addition, various standing committees such as the resource development committee, the administration committee, and the human resource committee, report to the tribal council.

ECONOMY

Government as Employer. Funding from various state and federal sources provides employment for tribal members in a number of social-service positions. The tribe employs a full-time community health representative whose position is funded through Indian Health Service funds. In addition the tribe employs an on-call magistrate and a full-time court clerk, a full-time resource teacher, and a part-time teacher's aide. Funding from the BIA supports three full-time conservation and preservation enforcement officers (game warden, chief game warden, and secretary-dispatcher). To assist the tribal council, the tribe employs a full-time tribal operations assistant and a full-time tribal programs coordinator.

Agriculture and Livestock. Although 1,900 acres of the reservation have been zoned for agricultural production, the tribe needs an adequate irrigation system to facilitate this development. The tribe sees agricultural development as an important economic strategy, potentially creating several types of skilled and unskilled jobs for tribal members.

Utilizing an agricultural method that involved flooding the river bottom ended traditional communal flood plain agriculture. Two hundred acres of Chemehuevi land are currently under experimental agricultural production. Recent efforts include an endeavor to improve soil quality through nitrogen fixation with alfalfa. There are also efforts to sustain traditional plant species by replanting mesquite trees. Approximately 1,000 acres of land are available for an agricultural lease.

Natural Resources. In 1998 the Chemehuevi Tribe entered into a 25-year lease that leased 5,000 acre-feet of the Colorado River per year to the Southeastern Nevada Water Company.

Gaming. The tribe owns the Havasu Landing Resort and Casino. It purchased the 6,000-square-foot facility in 1974. The casino offers 221 slots/VLTs, 5 table games, and a restaurant. The casino employs 90 people. The Resort and Casino also offers a full-service marina, grocery store, deli, year-round living, campground, and an RV park. Facilities also include a 5,000-foot paved runway for small aircraft and a tour boat that provides access to Lake Havasu City. The tribe also offers pull-tab gaming at its Havasu Landing Resort.

Construction. The tribally owned Chuckwalla Construction Company, a for-profit corporation, accepts contracts for construction projects throughout the area.

Real Estate/Commercial Development. Along the lake, the tribe also leases spaces for its Colony Mobile Home Park. These spaces may be rented annually or by the month. The tribe has recently increased the area of the park, adding 81 additional double-wide spaces. These leases account for a substantial part of the tribe's revenue.

Services and Retail. The tribe offers many retail services at the Havasu Landing Resort, including a newly expanded grocery story, a deli and gift shop, and gas stations. These facilities represent an important source of employment for the tribe and other area residents.

Tourism and Recreation. The Colorado River serves as a recreational haven for many sports and nature enthusiasts. The tribe has capitalized on the area's natural attractions by buying the Havasu Landing Resort. Located on the Colorado River's Havasu Lake, the resort offers year-round recreational activities, including boating; off-road recreational-vehicle riding; fishing; hunting for quail, dove, duck, and geese; and rock hunting. Many people also visit the area as a winter retreat. There are campgrounds, an RV park, a boathouse marina, and various other retail facilities. The resort, along with a smaller recreational center, Havasu Palms (located at Whipple Bay), provides the majority of the area's employment and tribal revenue.

The tribe's annual celebrations include Nuwuvii Days, held the first Friday in June, which is a celebration honoring the tribe's reinstatement, and Indian Days, which are observed on the third Friday and Saturday in September.

INFRASTRUCTURE

Electricity. Southern California Edison provides electricity to the reservation.

Water Supply. The community obtains its water from surface wells. Both the county and the tribe provide solid and liquid waste-disposal services.

Transportation. The tribe runs a passenger ferry that provides transportation across the Colorado River to Lake Havasu City, Arizona. Many of the resort's employees use this 48-person ferry as transportation to and from work. Lake Havasu Road provides access to the reservation from California Highway 95, which runs north-south 17 miles west of the reservation. In addition, the tribe's passenger ferry provides access to the reservation from Lake Havasu City, Arizona. The tribe is also developing an airport in the northern section of the reservation. Train, bus, air, and truck services are available in Needles, California, 20 miles to the north. Bus, commercial air, and trucking services are also available in Lake Havasu City, Arizona. Chemehuevi Valley Airport serves Chemehuevi Valley and San Bernardino County and is owned by the Chemehuevi Tribe. The paved runway extends for 5,000 feet. The facility is at an elevation of 631 feet at a distance of about four miles from Chemehuevi Valley.

Telecommunications. Continental Telephone serves the reservation's communication needs.

COMMUNITY FACILITIES AND SERVICES
There is a community service center located on the reservation. The reservation also has a post office, which is located near the Havasu Landing Resort.

Education. Elementary-school students attend a school located on the reservation, which offers bilingual educational services provided by community members. After fifth grade, middle school and high school students are bused to a school in nearby Needles, California. The Chemehuevi Indian Education Department Library, with a collection of around 1,780 volumes, is located in a temporary building on the northern end of the reservation. The library's computer lab offers six computers and serves students in grades K-5. The library also serves adult education needs, offering GED preparation classes and one-on-one computer training.

Health Care. Tribal members receive health care at the Chemehuevi Valley Medical Clinic.

Chicken Ranch

Total area *(BIA realty, 2003)*	50.58 acres
Total area *(Tribal source, 2005)*	700+ acres
Tribally owned	50.58 acres
(BIA realty, 2005)	
Federal trust lands	50 acres
(Tribal source, 2005)	
Tribally owned lands	2.85 acres
(Tribal source, 2005)	
Tribal enrollment *(BIA labor report, 2001)*	21
Total labor force *2000 census*	8
Total labor force *(BIA labor report, 2001)*	12
High school graduate or higher	70%
2000 census	
Bachelor's degree or higher	0%
2000 census	
Unemployment rate *2000 census*	0%

LOCATION AND LAND STATUS
The Chicken Ranch Rancheria is located in the foothills of the Motherlode, a section of the Sierra Nevada Mountains of northeastern California, in Tuolumne County. The tribe has 50 acres in trust lands in Jamestown where they built a casino on 2.85 acres. Tribe indicated that it has 700+ acres that are not in trust as of 2004.

ECONOMY
Although the tribe's main source of income is from its gaming facilities, many tribal members find employment in county and state highway jobs as well as with the U.S. Forest Service.
Gaming. The Chicken Ranch Bingo and Casino in Jamestown is owned by the tribe. The 30,000-square-foot facility offers 250 slots/VLTs, 900 bingo seats, and a restaurant. It employs about 120 people.

COMMUNITY FACILITIES AND SERVICES
Health Care. Health services are available through MACT Health Board. Clinics are located in Jackson, Tuolumne, Mariposa, Sonora, and West Point. Services include comprehensive medical, dental, community health, and behavioral health programs.

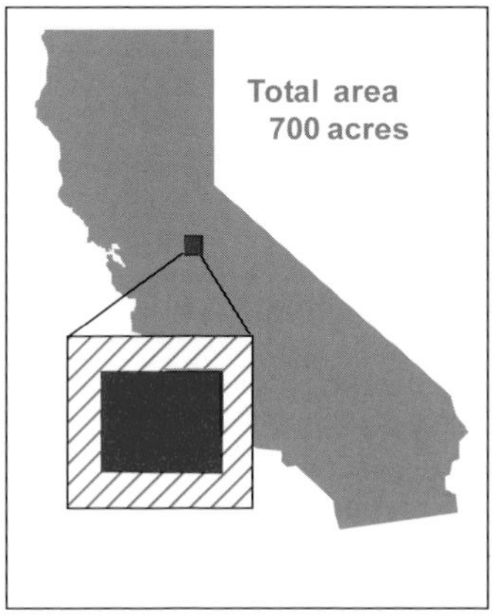

Chicken Ranch Rancheria
Federal reservation
Me-Wuk
Tuolumne County, California

Chicken Ranch Rancheria
P.O. Box 1159
Jamestown, CA 95327
    209-984-4806
    209-984-5606 Fax

Total area
700 acres

**Mechoopda Indian Tribe
of Chico Rancheria
Federal reservation
Mechoopda
Butte County, California**

Mechoopda Indian Tribe
of Chico Rancheria
125 Mission Ranch Blvd.
Chico, CA 95926
530-899-8922
530-899-8517 Fax
mechoopda.nsn

Total area *(Tribal source, 2004)*
690 acres

Total area *(BIA realty, 2003)*
0 acres

Tribal enrollment
(BIA labor report, 2001)
380

Tribal enrollment
(Tribal source, 2004)
413

Total labor force *2000 census*
1,566

Total labor force
(BIA labor report, 2001)
93

High school graduate or higher
2000 census
85%

Bachelor's degree or higher
2000 census
17.2%

Unemployment rate *2000 census*
9.6%

Unemployment rate
(BIA labor report, 2001)
27%

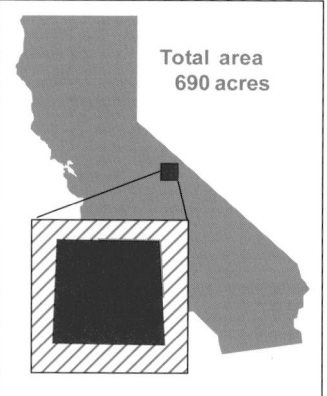

Total area
690 acres

LOCATION AND LAND STATUS

The Chico Rancheria is located in Chico, California, within the traditional territories of the Mechoopda Tribe. Since it received federal recognition in 1992, the tribe has purchased a number of parcels of land. In 1996 it purchased 40 acres, and in 2001 it acquired 650 acres south of Chico.

CULTURE AND HISTORY

Members of the Mechoopda Indian Tribe of Chico Rancheria have lived in the area of Chico, California, since time immemorial. The traditional language is related to Maidu. Early sustenance practices included hunting, fishing, and harvesting acorns. The Mechoopdas encountered Euro-Americans perhaps as early as 1828 when members of the Hudson Bay Company were trapping in the area's waterways. The tribe's central community was located on Little Butte Creek until 1850. At that time, John Bidwell acquired the Spanish land grant of Rancho Arroyo Chico. The tribe relocated to a former summer campsite south of Chico Creek, and later they moved further downstream nearer the Bidwell's residence. It is believed that Bidwell and a tribal member named Nuppani were married, thus establishing the foundation of a long-lasting relationship between the settler and the tribe. Tribal members participated in the agriculture, livestock, and mining industries as laborers for John Bidwell. In return, they were paid wages equal to their non-Native counterparts, and Bidwell extended his protection against federal intervention to the community. In 1851, the tribe reached a treaty agreement with the federal government. The tribe was provided with 200 head of cattle, 75 sacks of flour, sewing materials, iron, steel, mules, ploughs, milk cows, and other amenities, as well as a 227-square-mile tract of land. The U.S. government did not ratify the treaty, or others that had been negotiated with 18 California tribes. Policies of forced removal were subsequently initiated. The Mechoopdas likely did not face removal from tribal lands as they were associated with Bidwell's ranch and he continued to provide protection for them. During the process of forced removal, many Native peoples escaping from the tyranny sought and received refuge with the Mechoopda tribe at Bidwell's ranch. In 1868, the tribe established a community west of its present-day location. Members from many tribes and Native communities joined the Mechoopdas there.

The fate of Bidwell's marriage to Nuppani is unclear, but Bidwell married his second wife, Annie Kennedy, in 1868. Kennedy established a Christian church within the Mechoopda village, as well as a small school. She was an outspoken supporter of Native rights and, following Bidwell's death in 1910, she continued to support the Mechoopda community. Upon her death, the Bidwell lands were deeded to the Board of Home Missions of the Presbyterian Church as trustee for the Native residents and held in trust until the government conveyed the land into federal trust in 1939. This reservation consisted of 26 acres. All the lands were lost or sold through unscrupulous land transactions.

The tribe was terminated under the August 15, 1958, California Rancheria Act. In 1986, along with three other California rancherias, the Mechoopda Tribe filed a suit, *Scotts Valley v. United States*, challenging its unlawful termination. The tribe received federal recognition on January 6, 1992, and on May 4, 1992, the BIA served notice in the *Federal Register* that the tribe had been reinstated. The original rancheria was located in the center of Chico. California State University at Chico now occupies half of the original rancheria. The other half was divided into about 50 land parcels that were used for residential

and commercial purposes. The terms of the recognition prevented the tribe from establishing its former boundaries. In 1996 the tribe prepared a restoration plan that identified lands to purchase that would be placed into federal trust. In December 2001, the tribe purchased 650 acres about 10 miles from their former rancheria. This was the only purchase of land, with exception of the 40-acre almond grove purchased in 1996.

BUSINESS CORPORATION

The Mechoopda Economic Development Corporation oversees economic development projects on behalf of the tribe.

The Chico Rancheria Housing Corporation is a nonprofit tribal corporation. It is the tribe's tribally designated housing entity. The corporation provides home ownership and rental assistance to eligible tribal members. It also manages 30 lease-to-own housing units that the tribe owns in the City of Chico. The programs available through the corporation are funded in part by grants from HUD.

GOVERNMENT

The tribal government is organized according to the tribal constitution adopted on February 1, 1998, under the provisions of the Indian Reorganization Act of 1934. The tribe is governed by a general council composed of all tribal members and led by a tribal council comprised of a chairperson, a vice-chairperson, a secretary, a treasurer, and three members-at-large.

Government departments and programs include enrollment, personnel, education, housing, economic development, finance, environmental protection, and cultural.

ECONOMY

The tribal economy is supported by its enterprise in the agriculture industry and by leasing homes owned by the tribe. The Mechoopda Tribe is striving to achieve economic self-sufficiency.

Economic Development Projects. The tribe has initiated the process of developing a gaming facility. It expects that the revenue earned from this enterprise will bolster the tribal economy and provide additional funding for tribal programs.

Agriculture and Livestock. In 1996 the tribe purchased 40 acres of almond groves.

Gaming. The tribe has proposed the development of a gaming facility at Highway 99 and Highway 149 in Butte County.

Real Estate/Commercial Development. In 1997, the tribe purchased 4 homes in Chico and another 26 homes in 1998. The homes, managed by the Chico Rancheria Housing Corporation, are leased to tribal members.

COMMUNITY FACILITIES AND SERVICES

The tribe operates childcare payment assistance, low-income heating and energy assistance, and Indian Child Welfare Act programs. The tribe also offers a youth program that aims to increase the academic achievement and high school graduation rate among tribal youth.

The tribe owns and maintains a tribal cemetery on the lands of the original ranch. It also maintains a tribal office complex and a community building.

Education. The Mechoopda Education Department offers financial assistance, higher education, adult education, vocational training, and employment support programs to tribal members.

Health Care. Health services are available through Northern Valley Indian Health. Clinics are located in Willows and Chico.

Services include medical, dental, outreach, WIC, and behavioral services programs.

ENVIRONMENTAL CONCERNS
The tribe maintains an environmental protection agency. This department oversees the enforcement of environmental ordinances and land management plans for tribal lands.

loverdale

Total area *(BIA realty, 2003)*	12.56 acres	
Individually owned	12.56 acres	
(BIA realty, 2003)		
Tribal enrollment *(BIA labor report, 2001)*	427	
Total labor force *(BIA labor report, 2001)*	204	
Unemployment rate	18%	
(BIA labor report, 2001)		
Unemployment rate *(Tribe, 2004)*	40%	

LOCATION AND LAND STATUS
The Cloverdale Rancheria is located in Cloverdale, California.

PHYSICAL DESCRIPTION
The soil on the reservation is comprised of shale and adobe.

CULTURE AND HISTORY
The Pomos originated in northern California. Tribal members lived along the Pacific coast and relied primarily on gathering shellfish and fishing. Seven indigenous languages are spoken within the Pomo Tribe. Though they are mutually unintelligible, the languages share a common link to the Hokan language group.

During the course of contact with Euro-Americans, the Pomos have been divided into numerous communities. In the early 1900s, 12 landless families of Pomo Indians were allotted 27.5 acres of land on the outskirts of Cloverdale, California. The tribe was terminated by PL85-671 in 1958. They were then reinstated following *Tillie Hardwick v. The United States of America* in 1983.

Although the Cloverdale Tribe has experienced great financial strain, members continue to hold fast to the desire to become an established, self-reliant people.

GOVERNMENT
The Cloverdale Rancheria is governed by a tribal council whose members include a chairperson, a vice-chairperson, a secretary, a treasurer, and a tribal representative. The tribal government is recognized by the secretary of the interior and operates tribal programs through various grants.

ECONOMY
Tribal economy is unstable. The location of the reservation in rural California has made the successful operation of businesses difficult. There is a high rate of unemployment, poor health services, and few funds to provide tribal services. The greatest source of income for the tribe is federal grants.

Government as Employer. The tribe employs 10 people.

Agriculture and Livestock. Although the tribe has pursued such endeavors as orchards and vineyards, the soil on the reserva-

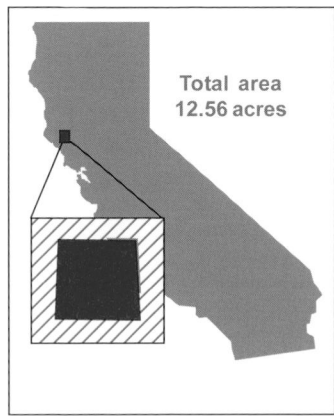

Total area
12.56 acres

Cloverdale Rancheria
of Pomo Indians
Federal reservation
Pomo
Sonoma County, California

Cloverdale Rancheria of Pomo
Indians
555 S. Cloverdale Blvd.
Suite A
Cloverdale, CA 95425
707-894-5775
707-894-5727 Fax

tion has proven to be inhospitable, and the crops did not yield any profits.

Gaming. The tribe has proposed the development of a casino on its tribal lands. The tribe is currently conducting an impact study of the proposed development to determine the best means to preserve water quality while still being able to complete the project.

INFRASTRUCTURE
The reservation is bisected by Highway 101.

COMMUNITY FACILITIES AND SERVICES
Education. Tribal youths attend schools in various counties.

Health Care. The tribe is part of the consortium of the Sonoma County Indian Health Project in Santa Rosa, California, and contracts with the BIA and Indian Health Services.

ENVIRONMENTAL CONCERNS
A city dump was developed on the northern border of the reservation. The presence of the disposal area has decreased property values and posed a threat to the health and well-being of reservation residents.

The tribe is currently exploring the possibility of establishing a casino on tribal lands. In this process, the tribe is participating in environmental impact studies. The site of the proposed casino is located by a tributary of the Russian River. The creek's water quality is being determined, and the effects that the casino would have on the water quality is also being explored.

Cold Springs

Cold Springs Rancheria
Federal reservation
Western Mono
Fresno County, California

Cold Springs Rancheria of
  Mono Indians of California
P.O. Box 209
32535 Sycamore Road
Tollhouse, CA 93667-0209
  559-855-5043
  559-855-4445 Fax

Total area *(BIA realty, 2003)*	154.65 acres
Total area *(Tribe, 2004)*	308 acres
Fed. Trust Lands *(Tribe, 2004)*	207 acres
Tribally owned *(Tribe,2004)*	25 acres
Allotted Lands *(Tribe, 2004)*	75 acres
Population *2000 census*	193
Population *(Tribe, 2004)*	185
Tribal enrollment *(BIA labor report, 2001)*	271
Total labor force *2000 census*	70
Total labor force *(Tribe, 2004)*	40
High school graduate or higher *2000 census*	59.8%
Bachelor's degree or higher *2000 census*	0%
Unemployment rate *2000 census*	5.71%
Unemployment rate *(Tribe, 2004)*	56%
Per capita income *2000 census*	$6,194

LOCATION AND LAND STATUS

The Cold Springs Rancheria is located in Fresno County. The rancheria is made up of 308 acres and 12 parcels. These parcels are actually in the city of Fresno. The rancheria sits in a remote valley called Sycamore Valley, near the Sierra Nevada foothills. The town of Tollhouse is nearby and Fresno is about 45 miles to the west. The Executive Order 2078 of November 10, 1914, established Cold Springs Rancheria. This order excluded Sierra National Forest lands.

CULTURE AND HISTORY

The Cold Springs Rancheria is mostly comprised of members of the Holkoma Band of Western Mono Tribe of Indians. One hundred years ago most of the Western Monos were still living on their ancestral homelands in the south-central Sierra Nevada of California. The tribe, like many other Native people in California, was considered "landless." About 1920, the federal government finally created three little rancherias for them. The allotment process allowed individual tribal members to acquire lands also.

The rancherias are very remote and therefore have never offered much economic opportunities for their inhabitants. The tribal men usually held jobs such as loggers, ranch hands, ropers, sheep shearers, miners, and woodchoppers. Tribal women often found employment in domestic jobs, hotels, hospitals, or convalescent facilities. Logging families in particular managed to sustain traditional gathering patterns because entire families would move to their logging homes during the summer and the Central Valley to pick crops during the reaping season. To this day Cold Spring inhabitants work in predominately lower-wage jobs.

In the 1950s many rancherias were terminated by the government, including two of the Mono's. Cold Springs, under the leadership of Frank Lee, not only maintained their federal status but positioned themselves to take advantage of new housing opportunities offered by HUD in the 1980s.

GOVERNMENT

All tribal members 18 years of age and older make up the general council of the Cold Springs Rancheria. The business council, made up of a chairperson, vice-chairperson, secretary-treasurer, and three members, is elected to staggered three-year terms. This council runs the affairs of the tribal government. The tribe is organized under a non-IRA constitution that was approved in 1980 and amended in 2001.

The tribal council duties include but are not limited to carrying out relations and agreements with other governments, economic development activities involving tribal resources, acquisition of new tribal territory, prescribing enrollment criteria, administering tribal assets and managing economic affairs and enterprises of the rancheria.

ECONOMY

The tribe has slowly been rebuilding its economic status, exploring enterprises that will yield profit for the tribe and assist in enhancing the well-being of tribal members. A steady source of employment on the reservation is provided by tribal, state, and federal agencies located there.

Government as Employer. A number of tribal members are employed by state, federal, and tribal government organizations. The tribal government employs a tribal administrator, fiscal officer, enrollment officer, ICWA director, social services intake worker, environmental director, environmental assistant/natural and cultural resources specialist, receptionist, health coordinator, community health representative, transporter, transportation planner, and transportation assistant. The California Indian Manpower Consortium employs about 15 people during the summer.

Agriculture and Livestock. The tribe believes the Cold Springs Rancheria is a good location for livestock projects, even though attempts to promote cattle raising have not been successful.

Economic Development. The tribe is continually looking for possible uses of tribal resources as well as economic development projects. Some options being considered include establishing a manufacturing and assembly plant or establishing a joint venture business relationship.

Manufacturing. Tribal members are employed in manufacturing jobs with firms such as Sierra Engineering. These jobs are not located on the reservation and require commuting. Because of the lack of local economic opportunities, in 1996 the tribe performed a study to find out if developing a small manufacturing and assembly plant on the rancheria was economically feasible. A plant has not been created at this time.

Industrial Parks. The tribe is striving to establish industrial development and increase tribal holdings by making contact with county, state, and federal representatives.

Tourism and Recreation. The Sierra Mono Museum, established in the 1970s, serves as an important source of cultural identity and practices for the region's Western Mono people. Located at North Fork, it maintains a number of collections and displays, supports demonstrations of traditional arts and skills, and gives classes in traditional culture such as basket making, beadwork, and language. The museum holds a popular event, the Annual Indian Fair Days, every August. It features traditional food, arts and crafts, dances and songs, and baseball games.

INFRASTRUCTURE

Currently the rancheria can be accessed off of State Highway 168. The tribe would like another access road and has been negotiating with the county supervisor and the Fresno Public Works Department.

Electricity. Electric power service is provided by Pacific Gas and Electric.

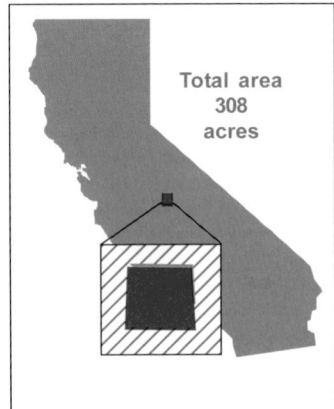

Total area
308
acres

Fuel. Bottled butane/propane is provided by suburban propane located in Auberry.
Water Supply. The rancheria owns the vast water system.

Transportation. As the nearest urban center, Fresno provides commercial bus, train, truck, and air service.

COMMUNITY FACILITIES AND SERVICES

Community facilities on the rancheria include a community center, the hub of the rancheria. The center houses the health project, Head Start program, and housing maintenance station. The tribal operations building houses tribal operations, social services programs, tribal environmental protection, and transportation. Other community facilities include a tribal fire and housing maintenance station, and a tribally owned church. The tribe is currently seeking funding for a multi-purpose facility which would include a gymnasium and offices. The rancheria receives federal assistance from the Bureau of Indian Affairs, Indian Health Service, and Environmental Protection Agency.

Education. Children attend Sierra Elementary School (Tollhouse), Foothill Middle School (Prather), and Sierra High School (Auberry); school buses provide transportation.

Health Care. Health care services are available to tribal members through Central Valley Indian Health. There are clinics located in Clovis, Prather, North Fork, and Lemoore. The IHS, in coordination with Clovis Central Valley Health Clinic, has provided funding for outpatient and transportation services to members. Fresno County Hospital also provides health care for tribal members.

Cold Springs

Colorado River

See Arizona

Colusa

Colusa

Total area *(Tribal source, 2004)*	573.22 acres
Federal trust lands	273.22 acres
Tribally owned lands	273.22 acres
(BIA realty, 2003)	
Population	20
Tribal enrollment *(BIA labor report, 2001)*	75
Total labor force *2000 census*	43
Total labor force *(BIA labor report, 2001)*	41
High school graduate or higher	70.3%
2000 census	
Bachelor's degree or higher	0%
2000 census	
Unemployment rate *2000 census*	16.3%
Unemployment rate	37%
(BIA labor report, 2001)	
Per capita income *2000 census*	$9,401

LOCATION AND LAND STATUS

The tribal lands of the Cachil Dehe Band of Wintun Indians of the Colusa Indian Community are located in central California. The reserved tribal lands consist of two parcels--the rancheria and the reservation. The first parcel, the rancheria, is over 60 acres. The second parcel, the reservation, comprises approximately 210 acres. The two areas are located four miles apart in the valley of the Sierra Mountains. They are approximately 200 miles inland from the Pacific coast. The tribe also purchased another 300 acres near the rancheria communities that is used for agricultural purposes.

CULTURE AND HISTORY

The residents of the Colusa Rancheria and Reservation are members the Cachil Dehe Band of the Wintun Indians Tribe. The tribe originated in the regions around the Sacramento River. The historic importance of the Sacramento River was as a provider of salmon, and as a meeting ground for exchange and trade. Currently, the Cachil Dehe Band is guaranteed the right to hunt and fish along the Sacramento River, which serves as the eastern boundary for the rancheria and is close to the reservation.

The Wintun people suffered devastating population losses due to the genocidal policies imposed upon them by Euro-American settlers. While the population of the tribe before European contact is estimated to be around 12,500, the 1990 census indicated that only 2,566 individuals claimed Wintun affiliation.

In addition to decimating Native populations, European arrival in southern California also brought negative effects upon the land. The introduction of cattle, hogs, and sheep destroyed numerous plant and bulb areas. Damage to streams and vegetation from copper-processing plants in the 1880s and early 1900s, and finally the inundation of lands by the construction of dams, dramatically decreased the Wintuns' ability to continue traditional subsistence practices.

Tribal members continue to practice numerous cultural traditions such as annual ceremonies, use of the roundhouse and sweat lodge on the reservation, healing ceremonies, and ceremonial dances. They also participate in other celebrations with the rancherias of Cortina, Rumsey, Grindstone, and Wintun. Members of these rancherias share a common cultural heritage in that they are all descended from the Wintun Tribe.

GOVERNMENT

The tribe is organized under an IRA constitution that was approved in 1941. The Colusa Rancheria is governed by the Colusa Indian Community Council. To vote in council elections, a community member must be at least 21 years old, have been a resident of the reservation or rancheria for at least one year, and be an enrolled member. The six-member tribal council is elected by the general council and is not financially compensated for its activities. The council is comprised of a chairman, a vice-chairman, and a secretary-treasurer. The tribal constitution allows for the creation of additional official positions. While the community has no tribal court or police force, they do employ an elaborate security force for the casino.

BUSINESS CORPORATION

The Tribal Economic Development Corporation is a tribally owned entity managed by tribal members, and reports to the tribal council. It oversees all water projects.

ECONOMY

Agriculture plays a significant part in the economic status of the tribe. The gaming industry has also become an essential factor to the tribe's income.

Agriculture and Livestock. Farming serves as an important source of tribal revenue and employment for the Colusa community. The tribe cultivates alfalfa, beans, wheat, and milo on 300 tribally owned acres. Individual tribal members also lease parcels of land from the tribe for agricultural purposes. The Sacramento

Cachil DeHe Band of Wintun Indians of the Colusa Indian Community
Federal reservation
Wintun
Colusa County, California

Cachil DeHe Band of Wintun Indians of the Colusa Indian Community
P.O. Box 8
Colusa, CA 95932
530-458-8231
530-458-2018 Fax

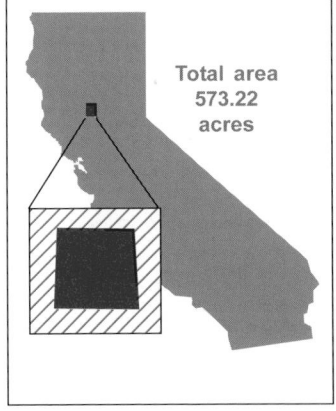

Total area
573.22
acres

Colusa

River supplies water used for irrigation purposes; this water is used to irrigate the community's 20-year-old English walnut orchard. The 300-acre parcel of community land has numerous irrigation ditches, supplied by groundwater pumps.

Gaming. Colusa Casino is a 50,000-square-foot gaming facility owned and operated by the tribe. It offers over 775 coin slot machines, 12 table games, 6 poker tables, and 850 bingo seats. The casino is the only one in Northern California to offer craps games. Facilities include a bar and grille, an entertainment showroom, and a gift and sundries shop. The casino employs 425 individuals. The tribe is in the process of developing improvement plans which will include expansion of the casino and construction of an adjacent hotel.

INFRASTRUCTURE
Interstate 5 and State highways 45 and 20 are the major routes to the Colusa Indian Community.

Electricity. Pacific Gas and Electric supplies electricity paid for by the community as a whole. Community homes are heated by wood and pellet stoves and by propane gas.

Water Supply. Water is available to rancheria members through a community water system. Three domestic wells comprise the system that serves two housing communities, the tribal administration complex, and the health center. The casino has a private well and wastewater system. All eight houses located on the rancheria utilize individual septic tanks. In 2002, the tribe hired an outside consultant to conduct a study of tribal water resources.

ENVIRONMENTAL CONCERNS
The Wintun's devout concern for protecting burial grounds and other sacred places is continually being challenged by developers of new subdivisions, highways, and general construction. The protection of Mount Shasta as a viable sacred place is a major issue for the Wintuns. Environmentalists have joined them in this concern to protect the mountain from development.

The study identified 4,511 acre-feet of groundwater storage beneath the rancheria. The water is hydraulically connected to the Sacramento River, and the activity on that river affects the flow to the rancheria.

Transportation. The towns of Colusa and Chico have small airports. The nearest major airport is located 60 miles south of Colusa in Sacramento. Bus service is available in Williams. The Southern Pacific Railroad stops in Colusa.

COMMUNITY FACILITIES AND SERVICES
A community center was completed in January 1995. The center was set to house a tribal health clinic, a conference room, and the library. The center is located on the reservation, and the tribal offices will remain in the casino. The tribe anticipates adding a playground to these facilities. The community also has a 500-gallon-capacity fire truck, and a volunteer firefighting force will be established.

Education. Children attend schools in the nearby Colusa.

Health Care. The Colusa Indian Health Community Council provides health services to the Cachil Dehe Band Wintun Colusa Community and the Colusa Indian Community. There are clinics in Arbuckle and Colusa. The tribe also operates a community health and wellness center, including a kidney dialysis center. Hospital, clinics, and dental facilities are also available in Colusa.

Housing. Homes on the rancheria were built by HUD in 1990 and 1994. Housing remains scarce, and many members live outside the rancheria and reservation.

Cortina

Cortina Indian Rancheria
Federal reservation
Cortina Band of Wintun Indians
Colusa County, California

Cortina Indian Rancheria
P.O. Box 1630
Williams, CA 95987
530-473-3274
530-473-3301 Fax

TRI-CA-017 Cortina Rancheria Sign

LOCATION AND LAND STATUS
The Cortina Indian Rancheria is located 70 miles northwest of Sacramento and 15 miles west of Arbuckle. The Cortina Rancheria was established by Order of the Secretary of the Interior on June 6, 1907, setting aside 160 acres for the exclusive use of this band of Wintun Indians. This action was pursuant to the Act of Congress of January 12, 1881, creating a Mission Indian Commission, which was charged with selecting a reservation for each band of Mission Indians residing in California. Subsequently, Cortina acquired an additional 480 acres by Order of the Secretary on July 20, 1907. A trust patent was issued on June 6, 1958, authorizing the U.S. government to hold the aggregate 640 acres in trust for the Cortina Band of Indians. This tribe is looking for additional suitable lands to purchase.

PHYSICAL DESCRIPTION
The Cortina Indian Rancheria spans 640 acres of steep, heavily wooded terrain. The far western section of the rancheria is bounded by Strode Canyon, which gradually descends toward relatively flat terrain.

CULTURE AND HISTORY
Cortina Rancheria tribal members are descendants of the Wintun Tribe, which traditionally occupied the greater Sacramento Valley region. The term "Wintun" is used to refer to the language group of Wintu, Nomlaki, and Patwin belonging to the Penutian linguistic family.

Early European contact in the region came when Spanish settlers arrived via Mexico by 1808. Hudson Bay Company trappers arrived sometime before 1832. As elsewhere, the imposi-

tion of European culture had devastating effects upon the Native people of the region. Tribal unity was destroyed by the taking of land and the destruction of traditional food and material-gathering areas. The introduction of cattle, hogs, and sheep destroyed numerous plant and bulb areas. Copper-processing plants in the 1880s and early 1900s, along with construction of dams, severely damaged streams and vegetation. These things took their toll on the health and survival of the Wintuns and other area tribes. In the early days of California statehood, Congress attempted to herd all the Indians onto four major reservations, against the wishes of the various tribes who had profound attachments to their Native areas.

Since the early 1970s, the Wintuns have achieved an incredible revitalization. While the tribe continues to strive for its own economic independence and development, it has managed to overturn the termination proceedings that were previously underway. Wintun groups are challenged by environmental issues, tribal reorganization and recognition, and the continuance of traditional and religious activities.

GOVERNMENT
The Cortina Indian Rancheria is governed by a general council composed of all tribal members 18 years and older. Thirty percent of the general council represents a quorum. The council's business committee is composed of five elected members and one member-at-large. A chairperson, vice-chairperson, secretary, and treasurer are officers of the business committee. The tribal constitution was developed under provisions of the IRA and approved in 1973. As a PL-638 nation, the tribe contracts

child care, housing, health, education, and roads services through the BIA.

The Cortina Environmental Court was established by the band to handle appeals from judicial actions or decisions made by the Wintun Environmental Protection Agency Board. The court exercises jurisdiction over matters as provided by tribal law. In accordance with the Cortina Band of Wintun Indians Rules of Procedure (2004), the environmental court possesses the authority to decide upon disagreements stemming from decisions of various tribal administrative agencies, as well as other matters that fall within its jurisdiction.

ECONOMY
The agricultural industry is the leading force in the local economy. Although the tribe does not maintain any operations in the industry, agriculture does provide the largest source of employment in the area.

Economic Development Projects. In 1994 Earthworks Industries completed a comprehensive environmental assessment for the Cortina Indian Rancheria, including environmental impact studies. As a result of this study, the tribe proposes: to continue focusing on developing the Cortina Integrated Waste Management and Recycling System; to create a multipurpose recreation, game, and exhibit field for activities and fund-raising projects; to develop an arts and crafts retail shop; and to pursue cultural preservation and enhancement projects, including classes in the various Native traditions and crafts. Of the 640 acres, approximately 200 acres, are available for economic development.

Agriculture and Livestock. The tribe does not operate any enterprises in the agricultural industry, though much of the land in Colusa county is devoted to agriculture, the primary industry and chief source of employment in the area. A wide variety of crops are produced in the county, including rice, tomatoes, sugar beets, prunes, and nuts. The highly mechanized nature of the area's agricultural sector has contributed to the region's decreasing employment opportunities. Agricultural development has been limited to small individual gardens located near the residential area.

INFRASTRUCTURE
The nearest major route is Interstate 5, east of the rancheria. State Highway 20 lies six miles to the northwest and connects with a new, all-weather road (Spring Valley Road) leading to Cortina Rancheria. State Route 16 lies 16 miles west and connects to Rumsey Rancheria.

Electricity. Pacific Gas and Electric provides electricity to the rancheria.

Fuel. There is no gas service to the rancheria. Residents use wood and bottled LP gas for heating and cooking.

Water Supply. In 2003, the community's water system was completely restructured. A water treatment plant was constructed, and a water storage tank with a capacity of 10,000 gallons was installed. A HUD Community Drinking Water System Grant has enabled the tribe to install a community drinking water reverse osmosis system on the reservation. Residents rely on separate septic tanks and drain field systems for sewage services.

Transportation. The Southern Pacific railroad line runs north-south through Arbuckle, 17 miles east. Air service is available in Sacramento, 70 miles from the rancheria, or in Redding, 120 miles away.

TRI-CA-018 Cortina Rancheria's Tribal Office

Telecommunications. With the help of the U.S. EPA, the community has a satellite dish for e-mail access and a wireless network for Internet capabilities. The tribe is currently researching the option of wireless phones.

COMMUNITY FACILITIES AND SERVICES
The rancheria offers members use of a community building, a utility trailer providing his/her bathroom and shower facilities, and a ceremonial prayer rock located near a year-round spring. A library is being built. An archaeologically sensitive bedrock mortar pit exists in upper Strode Canyon. In addition, a ceremonial roundhouse is located on the flat northeastern portion of the rancheria, near the community building.

Cortina Rancheria has received a portion of the Indian Housing Block Grant funds made available to California Native-American communities. During the late 1990s and early 2000s, the rancheria population increased from one to 26 people, tribal and non-tribal members. The tribe anticipates further growth and intends to increase the housing facilities from 10 to 15 homes in the near future. In 2000, the rancheria participated in California Federal Bank's Native-American Mortgage Program through the Native American Housing Assistance and Self-Determination Act of 1966 (NAHASDA) to assist tribal members with obtaining mortgages to buy homes off the reservation.

Education. Children attend schools in Williams. Language classes are offered at the community center.

Health Care. Northern Valley Indian Health serves the Cortina Indian Rancheria. Clinics are located in Willows and Chico. They provide dental, medical, behavioral health services, outreach, and WIC programs.

ENVIRONMENTAL CONCERNS
The Wintun Environmental Protection Agency (WEPA) serves to protect and improve the environmental and cultural resources of the tribe through collaboration and cooperation with local, state, tribal, and federal agencies. The tribe seeks to protect the environment within the boundaries of the rancheria and specifically seeks to prevent unreasonable air, ground, water, and soil pollution. The tribe has established a tribal environmental inventory and a tribal environmental plan to work toward these goals. WEPA oversees the EPA General Assistance Program, National Environmental Information Exchange Network, EPA Nonpoint Source, EPA Clean Water, EPA Clear Air Act, BIA Water Resources Management Planning, BOR Water Resource Study, HUD Community Drinking Water System, Natural Resources Conservation Services, and FEMA Chemical Emergency Response Planning grants. The agency maintains tribal air, watershed protection, pesticide, solid waste reduction and education, cultural resources management, and natural resources management programs.

Cortina

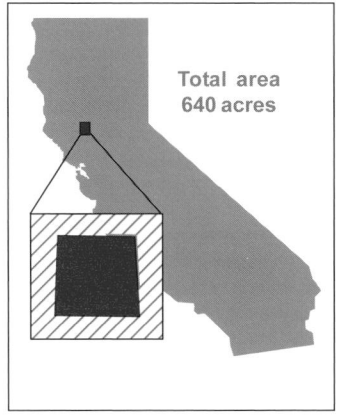

Total area
640 acres

Total area
(BIA realty, 2003)
640 acres

Tribally owned
(BIA realty, 2003)
640 acres

Population
29

Tribal enrollment
(BIA labor report, 2001)
136

Total labor force
2000 census
4

Total labor force
(BIA, 2001)
68

High school graduate or higher
2000 census
0%

Bachelor's degree or higher
2000 census
0%

Unemployment rate
(BiA labor report, 2001)
49%

Per capita income
2000 census
$17,350.00

Coyote Valley

Coyote Valley Band of Pomo Indians Reservation
Federal reservation
Pomo
Mendocino County, California

Coyote Valley Band of Pomo
Indians
7751 North State Street
P.O. Box 39
Redwood Valley, CA 95470
707-485-8723
707-485-1247 Fax

Total area *(Tribal source, 2004)*
76 acres

Total area *(BIA realty, 2003)*
71.76 acres

Tribally owned *(BIA realty, 2003)*
71.76 acres

Population *2000 census*
104

Tribal enrollment
(Tribal source, 2004)
350

Tribal enrollment
(BIA labor report, 2001)
358

Total labor force *2000 census*
34

Total labor force
(BIA labor report, 2001)
182

High school graduate or higher
2000 census
72.7%

Bachelor's degree or higher
2000 census
6.1%

Unemployment rate
2000 census
5.88%

Unemployment rate
(BIA labor report, 2001)
54%

Per capita income
2000 census
$10,948

LOCATION AND LAND STATUS

The Coyote Valley Reservation is located in northwestern California, 8 miles north of the town of Ukiah. It is bounded on the south and west by Forsythe Creek. U.S. Highway 101 runs along its northern border.

The original Coyote Valley Reservation, 101 acres reserved by an Executive Order in 1909, was purchased by the U.S. Army Corps of Engineers in 1957 for the Coyote Valley Dam site. Terminated at that time, the Coyote Valley Tribal Council reorganized in 1976 and purchased their current property using a community development block grant. The land was taken into federal trust status that same year.

CLIMATE

There is no climate data recorded for Redwood Valley, California; however, data was recorded for Calpella, a community located only three miles south of the reservation. Daily high temperatures average 74°F. Daily low temperatures average 43.6°F. The area receives just over 37 inches of precipitation annually, with less than an inch falling as snow.

CULTURE AND HISTORY

Residents of the Coyote Valley Reservation are descendants of the Shodakai Pomo who were living in Coyote Valley at the time of initial white contact in the early nineteenth century. The Pomo language belongs to the Hokan language family, which includes languages spoken by peoples from southern Oregon to southern Mexico.

Nineteenth-century settlers and the U.S. Department of War forced the Pomo people onto the Mendocino Reservation, at Fort Bragg, and later onto the reservation established at Round Valley. Their numbers and solidarity were disastrously affected by disease and enforced incarceration. Yet despite the odds against them, the Pomos on the Mendocino Reservation formed new coalitions in order to buy their land back during the late 1870s and 1880s.

One such group formed an organization called the Redwood Valley Tribe, which purchased seven acres of Coyote Valley land at the end of 1878. Usually no more than five or six households occupied the property at any one time, and the families would often have to travel long distances to obtain food by hunting and gathering. Unfortunately, this land was sold by a foreclosure action to the highest bidder, by order of the Mendocino County Superior Court in April 1928.

Land for the original Coyote Valley Reservation was purchased by the U.S. government in 1909 and held in federal trust status for the landless Pomos. The land consisted of 101 acres in three distinct sections: river bottom, sloping hillside, and flat terrace land overlooking the valley. The soils of the reservation were poor, and water for agricultural purposes was hard to obtain. Principal vegetation consisted of manzanita, brush oak, live oak, and poison oak.

Local Indians did not occupy the reservation until the late 1930s, when a number of families established homes and small garden plots. Because of the depletion of native plants and game, the Pomos turned to the wage economy rather than using traditional methods for subsistence. The men turned to working for others in agricultural labor, and the women often worked as domestics.

During a political climate of intense separatism and animosity toward indigenous peoples, the Coyote Valley Pomos actively used the courts to challenge local segregationist policies. In 1907,

an Eastern Pomo man, Ethan Anderson, won a court case giving non-reservation Indians the right to vote. In 1923, Stephan Knight of Mendocino County challenged the state school segregation laws, and in an out-of-court settlement forced a local public school to admit his daughter. Knight later took on the City of Ukiah, challenging the segregationist policy of the local movie theater, on behalf of his granddaughter.

When the Army Corps of Engineers offered to buy their land in 1949 for construction of the Coyote Valley Dam, tribal members were afraid that the probable condemnation of their land would drastically reduce its value; however, they had little choice but to accept. In 1957, each of the nine remaining assignees received a small amount of money for their land improvements and were required to leave. The reservation was terminated that year U.S. federal government.

In February 1976, the Pomos once again used the courts to protect their civil liberties in a successful attempt to reverse their terminated status. The two actions of *Eddie Knight, et al v. Thomas L. Kleppe, et al* in U.S. District Court concluded that the termination of the Coyote Valley Reservation in 1957 was invalid and that all dependent members were not terminated, and they were thus entitled, unless otherwise ineligible, to federal services provided to Indians. After this decision, the Coyote Valley Tribal Council reorganized (1976), and purchased a 57.76-acre parcel of land a few miles north of Ukiah in 1979.

Residents of the Coyote Valley Reservation strive to keep their traditional culture a part of their modern lives. Members participate in the Coyote Valley Kaiwia Dancers and have taken part in cultural, social, and ceremonial events throughout the state. Reservation children are taught the Pomo language.

GOVERNMENT

The Coyote Valley Band of Pomo Indians is governed by a seven-member elected tribal council, which includes a chairperson, vice-chairperson, secretary, historian, treasurer, and two members. The general council, comprised of all tribal members at least 18 years old, retains ultimate governmental authority and is led by an elected tribal chief. The tribe has its own tribal court of justice, initiated in September 2001, and it acts as the lead Tribe in a memorandum of agreement for a five-tribe consortium implementing the Indian Child Welfare Act. A youth court was in the planning stages in 2004. The tribe contracts many of the BIA's programs under PL-638. The tribe employs six full-time law enforcement officers, and in 2004 it was planning the development of fire protection services.

ECONOMY

Agriculture and Livestock. The tribe is considering the development of an organic native plant nursery which would provide seeds for native plants of the area to commercial markets.

Gaming. The 10,000-square-foot Coyote Valley Shodakai Casino, located in Redwood Valley just off Highway 101, features almost 400 slot machines, blackjack, and bingo. Tournament play is offered on a regular basis. There is a smoke shop on the casino premises, as well as a restaurant, gift shop, coffee bar, and cafe.

Services and Retail. The majority of employed tribal members work in the service industry. The tribe engages in gaming that features small retail services. It is considering the feasibility of opening a convenience store along U.S. 101, and it would like to

TRI-CA-019

TRI-CA-020

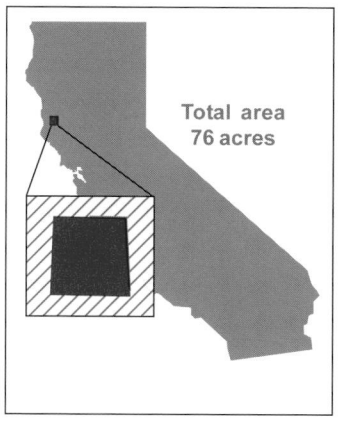

Coyote Valley

Total area
76 acres

TRI-CA-019 Coyote Valley Tribal Police Department

TRI-CA-020 Coyote Valley Tribal Housing Authority Logo on truck

buy a 10-acre vineyard. Four of the vineyard acres would be converted and used for building 10 additional housing units.

Tourism and Recreation. The scenic beauty of the Mendocino coastline draws many tourists to the area. At nearby Mendocino Lake, the former site of Coyote Valley Reservation, the tribe has a five-year lease with the U.S. Army Corps of Engineers to use the Lake Mendocino Interpretive Cultural and Visitor Center to present educational programs about the Pomos and other Native-American cultures. The annual Big Time event, similar to a festival, is celebrated with Pomo dancers, a salmon feed, and hand grass games.

INFRASTRUCTURE
U.S. Highway 101 borders the reservation on the west and serves as the main artery for the area. Bus and freight services are available in Ukiah, 8 miles away; there are no nearby commercial airports.

Water Supply. The reservation is served by community water facilities and by the Redwood Valley Water District. The tribe hopes to implement a Tribal Drinking Water Set Aside program in the future. There is a community sewer system on the reservation. Solid waste disposal is handled by Mendocino County.

COMMUNITY FACILITIES AND SERVICES
Community facilities on the reservation include a 30-unit housing project, a basketball court, a spa, weight room, community center, and a recreation and education facility. The community center has a gymnasium, swimming pool, locker room facilities, and a kitchen.

The California Indian Manpower Consortium provides employment services for all community members. Vocational training, money for uniforms, and equipment for individuals are all made available.

Education. Children attend area public schools. In addition, the tribe hosts a tribal learning center where adult literacy, computer training, and tutoring programs are available. There is a preschool daycare, and a California State-funded Indian Education Center, providing supplemental academic support to school aged youth on the reservation.

Health Care. The tribe is a member of the Consolidated Health Consortium which serves eight Mendocino County tribes at an Indian Health Service Clinic. Medical, mental health, and dental care services are provided.

ENVIRONMENTAL CONCERNS
The mission of the tribal environmental program is to "seek to plan environmental projects that will inform and inspire all tribal members; that are compatible with traditional tribal mores; that will bring tribal youth to full flower of their potential." During the summer of 2000, the regional water board staff worked in partnership with the Coyote Valley Tribal Environmental Protection Agency's Youth Program. It employed reservation youth from ages 14 to 21. The program's goals were to build leadership, provide environmental science and other employment skills, and demonstrate environmental projects that best protect tribal interests and needs. Together they established a water-sampling site on the West Fork Russian River in Ukiah; implemented a community recycling program; devised a solar street lighting project; built an electric vehicle in a special demonstration program; initiated erosion control techniques along Forsythe Creek, and mitigated vernal wetlands utilizing revegetation and trail maintenance techniques; monitored nonpoint source pollution; introduced programs toward the eradication of invasive species such as arundo donax and vinca; planted an organic garden; and furthered native species propagation and planting.

Coyote Valley Tribal EPA works with other agencies: the Mendocino County Water Agency, California Fish and Game, and the water quality control board, in an effort to protect ground and surface water and to restore and enhance aquatic habitats. The tribe is a member of the Forsyth Creek Restoration Steering Committee which is working to restore one-eighth mile of the Russian River, a critical habitat for coho salmon and trout. They are also currently working wth the U.S. EPA to acquire a new water storage tank and water treatment facilities for the reservation. Water quantity and quality remains the single most pressing environmental issue in Redwood Valley. Coyote Valley's EPA program was recognized as an "Honoree" in 2002 by Harvard University's Honoring Nations program.

Cuyapipe
See Ewiiaapaayp

Coyote Valley

Honoring Nations Honoree 2002

Text in its entirety from: The Harvard Project On American Indian Economic Development

John F. Kennedy School of Government Harvard University

Honoring Nations Honoree 2002

Coyote Valley Tribal EPA
Coyote Valley Band of Pomo Indians (Redwood Valley, California)

Established in 1991 with the cooperation of the US Environmental Protection Agency, the Coyote Valley Tribal EPA merges two important protection initiatives into a single, mutually reinforcing effort. By empowering youth through training in environmental protection, the Coyote Valley Band of Pomo Indians not only protects the reservation environment for future generations but also protects the Tribe's most precious resource: the Coyote Valley Pomo youth themselves.

The Coyote Valley Band of Pomo Indians believes that land and water are sacred and must be cared for with reverence. Regrettably, the Pomo Indians' determination to protect and preserve their traditional homelands has been thwarted since European contact-in the 1850s and 1860s, the Pomo were repeatedly dispossessed of their lands. Not surprisingly, this pattern struck at the population's vibrancy. According to the 1910 census, the once populous, prosperous people had been reduced to 1,200 survivors. Throughout these difficult years, the few Pomo bands that managed to stay on their original territories served as a source of strength and continuity for the larger community. The Coyote Valley Band was among these. However, the 1950s, a period in which federal policy emphasized the termination tribal rights, repeated the injustices of the previous century. The Coyote Valley Band was both terminated by the US government and, in 1957, dispossessed when the Army Corp of Engineers flooded its original reservation to create Lake Mendocino. Only in 1975 were the Coyote Valley Pomo finally able to restore their tribal rights and, in 1979, secure the eighty acres of land that comprise their current reservation.

Just as the pattern of dispossession took its toll on the Pomo during the late nineteenth century, the twentieth-century experience of termination and dispossession also left its mark-particularly in terms of environmental and social ills. For the Coyote Valley Band, environmental degradation has been among the most overt problems. In the past several decades, parts of the reservation were used as a dumping ground for discarded automobiles, littering was commonplace, and the creeks and streams running through the reservation were neglected. More serious still have been the social ills experienced by the Band's three hundred members, many of which have been most notable among tribal youth. Full-time attendance in the public school system has been low, and at a number of points over the last decade, Coyote Valley Pomo students have had a zero percent graduation rate. Drug and alcohol abuse have been widespread problems as well.

In 1991, the Band launched an innovate effort to combat both of these concerns. With funding from the US Environmental Protection Agency, the Band formed the Coyote Valley Tribal EPA, youth-focused tribal program that enables the Coyote Valley Pomo and the federal government's regional EPA office to partner in addressing water quality issues on the reservation. Since its inception, the Tribal EPA has grown from a summer water-testing program into a comprehensive program that educates Pomo youth in environmental monitoring skills and provides summer and after-school jobs for up to fifteen youth a year. Critically, the Tribal EPA is a means by which the Band can address youth problems directly by offering and encouraging productive activities. The Tribal EPA expects its youth employees and participants to attend school. It expects them to attend to their responsibilities on time, sober, and ready to learn. And, it teaches them

to look beyond themselves by addressing the environmental ills of the reservation. Youth who participate in the program gain both character education and practical science skills, as they become versed in recycling systems, water quality monitoring, erosion control, revegetation efforts, riverine habitat assessment, and air quality assessment.

Having first assumed responsibility for themselves, the Tribal EPA youth have in turn assumed responsibility for the reservation environment. Today, most discarded automobiles have been removed. The Tribal EPA's robust recycling program has positively changed community behavior, and the students are leading a successful effort to reduce littering on the reservation. In addition to participating in these efforts, the Tribal EPA youth monitor and maintain a stretch of Forsythe Creek that runs through the heart of the reservation. They concern themselves not only with water quality, but also with the preservation and protection of the surrounding banks. In addition, the Tribal EPA has produced four educational slide shows to promote local environmental protection titled "Recycle or Else," "The Wide, Wild, Wonderful World of Water and Waste," "The Gathering Garden," and "Lost Waters: The Restoration of Forsythe Creek."

Indeed, Tribal EPA youth are playing a crucial role in facilitating environmental improvement of reservation lands and waters. Significantly, new and productive government-to-government partnerships have made much of this work possible. The Coyote Valley Tribal EPA was founded through a Clean Water Act Grant from the US EPA in 1991. In 1998, it was awarded a General Assistance Program Grant from the Bureau of Indian Affair (BIA), in 2000, it received a BIA Water Studies grant award, and in 2002, it was awarded a Nonpoint Source Pollution Grant from the US EPA to implement stream restoration work on both Forsythe Creek and the Russian River. In addition to the US EPA and BIA, the Tribal EPA has worked with the Mendocino County Water Agency, the State Regional Water Quality Board, the California Department of Fish and Game, and the US Department of Agriculture's Soils and Water Conservation Service. The Band's intention to develop a Fisheries Management Plan has resulted in an additional partnership with the National Marine Fisheries Service.

The broader benefits of these partnerships mean that the impact of the Coyote Valley Tribal EPA extends well beyond its success in reversing serious environmental degradation on the reservation: The Tribal EPA has contributed to the strength of the Band as a whole. Partnerships have made it possible for Coyote Valley to initiate and operate the Tribal EPA - itself an expression of sovereignty that underscores the Band's commitment to self-governance. Additional government-strengthening benefits include enhanced interactions between the tribal government and other governments, expanded jurisdiction, and increased respect on behalf of state and federal agencies for the Band and its traditions. Moreover, Tribal EPA partnerships have resulted in the Band's involvement in environmental initiatives outside of the reservation's boundaries. For example, staff of the Tribal EPA sit on the executive committee of the Forsythe Creek Watershed Assessment, which brings together all stakeholders in watershed work; and in the near future, the Tribal EPA will participate in the Russian River Calibration Study. Additionally, tribal elders, Tribal Council members, Tribal EPA staff, and volunteer tribal youth have met twice with state and federal agency representatives to negotiate Band citizens' right to continue the traditional gathering and ceremonial use of fish that are listed as threatened or endangered by the US Fish and Wildlife Service.

Besides strengthening the Coyote Valley Band's government, these productive interactions endow Tribal EPA youth with respect for their government, increased confidence in their own abilities to act as citizens of a sovereign Indian nation, and a greater sense of empowerment through exposure to and mastery of challenging topics. This may be the Tribal EPA's greatest success-and it is achieved in very practical ways. Through the Tribal EPA, youth who may not have committed many hours to formal education find themselves in a learning environment that is, according to the monitoring coordinator of the Regional Water Board, a "cut above a classroom experience." Non-tribal conservationists and watershed experts hold the program in high regard for engaging youth, for teaching them scientific skills utilized by professionals on the job, and for providing a caring community apart from home and school. Non-Native parents familiar with the program are also enthusiastic about the program's ability to engage the youth. "I would love for my kids to have access to this program," one parent insisted. "The teenagers involved are excited about science and about learning. I wish my own children could be a part of something this interesting and educational."

By learning to respect and protect the environment, Tribal EPA youth are investing in their own futures and in the future of the Tribe. Working with the Regional Water Board to monitor water quality, the youth learn to focus intently on building the skills that the work demands. They no longer look upon their rivers as places to dump trash or to party. Instead, they have worked to restore Forsythe Creek, an effort that required careful planning, trail rebuilding and maintenance, the management of invasive flora, and the reintroduction of traditional willow and sedge. And, the teens' Tribal EPA work encourages them to look beyond

reservation boundaries to understand themselves and their efforts in a larger context. Each summer, for example, the Tribal EPA takes youth staff and volunteers to assess different riverine habitats in Mendocino County. They have visited the mouth of the Navarro River, the Big River tidal estuary, the Middle Fork of the Eel River, the salmon spawning grounds of the upper Noyo River, the ancient redwoods along the Albion River, and the Sinkyone Wilderness at Usal on the North coast. In shifting youth attitudes, the Tribe succeeds in protecting its own future.

Through the establishment of the Tribal EPA, the Coyote Valley Tribe effectively enhanced its own future by enlisting its youth in an effort to protect and preserve the reservation environment. Engaging youth in environmental protection has become, among the Pomo, one of the most effective strategies for protecting the youth themselves. It is a strategy that other governments - Indian and non-Indian alike - can learn from and be inspired by.

Lessons
Tribal governments that employ youth through after-school jobs and internships receive a dual benefit: they tap a pool of inexpensive talent whose work advances tribal interests, and they provide valuable "real-world" experience and training to future leaders and professionals.

Tribal governments should look to youth for fresh ideas and insights. Involving youth in planning, policy development, and policy implementation contributes to an environment that is able to attract and retain talent.

Non-Indian jurisdictions that surround or abut tribal communities can benefit from tribal input. Through participation in local and regional commissions, boards, and committees, tribal governments can share expertise, information, and resources - which helps build positive intergovernmental relations and fruitful partnerships.

Coyote Valley

Honoring Nations
Honoree 2002

Text in its entirety from:
The Harvard Project On
American Indian Economic
Development

John F. Kennedy School
of Government
Harvard University

Dry Creek

Dry Creek

LOCATION AND LAND STATUS
Dry Creek Rancheria is located in northern California, between Cloverdale and Healdsburg along the Russian River in Geyserville. Privately owned vineyards of the Alexander Valley, a valley known for its winemaking tradition, border some of the tribal lands. Dry Creek Valley lies between Porter Creek Fault and Mount Jackson Fault. The tribal and total acreage is 75, with no individual acreage. The area at one time consisted of 86,400 acres.

PHYSICAL DESRIPTION
Ridges with conifers on the highest crests; wet, low places; and deep ravines make up the topography. Soils vary from well-graded sandy gravels and fine gravel to slightly plastic silts and sandy clay.

CULTURE AND HISTORY
Dry Creek Valley is one of the traditional homes of the Pomo Indians. The Pomos are part of the Hokan language family and descendants of early inhabitants of the Alexander Valley who date back 12,000 years; as many as 200 Pomos are able to trace their ancestry back to these prehistoric residents. Seventy tribes have been linked to the Pomo Indians. The heritage of some of the Dry Creek Valley residents link directly to the ancient village site of Aca Modot, and the Mahikaune Pomo dialect is still in use.

The Dry Creek Rancheria was established in 1915 and has maintained its economic and demographic sovereignty into the twenty-first century. The tribe has a strong community, despite being assimilated into American society.

Several hundred regional plants and animals were relied on for food, with acorns as the main harvest. The creation of basketry allowed the Pomos to gather food and to supply cradles for babies. The basketry was intricate and to this day remains an important part of Pomo culture. Ornate jewelry was created for tribal ceremonies and for trade. Shaped clamshells were crafted for use as money and trade.

Europeans, Russians, and Americans exploited the Pomo Indians throughout the nineteenth and twentieth centuries. Tribal members refer to the "Death March" of the mid-1800s as the most destructive time in the tribe's history. During this time, the federal government relocated the Pomo Indians to two new reservations. They were forced to leave their land to make way for the large influx of American settlers in search of new lives and the prospect of California gold. For decades, the Pomos were forcibly relocated from area to area.

Construction of a dam that involved the Dry Creek Valley area was started in 1972. The Warm Springs/Lake Sonoma Project included an earth dam, a reservoir, spillways, a fish hatchery,

Dry Creek Rancheria
Federal reservation
Pomo
Sonoma County, California

Dry Creek Rancheria
3250 Hwy 128 E
P.O. Box 607
Geyserville, CA 95441
707-473-2178
707-473-2171 Fax
drycreekrancheria.org

Total area *(BIA realty, 2003)*
75 acres

Tribally owned *(BIA realty, 2003)*
75 acres

Population *2000 census*
53

Tribal enrollment
583

Dry Creek

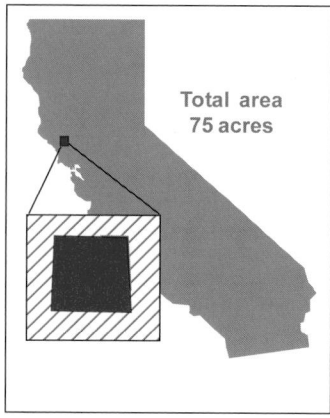

Total area
75 acres

Total labor force *2000 census*
20

High school graduate or higher
2000 census
41.7%

Bachelor's degree or higher
2000 census
0%

Unemployment rate
2000 census
20%

Per capita income
$5,702

recreational areas, and a visitors' building. A public hearing was held in 1976 to discuss protecting the natural resources that the Pomo Indians relied on, including the archeological significance of the Dry Creek Valley area. The Army Corps of Engineers agreed to relocate sedge, willow, lobatium, and angelica to areas unaffected by the project. Sedge and willow plants from the Dry Creek Valley area are used in making some of the finest baskets in the world. The protection of these plants allowed Pomo basket makers to continue their craft. The Indians held a ceremony to commemorate the process. Petroglyphs were relocated, and a critical habitat zone evaluation was started, as was a Pomo Food Interpretive Project. To help orient visitors to Pomo culture, a visitor center with an interpretive museum was built. A Pomo language project also was created. The original tribal territory, along with many of the 65 prehistoric and 45 historic sites, are now under water.

GOVERNMENT
The Dry Creek Rancheria is a member of the Intertribal Court of California (ICC). The ICC was chartered by a consortium of small Indian tribes to address legal issues best served by a tribal court authorized under their collective judicial authorities. The purpose of the court is to hear and settle on-reservation housing disputes and Indian child welfare cases. Mediation and peace-making services are also provided under the court's authority.

ECONOMY
A casino has bolstered the rancheria's economic base, allowing the tribe more opportunities for economic self-reliance.

Government as Employer. The Dry Creek Rancheria's tribal government employs five people.

Gaming. The River Rock Casino, located at 3250 Highway 128 East in Geyserville, California, is owned and operated by the Dry Creek Rancheria Band of Pomo Indians. It became fully operational in 2003. It is the closest casino to the Bay Area, "just over an hour north of the Golden Gate Bridge." The casino has 1,600 state-of-the-art slot machines; 16 table games featuring Pai Gow poker, blackjack, and three-card poker; and three restaurants. Approximately 550 people are employed by River Rock

Casino, making it one of the largest employers in the area. In 2003 it brought in $69 million, which created an estimated $26 million in local wages. Since the casino has prospered so well, it has become a large regional financial donor. It provides financial help to the local volunteer fire department, a local hospital, and the Geyserville Unified School District.

Manufacturing. Pomo Indians are known for their exquisite basket making. Historic and contemporary basketry is sold in the Spirit Gift Shop at the River Rock Casino.

Tourism and Recreation. Casino-bound motor coaches transport busloads of gamblers from the Bay Area to the rancheria's casino. The Wine Creek Room located at the casino features local wines from Alexander Valley wineries.

INFRASTRUCTURE
Fuel. Households in Dry Creek Rancheria are fueled by bottled, tank, or LP gas. There is no gas utility.

COMMUNITY FACILITIES AND SERVICES
Public Safety. The community has a volunteer fire department.

Education. Tribal members attend area schools and colleges. The tribe has agreed to donate $300,000 of the revenue from the River Rock Casino to the Geyserville Unified School District.

Health Care. Leaders from the Indian communities of Sonoma County established the Sonoma County Indian Health Project (SCIHP) in 1971 to provide accessible and high-quality healthcare to all Indians of Sonoma County. SCIHP subcontracts with the federal government through an agreement with the California Rural Indian Health Board. Services include medical, dental, nutritional, full-service pharmacy, behavioral health services, health education, and community health and outreach.

Housing. There are 15 total households in Dry Creek Rancheria living in 15 housing units, all occupied.

Elem Indian Colony

Sulphur Bank Rancheria
Federal reservation
Pomo
Lake County, California

Elem Indian Colony of Pomo
Indians
Sulphur Bank Rancheria
P.O. Box 618
Clearlake Oaks, CA 95423
707-995-2919
707-995-2853
707-995-2805 Fax

LOCATION AND LAND STATUS
Sulphur Bank Rancheria, or the Elem Indian Colony of Pomo Indians, is located in northern California's Lake County. The rancheria's 50 acres lie along the northwest side of Clear Lake. The Sulphur Bank Rancheria was established by court decree (Civil N; 4068-L) in January 1949. The U.S. holds the title in trust for the Sulphur Bank Band of the Pomo Indians.

The tribe is currently trying to regain ownership of Rattlesnake Island, an important ceremonial site located about 200 yards from the bank of the rancheria. Not only has the tribe held traditional ceremonies on these sacred grounds for centuries, the island continues to serve as an important source of many foods and medicines of value to the tribe. In the past, owners of the island have not always allowed the tribe to conduct ceremonies or gather herbs there. In 1995 Rattlesnake Island was currently for sale, and the tribe, with the aid of the California Indian Legal Services, was exploring options for acquiring the title.

PHYSICAL DESCRIPTION
The Sulphur Bank Rancheria is located along the shores of Clear Lake in Lake County, California. Clear Lake is the largest

natural freshwater lake within the state and is possibly the oldest lake in North America. It has been determined by the California Air Resources Board that Lake County has the best air quality in the state.

CULTURE AND HISTORY
Members of the Sulphur Bank Rancheria, or Elem Indian Colony, belong to the Southeastern Pomo tribes. The Southeastern Pomos are comprised of the Elem, Koi, and Koridot groups. Ancestral homelands of the Southeastern Pomos encompassed over one million acres of land and 50 miles of waterways in northern California. Archeological evidence supports the fact that an indigenous population resided at Clear Lake as many as 8,000 years ago. This evidence of human remains discovered along the shoreline are the oldest human remains ever discovered in California.

The tribe's indigenous language belongs to the Athabascan Hokan linguistic family, a designation given to speakers of seven related but mutually unintelligible languages. Pomo-speaking people have lived in what are now Lake, Mendocino, and Sonoma counties in northern California. For subsistence, these various bands utilized the bounty of their areas-hunting, fishing, and collecting native plants. *(For additional cultural information, see California introduction.)*

Traditional Pomo culture was irrevocably altered upon the arrival of European explorers and, later, of Euro-American settlers. Tribal populations were devastated by the introduction of European diseases, the enforced incarceration on reservations, and the further usurpation of tribal lands by settlers. The struggle for a permanent land base and tribal identity further characterized Pomo life in the twentieth century. In 1949 the Elem Colony lost over 80,000 acres of land, including the ceremonial grounds at Rattlesnake Island, as the result of false representation by their BIA agent. In addition to the ceremonial grounds, the tribe lost all mineral and water rights to the remaining tribal lands. The federal government then permitted outside entities to mine on the reservation. The mining operations destroyed the environment and created long-term pollution issues. In fact, the BIA renamed the tribe the Sulphur Bank Rancheria based upon the physical character of the reservation.

Throughout the twentieth century, Pomo tribes struggled to establish stable economies on their reservations. Many tribal members entered the wage economy and worked in the hop fields. Others earned money by cutting firewood for large buyers, such as the state hospital in Talmage. Women wove baskets for collectors and were employed as laundresses until they were displaced by Chinese laundries.

Pomo people are known for establishing their own independence and asserting their civil rights. For instance, after being displaced from their lands, many Mendocino Pomos collectively saved money to purchase these tracts of land back. In 1907 an Eastern Pomo, Ethan Anderson, won a court case giving nonreservation Indians the right to vote. Other Pomo actions have caused the reversal of the segregation list policies of California public schools and private facilities. Pan-Pomo projects include the establishment of the Ya-Ka-Ama Indian Center in Sonoma County. It has grown to be a model center with its native plant nursery, economic development projects, and educational and cultural programs.

The Elem Colony is the only Southeastern Pomo tribe with status as a federally recognized tribal government. The majority of voting members reluctantly adopted an IRA constitution in 1972 in order to assure that the BIA would continue to provide housing services to tribal members.

GOVERNMENT
In 1972, the Elem Colony approved a constitution created under the provisions of the Indian Reorganization Act. The constitution was accepted with great reluctance, as the reorganized tribal government does not represent the traditional matriarchal form of government. The tribal constitution was amended in 1977, and a bingo ordinance was passed in 1986.

The Elem Colony is governed by a general council composed of all eligible voters. The council's elected executive committee includes a chairperson, a vice-chairperson, a secretary-treasurer, and two members-at-large. Executive committee members are elected for two-year terms.

The tribal government includes the executive, bylaws, gaming commission, housing, education, tribal health, California Indian Manpower Consortium (CIMC), and ITCC committees.

ECONOMY
In the past, the tribal economy was supported by revenue generated from the rich mineral resources on tribal land at the Sulphur Bank Rancheria.

Agricultural activities serve as an important source of revenue for Lake County. Pears, cattle, walnuts, grapes, and hay represent the region's important products. In addition, the county's proximity to the San Francisco Bay Area combined with its variety of resorts and boating facilities make it a popular recreational area.

In the past few years, Lake County has experienced a dramatic population increase. This growth has led to an increase in the county's total wages and employment. Total wages and employment are projected to continue to rise as the economy is bolstered by increases in construction and mining, retail trade, and service industries.

Government as Employer. Government jobs represent the second-largest source of employment in the county.

Economic Development Projects. In 1995 the tribe began investigating the possibility of developing geothermal and wind energy facilities on the rancheria. To capitalize on the region's established tourist industry, the Elem Indian Colony is considering building a marina on Clear Lake. This marina would be located either on rancheria property or on an adjacent parcel. Along with the marina, the tribe is considering establishing an arts and crafts sale store, and a bait shop.

Gaming. The tribe is currently seeking investors to develop a gaming facility on the reservation. The tribe hopes that the facility will generate both desperately needed jobs and the tribal revenue to fund other economic development projects.

Mining. Mining operations on Elem Colony tribal lands began as early as 1865. Nontribal companies mined for mercury periodically until 1957. In 1949 the BIA reduced the size of the Elem Colony from over 80,000 acres to just 50 acres. At this time, the BIA also withdrew the tribe's mineral and water rights. The government allowed additional nontribal entities to establish mining operations on tribal lands. Although there have been no mining activities on the reservation since 1957, open mines, mine tailings, and waste rock are still located there. Water and soil contamination have been attributed to mining activity on tribal lands.

Tourism and Recreation. Lake County's most prominent geographical feature is Clear Lake which covers approximately five percent of the county's land area. The Sulphur Bank Rancheria lies along the northwestern edge of the lake. During the summer, many visitors are attracted to the lake's many recreational opportunities. Tourist attractions include opportunities for hiking, skydiving, cycling, golfing, sport fishing, sailing, water-skiing, boating, and wind surfing.

INFRASTRUCTURE
The rancheria is located two miles south of the intersection of State Highways 53 and 20.

Electricity. The Pacific Gas and Electric Company provides electric service to the rancheria.

Fuel. Residents use bottled butane for cooking and heating.

Transportation. Commercial air, train, and bus travel are available at Ukiah, 45 miles from the rancheria. Trucking lines and a private airport are located in Lakeport, 28 miles away.

COMMUNITY FACILITIES AND SERVICES
The Elem Indian Colony maintains a tribal office in nearby Clearlake Oaks.

Education. Children attend schools in the Konocti School District. In addition, the tribe provides tutorial services for these students.

Elem Indian Colony

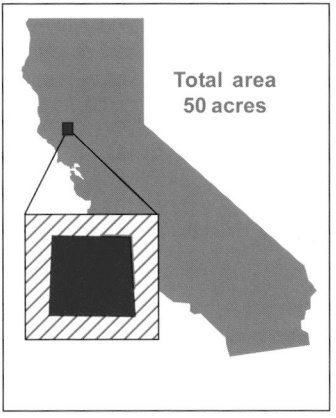

Total area
50 acres

Total area (BIA realty, 2003)
50 acres

Tribally owned (BIA realty, 2003)
50 acres

Population (Tribal source)
80

Tribal enrollment
(BIA labor report, 2001)
104

Tribal enrollment (Tribal source)
250

Total labor force 2000 census
20

Total labor force
(BIA labor report, 2001)
143

High school graduate or higher
2000 census
73.7%

Bachelor's degree or higher
2000 census
0%

Unemployment rate
2000 census
20%

Unemployment rate
(BIA labor report, 2001)
66%

Per capita income
2000 census
$3,428

Elem Indian Colony

Health Care. Tribal members may receive health services through the Lake County Tribal Health Consortium. Services include general medical, dental, community outreach, alcohol and drug prevention, and child and family programs. A clinic is available in Lakeport, 28 miles from the rancheria.

ENVIRONMENTAL CONCERNS

Years of mining activities conducted on tribal lands by non-Indian companies generated mercury and sulfur contamination of Clear Lake, and in turn, of the lake's fish and wildlife populations. The tribe initiated a task force, leading to the designation of the Sulfur Bank Mine as a U.S. EPA Superfund Hazardous Waste Site. However, the EPA did not include the tribe in the project.

The tribe has initiated development of the Turtle Bay Wetlands Restoration Plan. The plan will address hazardous contamination issues on tribal land. It also calls for the restoration of the wetlands at Rattlesnake Island, Buckeye Island, and Turtle Bay. The plan provides guidelines to control contaminated runoff reaching tribal land and waters, and to establish a cultural preservation program based on identifying and recording culturally significant sites in the Turtle Bay area.

Elk Valley

Elk Valley Rancheria
Federal reservation
Tolowa
Del Norte County, California

Elk Valley Tolowa Tribe
2332 Howland Hill Road
Crescent City, CA 95531
707-464-4680
707-464-4519 Fax
elk-valley.com

Total area *(BIA realty, 2003)*
21.72 acres

Individual allotments
(BIA realty, 2003)
21.72 acres

Total area *(Tribal source, 2004)*
640 acres

Trust acreage *(Tribal source, 2004)*
199

Tribally owned land
401 acres

Allotted
100 acres

Individual allotments
21.72 acres

Population *2000 census*
100

Tribal enrollment
(Tribal source)
98

Tribal enrollment
(BIA labor report, 2001)
100

LOCATION AND LAND STATUS

The Elk Valley Rancheria was established in 1906 under an appropriation act for "homeless" California Indians, but it was terminated in 1960, thus eliminating its land base. As a result of *Tillie Hardwick v. the United States of America*, the rancheria was reestablished, in 1983. Since about 1996, Elk Valley has purchased an additional 400 acres, which are not yet in trust status. The tribal offices are located in a beautiful new, redwood building in Crescent City, California, on a tiny spit of land jutting out into the Pacific Ocean, just south of the Oregon border.

PHYSICAL DESCRIPTION

The shoreline near the tribal offices is spectacularly immense and rocky, often rising steeply from sea level to nearly 2,000 feet above sea level. Both the Klamath River and the Smith River traverse the reservation on their way to the sea.

CLIMATE

Year-round daily high temperatures in Crescent City average 60°F. The highest temperature ever recorded was 92°F. The year-round daily low temperature is 45°F with the lowest temperature on record being 24°F. Crescent City, at an elevation of 56 feet above sea level, receives approximately 70 inches of precipitation annually, with only 1.2 inches falling as snow.

CULTURE AND HISTORY

The Elk Valley people are part of the Tolowa Tribe, members of the Athabascan language family. Their ancestral homelands span the coastal redwood forest region of what is now northern California and southern Oregon. The precontact Tolowas numbered about 4,000; by 1906 only 254 remained, having survived massacres by settlers, military destruction, diseases, and removal to the Siletz and Hoopa reservations during the mid-1800s. In the early years of the twenty-first century, the Tolowas number about 1,000, and the rancheria population consists of Tolowa, Yurok, and Kuroki tribal members. Elk Valley, along with another Tolowa reservation, Smith River, was terminated in 1960, thus losing its land base. During the 1970s, fellow tribesmen in the historic Tolowa fishing village of Nelechundun created the Nelechundun Business Council, a move that helped build momentum for federal re-recognition.

Traditional Tolowa culture, long repressed by white society, found religious expression in the Indian Shaker Church, imported from the Siletz Reservation in Oregon in 1927. The Tolowas found great solace in the healing and culturally inclusive practices of the "Shake," eventually adapting and hybridizing it. During the late 1960s, language preservation became a high priority, with Tolowa elders offering formal classes in the region's public schools. The late 1980s ushered in a period of optimism for the Tolowas, as accomplishments in the arenas of culture and health inspired confidence in the tribe's ability to meet economic and political challenges.

GOVERNMENT

The tribe is organized according to IRA rules and is governed by the nine-member Elk Valley Tribal Council, consisting of a chairperson, a vice-chairperson, a secretary, a treasurer and five members, each serving two-year terms. The tribe approved a constitution and bylaws in November 1994. The tribe is not yet a PL-638 self-governing tribal entity, although it contracts from the Bureau of Indian Affairs (BIA) for the provision of community fire protection, ICWA, social services, consolidated tribal government, general assistance, higher education and adult vocational, job placement, aid to tribal government, housing improvement and development, road maintenance, fire management, technical assistance, and other contract support.

The tribal council maintains a marketing and promotions department which oversees any promotions going on within tribal enterprises. Entertainment is booked through this department, as are golf tournaments, give-aways, and so on. This office purchases all print media for rancheria-owned businesses.

There are no tribal law enforcement or court systems, but there is a tribally operated environmental protection department, a finance department, a library, a government grants writer, a housing department and an education department. Work in these departments is accomplished with assistance from a business council, a cultural committee, an education committee, and a volunteers committee. Each committee, made up of tribal members, is headed by a council member.

ECONOMY

Elk Valley Enterprises consists of a diversified array of small businesses. The biggest enterprise is gaming. The largest employers are the casino and tribal government.

Government as Employer. In 2003, the tribe employed 250 people, making it the single largest employer in all of Del Norte County, California. Another 600 employees are anticipated with the future expansion of the casino, resort hotel, and golf course.

Economic Development Projects. In 2004 the tribe voiced plans for development of a larger golf course, with a recreational resort complex including a spa and performance art theater at the site. They are also considering the purchase of a liquor store in Smith River, California. Members would also like to offer guided whale-watching expeditions, white-water rafting tours, and tide-pool explorations. They have already applied to the BIA to have coastal lands in trust for these enterprises. With proceeds from these new ventures, the tribe hopes to fund stipends for community members to attend a computer program at the vocational high school.

Forestry. The timber industry represents another traditional component of the region's economy. National forests abound in this area, and logging, though somewhat diminished in recent years, remains a fundamental part of the area's economy.

Gaming. Elk Valley Casino opened in a triple-wide trailer in November 1995. Today, the new Elk Valley Casino is located along the coastline, nestled among giant redwoods. The 23,000-square-foot facility features 280 slot machines, 3 table games, 2 poker tables, and 250 bingo seats. There is a restaurant on-site as well as 6,000 square feet of convention and meeting space. The casino employs approximately 130 people, making it the second-largest private employer in Del Norte County, California, in 2004. The rancheria plans to build a larger beachfront casino, golf course, resort hotel, and entertainment venue along the major north-south thoroughfare, Highway 101.

In 2003, as a result of an aggressive economic development strategy, there were no rancheria members on public assistance, and proceeds from tribal investments were helping to fund many countywide initiatives, such as the Head Start program that serves 60 nontribal children and the annual Del Norte County Fourth of July fireworks show. The tribe also makes interest-free loans to the county's fair board. They will also donate certain sums toward programs for children, a new public-address system for the public school system, and scoreboards for athletic fields at the high school.

Fisheries. The economy of Crescent City and the surrounding region has historically been based heavily on the fishing industry. Commercial fishing remains a vital part of the region's economic base today, providing considerable revenues and employment for many area residents, including tribal members.

Services and Retail. Tsunami Lanes, a newly remodeled 16-lane bowling alley, features a full snack bar. Tsunami Sports Bar and Grill, purchased in November 2001, is a full-service restaurant and bar with six small televisions and a big screen. There is one liquor store. All businesses are located off-reservation.

Tourism and Recreation. Del Norte Golf Course is a nine-hole, par 71 course located in Crescent City, within walking distance of Redwoods National Park; the tribe purchased the golf course in September 2002. There is a restaurant, a full bar, and a pro shop on-site. The tribe enjoys an annual meeting in January that includes an employee appreciation dinner. In August and December, members attend cultural events held at the Smith River Reservation. A Golf Invitational is held annually in August, with proceeds benefiting athletic programs at the high school.

The rancheria lies within 25 miles of Lake Earl State Wildlife Area, Jedediah Smith Redwoods State Park, Redwoods National Park, and Six Rivers National Forest. The tribe operates the 120-site Hiouchi RV Resort inside the Redwood National Park. Crescent City operates a public swimming pool, and a privately owned gym is available to tribal members.

INFRASTRUCTURE
Scenic and historic U.S. Highway 101, also known as The Redwood Highway, passes through Crescent City in a north-south direction. Highway 197 enters Crescent City from the east. Jack McNamara Field in Crescent City allows commercial air and small passenger air traffic. Bus and trucking facilities are available in Crescent City, as well. The town also maintains a small harbor with abundant commercial shipping facilities. In 2003, the tribe was working with local government to improve the wastewater treatment plant to serve all county residents.

Electricity. Pacific Power provides electricity to the area.

Fuel. Gas service is provided by Blue Star and Suburban Propane.

Water Supply. Crescent City operates the sewer and water systems.

Telecommunications. Internet services are made available by Charter Cable.

COMMUNITY FACILITIES
In 1996 the tribe received a HUD grant to build a new community center, library, and Head Start facility. The original one-room library opened in 1998, and it moved to a new 2,000-square-foot space in August 2003, inside the newly constructed administrative office facility. The 6,757-square-foot building, made of redwood and river rock, is located on Howland Hill Road. The community room can seat 230 people for a banquet or 500 people in an audience seating arrangement. On display inside the facility are the rancheria's collection of baskets and a hand-carved redwood dugout canoe. The building also houses council chambers and has a kitchen, a computer lab, conference rooms, and office space for council members.

Not very many children live at the rancheria (approximately 16 in 2004); those that do attend public schools in Crescent City: Bess Maxwell Elementary, Pine Grove Elementary, Redwood School, Joe Hamilton School, Crescent Elk Jr. High, and Del Norte High School. College of the Redwoods is located in Crescent City as well. Two radio stations, neither tribally owned, serve the reservation area, and *The Daily Triplicate* newspaper is offered throughout the area.

Health Care. Health care is made available by United Indian Health Services.

ENVIRONMENTAL CONCERNS
The tribe has completed an environmental assessment. Combating wild fires and fire management (generally), earthquakes and severe winter rainstorms are the most pressing environmental issues for the tribe.

TRI-CA-021

TRI-CA-022

Elk Valley

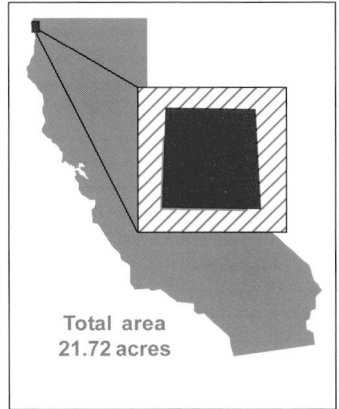

Total area
21.72 acres

Total labor force *2000 census*
24

Total labor force
(Tribal source, 2004)
186

High school graduate or higher
2000 census
71.7%

Bachelor's degree or higher
2000 census
4.3%

Unemployment rate
2000 census
29.17

Unemployment rate
(BIA labor report, 2001)
42%

Per capita income
2000 census
$11,435

TRI-CA-021 Elk Valley Casino

TRI-CA-022 Newly built Tribal Office Building

The Enterprise Rancheria
Federal reservation
Maidu
Butte County, California

The Enterprise Rancheria
of Maidu Indians
1940 Feather River Blvd.
Suite B
Oroville, CA 95965
530-532-9214
530-532-1768 Fax

Total area *(BIA realty, 2003)*
40 acres

Tribal enrollment
(Tribal source, 2003)
490

Population
(Tribal source, 2003)
490

Total labor force
(BIA labor report, 2001)
246

Unemployment rate
(Tribal source, 2003)
16%

Per capita income
2000 census
$5,400

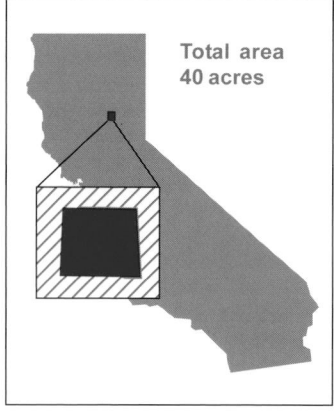

Total area
40 acres

LOCATION AND LAND STATUS
The Enterprise Rancheria is located in northern California in Butte County. The U.S. government purchased two 40-acre parcels of land for the Enterprise Rancheria in 1915 and 1916. The first parcel of land was called Enterprise 1 and was settled by the family that resided on the land at the time of purchase. On June 21, 1916, the U.S. government decided to purchase this parcel of land under the Homeless Indian Acts. The second parcel was appropriately named Enterprise 2. In 1965, Enterprise Rancheria 2 land was sold in a condemnation sale. Soon after, Oroville Dam was constructed, and the land was completely inundated by the Oroville Reservoir. The sale of the land was not by grant or by authority of the Rancheria Act. The tribe retained their federal status in 1995.

CULTURE AND HISTORY
The Enterprise Rancheria of Maidu Indians was established on April 20, 1915. Members of the Enterprise Rancheria consider the Feather River drainage their traditional homeland. The Maidus are of Penutian linguistic stock and originally inhabited the California area. The Maidus followed the traditional culture of the California region, practicing the Kuksu religion. Today the Maidus live in several reservations and communities in California, including Enterprise Rancheria.

Many tribal members settled on Enterprise 2 land when it was established in 1915. A good number of current tribal members were born and raised on Enterprise 2 land. The inundation of the land in 1965 with the construction of the Oroville Dam led to the loss of members' homes and communities. Families were forced to scatter to surrounding communities in search of employment and affordable housing.

On April 12, 1995, the Bureau of Indian Affairs (BIA) granted the Estom Yumeka Maidu of the Enterprise Rancheria federal recognition as a duly sanctioned governing body.

ECONOMY
The largest industries in the area include educational, health, and social services. Additional economic activity consists of retail, manufacturing, and construction.

Gaming. The Enterprise Rancheria applied to the BIA to purchase 40 acres in Yuba County to build a hotel and casino. The tribe plans to build a seven-story hotel with a 1,700-slot machine in a 150,000-square-foot casino. The tribe claims the casino will create 2,000 jobs in the area.

INFRASTRUCTURE
Electricity and Fuel. Pacifica Gas and Electric provides electricity and natural gas services for the rancheria.

Water Supply. The Yuba County Water Agency monitors, regulates, and provides irrigation water to the area.

Telecommunications. Pacific Telephone and Telegraph Company (Pacific Bell) currently provides local telephone service to the area.

COMMUNITY FACILITIES AND SERVICES
Public Safety. The Yuba County Sherriff's Department, headquartered in Marysville with substations in Brownsville, provides law enforcement for the area.

Fire protection in the area is currently provided by a combination of agencies including a volunteer fire department from the Plumas-Brophy Fire District, the California Department of Forestry and Fire Protection, and the U.S. Forest Service.

Education. Students residing on the Enterpirse Rancheria attend schools within the Plumas School District that operates the Plumas Elementary School, grades K-12. Yuba Community College provides people in the area with the opportunity for a postsecondary education.

Health Care. The rancheria receives health services from the Fremont-Rideout Health Group that operates hospitals in nearby Marysville and Yuba City. Bi-County Ambulance provides ambulatory services for the area. There are two additional hospitals located approximately 10 miles outside the rancheria.

LOCATION AND LAND STATUS

The Ewiiaapaayp Band of Kumeyaay Indians is a self-governing federally recognized Indian tribe exercising sovereign authority over the lands of the Ewiiaapaayp (Cuyapaipe) Indian Reservation. The Cuyapaipe Indian Reservation was established on February 10, 1891, following an Executive Order on January 12, 1891, and an Act of Congress.

The Ewiiaapaayp Indian Reservation consists of two sections, the 4,102.5-acre Ewiiaapaayp Indian Reservation in the Laguna Mountains and the 10-acre Little Ewiiaapaayp Indian Reservation located in the unincorporated community of Alpine in east San Diego County. The larger parcel is located near Mt. Laguna, approximately 47 miles east of San Diego and 19 miles east of Alpine. It was reserved in a trust patent in 1891. Most of the reservation (98 percent) consists of rocky ridges and steep hillsides between 5,000 and 6,500 feet high. The 10-acre Little Ewiiaapaayp Indian Reservation is located at 4054/4058 Willows Road in Alpine. This 10-acre section was reserved in a trust patent in 1986 (8.6 acres) and 1998 (1.4 acres). It is located approximately one-fourth mile east of the West Willows Road exit off of Interstate 8 in the community of Alpine.

The Ewiiaapaayp Band tribal government office currently resides on the Little Ewiiaapaayp Indian Reservation in Alpine, which is leased to the Southern Indian Health Council. On December 27, 2000, Congress enacted the California Indian Land Transfer Act of 2000 that added 1,360 acres to the Ewiiaapaayp Indian Reservation, representing a net addition of 432 acres following prior survey errors. All of the additional lands are on ridge tops or steep slopes.

The Ewiiaapaayp Band is listed in the *Federal Register* (Vol. 68, No. 234/Friday, December 5, 2003/Notices) as "The Ewiiaapaayp Band of Kumeyaay Indians, formerly the Cuyapaipe Community of Diegueño Mission Indians of the Cuyapaipe Reservation." The tribal affiliation is Kumeyaay, and it is one of the 12 Kumeyaay bands in San Diego County.

"Ewiiaapaayp" is the Kumeyaay language word meaning "leaning rock". This rock is on a high ridge on the Cuyapaipe Reservation, and it served as the touchstone and site-marker in the Kumeyaays' travels from the coast to the mountains and the desert beyond. The inland Kumeyaay bands were centered at the present-day Cuyapaipe Reservation.

CULTURE AND HISTORY

The Mission Indian Relief Act of 1891 enacted recommendations of the Jackson-Kinney Report stating, "The history of the Mission Indians for a century may be written in four words: conversion, civilization, neglect, outrage... . Justice and humanity alike demand the immediate action of Government to preserve for their occupation the fragments of land not already taken from them."

The late Tony J. Pinto (1914-2003), Ewiiaapaayp Tribal Chairman from 1967-2001, and his family members worked to preserve the cultural traditions of the Kumeyaays, including its Peon games and Bird Songs. As a part of the Mission Indian Federation, they opposed policies of the Bureau of Indian Affairs (BIA), which the traditional leaders believed would damage their people. Chairman Pinto participated in the Mission Indians Claims case and in the water claims settlement. He worked to protect sacred places and cemeteries from secular desecration, and he actively encouraged younger Kumeyaays to learn Bird Songs, play Peon, and become tribal cultural and political leaders. Chairman Pinto also brought the existence of the plight of the Paipai and

Kumeyaay Indians of northern Baja Mexico to the attention of the Mexican government. Rosalie Pinto Robertson and Christobal Pinto were past leaders of the Campo Band of Mission Indians.

Seven members are enrolled in the tribe. Due to the inaccessibility of the Ewiiaapaayp Reservation, the U.S. government established an Indian school (since closed) on the more accessible Campo Reservation. Ewiiaapaayp Band families with school-age children were relocated from the Ewiiaapaayp Reservation to the other reservations of Campo, La Posta, Laguna (since terminated), and Manzanita in order for children to attend the school. The relocation of the Ewiiaapaayp families with children to the other reservations, the subsequent disenrollments due to the lack of any utilities and adequate roads, and the lack of any kind of employment opportunity, are reasons the Ewiiaapaayp Band's enrollment consists of seven members today.

GOVERNMENT

The Ewiiaapaayp Band's tribal members govern themselves as a general council composed of all enrolled tribal members age 18 or above under its tribal constitution enacted and approved in 1973 and amended in 2002. Elected tribal officials are the chairman, vice-chairman, and treasurer/secretary.

The Ewiiaapaayp tribal government is a self-governing tribe in accordance with Indian Self-Determination and Education Assistance Act, PL 93-638, as amended. Social service and education programs are administered by the Southern California Tribal Chairman's Association, an intertribal association of 18 tribes in San Diego County, and the Southern Indian Health Council.

ECONOMY

Economic Development Projects. The Ewiiaapaayp Band is developing a wind turbine energy project that is a part of the largest renewable energy project in Indian country. The electricity generated will be sold to San Diego Gas and Electric to supply power for an equivalent of over 2,000 households per year.

Gaming. The Ewiiaapaayp Band signed a tribal-state compact on September 10, 1999. The compact was approved by the Assistant Secretary of Indian Affairs, Department of the Interior, on May 5, 2000. The tribe amended its compact on August 23, 2004, and it was ratified by the California legislature and signed by the governor on September 28, 2004.

INFRASTRUCTURE

There are no public utilities available on the reservation, including no telephone service, no mobile telephone or radio service, no electricity, no gas, and no treatment system for wastewater, solid waste, or drinking water.

COMMUNITY FACILITIES AND SERVICES

The tribe is planning the development of eight home-sites on the Ewiiaapaayp Indian Reservation. Currently three substandard houses exist, but they are not served by utilities of any kind.

Education. Tribal members attend local schools in east San Diego County.

Health Care. The Ewiiaapaayp Band's Little Ewiiaapaayp Reservation in Alpine, California, hosts the Southern Indian Health Council (SIHC), a California public benefit corporation whose membership and board of directors is composed of seven federally recognized Indian tribes located near San Diego, California.

Ewiiaapaayp Indian Reservation
Pronounced "Wee-a-pipe," Formerly Cuyapaipe, pronounced "Coo-ya-pipe"

Federal reservation
Diegueño and Kumeyaay
San Diego County, California

Ewiiaapaayp Band
   of Kumeyaay Indians
P.O. Box 2250
4054 Willows Road
Alpine, CA 91903-2250
   619-445-6315
   619-445-9126 Fax
leaningrock.org

Total area *(BIA realty, 2003)*
5,464.15 acres

Tribally owned
(BIA realty, 2003)
5,464.15 acres

Population
7

Total labor force
6

High school graduate or higher
5

Unemployment rate 33%

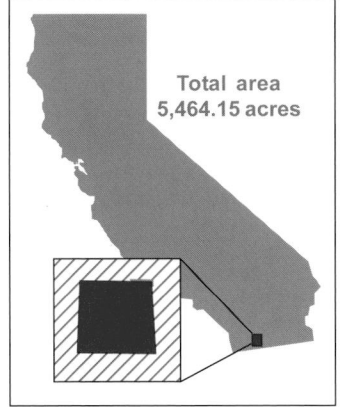

Total area
5,464.15 acres

Ewiiaapaayp

ENVIRONMENTAL CONCERNS

The tribe is working to mitigate the effects of erosion caused by the BIA's introduction of nonnative plant species after wildfires in the 1930s and 1940s. The tribe is also planning to develop roads and utilities.

TRI-CA-009-E

TRI-CA-010-E

TRI-CA-009-E Administration Building

TRI-CA-010-E Southern Indian Health Clinic

Only tribal contractors operate health programs from facilities owned by the tribes or health corporations, or leased from private sources. The SIHC serves Barona, Campo, Ewiiaapaayp, Jamul, La Posta, Manzanita, Viejas, and residents of East County. Programs and services offered are: medical and dental clinics, community health, social services, mental health, senior home, and substance abuse prevention. The SIHC also operates a satellite clinic on the Campo Reservation.

The SIHC began as a satellite operation of the Indian Health Council located in North County. It incorporated in 1982 as a nonprofit, public benefit corporation, and then moved to the Barona Reservation. In late 1987, the Ewiiaapaayp Band leased their Little Ewiiaapaayp Reservation in Alpine to SIHC, and the current permanent facility was built using two ICDBG funds awarded to the Ewiiaapaayp Band and one to the La Posta Band.

Fort Bidwell

Fort Bidwell Reservation
Federal reservation
Paiute
Modoc County, California

Fort Bidwell Indian Community
of Paiute Indians
P.O. Box 129
Fort Bidwell, CA 96112
530-279-6310
530-279-2233 Fax

Total area *(BIA realty, 2003)*	3,603.44 acres
Tribally owned	3,603.44 acres
(BIA realty, 2003)	
Population *2000 census*	108
Tribal enrollment	244
(BIA labor report, 2001)	
Total labor force *2000 census*	37
Total labor force *(BIA labor report, 2001)*	29
High school graduate or higher	67.2%
2000 census	
Bachelor's degree or higher	0%
2000 census	
Unemployment rate	35.1%
2000 census	
Unemployment rate	20%
(BIA labor report, 2001)	
Per capita income *2000 census*	$7,682

LOCATION AND LAND STATUS

The Fort Bidwell Reservation spans 3,334.97 acres along the eastern slope of the Warner Mountain range and the adjacent floor of northern Surprise Valley. The closest city is Alturas, the Modoc County seat, 50 miles away. Lakeview, Oregon, is also approximately 50 miles away, north of Fort Bidwell. The town of Fort Bidwell, adjacent to the reservation, has a population of approximately 300.

A joint resolution on January 30, 1879, authorized the secretary of the interior to use the abandoned Fort Bidwell Military Reserve for an Indian training school. An Act of Congress on January 27, 1913, granted land to the People's Church for a cemetery and right-of-way over the Fort Bidwell Indian School Reservation; the Indians were to have rights of interment therein. Executive Order 2679 on August 3, 1917, enlarged the reservation. The entire reservation is comprised of federal trust land.

PHYSICAL DESCRIPTION

Located in the extreme northwestern corner of California, the reservation's elevations range from about 4,550 to 7,000 feet.

CULTURE AND HISTORY

The residents of the Fort Bidwell Reservation belong to the Northern Paiute Tribe of the western Great Basin. The Northern Paiutes originally occupied a vast range along the eastern slopes of the Sierra Nevada and Cascade ranges from Mono Lake, California, to John Day River, Oregon. For subsistence, the Paiutes traditionally depended upon the region's ample resources of game and native plants.

By the early 1900s, Euro-American encroachment had eroded Paiute territory to less than five percent of its original size. Native Americans of this region actively resisted incursions on their traditional territories. Skirmishes culminated in the Modoc War, 1872-1873, when a group of about 70 dissident Modocs and their families held off hundreds of U.S. soldiers for several months in the Lava Beds area of northern California.

In 1864 the settlers of Surprise Valley appealed to the military for protection. Also, John Bidwell, Brigadier General of the California Militia, a prominent landholder, agriculturalist, and entrepreneur, appealed, with others, for protection of commerce along the roads in and out of Surprise Valley. In response, Fort Bidwell became one of a network of military posts established in the California-Nevada-Oregon border triangle area beginning in 1857. Until the end of the "frontier" period, Fort Bidwell was used for controlling Native populations.

When Fort Bidwell was turned into a Bureau of Indian Affairs boarding school in 1898, many Paiute people camped near the school until school officials determined that the presence of parents and relatives near the children was detrimental to the latter's becoming "civilized." These camps were forcibly evacuated around 1904.

Passage of the Dawes Act of 1887 provided for individual, rather than tribal, ownership of former Paiute lands. Between 1893 and

1897, 165 allotments were made to members of the Surprise Valley Paiute group in the vicinity of Cedarville and Fort Bidwell. The current reservation was established through Executive Orders in the beginning of the twentieth century.

Today the reservation contains many valuable archeological and historical sites, such as the ruins of the original fort. The current members of the Northern Paiute Tribe now ranch and farm along the California-Nevada state line.

GOVERNMENT
The tribe is organized under an IRA constitution approved in 1936 and amendments approved in 1940, 1942, and 1971. The reservation is governed by the Fort Bidwell Indian General Community Council which is composed of all eligible voters of the community and led by nine elected members including a chairperson, vice-chairperson, secretary, and treasurer. Council members serve two-year staggered terms.

ECONOMY
The area's economy is predominately dependent on agriculture, forestry, and other natural resources. The local economy is moderately seasonal in nature. Unemployment reaches its peak during winter months when inclement weather hampers outdoor activities.

Economic Development Projects. The tribe continues to explore and develop geothermal resources on the reservation. A feasibility study conducted by the Oregon Institute of Technology suggests that this energy source, if harnessed and developed, should be able to provide not only the energy requirements of the existing residential and commercial buildings and the aquiculture project, but also the requirements of eventual expansion. Moreover, the potential of hydropower has been identified as an additional source of energy. Construction of a hydropower plant began in 1995.

Agriculture and Livestock. The Fort Bidwell Reservation contains ample land for livestock grazing. The tribe leases the lower 500 acres of reservation pasture for cattle grazing.

Fisheries. In 1984 the tribe began a pilot aquiculture project to raise channel catfish. While still considered a viable economic project, the tribe needs funds to expand and renovate this facility.

Forestry. Timber serves as a valuable source of tribal revenue; half the tribal income is generated by forestry. The reservation's timber resources are primarily composed of pine-fir forests. Substantial logging activity has occurred on the reservation in the past. The tribe contracts with private lumber companies to harvest its timber.

Tourism and Recreation. Visitors may enjoy the various archeological and historical sites on the reservation. The ruins of the original fort are being considered for inclusion on the National Register of Historic Places. In addition, the tribal council supports the Native American seniors of Fort Bidwell in their annual pow-wow.

INFRASTRUCTURE
Water Supply. Water is available through a community water system. Most homes are connected to a community sewage system. Some homes remain on individual septic systems, and there are no plans to expand the community system. Households dispose of their own garbage at a local county landfill.

Transportation. Alturas is served by bus lines. The nearest truck line stop is in Cedarville, 40 miles from Fort Bidwell. Redding, 194 miles from the reservation, has the nearest available air and train services. There is also a private airstrip in Cedarville.

COMMUNITY FACILITIES AND SERVICES
Fort Bidwell Reservation's community facilities include a tribal gym, a firehouse, community center, and a clinic. The tribe provides tutoring to its children.

Health Care. The tribe operates a primary care facility through Warner Mountain Indian Health Clinic. The clinic provides general medical services to the community. In 1995 plans were in development to improve direct and contractual health services.

Fort Bidwell

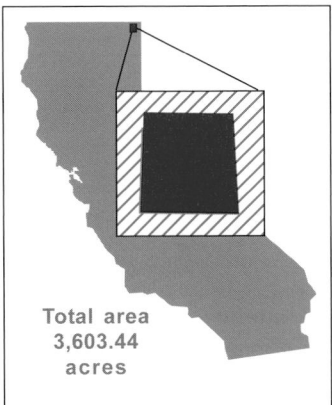

Total area
3,603.44
acres

Fort Independence

Ft Independence

Total area *(BIA realty, 2003)*	552.3 acres
Tribally owned	433.91 acres
(BIA realty, 2003)	
Individually owned	113.34 acres
(BIA realty, 2003)	
Federal trust *(BIA realty, 2003)*	5.05 acres
Population	58
Tribal enrollment *(BIA labor report, 2001)*	135
Tribal enrollment *(Tribal source, 2004)*	107
Total labor force *2000 census*	29
Total labor force *(BIA labor report, 2001)*	41
Total labor force *(Tribal source, 2004)*	20
High school graduate or higher	91.1%
2000 census	
Bachelor's degree or higher	13.3%
2000 census	
Unemployment rate *2000 census*	13.8%
Unemployment rate	34%
(BIA labor report, 2001)	
Per capita income *2000 census*	$20,086

LOCATION AND LAND STATUS
The Fort Independence Paiute Reservation is located in Inyo County, California. It consists of 552 acres of land. Two hundred acres have been acquired from the Bureau of Land Management (BLM) since 1999.

CULTURE AND HISTORY
Members of the Fort Independence Tribe are members of the Paiute Nation. Archeological findings include petroglyphs, obsidian chips, and house rings that indicate a Native population resided in the area at least 3,000 years ago. The Shoshonean-speaking Paiutes are linguistically related to the greater Uto-Aztecan language group. Now living on four small tracts of reserved lands, the Paiutes were not settled on reservations until after the turn of the twentieth century.

GOVERNMENT
The tribe is a PL-638 tribe. The cultural committee is an active branch of the tribal government. A new administration office building has been completed to house governmental programs.

Fort Independence Paiute Reservation
Federal reservation
Paiute
Inyo County, California

Fort Independence Paiute Reservation
P.O. Box 67
Independence, CA 93526
760-878-2126
760-878-2311 Fax

Ft Independence

ECONOMY
Government as Employer. The tribe employs 10 individuals.

Agriculture and Livestock. The tribe operates an irrigation system. One person is employed by the tribe in this industry.

Services and Retail. The tribe owns a staffing company.

Tourism and Recreation. The tribe owns a campground, which features a cultural interpretive trail.

INFRASTRUCTURE
Highway 395 runs through the reservation.

Water Supply. The tribe operates and maintains a domestic water system that services the reservation.

COMMUNITY FACILITIES AND SERVICES
The reservation houses one community building.

Health Care. Tribal members may receive health services through the Toiyabe Indian Health Project. Toiyabe Health offers clinics in the cities of Bishop, Lone Pine, and Coleville, California.

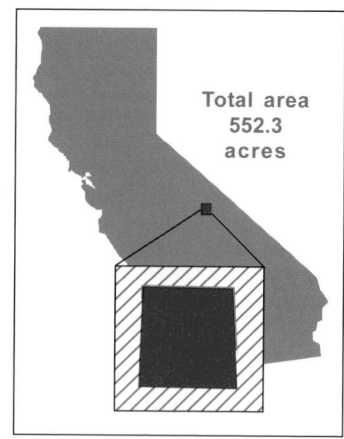

Total area
552.3
acres

Fort Mojave

Fort Mojave Reservation
Federal reservation
Mojave
Mohave County, Arizona; San Bernardino County, California; and Clark County, Nevada

Fort Mojave Tribal Council
500 Merriman Avenue
Needles, CA 92363
  760-629-4591
  760-629-5767 Fax
  itcaonline.com

LOCATION AND LAND STATUS
The Fort Mojave Indian Reservation stretches along the Colorado River in Mojave County, Arizona (23,669 acres), San Bernardino County, California (12,633 acres), and Clark County, Nevada (5,582 acres), at an altitude of between 480 and 550 feet above sea level. The nearest towns are Bullhead City and Topock, Arizona, and Needles, California. In August 1870, a U.S. Department of War General Order established this reservation; an Executive Order of February 1911 confirmed it.

CLIMATE
Summertime temperatures in Needles are often the hottest in the nation. At an elevation of only 490 feet, the area is a hot, dry basin, where summertime highs often hover in triple digits, and the average year-round high is 85°F. The hottest temperature ever recorded was 120°F. The average year-round low temperature is 60°F, with the lowest ever recorded being 21°F. The area receives less than five inches of precipitation annually.

CULTURE AND HISTORY
Since perhaps as early as 1150 AD, the Yuman-speaking Mojaves have inhabited an area of more than 200 miles along the Colorado River and the area surrounding Spirit Mountain, believed to be the tribe's place of origin. Archaeological evidence suggests ancestors of the modern Mojave Indians were in the area soon after the last ice age.

The Mojave Indians (Pipa Aha Makav, or "people who live along the river") still live on a portion of their aboriginal lands. The Mojaves are the largest of the Yuman-speaking tribes, which include the Yavapais, Maricopas, Quechans, Hualapais, and Havasupais. Specializing more in agriculture than other Yuman speakers, the Mojaves grew corn, pumpkins, melons, and other crops along the lush banks of the Colorado River. They also supplemented their diet by fishing, gathering wild fruits and vegetables, and occasionally by hunting.

The Mojaves were once organized into 22 patrilinear clans, with children taking their father's clan, even though women only used the clan name. In 2004, there were 18 clans. Families lived in sprawling, open settlements or neighborhoods, with people moving freely throughout the tribe's territory. The various settlements did not necessarily delineate a band or form a political or military force, as other Native peoples often did. While the nuclear family was the basis of Mojave society and there were several bands within the tribe, the Mojaves considered themselves one nation and acted in a unified manner against enemies. They governed themselves without a body comparable to a western administrative state; no one individual or group held a position of inherent authority over others. Hereditary chiefs, called "aha macav pima ta'ahon," along with leaders of the three bands, led by the respect accorded them by other Mojaves and by their moral strength, not by the authority of their post.

At least three bands existed within the tribe, with one in the north, one in the central region, and one in the south. Very active and well traveled, the Mojaves were recognized as great runners throughout the Southwest. They traded with the Havasupais, Hualapais, and some Californian tribes, creating a trail to the Pacific Coast via water sources and springs and through mountains and desert terrain. The knowledge of this trail was invaluable to early Spanish settlers. The Mojaves also very likely traded with the Navajos and Hopis.

As early as 1826, an American mountain man, Jedediah Smith, was leading Anglos into Mojave territory. An increase of immigrants to the West and advances in technology changed Arizona's territorial boundaries in 1850, and by 1858, the U.S. Army post of Fort Mohave was established to guard the river crossing along the old survey route. The American Civil War forced Army abandonment of Fort Mohave for a while in the 1860s; however, the Colorado Indian Reservation was established near Parker in March 1865, and many Mojaves were settled there.

The Fort Mojave Reservation was established in 1870 but it was not confirmed until February 1911. During the interim years, the encroachment of whites onto reservation lands continued unabated, with the completion of the Kingman and Needles section of the Santa Fe Railroad, which crossed through Mojave and Hualapai lands. Much of the land on the reservation around Fort Mojave became the property of the Santa Fe Railroad. This was not the first action to decrease Mojave territory, however. In 1860, the United States had persuaded some of the Mojaves to relocate farther south, although there was already an established population of Mojaves there, in the area designated as the Colorado River Indian Reservation in 1864. The majority of the Mojaves living in the north chose not to leave at that time; but the railroad and the population it supported led to a steady decrease in the amount of game and food plants available for Mojave use, causing a number of Mojaves to finally move south.

With no land of their own, many Mojaves found employment with the railroad which came to Needles in 1883. Others plied their trade selling beadwork or pottery dolls to tourists, worked in mines, or worked on riverboats. The Mojaves that stayed near Fort Mojave became known as Fort Mojaves in 1890, when 14,000 acres were transferred from the War Department to the Department of the Interior. The fort building became a boarding school for the Fort Mojaves and other regional tribal members. In 1905, Indian students at the boarding school were required to anglicize their names, and they were forbidden to utilize their traditional clan and individual names. Punishment for "Indianness" was severe.

The Mojaves were granted a reservation in 1911 consisting of areas historically referred to as hay and wood reserves, on both sides of the Colorado River in a checkerboard fashion. Land totaled approximately 31,300 acres; most of the remaining land was given to the railroad. In 1931 the boarding school closed and schoolchildren began attending public schools in Needles. In 1936 a flood washed out Indian homes along the riverbanks. They were not replaced until the tribe purchased land outside Needles in 1947 that became part of the reservation.

GOVERNMENT
Prior to the establishment of the reservation, the tribal chief informally discussed matters of importance with other prominent men from various settlements. In 1957 the tribe adopted a constitution. Its government consists of a tribal chairperson, an elected tribal council of seven, a trial and appellate court, a police force, and a housing authority. The Fort Mojave government must not only govern under tribal regulations set forth in their constitution and federal laws, but they must also consider the laws of California, Arizona, and Nevada.

The tribe, under PL-638, contracts with the BIA to administer key programs and services in Arizona. They are partially self-governing in California. The tribe has its own police department and tribal court system. A cultural preservation department operates a language program and a crafts program. The ranger department manages the tribe's natural resources, including enforcement of rules and regulations governing the use of its beaches, day-use areas, and campsites. This department issues hunting and fishing permits. It employs a licensed building inspector and has full-time staff positions in the real estate services department. There is a uniform commercial code, and a tribal tax commission administers the tax ordinance and bond issues. There is a tribal attorney. With increased revenues, the tribe has developed a plethora of social services for tribal members.

ECONOMY
Fort Mojave has moved from being almost totally dependent upon federal and state programs to increasing success in the cash economy via agriculture, gaming, retail sales, and natural resources development. Input/output analysis of the tribal economic contribution to the larger regional economy shows that the tribe, via its various enterprises, contributes approximately $250 million of economic output, along with over $140 million in income to the area. Ninety five million dollars of that is in wages earned.

Government as Employer. The tribe employs 3,000 people via its programs, services, and enterprises. The enterprises have created over 3,100 jobs in the southern Mojave Valley and account for seven percent of the total economy in Mohave County.

Agriculture and Livestock. By the 1960s, many Mojaves were able to lease reservation lands to large-scale farming operations, and within 10 years a majority of Mojave tribal income derived from agricultural and land leases. Today, the reservation has 15,000 acres under cultivation via the Avi Kwa 'Ame Farms, which grow genetically engineered, pest-resistant cotton, alfalfa, and wheat and a special weed-free species of hay. They also supply the turf-grass industry with Bermuda grass seed. Premium garbanzo beans, a staple on salad bars throughout the country, are raised here. Sudan grass is widely used in the Japanese beef industry to provide essential roughage for its cattle. The tribe is developing contracts throughout the Pacific Rim for export of this valuable commodity. During winter, cattle graze the hay fields.

Some farms are located in the California region of the reservation; the majority are found to the east of the Colorado River. With increased irrigation, the Fort Mojave Reservation has additional acres that could sustain agriculture, and it plans to develop between 7,000 and 12,000 acres of that land.

Gaming. Economic development projects resulted in a gaming compact with the State of Arizona for the operation of the 6,500-square-foot Spirit Mountain Casino in Mohave Valley, Arizona. In June 2004 the casino employed approximately 750 people. Following a master plan, the reservation's Nevada portion has built a hotel and casino as well. They operate the Avi Resort and Casino ("avi" means "money"), located in Laughlin, Nevada. A 250,000-square-foot facility opened in 1995 with 455 rooms, 29 spa suites, a 25,000-square-foot gaming area, and the largest beach lagoon on the Colorado River. The tribe operates a marina there with boat and personal watercraft rentals, a Texaco mini-mart and smoke shop, and an RV park. This facility offers hourly child care services. The tribe is also considering opening a gaming facility on its California lands.

Construction. The tribe operates Fort Mojave Construction, a licensed general contractor which built the water line to supply the Calpine Southpoint Power Plant on the Colorado River. Construction of the plant generated hundreds of jobs and stimulated growth in many other sectors, including the fast food industry, lodging, and gasoline. The tribe also operates a land-leveling company called Fort Mojave Construction. It also owns and leases two ready-mix concrete companies. Matco and Mesquite Creek are construction-related enterprises associated with residential development.

Services and Retail. The tribe operates casinos, resort hotels, the highest-grossing convenience store in Arizona, a mini-mart and smoke shop, a laundromat, a gas station and car wash, a JB's franchise restaurant, and housing developments for nontribal residents. There is a pizza place, and two popular franchises are represented on the reservation, Baskin Robbins and Subway. Smith's, a grocery chain, has a store on land owned by the tribe. The RV Supercenter operates near the RV campground at the Avi Resort and Casino. Off-reservation tribally owned enterprises include a Quick Lube, Valley Wheel and Tire located off Arizona I-95, and Fort Mojave Construction, specializing in defense contracting on Arizona's U.S. Air Force bases. There were a total of over 30 such enterprises in 2001. In June 2004 the tribe was planning the opening of The Corner Store, a feed, tack, and pet supply store.

Tourism and Recreation. The Colorado River offers year-round recreational and camping opportunities. Spirit Mountain Casino, Oatman Mines (where wild burros still visit regularly), and the former U.S. military outpost, Fort Mojave, also draw tourists. Hunters must obtain a tribal permit to hunt duck, goose, quail, dove, mule deer, and big horn sheep; fishermen must be permitted to fish the Colorado River. Nearby attractions include the Black Mountain Range, Lake Havasu State Park, and Lake

Fort Mojave

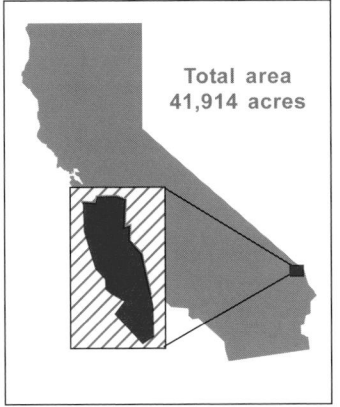

Total area
41,914 acres

Total area
(BIA realty, 2004)
41,914 acres

Total area Arizona
(BIA realty, 2004)
23,699 acres

Total area California
(BIA realty)
12,633 acres

Total area Nevada
(BIA realty)
5,582.15

Population *2000 census*
773

Tribal enrollment
(Tribal source, 2004)
1,150

Total labor force
2000 census
217

High school graduate or higher *2000 census*
71.8%

Bachelor's degree or higher
2000 census
8.2%

Unemployment rate
2000 census
4.9%

Per capita income
$13,221

Fort Mojave

Havasu National Wildlife Refuge. The tribe also operates an auto racetrack, the Mohave Valley Raceway. The community of Aha Macav in Nevada offers tourist lodging and recreational facilities.

The Colorado River flows for 17 miles through the reservation, running deep between channeled banks below Needles, California, offering fishing, water skiing, jet boarding, and water sports. In the Black Mountains, off-roading, hiking, photography, rock hounding, and exploring ghost towns are possible. In Lake Havasu State Park and Lake Havasu National Wildlife Refuge, tourists can explore rugged geological formations. Hikers enjoy wilderness trekking, and there are Indian ruins and abandoned mines to explore.

An array of dining experiences is available in the 450-room luxury Avi Resort and Casino complex, and there are three championship golf courses within 10 miles of the facility. The Arrow Weed Lounge, inside the resort hotel, features live entertainment. There is also a sports bar. In 1998 an RV campground and three restaurants were added. These facilities employ well over 1,000 employees.

INFRASTRUCTURE
Interstate 40 passes through the reservation, providing easy access to cities in both Arizona and California. There are airports in Bullhead City, Arizona, Needles, California, and Las Vegas, Nevada. The tribe leases an airfield to Radco Avionics, Tookies Flying Service, and Eagle Aviation.

Electricity. Electricity is provided on the reservation by tribally owned and operated Aha Macav Power Service. The tribe recently signed a lease with the Calpine Southpoint Power Plant, a 540-megawatt gas-fired electric generating facility.

Fuel. Southwest Gas Corporation provides natural gas.

Water Supply. Water and sewer services are provided by the Fort Mojave Tribal Utility Authority.

Telecommunications. Fort Mojave Telecommunications provides telephone, digital, Internet, and cable services.

Housing. The tribe constructed two long-term housing projects, in Arizona and California, for nontribal members.

COMMUNITY FACILITIES AND SERVICES
There is a community building, a gym, a youth shelter house, an administration building, a multipurpose childcare facility, and a 12,000-square-foot office building. The tribe has planned construction of an events center on their Arizona parcel, to include a 5,000-seat air-conditioned rodeo grounds and a 10,000-seat concert venue. Fort Mojave has a local newspaper, *The Mohave Valley News.* Several radio stations can be received from Kingman and Bullhead City, Arizona, and from Needles, California. Numerous television stations can be received from Phoenix and Las Vegas. The tribe publishes a newsletter, *Ech-Kah-Nav-Cha,* ("The Storyteller"), to publicize reservation business and significant community and regional events.

Public Safety. There is a tribal police department with 14 officers. A contract with local fire department provides fire protection for the reservation.

Education. Elementary and high school students attend public schools in Arizona or California. The Aha Makav Cultural Society provides Mojave language classes year-round.

Health Care. There are two hospital clinics in nearby Needles, California, along with a dentist, a social worker, and two counselors in the community operated tribal clinic.

ENVIRONMENTAL CONCERNS
Prior to extensive economic development, the tribe prepared a water budget for its water resources, maximizing the potential of the Colorado River's flow, while protecting diversion rights to 132,536 acre-feet per year. These first-call rights are protected from state regulation.

The tribe works with federal and state agencies to restore riparian habitats, wildlife travel corridors, and wetlands along the dammed-up Colorado River and its basin. Endangered species, such as the Southwestern desert willow flycatcher, the Yuma clapper rail, and the yellow-billed Cuckoo-find a home on the reservation. Tribally sponsored environmental educational opportunities are offered in local public schools and in public forums throughout the region.

Fort Yuma
See Arizona

LOCATION AND LAND STATUS

The Graton Rancheria was originally established in 1920 on 15.45 acres of land in northern California. The tribe's federal recognition was terminated in 1966 and all tribal lands were lost. When the tribe regained federal recognition, it received rights to the remainder of its tribal lands and the right to purchase additional acreage.

CULTURE AND HISTORY

The Graton Rancheria is home to members of the Coast Miwok and Southern Pomo cultural groups. The Marshall Indians, Marin Miwok, Tomales, Tomales Bay, Hookooeko, and Bodega/Bogeda or Olamentko bands comprise the Coast Miwok, and the Sebastopol Band comprises the Southern Pomo. Traditional homelands of the Miwoks ranged from the area of West Marin County to Bodega Bay, while the Southern Pomo ancestral lands encompassed the general area of the present-day rancheria. The Miwok and Pomo groups have historically maintained close connections and resided near one another.

The Miwok and Pomo groups encountered European explorers as early as 1579. As the Spanish, and later Mexican, colonists established communities in the area, they drew upon indigenous people to serve as a labor source. Many indigenous people were forced into servitude and their tribal lands seized on behalf of the Spanish crown. In the mid-1800s, a land grant was secured for the Coast Miwoks for the Olompali Village near Novato. In 1835 the Catholic Church granted the San Rafael Christian Indians 80,000 acres of mission lands near Nicasio. By 1850 the illegal confiscation of lands by Euro-Americans had decreased tribal land to less than 4,000 acres. In 1880 the tribe was forced to move when the County of Marin terminated all financial assistance to Native people who were not living at the Poor Farm, an established site for indigent people.

Although displaced from their ancestral lands, members of the Miwok and Pomo groups continued to live in surrounding communities. In May 1920, the BIA purchased a 15.45-acre parcel of land near the town of Graton and designated the area as a rancheria for the Marshall, Bodega, Tomales, and Sebastopol groups. The small size of the rancheria, combined with its harsh terrain and limited water supply, made it difficult to construct a community there. The BIA offered no assistance to tribal members. The area became a campsite of sorts, used by tribal members as a temporary home site during harvest seasons as they worked in the local agricultural industry.

In 1958 the BIA determined that the Graton Rancheria was to be terminated and the tribal assets dissolved. Although no longer federally recognized as a tribe, tribal members continued to assert their tribal identity and participate in cultural preservation programs and activities. During the 1970s, tribal members participated in the development of Kule Loklo, a Coast Miwok Cultural Exhibit at Point Reyes Seashore. Kule Loklo hosts the annual Strawberry and Acorn festivals. Tribal members continue to serve as cultural interpreters at Kule Loklo and at Olompali State Park. Tribal members have also assisted in the development of programs for the Marin Museum of the American Indian and the Bolinas Museum.

In 1990 the Cloverdale Pomo Tribe attempted to establish a reservation near the Marshall Cemetery located within Miwok traditional lands. Tribal members established the Federated Coast Miwok Cultural Preservation Association in order to assert their tribal identity and claim jurisdiction over ancestral territories. The organization evolved into the Federated Indians of Graton Rancheria to better reflect the tribal affiliations of its membership. The tribe's restoration as a federally recognized entity came in 2001 under the Omnibus Indian Advancement Act.

GOVERNMENT

The Graton Rancheria is governed by a tribal council consisting of seven members. There are four executive council officers and three council members, each elected to a two-year term. The tribe's general council includes all eligible tribal members. Government departments and programs include housing, membership, transportation, EPA, and cultural resources.

ECONOMY

Following the restoration of federal recognition, the tribe began to investigate methods to achieve economic independence. It has established organic food processing industries and a cheese factory. It is in the process of developing a gaming facility.

Gaming. The Federated Gratons have been negotiating a gaming agreement with the county and the neighboring city of Rohnert Park. In 2000 an agreement was made that allows for construction of a gaming facility outside of Rohnert Park. The tribe will distribute $200 million to the city over a period of 20 years and provide funds for police, fire, school, housing, nonprofit, and road improvement programs of the city. In addition, the tribe has agreed to donate 321 acres and its option to purchase up to 1,679 acres along Highway 37 to the county. The development of the tribe's casino is expected to create 750 construction jobs, 3,080 indirect jobs, and 2,200 direct jobs. The proposed facility will include a casino, hotel, and restaurant. It will be funded by Station Casinos of Nevada. In addition to the payments made to Rohnert Park, gaming revenue will be shared with the county, and the remainder will be diverted to support tribal programs.

Real Estate/Commercial Development. Land in Marin and Sonoma counties, the regions of the tribe's ancestral territories, is among the most costly in the country. The tribe has purchased housing for tribal members and 360 acres west of the city of Rohnert Park. It intends to construct a gaming facility on the lands. On its remaining lands, the tribe plans to restore 573 acres of wetlands and create preservation sites of two ancestral villages.

Tourism and Recreation. The Graton Rancheria hosts an annual picnic and an annual fundraising dinner.

COMMUNITY FACILITIES AND SERVICES

Members of the Graton group serve on Ya-Ka-Ama Indian Education and Development, Inc. Located on 125 acres near Graton, this nonprofit organization provides educational, employment, social, economic, and cultural development programs for local Native peoples.

Education. In 2003 the tribe donated $1.5 million to the Sonoma State University for an Endowed Chair in Native American Studies. An endowed chair is a faculty position that is funded in perpetuity. In addition, the tribe donated a $20,000 endowed student scholarship.

Health Care. Members of the Graton group participated in the establishment of the Sonoma County Indian Health Center, Sonoma County Indian Senior Site, and the California Rural Indian Health Board.

Graton Rancheria
Federal reservation
Coast Miwok and Southern Pomo
Sonoma County, California

Federated Indians of Graton Rancheria
P.O. Box 14428
Santa Rosa, CA 95402
  707-566-2288
  707-566-2291 Fax
  coastmiwok.com

Population
(Tribal source, 2004)
2

Tribal enrollment
(Tribal source, 2004)
568

Greenville Rancheria
Federal rancheria
Maidu and Wintun
Plumas, Shasta, and Tehama
counties, California

Greenville Rancheria
P.O. Box 279
410 Main Street
Greenville, CA 95947
530-284-7990
530-284-6612 Fax
greenvillerancheria.com

Total area *(BIA realty, 2003)*
1.8 acres

Tribally owned *(BIA realty, 2003)*
1.8 acres

Total area *(Tribal source, 2004)*
383.5 acres

Tribally owned lands
28.5 acres

Allotted lands
4 acres

Tribal enrollment
(Tribal source, 2004)
97

Total labor force *2000 census*
14

Total labor force
(Tribal source, 2004)
97

High school graduate or
higher *2000 census*
100%

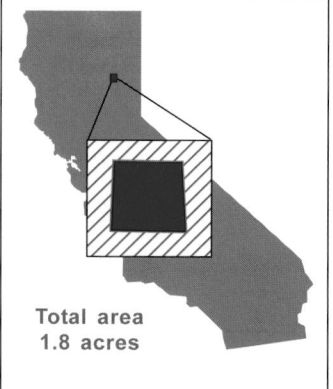

Total area
1.8 acres

LOCATION AND LAND STATUS

The rancheria is located 160 miles north of Sacramento and 60 miles west of the Nevada border, in northeastern California. The original rancheria land was in Greenville and called the Indian Mission. It was allotted land and many allotments were sold. The tribe was terminated in 1958 but was restored to federal recognition by the *Tillie Hardwick v. the United States of America* in 1983. Today, the Rancheria owns a total of 383.5 acres of which four are allotted the remaining not in trust.

CULTURE AND HISTORY

Tribal members of the Greenville Rancheria belong to the mountain Maidu Tribe, which consists of three bands in Plumas, Shasta, Tehama, and Lassen counties. The three groups are closely related culturally and linguistically. The Maidu language belongs to the Penutian language family which includes languages spoken by peoples from the northwest coast of Canada through the southwestern and southeast United States, as well as south to the Yucatan Peninsula. Ancestors of Greenville Rancheria tribal members resided in northern California as early as 1000 AD.

Spanish explorers arrived in California in the late 1500s. During the time of Spanish, and later Mexican, dominance in the territory, lands were seized from the Native populations and held in trust for the Spanish crown. Indigenous people were displaced, enslaved, and often murdered. Americans arrived in California in the mid-1800s, and they initiated a war with Mexico for rights to the California regions. The Spanish Mexicans were defeated, and in 1848 the Treaty of Guadalupe ended the Mexican-American War.

Upon the discovery of gold in northern California, Euro-Americans began arriving in the state in droves. In 1850, the California territory became a state and passed the Act for the Government and Protection of Indians. This act mandated the regulation of Indian affairs to the state, permitted Euro-Americans the right to assume custody of Native children, prohibited the use of Native testimony against a Euro-American charged with a crime, and permitted unemployed Native peoples to be arrested and hired out, a form of state-sanctioned indentured servitude. The state further protected prospectors and settlers as they encroached upon tribal territories and seized water sources in the area.

Between 1851 and 1853, Indian commissioners negotiated 18 treaties between the government and multiple Native groups. The agreements were to reserve over 7.5 million acres for various tribes across the state, but the senate did not ratify these Barbour Treaties. The tribes were not informed of this decision until the twentieth century, and they proceeded to live in agreement with the mandates outlined by the treaties. They ceded millions of acres of land to the government and confined themselves to the rancherias designated by the Barbour Treaties.

Local, state, and federal agencies condoned efforts to commit genocide against the Native people of California. Indigenous people were openly murdered, attacked, and enslaved. Atrocities committed against indigenous groups so outraged the Mexican government that officials crossed the U.S.-Mexico border to conduct investigations, and they threatened to bring arms against the citizens of California if the violence did not cease. The intervention on their behalf and their ability to isolate themselves in the mountainous regions of the state enabled some tribes to escape total decimation. However, the Native population was reduced from an estimated population of over 150,000 in 1845,

to less than 50,000 by 1855. By 1900, less than 16,000 indigenous people remained. The population of the Greenville Tribe in the early 1800s was about 4,000. By the end of the century, there were less than 500 tribal members.

The rancheria was terminated from federal status in 1958. Tribal lands were allotted and many allotments sold. Recognition was restored in 1983 pursuant to the *Tillie Hardwick Decision*. At that time, four of the original land allotments were also restored.

GOVERNMENT

The tribe is not organized under the Indian Reorganization Act of 1934. In 1996, a new constitution was drafted. The tribe is governed by a tribal council elected by the general membership. The tribal council consists of five members: a chairperson, a vice-chairperson, a secretary/treasurer, and two members-at-large. Officers serve four-year terms, while representatives serve two-year staggered terms. To vote in a tribal election, a voter must be a direct descendant of original landholders, be enrolled, and be 18 years of age or older. The tribe has 83 voting members.

The tribe has an administrative office and a medical director's office at the medical and dental facility in Red Bluff. It also has a housing commission. Under PL-638, the tribe contracts the Johnson O'Malley Scholarship Program, Indian Child Welfare Act services, an RATG Grant, a BIA Water Tech, and a BIA Transportation Planning and Development Grant.

ECONOMY

The forestry industry is a major contributor to the rancheria's economy. Although the tribe does not own or operate any facilities, many tribal members are employed with local companies. The tribe also provides a number of jobs in the community. The tribe is working on an economic development strategy with the help of CNIGA.

Government as Employer. The tribe employs 39 individuals: 25 at tribal headquarters and 14 at the Red Bluff Medical Clinic.

Forestry. Some tribal members work in the forestry industry off the rancheria. A private company is a major employer of tribal members. It is oriented toward providing services to the U.S. Forest Service, including firefighting.

Real Estate/Commercial Development. The tribe designated a 2.5-acre parcel of land on the rancheria for housing units. In 2003 it began accepting proposals from design firms and companies for the development of three units on the land. The completion date is 2005. The tribe also owns a duplex unit in Red Bluff and a quadplex unit in Redding.

INFRASTRUCTURE

Electricity. Pacific Gas and Electric provides electricity.

Fuel. Propane gas is purchased from various individual companies in the area.

Water Supply. The water supply comes from groundwater wells. There is a 35,000-gallon storage tank on the nearby mountaintop. Water and sewer services for the homes built in Tehama and Shasta counties are provided by the cities of Red Bluff and Redding. Greenville is the community Indian service district.

Transportation. The cities of Redding and Red Bluff, both approximately 110 miles from the rancheria, have commercial airports. Quincy and Plumas have small airports to accommodate jumper flights, as well as small aircraft facilities and rail and bus service. Bus service is also available in Quincy and Chester. California State Highways 36, 89, and 70 provide access to the rancheria.

Telecommunications. Internet access and cable service are available through Frontier. The local companies of Tehama, Plumas, and Shasta counties provide telephone service.

COMMUNITY FACILITIES AND SERVICES
Community centers for tribal members are located in Redding and Red Bluff. The tribe has a youth recreational program that offers seasonal activities such as ocean outings and basketball. The tribe also operates public-utility assistance, childcare, child welfare, and Tribal Assistance to Native American Family (TANAF) programs. The tribe sponsors the Maidu Cultural Development Group. The program provides language and cultural instruction and activities to tribal members.

Education. Children attend schools in the Plumas, Tehama, and Shasta Unified School Districts.

Health Care. The Greenville Rancheria owns and operates the Greenville Rancheria Medical and Dental Clinic in Greenville and the Red Bluff Medical Clinic in Red Bluff. Health programs at both clinics offer dentistry, medical, and mental health and substance abuse services. Both locations accept MediCal, Medicare, and commercial and private insurance plans. Transportation to and from the clinics is available to tribal members. Additional medical facilities are available in neighboring towns.

ENVIRONMENTAL CONCERNS
The tribe's environmental concerns include water, air quality, and soil contaminations caused by mining activities. The tribe is in the processing of setting up a tribal air monitoring station. The tribe is in complete compliance with all U.S. Environmental Protection Agency standards.

Greenville

Bachelor's degree or higher
2000 census
26.9%

Unemployment rate
2000 census
50%

Unemployment rate
(BIA labor report, 2001)
50-55%

Per capita income *2000 census*
$11,962

Grindstone

Grindstone

Total area *(BIA realty, 2003)*	100.03 acres
Tribally owned lands	100.03 acres
(BIA realty, 2003)	
Population *2000 census*	162
Tribal enrollment *(BIA labor report, 2001)*	157
Total labor force *2000 census*	54
Total labor force *(BIA labor report, 2001)*	87
High school graduate or higher	30.3%
2000 census	
Bachelor's degree or higher	0%
2000 census	
Unemployment rate *2000 census*	40.74
Unemployment rate	45%
(BIA labor report, 2001)	
Per capita income *2000 census*	$5,380

LOCATION AND LAND STATUS
The rancheria is located on a reservoir-fed creek about six miles from the small town of Elk Creek City and 32 miles west of Willows, in north-central California. The original land was purchased under the authorization of Acts on June 21, 1906, and April 1908, and by the secretary of the interior on January 7, 1909. Another 40 acres have since been purchased: 20 acres by the Modoc-Lassen Housing Authority, a consortium of several rancherias, for the purpose of a housing development; and 20 acres by the tribe.

CULTURE AND HISTORY
The Grindstone Indian Rancheria is composed of people affiliated with the Nomlaki and Wintun tribes. Their traditional languages belong to the Penutian language family, including languages spoken by peoples from coastal Canada to the southwestern and southeast United States, and south to the Yucatan Peninsula. The people resided in parts of the greater Sacramento Valley, with the Nomlaki people inhabiting parts of what are now Tehama and Glenn counties.

White contact, just before the turn of the twentieth century, caused the spread of diseases that devastated the Nomlaki population by at least 75 percent. This settlement process, with tribal lands confiscated and gathering areas of traditional foods and materials destroyed, also contributed to the disruption of tribal unity.

Moreover, the introduction of non-Native animals, such as hogs, cattle, and sheep, and the damaging effects of copper-processing plants during the 1880s and 1890s resulted in the destruction of numerous plant-food gathering areas.

In 1854 a 25,000-acre Nome Lackee Reservation was established by an Executive Order for several related peoples, but in 1863 the reservation was dissolved and the land was taken over by white immigrants. The Nomlaki people were then brutally removed to the Round Valley Reservation, and the Nome Lackee Reservation was closed.

After the turn of the twentieth century, the Grindstone Indian Rancheria finally offered a sanctuary for these people, which helped to stabilize the group. A sacred roundhouse, which still exists, was built on the rancheria; it is perhaps the oldest in use in California today. During the 1970s, the rancheria was able to rebuff a California water project, known as the Peripheral Canal Project, which planned to purchase rancheria property for a dam site.

GOVERNMENT
The tribe is governed by a general council composed of all members holding valid assignments 21 years or older. The council's business committee, composed of the tribal officers including a chairperson, vice-chairperson, and a secretary/treasurer, calls meetings. Members are elected for two-year terms.

ECONOMY
Economic Development Projects. The Grindstone Indian Rancheria is considering a number of economic-development projects that would utilize local resources. Under consideration is a gravel-processing business that would use gravel culled from the creek ruining through the rancheria. The tribe is also considering a small wood-finishing plant. The community would like to begin manufacturing mobile-home steps. Since the rancheria is located near the Mendocino National Forest, the rancheria is contemplating the feasibility of developing a hunters' retreat. This retreat would provide a storage area and showers for hunters, in addition to camper and trailer hookup facilities. There are no similar services available in the immediate area.

Grindstone Indian Rancheria
Federal reservation
Nomlaki and Wintun
Glenn County, California

Grindstone Indian Rancheria
of Wintun-Wailaki Indians
P.O. Box 63
Elk Creek, CA 95939
530-968-5365
530-968-5366 Fax

Grindstone

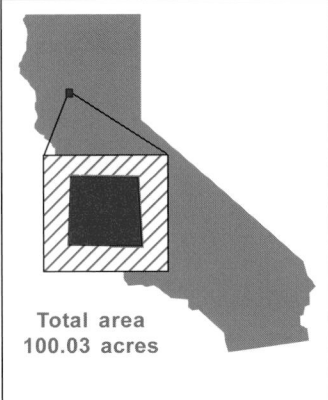

**Total area
100.03 acres**

Agriculture and Livestock. Agriculture serves as Glenn County's primary source of revenue. Grindstone Rancheria members gain seasonal employment by harvesting walnuts, pears, and prunes. Whole families are involved in the harvesting process.

The tribe would like to expand its own agricultural sector, which is based on 24 acres of arable land. The tribe intends to double crop this land, growing an early season of barley and a late season of mile.

Forestry. Three residents are employed by a local lumber mill. The timber used by the mill is harvested from the nearby Mendocino National Forest.

Services and Retail. Groceries and gasoline, as well as a restaurant, are available in the nearby town of Elk Creek.

INFRASTRUCTURE
The nearest major highway serving the community is Interstate 5, located 28 miles from the rancheria. A paved road leads into the reservation.

Electricity. Electricity is provided by Pacific Gas and Electric.

Water Supply. Residents draw water from a system installed by the U.S. Public Health Service. Septic tanks are utilized for sewage disposal. There are no trash disposal or pickup facilities on the rancheria.

Transportation. The town of Willows, 29 miles from the rancheria, offers a private airport, Amtrak rail service, bus service, and truck lines. Commercial air service is available in Chico, 53 miles away.

COMMUNITY FACILITIES AND SERVICES
Community buildings on the rancheria include a community center with a daycare facility inside, an administration building, and the Nomlaki Roundhouse. There is also a youth center, gymnasium, playing field, and ball diamond. The town of Elk Creek offers services such as fire protection and ambulance service. There is also a Temporary Aid for Needy Families (TANF) office.

Education. Tribal youth attend elementary, junior high, and senior high school in Elk Creek.

Health Care. Health services are available through Northern Valley Indian Health. Services include medical, dental, behavioral health, outreach, and women, infant, and child programs. Clinics are located in Willows and Chico.

Guidiville

**Guidiville Rancheria
Federal Reservation
Pomo
Mendocino County, California**

Guidiville Rancheria
P.O. Box 339
Talmage, CA 95481
707-462-3682
707-462-9183 Fax

Total area *(BIA realty, 2003)*	46.88 acres
Tribally owned	44.63 acres
(BIA realty, 2003)	
Individually owned	2.25 acres
(BIA realty, 2003)	
Tribal enrollment *(BIA labor report, 2001)*	114
Total labor force *(BIA labor report, 2001)*	79
Unemployment rate	16%
(BIA labor report, 2001)	

LOCATION AND LAND STATUS
The Guidiville Band occupied reservation lands in Mendocino County until 1961, when tribal lands were seized by the federal government. The tribe no longer has a land base.

CULTURE AND HISTORY
Members of the Guidiville Rancheria belong to the Pomo Tribe. (*See California introduction for additional cultural information.*)

GOVERNMENT
Tribal headquarters are located in Mendocino County.

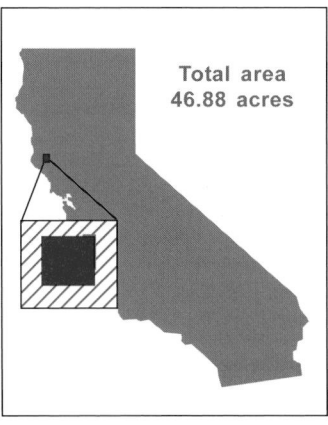

**Total area
46.88 acres**

ECONOMY
In the last few years, the band has been pursuing the development of gaming facilities. It has been seeking land to acquire and place in trust status for this purpose. To this point in time, its efforts have been unsuccessful.

Gaming. In 2004, the Guidiville Band proposed the construction of a resort and casino in San Francisco's East Bay. The proposed facility would be located on the site of a former navy fuel depot. It would include a 300,000 square foot shopping mall, a 1,100-room resort, a music auditorium, and a casino. The casino would offer 3,000 slot machines. However, the proposed project has met opposition from the Ione Band of Miwoks. The site is located at Point Molate overlooking the San Pablo Bay and Richmond-San Rafael Bridge.

In addition to the necessary BIA approval, the tribe's gaming ventures will be influenced by the state's decision in the pending gaming contract with the Lytton Band of Pomos. The proposed compact may grant the band exclusive rights to operate slot machines within a 35-mile radius of Casino San Pablo.

This is the second time that the Ione Band has opposed the Guidiville attempts to develop a casino. In 2003 the Ione Band claimed ancestral ties to Antioch, a site that the Guidivilles were proposing to develop. The plans were terminated. The Guidivilles also proposed developing a casino, hotel, and mall in Solano County, but the plan was rejected.

COMMUNITY FACILITIES AND SERVICES
Health Care. Health services are available through Consolidated Tribal Health. A clinic is located in Redwood Valley. Services include general medical and dental programs. An Indian Health Services behavioral health program is available in Talmage.

LOCATION AND LAND STATUS

The Hoopa Valley Reservation spans approximately 144 square miles in northeast Humboldt County along the Trinity River. San Francisco lies 300 miles north, Eureka 64 miles west. Land is either held in trust status or owned in fee status. Fee status lands were originally allotments on which deeds were granted; many of these lands were sold to non-Indians. Fee status land is also owned by many individual Indians as well as the Hoopa Tribe. Trust land is held in three ways: land in tribal trust, assignments to tribal members, or leases to tribal members.

The boundaries of the reservation were established by an Executive Order on June 23, 1876, pursuant to the Congressional Act of April 3, 1864. The boundaries were expanded by an Executive Order in 1891 to connect the old Klamath River (Yurok) Reservation to the Hoopa Valley Reservation. Further confirmation of the ownership by the Hupa Tribe of the Hoopa Valley Reservation came on October 31, 1988, through PL 100-580, the Hoops/Yurok Act.

The Hoopa Valley Reservation is the largest reservation in the state of California. It is located on approximately 50 percent of the tribe's traditional lands. The Hoopa Valley Reservation's seven districts (Campbell, Hostler-Matilton, Agency, Soctish-Chenone, Mesket, Norton, and Bald Hill) correspond with traditional Hupa villages.

CLIMATE

The mean annual temperature is 56.9°F. The annual rainfall is approximately 58 inches. The weather is generally wet and cool in the winter and dry in the summer.

CULTURE AND HISTORY

The Hupas (Hoopas) historically lived along the shores of Trinity River. The reservation, which covers about half of their traditional territory, contains several sites of historic and cultural significance. For many centuries the Trinity River, with its abundant runs of Chinook salmon and steelhead, served as the community center for the Hupa culture.

At the heart of the valley is the ancient village of Takimildin. This is "the center of the world" for the Hupa people, "the place where the trails return." Tributary streams divide the valley floor into six distinct fields, each corresponding to an ancient village site. For the purpose of dances and religious ceremonies, the land is divided into a northern and a southern unit, with Takimildin in the center. The Brush Dance, the White Deerskin Dance, and the Jump Dance are performed yearly.

Hupa people from the south fork of Trinity River call themselves Tsnungwe, whereas the Hoopa Valley Hupas refer to themselves as Natinook-wa. The Tsnungwes were relocated to their homeland in the 1880s and have since maintained tribal relations. The Tsnungwes are an unacknowledged tribe with a current enrollment of about 150, though federal acknowledgment is pending.

The Hoopa Valley Tribe encountered American trappers and gold miners in the early 1800s. They signed a Peace and Friendship Treaty with the federal government that designated the entire Hoopa Valley as tribal lands in 1864. The treaty was recognized by an Executive Order in 1876. In 1891 an Executive Order mandated the expansion of the reservation to connect to the old Klamath River (Yurok) Reservation. In 1896 the government began preparing an allotment list to be applied to the tribal lands. The list was not completed until 1923. The Hoopa Valley Tribe is one of the few Native nations to have been able to remain on traditional lands, and it is one of the first nations to have created a self-governance structure of government. Tribal members continue to live according to cultural traditions, speak the indigenous language, and participate in traditional spiritual customs.

GOVERNMENT

The non-IRA constitution and by-laws of the Hoopa Tribe were first approved on November 30, 1934. Revisions were adopted on September 4, 1952, August 9, 1963, and June 20, 1972. The Hoopa Valley Reservation is governed by an eight-member elected tribal council. Council members represent each of the seven districts. The districts correspond to the traditional village sites of the Hoopa Valley. The tribal council chairperson is elected by the council. A vice-chairperson is elected by the tribal council from within its membership; a secretary, a treasurer, a sergeant-at-arms, and other administrative employees are appointed by the council from outside its membership. Tribal council members are elected for two-year terms. The Hoopa Valley Tribe was one of the first Native communities to participate in the Self-Governance Demonstration Project. This tribe contracts all its governmental services under the PL-638 Self-Determination Act. It also has a comprehensive business code that defines tribal business standards.

The tribal government includes numerous entities including the self-governance office, recreation department, fiscal department, and elections department. The tribe has a tribal court system whose jurisdiction includes civil matters on the reservation. It is staffed with a judge, a bailiff and three clerks. In the planning stage is a juvenile wellness court, intended as a shelter for young offenders.

The tribe also has a police department with a chief, a lieutenant, a sergeant, a corporal, five officers, and a staff of eight. All tribal officers are graduates of state-approved police academies and are cross-deputized with Humboldt County. The reservation houses a city police substation. Tribal police also work with three natural resource officers, who protect the tribe's natural and cultural resources, and a school resource officer.

BUSINESS CORPORATIONS

The tribe owns California Indian Manpower Corporation. It provides employment services to tribes, organizations, and individuals. The company provides individual applicants with job training, referral, and assistance. It provides employers recruitment, interview, and referral assistance. The company provides tribes with organization and economic development assistance. Other company services include emergency services, a senior nutrition program, childcare services, and general community assistance services.

ECONOMY

The Hoopa Valley Tribe is the second-largest employer in the county. Timber is the reservation's primary natural resource, and a majority of the reservation is designated as commercial timberland. Through timber, some fishing and farming, and various retail enterprises, the Hoopa Valley Tribe is largely self-sufficient, despite the economic difficulties of the surrounding region. The tribe also engages in gaming.

Hoopa Valley Reservation
Federal reservation
Hupa (Hoopa)
Humboldt County, California

Hoopa Valley Tribe
P.O. Box 1348
Hoopa, CA 95546
530-625-4211
530-625-4594 Fax
hoopa-nsn.gov

Total area *(BIA realty, 2003)*
89,426.39 acres

Tribally owned lands
(BIA realty, 2003)
88,124.78 acres

Individually owned
(BIA realty, 2003)
1,301.61 acres

Allotted lands
2,250 acres

Population *2000 census*
2,051

Tribal enrollment
(BIA labor report, 2001)
1,893

Total labor force *2000 census*
1,001

Total labor force
(BIA labor report, 2001)
4,872

**High school graduate or
higher** *2000 census*
72.1%

Bachelor's degree or higher
2000 census
7.5%

Unemployment rate *2000 census*
24.3%

Unemployment rate
(BIA labor report, 2001)
40%

Per capita income
2000 census
$10,400

Hoopa Valley

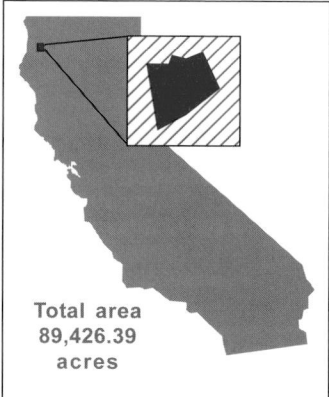

Total area
89,426.39
acres

Government as Employer. The Hoopa Valley Tribe employs over 450 people in 34 different tribal entities.

Economic Development Projects. The tribe is developing a manufacturing plant that will produce modular homes. The plant will employ approximately 145 individuals.

Agriculture and Livestock. Although a substantial amount of acreage is suitable for agricultural production, fragmented land ownership patterns prohibit large-scale commercial farming. At present, agricultural production is limited to small plot vegetable crops for household consumption, some grains, and native hay. Individuals also raise both horses and cattle on the reservation. In addition, the Hoopa Valley Reservation participates in the University of California's extension program.

Forestry. Since the end of World War II, the primary economic activity on the Hoopa Valley Reservation has been its timber industry. A total of 55,000 acres of forested land are classified as harvest areas on the reservation. Hoopa's dominant old-growth species is the Douglas fir. Since the late 1980s, the tribal government has managed its timber resources for a sustained yield harvest of approximately 12 million board feet, and it brings in between $4 and $6 million of annual revenue, depending on the timber market.

Hoopa Forest Industries (HFI), a division of the Hoopa Valley Development Enterprise, logs and markets tribal timber. HFI practices environmentally responsible logging and gives priority to hiring tribal members. HFI employs between 35 and 40 members full-time and provides 60 seasonal jobs. A new fire suppression facility was built in 2003. This forestry program has become a model for Indian forestry programs throughout Indian country.

Tsemeta Forest Regeneration Complex, a tribal enterprise, supplies seedlings for restocking reservation timberland, and sells seedlings to the Forest Service and other off-reservation entities. Employees harvest and maintain a seed bank using a local genetic base. This technique results in the production of superior quality trees that have a low mortality rate. The nursery is a certified organic producer of medicinal herbs. It also grows ornamental and native grasses and provides custom services, such as seed collection, cleaning, processing, stratification, and vegetative cutting and sprouting. The nursery's warehouse facility provides processing and packaging of specialty plant materials.

Gaming. The tribe owns the Lucky Bear Casino in Hoopa. The casino is a 5,000-square-foot facility that offers 85 slots/VLTs.

Fisheries. Hoopa Valley Tribal Fisheries is funded in part by the Bureau of Reclamation, the Bureau of Indian Affairs (BIA) Compact, and the National Marine Fisheries Service. Its functions include monitoring and reporting the fishery in the Trinity River Basin. Activities include fish tagging, weir operations, creel census, and net harvest monitoring. The department co-manages the Trinity River Hatchery with the California Department of Fish and Game.

Construction. Many tribal members are involved in the construction industry, working on both nonreservation and reservation sites.

Mining. The tribe owns and operates the Hoopa Valley Aggregates and Redi-Mix Enterprises, which consists of two production sites. A cement plant is located in Salyer, California, and an aggregate plant is located in Hoopa. In the past, both lode and placer deposits have been mined in Hoopa Valley. The reservation is exploring its other mineral reserves, as the reservation may contain viable copper and mercury reserves in lode deposits, as well as the potential for platinum and gold recovery from placer deposits.

Services and Retail. The tribe's Best Western Tsewenaldin Inn provides tourist information, limited tours, ride services, and continental breakfasts. The motel caters to both the vacation market and business travelers. Hotel facilities include conference rooms, an outdoor pool and spa, and a gift shop. The hotel overlooks Trinity River. The Hoopa Tribal Museum is adjacent to the hotel. The Inn serves as an important source of tribal revenue and employment.

The tribe's BP Station and mini-mart was built to replace an existing gas station. The facility offers a service bay for minor automotive work, a full line of convenience items, and gas, diesel, and propane fuel. The operation, which had a gross profit margin of over 30 percent in 1993, provides seven full-time and two part-time jobs. It also houses a Chester Fried franchise and serves as the drop-off site for Hoopa Tribal Fisheries data.

In addition, several new businesses have opened on the reservation. Services include a credit union, a hay and grain store, a laundromat, a computer store, a food and meat market, two pizza parlors, one breakfast and lunch restaurant, a delicatessen, and an office supply store. These businesses both promote the reservation's self-sufficiency and provide jobs for tribal members. A number of tribal members successfully market their artistry, both traditional and nontraditional.

Media and Communications. The tribe owns KIDE 91.3, a radio station that provides local, regional, and national programs and music to the community. It is associated with the National Federation of Community Broadcasters, American Indian Radio on Satellite, Corporation for Public Broadcasting, Rural Station Programming Initiative, and the Public Radio Satellite System. It has a staff of six, with five volunteers. The *Hoopa People Newspaper* is a biweekly publication serving the tribe. The tribe owns a cell tower and sells space to carriers.

Tourism and Recreation. The Hoopa Valley Tribal Museum is located adjacent to the Tswenaldin Inn in Hoopa. It is a nonprofit organization that displays collections of Hupa, Yurok, and Karuk artifacts. Many of the items on display, including Hupa dance regalia and basketry, are on loan from tribal members. Exhibits include a historical account of the reservation, Fort Gaston, and settlements in the area.

There are many sites of cultural, historic, and archeological significance on the Hoopa Valley Reservation. These sites include ceremonial dance grounds, aboriginal village sites, family cemeteries, and traditional camping and gathering areas. Traditional ceremonies and dances are also held annually and are open to the public. Other reservation events include the Logging Show (held in early May), the Whitewater Boat Race (held Mother's Day and Father's Day), the Hoopa Open Rodeo (held in late June), and the Fourth of July Celebration.

The tribe also sponsors an annual Sovereign Day Celebration in honor of the original treaty that established the reservation and the month when Congress recognized the tribe's ownership of the lands. Festivities include a parade, vendors, dancers, music, games, fireworks, and the All Indian Rodeo. It also sponsors the Coyote Run, the All Indian Basketball Tournament, a Christmas bazaar, and the Bald Hill Climb.

Aside from all the scheduled activities, tourists come to the reservation to enjoy its natural beauty. Outdoor enthusiasts enjoy swimming, hiking, fly fishing, rafting, and camping on the reservation. The tribe provides river tours and tours of the fishery and nursery by appointment.

INFRASTRUCTURE
State Highway 96, which runs north-south through the reserva-

TRI-CA-029

TRI-CA-030

TRI-CA-028

Hoopa Valley

TRI-CA-027

tion, serves as the chief access to the reservation. Highway 96 intersects with U.S. 299, 12 miles south of the reservation, and with Interstate 5. U.S. 101, the area's main artery, runs along the California coast 50 miles west of the reservation.

The Hoopa Valley Tribal Roads Department manages and maintains the 108 miles of roadways within the reservation. The department works in collaboration with the natural resources department to ensure that the construction and improvement of roads are sensitive to the ecosystem on the reservation.

Electricity. Pacific Gas and Electric supplies electricity.

Fuel. Gas is purchased from private vendors.

Water Supply. The Hoopa Valley Public Utilities District supplies reservation residencies with water services, solid waste collection, septic tank service, and general maintenance of water and sewer systems. A new water treatment facility is set to open in spring 2005. The tribe operates a full-service transfer station for solid waste disposal.

Transportation. Commercial air service is available at the Eureka/Arcata Airport. The tribe maintains a 2,022-foot runway used primarily for medical emergency transportation. UPS, the U.S. Postal Service, and Federal Express all serve the reservation daily, as do grocery supply trucks.

COMMUNITY FACILITIES AND SERVICES
The Neighborhood Facilities Building houses the tribe's recreation program and youth center. The complex includes a game room, a swimming pool and swimming lessons, a basketball court, and a tennis court. In addition, there are six churches on the reservation, and the Kim Yerton Memorial Library.

The Hoopa AmeriCorps on Native Lands Program assists community members in environmental projects specifically related to dwellings. Individuals may apply to serve as an AmeriCorps representative and receive the benefits of the position, including an education award of over $4,000 upon completion of the re-

quired 1,700 hours of service to the tribe. The program is only one of three tribal AmeriCorps programs in the nation. The tribe also operates the Tribal Civilian Community Corps.

Public Safety. The tribe provides emergency services to the reservation and nearby communities. Services include law enforcement, ambulance, volunteer fire department, and a wild land fire department. The tribe compacted the fire presuppression and suppression program through the BIA.

Education. The Klamath-Trinity Unified School District has offices and schools on the reservation. The College of the Redwoods maintains a branch community college in Hoops. Humboldt State University is located in Arcata.

The tribe provides various educational services for tribal members from infancy to adulthood. Programs include the Even Start Program, an Early Head Start program, and a Head Start program as well as adult education and GED classes. An education complex is under development and should be completed in summer 2005. Facilities will include an early childhood care building.

Health Care. The K'ima:w Medical Center is a tribally owned health center providing services to tribal members and nontribal members. In addition to medical services, the center provides community outreach programs addressing the prevention of injury and violence. It also operates the senior nutrition program and transportation services.

The K'ima:w Field Health and Outreach Department provides health screenings, home visits, health education, and support services for the community. The tribe also operates the dental clinic and K'ima:w Pharmacy.

The tribe's division of human services provides programs relating to mental health, drug and alcohol rehabilitation, domestic violence, child welfare, and community service. The Hoopa Tribe also provides its employees with insurance to assist in meeting medical needs.

TRI-CA-027 Welcome sign to Hoopa Valley Reservation

TRI-CA-028 The beautiful Hoopa River

TRI-CA-029 Hoopa Tribal Building

TRI-CA-030 Newly built Hoopa Valley Fire Department

ENVIRONMENTAL CONCERNS
The Tribal Environmental Protection Agency manages the tribe's environmental protection activities. The agency addresses issues such as water quality, air quality, hazardous waste, and pesticide contamination on the reservation.

Hopland

Hopland Reservation
Federal reservation
Pomo
Mendocino County, California

Hopland Band of Pomo
Indians
3000 Shanel Road
P.O. Box 610
Hopland, CA 95449
707-744-1647
707-744-1506 Fax
hoplandtribe.com

Total area (BIA realty, 2003)
371.94 acres

Tribally owned lands
(BIA realty, 2003)
285.49 acres

Individually owned
(BIA realty, 2003)
86.45 acres

Population
45

Tribal enrollment
(BIA labor report, 2001)
692

Tribal enrollment
(Tribal source 2004)
710

Total labor force
(BIA labor report, 2001)
363

**High school graduate or
higher**
2000 census
100%

Bachelor's degree or higher
2000 census
0%

Unemployment rate
(BIA labor report, 2001)
51%

Per capita income
2000 census
$18,000

LOCATION AND LAND STATUS

The Hopland Reservation is located 90 miles north of San Francisco, 13 miles south of Ukiah, and approximately 4 miles east of State Highway 101, along State Highway 175. The majority of the developed area of the reservation lies in a small valley and consists of about 500 acres of vineyards and homes. Approximately 350 acres of the reservation are held in federal trust status for the community, and the remainder is owned privately by Indian and non-Indian families alike.

The original rancheria (comprised of two tracts totaling 2,070 acres) was established by departmental order on June 18, 1907, and acts on June 21, 1906, and April 30, 1908. The rancheria was terminated under the California Rancheria Act, and deeds were issued to individuals. By 1978 only 184 acres of the original 2,070 acres remained in Indian hands. Pursuant to a judgment vesting title issued in *Daniels v. Andrus, No. CI 0661 WTS,* trust status has been reinstated to 350 acres of community lands and 64.53 acres of individually owned lands.

The decision as to whether individually owned lands would return to trust status was left up to the owner. Currently there are 38 parcels held in fee title by the tribe. An additional 250 acres have been purchased by the band. As a result of the effects of allotment and termination, the Hopland Reservation has a checkerboard landownership pattern.

CULTURE AND HISTORY

Members of the Hopland Reservation belong to the Pomo Tribe. Traditional homelands for the band include regions encompassing Humboldt County to San Pablo Bay. Tribal members made seasonal journeys to the Pacific Ocean on fishing and gathering excursions. The indigenous language belongs to the Hokan language family, which includes languages spoken by peoples living from southern Oregon to southern Mexico.

European settlement of the California territory disrupted Pomo culture through the spread of diseases, the usurpation of tribal lands, and forced incarceration on federal reservations. In response, the Pomos banded together in efforts to buy back their lands from the late 1870s through the 1890s. By the turn of the twentieth century, however, much of this land was confiscated through foreclosure settlements and mortgage debts.

Responding to public pressure, in 1905 Congress authorized an investigation of the living conditions of "landless" Indians. Beginning in 1906, legislation initiated by C. E. Kelsey, the lawyer and special agent appointed to lead the investigation, authorized annual appropriations for the purchase of Indian lands. Kelsey himself helped to found the Hopland Reservation.

During a period of intense separatism and animosity toward indigenous peoples, the Pomos actively used the courts to challenge local segregation policies. For instance, in 1907, an Eastern Pomo, Ethan Anderson, won a court case granting the right to vote to non-reservation Indians. In 1923 Stephan Knight, in Mendocino County, challenged the state school-segregation laws and, in an out-of-court settlement, forced a local public school to admit his daughter. Knight later took on the City of Ukiah, challenging the separatist policy of the local movie theater.

While traditionally subsisting on native plants, fish, and game, the Pomos were forced to enter the wage economy during the Depression. Many Pomo women moved to the San Francisco Bay

area and worked as domestics; there they were aided by the BIA. Pomo men, on the other hand, found local employment as migrant field workers and ranch laborers.

The Hopland Pomos strive to incorporate their traditional beliefs and practices into the context of their modern lives. They express their cultural heritage through their internationally recognized basketwork and through their ceremonial dancing.

GOVERNMENT

A seven-member elected tribal council governs the Hopland Reservation. The council includes a chairperson, a vice-chairperson, a secretary, and a treasurer. Officers are elected for two-year staggered terms. In addition, there is a general council of all tribal members, which meets annually.

Governmental departments include housing, police, health, and education. The tribe has a compact with the government, contracting: health services through the IHS; water and wastewater services through the EPA; housing services through HUD; and tribal police, road service, and housing through the BIA.

Contracted through the BIA, the tribe's law enforcement program includes a tribal court and a police department. Law enforcement officers are trained by the BIA or California state police academies.

BUSINESS CORPORATION

In 2000, the Economic Development Corporation became a separate entity of the tribe. The corporation oversees projects of economic development for the tribe and reports to the tribal council.

ECONOMY

Tribal economy is supported in large part by their casino. Other tribal enterprises include a vineyard and a party supply store.

Government as Employer. The tribe employs 60 individuals.

Economic Development Projects. The tribe is exploring the feasibility of developing an independent utility district, a power generator, and an alternate energy source for the reservation. As part of their development strategy, the Hopland people would like to develop a motel and restaurant complex on their land.

Agriculture and Livestock. The tribe has a 20-acre vineyard. Mendocino County's economic base is primarily agricultural. A number of Hopland men are employed at local ranches and farms.

Gaming. The tribe owns the Hopland Sho-Ka-Wah Casino in Hopland. The casino features 1,149 slots/VLTs and 16 table games. Facilities include a gift shop and two restaurants. The casino employs 313 individuals. Revenue generated by the casino is used to fund tribal programs and services. Monies have also been used to support political causes.

Real Estate/Commercial Development. The tribe owns property in the town of Hopland that is used for office space. The tribe assists members in purchasing homes. Land purchases made in the last decade have enabled the tribe to construct a casino, a parking lot, housing facilities, a water treatment plant, a wastewater treatment plant, vineyards, and roads.

TRI-CA-031

TRI-CA-032

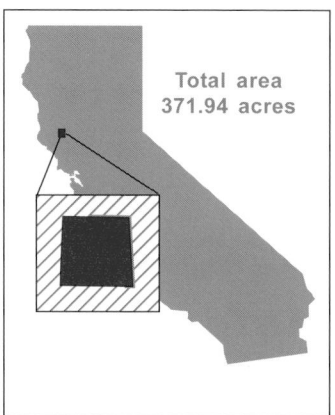

Total area
371.94 acres

Services and Retail. The tribe owns the Gala Customs and Party Supply Store located off the reservation. The store has two full-time employees.

The tribe also owns the Matuu Corporation. The corporation contracts economic development planning services to smaller tribes.

The tribe manages the ATM located at the casino, and it has an exclusive contract with the Bay Area Rapid Transit system (BART) to operate ATMs and kiosks at 18-20 BART stations.

There are a number of small businesses in the vicinity of the reservation. A number of Hopland women are employed as clerical workers in Ukiah.

TRI-CA-033

INFRASTRUCTURE
California State Highway 175 is the nearest major artery; it connects with U.S. 101 in the town of Hopland. All reservation roads are maintained by the county, except the road leading to the HUD housing project, which is maintained by the BIA.

Electricity. Electricity is provided to the rancheria by Pacific Gas and Electric.

Water Supply. The Hopland HUD housing project has its own sewage-collection facility and water system. Other residents rely on wells and septic tanks. Solid waste is handled by Empire Waste of Ukiah.

Transportation. Bus services are available on the rancheria, as are Federal Express and UPS. Railway access is available approximately three miles distant.

COMMUNITY FACILITIES AND SERVICES
The rancheria features a community center and gym.

The tribe provides its own fire protection through donations and agreements with local fire districts.

Education. The tribe operates an educational center that offers early childhood development programs, language and cultural activities, and educational support services. Children attend off-reservation public schools.

Health Care. Tribal members may receive health services through Consolidated Tribal Health. The clinic, located in Redwood Valley, California, offers general medical and dental services. The tribe serves as a board member of Consolidated Tribal Health. The Hopland tribe also has a CHC contract with IHS.

The tribe has received a grant to develop a wellness program that will incorporate traditional cultural elements into the prevention and treatment of substance abuse, domestic violence, and the victimization of children.

ENVIRONMENTAL CONCERNS
The tribe has identified solid waste removal, water-sewer cleanup, and air, water, and ground cleanup as areas of concern on the reservation.

TRI-CA-031 Hopland School located in tribal administrative complex

TRI-CA-032 Hopland Tribal Offices

TRI-CA-033 Hopland Tribal Police Car

Inaja-Cosmit Reservation
Federal reservation
Kumeyaay
Riverside County, California

Inaja-Cosmit Band of Mission
Indians
309 Maple Street
Escondido, CA 92025
760-737-7628
760-747-8568 Fax

Total area (Tribal source, 2004)		846.6 acres
Tribally owned (BIA, 2003)		851.81 acres
Population		1
Tribal enrollment (BIA labor report, 2001)		18
Tribal enrollment (Tribal source, 2004)		20
Total labor force (BIA labor report, 2001)		12
Unemployment rate		75%
(BIA labor report, 2001)		

LOCATION AND LAND STATUS

The Inaja-Cosmit Reservation is located 36 miles northeast of San Diego. It is accessible via Interstate 8 east and California Route 67 north. Tribal lands consist of two parcels of rather remote and somewhat inaccessible land at the base of Cuyamaca Peak. Deep winter snows and a lack of facilities make these locations inhospitable to all but the hardiest.

CULTURE AND HISTORY

Members of the Inaja-Cosmit Band belong to the Kumeyaay Nation. Tribal lands of the Kumeyaay Nation extend from San Diego and Imperial counties in California to territories 60 miles south of the Mexican border. The Kumeyaays are members of the Yuman-language branch of the Hokan linguistic group.

The Kumeyaays first encountered Spanish explorers in 1542. Over the next 200 years, the Spanish continued to arrive along the Pacific coast and to venture inland. Contact between the Spanish and Kumeyaays was violent, and the Kumeyaays managed to escape capture or confinement numerous times.

Americans arrived in the San Diego area in the 1840s. The Kumeyaay tribes offered assistance to the American military in efforts to overthrow the Spanish Mexican forces. The Spanish Mexicans were defeated, and in 1848 the Treaty of Guadalupe ended the Mexican-American War. Upon the discovery of gold in northern California, Euro-Americans began arriving in the state in droves. In 1850 the California territory became a state and passed the Act for the Government and Protection of Indians. This act mandated the regulation of Indian affairs to the state, permitted Euro-Americans the right to assume custody of Native children, prohibited the use of Native testimony against a Euro-American charged with a crime, and permitted unemployed Native peoples to be arrested and hired out, a form of state-sanctioned indentured servitude. The state further protected prospectors and settlers as they encroached upon tribal territories and seized water sources in the area.

In January 1852, the Treaty of Santa Ysabel was negotiated between the government and the Ipai and Tipai Kumeyaay bands. The treaty was one of 18 that would be negotiated between the government and multiple Native groups between 1851 and 1853. The agreements were to reserve 7.5 million acres for various tribes across the state, but the senate did not ratify the treaties. The Kumeyaays, and other affected tribes, were left vulnerable to forcible evictions and dislocation from remaining lands. Local, state, and federal agencies condoned the effort to commit genocide against the Native people of California. Indigenous people were openly murdered, attacked, and enslaved. Atrocities committed against indigenous groups so outraged the Mexican government that officials crossed the U.S.-Mexico border to conduct investigations, and they threatened to bring arms against the citizens of California if the violence did not cease. The intervention on their behalf and their ability to isolate themselves in the mountainous regions of the state enabled some tribes to escape total decimation. However, the Native population was reduced from an estimated population of over 150,000 in 1845, to less than 50,000 by 1855. By 1900, less than 16,000 indigenous people remained. The Kumeyaay tribes were fortunate in the relatively small number of losses they experienced until smallpox swept through the region in the 1860s, but the population of the clans was reduced from 2000 in 1850 to 200 by 1890.

Although reduced in size, and suffering from the loss of access to traditional water supplies and lands, the Kumeyaays continued to engage in conflict with the Americans throughout the latter half of the nineteenth century. In 1875 the Kumeyaay clans were excluded from an Executive Order that created reservations throughout San Diego. By 1890 the clans had become scattered and were suffering from continuing attacks by Americans, diseases, and starvation.

There are 13 federal reservations for the Kumeyaay Nation in the United States and three communities in Mexico. Members of the Kumeyaay Nation strive to maintain cultural traditions and elements. The Kumeyaay language has survived to this day in spite of strong pressure to suppress it. Now spoken mostly by elders, serious efforts are being made to teach the language to younger people. All speakers of Kumeyaay are also fluent in either English or Spanish, and sometimes other American Indian languages as well.

GOVERNMENT

The Inaja-Cosmits are governed by a tribal chairperson, and they maintain a tribal office in Escondido, California. Government programs include the Indian Child Welfare Act Committee and a Tribal Digital Village Representative.

ECONOMY

At this time, there is only one residency located on tribal lands and no businesses, enterprises, or other facilities.

Construction. The tribe is in the process of reconstructing homes that were destroyed in the wildfires of 2003.

INFRASTRUCTURE

The reservation is located in a remote setting at Cuyamaca Peak. It is accessible via Interstate 8 or California Route 67. There is only one residency on the reservation. No utilities are available to this home.

Water Supply. An individual well and an individual septic tank serve the single residency on this reservation.

COMMUNITY FACILITIES AND SERVICES

A tribal office is located in Escondido.

Health Care. The Indian Health Council (IHC) serves the Inaja-Cosmits with clinics in Valley Center. Services include general medicine, general dental, human services, and community outreach. The IHC also maintains a clinic in San Ysabel, which provides the same services as the Valley Center clinic.

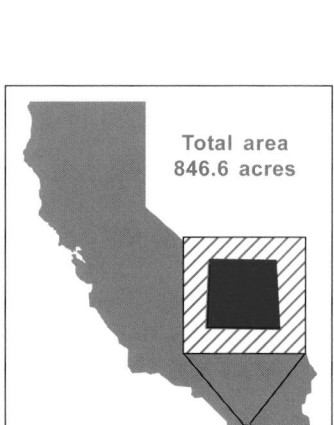

Total area
846.6 acres

LOCATION AND LAND STATUS

Tribal lands of the Ione Band of Miwok Indians are located near the town of Ione, about 40 miles east of Sacramento, California. The reservation was created in 1915 when 40 acres of land were purchased for the tribe's use.

CULTURE AND HISTORY

The Ione Band is a member of Nisenan- and Miwok-speaking people. Traditional homelands of the Miwoks encompassed northern California. The Miwoks were originally composed of three groups: the Sierra Miwoks, the Lake Miwoks, and the Coast Miwoks. The groups lived along the San Joaquin and Sacramento rivers between areas north of San Francisco Bay and the foothills of the Sierra Nevada Mountains. The Ione Band is descended from the Sierra Miwoks, whose traditional homelands included the Sierra Nevada Foothills.

When European explorers arrived in northern California, Miwok populations exceeded 20,000. The population was steadily reduced as a result of genocidal attacks and enslavement. The arrival of Euro-American settlers in the 1800s brought additional violence, as well as diseases, that further reduced the population.

The discovery of gold in northern California ushered in an era of great devastation for indigenous populations of northern California, including the Miwok tribes. Further attacks on tribal populations decimated several groups, and the seizure of traditional lands rendered many indigenous peoples homeless. The Miwok tribes were party to the Barbour Treaties that were negotiated with the federal government, in which many tribes ceded lands in return for permanent reservations. Congress failed to ratify these treaties, and though unaware, the affected tribes honored their promises and resigned themselves to designated areas and lived with little to no protection or assistance from the local, state, or federal governments. Many Miwok tribal members joined the communities of neighboring tribes, contributing to the creation of united groups of Native peoples with various tribal affiliations.

In 1915, the BIA identified a number of Miwok tribal members residing in or near Ione, California. These 101 individuals were later recognized as three distinct tribes, including the Ione Band of Miwok Indians, the Jackson Rancheria of Me-wuk Indians, and the Buena Vista Rancheria of Me-Wuk Indians. The U.S. promised to purchase 40 acres of land to create a permanent land base for the Ione Band and a number of tribal members relocated to the parcel. However, the lands were never designated a federal reservation, and in 1971 Miwok residents sought legal assistance. The parcel was eventually awarded to the ownership of the individuals named in the suit, but not to the tribe itself. In 1972 the BIA agreed to take the land into trust for the tribe, if the tribe could attain title to it. The tribe was unable to gain title to the lands because they were not a federally recognized tribe. In 1978 the tribe sought recognition under the Federal Acknowledgement Project, a process that would take several years. In 1994 the tribe was informed that it had received federal recognition in 1915, at the time when the 40-acre parcel was originally purchased. The BIA directed the tribe to organize a tribal council and membership roll based on the 1915 census and the 1972 judgment. A council was elected in 1996 and a tribal constitution adopted in September 2002.

In 2002, the Ione Band became the center of a widely publicized controversy. Against the wishes of tribal leaders, regional BIA officials opened tribal enrollment to include members from two other bands. Since that time, tribal enrollment has skyrocketed from 70 to over 500 members. None of the newly enrolled members are related to the original 70. Furthermore, a number of the newly enrolled members are BIA employees and their extended families. The BIA has denied requests that the matter be investigated.

The tribe has played a key role in obstructing the development of gaming facilities by other tribes in the Bay Area. In 2003, the Guidiville Band proposed the development of a facility at Antioch. The Ione Band claimed ancestral ties to the area, and the project was eventually terminated. The band has opposed a second proposal by the Guidiville Band at San Pablo Bay based on the assertion that the band has no ancestral claims to the land.

GOVERNMENT

The Ione Band government was organized in 1996 following the affirmation of recognition from the federal government in 1994. The tribe initially elected an interim tribal council, and it adopted a tribal council in September 2002. The first tribal elections were held in April 2003. The tribe is governed by a tribal council comprised of a chairperson, vice-chairperson, secretary, treasurer, and member-at-large. Each council member serves a three-year term. The mission of the Ione Band of Miwok Indians is to empower tribal members to achieve a better way of life and maintain tribal integrity and honor through a responsive government. The tribe is committed to preserving and exercising its sovereign rights in order to protect its cultural and historical integrity.

ECONOMY

The tribe's goal is to achieve true economic self-reliance. Increasing the tribal land base is key to achieving this goal, and the tribe is working toward this end. The tribe has received almost $2 million from the state's Tribal Revenue Sharing Trust Fund. The monies are being used to provide tribal members with emergency assistance for housing, health care, and energy bills. The Trust Fund is a program through which nongaming tribes in the state of California may receive funds contributed by gaming tribes.

Economic Development Projects. The tribe is proposing to develop a class III gaming facility on 220 acres along the outskirts of the town of Plymouth, California, and in the unincorporated area of Amador County. The 120,000-square-foot facility will offer 2,000 gaming machines, 40 tables, a restaurant, a buffet, a coffee shop, a snack bar, a retail center, an entertainment venue, a bingo hall, a convention center, meeting rooms, a day care facility, a video arcade, a lounge and bar, and administrative offices. The tribe will utilize revenue to fund tribal services and programs, such as health, education, and economic development. The casino will generate a great source of income and employment for local economies as well. The 220-acre parcel is in the process of being placed into federal trust status for the tribe.

COMMUNITY FACILITIES AND SERVICES

Health Care. Health services are available through the MACT Health Board. Clinics are located in Tuolumne, Sutter Creek, and Mariposa. Services include medical, dental, outreach, and substance abuse programs.

Ione Band of Miwok Indians
Reservation
Federal reservation
Miwok
Amador County, California

Ione Band of Miwok Indians
P.O. Box 1190
Ione, CA 95640
209-274-6753
209-274-6636 Fax

Total area
40 acres

Tribal enrollment
(BIA Labor Report, 2001)
536

Total labor force
2000 census
13

Total labor force
(BIA Labor Report, 2001)
370

High school graduate or higher
2000 census
66.7%

Bachelor's degree or higher
2000 census
0%

Unemployment rate
2000 census
0%

Unemployment rate
(BIA Labor Report, 2001)
43%

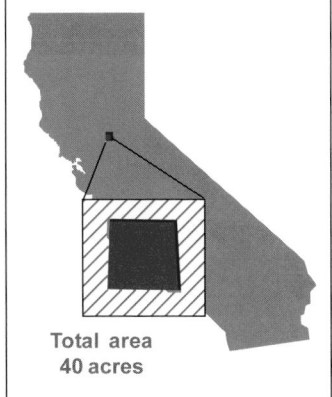

Total area
40 acres

Jackson

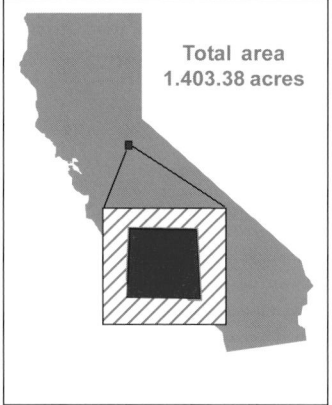

Total area
1.403.38 acres

LOCATION AND LAND STATUS
The Jackson Rancheria occupies approximately 1,330 acres in central California, in the foothills of the Sierra Nevada Mountains, about 50 miles southwest of Sacramento. It was initially established on January 7, 1895, after an Act on March 3, 1893, appropriated $10,000 to purchase land for the Digger Indians of Central California at Jackson.

PHYSICAL DESCRIPTION
The Jackson Rancheria is located in the foothills of the Sierra Nevada Mountains in northern California. The region is characterized by oak trees and grasslands.

CULTURE AND HISTORY
Members of the Jackson Rancheria belong to the Sierra Mi-Wuk Band of the Mi-Wuk Tribe. The tribe consists of two other bands: the Coast Mi-Wuk and the Lake Mi-Wuk. Traditional Mi-Wuk homelands encompassed lands along the foothills of the Sierra Nevada Mountains in central California. The present-day rancheria includes portions of the traditional lands. The Sierra Mi-wuks occupy three rancherias at Shingle Springs, Tuolumne, and Jackson, and three nontrust status communities at Sheep Ranch, Buena Vista, and Chicken Ranch.

For the Sierra Mi-wuks, white contact came with a fury in the wake of the California gold rush, which began in 1848. Prior to contact, Sierra Mi-wuks numbered about 8,000; by 1910 their numbers had dwindled to less than 700. The balance had succumbed to diseases and widespread killings, and most of the survivors fled into hiding.

Today, the Sierra Mi-wuks occupy a portion of their ancestral lands. The tribe has had to weather numerous struggles with the federal government over compensation for appropriated territories and for official recognition. The Mi-wuks, like other tribes, faced termination after the 1958 California Rancheria Act. The Jackson Rancheria escaped termination to remain one of only two federally recognized bands of Mi-wuks (the other being the Tuolumne Band).

GOVERNMENT
In 1995 the Jackson Rancheria was organized under a draft IRA constitution and bylaws, and it is governed by an interim council. The council officers include a chairperson, vice-chairperson, and a secretary-treasurer. The tribe operates a police department. Law enforcement officers are post-certified federal officers who meet all of the state's peace officer requirements.

ECONOMY
Tribal economy is largely supported by the tribe's gaming operations. The casino is the largest employer in the county and employs over 1,600 people. The tribe makes annual charitable donations. It focuses its philanthropic activity in Amador and Calaveras counties. The tribe has granted funds to community groups, schools, organizations, and projects benefiting children and elders. In 2004, the tribe donated $33,000 to the Amador High School to assist in the project to resurface the school track.

Government as Employer. Since the tribal government directly controls and operates the casino, most employed tribal members work for or through the tribal government. The casino employs ever 1,600 people.

Economic Development Projects. Revenue from the tribe's gaming operations has enabled the tribe to recover economically from its previous status as an impoverished community. The tribe has financed projects, tribal programs, and enterprises to sustain its success.

Gaming. The Jackson Indian Bingo facility opened in 1987. Since then, it has undergone reconfiguration and become the Jackson Rancheria Casino and Hotel. It employs over 1,600 people and is the largest employer in Amador County. The casino offers over 1,500 machines, 33 table games, and craps and roulette. The casino is a 130,000-square-foot facility that includes a convention center, two gift shops, seven restaurants, and two entertainment venues. The adjacent hotel has 146 guest rooms and a conference and banquet facility. The tribe has developed a daycare facility that serves families of casino employees.

The tribe has used income from its gaming operations to develop programs to help tribal members and various charities. Tribal members benefited from 17 housing units built; and local and Native American charities have benefited from The Giving Season program and Holiday Cheer Fund. The Giving Season program allots funds earned at the casino to go to charity. Recipients of the 2003 Giving Season were the Jackson Rancheria Activity Fund, the Interfaith Food Bank, the Calaveras Band of Mi-Wuk Indians, the American Indian Council of Mariposa, and the Sierra Native American Council.

Forestry. The densely forested land in and near Mi-Wuk territory has traditionally provided employment opportunities through lumber-related industries. However, the small size of the Jackson Rancheria strictly limits the tribe's timber resources.

Mining. Though the legendary California gold rush played itself out within a few years, the region remains a site for freelance prospectors, as well as for a few tourist ventures that advertise gold panning in area creeks and streams.

Services and Retail. The tribe has invested in off-reservation real estate, and in 2004 it constructed a 120-unit apartment complex in nearby Sutter Creek. This has helped to address a shortage of housing in Amador County.

INFRASTRUCTURE
Highway 88, which connects to Stockton 45 miles to the southwest, serves as the primary highway access to the rancheria. Highway 16 provides access to Sacramento.

Water Supply. The tribe operates its own wastewater treatment plants.

Transportation. Light commercial air service is available at a municipal airport located six miles from the rancheria. Bus service is available four miles away. Federal Express serves the nearby town of Jackson, while UPS serves the region.

COMMUNITY FACILITIES AND SERVICES
The tribe is currently developing new recreational facilities on recently acquired trust land. This includes the preservation of some newly discovered sacred sites.

Education. The town of Jackson provides public school services. Red Hawk School was established on the Rancheria to provide education to tribal members. This has allowed all tribal members the opportunity to earn a high school diploma.

Health Care. MACT Health Board provides services located on the rancheria.

LOCATION AND LAND STATUS

Jamul Indian Village is a small reservation located in rolling hills about 10 miles southeast of El Cajon in southern California, along State Highway 94 in San Diego County. In 1912 the San Diego Diocesan Office of Apostolic Ministry allowed Jamul Indian Village use of 2.34 acres of land for a cemetery; however, the Diocesan Office still retains ownership of the land. The Daley Corporation of San Diego deeded an additional 4.0 acres. The residents of Jamul Indian Village attained federally recognized reservation status in 1981.

The Jamul Tribe is working on the purchase of 101 more acres of land, and is waiting for the federal government to approve the federal trust status for the land. The tribe plans to use the land to house a tribal government administrative building, human resources building, parking structure, wastewater treatment plan, and tribal member housing. It will also be used to expand the tribe's gaming operation. Fifty of these acres will be dedicated to the tribe's nature conservation and preservation agenda. The tribe has come to an agreement with the Department of Fish and Game and the BIA (though the BIA is the only one who can make binding agreements) about conservation efforts that need to be adhered to, to protect the resources and beauty of the reservation and surrounding areas. The tribe, of course, also follows all the guidelines set by the county, state, and federal Multi-species Conservation Plan.

CULTURE AND HISTORY

The Jamul Tribe is part of the Kumeyaay or Diegueño Tribe of southern California. Their language belongs to the Hokan language group; languages included in this group are spoken by peoples from southern Oregon to southern Mexico. The Kumeyaay people are related to the Colorado River people, who are believed to have been the first Native Americans in the Southwest to come into contact with Europeans. The area's heavy concentration of Spanish missionaries, with their zeal for assimilation, adversely affected the Kumeyaay people's Native language and culture retention.

The Kumeyaays presently occupy eight of the 17 reservations in San Diego County. Prior to the Mexican-American War, the people freely traveled and lived in what is now southern San Diego County and northern Baja California, Mexico. Although the 1891 Act for the Relief of Mission Indians established a number of reservations for the Kumeyaay people, several small bands, including the Jamuls, remained landless.

During the early 1900s, many Jamul members worked for John Spreckels who owned the Jamul Rancho and was proprietor of Spreckels Sugar. They camped near their cemetery, which was close to a corner of the rancho. Spreckels assured them they would not be evicted, and in 1912 he deeded the San Diego Diocesan Office of Apostolic Ministry 2.5 acres of "cemetery and approaches." The Jamul community had a church there before the new Saint Pius Church was built.

Because of their lack of federal recognition, for many years, the Jamul Tribe was ineligible for many federal funds designed to aid Indian people. Through their efforts, and with the assistance of California Indian Legal Services, the tribe finally obtained federal recognition in 1981, receiving rights to certain BIA and other federal services. *(For additional cultural information, see California introduction.)*

GOVERNMENT

The federal government recognized the Jamul Indian Village's executive council as a tribal government in 1981. The Jamul tribal government operates under articles of association and bylaws that established an executive tribal council. The general tribal council is composed of the tribe's entire voting membership, and an executive tribal council, whose members are elected every two years. The six-member tribal council includes a chairperson, vice-chairperson, and a secretary-treasurer plus three executive council members. The executive council meets regularly or as necessary to conduct urgent business. The tribal council, which usually meets monthly, handles health matters, social services, drug prevention, housing, childcare, education, job training, and infrastructure.

The Jamul General Council established the Jamul Environmental Agency to implement policies to assist the Jamul Tribe in protecting, preserving, and enhancing Jamul Indian Village reservation lands.

ECONOMY

The Jamul Tribe is committed to building its own successful economic future, and it plans to do so through Indian gaming. The approval of a gaming compact with the State of California in 2000 represents a major step toward building an infrastructure; increasing employment opportunities, retail, services, and economic self-reliance; and improving the standard of living for the Jamul Indian Village Tribe.

Government as Employer. The tribal government currently employs four persons for administrative duties, one water quality person, one gaming person, one librarian, and three maintenance persons.

Economic Development Projects. The Jamul Tribe holds a signed compact with the State of California to allow Indian gaming on the reservation, and it plans to build its own gaming facility. The tribe is facing strong opposition from the State of California, but it does plan to exercise its sovereign right to the economic advantages that Indian gaming will provide for its members. In efforts to keep a harmonious relationship between governments, the tribe is studying the casino's economic impact before the development stage and final designs are complete.

Media and Communications. The Jamul Tribe has its own website at www.jamulindianvillage.com.

Tourism and Recreation. The Jamul Tribe pays homage to its ancestry and rich cultural heritage through a traveling exhibit called "Bringing the Past to Life." This 20-panel tribute portrays the past and present Kumeyaay and Jamul Indian Village culture. Panel scenes include food gathering, rock art, and basket weaving. The exhibit tours schools, colleges, universities, and museums in San Diego County.

The tribe would like to establish an outdoor museum. This would include a park setting, would feature cultural artifacts of the Kumeyaay and Jamul tribes, and would provide a testament to the tribe's continuous cultural preservation and natural conservation efforts. However, the land designated for the outdoor museum contains environmental wetlands that need to be preserved.

Jamul Indian Village
Federal reservation
Kumeyaay
San Diego County, California

Jamul Indian Village
P.O. Box 612
Jamul, CA 92035
   619-669-4785
   619-669-4817 Fax
   jamulindianvillage.com

Total area
(BIA realty, 2003)
6.04 acres

Federal trust lands
(Tribal source, 2004)
6.2 acres

Population
(BIA labor report, 2001)
56

Total labor force
2000 census
0

Total labor force
(BIA labor report, 2001)
36

Unemployment rate
(BIA labor report, 2001)
36%

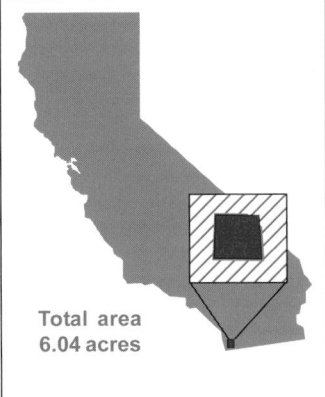

Total area
6.04 acres

Jamul

INFRASTRUCTURE

Jamul Indian Village sits adjoining State Route 94, which serves as the reservation's closest major artery. The road inside the reservation is paved. The nearest commercial airline service is in San Diego. Bus and freight services are available in nearby El Cajon.

Electricity. San Diego Gas and Electric supplies electricity.

Fuel. Proflame and Amerigas and various other businesses provide propane, the reservation's primary source of fuel.

Water Supply. The OTAY water district and a community well provide water. Sewage is disposed of by individual septic systems.

COMMUNITY FACILITIES AND SERVICES

A tribal hall, a small church, a library, a computer-learning center, a tribal cemetery and the Jamul Fire Station 66 are located on the reservation. The tribal hall, which is used for social gatherings, tribal meetings, and ceremonies, is located in a house with utilities and a kitchen available for use. The fire station currently sits on 0.82 acre that the tribe leases to the San Diego Rural Fire Protection District. A study conducted by the San Diego Rural Fire Protection District found the community had exceeded the capacity for the small station. The tribe plans to build a new fire station, which will be tribally owned, in the near future.

Education. Youth attend the Jamul/Dulzura School District. The Jamul Tribe has after-school tribal youth classes that help tribal youth learn about their cultural heritage and teach them the Kumeyaay language. The Kumeyaay Nation established a tribal college, formerly called D-Q University and now the Kumeyaay Community College, to provide tribal members and others the opportunity to be taught from the Native American perspective. The university teaches courses on the Kumeyaay language, the Kumeyaay culture, and issues facing Native America today. Young adults also may attend Cuyamaca College, Grossmont College, and San Diego State University.

Health Care. The Southern Indian Health Council is the primary provider of health care services for the Jamul Tribe. La Posta Outreach Substance Abuse Center provides outpatient substance abuse counseling and treatment sources. The Jamul Indian Village also has contract care; the tribe can be referred to other health care facilities or go to local emergency rooms, should the Southern Indian Health Council not be able to provide the necessary services.

ENVIRONMENTAL CONCERNS

The Jamul Tribe's main environmental concern is preservation of the reservation's natural environment and habitat. The tribe has proposed to set aside approximately 50 acres of land to be acquired under its upcoming "land into trust" application to serve as a conservation reserve. Currently the biggest pollution problem is the runoff from State Route 94, which includes oil and trash, that washes into the creek on the reservation. In the environmental plan, the tribe has to take care of this problem so that water leaves the reservation cleaner than when it arrived.

TRI-CA-011-J Jamul Tribal Office

TRI-CA-012-J Jamul Fire Station

TRI-CA-011-J

TRI-CA-012-J

Karuk

Karuk
Federal reservation
Karuk
Humboldt and Siskiyou counties, California

Karuk Tribe of California
P.O. Box 1016
Happy Camp, CA 96039
530-493-5305
800-505-2785
530-493-5322 Fax
karuk.us

LOCATION AND LAND STATUS

The Karuk Tribe of California is located in northwestern California. Currently tribal trust lands encompass approximately 601 acres. There are also 754 acres of private Indian allotments. The tribe's aboriginal territory covers an area of 1,048,818 acres. Federal landholdings within this territory account for 98 percent of ownership.

Tribal communities are situated in the towns of Happy Camp, Orleans, Somes Bar, and Yreka, California. These areas are within the ancestral lands of the Karuk Tribe. In 1979 the Orleans Karuk Council Corporation purchased 6.62 acres of land, which was then accepted into trust by the federal government. A gift deed on August 22, 1979, from the State of California granted 10.6 acres to the United States in trust for the Karuk Tribe of California. This land was accepted into trust on February 6, 1980.

PHYSICAL DESCRIPTION

Tribal lands are located in a central coastal region within Klamath Mountains in northern California. The terrain is characterized by steep mountains, forests, lakes, rivers, and streams. All tribal land, as well as most private property, are located adjacent to the Klamath River and its tributaries. The Klamath and Six Rivers National Forests comprise virtually all non-private land within the tribe's aboriginal territory.

CLIMATE

The region experiences moderate climates with summer highs near 90°F and winter highs near 50°F. Annual precipitation in the town of Orleans is about 50 inches.

CULTURE AND HISTORY

Archaeological and anthropological evidence supports the fact that ancestors of the Karuks occupied northwestern California by around 10,000 BC and perhaps much earlier. The traditional boundary of Karuk territory followed the watersheds bordering the Klamath River. Living in scattered villages along or near rivers and streams, the Karuks fished for salmon, a dietary staple, and hunted for elk, beaver, bear, deer, and small animals. The

Karuk language is related to the Hokan language group which includes languages spoken by peoples from southern Oregon into southern Mexico.

The General Allotment Act of 1887 declared all unallotted land to be public land available for homesteading. Only a handful of Karuks were able to file the necessary paperwork, and a majority of those that did file had their application denied. With virtually all of their land now declared public, most Karuks were forced to move from the river, in search for wage-earning employment in the agricultural valleys to the east and shipping centers on the coast to the west. In addition, many Karuk children were removed for long periods and sent to government boarding schools in Oregon, Nevada, southern California, and the Midwest.

In the 1850s, the tribe signed a peace treaty with the federal government. This treaty has never been ratified by the U.S. Congress. During the 1950s and 1960s, the Karuk people's interests were represented by nonprofit corporations, chartered by the State of California. Functioning in place of a tribal council, these Karuk organizations administered programs, purchased land, and operated under democratically elected boards of directors. Until 1979 the tribe remained unrecognized by the government. It had no formal reservation, though tribal members continued to reside on portions of their ancestral homelands throughout California. The tribe was recognized by the federal government in 1979. Its service region includes all of Siskiyou County and eastern Humboldt County, an area of approximately 4,000 square miles. Tribal communities are located in the towns of Happy Camp, Orleans, Somes Bar, and Yreka, California.

Although one of the largest tribes in California, with approximately 3,300 members, the Karuk Tribe has a small land base. Federal recognition only occurred in 1979, two years after a group of elders purchased a 6.6-acre parcel of land and placed it into trust status. This sequence of events qualified the tribe for establishment under the Indian Reorganization Act of 1934.

Various ceremonies remain an important aspect of the Karuk lifestyle; the Pick-ya-wish (World Renewal Ritual), the Jump Dance Ceremony, and the White Deerskin Ceremonies reiterate the Karuks' relationship with and appreciation for the natural world, and serve as a means of regulating social relations. (See California introduction for additional cultural information.)

GOVERNMENT
The Karuk people are governed by an elected nine-member tribal council whose membership includes a chairperson, vice-chairperson, a secretary, and a treasurer. Federal recognition was granted in February 1979, and the Karuk Tribe of California was constituted on April 6, 1985. A constitution, drafted under the authority of the Indian Reorganization Act of 1934 was approved on April 17, 1985.

The current tribal government is a consolidation of the autonomous political organizations that had represented the interests of Karuk individuals since the 1970s. The tribe is a self-governance tribe. Tribal headquarters are located in Happy Camp, California. Departments and programs include social services, environment, education, and health.

ECONOMY
The Karuk Tribe's mission is to establish a stable economy that will enhance its ability to exercise its rights as a self-governing nation.

Government as Employer. The tribe employs over 80 people to implement various federally funded programs (such as those from the BIA, HUD, and the Indian Health Service). The tribal council employs 12 people on a full-time basis and hires three to four others on a temporary basis each year. Services and pro-grams initiated by the U.S. Forest Service and the Department of Transportation provide limited and seasonal employment for tribal members.

Economic Development Projects. Karuk Community Development Corporation oversees tribal economic development projects. Current projects include a building-materials business, hardware employment through U.S. Forest Service contracts, and various consulting and business-development projects. The Yreka area is considered to have the best infrastructure for economic development.

Agriculture and Livestock. There is little agricultural use of land in the tribal territory, although the tribe does raise 40 acres of alfalfa. Some individuals also raise livestock.

Forestry. In 1994 the tribe entered into a partnership with the National Forest Service for the protection and restoration of the forests located within the tribe's ancestral lands. The tribe has secured over $1 million to assist efforts to revitalize the area. It has developed a comprehensive watershed restoration training and implementation program and a tribal restoration division.

Fisheries. The Karuk Tribe is currently only legally allowed to subsistence fish at one location using traditional methods. Because of the lack of habitat and poor water quality, the Fall Chinook run are the only fish with a population strong enough to be able to harvest without damaging the run. The sacred Spring run has been pushed to near-extinction above the confluence of the Trinity River, where the Karuks' aboriginal territory begins. The tribe operates a fisheries program as well as a watershed and water quality program to monitor and improve fish health.

Construction. Tribal members are employed in private construction enterprises. In addition, the tribe hires members for home-improvement jobs and housing construction.

Industrial Parks. The tribe is considering the feasibility of an industrial park.

Manufacturing. With the assistance of a $30,000 grant awarded in 1996, the tribe opened a furniture production company that uses Native designs. Karuk Tribal Design Works produces rustic furniture constructed from timber harvested from tribal forests in a sustainable manner. The tribe received a second grant of $65,000 in 1998 to continue development of the enterprise.

Services and Retail. As in most parts of the country, the service economy of the general area provides many jobs for tribal members. In addition, tribal members run a building materials business.

Tourism and Recreation. The beauty of the surrounding mountains and rivers attracts many tourists to the Klamath Mountain area each year. Individual members of the Karuk Tribe own RV parks and mobile-home parks. In addition, the Karuk Tribe holds a limited 51 percent interest in the Karuk-Beartooth Wilderness School, a Native American-owned rafting company and wilderness school in the Klamath River-Marble Mountain area. One of the tribe's priorities is to develop a replica of a Karuk fishing village, with planned commercial and recreational uses, about 70 miles southwest of Yreka.

INFRASTRUCTURE
Interstate 5 and California Highway 96 run north-south through the area; State Route 96 intersects Interstate 5 north of Yreka. Interstate 5 serves as the major transportation route in the area.

Transportation. There are noncommercial airports in Hoopa, Yreka, and Happy Camp. The nearest commercial airports are in Red ding and Eureka /Arcata. Siskiyou County is served by

Karuk

Total area (BIA realty, 2003)
596.07 acres

Tribally owned (BIA realty, 2003)
596.07 acres

Population 2000 census
276

Tribal enrollment
(BIA labor report, 2001)
3,165

Tribal enrollment
(Tribal source 2004)
3,371

Total labor force 2000 census
111

Total labor force
(Tribal source 2004)
3,371

High school graduate or higher 2000 census
79.5%

High school graduate or higher (Tribal source 2004)
74.4%

Bachelor's degree or higher
2000 census
10.6%

Unemployment rate
2000 census
19.82%

Unemployment rate
(Tribal source 2004)
25.5%

Per capita income
2000 census
$9,768

Karuk

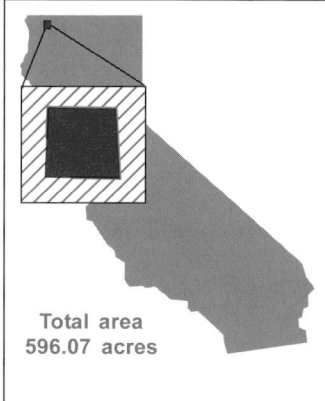

**Total area
596.07 acres**

bus lines and numerous truck lines. For the Humboldt County portion of Karuk territory, only State Highway 96 and a small county airport in Hoopa are available.

COMMUNITY FACILITIES AND SERVICES
The tribe provides a childcare voucher program, housing improvement programs, social services, and housing programs for tribal members. The tribe has three community centers. The center near Happy Camp occupies 11 acres of land.

Education. The tribe operates two Head Start programs, youth education services, and higher education and adult vocational training programs.

Health Care. The Karuk Tribal Health Program is governed by the tribe's health board. The board is comprised of nine elected members. The health program operates three clinics under a compact with Indian Health Services. A medical clinic is located in Orleans, a dental clinic is located in Happy Camp, and a medical and dental clinic is located in Yreka. The program also assumed operations of a medical clinic in Happy Camp in 2000. The clinics are licensed by the state and accredited by the Joint Commission on Accreditation of Healthcare Organizations. Available services include medical, dental, community outreach, public health, contract health, and HIV/AIDS programs.

ENVIRONMENTAL CONCERNS
Water quality and supply are primary concerns on the reservation. In 1997 the tribe prepared a Non-Point Source Pollution Assessment and Management Plan for Fiscal Year 1998, as well as Interim Water Quality Standards. In 2004, representatives from the Karuk, Yoruk, Hoopa, and Klamath tribes traveled to Glasgow, Scotland, to address environmental concerns at the headquarters of Scottish Power, a company responsible for damming the Klamath River and for the effects on the salmon population.

La Jolla

**La Jolla Reservation
Federal reservation
Luiseño
San Diego County, California**

La Jolla Band of Luiseño
Indians
22000 Highway 76
Pauma Valley, CA 92061
760-742-3771
760-742-1704 Fax
lajollaindians.com

Total area *(BIA realty, 2003)*
8,541.25 acres

Total area *(Tribal source2004)*
9,998 acres

Tribally owned *(BIA realty, 2003)*
7,957.31 acres

Individually owned
(BIA realty, 2003)
583.94 acres

Population *2000 census*
390

Tribal enrollment
(BIA labor report, 2001)
696

Tribal enrollment
(Tribal source2004)
403

Total labor force *2000 census*
187

LOCATION AND LAND STATUS
The La Jolla Reservation spans 8,541 acres along the southern slopes of Mount Palomar and descends in cascading terraces to the cool forests of the upper reaches of the San Luis Rey River. The reservation is located off State Highway 76, 25 miles east of Escondido and 60 miles northeast of San Diego. The La Jolla Reservation was first established by Executive Orders on December 27, 1875, and May 15, 1876. An Executive Order on May 3, 1877, returned some land to the public domain. The present reservation was established on September 13, 1892. A subsequent allotment consisted of 634 acres. The La Jolla Reservation lies within traditional Luiseño territory.

CULTURE AND HISTORY
Members of the La Jolla Band belong to the Luiseño Tribe. Tribal members have resided in the region for thousands of years. Luiseño traditional territory originally covered roughly 1,500 miles of southern California to the north of the Kumeyaays' land, including most of the San Luis Rey and Santa Margarita drainages. The Luiseño language is of the Cupan group of the Takic language, a subfamily of the greater Uto-Aztecan linguistic family. The term Luiseño is derived from the San Luis Rey Mission and has been used in Southern California to refer to those Takic-speaking people associated with the mission.

The Luiseño people first met European settlers when Gaspar de Portola's expedition arrived in 1796. The San Diego Mission was founded to the south two years later. Members of the La Jolla, Pala, Pauma, Rincon, and San Pasqual bands of the Luiseño Indians have resided in the San Luis Rey River Basin since the late 1800s. Historically the Luiseños relied on agriculture for subsistence, using sophisticated farming techniques to manage the area's natural resources. The Luiseño people continued their reliance upon agriculture until early in the twentieth century, when the City of Escondido built a dam above La Jolla, diverting all their water. Many Native people were forced to leave the reservation and seek work in the wage economy.

In 1951 a claim for the stolen reservation water was added to the Mission Indian Land Claim case. After a 1973 hearing, the Federal Power Commission required Escondido to regularly release six miner's inches from the dam. In 1988 a settlement was reached in the form of the San Luis Rey Indian Water Rights Settlement Act. The act authorized $30 million to be awarded to the Luiseño bands in compensation for the loss of water rights. In addition, the act mandates the delivery of water to tribal territories. The funds are used to promote economic development and to support the San Luis Rey Indian Water Authority.

GOVERNMENT
The reservation is a PL-638 tribe governed by a general council composed of all tribal members age 21 and older. The five-member elected tribal council includes a chairperson, a vice-chairperson, and a secretary-treasurer. The tribal council meets monthly and serves two-year terms. The tribe is organized under a non-IRA Articles of Association that was approved in 1962. The La Jolla Tribal Government developed one of the first tribal employment rights offices in California. Government departments include education and culture. The tribe does not maintain its own law enforcement department. However, it is in the process of developing a program through contracts with the BIA and the county sheriff's office currently provides services.

BUSINESS CORPORATION
The tribe is in the process of developing an ordinance to create the La Jolla Development Corporation Board of Directors which would oversee tribal economic activities. This type of corporation would encourage joint business ventures with the tribe.

ECONOMY
Employment on the reservation is primarily seasonal; the tribe's three enterprises operate only during the summer, although they averaged $800,000 in tribal revenue in 1994. The tribe maintains a store that sells camping supplies, a paintball-water park, and a speed track.

Government as Employer. Total tribal employees number 714.

Economic Development Projects. Projects that the tribe is exploring include a spring-water bottling plant, an off-road vehicle facility, an alternative energy power plant, and commercial businesses that would continue to enhance the area's recreational trade. The tribe also intends to purchase additional lands in the future.

TRI-CA-013-LJ LaJolla Trading Post

TRI-CA-014-LJ LaJolla Race Track

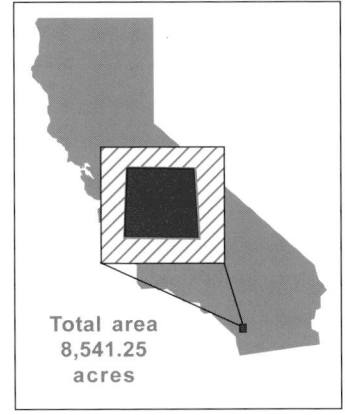

Total area
8,541.25
acres

Agriculture and Livestock. The tribe owns a herd of cattle and a grove.

Gaming. The La Jolla Tribe does not own a casino facility; however, it owns slot machines in its gas station facility.

Services and Retail. A service station with slot machines operates on the reservation. The store has gaming machines and sells camping wood. The Trading Post Store, one of three existing tribal enterprises, provides seasonal employment for tribal members, and is consistently profitable.

Tourism and Recreation. Excellent stream fishing is available at the La Jolla Indian Campground, which lies along the San Luis Rey River. The campground offers campsites and RV spaces. Attractions include fishing, hiking, mountain biking, inner tubing, swimming, a playground, and much more. The tribe intends to expand and upgrade this facility. The tribe owns and operates La Jolla Indian Water Park, also known as Sengme Oaks Family Water Park, which has been in operation since 1984. The park offers whitewater tubing on the San Luis Rey River. There is also limited camping space available to guests. Features include a sports bar, an arcade, and horseback riding opportunities. The tribe also owns a paintball facility and a speed track.

INFRASTRUCTURE
Escondido, 25 miles west of the reservation, has the nearest bus, train, and truck service. The reservation is accessed by Highway 76; Interstate 15 runs north-south about 15 miles west of the reservation. Interstate 5 runs north-south and lies approximately 30 miles west of the reservation.

Electricity. San Diego Gas and Electric provides electricity and gas to the area. The tribe is interested in using solar and wind energy as power sources.

Water Supply. A natural spring affords the reservation its own domestic water system. Septic tanks are used for sewage disposal.

Transportation. A tribal bus provides service on the reservation. The San Diego International Airport serves the region.

COMMUNITY FACILITIES AND SERVICES
The tribe has a multipurpose community building. The tribal hall houses a Head Start program.

Education. Children attend public schools in nearby Escondido. The tribe is exploring the possibility of developing an alternative tribal school program to better meet its children's needs. The county's extensive educational system includes 38 colleges and universities and five community college districts. The tribe provides culture classes for tribal members.

Health Care. The Indian Health Council serves the La Jolla Tribe, with clinics in Valley Center. Services include general medicine, general dental, human services, and community outreach. The IHC also maintains a clinic in San Ysabel, which provides the same services as the Valley Center clinic.

ENVIRONMENTAL CONCERNS
Tribal lands were ravaged by wildfires in 2003. The tribe is concerned with reforesting the affected lands. It is also concerned with preserving the checker-spotted butterfly.

Total labor force
(BIA labor report, 2001)
344

High school graduate or higher *2000 census*
68.6%

Bachelor's degree or higher
2000 census
8.4%

Unemployment rate *2000 census*
13.9%

Unemployment rate
(BIA labor report, 2001)
56%

Per capita income *2000 census*
$11,960

La Posta

Total area *(BIA realty, 2003)*	3,556.49 acres
Tribally owned	3,556.49 acres
(BIA realty, 2003)	
Tribal enrollment *(BIA labor report, 2001)*	20
Total labor force *2000 census*	9
Total labor force *(BIA labor report, 2001)*	11
High school graduate or higher	52.9%
2000 census	
Bachelor's degree or higher	0%
2000 census	
Unemployment rate *2000 census*	0%
Unemployment rate	27%
(BIA labor report, 2001)	
Per capita income *2000 census*	$6,610

LOCATION AND LAND STATUS
The La Posta Reservation spans 3,556.49 acres and is located in the Laguna Mountains, 56 miles east of San Diego and 46 miles west of El Centro. Located just west of the Manzanita and Campo Indian Reservations, the reservation is bordered on the southwest corner by Interstate 8.

The reservation was established on February 10, 1893, under the authority of the Act of January 12, 1891. In 1910 the Indian Office moved families with children from La Posta to the nearby Campo Reservation. The Bureau of Indian Affairs attempted to sell the land, believing that no descendants existed. In 1965 the descendants, who had been forcibly moved to Campo, came forward and reclaimed La Posta.

PHYSICAL DESCRIPTION
The La Posta Reservation is located in the high desert country of the Laguna Mountains in central California.

CULTURE AND HISTORY
The residents of La Posta Reservation are members of the

La Posta Reservation
Federal reservation
Kumeyaay
San Diego County, California

La Posta Band of Mission
Indians
1064 Barona Road
Lakeside, CA 92040
619-478-2113

431

La Posta

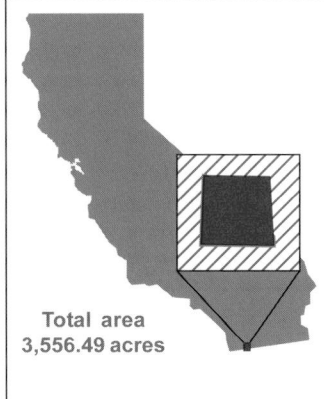

**Total area
3,556.49 acres**

Kumeyaay Tribe. The group's language belongs to the Yuman branch of the greater Hokan linguistic family. The Kumeyaays' traditional territory encompassed what is now San Diego County.

Since contact with European settlers, the Kumeyaay people have actively resisted encroachments on their lands and to their traditional lifestyles. The southern inland Kumeyaays avoided the Spanish troops and fought to free tribal members who were enslaved at the Mission San Diego. Eleven reservations were established under the Act for the Relief of Mission Indians in 1891. These reservations proved inadequate, and many Kumeyaays were forced to leave or else starved on the water-scarce lands. Public outcry forced the federal government to expand this territory.

In 1910, the federal government forcibly removed families with children from La Posta to the nearby Campo Reservation. In the 1960s, the BIA attempted to assert that the absence of tribal members indicated that there were no descendants to the land, and therefore the land could be sold. Tribal members returned from the Campo Reservation to reclaim their rights, and the reservation was reestablished. The La Posta Reservation has a small population, with some members residing on adjacent lands. In 1989 the tribe enrolled 14 new members, a historic event, considering that only a few years earlier the BIA couldn't locate any heirs for La Posta and sold the right-of-way for Interstate 8 without obtaining an on/off ramp for the reservation.

GOVERNMENT
The La Posta Reservation is governed by a general council. Elected council members include a chairperson, a vice-chair-person, and a business manager. Elected members serve two-year terms, and the general council meets twice a year. The band is organized under an IRA constitution that was approved on March 5, 1973.

ECONOMY
Gaming. In 2003 the tribe signed a gaming compact with the State of California. The agreement allows the tribe to develop gaming operations that offer 350 gaming devices.

Tourism and Recreation. The reservation's natural beauty serves as its greatest asset. La Posta is nestled under the shadow of 6,270-foot Mount Laguna at the eastern edge of Cleveland National Forest. In 1995 the tribe was exploring the possibility of opening a campground at Little La Posta.

INFRASTRUCTURE
La Posta's rugged terrain is accessible only by two narrow dirt roads. Interstates 8, 80 and U.S. 94 run near the reservation.

Water Supply. Individual wells provide water to the reservation's residents. Septic tanks are used for sewage disposal.

Transportation. The nearest airstrip is to the southeast in Jacumba; commercial air service is available in San Diego.

COMMUNITY FACILITIES AND SERVICES
The reservation houses La Posta Youth Regional Treatment Center.

Health Care. Health care is provided by the Indian Health Service Clinic in Alpine.

Laytonville

Laytonville Rancheria
Federal reservation
Cahto
Mendocino County, California

Cahto Indian Tribe
of Laytonville Rancheria
P.O. Box 1239
Laytonville, CA 95454
707-984-6197
707-984-6201 Fax

Total area *(BIA realty, 2003)*	200 acres
Tribally owned lands *(BIA realty, 2003)*	200 acres
Population *2000 census*	188
Tribal enrollment *(BIA labor report, 2001)*	81
Tribal enrollment *(Tribal source 2004)*	55
Total labor force *2000 census*	76
Total labor force *(BIA labor report, 2001)*	147
Total labor force *(Tribal source 2004)*	22
High school graduate or higher *2000 census*	62%
Bachelor's degree or higher *2000 census*	3.3%
Unemployment rate *2000 census*	26.3%
Unemployment rate *(BIA labor report, 2001)*	80%
Per capita income *2000 census*	$8,201

LOCATION AND LAND STATUS
The 200-acre Laytonville Rancheria is located in northwest California, approximately three miles west of the town of Laytonville and 26 miles north of Willits, on U.S. Highway 101.

The area was originally bought by missionaries for "landless" Indians, but when trouble developed regarding titles to the land, the Bureau of Indian Affairs purchased the 200 acres under authority of the Act of June 21, 1906. All the land is tribally owned. The rancheria is located within traditional Cahto territory.

PHYSICAL DESCRIPTION
The rancheria is covered with large pine trees, manzanita trees, and wild grass on rolling hills.

CULTURE AND HISTORY
Members of the Laytonville Rancheria belong to the Cahto Tribe. The Cahtos traditionally resided in the southernmost areas of northern California. The tribe's language belongs to the Athabascan family, and it is related to the languages of other groups living in the interior of Alaska and northern Canada, as well as to the Navajos and Apaches of the Southwest. The region's varied plant-food sources, primarily acorns, traditionally served as the tribe's dietary staple.

Concern over the welfare of the "landless" Cahtos propelled the area's missionaries to purchase land for the rancheria; a variety of title problems eventually convinced the federal government to take over the purchase by 1908. The confines of rancheria life, as well as the usurpation of their traditional lands, forced the Cahtos to join the wage economy at the turn of the last century. The hilly terrain of Mendocino County offered employment in the cattle- and sheep-ranching industries. Later in the twentieth century, the timber industry provided jobs.

The Cahto Tribe living on and near the Laytonville Rancheria remains a small, cohesive group. Since the 1950s the rancheria's population has dramatically increased, as more housing has become available. A cedar roundhouse stands in the center of the residential area and serves as a dance and meeting hall for the tribe.

GOVERNMENT

Laytonville Rancheria is governed by a general council, which is composed of all adult members of the tribe at least 21 years old. An executive committee is elected annually. The committee includes a chairperson, vice-chairperson, and a secretary-treasurer. Thirty percent of the general council represents a quorum. The general council meets three times annually, in March, August, and November. The tribe is organized under Articles of Association approved in July 1967 and amended in 1971.

The Laytonville Tribe is a PL-638 tribe. Government departments include housing, education, EPA, and police. The tribe contracts social services, education, transportation, community development, government, and resource management programs. The tribe has a police department and is recruiting law enforcement officers. The tribe is working in cooperation with other tribes and the county to develop a tribal court system. It hopes to develop a partnership with Coyote Valley on juvenile matters and advocacy, with the Pomo courts on referrals, and with the county on juvenile matters.

ECONOMY

A tribally owned casino generates income for the tribe. Tribal members continue to seek employment in the timber and agricultural sectors which provide Mendocino County's major employment opportunities. While the timber industry has been in decline, the majority of employed Cahto men still work in wood processing and related fields. Seasonal employment is also plentiful during the harvesting of the area's pears, grapes, prunes, and walnuts, especially for women, who can bring their children with them to the fields.

Tribal members participate in both Multi-Indian Tribes and its subsidiary, E.A.R.T.H. (Economic Advancement for Rural Tribal Habitats). E.A.R.T.H.'s planning component has aided the tribe with many aspects of their economic development program, including proposal writing, accounting and bookkeeping, grant writing and control, and project assistance.

Government as Employer. The tribe employs 14 people. A number of tribal members are employed through government-funded grants that provide necessary social services to tribal members. Some of these positions involve the administration of tribal services, rancheria maintenance, and educational programs.

Economic Development Projects. The tribe hopes to develop a gym, a movie theater, a golf driving range, and a ball field on the rancheria. It also is working toward organizing a community cemetery, developing additional housing, acquiring land, and protecting water resources. Plans to expand the casino are also under consideration.

Agriculture and Livestock. Laytonville members continue to provide inexpensive seasonal labor to the area's agricultural industry, as they have done throughout the century.

Forestry. Hundreds of acres of land within and adjacent to the rancheria are suitable for controlled timber farming. The tribe is currently considering the feasibility of developing this industry.

Gaming. The tribe owns and operates the Red Fox Casino. The facility offers 83 slots/VLTs and one restaurant. It also features a smoke shop.

Tourism and Recreation. The residents of the rancheria celebrate Big Day, an annual cultural event held the first weekend in June. It is open to the public.

INFRASTRUCTURE

U.S. Highway 101, the area's major artery, runs north-south five miles from the rancheria and passes through the town of Laytonville. The rancheria is connected to U.S. 101 by winding Branscomb Road.
Electricity. Pacific Gas and Electric provides electricity.

Water Supply. A 20,000-gallon holding tank supplies water for residents. Septic tanks are used for sewage disposal. There is a sewer system in place that serves 30 homes in the tribe's housing project.

Telecommunications. Verizon provides telephone service, and individually owned satellites are required for Internet access. Cellular towers are expected to be constructed in the area.

Transportation. Bus and truck lines stop in Laytonville, two miles from the rancheria. There are rail and freight services in Willits, 24 miles away. Willits also has an airstrip, but the nearest commercial air service is available in Ukiah, 59 miles from the rancheria.

COMMUNITY FACILITIES AND SERVICES

The Cahto Multi-Purpose Center contains tribal offices and serves as the rancheria's meeting hall. Tribal functions, cultural activities, and community meetings are held in the center. The tribe has received a federal grant to assist in the development of an anti-violence-against-women program. The tribe also partners with the City of Laytonville to provide programs and activities for children. The Red Road Program is a tribally sponsored substance abuse prevention and support group. It founded the Youth Red Road, which sponsors an annual Coast Walk. The Coast Walk is a 10-mile walk to the Pacific coast. The event is celebrated with a community barbeque and cultural activities.

Public Safety. The tribal fire department provides services for the rancheria and is certified by the state.

Education. Children attend both elementary and high school in the nearby town of Laytonville; a school bus provides transportation. A Youth Opportunity Group, the Laytonville Adult School, and the Community Day School are also available to tribal members. In addition, Mendocino Community College offers an extension program in Laytonville, through which area residents may earn associates degrees.

Health Care. The nearest health facility is the Long Valley Health Clinic in Laytonville, but most rancheria residents receive their health care from the consolidated tribal health project. The clinic is located in Calpella, California, approximately 50 miles from Laytonville. The rancheria also has the service of its own community health representative. The nearest hospital is in Ukiah.

ENVIRONMENTAL CONCERNS

The tribe has identified water quality, solid waste disposal, and landfill contamination as primary concerns to environmental health on the rancheria.

Laytonville

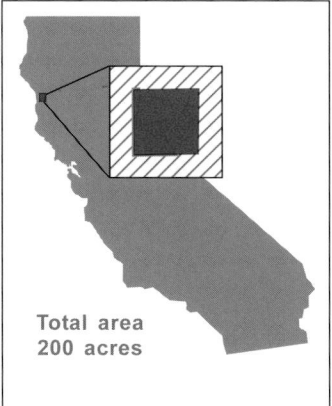

Total area
200 acres

Likely Rancheria
Federal reservation
Pit River
Modoc County, California

Pit River Tribe
37014 Main Street
Burney, CA 96013
530-335-5421
530-335-3140 Fax

Total area *(BIA realty, 2003)*	1.32 acres
Tribally owned *(BIA realty, 2003)*	1.32 acres

(See Pit River Tribe for further information on the following subjects: Culture and History, Government, Economy, and Community Facilities and Services)

LOCATION AND LAND STATUS
The Likely Rancheria is located in northeastern California, on the South Fork River near the South Warner Wilderness area.

This rancheria was purchased on June 26, 1922, by authority of acts on June 21, 1906, and April 30, 1908, on behalf of the Pit River Tribe. The tribe utilizes this parcel of land as a tribal cemetery.

INFRASTRUCTURE
Reno, Nevada, 169 miles from the Likely Rancheria, has the nearest commercial airline and train facilities. Bus and truck services are available in Likely, six miles away.

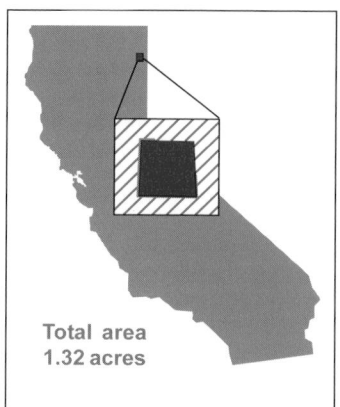

Total area
1.32 acres

Lone Pine Reservation
Federal reservation
Paiute and Shoshone
Inyo County, California

Paiute-Shoshone Indians
of the Lone Pine Community
P.O. Box 747
975 Teya Road
Lone Pine, CA 93545
760-876-1034
760-876-8302 Fax

Total area *(BIA realty, 2003)*	237 acres
Population *(Tribal source, 2005)*	236
Tribal enrollment *(Tribal source, 2004)*	1,400
Total labor force *2000 census*	82
High school graduate or higher *2000 census*	69.8%
High school graduate or higher *(Tribal source, 2005)*	98.4%
Bachelor's degree or higher *2000 census*	10.3%
Unemployment rate *2000 census*	8.54%
Per capita income *2000 census*	$14,126

LOCATION AND LAND STATUS
Lone Pine Reservation occupies 237.4 acres of the Owens Valley in south-central California on the eastern slope of the Sierra Nevada mountain range. It sits about five miles north of Owens Lake (a dry lake) and due east of Mount Whitney, the tallest mountain in the continental United States.

The original Lone Pine Reservation (along with the Bishop and Big Pine reservations) was established in 1912 by an Executive Order. The current reservation was acquired through a land exchange negotiated between the City of Los Angeles and the federal government in 1939, wherein 3,000 acres of trust land were exchanged for 1,391 acres of valley land, sites of the present-day Owens Valley reservations. An Act on April 20, 1937, authorized this exchange, which was made without water rights.

PHYSICAL DESCRIPTION
The reservation's topography consists of fairly flat, scrubby, high desert land. The elevation is 3,790 feet. The Owens River, when running, passes along Lone Pine on its course to Owens Lake.

CULTURE AND HISTORY
The people of the Lone Pine Reservation are members of the Owens Valley Paiute and Western Shoshone of the Great Basin. In the mid-nineteenth century this group controlled a 120-mile-long tract of land encompassing the Owens River on the eastern slope of the Sierra Nevada in south-central California. The Owens Valley Paiutes speak essentially the same language as that of the Mono Indians west of the Sierras, while their culture is quite similar to that of the Northern Paiutes of Nevada. *(For additional cultural information, see California introduction.)*

Like the valley's other reservations established during the early1900s, Lone Pine was too small for traditional hunting and gathering, and the land not conducive to full-scale farming or ranching. Hence, the residents relied on small-scale farming, gardening, and menial labor at area ranches and towns.

Motivated by a desire to control the Mono Lake Basin water rights, in 1937 the City of Los Angeles (through an Act of Congress) was empowered to exchange Owens Valley Reservation lands for 1,391 acres the tribe had previously owned. Los Angeles' domination of the region spelled the end of the farming and ranching economy. By the 1970s and 1980s, tourism had become a mainstay of the valley's economy.

GOVERNMENT
The tribe is governed by the tribal council, which consists of five elected officers--a chairperson, vice-chairperson, secretary, treasurer, and trustee. The tribal council, elected every two years in June, oversees tribal operations and prepares for the monthly meetings of the tribal general council, which includes all registered members of the tribe. The tribe is organized according to the Rehabilitation Trust Agreement of June 17,1939, and the Assignment Ordinance of April 17, 1939. Lone Pine is part of the Owens Valley Board of Trustees, a board comprised of representatives from each of the four Owens Valley tribes.

ECONOMY
The Owens Valley region has traditionally sustained ranching, limited agricultural activities, a little mining, and in more recent years, a good deal of tourism. At present, the reservation claims little in the way of economic resources.

Tourism and Recreation. The reservation's scenic location and pleasant weather are primary attributes for building a tourist trade. It sits 13 miles due east of Mount Whitney, west of Death Valley National Park, and seven miles south of Manzanar National Park. The region already has a thriving tourist trade; the tribe's challenge lies in capitalizing on this already-established tourism industry.

INFRASTRUCTURE
U.S. Highway 395 runs north-south through the reservation.

Electricity. The Los Angeles Department of Water and Power provides electric power.

Fuel. Local contractors provide propane.

Water Supply. A tribally owned groundwater system supplies water utilities for the reservation. Sewer lines are tapped into the Lone Pine Community Service District.

Transportation. The town of Bishop maintains a commercial airport, while private aircraft facilities are available in Lone Pine. Lone Pine also offers access to commercial train, bus, and trucking facilities.

Telecommunications. Verizon provides telephone service.

COMMUNITY FACILITIES AND SERVICES
A new community building houses tribal offices, a conference room where the general council meets, and an education center which offers tutoring for students. A library, available at the Lone Pine School, houses a collection of about 1,500 volumes and has a computer lab. The tribe also participates in the Youth Opportunity Program (YOP) and maintains a playground and a Little League baseball field.

Education. Tribal youth attend elementary and high school at the Lone Pine Unified School District.

Health Care. The Toiyabe Indian Health Project provides health care services. Services include medical, dental, community health, and family services programs. The project sponsors the American Indian Youth Challenge Program, the Tye-Duam Group, Indian Child Welfare Act youth groups, tobacco education presentations, and a Junior Youth Olympics. Clinics are located in Coleville, Bishop, and Lone Pine.

ENVIRONMENTAL CONCERNS
A critical concern for the tribe is the reservation's five-mile proximity to Owens Lake. This dry lakebed, artificially desiccated by the city of Los Angeles in the early twentieth century, now produces dust storms with the highest measurements of PM10 dust (a microscopic dust particle regulated by the EPA) pollution in the country. The tribe's environmental department has initiated aggressive steps to monitor and address this issue through such means as maintaining a meteorological station for tracking weather conditions as well as operating a Tapered Element Oscillating Microbalance (TEOM) 1400A for monitoring PM10 air pollution on the reservation. Another prime concern for the tribe has been the area's devegetation, arising from the exportation of Owens Valley water by the Los Angeles Department of Water and Power (LADWP). The LADWP is in the process of rewatering the Owens River through the Lower Owens River Project (LORP). The tribe is also concerned about the health risks posed by a county-run landfill one-fourth of a mile east of the reservation's boundaries. Additionally, the reservation's lack of water rights is a further focus of concern for the tribe.

Lone Pine

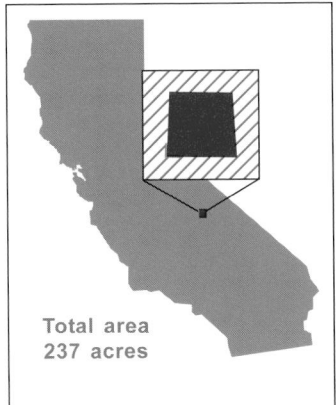

Total area
237 acres

Lookout

Lookout

Total area *(BIA realty, 2003)*		40 acres
Tribally owned *(BIA realty, 2003)*		40 acres
Population		62
Total labor force *2000 census*		2
High school graduate or higher *2000 census*		100%
Bachelor's degree or higher		0%
Unemployment rate *2000 census*		0%
Per capita income *2000 census*		$9,200

(See Pit River Tribe for further information on the following subjects: Culture and History, Government, and Community Facilities and Services)

LOCATION AND LAND STATUS
Lookout Rancheria spans 40 acres near the Pit River in Modoc County, partially surrounded by the Shasta National Forest. Adin, located on Highway 299, is the closest town to the rancheria. Bieber lies to the south of the rancheria.

Lookout Rancheria was purchased on October 11, 1913, by authority of Acts of Congress in 1906 and 1908, which appropriated funds for purchase of lands for California Indians.

ECONOMY
Since the mid-1970s, when the rancheria was almost deserted, Lookout has experienced substantial population growth. Even so, a lack of employment opportunities in the area has caused most of the Pit River people to move off their trust lands. In Modoc County, employment opportunities are primarily seasonal, with forest-related industries providing most of the jobs. The majority of the employed Lookout residents are engaged in the service economy.

Government as Employer. Federal and state jobs serve as an important source of employment for Modoc County residents.

Forestry. Because of the vast timber resources found in Modoc County, jobs created through lumber and wood-products businesses employ a substantial number of area residents, including tribal members.

Gaming. The Pit River Tribe has run a weekly bingo project since 1985. Profits from this endeavor have been invested in the construction of a permanent facility for the tribe's gaming operations. Profits are also used to fund tribal enterprises.

Services and Retail. In 1995 the tribe was considering the feasibility of building a combination truck stop, restaurant, and Indian gift shop. One possible site considered for this facility is at the four corners area (at the intersections of highways 89 and 299). Ownership of this intersection is currently being investigated.

Tourism and Recreation. Tourism accounts for a substantial amount of the area's revenues. Modoc County is primarily composed of national forest lands (the Modoc and Shasta national forests). Hunting and fishing are plentiful throughout the county, with deer hunting particularly rich in the southeastern portion of the county. Many visitors enjoy the county's Clear Lake National

Lookout Rancheria
Federal reservation
Pit River
Modoc County, California

Pit River Tribe
37014 Main Street
Burney, CA 96013
530-335-5421
530-335-3140 Fax

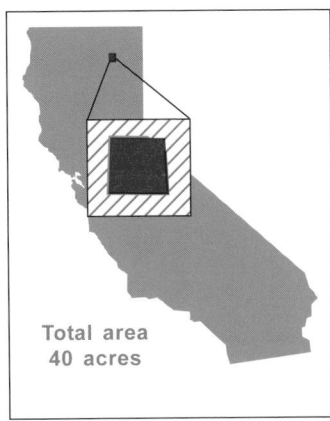

Total area
40 acres

435

Lookout

Wildlife Refuge and Cedar Pass (for winter sports). Other popular sites include Lassen Volcanic National Park, Lava Beds National Monument, and Burney Falls State Park. In 1995 the tribe was considering the development of an RV park along either Highway 299 or Highway 89. The tribe was also considering developing a campground or negotiating with the National Forest Service to manage an existing one.

INFRASTRUCTURE

Access to State Highway 299 is available six miles from the rancheria at the nearest town, Adin. State Highway 299, southbound, leads to the region's commercial hub, Redding, which is located 108 miles from the rancheria.

Electricity. Pacific Gas and Electric provides electricity.

Fuel. Individual homeowners purchase bottled gas.

Water Supply. The U.S. Public Health Service installed the water system. Residents use individual septic tanks for sewage disposal.

Transportation. Bus lines stop in Adin. Truck lines are available in Bieber, 12 miles from the rancheria. The closest rail service is available in Redding. A private airstrip is in Bieber.

COMMUNITY FACILITIES AND SERVICES

The Pit River Tribe's administrative headquarters are located in Burney.

Health Care. Tribal members may seek medical services through Pit River Health Service. Clinics are located in Burney and Alturas. They provide general medical, behavioral, and outreach programs. The Meyers Hospital in Fall River Mills, 32 miles from the rancheria, also offers medical services.

Los Coyotes

Los Coyotes Reservation
Federal reservation
Cahuilla and Cupeño
San Diego County, California

Los Coyotes Band of Indians
P.O. Box 189
Warner Springs, CA 92086
760-782-0711
760-782-2701 Fax

Total area *(BIA realty, 2003)*
25,049.63 acres

Tribally owned *(BIA realty, 2003)*
25,049.63 acres

Tribal enrollment
(BIA labor report, 2001)
286

Tribal enrollment
(Tribal source, 2004)
290

Total labor force *2000 census*
26

High school graduate or higher *2000 census*
46.3%

Bachelor's degree or higher
2000 census
0%

Unemployment rate *2000 census*
0%

Unemployment rate
(BIA labor report, 2001)
37%

LOCATION AND LAND STATUS

The Los Coyotes Reservation is located approximately 70 miles from San Diego, between the Cleveland National Forest and the Anza-Borrego Desert State Park, in scenic forested hills and valleys east of Mount Palomar and adjacent to a number of hot springs.

An Executive Order on May 5, 1889, set apart lands for this reservation, but it was not established until June 19, 1900, under the authority of an act on January 12, 1891. An Executive Order on April 13, 1914, transferred lands from the Cleveland National Forest to the Los Coyotes Reservation.

CULTURE AND HISTORY

Members of the Los Coyotes Band of Indians are descendants of the Cahuilla and Cupeño tribes. Ancestors of these groups originally occupied two village sites in the vicinity of the area's hot springs. Although from distinct tribes, both groups spoke a language belonging to the Takic branch of the larger Uto-Aztecan linguistic family; peoples speaking languages of these families live in areas from the Great Basin into central Mexico. While the Cupeños lived along what came to be known as Warner's Hot Springs, the Cahuillas resided in the hills to the immediate east. The latter location represents the present site of the Los Coyotes Reservation.

The area's hot springs have played a determining role in the history of the Los Coyotes people. Until the establishment of the local San Luis Rey and San Diego missions, the hot springs and the adjacent fertile lands served as the center of Cupeño life. Jonathan Trumbull (also known as Juan Jose Warner) acquired the springs and established a ranch there in 1844. Under Warner, the spring's hot mineral waters offered their restorative powers to passing visitors on the east-west Butterfield stages. Throughout this period, the indigenous people continued to live nearby, practicing a somewhat diminished version of their traditional subsistence patterns.

Bowing to commercial interests, however, the California Supreme Court decided in 1903 that the Cupeños had to leave their ancestral territory and move to the Pala Reservation. While the majority of the people were forced to live on the reservation, some remained in their traditional territory, coexisting with the neighboring Cahuilla Tribe. After their exile, a resort was built at the springs, and today the San Diego community uses these waters as a resource.

After joining the wage economy in the early part of the twentieth century, the region's Cahuilla people primarily sought income by working as ranch and farm hands. In addition, a number of Cahuilla people farmed and raised stock on their reservation lands. Since the 1950s, the majority of the Cahuillas have, out of necessity, sought employment in communities adjacent to their reservations. The labor trend at Los Coyotes certainly reflects this employment pattern.

Trying to combat the loss of cultural knowledge on their reservations, the Cahuilla people have been actively working to preserve their cultural heritage. Many tribal members serve on and chair various state preservation committees. In 1964, Cahuillas and others founded the Malki Museum on the Morongo Reservation as an archive and exhibition facility for Cahuilla cultural materials. While Native-language proficiency has decreased substantially over the past years, Cahuilla people continue to practice some forms of traditional music, including Bird and Peon Songs, which are performed regularly on social occasions.

GOVERNMENT

The Los Coyotes Reservation is governed by a general council, consisting of all members at least 21 years old; the tribe is organized by customs and traditions. Tribal officers include a spokesperson and five committee members. Tribal officers are elected for one-year terms. The tribal government is not organized under the Indian Reorganization Act of 1934.

The tribe is a PL-638 tribe. It contracts funding for tribal government, roads, natural resources, and water resources services. Tribal government programs include the Indian Child Welfare Act Committee, education, and a tribal digital village representative office. The tribe maintains a police department and a tribal court.

ECONOMY

The tribal economy is supported in large part by revenue generated from camping fees and Christmas tree sales.

Agriculture and Livestock. Introduced by the Spanish, pear and apple orchards thrived on much of the prime land on the Los Coyotes Reservation. The climate and terrain proved ideal, yielding healthy crops with little maintenance. The orchards are not managed. There is no open range on the reservation.

Tourism and Recreation. The reservation's proximity to the famous hot springs, coupled with the breathtaking scenery found on its extensive and primarily undeveloped lands, makes it a favorite camping spot for tourists. Two primitive campgrounds on the reservation provide access for exploring much of the reservation; they are in heavy use during summer weekends. Portable restroom and shower facilities are provided at one of the campgrounds. With a staff of four tribal members, the campground serves as a source of employment for the tribe. Profits from the campground are distributed to individual tribal members on a per capita basis. The tribe hosts the Los Coyotes Indian Reservation Explorer Run in August. The run is designed for 4x4 vehicles. Three off-road courses are available to participants across tribal lands.

INFRASTRUCTURE

State Highway 79, the area's main traffic artery, connects the reservation with the major metropolitan areas.

TRI-CA-016-LC Los Coyotes Band of Indians, Tribal Office & Community Center Sign

Electricity. San Diego Gas and Electric Company provides electricity.

Fuel. Residents purchase bottled gas. Many residents heat their homes with wood-burning stoves during the winter months.

Water Supply. The tribe provides water; individual septic tanks handle sewage disposal.

Transportation. Commercial air service is available in San Diego, train service is offered in Escondido, and bus service is available in the nearby town of Warner Springs. Trucking service is available in Ramona.

COMMUNITY FACILITIES AND SERVICES

The reservation houses a community hall.

Education. The tribe provides tutoring to students through the Johnson O'Malley Program at the public school in Warner Springs.

Health Care. Health care is provided in Rincon, 20 miles from the reservation. The Rincon Indian Health Council provides transportation to this facility. The Los Coyotes Tribe is also served by the Indian Health Council, which maintains clinics in Valley Center. Services include general medicine, general dental, human services, and community outreach. The IHC also maintains a clinic in San Ysabel, which provides the same services as the Valley Center clinic.

ENVIRONMENTAL CONCERNS

The tribe is investigating means to participate in the preservation and restoration of forests and wildlife populations on tribal lands. It is also concerned with illegal dumping and the pollution of regional streams.

Los Coyotes

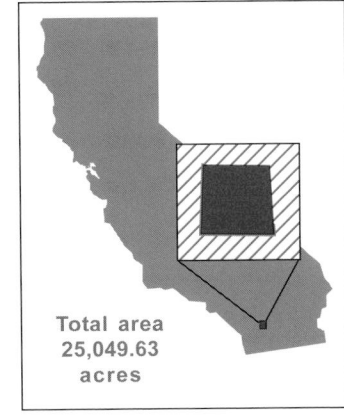

Total area
25,049.63
acres

Per capita income *2000 census*
$10,065

Per capita income
(Tribal source, 2004)
$25,000

Lower Lake

Lower Lake

LOCATION AND LAND STATUS

The Koi Tribe no longer had land after the Bureau of Indian Affairs (BIA) sold off 140 acres of the Lower Lake Rancheria, as approved by Congress in 1954, according to tribal sources. The communities of Lower Lake and Clearlake Heights were situated on either side of the rancheria. At that time most tribal members lived in the Bay Area. The tribe received federal recognition in 2000. At this time, it has no land base. The tribe is negotiating the placement of acreage in the Bay Area into federal trust status.

CULTURE AND HISTORY

The Lower Lake Rancheria Koi Nation is part of the Pomo Tribe. Pomo, the Nation's language, is a member of the Western Hokan group of languages. North-central California, between Mendocino County and the eastern shore of San Francisco Bay, was home to the Pomo Indians for millennia, as tribal history relates. When Europeans moved into the area, one of three separate tongues was used by each of 3,000 Pomo Indians.

Local plants and animals provided subsistence for the Southeastern Pomo people of Koi, a village situated on an island in Clear Lake. Although their renowned waterproof baskets featured both practicality and elaborate construction, other items manufactured by the Pomos that combined aesthetic values with a high degree of utility included arrowheads, knives, axe heads, scrapes, and personal adornments. One means of exchange

consisted of finely made clamshell and mineral beads. The area between San Francisco Bay's eastern shore north to what is today Mendocino County has yielded much ancient material that confirms that Pomos inhabited the area.

The world of California tribes altered dramatically when the nineteenth century brought a rush of Americans and Europeans into the region. Pomo territory, as delineated in documents agreed to in 1851 and 1852, was bounded by the eastern shores of both Clear Lake and San Francisco Bay. It extended westward to the Russian River. But half a century passed before these treaties were made public. California legislators had influenced the U.S. Congress to prevent ratification, the tribe relates.

The federal government permitted the Kois to continue living on their ancestral island, although other Pomo groups were relocated by force to the Indian reservation in Mendocino. The Kois, taken advantage of by the whites, were made to work for little pay.

When the celebrated two-year Ghost Dance took place in 1870, tribal history continues, the Kois left home and traveled to be present. When they returned, they found their dwellings had been destroyed by fire and confiscated. By 1901, homicide, forced labor, and sickness significantly reduced the population of the Kois and other Pomo groups.

Lower Lake Rancheria
Federal reservation
Pomo
Lake County, California

Lower Lake Rancheria
Koi Nation
360 Grand Ave., #249
Oakland, CA 94610
510-535-1900
koination.com

Total acres
(BIA realty, 2003)
0 acres

Tribal enrollment
(Tribal source, 2004)
53

Lower Lake

The communities of Lower Lake and Clearlake Heights were situated on either side of about 140 acres of land called Purvis Flat. To provide a place for the remaining Kois to live, the federal government acquired the land in 1916. Thirty-four years later, the population of the rancheria consisted of about seven families.

The rancheria received a proposal from Lake County in 1953, by which the county would pay $3,361 for 99 acres to be used for an airport. Although the tribe possessed no land after the 1956 sale of the rancheria, they continued to be officially recognized by the federal government. Nevertheless, aid generally provided to federally acknowledged tribes was withheld for many years, due to a BIA clerical error. Bay Area communities became home to most members of the Koi Nation. In 1975, however, a means for reversing government termination became available to tribes in the form of the Indian Self-Determination Act, a significant step toward the revival of California's Indian cultures. Other Pomo groups were recognized by the government early in the 1990s, the tribe notes, but the BIA, pointing to documentation errors, delayed reaffirmation for the Lower Lake Rancheria Koi National until December 29, 2000. *(See California introduction for additional cultural information.)*

GOVERNMENT

The tribal government consists of a tribal council, made up of three members, that decides on daily operational issues. Housing, health care, educational and vocational opportunities, and care for tribal elders are listed as the tribe's ultimate goals. Economic growth based on the acquisition of tribal lands is seen as the means for advancing towards such objectives, according to tribal sources.

ECONOMY

The lack of a land base has seriously impeded the tribe's economic progress. The tribe believes that reestablishment of its reservation will make further steps toward economic growth possible, it says. Pursuit of trust status for land in the Bay Area was reported in 2004, and a casino business is planned as the first project on the property. The tribe intends to use anticipated income generated from gaming to acquire additional acreage and to enhance the benefits it can provide to its members.

Gaming. In October 2004, the tribe initiated development of a gaming facility in Oakland. Crystal Bay Casino will be located near Oakland International Airport. The facility will feature 2,000 slot machines, making it one of the largest gaming facilities in northern California. Amenities will include a hotel, resort, and an entertainment venue. The casino is expected to create 4,400 jobs and generate over $1 billion in annual economic activity. The tribe has proposed to provide annual payments to the city, which will include funding for police and fire protection, compensation for lost taxes and parking tax revenue, and road and traffic improvement. The tribe's financial contributions will also be used to fund public programs, particularly those involved with youth education and violence prevention.

COMMUNITY FACILITIES AND SERVICES

Tribal education, health care, and vocational programs are among the services targeted to receive part of the anticipated income when the tribe's business plans are fully underway, according to the tribe.

Health Care. Health services are available through Lake County Tribal Health Clinic in Lakeport. Services include general medicine, dental care, community outreach, alcohol and drug abuse prevention, and family programs.

Manchester Point

Manchester Point Arena Rancheria
Federal reservation
Pomo
Mendocino County, California

Manchester Point Arena Band
of Pomo Indians
P.O. Box 232
Point Arena, CA 95468
707-882-2788
707-882-3417 Fax

Total area *(BIA realty, 2003)*	363.09	acres
Tribally owned	363.09	acres
(BIA realty, 2003)		
Population *2000 census*		197
Tribal enrollment *(BIA labor report, 2001)*		621
Total labor force *2000 census*		75
Total labor force *(BIA labor report, 2001)*		538
High school graduate or higher		60%
2000 census		
Bachelor's degree or higher		0%
2000 census		
Unemployment rate *2000 census*		13.3%
Unemployment rate		91%
(BIA labor report, 2001)		
Per capita income *2000 census*		$6,268

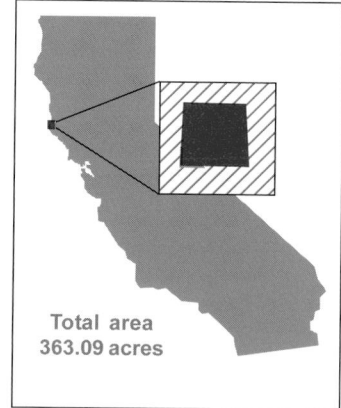

Total area
363.09 acres

LOCATION AND LAND STATUS

The Manchester Point Arena Rancheria is located in Mendocino County, California, near the town of Point Arena.

CULTURE AND HISTORY

Members of the Manchester Point Band belong to the Pomo Tribe. The Pomo people's ancestral homelands encompassed regions across northwestern California. The indigenous language belongs to the Hokan linguistic family. Traditional means of sustenance included fishing, gathering shellfish, and some hunting and gathering of acorns. Numerous rancherias throughout California are home to members of the Pomo Tribe.

Manzanita

Total area *(BIA realty, 2003)*	4,580.16 acres
Total area *(Tribal source 2004)*	4,580 acres
Tribally owned	4,580.16 acres
(BIA realty, 2003)	
Population *(EPA)*	67
Population *(Tribal source 2004)*	107
Tribal enrollment *(BIA labor report, 2001)*	98
Total labor force *2000 census*	33
Total labor force *(BIA labor report, 2001)*	72
High school graduate or higher	71.4%
2000 census	
Bachelor's degree or higher	20%
2000 census	
Unemployment rate *2000 census*	0%
Unemployment rate *(BIA labor report, 2001)*	32%
Per capita income *2000 census*	$14,825

LOCATION AND LAND STATUS

The Manzanita Reservation is located in southeastern San Diego County, California. Manzanita adjoins Campo Indian Reservation on the south and La Posta Reservation on the west. It is about 67 miles east of the city of San Diego on Interstate 8; the town of Boulevard is six miles away. The reservation lies within 10 miles of the U.S.-Mexico border. The reservation was established on 640 acres in 1893 under authority of an Executive Order of 1891. The land base was increased by Departmental Order in 1907, and it is held in trust by the U.S. government.

PHYSICAL DESCRIPTION

The Manzanita Reservation is located in the upland valleys and meadows of the western portions of the Carrizo Desert. There are 66 acres of forested lands and 21.3 acres of wetlands within reservation boundaries. Elevation ranges from 3,000 to 4,500 feet above sea level.

CULTURE AND HISTORY

Members of the Manzanita Band belong to the Kumeyaay Nation. The Kumeyaays' traditional territory extended north and south of the Mexican border from the Pacific coast almost to the Colorado River. The Kumeyaays are speakers of the Yuman branch of the greater Hokan linguistic family. *(See California introduction for additional cultural information.)*

Throughout the early part of the twentieth century, most Kumeyaays, living on inadequate reservations, sustained a few domestic animals, subsistence farms, and some cash crops. When forced to join the wage economy, the Kumeyaays worked for food or insubstantial wages on nearby ranches.

Current Kumeyaay groups work together to maintain the tribe's cultural integrity and political presence. The Kumeyaays, known for their basket weaving, practice private traditional ceremonies, including the blessing of new developments and the inauguration of officials with sage smoke and sacred songs. The seven southern bands joined to purchase centrally located land and to build the Southern Indian Health Council to serve members, maintaining a branch clinic at Campo.

GOVERNMENT

All tribal members 18 years and older make up the general council which governs the tribe. An executive committee, which consists of the tribal chairman, two committee members, and a secretary-treasurer, is elected by the general council to run the routine activities of the tribal government. The tribe is organized under an IRA constitution and bylaws approved in 1976. In addition to the administrative department, the tribe maintains a housing committee and grants management office.

BUSINESS CORPORATION

In 2002 the Manzanita Band approved the Articles of Incorporation of the Manzanita Economic Development Corporation (MEDCO), a tribally owned corporation, which focuses on economic and community development on the tribe's behalf. Governed by a board of directors, MEDCO has been aggressively seeking out economic development opportunities.

ECONOMY

The tribe is pursuing economic ventures to support its efforts to become a financially independent nation.

Economic Development Projects. A separate OEDP Committee focuses on economic development on the reservation. The band's resources have been spent mostly on reservation improvements such as new housing, electrical hookups and well drilling, governmental organization, maintenance of the fire station, and general infrastructural development. The reservation's geographic remoteness and the area's inadequate water supply make rapid development difficult.

In 2003 the tribe began development of a motorcross/off-road park. Although the project has been temporarily delayed due to legal issues, the tribe plans to resume development of the facility in the near future. The tribe's future projects also include a resort and casino facility located near El Centro, California.

Gaming. In 2003 the Manzanita Tribe proposed the construction of a resort and casino facility in an area approximately 50 miles from the reservation near El Centro, California. The development will include a casino, hotel, golf course, RV park, and a factory outlet center. The proposed project will be developed in partnership with the Viejas Band of Kumeyaay Indians, another tribe in the area, which operates a successful casino in Alpine, California. The project is awaiting approval from government agencies and neighboring tribes.

Tourism and Recreation. A horse camp and camground were created on the reservation in 1984. The location offers both primitive and full hookup campsites as well as horse facilities. Even though the campground provides only a small amount of income and a handful of jobs for the Manzanita Band, it provides important recreational opportunities for tribal and nontribal members.

INFRASTRUCTURE

The reservation is located 2.5 miles from the Crestwood exit off Interstate 8. U.S. Highways 80 and 94 also serve the area.

Electricity. San Diego Gas and Electric supplies electricity.

Water Supply. Individual wells provide water, and individual septic systems handle wastewater.

Transportation. The closest air and train services are in San Diego. Bus and trucking facilities are in Botievard and El Cajon.

Manzanita Reservation
Federal reservation
Kumeyaay
San Diego County, California

Manzanita Band of the
Kumeyaay Nation
6 Old Mine Road
P.O. Box 1302
Boulevard, CA 91905
619-766-4930
619-766-4957 Fax

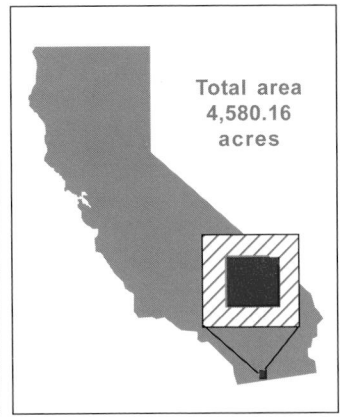

Total area
4,580.16
acres

Manzanita

COMMUNITY FACILITIES AND SERVICES

A tribal office on Manzanita Reservation serves as the band's administrative headquarters. The tribe also operates a language program, a recreation department, and an activity center and library on the reservation. The tribe maintains a Tribal Digital Village program. *Public Safety.* The band has its own fire department.

Education. Students attend the Mountain Empire School District.
Health Care. The tribe belongs to the Southern Indian Health Council, which maintains a branch clinic on the nearby Campo Reservation.

ENVIRONMENTAL CONCERNS

Primary environmental issues on the reservation are water supply and quality. The tribe conducted a water quality assessment in 1999 to identify priorities in regard to these issues.

Mesa Grande

Mesa Grande Reservation
Federal reservation
Diegueño
San Diego County, California

Mesa Grande Band of Mission
Indians
P.O. Box 270
Santa Ysabel, CA 92070
760-782-3818
760-782-9029 Fax

Total area *(BIA realty, 2003)*		1,802.80 acres
Total area *(Tribal source 2004)*		1,803 acres
Federal trust lands		1,803 acres
(Tribal source 2004)		
Tribally owned		1,802.80 acres
(BIA realty, 2003)		
Population		180
Tribal enrollment *(BIA labor report, 2001)*		628
Tribal enrollment *(Tribal source 2004)*		700
Total labor force **2000 census**		25
Total labor force *(BIA labor report, 2001)*		55
Total labor force *(Tribal source 2004)*		500
High school graduate or higher		46.9%
2000 census		
Bachelor's degree or higher **2000 census**		0%
Unemployment rate **2000 census**		8%
Unemployment rate		47%
(BIA labor report, 2001)		
Per capita income **2000 census**		$7,353

LOCATION AND LAND STATUS

The Mesa Grande Reservation is located on 1,803 acres in southern California. In 1998 the tribe purchased an additional 883 acres of land to be used for the construction of tribal housing.

PHYSICAL DESCRIPTION

The reservation is situated in a remote region of the hills above the forests of Black Canyon, within the Cleveland National Forest. Elevations range to 3,500 feet above sea level.

CULTURE AND HISTORY

The reservation was established in 1875.

GOVERNMENT

The tribe is governed by a tribal council that consists of a chairperson, a vice-chairperson, and three council members. Government departments include administration, housing, environmental protection, education, Indian Child Welfare services, and repatriation.

ECONOMY

A number of tribal members commute to nearby towns for employment. The tribe's largest source of income is from government grants.

Government as Employer. The tribal government employs five people within the tribal government offices.

Agriculture and Livestock. The tribe manages a herd of 40 bison. There are a few individually owned small farms located on the reservation.

Real Estate/Commerical Development. The tribe has constructed 22 HUD low-rental homes on a site in Black Canyon.

INFRASTRUCTURE

The reservation is accessible by Highways 78 and 79.

Electricity. San Diego Gas and Electric provides electricity.

Water Supply. Two community water systems and one community sewer system serve portions of the reservation, while other residencies rely upon individual wells for domestic water and individual septic systems for wastewater disposal.

Transportation. The nearest airport services are located at Lindberg Field in San Diego. UPS and FedEx service the reservation.

COMMUNITY FACILITIES AND SERVICES

The reservation houses a community swimming pool, a library, a Tribal Digital Village program, and a youth program.

Education. Tribal youth attend the Julian School and the Warner Unified School District. The tribe maintains a Native Pride program at the Warner schools.

Health Care. The tribe is a member of the Indian Health Council. Tribal members can receive medical care at the Santa Ysabel Clinic, which is operated by the Indian Health Consortium and is 14 miles away. A more fully staffed clinic is located in Rincon.

ENVIRONMENTAL CONCERNS

Environmental issues on the reservation include water quality and solid waste disposal.

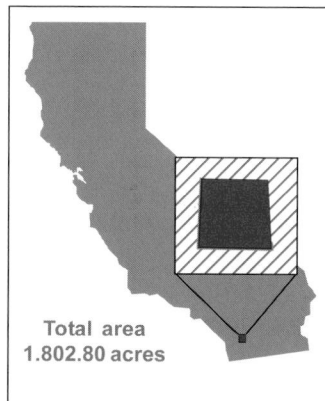

Total area
1.802.80 acres

LOCATION AND LAND STATUS

The Middletown Rancheria was established on July 30, 1910, by the secretary of the interior. The total acreage of rancheria lands held in trust is 108.70. Santa Rosa lies 40 miles southwest of the rancheria; the city of Ukiah is located 90 miles to the north.

CULTURE AND HISTORY

Although the tribal composition of Middletown Rancheria is predominantly Pomo, Wintun and Lake Miwok people were also moved onto this land when it was established for "landless" California Native people in 1910. *(For additional cultural information, see California introduction.)* At the turn of the century, people living on these isolated northern California rancherias had a difficult time entering the wage economy as the local communities were often extremely segregated. Many tribal men and women earned their livings by working in the hop fields. Others earned money by cutting firewood for large buyers. Women wove baskets and were employed as laundresses. During the Depression, some tribal women left the rancherias and sought employment in the San Francisco Bay Area where they were hired as domestics. Tribal men were able to find employment as migrant field workers and ranch laborers. During World War II era the men worked in war-related industries and served in the armed forces.

The Middletown tribal people are known for actively protecting their civil rights. Using the courts, the Middletown tribal leaders successfully fought to guarantee nonreservation Indians the right to vote and challenged the segregationist policies of public schools and private businesses. Middletown tribal people have maintained their culture and sense of identity through music, dance, and traditional crafts such as basketry.

A breakthrough legal case was won by the Middletown Rancheria in 2003 against Snow Lakes Vineyard and Lake County, California, according to tribal sources. Severe damage to 650 Lake County acres containing ecologically delicate locales and some of the tribe's gravesites was the motivation for the lawsuit. The California Environmental Quality Act and the Unfair Business Practices Act provided the basis for the suit, and an agreement was reached after 12 months. Snow Lake Vineyards agreed to protect identified sites relevant to Native American archaeology and to have any exposed sites professionally examined. A monitor from the tribe must be engaged to witness any actions that disturb the ground at a site. The tribe is to receive any tribal objects found at the sites and is allowed to perform established tribal rites at such locations. The vineyard will make efforts to reestablish normal plant cover and the tribe will have access to collect local plant materials in unused parts of the vineyard for their basket-making activities. The tribe expects native land rights for all groups and repatriation matters generally to be affected by this agreement, which the tribe views as a major success.

GOVERNMENT

The The Middletown Rancheria Band of California Pomo Indians was organized under the IRA. The tribe's first constitution is now under consideration, the tribe reports. The Middletown Rancheria is presently governed by a general council consisting of all adult members (18 years of age and older). They list a chairman, vice-chairman, secretary, treasurer, and representative as tribal officials. Elections are held in odd-numbered years in April.

ECONOMY

Its gaming operation is a keystone of the tribal economy. The tribe also reports acquisition of Middletown's Mount St. Helena Brewery.

Economic Development Projects. Funding is being sought for a hotel and permanent casino development and also for further real estate purchases, tribal sources report.

Gaming. The tribe opened a casino in 1994. With a staff of 205, this 2,500-square-foot facility is an important source of revenue. The Twin Pine Casino has slot machines/VLTs, a poker room and other table games. Nickel, quarter, one- and five-dollar slots; blackjack; and Pai-Gow poker are also available. Grand prize and hot seat drawings and an on-site restaurant are noted.

Tourism and Recreation. The area around the rancheria features a number of nearby attractions for visitors, the tribe reports, including three golf courses, six wineries, four museums, and a glider port. Clear Lake State Park and Lake Mendocino offer gold mine tours, geothermal features, nature paths, and equestrian facilities, among numerous outdoor recreational opportunities. Lakeport lies approximately 30 miles north of Middletown.

INFRASTRUCTURE

State Highways 29 and 53 serve the rancheria.

Electricity. Pacific Gas and Electric supplies electricity.

Middletown Rancheria
Federal reservation
Pomo, Wintun, and Lake
Miwok
Lake County, California

Middletown Rancheria Band
of California Pomo Indians
P.O. Box 1035
Middletown, CA 95461
707-987-3670
707-987-9091 Fax

Total area (BIA realty, 2003)
108.7 acres

Tribally owned (BIA realty, 2003)
108.7 acres

Population
161

Tribal enrollment
(BIA labor report, 2001)
88

Total labor force 2000 census
22

Total labor force
(BIA labor report, 2001)
36

High school graduate or
higher 2000 census
81.5%

Bachelor's degree or higher
2000 census
0%

Unemployment rate
2000 census
31.8%

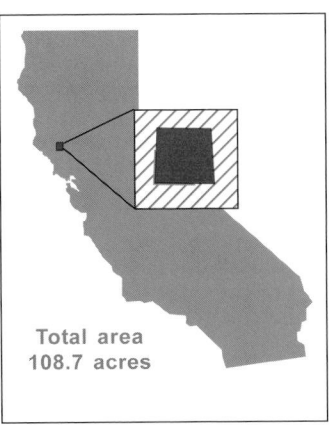

Total area
108.7 acres

TRI-CA-041 Middletown Tribal Building

TRI-CA-042 Middletown's Twin Pine Casino

Middletown

Fuel. Natural gas is used for heat, the tribe says.

Water Supply. The city of Middletown and private wells supply water to rancheria residents; septic tanks manage sewage disposal.

Transportation. Commercial air and bus lines are accessible in Ukiah, 90 miles from the rancheria. Train facilities are available in Santa Rosa, 30 miles west of the rancheria.

COMMUNITY FACILITIES AND SERVICES
The tribal center is housed in a traditional timber roundhouse built in 1993. The center houses general council meetings and other tribal governmental and community functions. A tribal elders and disability program receives tribal support for services to members, tribal sources say.

Education. Children attend Middletown Unified School District (Middletown Elementary, Middle, and High School), Coyote Valley Elementary, and Loconma, tribal sources say.

Health Care. Every tribal member of any age receives health insurance benefits, according to tribal sources. Medical, dental, vision, and life insurance benefits are among those named. Other sources of health services in the area include the Lake County Tribal Health Consortium and the Sonoma County Indian Health Services. A clinic is also available in Lakeport, the tribe notes.

ENVIRONMENTAL CONCERNS
The tribe has numerous environmental concerns and initiatives.

Montgomery Creek

Montgomery Creek Rancheria
Federal reservation
Pit River (Montgomery Creek)
Shasta County, California

Pit River Tribe
37014 Main Street
Burney, CA 96013
530-335-5421
530-335-3140 Fax

Total area *(BIA realty, 2003)*		108.44 acres
Population		8
Total labor force *2000 census*		0
High school graduate or higher *2000 census*		100%
Bachelor's degree or higher *2000 census*		0%
Per capita income *2000 census*		$445

(See Pit River Tribe for further information on the following subjects: Culture and History, Government, Economy, and Community Facilities and Services)

LOCATION AND LAND STATUS
The Montgomery Creek Rancheria is located 34 miles northeast of Redding, the region's primary trade and commerce center at the northern end of the Sacramento Valley and is partially surrounded by the Shasta-Trinity National Forest. The reservation was established by the secretary of the interior on October 13, 1915, under the authority of an Act on June 30,1913. The rancheria was set aside for homeless California Indians who had no prior land base. The rancheria was named in the act that terminated many California rancherias in the 1950s, but it was not terminated. Few people live on the Montgomery Creek Rancheria because of its isolated location and lack of utilities.

ECONOMY
Government as Employer. Federal and state jobs serve as an important source of employment for Shasta County residents, particularly in Redding.

Economic Development Projects. In 1995 the Pit River Tribe was considering development of an RV park along either Highway 299 or Highway 89. Another option under consideration was to build a campground or negotiate with the National Forest Service to manage an existing one.

Agriculture and Livestock. While there is currently no agricultural production on the rancheria, tribal members find employment in agriculture in the surrounding area; strawberries are a major crop in Shasta County and are exported to southern Europe.

Forestry. Because of the vast timber resources found in Shasta County, jobs created through lumber and wood-products businesses employ a substantial number of area residents, including tribal members.

Gaming. The Pit River Tribe has run a weekly bingo project since 1985. Profits from this endeavor are invested to be used for a future permanent bingo hall. Profits also are used to fund other tribal enterprises.

Services and Retail. In 1995 the tribe was considering the feasibility of building a combination truck stop, restaurant, and Indian gift shop. A possible site for the facility was the intersection of State Highways 89 and 299.

Tourism and Recreation. Tourism accounts for a substantial amount of the area's revenues. Much of Shasta County is covered by National Forest lands. Hunting and fishing opportunities are plentiful. Other popular recreational sites include Lassen Volcanic National Park, Lava Beds National Monument, and Burney Falls State Park.

INFRASTRUCTURE
The rancheria is located within a mile of State Highway 299. Redding lies 34 miles southwest on California Highway 299. The dirt road to the rancheria is three miles long and is impassable except by four-wheel drive vehicles during the winter.

Water Supply. Springs provide water for residents, and individual septic tanks handle sewage disposal.

Transportation. Redding has commercial air, train, truck, and bus services.

COMMUNITY FACILITIES AND SERVICES
Health Care. The Pit River Health Service provides medical services to residents of the Montgomery Creek Rancheria. The program services members of the Pit River Tribe residing within all tribal ancestral boundaries, including the reservations of Montgomery Creek Rancheria, Roaring Creek Rancheria, Burney Rancheria, Lookout Rancheria, XL Ranch Rancheria, Likely Rancheria, and Big Bend Rancheria. Services include medical, dental, behavioral, outreach, and environmental health. Transportation is available upon request. Hospitals and other medical care services are available in Redding.

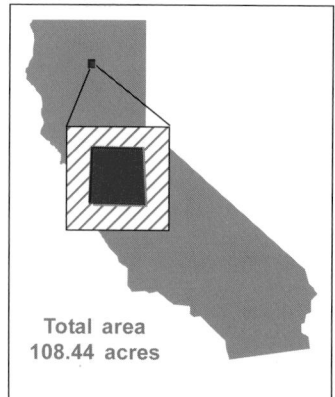

Total area
108.44 acres

Total area *(BIA realty, 2003)*		365.77 acres
Tribally owned *(BIA realty, 2003)*		346.08 acres
Individually owned		19.69 acres
(BIA realty, 2003)		
Population *2000 census*		166
Tribal enrollment *(BIA labor report, 2001)*		1,193
Total labor force *2000 census*		35
Total labor force *(BIA labor report, 2001)*		699
High school graduate or higher		74.3%
2000 census		
Bachelor's degree or higher		0%
2000 census		
Unemployment rate *2000 census*		17.1%
Unemployment rate		39%
(BIA labor report, 2001)		
Per capita income *2000 census*		$12,377

LOCATION AND LAND STATUS
The Mooretown Rancheria is located in north-central California, near Oroville.

CULTURE AND HISTORY
The Concow-Maidus of Mooretown Rancheria are descendants of the ancient Northwestern Maidus. The Northwestern Maidus, who migrated to the area now known as Butte County, California, about 1200 BC, settled on a ridge between the Middle Fork and South Fork of the Feather River. They practiced a subsistence lifestyle, practiced horticulture, and traded extensively with coastal tribes. The aboriginal hunting territory for these Maidus extended roughly from areas now known as Mount Lassen and Honey Lake, California, on the north, to the Cosumnes River on the south, between the Sacramento River and the Sierra Nevada Mountains. Despite persistent stories of European contact having been recorded in a Spanish document dated 1542 or 1559, the earliest verifiable contact occurred in 1800. By the 1820s and 1830s, when fur trapping brought an influx of strangers to their lands followed by waves of gold miners pouring into the region in the 1840s and 1850s, whole populations of the Concow-Maidus and other California Native people were decimated through war and disease. The railroads brought timber interests and agricultural and commercial development, and the Concow-Maidus were dispossessed of their homelands. During one removal to a reservation, in September 1863, 461 Concows left Chico, but only 277 survived the two-week trip to Round Valley.

Public outcry over the mistreatment of Indians led to the Rancheria Act of 1884; and in June 1894, one citizen, James T. Grubbs, relinquished 80 acres of his own land for the use and benefit of some Indian families. Their settlement consisted of four small cabins in the middle of about eight usable acres. The remaining 80 acres were of very poor quality, but these original settlement families lived there for the next 50 years, planting fruit trees and cultivating gardens.

The BIA purchased an additional 80 acres for the 53-member Frank Taylor Band of Indians, as they were named on a previous census document, in 1915. In 1924 Native Americans were granted citizenship and allowed to vote, and in 1928 they were granted the right to sue the federal government for redress. Three California tribes filed land claims in 1951. In 1958 the

Mooretown Rancheria was terminated, effective 1961. Mooretown Rancheria was one of three tribes that eventually received compensation for lost lands, but it was not distributed until December 1972. Furthermore, payment was made based upon the 1853 land value of 47 cents per acre. Federal recognition was restored on December 22, 1983. The tribe purchased 203 acres in 1990, near the historic Pence Ranch in Mesilla Valley, notorious as the gathering point for the Maidu Trail of Tears of 1853. The U.S. Department of Housing and Urban Development approved the building of 50 homes, and an additional 35 acres of land were purchased near Oroville in January 1992.

The tribe is working diligently to restore traces of their cultural heritage via the Mooretown Heritage Project, an initiative involving the collection of materials related to Mooretown and its members' ancestors and the original founders. The accumulated documents and photographs have been assembled into the Tribal Heritage Manual which, with other artifacts and collectibles, is housed in a newly constructed tribal library. The tribe is developing a Cultural Preservation Ordinance, and in 1997 was seeking funding to develop a Concow-Maidu Language Program.

GOVERNMENT
Mooretown Rancheria is a federally recognized tribal entity. Tribal council elections were held in October 1987, and a tribal constitution was adopted in November 1987. Tribal offices opened in June 1988.

ECONOMY
Gaming. The tribe opened Feather Falls Casino near Oroville, California, in February 1998. A spectacular 118,112-square-foot facility, it features 1,000 slot machines, 12 table games, 6 poker tables, 3 restaurants, and 3 entertainment venues, one of which, the Cascade Showroom, seats 900 guests. The facility employed approximately 477 people in 2004.

In fulfillment of the terms of the gaming compact, the tribe returns a portion of its gaming revenues to the community in which it operates. In 2004, Mooretown Rancheria donated $1,000 to the Chico High School Color Guard and gave $8,511 to the North Valley Animal Disaster Group, among others.

COMMUNITY FACILITIES AND SERVICES
There are 50 houses located on rancheria land, along with a newly constructed community center. The center houses various tribal offices, a day care center and an after-school classroom, a multipurpose meeting room, full kitchen facilities, and the community library.

Public Safety. Mooretown Rancheria has a 14-member fire department.

Education. Rancheria students attend local public schools.

Health Care. Feather River Tribal Health, with one branch clinic in Oroville, California, and another in Yuba City, provides medical services to members of several tribal communities throughout a three-county area, including the Mooretown Rancheria. Dental care and behavioral health programs, as well as outreach services are available to tribal members.

**Mooretown Rancheria
Federal reservation
Concow-Maidu
Butte County, California**

Mooretown Rancheria
#1 Alverda Drive
Oroville, CA 95966
530-533-3625
530-533-3680 Fax

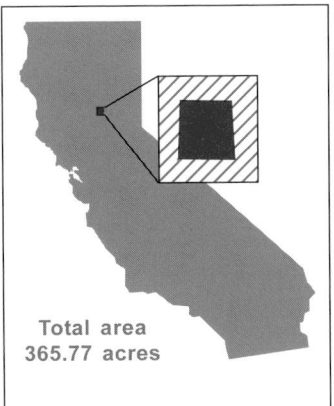

Total area
365.77 acres

Morongo

Morongo Reservation
Federal reservation
Cahuilla, Serrano, Cupeño,
and Chemehuevi
Riverside County, California

Morongo Band of Mission
Indians
11581 Potrero Road
Banning, CA 92220
951-755-5100
951-849-4697
951-849-4425 Fax
morongonation.org

Total area (BIA realty, 2003)
32,401.82 acres

Tribally owned (BIA realty, 2003)
31,123.73 acres

Individually owned
(BIA realty, 2003)
1,278.09 acres

Population 2000 census
954

Tribal enrollment
(Tribal source, 2004)
750

Tribal members on reserva-
tion
400

Total labor force
2000 census
230

High school graduate or
higher
2000 census
64.1%

Bachelor's degree or higher
2000 census
4.4%

Unemployment rate
2000 census
10%

Per capita income
$17,913

LOCATION AND LAND STATUS

The Morongo Reservation is located in south-central California along the Interstate 10 corridor, 80 miles east of Los Angeles, 22 miles northwest of Palm Springs, near the city of Banning. Lands for this reservation were set aside by Executive Orders on May 15, 1876, and March 9, 1881, and they were patented to the Morongo Band on December 14, 1908, by the secretary of the interior, under authority of an Act on March 1, 1907.

PHYSICAL DESCRIPTION

The reservation lies primarily within the foothills and lower portions of the San Bernardino Mountain range and borders the San Jacinto Mountains. The reservation land base includes 5,345 acres of forests and some 99.7 miles of streams. The upper portion, known as Burro Flats, is lush grassland that is grazed by reservation cattle.

CULTURE AND HISTORY

Residents of the Morongo Reservation are primarily members of the Cahuilla Tribe; the Serrano, Cupeño, and Chemehuevi tribes make up the remainder of the population. The Cahuillas and Cupeños have traditionally spoken languages belonging to the Takic branch, and the Chemehuevis the Numic branch, of the Uto-Aztecan language family. The Serranos' traditional language belongs to the Shoshonean branch.

In the early part of the twentieth century, the Morongo and other Cahuilla reservations retrieved some of the land that had been returned to the public domain by the 1891 Act for the Relief of Mission Indians. During this same general period, the Cahuillas made their living largely through farming, various types of wage labor, and raising stock on reservation lands. Serious farming was greatly hindered by a lack of water until the Indian Irrigation Service (an agency of the BIA) developed irrigation systems on some of the Cahuilla reservations, although these systems were rarely dependable. The Indians supplemented their efforts to make a living by harvesting reservation forests and selling hunting privileges, rights of way, and natural resources such as peat and asbestos.

Since the 1950s, many Cahuillas have found employment in careers such as educators, museum curators, authors, and businesspeople in the communities adjacent to their reservations. In 1970 the Morongo Indian Health Clinic opened, serving all the Riverside County reservations. The clinic's agenda has broadened considerably since then, to include the development of domestic water systems on the reservations and a focus on environmental health issues.

For Riverside County reservations, modern times have brought economic opportunities and their attendant controversies: whether to lease land for outside solid waste disposal, what kinds of commercial developments to pursue along the busy Interstate 10 corridor, and how to develop their gaming enterprise. Currently, Riverside County is one of the fastest-growing counties in California. The Morongo Reservation's lands were once considered a barren wasteland; but today the lands have become valuable real estate, being situated as they are along the I-10 corridor between famous tourist destinations from Los Angeles to Palm Springs and Phoenix, Arizona.

GOVERNMENT

Morongo tribal affairs are handled by the tribal council, elected by the general membership, which includes all tribal members 21 years of age and older. The council is comprised of seven members, one of whom serves as tribal chairman. Council mem-

bers serve two-year staggered terms. All council members serve on the overall economic development planning committee. The tribe offers the following services: natural resource management, social, realty, fire, community, and legal.

ECONOMY

Tribal government and gaming are major contributors to the tribe's economic self-reliance. The tribe's plans for further economic development include the promotion of tourism, recreation, and service and retail industries.

Government as Employer. The tribe is the largest employer in the San Gorgonio Pass area, employing more than 1,700 through its departments and business enterprises.

Economic Development Projects. In addition to opening the Morongo Casino, Resort, and Spa, construction is underway on a $26-million water-bottling plant on Morongo land in Cabazon. The new plant is expected to create over 200 employment opportunities. The 383,000-square-foot plant will be operated by Arrowhead Mountain Spring Water, a subsidiary of Perrier Group of America. The source will be natural spring water flowing from Millard Canyon, north of Cabazon and west of Kitching Peak. Morongo leaders purchased water rights to Millard Canyon water sources in June 2003 from the Cabazon County Water District, which serves about 800 customers. The land where the plant is being built lies within the Morongo Reservation. The plant plans to open with two production lines, and then expand to four production lines with a capacity for bottling up to 17 million cases of water annually in various container sizes. The plant has been designed to meet the U.S. Green Building Council's standards for environmentally-sustainable design and construction. Morongo officials conducted an environmental analysis and concluded there will be no adverse effects on the natural springs or other area water sources.

Other enterprises under consideration: Hadley Fruit Orchards (employs 18); Morongo Travel Center (employs 23); nationally franchised restaurants A&W Root Beer (employs 20) and Coco's (employs 250); and a world-class golf course, a theme park, shopping centers, an RV park, and a truck stop.

Agriculture and Livestock. A section of the upper portion of the reservation, Burro Flats, is used for cattle grazing.

Gaming. Casino Morongo, located in a tiny town near Banning, about 90 minutes' drive from Los Angeles, was the tribe's first gaming venture. The casino's relative success prompted the development of the Morongo Casino, Resort, and Spa on a spacious lot adjacent to the Casino Morongo. The $250-million, 44-acre resort was slated for completion in 2004. This 659,800-square-foot facility will host approximately 310 sleeping rooms, a lounge, buffet, a café, nightclub, steak house, other restaurants, a gift shop, conference room and small meeting room, and it will create some 1,200 new jobs. Revenue from the casino will be used for building a community center, street paving, educational scholarships, donations to the cities of Banning and Beaumont, community celebrations, Banning Skateboard Park, and Cabazon Community School playground equipment.

Services and Retail. A wide variety of services are available in nearby communities.

Tourism and Recreation. Striving to preserve traditional culture and practices, the Malki Museum on the Morongo Reservation presents an annual fiesta, maintains a Cahuilla archive, and exhibits Cahuilla cultural materials. With the completion of the new Morongo Casino, Resort and Spa, and plans for further destination resort amenities and attractions, Morongo Reservation expects to become a popular site for tourism, travel, and recreation.

INFRASTRUCTURE

Interstate 10 provides excellent road access to the reservation, and it transverses the reservation for approximately five miles, as do several miles of the Southern Pacific Railroad. Morongo Public Works provides maintenance of the reservation's paved roads. Bus, trucking, and private airport facilities are available in Banning, five miles from the reservation. The closest commercial airline facilities are in Palm Springs, about 22 miles to the northwest, and in San Bernardino, about 20 miles to the northwest. Freight service is provided by UPS, Federal Express, and Overnight Express.

Electricity. Electricity is provided to the reservation by Southern California Edison, and to Morongo Casino and Resort by the Morongo Cogeneration Facility.

Fuel. Gas is supplied to the reservation via Southern California Edison Gas Company.

Water Supply. Five wells supply water to reservation residents. Waste is taken care of by the Morongo wastewater treatment plant.

Telecommunications. The Morongo Tribe co-publishes the influential *Journal of California and Great Basin Anthropology* and provides the reservation with cable television service. Internet services are provided by Verizon Internet.

COMMUNITY FACILITIES AND SERVICES

The reservation houses the Morongo Administration Center, a community library, the Morongo Senior Center, Head Start, a tribal kitchen, a baseball field, and two churches. The Malki Museum is available for tribal language programs and cultural activities programs.

Public Safety. The tribe has a full-service fire department, and mutual aid agreements with the Riverside County Fire Department and the City of Banning. Law enforcement is provided by the reservation patrol.

Health Care. The Morongo Indian Health Clinic, operated by the U.S. Indian Health Service, serves the tribe during business hours. The tribe has a contract with the San Gorgonio Memorial Hospital, in Banning, to provide after-hours medical services.

ENVIRONMENTAL CONCERNS

The Morongo Reservation contains considerable quantities of high-quality water, which has become a precious commodity in southern California. Access to natural gas mains, running through its property, and vast acreages of undeveloped land have become valuable reservation resources. Given the value of these resources, one of the major current challenges to the people of Morongo is to maintain balance between economic growth and the preservation of their natural resources.

The tribe applied for and received a grant from the EPA's General Assistance Program (GAP) in 1994. The grant was used to develop initial environmental programs for the reservation focusing, initially, on water resource and solid waste management programs.

In 1994 the Morongo Indian Reservation published a Section 305(b) Water Quality Resources Assessment with assistance from the U.S. Geological Survey. At the time, little data was available for quantitative water quality assessments on tribal lands. While reservation drinking water met standards well below EPA maximum containment levels, the tribe viewed the assessment as an important first step in protecting its drinking water resources and in formulating initial efforts to prevent pollution of surface-water resources. Cattle waste matter appeared to be the main pollution threat to water quality. Additionally, a faulty well seal at one of the water-supply wells had allowed some surface contamination to enter the drinking water system. Due to some bacterial contamination, surface water did not fully support drinking water requirements. Also, no data was available for groundwater in an area close to an abandoned landfill. The primary potential sources of water pollution on the reservation were associated with agricultural activities in the Potrero Canyon area. It was felt that irrigation return-flow might also introduce salts, fertilizers, and pesticides into the groundwater system. The Morongo Community needed to implement monitoring networks and programs to assess water resources in order to manage and protect them. The 1994 Water Quality Assessment was the first step in this process.

One major concern regarding solid waste issues on the Morongo Reservation involved waste from clandestine drug labs found at illegal dumpsites in the area. In response to this, officials from state, county, and local law enforcement agencies established a fund to clean up any hazardous materials found on the reservation that were associated with illegal drug labs. When suspects were arrested for operating illegal labs and dumping the materials on reservation lands, the cost of cleanup activities would be part of the guilty parties' punishment and would be done without cost to the reservation. The improper dumping of green waste was also reduced by a permitting process for persons hauling waste and traveling on tribal roads. This process made it much easier to trace any illegal dumping activities and to pursue prosecution of violators of solid waste ordinances. Tribal authorities launched another successful program which used county prisoners for solid waste cleanup activities in an agreement with the Riverside County Sheriff's Department. Air quality in the region is also a concern for the tribe.

Morongo

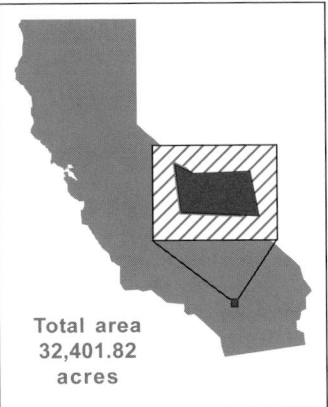

Total area
32,401.82
acres

**North Fork Rancheria
of Mono Indians
Federal reservation
Western Mono
Madera County, California**

North Fork Rancheria
of Mono Indians
33173 Road 222
P.O. Box 929
North Fork, CA 93643
559-877-2461
559-877-2467 Fax

Total area *(BIA realty, 2003)*
141.52 acres

Tribally owned *(BIA realty, 2003)*
61.52 acres

Individually owned
(BIA realty, 2003)
80 acres

Population *(BIA/SA)*
75

Tribal enrollment
(BIA labor report, 2001)
510

Tribal enrollment
(Tribal source, 2004)
1,345

Total labor force *2000 census*
4

Total labor force
(BIA labor report, 2001)
285

**High school degree or
higher** *2000 census*
100%

Bachelor's degree or higher
2000 census
0%

Unemployment rate
2000 census
75%

Unemployment rate
(BIA labor report, 2001)
13%

Per capita income
2000 census
$2,389

446

LOCATION AND LAND STATUS

The rancheria is located at the western edge of the Sierra National Forest in central California, about 50 miles northeast of Fresno. The reservation was terminated during the early 1950s, then it was restored to federal recognition under class action suit *Tillie Hardwick v. United States of America.* Judgment was filed on December 22, 1983. As a result, there are no tribally owned lands; however, 80 acres of individually owned lands have been restored to a trust status. Additionally, the tribe has acquired 61.5 acres that have been placed in trust.

CULTURE AND HISTORY

At the beginning of the twentieth century, a large percentage of the Western Mono Indians were still living in their ancestral homelands of the south-central Sierra Nevadas. Within a few short years, however, economic pressures and government policies had forced the Western Mono out of their mountain bastions and into the control of the dominant white culture.

The Northern California Indian Association lobbied for the creation of three small Mono rancherias during the 1920s, and they subsequently established a mission and boarding school for girls at North Fork. Meanwhile, the Baptist Mission Society set up churches and schools at the sites of other Mono rancherias. The rancherias themselves have never served as bases for significant economic enterprise. Male tribal members have typically found work in the region's logging industry, as well as in ranch labor and mining. Women have worked largely in local hotels, hospitals, and the like. *(For additional cultural information, see California's introduction.)*

GOVERNMENT

The rancheria is fully formed, with a constitution and governing statutes in place. The tribal office opened in North Fork, in November 1994. The tribe has three interim administrative positions: a spokesperson, a vice-spokesperson, and a secretary-treasurer. Recently the tribe established a tribal TANF (Temporary Assistance for Needy Families) program in the interest of Indian people in three counties: Madera, Mariposa, and Merced. Unique among TANF programs, the North Fork program is the only one in California set up independently, rather than as part of a consortium. The tribe, in conjunction with its Indian Housing Authority, has purchased an existing 6,000-square-foot building in North Fork and renovated it for use as their tribal government offices.

ECONOMY

The tribe is a recipient of various grants that represent a significant source of revenue.

Government as Employer. The tribe employs 20 people on a full-time basis, with others working on short-term grants.

Economic Development Projects. The tribe is in the process of developing a casino and resort complex.

Gaming. In 2004 the tribe began negotiations with local communities to develop a 200,000-square-foot casino and resort north of Madera. The tribe hopes to acquire a 300-acre parcel of land adjacent to State Route 99 and a 360-acre parcel on the west side of the highway to construct the facilities. It is estimated the casino will create over 1,700 direct jobs and another 2,000 indirect jobs. The project will be funded by Station Casinos and, pending agreements with government agencies and local communities, will be completed by 2007.

Tourism and Recreation.
The Sierra Mono Museum in North Fork is owned and operated by the Mono people. Aside from an array of displays and classes, it holds the Annual Indian Fair Days every August, featuring traditional food, arts and crafts, dances, and songs. The museum also features the Tettleton Wildlife Collection, regarded as one of the finest in the state. The tribe uses the museum for its council meetings. The rancheria lies near Yosemite National Park and the Sequoia National Forest. Hence, it is situated on the edge of one of the most heavily touristed regions of the country. It is located along the Sierra Vista National Scenic Byway, a seasonal route that permits visitors easy access to the natural surroundings in this area. The lakes, forests, and outdoor recreational areas draw a number of tourists to this region south of Yosemite. North Fork offers an array of tourist shops.

INFRASTRUCTURE

State Highway 41 serves as the rancheria's primary link Fresno to the south and Yosemite to the north.

Electricity. Electric power is provided by Pacific Gas and Electric.

Fuel. Propane is available through several wholesalers.

Water Supply. The water supply comes from individual wells. The sewage system relies on individual septic tanks.

Transportation. Commercial bus service is available in Auberry, 15 miles from the reservation. Fresno is the site of the nearest commercial airport. Federal Express serves the immediate vicinity.

Housing. Under the aegis of the North Fork Rancheria Indian Housing Authority, the tribe is currently installing the necessary infrastructure to support up to 54 homes.

COMMUNITY FACILITIES AND SERVICES

The tribe is currently building a community center.

Education. Public elementary and high schools are available in nearby Auberry. Head Start programs have been in operation on the reservation for over 20 years.

Health Care. The Central Valley Indian Health Service operates a clinic, along with shuttle services. Services are contracted through the California Rural Indian Health Board, that include comprehensive medical, dental, family wellness, mental health, and other social services.

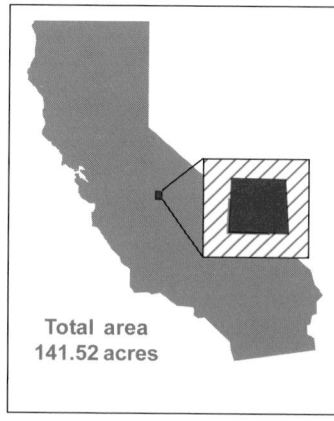

Total area
141.52 acres

LOCATION AND LAND STATUS

The Pala Reservation is located in southern California. It was established by the Executive Order of December 27, 1875. Executive Orders of May 3, 1877, and July 24, 1882, restored portions of it to public domain. A Congressional Act of May 27, 1902, appropriated $100,000 for the purchase of land for California Mission Indians. An Act of March 31, 1903, permitted the use of part of this money for removing the Indians to the purchased land. The Executive Order of December 20, 1973, returned the Mission Reserve, formerly controlled by the U.S. Bureau of Land Management, to the Pala Band of Mission Indians. The rancheria encompasses over 12,000 acres, including 4,000 acres of forests, 6 acres of wetlands, 8 acres of lake, and over 38 miles of streams. The San Luis Rey River courses through the center of the reservation.

CULTURE AND HISTORY

Members of the Pala Band belong to the Kuupangaxwichem, or Cupeño, and Luiseño tribes. The Pala Reservation represents one of the communities of Indians who were forced together by Spanish Franciscan missionaries during the 1800s. Although descendants of the Cupeño people form the majority, there has been a large degree of cultural integration between the groups.

The Luiseño people occupied about 1,500 square miles of coastal southern California, including the San Luis Rey River area where the Pala Reservation now exists. Living in small villages, they were farmers who used advanced agricultural techniques such as controlled burning, water and erosion management, and plant husbandry. In 1875, through the initiative of Chief Oligario Calac, the Luiseños petitioned the federal government to have their ancestral lands granted reservation status. The 1891 Act for the Relief of Mission Indians created five Luiseño reservations, including the Pala Reservation. Immediately after its creation, as decreed by the act, the reservation was divided into allotments.

In 1903 the Cupeño people joined the Luiseños on the reservation. Occupying two villages near Warner Springs, the Cupeños were forcibly moved from their farmland to Luiseño territory. In an attempt to retain their traditional land, the Cupeños, along with another band, fought their expulsion all the way to the Supreme Court. After they lost their case, the government purchased additional land that was added to the Pala Reservation to accommodate relocated tribal members. In addition to this acreage, the government promised to provide these displaced people with homes and infrastructural improvements. Unfortunately, the Cupeños received only temporary housing in the form of clapboard shacks and lean-tos. While the majority of the Cupeño refugees remained at the Pala Reservation, a significant number moved early in the twentieth century to the Morongo Indian Reservation. Both groups continued their agricultural traditions, raising fruit trees, market and subsistence crops, cattle, horses, chickens, and bees. Many Pala residents participated in the wage economy as ranch and farm laborers. By 1910, the average annual income of Pala residents either matched or exceeded that of the area's non-Indian farmers.

Throughout the reservation's existence, water issues have plagued Pala residents. Beginning in 1894, via a number of dishonest maneuvers, water has been consistently diverted from the Pala Reservation. In 1951 a claim for the stolen water was added to the Mission Indian Land Claim. It was not until 1985, however, when the Pala and other area reservations brought forth the San Luis Rey case, that an out-of-court settlement compensated these groups for water damages. The various bands received several million dollars for past damages, and the fed-

eral government promised that 16,000 acre-feet of other water would be made available to these groups. As of 1993, the water was yet to be provided.

People on the Pala Reservation continue to observe traditional cultural practices, such as rituals for the dead and playing a gambling game called "peon." Their settlement pattern, of a central-village type, reflects the housing arrangement of the Cupeño homeland at Warner Springs. *(For additional cultural information, see California introduction.)*

GOVERNMENT

The general council, composed of all adult members 18 years and older, governs the Pala Reservation. The council meets monthly, or the executive committee may call a special meeting. Executive committee members include a chairperson, a vice-chairperson, a secretary, and a treasurer. Members of the executive committee serve two-year terms. Tribal members must be at least 21 years old to run for office. The tribe is organized under Articles of Association approved in July 1961. These articles were amended in 1973 and 1980.

ECONOMY

The Pala Band of Mission Indians' tribal economy is supported in large part by its agricultural enterprises. Gaming facilities also contribute to the tribe's general fund.

Agriculture and Livestock. Projects designed to expand the tribe's agricultural sector represent its primary source of revenue and employment. While the tribe already grows about 125 acres of alfalfa, its largest endeavor is the Pala Avocado Project. Development of this orchard land was made possible by joint funding through a Comprehensive Employment and Training Act, Native American Stimulus Program, and an EDA Local Public Works Program. Pala is anticipating substantial returns. It lies within the fastest growing avocado area in the state. San Diego County leads the state in acreage and production of avocados.

Forestry. In 1996 the tribe considered the feasibility of developing forestry projects within Mission Reserves land. Under consideration were a limited wood products enterprise, a Christmas tree farm, and reforestation programs.

Gaming. In 1999 the tribe entered into a gaming compact with the State of California which permits class III gaming. The compact was renegotiated in 2004. The tribe owns the Pala Casino Resort and Spa, which is located in the Palomar Mountains overlooking a lake. It offers 2,000 slot machines, 77 table games, 8 restaurants, 5 entertainment venues, and 2 lounges. The hotel offers 507 guest rooms and a spa. The spa features 14 treatment rooms, a fitness center, a salon, and a retail boutique. The hotel also offers the services of a wedding coordinator to assist in arranging on-site weddings. The adjacent Pala Events Center can seat up to 2,000 guests.

Mining. The mining of sand and gravel represents a substantial portion of the tribe's revenue.

Manufacturing. The tribe owns a clay roofing-tile manufacturing business that employs 50 individuals.

Media and Communications. A tribal cable television enterprise provides cable television service to the reservation. The tribe employs a manager and two part-time workers. Two towers, each with six antennas, project the cable service.

Pala Reservation
Federal reservation
Luiseño, Cupeño
San Diego County, California

Pala Band of Mission Indians
PMB 50
35008 Pala-Temecula Rd.
Pala, CA 92059
   760-742-3784
   760-742-1411 Fax

Total area *(BIA realty, 2003)*
12,175.58 acres

Tribally owned *(BIA realty, 2003)*
11,043.54 acres

Individually owned
(BIA realty, 2003)
1,132.04 acres

Population *2000 census*
1,573

Population
1,125

Tribal enrollment
(BIA labor report, 2001)
891

Total labor force *2000 census*
493

Total labor force
(BIA labor report, 2001)
459

High school graduate or higher *2000 census*
52.3%

Bachelor's degree or higher
2000 census
8.4%

Unemployment rate *2000 census*
9.94%

Unemployment rate
(BIA labor report, 2001)
62%

Per capita income *2000 census*
$10,995

Pala

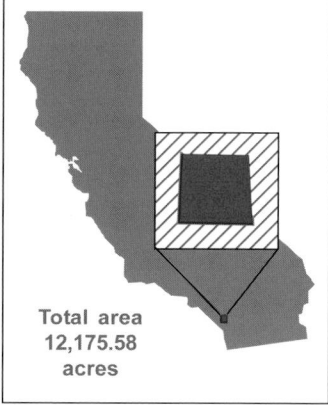

Total area
12,175.58
acres

Tourism and Recreation. The Pala Campground covers 20 acres of reservation land. Campground facilities include a children's playground, a softball diamond, and horseshoe pits. In 1996 the tribe was conducting tests to determine the feasibility of adding fishing ponds and a swimming pool to the campground site.

INFRASTRUCTURE
Interstate 15 (also known as State Highway 395) runs approximately six miles west of the center of the reservation and serves as an artery between the Los Angeles and San Diego urban complexes. The reservation has a paved access road to State Highway16 to the north and to east-west running State Highway 76.

Electricity and Fuel. San Diego Gas and Electric provides electricity. Reservation residents purchase bottled gas.

Water Supply. There are community water and sewer systems on the reservation.

Transportation. Bus and truck service is available in Fallbrook, approximately 20 miles from the reservation. A train station is located in Oceanside, 25 miles away. The nearest commercial air service is available in San Diego. There is a private airstrip six miles from the reservation.

COMMUNITY FACILITIES AND SERVICES
The Pala Reservation offers many community facilities, including the cultural center, a ballpark, tribal offices, a fire station, and a post office. The historic Pala Mission, a subsidiary of the Mission San Luis Rey, was established in 1815 and still serves the reservation's Catholics. The church maintains a museum that deals to some extent with Cupeño and Luiseño culture and history as well as with the history of the church.

Education. Children attend the Mission Parochial School through the eighth grade, while high school students must travel to nearby communities. Adults can receive instruction at the adult learning center.

Health Care. Health care services are available through Indian Health Council. Clinics are located in Valley Center and Santa Ysabel. Programs include general medicine, general dental, human services, and community outreach.

Paskenta Band

**Paskenta Band of Nomlaki
Indians Rancheria
Federally recognized
Nomlaki
Tehama County, California**

Paskenta Band of Nomlaki
Indians
P.O. Box 988
Williams, CA 95987
916-473-5196

Total area *(BIA realty, 2003)*
1,896.16 acres

**Tribally owned
1,896.16 acres**
(BIA realty, 2003)

Tribal enrollment
(BIA labor report, 2001)
282

Total labor force
(BIA labor report, 2001)
92

**Unemployment rate
28%**
(BIA labor report, 2001)

LOCATION AND LAND STATUS
The Paskenta Band of Nomlaki Indians Rancheria is located in Tehama County, California. When the band's federally recognized status was terminated in 1959, all tribal lands were dissolved. The tribe's status was restored in 1994, and in 2000 the tribe acquired 2,000 acres near Corning, California, to establish the present-day rancheria.

CULTURE AND HISTORY
The Paskenta Band of Nomlaki Indians' ancestral lands encompassed present-day Tehama County. The tribe's status as a federally recognized nation was terminated in 1959. The rancheria was sold to private landowners. Although no longer federally recognized, tribal members maintained their cultural identity as they worked toward restoration. Federal status was restored in 1994. In 2000 the tribe acquired a 2,000-acre parcel of land on which it established the rancheria.

GOVERNMENT
The tribal government is led by a chairperson. The tribe also maintains an economic development department.

ECONOMY
Since its restoration as a federally recognized tribe in 1994, the Paskenta Band has been working to regain its economic stability and tribal organization. It acquired 2,000 acres of land to establish a reservation, and it has initiated such projects as a casino. Construction of the tribe's casino generated 300 temporary jobs and 430 permanent positions. The tribe held job fairs in Corning and Chico to recruit casino employees.

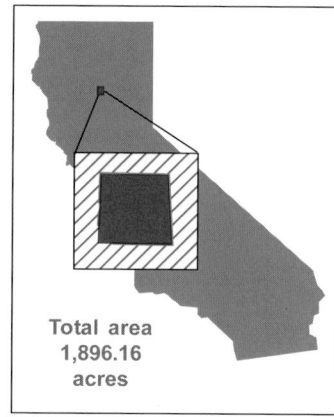

Total area
1,896.16
acres

Gaming. The tribe owns the Rolling Hills Casino in Corning, California, which opened in 2002. The casino offers 700 slot machines, 12 table games, 3 restaurants, and a lounge. There are also nonsmoking gaming areas and a video arcade. The adjacent hotel has 60 guest rooms. Revenue from gaming is used to support the tribe's health care, social services, educational, and cultural programs.

COMMUNITY FACILITIES AND SERVICES
Health Care. Northern Valley Indian Health provides health services. There are clinics in Willows and Chico. Available services include dental, medical, behavioral health, outreach, and Women, Infant, and Children (WIC) programs.

LOCATION AND LAND STATUS

The Pauma and Yuima Reservation lies in the northeastern corner of San Diego County, California, against the foothills of Mount Palomar. It is composed of four separate tracts of land totaling 5,877.25 acres. The residential portion of the reservation, 225 acres, is located 65 miles from metropolitan San Diego. The reservation was established on August 18, 1893, by an Executive Order. The Pauma Reservation proper totals 225 acres and serves as the community center for the reservation. Two 12.5-acre tracts located on the slopes of Mount Palomar are referred to as Yuima tracts 1 and 2. These tracts are approximately five miles from the main reservation and have tribal housing. In 1973 the Secretary of the Interior instructed the Bureau of Land Management to issue a trust patent to the Pauma Band of Mission Indians for the nearby Mission Reserve. This 5,627-acre parcel of land, composed of undeveloped wilderness, became the fourth tract of land in the Pauma Reservation.

CULTURE AND HISTORY

The Pauma and Yuima Indian Reservation is one of the homes of the Luiseño Tribe. Originally, the tribe occupied about 1,500 square miles of coastal southern California. Their language belongs to the Cupan group of the Takic language, a subfamily of the greater Uto-Aztecan linguistic family. *(For additional cultural information, see California introduction.)*

In the last 100 years, the history of the reservation has been closely linked to the water-use policies within the area. In 1916, the owner of the land surrounding the Pauma and Yuima Reservation subdivided the land and sold the orchards. Subsequently, non-Native orchardists appropriated a majority of the reservation's water supply, and the Pauma's prosperous orchards died.

By 1955, this lack of water forced most of the Pauma residents to seek employment off the reservation. In 1951, a claim for the stolen water was added to the docket of the Mission Indian Land Claim case. After a 1973 hearing, the Federal Power Commission required the city of Escondido to regularly release water from their dam for use by several reservations downstream. There was also some monetary compensation for the tribes involved, and the federal government promised 16,000 acre-feet of water to the reservations and rancherias involved in the lawsuit. However, as of 1933 much of the water still had not been provided. The settlement led to a small revitalization on the reservation, as a number of tribal members returned to live there. The tribes involved in the water rights battle formed the San Luis Rey Indian Water Authority to manage water, approve developments, and distribute benefits from the settlement for past damages.

GOVERNMENT

The Pauma Band of Mission Indians is governed by custom and tradition. The band is organized under the non-IRA Articles of Association, adopted by the group on March 17, 1966, and approved by the BIA on June 28, 1966. The general council serves as the reservation's governing body, and it consists of all enrolled members at least 21 years old. Elected tribal officials include a chairperson, a vice-chairperson, a secretary-treasurer, a tribal administrator, and a tribal council member. Tribal government departments will include administration, tribal administrative court, education K-12, after school care, fire station, library, natural resources (grove, land, air, and water), hazardous response crew, cultural committee, and law enforcement. The band will operate a police department that will have cross jurisdiction with the state of California. Once this is accomplished, the tribe will establish criminal and civil court.

ECONOMY

Gaming and agriculture are the main components of Pauma Band's economy. The fertile soil in the Pauma Valley, and the band's rights to Pauma Creek's surface water, make the reservation land valuable for agricultural, commercial, and residential uses. As the city of San Diego continues to expand in the direction of the Pauma Reservation, the land and its resources will correspondingly continue to become more valuable.

Economic Development Projects. Officials of Vegas-based Park Place Entertainment Corporation, which owns Caesars Palace and 28 other casinos, announced it was in negotiations with the Pauma Band of Mission Indians to build a $250 million Caesars Pauma resort and casino on the Pauma and Yuima Reservation, located off Highway 76 about 14 miles east of Interstate 15. The tribe hopes to complete the facility by 2005.

The band's future may include a full-scale Quick Mart and travel center offering all gasoline grade fuels, diesel, and a wide variety of snacks and beverages to all travelers.

Agriculture and Livestock. Twenty-five percent of the tribe's acreage has been devoted to growing lemons, oranges, and avocados. This project employs 30-50 seasonal employees.

Gaming. The Pauma Band operates the Pauma Casino. Located on Pauma Reservation Road, the 35,000-square-foot facility features 1,000 slots/VLTs and 25 table games, with poker tables. It also offers the Pauma Bay Buffet with its dramatic view of citrus groves and the Palomar Range Foothills, a deli, a pizzeria, and an entertainment venue. At present the casino employs 500 employees. The tribe plans to expand the casino to include a resort. Revenues from gaming are used for many tribal purposes, including the preservation and protection of the Pauma Creek economic and social growth.

Manufacturing. Native Threads, a clothing manufacturer, is owned and operated by the band. They are considering economic projects which include sand and gravel, forestry, and alternative power.

Tourism and Recreation. The tribe has created the Pauma Casino and, or course, want people to visit this as well as the spa and resort they plan to build in the future. However, the tribe does value privacy and does not allow visitors in other areas of the reservation.

INFRASTRUCTURE

State Highway 76, at Pauma Reservation Road, can easily access the Pauma and Yuima Reservation. The town of Oceanside, 25 miles to the west, provides train facilities; and the town of Escondido, also 25 miles from the reservation, offers truck and bus facilities. Commercial air service is available from San Diego International Airport, 70 miles distant. The band owns and operates its own heliport.

Electricity. San Diego Gas and Electric Company provides electrical service by resolution only. The band is seeking alternative electrical power sources.

Fuel. Escondido provides propane gas via a pipeline. Reservation residents must obtain permission from the tribe to receive propane.

Pauma and Yuima Reservation
Federal reservation
Luiseño
San Diego County, California

Pauma Band of Mission
   Indians
P.O. Box 369
Pauma Valley, CA 92061
760-742-3579
760-742-3422 Fax

Total area *(BIA realty, 2003)*
5,877.25 acres

Tribally owned
(BIA realty, 2003)
5,877.25 acres

Federal trust lands
(Tribal source, 2004)
5,088 acres

Population *2000 census*
186

Tribal enrollment
(BIA labor report, 2001)
32

Total labor force *2000 census*
48

Total labor force
(BIA labor report, 2001)
81

High school graduate or higher *2000 census*
97.1%

Bachelor's degree or higher
2000 census
18.6%

Unemployment rate
2000 census
0%

Unemployment rate
(BIA labor report, 2001)
40%

Per capita income
(BIA labor report, 2001)
$11,712

Pauma

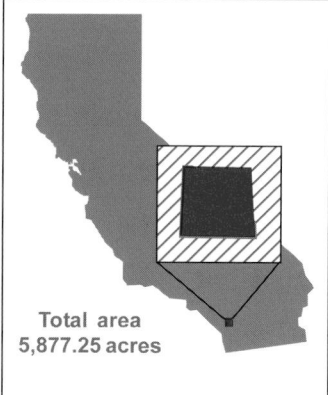

**Total area
5,877.25 acres**

Water Supply. Wells provide water for both domestic (two wells) and (four wells) irrigation use on the reservation. Individual septic tanks and a wastewater sewage plant are the primary means of sewage disposal, although the tribe is looking into the feasibility of switching to a system called Waste Water Management. The tribe has its own landfill.

Telecommunications. The Pauma Band has a monthly newsletter. A wireless hub receives its signals from their mountain (on the Mission Reserve) and transmits to the reservation. The band partners with Palomar communications, and plans to pursue future development in the telecommunications area. In the future the Pauma Band will develop a radio station to broadcast to tribal members day-to-day updates of what is going on in Indian country.

COMMUNITY FACILITIES AND SERVICES

The reservation is home to Pauma AA'Alvikat Library. Located in a newly expanded facility it shares with the Palomar College Education Center, the library offers collections of reference, Native American, and children's books. The library was established in the early 1980s and is one of seven tribal libraries of the San Diego Library Outreach Division Indian Library Services Project. Expansions included library furniture and media, provided by the Indian Library Services Project. The library publishes its own newsletter. An adobe-style tribal complex and adjacent adobe ruins, as well as a chapel, are also located on the reservation.

Education. Students attend local schools and colleges in the Pauma, Valley Center, Fallbrook, and Bonsall Union school districts. The Pauma Band is dedicated to preserving their language. In advancement of this effort they have participated in a Palomar College language class and begun a preservation program entitled First Voice. The program allows families who want to participate in the digital recording of the Pauma story to do so through a wireless Web hub. Tribal youth and seniors are especially encouraged to participate. Tribal youth are required to submit to the tribe proof of a high school or GED diploma with a five-year plan of what they will pursue as a career before they can receive any tribal trust money. The tribe has tribal higher education scholarships to assist tribal members in furthering their

education or career goals. The Pauma and Yuima Reservation is the northern satellite center for Palomar College, Cal State University San Marcos. The BVIA has used the Pauma's education facilities for fire crews, forestry, grove, and water and air monitoring training. The tribe encourages tribal youth to attain higher education and increase career options through education.

Health Care. The Indian Health Clinic provides tribal members with health care. Several tribal members still use traditional remedies to heal common illness. The band is acquiring a health care maintenance plan for its members.

ENVIRONMENTAL CONCERNS

The Pauma Band has water rights to divert surface water from Pauma Creek, which originates in the Palomar Mountain watershed. Preservation of Pauma Creek, often referred to as the lifeblood of the tribe for it's spiritual importance and a source of irrigation and drinking water, is the tribe's foremost environmental concern. In the mid-1990s, the Pauma Band, in conjunction with the BIA, began investigating and collecting data pertaining to this valuable natural resource, including seismic and magnetic studies to learn about the role of Pauma Creek in recharging local groundwater. To protect the purity of its drinking water, the Pauma Band developed a program to encourage proper pesticide use, storage, and disposal. The band brought in dumpsters to facilitate the removal of trash and other possible groundwater contaminants. Domestic wastewater is disposed of through individual septic tanks, while the larger system used to treat wastewater from the casino is reclaimed and used to irrigate the band's avocado and citrus groves. The Pauma Band is working hard toward establishing permanent measures that will ensure the long-term purity, protection, and preservation of Pauma Creek.

The band also has been involved in restoring the forested land destroyed in the California wildfires of 2003. As of 2004, they have replaced over 6,000 trees, created a fuel break around all of Mission Reserve, and have put an erosion control program into place. This program will safeguard the main road leading to the Mission Reserve for both the environmental and emergency response.

Pechanga

**Pechanga Reservation
Federal reservation
Luiseño
Riverside County, California**

Pechanga Band of Luiseño
 Mission Indians
P.O. Box 1477
Temecula, CA 92593
951-676-2768
951-676-1778 Fax
pechanga.com

Total area *(BIA realty, 2003)*	5,371.99 acres
Total area *(Tribal source, 2004)*	5,500 acres
Population *2000 census*	467
Population *(Tribal source, 2004)*	500
Tribal enrollment *(BIA labor report, 2001)*	1,372
Total labor force *2000 census*	150
Total labor force *(BIA labor report, 2001)*	833
High school graduate or higher *2000 census*	64.8%
Bachelor's degree or higher *2000 census*	3.7%
Unemployment rate *2000 census*	7.3%
Unemployment rate *(BIA labor report, 2001)*	0%
Per capita income *2000 census*	$13,248

LOCATION AND LAND STATUS

The Pechanga Reservation is located in southern California near the city of Temecula. The tribal headquarters are located off County Road S-16, south of Highway 79 at Temecula. President Chester Arthur's Executive Order established the Pechanga Indian Reservation on June 27, 1882. Under provisions of the General Allotment Act of 1887, 1,233 acres of the reservation were allotted in 1891, which increased the reservation's land base.

The allotments were not suitable for farming, and in 1907, tribal members petitioned the government for more suitable lands. Under PL 100-381, the Bureau of Land Management transferred a 235-acre parcel of land, named the Kelsey Tract, to the BIA in 1988, to be held in trust for the Pechanga Band. Also, in 1988, the Southern California Land Transfer Act (PL 100-581) added 303 acres to the reservation. In 2001, the tribe purchased 700 acres of its ancestral homelands at the Great Oak Ranch in California. The BIA placed the lands into federal trust in 2003. The Great Oak Tree is now under the tribe's protection.

PHYSICAL DESCRIPTION

The reservation is located 20 miles inland from the Pacific Ocean in the Temecula Valley. The oldest living coast live oak tree (Quercus agrifolia) in North America lives on tribal lands. It is estimated to be over 1,500 years old. The Great Oak stands more than 96 feet tall, and its trunk is 26 feet in diameter.

CULTURE AND HISTORY

The Pechanga Band has resided in the Temecula Valley for thousands of years. It is one of six bands of the Payomkawichum, or Luiseño, Tribe. Other bands are the Soboba, Pauma, Rincon, La Jolla, and Old Pala. The Luiseño Tribe is comprised of the indigenous groups that once inhabited the villages near the Mission San Luis Rey de Francia. The mission was founded in 1798 and served the ranchos of the Temecula Valley. These ranchos were established within boundaries of Native communities, and ranchers forced the indigenous residents into servitude for the mission.

In 1869 local ranchers petitioned the district court of California in San Francisco for a Decree of Ejection of Indians living in Temecula Valley. The court granted the decree in 1873, and in 1875 the tribe was forcibly removed from their ancestral lands, to which they held title. The band was moved to the hills south of the Temecula River near the eastern end of the present-day Temecula Creek Inn Golf Course.

GOVERNMENT
The Pechanga Band is governed by its general membership and led by a tribal council in accordance with its constitution and bylaws. The tribal council is comprised of seven members who serve two-year terms. The general membership also elects the tribal secretary and treasurer. It is a self-governing nation.

BUSINESS CORPORATION
The tribe has established the Pechanga Development Corporation and Pechanga Gaming Commission. The tribe's general membership elects members and officers for each entity.

ECONOMY
The Pechanga Band is committed to establishing a stable and successful tribal economy. The casino and RV park serve as the largest sources of revenue for the tribe and provide a number of job opportunities for tribal members as well as nonmembers.

Government as Employer. The Pechanga Band employs over 4,800 people.

Gaming. The Pechanga Casino opened its doors on July 1, 1995. Since that time, it has expanded to become the Pechanga Casino and Resort. The 88,000-square-foot, 14-story casino and resort offers 2,000 slot machines, 88 table games, a 27-table nonsmoking poker room, and 700 bingo seats. The resort is California's only AAA Four Diamond Resort. It offers 522 guest rooms overlooking the Temecula Valley wine country or the San Jacinto Mountains. Facilities include an outdoor pool and seven restaurants. The Pechanga Health Club occupies the third floor of the hotel and offers massages and related services. The Pechanga Spa offers a fitness center. There are also conference, banquet, and special-event rooms, and a 1,200-seat show room. The casino is one of the largest in the state of California.

Revenue from the tribe's gaming facilities is used to fund tribal services and programs, including road improvements, housing, water system, a wastewater system, public safety, and emergency services. As of June 2004, the tribe had voluntarily paid more than $8 million to the City of Temecula to offset the impact of its gaming facility. The payment helped to widen the Pechanga Parkway Bridge over Temecula Creek. The band also contributes funds to local communities.

Services and Retail. The Pechanga Gas Station offers gas services, a car wash, convenience store, an ATM, and a fresh-food center. The tribe also owns a Food Mart.

Tourism and Recreation. The tribe owns the Pechanga RV Resort located in the foothills of the Rainbow Gap in Temecula Valley. The park offers 168 full-service hookup sites and 25 pull-through sites. There are a clubhouse, barbeque facilities, a heated pool, and two spas. The clubhouse includes a recreation room and meeting rooms, each with a full-service kitchen, with a capacity for 160 people. The RV park is located adjacent to the resort and casino. Tribal lands house the former home of Erle Stanley Gardner, author of the famed Perry Mason novels. The reservation is also located near several tourist attractions. The nearby historic town of Temecula offers visitors golfing, shopping, and vineyards and wineries. The tribe hosts an annual powwow on the Fourth of July weekend. The event is free to the public and includes contest dancing and drumming.

INFRASTRUCTURE
The tribe has donated $4.4 million to the City of Temecula for the purpose of widening Pala Road. The road serves as the primary access to the tribe's casino.

Fuel. Propane is available to residents.

Water Supply. Eastern Municipal Water District provides sewer service.

Transportation. The reservation is located just off County Road S-16, south of the intersection with Highway 79.

Telecommunications. Telecom and Verizon provides telephone service.

COMMUNITY FACILITES AND SERVICES
The tribe maintains a cultural center on the reservation. The center provides after-school programs for tribal youth, recreational activities, the Pechanga Youth Center, and resource preservation programs. The center also features a nursery and displays of cultural artifacts. There is an outdoor Native village complex on the reservation.

Education. There is a tribal primary school located on the reservation. Tribal youth attend school at TVUSD. The tribe provides assistance to tribal members attending postsecondary programs.

Health Care. The Pechanga Health Care Center provides medical, mental health, chemical dependency, outreach, senior nutrition, and Meals on Wheels programs to tribal members.

Pechanga

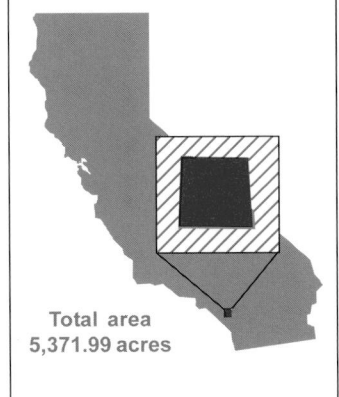

Total area
5,371.99 acres

Picayune

Picayune Rancheria
Federal reservation
Chukchansi
Madera County, California

Picayune Rancheria
46575 Road 417
Coarsegold, CA 93614
559-683-6633
559-683-0599 Fax
chukchansi.net

Total area *(BIA realty, 2003)*
28.76 acres

Total area *(Tribal source, 2004)*
160 acres

Federal trust lands
(Tribal source, 2004)
80 acres

Tribally owned lands
(Tribal source, 2004)
80 acres

Individually owned
(BIA realty, 2003)
28.76 acres

Population *(Tribal source, 2004)*
30

Tribal enrollment
(BIA labor report, 2001)
1,173

Total labor force *2000 census*
13

Total labor force
(BIA labor report, 2001)
936

High school graduate or
higher *2000 census*
100%

Bachelor's degree or higher
2000 census
38.5%

Unemployment rate *2000 census*
0%

Unemployment rate
(BIA labor report, 2001)
51%

Per capita income *2000 census*
$20,300

LOCATION AND LAND STATUS

The Picayune Rancheria, located 25 miles southwest of Yosemite National Park, was established by an Executive Order in 1912. Eighty acres of land were designated for the rancheria in Madera County, California. In 1958 the tribe was terminated from status as a federally recognized tribe, and its assets, including the 80-acre rancheria, were dissolved. When the tribe's status was restored in 1979, the lands were also restored. The tribe purchased an additional 80 acres between 1995 and 1996. Since 1996 the tribe has purchased more land, which is being used for low-density housing and cultural gatherings.

CULTURE AND HISTORY

Spanish explorers arrived in California in the late 1500s. During the time of Spanish, and later Mexican, dominance in the territory, lands were seized from the Native populations and held in trust for the Spanish crown. The indigenous people were displaced, enslaved, and often murdered. Americans arrived in California in the mid-1800s, and they initiated a war with Mexico for rights to the California regions. The Spanish Mexicans were defeated, and in 1848 the Treaty of Guadalupe ended the Mexican-American War.

Upon the discovery of gold in northern California, Euro-Americans began arriving in the state in droves. In 1850 the California territory became a state and passed the Act for the Government and Protection of Indians. This act mandated the regulation of Indian affairs to the state, permitted Euro-Americans the right to assume custody of Native children, prohibited the use of Native testimony against a Euro-American charged with a crime, and permitted unemployed Native peoples to be arrested and hired out, a form of state-sanctioned indentured servitude. The state further protected prospectors and settlers as they encroached upon tribal territories and seized water sources in the area.

Between 1851 and 1853, Indian commissioners negotiated 18 treaties between the government and multiple Native groups. The agreements were to reserve over 7.5 million acres for various tribes across the state, but the senate did not ratify these Barbour Treaties. The tribes were not informed of this decision until the twentieth century and proceeded to live in agreement with the mandates outlined by the treaties. They ceded millions of acres of land to the government and confined themselves to the reservations designated by the Barbour Treaties.

Local, state, and federal agencies condoned the effort to commit genocide against the Native people of California. Indigenous people were openly murdered, attacked, and enslaved. Atrocities committed against indigenous groups so outraged the Mexican government that officials crossed the U.S.-Mexico border to conduct investigations, and they threatened to bring arms against the citizens of California if the violence did not cease. The intervention on their behalf and their ability to isolate themselves in the mountainous regions of the state enabled some tribes to escape total decimation. However, from an estimated population of over 150,000 in 1845, the Native population was reduced to less than 50,000 by 1855. By 1900, less than 16,000 indigenous people remained.

The Picayune Rancheria was established by an Executive Order in 1912. Eighty acres were designated for the rancheria. In 1958 the tribe's status as a federally recognized tribe was terminated congruent to PL85-671. In 1979 the Picayune Rancheria joined 16 other California rancherias in a suit against the government in *Tillie Hardwick v. United States of America*. Federal status was restored to the rancherias and federal assistance and

services were permitted. In 1987 the Picayune Rancheria reached an agreement with Madera County restoring the rancheria's boundaries prior to termination.

GOVERNMENT

The Picayune Rancheria is governed by a tribal council. The seven members are elected annually by the general council which is comprised of all members of the tribe over the age of 18. Governmental departments and committees include the housing authority, natural resources, enrollment, the Indian Child Welfare Act, and the powwow committee.

The Chukchansi Indian Housing Authority is a tribal-designated housing entity. Its primary goals are to acquire suitable lands for housing developments for the tribe and to develop and improve upon the existing infrastructure. Program services include rental, relocation, rehabilitation, and utility assistance for tribal members.

ECONOMY

Revenue generated from the Chukchansi Gold Casino Resort supports the rancheria economy. It is the tribe's main source of income.

Government as Employer. The tribe employs over 30 individuals in its governmental departments and offices. The tribe operates the Chukchansi Gold Hotel Resort and Casino to assist tribal members in obtaining employment opportunities in the hotel and casino.

Gaming. The Chukchansi Gold Resort and Casino is owned by the Picayune Rancheria. It offers over 1,800 slot machines, 46 table games, and numerous other games. There are seven restaurants and one bakery located in the facilities as well as two entertainment venues. The adjacent hotel offers 192 guest rooms.

Real Estate/Commercial Development. A gas station and food mart are currently being built.

Media and Communications. The tribe produces the *Chukchansi Review* six times yearly. It is a newsletter distributed to tribal members that contains information specific to government activities, community events, and tribal services.

Tourism and Recreation. The tribe sponsors the annual Picayune Powwow during the first week of October. The annual powwow event is in its twelfth year.

INRASTRUCTURE

Highway 41 and Road 417 intersect on tribal lands. In 2000 the rancheria received $32,589 from the BIA Indian Reservation Fund. The tribe intended to use the funds to make improvements to the road system on the rancheria. The improvements are in progress.

Electricity. The tribe's electricity is furnished by Pacific Gas and Electric.

Transportation. The rancheria has bus service.

Telecommunications. Sierra Telephone provides telephone service to the rancheria.

COMMUNITY FACILITIES AND SERVICES

The tribe's Natural Resources Commission offers a cultural resource preservation program that processes repatriation claims, documents genealogies, secures funding for language retention programs and basket weaving grants, assists in the continuance of traditional basket weaving, and documents plant identification on tribal lands. The commission is also exploring the development of a tribal cultural center. The tribe operates a senior nutrition program under Title VI funds.

In 2004, the tribe donated new firefighting equipment to the California Department of Forestry. The equipment was designated for use by CDF Unit. No. 8 for fire prevention in northwestern Madera County and on the rancheria.

Education. Rancheria youth attend elementary school at Coarsegold Elementary and high school at Yosemite High School. The Child Care and Development Fund subsidizes childcare programs serving tribal children from infancy through age 12. The tribe is a recipient of a Title VII Formula Grant, which enables it to hire staff to provide tutoring services to tribal youth. The tribe participates in the Johnson O'Malley Grant; the Math,

Engineering, and Science Achievement program (MESA); and the Even Start Literacy Project. The tribe also operates an adult education program, a GED program, and a vocational training program. It provides scholarship assistance to tribal members seeking a postsecondary education.

Health Care. Health care services are available to the tribe through Central Valley Indian Health in Clovis.

ENVIRONMENTAL CONCERNS
The tribe actively works with community members, local residents, and government agencies to oversee the management and development of tribal lands. Its Natural Resource Commission serves as a liaison to the U.S. Forest Service and the CalTrans department to preserve and protect tribal resources, significant cultural sites, and plant and wildlife. The tribe's Environmental Protection Office was created in 1999 to address specific issues of environmental concern. Services include the water-testing program, environmental assessment, establishment of codes and ordinances, and dump site cleanup.

Picayune

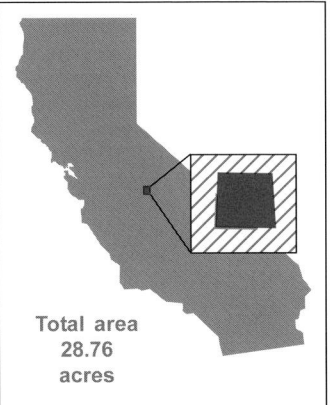

Total area
28.76
acres

Pinoleville

Pinoleville

Total area *(BIA realty, 2003)*		26.37 acres
Total area *(Tribal source)*		106.23 acres
Tribal owned lands		2.84 acres
(BIA realty, 2003)		
Individually owned		23.53 acres
(BIA realty, 2003)		
Population *2000 census*		136
Tribal enrollment *(BIA labor report, 2001)*		186
Total labor force *2000 census*		40
Total labor force *(BIA labor report, 2001)*		121
High school graduate or higher		79.7%
2000 census		
Bachelor's degree or higher		15.6%
2000 census		
Unemployment rate *2000 census*		17.5%
Unemployment rate		52%
(BIA labor report, 2001)		
Per capita income *2000 census*		$6,532

LOCATION AND LAND STATUS
The Pinoleville Rancheria is located in northern California. It consists of a parcel of 99.53 acres in Mendocino County, and a parcel of 6.7 acres in Lake County.

The rancheria was originally established at Pinoleville in 1911, but the tribe's federal recognition was terminated in 1966, and over 50 percent of tribal lands were lost. The rancheria regained federal recognition under the class action suit *Tillie Hardwick v. United States of America, C-79-1910SW.* Judgment was filed on December 22, 1983, and the tribe regained jurisdiction over the entire exterior boundaries of the reservation as they existed prior to termination. The larger parcel of tribal lands located in Mendocino County is located in the Russian River Valley. It is relatively flat and rural. It is an industrial zone although there are 12 residences on the parcel.

CULTURE AND HISTORY
The residents of the Pinoleville Rancheria belong to the Pomo Tribe and linguistic family. *(See California introduction for additional cultural information.)* The initial land purchase for the Pinoleville Rancheria (as well as many other reservations) came after the first of a series of congressional appropriation acts in 1906, which were designated for purchasing small parcels of

land for "homeless" California Indians. Given the small and isolated nature of most of these reservations, tribal members had few opportunities for earning money. These limitations were only compounded by the official segregation and prejudice against Indians that marked the provincial communities surrounding them. Many Pomo men and women labored in the region's hop fields or at wholesale woodcutting. Others worked in whatever service industry jobs they could find.

In 1958 the California termination bill passed, which allowed for the termination of numerous rancherias in exchange for land deeds and the promises of BIA-funded capital improvements. The failure of the federal government and the BIA to keep up their end of the bargain led to the historic *Tillie Hardwick v. United States of America* case for restoration argued before the U.S. Supreme Court. The case originated at the Pinoleville Rancheria (Hardwick was a tribal member), and ended in a judgment which restored federal recognition to 17 rancherias. Hence, the Pinoleville Rancheria figures prominently in the struggle for Indian rights and recognition.

GOVERNMENT
The tribe is organized under an IRA Constitution adopted on March 29, 1985. The rancheria is governed by the governing council, a seven-member body elected by the general voting membership to staggered two-year terms. Officers consist of a chairperson, a vice-chairperson, a secretary, and a treasurer. The council meets the first Sunday of each month, while the general membership meets semiannually on the second Sunday in January and July. The Pinoleville Band is a member of the Intertribal Court of California. This organization provides judicial services to member tribes. The court hears and settles matters of housing dispute and Indian child welfare cases and provides peacemaking/mediation services. The band also belongs to the Northern California Indian Development Council. This program provides assistance to the tribe for the organization of cultural events and activities.

ECONOMY
Government as Employer. In 1996 the tribal government employed five tribal members. Given the small rancheria population and workforce, this qualifies as a major employment source.

Pinoleville Rancheria
Federal reservation
Pomo
Mendocino County, Lake County, California

Pinoleville Rancheria
of Pomo Indians
367 North State Street
Suite 204
Ukiah, CA 95482
707-463-1454
707-463-6601 Fax
pinoleville.org

ENVIRONMENTAL CONCERNS
The Pinoleville tribal lands in Mendocino County have been zoned as an industrial area. This zoning allows for the operation of industrial plants and businesses that present a threat to water and soil quality on the reservation. In order to address these issues, the tribe is developing a general land-use plan and a comprehensive zoning ordinance.

Pinoleville

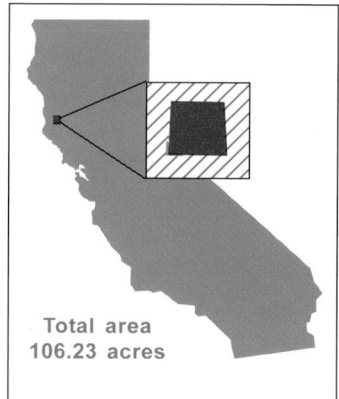

Total area
106.23 acres

Agriculture and Livestock. The region surrounding the rancheria remains a fertile agricultural zone; hence, agriculture and related industries might well provide future business and employment opportunities for the tribe.

Real Estate/Commercial Development. The tribe owns 6.7 acres of land on the western side of Clear Lake in Lake County, California. It has applied for placement of the land into trust status. The tribe plans to construct a housing development on the land. The tribe is in the process of developing a land-use plan and implementing ordinances on the tribal lands.

Services and Retail. Several small retail/service businesses exist on or near rancheria lands; three of these are Native-owned.

Tourism and Recreation. Given the rancheria's location in California's wine country, a well-heeled tourist contingent already patronizes the region. The tribe's challenge is to tap into this attractive pool of visitors. The tribe hosts an annual Big Time gathering. The celebration involves many tribes, dancing, and cultural festivities.

INFRASTRUCTURE
Tribal lands at the edge of the city of Ukiah in Mendocino County are a zoned industrial district located at the intersection of Orr Springs Road and U.S. 101. Highway 101 provides access to Ukiah, Santa Rosa, and San Francisco.

Electricity. Pacific Gas and Electric provides electricity to the rancheria.

Water Supply. Water service is provided by Millview County Water District in Ukiah.

Transportation. Commercial air, bus, and trucking service are available in Ukiah.

COMMUNITY FACILITIES AND SERVICES
The tribe maintains a social services department. It provides low-income home energy assistance, child care, general assistance, and Indian Child Welfare Act programs. The Pinoleville Tribal Library is funded by the Institute of Museum and Library Services and is housed in the tribe's social services department. The library offers a large collection of books and videos and Internet access. It houses the Resource and Reference Collection of the tribe's Cultural Preservation Project. The Resources and Reference Collection includes all tribal records, documents, and culturally significant media.

The Pinoleville Indian Reservation Vocational Rehabilitation Program provides job training, development, guidance, and counseling services to eligible tribal members.

Education. Ukiah Public Schools provide education facilities.

The Pinoleville Native American Head Start Program is available to tribal youths between the ages of three and five years old. In addition to the preschool program, Head Start offers programs in literacy development, first aid, home food budgets, parenting skills, health screening, and referral services. The KAWIA program offers tutoring, computer, and library programs to tribal youths. It is funded by the state through the Coyote Valley Reservation and is available through the Pinoleville Social Services Department.

Health Care. Health care is available through the Consolidated Tribal Health Project as well as the Ukiah Valley Medical Center.

PIT RIVER TRIBES

California Tribes

CULTURE AND HISTORY
The traditional territory of the Pit River people spanned throughout what are now called Lassen, Shasta, and Modoc counties of northern California. The Pit River Tribe is composed of 11 distinct bands whose contemporary tribal lands include the Alturas, Big Bend, Likely, Lookout, Montgomery Creek, Roaring Creek, and XL Ranch rancherias, as well as some allotted lands, and 79 acres in the northern California town of Burney These bands (Ajumawi, Aporidge, Astariwi, Atsuge, Atwamsini, Hammawi, Hewisedawi, Illmawi, Isatawi, Kosalektawi, and Madesi) traditionally spoke the Achumawi and Atsugewi languages, two closely related members of the Palaihnihan branch of the greater Hokan linguistic family, whose languages are, in turn, spoken by peoples from southern Oregon to southern Mexico.

The Pit River Tribe's post-contact history is characterized by a continued struggle for a permanent land base. While many of the Pit River people were forced to the Round Valley Reservation during the 19th century, others were able to resist this move and continued to live in marginalized groups along the fringes of their ancestral territory. It was not until the passage of the Dawes Act in 1887 that some members of the tribe were able to acquire land as individual allotments. Moreover, the tribe successfully garnered allotments that geographically resembled their traditional band divisions. The ability to live in more customary groupings reinforced band relationships and allowed the Pit River people to continue their usual subsistence practices.

The Pit River people, like many tribes "benefiting" from the allotment system, were unable to retain ownership of their allotted lands for a variety of reasons. Many allotments along the Pit River were acquired by representatives of the Pacific Gas and Electric Company between 1917 and 1930, prior to hydroelectric development, in ways the Pit River Tribe contends were questionable. By 1950 few of the former allotments remained.

A congressional act calling for the investigation of the status of California's "landless" Indians at the beginning of the 20th century led to the establishment of seven small rancherias in Pit River territory. None of these rancherias, including Big Bend, were suitable for intensive agriculture. The Atsugewi bands received no rancheria land.

Beginning in 1919, the Pit River Tribe attempted to gain compensation for land "ceded" to the U.S. government under unratified treaties. When a settlement was finally reached in 1959, many Pit River tribal members disagreed with the terms, which amounted to a compensation of $0.47 per acre of land unlawfully appropriated. After a BIA poll suggested that a majority of the tribe was willing to accept the terms, the Pit River Tribe was forced to agree to this settlement. Political activism instigated by younger members of the Pit River Tribe during the 1960s resulted in renewed cohesion among the different bands. Their activities focused on issues of tribal sovereignty, the free practice of Indian religion, and self-determination. *(See California introduction for additional cultural information.)*

GOVERNMENT

Recognized in 1976, the Pit River Tribe is governed by a tribal council which consists of an elected representative from each of the tribe's 11 bands. The executive department, composed of the tribe's officers, includes a chairperson, vice-chairperson, secretary, recording secretary, sergeant-at-arms, and treasurer. The tribe is organized under an IRA Constitution ratified on December 3, 1987. The constitution was amended for an Enrollment Ordinance in 1988, and a Land Assignment Ordinance in 1991. Tribal headquarters are located in the town of Burney.

ECONOMY

The Pit River Tribe's economy is largely dependent upon their enterprises in the gaming industry. The tourism and recreation industry also generates off-reservation revenue and employment opportunities for tribal members. There is currently no agricultural production on tribal lands but a number of tribal members find employment in the local agricultural and forestry industries. Strawberries are a major crop in Shasta County and are exported to southern Europe. Because of the vast timber resources found in Shasta County jobs created though lumber and wood products businesses employ a substantial number of area residents, including tribal members.

Economic Development. While the number of bands and the isolated location of the rancherias and trust lands pose many obstacles for the successful delivery of governmental services, the Pit River Tribal Council has been attempting, since its recognition in 1976, to develop a more permanent economic base on its tribal lands. In the mid-1990s, the Pit River Tribe was considering the development of an RV park along either Highway 299 or Highway 89. In 1995, the tribe was considering the feasibility of building a combination truck stop/restaurant/Indian gift shop. One possible site for this facility was at the "four corners" area (at the intersections of Highways 89 and 299). Ownership of this intersection is being investigated. The tribe was also considering the construction of a campground or negotiations with the National Forest Service to assume management of an existing site.

Government as Employer. Federal and state jobs serve as an important source of employment in both Modoc and Shasta counties, particularly in Redding.

Gaming. The tribe operates a number of gaming facilities. The Pit River Casino is located in Burney, California. It is an 8,600-square foot casino that offers patrons 108 slots and video lottery tables, 3 table games, and 70 bingo seats. The casino also has a restaurant. A second casino is located in Alturas. The tribe has also held a weekly bingo project since 1985. Profits from this endeavor have been invested in the construction of a permanent facility for the tribe's gaming operations, and to fund tribal enterprises.

Tourism and Recreation. Since the Shasta-Trinity National Forest covers much of Shasta County, tourism accounts for a substantial amount of the area's revenues. The region's plentiful hunting and fishing opportunities are an important tourist attraction, with deer hunting particularly rich in the southeastern portion of the county. The Sacramento River joins a network of rivers and streams to feed Shasta Lake in the Whiskeytown-Shasta-Trinity National Recreational Area, where many types of fish abound. Other popular sites include Lassen Volcanic National Park, Lava Beds National Monument, and Burney Falls State Park. Many visitors enjoy the county's Clear Lake National Wildlife Refuge and Cedar Pass (for winter sports).

COMMUNITY FACILITIES

The Pit River Tribe headquarters and health clinic are located in the town of Burney, California.

Health Care. The Pit River Health Service, Inc. provides medical services to its members residing within all tribal ancestral boundaries. The Burney Indian Health Clinic provides medical, dental, behavioral, outreach, environmental health, and WIC programs. Transportation is available to clients upon request. The XL Ranch Reservation Clinic is located in Alturas and provides referral and outreach services. For additional services, tribal members are referred to Mercy Medical Center Hospital in Redding.

Potter Valley

LOCATION AND LAND STATUS

The Potter Valley Rancheria is located in northern California, 18 miles northeast of the city of Ukiah. The tribal headquarters is located in Ukiah. The original rancheria was on Spring Valley Road, near the town of Potter Valley. The U.S. government purchased the land for the original rancheria under secretarial order on May 10,1909, with additional land being purchased under the authority of an Act on June 20, 1913 (38 Stat. 77, 86). The rancheria was originally for the "landless" California Indians, and at that time the land was vested to the U.S. in trust for the tribe. The tribe has purchased a four-acre parcel of land for housing in Redwood Valley. This land is also held in fee status.

The rancheria was formally terminated August 1, 1961, placing the land in fee simple status, and revoking the rancheria's federally recognized status. Throughout the termination era, individual Pomo people held 10 acres in fee status. In 1983, the U.S. District Court of Northern California ordered the full reinstatement of federal recognition for 17 Native American communities.

Of the original acreage that the tribe possessed in 1913, no lands remained in trust status for their benefit. The individual allotments retained by tribal members now comprise the current land base for the tribe; they are located southwest of the town of Potter Valley in Mendocino County.

CULTURE AND HISTORY

The Potter Valley Rancheria is the home of the Little Lake Pomo Band *(see California introduction).* Archaeological evidence suggests that Potter Valley has been inhabited for at least 5,000 years. In 1908 an ethnographic survey described 12 inhabited Pomo villages in Potter Valley, but by the middle of the twentieth century, only three villages remained. Since 1812, when the Russians established Fort Ross nearby, the lives of the indigenous people of Potter Valley have been continually disrupted by successive waves of immigrants. The gold rush in 1848, along with an increase in ranching shortly thereafter, brought a flood of non-Indians into the area, displacing Potter Valley's origi-

Potter Valley Rancheria
Federal reservation
Pomo
Mendocino County, California

Potter Valley Rancheria
112 N. School Street
Ukiah, CA 95482
  707-462-1213
  707-462-1240 Fax

Potter Valley

Total area (BIA realty, 2003)
0

Population
138

Tribal enrollment
(BIA labor report, 2001)
156

Total labor force
(BIA labor report, 2001)
117

High school graduate or higher
44%

Unemployment rate
(BIA labor report, 2001)
66%

nal inhabitants. In 1849 the U.S. Army moved the Potter Valley Indians to Covelo and the Round Valley Reservation; however, in 1856 most escaped confinement and returned to their homelands. In 1909 two rancherias were established for the Potter Valley Indians: a 16-acre parcel about a mile south of the original Pomo village and an 80-acre reservation in northeastern Potter Valley. The 80-acre site was sold at the time of termination and remains in private hands.

The most damaging result of the termination process was the alienation of the tribe's land base. After termination, much of the land obtained under the Plan for Distribution of Assets was either sold to meet subsistence needs, lost as collateral for loan encumbrances that could not be met, or lost for nonpayment of property taxes. During the termination period, many rancheria community members were forced to leave their homelands and migrated outward to surrounding towns in search of employment. Since its restoration in 1983, the tribe has adopted a constitution, developed a tribal government, and created basic services for tribal members. Today, the tribe's goals are acquiring land and providing additional housing for tribal members.

GOVERNMENT
The Potter Valley Rancheria is governed by a three-member tribal council compromised of a chairperson, a secretary, and a treasurer. They serve four-year staggered terms. The tribe's general council includes all tribal members 18 years or older. The tribe is organized under an IRA Constitution.

ECONOMY
The Potter Valley Rancheria, while occupying a modest amount of land, does have significant potential for economic development. The richness of Mendocino County can support a variety of industries, including commercial fishing, agriculture, and tourism. Although the rancheria does not operate any business, tribal members have formed companies outside the rancheria in retail and wholesale trade, the timber industry, commercial fishing, and construction. The lack of a large tribal land base is the primary constraint in developing the rancheria's economy.

INFRASTRUCTURE
Potter Valley Rancheria is located just south of the town, three and one half miles off State Highway 20. The rancheria is connected to the highway by three paved residential collector roads.

Electricity. The tribe's electricity is furnished by Pacific Gas and Electric.

Water Supply. Three wells and a pump house on the eastern portion of the rancheria provide water for residents. Individual septic tanks are the primary means of sewage disposal.

COMMUNITY FACILITIES AND SERVICES
Rancheria business is conducted at the tribal office.

Health Care. The tribe is a member of the Consolidated Tribal Health Program, which conducts an outreach program in nearby Ukiah. This program provides health services to Potter Valley Rancheria and other nearby rancherias.

Quartz Valley

Quartz Valley Indian Community
Federal reservation
Shasta, Upper Klamath, Karuk and Siskiyou County, California

Quartz Valley Indian
Community
13601 Quartz Valley Rd.
Fort Jones, CA 96032
530-468-5907
530-468-5908 Fax

Total area (BIA realty, 2003)	127.14 acres
Total area (Tribal source, 2004)	694 acres
Federal trust lands (Tribal source, 2004)	143.37 acres
Tribally owned lands (Tribal source, 2004)	143.37 acres
Allotted lands (Tribal source, 2004)	4.8 acres
Tribally owned (BIA realty, 2003)	103.12 acres
Individually owned (BIA realty, 2003)	24.02 acres
Population (Tribal source, 2004)	92
Tribal enrollment (Tribal source, 2004)	190
Total labor force 2000 census	45
Total labor force (BIA labor report, 2001)	121
High school graduate or higher 2000 census	86.8%
Bachelor's degree or higher 2000 census	3.9%
Unemployment rate 2000 census	22.2%
Unemployment rate (BIA labor report, 2001)	76%
Per capita income 2000 census	$12,241

LOCATION AND LAND STATUS
The original Quartz Valley Reservation was located in northwestern California, 8 miles from Greenview, 10 miles from Fort Jones, 16 miles from Etna, and 30 miles from the county seat of Yreka. The Scott River was 3 miles away. The two nearest urban areas with populations over 25,000 are Medford, Oregon (68 miles north), and Redding, California (110 miles to the south).

The original Quartz Valley Indian Reservation purchased by the United States in 1940 for certain Shasta, Karuk, and Upper Klamath Indians, consisted of 604 acres near Fort Jones in Siskiyou County. The reservation was terminated in 1967, under the California Rancheria Act of 1958. The tribe was reinstated on December 15, 1983, because of the class-action suit *Tillie Hardwick v. United States of America*, but it is still in the process of reacquiring land for the reservation. The original boundaries of the reservation were fully restored as Indian Country by court order, dated March 14, 1989. The tribe has added an additional 90 acres to its reservation, and the United States currently owns 143.37 acres in trust. Currently many tribal members live in or near the communities of Greenview, Fort Jones, and Etna.

CULTURE AND HISTORY
The people of Quartz Valley come from the Klamath River region of northern California and southern Oregon, some 30 miles from the location of the old reservation. Klamath belongs to the Penutian language family, other languages of which are spoken by peoples from coastal Canada to the Yucatan Peninsula, as well as in the southeastern United States. Shasta is a Hokan language, related to languages spoken by peoples from southern Oregon to southern Mexico. *(See California introduction for additional cultural information.)*

GOVERNMENT
Prior to termination, the tribe was governed under the provisions of a tribal constitution adopted on June 15, 1939. The constitution allowed the Quartz Valley Tribe to be governed by a general community council which consisted of all eligible adult tribal members. The business council, which oversees the day to day business of the tribe, is led by a chairman, a vice-chairman, and a secretary-treasurer, and five other representatives: council members one and two, and three additional at-large members, all elected from the general council membership.

ECONOMY
The tribe has a number of plans for economic development, but these depend on the acquisition of a suitable land base. The Quartz Valley Indian Reservation is funded through the BIA, Environmental Protection Agency, Indian Health Services, non-gaming distributions, the U.S. Department of Health and Human Services, and the U.S. Department of Housing and Urban Development.

Government as Employer. The tribe employs approximately 25 people: 10 full-time staff and 15 part-time seasonal staff.

INFRASTRUCTURE
Interstate 5, State Highway 3, Scott River Road, and Quartz Valley Road are the closest roads and highways.

Electricity. Provided by Pacific Power and Light Company.

Fuel. Wood-burning stoves heat most homes.

Water Supply. Water wells and septic tanks are used.

Transportation. Fort Jones Municipal Airport is 12 miles from the old reservation. The airport in Medford, Oregon, offers commercial flights. Local bus service is available in many nearby towns, as are freight services. Siskiyou County public transportation, The Stage, is expected to service Quartz Valley after 2005.

COMMUNITY FACILITIES AND SERVICES
The tribe has a family resource center with plans for a gymnasium and community center expansion. Cultural and language classes take place weekly. The city of Fort Jones has a community center and a family resource center.

Education. Tribal youth attend Fort Jones Preschool, Quartz Valley Elementary School, Etna High School, Etna Elementary School, and Scott Valley Junior High.

Health Care. A health clinic will be completed in 2005 and will bring expanded services. Until then, health services are provided for tribal members in an Indian Health Service facility shared with the Karuk Tribe in Yreka.

ENVIRONMENTAL CONCERNS
Environmental concerns facing the tribe are lack of water, fire danger, air quality, and emergency response capabilities.

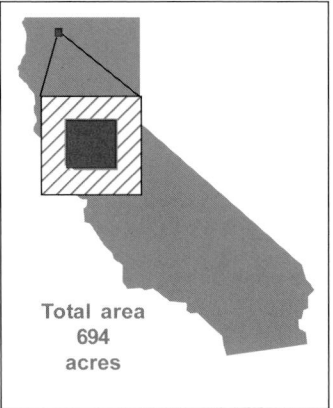

Total area
694
acres

Ramona

Total area *(BIA realty, 2003)*	560 acres
Tribally owned lands	560 acres
(BIA realty, 2003)	
Tribal enrollment *(BIA labor report, 2001)*	7
Total labor force **2000 census**	0
Total labor force *(BIA labor report, 2001)*	3
Unemployment rate	33%
(BIA labor report, 2001)	

LOCATION AND LAND STATUS
The Ramona Reservation is located in southern California.

CULTURE AND HISTORY
Members of the Ramona Band belong to the Cahuilla Tribe. Traditional homelands of the Cahuilla group encompassed territory ranging from the deserts to the mountainous regions of southern California.

ECONOMY
The Ramona Band is working on developing its economy.

Government as Employer. The tribe employs three individuals.

Economic Development Projects. The Ramona Band's economic development strategy is to establish a renewable energy-powered ecotourism industry on the reservation. In addition to creating a highly profitable industry, the tribe aims to demonstrate that renewable energy power systems can be used to eliminate the environmental impact of electric-grid power lines on Native American lands, National Forests, National Parks, protected areas, and rural environments. Wind and solar energy will provide the majority of the reservation's power, and propane will be used as a backup source. Research and fundraising for the project began in 2001. The tribe received a grant from the Department of Energy to pursue the project and is working in cooperation with HUD and the USDA. Projected facilities include a restaurant, a training center, a conference enter, eco-tents, a snack pavilion, and business offices.

Media and Communications. The Ramona Band maintains a website and is developing a newspaper.

Tourism and Recreation. The tribe is in the process of developing campgrounds on tribal lands.

INFRASTRUCURE
Water Supply. Individual wells and septic tanks serve residencies.

COMMUNITY FACILITIES AND SERVICES
Education. The tribe offers some educational grants for postsecondary education.

Health Care. Indian Health Council provides tribal members with health care services. Services include general medicine, general dental, human services, and community outreach programs. Clinics are located in Valley Center and Santa Ysabel.

ENVIRONMENTAL CONCERNS
The tribe is working toward restoring wetlands on tribal lands. It is also concerned with the effect of the Japanese beetle on tribal forests.

TRI-CA-Ra-017

**Ramona Reservation
Federal reservation
Cahuilla
Riverside County, California**

Ramona Band of Cahuilla
Indians
P.O. Box 391670
Anza, CA 92539
951-763-4105
951-763-4325 Fax
ramonatribe.com

TRI-CA-Ra-017 Sign for Anza Valley Center, Highway 371 and Ramona Tribal Office

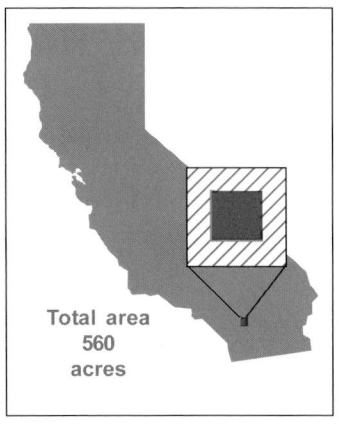

Total area
560
acres

Redding Rancheria
Federal reservation
Wintun, Pit River, and Yana
Shasta County, California

Redding Rancheria
2000 Rancheria Road
Redding, CA 96001-5528
539-225-8979
800-479-8979
530-241-1879 Fax
redding-rancheria.com

Total area *(BIA realty, 2003)*
13.40 acres

Tribally owned *(BIA realty, 2003)*
3.33 acres

Individually owned
(BIA realty, 2003)
10.07 acres

Population *2000 census*
72

Tribal enrollment
(BIA labor report, 2001)
281

Total labor force *2000 census*
8

Total labor force
(BIA labor report, 2001)
2,105

High school graduate or higher
2000 census
60.6%

Bachelor's degree or higher
2000 census
0%

Unemployment rate *2000 census*
0%

Unemployment rate
(BIA labor report, 2001)
17%

Per capita income *2000 census*
$6,925

LOCATION AND LAND STATUS

Redding Rancheria is located adjacent to the city of Redding, in north-central California. The rancheria was established in 1923, but when the tribe was terminated by the federal government in 1959, all tribal assets were dissolved. Federal recognition was restored on December 15, 1985, as a result of class action suit *Tillie Hardwick v. United States of America, C-79-I91OSW*, and tribal lands were returned.

PHYSICAL DESCRIPTION

The rancheria is located in north-central California. It is surrounded by waterways on three sides. Clear Creek runs through the rancheria.

CULTURE AND HISTORY

Members of the Redding Rancheria belong to the Pit River, Wintun, and Yana tribes. The rancheria was originally established for the groups in 1923. The Bureau of Indian Affairs (BIA) constructed a few very small homes on the rancheria, though many of them were constructed so poorly that they burned down. The BIA developed a water system, but tribal members were required to operate it. Although the BIA was obligated to complete road improvements on the rancheria, they were not completed until 1996.

The tribe was terminated in 1959 under the California Rancheria Act, and its lands were divided into individual parcels. Many members continued to reside on their allotted portions of the lands and, although no longer federally recognized, continued to maintain their tribal affiliation and cultural traditions. During the period of termination, tribal members saw their lands sold and water rights violated.

In 1983, *Tillie Hardwick v. United States of America* found that the BIA had failed to comply with provisions of the California Rancheria Act, thereby rendering the act invalid. Eighteen California tribes were restored to federal recognition status, including the Redding Rancheria. The rancheria's recognition was formally restored in 1985, and tribal lands were returned. At that time, there were 17 original distributees and their lineal heirs who comprised the Redding Rancheria population. Tribal enrollment now exceeds 200, and the tribe is well on its way to reaffirming itself as a self-sufficient entity.

GOVERNMENT

Redding Rancheria is governed by a seven-member tribal council. Council officers include a chairperson, a vice-chairperson, a secretary, a treasurer, and three members. Officers are elected for two-year staggered terms. The tribe is organized under a non-IRA constitution, which was approved in 1986. The constitution was later amended in 1989 for a gaming ordinance. The tribe has recently received a tribal court grant to develop its own court system.

BUSINESS CORPORATION

The tribe established the Redding Rancheria Economic Development Corporation (RREDC) in 1995. The corporation oversees the development and operation of tribal enterprises. In 1999 the tribe established the Redding Rancheria Gaming Commission which oversees the operation of the tribe's gaming facility. The commission has been recognized as a model for other tribes.

ECONOMY

Since restoration of its federal stature in 1985, the tribe has made great strides toward gaining financial independence and economic stability. It operates a casino, hotel, and a mini-mart, and has recently purchased a moving company. These ventures provide a great source of income to the tribe and contribute to the local economy as well. The tribe also contributes funds to local charities and, since its restoration, has contributed over $4-million dollars to surrounding communities.

Government as Employer. The tribal government employs many tribal members in administrative and service positions.

Gaming. The tribe owns the Win-River Casino. The casino offers 751 slots/VLTS, 18 table games, 300 bingo seats, one restaurant, and three entertainment venues. The casino, which employs 419 individuals, represents one of the rancheria's most lucrative tribal enterprises. The recently completed Hilton Garden Inn is adjacent to the casino and offers 100 guest rooms.

Services and Retail. The tribe has recently purchased a moving company that is operated out of Sacramento, California. The tribe owns and operates the Win-River Mini-Mart on the rancheria. It has also recently completed the Hilton Garden Inn located at the Win-River Casino.

INFRASTRUCTURE

Direct access in and out of the rancheria is achieved via one small road. The rancheria is located off Highway 273, running north-south, which branches off Interstate 5. Interstate 5 runs north-south two miles from the rancheria and serves as the primary interior artery in California.

Electricity. Pacific Gas and Electric provides for the rancheria's electric and gas needs.

Water Supply. Local wells provide water for rancheria members, and septic tanks handle sewage disposal.

Transportation. Air, bus, shipping, and trucking services are available in nearby Redding. Redding Municipal Airport offers commercial aviation and is located five miles from the rancheria. A railway line runs along the reservation.

COMMUNITY FACILITIES AND SERVICES

The rancheria houses a community center. It is planning to expand the facilities in the near future. The tribe offers a Native American Child Care Program at the tribe's Children's Center.

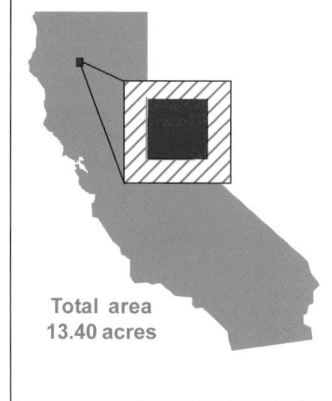

Total area
13.40 acres

This program offers financial assistance to tribal members seeking childcare services, and provides child care services for preschool age through fifth grade children. Transportation services are provided. The tribe also sponsors Camp Thunder, a summer day camp program for children.

Education. The Head Start program located on the rancheria is a nationally recognized program.

Health Care. The Redding Rancheria Indian Health Clinic offers comprehensive medical, dental, and community outreach programs to members. Services include well-care for all ages,

women's family planning, outpatient surgery, podiatry, acupuncture, laboratory, oral surgery, periodontics, operative dentistry, homebound services, mental health, nutrition, substance abuse, pharmacy, and health assessment programs. The clinic uses Contract Health Service funds for referrals and special services. A community health representative and a public health nutritionist are available to provide preventive services. The clinic employs 150 members. The tribe also offers the Redding Rancheria Tribal Health Program. The program is affiliated with the Wintun tribe. Ambulatory care, are available through the Redding Rancheria Indian Health Clinic and a satellite clinic in Weaverville. Hospitals in Redding and Weaverville also provide health care.

Redwood Valley

Redwood Valley

LOCATION AND LAND STATUS
The Redwood Valley Rancheria is located northeast of the town of Redwood Valley in Mendocino County, California, along the northeastern side of the Russian River Valley. The rancheria was established by Acts in 1906 and 1908, and the United States government purchased the land on July 19, 1909. However, the rancheria was terminated on August 1, 1961, along with 43 other California rancherias, according to the California Rancheria Act of 1958. The tribe was restored to federal recognition under provisions of *Tillie Hardwick v. United States of America* in 1983. Since then, the Redwood Valley Rancheria has rebuilt its land base through the addition of about 177 acres accepted into trust by the United States government in 1985.

CLIMATE
The Redwood Valley Rancheria is located in a transitional zone between coastal and interior climates. This climate zone consists of mild year-round temperatures with moist cool winters and warm dry summers. The annual rainfall in the area averages 35 inches.

CULTURE AND HISTORY
Members of the Redwood Valley Rancheria belong to the Northern Pomo Band. The Redwood Valley Pomos have traditionally lived in the Little River area northeast of the Clear Lake region. The arrival of European settlers in the nineteenth century completely disrupted the Pomo people's traditional lifestyle. *(For additional cultural information, see California introduction.)*

During the early 1900s, public outcry over the condition of California's "landless Indians" led Congress to authorize an investigation of their living conditions. C.E. Kelsey, an attorney from San Jose and an officer of the Northern California Indian Association, was the special agent appointed to investigate and develop a plan to improve their lives. Kelsey recommended that Congress purchase small parcels of land for these indigenous groups, with four criteria for the land: that there be sites for houses, that the land be irrigable, and that a proper supply of water and wood be available. A series of appropriation acts for land purchases were passed starting in 1906. Between 1906 and 1913, Kelsey himself purchased land in northern and central California pursuant to the acts, including the land for the Redwood Valley Rancheria. The rancheria was one of the many California Native land bases impacted by the California Rancheria Act of 1958. Termination of the Redwood Valley Rancheria caused many tribal members to migrate to surrounding towns and cities in search of employment, leaving behind only a few scattered Na-

tive American families on the rancheria. Since the rancheria's restoration in 1983, the tribe has formed a tribal government, acquired a land base, and initiated an overall economic development program.

GOVERNMENT
On June 20, 1987, the Little River Band of Pomo Indians adopted a constitution and bylaws pursuant to the Indian Reorganization Act of 1934. The Redwood Valley Rancheria is governed by a general council, consisting of all adult enrolled members, which elects a seven-member tribal council. The council includes a chairperson, a vice-chairperson, a secretary, and a treasurer. Elected members serve for two-year terms. The general council and the tribal council are supported by an administrative staff organization consisting of a tribal administrator, an ANA coordinator, a bookkeeper, and a secretary, in addition to several temporary and part-time employees.

The tribe is a member of the Intertribal Court of California. This entity hears housing disputes and Indian child welfare cases and provides mediation and peacemaking services for member tribes. There are presently nine member tribes.

ECONOMY
The rancheria's natural resources suggest that the greatest potential for economic development lies in the agriculture and tourism sectors. Its location along U.S. Highway 101 would provide the necessary access to the rancheria for future visitors. The tribe is emphasizing continued infrastructure development and is investigating the feasibility of acquiring more land for commercial uses.

Many rancheria residents commute to Ukiah for employment, and they participate in the area's mostly seasonal employment. The vast majority of total employment opportunities in Mendocino County are directly dependent on agriculture, forestry, fishing, and the lumber, wood processing, and food processing sectors of the manufacturing industry.

Agriculture and Livestock. Like much of the region, the rancheria's soils are particularly rich and fertile. Numerous vineyards throughout this area produce many varieties of grapes for the growing number of wineries throughout Napa, Sonoma, and Mendocino counties. The rancheria has 160 acres of undeveloped land.

Redwood Valley Rancheria
Federal reservation
Northern Pomo
Mendocino County, California

Redwood Valley Little River
 Band of Pomo Indians
3250 Road I
Redwood Valley, CA 95470
707-485-0361
707-485-5726 Fax

Total area (BIA realty, 2003)
176.52 acres

Tribally owned (BIA realty, 2003)
159.61 acres

Individually owned
(BIA realty, 2003)
16.91 acres

Population *2000 census*
263

Tribal enrollment (BIA, 2001)
156

Total labor force *2000 census*
132

Total labor force
(BIA labor report, 2001)
62

High school degree or higher
2000 census
78.3%

Bachelor's degree or higher
2000 census
6.7%

Redwood Valley

Unemployment rate *2000 census*
18.94%

Unemployment rate
(BIA labor report, 2001)
31%

Per capita income *2000 census*
$10,404

INFRASTRUCTURE

Redwood Valley Rancheria is located approximately 10 miles from the major north-south transportation route of U.S. Highway 101, and it is 20 miles north of the commercial center of the region, Ukiah. A major east-west transportation route, Highway 20, is located less than 10 miles to the south.

Water Supply. A community water system supplies the residents. Septic tanks serve as the primary means of sewage disposal.

Transportation. The nearest airport and railway facilities are located in Ukiah.

COMMUNITY FACILITIES AND SERVICES

The tribal offices are located at the main entrance to the rancheria, and they serve as the central location for the tribe's governmental, educational, cultural, social, and recreational activities. Facilities include a community center and an education building that houses the tribal Head Start program. New residential housing consisting of about 15 homes has been built since 2000.

Education. Children attend Mendocino County school.

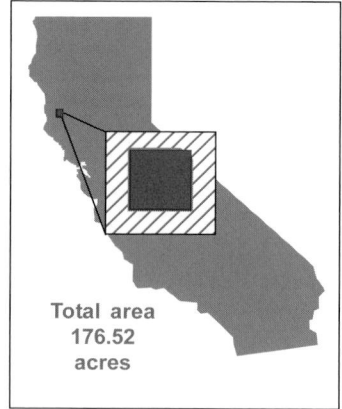

Total area
176.52
acres

Health Care. Tribal members may receive medical services from Consolidated Tribal Health. A clinic is located in Redwood Valley and provides general medical and dental services.

Resighini

Resighini Rancheria
Federal reservation
Yurok
Del Norte County, California

Coast Indian Community
P.O. Box 529
Klamath, CA 95548
707-482-2431
707-482-3425 Fax

Total area *(BIA realty, 2003)*
228.13 acres

Total area *(Tribal source, 2005)*
297 acres

Population *2000 census*
51

Population *(Tribal source, 2005)*
20

Tribal enrollment
(BIA labor report, 2001)
90

Tribal enrollment
(Tribal source, 2004)
101

Total labor force *2000 census*
20

Total labor force
(BIA labor report, 2001)
37

LOCATION AND LAND STATUS

The Resighini Rancheria spans 297 acres along the south shore of the mouth of the Klamath River, near Highway 101. The nearest city is Crescent City, 24 miles north. The land was purchased on January 7, 1938, by the secretary of the interior under the Wheeler Howard Act of 1934. It was deeded in trust to the Indians of Del Norte and Humboldt counties in 1938.

CULTURE AND HISTORY

Residents of the Resighini Rancheria are affiliated with the Yurok Tribe, who are Algonquin speakers. Historically, the Yuroks lived on the Lower Klamath River and the Pacific coast near its mouth. This area's ample reserves allowed the Yurok people to subsist primarily on fishing, hunting, and acorn gathering. *(For additional cultural information, see California introduction.)*

Since contact with Euro-American settlers, the Yuroks have been embroiled in conflict over their land. When territory set aside by President Pierce in 1855 for a Yurok Reservation came under debate, the matter was settled in 1891 by connecting their land, a 20-mile strip along the Lower Klamath River, with the fully authorized Hoopa Valley Reservation to the north. The extension was occupied primarily by the Yuroks, and it is now officially the Yurok Reservation. Three communal allotments were granted primarily to Yurok residents on the coast, one of which is the Resighini Rancheria.

The Yuroks have had to utilize the courts to prevent the desecration of their sacred territory. When a high-standard logging road was planned by the U.S. Forest Service to cross a Yurok cemetery, the Yuroks argued that this action was a violation of their freedom of religion. The federal government agreed to set aside that portion of the road as a wilderness area but refused to set a legal precedent for Native American religious rights.

In addition, the Yurok people have turned to the courts to protect their fishing rights and therefore to preserve their traditional way of life. Throughout the 1970s, the Yuroks fought a long battle over Native fishing rights, a dispute which was settled less than optimally in 1979. This settlement granted the Yuroks a mandated salmon harvest allocation.

The Resighini Rancheria was one of the tribal land bases impacted by the California Rancheria Act and was thus involved in termination proceedings throughout the 1970s. These proceedings were reversed by the class action suit *Tillie Hardwick v. United States of America, 1983.* Currently, the tribe is in the process of acquiring additional land along Resighini's borders.

GOVERNMENT

The tribe is organized under an IRA constitution, which was approved in 1975. A five-member business council serves as the governing body for the rancheria and includes a tribal manager, a secretary, an accountant, and a researcher. The officers' two-year terms are staggered, with elections held annually. Business council meetings are held quarterly. Governmental departments include administration, environment, housing, transportation, and social services. The tribe also has an ANA office on the reservation.

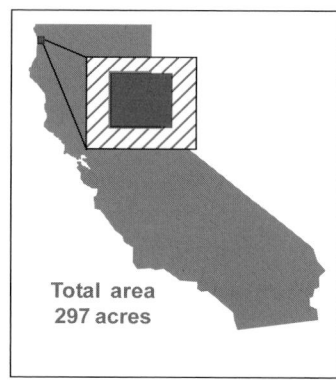

Total area
297 acres

TRI-CA-046 Resighini Tribal Office

ECONOMY

Up to this period, the tribe has been allocating their resources to develop the rancheria's infrastructure and improve residents' living conditions.

Economic Development Projects. The tribe owns RR Tobacco's Smoke Shop. In 1995 the tribe began exploring the feasibility of opening a mini-mart and gas station facility on rancheria property. In addition, the tribe planned to convert a tribally owned warehouse building into a boat dock and tackle shop.

Agriculture and Livestock. The tribe has experienced past successes with agricultural projects. In 1995 the tribe was planning to redevelop their berry production and potatoes enterprise.

Mining. In 1995 the tribe was working with the Army Corps of Engineers to acquire an Environmental Impact Statement permit. After gaining the permit, the tribe intends to begin gravel extraction on the rancheria.

Tourism and Recreation. Located near Northern California's Redwood National Park, the Pacific Ocean, and the Klamath River, the rancheria is ideally situated for recreational activities. Currently, the tribe runs the Chere Campground and RV Park. Fishing is allowed on the rancheria. This recreational facility is open from May to October. In addition, motels are located in nearby Klamath and Crescent City.

INFRASTRUCTURE

Electricity. Electricity is provided by Pacific Power and Light.

Transportation. Bus and train services are available in Crescent City.

COMMUNITY FACILITIES AND SERVICES

The tribal administration maintains a library. Tribal youths participate in the Yurok Boys and Girls Club. The tribe has a social services department providing assistance with the Indian Child Welfare Act, case management, assessment, and referrals. The department also issues tribal identification cards for members. The Intertribal Council of California "Taking Responsibility" program provides community education workshops, emergency services, and technical assistance in domestic violence prevention.

Education. Tribal youth attend the Del Norte County Unified School District. The tribe contracts the Johnson O'Malley programs through the schools.

Health Care. United Indian Health Services provides tribal members with health services. There are clinics in Crescent City and Klamath. The Crescent City clinic offers child and family welfare services and a community health and wellness program. The Klamath clinic also offers medical services.

Resighini

High school graduate or higher
2000 census
55.6%

Bachelor's degree *2000 census*
0%

Unemployment rate *2000 census*
20%

Unemployment rate
(BIA labor report, 2001)
57%

Per capita income *2000 census*
$6,925

Rincon

Rincon

LOCATION AND LAND STATUS

The Rincon Indian Reservation is in the northeastern corner of San Diego County, California, along the San Luis Rey River. The Rincon Reservation was established by an Executive Order on December 27, 1875. A second Executive Order on March 2, 1881, increased the land area of the reservation. The reservation was officially established on September 13, 1892, under the authority of the Act of 1891. Tribal headquarters are located in Valley Center, adjacent to Harrah's Rincon Casino.

CLIMATE

The Rincon Reservation has a moderate climate, with warm summers and mild winters. Average temperatures range from 22°F to 109°F. Annual rainfall averages approximately 12 inches. Precipitation occurs mostly from late fall to early spring.

CULTURE AND HISTORY

Members of the Rincon Band belong to the Luiseño Tribe. Since the founding of the Rincon Reservation more than a century ago, residents have utilized their fertile soil for agriculture and livestock. By 1910 the average annual income of the reservation matched or exceeded that of local non-Native farmers.

In 1924 a dam built upstream near La Jolla drastically reduced the amount of water available to the Rincon Reservation. The groundwater level dropped, and farming ceased. In 1951 a claim for reservation water was added to the Mission Indian Land Claim case. After a 1973 hearing, the Federal Power Commission required Escondido to regularly release six miner's inches from the dam for downstream reservations. The reserva-

tions involved in the lawsuit formed the San Luis Rey Indian Water Authority to manage water, approve developments, and distribute benefits from the settlement. As a provision of the Act for the Relief of Mission Indians, which established Rincon in 1891, the Bureau of Indian Affairs began allotting water to the Luiseño reservations. Members of the Rincon and La Jolla reservations protested this action, and the Mission Indian Federation sued to stop allotment and lost. The tribe is currently working toward buying the reservation lands that are no longer in trust.

GOVERNMENT

The tribe is organized under Articles of Association that were approved on March 15, 1960, by the secretary of the interior. A general council and a tribal business committee oversee the governing of the Rincon Reservation. The five-member elected business committee includes a chairperson, vice-chairperson, and three committee members. Council members serve two-year terms. Tribal government programs include an education committee and Indian Child Welfare Act Committee.

ECONOMY

The primary focus of the Rincon Reservation's economy is the gaming industry. The gaming facilities that the tribe co-owns contribute a great deal to the tribal economy, and the tribe intends to continue to develop other enterprises from gaming revenues.

Economic Development Projects. The tribe has turned its focus to the development of its gaming facilities in order to enhance the tribal economy. Expansions are being added to the existing ca-

Rincon Reservation
Federal reservation
Luiseño
San Diego County, California

Rincon Band of Luiseño Indians
P.O. Box 68
Valley Center, CA 92082
760-749-1051
760-749-8901 Fax

Total area *(BIA realty, 2003)*
4,269.52 acres

Tribally owned *(BIA realty, 2003)*
3,932.04 acres

Individually owned
(BIA realty, 2003)
337.48 acres

Population *2000 census*
1,495

Rincon

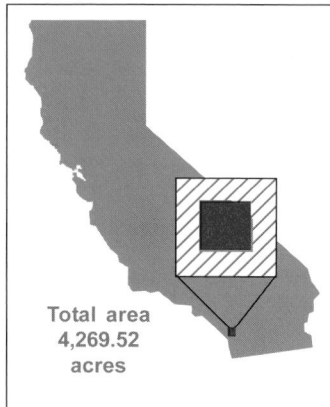

Total area
4,269.52
acres

TRI-CA-019-R Harrah's, Rincon Casino and Resort

TRI-CA-020-R Harrah's in Valley Center, 22 story hotel and Spa under construction

Tribal enrollment
(BIA labor report, 2001)
639

Total labor force *2000 census*
569

Total labor force
(BIA labor report, 2001)
436

High school diploma or higher
2000 census
56.6%

Bachelor's degree or higher
2000 census
4.8%

Unemployment rate *2000 census*
8.8%

Unemployment rate
(BIA labor report, 2001)
51%

Per capita income *2000 census*
$11,960

TRI-CA-019-R

TRI-CA-020-R

sino, and the tribe's overall goal for the project is to develop the complex into a destination resort.

Agriculture and Livestock. The area around the Rincon Reservation is considered one of the finest avocado and citrus climates in Southern California. The tribe owns a small citrus grove that employs 10 residents. A total of 150 acres of land are farmed, with orange orchards, small farms, and prickly pear cactus cultivation. The tribe's citrus and avocado groves are leased to private operators. The tribe also has 50 head of cattle.

Gaming. In partnership with Harrah's Entertainment, the tribe owns Harrah's Rincon Casino and Resort in Valley Center. The casino has 1,600 slots/VLTs, 42 table games, 200 hotel rooms, 6 restaurants, an entertainment venue, conference rooms, and a gift shop. The casino is undergoing renovations at this time. Expansions include a 22-story hotel and spa. Each tribal member receives approximately $1,500 per month from casino income.

Construction. The reservation has a public works crew that is employed locally.

Services and Retail. Several tribally owned and nontribal businesses are located on the reservation, including two gas stations and a trading post.

Media and Communications. The tribe produces a monthly newspaper, *Rincon Report*.

Tourism and Recreation. The Rincon San Luiseño Band of Mission Indians Museum is on the reservation. The museum features pottery, sculpture, and photographs of traditional clothing, baskets, and ceremonies. The museum's library emphasizes Native American news and culture. The museum hosts an artist in residency and offers culture classes.

INFRASTRUCTURE
The reservation is accessible via Highway 15 and Highway 76.

Electricity. San Diego Gas and Electric Company provides electricity.

Fuel. Natural gas is not available on the reservation; however, a tribally owned service station on the reservation provides LP gas.

Water Supply. Several wells, with water lines installed by the Bureau of Indian Affairs, provide water for residential use. The primary water source is Lake Henshaw, which is the headwaters of the San Luis Rey River; the riverbed courses through tribal lands. Septic tanks provide sewage disposal for residents. The tribe is working on a new wastewater treatment plant and a $10 million water project.

Transportation. The tribe owns a fleet of six buses. Service is provided for casino guests and tribal elders. The nearest national airport is in San Diego, 50 miles to the southwest. A seaport is also located in San Diego. County bus stops on the reservation serve Rincon residents. Freight railway services are available in Escondido, 17 miles to the southwest; a passenger railway is available in Oceanside, 30 miles to the west.

Telecommunications. Pacific Telephone Company provides telephone service.

COMMUNITY FACILITIES AND SERVICES
Community facilities on Rincon include a tribal hall, an Indian Education Center, athletic fields, a day care center, and a fire department. The tribe operates a Tribal Community Garden, the Rincon Museum and Library, and provides transportation services for tribal elders.

Education. Tribal youth attend Valley Center, Pauma Unified, and Escondido Union school districts. The tribe's education committee oversees the Rincon Indian Education Center on the reservation. The center houses Cyber High, Plato Educational System, adult education, higher education assistance, after-school tutorial, Luiseño Curriculum, early literacy, Summer Rez, soccer, and Tribal Digital Village programs. The tribe offers classes in the indigenous language. Classes are held at the tribal hall.

Health Care. Health services are available through Indian Health Council. Clinics are located in Valley Center and Santa Ysabel. Services include general medicine, general dental, and community outreach services.

ENVIRONMENTAL CONCERNS
The reservation is home to the arroyo toad, an endangered species. In order to secure lands to construct its casino, the tribe purchased lands near Bonall, California, and negotiated a land exchange with the State of California to ensure the protection of the species. The tribe does staff an environmental manager.

Roaring Creek

Total area *(BIA realty, 2003)*	80 acres
Tribally owned *(BIA realty, 2003)*	80 acres
Population	14
Per capita income **2000 census**	$45,000

(See Pit River Tribes for further information on the following subjects: Culture and History, Government, Economy, and Community Facilities and Services.)

LOCATION AND LAND STATUS
The Roaring Creek Rancheria is located in north-central California, 43 miles from the city of Redding, the area's commercial center. The rancheria lies in a valley, partially surrounded by the Shasta-Trinity National Forest. The land was purchased for "landless" California Indians who had no prior allotments, under the authority of the Wheeler Howard Act of August 31, 1915. There was no designation as to the occupying tribe.

CLIMATE
The weather is usually mild and sunny. Rainfall averages 10 inches yearly. Summer high temperatures may reach 98°F; winter low temperatures can drop below 20°F.

ECONOMY
Few people live on the Roaring Creek Rancheria due to its isolated location and lack of facilities. In addition there are few employment opportunities in rural areas of Shasta County, except those generated by seasonal work in the timber and agricultural sectors.

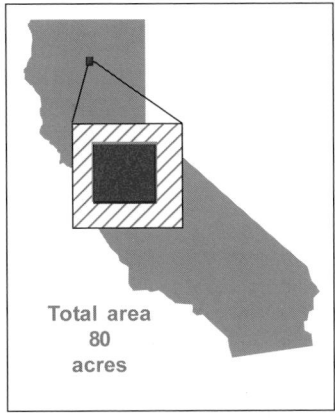

Total area
80
acres

INFRASTRUCTURE
An unpaved dirt road runs the two miles from the rancheria to Big Bend Road. Highway 299 is the nearest major highway.

Electricity. Pacific Gas and Electric provides electricity.

Water Supply. Area springs supply the rancheria's water.

Transportation. Commercial air, train, truck, and bus lines serve Redding, 43 miles from the rancheria.

COMMUNITY FACILITIES
Education. Rancheria children attend public schools in nearby communities.

Roaring Creek Rancheria
Federal reservation
Pit River
Shasta County, California

Pit River Tribe
37014 Main Street
Burney, CA 96013
530-335-5421
530-335-3140 Fax

Robinson

LOCATION AND LAND STATUS
The Robinson Rancheria is located halfway between the small towns of Nice and Upper Lake, approximately 110 miles northwest of Sacramento, California. Tribal lands consist of two sites in Lake County—the original rancheria site and the new rancheria site. The original rancheria was established on 88 acres in 1908, and an additional 80 acres were added in the 1920s. The original rancheria lies astride Highway 29, approximately 2.5 miles northwest of Clear Lake at an altitude of 1,310 feet.

The rancheria was terminated under the California Rancheria Act, and the distribution plan for its termination was approved February 25, 1960. Termination notices were published in the *Federal Register* on September 3, 1965, and 19 deeds were issued to distributees, turning their lands to fee status, to keep or sell as desired. Upon federal termination in 1965, the tribe lost all but 6.4 acres of its land base.

The tribe was restored to recognition in 1975. The court decision also restored 6.40 acres to trust status for individuals only. In 1982, the tribe purchased 107 acres to establish the new Robinson Rancheria. The new rancheria property lies astride Highway 20.

CLIMATE
The seasons in this geographical location are moderate, with temperatures ranging from a high of 90°F to a low of 30°F. The average rainfall is 17 inches per year.

CULTURE AND HISTORY
Residents of the Robinson Rancheria are members of the Pomo Tribe. The Pomo people's ancestral homelands encompassed regions across northwestern California. The indigenous language belongs to the Hokan linguistic family. Traditional means of sustenance included fishing, gathering shellfish, and some hunting and gathering of acorns. The arrival of European explorers and Euro-American settlers brought irreversible changes to the indigenous cultures of the California territory. Exposure to foreign diseases, usurpation of tribal lands, and forced incarceration on federal reservations resulted in near extermination for several tribal groups.

The original Robinson Rancheria was created in 1908. Under the provisions of the California Rancheria Act of 1958, the tribe was terminated from federal recognition in 1965. In 1975, in *Mabel Duncan, et al. v. the United States of America*, the court found that the tribe's termination had been illegal. The tribe's recognition was restored in 1981. Since its restoration, the tribe has been actively pursing means to increase its land base, develop a stable economy, and revitalize Pomo traditions within the community.

Robinson Rancheria
Federal reservation
Eastern Pomo
Lake County, California

Robinson Rancheria Tribe
of Pomo Indians
P.O. Box 1119
Nice, CA 95464
707-275-0527

Robinson

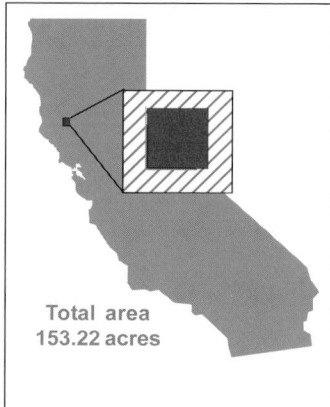

Total area
153.22 acres

TRI-CA-050 Sign for Robinson Rancheria

TRI-CA-051 Construction for expansion of
Robinson Casino

TRI-CA-052 View of Clear Lake from deck
of Tribal Office Building

Total area *(BIA realty, 2003)*
153.22 acres

Tribally owned *(BIA realty, 2003)*
143.28 acres

Individually owned
(BIA realty, 2003)
9.94 acres

Population *2000 census*
138

Tribal enrollment
(BIA labor report, 2001)
433

Total labor force
2000 census
42

Total labor force
(BIA labor report, 2001)
250

High school graduate or higher
2000 census
55.7%

Bachelor's degree or higher
2000 census
0%

Unemployment rate
2000 census
11.9%

TRI-CA-050

TRI-CA-051

TRI-CA-052

GOVERNMENT

The rancheria is governed by a six-member elected business council, which includes a chairperson, vice-chairperson, a secretary-treasurer, and three members-at-large. Business council members are elected annually for two-year terms by the tribal council. The tribal council includes all tribal members 18 years or older. Tribal council meetings are held quarterly. The tribe is organized under an IRA constitution and bylaws that were approved in 1980. Governmental departments include education and environment.

ECONOMY

Since its restoration in the early 1980s, the tribe has endeavored to develop a stable tribal economy to serve its members. The tribe owns a number of enterprises now, and in addition to supplementing its own tribal programs and services, it provides financial contributions to local schools and community organizations.

Government as Employer. The tribe employs over 200 people throughout its enterprises and governmental departments. Government jobs represent Lake County's second-largest employer. Housing projects, the bingo facility, and tribal administration provide short-term jobs for a number of tribal members.

Economic Development Projects. The new rancheria land base, located on a main transportation route and near Clear Lake, suggests many economic development potentials for the tribe. To take advantage of local and traveler traffic, the tribe is actively pursuing a commercial development on its acreage fronting Highway 20. This commercial center would include a 24-hour restaurant, a gas station, mini-mart, and a crafts store. The tribe is currently conducting feasibility studies for this project.

Agriculture and Livestock. The rancheria has approximately 34 acres of land that would be suitable for agricultural development. As Lake County's economy is based primarily on agriculture, the tribe is considering the feasibility of developing this property for agriculture.

Gaming. The Robinson Rancheria owns and operates Robinson Rancheria Casino and Bingo. Located on the north shore of Clear Lake in Nice, California, the casino offers 600 slots/VLTs, 10 table games, 530 bingo seats, and one restaurant. The casino employs 270 people. The casino hosts the annual California Indian Day (Big Time) celebrations in September and the National Indian Day in May. Expansions to the casino to be completed by the end of 2004 include a 50-room hotel, a sports bar, a coffee bar, a gift shop, and convention rooms with the capacity for 300. The tribe's high-stakes bingo operation, Kabatin Indian Bingo, has provided an important source of tribal revenue and employment. The bingo facility is located in a 1,600-person capacity building just off Highway 20. Kabatin Indian Bingo is open Thursday through Sunday.

Manufacturing. The tribe owns Solar Tactical. This company produces solar panels. The tribe also owns a plant that produces recyclable paint.

Real Estate/Commercial Development. The tribe is in the process of constructing 10 houses and 30 town homes on the reservation with the assistance of an Indian community development block grant. The tribe intends to purchase 720 acres of land. It will use the land for housing development and economic enterprises.

Services and Retail. The tribe owns and operates the Indian Arts and Crafts Store, a business that has employed three part-time workers and shown a consistent profit. The tribe intends to move this business to the planned commercial center.

Media and Communications. The tribe publishes a quarterly newsletter for tribal members.

Tourism and Recreation. The tribe owns the Aurora RV Marina and Park at Clear Lake. It features 60 hookup sites, a mini-mart, a clubroom, laundry room, showers, a boat ramp, and outdoor picnic and barbeque areas. In addition, the tribe holds two annual celebrations: Indian Cultural Day and Robinson Rancheria's Annual Track Meet. Native American dancers and performers come from throughout Lake County for Indian Cultural Day. At the Track Meet, participants age five to 18 are welcome to participate in this intertribal contest, with prizes awarded to all.

INFRASTRUCTURE

The rancheria lays astride Highway 20, which connects with Interstate 5 and U.S. 101, two of northern California's main corridors.

Electricity. Is provided by Pacific Gas and Electric.

Water Supply. The Nice Water Company provides water to residencies.

Transportation. Bus, trucking, and rail service are available in Ukiah, 30 miles from the rancheria. Lake Transit provides bus service to Clear Lake.

COMMUNITY FACILITIES AND SERVICES

Using HUD funds, the tribe has constructed a community center and an education and recreation facility. The education and recreation facility includes a half-court gymnasium, computer lab, and a daycare center. The tribe has applied for further funding to expand the building. The tribe also contracts a youth rogram from the U.S. Department of Justice.

Education. Tribal youth attend public schools in the town of Upper Lake. The tribe contracts funds for the Johnson O'Malley Program.

Health Care. Health services are available through the Lake County Tribal Health Consortium. Services include medical, dental, vision, community outreach, substance abuse prevention, and child and family programs. A clinic is located in Lakeport.

ENVIRONMENTAL CONCERNS

The tribe established an environmental center in 1996. The center's programs include a winter community garden, recycling buy-back center, GIS/GPS program, and cultural resource management. The center participates in California Adopt-a-Highway, Protection of California Native Oak Trees, and Lake County Discovery Center programs. It is responsible for developing environmental education programs, a tribal circuit court system, environmental ordinances, a website, and the tribal transportation plan. The department currently administers and implements grants from the U.S. EPA, the BIA, CTAA, National Park Service (NAGRPA grant), and the 7th Generation Fund. The department also represents the tribe on numerous local, county, state, and federal committees, consortia, and programs.

Robinson

Unemployment rate
(BIA labor report, 2001)
6%

Per capita income
2000 census
$8,177

Rohnerville

Total area *(BIA realty, 2003)*	62.16 acres
Tribally owned *(BIA realty, 2003)*	60 acres
Individually owned	2.16 acres
(BIA realty, 2003)	
Population 2000 census	6
Tribal enrollment *(Tribal source, 2004)*	241
Tribal enrollment *(BIA labor report, 2001)*	265
Total labor force *2000 census*	46
Total labor force *(Tribal source)*	80
Total labor force *(BIA labor report, 2001)*	98
High school graduate or higher	70.9%
2000 census	
Bachelor's degree or higher	3.6%
2000 census	
Unemployment rate *2000 census*	0%
Unemployment rate *(BIA realty, 2003)*	55%

LOCATION AND LAND STATUS

The Bear River Band of the Rohnerville Rancheria is located approximately one-quarter mile north of Fortuna, California, and two miles southeast of the town of Loleta. The historical rancheria, a 15,187-acre parcel of land located within Fortuna, was set aside for the tribe in 1910. When the tribe was terminated in 1962, the land was allotted to tribal members. By the time the tribe regained federal recognition in 1983, only 6.75 acres remained in individual ownership. The United States agreed to restore the original boundaries of the Rohnerville Rancheria as they existed immediately prior to the California Rancheria Act of 1958. The tribe purchased an additional 60 acres of land approximately six miles from the historical rancheria in 1991.

CULTURE AND HISTORY

The Bear River Band of the Rohnerville Rancheria is composed of three bands. They are the Mattale, Wiyot, and Bear River bands. During the occupation of present-day California by first Spanish and then United States forces, the Bear River Band suffered devastating social, cultural, and spiritual losses. The Spanish did not recognize tribal claims to land and proceeded to kill Native Americans residing in regions determined to be possessions of the Spanish crown. The Spanish also brought the first wave of Euro-American diseases to the Native people of the West Coast, and the population rapidly dwindled. When the United Sates gained control over the California territory in 1848, the federal government offered only minimal protection to the Native peoples. Settlers targeted tribal people to be enslaved, starved,

and ultimately eliminated. In 1850 the federal government authorized the sale of Native American people into slavery. In 1851 the government nullified Native land claims, and tribal lands became public domain.

In 1852 the government agreed to a series of treaties agreeing to reserve over 8.5 million acres of tribal lands for numerous California tribes in exchange for title to the lands. The federal government later refused to sign the treaties but failed to inform tribes of this decision. The tribes abided by the treaties and suffered loss of land, sovereignty, and well-being as a result. The federal government did not acknowledge the treaties until 1905. At that time, several rancherias were reserved for various groups.

In 1958 the U.S. Congress passed the California Rancheria Act. The act effectively terminated federal recognition of all 43 of California's rancheria tribes. The Bear River Band was formally terminated in 1962, and tribal lands were allotted to individual tribal members. The tribe did not regain federal recognition until 1983, and it was not until 1986 that the Rohnerville Rancheria was restored to the tribe.

GOVERNMENT

The tribe maintains its own law enforcement department but does not have a tribal court system.

ECONOMY

The tribe is currently pursuing the establishment of a gaming facility. Estimated revenue will be used to bolster the reservation's economy and enhance the services available to tribal members.

Government as Employer. The tribal government currently employs 22 individuals.

Gaming. The Bear River Band is in the process of developing a casino. The tribe submitted proposals for a class III gaming facility to be opened on 60 acres of land held in trust for the tribe north of the historical rancheria. The proposed complex is scheduled to open in 2005. The tribe intends to use revenue generated from their gaming enterprise to purchase lands, supplement the general budget, and enhance services available to tribal members.

INFRASTRUCTURE

Electricity. Pacific Gas and Electric provides electricity.

Bear River Band of the Rohnerville Rancheria
Federally recognized
Bear River, Mattale, and Wiyot
Humboldt County, California

Bear River Band of the
  Rohnerville Rancheria
27 Bear River Drive
Loleta, CA 95551
  707-733-1900
  707-733-1972 Fax

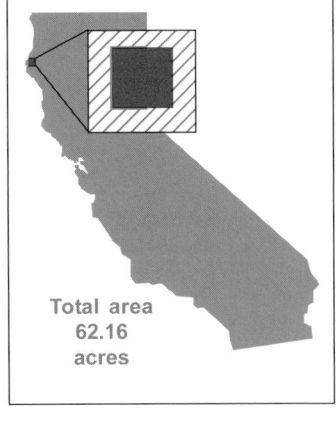

Total area
62.16
acres

Rohnerville

TRI-CA-053 Loleta Union Elementary School

TRI-CA-054 Loleta Family Fun Day in June

TRI-CA-053

TRI-CA-054

Fuel. Sequoia Gas and Amerigas supply fuel.

Water Supply. The tribe supplies domestic water to the reservation. The tribe also provides a sewer system.

Transportation. The tribe is in the process of buying two mini buses.

Telecommunications. Cox Communications provides cable television services.

COMMUNITY FACILITIES AND SERVICES
The tribe maintains a community center; facilities include a kitchen, council chambers, offices, a library, and a general meeting area. Tribal members actively promote the retention and vitalization of the Wiyot language, tribal ceremonies, and cultural traditions. Once a week a social luncheon is held for tribal elders.

Education. Tribal youth attend Loleta Elementary School and Fortuna High School. Nearby colleges include the College of the Redwoods and Humboldt State University.

Health Care. United Health Services provides health services. The company's clinics provide general medical, dental, and counseling programs. Full-service hospitals are available at nearby Redwood Memorial, St. Joseph's, and Mad River hospitals.

ENVIRONMENTAL CONCERNS
The tribe is concerned with issues of solid waste disposal, water quality, and soil erosion on the reservation.

Round Valley

Round Valley Indian Reservation
Federal reservation
Achomawi, Concow, Nomlaki, Wailaki, Wintun, Yuki, and Pomo
Mendocino County, California

Round Valley Indian Tribes
77826 Covelo Road
Covelo, CA 95428
707-983-6126
707-983-6128 Fax

LOCATION AND LAND STATUS
The Round Valley Indian Reservation is located in the northeastern part of Mendocino County. It is the second-largest reservation in California. The reservation was established by an Executive Order on November 18, 1858. A second Executive Order on March 30, 1870, enlarged the reservation, and the borders were further defined by a third Executive Order on May 18, 1875. The Camp Wright Military Reserve was added to the reservation in 1876. Old Fort Wright, which was added to the reservation, was abandoned in 1876 and converted into an Indian boarding school in 1883. Nothing remains of either, except a former officer's home.

Originally, the reservation covered over 102,000 acres. As a result of the General Allotment Act of 1887, tribal lands were significantly decreased. Today ownership of the land base is a mosaic divided between tribal lands under individual Indian family ownership and trust lands.

PHYSICAL DESCRIPTION
The reservation is located in a geographically round valley in Mendocino County. The isolated valley is situated within the second coastal mountain range, and it is approximately 60 miles inland from the Pacific Ocean.

CLIMATE
The Round Valley Indian Reservation is located in the transition zone between coastal and interior climates. Rainfall measures about 35 inches per year, and temperatures range from a low of 29°F to a high of 102°F.

CULTURE AND HISTORY
The Round Valley Reservation was created in 1856 as the Nome Cult Farm. It was originally designated for occupation by the Yuki Tribe of California. The Yuki people have lived in Round Valley for thousands of years. The reservation itself represents one of the oldest reservations in California. The large Nome Lackee Reservation was established in 1854 on the eastern foothills of the Coast Range, and the vestiges of many cultural groups living around Central Valley were removed to it. When Euro-American settlers claimed this land in 1863, these people were herded over the mountains to Round Valley, with considerable loss of life over the course of a two-week journey.

During the late nineteenth century, as Euro-American encroachment on tribal lands in California burgeoned, the federal government began to relocate members of other tribes to the reservation. Although many of the tribes were traditional rivals, the members were forced to share the tribal lands, and eventually they created a nation of confederated tribes that share a common experience and land base. Members of the Round Valley Indian Tribes are descended from the Yuki, Concow Maidu, Little Lake, Pomo, Nomlaki, Cahto, Wailaki, and Pit River groups of California. The tribe was initially referred to as the Covelo Indian Community, but later evolved into the Round Valley Indian Tribes.

GOVERNMENT
The tribe's constitution and bylaws, prepared according to the Indian Reorganization Act of 1934, were approved on December 16, 1936. The tribal charter was ratified the following year. The reservation is governed by the seven-member elected Covelo Indian Community Council, which includes a chairper-

son, vice-chairperson, secretary, treasurer, and sergeant-at-arms. Government programs include: cultural resource management, real estate, Indian Child Welfare Act, environmental protection, adult vocational training and higher education, early childhood education, senior center, law enforcement, and housing.

ECONOMY

The potentials for economic development on the Round Valley Indian Reservation lie in its rich natural resources. Within the valley, untapped reserves of fertile soil, water, and timber tracts provide potential areas of economic growth. Employment opportunities for tribal members are in the timber industry, tourism and recreation, agricultural projects, and the tribal government.

Government as Employer. Various sectors within the tribal government provide employment for tribal members, such as the tribal council, the career development center, and the Round Valley Health Center. Tribal government jobs account for approximately 26 percent of tribal employment.

Agriculture and Livestock. The reservation has a small fruit orchard and approximately 1,000 acres suitable for agricultural uses. Three percent of tribal members are employed in the agricultural industry. Approximately 750 acres of reservation land have been leased for cattle grazing. In addition, individual tribal members own cattle ranches on the reservation. There are a number of agricultural enterprises located in Round Valley. Live Power Community Farm, Tom Palley's Covelo Organic Vegetables, and Peaceful Glen Organics all operate in the area.

Forestry. Logging and milling serve as the primary source of employment for tribal members. The reservation has a small timber contracting company that employs tribal members and uses its own equipment (Cat, loader, and portable mill) for these projects. Other Round Valley residents work in the private sector for timber and milling businesses, including the Louisiana-Pacific Lumber Company, and for the Forest Service.

Industrial Parks. The Round Valley Indian Tribes own a sizable portion of land adjacent to the Round Valley Airport, which may be used for industrial development. This property is ideally suited to firms who wish to benefit from joint projects on Native American land. Access to water and low-cost utilities are available on this property.

Mining. The Tribal Sand and Gravel Company employs several tribal members. Because of the enterprise's financial success, the tribe is expanding the business by increasing equipment, office, and storage facilities.

Services and Retail. Numerous small businesses are located in Round Valley. The Round Valley Inn serves breakfast, lunch, and dinner menus. It also offers banquet facilities that seat up to 120 guests. The Burger Station offers casual meals and outdoor dining facilities. The North Fork Café offers locally produced foods and drinks. An adjacent lounge provides live entertainment and can be rented for events. The Drake Inn is located in Covelo and provides take-out dining services.

Tourism and Recreation. Due to the reservation's location, it has been referred to as the "gateway to Northern California's wilderness." The tribe runs the attractive Hidden Oaks Recreation Center on the reservation, which includes rodeo grounds, baseball diamonds, and a campground and recreational vehicle park. The tribe intends to expand this facility by supplementing existing hiking trails and campsites.

During the last weekend in September, the California Indian Days Celebration is held at the Hidden Oaks Recreational Park. A combined baseball tournament and powwow, the celebration also features arts and crafts, hand games, and a parade. In addition, the tribe hosts a summer camp at Hidden Oaks.

INFRASTRUCTURE

The Round Valley Reservation is accessible by a two-lane state highway off U.S. Highway 101.

Electricity. Pacific Gas and Electric Company provides electricity.

Fuel. Standard Oil sells gas to residents.

Water Supply. A water and wastewater system has been developed for the reservation through a Set-Aside Grant from the IHS. Tribal members have been trained and certified as State Certified Water Treatment Plant Operators.

Transportation. A 3,600-foot airstrip is located in Covelo and is operated by Mendocino County. The airport is illuminated, well-maintained, and includes gas and servicing facilities. Further commercial air service is available in Ukiah, which is located 70 miles away. Willits, the nearest city, lies some 45 miles from Round Valley and is served by commercial train and bus lines. Trucking service is available in Covelo, one mile from the reservation.

Telecommunications. In 1995 the tribe was developing a tribally managed radio station.

COMMUNITY FACILITIES AND SERVICES

There are a number of churches of varying denominations in Round Valley. There is also a public library and a community theater, as well as several animal rescue groups. In addition, community buildings on the reservation provide a meeting place for the tribal council and for the tribe's Head Start program. There is also a senior center. The Yuki Trails Transitional Living Center for young girls aged 12 to 18 was being built in 2004. The tribal career center serves the reservation population.

Round Valley

Total area *(BIA realty, 2003)*
31,751 acres

Tribally owned *(BIA realty, 2003)*
26,138.66 acres

Individually owned
(BIA realty, 2003)
5,612.34 acres

Population 2000 census
1,181

Tribal enrollment
(BIA labor report, 2001)
3,494

Total labor force 2000 census
86

Total labor force
(BIA labor report, 2001)
2,350

High school graduate or higher
2000 census
77.9%

Bachelor's degree or higher
2000 census
3.8%

Unemployment rate 2000 census
7%

Unemployment rate
(BIA labor report, 2001)
91%

Per capita income
2000 census
$10,336

TRI-CA-055 Welcome sign at Tribal Complex

TRI-CA-056 Round Valley Health Clinic

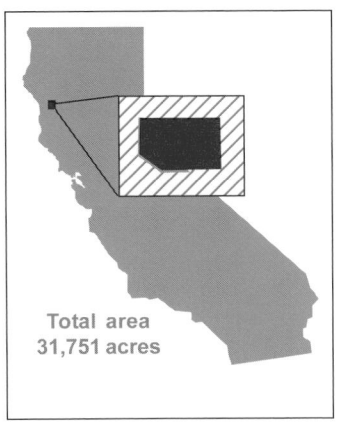
Total area
31,751 acres

Round Valley

Education. Tribal youth attend the Round Valley Unified School District. In addition to traditional elementary and secondary programs, the district offers the Eel River Charter School. The Round Valley Indian Education Center (RVIEC) is a resource center that provides programs to promote Native American student achievement. It offers instructional aide and student-parent advocacy services to participants. Programs include GED preparation; independent study; expulsion, suspension, and home study; academic counseling; and California high school proficiency examinations preparation. The center coordinates with the Round Valley Unified School District and the Eel River Charter School to better serve the individual needs of participating students.

Health Care. The Round Valley Indian Health Center has provided community, as well as the valley in general, a health unit that has become a model for rural health facilities. Programs include comprehensive medical, lab, well child, family planning, domestic abuse prevention, and dental services.

ENVIRONMENTAL CONCERNS

The tribe has established an environmental program with the assistance of the EPA, HUD, an Indian Community Development Block Grant, IHS, and the BIA. The program is part of a multimedia network of Native American tribes. The network helps participating tribes share information about grants, applications, and available resources. Through the network, the tribe is working to develop a Global Position and Satellite (GPS) and Geographic Information System (GIS) to be applied to tribal lands.

An area of concern to the tribe is soil contamination, particularly on the site of the former Louisiana-Pacific Mill. A review determined extensive contamination, and the company was required to remove 1,000 tons of soil.

Rumsey

Rumsey Indian Rancheria
Federal reservation
Wintun (Yocha Dehe) and
Penutian
Yolo County, California

Rumsey Indian Rancheria
P.O. Box 18
Brooks, CA 95606
530-796-3400
530-796-2143 Fax
cachecreek.com

LOCATION AND LAND STATUS

The Rumsey Rancheria covers just over 257 acres in the Coast Range of California, 45 miles northwest of Sacramento. The land on the eastern side of the Coast Range is hilly and dry. However, the reservation's position along Cache Creek (which drains Clear Lake) provides it with an abundance of water and vegetation. The rancheria is also just an hour's drive from Napa Valley. The original purchase of land for the reservation occurred in 1907 and 1908. The Secretary of the Interior and the Wheeler Howard Act (1934) authorized the purchase of additional lands. The reservation was moved in 1940 *(see Culture and History for additional information)*. In 1982 another 118 acres was purchased for the tribe.

CLIMATE

The climate is mild, sunny, and rather dry. Temperatures range from a low of 38°F to a high of 109°F. Average annual precipitation is 15 inches.

CULTURE AND HISTORY

Rumsey residents are affiliated with the Wintun Tribe, a band numbering about 12,000 in the early 1800s. Given the range of Wintun territory, their language (Wintu) evolved into a number of dialects. Early European contact in the region came through Spanish settlers who had arrived via Mexico by 1808. Hudson Bay Company trappers arrived sometime before 1832. As elsewhere, the imposition of European culture had devastating effects upon the Native people of the region. The pattern was a now-familiar one: tribal unity was destroyed by the taking of land and the destruction of traditional food-and material-gathering areas. Introduction of cattle, hogs, and sheep destroyed numerous plant and bulb areas. Copper processing plants in the 1880s and early 1900s, along with construction of dams, severely damaged streams and vegetation. These things took their toll on the health and survival of the Wintun and other area tribes.

In the early days of California statehood, Congress attempted to herd all the state's Indians onto four major reservations, against their wishes. The Wintuns struggled to return to their aboriginal lands. Finally in 1909 a reserve was set aside east of present-day Rumsey. The reservation was moved in 1940 to a 60-acre tract 15 miles south of Rumsey, part of the present-day site. By 1970 the rancheria had dwindled to only three members, and it was on the verge of termination under the Rancheria Act, Public Law 85-671. In 1982, 118 acres were added to the rancheria as it began acquiring new members. Later the tribe obtained financing for the construction of Cache Creek Indian Bingo and Casino. Culturally, the Wintuns continue to practice their traditional culture even as they continue to succeed within mainstream society. Many Wintuns continue to harvest traditional foods, most significantly acorns and salmon.

There are three divisions of the Wintun people: the Wintu, Nomlaki, and Patwin. Their traditional lands are located in the greater Sacramento Valley. The Sacramento River is a major feature of all the regions, from the Wintu Mountain rivers in the north, through the Nomlaki plains, to the marshes, valleys, and hills of the Patwin. Their languages are of the Penutian family, which includes a large group of central and northern California languages.

On the major rivers, the Wintun depended on the semiannual runs of king salmon, as well as on acorns with secondary use of other vegetable foods and game. Today there are approximately 2,500 people of Wintun descent; many live on the Colusa, Cortina, Grindstone Creek, Redding, and Rumsey rancherias, as well as on the Round Valley Reservation.

GOVERNMENT

The Rumsey Rancheria is governed by a tribal council, composed of five members elected by the Community Council, and it includes all qualified voters 18 years and older. Elected council members include a chairperson, a secretary, and a treasurer. Elections are held every three years in January. The tribe is organized under an IRA constitution that was approved in 1976.

ECONOMY

The region's economy since the late 1800s has been largely based on agriculture; over 80 percent of Yolo County is cultivated for various crops such as sugar beets and tomatoes. While the tribe derives some income from its agricultural leased land, since the mid-1980s the Cache Creek Indian Bingo and Casino has been a source of the rancheria's current relative prosperity. Real estate has been a recent economic endeavor for the tribe, which owns and leases major properties in various states. The beauty of the land also provides the prospect of directing a portion of the economy toward eco-tourism.

Agriculture and Livestock. Agriculture remains the primary land use, and it has passed historically through several distinct phases.

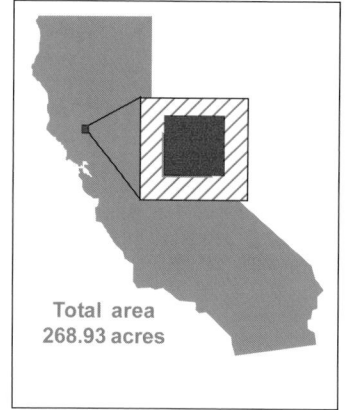

Total area
268.93 acres

TRI-CA-058

TRI-CA-057

TRI-CA-059

TRI-CA-060

Rumsey

TRI-CA-057 Parking structure at Casino Hotel

TRI-CA-058 Rumsey's Cache Creek Mini Mart at Casino Resort Complex

TRI-CA-059 Rumsey's new Tribal Building

TRI-CA-060 Newly planted vineyards in front of Casino

Fruit colonies established around 1900 gradually declined because local climate and soils do not favor commercial fruit production. Around 1920, farmers planted almond orchards, then shifted to the cultivation of walnuts. Other farmers continue to grow field crops, while ranchers graze livestock in the hills. The Rancheria has become a hub for organic produce cultivation, with two dozen organic fruit and vegetable growers currently expanding and diversifying operations. The tribe owns several parcels of agricultural land in Yolo County, with a full-time farm manager to oversee and maintain the farming of more than 1,500 acres.

Gaming. Cache Creek Casino Resort offers the ultimate gaming experience in its glamorous and exciting 66,000-square-foot casino. The casino is located in Brooks, California, and offers 1,762 slot machines, more than 120 table games, and bingo. Wide, free-flowing aisles, comfortable hydraulic-adjustable chairs, and a non-smoking area allow slot players to easily seek out and play their favorite games. In addition to blackjack and a smoke-free poker parlor, other table games include Pai Gow poker, mini-baccarat, California craps, California roulette, Texas hold'em, Caribbean stud, Let it ride, Casino war, and three-card poker.

The resort offers a 200-room luxury hotel and health spa, eight restaurants, Club 88 entertainment venue, a 20,000-square-foot event center, an outdoor swimming pool, a gift shop and a tribally operated mini-mart, gas station, and fire station.

Real Estate/Commercial Development. The tribe is the largest private owner of government-leased real estate in Springfield, Illinois. The Illinois Departments of Corrections, Public Health, Transportation and Community Services lease more than 600,000 square feet of office space. The tribe is involved in additional real estate, owning several buildings in Sacramento and contracting with well-known developers in many joint ventures. The tribe is working with the cities of Sacramento and West Sacramento on a master-planned residential, commercial, and office development project along the Sacramento riverfront.

Services and Retail. Rumsey Rancheria owns and operates a convenience store and service station in the Capay Valley. Rumsey Rancheria is the first Native entity in the United States to own an automobile dealership, which is located in Dallas, Texas.

Tourism and Recreation. Located only an hour from the scenic Napa Valley wine country and Clear Lake, the rancheria is positioned in a popular recreational region. In addition to the four-star accommodations found at the Cache Creek Casino Resort, there are hotels, motels, and bed-and-breakfasts located in surrounding areas.

The Capay Valley offers visitors an abundance of recreational activities from which to choose, including: gaming, fishing, rafting, camping, biking, wine tasting, farm tours, and the annual Almond Festival. Held the last Sunday in February, the festival is a celebration of the agricultural season and includes arts and crafts, wine tasting, a barbecue, and a classic car show.

INFRASTRUCTURE
Water Supply. Water and sewage services are provided by wells and septic tanks.

Transportation. The rancheria is accessed by Highway 16 which runs north-south along its front border. The rancheria's proximity to Sacramento International Airport as well as to two major interstates (5 and 80) places it at an important transportation hub.

COMMUNITY FACILITIES AND SERVICES
Health Care. Hospital facilities are available in Woodland. The Rumsey Rancheria Fire Department, Capay Valley Fire Protection District, and Esparto Fire Protection District provide world-class emergency response services to the people of Capay Valley.

Total area *(BIA realty, 2003)*
268.93 acres

Total area *(Tribal source, 2004)*
257 acres

Tribally owned *(BIA realty, 2003)*
268.93 acres

Population *(Tribal source, 2004)*
54

Tribal enrollment
(BIA labor force report, 2001)
44

Total labor force *2000 census*
5

Total labor force
(BIA labor force report, 2001)
23

High school graduate or higher
2000 census
68.8%

Bachelor's degree or higher
2000 census
0%

Unemployment rate *2000 census*
0%

Per capita income *2000 census*
$22,146

San Manuel

San Manuel Reservation
Federal reservation
Serrano
San Bernardino County,
California

San Manuel Band of Mission
Indians
P.O. Box 266
Patton, CA 92369
909-864-8933
909-864-3370 Fax
sanmanuel.com

Total area (BIA realty, 2003)
814.37 acres

Tribally owned (BIA realty, 2003)
814.37 acres

Tribal population
(Tribal source, 2004)
170

Tribal enrollment (BIA, 2001)
151

Total labor force 2000 census
20

High school graduate or higher
2000 census
97.9%

Bachelor's degree or higher
2000 census
0%

Unemployment rate
2000 census
0%

Per capita income 2000 census
$8,849

LOCATION AND LAND STATUS

The San Manuel Reservation is in southern California, four miles northeast of San Bernardino and just outside the city of Highland, along the foothills of the San Bernardino Mountains. Most of the land consists of large, rolling hills. The reservation was established on August 31, 1893, under authority of a Congressional Act on January 12, 1891.

CLIMATE

The climate is mild and reasonably moderate. Temperatures range from winter lows of 15°F to summer highs of 110°F. Average annual rainfall is less than five inches.

CULTURE AND HISTORY

San Manuel Reservation residents are primarily people of the Serrano Tribe. Their traditional language belongs to the Shoshonean division of the Uto-Aztecan linguistic family, which includes languages spoken by peoples from the Great Basin into central Mexico. The term "serrano," meaning "mountaineer," was initially used by Spanish settlers as a generic term of designation for otherwise "unnamed" Indians in the mountainous areas of southern California. Later the name came to refer only to that band whose territory extended roughly from Mount San Antonio in the San Gabriel Mountains to Cottonwood Springs in the Little San Bernardino Mountains. The Serranos originally occupied much of Mojave Desert and San Bernardino Mountains but had largely disappeared from both sectors by the twentieth century. The other Serrano base is the Morongo Reservation, about 30 miles to the east. In the wake of European contact, the Serrano population was dramatically reduced through disease, intermarriage, and killings.

Many Serranos were trained in agriculture at the Catholic missions in the area, and agriculture has been the region's economic mainstay from that time to the present, in the form of the citrus industry. Although the Serranos have yet to reap the benefits of the region's citrus industry, tribal members have often worked as independent farmers and cattlemen in the years since European contact. Traditionally, the Serranos were divided into two groups, or moieties, and marriage could occur only across group lines. Communities were typically villages of between 25 and 100 people. Today few people remain who speak the Serrano language and few ancestral rituals survive, although some people continue to sing traditional Bird Songs on special social occasions. Most of the few remaining Serranos today live on or near the reservation. Through the tribe's Cultural Awareness Program, the language and culture is being revived. The San Manuel Band has also been instrumental in shaping the school curriculum at both the local and statewide level to include lessons on tribes indigenous to California, and it annually hosts a conference for students at California State University, San Bernardino.

GOVERNMENT

The tribe is governed by a general council comprised of all members 21 years of age or over; 30 percent of the council is a quorum. The business committee includes a chairperson, a vice-chairperson, a secretary, a treasurer, and three at-large members. Elections are held every two years, as called by the business committee. The general council meets monthly. The tribe is organized under Articles of Association approved on December 1, 1966, with subsequent amendments.

Tribal government departments include administration, operations, water, fire, public safety, environmental, and project development.

ECONOMY

While Indian gaming is by far the largest contributor to the success and strength of the San Manuel Band's economy, the tribe is making great efforts to diversify its economic endeavors in industries such as real estate, manufacturing, and service and retail.

BUSINESS CORPORATION

The San Manuel Band joined forces with the Forest County Potawatomi Community, the Oneida Tribe, and the Viejas Band of Kumeyaay Indians, to form the Four Fires LLC. The corporation was set up to enable each tribe to increase and diversify their individual business holdings, assets, and revenue, and it is representative of the growing cooperation between tribes and the economic advantages created by such a union. This group of tribes invested in a Mariott Hotel in Washington, D.C., and three of the four tribes also invested in a Mariott Hotel in Sacramento, California.

Government as Employer. The City and County of San Bernardino, as well Norton Air Force Base, represent a significant source of the area's employment, including tribal members. Norton AFB closed in 1996 and no longer employs military and civilian personnel. As a result, the San Manuel Band is one of the largest local employers along with the County of San Bernardino. In total the tribe employs some 2,300 people in the community.

Economic Development Projects. The San Manuel Band and the other Four Fires LCC members are working in conjunction with Donohoe Development Companies to develop a 13-story luxury suite hotel in the heart of the nation's capital called The Residence Inn Capitol by Marriott. The completion of the project is slated for spring 2005. Members of the corporation are also cooperating to build a Marriott Hotel in Sacramento, California.

Agriculture and Livestock. Portions of the rugged reservation land are suitable for growing citrus, particularly in areas where there are several natural springs that can be used for irrigation. The tribe intends to seek funding for a feasibility study of such an enterprise.

Gaming. The San Manuel Indian Bingo and Casino is a 155,000-square-foot gaming facility originally built in 1986. It houses 2,000 slot machines, 54 table games including 25 poker tables, a 2,100-seat bingo hall, 2 restaurants, and an entertainment venue. San Manuel Indian Bingo and Casino is one of the largest employers in the Inland Empire area, providing employment for over 1,800 Native and non-Native people. Total tribal employment is closer to 2,300. The casino offers its staff first-class benefits including training seminars, first aid programs, scholarship opportunities, a 401K-retirement program, insurance coverage, and other programs. In January 2005 the tribe will replace the existing casino with a 465,000-square foot gaming complex. Amenities will include a six-level parking garage. The construction of the new facility has created over $250 million in economic stimulus to the local and state economies.

The tribe is also developing a 12-acre site in the city of Highland. The development will include a hotel with approximately 110 rooms and retail, office, and restaurant spaces. The tribe is considering developing a reservation-based museum.

The tribe donates revenues from gaming to local charities, schools, and universities. Recipients include UCLA Law School, YMCA, League of Women Voters, Little League Baseball, Feed the Children, Alternatives of Domestic Violence, Victory Outreach,

San Bernardino County Library, and other local groups and programs. In efforts to protect the reservation and surrounding areas from the delinquency often associated with gaming, the tribe also donates large amounts of monies to local community law enforcement agencies. It established a public safety department comprised of a 190-person staff which provides security and surveillance for the facility's premises.

Through the tribal-state compact, the tribe contributes to two additional funds. The first shares revenue with non-gaming tribes in the state, and the second, the Special Distribution Fund, funds local needs and projects. In 2002 the tribe donated a large sum of money to the White Mountain Apache Nation whose tribal lands were devastated by the Arizona wildfires of that year. In 2003 the tribe provided a large donation to the San Pasqual Tribe to assist in their recovery from wildfires that ravaged southern California that year.

Manufacturing. In April 2002, the San Manuel Band opened a water-bottling facility, which bottles water from the tribe's natural springs. The plant is able to produce 600 bottles of water per minute. The spring water is sold under the Big Bear Mountain brand to large retailers, including 7-11 and Target. The development of this enterprise earned the tribe a number of awards, including Exporter of the Year from the U.S. Department of Commerce.

Real Estate/Commercial Development. The San Manuel Band owns three office buildings; two are located in Irvine, California, and the other is in Washington, D.C. The tribe leases the buildings. The building in Washington, D.C. provides office and meeting space for the tribe's advocacy efforts. The tribe is now looking toward leasing additional space as a source of revenue. In partnership with the Oneida Tribe, the Forest County Potawatomi, and the Viejas Band of Kumeyaay Indians, the San Manuel Band of Mission Indians has created Four Fires LLC, a Delaware corporation. As a joint venture with The Donohue Development Companies of Washington, D.C., Four Fires LLC has built the Residence Inn Capitol, a hotel near the National Museum of the American Indian on the Mall in Washington. Four Fires owns a 59-percent stake in the 13-story Marriot Hotel. The hotel will be managed by Hospitality Partners of Bethesda, Maryland.

The tribe also owns parcels of land on and near the former Norton Air Force Base in San Bernardino, California. It is working with developers to maximize the use of these lands for economic growth and job creation.

Services and Retail. The San Manuel Band is the major partner in Twin Palms, an upscale restaurant in Pasadena, California, which has a celebrity clientele and hosts star-studded events such as Entertainment Tonight's Emmy party.

INFRASTRUCTURE
State Highway 30, a four-lane artery, runs just south of the reservation, connecting nearby Interstate 10 with Interstate 215, the Interstate 15 bypass.

Electricity. Southern California Edison provides electricity.

Fuel. Local vendors supply the reservation with fuel.

Water Supply. The East Valley Water District provides the reservation with water. The water is stored in large tanks on the reservation that are maintained by the tribal water department.

Transportation. The city of Ontario, 25 miles from the reservation, provides the nearest commercial airline facilities. A private airport, along with bus, train, and truck lines, are available in San Bernardino.

COMMUNITY FACILITIES AND SERVICES
The San Manuel Band has a computer learning center and a training library available to tribal members and employees. In 2003 the tribe opened a four-story community center. The center houses an educational and tutorial center, a basketball court, a fitness room, administrative offices, and tribal council chambers. A recreational park was opened across from the center in 2004. It offers tennis and basketball courts and barbeque and picnic areas.

Education. Tribal members attend local schools and universities. In 2004 the tribe donated a large sum of money to the UCLA Law School, and it is working with the university to establish a tribal learning and educational exchange center. The new center will offer courses on California Native issues, and will provide internships with tribes for UCLA students. Local colleges include California State University San Bernardino, University of California at Riverside, Redlands University, Crafton Hills College, San Bernardino Valley College, and Riverside Community College.

The tribe hosts an annual Native American Conference for school children and educators at California State University in San Bernardino. The tribe has also produced documentaries about the tribe for ICTN, the Cal State television station, and KVCR public television.

Health Care. Riverside-San Bernardino Indian Health serves the San Manuel Band. Tribal members visit the San Manuel Health Care Center for a range of affordable quality health-care services, including medical, dental, eye care, mental health, chemical dependency, pharmacy, complex laboratory, commodities, senior nutrition, Meals on Wheels, and an outreach program that offers transportation.

ENVIRONMENTAL CONCERNS
The San Manuel Band is primarily concerned with protecting and preserving tribal lands and their natural resources. The wildfires in October 2003 caused the loss of 98 percent of the vegetation on the San Manuel Reservation and left the reservation and its natural resources in an extremely vulnerable state. While the San Manuel Band worked hard to mitigate these damages, the wildfires underscored the fact that the San Manuel Reservation was, and still is, in imminent danger from wildfires, and the ensuing flooding and mudslides that these wildfires create. In December 2003, this threat was realized when heavy rains caused flooding and a release of massive debris on federal land just two miles from the reservation.

These two tragedies raised serious concerns for the tribe regarding the state of the reservation and the management of surrounding lands which are under the control of the U.S. Forest Service and the U.S. Bureau of Land Management. It has brought attention to the question of who is responsible for clearing these lands from the brush and debris that create a potential for future wildfires and flooding. The tribe is working with legislators to address these concerns and implement measures to prevent future tragedies of this nature.

San Manuel

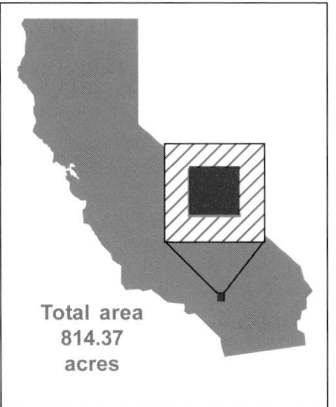

Total area
814.37
acres

San Pasqual

San Pasqual Reservation
Federal reservation
Kumeyaay
San Diego County, California

San Pasqual Band of
Diegueño Indians
P.O. Box 365
Valley Center, CA 92082-0365
760-749-3200
760-749-3876 Fax
sanpasqualindians.org

Total area *(BIA realty, 2003)*
1,379.58 acres

Tribally owned lands
(BIA realty, 2003)
1,379.58 acres

Population *2000 census*
487

Population
(Tribal source, 2004)
752

Tribal enrollment
(BIA labor report 2001)
529

Tribal enrollment
(Tribal source, 2004)
305

Total labor force *2000 census*
291

Total labor force
(BIA labor report 2001)
505

High school graduate or higher
2000 census
58.3%

Bachelor's degree or higher
2000 census
6.5%

Unemployment rate
2000 census
19.2%

Unemployment rate
(BIA labor report 2001)
39%

Per capita income *2000 census*
$9,237.00

LOCATION AND LAND STATUS

The current San Pasqual Reservation is comprised of five separate, noncontiguous tracts of dry, scrub-oak hill country in southern California. It adjoins the rural community of Valley Center approximately 40 miles north of San Diego, 12 miles from Escondido, and 25 miles inland from the Pacific Ocean. The original reservation was established July 1, 1910, under authority of an Act of January 12, 1891, as amended and supplemented. An Executive Order issued on April 15, 1911, set aside land for the reservation site, with an annex in 1972.

CULTURE AND HISTORY

Residents of the San Pasqual Reservation are members of the Kumeyaay Tribe. Their language belongs to the Yuman branch of the Hokan language family, other languages that are spoken by peoples from southern Oregon to southern Mexico. In 1769 Kumeyaay territory extended 50 to 75 miles both north and south of the Mexican border and from the California coast east nearly to the Colorado River. Prior to European contact, the tribe was divided into as many as 50 bands, but two tribal chiefs served to maintain cohesive intertribal relations.

Prior to 1870, the southern and interior Kumeyaays largely avoided repression by the mission at San Diego, even leading occasional revolts to free relatives who were in forced labor there. Only after 1870 was their land taken from them, as American immigrants moved into the area. Northern and coastal Kumeyaays, on the other hand, had early contact with the missions, thereby falling under Spanish domination. After their initial contact with Americans in 1846, they learned English as well as Spanish. These bands received reservations by Executive Order in 1875, and Indian agency schools were operating there shortly after. The 1891 Act for the Relief of Mission Indians set up 11 additional reservations, which proved to be pitifully small and inadequate, leaving many Kumeyaays without a home.

In 1901 the U.S. Supreme Court failed to uphold Indian land-rights treaties that had been established with the Mexican government in territory that was now part of the United States. As a result, the indigenous people were evicted. In 1903 the government purchased land at Pala and moved some of the Kumeyaays there (the San Felipe and Cupeno bands), while others fled elsewhere. In any event, the Kumeyaays largely starved on inadequate reservations or found menial labor on area ranches or in local homes. It was in 1910 that bad publicity finally forced the Indian Office (later to become the BIA) to enlarge certain reservations and establish some new ones, including the San Pasqual Reservation; conditions did improve marginally.

While most Kumeyaay reservations contained subsistence farms, marginal cash-cropping operations, and a few domestic animals, many were far from markets and had water routinely stolen or diverted. Additionally, non-Indian settlers staked claim to all the best farmland, most of it river-bottom land, in the area, leaving only the high rocky hills to the Indians. During the early twentieth century, organizations were established to oppose the BIA's authority. Then in 1953, PL-280 stripped the BIA of much of its authority, establishing it as merely the keeper of the reservation land's trust status. The vacuum created by PL-280 forced tribal leaders to face up to continuing problems in the areas of sovereignty, economics, education, and health. One result is that the Kumeyaays have revived the tribal-level organization, as it originally functioned, to manage tribal sacred places, focus on religious and cultural needs, and protect ancestral places. *(For additional cultural information, see California introduction.)*

GOVERNMENT

The San Pasqual Tribal Government operates under a constitution and bylaws approved January 14, 1971. The tribe is organized under the Indian Reorganization Act of 1934. The general council consists of all members 19 years of age and older; members elect a business committee which serves two-year terms and is comprised of a spokesman, a vice-spokesman, a secretary-treasurer, and two at-large members.

Tribal offices include housing and community development, fire, environment, community water, education, gaming, TERO, and finance. The housing and community development program provides a housing magistrate to rule on housing issues. It also offers the One Stop Mortgage Center which provides home buyer counseling, loan guarantee assistance, credit improvement, and real estate related services to tribal and nontribal members. The tribe is in the process of developing a tribal court system.

The tribe also participates in the Southern California Tribal Chairmen's Association, San Luis Rey Tribal Water Authority, Reservation Transportation Authority, All Mission Indian Housing Authority, Native American Environmental Protection Coalition, and Indian Health Council.

ECONOMY

The region's economy has been based largely on ranching and increasingly on agriculture, as irrigation techniques have improved. The seemingly endless southern California urban sprawl has stimulated real estate development, construction, and a burgeoning service industry. Gaming has bolstered the tribe's economy.

Economic Development Projects. The tribe's Economic Development Agency (EDA) is responsible for planning, implementing, and evaluating all development projects as approved by the general council. The EDA's board oversees the completion of projects. Over the next several years, the tribe hopes to develop a smoke shop, a convenience store and gas station, storage facilities, rental housing, fairgrounds, a hotel resort and golf course, a campground and equestrian park, and an outlet center and shopping mall.

Gaming. The Valley View Casino is the tribe's 40,900-square-foot gaming facility. The complex houses 1,350 slot machines, 12 table games, and 2 restaurants, and it has 1,100 parking spaces. The Valley View Casino provides employment for approximately 525 people. It is currently housed at a temporary site. A permanent site has been identified on 533 acres of land overlooking Lake Wohlford and southern California coastal areas.

Services and Retail. Several small businesses in the vicinity of the reservation provide employment opportunities for residents.

Media and Communications. The tribe owns a cellular communications tower. The tribe plans to lease the tower to cellular telephone providers. The casino publishes a newsletter.

Tourism and Recreation. The Bates Nut Farm, San Diego Wild Animal Park, and the Palomar Observatory are all located near the reservation.

INFRASTRUCTURE

California Highway S-6 links the reservation with Escondido from the south and continues to the north to connect with California 76. Old Castle Road and West Lilac Road provide access to the town of Valley Center from Interstate 15.

The tribe has an agreement with the Operating Engineers Training Trust of Southern California. Through this agreement, the Trust can conduct training operations on tribal lands, and the tribe receives grading, excavation, construction, and demolition services at little or no cost.

Electricity. San Diego Gas and Electric Company supplies the reservation's electricity.

Fuel. Various propane companies deliver fuel to the reservation. A natural gas line will be constructed near the reservation along Woods Valley Road within the next several years.

Water Supply. Two community domestic water systems and the Valley Center Municipal Water District serve the reservation. A wastewater treatment plant serves the casino. Sites for future sewage treatment facilities have been identified on tribal lands. The tribe's environmental program is planning to develop a waste transfer station and a recycling collection program.

Transportation. Commercial airline service is available in San Diego, 40 miles away. Nearby Escondido provides train, bus, and commercial trucking services.

Telecommunications. Television, cable, telephone, and Internet services are all available on the reservation.

COMMUNITY FACILITIES AND SERVICES
The reservation has a tribal hall which serves as the center of the tribe's community activities. Built in 1999, it is a 3,500-square-foot facility. The tribe also maintains an elders' center.

Education. Elementary and secondary students attend schools in Valley Center. The reservation maintains an education resource center, and the tribe operates a Head Start program. Palomar Community College is located in San Marcos, approximately 15 miles west of the reservation.

Health Care. The Indian Health Council serves the San Pasqual Reservation. Basic health and dental services can be obtained at the Valley Center Clinic, located on the Rincon Reservation. For health and dental needs not met by Valley Center, tribal members visit Palomar Hospital in Escondido.

ENVIRONMENTAL CONCERNS
A number of concerns have been raised as a result of the 2003 wildfires that destroyed 95 percent of tribal lands, including 30 percent of the homes located on the reservation. The presence of debris and the threat of flash flooding are major concerns. The tribe is also concerned with the cleanup of former dumpsites on tribal lands.

San Pasqual

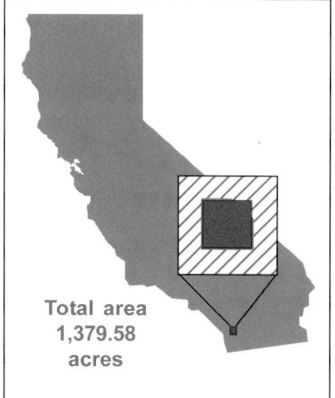

Total area
1,379.58
acres

Santa Rosa

Santa Rosa

Total area *(BIA realty, 2003)*	587.98 acres
Tribally owned	587.98 acres
(BIA realty, 2003)	
Population *2000 census*	517
Tribal enrollment *(BIA labor report, 2001)*	183
Total labor force *2000 census*	112
Total labor force *(BIA labor report, 2001)*	112
High school graduate or higher	48.1%
2000 census	
Bachelor's degree or higher *2000 census*	0%
Unemployment rate *2000 census*	25.9%
Unemployment rate	8.8%
(BIA labor report, 2001)	
Per capita income *2000 census*	$13,882.00

LOCATION AND LAND STATUS
The Santa Rosa Rancheria is located in south-central California, in the Tulare Lake Basin of the San Joaquin Valley just outside of Lemoore, 30 miles east of Visalia, and about halfway between Fresno and Bakersfield. U.S. District Court Decree 995 established the Rancheria on February 28, 1921. An additional purchase was finalized on July 28, 1938, under the Wheeler Howard Act of June 18, 1934.

CLIMATE
Summer temperatures may reach highs of 110°F, and winters may see lows of 20°F. Rainfall averages eight inches per year.

CULTURE AND HISTORY
The descendants of the Tachi, Wowol, and Chunut bands of the Yokuts Tribe presently live on the Santa Rosa Rancheria. Their traditional language belongs to the Penutian linguistic stock, which includes languages spoken by peoples from the Canadian coast to the Yucatan Peninsula, as well as in the southeastern U.S. Out of what was once approximately 60 Yokuts tribes, only a few still remain. The introduction of European culture and its attendant diseases and warfare is thought to have decreased the estimated aboriginal population by at least 75 percent. There are only three federally recognized rancherias and one reservation comprised of Yokuts descendants.

Following the General Allotment Act of 1887, many Yokuts people were displaced from their traditional tribal lands. Primary sources of employment for many Yokuts during this period and on into the early twentieth century included logging, working for livestock ranchers as ranch hands, and working as farm laborers in the fruit, vegetable, and cotton fields of the San Joaquin Valley.

Until the 1950s, many Yokuts children were sent to Indian boarding schools. During the 1960s, political activism took hold within the greater Native American community. One prominent manifestation of this activism was the Sierra Indian Center. It involved people from many area tribes and was pivotal in establishing other organizations, both local and statewide, which still exist today. The Sierra Indian Center's agenda, in part, involved revitalizing cultural practices. This mission stemmed from a recognition that adaptation to Euro-American culture and the intrusion of non-Indian schools and religion had altered or reduced many aspects of indigenous culture.

The March 1 Celebration stands as one example of continuing traditional cultural practices; it constitutes the Santa Rosa Rancheria's main tribal activity. It is a time that is dedicated to spiritual renewal and future prosperity. One of the Celebration's key events is the Roundhouse Sweat Ceremonies. Other rancheria cultural projects include a community dance group, composed of young people 8 to 16 years of age, which performs at schools and powwows. *(For additional cultural information, see California introduction.)*

GOVERNMENT
A general council composed of all tribal members 21 years or older governs the Santa Rosa Rancheria; 25 percent of the membership represents a quorum. A business committee is elected from the general council which includes a chairperson, vice-chairperson, secretary, treasurer, and a delegate. Business com

**Santa Rosa Rancheria
Federal reservation
Tache, Tachi, and Yokuts
Kings County, California**

Santa Rosa Indian Community
P.O. Box 8
Lemoore, CA 93245
559-924-1278
559-924-3583 Fax
tachi-yokut.com

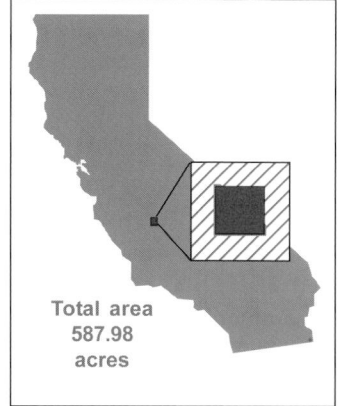

Total area
587.98
acres

Santa Rosa

mittee members are elected for two-year terms. The tribe is organized under approved Articles of Association.

ECONOMY
While many tribal members find employment in surrounding cities, tribal government, a small retail operation, and class I and class II gaming all contribute to the tribe's economy.

Gaming. The Santa Rosa Tribe operates a bingo parlor that features class I and class II bingo and pull-tabs. Revenues are low due to competitors in the area that feature class III gaming devices and card games.

Services and Retail. The rancheria operates a smoke shop that sells Indian jewelry and toys in addition to standard convenience-store goods.

Tourism and Recreation. The tribe welcomes visitors to its annual Santa Rosa Days Celebration on the last weekend of August. The celebration features Native food, song, and dance.

INFRASTRUCTURE
Access routes to the rancheria include Alkali Drive, which is paved, and State Highway 198, which runs five miles from the rancheria. California 41 runs north-south three miles away, and Interstate 5, one of the valley's major arteries, can be reached approximately 20 miles from the rancheria. The city of Visalia, 30 miles from the reservation, has commercial airline facilities. Train services are available in Hanford, 14 miles from the reservation. The town of Lemoore provides truck and bus services and also maintains a private airport.

Electricity. Pacific Gas and Electric Company provides electricity to the reservation.

Fuel. Southern California Gas Company provides natural gas.

Water Supply. Wells provide tribal members with their water supply. The tribe maintains its own sewer system, which is operated by a wastewater treatment specialist who is a tribal member.

COMMUNITY FACILITIES AND SERVICES
The rancheria has a recreation center that is used for various youth activities, a summer lunch program, an elders' hot-lunch program, and as a summer job site for youths.

Education. Tribal members attend local schools and colleges.

Health Care. The rancheria contracts for health-care services with Central Valley Indian Health Project, 50 miles from the rancheria in Clovis. A small clinic is located on the reservation. Hospital, clinic, and dental facilities are available in Hanford.

Santa Rosa

Santa Rosa Reservation
Federal reservation
Cahuilla
Kings County, California

Santa Rosa Band
of Mission Indians
P.O. Box 390611
Anza, CA 92539
951-658-5311
951-658-6711 Fax

Total area
11,092.60
acres

Total area *(BIA realty, 2003)*		11,092.60 acres
Tribally owned		11,092.60 acres
(BIA realty, 2003)		
Population *2000 Census*		65
Tribal enrollment *(BIA labor report, 2001)*		183
Total labor force *2000 Census*		11
Total labor force *(BIA labor report, 2001)*		11
High school graduate or higher		76%
2000 Census		
Bachelor's degree or higher		8%
2000 Census		
Unemployment rate *2000 Census*		0%
Unemployment rate		0%
(BIA labor report, 2001)		
Per capita income *2000 Census*		$16,122

LOCATION AND LAND STATUS
The Santa Rosa Reservation spans 11,092.60 acres in the Santa Rosa Mountains near Anza in Riverside County, California. Nearby cities include Palm Springs, 50 miles to the northeast, and Riverside, 60 miles to the northwest. While one of California's hottest, driest deserts lies 10 miles to the east, the reservation sits in the 5,000-foot Coachella Valley and hence is occasionally watered by clouds drawn to nearby 8,000-foot Santa Rosa Peak.

The reservation was established on February 2, 1907, under the authority of the Act of 1891 as amended. An Act on April 17, 1937, authorized the secretary of the interior to purchase 640 acres to be held in trust for the tribe. All reservation land is tribally owned and is not allotted, though some of the land is under assignment and has been passed from generation to generation under heirship.

CULTURE AND HISTORY
The Santa Rosa Band of Mission Indians is part of the Cahuilla Tribe, a group belonging to the Takic branch of the Uto-Aztecan linguistic family. The reservation is in an area that has been occupied by the Cahuillas for the past 1,000 years. Members of the Santa Rosa Band descend from the Mountain Cahuilla Band, which historically occupied the mountains south of San Jacinto Peak. Most Cahuillas are members of several reservations in inland southern California, though some live as far away as New York and Florida. The 1891 Act for the Relief of Mission Indians handed over much of the Cahuilla homelands to the public domain. The establishment of reservations during the first part of the twentieth century reclaimed some of these lands for the tribe. None of the reservations formed tribal governments that were organized under the rules of the 1934 IRA. During these years most Cahuillas subsisted on wage labor, farming, and raising stock. They supplemented their income through hunting fees, leasing forests, and selling resources such as peat, asbestos, and rights of way. The lack of water proved to be a major challenge, particularly for farming and grazing efforts. In response, the BIA installed irrigation projects on some of the Cahuilla reservations; unfortunately these systems were rarely dependable.

GOVERNMENT
The tribe is governed by a tribal council whose members are elected to two-year terms. Because of the very limited size of the Santa Rosa Band, the tribal council also acts as the planning committee.

ECONOMY
Many Cahuillas have developed professional careers in communities adjacent to their reservations. These positions include administrators, educators, museum curators, archaeologists, musicians, artists, and entrepreneurs. Commercial and tourist developments, bingo parlors, and leasing land for grazing and farming, comprise the primary sources of reservation income.

Government as Employer. The tribal government is a major source of revenue and employment for the tribe. BIA grants are an additional source of tribal funds.

Economic Development Projects. The tribe owns a parcel of land adjacent to Highway 79 that is a prime area for developing a campground or other type of tourist attraction. Development is still in the planning stage. The tribal council is also studying the feasibility of tribal enterprises based on cattle production and/or farming.

Agriculture and Livestock. Individual tribal members engage in farming and cattle-grazing activities. Potatoes and small grains serve as the region's primary crops. The tribe operates a small fruit orchard on reservation lands.

Forestry. Small amounts of timber can be found on 8,700-foot Toro Peak, located on the reservation. At present, this is not considered commercially viable.

Manufacturing. In recent times, nearby Hemet has seen growth in manufacturing and the reservation has benefited from this growth through occasional employment opportunities.

Media and Communications. The most significant tribal business revenues result from leasing sites atop Toro Peak for telecommunications relay stations. The tribe plans to expand leasing opportunities as growth in the telecommunications industry fuels demand for optimal relay and transmission sites.

Santa Ynez

LOCATION AND LAND STATUS

The Santa Ynez Reservation is located in south-central California, approximately 32 miles north of Santa Barbara and about 10 miles from the Pacific Ocean. The reservation was established on December 27, 1901, under authority of the act of January 12, 1891.

In 2004, 11.5 of 23.38 acres of land purchased by the tribe were placed in trust status. The parcel is located along a steep hillside. It unites the upper and lower portions of the reservation. The tribe has no plans to develop the area. The remaining nine acres border the reservation along Highway 246.

CLIMATE

High temperatures during July average 85°F, with overnight lows of 55. In January, highs average 55, with lows dipping down to 35. Average annual rainfall is about 13 inches.

CULTURE AND HISTORY

The residents of Santa Ynez Reservation are members of the Chumash Tribe whose language belongs to the Hokan language family. Other languages of the group are spoken by peoples from southern Oregon to southern Mexico. At the time of first Spanish contact in 1542, the Chumash were one of the most populous and highly developed of the California tribes; they occupied territory from San Luis Obispo to Malibu Canyon on the coast, the Santa Barbara Channel Islands, and inland to the western edge of the San Joaquin Valley.

The Chumash were the only California tribe to depend largely on ocean fishing for subsistence and, in fact, the tribe is known for its technological skill in the construction of ocean-going canoes. It is also known for its aesthetic contributions in the form of basketry and objects of shell and steatite.

In 1769 a Spanish land expedition led by Gaspar de Portola left Baja California and reached the Santa Barbara Channel. In short order five Spanish missions were established in Chumash territory, one-quarter of the number eventually established in all of California. Chumash population was decimated, largely due to the introduction of European diseases. By 1831 the number of mission-registered Chumash numbered only 2,788, down from pre-Spanish population estimates ranging as high as 22,000.

The modern-day towns of Santa Barbara, Montecito, Summerland, and Carpinteria were carved out of the old Chumash territory. The nucleus of the town of Santa Barbara began with Spanish soldiers who were granted small parcels of land by their commandant upon retiring from military service. After mission secularization in 1834, lands formerly under mission control were given to Spanish families loyal to the Mexican government, while other large tracts were sold or given to prominent individuals as land grants. With the Mexican authorities' failure to live up to promises of land distribution among surviving Chumash, the population continued to decline, both physically and spiritually.

By 1870 the region's now-dominant Anglo culture had begun to prosper economically. The Santa Barbara area had established itself as a mecca for health seekers, and by the turn of the century it became a haven for wealthy tourists and movie stars. By around 1880, the region had begun to establish itself as an important hub of agriculture and horticulture; most of the Chumash who remained in the area survived through menial work on area farms and ranches. During the 1890s Summerland experienced an oil and natural-gas boom adjacent to Highway 246 (a major tourist passage to and from Solvang).

The tribe struggled to establish a stable economy throughout the nineteenth century and most of the twentieth century as well. The development of its gaming operations in 1994 has become an abundant source of income that has enabled the tribe to begin to develop a stable economy and to provide tribal services and programs that it had previously been financially unable to provide. The most notable improvements on the reservation have been to tribal housing, educational programs, and cultural retention activities.

GOVERNMENT

A general council composed of all members 21 years old and older governs the Santa Ynez Reservation. Elected tribal officers constitute the business committee and include a chairperson, a vice-chairperson, and a secretary-treasurer. The tribal government is organized under the Indian Reorganization Act of 1934, with Articles of Association approved on February 7, 1964.

Tribal government departments and programs include education and environment. The tribe also maintains an elders council. The elders council is comprised of tribal members over the age of 50. The elders council is governed by a board of seven members and is responsible for the protection and preservation of cultural resources. Activities of the council include oversight of repatriation matters, monitoring of dig sites, developing relationships with outside agencies, entities, tribes, societies, and museums, and creating strong relationships with tribal youth. The elders council also provides employment opportunities for monitors.

Santa Ynez Reservation
Federal reservation
Chumash
Santa Barbara County,
California

Santa Ynez Band of Chumash
    Mission Indians
P.O. Box 517
Santa Ynez, CA 93460
805-688-7997
805-686-9678 Fax
santaynezchumash.org

Total area *(BIA realty, 2003)*
126.63 acres

Total area *(Tribal source)*
137 acres

Tribally owned *(BIA realty, 2003)*
126.63 acres

Population *2000 census*
122

Population *(Tribal source, 2004)*
283

Tribal enrollment
(BIA labor report, 2001)
159

Tribal enrollment
(Tribal source, 2004)
156

Total labor force *2000 census*
34

Santa Ynez

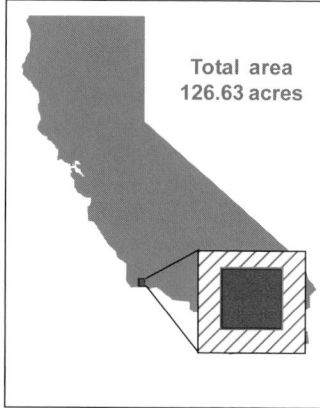

Total area
126.63 acres

Total labor force
(BIA labor report, 2001)
204

High school graduate or higher
2000 census
71.6%

Bachelor's degree or higher
2000 census
10.4%

Unemployment rate
2000 census
14.7%

Unemployment rate
(BIA labor report, 2001)
45%

Per capita income *2000 census*
$20,982

BUSINESS CORPORATIONS

The Santa Ynez Gaming Commission is a separate branch of the tribal government. It is overseen by a board of gaming commissioners. The commission is responsible for the development and operation of the tribe's gaming operations.

ECONOMY

The tribal economy is supported in large part by its gaming operations. The casino attracts approximately 6,000 visitors each day. The tribe has made the commitment to work together with surrounding towns to build a stronger local economy and community. The tribe intentionally patronizes local businesses and vendors in order to promote growth and stability in the local economy. In 2003 the casino payroll exceeded $24 million. The tribe paid over $2 million in payroll taxes and $3 million in benefits. It also paid $24 million to casino suppliers, 75 percent of whom are local vendors. The tribe itself is one of the largest employers in the county.

Government as Employer. The Santa Ynez Band is the largest employer in the Santa Ynez Valley. The casino and resort offer over 900 employment opportunities.

Gaming. The tribe owns the Chumash Casino Resort. It is a major employer in the Santa Ynez Valley and employs over 1,000 residents in Santa Barbara County. With revenues earned by the casino, the tribe has contributed over $5.5 million to the county. It has provided $1.5 million to fund a fire fighter/paramedic position in the Santa Barbara County Fire Department, $36,000 to purchase a search and rescue vehicle for the Santa Barbara County Sheriff's Department, $160,000 to purchase forensic equipment for various law enforcement agencies in the county, $2 million to fund road and infrastructure improvements to Highway 246 in Santa Ynez Valley, and millions of dollars to fund projects in the local schools and nonprofit organizations. The Santa Ynez casino is the only Native American-owned or Native Americcan-operated casino within a 150-mile radius.

The Chumash Casino Resort is located on the lower reservation. The casino offers 2,000 slot machines, 40 table games, a bingo hall, a gift shop, and five dining venues. Facilities include a five-level parking garage. Shuttle services are available from Santa Barbara, Lompoc, and Santa Maria for casino guests. The Chumash Casino Resort employs over 1,000 people.

A four-diamond rated, 106-room hotel was completed adjacent to the casino in Summer 2004. It offers a 5,000-square-foot full-service spa; luxury suites which feature balconies, whirlpools, and some fireplaces; a conference center; a hair salon; and a fitness center. The hotel offers full and part-time employment.

Tourism and Recreation. The tribe sponsors an annual pow-wow at the Live Oak Campground in Santa Ynez. It is a competitive powwow and attracts dance and drum competitors as well as food and craft vendors. Because of its proximity to Santa Barbara, the reservation is in a good position to capitalize on that city's well-established tourist trade.

INFRASTRUCTURE

California State Route 246 provides essentially all access to the reservation. The reservation lies adjacent to State Highway 246 and it is intersected by Zanja De Cota Creek. The reservation also contains individual driveways and roads as necessary for access to certain precincts and neighborhoods.

Electricity. Electricity is provided by the Pacific Gas and Electric Company.

Water Supply. The reservation obtains its water from a well provided by the Santa Ynez River Water Conservation Improvement District No. 1.

Transportation. Commercial transportation facilities are available in Santa Barbara. The nearest private airport is located in Santa Ynez, six miles from the reservation. U.S. Highway 101, the major north-south artery, is also six miles from the reservation.

COMMUNITY FACILITIES AND SERVICES

The tribe's education department provides recreational programs and events for tribal members. Programs include basketball, wrestling, horseback riding, whale watching, and organized field trips. It also coordinates monthly movie nights that feature films with Native American themes. In 2003 the department offered a summer program called "It Takes a Child to Build a Village" based upon the University of California at Santa Barbara (UCSB) program "Kids in Nature." In partnership with the UCSB, the tribe offered a six-week program that integrated tribal culture and environmental science. Activities included trips to UCSB touch tanks, Hollister Ranch tide pools, Knapp Painted Caves, and a jet-boat ride.

Education. Students attend school in the city of Santa Ynez. The tribe provides scholarships to tribal members participating in any post-secondary program. The scholarship provides assistance for tuition, books, supplies, housing, transportation, and other expenses related to obtaining a higher education. The tribe's education department offers an academic tutoring and mentoring program, vocational training programs, and a computer lab. In partnership with Allan Hancock College, the tribe offers ABE and GED programs. The tribe offers the Chumash Language Program, that provides instruction to tribal members in Chumash Inezeño.

Health Care. The Santa Ynez Tribal Health Clinic is a private, tribally governed facility that serves Native and non-Native clients. In 2002 the tribe constructed a new facility, doubling the amount of space available for programs. Services include medical, dental, mental health, and nursing programs. The clinic provides transportation services for clients. Hospital, clinic, dental, and U.S. Public Health Service facilities are also available in Santa Barbara.

ENVIRONMENTAL CONCERNS

The Santa Ynez Chumash Environmental Office was established in 1998. It oversees Emergency Management, Natural Resource Protection, Solid Waste Management, Tribal Land Use Enforcements, and Water Resource Protection programs.

Santa Ysabel

Total area *(BIA realty, 2003)*	15,526.78 acres	
Tribally owned	15,526.78 acres	
(BIA realty, 2003)		
Population *2000 census*		250
Population *(Tribal source)*		668
Tribal enrollment		936
(BIA labor report, 2001)		
Total labor force *2000 census*		82
Total labor force		439
(BIA labor report, 2001)		
High school graduate or higher		70.9%
2000 census		
Bachelor's degree or higher		3.4%
2000 census		
Unemployment rate *2000 census*		14.6%
Unemployment rate		84%
(BIA labor report, 2001)		
Per capita income *2000 census*		$14,332

LOCATION AND LAND STATUS

The Santa Ysabel Reservation is located about 40 miles east of Escondido, on Highway 76, south of Los Coyotes Reservation.

PHYSICAL DESCRIPTION

Santa Ysabel is situated on the slopes of the Volcan Mountains, at nearly 4,500 feet. The rugged, wooded area provides a sense of solitude for the reservation's residents.

CULTURE AND HISTORY

The Santa Ysabel Band is part of the Kumeyaay Nation, which extends from San Diego and Imperial counties in California to 60 miles south of the Mexican border. The Kumeyaays are members of the Yuman language branch of the Hokan group. Included with the Kumeyaays in the Yuman branch are the PaiPais, Kiliwas, Cocopas, Mojaves, Maricopas, Quechans, Yavapais, Havasupais, and Hualapais. The Hokan language group is wide ranging, covering most of the coastal lands of southern California. It includes tribes as far north as the Kuroks of Northern California.

The Kumeyaay language used to be called Diegueño because it was the language of the people in the neighborhood of Mission San Diego de Alcala. Kumeyaay consists of three very closely related languages–Iipai, Kumeyaay, and Tiipai–spoken in a great variety of dialects. Speakers of these languages understand each other without too much difficulty, but there are important differences between them. The term "Kumeyaay" (Diegueño) is used for the whole group of three languages. The Kumeyaay language has survived to this day and is mostly spoken by elders. Serious efforts are being made to teach the language to younger people. All speakers of Kumeyaay are fluent in either English, Spanish, or sometimes other American Indian language.

GOVERNMENT

The tribe is governed by a council comprised of a tribal spokesman, a vice-spokesman, a secretary, a treasurer, a councilman, and a councilwoman. The tribe is in the process of developing a tribal court system. Its police department currently shares cross-jurisdiction with the county's law enforcement officers.

ECONOMY

The Santa Ysabel Band is committed to economic growth and the overall economic well-being of its tribal members. The tribe provides scholarships for higher education and it is poised to secure future economic opportunities and success through gaming and the industries that support it.

Government as Employer. The Santa Ysabel Band employs 668 individuals throughout its tribal government and enterprises.

Economic Development Projects. The tribe is developing a gaming facility on the reservation, slated to open for operations in one to two years.

Forestry. The tribe provides local woodcutting services.

Gaming. In 2003 the tribe secured a gaming compact wit the State of California. It is now developing a mountaintop casino. The project is leading the second wave of smaller, more modest casinos expected to emerge in San Diego County. The 70,000-square-foot casino will be on Volcan Mountain overlooking Lake Henshaw. With no more than 349 slot machines, the tribe will continue to receive shared revenue from the larger casinos. The casino is expected to open for operations in one to two years. Majestic Gaming, a management team based in Arizona, will plan, finance, and operate the facility. The tribe has hired a Phoenix-based architect to design the facility.

Media and Communications. The tribe publishes the monthly *Santa Ysabel Newsletter.*

Tourism and Recreation. The reservation is home to the old Santa Ysabel Indian Mission, which was founded in 1818. The mission is still active and holds an annual Feast Day on November 14.

INFRASTRUCTURE

The Santa Ysabel Reservation is located off Highway 76 and is bisected by State Route 79. Commercial airline service is available in San Diego.

Electricity. San Diego Gas and Electric provides electricity and fuel.

Water Supply. A tribal well serves as the water source for the reservation.

Santa Ysabel Reservation
Federal reservation
Diegueño
San Diego County, California

Santa Ysabel Band of Diegueño Indians
P.O. Box 130
Santa Ysabel, CA 92070
760-765-0845
760-765-0320 Fax

TRI-CA-SY-022 Sign for the Indian Health Council, Inc.

TRI-CA-SY-023 Santa Ysabel Youth Complex

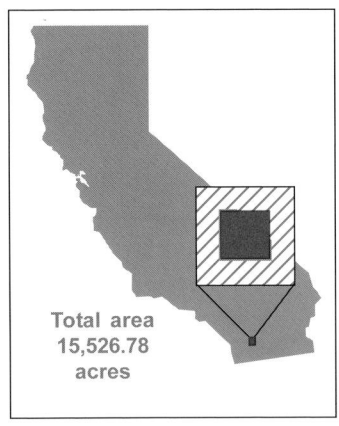

Total area
15,526.78
acres

TRI-CA-SY-022

TRI-CA-SY-023

Santa Ysabel

Transportation. Train, bus, and private airport services can be found in Escondido. Commercial trucking services are available in San Diego and Escondido.

COMMUNITY FACILITIES AND SERVICES

The tribe maintains a gym utilized by the youth program. The reservation also has a library called The El Ch' Qua-Nun Community Library. The library was established in January 1990, and it has a collection of approximately 2,500 titles. The tribe is applying for grants to further their library's collection and services. The library also sponsors a youth program for tribal youth.

Education. The tribe operates a Head Start program. It also provides a computer lab and a language class for tribal members. The Santa Ysabel Band is pushing hard to become one of the best-educated tribes in San Diego County. The tribe obtained federal grants in order to provide scholarships for tribal members who wish to attend trade schools, colleges, and universities including: University of Southern California, University of San Diego, University of California campuses at Irvine and Riverside, and California Polytechnic University Pomona.

Health Care. The Indian Health Council provides general health, dental, and community outreach services at the local clinic.

ENVIRONMENTAL CONCERNS

A primary concern to the tribe is the infestation of beetles in the surrounding forests. The beetles are rapidly destroying the trees.

Scotts Valley

Scotts Valley Band of Pomo Indians of the Sugar Bowl Rancheria
Federal reservation
Pomo and Wailaki
Lake County, California

Scotts Valley Band of Pomo
Indians of the Sugar Bowl
Rancheria
9700 Soda Bay Road
Kelseyville, CA 95451
707-277-8870
888-OKPOMO1
707-277-8874 Fax
svpomo.org

Total area *(BIA realty, 2003)*		.79 acres
Individually owned *(BIA realty, 2003)*		.79 acres
Tribal enrollment *(Tribal source, 2005)*		181
Tribal enrollment		147
(BIA labor report, 2001)		
Total labor force *(BIA labor report, 2001)*		76
Total labor force *(Tribal source, 2005)*		88
Unemployment rate		28%
(BIA labor report, 2001)		

LOCATION AND LAND STATUS

The Sugar Bowl Rancheria was established in 1909 on 56-acres in northern California. When the tribe's federal status was terminated, the land was distributed to individual tribal members. The lands eventually left tribal possession altogether. While federal status has been restored to the tribe, there is currently a very small land base. The tribe has received a number of grants to assist in the purchase of lands and intends to rebuild a tribal community.

CULTURE AND HISTORY

Members of the Scotts Valley Band belong to the Pomo Tribe. The Pomo traditionally occupied vast territories in northern California. Upon the arrival of European explorers, and later Euro-American settlers, the Pomo people were dislocated from their ancestral lands and forced to endure genocidal tactics that, although unsuccessful, did manage to greatly reduce the Pomo population.

In the 1850s, the U.S. government negotiated 18 separate treaties with California Native groups. Congress failed to ratify these treaties, known as the Barbour Treaties, though the Native people were never informed of this. Acting in good faith, the Native groups ceded millions of acres to the state and either confined themselves to small rancherias or were forced to abandon their communities altogether. Many Pomo people lived as squatters or workers at the local missions and ranches. The federal government finally acknowledged the Barbour Treaties in 1905 and appropriated funds to establish rancherias for the Native groups.

The Scotts Valley Tribe received the Sugar Bowl Rancheria, a 56-acre parcel of land, in 1909. The tribe was terminated from federal status under provisions of the California Rancheria Act of 1958, and tribal assets were dissolved. Tribal lands were distributed to individual tribal members, but over the course of time, all lands passed out of the hands of the Pomo tribe. Federal status was restored to the Scotts Valley Band in 1992, but there were no tribal lands to be returned to the tribe. The band has received a number of grants that will assist it in purchasing lands to reestablish a tribal community. A small portion of lands is currently in tribal fee status. The majority of Scotts Valley Pomos currently live in the San Francisco Bay Area or in Lake County and Mendocino County. Many tribal members plan to return to the tribal community once it is established.

In 2003 the tribe began the development of a gaming facility. In partnership with a Florida-based group, it has proposed two sites for the project. Negotiations on the first site fell through, and those on the second are still in progress.

GOVERNMENT

Rancheria members adopted a non-IRA constitution in 1992 and are governed by their seven-member general council. All council members serve four-year terms. The council meets monthly. Governmental programs include the youth activities program, health, environmental protection, and housing.

ECONOMY

Economic development is a difficult process for the Scotts Valley Band. With a very small land base and no central community, the tribe is seeking to purchase lands to establish a rancheria. The majority of tribal members live and work in the San Francisco Bay Area or in Lake and Mendocino Counties. Once a rancheria is re-established, economic viability becomes more certain.

Gaming. In 2003 the tribe proposed to develop a gaming facility at Terminal Three of the Port of Richmond in the San Francisco Bay Area. Negotiations with the City of Richmond stalled and the tribe pursued other options. In 2004 it identified a land parcel in the unincorporated area of North Richmond and has proposed construction of a gaming facility on that land. The tribe will have to enter into a years-long process in order to develop a casino, including placing the land in trust and negotiating a gaming compact with the state.

Tourism and Recreation. Local attractions include Clear Lake State Park and Lake Mendicino. Each offers numerous outdoor recreational opportunities and attracts a number of visitors to the area.

INFRASTRUCTURE

Tribal headquarters are located in Kelseyville, California. In 2001 the tribe began construction on of rental housing units in Kelseyville. The tribe's Environmental Protection Agency installed a new road and electrical system with funds secured from an Indian Community Block Grant (ICDGB). It plans to add four more units by the end of 2005.

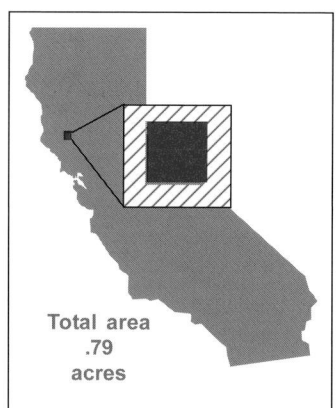

Total area
.79
acres

Transportation. The city of Lake Port has an airport; commercial flights are available in Oakland, 120 miles south of the tribal headquarters.

COMMUNITY FACILITIES AND SERVICES
Child care subsidies are available to families through the Scotts Valley Department of Health and Social Services. The tribe offers youth activities programs, sports and assistance with driver's education costs. The housing program offers rental assistance, emergency housing and repairs, and transitional housing programs funded by the Native American Housing and Self-Determination Act (NAHASDA). It also offers debt counseling and homeowner assistance programs. The tribe also pays all license renewal fees for tribal members working in professions that require licenses.

Education. The tribe provides stipends for books and equipment to members attending local colleges or vocational schools. It also provides graduation incentives to all tribal youth upon graduation from junior high, high school, and college. In addition, the tribe provides matching funds to tribal youth attending non-local schools. The tribe will match the funds provided by a student's family. The BIA provides tribal members with funds for adult education, job training, and scholarships.

Health Care. Health services are available to the Scotts Valley Band through Lake County Tribal Health Consortium located in Lakeport, California. Services include medical, dental, outreach, substance abuse counseling, and podiatry programs. The Scott Valley Health Department provides alcohol and substance abuse counseling, a community health worker, and social service assistance.

ENVIRONMENTAL CONCERNS
Although the current land base of the Scotts Valley Band is very small, the tribe has initiated several programs to ensure the environmental quality of the area. The tribe's environmental protection agency works cooperatively with other tribes in Lake County and the Lake County's board of supervisors. Programs include water resources, solid waste management, invasive weed management, and the tribal GIS database.

Scotts Valley

Sheep Ranch
See California Valley Miwok Tribe

Sherwood Valley

LOCATION AND LAND STATUS
The Sherwood Valley Rancheria is located in northwestern California on two sites near Willits, on U.S. Highway 101. Both of these sites, referred to as the old and new rancheria, have been converted to trust land. The original Sherwood Valley Rancheria was established by Executive Order on April 30, 1908, and purchased on May 10, 1909, for "homeless" California Indians, without tribal designation. Additional lands were purchased on June 10, 1916. The site is located 13 miles northwest of Willits and 150 miles north of San Francisco. The largely deforested rancheria lands range from 2,200 to 2,500 feet in elevation. Most of the county surrounding the original 298-acre rancheria is zoned by Mendocino County as "remote residential" and is characterized by scattered home sites on large parcels of land used primarily for livestock grazing.

Because the original land site is not considered developable due to lack of a sufficient water source and utility hookups, the tribe purchased a 58-acre parcel adjacent to the city of Willits in 1987. In 1988 it received a grant to improve roads and infrastructure needs for this new rancheria. In 1995 the tribe purchased an additional 160.8 acres through a Housing and Urban Development (HUD) Indian Community Development Block Grant (ICDBG) for land acquisition to support housing on the east side of Willits. Northern Circle Indian Housing Authority, as Sherwood Valley's Tribally Designated Housing Authority, will develop 15 housing units with funding from Traditional Indian Housing Development funds. Homes will be constructed in the central portion of the property in a grassy area located east of an existing pond, barn, greenhouse, and other agricultural facilities. The tribe has acquired other lands in the Willits area for housing and economic development. Approximately 75 acres have been purchased from a total of five parcels.

PHYSICAL DESCRIPTION
The new rancheria consists of rolling, undeveloped grasslands that rise westerly to the edge of two east-west ridges. Elevation rises from the eastern boundary of the property at approximately 1,400 to 1,650 feet at the northwestern boundary. Two creeks bisect the property, running downhill from west to east.

CULTURE AND HISTORY
Pomo-speaking people have traditionally occupied what is now Mendocino County, with other Pomos living in Sonoma and Lake Counties. Their language belongs to the Hokan language family, other languages of which are spoken by peoples from southern Oregon into southern Mexico. European settlement of these lands disrupted Pomo culture through the spread of diseases, the usurpation of tribal lands, and forced incarceration on federal reservations. In response, the Pomos banded together in efforts to buy back their lands from the late 1870s through the 1890s. By the beginning of the twentieth century, however, much of this land had been confiscated through foreclosure settlements and mortgage debts.

Responding to public pressure, Congress in 1905 authorized an investigation of the living conditions of "landless" Indians. Beginning in 1906, legislation initiated by C. E. Kelsey, the lawyer and special agent appointed to lead the investigation, authorized annual appropriations for the purchase of Indian lands. Kelsey himself helped in the founding of the Hopland Reservation.

During a period of intense separatism and animosity toward indigenous peoples, the Pomos actively used the courts to challenge local segregationalist policies. In 1907 an Eastern Pomo, Ethan Anderson, won a court case that gave the right to vote to non-reservation Indians. In 1923 Stephan Knight in Mendocino County challenged the state school-segregation laws and, in an out-of-court settlement, forced a local public school to admit his daughter. Knight later took on the City of Ukiah, challenging the separatist policy of the local movie theater.

While traditionally subsisting on native plants, fish, and game, the Pomos were forced to enter the wage economy during the Depression. Many Pomo women moved to the San Francisco Bay area and worked as domestics; there they were aided by the BIA. Pomo men, on the other hand, found local employment as migrant field workers and ranch laborers.

The Sherwood Valley Rancheria's original location and land quality restricted the tribe's ability to develop economically. The

Sherwood Valley Rancheria
Federal reservation
Pomo
Mendocino County, California

Sherwood Valley Rancheria
190 Sherwood Hill Drive
Willits, CA 95490
707-459-9690
707-459-6936 Fax

Total area *(BIA realty, 2003)*
510.45 acres

Tribally owned *(BIA realty, 2003)*
510.45 acres

Population *2000 census*
179

Tribal enrollment
(BIA labor report, 2001)
367

Total labor force *2000 census*
67

High school graduate or higher
2000 census
80.2%

Bachelor's degree or higher
2000 census
10.5%

Unemployment rate *2000 census*
12%

Per capita income *2000 census*
$11,087

Sherwood Valley

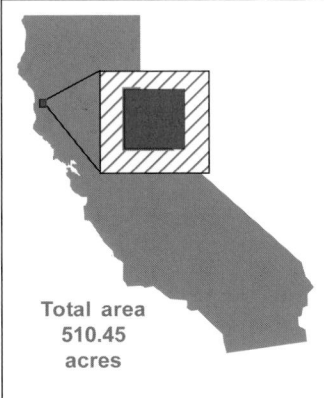

Total area
510.45
acres

group's new location has allowed tribal members to live in a tribal community, many for the first time, within easy commuting distance to a significant downtown area. Because of the new rancheria's small size, the tribe is attempting to purchase more property to enhance its economic potential. *(See California introduction for additional cultural information.)*

GOVERNMENT

The Sherwood Valley Rancheria is governed by a general council composed of all qualified voters at least 18 years old. A seven-member elected tribal council oversees the administration of the rancheria's business. Officers include a chairperson, a vice-chairperson, a secretary, a treasurer, two council members, and a parliamentarian. The general council meets annually in January, while the tribal council holds monthly meetings. The tribe is organized under a constitution that was approved in 1974. The tribal council serves two-year staggered terms, and elections are held annually. The tribal council also serves as the rancheria's economic development policy committee.

Some of the tribal government departments are adult education, water pollution control, public works program, woodland management, general assistance grant, summer food program, and low-income energy assistance.

The Sherwood Valley Rancheria is a member of the Intertribal Court of California (ICC). The ICC was chartered by member tribes to address legal issues that can be best served by a tribal court authorized under collective judicial authorities. The purpose of the court is to hear and settle on-reservation housing disputes and Indian child welfare cases. Mediation and peace-making services also are provided under the authority of the court.

BUSINESS CORPORATION

The tribe established the Economic Development Corporation to pursue economic development, vocational training, and education for the tribe. The Economic Development Corporation's main goal is to encourage outside businesses to engage in commercial activities with the tribe.

ECONOMY

The Sherwood Valley Rancheria is committed to the economic growth of the tribe and to improving the standard of living for all tribal members by providing programs and services addressing needs such as housing and food. Tribal government and gaming are the largest contributors to the tribe's economy, while capitalizing on the area's tourist appeal is under assessment for future economic endeavors of the tribe. The Sherwood Valley Tribe uses its economic success to help others in need, making charitable contributions to such projects as a skate park for youth in Willits and to local departments in surrounding areas including the Willits Fire Department.

According to the 2000 U.S. census, of the 105 people 16 years of age or older living on the rancheria, 67 are in the labor force. Twenty-three of the residents work in management, professional and related occupations; service occupations employ 15 people; and 15 residents are in sales and office occupations. Six residents are employed in construction, extraction, maintenance, production, transportation, and material moving occupations. The reservation has a 7.6 percent unemployment rate, with eight people unemployed.

Government as Employer. Of the 67 people in the labor force, tribal government provides employment for approximately 28 people through its different programs and services.

Economic Development Projects. The tribe established a separate Economic Development Corporation to encourage outside businesses to engage in commercial activities with the tribe. One

of the corporation's goals is to pursue economic development training and education for tribal members.

Gaming. The Sherwood Valley Band/Pomo Tribe's Black Bart Casino opened in 1996 and is located in Willits. The 5,000-square-foot casino employs 70 people. The casino has 184 slot machines, video lottery tables and one restaurant.

With revenues from its gaming enterprise, the Sherwood Rancheria has made charitable donations to local programs and activities, such as the Skate Park for the youth of Willits, and the Willits Fire Department.

Services and Retail. A tribally owned smoke shop/gift shop is located in Black Bart Casino. The smoke shop sells cigarettes, tobacco, jewelry, and other gift items. In 2004 it became a profitable addition to the tribe's revenues. The revenue is used primarily to help fund community services.

Media and Communications. The tribe has its own monthly publication called the *Sherwood Valley Tribal Environmental Newsletter.*

Tourism and Recreation. Since tourism is an important component of Mendocino County's economy, the tribe is considering ways of capitalizing on this market. Some possibilities are an outdoor amphitheater; a family arcade center (with miniature golf); a campground with a gift shop selling tribally produced crafts and food; and a fitness/wellness center which would include classes, a sweat lodge, the retail sale of traditional medicines, and health products produced from natural herbs.

INFRASTRUCTURE

The new rancheria is located approximately one-half mile from U.S. 101, which serves as the main transportation artery for the area. The new rancheria is also connected to State Highway 20 by a short series of paved residential roads. Sherwood Road, intersecting with Highway 1 outside of Willits, leads to the original rancheria land base. Access to the old rancheria is limited to a 10-mile partially paved road. The tribe is applying for a HUD ICDBG for the construction of the access road, Mitomki Way, which was added to the BIA Indian Reservation Roads System in 2003.

Electricity is used to heat 21.4 percent of the housing units; bottled, tank, or LP gas heats 19 percent of the housing units; and utility gas heats the remaining 16.7 percent. Plumbing facilities are available to 90.5 percent of the homes; 95 percent of households have complete kitchen facilities. Telephone service is available to 78.6 percent of households. There are no public services available at the old rancheria.

Electricity. The old rancheria relies on solar electricity.

Fuel. Rancheria residents used bottled, tank, and/or LP Gas.

Water Supply. Drilled horizontal wells supply the old rancheria's water. Wastewater is disposed of by individual septic tanks. The new rancheria is provided with sewer and water service by the City of Willits.

Transportation. The tribal environmental program provides transportation to assist tribal members with solid waste needs.

COMMUNITY FACILITIES AND SERVICES

The new Sherwood Rancheria is home to the tribe's community center and tribal government headquarters. The community center has helped the development of the tribe by providing services that are accessible to all tribal members.

The Sherwood Valley Food Program, sponsored by the U.S. Department of Agriculture and the Sherwood Valley Rancheria, provides government-issued commodities to eligible low-income Native individuals. This program is located in Willits in a newly renovated 12,000-square-foot metal building. This new facility is handicap accessible and energy efficient, and it helps the tribe to provide better service to more than 3,000 beneficiaries in three northern California counties.

Education. The Sherwood Valley Rancheria is part of the Johnson O'Malley program. Tribal members attend nearby schools and colleges. The tribe hosts after-school environmental conservation and cultural education through environmental activities programs for school-age tribal children. These include a summer program called the Hutton Junior Fisheries Biology Program for grades 10-12 and a hands-on program that teaches children how to restore oak tree orchards back to their original state.

Health Care. Sherwood Valley Rancheria is serviced by the Consolidated Tribal Health Clinic, located in Redwood Valley. Health care services provided by the clinic include general medicine and dental. For services not available at the clinic, tribal members visit health care facilities in Willits.

Housing. A 35-unit housing subdivision was completed in 1993. There are 46 households in Sherwood Valley Rancheria. Family households account for 35 of the 46 households. The average household size is 3.89 with the average family size being 4.29. Forty-nine housing units are located on the rancheria. The tribe has set 160 acres aside for 13 new homes that were slated for construction in 2004.

ENVIRONMENTAL CONCERNS

The Sherwood Valley Rancheria Tribe is very active in its environmental protection and conservation efforts. The tribe has a monthly publication called *The Sherwood Valley Tribal Environmental Newsletter* to help educate and inform tribal members about the state of their environment and what they can do to help preserve and protect it. The newsletter features information from the environmental director, recycling drop-off postings, and news about upcoming environmental programs and events.

A new grant will help the tribe to evaluate any pollutants that might be entering the community water system on the original rancheria. The grant by Source Water Assessment and Protection through the U.S. Environmental Protection Agency (EPA) was received in 2004. A second grant awarded in 2004 is the Woodland Management Program which allows tribal members on and off the reservation to remove trees for firewood. New trees will be planted to sustain the forest. Two older grants have received additional funding in 2004. The 106 Clean Water Act, Water Pollution Control Program through the EPA will create a water quality monitoring program to test water on federal lands of the rancheria. The environment also will benefit from new funding for the General Assistance Program through the EPA. The program aids the tribe in its environmental efforts through joint efforts with the education department. The program provides after school activities and projects pertaining to recycling, water pollution/conservation, endangered species, and cultural education through environmental activities. The tribe also has an agreement with the Willits Solid Waste Department to address sold waste disposal and recycling.

Shingle Springs

Total area *(BIA realty, 2003)*		160 acres
Tribally owned *(BIA realty, 2003)*		160 acres
Population *2000 census*		52
Tribal enrollment *(BIA labor report, 2001)*		310
Total labor force *2000 census*		25
Total labor force *(BIA labor report, 2001)*		169
High school graduate or higher		39.1%
2000 census		
Bachelor's degree or higher *2000 census*		0%
Unemployment rate *2000 census*		20%
Unemployment rate		23%
(BIA labor report, 2001)		
Per capita income *2000 census*		$9,892

LOCATION AND LAND STATUS

The Shingle Springs Rancheria is located in north-central California, 1 mile northeast of Shingle Springs, 6 miles southwest of Placerville, and 35 miles east of Sacramento, in the foothills of the Sierra Nevada.

The rancheria was established on December 16, 1916, under the authority of the Indian Homeless Acts of June 21, 1906, and April 30, 1908. It was created for the Sacramento/Verona Band of Homeless Indians. The original rancheria property of 80 acres was purchased in 1916, with an additional 160 acres purchased in March of 1920 by Executive Order. On July 1966, portions of the rancheria were sold or relinquished by the BIA, in part to accommodate the construction of U.S. Highway 50.

CULTURE AND HISTORY

Members of the Shingle Springs Band belong to the Sierra group of the Miwok Tribe and the Nisenan group of the Maidu Tribe.

Traditional homelands of the Sierra Miwoks encompassed territories in north-central California. The people lived in seasonal camps in the foothills or lowlands during the winter months and in the high Sierra Nevada Mountains in the summer months. The Nisenan people originally occupied territory in north-central California as well.

The town of Shingle Springs, noted for its shingle mill, was established in 1850. The areas surrounding the rancheria were virtually overwhelmed by gold miners during the 1850s when gold was discovered in California at Coloma, just 10 miles north of the rancheria near the center of Nisenan territory. A primary supply store for miners in the area was established about a mile from the present rancheria site in 1857. By 1859 the miners had constructed 5,729 miles of canals, ditches, and flumes throughout the area from the Yuba River to Mariposa. In 1865 a railroad was extended to Shingle Springs from Sacramento, making the town a railroad terminus. The influx of miners to the area devastated Maidu lands and culture.

The Shingle Springs population did not occupy rancheria lands until 1970 because the rancheria lacked the infrastructure necessary for housing developments until that time. The scarcity of water and physical access to the rancheria still constrain significant development.

GOVERNMENT

A seven-member elected tribal council governs the Shingle Springs Rancheria. The council includes a chairperson, a vice-chairperson, and a secretary/treasurer. The council meets monthly, and its members are elected for two- and three-year staggered terms. The tribe is organized under Articles of Association approved in December of 1976.

Shingle Springs Rancheria
Federal reservation
Miwok
El Dorado County, California

Shingle Springs Rancheria
P.O. Box 1340
Shingle Springs, CA 95682
530-676-8010
530-676-8033
shinglespringsrancheria.com

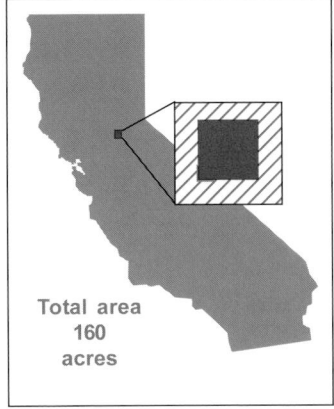

Total area
160
acres

ECONOMY

El Dorado County is part of the Sacramento Standard Metropolitan Statistical Area, one of the highest-valued commercial and residential markets in the United States. The region is known for its executive, high-priced, residential-home developments, and the rancheria is, in fact, located between two such areas. Aside from real-estate development, the area's primary industries include tourism, manufacturing, construction, mining, and agriculture (including apple orchards, wineries, and forests).

Government as Employer. Government-sponsored social service projects, funded through grants from the Administration for Native Americans, the U.S. Indian Health Service, and the Bureau of Indian Affairs Core Management Project provide significant employment and services to the rancheria.

Economic Development Projects. The rancheria has approximately five acres available for commercial development, earmarked for an eldercare facility, in a surrounding area of scarce and extremely expensive private land. Additional goals include the development of a cultural center, a mobile-home/RV park, and a mini-mart and gas station.

Gaming. The tribe has proposed the construction of a gaming facility on tribal lands. If approved, the hotel and casino complex will be a 381,250-square-foot structure that includes a gaming facility, 250-room hotel, and a 5-level parking garage. The complex would be the second largest building in the county, the tallest building in the county, and occupy 29 acres. Projected numbers include 3.7 million annual visitors and $194 million gross per year. The tribe is facing stern opposition in the development of this project from local residents. El Dorado County has filed two separate lawsuits in its attempt to halt the development. One lawsuit challenged the tribe's status as a federally recognized sovereign nation and the other challenged the environmental review of the proposed casino project. The courts have ruled in favor of the tribe on both matters.

Services and Retail. The local service economy provides many low-paying forms of employment for area tribal members.

INFRASTRUCTURE

U.S. Highway 50, an east-west artery, passes just south of the rancheria. Access is possible only by two private roads, owned by the Greenstone and Buckeye homeowners' associations, respectively.

Electricity. Local public utilities companies provide electricity and gas services.

Water Supply. Water is available to the rancheria only under agreement with the El Dorado Irrigation District. The rancheria maintains an on-site sewage disposal system.

COMMUNITY FACILITIES AND SERVICES

Fire protection is provided by a local volunteer fire department.

Health Care. The Shingle Springs Tribal Health Program includes a health clinic located in El Dorado County. Services include comprehensive medical, dental, outreach, chiropractic, behavioral health, orthodontic, and podiatry programs. The clinic will be adding telepsychiatry programs in the near future.

Smith River

Smith River Rancheria
Federal reservation
Tolowa
Curry, Coos, and Josephine counties, Oregon, and Del Norte and Humboldt counties, California

Smith River Rancheria
140 Rowdy Creek Road
Smith River, CA 95567
707-487-9255
707-487-0930 Fax
tolowa-nsn.gov

Total area *(BIA realty, 2003)*
89.17 acres

Total area *(Tribal source, 2004)*
100 acres

Tribally owned lands
(BIA realty, 2003)
39.84 acres

Individually owned lands
(BIA realty, 2003)
49.33 acres

LOCATION AND LAND STATUS

The Smith River Rancheria, the largest in northern California, is located very near the Pacific Ocean in the northwest tip of the state, three miles south of the Oregon border. Approximately 30 acres of land in Del Norte County are held by the tribe, awaiting trust status; however, the federally recognized service area includes Humboldt and Del Norte counties in northern California and Coos, Curry, and Josephine counties of southwestern Oregon, a total of approximately 6,947 square miles. Most tribal population is concentrated in a corridor stretching from Crescent City, California, to Brookings, Oregon. Rancheria property includes the shoreline opposite Prince Island in the Pacific, and the Island itself. The rancheria also encompasses a portion of the lower reaches of Lopez Creek and property along the northern shore of Smith River, near its mouth. In 2004, only 94 enrolled members lived on the reservation.

CLIMATE

The year-round daily high temperatures in Smith River, California, average 61.4°F. The year-round daily low temperatures average almost 46°F. The area receives over 78 inches of precipitation annually, with less than an inch falling as snow. Smith River sits at an elevation of 160 feet above sea level.

CULTURE AND HISTORY

The Deen-ni', or Tolowa, people thrived in the coastal regions of northern California and southwestern Oregon prior to contact with European settlers, with aboriginal territory extending from Wilson Creek in the northwest corner of California to Sixes River near Port Orford, Oregon, inland to the Applegate River. Their language is Athabascan, which is related to the Hupa language in the south. Historically, the Tolowa people resided in permanent plank villages along the Pacific coast in winter, moving inland for salmon, acorns, and other foodstuffs in the late summer. The rancheria is located within the Tolowa aboriginal territory, replete with culturally significant environmental resources, such as rivers, sacred sites and landscapes, and former settlements.

The Tolowas were very nearly completely eradicated by massacres, the Oregon Trail of Tears in the 1850s, the Termination Era of the 1950s, bounties placed upon Indians by the state and county governments, and forced assimilation through boarding schools and relocation. When Congress passed the Termination Act in 1954, federal recognition of the Smith River Rancheria ended and was not subsequently restored until *Tillie Hardwick v. United States* in 1983. Since 1987, when the tribal government was reinstituted, the rancheria has struggled to establish services for its people in the areas of housing, social services, child welfare, education, cultural development, and employment. Nevertheless, tribal government has progressed capably in the area of economic and community development.

GOVERNMENT

After the *Tillie Hardwick v. United States* ruling of December 15, 1983, the tribe was reinstated to federal recognition and adopted a constitution on June 27, 1987. They are a non-IRA tribe, governed by a seven-member tribal council that is composed of a chairperson, a vice-chairperson, a treasurer, a secretary and three members-at-large. The tribe employs a tribal administrator to manage tribal affairs.

The Smith River Rancheria, under PL-638, contracts with the Bureau of Indian Affairs for key programs and services. Governmental departments include a gaming commission, enrollment services, administration, maintenance, housing, forestry, economic development, Indian child welfare and social services, community and family services, environmental programs, election, fiscal and accounting, grants,contracts, and human resources. The tribe participates with the Northwest Inter-Tribal Court Systems wherein a tribal court judge rotates the location of court hearings throughout reservations and rancherias in the region on a weekly basis.

ECONOMY

Historically, the economy of northwest California and the coastal regions of Oregon have been reliant upon fishing, agriculture, timber industries, and tourism and related services. In 2004, the Smith River Rancheria's economy was dependent upon the rich regional tourism industry of northwest California and a small "non-gaming" tribally operated casino, named the Lucky 7, which employs 120 people from throughout the region.

Government as Employer. Via its various economic initiatives and programs, tribal government employed approximately 200 tribal members in May 2004.

Economic Development Projects. The tribe began a long-range planning process in 1996 that resulted in the formulation of Phase 2 of the Smith River Rancheria Master Plan, which helped to: determine the priorities of tribal members, establish a demographic profile of the membership, catalogue the rancheria's infrastructure assets, and identify community needs. Several long-range goals that emerged were to: 1) diversify an economic base, 2) increase on-reservation employment opportunities, 3) increase the land base, 4) develop and maintain a strong physical infrastructure, 5) preserve the tribe's historical and cultural heritage and language, 6) combat high teen pregnancy and single-parent households, and 7) improve the health of tribal members.

In 2004, the tribe had plans to add on to the gas station they already operate and to build an 80-room full-service hotel south of the casino with meeting space for conferences and conventions. They are also seeking additional land acquisitions.

Gaming. The 21,400-square-foot Lucky 7 Casino features 300 slot machines, 3 blackjack tables, and 150 bingo seats. The House of Howonquet, an American-style restaurant, and a bar called the Lounge are also located on the premises. In 2004, the Casino employed 120 people from throughout the region and had significantly contributed to improvements in the regional economy.

Construction. With the boom in economic development projects at the rancheria, an increasing number of tribal members have been employed in construction industries.

Services and Retail. There are a restaurant and bar at the casino, and the tribe operates a gas station and convenience store nearby.

Tourism and Recreation. The Smith River, with no dams from its headwaters to its mouth, is the largest undeveloped wild and scenic river in the continental United States. Famous for salmon and steelhead fishing, the Smith River area abounds in photographic opportunities, such as St. George's Reef and Battery Point Lighthouses. Smith River is also the Easter lily capital of the world. Pristine Pacific Ocean beaches and redwood national and state parks are major attractions. Visitors can access many area boat ramps and have a choice of hiking trails to take them deeper into the natural environment. There are opportunities for fishing, boating, biking, camping, RV camping, golfing, kite flying, crabbing, beach combing, river walks, and bird watching, in addition to the tribally operated Lucky 7 Casino. Also available are the Salmon Run Golf Course in Brookings and the Del Norte Golf Course on Highway 197 near Hiouchi.

Smith River, California, lies within 20 miles of the southern border to the Kalmiopsis Wilderness in Oregon, and within 5 miles of Pelican State Beach, California. The community of Smith River, location of tribal headquarters, is less than 10 miles north of the Jedediah Smith Redwoods State Park in California, along Highway 101.

INFRASTRUCTURE
California Coastal Highway 101 transects the rancheria in a north-south direction near the Pacific Ocean.

Water Supply. Tribally operated water and wastewater treatment facilities along with a water system provide services for the community of Smith River.

COMMUNITY FACILITIES AND SERVICES
The California Rural Indian Health Office operates a Head Start program at the rancheria, in a building the rancheria owns and maintains. The Howonquet Day Care Center serves all tribal children, including those of low-income tribal families and special needs children. A new community building, to be named Howonquet Hall, was completed in 2004. With over 8,000 square feet of space, the building houses the senior nutrition program, with a complete kitchen facility, classrooms, and meeting space. The structure's architectural design maintains the environmental aesthetic of rancheria community members.

Housing. There are six housing units for the elderly and disabled at the rancheria. Most tribal members live on individual allotments or in adjacent communities in nearby counties.

Health Care. Health care for the Tolowas is managed under the United Indian Health Services (UIHS) program, a consortium of 12 tribes. The program serves 12,000 patients annually.

Smith River

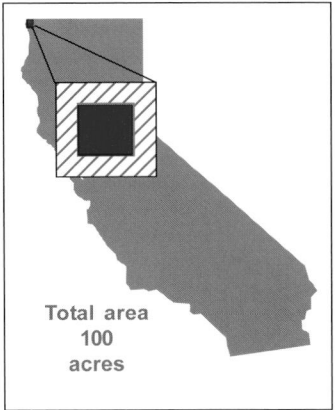

**Total area
100
acres**

Population *2000 census*
0

Tribal enrollment
(Tribal source, 2005)
941

Tribal enrollment
(BIA labor report, 2001)
896

Total labor force *2000 census*
31

High school graduate or higher
2000 census
52.8%

Bachelor's degree or higher
2000 census
3.8%

Unemployment rate *2000 census*
49.8%

Unemployment rate
(BIA labor report, 2001)
12%

Per capita income *2000 census*
$7,428

Soboba Band

Soboba Band of Luiseño Indians
Federal reservation
Luiseño
Riverside County, California

Soboba Band of Luiseño
Indians
P.O. Box 487
San Jacinto, CA 92581
951-654-2765
951-654-4198 Fax

Total area (BIA realty, 2003)
6,937.84 acres

Tribally owned (BIA realty, 2003)
6,937.84 acres

Population 2000 census
522

Tribal Enrollment
(BIA labor report, 2001)
802

Total labor force 2000 census
133

Total labor force
(BIA labor report, 2001)
458

High school graduate or higher
2000 census
72.5%

Bachelor's degree or higher
2000 census
5.7%

Unemployment rate 2000 census
26.3%

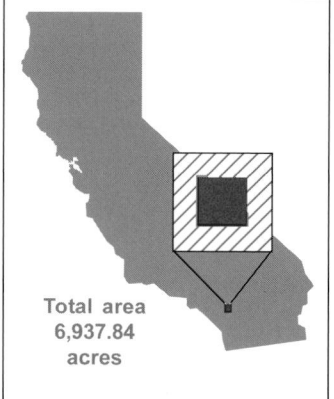

Total area
6,937.84
acres

LOCATION AND LAND STATUS
The Soboba Reservation is in eastern Riverside County, two miles east of the small town of San Jacinto and 35 miles from Riverside. The Soboba Reservation was created by an Executive Order on June 19, 1883. However, the reservation was not formally established until June 10, 1913, under the authority of the Act of 1891 as amended. The initial land grant did not include the tribe's primary village; this tract was added to the reservation at a later time.

PHYSICAL DESCRIPTION
The reservation is a large irregularly shaped block of land spanning 6,865.68 acres of rolling hills, deep ravines, a river valley, and several alluvial plains.

CULTURE AND HISTORY
The Soboba Reservation is home to the Luiseño Band of Mission Indians. Historically, the tribe occupied the territory south of Mt. San Jacinto extending to the Pacific Coast. Their language belongs to the Cupan group of the Takic subfamily. The term "Soboba" refers to a Luiseño place name. The Luiseños practiced sophisticated agricultural techniques including plant husbandry, inland corn agriculture, water and erosion management, and controlled burning. *(For additional cultural information, see California introduction.)*

Residents of the Soboba Reservation have continually fought to defend their water rights. It was not until 1908 that the U.S. government began to develop an irrigation system to support agricultural development. In 1933, after a tunnel was constructed through the San Jacinto Mountains for the purpose of diverting water from the Colorado River to Los Angeles, an underground river resulting from the construction drained all springs and streams on the Soboba Reservation. After approximately 30 years of litigation, the U.S. Claims Court finally entered a judgment granting the Soboba Band of Mission Indians $12 million. The tribe has come to a negotiated settlement with the water districts responsible for the draining of the springs and streams, from the digging of the San Jacinto tunnel, which left the reservations uplands unusable. This litigations agreement is being submitted to Congress for ratification of the terms of the agreement. The tribe this past year established a cultural center, Cham-Mix Poki', which means "Welcome to Our Culture." The cultural center houses a vast library full of books on the Luiseño and Cahuilla people as well as California Indians, many cultural items and historical pictures.

GOVERNMENT
The Soboba Reservation is governed by a general council composed of all voting members of the tribe. The five-member elected tribal council includes a chairperson, vice-chairperson, secretary, and treasurer. Council members serve two-year staggered terms. The council oversees a number of committees such as tribal administration, accounting, Administration for Native Americans (ANA), adult education, housing, and youth education.

ECONOMY
Gaming and its related industries are the major contributors to the Soboba Tribe's economy. Land leases and agriculture are also important to the tribe's economic self-reliance. To ensure a prosperous economic future, the Soboba Tribe plans to further cultivate the reservation's appeal as a luxury resort destination.

Government as Employer. A small number of residents are employed by the Soboba Reservation Tribal Government.

Economic Development Projects. The tribe is studying the feasibility of developing an RV resort and commercial development including a gas station, family restaurant, coffee shop, car wash, and commercial lease space. This area, if it proceeds as planned, will span 129.33 acres of tribal land and will include full hook-up sites. With the recent purchase of an 18-hole executive golf course, the tribe hopes to attract retired visitors for extended stays.

Agriculture and Livestock. The tribe leases land to both citrus producers and watermelon farmers. The land dedicated to agriculture, approximately 417 acres, is composed of both community-owned and individually assigned properties. In addition, the tribe has another 1,500 acres suitable for agricultural development.

Gaming. The tribe owns and operates a 74,000-square-foot gaming complex called Soboba Casino. The casino houses 2,000 slot machines, 21 table games, a 250-seat bingo hall, 4 restaurants, 2 entertainment venues, and 4,000 parking spaces. The Soboba Casino provides employment opportunities to approximately 900 tribal and nontribal members.

Mining. The Soboba Reservation leases land for surface sand and gravel mining. For the Soboba Reservation, the development of industrial minerals is important. As metropolitan areas zone out, build over, or mine out sand and gravel pits on public and private lands, reservation lands near these areas experience an increased demand for their resources.

Financial Institutions. The Soboba Band is the leading member of the California Indian Credit Consortium. This organization includes the Morongo Band of Mission Indians and Sycuan Band of Kumeyaay Indians. The consortium is in the process of developing the first Native American owned credit union in California. The credit union will offer checking and savings accounts, car loans, credit cards, emergency loans, home improvement loans, and financial education seminars. The California Indian Credit Consortium credit union project is still pending and in the process of securing a charter.

Tourism and Recreation. Located east of the San Bernardino National Forest and across the forest to the southwest from Palm Springs, the reservation is in a prime location for tapping into the tourism market. The tribe sponsors the Soboba Grand Prix, a motorcycle race that draws a regional audience. Gaming is a big tourist draw in the community.

INFRASTRUCTURE
The reservation is served by two paved roads, both of which are maintained by the county. State Highway 74 runs east-west through nearby San Jacinto.

Electricity. Southern California Edison provides electricity to residents.

Fuel. Southern California Edison is the reservation's main supplier of fuel, although some tribal members use bottled, tank, and LP gas as fuel sources.

Water Supply. Water is available to residents from wells located on the reservation. The tribe is currently having the existing water system upgraded to meet the expanding needs of additional agricultural production. Septic tanks serve as the primary means of sewage disposal.

Transportation. Hemet, seven miles from the reservation, has train services and a private airfield. Bus and trucking facilities are available in San Jacinto, located one mile from the reservation.

COMMUNITY FACILITIES AND SERVICES

The tribe has a sports complex that provides gymnasium facilities for tribal members. It includes health and fitness classes and a state-of-the-art weight room, cardio room, two softball fields, and a pool. The tribe offers an elders program for tribal members that schedules monthly meetings and luncheons, trips, and events during the year.

Education. Soboba junior high and high schoolers attend The Noli School which is run by the tribal government and located on the reservation adjacent to the sports complex. The tribe established the school in 1991, and the current facilities were built in 2001. They are still on the BIA waiting list for full construction funding. Tribal members also attend local schools in San Jacinto, both public and private; other high school age students attend San Jacinto High School. The tribe also established the Luiseño Indian Education for Adults Program to provide valuable training for tribal members. The tribe has a preschool that offers daycare and pre-school curriculum to prepare children to enter the school system. The preschool also offers cultural education including Luiseño language, traditional foods, and traditional games.

Health Care. The Soboba Tribe's health care needs are met by the Soboba Health Care Center, located in San Jacinto, California. The clinic provides medical, dental, eye care, mental health, chemical-dependency prevention, outreach, pharmacy, laboratory, and x-ray services.

ENVIRONMENTAL CONCERNS

The tribe is very concerned about water quality on the reservation and works diligently to ensure that water delivered to residents is free from bacteria and e-coli. The tribe recently hired a full-time water quality expert to take care of the water needs of reservation residents and visitors.

The tribe is also aware of the habitation of endangered species on certain parts of the reservation. It has worked with the U.S. Fish and Wildlife Service to protect these habitat areas, to ensure protection of those species.

Soboba Band

Unemployment rate
(BIA labor report, 2001)
85%

Per capita income *2000 census*
$18,481

Sulphur Bank
See Elem Indian Reservation

Susanville

LOCATION AND LAND STATUS

The Susanville Rancheria is located in northeastern California, at the juncture of the Cascade Range and the Sierra Nevada. It is situated approximately 70 miles from the Nevada border while Plumas National Forest is within 20 miles. Land access is obtained via State Highways 36 and 44 and U.S. Highway 395.

The original rancheria, consisting of about 30 acres, was purchased on August 15, 1923, for homeless California Indians, without designation of tribe. The Assignment Ordinance of 1963 allowed homeless Indians to acquire assignments on the rancheria and become members. PL 95-459, approved on October 14, 1978, provided for the United States of America to hold an additional 120 acres of land in trust for the rancheria.

In 2000 the tribe acquired the 72-acre Sierra Army Depot through a federal-to-federal transfer. It purchased another 3 acres that same year. In 2002 the tribe bought 875 acres to be used for tribal housing and tribal office buildings. In 2003 the tribe purchased an additional 160 acres with the intent of developing economic enterprises on the land and leaving some areas as designated open space. The rancheria is comprised of four community areas, including Upper Rancheria, Lower Rancheria, and Sierra housing. The fourth area is a 3-acre parcel of lands that has yet to be named or developed. The tribe has requested these lands to be placed in trust status.

PHYSICAL DESCRIPTION

Tribal lands are located on an earthquake fault line and within lava rock beds. There are large boulders scattered across the areas and the soil is clay.

CULTURE AND HISTORY

The people of Susanville Rancheria are descended from several different cultural and linguistic groups. Tribal members maintain affiliations with the Paiute, Maidu, Pit River, and Washoe groups, also known as the "Four Tribes." The area that is now the rancheria used to be a meeting place for the four tribes. The language of the Paiutes belongs to the Uto-Aztecan language family, relating them to peoples from the Great Basin south into central Mexico. The languages of the Pit River and Washoe peoples belong to the Hokan language family, as do the languages of peoples from southern Oregon to southern Mexico. The Maidu language belongs to the Penutian language family, related to languages spoken by peoples from the coast of Canada to the southeastern U.S. to the Yucatan Peninsula.

Spanish explorers arrived in California in the late 1500s. During the time of Spanish, and later Mexican, dominance in the territory, lands were seized from the Native populations and held in trust for the crown. The indigenous people were displaced, enslaved, and often murdered. Americans arrived in California in the mid-1800s and initiated a war with Mexico for rights to the California regions. The Spanish Mexicans were defeated, and in 1848 the Treaty of Guadalupe ended the Mexican-American War.

Upon the discovery of gold in northern California, Euro-Americans began arriving in the state in droves. In 1850 the California territory became a state and passed the Act for the Government and Protection of Indians. This act mandated the regulation of Indian affairs to the state, permitted Euro-Americans the right to assume custody of Native children, prohibited the use of Native testimony against a Euro-American charged with a crime, and permitted unemployed Native peoples to be arrested and hired out, a form of state-sanctioned indentured servitude. The state further protected prospectors and settlers as they encroached upon tribal territories and seized water sources in the area.

Between 1851 and 1853, Indian commissioners negotiated 18 treaties between the government and multiple Native groups. The agreements were to reserve over 7.5 million acres for various tribes across the state, but the Senate did not ratify the Barbour Treaties. The tribes were not informed of this decision until the twentieth century and proceeded to live in agreement with the mandates outlined by the treaties. They ceded millions of acres of land to the government and confined themselves to the reservations designated by the Barbour Treaties.

Local, state, and federal agencies condoned the effort to commit genocide against the Native people of California. Indigenous

Susanville Indian Rancheria
Federal reservation
Paiute, Maidu, Pit River, and
Washoe
Lassen County

Susanville Indian Rancheria
745 Joaquin Street
Susanville, CA 96130
530-257-6264
530-257-7986 Fax
sir.nsn-gov

Susanville

Total area *(BIA realty, 2003)*
224.88 acres

Total area *(Tribal source, 2004)*
1,341 acres

Trust acreage *(Tribal source, 2004)*
226 acres

Tribally owned *(BIA realty, 2003)*
224.88 acres

Population *2000 census*
298

Tribal enrollment
(BIA labor report, 2001)
360

Tribal enrollment
(Tribal source, 2004)
438

Total labor force *2000 census*
104

Total labor force
(BIA labor report, 2001)
1,126

Total labor force
(Tribal source, 2004)
1,130

High school graduate or higher
2000 census
68.5%

Bachelor's degree or higher
2000 census
5.6%

Unemployment rate
2000 census
11.6%

Unemployment rate
(BIA labor report, 2001)
26%

Per capita income *2000 census*
$7,693

people were openly murdered, attacked, and enslaved. The atrocities committed against the indigenous groups so outraged the Mexican government that officials crossed the U.S.-Mexico border to conduct investigations, and they threatened to bring arms against the citizens of California if the violence did not cease. The intervention on their behalf and their ability to isolate themselves in the mountainous regions of the state enabled some tribes to escape total decimation. However, from an estimated population of over 150,000 in 1845, the Native population was reduced to less than 50,000 by 1855. By 1900, less than 16,000 indigenous people remained.

In 1923 the federal government established the Susanville Rancheria on 39 acres in Lassen County. The rancheria was a nontribal-specific reservation, though members of the Susanville community claim tribal affiliation with the Paiute, Maidu, Pit River, and Washoe tribes of California.

Relations between the tribe and local government agencies are tenuous. In 2002 the tribe purchased 875 acres of land that the City of Susanville had hoped to develop into a 3,000-unit housing project. The tribe plans to leave the lands open to limited development. The city constructed a new hospital adjacent to tribal lands in 2000 and tapped into the tribe's water lines in order to access the shared water source. This was done without the tribe's permission. The city also circumvented the rancheria in order to extend its natural gas lines to the Herlong Prison. City and tribal representatives now meet under provisions of the Brown Act to negotiate on issues of common interest.

GOVERNMENT
The tribe is a PL-638 contract tribe governed by a tribal business council composed of seven elected tribal members; four members represent a quorum. The business council is presided over by an elected chairperson, vice-chairperson, and a secretary-treasurer. The tribal business council is elected by the general council which consists of all adult tribal members 18 years and older. The tribe is organized under the Indian Reorganization Act of 1934; its constitution and bylaws were approved on June 18, 2001. The tribe has established ordinances regarding property assignment, liquor sales, tort, environmental policy, and gaming. The tribal liaison committee handles cultural issues. City police and the Lassen County Sheriff's Department provide law enforcement for the reservation. There is no tribal court system.

The Susanville Indian Rancheria Housing Authority (SIRHA) is a very active department of the tribal government. In addition to acquiring lands for the tribe, it oversees the development and construction of housing units, the water and wastewater systems, and the roadways needed on tribal lands. SIRHA was organized under the Modoc-Lassen counties' housing division and became an independent entity in 2000.

ECONOMY
The tribal government, service industry, gaming, and agriculture all sustain the rancheria's economy. The tribe plans to increase its economic development without compromising the natural environment, including the land, air, water, minerals, and all living things on the reservation.

Government as Employer. The Aid to Tribal Government Program, funded by the Bureau of Indian Affairs, provides contract funds for various necessary governmental functions. A significant number of tribal members are employed in administrative, support, and service positions. The tribe employs 191 individuals throughout its governmental departments, programs, and businesses.

Gaming. In the 1990s, the State of California passed Proposition 5, allowing tribal governments to enter into gaming compacts with the state in order to develop gaming facilities on tribal lands.

Under provisions of the proposition, the Susanville Tribe opened the Diamond Mountain Casino in 1996. In 1999 the proposition was overturned after a number of Nevada-based casinos sued the state for allowing the establishment of Nevada-style gaming within California. In 2000, Proposition 1A was approved, and it overturned California's constitutional amendment that prohibited Nevada-style gaming in the state. Proposition 1A legalized the establishment of gaming facilities on tribal lands.

Since 2002, the number of clients the Diamond Mountain Casino serves has grown so rapidly that the casino has required remodeling and expansion to meet customers' needs. Improvements were made in 2002 and again in 2003. The Diamond Mountain Casino now encompasses 26,000 square feet and offers 208 slots/VLTs, blackjack tables, a sports bar, a 24-hour café with a nonsmoking area, a steak house-style restaurant called the Lava Rock Grill, a banquet room, and a gift shop. The casino sells beer and wine and serves complementary soft drinks. In addition to being a valuable source of employment, employing 135 people, casino revenues are used for donations to local area charities, for other beneficiaries, and to support the tribe's general fund.

Real Estate/Commercial Development. The tribe has purchased numerous tracts of lands in the past decade. It purchased 2.1 acres in 2000 to be used for housing, 875 acres in 2002 to be used for housing and tribal offices, and 160 acres in 2003 for designated open space. The purchase in 2000 of the 72-acre Sierra Army Depot in Herlong, California, included an administration building and 120 housing units. Over $1 million has been invested in improving the units, and the tribe estimates it will have to expend several hundreds of thousands of dollars more to bring the units up to state standards. The units are now being developed for a rental housing project. The youth treatment center facility on the site as well as the administration building are both available for rent.

The tribe has an easement agreement with non-Native residents living beyond the reservation. It allows them access to tribal roads in order to reach their homes. The tribe also has an easement agreement with a logging company working in timberlands beyond the reservation. The company is permitted to use tribal roads to access the forests and, in exchange, provides tribal members with wood.

Services and Retail. Diamond Mountain Mini-Mart, opened in April 2004, is a tribally owned and operated convenience store that employs people.

INFRASTRUCTURE
The tribe purchased three acres of land in 2002. It intends to construct tribal housing units on the land, which will necessitate the development of a water and wastewater system, roadways, and electric access. State Highways 44 and 36 pass near the rancheria, as does U.S. Highway 395.

Electricity. Lassen Municipal Utility District provides electricity.

Fuel. The city of Susanville sells natural gas, and a private provider supplies propane.

Water Supply. Susanville provides water to Upper Rancheria. The water is pumped through tribally owned and maintained water lines to a 100,000-gallon tank. Residents pay the tribe for water used, and the tribe in turn pays the city. A water system established by Indian Health Services in the 1970s services residencies in Lower Rancheria. The former army water system at the site serves the Sierra housing project, although a number of problems have arisen from the system's poor quality. A new system is being developed by the Herlong Utilities Company and will service the Sierra site.

Transportation. Reno, Nevada, 86 miles away, remains the nearest location for commercial air and train services. Bus and truck lines stop in Susanville, one mile from the reservation. Susanville Regional Airport serves the tribe, and Lassen Rural Bus service provides bus service. There are no railway connections to the reservation. The major freight carrier is UPS.

COMMUNITY FACILITIES AND SERVICES
Community centers include a gym, a tribal office, an elders' eatery, the community building for Head Start daycare, and educational tutoring.

Public Safety. The city provides fire protection for residential areas on the rancheria through a BIA-funded contract.

Education. Students attend Meadow View and McKinley elementary schools, Diamond View Middle School, Lassen High School and Lassen Community College. The rancheria provides tutoring during the school year and a cultural program during the summer. The tribe provides scholarship opportunities for members seeking post-secondary education and training.

Health Care. The Lassen Indian Health Center, which the rancheria oversees, has administered several different contracts

and grants to improve the health and welfare of tribal members. Some of the health center's services include medical, dental, social, mental, diabetic and public health education. Facilities include the Sierra Health Clinic and the Sierra Youth Residential Treatment Center. In addition to the health center on the rancheria, health care is available at hospitals in Redding or Reno and at the Lassen County Banner Hospital and Lassen County Health Clinic.

ENVIRONMENTAL CONCERNS
When the tribe purchased the Sierra Army Depot from the U.S. Army, it discovered that the water quality and the supply system were below standards. The Herlong Utilities Company was established to address the problems that the army's former system had created for the tribe, the city, the local prison, and other organizations within the system's jurisdiction. The tribe was unable to maintain its administration fee and was suspended from the company's board. The company elected to construct a new system and initiated the process in 2003. Both water and soil quality at the Sierra site remains a grave concern to the tribe. The environmental protection department of the rancheria is investigating future procedures.

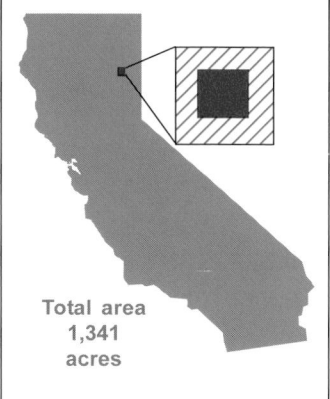

Total area
1,341
acres

S ycuan

LOCATION AND LAND STATUS
Sycuan Rancheria is located in southern California, six miles from El Cajon and within 20 miles of San Diego, off Highway 8 east. An Executive Order on December 27, 1875, set lands apart for this reservation. The secretary of the interior enlarged the Sycuan Reservation by 89.15 acres in November 2001 when it placed the Bradley and Big Oak Ranch properties into federal trust.

PHYSICAL DESCRIPTION
The reservation is located in the rolling hills amid oaks, cottonwoods, willows, chaparral, cactus, and wildflowers.

CULTURE AND HISTORY
Residents of the Sycuan Reservation are members of the Kumeyaay Tribe. Their language belongs to the Yuman branch of the Hokan language family, other languages are spoken by peoples from southern Oregon to southern Mexico. The Kumeyaays are also known as the Diegueños, named after the mission within their territory.

In 1769, Kumeyaay territory extended 50 to 75 miles both north and south of the Mexican border and from the California coast east nearly to the Colorado River. Prior to European contact, the tribe was divided into as many as 50 bands, but two tribal chiefs served to maintain cohesive intertribal relations.

Prior to 1870, the southern and interior Kumeyaays largely avoided repression by the mission at San Diego, even leading occasional revolts to free their relatives who were in forced labor there. Only after 1870 was their land taken from them as American immigrants moved into the area.

Northern and coastal Kumeyaays, on the other hand, had early contact with the missions, thereby falling under Spanish domination. After their initial contact with Euro-Americans in 1846, they learned English as well as Spanish. These bands, the Sycuan among them, received reservations by an Executive Order in 1875; Indian agency schools were operating there shortly after.

The 1891 Act for the Relief of Mission Indians set up 11 additional reservations, which proved to be pitifully small and inadequate, thus leaving many Kumeyaays without a home.

In 1901, the U.S. Supreme Court failed to uphold Indian land-rights treaties that had been established with the Mexican government in territory that was now part of the United States. As a result, the indigenous peoples were evicted. In 1903, the government purchased land at Pala and moved some of the Kumeyaays there (the San Felipe and Cupeno bands), while others fled elsewhere. Until 1910, the Kumeyaays suffered on inadequate reservations or found menial labor on area ranches or in local homes. It was in 1910 that bad publicity finally forced the Indian Office (later to become the BIA) to enlarge certain reservations and establish some new ones. While most Kumeyaay reservations contained subsistence farms, marginal cash-cropping operations, and a few domestic animals, many were far from markets and had water routinely stolen or diverted. Additionally non-Indian settlers staked claim to all the best farmland, most of it river-bottom land, in the area, leaving only the high rocky hills to the Indians.

During the early twentieth century, organizations were established to oppose the BIA's authority. In 1953, PL-280 stripped the BIA of much of its authority, establishing it as merely the keeper of the reservation land's trust status. The vacuum created by PL-280 forced tribal leaders to face up to continuing problems in the areas of sovereignty, economics, education, and health. One result is that the Kumeyaays have revived the tribal-level organization as it originally functioned, to manage tribal sacred places, focus on religious and cultural needs, and protect ancestral places.

GOVERNMENT
The Sycuan Reservation is governed by the seven-member elected Sycuan Business Committee. Tribal officials include a spokesperson, a vice-chairperson, a secretary, and a treasurer. The tribe is organized under Articles of Association approved in 1972. The tribe is a self-governing PL-638 tribe. The depart-

Sycuan Rancheria
Federal reservation
Kumeyaay (Diegueño)
San Diego County, California

Sycuan Band of Kumeyaay
5459 Sycuan Road
El Cajon, CA 92019
 619-445-2613
 619-445-1927 Fax
 sycuan.com

Total area *(BIA realty, 2003)*
808.43 acres

Tribally owned *(BIA realty, 2003)*
547.97 acres

Individually owned
(BIA realty, 2003)
260.46 acres

Population
70

Tribal enrollment
(BIA labor report, 2001)
67

Total labor force *2000 census*
28

Total labor force
(BIA labor report, 2001)
67

Sycuan

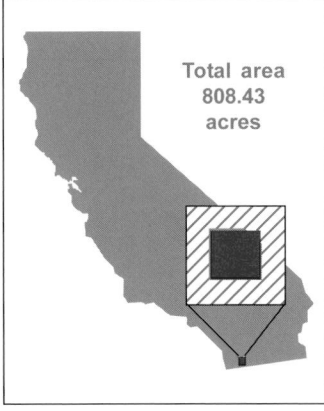

Total area
808.43
acres

High school graduate or higher
2000 census
53.1%

Bachelor's degree or higher
2000 census
9.4%

Unemployment rate *2000 census*
0%

Unemployment rate
(BIA labor report, 2001)
40%

Per capita income *2000 census*
$58,012

ENVIRONMENTAL CONCERNS
In 2004 the Sycuan Tribal Government developed the Sycuan Environmental Protection Agency to implement various tribal environmental ordinances and uphold federal and state environmental and health laws.

ments are: administration, accounting, construction, community development, environmental, landscape and janitorial, medical administration, senior citizen programs, medical and dental clinic, human resources, gaming commission, fire department, Kumeyaay Community College (formerly DQ University), learning center (H.S. satellite), daycare center, insurance and medical claims, tribal police, and the Sycuan Tribal Development Corporation.

The Sycuan Police Department is staffed full time and it enforces tribal and state law. The police department has cross jurisdiction with the State of California. Tribal police report directly to the Sycuan tribal government. The tribe does not have a tribal court.

BUSINESS CORPORATION
The Sycuan Tribal Development Corporation (STDC) was established in 2002 in order to further the tribe's economic development and prosperity. The STDC's plans include investing in industries such as real estate and hospitality, providing financial services to help individuals manage and protect their financial interests, and to improve the standard of living for all members.

ECONOMY
During the twenty-first century, the region's economy has been based largely on ranching and increasingly on agriculture, as irrigation techniques have improved. The seemingly endless southern California urban sprawl has stimulated real estate development, construction, and a burgeoning service industry. With its restaurants, casino, bingo, and off-track betting establishments, the Sycuan Rancheria represents one of the most economically vital portions of the Kumeyaay land bases. While Indian gaming is an integral part of Sycuan's economic base and a large contributor to the economies of surrounding cities, the Sycuan Tribe's strategy is one of economic diversification beyond the gaming industry in order to provide long-term stability for the tribal economy and tribal entities. The rancheria's biggest constraint is its lack of non-allotted tribal land.

Economic Development Projects. The STDC has established several development partnerships in National City and San Diego. Among the projects this partnership is undertaking are a $25 million project to revitalize National City's Waterfront, called the Marina Gateway project; the development of Hotel Solamar, a boutique hotel scheduled for completion in 2005; and the purchase of the historic U.S. Grant Hotel.

Gaming. The 305,000-square-foot Sycuan Resort and Casino opened in November 2000. The casino hosts 2,000 slots and video lottery tables, 60 table games, 17 poker tables, and 1,360 bingo seats. Gaming choices include slots, blackjack, Pai Gow, poker, craps, roulette, world poker tournament, bingo, and off-track betting. Five restaurants, including the buffet at Paipa's Oasis, dining at Wachena Falls Café, and specialty sandwiches from the Sunset Deli, are available for guests. Other features include a 54-hole golf course, tennis courts, 102 hotel rooms, one entertainment venue, and employs approximately 2,000.

Construction. Approximately 11 percent of the residents are employed in the construction industry.

Finance. The STDC created Sycuan Capital Management to serve as a mutual fund manager for tribal interests. The Sycuans became the first tribal nation to enter the financial services industry and is the first tribal-owned investment advisor. The Sycuan Band is a member of the California Indian Credit Consortium. This organization includes the Morongo Band of Mission Indians and Soboba Band of Luiseño Mission Indians. The consortium is in the process of developing the first Native American-owned credit union in California. The credit union will offer checking and savings accounts, car loans, credit cards, emergency loans, home improvement loans, and financial education seminars.

Services and Retail. The Sycuan Resort and Casino offers gaming, lodging, and entertainment. Arts, entertainment, recreation, accommodation, and food service industries employ 32 percent of the area's residents. Public administration professions employ 54 percent of area residents.

Tourism and Recreation. Aside from the gaming, lodging, and entertainment venues the reservation is home to the Singing Hills Country Club and Resort, which has 425 acres of picturesque terrain, two 18-hole championship golf courses, and 11 tournament tennis courts. The Showcase Theatre features concerts and shows and has seating for approximately 500. Many visitors attend the annual powwow.

In 2004 the Sycuan Tribe started a professional boxing promotions agency called Sycuan Ringside Promotions. The Sycuans are the first tribe or casino to do so. The tribe has signed an exclusive promotional agreement with the world junior featherweight champion, and it is in the process of securing other boxing champions to the agency.

INFRASTRUCTURE
U.S. Highway 80 passes four miles from the rancheria. Trucking, rail, and bus services are located in San Diego and El Cajon.

Electricity. San Diego Gas and Electric provides electricity. Approximately 37 percent of the homes are heated with electricity.

Fuel. San Diego Gas and Electric provides gas service. Approximately 10 percent of the homes are heated with utility gas, and 53 percent of the homes are heated with bottled, tank, or LP gas.

Water Supply. Wells provide water for the reservation. An SBR plant and home-owned septic systems treat the reservation's wastewater.

Transportation. The casino operates a shuttle service.

Telecommunications. Telephone service is available to 74 percent of the residences.

COMMUNITY FACILITIES AND SERVICES
A childcare program is available to the community. The tribe has a community center that is used for meetings, allowing residents and employees to join education and physical activities, including martial arts, basketball, arts and crafts, and exercise programs.

Public Safety. The Sycuan Fire Department provides assistance to the surrounding area with firefighting and emergency medical services.

Education. The Sycuan Learning Center is a satellite campus of the Mt. Empire Unified School District. The center provides independent study programs for adults and teenagers, and it also offers high school diploma courses. The center also provides tutoring and after-school programs for elementary school children. Kumeyaay Community College at Sycuan is an accredited two-year institution that focuses on teaching tribal members and non-Natives about the Kumeyaay culture and issues facing Native Americans today.

Health Care. The Sycuan Medical and Dental Center provides primary health care services to the tribe, Sycuan employees, and neighboring East Country residents. The facility includes a full-service pharmacy and employs medical and dental professionals. For health care needs not met by the Sycuan Medical and Dental Center, hospitals and clinics are available in El Cajon and San Diego. The nearest hospital is Grossmount Sharp Health Care in La Mesa, California.

Total area *(BIA realty, 2003)*	87.99 acres
Tribally owned *(BIA realty, 2003)*	87.99 acres
Population *2000 census*	300
Tribal enrollment *(BIA labor report, 2001)*	460
Tribal enrollment *(Tribal source, 2004)*	460
Total labor force *2000 census*	31
Total labor force *(BIA labor report, 2001)*	18
High school graduate or higher *2000 census*	75.7%
Bachelor's degree or higher *2000 census*	5.4%
Unemployment rate *2000 census*	38.7%
Unemployment rate *(BIA labor report, 2001)*	0%
Per capita income *2000 census*	$7,563

LOCATION AND LAND STATUS

The Table Bluff Reservation is located in Humboldt County, California. The tribe acquired 1.5 acres of ancestral homelands on Indian Island in 2001, and another 40 acres in 2004. The City of Eureka returned the land acquired in 2004 to the tribe by a unanimous vote of the city council. Eureka is the only city in California to return a sacred site to an indigenous group.

CLIMATE

The Table Bluff Reservation experiences mild, sunny weather. Temperatures range annually from a low of 38°F to 109°F. Average precipitation is 15 inches per year.

CULTURE AND HISTORY

Members of the Table Bluff community belong to the Wiyot Tribe. They have resided along the northern shores of California for thousands of years. Ancestral lands included Indian Island. On the mainland, homelands extended from the Little River to the Bear River and inland to the first range of mountains.

Wiyot contact with Euro-Americans has been brutal and devastating to the tribe. On February 26, 1860, a group of settlers massacred at least 100 tribal members on Indian Island. The majority of victims were women, children, and elders. Only one infant survived the slaughter. On that same evening, Wiyot villages on the mainland at Eel River and South Spit were attacked, and an estimated 100 more tribal members were murdered. The surviving Wiyot people were relocated to Fort Humboldt for their protection, and many were later dispersed to reservations throughout California, including the Klamath River Reservation. When floodwaters inundated the reservation, the residents were relocated to the Smith River, Hoopa, and Round Valley reservations. Precontact estimates place the Wiyot population between 1,500 and 2,000. By 1860, there were approximately 200 tribal members left. By 1910, there were less than 100 full-blood Wiyot people living within traditional Wiyot territory.

Throughout their experiences, the Wiyots continually attempted to return to their homelands, particularly to Indian Island. The island had served as a ceremonial site for countless years and is of great cultural significance to the Wiyot people. Tuluwat Village, on the island, contains a clamshell mound that measures over six acres in size. It is estimated to be at least 1,000 years old. The mound is known to contain artifacts of cultural importance, as well as burial sites. In addition to erosion of the mound by natural processes, Euro-American encroachment upon the mound has resulted in the desecration of many grave sites and the destruction of significant areas. In 2004, in a landmark decision, the City of Eureka, California, returned portions of Indian Island, including Tuluwat Village and the shell mound, to the Wiyot people. It is the first time in California that a city has restored a sacred site to a tribe. While the tribe remains concerned for the protection of this mound and the island itself, it is pleased and relieved to have the land back in tribal possession.

Years of racism and genocidal tactics have taken their toll on the Wiyots. In addition to reducing tribal population, there has been a stifling of the traditional culture that members are struggling to reverse. The 1860 massacred on Indian Island halted the annual renewal celebrations held there, an important facet of Wiyot spiritual practices and cultural beliefs. Tribal members are still fighting to retain traditional ceremonies, practices, and cultural elements. They hope the return of their sacred sites on Indian Island will mark the beginning of renewal of Wiyot traditions.

GOVERNMENT

The tribe is organized under provisions of the Indian Reorganization Act of 1934.

ECONOMY

Government as Employer. The Table Bluff Tribe employs 18 individuals.

Agriculture and Livestock. The tribe has a community garden.

INFRASTRUCTURE

Electricity. Pacific Electric and Gas provides electricity.

Fuel Supply. AmeriGas sells propane gas to residents.

Water Supply. Private water wells and individual septic tanks provide water to residences.

Table Bluff Reservation
Federal reservation
Wiyot
Humboldt County, California

Table Bluff Reservation-Wiyot Tribe
1000 Wiyot Drive
Loleta, CA 95551
707-733-5055
800 388-7633
707-733-5601 Fax
wiyot.com

TRI-CA-064 Sign for Table Bluff Rancheria

TRI-CA-063 Table Bluff Rancheria Office Building

TRI-CA-064

TRI-CA-063

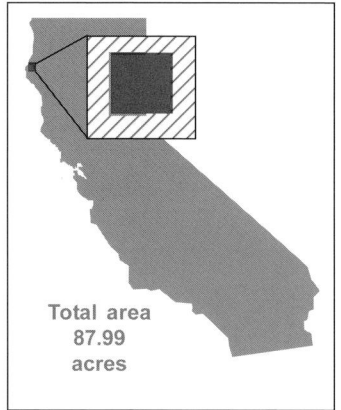

Total area
87.99
acres

Table Bluff

Transportation. Commercial airports are available in Eureka and Arcata, about 40 miles away. Freight carrier services are also available in Eureka. Bus services are available in nearby towns.

COMMUNITY FACILITIES AND SERVICES
The reservation offers a community center, a library which offers a fine collection of Native American history, reference materials, and general interest topics. Community services provided include community meal, blood pressure and blood sugar screenings, and an Indian Child Welfare Act program that provides childcare subsidies through a Child Care Development Fund Grant.

Education. Students attend elementary school, high school and colleges located off the reservation. The tribe contracts funds for a Johnson O'Malley Program from the BIA and administers funds to members for higher education, adult vocational training, and cultural programs.

Health Care. United Indian Health Services provides medical services, which include medical, child and family services, community health and wellness, dental, nutrition, and vision programs. Clinics are located in Arcata, Crescent City, Fortuna, Smith River, Klamath, and Hoopa.

ENVIRONMENTAL CONCERNS
The tribe is concerned with the protection of natural resources on tribal lands and with solid waste management. The tribe established an environmental department to address these issues. The department provides educational workshops, information, and events to the community. It also has developed an environmental inventory, and it is in the process of establishing a Tribal Environmental Plan. The IHS has provided funding to develop a recycling station on the reservation. The EPA funds the environmental program. The 1.5 acres the tribe purchased in 2001 include the site of an abandoned boatyard. The area will require over $1.5 million of cleanup of toxic chemical and debris.

Table Mountain

Table Mountain Rancheria
Federal reservation
Chukchanisi-Mono
Fresno County, California

Table Mountain Rancheria
23736 Sky Harbour Road
Friant, CA 93626
559-822-2587
559-822-2693 Fax

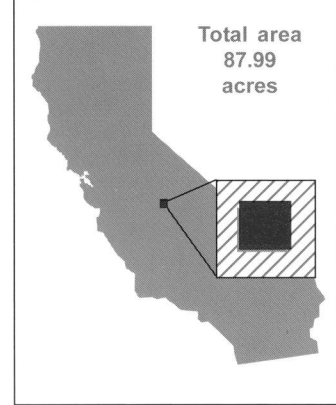

Total area
87.99
acres

Total area *(BIA realty, 2003)*		87.99 acres
Tribally owned *(BIA realty, 2003)*		87.99 acres
Population		81
Tribal enrollment *(BIA labor report, 2001)*		115
Total labor force *2000 census*		0
Total labor force *(BIA labor report, 2001)*		27
High school graduate or higher		100%
2000 census		
Bachelor's degree or higher *2000 census*		0%
Unemployment rate		30%
(BIA labor report, 2001)		
Per capita income *2000 census*		$146,000

LOCATION AND LAND STATUS
The Table Mountain Rancheria is located in the San Joaquin Valley in Friant, California. It was created in 1916 for dislocated Native families living in the Friant-Winchell Creek area. The Table Mountain community lost status as a federally recognized tribe in 1959, and tribal lands were dissolved. Recognition was restored in 1983, and the tribe regained its land base.

CULTURE AND HISTORY
Members of the Table Mountain Rancheria belong to various Native American groups, including the Chukchanisi and Monache tribes. The Table Mountain Tribe was created from the unification of multiple family groups relocated there in the early twentieth century. The rancheria's topography is such that residents were unable to rely upon it for sustenance. The rocky terrain and lack of water made farming impossible. Many tribal members worked as loggers, service workers, and migrant laborers. The tribe was terminated as a federally recognized nation in 1959, and tribal assets were dissolved. Status was restored in 1983, and the tribe has aimed to create a stable economy for its community. In 1987 it opened a bingo hall that has evolved into a casino. The success of its gaming operations has allowed the tribe to enhance tribal services and programs, and to offer employment to its members.

ECONOMY
The Table Mountain Rancheria is largely supported by revenue gained from their gaming operations. The tribe also owns a successful construction enterprise that generates a great source of income for the community. The tribe is one of the largest employers in Central Valley.

Gaming. The Table Mountain Casino originated as a bingo hall. Since its opening in 1987, it has developed into a 250,000-square-foot casino. It offers 2,000 slots/VLTs, 32 table games, 9 poker tables, 800 bingo seats, 2 restaurants, 1 entertainment venue, and a 12,844-square-foot convention center. The casino also has a seven-story parking garage. The casino is equipped with a high-tech security system that includes a networked video security and surveillance system.

Construction. The tribe owns Table Mountain Rancheria Enterprises. This company specializes in designing and constructing commercial projects. The company provides architectural, construction management, general contracting, and contract negotiation services to its clients. Projects have included the construction of the Crow Tribal Bank, court room addition, and community center; the Red Lodge Clinic; the Coast Guard's Loran-C Towers; Montana Bank; West Park Plaza; Boise Cascade Office Complex; Ford Truck Center; Pacific Iron and Steel; and a Quality Inn. Design projects have included the Westlake Village Plaza Hotel and wing additions; Sheraton Plaza ballroom addition; Desert Hot Springs Hotel and Spa remodel and additions; Westlake Medical; Bulldog Land Apartments; Bakersfield Imaging Facility; Fresno Lexus; Central Valley General Hospital emergency room and operating room HVAC remodel; and a Wells Fargo Bank.

Tourism and Recreation. In 1997 the tribe began the development of a cultural park on the reservation. Proposed amenities included a museum, a theater, gift shop, a park trail, and picnic facilities. The tribe intended to rebuild four buildings from Fort Miller at the site. Fort Miller was originally located in the San Joaquin Valley and served to protect and restrain the local Native people. The buildings from Fort Miller were disassembled in the early 1940s and placed in storage. When completed, the project would be the first restoration effort of its kind in California.

COMMUNITY FACILITIES AND SERVICES
Health Care. The Table Mountain Medical Clinic in Friant provides medical, dental, and vision programs. Health services are also available to tribal members through Central Valley Indian Health. Services include medical, dental, mental health, nutrition, outreach, podiatry, and substance abuse counseling programs. Clinics are available in Clovis, Prather, North Fork, and Lemoore.

LOCATION AND LAND STATUS

The Timbisha Shoshone Homelands are located in Death Valley National Park in the heart of legendary Death Valley, California. The tribe's central community is located on 313 acres near Furnace Creek. This spot is commonly known as Indian Village. Upon federal recognition in 1983, the tribe had no land base, though Congress authorized the acquisition of 40-40,000 acres for the tribe. In 2000, Congress approved an act to restore over 7,000 acres to the tribe.

PHYSICAL DESCRIPTION

Death Valley is located in south-central California, near the Nevada border. It includes the lowest spot in North America at 282 feet below sea level, and it comprises an austerely beautiful desert terrain.

CULTURE AND HISTORY

The Timbisha Shoshone group is a member of the Western Shoshone Nation. Prior to European contact, the Western Shoshones called themselves the Newe ("The people"). Their homelands ranged over much of the Great Basin, from southern Idaho to Death Valley and as far east as eastern Nevada. The Newes traditionally split off into small extended family groups who restricted their hunting and gathering to particular regions. The group that lived in the Death Valley region called themselves Timbisha, named after their Death Valley homelands. During the 1820s, white explorers gave the Newes the name "Shoshone"; the Nevada band was specified as "Western Shoshone."

At the beginning of the twentieth century, there was a single Western Shoshone Reservation located in Duck Valley along the Nevada-Idaho border. It was the BIA's plan to coerce all Shoshones of the Great Basin region to move there. However, only about one-third ultimately capitulated; so the government encouraged Northern Paiutes from Oregon and Nevada to join the Shoshones in Duck Valley. As for the remaining two-thirds of Western Shoshones still not living on reservation land, the government set aside thousands of acres for various colonies (in Nevada) and rancherias (in California) as alternatives to full-size reservations like Duck Valley.

In 1982 the tribe was federally recognized, although no boundaries were designated for tribal lands at the time. When Death Valley National Monument was established in 1993, it effectively encompassed the tribe's ancestral homelands and current community. The group continued to live within the park on approximately 40 acres near Furnace Creek. In 1994 a joint tribal-federal negotiating team drafted a plan to establish a homeland for the tribe. The plan would transfer five parcels of land to the tribe, including 7,540 acres to be placed in trust. When Death Valley National Monument became Death Valley National Park in 2000, Congress also passed the Timbisha Shoshone Homeland Act to restore over 7,000 acres to the tribe. The park service and land management are permitted to designate special use areas within the reserved land, and these portions remain in federal ownership. The tribe is able to use the land for low-impact, ecologically sustainable, traditional practices.

Like most American Indian tribes, the Western Shoshones have had their legal battles with the federal government over broken treaties. The Treaty of Ruby Valley in 1863, for instance, granted the tribe ownership of much of eastern Nevada. When, nearly a century later, the government agreed to pay $26 million in compensation, the tribe rejected the offer, insisting on a return of the land instead.

GOVERNMENT

The tribe was federally recognized on November 4, 1982. The general council approved a constitution on January 25, 1986. The tribe is governed by its tribal council comprised of five members elected to two-year staggered terms by the general council which in turn comprises all tribal members 16 years of age or older. Elections are held the second Tuesday in November. The tribal council meets the first Wednesday of each month, while the general council meets the last Saturday in October.

ECONOMY

Since its recognition in 1983, the tribe has focused on acquiring a land base for its community and developing a stable economy to serve its members. For many of the Western Shoshone bands, cattle ranching served as the main source of income during the twentieth century. But because of their limited land base, self-sufficiency remains an elusive goal, and unemployment remains high.

Government as Employer. The tribal government currently employs four to five people.

Economic Development Projects. The tribe plans to develop a museum and cultural center.

Gaming. In 2003 the tribe negotiated a gaming compact with the city of Hesperia, although it was met with great opposition from numerous interest groups. The primary argument of the interest groups was that the tribe's homelands did not extend to the city of Hesperia and that area should be considered off-reservation. The Department of the Interior upheld these arguments, and the proposed gaming site was not taken into trust for the tribe. However, in 2004 the tribe was able to purchase the lands from the city of Hesperia and will be able to develop a gaming operation on the site. The proposed facility will be located on 57 acres of land near Interstate 15 in the Mojave Desert. The complex will include a casino, a hotel, and a health spa. The casino is expected to generate 1,000 jobs. The tribe will provide $6.5 million per year to the city for the next 20 years: $2.8 million for a fire station and equipment, and $2.2 million for fees and permits. A compact must still be negotiated with the state.

Tourism and Recreation. Seasonal tourism already exists in Death Valley, the immediate vicinity of the tribe.

INFRASTRUCTURE

State Route 190 passes directly through the Timbisha lands.

Electricity. Southern California Edison provides electricity.

Fuel. Local vendors provide propane service.

Water Supply. Water comes from underground springs and is maintained by the Death Valley National Park Service. Septic tanks are used for sewage.

Transportation. Air service is available through the Death Valley airfield.

Telecommunications. Telephone service is provided by SBC.

COMMUNITY FACILITIES AND SERVICES

The tribe has a community building which houses their radio station, Timbisha Free Radio, and a small library of donated books. The tribe has received a Housing and Urban Development Community Development Block Grant to construct a new community building.

Timbisha Shoshone Reservation
Federal reservation
Western Shoshone
Inyo County, California

Death Valley Timbisha
   Shoshone Band
P.O. Box 206
Death Valley, CA 92328
760-786-2374
760-7862376 Fax
timbisha.org

Total area
7,753 acres

Population
(Tribal source, 2005)
34

Native population
200

High school graduate or higher
(Tribal source, 2005)
32%

Bachelor's degree or higher
(Tribal source, 2005)
9%

Unemployment rate
(Tribal source, 2005)
14%

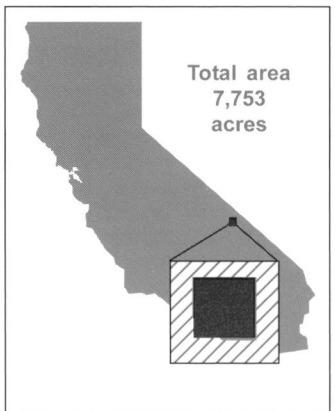

Total area
7,753
acres

Timbisha

Education. Children in grades 1-6 attend elementary school in Death Valley. High school students attend school in Beatty, Nevada (45 miles away) or Shoshone, California (60 miles away).

Health Care. The Toiyabe Indian Health Project provides medical services, which include ambulatory rural primary care. Clinics are located in Bishop, Coleville, and Lone Pine.

ENVIRONMENTAL CONCERNS
The tribe works with the National Park Service and Bureau of Land Management on maintaining the integrity of their surroundings and resolving environmental issues The restoration of a large tract of their homeland in 2000 has contributed to the tribe's increasing influence in regional environmental matters. The tribe currently seeks to further its ability to develop and establish criteria for determining the environmental impact of local projects and development, including assessing the effect of the Yucca Mountain project and several nearby military bases on their reservation. The unique conditions and challenges posed by living in Death Valley continue to be an important focus.

Torres Martinez

Torres Martinez Reservation
Federal reservation
Cahuilla
Imperial and Riverside counties, California

Torres Martinez Desert
Cahuilla Indians
P.O. Box 1160
Thermal, CA 92274
760-397-0300
760-397-8146 Fax

Total area *(BIA realty, 2003)*
23,842.83 acres

Total area *(Tribal source, 1994)*
24,024 acres

Tribally owned lands/
Riverside County *(BIA realty, 2003)*
9,748.06 acres

Tribally owned lands/
Imperial County *(BIA realty, 2003)*
8,485.1 acres

Individually owned lands/
Riverside County *(BIA realty, 2003)*
4,510.02 acres

Individually owned lands/
Imperial County *(BIA realty, 2003)*
1,099.65 acres

Population *2000 census*
4,146

Tribal enrollment
(BIA labor report, 2001)
532

Total labor force
(BIA labor report, 2001)
105

LOCATION AND LAND STATUS
The Torres Martinez Reservation was established by the Executive Order of May 15, 1876. Tribal lands are dispersed in a checkerboard pattern between Imperial and Riverside counties. From 1876 through June 6, 1910, Executive Orders granted approximately 24,000 acres to the tribe. The reservation is located in the eastern part of the Coachella Valley near Palm Springs. It is situated around and within a manmade body of water–the Salton Sea.

CULTURE AND HISTORY
The Cahuillas (pronounced Kah-we-ah), which means "masters" or powerful ones," are generally divided into three groups according to their geographic locations in the region: the Pass Cahuillas of the San Gorgonio Pass/Palm Springs area, the Mountain Cahuillas of the San Jacinto and Santa Rosa Mountains, and the Desert Cahuillas of the eastern Coachella Valley. The Desert Cahuilla people were the first known inhabitants that settled in the Coachella Valley and are the ancestors of the Torres Martinez Tribe. Tribal members are active in preserving their language and customs–through songs, dances, and educational and oral tradition.

During the period 1905-1907, over 11,000 acres of the reservation were inundated by water when a Colorado River irrigation aqueduct constructed by the Corps of Engineers broke and formed the Salton Sea. The remaining 13,800 acres are checkerboarded with agricultural lands. In 2002, after 90 years of litigation, the federal government agreed to compensate the tribe for the lost land.

The reservation has become a bedroom community to an estimated 16,000 workers in the construction, hospitality, and agricultural industries in neighboring communities. Although the tribe has the lowest priced electric rate in California, it does not have sewer and water infrastructure to meet the population growth of 5.5 percent. Torres Martinez Reservation is working with local and regional groups to create a solution that will better serve the reservation and surrounding communities.

GOVERNMENT
A tribal council–consisting of a chairperson, vice-chairperson, secretary, treasurer, four council members, and two proxy members–governs the tribe. Council members are elected to two-year terms. The tribal constitution of the Torres Martinez Desert Cahuilla Indians was adopted on November 9, 1997.

Law enforcement is provided by Riverside and Imperial County sheriff's departments. Fire protection is provided by Riverside and Imperial County fire departments and the California Department of Forestry (CDF). Governmental departments and programs include tribal housing, Tribal Employment Rights Ordinance (TERO), Tribal Environmental Protection Act (TEPA), planning, cultural resources, social services, property resources, education and daycare center, library, public works, and facilities management. Torres Martinez Reservation is active in the following organizations: Riverside/San Bernardino County Indian Health, California Indian Manpower Consortium, Coachella Valley Association of Governments, Tribal Alliance for Sovereign Indian Nations, California National Indian Gaming Association, Indian Child Family Services, Desert Alliance for Community Empowerment, and Inter-Tribal Council of California.

BUSINESS CORPORATION
The tribe has formed a corporation, Selnek-is-Ten-Al, which oversees all economic development on reservation lands. The tribe's economic development commission, a component of the corporation, reviews all economic development proposals.

ECONOMY
The Torres Martinez Tribe is in the process of improving its economy and enhancing programs and services available to tribal members. The tribe has formed a corporation, Selnek-is-Ten-Al, which is responsible for overseeing all economic development on reservation lands. The tribe's economic development commission reviews all economic development proposals.

Gaming. In 2003, after many years of negotiations, the tribe entered into a gaming compact with the State of California. The Torres Martinez Travel Center is under construction. It will have a state-of-the-art fueling system as well as convenience services for truckers and the traveling public. A small casino will be added. The tribe has the right to purchase an additional 640-acre parcel of land in Riverside County. It may be used to develop gaming operations. The Riverside County site will be located north of the reservation on Interstate 10 and will have 1,650 slot machines.

Tourism and Recreation. What is now Martinez Road was the original Bradshaw Trail. The Martinez Historic District has three buildings that are the oldest standing Indian Agency buildings in the state. The BIA schoolhouse, built in 1907, is still standing and serves as a center for tribal activities. The tribe recently received a grant to restore the structure. This site was one of the stopping points of the Bradshaw Wagon Company, the Pony Express, and other travelers.

The reservation also encompasses Travertine Point, Coachella Valley fish traps, Painted Canyon, and ecotourism for bird watchers. The tribe has an annual Su-Kutt Menyil Fiesta which brings together neighboring tribes and local communities to share in the Torres Martinez culture and traditions.

INFRASTRUCTURE

The reservation has 80 miles of roads maintained by the Reservation Transportation Authority, County of Riverside, and CalTrans. Three main arteries enter the reservation: 86 Expressway, also known as the NAFTA highway, which has opened economic opportunities for the tribe.

Electricity. Imperial Irrigation District provides electricity.

Water Supply. Water is in short supply on the reservation, and there is no sewer system. Reservation residents currently use septic systems.

COMMUNITY FACILITIES AND SERVICES

Programs available to tribal members include: housing improvement; an education and daycare center (which has a library for use by tribal and nontribal members); the Key Key Tum Park (which has a baseball field); and a swimming pool at tribal headquarters. The community at large has access to two places of worship, and there are three cemeteries.

Public Safety. The tribe has a community fire protection service.

Health Care. Health services are available through Riverside/San Bernardino County Health. The Torres Martinez Medical Center provides medical, dental, mental health, chemical dependency counseling, and outreach programs.

ENVIRONMENTAL CONCERNS

The Torres-Martinez Rancheria is exposed to a number of critical environmental issues. The tribe lost over 11,000 acres of land when contaminated waters inundated the region in 1909, creating the Salton Sea. The sea contains agricultural run-off, as well as an algae that exudes a noxious odor that can be smelled from as far as 30 miles away. The local bird population has been adversely affected by the creation of the sea. A Quantification Settlement has been reached by the states of California, Arizona, and Nevada. This agreement calls for the reduction of inflows into the Salton Sea as a result of water transfers. The reduction will result in the exposure of over 100 square miles of shoreline. Furthermore, the transferred water will be diverted to nearby tribal lands and communities. This water will contain selenium, arsenic, and heavy metals. The quality of air in the general region has long been a concern. The Coachella Valley is already in an unattainment status under the eight hour national standard rule. Air quality is expected to decrease as volatized sediments disperse in the valley. The increased traffic along Expressway 86 between the valley and the U.S.-Mexico border will generate pollution as vehicles make their way to the new international port south of Ensenada. The development of a railroad line between Mexicali and Calexico is also expected to impact air quality, as will increased use of tractor-trailers in the area. Air quality will be further impacted as a regional airport is currently being expanded into an international cargo airport. The expanded facility will provide an additional venue to transfer Pan Asian exports from the Mexican border.

The quality and availability of groundwater in the Coachella Valley has been a concern for at least 15 years. Over the last several years, the valley has experienced 18 percent growth. The population boom has created an overdraft of the groundwater aquifer. Additionally, the recharge from the Colorado River is expected to diminish water quality due to the presence of salts, selenium, perchlorate, and high TDS. It is also possible that the water will contain chromium VI, a pollutant that has been released into the Colorado River from the PG&E Topock Compressor Station. Further concerns include the high level of arsenic in tribal wells. Although arsenic is naturally present in the valley, thermal activity near and below the Salton Sea, as well as over extraction of the well water, has resulted in increased levels in both the wells and the aquifer.

The increased growth in the Coachella Valley has resulted in the increased production of solid waste at construction sites. Rather than paying the fees necessary to dispose of waste at public landfills, a number of contractors have been dumping their refuse on tribal lands. A simple solution would be for all contractors to provide proof or receipts of dumping activities, issued by landfill facilities. However, many general contractors do not require such documents and the county has not taken any action in the matter.

Human exposure to pesticides in the valley is also a concern. About 450 households occupy mobile homes in 35 different parks near or on tribal lands. These home sites in particular have been exposed to pesticides used by local agricultural operations. It is possible that residents may be exposed to air pollutants generated by the operations. The possibility of soil contamination exists as well. In addition to the exposure to pesticides, a number of the home sites are considered to be in substandard living conditions.

Torres Martinez

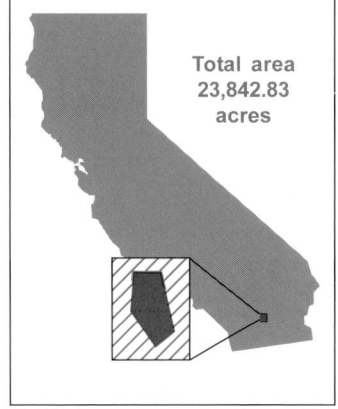

Total area
23,842.83
acres

Total labor force *2000 census*
1,730

High school graduate or higher
2000 census
19.4%

Bachelor's degree or higher
2000 census
1.5%

Unemployment rate *2000 census*
11.9%

Unemployment rate
(BIA labor report, 2001)
30%

Per capita income *2000 census*
$30,000

Trinidad

Trinidad

LOCATION AND LAND STATUS

The Trinidad Rancheria is located in northern California, just south of the Redwood National Park near U.S. Highway 101, about 25 miles north of Eureka and overlooking both the Trinidad Harbor and the Pacific Ocean.

The secretary of the interior established the rancheria in 1917. Congressional Acts of June 6, 1906, and April 30, 1908, appropriated funds for the purchase of lands for California Indians. The rancheria, which encompassed 60 acres along Highway 101, was purchased from the Vance Redwood Company, and it is entirely composed of trust property. The tribe has purchased additional lands in the nearby communities of Westhaven and McKinleyville.

PHYSICAL DESCRIPTION

The rancheria has a landscape of coastal bluffs, redwoods, and rocky shorelines between the Pacific Ocean and the Coast Range.

CULTURE AND HISTORY

Members of the Cher-ae Heights Indian Community descend from the Weott (Wiyot), Yurok, and Tolowa tribes. These groups share a similar cultural heritage. Traditionally, these groups lived throughout the coastal region of what is now northern California and southern Oregon, residing on lands from the Humboldt Bay area to the Oregon coast. The abundance of native plants including acorns and wild herbs, marine resources, and game provided a comfortable living. These tribes utilized their red-

Trinidad Rancheria
Federal reservation
Yurok, Weott (Wiyot), and
Tolowa
Humboldt County, California

Cher-ae Heights Indian
    Community of the Trinidad
    Rancheria
P.O. Box 630
Trinidad, CA 95570-0630
    707-677-0211
    707-677-3921 Fax
    trinidadrancheria.org

Trinidad

TRI-CA-066

TRI-CA-067

TRI-CA-066 Magnificent view of the Pacific Ocean along Highway 101 near Trinidad

TRI-CA-067 Pier at Seascape Restaurant in Trinidad (Photo by Christina Harrison)

TRI-CA-068 Cher-AE Heights Casino overlooks the Pacific Ocean

TRI-CA-065 Northern Coast Inn in Arcata off Highway 101

TRI-CA-068

TRI-CA-065

Total area (BIA realty, 2003)
83.15 acres

Tribally owned (BIA realty, 2003)
83.15 acres

Population
(Tribal source, 2004)
315

Total labor force 2000 census
14

Total labor force
(BIA labor report, 2001)
189

High school graduate or higher
2000 census
60%

Bachelor's degree or higher
17.1%

Unemployment rate
2000 census **78.6%**

Unemployment rate
(BIA labor report, 2001)
62%

Per capita income 2000 census
$5,602

Per capita income
(Tribal source, 2004)
$40,000

494

wood resources for building permanent homes and large, seaworthy canoes. The Weott and Yurok languages are related to the Algonquin languages, spoken by peoples over a vast expanse of eastern North America; the Tolowa language is Athabascan, related to languages spoken from the interior of Canada and Alaska to the southwestern United States.

The first land contact with Euro-Americans occurred in 1849, when the indigenous people of the region provided shelter and sustenance for the Josiah Gregg exploration party. Gregg was searching for the mouth of the Trinity River, wishing to establish an alternate route for the gold-mining business. After lending their hospitality, the local people showed the Gregg party the trail to Humboldt Bay. The Weott and Tolowa groups were nearly annihilated by subsequent immigrants. The present rancheria site is located near one of the largest precontact Yurok villages on the coast, called Tsurai, which was reduced to a single person by 1916. Some rancheria members trace their descent from former Tsurai residents.

Since the mid-1970s, when the rancheria was in the process of being terminated from its federally recognized status, the tribe has accomplished an enormous revitalization. After halting the termination procedures, the tribe has focused on improving its infrastructure, particularly its inadequate water supply; developing its housing facilities; and creating a stable economy to serve its members.

GOVERNMENT
The Trinidad Rancheria is governed by a community council, composed of all adult members; 51 percent of the members represent a quorum. A five-member elected business committee administers tribal programs and includes a chairperson, a vice-chairperson, a secretary-treasurer, and two members-at-large. The tribe is organized under Articles of Association approved in June 1961. Officers are elected for staggered two-year terms.

ECONOMY
The tribe endeavors to provide a stable economy for its tribal members, and it has achieved this by establishing numerous businesses and enterprises, including a casino, hotels, and res-

taurants. The tribe offers employment to all tribal members. It has become one of the largest employers in Humboldt County.

Government as Employer. The tribe is one of the largest employers in Humboldt County. It employs over 200 people in its casino operations, and with the assistance of federal grants, it supports a youth center staff and a librarian.

Economic Development Projects. The tribe's primary goals in developing its economy are to continue to improve and enhance the enterprises it owns and operates. The tribe plays a leading role in the tourism industry and strives to maintain its hold as a force in local tourism.

Gaming. The tribe owns and operates the Cher-ae Heights Casino in Trinidad. Overlooking the Pacific Ocean, the casino offers 349 slots/VLTs, 10 table games, 4 poker tables, 800 bingo seats, and the Sunset Restaurant, widely regarded as one of the finest in Humboldt County. The adjacent hotel features 78 guest rooms and 5 restaurants. The casino employs 218 people.

Construction. The local construction industry provides employment for a few rancheria members. In addition, various improvement projects on the rancheria itself, such as road paving, supply temporary employment for tribal members.

Services and Retail. Trinidad Rancheria owns a number of hotels and restaurants. In addition to the venues available at the casino, the tribe owns the North Coast Inn, known as the "Friendliest Inn on the Redwood Coast," located in Arcata. It houses the Wild Iris Restaurant, Acorn Café, and Grapevine Lounge. Purchased by the tribe in 1999, the inn features banquet halls and meeting rooms with a capacity of 500. Amenities include an indoor pool and spa and free shuttle service to the airport and tribal casino.

The Seascape Restaurant and Pier in Trinidad offers guests breakfast, lunch, and dinner menus. Its seaside location makes fishing charters, moorings, boat launchings, gift shops, bait and tackle shops, and skiff rental at the pier easily accessible. Local attractions include beaches, coves, trails, and the Humboldt State

University Marine Lab. The tribe purchased the property in 2000 from the Hallmark family to ensure that the business remains in local ownership. The tribe also owns Seascape House, a Cape Cod-style vacation house. Facilities include a main house, family room, a laundry room, a hot tub, housekeeping services, a full bath, and a handicap-accessible bath.

Tourism and Recreation. All of the tribe's enterprises are tourism-oriented. The North Coast Inn, many restaurants, and the casino operated by the tribe attract visitors wishing to enjoy the natural beauty of the area, gaming opportunities, fine dining, and recreational and commercial fishing activities.

INFRASTRUCTURE
U.S. Highway 101 runs north-south on the east side of the rancheria. Scenic Drive provides access to the rancheria from the highway.

Water Supply. The city of Trinidad supplies water to the rancheria. Private septic systems service all residencies. A privately owned company provides waste disposal services. A technologically advanced wastewater treatment plant that recycles about 70 percent of the treated wastewater services the casino.

Transportation. The nearest commercial airport is located approximately 8 miles away, in the town of McKinleyville.

COMMUNITY FACILITIES AND SERVICES
The tribe maintains a youth center on the rancheria. It offers after-school and summer youth activities that focus on cultural enrichment, environmental education, and tutoring services for tribal youth. In the same building is the rancheria library that provides collections for adults and children and offers a summer reading program.

Education. Children attend elementary and middle school in nearby Trinidad. While busing is provided for elementary school students, high school students must commute to McKinleyville High School. Advanced educational programs are available at the College of the Redwoods, located south of Eureka, and at Humboldt State University in Arcata.

Health Care. United Indian Health Services provides health services to tribal members. Services include medical, dental, vision, nutrition, pharmacy, and outreach programs. Clinics are located in Arcata, Klamath, Smith River, Fortuna, and Crescent City.

Trinidad

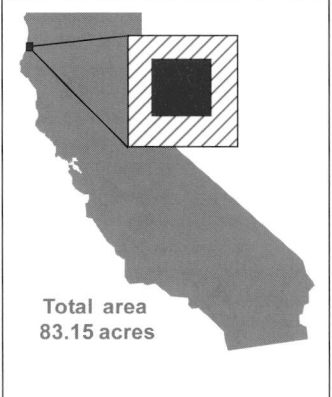

Total area
83.15 acres

Tule River

Tule River

LOCATION AND LAND STATUS
The Tule River Reservation is located in south-central California, approximately 20 miles east of the town of Porterville, which is 70 miles south of Fresno and 50 miles north of Bakersfield. The reservation spans mountainous forested foothills along the western edge of the Sierra Nevada and is almost surrounded by the Sequoia National Forest.

An Executive Order on January 9, 1873, established the reservation. An order on October 3, 1873, canceled the earlier order and reestablished the reservation 10 miles southeast of its former location. An act of May 17, 1923, changed the boundaries of the reservation, removing a 1,240-acre parcel of land; the U.S. Forest Service returned this land to the tribe in 1980.

CULTURE AND HISTORY
Members of the Tule River Tribe are descendants of the Tule-Kaweah Band of the Yokuts Tribe. The Band is composed of the Bokinuwas, Kawia, Wuchamni, Yausanchi, and Yokod groups. The Yokuts Tribe is comprised of 50 separate bands. The tribe's traditional homelands included territories across central California, including the foothills of Tehachapi, the foot of the Sierra Nevada Mountains, and the mouth of the San Joaquin River.

Prior to contact with Europeans and Euro-Americans, there were approximately 60 Yokuts tribes living in the area. It is estimated that by the late nineteenth century, 75 percent of the original population had been decimated, either by disease or warfare. Many Yokuts groups were forced together on the Tule River Reservation when it was established by Executive Order in 1873. The majority of tribal members live on or within five miles of the reservation.

Beginning in the twentieth century, the region's indigenous people joined the wage economy, working in the logging industry and on the area's ranches and farms. Many Tule River residents worked as ranch hands or as farm laborers in the fruit, vegetable, and cotton fields of the San Joaquin Valley. Currently the reservation's abundant timber resources serve as an important source of tribal revenue and employment.

In the 1900s, the region's Yokuts people pushed to revitalize some of their traditional cultural practices, many of which had been forgotten because of the public school system's efforts to assimilate tribal youth. Toward this end, several Yokuts tribes founded the Sierra Indian Center, which served as a hub for both political and cultural activism.

GOVERNMENT
The Tule River Reservation is governed by a nine-member elected tribal council, with six members representing a quorum. The council includes a chairperson, a vice-chairperson, a secretary, and a treasurer. Members serve two-year terms, and elections are held annually. The tribe is organized by a constitution drafted under the Indian Reorganization Act of 1934, approved in 1936. The Wukchumni Tribe, many of whose members reside on the Tule River Reservation, have their own tribal council, which is intensely involved in preserving traditional village sacred sites.

BUSINESS CORPORATION
Operating under tribal charter, the Tule River Economic Development Corporation (TREDC) negotiates the tribe's commercial ventures. The TREDC has office space in the town of Porterville, and it is managing preparations for the tribe's proposed industrial park, as well as actively pursuing trust status for another 40 acres of land designated for commercial development along California Highway 190. In 2003 the corporation received $400,000 from the Department of Housing and Urban Development (HUD), under its Rural Housing and Economic Development program, to develop a training center.

ECONOMY
The tribal economy is supported in large part by its endeavors in the forestry industry, the revenue earned from its gaming operations, and the support to tribal government from various federal government agencies.

Forestry. The 14,000 acres of conifers that lie within the reservation's boundaries provide the tribe with its principal source

Tule River Reservation
Federal reservation
Yokuts
Tulare County, California

Tule River Indian Tribe
P.O. Box 286
Porterville, CA 93258
209-781-4271
209-781-4610 Fax

Total area *(BIA realty, 2003)*
55,395.93 acres

Tribally owned *(BIA realty, 2003)*
55,395.93 acres

Population *2000 census*
566

Tribal enrollment
(BIA labor report, 2001)
1,425

Total labor force *2000 census*
197

Total labor force
(BIA labor report, 2001)
861

High school graduate or higher
2000 census
57.6%

Bachelor's degree or higher
2000 census
5%

495

Tule River

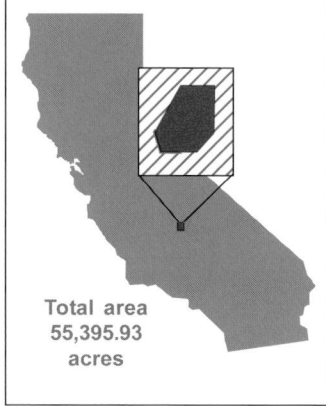

Total area
55,395.93
acres

Unemployment rate *2000 census*
10.7%

Unemployment rate
(BIA labor report, 2001)

48%
Per capita income *2000 census*
$9,674

ENVIRONMENTAL CONCERNS
The tribe's environmental program has developed a solid waste transfer station on the reservation in order to combat problems with illegal dumping and animal disturbance of waste disposal sites. Indian Health Services funded the construction. The program offers solid waste disposal and recycling bins.

of income. The tribe employs a timber management plan to actively protect and develop the forest area. The sustained-yield management principles instituted under this plan assure substantial revenues from alternate-year timber harvests. In addition, the tribe's natural resources department manages the reservation's Hunter, Smith Timber Mill.

Gaming. The tribe owns Eagle Mountain Casino in Porterville. The casino features 1,500 slots, 10 table games, 5 poker tables, and 2 restaurants. The casino employs 450 individuals. A bingo hall was constructed adjacent to the casino in 2000. It features 450 bingo seats, nonsmoking sections, and a snack park. Free park and ride service shuttles are available to guests. The tribe is considering the feasibility of developing a gaming facility off the reservation.

Fisheries. The tribe has completed feasibility studies that indicate the economic viability of a fish hatchery on the reservation.

Construction. The tribal public works department generates income for the tribe by using tribally owned equipment for road grading, hole digging, firebreak grading, and other earth-moving jobs. The equipment is also available for tribal members to rent for personal projects.

Industrial Parks. The tribe is developing 40 acres of tribally owned property to house the Porterville Air Industrial Park. This property, located near the airport, will be used for light industrial manufacturing, and it will house a U.S. Department of Agriculture warehouse and a quadruple lease facility. The tribe estimates that this industrial site could potentially employ as many as 245 people. In addition, the tribe has designated 160 acres within the reservation for industrial development.

Services and Retail. There are a variety of small businesses in the town of Porterville; in addition, the tribe has purchased a 40-acre parcel along California Highway 190, designated as the Foothill Scenic Development Corridor. This property is intended for commercial development, including a convenience store, a gas station, and a trading post.

Tourism and Recreation. The reservation is partially surrounded by the Sequoia National Park, which attracts more than a million visitors annually. There are public campgrounds and ski areas nearby, in addition to the archaeological Painted Rocks site, seven miles from the reservation entrance. The tribe has recently received a U.S. Forest Service grant to develop a campground on the reservation. To take advantage of the tourist activ-

ity, the proposed 40-acre commercial development parcel along Highway 190 will also house the Tule River Silversmith Guild and a gift shop where art and handcrafted items will be marketed. Since feasibility studies suggest that the area's greatest need is for a luxury motel and conference facilities, the tribe is planning to develop this type of facility and include a cultural center. Many visitors attend the Porterville Powwow which is held on the last weekend in September. This celebration features over 500 Indian dancers competing for prize money, over 75 art vendors, and Indian people demonstrating basketry, beadwork, soapstone carving, and Navajo weaving. Yearly activities on the reservation include the Elders' Gathering in August and San Juan's Day in June.

INFRASTRUCTURE
Access to the reservation is via Reservation Road which meanders along the South Fork of the Tule River from California Highway 190. Highway190, an east-west route, and California Highway 65, a north-south route, intersect in Porterville, approximately 20 miles west of the reservation. There are almost 150 miles of roads within reservation boundaries, although only about 10 miles are paved. The Tule River Tribal Council controls and maintains the road system. In addition, the tribe recently constructed two bridges that cross the Tule River leading to the Painted Rock site.

Water Supply. The reservation provides water; individual septic tanks are used for sewage disposal.

Transportation. All major transportation services are available in Visalia, about 50 miles from the reservation.

COMMUNITY FACILITIES AND SERVICES
Public Safety. The county sheriff's department provides law enforcement on the reservation.

Education. Reservation children attend public schools in Porterville. Reservation program services provide childcare, adult education, vocational and job training, and alcohol-abuse treatment.

Health Care. The Tule River Health Center is a nonprofit corporation that makes comprehensive medical care and ancillary services available to Native Americans in the region. The main clinic is located on the Tule River Reservation, and another site is located in Visalia, California. Services include medical, dental, optical, audiology, outreach, mental health, and social services programs.

Tuolumne

Tuolumne Rancheria
Federal reservation
Me-Wuk
Tuolumne County, California

Tuolumne Band of Me-Wuk
Indians
19595 Miwuk Street
Tuolumne, CA 95379
209-928-3475
209-928-1677 Fax

Total area *(BIA realty, 2003)*		392.11 acres
Total area *(EPA, 2004)*		324 acres
Tribally owned *(BIA realty, 2003)*		392.11 acres
Population *2000 census*		165
Population *(EPA, 2004)*		85
Tribal enrollment *(BIA labor report, 2001)*		350
Total labor force *2000 census*		86
Total labor force *(BIA labor report, 2001)*		1,680
High school graduate or higher *2000 census*		67.3
Bachelor's degree or higher *2000 census*		7.1%
Unemployment rate *2000 census*		34.9%

Unemployment rate	34%
(BIA labor report, 2001)	
Per capita income *2000 census*	$11,181

LOCATION AND LAND STATUS
The Tuolumne Rancheria is located in east-central California, in the western foothills of the Sierra Nevada near Yosemite National Park. It lies approximately120 miles southeast of Sacramento, 60 miles due east of Stockton, and is about a three-hour drive from San Francisco.

The original 289.52-acre purchase took place on October 25, 1910, under the authority of the Acts of June 21, 1906, and April 30, 1908. Executive Order 1517 of April 13,1912, added 33.58

acres, while an additional 12.67 acres were purchased on April 14, 1978, under the authority of the Act of June 18, 1934.

PHYSICAL DESCRIPTION
The Tuolumne Rancheria experiences summer temperatures that range between 88°F and 95°F and winter lows that range between 30°F and 45°F. Annual precipitation is about 13.8 inches.

CULTURE AND HISTORY
Members of the Tuolumne Rancheria descend from the Northern, Southern, and Central groups of the Sierra Me-Wuk Tribe. The traditional homelands of the Northern Me-Wuk surround much of the Central Sierra region and include present-day Amador and Calaveras counties. The Central Me-Wuk homelands encompassed southern Calaveras and Tuolumne in the Sierra Nevada, and the Southern Me-Wuk homelands included territory between Mariposa County and Yosemite National Park. Their traditional language belongs to the Penutian language family, other languages of which are spoken by peoples from the coast of Canada to the U.S. Southeast and south to the Yucatan Peninsula. The Tuolumne Rancheria is one of two federally recognized Miwok (or Me-Wuk) reservations.

The traditional territory of the Sierra Me-Wuks was the setting for the California gold rush; the fabled mother lode was discovered there in 1848. Contact with Euro-Americans during this disruptive period reduced the Sierra Me-Wuks from a once-thriving population of 8,000 to less than 700 by 1910. Foreign diseases and genocidal practices by Euro-American settlers account for this decline. Once the gold rush had run its course, logging of the dense forests in the region became a major industry, one in which many area residents found employment.

Today few tribal elders under the age of 60 speak the Me-Wuk language, largely because of the historic insistence by government Indian schools that students not speak their Native languages. Traditional Me-Wuk culture remains alive on the rancheria, however. The main cultural event of the year is the Acorn Festival, celebrated during the second week of September. This weekend of dance honors the acorn crop; the black acorn was once the main food staple of the Me-Wuks. Since the late 1970s, the Tuolumne Rancheria has expanded its land base and has looked largely toward the area's growing tourist market as a potentially fruitful arena of economic development.

GOVERNMENT
The Tuolumne Rancheria is governed by a community council composed of all qualified members. The council meets twice annually, with 35 percent of its membership constituting a quorum. Four tribal officers are elected from the council's membership for one-year terms. Officers include a chairperson, vice-chairperson, a secretary, and a treasurer. The tribe is organized under a constitution drafted under the Indian Reorganization Act of 1934; it was approved in January of 1936.

ECONOMY
The tribal economy is supported in large part by its gaming operations.

Agriculture and Livestock. The tribe is considering the feasibility of redeveloping the five to seven acres of apple orchards already existing on the rancheria.

Gaming. The tribe owns and operates the Black Oak Casino in Tuolumne. It offers 600 slots/VLTs, 6 table games, and 2 restau-

rants. The casino employs 350 people. Completion of expansions to the casino is scheduled for late 2004. Expansions will include 940 slot machines, 24 table games, a nonsmoking game area, three restaurants, two casino-floor bars, a sports bar, an entertainment lounge with a dance floor, and a gift shop. The new facilities will also feature an entire floor dedicated to family entertainment and dining, with a restaurant, a bowling center, and an arcade.

Construction. A number of developments in the rancheria's vicinity provide construction jobs for tribal members, with the clear potential for a significant increase in this kind of employment.

Tourism and Recreation. Tourism and recreation represent the area's most significant economic potential, according to the Central Sierra District Economic Development District. The tribe intends to capitalize on the area's recent and future growth in tourism, and it is investigating hotel and restaurant training programs for its members.

The tribe's annual Acorn Festival is held at the Tuolumne Rancheria in conjunction with an annual powwow held at the Westside Property. The powwow offers competitive dancing. The tribe's casino provides shuttle service between the festivities. The festival attracts approximately 2,000 people to the rancheria. The tribe acquired economic development administration funding to complete a large parking lot and toilet facilities specifically to enhance the feasibility of larger crowds at the festival. The tribe also sponsors an annual Indian Market in May. It features sales and demonstrations by California Native American artisans.

INFRASTRUCTURE
The rancheria is four miles from Tuolumne, off California Highway120 on Highway 108, just east of Highway 49.

Electricity. Pacific Gas and Electric provides the rancheria with electricity; only bottled gas is available to residents.

Transportation. Commercial bus service is available in Tuolumne. Sonora, 10 miles from the rancheria, has train and truck services. The nearest commercial air service is available in Stockton, 60 miles away.

COMMUNITY FACILITIES AND SERVICES
There are several roundhouses and a community building on the rancheria.

Education. Children attend school in the nearby town of Tuolumne.

Health Care. The Tuolumne Indian Health Center was established in 1969. The facility has provided medical assistance training that, over the years, has created many jobs for local people. MACT Health Board also provides health services, including comprehensive medical, dental, mental health, substance abuse prevention, community outreach, and laboratory. Clinics are located in Jackson, Tuolumne, Sonora, Westpoint, and Mariposa. A hospital and other major medical services are available about 10 miles away, in Sonora.

ENVIRONMENTAL CONCERNS
The tribe applied for General Assistance funding from the BIA for fiscal years 1997 through 2000 to develop an environmental and natural resources office. The tribe's primary concerns include illegal wood harvesting, which has led to the disruption of native species.

Tuolumne

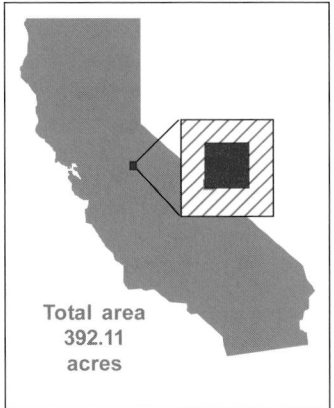

Total area
392.11
acres

Twenty-Nine Palms

**Twenty-Nine Palms
Reservation**
Federal reservation
Luiseño
**San Bernadino and Riverside
counties, California**

Twenty-Nine Palms Band
of Mission Indians
46-2000 Harrison Place
Coachella, CA 92236
760-863-2444
760-863-2449 Fax

Total area *(BIA realty, 2003)*	402.13 acres
Total area *(Tribal source, 2004)*	310 acres
Tribal enrollment *(BIA labor report, 2001)*	13
Total labor force *(BIA labor report, 2001)*	12
Unemployment rate	58%
(BIA labor report, 2001)	

LOCATION AND LAND STATUS
The Twenty-Nine Palms has a reservation of 160 acres, which is located in San Bernadino County, California. The other reservation, where the casino is located, is 150 acres in Riverside County, California.

CULTURE AND HISTORY
Members of the Twenty-Nine Palms Band of Mission Indians belong to the Chemehuevi groups. The Chemehuevi tribes traditionally occupied territories along the Colorado River.

GOVERNMENT
The Twenty-Nine Palms Band is a PL-638 tribe. Governmental departments include an Environmental Protection Agency.

ECONOMY
Economic Development Projects. The tribe is in the process of developing a resort.

Gaming. The tribe owns the Trump 29 Casino in partnership with Trump Hotels and Casino Resorts. The casino offers 2,000 slots/VLTs, 35 table games, 3 restaurants, 2 entertainment venues, and a banquet room. The tribe sponsors the annual 29 Palms Winter Gathering Powwow, and the Annual Theresa A. Mike Scholarship Fashion Show. The casino provides shuttle service. It employs 750 people.

Tourism and Recreation. The Twenty-Nine Palms Reservation is located near the well-known resort community of Palm Springs. The region attracts a number of visitors and is a force in the tourism industry in Southern California.

INFRASTRUCTURE
Electricity. Electricity is provided to the reservation by IDD.

Water Supply. The reservation water and sewer needs are serviced by the Coachella systems.

COMMUNITY FACILITIES
Health Care. Tribal members receive health care services through a self-insured health program.

ENVIRONMENTAL CONCERNS AND INITIATIVES
As for the desert tribes in the southern California, water is an all-consuming issue. On the Twenty-Nine Palms Reservation there is a state-certified laboratory that performs water-quality tests on water samples taken from the wells and waterways of the agricultural areas nearby. This tribally owned laboratory assists the region's other tribes with their water-quality testing.

Pesticide runoff from agricultural lands onto tribal lands is another problem facing Twenty-Nine Palms. Through the tribe's Environmental Protection Agency program, the tribe has the technical capability to deal with this issue. It works with other local water agencies, local governments and the federal agencies to tackle its environmental concerns.

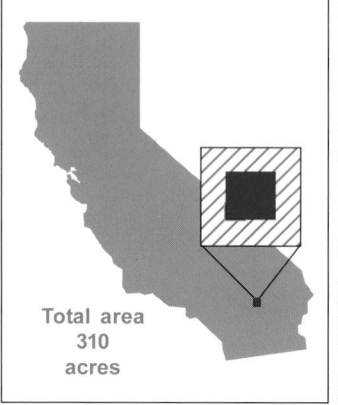

Total area
310
acres

TRI-CA-29Pm-025 29 Trump – Twenty-Nine Palms Casino

TRI-CA-29Pm-026 Entrance to the Trump Twenty-Nine Palms Casino

LOCATION AND LAND STATUS

The United Auburn Indian Community is located in the Sierra Nevada foothills near Auburn, California. A reservation was first established for the Auburn Band as the Auburn Rancheria when the federal government placed 20 acres of land into trust for the band. Although the tribe was terminated in the 1960s, some of the land was retained in private ownership.

In 1991 the band regained its federal recognition. The tribe had 2.84 acres of land returned to its ownership, and the tribe was permitted to purchase lands in Placer County to establish a reservation. In 2000 the tribe identified 1,100 acres of land to be used for residential and community purposes for the tribe and 58.3 acres to be used for development of a class II or class III gaming facility. It requested that the lands be placed in trust status with the federal government, and in 2002 the department of the interior placed a 49-acre parcel of land in trust for the community. In 2003 the tribe purchased the 1,100-acre parcel in northwest Placer County.

CLIMATE

The average summer weather in Placer County includes moderate, dry days and cool nights. The run-off from the snowfields of the Sierra Nevada Mountains serves as a primary water source during the summer. The months of November and April yield the heaviest rainfall.

CULTURE AND HISTORY

The United Auburn Indian Community is comprised primarily of members from the Miwok and Southern Maidu or Hill Nisenan tribes. There is also documentation indicating the presence of Pomo, Wailaki, and Tehama descendants on the reservation. The shared rancheria lies in the region where the ancestral Maidu lands adjoined the ancestral Miwok lands. Spanish explorers arrived in California beginning in the sixteenth century. The Spanish established 21 missions throughout the territory, and land was taken into possession for the crown of Spain. Native peoples were displaced, enslaved, or murdered. In addition to the ravages by the Spanish, the indigenous people were vulnerable to the diseases the foreigners brought, and Native populations began a rapid decline. The U.S. entered into war with Mexico over the California territory in the 1800s, and in 1848 the Treaty of Guadalupe Hildago brought an end to the Mexican-American War. California became a territory of the U.S. and a state in 1850. That same year, California passed the Act for the Government and Protection of Indians, which effectively sanctioned the subjugation of the Native population. In addition, tribal land claims were nullified, and their lands were opened to the public.

In early 1915, BIA acknowledged a village of United Auburn tribal members living outside Auburn. Twenty acres of land were placed in trust for the tribe in 1917. In 1934 the Auburn Band voted not to organize under the Indian Reorganization Act. In 1953 the tribe received another 20 acres of land to be placed in trust. Also in 1953, Congress passed Resolution 107, which called for the termination of federal responsibilities to tribes. In 1958, The Rancheria Act, Public Law 85-671, terminated federal recognition of 41 rancherias in California, including United Auburn. The government prepared the Distribution Plan for the rancheria in 1959, identifying specific tribal members and the intended termination procedure. The tribe was formally terminated in 1967.

In 1970, members of the Auburn Indian Community filed suit against the federal government demanding that the government fulfill promises agreed upon prior to termination. The community argued that only those members identified in the 1959 Distribution Plan were officially terminated. The remaining members were still "dependents" of the federal government and they demanded acknowledgment as a recognized tribe. As the tribe continued to fight for federal recognition during the 1980s, it did receive limited municipal and county support. However, in 1989 the City of Auburn attempted to annex the rancheria. The resolution did not pass, and the lands remained in private ownership.

In 1991, members of the Auburn Band adopted a constitution and requested that the federal government recognize them as the United Auburn Indian Community of the Auburn Rancheria. Formal recognition did not come until 1994 when the U.S. House of Representatives passed the Auburn Indian Restoration Act. The majority of lands established for the historical rancheria were lost by this time, having passed into the ownership of private parties. With federal recognition came the provision that the tribe may acquire land in Placer County, California, in order to establish a new reservation. In 2002, the federal government placed 49 acres of land into trust for the tribe. The tribe's intended purpose for the lands was to establish a gaming facility. The site for the casino is actually located on 49 acres of a 58-acre parcel. The undeveloped 9 acres have been left undisturbed to act as a buffer zone for regional wetlands. Under the provisions of its gaming compact with the state, the tribe received approval from the Placer County Board of Supervisors for this project. The tribe also entered into a Memorandum of Understanding with the county to: provide for all fire, emergency, and law enforcement services serving the casino; to employ county welfare-to-work participants; and make financial contributions to the county. The tribe agreed to: comply with county zoning ordinances; provide for road improvements necessitated by the casino; and contribute to Placer County's Open Space Preservation Program.

GOVERNMENT

The community has a tribal-state compact. The tribe is governed by a tribal council comprised of four officers and one member. The tribal government includes the education and environmental departments.

ECONOMY

The economy of the United Auburn Community relies primarily on the income gained from its enterprises in the gaming industry. Revenue from the casino is used to purchase lands, supplement the general budget, and improve services available to tribal members.

Gaming. The United Auburn Indian Community owns Thunder Valley Casino, which is located in Placer County. The casino is operated for the tribe by Casinos Inc. of Las Vegas. The casino complex includes gaming facilities, dining facilities, and entertainment venues. It is the first casino in Northern California to offer Las Vegas-style gaming. Amenities include slot machines/VLTs, 100 table games, and an Asian gaming parlor. There is a 500-capacity buffet, a food court, and three full-service restaurants. There is also a bar. The casino averages between 8,000 and 10,000 guests per day. Approximately 2,000 people are employed by the casino.

The tribe recently donated its installment of the $1 million it anticipates it will make annually to nonprofit organizations based in Placer County. Its community giving program offers funds to local educational, health, arts and humanities, environmental, community development, and social service projects. It will not fund

United Auburn Indian Community
Federal reservation
Miwok and Maidu
Placer County, California

United Auburn Indian
  Community
575 Menlo Drive, Suite 2
Rocklin, CA 95765
916-663-3720
916-663-3727 Fax
auburnrancheria.com

Total area *(BIA realty, 2003)*
49.21 acres

Total area *(Tribal source, 2004)*
1,158.3 acres

Tribally owned *(BIA realty, 2003)*
49.21 acres

Tribally owned lands
(Tribal source, 2004)
1,100 acres

Population
?

Tribal enrollment
(Tribal source, 2004)
247

Total labor force
(BIA labor report, 2001)
101

Unemployment rate
(BIA labor report 2001)
52%

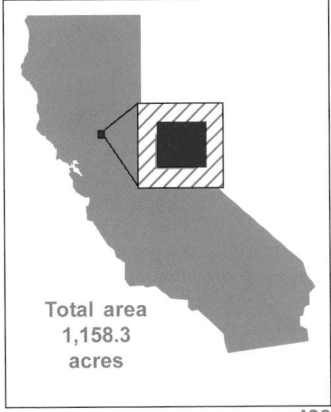

Total area
1,158.3
acres

United Auburn

loans, debts, retroactive funding, advertising, promotional sponsorships, religious-based projects, or political candidates, parties, or causes.

Real Estate/Commercial Development. The tribe recently purchased 1,100 acres of woodlands near the Camp Far West Reservoir. It plans to construct a housing development on the land. The proposed community will include approximately 93 five-acre home sites. Construction of the community will be especially sensitive to local wetlands and biological resources.

INFRASTRUCTURE
The reservation can be accessed from Highway 65. It is located on Athens Avenue in an unincorporated sector of Placer County. The tribe has provided the funds for road improvements in the area near the casino.

Transportation. Commercial air service is available in Sacramento, approximately 30 miles north of the reservation.

COMMUNITY FACILITIES AND SERVICES
The United Auburn Community is in the process of developing a community center at the historical rancheria. Housing grants are available to tribal members.

Education. The tribe has established an education center. The center's services include testing, tutoring, speech and language therapy, private teaching, and teacher consultation. GED classes, occupational therapy, and summer programs are in development. Over 20 tribal youth attend the center. The tribe also provides tuition for students at any educational level to any educational institution. Tribal youth attend public and private schools in the area.

Health Care. The tribe has established a medical, dental, and vision care plan for all tribal members. Services are provided through the Chapa de Indian Health Services.

ENVIRONMENTAL CONCERNS
The tribe operates an Environmental Protection Office. The tribe's foremost environmental concerns are the removal of abandoned and non-operational vehicles and the disposal of debris on the historic Auburn Rancheria. The tribe sponsored its first Community Clean-up Day in April 2004.

Upper Lake

Upper Lake Rancheria
Federally recognized tribe
Pomo
Lake County, California

Habematolel Pomo of Upper
Lake
P.O. Box 516
Upper Lake, CA 95845-0516
707-275-0737
877-543-5102
707-275-0757 Fax

Total area *(BIA realty, 2003)*
15.46 acres

Individually owned
(BIA realty, 2003)
15.46 acres

Tribally owned lands
(Tribal source, 2004)
249 acres

Population
70

Tribal enrollment
(BIA labor report, 2001)
145

Tribal enrollment
(Tribal source, 2004)
171

Total labor force *2000 census*
32

LOCATION AND LAND STATUS
Upper Lake Rancheria is located in northwestern California, one and a half miles from Upper Lake, 14 miles from the county seat of Lakeport, and 85 miles from the nearest urban center, Santa Rosa. The rancheria is divided into individually owned parcels and community property.

The secretary of the interior purchased the original 483.64 acres for the rancheria on February 15, 1907, and additional lands were purchased under the Indian Reorganization Act in 1934. The rancheria was terminated under the California Rancheria Act of 1958, but because of *Upper Lake v. Watt*, the tribe was given an option to elect "trust restoration". As of October 1984, 249 acres of individually owned lands were restored to trust. The Upper Lake Pomo Association holds the community lands in fee.

CULTURE AND HISTORY
Members of the Upper Lake Community belong to the Habematolel Band of the Pomo Tribe. The Pomos' ancestral homelands encompassed regions across northwestern California. The indigenous language belongs to the Hokan linguistic family. Traditional means of sustenance included fishing, gathering shellfish, and some hunting and gathering of acorns. The arrival of European explorers and Euro-American settlers brought irreversible changes to the indigenous cultures of the California territory. Exposure to foreign diseases, usurpation of tribal lands, and forced incarceration on federal reservations resulted in near-extermination for several tribal groups.

In response to the invasion upon their lands and ways of life, the Pomos banded together in efforts to buy back their lands. The tribe struggled to regain its land base from the late 1870s through the 1890s. By the turn of the twentieth century, however, much of this land was confiscated through foreclosure settlements and mortgage debts. Responding to public pressure, in 1905 Congress authorized an investigation of the living conditions of dislocated Indians. Beginning in 1906, legislation initiated by C. E. Kelsey, the lawyer and special agent appointed to lead the investigation, authorized annual appropriations for the purchase of Indian lands. With no, or very small, land bases, the Pomos were forced to enter the wage economy during the Depression.

Many Pomo women moved to the San Francisco Bay Area and worked as domestic laborers. Many Pomos were eligible for assistance through the BIA while there. Many Pomo men found local employment as migrant field workers and ranch laborers.

During a period of intense separatism and animosity toward indigenous peoples, the Pomos actively used the courts to challenge local segregation policies. In 1907 an Eastern Pomo, Ethan Anderson, won a court case granting the right to vote to non-reservation Indians. In 1923 Stephan Knight in Mendocino County challenged the state school segregation laws and, in an out-of-court settlement, forced a local public school to admit his daughter. Knight later took on the City of Ukiah, challenging the separatist policy of the local movie theater.

The tribe reorganized as the Habematolel Pomo of Upper Lake in 1998, and conducted a secretarial election to adopt its tribal constitution. It held its first executive council election on June 12, 2004, for seven members. The tribe's goals are to preserve the Pomo culture; to protect the interests of tribal youth; to use, conserve, and control its land and resources; to promote the stability and security of the tribe and tribal members; and to promote the social and economic well-being of tribal members. *(For additional cultural information, see California introduction.)*

GOVERNMENT
The Upper Lake Pomo Community was reorganized in 1998 as the Habematolel Pomo of Upper Lake. It is a corporate entity, established by a charter under the authority of the Act of June 18, 1934, and ratified February 15, 1942. The tribe is governed by a constitution and bylaws drawn up under the terms of the Indian Reorganization Act of 1934 and ratified in 1941. A seven-member elected executive council governs the tribe. The council includes a chairperson, vice-chairperson, secretary, treasurer, and three members at large

Governmental departments include environmental protection, housing, education, and administration. Upper Lake is a PL-638 tribe. It contracts its education and housing programs.

ECONOMY

The tribe is determined to develop a stable economy on the rancheria in order to allow its tribal members to live secure and comfortable lives there. Many job opportunities in the area require that residents travel long distances or reside away from the rancheria, at least part-time.

Economic Development Projects. The tribe is investigating projects to enhance economic conditions on the rancheria. Possible developments include a gaming facility.

Forestry. The timber industry provides jobs for residents of the entire northern California region.

Mining. The tribe has explored the feasibility of mining the gravel deposits located on the rancheria.

Tourism and Recreation. The rancheria's proximity to the Clear Lake recreational site makes it feasible to invest in camping facilities.

INFRASTRUCTURE

The rancheria is located 22 miles from U.S. Highway 101 and 68 miles from Interstate 5. Paved access roads lead to the rancheria.

Electricity. Is provided by Pacific Gas and Electric.

Water Supply. The rancheria provides water and sewer services to its residents. Individual septic tanks serve residencies.

Transportation. The nearest air service is available at the Lampson Airport in Lakeport, 15 miles from Upper Lake. Other transportation and freight facilities are located in Lakeport.

Telecommunications. SBC provides telephone service.

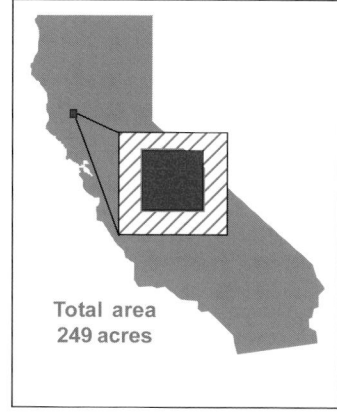

Total area
249 acres

COMMUNITY FACILITIES AND SERVICES
Tribal offices are located in Upper Lake.

Education. Children attend public schools in Upper Lake. The nearest postsecondary school is Mendocino Junior College, 32 miles away. The tribe provides educational services to its members, including tutoring, on-line tutoring, homework groups, computer access, computer software, books, Native American literature, math books, audio programs, and typing tutors. The tribe provides school supplies, lab fees, physical education clothing, test fees, and materials for students. The tribe also provides resources for financial aid, scholarships, and employment programs.

Health Care. Health services are available through the Lake County Tribal Health Clinic in Lakeport. Services include general medical, dental, community outreach, alcohol and drug abuse prevention, and child and family programs.

Upper Lake

Total labor force
(BIA labor report, 2001)
85

High school degree or higher
2000 census
64.6%

Bachelor's degree *2000 census*
4.6%

Unemployment rate *2000 census*
0%

Unemployment rate
(BIA labor report, 2001)
35%

Per capita income *2000 census*
$12,892

Viejas

Viejas

LOCATION AND LAND STATUS
The Viejas Reservation is located in southern California, 35 miles east of San Diego, north of Interstate 8 and the city of Alpine, approximately 30 miles north of the Mexican border. It is surrounded by the Cleveland National Forest. The reservation was established by an Executive Order in 1934.

On December 27, 1875, an Executive Order established the Capitan Grande Reservation on 15,573 acres. Kumeyaay tribal members resided at the Los Conejos and El Capitan communities within the reservation boundaries. In 1932 the City of San Diego proposed the creation of a dam on tribal lands and received congressional permission to forcibly relocate the Kumeyaay residents. The El Capitan Reservoir was completed in 1935 to feed the San Diego River. The reservoir, located on the Capitan Grande Indian Reservation, was removed from Viejas tribal ownership, and the City of San Diego awarded water rights. Tribal residents were forced to relocate to other lands. Members of the Los Conejos community purchased the Baron Long Ranch with money they received as compensation for their loss. In 1934 an Executive Order established the Viejas Reservation to the south of Capitan Grande on a 1,609-acre ranch formerly known as the Baron Long Ranch. The Capitan Grande Reservation remains jointly patented by the Viejas and Barona bands of the Kumeyaay tribe, though no tribal members reside there. The Viejas Band plans to purchase lands in order to increase its land base.

CULTURE AND HISTORY
The Viejas Band of Mission Indians is part of the Kumeyaay Indian Nation of southern California. Their language belongs to the Hokan language group; languages included in this group are spoken by peoples from southern Oregon to southern Mexico. The Viejas Band is one of 12 Kumeyaay bands. The others are Barona, Campo, Cyapaipe, Inaja-Cosmit, Jamul, La Posta, Manzanita, Mesa Grande, San Pasqual, Santa Ysabel, and Sycaun. Traditionally, the Kumeyaays depended upon the land for their subsistence, not only gathering the area's native plants and hunting wild game, but also farming within a complex system of agricultural landholdings. The area's heavy concentration of Spanish missionaries, with their zeal for assimilation, adversely affected the Kumeyaay people's Native language and culture retention.

Prior to the Mexican-American War, the Kumeyaay people traveled freely and lived in what is now southern San Diego County and northern Baja California, Mexico. Although the 1891 Act for the Relief of Mission Indians established a number of reservations for the Kumeyaay people, several small bands remained landless. The Kumeyaays presently occupy eight of the 17 reservations in San Diego County.

Viejas Reservation
Federal reservation
Kumeyaay
San Diego County, California

Viejas Band of the Kumeyaay
P.O. Box 908
Alpine, CA 92001
  619-445-3810
  619-445-5337 Fax
viejas.com

Viejas

Total area *(BIA realty, 2003)*
1,609 acres

Tribally owned lands
(BIA realty, 2003)
1,609 acres

Population *2000 census*
394

Native population
2000 census
146

Tribal enrollment
(BIA labor report, 2001)
268

Total labor force *2000 census*
129

Total labor force
(BIA labor report, 2001)
186

High school graduate or higher
2000 census
73.2%

Bachelor's degree or higher
2000 census
14.6%

Unemployment rate *2000 census*
10.9%

Unemployment rate
(BIA labor report, 2001)
68%

Unemployment rate
(Tribal source)
0%

Per capita income *2000 census*
$22,269

The Viejas Band of the Kumeyaays originally resided on El Capitan Indian Reservation, northwest of Alpine, California. The reservation was created in 1875 within the traditional Kumeyaay homelands. The reserved area encompassed 18,000 acres and was the largest in the county at the time. In 1932, the City of San Diego received approval from the U.S. Congress to forcibly remove the tribe from 2,800 acres in order to create a flood plain from the damming of the San Diego River. The tribe was compensated with $400,000. Using these funds, tribal members living in El Capitan bought a parcel of land to create the Barona Reservation, and members living in Los Conejos moved onto a 1,600-acre parcel of land to create the Viejas Reservation. The dam was consequently developed, and El Capitan Dam constitutes a 1,574-acre reservoir, the largest in the county, and a 190-square-mile watershed. In total, the tribe lost over 15,000 acres due to the dam's creation. Furthermore, the tribe was not permitted to retain any water rights to the area.

While the Viejas and Barona bands continue to share a joint-trust patent for the Capitan Grande Reservation, no tribal members reside there. Descendants of the former Capitan Grande communities now constitute the Viejas Band and the Barona Band.

The land continues to be of great value for the economic support of the Viejas people. While initially considered the least commercially attractive areas of the state, the Viejas land holdings have recently proven to be an extremely viable economic resource. The reservation's location, near Interstate 8 and within the pathway of the area's continuing urban sprawl, has provided the Viejas Band with a growing pool of people seeking recreational opportunities. The goal of the Viejas people is to capitalize on the economic value of their property without compromising their traditional cultural respect for the land.

GOVERNMENT

The Viejas Band is governed by a bi-level tribal government. The general council is comprised of all the tribe's adult voting members. The general council elects officers for the tribal council and votes on all land-use decisions. The tribal council is composed of a chairman, a vice-chairman, a secretary, and a treasurer, each elected to two-year terms. The tribal council serves as the executive, legislative, and judicial branches of the tribal government, and it serves as the director for the tribe's economic enterprises. The tribe is organized under a constitution drawn up under the Indian Reorganization Act of 1934.

The tribe has a law enforcement department. The tribal police force has cross-jurisdiction with the state, and the tribe has a tribal court. The tribe also maintains its own fully equipped fire station. The department employs a crew of 15 fire fighters and paramedics. An additional five fire fighters are available to provide fire prevention services to non-reservation rural area residents. The tribe is registered as a self-governing PL-638 tribe.

BUSINESS CORPORATION

Four Fires is an economic partnership of four member tribes: the Viejas Band of Kumeyaay Indians, the Forest County Potawatomi Community of Wisconsin, the Oneida Tribe of Indians of Wisconsin, and the San Manuel Band of Mission Indians of California. The partnership's first venture was the largest economic collaboration ever for American Indian governments. The project was the $43-million, 13-story, 233-suite Residence Inn by Marriott-Capitol in Washington, D.C. The hotel is situated in a prime location in the city, near the Smithsonian's National Museum of the American Indian.

ECONOMY

Since the loss of its original land base on the Capitan Grande Reservation, the Viejas Band has struggled to develop a secure and stable economy. In the last 20 years, it has done just that. On a foundation laid by its successful gaming operations, the tribe

has been able to fund the development of new economic projects and endeavors that have assisted it in reaching its goal of becoming a financially independent nation able to provide even the most basic services to its members.

In addition to the contributions the tribe makes to the local economy via employment opportunities, fees, and taxes paid, every year the Viejas Band makes philanthropic donations to hundreds of local community groups, service and civic organizations, schools, and charity events. Nearly $2 million was contributed in 2002. The support comes directly from the Viejas Tribal Council and its wholly owned business enterprises.

Government as Employer. The Viejas Band employs over 3,000 people. Its current payroll is about $72 million per year.

Economic Development Projects. The Viejas Band's mission is to continue to diversify its economy through the pursuit and development of economic projects in various fields and industries. A feasibility study regarding the formation of a renewable energy-based tribal utility is under way. The study will investigate which renewable energy technologies are optimal for the Viejas Reservation and the environment. The scheduled ending date for the study was December 2004.

The Viejas Band is currently negotiating a contract to purchase a cruise ship. The proposed project would create a partnership with Commodore Holdings to operate an 8,000-passenger cruise ship. The ship, to be named the Enchanted Sun, will provide day cruises from San Diego to Rosarito, Mexico. The ship will offer a 7,000-square-foot gaming area with Las Vegas-style slots, poker tables, craps, roulette, and Pai Gow. The cruise will also offer dining and entertainment to guests. The Viejas Band is the first California tribe to enter into the cruise line industry.

The tribe plans to develop a museum and an interactive representation of the Kumeyaay culture. The tribe hopes to eventually create a transportation system between the reservation and the city of San Diego. Further possibilities for the tribe include the development of a hotel and convention center in Viejas Valley. Should this project come to fruition, the complex will occupy an area that now houses tribal homes. In this case, the tribe would return to the available lands on the Capitan Grande Reservation.

Gaming. In September 1991, the band completed construction of the $4 million Viejas Casino and Turf Club. Open 24 hours and encompassing over 210,000 square feet, the gaming facility offers off-track horse betting, card and bingo games, video pull-tabs, and Indian blackjack. Other features include a 9,000-square-foot convention center, two entertainment venues, and five restaurants that offer a selection of dining tastes–Grove Steakhouse, the Harvest Buffet, the 24-hour Sunrise Diner, Tom Fat's China Camp Express, and the Viejas Deli Lounge. The casino has boosted the local economy, employing 2,400 people from the reservation and surrounding area. The casino is 30 minutes east of downtown San Diego.

The tribe has established the Viejas Casino Responsible Gaming Program and enforces policies and regulations to discourage gambling-addicted behavior in its patrons. All casino employees receive training to provide prevention support to clients, and the tribe supports anti-addiction programs as well.

Revenue generated by the tribe's gaming operations has been used to enhance tribal housing, community programs, health services, and tribal programs. In addition to creating a new community park, fire station, and senior citizens center, the tribe has also initiated a number of environmental projects to restore the integrity of tribal lands, watersheds, streams, and wetlands.

Financial Institutions. The tribe owns Borrego Springs Bank, N.A. The tribe purchased the bank in 1996, making it the first tribe to own a bank. The bank specializes in small business lending and was one of the 50 largest Small Business Administration lenders for three years. It has branches in Borrego Springs, La Mesa, and Alpine. The bank is designed to meet the needs of the entrepreneurial growth of Native American developmental projects.

Real Estate/Commercial Development. In partnership with the Oneida Tribe, the San Manuel Band of Mission Indians, and the Forest County Potawatomi, the Viejas Band of Kumeyaay Indians have created Four Fires LLC, a Delaware corporation. As a joint venture with The Donohue Development Companies of Washington, D.C., Four Fires LLC has built the Residence Inn Capitol, a hotel near the National Museum of the American Indian on the Mall in Washington. Four Fires owns a 59-percent stake in the 13-story Marriot Hotel. The hotel will be managed by Hospitality Partners of Bethesda, Maryland.

Services and Retail. Inspired by the design of an authentic Native American village, the Viejas Outlet Center provides 57 brand name stores, including a good selection of eateries. The grounds also feature Viejas Park, a center show court, a water court, and an air court. Entertainment shows and activities are held at these locations. The center is the only tribal business in San Diego County to collect sales and use tax. In 2002, it collected about $5 million. Over $600,000 was paid to the county, and the state allocated over $800,000 to county public safety, health, welfare, and transportation programs.

The Viejas Band's first business venture was the 133-acre Ma-Tar-Awa Recreational Vehicle Park, opening in 1976, at a construction cost of more than $1 million. Today, Ma-Tar-Awa features a clubhouse, a convenience store, a laundry facility, propane service, a swimming pool, 88 RV hookups, and campsites. In 1996, the Viejas Ban purchased Alpine Springs Recreational Vehicle Park 6. Features of the park include a clubhouse, a swimming pool, 96 full hookups, a group area with 17 electric and water hookups, and a laundry facility.

Media and Communications. The tribe publishes the *Viejas Newsletter.* The tribe also purchased KDI-TV, a 12,000-watt station based in National City, California.

Tourism and Recreation. The tribe owns the Viejas Concert in the Park Series. The series is held in Viejas Park, a 1,500-seat amphitheater park, usually during the late summer season. The concert series often features celebrity entertainers. The Viejas Casino and the Viejas Outlet Center are major attractions for visitors. The Ma-Tar-Awa Recreational Vehicle Park has successfully contributed to tribal employment and revenue since 1975.

INFRASTRUCTURE
Interstate 8 runs east-west, south of the reservation. A firebreak, which surrounds a portion of the reservation, protects it from the brush fires that can be so destructive in southern California.

Electricity. San Diego Gas and Electric Company provides gas and electricity.

Water Supply. The Viejas Band provides water to reservation residents by means of a recently completed underground water and sewer system. The tribe has also constructed a water-recycling center.

Transportation. Airline and train facilities are available 33 miles west of the reservation, in San Diego. In addition, bus and trucking services are available in Alpine and El Cajon.

COMMUNITY FACILITIES AND SERVICES
The tribe has recently completed a new community park, fire station, and senior citizens center on the reservation. The Viejas Management Internship Program (VMIP) provides interns with the opportunity to train in the management of every Viejas business. All tribal members are eligible to participate, and upon completion of the program most participants are placed in a management position with the tribal program of their choice.

Education. Tribal youth attend schools in the Alpine Union School District and the Grossmont High School District. The tribe has recently created the Viejas Learning Center. The center offers all tribal members supplemental educational programs, including a summer culture program, cultural preservation classes, an independent academic study program, family development classes, financial planning classes, and literacy workshops. Facilities include a college and career center and a computer lab. From the income created by its gaming operations, the tribe is now able to provide a full-scholarship program for all interested tribal members.

Health Care. The tribe provides health insurance to all tribal members. Southern Indian Health Council, located in Alpine, and Campo Medical/Dental Clinic, located in Campo, provide health care services. The Youth Regional Treatment Center in Boulevard provides medical monitoring and inpatient youth substance-abuse treatment. La Posta Outreach Substance Abuse Center in Boulevard provides outpatient substance-abuse counseling and treatment sources.

ENVIRONMENTAL CONCERNS
The tribe has implemented a series of multimillion-dollar projects on the reservation to provide environmental protection and restoration to its natural resources. Water supply is a primary concern in the area, and the tribe has developed a water recycling facility. The plant recycles water for non-domestic use.

Viejas

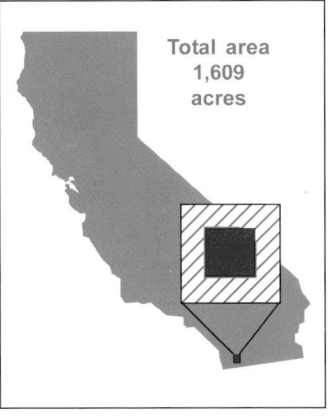

Total area
1,609
acres

Washoe

See Nevada

TRI-CA-Vj-029

TRI-CA-Vj-030

TRI-CA-Vj-029 Welcome Sign for the Viejas Outlet Center

TRI-CA-Vj-030 Viejas Outlet Mall - Patio

Bringing Financial and Business Expertise to Tribes, Borrego Springs Bank, Viejas Band of Kumeyaay Indians (La Mesa, California)

Honoring Nations Honoree 2002

Text in its entirety from: The Harvard Project On American Indian Economic Development

John F. Kennedy School of Government Harvard University

The first American Indian-owned bank in California, Borrego Springs Bank offers a full range of services to tribal governments, Native-owned businesses, and others in order to foster the economic self-sufficiency of American Indian nations and individuals, diversify the Viejas Tribe's economy, and improve Indian Country's access to financial services. With over $83 million in assets and three full-service branches that serve Indian and non-Indian clientele, the Bank is an impressive financial institution that provides fruitful lessons for other tribes.

For many Indians, obtaining even the most fundamental banking services is a difficult undertaking. A recent report by the US Department of the Treasury finds that Indians' lack of access to capital and financial services is a key barrier to economic advancement: 65 percent of Native survey respondents reported that conventional mortgages are difficult or impossible to obtain, and 66 percent stated that private equity is difficult or impossible to obtain for Native business owners. Trust-land issues, jurisdictional disputes, and cultural misunderstandings have long been identified as contributors to these problems. Yet without adequate access to capital and banking services, both Indian tribes and individuals have difficulty breaking cycles of poverty, fostering business activity, and achieving personal and community economic prosperity.

For the Viejas Band of Kumeyaay Indians, tribal gaming-introduced with the 1991 opening of the Viejas Casino and Turf Club-ushered in an era of economic hope for the Tribe's three hundred citizens. Located in the outskirts of San Diego, the Casino and Turf Club quickly became a major destination, and with its popularity came significant streams of revenue for the Tribe. The casino's success meant that Viejas leaders finally could address the longstanding problems of unemployment, substandard housing, and inadequate public services on the Tribe's 1,600-acre reservation. The Tribe built new homes, improved public works, built schools, invested in social services, and embarked on environmental enhancement projects. The Tribe also began to diversify its economy by building the multi-million dollar Viejas Outlet Center and the Alpine Recreational Vehicle Park. These efforts are paying off. Today, tribal unemployment is close to zero, and the Tribe's businesses employ well over two thousand people.

The Viejas Tribe's renaissance prompted tribal leaders to think strategically about the Tribe's economic future. They were convinced that achieving long-term economic prosperity required the Tribe not only to possess financial resources, but also to have the expertise to manage those resources. Tribal leaders concluded that one means of obtaining this expertise was through bank ownership.

The opportunity arose in 1995 when the Viejas Tribe learned that a small community bank in Borrego Springs serving several under-served rural communities in the California desert was in distress. By obtaining majority interest in the bank and turning it into a profitable institution, the Tribe could expand and diversify its economy, provide services that Indians had difficulty obtaining, and develop financial expertise that would enhance the Tribe's ability to be self-governing. After candid discussions about the risks and benefits of bank ownership, it decided to move forward. The parties crafted a purchase agreement, and

the bank filed an application with the state that would have led to the charter of the first tribally owned bank in California. However, opposition from the state's Attorney General delayed the deal, so the bank and the Tribe opted for an alternative strategy-a federal charter. In December 1996, the Viejas Tribe made a capital infusion of $2.4 million and became the majority owner of Borrego Springs Bank, a federally chartered financial institution.

With the Viejas Tribe's assistance, Borrego Springs Bank has developed an impressive array of services. These include business loans, government guaranteed programs, full business deposit services, money market sweep accounts, on-line banking, and computer cash management. The Bank also offers a full range of services tailored specifically to meet the needs of tribal governments, including credit counseling, minors and elders' trust assistance, housing programs, full deposit services, funds management assistance, infrastructure loans, consumer and credit repair loans, tax deferral programs, and federal lending programs. Additionally, Borrego Springs Bank possesses an Indian Gaming Services division, which partners with other Indian-owned financial institutions to facilitate "Indian-to-Indian" commerce and offers tribal casinos a full range of cash access services such as ATMs, credit and cash advances, and check cashing.

Borrego Springs Bank has proved that Indian-owned financial institutions can compete in an extremely competitive and intensely regulated market. The Bank provides all banking services for the Viejas Tribe and is a recognized leader in banking product development and programs. It now has three full service branches - located in Borrego Springs, La Mesa, and in Alpine (where the reservation is located) - and has opened twelve loan production offices around the United States. Its award-winning small business lending program serves six states and is consistently ranked among the top fifty lenders in the nation. Borrego Springs Bank's assets have grown tremendously-from $25 million in 1995 to more than $83 million in 2002-and it has earned steady profits. In other words, the Viejas have realized a significant increase in the value of their initial investment and have generated ongoing income for the Tribe. In addition to its success as a financial institution, Borrego Springs Bank and its owner, the Viejas Tribe, have gained widespread admiration. By rescuing the Bank from certain closure, the Viejas were viewed as expressing interest in the needs of neighboring non-Indian communities as well as in their own community. Indeed, the Bank has enhanced the Tribe's credibility in both financial and political circles.

But the Borrego Springs Bank has proven to be much more than a good investment-it also has had a direct impact on the lives of Viejas citizens through improved financial literacy and better access to financial opportunities. Prior to the Bank's incorporation into the community, the majority of tribal citizens functioned in cash only. For example, tribal per capita distributions were made in cash and most Viejas citizens did not have bank accounts or ready access to credit. Today, 75 percent of Viejas citizens have bank accounts and receive their revenue distributions through direct deposits into checking accounts. For tribal youth, the Bank partnered with the Tribe's government to design and implement a financial literacy course that is required of minors before they are allowed to access their tribal trust account. Borrego Springs Bank also assists tribal citizens with credit counseling and restructuring and works with individual entrepreneurs to develop and pursue business opportunities.

Additionally, the Bank is helping to develop a pool of financially savvy tribal leaders. Consistent with the Viejas' belief that self-governance requires leaders to possess financial resource management skills, four former Viejas tribal as well as the chairman of a neighboring tribe sit on the Bank's ten-member Board of Directors, which also includes business leaders and former bankers. As Board members, these tribal leaders are able to develop and refine their banking skills by gaining valuable experience in financial strategy and analysis, including program impact analysis, assessment of appropriate contingency reserves, and the balance between debt and equity financing. Not surprisingly, this has positively influenced all of the Tribe's government and business operations. A recent example is the formation of a four-tribe corporation to build and operate a hotel in Washington, DC which will be designed with a Native American theme and located only a few blocks from the Smithsonian Institution's new National Museum of the American Indian. This corporation once again demonstrates the Viejas Tribe's motivation and capacity to pursue opportunities that advance its economic independence.

Both Viejas leaders and Bank principals are committed to sharing the success of Borrego Springs Bank with other Indian nations. As noted, the Bank's tribal-specific programs, including credit counseling, tribal trust management, and programs offered by the Bank's Indian Gaming Services division, provide scores of tribes with services that are tailored to meet their needs. The Bank also has developed an innovative home loan program that allows rural California tribes to borrow against future income from gaming revenue-sharing (the most recent California tribal-state gaming compact guarantees such revenue sharing between gaming and non-gaming tribes). As a result, home construction efforts that would otherwise stretch over several years may be accomplished in a single season. Yet Borrego Springs Bank's investment in Indian Country extends well beyond its service offerings. Members of the Bank's Board of Directors educate other tribal governments by participating in conferences and seminars and providing pro bono advice about tribal financial resource management. The Bank is a leader in promoting Indian-to-Indian commerce. And finally, the Bank works with tribal governments, trade associations, lenders, legislators, and the federal government to revise rules, policies, and laws to improve access to financial services for Indians. In short, the Viejas are as concerned about helping others as they are about the Bank's bottom line.

The Viejas Tribe rightly considers its experience with the Borrego Springs Bank as establishing a pattern from which other tribes can and should learn. In July 2000, the Bank's president helped found the North American Native Bankers Association to further tribal participation in the commercial banking industry and hosted the Association's first conference to assist tribes that are consid-

ering establishing their own banks. For other Indian nations, the Viejas Tribe offers four lessons about what it takes to own and manage a commercial bank. First, banking requires a stable tribal government. The financial and political penalties for "not doing banking right" are severe, particularly given the regulations under which such enterprises operate. The second ingredient is a significant resource base. Both the purchase and on-going functioning of a bank require substantial investments, and while cumulative profits can be large, the margins are low. The third ingredient is a long-term outlook. It has taken Borrego Springs Bank seven years of unrelenting effort to achieve its present success. This type of venture is not well suited for tribes looking to make a quick profit. Finally, commercial banking requires highly skilled managers and staff who are able to work effectively in both the Indian and non-Indian worlds. Finding excellent staff who can work with tribal governments, regulatory agencies, auditors, and the community is imperative for success.

Driven by the idea that sovereignty and economic self-reliance go hand-in-hand, the Viejas Band of Kumeyaay Indians took a bold and calculated step in purchasing the Borrego Springs Bank. The Bank has become an innovative financial institution that effectively serves important individual and community needs. As an agent for economic, political, and social change for the Viejas and other tribes, the Bank is truly outstanding: Its presence will benefit generations to come. As a recognized leader in pushing the frontiers of self-sufficiency, the Viejas Tribe is showing Indian Country and the rest of America how to do banking right.

Lessons

Bank ownership is one way for an Indian nation to provide difficult-to-obtain financial services, develop internal financial expertise, and diversify the tribal economy. Ingredients for success in this extremely competitive and highly regulated industry include large sums of initial and working capital, a long-term outlook, and a highly skilled staff.

Providing financial literacy training to tribal citizens, youth, elected leadership, and public administrators (for example, in banking, credit, financial planning, investing, taxes, etc.) is a good investment for tribal governments. Such training allows individuals to make informed personal finance decisions and fortifies a tribe's ability to manage its resources effectively.

Tribal success in economic development creates new demand for tribal-specific services (for example, cash services for tribal gaming enterprises). Indian tribes and individuals can develop businesses to fill emerging market niches and thereby facilitate Indian-to-Indian commerce.

Honoring Nations
Honoree 2002

Text in its entirety from:
The Harvard Project On
American Indian Economic
Development

John F. Kennedy School
of Government
Harvard University

X-L Ranch

X-L Ranch Reservation
Federal reservation
Pit River (Achomawi)
Modoc County, California

Pit River Tribe
37014 Main Street
Burney, CA 96013
530-335-5421
530-335-3140 Fax

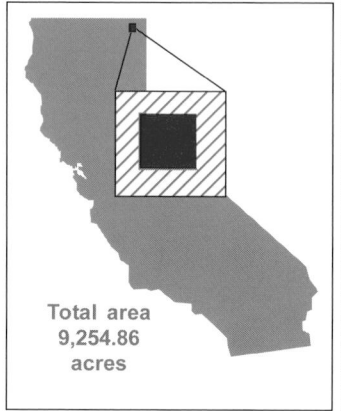

Total area
9,254.86
acres

Total area *(BIA realty, 2003)*		9,968.23 acres
Total area *(Tribal source, 2004)*		9,254.86 acres
Tribally owned		9,968.23 acres
(BIA realty, 2003)		
Population		23
Total labor force *2000 census*		3
High school graduate or higher		60%
2000 census		
Bachelor's degree or higher		0%
2000 census		
Unemployment rate *2000 census*		100%
Per capita income *2000 census*		8,140

(Please refer to the Pit River Tribe for further information regarding the following items: Culture and History, Government, and Community Facilities.)

LOCATION AND LAND STATUS
The X-L Ranch Reservation spans 9,254.86 acres of grazing and valley land in northeastern California. The reservation was established on October 13, 1938, for bands of the Pit River Indians of the State of California as designated by the Secretary of the Interior in accordance with the Act of 1934. The deed is held in trust by the United States Government.

GOVERNMENT
Tribal jurisdiction for the X-L Ranch Reservation was not restored until 1975, after an eleven-year legal battle pursued by the tribe and the California Indian Legal Services. The reservation was managed by the Bureau of Indian Affairs on behalf of the tribe until 1989.

ECONOMY
Because of the lack of local employment opportunities, most tribal members do not live on federal trust land or other tribally owned land. Primary employment opportunities in Modoc County are seasonal.

Agriculture and Livestock. While only one crop of hay is harvested each year on the X-L Ranch Reservation, there is a potential for two annual crops. The tribe currently leases a portion of the reservation for cattle grazing. This lease arrangement generates about $50,000 annually.

INFRASTRUCTURE
U.S. Highway 396 serves as the county's principle route and passes through Alturas. State Highway 299, running east-west, intersects U.S. 396 at Alturas and turns southwest at Canby. Several reservation roads and a bridge need repair.

Electricity. Electricity is provided by Pacific Gas and Electric.

Fuel. Only bottled gas is available.

Water Supply. Residents use individual septic tanks for sewage disposal and derive their water from both surface and subsurface wells.

Transportation. The closest bus and truck lines to the reservation are available in Alturas, which is located six miles from X-L Ranch. There are several private airstrips in the area; the closest commercial air service is available in Redding. The nearest train service is in Redding.

Yurok

Yurok Reservation
Federal reservation
Yurok
Humboldt and Del Norte counties, California

Yurok Tribe
P.O. Box 1027
Klamath, CA 95548
707-482-1350
707-482-1377 Fax
yuroktribe.org

LOCATION AND LAND STATUS
The Yurok Reservation is located near the Pacific Coast in northwestern California, about 30 miles south of the Oregon border. It is bisected by the Klamath River, dividing the reservation into upper and lower regions. Most of the reservation is located in a river gorge. Steep, rugged terrain and heavy precipitation produce considerable erosion throughout most of the reservation. The reservation spans from Del Norte to Humboldt counties, with the following population centers on or near the reservation– Weitchpec, Johnsons Village, and Klamath.

Of the approximately 5,500 acres within the reservation boundaries, about 85 percent remain outside of federal trust status, the vast majority of which is owned by Simpson Timber Company. A large portion of the tribe's land holdings are timberlands which the tribe's natural resource department manages.

What is now called the Yurok Reservation was established by President Harrison in 1891 as an extension to run between the Hoopa Valley Indian Reservation directly to the south (authorized by the U.S. Congress in 1864) and the disputed 1855 Klamath River Reservation to the north. This extension entails a narrow strip of land one mile in width on each side of the Klamath River. At the time of its formation, the extension consisted of 58,168 acres. By the following year, however, so-called "surplus" land within the reservation was opened to purchase (through questionable forced-fee patents) by immigrant interests, primarily timber companies. This action led to an eventual lawsuit filed on behalf of the Yuroks of Hoopa Square and the extension to recover proceeds from the sales that had long been held in escrow by the BIA. The Yuroks' persistence over this injustice has culminated in an historic agreement to amend the Hoopa/Yurok Settlement Act. This should have a large impact on the Yurok Tribe, both culturally and economically. The plan requires congressional approval.

CULTURE AND HISTORY
The Yuroks are indigenous to the Lower Klamath River and the Pacific Coast adjacent to its mouth. Prior to European contact, they comprised about 2,500 people living in more than 50 hamlets. The Yuroks are linked by a common language, customary law, and a reliance on salmon fishing, hunting, and acorn harvesting. Their traditional language is related to the Algonquian languages, spoken by peoples over vast areas of eastern North America.

The Gold Rush of 1849 brought the first non-Indian immigrants into Yurok territory. By 1851, Euro-American interests were already well enough established to defeat the ratification of a treaty that would have created a large Yurok reservation. Armed conflict between Yuroks and the settlers ensued in the wake of this defeat, continuing until the mid-1860s.

The Yurok population reached its ebb around 1910, when only 688 were counted, a 73 percent decline from the 1848 population. Out of this period arose the Yurok Tribal Organization, which sought relief from poverty and malnutrition for its constituents by working to guarantee access to aboriginal subsistence sites. Aside from these efforts, Yuroks found some wage labor in salmon canneries from the late 1800s through 1934, the same year all Indian commercial fishing and gill netting were banned. These rights were not restored until 1977. In addition to employment in commercial fishing and fish packing, Yuroks found work during the twentieth century primarily in the region's agricultural (hops and lily bulbs) and timber industries.

Around the turn of the twentieth century the government combined the Yuroks' land with the neighboring Hoopa Reservation. The two tribes operated under one tribal government until the passage of the Hoopa-Yurok Settlement Act of 1988. Yurok tribal members began the process of reestablishing a sovereign tribal government, a process that culminated on April 23, 1994, with the installation of the Yurok Tribal Council. Also beginning in the 1980s, the community has seen a revitalization of traditional Yurok renewal ceremonies (Jump Dances and Brush Dances). At the same time, what is perhaps the strongest Shaker church in California continues to thrive on the reservation. Preservation of the Yurok language, heritage, and traditional ways is very important to the tribe. In 2004, after 23 months of negotiations between the tribe and the Brooklyn Museum of Art, 11 cultural items were returned to the tribe after nearly 100 years of absence. The items were used in tribal ceremonial dances that were performed before the pioneer settlers outlawed the ceremonies.

GOVERNMENT
The Yurok Tribal Council consists of a tribal chair and a vice-chair elected at large, and seven council members elected on a district basis. Members are elected to three-year terms. The tribe is organized under a draft constitution. The tribe's staff moved into a new 30,000-square-foot office complex located in Klamath in September 2002.

ECONOMY
Government as Employer. Almost half of the people employed (47 percent) are government workers. Private wage and salary workers account for 46 percent of those employed, and the remaining 7 percent of workers are self-employed. Management, professional, and related occupations employ 28 percent of the workforce. The service industry employs 22 percent of the workforce, and 13 percent of the workforce is centered in farming, fishing, and forestry occupations. The median household income is $20,592.

Economic Development Projects. The tribal plan for the amendment to the Hoopa-Yurok Settlement Act focuses on the potential created by the reservation's natural resources. Management of a commercial timber harvest on a sustainable yield basis is planned. A financial boost would be provided for ongoing tribal enterprises that generate revenue to the tribe. Some enterprises would take advantage of the recreational opportunities in the Klamath River Basin. Business possibilities would include an eco-lodge, fishing, and RV resorts. A gravel operation is also planned. Federal funds are expected for the development of infrastructure on the reservation.

A large portion of the Klamath town site is owned by the tribe, as well as an RV resort located at the mouth of the Klamath River, in the village of Requa. A large-scale project of the Yurok Economic Development Corporation is planned to create a Yurok travel center in Klamath. Aside from the sale of gas, it would feature a smoke shop, sporting goods section, and an area for consignment sale of local arts and crafts.

Forestry. While the timber industry remains a major employer in the region and offers employment opportunities for tribal members, declining reserves and increasingly stringent environmental regulations mean that the industry may no longer be so singularly relied upon as a source of income. However, the amendment to the Hoopa-Yurok Settlement Act is expected to provide tribal management of a commercial timber harvest. This would be designed around a sustainable yield basis in accordance with scientifically established ecosystem management. This program would provide income and employment to the tribe, while overseeing forest management.

Fisheries. The native fishery (largely salmon-based) has been in a state of serious decline since the early 1980s, due to the continuing degradation of spawning habitat, dam diversions, and the cumulative effect of logging in the area. In the fall of 2002, an estimated 34,000 adult pre-spawning salmon and steelhead died in what some refer to as one of the worst fish kills in U.S. history. Man-made "low flows" in the river were cited as the cause. Significant numbers of tribal members continue to make their living from the salmon fishery. During the 1980s, two small Yurok-managed salmon hatcheries were established in the extension. Numerous projects were funded in 2000-2002: Pacific Coastal Salmon Recovery funds as well as tribal, state, and local funds benefited restoration and monitoring work on the Klamath River, in-stream survey work, and other projects designed to increase salmon survival.

Tourism and Recreation. With its proximity to Redwood National Park and the Pacific Ocean, as well its Klamath River resource, the Yurok Reservation is well situated for economic growth in the tourist sector. Thousands of travelers on Highway 101 pass by the town of Klamath daily. The Yurok Tribe is currently pursuing eco-tourism development in the Klamath area. The development would focus on recreation and tourist opportunities created by the surrounding Redwood National and State Parks. Site layouts include cabins, a restaurant, and a store. Other possible attractions include a smoked salmon and specialty food shop, river rafting, kayaking, guided fishing tours, and cultural demonstrations. Eventually the tribe would like to develop the Klamath location into a self-contained destination area, providing necessary services, such as a lodging facility, a gas station, a grocery store, and other businesses. The tribe is considering building a casino.

INFRASTRUCTURE
The single-lane State Route 169 serves as the primary access road to the reservation along the east side of the Klamath River, beginning at Weitchpec and ending at Johnsons Village. U.S. 101, the major highway in the area, crosses the reservation through the town of Klamath. The reservation also contains several state, county, and BIA roads. Reservation access from Johnsons Village to Klamath is only by boat along the Klamath River. Commercial bus service is available in the town of Klamath, while commercial air service and freight services are offered in Crescent City, approximately 20 miles north of the reservation. Because of the remote location of the upper reservation, infrastructure development has been minimal, leaving most of this land without power and phone service. The lower reservation, with its access to U.S. 101, provides most basic infrastructure services.

COMMUNITY FACILITIES AND SERVICES
Currently five small community water associations serve the Yurok Reservation; creation of a Public Utility District is anticipated. Other utilities are available from the city of Klamath. Most housing units are heated by wood. Heating for the 441 occupied housing units is as follows: 239 use wood; 100 use electricity; 59 use bottled, tank, or LP gas; 39 use fuel oil or kerosene; and 5 heat

Yurok

Total area *(BIA realty, 2003)*
5,490.50 acres

Total area
(Central California Agency, 2002)
5,489.50 acres

Tribally owned *(BIA realty, 2003)*
1,221.28 acres

Tribally owned lands
(Central California Agency, 2002)
1,221.28 acres

Individually owned
(BIA realty, 2003)
4,268.22 acres

Individually owned lands
(Central California Agency, 2002)
4,268.22 acres

Government owned
(BIA realty, 2003)
1 acre

Population
1,103
2000 census

Tribal enrollment
4,466

Total labor force on-reservation
2000 census
434

Total labor force
2,151

High school graduate or higher
2000 census
67.9%

Bachelor's degree or higher
2000 census
7.5%

Unemployment rate *2000 census*
24.9%

Per capita income *(1999)*
$10,881

Yurok

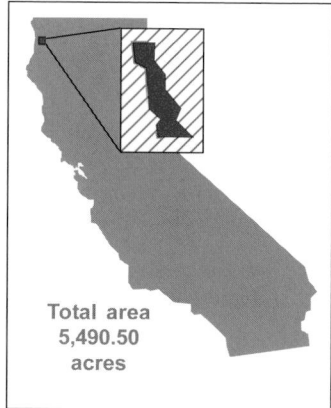

Total area
5,490.50
acres

with utility gas. Ninety percent of housing units have complete plumbing facilities; 92 percent of housing units have complete kitchen facilities; and 56 percent of housing units have telephone service.

The tribal plan for the amendment to the Hoopa-Yurok Settlement Act would provide federal funding for building and maintaining roads and providing electric and telephone service to members lacking these services. Funds also would be available for home construction, higher education, public buildings for residential care, community recreation, and cultural uses.

A few tribal members are developing a "Fish for Elders" program in which tribal youth process donated fish from other tribal fisherman. The fish would then be distributed to the tribal elders.

Education. Reservation students attend public schools in Klamath. The Yurok Magnet Elementary School in Weitchpec opened in 2003. The school is a partnership between the Yurok Tribe and the Klamath Trinity Joint Unified School District, providing education for grades K-3. Several educational programs are available to the tribe. Head Start enrolled over 60 students in their year-round program in 2003. The childcare program serves almost 70 children and families yearly. The Johnson O'Malley

Program provides cultural activities and tutoring to youth. Higher education scholarships were awarded to 125 students through the program for higher education, and 13 people were awarded adult vocational training scholarships. Eight master/apprentice teams have earned credentials from the Yurok Language Program. Adults are receiving vocational education from the College of the Redwoods and from local businesses. More than 150 students and almost 400 individual applications for people with disabilities seeking employment assistance have been served by these vocational programs.

Health Care. Yurok Reservation is serviced by United Indian Health Service in Arcata. In addition to the United Indian Health Service, the following six clinics also are available: Elk Valley Offices in Crescent City; Fortuna Health Center in Fortuna; Howonquet Health Center in Smith River; Klamath Health Center in Klamath; Weitchpec Health Center in Weitchpec Route; and Libby Nix Community Center in Hoopa. Services include medical, dental, pharmacy, vision, child and family, nutrition/WIC, and community health and wellness.

Plans for the construction of a reservation-based health clinic are in the process of being finalized.

TRI-CA-075 Community Center sign at Weitchpec, one of Yurok's communities

TRI-CA-076 River gorge scene near Weitchpec Community

TRI-CA-077 Yurok Tribal Office Building in Klamath, off State Route 169

TRI-CA-078 Boating and fishing on the Klamath River on Yurok Reservation

TRI-CA-075

TRI-CA-076

TRI-CA-077

TRI-CA-078

COLORADO

Photo Courtesy of National Park Service

Southern Ute

LOCATION AND LAND STATUS

The Southern Ute Indian Reservation covers approximately 309,000 acres in the southwestern corner of Colorado. The reservation features timbered ranges in the east and flat mesas in the west, and is crossed by seven rivers. Land use is divided into 25 percent irrigated farmland, 10 percent dry farm land and 65 percent timber and range land. The tribal headquarters of the reservation are located in Ignacio, 24 miles southeast of Durango.

The Ute Reservation was established in 1868 on 56 million acres in western Colorado. Treaties of 1873, 1880, and 1934 resulted in the reduction of the reservation to 553,600 acres. The Southern Ute Reservation was created in the late 1800s on a strip of land 15 miles wide and 110 miles long. It was a parcel of land that once belonged to the larger, original Ute Reservation but was subsequently designated for the Muaoche and Capote bands in 1895.

During the allotment process in the late 1800s, tribal lands were opened to the public. Tribal lands are now checkerboarded with Indian and non-Indian landholdings.

PHYSICAL DESRIPTION

The Southern Ute Reservation is located in southwestern Colorado. Tribal lands encompass forested mountains, semidesert grasslands, sagebrush savannas and flat mesas. The elevation ranges from 5,940 to 9,159 feet. Seven rivers: the San Juan, Piedra, Florida, La Plata, Navajo, Animas, and Los Pinos cross the reservation boundaries.

CULTURE AND HISTORY

Members of the Southern Ute Tribe belong to the Mouache and Capote bands of the Ute Nation. The Mouache Band traditionally lived along the eastern slopes of the Rocky Mountains from Denver to Las Vegas, New Mexico. The Capote Band lived in the San Luis Valley near the headwaters of the Rio Grande and in northern regions of New Mexico near present-day Chama and Tierra Amarilla.

The Ute Nation consists of seven individual bands. In addition to the Mouache and Capote, there are the Weeminuche, Tabeguache (Uncompahgre), Grand River Utes (Parianuche), Yamparicas (White River), and the Uintah bands. The Utes represent the oldest continuous residents of what is now Colorado. Traditional Ute territory encompassed most of Colorado and Utah and portions of New Mexico and Arizona. The language of the Utes is Shoshonean, which is a branch of the greater Uto-Aztecan linguistic family. The Utes were one of the first Native groups to use horses for subsistence and protection. By the late 1600s, the Utes were following buffalo herds on the plains and horse-packing their belongings.

Early relations between the Utes and the Mexican government were peaceful, resulting in the opening of the "Old Spanish Trail" as a regular trading route in the 1820s. In the 1830s, however, Mexican farmers tried to settle on Indian land, and the Utes and the Navajo joined forces, often raiding farming settlements in northern New Mexico.

The Utes' first encounter with Anglo-Americans was in 1806 when Lt. Zebulon Pike entered the San Luis Valley of Colorado. On December 30, 1849, a peace treaty was signed at Abiquiu, New Mexico with the United States government, in which the Utes recognized the sovereignty of the United States and established borders between the two nations. In 1863, a treaty was signed at Conejos that ended Ute claims to all mineral rights and lands that had been already been settled by Euro-Americans in the San Luis Valley.

The gold rush to the San Juan Mountains began almost immediately after the 1863 treaty. In the face of encroachment by miners, the Colorado Ute bands were persuaded to sign a treaty, the Brunot Agreement, in which they ceded the San Juan Mountains. This territory represented one-fourth of their reservation. The treaty resulted in the loss of their summer home and the majority of their deer harvest. The Hunter Act of 1895 allowed for the remainder of Ute territory, a strip of land 15 miles by 110 miles along the Colorado border, to be allotted. By April of 1896, 72,811 acres of this land were allotted to 371 Utes, the remainder being sold to non-Indians. The Weeminuche Ute Band refused to comply with the allotment scheme and instead retreated to the westernmost end of the reservation strip around Mesa Verde and Ute Mountain. The BIA was forced to leave the western reservation unallotted.

In 1896, Colorado's Southern Utes and Utah's Northern Utes organized the Confederated Bands of Ute Indians to seek financial compensation for the land taken from them. Reimbursement did not occur until 1910, when the U.S. Court of Claims awarded the Utes $3,300,000. In 1937, 222,000 acres of reservation land, about half of their original reservation, were restored to the tribe. These restored lands turned out to be energy rich, providing the contemporary Southern Utes with a valuable source of income.

The tribe is growing rapidly, with over half of the population under the age of 25. Approximately 25 percent of the membership lives off the reservation, mostly in larger metropolitan areas such as Denver, Albuquerque, and Phoenix.

GOVERNMENT

The tribal government is organized under provisions of the Indian Reorganization Act of 1934. The tribal council consists

Southern Ute Reservation
Federal reservation
Ute
La Plata, Archuleta counties,
Montezuma, Colorado

Southern Ute Indian Tribe
P.O. Box 737
Ignacio, CO 81137
970-563-0100
970-563-0396 Fax

Total area
(BIA realty, 2004)
314,995.89 acres

Total population
2000 census
11,159

Total population
(Tribal sources, 2004)
7,886

Tribal enrollment
(BIA labor report, 2001)
1,375

Tribal enrollment
(Tribal sources, 2004)
1,403

Southern Ute

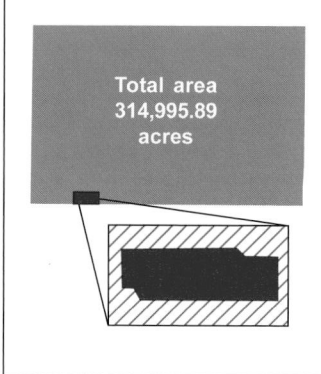

Total area
314,995.89
acres

Total labor force
2000 census
5,756

Total labor force
(BIA labor report, 2001)
1,584

Total labor force
(Tribal sources, 2004)
1,059

High school graduate or higher
2000 census
87.8%

Bachelor's degree or higher
2000 census
24.9%

Unemployment rate
2000 census
5%

Unemployment rate
(BIA labor report, 2001)
34%

Per capita income
2000 census
$18,552

Per capita income
(Tribal sources, 2004)
$6,240

of seven elected members; officers include the chairman, vice-chairman, and treasurer. The vice-chairman and treasurer are council members who are appointed by the chairman. Members serve for three-year staggered terms. The Southern Ute Indian Tribe approved its constitution and bylaws on November 4, 1936, and adopted revisions in September 1975.

The tribal government consists of numerous programs and departments. They include the division of gaming, tribal energy, natural resources, education, utilities, lands, wildlife, health, and administration.

The tribe manages its own judicial system with a tribal court, law enforcement officers, and legal services.

BUSINESS CORPORATIONS

The tribe developed the Red Willow Gathering Company in 1994. The company was formed to buy and operate gas wells and leases in order to increase the tribe's revenues from its energy resources. Red Willow oversees the tribe's investment in the Red Cedar Gathering Company. The tribe is a major partner in Red Cedar, one of the largest gathering companies of natural gas in Colorado. *(See Energy Exploration and Production below for complete details).*

ECONOMY

The tribal economy is supported in large part by the energy, gaming, tourism, government-sector development, and tribal enterprises. Major sources of income are from the energy and gaming sectors. The tribal government, City of Durango, and the Purgatory Ski Corporation provide employment opportunities for local residents.

Government as Employer. After the Purgatory Ski Corporation and the City of Durango, the tribe represents the most important source of employment for tribal members and is the largest employer in the county. The tribe employs approximately 900 individuals.

Economic Development Projects. In 1999 the Southern Ute Tribe initiated a financial plan. This plan provides for the development of four distinct funds: the Permanent Fund, Growth Fund, Revenue Fund, and Restricted Fund. These funding programs serve as the foundation of the tribe's economic development in the areas of energy, utilities, real estate, construction, mining, and tourism. *(See Investments below for more details).*

The tribe's business opportunity program, under the economic development division, assists tribal members in small-business development. This includes entrepreneurial training, a microenterprise loan program, technical assistance, business plan preparation, and development of business support services.

Agriculture and Livestock. The tribe operates the Custom Farm Department. Services include plowing, disking, leveling, planning (906 acres), and growing hay on 639 acres for tribal members and nonmembers alike.

Land use on the reservation is divided into 25 percent irrigated farmland, 10 percent dry farm land and 65 percent timber and rangeland.

The tribe manages a herd of bison through its bison management program. The program has implemented an irrigation and hay-production system and plans to develop production of buffalo products for resale.

Forestry. The reservation contains substantial stands of timber. The primary species are spruce, ponderosa pine, pinyon pine,

juniper, aspen, and oak. Total commercial timber acreage is 245,000, of which 76,066 acres are presently inaccessible. Total woodland acreage is 92,607. Approximately 7,794 cords are produced per year. The BIA employs eight permanent and six seasonal workers and the tribe employs six permanent and two to four seasonal employees.

Gaming. The Sky Ute Casino, Lodge, Conference Center and Dining is owned by the Southern Ute Tribe. It opened in September 1993. The facilities employ 350 individuals. The casino has class II gaming with bingo, class III gaming with over 400 slot machines, blackjack, poker, and bingo. In addition to the gaming facilities, the casino offers a gift shop and a museum/cultural center.

Fisheries. Lake Capote, now reconstructed under the U.S. Department of the Interior's Safety of Dams Program, is a tribal endeavor. The lake has been stocked by the tribe and was recently opened to the general public for trout fishing. Seven rivers run through the reservation: San Juan, Piedra, Florida, La Plata, Navajo, Animas and Los Pinos. Three of the rivers, the Los Pinos, Piedra and the Animas, are regularly stocked with cutthroat and rainbow trout. Fishing permit sales generate $30,000 annually.

Construction. The tribe owns the Mouache-Capote Construction Company. A major goal of the company is to train and employ Southern Ute tribal members. The company employs 4 permanent and 20 seasonal employees. Projects consist of fencing; roads and heavy construction; oil field site and road development, and municipal water, sewer, and irrigation system installation and maintenance.

Mining. The Southern Ute Tribe receives over 90 percent of its income from natural gas production on the reservation. *(See Energy Exploration and Production below).*

Sky Ute Sand and Gravel started operations in 2001 with one gravel pit located close to Ignacio. Today, Sky Ute Sand and Gravel produces concrete and aggregate and has four gravel pits located on and off the reservation in Colorado and New Mexico. It operates four ready-mix concrete plants in the Four Corners Region and is becoming the preferred concrete and aggregate supplier not only locally but on the Navajo Nation.

Energy Exploration and Production. The Southern Ute Tribe receives over 90 percent of its income from its natural gas production on the reservation. A majority of the wells are operated by nontribally owned companies, though operations are closely monitored by the tribe's department of energy. In the past few years, a dozen tribal members have gained employment with private gas companies.

The Southern Ute Tribe owns and operates the Aka Energy Group, Red Cedar Gathering Company, and the Red Willow Production Company. Aka Energy and Red Cedar are gathering companies of natural gas. Aka operates exclusively off-reservation while Red Cedar operates primarily on the reservation. Red Cedar Gathering Company is 51 percent tribally owned and is one of the largest gathering companies of natural gas in southern Colorado.

In February 1992, the Southern Ute Energy Resources Division started Red Willow Producing Company, a tribally owned oil and gas company that operates oil and gas wells on the reservation, in New Mexico, the Rocky Mountain region, Canada, several other southwestern states, and in the Gulf of Mexico. The company was formed mainly to buy and operate gas wells and leases to increase the tribe's revenues from its energy resources. In 1998, Red Willow joined a partnership with the Dominion Exploration and Production Company and the Ute Tribe in order to identify natural resources on that tribe's reservation in eastern Utah.

It is currently in the process of hiring tribal members to work on newly acquired properties.

Investment and Financial Planning. The tribe reached a significant level of financial success as a result of tribal control and operation of the energy resources found on the Southern Ute Reservation. The tribal council realized that these energy resources were finite and depletable. In 1999 the tribe initiated its financial plan with the mission statement: "To provide the tribe with an economic strategy which will ensure a core government and baseline per capita distribution in perpetuity, while at the same time optimizing available resources to achieve greater socioeconomic well being for the benefit of both current and future tribal members." The financial plan outlined the creation of four distinct funds: the Permanent Fund, the Growth Fund, the Revenue Fund and the Restricted Fund. Each fund was designed to meet different and distinct needs of the tribe.

Real Estate/Commercial Development. The GF Properties Group invests capital in commercial real estate ventures on behalf of the tribe. It is responsible for identifying, acquiring, and developing commercial real estate. The Tierra Group is a construction operation that has focused on residential home building in the past. While home construction is continuing on both a custom and a production level, they are now also involved in commercial construction and management. They also build residential and commercial buildings.

Services and Retail. The Sky Ute Lodge/Restaurant features 36 rooms; the restaurant serves a wide variety of authentic southwestern cuisine.

The Southern Ute Golden Sinew Arts Guild is a tribally owned art gallery and resale location. Tribal artists individually show and sell their work from the gallery.

Media and Communications. The tribe owns KSUT Four Corners Public Radio. The station is an award-winning NPR, PRI, and AIROS affiliate that broadcasts news, music, and public af-

TRI-CO-11

TRI-CO-9

TRI-CO-13

The Growth Fund Implementation Plan was approved by the tribal council on February 7, 2000. The primary purpose of the Growth Fund is to increase the tribe's wealth through the creation, purchase and operation of profit-generating businesses. The first part of this strategy is to replace the depleting energy resources on the reservation through the purchase and development of new resources both on and off the reservation. The second and longer-term portion of the plan is to methodically diversify away from the energy field into other areas such as real estate, private equity, construction, concrete and aggregate, and any other profitable ventures. Many gas wells are operated on the reservation by several large, nontribally owned energy companies. An integral part of the Growth Fund, the department of energy, provides energy and mineral land services that ensure that the tribe receives the maximum benefits from these resources. They are also responsible for minimizing the impacts of natural gas and oil extraction on tribal lands.

The Growth Fund currently operates nine enterprises on and off of the reservation: the Aka Energy Group, the Red Cedar Gathering Company, the Red Willow Production Company, the GF Private Equity Group, the GF Properties Group, the Tierra Group, the Sky Ute Sand and Gravel, the Southern Ute Utilities Division, and the Sky Ute Event Center. All of these enterprises and the Administration Group combined have a total of 377 employees, 63 of which are either Southern Ute Tribal Members or other Native Americans. One of the recent additions to the Growth Fund is the GF Private Equity Group. Their purpose is to invest capital in a variety of private equity funds, and more importantly, directly in other assets and companies. Their goal is to pursue above-average investment returns and to contribute to the diversification of the Growth Fund investment portfolio.

Industrial Parks. In 1995, the tribe was in the process of completing a feasibility and site analysis study for a business park.

TRI-CO-7

fairs programming. The station serves Durango, Pagosa Springs, Cortez, Mancos, Bayfield, Dolores, and Ignacio. It also serves the New Mexico towns of Farmington, Bloomfield, Aztec, and Gallup. KSUT operates a community station that broadcasts five days per week to Ignacio and Bayfield. This program provides Native American music, AIROS, and local programs. The tribe publishes the *Southern Ute Drum* newspaper.

Tourism and Recreation. The Sky Ute Event Center is the oldest tribal enterprise, constructed in 1971 as a high-altitude horse-training facility. The center now hosts cultural, social, and commercial events such as powwows, fairs, rodeos, and motorcycle rallies.

The Southern Ute Indian Reservation is within the outdoor recreation-tourism region of southwestern Colorado, a well-known major recreation area rich in scenery and history. The area's major tourist attractions are the San Juan Mountains, Mesa Verde National Park, and the Durango-Silverton Narrow Gauge Railroad. Other attractions include Navajo Lake, the Four Corners, Aztec Ruins National Monument, the forthcoming Mancos Canyon Indian Park (a Ute Mountain tribal enterprise), and numerous fishing lakes and streams that are used by residents and

TRI-CO-11 Tribal Council Chamber with pictures of former Tribal Chairmen

TRI-CO-9 Front Reception area inside Leonard Birch Tribal Administration Building

TRI-CO-7 Leonard Birch Tribal Administration Building and Parking area

TRI-CO-13 Vietnam Service Memorial at Southern Ute's Veteran's Memorial Park

Southern Ute

ENVIRONMENTAL CONCERNS
The Southern Ute tribe operates an environmental programs division that includes water quality, air quality, and general assistance. The division provides services for solid waste collection and recycling, domestic water testing, remediation guidance for petroleum and methane spills, and educational programs for community members, schools, government employees, and nontribal groups and organizations. The division houses an Environmental Programs Division Library that is open to the public.

visitors. The reservation's 33-acre Lake Capote offers some of the best trout fishing in southwestern Colorado. Renovated camping, a modern bathhouse with hot showers and flush toilets, and RV sites with water and electricity are planned upgrades at the lake.

The Southern Ute Cultural Center and Gallery represents the only Ute-funded and -operated Indian museum in Colorado. The Cultural Center features a multimedia production shown daily, depicting the early history of the Utes. Displays include examples of the beautiful beaded leatherwork for which the Utes are famous. During 1992, the Sky Ute Cultural Center and Museum acquired artifacts and equipment to aid in the preservation of museum resources. The Sky Ute Gallery adjoins the Cultural Center and features the finest in traditional and modern American Indian arts and crafts.

The newly remodeled Southern Ute Tourist and Convention Center includes a gaming facility and accommodates up to 300 people. The Bear Dance, Southern Ute Sun Dance, Southern Ute Fair, powwows, and the San Ignacio Fiesta provide visitors the opportunity to learn about Ute culture.

INFRASTRUCTURE
Highway 172 runs north and south through the Southern Ute Reservation. Highway 160 runs east-west, 25 miles northwest of Ignacio. Highway 550 runs east of Ignacio from Highway 172. The nearest commercial service is in Durango, Colorado, 25 miles northwest of Ignacio. Several motor freight carriers serve the reservation, including UPS, Kangaroo delivery from Durango, and RAC Transport. La Plata County Airport is located approximately 10 miles from Ignacio.

Fuel, Water and Waste Management. The Southern Ute Utilities Division, overseen by The Growth Fund, provides water, natural gas, and waste management services to the reservation and, in part, to the town of Ignacio. State-of-the-art water treatment and wastewater treatment plants with sufficient processing capacity were recently completed.

COMMUNITY FACILITIES AND SERVICES
Education. Tribal youth may attend the Ignacio Public School system in the town of Ignacio. Ignacio is an incorporated township located within the reservation boundaries.

The tribe's education department provides educational resources and assistance for tribal members at all stages. It initiated an educational excellence program that offers achievement incentives, internships, and scholarships.

The education department and Southwestern Indian Polytechnic Institute announced the creation of a certification program in art education in 2000. The program offers algebra, English, computer literacy, art education, drawing, painting, sculpture, ceramics, photography, and art marketing. Tribal members receive book deposits and activity fees.

Health Care. Tribal members receive health care services through the Southern Colorado Ute Service Unit (SCUSU). It provides ambulatory care services, including full-service medical, nursing, and dental programs. Other services include environmental health, social services, mental health, and women's health programs. Clinics are located in Towaoc and Ignacio, and a field station is open in White Mesa, Utah.

Community Health Representative programs are contracted by the tribe through Indian Health Services.

Ute Mountain

Ute Mountain Ute Reservation
Federal reservation
Ute
Montezuma, La Plata counties, Colorado
San Juan County, New Mexico
San Juan County, Utah

Ute Mountain Ute Indian Tribe
P.O. Box JJ
Towaoc, Colorado 81334
970-565-3751
970-564-5709 Fax

LOCATION AND LAND STATUS
The Ute Mountain Ute Reservation covers 597,288 acres of allotted and deeded lands, primarily in Colorado, but extending into New Mexico and Utah. The Ute Mountain Ute Reservation surrounds Mesa Verde National Park on three sides. The reservation is located 15 miles south of Cortez, Colorado, on the Navajo Trail. It was created in 1897 by the Weeminuche Band at the western portion of the federally designated Ute Reservation.

Towaoc is the only town on the reservation. It is the site of the Ute Mountain Indian Agency and the residence of most of the people on the reservation. The nearest large town is Cortez, Colorado, about 16 miles northeast of Towaoc, and is the principle market center for the area. South of the reservation in New Mexico are the towns of Shiprock, 30 miles from Towaoc, and Farmington, 29 miles east of Shiprock.

PHYSICAL DESCRIPTION
The topography of the reservation varies from approximately 4,600 feet near the Four Corners area to approximately 10,000 feet at the peak of the Sleeping Ute Mountain. The eastern half of the reservation is characterized by a high mesa cut by the canyon of the Mancos River and numerous side canyons. The western half of the reservation, with the exception of the

Sleeping Ute Mountain, is semidesert grassland. Lower elevations are characterized by sagebrush shrub lands, while the upper elevations contain ponderosa pine forests. The Mancos River and its tributaries, springs, and wetlands are all located within the reservation.

CULTURE AND HISTORY
Members of the Ute Mountain Ute Tribe belong to the Weeminuche Band of the Ute Nation. The Ute Nation consists of seven individual bands. In addition to the Weeminuche, there are the Mouache, Capote, Tabeguache (Uncompahgre), Grand River Utes (Parianuche), Yamparicas (White River), and the Uintah bands. The Utes represent the oldest continuous residents of what is now Colorado. Traditional Ute territory encompassed most of Colorado and Utah and portions of New Mexico and Arizona. The language of the Utes is Shoshonean, which is a branch of the greater Uto-Aztecan linguistic family. The Utes roamed from the Wasatch Range above the Salt Lake Valley east to the Great Plains, and from the Uintah Mountains at the rim of the Wyoming Basin south to the San Juan River and Santa Fe. The Utes shared many characteristics of the Plains Indians. In their early history they traveled by foot in small bands of 25 to 30 people. The sparse availability of resources required them to be highly mobile and

have efficient food-gathering techniques. The Utes were one of the first Native groups to use horses for subsistence and protection. By the late 1600s, the Utes were following buffalo herds on the plains and horse-packing their belongings.

The Utes' first encounter with Anglo-Americans was in 1806 when Lt. Zebulon Pike entered the San Luis Valley. On December 30, 1849, a peace treaty was signed at Abiquiu, New Mexico with the United States government, in which the Utes recognized the sovereignty of the United States and established borders between the two nations. In 1863, the Utes signed a treaty at Conejos that terminated their mineral rights and rights to mountainous areas of the San Luis Valley that had already been settled by Euro-Americans.

The gold rush to the San Juan Mountains began almost immediately after the 1863 treaty. In the face of encroachment by miners, the Colorado Ute bands were persuaded to sign a treaty, the Brunot Agreement, in which they ceded the San Juan Mountains. This territory represented one-fourth of their reservation; the treaty resulted in the loss of their summer home and the majority of their deer harvest. The Hunter Act of 1895 allowed for the remainder of Ute territory, a strip of land 15 miles by 110 miles along the Colorado border, to be allotted. By April of 1896, 72,811 acres of this land were allotted to 371 Utes, the remainder being sold to non-Indians.

While the Capote and Mouache bands agreed to the allotment process, the Weeminuche Ute Band refused to comply with the allotment scheme and instead retreated to the westernmost end of the reservation strip, around Mesa Verde and Ute Mountain. The BIA was forced to leave the western reservation unallotted and established an agency for the Weeminuches at Navajo Springs in 1897 (it was moved to Towaoc in 1914). This separation caused a regrouping of the three bands of Utes into two tribes. The Mouache and Capote bands became known as the Southern Utes, and the Weeminuche Band was referred to as the Ute Mountain Ute Tribe, in reference to the Sleeping Ute Mountain area of their settlement.

In 1896, Colorado's Southern Utes and Utah's Northern Utes organized the Confederated Bands of Ute Indians to seek financial compensation for the land taken from them. Reimbursement did not occur until 1901, when the U.S. Court of Claims awarded the Utes $3,300,000. In 1911, the Weeminuches provided acreage for Mesa Verde National Park, where the remains of Anasazi cliff dwellings exist. In exchange for the land provided for the park, the federal government granted the Utes other properties, including most of northern Ute Mountain. In 1938, the federal government returned 30,000 acres of appropriated lands to the tribe.

GOVERNMENT

The tribal government operates under a constitution, which provides for a tribal council of seven members, including a chairman, a vice-chairman, and a treasurer. The Ute Mountain Utes are a PL-638 tribe. As a self-governing Nation, the tribe contracts social services, public health services, vocational education, roads maintenance, aid to tribal government, higher education, and the Johnson O'Malley program. Government departments include health, education, justice, TERO, housing, planning and development, environmental, and energy.

In 2000, the tribe completed the Chief Ignacio Justice Center in Towaoc. The center houses the BIA police department, administrative support, adult and juvenile detention centers, and a treatment center.

ECONOMY

The tribal government is a major source of employment in the Four Corners region through its governmental departments, casino facilities, and various enterprises. The development of gaming operations on the reservation has served to increase employment opportunities in the region. Since the opening of the casino in 1992, the unemployment rate in Montezuma County has dropped by almost two percent.

The tribal economy is supported in large part by the revenue from coal and oil leases as well as the casino operations. Coal leases and oil and natural gas discoveries during the 1950s brought the tribe its first real income and provided for per capita payments to tribal members of up to $1,500 every 60 days. In addition, many Ute people began to raise cattle, gradually regaining some of the non-Indian allotted lands. In 1957, the tribe bought the 20,000-acre Pinecrest Ranch between Gunnison and Lake City for additional summer range.

Government as Employer. The Ute Mountain Ute Tribe employs 1,133 people.

Economic Development Projects. The tribe offers a series of classes designed to help tribal members and their spouses start businesses. Through structured course work, presentations by professionals, and classroom discussion, students gain practical knowledge in funding alternatives, business planning, personnel and accounting systems, marketing strategies, and inventory control.

Agriculture and Livestock. The Ute Mountain Ute Tribe's Farm and Ranch enterprise is an irrigated agricultural project, which encompasses over 7,640 acres of the tribe's reservation. The enterprise relies heavily upon the Dolores Irrigation Project, which delivers nearly 23,000 acre-feet of water annually to the reservation for agricultural development. The 125-acre demonstration farm is used for research in irrigation systems and crop adaptation. The farm features 109 center-pivot sprinkler plots with a range of 40-140 acres each. In addition, a new sweet corn production facility has been developed. It will allow the farming enterprise to market directly to retailers with its value-added product.

Currently the farm and ranch enterprise is operating 500 head of cattle and moving toward rebuilding range capacity of 1,000 head of cattle. The tribe's former herd was devastated in 2000-2003 by drought conditions. Also, the tribal cattlemen, approximately 50 to 55 ranch operators, are using the Ute Mountain rangelands. Since tribal member cattle operations represent just one facet of the range resource usage, the tribe is especially interested in enhancing the economic viability of its rangelands. Both the individual operators and the tribe use the ranches for summer range and the reservation for winter range. Range improvements on the ranches include water, irrigation ditches, fencing, and hay production. The concentrated and prioritized range management practices have produced greater revenues for the cattle operations.

Since 1986, the Ute Mountain Ute White Mesa Community, located in southeastern Utah, has owned and managed a cattle operation. Nearly 2,000 head of cattle graze on over 200,000 acres, which include tribal lands and public lands for which the tribe pays grazing fees. Revenues from annual calf sales support community services in White Mesa.

The Dolores Irrigation Project is a U.S. Bureau of Reclamation project that provides water storage and delivery for irrigation in southwest Colorado. The Towaoc Canal links the McPhee Reservoir to the Ute Mountain Ute Reservation and

Ute Mountain

Total area
(BIA realty, 2004)
606,218.48 acres

Population *2000 census*
1,687

Tribal enrollment
(BIA labor report, 2001)
2,012

Tribal enrollment
(Tribal sources, 2004)
2,053

Total labor force
2000 census
717

Total labor force
(BIA labor report, 2001)
1,584

Total labor force
(Tribal sources, 2004)
1,360

High school graduate or higher
2000 census
58.3%

Bachelor's degree or higher
2000 census
2.8%

Unemployment rate
2000 census
17.3%

Unemployment rate
(BIA labor report, 2001)
32%

Per capita income
2000 census
$8,159

Per capita income
(Tribal sources, 2004)
$4,839

Ute Mountain

TRI-CO-1A

TRI-CO-18A

TRI-CO-23A

TRI-CO-12A

TRI-CO-6

TRI-CO-23A Ute Mountain Travel Center & Gas Station at US Highway 160

TRI-CO-1A Tribal Administration-Tribal Office Complex

TRI-CO-18A Chief Ignacio Justice Center

TRI-CO-12A Child Development Center- "Nuruwachiu Pu O Kaan", Head Start & children's Program

TRI-CO-6 Front Entrance-Ute Mountain Casino - 11 miles from Cortez, CO on US 160/666

delivers approximately 23,000 acres of water for agricultural purposes. The project is the culmination of years of legal battles between the tribe and the state and affirms the tribe's water rights.

In 1994, the tribe began construction of the Solar Water Pumping Demonstration Project. Due for completion in 1997, the project would replace at least 35 wind pumps on water wells with photovoltaic pumps. The project was estimated to reduce the cost of well maintenance and increase the water yield.

Gaming. The Ute Mountain Casino opened in 1992. It is the largest casino in the Four Corners region. Ute Mountain Casino employs more than 430 people, over half of whom are tribal members. The casino complex is located on Highway 666. The casino provides shuttle service for guests and employees.

The casino features poker, blackjack, over 500 slot machines, keno, and bingo. There is one restaurant. Adjacent to the casino is the Sleeping Ute RV Park and Campground and the Indian Village. The Sleeping Ute R.V. Park and Campground offers pull-through RV spaces, tent sites, and tipi accommodations. Communal facilities include a playground, game room, indoor swimming pool, restrooms, showers, laundry, and a convenience store. The Indian Village is an outdoor plaza where cultural festivals, Native American dancing, and entertainment activities are held.

A hotel facility was completed at the casino in 2004. It offers guest accommodations, a conference center, and banquet rooms. The project has created 40 permanent jobs.

Revenues from the casino operations are utilized by the tribe to maintain the casino facilities and fund tribal programs and operations, education, economic development, and social and family programs. With the assistance of funds earned from the casino, the tribe has been able to develop a children's development center, education building, elder wellness center, rehab recreation facility, travel center, library, and computer lab on the reservation.

Construction. The Weeminuche Construction Authority has become one of the largest and most successful construction compa-

nies in the Four Corners area. The Weeminuche Construction Authority (WCA), a commercial construction enterprise, is owned and operated by the tribe. Through competitive bidding, it has provided broad-based construction services to clients including federal, state, and local municipalities; other tribes; oil and gas companies; and agricultural operations. WCA employs up to 216 employees, 57 of whom are tribal members. It owns over 400 pieces of major construction equipment. WCA has extensive experience in all facets of heavy construction, including site preparation, clearing, earthwork and grading, dams, drainage, canal work, utilities featuring all types of pipe and infrastructure, plus gravel, concrete and asphalt roads and surfacing. Capabilities in the construction of foundations and substructures include block, reinforced concrete, structural steel, masonry, wood, and timber frames. The WCA also has training in hazardous waste cleanup, which gives the company the ability to expand to more off- reservation projects. WCA has experience in gravel and sand operations and could help develop, as well as conserve, the mineral resources of the tribe. In 2003, the company successfully bid for and completed over $28 million in construction projects for the year. During the summer, the number of employees increased to 475.

Mining. There are 81 producing oil wells and 71 producing gas wells on the reservation. Sand and gravel deposits are also being developed, as well as coal, titanium, selenium, uranium, and bentonite. During the 1980s, the tribe negotiated a model mineral lease with the Wintershall Corporation. In addition to excellent financial terms, the company agreed to train Ute workers and to restrict activity in the Ute Mountain Tribal Park. In 1998, the tribe began mineral exploration of tribal lands in Utah. The tribe formed a partnership with the Red Company of the Southern Ute Tribe and the Dominion Exploration and Production Company in order to identify natural resources.

Manufacturing. The Ute Mountain Ute Pottery Plant is located in Towaoc and employs about 24 people. Up to 3,500 pieces of pottery are produced monthly and sold locally and in outlets across the country. Pieces are handcrafted. Pottery may be ordered through the company catalog, or purchased at the factory showroom or outlet store. Small groups are welcome to tour at any time; large groups should call for an appointment.

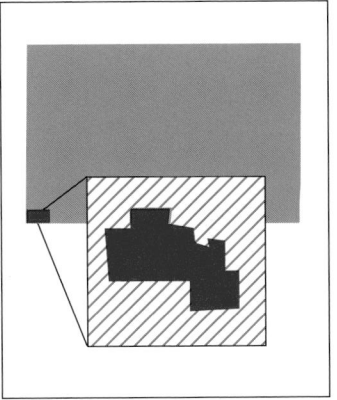

ndustrial Parks. In 2002, the Ute Mountain Tribe finished the infrastructure to accommodate industrial facilities. Currently, this Industrial Park has only one tenant, Weeminuche Construction Authority. The tribe is building a new maintenance and office facility for their use.

Services and Retail. The tribe operates two travel centers. The Ute Mountain Travel Center in Towaoc provides customers with gas services, a food court, a convenience store, snack bar, laundromat, and truck stop amenities. The White Mesa Travel Center in White Mesa, Utah was renovated in 1999 and now offers a convenience store, gas services, truck stop amenities, and a post office. It employs six people.

The tribe also owns the Sleeping Ute Pottery Factory Outlet. The store sells pottery inspired by the pottery-making traditions of the Anasazi people, produced by contemporary artists. The outlet employs 24 individuals, 90 percent of whom are tribal members.

Tourism and Recreation. Sleeping Ute RV Park opened in April 2004 and is operated by the Ute Mountain Casino. This 84-site RV Park hosts full service sites as well as tent and tipi areas. This tribal enterprise was originally funded partially by a BIA Indian Business Development Grant and Tribal Economic Development Trust Funds. This operation is a seasonal summer business and hires additional people as tourism grows. Occupancy rates have increased steadily since its opening, and the park often fills to near capacity during the summer months.

The Indian Village was constructed in the spring of 1995 and has served as a central tourist center by providing performances of traditional Native American dances and vendors of locally produced crafts during the summer months. Arts and crafts, traditional dances, stories, and ethnic foods have been highlights in the site. The facility has drawn more visitors and greater compliments than the other tourism services in the Commercial Center and Tribal Park.

The Ute Mountain Tribal Park has been a long-term development project for the Ute Mountain Ute Tribe. It has been developed using the theory of low-impact tourism. In 1995, over 3,215 tourists visited the park. This enterprise adds over $60,000 of income to the tribal park budget. Tours are available by reservation only and include the guidance of a required tribal guide. Overnight visits are also available. Each archeological site or area of interest visited within the park is interpreted for the visitor. At the entrance of the park an abandoned gas station has been established as the Tribal Park Tour Headquarters and contains a small museum, tour information, small gifts, books, and refreshments.

A nonprofit foundation, Adopt a Ruin, has done an intense marketing program for the tribal park. This foundation, created by the Colorado Commission of Indian Affairs and the Ute Mountain Ute Tribe, has raised monies for additional trails, ruins, and stabilization programs. This nonprofit organization finances repairs and programs. Contributors to the program are able to view their monies at work in the creation and improvement of park facilities, roads, and stabilization of archeological sites. One of the programs established by the foundation, Friends of the Park, has done many projects for the tribal park.

The tribal park currently employs four tribal members full time, with additional employees hired during the summer and tourist months to provide a quality experience for visitors the park. The tribal park is also working on a road development plan to better access a number of ruins that have not been accessed by visitors.

The Ute Mountain Tribal Park (Mancos Canyon area), which has been designated as a national historic district, is a special district of designated land use on the reservation. The district includes approximately 125,000 acres located south of Mesa Verde National Park and along both sides of the Mancos River Canyon. The area includes the mesa tops on each side of the Mancos River. The mesa is divided by a deep canyon with large caves and arches in the sandstones walls. This area holds the ruins of dwellings and kivas of the Anasazis (Ancient Ones), who inhabited the area between approximately AD 400-1100. The Anasazis hunted and farmed along the canyons and mesa tops. They grew in numbers and built great stone dwellings using stone tools. These villages were nestled into the cliff faces and under great ledges. The Anasazis were eventually devastated by severe drought and famine, which forced them to leave their great cliff palaces and stone towers. By the end of the thirteenth century, the canyons and mesas were empty of human life. Although natural forces have greatly eroded the sandstone dwellings of the Anasazis, there are a number of sites still intact in the area.

INFRASTRUCTURE

U.S. Highways 160 and 666 and State Highways 41 and 789 run through the reservation. Two maintained gravel roads cross the reservation: one follows the Mancos River canyon to the eastern part of the reservation then southward toward Farmington, NM; the other goes westward from Towaoc to the Cache Oil Field then on to Aneth, UT.

Electricity. The Western Area Power Association and the Empire Electric Association supply electricity to the Colorado reservation. Utah Power and Light supplies services to the White Mesa community.

Fuel Supply. Propane is provided by a propane delivery enterprise.

Water Supply. The BIA and U.S. Public Health Service installed the water and sewer systems that serve the reservation. Improvements were made to the systems in 1999, but the tribe hopes to develop its own water and wastewater utility programs. The programs will include further improvements to the current systems, creation of operating, maintaining, and monitoring schedules, and the development of additional treatment programs as needed. The White Mesa community receives its water from a two well system. The facilities are maintained by the tribe's public works department.

Transportation. Cortez, Colorado, is 16 miles from the reservation and has regularly scheduled air and truck services. The nearest commercial train service is located in Gallup, New Mexico. The nearest commercial bus service is in Durango, Colorado, about 60 miles east of the reservation. The main delivery service is by truck transportation from depots in Denver, Colorado; Albuquerque, New Mexico; and Salt Lake City, Utah.

The Ute Mountain Ute Tribe is in the vicinity of three commercial airports located at Cortez and Durango, Colorado, and Farmington, New Mexico. Great Lakes Aviation offers daily fights in and out of Durango, Cortez, and Farmington and links to air transport services in Denver, Colorado or Albuquerque, New Mexico.

Transportation is restricted on the reservation, with the main mode of transportation being the personnel car and the Tribal Transit Systems. The transit system consists of one van run on a fixed five-day schedule and the casino shuttle that provides services to casino employees.

Ute Mountain

Telecommunications. Cable services are available to the Towoac Community through Cable Enterprise, operated by the tribe's public works department. The tribe is currently negotiating with Charter Communications to secure high-speed Internet access on the reservation.

COMMUNITY FACILITIES AND SERVICES

A recreation center is located on the reservation and features a swimming pool, basketball court, and weight room. The council chambers are located in the tribal complex of the administration building in Towaoc, Colorado.

In 2002, the tribe received a grant to develop the Ute Mountain Ute Tribe Youth Opportunity Program. The program offers a center with career counseling, vocational training, and community support to tribal youth. The program works closely with local schools, the Upward and Outward Bound programs, talent search program, the tribal employee assistance program, and the Montezuma County Partners Program to provide school-to-career support and educational assistance to participants. The Crow Canyon Archeological Organization provides training in construction, instruction in creation of the atlatl, and elder-assisted instruction in basket making.

Education. Tribal youth attend secondary programs at Cortez High School, San Juan High School in White Mesa, Utah, and Southwest Open Alternative School. Post-secondary programs are available through Fort Lewis College and Pueblo College. tribal youth may also attend BIA boarding schools in California and Oklahoma.

The tribe's Culture and Language Program provides the community with different materials and workshops for both youth and adults to learn either the language or different cultural activities in the community. Basic Ute Language has been implemented in the tribal Head Start Program to give young children exposure to the indigenous language.

Health Care. Comprehensive medical and dental services are available through the Southern Colorado Ute Service Unit (SCUSU). SCUSU operates health centers in Towaoc and Ignacio and a field health station in White Mesa, Utah. In 2003, the tribe received an ambulance through the Indian Health Services to supplement its emergency services.

There is a U.S. Public Health Service clinic located in Towaoc; hospitals are located in Cortez and Shiprock, NM. White Mesa residents may seek emergency medical services in Monticello, Utah, over 40 miles from the community.

The Ute Mountain Ute Tribe is currently working with the Navajo Nation and private-sector investors to build a new hospital in the city of Blanding. The proposed medical center will provide health-care services to both Native and non-Native persons. It will be owned and operated by a Native corporation.

ENVIRONMENTAL CONCERNS

The Ute Mountain Ute environmental programs department provides water quality, water supply, and general assistance programs on the reservation. Environmental issues encountered by the tribe include the problem of illegal dumping. The Towaoc dump was closed in 1997 when a transfer station opened, but illegal dumping has continued.

M ashantucket Pequot

LOCATION AND LAND STATUS

The Mashantucket Pequot Reservation is located in southeastern Connecticut, northeast of New London near Ledyard. In 1985, the Bureau of Indian Affairs reported that both tribally owned and reservation land consisted of 1,201.39 acres. Since then the tribe has increased its off-reservation land holdings to more than 5,000 acres. The reservation alone consists of approximately 1,498 acres held in trust by the federal government.

CLIMATE

The Mashantucket Pequot Reservation experiences summer temperatures between 60°F and 80°F and winter temperatures between 18°F and 38°F.

CULTURE AND HISTORY

The Mashantucket Pequots have lived in southeastern Connecticut for thousands of years. Traditional lands consisted of a roughly 250-square-mile area between the Thames and Pawcatuck rivers, and along Long Island Sound. Prior to European contact, the tribal population exceeded 10,000. As a result of European diseases and wars, there were only approximately 2,500 tribal members by the 1700s.

The Pequots encountered English settlers in the early seventeenth century. In 1636, a militia from the Massachusetts Bay Colony traveled to Connecticut and burned two Pequot villages because the tribe had refused to provide retribution for a murder that a tribal member was involved in. The Pequots retaliated against the attack, seized Fort Saybrook, and cut off all river traffic at the mouth of the Connecticut River. The siege lasted until a troop of Massachusetts Bay soldiers arrived at the fort. On May 26, 1637, English soldiers and warriors from the Mohegans, Narragansetts, and Eastern Nianics raged an hour-long massacre on Pequot men, women, and children. The attack resulted in the deaths of 300-400 women, children, and elderly men. Attacks against the Pequots continued for the next several months. The Pequot people were hunted, enslaved, or executed, and they became what one historian describes as, "the first Indian nation to be terminated." The Pequots signed the Hartford/Tripartite Treaty, whereby the surviving tribal members were divided between the Mohegan and Narragansett tribes. The Mashantucket Pequots were forced to live within the Mohegan Nation while the Pawcatuck Pequots were forced to live within the Narragansett Nation. The Pequot Tribe was declared dissolved, and the colony forbade mention of its name.

The Pequots were eventually permitted to return to their homelands, settling first in New London and Groton, Connecticut, in 1650. In 1666, the Colony of Massachusetts set aside 2,500 acres for the tribe. From the seventeenth through the nineteenth centuries, the tribe's land was manipulated first by the settlers and the colony and then by the State of Connecticut and its authorities. In 1720, the tribe lost a 500-acre parcel. In 1761, another 1,000 acres was taken. By 1856 Pequot lands were reduced to 204 acres. By 1774 there were less than 200 tribal members living at the reservation, and by the early 1800s there were between 30 and 40 tribal members left on tribal lands.

The manner in which the State of Connecticut manipulated the economic and cultural aspects of the Mashantuckets hit a new low from the 1940s on. Tribal members were forbidden to hold gatherings or spend a night on their reservation without the expressed consent of the state welfare department. The economic hardships affecting life on the reservation forced them to seek employment and livelihood off the reservation By the 1970s, only two tribal members remained on the reservation-two sisters refusing to leave their ancestral homelands. By this point the reservation had been reduced to approximately 175 acres. When the sisters died, tribal members began to return to the reservation, hoping to restore their land base and community and rejuvenate their traditional culture. Tribal members began to establish numerous small business enterprises, construct housing, and work toward gaining federal recognition.

In 1976, the tribe received the assistance of the Native American Rights Fund and the Indian Rights Association to sue neighboring landowners in an attempt to recover tribal lands that had been illegally sold by the State of Connecticut. Within seven years, the landowners reached a settlement with the tribe, and as they agreed that the state's sale of lands had been illegal, they joined forces with tribal members to pressure the state to offer the tribe compensation. The State of Connecticut petitioned the federal government on the tribe's behalf, and in 1983 the tribe was granted recognition. In receiving recognition, the tribe was granted the right to repurchase the lands they had lost. The out-of-court monetary settlement required the State of Connecticut to pay $900,000 to the tribe (held in trust) and for the state to cede 20 acres to the tribe. The state further pledged to expend $200,000 on roads.

The Mashantucket Pequot Tribal Nation has successfully rebuilt its economy since the 1970s and has welcomed home hundreds of tribal members. The tribe has adopted the name "Fox People" as a reminder of the hardships that the people have endured.

Mashantucket Pequot

Mashantucket Pequot Reservation
Federal reservation
Pequot (Western)
New London County, Connecticut

Mashantucket Pequot Tribe
Indiantown Road
P.O. Box 3060
Mashantucket, CT 06339-3060
860-396-6500
860-396-6540 Fax

Total area *(BIA realty, 2005)*
1,403 acres

Federal trust *(BIA realty, 2005)*
1,403 acres

Tribally owned lands
(Tribal source)
5,000 acres (approx.)

Population *2000 census*
315

Tribal enrollment
(BIA labor report, 2001)
677

Total labor force *2000 census*
73

Total labor force
(BIA labor report, 2001)
212

Mashantucket Pequot

TRI-CT-21A

TRI-CT-12A

TRI-CT-14B

TRI-CT-14B Sculpture inside Foxwoods
Resort Casino

TRI-CT-21A Foxwoods Resort Casino

TRI-CT-12A Foxwoods Resort Casino

TRI-CT-23A Mashantucket Pequot
Museum and Research
Center

TRI-CT-22B Mashantucket Pequot
Museum and Research
Center

TRI-CT-24A Police and Fire Department

TRI-CT-23A

TRI-CT-22B

TRI-CT-24A

High school graduate or higher
2000 census
78%

Bachelor's degree or higher
2000 census
9.2%

Unemployment rate
2000 census
4.1%

Unemployment rate
(BIA labor report, 2001)
19%

Per capita income
2000 census
$27,261

GOVERNMENT

The reservation's governing body is a seven-person tribal council led by a chairperson. Members are elected to three-year terms. All tribal members over the age of 18 are eligible to vote in tribal elections. Government expenditures are funded primarily by gaming revenues and have enabled the tribe to exercise its sovereignty, not only through its zoning ordinances, but also through its self-governance, court system, police force, and health-care systems. Enrollment is based on the Indian Supplement to the 1900-1910 census and is extended to the descendants of enrolled members.

The tribal government provides an array of services ranging from police and fire protection to pre-school and after-school child development, snow removal, landscaping and park design and construction, and recreational services.

ECONOMY

The Pequot Tribe is one of the largest private employers in the state of Connecticut. In addition to providing employment opportunities for 12,000 people, the tribe has contributed to the region's economy through sizable donations, financing and funding assistance to organizations, businesses, and even townships. The tribe invested $700,000 in the movie *Naturally Native* in 1998. In the past, the tribe has also contributed to the Democratic National Committee and to the Republican National Committee. In 1995, the tribe donated $10 million to the National Museum of the American Indian campaign to assist in the construction of the National Museum of the American Indian, which opened in 2004. The donation

was the largest contribution awarded to the project and the largest ever made to the Smithsonian Institute. The tribe has also assisted in the construction of a baseball stadium in Norwich, enabled a regional school to assume ownership of the school facilities, provided funding for the Hartford Ballet production of *The Nutcracker*, and assisted in a waterfront rehabilitation project in Norwich. The Pequot Tribe has also made donations to the Mystic Marine Life Aquarium, Special Olympics World Games, Thames River Fireworks, YMCA of Southeastern Connecticut, and D.A.R.E. In 1996, tribal employees raised almost $200,000 for the United Way, and they have also supported fund-raising efforts for the March of Dimes and the American Cancer Society.

Gaming. The Mashantucket Pequots were the first tribe in Connecticut to operate a casino. In 1986 the tribe started its bingo operations. The casino opened its doors in 1992. The Foxwoods Resort Casino is a gaming complex that houses 6 casinos, 3 hotels, 30 dining venues, a 1,450-seat Fox Theater, the B.B. King Dance Club, the Hard Rock Café, and the Salon in the Woods and Spa. Facilities also include a business center, the Tree House-a two-story arcade and virtual reality game center, and a nonsmoking game room. There is also a shopping center located on the grounds, offering 17 specialty shops. The casino offers over 7,400 slot machines, 380 table games, keno, 3,500 bingo seats, the largest poker room on the East Coast, and greyhound and horse race betting. The Grand Pequot Tower, Great Cedar Hotel, and Two Trees Inn combined offer 1,400 guest accommodations. The resort offers 55,000 square feet of meeting space. Across the street from the resort, the tribe is currently building two 18-hole golf courses for the new Lake of Isles Golf Club and Resort. Slated to open in 2005, the championship courses are designed by well-known golf course architect Rees Jones and will be managed by Troon Golf.

The Foxwoods Resort Casino is the largest resort casino in the world. The resort has received 31 "Best of" awards by *Casino Player Magazine*, a 5 Star Platinum Dining Award, and AAA's 4 Stars for hotel accommodations. The tribe uses the monies earned from the gaming facilities to fund the tribal museum and to support cultural projects and institutions. When the federal government cut defense jobs in the late 1990s, southeastern Connecticut experienced a loss of 15,000 jobs. The combination of employment opportunities available at Foxwoods Resort Casino and at the Mohegan Sun Resort, owned by the Mohegan Tribe, exceeded that number and effectively offset the negative economic impact that surely would have been created.

Services and Retail. In addition to the many businesses located within the tribally owned resort and casino, the tribe owns the Pequot Pharmaceutical Network, a prescription drug distributor; Pequot Plus Health Benefits, a third-party health insurance administrator; the Spa at Norwich Inn in Norwich, Connecticut; the Hilton Mystic in Mystic, Connecticut; Randall's Ordinary, a restaurant and lodging facility in North Stonington, Connecticut; and the Foxwoods Country Club, an 18-hole golf course in Richmond, Rhode Island. The tribe also maintains its own branch of the U.S. Postal Service, which provides all standard post office amenities, including national and international services. The reservation was issued its own zip code in 2002.

Media and Communications. The tribe publishes *The Pequot Times*, a monthly, community newspaper that was established in 1992.

Tourism and Recreation. The 308,000-square-foot Mashantucket Pequot Museum and Research Center is located approximately one mile from the Foxwoods Resort Casino complex. The four-acre facility includes such exhibits as life-size, walk-through dioramas and permanent displays that feature 18,000 years of history. The museum also has two libraries, a restaurant, and a gift shop. The center hosts workshops, demonstrations, performances, and lectures by Native artisans, musicians, and scholars. In 2004, the museum received a grant from the Institute of Museum and Library Services. The grant will be used to develop relationships between Native American cultural institutions.

The Mashantucket Pequots host the annual Schemitzun Festival in honor of the traditional green corn festival. In 1992, the tribe opened the celebration to the public and integrated powwow festivities into the celebration. Held in August, the event is one of the largest powwows nationwide. The tribe also hosts Pau Was and Pequot Days.

INFRASTRUCTURE

Since 1991, the tribe has spent over $20 million in road improvement projects on state roads. Access to the Atlantic Ocean is available via the Thames River in New London, Connecticut.

Electricity. Connecticut Light and Power, a regional electrical utility, provides electricity.

Water Supply. The tribal nation owns a utilities and water department that supplies water service to the entire reservation. Furthermore, in 2003, the Connecticut Department of Public Health declared the tribe the exclusive water provider in an area adjacent to the reservation and overlapping the political boundaries of the cities of North Stonington, Preston, and Ledyard, Connecticut. A sewer treatment plant and additional roads were built for the casino.

Transportation. The tribe provides shuttle service to casino employees and for guests traveling within the resort and from the resort to the museum.

COMMUNITY FACILITIES AND SERVICES

The main tribal building houses the governmental offices and a gym and fitness center for tribal members. A baseball diamond near the tribal building hosts many games, including many with non-Mashantucket teams. The child development center provides tribal youth with general development skills and instruction and guidance in cultural traditions, history, and arts and crafts.

Education. The Pequot Academy provides specialized and general training for tribal members and employees. Tribal youth attend a variety of public and private schools off the reservation, predominantly in the local Ledyard School System.

Health Care. The tribe operates a health clinic through the U.S. Indian Health Services, which provides comprehensive medical services to tribal members from federally-and state-recognized tribes. The Nation also offers comprehensive health plan services to its members and employees as well as to off-reservation organizations and companies. The services include health plan management, pharmaceutical distribution, and a pharmacy benefits manager.

Mashantucket Pequot

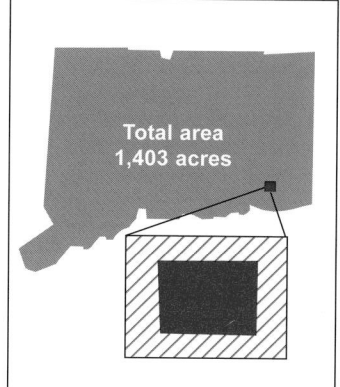

Total area
1,403 acres

M ohegan

Mohegan

LOCATION AND LAND STATUS

First recognized by the Colony of Connecticut in the seventeenth century, the original Mohegan Reservation consisted of approximately 2,700 acres in southeastern Connecticut. In 1861, the State of Connecticut disestablished the Mohegan Indian Reservation. The tribe retained only a small portion of its original land, however Mohegan tribal members continued to reside on or near the area.

In 1994, the United States formally recognized the Mohegan Tribe as a sovereign entity. A Land Claims Settlement Agreement gave the tribe the right to establish an 839-acre reservation in the town of Montville, Connecticut, and the tribe initially reacquired 240 acres of its ancestral homelands in Connecticut. Currently the United States has placed 406 acres of land into trust for the Mohegan Tribe, and 82 additional acres are pending.

The present-day reservation of the Mohegan Tribe is located

on the western bank of the Thames River in Uncasville, Connecticut. A number of tribal members have returned to the area and live on or near the Mohegan Indian Reservation.

PHYSICAL DESCRIPTION

The Mohegan Indian Reservation is situated 56 miles west of the state of Rhode Island and 53 miles from the city of Hartford, Connecticut. The reservation borders the Thames River. It is a saltwater river that is home to a number of migratory fish, including herring, alewives, and striped bass, and to quahogs and oysters. Birds in the area include the great blue heron and osprey. The region contains a variety of fresh and saltwater marshes and a groundwater aquifer.

Aside from a few isolated regions that retain the area's hilly, woodland terrain, the reservation is developed as a resort casino and the seat of the tribal government. The elevation ranges from sea level to 240 feet above sea level.

**Mohegan Indian Reservation
Federal reservation
Mohegan
New London County,
Connecticut**

Mohegan Tribe of Indians
of Connecticut
5 Crow Hill Road
Uncasville, CT 06382
860-862-6100
860-862-6025 Fax

Mohegan

TRI-CT-22A

TRI-CT-22A Mohegan Sun Casino

TRI-CT-14A Mohegan Sun Casino

TRI-CT-11A Sculpture in front of
Mohegan Sun Casino

TRI-CT-20A Sign at entrance to
Mohegan Sun Casino

Total area
(BIA realty, 2005)
406 acres

Federal trust lands
(BIA realty, 2005)
406 acres

Tribal enrollment
(Tribal source, 2005)
1,639

CULTURE AND HISTORY

The Mohegan people are descendants of the Lenni Lenape (Delaware) Wolf Clan. In the late 1500s and early 1600s, the Wolf Clan began a migratory trek northward. They temporarily settled in the area of present-day upstate New York, but eventually they continued on to southeastern Connecticut. Under the leadership of Sachem Uncas, the Mohegans settled along the Thames River in a community called Shantok. The tribe's friendship with British settlers of the area created conflict between the Mohegans and other local tribes, mainly the Pequots

TRI-CT-14A

TRI-CT-11A

TRI-CT-20A

and Narrangasetts. The Battle of the Great Plains over Yantic Falls in Norwich is the site of one of the most historical battles between the tribes, and it is commemorated by an historic marker. The conclusion of King Phillip's War in 1676 brought an end to the intertribal wars. Subsequently, the Mohegans lost their stature as military allies of the British colonies, and their socioeconomic livelihood began to suffer. The encroachment of colonists on Mohegan hunting grounds forced the tribe to seek subsistence in other areas. Thus the tribe began a shift toward an economy reliant on domestic livestock.

In the mid-1700s, Samson Occum, a member of the Mohegan Tribe, became the first ordained and trained Christian Indian minister. He succeeded in raising the funds necessary to establish an Indian academy. That academy later became the prestigious Dartmouth College. Frustrated by the socioeconomic conditions that Native people were forced to endure, Occum led a following of Native Americans from the various local tribes back to upstate New York. Although their journey was delayed by the outbreak of the American Revolution, the group did return to New York in 1784.

In 1790, in violation of the Federal Trade and Intercourse Act of 1790, the State of Connecticut permitted nontribal, state-appointed overseers to sell Mohegan lands to non-Indians. The tribally owned land base was significantly reduced. In 1861, the tribe requested that the majority of its reservation lands be transferred into fee status to avoid the corrupt practices of the state overseers. As a result, the tribe was dislocated from its original reservation. The Mohegans maintained a core land base in Uncasville, Connecticut, home of the Mohegan Church founded in 1831. The church proved to be of great significance when the Mohegans applied for federal recognition more than 150 years later. The church symbolized the continued existence of the Mohegans as a tribe. The Mohegan Tribe was granted federal recognition in 1994.

GOVERNMENT

The Colony of Connecticut recognized the Mohegan Tribe in the Treaty of 1638, and theState of Connecticut subsequently followed suit. After application in the 1980s, the tribe received federal recognition as a sovereign Indian nation in 1994.

Following federal recognition, the tribe established a government that would draw on the combined strengths of a tradi-

tional tribal government and a democratic constitution. The current constitution confers upon a seven-member council of elders authority over judicial and cultural matters and empowers a separate nine-member tribal council to serve as the legislative and executive branches of tribal government. Both councils are voted into office. Elections are held every two years, and members 18 years and older are eligible to vote.

The Mohegan Tribe also continues to honor the traditional roles of chief, medicine woman, and pipe carrier, and their contribution to the tribe's government. The tribe operates local government services from an annual budget funded by revenue from the tribe's business ventures. Tribal departments include: administration, cultural resources, historic preservation, development, gaming commission, courts, health and human services, housing authority, planning and development, public safety, public works, publications, and legal.

BUSINESS CORPORATION

The Mohegan Tribe has established several limited liability corporations. One of the first tribal corporations established was Little People, LLC. Little People's primary function is to ensure the integrity of all items sold at the Mohegan Sun Resort as Native American productions. Little People works in conjunction with the managers of Trading Cove, the Mohegan Tribe's retail outlet for all Native American artwork.

ECONOMY

Government as Employer. The tribe employs over 10,000 people at the Mohegan Sun Resort. During various stages of its construction, the tribe offered 2,000 jobs directly related to construction and 3,000 jobs indirectly related to construction.

The Mohegan Tribe and its members are subject to all applicable federal and state tax laws. As an employer, the tribe deducts all applicable federal and state income taxes, FICA payments, and FUTA taxes from all employee paychecks.

Gaming. In 1995, the Mohegan Tribe formed the Mohegan Tribal Gaming Authority (MTGA). The gaming authority financed the construction of a resort almost entirely through the sale of $175 million in bonds to Wall Street sources. The

Mohegan Sun Resort became the first Native-owned casino project to be funded by public capital markets.

The Mohegan Sun Resort opened in 1996. The facilities include an extensive gaming area, over 29 restaurants, over 30 gift shops and boutiques, convention and entertainment facilities, a planetarium dome, and a seven-story waterfall. It offers luxury hotel accommodations, a day spa, and the Kids Quest/Cyber Quest family entertainment facility. The Mohegan Sun Resort is home to the WNBA's Connecticut Sun team, and it hosts such events as arena football, professional boxing and kickboxing, numerous rock and music concerts, the WWE, the Mohegan Sun National Karate Championships, the Ultimate Fighting Championship, professional bowling association tournaments, rodeo and professional bull riding, and professional billiards tournaments.

The Mohegan Sun Resort is presently the second-largest casino in the United States. It receives an average of 35,000 visitors per day. When the federal government cut defense jobs in the late 1990s, Southeastern Connecticut experienced a loss of 15,000 jobs. The combination of employment opportunities available at the Mohegan Sun Resort and the Foxwoods Casino, owned by the Mashantucket Pequot Tribe, exceeded that number and effectively offset the negative economic impact that would have been created.

The Mohegan Sun Resort generates over $312 million, which is returned to the local economy on an annual basis. The tribe also pays 25 percent of its slot machine revenues to the State of Connecticut and $500,000 annually to the Town of Montville, Connecticut. Tribal revenues are used to fund tribal government, economic development projects, and charitable contributions. In 1997, the tribe returned $2.2 million to the Department of Housing and Urban Development, and it has returned other allotted federal funds for redistribution to other Native American tribes.

Real Estate/Commercial Development. The tribe is increasing development on the reservation, while establishing an economic partnership with tribes in Wisconsin and Washington, and pursuing a gaming project in Pennsylvania. The tribe wants to expand and diversify its economic base beyond the reservation borders so they can guarantee an ongoing success for the Mohegan people.

Tourism and Recreation. The tribe commissioned David Rockwell, International Designer of the Year of 1997, to create the resort's interior environment. Through his design, Mr. Rockwell incorporated traditional woodland tribal art and elements of historical and cultural significance to the Mohegan people. The result is a stunning décor that has been cited as "unbeatable."

The Ancient Mohegan Village site, a National Registered Historic Landmark within the reservation's boundaries, is currently being restored. The site marks the place where the Mohegan people first settled under the leadership of their Sachem Uncas in the seventeenth century, and it is the place from which Mohegan people draw their spiritual strength. The village of Shantok, adjacent to the ancient Mohegan Village, was the site of conflicts between the Mohegans and the neighboring Narragansett Tribe in the eighteenth century. The Royal Mohegan Burial Ground once spanned 16 acres in the center of Norwich, Connecticut. Only a few graves remain undisturbed. The burial ground is open to the public year round and can be accessed from Interstate 395 via exit 81E. The burial grounds lie on the hillside above Yantic Falls, an historic battleground. During the Battle of the Great Plains in the mid-seventeenth century, Mohegan Sachem Uncas leaped across the falls in pursuit of Narrangasett Sachem Miantonomo.

In 1831, Lucy Occum Tantaquidgeon, Lucy Tantaquidgeon Teecomwas, and Cynthia Teecomwas Hoscott of the Mohegan Tribe founded the Mohegan Church on lands they donated from their personal allotments. The Mohegan Church became the site of the first Mohegan school, and it continues to serve as the social and political center for the Mohegan people. A religious gathering site, the Mohegan Church also hosts tribal meetings and celebrations. The church is located on Mohegan Hill in Uncasville and is open to the public, except during the summer. Church services are still held every Sunday at 9:30 a.m. It can be reached via Route 32.

The Mohegan Tribe operates the oldest Native American-operated museum in the U.S. The Tantaquidgeon Indian Museum in Uncasville was founded in 1931. Permanent exhibits include woodland tribal artifacts, and featured exhibits include memorabilia from Southwest and Plains tribes. Contact the Mohegan Tribal Office for hours of operation. In August, the Mohegan Tribe hosts its annual Green Corn Festival, also called the "Wigwam." The Mohegan people have practiced this ceremony for centuries. It is a homecoming celebration for the Mohegans, and it is also open to the public. Vendors prepare clam chowder and succotash, and tribal artists from Mohegan and other tribes exhibit their artwork, beadwork, basketry, and woodcarving. There are also sessions of traditional Mohegan dancing and storytelling.

INFRASTRUCTURE

Bradley International Airport in Hartford is 53 miles distant. T.F. Green Airport in Providence, Rhode Island, is 56 miles away. Bus service is available in Norwich. U.S. interstates 95 and 395 are the nearest major highways. Central Vermont Railroad services the area railways. Major freight delivery services serve the reservation.

Water Supply. The Mohegan Tribe operates Mohegan Solid Waste (MSW), an integrated municipal solid waste management program. The program promotes waste reduction, reuse, and recycling in lieu of disposal options. It recycles over 44 percent of its solid waste, far surpassing the recycling rate of nonreservation towns and cities in Connecticut.

COMMUNITY FACILITIES AND SERVICES

Traditional cultural elements remain integral to contemporary tribal life. Mohegans continue to practice traditional spirituality, speak their language, and draw strength from lands that have been home to them for centuries. They encourage and support the maintenance of tribal traditions in daily living. Members continue to participate in ceremonies such as the Wigwam in August. Ceremonial sites are maintained on and off reservation lands. While a number of the sites are registered as National Historic Landmarks and are open to the general public, the tribe continues to conduct tribal meetings and celebrations on those grounds. Those sites include Cochegan Rock, Mohegan Congregational Church, and Fort Shantok.

ENVIRONMENTAL CONCERNS

The Mohegan Tribe operates a Tribal Pollution Prevention Team. This team is responsible for developing plans and strategies for the Mohegan Solid Waste (MSW) management program. The Mohegan Environmental Management Division (EMD) implements programs to ensure compliance with MSW standards. Programs are directed toward reducing waste and conserving water. The environmental management division promotes the use of indigenous plants for residential and commercial landscaping to reduce the use of chemicals, fertilizers, and pesticides. The environmental management division also conducts regular education programs to familiarize tribal members, employees, and off-reservation contractors with the tribe's policies and options to waste disposal in general.

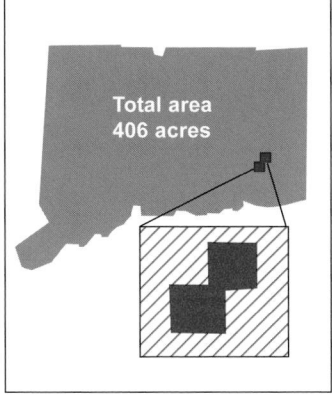

Total area 406 acres

FLORIDA

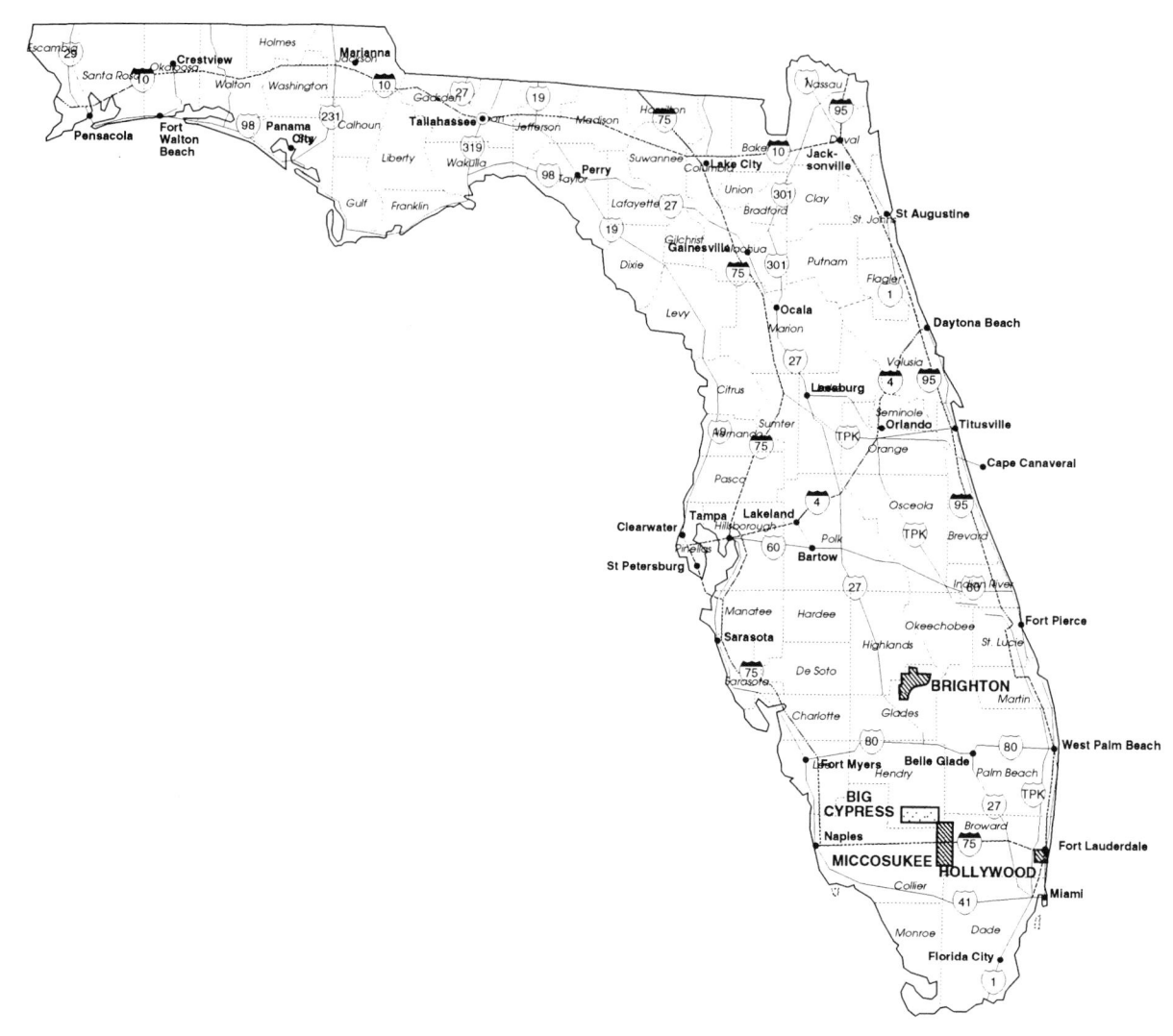

Map from Tiller's Guide to Indian Country (1996 edition)

SEMINOLE TRIBE OF FLORIDA

The state of Florida is home to two federally recognized tribes, the Seminole Tribe of Florida and the Miccosukee Tribe. While the groups are culturally related and share a common history, they have self-identified as two separate tribes. The Seminole Tribe is the largest tribe in Florida and occupies the greatest amount of reservation area. Tribal lands of the Seminoles are divided among six designated reservations and tribally owned parcels of land throughout Florida. For the purposes of this guide, the editor has created a single profile for the Miccosukee Tribe and its reservation at Alligator Alley, Tamiami Alley, and Krome Avenue. The Seminole tribes have individual profiles under each reservation's headings, Big Cypress, Brighton, Hollywood, Immokalee, Fort Pierce, and Tampa.

LOCATION AND LAND STATUS

The Seminole Tribe of Florida maintains tribal lands on over 90,000 acres throughout the southeastern portion of the state of Florida. The tribe's reserved lands include the Big Cypress Reservation, Brighton Reservation, Hollywood Reservation, Immokalee Reservation, Tampa Reservation, and Fort Pierce Reservation.

The majority of Seminole tribal lands lie within the swampy regions of the Everglades ecosystem. The Everglades, or the "River of Grass," has been the heart of Seminole culture for countless years. In addition to being part of the tribe's ancestral lands, the region has served as a sanctuary for tribal members during trying times over the course of the last two centuries. Tribal members have sought refuge in the swamplands following wars and conflicts, invasions and disturbances. There, the Seminole people have gathered strength to face the future and whatever it may bring.

The Everglades, characterized by miles of swamplands, is also home to numerous endangered plant and animal species. The Everglades is home to alligators, crocodiles, snakes, manatees, mosquitoes, bobcats, and numerous bird species. It provides sanctuary to 16 endangered and 6 threatened animal species. The Everglades is also home to the last known remaining population of the Florida panther, the most endangered mammal across the world. There is an estimated population of between 30 and 50 panthers, all living within the Everglades. The panther bears particular cultural significance to the Seminole people and is represented in the tribe's clan system.

The Everglades' endangered status is of concern to the tribe, who are inextricably connected to the lands. The health and well-being of their surroundings is critical to the well-being of the Seminole people themselves. The tribe has established programs that work toward protecting the natural resources and providing education to tribal and nontribal members regarding the area's significance to the larger ecosystem and to the Seminole people as well.

The tribe holds a water rights compact agreement with the State of Florida and the South Florida Water Management District. It allows the tribe to regulate surface water management, water use, and environmentally sensitive waters on tribal lands.

CULTURE AND HISTORY

Members of the Seminole Tribe lived in southeastern North America for thousands of years predating European arrival. Archeological evidence indicates that indigenous cultures occupied the area as many as 12,000 years ago. When Spanish explorers arrived in Florida in the early 1500s, the indigenous population was estimated at around 200,000. The arrival of the explorers drastically and permanently altered the lives of the indigenous groups. They suffered devastating losses caused by the rash of death brought on by European diseases foreign to their immune systems. Tribal lands were seized and tribal people targeted for extermination. Survivors from the Seminole Tribe moved toward the Florida peninsula, and they were living in that area in close proximity to members of the Euchee, Yamasee, Timugua, Tequesta, Abalachi, and Coça tribes, among others, almost two hundred years later when they encountered English settlers. The English identified all the Native Americans they encountered as members of one nation and referred to them as Seminolies, or Seminoles, their misinterpretation of the Maskókî word "yat'siminoli," or "free people."

In 1784, the American Revolution ended, and Euro-American settlers began to enter the southeastern United States in large numbers. The tension between Native nations and the settlers was exacerbated by the federal policy of taking or buying lands from the tribes and giving them to Euro-Americans. By 1813, the situation had escalated, and there began a series of conflicts throughout the region. The defeat of the Creek Nation in Alabama resulted in a flood of refugees into Florida. The Seminoles joined forces with the Creeks and other Native tribes in the area to resist Euro-American invasion.

In 1814, U.S. President Andrew Jackson authorized the destruction of Native communities in Florida and the murder of tribal leaders. The battles that ensued between the government and the tribes became known as the First Seminole War. In 1830, the federal government ordered the forced removal of Native Americans living east of the Mississippi River to Indian Territory west of the river. The Native people of the southeastern U.S. resisted the government's forced removal, and the Second Seminole War began in 1835. It continued until 1842. A number of tribes joined forces to fight the government, as did numbers of African-American slaves escaping slavery. The war was the longest, most expensive, and last of the wars fought between the U.S. and Native nations over the Indian Removal Act. In 1856, the Third Seminole War began when U.S. troops directly provoked Seminole leader Billy Bowlegs. Although no treaty was reached between the tribe and the federal government, the U.S. eventually declared victory.

By the 1860s, an estimated 3,000 Native Americans had been forcibly removed from Florida. Remaining numbers were approximated at 300 or less. Individuals who managed to escape removal sought refuge in the swamps of the Everglades and remained there relatively undisturbed until the late 1800s when, again, Euro-Americans began to encroach on their lands. The Seminole Tribe had no agreement with the federal government granting them reservation lands or protected status. Their land base dissipated as Euro-American settlements were established.

The years between 1870 and 1914 represent an era wherein the Seminoles relied on intensive hunting, trapping, and trading. Tribal members traded alligator hides, otter pelts, bird plumes, and the like for guns, ammunition, canned foods, clothing, and hand-cranked sewing machines. During this time, the Seminole people remained relatively undisturbed on their tribal lands, interacting with non-Natives primarily on the outskirts of the reservations. This relatively amicable balance was destroyed by the 1920s Florida "land boom," when Florida began to drain the Everglades and displace the tribe from its land.

During the Great Depression and on through World War II, most Seminoles eventually migrated to the federal reservations in south Florida. It was at this time that the tribe began to adopt cattle herding, wage labor, and non-Indian customs regarding schooling, health care, and religion. In the 1950s, the Seminole Tribe was targeted for federal termination. With the assistance of the state's congressional delegation, Indian rights advocates, and the National Congress of American Indians, the Seminoles evaded termination. Unprepared to assume sovereignty, however, the tribe agreed to surrender their traditional form of government and replace it with a congressionally approved system in order to maintain status as a federally recognized tribe. In 1953, the tribe adopted a constitution that was formally recognized in 1957. At that time, the Seminole Tribe of Florida was organized under the provisions of the Indian Reorganization Act of 1934. Reservation lands were established at Hollywood, Brighton, Big Cypress, and later, Immokalee, Tampa, and Fort Pierce.

The Seminole Tribe includes the majority of Seminole groups in Florida. The U. S. government had long identified numerous indigenous groups in the area as members of the Seminole Tribe regardless of tribal affiliations and self-identification. The Miccosukee Tribe, though members of the Creek Nation, were one of the tribes identified with the Seminoles. The Miccosukees formally separated from the Seminole Tribe in the 1960s. In 1962, it received federal recognition as a sovereign nation. A third group of Seminole people, the Independent or Traditional Seminole, have evolved into a separate entity from both the Seminole and Miccosukee tribes. This group does not recognize the authority of the federal government and is not a federally- or state-recognized nation.

During the past two decades, the Seminoles have grown into a strong sovereign force under an inspired and articulate leadership. Cultural elements are sustained in the form of special cultural events, language, clanship, and in the highly regarded Seminole arts and crafts tradition.

GOVERNMENT

The Seminole constitution, bylaws, and corporate charter were adopted on August 21, 1957, to establish the Seminole Tribe of Florida and the Seminole Tribe of Florida, Inc. The tribal council and board of directors oversee tribal operations. Both are elected by tribal members, and neither body is subservient to the other. The tribal council is responsible for most governmental activities, including the delivery of services to tribal members. The new governmental system replaced the traditional council of elders associated with the Corn Dance groups. The current tribal council consists of a chairman, a vice-chairman, a secretary, a treasurer, and representatives from the three big reservations: Hollywood, Big Cypress, and Brighton.

In 2003, the tribal constitution was amended to create two distinct tribal council offices of the tribal secretary and tribal treasurer. The tribe's growth since its incorporation in 1957 increased the tribe's command of its fiscal policies and financial procedures. The creation of a separate treasurer position was elemental to the tribe's fiscal management. The treasurer's office is

headquartered on the Hollywood Reservation, and satellite offices are located at Brighton and Big Cypress.

Governmental departments and programs include the office of planning development, credit and finance department, office of the executive administrator, office of education, office of health, office of recreation, office of purchasing, and the cattleman's program. The cattleman's program was established in the 1960s in cooperation with tribal cattle owners. The tribe's cattle operations and cow-calf productions are ranked fourth in the state and twelfth in the nation.

The tribe maintains a Governor's Council On Indian Affairs. This office is responsible for obtaining funds for the Seminole/Miccosukee Scholarship Program, organizing the tribe's participation in state programs, and monitoring state and federal legislation affecting Florida tribes.

The tribe maintains an extensive emergency care system, including police, fire, and emergency programs. There have been numerous devastating hurricanes during the tribe's recorded history, including Hurricane Andrew. In order to better prepare tribal members for hurricane season, the tribe has established an emergency management office. Its headquarters are located at the Brighton Reservation. The tribe's department of emergency services is a growing program, and additional personnel and equipment will be recruited by 2005.

The Seminole Police Department offers law enforcement services as well as numerous crime prevention, drug abuse prevention, child safety, community policing, and elders programs. It is affiliated with the Florida Department of Law Enforcement, the Secret Service, Homeland Security, the FBI, the BIA, the International Association of Chiefs of Police, and the Florida Police Accreditation Coalition.

The Hollywood Reservation serves as the seat of the Seminole Tribe. Tribal governmental departments and programs have their headquarters on that reservation, though a number of them maintain satellite offices throughout the tribe's reservations.

BUSINESS CORPORATION

In addition to its status as a federally recognized sovereign nation, the Seminole Tribe of Florida is a federally chartered corporation. The corporation is responsible for the tribe's economic development. A board of directors manages the corporation. The board consists of a president, a vice-president, and directors from the Brighton, Big Cypress, and Hollywood reservations. The president is the vice-chair of the tribal council, and the chairman of the council is the vice-president of the board of directors. Liaisons represent tribal members from Tampa, Trail, Naples, and Fort Pierce. A representative from Immokalee also sits on the board, but does not have voting authority. Each tribal member owns an equal share in the corporation.

The board oversees the operation of a number of tribal enterprises, including Seminole Wholesale Distributors,

Brighton Seminole Trading Post and Campground, tribal smoke shops, the tribe's sugarcane crops, the cattle program, and citrus groves.

ECONOMY

Since its inception as the Seminole Tribe of Florida, the tribe has made great strides in developing its economic base and furthering its efforts to establish itself as a sovereign nation. The tribe owns and operates several enterprises in various industries, including gaming, agriculture, services, and tourism. The Nation serves as a source of employment for tribal and nontribal members alike and is a formidable economic force in the region.

Government as Employer. The tribe employs a total of approximately 2,500 people, both Native and non-Native, through its various departments and reservations. These include road-building projects, renovation projects, administration of HUD and other federal contracts, health care, and childcare centers.

Agriculture and Livestock. Tribal operations in the agriculture and livestock industries serve as a major source of income and employment for the tribe and its members. The Seminole Tribe owns and operates citrus groves, sugarcane fields, and cattle ranches across its reservations. The tribe's largest reservations, Brighton and Big Cypress, host the cattle ranches and citrus farms. Both the cattle and citrus operations have state and national rankings. The tribe's sugarcane crops encompass 800 acres. The U.S. Sugar Corporation has been contracted to harvest the crops. The tribe plans to expand the production to 1,600 acres.

Gaming. The Seminole Tribe was the first tribe in the nation to open a large-stake bingo hall on tribal land. The first facility was opened in 1979 on the Hollywood Reservation and the second in 1982 on the Tampa Reservation. The tribe currently operates gaming facilities at Immokalee, Brighton, Coconut Creek, Hollywood, and Tampa. In addition to gaming operations, the facilities include restaurants, entertainment venues, and hotel accommodations.

The Seminole Casino at Coconut Creek is also an enterprise of the Seminole Tribe. It is situated on five acres of tribal lands in the city of Coconut Creek, Florida, in northern Broward County. The casino opened in 2000 in a 30,000-square-foot facility. It features over 800 pull-tab machines, bingo, and a card room. There is also a café and bar area. Future improvements to the casino include the addition of gaming space, restaurants, and hotel accommodations.

The income from the tribe's gaming facilities comprises over 90 percent of its income. In turn, gaming proceeds fund over 90 percent of the tribe's expenditures, including funds used for health care, social services, education, and economic development projects. Each member of the Seminole Tribe receives a monthly stipend earned from gaming operations as well. The local and state economies benefit significantly from the tribe's operations, too. The tribe employs thousands of Floridians, the majority of whom are non-Indian. In addition to the millions of dollars expended in payroll, payroll taxes, and unemployment insurance, the gaming operations purchase millions of dollars in goods and services from local and state vendors.

Construction. The tribe owns considerable heavy equipment for use in excavation, road building, and clearing reservation lands. Additionally, a number of tribal members make their living in the construction trade, some finding work through tribal renovation projects.

Mining. Mineral resources on Seminole tribal lands consist primarily of dolomite and high-quality sand.

Services and Retail. Seminole Wholesale Distribution began operations in 1982. The State of Florida passed legislation permitting state-licensed cigarette wholesalers to sell directly to Seminole retail shops. In 1980, the Seminole Tribe negotiated a joint enterprise with the largest wholesaler, and in 1982 it acquired the rights to exclusive distribution to the tribal shops on the Hollywood, Brighton, and Big Cypress reservations. In 1991 the Seminole Tribe owned the entire company, and it moved the operations to the Hollywood Reservation. The Davie Boulevard and Sample Road Shops, owned by the corporation, opened their doors in 1990 and 1991, respectively. Today the corporation owns seven other tribal smoke shops throughout its reservations.

Media and Communications. The Seminole Broadcasting Department is responsible for documenting and broadcasting newsworthy events. It also documents the life stories of tribal members and tribal celebrations, such as the Seminole Tribal Festival and Rodeo, Brighton Field Day and Rodeo, Veteran's Day Celebration, and Princess Pageant.

The tribe publishes *The Seminole Tribune*. It is published every two weeks and has a circulation of over 5,000. In 1989, *The Seminole Tribune* became the first Indian newspaper to win a Robert F. Kennedy Award. It was also nominated for the Pulitzer Prize that same year. The paper has been honored with numerous Native American Journalist Association awards, including Best Internet News Site, Best News Writing, Layout and Design, and General Excellence. In 1997, it was the most-awarded Native publication.

In addition to managing *The Seminole Tribune*, the tribe's communications department maintains three websites: seminoletribe.com, indiancircle.com, and seminoletribemotocross.com. It also provides graphic design services and manages the tribe's online marketplace.

Tourism and Recreation. The tourism industry has always served the Seminole Tribe well. During the early twentieth century, Seminole arts were highly sought after, particularly Seminole dolls. The demand for fine basketry, beadwork, and patchwork dresses has also allowed tribal members to use their artistic skills to draw visitors to the area and generate an income. The Seminoles continue to rely upon the tourism industry, though the largest source of income is now generated by the tribally owned campgrounds, safari parks, museums, and gaming facilities. Items produced in the traditional style are still available for sale and can be found at the tribe's online marketplace.

INFRASTRUCTURE

The Seminole Utilities Department provides water distribution, water treatment, wastewater treatment, sewage collection, and solid waste collection on each of the reservations. In addition, the department manages a capital improvement program which develops underground infrastructure, road improvements, housing construction, and tribal government facilities. The department's recent projects include the Big Cypress Water Treatment Plant, Big Cypress Master Planning, Brighton Waste Water Treatment Plant, Brighton Water and Sewer Mains, Immokalee Water and Wastewater Treatment Plant, Fort Pierce Housing Community, and widening State Road 7 at Hollywood. The department takes great pride in completing the road-widening project. Estimates placed completion at two years; however, under the department's management, the project was completed in six months.

COMMUNITY FACILITIES AND SERVICES

The Seminole Tribe was one of the first eight tribes in the country to join the Employment and Training Program under PL 102-477. The law allows for tribes to play a greater role in developing and regulating the program. The Seminole Tribe's program consists of four divisions: summer youth employment program, work experience program, adult vocational program, and adult ABE/GED program. Classes are offered at the Hollywood and Brighton reservations, and plans to expand to Big Cypress are in development.

The Seminole Tribe maintains its own library system. Public libraries are located at Brighton, Big Cypress, Hollywood, Immokalee, and Tampa. The library system offers an extensive collection of books, periodicals, photographs, and media resources. It participates in the Southwest Florida Library Network, enabling the libraries to share resources with libraries in six Florida counties. The library system serves over 20,000 clients each year.

The tribe's family services department provides student and parent school counseling and support services; oversees Indian Child Welfare services; manages elder programs; and provides mental health, substance abuse prevention, and outreach programs. Facilities are available on each of the tribe's reservations.

Housing. The Seminole Tribe Housing Authority has received HUD grants that have assisted in the development of the youth services program, economic development and supportive services, drug elimination program, family investment center, and community services offered by the tribe's law enforcement, recreation, and education departments. The housing authority also oversees the management and maintenance of all rental and homeownership properties on tribal lands.

Education. The tribe's education department manages the preschool program on the Big Cypress, Brighton, Hollywood, and Immokalee reservations; the Afhachkee School on the Big Cypress Reservation; and the education advisory program. Representatives of each of the Seminole reservations serve on the education advisory board. Members include representatives from the health department, recreation department, and parent advisory committees. The board meets twice each month to address educational matters affecting the tribe.

The tribe established a cultural education program in 1979. It offers programs and services to teach tribal youth all aspects of Seminole culture and tradition. The program provides instructional services at the preschool programs and through various community programs.

Health Care. The Seminole Health Department operates Indian Health Services primary care facilities at Brighton, Hollywood, and Big Cypress. The clinics provide medical, dental, environmental health, laboratory, and health education services, among others. The tribe has a health plan that oversees the administration of medical, dental, and vision insurance to tribal members and employees. The department employs a staff of seven.

Big Cypress

Big Cypress Reservation
Federal reservation
Seminole
Broward and Hendry counties, Florida

Seminole Tribe of Florida
6300 Stirling Road
Hollywood, FL 33024
800-683-7800
seminoletribe.com

Total area *(BIA realty, 2005)*
52,338 acres

Federal trust lands
(BIA realty, 2005)
52,338 acres

Tribally owned lands
(Tribal source, 1994)
52,337 acres

Population ***2000 census***
142

Total labor force ***2000 census***
66

High school graduate or higher
2000 census
100%

Bachelor's degree or higher
2000 census
16.1%

Unemployment rate
2000 census
13.6%

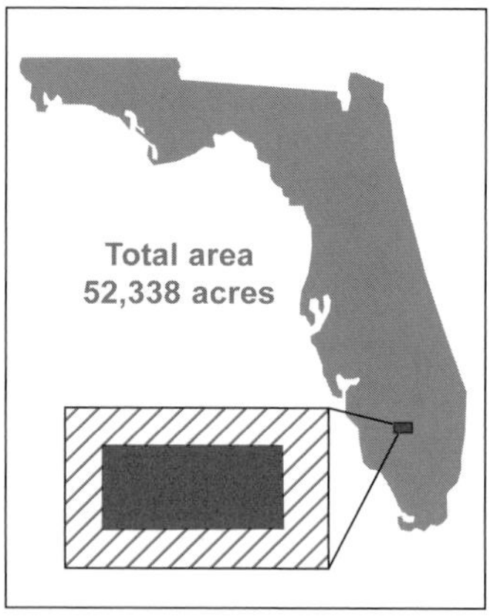

(Please see Seminole Tribe introduction for further detail on Culture and History, Government, Business Corporation, Economy, Infrastructure, and Community Facilities and Services.)

LOCATION AND LAND STATUS

The Big Cypress Reservation lies approximately 45 miles west of Fort Lauderdale. Big Cypress is one of six reservations of the Seminole Tribe of Florida and one of the first three to be consolidated for the Seminoles by the BIA in the 1930s.

In 1960, the State of Florida set aside 100,000 acres in the Florida Everglades for the Seminole and Miccosukee tribes. The northern portion is administered by the Seminole Tribe and is adjacent to the Big Cypress Reservation.

PHYSICAL DESCRIPTION

The Big Cypress Reservation is located adjacent to the Florida Everglades. The Everglades are home to an endangered ecosystem. Tribal members occupy less than two percent of the reservation; the remainder of the area is home to indigenous plant and animal species, many of them endangered.

ECONOMY

The economy of the Big Cypress Reservation is sustained primarily by the tribe's agricultural enterprises. There are also numerous tourist attractions that draw visitors to the reservation and supplement the tribe's income.

Agriculture and Livestock. The tribe operates citrus groves on the reservation. It is comprised of 1,600 acres. The groves produce a major portion of Florida's lemon crop. In 2003, the grapefruit crop was the earliest producing one in the state, bringing the tribe recognition for its successful practices.

The tribe manages a herd of cattle on the Big Cypress Reservation. Portions of the Everglades adjacent to the reservation were set in trust status for the tribe in the 1960s and are used for limited grazing by Native livestock owners.

Aviation. The tribe operates an aviation department. It provides safe, efficient, convenient, and cost-effective air transportation for tribal programs and medical travel requests. The tribe's fleet consists of twofixed-wing and two rotor-wing aircraft. The department also provides helicopter firefighting services to the BIA forestry program and conducts mosquito eradication for the Big Cypress, Brighton, and Immokalee reservations. A second helicopter is used to provide transportation to tribal programs. The airport is located in Big Cypress. The department employs five pilots, two maintenance technicians, a flight coordinator, a flight attendant, and three seasonal employees.

Services and Retail. There are several individually owned stores near the residential community.

Tourism and Recreation. The Ah-Tah-Thi-Ki Museum is located on the Big Cypress Reservation. The museum houses Seminole artifacts and serves to educate tribal members and non-Natives about the Seminole's history and culture. Exhibits include a full-scale re-creation of a traditional village, a 64-acre cypress dome, and over one mile of boardwalk nature trails. An important feature of the museum is the *We Seminoles* five-screen film. The museum houses exhibits on loan from the Smithsonian Institute and a growing collection of militaria dating from the period of the Seminole Wars. The museum also houses the tribe's historical preservation office and hosts two annual celebrations in particular. The American Indian Arts Celebration is held in November to commemorate Native American Month, and the Kissimmee Slough Shootout, a historic re-enactment based upon the Seminole Wars, is held the first weekend in February. The museum welcomes approximately 2,000 visitors each month.

The Billie Swamp Safari provides visitors with the opportunity to tour the swamp via buggy rides. It features a free herpetarium, an alligator and snake show, airboat rides, and an eco-tour. The safari houses alligator and crocodile breeding pens and is home to the largest known alligator in captivity-14 feet long. There are also campsites with traditional Seminole chickees available for overnight campers. The Safari has received international exposure, having been featured on nature shows on Animal Planet, ESPN, NBC, National Geographic, Telemundo, BBC, German, and Chinese television channels.

The Big Swamp Campgrounds is situated within the Everglades. Camping facilities are available, as are full-service RV hookup sites. There are also laundry facilities, a pool, cabin and trailer rentals, basketball courts, outdoor recreational facilities, and a camp store. The tribe offers animal hunts at Big Cypress Hunting Adventures. Hunting grounds encompass 3,000 acres of the reservation. Hunters may travel by foot or by the tribe's custom award-winning hunting vehicles. Tour guides are available. The tribe also operates the Seminole Tribe Motorcross.

Media and Telecommunications. The Seminole Tribe operates a broadcasting department which is housed on the Hollywood Reservation. The operation includes a broadcasting station with three sister sites in Big Cypress, Brighton, and Immokalee.

INFRASTRUCTURE

U.S. Interstate 75 crosses the reservation east-west, and Florida State Route 833 traverses it north-south.

Electricity. The Glades Cooperative supplies electricity on the reservation.

Water Supply. The tribe operates a water treatment and wastewater treatment plant on the reservation, and a new facility is in development. The water distribution system has recently been updated to accommodate new home sites on the reservation. A solid waste transfer center is currently under development.

Transportation. The Big Cypress Airstrip provides access to the reservation.

All transportation and shipping facilities are available in Fort Lauderdale, approximately 40 miles to the west, and in Miami, approximately 50 miles southeast.

COMMUNITY FACILITIES AND SERVICES

The community of Big Cypress has a new government center, the Henry Osceola Senior Citizen's Center, the Herman Osceola Gymnasium, the Ahfachkee School, two Baptist churches, a ball field, a branch of the Seminole Police Department, and the Willie Frank Memorial Library.

Education. The tribe owns and manages the Ahfachkee School on the Big Cypress Reservation. The school serves 150 students in preschool programs through 12th grade. The school is accredited by the Southern Association of Colleges and Schools. It offers a technologically supported curriculum that promotes a traditional program in addition to instruction in the Miccosukee language and Seminole culture and traditions. The program offers students small classes, extensive field trips, after-school learning activities, Title I services, an exceptional student education program, and counseling services.

The tribe's education division offers an adult education program, boarding school program, higher education program, preschool program, tutoring program, and numerous other programs facilitating educational training and opportunities for members.

Health Care. Health care is available at the Indian Health Services clinic.

ENVIRONMENTAL CONCERNS
The Big Cypress Reservation suffers from soil pollution because of agricultural practices in the region. In order to address this issue and other environmental concerns throughout the five Seminole reservations, the tribe has developed a nonpoint source management program.

Brighton

(Please see Seminole Tribe introduction for further detail on Culture and History, Government, Business Corporation, Economy, Infrastructure, and Community Facilities and Services.)

LOCATION AND LAND STATUS
The Brighton Reservation is located northwest of Lake Okeechobee in southern Florida, approximately 90 miles west of West Palm Beach. It is one of five reservations of the Seminole Tribe. Brighton Reservation is comprised of over 35,000 acres of land held in trust by the federal government. The BIA purchased the lands for the tribe in the 1930s.

ECONOMY
The Brighton Reservation's economy is supported largely by the tribe's agricultural and aquacultural enterprises. The tribe's casino and industrial park also generate income.

Agriculture and Livestock. The Brighton Reservation features the Brighton Citrus Farm. The farm occupies 150 acres and is home to over 18,900 living trees. Groves produce grapefruit, oranges, and tangelos. The tribe intends to expand the farm to incorporate an additional 85 acres. Tribal citrus crop sales generate approximately $4 million annually. The tribe has also recently entered into the aquaculture industry. Newly established enterprises include a turtle farm.

There are 42 cattle operators on the reservation whose cattle are run on over 12,000 acres of native Florida pastures and improved pasture. These operators belong to the tribe's cattleman's program. The program was established in the 1960s in cooperation with individual tribal cattle owners.

Gaming. The Brighton Reservation is home to the Seminole Casino. It is a class II gaming facility that features 540 bingo seats, 10 poker tables, and 240 gaming machines. There are also a restaurant and lounge. The casino, which first opened in 1999, employs approximately 105 individuals. Located 7 miles north of Lakeport and 28 miles west of Lake Okeechobee, the casino is situated near hotels, campgrounds, and RV parks.

Industrial Parks. The Brighton Reservation Industrial Park encompasses 10 acres, 1.5 acres of which are presently used for a 4-H complex and a half acre of which is used for a turtle farming and processing plant.

Services and Retail. The tribe owns and operates the Brighton Trading Post, a full-service gas station.

Media and Telecommunications. The Seminole Broadcasting Department includes a broadcasting station on the Hollywood Reservation and three sister sites on the Big Cypress, Brighton, and Immokalee reservations.

Tourism and Recreation. The Brighton Seminole Campground is situated three miles north of Lake Okeechobee. Campground facilities include a boat dock, an RV park with tent sites, a club house, a swimming pool, a bath house, and recreational activities. There is a private lake stocked with speckled perch, catfish, and bass. The tribe also owns the Brighton Rodeo Arena.

INFRASTRUCTURE
Florida State Route 721 traverses the reservation in a north-south direction.

Electricity. Glades Cooperative supplies electricity to the reservation.

Water Supply. The tribe operates a water and wastewater treatment plant in Brighton. New plants are currently under development. A new transfer station was recently completed to handle solid waste disposal on the reservation. Services include curbside pick-up.

Transportation. The Palm Beach International Airport is approximately 90 miles west of the reservation. Bus transportation is available in the town of Brighton, 8 miles north of the reservation.

COMMUNITY FACILITIES AND SERVICES
A community center and recreational activities are available to reservation residents.

Education. In cooperation with local public schools, the cultural education program has developed a program that allows tribal youth on the Brighton Reservation to remain on the reservation for one day a week in order to receive instruction in Seminole language, history, and crafts.

Health Care. The reservation houses a health clinic with a permanent staff of physicians.

Brighton Reservation
Federal reservation
Seminole
Glades County, Florida

Seminole Tribe
Route 6, Box 666
Okeechobee, FL 33472
863-763-4128
seminoletribe.com

Total area *(BIA realty, 2005)*
35,805 acres

Federal trust lands
(BIA realty, 2005)
35,805 acres

Population *2000 census*
566

Total labor force *2000 census*
212

High school graduate or higher
2000 census
75.5%

Bachelor's degree or higher
2000 census
10.9%

Unemployment rate *2000 census*
4.7%

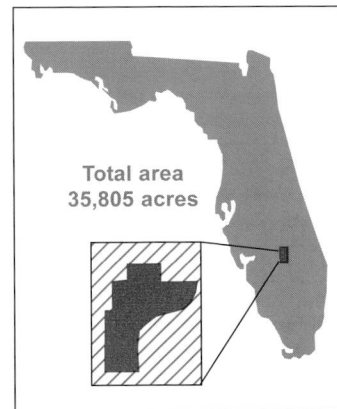

Total area
35,805 acres

Fort Pierce

Fort Pierce Reservation
Federal reservation
Seminole
St. Lucie County, Florida

Seminole Tribe of Florida
4150 E Okeechobee Rd.
Units E & F
Fort Pierce, FL 34945
772-467-2454
772-468-6690 Fax

Total area *(BIA realty, 2005)*		60 acres
Total area *(Indian Country, 2004)*		50 acres
Federal trust *(BIA realty, 2005)*		60 acres
Population *(Tribal source, 2005)*		0
Population		60
(St. Petersburg Times, 1998)		

(Please see Seminole Tribe introduction for further detail on Culture and History, Government, Business Corporation, Economy, Infrastructure, and Community Facilities and Services.)

LOCATION AND LAND STATUS
The Fort Pierce Seminole Reservation is about three miles southwest of downtown Fort Pierce, which is on Florida's east coast, and about two miles east of Interstate 95. Established in 1995, it is the newest and smallest of the six Florida Seminole reservations. At the present time no one lives on the reservation.

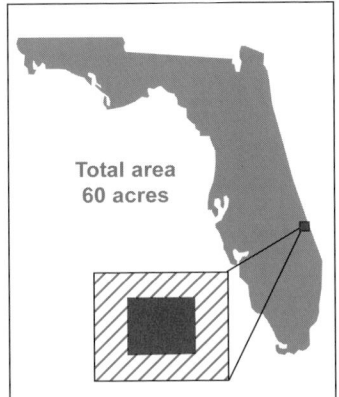

Total area
60 acres

Hollywood

Hollywood Reservation
Federal reservation
Seminole
Hendry County, Florida

Seminole Tribe of Florida
6300 Stirling Road
Hollywood, FL 33024
800-683-7800
seminoletribe.com

Total area *(BIA realty, 2005)*	497 acres
Federal trust *(BIA realty, 2005)*	497 acres
Population *2000 census*	2,051
Total labor force *2000 census*	729
High school graduate or higher *2000 census*	67.5%
Bachelor's degree or higher *2000 census*	6.8%
Unemployment rate *2000 census*	8.5%
Per capita income *2000 census*	$16,268

(Please see Seminole Tribe introduction for further detail on Culture and History, Government, Business Corporation, Economy, Infrastructure, and Community Facilities and Services.)

LOCATION AND LAND STATUS
The Hollywood Reservation is located south of Fort Lauderdale, Florida. It lies just west of Hollywood and the Atlantic Ocean. The Hollywood Reservation is one of five Seminole Tribe reservations.

GOVERNMENT
The Seminole Tribe headquarters is located on the Hollywood Reservation.

ECONOMY
During the late 1970s, tribal leadership moved the tribe into its most profitable enterprise-high-stakes bingo, which generates multimillion-dollar revenues annually. This, along with highly profitable cigarette sales, now underwrites many of the tribe's social services, as well as providing an annual cash dividend to tribal members.

Gaming. The Hollywood Reservation houses the Seminole Casino, a class II gaming facility. The casino includes 1,000 gaming machines, 800 bingo seats, 48 poker tables, and pull-tabs. There are three on-site snack-bar facilities. Opened in

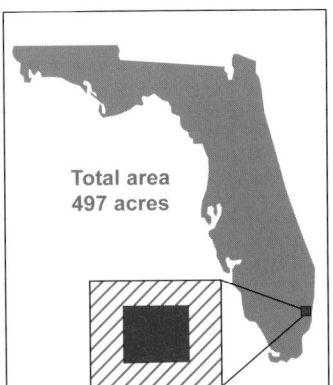

Total area
497 acres

1979, the casino was the first high-stakes operation in the country. Development of the Seminole Casino assisted in opening the industry to Native gaming facilities. The casino employs 770 people. It is located in Hollywood at the intersection of Stirling Road and State Road 7.

The tribe recently opened the Seminole Hard Rock Café Hotel and Casino, with one site on the Hollywood Reservation and one on the Tampa Reservation. The Hard Rock Café franchises are two of very few located on tribal lands across the nation. Nearby is the amphitheater where water events, including alligator wrestling, have become a regular attraction. In the fall of 2004, directly adjacent to the casino complex, a shopping mall complete with high-end fashion boutiques, brand-name retail stores, restaurants, and fast food restaurants was under construction and near completion.

Services and Retail. In 2004, the tribe opened the Seminole Paradise shopping center in Hollywood. Currently operating in the center are a hamburger diner, a coffee house, and 12 retail shops. Upon completion, the complex will feature 24 shops, 13 nightclubs, and entertainment venues. Seminole Paradise is adjacent to the Seminole Hard Rock Café Hotel and Casino.

The reservation's proximity to metropolitan Fort Lauderdale allows residents access to the many services and conveniences of city life. The region is saturated with tourist attractions and draws large numbers of visitors year round. Within the reservation, the tribe and tribal members own and operate a number of businesses, mainly about seven smoke shops that sell both wholesale and retail cigarettes and related products. Many of these smoke shops were started in the 1970s and early 1980s. One member owns and operates the Anhinga Indian Trading Post, while another owns a limousine service. The tribe owns Seminole Trailer Park, which is open to the public for rentals and leasing.

Media and Telecommunications. The Seminole Tribe operates a broadcasting department, which is housed on the Hollywood Reservation. The operation includes a broadcasting station with three sister sites in Big Cypress, Brighton, and Immokalee.

Tourism and Recreation. The reservation is home to the Seminole Indian Okalee Village and Museum, which is located within the Hard Rock Café Hotel and Casino. The village includes a reconstructed traditional village, and guided tours are available. The museum, a satellite of the Ah-Tah-Thi-Ki Museum on the Big Cypress Reservation, features a theater room, Seminole artifacts, and art exhibits. The site includes the Seminole Arts and Crafts Gift Shop and a refreshment venue. Off-site alligator wrestling shows are operated through the museum. Facilities are available for evening rental.

INFRASTRUCTURE

Major highways serving the various Seminole reservations include Interstate 75, the Tamiami Trail, Interstate 95, the Florida Turnpike, and Highway 27.

Electricity. Florida Power and Light provides electricity.

Water Supply. The tribe operates a water distribution system, water treatment, and wastewater treatment facilities on the reservation. A solid waste program is also in operation.

Transportation. Commercial air service is available at the Fort Lauderdale-Hollywood International Airport (5 miles from the Hollywood Reservation) and at an airstrip on Big Cypress. International airport and all commercial transportation and shipping facilities are available in Miami, approximately 20 miles south.

Commercial bus lines serve the Hollywood Reservation, as do rail facilities. Commercial trucking companies serve most areas of the Seminole tribal lands. Numerous canals and waterways intersect tribal lands, many of which are negotiable by boat. The tribe maintains a small fleet of school buses and employs several drivers.

Telecommunications. Southern Bell provides telephone service.

COMMUNITY FACILITIES AND SERVICES

The tribal community at Hollywood has access to many tribally operated community facilities. There is a community center, a fully-equipped gymnasium and swimming pool, a softball field, a playground, a youth center with a Boys and Girls Club, a senior citizens' center, and the three-story Dorothy Scott Osceola Education Building that also houses the Dorothy Scott Osceola Memorial Library and Archives. Library materials include archives of the *Seminole Tribune* and items relating to Seminole history.

Education. Children mostly attend area public schools, riding tribal school buses from 15 minutes to one hour, depending on the location.

Health Care. A health clinic with a staff of regular physicians is located on the Hollywood Reservation.

Immokalee

mmokalee

Total area *(BIA realty, 2005)*		600 acres
Federal trust lands		600 acres
(BIA realty, 2005)		
Total labor force *2000 census*		51
High school graduate or higher		59%
2000 census		
Bachelor's degree or higher		6.6%
2000 census		
Unemployment rate *2000 census*		27.45%
Per capita income *2000 census*		$8,554

(Please see Seminole Tribe introduction for further detail on Culture and History, Government, Business Corporation, Economy, Infrastructure, and Community Facilities and Services.)

LOCATION AND LAND STATUS

The Immokalee Reservation was created in the 1980s when the State of Florida accepted land into trust status for the Seminole Tribe. It is one of five reservations of the Seminole Tribe. It is located in the Everglades of Florida, near the town of Immokalee, approximately 30 miles southeast of Fort Myers.

The federal government holds approximately 599 acres of land held in trust for the Seminoles.

ECONOMY

The reservation's economy is supported in large part by the gaming facilities located there.

Gaming. The Immokalee Reservation is home to the Seminole Gaming Palace and Casino. It is the largest attraction in southwest Florida. The casino is a class II operation featuring 500 bingo seats, 525 slot machines, and 15 poker tables. There are also a full-service restaurant, a gift shop, and an entertainment venue. The facility is located in Immokalee, between Miami and Naples.

Services and Retail. The tribe operates Seminole Arts and Crafts Shop and Seminole Native Arts and Crafts. It also operates the Panther Hammock.

Media and Telecommunications. The tribe operates the Seminole Broadcasting Department which has a broadcasting station in Hollywood, Florida, and three sister stations in Big Cypress, Brighton, and Immokalee. The department provides technical training to its employees; it employs 20 members of the Seminole Tribe.

INFRASTRUCTURE

Water Supply. The Immokalee community has recently been connected to the new water treatment plant that the tribe constructed. A solid waste transfer center will be developed at the site.

COMMUNITY FACILITIES AND SERVICES

The reservation is home to a police station and the Immokalee Reservation Library. The library houses archives of the *Seminole Tribune* and numerous materials relating to Seminole history. The tribe maintains community centers and recreation facilities on each reservation.

Immokalee Reservation
Federal reservation
Seminole
Collier County, Florida

Seminole Tribe of Florida
6300 Stirling Road
Hollywood, FL 33024
800-683-7800
seminoletribe.com

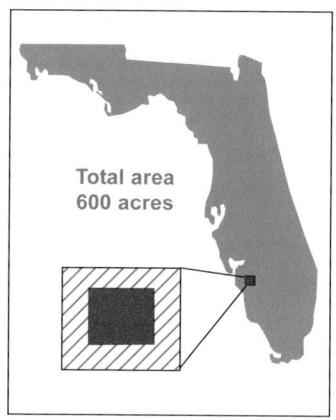

Total area
600 acres

Miccosukee

Miccosukee Reservation
Federal reservation
Miccosukee
Dade County, Florida

Miccosukee Tribe of Florida
Indians
P. O. Box 440021
Tamiami Station
Miami, FL 33144
305-223-8380
305-223-1011 Fax
miccosukeetribe.com

Total area (BIA realty, 2005)
79,711.44 acres

Federal trust lands
(BIA realty, 2005)
79,711.44 acres

Total reservation population
(EPA)
550

Tribal enrollment
(BIA labor report, 2001)
400

Total labor force
(BIA labor report, 2001)
332

High school graduate or higher
18.5%

Unemployment rate
(BIA labor report, 2001)
48%

Per capita income
$5,462

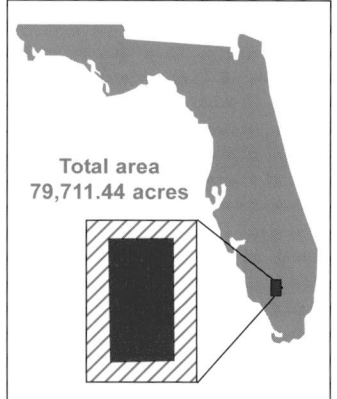

Total area
79,711.44 acres

LOCATION AND LAND STATUS

Tribal lands of the Miccosukee Tribe of Florida Indians consist of four reservations located within the state of Florida. Tamiami Trail Reservation is located approximately 40 miles west of Miami. It consists of 333 acres held by the tribe through a 50-year permit with the BIA and the National Park Service. The permit is due to expire in January 2014. This area is restricted from commercial development. The remaining portion of the Tamiami Trail Reservation is comprised of three parcels of land measuring approximately 600 by 65 feet. These lands have been used for commercial development.

The second reservation is the largest belonging to the tribe. Alligator Alley Reservation is located on 74,812 acres west of Fort Lauderdale. The third reservation is comprised of 25 acres in Miami on the northwest corner of the intersection of Krome Avenue and Tamiami Trail. The fourth reservation is 0.92 acres of land located on the southwest corner of the same intersection. This intersection is known as the Krome Avenue Reservation. The tribe has a perpetual lease from the State of Florida for 189,000 acres in southern Florida. This area is reserved for the purposes of hunting, fishing, frogging, subsistence agriculture, and traditional customs. In addition, the Miccosukee Tribe shares the Florida State Indian Reservation, dedicated in perpetuity by the state to the tribe.

PHYSICAL DESCRIPTION

Thirty-three acres of the Tamiami Trail Reservation lie within a national park and remain undisturbed by development. Alligator Alley Reservation contains approximately 55,000 acres of wetlands. The remaining portions of Miccosukee Reservation lands are urban sites already housing commercial developments or designated for such development.

CULTURE AND HISTORY

The Miccosukee Indians are descendants of the Creek Nation that once inhabited the regions of present-day Alabama and Georgia. Two groups composed the Nation, the Upper and Lower Creek. Although the groups shared a common heritage, they spoke mutually unintelligible dialects and often engaged in war with one another. The direct ancestors of the Miccosukee Tribe were the Lower Creeks, those members of the nation residing at the base of the mountains. Oral history suggests that the Miccosukees originated in northern Florida.

The tribe encountered Euro-Americans in the 1500s as the English, French, and Spanish began to arrive in what would become the southern United States. In the early 1700s, members of the Miccosukee Tribe left the area with Spanish forces. They settled the Florida peninsula around 1715. The tribe established communities in the Apalachee Bay region along the Chattahoochee and Apalachicola rivers. Conflicts between the tribe and Euro-American settlers eventually forced the Miccosukees to leave the area and settle in regions around Alachua.

In 1823, the tribe signed the Treaty of Moultrie Creek, agreeing to move tribal clans to a reservation in central Florida. The tribe remained undisturbed on the reservation for almost 20 years. In 1830, the United States adopted the Indian Removal Act. This law mandated that all Native Americans living east of the Mississippi River be relocated to Indian Territory west of the river. A number of Miccosukees escaped removal and sought refuge in the Everglades. In 1835, the Miccosukees joined other tribes of the Creek Nation in the Second Seminole War, and later participated in the Third Seminole War.

By the 1870s, identifiable Miccosukee communities began to reestablish on reservation lands. In the early twentieth century, the reservation experienced extensive intrusions. Canals were cut in order to create drainage of the Everglades for agricultural purposes. The canals depleted the reservation wetlands, greatly reducing fish and game populations. The construction of Tamiami Trail in 1928 allowed non-Indians access to tribal lands, and in 1947, the Department of the Interior declared that most of the Miccosukee ancestral lands were to become part of the Everglades National Park.

The Miccosukee Tribe was identified by the federal government as part of the Seminole Nation. The tribe remained allied with the Seminole Tribe until the mid-1900s when it chose to pursue its own independent status.

GOVERNMENT

The Miccosukees adopted their present constitution in 1961 when they separated from the Seminole Tribe. In 1962, the constitution was officially recognized by the Department of the Interior, in effect recognizing the tribe as a sovereign nation.

The Miccosukee Tribe is governed by the Miccosukee General Council. Members of the council include all adult members of the tribe. Officers of the tribe comprise the business council and serve in the positions of chairman, assistant chairman, treasurer, secretary, and lawmaker. The general council deals with tribal matters relating to membership, government, law and order, education, recreation, fiscal disbursement, and welfare. The business council deals with the development and management of resources.

Tribal departments include education, health, social services, tribal courts, housing, and natural resources. Tribal headquarters are located on the Tamiami Trail Reservation.

BUSINESS CORPORATION

The Miccosukee Corporation operates all programs and services provided for the community and formerly administered by the BIA. It receives and administers funds from private foundations and county, state, and federal agencies. The corporation disperses the funds to the tribe's educational, employment, housing, and social services programs.

ECONOMY

The tribal economy is largely supported by the revenue earned from leasing lands for cattle grazing. The addition of tribal casinos has bolstered the economy a great deal. The tribe also operates a number of tourist attractions.

Government as Employer. The tribal government employed four reservation residents in the early 1990s.

Economic Development Projects. Future endeavors for the tribe include further commercial and agricultural development, and construction of community facilities and housing developments.

Agriculture and Livestock. The Miccosukee Tribe leases 13,000 acres located in the Alligator Alley Reservation for cattle grazing.

Gaming. The Miccosukee Tribe owns and operates the Miccosukee Resort and Gaming Center on the Krome Avenue

Reservation in Miami. The site contains casino facilities, which feature 1,200 slot machines/VLTs, 58 poker tables, and 1,400 bingo seats. The adjacent hotel has 302 guest rooms, four restaurants, three lounges, and one entertainment venue. The Miccosukee Indian Gaming Facility is located on the Krome Reservation.

Services and Retail. The tribe owns and operates a gas station and service center on the Alligator Alley Reservation and the Miccosukee Smoke Shop on the Krome Avenue Reservation.

Tourism and Recreation. The tribe owns the Miccosukee Sports and Entertainment Dome. It hosts various sporting events and can seat up to 2,000 individuals. In 2001, the tribe purchased the Miami National Golf Club. Renamed the Miccosukee Golf and Country Club, the facilities feature a 27-hole course, tennis courts, swimming pools, banquet facilities, and a full-service golf shop. It has hosted a number of LPGA and PGA tournaments and events.

The tribe offers guided tours of the reservation's swampy areas through the Miccosukee Airboat Rides and Tours.

The Miccosukee Indian Village and Information Center is located on land that the tribe purchased from a private entity in the 1970s. The village is an authentic family camp that existed long before the Tamiami Trail was constructed. The tribe offers guided tours of the village, and has developed a museum, boardwalk, and alligator arena on the property.

Hunting and camping sites are available to the public but require occupancy and access permits issued by the tribe.

INFRASTRUCTURE
U.S. Highway 41 runs east to west through the Tamiami Trail Reservation. Highway 84 runs east to west through the Alligator Alley Reservation. The Krome Avenue Reservation occupies the northwest and southwest corners of the intersection of Krome Avenue and Tamiami Trail in Miami.

Electricity. Florida Power and Light Company provides electricity.

Water Supply. A community water system serves the residential units on the reservation. The U.S. Public Health Service built sewage facilities to serve the community.

Transportation. There is an international airport available in Miami, approximately 40 miles distant. Commercial bus lines serve the reservation; all other transportation and shipping services are available in Miami.

COMMUNITY FACILITIES AND SERVICES
Education. The tribe offers Head Start programs. It also sponsors services for elementary, secondary, post-secondary, adult, and vocational education students.

Health Care. The reservation has a clinic operated by the U.S. Public Health Service.

Miccosukee

Poarch Creek
See Alabama

Tampa

Tampa

(Please see Seminole Tribe introduction for further detail on Culture and History, Government, Business Corporation, Economy, Infrastructure, and Community Facilities and Services.)

LOCATION AND LAND STATUS
The Tampa Reservation is located on the eastern outskirts of Tampa, Florida. It lies at the intersection of U.S. Interstate 4 and Highway 92. The reservation is one of six reservations of the Seminole Tribe. The reservation was established for the Seminoles in 1985.

ECONOMY
During the late 1970s, tribal leadership moved the tribe into its most profitable enterprise-high-stakes bingo, which generates multimillion-dollar revenues annually. Bingo revenue and highly profitable cigarette sales now underwrite many of the tribe's social services, as well as providing an annual cash dividend to tribal members.

Gaming. The tribe operates the Seminole Hard Rock Café Hotel and Casino on the Tampa Reservation. Another site is located on the Hollywood Reservation. The Hard Rock Café Hotel and Casino at Tampa features over 1,800 gaming machines, 32 poker tables, and a bingo hall. Facilities include a bar and a multimedia tower.

INFRASTRUCTURE
The Tampa Reservation is located near the intersection of U.S. Interstate 4 and Highway 92.

Water Supply. A privately owned enterprise provides removal of solid waste from the reservation.

Transportation. The tribe maintains a small fleet of school buses and employs several drivers.

COMMUNITY FACILITIES AND SERVICES
The reservation is home to the Tampa Reservation Library. Library materials include archives of the *Seminole Tribune* and items relating to Seminole history. The tribe maintains community centers and recreation facilities on each reservation.

Tampa Reservation
Federal reservation
Seminole
Hillsborough County, Florida

Seminole Tribe of Florida
6300 Stirling Road
Hollywood, FL 33024
800-683-7800
seminoletribe.com

Total area (BIA realty, 2005)
39 acres

Federal trust (BIA realty, 2005)
39 acres

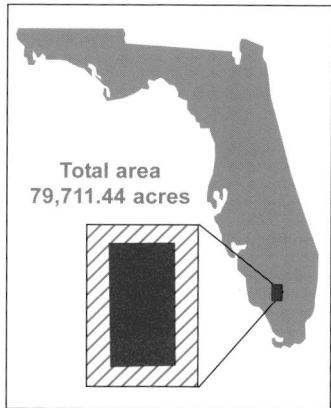

Total area
79,711.44 acres

IDAHO

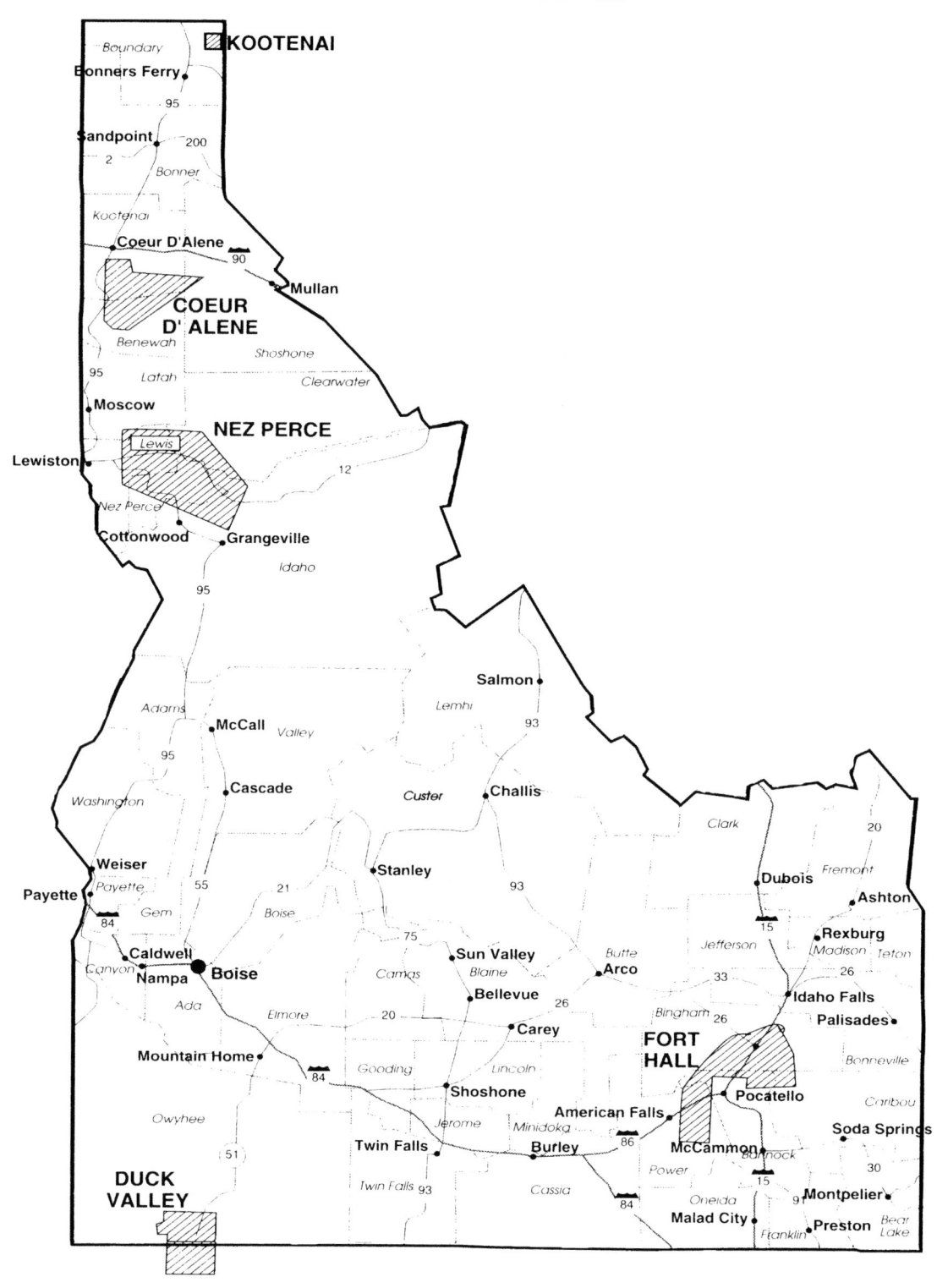

Map from Tiller's Guide to Indian Country (1996 edition)

Coeur d'Alene

Coeur d'Alene

LOCATION AND LAND STATUS
The Coeur d'Alene Indian Reservation is located in the Idaho panhandle, about 40 miles southwest of Coeur d'Alene, Idaho. Spokane, Washington, lies 40 miles to the west. Principal settlements on the reservation include Benewah, DeSmet, Plummer, and Tensed. Over 247,000 acres within the Coeur d'Alene Reservation are privately owned. The State of Idaho owns 12,640 acres, mostly in Heyburn State Park, which is situated at the south end of Lake Coeur d'Alene. The U.S. Forest Service owns 570 acres that are administered by Idaho Panhandle National Forests.

The reservation was officially established by an Executive Order in 1873. The reservation included almost 4,000,000 acres of the tribe's traditional territory, but it dwindled to its present size through treaties, forced sales, and the allotment process.

PHYSICAL DESCRIPTION
Reservation lands range from 2,200 to 2,600 feet above sea level. Mountain peaks rise to between 4,000 and 5,500 feet. The area consists of rolling hills and evergreen timber as well as wetlands and rangelands. Lake Coeur d'Alene and Black Lake are located in the southern regions of the reservation. Lake Coeur d'Alene is the region's major body of water. Several creeks and mountains are located in the northern quarter of the reservation. The St. Joe River and St. Maries River flow through the reservation.

CLIMATE
The average summer temperature on the reservation is 65ºF, while the average winter temperature is 31.2ºF. The annual precipitation is 10 inches and snowfall is 59.5 inches.

CULTURE AND HISTORY
The Schitsu'umsh, "Those who are found here," originated in the regions of present-day northwestern United States. The tribe is comprised of three family bands. The first band is made up of those families living along and near the Coeur d'Alene River; the second band is made up of those living along the St. Joe River; and the third band is made up those families living near Hayden Lake, Coeur d'Alene Lake, and Spokane River. Their ancestral lands encompassed nearly 5,000,000 acres in what are now Idaho, Washington, and Montana. The tribe traditionally hunted buffalo on the Montana plains, fished for salmon at Spokane Falls, and dug for cams and other wild root crops near Kalispel and present-day Palouse. Tribal members utilized the ancient trade routes between their homelands and those of other indigenous groups, including the Nez Perce, Shoshone, and Bannock. Members of the Schitsu'umsh tribe traveled as far west as the Pacific coast. The Schitsu'umsh became known as the Coeur d'Alene, "Heart of the Awl," following their encounter with French trappers.

The Coeur d'Alene band populations were decimated by the arrival of smallpox, measles, and other European diseases that came with Euro-American encroachment on tribal lands. Records indicate that in the late eighteenth century there were as many as 5,000 members of the Coeur d'Alene bands. In 1905, less than 200 years later, the population was recorded at only 490.

An Executive Order establishing the reservation was issued in 1873. In 1887 the tribe ceded nearly 3,500,000 acres in Washington, Idaho, and Montana to the U.S. government. Several thousand more acres were ceded in 1889 and 1894. Tribal lands were reduced from almost 4,000,000 acres to 345,000 acres.

Under the Homestead Act of 1909, over 80 percent of the reservation passed out of tribal ownership. Specifically, the tribe lost ownership of most of its land along Lake Coeur d'Alene through allotment and the opening of the reservation to non-Native settlers beginning that year. Moreover, the effects of the Homestead Act were gradual social, cultural, and economic degradation. The loss of a land base jeopardized tribal identity through forced acculturation, which in turn opened the door to many social problems. In response to this tragic downward spiral, the tribe filed a claim with the Indian Claims Commission on November 15, 1950, for compensation for the illegal confiscation of their traditional homelands. On May 6, 1958, the Commission awarded the tribe $4,342,778 on behalf of this claim. The tribe has subsequently pursued other claims and litigation, generally successfully. The proceeds from these awards have been applied toward economic development projects such as a gaming facility, which in turn have generated more profits, ultimately to be applied toward the general welfare of tribal members.

GOVERNMENT
The tribe's governing body is the Coeur d'Alene Tribal Council. The council has been empowered to act on behalf of the tribe under the terms of the revised constitution and bylaws, adopted on November 10, 1984, and approved by the secretary of the interior on December 21 of that year. The tribal council consists of seven members, each elected to three-year terms. Its officers include a chairman, a vice chairman, and a secretary-treasurer. The general council consists of all tribal members who are of voting age.

Tribal government is comprised of 18 departments. They include the gaming board, the housing advisory board, the health advisory board, the development advisory board, the law and order advisory board and the tribal school advisory board, each with their respective directors. There are also

Coeur d'Alene Reservation
Federal reservation
Benewah and Kootenai counties, Idaho

Coeur d'Alene Tribal Council
850 A Street.
P.O. Box 408
Plummer, ID 83851
  208-686-1800
  208-686-1182 Fax
  cdatribe-nsn.gov

Total area *(BIA realty, 2004)*
74,693 acres

Total area *(Tribal source, 2004)*
344,900 acres

Trust lands *(Tribal source, 2004)*
36,370 acres

Tribally owned *(BIA realty, 2004)*
30,559 acres

Tribally owned *(Tribal source, 2004)*
14,310 acres

Allotted lands *(Tribal source, 2004)*
22,060 acres

Individually owned
(BIA realty, 2004)
44,134 acres

Population *2000 census*
6,551

Tribal enrollment
(Tribal source, 2004)
1,907

Coeur d'Alene

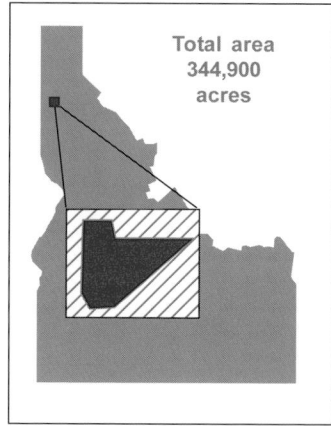

Total area
344,900
acres

Total labor force *2000 census*
3,032

Total labor force
(BIA labor report, 2001)
560

High school graduate or higher
2000 census
84.3%

Bachelor's degree or higher
2000 census
15.8%

Unemployment rate *2000 census*
12.7%

Unemployment rate
(BIA labor report, 2001)
67%

Per capita income *2000 census*
$16,421

the finance department, the grants office, the facilities department, human resources, social services, natural resources, and education. housing, planning, Benewah Medical Center, and law and order are also major programs in the tribal government.

The tribe maintains its own police force and court system. Jurisdiction over the reservation is concurrent with state and local law enforcement agencies. There is currently only once police station on the reservation, but plans to develop facilities in the lower third of Lake Coeur d'Alene are in progress.

BUSINESS CORPORATION
The tribe's federally chartered development corporation works in conjunction with the tribal council's planning department to initiate development projects for the tribe. The development corporation is responsible for daily bookkeeping duties, for conducting research into the feasibility of proposed economic development and business projects, and for conducting evaluations of current revenue-producing projects.

ECONOMY
The economy of the reservation is largely sustained by the tribe's enterprises in the logging and agriculture industries. The tribe's enterprises in the gaming industry are proving to be successful and generate a substantial amount of revenue, which the tribe uses in large part to fund the enhancement of the tribal services. The Coeur d'Alene tribal government is also a major force in the tribe's economic stability. It employs at least 1,000 people throughout the tribe's businesses and governmental departments.

Government as Employer. The tribe employs approximately 1,000 individuals throughout the tribal government and business enterprises.

Economic Development Projects. The Coeur d'AleneTribe's planning department is an essential part of the tribe's economic development. The planning department carries out long-range planning, comprehensive planning, site planning, coordination with all departments, land use codes development, and grant writing. With the oversight of the planning department, the tribe is in the process of developing numerous economic projects. They include the improvement of roadways that will enhance tourism and recreation in the region, the development of an industrial park, the development of a ferry system and an airport, and the development of educational tourist attractions to the region.

The tribe's most recent project was the Trail of the Coeur d'Alenes, approximately 15 miles of rail bed, converted to a multi-use trail within reservation boundaries. Construction began in spring 2001, and it was completed in summer 2003. A trailhead at Plummer marks the historical trail as the Trail of the Coeur d'Alenes, and it includes a tunnel under U.S. 95 that connects the trail to the tribal celebration grounds.

A 2004 comprehensive plan outlines the tribe's commitment to protecting the environment, managing and regulating natural resources, providing for the health, education and welfare of all tribal members, protecting religious freedoms, and making and enforcing laws. The comprehensive plan is designed to provide an official statement of growth and to serve as a guide to decisions about overall development.

Agriculture and Livestock. Agriculture provides 10 percent of the employment opportunities for tribal members, employing approximately 266 people. Tribal agricultural enterprises include a 6,000-acre farm. It produces wheat, barley, peas, lentils, and canola. Thirty thousand acres of tribal land produce

Kentucky bluegrass. Approximately 150,000 acres of tribal lands are occupied by privately owned farms.

Forestry. The reservation lies partially within national forest land in a region where the timber industry has been traditionally prominent. A limited amount of timber harvesting continues on tribal lands. Though a considerable number of tribal members find employment through this industry, many tribal members work through non-Indian timbering enterprises. Pacific Crown Timber Products is the largest private employer of tribal members within this domain. Over 180,000 acres of the reservation are forested. The tribe does not authorize clear cuts on tribal lands. All logging is done with selective cutting.

Gaming.. The Coeur d'Alene Casino Resort Hotel is located in Worley, Idaho. It offers over 1,400 slot machines, bingo, MegaBingo, off-track dog and horse betting, and video pull-tabs. There is also a non-smoking game area. The facilities include the adjacent resort, four restaurants, and an entertainment venue. The resort offers 202 guest rooms, a conference center, a video arcade, and daycare accommodations upon request. The resort offers transport to the Spokane airport for guests as well as daily shuttles to Spokane, Coeur d'Alene, and Post Falls.

The casino also sponsors a cruise boat on Lake Chatcolet. Cruise tours include brunch, lunch, dinner, special events, and special themed and private tours. There are facilities on the beaches of Lake Chatcolet for guests to enjoy recreational activities, seaplane tours, fishing, performances, and boating. The casino provides direct access to the Trail of the Coeur d'Alene, a scenic 73-mile paved trail that courses along the rivers and lakes of the Silver Valley in Idaho.

The Circling Raven Golf Club is located adjacent to the Casino Resort. It offers a par-72 championship golf course. The club is located in the forest meadows and wetlands of the tribe's recreation area. The club offers a School of Golf with classes, a Junior Golf Clinic, and one-day golf clinics with renowned golf instructors. The golf course opened in August 2003, and within four months it was honored as one of *Golf Magazine's* top 10 best new public courses is America. In 2004, it was honored by Audubon International by inclusion in the International Cooperative Sanctuary System.

The casino hosts numerous entertainment acts and events, including the PRCA Coeur d'Alene Casino Championship Rodeo Series and the July Coeur d'Alene Tribe Encampment and Powwow. The casino has been voted "#1 Casino in the Pacific Northwest" by the *Spokesman Reader Review* four years in a row.

Fisheries. The region surrounding the reservation is rich in streams, rivers, and lakes, most of which have excellent recreational fishing. Tribal members continue to fish on and beyond reservation boundaries. Coeur d'Alene Lake is a popular fishing spot, one that the tribe is seeking to regulate and enhance through its lake management policy.

Construction. In 1999, the Coeur d'Alene Tribal Housing Authority (THA) oversaw the construction of 221 homes on the reservation. An estimated 163 more will be needed by 2008. The primary aim of the THA is to administer the development of affordable housing for all tribal members.

The goal of the THA is to enhance the lives of all tribal members by anticipating and providing affordable housing opportunities to individuals in all walks of life. The THA administered 221 homes in 1999, and by 2008 an additional 163 homes will be required on the reservation.

Coeur d'Alene

TRI-ID-001

TRI-ID-002

TRI-ID-005

TRI-ID-003

TRI-ID-004

Manufacturing. The manufacturing industry is the second-largest source of employment among tribal members. As of 2004, manufacturing represented employment for 10 percent of the tribe's workforce, employing 268 tribal members. Except for the reservation-based cottage industry of traditional artisans, virtually all of these people work for enterprises located off the reservation.

Industrial Park. The tribe has proposed construction of the Coeur d'Alene ECO-Industrial Park on 24 acres south of Plummer. Development will include upgrading of the existing Union Pacific Railroad road, and construction of sidewalks, parking lots, walkways, and transit parking and boarding sites. Highway 95 and Agency Road will receive upgrades, and a bridge will be constructed at the existing culverts. Facilities will be constructed in three phases. Phase one will include construction of a business incubator building, a retail and light manufacturing building, and six cottage industry/residence units. Phase two includes two office buildings, and a manufacturing/warehouse building. Phase three will complete the complex with four additional office buildings, and a manufacturing /warehouse building.

Real Estate/Commercial Development. The tribe is in the process of constructing housing units at various sites across the reservation. The plans call for the construction of 17 units and include improvements to local roadways.

Services and Retail. The reservation hosts several businesses, including the Benewah Market, which employs about 20 people.

The Benewah Auto Center began by renovating an existing Exxon Station into a full-service automotive center. The auto center has expanded further into a convenience store and employs four people.

Media and Communications. The tribe publishes the *Coeur d'Alene/Schitsu'umsh Council Fires*, a monthly newspaper.

Tourism and Recreation. The Shadowy St. Joe Stream courses through the reservation to Lake Coeur d'Alene. It is considered one of North America's premier trout streams. It is the highest navigable stream in the world and serves as a waterway for tugboats working the Spokane River.

Upon completion of the Plummer-Mullan Rail Trail, the tribe plans to build an interpretive center and museum at the trailhead in the 45-acre area known as the Celebration Grounds. Other projects planned for the location are a longhouse, a war dance arena, an RV park, elderly housing, a vendors' building, a permanent sweat lodge, and recreational ball fields. The Celebration Grounds are ceremonial grounds used for tribal ceremonies and celebrations.

The historical Cataldo Mission is the oldest standing building in the state of Idaho. It was built in the mid-1840s to serve the Coeur d'Alene tribal people. In the 1870s, the mission was moved from the church site to a building in DeSmet when tensions between the tribe and Euro-American settlers began to rise. The historic Catholic mission and the adjacent Sisters' Building, built in 1880, serve as important cultural and religious gathering places.

Outdoor enthusiasts enjoy the reservation's abundant fishing, boating, and water sport activities. In the more remote regions to the east, hunters pursue big game such as bear, elk, and deer, as well as waterfowl. Golf, hiking, mountain climbing, and winter skiing are all quite popular. There are several camping areas on and adjacent to tribal lands.

INFRASTRUCTURE
U.S. Highway 95 is the main north-south road through the reservation, connecting with Interstate 90 to the north. Over 400 miles of county, local highway, and BIA roads traverse the reservation. The various governmental entities are responsible for maintaining the roadways. The tribe actively monitors and evaluates existing roads and determines the needs for additional roadways.

TRI-ID-001 Headquarters Sign at Coeur D'Alene Tribal Building

TRI-ID-002 Main entrance of Tribal Building complex

TRI-ID-005 Coeur D'Alene Casino Hotel US Highway 95 Worley, Idaho

TRI-ID-003 Tepees & Stagecoach Display in front of Trading Post off of Highway 95

TRI-ID-004 Back of Coeur D'Alene Tribal Wellness Center

Coeur d'Alene

Duck Valley

See Nevada

Electricity. Washington Power Company provides electricity.

Water Supply. Solid waste is collected by private contractors and transported to county landfills. The tribe is currently expanding landfill capacity on the reservation.

Transportation. The tribe's Transportation Plan 2003 addresses the motorized and non-motorized transportation issues of the tribe now and over the next 20 years. The tribe has identified the need for a public transit system on the reservation, a transit system for disabled tribal members, ferry transportation, and an airport.

The tribe is developing a ferry project that would provide east/west access to the eastern half of the reservation and Lake Coeur d'Alene. It is also developing plans for an airport near the Coeur d'Alene Casino and Resort. Furthermore, the tribe is in the process of developing the North U.S. 95 Casino Resort Corridor in collaboration with the cities of Worley and Coeur d'Alene, Kootenai County, and local businesses and residents. The corridor extends over five miles from Worley into the reservation

The nearest commercial airline service is in Spokane, 40 miles west. Commercial train and bus lines serve the city of Coeur d'Alene, about 25 miles from the reservation. Commercial truck lines serve the reservation directly. The tribe provides bus services for the tribal school.

COMMUNITY FACILITIES AND SERVICES

A wellness center provides community members with programs concerning wellness, recreation, fitness, pregnancy, child rearing, infant care, and general nutrition. The Youth Crisis Center is an emergency shelter available for tribal youth experiencing violent or potentially violent relationships in the home. There are also public libraries in Worley, DeSmet, and Plummer. The tribe operates a community center in DeSmet. The tribe sponsors an annual lottery for hunting moose on the reservation and in the ceded areas. The lottery is open to tribal members 14 years and older.

Public Safety. The reservation is serviced by volunteer fire departments from Worley, Plummer, Sorento, or Tensed.

Education. The tribal school system includes a Head Start program, a K-8 tribal school located in DeSmet, the Circling Raven Vo-Tech Program for adults, and a bachelor's degree program offered through Circling Raven and Lewis and Clark College.Tribal youth may attend the tribal school, public elementary and secondary schools, or a Christian academy located on the reservation. A new tribal school is currently under construction. The tribe offers instructional classes in the Schitsu'umsh language.

Health Care. The tribe operates the Benewah Medical Center in Plummer, Idaho. The center offers outpatient services, an in-house pharmacy, a laboratory, X-ray facilities, dental services, mental health programs, and community health outreach services for Native and non-Native community members. Programs of the center include various fitness and exercise classes, sports teams, alcohol recovery programs, and swimming classes. The center has been nationally awarded and recognized as a national model for Indian health care and rural health care. A contract health service provides ambulatory health care and hospital services. Additional medical facilities are available in Spokane, Washington, and Coeur d'Alene, Idaho.

ENVIRONMENTAL CONCERNS

The Coeur d'Alene Basin Restoration Project springs from the largest natural resource damage lawsuit in American history.

Over a 100-year period, the mining industry in Idaho's Silver Valley dumped 72 million tons of mine waste into the Coeur d'Alene watershed. As mining and smelting operations grew, they produced billions of dollars in silver, lead, and zinc. In the process, natural life in the Coeur d'Alene River was wiped out.

Today, the Silver Valley is the nation's second-largest Superfund site. The natural resource damages, however, extend upstream and far downstream from the 21-square mile "box" that is now under Superfund. The Superfund cleanup is expected to cost $200 million. The tribe's natural resource damage assessment for the river, its tributaries, the lateral lakes, and Lake Coeur d'Alene totals over $1 billion. The tribe, working with the U.S. Forest Service, the U.S. Fish and Wildlife Department, the Bureau of Land Management, and the U.S. Geological Survey, has taken the leading role in cleanup efforts and the leading role toward responsible stewardship of the basin.

The tribe took its case to court not only with a plea for environmental stewardship, but also with detailed and peer-reviewed science. The issue has become the Interior Department's number one priority for cleanup. The Justice Department followed the tribe's lead, and the United States government filed suit against the mines and Union Pacific Railroad in the spring of 1996, echoing almost verbatim the tribe's 1991 lawsuit. Union Pacific has since settled.

As the tribe works to create a basin cleanup, it also works to resolve ownership of Lake Coeur d'Alene. A lawsuit filed in October 1991 against the State of Idaho would enable the tribe to take the state into court and eventually prevent the state from interfering with tribal jurisdiction over Lake Coeur d'Alene, which is the heart of the tribe's homeland and reservation. The tribe's quest to resolve ownership was decided by the U.S. Supreme Court in 2001. The U.S. Supreme Court recognized that the tribe has always been the owner of the lower one-third of Lake Coeur d'Alene and other related waters.

Natural Resources. The tribe's natural resources department serves to enhance the quality of life for tribal members, to foster the development of social and economic benefits for the tribe, to protect and preserve natural resources on tribal lands, and to restore natural resources within the historical and traditional lands of the tribe. The department manages the forest management plan and lake management plan and is in the process of developing an environmental action plan. it is also creating a plan for the implementation of the tribe's comprehensive environmental statute.

The tribe is also a member of the Panhandle Lakes Resource Conservation and Development (RC&D)Area. A USDA project, the RC&D program facilitates community involvement in resolving environmental and economic problems. To date, over 300 projects have been completed in the area, with the emphasis shifting from traditional conservation practices to extensive involvement in rural economic development.

In addition, the tribal council enacted an Interim Land Use Ordinance in 1988 that enables the tribe to review and regulate development and land uses that threaten or result in significant social, environmental, or economic impact on the Coeur d'Alene Reservation.

The establishment of water quality standards protects the tribe's rights to water sources located on or bounded by the reservation.

Honoring Nations Honoree 1999

Coeur d'Alene Tribal Wellness Center, Coeur d'Alene Tribe (Plummer, Idaho)

Created in 1998, the Coeur d'Alene Wellness Center promotes healthy lifestyles by offering programs in fitness, aquatics, physical rehabilitation, childcare and community health to over 2,500 Indian and non-Indian clients. Utilizing a whole-life approach to health and focusing on preventative care, the Center complements acute and chronic illness care provided by the Benewah Medical Center, which was created in 1990 through a joint venture between the Tribe and the City of Plummer, Idaho. Together with the Medical Center, the multipurpose Wellness Center is the culmination of the Tribe's goal to provide reservation residents with affordable health care.

Until the 1990s, the Coeur d'Alene Tribe's health care services were clearly inadequate. The Tribe was served only by a small Indian Health Service (IHS) satellite clinic, which was located in a semi-condemned building. Additional barriers to quality health care included the long distance tribal members had to travel to access more comprehensive services and higher quality facilities, poor continuity of care, and the IHS's poor financial management, which resulted in tribal members' bills being turned over to collection agencies. Further, none of the ambulatory care facilities in the four surrounding counties provided services on a sliding fee schedule, which would allow for low-income users to pay lower medical fees.

In 1987, the Tribe began searching for ways to improve health care services offered on-reservation to its more than 6,000 resident members. The Tribe's efforts led to an innovative joint venture with the City of Plummer, in which the Tribe and the City together developed a rural outpatient health care delivery system for both Indians and non-Indians. Not only were the partners able to collectively secure construction funds from the state and federal governments for a new medical facility - the Benewah Medical Center (BMC), which opened in 1990 - but they also gained federal classification as a "Medically Underserved Population Area," a designation that increases BMC's operating revenues through additional cost reimbursement. These revenue gains have enabled BMC to bill its non-Native clients on a sliding fee scale, an important service given that approximately one-third of the eligible non-Native users in Benewah County qualify for reduced fees. Because of strong demand, BMC's 6,750 square foot building was expanded to 17,000 square feet in 1994, and medical exam rooms, a dental wing, pharmacy services and community health programs were added.

With its improved health care system in place, the Tribe began to think about how it could move the BMC toward a prevention and wellness focus. Of particular concern was the fact that community members had no access to a recreation or fitness facility. Therefore, the Tribe and the City of Plummer expanded the scope of their joint venture and opened the Tribal Wellness Center in July 1998. The 43,000 square foot, $5 million Wellness Center was built debt-free, using funding from a variety of sources, including federal, state, and private funds and BMC equity (tribal gaming revenue was not used). Today, the Wellness Center serves 2,500 users and provides a host of programs designed to improve mental, spiritual, emotional and physical health.

The Wellness Center's success is evident on several fronts. First, the Center addresses an important need in the community by enabling the BMC to complement its acute and chronic care services with preventative, wellness-based services. Programs and services are offered in aquatics, childcare, fitness, nutrition, physical therapy, cardiac rehabilitation, and community health. To promote these activities, the Wellness Center publishes a quarterly newsletter that informs the community about its programs and provides fitness and health tips. To improve the continuity of care between the Medical Center and the Wellness Center, staff members at the two organizations are encouraged to cross-train and to communicate regularly with each other. This way, care providers at the BMC can work cooperatively with experts at the Wellness Center on the best ways to meet specific patient needs. Given disproportionately higher incidence of chronic illness and preventable hospitalizations in the American Indian population (for example, American Indians' diabetes mortality rates are three times higher than the rates for whites), the various activities and initiatives offered through the Wellness Center have considerable potential to improve many individuals' lives.

Second, the Wellness Center's operations are impressive. Its Olympic-size recreational pool, therapy pool, gym, track and classrooms are state-of-the-art. The equipment is well maintained, and the Center's members and 30-member staff take great pride in keeping the facility as clean and functional as possible. In addition, the staff of both the BMC and Wellness Center has been proactive in making quality improvements: a full-time quality improvement director oversees safety, accreditation standards and other quality related matters. In fact, the BMC's and Wellness Center's leadeship chose to conform to rigorous accreditation standards as a means of maintaining superior service. This choice underscores the Tribe's commitment not just to having a wellness center, but to having one with high operational standards.

Moreover, the Wellness Center is well governed. A nine-member Health Board (comprised of two Tribal Council members, two tribal members, two non-Indian community members and three clinicians) oversees both the BMC and Wellness Center. The Board operates under its own by-laws and is autonomous from tribal politics - distance that has allowed its members to make important decisions about hiring, budgeting, and facility priorities in response to user needs, not political pressures. Interestingly, the Tribal Council is looking at the BMC/Wellness Center's board as a model for some of its other tribal departments. Such attention is well deserved.

In terms of the Wellness Center's operational funding, the Tribe has chosen to rely primarily on third party reimbursements rather than gaming revenues. While this choice may only be possible in service areas that possess a sufficient number of users with private insurance, it should be encouraging to non-gaming tribes to know that such impressive facilities can be established without significant infusions of casino revenues and without compromising quality. Further, this choice is a source of pride for the Wellness Center's management, and it is committed to ensuring the financial stability of the Center in this funding environment. The Wellness Center's response to the tribal government's request that it continue to offer childcare (because no other childcare services exist on the reservation) is an inspirational example of the management's commitment. They found a way to maintain the Wellness Center's childcare services, despite the fact that this service is expensive to sustain.

Honoring Nations
Honoree 1999

Text in its entirety from:
The Harvard Project On
American Indian Economic
Development

John F. Kennedy School
of Government
Harvard University

Health care service in the United States is steadily shifting toward a more preventative focus, and the Coeur d'Alene Wellness Center's focus on preventive health care and positive lifestyle behaviors is consistent with these trends. It is a critical shift in Native health care because of the importance of chronic disease management in American Indian communities. Clearly, the Coeur d'Alene Tribe realized the importance of building a healthy, fit community and of offering services that have long been available to non-Indians, and in so doing, it has begun to build a healthier society. Yet the tribal government deserves recognition not only for the size, quality and comprehensiveness of the facility it created, but also for its commitment to finding innovative solutions to potential organizational and funding barriers. Both the idea and its implementation warrant replication throughout Indian Country.

Lessons:
· Indian nations can complement acute and primary health care services with broader approaches that seek to promote healthy lifestyles. Such approaches are especially important given that American Indians suffer disproportionately from chronic diseases that can be ameliorate by behavioral change.
· Tribal medical and wellness centers should focus on quality of care. One way to ensure high quality services is to empower a board to make decisions based explicitly on user needs; another is to institutionalize quality control mechanisms.
· Wellness centers can operate without significant infusions of tribal revenue when a sufficient proportion of their clients possess private insurance. If neighboring communities have similar health care needs, tribes may consider joint ventures as an attractive option.

Fort Hall

Fort Hall Reservation
Federal reservation
Shoshone-Bannock Tribes
of the Fort Hall Indian
Reservation
Bannock, Bingham, Caribou,
and Power counties, Idaho

Shoshone-Bannock Tribes
of the Fort Hall Indian
Reservation
P.O. Box 306
Pima Drive
Fort Hall, ID 83203
888-297-1378
208-237-0797 Fax

Total area *(BIA realty, 2004)*
522,671.07 acres

Total area *(EPA)*
547,570 acres

Tribally owned
(BIA realty, 2004)
271,775.42 acres

Individually owned
(BIA realty, 2004)
218,263.77 acres

Federal trust
(BIA realty, 2004)
32,632.88 acres

Population *2000 census*
5,762

Tribal enrollment
(Tribal source, 2004)
4,673

LOCATION AND LAND STATUS
The Fort Hall Reservation is located in the eastern Snake River Plain of southeastern Idaho. It is comprised of two separate segments that lie north and west of the town of Pocatello. The Snake River, Blackfoot River, and the American Falls Reservoir border the reservation on the north and northwest.

The reservation was established by an Executive Order under the terms of the Fort Bridger Treaty of 1868. It originally contained 1.8 million acres, an amount that was reduced to 1.2 million acres in 1872 as a result of a survey error. The reservation was further reduced to its present size through subsequent legislation and the allotment process.

PHYSICAL DESCRIPTION
Topography ranges from relatively lush river valleys to rugged foothills and mountains. Elevations vary from 4,400 feet at the American Falls Reservoir to nearly 9,000 feet in the southern mountain areas.

CLIMATE
The nearby town of Pocatello experiences summer temperatures ranging between 68°F and 88°F. The winter temperature often drops into the low teens. Average rainfall is 11.5 inches per year. The snowy season lasts from September through May with an average of 43.3 inches annually.

CULTURE AND HISTORY
The Shoshone-Bannock Tribes of Fort Hall comprise members of the eastern and western bands of the Northern Shoshone and the Bannock, or Northern Paiute, bands. Ancestral lands of both tribes occupied vast regions of land encompassing present-day Idaho, Oregon, Nevada, Utah, Wyoming, Montana, and into Canada. The tribes are culturally related and, though both descend from the Numic family of the Uto-Aztecan linguistic phylum, their languages are dialectically separate. When the Northern Paiutes left the Nevada and Utah regions for southern Idaho in the 1600s, they began to travel with the Shoshones in pursuit of buffalo. They became known as the Bannocks then.

The tribes generally subsisted as hunters and gatherers, traveling during the spring and summer seasons, collecting foods for use during the winter months. They hunted wild game, fished the region's abundant and bountiful streams and rivers (primarily for salmon), and collected native plants and roots.

Buffalo served as the most significant source of food and raw material for the tribes. After the introduction of horses during the 1700s, hundreds of Idaho Indians of various tribal affiliations would ride into Montana on cooperative buffalo hunts. The last great hunt of this type occurred in 1864, signaling the end of a traditional way of life.

Fort Hall was established in 1834 as a trading post. It became a way station for settlers traveling along the Oregon and California trails that cut through tribal lands. Relations between the tribes and the Euro-American settlers were strained at best. In 1863 more than 200 Shoshones were massacred along the Bear River. The attack was led by volunteer soldiers from California, and it was one of the first and largest massacres of Native peoples west of the Mississippi River. In 1864 the government attempted to confine the tribes to a reservation with the Treaty of Soda Springs, but it failed to gain ratification. The Fort Hall Reservation was established for the tribes by an Executive Order in 1867. The 1868 Treaty of Fort Bridger confirmed the agreement. This treaty established both the Fort Hall Reservation in Idaho and the Wind River Reservation in Wyoming. The treaty stipulated the establishment of a separate reservation for the Bannock band, but the promises were breached and the band remained at Fort Hall with the Shoshones.

Although the tribes were initially permitted to leave reservation lands for summer hunting and gathering practices, settlers rallied against it, and the Bannock Wars of 1878 ensued. Tribal members participating in the conflict were returned to Fort Hall. The population of the reservation increased when other Northern Shoshone bands were forcibly moved to Fort Hall.

In 1888 the tribes were forced to cede over 1,800 acres of their 1.2 million-acre reservation to accommodate the development of the town of Pocatello located nearby. Around the turn of the century, Pocatello had grown so dramatically that the tribes were forced to agree to the cession of an additional 420,000 acres. For this they received approximately $600,000. The bulk of the lands were made available to the public through a land rush, a competition of sorts where individuals and families staked claim on designated lands during a race. On June 17, 1902, 6,000 settlers took part in the "Day of the Run" land rush of the Shoshone-Bannock lands.

The 1887 Dawes Severalty Act initiated the allotment of the reservation. This process was completed by 1914, with over 347,000 acres having been distributed among 1,863 individual allotments between 1911 and 1913 alone. By the time allotment of the tribal lands was terminated, nearly 36,000 acres had been alienated from Native ownership through sales, patents in fee, or certificates of competency. Surplus lands were ceded to Pocatello or sold to non-Natives, thus creating the checkerboard pattern of land ownership that now exists within the reservation boundaries.

In 1907, the Lehmi Reservation for the Lehmi Band of Shoshones was terminated. Remaining families were relocated to Fort Hall. In 1936, the tribes approved a constitution and bylaws for self-government under the provisions of the Indian Reorganization Act of 1934. The tribes ratified a corporate charter in 1937. As of 1992, 96 percent of the Fort Hall Reservation was once again under Indian control, either through federal trust or ownership by individual tribal members.

In 2002, the tribe hosted the Native American 2002 Foundation, a division of the Advisory Committee for Arts and Cultures of the Salt Lake Organization Committee for the 2002 Winter Olympics. The foundation was comprised of representatives of Native nations throughout the country serving to advise the committee on historical, political, and cultural matters pertaining to the depiction of the indigenous people of the United States.

In November 2002, the tribe hosted the Tribal Sovereignty Summit. Co-hosts were the Shoshone Paiute tribes and the United Vision for Idaho. The summit served to educate attendants on the historical and contemporary status of the Native nations of Idaho.

GOVERNMENT

The tribes are organized under the 1934 Indian Reorganization Act, and they operate under a constitution approved on April 30, 1936. The charter was ratified the following year.

The tribe is governed by the Fort Hall Business Council. The council includes seven members elected by the general membership to two-year terms. It maintains authority over all normal business procedures, including the development of lands and resources, and all matters of self-government.

The tribes operate numerous governmental departments and programs. They include the administration, credit energy, education, employment and training, election board, emergency management and response, enrollment, finance, property management, fire, fish and wildlife, Head Start and early childhood, land alliance, land use, transportation, tribal construction, health human services, T.E.R.O., tribal planning, utilities, and water resources departments, among others.

the tribes maintain their own judicial system with a law and order commission providing oversight, a tribal courts system, an attorney's office, and a police department. The federal government maintains authority over crimes that fall under the Major Crimes Act. The tribes may share jurisdiction over such matters. The State of Idaho exercises jurisdiction, under PL-280, over civil and criminal matters on the reservation such as truancy, juvenile delinquency, child welfare, matters of mental illness, public assistance, domestic relations, and matters involving motor vehicles. The tribes maintain jurisdiction over issues of personal property, water rights, ownership of property, treaty rights, and tribal land rights. The tribes are in the process of developing a tribal justice center to house all branches of the judicial system.

ECONOMY

The tribal economy is supported in large part from revenue earned from leasing agricultural lands and from gaming. Right-of-way agreements also contribute to the general fund. A large portion of monies is earned through taxes imposed upon utilities conducting business on tribal lands.

Government as Employer. Through various governmental programs and tribal enterprises, the Shoshone-Bannock tribes employ over 1,100 tribal members and 153 non-Native individuals. The beadwork industry is the largest employer, with 400 tribal members working in that industry. The tribal government and gaming enterprises offer the next highest number of employment opportunities.

Economic Development Projects. The Tribal Enterprise Board, a separate corporation from the tribal council, serves as the conduit for tribal commercial development. It coordinates all tribal projects including federally funded programs.

The reorganization of the Shoshone-Bannock Tribes' Economic Development Department resulted in the creation of the tribal planning department. A director was selected in 2001 and the existing staff was trained in the elements of planning. The primary goal of the planning department is to develop revisions to the tribe's comprehensive plan, which was first adopted in 1976. Other goals include providing technical support to tribal government departments, promoting economic development, and providing services to tribal members.

The tribes recently signed an agreement with Power County to work in cooperation toward economic development projects that will affect the tribes and the county. They hope to reach a similar agreement with Bingham County.

Additional projects being explored by the tribe include an RV park and the development of college credit courses in planning and management. The tribe also hopes to secure an agreement with the City of Pocatello and Power County to establish a foreign trade zone and an airfreight terminal at the Pocatello Airport.

Agriculture and Livestock. Shoshone-Bannock Buffalo Enterprises manages a herd of over 250 head of buffalo. The herd grazes on the bluffs of the Fort Hall Bottoms and Cedar areas. Buffalo meat is sold at tribal stores and restaurants and donated to tribal functions. Buffalo robes are also sold, as are live buffalos. The tribes also authorize buffalo hunts for a fee. The Buffalo Enterprise Committee advises the tribe on management and marketing practices.

The reservation lies in the heart of Idaho's prime agriculture land; principal crops grown in the area are potatoes, small grain, and alfalfa. While the major portion of the tribe's nearly 100,000 acres of irrigated land is leased to outside farming interests, the tribe continues to operate about 2,000 acres on its own. The tribe currently receives about $150 per acre of irrigated farmland that it leases and somewhat less for grazing land. In total, agriculture comprises one of the most significant sources of revenue on the reservation.

Forestry. The reservation contains relatively little in the way of forest, none of which is considered commercially viable.

Gaming. Shoshone-Bannock Gaming is located in Fort Hall at exit 80 on interstate Highway 15. It features 570 slots/VLTs, and high-stakes bingo, and it can hold up to 1,000 people. The building itself was constructed in 1992 as a multipurpose facility and thus serves as a venue for other community activities as well. The Bannock Peak Casino located on Interstate Highway 86 features 80 slot machines and one restaurant.

Fort Hall

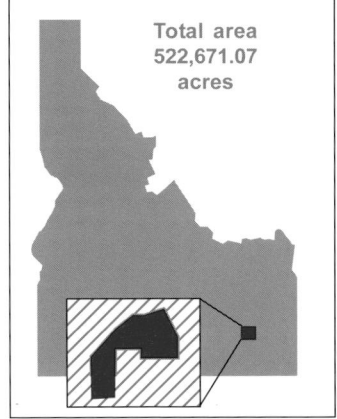

Total area
522,671.07
acres

Total labor force *2000 census*
2,363

High school graduate or higher
2000 census
73.3%

Bachelor's degree or higher
2000 census
6.3%

Unemployment rate *2000 census*
16.1%

Per capita income *2000 census*
$11,309

Fort Hall

Construction. The tribes own and operate a construction company that primarily employs tribal members. The company, founded during the 1970s and reactivated in 1992, does roadwork and builds commercial structures on the reservation.

Manufacturing. FMC/Astaris, a private, non-tribally owned company manufacturing phosphate-based products, was located on the reservation. The company closed its plant in 2001. Its plant site is now known as the Michaud Superfund Site. The tribes are taking a lead role in redeveloping this site.

Mining. The tribes possess right-of-way agreements with Northwest Pipeline, Williams Gas, and Idaho Power. These agreements generate income for the tribes. A non-Indian-owned phosphate mine that had been operating on the reservation since 1947 closed in 1993 due to diminishing recoverable reserves. This had been a source of significant employment for the tribe, and its closing has had a fairly severe impact.

Services and Retail. The tribes own a store, Indian Goods: The Corner Mercantile, located within the historic Fort Hall Trading Post. The store offers seed beads, cut beads, and traditionally tanned buckskin. It also sells handmade crafts, items for regalia, paintings, antique photographs, postcards, and music.

The Trading Post Grocery is located on the reservation and provides full supermarket services. It also contains a butcher shop that occasionally features buffalo meat from the tribe's herd. The grocery offers the largest, and lowest priced, tobacco products selection in the state of Idaho.

The Oregon Trail Restaurant serves buffalo stew, Indian tacos, and Indian fry bread in addition to traditional Euro-American foods.

The Trading Post Clothes Horse is a retail outlet and distribution center for craft work produced by the tribe. Clients can purchase hand-crafted and beaded moccasins, purses, bolo ties, belt buckles, hatbands, and jewelry as well as leather goods, porcupine quill work, and contemporary Native artwork. The store also sells books, jeans, shirts, and Pendleton brand clothing.

The Travel Plaza Fuel and Convenience store offers a full-service station that caters to travelers. Facilities include a lounge, shower facilities, office facilities, a restaurant, and grocery selection. It is located in the tribal enterprises complex off exit 80 on Interstate 15.

The Bannock Peak Fuel and Convenience store offers a full-service station as well as a deli and convenience store. It is located on Interstate 86.

The tribes maintain a number of businesses on the reservation. Among these are a small cabinet shop, an electrical contracting firm, a credit union, and a gas station and convenience store.

Media and Communications The tribes publish the *Sho-Ban News*, a weekly newspaper distributed nationwide and in several countries.

Tourism and Recreation. The tribes own the Shoshone-Bannock Tribal Museum, located on the reservation. The museum was initially opened in 1985 but closed for a number of years. It reopened in 1993 with the assistance of volunteers. The museum houses photos and artifacts donated by community members. The gift shop offers hand-made beaded items and buckskin crafts as well as books, posters, T-shirts, caps, and calendars. The museum sponsors daily tours of the Oregon Trail Crossroads.

The tribes host the Shoshone-Bannock Indian Festival in early August. Activities include art shows, a youth powwow, rodeo events, children's games, royalty competitions, traditional hand games, an NIAA softball tourney, a competitive powwow, and a parade. The Sho-Ban Golf Classic is held during the festival, as is the RMRIRA Rodeo. The tribes also host the Fort Bridger Treaty Day on July 3 to recognize the signing of the Fort Bridger Treaty.

Fort Hall Bottoms is a premier fishing ground that is located on the reservation. In addition to vast populations of fish, there are moose, elk, deer, wild horses, and buffalo in the area. The ecosystem at the Bottoms was in grave danger due to loss of vegetation, erosion of stream banks, warmer water temperature, and siltation in spawning gravels brought on by unrestricted grazing and rapid flooding. Restoration efforts have successfully revitalized the natural resources in this area. Fishing is permitted at the Bottoms with limited permits and adherence to strict regulations set forth by the tribes.

There are also historical sites of great interest near the reservation: the Old Fort Hall Monument at the original trading post site and The Oregon Trail.

INFRASTRUCTURE

Interstate 15 crosses the reservation north-south, while Highway 84/86 crosses in an east-west direction. The reservation is also crossed by the main line of the Union Pacific Railroad and a north-south line connecting to Montana and Utah.

The Pocatello Airport, located on reservation land that was alienated under the World War Two Powers Act, provides an all-weather instrument-certified runway for large commercial aircraft.

Electricity. Electricity is provided by Idaho Power Company.

Fuel. Natural gas is supplied by Intermountain Gas Company.

Water Supply. The Fort Hall Water and Sewer District supplies the reservation with water and sewer service in the form of a large lagoon located north of the Fort Hall town site. Because of agricultural chemical contamination of much of the reservation's groundwater, a domestic water supply system is being constructed to serve the core area of the reservation. Outlying residents rely on wells and septic tanks.

Transportation. The tribes have contracted with the BIA for their roads program, including planning, maintenance, and construction. The tribes maintain a number of school buses to transport students to schools within the tribal school district. Commercial air service is available at the Pocatello Municipal Airport on the reservation. Commercial bus lines also serve the reservation directly, as do the Union Pacific Railroad and numerous truck lines.

Telecommunications. A site on Ferry Butte, north of Fort Hall, commanding a 50-mile radius, is leased out to communications service providers and is used for police, fire, and public safety communications.

COMMUNITY FACILITIES AND SERVICES

The tribes maintain a Human Resource Center, a Tribal Business Center, and a Multipurpose Center for various tribal activities and meetings.

Education. Students attend schools on the reservation that are operated under the tribal school district. A new high school was built in 1992.

Health Care. The Indian Health Service runs a large health clinic at Fort Hall, and there are hospitals in Pocatello and Blackfoot. Traditional healing medicines and ceremonies continue to be honored by many tribal members. Medicine persons are still consulted and often collaborate with Euro-American medical practitioners to treat Native patients.

TRI-ID-010

TRI-ID-013

TRI-ID-012

TRI-ID-011

TRI-ID-014

TRI-ID-015

ENVIRONMENTAL CONCERNS

The tribes participate in the Snake River Sockeye Salmon Enhancement Program. The program aims to restock the river and Redfish Lake with the endangered sockeye salmon. The installation of dams along the river has reduced the salmons' ability to return to the lake to spawn, thus creating a vast reduction in population. The tribes support breaching the dams to restore the natural ecosystem.

In 2002, the tribes initiated a research project in their agricultural enterprises. The Alternative Potato Rotation Technique uses radish and mustard crops to fertilize the soil in potato fields. The hope is that the technique will reduce the amount of pesticides required to grow potato crops, thus reducing the amount of chemicals being absorbed into the soil and making the potatoes safer for human consumption.

Natural Resources. In 1998, the Fort Hall Indian Mineral Resources Agreement was finalized. The agreement recognizes the tribes' water claims to the Snake River Basin in Idaho. This includes the natural flow, groundwater, and federal contract storage water. The agreement further stipulates access to storage water in American Falls Reservoir and access to a specific amount of storage water in the Blackfoot Reservoir and Grays Lake to maintain and improve regional ecosystems. The tribes received funds for water management, grazing rights, enhancing the Fort Hall Irrigation Project, and BIA purchase of lands.

TRI-ID-010 Shoshone Bannock Junior-Senior High School

TRI-ID-013 Trading Post "Clothes Horse" off Highway 15

TRI-ID-012 Covered walkway -Playground at Day Care/Early Childhood Center

TRI-ID-011 Day Care/Early Childhood Center Building

TRI-ID-014 Fort Hall Rodeo Grounds

TRI-ID-015 Front entrance, Shoshone Bannock Gaming Casino

Kootenai

Kootenai Reservation
Federal reservation
Kootenai
Kootenai Boundary County,
Idaho

Kootenai Tribe of Idaho
County Road 38A
P.O. Box 1269
Bonners Ferry, ID 83805
208-267-3519
208-267-2960 Fax

Total area *(BIA realty, 2004)*
1,974.77 acres

Tribally owned *(BIA realty, 2004)*
72.66 acres

Individually owned
(BIA realty, 2004)
1,902.11

Population *2000 census*
71

Tribal enrollment
(Tribal source, 2004)
165

Tribal enrollment
(BIA labor report, 2001)
121

Total labor force *2000 census*
32

Total labor force
(BIA labor report, 2001)
289

High school graduate or higher
2000 census
90.7%

Bachelor's degree or higher
2000 census
20.9%

Unemployment rate
2000 census
3.13%

Unemployment rate
(BIA labor report, 2001)
11%

Per capita income *2000 census*
$16,291

LOCATION AND LAND STATUS

The Kootenai Reservation is located in the northern tip of the Idaho panhandle, about 30 miles from the Canadian border. The reservation has 250 acres in federal trust, with approximately 2,000 additional acres allotted to individual tribal members. The Kootenais refused to participate in the 1855 Hellgate Council called by Washington Territorial Governor Isaac Stevens. Throughout the next decade, the tribe resisted all attempts to move it to the Flathead Reservation in Montana. In the early 1900s, the federal government finally set aside 8,000 acres for the Kootenais, with each recognized tribal member receiving a plot of 160 acres. Having little experience with farming, however, most tribal members failed to cultivate the land, and the majority of it was eventually leased to white settlers. Today, the Kootenais still have a very small community land base, consisting of little more than the tract upon which their tribal headquarters, community center, and a tribal housing project are situated.

CLIMATE

Annual rainfall on the Kootenai Reservation is 24.5 inches. The average temperatures range between 26°F and 68°F.

CULTURE AND HISTORY

The Kootenai Tribe of Idaho is one of six bands of the greater Kootenai Nation. Aside from the Idaho band, the Kootenai people may be found in British Columbia and northwestern Montana. The Kootenais traditionally relied on the region's rivers, lakes, prairies, and mountain forests for their sustenance.

Fur traders were the first Euro-Americans to appear on Kootenai lands, arriving in the 1830s. Within a decade, Jesuit missionaries began arriving, and shortly thereafter, homesteaders began to appear, crossing through or settling on Kootenai lands.

The ambitious Washington territorial governor, Isaac Stevens, was determined to open the Northwest to the railroad and agricultural development. This ambition spurred him to call for the 1855 Council at Hellgate, Montana. At the council, Stevens offered reserved lands and protection from further encroachment to the various bands of Salish and Kootenai in attendance. Several of the bands agreed and were placed on the Flathead Reservation, but the Idaho Kootenais had refused to even participate in or attend the council.

After losing its land to allotment, the tribe was dealt a further series of blows. First, in 1930 the Grand Coulee Dam was constructed, destroying the salmon runs upon which the tribe had depended for centuries. Then in the 1940s, non-Indian landowners refused to allow the tribe to work its traditional fishing areas along the Kootenai River. The third strike came later in that decade when the Idaho Department of Fish and Game forbade the Kootenais to hunt in their traditional areas. This decision was revised three decades later when in 1976 the Idaho Supreme Court ruled that the Hellgate Treaty of 1855 guaranteed the tribe's hunting rights on state and federal lands. In 1947, the tribe established its own government, though they had essentially no land base. In 1974, after decades of frustration, the tribe declared war on the U.S. government in an attempt to force the BIA to fulfill its trust responsibilities and provide a reservation. Tribal members turned the road through the minuscule reservation into a toll road, charging vehicles 10 cents each, and demanded that the U.S.

enter negotiations with them. Hostilities ceased when the tribe received assurances that negotiations would be forthcoming. The federal government finally fulfilled their obligations and deeded the tribe 12.5 acres.

Today the tribe is actively engaged in preserving its traditions and heritage, which have been so integral to its survival. Elders continue to speak the Native language, with some informal teaching it to the young people. The Kootenais remain a small, tenacious band that continues to hold fast to its sovereignty and pursue its goal of expanding its land base.

GOVERNMENT

Historically, the Kootenai Tribe was governed by a hereditary chief. The tribe's existing constitution was ratified on July 16, 1947, and structured according to the provisions of the 1934 Indian Reorganization Act, which established the tribal council as the tribe's governing body. The five-member tribal council consists of a chief (elected for life), and a chairman, a vice-chairman, a secretary, and a treasurer, all elected to staggered three-year terms. The general membership meets annually, while the tribal council meets weekly or as needed. Voting membership can legislate by initiative or referendum. The tribal government oversees health, housing, job training, environmental, fish and wildlife, health, and education programs for the Kootenai people.

The Kootenai Tribe has its own tribal court, which is overseen by the tribal council. The tribal court has exclusive jurisdiction over all judicial matters occurring on the reservation involving Indians and non-Indians to the full extent allowed by federal law.

ECONOMY

Tribal government, agriculture, gaming, and tourism are the major components of the Kootenai economy. The tribe is actively pursuing additional economic development projects and tax incentive programs to attract new industries to the reservation.

Government as Employer. The numerous departments and programs of the Kootenai tribal government provide employment opportunities for approximately 32 tribal members. Four people are employed by the environmental program and eight are employed in the administration and finance division.

Economic Development Projects. The Kootenai Tribe of Idaho is a member of the Panhandle Lakes Resource Conservation and Development (RC&D) Area. A USDA project, the RC&D program facilitates community involvement in resolving environmental and economic problems. To date, over 300 projects have been completed in the area, with the emphasis shifting from traditional conservation practices to extensive involvement in rural economic development.

Agriculture and Livestock. Most of the 250 acres of tribal lands are under agricultural use, primarily in wheat and barley cultivation. Additionally, a number of individual tribal members lease land to outside agricultural interests. The tribe realizes approximately $20,000 annually from agriculture.

Forestry. There is a fair amount of forested acreage on tribally affiliated land, though very little is presently under commercial development.

Gaming. The tribe's Kootenai River Inn and Casino is a 30,000-square-foot resort, with a class II and class III gaming facility. The casino features over 400 slot machines, a 250-seat bingo hall, a restaurant, and a hotel. There are several small retail and service establishments at the Kootenai River Inn and Casino resort. The Best Western Motel franchise has 65 hotel rooms and houses the Springs Restaurant, a 24-hour deli, a video arcade, and a recreation facility featuring an indoor/outdoor swimming pool, an exercise room, a sauna, and a Jacuzzi. The facility is currently under renovation and will include a spa facility including four massage rooms, a flow- through tub, facials, manicures, pedicures, and a hair salon. The Kootenai River Inn and Casino is situated on the scenic Kootenai River in Bonners Ferry and does a thriving, though largely seasonal, business.

The Kootenai River Inn and Casino employs approximately 160 people. Revenue from the casino has funded the development of the tribal medical center, scholarships for tribal members, various tribal programs, and generous donations to the local schools in the district.

Fisheries. The tribal hatchery is co-managing a project with the Idaho Fish and Gaming Department designed to repopulate the Kootenai River with sturgeon, a fish of spiritual significance to the tribe. The project employs about six tribal members and six non-Indians. Other divisions of the tribe's fish and wildlife program include: improving the Kootenai River ecosystem, the wildlife mitigation project, wetland conservation, andTrout Creek biological assessment.

Construction. A number of tribal members find employment through the construction industry. The tribal government has successfully created construction jobs for its members through development projects like the Kootenai River Inn.

Tourism and Recreation. The Bonners Ferry region is extremely popular with outdoors enthusiasts year round, featuring excellent hiking, boating, fishing, swimming, skiing, snowmobiling, mountain climbing, and more.

INFRASTRUCTURE
The primary road access to the reservation is provided by Highway 95 (running north-south) and Highway 2 (running east-west).

Electricity. The Northern Lights Power Company provides electricity to the area.

Water Supply. The Bonners Ferry municipal system supplies water. The reservation's lagoon and individual septic tanks provide wastewater service.

Transportation. The nearest commercial air service may be found at the Coeur D'Alene municipal airport, 90 miles away, and at the Spokane International Airport, about 120 miles distant. Additionally, there is a small private airport in Bonners Ferry. Commercial truck, bus, and rail freight lines serve Bonners Ferry, while Amtrak passenger rail service is available 30 miles south of the reservation.

The Kootenai Tribe provides a 24-hour transportation service for elderly tribal members.

Telecommunications. AT&T provides local telephone service.

COMMUNITY FACILITIES AND SERVICES
The tribe maintains a community center at its tribal headquarters, three miles west of Bonners Ferry.

Education. The Kootenai Tribal School serves about 36 students in grades K-12. The school has a staff of three teachers, a counselor, a teacher's aide, a language teacher, a general assistant, a cultural teacher, and an administrator. Tribal elders often volunteer to lead classes in the Kootenai language. Students may also attend the local public school system.

Health Care. The tribe owns and operates the Kootenai Tribal Clinic, located at tribal headquarters. The facility has a physician, a nurse practitioner, a community health representative, and a mental health counselor as well as two contract administrative health employees. These positions are direct tribal hires. A public health nurse also provides services once a month. Community health services include a well child program, diabetes, woman's health, and an immunization program as well as mental health counseling. The clinic also provides transportation and billing assistance. For health care services not provided by the clinic, tribal members are referred to outside providers in the surrounding area whose services are covered by contract health. The clinic includes two exam rooms, a laboratory, four business offices, a medical records room, and a reception lobby area covering approximately 720 square feet.

ENVIRONMENTAL CONCERNS
The tribe maintains an environmental program that monitors air and water quality on tribal lands. The program has a staff of six. The program also assists in improving water quality for the Kootenai River, located within the tribe's ancestral lands. The tribe's environmental department also includes an environmental health program. The Panhandle Lakes Resource Conservation and Development Area projects include fuel for schools, community forestry assistance, noxious weed control efforts, a seedling and seed bank program, and a forestry assistance directory.

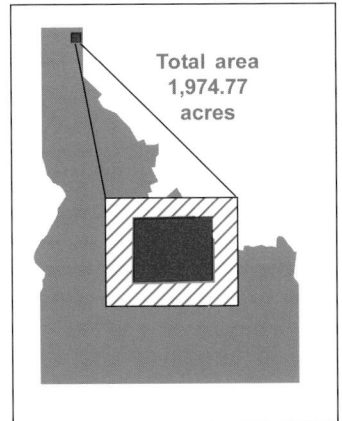

Total area 1,974.77 acres

Nez Perce

Nez Perce Reservation
Federal reservation
Nez Perce
Nez Perce, Clearwater, Idaho,
Latah, and Lewis counties,
Idaho

Nez Perce Tribe of Idaho
P.O. Box 305
Lapwai, ID 83540-0305
208-843-2253
208-843-7354 Fax
nezperce.org

Total area (BIA realty, 2004)
108,534.78 acres

Total area (Tribal source, 2004)
770,453 acres

Tribally owned (BIA realty, 2004)
42,767.84 acres

Individually owned
(BIA realty, 2004)
46,268.49 acres

Federal trust (BIA realty, 2004)
19,489.45 acres

Individual-Indian trust lands
(Tribal source, 2004)
46,250 acres

Tribal trust lands
(Tribal source, 2004)
43,106 acres

Tribal fee lands
(Tribal source, 2004)
11,365 acres

Fee title lands
(Tribal source, 2004)
643,565 acres

**Tribal fee land
outside reservation**
(Tribal source, 2004)
44,293 acres

LOCATION AND LAND STATUS

The Nez Perce Reservation is located in north-central Idaho and encompasses five counties. Several small towns are located within the boundaries of the reservation; Lapwai, on the reservation's western edge, serves as the tribal headquarters and is home to the largest population of tribal members. Kamiah, on the reservation's eastern boundary, contains the second-highest concentration of tribal members and provides social services through the Wa A'Yas Community Building. Other towns within the reservation are predominantly non-Indian.

The Treaty of June 11, 1855, established a reservation of some 7.5 million acres. However, the United States reduced the size of the Nez Perce Reservation to 750,000 acres in 1863 after the discovery of gold in the region. An additional 542,000 acres were lost to individual and non-Native ownership as a direct result of the Allotment Act of 1877. Today about 12 percent of the land within the reservation is owned by the Nez Perce Tribe or tribal members. The Nez Perce Tribe is currently raising funds to acquire 60 acres of land in Wallowa County, Oregon. The lands are the site of a proposed housing development adjacent to Old Chief Joseph Cemetery. The area is known to contain at least two archeological finds and is of great cultural and historical importance to the tribe.

CLIMATE

The reservation experiences an average temperature of 43°F. The annual rainfall averages 21.6 inches, and snowfall 61 inches.

CULTURE AND HISTORY

The Nimilpuus originated in the northwest region of the United States. Their ancestral homelands encompassed present-day north-central Idaho, northeastern Oregon, and southeastern Washington. Carbon dating of village sites along the Snake River and its tributaries indicates that the Nimilpuus occupied these regions as long as 11,000 years ago. There are indications of even older settlements. The Nimilpuus encountered the Lewis and Clark Expedition in 1805. Translators from that group identified the people as Nez Perce, or "pierced nose" (French). The assignment of this term to the Nimilpuus is not clear as the tribe did not practice nose piercing. However, the name was accepted and the tribe became known as the Nez Perce Tribe of Idaho.

In the early nineteenth century, the tribe participated in the fur trade with both Great Britain and America. As more and more settlers began to encroach upon the region, the tension between the Native population and the Euro-American newcomers escalated into violent conflicts. In June 1855 the Nez Perce agreed to cede several million acres to the United States in return for an approximate 7.5 million-acre reservation. In 1863 a new treaty was signed mandating a reduction in the tribe's lands to just 750,000 acres. Often called the "steal treaty", it stripped the Nez Perce of the Wallowa and Imnaha valleys and the land at the confluence of the Snake and Clearwater rivers, the site of the present-day towns of Lewiston and Clarkston. A number of Nez Perce bands refused to sign the treaty, including the Wallowa Valley Band led by Chief Joseph. A war ensued and resulted in the eventual surrender of the Nez Perce in 1877. Members of the Wallowa Band, among others, retreated north to Canada for a period of four months. Upon their return, the Nez Perce were confined to the new reservation lands. The reservation was further reduced by the

effects of the Allotment Act of 1877. In 1893, the federal government opened all non-allotted Nez Perce lands to the public. These actions resulted in the loss of 542,000 acres of tribal lands. In 1948, the tribe became a self-governing Nation under an adopted constitution and bylaws. As with many other tribes, the Nez Perce have experienced a cultural renaissance during the past half century. A revival of traditional arts and crafts, dance, and religion has been ongoing since the 1940s. Today, the Nez Perce are involved in writing their own history and reviving the Nez Perce language.

GOVERNMENT

The Nez Perce Tribal Executive Committee, a nine-member body elected at large, manages economic development, tribal social service programs, natural resources, and tribal investments. Committee members serve three-year terms, with elections occurring annually. The tribe did not accept the provisions of the Indian Reorganization Act of 1934 and is a self-governing nation. The current constitution and bylaws were adopted on April 2, 1948.

The Nez Perce Tribal Court is involved in implementing and activating laws as set out in the Law and Order Code. The court maintains jurisdiction over most criminal, civil, juvenile, and domestic matters within the reservation. A part-time public defender provides services for tribal members in adult criminal matters, as well as for a few juvenile cases. The University of Idaho provides legal aid interns to practice in the Nez Perce Tribal Court. They provide representation in criminal and juvenile matters. Both of these services are provided at no cost to the clients.

The Nez Perce Tribe has numerous governmental departments and programs. They include human resources, law and order, youth affairs, land commission, budget and finance/credit, natural resources, the court system, enterprise system, and office of the prosecutor, law enforcement, executive direction, and office of legal counsel. The tribe also has the following boards and authorities and, commissions: TERO Commission, NPT Housing Authority, utility board, gaming commission, NMP Health Authority, enterprise board, F&W Commission, LCBC Advisory Committee, foundation board, and retirement board.

The Lewis and Clark Program of the tribal government serves to represent the tribe during the Lewis and Clark Corps of Discovery Bicentennial Commemoration between 2003 - 2006. The program works with other tribal, federal, and state agencies to provide accurate and appropriate information about the Nez Perce Tribe and to protect the cultural properties of the tribe in this matter. Projects within the program include oral history and Native traditions, archaeology and historic preservation, ERWM cultural resources, the Nimiipuu language, archival, and the Lapwai Arts Council.

ECONOMY

The tribe's economy is sustained by revenue earned through its many businesses. Enterprises of the tribe include Nez Perce Tribal Gaming, the Nez Perce Express Store, Aht'wy Plaza RV Park, and the Nez Perce Forest Products. The Nez Perce tribal government contributes greatly to the economy of the reservation as well. The government employs over 1,000 individuals throughout the various tribal businesses and services. Over 700 people are employed by governmental departments and programs.

Government as Employer. The Nez Perce Tribe employs a total of 1,145 employees in its tribal government and various enterprises. Of this number, 526 are tribal members, 501 are non-tribal and 118 are from other tribes. The tribal government employs 742 persons.

Economic Development Projects. The Nez Perce Department of Economic and Community Development Program provides management of economic, community, and transportation planning for the tribe. Some current projects of the department include an annual update of the Comprehensive Economic Strategy (CEDS), development of a tourism plan, and development of funding sources for small business on the reservation. This program also investigates new business development such as industrial parks, natural resource development, added-value businesses, and related private business development.

The Aht'way Commercial Plaza is under construction near Lewiston, Idaho. The tribe is also considering a proposal to establish a polyethylene plastics recycling plant on or near the reservation.

Agriculture and Livestock. The tribe cultivates 37,639 acres of reservation land; wheat is the major crop. Other crops include barley, dry peas, lentils, canola, bluegrass seed, alfalfa, and hay. The tribe also raises some cattle.

The tribe's herd of horses produces an Appaloosa - Akahl-Teke cross. The tribe hopes that through the breeding process, it will reestablish its line of horses that dominated the tribal herds prior to American contact in 1806. The Nez Perce horse program is administered by the Nez Perce Tribe. The program teaches tribal youth ages 14 - 21 about horsemanship, management practices, and economic opportunities available in the horse industry.

Forestry. The Nez Perce Forest Resource Management Program manages 40,203 acres of tribally owned timberland, harvesting approximately 7,000 MBF annually on a sustained-yield basis. The forest is primarily composed of mixed conifers. The Nez Perce Forest Products Enterprise conducts harvesting, marketing, and replanting of tribally owned timber.

Gaming. The Clearwater River Casino is located in Lewiston. It is an 18,000-square-foot facility that features video lottery machines, bingo, and over 400 video terminals. Amenities include a grille, a gift shop, and an adjacent RV park. The It'Se-Ye-Ye Bingo and Casino is located in Kamiah. It offers over 100 video lottery machines and electronic bingo. Combined, the casinos employ approximately 250 individuals. The average net revenue is between $2 and $3 million. The tribe infuses the funds into the general budget, economic development projects, and services for tribal members. The revenue is also used to donate sums to local police and fire services, charitable organizations, and local schools. Although the tribe has encountered some legal issues concerning electronic gaming machines, it is moving forward with plans for expanding the gaming facilities.

Fisheries. The tribe's department of fisheries resources management is an extensive program that is responsible for the restoration and recovery of watershed environments and fish populations. It works to ensure that the harvest and conservation actions taken by any tribal or non-tribal entity comply with all tribal laws and regulations. The department currently oversees 17 watershed projects. The tribe manages three tribal fish hatcheries, site management, fish recovery, and restoration plans.

Mining. The tribe is currently studying the feasibility of re-opening the Mission Creek Quarry and developing a new mining and basalt plan to improve efficiency at the quarry. Early studies indicate a high quality limestone and basalt deposit on the reservation.

Services and Retail. The Nez Perce Express Enterprise includes one full service convenience store. The Express II is a 5,400-square-foot store that offers tobacco products, a full deli, groceries, gift selections, automotive supplies, housewares, and bakery items. The store has recently added petroleum products for tribal programs and the general public.

Tourism and Recreation. The tribe hopes to expand its involvement in the local tourism and recreation market. Currently the Nez Perce National Park, partially located on tribal land, attracts over 36,000 visitors annually. The tribe is presently developing a brochure that will present tribal stories about rock formations on the Snake, Clearwater, and Columbia rivers to tourists and will serve as a reservation road map for visitors. The Nez Perce Reservation lies in the proximity of several outdoor recreational areas, including Hell's Canyon, Clearwater River, Clearwater National Forest, and the Nez Perce National Forest. Five Idaho state parks are also located near the reservation. The Aht'wy Plaza RV Park has 33 hookups, 10 dry camps, 15 tent sites, restrooms and shower facilities, a coin-operated laundry, vending machines, a heated pool, and a picnic area. It is located within walking distance of the casino.

The tribe participates in the operation of the Nez Perce Cultural Museum at Spalding, Idaho where Nez Perce artisans sell cornhusk weaving, jewelry, and other crafts.

INFRASTRUCTURE
U.S. Highways 12 and 95 run through the reservation.

Electricity. Electricity is provided to the reservation by Washington Water Power and Clearwater Power.

Fuel. Natural gas service is available through Washington Water Power.

Water Supply. Groundwater wells provide water.

Transportation. Commercial airlines serve Lewiston Airport, located in Lewiston. Several truck lines service the area via Lewiston, including United Parcel Service, Pony Express, Federal Express, Quick Delivery, Broadway Package Service, and Viking. Camas Prairie, Union Pacific, and Burlington Northern railway services are available in Lewiston. Several freight barge companies operate out of the Port of Lewiston, including Lewiston Tidewater Barge Lines, Brix Maritime, and Gem Chip Trading Company. Nez Perce Municipal Airport serves Nez Perce and Lewis counties. It is owned by the City of Nez Perce. The paved runway extends for 2,000 feet. The facility is at an elevation of 3,201 feet at a distance of about a mile or less from Nez Perce.

Telecommunications. The reservation is served by U.S. West Communications and Northwest Communications.

COMMUNITY FACILITIES AND SERVICES
The Nez Perce Tribe Teweepuu Community Center and the Wa-a'yas Community Center provide recreation, sports, and educational and cultural activities for tribal members. The Teweepuu Center served as the host to the Governor's Lewis and Clark Bicentennial Trail Committee meeting. The Wa-a'yas Center sponsors the annual Turkey Shootout, Community Christmas Dinner, and ECHDP Powwow. The Pi Nee Waus Community Center serves as the host for the annual Halloween party

Nez Perce

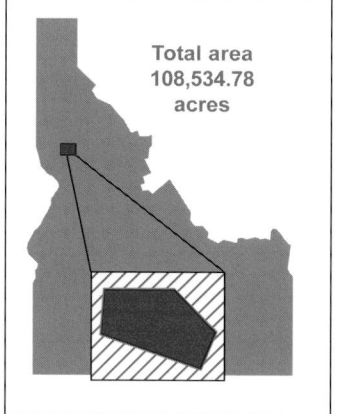

Total area
108,534.78
acres

Population *2000 census*
17,959

Tribal enrollment *(Tribal sources)*
3,872

Total labor force *2000 census*
7,737

High school graduate or higher
2000 census
81.6%

Bachelor's degree or higher
2000 census
14%

Unemployment rate *2000 census*
9.2%

Unemployment rate
(BIA labor report, 2001)
64%

Unemployment rate
(Tribal sources)
39%

Per capita income
(Tribal sources)
$21,620

Nez Perce

TRI-ID-007

TRI-ID-009

TRI-ID- 006

TRI-ID-016

TRI-ID-008

TRI-ID-007 Directional sign to: PI-NEE-WAUS Community Center & Tribal Headquarters

TRI-ID-009 The Nez Perce Tribe Horse Registry's logo painted on horse barn

TRI-ID-016 Limestone Compound Young Horsemen Bicentennial

TRI-ID-008 Registered Appaloosa Stallion

TRI-ID- 006 Nez Perce Housing Authority Sign

and activities in the summer for the youth. They also facilitate numerous events, such as tournaments, Christmas dinners, pow-wows, and employee fitness.

In 2003 the tribe established the Nez Perce Tribal Children's Trust Fund. The organization provides funding for the Nez Perce Tribal Children's Home and Advocacy Center, Child Protection Services, Foster Care Placement, supportive services, and youth development programs. Future programs will include internships and college scholarships for specific social service needs. The tribe's hope is that the trust fund will become a self-sustaining children's service program that will exist indefinitely to serve the needs of tribal youth.

The tribe offers the Students for Success program to tribal youth. The program aims to provide participants with the personal strength and ability to achieve educational, career, and personal goals. The program provides educational and support services toward the prevention of substance abuse and HIV. The program is a recipient of the Drug-free Communities Support Program Grant, the HIV Prevention Grant, and the Spirit of Eagles Grant, the Increase Resiliency and Development Assists in our tribal Youth to Prevent, Reduce or Delay Onset of Alcohol, Tobacco, and Other Drugs (ATOD) use for Native American youth, age 9-18. The infusion of cultural practices and knowledge is the main strategy of the program. The Boys & Girls Clubs of the Lewis Clark Valley provide recreational and after-school activates for community youth. The program is located on the reservation in Lapwai at its Lapwai Club unit, which features a 10,300-square-foot facility with gymnasium, technology center, arts and crafts, and teen center.

Education. There are five public schools, a tribal Head Start program, and the Nez Perce Tribal Employment and Training Department on the reservation. The tribe provides financial assistance to students seeking postsecondary and vocational education. The tribe offers instructional classes in the indigenous language and a cultural camp for children between the ages of 4 and 12 years.

Health Care. Under the provision of PL 93-638 in 1997, the tribe assumed operation of the Nimilpuus health programs, which

include health clinics in Lapwai and Kamiah. Both clinics are ambulatory facilities that offer medical, pharmacy, lab and X-ray, dental, behavioral health, and community health services. Offices for behavioral health and community health services are located at separate sites.

The tribe is in the process of building a 42,000-square-foot facility that will put all health programs under one roof. Under the Self-Governance Compact of 2002, the tribe has gained greater autonomy, allowing it the ability to reallocate funds to best suit the needs of its population. The tribe also has better access to other sources of funding such as grants for program expansion and construction. Health care is also available at St. Joseph's and Tri-State hospitals in Lewiston

ENVIRONMENTAL CONCERNS

The tribe has been the leading force in the statewide recovery of the endangered Idaho gray wolf. The program is headed by the tribe's wildlife program. The tribe is working to reestablish the gray wolf population in a 13,000,000-acre area in central Idaho. Operations of the program include monitoring the wolf population, providing public education, population management and control, and research. In 2000 the project received the Honoring Nations/Ford Foundation Award administered by the Harvard Project on American Indian Economic Development at the John F. Kennedy School of Government. In 1999, the tribe began the development of a Memorandum of Understanding with local and state officials to address the issue of illegal dumping on tribal lands. Illegal dumping by non-tribal entities has become a serious issue on the reservation.

The tribe is also involved in the management of its surface and groundwater sources, resources to which the tribe's rights have been reserved by treaties with the federal government. The U.S. EPA awarded the tribe a grant in order to develop a wetland management, restoration, enhancement and protection program. The methodology will establish a process by which wetlands will be identified for preservation activity in order to restore a watershed level and facilitate the total maximum daily load implementation.

Honoring Nations Honoree 1999

Idaho Gray Wolf Recovery Wildlife Program, Nez Perce Tribe

In 1995 the United States Fish and Wildlife Service (USFWS) resolved to reintroduce gray wolves to their traditional habitat in the northern Rocky Mountains. State governments are the Fish and Wildlife Service's traditional partners in such efforts, but giving substance to local opinion, the governments of Idaho, Montana, and Wyoming declined to participate in the wolf recovery program. USFWS remained committed to working with the states in the future, but their present non-participation created a vacuum-the Service needed to find an alternate partner to take responsibility for implementation.

The Nez Perce Tribe (headquartered in Lapwai, Idaho) was one possibility. Many of the Tribe's members were in favor of wolf reintroduction, and the Tribe itself had sought and gained the right to participate in an earlier stage of the recovery program, the drafting of the environmental impact statement. Yet the Tribe's leaders knew that further involvement would require both technical capacity and political courage. The implementation agent would have to be able to monitor and manage the wolf population across a vast, rugged, and largely roadless wilderness area encompassing nearly 13 million acres of central Idaho. And, management would have to occur in the face of strong opposition from powerful rancher and hunter organizations and from states rights advocates. Professional wildlife staff, access to appropriate equipment, and a willingness to be "wolf ambassadors" would be vital components of any implementation plan.

Instead of tackling these challenges independently, the Nez Perce Tribe had hoped to partner with the State of Idaho in the recovery effort. With that possibility no longer available, the Nez Perce became determined to gain the opportunity to manage wolf recovery themselves. To that end, they entered into partnership talks with the USFWS-but they did so with forethought and strategy. In particular, the Tribe's Executive Committee believed their staff's experience with other recovery efforts would give them expertise on the technical aspects of the wolf recovery, and they chose to view the political situation as an opportunity to strengthen external relationships. Several concrete steps followed: the Tribe signed a cooperative agreement with the USFWS, developed a Gray Wolf Recovery and Management Plan for Idaho, and gained approval of that plan from the USFWS.

While the USFWS retains ultimate responsibility for wolf recovery, the Nez Perce plan adopts an innovative team approach to accomplish the program's four key tasks-monitoring, wolf management and control, research, and education and outreach. The Tribe is primarily responsible for monitoring the wolves. Tribal biologists gather data about the wolves' movements, food habits, habitat use, and reproductive success. Wolf management and control is a team responsibility. Wildlife Services, a Division of the United States Department of Agriculture, is under the direction of the USFWS to determine if depredations on livestock are caused by wolves. After verification, tribal biologists capture and relocate the wolves to which attacks have been attributed. The USFWS handles law enforcement, addresses policy issues, and when necessary, authorizes lethal control measures. Research and education and outreach are conducted by an even larger group of program cooperators. The Tribe, federal agencies, special interest groups, and affected parties together conduct research and address public concerns about the effects of wolves on livestock and game populations.

After only four and a half years of implementation, the Program is a success on all fronts. From the standpoint of biology, the packs are healthy, and because the number of breeding pairs in Idaho has reached the target level, talks are underway to start the next phase of the reintroduction process-delisting.

The Tribe also has adeptly addressed the political sensitivities of wolf recovery. Through an effective combination of outreach, communication, and coalition building, the Tribe's recovery program has been able to make substantial progress in responding to livestock producers' concerns. In its work with these and other stakeholders, the Tribe has effectively coupled a neutral political position with an active commitment to answer concerns, develop solutions, and defuse conflicts-an accomplishment that has won the Nez Perce respect in many circles. Similarly, in its work with the general public, the Tribe's goal has been to educate and assuage concerns. For example, the Tribe works with the Wolf Education and Research Center, a non?profit outreach organization, to provide a broad dissemination of information about wolves, the reintroduction program, and the Nez Perce role in the wolf recovery.

Cultural benefits are another measure of the Recovery Program's successes. Being Nez Perce entails respecting and celebrating wolves, and in the future, it will even mean harvesting wolves. This aspect of Nez Perce culture had languished as local populations of wolves disappeared, but it has been refreshed through wolf reintroduction. Today, wolf legends that had been sequestered within families are shared widely in the Tribe, baby naming ceremonies include wolf names, and dancers are once again using wolf pelts as part of their regalia.

Finally, and significantly, the Gray Wolf Recovery Program has been a success in terms of tribal self?determination and tribal sovereignty. The Nez Perce were able to make a credible offer to implement wolf recovery because of the expertise, track record, and reputation the Tribe had earned in earlier wildlife management efforts. Just as these investments in institutional effectiveness and technical capacity enabled the Nez Perce to seize an opportunity for increased self?determination, its effective management of wolf recovery is now opening even more doors-proof that good governance and enhanced self-determination go hand-in-hand. The Tribe's entrepreneurial involvement in wildlife management has similarly increased tribal sovereignty. The Wolf Recovery Plan gives the Tribe a new measure of responsibility over off?reservation treaty lands (on which Indian jurisdiction is otherwise limited) and promotes sovereign, government-to-citizen or government -to- government relationships between the Tribe and private land owners, the State of Idaho, and other governmental entities.

Today the Nez Perce people draw parallels between the wolves' fate and their own. Both were deprived of habitat necessary for their traditional means of support, and both were systematically driven off their land at a great cost of life. Thus, it is not surprising that the wolf recovery is intertwined in many tribal members' minds with Nez Perce survival and resurgence. The Wolf Recovery Program is an exercise in effective tribal administration, but it is also an investment in culture, community, and nationhood.

Honoring Nations
Honoree 1999

Text in its entirety from:
The Harvard Project On
American Indian Economic
Development

John F. Kennedy School
of Government
Harvard University

IOWA

Map from Tiller's Guide to Indian Country (1996 edition)

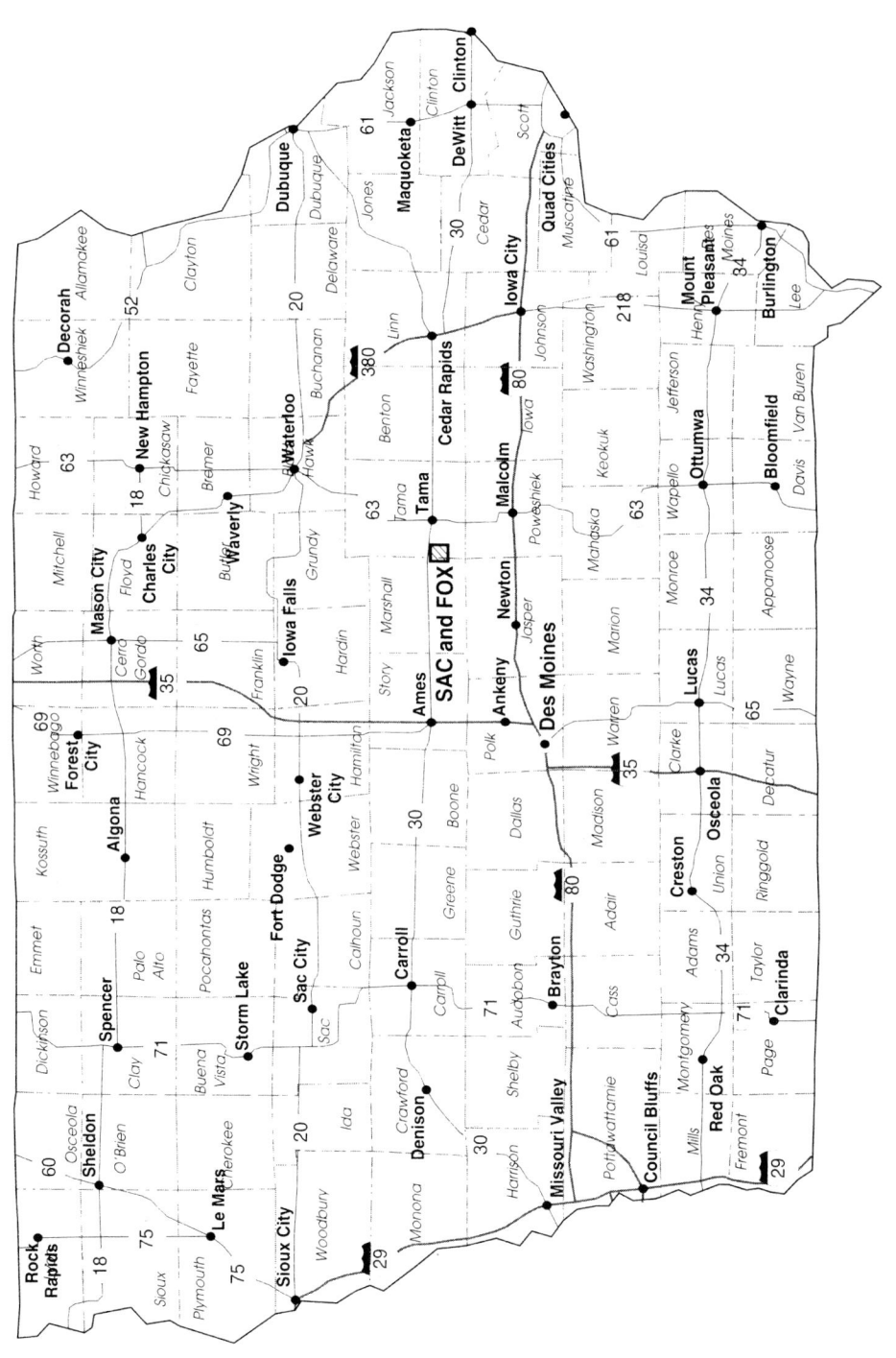

Sac and Fox

LOCATION AND LAND STATUS

Formerly known as the Meskwaki Indian Settlement, the reservation lands of the Sac and Fox Tribe of the Mississippi in Iowa are located in the south-central region of Tama County, Iowa. Lands of the now federally recognized tribe are approximately 130 miles from the Mississippi River, the state's eastern border. The Iowa River enters the reservation at its eastern edge and continues through to the reservation's southeast corner. While the tribal lands are held in federal trust, the tribe has purchased all acreage. The reservation has grown from an original settlement of 84 acres purchased in 1857, to about 3,500 acres in trust plus another 700 acres subject to life estate. The Meskwakis purchased additional acreage. All lands are commonly owned, with no individual allotments.

CLIMATE

The elevation in Tama, Iowa, is 890 feet above sea level. The year-round average daily high temperature in Tama is 58°F, with the highest temperature on record as 109°F. The year-round average daily low temperature is approximately 36°F, with the lowest temperature recorded being -34°F. The area receives approximately 34 inches of precipitation annually, with 25 inches falling as snowfall.

CULTURE AND HISTORY

As members of the Algonquian confederacy, ancestors of the modern Sac and Fox Tribe of the Mississippi in Iowa were originally two separate tribes who lived along the Eastern Seaboard: the Fox, or Meskwaki, and the Sauk, or Sac. Pressure from white settlers and encroachment from other tribes forced a migration to areas around Lake Michigan. The two tribes were related and spoke the same language, but originally they had independent political leadership from one another.

The Meskwakis (formerly spelled Mesquakie, pronounced "mesk-wah-kee"), or "Red Earth People," traditionally occupied permanent villages of rectangular, bark-covered houses. They practiced a subsistence lifestyle, raising summer crops and following the herds in the winter for meat. During the winter hunts, they lived in dome-shaped portable wigwams. They made and utilized both birch-bark and dugout canoes for river transportation. Toward the end of the eighteenth century, the tribe moved permanently west and settled along the Mississippi River, becoming allied with the Iroquois and later with the Five Nations in the French and Indian Wars. After a bitter war between the Fox Tribe and the French, the Sauks sheltered the surviving Fox Indians, and the two tribes largely merged. After moving across the river from the Sauk (Sac) group, around what is now Rock Island, Illinois, both groups were referred to by the federal government as "Sac and Fox", thus consolidating their identities.

After the Blackhawk Wars in 1842, the Meskwakis were forcibly removed to a reservation in Kansas. To prevent yet another forced resettlement to Indian Territory in Oklahoma, the tribe returned to the Mississippi River Valley in Iowa and purchased its own land. This property, originally consisting of 84 acres, was placed in trust with the governor of Iowa. In 1896, the Bureau of Indian Affairs (BIA) assumed jurisdiction over the tribe, and today the United States government holds the land in trust.

The Meskwakis, one of three federally recognized bands of Sac and Fox people, consider themselves a conservative people and are currently attempting to integrate economic development without corrupting their traditional culture. Today, 80-90 percent of the Sac and Fox people continue to speak the Meskwaki language. For more than 75 years, the tribe has hosted an annual powwow where numerous indigenous groups meet to celebrate their heritage and express their spirituality.

GOVERNMENT

The Sac and Fox Tribe of Mississippi is governed by a seven-member tribal council which consists of a chief of the council, an assistant chief of the council, a secretary, and a treasurer, with all members elected to four-year staggered terms. The tribal constitution and bylaws were ratified on November 13, 1937, and approved on December 20, 1937, by the BIA, in accordance with the Indian Reorganization Act of June 18, 1934. The tribe, under PL-638, contracts with the BIA to administer key programs and services. While there are no tribal police on the reservation, an annual stipend from the Iowa legislature provides funds for a part-time sheriff.

BUSINESS CORPORATION

The tribal council chartered the Meskwaki Enterprise Corporation, headed by a seven-member board of directors, to direct the Meskwaki Tribe's economic development. The tribal council appoints four of the members, while representatives from area businesses and professional corporations fill the remaining three seats.

ECONOMY

Agriculture and Livestock. While the majority of the settlement's tillable land is not under cultivation, the tribe leases 520 acres of farmland to farmers who raise corn and soybeans. The tribe earns an annual income from these leases. In addition, individual tribal members use agricultural land for both farming and pasture. Many residents tend small gardens, up to one acre, which accounts for the remaining tillable land in use.

Sac and Fox Reservation
Federal reservation
Meskwaki
Tama County, Iowa

Sac and Fox Tribal Office
349 Meskwaki Road
Tama, IA 52339
641-484-4678
641-484-5424 Fax

Total area (BIA)
6,156.99 acres

Federal trust lands (BIA)
5 acres

Tribally owned lands (BIA)
6,151.99 acres

Population 2000 census
761

Tribal enrollment
(BIA labor report, 2001)
1,260

Tribal enrollment
(Tribal source, 2003)
1,293

Total labor force 2000 census
277

High school graduate or higher
2000 census
67.4%

Bachelor's degree or higher
2000 census
6%

Unemployment rate 2000 census
14.8%

Unemployment rate
(BIA labor report, 2001)
56%

Per capita income 2000 census
$7,508

Sac and Fox

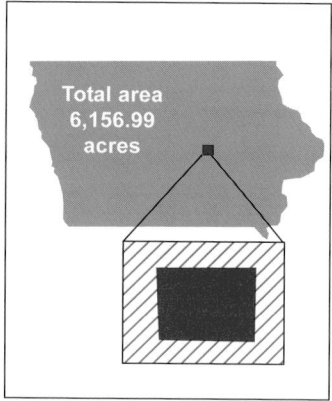

Total area
6,156.99
acres

Forestry. The settlement lands are scattered, with approximately 1,400 acres of timber woods, primarily high-grade walnut, black oak, hard and soft maple, and white pine.

Gaming. The tribe first entered the gaming industry with a bingo hall in 1992. It entered into a class III gaming compact with the State of Iowa in 1995, and it opened the Meskwaki Bingo Casino in 1998. The casino is located along Highway 30, three miles west of Tama, and in 2004, it represented the tribe's primary revenue source. The 127,669-square-foot Meskwaki Bingo Casino and Hotel features 1,381 slot machines, 28 table games, a 498-seat bingo hall, eight poker tables, keno, and a race book. The casino complex includes two entertainment venues, four restaurants, the River's Edge Gift Shop, and a 206-room hotel with whirlpool suites. There are approximately 1,200 employees.

Services and Retail. The Meskwaki Enterprise Group operates the Meskwaki Trading Post, a convenience store and gas station. The store is located on the reservation approximately five miles west of Tama, along Highway 30. Operating under a franchise from the Car-Go Convenience Store operation, the Meskwaki Trading Post offers sheltered pump service including diesel fuel, the usual food and drink items, Indian fry bread, and souvenirs.

Tourism and Recreation. The tribe sponsors two annual powwows and operates the casino to attract tourism to the reservation. Tama, Iowa, offers recreational opportunities also, with an annual Lincoln Highway Bridge Festival and Parade, a farmer's market, and the Tama County Museum.

INFRASTRUCTURE

One major gravel road traverses the reservation lands and connects with Highway 30. While there are numerous gravel roads and lanes branching off, they can be impassable during the spring and winter months. Interstate 80 lies 25 miles to the south of the reservation, while Interstate 35, which connects Minneapolis/St. Paul and Kansas City, lies 35 miles to the west.

Water Supply. The tribe installed a deep, fresh-water well; a pumping station; and a 30,000-gallon reservoir in 1983. Some residents continue to rely on shallow wells for their water supply. An underground aeration system provides sewage treatment for reservation homes, gaming facilities and the trading post.

Transportation. The closest rail and bus services are available in Tama, three miles to the east. Tama also has a small, sod-surfaced runway to accommodate small aircraft. The nearest commercial airports are in Waterloo and Cedar Rapids.

COMMUNITY FACILITIES AND SERVICES

The tribe maintains a community powwow grounds.

Education. Reservation children attend school, pre-kindergarten through eighth grade, on the Meskwaki Indian Settlement.

Health Care. The tribe provides for the health of its residents under contract with the Indian Health Service. An appointed director of health care services oversees the reservation's medical clinic and its other health care programs which employ a full-time family physician and a part-time podiatrist. The tribe has also provided a 20-room apartment complex for its elderly residents.

ENVIRONMENTAL CONCERNS

The tribe has been working on an emergency stream bank stabilization project to mitigate damages to powwow grounds and other tribal lands, with funding obtained via programs that provide planning and management assistance to states and flood plain areas. A flood plain study of tribal lands was completed in 1998. Grounds are threatened by inundation, erosion, and a potential channel change.

KANSAS

Iowa Tribe

Total area *(BIA realty, 2003)*	2,771.65 acres
Total area *(Tribal source, 2004)*	2,747.37 acres
Tribally owned	2,380.58 acres
(BIA realty, 2003)	
Individually owned	391.07 acres
(BIA realty, 2003)	
Population *2000 Census*	640
Tribal enrollment	3,100
(Tribal source, 2004)	
Total labor force *2000 Census*	95
High school graduate or higher	82.9%
2000 Census	
Bachelor's degree or higher *2000 Census*	2%
Unemployment rate *2000 Census*	4.2%
Per capita income *2000 Census*	$6,336

LOCATION AND LAND STATUS

The Iowa Tribe's reservation straddles two states. The 2,747.37-acre reservation is located in northeastern Kansas in Brown and Doniphan counties and in the southeastern corner of Nebraska in Richardson County. In Kansas the tribe owns 2,253.85 acres, and 181.01 acres of individual allotments. In Nebraska it owns 493.52 acres of tribal lands and 210.06 acres of individual allotments. Tribal headquarters are located west of White Cloud on Highway 7.

CULTURE AND HISTORY

The Iowa Indians speak Chiwere, a Siouan language. They are closely related to the Winnebago, Otoe, and Missouri tribes, whose combined aboriginal lands were located on the Mississippi River along the Upper Iowa River. In the mid-1700s, the Iowa peoples moved into the area along the Mississippi between the Iowa and Des Moines rivers. The Iowa Nation signed numerous treaties with the United States, often in association with neighboring tribes, including the Sac and Fox of Missouri Tribe. The treaties of 1816, 1824, 1825, 1830, 1836, 1837, and 1838, were all treaties of land cession. The original Iowa Reservation was established by treaty in 1836, only to be reduced by the treaties of May 17, 1854, and March 6, 1861. The 1854 treaty ceded a portion of the reservation for the Sac and Fox of Missouri Indian Tribe. Both of these tribes ceded the majority of their adjoining reservation to the United States in 1861. At the end of the Civil War, the Iowa Tribe was separated into two divisions; one group moved to Indian territory (Oklahoma) and became the Iowa Tribe of Oklahoma. The Iowa Reservation was allotted in 1885 and in 1887 with surplus lands sold in the 1890s. The remaining lands, which approximated 1,500 acres in the late 1980s, have been increased under the tribe's program of land acquisitions. In 1995, the BIA indicated that there were 1,618.7 acres of Iowa tribal lands in trust status.

GOVERNMENT

The Iowa Tribe is organized and chartered under the Indian Reorganization Act of 1934. Its constitution and bylaws were adopted on November 6, 1937. The Executive Committee is the tribe's governing body. It consists of a chairman, a vice-chairman, a secretary, a treasurer and one member; each serves a three-year term. Tribal departments include the police, fire, health, and a tribal court. Social services are provided to tribal members through Native American Family Services located in Hiawatha, Kansas.

ECONOMY

Agriculture, tribal government, and gaming are the major elements of the tribe's economy, although the tribe is looking toward tourism and recreation as a possible source for further economic development.

Government as Employer. The Iowa tribal government is one of the largest employers of tribal members, employing 110 people.

Economic Development Projects. The reservation's abundance of small game and fishing holes could allow for future economic endeavors in the tourism and recreation industry. The tribe is considering constructing cabins and hunting lodges as a way to capitalize on the reservation's beauty and wealth of wild game.

Agriculture. The Iowa Tribe has a successful farming business, including 1,077 acres planted in row crops, and additional acres held in CRP programs consisting of pastures, woods, and hay ground that support 150 head of cattle.

Gaming. Casino White Cloud is a full-fledge gaming facility with bingo and a buffet. The casino employs 145 people.

Services and Retail. The tribe owns and operates the Grandview Oil Service Station and Convenience Store.

Tourism and Recreation. The Missouri River runs through tribal land, making the reservation a haven for hunting and fishing. Small game includes turkey, whitetail deer, rabbits, quail, and pheasants. The tribe also has a number of annual events, including the All Encampment Powwow in September, the Chief White Cloud Rodeo in June, and the Demolition Derby in August.

INFRASTRUCTURE

The reservation has a sanitation service route, 28 miles of paved roads, and 14 miles of public water systems, all built and maintained by the tribe.

Iowa Tribe of Kansas and Nebraska Reservation
Federal reservation
Iowa
Richardson County, Nebraska, and Brown and Doniphan counties, Kansas

Iowa Tribe of Kansas and Nebraska
3345 B Thrasher Road
White Cloud, KS 66094
785-595-3258
785-595-6610 Fax

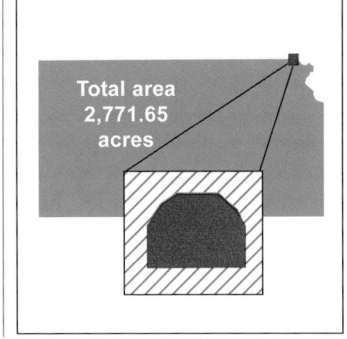

Total area
2,771.65
acres

Iowa Tribe

TRI-KS-052

TRI-KS-051

TRI-KS-052 Iowa Tribe of Kansas & Nebraska sign with listing of offices

TRI-KS-051Signs at crossroads to White-Cloud Casino

COMMUNITY FACILITIES AND SERVICES

The Iowa Reservation Complex is home to the United Tribes, a consortium of the Iowas and the Sac and Fox Nation of Missouri. The United Tribes administer a summer Youth Work Program, a commodity program, and a Low-Income Energy Assistance Program. The reservation also has its own fire station, day care, youth group, and senior citizen center. A meal site and meal delivery service is available for elders.

Education. College scholarships and grants for higher education are available to eligible tribal members upon graduation from high school.

Health Care. Tribal members get their health care needs met at the Indian Health Service operated health clinic. The tribe also has a community health representative.

Kickapoo

Kickapoo Reservation
Federal reservation
Kickapoo
Brown County, Kansas

Kickapoo Tribe of Kansas
1107 Goldfinch Road
Horton, KS 66439
785-486-2131
785-486-2801 Fax
ktik.org

Total area *(BIA realty, 2003)*
6,441.06 acres

Total area *(Tribal source, 2004)*
19,200 acres

Federal trust lands
(Tribal source, 2004)
9,100 acres

Federal trust *(BIA realty, 2003)*
1 acre

Tribally owned *(BIA realty, 2003)*
3,702.94 acres

Tribally owned
(Tribal source, 2004)
3,800 acres

LOCATION AND LAND STATUS

The Kickapoo Reservation is located in far northeastern Kansas, along the Delaware River, just off State Highway 75. The reservation is checkerboarded with non-Indian lands as a result of allotments that began as early as the 1830s. Tribal headquarters are located about six miles west of Horton, Kansas, on Highway 20. The tribe continues to increase its land base, using newly acquired parcels primarily for farming purposes.

PHYSICAL DESCRIPTION

The Kickapoo Reservation is mainly comprised of relatively flat farmlands, rolling grassy hills, and several small rivers and streams.

CLIMATE

Horton, Kansas, lies at an elevation of 1,134 feet above sea level, with climate patterns typical of the south-central plains. Year-round daily high temperatures average 65°F, with the highest temperature ever recorded being 112°F. Year-round daily low temperatures average 42°F, with the lowest temperature ever recorded being -33°F. The area receives approximately 33.3 inches of precipitation annually, with 22.6 inches falling as snow.

CULTURE AND HISTORY

Linguistically, the Kickapoos, from the Algonquin, Kiwigapawa (he who moves about, stand now here, now there), are related to the Mascouten, Shawnee, and Sac and Fox tribes of the central plains states. Like the Shawnees, the Kickapoos were skilled farmers. They constructed longhouses and lived in fixed villages throughout the summer months, separating into smaller communities after the autumn harvest and communal buffalo hunts. They enjoyed a subsistence lifestyle with a diet consisting of beans, corn, and squash, supplemented by meat. Early Indian agents in the territory now known as Illinois reported the Kickapoos using horses for buffalo hunts before contact with western plains tribes had been made. Culturally, the Kickapoos trace their descent paternally, though with special responsibilities ascribed to maternal aunts and uncles in the upbringing of children.

In the early 1700s the Kickapoos, estimated to have numbered between 2,000 and 4,000 at the time, were pushed out of their aboriginal territory throughout the St. Lawrence River Valley into Wisconsin, and by the 1800s they were occupying southern Wisconsin and Illinois. They signed their first treaty with the United States government at Greenville, Ohio, in 1795. In 1809 and 1819 they ceded their lands in Illinois to the United States and relocated near the Osage River in Missouri. White encroachment on their Missouri lands caused them to petition the government for lands in Kansas in the 1830s, but these too were ceded to the United States for 768,000 acres in northeastern Kansas by 1832. Among these treaty signers were the famous Kickapoo prophet, Kennakuk, and Pa-sha-cha-hah (Jumping Fish).

In 1852, a number of Kickapoos moved to Mexico and have become known as the Mexican Kickapoos. On March 16, 1854, another 618,000 acres were ceded to the United States. In the Treaty of June 28, 1862, Kickapoo lands were allotted to 351 individuals, creating a checkerboard pattern to their lands. By 1873 many Kickapoos had returned to the United States, to Oklahoma and the Kansas Reservation; others remained in or near the Santa Rosa Mountains of eastern Chihuahua and western Coahuila. A reservation consisting of 100,000 acres was assigned to the Kickapoos who returned from Mexico in 1883, but in the interim, nearly all of the land located near McCloud, Oklahoma, had been absorbed by non-Indians.

GOVERNMENT

The tribe is organized under the Indian Reorganization Act of 1934, with a constitution and bylaws adopted in February 1937. The governing body consists of a seven-member tribal council with officers elected from its membership. The tribal chairperson acts as the tribe's administrative head. The chairperson, officers and at-large council members serve staggered two-year terms.

Tribal government operates the tribal employment rights office, founded in 2002, to assure Indian preference in hiring,

TRI-KS-043

TRI-KS-046

TRI-KS-048

TRI-KS-041

Kickapoo

training, and promotion, and to increase the skilled Indian workforce throughout the Kickapoo Reservation. This office strives to create jobs and training opportunities for its own members and Indians of other tribes, and to prevent discrimination against all Indian people.

ECONOMY

The Kickapoo economy is based largely upon the agricultural industry. Revenues are derived from leasing agricultural lands and from a tribal farming operation. Gaming and tribal government also provide employment opportunities, and they are important sources of revenue for the Kickapoos' future economic development plans.

Government as Employer. The tribal government employs 133 people via its departments and programs.

Agriculture and Livestock. A tribal farming operation raises crops such as wheat, corn, soybeans, and milo. The Kickapoos have devoted 3,051 acres to agriculture and another 1,936 acres for cattle grazing, and 221 acres are forested timberlands.

Gaming. The Kickapoo Tribe owns and operates the Golden Eagle Casino, which opened in May 1996, in Horton, Kansas. The 25,000-square-foot casino was expanded to 55,000 square feet in 1998. The facility houses slot machines, table games, a restaurant, and a 550-seat showroom. Revenue from the tribe's gaming industry is used for tribal government, education, health clinics and services, land purchase, bills and programs for tribal elders, youth organizations and programs, and general economic development.

Construction. The tribe owns the Kickapoo Construction Company. It employs eight people and provides construction services to customers on and off the reservation.

Services and Retail. Kickapoo Trading Post, located directly south of the Golden Eagle Casino, is home to a tribally owned gas station and convenience store. A tribally owned tire shop is nearby. Kickapoo Truck Plaza, located near the crossroads

of highways 75 and 20, opened in 1999, and it offers services to truckers such as showers, telephones, TV, and a laundromat. Kickapoo Truck Plaza also has a convenience store and 20 regular and diesel gasoline pumps.

Tourism and Recreation. The Annual Kickapoo Powwow takes place the third weekend in July. Fishing and camping are available at the nearby Delaware River.

INFRASTRUCTURE

Kansas State Highway 20 runs east-west across the southern portion of the reservation, and U.S. Highway 75 runs north-south, just one mile west of the western border of the reservation. The reservation lands are crisscrossed with county roads running in approximate one-square-mile increments. The nearest airport is located in Topeka, Kansas. The nearest bus service is in Hiawatha, Kansas. Federal Express and UPS offer one-day delivery.

Electricity. The Brown Achison Electric Company provides electricity.

Fuel. B&P supplies propane.

Water Supply. The Kickapoos have a tribally owned and operated water and sewer system.

Telecommunications. Sprint provides the tribe's telephone service. The Golden Eagle Casino has Internet service at the Sky Caster Internet café.

COMMUNITY FACILITIES AND SERVICES

The Kickapoos have a tribal administrative building, a community center, a senior center, and a Boys and Girls Club. The Kickapoo Powwow Grounds are tribally owned and have dancing grounds, bathrooms, an arbor, bleachers, and a covered barbeque area.

Education. Students attend the Kickapoo Nation School. The school teaches the Kickapoo language. The tribe maintains a Head Start program.

TRI-KS-043 Kickapoo Tribes Gaming Commission office

TRI-KS-046 Kickapoo Nation Health Center

TRI-KS-048 Kicakapoo Headstart Bus

TRI-KS-041 Kickapoo Truck Plaza

Kickapoo

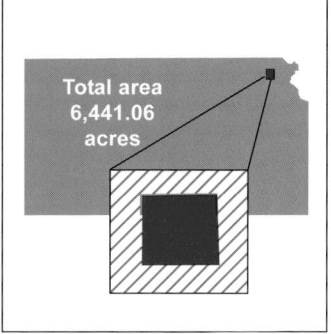

Total area
6,441.06
acres

Health Care. The Holton Health Center, located approximately 30 miles north of Topeka, serves four small reservations, including the Kickapoo. Originally built by the Sac and Fox Tribe of Missouri, the Iowa Tribe of Kansas and Nebraska, and the Prairie Band Potawatomi Tribe of Kansas, the facility is leased to the Public Health Service. The Kickapoo Clinic provides basic health care needs such as checkups, blood testing, and pharmaceuticals, as well as diabetic services and counseling. For services not provided by the clinics, tribal members can receive care at local facilities such as Horton Hospital, Stormont-Vail Healthcare, and St. Francis Hospital.

ENVIRONMENTAL CONCERNS
In the last several decades, one of the most significant issues to challenge the tribe has been the limited water supply available to the reservation. The tribe relies primarily on the Delaware River and its tributaries to support its water system, but severe drought conditions not uncommon to the region have greatly reduced the amount and quality of the water supply. The tribe has developed a plan to construct the Plum Creek Reservoir, a 400-acre water surface area and 1,200-acre land area, a multi-use reservoir that would meet the reservation's current and future needs. In 1994, the tribe entered into agreements with the Nemaha-Brown Watershed District and the Natural Resource Conservation Service (NRCS) to develop the Upper Delaware Watershed. However, despite these agreements, the project has been delayed by the district's and NRCS's refusal to address the tribe's eminent domain request necessary to acquire the nontribal lands involved. In the meantime, the reservation continues to suffer under the lack of a sufficient and suitable water supply. The tribe produced *Plum Creek: Water Is Life*, a film documenting the situation. The film was nominated for the Best Industrial Film at the American Indian Film Festival of 2004.

Other issues concerning the tribe include water quality management programs to address agricultural runoff, riverbank erosion, wetland drainage, and water use restrictions. The tribe cooperates with the Brown County Kansas Conservation District to build water diversion terraces and to replant grass along waterways. In 1996, tribal environmental staff identified the closure, cleanup, and monitoring of the solid waste landfill as another primary environmental problem. The Topeka shiner, a minnow, was declared an endangered species in 1999, placing water use restrictions on the tribe.

Prairie Band

Prairie Band Potawatomi Nation
Federal reservation
Potawatomi Tribe
Jackson County, Kansas

Prairie Band Potawatomi
Nation
16281 Q Road
Mayetta, KS 66509
785-966-4000
785-966-4035 Fax
pbpnation.org

LOCATION AND LAND STATUS
The Prairie Band of Potawatomi Indians Reservation is located in northeastern Kansas, about 20 miles north of Topeka and 80 miles northwest of Kansas City. The reservation was established by an Executive Order in 1864 after the band had migrated to the region from the southern Great Lakes area in 1847. By 1895, the Dawes Act of 1887 had forced nearly all of the tribal members to accept individual allotments. By the 1960s, only about 20 percent of the tribe's former 121-square-mile land base remained in Indian hands, with much of this remainder belonging to absentee Potawatomis who leased their allotments to non-Indians.

By the late 1970s, tribal land holdings totaled only 890 acres, or little more than one percent of the original reservation. Nevertheless, approximately 20 percent of the former reservation had been returned to Indian hands by 1977, though mostly in noncontiguous allotments. Moreover, the tribe has been working on expanding its land base, purchasing 1,500 acres of its former land in 1982, for instance. Today about 60 percent of the reservation area remains in non-Indian hands, with tribal lands arranged in a checkerboard pattern. The tribe has a goal of purchasing lands within and adjacent to the reservation for future development.

CLIMATE
Weather data has not been recorded for Mayetta, Kansas, the location of tribal headquarters. However, data exists for Topeka, Kansas, which lies only 20 miles south. The year-round average temperature in Topeka is 55°F, with highs averaging 65°F. Year-round daily low temperatures average 43°F. The area receives approximately 35 inches of precipitation annually, with 21 inches falling as snow. Dramatic prairie thundershowers, high winds, and tornados are common.

CULTURE AND HISTORY
The Prairie Band of Potawatomi has its roots in the southern Great Lakes region, where it is believed they first arrived in the 1400s along with people now known as Odawas and Ojibwas. Following first contact with white traders in 1641, they moved westward into what is now Wisconsin. A series of cession ancestors were forcibly removed from northern Indiana beginning in 1838. The forced emigration, which eventually brought them to Jackson County, Kansas, was dubbed the "Trail of Death" because so many Indians died along the way and were buried in unmarked graves by the roadside.

The tribe fiercely resisted the Dawes Act of 1887, which all but decimated the tribal land base. For the first part of the twentieth century, the Potawatomis subsisted on farming, hunting and trapping, wage labor, and leasing their lands, suffering greatly during the Great Depression and the accompanying drought of the 1930s. During this period, the tribal government acted as little more than an advisory council to the BIA superintendent, while also pursuing land claims against the U.S. government.

In August 1953, the tribe was singled out for termination; however, thanks to intense opposition by tribal leadership, in solidarity with the neighboring Kansas Kickapoos, the Kansas tribes escaped this fate. This successful resistance set a precedent for continuing tribal activism, which, by the early 1970s, saw many of the Prairie Band enmeshed in local and national Indian affairs such as the fight for state approval for hunting and fishing rights. In 1972, in response to the tribe's activism and increasing factionalism, the BIA suspended the band's constitution and placed it under its direct control. On February 19, 1976 the band was finally able to adopt a new constitution and seat a new tribal council.

Culturally, the Prairie Band remains rather traditional, with a significant proportion of the members fluent in their Native language and most members participating in either the Drum Religion or the Native American Church. The band created a language preservation department, with classes for young and old alike, in order to restore, revive, and preserve the Native language.

GOVERNMENT

The band rejected the 1934 Indian Reorganization Act. After defeating the government's attempt to terminate them, the membership ratified a modernized constitution in 1961. On February 19, 1976, the band adopted its new constitution and bylaws and established a new tribal council. This constitution was amended on August 28, 1985. The council is composed of seven members elected to staggered four-year terms. Officers include a chairperson and a vice-chairperson. The tribal council has three committees, three boards, and the Nation attorney's office as part of its governing body. Tribal council created a tribal administration to carry out its laws and policies. In 2004 it had five major departments: protective services, public works, special member services, administrative services and community services. These departments are

TRI-KS-032

headed up by an executive director, who also serves as a liaison between the council and the departments. In addition to these administrative offices, there are also a four-member gaming commission and the PBP Nation Enterprises that oversees the tribe's commercial enterprises.

The Prairie Band Potawatomi Tribal Police Department is a full-service law enforcement agency. Officers enforce tribal codes, citing Native American offenders to appear in tribal court; and as certified Kansas law enforcement officers, they cite non-Native offenders into the Kansas court system. Some tribal officers hold a federal commission as special deputy for the BIA, empowered to enforce federal codes including, the Title 18 Major Crimes Act and the Title 25 Crimes against Children, and Indian Family protection laws.

The tribal court is a general jurisdiction court of record that hears all tribal matters. It consists of an administrative judge, a judicial administrator, three appellate judges, one tribal district judge, a court clerk, and a deputy court clerk. The tribe's Law and Order Code consists of 24 titles that govern issues like crimes, motor vehicles, and family codes. Its jurisdiction extends to people and activities within the boundaries of the reservation.

Governmental departments include constitution, enrollment review, grievance, Head Start policy, natural resource, parent advisory, personnel policy, planning, Soldier Creek watershed partnership, interagency coordinating council, tribal emergency response, and tribal review. Tribal members serve on the Native American Tribal Gambling Commission and the joint committee on state-tribal relations.

ECONOMY

Economic opportunities have been increasing on the reservation, with casino revenues fueling an improving economy since the late 1980s.

Government as Employer. The tribal government, via its various economic initiatives and social services, is the largest source of employment on the reservation. The tribal government employed 359 people in 2004.

Economic Development Projects. The band completed a comprehensive economic development management plan listing measures by which they will gauge success and objectives by which they will reach both short-term, mid-range, and longer-range goals. Operating within this framework, the band seeks to develop resources that will lead to a higher standard of living, increased cultural vitality, and greater self-sufficiency for individual tribal members, families, entire communities, and business enterprises. Toward these ends, the Potawatomi Tribal Council mandated that 43 percent of all gaming revenues go toward economic development, with an emphasis on creating infrastructure that will facilitate further future growth and with an eye toward their impact on the larger society.

TRI-KS-024

Agriculture and Livestock. Tribal agricultural lands number approximately 2,500 acres of corn, beans, wheat, and hay. Significant acreage is leased to outside agricultural interests as pastureland, providing considerable annual revenues for individual members. The tribe also maintains a communally owned orchard.

A Buffalo Stocking Program began in 1981 with a donation of three buffalos from the Kickapoo Nation. By 1993, the Nation had joined the Inter-Tribal Bison Cooperative, and in 2004, the herd was comprised of 100 buffalo, with 8 -12 animals harvested annually for use in tribal celebrations.

Forestry. Reservation lands include a modest amount of timber, none of which is considered viable for commercial development.

Gaming. In 1997, the Nation entered into a gaming compact with the State of Kansas, and in 1998, it opened Harrah's Prairie Band Casino, a 63,000-square-foot entertainment complex, now the largest employer in Jackson County, Kansas, with annual payrolls of $23 million in 1998 and $23.5 in 1999. The facility features 970 slot machines, 30 table games, a 350-seat bingo hall, a restaurant, a lounge, a gift shop, and a hotel. The casino has created over 1,550 jobs and generated millions in revenue to fund tribal economic initiatives and social services.

A four-member casino management committee manages operations at the casino, including approval and monitoring of the annual operating budget, and preparation of the monthly financial reports to the tribal council.

The tribal bingo operation returned to full operation in its former location at 162 and Q Road next to the Tribal Governmental Center in January 2000. In August 2004, the Nation celebrated the opening of a steakhouse, the grand opening of an expansion of the 100-room motel to a three-story hotel with 298 rooms, a coffee shop and gift shop in the lobby, a 12,000-square-foot convention center and meeting space at the casino complex, and a state-of-the-art RV park with 75 fully paved spaces, with shower and laundromat facilities, picnic areas, and optional Internet and cable TV access.

Prairie Band

Total area *(BIA realty, 2003)*
22,694.45 acres

Tribally owned trust acreage
(Tribal source, 2004)
4,273 acres

Tribally owned not in trust
(Tribal source, 2004)
9,229 acres

Tribally owned
(BIA realty, 2003)
3,623.35 acres

Individually owned
(BIA realty, 2003)
19,072.10 acres

Population *2000 Census*
1,191

Tribal enrollment
(BIA labor report, 2001)
4,870

Tribal enrollment
(Tribal source, 2004)
4,857

Total labor force *2000 Census*
579

High school graduate or higher
2000 Census
89.2%

Bachelor's degree or higher
2000 Census
8.4%

Unemployment rate
2000 Census
4.3%

Per capita income
2000 Census
$15,372

TRI-KS-032 Harrah's Prairie Band Casino entrance

TRI-KS-024 Harrah's Prairie Band Casino

555

Prairie Band

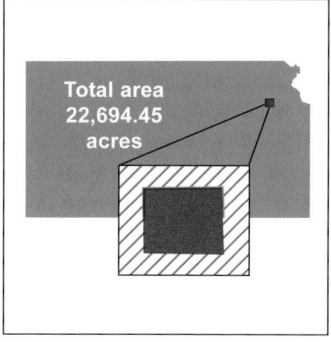

Total area
22,694.45
acres

Gaming has provided the financial stimulus for a host of development-related projects: ongoing land acquisition, construction of a government center (1999), a senior citizen building (2000), a fire station (2001), a police station (1998), and the remodeling of the bingo hall (2000). Since 2000, they have built a social services building, a convenience store and a craft shop, expanded the food distribution warehouse and the Boys and Girls Club facilities, made improvements to reservation churches, and opened a cultural interpretive site and museum. The band built housing units for the elderly, added on to the existing childcare center, constructed a wastewater treatment facility at the government center complex, and made other improvements to the water system. Between 2000 and 2003, they added tribal member housing units (six duplexes and two eight-unit apartment buildings), undertook a five-year road paving project, built a maintenance building (2002), a lands management building (2002), and renovated the powwow grounds. These initiatives created 1,300 new reservation jobs and permitted the expansion of tribal services.

Fisheries. Tribal lands include several small ponds that provide good recreational fishing.

Construction. Various construction industries are well represented on the reservation due to the economic development activities undertaken since 1996.

Mining. During the early 1970s, there was limited natural gas development on tribal lands, though that activity has been discontinued for the time being. The potential for renewed development remains possible.

Services and Retail. An 8,400-square-foot convenience store and gas station, called the Nation's Station, was opened near the casino on September 30, 1999. It sells fuel, cigarettes, food, snacks, and other merchandise. This enterprise employed 11 people in 2004. The Prairie Band Gift Shop, located within Harrah's Prairie Band Casino, features a variety of Native American handcrafted gift items, including beadwork, moccasins, jewelry, Pendleton blankets, and a selection of clothing. It employs seven people.

Tourism and Recreation. The tribal hunting preserve is quite popular among the region's hunters. Bingo is also a major attraction for outside visitors. Additionally, the band hosts a number of powwows and ceremonies each year, some of which are open to outsiders. In 2002, the Nation renovated the People's Park, which includes a new arbor, shelter houses with picnic tables, new lighting, more parking areas, and an expanded campground with more trees.

INFRASTRUCTURE
Major highways are U.S. Highway 75 (north-south), Interstate 70, and U.S. Highways 24 and 40. Commercial air service is available in Topeka (20 miles distant) and Kansas City (80 miles away). Commercial bus service is available in Topeka, and commercial truck lines, including UPS and Federal Express, serve the reservation directly. Commercial and freight rail lines are available in Kansas City. Seven new bridges have been constructed on the reservation. the road and bridge department is responsible for maintaining 118 miles of roads on tribal lands, 44 of them improved by blacktop or chip/seal.

Electricity. Electricity is provided through Kansas Power & Light, the Brown-Atchison Cooperative, and Kaw Valley Electric Company.

Fuel. Propane service is furnished through a local distributor.

Water Supply. Water service is provided via Jackson County's Rural Water Districts and privately owned wells. In June 2004, a new water storage tower was nearing completion. A newly constructed 60,000-gallon capacity wastewater treatment facility provides sewage treatment for all tribal buildings along K Road and a 30-unit housing subdivision.

Telecommunications. As of 2004, the tribe has dial-up Internet services via a tribally owned PBP Net, and Sprint's high-speed DSL services are available in some areas of the reservation. Mobile phone service is also offered through Sprint, with antennae placed on the PBPN communications tower providing a good coverage base for the surrounding areas. The Prairie Band Potawatomi Nation has published a bimonthly community newspaper, the *Prairie Band Potawatomi News*, since 1998 and now hosts their own web site at www.pbpindiantribe.com.

Housing. The tribal housing authority provides affordable housing via 35 low-rent units and 95 mutual-help homes. Renovation and rehabilitation of existing housing is permitted via the Native American Housing Assistance and Self-Determination Act of 1996. In June 2004, the tribe celebrated groundbreaking for Prairie Village Garden Apartments, a complex for senior citizens to be composed of three five-unit buildings, a community multipurpose room, and a whirlpool.

COMMUNITY FACILITIES AND SERVICES
Between 1999 and 2004, the Nation built: a new $1.5 million, 36,600-square-foot government center complete with office space and a conference room; a new tribal police station; a new childcare center; a new fire station that houses a new fire engine, tankers, trucks, and two ambulances. The tribe also built a $5.4 million health center and the 11,000-square-foot Fire Keeps Elder Center with a dining room capacity of 96 and all types of recreational amenities. The center opened in December 2000, and delivers meals to homebound seniors and provides transportation services for grocery shopping and other outings.

The Boys and Girls Club replaced the former youth program and their facility includes an indoor swimming pool, library, study rooms, language training, arts and crafts, a gymnasium, a kitchen, multipurpose rooms and a new computer lab, equipped with 12 computers .Wa Ta Se, American Legion Post 410, made up of 57 members of the tribe, is active in the community.

Education. The tribe runs Head Start and Early Intervention programs and older students attend the Mayetta and Hoyt public schools. There is also a college in Topeka attended by tribal members. The tribal education department operates projects funded by the Johnson O'Malley Act of 1934, adult education; adult vocational training; higher education scholarships; tribal education and training assistance; graduate student scholarships; and job skills. Some scholarship monies are also available to tribal members from Harrah's, the company contracted for casino management.

Health Care. In addition to a new health clinic to be built in March 2005, there is also a Potawatomi/Sac and Fox Health and Wellness clinic located in Holton, Kansas. The Health and Wellness Center is the only 638 contract the tribe has. The tribe operates a community health program, providing home visitation, blood pressure readings, and referrals to other health facilities and transportation to medical appointments. Ambulance services and emergency care, prevention education, home safety inspections, and blood pressure checks are provided by the tribal emergency services department. The Nation operates an alcohol and drug program including individual counseling, outreach programs, referrals, assessments and post-treatment guidance; and it also owns Parr Ranch, an assistance program for recovering alcoholics. Medical assistance is also provided by the Holton Health Center located approximately 30 miles north of Topeka. Full-service medical care is referred to hospitals in Topeka.

ENVIRONMENTAL CONCERNS

The tribe has its own department of planning and environmental protection to carry out community planning, provide environmental services, and protect the health of individuals, wildlife habitats, and natural resources from environmental threats. The department oversees the monitoring of water resources, oversees the restoration and conservation of tribal land, and conducts environmental educational opportunities for the entire tribal community. This department has been responsible for developing the land use plan that addresses community growth, a wetlands conservation plan, a watershed management plan, a pesticide management plan, a solid waste management plan, and the tribal zoning regulations. They conduct indoor air-quality testing, maintain a GIS database, oversee management of the orchard, and provide landscape planning assistance for facilities on the reservation.

Waste Management. The environmental department implemented a solid waste management program and developed a solid waste service and recycling program for the entire community, providing a composting service that supports wastewater needs and recycling as a way of generating revenues from across the United States.

Sac and Fox

Sac and Fox

LOCATION AND LAND STATUS

The Sac and Fox Reservation is located three miles south of the Nebraska/Kansas border, near the Missouri River, off U.S. Highway 73. Sac and Fox territory stretches across the border into Nebraska, with the western boundary adjoining the Iowa Nation of Kansas and Nebraska Reservation.

The reservation was established by treaty in 1861, originally containing nearly 8,000 acres in 131 allotments. The vast majority (close to 99 percent) of that land has been alienated from Indian ownership since that time, with the remaining Indian lands now checkerboarded throughout the region's non-Indian community.

CLIMATE

The year-round daily high temperature averages 63.5°F. Daily low temperatures average 40.2°F. The area receives just over 34 inches of precipitation annually.

CULTURE AND HISTORY

The Ne ma ha ha ki, or Sac and Fox Nation of Missouri in Kansas and Nebraska, is one of three bands of the Sac and Fox Nation. The other bands constitute the Meskwaki Sac and Fox Tribe of Mississippi in Iowa and the Sa ki wa ki Sac and Fox Nation of Oklahoma. Each band is a federally recognized sovereign nation with its own governing system, enrollment process, and land base. Ancestral lands of the Sac and Fox, also known as the Sauk and Fox, encompassed territories in Canada, Michigan, Wisconsin, Illinois, Iowa, Missouri, Kansas, and Nebraska. Osakiwug, or Sac ("people of the outlet" or "people of the yellow earth") and Meshkwakihug, or Fox ("red earth people") are culturally related to the Kickapoo and Potawatomi tribes and spoke an Algonquian-based language.

The Sac and Fox tribes lived in separate tribal communities, subsisting primarily on cultivated produce and wild rice, fish, and buffalo. The tribes developed an alliance during the 1700s when French attacks on the Fox people motivated the tribes to join forces The tribes migrated west to the Green Bay area of what is now Wisconsin. There they first encountered European settlers in about 1635 in the form of French trappers and traders. Feeling the pressure of encroachment by settlers, the tribes began moving south and west, fighting a war to preserve tribal lands throughout what are now the present-day states of Illinois, Wisconsin, and Iowa.

Between 1804 and 1810, bands of the Sac and Fox Tribe began to separate from one another. Bands comprising the Sac and Fox Tribe of Missouri settled near the Osage River. The federal government recognized them as a separate tribe in 1815. The Sac and Fox Tribe of Missouri continued to migrate across the state of Missouri between 1917 and 1824. Tribal members eventually settled in the Platte Purchase area in northwestern Missouri. The tribe remained there until 1837, when they were forced to relocate to the present-day reservation in southeastern Nebraska and northeastern Kansas.

By 1850, most of the tribe's Kansas land had been forcibly ceded as well, and the Sac and Fox Tribe moved down into Indian Territory (present-day Oklahoma). Eventually, a small band of tribe members returned to Iowa and Kansas, taking up land in severalty in 1889 and selling surplus territories to the U.S. government.

Remnants of the Sac and Fox traditional cultures may still be seen in their highly regarded beadwork, silverwork, and weaving. Although there are no Native speakers, language tapes are available at the Sac and Fox Nation of Missouri Tribal Museum.

GOVERNMENT

The Sac and Fox tribal government is administered by a five-member tribal council whose members are elected to staggered four-year terms by the general council. The general council consists of all enrolled tribal members over the age of 18. Elections are held every two years. The tribe adopted its constitution and bylaws on September 15, 1980, but its IRA charter had been ratified on June 13, 1937. The constitution was written and established under provisions of the 1934 Indian Reorganization Act.

The tribe has a PL-638 contract with the BIA under which key programs and services, such as education, a community health representative, and roads are administered. Tribal government programs include elderly assistance, school allowance, higher education, adult education, domestic violence, language, and burial assistance. A social worker conducts Indian Child Welfare Act investigations. In 2004, the tribal government added departments for environmental protection, tribal court, police, fire, housing, enrollment, and a museum. The tribe has a housing authority to assist residents with housing needs.

Sac and Fox Reservation
Federal reservation
Sac and Fox
Brown County, Kansas, and
Richardson County, Nebraska

Sac and Fox Tribe of Missouri
in Kansas and Nebraska
305 N. Main
Reserve, KS 66434
785-742-7471
785-742-3785 Fax

Total area *(BIA realty, 2003)*
549.01 acres

Total area *(Tribal source, 2004)*
12,000 acres

Tribally owned lands
(BIA realty, 2003)
486.84 acres

Tribally owned lands
(Tribal source, 2004)
550 acres

Individually owned
(BIA realty, 2003)
62.17 acres

Allotted lands
(Tribal source, 2004)
44.60 acres

Sac and Fox

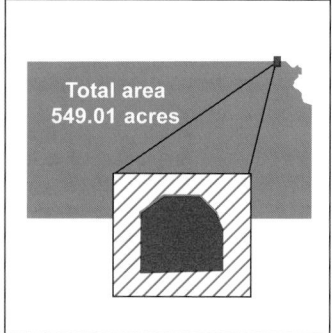

Total area
549.01 acres

Population *2000 census*
199

Tribal enrollment
(Tribal source, 2004)
440

Total labor force *2000 census*
107

**High school graduate or
higher** *2000 census*
87.1%

Bachelor's degree or higher
2000 census
8.1%

Unemployment rate *2000 census*
1.9%

Per capita income *2000 census*
$12,614

The Nation's Tribal Court System exercises jurisdiction over tribal land, tribal members, and individuals whose cause of action began on tribal lands. It deals with civil, criminal, juvenile, small claims, and traffic matters.

ECONOMY
Gaming revenues have largely replaced federal contracts and grants as the tribe's primary source of income, but the tribe's economy still depends on its tribal operations and its small retail businesses.

Government as Employer. Approximately 54 tribal members are employed in the various departments of the tribal government. In 2004, the Sac and Fox Casino employed 380 people.

Agriculture and Livestock. There are 1,446 acres of tribally affiliated lands under lease for farming activities. In 2003, the tribe established a buffalo herd with one bull and five cows.

Gaming. The Sac and Fox Casino is located in Powhattan, Kansas, along U.S. Highway 75 in northeast Kansas. The facility features 370 slot machines, roulette, craps, blackjack, and other table games. The complex has a gift shop that features handcrafted items from Native American artisans around the country. There is a full-service buffet and steak house on the premises, along with a snack deli. The casino hosts an Annual Pro Bull Riding event.

Located near the complex, an Event Center seats up to 500 people; there is also an RV park, a golf driving range, and a 24-hour convenience store and gas station.

Services and Retail. In addition to the services at the casino complex, the tribe owns and operates the Sac and Fox Tradin' Post, a combination smoke shop and gas station, a truck stop, and the Red Earth Cafe.

Media and Communications. The tribe publishes a quarterly newsletter called *Tribal Talk*, which features community news and services, upcoming events, and employment opportunities.

Tourism and Recreation. The Sac and Fox Nation of Missouri Tribal Museum, located along Highway 73 in Reserve, Kansas, was opened in April 1996. The museum houses tribal members' and other Native American regalia. In 2004, the museum began the development of a Veterans wall outside the museum, and a complementary wall inside the facility.

Tourists can also enjoy the tribally owned golf course and RV park, both located near the casino. The tribe hosts the Annual Sac and Fox Nation of Missouri Powwow. The powwow is held the last full week in August and is open to the public. Activities include competitive dancing and drumming, pageantry, and vending.

INFRASTRUCTURE
U.S. Highway 73 dissects the reservation, providing the primary road access from the outside. The nearest full-service airports are located in Kansas City and Topeka.

Electricity. West Star Energy, formerly known as Topeka Gas and Electric, provides electricity to individual residences.

Fuel. West Star Energy provides natural gas. Local distributors supply propane.

Water Supply. The rural water system furnishes water service and is supplemented by wells. Each resident has an individual septic tank for wastewater purposes.

A wastewater treatment facility serves portions of the reservation with two treatment lagoons. In 2004, the tribe initiated the use of wetlands near the treatment center as a tertiary wastewater treatment system. The process will further treat wastewater, relying on the natural processes of plant intake and sediment deposition to turn the waste into food for the plants.

Transportation. The closest regional air service is in St. Joseph, Missouri, approximately 40 miles away. Commercial bus service is available in Hiawatha, nine miles from the reservation. Commercial truck lines serve the reservation directly.

Telecommunications. Sprint and Giant Corporation supply telephone service. Cable, satellite, and direct TV services are available.

COMMUNITY FACILITIES AND SERVICES
The tribe has its own community center at its tribal offices in Reserve, Kansas. The center was purchased in the 1980s, and it was renovated with HUD funds. The Sac and Fox Tribe also has its own gymnasium and an event center located near the casino. The event center can be reserved for private functions and holds up 500 people.

The tribe offers a domestic violence services program. Services include victim's assistance, community resources, and support groups.

Education. Tribal members of school age attend area public schools approximately 10 miles from the reservation.

Health Care. Tribal members' health care needs are served by the Holton Health Center, located approximately 30 miles north of Topeka. The Sac and Fox Tribe of Missouri, the Iowa Tribe of Kansas and Nebraska, and the Prairie Band Potawatomi Tribe of Kansas built the original clinic. These tribes now lease the clinic to the Public Health Service. The Sac and Fox, the Potawatomis, and two other tribes share the facility.

The Kanza Mental Health Center, in Hiawatha, Kansas, serves tribal members with mental health and substance abuse issues at four area locations. Tribal members also have access to a community health representative who can provide basic services, such as blood pressure screenings, and transportation to the health clinic. The tribal government offers assistance with eyeglasses, dental care, and hearing aids.

The tribal health program hosts an Annual Health Fair, offering vendors, a blood drive, and on-site medical services.

ENVIRONMENTAL CONCERNS
Three of the tribe's major environmental concerns are the use of pesticides and herbicides, trains transporting hazardous waste through the area that pose the threat of chemical spills, and issues regarding waste and recycling. To address the tribe's concerns about waste and recycling, the environmental protection department has developed a solid waste and recycling program that educates community members about the problems regarding waste and the methods and benefits of recycling.

The tribe also celebrates the Sac and Fox Nation of Missouri Earth Day in April. The day includes activities and events geared toward environmental and cultural awareness. The day also serves to provide reservation residents the opportunity to have solid waste items picked up at their homes.

Chitimacha

LOCATION AND LAND STATUS

The Chitimacha Reservation is located in south central Louisiana, near the town of Charenton southeast of Lafayette. In 1767, the Spanish granted land to the Chitimachas.

In 1855 a large tract of land in the vicinity of Charenton was patented to the "Chettimachas Nation or Tribe of Indians" by the federal government. From time to time, land was sold to cover debts, so that by 1914, there were just 261.54 acres left in tribal control. In 1914, a private investor purchased the last tribal lands at a sheriff's auction. This title was later sold to the federal government, who placed the land in trust status for the tribe. Though vastly diminished in size, the present-day reservation occupies areas that were once part of the Chitimachas' ancestral lands. They are one of the few tribes in the nation that still maintain ownership of traditional land bases.

During the 1970s, the tribe filed a series of land claims to the rich Atchafalaya wetlands. These claims were dismissed by the courts.

CULTURE AND HISTORY

The Chitimacha Tribe originated in territories that lie within the contemporary geographical markers of: Maringouin, Louisiana in the north; regions southeast of New Orleans, to the mouth of the Mississippi River; and near Gueydon, Louisiana in the west. The Chitimacha Tribe was comprised of four bands-the Chitimacha, Yagenechito (eastern Chitimacha), Chawasha, and Washa. Tribal members established many villages, fifteen of which were recorded as permanent villages by European cartographers. Archeological evidence dating to 6,000 years before the present has been unearthed in the ancestral lands, and oral history indicates that the tribe has "always been here."

The French and their allies regularly forced Chitimacha tribal members into slavery during their domination in Louisiana. Women in particular were sought after to supply troops with female "companionship." In the early 1700s, the Chitimachas revolted against the slave trade and killed French missionary Jean Francois Buisson de St. Cosme and two other Frenchmen. The French government ordered immediate action against the Chitimachas and enlisted the assistance of other tribes in the area. Traditional enemies such as the Acolapissas, Bayougoulas, Biloxis, Choctaws, Houmas, Natchitoches, Pascagoulas, Taensas, and even traditional allies such as the Chawashas, joined the French in leading a campaign against the Chitimachas. The war lasted for 12 years, and the Chitimachas were eventually defeated. The tribe suffered the deaths of numerous warriors and lost many women and children to slavery.

In 1718, the Chitimachas signed a treaty with the French agreeing to reside on lands designated for them along the Mississippi River near the entrance to Bayou Lafourche. In the meantime, the Chawasha and Washa bands were suffering devastating losses. No longer allies to the French, by the mid 1700s the Chawashas were targeted for destruction. Following an attack by French-African slaves, the remaining Chawashas joined forces with the Washas. The bands lived in a single village on the west bank of the Mississippi River above New Orleans. The last reports of the village were recorded in 1758. It is believed that remaining individuals were absorbed into the Chitimacha Tribe.

When the Spanish regained control of the territory in the 1750s, it renewed its recognition of the Chitimacha Tribe and issued another land grant. The Mississippi Band continued to reside along the river in the villages of Bayou Lafourche and Point Coupee. The Spanish government relocated the groups to a single village near Plaquemine.

As Euro-American presence in the territory increased in the late 1700s, members of the Chitimachas at Bayou Teche began to intermarry with Acadians. Many tribal members converted to Christianity, and in time the indigenous spirituality and many cultural traditions were lost. The language was replaced by Cajun French. During this time, the Chitimacha Tribe retained ownership of their tribal lands. However, they were forced to sell portions over the years.

The Spanish sold Louisiana back to France in 1800, and France proceeded to sell it to the United States in 1803. Government surveys found two villages of Chitimachas intact, with a combined population of 100. The government was certain that the tribe was near extinction and did not want to enter into a treaty agreement. However, in the 1830s the Chitimachas filed for recognition of their Spanish land grant and title to the lands. The government established a reservation for the tribe on 1,062 acres of land that remained from the grant, but it continued to refuse to sign a treaty.

The U.S. Census of 1900 indicates that only six Chitimacha families, for a total of 55 people, were living on reservation lands at Grand Lake. Only three of those individuals met the criteria for full-blood status. As with the population, the tribe's land base continued to decrease. In June 1905, 300 acres on the south side of Bayou Teche were adjudicated to the sate of Louisiana for payment of back taxes. A 1913 letter indicates that a lawsuit divided what remained of the reservation into 4/9ths and 5/9ths, leaving the tribe with 261.54 acres of land in their possession.

Chitimacha Reservation
Federal reservation
Chitimacha
Saint Mary Parish, Louisiana

Chitimacha Tribe of Louisiana
P.O. Box 661
Charenton, LA 70523
337-923-4973
337-923-6848 Fax
chitimacha.com

Total area *(BIA realty, 2005)*
445 acres

Federal trust lands
(BIA realty, 2005)
445 acres

Tribal enrollment
(BIA labor report, 2001)
1,070

Total labor force *2000 census*
200

Total labor force
(BIA labor report, 2001)
165

High school graduate or higher
2000 census
61.9%

Bachelor's degree or higher
2000 census
5.7%

Unemployment rate
2000 census
4%

Unemployment rate
(BIA labor report, 2001)
11%

Per capita income *2000 census*
$19,126

Chitimacha

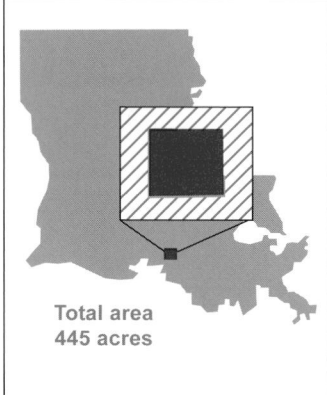

**Total area
445 acres**

In 1914, Sarah Avery McIlhenney, a private investor and friend of the women of the Chitimacha Tribe, purchased the remaining tribal lands at a sheriff's auction. She then sold the lands to the federal government, and the land was placed in trust for the tribe.

In 1916, the Chitimacha Tribe became the first Louisiana tribe to receive formal federal recognition. The tribal government organized under the provisions of the Indian Reorganization Act of 1934, but it was targeted for termination in the 1950s. The tribe was able to retain its status, and its constitution and bylaws were approved in 1971.

GOVERNMENT

The Chitimacha constitution and bylaws have been in place since January of 1971. The tribe is governed by a council comprised of a chairman, vice-chairman, secretary, and two other members, all elected to two-year terms. Over the years, the tribal government has been largely concerned with providing services to tribal members and preserving culture and maintaining tribal sovereignty.

BUSINESS CORPORATION

The tribe established the Chitimacha Development Corporation, an enterprise responsible for matters of economic development.

ECONOMY

Tribal economy is sustained by the tribe's enterprises in the agricultural, fishing, and gaming industries.

Government as Employer. In addition to the number of people employed by the casino, the tribe currently employs a total of 80 people in its various departments and operations.

Economic Development Projects. The tribe is in the process of expanding its casino facilities. Expansions will include a hotel, an RV park, and additional gaming venues.

Gaming. The tribe owns the Cypress Bayou Casino in Charenton, Louisiana. The casino is a class III facility that features 1,200 slots and numerous table games. The casino includes a nonsmoking game area, three eateries, and a lounge. The casino employs 850 individuals.

The Chitimacha Tribe is in the process of expanding the casino. Expanded facilities will include an entertainment venue (night club), off track betting, poker, a coffee shop, and two restaurants.

Construction. A construction company owned and operated by a tribal member maintains various types of heavy equipment for use on construction projects.

Mining. The tribe leases a small portion of land for oil mining. During the oil boom years prior to 1980, most tribal members found work in the offshore oilfields as laborers, drillers, and foremen. This remains the case today as the domestic oil industry stabilizes somewhat.

Real Estate/Commercial Development. The tribe recently began construction of Raintree Village, a master planned residential community on 500 acres in the bayou country of Louisiana. In 2003 the first phase of homes was completed. The community, once complete, will include 1,300 home sites, apartments, parks, and a community shopping mall. The project was developed in partnership with the State of Louisiana, St. Mary Parish, and the City of Baldwin and is not located on trust lands.

Services and Retail. In addition to the gaming complex and affiliated facilities, tribally affiliated businesses include a gas station, a convenience store, a recreation/fitness complex, and a museum with a gift shop.

Tourism and Recreation. The reservation is near lakes and bayous with fishing and boating opportunities and boat launch facilities, archeological sites, hunting, and a number of cultural events. The tribe also maintains the Chitimacha Museum and a gift shop that sells handcrafted tribal items.

INFRASTRUCTURE

Road access is provided by U.S. Highway 90, which runs east-west three miles from the reservation, and State Highway 182, about two miles from the reservation. These two roadways are connected to the reservation by the Ralph Darden Memorial Parkway.

Electricity. Central Louisiana Electric Company provides electricity.

Fuel. Natural gas service is available from Atmos Energy.

Water Supply. The Charenton municipal system furnishes water. A tribal system provides sewer service, presently serving 130 residences.

Transportation. Commercial air service is available in Lafayette (about 45 miles away), Baton Rouge, and New Orleans. Commercial bus lines also serve Lafayette. Southern Pacific Railroad serves the area directly, though there is no spur on the reservation. Commercial truck lines serve the reservation directly. As for water transport, the reservation is located on Bayou Teche, eight miles from the Gulf of Mexico, near the Port of West St. Mary.

COMMUNITY FACILITIES AND SERVICES

The tribe recently completed construction of a health clinic, Yamahana-an early learning facility (daycare), a sports complex, and an elderly assisted living facility called River Cane. Recreation facilities include a swimming pool.

Education. The Chitimacha Day School, a school for K-8 students, is located on the reservation. It is the only Indian school in the state. Middle school and high school students attend local public and private schools, or attend Indian boarding schools.

Health Care. Health care is partially funded through federal grants at the Chitimacha Health Clinic, which provide for a nurse and an ambulance. A general practitioner, nurses, dialysis, pharmacy, x-ray, and dental services are available. Hospitals and clinics are also located in nearby Franklin.

Total area *(Tribal source, 2004)*	683 acres
Federal trust *(BIA realty, 2005)*	684 acres
Federal trust lands	683 acres
(Tribal source, 2004)	
Fee lands	2,898 acres
(Tribal source, 2004)	
Population *(Tribal source, 2004)*	462
Tribal enrollment *(BIA labor report, 2001)*	835
Total labor force *2000 census*	7
Total labor force *(BIA labor report, 2001)*	237
High school graduate or higher	0%
2000 census	
Bachelor's degree or higher *2000 census*	0%
Unemployment rate *2000 census*	0%
Unemployment rate	15%
(BIA labor report, 2001)	
Per capita income *2000 census*	$16,828

LOCATION AND LAND STATUS

The Coushatta Reservation is located three miles north of Elton, Louisiana. In 1975, the federal government established a 15-acre reservation for the tribe. In 1980, by another federal proclamation, 160 acres were set aside for the Coushattas. In 1992, the tribe purchased an additional 80 acres.

The federal government first placed Coushatta tribal land in trust in 1898. The BIA held 160 acres of land in trust for the tribe. When recognition was terminated in 1953, the lands were removed from trust status.

CULTURE AND HISTORY

The Coushatta Tribe is descended from the Muskogean tribes that once resided in the southeastern United States. The tribe once belonged to the Creek Confederacy and lived a somewhat stationary lifestyle in the Tennessee River country of Alabama. The people relied upon local agriculture, hunting, fishing, and trade to sustain their economy.

The Coushatta Tribe encountered Spanish explorers in 1540. The tribe maintained a civil coexistence with the Euro-American settlers until the United States government began to initiate its policies to remove Native Americans from their homelands. In 1783, the Coushatta Tribe lost over 800 square miles of land to the State of Georgia. The loss set in motion a series of conflicts and treaties that eventually drove the Coushattas out of their ancestral lands. Tribal members were dispersed across the southeastern United States into Georgia, Alabama, Mississippi, Louisiana, and even Texas.

Remaining members of the Coushatta Tribe participated in the Creek War of 1813. Over 3,000 Native Americans were killed during this conflict, and 22 million acres of ancestral lands were ceded to the federal government. Bands of the Coushatta Tribe moved south out of the Alabama and Georgia regions to settle in the lower reaches of the Red River in Louisiana. By 1861, approximately 250 tribal peoples had settled near Kinder. Continued Euro-American encroachment pushed the Coushattas east of the Calcasieu River. The tribe purchased a parcel of land there and established a community.

In 1898, the United States placed 160 acres of land in trust for the Coushattas, and the BIA provided funding to educate tribal youth. However, in 1953, the tribe was targeted for termination. The BIA discontinued holding the Coushatta lands in trust status and discontinued providing services to tribal members. In the eyes of the federal government, the Coushatta Tribe no longer existed.

In 1956, the tribe established the Coushatta Indians of Allen Parish. The organization was to serve primarily as a business enterprise that would manage the sale and production of tribal arts and crafts. The corporation served as a means for tribal members to organize as a unit and begin the process of regaining federal recognition. When the tribe received Louisiana state recognition in 1972, it formed the Coushatta Alliance and drafted a constitution and bylaws while pursuing federal assistance and federal recognition. The Coushatta Tribe received federal recognition in 1973.

Tribal members continue to practice traditional cultural and spiritual ways. The dialect of the Muskogee parent language spoken by the Coushatta Tribe is considered unique as it has remained virtually unchanged over the course of several hundred years.

GOVERNMENT

The tribe received federal recognition in 1973 under provisions of the Indian Reorganization Act of 1934. It is governed by a popularly elected tribal chairperson and a five-member tribal council. The tribe maintains programs such as health, education, social services, and administration. The tribe also maintains its own judicial system.

ECONOMY

In the early and mid-1900s, the Coushatta economy relied heavily upon the production and sale of arts and crafts items to tourists. Farming enterprises have also contributed to the economy, but the largest source of revenue for the tribe has become the gaming facilities it owns and operates. The tribe's expansion efforts into the gaming industry have generated income that is used to promote social services and support the general needs of the reservation population.

Economic Development Projects. The tribe is in the process of developing a cattle-raising enterprise. The Coushatta Tribe operates Coushatta Millworks. This plant offers all-architectural mill works, and produces cabinetry for residential and commercial use.

Agriculture and Livestock. The tribe utilizes a large portion of its land base for rice farming and cattle grazing.

Gaming. The Coushatta Tribe owns and operates the Grand Casino Coushatta in Kinder, Louisiana. Casino facilities include 3,200 slot machines and 80 table games. On-site guest services include a video arcade, a childcare center, a gift shop, an indoor play area, and nonsmoking gaming areas. There are also a number of lounges and entertainment venues. The casino employs 3,000 individuals. Three hotels and six restaurants are associated with the casino complex. The Coushatta Grand Hotel is adjacent to the casino and features 223 guest rooms. Facilities include several conference rooms, a fitness center, and an indoor pool. The Grand Casino Coushatta Luxury RV Resort is also adjacent to the casino. It includes 156 hookup sites, 50 cottage accommodations, a basketball court, a convenience store, laundry facilities, a guest lounge, a playground pool, tennis courts, volleyball courts, horseshoe pits, and shuffleboard courts.

Coushatta Reservation
Federal reservation
Coushatta
Allen Parish, Louisiana

Coushatta Tribe of Louisiana
P.O. Box 818
Elton, LA 70532
337-584-2261
337-584-2998 Fax
coushattatribela.org

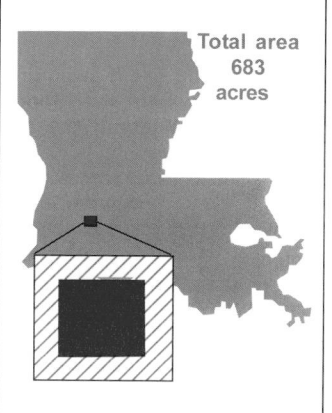

Total area
683
acres

Jena Band

Jena Band of Choctaw Reservation
Federal reservation
Choctaw
LaSalle and Grant parishes, Louisiana

Jena Band of Choctaw
P.O. Box 14
Jena, LA 71342
318-992-2717
318-992-8244 Fax
jenachoctaw.org

Federal trust *(BIA realty, 2005)*
62.63 acres

Population *2000 census*
59,992

Tribal enrollment
(BIA labor report, 2001)
250

Total labor force
2000 census
26,115

Total labor force
(BIA labor report, 2001)
69

High school graduate or higher
2000 census
74.7%

Bachelor's degree or higher
2000 census
14.8%

Unemployment rate
2000 census
3.7%

Unemployment rate
(BIA labor report, 2001)
36%

Per capita income *2000 census*
$15,727

LOCATION AND LAND STATUS

The Jena Band of Choctaw has one small tract of federal trust land, approximately 60 acres, located in Grant Parish. The members of the Jena Band of Choctaw are located in separate communities scattered throughout north-central Louisiana, centered largely in the town of Jena, Louisiana. According to the Office of Federal Acknowledgement, U.S. Department of the Interior, 53 percent of all enrolled tribal members live within 20 miles of the community; 72 percent live within 30 miles.

CLIMATE

There is no climate information recorded for Jena, Louisiana; however, there is data for Alexandria, Louisiana, approximately 30 miles distant. The year-round average daily high temperature at Alexandria is 77°F, with the highest on record as 105°F. The year-round average daily low temperature is 56°F, with the lowest ever recorded temperature being 10°F. The area receives approximately 52 inches of precipitation annually, with only 1 inch falling as snow.

CULTURE AND HISTORY

The ancestors of modern Choctaws have lived in the southeastern part of the North American continent since prehistory. The aboriginal territory of the Jena Band extended from the east-central region of what is now the state of Mississippi in the east, to the Mississippi River, and slightly beyond, to the west. Prior to the American Revolution and the Louisiana Purchase in 1803, the British, French, and Spanish governments colonized the area. The band was beset by conflicts with white settlers, diseases, and war with other tribes.

A treaty of peace between the new United States and the Choctaws was first entered into at Hopewell, South Carolina, in 1786, wherein the fledging U.S. government promised them protection. Following the Treaty of Doak's Stand in 1820, wherein the Choctaws ceded 5.2 million acres of land in Mississippi in exchange for 13 million acres in what is now southern Oklahoma, the United States government sought to remove the Choctaws of Louisiana to more western territories. In 1830 Congress passed the Indian Removal Act. The Mississippi state legislature followed suit by passing a series of laws abolishing tribal governments within their state. Some Choctaws migrated west on their own, but many more, approximately 5,000, were forcibly removed between 1831 and 1834, and again from 1844 to 1847. Many actively resisted removal. In an 1856 census of Choctaws living east of the Mississippi, there were 2,068 remaining. While there is no recorded evidence of Choctaws settling near Jena during the removals, there is much evidence to suggest that there were well-known trails in the area of Catahoula Parish near Trout Creek that had been well-traversed by many bands of Choctaws. Principal settlements were established on Trout Creek in LaSalle Parish and Bear Creek in Grant Parish.

The first recorded evidence of a settlement at Jena is found in the 1880 Federal Census which listed four families living there. There were a total of 34 Indians recorded in Catahoula Parish in the 1890 census. These families contributed to Jena's economy, trading skins and cured hides in exchange for goods at the local dry goods market. Some worked as day laborers on farms or lumber mills or as household help to white families in the area. The Penick Indian School, which operated between 1932 and 1938, served Indian school children. Fol-lowing World War II, school children began attending local public schools, where they experienced discrimination and alienation from white students. After incorporation in 1974, the band built a tribal center, completed in 1977, which housed various tribal social service programs, community activities, and language and cultural education classes. In 2004 only a few Native speakers remained; consequently, emphasis is placed on teaching and maintaining a strong sense of Indian identity and reintroducing the language to daily use. The center also houses tribal art and artifacts and has a full-service kitchen; and there are basketball and tennis courts and BBQ facilities located on the grounds outside the facility.

The band's petition for federal recognition was granted in May 1995 and was celebrated with a signing ceremony. The recognition became official on August 29, 1995.

GOVERNMENT

The Jena Band of Choctaw Indians of Louisiana was incorporated as a state-recognized tribe on April 20, 1974, with a five-member board of trustees. Trustees serve three-year terms. The tribal constitution was adopted December 20, 1990, changing the structure of the governing body to a four-member tribal council, each serving four-year terms. The tribal council makes the following departments or offices, programs or services available to all tribal members: health, social service, environment, transportation, education, activities, and housing. The band's housing department oversees construction of housing for low-income tribal members, provides inspections and maintenance, and furnishes sewage services for those homes.

The Jena Band is a member of the Louisiana Intertribal Council which has an office in Baton Rouge. The intertribal council serves as headquarters for programs and activities to assist the member tribes.

ECONOMY

As a former "landless tribe," the Jena Band has no economy of their own. Historically, as members left agricultural work, they migrated to areas where wage labor jobs could be obtained. Some members stayed near Jena and worked as day laborers in lumber mills or as household help.

In 2004 the band was seeking a compact with the State of Louisiana in order to build a casino on a small tract of tribally owned land located in Grant Parish. Many members work either for the tribe, for the state government, or for gas and oil companies located offshore.

Gaming. The tribe has wanted to open a casino on federal trust land in Grant Parish near the Alabama state line; however, in 2004 the governor of Louisiana had not yet approved the class III gaming compact.

Tourism and Recreation. The band has an activities department to plan and organize special events for tribal members, such as the annual Princess Pageant, Christmas parties, the Thanksgiving Celebration, and Valentine banquets.

The Jena Band Reservation is within 25 miles of the Kisatchie National Forest and the Catahoula National Wildlife Refuge and Catahoula Lake.

INFRASTRUCTURE

Transportation. The band's department of transportation was established through the Bureau of Indian Affair's Eastern Regional Office to provide the network of transportation and infrastructure needed to establish self-sufficiency for the tribe and all tribal members.

COMMUNITY FACILITIES AND SERVICES

The White Rock Indian Cemetery in Jena serves as an education and cultural community resource for the band. The tribe maintains it as an ongoing educational project of the history classes taught at the center.There is an activities gym used for tribal meetings, the annual Princess Pageant, after-school tutoring, basketball, volleyball, meetings, and other social activities. The cemetery is a focal point for community social events.

Education. Choctaw language and history classes are offered to tribal members at the center. The tribal council participates with the LaSalle Parish School District to make GED classes available to all members.

ENVIRONMENTAL CONCERNS

The band has an environmental department funded by a U.S. Environmental Protection Agency General Assistance Program grant, to protect and monitor environmental issues concerning all tribal lands and resources. It was established in November of 2000. Programs currently under development include: educational outreach and protection, environmental reviews and assessments, emergency response, recycling, GIS/GPS, wastewater, and water and air quality. Potential programs for the future include: lead-based paint, radon testing, endangered species and wetland protection. In addition to these programs, the band operates an American Red Cross Shelter, to be open only in disasters declared by the Red Cross, the first of its kind in LaSalle Parish.

Jena Band

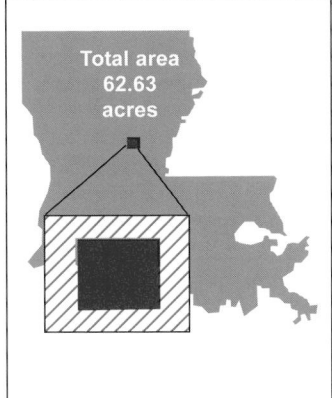

Total area
62.63
acres

Tunica-Biloxi

LOCATION AND LAND STATUS

The Tunica-Biloxi Reservation is located in east-central Louisiana near the town of Marksville. The reservation lies 25 miles west of the Mississippi River. The present-day reservation occupies a land base that has served as tribal lands since given to the Tunica Tribe in the 1780s by Spanish colonist Bernardo de Galvez.

CULTURE AND HISTORY

The Tunica-Biloxi Reservation is home to descendants of the Tunica and the Biloxi tribes. Although they speak unrelated languages, both these groups are descendants of the ancient Mound People of the area. The tribes have lived on the reservation for the past two centuries, during which time they became unified by intermarriages.

The Tunica Tribe originated in northern Mississippi and exercised great influence over vast amounts of territory across present-day Arkansas, Oklahoma, Missouri, Tennessee, Louisiana, Alabama, and Florida, from their central settlement of Quizquiz. The Tunicas encountered Spanish explorers in 1541, and the ensuing threat of diseases, famine, and warfare forced the tribe to begin a migration southward along the Mississippi River.

The Biloxi Tribe originated along the Mississippi Gulf Coast near present-day Biloxi, Mississippi. They encountered French explorers in 1669.

Spanish colonizers gave the land encompassing the present-day Tunica-Biloxi Reservation to the Tunica Tribe. The Tunica and Biloxi tribes resided together on the lands, and they united for political reasons during the 1920s.

The tribe was incorporated in 1976 and received state recognition the same year. The U.S. government did not grant federal recognition until 1981.Since the 1960s, the tribe has been particularly active in local and national politics, often forming political coalitions with other Louisiana indigenous groups to further their shared agenda. Tribal members strive to achieve financial sovereignty, while at the same time retaining and nourishing their traditional culture and values.

GOVERNMENT

The Tunica-Biloxi government is led by a seven-member elected tribal council. Council members include a chairperson, a vice-chairperson, a secretary-treasurer, and four members-at-large.

The tribe has a number of departments to serve the needs of its members. Departments and programs include the housing authority, historic preservation, health services, social services, environmental protection, geographic information systems, surveying, health and sanitation, water quality, natural resources, grants administration, and information systems. The tribe maintains its own judicial system with a tribal court and tribal police. Tribal courts exercise jurisdiction over civil and criminal matters.

ECONOMY

The expansion of tribal enterprises into the gaming industry has bolstered the tribe's economy a great deal and enabled the tribe to provide more, and improved, services and facilities to tribal members. The Tunica-Biloxi Tribe provides a major source of employment for residents of central Louisiana. The majority of its employees are non-tribal residents of Avoyelles and nearby parishes.

Government as Employer. The tribe is one of the largest employers in the region with 1,600 employees serving throughout its government departments and enterprises.

Economic Development Projects. The tribe's recently opened gaming venue represents its current economic development ventures. The Tunica-Biloxi Tribe abides by its motto "Cherishing Our Past, Building for Our Future." It aims to create opportunities that will enhance the lives of tribal members as well as members of the surrounding communities. The tribe has created a donations program to benefit nonprofit groups, scholarship programs, and local programs and activities. It is dedicated to serving the community, promoting economic stimulus, and heightening cultural exchanges.

Gaming. The tribe established the Tunica-Biloxi Tribal Gaming Commission under Tribal Resolution #09-94B. The com-

Tunica-Biloxi Reservation
Federal reservation
Tunica and Biloxi
Avoyelles Parish, Louisiana

Tunica-Biloxi Tribe
P.O. Box 1589
Marksville, LA 71351
 318-253-9767
 318-253-9791 Fax
tunica.org

Total area *(Tribal source, 2004)*
1,462 acres

Federal trust lands
(BIA realty, 2005)
725.61 acres

Tribal enrollment
(BIA labor report, 2001)
920

Total labor force *2000 census*
50

Total labor force
(BIA labor report, 2001)
138

High school graduate or higher
2000 census
51%

Bachelor's degree or higher
2000 census
8.2%

Tunica-Biloxi

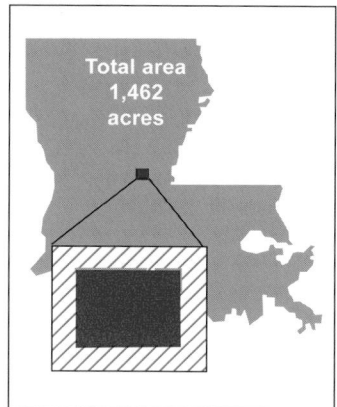

Total area
1,462
acres

Unemployment rate
2000 census
14%

Unemployment rate
(BIA labor report, 2001)
0%

Per capita income *2000 census*
$14, 230

mission is in charge of regulating the conduct of all class III gaming activities conducted on tribal lands.

The Tunica-Biloxi Tribe owns and operates the Paragon Casino Resort in Marksville.Casino facilities include 2,100 slot machines/VLTs, 46 gaming tables, and 11 poker tables. The adjacent hotel offers 335 guest rooms, 5 restaurants, and 2 entertainment venues. Employing 1,800 people, the casino represents the largest private employer in Avoyelles Parish.

The Paragon Casino Resort Hotel, adjacent to the casino, offers hotel accommodations, cabins, and RV facilities. Guests opting to stay in an outdoor cabin can choose between one- and two-bedroom cabins. The RV Resort includes 166 hookup sites, a guest lodge, a swimming pool, laundry and bath facilities, and recreational activities.

Services and Retail. The tribe owns and operates four franchises of the Burger King fast food chain.

Tourism and Recreation. The tribe owns and operates the Tamahka Trails golf course. Amenities include an 18-hole golf course, a full-service pro shop, a full-service clubhouse, practice facilities, and lessons. The golf course is also a member of the Louisiana Audubon Trail. The tribe will begin construction of a cultural and educational resources center on the reservation in 2005. The center will be located on the grounds of the former tribal museum. It will occupy 40,000 square feet and will include a museum, a gift shop, a conservation and restoration laboratory, a library, a traveling exhibit gallery, an auditorium, educational classrooms, and office space. The tribe hosts a powwow in the spring that is open to the public.

INFRASTRUCTURE
Louisiana Highway 1 crosses the reservation property and continues northeast to the city of Alexandria. Interstate 49 runs north-south 20 miles south of the reservation.

Electricity. Louisiana Power and Light and the Central Louisiana Electric Company provide electricity.

Water Supply. A tribal water tower provides 750,000 gallons of water to numerous entities on the reservation. The town of Marksville also provides water and sewerage facilities. The tribe has initiated the development of a three-cell oxidation pond on lands it purchased. The nearby City of Marksville will utilize the ponds in order to provide sewer services to residents of the Tunic-Biloxi Reservation. Additionally, the tribe provided funding, labor, material, and rights of way for the installation of a sewer force main between the oxidation pond and the tribal casino.

Transportation. Commercial air service is available in Alexandria, Baton Rouge, and Lafayette. Shipping and trucking service is available in the adjacent city of Marksville, a quarter of a mile from the reservation. Bus service is available in Alexandria. UPS and Federal Express serve the reservation directly; railway freight lines are about 10 miles away.

COMMUNITY FACILITIES AND SERVICES
The reservation has many community buildings, including the tribal center administration headquarters, and the Tunica-Biloxi Regional Indian Center and Museum. The reservation also provides a recreational area for its children.

The tribe has been recognized for its basketry and has implemented an apprenticeship program to guarantee the continuance of this art.

Education. Tribal youth may attend public schools located in Marksville.

Health Care. Health care and social services are provided through a contract with the Indian Health Services. Hospital services are available in Marksville.

MAINE

INTRODUCTION

PASSAMAQUODDY TRIBE OF MAINE

LOCATION AND LAND STATUS

The Passamaquoddy Tribe occupies two reservations in northeastern Maine. The Indian Township and Pleasant Point reservations are situated about 50 miles apart near the Eastern Seaboard. Under provisions of the Maine Indian Claims Settlement Act of 1980, the tribe owns eight widely scattered parcels of land throughout the state, totaling 108,900 acres.

CULTURE AND HISTORY

The Passamaquoddy Tribe has lived in the northeastern United States for several thousand years. They are an Eastern Woodlands tribe and are closely related to the Penobscot, Maliseet, Micmac, and Abenaki tribes. The Passamaquoddy Tribe is one of several members of the Wabenaki Confederacy, an alliance formed among local tribes in the eighteenth century. The tribe's indigenous language is an Algonquian dialect. The tribe is the largest federally recognized Native American nation in New England.

During the colonial period, traditional Passamaquoddy land and resources became a point of dispute as both the French and the English attempted to gain control of the area. This competition escalated into the French and Indian Wars. The indigenous groups in Maine generally sided with the French, as the French tended to treat the Native people better. The Passamaquoddy people generally disliked and distrusted the English settlers, perhaps fueling their decision to support American colonists during the Revolutionary War.

During the Revolutionary War, Passamaquoddy Chief Francis Joseph Neptune led a party of tribal members in the efforts to turn back British forces in eastern Maine. The tribe further assisted the Americans in a naval attack at Machias, Maine, in 1777. The Passamaquoddy Tribe's efforts were acknowledged in a letter that George Washington sent to the tribe, proclaiming a pledge of friendship between the Americans and the Passamaquoddy people.

The tribe entered into a treaty agreement with the Commonwealth of Massachusetts in 1794. The tribe agreed to cede all ancestral lands in return for 10 acres at Pleasant Point, 23,000 acres north of the present-day town of Princeton, Maine, and a number of islands in the Schoodic (St. Croix) River. The local government finally recognized tribal ownership of the lands when Maine gained statehood in 1820. At that time, Maine's government began to sell portions of Passamaquoddy

lands at Indian Township. The sale of tribal lands continued for a number of years as the tribe had no means to challenge or stop the actions.

The State of Maine established the Passamaquoddy Trust Fund in 1856 with funds earned from the sale of timber and resources from tribal lands. The fund was intended to provide emergency assistance to eligible tribal members. The lack of employment opportunities near the Pleasant Point and Indian Township communities contributed to the large number of people requiring financial assistance. By the turn of the century, tribal members at both reservations sought employment as migrant laborers. A number of members constructed and sold baskets, furniture, canoe paddles, axe handles, moccasins, Christmas wreaths, and snowshoes. Residents at Pleasant Point also relied on weir fishing, clamming, seal and porpoise hunting, and lobstering for sustenance. Residents of Indian Township relied primarily on hunting and trapping, though some members also farmed, logged, and served as guides to sportsmen.

By the 1960s, many tribal members were forced to leave the region in search of work. Less than 600 residents remained at the reservations. During that time, the tribe considered legal recourse for the loss of tribal lands and sued the State of Maine. The Maine Indian Land Claim Settlement Act of 1980 was eventually negotiated between the Passamaquoddy Tribe, Penobscot Tribe, and Maine. Under the act, the tribes were able to buy back tribal lands at fair market value and to invest in various business ventures. The act also created a trust fund from which tribal members will be paid.

Since the 1980s, the tribe has purchased almost 134,000 acres of lands that have been placed in trust status. These lands include a 1,000-acre parcel adjacent to Pleasant Point, 6,000 acres of blueberry barrens, and forested lands northwest of Indian Township, as well as portions of western Maine. Access to federal assistance has allowed the tribe to fund the development of new administrative offices at each community, in addition to a health center, an elementary school, and tribal housing. Improved conditions and enhanced services have drawn a number of tribal members back to the reservations.

GOVERNMENT

The Indian Township and Pleasant Point reservations

are governed by individual tribal councils. Each tribal council consists of a governor, a lieutenant governor, and six council members, each elected to four-year terms. Each council maintains jurisdiction over its own reservation and, together, they serve as the Passamaquoddy Joint Tribal Council. The joint tribal council is responsible for issues that affect both groups, such as jointly owned businesses, tribal land issues, and trust responsibility concerns. Since 1820, a tribal representative has been sent to the Maine State Legislature. The representative is elected every four years, and alternates between the reservations.

ECONOMY

Jointly owned businesses serve to generate income for both tribal communities. In the early 1980s, the tribe purchased the Dragon Cement Company for $28 million. It later sold the company to a Spanish cement consortium for $81 million.

Economic Development Projects. Currently, the tribe is exploring a number of economic development projects, including the development of a casino and resort complex in the town of Calais, Maine. The tribe aims to expand its agricultural base and renovate existing agricultural infrastructure. It is also considering starting a value-added salmon products business.

Agriculture and Livestock. The tribe owns Northeast Blueberry Company, the third-largest producer of blueberries in the nation. The company also produces cranberries. It employs a full-time staff of 5 and up to 160 seasonal workers. The tribe harvests about 300 acres of alfalfa from tribal lands in the Town of Perry. The hay is used to feed tribally owned cattle and horses.

Gaming. The Passamaquoddy Tribe must receive permission from the State of Maine prior to developing gaming facilities on tribal lands. The state has been reluctant to allow the development of casinos on Native American reservations, and thus far, the tribe has not been permitted to conduct gaming operations at either Indian Township or Pleasant Point. There are a number of high-stake bingo halls on the reservations.

Media and Communications. The Passamaquoddy Tribe owns two radio stations.

Tourism and Recreation. Tourist attractions to the area include the Waponhki Museum in Pleasant Point and the annual Indian Days festivities. Indian Days celebrations have been held at both reservations since 1965 and include ceremonial dances, crafts sales, and traditional food.

INFRASTRUCTURE

Both Indian Township and Pleasant Point are accessible via U.S. Route 1. The town of Calais, Maine, is located midway between the communities and is the primary service center for the area. The highway runs east along the southern portion of Maine and continues north along the Canadian border. Four points of entry to Canada are located within a few miles of the reservations.

Electricity. Bangor Hydroelectric Company provides electric service to tribal members.

Fuel. The Deep River Fuel Company and Ramsdell Fuel furnish propane gas.

Transportation. The Eastport Municipal Airport is located six miles from the Pleasant Point Reservation. The nearest commercial airport is located in Bangor. West's Transportation Van provides bus transportation to the area. UPS and FedEx provide shipping services to the reservations. The tribal pier and the privately owned Rockland Pier and Eastport Port Authority provide access to water transportation routes.

Water Supply. The Passamaquoddy Water District and a tribally owned municipal system provide water to residents of both reservations. The tribally owned municipal sewer system and treatment plant provide sewage treatment services.

ENVIRONMENTAL CONCERNS

The Passamaquoddy Tribe is committed to providing a clean and healthy environment for its residents. In 1999, it entered into a tribal environmental agreement with the EPA toward the goal of fulfilling this mission at both the Indian Township and Pleasant Point reservations.

A roostook

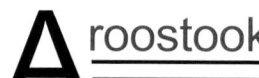

Aroostook Band of Micmac Indians
Federal reservation
Micmac
Aroostook County, Maine

Aroostook Band of Micmac
Indians
7 Northern Road
Presque Isle, ME 04769
207-764-1972
207-764-7664 Fax
micmac.org

Total area *(BIA realty, 2005)*
314.38 acres

Total area *(Tribal source, 2004)*
1,353 acres

Federal trust
(Tribal source, 2004)
302 acres

Tribally owned, non-trust lands
(Tribal source, 2004)
1,051 acres

Tribal enrollment *(Tribal source, 2004)*
847

Tribal enrollment
(BIA labor report, 2001)
1,180

LOCATION AND LAND STATUS

The U.S. government recognized the Aroostook Band of Micmacs on November 26, 1991. Since their recognition, the tribe has acquired over 1,300 acres of land. In 1996, 189 acres were purchased at Powers Michaud and are reserved for commercial use. In 1977, 80 acres were purchased at Spruce Haven and are used for cultural and economic purposes. Between 1997 and 2004, 658 acres were acquired at the former Loring Air Force Base; these lands contain forests and natural resources, and portions are used for industrial and commercial purposes. In 1998, 19 acres were purchased at Bridgewater and are reserved for cultural and health use. In 2001, 104 acres were purchased at Littleton, and they have been used for housing, a health clinic, and community services. In 2003, 264 acres were purchased at Inoo'agati, and the tribe has reserved those lands for housing, cultural, agricultural, and commercial use. The Aroostook Band intends to continue to increase its land base.

The majority of tribal members reside in the cities of Presque Isle, Caribou, and Houlton, Maine. Tribal members also reside throughout towns in central, northern, and southern Aroostook County. Tribal headquarters are located in Presque Isle, and satellite offices are located in Littleton, Maine.

CLIMATE

The general area where tribal lands are located receives about 39 inches of annual precipitation. The mean annual snowfall may reach as high as 100.1 inches. The average summer high temperature is 99°F, while the average winter temperature often falls to around -49°F.

CULTURE AND HISTORY

The Aroostook Band of Micmac Indians and 28 other bands that are based in Canada comprise the Micmac Nation. The Micmacs are members of the Wabenaki Confederacy, an alliance that was forged among the Maliseet, Passamaquoddy, Penobscot, and Abenaki tribes in the eighteenth century. Members of the Aroostook Band have free border-crossing rights guaranteed under the Jay Treaty. Traditionally, the Micmac people have lived along the 400-mile-long St. John River, which runs along the Canadian border in northern Maine. Archeological evidence suggests that Native gather-

ers inhabited this region as early as 12,000 years ago. Tribal history and place names suggest that the Micmac and the Maliseet peoples jointly inhabited this area for at least several thousand years.

As early as 1607, the Micmac people participated in the fur trade with French traders who depended upon the Native people's hunting skills. The Micmacs served as the first middlemen to the interior Native population for the European fur trade. Competition stemming from the fur trade served to intensify existing rivalries between the Micmacs and the neighboring Abenaki people. The introduction of guns by the French resulted in a level of fatalities between the groups, which had rarely occurred previously. While the colonial governments eventually attempted to limit the gun trade, the already-established pattern of trading furs for guns to better compete resulted in a deadly cycle for the area's Native people.

Between 1678 and 1752, the Micmacs signed numerous treaties with the newly founded Colony of Massachusetts. In July 1776, the Commonwealth of Massachusetts, which at that time included what is now the State of Maine, formed a specific treaty on behalf of the United Colonies of America with the Micmac and Maliseet tribes wherein the tribes agreed to support the American revolutionary forces against the British.

A migratory people, the Micmacs traditionally subsisted on hunting and fishing. By the early 1900s, many of the migratory Micmacs had settled in more or less permanent residences in various Indian reserves, in off-reservation towns and in rural hamlets. Throughout the twentieth century, the Micmacs supported themselves through seasonal labor and by selling crafts, particularly splint basketry. Micmac people have participated in the logging industries, river driving, blueberry raking, and potato picking, often crossing into Canada to seek employment.

In 1970, with other off-reservation Natives, the tribe formed the Association of Aroostook Indians (AAI) to combat poverty and discrimination. Lobbying for their Native rights, they gained state recognition of their tribal status in 1973, becoming eligible for Maine's Department of Indian Affairs services, In-

TRI-ME-1741

TRI-ME-1765

TRI-ME-1743

TRI-ME-1753

TRI-ME-1745

TRI-ME-1749

Aroostook

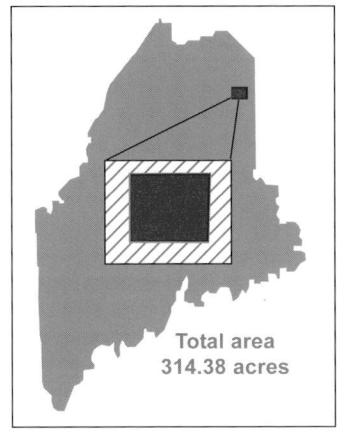

Total area
314.38 acres

Total labor force *2000 census*
4,463

Total labor force
(Tribal source, 2004)
551

High school graduate or higher
2000 census
78.6%

Bachelor's degree or higher
2000 census
21.2%

Unemployment rate *2000 census*
7.7%

Unemployment rate
(BIA labor report, 2001)
92%

dian scholarships, and free hunting and fishing licenses. Due to inadequate resources, documentation of Micmac history in Maine was not available when the state's other tribes participated in the 1980 settlement of the Maine Indian land claims, and the Aroostook Band was unable to benefit from the agreement. After dissolving the AAI, the band incorporated the Aroostook Micmac Council in 1982, which is headquartered in Presque Isle.

Without reservation status, tribal members learned to retain their tribal heritage while residing in Euro-American communities. The Micmacs continue to speak their Native language, which is part of the Algonquian linguistic group, and have sponsored a documentary film about their community.

Manufacturing. Manufacturing is an important and valuable part of the tribe's economy. Aroostook Generators is owned by tribal member David Gould and is a generator-manufacturing company. Benjamin E. Small and Anything Wood are manufacturers of wooden art and craft products. Other enterprises owned by Micmac tribal members include manufactures and retailers of Native arts and crafts, such as Micmac Traditions, Young Eagle Native Arts, Liz's Custom Native Clothing, and Native Jewel. Tribal members harvest ash trees, which are used to manufacture their popular basketry. The Micmacs sell these baskets through successful mail order and Internet based businesses.

Real Estate/Commercial Development. Since 1995, the tribe has seen a lot of growth in the area of housing, including 21 home ownership units and 19 rental units with nine located in Caribou, Maine, and ten located in Littleton, Maine.

Services and Retail. Micmac people manage and own a number of retail businesses. Liz's Custom Native Clothing, established in 1998, is a source for beautifully handcrafted Native dress. Native Jewel is a retailer of a fine line of gift items for the home. Young Eagle Native Arts and Micmac Traditions are Internet-based retailers of Native arts and crafts. The avid fisherman can find what he needs at Brewer Fly-Tying Service, a specialty supplier of fishing tackle and accessories. Gary's Hot Coating provides auto body paint coating and repair services. Pine Tree Legal Assistance publishes a legal assistance newspaper, called *Wabanaki Legal News*, and hosts a low-income taxpayer clinic. Future plans for additional services include developing a tribally owned day care center.

Transportation. The reservation has two transportation companies with a commercial drivers license. Murray's Trucking, established in 1997, is an independent company offering transportation of products. A&S Transport is a privately owned transportation company that offers long-haul transport services for goods going in and out of Maine.

TRI-ME-1741 Entrance view of Aroostook reservation

TRI-ME-1765 Aroostook Tribal office building

TRI-ME-1743 Front entrance to tribal offices building

TRI-ME-1753 Penobscot Hall

TRI-ME-1745 Tribal Administrator, with her daughter and TRI field researcher

TRI-ME-1749 Daycare classroom

TRI-ME-1769

TRI-ME-1766

TRI-ME-1763

TRI-ME-1795

TRI-ME-1767

TRI-ME-1769 Health clinic exercise room

TRI-ME-1766 Micmac Health Department sign in front of clinic

TRI-ME-1763 Canoe on display at tribal museum

TRI-ME-1795 View of college campus from window of 2nd story level of the Micmac Health Clinic. Campus is across the street.

TRI-ME-1767 Fronit view of the Micmac Health Clinic

Tourism and Recreation. In August 1994, the tribe hosted its first annual powwow a three-day festival known as Mawiomi of tribes that celebrates the traditions of the Micmacs through song, dance, food, and ceremonies. The reservation is also host to a variety of outdoor recreation activities. Fishing and deer hunting are popular draws.

INFRASTRUCTURE
U.S. Highway 1 runs along the Canadian border in northern Maine, and it is one of the area's main arteries. Presque Isle Municipal Airport serves the general area. The Aroostook Railroad and bus service are both available in Houlton.

Electricity. The reservation's electricity is supplied by Maine Public Service Company.

Fuel. Tribal members purchase propane gas and #2 fuel oil.

Water Supply. Water is supplied through the Caribou Utilities District, the Presque Isle Water District, and the Houlton Water Company. The Public Utilities Commission provides wastewater services.

Transportation. UPS and Federal Express provide freight service to the region, along with a number of trucking companies.

COMMUNITY FACILITIES AND SERVICES
Tribal council meetings are held in its headquarters in the Micmac Cultural, Community, and Education Services Center in Presque Isle, which also houses the tribal library, computer learning lab, and tribal administration programs. Spruce Haven in Caribou, Maine, is the site of most community meet-

ings and the annual Mawiomi. The tribe has satellite offices and clinic facilities in Littleton. Other tribally owned facilities include the Micmac Family Clinic and the Pi'gunjigi Little Feathers Head Start.

Health Care. Health service is available at the Aroostook Medical Center and is contracted with Indian Health Service. Members also use the Cary Medical Center. The Micmac Family Clinic has a doctor, a nurse, a nutritionist, and a counselor, and it offers such services as surgery referrals, pharmaceuticals, screening, testing, disease prevention, and transportation services to its members. The health newsletter called the *Micmac Health News* provides helpful information and addresses current health-related issues.

ENVIRONMENTAL CONCERNS
Due to the reservation's abundance of water and the popularity of fishing, the tribe's primary environmental concern is water pollution. The Micmac Environmental Health Department administers environmental health programs, including clean water, clean air, and natural resource management for tribally owned properties. These tests are performed at The Micmac Environmental Laboratory. The laboratory, built in 1999, is owned and operated by the Aroostook Band of Micmacs Tribal Government. The laboratory was established by the tribe to support the environmental health programs, clean water, clean air, and natural resource management programs for tribally owned properties. The laboratory is equipped with state of the art laboratory equipment and instrumentation. It performs all analytical work using the Environmental Protection Agency (EPA) and Maine Department of Environmental Protection (MDEP) approved drinking water analysis methods.

Maliseet

LOCATION AND LAND STATUS

The Houlton Band of Maliseet Indians was federally recognized in 1980, and 800 acres were set aside for its reservation in northwestern Maine. The Maliseet Reservation is located in eastern Houlton, overlooking the river valley to the west. The tribe intends to continue to increase its land base. Houlton is south of U.S. I-95, off Highway 1.

PHYSICAL DESCRIPTION

Over 500 acres of tribal lands are forested, primarily of northern hardwoods, such as spruce fir, pine, and hemlock. Tribally owned lands also contain agricultural fields, wetlands, a small pond, and a number of gravel pits. Approximately three miles of the Meduxnekeag River flows through tribal lands.

CULTURE AND HISTORY

The Houlton Band of Maliseet Indians has resided in the regions of present-day New England and southeastern Canada for countless years. There are seven bands in the Maliseet Nation, six of them based in Canada. The indigenous language of the Maliseet is an Algonquin dialect. Traditional means of sustenance have included hunting, gathering, and salmon harvesting. The tribe belongs to the Wabanaki Confederacy, an alliance that was forged among the Penobscot, Passamaquoddy, Micmac, and Abenaki Tribes in the eighteenth century.

The indigenous peoples of the northeastern United States encountered Europeans in the late seventeenth century. The arrival of settlers brought scourges of smallpox and other European diseases. Tribal populations, including that of the Maliseet, were devastated. The Maliseet Tribe was a party to the Jay Treaty of 1794. This treaty granted tribal members the right to travel freely between the United States and Canada.

In 1970, the Houlton Band and members of other non-reservation tribes organized the Association of Aroostook Indians to promote the recognition of their Native status. In 1973, the group was awarded access to services provided by Maine's Department of Indian Affairs. The group eventually dissolved, and the Maliseets reorganized as the Houlton Band of Maliseet Indians. In 1980, the band was recognized in the Maine Indian Land Claim Settlement Act as the sole successor of the Maliseet Nation within the United States. The band was allotted $900,000 to buy up to 5,000 acres of trust lands. The band was also granted access to federal services. Although a federally recognized tribe, the Houlton Band remains under the jurisdiction of the State of Maine. The band is required to make payments to the state in lieu of paying taxes.

As in many New England indigenous communities, the art of basketry continues to be practiced among the Maliseets. Artists are renowned for their intricate techniques and fine products.

GOVERNMENT

The tribe has a council composed of six members, headed by a chief. Council members are elected to four-year terms. The executive director oversees the daily administration business. The Maliseet Tribe is a self-governance tribe and has a resolution form of government.

The tribe contracts Indian child welfare, real estate, forestry, social services, education, Johnson O'Malley, planning, health, and aid to tribal government programs. The Maliseet Tribe is in the process of creating a tribal law enforcement department. Currently, a single officer provides law enforcement needs. Court matters are handled through the Maine District Court System.

ECONOMY

Agricultural lease payments are the tribe's main source of revenue. Revenue earned from its enterprise, the Maliseet Gardens, also contributes to the tribal economy.

Government as Employer. The tribal government is the biggest employer of the Maliseets. The government has more than 12 departments and employs 60 persons. Up to 10 additional workers are employed during the summer months.

Agriculture and Livestock. Over 300 acres of tribal lands are tillable. The tribe leases their fertile lands to farmers, who raise potatoes, peas, barley, and fiddleheads.

Construction. Fifty HUD homes were built on the reservation just east of the river in the early 1990s. Construction of a bridge

Maliseet Reservation
Federal reservation
Aroostook County, Maine

Houlton Band of Maliseet
  Indians
88 Bell Road
Littleton, ME 04730
  207-532-4273
  207-532-2660 Fax

Total area *(BIA realty, 2005)*
850 acres

Total area *(Tribal source, 2004)*
856 acres

Total population *2000 census*
136

Tribal enrollment
(Tribal source, 2004)
831

Tribal enrollment
(BIA labor report, 2001)
741

Total labor force *2000 census*
56

Total labor force
(Tribal source, 2004)
184

High school graduate or higher
2000 census
72.9%

Bachelor's degree or higher
2000 census
0%

Unemployment rate
2000 census
10.7%

Unemployment rate
(BIA labor report, 2001)
0%

Per capita income *2000 census*
$8,188

TRI-ME-1804

TRI-ME-1858

TRI-ME-1804 Maliseet Tribal office directional sign

TRI-ME-1858 The Meduxnekeag River flows through the reservation for about 3 miles

Maliseet

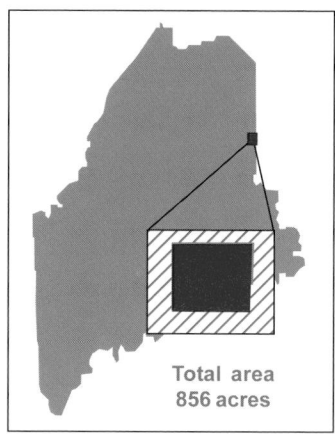

Total area
856 acres

TRI-ME-1809

TRI-ME-1826

TRI-ME-1844

TRI-ME-1829

TRI-ME-1809 Maliseet Tribal office building

TRI-ME-1826 Maliseet Indian Health Clinic

TRI-ME-1844 Old Maliseet Indians abandoned school bus

TRI-ME-1829 Maliseet Housing Authority Offices

coincided with the housing development. Non-Indian town residents vehemently opposed the bridge; upon completion, traffic increased in the area.

In the last decade, the tribe has constructed a number of tribal facilities, including a new health department building, a gymnasium, and a Head Start daycare facility. A number of new housing units have also been constructed. The tribe has completed repairs to existing roadways and developed new ones.

Real Estate/Commercial Development. The tribe owns Maliseet Gardens in Bangor, Maine. This facility features congregate housing and commercial retail space.

INFRASTRUCTURE
Electricity. The City of Houlton provides electric services.

Water Supply. The Houlton Water Company provides water, and homes are linked to a central septic system.

Transportation. Bus services are available in Houlton. A commercial airport is located about 120 miles from the reservation. Freight carriers serve the area. The tribe also provides transportation for tribal members to and from medical appointments at the health clinic.

Telecommunications. Local retailers provide Internet access and cable services.

COMMUNITY FACILITIES AND SERVICES
Tribal headquarters are located in Houlton, Maine. The tribe maintains tribal offices, a gym, a Head Start facility, tribal housing,

and a clinic. The tribe is developing a culture and language revitalization program to be implemented on the reservation.

Education. The tribe offers a Head Start program. Tribal youth attend schools in Houlton. The Northern Maine Technical College and University of Maine provide postsecondary programs in the region.

Health Care. Health services are available through the tribal health clinic. Services include medical, nutrition, laboratory, mental health, substance abuse, domestic violence, and education programs. Transportation is available for medical appointments. Contracted through the Indian Health Service, the clinic employs three doctors and a nurse practitioner. Dental services are contracted through local providers. Additional medical services are available through the Houlton Regional Hospital and the Eastern Maine Regional Hospital.

ENVIRONMENTAL CONCERNS
The tribe's primary environmental concerns include protecting the Meduxnekeag River watershed. The tribe hopes that restoring a clean water source will encourage the revitalization of the fish populations and the Bald Eagle population of the watershed. A Watershed Protection Plan and Environmental Assessment and a Non Point Source Assessment and Management Plan have been implemented. The tribe's programs include agricultural conversion, environmental quality incentive, and conservation reserve. The tribe is also a member of the Meduxnekeag Watershed Coalition.

Total area (BIA realty, 2005)	24,570 acres
Federal trust (BIA realty, 2005)	24,570 acres
Joint federal trust	47371 acres
(BIA realty, 2005)	
Total population 2000 census	676
Tribal enrollment (BIA labor report, 2001)	1,314
Total labor force 2000 census	276
Total labor force (BIA labor report, 2001)	367
High school graduate or higher	76.4%
2000 census	
Bachelor's degree or higher	11.7%
2000 census	
Unemployment rate 2000 census	21%
Unemployment rate	69%
(BIA labor report, 2001)	
Per capita income 2000 census	$10,808

(Please see Passamaquoddy introduction for further information on Location and Land Status, Culture and History, Government, Economy, Infrastructure, and Environmental Concerns.)

LOCATION AND LAND STATUS

The Indian Township Reservation is the largest Native American reservation in the state of Maine. Indian Township consists of two neighborhoods separated by a seven-mile paved road. Peter Dana Point is located at Big Lake, and the Indian Township strip overlooks Lewy Lake.

The Treaty of 1794 between the tribe and Commonwealth of Massachusetts established the Indian Township Reservation. During World War II, the federal government took parcels of reservation lands and established a German prisoner-of-war camp. The land was later sold to nontribal parties.

PHYSICAL DESCRIPTION

The Indian Township Reservation is situated 50 miles inland from Pleasant Point. This reservation spans 23,000 acres of thick forest on the chain of lakes that includes Schoodic Lake.

CULTURE AND HISTORY
(Please see Passamaquoddy introduction for further information.)

GOVERNMENT

The Indian Township Reservation is governed by a six-member council, which is led by a governor and lieutenant governor. The council represents the reservation on the Passamaquoddy Joint Tribal Council.

Tribal government departments at Indian Township include public works, fire, social services, home improvement, purchasing, tribal clerk and census, forestry, environmental, personnel, education, and finances.

ECONOMY

The Indian Township Reservation economy is supported in large part by revenue earned from enterprises that are jointly owned with the Pleasant Point Reservation. Together, the tribes own the Northeast Blueberry Company, the nation's third-largest producer of blueberries. Employment opportunities are available in government offices and programs and in tribally owned enterprises.

Government as Employer. The tribe employs approximately 175 individuals throughout its government offices and programs.

Indian Township Reservation
Federal reservation
Passamaquoddy
Washington County, Maine

Passamaquoddy Tribe
P.O. Box 301
Princeton, ME 04668
    207-796-2301
    207-796-5256
    passamaquoddy.com

TRI-ME-2041 Indian Township Health Clinic

TRI-ME-1989 Indian Township Tribal Government office building

TRI-ME-1990 Indian Township Tribal Government entrance sign

TRI-ME-2031 Daycare Center

TRI-ME-2043 Forest Department Office

TRI-ME-2041

TRI-ME-1989

TRI-ME-1990

TRI-ME-2031

TRI-ME-2043

Indian Township

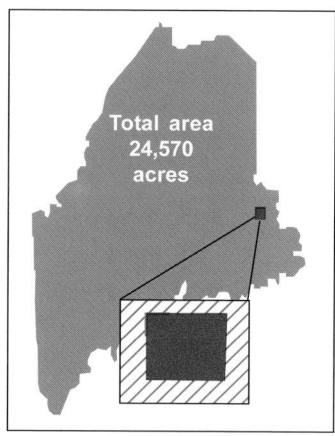
Total area
24,570
acres

TRI-ME-2020

TRI-ME-2002

Manufacturing. Indian Township is the major shareholder of Creative Apparel Associates. The company is contracted by the U.S. Department of Defense to manufacture military apparel, including firefighting gear and fire-resistant flight jackets. It has also begun manufacturing chemical protective suits for the military. The tribe would like to attract more joint ventures to the Indian Township Reservation.

Services and Retail. The tribe operates Bowling Lanes, an eight-pin bowling alley. The alley features a lunch counter.

COMMUNITY FACILITIES AND SERVICES
Numerous tribal community facilities are located on reservation land, including the tribal youth center, the Nation House, the tribal administration building, a recreation center, a police and fire stations school, and the forestry resources building.

TRI-ME-2020 Creative Apparel Associates manufacting building

TRI-ME-2002 Creative Apparel factory workers

TRI-ME-2007 Factory worker assembling military apparel

Education. The Washington County Community College is located in Calais.

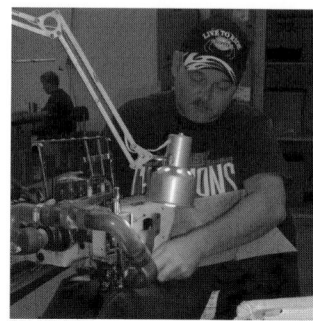
TRI-ME-2007

Health Care. Health services are available at a local clinic. There is also a 75-bed hospital located in Calais.

Penobscot

Penobscot Reservation
Federal reservation
Penobscot
Penobscot County, Maine

Penobscot Indian Nation
12 Wabanaki Way
Indian Island, ME 04468
207-827-7776
207-827-6042 Fax
penobscotnation.org

LOCATION AND LAND STATUS
The Penobscot Nation owns approximately 148,525 acres of land in Maine. Of this acreage, 4,841 acres include almost 200 islands on the Penobscot River. These islands, which include the tribe's activity center on Indian Island, represent a portion of the Penobscot Nation's traditional pre-colonial territory. The remaining lands were purchased through the tribe's Land Acquisition Fund, which was established through a federal appropriations bill signed by President Carter in 1980.

Tribal headquarters are located on Indian Island Reservation near Old Town, Maine. While the tribe has grown dramatically in size in the last decade, only 25 percent of its members live on the reservation.

CULTURE AND HISTORY
The ancestral home of the Penobscot Nation covered the entire Penobscot River Watershed in eastern Maine. The rich resources of the area amply supplied the early Penobscot people with fish, game, and native plants. Culturally, the Penobscots are one of the four tribes of the original Eastern Abenaki group. The tribe is a member of the Wabenaki Confederacy. The members of the Penobscot Indian Nation speak a dialect of the Eastern Algonquian language. This language was shared by residents of all but one of the coastal river drainages from North Carolina to Nova Scotia.

Beginning in 1615, European diseases ravaged the population of the Eastern Abenaki and other New England tribes. Alternating epidemics of smallpox, measles, and the plague reduced the Eastern Abenaki population by three-fourths. Whole villages were abandoned and family units shattered.

The Penobscots actively supported the rebel colonists during the Revolutionary War, partly on the basis of assurances from the fledgling Provincial Congress of Massachusetts that their territorial rights to the upper Penobscot River drainage would be preserved. The Penobscots fought alongside the colonists in several local engagements, and joined the Passamaquoddy, Maliseet, and Micmac in securing the town of Machias, Maine against British attack in 1777. This victory represented America's first naval success, and secured the northern boundary of the colonies for the rest of the Revolutionary War. Predictably, these alliances were abandoned at the end of the war. Early agreements with the Penobscot Nation were never ratified by Congress, and repeated petitions for federal aid were rejected. Massachusetts used a misinterpretation of earlier pledges to wrest most of the middle of the Penobscot River drainage away from the tribe.

The limits of this cession were defined in 1786 and clarified in 1796. These treaties left the Penobscots with only the islands in the river from their main village at Old Town for thirty miles, two small islands in Penobscot Bay, and the hunting grounds in the uppermost portion of the river drainage. When the State of Maine was organized in 1820, the tribe fell under its jurisdiction. In 1833, the state sold about 100,000 acres of Penobscot lands. Less than 5,000 acres remained in tribal ownership. The proceeds from the sale of tribal lands and resources were controlled and dispersed by the State of Maine.

With the loss of ancestral lands and hunting territories, tribal members were forced to seek other means of sustenance. By the turn of the century, a number of Penobscots were seeking work as seasonal laborers and hunting guides. A number of tribal members also made a living selling handmade items such as baskets, canoes, moccasins, snowshoes, and various arts and crafts. The local lumber and manufacturing industries also provided employment opportunities for tribal members. The tribe promoted tourism to the reservation. During the 1920s, it hosted elaborately staged Indian pageants, with tribal members sporting special costumes and participating in special dances.

The Penobscots did not receive federal recognition until late in the 20th century. The U.S. District Court ruled that the Nonintercourse Act was applicable to the Penobscot and Passamaquoddy tribes, despite the previous lack of federal recognition. This ruling established a trust relationship with the United States and in effect ordered the federal government to litigate a Non-intercourse Act claim against the State of Maine for damages arising from the illegal taking of Indian lands. The decision also made the Maine tribes eligible for federal benefits such as housing, education, health care, and other social services. In April of 1980, the Maine legislature adopted the Maine Implementing Act, settling the outstanding land claims. Six months later, the U.S. Congress approved the corresponding federal legislation. President Carter signed the measure on October 10, 1980, thereby establishing an appropriations bill setting aside $81,500,000 for the two tribes. As a result of this complex settlement, the Penobscot Nation is recognized as a sovereign, federally recognized Indian tribe, a municipality under state law, and a business entity.

GOVERNMENT
The Penobscot Nation is led by a governor, lieutenant governor, and a 12-member council elected biennially by the tribe. The tribe's OEDP Committee is composed of eight members.

Tribal government departments include natural resources, health, forestry, finance, grants/contracts, legal, housing, human services, public safety, and education.

The Penobscot Nation Police Department, a division of the department of public safety, provides law enforcement on the reservation. The tribe also has a tribal court system. Under provisions of the Main Indian Land Claims Act, the court exercises jurisdiction over criminal and civil matters on the reservation and tribal trust lands.

ECONOMY
The tribal economy is supported in large part by the tribe's activity in the tourism, manufacturing, gaming, and forestry industries.

Government as Employer. Through the administration of several social service programs, the tribal government functions as an important employment source for tribal members.

Economic Development Project. The tribe is exploring the feasibility of developing a year-round recreational facility on tribal lands. The proposed site is located at Mattagamon, adjacent

to Baxter State Park. The park is one of the area's most vital tourist attractions. The tribe also hopes to expand the museum and archives, and to develop a cultural center.

Forestry. The majority of the Penobscot land base is covered with a combination of hardwood and softwood timber. Totaling over 100,000 acres, this forestland offers just over 2.5 million cords of standing timber. Overall, the timber ands are of good to excellent quality, averaging about 18.7 cords per acre. Between 1983 and 1987, the Penobscot Nation generated a gross annual income of around $635,000 from timber harvesting. More recently, annual timber revenues (stumpage) have averaged around $450,000.

Gaming. The tribe owns the Sockalexis Bingo Palace on Indian Island. The tribe has been operating high stakes bingo since 1987.

Manufacturing. The Penobscot Nation owns and operates Olamon Industries, a manufacturing facility. The main product is audio media, but the facility also produces automotive, building, construction, toy, and information technology parts. It is situated in a 33,000 square foot facility and provides full assembly, packaging, and shipping services. The goal of the company is to become involved in divergent technologies, and to enhance employment opportunities for Native Americans. The plant employs over 150 individuals. Unemployment in the area has been reduced from 35 to 15 percent as a direct result of the opportunities available at the facility.

Media and Communications. The tribe produces the Community Flyer. This monthly publication provides tribal members with information and updates from tribal services as well as community advertisements.

Tourism and Recreation. The tribe operates the Penobscot Nation Museum on Indian Island. The museum displays tribal artifacts, contemporary Wabanaki art, and regional artifacts. It also houses research materials, outreach programs, and a gift shop.

Deer, duck, bear, and small game hunting, as well as eel trapping, are permitted on tribal lands. A permit must be attained through the tribe's department of natural resources.

INFRASTRUCTURE
Interstate 95 serves as a major north-south artery throughout the Penobscot lands. U.S. Highway 2 (east-west) also crosses the reservation.

Electricity. Electricity is provided to the region by the Hydroelectric Company.

Water Supply. Water and wastewater services are provided by the tribe.

Transportation. Commercial air, bus, and truck lines are available in Bangor, located 12 miles from the reservation. The nearest available train service is in Boston, Massachusetts, 275 miles from the reservation.

Telecommunications. Cable services are available through Adelphi Cable Communications.

COMMUNITY FACILITES AND SERVICES
There are a number of community facilities within the Penobscot lands, most of which are located in Old Town, including a small museum, a community center, the Penobscot Nation Health and Fitness Center, and a parish hall. The reservation is home to the Penobscot Nation Boys and Girls Club.

Penobscot

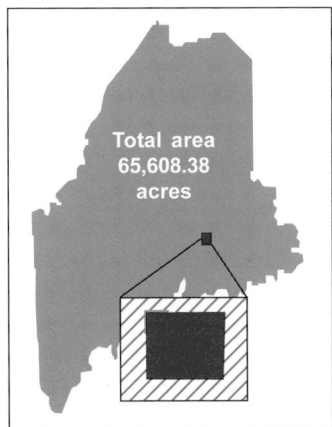

Total area *(BIA realty, 2005)*
65,608.38 acres

Federal trust *(BIA realty, 2005)*
65,608.38 acres

Total population *2000 census*
562

Tribal enrollment
(BIA labor report, 2001)
2,194

Total labor force *2000 census*
248

Total labor force
(BIA labor report, 2001)
446

High school graduate or higher
2000 census
88.1%

Bachelor's degree or higher
2000 census
11.1%

Unemployment rate *2000 census*
13.3%

Unemployment rate
(BIA labor report, 2001)
27%

Per capita income *2000 census*
$13,704

Penobscot

TRI-ME-1867

TRI-ME-1893

TRI-ME-1943

TRI-ME-1895

TRI-ME-1935

TRI-ME-1896

TRI-ME-1921

TRI-ME-1867 Penobscot Tribal office building

TRI-ME-1893 Penobscot Police Department Building

TRI-ME-1943 Traditional hand crafted Penobscot canoe to be part of the grand opening for the 2004 National Museum of the American Indian in Washington, DC

TRI-ME-1895 Penobscot fire truck

TRI-ME-1935 Traditional canoe crafting art studio

TRI-ME-1896 Tribal Court sign

TRI-ME-1921 Water system under construction, summer 2004

Education. Tribal youth attend the tribal school, which serves students in grades preschool through eighth. The tribe offers an education and career services center. Programs include the workforce investment and vocational education training programs. The tribe provides scholarships for eligible tribal members in pursuit of a post-secondary education. Career counseling services and courses are offered through the Penobscot Learning Center.

The Indian Island School offers classes in cultural arts and the indigenous language. Tribal elders lead the classes and utilize the Penobscot Dictionary in instruction.

Health Care. The Penobscot Community Health Center, located on Indian Island, provides medical services to tribal members. Services are contracted through Indian Health Service and include comprehensive medical, lab, pharmacy, counseling, diabetes control, community outreach, nutrition, and environmental health programs. Transportation services are available to tribal members. The tribe also provides contract services for eye care. The tribe leases a 6,600-square-foot facility across the street from the health center. It houses a dental clinic with 12 dental operatories. The clinic has the capability to expand to 18 operatories, which would make it the largest general practice dental clinic in the state.

The tribe is constructing an assisted elder care living facility on the reservation. It is expected to be completed in early 2005.

ENVIRONMENTAL CONCERNS

The tribe's department of natural resources is charged with the management, preservation, and restoration of tribal lands and resources. Programs include fisheries, water quality, water resources, air quality, and forestry. The department publishes a newsletter and provides educational workshops for the community. Environmental concerns of the tribe include water quality and air quality. The tribe is active in the efforts to restore and preserve the quality of water in the Penobscot River. The high level of dioxins and dioxin-like substances released in the river by paper mills has become a critical concern. The natural resources department monitors the water regularly.

In 2004, the tribe filed suit in response to the U.S. EPA's decision to relinquish authority for clean water enforcement policies on tribal lands to the State of Maine. The decision is reflective of the fact that although a federally recognized tribe, the Penobscot Nation remains under the jurisdiction of the state and is not afforded government-to-government relations with the federal government or its departments.

Total area *(BIA realty, 2005)*	61,776	acres
Federal trust *(BIA realty, 2005)*	61,776	acres
Total population *(Tribal source, 2004)*		542
Total population *2000 census*		640
Tribal enrollment *(Tribal source, 2004)*		1,158
Tribal enrollment *(BIA labor report, 2001)*		1,927
Total labor force *2000 census*		250
Total labor force *(Tribal source, 2004)*		174
High school graduate or higher *2000 census*		72%
High school graduate or higher *(Tribal source, 2004)*		57.4%
Bachelor's degree or higher *2000 census*		8.8%
Unemployment rate *(Tribal source, 2004)*		8.6%
Unemployment rate *2000 census*		21.2%
Per capita income *(Tribal source, 2004)*		$6,531
Per capita income *2000 census*		$9,096

(Please see Passamaquoddy introduction for further information on Location and Land Status, Culture and History, Government, Economy, Infrastructure, and Environmental Concerns.)

LOCATION AND LAND STATUS

The Pleasant Point Reservation consists of its original 100 acres plus 112 acres of annexed land authorized by the State of Maine. Sipayik, the main Passamaquoddy village since 1770, is located at the Pleasant Point Reservation. It is situated on a promontory in Passamaquoddy Bay, which leads to the island community of Eastport, the easternmost town in the continental United States.

CULTURE AND HISTORY
(Please see Passamaquoddy introduction for further information.)

GOVERNMENT

The Pleasant Point Reservation is governed by a tribal council consisting of a governor, a lieutenant governor, and six council members under provisions of the Constitution of the Sipayik Members of the Passamaquoddy Tribe. The Pleasant Point community adopted its constitution in 1990; the Indian Township Reservation did not adopt the constitution. The council represents the reservation in the Passamaquoddy Joint Tribal Council. Tribal government departments include health, human services, housing, economic development and planning, finance, census, education, child welfare, social services, information and computer technology, domestic violence, personnel, public works, youth and recreation, and elderly.

The reservation is served by its own fire, warden, and police departments, as well as its own tribal court system. The police department offers law enforcement, crime prevention, education, K-9, school resources, and disaster preparedness programs, among others. The tribal court exercises jurisdiction over matters involving the reservations and tribal members. The State of Maine maintains jurisdiction over all nontribal members.

ECONOMY

The Pleasant Point Reservation's economy is supported in large part by the revenue generated by enterprises that are jointly owned with the Indian Township Reservation, including the Northeast Blueberry Company. Employment opportunities are available in government programs and offices, as well as in the local gaming, tourism, agriculture, forestry, and manufacturing industries.

Government as Employer. The tribal government serves as the largest employer on the reservation with about 170 employees.

Pleasant Point Reservation
Federal reservation
Passamaquoddy
Washington County, Maine

Passamaquoddy Tribe
of Pleasant Point
P.O. Box 343
Perry, ME 04667-0343
207-853-2600
207-853-6039 Fax
wabanaki.com

TRI-ME-1985 Tribally owned gas station and gift shop

TRI-ME-1945 Passamaquoddy Tribal Office Building

TRI-ME-1949 Totem pole at the entrance to the tribal building

TRI-ME-1975 Waponahki Museum

TRI-ME-1956 School

TRI-ME-1985

TRI-ME-1945

TRI-ME-1949

TRI-ME-1975

TRI-ME-1956

Pleasant Point

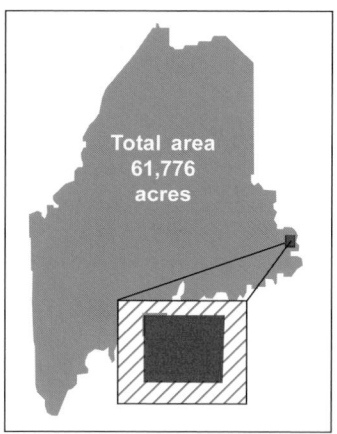

Total area
61,776
acres

TRI-ME-1981

TRI-ME-1982

TRI-ME-1971

TRI-ME-1965

TRI-ME-1981 A view of Passamaquoddy Bay

TRI-ME-1982 Boys & Girls Club of Passamaquoddy sign

TRI-ME-1971 Pleasant Point Health Center

TRI-ME-1965 Tribal court chambers

Services and Retail. The Sipayik Corner Store is a tribally owned enterprise. The tribe also owns the Wabanaki Mall, a gas station, and a restaurant.

Media and Communications. The reservation publishes the *Sipayik Newsletter*, a weekly newsletter. The graphics studio, a division of the newsletter, produces advertising, design and production materials. The copy center division handles reproduction services for the tribe, BIA programs, Indian Health Service, and other entities.

The housing authority and volunteers operate the Passamaquoddy tribal television system, a closed-circuit community access cable system. The signal originates from the Pleasant Point Housing and Elderly Complex, and it is received within the Pleasant Point community.

Tourism and Recreation. The Waponahki Museum and Resource Center is located at Pleasant Point. It was established in 1987 and features tribal photos, artifacts, and arts and crafts. Classes in the indigenous language are available at the museum. The Daughters of the American Revolution have erected at the reservation a monument honoring Passamaquoddy warriors who fought against the British during the Revolutionary War.

Attractions to the area include the Quoddy Loop at the Bay of Fundy and Old Sow, the largest tidal whirlpool in the Western hemisphere. The Quoddy Maritime Museum in Eastport also draws visitors. The Sipayik Trail project was recently completed on the reservation. This project transformed an old railroad bed into a three-mile, paved walking and biking path.

COMMUNITY FACILITIES AND SERVICES

The reservation is home to the Passamaquoddy Peaceful Relations Domestic Violence Response Program. It provides a 24-hour hotline, crisis intervention, emergency assistance, information referrals, advocacy, support, and community education services. The human services department at Pleasant Point provides victim advocacy, child welfare, farm share, and general assistance services to reservation residents.

The reservation is also home to the Sipayik's Boys and Girls Club and a daycare facility. Tribal elders may live at The Elderly, a complex that provides housing, a meal program, and social activities for elders.

Education. The tribe contracts with the BIA to fund operation of the Beatrice Rafferty School at the Pleasant Point Reservation. The school serves students in grades K-8. It also houses a Head Start program. High school students attend secondary programs in Eastport and Calais. The Washington County Community College in Calais also serves tribal members.

Health Care. The Pleasant Point Health Center provides on-site medical, mental health, dental, and nutritional services to members of federally recognized Native American nations residing in its service area. Other services include contract health care, education, screening, prevention programs, and a number of specialty clinics. Medical services are also available in Machais, Calais, and Bangor.

LOCATION AND LAND STATUS

The Wampanoag trust lands are located at the southwestern portion of Martha's Vineyard Island, a 93-square-mile island located six miles off the coast of southern Massachusetts. In accordance with the Wampanoag Tribal Council of Gay Head (Aquinnah) Indian Claims Settlement Act of 1987, there are approximately 485 acres (160 acres private and approximately 325 acres common lands) of tribally owned land. Tribal common lands include the Gay Head Cliffs, Lobsterville, and parcels of land in Christiantown.

CULTURE AND HISTORY

The Aquinnah Wampanoag people have lived in Aquinnah (the City of Gay Head) on the island of Noepe (present-day Martha's Vineyard Island) for at least 10,000 years. Tribal lands once encompassed the mainland of southern Massachusetts and eastern Rhode Island. Of eastern Algonquian linguistic stock, the Wampanoags were referred to as the Pokanokets in early documents. A horticultural people, during the early seventeenth century the Wampanoags occupied approximately 30 villages in this region. Best known in the literature for their relationship with the Plymouth Pilgrims, the Wampanoags' leader, Massasoit, welcomed the English and remained at peace with them until his death in 1661. By that time the Wampanoags had suffered grave population losses due to the introduction of epidemic-causing diseases and the usurpation of much of their ancestral land.

In retaliation for these losses, Massasoit's son, Metacom, led a coalition of New England Native people against the colonists in 1675. Known as the King Philip War, referring to the title given to Metacom by the English, the Native people were initially successful, attacking 52 of the 90 white settlements in Indian territory and wiping out 12 of them. But Metacom, who did not command the wide respect that his father had, faced trouble in keeping together his coalition of New England tribes. The English suffered heavy losses before the Indians were finally defeated and Metacom was killed in 1676.

By 1800, only three Wampanoag communities remained at Aquinnah, Christiantown, and Chappaquiddick. The Aquinnah community was the only one able to maintain control over their lands and demand recognition as a sovereign nation. The Wampanoag Nation was established in 1928 through the involvement of two Mashpee men, Eben Queppish and Nelson Simons, in the Pan-Indian movement in the early part of this century.

In 1972, the Wampanoag Tribal Council of Gay Head was established. The corporation fought for the recognition of tribal status, the preservation of Wampanoag culture and history, and the restoration of tribal lands. In 1987, the Wampanoag Tribe of Gay Head (Aquinnah) received federal recognition. The Wampanoags of Gay Head (Aquinnah) represent the only tribe of the Wampanoag Nation that has gained federal recognition. The Wampanoag term "Aquinnah" refers to the Gay Head region of the island. While Gay Head is the largest and most socially and politically active of the Wampanoag tribes, some of the other four autonomous groups are currently seeking federal recognition.

GOVERNMENT

The Wampanoag Tribe of Gay Head (Aquinnah) is governed by a popularly elected representative tribal council. The 11-member council is elected for three-year staggered terms and includes a chairperson, a vice-chairperson, a secretary and a treasurer. In addition, a traditional chief and medicine man are council members. Meetings are open to all tribal members.

There are a number of departments maintained by the tribal government. They include education, natural resources, historic preservation, health, human services and housing authority, among others.

The Wampanoag Aquinnah Ranger Service patrols tribal lands. The rangers are trained in natural resources management, environmental law enforcement, emergency medical response, and archeological resources protection. Rangers also participate in search and rescue operations. The rangers provide educational programs to the public regarding the tribe's natural landmarks, such as the Aquinnah Cliffs.

The tribe has initiated the Wampanoag Judicial Project with the assistance of an Administration for Native Americans grant. The project will include creating a judicial task force, drafting and adopting a judicial code, and developing an effective judicial system to service the needs of the tribe.

ECONOMY

Tourism has become one of the major island businesses, and individual families run some of the many snack bars and shops up at the cliffs. Other occupations held by tribal members are plumbers, landscapers, and electricians.

Government as Employer. Consolidated tribal government programs provide important employment opportunities for tribal members. Moreover, the tribal council oversees a WorkLearn program that places young tribal members in employment positions throughout the community.

Economic Development Projects. The tribe's planning depart-

Gay Head Reservation
Federal reservation
Wampanoag (Aquinnah)
Dukes County, Massachusetts

Wampanoag Tribe of Gay Head (Aquinnah)
20 Black Brook Road
Aquinnah, MA 02535-1546
508-645-9265
508-645-3790 Fax
wampanoagtribe.net

Total area *(BIA realty, 2005)*
485 acres

Federal trust *(BIA realty, 2005*
466.70 acres

Population *2000 census*
260

Tribal enrollment
(BIA labor report, 2001)
1,001

Total labor force *2000 census*
43

Total labor force
(BIA labor report, 2001)
203

High school graduate or higher
2000 census
82.6%

Bachelor's degree or higher
2000 census
10.9%

Unemployment rate *2000 census*
4.7%

Unemployment rate
(BIA labor report, 2001)
44%

Per capita income *2000 census*
$11,126

Gay Head

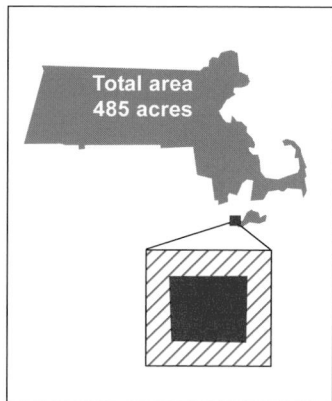

Total area 485 acres

TRI-MA-0448

TRI-MA-0451

TRI-MA-0452

TRI-MA-0450

TRI-MA-0448 Wampanoag Tribal office building

TRI-MA-0451 Tribal housing

TRI-MA-0452 Tribal housing

TRI-MA-0450 Tribal housing and playground

ment is responsible for identifying and administering private and public funds necessary to accomplish proposed developments. The department conducts surveys, collects demographic information, seeks direction from tribal members and the tribal government, and conducts various planning initiatives in order to successfully serve the community's development needs.

Since their successful bid for recognition in 1987, the Gay Head Wampanoags have actively pursued various economic development projects. The completion of the tribe's multipurpose building and first tribally owned residences represents the first phase of the tribe's plans for geographic unification. A community building is also being built in a joint effort between the tribe and the U.S. Air Force, which is supplying the labor.

Gaming. In the 1990s, the tribe began negotiations with the Commonwealth of Massachusetts over a proposed casino compact. As of this time there has not been any significant progress toward a gaming facility.

Fisheries. The tribe leases Herring Creek to a tribal member and operates a natural herring fishery at the creek. The fishery operations include monitoring fishing activities and enforcing practices to ensure the viability of the herring population. The herring are harvested by tribal fisherman and sold for consumption to serve as lobster bait and crab bait.

The tribe operates the Wampanoag Aquinnah Shellfish Hatchery (WASH). WASH produces native species of bay scallops, quahogs, and American oysters. Seed shellfish is sold to municipal agencies, private aquaculturalists, and the wholesale shellfish market. The hatchery restocks traditional native fisheries utilized by tribal fishermen. Oyster production has significantly increased and the tribe is now providing oysters to the Fulton Fish Market in New York City, serving them at the Democratic Convention in Boston, and negotiating to sell them overseas.

Services and Retail. The Wampanoag Tribal Store offers t-shirts, sweatshirts, hats, calendars, and additional merchandise with the tribal logo. The store can be accessed at the tribe's website.

Tourism and Recreation. The general public is restricted access to tribal lands. Tours and visits to tribal lands must be arranged and approved by the tribe. The Aquinnah Conservation Rangers are available to lead groups on interpretive tours.

The Gay Head tribal lands offer many spectacular landscapes for outdoor enthusiasts, including the multicolored clay cliffs of Gay Head. The tribe collaborates with the Martha's Vineyard Land Bank and the Massachusetts Audubon Society to provide visitor services. Their services include monitoring use of the beach, developing interpretive programs, and maintaining visitor facilities.

Wampanoag tribal members operate two fishing charter boats, *The Tomahawk* can be reserved for bass fishing, and *The Conomo* provides fishermen the opportunity to harvest striped bass and blue fish. *The Conomo* is also available for sunset charters.

Cranberry Day is an annual tribal celebration that the tribe has hosted for over 100 years. Cranberry Day begins when Gay Headers go down to their bogs to spiritually give thanks for the berries they are about to harvest. This private ritual is followed by a public display when the Native people return to tribal headquarters, baskets filled with berries, for an afternoon of feasting, dancing, and drumming. Cranberry Day is usually held the second Tuesday in October.

The tribe hosts the annual Spring Social. It is a dance social that features performances of Native American musicians. Native people from all over the Northeast pertaicipate. It is usually held the last Sunday in April.

Thte "Stories of Moshup" is an annual performance usually held in August on tribal lands at sunset. It is a reenactment of the life of Moshup, a giant who brought his people, the Wampanoags, to Martha's Vineyard island.

Service and retail jobs supporting the tourism market are not only the most significant revenue source for Martha's Vineyard, but they also provide employment for tribal members. Visitors are drawn to the island's beautiful beaches, secluded appeal, and the state forest that covers much of the island.

There are tourist accommodations throughout the area, including the Martha's Vineyard Family Campground, located one mile from the Vineyard Haven ferry terminal. The campground offers full-service tent and RV sites. Additional accommodations are available in Woods Hole, the mainland town adjacent to the island. Woods Hole is also the site of the Woods Hole Oceanographic Institute and the Massachusetts State Aquarium.

The tribe produces "Wampanoag Way: An Aquinnah Cultural Trail." It is a map available to tourists visiting the island and desiring to learn more about the Wampanoag Tribe.

INFRASTRUCTURE
The tribe has recently completed a main access road leading to its new multipurpose building. The BIA funded this road.

Transportation. The Martha's Vineyard and Nantucket Steamship Authority provides the most commonly used transportation onto the island. The ferry, which travels across Vineyard Sound from the town of Woods Hole, runs hourly, and trips last approximately 45 minutes. Car reservations may be made in advance.

COMMUNITY FACILITIES AND SERVICES
In addition to general library services, the tribal library is the home of the Jennings Collection. The collection is an extensive source of information regarding the history, cultural traditions, folklore, arts and crafts, and literature of the Wampanoags.

The tribe contracts police, fire, and medical personnel and resources through the Town of Aquinnah.

The Aquinnah Turtle program provides tribal youth with a seven-week program that includes fishing trips, beach cleanups, gardening, cliff walks, beach plum picking, jewelry making, genealogy projects, and most importantly, learning the Wampanoag language.

The tribe offers an elders program, a family and community services program, and a childcare and development program to tribal members.

The tribe is developing the Aquinnah Cultural Center. The center will include a child daycare center, classrooms, cultural arts and education, an elder day center, a full kitchen, a community gymnasium, after-school programs, and facilities to host large community events.

Education. Tribal youth attend public schools on the island. The director of the tribe's education department represents the tribe on various local school advisory boards and committees. The department also provides consultation services, develops curriculum supplements, and conducts cultural and historical presentations in the local schools and at the tribal center.

The tribe offers a higher education scholarship program to tribal members pursuing a bachelor's degree or higher through BIA grants.

The Work/Learn program available through the tribe provides eight weeks of employment during the summer months to tribal members between the ages of 15 and 23.

A summer cultural education program is offered to tribal members. The program provides activities in traditional arts, dancing, music, games, and foods.

The adult vocational training program provides funding for tribal members over the age of 18 to achieve vocational skills training certification and complete skill-enhancing courses.

Health Care. Member health care is available through the Wampanoag Health Service. The primary service is contract health services. Through this program, tribal members residing on Martha's Vineyard may be eligible to receive comprehensive health services as a supplement to personal health insurance coverage through contract health providers.

The community health nurse for the tribe provides home- and community-based nursing services. Health risk screening, counseling, and consultation services are available through this program.

The tribe's community health coordinator serves as an advocate for tribal members who are seeking access to the health care system. The coordinator provides information for tribal members and guidance in attaining health care. The coordinator is also responsible for the Safe Kids program and other home and community safety and injury programs.

ENVIRONMENTAL CONCERNS
The tribe has been vocal concerning the inadequate cleanup activities of the bombing range on Nomans Island National Wildlife Refuge in Chilmark, Massachusetts. The U.S. Department of Defense failed to provide adequate cleanup of harmful materials on the island. The inadequate removal of the materials resulted in contamination of the island ponds, which has left the waters void of all life, and there is probable cause to believe that the remaining water sources are threatened by contamination.

Because of sensitivity to the area's wetlands and historical and archeological sites, only 97.49 acres of the Wampanoag land are developable. Through joint efforts by the tribe, the Center for Economic Development, the University of Massachusetts, and the Development Studio, Landscape Architecture Program, Graduate School of Design, Harvard University, a careful land development plan has been established.

Tribal lands and resources contained within them are managed for the sole use and benefit of tribal members. Access to tribal lands is restricted to tribal members only. The tribe offers an annual deer hunting season, a game check station, and waterfowl hunting seasons. The goals and programs of the tribe's natural resource department reflect the maintenance of traditional hunting and fishing practices and an effective wildlife management project.

The tribe in the past has purchased 100 bobwhite quail and 215 ring-necked pheasant for release on tribal lands. The aim of the project is to restore self-sustaining population of ground-nesting birds on the reservation.

MICHIGAN

Map from Tiller's Guide to Indian Country (1996 edition)

Photo Courtesy of National Park Service

MICHIGAN

Bay Mills

LOCATION AND LAND STATUS

The Bay Mills Indian Community is located approximately 15 miles west and southwest of Sault Ste. Marie, Michigan. The community's land consists of two separate areas, both of which are granted U.S. trust status. The majority of the land base lies northwest of Brimley, Michigan, while the remainder, approximately 600 acres, exists on Sugar Island in St. Mary's River. The community obtained additional land, increasing the land base from 2,209.47 acres to approximately 3,494 acres, of which 3,109 acres are in trust.

CULTURE AND HISTORY

The Bay Mills Indian Community is part of the larger Chippewa or Ojibwa population, which through a series of alliances once predominated over a vast territory in the Great Lakes Region, extending as far west as the Turtle Mountains of North Dakota. In alliance with early French in the region, they pushed the Sioux Tribes further west; in alliance with Pontiac's Rebellion in 1763, they drove the British from all their western outposts except Fort Pitt and Detroit. Later, Ojibwa warriors fought with Tecumseh in the last great Indian allied military campaign in the upper midwest region. After the defeat of Tecumseh in 1813, the various Chippewa Bands entered into a series of more than 30 treaties with the U.S., with the last treaty made in 1864.

The first land set-aside exclusively for the Bay Mills Indian Community was purchased by the Methodist Mission Society. The treaty of July 1, 1855, authorized the establishment of the reservation, and the U.S. Congress established the Bay Mills Reservation by the Appropriations Act of June 19, 1860.

Prior to the arrival of the Europeans and the ascent of the fur trade, the Bay Mills Chippewas subsisted primarily by hunting and fishing, along with some agricultural pursuits. The Chippewas turned to the fur trade as a means of acquiring items to barter and of solidifying military alliances.

The Bay Mills Community continues to assert its traditional and treaty rights and enjoys treaty-fishing rights in Lake Superior, Lake Huron, and Lake Michigan. As a result of resources reaped from recent economic successes, the community provides Ojibwa language classes through the tribal college.

GOVERNMENT

The government of the Bay Mills Indian Community is carried out according to a constitution adopted by the membership on August 8, 1936, and approved by the secretary of the interior on November 14, 1936, pursuant to the Indian Reorganization Act of 1934. The governing body is composed of a five-member executive council elected by the membership at large to two-year terms.

In addition to the executive council, the Bay Mills Indian Community has a tribal court whose jurisdiction covers the reservation. Court facilities include a courtroom, a jury deliberation room, a judge's chambers, a clerk's office, and a law library. Recently, all court cases were organized and maintained through a computerized network.

The Bay Mills Indian Community's law enforcement department has a two-component police force consisting of police and conservation officers. Each component is responsible for separate duties with police officers enforcing tribal, federal, and state criminal and civil laws, and conservation officers enforcing the fishing, hunting, and trapping laws of the Bay Mills Indian Community.

Other tribal government departments provide services, including health planning, substance abuse counseling and treatment, fire protection, educational services, social services, college administration, and financial and fiscal management.

ECONOMY

The Bay Mills' Indian Casino and Resort and the King's Club Casino are the primary forces that fuel the community economy, which branches into dependent service sector operations comprised of casino restaurants, tourist gift shops, a banquet and business conference center, and resort lodging. Additional economic activity in the community includes government operations and small private businesses comprised of grocery stores, small markets, banks, community restaurants, and additional lodging facilities.

Government as Employer. A significant source of employment for tribal members is in the public sector. The State of Michigan employs about 20 men and women on the reservation, and the federal government employees two tribal members.

Agriculture and Livestock. Bay Mills Indian Community has 770 acres of wetlands located in the eastern Upper Peninsula of Michigan. Four hundred and sixty acres were set-aside in October 1996 for a wetland preserve. Bay Mills Indian Community decided to utilize these wetlands for cultivating wild rice. In 1997 alone, tribal staff seeded 1,000 pounds of wild rice. The cultivation of wild rice is an increasingly innovative agricultural endeavor at the wetlands within the Bay Mills Indian Community.

Forestry. Thirteen hundred and ninety acres of the reservation are forested, with stands of pine, aspen, red oak, and maple predominating. Some 100 acres of the reservation have been harvested for timber.

Gaming. The Bay Mills Indian Community owns and operates the Bay Mills Resort and Casino and the King's Club Casino.

Bay Mills Indian Community
Federal reservation
Ojibwa (Chippewa)
Chippewa County, Michigan

Bay Mills Indian Community
of Michigan
12140 W. Lakeshore Drive
Brimley, MI 49715
906-248-3241
906-248-3283 Fax

Total area *(EPA data, 2004)*
3,185.48 acres

Federal trust lands
(EPA data, 2004)
3,109 acres

Population *(Tribal source, 2004)*
1,013

Tribal enrollment
(Tribal source, 2004)
1,610

Total labor force *2000 census*
462

Total labor force
(BIA labor report, 2001)
648

High school graduate or higher
2000 census
79.9%

Bachelor's degree or higher
2000 census
4.4%

Unemployment rate *2000 census*
10%

Unemployment rate
(BIA labor report, 2001)
7%

Per capita income *2000 census*
$12,948

Bay Mills

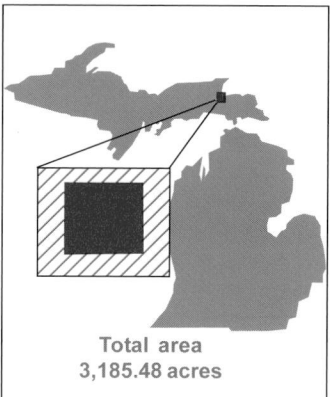

Total area
3,185.48 acres

The Bay Mills Resort and Casino is a class III casino with a 15,000-square-foot gaming floor filled with nearly 1,000 slot machines and 15 table games, including blackjack, roulette, craps, Let It Roll, Caribbean stud, and three card poker. The resort offers customers a 144-room hotel, two gaming areas, a conference center, three restaurants, a gift shop, and a sports bar with large golf simulators. For those who prefer live golf, the Wild Bluff Golf Course located adjacent to the resort offers 18 holes of championship golf.

Located two miles north from the Bay Mills Resort and Casino is the King's Club Casino. A class II casino opened in 1984, the smaller 7,400-square-foot gaming floor at the King's Club Casino offers 300 slot machines. A shuttle bus service is available, transporting customers back and forth between the two casinos.

Construction. The tribally owned Bay Mills Construction Company provides local excavation, dirt moving, and snow removal operations with a yard of tribally owned vehicles including backhoes, graders, tractors, and snow plows.

Services and Retail. In addition to the three restaurants located at the Bay Mills Resort and Casino, visitors may also dine at Chubby's Pizza, Willabee's Restaurant and Lounge, Van's Restaurant, and Wilcox Fish House Restaurant. The Brim-O-Bay Motel and the Cozy Inn provide additional lodging for visitors. The Brimcor Party Store and Gas provides convenience store services. Other stores include a hardware store, a carwash, a fireworks store, three markets, and a grocery store. There is also a credit union with a 24-hour ATM. The tribe owns and operates its own gas and convenience station.

Tourism and Recreation. The Bay Mills Indian Community owns an RV park for visitors and tourists as an additional component to the 144-room Bay Mills Hotel Resort. The Bay Mills RV Park has a 76-trailer capacity and provides each vehicle with a space that is 30 feet wide and 58 feet long, complete with water, electric, and cable hookups to meet the needs of RV travelers. The 18-hole Wild Bluff Golf Course, also located at the Bay Mills Resort, offers visitors a world-class double-teed driving range, two practice putting greens, and one green for brushing up on your chipping and bunker play. The Minnow Lake Campground and the Monocle Lake Campground provide travelers a scenic place to camp. Museum attractions in the area include the Wheels of History Museum and the Iroquois Point Lighthouse and Museum. The magnificent north woods of Michigan, the St. Mary's waterway, the island woodlands of the international boundary waters, a location in close vicinity to the Canadian province of Ontario, tribally provided boating opportunities, and exciting casino gaming opportunities make Bay Mills an attractive destination.

INFRASTRUCTURE
Electricity. Electric power is provided to 300 households by a federal cooperative that the homeowners pay directly.

Fuel. Natural gas is offered throughout the reservation. Some households still use individual propane tanks.

Transportation. The Chippewa County International Airport, served by commuter airlines, is located 25 miles from the reservation. Interstate 75 runs 20 miles east of the reservation, and

State Highway 28 runs 7 miles from the reservation. There is no rail or commercial bus service convenient to the reservation, but all the major freight carriers provide routine service.

Water Supply. A solid waste transfer station serves the needs of the Bay Mills Indian Community. The eastern end of the reservation is served by a sewage system, but homes and buildings on the western end are tied to septic tanks.

Telecommunications. A private phone company provides telephone service.

COMMUNITY FACILITIES AND SERVICES
The Bay Mills Indian Community maintains a community center for tribal members, along with outdoor recreational facilities. The Bay Mills Indian Community Recreation Department operates the Bay Mills Boys and Girls Club and Bay Mills Boxing Club. In 2001, the tribe opened The Armella LeBlanc Parker Center, a tribal elder's facility. In 2003, the tribe opened the new Commodity Foods Building, next to the elder's facility.

Education. Children residing at Bay Mills attend school at the Brimley Public School or the tribally operated Ojibwa Charter School, which opened in 2003. Bay Mills Community College, first established in 1984 as a vocational school, provides the community with the opportunity for postsecondary education. Bay Mills Community College has established North Central Accreditation and offers a thriving LPN nursing program, Anishnabek Ojibwa language program, and a newly introduced teacher education program, which is operated in conjunction with Ferris State University of Big Rapids, Michigan. The old Iroquois Lodge, located near the reservation, was recently purchased by the tribe and leased to Bay Mills Community College. After renovations are completed it will be used simultaneously as classroom space for the college's cultural and language programs, and as a home for the tribe's cultural programs. In 2004 the college will also begin offering a building trades program. This program will be located in a new building adjacent to the lodge.

Health Care. The Ellen Marshall Memorial Building, opened in 1997, serves as the location for the Bay Mills community health center and the Bay Mills dental clinic. The community health center offers all members of Bay Mills Indian Community affordable quality health care services. The health service staff provides up-to-date health care services to the community without sacrificing respect for traditional ways of healing. The Bay Mills dental clinic offers members various services such as exams, x-rays, cleanings, fillings, and treatments for jaw joint problems. Other health services include a 24-hour emergency medical service with EMT-basics, EMT-specialists, and EMT-paramedics on staff.

ENVIRONMENTAL CONCERNS
The Bay Mills Indian Community has concerns regarding the purity of their water. In 2001, the Bay Mills Indian Community conducted a study on the Waishkey River Watershed to assess the suspended sediments and water chemistry within the watershed. The test measured suspended sediments, flow rate, pH, ammonia-nitrogen, nitrite-nitrogen, alkalinity, carbon dioxide, chloride, hardness, and dissolved oxygen. Results of the test were then merged into a larger analysis.

LOCATION AND LAND STATUS

The Grand Traverse Band of Ottawa and Chippewa Indians has land holdings in six counties in the northwestern area of Michigan's Lower Peninsula. The majority of tribal members live in Peshawbestown, a community perched on the edge of Grand Traverse Bay, 23 miles north of Traverse City in Leelanau County. Tribal administrative offices are located in Peshawbestown, accounting for a majority of the tribal land base. Additional acreage, totaling approximately 10 acres on the eastern edge of Michigan's Upper Peninsula, is held in federal trust.

In an 1855 treaty, the eastern two-thirds of Leelanau County were ceded to the Indians of the area. Over time this land was lost, piece-by-piece, to fraudulent land schemes and legalized government appropriation, such as the Homestead Act. In 1934, the Grand Traverse Band petitioned the federal government for recognition under the Indian Reorganization Act; the petition was denied due to lack of funds from the BIA. Again in 1943, the band was denied federal recognition; however, in 1949, Leelanau County obtained 172 acres from the Michigan State Department of Conservation to be taken in trust for "Indian community purposes." Federal recognition of the band was not granted until May 27, 1980, despite clear references to the Ottawa people of the area in several nineteenth-century treaties and the strong Indian presence throughout the Leelanau Peninsula. Since its official recognition, the band has concentrated on improving the quality of life for all tribal members while expanding its land base. There are members living on tribal land in all six counties.

CLIMATE

Climate data is available for Traverse City, only 23 miles from Peshawbestown. Weather patterns in the area are typical of the midwest, heavily influenced by the Great Lakes. The average year-round daily high temperature is 55°F; the highest temperature on record is 105°F. The average year-round daily low temperature is 36°F. Winters are often harsh, with annual snowfalls of approximately 78 inches. The area receives an average total of 29 inches of rain annually.

CULTURE AND HISTORY

Historically, Michigan's Native population included three tribes, which made up the Three Fires Confederacy: the Odawas, or Ottawas; the Oda'Wa-Tomis, or Potawatomis; and the Anishinaabegs, or Ojibwas or Chippewas. These peoples lived by hunting and fishing in the game-rich forests surrounding the Great Lakes. Following the conflict between the French and British settlers for control of the North American colonies, known in the U.S. as the French and Indian Wars, contact with European settlers in the late eighteenth and early nineteenth centuries brought about declines in hunting and fishing. Farming, manufacturing, and wage work increased with the influx of settlers.

In spite of outside influences, the band's settlement areas on the Leelanau Peninsula remained constant and populated. Traditional lifestyles remained intact; elders in the community still speak Odawa, properly called Anishnabemowin, the original people's language, and many Ottawa customs are still practiced.

Life was difficult, particularly before federal re-recognition on May 27, 1980, when government assistance was not available. Since 1980, however, the Ottawas-Chippewas have made great strides; the band initiated several programs and established an economic development corporation to bring businesses to the reservation. Enormous improvements in all aspects of tribal life have been achieved, and the band works diligently to ensure its future stability. The band's gaming operation is very successful, and it has enabled the band to acquire a land base by repatriating some of its aboriginal territory.

GOVERNMENT

The Grand Traverse Band is governed by a popularly elected tribal council consisting of a chairperson and six council members, who function with the assistance of several advising subcommittees. A constitution, adopted in 1988, mandates a separate judiciary branch, to include the tribal court, the conservation court, and law enforcement services. The Grand Traverse Band tribal police have a mutual assistance agreement with the Leelanau County Sheriff's Department, patrolling and enforcing tribal law on reservation lands. The tribe, under PL-638, contracts with the BIA to administer key programs and services.

BUSINESS CORPORATION

The band formed an economic development corporation in 1983. The corporation functions as the governing body for the band's increasing tourism and recreational enterprise industry, especially the Grand Traverse Resort and Casino.

ECONOMY

The Grand Traverse Reservation's economy is primarily dependent upon its gaming enterprises, although there are still a small number of band members employed in the commercial fishing industry on Lake Michigan. Many are now employed in other small business enterprises, which have sprung up in support of the increased tourism and recreation and gaming market.

Government as Employer. Tribal government and gaming operations employ 1,090 people.

Gaming. The Grand Traverse Band was one of the first tribal entities in the U.S. to initiate gaming, opening the Super Bingo Palace in 1984. With considerable success over time, the band expanded its gaming opportunities, and it now has two gaming facilities. The Leelanau Sands Casino, in Peshawbestown, is one of the area's major employers. This casino, renovated in the mid-1990s, features over 30,000 square feet of gaming space, with 825 slot machines, 16 table games, 2 poker tables, and an entertainment venue. There is a 51-room hotel at the casino complex, the Leelanau Sands Casino Lodge, and the Eagles Ridge Conference Center with two restaurants.

The 39,014-square-foot Turtle Creek Casino, in Williamsburg, Michigan, offers 1,239 slot machines, 25 table games, 4 poker tables, and 2 restaurants. This facility employs 573 people. The 669-room Grand Traverse Resort and Spa, located next to the casino, offers luxury accommodations overlooking East Grand Traverse Bay on Lake Michigan, 85,000 square feet of convention and meeting space, a championship golf course, full-service spa facilities, and shopping, dining, and entertainment opportunities.

The band has offered more than the required two percent of its gaming revenues back to the communities within which the casinos are operating. Twenty-five percent of revenues go into tribal programs as a supplement, 15 percent of revenues go into economic development, 10 percent into long-term investment, and 50 percent into per capita distribution to tribal members.

Fisheries. A small number of band members rely on commercial fishing in Lake Michigan for self-employment.

Grand Traverse Band of Ottawa and Chippewa Indians Reservation
Federal reservation
Ottawa-Chippewa
Antrim, Benzie, Charlevoix, Grand Traverse, Leelanau, and Manistee counties, Michigan

Grand Traverse Band
of Ottawa and Chippewa
Indians
2605 N. West Bayshore Drive
Peshawbestown, MI 49682
231-534-7750
231-534-7568 Fax
gtb.nsn.us

Total area *(Tribal source, 2004)*
2,369 acres

Tribally owned lands
(Tribal source, 2004)
1,658 acres

Federal trust lands
(Tribal source, 2004)
711 acres

Population *(Tribal source, 2004)*
1,596

Tribal enrollment
(Tribal source, 2004)
3,986

Total labor force *2000 census*
254

Total labor force
(Tribal source, 2004)
1,090

High school graduate or higher
2000 census
75.8%

Bachelor's degree or higher
2000 census
4.8%

Unemployment rate *2000 census*
12.6%

Unemployment rate
(BIA labor report, 2001)
47%

Per capita income *2000 census*
$13,480

Grand Traverse

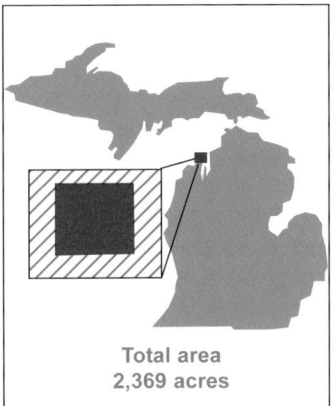

Total area
2,369 acres

Industrial Parks. An industrial park in the Peshawbestown area was under development in 1996. The park roads have been completed. The Benodjenh Childcare Center and the Strongheart Sports Complex are two new buildings that were constructed.

Services and Retail. In addition to the services and retail opportunities associated with the casinos, the band built The Lodge, offering affordable accommodations in a peaceful woodlands setting behind the Leelanau Sands Casino, and The Chalet, a remodeled beach house located on Grand Traverse Bay, across from the casino. Cedar View is a remodeled cottage located on Lake Michigan that offers accommodations for groups of eight. There is also the Eagle Town Market gas and convenience store.

Insurance. The tribe offers Blue Cross Blue Shield of Michigan coverage for government and gaming employees.

Media and Communication. The tribe publishes a monthly newsletter which is posted on their website.

Tourism and Recreation. In addition to the gaming facilities found at the reservation and the other resort and recreational amenities associated with the casinos, the reservation lies less than 25 miles from the Sleeping Bear Dunes National Lakeshore on Lake Michigan, a popular summertime tourist destination. Lake Michigan itself holds tremendous recreational opportunities for travelers, photographers, and wildlife enthusiasts. The band holds an annual powwow in Peshawbestown, drawing Native American and non-Native travelers from around the country.

In 2003, the band purchased a resort and spa in Traverse City, Michigan, from KSL Recreation. The facility, renamed the Grand Traverse Resort and Spa, features three nationally acclaimed golf courses and other luxury accommodations and facilities for travelers. There are plans to develop a skeet-shooting range on a 168-acre parcel of land the band owns near the resort. The Boardman River, a blue ribbon trout stream that drains into Grand Traverse Bay in Traverse City, flows through reservation lands near the resort. The band hopes to capitalize on area fly-fishing to supplement the attraction of the shooting range and golfing opportunities at their resort, already an accredited Orvis lodge. The band believes that with the addition of this non-gaming-based enterprise, their economic stability is better guaranteed over the next several years, as more and more tribal entities and non-Native entrepreneurs enter the gaming market.

INFRASTRUCTURE

Tribal administrative offices are located primarily in Peshawbestown, though there are also offices in Grand Traverse County.

Electricity. The regional supplier in each of the six counties provides electricity.

Fuel. Regional companies supply natural gas or propane; tribal members are responsible for their own utilities.

Water Supply. A well supplies water in the Peshawbestown area. A multimillion-dollar sewage treatment plant was completed in Peshawbestown in 1995 to serve the area.

Transportation. Peshawbestown is on M 22 (West Bay View Drive) between Northport and Sutton's Bay, 23 miles north of Traverse City. Regional public transportation serves the area. There is an international airport in Traverse City, as well as freight rail service and a bus station. There are casino shuttle buses and Bata Bus. Commercial trucking companies and UPS serve the reservation directly. The tribe owns two full-size school buses, which service the childcare center.

Telecommunications. Four telephone services provide for the six counties.

COMMUNITY FACILITIES AND SERVICES

The band has community centers in Peshawbestown, Benzie, Traverse City, and in Charlevoix County.

Public Safety. There is a volunteer fire department, and the seven officers of the tribal police are cross-trained as fire fighters and EMTs.

Education. The tribe has a Head Start program, with a new building of its own completed in 2001-the Benodjenh Childcare Center. Elementary through high school children attend area schools. The Johnson O'Malley Program supplements educational opportunities for all tribal schoolchildren in the six-county reservation area. The State of Michigan offers a free higher education tuition program for qualifying Native Americans.

The Grand Traverse Band Education Department offers the Anishinaabemowin (language) Program at two locations throughout the reservation so future generations will maintain language skills in the Native tongue. Four learning centers in separate reservation communities offer adult education and literacy programs, including GED prep courses, computer training, and career planning services. A satellite of Bay Mills Community College is located in various locations within the reservation.

Health Care. The tribe has its own health clinic funded in part by Indian Health Service. It has three part-time doctors, a nursing staff, and physicians aides. An expanded health care facility is being developed. More comprehensive medical care is available in Traverse City.

ENVIRONMENTAL CONCERNS

The 287-square-mile Boardman-Charlevoix River Watershed, which makes up large portions of Grand Traverse and Kalkaska counties in northwest Lower Michigan, and the Betsie-Platte Watershed combine to form the larger Grand Traverse Bay Watershed. Under threat from shoreline development, the watershed's water resources and wildlife are protected on tribal wetlands. Under an environmental agreement with the U.S. EPA, the band monitors groundwater recharge, and in cooperation with the Inter-Tribal Council of Michigan, it works to ensure water quality improvements and protects against erosion and other degradations to surface water quality.

In 1999, the band finalized a Wetland Conservation Plan as part of their Unified Watershed Assessment for the Environmental Protection Agency, Region 5. Protection of water quality is the band's highest environmental priority; however, in their 1999-2001 Tribal Environmental Agreement with the U.S. EPA, the band stated a desire to implement air quality management programs as well. In 1998, the band developed a recycling program for the six-county service area of the reservation.

Land Claims Distribution Trust Fund, Office of the Chairman, Grand Traverse
Band of Ottawa and Chippewa Indians

In 1971, the Indian Claims Commission settled a 1948 case against the U.S. government by awarding the Michigan Chippewa and Ottawa Indians $10.3 million in just compensation for ceded lands. However, the settlement money could not exit Federal government coffers until the tribes decided on a distribution formula, and inter-tribal disagreements prevented its transfer for two and a half more decades.

By the mid-1990s, the settlement fund had grown to more than $70 million. Appreciative of the benefits that this amount of money could generate for the disputing tribes, the Tribal Chairman of the Grand Traverse Band of the Ottawa and Chippewa Indians (GTB), undertook to bring the tribes to the negotiating table and begin work in earnest. The GTB Chairman's efforts created momentum and one year later, the tribes' decision was imbedded in the Michigan Indian Claims Settlement Act.

The Act establishes each tribe's portion of the settlement money and outlines parameters for its expenditure. For tribes prepared with an expenditure plan, the legislation actually specifies how the settlement money will be used. For tribes unprepared to embed an expenditure plan in law, the legislation gives the Secretary of the Interior the authority to approve both the process used to develop a plan and the plan itself. The proactive work of Grand Traverse's negotiators placed GTB among the first group, thus promoting the Band's self-determination over their money's use.

The GTB government's commitment to and "readiness" in the settlement process is commendable, but it is the Band's expenditure plan that is an even more important contribution to good governance. Whether Indian nations receive substantial financial settlements for claims against other governments, as in this case, or whether they earn substantial profits from the development if unique resources or market niches, American Indian governments are sometimes in the position of managing sudden and large monetary gains. On the one hand, the difficult present circumstances of many tribal members make immediate per capita distributions of this type of tribal income attractive; on the other hand, such distributions limit future generation's benefits. Remarkably, the Grand Traverse Band's innovative spending program makes it possible for the

tribal government to meet both short term pressure for per capita distribution and long-term fiduciary obligations. Eventually, it will even enable them to provide ongoing income support to tribal elders-a group whose economic security is of concern to many tribes.

In particular, the spending plan specifies that the Band's portion of the settlement be transferred to a Land Claims Distribution Fund and that the entire amount be invested (with an appropriate balance between income potential and wealth protection). The plan further directs the Band to post 80 percent of the investment principal as collateral for a loan and to distribute loan proceeds on a per capita basis to all eligible members. Income from the Fund's invested principal is to be applied to debt service until the loan is retired, and at that point, a permanent distribution fund for elders is to be established. After an initial fixed distribution, the plan calls for only 90 percent of the investment income from the Elders' Land Claim Distribution Fund to be distributed. The remaining 10 percent of the investment income is to be reinvested in order to maintain-and ever increase-the Fund's value. In essence, the Elder's Fund will behave like a tribal social security fund, but with benefits based on the Fund's returns and size, not on individual contributions. While the Band's Council may add to the Fund as it sees fit, the principal can never be distributed on a per capita basis. Finally, to further solidify the Band's self-determination over the settlement money, the law specifies that the Secretary of the Interior will have no trust responsibility for the Funds.

By, 1998, GTB had implemented the first stages of the spending plan. Favorable market conditions were enabling the Band's Land Claims Distribution Fund managers to accelerate loan repayment and to move even more quickly toward establishment of the Elder's Fund. The Band's Council, Chairmen, and citizenry continue to be supportive of the spending plan and of the opportunity it now presents to substantively honor tribal elders' lifetime contributions to and sacrifices for the community. And, because GTB's settlement negotiator had the foresight to "lock-in" self-determination, the Band will be able to continue to effectively manage its own settlement award, rather than see it be subject to the vagaries of Federal administration.

Honoring Nations
Honoree 1999

Text in its entirety from:
The Harvard Project On
American Indian Economic
Development

John F. Kennedy School
of Government
Harvard University

Honoring Nations Honoree 2000

Tribal Court, Grand Traverse Band of Ottawa and Chippewa Indians

The vagaries of U.S. government policy toward American Indian nations in the 1900s had a particularly damaging effect on the Grand Traverse Band of Ottawa and Chippewa Indians (GTB). During various and overlapping periods, they existed as a self-governing Indian community, a non-profit corporation, and a state-recognized Band with lands held by the local county government to meet the housing needs of the immediate Indian community. Finally, in 1980, the Band obtained federal recognition and, in 1988, developed a constitutional government.

In this process, GTB's leaders were acutely aware that developing a constitutional government was not about constitution writing alone. The challenge was also to develop a government that accorded with community members' beliefs about who should hold authority and how it should be exercised, so that the system outlined in the written constitution would be both workable and sustainable. For example, GTB leaders involved in the development of the Band's constitutional government felt there was substantial value in having a separate and independent tribal judiciary, and therefore wrote provi-

Grand Traverse

Honoring Nations
Honoree 2000

Text in its entirety from
The Harvard Project On
American Indian Economic
Development

John F. Kennedy School
of Government
Harvard University

sions for one into the Band's constitution. But for the Court truly to operate as the fundamental institution of government envisioned by its founders, it would need to be used by tribal members, operate in a way tribal members appreciated, and be able to exercise its independence effectively. This "constitutionalization" of the Court is occurring at Grand Traverse and deserves recognition.

When the GTB Tribal Court opened its doors in 1988, it heard very few cases. The Chief Judge worked only part-time in the evenings, with little or no staff. Just over ten years later, the Court has grown into a well-functioning and oft-used institution, hearing as many as 500 cases a year. The Chief Judge now works full time, as does his staff, which includes an Associate Judge, three court clerks, and a tribal court administrator. The Band also has established an Appellate Court, comprised of three appellate justices.

Despite this remarkable maturation, the Chief Judge became concerned that, in some cases, the Court's western dispute resolution mechanisms did not serve the community well. His experiences on the bench convinced him that tribal members would value a system that relied on more indigenous practices. Thus, the GTB Court has recently begun to incorporate Ottawa and Chippewa culture into the legal system through Peacemaker Courts. As in other communities, peacemaking is a non-adversarial, traditionally based process of conflict resolution. At GTB, the procedure is for two peacemakers to be present to facilitate the session, but not to decide issues in the case; for all parties to the dispute to participate; and for participants to rely on and use emblems of blessing, comfort, open conversation, listening, wisdom, and peace in their conversation.

While the Peacemaker Court is still in its development phases,

the peacemakers themselves already have had an impact on the community. Because their initial jurisdiction involved juvenile offenses, they have worked to become more involved with GTB youth. In 1999, for example, the director of the Peacemakers and the tribal prosecutor conducted a 150-mile canoe trip for at-risk youth, to help them develop social skills and confidence. At the end of the trip, the peacemaker asked each participant to become the "caretaker" of an eagle feather, in an effort to remind the youths to be good stewards of the community's values. Later, when one trip participant ran afoul of the law, the Court was able to officially remind him of his stewardship responsibilities-evidence of a creative synergy between the western-style court and the peacemakers' preventative work.

Finally, and perhaps most importantly, the GTB Court is effectively establishing its independence. A true separation of powers, in which the branches of government serve as a check on the actions of the others, is difficult for many governments to achieve. All too often, American Indian nations' judiciaries succumb to the volatile influences of tribal politics. But the Grand Traverse Tribal Court is achieving status as a separate and independent branch of government. Rulings that adversely affect the Tribal Council have been respected and followed by the elected leadership, instead of devolving into a political tugs-of-war. While building precedents in the area of political-judicial relations takes time, the GTB Court and Council are laying a strong foundation for government constituted on a respectful separation of powers.

The Grand Traverse Tribal Court is growing, adapting to tribal culture by pursuing Ottawa and Chippewa approaches to conflict resolution, and establishing itself as a strong, separate and independent branch of government-a combination that has, and will continue to, serve the Grand Traverse Band well.

Hannahville

Hannahville Reservation
Federal reservation
Potawatomi
Menominee County, Michigan

Hannahville Indian Community
N14911 Hannahville B-1 Road
Wilson, MI 49896
906-466-2932
906-466-2001 Fax
hannahville.org

LOCATION AND LAND STATUS
The Hannahville Reservation spans 5,962 acres of Michigan's Upper Peninsula, near the Green Bay section of Lake Michigan, approximately 60 miles north of the Wisconsin line. A Congressional Act established the reservation on June 30, 1913. The land consisted of small parcels scattered among non-Indian holdings around the towns of Harris and Wilson, Michigan. Since the late 1990s, the tribe has purchased additional lands for housing development, cultural activities, and general future development.

CULTURE AND HISTORY
The Hannahville Potawatomis originally lived in the region of Michigan, Wisconsin, Illinois, Indiana, and Ohio. They had settlements that surrounded Lake Michigan and bordered the U.S. Michigan side of the St. Claire River and Lake St. Claire. While the 1833 Treaty of Chicago called for the Wisconsin Potawatomis to move west of the Mississippi River, the band that would become the Hannahville Potawatomis declined to move. The tribe receded into the most remote areas of their territories, into Door Peninsula and crossing into Michigan's Upper Peninsula, mostly the Cedar River area. In 1883, a Chippewa preacher named Peter Marksman took note of the refugees' plight, and lent the group money to begin building a permanent settlement near the town of Harris (near the site of the present-day Hannahville Reservation). In 1913 the U.S. Congress formally recognized the community's existence by purchasing numerous small parcels of land for it around the towns of Harris and Wilson.

During the late nineteenth century, members of the Hannahville Community subsisted largely on small-scale farming. Primary crops included corn, squash, beans, pumpkins, potatoes, and other vegetables. Tribal members also worked seasonally in the region's lumber industry. By the early part of the twentieth century, their fields were declining in fertility and the best quality timber had been harvested. At the same time, state and federal governments grossly neglected the tribe, leaving it without health care and with very poor infrastructure income. Impoverished conditions bred disease, and during the 1940s and early 1950s tuberculosis was a major health problem among the tribe.

It was not until the 1960s and 1970s that conditions began to improve noticeably. The Hannahville Potawatomi Tribal Council began taking bold initiatives, working with the Michigan Agency to devise economic development plans, which allowed the tribe sovereignty over its forest, wildlife, and human resources. They also created social programs such as alcohol treatment, legal aid, housing assistance, and educational services. The real economic turning point for the tribe came in 1990 when it opened its casino, providing tribal members with employment opportunities on the reservation. The tribe has consistently emphasized the value of the Potawatomi language, traditional customs, and reverence for the environment. For nearly 20 years now, the tribe has hosted the Great Lakes Powwow, celebrating Potawatomi traditions in song, dance, and art.

GOVERNMENT

The tribe reorganized under the 1934 IRA, adopting a constitution and bylaws on July 23, 1936. The tribe is a 638 self-governance tribe with a tribal council of 12 people, with two alternatives that are elected to three-year terms. Officers include a chairperson, a vice-chairperson, a secretary, and a treasurer. Tribal government agencies include law enforcement, a judicial branch, social services, higher education, employment assistance, adult education, Johnson O'Malley, Indian Child Welfare, general assistance, and housing improvement.

ECONOMY

The Hannahville Chip-In's Resort and Casino contributes the largest amount of revenue and employment opportunities to the Hannahville Indian Community's economy. The tribal government, the service sector, and a construction company are the driving forces for the remainder of the economy.

Government as Employer. The Hannahville Potawatomi Tribe reports that the tribal government employs a total of 900 people. The law enforcement department employs 13 people, and the tribal court employs six people.

Economic Development Projects. The Hannahville Indian Community plans to expand its industrial base with a 1,000-megawatt coal-burning power plant and a new ethanol plant. Currently these plans are in the design phase. The $1.3 billion project is scheduled for completion in 2007.

Forestry. In collaboration with the BIA, the tribe is developing a forestry management plan. A BIA forester works with the tribe in managing its forestlands. At the present, there are 4,000 acres of timberland with mixed and hardwood pine.

Gaming. The Hannahville Potawatomis own and operate the Chip-In's Island Resort and Casino. The class III 55,000-square-foot facility has a gaming floor consisting of 2 craps tables, 20 blackjack tables, 2 Let-It-Ride tables, Spanish 21, roulette, three-card poker, four-card poker, live keno, live poker, and over 970 slot machines. There are also various gaming tournaments and bingo seven-days a week. Chip-In's Resort offers two fine dining locations, an ice creamery, and resort lodging. Originally opened in 1985 as the Hannahville Casino, Chip-In's Island Resort has been renovated various times, the most recent major addition being a convention center in 1999, prior to becoming the facility that stands today. The tribe has begun an expansion project of its gaming operation. This $40,000,000 project will increase the gaming areas, add a new restaurant, add a larger theater, double the capacity of the convention center, and add 229 new hotel rooms, including a floor of suites. It is expected to be completed in the fall of 2006.

Two percent of gaming revenues go directly to local governments according to the gaming compact. Gaming revenues contributed to the expansion of Hannahville's infrastructure, including renovation of the Tribal Administration Center in 1994, the construction of Hannahville's Medical Center in 1997, and funding support for the dialysis center at the OSF St. Francis Hospital in nearby Escanaba, Michigan.

Construction. The Hannahville Construction Company is a tribally owned enterprise, which has focused on reservation-based projects. The company's minority status is pending, whereupon it will begin pursuing outside contracts as well. The company employs 14 tribal members.

Mining. Some sand and gravel mines are located on the reservation. The products of these mines are primarily used for on-reservation maintenance and construction purposes.

Services and Retail. The Hannahville Chip-In's Island Resort and Casino features a full all-you-can-eat buffet at the Firekeeper's Restaurant, fine dining at the Coral Reef Grille, and gourmet ice cream at Thornbury's Frozen Custard Creamery. There is also a dinner-theater style show lounge and a retail shop located inside the resort. Chip-In's Resort offers 113 rooms of luxurious lodging that include queen, king, and Jacuzzi suites. The Island Oasis, a full-service convenience store, provides visitors with a gas station and a place to pick up a snack.

Tourism and Recreation. In addition to the Hannahville's Chip-In's Casino and Resort, the community offers visitors a recreational park with an RV park and campsites. There is also an amphitheater that provides a facility for entertainment venues. The Hannahville Indian Community holds their annual powwow in the summer each year; the event is open to the public and features traditional dances, ceremonies, and crafts.

INFRASTRUCTURE

Electricity. Wisconsin Electric and Alger, and Delta Cooperative Electrical Association provide electricity.

Fuel. MichCon provides the reservation with natural gas.

Water Supply. The Hannahville Potawatomi Tribe owns and operates the reservation's water and wastewater utilities.

Transportation. The community is accessible via U.S. Highway 2 and U.S. Highway 41. Delta County Airport provides the area with air travel opportunities and makes Hannahville a global destination.

Telecommunications. Ameritech provides the reservation with telephone service. Charter Communications provides the area with cable television, Internet, and broadband services.

COMMUNITY FACILITIES AND SERVICES

The tribe's Community Tribal Center is the center of community activity.

Education. Children residing in the community attend the Hannahville School, which provides K-12 education and child care for children of all ages.

Health Care. Using revenue from the community's gaming industry, the Hannahville Indian Community opened the Hannahville Medical Center in 1997. The tribe's department of health and human services operates the Medical Center, which provides services including outpatient physician, dental, pharmacy, laboratory, and outreach nursing. The department also provides mental health, substance abuse, and family social services. All medical services are offered in conjunction with traditional healing methods.

Hannahville

Total area *(Tribal source, 2004)*
5,856.13 acres

Federal trust lands
(Tribal source, 2004)
5923.88 acres

Population *2000 census*
395

Tribal enrollment
(Tribal source, 2004)
754

Total labor force *2000 census*
136

High school graduate or higher
2000 census
81.5%

High school graduate or higher
(Tribal source, 2004)
70%

Bachelor's degree or higher
2000 census
2.3%

Unemployment rate *2000 census*
14%

Unemployment rate
(BIA labor report, 2001)
44%

Per capita income *2000 census*
$9,969

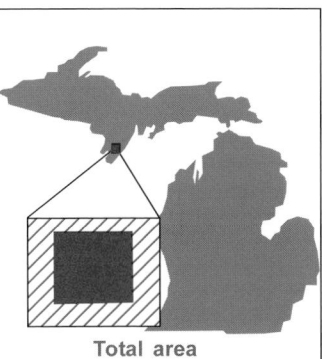

Total area
5,856.13 acres

Pine Creek

Pine Creek Reservation
Federal reservation
Nottawaseppi Huron Band
of Potawatomi
Calhoun County, Michigan

Huron Potawatomi, Inc.
2221 11/2 Mile Road
Fulton, MI 49052
269-729-5151
269-729-5920 Fax
nhbpi.com

Total area *(Tribal source, 2004)*
370 acres

Tribally owned lands
(Tribal source, 2004)
370 acres

State trust lands
(Tribal source, 2004)
120 acres

Population *(Tribal source, 2004)*
666

Tribal enrollment
(Tribal source, 2004)
666

Tribal enrollment
(BIA labor report, 2001)
428

Total labor force *2000 census*
6

Total labor force
(BIA labor report, 2001)
192

High school degree or higher
2000 census
100%

Bachelor's degree or higher
2000 census
30%

Unemployment rate
2000 census
0%

Unemployment rate
(BIA labor report, 2001)
40%

Per capita income *2000 census*
$25,569

LOCATION AND LAND STATUS

The Pine Creek Reservation is located in southwestern central Michigan near the towns of Athens and Fulton, with tribal headquarters in Fulton. They also maintain satellite offices in Grand Rapids, Michigan, 55 miles north of the Indiana border and Wyoming, Michigan, a suburb of Grand Rapids. The Pine Creek River, after which the reservation is named, runs through reservation lands near Athens. Battle Creek, Michigan, the closest urban hub, lies 14 miles north of the reservation via State Road 66.

In 1845, William and Louise Booth, in conjunction with Michigan Governor John Barry, established a 40-acre land trust along Pine Creek River in Calhoun and Barry counties on behalf of the Nottawaseppi Huron Band. In 1848 President James K. Polk conveyed another 80 acres to the state reservation. These lands have remained in state trust and are classified as a tax-exempt Indian reservation. These original 120 acres became the Pine Creek Reservation.

CLIMATE

There is no climate data recorded for Fulton, Michigan, the location of tribal headquarters; however, there is information for Battle Creek, Michigan, only 14 miles north of reservation lands. The average year-round daily high temperature at Battle Creek is 58°F, with the highest temperature ever recorded of 104°F. The average year-round daily low temperature is 39°F, with the lowest temperature on record of -24°F. The area receives approximately 33 inches of rain annually, and 40 inches of snow.

CULTURE AND HISTORY

The Nottawaseppi Huron Potawatomis are descendants of the Algonquian Potawatomi people, a Great Lakes tribe closely related to the Ojibwes and Ottawas. The Potawatomis hunted for elk, deer, beaver, and bear, and fished along the shores of Lake Superior and Lake Michigan in the area of the present-day state of Michigan, and they raised beans, squash, peas, melons, and other food crops. They also tapped maple trees for syrup to make sugar. During the seventeenth century fur trade wars, the Potawatomis gradually moved further west under pressure from other tribes fleeing Iroquois war parties. Throughout the eighteenth century, the British and French struggled for hegemony in North America, largely within Potawatomi territory; the Potawatomis participated in the failed Pontiac Rebellion against the British, which flared from 1763 to 1769.

It was the fledgling U.S. that eventually ended Potawatomi autonomy. The treaties of 1807 and 1821 restricted Potawatomi territory to southwestern Michigan. The 1833 Treaty of Chicago, a land-cession treaty, forcibly removed many Potawatomis to lands west of the Mississippi River. In 1839, the U.S. Army forcibly relocated many Potawatomis to Oklahoma and Kansas; these people became known as the Citizens' Band of Potawatomis in Oklahoma and the Prairie Band of Potawatomis, located primarily in Horton, Kansas. Resistance to this forced relocation resulted in the political and geographical disintegration of the Potawatomi Nation. A small number of Potawatomis had fled to nearby Illinois and Canada, then went home as soon as it was safe to do so. Two of these returning band members purchased 80 acres, then convinced the State of Michigan to donate another 40 acres. These 120 acres became the original reservation, thereby making the Nottawaseppi Huron Band of Potawatomis one of three Potawatomi bands to remain in Michigan. The band purchased an additional 132 acres near the

original reservation in order to continue tribal development, and it is seeking federal trust status for a 79-acre parcel of land to construct a casino near Battle Creek.

Today, members of the Nottawaseppi Huron Band of Potawatomis are dispersed throughout a seven-county area of southern Michigan and the remaining U.S. The tribe received federal recognition on December 19, 1995.

GOVERNMENT

The Huron Potawatomi's Pine Creek Reservation is governed by a five-member tribal council composed of a chairperson, a vice-chairperson, a treasurer, a secretary, and a sergeant-at-arms. The tribe's constitution and bylaws were ratified on July 17, 1970, under a State of Michigan corporate charter. The following departments provide services to band members: education, enrollment, operations and finance, housing, health and human services, and environmental. Throughout 2004 and 2005, the band is developing its own tribal court with assistance from a planning and development grant provided by the office of justice programs. Codes and ordinances are being drafted.

The band has formulated a tribal strategic plan to guide program, planning, and development objectives, to formulate grant applications, and to consolidate ongoing program evaluation efforts through 2008. The tribal council evaluates the entire strategic plan annually, conducts community gatherings to update community needs information, and changes the plan as needed.

Beginning in 1997, the Nottawaseppi Huron Band of Potawatomi Indian Housing Authority received a development grant that provides funding for the position of housing director. The award also provides funding for housing rehabilitation, emergency assistance, new construction, and demolition of unsafe housing on reservation lands. Funds provided by an Indian housing block grant are used for rehabilitation, new construction, and emergency assistance as well. These monies also provide a Traineeship and Apprenticeship Program (TAP). A separate low-income energy grant, administered by the Inter-Tribal Council of Michigan, provides emergency home energy assistance to band members threatened with final notice of heat shut-off.

BUSINESS CORPORATION

The band conducts business under the name Huron Potawatomi, Inc.

ECONOMY

Because there is no federal reservation, there is no consolidated local economy for the Pine Creek Reservation. Unemployment among the dispersed band members remains high, approximately 40 percent in the 2000 census. Most working band members are employed in the wage economy of their local communities, including Fulton, Athens, Battle Creek, and Grand Rapids, Michigan.

Government as Employer. In 2004, tribal government employed a total of 30 band members.

Gaming. In 2004, the band had plans for a 200,000-square-foot casino, to be built on 79 acres of trust lands located along I-94 at 11 Mile Road (Exit 104) in Emmet Township, Michigan. To be named the FireKeepers Casino, it would be located seven miles from downtown Battle Creek. It is anticipated that the development will add more than 2,000 jobs to the Calhoun County economy; 700 of them would be permanent positions within the casino once it opened. The band has projected 2.9 million visitors per year to create expected revenues totaling more than $100 million annually.

The band received State of Michigan approval to build and operate a casino when the legislature approved the class II and class III Gaming Compact in 1998. Under the compact's terms, the band would be required to pay: $50,000 annually to the State of Michigan for oversight services; eight percent of their slot machine and video gaming proceeds to the Michigan Strategic Fund; and two percent of revenues to the community in which the facility operates, in the form of tax-exempt, charitable contributions. In April 2004, the District of Columbia Federal District Court dismissed legal challenges to the development.

INFRASTRUCTURE

Tribal headquarters at Fulton and reservation lands are accessible via north-south State Route 66 and east-west via State Route 60/66. Interstate 94 passes east-west 13 miles north of the reservation.

Electricity. Regional electricity providers supply electricity to individual tribal members.

Fuel. Regional providers offer gas service.

Water Supply. Five wells provide water, and septic tanks handle waste for on-reservation facilities.

Transportation. Commercial and private air services are available in Kalamazoo, 30 miles northwest and in Battle Creek, 14 miles north. Major trucking companies and express package carriers serve Battle Creek, as do commercial bus lines. From 2000 throughout 2004, the band received funding for transportation planning. It was converted to a construction contract in 2003, in order to build the Pine Creek Reservation Trailway.

COMMUNITY FACILITIES AND SERVICES

The tribe maintains an administration building located in Fulton. The band receives a community services block grant, administered through the housing department, which provides food, clothing, and other miscellaneous financial assistance for qualified members.

Education. Children attend public schools in the Battle Creek and Athens school districts. In 2004, in collaboration with the Gun Lake and the Pokagon bands, the Huron Band received a three-year grant via the Administration for Native Americans to implement a language preservation program for the Potawatomi language.

The band received a library grant in 2003 to preserve old tribal photographs on CD-ROM. Another library grant in 2004 provided for the purchase of Native American resource materials for use by the education department.

Health Care. Two health offices serve band members; one is located in Battle Creek, the other is located in Grand Rapids. The annual funding agreement with the U.S. Indian Health Service provides a community health representative, a behavioral health component, along with an administrative assistant, a community health nurse, a part-time case manager, a part-time planner, a nurse practitioner, and a health director. The reservation is also served by private physicians in Athens and Union City and hospitals in Battle Creek.

Multiyear grants help to fund several programs, services, and the medical providers necessary to operate them. A STEPS grant pays for a health educator to provide diabetes, asthma, and obesity education and prevention services. Another diabetes program focuses on nutrition services and exercise programs, supplemented by a Title VI nutrition grant for band members 55 years of age and older. This program provides a dietician to offer nutritional consultation and monetary assistance in the form of grocery vouchers for band elders. A one-year injury prevention project award will provide smoke detectors, carbon monoxide detectors, fire escape ladders, and home injury prevention educational services to band members.

ENVIRONMENTAL CONCERNS

In December 2003, the EPA designated Calhoun County, Michigan, and all tribal lands therein, a non-attainment area under Section 107(d)(1) of the Clean Air Act for failing to meet the eight-hour ozone health standard required by the act. In 2004, the band listed water quality and wetlands as their highest environmental priority, followed by air quality and preservation of natural resources.

In May 2004, the leaders of 12 Michigan tribes, including the Nottawaseppi Huron Band of Potawatomis, and the State of Michigan entered into an intergovernmental agreement wherein they pledged mutual support of one another and to work in partnership to clean up pollution and eliminate non-native fish species from Michigan lakes and waterways.

The band's environmental department received General Assistance Program (GAP) funding for the environmental director's position to oversee projects such as water monitoring, solid waste, and cultural plant repropagation. They received a tribal wildlife grant to develop a wildlife habitat assessment and restoration plan, to establish a greenhouse for plant repropagation and beetle production, and to eliminate and control invasive plant species and conduct revegetation projects. An EPA pesticide grant permits testing of band members' wells for contamination.

The band received an EPA clean air grant to implement initiatives designed to identify sources of outdoor air pollution, to assess and monitor air quality, and to test indoor air quality (radon detection) in band members' homes. There are two air quality specialists on staff. In 2003-2004, a solid waste grant, also from the EPA, was being used to develop a solid waste management plan. In 2004, the band was completing a draft Tribal Brownfield Program with an EPA-Brownfields planning grant.

Pine Creek

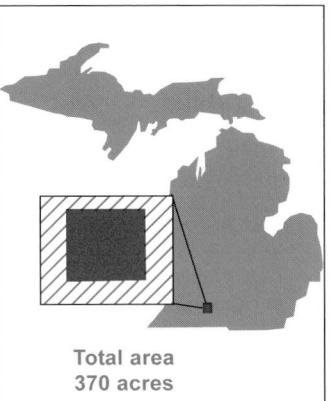

**Total area
370 acres**

Isabella Reservation
Federal reservation
Anishinabe (Chippewa)
Isabella County, Michigan

Saginaw Chippewa Tribe
7070 East Broadway
Mt. Pleasant, MI 48858
989-775-4000
989-772-3508 Fax
sagchip.org

Total area (Tribal source, 2004)
1,415 acres

Federal trust lands
(Tribal source, 2004)
1,415 acres

Tribally owned lands
(Tribal source, 2004)
1,261 acres

Population 2000 census
25,822

Tribal enrollment
(BIA labor report, 2003)
3,016

Total labor force 2000 census
13,768

High school graduate or higher
2000 census
85%

Bachelor's degree or higher
2000 census
24.4%

Unemployment rate
2000 census
5.69%

Unemployment rate
(BIA labor report, 2001)
19%

Per capita income 2000 census
$18,862

LOCATION AND LAND STATUS

The Isabella Reservation is still comprised of the same 138,240 acres ceded by the U.S. in the Treaty of 1864. The reservation is near the geographic center of Michigan's lower peninsula, and the northern portion of the city of Mount Pleasant lies within its boundaries; thus the reservation's population is notably large.

The Saginaw, Swan Lake, and Black River Chippewas signed two prior land cession treaties on May 9, 1836, and January 14, 1837. On August 2, 1855, the three parties signed another treaty, and the U.S. granted them allotted lands in several townships. However, in a treaty signed on October 18, 1864, the tribes relinquished still more land, and those that had selected land in a township at Saginaw Bay had to move to the Isabella Reservation. Land was allotted among tribal members in varying amounts; this allotment process preceded the General Allotment Act of 1887. There are 22 allotment parcels left that total 723 acres.

CULTURE AND HISTORY

The Saginaw Chippewa Indian Tribe traces its roots to three bands of Chippewas or Ojibwas that once occupied most of the northeastern and southern portions of Michigan's lower peninsula. These three bands were the Saginaw, Swan Creek, and Black River bands of Chippewas. In Ojibwe, the language of the Saginaw Chippewa Tribe, their name is Anishinabe, meaning "the First People" or "the People." The bands were involved in about 30 treaties with the federal government beginning in 1795 and ending with the treaty of 1864. Allotment schemes implemented during the 1850s and 1860s defrauded the Indians out of much of the land promised them in these treaties. By the beginning of the twentieth century, the individual bands owned little of the trust property once reserved for them. The Isabella Reservation, for instance, before 1864 entailed approximately 138,000 acres, while in the 1990s tribal and allotted lands comprise 1,467 acres. As the tribe lost its land base during the late 1800s, the federal government gradually abandoned its responsibilities for maintaining its end of the trust relationship. During the twentieth century, the tribe spent a tremendous amount of energy and resources reestablishing its right to self-government. The Saginaw Tribe agreed to the terms of the 1934 IRA and accepted government promises that this would grant the tribe access to federal programs and would relieve the suffering and poverty it was experiencing during the Great Depression.

During WWII many Anishinabe men served in the U.S. armed forces. Later other members found themselves able to secure decent wage jobs that had previously been closed to them. During the 1950s and 1960s, the tribal government focused intently on raising standards of living on their respective reservations. State and federal grant funds proved instrumental in this regard, as did the revenues from gaming. The tribe won control of a $10 million judgment fund as a result of congressional legislation on June 30, 1986, and it succeeded in further reestablishing its right to self-government. On August 20, 1993, the gaming compact between the State of Michigan and the Saginaw Chippewa Tribe was signed.

The tribe maintains its strong Anishinabe culture through participation in intertribal powwows, sweat lodges, and talking circles, as well as Big Drum ceremonies. Ojibway, the language of the Saginaws, is still spoken and is passed on to younger generations.

GOVERNMENT

The tribe reorganized on May 6, 1937, under the provisions of the 1934 Indian Reorganization Act. It amended its constitution and bylaws; they were approved on November 4, 1986. The tribal government is administered by the tribal council, which is comprised of 12 members, each elected to two-year terms and each representing one of the three electoral districts. The council includes 10 representatives from District 1 (the Isabella Reservation) and one representative each from District 2 (Saganing) and District 3 (members at large). Tribal council members are elected by registered voters in their respective districts. The council then selects its executive officers, the chief, subchief, secretary, and treasurer. Enrolled members 18 years and older may vote for their district representative. Officers include a chief, a subchief, a treasurer, and a secretary. The tribal council has allocated generous funds to improve the community and infrastructure. The tribal court maintains law and order within the Isabella Reservation and the Saganing district. The tribe has over 30 different departments in tribal government alone, including police, fire, courts, accounting, health/clinic, human resources, elders, education, public relations, planning/housing/environmental, cultural preservation, administration, utilities, facilities management, education, and tribal college.

The tribal social services department, which operates under the title "Helping Our Families," provides various programs including a family-counseling program called Families First. The department also offers the Indian child welfare program and provides parenting education, child development classes, family advocacy, individual counseling, and home maintenance skills. The department's general assistance program supports unemployed workers actively seeking employment.

The information technology department supports the tribe's technological needs. The department has various duties, including computer workstation maintenance, telephone connection, tribal computer networking, systems security, tribal electronic publishing, and providing tribal offices with the latest software applications. The planning department administers the tribal building code. Department duties include inspecting and enforcing code to ensure safety in all construction endeavors on the reservation.

ECONOMY

The gaming industry drives the economy of the Isabella Reservation with constant increasing momentum. The Soaring Eagle Casino employs 4,000 people in its various operations, which include casino floor gaming, dining, lodging, retail, and operation of a museum. Along with gaming, state and federal grants, and the tribe's investment portfolio provide major sources of revenue. Agriculture, construction, government operations, and tourism comprise additional economic activity on the reservation.

Government as Employer. The tribal government employs 3,909 tribal members and is a major source of employment on the reservation. These positions range from administrative to judicial and law enforcement, from grant writing to child welfare, from health care operations to staffing the education department.

Agriculture and Livestock. The tribe is looking into possible uses for its 550 tillable acres of farmland. Some of the options include organic farming and reforestation initiatives. The tribe is also fighting the outbreak of the emerald ash borer, which is threatening to decimate the ash population. The ash trees are important to the tribe culturally, as well as being an important source of basket making materials.

Forestry. Tribal lands contain approximately 150 acres of noncommercial forest; these are mainly oak, beech, and maple trees.

Gaming. The Saginaw Chippewa Tribe owns The Soaring Eagle Casino and Resort, one of the largest gaming destinations in the Midwest. The 210,000-square-foot facility consists of 4,704 slots, 67 table games, and 928 bingo seats. The resort offers guests 512 luxurious rooms, 26,000 square feet of meeting, conference and entertainment space, a complete spa with a health club, and an indoor pool. The resort offers dining at the Water Lily Restaurant, and at the Sinii Kaung Steak and Chop House. Visitors may attain a less formal meal at the Little Eagle Café, which offers pizza, French fries, hot dogs, nachos, soups, and sandwiches. Cocktails are served at the Water Lily Lounge. The Ziimiwing Cultural Society's Naanooshke (hummingbird) Gallery within the Soaring Eagle Resort gives visitors an opportunity to view true Native American fine art. There are also two gift shops. The enterprise employs 4,000 people.

Construction. Until 1995 the tribe owned a construction company, which employed six tribal members. A joint venture construction firm between the tribe and another party employs 12 people. A new water tower was under construction during the summer of 1995. Completed in the same year was the tribe's new public safety building. The tribal council also built homes for several families on the reservation during 1995.

Mining. Extensive oil and gas exploration is underway within the reservation boundaries, including on some allotted lands.

Services and Retail. The Saginaw Chippewa Indian Tribe of Michigan's Ziibiwing Cultural Society owns NativeDirect, an enterprise that consists of two gift shops and a gallery. The Dawe-Wi-Gamigoonse (Little Store) Gift Shop, located inside the Soaring Eagle Casino, offers visitors handmade Native American crafts, Soaring Eagle souvenirs and clothing, contemporary Native American clothing, handmade Native American jewelry, and discount cigars and cigarettes. The Jeemon-aince (Little Canoe) Gift Shop, located across the street from the resort casino, features similar products to purchase.

Media and Communications. The Tribal Observer is the tribal newspaper.

Tourism and Recreation. In addition to the Soaring Eagle Resort and Casino, the tribe operates the Saginaw-Chippewa Campground, featuring 64 attractive, semi-wooded sites (with 45 full hookups). Amenities include a swimming pool and a picnic area. The Little Elk's Retreat Tribal Powwow is held annually during the first weekend in August; Central Michigan University sponsors a powwow every April.

INFRASTRUCTURE
Electricity. Consumer's Energy provides electricity on an individual basis to over 200 homes in the tribal community.

Fuel. Local distributors provide natural gas.

Water Supply. The tribe owns three community wells, which furnish water to its members. The tribe constructed a water tower in 1995. It also maintains a tribal sewage system that provides service to the over 200 homes in the tribal community.

Transportation. Road access to the reservation is provided by U.S. 27 (north-south) and State Highway 20 (east-west). Commercial air service is available at the Mt. Pleasant Municipal Airport, less than three miles from the reservation. For additional service, the Tri-Cities Airport in Saginaw is about 45 miles away. The tribe owns a shuttle bus as part of its gaming operations, two

small school buses, a 16-passenger van for its childcare program, and a 66-passenger school bus.

Telecommunications. The tribe operates Telecommunications Group, which provide telephone, modem, cell phone, and pager services to the Saginaw Chippewa Indian Tribe. Telecommunications Group works with external private contractors to ensure proper wiring and connection installation to guarantee user access to voice, data, and networking resources for all newly constructed buildings on the reservation. The tribe has also partnered with Alltel to provide local cellular telephone service.

COMMUNITY FACILITIES AND SERVICES
The tribe maintains the tribal operations building, the Ziibiwing Cultural Center And Museum, the Elijiah Elk Cultural Center, and the Nimkee Fitness Center. The tribe also owns a behavioral health center, which has a residential treatment center for substance abuse and a shelter for abused individuals. The senior community gathers at the Sowmick Senior Center, which provides daily activities and meals. The Sowmick Senior Center also provides a home for several seniors.

Public Safety. A tribal fire and tribal police department serve the community.

Education. The Mt. Pleasant Public Schools provide K-12 facilities for community students. The tribe owns and operates the Saginaw Chippewa Academy Parent Child Center for tribal children ages 0-3 years and the Saginaw Chippewa Academy Binoojiinh Montessori School for preprimary and elementary students.

The tribe's education department, with a staff of about 20 employees, oversees the tribe's scholarship program, an adult education program, a parent-student advocate program, and the Ojibwe bilingual program. It also administers the tribe's tribal library. This department works closely with the Saginaw Chippewa Tribal College, which offers special courses that address the tribe's cultural, historical, and tribal governmental administrative needs. University and Mid-Michigan Community College are also located within four miles of the reservation.

Health Care. The Nimkee Memorial Wellness Center in Mt. Pleasant, Michigan, is the primary health facility on the reservation, complete with a medical and ambulatory care clinic, a dental clinic, a pharmacy, and a public health department. The Nimkee Memorial Clinic provides medical care, with three physicians, a nurse practitioner, and an experienced support staff of nurses and assistants. There is also a pharmacy in this clinic. All Saginaw Chippewa Indian Tribal members have a free membership to the Nimkee Fitness Center, which is located on the east side of the wellness center.

ENVIRONMENTAL CONCERNS
Critical environmental issues for the tribe include groundwater availability and source protection. Due to an increase in industry in the area, there is concern in the community about water quality and purity levels. The U.S. EPA conducted a test in 2000 and found no toxins in the water. However, the community is still concerned about unknown substances contaminating the water supply and has requested further testing by the U.S. EPA. A hydrogeological study has been funded by the tribe. This tribe feels aquifers will be critical to their future growth and development, so this study will map and identify potential sources, which can be used. A yearlong study is being conducted by the tribe regarding the practicality of using wind power to satisfy energy needs.

Isabella

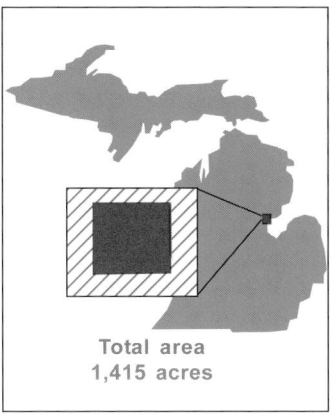

**Total area
1,415 acres**

Lac Vieux Desert

Lac Vieux Desert Reservation
Federal reservation
Lake Superior Chippewa
Gogebic County, Michigan

Lac Vieux Desert Band of Lake
Superior Chippewa
P.O. Box 446
Watersmeet, MI 49969
906-358-4577
906-358-4785 Fax

Total area *(Tribal source, 2004)*
300.37 acres

Tribal enrollment
(BIA labor report, 2001)
442

Population *2000 census*
135

Total labor force *2000 census*
64

High school or higher
2000 census
61.5%

Bachelor's degree or higher
2000 census
3.8%

Unemployment rate
2000 census
7.8%

Unemployment rate
(BIA labor report, 2001)
9%

Per capita income *2000 census*
$7,766

LOCATION AND LAND STATUS

The Lac Vieux Reservation covers 295 acres at the western edge of Michigan's Upper Peninsula, spanning two different sites. The reservation is located near the town of Watersmeet, a few miles north of the Wisconsin border, in the Ottawa National Forest. The reservation was established by PL 100-420 in 1988. This legislative action represented a comeback for the band, which, like most of the Michigan Chippewa, had lost essentially all of its land base by the beginning of the twentieth century through fraudulent allotment schemes during the late 1800s.

CULTURE AND HISTORY

The Chippewa Tribe descend from the Algonquian linguistic family and was once among the largest tribes in North America, with tribal lands spanning both sides of Lakes Huron and Superior westward to the Turtle Mountains of North Dakota. Seven distinct tribes comprise the twentieth-century Michigan Chippewas. The Upper Peninsula of Michigan holds the largest number of Chippewas, with four discrete bands, the Lac Vieux Desert being one of them. Between 1795 and 1864, the Michigan Chippewas signed a number of treaties in which they ceded title to their traditional land bases in exchange for specific rights and properties. Allotment programs during the 1850s and 1860s served primarily to defraud the Indians out of even these treaty-reserved lands, leading to land-claims cases that continue to this day. In any case, by the early 1900s, the Michigan Chippewas had lost nearly their entire land base. The 1934 Indian Reorganization Act (IRA) had the effect not only of somewhat alleviating the tribes' economic suffering, but also of reestablishing the federal trust and restoring a government-to-government relationship with the U.S. As a result of the IRA, the U.S. government purchased and took land into trust, providing bands that had lost their land base with a center for economic, cultural, and political activities. For the Lac Vieux Desert Band, an autonomous land base came even later than for the other Michigan Chippewas. It was not until 1989 that the band was formally recognized as separate from the Keweenaw Bay Band.

The Lac Vieux Desert Band has, since its federal recognition, been actively involved in economic development projects, including a health clinic, an elders facility, child care and daycare, a golf course, a public water and wastewater utility, a construction company, a motel, a restaurant, and a casino and bingo. Traditional culture continues to thrive through an active program of intertribal powwows, sweat lodges, Big Drum ceremonies, and the like. The Lac Vieux Desert Band has established a tribal historic preservation office guided by their cultural committee. Activities such as hunting, trapping, and native food gathering remain popular as well.

GOVERNMENT

The Lac Vieux Desert Band was until very recently considered part of the Keweenaw Bay Indian Community. Keweenaw Bay, like the rest of the Upper Peninsula Chippewas, wrote its constitution and established a tribal government under provisions of the 1934 IRA. In 1991 the U.S. Congress finalized formal recognition of the Lac Vieux Desert Band as a tribe separate from the Keewenaw Bay Community, allowing them to establish their own independent government. The tribal government is administered by a nine-member elected tribal council, operating under an interim constitution approved in 1986. The Lac Vieux tribal government consists of various departments, including administration, the social services, planning and environmental, accounting, tribal grounds maintenance, and heavy equipment.

The Lac Vieux Desert Band's social services department operates various programs. The general assistance program provides financial assistance to the unemployed who are actively seeking employment. Other assistance programs include a low-income energy program, an emergency assistance program, and a commodity food item program. The department also offers an Indian child welfare program, child protective services, a crime victim advocacy group, in-home child care grants, and an emergency assistance program offered to families with loved ones who are terminally ill.

The Lac Vieux Desert tribal government's judicial branch consists of a criminal and civil court, and it also offers mediation dispute resolution.

There is a tribal police department that operates within a 6,000-square-foot correctional facility. The department's officers are deputies in multiple jurisdictions, allowing them to write state, federal, or tribal tickets determined by the jurisdiction of the offense.

BUSINESS CORPORATION

The Katikitegon Community Development Corporation, a 501(c)(3) organization, has been chartered by the Lac Band. This corporation, with the support of the U.S. Treasury, is developing a CDFI. The tribe created the White Birch Park on land they had purchased for economic development projects. The tribe is trying to have this land put into trust status.

ECONOMY

The Lac Vieux Desert Reservation economy makes a presence in the region with its gaming industry. The Lac Vieux Desert Casino and Resort is the focus of economic activity in the community, with service sector businesses relying on the flow of visiting gaming consumers. The tribal government, construction, and tourism comprise additional economic activity in the community. The tribe's investment in labor force skills training with an emphasis on construction is reaping benefits with the establishment of new facilities on the reservation.

Government as Employer. The tribal government directly employs 20 tribal members in administration and other operations.

Agriculture and Livestock. The Lac Vieux Desert Band, in cooperation with the Great Lakes Indian Fish and Wildlife Commission and the Ottawa National Forest, has been attempting to cultivate wild rice along the bays of the reservation. Since 1991, the tribe has annually planted 500 pounds of rice in Misery Bay, Rice Bay, and Slaughter Bay. This effort met challenges throughout the 1990s since water levels in the lake exceeded the proper depth for effective rice cultivation. In response, the tribe has sought licensing authority of dam operations, which control Lac Vieux Desert lake water levels.

Forestry. The reservation lies in the Ottawa National Forest and thus contains nearly 250 acres of forested land, primarily maple, pine, birch, and cherry trees.

Gaming. The Lac Vieux Desert Tribe owns the Lac Vieux Desert Casino and Resort. The 25,000-square-foot facility offers 693 slot machines, 14 table games, 4 poker tables, and 500 bingo seats. The resort offers dining at the Katikegoning Restaurant and the opportunity to grab a snack at their resort snack bar. The resort has 138 luxury rooms and includes a 100,000-square-foot convention center for business or entertainment gatherings, and it also offers a gift shop. The Lac Vieux Desert Golf Coarse is a 9-hole golf course adjacent to the casino and resort.

Fisheries. Four and a half million walleye fry have been hatched by Lac Vieux Hatchery and returned to the lakes the eggs originally came from. The rest of the fry were put in local ponds until they were fingerlings. Approximately 1,745 of those that reached fingerling size were then released in local lakes that stock walleye. Though the region is rich in fisheries, the limited land base of the Lac Vieux Desert Reservation does not presently allow for more than recreational fishing. There are excellent fishing lakes nearby, however.

Construction. The tribe operates an educational class entitled Building Trades, which offers hands-on construction training. Over the years, program participants have built numerous homes, garages, storage sheds, additions, business buildings and other work orders. The program is an investment in the labor force that provides the community with knowledge, skills, and experience in all aspects of the construction industry.

Services and Retail. In addition to the conveniences at the Lac Vieux Desert Casino and Resort, other services in the area include a Co-op Credit Union, a check cashing enterprise, and a tribal gas station with a convenience store. The tribe owns and operates The Lac Vieux Desert Arts and Crafts Store. The enterprise features handmade Native items and is located at the resort complex. All services and retail, other than the credit union and check cashing are tribal owned. Check cashing is a tribal member business.

Tourism and Recreation. There are 320 lakes in the immediate vicinity of the reservation that provide excellent fishing opportunities, as well as an outlet for boating, canoeing, swimming, and other water activities. Hunting, snowmobiling, and skiing are also extremely popular. Additionally, the tribe holds its annual pow-wow during the last weekend in August. The Lac Vieux Desert Golf Course is spread out into 100 acres in the Ottawa National Forest, and it offers visitors nine holes of golf among five ponds, a running stream, and woodlands surrounding the course.

INFRASTRUCTURE
Electricity. Electricity is supplied by Wisconsin Electric.

Fuel. Semco Energy supplies natural gas.

Water Supply. Water is supplied through two community wells operated and maintained by Lac Vieux Utilities and eight other individual wells. Sewer service is furnished through individual septic tanks and a lagoon system operated and maintained by Lac Vieux Desert Utilities.

Transportation. The tribe owns a bus for its Head Start program, as well as several service and maintenance vans. U.S. highways 2 and 45 provide road access to the reservation. Commercial air service is available at the Gogebic County Airport, about 55 miles away. Commercial truck lines serve the reservation directly. Commercial bus lines are available in Ironwood, Michigan.

COMMUNITY FACILITIES AND SERVICES
The tribe maintains a new community center, along with a variety of recreational facilities.

Education. Students attend the Watersmeet public schools. There is a child development center that offers a Head Start program, an Early Head Start program, and childcare. The Head Start and Early Head Start programs provide bus transportation for the children to and from school.

Health Care. The Lac Vieux Desert Health Clinic provides medical and mental health services to the community. The tribe also operates a pharmacy.

Lac Vieux Desert

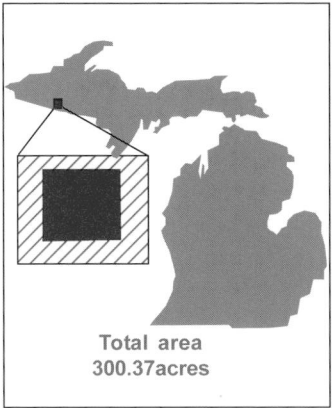

Total area
300.37 acres

L 'Anse
(Keweenaw Bay)

LOCATION AND LAND STATUS
This checkerboarded reservation is located in northern Michigan, on the shores of Lake Superior, approximately 65 miles northwest of Marquette. Baraga is the tribe's headquarters. L'Anse Reservation was established in 1854 by treaty. The reservation has approximately 54,561 acres. Ontonagon Reservation, west of Houghton is part of L'Anse. It is a 620-acre forested area that has no permanent residents.

PHYSICAL DESCRIPTION
The reservation is approximately one-quarter forest with hardwoods and evergreens, and one-third wetlands and shoreline on Lake Superior.

CULTURE AND HISTORY
The Lake Superior Band of the Chippewa Tribe is part of the vast Ojibwa Nation, which originally occupied the mid-north of the North American continent. The Ojibwas (Chippewas) are a member of the Algonquian linguistic family and one of the largest tribes north of Mexico. Decades of organized resistance to Euro-American takeover ended in a peace treaty signed with the U.S. government in 1815. The present reservation site was recognized by the Treaty of 1854 between the Chippewas and the U.S.

GOVERNMENT
The tribe adopted a constitution and bylaws in 1936, which the secretary of the interior approved the same year, pursuant to the Indian Reorganization Act of 1934. A tribal council has 12 members, including a chairperson, a vice-chairperson, a secretary, an assistant secretary, and a treasurer, all elected to three-year terms. The tribal government has various departments, including social services, natural resources, and planning and development that includes the tribal roads department, grants and funding, and economic development. The tribe also operates a housing authority and a TERO office.

The Keweenaw Bay Indian Community's social services department offers prevention services with family education, child protective services, foster care and adoption services, and juvenile justice services. The social services department sponsors a program entitled "Families First," an intensive, four-week, crisis intervention program.

L'Anse
(Keweenaw Bay)

**L'Anse Reservation
(Keweenaw Bay)
Federal reservation
Chippewa (Lake Superior
Band)
Baraga County, Michigan**

Keweenaw Bay Indian
    Community
Keweenaw Bay Tribal Center
107 Beartown Road
Baraga, MI 49908
    906-353-6623
    906-353-7540 Fax
    kbic-nsn.gov

L'Anse
(Keweenaw Bay)

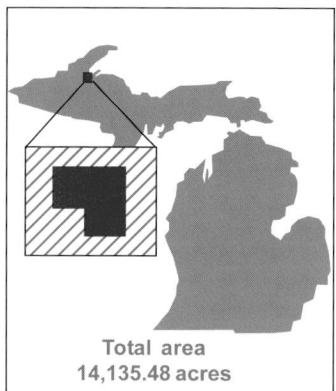

Total area
14,135.48 acres

Total area *(EPA data)*
14,135.48 acres

Population *2000 census*
3,672

Tribal enrollment
(BIA labor report, 2001)
3,120

Total labor force *2000 census*
1,738

Total labor force
(BIA labor report, 2001)
834

High school graduate or higher
2000 census
78.9%

Bachelor's degree or higher
2000 census
9.7%

Unemployment rate
2000 census
9.95%

Unemployment rate
(BIA labor report, 2001)
36%

Per capita income *2000 census*
$15,656

The natural resources department provides programs for the Keweenaw Bay Indian Community that include fishery assessments in Lake Superior, stream assessments in Baraga County, surface water and groundwater monitoring, air and radon studies, and fish stocking into tribal hatcheries.

The Keweenaw Bay Indian Community has its own tribal police department and a type 2 wildland fire fighter hand crew in cooperation with the BIA.

ECONOMY
The L'Anse Reservation economy is primarily driven by the gaming industry. Additional economic activity on the reservation includes government operations, construction, and service sector retail.

Government as Employer. Tribal government employs 375 people. The tribally owned resort employs 110 Indians and 120 non-Indians. State and federal governments employ 12 people on the reservation.

Agriculture and Livestock. The Keweenaw Bay Indian Community annually plants several hundred pounds of wild rice seed at Sand Point, Pinery Lakes, and Mud Lakes.

Forestry. The reservation forests 14,000 acres; hardwoods are logged at L'Anse but not on the Otonagon parcel.

Gaming. The Keweenaw Bay Indian Community owns the Ojibwa Casino and Resort Baraga, and the Ojibwa Casino Marquette. The Ojibwa Casino Resort in Baraga offers visitors 17,000 square feet of gaming, dining, and luxury lodging. The gaming floor offers 400 slots, 12 table games, and 450 bingo seats. The resort offers 40 rooms including suites with a private spa. Visitors may dine at the Ojibwa Four Star Family Restaurant and Pancake House located across from the lobby of the hotel. The casino and resort employs 300 people. The Ojibwa Casino Marquette is a 10,000-square-foot casino that offers visitors 350 slots and 10 table games including blackjack, roulette, craps, and three-card poker.

Fisheries. A fish hatchery is located on tribal land.

Construction. A tribal construction company employs 20 to 30 people seasonally.

Industrial Parks. The tribe owns an industrial park that houses the USDA, tribal housing, tribal maintenance, Great Lakes Indian Fish and Wildlife, CJ's Auto Body, tribal police, and Keweenaw Bay Indian Community.

Services and Retail. In addition to the Ojibwa Baraga and Marquette casinos, the tribe owns the Ojibwa Resort Motel located next to the Baraga casino. The Pressbox Lanes and Lounge provides live entertainment every weekend and eight lanes of bowling. KBIC Tire and Flatproof services everything from wheelbarrows to tractor-trailers. Wildcat Fence is a full-service fence contractor with over 27 years of experience. The Pine Convenience Store and Smokeshop in Baraga offers visitors an opportunity to quickly purchase a snack or necessity. All businesses listed above are tribally owned.

Tourism and Recreation. The Ojibwa recreation area serves as an additional tourist attraction away from casino action. The recreation area is located along the shores of Lake Superior and includes a campground, a marina, and a lighthouse. The Ojibwa campground offers visitors a secluded environment with amenities including restrooms with showers, fire pits, an RV dump station, electrical outlets, a playground, and pavilions to host family reunions. The campground is also the site for the annual

Keweenaw Bay Maawanji-iding, or powwow, held every July. The marina is located along the shores of the Keweenaw Bay and offers visitors a place to launch private boats for a day of fishing and sailing. Another attraction is the historic Sand Point Lighthouse also located on the Keweenaw Bay shore.

INFRASTRUCTURE
Electricity. A local cooperative provides electricity.

Water Supply. In 2005, a new water line is scheduled to be installed on old U.S. Highway 41 in Baraga. Septic tanks and municipal facilities provide sewage disposal.

Transportation. Scheduled for reconstruction in 2005, U.S. Highway 41 traverses the reservation north to south. Michigan State Highway 38 accesses the reservation town of Baraga. UPS, Federal Express, Airborne Express, and other shippers serve the reservation. A commercial airport is available 40 miles distant, in Houghton, Michigan. Commercial bus lines serve L'Anse, three miles from the reservation.

Media and Communications. The tribe owns two radio stations, WCUP-FM Eagle Country and WGLI-FM The Rockin' Eagle.

COMMUNITY FACILITIES AND SERVICES
The tribe has a library and two community centers. The Ojibwa senior citizens center and the Keweenaw Bay tribal center are foci of activity. The Keweenaw Reservation youth club serves as a gathering area for children and adolescents in the community, and it funds up to $100 per child for extracurricular sports, athletic equipment, camps, and other school-related activities.

Education. There is a daycare center and a Head Start program that serves the community. The Keweenaw Bay Indian community operates an education department that provides financial, personal, education, and retention services to individuals pursuing postsecondary and other educational opportunities. The Keweenaw Bay Community College, chartered on July 12, 1975, gives members of the community an opportunity for a postsecondary education; it offers arts and sciences, and business courses.

Health Care. A health department operates within the Keweenaw Bay Indian community. U.S. Public Health Service health care is available, and there is a tribal outpatient medical and dental health clinic. There is also a New Day Treatment Center located on the reservation.

ENVIRONMENTAL CONCERNS
The Keweenaw Indian community confronts an epidemic of illegal dumping of waste materials on unauthorized areas of the land. Both tribal and nontribal members disposing household garbage, automobile parts, and other products on illegal dumpsites characterize the problem. Recent efforts to battle this problem include the tribe using EPA money to clean up existing illegal dumpsites. These cleanup efforts have seen relative success, but the problem persists on other parts of the reservation. Local government officials have attempted to increase the penalty for illegal littering on tribal land, and they have initiated a literature campaign discouraging illegal dumping.

The Keweenaw Bay Indian community has taken action to protect the waterfowl populations that inhabit the reservation's wetlands. The tribe has invested nearly $171,000 to improve the waterfowl habitat on the reservation. Efforts include analysis and water level maintenance of the reservation's three wetlands, including Sand Point Sloughs, Pinery Lakes, and Mud Lakes. The tribe has also planted wild rice on these wetlands.

LOCATION AND LAND STATUS

The Little River Band of Ottawa Indians was reaffirmed and restored to federal recognition on September 21, 1994 pursuant to PL 103-324 (the Little River Act). The 1836 Treaty of Washington reserved land for the tribe's political predecessors in what is now Manistee County, Michigan. The 1855 Treaty of Detroit reserved additional lands for the tribe's predecessors in Mason County, Michigan. Section 6 of the Little River Act provides for the restoration of lands to the tribe by requiring the secretary of the interior to accept lands in trust for the tribe in Manistee and Mason counties, and it provides that lands accepted in trust "shall become a part of the bands' reservation." The Little River Act recognized that many tribe members continued to reside within or near the lands reserved for the tribe's political predecessors in 1836 and 1855.

The U.S. currently holds approximately 512 acres of land in trust for the tribe within the historic treaty reservations described in the 1836 and 1855 treaties within Manistee and Mason counties. These lands are part of the tribe's reservation under the Little River Act and therefore constitute Indian country. The tribe has applied to transfer additional lands to the U.S. under the Little River Act to be held in trust for the tribe within Manistee and Mason counties. These additional lands that the tribe currently owns in fee include: one 612-acre tract in Custer Township in Mason County, two parcels near the trust land in Manistee County (229 acres total), seven parcels within the city of Manistee (of unknown size), one parcel in the Village of East Lake in Manistee County (32.67 acres), and 23 other parcels in Manistee County, totaling approximately 1,377 acres. Upon acceptance in trust, those lands will also become part of the tribe's reservation and constitute Indian country.

The tribe believes all lands within the exterior boundaries of the area reserved by the tribe's predecessors in Articles Second of the 1836 Treaty, an approximately 70,000-acre area known as the Manistee Reserve, and all lands within the northern portion of the lands reserved in Article 1, Paragraph Sixth of the 1855 Treaty, consisting of Custer and Eden Townships in Mason County, Michigan, continue to have reservation and, therefore, Indian country status. The tribe's constitution, which was approved by the Department of the Interior on July 10, 1998, asserts territorial jurisdiction within these historic reservation areas, and the tribe has enacted ordinances that assert regulatory authority over tribe members within these areas. The tribe is currently consulting with the Department of the Interior to clarify the legal issues relating to its reservations.

PHYSICAL DESCRIPTION

A large part of the tribe's lands are commercial in nature, including an office building, an administrative building, a clinic, and four rental housing units in the city of Manistee, and a casino and resort site at the intersection of U.S. 31 and Michigan Rt. 22, northeast of the city.

The Manistee Forge land in East Lake is a former industrial site, which the tribe purchased in 1998 after conducting an environmental assessment. In the past century, the site has been used for a number of industrial purposes, including a lumber mill, salt and chemical operations, metal forging, hydraulic lift manufacturing, and fiberglass fabrication. The assessment found soil contamination and indicated the potential presence of a mixture of metals, petroleum products, and lubricants as well as chemicals associated with the production of salt and bromide products. It has been designated a "Brownfields" site by the Environmental Protection Agency, and in May 2002 the EPA selected it for an Assessment Pilot. The Pilot targeted this site for redevelopment into housing for tribal members, a marina, and a manufactured home construction business.

CULTURE AND HISTORY

The Ottawas are an Algonquin people, the smallest of the Three Fires Confederacy of the Great Lakes, together with the Ojibwes or Chippewas ("older brothers") and the Bodwe'aadamiinh or Potawatomis ("younger brother"). The name Ottawa comes from the Algonquin word *adawe*, which means "to trade" and originates from their role as traders even before contact with Europeans. The Ottawas became so important in the French fur trade that, before 1670, it was common practice in Quebec to call any Algonquin from the Great Lakes an Ottawa. In their own language, the Ottawas (like the Ojibwes) refer to themselves as *Anishinabe* ("the people"). The Ottawas speak Central Algonquin-Anishinaabemowin-which is the same as Ojibwe and similar to Potawatomi. In Algonquin, the tribe calls itself *Ga Ching Ziibi Dawaa Anishinaabek* ("The Little River Band of Ottawa Indians").

The Ottawas were businessmen before they ever met a European, so when the French arrived in 1615 they immediately recognized the opportunity presented by the fur trade with the French. Between 1615 and 1763, the Ottawas were one of the most important tribes in North America. Paddling their birch-bark canoes for great distances, the Ottawas became the intermediaries with other Algonquins in the Great Lakes, and they brought the furs they collected to the French at various Huron villages. The Hurons provided warehouse space and protection from the Iroquois, but it was the Ottawas who went out and acquired the furs. By the 1620s, French trade goods were reaching the Ojibwes at Sault Ste. Marie and the Crees to the north in the Hudson Bay watershed. The Iroquois pushed the Ottawas west, but business continued as usual for the Ottawas. By 1685 Ottawa middlemen were supplying two-thirds of the fur at Montreal, and by the end of the seventeenth century they had moved back east to Mackinac on Michigan's Upper Peninsula and to Detroit, where they became the dominant tribe. The Mackinac Ottawas moved to the northwest part of Michigan's Lower Peninsula in the mid-1700s. These were the ancestors of the Little River Band. Although Ottawa power declined after the British takeover of the Great Lakes in 1760, they remained influential. The Detroit Ottawa chief Pontiac was able to organize an alliance against the British in 1763, but it did not include the Ottawas of northern Michigan.

The Ottawas of northern Michigan were remote from the American Revolution, and they were not involved except for occasional support for their Detroit relatives. With the end of the Revolution, American settlers poured across the Appalachians, and by the end of the War of 1812 the tribes of the Old Northwest no longer had the strength to resist them.

In 1821, a single Grand River Ottawa leader, without the consent of his people, signed the 1821 Treaty of Chicago, which resulted in the cession of all Ottawa lands south of the Grand River. In 1836 the Ottawas and Chippewas of Michigan ceded most of their remaining land in upper and lower Michigan, but they retained land reservations and also reserved the right to continue hunting, fishing, and gathering on the lands they ceded. The Grand River Ottawa Bands, including the bands now comprising the Little River Band, retained a large reservation along the Manistee River, referred to as the Manistee Reserve.

Little River Band Reservation
Federal reservation
Ottawa
Manistee and Mason, Lake, and Wexford counties, Michigan

Little River Band of Ottawa
  Indians
375 River Street
Manistee, MI 49660
  888-723-8288
  231-723-8020 Fax
lrboi.com

Total area *(Tribal source, 2004)*
2,763 acres

Federal trust lands
(Tribal source, 2004)
512 acres

Tribally owned lands
(not including property within the city of Manistee)
2,251 acres

Tribal enrollment
(BIA labor report, 2001)
3,058

Total labor force *2000 census*
0

Total labor force
(BIA labor report, 2001)
1,050

Unemployment rate
(BIA labor report, 2001)
63%

Little River Band

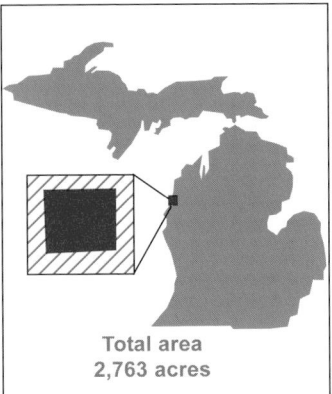

Total area
2,763 acres

Then in 1855, the Treaty of Detroit was negotiated, which reserved additional lands for regional groups of Ottawa and Chippewa bands. The 1855 treaty also included a provision that dissolved the fictitious "Ottawa and Chippewa Nation," which U.S. negotiators of the 1836 treaty had created in order to ensure the cession of land by the various Ottawa and Chippewa bands. Federal officials later misinterpreted this provision as having dissolved the tribal status of the individual bands. The 1855 treaty also provided for the allotment of lands reserved under the 1836 treaty. Many residents of the Manistee Reserve relocated to the new reservation in Mason County but later moved back to the Manistee Reserve when families lost their allotments due to fraud and illegal taxation.

By the mid-1870s, the Ottawas had lost title to nearly all of the lands within their reservations. The frauds became so obvious that the federal government initiated investigations and, in some instances, commenced litigation to recover Ottawa lands. Unfortunately the erroneous interpretation of the 1855 treaty provision dissolving the artificial Ottawa and Chippewa Nation resulted in the federal government abandoning its efforts to protect the Ottawa reservations and resulted in the de facto termination of the federal government's trust relationship with the Ottawas. The Ottawas continued to file petitions with the U.S. and pursued litigation to assert their treaty-reserved rights.

Finally, in 1994, the U.S. Congress enacted the Little River Act, which acknowledged the U.S's fault in terminating its recognition of the tribe's sovereign status. The Little River Act recognized the tribe and reaffirmed the band's rights and privileges. The statute acknowledged that many tribe members now lived near or within the boundaries of the tribe's treaty reservations in Manistee and Mason counties. Other members live throughout northern lower Michigan.

GOVERNMENT
The tribe is governed by an elected *Ogema* (chief executive officer) and a nine-member tribal council. Government departments include training and development, housing (which operates elder housing and supports low-income members), member's assistance (which provides financial assistance to low-income members), commodities (which provides in-kind food distribution), health (which provides a clinic and insurance), family services, wastewater and utilities, natural resources conservation, maintenance, public safety, education, and *Be-da-bin* behavioral health. There is also an elder's coordinator and an enrollment officer. As a self-governing tribe, it provides most services funded by the BIA.

The tribal court has a chief judge and an associate judge at the trial court level and a three-judge appellate panel. The tribal court can hear a wide range of civil matters, including divorces, child custody disputes, and small claims. The court can issue a personal protection order to help someone in an abusive relationship or in dealing with harassment. It also has two "Peacemakers," who deal mainly with juveniles but are also available to help solve differences between people using traditional dispute resolution methods. They have been used successfully in employment conflicts and child custody mediations.

ECONOMY
Before opening a casino in 1999, the area's economic base had declined with the closure and relocation of lumbering and salt mining industries. About 1,200 of the 2,728 tribe members reside in the four-county area. Of these, approximately 41 percent previously lived in households with incomes below the poverty rate and about 60 percent were unemployed. With the opening of the casino, the tribe has expanded local employment opportunities, but new housing and jobs are needed as more tribal members return to the reservation.

Economic Development Projects. As of 2004, the tribe's economic development activities were centered on expanding the casino into a multifunction resort and entertainment venue and on reclaiming and subsequently developing industry on the Manistee Forge land in East Lake. A tax agreement with the State of Michigan helps to promote tribal members' economic development and the tribe's economic diversification.

Gaming. The tribe owns and operates the Little River Casino Resort in Manistee County at the intersection of U.S. Highway 31 and Michigan Highway 22. The casino can be reached without difficulty from Traverse City, Cadillac, Muskegon, and Grand Rapids. It offers more than 1,300 slot machines, 32 table games, and a live poker room. In addition to gaming, it offers family and fine dining, a hotel with 12 suites and 88 guest rooms, a 45-space RV park, and a 9,000-square-foot conference center. It also hosts bus tours from several locations in Michigan, Chicago, Ohio, and Ontario. With more than 800 employees, the casino is the largest employer in the four-county area.

The tribe negotiated a gaming compact with the State of Michigan in 1997, which the Michigan Legislature ratified in 1998. The compact was challenged in court on the grounds that it required the enactment of a statute rather than only concurrent resolutions, but in 2004 the Supreme Court of Michigan upheld the compact, stating it was no different from any other state contract requiring legislative approval by concurrent resolutions. The casino opened in July 1999, and it was significantly expanded in December 1999, and in 2001. As part of the compact, the tribe was required to distribute two percent of its casino profits to local schools and government organizations in communities affected by the casino and eight percent of its casino profits to the Michigan Renaissance Fund. If any person besides other federally recognized Indian tribes and the three existing Detroit casinos operate commercial casino games or electronic games of chance, then the tribe is released from sharing revenues with the Michigan Renaissance Fund.

In fall 2004, the tribe began construction to expand the casino and resort to include additional hotel rooms and an entertainment venue, and began remodeling existing facilities to accommodate an indoor atrium and additional retail space and connections between new and existing facilities, which will house cultural presentations.

Fisheries. For many years, the establishment of fishing rights under the Treaty of 1836 was a major source of contention between the Indians of Michigan and the state. Following a 1979 U.S. District Court decision recognizing tribal treaty fishing rights, the major fishing tribes organized the Chippewa Ottawa Treaty Fishery Management Authority, now called the Chippewa Ottawa Resource Authority (CORA). The Little River Band joined in 1998. Under consent orders entered in 1985 and 2000, CORA shares responsibility for fisheries management with state and federal fisheries officials. In 2001, the tribe began commercial netting operations in Lake Michigan with one boat trap netting for whitefish along the shore. Other boats with small-mesh gill nets catch chubs in deep water. The tribe's conservation department also sets large-mesh gill nets as part of a study of lake trout populations in northern Lake Michigan. The tribe received four vessels from the state government, including two trap-net fishing boats and two gillnetting tugs as compensation for agreeing not to authorize the use of large-mesh gill nets by commercial fishers during the term of the 2000 consent order. The tribes and CORA support fisheries research and education. Technical fisheries committees comprised of tribal, state, and federal biologists develop harvest guidelines or, if necessary, harvest limits. Tribal fishers and staff work with the sport and charter fishing community to provide sport fishers with information regarding net locations, net marking, and how to avoid fishing nets so commercial and sport fishers can safely coexist. Tampering with tribal fishing nets is a federal offense.

Construction. The tribe is currently planning to build community facilities at the site of its housing subdivision and government facilities on nearby tribal lands. The tribe is also considering construction of a business park and a redevelopment and reuse plan for the reclaimed Manistee Forge site.

Services and Retail. See the discussion of the Little River Casino and Resort, above.

Tourism and Recreation. In addition to expanding the Little River Casino and Resort, the tribe will explore the feasibility of building a marina on the reclaimed Manistee Forge site based on the results of the environmental assessments conducted under the tribe's "Brownfields Pilot" project.

INFRASTRUCTURE
The tribe constructed a water supply system and wastewater treatment facility, which serve the Casino Resort and Akimaadiziwin housing development. These utilities will also serve the community and governmental facilities planned for nearby tribal lands on the Manistee Reserve. Other tribal facilities are served by a combination of tribal and local government services.

COMMUNITY FACILITIES AND SERVICES
The tribe's government offices are located in the tribally owned National Bank Building in Manistee. The Administration Building and Community Center are also located in Manistee. The Newland Building houses the public safety department and the tribal court. The Natural Resources Building is located in Manistee County near the city.

Education. Little River Band students attend the public schools in the districts in which they live. The tribe's education department provides financial support and cultural instruction.

Health Care. The Tribal Health Clinic in the city of Manistee, an IHS-recognized Indian Health Center, serves the tribe's health care needs.

ENVIRONMENTAL CONCERNS
The tribe considers itself to be the natural environmental custodian of the Manistee River basin and nearby Lake Michigan. It is concerned with the impact of pollution on its own lands, on fishing in Lake Michigan and in the Manistee River watershed, and generally throughout northwestern lower Michigan.

In 2004, the Environmental Protection Agency selected the tribe for a Brownfields Assessment Pilot. The tribe also was selected to receive additional funding for assessments at Brownfields properties to be used for Greenspace purposes. The tribe has targeted the 32-acre Manistee Forge Corporation East Lake plant site, suffering from soil contamination and the potential presence of a mixture of metals, petroleum products, and lubricants as well as chemicals associated with the production of salt and bromide products. In the past century, the site has been used for a number of industrial purposes, including a lumber mill, salt and chemical operations, metal forging, hydraulic lift manufacturing, and fiberglass fabrication. As part of the Brownfields Assessment Pilot, the tribe will identify proposed uses for this site, and a reuse and redevelopment plan will be prepared. The reclamation and redevelopment of this site is projected to be accomplished by 2006.

Also in 2004, the tribe signed an environmental agreement with the other Indian tribes in Michigan and the state, committing the state and tribal governments to work together to clean up the pollutants in the waters, eliminate exotic species, maintain and preserve diverse water resource habitats, and prevent future contaminants, exotics, and depletion of the waters. The tribe has proposed building an environmentally sensitive alternative energy project based on wind, ethanol, and biomass. This was in response to a proposed coal-fired plant proposed for Manistee County that area residents successfully resisted.

Little Traverse

LOCATION AND LAND STATUS
The Little Traverse Bay Bands of Indians (LTBB) Housing Reservation is located seven miles north of Harbor Springs, Michigan. The tribe has a small land base of 40 acres, purchased on a land contract and lying within ancestral lands. No residents occupy the reservation; the tribal community is made up of those members living on or near the tribe's ancestral homeland, an area including Emmet, Charlevoix, Delta, and Schoolcraft counties of northern Michigan. This tribe was a signatory to the 1855 Treaty of Detroit.

PHYSICAL DESCRIPTION
The tribal properties are forested with hardwoods in a rural setting. The reservation features three rivers, about 18 inland lakes, and numerous streams and wetlands. The waters of Lake Michigan border tribal lands.

CULTURE AND HISTORY
The Little Traverse Bay Bands of Odawa Indians, or Ottawa, inhabited the geographical region of the present-day state of Michigan for centuries prior to the arrival of Europeans. Historically, the Odawas were a migratory group, traveling from Michigan's Upper Peninsula and the northern area tip of Michigan in the fall, to southern Michigan during the winter months. The people returned to their homelands in the spring to collect maple syrup, to fish, and to plant crops.

The tribe reorganized as the Little Traverse Bay Bands in November 1982, and the federal government recognized them on September 21, 1994. This was an important step toward the tribe's goal of self-sufficiency.

GOVERNMENT
The Little Traverse Bay Bands are governed by a tribal council. The council consists of a chairman, an executive assistant, and five other members. Each of the seven members serve staggered terms. Tribal headquarters are located in Harbor Springs, Michigan.

Tribal government departments and programs include health, human services, education, housing, enrollment, law enforcement, and natural resources. The tribe also offers archives and records, communications, facilities, elders' services, manage-

Little Traverse Bay Bands Reservation
Federal reservation
Odawa
Emmet, Charlevoix, Delta, and Schoolcraft counties, Michigan

Little Traverse Bay Bands
of Odawa Indians
7500 Odawa Circle
Harbor Springs, MI 49740
231-242-1400
231-242-1430 Fax

Little Traverse

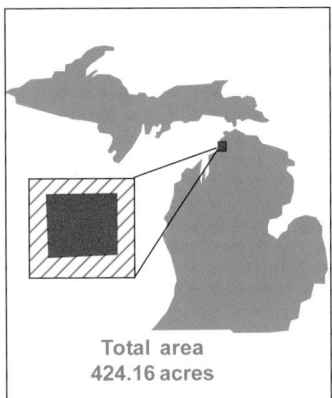

Total area
424.16 acres

Total area *(Tribal source, 2004)*
424.16 acres

Tribal enrollment
(Tribal source, 2004)
3,900

Tribal enrollment
(BIA labor report, 2001)
3,521

Total labor force *2000 census*
0

Total labor force
(BIA labor report, 2001)
785

Unemployment rate
(BIA labor report, 2001)
72%

ment information systems, culture and historic preservation/ NAGPRA, and contract management programs.

The tribe maintains a police department and contracts jail space from the Charlevoix and Cheboygan county sheriff departments. Tribal law enforcement was deputized by Emmet and Charlevoix counties in 2003. The tribal court consists of one chief judge, three appellate judges, one probation officer, one court administrator, and one administrative assistant. The system includes a tribal court, an appellate court, and a children's court. In addition to judicial matters, the court oversees the Odawa Youth Healing to Wellness Drug Court Program.

ECONOMY
The tribal economy is supported in large part through the revenue earned by its enterprises in the gaming industry.

Economic Development Projects. The tribe maintains an economic development department that oversees the identification and implementation of economic development projects on the tribe's behalf.

Gaming. The tribe owns the Victories Casino and Hotel in Petoskey, Michigan. The casino offers over 850 slots and video poker machines. Table games include craps, blackjack, roulette, three-card poker, Let It Ride, and Caribbean stud poker. The hotel offers 10 suites, 128 standard rooms, an indoor pool, a hot tub, a lounge, a restaurant, a sports lounge, and a deli. It also features a banquet hall with a capacity for 225 guests.

Real Estate/Commercial Development. The housing department is in the process of developing the first Odawa Housing Development. The community will be developed on 80 acres located north of Harbor Springs. It will offer 30 home sites and a rental housing complex for elders that will include six duplexes.

Media and Communications. The tribe's communications department publishes *The Odawa Trails*, a monthly newsletter.

Tourism and Recreation. Hunting and fishing are permitted on tribal lands. Permits are required and may be attained through the tribe's natural resources department.

Northwestern Michigan is home to numerous championship golf and ski resorts, including Boyne Mountain, Boyne Highlands, and Nubs Nob.

INFRASTRUCTURE
Little Traverse Bay Bands' tribal land base is 30 miles west of Interstate 75. U.S. 31 and U.S. 131 are major state highways that intersect in the community of Harbor Springs. The Mackinac Bridge links the upper and lower Michigan Peninsula and is a nearby landmark.

Water Supply. Groundwater from the city of Petoskey, Michigan, supplies water to the reservation.

COMMUNITY FACILITIES AND SERVICES
Tribal programs are available to tribal members residing within a 70-mile radius of the tribal headquarters in Harbor Springs. The tribe's human services department provides child welfare, social services, food distribution, low-income energy assistance, and child care development fund programs.

The tribe offers an elders program which is funded by grants through the Association on Aging and the Enterprise Revenue. The elders program services include a meal program. The tribe's archives and records program collects, documents, and preserves material pertaining to tribal history and culture. It organizes exhibits, educational presentations, and publications. Collections are available to the general public for research and reference. A community library located in the tribe's education department offers a collection that focuses on Native American literature, cultures, history, and languages.

Education. The tribe offers eligible members higher education merit, higher education emergency assistance, adult vocational training, direct employment, and K-12 education financial assistance programs. It also manages BIA-funded adult education and higher education scholarships. Through a program funded by the U.S. Department of Education, the tribe offers a Certificate in Clerical Technology at Bay Mills Community College. Courses are taught at the tribe's education department.

Health Care. The tribe maintains the Mskiki Gumik Clinic, contract health, a community outreach program, the Maajitaag Mnobmaabzid: Healthy Start Program, and a diabetes self-management program. The tribe maintains a substance abuse program that offers outreach, education, assessment, referrals, outpatient therapy, case management, crisis intervention, child abuse evaluation and therapy, and season encampment services. These services are based in traditional and culturally sensitive methods.

The tribe also offers the Biinoogiiyuk Guh Niigaanziiwaad (Mental Health Youth Initiative). It coordinates services for children and youth, including outreach and referrals.

ENVIRONMENTAL CONCERNS
The tribe's primary environmental concerns are related to the quality of water within the region's lakes, streams, rivers, and wetlands. It is also concerned with preserving fish and wildlife habitats in the area. The encroachment of development and the influx of summer tourists to the area pose serious threats to the local ecosystem.

Match-E-Be-Nash-She-Wish

Match-E-Be-Nash-She-Wish
 Band of Pottawatomi
 Indians of Michigan
Pottawatomi
Allegan County, Michigan

Match-E-Be-Nash-She-Wish
 Band of Pottawatomi Indians
 of Michigan
1743 142nd Ave.
P.O. Box 218
Dorr, MI 49323
 616-681-8830
 866-564-7429
 616-681-8836 Fax
 mbpi.org

Tribal enrollment
(BIA labor report, 2001)
276

Total labor force
(BIA labor report, 2001)
94

Unemployment rate
(BIA labor report, 2001)
24%

LOCATION AND LAND STATUS

The Match-E-Be-Nash-She-Wish Tribe is commonly known as the Gun Lake Tribe. Their tribal headquarters are located in Dorr, Michigan. This tribe was given federal recognition on October 14, 1998. It has petitioned the BIA to take a 145-acre site into trust, and in March 2004, the BIA issued a finding of no significant impact. As of December 2004 this issue remains unresolved.

CULTURE AND HISTORY

The Match-E-Be-Nash-She-Wish Band of Pottawatomi Indians of Michigan is the northernmost band of the Pottawatomi Nation on Michigan's Lower Peninsula. The Pottowatomis are an Algonquin people, one of the "Three Fires" of the Great Lakes, together with the Ojibwes (Chippewas) and Ottawas. They speak Central Algonquin, which is very similar to Ojibwe and Ottawa.

Important to the tribe's survival has been its association since 1836 with Christian (Episcopalian, then Methodist) Indian missions in what are now Bradley and Salem, Michigan. During much of this period, indigenous lay preachers served as the tribe's leaders, and the mission served as a central location for tribe members who might otherwise have scattered, been absorbed into other tribes, or been absorbed by the non-Indian community. Remaining identified as an Indian colony, both by themselves and by the surrounding non-Indian community, helped to preserve their history and cultural heritage. Of note, certain families still make the tribe's traditional black ash baskets.

In the eighteenth century, the tribe had villages located on the Grand, Thornapple, and Kalamazoo rivers in southeast Michigan. In 1795 the first chief known to have had extensive relations with non-Indians, Match-E-Be-Nash-She-Wish, signed the Treaty of Greenville on behalf of the Ojibwe (Chippewa), Ottawa, and Pottawatomi nations. For many years, Chief Match-E-Be-Nash-She-Wish was a leading spokesman for all three central Algonquin nations, and non-Indians frequently identified him as Ottawa or Ojibwe rather than as Pottawatomi. By 1820 the tribe's primary village was located at the head of the Kalamazoo River, and under the 1821 Treaty of Chicago the tribe retained a three-mile-square reservation located in what is now downtown Kalamazoo. Under the 1833 Treaty of Chicago, a dummy tribe called the "United Nations of Chippewa, Ottawa, and Pottawatomi" sold five million acres of land in Michigan for $100,000, and the nations purportedly agreed to move west of the Mississippi River. This fraud was so blatant that the federal government did not try to enforce removal for several years. In 1838 the federal government entered into compacts with Michigan Indian tribes under which annuity payments were to be made for 20 years. Because of its northern location, the tribe was attached to the Grand River Ottawas for administrative purposes, which led to confusion as to the tribe's identity for the next 150 years.

The tribe avoided removal by moving to an Episcopalian Indian mission in Allegan County. This became known as the Griswold or Bradley Colony. In 1855 the Grand River Band of Ottawa signed a new treaty granting it land to the north in Oceana County. Much of the tribe moved north, but within 15 years many families had moved back to the Bradley Colony because the federal government failed to implement the provisions of the 1855 treaty. In the 1870s the Bradley Colony became Methodist. In 1890, leaders of the Bradley Colony joined with other Pottawatomi groups filing claims against the United States for unpaid treaty annuities. Litigation continued in one form or another for another century.

In 1894 the trust that owned the land on which the Bradley Colony was located was dissolved, and the land was conveyed in fee to 19 descendants of Chief Match-E-Be-Nash-She-Wish. Most land was lost due to tax liens, but the tribe remained stable. A "daughter" Indian mission was established in Salem, about 10 miles west of Bradley. In 1939 the tribe was denied reorganization under the Indian Reorganization Act. By the 1950s, many members of the tribe had left Bradley to find employment. Claims against the federal government were revived under the Indian Claims Commission Act, and a member of the tribe was elected head of the Northern Michigan Ottawa Claims Organization. In 1959 the Indian Claims Commission ruled that the tribe was to be paid separately from the Ottawas, and the tribe began to pursue its claim based on the three-mile-square Kalamazoo reservation land; as of 2004 that claim was unresolved. In the 1990s, the tribe organized itself on a tribal government basis and petitioned for federal acknowledgment. The BIA recognized the tribe on October 14, 1998, finding that the residents of the Bradley community had been consistently identified since the mid-1800s as descendants of Match-E-Be-Nash-She-Wish's band of Pottawatomi Indians.

GOVERNMENT

The seven-member tribal council has three members elected from the Bradley voting district, two members from the Salem voting district, and two members from the at-large voting district. As of 2004, two of the council members were also full-time tribal staff employees, and one was the chief executive officer of the tribe's economic development corporation.

Governmental departments (some of which have only one employee) include environmental, finance, housing, member services, and health and human services. The environmental department deals with grant applications, Emerald Ash Borer concerns, wetlands, soil erosion and sedimentation of inland lakes, air quality issues, land-use issues, recycling, and tribal places of residence during the last 300 years. The housing department handles a home improvement program, college student rental assistance, down payment assistance, and weatherization assistance. The member services department administers enrollment, educational matters, college scholarships, vocational training assistance, employment assistance, Title VI nutrition grant, notary public, and the monthly newsletter. The health and human services department focuses on assessment and case management, children and family services, crisis intervention, information and referral, and prevention and protective services.

Under PL-638 the tribe administers federally funded college scholarship and vocational training programs and health coverage. Until the proposed casino is in operation, most of the financing for the tribe's operations will come from federal and state grants. The tribe received new tribe funding from the BIA for fiscal years 2000 to 2002, and will moved into base funding in 2003. Since 2003, the tribe received funds from the Indian Housing Block Grant and an EPA grant for projects to restore the Kalamazoo River watershed in southwest Michigan.

BUSINESS CORPORATION

The MBPI is the tribe's economic development corporation.

ECONOMY

As of 2004, the tribe had no separate economy but was fully integrated with the surrounding non-Indian communities. Economic development is focused on gaming.

Match-E-Be-Nash-She-Wish

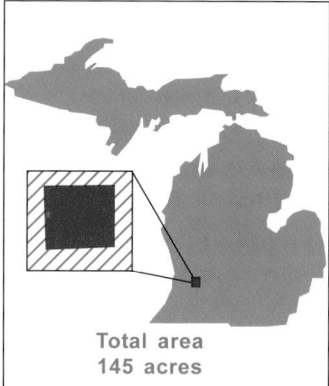

Total area
145 acres

Gaming. The tribe has proposed opening a casino and entertainment complex on approximately 145 acres on Highway 131 approximately 25 miles north of Kalamazoo and 25 miles south of Grand Rapids. Planning in 2002 envisioned a complex that would include a 193,000-square-foot gaming facility with up to 2,500 slot machines and 75 table games, a buffet restaurant seating 300, a 125-seat coffee shop, a 150-seat steakhouse, and an entertainment venue. Plans are to convert an existing 193,000-square-foot building into the entertainment facility. The tribe estimated that as many as 4,300 jobs would be created.

The tribe entered into a management agreement with Station Casinos, a Las Vegas, Nevada, casino owner and operator that also manages the Thunder Valley Casino in Sacramento, California, for the United Auburn Indian Community. Station Casinos paid $6 million for its interest, and it will arrange or provide financing of development and construction. Station Casinos expected to advance $10 to $15 million to the tribe for the acquisition of land and other development costs, and the overall cost would be between $100 and 200 million. The management fee is 30 percent of net income, of which Station Casinos is to receive 50 percent of the first $24 million, 83 percent of the next $24 million, and 93 percent of amounts above $48 million.

In 2003 the tribe and Stations Casinos expected to have the casino operational in 2005, but it hit a major roadblock. Although Michigan's legislature had approved a compact in 2002, and then-Governor Engler recommended approval, the compact hit a major snag owing to a potential conflict of interest. Engler's successor, Governor Granholm, had not signed the compact as of 2004, and the Michigan senate rescinded its approval in December 2004. Governor Granholm has stated that the compact remains under review, and the effect of the senate's action on the compact is unknown. While the tribe will be able to open the casino under federal law irrespective of the state's consent, this will almost certainly delay the process.

INFRASTRUCTURE
The tribe is dependent on the infrastructure of the surrounding communities.

COMMUNITY FACILITIES AND SERVICES
Other than its administrative offices in Dorr, Michigan, the tribe has no community facilities. The tribe is in the planning process for a tribal community center that will open in 2005.

Health Care. A community health representative and a community health nurse and diabetes coordinator are on staff at the tribal administrative offices. Indian Health Services recognizes that location as an Indian Health Center.

ENVIRONMENTAL CONCERNS
In addition to Emerald Ash Borer concerns, wetlands, soil erosion and sedimentation of inland lakes, air quality issues, land-use issues, and recycling, the tribe is particularly concerned about the Kalamazoo River and its watershed. The tribe is leading efforts to reduce agricultural runoff by developing a pollutant-trading program.

Pokagon Township

Pokagon Township Reservation
Federal reservation
Bode'wadmi or Potawatomi
Berrian, Cass, and Van Buren
counties, Michigan; and St.
Joseph's County, Indiana

Potawatomi Indian Nation
58620 Sink Road
Dowagiac, MI 49047
269-782-6323
269-782-9625 Fax
pokagon.com

Total area *(Tribal source, 2004)*
4,700 acres

Tribally owned land
(Tribal source, 2004)
4,700 acres

Population *(BIA labor report, 2001)*
1025

Tribal enrollment
(BIA labor report, 2001)
2,730

LOCATION AND LAND STATUS
During the eighteenth and nineteenth centuries, the Pokagon Band signed 11 treaties with the United States establishing the band's right to remain in Michigan. In the mid 1800s, therefore, the Pokagon and the Huron bands refused to leave their Michigan villages and territories for a Kansas reservation that the federal government had arranged for the greater Potawatomi Tribe.

The Pokagons have traditionally lived in two communities built on land purchased by band members at Silver Creek, near Dowagiac, and at Rush River, north of Watervliet. In September 1994 the band finally won its 60-year struggle for federal recognition, and it now has a land base of 4,700 acres which the band purchased at three different sites for reservation development in 1997. Tribal headquarters are located in Dowagiac, Michigan; however, most members live within a 10-county service area of Indiana and Michigan.

CLIMATE
The elevation at Dowagiac, Michigan, is 740 feet above sea level. The year-round average daily high temperature is 58°F, with the highest temperature ever recorded being 103°F. The year-round average daily low temperature is 37°F, with the lowest temperature on record being -23°F. The area receives approximately 39 inches of precipitation annually, with 68 inches of snowfall.

CULTURE AND HISTORY
Ancestors of the modern-day Pokagon Band of Potawatomi have been living in the area of what are now the states of Michigan, Indiana, Illinois, and Wisconsin for over 500 years. The Potawatomis are Anishnabeks, ("People of the Fire" or "Keepers of the Sacred Fire"). They are of the Algonquian linguistic stock and call themselves simply Nishnabek, or "The People." Together with two other tribes, the Ojibwas and Ottawas, they formed the Council of the Three Fires and cooperated for mutual protection and trade. They were organized into family clans and lived a subsistence lifestyle consisting of hunting, fishing, gathering, and horticulture. They supplemented these activities as French fur trappers brought trade goods in exchange for furs. They first encountered the French explorer Jean Nicolet in 1634 and referred to the French as "hairy faces" or Wemitigoji.

After the American Revolution and the westward migration of white settlers, the Potawatomis were party to 11 treaties with the federal government. The primary land cession treaty was the Treaty of Chicago, signed in 1833 during the Jackson removal era, when all Indians living east of the Mississippi were scheduled for relocation either to Kansas or Oklahoma. The Potawatomi Nation as a whole, but not the Pokagon Band, were hurt much more by the Removal Policy than were their two council brethren, the Ottawas and Ojibwas. Chief Leopold Pokagon was able to negotiate with the federal government to keep his band of 280 people in southwestern Michigan, becoming the only Potawatomis to reside legally in the state of Michigan at that time. Thus, this group became known as the Pokagon Band of Potawatomi.

The band practiced a subsistence lifestyle throughout the nineteenth and the early part of the twentieth centuries, when they began hiring out as wage laborers on farms owned by non-Indian neighbors. In the wake of World War I, a number of Pokagons found employment in burgeoning area industries, though the number of band members looking beyond their home-grown rural economy remained quite limited until World War II, after which band members branched out widely into the region's booming industrial economy, headed up by the auto industry and tangential businesses such as plastic molding factories and die-casting industries. This continues today.

Establishing federal recognition was the most consuming political struggle facing the Pokagons during the twentieth century, a process begun in 1934 when the band informed the U.S. government of its desire to organize a tribal government under the Wheeler-Howard Act. However, the federal government made an administrative decision to limit the number of non-reservation tribes officially recognized under Wheeler-Howard, and the band's request was denied. The Federal Acknowledgment Project, within the BIA, breathed new life into the Pokagons' quest, with recognition finally being granted in September 1994. With recognition, the band has become eligible for federal programs and it will be able to promote self-sufficiency through economic development and to reassume control over its own destiny.

The Catholic Church has long served as a center for social and political gatherings for the Pokagons, providing opportunities for socialization that have kept the Potawatomi traditions and identity alive. Present-day Pokagons are highly concerned with maintaining their distinct cultural identity, particularly via ceremonies, art, and the use of their Native language that symbolizes the Potawatomi worldview. To this end, the sacred longhouse ceremonies, sweat lodges, and powwows have returned to occupy a more central position in the Pokagon culture than they have for many decades. Moreover, the present-day tribal government emphasizes education, continued diversity, and expansion of economic development.

GOVERNMENT
As early as 1866, the Pokagon Band established a formal government with an elected seven-member business council headed by a chairman and a chief dedicated to pursuing various claims against the U.S. government. The present-day business council is an active agency working within the community to meet the needs of its members. The council focuses primarily on human services, having established departments and/or programs such as, social services, education, health services, behavioral health and substance abuse services, child welfare and protection, and tribal courts and tribal law enforcement. The social services department works in conjunction with community prevention and outreach services to meet the needs of tribal families and individuals. The Indian Child Welfare Commission was established to work with the Pokagon Band Tribal Council, tribal court, social services department, and state judicial systems. Financial assistance for child care, food commodities, and the low-income home energy assistance programs are available via the social services department as well.

ECONOMY
Gaming. The band entered into a class III gaming compact with the State of Michigan on December 3, 1998.

Fisheries. There are recreational and commercial fishing possibilities in Lake Michigan, 25 miles west of tribal lands.

Manufacturing. Though the Pokagons currently have no tribal manufacturing enterprises, the region's manufacturing industry has traditionally been a strong source of employment for tribal members and nonmembers alike, much of it in automobile manufacturing and its ancillary industries.

Services and Retail. Tribal members engage in a variety of business enterprises, including arts and crafts shops, traveling vendors on the powwow circuit, accounting businesses, and law firms.

Tourism and Recreation. The tribe sponsors several annual events including the Kee-Boon-Meinkaa Powwow over Labor Day weekend. This event features much in the way of arts, crafts, and Native foods.

INFRASTRUCTURE
Interstate 94, along with Route 57 and the Indiana Toll Road, provide road access to the tribal community.

Electricity. The Indiana/Michigan Power Company and Fruit Belt Electric provide electricity.

Fuel. Michigan Gas Company furnishes natural gas service.

Water Supply. The Dowagiac municipal systems provide water and sewer services.

Transportation. Commercial air service is available approximately 25 miles distant in South Bend, Indiana. There is also a small private airport in Dowagiac. Commercial bus service is available at Benton Harbor, 20 miles from tribal headquarters. Amtrak serves Dowagiac directly, as do commercial truck lines. The St. Joe River provides for some water-based transportation.

Telecommunications. GTE and Michigan Bell supply telephone service.

COMMUNITY FACILITIES AND SERVICES
The tribal hall was built at Dowagiac in 1987, with offices, meeting rooms, and a weekly language class. The education department sponsors a full-service computer lab at the tribal hall, with instruction available in desktop publishing, typing, and Internet access. The National Society for American Indian Elderly, a national nonprofit organization, provides senior services for tribal elders.

Education. Children attend the local public schools. The tribe provides language classes at the tribal center.

Health Care. There are several local, nontribal clinics and a number of area hospitals, all of which are private contractors.

Pokagon Township

Total labor force
2000 census
17,375

Total labor force-Michigan
(BIA labor report, 2001)
562

Total labor force-Indiana
(BIA labor report, 2001)
295

High school graduate or higher
2000 census
80.2%

Bachelor's degree or higher
2000 census
12%

Unemployment rate
2000 census
7.4%

Unemployment rate-Michigan
(BIA labor report, 2001)
12%

Unemployment rate-Indiana
(BIA labor report, 2001)
71%

Total area
4,700 acres

Sault Ste. Marie

Sault Ste. Marie Reservation
Federal reservation
Ojibwa (Chippewa)
Chippewa County, Michigan

The Sault Ste. Marie Tribe of
Chippewa Indians
523 Ashmun St.
Sault Ste. Marie, MI 49783
906-635-6050
906-635-6050 Fax
sootribe.org

Federal trust lands
(Tribal source, 2004)
1,608.13 acres

Population *2000 census*
1,676

Tribal enrollment
(Tribal source, 2004)
31,538

Total labor force *2000 census*
648

Total labor force
(BIA labor report, 2001)
12,816

High school graduate or higher
2000 census
74.9%

High school graduate or higher
(Tribal source, 2002)
85.6%

Bachelor's degree or higher
2000 census
8.9%

Bachelor's degree or higher
(Tribal source, 2002)
16.4%

Unemployment rate
2000 census
17%

Unemployment rate
(BIA labor report, 2001)
72%

Unemployment rate
(Tribal source, 2002)
19.3%

Per capita income *2000 census*
$7,115

LOCATION AND LAND STATUS

The Sault Ste. Marie Reservation is located east of the city of Sault Ste. Marie, at the extreme eastern end of the Michigan Peninsula, near the Canadian border. The reservation was established by proclamation of the secretary of the interior in 1974. While 1,265 acres are held in federal trust for the tribe, its service area encompasses the seven counties at the east end of Michigan's Upper Peninsula. The tribe's headquarters are located in Sault Ste. Marie.

CULTURE AND HISTORY

The original bands of Sault Ste. Marie Chippewa Indians were an identifiable tribal entity long before their first contract with white explorers. Between 1795 and 1864, the Michigan Chippewas were party to treaties that ceded title to their land and that reserved specific rights and properties for the individual bands. Allotment schemes implemented during the 1850s and 1860s defrauded the Indians out of much of the land promised them in these treaties. By the beginning of the twentieth century, the individual Chippewa bands owned little of the trust property once reserved for them. As the tribe lost its land base during the late 1800s, the federal government gradually abandoned its responsibilities for maintaining its end of the trust relationship. During the twentieth century, the Chippewa tribes spent a tremendous amount of energy and resources reestablishing their right to self-government.

In the wake of the Revolutionary War, the U.S. government continued the precedent established by the British and the French of dealing with the various bands in the area as one tribal entity. The Sault Ste. Maries were part of the treaty of July 31, 1855, which placed the Michigan Chippewas on several large reservations extending across the eastern portion of the Upper Peninsula. During the 1930s, the Sault Ste. Marie band members comprised one of the most depressed segments of that area's population. Passage of the 1934 Indian Reorganization Act offered some hope of reversing this negative trend, though for various reasons it ultimately did little to reverse the band's slide into poverty. By the late 1950s, the bands had compiled membership rolls, along with a synopsis of their history, and they were preparing to bring their case for recognition before the federal government, in spite of the congressional trend toward termination. In 1972, a delegation of the Original Bands of the Sault Ste. Marie Chippewa Indians met in Washington with the U.S. Interior's Commissioner of Indian Affairs. The commissioner agreed that the bands were in fact eligible for federal recognition, signing a memorandum to this effect on September 7, 1972. This memo paved the way for the tribe's acquisition of trust land, which the federal government subsequently accepted on March 17, 1974. The Sault Ste. Marie Band, like other Michigan Chippewa tribes, maintains strong links to the culture and worldview of its ancestors.

GOVERNMENT

The tribe established its constitution and bylaws under the provisions of the 1934 Indian Reorganization Act, which were approved by the secretary of the interior in November 1975. The tribal government is governed by a 12-member board of directors and a chairperson elected at large by the people every four years. The board of directors serves a four-year term, and half of its membership are up for election every two years. As of 2000, the tribal government administered 82 membership services and operated five gaming and 27 nongaming enterprises.

Tribal government departments include human resources, accounting, communications, enrollment, economic development commission, investment, gaming commission, legal, enterprises, and housing authority. Other tribal government departments include management information services, which maintains the tribe's computer network, management and budget, planning, public safety, purchasing, and video.

The Sault Ste. Marie Tribe's law enforcement department, with 19 sworn police officers, has a main office in Sault Ste. Marie, and satellite offices in Kincheloe, St. Ignace, and Manistique, and it provides public safety to all communities within the reservation. A 24-bed juvenile detention facility in St. Ignace, Michigan is also operated by the law enforcement department. The judicial branch consists of a tribal court consisting of one chief judge who is appointed by the tribal council and a magistrate. The appellate court has one chief judge and four associate judges comprised of one attorney and three tribal lay judges, also appointed by the tribal council. A victim's advocate program and a Woman's Gathering Lodge provide services to the community and function in close association with law enforcement and the judiciary.

ECONOMY

The gaming industry drives the Sault Ste. Marie Tribe's business-based economy. Other economic activities on and near the reservation include tribal government operations, construction, real estate and commercial development, and service sector businesses. Since the late 1990s, the tribe has developed its economy, with its businesses as the major sector, to supplement federal appropriations and to increase its governmental services to its membership through building health centers and expanding its housing construction. A large percentage of gaming revenues are used to fund government operations, to support member services and community projects, and to expand tribal business enterprises.

Government as Employer. As of 2004, the tribal government, its programs, and enterprises employed 908 people in all its programs and divisions. Division/department breakdowns are as follows: human services (65), housing (100), health (203), elder programs (22), recreation (43), education (73), governmental services (87), internal services (211), employment programs (79), and governmental activities (25).

The casinos have collectively provided work for 1,323 people. Tribal enterprises employed 77 people.

Economic Development Projects. Economic development projects are handled by the tribe's board of directors. One current project is the development of a resort and casino in the St. Ignace area on trust land.

Gaming. The Sault Ste. Marie Tribe of Chippewa Indians owns and operates five casinos in the upper peninsula of Michigan. These include casinos in Christmas, Hessel, Manistique, St. Ignace, and the flagship casino in Sault Ste. Marie.

The Kewadin Casino Christmas is located on M-28 just west of the town of Munising. The 22,000-square-foot casino has a gaming floor featuring 215 slot machines and 6 table games, including blackjack, two-deck pitch, and three-card poker. Christmas Casino has one restaurant, Frosty's Bar and Grill, and the Northern Lights gift shop.

The Kewadin Casino Hessel is located three miles from the Les Cheneaux Islands and Lake Huron. Surrounded by a small town environment, the 6,400-square-foot-casino offers a gaming floor with 111 slot machines. Customers may eat at the casino deli.

The Kewadin Casino Manistique is located on US-2 west of Mackinaw Bridge. The 25,000-square-foot casino offers 264 slot machines, 9 table games including blackjack, roulette, craps, three-card poker, two-deck pitch, and Let It Ride, and 50 bingo seats. Visitors may dine at the Mariner's Cove restaurant and visit the Team Spirits Sports Bar inside the casino.

The Kewadin Casino St. Ignace, also known as The Shores, is located on the Mackinac Trail along the picturesque Straits of Mackinac. The 47,036-square-foot casino offers 998 slots, 24 table games, and 4 poker tables. Take a break for a meal at the Market Square Buffet Restaurant located inside the casino. Visitors also have the opportunity to pick up a souvenir at the gift shop.

The Kewadin Vegas Casino Sault Ste. Marie, located in the heart of Michigan's Upper Peninsula, offers a 39,000-square-foot facility with 934 slot machines, 22 table games, and 200 bingo seats. The Kewadin Casino Hotel features 318 rooms and a 22,000-square-foot convention center. Visitors may dine at the Dream Catcher's restaurant that offers a buffet for every meal.

The tribe also operates a casino in Detroit, Michigan's high-energy Greektown District. The Greektown Casino offers 75,000 square feet of action with a gaming floor featuring 2,552 slot machines, 86 table games, and 8 poker tables. Greektown features 22 restaurants, including the Alley Grille Steakhouse and the Grapevine Café. Find entertainment at the Apollo Lounge, or plan your next business or reception gathering at the 2,700-square-foot Olive Convention Room. The Greektown Casino is regulated as a Michigan Limited Liability Corporation by the Greektown Gaming Management Board. This board is made up of members of the Sault Tribe Board of Directors.

Fisheries. Fisheries currently employ 150 tribal members as captains and helpers. More tribal members are employed on the dockside. A new commercial fishing agreement with the state was negotiated in 2000 recognizing the Indian tribes commercial fishing rights preserved under the 1836 treaty. The tribe's 1985 consent order was negotiated into this new agreement. The provisions of this new agreement will impact all of the tribe's fisheries.

The Sault Ste Marie Tribe is a member of the Chippewa-Ottawa Resource Authority (CORA), which consists of four other tribes in Michigan. CORA monitors tribal fish hatcheries for water quality, tests for contaminants, and keeps track of catch limits.

Construction. There is a tribally owned enterprise called the Sault Tribe Construction Company. In 2004 it employed 34 people. This company was merged with the former Chi Chunk Construction and another firm. The new company works exclusively on tribal housing, community and business projects throughout the seven-country tribal service area.

Real Estate/Commercial Development. The Sault Ste. Marie Chippewa Tribe operates DeMawating Sales and Development, which rents and sells 212 single-family and two-family homes that once served as military housing for Kincheloe Air Force Base, which closed in 1977. The tribe also owns and rents the Eagle Ridge Apartments.

The tribe owns commercial properties near and off the reservation, including the 46-room Kewadin Inns in Sault Ste. Marie, a 70-room motel in St. Ignace, and four other hotel properties,

including a former Ramada Inn in Mantistique, a former Holiday Inn in Orilla, Ontario, near the popular RAMA Casino, a Roadway Inn in Mackinaw City, and Georgian House in St. Ignace. The tribe has the controlling interest in the Courtyard by Marriott Hotel in Grand Rapids near Michigan's largest airport.

Services and Retail. There is a plethora of tribally owned or affiliated businesses in the Sault Ste. Marie tribal service area. A partial list includes the following: Chippewa Service and Supply, a janitorial service and supply company; two or more convenience stores; a charter air service; a furniture, carpeting, art, and graphics company; several restaurants; a real estate sales and rental agency; a gift shop; a nonprofit finance company; and a health and recreation center.

Kewadin Village is a tribally owned travelers center and convenience store with a full-service RV campground and trout pond. The tribe also owns the Midjim Stores, which provide basic food, health, and other items to members living on the reservation in St. Ignace and Sault Ste. Marie. Northern Hospitality opened as a wholesale supplier of flooring and furnishings to serve tribal enterprises in 1993. In 1995 it opened a retail storefront to sell to the public. Today this company designs and installs home and business interiors. The tribe's gaming properties, offices, and businesses, including Greektown, are still its major customers.

Media and Communications. The tribal communication department publishes the tribal newspaper, *The Sault Tribe News*, it is published every three weeks and delivered to tribal members all over the world. The tribe also produces three radio shows that air on local stations each week.

The communications department also houses the tribe's public relations office.

Tourism and Recreation. Tourism centers on the tribal gaming enterprises and the Kewadin Inn. The tribe owns an RV park. Additionally, the region features excellent fishing, boating, hiking, camping, and during the winter, cross-country skiing and snowmobiling. The Hessel Powwow, the annual Gathering of the Eagles Honoring Mother Earth, takes place in late August in Hessel, Michigan.

INFRASTRUCTURE
Electricity. The regional utilities provide electricity and gas service on an individual residential basis

Water Supply. Municipal systems supplemented by wells and septic tanks in the outlying areas provide water and sewer service.

Transportation. Road access to the reservation is provided by Interstate 75, which ends in the city of Sault Ste. Marie near the tribal community. Commercial air, bus, and truck lines serve Sault Ste. Marie. There is a tribally affiliated air charter service as well.

Telecommunications. The Sault Ste. Marie Tribe communications department manages the tribe's web pages: Kewadin.com and saulttribe.org.

The former Northstar Neon Company closed in 1998, but a portion of the building is leased to a high-tech computer company in Sault Ste. Marie.

COMMUNITY FACILITIES AND SERVICES
The tribe owns the 150,000-square-foot Chi Mukwa Health and Recreation Center, giving tribal members free access to fitness and recreation programs. The facility operates two ice arenas, basketball and volleyball courts, a pro shop, a health center, public skating, hockey, and figure skating camps.

Sault Ste. Marie

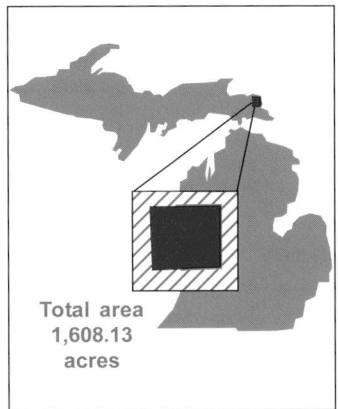

Total area
1,608.13
acres

Sault Ste. Marie

Education. The tribe operates the Bahweting Anishinabe School for kindergarten through eight graders. It is a chartered BIA school that was established in 1993. Attending the Joseph K. Lumsden state chartered elementary school is an option for tribal children. Since this school has limited enrollment the rest of the children attend various schools throughout the area. The tribe maintains an education division under its department of membership services, which oversees both youth and adult education protocol. The department offers both a Head Start program and an Early Head Start program. The Early Head Start program offers qualified families free medical and dental care. The Early Head Start program is annually open for 50 infants and their families. Activities provide new parents with basic child care skills, while offering supplemental parenting courses from the Parents as Teacher's curriculum. Early Head Start mothers receive hands-on family training within the privacy of their homes. The Head Start program offers two classes comprised of 20 students each in Sault Ste. Marie, and one class of 20 students in St. Ignace.

Health Care. The tribe's single most expensive budget item is its health department. In 2004 it allocated $24.3 million to provide quality health care to its members. The tribe's main health facility is located in Sault Ste. Marie at the Community Health and Human Service Center. The clinic provides health care for all tribal members. The clinic offers services such as ambulatory services, medical, dental, pharmacy, laboratory, radiology, optical, community health services, contract health services, enrollment, traditional medicine, and environmental health.

The tribe operates six ambulatory care clinics in Sault Ste. Marie, Kinross, St. Ignace, Manistique, Munising, and Detour. It also operates one urgent care clinic in Sault Ste. Marie. Health services are also provided at three outlying tribal community centers located in Hessel, Newberry, and Escanaba.

ENVIRONMENTAL CONCERNS

There are several environmental issues currently facing the tribe. The largest threat is posed to the fisheries by an invasion of non-native species, specifically zebra mussels. The tribe has received a grant that they will use to attend to this issue. Some aquifers in Sault St. Marie and in Kinross have become contaminated and the tribe is looking for ways to fix this. There have also been some issues with land contamination in Kinross by solvent, and in Marquette by jet fuel. The old dump site located on casino property in Sault St. Marie is also a potential hazard. A worm farm is being discussed as a potential project to compost food wastes in the area.

Bois Forte

Bois Forte

LOCATION AND LAND STATUS

The Bois Forte Reservation is divided into three sections: Nett Lake, the largest and the location of Bois Forte tribal headquarters; Deer Creek, in Itasca County; and Vermilion. Tribal members currently live in the Vermilion and Nett Lake sectors, and on trust lands. The reservation lies 75 miles south of the Canadian border in Minnesota.

Originally spanning 103,863 acres, the Bois Forte Reservation was established by treaty in 1866. An executive order on December 30, 1881, set aside additional parcels for the "use and residence of the Bois Forte Band of Chippewas." Currently, the reservation totals 132,000 acres; approximately 11,500 acres of the land base are allotted.

PHYSICAL DESCRIPTION

The Nett Lake sector straddles the Koochiching and St. Louis county line; both the Nett Lake River and the Little Fork River intersect the Nett Lake sector. The Deer Creek sector lies in Itasca County and is crossed by the Big Fork River. The Vermilion sector lies within a peninsula on Lake Vermilion. Nett Lake contains the largest contiguous wild rice (manoomin) beds in the world, totaling almost 8,000 acres near Spirit Island.

CLIMATE

There is no climate information recorded for Nett Lake, Minnesota. However, the community lies approximately 40 miles south of International Falls and temperatures would not differ significantly. The year-round average daily high temperature at International Falls is 48°F, with the highest temperature ever recorded of 99°F. The year-round average daily low is 26°F. The lowest temperature on record is -46°F. The area receives approximately 24 inches of rain annually and 64 inches of snow.

CULTURE AND HISTORY

Ojibway is generally interpreted as "To roast till puckered up," referring to the puckered seams of moccasins, or as a mispronunciation of O-jib-i-weg, "Those who make pictographs." The name Chippewa, widely used in treaties and other official documents, is a corruption of the early spellings of Ojibway or Otchipwe. Anishinabe (Anishinabeg, plural) is the name by which the people call themselves, and it indicates "Original or Spontaneous Man" or "The People." Bois Forte, a French phrase translates as "Strong men (or Strength) of the woods," Chippewas speak an Algonquian based language.

The Bois Fortes originally lived in small self-governing villages in Canada. The tribe first encountered French explorers in the 1600s near Sault Sainte Marie, Canada. Later, they prospered in the fur trade and expanded their population and territory. By the late eighteenth century, the Iroquois had driven the Chippewas out of the Ontario peninsula, and they began to move into western Wisconsin and northeastern Minnesota. Arriving in what is now Minnesota, the Chippewas encountered the powerful Santee Sioux. Conflicts between the two tribes persisted until the Chippewas successfully drove the Sioux westward. When Euro-American settlers arrived, the Chippewas occupied more than half the state. The Minnesota Chippewas lived in four great divisions, each containing a number of bands.

Living in isolated villages throughout the early nineteenth century, the Chippewas were able to avoid the increasing number of westward-moving settlers. In the March 19, 1867 Treaty, the 10 chiefs of the Chippewa of the Mississippi ceded their treaty rights to land that extended northwest to Thief River and north to Turtle Lake. They retained land in an area quite similar to the present Leech Lake Reservation boundaries. The 1889 Nelson Act designated that all Chippewas living in Minnesota be moved to the White Earth Reservation. The Native people resisted this decree, and finally the U.S. Chippewa Commission was directed to negotiate for the complete cession of all lands belonging to the different bands except for the Red Lake and White Earth reservations. The Chippewas were able to retain seven reservations in Minnesota: Bois Forte, Fond du Lac, Grand Portage, Leech Lake, Mille Lacs, White Earth, and Red Lake, all located in the northern half of the state. Land losses by the turn of the twentieth century as a result of allotments were so massive that today the reservations are a fraction of their original size.

Chippewas in the twenty-first century are a diverse group active in contemporary society. Determined to maintain their culture and improve the living conditions of tribal members, the Minnesota Chippewas have a long tradition of political and legal activity to reclaim lost lands. Many contemporary members excel and have received national recognition in the visual, literary, and traditional arts.

GOVERNMENT

The original constitution and bylaws of the Minnesota Chippewa Tribe were ratified in 1936, in accordance with the Indian Reorganization Act. The six member reservations of the Minnesota Chippewa Tribe sought a single consolidated tribal government without relinquishing governance at the local level. Each member reservation elects its own tribal government, the Reservation Business Committee, which governs locally as well as provides representation to the consolidated organization, which is governed by a tribal executive committee. The headquarters of the Minnesota Chippewa Tribe are located in the community of Cass Lake, on the Leech Lake Reservation. Enrolled members in the Minnesota Chippewa Tribe totaled 40,000 in 1993.

The Bois Forte Reservation is governed by a five-member elected tribal council, each member serving staggered four-year

Bois Forte Reservation
Federal reservation
Chippewa or Ojibway
Koochiching, Itasca, Lake, St.
Louis and Cook counties,
Minnesota

Bois Forte Band of Chippewa
P.O. Box 16
Nett Lake, MN 55772
218-757-3261
218-757-3312 Fax
boisforte.com

Total area (BIA realty, 2004)
43,789 acres

Tribally owned (BIA realty, 2004)
31,624 acres

Individually owned
(BIA realty, 2004)
12,160 acres

Population 2000 census
717

Tribal enrollment
(BIA labor report, 2001)
2,857

Total labor force 2000 census
315

Total labor force
(BIA labor report, 2001)
1,069

High school graduate or higher
2000 census
80%

Bois Forte

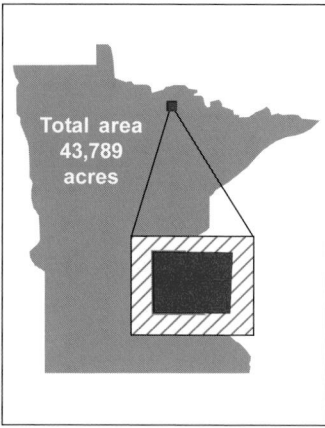

Total area
43,789
acres

Bachelor's degree or higher
2000 census
11.3%

Unemployment rate *2000 census*
7.9%

Unemployment rate
(BIA labor report, 2001)
5%

Per capita income *2000 census*
$11,790

terms. The council includes a chairman, a secretary-treasurer, and district representatives.

The tribal council operates Head Start and other childcare programs, conservation enforcement programs, roads and community maintenance, tribally owned enterprises, and central administration. They have their own criminal and judicial court system. The community maintenance program provides street and road maintenance, public building maintenance, and general community grounds upkeep and beautification.

The tribe, under PL-638, contracts with the BIA to administer key programs and services, such as the Indian Health Service clinic. The Bois Forte Tribal Council participates with that of Grand Portage in the 1854 Authority, an entity that regulates off-reservation tribal hunting, fishing, and gathering rights stemming from the 1854 treaty.

BUSINESS CORPORATION
In 1992, the tribe formed the Bois Forte Business Development Program, which provides loans for tribally owned small businesses.

ECONOMY
The Fortune Bay Casino has become a mainstay of the tribal economy. However, many tribal members are engaged in the cultivation of zizania aquatica, an aquatic grass better known as wild rice. Nett Lake is the largest contiguous wild rice bed in the world; there are approximately 8,000 acres growing naturally. It is harvested by canoe by Bois Forte tribal members from late August to early October. Approximately 100,000 pounds of finished product is sold annually by individual band members or used for personal consumption. Also, finished lumber products from the Bois Forte Sawmill are marketed throughout the upper midwest and Canada. There is a growing tourism market on the reservation drawn by the Fortune Bay Casino.

Government as Employer. Tribal government employs people at the Fortune Bay Casino, the Bois Forte Sawmill, the Multi-Service Center, and through various tribal programs and services, such as the elderly nutrition program, Head Start, and Nett Lake Elementary School.

Gaming. The Fortune Bay Resort Casino opened in December 1985 on the detached Vermillion parcel, 70 miles from the main reservation, near Tower, Minnesota. It is a primary source of tribal revenue and employment. The 50,000-square-foot gaming facility features 800 slot machines, 12 table games, a 300-seat bingo hall, 2 restaurants, an entertainment venue, and 5,200 square feet of convention and meeting space located on the shore of Lake Vermilion. In 2004 the casino employed 450 people. The casino and its board report directly to the reservation tribal council for policy and procedural approval.

Services and Retail. The tribally owned Multi-Service Center (M.S.C. Foods) is a convenience store, providing grocery items for members of the Bois Forte community, elderly nutrition program, Head Start, and Nett Lake Elementary School. Other businesses on the reservation include Voyager Trucking, six logging businesses, Strongs Wild Rice, and Summertime Painting and Sign.

Tourism and Recreation. Nett Lake's location within the northern duck and goose flyway makes it one of North America's best duck hunting lakes. A number of reservation residents earn a seasonal supplemental income providing guide services to non-Indian licensed hunters. Guide service is also provided for deer and moose hunting. Non-Indian hunting within the boundaries of the reservation is restricted to Nett Lake itself and is regulated by the Bois Forte conservation code. Other outdoor activities, such as hiking, biking, and winter snow sports, are also permitted.

The Anishinabe Mikana committee sponsors two powwows yearly, attracting drummers, singers, and dancers from the Great Lakes area, Canada, and North Dakota. Traditional foods are served. A marina on Lake Vermilion and an RV park are open to serve the Fortune Bay Resort Casino patrons and other tourists, along with a banquet and ballroom/conference center with meeting rooms and exhibition space. The new 3,000-square-foot Heritage Center and Cultural Museum, Atisokanigamig, or "Legend House" is open as well, with exhibits explaining traditional activities, such as net fishing, and harvesting and parching wild rice, and describing the history of the Chippewa people. A gift shop on-site features locally handcrafted Native American arts and crafts. The Wilderness, an 18-hole golf course at Fortune Bay Resort Casino, was scheduled to open spring 2004. Accommodations can be found at the resort hotel, featuring whirlpool and fireplace suites, dining and shopping opportunities, a fitness room, an indoor pool, a game room, and daycare. Cozier lodging can be obtained at Hideaway Pines, a rustic lodge accommodating up to eight people, with direct access to Arrowhead Trail and hundreds of miles of scenic hiking and snowmobile paths.

INFRASTRUCTURE
The community of Bois Forte, in the Nett Lake sector, lies along State Highway 65 and State Highway 23, the latter leading to the eastern edge of Nett Lake. State Highway 1 crosses the Deer Creek sector and intersects west of Deer Creek at the town of Effie with Highway 38. The Vermilion sector may be accessed from State Highway 17 off of Highway 169.

Water Supply. Water and sewage systems are provided by the Bois Forte Water and Sanitation Department.

Transportation. Falls International Airport, 80 miles northwest of Nett Lake, provides the closest commercial air service. The City of Orr, 20 miles from Nett Lake, has commercial train and bus services. The nearest truck line stops in Cook, 36 miles from Nett Lake. The Chishom Hibbing Airport lies southwest of the Vermilion Sector.

COMMUNITY FACILITIES AND SERVICES
The tribal community center provides a gathering place for special events, and it houses the elderly nutrition program and other senior events. The Nett Lake recreational area has facilities for softball and skating, as well as a permanent powwow grounds. The Nett Lake Post Office is located in the Bois Forte Reservation Tribal Office Building.

Education. Reservation students (grades K-12) are enrolled in Nett Lake School, Independent School District #707. Younger children may attend the Head Start program and the Bois Forte Reservation Daycare Center. The tribe's adult basic education program provides GED testing and a comprehensive adult curriculum. The Bois Forte Reservation Tribal Academic Scholarship Program awards scholarships to graduating seniors at both Orr and Tower high schools.

Health Care. Nett Lake Health Center (full-time) and Vermilion Lake Health Station (two days a week) are staffed by a full-time physician, physician's assistant, registered nurse, LPN, and part-time lab technician. Community Health representatives provide liaison and follow-up services. Community Health Nursing employs one community health nurse, and it emphasizes early detection of illness and preventative health services. Emergency medical service is provided by the tribally operated, licensed ambulance program. The mental health department provides mental health and social services. The child welfare program provides children's advocacy services in abuse and custody situations. There is a dental clinic with a tribally hired dentist, dental assistant, and dental assistant/receptionist.

ENVIRONMENTAL CONCERNS

The tribe's department of natural resources has an environmental services division responsible for comprehensive management, planning, and regulatory compliance in the areas of solid waste, public water and sewer systems, underground storage tanks, emergency response, and environmental assessments. A water resources program researches, manages and protects over 10,000 acres of lakes, 60,000 acres of wetlands, and 45 miles of rivers and streams on the Bois Forte Reservation.

As part of the Circle of Flight Tribal Wetland and Waterfowl Enhancement Initiative in January 1998, the Bois Forte Department of Natural Resources focused attention toward developing land-based feeding plots for waterfowl, and toward developing and enhancing the Nett Lake wild rice restoration program. In 1999-2001, the tribe listed surface water quality as the top environmental priority.

Fond du Lac

LOCATION AND LAND STATUS

The Fond du Lac Reservation is composed of three districts: Cloquet, Sawyer, and Brookston, and is located in east-central Minnesota, about 15 miles west of Duluth. The western edge of Lake Superior lies due east of the reservation. The St. Louis River, the largest tributary to Lake Superior on the United States side, forms the reservation's northern and eastern boundaries.

The original reservation was established by the Treaty of LaPointe in 1854 and at the time comprised 100,000 acres. As a result of federal allotment policies, by the 1980s only about 4,800 acres remain as tribal community lands, and with 17,034 acres of allotted land held for individual tribal members. Beginning in the 1990s, the Reservation Business Committee (tribal council) has begun to use casino profits to reacquire reservation fee lands as they become available. Today, the Fond du Lac Band directly owns approximately 13,000 acres of the reservation.

PHYSICAL DESCRIPTION

Reservation lands are predominantly flat and moderately lush in vegetation, including about 54,000 acres of forest, rich with birch, aspen, jackpine, Norway pine, oak, and maple, and approximately 44,000 acres of wetlands, some of which are wild rice waters. There are 96 miles of rivers and streams crisscrossing the reservation.

CLIMATE

The year-round average high temperature in Cloquet, Minnesota, is 51°F, with the highest temperature on record as 105°F. The year-round average low temperature is 28°F, with the lowest temperature on record as -45°F. The area receives approximately 31 inches of rain annually, and 67.5 inches of snow.

CULTURE AND HISTORY

The Fond du Lac Reservation is a member reservation of the Minnesota Chippewa Tribe, a confederation of six Minnesota reservations all located in the northern half of the state. 'Chippewa', the term generally used in treaties and official documents, is a corruption of the early spellings of 'Ojibway.' The Ojibwe were once one of the largest Indian nations north of Mexico, controlling lands that ranged from both shores of Lakes Huron and Superior in the east to what is now the state of North Dakota in the west. They were a nomadic timber people who engaged in subsistence hunting and fishing, gathering fruits and wild rice, and some agriculture. Their tendency to remain in the native forests and avoid the prized farming areas lessened the impact of white encroachment upon the tribe. The tribe has been officially at peace with the U.S. government since 1815 and thus experienced less dislocation than many other tribes.

The original constitution and bylaws of the Minnesota Chippewa Tribe were ratified in 1936, greatly influenced by the Indian Reorganization Act of 1934. The structure allows for a consolidated tribal government without relinquishment of control at the local level. Each member reservation elects its own business committee, which governs locally as well as furnishing representation to the larger tribal organization that is in turn governed by a tribal executive committee. The modern-day Minnesota Chippewas are a highly diverse group, maintaining aspects of their separate traditional cultures while improving economic and social conditions on behalf of the member reservations collectively.

The Fond du Lac Band holds powwows, exhibitions, and storytelling throughout the state. The Ojibwe language, once close to extinction, is now taught both on and off the reservations in a number of area schools and colleges.

GOVERNMENT

The Fond du Lac Band is governed by the Reservation Business Committee, which was established by the Minnesota Chippewa Tribe Constitution subsequent to the 1934 Indian Reorganization Act. Records indicate that the Fond du Lac Band ratified the Minnesota Chippewa Tribe Constitution in 1936, but voted against the Minnesota Chippewa Tribe Corporate Charter. However, several senior band members insist that the Fond du Lac Band actually voted against both the Minnesota Chippewa Tribe Constitution and Corporate Charter, and was made a part of the Minnesota Chippewa Tribe without band consent (the Minnesota Chippewa Tribe Corporate Charter was rescinded by Congress in 1996 at the tribe's request).

The Fond du Lac Reservation Business Committee is comprised of five elected officials, three of whom represent the reservation's three districts, and two at-large positions. The committee serves as the band's legislative governing body and oversees all band programs and businesses. The band operates over 40 separate programs in areas such as education, social and health services, conservation, and economic development. The tribe also maintains its own court system.

Criminal jurisdiction on the reservation and state court jurisdiction over civil matters involving band members was transferred to the State of Minnesota under federal law PL-280. The band has a tribal court and its own police department.

The Fond du Lac Band, under PL-638, contracts with the BIA to administer key programs and services. The band has a division of resource management, which operates an environmental program, forestry department, natural resources department and conservation department, and human services department, and operates childcare and health, Head Start, and WIC programs.

ECONOMY

The band operates two casinos, a hotel, a golf course, a gas station and convenience store, a construction company, and a propane distribution company. A tribal gift shop in the casino complex provides an outlet for tribal arts and crafts.

Fond du Lac Reservation
Federal reservation
Chippewa
Carlton and St. Louis counties, Minnesota

Fond du Lac Band of Lake Superior Chippewa
1720 Big Lake Road
Cloquet, MN 55720
218-879-4593
218-879-4146 Fax
fdlrez.com

Total area (BIA realty, 2004)
22,902.23 acres

Tribally owned (BIA realty, 2004)
5,633.89 acres

Individually owned
(BIA realty, 2004)
17,268.34 acres

Population 2000 census
3,728

Population
3,211

Tribal enrollment
3,729

Tribal enrollment
(BIA labor report, 2001)
3,905

Total labor force 2000 census
1,729

Total labor force
(BIA labor report, 2001)
1,826

Fond du Lac

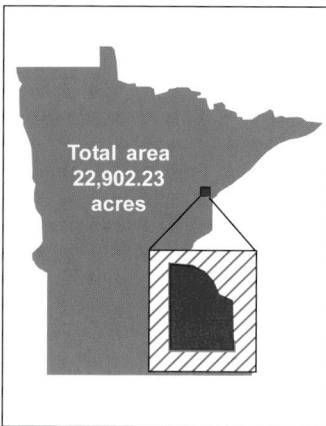

Total area
22,902.23
acres

High school graduate or higher
2000 census
82.8%

Bachelor's degree or higher
2000 census
9.6%

Unemployment rate *2000 census*
8.9%

Unemployment rate
(BIA labor report, 2001)
25%

Per capita income *2000 census*
$15,551

Government as Employer. The band, via its various business enterprises, and education and human service programs, employs nearly 2,000 people. The band is the largest employer in Carlton County, Minnesota.

Gaming. The band operates two gaming facilities. Originally opened as the Fond du Lac Big Bucks Bingo Parlor (near Cloquet), the tribe then constructed the Black Bear Casino and Hotel in 1993, and added a hotel in 1995. Games in the 60,000-square-foot facility include 1,258 slot machines, 12 table games, 4 poker tables, and 350 bingo seats. There are 218 rooms in the hotel. An entertainment venue and a conference center are also located in the casino complex. The facility is slated for additional expansion, to be completed by 2006. The Fond du Luth Casino opened in Duluth in 1986, providing employment to approximately 300 persons, half of whom are non-Indians. The 20,000-square-foot Fond du Luth Casino features 12 blackjack tables and 510 slot machines.

Fisheries. Fishing on and around the reservation is quite popular, primarily with tribal members, but also with nonmembers. Lake Superior is 20 miles to the east, offering a wide variety of recreational and commercial fishing options.

Real Estate/Commercial Development. The band has a planning department, which coordinates all new projects. In addition, the band provides funding and support services for business enterprises by individual band members.

Services and Retail. At the Black Bear Casino, there is a gift shop, two restaurants, a lounge, Bear's Touch Massage Therapy, and La Stone Therapy.

Transportation. The band operates a casino shuttle service, along with several buses for the Fond du Lac School.

Tourism and Recreation. The gaming facilities are the reservation's biggest tourist attraction. In a more traditional vein, the band sponsors various cultural events, such as the annual powwow, held in July, featuring Native dancing, and arts and crafts. They also have a cultural center and museum in Cloquet and an 18-hole championship golf course located next to the Black Bear Casino and Hotel in Carlton. The Black Bear Hotel features a 10,000-square-foot indoor swimming pool, with a kiddy wading pool, sauna, two hot tubs, and other amenities. There is a video game arcade inside the hotel complex, along with the Buckskin and Beads gift shop.

INFRASTRUCTURE
Interstate 35 and State Highways 2 and 210 provide road access to the reservation.

Electricity. Minnesota Power and Light and Lake Country Power provide electricity to the reservation.

Fuel. Northwestern Power and Gas Company furnishes natural gas, while local distributors sell propane and fuel oil.

Water Supply. There are three public water supply systems on the reservation. Individual wells provide water to residences; individual septic tanks provide sewer service, though a few homes are connected to the Cloquet community system. The Fond du Lac Reservation, in conjunction with the City of Cloquet and the City of Carlton, constructed a sewer and water system to the Western Lake Superior Sanitary District in 1995 and 1997.

Transportation. Cloquet Airport is located on the reservation; nearby Duluth also provides commercial air service. Commercial bus and truck lines serve Cloquet and the reservation directly. St. Louis River passes through the reservation, while full port services are available at Duluth.

Telecommunications. Qwest and AT&T provide local telephone service.

COMMUNITY FACILITIES AND SERVICES
The reservation maintains three community centers, which feature a wide variety of facilities.

The natural resource management division has a building in Cloquet, and the human services and health clinic programs are housed in the Min-No-Aya-Win Center for Human Services, which underwent renovation and expansion in 1995 and again in 2003. A unique nonprofit licensing and placement agency, operated under the auspices of the human services department, coordinates foster care for off-reservation Indian children.

Education. The Fond du Lacs operate their own branch of the Ojibwe School Board, which administers the Ojibwe Spotted Eagle School (K-12), a Head Start program, and Fond du Lac Community College, a unique blend of tribal college and state community college, accredited by the Higher Learning Commission of the North Central Association of Colleges and Schools. A housing dormitory was added to the campus in August 1999, many buildings were renovated, and new buildings were added and opened in August 2003. Other school-age students attend schools in one of four Minnesota public school districts on the reservation, or the new Fond du Lac School, an 85,000-square-foot K-12 facility completed in 2002. The education division operates a website and posts the Anish School newspaper online.

Health Care. The band operates its own health clinic, featuring holistic and culturally sensitive care. The clinic provides comprehensive outpatient care, family medicine services, and pharmacies in two locations. 'Mash-Ka-Wisen,' the Nation's first Indian-owned and operated residential, primary treatment facility for chemical dependency, is located in Sawyer.

ENVIRONMENTAL CONCERNS
The EPA's Region 5 office recognized the Fond du Lac Band as the first band in the region to be granted authority to administer parts of the Clean Air Act. The Minnesota Pollution Control Agency and the Wisconsin Department of Natural Resources must give the band advance notice of any Clean Air Act Title V operating permit applications it receives for potential pollutant sources within a 50-mile radius of reservation boundaries. The band may review and offer comments on these permits prior to issuance, a key step in protecting air quality throughout the reservation. The Fond du Lac Reservation has an air quality monitoring station to monitor for airborne mercury, acid rain, and particulates.

Long prone to devastating wildfires, vegetation on the reservation includes large stands of over-mature aspen and paper-birch trees. Many other sections of forested acreage are also in poor health due to insects, disease, and drought. To counter the dangers presented by these areas, the Fond du Lac Forestry Office, initiated a fuel-reduction program in the early 1990s and undertook fire preparedness activities and protection responsibilities on all land ownerships within the boundaries of the reservation in 1997. They also cooperate with the Minnesota Department of Natural Resources (MDNR), the U.S. Forest Service, and other agencies in a statewide fire management program focused on educating homeowners and residents about reducing the threat of wildfires by eliminating the fuel around their homes.

In 2003 the forestry office created a full-time fire prevention position responsible for overseeing the firewise program and developed a Firewise Community Board, which conducted public meetings soliciting community volunteers to distribute educational materials at powwows, schools, residential neighborhoods, health fairs, and other community activities, such as designated fire prevention days. As environmental priorities, the band is concerned about comprehensive watershed management, Great

Lakes planning activities, mercury contamination in fish, and well-head protection. With EPA funding, the band obtained help with watershed protection and surface water monitoring, including the development of water quality standards for reservation lands. The water quality monitoring plan was implemented in 1999. They have also collaborated with the Minnesota Pollution Control Agency to protect special wild rice lakes and rivers.

The band participated in a cooperative effort with the MDNR and Ducks Unlimited (the Hay Lake Waterfowl and Wild Rice Enhancement Project) to build a water control structure on Hay Lake near Aurora, Minnesota, in the band's ceded territory. Regulating water supply to the area will allow rice reseeding and will encourage migratory waterfowl nesting. They also participated with the MDNR to create the Pike Bay Wildlife Management Area Project, restoring a 40-acre marsh located on Lake Vermillion near Tower, Minnesota, in the band's ceded territory. The Wild Rice and Wetland Restoration Project was implemented on drained portions of Rice Portage Lake and Deadfish Lake to mediate the historical effects of the judicial ditch, a drainage canal dug through the lakes between 1916 and 1922. The goal is to enhance wild rice growth and create waterfowl habitat.

TRI-MN-FdL-130 Front entrance of The Black Bear Casino in Cloquet

TRI-MN-FdL-129 The Black Bear Casino in Cloquet

TRI-MN-FdL-130

TRI-MN-FdL-129

Honoring Nations Honoree 1999

Off-Reservation Indian Foster Care, Human Services Division, Fond du Lac Lake Superior Band of Chippewa

In 1991, only 30 percent of children in foster care in Saint Louis County, MN were in Indian homes, despite the legislative attempt of the Indian Child Welfare Act to improve this statistic. Many of these children lived with families who were residents of the Fond du Lac Indian Reservation, which lies primarily in Saint Louis County. Understandably, the staff responsible for social services at Fond du Lac were concerned about the number of Indian children they could not serve. But by 1990, there were 12 Indian foster homes per 1,000 persons on the Reservation, as contrasted with only one non-Indian foster home per 1,000 persons in the surrounding county. In other words, the Fond du Lac Band had reached a saturation point for eligible foster homes, and if more Indian children in need of foster care were to receive the benefits of placement with cultural integrity, those placements could not occur on the reservation. It was vital for Indian children to be placed in off-reservation Indian homes.

Unfortunately, off-reservation non-Indian agencies had difficulty recruiting Indian families. In 1991, for instance, there were no Indian foster care homes in Saint Louis County. This poor record was largely attributable to a lack of trust and understanding between Indian families and county and state government representatives. In particular, Indian families were concerned that cultural misunderstanding or even racism would cause non-Indian licensing officials to mis-assess their ability to care for foster children.

Fond du Lac's directors of human and social services believed the answer to this problem would be for the band to license off-reservation Indian foster parents. But the idea raised a second problem: The band's government was able to exercise licensing authority within reservation boundaries, but lacked authority outside those boundaries.

The Fond du Lac Foster Care Licensing and Placement Agency was the solution to both the jurisdictional and recruitment problems. By establishing a separate non-profit entity, chartered under state laws, which then contracted the Fond du Lac government's Division of Human Services to provide all programmatic and administrative services, the Band could legitimately work toward expanding the availability of Indian foster homes in northeastern Minnesota.

With the establishment of the off-reservation placement agency, many Indian families stepped forward to be considered for their licensure. In fact, before the Agency even opened its doors, interested parents were calling to ask how to being the application and review process. The instincts of the staff had been correct - Indian families were more comfortable working with the Band. Discussing her family's decision to become a foster family and their choices of the Fond du Lac off-reservation program as the licensing body, one mother said, "We don't have to explain (to the Fond du Lac program) why we live the way we do, why we smudge the house down with sage or why we go to Canada for a pow-wow."

In the last decade, the Fond du Lac Foster Care Licensing and Placement Agency has helped assure that fewer Indian children in Minnesota grow up in non-Indian homes, with little or no cultural contact. Statistics attest to specific program successes: The Agency has licensed 58 off-reservation Indian homes since its inception; it has placed more than 70 children each year since 1995; and, today, some 60 percent of the Indian children in out-of-home placement in St. Louis County are in Indian homes.

And there is more to the Agency's success story. For instance, the program has brought foster families closer to their roots, a

Fond du Lac

Honoring Nations
Honoree 1999

Text in its entirety from:
The Harvard Project On
American Indian Economic
Development

John F. Kennedy School
of Government
Harvard University

process facilitated in particular by the Agency's cultural advisor, who arranges training and cultural events and is on call for emergency situations. The Agency also has helped the on-reservation foster care program, tribal administrators realized the Band could petition the state for reimbursement for reservation-based foster care as well. In combination, the programs channeled more that 41.9 million to Indian foster families over the period 1991-1996. Finally, the Agency is having a catalytic effect on Indian foster care provision across Minnesota. For example, one family has volunteered to develop a home for 16 teenage girls, and state officials are so pleased with the Program's overall success that they are encouraging other bands and tribes to develop similar agencies.

For tribes nationwide, the most important aspect of the success of the Fond du Lac Foster Care initiative is that it enhances tribal self-determination and self-governance - an Indian foster care licensing and placement agency, together with a tribal government, is licensing and placing children in Indian foster homes outside the reservation boundaries. On a basic legal level. This

extension of jurisdiction is an important accession of tribal sovereignty. On a more conceptual level, the Band's degree of self-government has increased because it is better able to promote the rights and interests of all its citizens. Because of the Fond du Lac Foster Care Licensing and Placement Agency, Indian youth are much less likely to be "lost" in the non-Indian foster care system, and are increasingly afforded the protection of the Band despite their location off of the reservation. In protecting youth, the Band also helps assure future self-determination.

Several keys to the success of the Fond du Lac Foster Care Licensing and Placement Agency deserve mention. Most notably, the Fond du Lac Band tribal government has been extremely committed to the Program's success. The Band's directors of human and social services insisted on hiring highly qualified employees, creating good working relationships with county social workers, winning the support of the state government, and, in general, running an exemplary program. Because of these commitments, other tribal communities have the opportunity to similarly extend their self-governance and achieve similar success.

Honoring Nations Honoree 2000

Pharmacy On-Line Billing Initiative, Human Services Division, Fond du Lac Band of Lake Superior Chippewa

Challenged to provide all of the pharmaceuticals needed by Band members and faced with an inability to bill and collect from third-party insurers, the Fond du Lac Human Services Division contracted with a private sector firm to implement a computerized billing system. The first of its kind for Indian Country, the on-line system interfaces with the Indian Health Service's Resource Patient Management System, speeds and enhances the Division's pharmaceutical billing capacity, increases Human Services revenues and improves the quality of care offered to Fond du Lac Band members.

In 1994, the Fond du Lac Human Services Division's pharmacy program faced a financial challenge. Without the capacity to electronically bill third-party payers (private insurers and government programs such as Medicare and Medicaid), the division would be unable to continue providing adequate service to Fond du Lac Band members. The problem stemmed from the fact that Congress had given the Indian Health Service (IHS) authority to collect third-party payments and, subsequently, counted these funds against the IHS's budget - but the IHS never actively pursued collections, leaving tribes to fend for themselves. The IHS's patient record-keeping system (the Resource Patient Management System, or RPMS) was itself a prominent barrier to collections. While effective for health data collection, the RPMS was not designed to deal with billing. As a result, the IHS's direct service clinics and contracted/compacted programs, like Fond du Lac's, lost money on every obligation they failed to collect. The situation worsened as many third-party payers moved to on-line billing systems. Even clinics and programs that had managed to submit bills on paper were suddenly confronted with "wired" payers who found it inconvenient and difficult to respond to paper bills. These collection problems were particularly acute for Indian pharmacies reliant on IHS funding - their budget allocations suffered a double blow from the challenges of electronic billing and rampant pharmaceutical cost inflation.

Fond du Lac responded to this financial challenge with aggressive action. The Band's Human Services Division applied for

and was awarded an Indian Health Service Tribal Management Grant to support the purchase of a computerized pharmaceutical record-keeping and billing system from the private sector. Then the Band sought out a vendor, worked with that company to develop a system with the necessary attributes, and installed, tested and implemented the new software. A single year later, the Fond du Lac Human Services Division had in place an on-line pharmacy billing system that both served the Band's financial needs and was compatible with the IHS's RPMS (which was necessary because the Band was obligated to provide data to the IHS in order to continue to receive funding).

At its most basic level, the pharmacy on-line billing system uses an internet connection to automatically bill third-party payers as prescriptions are entered into the computer system by the Band's pharmacy staff. In addition to its billing capabilities, however, the electronic system provides dosing, cost and generic drug substitution information, warns pharmacists of potential allergic and/or adverse drug reactions based on the patient's medical history, updates insurers' formulary lists and creates a printout of these data for pharmacists and patients. Unlike the Indian Health Service's RPMS, the Fond du Lac system was conceived with multiple purposes in mind and, therefore, is more useful from both a financial and a healthcare perspective.

The impacts of the Band's innovation are substantial and wide-ranging. The most direct impact has been on the Human Services Division's finances. Since installing the system, the Band's pharmacy has been able to collect payments for thousands of prescriptions that it would have been unable to collect without on-line billing capacity. The system generated nearly $37,000 in new revenue in its first year alone (1995) and more than $625,000 over its first five years of operation. These monies in turn support an expanded pharmacy program and additional, unrelated Human Services programs (such as the Band's optometry clinic and summer day camp), investments that generate a second impact of the billing system - a healthier tribal population. The Fond du Lac pharmacy is able to fill more of the prescriptions its service population needs, is better able to avoid adverse drug reactions, can commit more pharmacist time to patient counseling and fund programs that support diverse aspects of Band members' health. Both of these impacts - on Division finances and citizen health - have been magnified as the pharmacy's success has inspired the Human Services Division to pursue similar technological developments in the Dentistry and Public Health Nursing Departments.

Another significant effect of Fond du Lac's Pharmacy On-Line Billing Initiative has been on the Indian Health Service. According to the IHS Bemidji Area Director, in identifying a problem and seeking an innovative technological solution, Fond du Lac's leadership sparked awareness in the IHS to what was possible and, indeed, what was necessary. Today, the IHS is striving to make its systems capable of meeting the standards set by Fond du Lac.

Yet many tribes have not waited for the IHS system to catch up. Viking Computer Systems, the private sector vendor contracted by Fond du Lac for system development, reports that 50 tribal and IHS pharmacies have purchased and implemented its RPMS-compatible program. This is not surprising given Fond du Lac's experience. The Human Services Division reports that payback on the initial system purchase and on-going system maintenance contracts occurred quickly, that training took a minimal amount of time and that the computerized system sped up service delivery significantly. The only caution to potential tribal purchasers is that market analysis should precede purchase: third-party billing systems pay for themselves only when a critical mass of a pharmacy's or clinic's service population has third-party insurance.

Several factors underlie the Fond du Lac pharmacy program's success. The first is the Band's willingness to exercise real self-determination over healthcare. Rather than being a mere recipient of funds and services, and rather than having the federal government dictate the way in which its health systems would be managed, Fond du Lac made a sovereign, strategic choice to create its own billing and patient record management system. Further, the Band used this decision to reinforce its government-to-government relationship with the IHS. Instead of taking the

minimum steps necessary to maintain Indian Health Service funding, the Fond du Lac Human Services Division sought input from and shared results with the IHS throughout the system development process. Today, the IHS sees Fond du Lac not only as a partner, but also as a leader in health care innovation, an outlook and attitude that can only benefit the Band's ongoing and future health services work.

A second factor in the pharmacy program's success is that the political and institutional culture at Fond du Lac supports initiative and experimentation. The Human Services Division encourages staff at all levels to be innovative, obtain additional training and to engage management. The record of the Reservation Business Committee (tribal government) is also one of helpfulness - it gave the Division the freedom to question IHS practices, to commit staff time and Division resources to a solution whose success potential was unknown, and to negotiate with the private sector vendor without political interference, which greatly eased the vendor's early concerns about working with a tribal entity.

In sum, the Fond du Lac Pharmacy On-Line Billing Initiative is remarkable for the way it challenged the Indian Health Service's standard operating procedures and for the way it harnessed modern technology to increase the Human Service Division's revenues, which improved healthcare. The Initiative's spillover effects - which include an increased technological capacity across the Division and improved prospects for other Indian health clinics - stand as further proof that the Fond du Lac Band is a true leader in Indian and non-Indian health and social services provision.

Lessons:
· Base funding from the federal government does not have to limit the operational capacities of tribes' health care programs. Innovative policy changes may increase revenues and improve service offerings.
· Partnerships between tribes and the private sector can serve as productive avenues for innovation and may offer tribes new resources and opportunities.
· Innovation in tribal government thrives where there is a trust of program staff and a willingness to challenge the status quo and take risks.

Fond du Lac

Honoring Nations Honoree 2000

Text in its entirety from: The Harvard Project On American Indian Economic Development

John F. Kennedy School of Government Harvard University

G rand Portage

LAND AND LOCATION STATUS
The Grand Portage Reservation is located in extreme northeastern Minnesota, bordered on the north by Canada, on the south and east by Lake Superior, and on the west by the Grand Portage State Forest. The reservation lies approximately 150 miles northeast of Duluth and spans approximately 48,234 acres of largely forested land, of which a little over 7,000 acres are allotted. The forests include birch and pine, and some of the wildlife includes moose, lynx, and deer. It also features approximately 24 miles of irregular shoreline along the shores of Lake Superior. The elevation of the area rises from 602 to 1,814 feet above sea level. The reservation extends approximately 18 miles along the Lake Superior shore and from one-quarter of a mile to 9 miles inland. The Grand Portage village is the site of the majority of tribal buildings and homes. The nearest American city is Grand Marais, 36 miles to the southwest. The nearest northern city lies in Thunder Bay, Canada, approximately 37 miles away.

In the early 1700s, the Grand Portage region was used first by the French and then the British fur traders. The Ojibwa people

participated in the trade business with both the French and the British. By the mid-1830s, they were conducting their business primarily with British Canadians. The Ojibwas were members of the Lake Superior Band, but they were excluded from the treaties between the Lake Superior Band and the U.S. government. After protesting the 1842 treaty, the band received annuity rights and in the 1854 treaty, they accepted the Grand Portage Reservation, in turn ceding their lands in the Arrowhead region of Minnesota. At the time of its creation in 1854, the Grand Portage Reservation comprised 56,512 acres. Revenue from its gaming enterprises has enabled the tribe to consistently acquire land. The tribe now owns approximately 95 percent of its land.

CULTURE AND HISTORY
The Grand Portage Reservation is a member reservation of the Minnesota Chippewa Tribe, a group comprising six Minnesota reservations, all located in the northern portion of the state. The name "Chippewa," generally used in treaties and official documents, is a corruption of the early spellings of "Ojibwa." The Ojibwas were once one of the largest Native American nations

**Grand Portage Reservation
Federal reservation
Chippewa
Chippewa Cook County, Minnesota**

Grand Portage Reservation
Tribal Council
P.O. Box 428
Grand Portage, MN 55605
   218-475-2277
   218-475-2284 Fax

Grand Portage

Total area *(BIA realty, 2004)*
46,131.48 acres

Tribally owned *(BIA realty, 2004)*
37,966.28 acres

Individually owned
(BIA realty, 2004)
7,086.10 acres

Population *2000 census*
557

Population *(Tribal source, 2004)*
508

Total labor force *2000 census*
327

Total labor force
(BIA labor report, 2001)
397

Total labor force
(Tribal source, 2004)
313

High school graduate or higher
2000 census
78%

Bachelor's degree or higher
2000 census
10.6%

Unemployment rate *2000 census*
10.7%

Unemployment rate
(Tribal source, 2004)
5%

Per capita income *2000 census*
$15,78

north of Mexico, controlling lands that ranged from both shores of Lakes Huron and Superior in the east to North Dakota in the west. The tribe, known as a timber people, maintained a nomadic lifestyle and engaged primarily in hunting and fishing, gathering fruits and wild rice, and some agriculture. Their tendency to remain in the native forests and avoid the farming areas prized by European settlers lessened the effects of white encroachment upon the tribe. The tribe has been officially at peace with the U.S. government since 1815 and hence has experienced less dislocation than many other tribes.

The original constitution and bylaws of the Minnesota Chippewa Tribe were ratified in 1936, greatly influenced by the Indian Reorganization Act of 1934. The structure they arrived at allowed for a consolidated tribal government without the individual bands relinquishing control at the local level. Each member reservation elects its own business committee, which governs locally as well as furnishes representation to the larger tribal organization, which is in turn governed by a tribal executive committee.

The modern-day Minnesota Chippewas are a highly diverse group, intent on maintaining aspects of their traditional culture while improving their economic and social conditions. The Grand Portages have staked much of their immediate economic future on commercial gaming operations. The tribe continues to rely on the region's abundant timber as an important aspect of its economy. The band maintains connection with Ojibwa traditions by participating in powwows, storytelling ceremonies, and other exhibitions in conjunction with the larger Minnesota Chippewa Tribe.

GOVERNMENT
The Grand Portage Reservation is governed by its five-member business committee, under a constitution ratified in 1937 under the 1934 Indian Reorganization Act. Committee members are elected to staggered four-year terms. As a member reservation in the Minnesota Chippewa Tribe, the chairperson and secretary of the Grand Portage Business Committee sit on the tribe's 12-member tribal executive committee. This overall executive committee has the power to administer funds, manage tribal resources, pass laws regulating the use of lands under its jurisdiction, and conduct business to promote the interests of its member reservations.

The business committee operates a number of departments. These include health services, social services, education, community services, environmental, natural resources, tribal courts, conservation, fire department, emergency medical services, and GIS services. The governmental departments employ approximately 125 people.

Criminal matters and various civil matters on the reservation are under the jurisdiction of the State of Minnesota. The tribe established its own court in 1997 and maintains jurisdiction over some civil matters. Hunting and fishing rights of tribal members are regulated under tribal code and enforced by the 1854 Authority.

ECONOMY
The Grand Portage community maintains a strong and profitable economy. The tribe successfully operates a sawmill, pallet plant, 12 blackjack tables, and a construction company. Tribal members continue to achieve financial security through logging and fishery. The Grand Portage Tribe has achieved its greatest economic security through the gaming and tourism industries. It operates a successful hotel and casino, a marina, and an RV park. It owns and participates in the management of a national park and the programs available through the park centers.

Government as Employer. At the present time, approximately 312 members are employed through the tribal government. This figure represents employment under the various administrative and tribal service programs. The Grand Portage Lodge and Casino employ approximately 175 people.

Forestry. The vast majority of the reservation is made up of densely forested lands, mostly birch and poplar. A half-dozen or so tribal members make their living logging these lands.

Gaming. The Grand Portage Lodge and Casino opened for business in 1975. It was refurbished in 1990 and now includes both hotel and casino facilities. The casino features 500 slot machines, 300 bingo seats, and pull-tabs. The lodge features 100 rooms, conference facilities, an indoor pool, tennis courts, lawn games, and a gift shop. The lodge also features a restaurant specializing in Lake Superior fish. The enterprise presently employs about 175 people, nearly half of them Native American, and it is managed directly by the Grand Portage Band. It serves as the reservation's largest single employment source. The revenue from the casino has made it possible for the tribe to establish an endowment fund. These monies provide financial security for the possibility of a drop-off in casino business.

Fisheries. Some excellent recreational and commercial fishing opportunities exist on and around the reservation. At present, five tribal members are employed as commercial fishermen, primarily working the waters of Lake Superior, which form the reservation's southern and eastern borders. The tribe has restocked the lake with its native Coaster Brook Trout. This project received national attention and supports the tribe's ongoing efforts to revitalize the indigenous wildlife. The tribe is a member of the Great Lakes Indian Fishery and Wildlife Commission.

Construction. The Grand Portage Band owns and operates its own construction company, including some heavy equipment. The enterprise employs 25 people, largely tribal members.

Real Estate/Commercial Development. The tribe continues to purchase lands and increase its tribally owned land holdings. Uses for the acquired lands are various. One of the purposes is to restore and revitalize indigenous wetlands and wild rice. Overall, the tribe does not wish to introduce industrialization to the reservation, seeking instead to preserve the land they possess and draw on its resources as minimally and as responsibly as possible. In 2001, the tribe received ownership of the 300-acre Grand Portage State Park. The tribe now leases the land to the Minnesota Department of Natural Resources so that it may be maintained as a state park. The revenue from the lease is small, but the significance of the agreement is monumental. It recognizes the relationship between the community and the land and acknowledges their right to determine its uses. While the development of tourist attractions within the park continues, the overriding goal is preservation of the resources it contains.

Services and Retail. The band operates the Grand Portage Trading Post, the Grand Portage Marina and RV Park, with dock rentals, launching facilities, and 30 RV sites, and the Grand Portage Lodge and Conference Center.

Tourism and Recreation. Water activities along the scenic Lake Superior coast, particularly boating and fishing, are quite popular with seasonal visitors. The Grand Portage Marina is readily equipped to serve these needs. Boat trips to Isle Royale National Park run regularly during the summer.

Located within the reservation is the Grand Portage State Park. It is home to High Falls, the highest falls in the state of Minnesota. The park attracts a vast number of visitors to enjoy the historical significance of the area, hiking trails, photography opportunities, and educational day trips. Within the park are the archeological remains of the Northwest Company Depot and a fully restored town site containing the trading post, stockade and Great Hall. The tribe also owns the land where the 300-year-old cedar tree known as Manito Geezhigaynce lives. This tree is of great cultural significance to the tribe and historical significance to local non-Natives. The tribe permits visitors but only those accompanied by a tribal guide. The tribe sponsors a number of annual celebrations open to tribal and nontribal members, including pow-wows, celebrations, storytelling events, and concerts. It sponsors the Summer Rendezvous Days, which features traditional dance, singing, and Native foods. During the festivities, the tribe re-creates and reinterprets the annual fur trade rendezvous held in the 1700s and 1800s. It also sponsors the Winter Frolic, which showcases winter life at the Northwest Company Depot. Future additions to tourist attractions include the conversion of the original log school building to a museum. Grand Portage children attended the log school from the early 1930s until 1997. It is the only log school in the state of Minnesota.

INFRASTRUCTURE
Electricity. Electricity is provided to by Arrowhead Electrical Co-operation.

Fuel. Propane service is available through local distributors.

Water Supply. The tribe is serviced by the community water and sewer system.

Transportation. Highway 61 provides road access to the reservation, following along the shoreline of Lake Superior. The nearest commercial air service is in Grand Marais, 36 miles from the reservation, with more comprehensive service in Duluth, 150 miles to the south along Route 61. Commercial bus and truck lines serve the reservation community directly. Lake Superior provides water access to anywhere in the Great Lakes.

Telecommunications. Local telephone services are available to community members through Centurytel.

COMMUNITY FACILITIES AND SERVICES
The band maintains the Gitchi Onigaming Community Center. It offers recreational activities, a swimming pool, a senior center, a youth center, a media center, and a daycare program. It is also home to a Head Start program. The grounds at the center is designated specifically for powwows. The tribe also offers rental housing for casino and lodge staff.

Education. In 1997, the tribe closed the doors of the original log school building. The new school was leased to the Cook County Public School System and operates as a state public school under special legislation. Children in grades K-3 attend the new elementary school, while students in grades 4-12 travel to Grand Marais. The tribe provides full college scholarships to its members.

Health Care. Health care is provided through the tribal clinic. The nearest hospital is located approximately 36 miles away in Grand Marais, Minnesota. The tribe maintains an ambulance service and a volunteer fire department.

ENVIRONMENTAL CONCERNS
In 1996, the tribe established a land use ordinance that designates land use according to the tribe's priorities for wildlife habitat, timber production, and for recreational purposes. In 1997, the tribe built a dam that restored the 60-acre Dutchman Wetland for migratory waterfowl. In 1997, the tribe also completed the preparation of the Little Lake Wetland Enhancement. In 1998, the Mount Maud Lake Wild Rice Restoration was initiated to restore the lake to historic water levels, and to restore 79 acres of wild rice beds for waterfowl and subsistence use. In 2003, the Grand Portage community received a Tribal Wildlife Grant to assess and promote the rehabilitation of the indigenous wildlife of Lake Superior and adjoining tributaries. It also received a Tribal Owner Incentive Program grant in the amount of $84,911 to be used towards restoring wetlands and wild rice on the land.

The tribe is working with the Ashland Fishery Resources Office to assess and protect wildlife within the reservation. The tribe has successfully restored the Grand Portage Creek Fish Passage, securing safe passage for fish from the stream to Lake Superior. This improvement will greatly benefit the production of local fish and the success of regional fishery. With EPA assistance, the tribe continues to develop its water quality management program. 1n 1996, the EPA approved a joint water quality agreement with the tribe acknowledging that the tribe possesses the technical capabilities necessary to conduct the scientific monitoring for the protection of groundwater, rivers, and lakes. Most significantly, the agreement recognizes the tribe's ability to participate in the protection of the Lake Superior fish from foreign invaders entering the lake via freighters docking in the ports of Duluth and Superior. The tribe also participates in a joint air pollution monitoring system with the Minnesota Pollution Agency to monitor air quality and to participate in community education programs.

Grand Portage

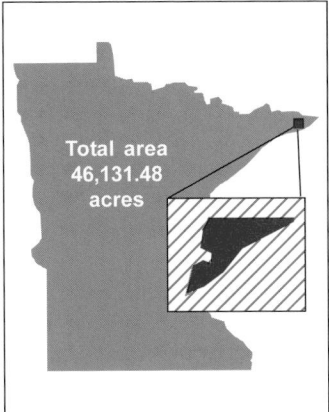

Total area
46,131.48
acres

Leech Lake

Leech Lake

LOCATION AND LAND STATUS
The Leech Lake Reservation encompasses over 600,000 acres in north-central Minnesota. Tribal headquarters are located in Cass Lake, Minnesota, the reservation's population center. In addition to Cass Lake there are 16 other communities on reservation land: Ball Club, Bena, Inger, Onigum, Mission, Pennington, Smokey Point, Sugar Point, Mission, Deer River, Kego Lake, Winnie Dam, Buck Lake, Boy Lake, Squaw Lake, and Squaw Point, which was renamed Oak Point in 1995.

The reservation was established by the treaties of February 22, 1855, and May 1, 1867, and by the Executive Orders of October 28, 1873, and May 26, 1874. Tribal lands included 677,099 acres. The original acreage was gradually reduced in size by congressional acts, including the Dawes General Allotment Act of 1887. The population of Leech Lake was forced to relocate to the

White Earth Reservation by the Nelson Act. This act also allowed all the tribal lands to be seized.

The majority of the reservation is owned by either the county, state, or federal government. In total these agencies own over 332,804 acres, which leaves the tribe only a small portion. The tribe has retained control over aquaculture activities on the reservation's interior and boundary waters. They have also retained the rights to hunting, fishing, and wild rice harvesting.

PHYSICAL DESCRIPTION
The reservation lies 225 miles from Minneapolis/St. Paul and 135 miles from Duluth, in the pine forests of north-central Minnesota. Reservation lands lie within the headwaters of three major watersheds and are generally swampy. There are 208 miles of

Leech Lake Reservation
Federal reservation
Ojibwe
Beltrami, Cass, Hubbard, and
Itasca counties, Minnesota

Leech Lake Band of Ojibwe
115 6th Street S.E., Suite E
Cass Lake, MN 56633
  218-335-8200
  218-335-8309 Fax

Leech Lake

Total area *(BIA realty, 2004)*
27,560.74 acres

Individually owned
(BIA realty, 2004)
10,916.31 acres

Population *2000 census*
10,205

Population
(Tribal source, 2004)
5,185

Tribal enrollment
(Tribal source, 2004)
7,948

Tribal enrollment
(BIA labor report, 2001)
8,294

Total labor force *2000 census*
4,341

Total labor force
(BIA labor report, 2001)
3,839

High school graduate or higher
2000 census
79.7%

Bachelor's degree or higher
2000 census
11.8%

Unemployment rate *2000 census*
10.7%

Unemployment rate
(BIA labor report, 2001)
26%

Per capita income *2000 census*
$13,103

rivers and streams; 232 named and unnamed lakes, including Leech Lake, Lake Winnibigoshish, and Cass Lake; and 150,000 acres of wetlands, many of which produce wild rice. Seventy-five percent of the National Chippewa Forest lies within reservation boundaries. Three major lakes comprise 212,000 acres of the reservation's surface area.

CLIMATE
The community of Cass Lake, Minnesota, sits at an elevation of 1,296 feet above sea level. The year-round daily high temperatures average 50.1°F, with the highest on record as 104°F. The year-round daily low temperatures average 25.6°F; the lowest temperature on record is -48°F. The area receives approximately 26 inches of precipitation annually, with 44 inches falling as snow.

CULTURE AND HISTORY
The Leech Lake Band is compromised of people belonging to the Minnesota Chippewa or Ojibwe Tribe. Leech Lake has been home to the Ojibwe peoples since early in the sixteenth century. The traditional homelands of these people covered most of what is now Minnesota and Wisconsin and reaching north into Canada. The Leech Lake Band speaks an Algonquian language and originally lived in small self-governing villages in Canada. The name Ojibwe is favored in Canada and by the Leech Lake people, but Chippewa is commonly used in the United States.

The tribe first encountered French explorers in the 1600s near Sault Ste. Marie, Canada. Later, they prospered in the fur trade and expanded their population and territory. By the late eighteenth century the Iroquois had driven the Ojibwes out of the Ontario peninsula, and they began to move into western Wisconsin and northeastern Minnesota. Arriving in what is now Minnesota, the Ojibwes encountered the powerful Santee Sioux, and conflicts between the two tribes persisted until the Ojibwes successfully drove the Sioux westward. When the Euro-American settlers arrived, the Ojibwes occupied more than half the state, living in four great divisions, each containing a number of bands.

By living in isolated villages throughout the early nineteenth century, the Ojibwes were largely able to avoid the increasing number of westward-moving settlers. By the Treaty of March 19, 1867, the 10 chiefs of the Chippewa of the Mississippi ceded their treaty rights to land extending northwest to the Thief River and north to Turtle Lake. They retained land in an area quite similar to the present Leech Lake Reservation boundaries. The 1889 Nelson Act designated that all Chippewas living in Minnesota be moved to the White Earth Reservation. The Native people resisted this decree, and finally the United States. Chippewa Commission was directed to negotiate for the complete cession of all lands belonging to the different bands except for the Red Lake and White Earth reservations. Moreover, it attempted to break up these reservations into allotments, thereby decreasing their size. Despite these numerous attempts, the Leech Lake Reservation has not been eliminated.

The Leech Lake Band of Ojibwe has been able to reverse the trend leading toward the reservation's termination by actively pursuing a policy of self-determination and utilizing the court system to restore its treaty rights and jurisdiction. Notably, the hunting and fishing suit argued in federal court in 1969 not only guaranteed the band these rights but also asserted its right of self-governance and recognized the validity of its treaty rights. Today, the Ojibwes of the area continue their traditional autumn harvest of the wild rice beds, which are plentiful in the area's lakes, streams, and rivers. They also maintain many other traditional practices such as woodcraft skills and the use of birch bark canoes.

GOVERNMENT
The Leech Lake Reservation is governed by a five-member elected Reservation Tribal Council with officers serving staggered four-year terms. Members include a chairperson, a secretary-treasurer, and representatives from three districts. The tribe's constitution was approved in 1937. The reservation is one of six Chippewa reservations in the state that were organized to form the Minnesota Chippewa Tribe under the 1934 Indian Reorganization Act.

In 1991 under PL 101-413, an amendment to the PL-638 Act, Leech Lake became a self-governance tribe. A major feature of this amendment allowed the tribe to manage its own trust resources. Now the tribe has exclusive authority to regulate bait netting and other netting activities from reservation waters, wild rice harvesting, and the licensing of band and non-band members to use the resources. The tribal government, under PL-638, contracts with the BIA to administer key programs and services. They have a health division and a social services division. The band participates in a cooperative agreement with six agencies to provide concurrent jurisdiction law enforcement services and police protection. They also have an environmental protection office that operates programs within the division of resources management, which was established in 1992, and a housing authority, which managed 496 housing units in 2000 with 20-30 more developed annually. The tribal council has developed a division of economic development to guide the tribal economy toward self-sufficiency and prosperity for all members and a heritage sites division to protect cultural resources. The tribe also operates roads, accounting services, and emergency response departments.

Leech Lake Gaming Division is a separate tribal entity. It oversees the management of the tribe's gaming facilities, including the Northern Lights Casino, White Oak Casino, Palace Casino and Hotel, and the forthcoming Shingobee Marina.

ECONOMY
The tribe's economy is tied to the regional economy, which is based on tourism, the wood products industry, and government. The band's primary source of revenue is gaming. The tribe owns several retail enterprises that capitalize on the local tourism industry. The tribe also owns other service retail establishments, including an office supply store, Che Wa Ka E Gon Convenience Store, and the Leech Lake Wild Rice Company.

Government as Employer. Government is a major employer in the region, including the federal, state, and county government and municipalities, and the various school systems. Among this sector is the Leech Lake Reservation Tribal Council, the major employer on the reservation. In 2004, tribal government employed 871 people and its casinos provided jobs for 1,139 people. The Indian Health Service and the tribe's health department employ over 200 people. Contributing to the employment picture is the BIA's regional field office in Cass Lake, where its administration and forestry offices are located.

Economic Development Projects. The Leech Lake Economic Development Division is the tribe's business arm. The mission for the economic development division is to improve the economic well being of its tribal members and to move the Leech Lake Band of Ojibwe toward self-sufficiency through the development of new business and the efficient operation of existing programs and businesses.

The reservation offers many incentives for commercial development. Included in these incentives is the Leech Lake retail center, a small business micro-loan program. Emphasis is given to businesses that specialize in value-added processing of renewable natural resources. The tribe offers various tax incentives to prospective investors to encourage economic development within reservation boundaries.

To encourage retail businesses on the reservation, the Leech Lake Reservation Tribal Council has established the Leech Lake Business Incubator Center, which is located in a former bowling alley at Cass Lake. The building contains approximately 6,110 square feet of rentable space for developing small businesses. Tenants are provided with management and technical assistance in an effort to address problems commonly experienced by new and expanding businesses. Of utmost concern to tribal government is the need for additional lands to support tribal economic development. The tribe is pursuing a plan to acquire more lands. The band has a land-leasing program from which revenues are designated for land acquisitions.

Agriculture and Livestock. One economic development project created by the tribe is raising Galerucella beetles to be sold as an alternative to pesticide. They began growing purple loosestrife plants in a greenhouse in 1996 and released the beetles on the plants. The tribe anticipates this project will eventually become a large-scale operation.

Leech Lake Reservation is by far the largest natural wild rice producer in the United States, with approximately 10,000 acres of natural wild rice stands. The Leech Lake Band has jurisdiction on all the reservation's interior waters and boundary waters for the management of wild rice. The band harvests wild rice stands on 55 lakes over 10 acres in size. The Leech Lake Wild Rice Company packages and sells rice produced from the tribe's rice paddies. The band is working to further develop the Leech Lake Reservation's wild rice harvest.

Forestry. In the early part of the twentieth century, the people of Leech Lake were forced to move to the White Earth Reservation by the Nelson Act. The railroad and timber companies were then allowed control of the tribal lands. These companies destroyed many of the reservations' natural forests. The forests have been re-established and today about 20,000 acres of tribal lands are forested and an additional 500,000 forested acres are considered public domain.

Although the wood-products industry is a major contributor to the region's economy, benefits to the tribe are miniscule. Over 74 percent of all reservation land is covered in commercial-grade timber, aspen or northern hardwoods. In those areas heavily harvested in the past, pine species predominate.

Gaming. The tribe owns Leech Lake Palace Casino and Hotel located near Cass Lake; the Northern Lights Casino, Hotel and Events Center near Walker; and the White Oak Casino west of Deer River, Minnesota. The gaming division, operated by the tribal council, oversees the tribe's three casinos.

The 10,000-square-foot Palace Casino features 560 slot machines, 6 table games, and a 650-seat bingo hall. The Palace Casino Hotel offers 80 rooms including 16 Jacuzzi suites, an indoor swimming pool, 6,000 square feet of convention space and meeting rooms, the Garden Restaurant, 2 hot tubs, an arcade room, and a gift shop featuring locally handcrafted arts and crafts. Limited overnight RV parking sites are available for rent. The 40,000-square-foot Northern Lights Casino features 1,003 slot machines, 12 live blackjack games, 5 poker tables, a full-service restaurant, and the River of Stars Cabaret, a lounge, and live entertainment venue. Northern Lights Casino Hotel features 9,000 square feet of convention space, 5,000 square feet of pool and water features, a 5,000-square-foot arcade room, 105 spacious guest rooms, 3 restaurants, and 2 entertainment

venues, employing a total of over 600 Native and non-Native people. There are over 3,000 square feet of retail space available for rent within the casino and hotel complex and 1,500 square feet of Ojibwe cultural display areas.

The White Oak Casino opened in 2000 and offers over 200 slots, 2 blackjack tables, a gift-shop, a bar, and a snack shop. The 12,780-square-foot facility, located at the junction of U.S. Highway 2 and Minnesota Highway 46, was named in honor of the White Oak Point Band of Ojibwe who lived in the area for centuries. It employs 169 people.

In 2004, another facility was in the planning and development phase. It will be located on Leech Lake, near Walker, Minnesota. When finished, the Shingobee Marina will consist of a 9,000-square-foot building with a convenience store, bait shop, snack bar, boat slip rental, and boat gas service.

Fisheries. Within the Leech Lake Reservation boundaries, there are 108 miles of rivers and streams, including a segment of the Mississippi River, and 256 fishable lakes covering 246,000 surface acres of water. The largest surface water lakes, Leech, Winnibigoshish, and Cass, support over 2.5 million recreational angler hours annually, a tribal commercial fishery, and tribal subsistence fishing. Tribal commercial fishermen annually harvest 10,000 to 30,000 pounds of whitefish and 10,000 to 40,000 pounds of Cisco, the two primary commercial species, and they are processed through the Ojibwe Fisheries processing facility. The annual take for subsistence fishing is estimated at about 10 percent of the state recreational game fish. DRM permits, regulates, and monitors the aquatic bait consisting of minnows and bait leeches. In 1999 approximately 6,000 pounds of both types of bait were harvested from reservation waters.

The tribal hatchery has a small visitor's center exhibiting its fish management and hatchery activities and an interpretive nature trail at Winnie Fish Pond. Leech Lake Reservation has a cooperative rearing agreement with the White Earth Reservation Fisheries for the stocking of reservation waters. It has a series of rearing ponds including those below the Winnibigoshish Dam. Fishing-related businesses employ approximately 600 seasonal workers.

Manufacturing. There are a few manufacturing businesses located on the reservation, including an electronics parts firm and some small private sawmills, which are not tribally owned. The region has a large wood-manufacturing base, including paper mills, oxboard and hardboard plants, laminated timber, and a dimension wood plant.

Services and Retail. There are many retail businesses on the reservation, including 10 groceries, 16 convenience stores, a hardware, and gift shops. The tribe owns the Che Wa Ka E Gon Complex, a gift shop, restaurant, and convenience store and gas station. Tribally owned Ojibwe Foods specializes in buying and marketing maple syrup. The tribe also owns Che We Office Supply and the Leech Lake Wild Rice Company.

Tourism and Recreation. The tourism and recreation market accounts for a formidable percentage of the area's economy. The sport fishing industry is a major attraction in the area. There are 232 lakes and 68 miles of the Mississippi River to draw tourists to the reservation. While the industry provides over 8,000 jobs on the reservation, very few tribal members are employed in local businesses, and only a small percentage of the revenue generated by the industry belongs to the tribe. The tribe is in the process of developing projects to enter the industry.

The Chippewa National Forest attracts approximately 1.5 million people each year, with 75 percent of these visits within the reservation boundaries. The reservation, including facilities in the

Leech Lake

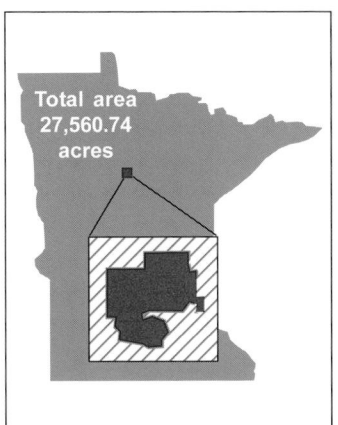

Total area
27,560.74
acres

Leech Lake

TRI-MN-LL-003

TRI-MN-LL-002

TRI-MN-LL-001

TRI-MN-LL-003 Entrance sign to Northern Lights Casino

TRI-MN-LL-002 Leech Lake Palace Casino and Hotel in Cass Lake

TRI-MN-LL-001 Business Corporation Leech Lake Band of Ojibwe

Chippewa National Forest, offers a variety of outdoor recreational and interpretive programs. For instance, the community of Walker hosts an annual Eelpout Festival on the ice of Leech Lake, attracting thousands of competitive anglers. During the summer, Walker also hosts the annual Leech Lake Regatta. Within the reservation, 136 resorts offer lodge accommodations, hunting, fishing, water-skiing, golfing, hiking, and horseback riding. In addition, the tribe operates a recreational land-leasing program.

Along with the area's many outdoor sporting opportunities, there are several historical and archeological sites located on the reservation, and the band holds six annual powwows. The tribe sponsors the annual Leech Lake Nation Spring Powwow held at the Veterans Memorial Powwow Grounds. They also host an annual Memorial Day Powwow, Fourth of July Powwow, and Labor Day Powwow.

INFRASTRUCTURE

Federal Highway 2 runs east-west through the reservation and connects the reservation to Duluth. Federal Highway 371 enters the southern end of the reservation, ending at Cass Lake. State Highways 200 and 34 cross the reservation, and I-30 runs 130 miles from Leech Lake. In 2001, tribal roads on the reservation were repaired and upgraded with assistance from the U.S. Navy Seabees through the Military Reserve Command's infrastructure-building program.

Electricity. Minnesota Power and Light, Ottertail Power, Dairyland Electric Co-op, and Beltrami Electric Co-op provide electric service.

Water Supply. Both municipal and private water and sewage systems serve reservation residents. In the Comprehensive Overall Economic Development Plan of April 2000, the tribe acknowledged the need to expand and upgrade both water and sewer systems throughout the reservation.

Transportation. Rail service is provided by Burlington Northern line, which bisects the reservation east-west and stops three times a week. A variety of truck lines are available in the vicinity. The nearest commercial airport is in Bemidji, 17 miles from the reservation. The Grand Rapids (Itasca County) Airport, located approximately one-half mile from the reservation, offers charter service. Greyhound bus service is available in Cass Lake. The tribe operates six 15-passenger shuttles for 24-hour employee and customer transportation services to the casinos. The shuttle services include a bingo shuttle for elders and medical transit services for any tribal member throughout Minnesota.

Telecommunications. Development of technology services has been tied to casino construction and other economic development projects, primarily along Highway 2. The reservation is now Internet accessible, and fiber optic cables installation was planned prior to 2002.

COMMUNITY FACILITIES AND SERVICES

Eight municipal community centers and 10 tribal centers are located at Leech Lake Reservation. In addition to the local school systems, the tribe operates its own Head Start program and has a social services division, offering a number of services, including Meals on Wheels for elders, the WIC nutritional programs, and Boys and Girls Clubs for reservation youth. The band maintains a powwow grounds. The tribe participates in the Cass County-Leech Lake Reservation Children's Initiative. The organization strives to provide guidance to tribal youth.

Education. The reservation is served by seven independent school districts on the reservation and in outlying regions. The Cass Lake-Bena Elementary School is located in the Cass Lake within the reservation's boundaries. The school serves tribal and nontribal youth. The tribe operates the Bug-O-Nah-Ge-Shig K-12 school system on the reservation. The school offers cultural camps and summer programs. Bug-O-Nay-Ge-Shig School offers free tuition for the area's Native people.

Leech Lake Tribal College was established by the tribe to provide higher education opportunities on the reservation. The college offers associate's degree and certification programs. The curriculum includes courses to enhance and maintain traditional culture and language. Other education and training programs are offered via the tribal government, including the Jobs Training Program, the Native Employment and Work Program, and the Work Readiness Program. The Bemidji and Grand Rapids Technical Colleges and Bemidji State University also offer postsecondary educational programs.

Health Care. The Leech Lake Band's medical system includes a network of six satellite outpatient clinics located in Cass Lake, Inger, Ball Club, Onigum, Bemidji and at the Bug-O-Nay-Ge-Shig School. They are staffed by tribal and Indian Health Service professionals, and they offer a full range of acute and ambulatory care services, along with educational and prevention programs. Cass Lake Indian Hospital and Clinic provides free medical services to anyone who is an enrolled member of any federally recognized Indian tribe. Dental services are available at this facility. The Leech Lake Health Department employed a total of 200 people in 2000. The tribal health department provides medical transit services to tribal members for travel throughout the state. It maintains a staff of four full-time drivers who operate a fleet of minivans and cars with handicap access.

The tribe plans to develop a tele-wellness network involving medical specialists and ambulatory care providers from the six satellite clinics, as well as a home health service. The proposed program will enhance services to tribal members unable to make regular visits to the clinic sites. A partnership has been developed with several hospitals and medical facilities to offer them commuter services. Hospitals are located in Cass Lake, Bemidji, and Grand Rapids. Medical and dental health care is available in Cass Lake, Bemidji, Deer River, Grand Rapids, and Walker.

ENVIRONMENTAL CONCERNS
In 1992 the tribe established the Gull and Pelican Islands Bird Sanctuary to encourage breeding and to protect species common to the area, including the northern goshawk and the common tern. In 1994, the tribe took over management and operations of the Winnibigoshish Fish and Wildlife Management Area, an 80-acre water impoundment site originally constructed and utilized as a fish hatchery by the Minnesota Department of Natural Resources. With funding provided by the Bizhibayash Circle

of Flight Tribal Wetland and Waterfowl Enhancement Initiative and in cooperation with the U. S. Army Corps of Engineers, Chippewa National Forest, and the Minnesota Department of Natural Resources, the tribe has improved and dedicated a majority of the wetland area to waterfowl enhancement and to the proliferation of game and nongame wildlife species. Only half of one of the four originally constructed ponds has been retained for fish production. An interpretive trail, including observation platforms, was constructed in 1995 throughout the area to encourage ecotourism. There were no solid waste disposal sites located on reservation lands in 2000. The tribe recognizes the hazards of potential groundwater contamination by the illegal dumping encouraged by the dearth of landfills, and it has placed waste reduction, recycling, and development of a solid waste infrastructure as its number one environmental priority.

Lower Sioux

LOCATION AND STATUS
The Lower Sioux Reservation spans 1,743 acres in southwestern Minnesota, approximately 100 miles southwest of Minneapolis. It is located on Redwood County Highway 2 and is nine miles east of Redwood Falls and two miles south of Morton. The Lower Sioux tribal lands lay on the south side of the Minnesota River. The region is dotted with rivers, wooded areas, and state parks. While the original reservation, established on June 29, 1888, entailed only 623 acres, the 1934 Indian Reorganization Act provided for the purchase of another 1,120 acres. Although some of this land has been assigned to individuals for home sites, the tribe owns the entire reservation.

CULTURE AND HISTORY
Two French explorers in 1660 first encountered the Minnesota Dakotas who were living in northern Wisconsin. The two Frenchmen helped some missionaries negotiate a working relationship with the Dakota people. During this time the first recorded written history of the Dakotas was made. In 1750, the Dakotas lived in the Mille Lacs Lake region until they were driven away from their aboriginal lands by the Ojibwas in the Battle of Kathio. The Dakotas were always migrating, and had lived by the Mississippi, Minnesota, and St. Croix rivers in the 1830s. This displacement was only temporary, however; in the treaties of 1851 and 1858, the Dakotas were moved to a reservation that was far from providing an economy or livelihood like the forests they were familiar with.

The Minnesota Sioux Reservation was set up to accommodate the "cuthairs" who were friendly to non-Indians during the Minnesota Sioux War of 1862. The 1,151 acres was placed under federal trust at five separate locations for tribal family heads to occupy by assignment. The Lower Sioux community comprised the largest of these five assignment areas, occupying about 623 acres initially. All five of the communities were tied to the Pipestone Indian School Agency from the time of their inception until 1952. Because these bands were deemed "citizens amenable to the laws of Minnesota," their privileges included land assignments, education, health and dental care, and occasionally loans and payments due them through the 1863 Forfeiture Act.

Most of the Minnesota Sioux worked for wages in the local farm and service economy, tended subsistence gardens, and applied for county benefits to supplement these and other sources of income. The 1934 Indian Reorganization Act provided for the purchase of an additional 1,120 acres for the Lower Sioux com-

munity, a move that expanded the number of home sites and farmland under cultivation. During the 1960s, the tribe benefited from Great Society programs, receiving grants for its budding gravel pit and pottery manufacturing operations. This period also saw a resurgence of tribal interests in traditional culture, particularly in regard to the Sacred Pipe Religion and the Native American Church. Finally, the emergence of gaming operations in the mid-1980s significantly enhanced the tribe's economic fortunes.

PHYSICAL DESCRIPTION
There is much scenic beauty in the flood plains of the Minnesota River Valley with its shaded, wooded bluffs and rich agricultural lands. There are areas with restored prairie, and sceneries of wide valleys on the banks of the river.

GOVERNMENT
The tribe is organized under the 1934 Indian Reorganization Act, and it approved a constitution and bylaws in 1936. The general membership of the tribe approved the corporate charter in 1937. The governing body is named the Community Council of the Lower Sioux Indian Reservation and it is administered by five members: a chairperson, a vice-chairperson, a secretary, and a treasurer. Council members are elected by the general membership and serve two-year terms. The community council appoints a land chairman, an agricultural chairman, a forest and conservation chairman, and a public welfare chairman.

The tribal court was established in 1993, and cases are heard on contract law, worker's compensation, and tribal governance matters. Tribal programs in social services and community health services are overseen by the council and funded by the tribe or other federal government agencies.

ECONOMY
The reservation is a growing community of people with the need for services. The largest employer, the Jackpot Junction Casino, has help to meet most of the needs of the community tribal members. The casino also has benefited the southern area of Minnesota economically.

Government as Employer. Employment gained through government efforts is mainly from the Jackpot Junction Casino Hotel with 1,000 employees, making it one of southern Minnesota's biggest employers.

Lower Sioux Reservation
Federal reservation
Mdewakantonsh Sioux
Redwood County, Minnesota

Lower Sioux Reservation
RR 1, Box 308
Morton, MN 56270-9801
507-697-6185
507-637-4380 Fax

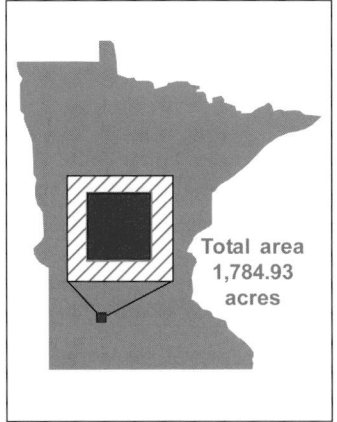

Total area
1,784.93
acres

Lower Sioux

TRI-MN-LSx-244

TRI-MN-LSx-243

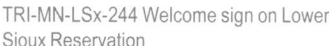

TRI-MN-LSx-244 Welcome sign on Lower Sioux Reservation

TRI-MN-LSx-243 Lower Sioux Community Center Sign

TRI-MN-LSx-247 The Water Tower with tribal logo

TRI-MN-LSx-246 A car window view of the Lower Sioux Community Center

TRI-MN-LSx-247

TRI-MN-LSx-246

Total area *(BIA realty, 2004)*
1,784.93 acres

Tribally owned
(BIA realty, 2004)
1,784.93 acres

Population *2000 census*
335

Total labor force *2000 census*
84

Total labor force
(BIA labor report, 2001)
341

High school graduate or higher
2000 census
75.3%

Bachelor's degree or higher
2000 census
3.2%

Bachelor's degree or higher
(BIA labor report, 2001)
1.2%

Unemployment rate *2000 census*
10.7%

Per capita income *2000 census*
$26,181

Agriculture. Individual tribal members raise approximately 300 acres of corn and soybeans, making agriculture a significant source of tribal income.

Gaming. The tribe operates the Jackpot Junction Casino, which serves as the single-most important source of tribal revenue and employment. The 40,000-square-foot facility includes 1,650 slot machines, 6 blackjack tables, 375 bingo seats, 38 table games, 276 hotel rooms, 4 restaurants, entertainment venues, and a 36,000-square-foot convention center. The Jackpot Junction Casino and Resort has four food outlets, four full-service bars and live entertainment, a 276-room hotel rated AAA Three Diamond, the Dacotah Ridge Golf Club, New Horizon Kids Quest Child Care, the Dacotah Gift Shop, an indoor heated pool, a spa and sauna, video game room, and a fitness center for the health-minded individual.

An airfield also routinely receives planeloads of casino visitors from Minneapolis and elsewhere. A shuttle service brings visitors to the casino from the airfield. This casino has helped the community realize financial independence, and the tribal government sees a promising future.

Mining. The government has leased lands for a gravel pit operation, and considerable revenue is made on this venture. Much of the mined gravel is used for maintenance and infrastructure on the reservation, while the excess is sold locally.

Manufacturing. The Tipi Maka Duta Lower Sioux Trading Post produces local, handmade pottery depicting modern-day art and techniques used for generations. These traditional works of art use a renowned art form, the hand-thrown process. Tribal members produce Lower Sioux pottery fired in kilns.

Services and Retail. The Tipi Maka Duta sells small gift items and handmade pottery.

The Dakota Inn located in Redwood is five miles from the Jackpot Junction Casino and has 119 guest rooms, continental breakfast, a pool, a spa, and a game room. Shuttle service is provided to the casino.

Cornelia's Church Mission is located on the reservation and has much historical significance.

Insurance. The tribe's members and employees have access to an insurance policy covering medical costs.

Tourism and Recreation. The Lower Sioux Agency State Park is located just outside the reservation boundary. The tribe also maintains an RV park, located next to the casino, which is open from mid-April to mid-October. There are 40 full hookup sites for water, electricity, and sewer service. The park also has restrooms and shower facilities, picnic tables, and a shelter house. An annual "wacipi" or powwow is held the second week of June and features traditional dancing, ceremonies, crafts, and concessions. Family, friends, and tourists visit, and new friends are made in one of the largest traditional powwows with over 800 dancers and drum groups. The traditional regalia are colorful and the culture rich with pride.

The Dacotah Ridge Golf Club has 7,100 yards of diverse terrain with the Wabasha Creek tributaries all around the golf area. It was voted one of the best courses in Minnesota for 2003-2004.

Kids Quest Child Care includes Barbie Land, a construction quarry, The Quest, TechnoQuest Video Adventure, a karaoke star stage, a movie, and quiet zone. Children six weeks and up can enjoy Kids Quest while the adults take in the casino fun, entertainment, and golfing.

INFRASTRUCTURE
Major throughways exist for vehicles, trucks, and airplanes, or are near the communities. Other services are obtained from local companies and distributors.

Electricity. The Lower Sioux Reservation is served by the Northern Lights Power Company.

Fuel. Local distributors are the main suppliers of gas and propane for fuel.

Water Supply. A community water system is utilized for water.

Transportation. Two major highways run through the reservation: Highway 71 runs north to south, and Highway 19 runs east to west. Interstates 90 and 94 each serve the general vicinity. Several commercial truck companies serve the area, while a railway train system passes near reservation boundaries. Full-service commercial air facilities are available in Minneapolis and St. Paul, about 100 miles away. A small airport serves nearby Redwood Falls.

COMMUNITY FACILITIES AND SERVICES

The tribal community center houses government offices, a health center, and a clinic for the local populace.

Education. The tribe operates the Dakota Open School, a charter high school. Additional public high schools and elementary schools are located in Redwood Falls and Morton.

Health Care. The Lower Sioux Tribe has a health center and clinic, with other hospitals and clinics located in Redwood Falls. Members enjoy a tribal-funded health insurance plan.

Mille Lacs

LOCATION AND LAND STATUS

The Mille Lacs Reservation is located in east-central Minnesota, in three parcels scattered within Aitkin, Pine, Crow Wing, and Mille Lacs counties. Tribal headquarters are located on the south end of Lake Mille Lacs, approximately an hour and a half north of Minneapolis/St. Paul. Reservation population is centered in Vineland, the largest Indian community within the reservation and the location of the band's government center.

The reservation was established by treaty in 1855, though much of its land base has been taken through legislative measures. Of the original 61,000 acres, only about 5 percent remains in tribal possession, consisting largely of parcels held in federal trust, tribally owned lands, and land owned by individual tribal members.

The band is involved in various legal actions to regain and preserve its land base, along with its water, hunting, fishing, and gathering rights. One such lawsuit, brought in federal court by Mille Lacs County in 2002, challenges the band's claims to their original 61,000 acres, which include the towns of Isle, Wahkon, and Onamia and account for more than two percent of the tax base. In 2004, the case was on appeal to the U.S. Supreme Court.

PHYSICAL DESCRIPTION

The Mille Lacs Reservation is divided into three distinct parcels or districts. District I, on Mille Lacs Lake, is a population center for the band; the Grand Casino Mille Lacs is located there, as is the newly constructed government center. District II incorporates the cities of McGregor and Isle, Minnesota. District III, near Hinckley, is where the Grand Casino Hinckley is located. Most all other reservation lands consist mainly of second-growth forest, swampy tracts, and countless lakes and streams.

CLIMATE

There is no climate data recorded for Onamia, Minnesota. However, St. Cloud, Minnesota, is 50 miles south and west, and temperatures would not differ significantly. The year-round average high temperature at St. Cloud, Minnesota, is 53°F; the highest temperature on record is 102°F. The year-round average low temperature is 31°F, with the lowest temperature on record -43°F. The area receives approximately 27.5 inches of precipitation annually, with 44.5 inches falling as snow.

CULTURE AND HISTORY

According to the band's oral tradition, ancestors of today's Ojibwe (Chippewa or Anishinabe, meaning "Spontaneously created" or "Original man") began migrating west from near the Atlantic Ocean about 500 years ago. In the late 1600s, these people split into two groups: one moved north into Canada, and a larger group moved along the south shore of Lake Superior into the northern sections of what is now Wisconsin, Minnesota, and Michigan's Upper Peninsula. The Mille Lacs Band descends from this second group. By the mid-eighteenth century, the ancestors of the Mille Lacs Band had established a nomadic subsistence lifestyle in the region around Mille Lacs Lake in central Minnesota, hunting the area's abundant bear, moose, deer, and waterfowl. They also relied on fishing, gathering wild rice, berries, and maple sugar, and cultivating small crops.

Everything changed for the Ojibwe with the coming of French fur traders (around 1640), who were soon followed by a plethora of other Europeans demanding land and natural resources. The band began negotiating for land by treaty during the 1830s. In 1855, a Mille Lacs chief named Shawbashkung signed the Treaty of Peace and Friendship, establishing a permanent home for the band called the Mille Lacs Reservation in exchange for promises not to harm or interfere with increasing numbers of white settlers. The promise was kept, even during the Dakota Conflict of 1862, after which their good conduct prevented them from being removed from their homeland near Mille Lacs Lake when the federal government forced the tribe to move.

These treaties were promptly violated by the federal government, and the band remained in poverty throughout most of the twentieth century, as its hunting, fishing, and gathering economy had been virtually destroyed. In 1988, however, the U.S. Congress passed the Indian Gaming Regulatory Act, which proved a turning point for the Mille Lacs Band and countless other tribes.

Anishnaabemowin, the Ojibwe language, has been carefully preserved. The band funded a tribal recording project that produced a dictionary of Minnesota Ojibwe, contributed to the development of a computerized language database, and subsidized printing costs of the text. They have also produced a Woodlands Video and Teacher's Guide, and two educational comic book series, called "Dreams of Looking Up" and "A Hero's Voice." This language program has been honored for its successes in reintroducing the language into everyday life. Singers and drum groups also help to preserve tribal culture by playing for dances and powwows and by recording traditional songs and ceremonies. Elders pass along traditional customs and information about tribal culture, and sweat lodges are used for personal purification and spiritual cleansing.

GOVERNMENT

The Mille Lacs Band is one of six member tribes organized into the Minnesota Chippewa Tribe in Minnesota under the 1934 Indian Reorganization Act. In 1939, the Minnesota Chippewa Tribe formally approved a constitution and bylaws. Subsequently, a reservation business committee was formed to represent the Non-Removable Band of Mille Lacs Ojibwe in the Minnesota

Mille Lacs Reservation
Federal reservation
Ojibwe (Chippewa)
Mille Lacs, Aitkin, Crow Wing, and Pine counties, Minnesota

The Mille Lacs Band of Ojibwe
43408 Oodena Drive
Onamia, MN 56359
320-532-4181
800-709-6445
320-532-4209 Fax
millelacsojibwe.org

Total area *(BIA realty, 2004)*
4,107.80 acres

Tribally owned *(BIA realty, 2004)*
3,967.45 acres

Individually owned
(BIA realty, 2004)
140.35 acres

Total labor force *2000 census*
2,004

High school graduate or higher
2000 census
80.5%

Bachelor's degree or higher
2000 census
13.8%

Unemployment rate *2000 census*
9.9%

Mille Lacs

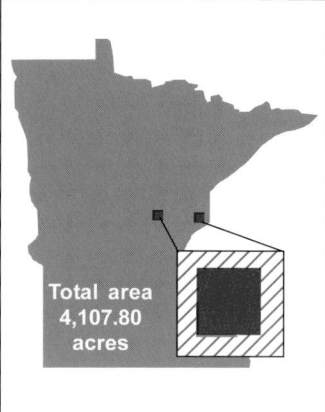

Total area
4,107.80
acres

Chippewa tribal system. This form of government set the stage for a new and more promising relationship with the State of Minnesota and the federal government. The Mille Lacs business committee consists of five members, elected on a staggered basis to four-year terms. The chairman and secretary of the Mille Lacs Band (as well as the other five bands) form the 12-member tribal Executive Committee of the Minnesota Chippewa Tribe.

Tribal government consists of executive, legislative, and judicial branches. The legislative branch, called the Band Assembly, consists of a representative from each of the three districts, their assistants, and a secretary/treasurer who presides over the assembly. Each representative is elected to four-year terms by the people in that district, and the secretary/treasurer is elected by members in all three districts. The commissioner of finance also serves in the legislative branch. The legislative branch passes tribal resolutions and appropriates funding for tribal programs.

The executive branch is headed by the chief executive, elected at large for a four-year term. The chief executive appoints commissioners to direct major tribal departments. A solicitor general serves as the director of public safety; there are also commissioners of corporate affairs, administration, community development, natural resources, education, and health and human services. There is also an assistant commissioner of administration. The administrative policy board, composed of the commissioners of administration, education, natural resources, health and human services, and the assistant commissioner of administration, prepares the budget, oversees personnel matters, and sets personnel policies.

The judicial branch consists of a chief justice and the court of central jurisdiction, consisting of four associate justices and two district judges.

The tribe, under PL-638, contracts with the BIA to administer key programs and services. They have a full-time tribal police department, with concurrent jurisdiction in Mille Lacs County. The police department does not have a substation in Hinckley, so Grand Casino Hinckley contributes $92,000 annually to the Pine County Sheriff's Office to offset law enforcement and public safety costs.

BUSINESS CORPORATION

A corporate commission oversees the band's gaming enterprises and related businesses. It also supervises all of the band's investments in local, regional, and national companies and businesses. The corporate commission provides low-interest loans, business management classes, and technical assistance to any band member opening their own businesses via the small business development program.

ECONOMY

Economy consists of the gaming industry, small retail businesses, banking, tourism, and the tribal governmental services. Economic growth on the reservation, fueled primarily with investment revenues earned from tribal gaming facilities, has become more diversified since 1995. Revenues from these sources are invested in tribally provided government services such as health care, education, law enforcement, economic development, cultural preservation, and land acquisition, and in infrastructure such as wastewater treatment plants that benefit a larger region. The regional economy has experienced a boost in job opportunities created by the development of more than 40 tourism-related industries associated with the casinos. The ancillary businesses include fast food franchises, restaurants, hotels, gas stations, and convenience stores.

Government as Employer. Tribal government employs a total of 490 people through its various departments, including administration, education, health and human services, and community

development. This number includes approximately 130 people employed at the band's Nay Ah Shing schools.

Gaming. The Mille Lacs Band owns two casino/resorts, Grand Casino Hinckley at Hinckley and Grand Casino Mille Lacs at Onamia. Each casino has its own hotel, events and convention centers, restaurants, shops, and recreational and entertainment centers. The 54,800-square-foot Grand Casino Hinckley, featuring 2,144 slot machines and 28 table games, is located halfway between Minneapolis/St. Paul and the twin ports of Duluth and Superior, with free 24-hour shuttle service to most area hotels. Within this casino complex is the Grand Casino Hinckley Hotel, a 281-room luxury facility with parlor suites, a heated indoor pool, five restaurants, retail shops, an exercise room, a Kids Quest recreation area, pet boarding, and three entertainment venues. The Grand Casino Hinckley events and convention center has 10,425 square feet of convention and meeting space. Nearby the casino are the 222-site Grand Casino Hinkley RV Resort and Chalets and the Grand Casino Hinckley Amphitheater.

The 42,000-square-foot Grand Casino Mille Lacs, in Onamia, Minnesota, is an alcohol-free gaming facility featuring 1,550 slot machines, 29 table games, and a 350-seat bingo hall. There are 26,043 square feet of convention and meeting space at the Grand Casino Mille Lac events and convention center, as well as retail shops, pet boarding, four restaurants, and an entertainment venue featuring nationally known musicians and entertainers. The Grand Casino Mille Lacs Hotel is a 363-room luxury hotel with all the amenities.

Prior to the opening of the Grand Casino Mille Lacs, tribal unemployment stood at about 45 percent. After the casino's opening in April 1991, the unemployment rate dropped dramatically. A year later when Grand Casino Hinckley opened, the rate dropped to near zero. The casinos employ approximately 2,950 people, of whom about 90 percent are non-Indian, and they have spent millions of dollars in capital construction since opening. In 2003, the Mille Lacs Band, the corporate commission, and Grand Casino Mille Lacs paid $228,105 in property taxes to Mille Lacs County and $777,715 in property taxes to Pine County (for Grand Casino Hinckley). The two casinos have generated more than $49 million in federal and state taxes through wages paid to employees since 1991, and they have given millions of dollars to community programs and nonprofit or governmental agencies.

The phenomenal success of the two Mille Lacs casinos has single-handedly pulled the tribe out of poverty and unemployment, serving to fund numerous social welfare projects on the reservation, and community projects in the various population centers as well. Of particular pride are the new schools, built with casino-backed bonds, featuring curricula that emphasize tribal history and language and that foster an enhancement of cultural traditions. Other community improvements funded by casino revenues include a new medical clinic, two ceremonial buildings, two community centers, wastewater and water treatment facilities, improved roads, and new housing units.

Fisheries. The reservation's abundance of relatively clean lakes and streams provides excellent sport and recreational fishing opportunities. Tribal revenues from this activity are quite modest, however.

Banking. The Woodlands National Bank in Onamia and its branches at Hinckley and Sturgeon Lake are 100 percent owned by the band. This bank is a full-service commercial bank and one of the few Indian-owned banks in the United States.

Services and Retail. In addition to the ancillary businesses associated with the casino complex, other small retail businesses owned by the tribe include three more hotels, the Grand Hinckley

Inn, the Grand Northern Inn, and the Waterfront Hotel at Eddy's Resort, the Lake Mille Lacs Bakery, three Conoco gas stations and convenience stores, two laundromats, and a Subway restaurant.

The Grand Hinckley Inn, a 154-room hotel, is located near the casino. This facility offers Jacuzzi suites and a 10,000-square-foot domed indoor pool with hot tub and sauna. There are also several one- and two-bedroom chalets available for extended stays. At the Grand Northern Inn, the newest facility at the Hinckley Casino complex, there are 101 rooms and an indoor swimming pool spa and sauna. Eddy's Lake Mille Lacs Resort is located on Lake Mille Lacs. The Waterfront Hotel at the resort offers 80 rooms and two restaurants and banquet facilities. It also offers the area's largest fleet of fishing launches and ice fishing.

A new grocery store, the Grand Market, opened in 2004 next to the Grand Casino Mille Lacs. Twenty-nine band members currently operate small businesses including: a coffee shop, a styling salon, a horse breeding business, a gift shop, a sign company, a sewing and quilt shop, a lawn care and snow-removal service, and various construction companies.

Media and Communications. The band publishes a monthly newspaper, the *Ojibwe Inaajimowin,* meaning, "The story as it's told." They also publish a 22-page magazine-style educational brochure, *Walking Forward, Looking Back,* to acquaint non-Indians with tribal culture and raise awareness regarding tribal contributions to the larger, regional economy of central Minnesota. Radio stations KKIN 94.3 FM and KBEK 95.5 FM feature weekly Native talk radio and tribally inspired music from the region.

Tourism and Recreation. The two casinos bring an estimated five million visitors to the region annually, many from outside of Minnesota, adding tens of millions of dollars to the local economy. There are many recreational opportunities offered at both of the casino resort complexes at Onamia and Hinckley. Golfing is available at the tribally owned Mille Lacs Golf Resort in Garrison or the Grand National Golf Club in Hinckley, Minnesota.

Opportunities for hunting, fishing, boating, and recreational harvesting of wild rice abound throughout the reservation. In addition, the tribe holds several annual ceremonial events, including their traditional powwow during the last weekend of August and the Grand Celebration featuring a contest powwow and a boxing exhibition.

The Mille Lacs Indian Museum and Trading Post, which opened in May 1996, is located near the Grand Casino Mille Lacs near Onamia, Minnesota. The interactive museum features a collection of Ojibwe and Dakota art and artifacts, a crafts room, a restored trading post, and other exhibits.

Near the reservation lands in Hinckley, there are several attractions: Banning State Park, Moose Lake State Park, St. Croix State Park, and the Willard Munger Trail, the longest paved recreational trail in the United States. At Mille Lacs, tourists enjoy hiking, biking, and fishing at Eddy's Lake Mille Lacs Resort, and all the outdoor facilities associated with Brainerd Lakes, Father Hennepin State Park, and the Mille Lacs Kathio State Park. In the winter, ice fishing is a popular pastime for locals and tourists alike.

INFRASTRUCTURE
U.S. Highway 169 serves as the primary road access to the Mille Lacs Lake section of the reservation, while I-35 to Highway 48 reaches the Hinckley section. The East Lake Community, of District II, may be accessed by County Highway 65. The nearest commercial air service is available at Brainerd, about 30 miles from the reservation, and the international airport at Minne-apolis/St. Paul is approximately 115 miles away. Commercial bus and truck lines serve Onamia directly.

Electricity. Electricity is provided to the reservation by the Mille Lacs Electric Cooperative.

Fuel. Propane is available from local distributors. Natural gas was introduced in 1995.

Water Supply. Water for the tribal community is provided through a community well system. Sewer service is furnished through the tribally owned public sewer system, with outlying areas making use of septic tanks.

With revenues from gaming, the band has improved various aspects of the reservation's infrastructure, thereby benefiting surrounding communities as well. They constructed two new water storage towers, built a new water treatment plant, and formed a nonprofit corporation in partnership with the Garrison Kathio West Mille Lacs Lake sanitary district to provide wastewater treatment services to the West Mille Lacs region.

The nonprofit organization, ML Wastewater Management, is owned by the Mille Lacs Band's corporate commission. The band constructed the new wastewater treatment plant, which began operations in May 2004, with a capacity to handle 625,000 gallons of sewage per day from a 30-square-mile area. The plant, located in Vineland, Minnesota, when fully operational, will serve over 10,000 residents from the City of Garrison, the Mille Lacs Reservation, and the townships of Garrison and Kathio.

Telecommunications. GTE provides telephone service.

Housing. Since 1991, the band's housing authority has built over 200 new homes for tribal members, renovated many existing homes, built garages and installed air conditioning for elders' homes, and developed a transitional housing program. The housing authority maintains over 525 homes on or near the reservation. In 2003 alone, the housing authority renovated 73 homes for elders and completed 14 rehabilitation projects for handicapped family members. That same year, the band provided 60 families with emergency rental assistance.

With the expansion of its home loan program in 2002, the band added $5 million to it budget, offering home improvement loans to 30 band members in 2003, and renovating five homes through its own home improvement program. Home sales throughout the region are up due to increases in the job market, an economic trend the band credits to its grand casinos. Local property market values are up by 435 percent since the opening of the casino in Hinckley, and by 150 percent since the opening of the casino in Mille Lacs.

COMMUNITY FACILITIES AND SERVICES
The band was the first Indian tribe in the United States to use casino revenues to back a bond issue, raising more than $20 million for improvements to its community facilities, which included construction of two new schools, a government center, three ceremonial buildings, two new medical clinics, four community centers, language and cultural immersion grounds, a water treatment plant, two powwow celebration grounds, the Shaw Bash Kung Elderly Center, and the Mille Lacs Indian Museum and Trading Post. They built a new office building for the corporate commission and renovated the Department of Natural Resources facility.

Education. Students on the reservation attend the BIA-affiliated Nay-Ah-Shing Abinoojiiyag Lower School (preschool through fourth grade) and the Nay-Ah-Shing Abinoojiiyag Upper School (grades 5-12). Both schools are located north of Onamia, Minne-

Mille Lacs

TRI-MN-ML-121

TRI-MN-ML-113

TRI-MN-ML-116

TRI-MN-ML-124

TRI-MN-ML-115

TRI-MN-ML-116 Grand Casino Mille Lacs sign

TRI-MN-ML-121 The Mille Lacs Indian Museum

TRI-MN-ML-113 The new Mille Lacs Grand Market opened in 2004

TRI-MN-ML-124 The Woodlands National Bank in Onamia is 100% by Mille Lacs Tribe . It has branches in Hinckley and Sturgeon Lake.

TRI-MN-ML-115 Grand Casino Mille Lacs was under construction in summer, 2004

sota. First opened in 1975, both grade divisions are in new buildings built in the mid-1990s, funded by casino revenues. The schools offer standard academic coursework and Ojibwe culture, history, and language studies. The band also maintains an early education program that consists of Early Head Start for children ages newborn to three, Head Start for children ages 3-5, and affordable child care at the beginning and end of each day for infants, toddlers, and preschoolers.

The Mille Lacs Band offers a scholarship program for any band member desiring higher education and/or training and career programs to help prepare members for management positions in all of its business enterprises. The band also has partnerships with Central Lakes College and Fond du Lac Community College to offer college courses on the reservation.

Health Care. Health care is provided through three new state-of-the-art clinics, also funded through casino-backed bonds. The Ne-Ia-Shing Clinic, located near Onamia, and the Aazhoomog Clinic, near Hinckley, provide a broad range of health and dental services, including pharmacy, chemical dependency programs, and a laboratory. The band also offers clinic services at its East Lake Community Center near McGregor.

Culturally sensitive assisted living units have been built for elders, and a nonprofit tribal health insurance corporation, Circle of Health, ensures that all band members and their families have access to good medical care. Circle of Health supplements existing coverage to help band members cover the costs of co-pays for prescription drugs and medical visits, co-premium payments for single or family coverage, Medicare supplemental coverage and Part B premiums, and upgrades for durable medical equipment.

The band operates a Workforce Education and Development Center for members looking for work or in need of financial assistance, and family services such as a foster care program, an

anger intervention group, child welfare services, and an adolescent group home. Community support services such as emergency assistance and chemical dependency services are also available. They operate the area's first home for non-Indian and Indian battered women and children, and a series of educational community youth services recreation programs. A complete list of the Mille Lacs Band's tribal programs and services is found on the Internet. The band publishes a 46-page comprehensive directory of all programs and services.

ENVIRONMENTAL CONCERNS
Assertion of the band's treaty rights in the territory ceded to the United States in the Treaty of 1837 remains an environmental priority in the regulation of hunting and fishing activities on those lands. Contested largely by sport fishermen who object to traditional Ojibwe net- and spear-fishing methods, the band has utilized the courts to reaffirm hunting, fishing, and gathering rights, and it has produced a lengthy conservation code establishing hunting and fishing seasons, the regulation of licenses, and bag-and-catch limits. Working with the Great Lakes Indian Fish and Wildlife Commission and the State of Minnesota's conservation officers, the band published the Mille Lacs Band of Chippewa 1837 Ceded Territory Conservation Code, delineating enforcement measures for band members and non-members.

The band's Department of Natural Resources Wildlife Program initiated waterfowl enhancement activities on 3,000 acres of land purchased in Morrison County in 1995. Using existing wetlands, they constructed open water areas, built wood duck nesting boxes and predator-proof goose nests, installed beaver baffles, and improved access road and trail maintenance to the areas. A similar effort was made on a 2,000-acre parcel managed for hunting and gathering. In partnership with the U.S. Fish and Wildlife Service, the Two Island Wetland Restoration Project restored wetlands to encourage the return of manoomin (wild rice) and waterfowl.

Honoring Nations Honoree 1999

Minnesota 1837 Ceded Territory Conservation Code, Department of Natural Resources, Mille Lacs Band of Ojibwe

Fishing, hunting, and gathering have long been central to the Mille Lacs Band of Ojibwe's collective identity. So when the Band yielded a large amount of territory to the United States government in Treaty of 1837, its members retained hunting, fishing, and gathering privileges on the ceded land. Unfortunately, ongoing treaty rights violations-and the mere passage of time-left Band members with a limited ability to exercise their rights. Although they continued to hunt and fish in the Treaty area according to Ojibwe tradition, they did so hesitantly and with a certain degree of fear. Their practices were inconsistent with State of Minnesota regulations, and without the protection of clearly enunciated treaty law, Band members were subject to gear seizure, hefty fines, and possible arrest by State game wardens.

A dramatic turnaround occurred in the 1980s when the Band began to investigate its treaty rights. In 1990, the Mille Lacs filed suit against the State of Minnesota in federal district court to halt State regulation, protect the Band's treaty rights, and gain control of the right to regulate members' hunting and fishing. A series of negotiations, State legislature votes, and court challenges ensued. Responding to the concerns of the anti-treaty lobby (largely sport fishermen), the State legislature, and Band members themselves, tribal negotiators eventually produced a 200-point document stipulating the Band's rights and responsibilities regarding the major issues in dispute-conservation and public safety. As decisions of the U.S. District Court, Court of Appeals, and Supreme Court affirmed Band members' rights to hunt, fish, and gather in east-central Minnesota, the document solidified as the Mille Lacs Band of Chippewa 1837 Ceded Territory Conservation Code.

The 111-page Code addresses a wide range of issues and governs treaty hunting, fishing, and gathering activities of Band members. For example, the Code establishes hunting and fishing seasons, regulates hunting and fishing licenses, sets bag limits, and requires hunters and fishermen to report their takings from the treaty area. Band officials, the Great Lakes Indian Fish and Wildlife Commission, and State conservation officers coordinate enforcement cooperatively.

The Code's careful enunciation and enforcement of rights serves both Band members and non-members well. Most basically, it allows Band members to exercise their hunting and fishing rights without fear. By protecting traditional territory and practices, the Code also affirms the Ojibwe lifestyle and, with its strong emphasis on conservation, provides a means for the continued practice of Ojibwe traditions. Among non-Indians, the Code has assuaged fears that Band members will over-hunt or over-fish shared resources. In fact, the enforcement and information mechanisms put in place by the Code show that in the year following its adoption, Band members took only 140 of the 900 deer and 37,000 of the 40,000 pounds of fish they were allowed.

In addition to these virtues, the Conservation Code stands as an example of the methods and benefits of effective government-to-government negotiation. For instance, the Band's Chief Executive insisted on maintaining transparency in the process of Code development-a decision which was intended to, and succeeded in, averting violence of the type that had erupted over similar tribal-state hunting and fishing disputes in Wisconsin. The Band held meetings for State law enforcement officers to educate them about the Code and to discuss enforcement options. Similarly, they used open hearings to educate, gather input, and garner support from the public overall. This diligence paid off. The negotiation process leading up to the Code was able to replace historical disregard with positive tribal-state relations in the area of resource use and management. The Code has been particularly instrumental in forging a strong working relationship between tribal conservation officers and State game wardens.

Many American Indian nations face dilemmas over the use of resources shared with other governments. Against this backdrop, the Mille Lacs Band's Ceded Territory Conservation Code demonstrates that Indian tribes can successfully develop, implement, and monitor important natural resource programs in cooperation with non-Indian governments, and it stands as a model of effective government-to-government relations.

Honoring Nations
Honoree 1999

Text in its entirety from:
The Harvard Project On
American Indian Economic
Development

John F. Kennedy School
of Government
Harvard University

Honoring Nations Honoree 1999

Ojibwe Language Program, Department of Education, Mille Lacs Band of Ojibwe

In 1994, only 10 percent of the members of the Mille Lacs Band of Ojibwe were fluent in the Band's native language, and the youngest native speaker was 37. Faced with these statistics, tribal leaders had great cause for concern-declining language use was a disturbing indicator of the loss of tribal traditions. The Band's Chief Executive summarized her colleagues' sentiment: "Our families were not engaging in our traditions, our children were turning away from our values, and little by little we were losing the battle to protect the uniqueness of our culture." If allowed to continue, the effects of this change would be broad sweeping. For example, because Band members had long considered knowledge of Ojibwe traditions a prerequisite to leadership, few in the succeeding generations would be prepared to step into leadership roles.

Educators working at the Band's Nay Ah Shing School were the first to take action against this problem. Since its founding in 1978, the tribal school had served Ojibwe families who preferred a Band-controlled, reservation-based education for their children. While it was successful in providing this choice, the School had yet to actively incorporate Ojibwe culture and language into its curriculum and activities. But in 1995, recognizing the dangers implied by the Band's loss of traditional knowledge, school staff members changed that. They created an Elders Advisory Board, invited five traditionalists to serve on it, and gave them a charge-to help the School structure an Ojibwe language and culture program.

Today, the tribally funded Ojibwe Language Program serves 350 students, from toddlers to teenagers. The very youngest

students-those in Head Start and day care programs across the reservation-spend four to eight hours a day with a fluent Ojibwe instructor. Kindergarten to twelfth-grade students at the Nay Ah Shing School attend daily 35-45 minute Ojibwe language classes. Even Band members attending non-tribal public schools have the opportunity to benefit from the Program, as the high school language classes at Nay Ah Shing are broadcast on interactive television to them.

Program pedagogy places a strong emphasis on usefulness and fun. The teachers and elders who designed the Program believe strongly that Ojibwe will take root among the young only if language learning is relevant and enjoyable. To accomplish these goals, language instructors rely on conversation, class-room interaction, singing, and comic books. To demonstrate that Ojibwe is a living language, for example, K-12 classes are taught by two speakers, so that students can hear actual, fluent, and complete conversations in Ojibwe. And, with elders as instructors, student-teacher conversations become a means not only of language instruction, but also of satisfying students' curiosity about cultural practices and values. The music teacher and students write songs in Ojibwe to be sung by the Nay Ah Shing choir. The choir has become so popular that, despite recess-time rehearsals, almost all students participate. The Program's comic books teach language in an amusing format while tackling important contemporary issues. For instance, the book "Dreams of Looking Up" discusses the challenging concept of American Indian nations' sovereignty.

Although the Program is young, its success is already apparent. Last year, every Nay Ah Shing fourth grader gave a short "graduation" speech in Ojibwe. School music and video projects have helped make it "cool" for youth to speak to each other in Ojibwe, and some students have even composed Ojibwe "rap" songs. Hearing their children speak, many parents have expressed a desire to learn to speak the language with their children, and plans are underway to make this Program growth possible. In sum, the Program has increased the pride that Mille Lacs Band members, young and old, feel in knowing their language and practicing their traditions.

An additional Program success has come from the Band's wide distribution of the comic book "Dreams of Looking Up." Many Minnesota educators, librarians, media representatives, legislators, and especially students have read and are using the Mille Lacs book, making it an important tool for communication between Indians and non-Indians about the often-confusing issue of tribal sovereignty.

Language and other traditional knowledge sustain American Indian nations-they are an integral part of the fabric that binds a Native society together. The Ojibwe Language Program strengthens the Mille Lacs Band's unique cultural resources and thus strengthens the nation. In particular, the Language Program gives Mille Lacs youth the self-confidence and cultural pride necessary for them to become the Band's next generation of leaders.

Honoring Nations Honoree 2000

Small Business Development Program, Corporate Commission, Mille Lacs Band of Ojibwe Indians (Onamia, Minnesota)

The Small Business Development Program promotes the Mille Lacs Band's private sector economy by providing technical assistance, training and low-interest loans to Band-member-owned businesses located in Minnesota or within 50 miles of the eastern Reservation community of Lake Lena. Since its inception in 1996, the Program has provided loans to more than 30 businesses, including agricultural, construction, service, retail and home-based enterprises.

Since the early 1990s, the Mille Lacs Band of Ojibwe has operated two of the most successful gaming enterprises in the State of Minnesota, and income from these ventures has helped the Band begin to address the difficult social and economic conditions in which many of its citizens live. For example, prior to the Band's entry into the gaming business, tribal unemployment was nearly 45 percent; after the development of gaming, unemployment has been in the single digits.

The Band's government was eager to see the Mille Lacs economy continue to support such positive change, but by the mid-1990s, several economic realities were of great concern. First, the Band's political leaders and economic experts were convinced that while gaming revenues had given their economy a necessary kick-start, reliance on this tribal government-managed industry would be imprudent. Instead, they felt that increased economic diversity was desirable along two dimensions - increased private business ownership and increased non-gaming business activity. Second, population statistics showed that 1,100 Band members were under the age of 18 and that significant numbers of adult Band members were moving back to the reservation. The reservation economy would have to be able to generate new jobs for this growing labor force. Third, with large

numbers of Band members living near but not on tribal land, reservation-based business development alone was likely to be inadequate. Finally, while individual entrepreneurs would be key partners in the creation of a diverse, healthy regional economy, many of Mille Lacs' citizens lacked the finances and the skills necessary to make their business dreams a reality.

As a direct response to these concerns, the Band created the Small Business Development Program (SBDP) in 1996. The SBDP's mission is to provide technical assistance, training and low-interest loans to the Band's entrepreneurial members. Specifically, the Program provides technical assistance and training in market analysis, business plan development, accounting, management, marketing and financing. Similarly, the SBDP's loan options target several different entrepreneurial needs. The Program offers "micro" loans (up to $5,000) to serve as seed money for cottage industry/home-based business development, and "macro" loans (up to $75,000) for more extensive start-ups and expansions. Loans are available to businesses that are actively managed and controlled by a Band member (businesses must be at least 60 percent Band-member owned) and that are located in Minnesota or within 50 miles of the eastern Reservation community of Lake Lena.

Organizationally, the SBDP is part of the Mille Lacs Band of Ojibwe Corporate Commission, a tribal corporation charged with the development and management of the Band's economy. The Corporate Commission employs SBDP staff (a coordinator, accountant and a marketing specialist) and provides office space, operating resources and capital for the loan fund. In addition to these direct forms of support, the Corporate Commission has found other ways to promote the SBDP's activities. For example, its research staff provides the Program with specialty assistance on a pro bono basis, and it has made retail space in the Band's casinos available for SBDP participants to lease.

By the end of its first four years of operation, the SBDP had loaned nearly $1.2 million to Mille Lacs Band entrepreneurs and aided in the start up of more than 30 new businesses (through 16 micro loans and 18 macro loans). Sixty percent of the funded businesses are still in operation (a figure that compares well with the non-Indian small business survival rate), and 18 percent of the loans have been repaid in full. In 1999, businesses that had received financial or technical support from the SBDP circulated over $2 million in gross sales in the Mille Lacs Band economy. Yet statistics do not capture the full measure of the Program's success. By funding both new businesses and business expansions, the Program has led to a substantial increase in the variety and vitality of Indian-owned businesses in the Mille Lacs community. And, through these businesses, it has reached out to a broad range of Band citizens. The Program improves all Band members' employment opportunities, offers models of entrepreneurial success, and generates the economic, educational and social benefits of locally produced goods and services.

The reasons for the SBDP's success are varied. For one, the Program has received consistent financial and operational support from the Mille Lacs Band's leaders. The Band government understands that entrepreneurs are important players in the fulfillment of the Band's long-term economic development goals. This strong tribal commitment sustains the Program, attracts competent and skilled staff members, and ensures the quality of Program services.

The SBDP's success also can be attributed to the vigilance exercised in loan making and monitoring. All prospective loans undergo strict market and financial analysis in order to identify potential problems and to help determine the true feasibility of entrepreneurs' business ideas. As desired, the SBDP's low interest rates attract a larger pool of applicants than traditional programs, but the loan approval process has advanced only those business ideas with a reasonable chance of surviving the rigors of the market.

A final reason for the Program's success is its ability to adapt administratively. The Program's adjustment to early growing pains is an instructive example. The SBDP was originally staffed by only one person and, due to a higher-than-anticipated demand for Program services, it became difficult for him to administer and perform all SBDP activities. Loans fell into delinquency, and en-

trepreneurs were unable to obtain the technical assistance they needed and expected. After analyzing current and future demand, the SBDP and Corporate Commission together determined that two additional staff members were needed. The Corporate Commission committed the funds, and the new staff were recruited and hired. As a result, the Program has been able to return a large number of delinquent loans to repayment status, increase its technical and administrative capabilities, and expand its service offerings.

Looking to the future, Program principals are considering yet another administrative challenge - they are analyzing the desirability of reorganizing as a nonprofit entity. It is possible that nonprofit status would allow the SBDP to leverage additional funds and, thus, expand the Program's capabilities. With more capital, the Program could raise its maximum loan amount and work with businesses whose start-up and expansion needs exceed $75,000. Additional funds would also support more extensive training and technical assistance services. Certainly, the willingness to watch for and analyze such opportunities is an important factor in the Program's achievements.

The Mille Lacs Band Small Business Development Program was created because the Band government realized that its economy would continue to grow only if citizens had the resources, skills and tenacity to pursue business opportunities. The SBDP's aim is to cultivate businesspeople who will both generate private sector growth and acquire the skills necessary to manage those enterprises. In sum, the Band, through the Corporate Commission, has brought its financial and technical capacities to bear on the vital problems of grassroots business development and entrepreneurship training.

Lessons:

·   Gaming tribes that have the resources to promote a broad base of economic growth can do so by providing support for tribal citizen-driven private sector development.

·   In building a private sector economy, it is important for tribal leadership, program staff and entrepreneurs to recognize that business endeavors must be feasible. New businesses must be marketable and financially self-sufficient.

·   New entrepreneurs and businesses may need on-going assistance in order to develop successfully. Assistance might include market analysis, business feasibility analysis, business plan development, management and business skills training, and guidance in overcoming obstacles.

Honoring Nations Honoree 2000

Text in its entirety from: The Harvard Project On American Indian Economic Development

John F. Kennedy School of Government Harvard University

Prairie Island

LOCATION AND LAND STATUS

The Prairie Island Reservation is approximately 30 miles southeast of St. Paul, Minnesota, along the Mississippi River, near Red Wing, Minnesota. The reservation encompasses approximately 534 noncontiguous acres in southeastern Minnesota. The Prairie Island Reservation was established by an Act of Congress on March 2, 1889. In 1936, the government recognized the Prairie Island Indian Community as a nation and allotted 534 acres of the island to serve as its reservation.

In 1996, the tribe entered an agreement with Xcel Energy (formerly known as Northern States Power Company) meant to give the tribe 1,750 acres of trust land. The agreement allowed Xcel Energy to continue to store nuclear waste at the plant located on the island in return for land and monetary compensa-

tion. The land was to be held in trust for tribal members wishing to relocate from the island. The agreement was contingent upon the passage of legislation that would allow the company to forgo the search for alternative waste storage sites. The legislations failed to pass, and the tribe did not receive either lands or compensation. The plant was permitted to continue storing waste at their site, which lies within a quarter mile of the reservation.

In 2003, the tribe reached an agreement with the State of Minnesota and Xcel Energy regarding additional dry cask storage at the nuclear generating plant. Their proximity makes the Prairie Island Indian Community the closest community in the Nation to a nuclear generating plant and dry cask storage waste. Moreover, there is currently only one evacuation route off the island,

Prairie Island Reservation
Federal reservation
Mdewakanton Sioux
Goodhue County, Minnesota

Prairie Island Indian Community
5636 Sturgeon Lake Road
Welch, MN 55089
    651-385-2554
    800-554-5473
    651-385-2980 Fax
    prairieisland.org

Prairie Island

Total area (BIA realty, 2004)
1,192.30 acres

Total area (Tribal source, 2004)
534 acres

Tribally owned
(BIA realty, 2004)
1,192.30 acres

Population, on- and off-reservation 2000 census
199

Population, on reservation 2000 census
177

Population (Tribal source, 2004)
684

Total labor force 2000 census
62

Total labor force
(BIA labor report, 2001)
378 .

High school graduate or higher 2000 census
75.8%

Bachelor's degree or higher 2000 census
6.1%

Unemployment rate 2000 census
1.6%

Unemployment rate
(BIA labor report, 2001)
76%

Per capita income, on- and off-reservation 2000 census
$26,955

Per capita income, on-reservation 2000 census
$28,479

Per capita income, off-reservation 2000 census
$17,713

and passing trains frequently block it. This agreement provides the tribe with about $2.3 million annually for the next 10 years and lesser amounts after that. The majority of these funds will be used for a tribal health study, an improved emergency evacuation route from the island, and the purchase of land so some members can move away from the nuclear plant.

PHYSICAL DESCRIPTION
The reservation lies approximately 30 miles southeast of St. Paul, Minnesota. It is located along the banks of the Mississippi River, near the town of Red Wing, Minnesota. The community is located on Prairie Island, where the Mississippi meets the Vermillion River. The community may be reached by following U.S. Highway 61 or by boat one mile north of lock and dam #3 on the Mississippi River.

Backwater lakes and wetland areas surround reservation and trust lands. When the U.S. Army Corps of Engineers built lock and dam #3 on the Mississippi River, it flooded a portion of tribal land, including ancestral burial grounds. It also created a larger floodplain, reducing the amount of the tribe's usable land area.

CLIMATE
Winter in the region is primarily cold and dry, with infrequent milder air. The summer is often hot and humid, influenced by tropical air moving northward from the warm, moist area of the Gulf of Mexico. The area normally receives approximately 27.01 inches of precipitation per year.

CULTURE AND HISTORY
The Mdewakanton Dakotas (Sioux) are descendants of the Mdewakanton and Wahpekute Bands of Eastern Dakota, also referred to as the Mississippi or Minnesota Sioux. Their traditional homelands included areas from the upper midwest to the shores of Lake Superior. The name "Mdewakanton" refers to the tribal homeland, meaning "Those Who Were Born of the Waters." Intertribal conflict during the eighteenth century drove the Mdewakanton Dakotas further south into the Mississippi and Minnesota river valleys.

In 1805, the Mdewakantons signed the first of a series of treaties, which transferred 36,000,000 acres of tribal land to the U.S. government and limited their access to traditional hunting and fishing grounds. The tribe was eventually limited to a 10-mile strip along the Minnesota River. In 1862, over 1,700 tribe members were imprisoned at Fort Snelling under suspicion of having fought in the Dakota War against the federal government. The prisoners were relocated to reservations in South Dakota and Nebraska. No Mdewakantons remained on the island. By 1880, a few families had begun to return, literally walking back to their homelands and then buying back land on the island. The Prairie Island Reservation was established for the Mdewakantons on the banks of the Mississippi River by an Act of Congress on March 2, 1889. The tribe organized under the Indian Reorganization Act in 1936 as the Prairie Island Indian Community.

The Prairie Island Indian Community continues to uphold the values of their Mdewakanton heritage. Tribal members still practice traditional spiritual beliefs, participate in ceremonies, and speak the indigenous language.

GOVERNMENT
In 1936, the tribe became a limited self-governing tribe with the formation of its constitution and bylaws. The constitution and bylaws are amended regularly to reflect the needs of the people. The community votes on amendments, but the BIA must approve them before changes become effective.

The Prairie Island Tribe is governed by a five-member tribal council. Members are elected to two-year terms. The council is advised by a number of committees, including enrollment, consti-

tutional revision, and powwow. Committee members volunteer and are approved by the tribal council.

The tribe maintains a tribal court and a tribal appellate court. The courts have jurisdiction over civil matters contained in the tribe's constitution and bylaws. Based upon a crime's severity, criminal matters fall under the jurisdiction of Goodhue County, the State of Minnesota, or the Federal Bureau of Investigation.

ECONOMY
The tribally owned and operated Treasure Island Resort and Casino represents the tribe's major source of income. The majority of these revenues are invested in social services, including tribal housing, health care, and sewer and water facilities. The casino is the largest employer in Goodhue County, and it provides employment opportunities for tribal and nontribal members. In addition to the resort and casino, the facility is home to a marina, an RV park, a golf course, a river cruise operation, several restaurants, and a smoke and gift shop. At present, the resort and casino serves as the foundation of the tribe's economy.

Government as Employer. The tribal government employs 100 persons. Tribal businesses employ an additional 1,550 people.

Agriculture and Livestock. The tribe is in the process of repurposing lands that were once used for agricultural production. In association with the Circle of Flight preservation programs, they are restoring traditional flood plains for waterfowl habitats and reestablishing prairie lands to be used for bison grazing. In fact, the tribe owns and manages a buffalo herd on this land.

Gaming. The Prairie Island Indian Community operates the Treasure Island Resort and Casino. It is located on Sturgeon Lake Road on Prairie Island. The casino offers 7 separate, themed gaming areas that include 2,500 slot machines, video poker, video keno, bingo, and 44 blackjack tables. The hotel area offers 250 guest rooms, a fitness center, an indoor pool, hot tubs, a daycare facility, and a video arcade. There are also 5 restaurants and a smoke and gift shop. The facilities include 9 conference halls/banquet rooms and a facility to host entertainment acts.

The Prairie Island Indian Community's casino has been credited with creating over 1,500 jobs in southern Minnesota and with helping to reduce the number of local residents on welfare by approximately 67 percent. In 2004, the Prairie Island Indian Community spent $44 million with vendors. The casino is the largest employer in Goodhue County. Revenue generated by the casino has permitted the tribe to implement a number of services. The tribe is now able to provide educational programs, scholarships, social services, financial planning services, improved water and waste systems, a water treatment facility, a health care facility, a community center, a library, a tribal government center, and exercise facilities. The tribe also makes annual donations to the March of Dimes, Salvation Army, American Red Cross, diabetes organizations, Special Olympics, veteran organizations, Toys for Tots, and hundreds of local hospitals, schools, preservation groups, and organizations. In 1999, the tribe was able to assist the Pine Ridge Indian Reservation in South Dakota when they were victim to devastating tornadoes.

Services and Retail. Located within the Treasure Island Resort and Casino are Java's Casual Dining, Tradewinds Buffet, Prime Thyme, Mongo Bay Grill, and Blue Lagoon restaurants. The casino has four bars: Toucan Harry's, Bongos, Barracudas, and Emerald Bay Lounge. The resort is also home to a smoke and gift shop. Nine automated teller machines (ATMs), check cashing services, and a video arcade are located on-site. The associated marina has fuel and a ship store, and the golf course has a pro shop.

Prairie Island

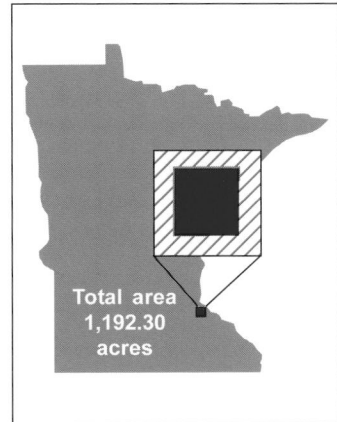

Total area
1,192.30
acres

Tourism and Recreation. As a part of the Treasure Island Resort and Casino, the tribe operates a marina, an RV park, a golf course, and Dakota Station, a gas and convenience store. The marina has 137 slips, which include water and electric hookups, pump-out service, gas and diesel, shower and laundry facilities, and a ship store. The marina allows access to the Mississippi River. The RV park maintains 95 sites with water, sewer, and electric hookup. It also provides bathrooms, showers, laundry facilities, and picnic areas. Treasure Island's Mount Frontenac Golf Course is located south of Red Wing and includes a lounge, restaurant, pro shop, and space available for events and programs. In addition to the facilities and activities available at the resort and casino, the tribe holds an annual powwow during early July.

INFRASTRUCTURE

Sturgeon Lake Road provides the only roadway access to Prairie Island from the mainland. In 1998, the tribe worked in conjunction with the county to raise the road's elevation above flood level. The road is regularly blocked as a result of the passage of over 20 trains per day across the tracks that cross the island. The tribe is pursuing development of additional roadways and is working with the U.S. Army Corps of Engineers to raise Church Road above flood level as well. The primary concern with the reservation's limited roadways is the event of a derailment of trains carrying hazardous waste or a crisis at the nuclear plant an emergency evacuation of the island will be required. The tribe is working with the Federal Emergency Management Agency to develop an emergency evacuation plan.

Electricity. Local providers supply electrical services to reservation residents.

Fuel. Local distributors provide propane to homes.

Water Supply. The tribe provides water and sewer services for residents. There is one public water supply system, eight class V underground injection control wells, and a wastewater facility on the reservation. The tribe operates all utilities in accordance with the tribal environmental agreement.

Transportation. Commercial air service is available at Minneapolis-St. Paul International Airport (40 miles northwest). Tour buses serve the casino and tribal headquarters. Passenger bus lines serve the Minneapolis-St. Paul area, as do UPS, FedEx, and many other freight carriers. The tribe provides shuttle services for guests of the Treasure Island Resort and Casino.

Telecommunications. U.S. West provides telephone services.

COMMUNITY FACILITIES AND SERVICES

The tribe maintains a community center that features a meeting area, an exercise room, and facilities for the tribal government. Programs and dining activities are available to tribal elders at the casino.

Education. Elementary and secondary students attend the Red Wing School District. The tribe provides scholarships for tribal members wishing to pursue a postsecondary education.

Health Care. The tribe is self-insured and provides tribally paid health insurance coverage to tribal members and casino employees. The tribe and Indian Health Service contract physicians from the renowned Mayo Clinics to visit the community health clinic one day a week. In addition, the health clinic has both registered nurses and certified nursing assistants on staff, as well as specialists who visit on a regular basis. The nearest full-service hospital is located in the nearby Red Wing.

ENVIRONMENTAL CONCERNS

The Prairie Island Tribe maintains a tribal environmental agreement with EPA to identify tribal environmental concerns and to implement programs to address them. The Prairie Island identified four priorities in 2001-2003: radiological monitoring, a surface and groundwater monitoring system, an emergency preparedness program, and a data management program. The foremost environmental concern for the Prairie Island is its proximity (within 500 yards) to the Prairie Island Nuclear Generating Plant, owned and operated by Nuclear Management Company and Xcel Energy. The disposal of nuclear waste has become a very troublesome issue. The state and federal governments have permitted the plant to continue storing waste at the facility. The tribe pursued legal action to ensure that the facility is operated under EPA. Although the tribe's concerns have often been overlooked, it continues to remind the governments of its past and future responsibilities. EPA has assisted the tribe in establishing air quality programs that meet Nuclear Regulatory Commission standards, in helping the tribe determine the impacts on community health, and in creating educational programs.

The tribe is also concerned about the threat of nuclear contamination to its water quality in the various bodies of water on and off reservation lands. The wetlands adjacent to the Mississippi and Vermillion rivers provide habitat for waterfowl and medicinal plants. The tribe's goal is to restore these rivers to assure that the consumption of fish, plants, and other wildlife are safe. To revitalize the wetlands, the tribe reseeded over 30 acres of tribal land to bolster wild rice beds that are important for migratory waterfowl, amphibians, reptiles, fish, and other wildlife.

TRI-MN-PI-001

TRI-MN-PI-002

TRI-MN-PI-001 Treasure Island Casino and Hotel

TRI-MN-PI-002 Front view of the Treasure Island Casino and Hotel

Red Lake Band Reservation
Federal reservation
Chippewa
Beltrami and Clearwater counties, Minnesota

Red Lake Band of Chippewa Indians
P.O. Box 550
Red Lake, MN 56671
218-679-3341
218-679-3378 Fax

Total area (BIA realty, 2004)
806,698.49 acres

Tribally owned (BIA realty, 2004)
806.698.49 acres

Allotted lands
(Tribal source, 2004)
803,720 acres

Population 2000 census
5,162

Tribal enrollment
(BIA labor report, 2001)
9,610

Tribal enrollment
(Tribal source, 2004)
2,761

Total labor force 2000 census
1,745

Total labor force
(Tribal source, 2004)
871

High school graduate or higher
2000 census
61.5%

Bachelor's degree or higher
2000 census
2%

Unemployment rate 2000 census
23.7%

TRI-MN-RL-001 The reservation boundary sign

TRI-MN-RL-002 Red Lake Foods Supermarket

LOCATION AND LAND STATUS

Lower Red Lake and Upper Red Lake cover over one-third of the Red Lake Band Reservation's land surface area in the northwest corner of Minnesota, 100 miles south of the Canadian border. The two closest cities are Bemidji, which is 35 miles to the south, and Thief River Falls, which is 70 miles to the west.

The tribe owns scattered holdings and fee status lands up to the Canadian border, totaling over 156,690 acres in addition to the main tribal area. Tribal headquarters are in Red Lake. Due to aboriginal land and unceded land holdings, 407,730 acres surround Lower Red Lake and Upper Red Lake. The tribe also has 229,300 acres of surface rights on both lakes. Four districts make up the Red Lake tribal lands. On the south shore of the two freshwater lakes are the communities of Little Rock, Red Lake, and Redby. Ponemah resides on a peninsula on the northern side of the lakes.

The village of Redby is the only place on the reservation that has some taxable land under private ownership by non-Indians.

PHYSICAL DESCRIPTION

Red Lake tribal lands are rural, and there are abundant shorelines that attract many types of animals, such as, bears, moose, and deer from the forests. There are hills with lakes, prairies, and swamps.

CULTURE AND HISTORY

The Chippewa, or Ojibwe, form one of the principal branches of the Algonquian family of aboriginal Indians. The Grand Medicine Society controls the tribe's movements. The Red Lake Chippewas have lived on the shores of their lakes since the early 1700s. The Chippewas were timber people and engaged primarily in hunting and fishing. They supplemented these occupations with gathering fruits and cultivating wild rice. They lived in wigwams and traveled in canoes.

The Chippewas were among the largest tribes north of Mexico, with lands extending along both shores of Lakes Huron and Superior and westward through Minnesota to the Turtle Mountains of North Dakota. They migrated to this area in the midseventeenth century, having been driven by the Iroquois from an area further to the northeast. The Chippewas pushed the Sioux west. The Chippewas in the United States have been at peace with the federal government since 1815, and they have experienced less dislocation than many other tribes.

The Red Lake Reservation was reserved by the band when they ceded some 2.9 million acres of surrounding lands to the United States in 1889 to be held in trust. The ceded lands were to be disposed of by the government in 40-acre parcels, with the proceeds paid into a trust fund for the band. The resulting disposition of the ceded lands was a source of continuing scandal investigated by the federal government for many years, extending well into the twentieth century. Alone, the Red Lake Band successfully resisted the allotment policy of the late nineteenth century that resulted in the other Chippewa Bands of Minnesota ultimately losing most of the lands they had not ceded to the United States. This resistance to the allotment policy maintained tribal ownership of more than 1,000 square miles of northern Minnesota with land holdings surrounding Red Lake itself, and a reservation parcel around Lake of the Woods near the Canadian border.

The first real fur trading post was built in 1732 and was located in the Northwest Angle. Red Lake is the oldest village in northwest Minnesota; the Northwest Fur Company had a trading post there in the early 1800s. It was the site of the first post office in Beltrami County in 1875, before the county was organized.

In the village of Ponemah, the second bridge spanning Battle River was the site of a fierce battle in 1765 between the Sioux and the Chippewas, resulting in the Chippewas gaining control of the region. The southeastern shore of Lower Red Lake was the scene of many such battles between these tribes, and arrowheads can still be found there.

GOVERNMENT

The Red Lake Tribal Council consists of 11 members, a chairman, a secretary, and a treasurer who are elected at large by members of the tribe. Eight councilmen are elected from the four districts and two represent each district. Hereditary chiefs provide advice to the tribal council on matters involving preservation of traditional and cultural values of the band. The Red Lake Tribe is not subject to state law and is accorded full sovereign rights; however, the federal government has jurisdiction over major crimes. Other crimes on tribal lands are the responsibility of the tribal courts and police. For police protection, the tribe administers a self-governance contract with the BIA.

The tribe's constitution allows for a three-member business council and a five-member gaming commission.

ECONOMY

The reservation's abundance of natural resources allows for an economy based on industries such as agriculture, forestry, fisheries, tourism, and recreation. Gaming, construction, and manufacturing are also important parts of the tribe's economic portfolio. The tribal government is actively seeking to provide employment for tribal members through various tribally owned business and government services, such as the Red Lake Hospital, and

TRI-MN-RL-001

TRI-MN-RL-002

is aggressive in planning and implementing economic and community development initiatives.

Agriculture and Livestock. Wild rice became a commercial tribal enterprise in 1968 with the purchase of a rice paddy farm. The tribe has developed and reclaimed wasteland by flooding and growing wild rice. There are 300 acres in production, and an estimated 55,000 acres are suitable for cultivation. The tribe is also experimenting with the cultivation of cranberries.

Red Lake Nation Foods is owned by the tribe and is a specialty food business that is "100 percent Natural-Indian Grown, Indian Harvested."

Forestry. Timber is the reservation's primary natural resource. Commercial timberlands occupy approximately 330,000 acres on the reservation. The tribe has the Red Lake Sawmill and operates two allied wood-products manufacturing plants: the Red Lake Chippewa Cedar Fence Plant and the Red Lake Pre-Fabricated Housing Plant.

Gaming. The band operates three small casinos including one at Red Lake, War Road, and Thief River Falls. The 12,000-square-foot Thief River Falls Casino has the world's largest indoor water park, 151 guest cottage style rooms, a gift shop, the Triple Seven Malt Shop, 3 restaurants, and a meeting center. Casino games include video keno, poker, 750 slots, 9 blackjack tables, and the Players Club. The Red Lake Seven Clans Casino is approximately 30 miles north of Bemidji on Highway 89, with over 200 machines, blackjack tables, 400 bingo seats, and 150 employees. There is a gift shop and a snack bar. The Warroad Casino has a Super 8 Motel, Lakeview Restaurant, and Warroad Estates Golf Course. Lake of the Woods community is located on Warroad on the Canadian border. The casino has 13,600 square feet with 7 lucky blackjack tables, 534 slots, video games, and bingo. Also available are a restaurant, a bait shop, and a launching service.

Fisheries. The Red Lake Fisheries Association was established in 1929 and has between 300 and 500 members, depending on the season. It serves as a cooperative for tribal members to process and market fish that are filleted and sold fresh from the lake or flash-frozen. In addition, the band operates the Red Lake Hatchery to maintain stocks of commercial species of fish from Red Lake.

Construction. Red Lake Builders is a commercial and residential construction business that is owned by the tribe. They build custom homes and major government facilities. They are also in the highway and heavy construction business on the reservation.

Manufacturing. The Red Lake water bottling plant, Nibi, makes bottled water available through a retail distribution network in northern Minnesota. The water is supplied by an aquifer located on the reservation. Red Lake Custom Doors is a tribally owned and operated manufacturer of high-quality custom doors, specializing in doors with an antique look.

Services and Retail. Red Lake retail stores include Beaulieu's Café, Elderly Nutrition, L&L Drive In, The Other Store, Thunder Café, the Chippewa Trading Post, and Westbrook Pizza. Native arts and crafts can be purchased at St. Mary's Mission and Indian Handicraft. There is a gasoline and convenience store in the nearby village of Ponemah. Post offices are located at Redby, Red Lake, and Ponemah.

Tourism and Recreation. Scenic areas, trails, hunting, and freshwater fishing are abundant on the reservation. Big game animals include deer, moose, and bear. Red Lake and other surrounding lakes offer fishing and waterfowl-hunting opportunities. The reservation's wild rice paddies provide recreational duck hunting and trapping sites. The reservation has several campgrounds.

INFRASTRUCTURE
State Highway 1 is the east-west route through the reservation. State Highway 89 crosses the reservation north and south. Commercial air, bus, and truck services are available in Bemidji, 32 miles from Red Lake.

Electricity. The Beltrami Electric Cooperative Association provides electricity to the reservation.

Fuel. Only bottled gas is available to residents.

Water Supply. Wells supply the water for the reservation.

COMMUNITY FACILITIES AND SERVICES
The Red Lake Tribal Information Center, Archives, and Library were built to store tribal history on treaties, government, music, artwork, photographs, and other artifacts.

Education. Students attend the state public school, Red Lake School for K-12.

Health Care. Top-level health care services are available at the Red Lake Hospital and Health Care, which the tribe designed and constructed. Tours of the hospital are available. The Jourdain/Perpich Extended Care Facility serves members of the tribe and offers its residents assisted living; it has 47 beds. The residents have access to other services such as primary care, dental, laboratories, x-rays, vision and hearing, and beauty and barber services. Residents are provided with a culturally sensitive environment and care.

ENVIRONMENTAL CONCERNS
The Red Lake Band has many of the main concerns of those living around water and maintaining the integrity of their environment. Many of the environmental concerns are being addressed, such as the Brownsfield Project, with the U.S. EPA. A tribal energy program was begun in 2003 to address the use of biomass resources. This project studies the feasibility of power generation, biomass for thermal needs, bio-fuel production, and bio-products. The result will be a business plan for sustainable bio-products industries. Also established in 2004 is the Waterfowl Enhancements at Good Lake, which will mitigate downstream flooding to increase the waterfowl area and to improve access to the impoundment for nesting and migratory seasons.

Red Lake Band

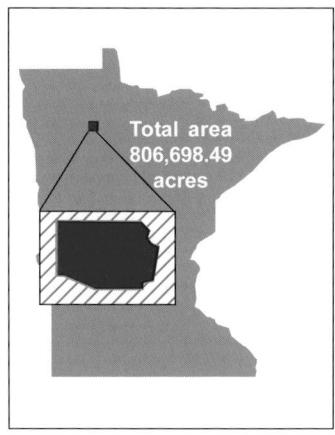

Total area
806,698.49
acres

TRI-MN-RL-003

TRI-MN-RL-004

TRI-MN-RL-003 Red Lake Fisheries Office

TRI-MN-RL-004 Tree Nursery for the Forestry Department

Shakopee

Shakopee Mdewakanton Sioux Community
Federal reservation
Mdewakanton Dakota
Carver and Scott counties, Minnesota

Shakopee Mdewakanton Sioux Community
2330 Sioux Trail NW
Prior Lake, MN 55372
952-445-8900
952-445-8906 Fax
shakopeedakota.org

Total area (BIA realty, 2004)
661.25 acres

Tribally owned (BIA realty, 2004)
661.25 acres

Total labor force 2000 census
118

High school graduate or higher
2000 census
87.3%

Bachelor's degree or higher
2000 census
5.4%

Unemployment rate 2000 census
7.6%

LOCATION AND LAND STATUS

The Shakopee Mdewakanton Sioux Community's reservation lands are located in southeastern Minnesota, near the Minnesota River, southwest of the suburbs of Minneapolis. The reservation boundaries encompass some 2,000 acres in Scott County, in Shakopee, Minnesota, and Prior Lake, Minnesota, the location of tribal headquarters. All acreage is near the original 250-acre reservation established for the tribe in the 1880s. Minneapolis/St. Paul lies 25 miles to the north and east. The Shakopee Reservation was reserved by federal acts in 1888 and 1889. The Mdewakanton Sioux were officially reincorporated in 1969 as the Shakopee Mdewakanton Sioux Community. Throughout 2000-2003, the community purchased 526.5 acres of land for construction of tribal housing, tribal offices, rights-of-way, land exchanges, golf courses, and powwow grounds.

PHYSICAL DESCRIPTION

The reservation contains several small lakes suitable for fishing and swimming. Most reservation acreage, however, lies within small population centers.

CLIMATE

There is no climate data recorded for Prior Lake, Minnesota; however, the community lies only 26 miles south of Minneapolis, Minnesota and the temperatures would not differ significantly. The year-round average daily high temperature at Minneapolis is 54°F, with the highest temperature on record as 105°F. The year-round average daily low temperature is 36°F, with the lowest temperature on record as -34°F. The area receives approximately 27 inches of rain annually, and almost 50 inches of snow.

CULTURE AND HISTORY

The Mdewakanton Dakotas are descendants of an eastern woodland band of the Dakota Nation who once roamed the upper midwest and the shores of Lake Superior. The name Mdewakanton refers to the tribal homeland, meaning "Those who dwelt at Spirit Lake." The name Shakopee derives from the chief (Sakpe, pronounced Shock-pay) who was the spokesperson for a village once located near what is now the city of Shakopee. As intertribal conflict during the eighteenth century drove the Mdewakanton Dakotas further south into the Mississippi and Minnesota river valleys, the larger group, led by Chief Sakpe, settled along the south shore of the Minnesota River.

In 1805, the Mdewakantons signed the first of a series of treaties, which transferred 36,000,000 acres of tribal land to the U.S. government and limited their access to traditional hunting and fishing grounds. The Mdewakantons participated in the Santee Sioux uprising of 1862. Following their defeat, 38 Mdewakantons were executed and many others were banished to the reservation at Santee, Nebraska. A few Mdewakantons remained in the Prior Lake area, while others relocated to the Lower Sioux Agency at Morton and the Upper Sioux Agency at Granite Falls. The tribe was eventually limited to a 10-mile strip along the Minnesota River.

The tribe organized under the Indian Reorganization in 1934 and reincorporated with a new constitution in 1969, becoming Minnesota's newest and smallest reservation. During the 1980s, this smallest of Minnesota's reservations became one of the state's most economically successful with the introduction of high-stakes gaming in 1982. Completed in 1992, the Mystic Lake Casino, with its teepee-shaped array of spotlights, represents at once a substantial financial resource and a visible symbol of the tribe's resilience. All tribal members are shareholders of the casino-operating corporation, Little Six. The tribe has reinvested a substantial portion of the revenues earned by the casino in the construction of tribal housing, water and sewer projects, and ambitious tribal enterprises.

The tribe sponsors traditional dance exhibitions and contests with tribal singers and drum groups in August every year to celebrate the Shakopee Mdewakanton Sioux Community Wacipi, or powwow. Events are open to the public.

The tribe has initiated a mapping and database project to illustrate the historical presence of the Dakotas within the Mississippi and Minnesota river valleys. "The Dakota Presence in the River Valley" is updated regularly to reflect recent discoveries of sacred sites, earthworks, or sites where contact with Europeans was first made.

GOVERNMENT

The Mdewakanton Dakotas reorganized in 1934 under the Indian Reorganization Act and received federal recognition in 1969. That year, the tribe approved a constitution establishing a tribal chairman elected by a general council composed of all enrolled tribal members over the age of 18. The tribe is also represented by a three-member business council elected by the general council. The business council consists of a chairperson, a vice-chairperson, and a secretary/treasurer. A gaming commission is made up of five popularly elected commissioners.

The tribe, under PL-638, contracts with the BIA to administer key programs and services, such as a full range of social services, health and dental care, education, administration, and public works services. Utilizing revenues from gaming and non-gaming sources, the tribe builds, maintains, and plows snowy roads and streets; constructs and operates water and sewer systems; provides educational programs for youth; safeguards the environment by monitoring wildlife and wetland conditions; and evaluates alternative energy sources. They participate in intergovernmental agreements for other projects with the City of Prior Lake and Scott County. In 2003, the tribe opened the Mdewakanton Fire Department, which has responded to an average of 100 calls a month since that time. They pay fees to local governments for police protection.

The community has developed a cultural resources department and operates language preservation and other programs designed to preserve the unique cultural heritage of the Shakopee Mdewakanton Sioux. The health department provides medical services to the tribal community and hosts health-related conferences on a regular basis. The Mdewakanton Fire Department has full-time professionally trained fire fighters and emergency response personnel. A legal department, consisting of two attorneys and a support staff person, provide legal guidance to the business and general council, all tribal departments, and tribally owned enterprises. In 2003, the maintenance department was staffed by 11 employees. Public works ensures the quality of the water supply. Other departments include: land, community health, education, networks employee services, family and children services, finance, marketing, and MIS.

BUSINESS CORPORATION

Three separate and distinct tribal entities, the SMSC Business Council, Little Six Incorporated (LSI), and the gaming commission, operate the community's gaming and non-gaming activities on a day-to-day basis. As stated in the community's public relations literature, "the Business Council governs, the LSI manages, and the Gaming Commission regulates gaming operations." The LSI was chartered in May 1991 and is managed by a six-member board of directors, who are licensed by the gaming commission and serve staggered two-year terms. The LSI serves as the corporate body of SMSC and owns Mystic Lake Casino Hotel and Little Six Casino.

ECONOMY

Fueled primarily with revenues from gaming, the tribe has developed other economic enterprises that diversify their economy beyond dependence upon gaming as a sole source. The general council encourages members to open small businesses by offering a growth fund loan program. Since initiating this program in 1993, over 37 member-owned businesses have been started.

Government as Employer. The tribal government, via its various economic enterprises and tribal programs and services, was the largest employer in Scott County, Minnesota in 2004, employing over 4,477 Native and non-Native people.

Gaming. The tribe operates both the Little Six Casino and the Mystic Lake Casino under a 10-year master plan approved in 2002. The 19,000-square-foot Little Six Casino, in Prior Lake, Minnesota, offers 590 slot machines, 8 table games, and a restaurant. Little Six Casino employed approximately 280 people in 2004. The 125,000-square-foot Mystic Lake Casino and Hotel complex, also located in Prior Lake, features 3,700 slots, 88 table games, an 850-seat bingo hall, and the 20,000-square-foot Playworks LINK event center, a convention/banquet hall and meeting facility. There are 4 restaurants and 2 entertainment venues on-site. The facility employs approximately 4,000 Native and non-Native employees. New parking lots and garages at the casino complex have been constructed. A number of other businesses have been developed in the area in support of the increased traffic brought on by the casinos, creating an estimated economic impact of greater than $189 million annually in Scott County and $271.9 for the State of Minnesota for 2002. In addition to supporting tribal programs and services, with revenues earned primarily from its gaming facilities the community also makes sizeable donations to other tribes in the Great Plains and Great Lakes areas for health care, education, infrastructure improvements, and economic development projects.

In 2003 alone, they contributed almost $8 million to various schools, community groups, and organizations. They have extended over $119 million in loans since 1998, with dozens of tribes, schools, health care facilities, and 30 Native American tribes and other charities benefiting. With its gaming revenues, the tribe has made a difference throughout Indian country. According to a tribal press release, "in fiscal year 2004, the Shakopee Mdewakanton Sioux Community has made these donations to tribes: $579,377 to the Santee Sioux Tribe (Nebraska) for economic development and community improvement; $57,945 to the Turtle Mountain Tribe (North Dakota) for a nursing home on the reservation; $163,422 to the Lower Brule Sioux Tribe (South Dakota) for a Buffalo Interpretive Center and tribal farm; $1 million to the Lower Sioux Community (Minnesota) for a community center; $416,000 to the Spirit Lake Sioux Tribe (North Dakota) to move homes onto the reservation from an Air Force Base; $500,000 to the Leech Lake Band of Ojibwe (Minnesota) for a well-drilling truck; $500,000 to the Red Lake Band of Chippewa (Minnesota) for St. Mary's School; $500,000 to the Grand Portage Band of Ojibwe (Minnesota) for economic development; $103,700 to the Oglala Sioux Tribe Woitancan Empowerment Zone (South Dakota) for propane trucks; $10,000 to the Oglala Sioux Tribe for propane tanks; $5,000 to the Sisseton Wahpeton Oyate (South Dakota) for the elderly program; $337,939 to the Crow Creek Sioux Tribe (South Dakota) for the tribal school and Christmas gifts; and $8,400 to the Wind River Reservation for the Children and Family's Program."

Banking. South Metro Federal Credit Union is a community-chartered federal credit union sponsored by the tribe. It provides financial services to anyone living or working in Scott County, Minnesota. It is located in the Dakota Mall, offering a range of financial services to members from travelers and check cards to signature guarantee program for securities and bonds, home improvement loans, new home mortgages, and an array of online banking. South Metro's ATMs are found throughout the area. In 2003 a second SmartBranch was opened at the South Bridge Crossing Shopping Center in the Shakopee/Savage area. In 2002 this credit union was named one of the top 100 fastest-growing credit unions in the U.S. for a second year in a row. This credit union will celebrate its twelfth anniversary in August 2005.

Services and Retail. The tribe owns a number of retail and service enterprises. The Dakota Mall/Shopping Center is home to the Shakopee Convenience Store, the credit union, a travel agency, and a salon and spa. Shakopee Travel, owned by a tribal member, provides travel and tour services. Mystic Lake Store, a marketing tool for the Mystic Lake Casino Hotel, opened in the Mall of America in Minneapolis on May 23, 2001. The store serves as a reservation desk for the hotel and a ticket outlet for events held at the casino complex entertainment venues.

The Dakota Meadows Mini Storage facility is located in Prior Lake. The Dakota Meadows RV Park and Campground is located adjacent to the casino, offering campsites, teepee rental, shower and laundry facilities, a self-service fuel facility, and shuttle services to other tribally owned recreational facilities.

Dakotah! Sport and Fitness, operated by the community in Prior Lake, is an aquatic recreation center, with swimming pools and slides, a fitness center with weight machines and aerobic exercise equipment, and a whirlpool. The Dakotah! training center, based in the ice arena at Dakotah! Sport and Fitness, provides facilities and equipment for skaters and their families, a gymnasium, racquetball and squash courts, an indoor firing range, an ice arena, and an indoor running track. Playworks, for children, is a favorite feature of the facility, offering supervised playtime fitness activities for the youngsters while adults work out in other areas of the building.

Tourism and Recreation. Gaming draws the largest number of visitors to the reservation, and a large number of ancillary businesses have been developed in support of gaming and tourism. The tribe hosts a Fourth of July fireworks annually and wacipi, the Shakopee Mdewakanton Dakota Community Powwow, every August. The tribe is also planning the construction of a cultural heritage museum. In 2004 the Lone Pine Golf Course was closed for rehabilitation and expansion but it is scheduled for a grand reopening in June 2005.

The Dakotah Meadows Campground, selected by readers of *Midwest Gaming and Travel Magazine* as the best RV park in Minnesota, provides 48 full-service RV hookups, showers and laundry facilities, with free shuttles to the Sport and Fitness Center, the casinos, and Playworks for children. The community provides a self-serve fuel facility at the campground for convenience to campers, and a unique, self-serve cleaning station with a catwalk for washing any size RV or camper. There are also individual family-camping teepees on site for a more rustic camping experience.

INFRASTRUCTURE

The Shakopee Mdewakanton Community is bounded on the north by Minnesota County Road 42, on the south by County Road 82, and by County Road 21 on the east. The reservation is 25 miles south of Minneapolis via Interstate-35.

Electricity. The reservation receives electricity via a new MVEC power substation located on tribal land.

Shakopee

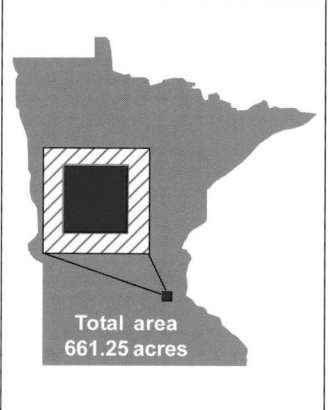

Total area 661.25 acres

ENVIRONMENTAL CONCERNS

Long considered a sacred site among the regional tribes, the Ma-Ka Yu-So-Ta Boiling Springs on Eagle Creek, near Savage, Minnesota, were under threat of development in the early 1990s. The community adopted a resolution in November 1994, calling for the preservation of the boiling springs as a cultural site. With assistance from the Minnesota Department of Natural Resources, they created an aquatic management area along a 400-foot wide corridor of Eagle Creek; the environmental and spiritual significance of the site are now protected from development.

In other ongoing wetland restoration projects, the community administers 1,600 acres of tribal lands in a prairie pothole region of the Minnesota River Valley, where unique hydrological and topographical features (potholes) remain protected for migratory waterfowl habitat.

Shakopee

Water Supply. In 1989, the tribal public works department undertook a $3 million program to improve sewer and water services. The public works department finished construction of a third well on the reservation and installed a 1,000,000-gallon water tank and tower to serve the needs of residents and businesses. These internal improvements resulted in the Shakopee Mdewakanton Community being recognized for having the best small water system in Minnesota.

Transportation. Major railways, bus services, and parcel delivery companies serve the Twin Cities area. Commercial air service is available at Twin Cities International Airport, minutes north of the reservation.

Housing. Since January 2000, the community has added 29 home sites to meet the needs of their growing tribal community. Community home improvement loans are made available by the general council to any member whose home needs renovation.

COMMUNITY FACILITIES AND SERVICES

The tribe built a new community center, which houses the tribal government as well as existing programs in medical and dental care, social services, education, and public works. The Oicimani Media Center, a collection of over 3,700 books about, by, and for Native Americans, is housed at the community center. The tribal fire department built a state-of-the art building in 2003, and offers fire protection and emergency medical services to surrounding communities. A free monthly tabloid newspaper, *The Circle*, is available throughout Prior Lake, featuring articles about all regional tribes.

Education. The community operates the nationally accredited Koda Cistina early childhood program and the Maga Hota preschool. A kindergarten enrichment center features a curriculum focusing on the arts, music, literature, cooking, science, language, and math skills. School-age children of the community attend Prior Lake and Shakopee public schools. The tribal education department supports its students with three home school coordinators working in area schools. The education center works in cooperation with Mankato State University and the University of Minnesota to bring college-level courses to the community center. A GED and diploma program also operates through the community center. Children's educational programs and activities are offered at Playworks, inside the Dakotah! Sport and Fitness Center. They include programs, such as Young Native Pride, an annual theater and dance group, and summer camps. The Tiowakan Spiritual Center, used for weddings, funerals, and other gatherings, opened in April 2000, housing the Ho Waste Parish, an independent, non-denomination church group.

Upper Sioux

Upper Sioux Community
Federal reservation
Sioux
Yellow Medicine County,
Minnesota

Upper Sioux Community
P.O. Box 147
Granite Falls, MN 56241
320-564-3853
320-564-4482 Fax
uppersiouxcommunity.org

Total area *(BIA realty, 2004)*
1,200.65 acres

Federal trust *(BIA realty, 2004)*
1,200.65 acres

Population
(Tribal source, 2004)
413

Total labor force *2000 census*
30

LOCATION AND LAND STATUS

The Upper Sioux Community Reservation is located on 1,250 acres in southwestern Minnesota, approximately 115 miles west of the state capital of Minneapolis. It is nestled in the scenic Minnesota River Valley. Ninety percent of the land is located in a flood plain while the remaining acreage is located in a heavily forested, hilly terrain. Established during the early 1800s, the original reservation boundaries extended 10 miles in each direction from the Minnesota River. In accordance with the Treaty of 1837, the Sioux agreed to sell their lands in order to pay their debts to local traders. Following an uprising in 1862, the U.S. Congress assumed ownership of the tribe's lands and annuities. In 1935, the secretary of the interior proclaimed that a reservation would be established for this group of Mdewakantan, Sisseton, and Santee Sioux from certain lands held in trust.

In February 1995, the Upper Sioux Community purchased approximately 160 acres. The area has been used as a housing development that includes a multipurpose gym, 12 housing units, 2 duplexes, a park, and a water tower. Since 1995, the tribe has purchased additional acreage. The tribe intends to utilize this land for housing and business as well as infrastructure developments.

PHYSICAL DESCRIPTION

Within the tribe's landholdings lie approximately 200 acres that remain completely undeveloped. They are heavily forested with a variety of species, including willow, Osier dogwood, cherry, red oak, white oak, and Black Hills spruce.

CULTURE AND HISTORY

The Sioux Indians continued to occupy village sites near Spirit Lake and carry on their hunting, fishing, and planting activities along the Minnesota-Wisconsin border for as long as a century after the initial appearance of white settlers. Several times a year the various bands of Sioux would gather for seasonal use of a 100-million-acre ancestral hunting area. By the mid-nineteenth century, a number of treaties were propagated due to the increased encroachment by non-Indians. Tension from this encroachment finally erupted into full-scale violence in the Minnesota Sioux War of 1862. This tragic affair ended with the conviction of approximately 300 Lakota Sioux men, the subsequent hanging of 38 at Mankato, Minnesota, and the imprisonment of many others. The Forfeiture Act of 1863 formally negated prior established treaty rights and allowed for the confiscation of all tribal lands and the expulsion of remaining tribe members from Minnesota. Many sought refuge in Canada. In subsequent years, some tribal members chose to reside in Canada and formed small reserves, while others eventually returned to the United States and were placed on the Santee Reservation. From there, small groups migrated eastward, some of them to Minnesota.

During the 1880s, Congress set aside small trust areas for those Indians "peaceably" disposed during the 1862 war. Eventually, they dispersed into five Minnesota communities, one of which was the Upper Sioux Reservation. Pe-Zi-Hu-Ta Zi-Zi Ka-Pi Ma-Ko-Ce, meaning "Land where they dig the yellow medicine," is the ancient Dakota name for this area. For years, the only work for the Upper Sioux was to be found in nearby non-Indian communities, mostly in farming and some in construction. A number of band members are still engaged in these activities today. The establishment of the tribal casino in 1990, however, totally revamped the tribal economy. Today this small Sioux community has nearly full employment and a healthy source of tribal revenue.

GOVERNMENT

The Upper Sioux tribal government is administered by the Upper Sioux Board of Trustees, which comprises five elected positions: tribal chairman, vice-chairman, secretary, treasurer, and member at large. The government was established as a board of trustees in 1942, operating under provisions provided for them through the BIA and adopted by the community. These provisions were revised in November 1974, and action is underway to provide the community with a constitution and bylaws. The Upper Sioux Community maintains a number of governmental departments. They include health administration, child welfare services, maintenance, finance, summer youth program and family health services. The board of trustees also oversees a number of programs for the Upper Sioux Community, including the housing improvement program, emergency energy conservation program, BIA youth programs, adult education, farm account, and youth employment.

As a self-governing tribe (as defined by PL-638), the Upper Sioux Community contracts a number of its governmental services. These services include, but are not limited to, BIA road maintenance, social services, job placement and training, transportation planning and administrative capacity building, tribal court; and bioterrorism preparedness and response programs. The tribe is in the process of negotiating contracts for administration for Native Americans and law enforcement programs.

The tribe maintains a BIA tribal court. The court presides over civil issues between tribal and nontribal members. It is in the process of negotiating contracts for law enforcement, but criminal actions currently lie outside its jurisdiction.

ECONOMY
The tribe operates the Prairie's Edge Casino and Resort, Prairie's Edge Convenience Store, and USC Propane.

Government as Employer. The tribal government employs 43 tribal members in areas such as health administration, child welfare, maintenance, finance, and others. In addition, a summer youth program employs a number of individuals on a seasonal basis. The tribal government operates on funds earned primarily by federal grants, leases, contracts, and tribal businesses.

Economic Development Projects. The Upper Sioux Community is pursuing venues to begin a housing development project, a regional tourism location, and an Indian interpretive center. Further projects include a credit union and bank, a telecommunications business, a health clinic, and a walking and biking trail between Montevideo/Granite Falls and Upper Sioux State Park. There are also plans to solicit an international fast-food chain and a retail outlet.

Agriculture and Livestock. The tribe has an estimated 250 acres currently under cultivation. Crops include soybeans, sugar beets, and corn.

Gaming. In 1990, the tribe built the Firefly Creek Casino, a class II gaming facility, with ATM machines and a restaurant that seating 140; the operation was expanded in 1992. The facility employed 29 tribal members and 133 non-members. Within five years of its opening, the casino was averaging $7.2 million in revenues. By 1995, it served as the reservation's largest employer and source of revenue. This casino is no longer in operation.

In March 2003, the Upper Sioux Community opened the Prairie's Edge Casino and Resort. Within its 27,000-square-foot area, the casino operates 600 slots/VLTs and 8 table games. The resort boasts 80 rooms, 2 restaurants, a lounge, a gift shop, a deli, a swimming pool and spa, a sauna, an exercise room, and an arcade. Adjacent to the hotel is the 15,000-square-foot conference center. It employs approximately 350 people, 90 percent of whom are non-Indian. It regularly hosts conferences, entertainment acts, tribal celebrations, powwows, and numerous events that draw visitors from throughout the Nation. The tribe is adding a nonsmoking facility adjacent to the Prairie's Edge Casino. The casino provides employment opportunities to the community members and has enabled the tribe to provide basic services such as water, sanitation, and housing. Recently, when local government aid was reduced in Minnesota, Prairie's Edge Casino further increased its contributions to the Indian and non-Indian communities. It provided funding to county and state programs and school systems. It also financed the purchase of a squad car for local law enforcement personnel.
Future improvements to the casino include interior development, increased entertainment, and strengthening the daycare program available to casino employees.

Fisheries. At this time, the tribe has no commercial fishing industry, though the Minnesota River and other bodies of water on and around the reservation provide recreational fishing opportunities.

Construction. The Upper Sioux Community Housing Program consists of seven full-time employees. The company owns a pay loader, a grader, and other equipment. The crew does regular contracting with the tribal casino and participates in a tribal employee-training program.

Real Estate/Commercial Development. The Upper Sioux Community intends to continue to increase their landholdings. Commercial plans for the land include housing developments (including apartment complexes), industrial parks, and retail services.

Services and Retail. The tribe operates a smoke shop that sells tobacco products, some local Native American crafts, and other merchandise. It also operates a convenience store. There are two restaurants and a gift shop located within the Prairie's Edge Casino. An RV park and a museum and interpretive center are currently under development.

Tourism and Recreation. Prairie's Edge Casino offers a regular venue of entertainment and conferences. Annually, it hosts Edgefest, a summer celebration of country music. In addition to events hosted at the casino, the tribe hosts a number of celebrations and ceremonies, such as the Annual Dakota Wacipi (pow-

Upper Sioux

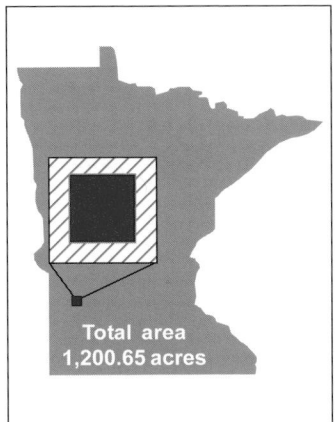

Total area
1,200.65 acres

Total labor force
(BIA labor report, 2001)
127

High school graduate or higher
2000 census
80.4%

Bachelor's degree or higher
2000 census
17.6%

Unemployment rate
2000 census
13.3%

Unemployment rate
(BIA labor report, 2001)
46%

Per capita income
2000 census
$14,815

Per capita income
(Tribal source, 2004)
$24,000

TRI-MN-USx-006

TRI-MN-USx-005

TRI-MN-USx-006; TRI-MN-USx-005
The Prairie's Edge Casino and Resort

633

Upper Sioux

wow). The tribe also holds an annual dignitaries dinner and numerous special awards and recognition events. The tribe also supports the Upper Sioux Agency State Park and Horse Camp. Hunting is quite popular with visitors to the area though the Upper Sioux Community has banned hunting on the reservation without a tribally issued license.

Local attractions include Hazelwood Mission, Langmaid Farmhouse, Dakota Wacipi, and the Upper Sioux Agency State Park and Horse Camp. The park is home to an extensive and diverse trail system. It is a multiuse system and is open to hikers, horseback riders, and in the winter, snowmobiles. There are also two miles of trails groomed specifically for cross-country skiing. The park features a number of picnic, camping, and recreation sites.

INFRASTRUCTURE

Highway 67 runs through the reservation community and provides access to and from Minneapolis via Highway 212, 120 miles to the east. The nearest commercial airport is two miles from the reservation. Full air service is located in Minneapolis. The community of Granite Falls has local bus service and commercial truck lines.

Electricity. Electricity is provided by Excel Energy and Minnesota Valley Light and Power Association.

Fuel. Tri-county Cooperative and Natrogas provide natural gas service. The tribe has recently formed USC Propane, and it will begin servicing reservation residents.

Water Supply. The tribe operates a water and wastewater system that services a number of reservation homes. However, some community residents continue to receive their water supply from individual wells. The tribe supplements the cost of maintaining the wells by 50 percent. Residencies not serviced by the sewer system maintain individual septic tanks.

Transportation. Although there are no extensive bus or cab services available in the county, the tribe provides transportation to tribal elders through its family health services department. The Prairie's Edge Casino provides shuttle service for its clients. The nearby City of Granite Falls, Minnesota, provides city bus routes. Greyhound Busline is also located in Granite Falls and is available for long-distance commuting.

Telecommunications. The Upper Sioux Community receives Internet access. It is not in a service area to receive cable television, and residents must individually purchase satellite systems to increase their reception.

COMMUNITY FACILITIES AND SERVICES

The Upper Sioux Community maintains a community center with a number of facilities. It operates an elder's meal site and a multipurpose gym, with full kitchen facilities, an exercise room, and public showers. The tribe has initiated a language revitalization program. The program promotes language and cultural retention and aids in strengthening the bonds between tribal members. The tribe operates Wellbriety, a program that promotes sobriety and healthy living. The tribe also supports Project Turnabout, an addiction treatment facility that serves a local and national clientele. It employs approximately 118 full- or part-time employees and offers detoxification programs, preventive education, a women's center, family support programs, and community education programs. It also provides its clients with Christian, Jewish, and traditional Native spiritual programs and support.

Education. Students of the Upper Sioux Community attend Yellow Medicine East, part of the Granite Falls/Clarkfield Public School System. These facilities are located approximately five miles from the reservation. Ridgewater College in nearby Willmar, Minnesota, is a local junior college and hosts activities and events that are open to the public (including Native American Awareness Gathering Children's Day, lectures, and programs).

Health Care. The tribe provides a self-funded health insurance program to its members and employees. There is no on-reservation health clinic, but the tribe receives available services through the reservation-based community health representative, diabetes coordinator, and family health services. There are hospital services available in the nearby town of Granite Falls, and the renowned Mayo Clinic is located in Rochester.

ENVIRONMENTAL CONCERNS

In negotiations with the Emergency Wetland Reserve Program, the tribe has been able to place 299 acres of recently acquired lands and adjacent uplands on the list of protected wetlands. In addition to preserving their lands, the tribe is concerned with water quality and erosion control. The restoration of watersheds has become a high priority for the tribe. In the Clean Water Action Plan of 1999/2000, the tribe made the commitment to continue working with state, local, federal, and nongovernmental entities to address watershed concerns. The tribe aims to continue the development of a tribal geographic information system, to continue wetland restoration and protection, to complete the planning process for a wastewater treatment facility, to develop tribal water quality standards, and to develop a tribal pesticide code.

TRI-MN-USx-007 Top portion of the Statue of a buffalo hunter in front of the Prairie's Edge Casino and Resort

TRI-MN-USx-008 Bottom portion of the Statue of a buffalo hunter in front of the Prairie's Edge Casino and Resort

TRI-MN-USx-007

TRI-MN-USx-008

LOCATION AND LAND STATUS

The White Earth Reservation is located in northwestern Minnesota, on the edge of the Red River Valley, approximately 68 miles from Fargo, North Dakota, and 225 miles from Minneapolis/St. Paul, Minnesota. The reservation's boundary encompasses 36 townships, or about 1,300 square miles, within three Minnesota counties: northern Becker, northeastern Clearwater, and all of Mahnomen. There are five incorporated cities within the White Earth Reservation, all located along U.S. Highway 59; the cities are Callaway, Ogema, Waubun, Mahnomen, and Bejou. Tribal headquarters are located in White Earth, with additional offices in Mahnomen. There are several other small communities throughout the reservation, with populations ranging from several hundred to fewer than 100 people. Major Minnesota cities near the reservation include Detroit Lakes (10 miles south), Bemidji, and Park Rapids.

The White Earth Reservation was established by the Treaty of March 19, 1867. By the 1887 Dawes Act and the subsequent Nelson Act of 1889, the communally owned reservation land was parceled into 20-acre individual Indian allotments. Parcels were then claimed by the government, and Indian owners were defrauded in unscrupulous business deals, resulting in many White Earth tribal members being dispossessed of their lands. This dispossession continued largely unabated until the 1980s when the White Earth Land Settlement Agreement allotted 10,000 acres to the tribe, in privately owned parcels. Nonetheless, the land within the reservation's borders is 90 percent privately owned by non-Indians; only 10 percent is owned by the tribe. Government lands held within the boundary of the reservation continue to be contested by the tribe in partnership with the White Earth Land Recovery Project, a nonprofit advocacy group seeking to regain tribal lands lost through tax foreclosures, treaty abrogations, and theft. Continuing land purchases are planned for the construction of housing, schools, additional economic development initiatives, and wildlife protection.

PHYSICAL DESCRIPTION

Outside the communities, much of the land is forested with aspen, white pines, basswood, oak, and spruce, broken by stretches of rich, fertile farmland and pasture.

CLIMATE

Climate data has not been recorded for White Earth, the location of tribal headquarters. However, there is data available for the city of Mahnomen, only 20 miles west and north of White Earth. The year-round average daily high temperature in Mahnomen is 51°F. The highest temperature ever recorded was 103°F. The year-round average daily low temperature is 28.8°F, with the lowest temperature on record as -48°F. The area receives over 23 inches of rain annually, and 42.2 inches of snow.

CULTURE AND HISTORY

The White Earth Ojibwas (Chippewas) speak an Algonquian-based language called Anishinabemowin, and the people call themselves Anishinabe (Anishinaabeg). The term Chippewa, widely used in treaties and other documents, is a corruption of the early spellings Ojibway or Otchipwe. The people originally lived in small, self-governing villages in Canada, where they first encountered French explorers in the 1600s near Sault Ste. Marie.

Later, they prospered in the fur trade and expanded their population and territory. By the late eighteenth century, the Iroquois had driven the Ojibwas out of the Ontario peninsula, and they began to move into western Wisconsin and northeastern Minnesota. Arriving in what is now Minnesota, the Ojibwas encoun-

tered the powerful Santee Sioux. Conflicts between the two tribes persisted until the Ojibwas successfully drove the Sioux westward.

When the Euro-American settlers arrived, the Ojibwas occupied more than half the state, gathered into four great divisions, each containing a number of smaller bands. By living in isolated villages throughout the early nineteenth century, the Ojibwas had been able to avoid the increasing number of westward-moving settlers. However, by treaties signed in 1854 and 1855, the Lake Superior and Mississippi bands were pressured into ceding huge tracts of land in north-central and northeastern Minnesota in exchange for meager sums of cash and subsistence trade items. The treaties created reservations in the regions near Grand Portage, Fond du Lac, Mille Lacs, Sandy Lake, Rabbit Lake, Gull Lake, Cass Lake, Lake Pokegama, and Lake Winnibigoshish. Then, in the March 19, 1867 treaty, the 10 chiefs of the Chippewas of the Mississippi ceded their treaty rights to lands that extended northwest to Thief River and north to Turtle Lake. The 1889 Nelson Act designated that all Chippewas living in Minnesota be moved to the White Earth Reservation, originally consisting of 837,120 acres. The Native people resisted this decree, and finally the U.S. Chippewa Commission was directed to negotiate for the complete cession of all lands belonging to the different bands except for the Red Lake and White Earth reservations. Moreover, it attempted to break up these reservations into allotments, thereby decreasing their size. These land losses were so massive that, by the turn of the twentieth century, only a fraction of the White Earth Reservation remained in tribal hands.

Today the Anishinabes of the area continue their traditional autumn harvest of wild rice beds, which are plentiful in the area's lakes, streams, and rivers. They have also maintained many other traditional practices such as woodcraft skills and the use of birch bark canoes. In addition, the Anishinabemowin language, once slated for extinction, is currently taught both on- and off-reservation at a number of schools and colleges.

GOVERNMENT

A reservation tribal council, composed of a chairperson, a secretary/treasurer, and a representative from each of the three districts, serves as the elected governing body for the enrolled members. Council members are elected for staggered four-year terms, with elections occurring every two years. Tribal business is conducted by the White Earth Reservation Business Committee.

The White Earth Band of Chippewas, a PL-280 tribe within the state of Minnesota, are members of the six-member Minnesota Chippewa Tribe (MCT), who sought a single consolidated tribal government without relinquishing governance at the local level. The original constitution and bylaws of the Minnesota Chippewa Tribe were ratified in 1936, according to the Indian Reorganization Act of 1934. They are governed by an executive committee with each band chairperson acting as a member of the committee.

The band has its own tribal court system, consisting of a chief judge and two associate judges, to enforce the judicial code and ordinances. They also have a separate juvenile justice code, and they use a juvenile tribal court advocate who serves as a probation officer and counselor to youth. The juvenile court utilizes Sentencing Circles, a model of sentencing in which the offending juvenile agrees to participate in a process recommending disposition to the court. As part of the juvenile justice program,

White Earth Reservation
Federal reservation
Anishinabe (Chippewa)
Mahnomen, Becker, and
Clearwater counties, Minnesota

White Earth Band of Chippewa
P.O. Box 418
White Earth, MN 56591
   218-983-3285
   218-983-3641 Fax

Total area (BIA realty, 2004)
77,220.35 acres

Total area (Tribal source, 2004)
837,425 acres

Tribally owned
(BIA realty, 2004)
75,267.52 acres

Individually owned
(BIA realty, 2004)
1,952.83 acres

Population 2000 census
2,759

Population
(Tribal source, 2004)
9,192

Tribal enrollment
(BIA labor report, 2001)
20,820

Tribal enrollment
(Tribal source, 2004)
19,629

Total labor force 2000 census
3,968

Total labor force
(Tribal source, 2004)
4,266

High school degree or higher
2000 census
75.8%

Bachelor's degree or higher
2000 census
10.9%

Unemployment rate 2000 census
8.2%

Unemployment rate
(BIA labor report, 2001)
51%

Per capita income 2000 census
$12,786

White Earth

TRI-MN-WE-99

TRI-MN-WE-98

TRI-MN-WE-97

RI-MN-WE-97 Sign for the Shooting Star Casino

TRI-MN-WE-99 The Shooting Star Casino, Hotel and Event Center, in Mahnomen

TRI-MN-WE-98 Sideview of the Shooting Star Casino

the tribe operates a tribal youth program to counter soaring rates of tobacco use, alcohol and drug use, violence, truancy, and school dropouts among its young people. The tribal law enforcement department has cross-jurisdiction with the State of Minnesota.

ECONOMY
The economy consists of gaming, small retail businesses, manufacturing, and governmental services.

Government as Employer. The White Earth Tribal Council is the largest employer in the three counties that lie, either in part or totally, within the boundaries of the White Earth Reservation. The tribal council administers federal, state, and private funds to operate over 115 programs in the areas of education, health and human services, public facilities, and economic development. Government services and programs employ approximately 464 tribal members, while the casino and hotel complex and other tribal enterprises employ a total of approximately 1,500 people, including both Native and non-Native individuals.

Economic Development Projects. The tribe adopted a strategic plan in February 2002. One of the stated goals in this plan is the diversification of employment opportunities for its members, beyond gaming and tribal government programs and services. A Comprehensive Economic Development Strategy Task Force, initiated in 2003, is implementing the strategic plan, utilizing the already-existing city of Mahnomen industrial park infrastructure to recruit new employers to the reservation and to seek high tech and other growth industries.

Agriculture and Livestock. There are 2,537 acres of tribally owned agricultural land. Tribal land for agriculture is leased on a yearly basis, not to exceed a five-year option. A tribal organization called the White Earth Aki Planning Circle (Aki means "small plot of land" in the Ojibwa language), promotes cultural traditions in agriculture by promoting reservation-wide community gardening, in conjunction with health and wellness goals. They incorporate ancient values with teaching modern technology in the growth, harvest, and preservation of food. The project pairs tribal elders with Head Start participants and other young people to plant seedling trees, build and plant raised seed beds for the disabled, conduct community education programs, and promote the use of native seeds in gardens, while tending to over 420 individual gardens and seven community gardens. The project gardens serve as outdoor grow labs for teachers to: teach plant science, gardening, health, and nutrition to tribal youth; produce vegetables and fruits used in elderly nutrition programs; and instill a sense of community service in all participants.

A tribally affiliated nonprofit advocacy organization, the White Earth Land Recovery Project, operates Native Harvest, on the reservation. The organization markets wild rice, hominy, maple syrup, corn, and other products to fund its various community-

organizing and land-recovery efforts. The group promotes sustainable agriculture practices to a larger region within the state of Minnesota. The products are an alternative source of forestry revenue and are designed to demonstrate the value of forests other than for harvesting.

Forestry. According to the BIA Forestry Department, 60,000 acres of the White Earth Indian Reservation are forested with aspen, some maple, basswood, oak, white pine, and spruce.

Gaming. Two tribally owned gaming facilities are located on the reservation. The Shooting Star Casino, Hotel and Event Center, in Mahnomen, Minnesota, employs 1,064 people, 70 percent of whom are Native American. The gaming facility features 1,100 slot machines, poker and blackjack tables, 4 restaurants, the Mustang Lounge, a concert venue, and a karaoke bar. On the premises, the tribe operates an RV park with 47 hookups with water, sewer, and electric services, horseshoe pits, an indoor swimming pool, volleyball courts, and complete shower and laundry facilities. The 368-room hotel supports operations at the event center, offering over 25,800 square feet of convention and meeting space. The complex includes the Northern Lights gift shop and the Star Adventure Kids Center, a licensed daycare facility. In addition, the tribe operates the Golden Eagle Bingo Hall.

Fisheries. The White Earth Band, in an agreement with the U.S. Fish and Wildlife Service and the Minnesota Department of Natural Resources, has reintroduced lake sturgeon, a primitive fish once common in regional waters, into White Earth Lake and Round Lake on the reservation. The lake sturgeon is considered a culturally relevant species to the White Earth Band since ancestral Native American cultures depended on the harvest of this fish to supplement subsistence diets. However, since the early 1900s, schools of the fish have declined in size due to the construction of dams and water-quality problems associated with agriculture and erosion. There had not been a recorded catch of a lake sturgeon since 1957, pulled from Lake Lida. The Rainy River First Nation Tribe of Canada assists the project by raising the fingerlings at their hatchery before turning them over to the White Earth Band for reintroduction. The goal is to stock 8,000 fingerlings annually.

Construction. Within the reservation boundaries there are private enterprises engaged in steel manufacturing, plumbing, heating, welding, carpentry, masonry, painting and drywall, electrical, and many other aspects of construction work.

Manufacturing. There are several manufacturing enterprises located on the reservation. The tribe owns a retail lumber business, the Ojibway Lumber and Building Supply Company. Waubun Steel, a privately owned business, produces custom steel orders such as docks and trailers. This company employs about eight people. Another privately owned business mills approximately 50,000 pounds of wild rice per year.

Industrial Parks. An industrial park with full infrastructure is located in the city of Mahnomen. Additional industrial park sites have been identified at nearby Callaway and Waubun.

Real Estate/Commercial Development. Manitok Mall, a 16,000-square-foot shopping facility, jointly owned by the White Earth Reservation Tribal Council and a private company, opened in the spring of 1995. The facility is currently managed by the casino. It contains a convenience store, the tribal credit union, a fitness center, a liquor store, a daycare center, and an optometrist office.

Services and Retail. Tribally owned businesses include a limousine company, an office supply store, an insurance processing center, various construction-related businesses, a fish hatchery, a freeze-dried bait operation, a firewood-processing company, and a garage.

Transportation. There are several private trucking companies located on the reservation. Private and tribal limousine services serve the Shooting Star Casino.

Media and Communications. The band publishes a newspaper, the *Anishinaabeg Today*; and *Ojibwe Akiing*, a publication of the Anishinabe Akeen Dabajimowad of Reserve, Wisconsin is distributed to various locations throughout the reservation. *News from Indian Country: The Independent Native Journal*, a monthly publication, is also available.

Tourism and Recreation. Tourists enjoy the accommodations of the Shooting Star Hotel/RV Lodge, which include gift shops and an indoor swimming pool. Small gift shops and craft shops feature hand-harvested wild rice grown on the reservation, as well as beautifully beaded items, basketry, quilts, and other handmade items produced by local people. The pristine lakes of the White Earth Reservation invite residents and tourists alike to enjoy swimming, canoeing, boating, water skiing, and fishing during the summer months. In winter, ice fishing, snowmobiling, and cross-country skiing are available. Abundant wildlife, waterfowl, excellent fishing, and campsites attract sportsmen and naturalists alike.

Other nearby attractions include: Itasca State Park, home to the headwaters of the Mississippi River, adjacent to the eastern boundary of the reservation; Tamarac National Wildlife Refuge; White Earth State Forest; Elbow Lake State Park; and St. Benedicts Mission, an historic site.

The White Earth Powwow, which is held each year on the weekend closest to June 14, celebrates the Indian heritage of the people on this reservation. Other events include golf tournaments, ice and fishing derbies, snowmobile races, and county fairs.

INFRASTRUCTURE
Minnesota Highways 113 and 200 and U.S. 59 run through the reservation.

Electricity. Electricity is provided by Otter Tail Power Company, Wild Rice Electric Cooperative, Itaska-Mantrap Electric Cooperative, and Clearwater-Polk Electric Cooperative.

Fuel. No natural gas service is available.

Water Supply. Incorporated cities, villages, and community housing projects have water and sewer services. Scattered single-family housing sites utilize private wells and septic systems.

The White Earth Tribal Council operates a solid waste management program that includes fee-based residential garbage pickup. They also operate five solid waste transfer stations.

Transportation. Private air facilities are located at Mahnomen and Detroit Lakes; commercial air service is available at the Hector International Airport, located in Fargo, North Dakota, 63 miles from White Earth. Greyhound bus service is available in Detroit Lakes, 11 miles distant. Many truck lines service the area, including UPS, Winter Truck Lines, Haider Truck Lines, and Ingebrigtson Trucking. Both Amtrak Passenger Service and the Burlington Northern Rail Line are available in Detroit Lakes. C. P. Rail Lines run north-south through the White Earth Reservation, with stops at Callaway, Ogema, Waubun, and Mahnomen to pick up grain and freight.

Housing. The White Earth Reservation became the first in the Nation to have a congregate housing complex. It was built in 1983. In 2003, the band's housing authority received a $3.1 million grant from HUD to provide essential community housing and revitalization projects. The money will be used to modernize older housing units, to construct new low-income housing units, and to provide ongoing housing assistance to tribal members seeking to become homeowners for the first time. The monies were awarded via the Indian Housing Block Grant under the Native American Housing and Self-Determination Act.

COMMUNITY FACILITIES AND SERVICES
Community centers are located at Callaway, Ogema, Waubun, Rice Lake, Pine Point, Elbow Lake, and Naytahwaush. Another will open in the community of White Earth sometime in 2005 or 2006. Five financial institutions are located on the reservation, including a credit union and a community development bank.

The tribe operates a child care program that provides licensing support services for child care centers, in-home caregivers, and relative-care financial assistance programs and other services through the Child Care Assistance Program.

Education. There are six public elementary schools, two public junior highs, two public high schools, two private schools, and four Head Start programs within the reservation. In addition, a vocational branch and extension courses are available through Moorhead State University. The tribe operates the White Earth Tribal and Community College in Mahnomen, Minnesota. It is currently seeking accreditation. A temporary campus, scattered among various buildings in downtown Mahnomen, will be replaced by a permanent campus. There are technical schools located in Detroit Lakes, Bemidji, Moorhead, Thief River Fall, and Crookston. The Minnesota State College system operates campuses in Bemidji and Moorhead, and a vocational rehabilitation center is located in Naytahwaush, Minnesota. The tribally owned and operated Ojibwa Building Supply offers carpentry classes.

Health Care. The Indian Health Service operates clinics in White Earth, Naytahwaush, and Ponsford. Ambulance service is available through the tribal health department. Private physicians, hospitals, and clinics are available in Mahnomen and Detroit Lakes. In addition, there are many hospitals, including the Veterans Administration, located in Fargo, North Dakota.

The White Earth Reservation's Health Services Department operates an elderly nutrition program, providing hot home-delivered meals to seniors, with four nutrition centers: Rice Lake, Naytahwaush, Elbow Lake Village, and White Earth. Another nutrition center in Pine Point is administrated through the Minnesota Chippewa Tribe. Community health representatives are available in five communities on the reservation, offering assistance with transportation needs and other types of outreach services to medical care. The substance abuse program is located in White Earth and serves the entire reservation, with a choice of traditional and Indian cultural treatment approaches. The facility offers both outpatient and inpatient admission and an after-care program. The White Earth Home Health Agency provides nursing and homemaker services to the Indian and non-

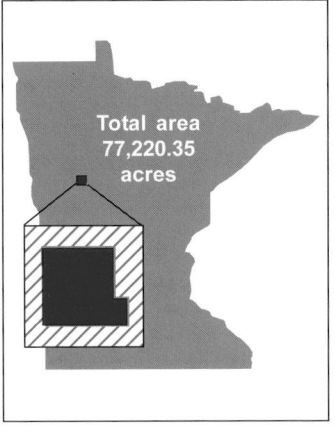

Total area
77,220.35
acres

White Earth

Indian homebound residents of the reservation. A mental health program provides comprehensive counseling, education, and support services for the treatment of depression, family conflict, stress management, grief, child abuse, including adult survivors, separation and loss, suicide prevention, and anger management. The Community Health Education Program supports prevention education and lifestyle interventions for reducing the risk of certain preventable diseases. The tribe offers WIC nutritional services to pregnant and lactating women and mothers of young babies, and the diabetes project makes prevention education, nutritional counseling, and fitness information available to all tribal members, beginning at very early ages. In 2004, the diabetes project operated five community fitness and wellness centers in White Earth, Naytahwaush, Pine Point, Mahnomen, and Rice Lake. The emergency medical services owns two ambulances to meet emergency medical needs. They are dispatched from the tribal communications center.

ENVIRONMENTAL CONCERNS

In 2001, the White Earth Band negotiated with the State of Minnesota's Department of Natural Resources to adopt hunting and fishing regulations that would allow the band to receive 2.5 percent of the revenues from hunting and fishing licenses, or approximately $1.2 million annually.

The band's biology department participates in a joint initiative along with the Minnesota Department of Natural Resources and the Wild Rice Watershed District in maintaining a fish passage structure on the Wild Rice River near Twin Valley, Minnesota. The Wild Rice River, a tributary to the Red River of the North, has numerous dams and barriers limiting natural fish migration. The structure permits safe passage past the Heiberg Dam to 120 miles of watershed spawning grounds farther upriver, promoting species diversity and preservation. The structure is built of boulders arranged to create stair step rapids for fish to navigate, a simulated rapid run.

Initiatives to clean up the White Earth Reservation have been successful. Over 350 abandoned vehicles have been removed, junk house trailers have been hauled away, and there are plans for new parks and recreation trails in several of the villages. The revitalization efforts included putting welcome signs at the entrance to each village, planting trees and shrubs, and installing street signs and lighting. The project is sponsored by the White Earth Investment Initiative, a nonprofit subsidiary of the Midwest Minnesota Development Corporation, located in Detroit Lakes. The mission of the organization is to make the reservation more attractive to potential investors.

In a separate initiative aimed at removing unsightly illegal dumpsites, a multiagency task force headed by the White Earth Reservation Tribal Council, cleaned up a site along Cherry Lake Road in 2000. The site threatened a wetlands area. With funding obtained from the Tribal Solid Waste Interagency Workgroup, a consortium of agencies that includes the U.S. EPA, the BIA, and the Indian Health Service, a contractor was hired to accomplish excavation and removal of over 1,500 tons of debris. The Minnesota Department of Natural Resources donated 1,000 trees for replanting the damaged area to prevent erosion. In ongoing efforts, the tribe has created recycling sheds and household hazardous waste collection events to encourage proper waste disposal, and it conducts educational programs to motivate tribal members toward long-term behavior change regarding illegal dumping.

In an innovative approach to math and science instruction, White Earth Reservation Natural Resource Department managers, teachers from the reservation's Circle of Life School, and tribal elders, in cooperation with University of Minnesota (volunteer) faculty, created a six-week summer program in 1999 to improve the academic performance of tribal youth while maintaining strong cultural foundations of the Ojibwa traditions. Utilizing the reservation's already-existing resources-the waters, birds, plants, and trees-an outdoor math and science laboratory was created, wherein students realized the everyday usefulness of math and science skills via practical applications such as soil testing, water quality monitoring, forestry measurements of standing trees and harvested timber products, stream sampling for aquatic life, observations (and counts) of wildlife species, and various land use issues. Field trips exposed students to various aspects of natural diversity throughout the reservation, and career options using lessons learned were discussed during each session. The program was such a success that it has been continued, and the band is exploring opportunities to develop a year-round environmental learning center to further enhance the educational experience of tribal youth and young people from surrounding areas.

Throughout the years 1991 through 2003, the White Earth Reservation Natural Resources Department Wildlife Program was involved in prairie and wetlands restoration projects aimed at promoting the prairie ecosystem and eliminating noxious weeds. During this period, a total of 2,225 acres were restored to natural conditions and enhanced for wetlands or upland nesting and/or migrational habitats. There were another 820 acres treated for noxious weeds. Additional eventual goals to be realized by the projects will include restoration of northern tallgrass to reservation prairie lands, flood abatement, and improvements in quality of surface waters.

Honoring Nations Honoree 2000

White Earth Suicide Intervention Team, White Earth Chippewa Tribe

The White Earth Suicide Intervention Team was created in 1990 in response to an extraordinarily high rate of suicide attempts and completions on the White Earth Reservation. The all-volunteer team provides many services previously absent or lacking, including 24-hour support for the attempter and his or her family, encouragement of voluntary or involuntary hospital admission for all attempters, referrals to mental health services and suicide education.

In 1990, the citizens of the White Earth Reservation faced a severe mental health crisis. Four tribal members had committed suicide within a several week period and the community feared that a cluster of copycat suicide attempts (and completions) might follow. To put the problem in perspective, White Earth had suffered an average of only one suicide per year over the previous five years, and although American Indians experience higher rates of suicide than members of the U.S. population overall, the 1990 suicide rate at White Earth had reached a level 8.5 times higher than the American Indian average.

The suicides rocked the tight-knit community. Overcoming the denial, fear and shame frequently associated with suicide, dozens of tribal members spoke out at an open-mike event sponsored by the Tribal Council. Besides helping individuals and families deal with their losses, the event led to a great upsurge of grassroots support for community action. After the meetings, a group of community members came together and, with the Council's official support (expressed through the passage of a tribal resolution), the White Earth Suicide Intervention Team (WESIT) was formed.

The Team chose to focus their efforts on suicide intervention because they believed that, with limited time and scarce financial resources, this was an area in which their work could have the most impact. Examining the situation, the Team identified a number of systemic, but rectifiable problems associated with the methods of suicide response at White Earth. For instance, few survivors were hospitalized for the recommended 72-hour period immediately after their attempts - most were simply examined and released from local hospitals' emergency rooms. Prior to the establishment of WESIT, emergency response personnel had no one to contact for support and direction in dealing with suicide attempts and completions. Beyond an ability to attend to victims' immediate medical needs, even hospital staff lacked information about how to best deal with individuals who attempted suicide. Further, because individuals responding to each crisis were focused mainly on the victim, the mental health needs of families and friends on the scene were often left unattended.

WESIT is a highly creative and effective institutional response to these needs. It is an all-volunteer organization, composed of Indian Health Service (IHS) and Tribal Mental Health staffers, concerned community members, and clergy and spiritual leaders. The 20-plus member team works closely with tribal dispatchers and emergency medical technicians (EMTs), tribal police, non-Indian local law enforcement officials, and emergency room staff at area hospitals to support suicide victims within the White Earth tribal community. The Team's on-call members accompany tribal EMTs and police officers to the scene of a suicide attempt or completion, or to the hospital, and intercede on behalf of victims and their families. In the case of an attempted suicide, WESIT has been instrumental in compelling the non-Indian hos-

pitals that serve White Earth members (White Earth does not have its own hospital) to admit victims for 72-hour holds. In the case of a completed suicide, WESIT provides immediate, on-the-scene counseling to friends and family and lays the groundwork for further mental health care by providing referrals to other social services. The Team is able to respond 24 hours a day through an agreement brokered with the IHS's and Tribe's health programs- Team members who work for the IHS or for Tribal Mental Health cover daytime calls, while a rotating on-call team member handles calls during nights and weekends.

WESIT complements these direct intervention activities with a variety of other activities undertaken at its monthly meetings. In particular, the Team uses these meetings to debrief, discuss issues of concern, strategize, craft policy, train and introduce themselves to the continually changing set of individuals and organizations with which they work.

Statistically, WESIT's effectiveness can best be demonstrated by the impact its efforts have had on post-attempt hospitalizations. In 1990, 77 percent of the resident White Earth tribal members who attempted suicide were released from emergency rooms within hours after arrival. By 1996, as a direct result of the Team's interventions, the number had fallen to 6 percent. These holds are significant, since research shows that most terminal suicide re-attempts occur in the 72-hour period following the first attempt. Thus, WESIT's success in increasing hospitalization rates has dramatically decreased the number of suicide completions resulting from repeated attempts.

WESIT's effectiveness is also demonstrated through the partnerships it has created with on- and off-reservation emergency response and health care providers. The tribal emergency medical technicians and dispatchers, local law enforcement officers, and emergency room nurses with whom WESIT works all attest to the Team's effectiveness as a partner in health care provision. These professionals note especially that, because of the WESIT members' comprehensive training and personal knowledge, the volunteers are able to assist in the care of victims, family and friends in a way that helps the partners perform their own jobs better.

Finally, WESIT has been a catalyst in renewing community hope. In 1990, there was great despair at White Earth, and the community feared that it might not be able to overcome this difficult problem. While it is impossible to eliminate all suicides in any community, WESIT has turned the tide of opinion at White Earth, showing that something can be done in terms of intervention at the most critical moments. Especially since the "degrees of separation" between individuals in the community are small, helping just one family through a suicide attempt or completion has positive reverberations throughout the entire Tribe.

There are numerous reasons why the White Earth Suicide Intervention Team works so well. For one, WESIT keeps its focus narrow. The emphasis on intervention keeps everyone's goal simple and helps ensure that the Team's time, energy, and financial resources are put to their best use. Second, WESIT has substantial political support. Despite several leadership changes over the last decade, WESIT has retained support of the tribe's politicians, as evidenced by their public statements and resolutions. Third, WESIT emphasizes training. WESIT's distributes a

Honoring Nations
Honoree 2000

Text in its entirety from:
The Harvard Project On
American Indian Economic
Development

John F. Kennedy School
of Government
Harvard University

White Earth

Honoring Nations
Honoree 2000

Text in its entirety from:
The Harvard Project On
American Indian Economic
Development

John F. Kennedy School
of Government
Harvard University

comprehensive training manual to its members and conducts on-going training at its monthly meetings. The later consists of everything from presentations on the latest research information about effective suicide intervention techniques to the introduction of new nurses in the emergency room of a local hospital. In addition to being educational, such training has the added benefit of sustaining WESIT by convincing the ever-changing group of players that the Team is itself a legitimate, useful and professionally competent partner. Fourth, WESIT practices on-going recruitment. This is necessary because, as an all-volunteer entity, it is no one's paid job to be part of WESIT. Recruitment also provides respite, as it keeps the group large enough to allow committed Team members to rotate between on-call and non-call positions. Finally, while some would see the Team's all-volunteer staff as a weakness, WESIT members themselves cite this status as a strength and a major component of their success. For example, clients know Team members do the work because they really care - no one "forces" them to be there, which makes their messages, especially the more difficult ones (such as, "You have to stay in the hospital for the next three days") easier to hear.

Significantly, this program has promoted the White Earth Tribe's capacity for self-determination and self-governance. Most striking is how WESIT proves that tribes can, on their own, do something to combat one of the most serious social problems in Indian Country. As one WESIT member stated, WESIT "is not a federal or state program. It was not mandated by any agency. It has no outside program funding. The need existed simply to do something for our people to reduce the threat of suicide and to preserve our people." Further, as this quote implies, self-determination and self-governance proceed only with the preservation of the people. Not only are many people alive today as a result of WESIT's efforts, but by helping to improve the physical and mental health of White Earth's citizens, the Team preserves and promotes a sense of positive accomplishment and pride. A final way WESIT promotes self-determination and self-governance is by fostering fruitful partnerships with non-tribal entities. WESIT has compelled non-tribal emergency service and health care providers to address the needs of their Indian clients, and by being

good "ambassadors" for the Tribe, WESIT has accomplished this difficult task in a way that has improved government-to-government and agency-to-agency relationships.

Two aspects of the WESIT approach suggest that many other communities in Indian Country could benefit through replication of this program. First and most regrettably, WESIT addresses a problem shared by much of Native America. Thus, the program's potential for replication is supported by a great need. Second, WESIT is inexpensive. The volunteer team relies on tribal funds alone, and this funding is minimal. The White Earth Tribal Council provides a room for the team's monthly meeting, pays for their lunch, and has provided radios so that on-call team members can be in better contact with tribal dispatchers. (Of course, this final investment is critical. As one member states, "Our radios are our lifeline when going out on a call.") But team members donate their time and even mileage, so costs are kept low.

The White Earth Suicide Intervention Team is a low-cost, fully volunteer effort to address one of the most pressing social and health problems in Indian Country - suicide. Too often, communities (Indian or non-Indian) assume that without a large expenditure and without help from outside, progress against important social problems is not possible. WESIT provides compelling evidence to the contrary.

Lessons:

· Grassroots movements and community-based organizations can help tribal governments make important advances against critical social problems.

· There can be benefits to limiting the scope of an organization's mission. A narrow focus can help maintain volunteers, promote the best use of limited resources and maximize a group's impact.

· Well-trained and qualified staff, volunteer or paid, have a dual payoff for any organization - they do their work more effectively and they garner respect for the organization from the outside world

Photo Courtesy of National Park Service

Choctaw

Choctaw

LOCATION AND LAND STATUS

The Choctaw Reservation encompasses nine communities within the eastern central part of the state. They are Pearl River, Bogue Chitto, Tucker, Red Water, Standing Pine, Conehatta, Crystal Ridge, Bogue Homa, and Ocean Springs. Reservation lands are checkerboarded with non-Indian lands.

The reservation was established for members of the Choctaw Nation who refused to leave Mississippi during the 1830 removal efforts. Those remaining were awarded 104,320 acres. In 1918, the band was recognized by the federal government. By 1918, only one of 163 sections remained in Indian ownership. In 1944, the U.S. government sponsored a land-purchase program and acquired 16,805 acres in nine counties for the Choctaws. The title is held in trust by the United States.

CULTURE AND HISTORY

The Mississippi Band of Choctaw Indians is a member of the Choctaw Nation. The Choctaws have lived in the regions of present-day Mississippi and western Alabama for several hundred years. The Mississippi Band of Choctaw Indians are descendants of the relatively few Choctaw Indians who escaped the tribe's forced removal to Oklahoma in the 1830s. The band members sought refuge in the forests and swamplands, determined to remain in their ancestral territory.

Prior to the federal removal policy, Choctaw people lived throughout the Mississippi and Alabama region, farming the area's rich soil for subsistence in addition to hunting. Today, Choctaw people live in both Mississippi and Oklahoma, with the minority of the population residing in Mississippi. The Choctaws, whose name is an anglicized version of the word "Chahta," speak a Muskogean language. The Choctaws' first interaction with European explorers occurred in 1540 when the de Soto Expedition marched northwest across the continent. Though the Choctaws experienced a 150-year reprieve from foreign invaders after Hernando deSoto left, the encounter resulted in a bloody battle culminating in the deaths of 1,500 to 3,000 Choctaw people. Toward the end of the seventeenth century, French and English traders began to encroach upon Choctaw lands, with the French sending missionaries from its settlement at Biloxi to proselytize the Choctaws in 1699. While the region stood at the center of the geopolitical conflicts between the French, English, Spanish, and American governments, the Choctaws sided primarily with the French in the regional power struggle.

After American independence, the Choctaws signed the Treaty of Hopewell in 1785, which provided federal recognition of Choctaw sovereignty and established borders between the two nations. The parameters of this treaty were essentially voided by the steady influx of settlers onto Choctaw land. Subsequent treaties and Mississippi's ascension to statehood increased the pressure on Choctaw land. The situation culminated in President Andrew Jackson's policy of removing southeastern Native people to the newly proposed Indian Territory in Oklahoma. Despite internal dissent, but perhaps bowing to the inevitable, Chief Leflore of the Choctaws proposed a treaty to President Jackson for the westward removal of the tribe. The historic Treaty of Dancing Rabbit Creek, signed in 1830, called for the removal of the Choctaws from their ancestral homeland to Oklahoma. Article 14 of the treaty deemed removal voluntary and provided for land grants and citizenship for those Choctaws who chose to remain in Mississippi.

Approximately 5,000 Choctaws decided to stay in Mississippi. These were the most traditional members of the tribe, and they fell victim to pervasive land fraud and governmental corruption. Most of the remaining Choctaws found it necessary to withdraw to the region's hills and swamps where they lived as squatters on land to which they held no title. Seven communities, which coincide with the reservation's current community centers, grew from where these Choctaws congregated. The band's initial isolation largely accounts for the persistent use of Native language and their community identity. At least 90 percent of the Mississippi Band of Choctaw Indians' tribal members continue to speak the indigenous language, while English serves as the second language. Tribal members continue to practice traditional cultural elements.

A series of congressional hearings investigating the conditions of the Mississippi Choctaws resulted from a second attempt to remove the band to Oklahoma. The hearings led to the establishment, in 1918, of the Choctaw Agency on Indian Affairs in Philadelphia, Mississippi, and the provision of federal funds for both education and land purchase. The agency's establishment represented the first official recognition of the Choctaws living within Mississippi. In December 1944, reservations were created around the existing communities, the largest of which was at Pearl River. Following the reconstruction, the Choctaws drastically changed their mode of living and worked as sharecroppers on non-Indian-owned land. This semi-stable economic practice continued until the mechanization of farming during the 1950s made sharecropping obsolete. The 1950s represented a time of increased dependence on the federal government by the Choctaw people as local jobs in manufacturing proved unattainable. Many Choctaws worked as underpaid farm laborers until the Civil Rights Act of 1964, which opened up employment opportunities within the manufacturing industry. Many Choctaw women began to participate in the manufacturing industry toward the end of the 1960s.

Mississippi Band of Choctaw Indians Reservation
Federal reservation
Choctaw
Neshoba, Newton, Leake, Scott, Jones, Attala, Kemper, Jackson, and Winston counties, Mississippi

Mississippi Band of Choctaw Indians
101 Industrial Road
Choctaw, MS 39350
601-656-5251
601-650-3684 Fax
choctaw.org

Total area *(BIA realty, 2004)*
28,402.26 acres

Total area *(Tribal source, 2005)*
37,000 acres

Federal trust *(BIA realty, 2004)*
28,402.26 acres

Population *2000 census*
4,311

Tribal enrollment
(BIA labor report, 2001)
8,823

Tribal enrollment
(Tribal source, 2004)
9,100

Total labor force
2000 census
2,000

Total labor force
(BIA labor report, 2001)
4,868

Choctaw

High school graduate or higher
2000 census
59.3%

Bachelor's degree or higher
2000 census
5.8%

Unemployment rate *2000 census*
12.2%

Unemployment rate
(Tribal source, 2004)
1.2%

Per capita income *2000 census*
$7,444

Per capita income
(Tribal source, 2004)
$22,407

Since 1979, the Choctaws have experienced phenomenal economic growth, unparalleled by that of any community in Mississippi. Prior to their strides in developing industrial facilities on the reservation, the tribe often suffered an unemployment rate in excess of 75 percent. Today, Choctaw commercial and industrial facilities employ over 6,000 people, and the rate of unemployment on the reservation has dropped to less than 30 percent.

GOVERNMENT

The Choctaw Reservation is governed by a 16-member tribal council, which is elected from the nine major communities on the reservation. The council serves staggered, four-year terms. The chief of the Choctaw Reservation, who is elected at large from the entire reservation, serves for four years and presides over council meetings, serving as chief executive and administrative officer. Other officers include a vice-chief and a secretary-treasurer, elected by the council members. The council meets four times annually, with additional meetings called when necessary. The tribal council has been organized into a committee system composed of the following standing committees: health, education, governmental affairs, budget and finance, community development, economic development, and judicial affairs. The governmental headquarters are located in Pearl River, seven miles west of Philadelphia, Mississippi.

The Choctaw Tribal Constitution was adopted in 1945 under the terms of the Indian Reorganization Act. Prior to this constitution, a business committee, formed after the Indian Reorganization Act of 1934, managed tribal funds and made economic decisions.

The tribal police department employs 71-72 full-time law enforcement officers. The police department provides law enforcement on tribal lands. The tribe's judicial system exercises subject-matter jurisdiction over misdemeanors and civil matters. Felonies are under the jurisdiction of the federal government. The tribe is in the processing of getting a presiding federal magistrate. In 2004 a judicial building was built. It houses a jail and courts.

BUSINESS CORPORATION

The Mississippi Band of Choctaw Indians established the Choctaw Resort Development Enterprise. It owns and manages the Pearl River Resort in Choctaw. The resort is comprised of the tribes' Silver Star Hotel and Casino, the Dancing Rabbit Golf Club, and the Golden Moon Hotel and Casino. It also offers Geyser Falls Water Theme Park, Clearwater Key Beach, and the world's first Hard Rock Beach Club.

The Choctaw Shopping Center Enterprise oversees the operation of retail and residential developments on the reservation. Operations under its management include the Choctaw Office Supply, Ace Hardware, Conehatta Exxon, and Pearl River Exxon. This enterprise also manages an office and medical park, community shopping center, and a mixed-use retail, dining, and entertainment district. It also oversees timber management services available to commercial and private sector clients.

ECONOMY

In 2002, the Mississippi Choctaw Tribe was the second-largest employer in the state and the single largest employer in Neshoba County. In recent years, tribal industries alone have created over 9,300 permanent full-time jobs, with half of those going to non-Indians. In addition to its very lucrative gaming operations, the tribe operates a number of businesses that help sustain its growing economy. The Mississippi Choctaws have become a formidable economic force in the region and have extended their pursuits into international markets, including a wire harness plant in Mexico, which employs about 1,300 people.

Government as Employer. The tribe employs over 1,800 individuals in its governmental departments and programs and over 7,500 individuals throughout its businesses and organizations.

Economic Development Projects. The Mississippi Band of Choctaw Indians is in the process of developing the Choctaw Town Center. The center is a master-planned business district in Pearl River, Mississippi. Phase I of the project has been completed and houses a Piggly Wiggly, Dollar General, ACE Hardware, Exxon, and several other businesses. Phase II will include a video rental store, clothing outlet, and dry cleaners. Future expansions will include an elderly activity center for elders, a 300-acre lake, an exercise trail, a restaurant row, a hotel, and a mixed-use retail, residential, and entertainment area.

In 2002, the tribe received a grant from the Department of Energy to conduct a feasibility study for alternative energy sources on the reservation.

Agriculture and Livestock. The tribe's department of agriculture and rural development operates a tribal farm, which hosts a Farmer's Market, a community gardening program, a 4-H Youth Development Program, and numerous community activities and services geared to promoting health and nutrition.

Forestry. The tribal forestry program manages the tribe's timber resources. Program services include conducting prescribed burns, herbicide applications for site preparation, reforestation, timber stand improvements, and forest pest management.

Gaming. The Choctaw Resort Development Enterprise owns and manages the Pearl River Resort in Choctaw. The resort is comprised of the tribes' Silver Star Hotel and Casino, the Dancing Rabbit Golf Club, and the Golden Moon Hotel and Casino. It also offers Geyser Falls Water Theme Park, Clearwater Key Beach, and the world's first Hard Rock Beach Club. Plans for expansion include the construction of a fairground, an expo hall, and a stadium that can seat 10,000 people. Those venues will be open by the end of 2005. The Mississippi Choctaw gaming facilities are the only casinos in Mississippi located on tribal lands.

The Silver Star Resort and Casino was the tribe's first gaming facility. It opened in July 1994. It is open 24 hours a day and employs 2,400 people. The casino offers over 3,020 slot machines, 100 table games, and 12 poker tables. Facilities include six restaurants, six bars, six retail shops, a conference center, a parking garbage, and a hotel. The hotel is a 12-story-high structure that features 500 guest rooms. The complex also includes the Star Car Autotorium and the Startacular pyrotechnic facility. The casino is connected to the Golden Moon Hotel and Casino by a sky bridge that crosses Highway 16.

The Golden Moon Hotel and Casino offers 1,750 slots/VLTs and 39 table games. The adjacent hotel offers a convention center, 572 guest rooms, 6 restaurants, and 2 entertainment venues. It features a fitness center, a health spa, a beauty salon, a barbershop, and indoor and outdoor swimming facilities. The hotel tower is 28 stories high, and the main entry features a 20-foot waterfall.

Dancing Rabbit Golf Club, also adjacent to the Silver Star Resort and Casino, offers a 36-hole golf course that has rated one of the top 100 courses in the nation by *Golf Digest*, *Golf and Travel*, and *Golf Magazine*. Located in a breathtaking natural setting, the club contains over two miles of creeks and streams that weave through the course. The clubhouse offers a pro shop, restaurant, full locker facilities, and eight luxurious guest rooms.

Construction. The tribe owns the Choctaw Development Enterprise, the Choctaw Construction Enterprise, and the Chahta Development Company, all enterprises in the construction industry.

Choctaw Development Enterprise contracts for roads, bridges, schools, sports arenas, factories, and several other construction opportunities. It employs up to 250 people per project. Choctaw Construction Enterprise, formerly Choctaw/Yates Construction Enterprise, contracts on national construction projects, including casinos, hotels, and office buildings.

The Chahta Development Company, a construction contractor, employs 70 people and generates $4.5 million annually in construction contracts. A private stock company directed by a volunteer Choctaw board, the Chahta Development Company has undertaken a number of construction projects throughout the community. This company was established in 1969 and reinvests its profits in new projects rather than distributing them to stockholders.

Manufacturing. The tribe operates numerous manufacturing facilities throughout the reservation, including Chahta Enterprise, Choctaw Manufacturing Enterprise, First American Plastic Molding Enterprise, First American Printing and Direct Mail, Choctaw Electronics, and American Greetings Enterprise.

Chahta Enterprise, located in Pearl River, produces wiring harnesses for the automotive industry. With plants throughout Mississippi and in the Enpalme Industrial Park in the state of Sonora, Mexico, Chahta Enterprise has 200 employees in Mississippi and over 1,900 in Mexico. Operations generate over $80 million in annual sales. Major clients include Ford Motor Company, Delphi Packard, and Matrix Systems.

First American Plastic Molding, located in Ocean Springs, manufactures plastic injection molding. Plants are located in Ocean Springs, South Beloit, Illinois, and El Paso, Texas. The company employs over 100 people. It is a joint venture between the tribe and Quad, Inc. whose major clients are McDonald's, Harman-Becker International, Pepsi, and Panasonic. The company generates in excess of $10 million per year. First American Printing and Direct Mail, also located in Ocean Springs, produces commercial printing, direct mail, and inquiry fulfillment materials. The company employs approximately 95 individuals. It is the largest commercial printer in the Mississippi Gulf Coast area, and generates almost $7 million in annual sales.

Choctaw Electronics is located in Pearl River. It manufactures automotive speakers. An additional plant was opened in the Enpalme Industrial Park in the state of Sonora, Mexico in 1999. The company employs over 200 people in both countries. This company is a joint venture with Harman-Becker International. American Greetings, located in Pearl River, produces hand-finished greeting cards. The company's major clients are Wal-Mart and Kmart. It employs almost 200 people. American Greetings was created in 1981 and financed by an industrial revenue bond issued by the local non-Indian government. This contract was a first for tribal enterprises.

Industrial Parks. In 1971 the tribe completed the first phase of what has become an 80-acre industrial park. The Choctaw Industrial Park includes 512,000 square feet of operational manufacturing space. The park offers a paved access road, paved and divided parking facilities, lighting, fencing, an elevated water tank and water connections, and sewage facilities. The park

houses Packard Electric Division of General Motors, a Ford Motors factory, and the Oxford Speaker Company.

Real Estate/Commercial Development. The tribal estate program manages land leases of tribal lands to tribal members and entities. Services include a survey plan and a description for each lease. The program also provides vehicle affidavit services to reservation residents.

The Choctaw Housing Authority has completed the construction of almost 800 homes on the reservation in the past 15 years. In 2002, it completed the River Oaks Place development. The subdivision features a play area, an athletic course, and picnic areas.

In 2004, the tribe was constructing a corporate apartment development within the Town Center development. The Town Center Villas will offer one and two bedroom, one and two story units. Pre-leasing efforts are currently in operation.

Services and Retail. The tribe owns the Choctaw Shopping Center in Pearl River. The tribe owns 80,571 square feet of commercial service and retail space and is continuously looking for ways to grow in this area.

Tourism and Recreation. The tribe hosts the annual Choctaw Indian Fair. Festivities include the World Series of Stickball. This celebration began in 1949. It is organized by the tribe's committee on economic development. The Choctaw Cultural Center opened in 2000. It features cultural artifacts and educational displays.

The reservation is located near numerous tourist attractions. Areas of interest include Nanih Waiya Cave and Mound, Indian Mission Site, Philadelphia Historic District, Williams Brothers Store, and the Neshoba County Fair Grounds.

INFRASTRUCTURE

The reservation is located on Highway 16 with Interstate 20 (east-west) and 55 (north-south) running approximately 50 miles from the reservation. The Natchez Trace Parkway, a major tourist route, is only 27 miles west of the Choctaw Industrial Park.

Water Supply. The tribe's public works department operates and maintains water treatment facilities in the communities of Pearl River, Bogue Chitto, and Conehatta. Approximately 1,170 residential units, 3,500 to 4,000 individuals, are served by the water system. The department is staffed by 12 employees and is located in Pearl River.

The Pearl River system consists of two water wells ranging from 930 to 1,120 feet deep. A third well, that exceeds 1,100 feet in depth, is currently under construction and should be operational in spring 2005. Elevated tanks in the community pressurize the system and provide over one million gallons of storage capacity.

The Bogue Chitto system consists of two wells ranging from 320 to 370 feet deep. Each is capable of producing up to 260 gallons per minute. One elevated storage tank pressurizes the system and provides over 130,000 gallons of storage capacity.

The Conehatta system consists of two wells ranging from 625 to 638 feet deep. The wells have the capacity to produce up to 200 gallons per minute. Wastewater collection and treatment facilities are located in Pearl River, Bogue Chitto, Conehatta, Crystal Ridge, Standing Pine, and Tucker. They serve approximately 1,400 homes. The wastewater system in Pearl River consists of

Choctaw

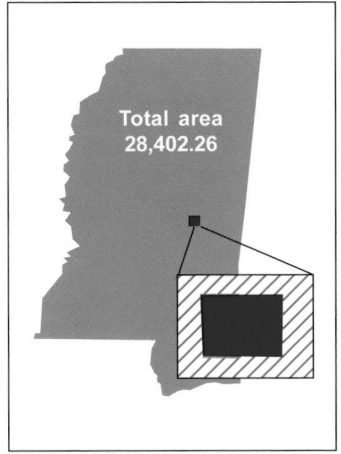

Total area
28,402.26

a treatment facility and wastewater lagoon. The Conehatta system consists of three wastewater lagoons and a small package plant. The Tucker community is served by a lagoon and package plant. Bogue Chitto and Crystal Ridge are served by wastewater lagoons.

Transportation. Air service is available in Philadelphia, four miles from the reservation; in Meridian, 50 miles southeast of the reservation; and in Jackson, 65 miles west of the reservation. The tribe has its own bus system, the Choctaw Transit Authority, which links six of the communities and transports tribal members to the industrial park. Merchants Truck Line, Shippers Express, Olen Burrage Trucking Company, and Spector Freight System provide motor freight service to the area. Illinois Central Gulf provides rail freight service from the nearby town of Philadelphia. The industrial park is also 10 miles from the port of Pascagoula, which has access to deepwater world shipping lanes.

COMMUNITY FACILITIES AND SERVICES
The tribe operates daycare centers in all of the reservation communities. There are community centers in each of the nine communities within the reservation. New facilities were completed in Bogue Homa, Crystal Ridge, and Standing Pine in 2002. Community programs include the tribal youth program, summer youth programs, Save the Children program, and youth recreation programs. The family and community services department oversees the behavioral health, family emergency assistance, food distribution, social and elderly nutrition, and social services programs. The tribal office complex and council building are located in Pearl River. In addition, the tribe operates a juvenile detention center.

Public Safety. The tribe operates its own fire department.

Education. The tribe operates the Choctaw Tribal School System on the reservation. The system includes six elementary schools, a middle school, and one boarding high school under contract with the BIA. All tribal schools are fully accredited by the state and the Southern Association of Colleges and Schools. The Choctaw Tribal School System serves more than 1,700 students and is the largest unified and locally controlled Native

American school system in the country. The tribe also provides preschool, childcare, adult education, vocational, and postsecondary education programs. Scholarships are available for tribal members attending postsecondary programs. In addition to financial assistance, the tribe's scholarship program provides pre-counseling services that include advising and assistance with applications and enrollment procedures.

The tribe was the first in the United States to endorse Education 2000 and the first to join NASA to provide a Teacher Enhancement Center.

Health Care. In 1994, the tribe entered into a self-governance compact with the federal government for its health care services. The compact allowed for the tribe to assume control over the health services provided to tribal members. The tribe operates a health care system that includes an 18-bed inpatient facility, an outpatient center, a women's wellness center, a dental clinic, and a diabetic clinic. Services also include a Tuberculosis control and eradication team, a pre- and post-partum care system, an HIV/AIDS education program, mammography services, and disability determination clinics. The Choctaw Health Center was a finalist for the 1999 Honoring Contributions in the Governance of American Indian Nations Award.

The tribe also owns and operates the Choctaw Residential Center. It is a 120-bed licensed nursing facility that provides comprehensive nursing care to tribal and non-tribal members. The center is located on 10 lakeside acres. It employs 119 people. A kidney dialysis center services tribal members.

ENVIRONMENTAL CONCERNS
The tribe's environmental program office strives to provide services that protect the environment while incorporating traditional values and culture. It coordinates reservation-wide testing of tribal homes and buildings for radon gas. (A federal environmental program funds this project). The tribe's environmental program also operates a recycling program in the Pearl River community. It is successful and generates substantial income for the tribe.

Honoring Nations Honoree 1999

Choctaw Health Center, Mississippi Band of Choctaw Indians

In the 1960s, members of the Mississippi Band of Choctaw subsisted in miserable economic and health conditions. Nearly all tribal housing was substandard (90 percent of tribal members lived in units with no plumbing and 30 percent had no electricity), life expectancy was less than 50 years of age, and the Tribe's infant mortality rate was among the highest in the United States.

At that time, the Indian Health Services (IHS) was the primary provider of reservation health care services and spent approximately $1,000 per tribal member per year on physical, mental, and dental health care. But by the early 1970s, the Choctaw tribal government determined that it would be better for the Tribe to work on its own to find solutions to its citizens' health problems. Over the next decade, the Tribe worked consistently to contract with the IHS to take over management control of reservation health programs. It obtained IHS funds to build a new hospital (the 58,800 square foot Choctaw Health Center in

Philadelphia, MS opened in 1975) and had contracted all of the IHS's public health programs, some critical support services, and a few direct medical care activities. Still, it was not until the mid-1980s that the Tribe was able to take over the management of all health services: On January 1, 1984, the Mississippi Band of Choctaw became one of the first Indian nations to assume responsibility for the management of a complete tribal health care system.

Despite this high degree of management control, health conditions among the Choctaw had improved only marginally since the 1960s. Health system managers pointed to funding as one of their main problems. For example, even though the Tribe had contracted for control of the hospital, IHS funding covered only 38 percent of the community's established need. At a deeper level, the problem lay in the stipulations of Public Law 93-638, the act that allows tribes to contract with the federal government to take over management of service programs. Under the law, an existing program's budget defines the parameters of a "638" contract. This restriction made it difficult for the Choctaw to create new programs and to move funds between programs in response to need or according to tribal priorities - and left many vital programs underfunded.

Therefore, in 1994, the Tribe took the final step in breaking away from the restraints of federal government control: It entered into a self-governance compact for all health care services and funds designated for the Choctaw. Essentially, self-governance compacts are block grants to tribes. They transfer all of the federal government's budget in a particular service area to a tribe without stipulating the specific programs in which the money must be used. Under a compact, a tribe can set its own priorities, develop its own programs, and create a truly indigenous system of service provision. Ideally, compacts free Indian nations' program planners from thinking in the same boxes that federal program developers do. While there are drawbacks to compacts (in particular, the negotiation phase can be more difficult), the Choctaw felt that having tried self-management, self-governance of health care would be an even better option.

Indeed, the Choctaw's five years of self-governance over health care have built successfully on the previous two decades of self-management. Since compacting, the Tribe has achieved tremendous strides against the health problems that have plagued community members, and it has put in place a health system specifically designed to meet members' needs. For example, the Choctaw Health Center's programs have

helped to improve the Tribe's immunization rate for children (from 70 percent in 1990 to 95 percent in 1999) and to increase the average life span for tribal citizens (which reach 68 years in 1999). With seven full time physicians and over 240 employees, the Health Center's services now include a 18-bed inpatient acute care unit, a 24-hour emergency medical services department, outpatient and dental clinics, a mental health center, a diabetes clinic, a disability clinic, a women's wellness center, and a variety of preventative programs.

In addition to these improved and expanded service offerings, the Tribe has implemented an efficient billing and records system and reduced the red tape typically associated with third party billing.

The Mississippi Band of Choctaw's methodical take over of federally funded health care programs and it systematic development of the Choctaw Health Center are a model of the opportunities presented by the U.S. government's self-determination and self-governance legislation. Today, the Tribe - not the Indian Health Service or other federal agencies - "calls the shots" in its health care delivery system. The Tribe hires the providers it chooses. It contracts with off-reservation providers for specialized care. Choctaw children are born in state-of-the-art local facilities instead of low-income patient wards in urban hospitals, and the Tribe has developed many other preventative and direct-care health programs that are specifically suited to member needs. Because the Mississippi Band of Choctaw Indians sets its own priorities in health care, it has been able to significantly improve health conditions among its citizens - a remarkable example of the effective exercise of sovereignty.

Choctaw

Honoring Nations
Honoree 1999

Text in its entirety from:
The Harvard Project On
American Indian Economic
Development

John F. Kennedy School
of Government
Harvard University

H onoring Nations Honoree 2003

Choctaw Community Injury Prevention Program, Choctaw Health Center
Mississippi Band of Choctaw Indians, Choctaw, MS

In 2000, two Mississippi Choctaw citizens organized the Choctaw Community Injury Prevention Program to combat the reservation community's rising level of preventable injuries and accidental deaths. In hopes of significantly reducing emergency room visits, their efforts-as well as the efforts of other volunteers inspired by their example-have introduced thousands of Choctaw children and adults to safety education and resulted in the distribution of hundreds of child safety seats and bicycle helmets. The Choctaw Community Injury Prevention Program proves that the programmatic efforts of concerned individuals can make headway against one of Indian Country's most pervasive and daunting problems.

Accidental deaths and preventable injuries exact an enormous toll on American Indian communities. For example, American Indian deaths from motor vehicle accidents occur at over twice the rate of such deaths in the US generally. The overall accidental death rate among American Indians is nearly twice that among the US population at-large. The Mississippi Band of Choctaw has not been exempt from these sobering statistics. In 1996, 11 percent of Mississippi Choctaw men and 14 percent of women had experienced an accidental death in their family. In addition, approximately 10 percent of all adults

reported that a household member had been injured as a result of a motor vehicle accident.

At Mississippi Choctaw in the late 1990s, several of the causes of these accidental deaths and preventable injuries were easily identifiable. The reservation's many dark, winding, and unpaved roads resulted in frequent single car accidents. The Tribe's phenomenal economic success brought thousands of employees and visitors to the reservation each day, creating traffic congestion and stressful road conditions. In spite of these dangers, only 30 percent of male and 26 percent of female tribal members used seat belts while riding in or operating a motor vehicle. The resulting injuries and deaths had a devastating impact upon individuals and families and took an increasingly high toll on the Choctaw community in the form of escalating health care costs. As early as 1992, injury rates were identified as one of the leading causes of health care cost increases on the reservation.

Despite the enormity of these problems, the Tribe lacked any programmatic means to address preventable injuries and accidental deaths; indeed, such programs are rare in Indian Country.

Honoring Nations
Honoree 2003

Text in its entirety from:
The Harvard Project On
American Indian Economic
Development

John F. Kennedy School
of Government
Harvard University

Choctaw

Honoring Nations
Honoree 2003

Text in its entirety from:
The Harvard Project On
American Indian Economic
Development

John F. Kennedy School
of Government
Harvard University

In 2000, two Choctaw citizens who were deeply troubled by a series of accidents that killed or injured young children on the reservation set out to make a change. Under the supervision of the director of the Community Health Services Department, and working within the Choctaw Health Center, they established the Choctaw Community Injury Prevention Program. From the initial efforts of these two citizens, the Program now relies on more than fifty volunteers who educate parents, children, teachers, health providers, law enforcement officials, tribal leaders, and other individuals and organizations in injury and accidental death prevention. Volunteers host injury awareness and prevention activities within the seven Choctaw tribal schools for the benefit of children. At the same time, the Program works through Choctaw community groups, the Choctaw Newspaper, Choctaw Cable, and other public forums to reach the population at-large.

The Program pursues a number of clear objectives. It works to improve the use of seatbelts among Choctaw drivers and to secure adult participation in ensuring that all passengers wear seatbelts or are secured in appropriate child safety seats. The Program also seeks to reduce the DUI/DWI rates among tribal citizens and to enhance the enforcement of the Mississippi Department of Highway Safety and Passenger Restraint Laws on the reservation. As its successes in improving transportation safety have grown, the Program has expanded its focus to include bicycle safety, home safety, and poison control.

The Choctaw Community Injury Prevention Program has realized impressive and measurable successes. The Program has instructed over sixteen hundred Choctaw children up to age eighteen in safety awareness and injury prevention. It has distributed over two thousand toddler and infant safety seats to Choctaw and non-Indian parents across the state of Mississippi, and assisted other state programs in raising awareness. Utilizing funds from a grant, the Program has established the first and only designated safety seat Fitting Station in Mississippi. It has encouraged a year of "Click It or Ticket" checks to ensure the appropriate use of safety equipment. And, by the end of 2004, Program inspectors will have visited over two hundred homes of children fourteen and younger to install needed fire alarms, fire extinguishers, carbon monoxide alarms, door latches, outlet covers, and other safety devices.

These preventative measures are enhancing the safety of Choctaw citizens. Through the Program's public education, more Choctaw adults are now aware of the importance of using seat belts and child restraint seats in motor vehicles. "Click It or Ticket" inspections of 3,210 cars measured an increase in child seat belt and safety seat use from 63 to 78 percent over a ten month period. Emergency room statistics are equally impressive. Between 1998 and 2002, emergency room visits for preventable injuries dropped by more than 25 percent (from 4,106 to 3,012), while injuries resulting from motor vehicle accidents between 1999 and 2002 were cut in half (from 533 to 272).

These successes are particularly notable considering the Program's structure. The Program's extensive volunteer network stands in stark contrast to an earlier effort when, in 1992, the Choctaw Health Center's Community Health Services Department received an IHS Community Injury Prevention Program grant and staffed a small office to conduct all prevention activities. Prevention by nature, however, requires broad informational outreach that is impossible to achieve with limited funding and employee efforts alone. Thus, in 2000, it was the passionate investment of volunteers that reestablished the Choctaw Community Injury Prevention Program as an ongoing concern. Two dedicated citizens have inspired years of service from dozens of additional volunteers who work through various tribal and non-tribal entities. Not only does this volunteer commitment ensure the long-term sustainability of the Program, but it also serves as an inspiration throughout the Choctaw community which sees, first-hand, that volunteers can bring about widespread positive change.

The Choctaw Community Injury Prevention Program also convincingly demonstrates that concerned community members are among those best positioned to respond to community crises. The early volunteers' familiarity with the Choctaw community, combined with their ability to draw judiciously from non-Choctaw injury prevention programs, resulted in remarkably productive tribal-non-tribal partnerships. For example, the Program adapted the Mississippi SafeKids program to meet the Tribe's specific needs and quickly maximized Choctaw participation in the SafeKids model. This partnership enables the Mississippi Choctaw to leverage the resources, expertise, and funding sources of a larger prevention effort. The Program receives continuing support from Mississippi SafeKids, the Office of Public Highway Safety, Ford Motor Company, General Motors, the United Auto Workers, and National SafeKids. It initially secured a grant to distribute one thousand booster seats through the efforts of the Mississippi SafeKids director and is eligible for still other grants as a SafeKids coalition member. Its volunteers have a statewide professional network available for their assistance.

Finally, it should be noted that the Program's significant reduction of preventable injuries and accidental deaths through community awareness activities has lessened the financial burden accidents place on the Choctaw health care system. The IHS has never sufficiently covered the costs of building, maintaining, and staffing adequate health facilities in Indian Country, and tribes have felt pressured to raise supplementary resources or limit their service offerings. Through the success of its Injury Prevention Program, however, the Mississippi Choctaw Tribe is experiencing less of this pressure from unmet needs. Their accident prevention has reduced demands on the tribal health care system and promoted a more optimal distribution of health care resources. The Program's strategic efforts mean these benefits will continue: it works closely with other tribal and non-tribal health programs and integrates its injury prevention education with the full range of community health and treatment programs.

Accidents are the leading cause of death among American Indians. Through the Choctaw Community Injury Prevention Program, the Mississippi Choctaw have begun to address this devastating problem. The passionate efforts of volunteers and the partnerships they have formed with tribal schools, community clubs, the Choctaw newspaper, Choctaw cable station, and non-tribal injury prevention programs have resulted in the education of community members in safety awareness and in measurable decreases in preventable injuries and accidental deaths. Every success the Program enjoys is a celebration of prolonged and protected Choctaw lives.

Honoring Nations Honoree 2003

Family Violence and Victim's Services, Department of Family and Community Services, The Mississippi Band of Choctaw Indians, Choctaw, MS

Responding to the alarming frequency of domestic abuse and sexual assault among the Mississippi Band of Choctaw Indians, the Tribe's Department of Family and Community Services created the Family Violence and Victim's Services Program (FVVS) in 1999. By coordinating various agencies-including Choctaw Law & Order, Choctaw Social Services, Choctaw Behavioral Health, and the US Attorney's Office-FVVS ensures that victims receive comprehensive care and that perpetrators are dealt with appropriately. Just as essential as promoting the overall physical and emotional health of the Tribe, FVVS is changing the citizens' attitude about an important topic that often remains unaddressed.

Although the Mississippi Band of Choctaw Indians' 30-year economic renaissance is widely cited as being one of Indian Country's greatest success stories, several aspects of the Tribe's social health have been slow to improve. In the late 1990s the Tribe commissioned a Mississippi State University study which found that a surprisingly high number of Choctaw homes experienced serious social problems including poor marital relations, verbal and physical aggression, sexual abuse, substance abuse, mental illness, and the intergenerational transmission of trauma resulting from cultural genocide. All of these problems contributed to a disturbing pattern of domestic violence.

Domestic violence was rising to epidemic levels among the Mississippi Choctaw. It was also one of the most underreported crimes. Many Choctaw offenders considered domestic violence to be an "internal family matter" rather than a criminal offense. Sadly, violence in the household is frequently tolerated and a pervasive attitude exists that there is nothing unusual or wrong about abusing family members. Not surprisingly, victims often remain silent. They may fear a stigma for attempting to end violent relationships or for carrying family matters into the courts. Victims also might feel that domestic abuse is not their problem, but the perpetrator's. Or, they become convinced that violence is an acceptable method of marital and familial interaction. As one Choctaw woman learned from her mother-in-law: "Your husband only does this to you because he loves you and wants you to stay."

Such learned attitudes-which, it should be noted, are typical in Native and non-Native communities everywhere-allow domestic violence to quietly fester. Unfortunately, the intergenerational toll of domestic violence is high; research finds that children who grow up in homes wracked by violence are more likely to become victims or perpetrators of violence in their own homes.

In 1999, the Mississippi Band of Choctaw Indians' tribal government decided that something had to be done to abate domestic violence. It decided to launch a domestic violence prevention program that would protect victims, monitor and reeducate perpetrators, and break the cycle of silence. Thus, the Family Violence and Victim's Services Program (FVVS) was born. Administered under the Band's Department of Family and Community Services, the Program brings together the financial, human, and technical resources of five different grant projects. It is staffed by a program director (who is also an attorney), a legal secretary, a victim assistance coordinator, a women's advocate, a victim assistance therapist, and a family violence counselor.

The Program works through several complementary strategies to combat domestic violence and its aftermath. Drawing upon the legal expertise of the staff, FVVS drafts and helps enforce laws that can help stem family violence. In 2000, for example, it drafted a Choctaw domestic violence code that was subsequently enacted by the Tribal Council. Since then, FVVS has consistently worked to expand the code's reach and effectiveness in combating domestic violence; in both 2002 and 2003, it augmented and revised the code. Based upon these successes, FVVS is part of a committee that is now drafting a complementary code that will protect the rights of vulnerable adults, particularly the elderly and infirm.

FVVS staff works to offer victims of domestic violence the kind of support and protection that was once lacking. For example, FVVS initiates one-on-one contact with all victims of domestic violence or sexual assault who are either identified in police reports or approach the Program for services. It offers legal representation for those victims who seek protection orders against their abusers. The Program provides victims assistance in identifying alternate housing, finding employment, accessing transportation to court or to a shelter, and receiving translation during court proceedings. Counseling and therapy are offered to both victims and perpetrators, serving the latter largely through a court-mandated Batterer's Reeducation Program which it supervises.

While tailored to the needs of the Choctaw community, FVVS offers more services than most programs in the state of Mississippi. This is the result, in part, of FVVS's extensive coordination with relevant agencies, including the Choctaw Social Services, Choctaw Health Center, Choctaw Behavioral Health, Choctaw Law and Order, and the Choctaw Attorney General's Office. This collaboration ensures that FVVS readily addresses victims' physical, emotional, and legal needs under a single roof. Regular meetings of representatives allow for a review of each month's challenges and successes in order to continue to enhance victims' services. Interagency cooperation also provides necessary cross-discipline expertise. For example, Choctaw Health Center nurses now possess excellent equipment for documenting abuse and are trained to take photos that meet court standards. Such collaboration reduces frictions among agencies, allowing all professionals to focus on victims' needs. This is especially critical to Choctaw victims who may request services from any one of the Tribe's seven communities within ten counties.

The Program also works to raise community awareness. For instance, FVVS established resource centers, in partner facilities, that provide information about its services and educational booklets on topics such as domestic violence, rape, sexual assault, and elder abuse. Further awareness is cultivated through an in-house resource center that consists of educational booklets, videos, and children's games dealing with family violence and anger. Every October FVVS marks Domestic Violence Awareness Month by sponsoring events and hanging "Stop Domestic Violence" banners in each Choctaw community. The Program routinely publishes ar-

Honoring Nations
Honoree 2003

Text in its entirety from:
The Harvard Project On
American Indian Economic
Development

John F. Kennedy School
of Government
Harvard University

Choctaw

Honoring Nations
Honoree 2003

Text in its entirety from:
The Harvard Project On
American Indian Economic
Development

John F. Kennedy School
of Government
Harvard University

ticles in the Choctaw Community News and disseminates flyers, posters, brochures, and promotional items.

FVVS's commitment to drafting strict domestic violence codes, supporting victims through effective interagency collaboration, and raising public awareness has produced remarkable successes. Most notably, the Tribe has realized a significant increase in the identification and reporting of domestic violence crimes. In 1998 and 1999, Choctaw Law and Order received 542 calls reporting domestic violence. In 2000, 2001, and 2002, however, following the establishment of FVVS, it received 1,111 calls. These calls resulted in 457 arrests for domestic violence crimes and over 682 FVVS follow-up contacts with domestic violence victims. FVVS obtained more than 250 court orders for clients seeking protection from their abusers and graduated more than 200 perpetrators from their Batterer's Reeducation Program.

Behind the numbers, Family Violence and Victim's Services positively changes people's lives. For example, one Batterer's Reeducation Program participant reflected that he never realized he was part of the cycle of continued violence. He truly thought that domestic violence was a part of life. However, with the assistance of FVVS, he now understands why domestic violence is not acceptable and sees how he can change his behaviors.

These numbers and similar rehabilitation stories offer compelling evidence that FVVS is succeeding in changing Choctaw perceptions of domestic violence. FVVS is shifting Choctaw citizens' tendency to willfully ignore or dismiss incidents of domestic violence. Now, tribal citizens discuss and report its occurrence more openly. While domestic violence was once a private family matter, it is increasingly viewed as a serious public health issue that affects the entire tribal community. FVVS is moving rapidly toward the realization of one of its long-term goals: that every Choctaw citizen embraces a zero-tolerance attitude with respect to domestic violence. Not only the collaborating agencies, but also the tribal government offers its support of this agenda. With this vital support, the Program's activities and actions command respect.

These accomplishments are the result of four strategic decisions that can inform other Indian nations' efforts to develop their own violence prevention programs. First, FVVS is the result of an impressive coordination of tribal revenue and five funding sources, ranging from the US Department of Justice's STOP Violence Against Indian Women grant program to the state of Mississippi's Department of Public Safety, which administers a fund through the State's Victims of Crime Act. While seeking and maintaining financing for a multi-function violence prevention program is challenging, it generates distinct advantages for Choctaw citizens. Rather than seeking services from separate organizations, they can access a variety of victim-oriented services from a single operation. And FVVS is better able to synchronize its services, which helps it most effectively promote the safety, health, and autonomy of domestic violence victims and their families.

Second, FVVS replicates this focus on coordination in its interagency partnerships-partnerships that are vital for serving victims' interests and to the overall success of the Program. For example, FVVS is an active member of the Protocol Committee charged with the task of developing the procedures that guide interagency coordination. The Committee's monthly meetings refine the effectiveness of sharing information, strengthening communication, increasing efficiency, and providing maximum protection for domestic violence victims. Through such procedures and protocols, and through less formal outreach, FVVS is able to work in conjunction with Choctaw law enforcement agencies, health services, and the judiciary. These forms of inter-agency familiarity and reliance make law enforcement and case management more efficient and comprehensive, and enhance their abilities to tailor services to individual victims and offenders. For instance, Choctaw Law and Order alerts FVVS of the arrest of an offender who has repeatedly been released on bail, FVVS may contact the tribal attorney general who may, in turn, alert the judge to the offender's criminal history and request that bail be denied.

Third, FVVS has undertaken important government-building work in drafting and enacting the Choctaw domestic violence code. Through its grounding in Choctaw culture, the code is both enforceable and effective. It clearly states that "violence against family members is not in keeping with Choctaw values...that hold the family sacred." Accordingly, the code contains strict guidelines for the treatment of domestic violence crimes including mandatory arrest, a twenty-four hour holding period, and a mandatory twenty-six week Batterer's Reeducation Program for offenders, a firearms prohibition and enhanced sentencing for repeat offenders, and a no-drop policy for the prosecution. Initially mirroring federal law, these guidelines now acknowledge Choctaw cultural realities. For example, the firearms prohibition modification takes tribal hunting needs into account, and the reeducation program eliminated negative reinforcement already influencing offenders in their daily lives. Notably, the code also formalizes the roles of FVVS' partners, and complements and enhances the partnerships noted above. Rightly, the Choctaw domestic violence code has become a model for other tribes to learn from.

Fourth, FVVS strengthens the self-determination of the Mississippi Choctaw by strengthening its individual citizens. By assisting individuals and families to overcome a problem that is connected to other debilitating social problems, the Tribe is addressing a national crisis. The Program offers holistic and accessible services that foster a sense of empowerment in former victims, enabling them to make better choices for themselves and their families. FVVS's Batterer's Reeducation Program encourages offenders to evaluate and learn from their behaviors. As one offender contemplated his life before the Program, he remarked: "I suppose either I or someone else would be dead." FVVS literally helps the Mississippi Band of Choctaw to build human capital through healing and also prevents victimization and/or loss of tribal citizens.

An Indian nation's human capital deserves such an investment. In changing community attitudes toward domestic violence, FVVS enhances its own citizens' respect for their own and other individuals' worth. The community-wide zero-tolerance attitude FVVS is striving for will undoubtedly result in further decreases in domestic violence crimes, and in turn, increase the health and productivity of the Mississippi Band of Choctaw Indian's most precious resource: its own people.

MONTANA

Blackfeet

Blackfeet

LOCATION AND LAND STATUS

The Blackfeet Reservation is located in northwestern Montana near the United States/Canada border. The reservation's present size represents a significant depletion of the original Blackfeet territory. In 1855, Blackfeet lands extended through much of northern Montana west of the Rockies. The first treaty to affect the Blackfeet was the 1851 Treaty of Fort Laramie in which, despite the absence of any Blackfeet negotiators, the boundaries of the Blackfeet Nation were limited and set. In 1888, Congress ratified and confirmed the Sweetgrass Hills Treaty, which established the bulk of the reservation and also introduced the allotment system of individual land ownership. In an 1896 treaty, the Blackfeet ceded land, which was later to become Glacier National Park.

PHYSICAL DESCRIPTION

The Blackfeet Reservation is bordered by the Province of Alberta, Canada, on the north and Glacier National Park and Lewis and Clark National Forest on the west. It is bordered by Birch Creek on the south and Cut Bank Creek on the east. The general topography consists of rolling plains rising westward to the forests of the Continental Divide. The average elevation ranges from 4,000 to 5,000 feet; the highest elevation is 9,000 feet at Chief Mountain on the northwest boundary.

CULTURE AND HISTORY

The Blackfeet Nation consists of Pikuni/Peigan, North Peigan Pikuni, Blood/Kaini, and Blackfoot/Siksika people. The groups are all members of the greater Algonquian linguistic family, and they share common cultural and religious beliefs as well. The Blackfeet of Montana are the only Plains group to have a reservation in the United States; the other three groups occupy reserves in southern Alberta, Canada. Initial contact between the Montana band of Blackfeet and Euro-American settlers occurred during the mid-1700s as fur traders and, later, railroad men began exploring the region. In exchange for their land, the federal government made treaties with the Blackfeet that promised peace, protection, agricultural goods, money, and inviolate reservations, all promises that were eventually breached.

Traditionally, buffalos represented an essential resource for the Blackfeet, providing food and materials for clothing, lodging, and tool making. In 1874 the northwest buffalo herd was estimated at four million; five years later the vast majority had been exterminated, largely by white traders and settlers. With their traditional economy devastated, the Blackfeet became dependent upon the federal government for food and supplies, and hence suffered greatly, both materially and spiritually. By 1900 approximately 2,000 Blackfeet lived near Badger Creek, the site of the Blackfeet Agency. Catholic missionaries, who introduced Euro-American educational systems and Catholic religious practices to the tribe as early as 1859, were joined by the government in these education efforts. By the early 1900s, a government boarding school and day schools were established. During this period the government began pressuring tribal members to embrace farming for subsistence, though by 1915 the government was emphasizing raising livestock instead. Unfortunately, a 1919 drought, coupled with low beef prices, forced many Blackfeet to sell or give up their allotted lands because of nonpayment of taxes. Prospects improved somewhat during the 1920s when a forward-thinking superintendent implemented a five-year industrial program, which emphasized small, manageable farming ventures of grains and vegetables. The Indian Reorganization Act of 1934 stemmed the tide of Blackfeet land losses by placing most Indian land into trust status. In the years since the Indian Reorganization Act, the tribe has steadily progressed in terms of economics, health, education, and housing standards. The modest development of coal, oil, and natural gas reserves on the reservation has raised expectations even more, as have the establishment of two manufacturing concerns, an industrial park, and numerous small businesses.

People of the Blackfeet Nation continue to practice traditional cultural and religious ceremonies like the Sun Dance and sweat lodges. Members also continue to speak the indigenous languages, and tribal scholars encourage language revitalization programs.

GOVERNMENT

Under the Indian Reorganization Act of 1934, the tribe adopted a new tribal council and bylaws. It is recognized as a "domestic sovereign" nation by the federal government. The reservation is governed by a popularly elected tribal business council, which consists of nine members elected to four-year, staggered terms. Five members will be up for reelection in 2006, and four will be up in 2008. The business council nominates executive officers (a chairman, vice-chairman, and secretary). The reservation is divided into four districts, each represented by two council members, except for the Browning District, which has three representatives.

The Blackfeet Nation operates a number of governmental entities that provide essential services to tribal members. Among them are the procurement department, cultural department, fish, wildlife parks, and tribal planning depart-

Blackfeet Reservation
Federal reservation
Blackfeet
Glacier and Pondera counties, Montana

Blackfeet Reservation
P.O. Box 850
Browning, MT 59417
406-338-7521
406-338-7522 Fax
blackfeetnation.com

Total area *(BIA realty, 2004)*
1,010,472.63 acres

Tribally owned
(BIA realty, 2004)
311,356.27 acres

Individually owned
(BIA realty, 2004)
696,549.08 acres

Government trust lands
(BIA realty, 2004)
1,814.46 acres

Population *2000 census*
10,000

Total labor force *2000 census*
4,066

High school graduate or higher *2000 census*
74.4%

Bachelor's degree or higher
2000 census
13.5%

Unemployment rate *2000 census*
22.6%

Unemployment rate
(BIA labor report, 2001)
70%

Per capita income *2000 census*
$9,751

Blackfeet

TRI-MT-001

TRI-MT-003

TRI-MT-002

TRI-MT-004

TRI-MT-005

TRI-MT-006

TRI-MT-001 Welcome sign at entrance to reservation

RI-MT-003 View of Blackfeet Community College entering Browning

TRI-MT-002 The Native American National Bank, NANB

TRI-MT-004 Siyeh Development, Inc, a tribal enterprise

TRI-MT-005 Blackfeet Heritage Center & Art Gallery

TRI-MT-006 Tepees at fairgrounds- Annual Pow Wow & Rodeo

ment. The tribe also employs a livestock inspector. The tribe operates its own facility management department. This program is responsible for the maintenance, care, and planning of all tribal facilities The tribe's legal department represents the Blackfeet Nation in tribal, federal, and state matters as well as commercial and economic developments. It is responsible for drafting legal documents such as laws, rules, regulations, and ordinances.

The tribal documents and processing department is responsible for keeping minutes of the tribal council and some committee meetings. It also maintains records of tribal resolutions and election records. The department conducts research of documented tribal history since the 1930s. The Blackfeet Enrollment Department assists the Blackfeet Tribal Council in developing and maintaining membership rolls for the tribe. It provides enrollment assistance, provides certification to eligible individuals, and maintains vital records for all enrolled tribal members. It maintains genealogical records of enrolled members and non-enrolled descendants of enrolled tribal members. The department is also responsible for maintaining accurate information to be provided to tribal, state, and federal programs.

The Blackfeet Tribe operates its own finance department. It provides accounting services for all reservation-based federal, state, local, and tribal programs. It also processes vouchers, checks, reports, and financial statements for the aforementioned organizations, as well as for tribal members and funding

agencies. The tribe's revenue department manages the tribe's income. It is responsible for assessing taxes, collecting fees, and issuing permits and licenses. This department strives to assist the tribe in attaining self-sufficiency and economic freedom.

In addition to a personnel department, the tribe operates a tribal employment rights office. This office is responsible for ensuring that tribal members are provided with the opportunity to participate in the economic activity on the reservation. In addition to contracting with the federal Equal Employment Opportunity Commission, the tribe has passed its own Tribal Employment Rights Ordinance. The mission of the ordinance is to ensure that all business operations on the reservation afford Native people preference in all contracting, employment and training opportunities.

Having a reservation of considerable size, the tribe operates a tribal land department. The department works with the land committee, the business council, the BIA, Glacier County, Pondera County, tribal Indian housing authority, the local school district, Indian Health Service, farm service agency, and the State of Montana in reference to the Blackfeet Reservation land base. They provide assistance to the public in matters regarding home-site leases, farm leases, pasture leases, commercial leases, recreation leases and land-use permits, and rights-of-way permits. The office also deals with matters of land acquisition on the tribe's behalf, and permission for exploration and removal must be sought from the office when archeological sites are located on tribal lands.

ECONOMY

The Blackfeet Nation possesses a strong economy supported by a number of businesses and programs. The tribe owns and operates a variety of businesses, and members are employed in agricultural production, livestock farming, and mining. However, the tribal government is the primary source of employment on the reservation, providing opportunities for tribal members in the numerous departments and programs it maintains.

Government as Employer. As on many reservations, government jobs serve as a major source of employment on the Blackfeet Reservation. Presently, 31 percent of all employed tribal members work for the tribal government, and 38 percent of jobs are linked to federal programs.

Economic Development Projects. The tribe has been working with the Museum of the Rockies in Bozeman, Montana, in archeological searches on reservation land. Dinosaur fossils have been located and, with the tribe's permission, removed for further study. The tribe plans to develop a museum where fossils may be displayed. In the past, the tribe has also offered a portion of found fossils for sale to private collectors and public institutions.

Agriculture and Livestock. Blackfeet members produce a variety of crops on their approximately 185,000 acres of rich farmland. These include spring and winter wheat, oats, barley, and alfalfa. Slightly over 20 percent of this acreage is presently irrigated.

Tribal members also raise a significant amount of livestock including approximately 23,000 head of cattle, 6,500 sheep, 3,000 horses, and several dozen bison. Over 640,000 acres of reservation land are used for grazing purposes. The tribe operates a tribal ranch with an annual income of $500,000.00, with over 150 buffalo and 300 cattle and both dry land and irrigated farming.

Forestry. Nearly 10 percent of the reservation is forested, with about 4 percent of the total land area designated as commercial timberland. Forested lands primarily feature conifers, lodgepole pine, spruce, alpine fir, and Douglas fir. A significant number of tribal members are employed by the timber industry.

Gaming. The Blackfeet Tribe owns and operates the Discovery Lodge Casino two miles west of Cut Bank, Montana. The casino has 30 class II gaming machines and one restaurant. The Glacier Peaks Bingo and Casino, the tribe's largest casino, is located in Browning. Glacier Peaks has 70 class II gaming machines, a small restaurant, and provides nightly bingo. The tribe recently secured a $3.5 million loan for a new casino to be located near the Museum of the Plains Indians in Browning.

Construction. Numerous construction contractors located within the reservation employ more than 180 tribal members. Individual contractors have been very active due to a recent increase in housing construction, including a HUD-funded home project.

Mining. Coal, oil, and natural gas represent the three dominant mineral resources on the reservation. Approximately 90 percent of the tribe's annual income is generated from the sale of oil and gas. The tribe leases oil fields to national and international companies and participates in management decisions as well as profit sharing on most agreements. The Blackfeet Coalfield is approximately 12 miles long by one mile wide. It is estimated to contain 30 to 50 million tons of bituminous coal. The field remains essentially undeveloped at the present time. Two oil and gas fields lay partially within reservation boundaries, while a third field lies wholly within the reservation. Though these fields have been actively developed since the 1950s, substantial reserves remain. Other reservation mineral reserves with development potential include titaniferous magnetite, gold, silver, lead, and zinc.

There are also a number of extensive deposits of sand and gravel that may serve as potential sources of industrial aggregate. At present, there are 58 gravel pits on the reservation, though fewer than 5 are operating.

Manufacturing. The Blackfeet Tribe recently created Pikuni Industries, a 100 percent tribally owned modular home and general contracting company with 8(a) status. Pikuni recently completed a $2.5 million project at the Port of Piegan for the general services administration on the reservation's border with Canada. Pikuni will construct the tribe's new casino.

Heart-Butte Industries produces tepees and canvas carrying bags on a limited piecework basis (generally 8 to 10 employees). The nation operates Kimi Mountain Spring Water, a company that makes bottled natural spring water available to local residents.

Industrial Parks. The tribe maintains the 67-acre Blackfeet Industrial Park, which offers full utility services including security fencing and railroad sidings. It currently has abundant building and warehouse space available for the establishment of business enterprises, and the tribe is actively seeking joint ventures.

Credit Unions. The tribe operates a tribal credit program, which provides funds to eligible members who qualify for the lease income and payroll loan program.

Services and Retail. As of 1990, there were 360 consumer and retail businesses located on the reservation, with 109 of these located in Browning. These businesses include restaurants, bars, grocery stores, gas stations, and video rentals. Other businesses include oil well operators, construction contractors, logging enterprises, lumber and hardware stores, and excavation services. Though not all are Indian-owned, these businesses provide considerable employment for tribal members and generate vast revenues.

The nation operates Blackfeet Coins, which sells coins that commemorate the 200th anniversary of the Lewis and Clark Expedition. The explorers crossed Blackfeet lands in 1806 and, in fact, killed two Piegans during their encounter with Blackfeet people. The nation offers the coins as an acknowledgment of historical events that greatly influenced relations between the Blackfeet people and Euro-Americans.

Media and Communications. The tribe operates Starlink Cable, which provides cable television service to Browning and East Glacier. The Blackfeet Tribe also has recently opened an advertising company.

Tourism and Recreation. The reservation contains eight major lakes and over 175 miles of fishing streams. It is home to a number of wildlife as well. Fishing and hunting are permitted with a tribally issued license. The tribe also maintains four campgrounds. Glacier National Park, bordering the reservation on the west, attracts two million visitors annually. The park features a number of lakes, streams, campgrounds and hiking trails.

Blackfeet

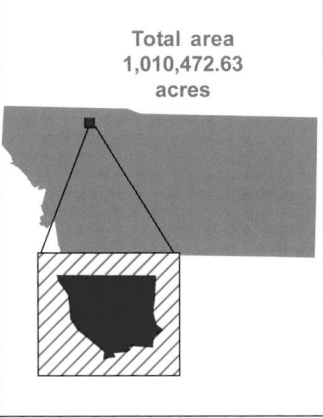

Total area
1,010,472.63
acres

Blackfeet

The northernmost point of the Lewis and Clark expedition lies only 12 miles outside of Browning. The nearby town of Cut Bank hosts Lewis and Clark Days activities. The Museum of the Plains Indian features regular art exhibits as well as artifacts of the Northern Plains peoples. The museum contains a gift shop. The exhibit "In the Footsteps of the Blackfeet," a recreation of a traditional camp, sits adjacent to the museum. The museum serves as the beginning of the Blackfeet Historic Site Tour that allows guests tours of the reservation and the Head Smashed in Buffalo Jump site. The museum is located in Browning along U.S. 89.

The Blackfeet Nation operates the Manista'mi Gallery ki Aka'pioyiss, the Lodgepole Gallery and Tipi Village, just 2.5 miles west of Browning, Montana, and a few miles east of Glacier National Park. The gallery provides guests with lodging in traditional Blackfeet canvas teepees and offers traditional and gourmet meals for dining. Facilities include an art gallery and studio. The experience also includes historic sights, seasonal powwows, visits to the nearby Museum of the Plains Indian, horseback riding, and fishing. Overnight guests are invited to share in campfire storytelling, drumming, singing, and introductions to Blackfeet history and culture.

The tribe also operates a Sun Child Recreation Camp. The camp provides guests the opportunity to experience overnight stays with tepees and traditional Blackfeet meals. The nation also hosts the North American Indian Days in late summer. This celebration includes powwow activities, traditional dances, ceremonies, and a rodeo.

INFRASTRUCTURE

The nearest interstate highway is I-15, a north-south route located about 60 miles east of Browning. U.S. highways 89 and 2 directly serve the reservation, both providing access to and from Glacier National Park. Browning is served by train lines (including Amtrak and Burlington Northern) and two trucking companies. Commercial air transportation is available in Kalispel (95 miles distant) and Great Falls (130 miles distant), while a small public airport is located about 35 miles from Browning.

The tribe has created a transportation-planning department to address the pertinent issues on the reservation. The department will develop a transportation improvement plan to identify transportation needs, prioritize funding, and initiate improvement of the road system.

Electricity. Glacier Cooperative provides electricity.

Fuel. Montana Power Company provides natural gas.

Wind Energy. The tribe is in the process of building a wind energy facility to be called Blackfeet I. This facility will generate between 36 and 66 megawatts of power.

Water Supply. The Blackfeet Utilities Commission operates five water and wastewater systems that service the Seville, Heart Butte, Star School, Glacier Homes, and Babb communities located throughout the reservation. Septic tanks are used in more remote regions. Browning has a municipal water system; wells are utilized in most other locations.

Solid Waste Facilities. The Blackfeet Tribe operates a solid waste system. It provides garbage collection services on the reservation and operates a landfill.

Transportation. Various tribal programs offer transportation services to members. Services are available for medical appointments, home-to-work transport, and elderly transport.

Telecommunications. Three River Telephone Company and Mountain Bell provide telephone service. The tribally owned and operated Starlink Cable Company offers cable television service to residents of Browning and East Glacier.

COMMUNITY FACILITIES AND SERVICES

The tribe operates a community swimming facility that includes an Olympic-sized swimming pool, a wading pool, saunas, locker rooms, a weight and exercise room, a whirlpool, a racquetball court, and indoor walking and jogging areas. The tribe also offers numerous social services, educational programs, and resources to tribal members of all ages. The tribe makes a concerted effort to provide assistance and tools to its members in an effort to improve the well being of individual members and the tribe as a whole.

The tribe offers a 24-hour emergency shelter for victims of floods and fires, the homeless, and travelers. The center, Medicine Bear Shelter, offers meals, GED courses, social services, referrals, resume writing assistance, employment counseling, elderly transport, home-to-work transport, counseling, and educational workshops. The Blackfeet Personal Care Program trains personal care attendants and assigns them to provide in-home assistance to handicapped and disabled clients eligible for Medicaid. There are 89 contracted attendants at this time.

The Blackfeet Nurturing Center provides shelter for abused, neglected, and abandoned children. The Blackfeet Youth Initiative provides elementary and high school students with summer camp activities designed to strengthen young people's abilities and understanding of community health and safety issues, writing, art, and sports. Students participate as co-counselors, helping to create the curriculum and courses. The program nurtures self-confidence, cultural pride, and community service.

Tribal elders may receive the services of the Eagle Shields Senior Center. This program provides meals, social events, and access to other tribal services. The center also hosts community health activities, income tax preparation assistance, information and referral services for elders, and daily social events. The tribe's personal care attendants, green thumb volunteers, and volunteers for the visually impaired are located within the center. Facilities at the center are also available for private functions.

The Blackfeet Tribal Manpower Department promotes employability of tribal members by providing education, training, and additional support services to Native American clients and Blackfeet tribal members with disabilities.

Education. Five K-12 schools are located in Browning. K-8 students also attend schools in East Glacier, Heart Butte, and Babb. The Blackfeet Tribe operates Blackfeet Community College, which is located in Browning. It currently offers associate degrees in the arts and sciences. The tribe also has a higher education department on the reservation. This department provides members currently in postsecondary programs with academic and career counseling and financial assistance. It administers the higher education grant assistance program and the adult vocational training grant assistance program.

Health Care. The Blackfeet Community Health Representative Department provides a number of services to the community including assessment and evaluation, education and awareness programs, and follow-up care. The office also serves as a liaison between the tribe and Indian Health Service and provides language interpreters for tribal members. Transportation for medical appointments and limited in-home services are also available.

The tribe operates the Blackfeet Tribal EMS Program. It provides reservation residents with emergency care and transportation. The tribe also maintains a health clinic in Browning with seven doctors and three dentists, a hospital run by the Indian Health Service and U.S. Public Health Service.

ENVIRONMENTAL CONCERNS

The Blackfeet Environment Office operates on federal grants. It manages programs of water quality, air quality, wetlands, lead-based paint, open dump, radon, solid waste, GAP, and NPEDS. It enforces tribal ordinances pertaining to aquatic lands, solid waste, and air quality, and it is in the process of developing water quality standards. There are also plans to develop a junk car ordinance, pesticides inventory and assessment, and a comprehensive environmental management plan. Representatives from the office teach a course at the Blackfeet Community College; conduct educational seminars at the elementary, middle, and high school levels; and serve as mentors and/or judges for science programs in the schools. The department is staffed by 12 employees.

Each year the Blackfeet Utilities Commission sponsors an annual cleanup. During this scheduled time, tribal residents, businesses, and government entities join efforts to bolster cleanup efforts on the reservation. Specific areas may be targeted for cleanup and assistance may be provided for removing large items and hauling refuse to the landfill. The commission is presently pursuing options to improve the services it provides to the community in order to best serve reservation residents and provide a clean and healthy environment for tribal members.

The nation is also involved in revitalizing the swift fox population on the reservation. They have joined with the Defenders of Wildlife and the Cochrane Ecological Institute to create an environment that fosters the return of these animals.

Crow

LOCATION AND LAND STATUS

The Crow Reservation is located in south-central Montana. It lies within Big Horn, Carbon, Treasure, and Yellowstone counties in Montana and Big Horn and Sheridan counties in Wyoming. The reservation is bordered on the east by the Northern Cheyenne Reservation. It is approximately 60 miles wide and 40 miles long.

After treaties were signed in 1825 and 1851 with the U.S. government, a final treaty in 1880 reduced the reservation to its current size. Allotments were issued to tribal members after the 1887 Allotment Act, and from 1922 until 1962 allotment holders of the reservation sold land mostly along the three rivers that run through it. The tribe has mineral rights to 1.1 million acres near Billings and Hardin, Montana, and near Sheridan, Wyoming.

PHYSICAL DESCRIPTION

The Crow Reservation contains wooded valleys, piney bluffs and grassy plains. The Big Horn Canyon lies within reservation boundaries, as does the Yellowtail Dam. The three principal mountain ranges on the reservation are the Wolf Mountains in the east and the Big Horn Mountains and Pryor Mountains in the south. The reservation lies primarily in the plains where the altitude varies from 3,000 to 4,500 feet. The alluvial bottomlands lie along the Big Horn River, Little Big Horn River, and Pryor Creek drainage systems.

CLIMATE

The reservation experiences mild weather. The mean annual temperature is 45.5°F, with summer highs of 110°F and winter lows of -48°F. Snow seldom accumulates and precipitation varies from 12 to 18 inches per year.

CULTURE AND HISTORY

The Crow Indians are known to have had their origins prior to the 1300s in the Mississippi headwaters and as far as north as Lake Winnipeg, Canada. They made incremental migrations through North Dakota, first entering Montana in the 1600s. They were part of the Hidatsas, with whom they had a sedentary life, raising crops and hunting buffalo, deer, and elk. But they turned more to hunting, and eventually they separated themselves from the Hidatsas and became a nomadic people, with their lives built around the buffalo. They were excellent horsemen and a prosperous people. In Hidatsan, the Crow are called *Apsáalooke*, literally translated, "children of the large beaked bird." White explorers misinterpreted it to mean, "the flapping of one's hands like the wings of a bird in flight" and just called them Crow.

From their first encounter with Europeans in 1740, the Crow Nation has attempted to foster amiable relations with non-Indian cultures. Treaties with the U.S. government were signed as early as 1825, and the treaty of 1880 established their reservation as it is currently defined. In 1869, a famous Crow chief, Chief Plenty Coups, emerged as a major leader and negotiator with the federal government, and he required the BIA to provide education to the people.

The Crow people maintain traditional cultural elements and practices. Eighty-two percent of Crow tribal members still speak the Crow language, and many tribal entities conduct business in the language. Within the Crow culture, the clan is almost as important as the family. Crow people are born into the clan of their mothers, and they are children of their father's clan. The tribe consists of six active clans. The Crow clan system is one of their religions; it is also used as a social control. It builds character, instills morale, boosts self-esteem, develops respect, and motivates self-control, especially when intimidated by a teasing clan. The Crow clan fathers and mothers build the people up, and the teasing clan tears them down to avoid being intoxicated by status. The Crow people are taught to respect all members of the tribal membership, especially the members of their father's clan; they only terrorize members of their teasing clan (which is male members of their father's clan). In days of old their ancestors would address their creator as First Maker, My Clan Father, and The One Riding the Red Paint Horse. When they call upon their clan fathers, they are calling upon their creator in a worldly manner. That is why it is said, "What the clan fathers ask for the clan child always comes true."

Crow Indian Reservation
Federal reservation
Apsalooke (Crow)
Big Horn, Yellowstone, and Carbon counties, Montana

Crow Nation
Bacheeiche Avenue
Box 159
Crow Agency, MT 59022
406-638-3841
406-638-3890 Fax
crownations.net

Total area *(BIA realty, 2004)*
1,536,317.84 acres

Tribally owned
(BIA realty, 2004)
554,559.02 acres

Individually owned
(BIA realty, 2004)
980,358.23 acres

Government Trust Lands
(BIA realty, 2004)
1,400.59 acres

Population *2000 census*
6,894

Total labor force *2000 census*
2,786

Total labor force
(BIA labor report, 2001)
4,606

Crow

TRI-MT-007

TRI-MT-011

TRI-MT-010

TRI-MT-009

TRI-MT-008

TRI-MT-007 Sign in front of Tribal Administration Building

TRI-MT-009 Apsaalooke Visitors Center at intersection

TRI-MT-010 Little Big Horn Casino & Bingo

TRI-MT-011 View of Ihkasahpua Seven Stars Learning Center, Little Big Horn College, 2004

TRI-MT-008 Street view of Crow Tribe's Veterans Memorial Park

High school graduate or higher *2000 census*
77.2%

Bachelor's degree or higher
2000 census
13.8%

Unemployment rate *2000 census*
17.1%

Unemployment rate
(BIA labor report, 2001)
60%

Per capita income *2000 census*
$9,440

In 2000, the 9th U.S. Circuit Court of Appeals dealt the tribe a major setback in their ongoing efforts to establish economic freedom and sovereignty. The tribe had imposed a tax on Big Horn County Electricity for utilization of reservation resources. The Court of Appeals ruled that the tribe had no authority to impose the tax. It also overturned a 1991 decision that allowed the tribe to impose similar taxes on Burlington Northern Railroad and other utility companies that operate within reservation boundaries. The decision limits the tribe's ability to gain economic wealth from taxation of the companies, and it also limits it's the tribe's ability to exercise authority over issues that pertain to its natural resources.

GOVERNMENT

The Crow Tribe did not choose to reorganize under the 1934 Indian Reorganization Act, but adopted its own constitution in 1948. A new constitution and bylaws, adopted in 2001, provides for a more stable government system as well as giving tribal members access to due process and equal rights. This improved government consists of three branches: the executive, the legislative, and the judicial. This structure balances the branches and allows for an independent tribal court. The new terms of office, except in the judicial branch, are four years long, which will enhance the stability even further. Executive branch officials include a chairman, vice-chairman, secretary, and vice-secretary. Executive branch officials include a chairman, vice-chairman, secretary, and vice-secretary.

The tribe operates a number of departments and programs to serve the needs of reservation residents and tribal members. Among them are the cultural committee, legal office, natural resources, grants and contracts, education, Head Start, health, transportation, credit, social services, economic development, Tribal Employment Rights Office, finance, home renovation, Work Investment Act Abandon Land Mines, and fish and game. The tribe also houses representatives of the BIA, EPA, FSA, and NRCS. The Crow Housing Authority manages housing in the district communities and outlying rural areas through HUD low rent and mutual help programs.

The Crow Tribe also manages a number of programs and services through BIA and Indian Health Service under PL 93-638 contracts. BIA contracts include: higher education and scholarship, Indian Child Welfare, home improvement, job placement and training, and judicial services. Indian Health Service contracts include: substance abuse, hospital security, lawn maintenance, and water and sewer systems.

In 2003 when the Crow Nation began managing a tribal appraisal program under a PL 93-638 contract that had never been done by a tribe. These appraisal services are offered to tribal members by a tribal member.

ECONOMY

The Crow Nation's economy is largely supported by revenues from the mining industry. The reservation lands are rich in coal, gas, and oil. The tribe benefits from leasing these lands. The tourism industry also provides the tribe with an ample source of income. Historic sites, national parks, and tribal festivities draw a large number of visitors to the reservation.

Government as Employer. The tribe serves as a major source of employment on the reservation. Other employers include on-reservation public and private schools, the Crow/Northern Cheyenne Hospital, Indian Health Service, the BIA agency, National Park Services, Big Horn County, and Little Big Horn Community College.

Agriculture and Livestock. The Crow Tribe manages a buffalo heard of over 1,400. The tribe and individual tribal members lease a large portion of reservation land to non-Indian entities. Approximately 1.2 million acres of grazing lands, 150,000 acres of dry-land farming land, and 30,000 acres of irrigated farming land are leased.

Gaming. The tribe owns and operates the Little Bighorn Casino in Crow Agency. The casino operates 100 slots/VLTs, 200 bingo seats, and 1 restaurant. It employs 49 individuals

Mining. Primary sources of income for the tribe are coal, gas, and oil leases. Since 1920, coal has been mined on the reservation. The eastern part of the reservation contains billions of tons of coal, and the Absloka Mine strips coal from the ceded strip northeast of the reservation. The mine has the capacity to supply 11 million tons of low-sulfur, subbituminous coal annually. Oil and gas have been produced on the Crow Reservation since 1930. In 1984, tribal lands produced nearly 18,000 barrels of oil, and allotted lands produced over 24,000 barrels. In 1985, 20 companies had 709 oil and gas leases. The reservation's mineral resources also include potential sources of industrial aggregate in the form of terrace deposits along the Bighorn River.

Services and Retail. Limited service businesses exist in the small communities of Lodge Grass, Crow Agency, and Pryor. Necessities may be purchased at local stores, but travel into Billings nearly 65 miles away is necessary for major shopping.

Tourism and Recreation. The Crow Indian Reservation provides a setting for recreational activities, such as hunting, fishing, boating, camping, picnicking, hiking, and backpacking. The Crow Tribe requires nontribal members to obtain licenses and permits for recreation on reservation lands. Bighorn Canyon National Recreation Area and Yellowtail Dam offer fishing, water sports, and camping sites.

The historic site of the Battle of Little Big Horn National Monument is located near the reservation and draws over 400 tourists annually. A re-enactment of the battle is a major event. Chief Plenty Coups State Park is located in Pryor. There are picnic areas as well as a display of Crow artifacts. The tribe also offers numerous tour programs to allow guests to visit historical sites, tour the reservation, and gain an understanding of Crow culture and history.

The tribe hosts the annual Crow Fair off Interstate 90 and U.S. 212. Crow Fair, "Chichiáxxaawasuua," provides the Crow people from on and off the reservation an opportunity to gather in celebration of Crow cultures and traditions. Over 10,000 Crow people set up camp in tepees and tents. Local families relocate their entire households to the site. Crow people are welcome to participate in a parade, rodeo, race meet, and intertribal powwow. The festivities provide Crow people the opportunity to share in the celebration of language, spirituality, homelands, and culture.

In late June, the tribe hosts Crow Native Days, which is becoming a major event with parades, dancing, and battle reenactment.

Another popular event during this time is the "Ultimate Warrior Challenge," which features men and women categories on a three-member team in a canoe race, followed by a three-mile race on foot, and ending with an Indian relay. Other activities include arrow throwing, horseshoe throwing, and hand games. Food and merchandise vendors are also available.

INFRASTRUCTURE
A major highway connects Lodge Grass and Crow Agency with Billings, Montana. Secondary roads connect other communities in the sparsely populated area. The Burlington Northern Railroad runs parallel to the Little Bighorn Valley in its route between Billings and Montana.

COMMUNITY FACILITIES AND SERVICES
Awe Kualawaache Care Center, located in Crow Agency, provides inpatient elder care services for Natives who require 24-hour medical attention.

Education. Tribal youth attend eight elementary schools and three high schools located throughout the reservation. With the benefit of coal-mining revenues, the schools at Hardin and Lodge Grass are two of the wealthiest in the state.

The closest nonreservation towns of Billings and Hardin boast public elementary and secondary schools as well as Montana State University, Rocky Mountain College, MSU College of Technology, two technology colleges, and two schools of cosmetology.

The tribally owned and administered Little Bighorn Community College is located in Crow Agency. It is a 1994 Land Grand Institution. It offers associate's degrees in nine academic areas. The college offers courses directed to the economic and employment opportunities in the area. Approximately 90 percent of the student body are members of the Crow Tribe. The college conducts student services and business functions in the Crow language. It is home to an extensive library and the Crow Archives. The college facilities include Internet access, computer labs, science labs, a building trades lab, and a daycare.

Health Care. The tribe maintains the Crow/Northern Cheyenne Hospital in Crow Agency, the Lodge Grass Health Center in Lodge Grass, and the Pryor Health Station in Pryor. Additional medical facilities are located in Billings, approximately 65 miles from the reservation's central town of Crow Agency.

Crow

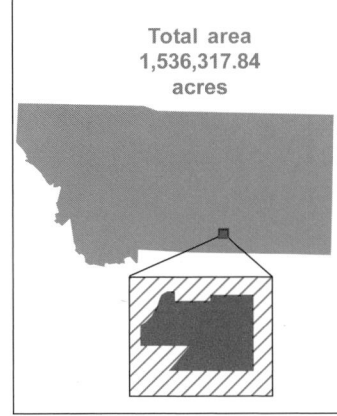

Total area
1,536,317.84
acres

ENVIRONMENTAL CONCERNS
The tribe operates the Brownsfield Assessment Program. This program tests soil, groundwater, and asbestos levels throughout the reservation. The tribe has identified surface water contamination and is working toward establishing water quality standards and regulations.

Flathead

Flathead

LOCATION AND LAND STATUS
Situated in northwestern Montana south of Kalispel and north of Missoula, the Flathead Reservation is 60 miles long and 40 miles wide. The towns of Polson, Pablo, Ronan, and St. Ignatius are on the reservation. The Flathead Lake, the largest freshwater lake in the United States, borders the reservation, and the tribes control about one-half of its shoreline.

CULTURE AND HISTORY
The reservation was founded when representatives of the Salish, the Kootenai, and the Pend d'Oreilles Indians signed the 1855 Hellgate Treaty, ceding some 20 million acres of ancestral land to the U.S. government and retaining title over 1.3 million acres as their homeland. In 1904, land parcels within the reservation were allotted to Indians and others. Since the 1940s the resident tribes have been

buying back reservation lands; over 65 percent was tribally owned by 2000.

GOVERNMENT
The Confederated Salish and Kootenai Tribes have a 10-member tribal council, with members representing each of the 8 reservation districts. The tribal council elects a tribal chairperson and vice-chairperson from its membership. The council appoints a secretary, a treasurer, a sergeant-at-arms, and other offices and committees from within or outside of the tribal council.

The Confederated Salish and Kootenai Tribes were one of the first 10 Native American nations choosing to participate in the 1988 Self-Governance Demonstration Project. Their efforts were successful, and the federal government rec-

Flathead Reservation
Federal reservation
Salish and Kootenai
Lake, Sanders, Missoula, and
Flathead Counties, Montana

Confederated Salish and
 Kootenai Tribes
P.O. Box 278
Pablo, MT 59855
406-675-2700
406-675-2806 Fax
cskt.org

Flathead

Total area *(BIA realty, 2004)*
817,631.56 acres

Total area *(Tribal source, 2004)*
1,317,000 acres

Tribally owned *(BIA realty, 2004)*
775,956.64 acres

Tribally owned trust
(Tribal source, 2004)
70,000 acres

Tribally owned in fee status
(Tribal source, 2004)
71,000 acres

Individually owned
(BIA realty, 2004)
40,942.80 acres

Federal trust *(BIA realty, 2004)*
732.12 acres

Federal trust *(Tribal source, 2004)*
700,000 acres

Population *2000 census*
26,172

Tribal enrollment
(Tribal source, 2004)
7,005

Percent Native *2000 census*
26.7%

Total labor force *2000 census*
11,878

**High school graduate or
higher** *2000 census*
83.4%

Bachelor's degree or higher
2000 census
20.8%

Unemployment rate *2000 census*
7.9%

Unemployment rate
(BIA labor report, 2001)
36%

Per capita income *2000 census*
$14,503

ognized the nation's self-governance rights in 1993. Their achievements as a self-governing nation have been honored by the Harvard University Kennedy School of Government Honoring Nations Program. The tribes recently completed construction of a new $3.5 million governmental offices complex that serves as tribal headquarters. This new facility houses various tribal governmental departments, including administration, accounting, personnel, education, cultural resources, and tribal lands.

The Salish/Pend d'Oreille Culture Committee is responsible for facilitating the preservation, protection, and perpetuation of the traditional and living cultures. The committee works on projects such as language retention and documentation and culture preservation. The committee archives include several hundred audiotapes, videotapes, books, slides, photos, individual accounts, and other media. It conducts annual language and cultural camps. The committee employs approximately nine individuals.

The Kootenai Culture Committee functions independently from the tribal organization. It advises the tribal council on matters that affect policy and program development. The committee confers with the Kootenai Elders Committee on all issues pertaining to traditions and cultures. The committee employs six individuals.

The Confederated Salish and Kootenai Department of Human Resources is a large governmental office that manages numerous programs. The majority of the programs serve the social services needs of tribal members. Most of the services are available to members who meet specific income criteria, live at or below the poverty level, and require public assistance. The Confederated Salish and Kootenai Tribes were the first tribe in Montana to contract with the TANF program, a federal program under the Administration for Native Americans that is division of the Administration for Children and Families. The program offers services and assistance pertaining to welfare issues.

The tribes operate a tribal court and tribal court of appeals. These bodies exercise jurisdiction over tribal matters as outlined in the tribal constitution. The Tribal Defenders Office provides legal representation to any enrolled member of a federally recognized tribe in matters that come before the Confederated Salish and Kootenai Tribal Court and any Montana State Court. The tribal law and order department provides law enforcement-related services on the reservation. In 2002, the department began a training program to prepare community service officers to assist the department by providing additional security at school functions and social events. The department also houses the drug task force. Task force officers serve the reservation and also respond as part of the Northwest Drug Task Force, which covers a five-county area in western Montana.

BUSINESS CORPORATION

The tribes have four business corporations. One of the tribes' development corporation, S&K Holding Company, coordinates with the tribes' economic development director to develop and manage tribal enterprises, provide planning and technical assistance to members starting or expanding businesses, and review outside business proposals. S&K Holding Company is currently exploring market opportunities for botanical product production, the Intertribal Agricultural Council foreign marketing program, food production, and native plant production. S&K Holding also provides management oversight to three tribal enterprises: S&K Marina, Flathead Sticker and Lath, and Native Timber Log Furniture.

The tribes also own and manage three other corporations: S&K Technologies Corporation, which provides information technology services to government agencies and private-sector clientele; S&K Electronics Corporation, which produces electronic equipment for worldwide distribution; and S&K Banking Corporation, which manages the tribes' endeavors in the banking industry. A bank is planned with an opening date of May 2005.

ECONOMY

The Confederated Salish and Kootenai Tribes have developed their reservation economy into a diversified economic powerhouse, generating revenues from its four business corporations and their subsidiaries, which include gaming, manufacturing, retail service enterprises, banking, technology, and electric utilities. Tribal land is the dominant source of timber for the region's lumber industry. The tribes also receive revenue from fishing, hunting, and camping fees. Individual tribal members own approximately 125 non-farm businesses and 20 construction companies in the region. The tribes continue to look at viable economic opportunities and to develop projects that will help them to diversify their investment portfolio.

Government as Employer. The Confederated Salish and Kootenai Tribes are the largest employer in northwestern Montana. It employs approximately 1,000 individuals. The tribes manage a budget of $180 million annually. Employment opportunities are available in tribal government, wildlife management, unionized electrical work, public safety, education, resort and casino work, and many other fields in which the tribes serve as active business leaders. Approximately 20 percent of the tribes' employees are nontribal members.

The Confederated Tribes are actively engaged in economic development research. Strategies are being developed to deal with the fact that tribal members are largely engulfed by non-Indian economic enterprises within the reservation and in the region, which was experiencing strong economic growth well into the twenty-first century. Recognizing that the future of reservation economic growth no longer lies in forestry, agriculture, and mining, the Confederated Tribes' strategy is to direct the reservation's economic growth to benefit tribal members, to create tribal enterprises based on reservation natural resources, to set up enterprise boards to separate tribal government from business development, to encourage individual Indian entrepreneurship, to develop tourism and recreation, and to provide incentives for Indian business growth.

Agriculture and Livestock. The Confederated Tribes control approximately 400,000 acres of nonirrigated grazing land within the reservation, as well as approximately 15,500 acres of cropland. The tribes lease a large portion of its farmland.

The tribes participate in the Agricultural Extension Program through Montana State University. Members may be eligible for involvement in programs such as the Crop Loss Disaster Program, Future Farmers of America, the Intertribal Agricultural Council, the Indian Livestock Feed Program, and the Water Quality Education Project. The tribes produce Crooked Bow Smoked Beef Strips for sale through the Flathead Native Agricultural Cooperative.

The Confederated Tribes are currently negotiating an agreement with the federal government to acknowledge the tribe's role in the management of the National Bison Range. The title to the lands would remain unchanged, and the federal government would oversee management of the site. The National Bison Range is located on approximately 18,500 acres that were originally

TRI-MT-012

TRI-MT-013

Flathead

TRI-MT-014

TRI-MT-017

TRI-MT-016

taken from the tribe by the federal government. The herd is descended from the bison preserved by the tribes as many as 130 years ago.

Forestry. The Tribal Forestry Program manages the tribes' timber. They sell a sustainable 14 million board feet annually.

Gaming. The tribes own the Best Western Kwa Taq Nuk Resort in Polson, Montana. Resort facilities include 117 guest rooms, a restaurant, and a lounge. The casino has 41 gaming machines. There are plans in development to expand the facilities. Currently, revenue from the casino is used to supplement the tribes' general fund, health care services, and other tribal programs.

Construction. There are 20 individually owned construction firms located within reservation boundaries. Combined, the companies employ over 100 people.

Mining. The development of mineral resources is under study by the Confederated Tribes.

Manufacturing. S&K Electronics, one of the first electronics firms in Indian country, celebrated its twentieth anniversary in 2004. It has successfully graduated from an 8(a) program. S&K Electronics Corporation produces electronic equipment for worldwide distribution. In 2003, the corporation entered into a multiyear contract with Lockheed Martin to produce assemblies for the F16 fighter. S&K Electronics was awarded the 2003 SBA Business of the year and the Rockwell-Collins Preferred Supplier Award in 2003.

S&K Holding Company manages Native Timber Log Furniture, which produces log furniture designed and created by local artists. Natural resources from the reservation are used to produce the custom furniture. The tribe also operates Flathead Sticker and Lath, which is a subsidiary of S&K Holding. The company manufactures wood lath, kiln stick, and shipping batons for regional sawmills and survey stakes for surveyors and construction firms. The company also produces wooden dowels.

Real Estate/Commercial Development. Around 1999, the housing authority completed construction on 20 new lease-to-own homes. The project was completed through the Federal Home Loan Bank of Seattle Affordable Housing Program and the lease purchase provision of the Low-Income Housing Tax Credit and permanent financing. The housing authority manages over 800 housing units throughout the reservation, as well as the community water and sewer systems.

Services and Retail*. The tribes' S&K Holding Company sells a number of retail products. They include Morel Mushrooms; St. John's Wort supplements, Native American art and jewelry, tepees, and hand-stitched horsehair head stalls.

Technology. The tribe owns S&K Technology. Its services are extensive and include the development of electronic technology manuals, website design, system management, logistic support, and software development. Current S&K Technologies projects include the Integrated Collaborative Environment Toolkit as part of the U.S. Air Force Predator Project; the Multinational Aircraft Repair and Return Project; Fleet Readiness for the U.S. Air Force; geographical information system implementation and mapping for the Farm Service Agency; and medical management systems for various health management organizations. S&K Technologies also operates three aerospace service sites out of Georgia, Ohio, and Texas.

Media and Communications. The *Char-Costa News* is a weekly newspaper published by the tribe. The Salish Kootenai College has a TV station, KSKC TV.

Tourism and Recreation. The Confederate Tribes are the first Native Nation to designate its own wilderness area. It designated the Mission Mountain Wilderness Area in Montana. The State of Montana has designated the Ninepipe National Wildlife Refuge and State Wildlife Management Area as a wildlife viewing area. It contains an exceptional wetland and bird-watching opportunities. The National Bison Range/Pablo National Wildlife Refuge is home to over 500 bison and herds of deer, elk, bighorn sheep, and antelope. Visitors may tour the 20,000-acre refuge year-round.

TRI-MT-012 Scenic view and rest area, Old "Welcome" sign for the Flathead Nation with Tribal directory across from National Bison Range

TRI-MT-013 Highway view of Salish Kootenai College sign

TRI-MT-014 Metal Statue of Eagle & Man at Salish Kootenai College Campus

TRI-MT-017 - Old Tribal Office Complex

TRI-MT-016 - Dome of new Flathead tribal administration building

657

Flathead

TRI-MT-020

TRI-MT-018

TRI-MT-021

TRI-MT-020 Exist water from Kerr Dam by hydroelectric poser plant

TRI-MT-018 View of Flathead Lake and Sign

TRI-MT-021 Water flowing out of Kerr Dam & Montana Power Company

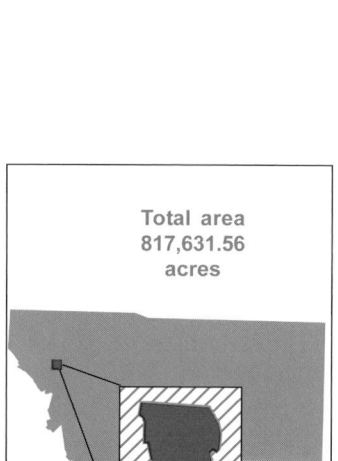

Total area
817,631.56
acres

Native Americans built St. Ignatius Mission in 1854 under the direction of Catholic missionaries. The mission is surrounded by the Mission Range of the Rocky Mountains. Adjacent to the mission are the St. Ignatius Campground and Hostel. A tribal member operates the Eagle Nest RV Resort at Polson. The People Center Museum exhibits Native American crafts, memorabilia, and locally manufactured Native products.

The tribes also host a number of events that draw visitors to the area. Those include the annual Fourth of July celebration, the Standing Arrow Powwow, Live History Day, Flathead Lake Hoop Fest, Native American Awareness Week festivities, and the Ninepipe Museum Black Tie Benefit Dinner. In the spring, the tribes host a River Honoring Celebration for the Flathead River; it is attended by local school children, the elders, and community members. There is also an Annual Bitterroot Feast, a root-gathering event that pays homage to the elders.

Banking. S&K Banking Corporation, one of the tribes' business corporations, is in the process of developing a tribally owned bank. The BIA has approved a Section 17 Bank Holding Corporation, the Salish and Kootenai Bancorporation.

INFRASTRUCTURE
The reservation is traversed north-south by U.S. Highway 93 and east-west by Montana State Highway 200.

Electricity. The Confederated Tribes manage the Mission Valley Power Electric Utility under a contract with the U.S. Department of the Interior, serving over 15,000 commercial and residential customers. The tribal council appoints the utility's five-member board and seven-member consumer council. The Nation assumed management of the Safety of Dams Program from the Bureau of Reclamation in 1989. Since that time, the Confederated Tribes have met project goals more expediently and cost-efficiently than estimated. The tribes will have the opportunity to fully operate the dam.

Water Supply. The Confederated Tribes' Housing Authority operates over 20 water systems and 20 community sewer systems throughout the reservation.

Transportation. Bus service is available through the reservation. Motor freight and carrier services serve the area. Airport facilities are available in Kalispell and Missoula, both approximately 60 miles from the reservation. Three small airports in

Polson, Ronan, and St. Ignatius provide facilities for freight and private planes, including the one used by the tribal game and fish department.

COMMUNITY FACILITIES AND SERVICES
The nation manages the People's Center cultural center. It provides educational programs, Native Ed-Ventures tours, and supplies for local Native artists. Facilities include a museum, art gallery, and gift shop.

The Kicking Horse Job Corps Center is contracted through the Department of Labor and offers career development training to Native Americans aged 16 through 24.

Education. The tribes operate six Head Start centers, including those at Elmo, Arlee, St. Ignatius, Ronan, Pablo, and Paulson, along with 11 public elementary schools, six high schools, a private Christian academy, and the tribes' college. The tribes also operate Two Eagle River High School, which was created in 1974 to serve as an alternative high school for tribal youth. It includes 31,728 square feet of facilities for grades 7-12, an administration building, vocational shops, library, kitchen, cafeteria, and gymnasium.

The Salish Kootenai College offers bachelor's degree programs, associate's degree programs, certificate programs, and a registered nursing program. It is a member of the American Indian Higher Education Consortium. Facilities include a fine arts center, science facility, and golf course. Eleven hundred students were in enrolled in 2004.

Health Care. The tribe operates a full health care service program, including medical, dental, pharmacy, and public health nursing services. Services are contracted through the Indian Health Service.

ENVIRONMENTAL CONCERNS
The Division of Environmental Protection is a program of the Confederated Salish and Kootenai Tribes' Natural Resources Department. This division includes air quality, water quality, shoreline and aquatic lands protection, and solid and hazardous waste programs. The tribes have fish, wildlife, recreation, and conservation programs housed under the natural resource department as well. These programs aim to manage resources and public education. The water management program is responsible for quantifying, evaluating, and assisting in managing water resources on the reservation.

Trust Resource Management, Office of Support Services, Confederated Salish & Kootenai Tribes, Pablo, MT

In the mid-1970s, the Confederated Salish and Kootenai Tribes of western Montana decided to assume the management of their natural resources. Consciously avoiding haphazard takeovers of existing programs, the Tribes strategically built the necessary infrastructure and developed the necessary expertise to enact a gradual assertion of self-governance. Now, with the management of trust resources firmly under their control, the Confederated Salish and Kootenai Tribes understand that the ability to establish priorities, set goals, and address the economic and cultural needs of their citizens through effective and efficient management is indispensable to the fullest possible exercise of tribal sovereignty.

As a result of the 1855 Hellgate Treaty, the Confederated Salish and Kootenai Tribes (CSKT) became the holders of a 1.25 million acre land base. Their natural resources included mountain forests, grasslands, an extensive river corridor, the southern half of Flathead Lake, and a diverse array of wildlife and fisheries. Since the signing of that treaty, natural resources have been the cornerstone of CSKT revenue. Regrettably, the Tribes did not exercise control over these resources for over a century while the federal government held them in trust.

Indian trust was born out of the explicit language used in the government-to-government treaties the US made with various tribes. Eventually, it became a fiduciary responsibility in which the US government was to protect all Indian tribes' lands, assets, resources, and the right to self-governance. Many tribes and individual Indians view the trust relationship with great suspicion, however. And rightly so. The trust relationship has too often morphed into the paternalistic idea that the federal government can manage Indian resources more effectively than the tribes themselves. Perhaps worse, the federal government's trust responsibilities have been-and continue to be-characterized by chronic mismanagement, a topic that has received much attention in recent years.

The CSKT have suffered from trust mismanagement. By the 1930s, homesteading and allotment resulting from the Dawes Act had eroded their treaty lands and attendant natural resources by 70 percent. This loss created a checkerboard-effect of federal Indian and non-Indian lands on the reservation and compromised the possibility of effective tribal management of what remained. The Tribes currently own 60 percent of their total treaty reservation lands and enrolled tribal members comprise only 17 percent of the total reservation population. Checkerboard land ownership and a significant non-tribal population mean that CSKT resources that might have been managed solely by the Tribes themselves must now be managed in consultation with municipal, county, state, and federal governments. Nevertheless, the costs of challenging resource management were hardly as daunting as the costs of continued mismanagement. In the early 1970s, the Tribes were determined to fight for their survival as a sovereign nation by assuming the management of their own land base and natural resources in the new and changing conditions of a dominant non-Indian world.

In fact, the Tribes began assuming this management even before the Indian Self-Determination and Education Assistance Act of 1975 ushered in a new era of self-governance. In the 1930s, the Tribes recognized that control of their land base was critical to effective natural resource management. Between 1934, when they organized themselves under an Indian Reorganization Act constitution, and the 1970s, the CSKT set about establishing formal processes for land management.

In 1969, the Tribes began laying down the foundation that would sustain the eventual control of their trust resources. In that year, they established the Tribal Realty Office and started issuing home site leases. The Tribal Forest Management Enterprise was created a few years later to administer permits and forest improvement projects such as thinning and reforestation. These programs expanded in 1990 and 1995, respectively, when the Tribes assumed complete management of BIA Realty and BIA Forestry under PL 93-638 contracts. In the early 1980s, the Tribes developed an Earth Resources Program and Tribal Water Rights & Administration to provide vital support of their natural resource management. Also, in conjunction with the University of Montana, they designed a Wilderness Program. Finally, they undertook management of Mission Valley Power, the electric utility formerly overseen by the BIA.

Even then, the CSKT were only getting started. By the 1990s, the Tribes' experience in managing their natural resources had strengthened their commitment to total resource management. During this decade, the Tribes took over the management of all federal programs under the direction of the Bureau of Indian Affairs and the Indian Health Service through PL 93-638 contracts. They procured community health programs, higher education, vocational training, and social services. In 1998, the Tribes were among the first to administer a Temporary Assistance for Needy Families program through an agreement with the state of Montana.

Importantly, the Tribes were not just assuming the management of their natural and human resources, they were succeeding. The CSKT's goal of self-governance demanded the development and maintenance of a stable management infrastructure. They created the Tribal Lands Department to coordinate the efforts of the varied natural resource programs. With the support of this institutional home, the Tribes established a record of responsible program administration and moved closer to greater economic self-sufficiency through enterprise development.

For example, under the administration of the Tribal Lands Department, the Tribes now manage their own real estate and land resources as well as those of individual trust landowners. The Department successfully completes thousands of land transactions including appraisals, leases, permits, easements, purchases, deeds, wills, and probates. It also develops and processes hundreds of farm and pasture leases and home site lots and maintains title management from tracking ownership and filing subdivision plats to recording property encumbrances and

Honoring Nations Honoree 2003

Text in its entirety from: The Harvard Project On American Indian Economic Development

John F. Kennedy School of Government Harvard University

Flathead

Honoring Nations
Honoree 2003

Text in its entirety from:
The Harvard Project On
American Indian Economic
Development

John F. Kennedy School
of Government
Harvard University

modifications. The Department is a leader in the automation of leasing contract management including the distribution of payments to trust land owners.

The tribal management of Mission Valley Power has been similarly successful. Power rates among the CSKT are some of the lowest in the Northwest and their utility system is one of the best maintained. The Tribes' ten-year improvement plans are enhancing power delivery and reliability as well as preparing for future load growth. In 2000, a survey of fifteen hundred customers revealed that 75 to 79 percent of respondents considered their service excellent and 20 to 24 percent considered it satisfactory. Less than 1 percent of respondents were dissatisfied.

In 2002, the CSKT realized annual revenues of over two million dollars from their natural resources and six hundred seventy-seven thousand dollars from land leases. That same year, the Kerr Dam lease revenue brought in over thirteen million dollars. A portion of these revenues are reinvested in securing the Tribes' continuing self-governance. For example, three to five million dollars are budgeted annually for the acquisition of reservation lands.

The significance of the CSKT's successes, however, should not be measured in revenues alone. Tribes contemplating the management of their own natural resources may learn from the following two examples. First, by systematically putting themselves in charge of their resources and programs, the CSKT corrected the fundamental accountability problem that has persisted in Indian Country for hundreds of years. Today, their tribal government, not the federal government, presides over the Flathead Reservation. Even though the configuration of their reservation dictates that the tribal government must interact with municipal, county, state, and federal government agencies, the Tribes have, to the maximum extent possible, achieved self-governance over their lands, resources, and citizens. Secondly, as the Tribes come to hold increasingly direct control over their resources, they have created a national ethos of accountability for their management actions. Both the Tribes' employees and its citizens expect the tribal government to perform at the highest level in meeting the CSKT's needs. For the CSKT, this accountability has been an enormous asset. The CSKT have improved the lives of those on the reservation, and they have gained recognition from local, state, and federal governments for CSKT's capabilities and built awareness within these governments of CSKT's resource management goals and priorities.

Not only have the Tribes established first-rate organizational and managerial systems, but they have established it in a strategic and self-determined manner. The CSKT were motivated to assume the management of their lands and resources because they had a clear vision of what their tribal government should accomplish. The Tribes' traditional beliefs place priority on the respectful care of the natural world. Acknowledging that water, forest, and land resources are the cornerstones of their tribal revenues, the CSKT desired to strike a "careful balance" between "properly utilizing resources and ensuring that abuse and waste is minimal." Tribal governments that effectively assert their sovereignty, like the CSKT, are among those best positioned to develop laws and policies that protect and advance the interests of their people.

The Tribes' understanding of, and commitment to, building their capacity for self-governance made their vision possible. They cultivated their human resources, hiring tribal members to manage their natural resources and ensuring that these

individuals met the standards of state and federal government agencies by providing opportunities for degree completion and necessary licensure. Additionally, the Tribes opened management opportunities to their staff members and maintained an environment where the management of natural resource programs is independent of tribal government politics. They also invested in their trust resources. For example, the Tribal Lands Department has assisted Indian and non-Indian livestock producers in accessing aid through the American Indian Livestock Feed Program; treated nearly twenty-five thousand acres of noxious weeds; and, in collaboration with the National Bison Range, released bio-control agents on and around the Bison Range. Recognizing that their success in natural resource management is a direct result of their capacity, the Tribes have formed working relationships-occasionally formalized through Memoranda of Understanding-with municipalities, county governments, multiple state and federal agencies, real estate brokers, title insurance companies, utilities, universities, and surveyors.

Lastly, the Tribes' establishment of an accountable system of self-governance is, because of its strategic, self-determined quality, remarkably efficient. The CSKT refused to assume management of any program until they were convinced they could manage these resources more effectively than the previous provider. As a result, the Tribes' management operations-from ordinances to policies and procedures-are model tribal programs. The Tribal Forestry program enacts less restrictive purchasing procedures than were previously required. There is also greater freedom to allocate financial resources to changing priorities. The staff of the Tribal Lands Department is dedicated to quality customer service and familiar with the status of the lands. Thus, it can process the Tribes' titles locally, rather than submit them to a regional BIA office. The Lands Department also manages Individual Indian Money Accounts, depositing funds into individual accounts within twenty-four hours of their receipt. These enhancements exist not only at the program level, but also at the tribal level. As manager of all tribal natural resources, the CSKT are able to integrate technical and human resources more effectively than partial managers such as the BIA. The Tribes exceed previous efforts even to the extent of meeting requirements of previously "unfunded mandates," such as the protection of threatened and endangered species and National Environmental Policy Act compliance, which exist in federal programs.

The Confederated Salish and Kootenai Tribes have understood the benefits that would result from self-governance. Even before the era of self-determination, they were committed to assuming management of their trust resources and to acquiring this responsibility strategically. Self-governance is an imperative for Indian nations. However, it is equally as important that this self-governance be exercised effectively. Across the board, the Tribes set their own goals and priorities, develop laws and policies that support tribal sovereignty and effective programs to meet tribal needs, demand that their programs perform at a high standard, and hold themselves accountable for outcomes. They have made enormous progress in restoring the 1885 land base by acquiring major pieces of land, and have proven themselves to be among the best land managers in the country.

LOCATION AND LAND STATUS

Located in north-central Montana, the Fort Belknap Reservation is the fourth largest reservation in the state and covers an area of 652,593 acres. Rectangular in shape, the reservation has an average east-west width of 28 miles, and an average length of 40 miles. The Fort Belknap Agency is the central community on the reservation and is located three miles southeast of Harlem, Montana, along U.S. Highway 2.There are four major communities at Fort Belknap: Fort Belknap Agency in the northwest corner of the reservation, Hays, Lodgepole, and Milk River Valley. Harlem, which lies outside the reservation boundaries northwest of Fort Belknap Agency, also has a large Indian population.

Fort Belknap was established in 1869 near the present town of Chinook, Montana. The new fort served as a trading post and became the government agency for the Gros Ventre and Assiniboine Indians living in the area. On May 1, 1888, by an Act of Congress, the Blackfeet, Flathead, and Nez Perce tribes were forced to cede 17,500,000 acres of their joint reservation and relocate to three smaller reservations: the Blackfeet Reservation, Fort Peck Reservation, and Fort Belknap Reservation. The Gros Ventres had signed the treaty as part of the Blackfeet Nation. The Gros Ventres and the Assiniboines were relocated to the Fort Belknap Reservation. The same year, the agency moved from Chinook to its present location five miles east of Harlem, on the northwest corner of the reservation.

PHYSICAL DESCRIPTION

The Fort Belknap Reservation spans alluvial bottomland, glacial till plains, and the Bearpaw and Little Rocky mountain ranges. The northern portion of the reservation drains into the Milk River, while the southern portion drains into the Missouri River. The Bearpaw and Little Rocky mountain ranges reach an elevation of approximately 6,000 feet.

CLIMATE

The reservation experiences semiarid weather. Temperatures range from highs of over 100°F in the summer to below -50°F in the winter. Annual precipitation averages between 10 and 16 inches.

CULTURE AND HISTORY

Fort Belknap Indian Reservation is populated by members of the Gros Ventre (pronounced Gro Von,) and Assiniboine tribes. The Assiniboines speak a Siouan dialect, while the Gros Ventre language belongs to the greater Algonquian linguistic family. Traditionally belonging to the Yanktonai Sioux group, the Assiniboines are believed to have separated from the tribe in the early 1600s due to internal strife. The Assiniboines, whose tribal name is Nakota, "The Peaceful Ones," moved westward from the Rainy Lake and Lake of the Woods area along the Canadian border to the northern plains region in the early 1700s. To facilitate hunting, the tribe broke into two bands, one group remaining in the northern plains to hunt bison. Before 1774, the Assiniboines divided again, with some moving south and west along the Missouri River. Epidemics ravaged their numbers, necessitating an alliance with the Crees against their common enemy, the Blackfeet. The Assiniboines agreed to the Fort Laramie Treaty of 1851, as the treaty provided them with hunting territory. The Assiniboines were traditionally considered excellent hunters and horsemen.

They shared hunting rights with the Gros Ventre tribe on lands that would become the Fort Belknap Reservation.

The Gros Ventres, whose traditional name is Aa'ninin, "White Clay People," formerly lived in the Red River Valley in what is now North Dakota. In the sixteenth century, the tribe began to move westward and divided into two groups. One group continued to move southward and formed the Arapaho Tribe, while the other group moved northward to Montana. This group forged alliances with the Blackfeet Tribe in Montana.

Their relationship with the Blackfeet remained solid until the mid-1800s, when a number of cultural and social factors caused the Blackfeet and the Gros Ventre people to wage war against each other. After losing a major battle against the Blackfeet in 1867, the Gros Ventres became close allies with the Assiniboines, and they began living together in the Milk River country.

When the Gros Ventre Tribe agreed in 1888 to give up their larger territorial rights and settle for a reservation land base, the federal government intended this reservation to also house other indigenous groups. The Gros Ventre and the Assiniboine people vehemently opposed the sale of the mountains, which federal commissioners who were assigned to negotiate the sale of the gold-mining country advocated in 1896. Advising the impoverished Indians that they would starve in two years if they did not make an agreement with the government, the commissioners convinced tribal representatives to sell a strip of land, seven miles long and four miles wide, for $360,000. Pegasus Gold Company now mines this site, with heavy opposition from some tribal members. The opposition is compounded by the current reality of contaminated land and water and the accompanying health risks to the reservation people.

GOVERNMENT

The Fort Belknap Community Council was organized under the 1934 Indian Reorganization Act. Its constitution and bylaws were approved in 1935, and a corporate charter was ratified in 1937. The tribal council is composed of 12 members, six Gros Ventres and six Assiniboines, elected by the community at large, with three officers elected by the council. Council members serve for four-year staggered terms.
The tribe maintains jurisdiction within reservation boundaries on matters of rights-of-way, waterways, watercourses, and streams.

ECONOMY

Reservation economy relies on a number of entities. The tribe has a strong agricultural industry; including ranching and leasing tribally owned lands. There are mining ventures and lumber operations on the reservation as well.

In 2003 the tribe reached an agreement with the State of Montana regarding the distribution of taxes collected from the sale of cigarettes and tobacco products on the reservation. The state agreed to pay the tribe 150 percent of the state per capita tobacco taxes for each enrolled tribal member living on the reservation. The tribes estimated revenue for the quarters of July 1, 2004, through June 30, 2005, were $150,000.

Fort Belknap Reservation
Federal reservation
Blaine and Phillips counties,
Montana

Fort Belknap Indian Community
Gros Ventre and Assiniboine
Tribes
R.R. 1, Box 66
Harlem, MT 59526
406-353-2205
406-353-2797 Fax
usgennet.org

Total area *(BIA realty, 2004)*
619,035.71 acres

Tribally owned
(BIA realty, 2004)
238,668.84 acres

Individually owned
(BIA realty, 2004)
376,058.38 acres

Federal trust *(BIA realty, 2004)*
4,308.49 acres

Population *2000 census*
2,959

Fort Belknap

Total labor force *2000 census*
1,086

Total labor force
(BIA labor report, 2001)
3,039

High school graduate or
higher *2000 census*
75.1%

Bachelor's degree or higher
2000 census
12.5%

Total labor force *2000 census*
23%

Unemployment rate
(BIA labor report, 2001)
71%

Per capita income *2000 census*
$8,150

TRI-MT-023

TRI-MT-025

TRI-MT-024

TRI-MT-026

TRI-MT-027

TRI-MT-028

TRI-MT-023 Sign: "Welcome to Fort Belknap Agency, Home of the Gros Ventre & Assiniboine Tribes"

TRI-MT-025 Tribal Radio Station "KGBA 88.1 FM"

TRI-MT-024 Tribal Beef & Buffalo Meat Packing Co.

TRI-MT-026 Fort Belknap Kwik Stop, Gas Station & Convenient Store

TRI-MT-027 Seal of the Fort Belknap Reservation hand-painted Buffalo Skin inside Council Chambers

TRI-MT-028 Fort Belknap College, Little River Learning Lodge, "Wakpa Juk'an Wasnokya Tibi"

Government as Employer. The Fort Belknap Tribal Council, BIA, and Indian Health Service serve as the primary employers and vocational training sources for local residents. While many of these jobs have been permanent, such as employment through the Hays/Lodge Pole School Systems, the majority of the employment opportunities have been sporadic and temporary, such as jobs through housing and urban development programs.

Agriculture and Livestock. Fort Belknap has an agriculturally based economy, which includes farming, ranching, and leasing lands. Approximately 40,000 acres are used for dry land farming. The reservation leases both irrigated and dry farmland, totaling 85,386 acres. Important crops grown on the reservation include wheat, hay, and barley.

Grazing permits represent a substantial percentage of the tribe's annual revenue. The "right to do business" fee, as the grazing tax is called, is one dollar per animal. The tax is waived for the first 300 head of tribal member-owned cattle.

The tribe operates Little Rockies Meat Packing. Formerly Hi Line Packing/Big Sky Beef, the tribe purchased the company in 2002, and it is the only tribally owned, USDA-certified meatpacking facility in the United States. It serves the meatpacking needs of local industry, and it specializes in

custom meat cutting and processing of beef and buffalo. The tribe manages a heard of 300 buffalo.

Forestry. Fort Belknap's timber reserves lie in the southern part of the reservation in the Little Rocky Mountains. The tribe currently maintains 33,700 acres of wooded land through a 10-year forest management plan. The timber's potential, at this time, seems limited to a small post and pole operation. After approximately 15 more years of managed growth, the timber could support commercial sales and a larger scale harvest. Pine is predominant.

Mining. Mineral production on the Fort Belknap Reservation has been limited primarily to traprock for local use in constructing and maintaining the Fort Peck Dam. The rock quarry at Snake Butte, 12 miles south of Harlem, still contains millions of tons of easily accessible rock. While geological formations would indicate the presence of natural gas, oil, or coal on the reservation, none has been discovered at this point. Limestone deposits are readily accessible in the southern part of the Fort Belknap Reservation.

Industrial Parks. The tribe intends to use the tribally owned Fort Belknap Builders Building for industrial purposes. At 180 x 420 feet, this steel building offers plumbing, electricity, and office space.

Tourism and Recreation. The Fort Belknap Tourism Office and Information Center provides tourism information for interested parties. Fort Belknap Ventures, located within the center, features Native American arts and crafts. St. Paul's Mission Church is located in Hays. It is a historic site that currently operates as an elementary school for tribal youth.

RV parking, showers, and picnic grounds are available. Opportunities are also available for visitors to take guided tours of Mission Canyon, Snake Butte, ancient tepee rings, and the tribal buffalo pasture. Mission Canyon, located south of Hays, offers several natural attractions and recreational sites. Picnic and camping areas are located within the park.

Both trout fishing and hunting are abundant on the reservation. Mule deer, whitetail deer, antelope, and some migratory waterfowl are hunted seasonally. Fishing and hunting licenses issued by the tribe and a tribal guide for hunting parties are required on reservation lands.

Three major celebrations are held on the reservation, the Fort Belknap Indian Days celebration in July, the Chief Joseph Memorial Dance in October, and the Mid-Winter Fair in February. The tribe also hosts the Arts and Crafts Fair and Cultural Food Festival, the Milk River Indian Days, and the Hays Powwow.

INFRASTRUCTURE
Both the Burlington Northern Railroad and U.S. Highway 2 cross the reservation, providing east-west access. State Highway 66, on the other hand, offers a north-south transportation route. Air, bus, and trucking services are available in Havre, which is located 47 miles from the reservation. There is no form of public transportation on the reservation, although it
does have a small airstrip.

Electricity. North West Energy Company supplies electricity in the Fort Belknap Agency area of the reservation, while the Big Flat Rural Electric Cooperative supplies electricity to the Lodge Pole and Hays area.
Water Supply. The Fort Belknap Tribal Utilities Company provides water and sewage treatment to the reservation. The EPA has issued a permit allowing the operation of wastewater lagoon systems to treat most domestic sewage on the reservation.

Telecommunications. Central Montana Communications and Triangle Telephone Cooperative, which own the area's telephone equipment, both provide service to Fort Belknap Reservation.

Cable television is available in some areas of the reservation, though satellites are required for reception in others. Most residencies are equipped with radios that receive reception from Havre and Great Falls stations, and with transreceivers that allow for communication between Hays, Fort Belknap Agency, and the tribal police station.

COMMUNITY FACILITIES AND SERVICES
The tribe operates a recreational complex that offers indoor swimming, weight training, and basketball facilities. The tribe provides an Elderly Nutrition Program and a Youth Cultural and Recreational Activities Program.

Education. The Fort Belknap Education Department was established in 1977. The area's children attend public schools in Lodgepole, Hays, Harlem, and Dodson. Some reservation children attend off-reservation boarding schools. St. Paul's Mission, a Catholic school, established as a boarding school, September 14, 1886, continues as a day school, educating grades K-6 in the community of Hays, at the southern boundary of the reservation.

The Fort Belknap Community College opened in 1984. The college offers associate's degrees in the arts and sciences. Campus facilities include a library and tribal archives. Montana State University/Northern is located approximately one hour from the reservation in Havre.

Health Care. The recently constructed hospital and health center in Hays provides tribal members with health and dental services. It is operated by Indian Health Service. The tribe's health department operates a health education program and employs a community health representative. The tribe also offers ambulance services to residents of the reservation.

ENVIRONMENTAL CONCERNS
The tribe received a Clean Water Act Section 104 (b)(#) Wetlands Program grant in 1996. An initial inventory of wetland areas was completed. The tribe completed a 5-Year Strategic Plan for the Wetlands Program in 1999. This strategy contributes to the goal of preserving the reservation's wetlands.

The tribe has identified water source contamination on the reservation. A number of the rivers and tributaries were found to have been affected by mining activities upstream. With the assistance of the Environmental Protection Agency, the tribe hopes to offset the impact of the contamination.

Fort Belknap

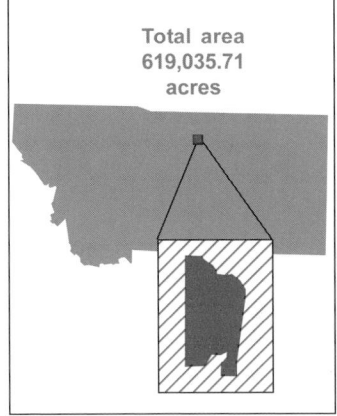

Total area
619,035.71
acres

Fort Peck

Fort Peck Indian Reservation
Federal reservation
Assiniboine and Sioux
Roosevelt, Daniels, Valley, and
Sheridan counties, Montana

Fort Peck Assiniboine and
Sioux Tribes
P.O. Box 1027
Poplar, MT 59255
406-768-5155
406-768-5478 Fax

Total area *(BIA realty, 2004)*
937,046.28 acres

Tribally owned *(BIA realty, 2004)*
402,730.05 acres

Individually owned
(BIA realty, 2004)
534,6316.23 acres

Population *2000 census*
10,321

Population *(Tribal source)*
10,321

Total labor force *2000 census*
4,378

**High school graduate or
higher** *2000 census*
80.5%

Bachelor's degree or higher
2000 census
14.6%

Unemployment rate *2000 census*
17.5%

Unemployment rate *(BIA labor
report, 2001)*
63%

Per capita income *2000 census*
$10,691

LOCATION AND LAND STATUS

The Fort Peck Indian Reservation lies in northeastern Montana, primarily in Roosevelt County, although small portions lie in Valley, Daniels, and Sheridan counties. The reservation is bordered on the south by the Missouri River, on the east by the Big Muddy Creek, and on the west by the Porcupine Creek. The largest community on the reservation is Wolf Point, which is also the Roosevelt County seat. Tribal headquarters are located in Poplar.

The reservation was established in 1871 by an Executive Order. Over time, Congress authorized the sale of large portions of tribal lands. The Dawes Act of 1887 authorized the division of tribal lands into parcels to be given to individuals. The Allotment Act of 1908 dictated that each tribal member receive 320 acres, in addition to 40 acres of irrigable land. Heads of families also received 20 acres of timberland. In 1913, over one million acres of unallotted or tribal unreserved lands were made available to non-Native homesteaders. In 1917, a portion of tribally owned and allotted lands was sold to railroad interests. In 1946, Congress authorized the sale of lands for the Fort Peck project, and any lands no longer required for use were to revert into trust status.

In addition to the land held in trust, the tribe retains control of 85,000 acres of submarginal land through a lease agreement with the U.S. Department of the Interior. Title to the Indian-owned land is complicated due to multiple inheritances. As a result of the Dawes Act of 1887, there is a checkerboarding between Indian-owned land allotments, tribally owned land, and land owned by non-Indians (an estimated 55 percent of the reservation).

An estimated 6,499 enrolled tribal members live on the reservation while approximately 3,900 live in off-reservation areas. Tribal enrollment increased by 1,247 enrolled members from 1994 to 2003. Increase of enrolled population is about 1.4 percent per year; using a conservative 1 percent per year growth, tribal enrollment will increase to 12,560 by 2012. Approximately 500 members of other Native American tribes live within reservation boundaries as well. These include Chippewa, Cree, and Teton Sioux people.

PHYSICAL DESCRIPTION

The Fort Peck Indian Reservation lies in regions of rolling hills, glacial till, and river valleys. There are woodlands near the rivers and stock dams.

CLIMATE

The reservation experiences an average of 16 to 17 inches of rain during the summer months. The temperature during the summer ranges from 69°F to 110°F. Winter temperatures range from -30°F to +25°F. Snowfall averages between moderate and heavy. The wind averages 14 miles per hour daily year round.

CULTURE AND HISTORY

Within the Assiniboine and Sioux Tribe are several smaller bands. The Sioux Bands on the reservation are the Sisseton/Wahpeton, Yantonai, Cuthead, Oglala, and the Teton Hunkpapa. The Assiniboine Bands include the Canoe Paddler and Red Bottom. The Assiniboines occupied the region surrounding the present-day reservation as early as the late 1600s. Their winter grounds included the Saskatchewan River country, and they ventured as far south as the Missouri River. The tribe gradually moved out of the woodlands into the prairies. They participated in fur trading with French-Canadian trappers and were allies with the Crees, Chippewas, and Monsonis against Sioux, Arikaras, Cheyenne,

Blackfeet, and Gros Ventre tribes. The Assiniboines were a strong presence in the region and very competitive in the fur trading industry. Although they suffered great losses in smallpox epidemics in 1780 and 1800, the Assiniboines managed to remain a central force in the fur trade industry for a number of years. In 1827, the American Fur Company built Fort Union at the confluence of the Missouri and White Earth rivers. Fort Union became the primary institution servicing the Assiniboine traders.

In 1851, the Assiniboine Tribe attended the Fort Laramie Treaty Council meeting along with representatives of the Great Sioux Nation, the Blackfeet Nation and the U.S. government. The boundaries for lands were delineated for the tribes represented, and chiefs were named. The Assiniboines claimed lands south of the Missouri River, the Sioux claimed what is now North Dakota and South Dakota, and the Blackfeet were assigned an area north of the Missouri River from the Rocky Mountains to the western boundaries of the present-day Fort Peck Reservation.

During the mid-1850s, various bands of the Sioux Nation began to enter the Assiniboine's region, remaining for longer periods of time as the game in their traditional hunting grounds became depleted. In 1862, a large number of eastern Sioux refugees fled from the conflicts arising in Minnesota. Assiniboine Bands offered refuge to the Sioux and began to serve as mediators between Sioux tribal members, government agents, and traders. The bond between the tribes was strengthened by the increase of intermarriage.

Various conflicts, further depletion of natural resources, and encroachment of Euro-American settlers created an influx of Sioux Bands to the area. The arrival of more Siouan Bands to the region began to deplete the resources of the local government agency. In 1872, a new Fort Peck Indian Agency was established to specifically serve the Assiniboine and Sioux Indians. It was located within the old Fort Peck stockade. In 1878, the agency was relocated to present-day Poplar because of annual flooding to the area.

Each tribe maintains cultural and spiritual traditions. Indigenous languages are still spoken by tribal members and religious ceremonies are practiced as well.

GOVERNMENT

The Fort Peck tribes adopted their first written constitution in 1927 and amended in 1952. It established a representative form of government, and the department of the interior granted it formal recognition in 1960. The Fort Peck tribal constitution remains one of the few modern tribal constitutions that retains provisions for a general council, the traditional form of government. The council includes a chairperson, vice-chairperson, secretary-accountant, sergeant-at-arms, and 12 voting members. Council officers and members are elected at large and serve two-year terms. Council members preside over nine business committees, each dealing with tribal policy and business management.

The tribes participate in the Tribal Strategies Against Violence (TSAV) program. The program provides assistance to Native American reservations as they develop community-based programs to address issues of crime, violence, and substance abuse. The Fort Peck division of TSAV established a planning team consisting of representatives from law enforcement, court system, child protective services, education, and business entities. Spiritual leaders and community members are also on the team. The team's primary goals include strengthening community part-

TRI-MT-029

TRI-MT-030

TRI-MT-031

TRI-MT-032

TRI-MT-033

TRI-MT-034

Fort Peck

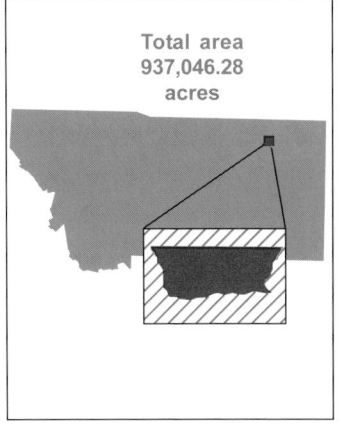

Total area
937,046.28
acres

nerships to create comprehensive service delivery, enhancing prosecution, initiating community policing, and reducing child-to-child violence. In 1996, six law enforcement agencies joined with the Fort Peck TSAV team to create a task force that discussed multijurisdictional matters, provided educational programs, coordinated investigative procedures between agencies, and rewrote the tribal juvenile code.

ECONOMY

The reservation maintains a stable economy that is largely reliant on the agriculture industry. As the tribe faces concerns with water quality and supply, however, it is turning to other sources to support its economies. Manufacturing and mining provide great opportunities for the tribe.

The tribes are currently working on an Indian Community Development Block Grant. The grant would support development of viable Indian communities by creating decent housing, suitable living environments, and economic opportunities.

Government as Employer. The Assiniboine and Sioux Tribes serve as the largest employers on the reservation. Fort Peck Community College, the BIA, and Indian Health Service also provide substantial employment opportunities.

Economic Development Projects. The tribe receives annual planning grants from the economic development administration as well as a five-year BIA Community and Economic Development Grant. The tribe created an economic development commission to determine the area's economic needs and the means to meet those needs. Proposed economic ventures for the community include Looking Eagle Manufacturing, Silverwolf Casino, Tribal Express, and Nakoda Trails.

Agriculture and Livestock. The reservation lies within an agricultural region. Important crops grown in the area include cereals and feed grains, hay silage, and grasses. Dryland farming, mostly in spring wheat, accounts for about 75 percent of all harvested acreage. Eight grain elevators are located on the reservation. Currently, the tribe is attempting to update its irrigation system, which was constructed in 1908. Located along the Missouri River Valley between Frazer and Wolf Point, this irrigation system services approximately 18,500 acres. Only about 22 percent of these irrigated lands are operated by Indians. In total, tribal members operate about 155,072 acres of the reservation's farmlands, while 106,522 acres are leased to non-Indians. There are 188,702 acres of tribally owned and 198,526 acres of individually owned land dedicated to rangeland. The tribes have been operating their own buffalo ranch since 2001.

Mining. The Assiniboine and Sioux Tribes of the Fort Peck Reservation are one of the first Native American nations in the United States to develop jointly and wholly owned oil wells.

TRI-MT-029 Directional Sign to "Fort Peck Tribes Museum, Dakota & Dakoda"

TRI-MT-030 Administration Building, Fort Peck Community College

TRI-MT-031 Tribal Administration & BIA Office Building Complex on Hilltop

TRI-MT-032 West Electronics, Inc. Fort Peck Industrial Park Popular, MT

TRI-MT-033 Assembly workers inside West Electronics, Inc.

TRI-MT-034 A & S Tribal Industries, Inc. Popular, MT

Fort Peck

There are 32 oil fields, 22 of which have 168 producing wells. The reservation has an abundance of coal-bearing rocks, which lie between the Poplar River and Big Muddy Creek. Coal resources were mined on the reservation as late as 1960, when the Wolf Creek mine closed. The present status of the coal market, coupled with evolving tribal perspectives on environmental preservation, preclude further coal development in the near term. The tribes are, however, currently soliciting proposals from natural gas companies to develop their vast reserves of shallow natural gas found in the reservations Cretaceous-age rocks. Sand and gravel deposits are also widespread throughout the reservation and are utilized locally for road construction and sanding. In addition, numerous deposit beds of bentonite, a clay mineral used mainly in the manufacture of iron ore pellets, are located in the western and southwestern part of the reservation.

Manufacturing. A number of manufacturing enterprises are located on the reservation. Fort Peck Tribes own A&S Tribal Industries (A&S), which is operated as a joint venture through a management contract with Brunswick Industries. A&S specializes in department of defense product lines, including camouflage netting and deep draw metal fabrications for military chests. A&S has recently been developing nonmilitary product lines as well. A&S has the potential to become the largest private employer in Montana. Tribally owned West Electronics also specializes in military contracts, producing printed circuit cards and laced cable harnesses. The company has recently redesigned and tested a security alarm control box system and is marketing the product to National Guard installations. WPCO/Great Divide Manufacturing Company is another tribally owned firm.

Industrial Parks. The tribe manages a prosperous industrial park in Poplar, Montana. The park houses a metal fabrication plant and a sewing factory, among other enterprises. The park is one of the largest employers in the state. West Electronics, a tribally owned manufacturing plant, is also located in the industrial park and provides a large source of employment and revenue to the tribe. It produces electronic equipment for government and private sector clientele.

Services and Retail. There are a number of privately owned businesses located on the reservation. They include a convenience store, gas stations, restaurants, a laundromat, an auto repair shop, a video arcade/fast food business, and an arts and crafts store.

Tourism and Recreation. The Fort Peck Assiniboine and Sioux Culture Center and Museum are located in Poplar. The center features exhibits of Assiniboine and Sioux heritage, arts, and crafts. The Fort Peck Tribes also host wild game hunters and fishermen from all over the country and Canada. Licenses for nonmembers can be purchased for $15.

On May 6-9, 2004, there was a Corps of Discovery II Celebration in Poplar. This Lewis and Clark event entailed three days of activities. Weekend-long powwows are held throughout the summer. The Poplar Indian Days held over Labor Day weekend is the largest powwow and draws a number of visitors to the area. The powwow includes dancing competitions as well as honoring ceremonies. The Wolf Point Wild Horse Stampede occurs every second weekend of July. This PRCA Rodeo attracts cowboys from all over the country.

INFRASTRUCTURE

Running east-west along the south end of the reservation, U.S. Route 2 serves as the reservation's primary highway. Running north-south, State Route 13 bisects the reservation between Wolf Point and Poplar. The nearest interstate highway is I-94, which lies approximately 90 miles south of the Fort Peck area.

Electricity. Montana Dakota Utilities, Sheridan Electric, Northern Electric, Valley Electric, and McCone Electric provide electricity to the reservation. The tribe has contracted power from the Western Area Power Administration for irrigation purposes.

Water Supply. Water quality and supply are critical issues. The tribe has initiated a Municipal and Industrial Rural Drinking Water Program, which will be responsible for an irrigation system along the Missouri River. The tribe hopes the project will help stabilize the water supply and, in turn, better serve the reservation's domestic and commercial needs. The intake construction phase began in 2003, and it is near completion. The whole project is estimated to take 10 years.

Transportation. Freight delivery, rental car service, a UPS operations center, and AMTRAK rail service are all available at Wolf Point. The Burlington Northern Railroad provides rail freight service to the area, with service provided to the Fort Peck Industrial Park via a rail spur line. Both the Wolf Point International Airport and the nearby Glasgow International Airport offer daily commercial flights. Additionally, there is a small general aviation airport located in Poplar. The Fort Peck Transportation System provides commuter bus service, transporting t college students and workers from outlying reservation communities into Poplar as well as serving the elderly and handicapped.

Telecommunications. Nemont Telephone Company provides telephone services to reservation residents.

COMMUNITY FACILITIES AND SERVICES

The tribe provides an elderly nutrition program and youth cultural and recreational activities. The Saddle Club of Poplar and the Stampede Committee of Wolf Point organize rodeos in their communities. Four of the six communities on Fort Peck operate their own Boys and Girls Clubs.

Education. Tribal youth attend five public school districts on the reservation. The tribe operates a Head Start program, Fort Peck Community College, and Native American Education Service College. Fort Peck Community College is a fully accredited community college and offers associates of arts and technical degrees. Native American Education Service College offers a bachelor's degree program and maintains one of the strongest tribal studies programs in the United States. The tribe maintains a scholarship program and enrolled members are eligible to attend college on or off the reservation.

Health Care. Health care services are contracted through Indian Health Service. Facilities on the reservation include the Verne E. Gibbs Health Center in Poplar and the Chief Redstone Clinic in Wolf Point, and there is a reservation-wide ambulance service. The health department provides a community health representative program, mental health, dental services and eye care.

ENVIRONMENTAL CONCERNS

Water quality and supply are of major concern on the Fort Peck Reservation. In 2000, the tribe began discussions with the nearby towns of Plentywood and Peerless to work toward the development of a $180 million water project to serve all three communities. The Fort Peck Reservation is not immune to the effects of global warming. The tribe will need to begin extensive long-term planning for their land and water resources.

LOCATION AND LAND STATUS

The Northern Cheyenne Reservation spans nearly 450,000 acres of southeastern Montana. It is situated about 100 miles east of Billings, Montana, and 75 miles due north of Sheridan, Wyoming. The reservation is bordered on the east by the Tongue River and on the west by the Crow Reservation. The reservation was established by an Executive Order in November 1884.

The tribe has purchased 560 acres adjacent to the Bear Butte State Park in South Dakota, 5,000 acres adjacent to the southern boundaries of the reservation, and 554 acres of land near the Tongue River Dam.

PHYSICAL DESCRIPTION

Terrain on the reservation varies from low, grass-covered hills to high, steep outcroppings to narrow valleys. Elevations range from approximately 3,000 to 5,000 feet. Rocky areas on the reservation comprise the Fort Union Formation. The formation consists of alternating layers of sandstone, shale, and coal beds and has been dated to the Paleocene Era. Plant and animal fossils are apparent.

CLIMATE

The reservation experiences average temperatures of 46°F. Snow is often heavy during winters, and roads may become impassable in places. Average relative humidity is between 25 and 35 percent.

CULTURE AND HISTORY

Members of the Northern Cheyenne Tribe are descendants of the Tsi'sti'stas and Suh'tio peoples. Their traditional homelands incorporated the Great Lakes region to lands in the Mississippi River country. It is believed that the people once inhabited areas as far north as northeastern Canada. During the 1600s, the Cheyennes began to move westward from the Great Lakes toward the Missouri River to avoid contact with Euro-American settlers. The people began to rely on the buffalo of the plains to support their livelihood.

By the 1800s, the Cheyenne people began to participate in the fur trading industry. They encountered the Lewis and Clark Expedition in 1804. In the 1830s, the tribe divided into two bands, the Northern Cheyenne and the Southern Cheyenne. The Northern Cheyennes remained in the northern territories near their Lakota relatives and the Black Hills and Tongue River regions. The Southern Cheyennes moved southward toward the Colorado Territory.

Although the Northern Cheyennes willingly signed treaties with the federal government, the government failed to uphold those agreements. Conflicts arose and the Cheyennes were eventually confined to the Tongue River Reservation in southeastern Montana Territory. Once confined to the reservation, the Northern Cheyennes experienced almost total devastation of their traditional ways. Euro-American encroachment destroyed the buffalo herds and the independence that livelihood yielded. As happened throughout the country, federal agencies and religious groups further attempted to eradicate Cheyenne ways through policies, regulations, and laws.

The Cheyenne people continue to struggle to repair the damage created. They are actively working toward retrieving their indigenous language, spiritual beliefs, and cultural traditions. In 2003, the tribe entered into nonviolent conflict with the St. Labre Mission. The tribe requested that the Catholic Church discontinue use of the Northern Cheyenne name to raise monies that would not be dispersed to the tribe. While the church initially denied any wrongdoing, it did eventually agree to compensate the tribe. The tribe hopes to reconcile with the Church under new terms that will recognize the tribe as a sovereign nation with property and intellectual property rights, and will promote and support economic growth for the tribe. Currently, Northern Cheyenne tribal member Ben Nighthorse Campbell serves as a United States Senator.

GOVERNMENT

The Northern Cheyenne Tribe was recognized as a sovereign nation under an amended constitution, and bylaws and corporate charter were approved pursuant to the Indian Reorganization act of 1934. The tribe adopted a constitution and bylaws in 1936 and amended them in 1960.

The tribal council serves as the governing body, consisting of the president, vice-president, sergeant-at-arms, secretary, treasurer, and one representative for every 200 enrolled tribal members. The president is elected at large; representatives are elected from each of the five districts on the reservation; the vice-president and sergeant-at-arms are elected by the council; and the secretary and treasurer are appointed. The secretary and treasurer have no voting powers on the council.

The tribe operates a number of programs. Departments include air quality, child care, community health representative, commodity, community health, elderly, environmental protection, M.S.U. extension, natural resources, personnel, Sand Creek Offices, tribal employment rights, fish and wildlife, Title IV-E, education, forestry, health, enrollment services, WIC, and work investment act.

The tribal constitution created a judicial branch of the tribal government. It consists of all the tribal courts. The courts exercise authority over decisions regarding the constitutionality of council enactments and resolutions; they also exercise authority over criminal and civil matters within the tribe's jurisdiction. The Comprehensive Indian Resources for Community and Law Enforcement is funded through the U.S. Department of Justice. Program goals include building a youth services center, a detention center, a group home, an alternative school, a juvenile mentoring program and a number of other social services related to crime prevention.

BUSINESS CORPORATION

The Northern Cheyenne Tribe operates tribal government enterprises.

ECONOMY

Government as Employer. The tribe employs about 300 of its members in various capacities, including social services, health care, forestry, and the casino.

Economic Development Projects. The tribe operates an economic development administration and adopted a Comprehensive Economic Development Strategies Planning Document in 2001. This program is funded by the U.S. Department of Commerce and serves to assist the tribe in meeting the socioeconomic needs on the reservation.

The tribal fire department contracts with the State of Montana to dispatch fire fighter crews throughout the region as needed. In 2000, the state used 58 Northern Cheyenne fire crews. Fees amounted to $956,468 in payroll.

Northern Cheyenne Reservation
Federal reservation
Northern Cheyenne
Big Horn and Rosebud counties, Montana

Northern Cheyenne Tribe
P.O. Box 128
Lame Deer, MT 59043
406-477-6284
406-477-6210 Fax
ncheyenne.net

Total area *(BIA realty, 2004)*
440,882.43 acres

Tribally owned *(BIA realty, 2004)*
339,888.31 acres

Individually owned
(BIA realty, 2004)
100,993.44 acres

Federal trust *(BIA realty, 2004)*
.68 acres

Population *2000 census*
4,470

Total labor force *2000 census*
1,567

Total labor force
(BIA labor report, 2001)
1,618

High school graduate or higher *2000 census*
74.6%

Bachelor's degree or higher
2000 census
13.5%

Unemployment rate *2000 census*
19.5%

Unemployment rate
(BIA labor report, 2001)
27%

Per capita income *2000 census*
$7,736

Northern Cheyenne

TRI-MT-043

TRI-MT-036

TRI-MT-037

TRI-MT-038

TRI-MT-043 Lame Deer High School, Courtesy of Weller Architects, Albuquerque, NM

TRI-MT-036 Front Entrance of Northern Cheyenne Law Enforcement Center

TRI-MT-037 Sign in front of Northern Cheyenne Community Health Center

TRI-MT-038 Front view of "Northern Cheyenne Community Health Center"

Agriculture and Livestock. Approximately 27,000 acres of reservation lands are presently under cultivation, the vast majority of this in dry land farming efforts. These primarily entail hay, wheat, barley, and small grains. Annual revenues generated by farming total about $2.5 million.

Reservation lands support a strong livestock industry. The tribe leases almost 100 percent of its rangeland to the Northern Cheyenne Livestock Association. The association has, in turn, leased the range permits. Livestock have unrestricted access on the ranges and are able to enter riparian areas, which has resulted in major damage to the wetlands of the region. Individual tribal members own an estimated 12,000 to 15,000 head of cattle which, on the open market, would presently be worth somewhere in the range of $12 million. The tribe also purchased a herd of buffalo in 1974. The herd draws tourists and is also a potential source of food for tribal members.

Forestry. The tribe purchased the Tongue River Lumber Company in 1998. It produced boards, dimensional lumber, shop molding, and laminated products. It also sold residual chips shavings and bark. Due to financial setbacks, the company was temporarily closed in 2001 and voluntarily dissolved in 2004.

Gaming. The tribe owns and operates the Charging Horse Casino. The casino features 100 slots/VLTs, 500 bingo seats, and one restaurant. It employs 33 individuals. A building loan has recently been approved and the facility will be expanded.

Construction. Several tribal members are contractors and subcontractors. Reservation-based construction firms are regularly contracted for tribal projects.

Mining. Geological studies show that reservation lands contain approximately 55 billion tons of low-sulfur coal reserves; of these, about 35 billion tons are readily extractable. Additionally, Atlantic Richfield (ARCO) has explored for oil and gas reserves on tribal lands, given the reservation's proximity to a number of proven reserves.

Manufacturing. The reservation hosts several manufacturing concerns, including Northern Cheyenne Industries, which produces tepees and other traditional articles, and Cheyano Designs, which manufactures designer clothing.

Industrial Parks. A 30-acre site for a coal-based cogeneration power plant is planned in anticipation of the development of tribal coal reserves.

Real Estate/Commercial Development. Two proposed sites for housing developments are under consideration. The first project will include up to 100 housing units on 140 acres. The second will include 48 units donated by the Air Force on tribal lands.

Services and Retail. There are presently a total of 44 small businesses on the reservation, the majority of them Indian owned. These include laundromats, restaurants, gas stations, grocery stores, and Indian arts and crafts outlets.

Media and Communications. The tribe owns the Northern Cheyenne Tribe Internet Service Provider. It provides Internet access to reservation residencies.

Tourism and Recreation. The reservation is located near several historic sites that draw numerous visitors. The Chief Two Moons Monument located in Busby, the Battle of Little Bighorn Monument, the Decker Coal Mine, and the Tongue River Reservoir all offer tourist attractions. The St. Labre Indian School facilities in Ashland include a visitor center, a museum, and a gallery that features Native American memorabilia and artifacts The tribe also operates the Northern Cheyenne Tribal Museum in Lame Deer.

Camping facilities exist at the Northern Cheyenne Craft Center in Lame Deer and at the Morning Star View Campgrounds. Crazyhead Springs Recreation Area is a lovely spot for swimming, camping, and picnicking or skiing, snowshoeing, and snowmobiling as seasons permit. Tribal elk and buffalo herds are pastured near Lame Deer Ice Well Campgrounds. The tribe holds a celebrated and widely attended Fourth of July Powwow.

INFRASTRUCTURE

U.S. Highway 212 passes east-west through the reservation, while Route 315 also directly serves the reservation. Road 39 provides access from Lame Deer to Forsyth, Montana, and a paved road maintained by the BIA provides access from Ashland to Birney, Montana. During winter months, roads may become snowbound and icy, often impassable. The Highway Department is responsible for clearing obstructions and maintaining safe passageways.

Electricity. Pacific Power and Light provides electricity to the reservation. It has a coal powered electric-generating facility 21 miles north of Lame Deer.

Water Supply. The Northern Cheyenne Utilities Commission supplies domestic water to residents within population centers on the reservation. Wells located on individual lands or a district well, supply water to outlying residencies.

Each district maintains a central sewage system that services residences within population centers. Individually owned septic tanks service outlying residencies. The Indian Health Service and the Tribal Utilities Commission retain responsibility for maintaining and operating the water and sewage systems. Solid waste is transported to transfer sites located near population centers in each reservation district and then on to the Rosebud County or Bighorn County landfills.

Transportation. The nearest commercial bus services are available in Crow Agency, 45 miles from the reservation, and in Forsyth, 58 miles away. The Catholic Church maintains a private airstrip on the reservation. Billings and Sheridan, Wyoming, offer the nearest commercial air service. A railroad spur 20 miles north of the reservation connects with Burlington Northern rail lines.

Telecommunications. Range Telephone provides telephone service to the reservation. Northern Cheyenne Tribe Internet Service Provider furnishes Internet services. Several commercial television and radio stations serve the region.

COMMUNITY FACILITIES AND SERVICES

The tribe operates several community programs, including the Boys and Girls Club, a child care program, Healing Hearts, and the Recovery Program. Facilities include the fitness center. The Boys and Girls Club sponsors three sites on the Northern Cheyenne Reservation. It offers a technology center, Torch Club, Youth of the Year, CLUBService, Power Hour, Career Explorers Club, Junior Staff Career Development, SMARTMoves, Fine Arts Exhibit Program, NIKE Girls Sports, Challenges and SWOOSH clubs, and an after-school meal program, among many other programs and activities. The Boys and Girls Club provides support, education, and healthy alternatives for youth on the reservation. The club sponsors an annual youth powwow.

Native Action is a community-based organization that works together with the Northern Cheyennes and other tribes to promote and protect the community's needs. They strive to raise awareness of social issues and to empower tribal members to actively participate in the political, social, and economic processes on the reservation.

Public Safety. The tribe manages a volunteer fire department.

Education. The reservation maintains a Head Start program with nine sites throughout the reservation. The program received an award to initiate a Head Start curriculum in conjunction with Dull Knife Community College. The curriculum, "Identity-based Education: The Role of Culture in Helping People Become More Socially Competent" is funded by the Administration for Youth,

Families, and Children and by the American Indian Program Branch of the Head Start Bureau. Another award was granted to establish the "Healthy Children, Healthy Families, Healthy Communities" curriculum to address diabetes among Head Start children, families, and staff.

The tribe has an elementary school and a public high school. The Catholic Church operates the K-12 St. Labre Catholic Indian School on the eastern border of the reservation. It is a private school that provides boarding and day school services to students primarily from the Crow and Cheyenne reservations.

The tribe also operates the Dull Knife Memorial Community College. It is a fully accredited college and offers associate's degree programs in the arts and sciences. The college sponsors the Junior Path Makers school-to-work program. The program serves as a mentoring network to guide students in their career paths. The program sponsors a summer bridge heritage camp each summer. Program volunteers also actively contribute to the revitalizing the indigenous language through awareness programs sponsored in the local elementary and secondary schools.

Health Care. The Northern Cheyenne Community Health Center provides Indian Health Services to the reservation. The center employs five physicians and seven nurses, and it has an emergency room. The Northern Cheyenne Ambulance Service provides ambulance services to the center. Full-service facilities are available at the Crow Indian Health Service Indian Hospital and hospitals in Billings or Sheridan.

The Northern Cheyenne Tribal Health Department operates a number of programs to serve tribal members. Services range from health and nutrition education to alcohol and drug abuse treatment programs to cancer screening and support services. There are nine community-oriented programs in total, with three support programs and 40 permanent employees. The tribe's diabetes program is perhaps the department's most vital program. Diabetes is the fourth leading cause of death among the Northern Cheyenne, and the incidence continues to increase. Projections indicate that by 2005, 948 tribal members will be living with diabetes. The program provides education, screening, and assessment; conducts home visits and hospital follow-up visits; reviews lab data; and monitors blood sugar levels.

ENVIRONMENTAL CONCERNS

Managing water resources is a primary concern for the Northern Cheyennes. Because grazing lands on the reservation are open range, there has been extensive damage done to water sources and wetlands. Surface water on the reservation has been determined unsuitable for human consumption.

The reservation is home to numerous endangered species, including the bald eagle, peregrine falcon, swift fox, mountain plover, and black-footed ferret. Although the economic benefits of mining coal and extracting oil are vast, the tribe is reluctant to initiate such projects. It remains concerned for the status of natural resources and the ecosystem. Concerns about pollution, contamination, and degradation of natural resources are abundant. In addition, the tribe continues to hold sacred many bodies of water and areas of land on the reservation. The people maintain strong spiritual relationships with these areas and do not want to see them desecrated.

Northern Cheyenne

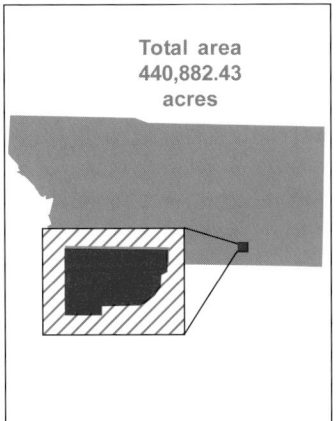

Total area
440,882.43
acres

Rocky Boy's

Rocky Boy's Reservation
Federal reservation
Chippewa-Cree
Chouteau and Hill counties,
Montana

Chippewa-Cree Tribe
RR1, P.O. Box 544
Box Elder, MT 59521
406-395-4210
406-395-4497 Fax

Total area (BIA realty, 2004)
110,950.20 acres

Tribally owned (BIA realty, 2004)
110,950.20 acres

Population 2000 census
5,008

Population (Tribal source, 2005)
6,179

Total labor force 2000 census
955

Total labor force
(BIA labor report, 2001)
2,846

High school graduate or higher 2000 census
80.9%

Bachelor's degree or higher
2000 census
11.8%

Unemployment rate
2000 census
28.3%

Unemployment rate
(BIA labor report, 2001)
76%

Per capita income 2000 census
$8,210

LOCATION AND LAND STATUS

The Rocky Boy's Reservation is located in north-central Montana. The reservation lies 70 miles south of the Canadian border. The nearest town is Havre, Montana, 32 miles to the north. The nearest urban center is Great Falls, 100 miles southwest of the reservation. The reservation was established in April 1916, when Congress set aside 56,035 acres for the Chippewa and Cree bands of Chief Rocky Boy. In 1947 the reservation was expanded by 45,523 acres. None of the land has been allotted, though some individual assignments have been made. The Rocky Boy's Reservation is the smallest Native American reservation in the State of Montana.

PHYSICAL DESCRIPTION

The reservation spans rolling high-plains grasslands to the sub-alpine environment of the Bear Paw Mountains.

CLIMATE

The reservation experiences relatively mild springs and summers. Average rainfall during those seasons is 8 inches, and the temperature rarely reaches 100°F. Winter temperatures drop to as low as -40°F, and there are frequent winds.

CULTURE AND HISTORY

Following the Riel Rebellion in 1885, a band of Cree people migrated south from their Canadian homelands into northern Montana. The Crees became allies of a group of Chippewa people led by Stone Child, or Rocky Boy. This group of Chippewas had left their designated reservation lands in North Dakota in the late nineteenth century. The tribes remained unassociated with any particular parcel of land until 1915, when a reservation was created for them in the southernmost portion of the former Fort Assiniboine Military Reservation.

The Native community on the Rocky Boy's Reservation shares a rich variety of cultures, spiritual beliefs, and traditions. Members continue to live and practice elements of their Cree, Chippewa, Assiniboine, and Metis heritages. Cree, an Algonquian language, is still spoken, and some tribal members continue to participate in the Sun Dance and sweat lodge ceremonies. Additionally, many members are active in the Native American Church.

GOVERNMENT

The Chippewa-Cree Tribe of the Rocky Boy's Reservation was organized under the Indian Reorganization Act of 1934. Tribal members adopted a constitution in 1935, ratifying their charter the following year. The constitution was amended in 1973. The governing body comprises a nine-member business committee, elected by popular vote from the reservation's five districts.

The tribal government includes the Rocky Boy Housing Authority, Indian Child Welfare Act Department, health department, and business committee. The tribe also maintains an agricultural credit program, cultural committee, environmental department, home improvement program, natural resources department, public schools department, and social services department. It employs a BIA representative, an EDA planner, a lease compliance officer, a soil conservationist, and an EPA representative.

ECONOMY

The Chippewa-Cree Tribe has faced serious economic hardships over the years, and while poverty and unemployment remain a challenge, the reservation economy steadily strengthens. Cattle grazing, wheat and barley production, development of timber and mineral resources, and tourism all represent solid sources of tribal income and employment today.

Government as Employer. The government and local schools serve as the largest employers on the reservation. The Chippewa-Cree Tribe became self-governing in 1993 and has contracted with BIA and Indian Health Service.

Economic Development Projects. The tribe is considering the development of a scenic byway through reservation lands. Possible funding sources include the monies made available by the Internodal Surface Transportation Efficiency Act.

Agriculture and Livestock. Wheat, barley, and cattle are raised on the tribally owned Dry Fork Farm and Ranch. The tribe also owns and operates the Stone Man Farms. The tribe initiated the Stone Man Agriculture Incentive and Education Project. The goal of this long-term project is to teach tribal members effective land management practices. Ten tribal members are chosen to participate in the project and are given both economic aid and educational opportunities to pursue a career in agriculture. The tribe also manages a herd of buffalo.

Forestry. An estimated 175,000,000 board feet of timber is located on 16,000 acres of forested lands on the Rocky Boy's Reservation. The tribe allows 5,000,000 board feet of timber to be cut on an annual basis. The Rocky Boy's forest project department uses the reservation's abundant lodge pole pine for posts and poles, saw log, house logs, and firewood. Douglas fir and ponderosa pine are also used for saw logs and firewood.

The tribe receives FY1992 funding from the BIA for its Woodlands Management Program. The program's purpose is to seek out means of effectively using the reservation's woodland and hardwood resources. For example, the Woodlands Management Program initiated the tribe's marketing and production of handcrafted rustic furnishings.

Gaming. The tribe operates the Four C's Café and Casino in Box Elder, Montana. The casino has 59 slots/VLTs, one restaurant, and 13 employees.

Construction. Tribal members are employed by the BIA Road Construction Department, which is responsible for constructing and maintaining the reservation road system. Employment varies depending on the project. The tribe is currently involved in road construction and in building homes and dams.

Mining. While the tribe is not presently involved in mining on reservation lands, the U.S. Bureau of Mines conducted a phase III study to determine the content and mining feasibility of minerals on the reservation. Minerals present with mining potential include: gold, silver, copper, iron, lead, and zinc. The bureau also discovered rare earth minerals, such as thorium, niobium, lanthanum, scandium, neodymium, and yttrium upon the reservation. The results of past oil exploration on the reservation suggest the likelihood of oil reserves. The tribe is presently seeking further seismic studies and oil exploration. The tribe leases 10 producing natural gas wells to the Montana Power Company. At least three other wells on reservation lands are capable of production.

Media and Communications. The tribe holds several leases with local broadcasters who operate antennas on Bowery Peak and Centennial Mountain.

TRI-MT-039

TRI-MT-042

TRI-MT-041

TRI-MT-040

Rocky Boy's

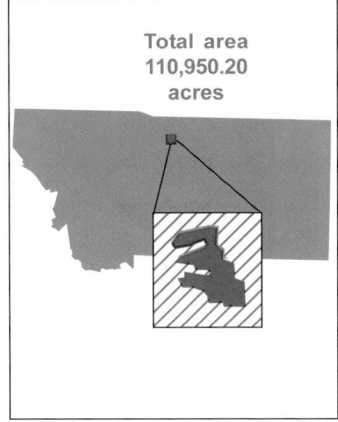

Total area
110,950.20
acres

Tourism and Recreation. The Chippewa-Cree Recreation Area provides several outdoor recreational resources. Located in the Bear Paws Mountains, the area contains the tribally owned Bear Paw Ski Bowl. The Baldy Butte Ski Resort draws visitors during the winter months, and hunting, fishing, camping, and hiking opportunities are also available.

INFRASTRUCTURE
U.S. Highway 87, between Havre and Great Falls, intersects the reservation at Box Elder. Reservation roads total 216 miles, with 62 of them providing well-paved easy access to major points throughout the reservation.

Electricity. Hill County Electrical Co-op supplies electricity to the reservation.

Transportation. Great Falls furnishes commercial airline services. Rail service, including Amtrak, is available in Havre on the main east-west line of the Burlington Northern Railroad. A southern spur adjoins the reservation.

COMMUNITY FACILITIES AND SERVICES
The tribe is currently building the Chippewa-Cree Wellness Center. Funded by the Indian Health Service, the USDA, and a HUD Grant, its facilities will include a swimming pool, a sauna, and a whirlpool.

The Boys and Girls Club, in cooperation with the Christian Children's Fund and the tribe, established the Boys and Girls Club of Bear's Paw. The tribe provides facilities for two locations. The club sponsors the TEENSupreme Keystone Club and is hoping to establish a SMART Moves program as well.

Education. A Head Start program, elementary, secondary, and high schools are located within the reservation.

Stone Child College, a tribal community college, is located in Rocky Boy and is dedicated to maintaining and enhancing tribal culture and tradition. The college currently offers associate's degree programs in the arts and sciences.

Health Care. As a self-governing Nation, the tribe contracts health services through the Indian Health Services. The Rocky Boy's Clinic and Chippewa-Cree Health Center is located on the reservation. It provides medical, dental, and optometry clinics as well as laboratory and x-ray services. Full-service medical facilities are available in neighboring communities.

ENVIRONMENTAL CONCERNS
The tribe has identified the water supply on the Rocky Boy's Reservation as a major environmental concern. Access to water sources has been limited in the past, and the tribe has had to work hard to establish water rights.

In 2001, a bill was proposed to authorize the federal government to begin development of the Rocky Boy's North Central Montana Regional Water Authority. The system would include a surface water treatment plant, hundreds of miles of pipeline, storage reservoirs, pumping stations, and electrical transmission lines. The project will move water from Lake Elwell to 7,000 homes on the reservation and in the communities of Chouteau, Hill, Liberty, Toole, Pondera, and Teton counties. The bill authorizes the federal government to pay 100 percent of the tribe's costs.

TRI-MT-039 Entrance welcome sign to Rocky Boy, Home of the Chippewa Cree Tribe

TRI-MT-040 Directional sign - "Chippewa Cree Tribal Operations"

TRI-MT-041 Rocky Boy's Community College

TRI-MT-042 Rocky Boy's Utility Commission Building

671

Nebraska

From <u>1996</u> edition of Tiller's Guide to Indian Country.

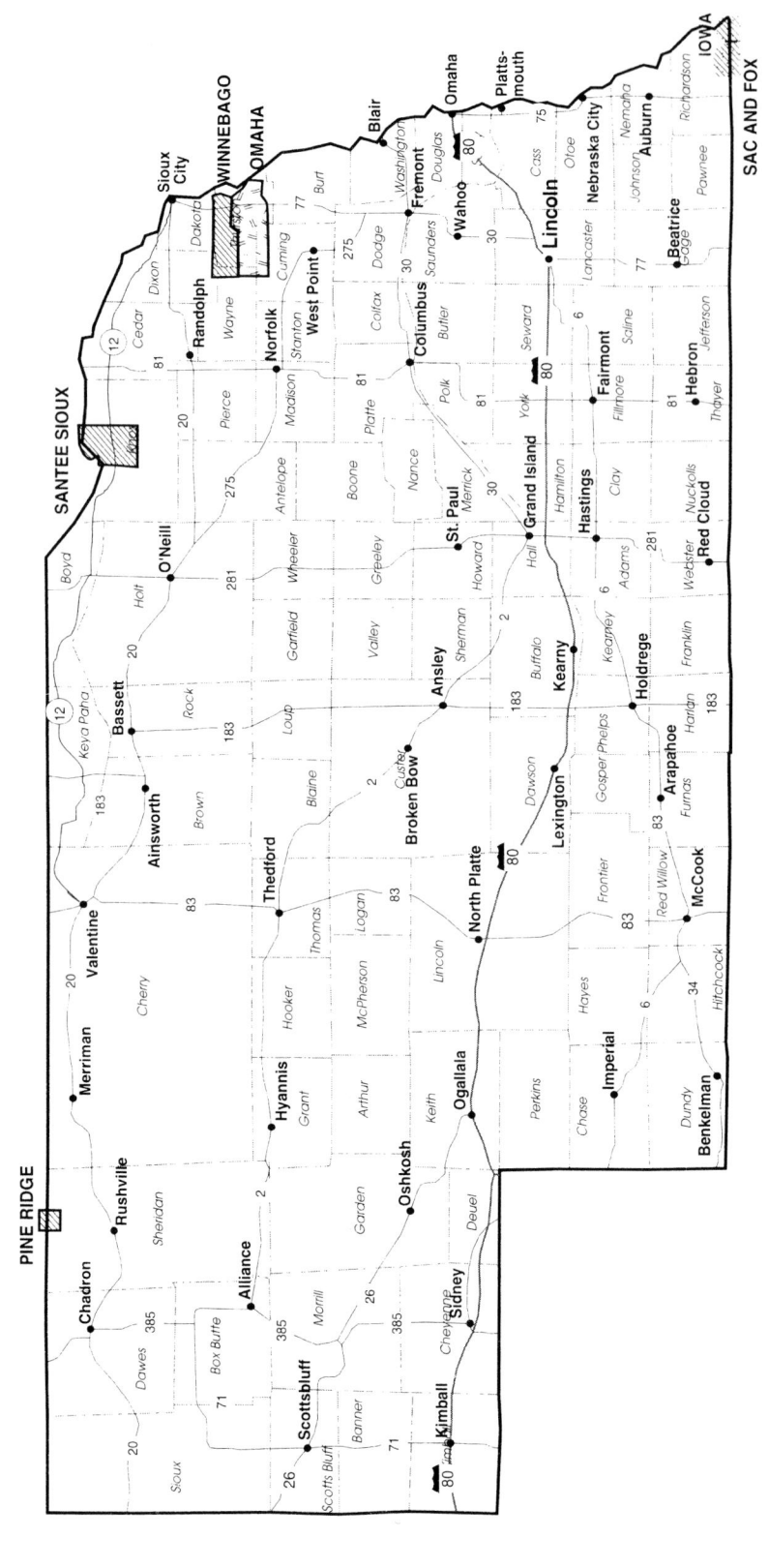

NEBRASKA

Omaha

LOCATION AND LAND STATUS

On March 6, 1854, the Omaha Tribe was granted reservation land along the Missouri River. The Omaha Indian Reservation is located in the northeastern corner of Nebraska, just 26 miles southeast of Sioux City, Iowa, and 70 miles north of Omaha, Nebraska, off State Highways 75 and 77. The reservation is bordered by the Missouri River on the eastern side and the Winnebago River on the northern side. The Omaha Tribe's headquarters is located in Macy, Nebraska.

PHYSICAL DESCRIPTION

The Omaha Tribe and its tribal members own over 93 percent of the reservation. The 29,255 acres of the reservation include rolling hills, marked by creeks and streams, which level off into agricultural land. Cottonwoods and various brush and shrub can be found in the reservation's wooded areas along the Missouri River.

CLIMATE

The Omaha Indian Reservation experiences unpredictable weather patterns from season to season. The average temperature in the region is approximately 49°F. In the winter, the average temperature ranges from 10°F to -25°F. A typical winter often includes heavy snowfalls, strong winds, and blizzard conditions. Summers, on the other hand, are hot and humid and are often accompanied by severe thunderstorms with occurrences of tornados and hail. The spring and fall seasons are relatively pleasant. The area experiences its rainy season between April and September, with an annual precipitation rate of 26 inches.

CULTURE AND HISTORY

The Omaha Tribe may have originally been part of another larger Indian tribe, possibly the Ponca Tribe, and may have originally lived on the Atlantic coast at the mouth of the Ohio River. The Omaha Tribe's language, the Dhegiha division of the Siouan linguistic stock, is similar to the language spoken by the Ponca tribes. The oral stories within the tribal community have interpreted the name "Omaha" to mean "Those going against the wind or current." The stories hold that the Omaha Tribe received its name when it moved up the Mississippi River to the Missouri River to settle the area from the mouth of the Platte River up to the Cheyenne River, in what is now South Dakota. The oral stories of the Ponca Tribe suggest that the Omaha and Ponca tribes split up after a quarrel and then formed new tribes before the 1800s, each going its separate ways. The Dakota Indians eventually drove the Omaha tribes out of the South Dakota area.

Around the middle of the 1700s, the Omaha Tribe settled the shores of the Missouri River in eastern Nebraska. Here, they lived subordinate to the Pawnee Indians, who had claims to the whole Platte region. It was during this time that the Omahas learned how to build earth lodges-winter homes that were eight feet high with dome-shaped roofs, from the Arikara, a Pawnee

Tribe living along the upper Missouri. Although the Omahas are believed to have played a subordinate role to the Pawnee and Ponca tribes, historically, the Omaha Tribe's determination to preserve and maintain their separate and unique heritage and culture was apparent even then. The Omaha Tribe built its earth lodges in accordance with their own tribal interests and did not perform the religious or ceremonial rituals that the Pawnee observed in building their earth lodges.

On March 16, 1854, the Omaha Tribe entered into a treaty with the United States, in which the tribe was granted reservation land along the Missouri River. In order to survive the early years on the reservation, the Omahas began to assimilate to white culture by adopting the white man's outward appearance. As a projection of the Omaha Tribe's sense of business enterprise, the tribe sold a majority of their hunting lands to the U.S. government for $850,000 in 1854. The tribe's assimilation into white culture was intended to help their people continue to survive and become self-sufficient. The assimilation process resulted in their one tribal member, Susan La Flesche, becoming the first Indian female physician and; another, her sister Susette (Bright Eyes) La Flesche, being offered the opportunity to play a major role in the trial of Standing Bear in 1879.

The Omaha people were traditionally hunters and farmers. Each member of the tribe had a working role in the tribe whether an adult, a female, a male, an elderly member, or a child. The men would hunt; the women would gather roots and plants, make pots, weave baskets, and make tools; and the children would learn how to do what the adults did. The tribe had a structured class system that included chiefs, priests, physicians, and commoners. The Omaha clans performed various functions for the tribe. For instance, the earth clans were responsible for holding and creating ceremonies that related to the supernatural. Overall, the tribe was musically inclined and taught their children the art of music at an early age. The powwow was the highlight of their social gatherings. Today, the Omahas preserve their culture and history through music and oral traditions. Omaha, Nebraska's largest city was named after the Omaha Tribe.

GOVERNMENT

Although the Omaha Tribe has not been a prominent part of history due to the subordinate role they played in other Indian tribes' histories, the Omahas have always been a self-governing people. The tribe operates under its own constitution, consistent with the Indian Reorganization Act of June 18, 1934. The Omaha Tribe has a tribal council, a tribal court, and a law enforcement department.

The tribal council consists of a tribal chairman, who is also the tribe's administrative head, a vice-chair, a secretary, a treasurer, and three additional councilmen who are elected by the

Omaha Tribe of Nebraska Reservation
Federal reservation
Omaha
Thurston, Burt, Wayne, and Cuming counties, Nebraska

Omaha Tribe of Nebraska and Iowa
P.O. Box 368
Macy, Nebraska 68039
402-837-5391
402-837-5239 Fax
omahatribe.com

Total area (BIA realty, 2003)
26,911.50 acres

Total area (Tribal source, 2004)
31,148 acres

Tribally owned (BIA realty, 2003)
9,756.05 acres

Tribally owned (Tribal source, 2004)
17,155 acres

Federal trust (Tribal source, 2004)
12,000 acres

Individually owned
(BIA realty, 2003)
17,155.45 acres

Allotted (Tribal source, 2004)
29,148 acres

Population 2000 census
5,194

Tribal enrollment
(BIA labor report, 2001)
5,427

Iowa Tribe

See Kansas

Omaha

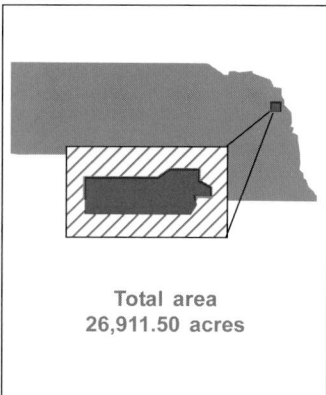

Total area
26,911.50 acres

Tribal enrollment
(Tribal source, 2004)
12,000

Total labor force *2000 census*
2,197

Total labor force
(Tribal source, 2004)
600

High school graduate or higher
2000 census
80.4%

Bachelor's degree or higher
2000 census
13.2%

Unemployment rate *2000 census*
11.8%

Unemployment rate
(BIA labor report, 2001)
47%

Per capita income *2000 census*
$11,708

Pine Ridge

See South Dakota

tribal members. The tribal chair, vice-chair, and councilmen each serve a term of three years. The tribal court consists of two magistrates, one prosecutor, one public defender, and a bailiff. The law enforcement department has cross jurisdiction with the state of Nebraska, and it has 16 acting officers, 6 jailors, 4 dispatchers, and 3 individual staff personnel. The Omaha Housing Authority manages a number of housing units in the Macy and Walt Hill communities. The Omaha Housing Authority also manages the tribe's scattered, rural sites by implementing HUD low rent and Mutual Help home ownership housing programs. The BIA and the Indian Health Service offer housing to their employees. In May 2004, the U. S. State Department of Economic Development granted $40,000 to the Nebraska Commission on Indian Affairs that the commission will use to hire consultants and support further efforts to provide affordable housing for the Omaha Tribe and other Nebraska tribes.

ECONOMY

The Omaha tribal community's economy is facilitated through tribal and federal administration. The major contributors to the Omaha economy are tribal government, the BIA, the Omaha Casino, and the tribally owned and operated Carl T. Curtis Health Center.

Economic Development Projects. The Omaha Tribe and the Winnebago Tribe dedicated $48 million to building a new health care facility in Winnebago, Nebraska. The new facility will provide over 10,000 Indians in Winnebago with needed health care services. Construction on the new facility began in 2000 with renovations of the old hospital. Plans for the new facility include a drug dependency unit and a birthing center, which will be the first of its kind for the Omaha and Winnebago communities. The new facility will be 100,000 square feet in size and is projected to provide 8,000 inpatient visits and 25,000 primary care provider visits per year. The new facility will provide 147 new staffing positions.

Other economic development plans include developing tourism to strengthen the economy on the reservation. The Omaha Tribe initiates these plans with the hope of increasing the tribe's and its members' self-sufficiency and business opportunities, while maintaining the tribal culture for future generations.

Agriculture and Livestock. The Omaha Indian Reservation has approximately 14,784 acres devoted to agricultural use. The tribe also uses 2,446 acres for grazing.

Forestry. The tribe has 4,042 acres of forested land.

Gaming. The Casino of Omaha is a major employer and source of revenue for the Omaha Tribe. Located just west of Onawa, Iowa, off I-29 at exit 112, the Omaha Casino features slot machines, blackjack, poker, craps, roulette, a restaurant, and a lounge. The gaming facility's theme is the roaring '20s, and details such as neon palm trees and mirrored sand dunes help create the casino's entertainment appeal. The Omaha Casino is considered the "Hot Spot for Fun" in the Omaha region.

Services and Retail. The Omaha tribal community is home to a number of commercial businesses, including one gas station, two grocery stores, a bait shop, and shops that sell Native arts and crafts.

Tourism and Recreation. The Omaha Indian Reservation has many outdoor and cultural activities. In August, the Omaha Tribe hosts an annual powwow event in Macy, Nebraska. Year round, tourists can visit the Big Elk Park or Hole in the Rock recreation areas for fishing, hiking, camping, or nature observation.

INFRASTRUCTURE

There are three major highways accessible to and from the reservation; Highway 77 runs through the center of the reservation, and Highway 75 and I-29 run through the reservation's eastern boundary. The nearest airports and bus services are located 30 miles to the north, in Sioux City, Iowa, or 70 miles to the south, in Omaha, Nebraska. There is a motor freight carrier in the area and a railway system that runs north-south through the reservation.

Electricity. The Burt County Public Powers Electric Company provides electricity to the reservation.

Fuel. The Aquila Gas Company is the main source of fuel for the Omaha community.

Water Supply. The Omaha Tribal Utilities Department provides the reservation with water and wastewater services.

Telecommunications. The Huntel Telephone Company provides commercial and residential telephone service.

COMMUNITY FACILILTIES AND SERVICES

The Omaha Indian Reservation houses many community facilities and services to promote the education, religion, communication, and the health and wellness of the Omaha Indian people. The reservation has a post office, three churches, and a community center that is often used as the location for funerals, dances, and other Indian ceremonies. The Omaha Tribe has its own youth shelter/group home to provide a safe haven for youth at risk.

Public Safety. In order to protect and preserve the safety of the tribal community, the Omaha Tribe has its own local fire department and police force. Volunteers in the community form the local fire department.

Education. Residents of the Omaha Tribe attend public schools and colleges. In order to continue to create self-sufficiency among its tribal member and expand business opportunities for both the tribe and its members, the Omaha Tribe provides educational scholarship funds for tribal members.

Health Care. The Omaha Tribe independently owns and manages the Carl T. Curtis Health Center in Macy, Nebraska. The Omaha tribal health center provides numerous services to its tribal members that include an elderly nutrition program and a youth recreational activities program. Other health care services are provided by the Indian Health Service hospital in Winnebago, Nebraska. Indian Health Service provides ambulance services for nursing home patients and outpatient referrals for patients at the Omaha tribal health center. Recently, the Omaha and Winnebago tribes dedicated $48 million to developing a new facility in Winnebago, Nebraska.

Tribal members receive care for services, such as surgery, that are not provided for by the tribal clinic, in Sioux City, Iowa. The Inter-Tribal Elderly Program provides transportation for elderly tribal members to the numerous health facilities. Macy Industries provides transportation services for tribal members without means of transportation to purchase shopping necessities.

ENVIRONMENTAL CONCERNS

As of 1996, the tribe's major environmental concern was its inability to perform baseline data gathering to quantify environmental resources and to identify hazardous environmental problems in order to protect the reservation's residents.

LOCATION AND LAND STATUS

The Ponca Tribe of Nebraska's tribal lands are located near the Missouri River in Nebraska. In 1879, a number of Ponca tribal members returned from the Oklahoma Territory, where they had been forcibly moved in the previous decade. They were eventually awarded tribal lands on a 26,236-acre reservation in Knox County, Nebraska. The Dawes Act of 1887 initiated the allotment of this reservation to individual members, however, seriously weakening the group's coherence and structure. By the mid-1900s, the reservation had been reduced to 834 acres. The tribe remained on what was left of their reservation until they were terminated by the federal government in 1966. In 1990 the Poncas regained federal status under the Ponca Restoration Act, and they are currently in the process of reacquiring their former reservation lands.

CULTURE AND HISTORY

Historically, the Poncas have been described as a small prairie-plains tribe. They descend from the Dhegiha group within the Siouan linguistic family. The heart of the traditional Ponca homeland is situated along the confluence of the Niobrara and Missouri rivers in northeastern Nebraska and southern South Dakota, and east to Sioux City, Iowa. The tribe was a relative latecomer to the Central Plains, with most estimates placing the time of their arrival in the Nebraska area in the seventeenth or early eighteenth century.

Four treaties were negotiated between the federal government and the Poncas, with the second one resulting in the exchange of their 2.3 million acres of tribal land for a 96,000-acre reservation. During the Fort Laramie Treaty of 1868, even that land was lost, as it was inadvertently assigned to the Sioux. Subsequently, the Poncas were ordered to move to Indian Territory in Oklahoma in 1876. A resistant band decided to return to its former homeland, defying government orders and heading north. The band was arrested and placed into detention on the Omaha Reservation in Nebraska. The Ponca chief, Standing Bear, sued the federal government to allow the tribe to return to their homelands. In the famous Trial of Standing Bear in 1879, the U.S. District Court found in favor of Chief Standing Bear, and in 1880 the U.S. Supreme Court dismissed the case. The Ponca Band was free to return home, and 26,236 acres in Knox County were restored to the tribe in 1881. Ponca tribal members who returned to Nebraska became known as the Northern Poncas, while those who remained in Oklahoma became the Southern Poncas.

In 1962 the federal government targeted the Northern Poncas for termination. The tribe was formally terminated in 1966 and their tribal assets dissolved. In 1987 the tribe incorporated the nonprofit organization of the Northern Ponca Restoration Committee to organize its efforts to regain recognition. In 1988, the State of Nebraska recognized the tribe, and in 1990 the U.S. Congress passed the Ponca Restoration Act, restoring the tribe to federal status.

GOVERNMENT

The Ponca Tribe is organized under the provisions of the Indian Reorganization Act of 1934. The tribe is governed by a tribal council according to its tribal constitution. The council is comprised of a chairman, a vice-chairman, a secretary, a treasurer, and three councilmen. Government departments include housing authority, cultural affairs, and environment. Cultural affairs houses the cultural committee, powwow committee, and cemetery committee. The cultural affairs department is very active in promoting cultural retention and revitalization.

ECONOMY

The tribe's primary source of income is from federal contracts, grants, and a number of land leases.

Government as Employer. In 1995, the tribal government employed 43 tribal members through its various departments, including the departments of health, human services, education, and economic development.

Economic Development Projects. The tribe is primarily concerned with economic development and the reacquisition of its former reservation land base. It reacquired 413 acres, and it is actively engaged in obtaining two additional tracts, which also total about 413 acres. The Ponca Tribe of Nebraska holds the status of "nonresident tribe," with designated service areas in each of six different counties.

Agriculture and Livestock. Ponca territory lies in the heart of the great American grain belt, with corn and wheat being of particular importance. Many tribal members make their living through some affiliation with the region's agriculture industry.

Industrial Parks. In 1995, the tribe was in the process of developing an industrial park.

Services and Retail. With the tribal area spanning a broad region of northeastern Nebraska, there are countless businesses within the area, a number of which are either owned by tribal members or serve as a source of employment. In 1995 the tribe's business authority was in the process of developing feasibility studies for various businesses in each tribal service area.

Real Estate/Commercial Development. The Northern Ponca Housing Authority (NPHA) owns and manages 120 housing units. There are 16 tax-credit homes located in Omaha and Lincoln, a fourplex in Creighton, and two homes in Bloomfield. HUD has approved the NPHA as a housing counseling agency and provides services to tribal members and other Native Americans.

Tourism and Recreation. In 2003, the tribe began construction of a traditional earthen lodge outside of Niobrara, Nebraska. The lodge is built of red cedar trees, green willow branches, brome grass, and soil in the technique that Ponca tribal members have used for centuries. The tribe planned to add a traditional garden and integrate interpretive materials into the exhibit. The site will be featured in the Lewis and Clark Bicentennial Commemoration activities and will serve as an educational and cultural resource for tribal members. The tribe also operates a tribal museum.

The Ponca State Park is located near the reservation. It offers numerous outdoor recreational activities, including horseback riding, pleasure boating, hiking, camping, and fishing. There are also campsites, lodging facilities, and a golf course within the park. The park houses an exhibit honoring the Ponca Chief Standing Bear. The tribe hosts an annual powwow at the Old Agency Building in Niobrara, along with several other special events that attract considerable numbers of visitors.

INFRASTRUCTURE

Interstate 29 traverses the reservation north-south, as does Highway 81. Interstate 80 traverses the reservation east-west.

Electricity. North Central Public Power District services reservation lands in Niobrara, Nebraska Public Power District services

---

Ponca Tribe of Nebraska Reservation
Federal reservation
Douglas, Knox, Lancaster, and Madison counties, Nebraska
Charles Mix County, South Dakota

Ponca Tribe of Nebraska
1701 E Street
Lincoln, NE 68508
402-438-9222
402-438-9226 Fax
poncatribe-ne.org

Total area *(BIA realty, 2003)*
725.84 acres

Tribally owned *(BIA realty, 2003)*
725.84 acres

Population *(Tribal source, 2004)*
30

Tribal enrollment
(BIA labor report, 2001)
2,095

Total labor force
(BIA labor report, 2001)
1, 687

Unemployment rate
(BIA labor report, 2001)
54%

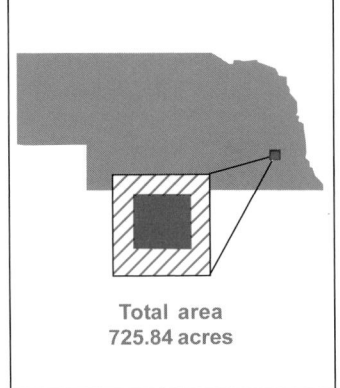

Total area
725.84 acres

Ponca Tribe

lands in Norfolk, Lincoln Electric Service services lands in Lincoln, and Omaha Public Power District services lands in Omaha.

Transportation. The nearest commercial air service is located in Sioux City, Iowa, and Yankton, South Dakota. Commercial bus and trucking lines serve the region, while the Missouri River (at the border of Nebraska and South Dakota) provides for some water-based transportation opportunities.

COMMUNITY FACILITIES AND SERVICES

The tribal community center located in Niobrara is scheduled for renovation. The tribe received a $300,000 grant from the Denver HUD offices to make improvements on the building. The tribe operates a transitional living center in Lincoln. It also maintains powwow grounds and a cemetery in Niobrara.

Education. Students attend local public schools.

Health Care. A tribally owned clinic in Omaha provides health care for Ponca members.

ENVIRONMENTAL CONCERNS

In 1996, the tribe identified groundwater and surface water contamination as the primary environmental concern at Ponca Agency.

Sac and Fox

See Kansas

Santee Sioux

Santee Sioux Indian Reservation
Federal reservation
Sioux
Knox County, Nebraska

Santee Sioux Nation
425 Frazier Ave. N, Ste. 2
Niobrara, NE 68760
402-857-2302
402-857-2307 Fax
santeedakota.org

Total area *(BIA realty, 2003)*		10,198.06 acres
Tribally owned		7,782.77 acres
(BIA realty, 2003)		
Individually owned		2,415.29 acres
(BIA realty, 2003)		
Population *2000 census*		878
Tribal enrollment		2,662
(BIA labor report, 2001)		
Total labor force *2000 census*		397
Total labor force *(BIA labor report, 2001)*		355
High school graduate or higher		81.1%
2000 census		
Bachelor's degree or higher		9.6%
2000 census		
Unemployment rate *2000 census*		7.6%
Unemployment rate		73%
(BIA labor report, 2001)		
Per capita income *2000 census*		$9,532

LOCATION AND LAND STATUS

The Santee Sioux Indian Reservation is on the northeastern Nebraska-South Dakota border, approximately 110 miles northwest of Sioux City. It is on the shores of the Lewis and Clark Lake, which is formed by the Niobrara River. An Act of Congress established the reservation in 1869.

The village of Santee is on the reservation and is an incorporated village like other Nebraska villages of similar size. The village is governed by a board that is responsible for the day-to-day operation of the fire and police departments, utilities, schools, and other village entities.

PHYSICAL DESCRIPTION

Tribal lands encompass the rolling hills of northeast Nebraska. Niobrara is located 1,318 feet above sea level. There are 9,621 acres of lakes on the reservation, 2,286 acres of wetlands, and 20,483 acres of forests.

CLIMATE

The annual precipitation for Niobrara averages 22 inches. Annual temperature ranges from 9°F in the winter to 89°F in the summer.

CULTURE AND HISTORY

The Santee Sioux Tribe of Nebraska are members of the Great Sioux Nation. They are descended from Mdewakanton and Isanti bands of the Dakota Sioux. Traditional homelands of the Santee Sioux extended from present-day Minnesota to the Rocky Mountains of Montana and as far south as northwestern Nebraska. In 1837, the Great Sioux Nation agreed to a treaty that ceded all lands east of the Mississippi River. In 1862 the Sisseton, Wahpeton, Mdewakanton, and Wahpekute bands of the Sioux joined in an uprising against the government. The government proceeded to annul all treaties that it had formerly made with all tribes of the Great Sioux Nation. The Santee Sioux were moved from Minnesota to Crow Creek, South Dakota, and again to the current reservation in northeastern Nebraska. The reservation was established by an Executive Order in 1869.

GOVERNMENT

The Santee Sioux Tribe is organized as a federal corporation; its constitution and bylaws were ratified in 1936, pursuant to the Indian Reorganization Act. The tribal charter was ratified in 1936. An elected tribal council of eight members governs the tribe. The council has a chairperson, vice-chairperson, secretary, and treasurer elected at large. Council members represent the Santee, Hobu Creek, Howe Creek, and Bazile Creek districts of the reservation. All terms are for four years. Government branches include social services, education, health center, parks and wildlife, credit and finance, transportation, land management, law enforcement, and a tribal court. The police force consists of six officers. The tribe has a PL-638 contract with the BIA and the Indian Health Service for various governmental programs.

BUSINESS CORPORATION

The Santee Sioux own the Feather Hill Development Corporation. The corporation has been aggressively pursuing businesses that generate income for the Nation to benefit tribal members and to cover unmet needs.

ECONOMY

Economic Development Projects. The Santee Sioux Nation currently owns and operates two gas station/convenience stores. The Pony Express is located on the reservation, and the Shop EZ is located off-reservation on Highway 81 south of Yankton, South Dakota.

Agriculture and Livestock. The tribe operates a tribal cattle ranch and conducts farming operations on 3,245 acres of the reservation. In the summer of 2004, the cattle herd numbered 750. The ranch produces corn and alfalfa for the tribal ranch. There are also 23,000 acres of pasturelands on the reservation. The tribe strives to acquire neighboring ranch lands and farmlands to increase its agricultural and livestock enterprises. The Santee Sioux also own a herd of 40 buffalo, which is mainly kept for ceremonial and community gatherings. Tribal members also own five private cattle operations.

TRI-NE-SSx-004

TRI-NE-SSx-081

Santee Sioux

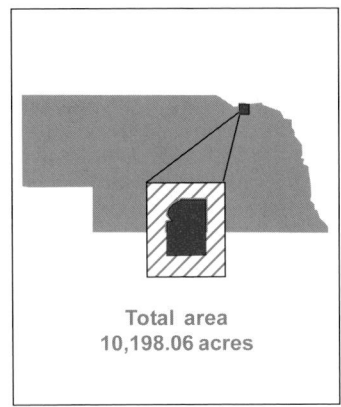

Total area
10,198.06 acres

TRI-NE-SSx-075

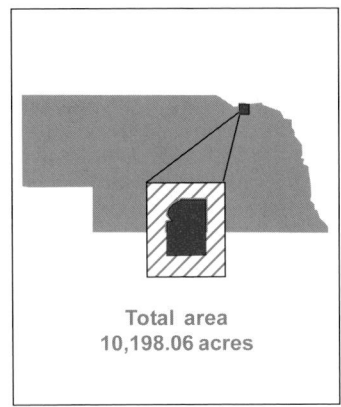

TRI-NE-SSx-080

Forestry. The tribe has entered into the forestry industry by initiating woodcutting operations on the reservation. It also operates a reseeding program to restore cottonwood trees on the tribal lands.

Gaming. The Santee Sioux Nation owns the Ohiya Casino on the reservation along Highway 12. The casino occupies 12,000 square feet. Facilities include 80 slots/VLTs, 100 bingo seats, and pickle machines. Amenities include a restaurant, a gas station, and an adjacent RV park. The tribe is studying the feasibility of adding a hotel, 18-hole golf course, and other recreational activities to attract more business. They are also planning to try to better use the existing community amenities, such as tubing, canoeing, rafting, fishing, and hunting, to their advantage.

Mining. Lime, gravel, and sand deposits exist and had not been developed as of the mid-1990s.

Real Estate/Commercial Development. The tribe has constructed 121 single-family dwellings, four duplexes, and a housing facility for the elderly on tribal lands.

INFRASTUCTURE
Nebraska State Highway 12 runs east-west through the reservation, intersecting with north-south U.S. Highway 81 approximately 32 miles east. State Road S-54D connects Highway 12 with the village of Santee.

Electricity. The North Central Public Power District supplies the reservation with electricity.

Water Supply. The reservations own municipal water system serves the community at Santee. Wells provide water to rural residents for their households and livestock. The tribe is expecting to build a $32 million water treatment facility in the coming year.

Transportation. There is no public transportation on the reservation; the nearest bus service is in Sioux City, Iowa located 110 miles to the east. Commercial air and rail services are 40 miles distant, in Yankton, South Dakota.

COMMUNITY FACILITIES AND SERVICES
The reservation houses a community center and library for tribal members. There are also three churches in the reservation communities.

Education. The tribe operates a Head Start program, the Takoja Tipi Day Care Center, and a K-12 program at the Santee Public School District. The tribe also owns Nebraska Indian Community College.

Health Care. The tribe houses a health center, which features a nutrition center, an alcoholism program, a heart program, and a social services program.

Winnebago

Winnebago Indian Reservation
Federal reservation
Winnebago
Thurston County, Nebraska
Woodbury County, Iowa

Winnebago Tribe of Nebraska
P.O. Box 687
Winnebago, NE 68071
402-878-2272
402-878-2938 Fax
winnebagotribe.com

Total area *(BIA realty, 2003)*
28,167.08 acres

Tribally owned *(BIA realty, 2003)*
4,987.89 acres

Individually owned
(BIA realty, 2003)
23,172.40 acres

Federal trust *(BIA realty, 2003)*
6.79 acres

Population *2000 census*
2,588

Tribal enrollment
(BIA labor report, 2001)
4,033

LOCATION AND LAND STATUS

The Winnebago Indian Reservation spans 120,000 acres of cropland, woods, and prairie pastureland in northeastern Nebraska. Of this total, over 20,000 acres are individually allotted to tribal members. Located 72 miles north of Omaha and 20 miles south of Sioux City, Iowa, the reservation is bordered by the Missouri River to the east (which also defines the Iowa state line on the east) and the Omaha Indian Reservation to the south. The Dakota-Thurston county line forms the reservation's northern boundary. The largest community is the village of Winnebago, where 30 percent of the reservation population is centered.

The reservation was created by treaties in 1865 and 1874. The treaty agreements recognized the tribe's rights-of-way, waterways, watercourses, and streams located on any part of existing or future tribal lands. In 2001, the tribe purchased 400 acres south of Winnebago. It intends to construct a housing division with over 100 home sites on the land.

PHYSICAL DESCRIPTION

Located in northeastern Nebraska, the Winnebago Reservation is characterized by low, rolling hills, creeks, and underbrush. The Missouri River borders the reservation on the eastern side, and cottonwood, brush, and shrubs grow along its shores.

CLIMATE

The average daily temperature on the reservation is 49°F. Winters bring blizzard conditions, heavy snowfall, and temperatures ranging from 10°F to -25°F. Summers are often hot and humid during daylight hours and cooler in the evenings. Summer also brings severe thunderstorms, hail storms, and tornadoes.

CULTURE AND HISTORY

The Ho-Chungras, or "people of the parent speech" or "people of the big voices," constitute the Winnebago Tribe of Nebraska. The Winnebagos are part of the Chiwere Siouan linguistic family. The Winnebago's presence in North America has been traced as far back as 500 BC in the region of present-day Kentucky. They arrived in Wisconsin by 400 AD and identify this region as their ancestral homelands. The Winnebagos dominated the area from upper Michigan south to present-day Milwaukee, Wisconsin, and westward to the Mississippi River.

During the seventeenth century, Algonquin refugees from the Beaver Wars sought refuge in Wisconsin. Their presence resulted in intertribal warfare, but more devastating was the arrival of the illnesses and disease foreign to the Native tribes. Both the Winnebago and Menominee tribes suffered vast losses and, in fact, faced near extinction. By 1665, when French explorers returned to the area now known as Wisconsin, the Winnebagos numbered approximately 500.

A series of treaties signed with the United States, beginning in 1816, resulted in their removal to a series of reservations in Iowa, Minnesota, and South Dakota. They remained near Blue Earth County, Minnesota, until after the Sioux uprising of 1862. Since their War Chief Little Priest participated with the Sioux in two battles, the United States removed the Winnebagos to a reservation established for the Yankton Sioux in South Dakota. Many rebelled and returned "home," others traveled the Missouri River to the Omaha Reservation in Nebraska. The 40,000-acre Winnebago Indian Reservation was established by the treaties of March 8, 1865, and June 22, 1874.

During the 1880s, half of the tribe moved back to Wisconsin. The tribe lost two-thirds of its Nebraska reservation land due to the General Allotment Act of 1887. In 1975 the Indian Claims Commission awarded the tribe $4.6 million for the land it lost in 1837; the tribe decided to use some of the award monies for per capita payments and a wake and burial program. In 1986, the tribe reestablished its sovereignty via the legal system, and the tribal court system now has jurisdiction over misdemeanor criminal and concurrent civil matters within tribal boundaries.

The region surrounding the Winnebago Indian Reservation has traditionally supported agriculture, and it remains a significant source of tribal income today. Otherwise, tribal businesses, particularly the casino, provide for much of the employment among members. Traditional culture remains relatively vital with many members belonging to the Native American Church and approximately 10 percent continuing to use the language.

GOVERNMENT

The tribe is organized under the provisions of the Indian Reorganization Act of 1934. A constitution and bylaws were adopted in 1936 and amended in 1968. The tribal council is composed of nine elected members. All council members are elected to serve three-year terms. Council officers are elected each year following the general election and perform their duties for one-year terms.

The tribe operates its own tribal court system to enforce criminal codes and resolve civil conflicts; it is staffed by a judge, a prosecutor, and a chief clerk/administrator. There are codes governing traffic; health, safety, and welfare; natural resources; civil trespass; gaming; taxation; business corporation; and the Industrial Development Financial Service Act. The tribe operates the following offices, programs, and services on behalf of its members: community health representative, environmental health, environmental protection, alcohol, land management, health education, heritage, enrollment, dental clinic, land operations, higher education, human, mental health, forestry, roads, water resources, youth development, wildlife and parks, among others.

BUSINESS CORPORATION

The tribe has established Ho-Chunk, a corporation that oversees the development and operation of business ventures on the tribe's behalf. Ho-Chunk is the parent company of Allnative.com, Indianz.com, All Native Systems, Heritage Express, Ho-Chunk Community Development Corporation, HCI Capital, HCI Distribution, Dynamic Homes, and HCI Construction Company. Ho-Chunk has received numerous honors awarded by national and private institutions.

In 2001, in collaboration with representatives of the Winnebago tribal government, Ho-Chunk successfully negotiated a tax agreement with the State of Nebraska. The agreement recognizes the tribe's right to implement gasoline excise taxes at locations within its jurisdiction.

ECONOMY

The Winnebago Tribe continues to develop into a formidable economic force in the region and throughout the midwest. It owns and operates numerous businesses on and off the reservation, and through its commercial activities, it contributes a great deal to tribal, local, and regional economies. The tribe's retail operations serve as the largest local private employers, and they are the largest customer of HCI Distribution.

Important sectors of employment on the reservation include health and education services, manufacturing, agriculture, public administration, and retail trade. It is the WinneVegas Casino; however, that has resulted in most of the tribe's economic advances since 1995 when it first opened. In 1994, reservation unemployment was 65 percent, dropping to 10 percent by 2002, though this change cannot be solely accredited to the casino. In 2001, gross revenues exceeded $50 million annually.

Economic Development Projects. Tribal economic development and planning is conducted through its business corporation, Ho-Chunk. Ho-Chunk aims to further the tribe's investments in retail, distribution, housing, construction, technology, hotels, and passive investments in order to provide for a stable tribal economy. Ho-Chunk Community Development Corporation is a 501 (c)(3) nonprofit organization that identifies federal grants, low-interest loans, government certifications, and business planning and development programs that the tribe may be eligible to receive.

The federal government and the state of Nebraska have designated the reservation an economic development zone, thus providing incentives for businesses and manufacturers to locate there. In 1995, the tribe, in conjunction with the town of Winnebago, was developing private-sector housing and a 75,000-square-foot strip mall. These projects were expected to employ significant numbers of tribal members.

The Winnebago Tribe participates in WinComp, a computer manufacturing joint venture with Density Marketing. In 2002, Ho-Chunk also entered into partnership with the Shakopee Tribe and the Santee Sioux to establish the Pony Express motor fuel plaza on the Santee Sioux Reservation. Ho-Chunk manages the operation, furnishing both employee training and fuel.

Financial Institutions. Native American Housing Company, a Ho-Chunk affiliate, is a shareholder in Liberty National Bank in Sioux City.

Agriculture and Livestock. The tribe manages a herd of 60 bison. The herd is grazed in ranges located near the newly constructed Ho-Chunk Village.

Forestry. The tribe maintains a forest preserve in excess of 200 acres along the Missouri River.

Gaming. The tribally owned and operated WinneVegas Casino, located 20 miles south of Sioux City, Iowa, in Sloan, Nebraska, was the largest employer on the reservation. After opening in doublewide trailers in 1992, a permanent (larger) facility was finished by 1993. Expansions since that time have included the addition of the Flower Islands Restaurant and Buffet, a 400-seat bingo hall, and a 900-seat entertainment venue. The facility now boasts 630 slot machines, table games including craps and roulette, a six-table live-action poker room, and bingo.

The future of gaming for the Winnebago Tribe is under attack by the Iowa legislature, which passed a law in spring 2004 prohibiting gambling by individuals less than 21 years of age, even at Indian casinos, which were previously exempt from such age restrictions. The tribe contends that the legislature may not change the terms of their gaming compact with the State of Iowa simply by passing a law without consultation with or notice to the Winnebago Tribe.

Construction. HCI Construction is a full-service individual and commercial building construction company.

Industrial Parks. In 1996, the tribe was setting acreage aside for anticipated development of an industrial park.

Real Estate/Commercial Development. The tribe owns HCI Capital, the parent company of HCI Real Estate, HCI Investments, Native American Housing, and HCI Leasing. These companies invest in real estate ventures on the tribe's behalf.

In 2000, Ho-Chunk purchased controlling interest in Dynamic Homes, an enterprise worth $12 million. Dynamic Homes markets modular homes throughout the upper midwest, including North Dakota, South Dakota, Minnesota, Iowa, and Wisconsin. No longer building only single-family dwellings, the tribe has expanded its product line to include duplexes, fourplexes, apartments, hotels, banks, and office buildings. In 2001, the company employed 100 people. The largest projects completed by Dynamic Homes include 109 housing units, 20 motel and casino units, and 1 classroom unit for the Leech Lake Band of Chippewa Indians; 88 housing units for the Three Affiliated Tribes at Fort Berthold; 76 housing units for the Turtle Mountain Band of Chippewa Indians; and 56 motel units and 18 motel and casino units for the Lower Sioux Mdewakanton Dakota. Dynamic Homes is also constructing the homes and buildings located at Ho-Chunk Village.

In 2003 the Winnebago Housing and Development Commission (WHDC), in partnership with HCI, began construction on a 40-acre mixed residential, commercial, and industrial property. By fall 2004, four homes, an office building, and a Dollar General store were completed. Up to 110 three-bedroom modular housing units are to be built at the location, to be known as Ho-Chunk Village, somewhat alleviating the housing shortage on reservation lands, with another 180 units planned to be completed by the end of the decade. Seventy of these units will be specifically for low-income tribal members. Integrating healthy lifestyles into the design of the largely residential community, with walking trails, a new hospital, and the cultural center, the tribe has planned business and economic development for Ho-Chunk Village around the concepts of active living promoted by the Whirling Thunder Wellness Program.

To facilitate home ownership and build an unsubsidized housing market on reservation lands, the WHDC sponsors a homebuyer's education program, which offers a $5,000 grant toward a down payment to income-eligible members and families; in this program a group of tribal members may work together to build their homes-rent-to-own units south of Winnebago-using credits from the Nebraska Investment Finance Authority. The WHDC plans to seek a USDA Rural Development Grant for a self-help construction program. Ho-Chunk Community Development Corporation, the nonprofit arm of the Ho-Chunk, offers first-time homebuyers a 10-year, $15,000 loan, regardless of income, pending completion of the homebuyer's education program. Recipients may use the loan toward purchase of a new house on the reservation, and the loans are forgiven with 10-year occupation.

Services and Retail. The tribe owns and operates numerous businesses on and off the reservation. Many of them are managed by Ho-Chunk. There are 10 franchises of Heritage Express convenience stores throughout northeastern Nebraska and western Iowa. The stores offer general goods, tribally or Native American-produced tobacco products, and gasoline gathered from the Winnebago Reservation. HCI Distribution Company sells Native American tobacco products and gasoline products blended on the reservation. It is the most successful corporation of Ho-Chunk.

Media and Telecommunications. The tribe owns Allnative.com, an e-commerce company that provides web design services, and Indianz.com, the largest Native American news and information website. In 2004, the two companies merged operations.

Winnebago

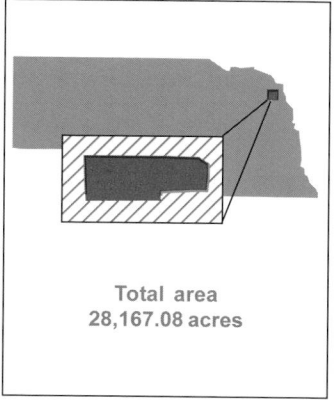

**Total area
28,167.08 acres**

Total labor force
2000 census
1,079

Total labor force
(BIA labor report, 2001)
913

High school graduate or higher
2000 census
81.1%

Bachelor's degree or higher
2000 census
11.1%

Unemployment rate
2000 census
10.7%

Unemployment rate
(BIA labor report, 2001)
59%

Per capita income
2000 census
$10,091

Winnebago

TRI-NE-001

TRI-NE-002

TRI-NE-005

TRI-NE-003

TRI-NE-004

TRI-NE-001 Winnebago Veterans Association Headquarters

TRI-NE-002 Winnebago Headstart

TRI-NE-005 Sign for Winnebago Police Department

TRI-NE-003 sign for Winnebago Health Administration Building

TRI-NE-004 Street view of Winnebago School

The tribe also owns All Native Systems, a government technology and sales company. Ho-Chunk manages all three entities. In addition, the tribe is a passive investor in Lakota Express, a telemarketing company owned by the Pine Ridge Lakota Tribe; Native American Systems, a Native-owned technology company; and HorseZone.com, an e-commerce site.

Tourism and Recreation. Wild turkey, pheasant, and white-tailed deer hunting, with a limited number of permits issued by the Tribe's Wildlife and Parks Department, attract hunters from across the United States. The reservation is located along the Lewis and Clark Byway. The tribe manages the Winnebago Museum and Culture Center located at the Little Priest Tribal College. The Homecoming Powwow, held annually in July, remains the tribe's primary tourist attraction and draws thousands of spectators.

INFRASTRUCTURE
The reservation is on U.S. Highway 75 and Nebraska State Highway 9 which connects with Highway 77 in the town of Winnebago. The nearest commercial air service is in Sioux City, 23 miles to the north.

Electricity. The Electric Cooperative provides electricity.

Water Supply. The Village of Winnebago maintains its own water and sewage systems.

Transportation. The tribe contracts with Arrow Stage Lines to provide bus service for WinneVegas employees to commute to the casino, located 40 miles from the village of Winnebago. Commercial rail freight service is available on the reservation. Several commercial trucking companies serve the town of Winnebago. Commercial barge service is available on the Missouri River, which runs through the reservation.

Telecommunications. The Eastern Nebraska Telephone Company provides telephone and Internet service.

COMMUNITY FACILITIES AND SERVICES
The Blackhawk Community Center houses some of the tribal offices, a gymnasium, meeting rooms, a post office, a police station, a swimming pool, and a dental clinic. The Winnebago Senior Citizen Center serves Native American and elderly members in the community by providing hot meals and transportation, acting as a protective payee, and arranging monthly field trips and shopping errands. A Winnebago Cultural Center and Museum is located on the Little Priest Tribal College campus, and a new 7,000-square-foot library on the Little Priest campus is open to the community.

Education. The tribe operates a Head Start program, the Little Bear Day Care Center, and the Little Hill Day Care Center. Tribal youth attend the Winnebago Public Schools (K-12) and St. Augustine Indian School (K-8), which are both located on the reservation. Both school sites underwent major renovations in 2001.

The tribe chartered the Little Priest Tribal College in 1996. It offers associate of arts and associate of science programs, two diploma programs, and a certification program. Enrollment generally exceeds over 100 students per year. The tribe sponsors several scholarship and other financial aid programs for any tribal member going on to higher education.

Health Care. A new U.S. Public Health Service hospital built on the reservation, the Winnebago-Omaha Comprehensive Health Care Facility, provides health care for the community. Opened in April 2004 and operated by the Indian Health Service Omaha-Winnebago Service Unit, this new facility has 32 beds, a laboratory, emergency services, radiology, podiatry, optometry, diabetes prevention and treatment, behavioral health, public health, nutrition and health education, and a helicopter landing pad. This new 100,000-square-foot hospital replaces the previous, 60-year-old facility.

Economic Development Corporation: Ho-Chunk Inc., Ho-Chunk, Inc. Winnebego Tribe of Nebraska

Chartered under the laws of the Winnebago Tribe and wholly owned by the Tribe, Ho-Chunk, Inc. was launched in 1994 to diversify the Tribe's business interests while maintaining a separation between business and tribal government. The general purpose company promotes economic self-sufficiency and creates jobs through its actively managed enterprises, joint ventures and passive investments, which include hotels, convenience stores, websites and an order fulfillment center.

The Winnebago Reservation lies in one of the most economically depressed counties in Nebraska. Like many other Indian nations, the Winnebago Tribe does not have an adequate tax system, and historically it has had little income to fund its operations. In fact, as recently as the 1980s, the sole source of tribal income was derived from land leases, which amounted to less that $180,000 per year. In the early 1990s, the Tribe established its WinneVegas casino on tribal trust land in Sloan, Iowa, and the tribal budget expanded significantly. Soon, however, the Iowa laws that allowed riverboat gaming near the Tribe were liberalized, posing an imminent threat to the Tribe's casino revenues. Tribal leadership saw that it would have to diversify its economy beyond gaming and into long-term self-sustaining endeavors within a period of two years or less.

Considering the Tribe's economic future, elected officials reached several critical conclusions. They understood that simply starting a tribal business - or even several businesses - would not ensure a strong economy over the long term. They wanted to create an environment in which businesses could flourish as sustainable and profitable enterprises, and where the Tribe could maximize the benefits of its sovereign immunity, federal tax immunity and civil regulatory authority. Having learned from other tribes' efforts at economic development, tribal leaders also knew that mixing business and politics needlessly puts the profits - and ultimately the viability - of enterprises at risk.

The Tribe's first step in building a sustainable and diversified economy was to incorporate these lessons into a tribal business code. In 1994, the Tribe wrote and enacted the Winnebago Business Code, which allows for the formation of wholly owned tribal corporations. It gives the Tribe the option of bestowing all privileges and immunities of the Tribe on tribally owned corporations, including sovereign immunity and all applicable tax immunities. In September, the Tribe chartered Ho-Chunk, Inc., an economic development corporation wholly owned by the Winnebago. Roughly translated, Ho-Chunk, Inc. means "The People Incorporated."

Ho-Chunk, Inc. (HCI) has a simple mission: to use the Tribe's various economic and legal advantages to develop and operate successful tribally owned businesses and to provide jobs and opportunities for tribal members. In its initial two years (1995-96), HCI was supported by casino revenue, which allowed it to develop a diversified investment and development portfolio. Freed from any requirement to pay dividends (freed, that is, from the requirement to contribute to the Tribe's general fund) in its first five years, HCI reinvested its profits and now possesses an impressive portfolio of active and passive investments both on and off the reservation. In the area of active investments, HCI developed and operates four hotels in Nebraska and Iowa, plus numerous retail grocery and convenience stores; it created HCI Distribution, a Native American tobacco and gasoline distribution company with over 25 tribes as customers; and it purchased and

expanded two Indian websites. In the area of joint ventures, HCI is the majority owner of a temporary labor service provider with six offices in three states, and is also the majority owner of a telecommunications, computer and networking equipment company. As a limited partner, HCI has invested in eleven hotels, apartment complexes, a small business venture capital fund, a now publicly traded internet news and search company (Indianz.com), an e-commerce company (AllNative.com), and a housing manufacturing company.

"Winnebago on a Roll to a Financial Empire," read the headline in a recent issue of the newspaper Indian Country Today (January 3, 2001). It summarizes Ho-Chunk's economic success well. HCI has enjoyed profitability over its entire life, although its growth rate and recent success are most remarkable. In 2000, the company's revenue was $25 million, operating cash flow was $1.5 million, and net income was $1.2 million. And, HCI made a dividend payment to the Tribe of $120,000 (or 10% of net income). Importantly, HCI now employs 250 employees, and nearly all of the employees in Winnebago, Nebraska are American Indian.

Another hallmark of HCI's effectiveness is that the company, through its many accomplishments, invigorates tribal pride. The tribal government and tribal members are proud, for example, that what appeared to be a cloud of doom - the collapse of gaming revenue - turned into a demonstration of flexibility and strength. Similarly, when the Omaha Tribe closed its cigarette plant, HCI lost its main and original supplier of cigarettes. Because HCI was able to diversify quickly into other brands of Indian-made cigarettes, however, its distribution company, smoke shops and convenience stores hardly suffered. The rapid development of Indianz.com and AllNative.Com generated a flurry of press attention. The community can also be proud of the innovative use HCI has made of tribal sovereignty. By engaging in gasoline wholesaling and adding value on the reservation to motor fuels and Indian-made cigarettes, the Tribe retains its inherent tax-setting power.

A primary factor in Ho-Chunk, Inc.'s success is the Tribe's conscious decision to separate business from politics. Too often in Indian Country, tribally owned businesses fall prey to political favoritism. Elected officials tend to meddle in day-to-day operations, and governmental red tape threatens efficiency and profitability. All of this has been minimized, and indeed, largely avoided at Ho-Chunk, Inc. The founding document of the corporation minces no words: "Ho-Chunk, Inc. was established so that tribal business operations would be free from political influence and outside the bureaucratic process of the government."

HCI's five-member Board of Directors (two of whom are Tribal Council members) acts independently of the Council to select Ho-Chunk, Inc.'s Chief Executive Officer, who oversees day-to-day management and makes all major strategic decisions for the Corporation. The Board is also responsible for providing the Tribal Council with an annual report, audited financial statements and an annual development plan. For its part, the Tribal Council appoints Board members, formulates the long-term development plan of the Corporation, and approves annual operating plans. The Tribal Council understands that they need to protect HCI's autonomy to ensure its success. Therefore, the Council defers to the CEO and Board, allowing them to make decisions based upon economic prudence-not on the basis of minimizing political

**Honoring Nations
Honoree 2000**

**Text in its entirety from:
The Harvard Project On
American Indian Economic
Development**

**John F. Kennedy School
of Government
Harvard University**

681

Winnebago

**Honoring Nations
Honoree 2000**

**Text in its entirety from:
The Harvard Project On
American Indian Economic
Development**

**John F. Kennedy School
of Government
Harvard University**

risk. This separation of business from politics, or division of labor, frees Tribal Council members to focus on questions of governance and enables the business experts at HCI to focus on maximizing the profitability of the Corporation.

The Council's hands-off approach results not just from institutionalizing its relationship with HCI, but also from careful cultivation of the relationship by HCI and the Board. Newly elected Council members receive a daylong tour of HCI operations and an introduction to the by-laws, plans and financial reporting. In addition, the Council and Board practice deliberate communication that keeps the Council informed of current developments in the Corporation while minimizing the amount of pressure the Council can exert on the CEO. It should be noted that the arrangement neither gives HCI a "blank check" to do whatever it wants, nor elevates the Board to an equal position with the Council. The Corporation is tribally owned and the Council has ultimate authority over its assets and strategy. In other words, the Council has every legal right to intervene in the Corporation if it finds reason to do so.

For Indian nations considering the creation of economic development corporations, Ho-Chunk, Inc. is also instructive in many other ways. For example, HCI chose to pursue what it calls an "outside-in" approach to business development: it took advantage of opportunities where the economic conditions were the most favorable, regardless of whether they were on the reservation or not. This approach was based upon the assumption, at least initially, that HCI's chances of success were much higher in off-reservation, metropolitan areas. Before HCI was formed, it was common for reservation-based businesses to yield little or no investment return. Lacking appropriate guidance or market access, for example, they frequently faltered or failed. However, once HCI created a stable income stream from its off-reservation investments (which include investments in Oregon, Colorado, Minnesota, Utah, Kansas, Oklahoma, Wisconsin, Texas and New Jersey), it was able to leverage its existing businesses to create solid on-reservation development. In other words, the company's off-reservation experience gave it the expertise and resources to better guide on-reservation business concerns. Needless to say, not only has the "outside-in" approach placed HCI in a position of strength, but it has paid off: Today, the majority of HCI's development is reservation-based, and most of its off-reservation development directly or indirectly creates employment on the reservation.

Another ingredient of HCI's success is that it started small. HCI avoided debt-based growth, which would have allowed it to move quickly into bigger business endeavors. The strategy both minimized risk to the Tribe and meant that HCI could borrow

against its assets in the future if the Tribe were to fall on hard times. In addition, this self-constrained capital approach meant that the managerial staff could grow with the Corporation's success. In fact, HCI made a strategic decision to begin its development activities in the franchise business (hotels) so that it could develop managerial talent under the tutelage of an experienced franchiser and eventually move to more sophisticated business activities. This is starting to take place as HCI has begun to exit some of its hotel investments and focus on its distribution, internet, technology and retail businesses. This "learn by doing" approach has resulted in better business managers and, again, enables the Corporation to build off its successes.

Finally, Ho-Chunk, Inc.'s investments complement each other. Most of its companies are vertically integrated; that is, they sell each other intermediate goods and services in a production chain. Its tobacco and gasoline distribution company sells tobacco products to AllNative.com, the Smoke Signals cigarette outlet, and the Heritage convenience stores, and it also sells gasoline to the Heritage stores. As a result, each time HCI expands the number of its convenience stores, HCI Distribution gains additional tobacco and gasoline customers. Generally speaking, vertical integration is not always profitable, yet HCI has identified where the strategy of complementary investing has long-term economic advantages.

The ultimate objective of Ho-Chunk, Inc. is to make the Winnebago Tribe self-sufficient and to provide job opportunities for tribal members. In its six short years of existence the company is making headway on both counts. As tribal leaders throughout Indian Country know, economic diversification and sustainable tribal enterprise development are as difficult as they are necessary. Ho-Chunk, Inc. is a shining example of an economic development corporation that others can learn from and be inspired by.

Lessons:

·   Successful economic development requires a firm commitment to separating business from politics, one that is not just enshrined in governing documents but is cultivated and reinforced in ongoing relationships and processes.

·   While employment of reservation members is a worthwhile goal, it makes sense to focus first on profitability. In shifting focus, however, the pursuit of short-term gains should not come at the expense of sustained profitability.

·   Business success breeds additional success. There are benefits to starting small and building managerial talent.

NEVADA

Battle Mountain

Battle Mountain

LOCATION AND LAND STATUS
The two separate parcels of land that make up the Battle Mountain Colony are located one mile west of the city limits of Battle Mountain, Nevada, near Interstate 80. The original 677.05-acre colony site was established by Executive Order on June 18, 1917, for Shoshones living near Winnemucca and Battle Mountain. By an Act of Congress on August 21, 1967, an additional 6.25 acres were added to reservation lands. The band plans additional land purchases. The Battle Mountain Colony is the only Te-Moak Tribe community not located within Elko County, Nevada.

PHYSICAL DESCRIPTION
Reservation lands are typical of the high altitude desert topography of the Great Basin region of the United States, with Nevada being the most arid state. The Humboldt River is the only significant body of water located within the reservation, although there are a few other small surface waters such as springs, seeps, and creeks.

CLIMATE
The elevation at Battle Mountain, Nevada, is 4,533 feet above sea level. The year-round average daily high temperature is 65°F, with the highest temperature recorded being 106°F. The year-round average daily low temperature is 30°F, with the lowest on record being -35°F. The area receives approximately 7 inches of precipitation annually, with almost 20 inches falling as snow.

CULTURE AND HISTORY
The Battle Mountain Band is one of four separate colonies that comprise the Te-Moak Tribe of Western Shoshone Indians. The 1870s saw the coming of the Central Pacific Railroad to Nevada, and soon thereafter the small mining town of Battle Mountain was founded. After the 1880s, the Newes continued to live on the outskirts of town, finding work at the ranches, raising agricultural products and hunting game to supply the mining camps, delivering mail, or cutting wood. Some band members worked in the mines, as well.

On June 18, 1917, the Battle Mountain Band received official recognition for its lands, and by the 1930s the band had begun building residential homes and a community center. Community development continued in the 1970s with the purchase and renovation of houses from the Getchell Mine near Winnemucca, Nevada. Later, the community center was renovated and expanded with the addition of a playground, a park, and picnic grounds.

GOVERNMENT
The Te-Moak Tribe of Western Shoshone Indians of Nevada, comprised of four constituent bands, the Elko, the South Fork, the Wells, and the Battle Mountain Bands.

The Battle Mountain Band Council, consisting of a chairman, a vice-chairman, and four council members, is organized under a constitution and bylaws of the Te-Moak Tribe of Western Shoshone Indians, approved on August 24, 1938, pursuant to the Indian Reorganization Act of 1934. All council members serve three-year terms of office. The constitution was amended and sanctioned on August 26, 1982, and the charter was ratified on December 12, 1938. The Te-Moak Tribal Council has total jurisdiction over all tribal lands, though each band, formerly referred to as colonies, retain sovereignty over all other individual band affairs.

The tribe, under PL-638, contracts with the BIA to administer key programs and services. The following departments or offices have been created within tribal governmental structure to serve the needs of band members: administration, education, environmental, finance, health, library, maintenance, social services, senior center, and taxation. BIA police officers provide law enforcement, and the Te-Moak Tribal Courts located in Elko, Nevada, 75 miles distant, serve the band. In the early 1970s, with funds from interstate highway right-of-way leases, the colony purchased about 17 homes from the Getchell Mines (no longer operating) and relocated them to reservation lands. Using other federal program monies, the Te-Moak Housing Authority has assisted tribal members with obtaining additional housing. The tribe also provides a housing improvement program.

ECONOMY
There is relatively little economic activity on the reservation due to its demographic isolation. One source of tribal income is a smoke shop and convenience store. The government has federal contracts that employ members of the tribe.

Government as Employer. The Battle Mountain Band tribal government employs 40 people via its various programs and services.

Economic Development Projects. Tax revenues resulting from the sale of tobacco products at the tribal smoke shop yielded over $125,000 in 2001. Development plans are underway to construct a truck stop near I-80.

Mining. Although the band does not have mining operations on reservation lands, the region occupied by the Western Shoshone people has produced approximately 10 percent of the world's gold supply. Mining is an industry of continuing concern for the Battle Mountain Band as it struggles to preserve ancestral and culturally valued sites, protect water quality and quantity, and safeguard wildlife species within the natu-

Battle Mountain Colony
Federal reservation
Western Shoshone
Lander County, Nevada

Battle Mountain Band
37 Mountain View Dr.
Battle Mountain, NV 89820
775-635-2004
775-635-8016 Fax

Total area *(BIA realty, 2004)*
691.25 acres

Total area *(Tribal source, 2004)*
683.3 acres

Tribally owned *(BIA realty, 2004)*
691.25 acres

Tribally owned *(Tribal source, 2004)*
683.3 acres

Population *2000 census*
124

Tribal enrollment
(Tribal source, 2004)
575

Total labor force *2000 census*
42

Total labor force
(Tribal source, 2004)
75

Battle Mountain

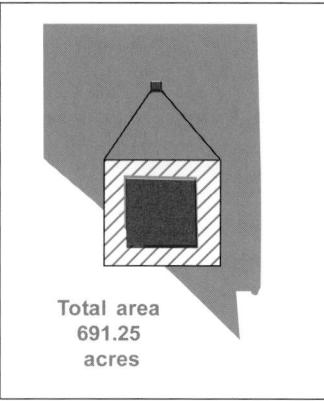

Total area
691.25
acres

High school graduate or higher
2000 census
41.5%

Bachelor's degree or higher *2000 census*
0%

Unemployment rate
2000 census
2.4%

Per capita income *2000 census*
$13,084

TRI-NV-001 - Battle Mountain Smoke Shop and Gas Station

ral environment for future generations in the face of expanding local mine operations. Although state and local governments within Nevada receive a "mine proceeds tax" from mining companies, the Battle Mountain Band and other Native American populations do not.

Services and Retail. The colony's primary source of revenue is the smoke shop and convenience store. These enterprises employ nine people selling gasoline, snacks, fireworks, and an assortment of dry goods.

Media and Communications. Residents of the Battle Mountain Colony have access to the *Battle Mountain Bugle* and the *Elko Daily Free Press,* and the *Nevada State Journal.*

Tourism and Recreation. The area of Battle Mountain, Nevada, offers a plethora of outdoor recreational activities, including, fishing, hunting, motocross and mountain biking, hiking, and wildlife watching, with year-round access to public lands. The reservation is 75 miles southeast of the Sheldon National Wildlife Refuge. Battle Mountain has public parks, an auto raceway, an outdoor skate park, tennis courts, a nine-hole golf course, and a livestock center with shows and rodeos. There are also historical sites, such as Carter's Monument, museums, and other sites of interest to tourists in the area. An Annual Powered Speed Challenge is held in September, and the Pony Express Open Road Car Race and Fourth of July celebrations are in July. The Basque Festival is held each August.

INFRASTRUCTURE
I-80 intersects the Battle Mountain Colony. State Highway 305 is the area's north-south route. Highway 50 runs east-west in the southern portion of the county.

Electricity. Sierra Pacific Power Company provides electricity to the area.

Fuel. Southwest Gas Corporation provides natural gas to the area, and two local suppliers provide propane.

Water Supply. The band provides sewer and water services to reservation housing and public facilities.

Transportation. Commercial air service is provided in Elko, 60 miles away; the nearby Battle Mountain/Lander County Airport has two lighted runways and two helipads. Train, bus, and truck service is available in Battle Mountain, and Amtrak passenger service is provided in Carlin or Winnemucca. Union Pacific and the Burlington Northern Santa Fe railways provide rail freight services.

Telecommunications. SBC provides telephone service. There is Internet access at the reservation, but no cable services.

COMMUNITY FACILITIES AND SERVICES
The band's administrative offices also serve as a community center and senior's center.

Education. Tribal children attend public schools in the Humboldt County School District facilities located at Battle Mountain. For those interested in pursuing a college degree, there is the Battle Mountain Campus of Great Basin College. Members of the tribe are taught the Shoshone language and basket weaving in the Tribal Language and Cultural Activities Programs.

Health Care. An Indian Health Service field medical team, a state public health nurse, and an Indian Health Service community health representative provide medical services to the reservation. Medical services are also available at the Lander County Hospital and at the Indian Health Service facilities in Elko, Nevada.

ENVIRONMENTAL CONCERNS
Decreases in the quantity of water, degradations to water quality, and depreciation of the reservation's other natural resources, are of primary environmental concern to the band. Gold mining in the region, which has historically benefited only non-reservation corporate interests, has exacted an ever-increasing toll on the area's surface and subsurface resources, draining an already-arid landscape of much needed water and contaminating the remaining streams, springs, and ponds. Lands utilized for livestock grazing and other cattle operations have been decreased by interruptions to the topography to accommodate mine operations. Open pits, heap leach pads, and mine tailings abound in the region; some are only thinly revegetated, creating the potential for future toxic air quality. Protecting against further mine development is a priority.

TRI-NV-001

Carson Colony

Carson Colony
Federal reservation
Washoe
Ormsby County, Nevada

Carson Colony Community Council
3311 Paiute Street
Carson City, NV 89703
775-265-5645
775-265-6240 Fax

Total area *(BIA realty, 2004)*		160.91 acres
Tribally owned		160.91 acres
(BIA realty, 2004)		
Total population *2000 census*		265
Total labor force *2000 census*		129
High school graduate or higher		72.1%
2000 census		
Bachelor's degree or higher		5.5%
2000 census		
Unemployment rate *2000 census*		7%
Per capita income *2000 census*		$7,830

LOCATION AND LAND STATUS
The 160-acre Carson Colony is located near Carson City, Nevada. It was established by the Act of May 18, 1916, which authorized the purchase of lands for Nevada's non-reservation Indians and the Washoe Tribe of Indians.

CULTURE AND HISTORY
Carson Colony is a part of the Washoe Reservation. The first lands of the greater Washoe Reservation were officially established in 1917 when the Washoe Tribe, after submitting countless petitions, finally received the Carson and

Dresslerville colonies. These colonies retained separate councils. In 1967, Washoe residents of the Woodfords, Carson, and Dresslerville colonies consolidated to become the Washoe Tribe of Nevada and California. They were joined in the early 1980s by the former BIA Stewart Indian School lands, or Stewart Colony. *(Please see Washoe Tribe profile in this chapter for further information.)*

GOVERNMENT
Carson Colony's constitution and bylaws were authorized by the Indian Reorganization Act of 1934 and approved in 1936. They were revised in 1966 and adopted on June 16, 1967, under the Washoe Tribe of Nevada and California's Articles of Association. The colony has a community council consisting of a chairperson-secretary-treasurer, a vice-chairperson, and three council members, each serving a four-year term.

INFRASTRUCTURE
U.S. Highway 395 runs north-south through the reservation. Commercial transportation and shipping are available in Reno, 34 miles distant; buses and trucks stop in Carson City, two miles from the colony.

Electricity. The Sierra Pacific Power Company sells electricity to the colony.

Water Supply. The tribe owns water and sewage facilities.

COMMUNITY FACILITIES AND SERVICES
Health Care. Health care through the BIA is available at Stewart.

TRI-NV-002

Carson Colony

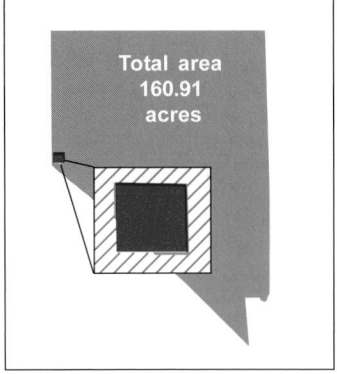

Total area
160.91
acres

TRI-NV-002 Carson Colony Youth Center and Colony Offices

Dresslerville

Dresslerville

Total area *(BIA realty, 2004)*	39.8 acres
Tribally owned *(BIA realty, 2004)*	39.8 acres
Total area *(Tribal source, 2004)*	795 acres
Population *2000 census*	321
Total labor force *2000 census*	90
High school graduate or higher *2000 census*	62%
Bachelor's degree or higher *2000 census*	5.9%
Unemployment rate *2000 census*	5.6%
Per capita income *2000 census*	$9,440

LOCATION AND LAND STATUS
Dresslerville Colony is adjacent to the Washoe Reservation, south of Gardnerville, Nevada. The colony is a part of the Washoe Reservation. By the Act of May 18, 1916, Congress authorized the purchase of lands for the Indians living near Dresslerville. It is said that the U.S. government purchased the acreage from the Dresslers of Gardnerville with $10 worth of gold. The metes and bound survey of Dresslerville was completed in 1973. The greater Washoe Reservation was officially established in 1917 when the Washoe Tribe, after submitting countless petitions, finally received the Carson and Dresslerville colonies. These colonies retained separate councils. In 1967, Washoe residents of the Woodfords, Carson, and Dresslerville colonies consolidated to become the Washoe Tribe of Nevada and California. They were joined in the early 1980s by the former BIA Stewart Indian School lands, or Stewart Colony. The colony became a member of the Washoe Tribe under the Articles of Association adopted on November 14, 1969. *(Please see Washoe Tribe profile in this chapter for further information.)*

CULTURE AND HISTORY
The Carson River Basin has been home to the Washoe Tribe for thousands of years. The region is rich in resources that have benefited tribal members. The Carson River courses in channels and wetlands on tribal lands, contributing to the creation of fertile farmland and wildlife habitats. The natural aquifer is a critical element in tribal life in the deserts of the Great Basin.

GOVERNMENT
The tribe is governed by the Dresslerville Community Council.

ECONOMY
Tribal lands are rich in natural resources and are situated in areas that lend themselves to development and growth. The reservation currently contains ranches, farmlands, and grazing lands. The tribe is concerned, however, with the impact of economic development on its natural resources.

Agriculture and Livestock. Natural resources in the area include fertile farmlands and an abundant source of water. With proper management, tribally owned farms may produce high yields with a limited impact on energy and resources.

Fisheries. The reservation is home to one of the best trout habitats in the Carson Valley. As a result, the tribal fishery is thriving.

Construction. Growth on the reservation is increasing. The construction of housing is steady and the tribe anticipates continual development in the coming years.

INFRASTRUCTURE
Highway 395 runs through the reservation in a north-south direction. Trucking and bus services are available in nearby Gardnerville. Air transportation is available 60 miles away in Reno.

Electricity. Sierra Pacific Power Company provides electricity.

Water Supply. The tribe owns water and sewer services.

COMMUNITY FACILITIES AND SERVICES
The Washoe Tribe provides most community services and facilities.

Health Care. Tribal members can obtain medical services at the USPHS hospital in Schurz and the clinic at Gardnerville.

**Dresslerville Colony
Federal reservation
Washoe
Douglas County, Nevada**

Dresslerville Colony
1585 Watsheamu Drive
Gardnerville, NV 89410
775-265-5845
775-883-6467 Fax
itcn.org

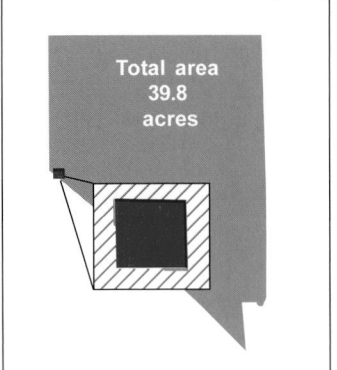

Total area
39.8
acres

Dresslerville

The quality and quantity of water resources are key issues on the reservation. The tribe carefully monitors the water in order to preserve their resources. Rapid development and growth in the area place a strain on natural resources in the region. Recent droughts have also resulted in higher demands upon surface and groundwater. In many instances, water is being extracted faster than it is being replenished. Droughts have resulted in the illegal exportation of water, which threatens the tribe's supply. In addition, the contamination of groundwater is a threat that has resulted in the closure of a local landfill. Another issue of concern in the region is the possibility of a severe earthquake. Four earthquake faults lie beneath Carson Valley.

Duck Valley

Duck Valley Reservation
Federal reservation
Shoshone, Paiute
Elko County, Nevada; Owyhee
County, Idaho

Duck Valley Shoshone Paiute
Tribal Council
P.O. Box 219
Owyhee, NV 89832
208-759-3100
208-759-3102 Fax

Total area *(BIA realty, 2004)*
297,786.97 acres

Federal trust *(BIA realty, 2004)*
3,981.68 acres

Tribally owned *(BIA realty, 2004)*
293,805.29 acres

Population *2000 census*
1,265

Tribal enrollment
(BIA labor report, 2001)
1,888

Total labor force *2000 census*
430

Total labor force
(BIA labor report, 2001)
1,165

High school graduate or higher
2000 census
73.4%

Bachelor's degree or higher
2000 census
12.1%

Unemployment rate *2000 census*
21.6%

Per capita income *2000 census*
$9,810

LOCATION AND LAND STATUS

Duck Valley Reservation straddles the state line of southern Idaho and northern Nevada, approximately 100 miles north of Elko, Nevada and 100 miles south of Mountain Home, Idaho. Owyhee ("Oh-Why-He") is the location of tribal headquarters, 142 miles southwest of Boise, Idaho. The reservation was established by the Executive Orders of April 16, 1877, May 4, 1886, and July 1, 1910, and by an Act of Congress of June 18, 1934. Reservation lands are all contiguous in a near block with the exception of the 3,981.68 federally owned acres at the Wildhorse Reservoir. There are 144,274.3 acres of tribal lands in Nevada and 145,545 acres in Idaho. Owyhee is the commercial and social center of the reservation. The tribe is seeking the return of some ancestral lands in southern Idaho along the Oregon Trail route for economic development.

PHYSICAL DESCRIPTION

The diverse land extends from the Owyhee River Valley into high desert country with elevations ranging from 5,200 to nearly 9,000 feet above sea level. Soil deposits up to 300 feet deep are common in the Blue Creek Valleys. The Ohwyhee River runs through the southeast portion of reservation lands, existing to the northwest, into Idaho's Snake River. Most of the highland areas are rangeland; the western and northeastern areas are rolling volcanic plateaus and tablelands. Basalt and rhyolite are common bedrock in these areas. The central portion of the reservation consists of largely wide, open lowlands: Blue Creek and Owyhee River valleys with associated wetland areas. Approximately 87,000 acres are suitable for irrigated agriculture.

CLIMATE

Annual precipitation is approximately 14 inches, with 62 inches of snowfall. The average high temperature is 80°F with the average high winter temperature at 40°F. Summers tend to be short and dry, winters long and fairly cold.

CULTURE AND HISTORY

The federally recognized Duck Valley Reservation is home to Shoshone Indians, descendants of the Newe people, as well as being home to Paiutes, descendants of the Numa. The Duck Valley Reservation dates back to the Treaty of Ruby Valley signed by the United States and the Western Shoshone Tribes in 1863. Ancestral lands of the Western Shoshone and Northern Paiute tribes make up the present day Duck Valley Reservation. In the 1800's Euro-Americans moved onto the lands of the bands and extended families.

A Shoshone leader named Captain Sam, looking for a home for his people, inspected the Duck Valley region in 1870 and recommended to the federal government that they be allowed to settle there. The government supported his request, establishing the reservation by Executive Order in 1877, and ordering the few white settlers who lived on the land to vacate; they were compensated for the land they had claimed.

Shoshone occupied the land but soon faced a crisis brought about by a severe winter. Federal government inattention to the resulting illnesses forced many Shoshones to leave Duck Valley, and in 1884 a special Indian agent called the Indians together in council to request their removal to Idaho. Captain Sam and other Indians argued earnestly against removal, and the government acquiesced. In 1885 a band of about 60 Paiutes arrived at Duck Valley with a letter from an Indian agent recommending that they be allowed to settle there. In 1886 President Cleveland issued an executive order adding land to the Duck Valley Reservation for the use of the Paiutes. President Taft added additional acreage to the reservation in 1910. The two tribes share the reservation to this day.

GOVERNMENT

A constitution and bylaws were approved and adopted on April 20, 1936, under the provisions of the Indian Reorganization Act of 1934. The constitution was amended May 20, 1966. The reservation is governed by a tribal business council consisting of a chairperson, a vice-chairperson, and five council members, all of who serve three-year terms. The council meets monthly. The tribal chairman and the chief executive officer report directly to the tribal business council.

The tribe, under PL-638, contracts with the BIA to administer key programs or services. Tribal government departments include: health and human services, business development, education, housing, support services, and the judicial department, which operates the Duck Valley Tribal Court. The BIA provides police and fire services. The tribal court system is operated by a court administrator. Judges are elected to three-year terms by the membership. There is a separation of power from the business council. The business council enacts laws into the law and order code.

The Duck Valley Reservation also has its own housing authority, and there are two tribal members on staff at the Owyhee branch of the Nevada Bank and Trust, who are experts in the federal government's housing and loan programs. A credit co-op, operated in conjunction with Nevada Bank and Trust in space leased by the tribe, is facilitating first-time homeownership for many tribal members. The housing authority, which reports directly to the tribal business council, also supervises a home improvement program and manages a total of 445 homes throughout the Duck Valley Reservation.

BUSINESS CORPORATION

In 1999 the economic development planning committee, a part of the business council of the Shoshone-Paiute tribes, wrote a 10-year economic development strategic plan reflecting tribal values and preserving traditional heritage, while protecting the environment with a firm commitment to sustainable development. Expanding economic and educational opportunities are key priorities. Economic development programs are administered by the tribal programs/enterprise administrator. Fourteen separate tribal departments or offices report to the administrator.

ECONOMY

Unemployment among tribal members remains high. A small but steady source of tribal income results from the sale of fishing permits for the two reservoirs. A marina and store provide income, as do business leases, land leases, and livestock grazing permits, but cattle and agriculture remain the mainstay of the economy. In their economic development strategic plan, the tribes' focus will be on the enhancement of resources to support economic diversification, while developing more enterprises.

Government as Employer. The largest employer on the reservation is the Shoshone-Paiute Tribal Government through the expansion of the Owyhee Community Health Facility, new home construction, and the BIA. Approximately 240 employees are working in tribal services. Wildlands firefighting crews number about 70 people during the summer.

Economic Development Projects. The development of tribal enterprises in six key areas is a high priority for the tribes. The Economic Development Strategic Plan of 1999-2009 lists: 1) agriculture and ranching, 2) gaming, 3) outdoor recreation and tourism, 4) downtown revitalization, 5) community services, and 6) alternative energy as the most viable opportunities for future development. The tribes also emphasize natural resource industries and general business goods and services. A strip mall is planned to include space for a branch of the Nevada Bank and Trust.

Commercial and light industrial development is planned in two locations. Toward this end, the tribes have improved roads and utilities to attract business investment. The government has designated lands for development within Owyhee City limits and on a 200-acre site near the tribal headquarters. In recent years, a 280-acre tribal ranch was purchased. In 2004, one tribe opened a tribal travel center.

Agriculture and Livestock. Twelve thousand acres were in agricultural use as of 2004, and another 269,000 acres of rangeland are used for grazing cattle and horses. Tribal members have between 4,000-5,000 head of cattle. The opportunity for development of tribally-operated value-added beef production is being considered. Pivot irrigation and the completion of the Wild Horse Dam have boosted livestock capacity by increasing the amount of irrigated land; the reservoir's capacity is 73,500 acre-feet of water. The Duck Valley Tribal Farm, leased to a contractor for harvesting, raises grass and alfalfa hay to sell to the various cattle operations. Irrigated agriculture and mineral extraction have potential for expansion on tribal lands.

Forestry. The feasibility of a hybrid poplar tree farm is under consideration, as is the cultivation of a native plant seed collection enterprise.

Gaming. The tribe is interested in establishing a gaming facility on reservation land. Although the reservation is isolated geographically, residents from Boise, Idaho, already travel through the reservation to gamble in Elko, Nevada. Locating a casino at Owyhee would increase the flexibility in the classes of gaming being provided. Research is underway to identify potential private industry or Native American joint-venture partners who would assume part of the financial and development risks associated with a gaming initiative.

Fisheries. There are four sport fisheries on the reservation: Sheep Creek, Wild Horse, Mountain View, and Billy Shaw reservoirs. The Owyhee River also provides fishing opportunities.

Construction. Gah Nee Construction is an enterprise that builds homes for employees, whether they are from the tribal membership or those hired to work for the government. It is not viewed as a for-profit enterprise.

Services and Retail. Local businesses include a motel, a laundromat, a general store, two cafés, a gas station, a tire repair shop, and a marina. In addition, there is a post office in Owyhee. There is an increasing number of retail services available surrounding the reservoirs, in support of the increasing tourism market. (*See also, Tourism and Recreation, below.*) The community seeks additional retail stores selling basic necessities such as food and clothing. The business committee pursues a motel, drug store, and other retail outlets (such as an automobile service center; a hardware store; and a movie theater) by making land and utilities available for business site leases on tribal lands. The tribes also hope to develop a trading post where local handmade arts and crafts could be marketed by tribal members. To date, artisans have been selling their work privately.

Media and Communications. The tribe publishes the *Sho-Pai News.*

Tourism and Recreation. Outdoor recreation is Duck Valley's primary tourism development activity. Duck Valley, located in the Pacific Flyway, is well known for its extraordinary populations of pelicans and other migratory birds, which attract tourists to bird-watching and photography opportunities. Recreational fishing is available at four reservoirs on the reservation: Mountain View, Sheep Creek, Wildhorse, and Billy Shaw, as well as Owyhee River. A marina, campground, RV hookups, and picnic area are available at the Wildhorse Reservoir. There are 15 campsites at Mountain View, 28 at Wildhorse, and 25 at Sheep Creek. The tribe is working on facilities upgrades such as additional RV hookups, showers at the campground facilities, boat rentals, and fish cleaning stations. The Wildhorse Marina and Saloon can be rented for private functions for a small fee.

There are plans for development and construction of additional recreational opportunities including hiking/biking trails with interpretive signs; a dude ranch; a youth camp; a rodeo, powwow, and ceremonial grounds; lodging, guided fishing and hunting trips; and restaurants to support the growing tourism industry at the reservation. The tribes built the human development center, a community recreational gymnasium and education facility in Owyhee. They are planning to utilize the old gym building in Owyhee for their cultural center. The tribe holds powwows each Fourth of July and Veterans Day.

INFRASTRUCTURE

Nevada State Highway 225, which becomes Idaho State Highway 51, runs north-south through the reservation. In recent years, existing roads have been improved, and about two-thirds were paved for a bus route. There is also a new road to the juvenile detention center. The BIA maintains tribal roads. The states of Idaho and Nevada maintain the highway, which passes through the reservation.

Electricity. Idaho Power Company supplies electricity to the tribe. The tribes have invested in substantial power supply system upgrades so that a reliable source of electricity is available to all reservation housing and all present and future enterprises.

Duck Valley

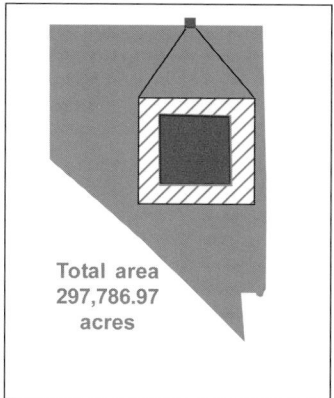

**Total area
297,786.97
acres**

Duck Valley

Fuel. The 1999 economic development strategic plan cited a need for development of alternative energy resources on the reservation. The tribes hope to integrate creation of wind, solar, and water-generated power sources in all future economic development initiatives.

Water Supply. Approximately half of the reservation's homes are serviced by the tribe's water and sewage system. Water is provided by wells, then pumped into three storage tanks. The BIA recently extended water mains in the area to accommodate new housing development and proposed economic development projects. Some tribal members continue to rely on private water wells. A gravity-flow/lagoon sewage system serves the community of Owyhee; most reservation residents use septic tanks.

Transportation. In the 1999 economic development strategic plan, a vast majority of all tribal members expressed a need for public transportation/van pool at the reservation, to increase access to medical and dental services and to off-reservation employment and economic opportunities. Public transportation, commercial shipping, and airport facilities are available in Elko, approximately 100 miles south. The tribe is serviced by UPS and FedEx. The tribe owns a senior citizens bus for transporting its elders.

Telecommunications. Telephone services are provided by Century Telephone Company. Central Communications provides analog voice and data communication services. The tribal headquarters, the school, and the hospital receive high speed Internet through Glen Optic Service.

COMMUNITY FACILITIES AND SERVICES

A community government complex was built on a 10-acre site north of Newtown, Nevada. There are 14 tribal community buildings housing the Duck Valley Tribal Court, BIA police and fire departments, Indian Health Services, Duck Valley Housing Authority, and the Owyhee schools. Human services are provided by the Shoshone-Paiute social services, and housing services are available via the Duck Valley Housing Authority. Since 1996, two modular office buildings have been constructed. They house the fire station, community education center, juvenile detention center, and a household hazardous-waste facility. The tribe also has a senior center.

The Duck Valley Housing Authority built 20 homes in 2000 and three annually since then. In addition, a 12-unit apartment complex has been built.

Education. The local school system, the Owyhee Combined Schools, is operated by the Elko County School District. It serves approximately 348 children in grades K-12, including children from off the reservation. Vocational, GED, and college courses are available on the reservation from Great Basin Community College in Elko. Grants for higher educa-

tion and adult vocational training are available to all tribal members. In their 1999 economic development strategic plan, the tribes' goals included expansion of vocational and continuing education and distance learning opportunities, and their availability to all tribal members. Tribal youth occasionally are offered classes in language or other culturally-sensitive subjects such as tribal arts and crafts.

Health Care. Owyhee has two health care centers: the recently-completed Owyhee Community Health Facility and the Owyhee Public Health Service Indian Hospital. The tribe also has a community health representative. Telemedicine technology is now available at the hospital and offers patients specialized services by use of high-speed Internet. The economic development strategic plan of 1999 prioritized increased access to health care, including the creation of more extensive specialized services such as an alcohol/drug abuse center, a nursing home for elders, home health care services, and a domestic violence safe house. Emergency medical services are provided 24 hours a day.

ENVIRONMENTAL CONCERNS

The release of fuel oils and gasoline in Owyhee has contaminated the groundwater. It is believed that a BIA fuel storage system is the likely source. Until the fuel oil spill is cleaned up, it will be extremely difficult to attract new businesses to the area because traditional financing is not available while underlying groundwater is contaminated. This problem has inhibited economic development opportunities in Owyhee.

A concern of the tribe is acid mine drainage from an abandoned copper mine located just off the reservation. Heavy metals have entered the reservation water system. Remediation and clean-up efforts are supported by the tribes in working with the EPA, the State of Nevada, U.S. Forest Service, U.S. Fish and Wildlife Service and the previous owners of the property.

Waste disposal on the reservation had been an environmental issue. Residents were burning trash in barrels and using open-pit dumps. Toxic smoke and ash contaminated air quality, and the illegal dumps threatened ground and surface water quality. The tribes' integrated solid-waste management program, which includes operation of a solid-waste transfer station, construction of a recycling and environmental education center, educational emphasis on reduced waste production, and successful marketing of the recyclables has dramatically improved the situation. EPA Region 9 Office recognized Duck Valley Reservation success with an outstanding environmental achievement award in 1999.

Much of the reservation lands are natural wetlands. The tribe is in the planning stage of preserving and enhancing those lands. In addition, the tribe has protected spring heads in mountain and rangeland areas.

Total area *(BIA realty, 2004)*   3,854.52 acres
Tribally owned *(BIA realty, 2004)*   3,814 acres
Federal trust *(BIA realty, 2004)*   40 acres
Population *(Tribal source, 2005)*   149
Tribal enrollment *(Tribal source, 2005)*   355
Total labor force **2000 census**   72
High school graduate or higher   73.7%
   2000 census
Bachelor's degree or higher   11.8%
   2000 census
Unemployment rate **2000 census**   9.7%
Per capita income **2000 census** $13,110

LOCATION AND LAND STATUS

Duckwater Reservation is located in east-central Nevada, approximately 225 miles southeast of Elko. This reservation was established under the Proclamation of November 13, 1940, by authority of the Indian Reorganization Act of 1934; 3,273.26 acres were purchased at that time. On December 22, 1943, by the Act of June 28, 1941, another 398.76 acres were purchased. The last 142.5 acres of tax deed land were purchased by authority of the Indian Reorganization Act, on January 22, 1955.

CULTURE AND HISTORY

Duckwater Reservation residents are descended from the Newe people, whose modern tribal name is Shoshone. A natural mineral spring, Duckwater Springs, gave the area its name. The Duckwater region features much fertile farmland. As Euro-American settlers took the choicest lands, many Newes moved to reservations in northern Nevada, while some remained in hopes of reclaiming their land. Learning that a large ranch was for sale in the region, Indian leaders petitioned the BIA to purchase it for a reservation. The Indians prevailed, and between 1940 and 1944 they purchased nearly 4,000 acres for the reservation. With government loans, the Duckwater Indians began to buy horses and milk cows and work the land. Duckwater Reservation children attended an Indian School in Carson City until 1973 when the residents opened their own school.

GOVERNMENT

The Duckwater Reservation adopted a constitution and by-laws on November 11, 1940. The tribal council consists of a chairperson, a vice-chairperson, and three members, all of whom serve three-year terms. The reservation has a tribal court that consists of a chief judge and a county clerk.

The Shosone-Pauite Social Services serves Duck Valley Reservation areas as well as parts of Idaho, and the Duckwater Health and Social Services Department also serves the Duckwater Reservation. The Duckwater Housing Committee is the reservation's housing authority. The Duckwater Police Department employs one police office and a part-time probation officer.

ECONOMY

A tribally operated catfish farm provides revenue to the tribe. A tribally owned cattle herd employs one person full-time and six more on a seasonal basis.

Government as Employer. Self-governance BIA and Indian Health Service programs employ 63 persons.

Agriculture and Livestock. There are 930 acres of irrigated agricultural land. The tribe purchased 500 head of cattle in 1988, and due to the falling cattle market sold all the cattle except for 99 bulls in 2002. Tribal livestock graze on 340,000 acres of public domain land. Individual tribal members also own small-to-medium-sized herds.

Fisheries. In collaboration with the U.S. Fish and Wildlife Service, the tribe is restoring a large geothermal spring and in-stream habitat, which is home to the ESA-listed Railroad Valley Springfish. The restoration project was initiated in 2004 with the decommissioning of a catfish farm.

Construction. The tribal construction company, now six years old, provides excavation, trucking, and oil field services. The tribe also operates a greenhouse business that provides a specialized mine reclamation service, growing and planting native sagebrush and other native seedlings on reclaimed lands and noxious weed areas. The tribal enterprises contract with 13 CDL truck drivers.

INFRASTRUCTURE

Duckwater is approximately 18 miles northwest of Nevada State Highway 6, a major east-west corridor. State Highway 379 traverses the reservation in an east-west direction. An airport and commercial trucking facilities are available in Ely, approximately 75 miles northeast.

Electricity. Mount Wheeler Power Company sells electricity to the reservation.

Water Supply. Tribal water and septic systems serve the school, tribal government building, health clinic, maintenance and fire engine buildings, and 48 residences.

COMMUNITY FACILITIES AND SERVICES

The reservation has a gymnasium, a K-8 school building, a health department and clinic, a ballpark with a concession building, a maintenance shop, and a senior center as well as a tribal government building. Tribal police provide law enforcement, and the Indian Health Service provides emergency services. There is also a volunteer firefighter unit on hand.

Education. Tribal children in grades K-8 attend school at Duckwater Shoshone Elementary School. Others attend the Nye County Public School, three miles south of the reservation, or the Eureka Middle School. High school students attend Eureka High School, which is 50 miles away.

Health Care. The Duckwater Shoshone Tribe maintains a clinic with a full-time physician. The tribe has a self-governance compact with Indian Health Service that provides medical and social services to the tribe.

Duckwater Reservation
Federal reservation
Shoshone
White Pine and Nye counties,
Nevada

Duckwater Shoshone Tribe
P.O. Box 140068
Duckwater, NV 89314
   775-738-0569
   775-863-0301 Fax

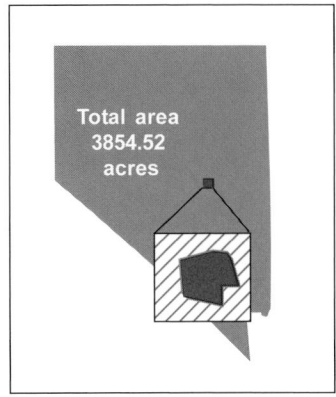

Total area
3854.52
acres

Elko Colony

Elko Colony
Federal reservation
Western Shoshone
Elko County, Nevada

Elko Band Council
1745 Silver Eagle Drive
Elko, NV 89801
775-738-8889
775-753-5439 Fax

Total area (BIA realty, 2004)
192.80 acres

Tribally owned (BIA realty, 2004)
160 acres

Tribal enrollment
(BIA labor report, 2001)
1,594

Total labor force 2000 census
316

Total labor force
(BIA labor report, 2001)
1,044

High school graduate or higher
(BIA realty, 2004)
81.6%

Bachelor's degree or higher
(BIA realty, 2004)
2.5%

TRI-NV-005 Elko Band Administration
Building

TRI-NV-006 Elko Smoke Shop and
Sinclair Gas Station

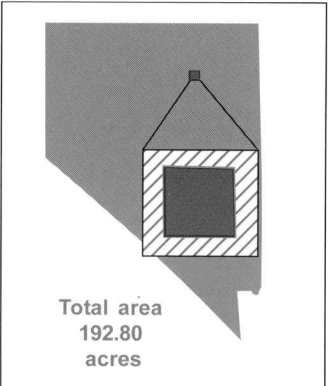

Total area
192.80
acres

LOCATION AND LAND STATUS

The Elko Colony, part of the Te-Moak Tribe of Western Shoshone Indians of Nevada, is located in northeastern Nevada near the Humboldt River. The reservation was established by Executive Order on March 23, 1931, on 160 acres near Elko. An additional 32.8 acres were purchased by warranty deed on April 22, 1931. Tribal lands consist of two separate parcels divided by I-80. The lands are zoned for institutional, commercial, and residential uses. The lands have almost reached development capacity, creating constraints for further commercial development. In the past decade, the band has attempted to acquire further lands, but to no avail. It is currently attempting to acquire lands again. The Elko Colony is the most populous of the Te-Moak Tribe communities and is the tribal headquarters for the Te-Moak Tribe of the Western Shoshone Indians of Nevada.

CLIMATE

The Elko Band reservation is located in the high desert. The region experiences an average rainfall of 3 inches and an average snowfall of 19.9 inches per year. The average temperature is 62.4°F. The reservation is located 5,050 feet above sea level.

CULTURE AND HISTORY

The Elko Band is a member of the Te-Moak Tribe of Western Shoshone Indians of Nevada. They are one of four separate constituent bands of the nation. The Battle Mountain, South Fork, and Wells bands are the other three bands of the Te-Moak Tribe. *(Please refer to Te-Moak Tribe introduction for further information.)*

GOVERNMENT

The Elko Colony was established by Executive Order in 1931. The Elko Band is organized under provisions of the Indian Reorganization Act of 1934 as a government entity on a "reservation-basis" only. It is governed by the Te-Moak Tribe constitution, which was adopted in 1938 and amended in 1982. The band is governed by the Elko Band Council. The council is comprised of seven members led by a chairman. The band also elects two representatives to serve on the Te-Moak Council and the Inter-Tribal Council of Nevada. The Te-Moak tribal administrative offices are located at the Elko Colony.

The Te-Moak Tribal Police and the Te-Moak Bands Tribal Court provide law enforcement on the reservation. The Te-Moak Tribe provides the Western Shoshone Social Services program and the Te-Moak Housing Authority for members of all four bands.

ECONOMY

For many of the Western Shoshone bands, cattle ranching served as the main source of income during the twentieth century.

Government as Employer. The Elko Band Council employs approximately 28 people to provide a variety of administrative and social service programs such as a child care center, an alcohol and drug abuse prevention program, a senior center, and an environmental department.

Services and Retail. The tribe operates a smoke shop and convenience store and a gas station at the Elko Colony. It provides the only nonfederal income source for community operations.

INFRASTRUCTURE

The Elko Colony is surrounded by the City of Elko, which is the county seat of Elko County, Nevada. Nevada State Highway 228 runs south from the Elko Colony, and Highway 275 runs north. Interstate 80 runs through the Elko Band community in an east-west direction.

Electricity. Sierra Pacific Power Company, state-appointed provider of last resort, provides electricity to the Elko Colony.

Fuel. Southwest Gas Corporation provides the colony with natural gas for heating and other uses.

Water Supply. The City of Elko provides municipal water and sewer services to the Elko Band Colony. A municipal solid waste landfill is located five miles south of the reservation, and many tribal members transport domestic waste to the site. The tribe does provide pickup and disposal services for a fee.

Transportation. A regional airport is located in the City of Elko, approximately 10 miles from the Elko Band Colony. Union Pacific provides limited passenger train service, with a pickup point located in downtown Elko. There is no public transportation service available in Elko or within the Elko Band Colony.

Telecommunications. Frontier, a Citizens Communication company, provides telephone and DSL services. Cellular One and Verizon furnish cell phone service.

COMMUNITY FACILITIES AND SERVICES

Community facilities at the Elko Colony include the Elko Colony Gym, a senior citizens center, daycare and ABC Preschool Center, the Elko Band Wellness Center, and the Shoshone Welcome Center.

TRI-NV-005

TRI-NV-006

Education. Elko Band children attend public school in the Elko County School District system. Grammar No. 2 Elementary School, Elko Junior High School, and Elko High School are all located within five miles of the Elko Colony. A four-year state college, Great Basin College, is also within five miles. The ABC Preschool is located at the Elko Colony.

Health Care. Elko Band members may receive health care services through the Indian Health Services Southern Bands Clinic located at the Elko Colony. An Indian Health Service hospital is located about 100 miles away at the Owyhee Indian Reservation.

ENVIRONMENTAL CONCERNS
The Elko Band Environmental Services Department has identified a number of its environmental concerns. They include the transportation of hazardous materials through tribal lands via I-80, vehicle emissions, noise pollution, mining emissions, pesticides, poor drainage, and solid waste disposal. The band is concerned with the safety of homes and offices, especially the use of lead in plumbing systems. It intends to explore the levels of radon and asbestos in its facilities. The environmental services department is currently completing an emergency preparedness plan to tie in with the Elko County Plan.

Elko Colony

Unemployment rate
(BIA realty, 2004)
14.9%

Unemployment rate
(BIA labor report, 2001)
61%

Per capita income *2000 census*
$11,554

Ely Shoshone

Ely Shoshone

LOCATION AND LAND STATUS
The Ely Shoshone Reservation, formerly known as the Ely Colony, is situated at 6,600 feet in Nevada's high desert, along the western edge of the Steptoe Valley in east-central Nevada. It is located in one of the more isolated areas of the continental United States. The nearest population centers are Salt Lake City, Utah, and Las Vegas, Nevada, 250 miles east and south, respectively. The reservation spans 111 acres on 3 separate parcels, all within 1 mile of each other. The colony was established by the Act of June 27, 1930, which authorized an appropriation of $1,000 for the purchase of 10 acres already occupied as a camp by the Shoshone Indian Colony near Ely, Nevada. The act authorized an additional $600 to connect the camp with the city water service. During the mid-1970s, the colony obtained 11 additional acres through a lease with White Pine County, Nevada, upon which 17 HUD homes were constructed. The tribe purchased this land outright in 1992. The tribe has also acquired a 90-acre tract of land known as the Pioche Highway Parcel for a community center, health center, and law enforcement office, the tribe says, and to provide housing for about 45 families. A 20,000-acre increase in tribal land has been proposed to the Bureau of Land Management.

CULTURE AND HISTORY
At the turn of the twentieth century there was only one reservation for the Western Shoshones. It was located in Duck Valley along the Nevada-Idaho border and was called the Western Shoshone Reservation. The BIA initially planned to induce all the Great Basin Shoshones to move to this reservation. During the early 1900s, the federal government established the Colony Program for Nevada Indians, setting aside small colonies on the outskirts of Nevada towns. The colonies were intended to accommodate only small numbers of families who worked in the adjacent communities. The Ely Colony was one of these, being established in 1930. For many of the Western Shoshone bands, cattle ranching has served as the main source of income during the twentieth century. The Ely Shoshone Tribe, however, has an insufficient land base for cattle grazing and has thus turned its sights elsewhere. Some traditional crafts are practiced and marketed, while several service businesses also generate tribal revenues.

GOVERNMENT
The Ely Colony ratified its constitution and bylaws on April 8, 1966. It is governed by the council, which consists of five members, elected to two-year terms. Officers include a chairperson and vice-chairperson. The council meets the second Tuesday of each month. The Ely Shoshone Tribe provides social services. A supervisor and two deputies make up tribal law enforcement and tribal court.

ECONOMY
A self-governance compact from Indian Health Service and the BIA is the financial source for the Ely Shoshone Tribe. The tribe believes that, through self-rule, its programs can grow to their full extent and target the most urgent priorities.

Government as Employer. The tribal government presently employs 52 staff members in its administrative and operations capacities.

Economic Development Projects. The tribe is starting a greenhouse that will provide Native plants for mining reclamation. Gaming is also a subject of study, tribal sources state.

Forestry. Some 50 acres of undeveloped piñon, juniper, and sage compose a portion of the tribe's land holdings. None of this is considered viable for commercial timber development.

Manufacturing. Purses, duffle bags, travel bags, gun and archery cases, bat bags, briefcases, and various other specialty products are listed as products manufactured by Shoshone Cloth Industries. Fabric used by this 10-person tribal business is superior and long lasting. A broader customer base is a goal, although current business is primarily single purchases, according to the tribe.

Services and Retail. Silver Sage Travel Center, the tribe's new retail operation on Highway 6/50/93, was constructed using funds from the tribe, the U.S. Department of Commerce Economic Development Administration, and HUD. The Silver Sage facility consists of a convenience store, gasoline station, smoke shop, Shoshone Cloth Industries, deli, and amenities for truckers, including showers, lounge, phones, and laundry facilities, according to the tribe.

Tourism and Recreation. The tribe holds a traditional fandango the second weekend in July.

INFRASTRUCTURE
U.S. Highway 50 bisects the reservation, providing easy access from points east and west. The local north-south highway is Route 6. Commercial air, bus, and truck lines are located in the town of Ely.

Ely Shoshone Reservation
Federal reservation
Western Shoshone
White Pine County, Nevada

Ely Shoshone Tribe
16 Shoshone Circle
Ely, NV 89301
775-289-3013
775-289-3156 Fax

Total area *2000 census*
282.32 acres

Total area *(Tribal source, 2004)*
111 acres

Individually owned
(BIA realty, 2004)
160 acres

Total population *2000 census*
85

Tribal enrollment
(Tribal source, 2004)
504

Total labor force *2000 census*
71

High school graduate or higher
2000 census
80.7%

Bachelor's degree or higher
2000 census
0%

Unemployment rate *2000 census*
7%

Per capita income *2000 census*
$4,819

Ely Shoshone

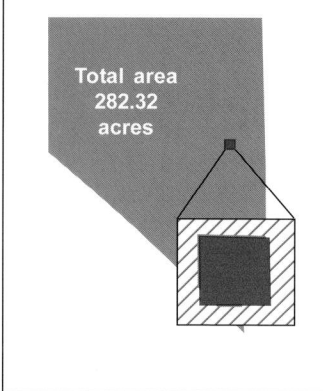

Total area
282.32
acres

Electricity. Mount Wheeler Power furnishes electricity.
Water Supply. The Ely Water District provides the reservation with water and sewage service. White Pine Community Landfill provides solid waste disposal service.

Transportation. The nearest airport is five miles from the reservation. Bus service is available in Ely. Motor freight service is available from UPS and Motor Cargo.

Telecommunications. Is provided by Internet Services, SBC, Mount Wheeler Power, and Precis Cable.

COMMUNITY FACILITIES AND SERVICES
There is a tribal community center on the reservation where tribal offices and activities are centered. The HUD ICDBG and tribally built multi-purpose center contains the education center, library, elders' dining room/recreation room, kitchen, and a multipurpose room. Other community uses listed by the tribe are: providing the educational components of preschool, tutoring children from grades K-12, promoting higher education, and fulfilling other alternatives for completing their education. Socialization, activities, and meals at the center meet the needs of the elders. The multi-purpose center also provides space for tribal council meetings, training events, and community events. The tribe's administrative office houses

a gymnasium on its lower level, the tribe notes.

Public Safety. Tribal police provide law enforcement. The White Pine Sheriff and Ely provide emergency services.

Education. Tribal children from three to five attend the tribe's own preschool. The elementary, middle school, and high school children attend Ely public schools. Great Basin College is located in Ely. The Administration for Native Americans provided the Ely Shoshone Tribe with funds that initiated a program for language preservation.

Health Care. A significant community medical resource, the Newe Tribal Medical Clinic, the tribe notes, is provided to the Indian Health Service without charge by the tribe. The clinic was funded by the tribe and HUD ICDBG. It provides the Ely Shoshone with a tribal nurse practitioner and three federal health workers. Health care is also available in the area at William Bee Ririe Clinic and Hospital as well as clinics and hospitals in Salt Lake City, Las Vegas, and Reno.

ENVIRONMENTAL CONCERNS
The major environmental issues facing the tribe are maintaining water quality, transportation of low- and high-level hazardous waste, and air quality.

Fallon

Fallon Reservation and Colony
Federal reservation
Paiute and Shoshone
Churchill County, Nevada

Fallon Paiute-Shoshone Tribe
565 Rio Vista Dr.
Fallon, NV 89406
702-423-6075
702-423-5202 Fax

LOCATION AND LAND STATUS
The Fallon Reservation and Colony spans approximately 8,218.38 acres in the high desert of west-central Nevada, southwest of the Carson Sink. The reservation lies entirely within Churchill County, Nevada, and it encompasses the township of Fallon, Nevada, which serves as the tribal headquarters. Stillwater, Nevada lies 6 miles west of the reservation, along State Road 116. Major Nevada cities near the reservation include Reno (65 miles west) and Carson City (65 miles southwest). The Fallon Reservation was established under the 1890 allotment schedule approved by the secretary of the interior. Fifty allotments, each 160 acres, were made under the General Allotment Act of February 8, 1887. Today, individual tribe members own 4,640 acres of allotted land. Some 865 acres remain as tribal trust land, divided between the Fallon Reservation and the Fallon Colony, outside the town of Fallon.

CULTURE AND HISTORY
The ancestors of present-day Fallon Paiute-Shoshone tribal members were primarily Northern Paiutes (Numas) of the Toi Ticutta (tule eaters) and Koosi Pah Ticutta (muddy water eaters) bands who roamed the marshy lakebeds of the Carson and Humboldt sinks from prehistoric times into the nineteenth century, subsisting on a diet of fish, pine nuts, waterfowl eggs, and small game. The benevolent marshes also provided the Numas with material for making shelters, clothing, and tools. A short growing season prevented them from practicing horticulture.

The blazing of the California Trail during the 1840s brought the Northern Paiutes into increasing contact with Euro-American settlers. The Toi Ticuttas clashed with a force of U.S. Army volunteers in 1860, near Pyramid Lake. Soon after, the U.S. Army increased its presence in the area by establishing Fort Churchill, 35 miles southwest of present-day Fallon. Numerous small conflicts arose between the army and the Toi Ticuttas. Simultaneously, the Koosi Pahs were permanently displaced by Euro-American farmers moving into the Lahontan Valley. Both bands of Numas fled to the marshes and joined together.

In the early 1890s, the U.S. government moved individual Numa families to a reservation divided into 160-acre plots near present-day Fallon. As settlers began moving into the area, they realized that the Numa land was valuable for agriculture, and they urged the federal government to take away reservation land. In 1902 the federal government asked the Numa people to relinquish their 160-acre allotments in exchange for 10-acre allotments with water rights, with the underlying threat that those who didn't relinquish their acreage would not receive water from the new dam. Lacking irrigation ditches, most land owners had to relent to the Newland Project of 1906, thus receiving irrigation ditches and water rights for the relinquishment of their land. Many of these families were pressured off their land by white farmers, and they moved nearer the town of Fallon. In 1908, the Indian Service established an Indian school 10 miles east of Fallon and built 30 homes for the Toi Ticuttas. The Toi Ticuttas also received additional irrigable land from the federal government.

In 1958, the Toi Ticuttas and Shoshones who moved to the Stillwater area incorporated as the Fallon Paiute-Shoshone Tribe, adopting a constitution and bylaws outlining tribal duties and authority.

GOVERNMENT
The original constitution and bylaws of the Fallon Paiute-Shoshone Tribe were ratified on June 12, 1964, and amended in 1971 and 1980. The tribal council is the tribe's governing body and is composed of a chairperson, a vice-chairperson, a secretary/treasurer, and four members each elected to two-year terms, with elections occurring every year. The tribal council also serves as the Fallon Business Council.

The tribal government includes the Paiute-Shoshone Tribal Court and the following departments: police, fire, environmental protection, housing authority, education, finance, health, Indian Child Welfare, mental health, substance abuse prevention and counseling, child care development, domestic violence, senior center, employment development, and general assistance. The Fallon

BIA law enforcement department is situated in Churchill in the middle of the reservation. The department is designed to uphold the laws of the reservation and colony. This department is a 24-hour operation.

The Fallon Paiute Shoshone Tribe is also a member of the Native American Graves Protection and Reparation Act (NAGPRA) Coalition. The NAGPRA is a federal law that was passed in 1990 to aid Native Americans in their quest to repatriate human remains, funerary objects, sacred objects, and objects of cultural patrimony from museums and other federal agencies.

BUSINESS CORPORATION
The Fallon Business Council created the Fox Peak Economic Development Corporation to manage tribal businesses and to work toward the goal of economic self-sufficiency. The corporation oversees the economic development pursuits, health, safety, and general welfare of Fallon Paiute-Shoshone tribal members. The council meets on the second and fourth Tuesday of each month.

ECONOMY
The Fallon Paiute-Shoshone Tribe's economy is largely supported by the tribal government. Agriculture, service and retail businesses, and recreation and tourism also contribute. The tribe's main economic development goals are to expand job opportunities and to provide affordable housing for tribal members, and with the aid of the Fox Peak Development Corporation and the housing authority, they are on their way to meeting these goals.

Government as Employer. The tribal government employs approximately 55 persons in tribal offices and the health clinic. Job opportunities exist through direct employment by the tribe and by the BIA contract services.

Economic Development Projects. Economic development plans include a trap shoot, a skeet shoot, rifle ranges, fishing accommodations, and possibly a clubhouse.

Agriculture and Livestock. Some 2,800 allotted acres of irrigable land are currently in agricultural production. Most tribal members work in agricultural production on irrigated, allotted land.

Real Estate/Commercial Development. The tribe is planning the development of a 24-acre retail, commercial, and professional office development located on a 24-acre lot off of Highway 50 called the Fox Peak Centre. The center will consist of a 250,000-square-foot retail establishment and a 70,000-square-foot medical and professional office building. A modern Native American theme will be carried throughout the development. The tribe is planning to provide tax incentives such as accelerated depreciation and employment tax credits to draw businesses and investors to the facility.

Services and Retail. The Fox Peak Development Corporation owns and operates a smoke shop and gift shop located at Fallon Colony. The facility includes a convenience store, a snack bar, and a small gift shop that sells arts and crafts made by tribal members. A privately owned gallery located in Fallon sells Indian-made arts and crafts fashioned from stone, wood, and metal. The owner conducts guided tours of the gallery and museum.

Transportation. As part of the youth summer program, government transportation services are available to tribal youth during the summer months. The Fallon Tribal Health Center provides transportation to and from medical appointments.

Tourism and Recreation. The tribe holds the Annual Fallon All-Indian Stampede and Powwow in mid-July. This family event features a rodeo and dancing. The tribe also maintains the Pheasant Club, a commercial hunting club. The reservation lies some 10 miles south of the Fallon National Wildlife Refuge, a prime site for observing numerous species of waterfowl.

INFRASTRUCTURE
The Fallon Reservation and Colony lies along State Road 116 near the intersection of U.S. Highway 95 and Highway 50 near Fallon, Nevada. There is a small municipal airport adjacent to tribal lands. Commercial air service is available in Reno, 65 miles west. No public transportation companies serve the reservation directly. However, four major trucking lines, the Southern Pacific Railroad, and Greyhound, Nevada Central, and Las Vegas-Tonopah-Reno bus lines serve the reservation area via the City of Fallon.

Electricity. Sierra Pacific Power Company services the area.

Fuel. Sierra Pacific Power Company provides natural gas.

Water Supply. A community well and a 250,000-gallon storage tank from the colony's water resources serve the reservation and colony.

Telecommunications. Churchill County provides and services the telecommunications needs of the colony and reservation.

Housing. The housing authority, formed through Tribal Ordinance No. 1-67 in 1966, was established to provide sanitary housing and promote economic independence of tribal members. The housing authority has five employees and manages 235 HUD, housing improvement program, and rental housing units on the reservation and colony. In May 2003, the housing authority began construction of a phased energy-efficient home project west of Reservation Road. The tribe received NAHASDA block funding for this project. Additionally, a Title VI grant is enabling the housing authority to build approximately 15 houses in various locations on the reservation, due to begin construction by 2004.

Fallon

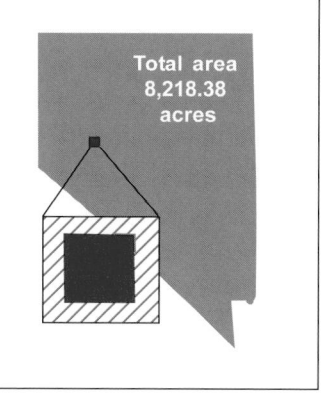

Total area
8,218.38
acres

Total area *(BIA realty, 2004)*
8,218.38 acres

Tribally owned *(BIA realty, 2004)*
3578.38 acres

Individually owned
(BIA realty, 2004)
4,640 acres

Population *2000 census*
1,002

Total labor force *2000 census*
288

High school graduate or higher
2000 census
76.7%

Bachelor's degree or higher
2000 census
6.2%

Unemployment rate *2000 census*
14.6%

Per capita income *2000 census*
$10,090

TRI-NV-007

TRI-NV-008

TRI-NV-007 Sign for Fallon Paiute-Shoshone Administration Building

TRI-NV-008 Front view of Fallon Headstart Building

Fallon

COMMUNITY FACILITIES AND SERVICES

The tribe has a community complex located on the colony site. The complex has an adjoining senior center that offers many services to handicapped and tribal elders, including nutritious meals, meal delivery, trips to surrounding areas and other senior centers, traditional crafts, and other cultural activities. During the months of June-August, the tribal recreation program involves children ages K-16 in activities such as swimming, movies, arts and crafts, sports, games, and field trips to nearby places. The tribe also has a group home for Native American children in need called The Stepping Stones Tribal Youth Shelter. The shelter provides a nurturing home environment for at-risk Native American teenagers.

Education. Tribal youth attend public schools in the Fallon and Stillwater area. The tribe's higher education program provides scholarships for full-time students enrolled in an accredited college in pursuit of a degree. The enrichment program caters to those tribal members who are not enrolled full-time, but need credits to upgrade their job or are earning credits toward a degree. The adult vocational training program is available to tribal members who want to attend technical schools and learn a trade. Courses may be taken in the trade of choice, but students are only allowed to enroll in this program once.

Health Care. The Fallon Paiute-Shoshone Tribe has contracts through the Indian Health Service to provide ambulatory health care, and alcohol and substance-abuse prevention and counseling. The 13,550 square-foot health care clinic was built in 1997; it is an outpatient facility that provides primary care services including: general medicine and pediatrics, women's health, allergy testing, diabetes education, dental, optometry, mental health, community health outreach, substance abuse coun-

seling, a pregnancy program, and a car seat and booster seat program. The clinic has five exam rooms, two treatment rooms, and an in-house pharmacy with contracts for laboratory services. The health center has two registered nurses, one licensed practical nurse, a health services director, and three health community representatives. The community health representatives provide limited in-home care, domestic care, patient education, and transportation. The clinic has a fleet of sedans and minivans, and a wheelchair-lift-equipped bus to provide service for medical appointments and limited shopping in the nearby Fallon community. The closest hospitals are located in Fallon, Reno, and Carson City, Nevada. Tribal members in need of these services can use private insurance, Medicaid, Medicare, and other types of billable insurance plans.

ENVIRONMENTAL CONCERNS

The tribe's goal is to increase awareness and to protect the environment using the laws and regulations of the Clean Water Act, solid waste program, air quality program, and chemical and hazardous materials program. Contamination of the reservation and colony's water is of particular concern to the tribe. The Paiute-Fallon Environmental Department receives funding under the Clean Water Act of 106, and 319 grants to address these concerns. The EPA has a pesticides program to assess the impact of upstream pesticides on tribal groundwater and determine whether these pesticides can be found in tribal drinking water. The EPA's Environmental Justice Grant is working to determine whether the tribal wastewater lagoon system is contaminating the reservation's groundwater. A USDOT HAZMAT preparedness grant is being used to develop emergency response plans for the Fallon Reservation and Colony.

Fort McDermitt

Fort McDermitt Reservation
Federal reservation
Numa
Humboldt County, Nevada
Malheur County, Oregon

Fort McDermitt Paiute and
Shoshone Tribe
P.O. Box 457
McDermitt, NV 89421
775-532-8259
775-532-8487 Fax

Total area *(BIA realty, 2004)*	34,604.36 acres	
Tribally owned	34,459.36 acres	
(BIA realty, 2004)		
Population *2000 census*	309	
Population *(Tribal source, 2005)*	335	
Tribal enrollment *(BIA labor report, 2001)*	928	
Tribal enrollment *(Tribal source, 2005)*	1,002	
Total labor force *2000 census*	94	
Total labor force *(BIA labor report, 2001)*	385	
High school graduate or higher	49.4%	
2000 census		
Bachelor's degree or higher	1.2%	
2000 census		
Unemployment rate *2000 census*	46.81%	
Unemployment rate *(BIA labor report, 2001)*	7%	
Per capita income	$6,322	
(BIA labor report, 2001)		

LOCATION AND LAND STATUS

The Fort McDermitt Reservation is located on the remote Oregon-Nevada border, approximately 75 miles north of Winnemucca, Nevada. Sixteen thousand acres of the reservation lay in Humboldt County, Nevada, and 18,000 acres are located in Malheur County, Oregon. The town of McDermitt, Nevada, is adjacent to the northern part of the reservation. The reservation is on land established by an Executive Order

on September 3, 1867, which set aside lands as the Camp McDermitt Military Reservation.

Another Executive Order in 1889 transferred these lands to the secretary of the interior, making the area public domain land. An Act of Congress on August 1, 1890, authorized the disposition of this land under the Homestead Law, and in 1892 parcels of it were allotted to Indian residents under the General Allotment Act of 1887.

A host of congressional acts authorized by the Indian Reorganization Act of 1934 have added lands to the reservation in both Nevada and Oregon; the Act of January 17, 1936, set aside 20,414.46 acres. This was followed by the Act of November 16, 1946, for 1,554.35 acres; the Act of November 9, 1940, for 3,542.40 acres; the Act of July 18, 1941, for 1,240 acres; the Act of February 24, 1943, for 3,919.37 acres; and the Act of June 16, 1944, for 449.92 acres.

The Indian Reorganization Act has a provision that gives tribes the opportunity to purchase lands near their reservations. Taking advantage of this provision, the Fort McDermitt Tribe purchased 160 acres on February 3, 1956. In addition, many tribal members relinquished their individual private allotments to tribal ownership, also under authority of the Indian Reorganization Act. Between 1949 and 1957, about 3,900.10 acres of relinquished allotments were added to the reservation. From 1960 to 1973, 162.63 acres were also added to the reservation land base.

CULTURE AND HISTORY

The descendants of the people known as the Numas now inhabit the Fort McDermitt Reservation. Their ancestors once roamed northern Nevada and southern Oregon. The 1860s were marked by hostilities between Indians and Euro-American settlers in the area, and Fort McDermitt was originally set up as a camp to protect white settlers and travelers.

After the Bannock and Paiute War of 1878, many Numas of the Paiute and Shoshone tribes were rounded up and forced to march over 400 miles to the Yakama Indian Agency in northern Washington. After several years of living under adverse conditions in Yakama and petitioning the authorities to allow them to leave, the Indians left the area in 1883 without permission and were apparently unopposed by the government. Some of the Indian families who left settled at Fort McDermitt, where they were assigned land parcels by federal allotment, drawing numbers from an Indian agent's hat. The land thus assigned to them proved inadequate for subsistence farming, and in 1934, under the Indian Reorganization Act, the federal government purchased neighboring farmland and transferred it to the tribe. Land transfers from the federal government have continued to bring the reservation to its present size. Today, along with the continuing use of the Paiute language, the tribe maintains a distinct, thriving Indian culture at Fort McDermitt.

GOVERNMENT

The Fort McDermitt Paiute and Shoshone Tribe is governed by a tribal constitution and bylaws that were approved and adopted on July 2, 1936, under the Indian Reorganization Act of 1934. The Fort McDermitt Tribal Council officers, who hold four-year terms, include a chairperson, a vice-chairperson, a treasurer, and five council members; a secretary is appointed. The council meets monthly for important governmental concerns such as negotiating with the federal, state, and local governments regarding tribal interests, managing tribal programs, and overseeing tribal economic enterprises.

Government departments include the tribal court, police, ambulance, social services, Indian child welfare advocacy, Head Start, health, housing, and education. Currently, the tribal government employs 10 aides, the tribal court employs 1 clerk, social services employs 10 workers, the Indian Health Services employs 10 people, and the Inter-Tribal Council of Nevada Head Start program along with workforce development employ 8 individuals.

ECONOMY

The major sources of tribal revenue are the tribal government and agriculture. Possible avenues for economic development include manufacturing and exporting durable goods, and developing business, repair, entertainment, and recreation services.

Economic Development Projects. The tribe is planning to construct a truck stop, convenience store, and casino complex on the reservation adjacent to U.S. Highway 95, to be opened in early 2006.

Agriculture and Livestock. Some specialized agricultural crops, such as potatoes, provide seasonal employment on the reservation. Leasing hay land and cattle grazing pastures are additional sources of tribal revenue. The tribe leases the Hog John Ranch, situated 54 miles west of the reservation; however, the water rights were transferred or sold to ranches in the upper valleys of Quinn and King Rivers, limiting development of the ranch and surrounding area. A small diversion dam on the Quinn River provides some irrigation. The tribe also owns ranch lands suitable for running 2,000 head of cattle.

INFRASTRUCTURE

Due to this community's geographic isolation, the infrastructure is not developed extensively. U.S. Highway 95 passes in a north-south direction through the reservation. The closest trade centers are Winnemucca, and Boise, Idaho. Commercial air and train service are available in Winnemucca, 75 miles distant. Buses and commercial trucking serve the reservation.

Electricity. Harney Electric Cooperative provides electricity.

Water Supply. Tribally owned water and wastewater facilities on the reservation serve residents.

Telecommunications. Humboldt Telephone Company provides telephone and Internet service.

COMMUNITY FACILITIES AND SERVICES

The tribe's community center, the Tribal Youth and Wellness Center, offers a variety of social activities and programs, including Head Start, the senior citizen's program, and a wellness program.

Education. Tribal youth attend elementary and high school at McDermitt Combined School, which is five miles away in the Town of McDermitt. The tribe also offers a program for tribal youth called Learn 'n Serve. In this program, which is administered by the McDermitt Combined School, participants research and design economic development projects for the reservation.

Health Care. The Fort McDermitt Health Clinic, which is funded by Indian Health Service, is adjacent to the tribal administration building. The clinic provides basic medical care, a WIC clinic, nutrition counseling, a diabetes program, and a substance-abuse program.

ENVIRONMENTAL CONCERNS

The tribe is currently working with the EPA to develop a plan to clean up a landfill located on the reservation. The tribe also conducts monthly testing of their potable water supply for traces of bacteria, and it is seeking a EPA grant to repair two pumps at a lake on the reservation.

Fort McDermitt

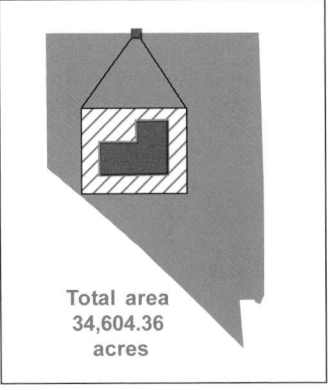

Total area
34,604.36
acres

Goshute Pauite

See Utah

Las Vegas Paiute

Las Vegas Paiute Colony
Federal reservation
Paiute
Clark County, Nevada

Las Vegas Paiute Tribe
No. 1 Paiute Drive
Las Vegas, NV 89106
702-386-3926
702-383-4019 Fax
lvpaiute.com

Total area *(BIA realty, 2004)*
3,852.68 acres

Tribally owned *(BIA realty, 2004)*
3,852.68 acres

Population *2000 census*
108

Enrollment *(Tribal source, 2004)*
56

Total labor force *2000 census*
33

Total labor force *(BIA, 2001)*
62

High school graduate or higher
2000 census
77%

Bachelor's degree or higher
2000 census
0%

Unemployment rate *2000 census*
3%

Unemployment rate *(BIA, 2001)*
20%

Per capita income *(BIA, 2001)*
$8,529

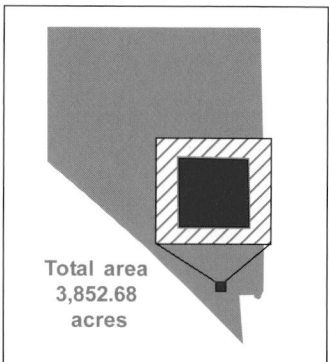

Total area
3,852.68
acres

LOCATION AND STATUS
The original 16-acre Las Vegas Paiute Colony was established in what was primarily a residential community of Las Vegas, Nevada, on March 3, 1911, via a Congressional Appropriations Act when Helen J. Steward, a benefactor, sold 10 acres to the federal government in 1911 for the tribe's use. Presently 2.54 acres are set aside for business enterprises, 3.63 acres are for residential or new commercial development, and 10 acres are for residential and tribal administration buildings.

The remainder of the tribe's land was acquired on December 2, 1983, through PL 98-203; it totals 3,850.15 acres at Snow Mountain, just north of Las Vegas along the Reno-Tonopah Highway, near the Charleston turnoff. This turnoff, a major highway interchange, connects with East Snow Mountain to the west of the reservation for easy accessibility.

CULTURE AND HISTORY
The Paiutes are descended from the Nuwuvi people, who lived in a large area of the southwest and east of the Colorado River. The Nuwuvis were hunters and gatherers who existed in family units and gathered together into loose bands. As the Euro-American invasion progressed, the Nuwuvis gathered into larger and larger bands for survival. The Las Vegas area was long the home of many bands of Nuwuvis, many of whom had left the nearby Moapa Reservation when it fell into mismanagement and decline. As more trappers and traders arrived and crossed the aboriginal lands in 1826, the trails from New Mexico to California became known as the Old Spanish Trail, and in 1848 the U.S. government took over the area.

In 1857, Nuwuvis who converged on Las Vegas gathered and successfully drove out a Mormon settlement there. In the years that followed, Nuwuvis from different regions began to make their way to Las Vegas, some becoming employed at the ranches of the few white settlers who did not leave with the Mormons. The white settlement grew steadily, and in 1911 Helen J. Stewart sold a 10-acre lot to the federal government with the provision that it be exclusively for Indian use. Housing and a day school were constructed, and the tract became a colony for Indian families, but its farmland was poor. In spite of the efforts of local townspeople to help with irrigating and developing the camp, by 1953 the BIA was considering closing it and relocating its residents. Efforts to sell the land continued until 1970, when the residents at last formed a government with a constitution and bylaws. The tribe acquired an additional 3,840.15 acres at Snow Mountain, north of Las Vegas.

GOVERNMENT
Under the terms of the Indian Reorganization Act of June 18, 1934, the Secretary of the Interior approved the Las Vegas Paiute tribal constitution and bylaws on June 24, 1970. The tribal council consists of a chairperson, a vice-chairperson, and five members, all of whom serve two-year terms.

The tribe, under PL-638, contracts with the BIA to administer key programs and services. These include law enforcement, judicial, social, welfare assistance, water rights negotiation and litigation, and the Indian Child Welfare Act. They contract with the Indian Health Service to provide contract health service, community health representatives, mental and substance abuse, health care delivery, outpatient health, a child development center, and a vocational rehabilitation center. The tribe receives grants to operate various law enforcement programs

on the reservation. The tribe also has its own housing office, which has constructed 35 tribal housing units.

ECONOMY
Because of the Las Vegas Colony's urban residential location, the tribe's economic activities are largely integrated with those of the City of Las Vegas. Tourism, retail, and manufacturing are the major contributors to the tribe's economic stability and success.

Economic Development Projects. The tribe operates two smoke shops, a mini-mart, and a gas station.

Manufacturing. Tribal enterprises include a technology manufacturing company and a clothes fabrication operation.

Real Estate/Commercial Development. The tribe has 16 acres of land in downtown Las Vegas, including 2.5 acres intended to be used for a business enterprise, and 3.6 acres to be used either to expand residential or for new commercial development.

Services and Retail. The Las Vegas Paiute Tribal Smoke Shop is America's largest single retailer of cigarettes in the United States, and it is among the top 10 nongaming businesses in Nevada.

Tourism and Recreation. Las Vegas has abundant casinos, theme parks, hotels and motels, and thousands of other attractions. And for those who want to get away from the city's fast-paced environment for the day, Snow Mountain, 20 minutes northwest of Las Vegas, is home to the Las Vegas Paiute Golf Resort. The resort features three championship golf courses, a restaurant, a pro shop, and a practice facility.

INFRASTRUCTURE
U.S. Interstate 15 and U.S. Highway 95 intersect in Las Vegas. A major arterial interchange connecting the west and east sides of Snow Mountain was completed in fall 1994.

Electricity. Tribal members who reside within the Las Vegas city limits have access to utilities through the Las Vegas Civic Utility Services.

Water Supply. The tribe does not have its own water and power lines due to prohibitive costs. Las Vegas Civic Utility Services provides utilities to tribal members who reside within the Las Vegas city limits.

Transportation. Commercial transportation and shipping facilities are available in Las Vegas. The Las Vegas airport is 6 miles from the Colony, and 18 miles from the Snow Mountain lands.

COMMUNITY FACILITIES AND SERVICES
The Las Vegas Paiute Tribe has its own child development center, which opened in November 2000 to all tribal members and tribal employees. The center's programs serve children aged 2-12, and it has a capacity for 40 children. There are recreation fields, community health facilities, public safety, maintenance, and administration buildings located in the tribal complex.

Education. Las Vegas offers many public and private educational opportunities for the youth and adults of the Las Vegas Paiute Tribe, including the University of Nevada at Las Vegas. The tribe operates a self-funded scholarship program for its members.

Health Care. A community health services program operates under a joint resolution between the Las Vegas and Moapa Paiute tribal councils. These services, available to tribal members in Las Vegas, Moapa, and the rest of Clark County, are funded by Indian Health Services. Contract health services include health care, counseling, substance abuse prevention, mental health, delivery, outpatient, referrals, and a community health representative. There is a transportation service for tribal members who are without a vehicle or unable to drive.

Housing. The Las Vegas Paiute Tribe has 35 housing units constructed under the housing improvement program. These units are held to a high standard in providing safe and healthy housing for tribal members. As of 2004, there were no plans to construct additional housing units.

ENVIRONMENTAL CONCERNS

The Las Vegas Paiutes are focused upon improving the desert environment, maintaining water rights, and increasing stakeholder participation in air quality.

Lovelock

Total area *(BIA realty, 2004)*		20 acres
Tribally owned *(BIA realty, 2004)*		20 acres
Population *2000 census*		103
Tribal enrollment		369
(BIA labor report, 2001)		
Tribal enrollment *(Tribal source, 2004)*		292
Total labor force *2000 census*		28
Total labor force *(Tribal source, 2004)*		298
High school graduate or higher		57.1%
2000 census		
Bachelor's degree or higher		4.8%
2000 census		
Unemployment rate *2000 census*		17.7%
Unemployment rate		46%
(BIA labor report, 2001)		
Per capita income *2000 census*		$7,020

LOCATION AND LAND STATUS

Lovelock Colony is located in west-central Nevada, on the outskirts of the town of Lovelock, approximately 90 miles northeast of Reno. Two acres of land were first purchased for construction of a school on the tribe's behalf in September 1907, and the colony was officially established on November 1, 1910, when 18 more acres were purchased and the secretary of the interior allotted the total 20 acres as a reservation. The tribe owns this acreage and uses it for residential purposes for tribal members. In 2004 the tribe was considering purchasing additional land.

CLIMATE

Lovelock, Nevada, sits at an elevation of 3,980 feet above sea level. The year-round daily high temperatures average 67.8°F, and the year-round low temperatures average 35°F. The area receives approximately 5.3 inches of rain and 6.9 inches of snow annually.

CULTURE AND HISTORY

The Paiute Indians at the Lovelock Colony are descendants of the Numas, a people who once lived in much of what are now the states of Nevada, Oregon, Idaho, and California. Hunters, gatherers, and farmers, the Numas could no longer find enough food when Euro-American settlers encroached upon traditional lands. The Numas (Paiutes) living near Lovelock, Nevada, traditionally called themselves Koop Ticutta, or "ground-squirrel eaters."

Some Koop Ticutta joined in the 1860 Pyramid Lake War against Euro-American occupation, and when defeated, they camped near Lovelock and avoided all contact with settlers. In 1907 a local politician, William Pitt, and his wife, Capitola, sold two acres of land to the federal government, with the provision that it be reserved for building an Indian school that would prevent the integration of whites and Indians in public schools. In 1910 the Pitts sold an additional 18 acres to the government for Indian use, and this acreage became the site of the Lovelock Colony, decreed an Indian reservation by the secretary of the interior.

GOVERNMENT

Tribal government was organized under the Indian Reorganization Act of 1934, with a constitution and bylaws approved and adopted on March 14, 1968. The tribal council consists of a chairperson, a vice-chairperson, and three members, all of whom serve two-year terms.

The tribe, under PL-638, contracts with the BIA to administer key programs and services. Programs contracted by the tribe include enrollment/ATG, tribal court, social services/ICWA, Johnson O'Malley, road maintenance, law enforcement, and home improvement. It contracts CHR, IHHA, and a van driver through the Indian Health Service, and it contracts Head Start, child care, elder's lunch, summer youth, and domestic violence programs through the Inter-Tribal Council of Nevada. The tribal government also operates language and cultural programs.

ECONOMY

Tribal members are employed in agriculture, mining, and retail commercial establishments within commuting distance.

Government as Employer. Tribal government, via its various programs, employed approximately 21 people in 2004.

Economic Development Projects. The tribe has recently submitted a proposal to develop a consortium for health care services with three other tribes.

INFRASTRUCTURE

I-80 crosses the reservation in an east-west direction.

Electricity. Sierra Pacific Power Company provides electricity.

Fuel. Southwest Gas Company provides gas service.

Water Supply. The city of Lovelock provides water and sewer systems.

Transportation. Commercial truck transportation and shipping are available in Lovelock, one mile from the reservation, and

Lovelock Colony
Federal reservation
Paiute
Pershing County, Nevada

Lovelock Paiute Tribe
P.O. Box 878
Lovelock, NV 89419
775-273-7861
775-273-1144 Fax

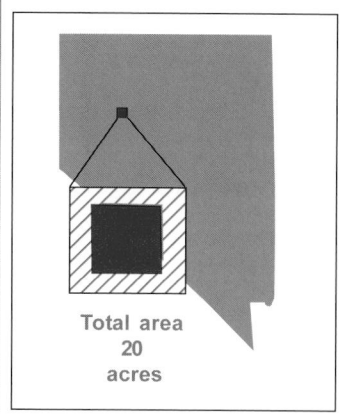

Total area
20
acres

Lovelock

TRI-NV-009

TRI-NV-010

TRI-NV-009 Sign in front of Lovelock Paiute Tribal Offices

TRI-NV-0010 Lovelock Recreation Center and Boxing Facility

air services are available at the Reno International Airport, 92 miles distant. The Union Pacific Railroad has a connection to the Colony.

Telecommunications. GBIS provides Internet service.

COMMUNITY FACILITIES AND SERVICES
The tribe owns a community hall for sports and social events. A number of social services are available via the Fallon Paiute-Shoshone Social Services organization in Fallon, Nevada.

Public Safety. Lovelock provides fire and ambulance services.

Education. Tribal youth attend preschool, elementary, and secondary schools operated by the county.

Health Care. Tribal members have access to the Fallon Tribal Clinic, an Indian Health Service facility, in Fallon, Nevada, where general medical services, a dental clinic, and a community health representative are available. The tribe operates a diabetes prevention program. Full-service medical and surgical care is available at the Washoe Medical Center or St. Mary's Hospital in Reno, Nevada. In June 2004, a proposal to form a health consortium with three other tribes was pending approval.

ENVIRONMENTAL CONCERNS
In June 2004, the tribe listed radon gas and solid waste disposal as high environmental priorities, followed by overall air quality, and an increased use of herbicides and pesticides in the surrounding region. The water system serving the colony is old, and some tribal members distrust the water quality.

Moapa

Moapa Reservation
Federal reservation
Nuwuvi
Clark County, Nevada

Moapa Band of Paiute Indians
P.O. Box 340
Moapa, NV 89025
    702-865-2787
    702-865-2875 Fax

LOCATION AND LAND STATUS
The Moapa Reservation is located 55 miles northeast of Las Vegas, Nevada, on I-15 and State Route 168. Moapa, Nevada, serves as the tribal headquarters. The 71,954-acre reservation, composed of alternating desert and range, lies approximately 24 miles east of the Nevada Test Sight and approximately 12 miles north of the Lake Mead National Recreational Area. Towns near the reservation include Logandale and Overton, 6 and 12 miles south, respectively, via State Road 169. Glendale is located 8 miles to the west. The Moapa Reservation was established by an Executive Order on March 12, 1873, on 2,000,000 acres; it was, however, reduced to 1,000 acres in 1875. In 1981, an Act of Congress restored 70,565 acres to the reservation.

CULTLURE AND HISTORY
The Moapa Band of Paiutes or "Nuwuvi" are part of the Southern Paiute Nation, whose traditional territory covered much of present southern Nevada, northern Arizona, and southern Utah. The Moapa Band hunted small game and gathered plant foods in southern Nevada's Moapa Valley; this prehistoric flood plain of the Muddy River today flows southward through the valley and drains into Lake Mead. The Moapa Paiutes' first contact with Euro-Americans occurred after the blazing of the Old Spanish Trail through their territory in 1830. Until the Mexican-American War, this trade route between the Mexican provinces of New Mexico and California afforded Mexican slave owners the opportunity to raid Paiute settlements for slaves. American explorer John C. Fremont encountered a Moapa war party during his passage through the Moapa Valley in 1844. The Moapa Paiutes were subsequently regarded as the most hostile Nuwuvi band. However, Mormon missionaries entered the Moapa Valley during the 1850s and found the Moapa people friendly and courteous. Prior to the

invasion of Mormon settlers, New Mexicans, and other emigrants, the Moapas had adapted to hunting and gathering with great ingenuity. They were skilled in using the land's natural resources, such as animal skins and plants. Plants were used for medicinal purposes and basketry, and leather was used for shoes.

Under pressure to open Paiute lands for white settlement, the U.S. government confined the Moapa Band to a 70,565.7-acre reservation in 1873. Two years later, the reservation was reduced in size to 1,000 acres. This reduction was followed by 60 years of Indian service neglect and white theft from the reservation. The cultural disruption by foreigners in the area all but destroyed the legends, songs, and dances of the Moapas by the early 1900s. Furthermore, individual allotments were too small to farm economically. As a result, many people fled the reservation or began to live on low wages farming for others. Tuberculosis and whooping cough wracked the remaining population during the 1920s and 1930s.

In 1951, the Southern Paiute Tribe filed a claim with the Indian Claims Commission, and they won a settlement in 1965 of $7,253,165.19. In 1981, Congress restored 70,565 acres to the Moapa Reservation. The Moapa Band's motto, "To advance the Moapa Bands of Paiutes and preserve our homeland by building an independent and self-governing community that provides an opportunity for all peoples who have made a commitment to this mission. Traditional, Contemporary, Progressive," describes their outlook. Today, the tribe strives to improve the well-being of members through social services and economic development while maintaining a firm grasp on Paiute culture and heritage.

GOVERNMENT

The tribe ratified a constitution and bylaws on April 17, 1942, in accordance with the Indian Reorganization Act. The Moapa Business Council serves as the governing body for the Moapa Band, and it is composed of a chairperson, a vice-chairperson, a secretary, and three members. Council members serve staggered three-year terms, with two council members elected every year. The business council oversees the tribal courts; the police, fire, ambulance, and health and human services departments; the Boys and Girls Club; and the water quality, and housing programs, and business enterprises.

BUSINESS CORPORATION

Under the supervision of the Moapa Business Council, the Moapa Paiutes used money awarded to them from a suit with the Indian Claims Commission to establish a perpetual capital fund for improvements and economic development. This corporation was the major employer of tribal members.

ECONOMY

Government as Employer. The tribal government employs 24 people in various departments. The tribal government serves as the major employer of tribal members. During peak periods, the tribal government employs over 100 people.

Economic Development Projects. Plans are being developed to expand the Paiute Travel Plaza near the Valley of Fire exit, including a residential community, an RV park, and a hotel and casino on the reservation near I-15. An electric generating station was proposed in partnership with Calpine Corporation and is still in the developmental stage. This project may produce $200 million in revenue for over 35 years in property and excise taxes and land and water leases. The Moapa Band plans to seek 7,000 acre-feet of water to cool the power plant. Union Pacific Railroad crosses over this land mass, and I-15 straddles it with off ramps, increasing tribal development. A cement plant is being proposed on the reservation. This will be the first of its kind on any Indian reservation.

Agriculture and Livestock. The tribe has approximately 460 acres of alfalfa under cultivation, which is marketed in the Las Vegas area. Some land is used for ranching. The tribe raises Black Angus beef and when the herd is ready for market they will be sold.

Gaming. Moapa Tribal Enterprises operates 90 slots at the tribal store on I-15 at exit 75. The Moapa Tribal Casino is 2,500 square feet, with 50 parking spaces; it contributes approximately 90 percent of the tribe's revenues. The casino employs eight staff.

Real Estate/Commercial Development. The tribe is proposing to develop 70,000 acres for industrial, commercial, recreational purposes, including negotiations to build a dude ranch. Construction of a gymnasium and multipurpose facility was completed for use by tribal members on the reservation. The tribe continues to rehabilitate residential homes located on the reservation.

Services and Retail. The tribe operates a gift and tobacco shop along I-15 that sells gas, fireworks, souvenirs, food, beer, and arts and crafts. A tribally owned convenience store sells food and dry goods near Hidden Valley. The tribe also owns a gas station and truck stop.

Tourism and Recreation. The tribe has plans to open a resort complex on reservation land. The reservation lies 12 miles west of the popular Lake Mead National Recreational Area and the Valley of Fire in Moapa Valley. The camping facilities have restrooms and showers with electricity, hiking trails, picnic areas, and plaques with explanations of the trapping days of the old west and other historical information.

INFRASTRUCTURE

The Moapa Reservation straddles I-15, which runs north-south. The reservation is also accessible from Logandale and Overton via State Route 169. Commercial and private air carrier services are available in Las Vegas, the boundary of the reservation is 30 miles to the southwest, as are passenger bus lines, trucking lines, and express package services. The Union Pacific Railroad crosses the Moapa Reservation, providing access to a railroad spur line.

Electricity. Overton Power Company serves this area.

Water Supply. The tribal sewer and water system serves reservation homes.

Telecommunications. A high-speed line has made the Internet accessible to the Indian Health Service, tribal government, and business services.

COMMUNITY FACILITIES AND SERVICES

The Moapa Reservation has a gymnasium and multipurpose building for the tribe's recreational and community service needs. The community also has a volunteer fire department, multipurpose building, daycare and senior citizen center.

Education. Tribal youth attend public schools in the Moapa Valley area. A preschool center and a Boys and Girls Club offer many educational activities.

Health Care. The Moapa Tribe provides health care under an Indian Health Service contract. Contract clinic facilities are located in Las Vegas. Hospitalization and acute care services are available at hospitals in Las Vegas, Mesquite, and at the Indian Health Service Hospital in Walker River.

ENVIRONMENTAL CONCERNS

High-level nuclear waste crossing tribal lands is of utmost importance. The Moapa Department of Environmental Protection states that tribal preparedness for a nuclear waste disaster will have an impact on the tribe's economy, community, social well-being, and spiritual values. The impact would lose revenues, close highways, increase insurance rates, and adversely impact health, among other negative costs due to contamination from this hazardous substance. The tribe understands the importance of protecting the land, water, and environment, not only for today, but for future generations.

Moapa

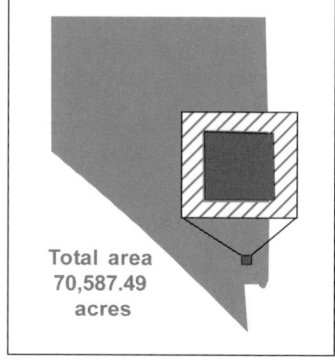

Total area
70,587.49
acres

Total area *(BIA realty, 2004)*
70,587.49 acres

Tribally owned *(BIA realty, 2004)*
70,587.49 acres

Population *2000 census*
295

Total labor force *2000 census*
96

Total labor force
(BIA labor report, 2001)
199

High school graduate or higher
2000 census
60.3%

Bachelor's degree or higher
2000 census
0.7%

Unemployment rate *2000 census*
11.5%

Per capita income *2000 census*
$12,255

Pyramid Lake

Pyramid Lake Reservation
Federal reservation
Paiute
Washoe, Lyon, and Stoney counties, Nevada

Pyramid Lake Paiute Tribe
208 Capitol Hill Dr.
Nixon, NV 89424
775-574-1000
775-574-1008 Fax
plpt.nsn.us

Total area (BIA realty, 2004)
479,741.92 acres

Total area (Tribal source, 2005)
476,689 acres

Tribally owned (BIA realty, 2004)
479,741.92 acres

Population 2000 census
1,734

Population (Tribal source, 2005)
2,137

Tribal enrollment
(Tribal source, 2005)
2,167

Total labor force 2000 census
770
Total labor force
BIA labor report, 2001)
1,197

High school graduate or higher
2000 census
73.6%

Bachelor's degree or higher
2000 census
8%

Unemployment rate 2000 census
10.5%

Unemployment rate
(BIA labor report, 2001)
39%

Per capita income 2000 census
$13,239

LOCATION AND LAND STATUS

The Pyramid Lake Reservation is located in a relatively isolated area of west-central Nevada, approximately 40 miles northeast of Reno. The communities of Nixon, Sutcliffe, and Wadsworth exist within the reservation, and Fernely is three miles south. The federal government ordered the site reserved for Indian use in 1859, and its reservation status was confirmed by Executive Order in 1874.

PHYSICAL DESCRIPTION

Reservation lands include parts of Washoe, Lyon, and Stoney counties, Nevada. Much of the land is arid high desert, largely devoid of foliage except sagebrush and scrub; however, 112,000 surface acres consist of a terminal desert lake, Pyramid Lake, the state's largest natural lake, which is 30 miles long and 11 miles at its widest point, and is fed by the Truckee River flowing out of Lake Tahoe in the Sierra Nevada Mountains. Ancient tufa rock formations, composed of calcium carbonate deposits, rim the lake's shorelines, creating stone sculptures of distinctive size and shape. Anaho Island, visible from the shore, is a bird sanctuary, harboring the largest nesting colony of white pelicans in the nation. The elevation at Nixon, Nevada, the location of tribal headquarters, is 3,880 feet above sea level.

CLIMATE

The average daily year-round high temperature is 65.1°F. The average daily year-round low temperature is 43.8°F. The area receives approximately 8.1 inches of precipitation annually; virtually all of this, 7 inches, falls as snow.

CULTURE AND HISTORY

The people inhabiting Pyramid Lake Reservation are known as Cu-Yui Ticutta, or Kuyuidokado, "eaters of cui-ui," a unique species of lakesucker fish that inhabits Pyramid Lake and is found nowhere else in the world. The tribe is a subdivision of the ancient Numa people who once roamed northern Nevada and southern Oregon. In January 1854 the explorer John Charles Fremont arrived at Pyramid Lake, where the Cu-Yui Ticutta gave him food and hospitality, but hostilities between settlers and Indians ensued. In 1859 the General Land Office ordered the establishment of the reservation, and the area was withdrawn from sale and settlement in 1861. President Grant issued an executive order confirming the Pyramid Lake Reservation in 1874. A school for children was established at the reservation as early as 1879, and a sawmill was built in late 1884. The tribe, which has never signed a treaty with the U.S. government, is incorporated and owns its reservation land. Fishing was long the major income-producing activity for the Cu-Yui Ticutta, but by the early 1940s fish were nearly extinct in Pyramid Lake, largely because of federal water projects upstream. Three fish hatcheries still exist.

GOVERNMENT

The tribe operates under an Indian Reorganization Act constitution that was approved on January 26, 1936. The Pyramid Lake Paiute Council, composed of 10 members elected biannually in December for staggered two-year terms, governs the tribe. The council, under PL-638, contracts with the BIA to administer key programs and services.

The Pyramid Lake Tribal Court operates the judicial services department, which is composed of a chief judge, two associate judges, a court administrator, a prosecutor, a defense advocate, a wellness court coordinator, a juvenile probation officer, a wellness court clerk, and an adult probation officer. This court officiates all criminal, civil, juvenile, traffic, and fishing and hunting cases.

Enrollment services maintains membership rolls by compiling and documenting all approvals, disapprovals, relinquishments, and disenrollments in as timely manner as possible and maintains the BIAs' IRMS People System database. This office issues tribal membership and identification cards. The tribal human services department manages all aspects of employment on the reservation and maintains a current list of job openings. The tribe also has a technology services department, a tax department, parks and recreation, law enforcement, and a maintenance department. (*See below, Environmental Concerns, for information regarding the tribal environment department and water resource department.*)

ECONOMY

The reservation's economy is based primarily on livestock and hay production, construction, and repair projects. Fishing and recreation enterprises relating to the use of Pyramid Lake and tribal government also support the economy.

Government as Employer. Tribal government employs approximately 158 people.

Economic Development Projects. The tribal economic development department focuses its energies on fostering business growth and developing employment opportunities on or near the reservation lands. A comprehensive economic development plan was developed in 2004. In 2004 the tribe released two requests for proposals: one for a resort to be developed near Pyramid Lake, and a second to increase commercial activity along I-80.

Agriculture and Livestock. Approximately 366,600 acres of the reservation's high desert lands are devoted to grazing livestock, an enterprise operated and managed by tribal cattlemen. Many of the cattlemen belong to the Pyramid Lake Cattleman's Cooperative Association. There are 1,093 acres planted in irrigated hay pasture and forage.

Fisheries. Pyramid Lake Fisheries, operating since 1974, now has three facilities on the reservation. The fisheries are nationally and internationally acclaimed for the Lahontan cutthroat trout and for restoring the cui-ui, an endangered fish species. Via cooperative agreement with the U.S. Fish and Wildlife Service, the fisheries supply approximately 450,000 cutthroat fingerlings annually to programs throughout the United States. Utilizing state-of-the-art environmental technologies, the fisheries successfully recycle 95 percent of all fresh water used in its operations. The fisheries employ approximately 19 people.

Mining. Sand and gravel are mined on a tribally operated lease in Wadsworth.

Services and Retail. Tribal businesses include a smoke shop, campground, and the Pyramid Lake Marina. There is also an Indian-owned combination service station and trading post.

Media and Communications. Pyramid Lake Junior/Senior High School publishes a small newsletter, *Ho Ma Ne Wan*, with an

TRI-NV-012

TRI-NV-014

TRI-NV-015

TRI-NV-013

TRI-NV-016

extensive calendar of upcoming events and various extracurricular educational opportunities.

Tourism and Recreation. Near the large population center of Reno, Pyramid Lake is rated one of the top trophy trout fisheries in the world and is therefore a major draw for sport fishermen. Other water-based recreation, such as water skiing and jet skiing, are popular, as are camping, wildlife observation, and hiking along its shores. The tribe operates a museum, multiple visitors' centers, and other facilities for tourists, including a marina in Sutcliffe, Nevada, convenience stores, gas stations, campgrounds, and an RV park. Beaches at Pelican Point and Warrior Point are noted visitor attractions. The nearby tribally operated Pyramid Lake Ranger Station manages the marina, RV park, and a dry storage facility at the lake.

The Scenic Byway Visitor Center and Tribal Museum sit along the Pyramid Lake Scenic Byway, an interconnected system of reservation roads known for its archeological and natural and scenic attractions. Numana Hatchery Visitor Center is located along Route 447, and the wetlands of the Truckee River, slightly north of West Wadsworth.

INFRASTRUCTURE
Electricity. Sierra Pacific Power Company supplies electricity.

Fuel. Natural gas and propane companies in Fernley and Reno supply heating fuel. Off-reservation companies supply gas and diesel.

Water Supply. The tribe owns its own water system.

Transportation. The reservation is located between State Highways, 33 and 34, which bound it on the east and west and connects with I-80. Commercial transportation of all types is available in Reno, approximately 40 miles distant.

Telecommunications. SBC supplies the telephone systems on the reservation.

COMMUNITY FACILITIES AND SERVICES
Various sports activities are held in a tribal gym and community hall. The community library boasts an exclusive collection of Native American sources, links to databases through the Nevada State Library system, and offers high-speed Internet access and multimedia equipment. The Numaga Senior Center, named after a Paiute leader whose name meant, "Give Food," provides various services to tribal members over 60 years of age. The center provides one daily hot meal, and offers transportation for other meals, shopping, and special activities; and collaborates with other reservation and local and community agencies to provide support for senior citizens.

Education. Two Head Start centers, two elementary schools, three middle schools, and three high schools provide public education for reservation children. The Johnson O'Malley Program supports students in all grades by providing funding for special services such as educational field trips, Paiute language coursework, and correspondence courses. The tribe operates a school-based and community language preservation and cultural program to revive and perpetuate the use of the Kooyooe Tukadu dialect and tribal traditions.

The Pyramid Lake Paiute Tribe Higher Education Office oversees a higher education grant program, which provides funding to tribal members desiring college education. There is also funding available for those seeking adult vocational training. The higher education office oversees the activities of the 21st Century Community Learning Center, an after-school and summer camp academic enrichment program for middle and high school students. The center serves as the distance-learning site for students taking web-based coursework via Truckee Meadows Community College and/or the University of Nevada at Reno. The center offers weekly computer classes that are open to the community, tutoring, Paiute language classes, and GED courses for the public.

Health Care. The newly constructed Pyramid Lake Health Clinic provides a full range of general and specialty medical services to tribal members: well-child clinics, diabetes prevention education and specialized services, immunizations, an allergy clinic, podiatry care, mental health counseling, laboratory, nutrition and weight-loss clinics, pharmacy, optometry,

TRI-NV-012 Directional sign for the Numana Hatchery Visitors Center

TRI-NV-014 Hatchery tanks at Numana Hatchery

TRI-NV-013 Mural inside Numana Hatchery Visitors Center

TRI-NV-016 View of Pyramid Rock on Pyramid Lake

TRI-NV-015 Pyramid Lake Museum and Visitors Center

Pyramid Lake

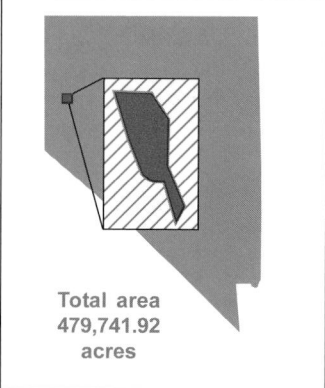

Total area
479,741.92
acres

and a comprehensive dental care clinic. A community health worker provides transportation and medical outreach. Substance abuse treatment and counseling services are offered via the clinic's Sumunumu Substance Abuse Program. The Indian Health Service operates a hospital in Schurz, Nevada, with a full range of emergency and surgical services.

ENVIRONMENTAL CONCERNS

The Pyramid Lake Paiute Tribe has its own environment department which participates in a cooperative agreement with the U.S. Department of Defense and Army Corps of Engineers to oversee federally funded mitigation programs such as the Native American Lands Environmental Mitigation Program. In 2004 this partnership was working to remove contamination on a privately owned portion of land adjacent to the reservation, known as the Pyramid Lake Ranch, the site of a torpedo and bombing practice range used during World War II. They were also investigating potential impacts of a 1988 military plane crash in Pyramid Lake, low-level flyovers by jets stationed at the naval air station in Fallon, Nevada, and potential air quality degradation caused by emissions resulting from the destruction of munitions at the Sierra Army Depot located in Herlong, California.

The environment department manages various land and cultural preservation activities, and it governs tribal land management issues such as those pertaining to grazing and noxious

weed control. Since 2003 the environment department has managed a breeding program for the northern leopard frog, a threatened frog species now found only in the reservation's portions of the wetlands along the Truckee River. The program also raises spade foot toads, western toads, and Pacific tree frogs from eggs, distributing tadpoles to various environmentally suitable habitats such as desert springs and mountain seeps throughout the reservation lands. It also works to reconstruct and preserve the oxbow lakes and ponds suitable for breeding and living habitats.

A separate department of water resources was created in 1990 to implement PL 101-618, also known as the Pyramid Lake/Truckee-Carson Water Rights Settlement Act, which implemented a multitude of provisions impacting tribal endangered species, wetlands, and wildlife. The water resources department has been negotiating a reasonable water rights settlement in order to stabilize lake levels and provide sufficient flows to maintain tribal fisheries. The settlement will eventually provide funding for an economic development fund to meet future needs on the Pyramid Lake Reservation. This department also manages irrigation waters in accordance with the 1944 Orr Ditch Decree for farmers on the reservation and is working on a draft Truckee River Operating Agreement for use with off-reservation entities in controlling water for the maintenance of Pyramid Lake and surrounding wetlands.

Reno-Sparks

Reno-Sparks Indian Colony
Federal reservation
Washoe and Paiute
Washoe County, Nevada

Reno-Sparks Indian Colony
98 Colony Road
Reno, NV 89502
775-785-1363
775-789-5652 Fax

LOCATION AND LAND STATUS

Located in the City of Reno, in western Nevada near the California border, the Reno-Sparks Indian Colony comprises 70 acres in downtown Reno, along with 1,920 acres in nearby Hungry Valley, and an additional 40 acres just south of Reno. The original Reno-Sparks Colony, consisting of 20 acres, was established on April 13, 1917, by authority of the Act of May 18, 1916. On July 23, 1926, by authority of the Act of May 10, 1926, 8.38 acres were purchased for the tribe. Again on August 23, 1986, the tribe acquired 1,949.39 acres under the Act of August 23, 1986.

CULTURE AND HISTORY

The Reno-Sparks Indian Colony is composed of three tribal groups: the Washoes, the Paiutes, and the Shoshones. Indians who were displaced throughout Nevada were assigned to a few urban colonies, including the Reno-Sparks Colony in 1917. The colony has operated for nearly a century as an urban tribe.

GOVERNMENT

The colony's government is organized under the provisions of the 1934 Indian Reorganization Act. It adopted its constitution and bylaws on January 15, 1936, and it amended them on January 8, 1971. The colony is governed by the Reno-Sparks Tribal Council, a nine-member elected body. Members serve two-year terms. Officers include a chairperson, a vice-chairperson, a secretary, and a finance officer.

The tribe also maintains a tribal court system, a police force, and a health clinic, and it provides full government services to its membership. The tribe's other governmental departments include administration, education, public works, social services, utility district, planning, prevention coalition, enrollment, human resources, economic development, and the chairman's department. The tribal court has a judge, a clerk, an appeals clerk, a bailiff, and three other administrators who provide judicial services for criminal and civil proceedings pertaining to

the tribe's jurisdiction and the enforcement of tribal ordinances. This court manages the Tribal Court Advocate Services, which provides advocates to members accused of violating tribal laws. Its appeal procedure is handled by the Inter-Tribal Appellate Court of Nevada, which consists of a three-justice panel that meets each quarter during the year. It also has a probation program to supervise juvenile offenders. The police force shares cross-jurisdiction with the State of Nevada.

ECONOMY

Since 1985 the Reno-Sparks Indian Colony has contributed to the general economy of the Reno-Sparks area and has supported its tribal economy through ownership of five smoke shops and several other retail businesses and through leasing commercial properties. The tribe holds a dominant share of the northern Nevada market in cartons sold. They are the second-largest tribal retailer in Nevada. Tax revenues from these enterprises support tribal governmental services. The tribe does not have a gaming facility. In 2004 the tribe entered into an agreement with the Nevada Tax Commission regarding a tax sharing arrangement for a Mercedes-Benz dealership located on colony lands. The colony's 1991 Intergovernmental Tax Agreement with the State Tax Commission governs sales tax collections from business located on the reservation. Nevada recognizes the colony's right to collect and keep such taxes as long as the tax rate (currently 7.375 percent) is not lower than Nevada's going tax rate. The agreement on Mercedes-Benz of Reno clarified the state's right to collect a use tax on auto leases but not a sales tax on auto purchases. This agreement does not just apply to the Mercedes dealership.

Government as Employer. The tribal government and its enterprises employ 270 people: 65 in the health clinic, 45 in the smoke shops, and 110 in the general government. The colony employs both Native and non-Native Americans.

Construction. A tribal construction crew does work for the public works department. The colony recently completed an expansion of criminal justice and court facilities, and they finished a new water distribution system in Hungry Valley in 2004.

Real Estate/Commercial Development. The tribe leases to 44 non-Indian businesses, including a Mercedes-Benz dealership. Other businesses are: Reno Toyota Mazda Used Cars, Springtime Gardens Nursery, Wright Outdoor Center, Dayton Valley Turf, Blue Corn Gallery, Featherlite Trailers, Taco Bell, Oxborrow Trucking, and Golden Eagle Press.

Services and Retail. The tribe operates five smoke shops.

Tourism and Recreation. The reservation is located, in part, in downtown Reno, a major gambling resort and site of top-name entertainment acts and other facilities. Additionally, tribal lands sit on the eastern slope of the Sierra Nevada Mountains, in close proximity to Lake Tahoe, an area extremely popular with skiers, hikers, fishermen, and mountaineers. The tribe hosts special events including the Numaga Indian Days Celebration over Labor Day Weekend and a Christmas crafts sale in early December.

INFRASTRUCTURE

I-80 crosses the reservation east-west, while I-395 runs off to the north from Reno. Commercial air, bus, truck, and train lines all serve Reno.

Electricity. Sierra Pacific Power Company provides electricity and gas.

Water Supply. Reno and the Hungry Valley Utility District provide water and sewer systems.

Transportation. A van service provides regular service throughout the community.

COMMUNITY FACILITIES AND SERVICES

The tribe maintains two community centers, a library, a child care center, and a senior center. The Reno-Sparks Indian Colony Records Center operates an archives and records management program. The senior center has an elders' advisory committee, which makes recommendations for the center's management and its programs, which consist of food service, health awareness, and social and cultural activities. The recreation department offers a wide selection of activities for all age groups. The tribe has recently received a grant from the substance abuse and mental health services administration. The tribe will use this grant to create a series of coalitions that will focus on promoting mental health and decreasing violence and substance abuse. The colony established a cultural department in 2004, and currently offers language classes in Paiute, Washoe, and Shoshone.

Public Safety. The tribal police department employs engage in community policing and employs 11 officers. Reno provides emergency and fire services, as does the Hungry Valley Volunteer Fire Department.

Education. Students primarily attend the Washoe County schools. The tribe provides a tutoring service for students as well as a higher education program, which offers assistance to those who wish to attend college or trade schools.

Health Care. The tribe provides health care at the Reno-Sparks Indian Colony Health and Human Services Clinic. In addition to medical services, it offers dental services, a public health nurse, a community health representative, mental health and substance abuse services, optometry services, a laboratory, a pharmacy, and several other specialized health programs. An $18.5 million clinic project is scheduled to begin in early 2005. The new two-story tribally operated 65,000-square-foot clinic is to be located along the Truckee River in central Reno. It will house general medical, dental, optometry, pharmacy, mental health, diabetes, and community health services. It will also serve the Native American population throughout Washoe County. If tribal members need services not offered at the clinic, they can go to the Phoenix Indian Health Service Center or one of the four area hospitals.

ENVIRONMENTAL CONCERNS

The tribe must closely oversee their business tenants' use and disposal of materials to ensure that they will not have problems with this in the future. There is also a concern about controlling the Mormon cricket population within the reservation and surrounding areas.

Reno-Sparks

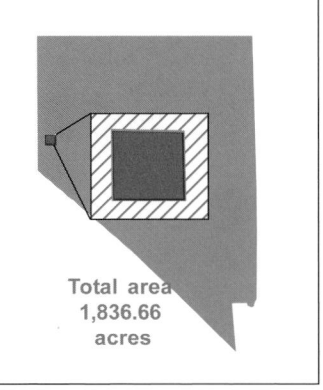

Total area
1,836.66
acres

Total area *(BIA realty, 2004)*
1,836.66 acres

Tribally owned *(BIA realty, 2004)*
1,836.66 acres

Population *(Tribal source, 2004)*
1,400

Tribal enrollment
(Tribal source, 2004)
771

Total labor force *2000 census*
382

High school graduate or higher
2000 census
73.6%

Bachelor's degree or higher
2000 census
4.3%

Unemployment rate *2000 census*
13.6%

Per capita income *2000 census*
$11,927

TRI-NV-017

TRI-NV-018

TRI-NV-017 Front view of Reno-Sparks Colony Smoke Shop in Reno, Nevada

TRI-NV-018 View of Mercedes-Benz dealership located in Reno on land owned and leased by Reno-Sparks Colony

South Fork

outh Fork

South Fork Band Colony
Federal reservation
Western Shoshone
Elko County, Nevada

South Fork Band
21 Lee, Unit B-13
Spring Creek, NV 89815
775-744-4273
775-744-4523 Fax

Total area *(BIA realty, 2004)*
13,913.34 acres

Total area *(Tribal source, 2004)*
13,050 acres

Tribally owned *(BIA realty, 2004)*
13,913.34 acres

Population *(Tribal source, 2004)*
120

Tribal enrollment
(Tribal source, 2004)
220

Tribal enrollment
(BIA labor report, 2001)
226

Total labor force *2000 census*
52

Total labor force
(BIA labor report, 2001)
191

High school graduate or higher
2000 census
63.9%

Bachelor's degree or higher
2000 census
0%

Unemployment rate *2000 census*
5.8%

Unemployment rate
(BIA labor report, 2001)
80%

Per capita income *2000 census*
$11,906

TRI-NV-021 South Fork Hay field
TRI-NV-020 South Fork Admin. Bldg.
TRI-NV-022 Cattle herd on Colony lands

LOCATION AND LAND STATUS

The South Fork Band Colony encompasses over 13,000 acres in northeastern Nevada. It is situated 28 miles south of the city of Elko. It is located just west of the Humboldt National Forest and in the foothills of the Ruby Mountains.

The reservation was established by Executive Order in 1941 under the provisions of the 1934 Indian Reorganization Act. Land purchases between 1937 and 1939, totaling 9,500 acres, were put toward the band's land base. Subsequent land purchases brought the colony to its present size.

PHYSICAL DESCRIPTION

The reservation is located in the foothills of the Ruby Mountains. It sits on rugged high desert terrain typical of northern Nevada and Utah. The south fork of the Humboldt River is located within tribal lands. Elevations range from 5,500 to 6,000 feet above sea level. Annual precipitation is approximately nine inches. The region often experiences high winds, dust storms, and blizzards over the course of a year. Temperatures vary between a high of 107°F in July to a low of 13.2°F in winter.

CULTURE AND HISTORY

The South Fork Band is one of four bands comprising the Te-Moak Tribe of Western Shoshone Indians. Other bands include the Battle Mountain Band, Elko Band, and Wells Band. The South Fork Band was one of the groups of Western Shoshones that refused to move to Duck Valley and remained living at the headwaters of the Reese River near the present Battle Mountain Colony until lands in that area were purchased for them in 1937. *(Please refer to the Te-Moak Tribe profile for further information.)*

GOVERNMENT

The South Fork Band Colony is under the overall governance of the Te-Moak Tribe of Western Shoshone Indians. The Te-Moak Tribal Council has total jurisdiction over all tribal lands, though the colonies retain sovereignty over all other affairs. The South Fork Band has its own council as well, composed of seven members. Members include a chairperson, a vice-chairperson, and five other members. All council members serve three-year terms. The corporate charter was ratified on December 12, 1938, while the band's constitution and bylaws were ratified on August 26, 1982. The South Fork Band also belongs to the Inter-Tribal Council of Nevada.

The tribe is a PL-638 tribe and contracts a number of programs to service the community. These include social services, law enforcement, Johnson O'Malley, higher education, adult vocational training, EPA, general assistance, parks and recreation, and agriculture and range programs.

The tribe does not maintain a tribal court, but judicial matters are heard in a CFR Court of the Te-Moak Bands Tribal Court system. The South Fork Police Department provides police protection. Housing services are available through the Te-Moak Housing Authority, and the South Fork Social Services Department provides social services.

ECONOMY

The tribal economy is supported primarily through federal contracts and the tribe's enterprises in the livestock industry.

Government as Employer. The tribal government employs 11 people in the following departments and programs: The EPA/ GAP program employs two individuals; solid waste employs one; finance employs one; social services employs one; clean water employs one; law enforcement employs two; latch key employs one; and pesticide employs one.

Agriculture and Livestock. The tribe manages a herd of 900. The herd is comprised of both cattle and horses. The tribe cultivates 2,800 acres of tribal lands, primarily to produce hay to sustain its herd of livestock.

Fisheries. The band is considering the development of a recreational fishing industry on the reservation. It has also directed some research into the region's fisheries for the Nevada Fish and Game Commission.

Construction. The tribe owns a military surplus grader and a backhoe which are occasionally used for maintenance projects on the reservation.

Tourism and Recreation. Local reservoirs on the south fork of the Humboldt River provide areas for fishing, swimming, and recreational boating.

INFRASTRUCTURE

Electricity. Wells Rural Electric provides electricity.

TRI-NV-021

TRI-NV-020

TRI-NV-022

Fuel. Wells Propane and Suburban Propane provide service.

Water Supply. The Te-Moak Housing Authority provides water to the housing development located on the reservation; private wells serve residencies outside the development. Reservoirs along the south fork of the Humboldt River serve as water sources for irrigation and ranches. Homes are served by individually owned septic tanks.

Transportation. The nearest air and rail service is located in Elko. UPS and other trucking companies provide direct service to the tribal community.

COMMUNITY FACILITIES AND SERVICES
A tribal community center in Lee, Nevada, was constructed in the 1970s, and it houses a small gymnasium, a seniors' kitchen, a council meeting room, and an after-school latch key program.

Public Safety. A volunteer fire department serves the reservation, and BIA Dispatch provides ambulance service.

Education. Students on the reservation attend public schools in Elko. Postsecondary programs are available at the Great Basin Community College in Elko.

Health Care. Indian Health Services provide comprehensive health care services. Tribal members may receive services at the Southern Bands Health Clinic. A community health representative also serves the reservation. Te-Moak Tribal Health Authority also provides a community health representative to serve the reservation.

ENVIRONMENTAL CONCERNS
The tribe is concerned with lead contamination of rivers within tribal lands. The American Beauty Mine located in the Ruby Mountains is the primary source of pollution. The tribe has instituted a water-monitoring program in order to assess the problem. The tribe has also closed its dumpsite. The nearest landfill is almost 30 miles away, and illegal dumping on tribal lands has increased. A solid waste transfer station has been proposed.

South Fork

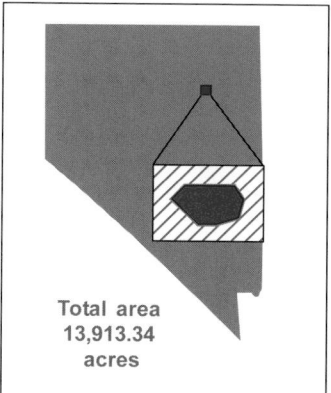

Total area
13,913.34
acres

Stewart

Stewart

Population *2000 census*	196
Per capita income *2000 census*	$12,220
Total labor force *2000 census*	98
High school graduate or higher *2000 census*	85.7%
Bachelor's degree or higher *2000 census*	3.6%
Unemployment rate *2000 census*	11.2%

LOCATION AND LAND STATUS
Stewart Indian Colony is located on a small tract of land within the town of Stewart, Nevada. An Act of Congress on May 18, 1916, established this colony. The Stewart Colony became part of the Washoe Reservation in 1980. *(Please see Washoe Tribe profile in this section for further information.)*

GOVERNMENT
The Stewart Colony is governed by the Washoe Reservation Tribal Council, and it has two representatives on the council. The Stewart Colony Indians are a colony band, and it adopted its Articles of Association under the Washoe Tribe of Nevada and California in 1990.

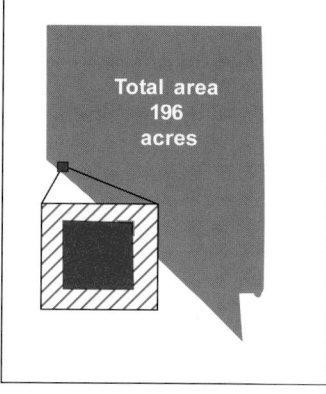

Total area
196
acres

Stewart Indian Colony
Federal reservation
Washoe
Douglas County, Nevada

Stewart Indian Colony
5300 Snyder Ave.
Carson City, NV 89701
775-265-8600
775-883-5679 Fax

COMMUNITY FACILITIES AND SERVICES
Education. The Washoe Tribe manages a Head Start center in the community.

Summit Lake

Summit Lake

Total area *(BIA realty, 2004)*	10,862.91 acres
Tribally owned *(BIA realty, 2004)*	10,097.97 acres
Individually owned *(BIA realty, 2004)*	764.94 acres
Population *2000 census*	16
Tribal enrollment *(BIA labor report, 2001)*	94
Total labor force *2000 census*	8
High school graduate or higher *2000 census*	50%
Bachelor's degree or higher *2000 census*	0%
Unemployment rate *2000 census*	0%
Per capita income *2000 census*	$25,050

LOCATION AND LAND STATUS
The Summit Lake Paiute Reservation encompasses 11,591 acres in northwestern Nevada, including 560 surface acres of Summit Lake. It is located near the city of Winnemucca at the site of the former Camp McGarry Military Reserve. The reservation was established by Executive Order on January 14, 1913. In 1959 the tribe received 9,489 acres.

CLIMATE
The area near Winnemucca, Nevada, experiences temperatures that range from the low teens in winter to as high as 95°F in summer. The average precipitation is eight inches per year.

Summit Lake Paiute
Reservation
Federal reservation
Paiute
Humboldt County, Nevada

Summit Lake Paiute Tribe
653 Anderson Street
Winnemucca, NV 89445
775-623-5151
775-623-0558 Fax

Summit Lake

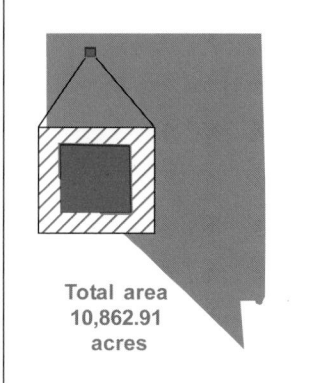

Total area
10,862.91
acres

CULTURE AND HISTORY

The Summit Lake Band is part of the Northern Paiute Tribe, a term generally applied to both a linguistic and cultural group in the western Great Basin. During the early nineteenth century, the Northern Paiute people occupied a large region that paralleled the eastern slopes of the Sierra and Cascade ranges from roughly Mono Lake in California to the John Day River in Oregon. By the mid- to late-nineteenth century, this large region was being systematically eroded by the encroachment of white settlers and the establishment of federal reservations. By the beginning of the twentieth century, less than five percent of the original ancestral lands remained in Paiute control. The government hoped to settle all of the Northern Paiute people on four large reservations it had established at Pyramid Lake, Walker River, Stillwater, and Malheur, but many of the bands refused to abandon their traditional territories. Most of these groups remained on their traditional land base, and some groups established small settlements on the outskirts of towns in the region. Many tribal members worked a variety of wage jobs for town residents and businesspeople. The Summit Lake Reservation was established for the Summit Lake Band by Executive Order in 1913. The tribe has never concluded a treaty with the federal government.

GOVERNMENT

The tribe is organized under the provisions of the 1934 Indian Reorganization Act and is governed by the Summit Lake Business Council according to the tribal constitution as approved on January 8, 1965. The council is composed of five members who are elected to three-year terms. Officers include a chairperson, a vice-chairperson, and a secretary-treasurer. The tribal departments are health, social services, and housing. The BIA provides law enforcement and fire prevention services.

ECONOMY

The lease of tribal lands generates a substantial source of income for the tribe. The tribe also maintains exclusive commercial fishing rights in Summit Lake.

Government as Employer. The tribal government employs approximately six people in its administration of seasonal grazing leases and in related maintenance of these lands.

Agriculture and Livestock. The tribe generates meaningful income from selling and leasing grazing permits to area livestock interests. The leases pertain both to grazing and to cultivating hay on tribal lands.

Fisheries. Fishing at Summit Lake is open only to tribal members. The tribe realizes significant annual revenues from its catch, which is marketed locally.

INFRASTRUCTURE

State Route 140 and an unimproved road, 8A, provide access to tribal lands.

Electricity. The regional electric utility provides electricity on an individual basis to the five residences on the reservation.

Fuel. A local distributor provides propane service.

Water Supply. A spring near the community provides water.

Transportation. The relatively near city of Winnemucca provides commercial bus and truck lines. The nearest commercial air and train service is in the Reno-Sparks area, about 180 miles to the west.

COMMUNITY FACILITIES AND SERVICES

Education. The nearest schools are located in Winnemucca.

Health Care. Health care is provided through representatives of the Indian Health Service, while more comprehensive treatment is available in Winnemucca.

ENVIRONMENTAL CONCERNS

Summit Lake, and the Lohontan cutthroat trout that live in it, are extremely important to the tribe for economic and cultural reasons. The lake is also important to the trout, which are on the threatened species list. Because of this, Summit Lake has been categorized as category II, watersheds meeting goals, including those requiring action to sustain water quality. The water quality increases or decreases depending on how dry the season is. The tribe is preparing a water quality sampling and analysis plan to guide the future protection measures.

Te-Moak

**Te-Moak Tribe of Western
Shoshone Indians
of Nevada**
525 Sunset Street
Elko, NV 89801
775-738-9251
775-738-2345 Fax

*See Also
Battle Mountain, Elko Colony,
South Fork, and Wells Colony*

CULTURE AND HISTORY

The Te-Moak Tribe of Western Shoshone Indians of Nevada consists of four separate constituent bands of the nation. The Elko, Battle Mountain, South Fork, and Wells bands represent the tribe, and each band constitutes a separate reservation, or colony. Western Shoshone Indians are the descendants of an ancient widespread people whose name is "Newe," meaning "The People." The traditional Western Shoshone territory covered southern Idaho, the central part of Nevada, portions of northwestern Utah, and the Death Valley region of southern California. This vast land of mountains, valleys, deserts, rivers, and lakes offered an abundance of wildlife and plants for the Shoshones to hunt, fish, and gather. The Newes knew their lands and cared for its natural balance; for them it was a land of plenty.

Prior to contact with white culture, the Newes divided themselves into small extended family groups who confined themselves to specific areas for hunting and gathering. Several Newe bands lived in the region, a communal area for hunting rabbit and antelope, gathering pine nuts, and other subsistence activities. An influx of fur-trapping whites soon claimed the fertile regions along the Humboldt River and its tributaries, and by 1848, with the discovery of gold in California, an estimated 300,000 immigrants carrying their belongings and trailing their livestock behind them had trampled and depleted much of the land's and river's resources that provided food for the Shoshones. Subsequent clashes between the Shoshone people and military troops, sent to the area to protect the wagon trains, resulted in much Indian loss of life. In October 1863, tribal representatives and the United States signed the Treaty of Ruby Valley, otherwise known as the "Treaty of Peace and Friendship." Although this treaty ceded no land, the treaty was much to the benefit of the United States, as it included a "permit to prospect and mine" and certain other privileges at the expense of the Indians. The federal government overtly ignored the agreements ratified by the treaty, which are still in dispute today. When, nearly a century later, the government agreed to pay $26 million in compensation, the tribe rejected the offer, insisting on a return of the land instead.

At the beginning of the twentieth century there was but a single Western Shoshone reservation, located in Duck Valley along the Nevada-Idaho border. The BIA planned to coerce all the Shoshones of the Great Basin region to move there. Ultimately, less than one-third of them agreed to this arrangement, so the government encouraged Northern Paiutes from Oregon and Nevada to join the Shoshones in Duck Valley. As for the remaining two-thirds of Western Shoshones still not living on reservation land, the government set aside thousands of acres for various colonies (in Nevada) and rancherias (in California) as alternatives to full-size reservations like Duck Valley.

GOVERNMENT

The Te-Moak Tribe of Western Shoshone Indians of Nevada is a coalition government with headquarters in Elko. The tribal government serves the four distinct Shoshone colonies in Nevada: Battle Mountain Colony, Elko Colony, South Fork Band Colony, and Wells Colony. The Te-Moak Tribal Council has total jurisdiction over all tribal lands, though the colonies retain sovereignty over all other affairs, and each band has its own separate governing council. The Te-Moak Tribe's constitution and bylaws were adopted and approved in 1938 and amended in 1982.

Walker River

LOCATION AND LAND STATUS

Walker River Reservation is located in the northeastern part of Nevada's Walker River Valley, approximately 105 miles south of Reno. In 1859 the General Land Office recommended establishing the reservation, and an Executive Order confirmed it in 1874. Reservation lands are located within the tribe's traditional wintering grounds.

PHYSICAL DESCRIPTION

The Walker River Indian Reservation contains mountains, wetlands, desert terrain, and the freshwater terminal lake, Walker Lake. This is one of only six freshwater terminal lakes (a terminal lake is a lake with no outlet) in the world. It has a huge impact on the tribe's future, and it is currently in danger of being destroyed. (See Environmental Concerns section for more information.)

CULTURE AND HISTORY

The Agai Dicutta Yaduas, or "Trout Eaters Speakers," have lived on the eastern side of the Sierra Nevada Mountain Range for thousands of years. They are a band of the Northern Paiute Nation, and they traveled extensively throughout the Pacific Northwest prior to European contact. Walker Lake was known in the Numa language as Agai Pah, or "Trout Lake." The tribes, which traditionally lived on the lakeshores, were known as the Agai Dicutta (Trout Eaters, north end) and the Pugwi Ticutta (Fish Eaters, south end).

The Northern Paiutes first encountered Euro-Americans during the early 1800s, when trappers crossed tribal lands. When gold was discovered in California in 1849, vast amounts of American settlers began to travel through Nevada, and they eventually established communities upon tribal territory. The entire region was highly desired by generations of settlers for many uses, and Indian claim to the land was much contested. An 1859 land office order established the reservation, which President Grant's 1874 Executive Order formally recognized.

In the 1880s the Carson and Colorado Railroad Company managed to buy a right-of-way through the reservation, and in 1882 the company had legislation introduced to remove the Walker River Numas to the Pyramid Lake Reservation. Strong Indian opposition backed by white legislators defeated the move. The tribe remained at Walker River, but under provisions of the Allotment Act, tribal lands were greatly reduced. A Presidential Proclamation in 1906 further reduced its area to less than 86,000 acres, took away Indian title to the lake itself, and opened the area to settlement.

In 1890, tribal member Wovoka initiated the Ghost Dance religion. The religion called for the unification of indigenous people across the nation to rally for the revitalization of indigenous languages, cultures, and spiritual beliefs, and for the restoration of tribal lands and rights. The religion drew a number of Native people, and the force of its following propelled the federal government to outlaw all Native religious practices and ceremonies. Wovoka died in 1932 and is buried on the Walker River Reservation. Although the BIA introduced numerous western religions to the reservation, a small number of tribal members continue to practice the Ghost Dance religion.

Between 1928 and 1936 Acts of Congress and an Executive Order restored the Walker River Reservation to approximately 323,000 acres. Water issues became troublesome to Indian farming efforts when Walker River spring runoff destroyed dams and summer water shortages threatened crops. Even though a dam completed at Weber in 1937 helped alleviate the problem, legal action had to be taken to assure Walker River Reservation's water rights. During the 1990s, the federal government opened the dam. When the reservoir was drained, it effectively cut off the water supply the tribe used to irrigate crops and water cattle. In 2002, the tribe began a series of appeals through the Department of the Interior to reverse the decision to drain the Weber Reservoir. The tribe is seeking storage rights for Weber Reservoir, water rights for the Walker River Basin, and water rights for lands that were returned to the reservation in 1936.

GOVERNMENT

The Walker River tribal government is organized under the provisions of the Indian Reorganization Act of 1934. In 1937 a tribal constitution was adopted. The reservation is governed by a tribal council, which meets once a month. It consists of a chairperson, a vice-chairperson, a secretary, a treasurer, and three members. The tribal government houses several departments and programs, including housing, clinic, environmental, cultural and language, human resources, tribal court, law enforcement, recreation, education, social services, taxation, tribal employment rights office, VOCA, fitness center, diabetes, safety of dams, water resources, roads, utilities, tribal enrollment, and accounting.

ECONOMY

Government as Employer. The tribal government employs a large number of tribal members, as does the Indian Health Services.

Economic Development Projects. The tribe owns a gas station and convenience store and leases a hay-growing operation. Seasonal work opportunities are tied to reservation construction projects. Taxes and hunting and fishing permits are a source of tribal income. The tribe's future projects include

Walker River Reservation
Federal reservation
Northern Paiute
Churchill, Lyon, and Mineral
counties, Nevada

Walker River Paiute Tribe
1022 Hospital Road
P.O. Box 220
Schurz, NV 89427
775-773-2306
775-773-2585 Fax
walkerriverpaiutetribe.com

Total area (BIA realty, 2004)
323,386.35 acres

Tribally owned (BIA realty, 2004)
313,690.34 acres

Federal trust (BIA realty, 2004)
964.23 acres

Individually owned
(BIA realty, 2004)
8,731.78 acres

Population 2000 census
853

Tribal enrollment
(BIA labor report, 2001)
2,219

Tribal enrollment
(Tribal source, 2003)
3,000

Total labor force 2000 census
341

Total labor force
(BIA labor report, 2001)
584

Walker River

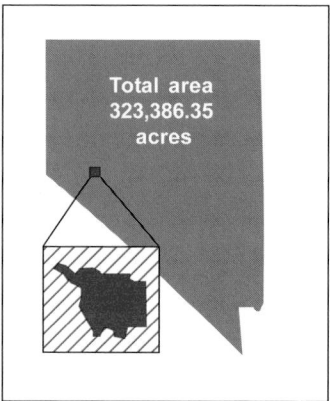

Total area
323,386.35
acres

TRI-NV-023

TRI-NV-024

TRI-NV-025

TRI-NV-026

High school graduate or higher
2000 census
67.9%

Bachelor's degree or higher
2000 census
5.1%

Unemployment rate *2000 census*
22.6%

Unemployment rate
(BIA labor report, 2001)
77%

Per capita income *2000 census*
$10,092

TRI-NV-023 Sign for Walker River Paiute Tribal Administration Building

TRI-NV-024 Agai Dicutta Elders of Walker River, Inc. Senior's Center

TRI-NV-025 Walker River Taxation Department Building

TRI-NV-026 Walker River Tribal School

developing a Wovoka Museum, establishing a Boys and Girls Club, and rebuilding Weber Reservoir.

Agriculture and Livestock. The tribal government views developing the unexploited agricultural resources on the reservation as a top priority. Currently they lease several hay producing operations. They would also like to begin making use of a tribally owned feedlot, with a capacity for 3,000 calves or horse, and the 10,000 acres of irrigable reservation farmland.

Construction. In November 2004, the tribe completed a community facility that includes a senior center and a community center. In 2005, the tribe will complete a new dental center and a Girls and Boys Club. The convenience store will be moved to the truck stop after renovations. The Safety of Dams Program will begin construction on the Weber Reservoir under the Safety of Dams Program.

Services and Retail. The tribe owns the Four Seasons Market that markets tobacco produces, Native American jewelry, groceries, gasoline, and fireworks. The tribe also owns the Black Mountain Restaurant and Truck Stop.

Tourism and Recreation. Walker Lake, a recreational destination for fishing, boating, and camping, lies on the southern end of the reservation. Weber Reservoir is a popular fishing and camping area.

The tribe hosts the Annual Pinenut Festival and All-Indian Rodeo in September. Festivities include the traditional Pinenut Blessing Ceremony, the Miss Walker River and Lil' Miss Pinenut Festival pageants, a talent show, a fun run, a car contest and parade, a fry bread contest, a cradleboard contest, a Little League tournament, a traditional hand game tournament, a horseshoe tournament, and various activities for children.

INFRASTRUCTURE
Water Supply. The tribe owns and operates its own water, sewer, and solid waste disposal facilities.

Transportation. Interstate 95 runs north-south through the reservation and connects with U.S. Alternate 95 within the center of the reservation.

Telecommunications. The tribe owns and operates its own television translators for local programming from Reno, Nevada. The tribe has installed a T-1 computer line.

COMMUNITY FACILITIES AND SERVICES
The tribe offers a senior center, a Summer Youth Employment program, a vocational training center, a daycare center, the Schurz Walker River Youth Group, an education and learning center and manages the Agai-Dicutta Language project.

Education. The tribe operates a Head Start program. Tribal youth attend elementary school at a public school located on the reservation. High school students attend public schools in the towns of Yerington or Hawthorne. The tribe is working on a distance-learning project through the University of Nevada for university and community college-level students.

Health Care. The Walker River Tribal Health Center provides medical services, including dental, mental health, optometry, diabetes, substance abuse, and emergency medical services. Contract health services are also available at the clinic.

ENVIRONMENTAL CONCERNS
The tribe maintains an environmental department to address issues of concern on the reservation. Air quality is a key concern to the tribe, and a tribal air program has been established. The program was developed with the assistance of a U.S. Clean Air Act Grant in 1999.

The tribe attaches culture significance to Walker Lake and has the oldest water rights to this area. Because of a five-year drought, irrigation water levels are down. The tribe has been forced to divert water from Weber Reservoir for crops and cattle.

Twenty-five miles up the Walker River is the Anaconda Copper Mine. This abandoned mine has caused so much damage to Walker River's groundwater and ecosystem, it is considered a Superfund Site by the U.S. EPA.

LOCATION AND LAND STATUS

The Washoe Reservation is located in both western Nevada and eastern California. It entails at least 10 geographically distinct tracts of land, which comprise a number of separate colonies near Reno, Nevada, and the Lake Tahoe area. These colonies include Carson, Dresslerville, Stewart, Washoe, Reno-Sparks, and Woodfords. The combined trust area of the colonies totals 4,320 acres. Individual allotments belonging to tribal members total over 61,000 acres.

The reservation was established in 1917 with tribal lands located in Carson and Reno. Lands donated by a rancher in Dresslerville were integrated into the reservation, and the Dresslerville parcel was expanded in 1936. In 1970 the Bureau of Land Management acquired 80 acres for the tribe and established the Woodfords Colony for tribal members who had been living on allotments in Alpine County. The Alpine County allotments, or the Wade Property, were converted to fee land and deeded to the tribe in 1976. In the 1980s, the majority of the former Stewart Indian School lands were transferred to the Washoe Tribe. Communities within this area include Stewart Ranch, Silverado, Upper and Lower Clear Creek, and Stewart. The tribe also purchased 11 acres of individual allotments in the Pine Nut Mountains in 1994.

PHYSICAL DESCRIPTION

Located in both California and Nevada, the Washoe Reservation includes rangeland and geothermal springs. Topographically, reservation lands fall on the western edge of the Great Basin, bounded on the west by the Sierra Nevada Mountains and on the east by the Pine Nut Mountains. Community elevations average in the 4,600- to 5,000-foot range.

CULTURE AND HISTORY

The Washoe Tribe's history has been centered around Lake Tahoe, Nevada, for at least 400 generations. Ancestral lands extended from the lake into the Sierra Nevada mountain range, south into the valleys that now include the cities of Reno, Carson City, and Minden, and east into the Pine Nut Mountains.

The Washoes encountered Euro-American settlers in the mid-1800s after gold was discovered in California. The tribe's homelands were directly in the path that many immigrants used to reach California, and in 1849, Virginia City, Nevada, was established in Washoe territory. The tribe's population at the time of Euro-American contact is estimated at about 1,500. By the turn of the twentieth century, the population ranged between 150 and 800. These latter figures demonstrate the effects of disease and starvation brought about through Euro-American settlement.

The tribe was never formally given a reservation or the protection of a treaty. As Euro-Americans encroached upon tribal lands, the Washoes were forced to move from communities they had resided in for hundreds of years. The tribe remained essentially landless until scattered allotments were awarded through the Dawes Act of 1887. Most of these tracts lay in the most desolate and arid sections of the Pine Nut Mountains. In 1917 the federal government purchased 156 acres for the Carson City Colony. A private rancher donated 40 acres for what would become the Colony of Dresslerville. Land was later added to the Dresslerville Colony with the purchase of Carson River bottomland, or the Washoe Ranch. Another 28 acres were acquired in Reno, and the Reno-Sparks Colony was established there. In 1970 the tribe received the deed to 80 acres in Alpine County, and in the 1980s, the communities of Stewart Ranch, Silverado, Upper and Lower Clear Creek, and Stewart were added to the reservation.

Throughout the first half of the twentieth century, many Washoe families lived in camps on the ranches of white settlers, with the women serving as cooks and laundresses and the men as laborers and cowhands. The tribal population became increasingly concentrated in the Carson City area, though a number of small groups continued living in traditional areas along the headwaters of the Truckee River, in Truckee Meadows near Reno, and in the Sierra Valley to the north. The Washoes finally received citizenship in 1924, though they continued to suffer the effects of segregation until the 1950s. In 1951 a claim was filed before the Indian Claims Commission on behalf of the Washoe Tribe of Nevada and California asking for $42.8 million in compensation for nearly 10,000 square miles of appropriated land and resources. In 1970 the claim was settled for $5 million. Most of this amount was invested in tribal development and education programs, with the remainder being distributed as per capita shares.

In 1966 the Washoe Tribe was reorganized under the provisions of the Indian Reorganization Act of 1934. Its colonies were consolidated to create the existing nation. Today the Washoes are in the process of recreating a land base from the remnants of their former territory: noncontiguous lands that they now refer to as the Washoe Reservation. A new, full-service tribal headquarters was constructed just south of Gardnerville.

GOVERNMENT

The tribe is organized under the 1934 Indian Reorganization Act. Tribal members approved their constitution and bylaws on January 24, 1936, amending them three times between then and 1990. The tribe is governed by the Washoe Tribal Council, composed of 14 members elected to four-year terms. The council is comprised of two representatives from Dresslerville, Carson, Woodfords, and Stewart; one representative from Reno-Sparks; and two representatives of the off-reservation population. Officers include a chairperson, a vice-chairperson, and a secretary-treasurer. Each colony also has an elected council that addresses community-specific issues. The tribe maintains its own police force and tribal court.

The Washoe Cultural Resource Program was established in response to the decline in the practice of the Washoe language and traditions. Among other objectives, this program has focused on identifying and documenting historical and sacred sites increasingly endangered by the pressure of real estate development. The program also sponsors classes in the Washoe language, in preparing and procuring native foods and medicinal herbs, and in other traditional crafts.

BUSINESS CORPORATION

The tribe owns the Washoe Development Corporation.

ECONOMY

The tribe is currently attempting to expand its economic base through the promotion of commercial enterprises on tribal properties geared to the region's thriving tourism and service economies. The tribe is paying special attention to enhancing tribal members' vocational opportunities and skills by employing tribal members in new projects.

Washoe Reservation
Federal reservation
Washoe
Douglas and Carson counties, Nevada
Alpine County, California

Washoe Tribe of Nevada and California
919 Highway 395 South
Gardnerville, NV 89410
775-265-8600
775-265-6240 Fax

Total area *(BIA realty, 2004)*
3,480.76 acres

Tribally owned *(BIA realty, 2004)*
3,480.76 acres

Population *2000 census*
1,300

Tribal enrollment
(BIA labor report, 2001)
1,582

Total labor force
(Tribal source, 2004)
33

High school graduate or higher
(Tribal source, 2004)
54.5%

Per capita income
(Tribal source, 2004)
$5,870

Washoe

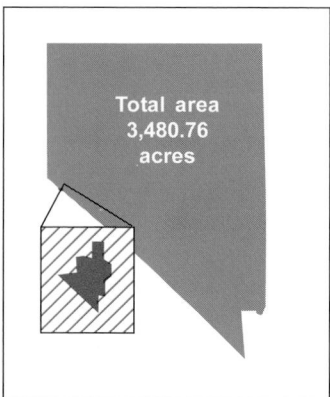

Total area
3,480.76
acres

TRI-NV-027

TRI-NV-028

TRI-NV-027 Sign for Washoe Tribal Head-quarters off HIghway 395, south Gardner-ville, Nevada

TRI-NV-028 View of reservation from tribal headquarters building

Government as Employer. In 1995 the tribal government employed approximately 85 tribal members in administrative and operations capacities. The tribe's main source of revenue comes through federal contracts, sales and excise taxes, grants, and land leases.

Economic Development Projects. The tribe encourages businesses to relocate to tribal lands. It offers technical assistance and numerous financial motives to business owners. The reservation does not levy corporate, personal severance, unitary, or franchise taxes.

Agriculture and Livestock. The tribal council is responsible for operations of the tribal cattle herd and cropland. This includes a 2,500-head capacity feedlot that feeds both tribally owned and custom cattle, averaging about 300 head in occupancy at any given time. Geothermal water sources are present on the feedlot property. Tribally affiliated lands also include over 300 acres of rangeland that support about 100 head of cattle. A tribal farm comprises about 1,200 acres of alfalfa and irrigated pasturelands, along with 40 acres leased out for garlic cultivation.

Forestry. Tribal lands contain about 160 acres of forest preserve.

Construction. The tribe runs a heavy-equipment vocational training program that awards attendees credits toward union apprenticeships.

Industrial Parks. The tribe owns two tracts of highway frontage property totaling 660 acres, which have been proposed for commercial and industrial development. It also owns a 24-acre site that it currently leases for light industrial usage.

Services and Retail. The tribe operates numerous small business enterprises including two smoke shops, an auto body repair business, a tribal trailer park, an arts and crafts store, a shopping mall in Reno, and a child care facility.

Tourism and Recreation. The tribe sponsors various powwows, including the Nevada Day Powwow on October 31 and the Annual Wa She Shu Eden festival at Lake Tahoe during the last weekend in July.

The Washoe colonies are located in regions that are extremely popular and varied in terms of tourist activities. The nearby Sierra Nevada Mountains offer hiking, mountain climbing, skiing, and camping; the colonies operate commercial camping facilities. The region supports strong recreational fishing opportunities within its abundant lakes (including Lake Tahoe), rivers, and streams.

INFRASTRUCTURE
Tribal lands are accessible by two major highways, and an international airport is within a 45-minute drive.

Water Supply. The Washoe Utility Management agency provides water to the Carson Colony, and the Carson City Sewer System provides sewer service. The Gardnerville Ranchos General Improvement District and the Washoe Utility Management Agency provide water and waste services to the Dresslerville Colony. A community well provides water for the Stewart Colony; Carson City owns and operates its wastewater system. Individual septic systems serve the Stewart Ranch community. Domestic wells and individual septic systems provide water and sewer services for the Wade Parcel. A community well associated with facilities operated by the Washoe Utility Management Association serves the Woodfords Colony.

ENVIRONMENTAL CONCERNS
The tribe has established a non-point source pollution management program to address water quality issues on the reservation. The program's goals include: adopting water quality standards, installing effective management procedures, implementing traditional stewardship practices, implementing a long-term program, providing education to the public, and coordinating services with local, state, and federal agencies and land managers.

LOCATION AND LAND STATUS

The Wells Band Colony is located in the high desert of northeastern Nevada, just one-quarter mile west of the city of Wells, in Elko County. Elko, the major population center in northeastern Nevada, lies approximately 45 miles southwest of the Wells Band Colony via I-80.

The reservation was established by an Act of Congress on October 15, 1977, by authority of PL 95-133. This public law set aside 80 acres of federal trust land for the Wells Band of Western Shoshone Indians. The band has identified Bureau of Land Management disposal lands, 80 acres north of the Wells Band Colony, 80 acres south of the colony, and another 440 acres northeast of the colony-for community expansion.

CULTURE AND HISTORY

The Wells Band Colony is one of four separate colonies that comprise the Te-Moak Tribe of Western Shoshone Indians. Members of the Wells Band of Western Shoshones, or Newes ("The People"), are descendants of several Newe bands, which once hunted and gathered food throughout the valleys, near the present-day Town of Wells. They named themselves Kuiyudika, after a desert plant used for food; within this group were at least two other smaller groups, the Doyogadzu Newenees (end-of-the-mountain people) and the Waiha-Muta Newenees (fire-burning-on ridge people). Clover Valley served as a rendezvous spot among these small Newe bands. The arrival of Euro-Americans in the middle nineteenth century brought an end to the Newe's seminomadic life-style.

Although they were not members of the Te-Moak Tribe, the Kuiyudikas were included in the Ruby Valley Treaty of 1863 between the United States and the Te-Moak Tribe of Western Shoshone Indians, which ceded most Newe land to the United States. Newe people lived and worked in Wells from its beginning as a railroad station in 1870. For many years, the Wells area Newe people languished due to an insufficient land base, low wages, and poor living conditions. During the 1970s, the Wells Band organized the Wells Community Council to address these issues. In 1976, the Te-Moak Tribe of Western Shoshone Indians recognized the community council as a committee. Congress established the Wells Band Colony on 80 acres in 1977. Since then, the Te-Moak and Wells bands have worked to improve conditions at the Wells Band Colony by supplementing the land base with acreage from the Bureau of Land Management and improving on-reservation facilities.

GOVERNMENT

A constitution and bylaws, approved in 1982, established the Te-Moak Western Shoshone Council, of which the Wells Band Colony is a member. The Wells Band Colony participates in the council, which has total jurisdiction over all tribal lands; the Wells Band Colony retains sovereignty over all other affairs. The governing body within the Wells Band Colony is the Wells Band Council, which is comprised of a chairperson, a vice-chairperson, and five members, all of whom serve three-year terms.

The Wells Band Council, organized under the constitution and bylaws of the Te-Moak Tribe of Western Shoshone Indians (which was organized under the Indian Reorganization Act of 1934), was approved on August 24, 1938, and amended in August of 1982. The tribal government departments and programs include social services, the housing improvement program, aid to tribal government, alcohol and substance abuse prevention, health care, a community health representative, and a tribal law enforcement department. The Wells Band Colony Tribal Police Department has two police officers and is charged with upholding the Articles of the Tribal Constitution and applicable portions of the U.S. Code of Federal Regulations. The police department operates with direction from the tribal chairman, the tribal council, and the BIA.

ECONOMY

The tribal economy is supported in large part by a tribally owned smoke shop and its tribal operations.

The economy of Wells Band Colony is small but is growing due to the population increase and subsequent need for additional services and employment. The tribal council sees community growth as one of its priority issues.

Government as Employer. The Wells Band Council employs approximately 12 persons, including two law enforcement officers, a community health representative, a social service worker, a environmental protection services employee, and six administrative and support staff. The USDA Forest Service provides seasonal work for tribal members as firefighters.

Economic Development Projects. Future economic development projects include developing a convenience store and gas station, organizing a police department, creating a waste disposal program, and establishing new sites for recreational and spiritual use, as well as a tribal cemetery.

Services and Retail. A discount tobacco and smoke shop and a souvenir gift shop exist within the small community. The smoke shop employs two people.

Tourism and Recreation. Recreational areas near the Wells Band Colony include Humboldt National Forest picnic and camping areas, and the scenic Hole-in-the-Mountain Peak. The tribal powwow is held annually and is a celebration filled with Native song, dance, art, and food. This event is open to the general public. The tribe is planning to have more cultural activities in the near future.

INFRASTRUCTURE

The Wells Band Colony is located near the intersection of north-south U.S. 93 and east-west I-80. Private air service is available in Wells. Wells has UPS package delivery service. Union Pacific and Southern Pacific Railways provide freight-hauling services to the Wells area.

Electricity. The city of Wells Rural Electric Services provides electrical power.

Water Supply. The city of Wells also provides water and wastewater services.

Telecommunications. Frontier.net provides Internet access to the tribe, and Charter Communications provides cable services.

COMMUNITY FACILITIES AND SERVICES

The Wells Band Colony maintains a small park and plans to build a community center for elders and tribal youth. The alcohol and substance abuse program built a sweat lodge for community use and healing.

Wells Band Colony
Federal reservation
Western Shoshone
Elko County, Nevada

Wells Band Council
P.O. Box 809
1755 Mountain View Drive
Wells, NV 89835
775-752-3045
775-752-2179 Fax

Total area *(BIA realty, 2004)*
80 acres

Tribally owned *(BIA realty, 2004)*
80 acres

Population *2000 census*
34

Tribal enrollment
(Tribal source, 2004)
203

Total labor force *2000 census*
34

Total labor force
(BIA labor report, 2001)
144

High school graduate or higher
2000 census
85%

Bachelor's degree or higher
2000 census
0%

Unemployment rate *2000 census*
5.9%

Unemployment rate
(BIA labor report, 2001)
81%

Per capita income *2000 census*
$11,025

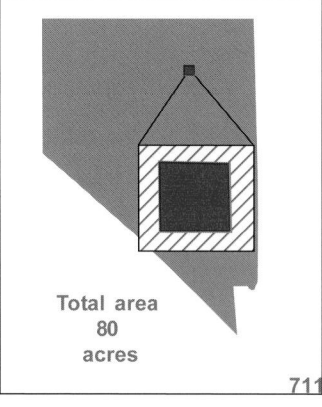

Total area
80
acres

Wells Band

TRI-NV-035

TRI-NV-035 Wells Colony Housing Unit

Education. Wells Band Colony tribal youth attend Wells Grammar School and Wells High School.

Health Care. Health care is provided for tribal members through the Indian Health Service, Southern Band Clinic in Elko. The tribe has a community health representative who provides basic health services to tribal members. One private physician serves the Town of Wells. The Elko General Hospital and Regional Clinic is 50 miles southwest of Wells. Major surgeries and emergencies are covered under Indian Health Service contract with the Washoe Medical Center in Reno; Northeastern Nevada Regional Hospital in Elko, and the University of Utah Medical Center in Salt Lake City, Utah.

Winnemucca

Winnemucca Indian Colony
Federal reservation
Paiute and Shoshone
Humboldt County, Nevada

Winnemucca Indian Colony
P.O. Box 1370
Winnemucca, NV 89446
775-623-0888
775-623-6918 Fax

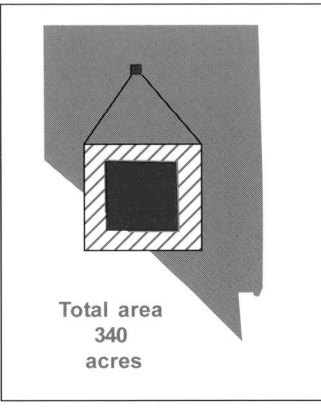

Total area
340
acres

Total area *(BIA realty, 2004)*	340 acres
Individually owned *(BIA realty, 2004)*	340 acres
Population *2000 census*	61
Tribal enrollment	77
(BIA labor report, 2001)	
Total labor force *2000 census*	33
Total labor force *(BIA labor report, 2001)*	31
High school graduate or higher	76.9%
2000 census	
Bachelor's degree or higher	0%
2000 census	
Unemployment rate *2000 census*	21.2%
Unemployment rate	23%
(BIA labor report, 2001)	
Per capita income *2000 census*	$12,268

LOCATION AND LAND STATUS

Winnemucca Indian Colony covers 340 acres in and near the Town of Winnemucca in north-central Nevada. A small tract is within the town and a larger noncontiguous one is just outside. A 60-acre reservation was established by an Executive Order on June 18, 1917. By Executive Order on February 8, 1918, another 60 acres were added. Acts on May 21, 1928, and May 29, 1928, added 20 more acres.

CULTURE AND HISTORY

The Winnemucca Indian Colony was originally established by an Executive Order on June 18, 1917, as a reservation for homeless Shoshones, descended from the Newes, a word that means "the People." The original inhabitants were members of three bands of Shoshones living near Winnemucca and Battle Mountain. A number of Paiute tribal members relocated to the Winnemucca Colony from the Fort McDermitt Reservation at the Nevada-Oregon border. Today the colony is home to more Paiutes than Shoshones.

GOVERNMENT

The Winnemucca Indian Colony is organized under provisions of the Indian Reorganization Act of 1934. The secretary of the interior approved the band's constitution on March 5, 1971. The governing body is a de facto tribal council composed of a chairperson, a vice-chairperson, a secretary, and two members. The council meets monthly; officers serve two-year terms.

The BIA provides law enforcement to the colony. The city of Winnemucca provides emergency and fire prevention services. Social services are provided through the Fort McDermitt Indian Health Clinic.

ECONOMY

Service and Retail. The tribe owns the Winnemucca Smoke Shop, which is located in Winnemucca.

INFRASTRUCTURE

Electricity. Sierra Pacific Power Company supplies electricity to the colony.

Water Supply. The city water and sewer system serve the colony.

Transportation. Taxi service is available in Winnemucca, one mile from the colony. The nearest airport is in Elko, 130 miles east; another airport and a large variety of services are available in Reno, 165 miles southwest.

COMMUNITY FACILITIES AND SERVICES

Education. Tribal youth attend public schools.

Health Care. Health care and social services for the reservation are provided by contract health services at Indian Health Service facilities at the Fort McDermitt Reservation, approximately 70 miles north.

TRI-NV-029

TRI-NV-029 Winnemucca Smoke Shop in Winnemucca, Nevada

Woodfords

Total area *(Tribal source, 2004)*	80 acres
Population *2000 census*	219
Total labor force *2000 census*	91
High school degree or higher *2000 census*	67.2%
Bachelor's degree or higher *2000 census*	9%
Unemployment rate *2000 census*	22%
Per capita income *2000 census*	$8,172

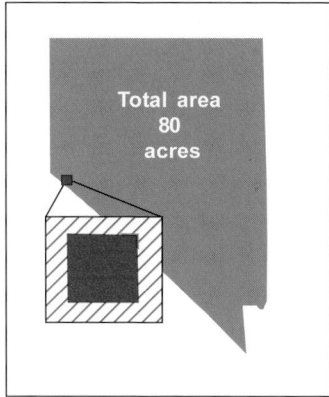

Total area
80
acres

Woodfords Community
Federal reservation
Washoe
Alpine County, Nevada

Woodfords Community Council
96 Washoe Blvd.
Markleeville, NV 96120
530-694-2170
530-887-3531 Fax

LOCATION AND LAND STATUS
Woodfords Indian Community occupies 80 acres of the Washoe Tribe of Nevada and California tribal lands. The community is situated approximately 60 miles south of South Lake Tahoe, California, near the Nevada border.

The Washoe Tribe owns 4,234 acres; 3,384 acres are located in Nevada and 400 acres are located in California. An Act of Congress on July 31, 1970, set aside 80 acres for the Woodfords Community. Woodfords Community became part of the Washoe Reservation in 1980.

CULTURE AND HISTORY
Members of the Woodfords Washoe Community belong to the Southern Band (Hung-A-Lel-Ti) of the Washoe Tribe of Nevada and California. Other communities of the tribe include the Carson Colony in Carson City, Nevada; Dresslerville Colony in Douglas, Nevada; and Stewart Colony in Carson, Nevada. *(Please see Washoe Tribe profile for further information.)*

GOVERNMENT
The Woodfords Community is governed by the Washoe Reservation Tribal Council, on which it has two representatives. The Woodfords Community Indians are a colony band whose charter is under the Washoe Tribe of Nevada and California.

COMMUNITY FACILITIES AND SERVICES
The band operates the Woodfords Indian Education Center on the reservation. It houses the Hungalelti Library, a computer lab, and a community kitchen. Services available through the center include family outreach, job coordination, financial aid, college preparation, and tutoring programs. A parent advisory committee provides direction for the center's activities.

Health Care. In 2002 the Washoe Tribe began development of a new clinic at the Dresslerville Colony. The new facility is to be a 15,000-square-foot, $2.2 million project to serve Native Americans living in the service area.

Yerington

LOCATION AND LAND STATUS
The Yerington Colony and Reservation's tribal lands consist of 22.336 acres adjacent to Yerington, Nevada, and a ranch comprised of 1,633 acres about 10 miles north of Yerington. A Congressional Act on May 18, 1916, established the Colony on 9.456 acres. An additional 12.91 acres were purchased on January 16, 1978. The ranch was created with 1,018.88 acres by authority of the Indian Reorganization Act on December 10, 1936. In 1941, 120 acres were added, and another 480 acres were purchased in 1979. Tribal lands are situated about 55 miles southeast of Carson City and about 80 miles southeast of Reno. Tribal headquarters are located eight miles north of Yerington in Lyon County.

CULTURE AND HISTORY
The people of Yerington Colony and Reservation are part of the Northern Paiute Tribe, a term generally applied to both a linguistic and a cultural group in the western Great Basin. During the early nineteenth century, the Northern Paiute people inhabited a large region, which ran roughly parallel to the eastern slopes of the Sierra and Cascade ranges from approximately Mono Lake in California to the John Day River in Oregon. By the mid- to late-nineteenth century, the encroachment of white settlers and the establishment of federal reservations were systematically eroding this large region. By the beginning of the twentieth century, less than five percent of the original ancestral lands remained in Indian hands. The government harbored designs to settle all of the Northern Paiute people on four large reservations it had established (Pyramid Lake, Walker River, Stillwater, and Malheur), but many of the bands refused to abandon their traditional territories. Given the limited size of most of these bands, it was not in the government's interest to forcibly relocate them. Most of these groups simply stayed put, with some establishing small settlements on the outskirts of towns in the region, working a variety of wage jobs for town residents and businesspeople. This was the case with the Yerington Band, though the remote location and small size of the neighboring town has meant a dearth of economic opportunity, a situation that continues to the present day.

GOVERNMENT
The tribe is organized under provisions of the 1934 Indian Reorganization Act. The tribe ratified its constitution and bylaws

Yerington Colony
and Reservation
Federal reservation
Paiute
Lyon County, Nevada

Yerington Paiute Tribe
171 Campbell Lane
Yerington, NV 89447
775-463-3301
775-463-2416 Fax

Yerington

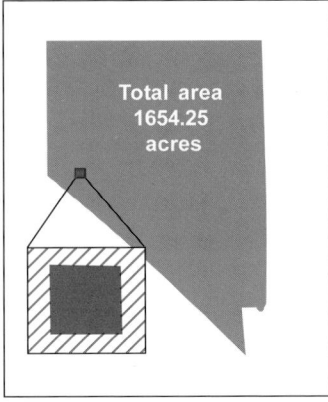

Total area
1654.25
acres

TRI-NV-030

TRI-NV-033

TRI-NV-032

TRI-NV-034

TRI-NV-030 Sign for tribal enterprises

TRI-NV-033 Arrowhead Market & Gas

TRI-NV-032 Arrowhead Market & Gas sign

TRI-NV-034 Tribal alfalfa fields & hay cutting

Total area *(BIA realty, 2004)*
1,654.25 acres

Tribally owned *(BIA realty, 2004)*
1,654.25 acres

Population *2000 census*
139

Tribal enrollment
(BIA labor report, 2003)
1,017

Total labor force *2000 census*
33

Total labor force
(BIA labor report, 2001)
302

High school graduate or higher
2000 census
70.3%

Bachelor's degree or higher
2000 census
0%

Unemployment rate *2000 census*
9.09%

Per capita income *2000 census*
$6,705

in 1937. The tribe's governing body is the Yerington Paiute Tribal Council, comprising seven members elected to three-year, non-staggered terms. Officers include a chairperson and a vice-chairperson. Tribal government departments and programs include housing, health, law enforcement, social services, and education. The tribe also maintains its own court system. Lyon County provides emergency and fire prevention services.

In 1992 the tribe became the first in Nevada to adjust its bylaws to accommodate Section 184 of the HUD program. The program guarantees loans for homebuyers and enables Native American homebuyers to secure mortgage loans from any financial institution with less difficulty than in the past. The program requires that tribal laws recognize the possibilities of bankruptcy or the inability to repay a loan. The Yerington Paiute Tribal Council-Yerington Housing Authority became the first in the state to sign a memorandum of agreement with Citizens for Affordable Homes, a non-profit housing development organization and Nevada's largest builder of self-help homes. The 2004 agreement allows for eight self-help homes to be constructed on tribal lands. If this project is a success, the tribe and Citizens for Affordable Homes will consider building another 30 homes near Campbell Ranch.

ECONOMY
The tribe has successfully developed several businesses including a small ranch and three retail operations.

Government as Employer. The tribal government employs six people.

Agriculture and Livestock. The tribe operates a 250-acre ranch, run by two full-time employees, upon which they cultivate alfalfa and winter wheat.

Construction. A new tribal clinic was under development in the mid-1990s, employing tribal members during the construction process. Currently the tribe is in the beginning stages of expanding its tribal clinic to meet the growing need for additional services that it may offer to its tribal membership.

Services and Retail. The tribe operates three small businesses: Arrowhead Market, Yerington Paiute Tribal Smoke Shop, and

Arrowhead Ranch. It also leases two properties to Rite of Passage and Subway.

Media and Communications. The tribe publishes the *Yerington Paiute Tribal Newsletter* on a monthly basis. During the 1980s the tribe produced a number of publications that tell of the tribe's history. Some of these books include a Paiute grammar book, *Let Me Tell You a Story, Nevada Tribal History and Government, Paiute Dictionary, Wovoka and the Ghost Dance*, and *Corbett Mack*.

Tourism and Recreation. With the colony and reservation's proximity to Carson City, Reno, and Lake Tahoe, there are numerous destinations for tourists within an hour or so of the tribal area. However, this rather remote reservation features little in the way of recreational facilities or attractions for visitors.

INFRASTRUCTURE
Highway 95A provides road access to the colony and reservation, intersecting with Highway 50 and I-80 to the north.

Electricity. Sierra Pacific Power Company provides electricity.

Fuel. A local distributor provides gas.

Water Supply. Yerington's water and sewage systems are connected to the colony, and the reservation has a local water system.

Transportation. The nearest commercial air and train service is in Reno, approximately 80 miles away. Commercial bus lines serve Yerington. Commercial truck lines serve Yerington and the reservation itself.

COMMUNITY FACILITIES AND SERVICES
The Yerington Paiute Social Services program provides social services for Yerington Colony, Campbell Ranch, Smith Valley, and Yerington. The tribe maintains a wellness center. Services at the center include health education workshops, summer youth programs, field trips, and a fitness center.

Health Care. Provided by the Yerington Health Clinic.

Total area *(BIA realty, 2004)*		4,718 acres
Tribally owned *(BIA realty, 2004)*		4,718 acres
Population *2000 census*		206
Tribal enrollment *(BIA labor report, 2001)*		205
Tribal enrollment *(Tribal source, 2005)*		111
Total labor force *2000 census*		45
Total labor force *(BIA labor report, 2001)*		63
High school graduate or higher *2000 census*		79.5%
Bachelor's degree or higher *2000 census*		6.8%
Unemployment rate *2000 census*		6.7%
Unemployment rate *(BIA labor report, 2001)*		41%
Per capita income *2000 census*		$11,110

LOCATION AND LAND STATUS

The Yomba Colony is in central Nevada, in the Shoshone Mountains region, near the town of Austin in the Reese River Valley, approximately 180 miles east of Carson City. The reservation was established by an Act of Congress on June 18, 1934. It is comprised of the three separate properties of Doyle Ranch, Dieringer-Worthington Ranch, and Bowler Ranch.

PHYSICAL DESCRIPTION

The reservation is bordered on the west by the Shoshone Mountains and on the east by the Toiyabe Mountains. Elevations on tribal lands range from 6,320 to 7,030 feet above sea level. The reservation features over 24 miles of streams, an acre of lake property, and 113 acres of wetlands. It also contains 371 acres of forested lands. The terrain includes river and creek bottomlands, irrigated lands, and open range.

CLIMATE

The average precipitation on the reservation is 12.9 inches annually, with an average snowfall of 69.5 inches. Temperatures range 18ºF in January to highs of 80ºF in July.

CULTURE AND HISTORY

The Yomba Colony is home to descendants of Western Shoshones who refused to move to federal reservations when treaties were written in 1863. They lived independently in the region until a reservation was established for them in 1937.

GOVERNMENT

The Yomba Colony has a tribal council whose constitution and charter were approved in 1939 under the Indian Reorganization Act. The council has a chairperson, a vice-chairperson, a secretary, a treasurer, and four members, all of whom serve three-year terms. Government departments include tribal court, housing, and social services. The tribe maintains a tribal court. The city of Gabbs and Nye County provide police, fire, and ambulance services.

ECONOMY

Agriculture and Livestock. Individual tribal members operate a limited cattle operation on Bureau of Land Management and U.S. Forest Service land near the reservation. Some natural grasses are irrigated and harvested as hay for the livestock.

Services and Retail. The tribe operates the Yomba Shoshone Convenience Store.

INFRASTRUCTURE

The Yomba Colony is located near the intersection of U.S. Highway 50 and Nevada State Highways 305 and 376. It is accessible from Austin, Nevada, via State Route 21.

Transportation. Commercial air and train facilities are available in Reno, 180 miles distant; bus and truck services are available in Austin, 35 miles from the colony.

COMMUNITY FACILITIES AND SERVICES

There is a community building on the reservation.

Education. Reservation youth attend local public schools.

Health Care. Health services are provided by a community health services representative contracted by the tribe and by Indian Health Services personnel.

Yomba Shoshone Reservation
Federal reservation
Shoshone
Lander County, Nevada

Yomba Shoshone Tribe
HC 61 Box 6275
Austin, NV 89310
775-964-2463
775-964-2443 Fax

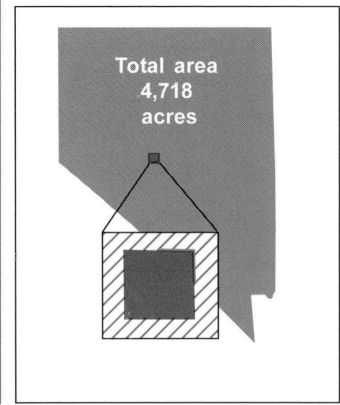

Total area
4,718
acres

New Mexico

From <u>1996</u> edition of Tiller's Guide to Indian Country

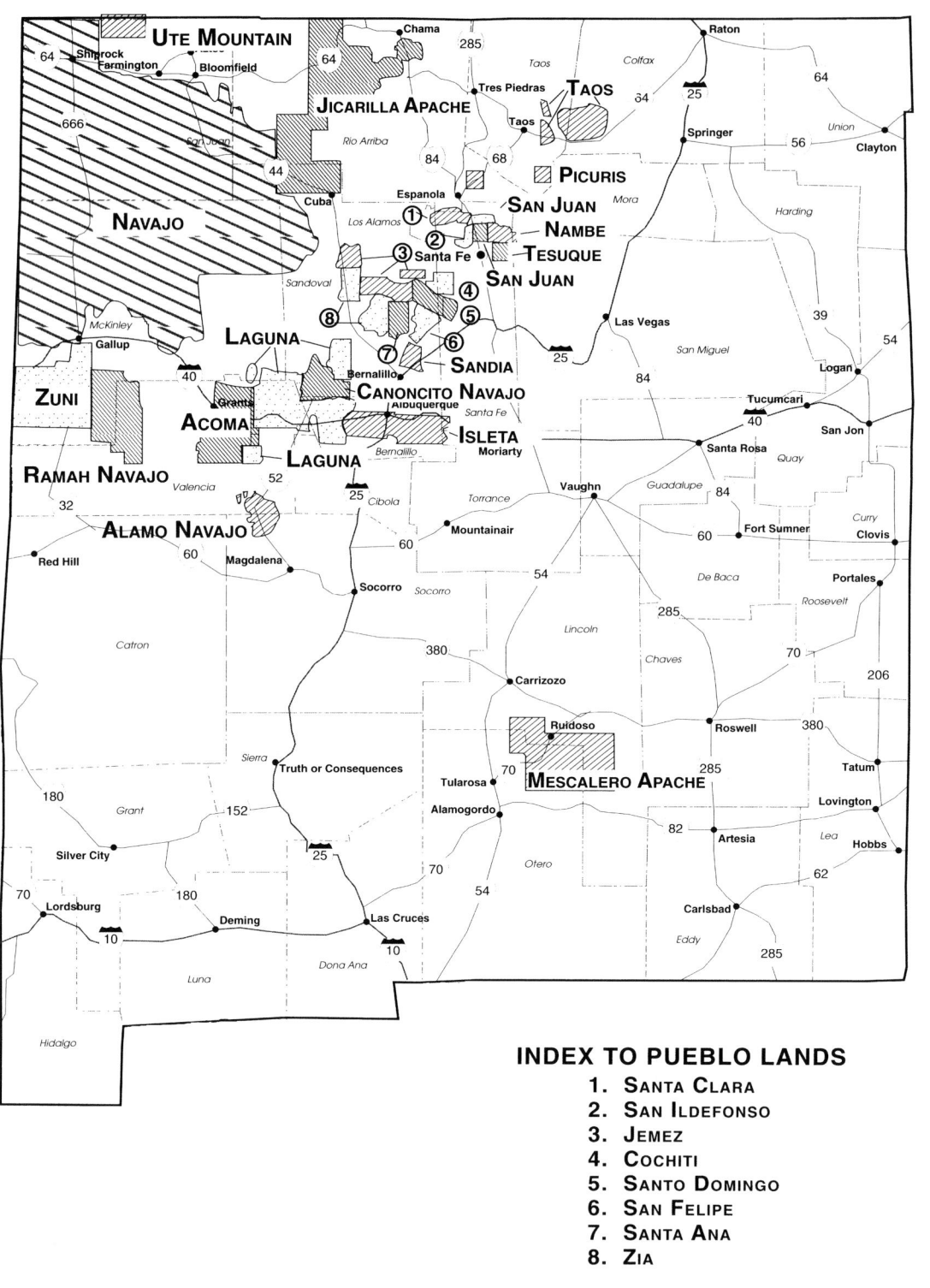

INDEX TO PUEBLO LANDS

1. **Santa Clara**
2. **San Ildefonso**
3. **Jemez**
4. **Cochiti**
5. **Santo Domingo**
6. **San Felipe**
7. **Santa Ana**
8. **Zia**

NEW MEXICO

A coma

Acoma

LOCATION AND LAND STATUS

The Pueblo of Acoma is located in the northwest corner of Cibola County, New Mexico. The pueblo is 120 miles from Santa Fe, 56 miles west of Albuquerque, and 15 miles east of Grants. Adjacent to the Pueblo of Laguna, the reservation spans approximately 448,037 acres. Most of the reservation lies south of I-40 between Grants and Albuquerque. The reservation includes the villages of Acomita, McCartys, Shutivaville, Anzac, and Old Acoma. Old Acoma, or Haaku, often referred to as "Sky City" by Americans, lies atop a 365-foot mesa above the surrounding valley of sparse, dry farmland with its mixture of piñon and juniper growth. The original pueblo consists of 250 dwellings, none of which have running water or sewer service. Fewer than 50 families continue to reside in Old Acoma. The Spanish made the original land grant to the Pueblo of Acoma on September 20, 1689. President Hayes confirmed the grant by a patent, which was issued on November 19, 1877.

CLIMATE

The area receives about 9.58 inches of precipitation each year with an average temperature range of 76ºF in summer and 35ºF in winter.

CULTURE AND HISTORY

Haaku is among the oldest inhabited sites in the United States. Fray Marcos de Niza visited Haaku in 1539 and Francisco de Coronado's army visited in 1540. The Spanish title "Kingdom of Acu" originated through these and subsequent encounters during the sixteenth century.

Early descriptions supported the Pueblo of Acoma's claims to traditional lands comprising some 1.5 million acres and numerous villages throughout the Acoma province. The vast majority of Acoma's aboriginal lands were taken from them. The Pueblo of Acoma has been on a 100-year land recovery program. It began in 1877 when the United States measured off the Acoma Grant erroneously. As a result of this, the Spanish land grant was all Acoma had in its legal possession until 1928. The Pueblo of Acoma was compensated for its land claims case against the federal government, but it resulted in the loss of much of its aboriginal land. In 1987 the tribe vigorously opposed the federal government in declaring El Malpais a national monument because that continued to confirm the taking of tribal land. Today the pueblo land base has grown by almost 400 percent. The Pueblo of Acoma has recovered almost half a million acres of what was once the Acoma province by purchasing ranches and properties bordering its present reservation.

In 1977 the tribe purchased the Berryhill Ranch, which includes 3,972 acres to the west of the reservation. The Berryhill purchase was followed by the acquisition of 84 acres of the Kowina

Foundation. This purchase in 1979 included extensive ancestral ruins and a museum complex.

In 1978 the Pueblo of Acoma purchased the large Wilson Ranch, known locally as Bar-15, southeast of the reservation. In 1982 the tribe added 292 acres to the west by purchasing a farm from Pete Baca, Jr. In 1983 the tribe bought the Los Cerritos property, which consisted of 236 acres north of the reservation. The Los Cerritos purchase included a business complex comprising a trading post, warehouse, restaurant, a 25-unit mobile home and RV park, and a Chevron service station. Former Governor Merle L. Garcia championed the purchase of this area because of its potential to become the cornerstone of the Pueblo of Acoma's economic development efforts.

The largest land purchase occurred in 1989 when tribal Governor Ray A. Histia finalized the Red Lake Ranch purchase of 114,342 acres south of the reservation. The tribe retrieved valuable religious sites through these purchases.

During the past 37 years, the Pueblo of Acoma has moved from a primarily agrarian-based economy and an economy dependent upon regional mining activities and federal dollars to one based upon tribal business entrepreneurship. Local farming has dwindled over the past 50 years due to increased pollution of the Rio San Jose waters caused by the growing town of Grants. Tribal business ranching has increased significantly. Community development activities during this period have stressed the need for providing basic community services.

GOVERNMENT

The Pueblo of Acoma is governed by a 12-member tribal council and 5 tribal administrative officers. The tribal governor, first and second lieutenant governors, tribal secretary, and tribal interpreter constitute the tribal administration. The Acoma Tribal Administration and the Acoma Tribal Council are appointed through a traditional, cultural leadership process.

In 1863 President Lincoln presented a silver-headed cane to Acoma and several other pueblo groups in New Mexico in recognition of their political and legal right to land and self-government. Traditionally, the governors of each pueblo keep their cane as a symbol of their authority during their terms of office. Although the tribe is organized under the Indian Reorganization Act of 1934, Pueblo of Acoma chose not to adopt a constitution or charter. Acoma's traditional government serves as a stabilizing force for the community.

The Pueblo of Acoma has an established tribal court system with an independent and separate trial court. The tribal council cur-

Acoma Pueblo
Federal reservation
Keresan
Cibola County, New Mexico

Pueblo of Acoma
P.O. Box 309
Acomita, NM 87034
505-552-6604
505-552-7204 Fax

Total area *(BIA realty, 2004)*
378,262.41 acres

Total area *(Tribal source, 2004)*
448,037 acres

Population *2000 census*
2,802

Tribal enrollment
(Tribal source, 2004)
4,754

Tribal enrollment *2000 census*
2,802

Total labor force *2000 census*
793

Total labor force *(BIA, 2001)*
1,394

High school graduate or higher
2000 census
73%

Bachelor's degree or higher
2000 census
8.5%

Per capita income *2000 census*
$8,794

717

Acoma

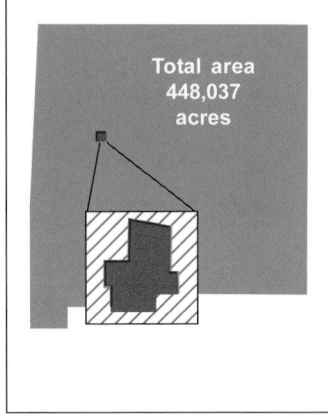

Total area
448,037
acres

rently serves as the appellate court. The Pueblo of Acoma is a member of the recently constituted Southwest Inter-Tribal Court of Appeals. The pueblo has adopted a business property tax and a gaming ordinance, which regulates business development for the Sky City Junction.

ECONOMY

Funding for tribal programs and services are supported by federal contracts and grants. Infrastructure improvements and tribal government operations are sustained by revenues generated from gaming and other business enterprises.

Government as Employer. Fifty-one percent of the tribal workforce stems from tribal government service, currently with 247 employees. Acoma Business Enterprises currently employ 703 individuals. Other employers are the BIA, the Indian Health Service, Pueblo of Laguna, Mesa Transportation, Grants Public School District, and the NM State Highway Department.

Economic Development Projects. The Pueblo of Acoma Tribal Council and Tribal Administration approved and adopted the master plan for the Sky City Junction on March 3, 2004, as the catalyst for orderly development and use of 437 acres of land zoned for commercial and economic development uses. Development efforts focus on establishing a well-balanced economic base that will provide job opportunities using the pueblo's resources to their highest advantage and will enable those people who wish to live and work on the pueblo to do so without sacrificing their earning capacity or quality of life.

Agriculture and Livestock. The reservation contains 2,000 acres of irrigable farmlands. Residential farming areas are located in the San Jose River Valley. Approximately 238 acres of the reservation are farmed. The Acoma Land and Cattle Company is a commercial cattle operation with three ranches that together cover some 230,000 acres. The Acoma Land and Cattle Company is grazing 2,000 head of cattle on the Bar-15 Ranch, the Red Lake Ranch, and the Pick Martin Ranch. Bar-15 has received several stewardship awards and is becoming famous for its Hereford cattle operation. Approximately 125 Acoma families are involved in ranching and/or farming. These tribal members are invited to join the Acoma Cattle Association and the Acoma Livestock Growers Organization in an effort to better manage reservation grazing areas and their herds.

Forestry. The reservation contains 178,396 acres of forested land of which 4,500 are used for commercial purposes. Tribal members use fuel wood for both personal consumption and sale. The pueblo operates a fuel wood business, which was started in 1992 with the assistance of the BIA. In another BIA-assisted venture, the tribe started a woodland specialty project in 1993. They subsequently purchased a chipper and have shredded and sold 450 cubic feet of piñon-juniper. In 1994 the pueblo sold 1,277,087 board feet of saw logs, wood logs, and pulpwood material for a total of $268,894. Timber species on the reservation include piñon, juniper, ponderosa pine, and Gambel oak.

Gaming. The Sky City Casino Hotel and Conference Center offers its guests 750 slots, 14 table games, and a bingo hall that seats 500. The Huwak'a Restaurant offers a variety of meals and a buffet including traditional Acoma foods. The 134-room hotel features beautiful southwestern décor with wood furniture designed and made by Acoma tribal members who are employees of the Acoma Business Enterprises.

Mining. Natural resources such as coal, oil, natural gas, uranium, rock, clay, sand, and gravel are available; however, mining these resources is limited to rock, clay, and gravel. Geothermal water resources are available and have not yet been developed. One site has shown water temperatures varying from 82°F to 134°F.

Industrial Parks. There are no industrial zoned lands on the Acoma Pueblo. The tribe is conducting the due diligence necessary to use railroad spurs from the Burlington Santa Fe Railroad for future economic opportunities.

Services and Retail. The pueblo owns the Flower Mountain Travel Center at the Sky City Junction near Exit 102, off I-40. This travel center consists of a convenience store and gasoline islands for the community and the traveling public. It also houses a nonsmoking slot machine area. Expansions for truck driver accommodations at the center have been made. This expansion included the installation of showers, a laundry room, and a lounge. The plans for developing a McDonald's franchise are presently being finalized. Construction will begin in 2005. The single largest private business sector at Acoma is pottery making. In 1990 it was estimated that there were over 120 self-employed potters. Pottery can be purchased at the Tourist Visitor's Center or directly from vendors at the nearby open market.

Tourism and Recreation. Old Acoma, or "Sky City," among the oldest continuously inhabited cities in the United States, is very popular with visitors. Tours are offered daily, except for July 10 through July 13, and on either the first or second weekend of October. Enchanted Mesa is a monolith standing a few miles east of Acoma, rising nearly 400 feet above the valley and looming large in Acoma history. Acoma legend teaches that tribal ancestors inhabited the mesa. The San Esteban del Rey Mission shares the massive sandstone mesa with the old village. The mission was completed in 1640 on the site of a previous village, and it is registered as a National Historic Landmark. The new Sky City Cultural Center, which is under construction is expected to be completed in June 2005. This two-story structure will have a lobby, gift shop, multipurpose room, theater, café, restrooms, and a museum on the ground floor; administrative offices, a research library, a conference room, and an employee break room on the top floor. The basement will be reserved for artifact storage and a repatriation area for cultural artifacts. Hotels are located 15 miles from the reservation in nearby Grants.

Acoma trophy hunts are offered through the game and fish enterprise. Participants hunt for elk, which are populous on the reservation.

There are many festivals and celebrations at Acoma Pueblo, including the Governors Feast, Santa Maria Feast, Feast of Saint Lawrence, and the annual Feast of San Estevan del Rey, which are open to the general public. There are also cultural celebrations throughout the year, which are closed to the general public. While visitors are welcome at a number of these celebrations, no camera or video use is allowed at ceremonies or dances. Visitors must check in at the visitor center upon arrival.

INFRASTRUCTURE

The pueblo is traversed by I-40. An international airport, passenger rail, Greyhound and Trailways bus service is located in Albuquerque about 60 miles to the east. Delivery service is available through UPS and FedEx.

Electricity. The Continental Divide Electric Cooperative supplies electricity.

Fuel. The Gas Company of New Mexico provides gas service.

Water Supply. The tribe maintains two standard lagoon sewage systems. Recent construction of an extended aeration wastewater treatment plant on the eastern part of the reservation improved the existing system.

Telecommunications. Tribal members have access to cable television service and three local radio stations.

COMMUNITY FACILITIES AND SERVICES

Education. Educational opportunities available on pueblo lands include the Sky City Community School operated by the BIA, and the Haaku Learning Center which is a preschool education facility owned and operated by the pueblo. Acoma students also attend Cubero Elementary School, Los Alamitos Middle School, Laguna-Acoma High School, Grants High School, Santa Fe Indian School, and private schools, all of which are off the reservation. There are many postsecondary education institutions located off the reservation that serve Acoma students. Some postsecondary education students attend the Grants branch of New Mexico State University, which offers vocational and technical training.

Health Care. The Acoma-Canoncito-Laguna Hospital provides health care to tribal members from Acoma, the Pueblo of Laguna, and the Canoncito Band of Navajos. A dialysis center is located adjacent to the Acoma-Canoncito Laguna Hospital that serves members from the three tribes.

ENVIRONMENTAL CONCERNS

The pueblo is working on long-range environmental goals, to be met by 2007, which address environmental concerns including air and water quality, climate change risk reduction, healthy terrestrial ecosystems, healthy indoor environments, safe drinking water, waste management, and restoration of contaminated sites. Six sites on the pueblo have been selected for EPA's preliminary assessment in the Superfund Program.

lamo

LOCATION AND LAND STATUS

The Alamo Navajo Chapter is situated 220 miles southeast of the Navajo Nation's capital of Window Rock, Arizona. It is 30 miles northwest of Magdalena, New Mexico, on State Road 169. The nearest city is Socorro, New Mexico, 57 miles to the southeast. Adjoining the reservation to the northwest is off-reservation trust land of the Acoma Pueblo, and to the south is part of the Cibola National Forest. Alamo is one of three satellite reservations of the Navajo Nation in New Mexico. It has also been known as the Puertocito Indian Reservation. The reservation was created by statute in 1964, at which time the chapter was known as the Alamo Band of Puertocito Navajo Indians.

In the early 1990s, the Navajo Nation Council purchased land adjacent to the Alamo Reservation, a 58,702-acre tract referred to as Slash-B/LaJara Ranch, which is not included in the land totals above. Of this land, the Navajo Nation (not the chapter) owns 29,483 acres in fee; 15,680 acres are leased from the BLM; and 13,539 acres are leased from the state of New Mexico.

PHYSICAL DESCRIPTION

The reservation ranges from the northern plains through mesa and valley terrain to the forested Gallina Mountains. The land is generally semiarid rangeland, with some rolling hills, badlands, volcanic rock formations, and mountains.

CULTURE AND HISTORY

The Alamo Chapter of the Navajo Nation descends from the nomadic Apache de Navajo. The Navajo name for the chapter is T'iistsoh sikaadi, or "big cottonwood spreading." The chapter was certified in 1957, and the reservation was created by statute in 1964. Isolation is felt to be the main drawback on the reservation. This has hurt education and socioeconomic conditions on the reservation and created barriers between the chapter and the Navajo Nation, as well as between the chapter and the American mainstream. Progress on the reservation in the last decade is credited to the Alamo Navajo School Board, a private local nonprofit organization that was instrumental in establishing a high school, a radio station, a new chapter house, and increased health services.

On the Alamo Reservation, 17.9 percent of the 1,964 people five years of age and over are monolingual in English, 82.1 percent speak Navajo, and 54.0 percent speak English less than "very well" according to the 2000 census. The Alamo dialect of Navajo is an oral language only, and most people who speak the Alamo dialect do not know how to read or write in Navajo. A 2003 survey found that about half of Navajo students attending the Magdalena public schools were classified as "limited English

proficient." *(See the Navajo Nation listing in the Arizona section for further information.)*

GOVERNMENT

The Alamo Navajo Chapter is a federally recognized subunit of the Navajo Nation. It has a council led by an elected chairman. It is administratively under the Navajo Area BIA and Albuquerque Indian Health Service area offices. It is recognized as a self-governing tribe for PL-638 contracting purposes, and it is eligible to apply for and receive direct funding of federal programs. The Alamo Circuit Court is a satellite court of the Ramah District of the Navajo Nation Tribal Courts.

ECONOMY

The reservation has no economy other than federal, state, and Navajo Nation-funded government and quasi-government operations. The Navajo Nation's Division of Economic Development is working toward establishing a mini-mart on the reservation, but as of 2004 the project was still in the planning stage. The chapter received a USDA Rural Business Enterprise Grant in 2002 for technical assistance to pay architectural and engineering design fees for the mini-mart.

Agriculture and Livestock. Two cooperative farming operations, the Blue Corn Demo Farm and the Chapter Demo Ranch, were established in the late 1980s. The former is no longer operational.

INFRASTRUCTURE

Electricity. Public Service Company of New Mexico provides electricity. The chapter also buys bulk hydroelectric power from the Western Area Power Administration of the U.S. Department of Energy.

Fuel. Public Service Company of New Mexico provides natural gas.

Water Supply. In 2003 the chapter experienced well failure in its water system that required the National Guard to haul water to the community.

Transportation. The main highways through the area are State Route 169 and Navajo Route 55. A new paved road was constructed between Alamo and Magdalena. A 45-mile road, which will connect the reservation with I-40, is being planned.

Telecommunications. Reservation residents can receive direct transmissions from three Albuquerque television stations, and

Alamo Reservation
Federal reservation
Navajo
Socorro County, New Mexico

Alamo Navajo Chapter
P.O. Box 827
Magdalena, NM 87825
505-854-2686
505-854-2685 Fax
alamo.nndes.org

Total area *(Tribal source, 2004)*
65,028 acres

Population *2000 census*
2,072

Population *(Tribal source, 2003)*
2,187

Total labor force *2000 census*
548

Total labor force
(Tribal source, 2003)
668

High school graduate or higher
2000 census
61.9%

Bachelor's degree or higher
2000 census
6.9%

Unemployment rate
(Tribal source, 2003)
64.2%

Unemployment rate *2000 census*
35.9%

Per capita income *2000 census*
$6,528

Alamo

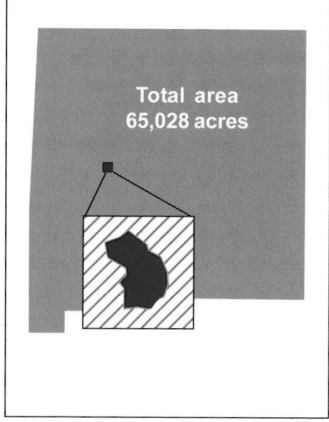

Total area
65,028 acres

they can clearly receive one FM and four AM radio stations. Alamo Navajo School Board operates a public radio station in the AM band, and it has petitioned the Federal Communications Commission for allocation of an FM transmission frequency.

COMMUNITY FACILITIES AND SERVICES

Largely through the efforts of Alamo Navajo School Board, the chapter has a senior citizens center, a community center, a child daycare center, a fitness center, a warehouse, a multipurpose building, and offices for the chapter administration. Recreational facilities include a park, a baseball field, outside basketball courts, tennis courts, a library, a general recreation building, the fairgrounds, and the rodeo arena. The Alamo Reservation has a

Navajo police substation with two officers from the Crownpoint District.

Education. Alamo Navajo School Board is a private nonprofit organization that operates the BIA-funded Alamo Navajo Community School; it had 380 students in grades K-12 in fall 2003. The school board also hosts extensive early childhood education programs; and it provides postsecondary education, with 300 students enrolled in fall 2003.

Until 1979, all school age Alamo Navajo children were sent away to boarding school as they had been for a century. Government policy was to assimilate Indians by removing the children from their families and culture for most of their growing years. With the closing of the boarding school, chapter members created a six-member school board, secured funding, and built the up-to-date community school on the reservation. For the last 20 years, they have been working on bilingual education, and they have created an effective school-to-work program beginning at the middle school level. Chapter children also attend the public schools in Magdalena. Forty-four percent (approximately 160) of Magdalena students are from the Alamo Chapter.

Health Care. The chapter has assumed full control under PL 93-638 of all operations of the Alamo Navajo Health Center, which provides basic health care. It is supported by the Albuquerque Service Unit of the Indian Health Service, which operates the 28-bed Albuquerque Indian Hospital. This hospital provides general inpatient care, with intensive care, surgery, and obstetric services contracted with the adjacent University of New Mexico Hospital and several private hospitals. Serious cases may also be referred to the Socorro Hospital in Socorro.

Cañoncito
Navajo Chapter

See To'Hajiilee

Cochiti

Pueblo of Cochiti
Federal Reservation
Pueblo of Cochiti
Sandoval and Santa Fe
counties, New Mexico

Pueblo of Cochiti
P.O. Box 70
Cochiti, NM 87072
505-465-2244
505-465-1135 Fax
pueblodecochiti.org

LOCATION AND LAND STATUS

The Pueblo de Cochiti, (Cochiti), is contained within 53,779 acres of reservation land in north central New Mexico. It is the northernmost Keresan Pueblo in New Mexico and is located approximately 13 miles northwest of I-25. It is 55 miles north of Albuquerque, New Mexico, and 35 miles southwest of Santa Fe, New Mexico. The Keresan people have resided at the Cochiti Pueblo for at least several hundred years. In 1689, the Spanish government established the original pueblo land grant. In 1864, the grant was recognized by the U.S. government.

PHYSICAL DESCRIPTION

The elevation ranges between 5,300 and 6,800 feet above sea level. There are 4,443 acres of lakes and wetlands and 41,424 acres of rangeland, portions of which contain piñon and juniper forests. The Rio Grande and Santa Fe rivers course through tribal lands and the Cochiti Dam is located north of the pueblo.

CULTURE AND HISTORY

The Cochiti are a member of the Eastern Keresan language group. Speakers of the Keresan language reside in five New Mexican pueblos. It is generally agreed that the Cochiti lived at Frijoles Canyon until a few centuries before the beginning of the Spanish colonial era in the 1590s. The band has occupied the site of the present-day pueblo for at least 700 years. The present Cochiti village lies near the center of the reservation, a tract of land situated along the Rio Grande. It is the northernmost Keresan Pueblo in New Mexico.

The pueblo site has been occupied by a band of Keresan Indians since prior to the arrival of the Spanish in the year 1540.

Because Cochiti lies west of the Rio Grande and away from the primary Spanish routes, the pueblo was not often visited by outsiders until after 1581. In 1680, the Pueblo Revolt resulted in the expulsion of the Spanish colonists from the area north of the Rio Grande. The Pueblo Indians maintained their independence, and in 1689 the Spanish Crown established the original pueblo land grant. Cochiti Pueblo enjoyed independence until 1821, when the Mexican government gained control over New Mexico and declared the people citizens of Mexico. In 1846, the United States gained control over New Mexico. The 1848 Treaty of Guadalupe Hidalgo confirmed the traditional Indian land grants. In 1864, the U.S. Congress patented the original Cochiti land grant from the Spanish Crown.

Today, the people of Cochiti continue to practice traditional cultural elements and speak the indigenous Keres language. The traditional patrilineal moiety and matrilineal clan systems remain in tact at the pueblo. The tribe is committed to the perpetuation and preservation of its traditions and has implemented programs towards this end.

GOVERNMENT

The tribe is governed under a traditional system. Each year, the tribal *cacique* appoints a war chief, lieutenant war chief, governor, lieutenant governor, major *fiscale*, and lieutenant *fiscale*. Six minor officials are appointed to represent the two tribal moieties. The war chief and lieutenant war chief are responsible for cultural and ceremonial issues of the tribe while the governor, lieutenant governor, and *fiscales* oversee the daily operations of the tribal government, including economic, political, administrative,

TRI-NM-Co-001

TRI-NM-Co-004

and legal matters. Former tribal officials serve life terms on the Cochiti Pueblo Council and are responsible for policy development and matters that require consensus decision-making. The pueblo maintains its own tribal court system.

BUSINESS CORPORATION
The tribe owns the Cochiti Community Development Corporation (CCDC). Established in 1995, the CCDC employs about 40 people. It conducts business primarily in the construction and service industries. Operations are overseen by a board of directors appointed by the Cochiti Pueblo Council.

This enterprise manages the 600-acre Cochiti Lake residential development, a golf course, marina, recreation center, commercial center, and farm enterprise on behalf of the tribe. The corporation is also co-manager of the Tent Rocks National Monument.

ECONOMY
The tribal economy is supported in large part by tribally owned enterprises in the retail, tourism, and agricultural industries. The largest source of revenue is the tribally owned Cochiti Lake, a man-made lake on tribal lands. In addition, leasing of tribal lands provides the tribe with a significant portion of its annual income.

Government as Employer. A significant number of tribal members are employed in various facets of the tribal government, including public administration, health services, environmental offices, and educational services.

Agriculture and Livestock. While pueblo residents traditionally relied primarily upon agriculture, today this activity plays a minor role in the tribal economy. Just over 880 acres of tribal land are designated for farming. Another 424 acres are utilized for grazing. In 1994, the tribe established the Farm Enterprise. This entity is responsible for the restoration of traditional farmlands. Once inundated by the Cochiti Dam, the lands were reclaimed with the assistance of the U.S. Army Corps of Engineers. The enterprise also manages 250 acres of tribal lands, upon which it grows alfalfa.

Fisheries. The tribe owns a hatchery on the Santa Fe River. Fish are transplanted from the hatchery to lakes throughout New Mexico.

Construction. There are individually owned construction firms located at the pueblo. Between 1997 and 1998, the tribe constructed 40 new homes on tribal lands. It is planning to construct additional housing and a youth center in the future.

Mining. Low-grade deposits of gold and silver on tribal lands have supported limited mining activities in the past. The reservation also holds deposits of pumice, gypsum, and clay. Approximately 20 miles east of Cochiti is the Cerrillos District, where veins of turquoise have been mined for centuries.

Services and Retail. There are a variety of businesses either operated by or affiliated with the pueblo. These include a boat rental operation on Cochiti Lake, a glass company, a laundromat, and a residential sub-leasing business. A restaurant, the Cochiti Convenience Store, and a pizzeria/deli are located near the Cochiti Lake, three miles from the village. There is also a Quintana's located in the pueblo.

The pueblo is also home to a number of artisans. Cochiti tribal members are renown for their jewelry, pottery, and drums. The world-recognized storyteller figure is an image first produced by Cochiti artist Helen Cordero. In order to protect the rights of artisans and the integrity of the traditional culture, the tribe has created an official directory of artisans within the tribe. This directory helps to assure that products sold as Cochiti items are indeed created by Cochiti tribal members.

Tourism and Recreation. The tribe hosts a number of annual festivities and ceremonies, many of which are open to the public, including San Buenaventura Feast Day (July 14) in honor of the patron saint of the pueblo. The tribe welcomes visitors to the pueblo, but expects that all guidelines and restrictions will be adhered to. Visitors may not enter ceremonial buildings, private homes, or other restricted areas. Photos, videos, and other recordings are not permitted without prior permission.

A number of the facilities associated with the Cochiti Community Development Corporation serve as first-rate tourist and recreational attractions. The Cochiti Lake Marina provides boat rentals for a variety of water sports. The lake itself has areas for camping, swimming, fishing, hiking, and picnicking. In addition, the Cochiti Recreation Center offers tennis courts, a swimming pool, bingo, volleyball, and more.

The Pueblo de Cochiti Golf Course has been ranked by *Golf Digest* as one of the country's top 25 public courses. This spectacular high desert course is carved among the cedars, piñons, and natural arroyos. A pro shop, golf lessons from PGA golf professionals or assistants, tournaments, and a snack bar are all available at the course. The course is a par 72 and plays to 6,500 yards. Recent upgrades to the facility include the addition of new tee boxes, cart paths, and renovation of all the lakes.

In partnership with the Bureau of Land Management, University of New Mexico, and Sandoval County, the tribe co-manages the Kasha-Katuwe Tent Rocks National Monument on the western edge of the pueblo. The geological formations at the monument are the result of volcanic eruptions over 6 million years ago. The site is of cultural significance to the tribe and continues to be used in traditional ceremonies.

INFRASTRUCTURE
Road access to the reservation is provided by Routes 22 and 16, both of which intersect with I-25, about 15 miles away.

Electricity. Electricity and gas is provided by the Public Service Company of New Mexico.

TRI-NM-Co-001 Marina at Cochiti Lake

TRI-NM-Co-004 Pueblo de Cochiti Golf Course

Total area *(BIA realty, 2004)*
50,681.46 acres

Total area *(Tribal source, 2005)*
53,779

Tribally owned
(Tribal source, 2005)
53,999

Total population *2000 census*
1,502

Tribal enrollment *(BIA, 2001)*
1,189

Total labor force *2000 census*
585

High school graduate or higher
2000 census
81.9%

Bachelor's degree or higher
2000 census
27.2%

Unemployment rate
2000 census
4.4%

Per capita income
2000 census
$15,363

Cochiti

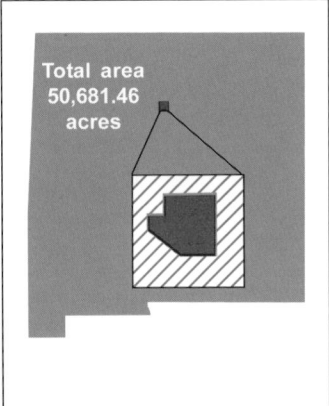

Total area
50,681.46
acres

Fuel. The Public Service Company of New Mexico provides gas service to the pueblo.

Water Supply. Cochiti has its own water and sewage systems.

Transportation. The nearest commercial airport is in Santa Fe, about 35 miles away, while Albuquerque International Sunport lies approximately 55 miles to the south. The major bus lines serve both of those cities; commercial train service is available in Lamy, about 30 miles away. Trucking companies serve the reservation directly.

Telecommunications. Radio and television are all available through Santa Fe and Albuquerque media sources.

COMMUNITY FACILITIES AND SERVICES

The Pueblo de Cochiti administration compound, which houses tribal government offices, a dental and health clinic, substance abuse program, pueblo financial services, education department. The CHR office, the post office, and a library are also located at this site. The tribe maintains a language and culture program.

Education. The pueblo operates a Head Start program and the Bernalillo Public School District administers an elementary school at the pueblo. High school students attend schools in Bernalillo, Santa Fe, and Albuquerque.

Health Care. Health services are available through a public health services clinic located at the pueblo. Medical care and hospital services are also available in Santa Fe and Albuquerque.

ENVIRONMENTAL CONCERNS

The tribe is concerned with the protection and preservation of natural resources on tribal lands and in the surrounding areas. The pueblo's location in the heart of Cochiti ancestral lands is vital to the tribal culture, spirituality, and customs. The tribe has proposed a study of the impacts of the Cochiti Dam and Cochiti Lake on tribal resources.

Isleta

Isleta Pueblo
Federal reservation
Tano-Tigua
Bernalillo and Valencia
counties, New Mexico

Pueblo of Isleta
P.O. Box 1270
Isleta Pueblo, NM 87022
505-869-3111
505-869-4236 Fax
isletapueblo.com

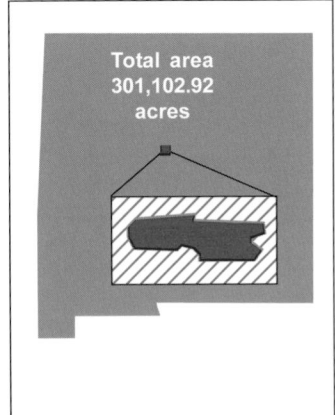

Total area
301,102.92
acres

LOCATION AND LAND STATUS

Isleta Pueblo is located approximately 15 miles south of Albuquerque. It is one of the largest pueblos in New Mexico, covering more than 329 square miles. Its terrain is diverse, extending from the forested Manzano Mountains in the east, to the mesa lands of the Rio Puerco in the west. The principal village of Isleta lies in the Rio Grande Valley. The pueblo has occupied its present site for at least 450 years. In 1855, the U.S. Congress confirmed the Spanish land grant to Isleta's inhabitants, which was reconfirmed and patented in 1864. The tribe has recently purchased several thousand acres formerly used for military testing sites.

PHYSICAL DESCRIPTION

The Isleta Pueblo is located in the diverse New Mexican terrain south of Albuquerque. Tribal lands feature the forested Manzano Mountain and mesa lands. There are over 500 acres of lakes and 545 acres of wetlands on the reservation. Elevations range from 5,100 to 7,800 feet above sea level.

CLIMATE

The average temperature on the pueblo ranges from 23°F in January to 92°F in July. The annual precipitation is 8.5 inches.

CULTURE AND HISTORY

Members of the Tue-i, or Isleta, Tribe were residing at the Isleta Pueblo in its present location when Francisco de Coronado first explored the area in the 1540s. Traditionally an agricultural society, the tribe's principal crop was corn. Irrigation systems were developed using water from the Rio Grande. Isletans speak Tiwa, a dialect of Tanoan. Spanish colonists returned in 1598, led by Juan de Oñate. Harsh Spanish rule devastated pueblo life over the next 80 years. The Mission of San Antonio, constructed in 1613 in the village of Isleta, was part of the Spanish colonists' system of forced religious conversion. In 1680, residents of numerous New Mexican pueblos participated in the Pueblo Revolt, during which the Spanish settlers were defeated and forced to vacate the area for a number of years. Though the Isletans did not actively participate in the Pueblo Revolt of 1680, the Spaniards took hundreds prisoner and the remaining population was forced to flee westward to Hopi territory. The pueblo was repopulated in the early 1700s.

During the 1800s, members of the Laguna and Acoma pueblos relocated to the Isleta community. Despite differences in language, Pueblo of Isleta shares many cultural similarities with the Acoma and Laguna pueblos due to prolonged periods of contact. The main communities within the pueblo today are Oraibe, Chicale, and Isleta.

In their matrilineal culture, Isletans belong to their mother's clan, or corn group. Pueblo of Isleta has five corn groups. In addition, tribal members belong to one of two moieties, the Shifun (Black Eye) and the Shure (Red Eye). Each moiety is responsible for executing one major ceremonial dance per year. As in many pueblo cultures, religious ceremony is an integral part of everyday life among Isleta's people.

GOVERNMENT

The tribe adopted a constitution in 1947, which was replaced in 1970 by a new constitution. The tribe is governed by a tribal council of six members and led by a governor and lieutenant governor. Government departments include administration, education, environment, and health. The tribe maintains a police department. Law enforcement officers exercise jurisdiction over the people and property of Isleta Pueblo.

ECONOMY

The tribal economy is supported in large part by its governmental operations, agriculture, its tourism industry, and its gaming enterprises.

Government as Employer. The tribe provides numerous employment opportunities throughout government programs and tribally owned enterprises. Significant among these is the Community Health Representative Program, which employs and trains pueblo residents to work in a variety of health care occupations.

Agriculture and Livestock. Roughly 4,500 acres of land are under cultivation. Fewer than 10 percent of the people employed on the reservation have jobs in commercial farming and ranching. Woodlands are used for grazing, hunting, and harvesting piñon nuts. The Isleta Pueblo Farming Enterprise assists Isleta farmers with agricultural equipment, laser land leveling, and irrigation systems maintenance and improvement.

TRI-NM-Is-001 View of Isleta Lakes

TRI-NM-Is-002 Old church in the village

Forestry. Over 750 acres of commercial timber stand in the Manzano Mountains are periodically thinned for the sale of timber and firewood. The timber harvesting enterprise began in 1987.

Gaming. The tribe owns and operates the 100,000-square-foot Isleta Casino Resort in Albuquerque. It offers 1,700 slots/VLTs, 30 table games, 6 poker tables, 1,200 bingo seats, 5 restaurants, and 3 entertainment venues. It has 900 parking spaces. The casino employs 1,000 individuals. The tribe also owns Palace West at the intersection of Coors Boulevard and Isleta Road south of Albuquerque.

Fisheries. The Isleta Lakes, stocked with trout and channel catfish, provide good recreational fishing.

Services and Retail. The tribe recently opened the Isleta Convenience Store. Tribal retail businesses include a small supermarket, a gas station, and a gift shop that sells locally produced arts and crafts. Many artisans within the community have their own shops.

Tourism and Recreation. New Mexico attracts numerous visitors year round. Tourists come to enjoy the outdoor recreational opportunities, rich cultural environment, and entertainment venues available throughout the region. Easy access to the pueblo makes it appealing to tourists interested in enjoying the gaming, golfing, outdoor recreation, and cultural celebrations that the tribe hosts.

Isleta Pueblo began to develop its tourism industry in the late 1970s by establishing a fishing park and recreation area. Facilities include Bass, Turtle, and Sunrise lakes, a picnic area, a playground, and a campground. The lakes are stocked with trout and catfish.

The tribe's casino attracts many visitors, averaging a daily attendance of 2,000 people. The tribe also owns Isleta Eagle Golf Course. It is a championship 27-hole course with three lakes. Facilities include the Eagle's Nest Restaurant and the Isleta Eagle Golf Shop. The golf course is situated just south of Albuquerque.

The Village of Isleta is of architectural interest. Visitors are welcome to visit the Isleta mission church, constructed in the early 1600s, which presides over the pueblo's historic plaza. A small museum is located adjacent to the church. The tribe also hosts a number of ceremonial dances that are open to the public.

INFRASTRUCTURE
Electricity. The Public Service Company of New Mexico provides electricity.

Water Supply. Seven wells that draw upon aquifers in Los Charcos, Chical, Los Padillas, and Lobumtee provide domestic water. Individual septic tanks provide sewer service.

Transportation. Isleta Pueblo is located 13 miles south of Albuquerque on I-25. Airport service is available at Albuquerque International Sunport. A freight railway runs north-south through the reservation along the Rio Grande corridor. Bus and passenger service is available in Albuquerque, and trucks serve the reservation directly.

Telecommunications. In 1999, the Solecteck Corporation and Excel Communications Corporation constructed two 100-foot towers that linked up the pueblo with a data communications network. This system integrated voice, data, and wireless and video communications for the pueblos' business offices. Services are linked with the police, emergency medical services, the recreation center, the hospital, the casino, the golf course, and the convenience store. The system was upgraded in 2002 to a more efficient and powerful network.

COMMUNITY FACILTIES AND SERVICES
A multipurpose complex (housing a recreation center, a health center, and an education center) was under development in 1995. The recreation center was to feature a swimming pool, a gymnasium, and weight training and aerobics facilities. In 2004 the tribe opened a new facility to house its Head Start, child care, and family counseling programs. The building's architectural and interior design reflect Isleta cultural elements.

The tribe maintains the Isleta Library and Resource Center. It offers 12 computers and Internet access. Computers and video equipment were purchased with the assistance of the Gates Library Foundation. The Isleta Library is a public library and part of the New Mexico State Library System.

The tribe sponsors the Isleta Parent Pride cultural program. Services include support groups, traditional parenting, Native language, home management skills, traditional crafts, and counseling workshops. Tribal elders provide assistance in developing and instructing classes.

Education. The tribe's Head Start program serves children between the ages of three and five. The child care program serves children between the ages of 6 months and 3 years. Isleta Pueblo has one elementary school. Older students attend schools in Albuquerque and Los Lunas. The tribe contracts the Johnson O'Malley program for tribal student services in the Albuquerque and Los Lunas school districts.

The Isleta Department of Education offers adult basic education and vocational and career counseling. There is a computer laboratory located in the education building. Numerous postsecondary institutions and programs are available in the nearby City of Albuquerque; the tribe offers financial assistance for tribal members pursuing a postsecondary education.

Total area *(BIA realty, 2004)*
301,102.92 acres

Population *2000 census*
3,166

Tribal enrollment
(BIA labor report, 2001)
4,441

Total labor force
2000 census
1,316

Total labor force
(BIA labor report, 2001)
2,595

High school graduate or higher
2000 census
72.9%

Bachelor's degree or higher
2000 census
6.1%

Unemployment rate
2000 census
9.6%

Unemployment rate
(BIA labor report, 2001)
12%

Per capita income
2000 census
$11,438

Isleta

Health Care. A small pueblo-owned health clinic provides both basic and emergency care. The pueblo also runs its own ambulance service. The tribally operated Community Health Representative Program provides a variety of health services to members, including nutrition, counseling, and maternity and child care. Additionally, the pueblo operates the Cottonwood de Isleta Rehabilitation Center, a 65-bed inpatient facility on a 26-acre site. There are a number of community service projects being planned in the pueblo.

ENVIRONMENTAL CONCERNS

The All-Indian Pueblo Council conducted an environmental needs assessment on the tribe's behalf to submit to the U.S. EPA. The findings indicated that the tribe's priorities are water quality, air pollution, and hazardous waste use and disposal. Noise pollution is also an issue for the tribe as it is in the fly zone of nearby military bases.

The U.S. Fish and Wildlife Service awarded the tribe a $150,000 grant in 2004. The tribe will use the grant to design and build a habitat to raise the endangered Rio Grande silvery minnow.

Jemez

Pueblo of Jemez
Federal reservation
Tano-Jemez
Sandoval County, New Mexico

P.O. Box 100
Jemez Pueblo, NM 87024
505-834-7359
505-834-7331 Fax
jemezpueblo.org

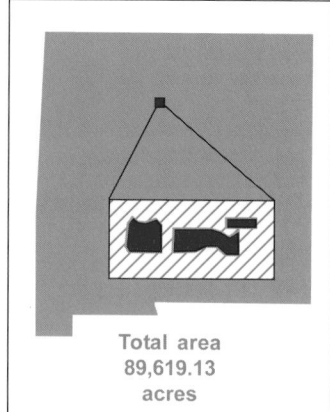

Total area
89,619.13
acres

LOCATION AND LAND STATUS

The Jemez Reservation is located in north-central New Mexico, within the southern end of the Canon de San Diego, about 50 miles northwest of Albuquerque and 75 miles southwest of Santa Fe. The reservation covers just under 90,000 acres. Most tribal members reside in the village known as Walatowa *(a Towa word meaning "this is THE place")*.

The original Spanish land grant to the pueblo was made on September 20, 1689. The U.S. Congress confirmed the grant on December 22, 1858. President Lincoln issued a patent to cover the grant on November 1, 1864. Ancestors of the Jemez migrated to the pueblo's present location from the four-corners area during the late fourteenth century.

CULTURE AND HISTORY

The Pueblo of Jemez is the only remaining village of the Towa-speaking pueblos in New Mexico. Oral history holds that ancestors of the present-day Jemez people originated in a place called "Hua-na-tota." The tribe migrated to the Canon de San Diego region in the fourteenth century and became one of the largest and most powerful of the pueblo cultures by the time of European contact in 1541. They traditionally relied on hunting, gathering, and farming for their subsistence. The pueblo's first contact with Europeans came with the Coronado Expedition. Following the Coronado Expedition, the tribe was left in peace for 40 years until the next wave of Spanish explorers arrived. During the next 80 years, the Jemez people carried out numerous revolts and uprisings in response to Spanish attempts to forcibly Christianize them. These activities culminated in the Pueblo Revolt of 1680, during which the Spanish were expelled from the New Mexico Province by the collaborative efforts of all the Pueblo Nations. By 1688, the Spanish had begun their reconquest and by 1696 finally succeeded in subduing the Jemez Nation and concentrating the tribe into the Village of Walatowa, where they reside today. In 1838, the Towa-speaking people from the Pueblo of Pecos (located just east of Santa Fe) requested to be taken in by Jemez and to resettle at the Jemez Pueblo in order to escape harassment by the Spanish and Comanches. In 1936, the two tribes were merged by an Act of Congress.

Traditional culture remains vital at Jemez, with many dances and ceremonies held throughout the year, most of which remain closed to the public. Today, farming still serves as an important source of tribal income, with corn and chili crops being particularly well-respected. In addition, many tribal members now also work in the region's timber industry and in the reservation's thriving and internationally renowned arts and crafts cottage industry. Other members find employment off the reservation at the Los Alamos National Laboratory, and in Albuquerque and Santa Fe.

GOVERNMENT

The Pueblo of Jemez is a sovereign nation with an independent government and tribal court system. The secular tribal government includes the tribal council, the Jemez Governor, two lieutenant governors, two *fiscales*, and a sheriff. The tribal council is composed of 14 members, with the presence of 8 required for a quorum. Council members are former governors and serve life terms. Officers are appointed to one-year terms by the *cacique*, the highest religious leader. New officers are sworn in on January 1. Traditional matters are still handled through a separate governing body. The traditional government includes the spiritual and society leaders, a war captain, and a lieutenant war captain. There is also a tribal administrator as well as professional staff who ensure continuity from one administration to the next.

BUSINESS CORPORATION

The Jemez Community Development Corporation (JCDC) was established in 2003 to oversee all of the tribe's economic and business development activities, to create employment opportunities for its membership, and increase tribal revenues without compromising the Jemez way of life. JCDC is governed by a board of directors. It works in close conjunction with the tribal council, the office of the governor, and the economic development department.

ECONOMY

The pueblo has a strong and diverse economy. Tribal government, agriculture, forestry, and tourism, are only a handful of the various contributors to the tribe's economic success. The tribe's thriving economy and plans for future economic endeavors ensure a bright economic outlook for the Jemez Pueblo.

Government as Employer. A large number of tribal members are employed by the tribal government's various departments, including law enforcement and the tribal court system, health, education administration, and other operations. The BIA and the U.S. Forest Service also provide employment to a number of tribal members.

Agriculture and Livestock. Agriculture and livestock represent a major source of livelihood on the reservation. The Jemez people are particularly known for their corn and chili crops.

Forestry. Timber resources on the reservation are valuable, both for saw timber and fuel wood. Tribal timber sales since 1957 have totaled nearly six million board feet of ponderosa pine and Douglas fir. The reservation is home to many high-risk, over-mature trees which the tribe would like to market. The tribe is also instituting a fuel wood permit system for sales of logging slash and piñon-juniper to the general public.

Jemez

TRI-NM-Jz-016

TRI-NM-Jz-009

TRI-NM-Jz-003

TRI-NM-Jz-005

TRI-NM-Jz-016 Scenic view on Highway 25

TRI-NM-Jz-009 Outside Indian Oven

TRI-NM-Jz-003 Side view of Walatowa Visitor Center and Malatoma Gift Shop

TRI-NM-Jz-005 Wall mural at the Walatowa Visitor Center

TRI-NM-Jz-013 Wood cutting equipment

TRI-NM-Jz-010 Sign for Walatowa Woodlands Initiative/Lumber Yard

TRI-NM-Jz-013

TRI-NM-Jz-010

Total area (BIA realty, 2004)
89,619.13 acres

Population *2000 census*
1,958

Tribal enrollment (BIA, 2001)
3,486

Total labor force *2000 census*
685

Total labor force (BIA, 2001)
1,966

High school graduate or higher
2000 census
71.7%

Bachelor's degree or higher
2000 census
7.6%

Unemployment rate
2000 census
20.6%

Unemployment rate (BIA, 2001)
27%

Per capita income *2000 census*
$8,045

The pueblo founded the Walatowa Woodlands Initiative in 1999. This tribally-owned enterprise works in partnership with the U.S. Forest Service, the Bureau of Land Management, and the BIA to restore the tribal forest through professional and ecologically sound forest management practices such as thinning for timber stand improvement and fire prevention. The enterprise engages in logging and their mill produces milled lumber of various sizes, custom beams and boards, ponderosa pine *vigas*, and peeled poles for *latillas* and fence poles. It also bids on forest thinning and restoration projects. The enterprise employs about 14 people.

Services and Retail. The Puebloan Gift Shop features Native arts and crafts and provides a major source of employment and income for the tribe. The Jemez are internationally known for their traditional polychrome pottery, woven cloths, stone sculptures, moccasins, jewelry, and basketry. The pueblo also operates a convenience store/gas station at the village.

Tourism and Recreation. The Walatowa Visitors Center features the Pueblo's Museum of History, a one-of-a-kind museum, a replica of a traditional field house landscaped by Native plants, and a gift shop. The center offers the Walatowa Cultural Ed-Ventures, which is a guided tour for visitors interested in the

prehistory and culture of the Jemez people. It also offers bread baking demonstrations, traditional feasts, artisan demonstrations, and traditional dances. The pueblo celebrates a number of feast days and ceremonies throughout the year. Visitors are welcome at some of these events.

The Towa Arts and Crafts Committee in coordination with the Walatowa Visitors Center sponsors the annual Jemez Red Rock Arts and Crafts Show where tourists can purchase traditional foods and native arts and crafts from tribal members at roadside stands, located across from the Walatowa Center during the summer months.

The Jemez State Monument, located in Jemez Springs, is home to the 700 year old ruins of the ancestral Jemez Village of "Guisewa,"-place of the boiling waters. Along with the ruins, people can see a seventeenth century Spanish Mission, and a small museum display. The Walatowa Visitor's Center promotes the area's attractions by cooperating with the U.S. Forest Service for the Jemez District to distribute literature on the Santa Fe National Forest, the Jemez Mountain Trail which was designated as a National Scenic and Historic Byway in 1998, the Jemez Mountain National Recreation area, and the Valles Caldera National Preserve. The Jemez Mountains offer an abun-

Jemez

dance of activities for the outdoor enthusiast. Hiking, mountain climbing, and winter cross-country skiing are quite popular. Numerous hot springs can also be found throughout the region, excellent for soaking, with camping nearby.

INFRASTRUCTURE

State Highway 550 connects the reservation to I-25 and Albuquerque to the southeast and to Farmington to the northwest. Highway 4 runs up the Jemez Canyon and then east to Los Alamos. Commercial bus service is available in San Ysidro, 5 miles from the pueblo. Commercial train lines serve Bernalillo, 35 miles away. Truck lines serve the reservation directly.

Electricity. Electricity is provided by the Jemez Mountain Cooperative.

Water Supply. Water and sewer systems are provided by the Pueblo of Jemez Public Works Department.

COMMUNITY FACILITIES AND SERVICES

Jemez Pueblo offers an array of facilities and services to its members through its tribal governmental departments. The pueblo's department of education oversees the library, the higher education center, the creative learning center, and the Walatowa Child Care Center. The Jemez Pueblo Community Library has over 16,000 books, 1,1000 videos, and a special children's section. The higher education center and the creative learning center serve as support centers for a multitude of services in the educational arena. All three programs offer advanced technology access and maintain expanded technological capabilities that includes an access grid.

The Walatowa Child Care Center has an infant room, a toddler room, and offers an after school program. It provides developmentally appropriate child care services for working parents who are either in school or in the workforce. The child care center is planning to expand its services in 2005. Plans are also underway to construct a community resource center that will bring the senior citizens' and the early childhood programs together, via a facility that will cater to all community members with programming focused on intergenerational teaching and learning. The pueblo provides a growing number of services at its senior center including rehabilitative physical therapy, massage therapy, and an exercise and nutrition program

The senior citizens program has a responsibility to serve the pueblo's aging population, with programs such as the home de-

livery of nutritious meals; supportive social outreach activities, recreation, health promotion, education, and transportation. The senior program recently opened a new center with state appropriation funds supplemented with federal and other funding sources.

Through the Health and Human Services Department, a community wellness center and youth center offer an array of health education and physical fitness programs. The community wellness center, with its state-of-the-art exercise equipment, offers weight training and health education. The Walatowa Youth Center has after school program, an intramural sports program that collaborates with the community schools in offering physical education and in sponsoring sporting events and summer recreational activities.

Education. All students from the Pueblo of Jemez attend a variety of schools, ranging from public to privately chartered schools. The on-reservation schools are the Walatowa Head Start, Jemez Day School (K-6), San Diego Riverside Charter School (K-8) and the Walatowa High Charter School (9-12). San Diego Riverside and Walatowa High are the only two tribal schools in the state that have been chartered under the New Mexico Charter School Act, making Jemez the only New Mexico tribe to establish its own charter schools. Jemez strives to develop and implement culturally appropriate curriculums in all its schools. Pueblo students have the option to attend the off-reservation schools in the Jemez Valley School district, the Santa Fe Indian School, or the Sandoval and Bernalillo County schools.

Health Care. The Jemez Comprehensive Health Clinic provides primary care, family medicine, dental, optometry, podiatry, audiology, and clinical social work. It has pharmacy and a laboratory. Its community-oriented primary care program offers diabetes prevention and treatment, at the clinic, in the schools, and in the community. The clinic also provides outpatient, behavioral health, social and family services and long-term care through its accredited mental health and substance abuse facilities. The pueblo has an emergency medical service. In 2005 it will add one more ambulance and will have a staff fully trained and certified in advance life support. The health department complements the school's nursing program with the annual fitness testing and nutrition education. This department employs 90 full-time employees and approximately 5 full-time contract professionals. Contract health care is also available by local referral at IHS in Santa Fe and Albuquerque, and the private sector. The Pueblo is working toward accreditation for ambulatory health care in the spring of 2006.

TRI-NM-Jz-018

TRI-NM-Jz-015

TRI-NM-Jz-018 - Heavy equipment at the future airport site

TRI-NM-Jz-015 – Metal Building at the new airport site

LOCATION AND LAND STATUS

The Jicarilla Apache Reservation spans 879,917 acres of scenic terrain in north-central New Mexico, on the eastern edge of the San Juan Basin. Approximately in the center of New Mexico's east and west boundaries, the reservation's northern boundary borders the Colorado line. The town of Dulce is the tribal center of government, education, and commerce.

The northern portion of the Jicarilla Apache Reservation, consisting of approximately 416,000 acres, was created by an Executive Order on February 11, 1887, and enlarged by almost 300,000 acres by Executive Orders of November 11, 1907 and January 28, 1908. Since the 1970s, the tribe has purchased three ranches, Theis, El Poso, and Willow Creek-consisting of 95,207 acres with direct access to significant water resources, including the Rio Chama, Willow Creek, and the Heron and El Vado reservoirs. In 1992, the Nation secured 40,000 acre feet of surface water per annum through the first congressional approved Indian water rights settlement in the State of New Mexico. The ranches are used primarily for grazing, hay production, and hunting. In 1995 the tribe purchased the 25,000-acre Chama Land and Cattle Company where the Running Elk Ranch is located. The tribe has also acquired the Mundo property, formerly the Gomez Ranch. Development on the parcel will include tribal housing.

PHYSICAL DESCRIPTION

The reservation's geography varies from high desert at the south boundary, at about 6,500 feet in elevation, to mountainous areas of over 11,400 feet in elevation in the north. Tribal lands are abundant with natural resources, including forests, woodlands, lakes, streams, rivers, and agricultural and range lands. Navajo River, Willow Creek, Rio Chama, Dulce Lake, Mundo Lake, Horse Lake, La Jara Lake, and Stone Lake are all within reservation boundaries. Ponderosa pine is the most represented tree species on the reservation. A rich diversity of wildlife also resides on the reservation, including many species of furbearers, small game, and birds. A number of endangered or threatened species also occupy tribal lands, including the peregrine falcon, Mexican spotted owl, and bald eagle.

CLIMATE

The average temperature on the reservation ranges from 32°F in winter to 70°F in summer. The average rainfall is about 17.4 and the average snowfall is about 24 inches annually.

CULTURE AND HISTORY

Scholars believe that Apache people migrated from arctic regions of western Canada to the desert southwest of the United States between the late thirteenth and sixteenth centuries. The Jicarilla Apache people's traditional lands spanned more than 50 million acres and were bounded by four sacred rivers. Traditional territories included portions of Texas, Colorado, and New Mexico. The area's geography, with its variety of terrain and ecosystems, afforded the Jicarillas a lifestyle of hunting, fishing, and agricultural development. The Apache people, including those on the Jicarilla Apache Reservation, are linguistically related to the greater Na-Dene language family.

The Apaches vehemently resisted the encroachment upon their traditional lands by Spanish, Mexican, and American settlers and military forces. But by the mid-1880s, Apaches were consolidated on various southwestern Indian reservations. The Jicarillas were sent to the Mescalero Apache Reservation in southeastern New Mexico.

Jicarilla tribal leadership, stepping outside the bounds of traditional channels, sought to win the support of New Mexico Territorial Governor Ross in 1886, in an attempt to regain their northern reservation. Ross's influential coalition convinced the president to sign the Executive Order of February 8, 1887, which created the permanent site of the Jicarilla Apache Reservation. In an effort to create self-sufficiency among the Jicarilla Apaches, the U.S. government expanded the reservation in 1907 and encouraged the Jicarillas to raise livestock.

The reservation's ample natural resources have proven to be the tribe's greatest economic asset. Currently, fees from hunting and fishing, livestock production, and particularly the vast oil and gas reserves located in the San Juan Basin have provided valuable sources of tribal revenue. Protecting these assets continues to be the Jicarilla people's greatest challenge. Since the 1970s, considerable tribal funds have been spent in resolving legal issues relevant to natural resources.

The tribe brought suits against a number of oil companies and the secretary of the interior. While many of the oil companies were quick to settle, the U.S. government proved to be the most intractable. The Secretary of the Interior refused to sign any new agreements unless the tribe agreed to drop its case. For expediency's sake, the tribe agreed; yet this action signaled a new relationship between the tribe and the U.S. Department of the Interior, with the tribe taking the initiative in forging increasingly sophisticated agreements with industry partners.

In 1976 the tribe entered into a joint contract with the Palmer Oil Company of Billings, Montana, to develop oil and gas. The tribe bought out Palmer's interests in 1977 and became the first tribe in the country to own and operate oil and gas wells. The tribe also formed the Jicarilla Oil and Gas Administration, which successfully petitioned to withdraw its royalty gas from interstate commerce, acquired a small-producer's certificate in its own name, and began marketing its gas in New Mexico.

In addition to this shift in control over their natural reserves, the Jicarilla Apaches won the right, in a decision by the U.S. Supreme Court in the early 1980s, to act as a sovereign entity and impose a severance tax on minerals extracted from tribal lands.

GOVERNMENT

The Jicarilla Apaches adopted their original constitution and by-laws on August 4, 1937 under the terms of the Indian Reorganization Act. This constitution was revised in 1968. The tribe also holds a federal corporate charter. In 2000 the Jicarilla Apache Tribe officially changed its name to the Jicarilla Apache Nation through its tribal ordinance that was approved by the secretary of the interior. This notice was published in the *Federal Register.*

The Jicarilla Apache tribal government consists of three branches, the legislative, executive, and judicial. The legislative branch is composed of a legislative council consisting of eight members who serve staggered terms of four years. The executive branch consists of a president and vice-president, who are also elected every four years by tribal members 18 years and over. The secretary and treasurer are appointed by the president. The judiciary branch consists of a tribal court with up to two judges appointed by the president and an appellate court consisting of three members of the legislative council also appointed by the president.

Jicarilla Apache Reservation
Federal reservation
Jicarilla Apache
Rio Arriba and Sandoval
counties, New Mexico

Jicarilla Apache Nation
P.O. Box 507
Dulce, NM 87528
505-759-3242
505-759-3005 Fax
jicarillaonline.com
jicarilla.net

Total area *(BIA realty, 2004)*
879,917 acres

Population *2000 census*
2,755

Tribal enrollment
(BIA labor report, 2001)
3,403

Tribal enrollment
(Tribal source, 2005)
3,539

Total labor force *2000 census*
1,051

Total labor force
(BIA labor report, 2001)
1,666

High school graduate or higher
2000 census
77.6%

Bachelor's degree or higher
2000 census
13.9%

Unemployment rate *2000 census*
14.2%

Unemployment rate
(BIA labor report, 2001)
33%

Per capita income
2000 census
$10,136

Jicarilla Apache

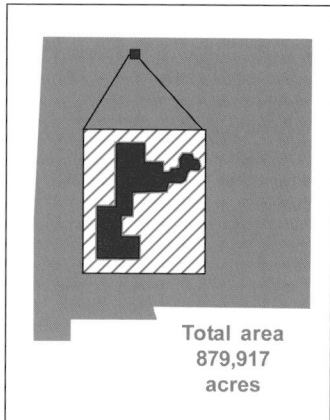

Total area
879,917
acres

TRI-NM-jan-026

TRI-NM-jan-023

TRI-NM-jan-029

TRI-NM-jan-028

TRI-NM-jan-026 View of Ishoteen Judicial Complex below Dulce Rock

TRI-NM-jan-023 Fire trucks in front of the Dulce Fire Department

TRI-NM-jan-029 Street view of Dulce Junior High School and School Administration Building

TRI-NM-jan-028 Street view of the Senior Citizen Building

Tribal government departments include health and human services, education and recreation, public works, public safety, natural resources, and labor. Divisions include community development, health and welfare, senior citizens, mental health and social services, community center, youth, language and culture, library, construction, roads, law and order, game and fish, agriculture, tribal realty, forest development, environmental protection, and JTPA, among many others.

The tribe's culture committee is comprised of traditional and spiritual leaders. These elders provide guidance and advice to the tribe in matters before the council.

The tribe funds and operates its law enforcement program and tribal court. Both the tribal court and the police department, with its corrections department, will move to a new judicial complex in 2005. The $14.3 million dollar Ishkoteen Center will occupy approximately 98,000 square feet. The facility will also house various other tribal government departments, including social services. The tribal court consists of a judge, two associate judges, several contract judges, a prosecutor, and three administrative clerks. The court has jurisdiction over reservation domestic, criminal and civil, and child welfare cases. The tribal council is the appellate court.

The police department has a roster of over 100 employees including the chief of police, 2 lieutenants, a criminal investigator, juvenile justice officers, and about 40 patrol officers. The administrative staff consists of 2 administrative secretaries, 3 dispatchers, a 4-person corrections department, a cook, a squad of fire fighters, and about 10 emergency medical services personnel. There is also a police substation at the Apache Nugget Casino at the junction of state highways 550 and 537.

BUSINESS CORPORATION

The Jicarilla Apache Tribe has had a federal corporate charter since 1937 under the Indian Reorganization Act of 1934. In addition, several business corporations have been established since the early 1990s. The Running Elk Corporation was established to manage the Chama Land and Cattle Company in Chama,

New Mexico. The Apache Nugget Casino is also organized as a corporation with a board of directors consisting of a president, vice-president, and four board members, each serving a term of four years.

ECONOMY

The tribe operates a number of enterprises that contribute to the tribal economy. Its ventures in the agriculture, forestry, gaming, mining, retail, and tourism industries provide a great source of income for the tribe and help support both the tribal and local economies.

Government as Employer. Government jobs account for 53 percent (429 of 802) of the employment for tribal members. Local government supports 57 percent (227) of the jobs; state government, 18 percent (95); and the federal government, 24 percent (76 of 111).

Economic Development Projects. The Jicarilla Apaches have two development groups that advise the tribe on economic issues. The Integrated Resource Management Plan (IRMP) and its committee supply the tribe with a comprehensive assessment of the tribe's resources. The IRMP has been developed through a cooperative tribal and federal interdisciplinary planning team. Its goals are to ensure and develop a direction for sustainable growth and to protect the reservation's resources compatibly with the traditional values of the tribe.

Future projects include an expansion of the casino, developing a truck stop at the intersection of highways 550 and 537 and completing a mini-mall. Future community-based projects include developing a comprehensive economic development plan; developing a master land use plan for the Mundo subdivision; developing a community development plan; constructing an elderly care facility; expanding hospital, emergency medical services, and detention facilities; developing the Horse Lake Mesa Game Park; expanding educational services; improving water and wastewater systems; developing an artisan's guild; developing a recycling center; and constructing a youth facility.

Jicarilla Apache

TRI-NM-jan-025

TRI-NM-jan-027

TRI-NM-jan-031

TRI-NM-jan-033

Agriculture and Livestock. The livestock industry has been a primary use of reservation land since 1890. Ranching serves as the primary agricultural enterprise on the Jicarilla Apache Reservation and features many family-operated cow-calf operations. Raising sheep dominated this industry until 1960 when cattle raising increased. Ranching enterprises on the reservation consist of range units of 1,460 acres to 24,841 acres, each capable of sustaining 11 to 376 animal units during the grazing season.

Although there are approximately 58,000 acres of irrigable land on the reservation, currently only 6,496 acres of dry farming land and 1,000 acres of irrigated land are in use. The 1990 crop production was valued at $365,000, and the tribe anticipates the expansion of its agricultural output.

In the mid-1990s, the tribe acquired the Willow Creek Ranch. Located at the eastern edge of the reservation, the ranch has been developed as a tribal enterprise. The site is utilized as an agricultural career development, training, and research center. It is a joint effort involving the tribe, New Mexico State University, the U.S. Department of Agriculture, and the BIA Branch of Natural Resources. The site will also include a 1,000-acre irrigation project.

Forestry. Nearly 50 percent, or 404,837 acres, of the reservation is forested. This acreage comprises 184,282 acres of timberland and 270,857 acres of woodland. Ponderosa pine represents the majority (over 90 percent) of commercial tree species. Harvesting occurs on the northern half of the reservation. The tribe's timber harvest and management began in the early part of the century. Modern forest management planning by the BIA began in 1993. For ten years, ending in 2002, over 74 million board feet has been cut from the reservation forestlands. The tribal forestry committee serves as the tribe's policy advisor on forest and woodland management matters. The committee reviews forest management plans, timber sales, and management practices of the BIA Jicarilla Agency Branch of Forestry.

Natural Resources. The Jicarilla Apache's tribal economy has long relied upon the use of the tribe's natural resources as the major source of revenue and employment. Harvesting oil, gas,

and timber; ranching; tourism; and hunting and fishing are the cornerstone of the tribal economy. Tribal lands contain abundant sources of woodlands, water sources, minerals, oil, gas, and wildlife. The tribe has utilized these resources well in order to promote a self-sustaining economy.

The Jicarillas are intent on managing their resources in the best possible manner in order to secure a productive land base for future generations while sensibly preserving the delicate ecosystem of tribal lands.

The tribe has been very active in preserving and restoring natural resources on tribal lands for a number of years. Projects include reintroducing wildlife, improving and restoring wildlife habitats, and excellently managing all wildlife resources. The tribe practices comprehensive forest management, including prescribed burn, development backlog, and reforestation methods. Soil erosion and contamination is closely monitored on the reservation, and the tribe intends to develop a system of policies and procedures to address this issue. Mining operations yield the tribe's greatest source of revenue, and although the resources are abundant on tribal lands, the tribe is adamant about providing for a sensible and efficient manner of extraction. A series of plans, guidelines, codes, and ordinances are in effect.

Gaming. In 2004 the Apache Nugget Casino opened its doors to business at the junction of State Highways 550 and 537. The casino is approximately 21,000 square feet, and it has offices for EMS, a fire department, tribal police, and a conference room. The casino offers 200 slot machines and six table games. It also has a snack bar and restaurant. A small casino is also housed at the Jicarilla Inn in Dulce.

Fisheries. Harvard University Honoring Nations Program recognized the tribe's wildlife and fisheries program in 1999. The program is one of the largest and most respected fish and wildlife management initiatives on the continent. It manages a 14,500-acre game park and has implemented a number of projects that preserve the wildlife population and, at the same time, create a significant source of revenue for the tribe. The fish stock in tribal waters include rainbow, brook, brown, and cutthroat trout;

TRI-NM-jan-025 Eastern view of the new Jicarilla Student Residence

TRI-NM-jan-027 Ishoteen Judicial Complex under construction, 2004

TRI-NM-jan-031 Street view of Jicarilla Apache Supermarket Complex

TRI-NM-jan-033 Street entrance to Best Western-Jicarilla Inn

729

Jicarilla Apache

bluehead sucker, flannelmouth sucker, speckled dace, and mottled scuplin. Reservation lakes are restocked annually with about 100,000 fish, and the larger lakes are managed as "put, grow, and take" sites. Annual gill netting surveys are conducted at the lakes, and populations are monitored closely.

Construction. The tribal public works department and the Jicarilla Construction Company support construction on the reservation and focus on community development projects.

Mining. The Jicarilla Apache Reservation is geographically situated in the resource-rich San Juan Basin, which contains the second-largest gas field in the continental United States and is the largest producer of oil of any basin in the Rocky Mountains. The basin contains large amounts of oil, gas, coal, uranium, and geothermal reserves. Coal underlies nearly all of the reservation, and oil and gas pools underlie the southern portion of the reservation. Crude oil accounts for 25 percent of the mineral revenues and natural gas 75 percent. Two recent discoveries highlight the new potential of this mature basin: gas from the Fruitland coal seam has more than doubled the basin's gas production. Additionally, an estimated 5- to 10-million barrel reservoir was discovered on the relatively unexplored northern half of the reservation.

The Jicarilla Apache Tribe was the first tribe in the United States to acquire and operate its own oil and gas production company. The tribe bought out the interests of a private sector partner in 1977, becoming the sole owner of the company. The Jicarilla Apache Tribe is the single largest mineral owner in the San Juan Basin, excluding the U.S. government. During more than 35 years of gas and oil activity on the reservation, over 2,700 wells have been drilled. The 1993 production from 2,200 active wells was nearly 900,000 barrels of oil and 30 cubic feet of gas. The tribe's most important source of tribal revenue stems from its mineral reserves.

The tribe has two offices that manage oil and gas resources. The tribal oil and gas administration is responsible for inspecting tribal wells, monitoring lease compliance, overseeing exploration, negotiating new oil and gas projects and proposals, and monitoring permittees. The oil and gas accounting office, separate from the oil and gas administration, performs minerals accounting, production reports, and auditing.

Services and Retail. The service industry represents a substantial percentage of tribal employment. All businesses located within the town of Dulce are tribally owned. Several new buildings were built and opened in 2004. The newly built and modern Jicarilla Apache Supermarket has a deli-café, a bakery, a Wells Fargo Bank branch, and a community meeting room. A new hardware store affiliated with TruValue also opened in 2004. Apache House of Liquors, a Conoco station with a convenience store and the Jicarilla station, and the Best Western Jicarilla Inn are long-standing businesses. The inn offers excellent accommodations, with a restaurant and lounge, and a gift shop with original arts and crafts. The tribe also operates the Jicarilla Shopping Center and the Willow Creek Ranch.

The tribe owns the Lodge at Chama, a 32,000-acre ranch situated in the San Juan Mountains. Visits to the lodge include access to recreational opportunities including fishing, hunting, hiking, horseback riding, snowshoeing, skiing, snowmobiling, wildlife touring, and winter sleigh riding. Guests may also observe day-to-day ranch operations, visit with cowboys, and participate in cattle drives. Tribal revenues also stem from a number of off-reservation endeavors such as ownership of the Floridian Hotel in Orlando, Florida; funding of time-share properties in Orlando; and partnership in time-share lodges in Jackson Hole, Wyoming; and the Whitney Mountain Lodge in Rogers, Arkansas.

Media and Communications. The tribe owns radio station KCIE 90.5 which was established in the early 1980s. The *Jicarilla Chieftain* is the tribe's official newspaper.

Tourism and Recreation. The Jicarilla Apache Reservation is located in a major regional, growing, multi-season recreation and tourism zone. The reservation offers the outdoor enthusiast and tourist some of the most spectacular vacation, sightseeing, sports, hunting, and fishing opportunities in the southwestern United States. For the sportsman, hunting on the reservation is considered some of the best in the United Sates, drawing hunters and sightseers worldwide. Five major big game migration corridors cross the reservation. Game includes elk, deer, black bear, mountain lion, turkey, and Canadian geese. In addition, 7 of the tribe's 15 mountain lakes are stocked with rainbow, brown, and cutthroat trout. Fishing is permitted at Dulce, Enbom, Hayden, Horse, La Jara, Mundo, and Stone lakes, and the Navajo River. Tribally issued permits are required and may be secured from the Jicarilla Game and Fish Department. Boaters are also permitted on tribal lakes. The tribe welcomes all visitors, but it requires that they abide by guidelines and restrictions intended to protect and preserve natural resources. Guidelines are available through the game and fish department.

Camping and picnicking are permitted around the reservation lakes where picnic tables, grills, and shelters are available. Many visitors also enjoy hiking, exploring, and taking trail rides through the reservation. With an archeological site density of approximately 25 sites per square mile, there are many cultural attractions on the reservation. These include two major archeological sites: the La Jara Cliff Dwellings and Cordova Canyon Cliff Dwellings.

Jicarilla Apache Arts and Crafts Museum is a tribal department that promotes the preservation of traditional arts and crafts through employing training Apache artisans and through its sales. It exhibits historical baskets, photographs, paintings, and clothing.

A number of the Jicarilla Apaches' annual celebrations are open to the public, including the Little Beaver Round-Up held the third weekend in July. This event is considered a high point of the midsummer season and includes the Pro-Indian Open Rodeo, Pony Express Race, 5K Run/Walk, a powwow, a parade, traditional dances, and a carnival. In addition, Go-Jii-Yah Feast, an annual harvest festival, is held on September 14-15. It has been a part of the Jicarilla culture for hundreds of years. Clan racing, a rodeo, and traditional dances are part of this event. The tribe also hosts the Jicarilla Day Powwow in February.

INFRASTRUCTURE
Most of the Jicarilla Apache Reservation lies north of Highway 550, which is the main route to the Four Corners area, and it is bisected north-south by State Road 536. Highway 64 to Aztec and Farmington, Highway 64/84 to Chama, and Highway 84 to Pagosa Springs, Colorado, complete the major transportation corridors. There are 884 miles of surface roads on the reservation, ranging from paved to unimproved earth. There is access to the reservation via state highways 550 and 537, but U.S. 64/84, the corridor to the northeast through New Mexico and southern Colorado, carries most of the regional traffic, which bypasses the reservation.

In efforts to promote safety, accessibility, and economic development, the tribe plans to develop standards for road construction and design, create a five-year organizational strategic plan for the roads department, and complete the east-west road from the Heron and El Vado reservoirs to Highway 537. Future projects also include a coordinated public transportation system and upgrades to the Dulce street system.

TRI-NM-jan-035

TRI-NM-jan-036

TRI-NM-jan-038

TRI-NM-jan-024

Electricity. The Northern Rio Arriba Electric Cooperative serves the northern portion of the Jicarilla Apache Reservation. The Jemez Mountains Electric Cooperative serves the southern portion of the reservation.

Fuel. The Public Service Company of New Mexico supplies natural gas to the community of Dulce.

Water Supply. The Jicarilla Apache Community Water System serves the Town of Dulce and its surrounding areas. The Navajo River runs north of Dulce, providing the community with its domestic water supply. The current water and sewer system in Dulce, funded by the BIA and the Indian Health Service, is outdated and has proven inadequate as the community grows and, at this time, is hindering development. A wastewater treatment system built by the BIA serves Dulce. The facility was constructed in the 1930s and was updated regularly between the 1960s and 1990s. The system requires major improvements.

In 1997 the tribe received a $550,000 Tribal Integrated Waste Management Award from the U.S. EPA to fund a two-year development project for waste management. The tribal landfill is expected to meet demand within the next five years. The tribe is investigating the development of a regional landfill.

Transportation. The nearest rail service is 135 miles away in Santa Fe. Commercial air service is available in Farmington, 90 miles from Dulce, although there is a tribally owned 5,000-foot paved and lighted airstrip with a navigational beacon on the reservation. A new airport funded by the Federal Aviation Administration was built in 2001, and it is 11 miles south of Dulce. Several truck lines and UPS service the area. Para-transit service exists for the elderly and disabled. Three school districts that serve the reservation provide school transportation.

Telecommunications. GTE-Midwest Region supplies telephone service. The reservation receives both network and cable television broadcasts.

COMMUNITY FACILITIES AND SERVICES

The community of Dulce has a multipurpose community center that houses tribal offices, a bowling alley, a swimming pool, and a gymnasium. There is a senior citizens center with dining facilities, meeting space, and an office. A cultural center with a gift shop is located in an office in the historic district. Recreational facilities include a lighted rodeo arena with nearby camping facilities, a lighted baseball field, and a park. A new fully equipped health fitness center opened in 2000. Many recreational facilities are shared with the local public school, such as the football stadium with a padded track for field sports and recreational walking. Wells Fargo Bank has a branch in Dulce. The U.S. Post Office built a new post office in 2002. There are also a fire department and a library. The tribe sponsors a Young Men's Summer and Winter Camp. Tribal youth, or those affiliated through lineage, ages 7-14, and their fathers may participate in the three-day camping trip.

Education. Jicarilla youth in grades K-12 attend the local public elementary, middle, and high schools in the Dulce School District. Each school has its own buildings in adjoining school campuses. A new elementary school was completed in 2003. In the last 10 years, the school district has funded the renovation and building of new facilities, including a state-of-the-art sports gymnasium, cafeteria, and Head Start facilities. Many students attend St. Francis Catholic School in nearby Lumberton, while others choose Santa Fe Indian School. A small number of Jicarilla students living in the southern portion of the reservation attend schools in Gallina and Cuba.

The tribe has an education department that sponsors programs such as higher education, adult education, cultural and language preservation, a library, and federal programs. The tribe began the Chester E. Faris Scholarship program for higher education in 1952 with its first proceeds from the discovery of oil and gas. In 2002, in honor of a venerated elder, the scholarship program changed its name to the Norman TeCube Sr. Scholarship Fund.

TRI-NM-jan-035 Outside view of classrooms of Dulce Elementary School

TRI-NM-jan-036 Sign in front of Dulce Elementary School, Home of the Warriors

TRI-NM-jan-038 Driveway to Nzhonach'idele'ee, (a place to get well) Jicarilla Apache Health Care Facility

TRI-NM-jan-024 Sign & front entrance of the Jicarilla Student Residence

Jicarilla Apache

TRI-NM-jan-042

TRI-NM-jan-049

TRI-NM-jan-042 Dulce Athletic Complex

TRI-NM-jan-049 Side View of the Apache Nugget Casino at the intersection of Hwy. 550 and 537

TRI-NM-jan-041 Jicarilla Child Development Center

TRI-NM-jan-051 Gas Well on the southern part of the reservation

TRI-NM-jan-003 Buffalos grazing at Chama ranch

TRI-NM-jan-004 Buffalos herd grazing at Chama Ranch

TRI-NM-jan-041

TRI-NM-jan-051

TRI-NM-jan-003

TRI-NM-jan-004

The department also provides a cultural preservation program. The program's goals are to promote language retention, develop curriculum, and teach cultural crafts and stories. Language, art, and culture classes are offered in the Dulce school system, St. Francis School, and the tribal education programs. A language immersion program is held in the Dulce Day Care Center. The program's other projects include language classes, a culture camp, Jicarilla language project, an ethnobotany study, video documentation, and inventory of cultural items.

Health Care. The community is served by the Dulce Indian Health Service Clinic. In 2005 a new health ambulatory health facility will open near the elementary school on the newly acquired Gomez Ranch property on the road to Mundo Lake. Facilities will include a morgue, a pharmacy, and a housing complex for health services employees. This $11.5 million dollar, 61,000+ square feet, facility will be leased to the Indian Health Service by the Nation. The tribe operates a health and fitness center. Amenities include a cardio workout room with state-of-the art equipment.

ENVIRONMENTAL CONCERNS

The tribe is committed to providing a safe environment and productive land base for current and future tribal populations. The majority of the Jicarilla Apache Tribe's environmental concerns stem from the effects of clear-cut logging, overgrazing, poorly managed gas and oil harvesting, and the construction of roads and railroads on tribal lands over the years. These activities have resulted in soil erosion, watershed pollution, and timberland damage. In 2002 the tribe proposed the Jicarilla Apache Lands Restoration Project to address these issues. The project called for a two-year service period during which the tribe would receive federal assistance to analyze the extent of the damages to tribal lands, determine agency responsibility, and determine the cost of a restoration program. Activities would include creating a tribal historical record and identifying archeological sites.

The Mt. Archuleta Fire of 1996 destroyed a large portion of the Navajo River watershed and riparian area located on tribal lands. The resulting ash, debris, and sediment have adversely affected the aquatic habitat and fishery resources.

Honoring Nations Honoree 1999

Wildlife and Fisheries Management Program, Game and Fish Department,
Jicarilla Apache Tribe

The land base of the Jicarilla Apache Tribe boasts numerous quality fishing lakes and is home to some of North America's largest populations of elk and mule deer. Until early 1980s, however, the Jicarilla Tribe had only partial jurisdiction over these resources and virtually no money to manage them appropriately. State of New Mexico game and fish regulations applied on tribal land, and yet the State gave tribes no financial or biological support for wildlife management. Nor had the Bureau of Indian Affairs (BIA) actively supported tribal wildlife programs.

Acutely aware that appropriate management of their valuable game and fish resources required better financing, members of the tribal government convinced the BIA to establish a small wildlife and parks program at Jicarilla in 1982. The Tribe immediately initiated an agreement with the Bureau to take over this funding stream-and thus secured the seed money needed to operate a program of their own. Fortuitously, the United States Supreme Court ruled in that same year (in a suit that the Jicarilla Apache had joined) that American Indian tribes could assert full jurisdiction over hunting and fishing on reservation lands. The Tribe's diligence in pursuing both de facto and de jure rights over wildlife management had paid off.

Initial funding for the Jicarilla Fish and Wildlife Management Program was sufficient to hire only one wildlife biologist and to establish a small operating budget, but from these humble beginnings, the Program has evolved into one of the largest and most respected fish and wildlife management initiatives on the continent. Operating under the auspices of the Tribe's Game and Fish Department, the Program manages a 14,500-acre game park and has implemented a series of projects that have been extremely successful in both preserving the Tribe's wildlife population and creating a significant revenue source for the Tribe.

Information systems for tracking and managing animal populations and innovative environmental science projects are two keys to the Program's success. The Game and Fish Department strictly limits the number of hunting and fishing permits and requires all harvesters to report their takings before leaving the reservation. Permit and catch data (including DNA information for tribally owned large game) are then tracked in the Program's computerized management information system, which tribal biologists rely on to monitor the size, composition, and health of reservation fish and wildlife populations. When necessary, the Program intervenes to thwart threats to the Tribe's game and fish resources. In 1987, for example, the Program suspended all mule deer hunting for three years to allow population recovery, which, in conjunction with habitat improvement and predator management projects, has helped the Jicarilla reservation produce more trophy mule deer than any other comparably sized area in North America. In 1993, the Program completed a chemical treatment

of one of the Tribe's largest lakes to prevent it from being overtaken by carp-the first successful project of its type in New Mexico in 25 years. In the late 1990s, the Program completed the United States' first-ever eradication of brucellosis from a captive elk herd.

Strong administrative enforcement mechanisms are a third key to the Program's success. The Tribe's Game and Fish Code, which regulates hunting and fishing on reservation land, is one of the most comprehensive and severe law enforcement codes in Indian Country. Poachers and others who illegally harvest Jicarilla wildlife face a mandatory $10,000 fine and confiscation of their vehicles and weapons. If questioned, decisions regarding code violators are reviewed and enforced by the Jicarilla Tribal Court.

Together, these measures have resulted in a tripling of the Tribe's elk and deer populations and in the reemergence of a once-endangered trout population. They have also underwritten the Program's financial success. Jicarilla's reputation for prize-winning populations of elk, mule deer, and trout has led to a substantial increase in revenue from permits and fees. The Program currently enjoys a net profit of approximately $500,000 per year-money that helps support other tribal programs.

The Tribe has taken numerous steps to ensure the long-term sustainability of the Fish and Wildlife Management Program. Politically, the Jicarilla Tribal Council has supported the efforts of the Game and Fish Department and has allowed it considerable decision-making autonomy. In the 1980s, the Tribe also successfully fought several lawsuits against attempts by the State of New Mexico to intervene in tribal wildlife management. Financially, the Council has supported the Department's creation of a Wildlife Management Fund, into which the Department transfers 10 percent of all revenue from the sale of hunting and fishing licenses. Fund monies are earmarked for projects such as drainage, prescribed burning, and predator control-habitat enhancement activities that will help assure program success well into the future.

Significantly, the Program has already begun to share its learning. Representatives from a number of American Indian nations and Canadian First Nations have toured the Department's facilities to learn more about the Program. Members of the Department have held an elk ranching seminar for other tribal wildlife managers. And, recently, the State of New Mexico requested the Jicarilla Game and Fish Department's assistance with the management of its own mule deer population.

Through a combination of political will, long-term planning, commitment to scientific innovation, and attention to administrative detail, the Jicarilla Apache's Fish and Wildlife Management Program has served-and should continue to serve-as a model for government programs both within and outside Indian Country.

Honoring Nations
Honoree 1999

Text in its entirety from:
The Harvard Project On
American Indian Economic
Development

John F. Kennedy School
of Government
Harvard University

Laguna

Laguna Pueblo
Federal reservation
Keresan
Valencia, Bernalillo, and
Sandoval counties, New
Mexico

Pueblo of Laguna
P.O. Box 194
Laguna, NM 87026
505-552-6654
505-552-6941 Fax

Total area *(BIA realty, 2004)*
495,442.66 acres

Total area *(Tribal Source, 2004)*
533,000 acres

Total population *2000 census*
3,815

Tribal membership *(BIA, 2001)*
7,825

Total labor force *2000 census*
1,288

Total labor force *(BIA, 2001)*
3,393

High school graduate or higher
2000 census
79.4%

Bachelor's degree or higher
2000 census
7.5%

Unemployment rate *2000 census*
16.1%

Per capita income *2000 census*
$8,773

LOCATION AND LAND STATUS

The Laguna Pueblo is located about 45 miles west of Albuquerque in west-central New Mexico. The pueblo consists of six separate villages located along the Rio San Jose Valley: Laguna/Old Laguna, Encinal, Mesita, Paguate, Paraje (Casa Blanca), and Seama. Tribal headquarters are located in Old Laguna. Reservation lands total 533,000 acres in three locations, with the two smaller segments situated southwest and northwest of the main reservation. The Village of Old Laguna was originally recognized through Spanish land grants in 1699, while studies suggest habitation well before this date. Acts of Congress in 1858 and 1869 confirmed the original Spanish land grants of all the existing New Mexico pueblos except for Laguna and Zuni. Laguna Pueblo's land grant was not officially confirmed and patented until November 7, 1906.

PHYSICAL DESCRIPTION

The land is semiarid and marked by buttes, mountains, and high desert terrain. Elevations range from just over 5,000 feet at the junction of the Rio Puerco and Rio San Jose, to a high of nearly 8,500 feet at the foothills of Mt. Taylor.

CULTURE AND HISTORY

The Pueblo of Laguna is one of the largest of the Keresan-speaking villages. Laguna ancestors migrated from the north, eventually settling in their present location. They are thought to be closely related to the people of Acoma. Living in villages, the Lagunas cultivated small areas of land around their villages and collected clay from the surrounding areas. First pueblo contact with European settlers came during the sixteenth century, when Spaniards arrived in the Rio Grande Valley. Until this time, the Laguna people had relied primarily on farming, but with the Spanish introduction of livestock, many became herders. When the region passed from Spanish to Mexican hands in 1821, the Laguna's status, as it existed under Spanish domination, was retained under Mexican law. At the end of the Mexican-American War, the southwest came under the sovereignty of the United States. The United States failed, however, to adequately define pueblo rights and the status of their land claims, thereby creating an ongoing source of contention. A U.S. Supreme Court ruling in 1876 deprived the pueblos of federal land protection, thus allowing thousands of non-Indians to settle on pueblo lands. In an attempt to unravel the morass of ensuing land title issues, Congress created the Court of Private Land Claims in 1891. On April 20, 1898, this court confirmed the original land grant to the Pueblo of Laguna, though a land patent was not finally issued until November 7, 1906. In 1922, a bill was introduced before Congress that would have allowed non-Indians to gain title to lands within the pueblos. This threat led to the founding of the All Indian Pueblo Council that same year. The council and its supporters successfully lobbied for the passage of the Pueblo Lands Act on June 7, 1924, which created the Pueblo Land Board to settle lingering and future land controversies.

The 1934 Indian Reorganization Act repudiated the allotment law (Dawes Act of 1887) in favor of a new policy designed to safeguard Indian lands. The Lagunas, poor in resources (particularly water) and impoverished by lack of federal recognition, did not accept the Indian Reorganization Act until 1949. After World War II, an increase in wage work and tourism, coupled with the tribe's new Indian Reorganization Act status, provided some relief to the Lagunas. In 1952, with BIA assistance, Laguna Pueblo signed a lease with the Anaconda Company to develop the reservation's uranium deposits, thus leading to a period of relative prosperity for the tribe. Until 1982, Anaconda employed up to 800 workers in and around the Laguna area. Though the

company ceased its mining operations that year, it continues to fund a $45 million reclamation project. Today, other sources of employment in the pueblo include a tribally owned shopping center, Laguna Industries, Laguna Construction Company, civic positions in the tribal police department and high school, and the Laguna Rainbow Center, a facility for elders.

Culturally, the Lagunas maintain an extraordinary tradition of ceremonies and customs. Ancient dances and village feast days are held as part of an ongoing celebration of life. Each of the six villages has a Catholic mission named for its patron saint, and each hold an annual feast in honor of that saint. Additionally, the pueblo supports a thriving arts community that comprises painters, silversmiths, potters, and makers of traditional clothing.

GOVERNMENT

The Pueblo of Laguna's constitution was adopted in revised form in 1958 following the Indian Reorganization Act. The constitution was revised again in 1982. The tribal government consists of a 21-member council, composed of two members elected from each village and nine staff members elected at large. Terms of office are staggered, each member serving a two-year term. The council members include a governor, first lieutenant governor, second lieutenant governor, head *fiscale*, second *fiscale*, treasurer, secretary, and interpreter. The council holds meetings weekly. Additionally, each village holds a weekly meeting to determine its position on upcoming council decisions. All men 18 years of age and over are required to attend village meetings and functions. The tribal government also maintains its own judicial system.

ECONOMY

Federal funding for tribal programs and infrastructure and revenues from tribal gaming and other business enterprises are the main components of the tribe's economy.

Government as Employer. The tribal government provides employment for 192 tribal members through administration, operations, health care, and its enterprises. The Laguna Rainbow Center, a nursing home and long-term care facility employs 45 tribal members, and is on the verge of doubling its capacity from 25 to 50 beds. The Acoma-Cañoncito-Laguna Hospital employs about 150 persons. Additionally, a number of members find employment through the New Mexico State Highway Department and other state agencies.

Agriculture and Livestock. Once primarily a livestock-grazing region, the reservation continues to support some grazing and agricultural activities. At least five ranches, ranging in size from 2,200 acres to nearly 252,000 acres, operate on pueblo lands.

Gaming. The tribe owns three casinos, all accessible from I-40. Route 66 Casino is their newest gaming facility, and it is located off of I-40 on the Rio Puerco River. It features 1,250 slots, 20 table games, a 750-seat bingo hall, an entertainment venue, a restaurant, and a nightclub. It is 50,000 square feet and employs 1,200 people. Dancing Eagle Casino, located at the village of Casa Blanca, has 500 slots, 8 poker tables, one table game, and a restaurant. The complex is 31,000 square feet and employs 350 people. Casino Express is a small annex casino located at the travel center near the Route 66 Casino.

Construction. The Laguna Construction Company figures as a major employer and generator of revenues for the tribe. It specializes in land reclamation, heavy construction operations, engineering, and construction management. The company has a current labor force of 80 people, largely tribal members, who are skilled in engineering, heavy equipment operation, and other technical positions.

Mining. The Laguna Construction Company is managing and overseeing the $45 million Laguna Reclamation Project that is restoring a uranium mining site that the Anaconda Mining Company operated on the reservation until 1982. This project employs significant numbers of tribal members and was expected to take until at least 1999 to complete.

Manufacturing. Laguna Industries is now the largest single source of employment on the reservation. The company, which was established in 1980, currently employs 220 persons, 85 percent of them Native Americans, and generates over $15 million in annual revenues. The company is involved in manufacturing sheet metal components, electrical cables and harnesses, electrical mechanical assemblies, mini-intercom components, and other high technology and communications products contracted by the Defense Department. The company has been garnering more and more contracts within the private sector. Laguna Industries is now a key supplier for major concerns such as GTE, General Dynamics of San Diego, Hughes Aircraft, Digital Equipment Corporation, Hewlett-Packard, and Sandia and Los Alamos National Laboratory. The company continues to grow, and the Pueblo of Laguna (with assistance from EDA) added approximately 50,000 square feet of manufacturing and office space during 1991.

Services and Retail. The Laguna Commercial Enterprise operates the Casa Blanca Market Plaza, which consists of a major supermarket and a gas station. The Market Plaza also contains five smaller shops that are leased to local businesses. The enterprise employs a total of 42 people. Laguna people sell their arts and crafts, such as Indian belts, pottery, jewelry, baskets, and paintings, at the Market Plaza.

Tourism and Recreation. The largest celebration and tourist attraction at Laguna Pueblo is the Feast of Old Laguna, held annually on September 19 in celebration of St. Joseph (Old Laguna also continues to celebrate the original St. Joseph Feast Day on March 19). Various Indian dances are held throughout the day in front of a shrine specifically erected for the event. Local and regional artists and crafts people sell their work, and every house bustles with visitors partaking of traditional foods. Each of the six villages also celebrates its own feast day, called Grab Days because people with the names of patron saints throw small wares or baked goods from the rooftops of their homes to the people below.

Ceremonial dances are held throughout the year. Many visitors enjoy visiting the St. Joseph's Mission, a National Register site, which Friar Antonio de Miranda, an early Franciscan missionary, had built in 1699. The mission was recently restored and is open to visitors on weekdays. Elk and deer hunting and fishing are also extremely popular on the reservation.

INFRASTRUCTURE

Interstate 40 and the old Route 66 pass east-west through the reservation. The tribal roads department maintains the secondary roads on the reservation. Commercial air service is available at Albuquerque International Sunport, 45 miles to the east. Numerous commercial truck lines serve the reservation directly. The Santa Fe Railroad has a currently unused rail spur in the Village of Laguna, while the company offers commercial rail service in Albuquerque. Commercial bus service is available in Grants, 30 miles to the west.

Electricity. Continental Divide Electric Cooperative in Grants, New Mexico, provides electricity.

Fuel. Union Gas Company provides gas service.

Water Supply. The tribe maintains its own water and sewer system.

Telecommunications. The reservation receives radio, television, and cable services out of Albuquerque.

COMMUNITY FACILITIES AND SERVICES

The community center and tribal offices are located in the Old Laguna.

Education. Laguna Pueblo has its own department of education, created in 1992, and operates Head Start and daycare programs. The pueblo hosts the Laguna Elementary School (run by the BIA) and a newly built junior high school. Older students attend the Laguna-Acoma High School, which is operated by Cibola County. The Laguna Higher Education program assists eligible Laguna students pursuing postsecondary degrees at accredited institutions, as well as those pursuing certification at vocational schools. The pueblo also has a scholarship program to serve its members.

Health Care. The Acoma-Cañoncito-Laguna Hospital furnishes local health care. The Laguna Rainbow Center provides long-term care for the tribe's elderly.

Laguna

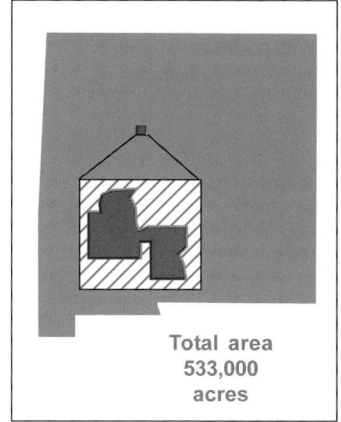

Total area
533,000
acres

TRI-NM-Lg-014 The Route 66 Casino, the newest gaming facility

TRI-NM-Lg-005 The Route 66 Travel Center

TRI-NM-Lg-003 Route 66 Travel Center sign

TRI-NM-Lg-014

TRI-NM-Lg-005

TRI-NM-Lg-003

Mescalero Apache

Mescalero Apache Reservation
Federal reservation
Mescalero Apache
Otero County, New Mexico

Mescalero Apache
Reservation
P.O. Box 227
Mescalero, NM 88340
505-671-4494
505-464-9191 Fax

Total area *(BIA realty, 2004)*
460,769.30 acres

Total area *(Tribal Source, 2004)*
460,679 acres

Population *2000 census*
3,156

Tribal enrollment
(BIA labor report, 2001)
3,979

Total labor force *2000 census*
1,076

Total labor force
(BIA labor report, 2001)
2,083

High school graduate or higher
2000 census
72.6%

Bachelor's degree or higher
2000 census
6.4%

Unemployment rate
2000 census
16%

Unemployment rate
(BIA labor report, 2001)
62%

Per capita income
2000 census
$8,118

LOCATION AND LAND STATUS
The Mescalero Apache Reservation sprawls across some 460,679 acres in southeastern New Mexico and lies entirely within Otero County. Tribal headquarters are located in the incorporated town of Mescalero. The Mescalero Apache Reservation was established by treaty on July 1, 1852. Executive orders were issued in 1873, 1874, 1875, 1882, and 1883, further extending the reservation's boundaries.

PHYSICAL DESCRIPTION
The reservation extends from the arid Tularosa Basin on the western boundary to the densely forested peaks and valleys of the Sacramento Mountains. Presiding over this vast expanse is the 12,003-foot Sierra Blanca, sacred peak of the Mescalero Apache. The reservation borders the Lincoln National Forest on the north and south.

CULTURE AND HISTORY
The name "Mescalero" (Spanish for "eater of Mescal") applies to one branch of the Eastern Apache people or culture. The Mescalero Apache Reservation is home to three Apache bands-the Mescalero, Lipan, and Chiricahua Apache, which collectively organized in 1936 under the Indian Reorganization Act as the Mescalero Apache Tribe. Most tribal members, however, are members of the Mescalero Band.

From the time of pre-European contact through the mid-nineteenth century, the Mescalero and Lipan Apaches hunted and gathered in a vast area stretching from present-day Santa Fe, New Mexico, in the north, to Chihuahua City, Mexico, in the south. Primarily desert dwellers, the Chiricahuas and Lipans subsisted on buffalo, antelope, and various desert flora while the Mescaleros resided in the mountainous and plains areas. They made frequent forays into several mountain ranges, including the Sacramento, to hunt game and cut tepee lodge poles. The Mescalero lifestyle was much more reflective of the Plains people's styles, including the traditional dress.

The Mescaleros and Lipans remained relatively autonomous during the Spanish and Mexican periods of southwestern occupation. Establishment of the New Mexico Territory in 1850 brought them into increasing conflict with the U.S. Army and Euro-American settlers encroaching upon their domain. Following hostilities, the Mescaleros signed a treaty in 1852, which confined them to a small reservation at the Bosque Redondo. Poor conditions spurred many Mescalero families to flee, but most returned by 1864. An 1873 Executive Order established a reservation for the Mescaleros in the Sacramento Mountains. Subsequent executive orders expanded the reservation's boundaries, and in 1889 the U.S. Army relocated several bands of Lipan Apaches and some of Geronimo's Chiricahuas to the Mescalero Reservation. The Mescaleros, Lipans, and Chiricahuas languished throughout the early twentieth century under Indian Service pressure to become farmers. After incorporation in 1936, the Mescalero Apache Tribe initiated a long-term program of economic development and diversification.

In recent decades, the Mescalero Apache Tribe has been referred to as one of the most ambitious tribes in the United States. The diverse tribal economy rests upon an expanding wood products enterprise and a thriving tourism industry.

GOVERNMENT
The Mescalero Apache Tribal Council, composed of a president, a vice-president, and eight at-large members, serves as the governing body for enrolled tribal members. Council members are elected to two-year terms, with elections occurring annually. The original constitution and bylaws of the Mescalero Apache Tribe were ratified on March 25, 1936, in accordance with the Indian Reorganization Act. The tribe adopted a revision on December 18, 1964. Tribal law was consolidated and codified under the Mescalero Tribal Code, approved on January 13, 1984. Long-range planning is directed by the tribe's overall economic development plan, adopted September 8, 1961, and periodically amended under the direction of a tribal staff.

The tribe contracts numerous programs through the BIA. They include law enforcement, forestry, youth development, natural resources, and social services. The tribe also maintains a tribal court, a law and order office, a drug court, human services, resource management and protection, historic preservation, and conservation programs. The Mescalero Tribal Court exercises jurisdiction over crimes committed on the reservation. The court is guided by the tribal civil and penal laws.

The tribe's resort enterprises are operated by the unincorporated entity, Inn of the Mountain Gods Resort and Casino. It oversees Casino Apache, Casino Apache Travel Center, Ski Apache, and Inn of the Mountain Gods Resort and Casino. It also manages the development of the tribe's new ventures.

ECONOMY
The tribal economy is supported in large part through the tribe's enterprises in the tourism industry. The tribe operates a ski resort, a luxury resort complex, gaming facilities, and several recreational areas.

Government as Employer. The tribe offers employment in several sectors of tribal government, including forestry and natural resources, social services, law enforcement, roads, recreation, and administration. The Inn of the Mountain Gods Resort employs 355 people on a seasonal basis. Ski Apache employs 350 people during the ski season. Mescalero Forest Products employs 89 people. The BIA employs 79 people on the reservation. The on-reservation Indian Health Service clinic employs 68 people.

Economic Development Projects. The tribe is constructing a new resort facility that will include a 273-room hotel, fitness center, convention hall, special events center, an indoor swimming pool, and a casino that will replace the existing Casino Apache.

Agriculture and Livestock. In 2004, poor market conditions and a reduction in livestock influenced the tribe's decision to purchase all the shares in the Mescalero Cattle Grower's Association and assume control of operations. The tribe is in the process of developing a ranching enterprise to focus on restoring grazing lands through vegetative management and watershed improvements.

Forestry. The Mescalero Apache Reservation encompasses some 175,000 acres of forested land composed primarily of ponderosa pine, Douglas fir, southwestern white pine, and white fir. The tribally owned Mescalero Forest Products contracts for direct sales of unprocessed timber. The Mescalero Forest Products sawmill, employing 80 people, processes lumber for sale throughout the Southwest. Mescalero Forest Products and the BIA forestry branch jointly harvest approximately 20 million board feet of timber, employing model uneven-age silvicultural management. The tribe is considering the development of a biomass cogeneration plant at the mill.

TRI-NM-Mes-005

TRI-NM-Mes-007

In 2004, the tribe purchased the former White Sands Forest Products in Alamogordo, New Mexico. Renamed Mescalero Forest Products II, the mill produces 2x4 and 2x6 studs as well as poles and posts. It employs about 80 people.

Gaming. The tribe owns and operates Inn of the Mountain Gods Resort and Casino just outside of Ruidoso, New Mexico. The resort offers a luxury hotel, a casino, golf course, and banquet halls. The casino features 1,000 slot machines and 34 table games. The facilities also include a sports bar and nightclub with live entertainment and a dance floor. The inn offers a number of dining venues: Wendell's Lounge, Gathering Nations Buffet, Big Game Sports Bar, and Apache Tee Bar and Grill provide a wide array of selections. The hotel at the inn features 273 luxury rooms and suites, 40,000 square feet of meeting space, an indoor pool, and a fitness center. The inn also features an 18-hole championship golf course that was rated one of the 35 best courses in the nation by *Golf Week Magazine*. It is scheduled to host the New Mexico Pro-Am Golf Tournament in September 2005. The inn offers fishing, tennis, and horseback riding opportunities for guests. The tribe holds the annual Wendell Chino Golf Classic each May. Big game hunts are also organized through the Inn of the Mountain of Gods.

The tribe owns and operates Casino Apache in Mescalero. It offers 1,200 slots/VLTs, 40 table games, and 1 restaurant. It also features a smoke shop and convenience store. Casino Apache will be replaced by a new casino currently in development. The tribe also owns and operates the Casino Apache Travel Center in Ruidoso. The casino offers 415 slots/VLTs and 30 table games.

In 2004 the U.S. Department of the Interior provided closure to a long-standing feud between the tribe and the State of New Mexico. The department approved a gaming compact between the two. The compact calls for the tribe to pay $25 million in back payments and to share eight percent of its revenues from Casino Apache with the state.

Fisheries. The hatchery was closed by the U.S. Fish and Wildlife Service following watershed fires and regional flooding in 1999. Since that time, the Mescalero Apache Tribe has assumed control of the facility. In 2004, functions were restored and the cultivation of the Rainbow trout resumed. Plans for renovation include updating equipment in order to increase production. The tribe also plans to initiate propagation of the Rio Grande Cutthroat Trout. The tribe is a member of the Southwest Tribal Fisheries Commission.

Construction. The tribe owns heavy equipment suitable for land clearing and road construction.

Industrial Parks. Opportunities for business ventures are available at the 68,000-square-foot Mescalero industrial site.

Services and Retail. The Mescalero Apache Tribal Store sells groceries, dry goods, and gas. The tribe also operates the Mescalero Tribal Lounge and Package Store.

Media and Communications. The tribe owns Mescalero Apache Telecom. Telephone, Internet, and broadband services are available. It also provides web design, website hosting, and technical support. The company serves approximately 1,000 customers.

Tourism and Recreation. In addition to the Inn of the Mountain Gods Resort and Casino and other tribal gaming facilities, the tribe offers several attractions that appeal to visitors. Ski Apache is southern New Mexico's premier ski area, with high-speed quad chairs and the state's only gondola. Located in the Sacramento Mountains, Ski Apache opened in 1961. It offers guests a certified ski school for all abilities, ski and snowboard rentals, round-tribe scenic rides for non-skiers, and the Kiddie Korral for small children.

Mescalero Big Game Hunts provides clients with the opportunity to experience the hunting of bull elk, cow elk, bear, and wild birds. The Big Game Hunting Lodge also offers the Sporting Clay Range. The tribe also operates the Silver Lake, Eagle Creek, and Ruidoso recreation areas. Silver Creek, located at the southern end of the reservation along State Route 244, and Eagle Creek, located at the northern end of the reservation along the ski road, offer full RV hookups, tent sites, picnic areas, and fishing. Ruidoso recreation area, located west of Ruidoso in the Upper Canyon region, offers tent sites, picnic areas, and fishing.

St. Joseph's Church on the reservation is also an attraction to many visitors. The structure took 23 years to complete. It is currently undergoing restoration, and a request has been submitted to the National Park Service to add the church to the National Register of Historic Places. No cameras are permitted on the premises. The Mahi Ke Daada Haax Art Gallery is also located on the reservation. It features original fine art by Mescalero Apache tribal members. The gallery offers a coffee bar and bakery. The tribe also operates the Mescalero Cultural Center.

The tribe hosts the Mescalero Apache Ceremonial and Rodeo in July of each year. Festivities include four days and nights of dancing, eating, and paying tribute to young maidens undergoing tribal puberty rites. In cooperation with the state, the tribe co-hosts the annual Mescal Roast and Celebration at the Living Desert State Park outside Carlsbad, New Mexico.

INFRASTRUCTURE

U.S. Highway 70 bisects the Mescalero Apache Reservation, connecting Tularosa (18 miles west) and the resort town of Ruidoso (2 miles north), and passing through the town of Mescalero. U.S. Highway 70 serves as the major transportation corridor through the Mescalero Apache Reservation. State Highway 244 connects the reservation with Cloudcroft to the south.

Electricity. Otero County Electric provides electricity.

TRI-NM-Mes-006

TRI-NM-Mes-005 Lakeview of the golf course

TRI-NM-Mes-007 Evening view from the Inn of the Mountain Gods Resort and Casino

TRI-NM-Mes-006 Golf ball with logo of resort and casino

Mescalero Apache

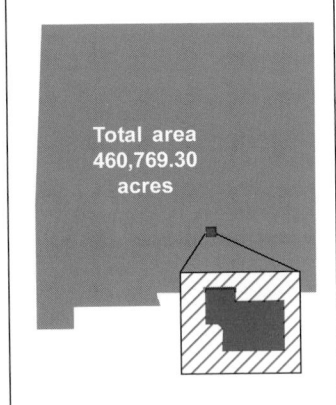

Total area
460,769.30
acres

Fuel. Natural gas is not used on most of the reservation, but lines do supply the Inn of the Mountain Gods Resort and Casino. Liquid propane gas is also available.

Water Supply. The tribal utility department, established in 2000, provides water service. The tribe operates 14 public water supply systems throughout the reservation. Of the 900 homes on the reservation, approximately half are served by the tribal sewer system and half utilize individual septic tanks.

Transportation. A privately owned school bus company transports children to area schools. Individual tribal members also own log trucking companies. Ruidoso Municipal Airport and Alamogordo Regional Airport provide private and commercial air service. Commercial air service is also available at El Paso International Airport (125 miles southwest). TNMO Buslines makes stops in Mescalero. Several major trucking lines also service the reservation. The Southern Pacific Railway provides commercial service through Tularosa (18 miles west).

Telecommunications. GTE West provides telephone service. The tribally owned Mescalero Apache Telecom provides service to about 1,000 residencies on the reservation.

COMMUNITY FACILITIES AND SERVICES

The tribe maintains a community center in Mescalero, complete with swimming pool, gymnasium, weight room, library, snack bar, and bowling alley. The Boys and Girls Club, the high school, and the library share this space. The tribe chartered the Mescalero Boys and Girls Club in 1994. It provides tribal youth with many recreational, athletic, cultural, and social activities. It sponsors an annual triathlon and hopes to sponsor a powwow and a little league bowling team in the near future. The Mescalero Apache Library offers an extensive collection of fiction, nonfiction, reference, and video materials. It also has a digitized artifact collection of the tribal museum. The tribe maintains an elderly center, a fire department, and a care center. In 1948 the tribe

organized Red Hats, the first firefighting group in the western United States.

Education. The tribe opened the Mescalero Apache School in 2003. It offers programs for tribal youth in grades K-12. The facility includes two gyms, an auditorium, metal and wood shops, and computer labs. The school is capable of serving up to 1,600 students. The curriculum at the school includes forestry and agriculture courses. College courses are available through Eastern New Mexico University's Ruidoso branch campus and the Alamogordo branch campus of New Mexico State University. Future plans call for the construction of a community college on the reservation. The tribe maintains an education center. The tribe also offers Head Start and early childhood programs.

Health Care. Health services are available through the Mescalero Service Unit. The unit includes a 13-bed Mescalero Indian Hospital and a field health program. Services include inpatient and outpatient medical, dental, lab, psychology, nutrition, pharmacy, social work, and substance abuse programs. Field health programs include surveys, clinics, environmental health, and sanitary facility construction projects. Additional health services are located in Ruidoso and Alamogordo. The tribe opened an elderly care center in 2003. It offers a 40-bed nursing home, an assisted living center with eight apartments, and a dialysis treatment facility.

ENVIRONMENTAL CONCERNS

The tribe is currently developing a long-range plan to reduce hazardous fuels and to prevent wildfires within tribal lands, the Lincoln National Forest, the Village of Ruidoso, Ruidoso Downs, and Cloudcroft. The protection of water sources is also a concern to the tribe and is being incorporated into the plan. The tribe has received program authorization under Sections 106 and 319 of the Clean Water Act. The EPA is currently reviewing the tribe's water quality standards. In 2004, the tribe received national recognition as a firewise community.

Nambé

**Nambé Pueblo
Federal reservation
Tewa
Santa Fe County, New Mexico**

Nambé Pueblo
Route 1, Box 117-BB
Santa Fe, NM 87506
505-455-2036
505-455-2038 Fax
505-455-7450 Fax

LOCATION AND LAND STATUS

Nambé Pueblo is located in northern New Mexico, 16 miles north of the state capitol of Santa Fe. The Pueblo of Nambé has been home to the tribe since around the year 1300. Its residents were declared citizens of Mexico when that country won its independence from Spain. Although the tribe had no documentary evidence of its land grant from the Spanish government, after testimony from tribal elders, the U.S. Surveyor General confirmed the grant in 1858. The grant was then patented in 1864. The pueblo is now registered as a National Historic Landmark.

PHYSICAL DESCRIPTION

The pueblo is surrounded by national forest and lies at the base of the Sangre de Cristo Mountains. Its terrain is scenic and striking, featuring waterfalls, lakes, and mountainous areas.

CULTURE AND HISTORY

The Nambé Pueblo is one of the Tewa pueblos of the northern Rio Grande region. The name is a Spanish interpretation of the Tewa word "nanbe," which roughly translates as "earth roundness." Prior to the arrival of Spanish explorers, Nambé Pueblo served as the primary cultural and religious center for the northern New Mexican pueblo communities. As such, it was of particular interest to the Spanish in their efforts to destroy the indigenous cultures of New Mexico.

In 1620, the King of Spain ordered the New Mexico pueblos to choose civil officials by popular vote to govern each pueblo. The tribes adopted the new form of government and integrated it into the traditional systems. The right of each pueblo to self-govern was subsequently recognized by the crown, and later, by Mexico and the United States. The state of New Mexico and the federal government have repeatedly recognized the status of the pueblos as sovereign nations. Over the years, the pueblo has become largely Hispanicized, though there has been a resurgence of interest in the indigenous culture within the pueblo community.

As with most of the other northern pueblo tribes, land and water rights have figured as the most critical issues facing the Nambés. The tribe petitioned the Indian Claims Commission for the return of 45,000 acres bordering the Santa Fe Ski Basin they claim were illegally taken from them by Santa Fe County in 1905 and declared part of the National Forest. After painstaking legal work, tribal counsel won a favorable ruling from the commission, which then began proceedings to determine the fair-market value of the land at the time of its confiscation. The tribe, however, rejected the government's offer of a cash payment in 1976, holding out for the land instead. This hope has yet to be realized.

The tribe was the first pueblo to accept HUD assistance for the construction of residential buildings, doing so initially in 1967. In

TRI-NM-Nbe-002

TRI-NM-Nbe-003

Nambé

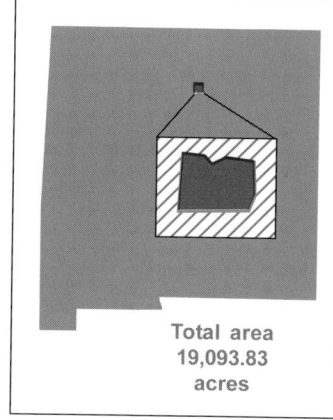

Total area
19,093.83
acres

2004, the tribe received $662,207 from HUD to be used for housing construction and management. Tribal housing continues to be comprised of traditional homes, some as many as several hundred years old, as well as contemporary structures.

In 2003, the pueblo became one of two in New Mexico authorized by the New Mexico State Legislature to sell gasoline wholesale. The impact of this arrangement resulted in the state losing over $12 million in tax revenue. The state sought to reverse the arrangement but was unable to do so. The tribe proposed a joint tax-sharing bill, which was approved. The bill mandates a 60/40 division of tax revenue. The tribe will receive $2.1 million per year and the state $3 million over the next 10 years.

GOVERNMENT

The tribal government, as with a number of the other northern pueblos, is fairly traditional in structure. The tribal council, the governing body, comprises past governors, along with two at-large elected members. Council officials are elected to two-year terms and include a governor, a lieutenant governor, a secretary-treasurer, and associated officers. The tribal council meets bimonthly. The tribe has no constitution or charter.

BUSINESS CORPORATION

In August 1994, the Nambé Pueblo was granted a federal charter and formed the Nambé Pueblo Development Corporation (NPDC). NPDC serves as the primary business arm of the tribe. Its focus is non-gaming related economic development projects. NPDC is overseen by a board of directors that includes officers, members, a chief executive officer, and support staff. Projects of the corporation include wholesale and retail gas sales and warehouse developments. Land leasing projects have included a 500 home site development for nontribal use. Future projects include a municipal solid waste landfill and recycling center and a bottled water company.

The tribe is a member of the Eight Northern Indian Pueblos Council (ENIPC), a nonprofit organization that provides community-based services to Nambé, Taos, Picuris, San Juan, Santa Clara, San Ildefonso, Pojoaque, and Tesuque Pueblos. ENIPC is the host of the Annual ENIPC Arts and Crafts Show. A collaboration of the eight northern tribes in New Mexico, the show is the largest Indian-owned and managed art show in the United States. Approximately 40,000 visitors enjoy over 500 booths featuring the works of over 1,000 local and national artists.

ECONOMY

The tribal economy is supported in large part from the tribe's agricultural enterprises. However, the pueblo's primary source of income today is wage work. Many tribal members find employment at Los Alamos National Laboratory, in Santa Fe and Española, and for the ENIPC (located at San Juan Pueblo). Local companies, such as The Yellow Leaf Trading Company, also offer employment opportunities. The tribe also benefits from its decision to opt out of the gasoline selling business.

Government as Employer. Funds derived from federal grants and contracts are used to administer the tribal government and other specific programs. These comprise a major source of tribal income and a significant source of tribal employment. At present, tribal administration employs five full galleries or studios, which employ tribal members.

Economic Development Projects. In October 2004, tribal members voted to enter the gaming industry. A proposed casino will be constructed on 15 acres between the Tesuque and Pojoaque pueblos along U.S. Highway 84/285. Tentatively called Nambé Stargate Casino, the 50,000-square-foot facility will be an outer space-themed family entertainment and gaming complex. It will include water slides, go-carts, and an indoor arcade. The casino will create a projected 400-500 jobs. The tribe expects casino revenue to provide competitive-paying jobs for tribal members, and to enable the tribe to develop an assisted living center for seniors and further educational programs for tribal members. The casino will be developed in partnership with an outside gaming management team. Plans are also underway to construct the Inn at Nambé, a bed-and-breakfast that will accommodate up to 32 visitors.

The pueblo is active in efforts to establish a national/international center in Santa Fe called the United First Nations Assembly for all Native Tribes. The mission of the center is to provide a more formal venue for tribal nations as they work towards the promotion of tribal sovereignty. The center will feature a general assembly, hall of honors, Native American Veterans Memorial, Jim Thorpe Sports Center, botanic garden, bison ranch, national gallery, and Imax theater. The proposed facility will also offer a performing arts center, a five-star hotel, and food courts. First Nations Fund Corporation, a nonprofit organization, has secured a loan commitment to initiate the project.

Agriculture and Livestock. There are close to 200 acres of agricultural lands under cultivation on the reservation, served by almost 17 miles of irrigation ditch. An additional 435 acres are available for further agricultural development. Crops grown include alfalfa, other hay crops, irrigated pasture, and vegetables. All are grown for personal or tribal consumption. The reservation also contains over 18,000 acres of rangeland, of which about half are grazeable woodland. The tribe has about 72 head of cattle and 20 horses.

Forestry. Though the pueblo sits on the edge of a national forest, the forest does not at present support any commercial timbering activities by the tribe.

Fisheries. The pueblo contains the 56-acre Nambé Lake, used extensively for recreational and sport fishing, which generates a modest amount of tribal revenue each season. The lake's fish population has had to be restocked because of the negative impact of sediment that settled in the lake as a result of the Molina Complex Fire of 2003. The U.S. Fish and Wildlife Service do-

TRI-NM-Nbe-002 Nambe Falls Recreation Area

TRI-NM-Nbe-003 Nambe tours and visitors parking sign

Total area *(BIA realty, 2004)*
19,093.83 acres

Population *2000 census*
1,764

Tribal enrollment
(BIA labor report, 2001)
643

Total labor force *2000 census*
670

Total labor force
(BIA labor report, 2001)
242

High school graduate or higher
2000 census
82.7%

Bachelor's degree or higher
2000 census
21%

Unemployment rate
2000 census
4.6%

Unemployment rate
(BIA labor report, 2001)
35%

Per capita income *2000 census*
$16, 543

Nambé

TRI-NM-Nbe-004

TRI-NM-Nbe-001

TRI-NM-Nbe-004 Nambé Lake offers fishing opportunities to tourists

TRI-NM-Nbe-001 Scenic view of Nambe Lake

nated 4,500 rainbow trout, and the tribe was able to open the lake for fishers in June 2004. However, 260 acres of tribal lands surrounding the lake were damaged from the Molina Complex Fire in 2003 and subsequent rainstorms.

Construction. A number of tribal members find employment through the region's busy construction industry. Some members are highly skilled, and others work as unskilled laborers.

Tourism and Recreation. The pueblo is a registered National Historic Landmark and is a major tourist attraction. Nambé Pueblo Tours was the only Indian-owned and operated tour company in New Mexico, providing day tours, group tours, and package tours throughout the northern pueblos. The operation has closed, but the tribe hopes to reopen it in the future.

Nambé Lake offers fishing opportunities to tourists. Nambé Falls Recreation Area is a popular summertime location for camping, picnics, and organizational gatherings. The pueblo has hosted two annual reggae concerts, a low-rider car show, hip-hop concerts, and family fun events at its waterfall recreation area. The scenic Nambé Rock Formations are popular with tourists and as a movie site. The films *City Slickers* and *Vampires* were shot at the pueblo. The tribe continues to invite film producers to consider filming movies on its lands.

The tribe hosts a number of ceremonial dances that are open to the public. The most popular occur on the Fourth of July and St. Francis of Assisi Feast Day in October.

INFRASTRUCTURE

Road access to the pueblo is provided by State Highway 503, which traverses the reservation; U.S. Highway 84/285 in the western part of the reservation; and I-25, which runs north-south within 25 miles of the reservation.

Electricity. The Jemez Mountain Electric Cooperative provides electricity throughout the reservation.

Fuel. The Gas Company of New Mexico furnishes natural gas.

Water Supply. The tribe maintains its own water and sewer systems, though some areas of the pueblo still rely on septic tanks.

Transportation. Commercial air service is available at the nearby Santa Fe and Española airports (for small craft), and at Albuquerque International Sunport, 90 miles to the south. Commercial bus lines serve Pojoaque, 6 miles from the reservation, while commercial truck lines serve the reservation directly. Passenger rail service is available in Lamy (35 miles away), while passenger service can be found in Santa Fe.

COMMUNITY FACILITIES

The tribe has a community center, which houses the tribal administration, the community health representative, and an Indian Health Service alcoholism program, among other services.

The tribe is a member of the All Indian Pueblo Council. The council is comprised of all 19 New Mexico pueblos and has been a recognized consortium since 1958. It serves as a unifying political and economic entity for the pueblos. The council's enterprises include the Santa Fe Indian School, the Indian Pueblos Federal Development Corporation (IPFDC), and the Indian Pueblo Cultural Center in Albuquerque, New Mexico. The center is co-owned by all 19 New Mexico pueblos. The Indian Pueblo Cultural Center offers demonstrations, workshops, functions, and a café that reflect all 19 pueblos. Thousands of people visit the center each year. The Santa Fe Indian School is a former BIA facility, but ownership of the school was granted to the 19 pueblos during the Clinton administration. The tribes co-manage the school, which is located on over 100 acres of trust lands in Santa Fe. IPFDC oversees major commercial developments on behalf of the member tribes. Projects have included the construction of a $30 million building for the federal government. It will begin construction of another $30 million building for lease to the government in 2005.

The pueblo is also a member of the National Congress of American Indians (NCAI). Founded in 1944, the goal of NCAI is to increase the knowledge of both the public and the federal government on issues of treaty rights, federal policy as it pertains to tribes, and tribal sovereignty. NCAI is the largest and oldest tribal government organization in the nation.

Education. Students in the pueblo attend elementary and secondary school in Pojoaque. Postsecondary educational opportunities are available at New Mexico Community College in Española and the University of New Mexico Los Alamos Branch campus. The state capitol of Santa Fe is approximately 16 miles south of the pueblo and offers a number of post-secondary education programs.

The tribe offers the Indigenous Language Institute, a nonprofit organization whose mission is to help indigenous communities restore their native languages. Classes in both the indigenous language and traditional crafts are available.

Health Care. Health care is available through Indian Health Service, Santa Clara Clinic, Santa Fe Indian Hospital, and St. Vincent Hospital in Santa Fe. A community health representative provides assistance to tribal members in attaining health services and the tribe operates its own ambulance service.

Navajo

See Arizona

LOCATION AND LAND STATUS

This remote pueblo sits high in the Sangre de Cristo Mountains of northern New Mexico, 24 miles southeast of Taos and about 50 miles north of Santa Fe. The reservation spans over 15,000 acres. All of the land is tribally owned. Picurís was founded between the years 1250 and 1300 AD. In 1864 the U.S. Congress confirmed and patented the 1689 Spanish land grant to the tribe.

PHYSICAL DESCRIPTION

Situated in the foothills of the Sangre de Cristo Mountains, Picurís Pueblo enjoys a remote and secluded location. Even today, the Picuris people often refer to themselves as the "People of the Hidden Valley." The community is located along the banks of the Rio Pueblo and is home to two lakes. Picurís is surrounded by about 12 non-Native, Hispanic villages, the largest being Peñasco, New Mexico. Many of these communities encroach upon tribal land. The community center of Picurís is defined by a clustering of adobe houses around a church, a *placita*, and a cemetery. The pueblo is bounded by a fence.

CULTURE AND HISTORY

The Picurís people have lived at their current pueblo in northern New Mexico for at least 750 years. The tribe originated in the Pot Creek area and migrated to their current site around 1250 AD. Presently, the smallest of New Mexico's northern pueblos, Picurís is believed to have been the largest at the time of Spanish contact. Due to its geographical isolation, the pueblo was missed entirely by the Coronado Expedition of 1540 and by various other expeditions. It remained undisturbed by explorers until Gaspar Castaño de Sosa's 1591 expedition. In 1680, the year of the Pueblo Revolt, the population was estimated at around 3,000. Further revolts against the Spanish led to the evacuation of the pueblo in 1696. In 1706 the Spanish returned about 300 Picuris people to the reservation from the plains.

The tribe traditionally relied on farming, raising stock, and hunting for their subsistence, but today these activities have been almost entirely abandoned. There has been a steady exodus from the reservation in recent years as members seek outside wage work on a permanent or semi-permanent basis. The sale of their traditional and fine micaceous pottery, coupled with federal aid and assistance programs, now serve as the primary sources of tribal revenue. Picurís artisans are internationally known for their pottery. Tribal members have traditionally gathered the clay used for potting from a sacred site located approximately four miles from the community. The site is currently the center of a legal suit that the tribe filed in its attempt to regain ownership of the land.

During the 1940s and 1950s, Picuris was a rather desperate place, both culturally and economically. On occasion, the BIA and Red Cross arrived to distribute emergency rations of food and clothing. During the 1960s, the pueblo's fortunes began to turn, due to the tribal council's avid pursuit of federal aid and other assistance programs. An excavation project was undertaken at the old village site, which uncovered an ancient kiva along with an astounding array of artifacts, which are now on display in the tribal museum. The tribe has also opened a restaurant serving traditional foods, is a partner in a luxury hotel in Santa Fe, and has produced a commercial video venture promoting its traditional dance ceremonies. In 1992 the tribe contracted with a small college in the eastern United States to hold its anthropological field school at the pueblo.

GOVERNMENT

While the people of Picurís recognized the 1934 Indian Reorganization Act, they have not adopted a constitution or a charter. The traditional council of ceremonial leaders was replaced in the 1960s by one in which the governor is the pueblo's chief officer. Other tribal officials include a lieutenant governor, a secretary-treasurer, a sheriff, a war captain, two war chiefs, and two *fiscales*. The tribal council meets once a week. The general council is still composed of only male tribal members, 18 years of age and over.

The tribal government maintains a law enforcement staff, a tribal court system, a parks and wildlife office, a Johnson-O'Malley staff, and an accounting and census office.

ECONOMY

Maintaining cultural beliefs, tribal practices, and the indigenous language is paramount to the tribe. As it works toward establishing a stable tribal economy, the tribe adheres to its commitment to preserving traditional cultural ways and developing environmentally sensitive enterprises. The tribe owns and operates a number of small businesses within the pueblo, including campgrounds, a museum, gift shop, and a restaurant. It is also the major partner in a luxury hotel.

Government as Employer. Various federal agencies, including the Bureau of Land Management, the BIA, and the National Forest Service, serve as the primary sources of employment on the reservation.

Agriculture and Livestock. The reservation contains 215 acres of agricultural land served by 4 miles of irrigation ditch, along with an additional 55 acres of potential agricultural land. Crops include alfalfa, timothy hay, and vegetables for home consumption.

There are nearly 8,500 acres of rangeland under study for development for commercial grazing. Picuris is a member of the Inter-Tribal Bison Cooperative and is presently managing a nucleus herd of eight buffalo. As a result of the bison program, some idle lands are being cultivated and irrigation ditches are being improved.

Forestry. In 2002 the tribe received a $200,000 Forest Service grant to develop a forest restoration program. The program, created in partnership with Sustainable Communities/Zeri, promotes the production of environmentally sensitive materials from the tribe's overgrown forests. The tribe thins the forests and uses the removed trees to produce charcoal. Smoke generated from the process preserves lumber to be used for construction. Those trees that cannot be burned for charcoal, preserved as lumber, or used for firewood, are chipped and inoculated with oyster mushroom fungicide. The fungi help to break down the wood, and the mushrooms are harvested for resale. Up to 20 percent of the fungus-woodchip mix can be used as feed for the tribe's bison herd. The tribe is investigating the possibility of using wood resins as a natural fungicide.

Fisheries. The Sangre de Cristo Mountains have a fairly healthy recreational fishery, which is popular with both tourists and local fishermen. The pueblo maintains two fishing ponds which are used extensively by non-Indians, and which generate nominal tribal revenues.

Picurís Pueblo
Federal reservation
Tano-Tigua
Taos County, New Mexico

Picurís Pueblo
P.O. Box 127
Peñasco, NM 87553
505-587-2519
505-587-1071 Fax

Total area *(BIA realty, 2004)*
15,034.49 acres

Population *2000 census*
1,801

Tribal enrollment
(BIA labor report, 2001)
324

Total labor force *2000 census*
692

Total labor force
(BIA labor report, 2001)
211

High school graduate or higher
2000 census
70.3%

Bachelor's degree or higher
2000 census
14.6%

Unemployment rate *2000 census*
9.3%

Unemployment rate
(BIA labor report, 2001)
35%

Per capita income *2000 census*
$10, 970

Picurís

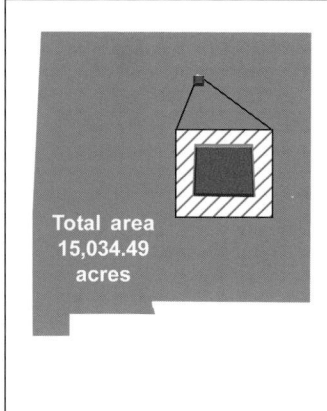

Total area
15,034.49
acres

Mining. In February 2004, the tribe filed an aboriginal title claim in the New Mexico District Court for the return of approximately 200 acres located near the pueblo. The area has served as a sacred site and a source for the clay that tribal members used for making pottery for at least 1,000 years. The tribe has never ceded ownership of the land, and the federal government has never lawfully terminated its right to title. Since the 1960s, mining companies have been permitted to mine mica at the site, steadily causing the destruction of the area and limiting tribal members' access to the clay supply. The current mine, located outside of the tribe's grant boundary at U.S. Hills, is the largest mica mine west of the Mississippi River. The suit names the current owners of the mine, Oglebay Norton Specialty Minerals, and all companies that have owned or operated mines in the area since the 1960s. The tribe is seeking restoration of the land and financial compensation. It is also hoping that this will bring attention to the efforts of Native American groups to overturn the 1872 Mining Act. This legislation has allowed mining companies to have access to tribal lands for as little as five dollars an acre.

Services and Retail. The Hidden Valley Shop and Restaurant includes a convenience store and gift shop that sells fishing equipment and licenses, souvenirs, and authentic Native American-made crafts and jewelry. The restaurant features Native Picurís and American-style dishes. The shop and restaurant are located within the Picurís Pueblo Museum. The Picurís Enterprise Board runs the tribally owned restaurant, museum, and gift shop.

Tourism and Recreation. The tribe has restored the San Lorenzo Mission located in the community. The 200-year old structure was restored using original building methods, hand-hewn corbels, vigas, handmade adobe bricks, and artifacts discovered during excavation. The tribe also provides guided tours to the ancient Village of Pot Creek, located near the current pueblo. Tours may include a traditional meal. Reservations are required. The tribe operates a museum overlooking a small lake. The museum offers exhibits of prehistoric artifacts, photographs, and art produced by regional artists. A gift shop and restaurant are located within the museum. The museum maintains the pueblo ruins, the mission, the scalp house, and several restored kivas within the pueblo. In addition, the tribe maintains two regularly stocked fishing ponds, picnic areas, and campsites.

The tribe has entered into a partnership with the Santa Fe Hospitality Company to own and operate the Hotel Santa Fe. The tribe is the majority owner of the luxury Santa Fe hotel. It features a Picurís theme and offers guests every conceivable amenity. It features 40 rooms, 91 suites, shuttle service, a swimming pool and hot tub, a café, and meeting facilities with a capacity for 120 people. The hotel provides job opportunities for tribal members and acts as a major referral source for tourists otherwise unfamiliar with the Picurís Pueblo. Hotel Santa Fe is located in the downtown historical district of the state capitol of Santa Fe.

The Picurís people celebrate numerous ceremonies and dances, many of which are open to the public, including the Sunset Dance (August 9), the San Lorenzo Feast Day (August 10), the Procession of the Virgin (held on Christmas Eve), the Matachine Dance (December 25), and the Annual Feast Day (January 25). It also hosts the High Country Arts and Crafts Festival during the month of July.

INFRASTRUCTURE

The Picurís Pueblo is accessible from Service Route 203 northeast of Highway 75.

Electricity. The Kit Carson Electric Cooperative supplies electricity.

Fuel Supply. Local distributors supply bottled gas.

Water Supply. Reservation wells supply water. A central sewer system handles sewage.

Transportation. The nearest commercial bus and air services are located in Taos and Santa Fe, though there is a small landing strip less than a mile from the pueblo. The nearest passenger train service is in Lamy, south of Santa Fe.

COMMUNITY FACILITIES AND SERVICES

The tribe belongs to the Eight Northern Pueblos Indian Council (ENPIC). ENPIC is an intertribal chartered, nonprofit organization that provides community-based services in the areas of economic development, community services, social services, employment, and training. Other members of the council include the Taos, San Juan, Santa Clara, San Ildefonso, Nambe, Pojoaque, and Tesuque pueblos.

Groundbreaking for the construction of a $1.5 million community center, equipped with a gymnasium, classrooms, and a library was scheduled for fall 1995.

Education. Children in the pueblo attend Peñasco public schools.

Health Care. Health services are available at the Taos/Picurís Indian Health Center in Taos. Formerly a member of the Santa Fe Service Unit, the center provides comprehensive medical, dental, community health, and social services programs. The seriously ill must be transported to Taos or to the USPHS Indian Hospital in Santa Fe.

ENVIRONMENTAL CONCERNS

The tribe's primary environmental concern is the protection of sacred sites within and near the pueblo. Nearby mining activities in the area have taken their toll on the land and water supply. The tribe has recently filed for the restoration of some of these areas to tribal ownership.

LOCATION AND LAND STATUS

The Pojoaque Pueblo was inhabited long before occupation by the Spanish, which began during the 1500s. Archeological studies indicate that the pueblo community was established by 900 AD. It was abandoned, however, after the Pueblo Revolt of 1680. Five families resettled there in 1706. During the first half of the 1800s, the population was greatly reduced by Mexican encroachment. The original land grant and water rights document has disappeared; hence, after the United States took over the region with the 1848 Treaty of Guadalupe Hidalgo, the tribe had to make a plea to the surveyor general of the United States to claim title to the original land grant of 13,250 acres. President Lincoln patented the grant in 1864. By 1912, the pueblo had fallen into disarray-the governor having deserted the reservation for outside employment-and tribal lands were being openly used for grazing by non-Indian ranchers. Under the 1934 Indian Reorganization Act, the land was retrieved for the tribe, and in 1946 the pueblo was finally recognized as a federal reservation. Today the pueblo covers 12,004.02 acres; this includes 36.7 miles of streams and 278 acres of forest. It is located in northern New Mexico, approximately 16 miles north of Santa Fe, near the junction of U.S. Highway 285 and State Route 64. It is the smallest of the New Mexico pueblos.

CLIMATE

The pueblo enjoys a mild climate with generally dry, sunny weather with temperature ranges from 82.4°F in summer to 56.8°F in winter. The average annual precipitation is 13.83 inches.

CULTURE AND HISTORY

Pojoaque means "Water Drinking Place," and the pueblo is one of the eight northern Tewa pueblos of New Mexico. It was once the center for all the surrounding Tewa pueblos and had ample resources to sustain both its agriculturally based economy and its cultural and religious independence. Oppression by the Spanish colonists led to the 1680 Pueblo Revolt, which successfully, if temporarily, removed the Spanish from the Rio Grande Valley. When Spanish rule was reestablished during the early 1690s, the Pojoaque people scattered to escape retribution for their participation in the revolt. By 1712, Pojoaque Pueblo's population had declined to 79; and by 1890 the pueblo had only 40 residents, a small fraction of its precontact population. During the nineteenth century, Pojoaque Pueblo was further devastated by a smallpox epidemic, lack of water, and a drastically diminished agricultural base due to encroachment by non-Indians. The pueblo virtually disappeared as an organized entity during the early twentieth century, but in 1934, after a tenacious struggle by tribal member Antonio Jose Tapia, the Commissioner of Indian Affairs called for all tribal members to return to the reservation. Under that year's Indian Reorganization Act, 14 members of tribal families were awarded lands that had passed into the hands of Mexican families.

Since that time, particularly over the past 25 years, the tribe's reliance on agriculture has diminished as the Pojoaques have focused on developing a long-term land use plan. The plan calls for a strategy of commercial development and leasing the pueblo's commercially desirable lands. This strategy has already begun paying off rather handsomely, with the phenomenal growth of the Santa Fe area and the strip along Route 84/285 to Española. Along with their other businesses, the tribe's official state tourist center and its Poeh Cultural Center and Museum have been particularly welcome signs of a successful merging of commerce with traditional tribal culture.

GOVERNMENT

The Pojoaque tribal government conforms to the provisions of the 1934 Indian Reorganization Act. It consists of a general council, which comprises all enrolled members, and a regular council, made up of elected officials. Officials include a governor, a lieutenant governor, a secretary, a treasurer, and other council members. The officials are elected to two-year terms; all enrolled tribal members 18 years of age and above are eligible to vote in council elections. The governor and his/her staff are responsible for the administration of civil and tribal law enforcement, social services, and tribal health, education, and welfare programs. The pueblo maintains a separate tribal court and has adopted a civil and criminal code.

ECONOMY

The main vehicles of the pueblo's economy are revenues from various business enterprises and federal funding of tribal programs. Aggressive economic development has helped rebuild the population at the Pojoaque Pueblo.

Government as Employer. While the tribal government directly employs a fairly modest number of tribal members, the numerous enterprises owned and operated through the tribal government employ about 720 people. Revenues from leased properties provide the largest source of funding for tribal government administration and operations.

Economic Development Projects. Pojoaque's land base is located in proximity to major Highway Route 285, and to the cities of Santa Fe and Española. Land fronting Highway 285 in the Pojoaque Pueblo Plaza is currently leased to outside commercial interests, providing dependable revenue for the pueblo. Further leasing and development projects are in the works. The pueblo is also considering a joint venture with the Hilton Hotel Corporation to build a large resort hotel. In October 1995 the pueblo purchased Santa Fe Downs, a major racetrack south of Santa Fe (off I-25); however, the pueblo's plan to reinstate quarter horse and thoroughbred racing continues to be on hold.

Agriculture and Livestock. Farming on the reservation is presently limited to about 40 acres, which are served by 2.7 miles of irrigation ditch. An additional 144 acres are available for further agricultural development. Crops produced are primarily vegetables and hay for home use. The reservation also has nearly 11,500 acres that are designated as rangeland.

Gaming. The pueblo operates the Cities of Gold Casino, a 40,000-square-foot facility with 650 slots and a 300-seat bingo hall, 2 entertainment venues, a restaurant, and 1,500 square feet of convention space. Adjacent to the casino is the 125-room Cities of Gold Hotel and the Gold Dust Restaurant. The tribe runs a shuttle service for patrons of its gaming facilities.

Construction. The tribe operates Pojoaque Pueblo Construction Services, a construction contracting company that employs about 15 tribal members. The tribe recently incorporated a manufacturing corporation, to be located in a planned industrial/business park.

Services and Retail. The tribe has a variety of businesses, including the Pojoaque Pueblo Supermarket, the Pojoaque Pueblo Plaza Shopping Center, a True Value Hardware Store franchise, and an automotive center, a home decorating center, the Po Suwae Geh Restaurant, a gravel business, a mobile home park, and a real estate office.

Pojoaque Pueblo
Federal reservation
Tewa
Santa Fe County, New Mexico

Pueblo of Pojoaque
Route 11, Box 71
Santa Fe, NM 87501

Governor's Office
17746 US 84/285
Santa Fe, NM 87506
505-455-3901
505-455-3363 Fax

Total area *(BIA realty, 2004)*
12,004.20 acres

Population *2000 census*
2,712

Tribal enrollment *(BIA, 2001)*
327

Total labor force *2000 census*
1,366

Total labor force *(BIA, 2001)*
117

High school graduate or higher
2000 census
81.8%

Bachelor's degree or higher
2000 census
23.7%

Unemployment rate *2000 census*
2.4%

Per capita income *2000 census*
$17,348

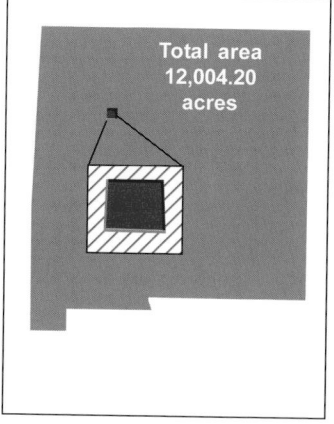

Pojoaque

TRI-NM-Poj-006

TRI-NM-Poj-005

TRI-NM-Poj-004

TRI-NM-Poj-001

TRI-NM-Poj-003

TRI-NM-Poj-004 Sign for the Poeh Center, Poeh Gallery

TRI-NM-Poj-006 Pojoaque Supermarket

TRI-NM-Poj-005 Cities of Gold Hotel with panoramic view of mountains in the background

TRI-NM-Poj-001 Gold Dust Restaurant

TRI-NM-Poj-003 The Poeh Museum and Cultural Center offers classes in traditional dance, singing, and costume making

The pueblo also owns the Cities of Gold Sports Bar, which houses a small annex casino. The Lucky Buffalo Gift Shop offers a wide range of merchandise. Additionally, the tribe leases land to a good number of non-Indian businesses.

Tourism and Recreation. Golf enthusiasts can enjoy the Towa Golf Course. The course offers 36 holes surrounded by amazing southwestern vistas. The tribe also operates a Tourist Information Center, which also sells art, pottery, jewelry, rugs, and crafts from all of the 19 New Mexico pueblos. The facility serves as a Tewa resource center for the Northern Pueblos; their vision is to create a place for the artisans of the Northern Pueblos to recreate their traditional ties to the Tewa culture and beliefs and to express these through their arts. The Poeh Museum and Cultural Center offers classes in traditional dance, singing, and costume making.

The pueblo also hosts a variety of celebrations and dances throughout the year, including the Pueblo Plaza Fiesta the first week in August, Our Lady of Guadalupe Feast Day on December 12, and The Reyes Day Dances on January 12.

INFRASTRUCTURE

The pueblo is situated on busy Highway 84/285, the major route between Santa Fe, Española, and Taos. The nearest commercial air service is located in Santa Fe, while full air service is available at Albuquerque International Sunport, about 75 miles to the south. Commercial bus and truck lines are available in Santa Fe. The nearest passenger rail service is in Lamy, 30 miles south of the reservation.

Electricity. The Jemez Mountain Electric Cooperative provides electricity.

Fuel. The Gas Company of New Mexico provides natural gas service. A local distributor provides butane.

Water Supply. The pueblo maintains its own community water system (a certified class III operator), as well as its own sewer system in the form of a total retention lagoon station

COMMUNITY FACILITIES AND SERVICES

The pueblo has a community center with tribal offices and other facilities. The Wellness Center, completed in 2002, has a gym, a library, and a senior citizen center. The pueblo also has a Boys and Girls Club. The Poeh Cultural Center is responsible for cultural regeneration. Native studio art is offered to students as part of a vocational education program.

Education. Students in the pueblo attend either the public school at Pojoaque or the Santa Fe Indian School.

Health Care. Health care is furnished through the USPHS hospital in Santa Fe. The tribe also has a community health representative, a community health resources program, and a wellness center.

ENVIRONMENTAL CONCERNS

The pueblo's major environmental concern is the possible pollution of water resources by hazardous material dumped in a landfill. The tribe's environmental office is also involved in assessing the impacts of economic development ventures.

The Pueblo of Pojoaque created the for-profit Pojoaque Pueblo Construction Services Corporation in 1993 specifically to generate revenues for and to oversee the construction and maintenance of the Pueblo's non-profit Poeh Cultural Center and Museum. By blending cultural revitalization and economic development into a unique partnership, the Pueblo is creating new revenues and employment opportunities through its construction company, and is regaining control over its cultural future through the promise of a sustained funding stream for cultural and artistic activities.

Located in northern New Mexico, at the confluence of three rivers, the Pueblo of Pojoaque is known in the native Tewa language as Po-suwae-geh, or "water-drinking place." Historically, the Pueblo was a pla ce for travelers to stop and drink water, and a cultural hub for the Tewa people. It is also a place widely known for its rich artistic tradition. Pojoaque artists have long been recognized as producers of exquisite baskets, stone carvings and polychrome pottery. Indeed, artistic expression is of central importance to Pueblo history, and Pojoaque citizens have traditionally relied on art both as a means of employment and as a cultural staple.

Pojoaque's cultural and traditional legacies have faced serious challenges throughout history. The combined consequences of small pox, Spanish conquest, lack of water and a diminished land base reduced Pojoaque's population to a mere 20 citizens by the end of the nineteenth century. As Pueblo citizens fled their homelands, its feasts and dances went into hibernation, and its unique art techniques were threatened by extinction. A turnaround began in the 1930s, however, when several families returned to Pojoaque, and the Pueblo received permanent federal recognition as part of the Indian Reorganization Act. This sparked a political, economic and cultural resurgence, which gained momentum in subsequent decades. The Pueblo's revival accelerated further in 1973 with the reintroduction of its ceremonial dance after over 100 years of dormancy. Its leaders vowed to return economic prosperity and cultural health back to the people.

By the 1980s, art and culture had become important vehicles for the advancement of Pojoaque's self-determination, and as a part of this effort, the Poeh Cultural Center was established in 1988. With nearly 900 artists and artisans living among the eight northern Pueblos, the Center provided a space where artists could display and sell their work. In 1990, Pojoaque established an educational division, Poeh Arts, to teach traditional Pueblo art forms and to provide artists with the necessary marketing skills to achieve greater economic self-sufficiency for themselves and their families. Soon, the non-profit Poeh Center became the focal point for cultural preservation and revitalization within the Tewa and Tiwa-speaking communities. Encouraged by the Center's early success and the community's support, Pojoaque's leadership embraced the vision of constructing an educational complex and major museum based upon Pueblo beliefs and perspectives, and designed and operated by Pueblo people.

As a first step, the Poeh Center opened a temporary museum in a 1,200 square foot storefront. The Center then began seeking ways to build and fund a permanent venue which could house all of the Center's programming, including a state-of-the-art museum, archives, classrooms and studio space. But making this

dream a reality would not be easy. The Center encountered a challenge familiar to art and cultural institutions everywhere - obtaining the necessary funds for facilities construction and operation. The majority of federal, state and private funding sources that support the arts and humanities tend to offer funding for programs, rather than for construction and maintenance of arts facilities. Consequently, the Pueblo considered ways to combine cultural preservation and economic development into a mutually beneficial relationship. Pojoaque's solution exemplifies creative and pragmatic vision.

In 1993, the Tribal Council created and incorporated the Pojoaque Pueblo Construction Services Corporation (PPCSC), using a two-year grant from the Administration for Native Americans for start-up costs. The tribally owned construction company was directed to work on a variety of commercial construction projects throughout New Mexico, and to use the profits for the construction and on-going maintenance of the Poeh Center's facilities. Specifically, the tribal resolution that chartered the corporation states that PPCSC's purposes are to "garner revenues and allocate thirty-five percent of the total net profits from such revenues to cultural activities including, but not limited to, the Pojoaque Pueblo Cultural Center and Museum and development of a traditional Tewa cultural center."

This unique cross-sector collaboration has been successful on many fronts. First, consistent with its original goal, the fiscal partnership provides the Poeh Center with a sustainable revenue stream. At present, the Poeh Center receives about $85,000 per year from PPCSC, funds it is using to build a new museum, which is set to open in 2002. PPCSC has also given the Center $30,000 to start an endowment. These monies - combined with the subsequently obtained matching funds, private funding and direct tribal investment - have placed the Poeh Center in good financial health. With PPCSC's growing number of contracts, the Center stands to receive substantial on-going support. Equally important, as a construction company that specializes in adobe structures, the PPCSC is building and expanding the Center and Museum, which it does without charging administrative fees or taking a profit. Since 1993, PPCSC has contributed over $300,000 in construction services, virtually eliminating the need for outside construction support. The synergistic relationship between the Poeh Center and PPCSC does not end there, however, as the Corporation's leadership believes that working on the Center has led to increased demand for PPCSC's services elsewhere.

Second, PPCSC is itself impressive. The Pueblo-owned corporation was built debt-free, is Native operated and governed, and is incorporated by the Pueblo as a New Mexico corporation under foreign corporation status. While the company was created specifically to support the Poeh Center and other cultural activities, it has accomplished this goal and much more. In its early years, PPCSC obtained contracts to construct public facilities and roads at Pojoaque; eventually it began serving all eight northern Pueblos. As the second tribal corporation in New Mexico to receive its 8(a) certification from the Small Business Administration, PPCSC bids on construction projects throughout the state. As of January 2001, PPCSC has completed 26 construction projects and had contracts for seven new contracts with a total value of $3.3 million. The company employs one tribal member full time, possesses a 13-member base crew and maintains up to

Honoring Nations
Honoree 2000

Text in its entirety from:
The Harvard Project On
American Indian Economic
Development

John F. Kennedy School
of Government
Harvard University

Pojoaque

Honoring Nations
Honoree 2000

Text in its entirety from
The Harvard Project On
American Indian Economic
Development

John F. Kennedy School
of Government
Harvard University

a 63-member crew (predominantly Native) for construction projects. Additionally, PPCSC has taught 24 residents how to build their own adobe homes and has recently been granted funding to teach seven young apprentices. Clearly, PPCSC seeks much more than profit generation and is constantly looking for ways to improve the livelihood of residents of the Pueblo of Pojoaque.

Third, from an educational and cultural preservation standpoint, the win-win relationship between the Poeh Center and PPCSC has produced remarkable results. The 26,500 square foot Poeh Center is traditionally constructed, yet possesses the latest in technology, from T1 computer lines to state-of-the-art ventilation systems and art repositories. The Center's classrooms attract hundreds of students, many of whom receive academic credit for their work through a partnership that the Center formed with Northern New Mexico Community College. The Center's instructors provide tutelage in ancient and modern techniques, as well as computer skills, and they even offer their students marketing advice. The Center also brings in children from local schools and the Pueblo's Boys and Girls Club to learn about and create art.

Finally, the Pueblo of Pojoaque's business and cultural investments are transforming the community. Not only does the Poeh Center serve as the eight Northern Pueblos' repository for repatriated sacred objects, but it is also gives community members a venue through which they can express their culture, gain additional training and even launch careers. Indeed, community members share great pride in Pojoaque's commitment to the arts. And the Poeh Center is educating the wider community about Pueblo culture. Its new museum has an anticipated annual audience of 45,000 visitors, plus an unlimited worldwide virtual audience through its on-line exhibits and collections.

In short, the Poeh Cultural Center and Museum have become what countless Pueblo citizens could only once dream of - a veritable showcase of Tewa culture and history, blending past and present in a facility that again makes Pojoaque the cultural hub of the eight Northern Pueblos. This dream became a reality because of the Pueblo of Pojoaque's strategic establishment of PPCSC, a corporation that meets the construction needs of the community and the State, serves as an important source of employment and profit, and embraces a socially responsible mission that benefits Pojoaque, other Pueblos and their non-Indian visitors.

For other American Indian nations, the Poeh Center's partnership with PPCSC serves as an inspiring example. Rather than giving up on their vision, or continue fighting an uphill battle to find private or public funds to undertake museum construction and maintenance, the Pueblo looked within itself for an innovative solution. In addition, the partnership provides a new model of how economic development and cultural revitalization can work together. Throughout Indian Country, the 1980s and 1990s have witnessed a swell in the number of tribally chartered corporations; likewise, a growing number of tribes are actively pursuing the creation or expansion of nonprofit cultural centers and museums. Few tribes, however, have integrated economic development and cultural revitalization as explicitly - or as successfully - as the Pueblo of Pojoaque.

Importantly, the experience of Pojoaque also demonstrates how the arts can serve as the vehicle for advancing self-determination. The Pueblo is cultivating new generations of artists skilled in ancient techniques and trained in modern technologies. These artists are showcasing their culture in ways that the community finds appropriate, and they are building greater knowledge and appreciation of the important contributions Pueblo people have made throughout history. Through these efforts, Pojoaque has seized control of its cultural future. The importance of such self-determination is particularly pronounced given the federal government's historical policies of assimilation and acculturation, which resulted in the loss of Native languages, traditional practices and indigenous knowledge. In stark contrast, the Poeh Center is a focal point of cultural revitalization and plays a central role in building a positive social, economic and cultural environment of which its citizens and the surrounding communities can be proud.

Lessons:
·   Cross-sector collaboration is at the cutting edge of governing, and tribal governments should seek win-win partnerships with the private and nonprofit sectors. Such partnerships can be especially fruitful for tribal art and cultural institutions.
·   Economic development and cultural revitalization can complement each other. Tribal governments have the ability to charter corporations that have both a profit motive and a social responsibility.
·   Cultural preservation and revitalization are important expressions of self-determination. Tribally owned and operated museums, cultural centers and art institutions maximize a tribe's ability to present its culture in ways it finds most appropriate.

amah

Ramah Navajo Reservation
Federal reservation
Navajo
McKinley and Cibola counties,
New Mexico

Ramah Navajo Chapter
Route 2, Box 13
Ramah, NM 87321
505-775-7140/7141
505-775-7137 Fax
ramahnavajo.com

LOCATION AND LAND STATUS
The Ramah Navajo Reservation lands lie 71 miles west of Albuquerque, New Mexico, in arid plateau country on NM Route 53 east of its intersection with NM Route 36. The lands cover 146,953 acres and are at an elevation of 7,000 feet. They are adjacent to the Zuni Reservation, El Morro and El Malpais national monuments, and the Cibola National Forest. The present outline of the Ramah lands began to take shape in the 1940s, although some individual allotments existed in the area before then. While the lands covered by this profile are often referred to as the Ramah Navajo "Reservation," it is not part of the formal Navajo Nation Reservation created by treaty in 1868. They consist of a checkerboard of lands owned by the Ramah Navajo Chapter-by individual Navajos, by the Navajo Tribe, by the State of New Mexico, and by the federal government. Irrespective of its status as a reservation, the Ramah Chapter's lands are regarded as "Indian Country" for jurisdictional purposes by the Navajo, state,

and federal governments. The chapter has a land acquisition policy intended to enhance economic development and community security by recovering traditional use areas and exploiting opportunities to purchase, exchange, and consolidate land.

PHYSICAL DESCRIPTION
Much of the land included in the Ramah Reservation is "malpais" (lava fields), unsuited for farming or grazing. The balance is generally piñon and juniper forest.

CULTURE AND HISTORY
The Ramah Navajos-the Tl'ochini Diné'e (People of the Wild Onion) were removed in the Long Walk of 1863. When released in 1868, seven families returned to the Ramah area, even though it was not part of the new Navajo Reservation set out in the treaty, thus reuniting with relatives who had avoided removal. The land

remaining after non-Indian settlement was poor and not fertile enough to sustain the level of farming enjoyed before the Long Walk, so the families dispersed to take advantage of what grazing existed. In 1934 a member donated eight acres of land in Mountain View to the BIA to use for a school. In 1964 the BIA conveyed the same land back to the Ramah Navajo Chapter. The BIA recognized the chapter as a subdivision of the Navajo Nation in 1955, and the Navajo Tribal Council recognized the chapter in 1957. However, the chapter perceived itself as being ignored by the tribal government and the Navajo Agency of the BIA, so it developed a practice of self-determination and government-to-government relationships in the 1970s. In 1972 the BIA established a separate agency for the Ramah Navajo Chapter under the Southwest Region rather than under the Navajo Region.

On the Ramah Reservation, as of the 2000 census, about one-third of the people are monolingual in English, about one-third are bilingual Navajo-English, and about one-third are primarily Navajo speakers. *(See the Navajo Nation listing in the Arizona section for further information on Navajo culture and early history.)*

GOVERNMENT

The Ramah Navajo Chapter's governing body consists of five members, elected every four years. Chapter officials include a president, vice-president, secretary-treasurer, land board member, and tribal council delegate. At one point, the president and the council delegate were also members of the Ramah Navajo School Board. The two governing bodies are closely coordinated. Chapter government emphasis is on self-determination and self-sufficiency, particularly in the areas of education and economic development.

As a practical matter, the federal government recognizes the Ramah Navajo community as a band of Indians separate from the Navajo Nation. Through the chapter or the Ramah Navajo School Board, the tribal government can apply directly for federal resources like Work Force Services and Title IV funding. As a separate agency under the BIA Southwest Region and a separate service unit under the Indian Health Service's Albuquerque Area office, Ramah Navajo Chapter receives funding directly from these federal sources and not through the Navajo Nation. The Navajo Nation funds some activities, including chapter government operations, the community services program staff, chapter official stipends, and the Navajo Nation Council delegate. However, most activities are directly federally funded.

Chapter government departments include the administrative office, tribal census office, Native American Housing and Self-Determination Act office, office of grants and contracts, community resources, facilities management, finance office and property, law enforcement and detention, office of trust services, and the chapter house. Tribal government units supporting the people of the chapter but not under chapter control are the Navajo housing authority, tribal court, and Navajo utility authority. The Navajo Nation Tribal Court, Ramah Judicial District, holds jurisdiction over criminal and civil cases in the Ramah Navajo community.

In 1970 the Ramah Navajo School Board (RNSB) was established and incorporated as a nonprofit organization to provide educational services. RNSB has four divisions: educational services, community services, health and human services, and administrative services. Beyond education, RNSB provides behavioral health, clinic, daycare, public health, emergency medical services, family services, vector control, public radio broadcasting, and wellness services to the entire community.

As a self-governing tribe (as defined by PL-638), the chapter and RNSB administer more than 20 federal programs between them. The chapter operates realty services, natural resources

and agriculture, public safety, facilities management, and administrative services. The Ramah BIA Navajo Agency still operates branch of roads, branch of forestry, and some administrative services not subcontracted with the chapter's PL-638 programs.

ECONOMY

Government as Employer. Tribal government is the largest employer on the reservation. The school board has more than 250 full-time employees; the chapter government, 50; and federal agencies, approximately 25.

Economic Development Projects. The chapter's economic policy emphasizes self-determination and self-sufficiency.

Agriculture and Livestock. The chapter has an estimated 157 family farms.

Forestry. The Ramah Navajo Chapter is developing its Woodland Project. The enterprise includes harvesting, packaging, and marketing wood products.

Mining. Because it is part of the Navajo Nation, the Ramah Navajo Chapter receives a portion of the Navajo Tribe's revenues, which are largely proceeds from mining and mineral sales. Mineral resources on the Ramah Reservation are not being exploited at this time.

Manufacturing. The reservation features the tribally run Saddle Shop, which develops a variety of leather products for marketing. The school board established Turquoise Mountain Woodworks, which designs and manufactures cabinetry and furniture. It targets wholesale markets in the southwest. The Ramah Navajo Weavers Association is a cooperative that makes traditional hand-spun and hand-woven Navajo rugs.

Real Estate/Commercial Development. The chapter-developed Pine Hill Shopping Center, which has three businesses: a gas station and convenience store, a variety store, and a self-service laundry.

Services and Retail. The chapter has five restaurants, four gas stations, four convenience stores, two trading posts, three video shops, and a self-service laundry.

Tourism and Recreation. There are several cliff dwellings in the area, as well as an ancient pueblo ruin. El Morro National Monument draws many tourists. El Morro is a rock that bears Spanish inscriptions dating from 1603, as well as more ancient Indian inscriptions. El Malpais National Monument, an area of 115,000 acres of extinct volcanoes, is nearby, as are the adjacent Zuni Reservation and the Zuni Mountains, with fishing at Ramah, McGaffee, and Bluewater lakes. Near Ramah, the chapter owns and operates the El Morro RV Park. The community hosts an annual fair, rodeo, and powwow in September, and traditional Indian ceremonies throughout the year.

INFRASTRUCTURE

Electricity. Public Service Company of New Mexico provides electricity.

Fuel. Public Service Company of New Mexico provides natural gas.

Water Supply. Water supply and waste disposal infrastructures are in place.

Transportation. State Highway 53 runs through the chapter's lands northeast to Grants, 48 miles away, where it connects with I-40, the area's principal east-west corridor. Navajo Route 125 also runs through the chapter's lands. Commercial air, bus, and rail services are available in Albuquerque, 70 miles east.

Ramah

Total area (BIA realty, 2004)
146,953.73 acres

Total area (Tribal source, 2004)
146,953 acres

Population 2000 census
2,167

Tribal enrollment
(BIA labor report, 2001)
2,463

Total labor force 2000 census
642

Total labor force
(BIA labor report, 2001)
1,334

Unemployment rate 2000 census
17.9%

Unemployment rate
(BIA labor report, 2001)
69%

High school graduate or higher
2000 census
67.1%

Bachelor's degree or higher
2000 census
15.7%

Per capita income 2000 census
$8,187

Ramah

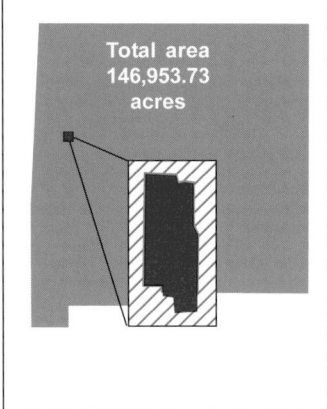

Total area
146,953.73
acres

Telecommunications. The chapter area directly receives broadcasts of five television stations from Albuquerque, three clear AM stations, and three clear FM stations. Many chapter residents have satellite dishes for direct television.

COMMUNITY FACILITIES AND SERVICES

The community operates a full array of public services and facilities largely funded by the federal government, including education, health care, law enforcement, natural resources conservation and development, and a land status management system. There are a public radio station, vocational training programs, a daycare center, a substance abuse counseling center, traditional peacemaking services, and a community planning and development program. The Chapter House is the chapter's political and administrative center. The senior citizen center, built in 1993, serves an average of 60 seniors. It has complete kitchen facilities, rest rooms with showers, and a living room with a fireplace.

Education. The Ramah Navajo School Board (RNSB) operates the Pine Hill and Ramah elementary and high schools. The schools are fully supported with school buses and facilities management. Educational services provided by RNSB include Head Start and several other early childhood programs. The University of New Mexico at Gallup and New Mexico State University at Grants provide extension courses at the Pine Hill School campus for continuing education.

The Ramah Navajo High School was dedicated in 1970, the first Indian-controlled school in the country. In 1974, new high school, elementary school, and gymnasium buildings were completed in Pine Hill, 20 miles southeast of the Ramah Village. A kindergarten

building was completed in 1976, and the library and media center built in 1980. In 1989 a new middle school and multipurpose building were constructed, and staff housing units were completed in 1995.

Pine Hill School also has a football and track stadium, a school farm with a fairground and rodeo arena, and the Pine Hill Health Center. Pine Hill School provides educational services to almost 600 students in grades K-12. Pine Hill School is fully accredited both by the State of New Mexico and the North Central Association Commission on Schools. All course offerings meet state standards. Above and beyond state requirements, a Pine Hill School student must have two more units to graduate than required by the state. In addition to the standard requirements in English, social studies, math, science, and physical education, students are required to take the Navajo language course.

Health Care. The Pine Hill Health Center was the first community-controlled health care system in the United States to function under PL 93-638. It is supervised and supported by the Ramah Navajo School Board. Services offered include outpatient, dental and field health care, and ambulance and EMT, with laboratory services on-site. The center is backed by the Black Rock Indian Medical Center in Zuni, a 45-bed general medical hospital that provides a full range of outpatient services. The hospital has 37 medical/surgical and pediatric beds and 8 obstetrical beds. The facility also houses a research center, staffed by the University of New Mexico's Departments for Pediatrics, Communicative Disorders and Medicine. Full outpatient diagnostic and treatment facilities include emergency treatment and a casting room as well as specialty services such as well baby, family planning, and mental health clinics, and substance abuse and nutrition services.

San Felipe

San Felipe Pueblo
Federal reservation
Keresan
Sandoval County, New Mexico

Pueblo of San Felipe
P.O. Box 4339
San Felipe Pueblo, NM 87001
505-867-3381
505-867-3383 Fax

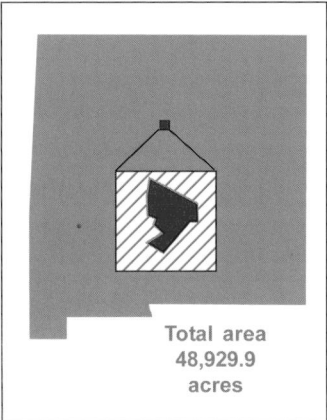

Total area
48,929.9
acres

LOCATION AND LAND STATUS

San Felipe Pueblo covers an area of 76.4 miles in Sandoval County, New Mexico, on the west bank of the Rio Grande. Albuquerque lies about 25 miles south of the pueblo; Santa Fe is about 30 miles north.

Under the provisions of the 1848 Treaty of Guadalupe Hidalgo, the United States confirmed and ratified the rights of the inhabitants of San Felipe Pueblo as Mexican citizens. Congress confirmed and patented Spain's original land grant of 30,000 acres to the tribe in 1864.

CULTURE AND HISTORY

Katishtya, or the San Felipe Pueblo, was established at its current site in northern New Mexico in 1706. Tradition has it that enemies drove the people of San Felipe to the banks of the Rio Grande from their home on the Pajarito Plateau. The people of San Felipe Pueblo speak an eastern dialect of Keres. Their identity as a people is very strong, and they consider their privacy integral to maintaining their traditional lifestyle. Ceremonial dances are held throughout the year, and the Native language is still spoken.

GOVERNMENT

The tribe was organized under the Indian Reorganization Act, but considers itself a traditionally organized tribe as well. The pueblo's governing body is the 42-member tribal council. Officers of the tribal council serve one-year terms; tribal council members (who include former governors, war chiefs, and *fiscales*) serve life terms. In 1864 San Felipe Pueblo was among those presented with a silver-headed cane by President Lincoln as a token of government-to-government recognition. The governor

keeps the cane during his term of office. The governor is appointed by the *caciques*, who also oversee traditional matters.

BUSINESS CORPORATION

The San Felipe Enterprise Board operates the tribe's casino complex with its casino, entertainment arena, and travel center.

ECONOMY

In the last decade, the tribe has entered into the gaming and tourism industries in full force. It has developed a casino complex that includes a travel center and entertainment arena. The complex attracts numerous visitors and generates a great source of revenue for the tribe. The development of the project has assisted the tribe in achieving economic self-sufficiency. The tribal economy is also supported by agricultural and mining enterprises. It also benefits from the demand for authentic, high-quality Indian jewelry that has brought national attention to the fine work produced by San Felipe artisans.

Agriculture and Livestock. The BIA aided in the development of a 12-acre tribal farm. The farm produces nearly 600 tons of alfalfa hay every year, generating between $44,000 and $48,000 annually, and it seasonally employs 4 people. Ranching and farming are important sources of income engaged in by 45 families. A total of 1,670 acres of farmland are in use.

Gaming. The tribe owns and operates San Felipe's Casino Hollywood just east of I-25 on Exit 252 between Albuquerque and Santa Fe. The casino offers 800 slots/VLTs, 15 table games, 2 restaurants, a gift shop, a video arcade, and 2 entertainment venues. A 35,000-square-foot amphitheater was recently com-

TRI-NM-SFpe-001

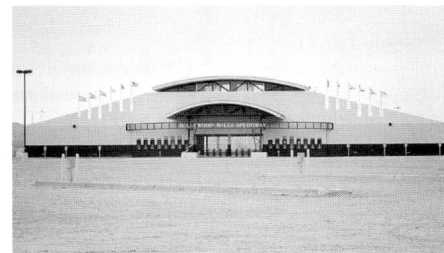

TRI-NM-SFpe-003

pleted at the casino. It seats 1,250 people. The casino employs 350 people, over 65 percent of whom are Native American. The San Felipe Travel Center and Speedway are adjacent to the casino.

Mining. The pueblo's mineral resources include gypsum, clay, scoria, coal, oil and gas, uranium, sand, and gravel. The pueblo realizes production royalties from a sand and gravel permit with San Felipe Rock and Sand Company, granted in 1986.

Services and Retail. The Travel Center, next to the casino, is a 24-hour convenience store and gas station. Amenities include a full-service truckers' lounge with showers and laundry facilities. The center offers discount gas days on Tuesdays and Fridays and provides commercial drivers with bonus coupons and discounts.

Tourism and Recreation. The tribe opened the Hollywood Hills Speedway in the spring of 2002. Adjacent to the casino, this facility is an outdoor multi-sports and entertainment venue. Facilities include an arena with a capacity for over 10,000 spectators, VIP suites, and pit access. It also features an RV park with 100 full-service hookup sites. It hosts local, regional, and national specialty events such as monster trucks, powwows, motor cross, rodeos, and concerts. The Hollywood Hills Speedway is the only casino and racetrack combination in New Mexico. The tribe projects that it can gross over $200,000 per event, and it plans to host an average of 30 events per year. Annual revenue is expected to exceed $5 million.

The tribe hosts an annual arts and crafts show in October. Vendors offer traditional foods, jewelry, arts, and crafts. San Felipe artisans are renowned for their pottery and silversmithing. They are also known for their intricate beadwork using heishe, handcut beads made of semiprecious stones, turquoise, shell, and red coral.

The pueblo hosts numerous ceremonies and dances throughout the year, many of which are open to the public, including the

Green Corn Dance held during St. Philip's Feast Day in May. The San Felipe Church is an outstanding example of early Franciscan mission architecture, and the town's unique sunken plaza provides an unusual setting for dances.

INFRASTRUCTURE

Interstate 25, the region's main north-south artery, is about five miles southeast of San Felipe Pueblo.

Electricity. Public Service Company of New Mexico supplies electricity.

Fuel. Residents purchase bottled gas.

Transportation. Passenger rail and bus service are available in Bernalillo, 13 miles south. The nearest commercial air service is at Albuquerque International Sunport, 30 miles south.

COMMUNITY FACILITIES AND SERVICES

The tribe operates a disabled and elderly program, senior companion program, and senior outreach program, each offering a range of services for tribal elders. Traditional activities are held in a tribal building in the village.

Education. San Felipe Elementary, a BIA school, sees to educational needs through the sixth grade. Junior high and high school-aged tribal members attend Bernalillo public schools. The tribe also maintains a Head Start program. The tribe maintains a program that brings school children and tribal elders together in order to perpetuate the cultural teaching traditions.

Health Care. Services are available to tribal members through the Santa Fe Service Unit. With clinics located in the Santa Fe, Santa Clara, Santo Domingo, and Cochiti pueblos, the program offers comprehensive medical, dental, community outreach, and behavioral services. Inpatient care is provided by the Santa Fe Indian Hospital in Santa Fe and the University of New Mexico Indian Hospital.

TRI-NM-SFpe-001 Speedway viewing stand near Hollywood Casino

TRI-NM-SFpe-003 The Hollywood Hills Speedway is the only casino and racetrack combination in New Mexico

Total area *(BIA realty, 2004)*
48,929.9 acres

Population *2000 census*
3,185

Tribal enrollment
(BIA labor report, 2001)
3,131

Total labor force *2000 census*
690

Total labor force
(BIA labor report, 2001)
1,544

High school graduate or higher
2000 census
68.3%

Bachelor's degree or higher
2000 census
6%

Unemployment rate *2000 census*
17.8%

Unemployment rate
(BIA labor report, 2001)
34%

Per capita income *2000 census*
$9,266

San Ildefonso

Pueblo of San Ildefonso
Federal reservation
Tewa
Santa Fe County, New Mexico

San Ildefonso Pueblo
Route 5, Box 315-A
Santa Fe, NM 87501
505-455-2273
505-455-7351 Fax

Total area *(BIA realty, 2004)*
28,179.92 acres

Total area *(Tribal Source, 2004)*
26,198 acres

Total population *2000 census*
1,524

Tribal enrollment
(BIA labor report, 2001)
628

Total labor force *2000 census*
731

Total labor force
(BIA labor report, 2001)
383

High school graduate or higher
2000 census
82.9%

Bachelor's degree or higher
2000 census
21.7%

Unemployment rate *2000 census*
6.4%

Unemployment rate
(BIA labor report, 2001)
20%

Per capita income *2000 census*
$14,888

LOCATION AND LAND STATUS

The Pueblo of San Ildefonso spans some 26,198 acres in northern New Mexico, about 18 miles northwest of Santa Fe, on the Parijito Plateau, which rests upon the eastern apron of the Jemez Mountains. The Rio Grande cuts through pueblo land, providing irrigation to the reservation's low-lying fields. The pueblo's most striking topographical feature is Black Mesa, which rises dramatically to separate the Pueblo of San Ildefonso from the Pueblo of Santa Clara.

Like most of the other New Mexican pueblo tribes, the San Ildefonso Tewas' rights were recognized and confirmed under the Treaty of Guadalupe Hidalgo between the United States and Mexico in 1848. The surveyor general for the United States confirmed the grant of 17,292 acres in 1858. The grant was patented in 1864. Since that time, additions to the reservation have been made by congressional acts.

CULTURE AND HISTORY

The Tewa Indians of San Ildefonso settled near the site of the present-day pueblo around the year 1300, occupying villages known today as the ruins of Sankewi, Otowi, and Potsuwi. After the 1694 attack by the Spanish General Don Diego de Vargas, the tribe sought refuge atop Black Mesa, where it heroically repelled repeated attacks and withstood captivity. After two years, the tribe surrendered and resettled just north of their previous home. European contact brought diseases that decimated their numbers. By 1864, census figures showed only 161 remaining pueblo residents. By the early twentieth century, factionalism between the tribe's summer and winter clans resulted in partitioning the tribe into the North and South Plaza People, each maintaining their own secular and religious officers.

Prior to 1848 and the Treaty of Guadalupe Hidalgo, the tribe subsisted on agriculture and hunting, with the barter system serving as their primary method of exchange. In the wake of the treaty, the entire southwestern United States experienced a great influx of traders and merchants, who introduced a cash and wage economy. This trend continued, and by World War II many tribal members sought work off the reservation, with a number employed at the laboratories in nearby Los Alamos or in Santa Fe. This remains the case today, though the emergence of a pueblo-based arts and crafts cottage industry has arrested the trend to a degree.

Pottery, the backbone of the tribe's arts and crafts market, has held great significance for the tribe for many centuries. By the late 1800s, potters at San Ildefonso were well-known for creating a highly regarded polychrome variety. By the 1920s, a pair of tribal members, Maria and Julian Martinez, developed a new strain of pottery, which was inspired by shards of ancient pottery excavated by archaeologists at a nearby ruin. This new highly polished black or red ware has become a lucrative source of income today for many tribal craftspeople, as well as a source of community pride.

GOVERNMENT

The tribal council is composed of appointed officials, though the governor is elected to a two-year term. It is the governor's job to mediate relationships with the outside world, as well as to mediate internal disputes. Council members also include first and second lieutenant governors, the sheriff, the deputy sheriff, the first and second war captains, the assistant war captains, and the two *fiscales*. The council meets monthly.

San Ildefonso Pueblo is also a member of the Eight Northern Indian Pueblos Council (ENIPC), which is located at San Juan Pueblo, the headquarters for the association. The ENIPC was established to assist the northern pueblos in the areas of health, education, welfare, and economic development.

ECONOMY

Due to the historic nature of the Pueblo of San Ildefonso, tourism, recreation, and retail services are major contributors to the tribe's economy. Tribal government, agriculture, livestock, and mining the pueblo's mineral resources round out the San Ildefonso Tribe's successful economic portfolio.

Government as Employer. The tribal government employs close to 30 tribal members through its various facets, including administration, educational services, and other operations. The ENIPC is also a limited source of employment, administering the pueblo's senior center, for instance.

Agriculture and Livestock. There are approximately 500 acres of developed agricultural lands on the reservation, served by over 11 miles of irrigation ditches. An additional 700 acres of land are suitable for agricultural development. Crops include alfalfa and other hay crops, vegetables, and some fruit, generally for personal consumption. Additionally, the reservation has approximately 25,000 acres of rangeland, of which just over half are grazeable woodlands. The tribe has approximately 250-300 head of cattle, most of which are sold at local auction.

Forestry. While nearly half of the reservation's acreage comprises woodlands, only about 700 acres comprise commercial timberlands. There is presently little in the way of development taking place.

Fisheries. The reservation contains the 4.5-acre San Ildefonso Lake, which is well-stocked with rainbow trout and catfish from the Mescalero National Fishing Hatchery. Permits sold through the tribal office generate modest annual revenues.

Mining. Commercial mineral resources on the reservation include sand, gravel, and pumice.

Manufacturing. Aside from the manufacturing jobs that employ a number of tribal members outside the reservation (mostly in Los Alamos and Santa Fe), San Ildefonso Pueblo is well-known for its skilled craftspeople, who produce pottery, embroidery, paintings, and clothing. Of these, the pueblo's matte black-on-black pottery, with its traditional designs featuring a water serpent or feathers, is the most highly regarded. The reservation houses numerous pottery studios.

Services and Retail. Service outlets for the pueblo's considerable production of arts and crafts comprise the bulk of the retail and wholesale business sector on the reservation. Some of these businesses include Aguilar Arts, which specializes in red and black pottery; Popovi Da Studio of Indian Arts, which offers pottery, paintings, and kachinas; and Juan Tafoya Pottery and Torres Indian Arts, both of which feature the local pottery. The pueblo's Visitor and Information Center houses a gift shop, which features local pottery, embroidery, and other Native arts and crafts. The tribe also owns and operates the White Rock Shell Service Station and convenience store.

TRI-NM-Si-076

TRI-NM-Si-079

TRI-NM-Si-073

TRI-NM-Si-080

TRI-NM-Si-082

TRI-NM-Si-077

San Ildefonso

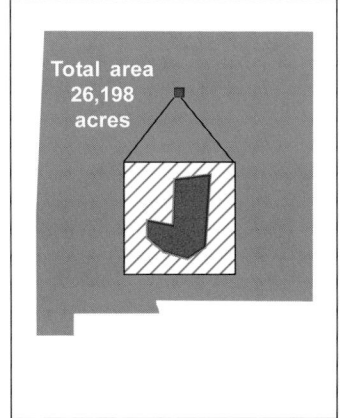

Total area
26,198
acres

TRI-NM-Si-076 Historic Marker for the Pueblo of San Ildefonso

TRI-NM-Si-079 Scenic view of Black Mesa

TRI-NM-Si-073 Village houses, shops and tree

TRI-NM-Si-080 Village at San Ildefonso

TRI-NM-Si-082 Side view of San Ildefonso Pueblo Church

TRI-NM-Si-077 South Kiva at San Ildefonso Pueblo

Tourism and Recreation. The pueblo, listed as an historic district on the National Register of Historic Places, is a popular tourist attraction; the tribe realizes considerable revenues from entrance fees. The San Ildefonso Pueblo Museum, located at the governor's office, features exhibits of local arts, embroidery, and the renowned pottery-making process. In addition, the tribe celebrates numerous dances and feast days throughout the year, including San Ildefonso Feast Day on January 23, St. Anthony's Feast Day in mid-June, Corn Dances in early September, and the Matachine Dance on December 25. Finally, the Annual Northern Pueblo Artist and Craftsman Show, featuring outstanding displays of artistic talent and drawing people from around the country, takes place the third weekend in July. The tribe's fishing lake is open on a seasonal basis, and picnic facilities are available.

INFRASTRUCTURE
Road access to the reservation is provided by State Roads 502 and 30, which cross it directly. The busy U.S. Highway 285 runs north-south about 10 miles east of the reservation. Limited commercial air service is available in nearby Santa Fe, while Albuquerque International Sunport (about 80 miles south) offers flights and connections to anywhere in the world. Commercial bus and train lines are available in Santa Fe, while truck lines serve the pueblo directly.

Electricity. The Jemez Mountain Cooperative provides electricity to the pueblo.

Fuel. The Gas Company of New Mexico provides gas service.

Water Supply. Wells provide water, and U.S. Public Health Service septic tanks provide sewer service.

COMMUNITY FACILITIES AND SERVICES
The tribe operates the Tewa Community Center and a senior citizens center and program, which are administered through ENIPC.

Education. The pueblo hosts a BIA elementary school, though a number of tribal children attend the Pojoaque Valley Schools. Junior high and high school students attend either the Pojoaque public schools, St. Catherine's in Santa Fe, or the Santa Fe Indian School. A majority of high school graduates attend postsecondary or vocational schools.

Health Care. Tribal members obtain health care through the USPHS Hospital in Santa Fe and the Santa Clara Health Clinic. The pueblo community also maintains a community health representative to assist individuals in obtaining medical services.

ENVIRONMENTAL CONCERNS
The tribe's environmental office is funded under a grant from EPA; programs include air and water quality. The pueblo is situated along the transportation corridor of nuclear waste shipments from Los Alamos National Laboratory to the repository in Carlsbad, New Mexico, and it receives funding from the U.S. Department of Energy.

San Juan

San Juan Pueblo
Federal reservation
Tewa
Rio Arriba County, New Mexico

Pueblo of San Juan
Governor's Office
P.O. Box 1099
Santa Fe, NM 87566
505-852-4400
505-852-4820 Fax

Total area (BIA realty, 2004)
12,236.33 acres

Total area (Tribal source, 2004)
12,237 acres

Population 2000 census
6,748

Population
(Tribal source/BIA labor report, 2001)
2,723

Total labor force 2000 census
2,951

Total labor force
(Tribal source, 2004)
974

High school graduate or higher
2000 census
68.8%

High school graduate or higher
(Tribal source, 2004)
31.8%

Bachelor's degree or higher
2000 census
8.5%

Unemployment rate 2000 census
7.6%

Per capita income 2000 census
$12,083

LOCATION AND LAND STATUS

San Juan Pueblo spans 12,237 acres in Rio Arriba County, approximately 30 miles north of Santa Fe. It sits in the Rio Grande Valley, along the Rio Grande, and features an abundance of relatively flat farmland. The tribe has occupied the site of the pueblo for at least 700 years. The original Spanish land grant to the pueblo was confirmed in 1689. The United States reconfirmed this grant (then an area of 16,174 acres) in 1858 and patented it in 1864.

CULTURE AND HISTORY

The Ohkay Owingeh, also known as San Juan Pueblo, is the largest of the six Tewa-speaking villages and is known as the "mother village of the Tewa Nation." The Spanish named it San Juan Bautista (St. John the Baptist) in 1598; in the same year they established the first Spanish capitol in New Mexico at the site of the old Tewa Pueblo on San Juan Pueblo land. In 1689, the Spanish officially confirmed the pueblo by designating 17,544 acres as the San Juan Pueblo Land Grant. Though the Treaty of Guadalupe Hidalgo guaranteed the tribe's title to this land in 1848, the land base steadily decreased through the late nineteenth and early twentieth centuries due to encroachment by outsiders. The Pueblo Lands Act of 1924 reduced it further, to 12,234 acres. Though all the land is considered trust land, individual pueblo families were assigned pieces of land during the 1930s, which could be left to descendants or sold or traded to other pueblo residents living in the village. Some of the pueblo lands were left as common grazing lands.

Until World War II, farming, raising cattle, and trade had served as the backbone of the San Juan tribal economy. By the 1960s, wage work, mostly in Santa Fe, Espanola, or Los Alamos, had become dominant. In 1965 the Eight Northern Pueblos Community Action Program was created, by which the San Juan Pueblo obtained various grants for construction projects. The projects included a youth center, a senior center, tribal offices, a tribal court, a warehouse, and a post office. A federal grant funded the Eight Northern Pueblos Artisans Guild at San Juan from 1972 to 1982. Many tribal members support themselves as independent artists and craftspeople. Tribal members operate and staff the Oke Oweenge Cooperative, an enterprise that holds art classes and workshops, as well as studio, gallery, and retail sales space. The tribe continues to host traditional ceremonies, some open to the public and some reserved for pueblo members only. San Juan tribal culture, as a whole, follows this pattern, with the members maintaining the most meaningful parts of their traditional culture while adapting aspects of Anglo culture that enhance their ability to survive and prosper.

GOVERNMENT

The San Juan Pueblo Tribe has no charter or constitution. The tribal government comprises three kinds of officials: civil officers, tribal religious leaders, and Catholic Church officers. The Spanish established the civil government in the early 1600s, and it includes a governor, two lieutenant governors, and a sheriff. These officials are appointed to one-year terms by the tribal religious leaders and may be appointed any number of times. The tribal council is comprised of the present governor, lieutenant governors, a sheriff, all former governors, and the heads of the religious societies of the village. A personnel selection committee selects various tribal program administrators. Active religious leaders are responsible for selecting other Native officers, as well as the civil and Catholic officers. In 1976, the tribe established a tribal court. Federal and BIA grants over the past two

decades have resulted in the construction of numerous tribal facilities and projects. These projects have been a source of employment for a number of tribal members.

ECONOMY

Tribal government, agriculture, livestock, gaming, and tourism are the mainstays of the San Juan Pueblo's economy. Construction of an airport and plans for an industrial park are two of the ways that the tribe is working toward economic growth and attracting more industries to the pueblo.

Government as Employer. The Eight Northern Pueblos Indian Council Offices, located in San Juan Pueblo, employs approximately 34 persons. Various tribal businesses employ around 40 people. The tribal government directly employs 33 tribal members. The tribal education and health departments also employ a large number of members.

Economic Development Projects. The pueblo is planning a 500-acre industrial park. In 2004, construction began on an airport to accommodate private planes and jets.

Agriculture and Livestock. The San Juan Pueblo consists of about 1,200 acres of agricultural lands, served by 13 miles of irrigation ditch, and an additional 800 acres available for agricultural development. Crops include chili, vegetables, alfalfa hay, and orchard fruit. Much of these are consumed within the pueblo, though some are sold at area farmers' markets. The pueblo also has about 10,000 acres of rangeland, with an additional 1,000 acres of grazeable woodlands. The tribe has about 50 head of cattle.

Forestry. The reservation has over 1,000 acres of woodlands, which are not presently considered a viable commercial resource.

Gaming. The tribe owns and operates the Best Western Ohkay Casino Resort, located about two miles north of Española. The 30,000-square-foot establishment employs 450 people. It offers 700 slots and 4 table games in its gaming facility; 20,000 square feet of convention space; and a 101-room hotel including 24 luxury suites, a restaurant, a gift shop, and entertainment. The tribe also owns and operates two bingo halls: Indian Country Bingo and Stroud Bingo.

Fisheries. The San Juan Tribal Lakes and the pueblo's eight miles of streams provide excellent recreational fishing opportunities.

Construction. In 1995 the pueblo established Tsay Construction, which specializes in building custom homes and in decommissioning and demolition projects at Los Alamos National Laboratory.

Mining. The only commercially viable mineral resources on the pueblo are sand, gravel, and adobe materials.

Services and Retail. Tribally owned businesses include the Shell Service Station and convenience store, Aguino's Arts and Crafts Shop, Walk-In-Beauty Fiber Arts clothing store, an RV park, and a travel center. Additionally, over 100 tribal members work independently as artists and craftspeople, and selling their work through the Oke Oweenge Cooperative.

Tourism and Recreation. The San Juan Tribal Lakes provide excellent fishing and picnicking opportunities. The Oke Oweenge artisans' cooperative features locally produced art of all kinds. The tribe also hosts numerous dances and ceremonies throughout the year. These include the Buffalo, Deer, and Animal Dances in February; San Antonio's Feast Day on June 13; San Juan's Feast Day on June 23-24; Harvest Dances in September; the Matachina Dance on December 28-29; and the Turtle Dance on December 26. The pueblo is a stunning historical and archeological site and a popular spot for visitors at any time of year.

INFRASTRUCTURE

Electricity. Provided by The Jemez Mountain Cooperative.

Fuel. Public Service Company of New Mexico and Snow Bird Enterprise gas line stations supply the pueblo's fuel.

Water Supply. The pueblo's utility board provides the pueblo with water and a sewer system.

Transportation. Santa Fe, 24 miles to the south, provides full commercial air service and commercial bus and truck lines. Bus and truck service is also available in nearby Española. The Santa Fe Railroad serves the entire area.

COMMUNITY FACILITIES AND SERVICES

Community facilities include the Tribal Lakes Recreation Area and the Blue Rock Office Complex, which serves as the headquarters of the Northern Pueblos Agency of the BIA. This facility also serves the eight northern Indian pueblos.

Education. The pueblo has a Head Start program, a BIA day school and a public day school, and two grade schools. Junior high and high school students largely attend the public schools in Española, Pojoaque, Mesa Vista, and McCardy, while some go to boarding school at the Santa Fe Indian School in Santa Fe.

Health Care. Tribal residents receive full-service health care through the USPHS Hospital in Santa Fe. Since 1970, San Juan Pueblo has had a community health representative program funded by Indian Health Service. The New Moon Lodge, an alcohol-treatment center, has been located in the pueblo for about 10 years.

ENVIRONMENTAL CONCERNS

San Juan Pueblo is concerned with preatrophyte removal of non-Native tree species, illegal dumping, floor control, and water quality. The pueblo is working collaboratively the Corps of Engineers, Bureau of Reclamation, BIA, U.S. Forest Service, and NEA to address these concerns.

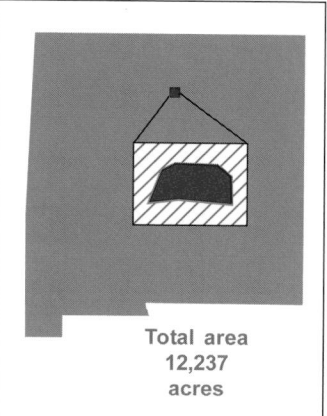

Total area
12,237
acres

Sandia

Sandia

LOCATION AND LAND STATUS

Sandia Pueblo spans approximately 23,000 acres in north-central New Mexico, north of the city of Albuquerque. The reservation lies on the east side of the Rio Grande Valley and the western side of the Sandia Mountains.

The U.S. Congress confirmed the original Spanish land grant of 1748 to the tribe in 1858 and patented it in 1864. However, the official government surveyor only surveyed the land to the foothills of the Sandia Mountains, rather than to the crest, the "Sierra Madre" or main ridge, as defined in the original land grant. Congress thus granted the tribe a reduced land base, setting the stage for ongoing attempts during the twentieth century to recover access to these thousands of acres of lost land.

To help resolve this issue, the United States Congress passed the T'uf Shur Bien Preservation Trust Act in 2003. The Act establishes the 9,890-acre T'uf Shur Bien Preservation Trust Area within the Cibola National Forest and Sandia Mountain Wilderness. Although the U.S. Forest Service continues to administer the area, the pueblo's rights and interests are to be recognized and protected in perpetuity. The pueblo may practice traditional and cultural uses in the area, and the U.S. Forest Service must consult with the pueblo regarding any new uses.

PHYSICAL DESCRIPTION

The rugged west face of these 10,700-foot Sandia Mountains and the Rio Grande are the reservation's most prominent physical features. Much of the remaining topography consists of brush- and piñon-covered foothills and a sandy plain that slopes gradually to the fertile agricultural lands along the Rio Grande.

CULTURE AND HISTORY

The Sandia people have resided at T'uf Shur Tu', "Green Reed Place," since at least 1300 AD. Originally, Sandia Pueblo was one of approximately 20 pueblo cultures stretching south along the Rio Grande in the province that Spanish explorer Coronado called Tiguex. Sandia was not identified by its current name until the seventeenth century when Spanish settlers dubbed it Sandia ("watermelon" in Spanish) in reference to the deep red color that the mountains often appear at sunset. Sandia became a Spanish settlement during the 1600s, when the Mission San Francisco de Sandia was established.

The many villages of the Tiguex suffered under Spanish occupation, with many sites becoming depopulated and reduced in geographical extent. In response to its mistreatment, Sandia participated in the Pueblo Revolt of 1680. The Spanish burned the pueblo as they retreated, and Governor Antonio de Otermin burned it again during early attempts at reconquest. The people of Sandia sought refuge with the Hopis, and they temporarily settled in the Village of Payupki on Second Mesa. The Sandia people were finally granted their petition to resettle in their traditional territory in 1748, when a land grant established the boundaries of the pueblo.

The pueblo's old village has a central plaza. New housing units have been built on the hills to the east of the old village. Many families maintain a home in the village, which they use during feast days, and another home in the newer residential areas. The original site of the San Francisco de Sandia mission now serves as the pueblo's cemetery. The second mission church, Nuestra Señora de Los Dolores y San Antonio de Sandia, is located at the northern end of the old pueblo. A third church, San Antonio de Padua, built in 2001, has received architectural awards.

Traditional practices are maintained, and the Tiwa language is taught to tribal youth. Some tribal elders are trilingual, speaking Tiwa, Spanish, and English.

Sandia Pueblo
Federal reservation
Bernalillo and Sandoval
counties, New Mexico

Pueblo of Sandia
481 Sandia Loop
Bernalillo, NM 87004
505-867-3317
505-867-9235 Fax
sandiapueblo.nsn.us

Sandia

Total area *(BIA realty, 2004)*
22,890.28 acres

Population *2000 census*
379

Tribal enrollment
(BIA labor report, 2001)
485

Total labor force *2000 census*
1,924

Total labor force
(BIA labor report, 2001)
252

High school graduate or higher
2000 census
67.1%

Bachelor's degree or higher
2000 census
9.6%

Unemployment rate *2000 census*
5.5%

Unemployment rate
(BIA labor report, 2001)
1%

Per capita income *2000 census*
$11,508

TRI-NM-San-002

TRI-NM-San-003

TRI-NM-San-005

TRI-NM-San-004

TRI-NM-San-002 hayfield with the colorful Sandias in the background

TRI-NM-San-003 Serene fishing spot at Sandia Lakes

TRI-NM-San-005 Hotel construction in process at Sandia Casino Resort

TRI-NM-San-004 The Bien Mur Indian Arts and Crafts Market, a wholesale and retail outlet of Native American goods

GOVERNMENT

The Pueblo of Sandia continues to honor traditional governing roles. The tribe is governed by a governor, a lieutenant governor, and governing staff. A war chief and lieutenant war chief also exercise authority within the pueblo and are responsible for all religious and ceremonial activities.

The tribe has a tribal council composed of former governors and war chiefs, who serve life terms. The governor, lieutenant governor, war chief, and lieutenant war chief are appointed for one-year terms. The selection process usually occurs around December 28 of each year, with new officers being sworn in on January 1. The pueblo also maintains its own court system (with the lieutenant governor serving as chief judge) and law enforcement department.

ECONOMY

The tribal economy is supported by leasing tribal lands, by tribal retail enterprises and, most significantly, by tribal gaming facilities. One of the pueblo's objectives is to increase its economic base by developing businesses on the reservation's southern boundary where it meets the expanding metropolitan area. The southern border area consists of approximately 1,550 acres of land held in trust by the federal government and 450 acres of land held in fee simple by the pueblo. This area has been planned for retail, commercial, industrial, recreational, and residential development.

In 2003 the tribal council adopted development guidance standards for the southern border area. The development guidance standards include standards and guidelines for site planning and design, and they define the process by which development occurs. The pueblo requires that all proposed developments go through a process that includes review by staff, the pueblo governor, and the tribal council.

Government as Employer. Sandia Casino employs approximately 1,450 people; tribal administration employs an additional 300 people. The casino alone was one of the top 20 employers in the Albuquerque metropolitan area in 2004. In fall 2005, the pueblo will be opening a hotel and new restaurants associated with the casino, and it will be hiring at least 400 new employees. In addition to the direct employment that these enterprises provide, and the revenue the pueblo shares per its compact with the state, the Albuquerque metropolitan area and the state of New Mexico also benefit from the economic multiplier effect created by jobs and commerce.

Agriculture and Livestock. Agriculture and livestock continue to be major sources of income for some tribal families. The pueblo is in the process of implementing a range management technique known as the savory grazing method' to improve overall range and cattle management. This technique is designed to improve natural vegetation cover to the surface area without a decrease in livestock numbers. The tribe operates a buffalo preserve and manages a small herd. The 107-acre site is located across from the tribal casino off I-25 and Tramway Road in Albuquerque.

Gaming. The tribe owns and operates Sandia Casino, just north of Albuquerque. The casino is a successful gaming enterprise that employs about 1,450 persons. It offers over 1,700 slot machines/VLTs, table games such as blackjack, roulette, craps, Pai Gow poker, and mini baccarat, and features the largest poker room in New Mexico. The casino also offers bingo and keno. The casino houses an all-you-can-eat buffet, fine dining at Bien Shur restaurant, a snack bar, and banquet facilities for up to 300 guests. Sandia Casino's outdoor amphitheater hosts local and national entertainment. The amphitheater offers tiered seating, excellent sight lines, and a view of the Sandia Mountains as a backdrop. Sandia Casino sponsored the third annual Native American Music Awards in 2003.

Sandia Casino will become the Sandia Casino Resort with the opening of a 228-room resort hotel in late 2005. Rooms will reflect the pueblo's heritage, and they will feature views of the Albuquerque skyline and Sandia Mountains. The resort will also include more than 35,000 square feet of meeting, convention, and entertainment space; a new steak-house restaurant, a roof-top restaurant and lounge, an expanded buffet; and a 12,000-square-foot spa. Sandia Casino Resort will be associated with a championship 18-hole public golf course designed by Scott Miller and managed by OB Sports.

The Pueblo of Sandia's gaming enterprises have a substantial impact on the regional economy. Sandia Casino and the Pueblo of Sandia also have an active giving program to support local and national charities, sports, and the arts. Support has been provided to the American Diabetes Association, Albuquerque Public Schools Character Counts program, the Hispano Chamber of Commerce, the Muscular Dystrophy Association Telethon, the Multiple Sclerosis Society, and the Presbyterian Ear Institute.

Real Estate/Commercial Development. Pueblo of Sandia also realizes income from leasing of land to various interests. A partial listing of lessees includes Sandia Peak Tram Company; Clear Channel Outdoor; and Los Amigos Round-Up, an off-site entertainment venue and western banquet barn.

Services and Retail. The tribe owns the Bien Mur Indian Arts and Crafts Market, a wholesale and retail outlet of Native American goods. The market is one of largest Native American-owned and operated stores in the southwest. The Bien Mur Travel Center, which offers gasoline and diesel fuel, a deli and convenience store, discount cigarette sales, and an automatic car wash, opened in fall 2003.

There are also tribally owned or tribally affiliated businesses on the reservation. These include: Tiwa 66, a privately owned gas station, convenience store, smoke shop, and gift shop, employing 12 people; and Jack's Smokeshop, a retail tobacco products outlet employing four people.

Tourism and Recreation. In addition to the upcoming Sandia Casino Resort and Golf Course, the tribe operates the Sandia Lakes Recreation Area, a 70-acre area that includes three fishing lakes stocked with trout and catfish, picnic areas, meeting space, a playground, shelters, a bait and tackle shop, and a natural trail along the Rio Grande *Bosque* (woodlands).

The tribe hosts several dances and celebrations throughout the year. Events that are open to the public include King's Day on January 6, and the Feast of St. Anthony (honoring the pueblo's patron saint) on June 13.

INFRASTRUCTURE
Electricity. The Public Service Company of New Mexico provides electricity.

Fuel. The Public Service Company of New Mexico furnishes gas service.

Water Supply. The pueblo provides water and sewer services to the tribal residential and business community. Irrigation water, stored at El Vado Lake, flows into the Rio Grande from which it is fed into irrigation canals for use by the pueblo's farmers.

Transportation. Road access to Sandia Pueblo is convenient, as I-25 cuts through the reservation in a north-south direction with one major exit and entry point. I-40 runs east-west about six miles south of the reservation. Commercial air service is available at nearby Albuquerque International Sunport. Albuquerque also features a full range of commercial bus and trucking services. Amtrak operates a passenger terminal in Albuquerque, while rail freight service is available from the Atchison, Topeka, and Santa Fe railroads.

COMMUNITY FACILITIES AND SERVICES
Quality of life has improved greatly in recent years, with the assistance of gaming revenues. Sandia Pueblo maintains a wellness center, a swimming pool, tribal government offices, and an elderly center. The Sandia Wellness Center includes a weight room, swimming pool, computer room, photography darkroom, and a gym. The tribe also operates a child care center for infants and children to age three.

Education. Tribal youth are able to attend the school of their choice from grades kindergarten through college, grades permitting, and using funds from a tribal scholarship program.

Health Care. The Sandia Pueblo Medical and Dental Clinic, a 10,400-square-foot facility built primarily with gaming revenues, offers medical, chiropractic, acupuncture, and dental services to the Sandia and Santa Ana pueblos. The Kellogg Foundation honored the facility as a model of rural health services. Health care is also available through the Indian Health Service and a wide variety of area health care providers including clinics and hospitals in metropolitan Albuquerque.

ENVIRONMENTAL CONCERNS
The deterioration of the Rio Grande is of major concern to the Pueblo of Sandia. In the past several decades, the river has become one of the most endangered rivers in the country. While the tribe has traditionally relied upon the river for agricultural, recreational, and cultural uses, the appearance of fish mutations, foul odors, discolored water, and the erosion of native vegetation forced the tribe to stop using the river altogether. In 1991 the tribe became the first in the nation to apply for water quality standards under the Clean Water Act. EPA approved the pueblo's standards in 1993. The tribe's water quality program is all-encompassing, involving the tribe's environmental department, community members, and even tribal youth in protecting and restoring the water supply. The John F. Kennedy School of Government at Harvard University and the EPA have honored the tribe's program.

Sandia

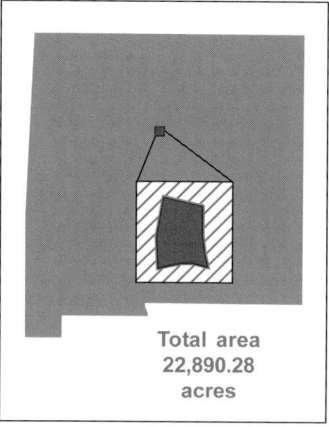

**Total area
22,890.28
acres**

Honoring Nations Honoree 1999

Water Quality Standards, Environmental Department, Pueblo of Sandia

**Honoring Nations
Honoree 1999**

**Text in its entirety from:
The Harvard Project On
American Indian Economic
Development**

**John F. Kennedy School
of Government
Harvard University**

The Rio Grande River has always played a crucial role in daily life at the Pueblo of Sandia. For centuries, members relied on the river for agricultural, recreational, and traditional uses. Over the past several decades, however, rapid industrial growth and lax state and federal environmental enforcement have resulted in the River's deterioration - making it one of the most polluted and endangered rivers in the United States. During the 1970s and 1980s, the appearance of fish mutations, foul smells, discolored water and the erosion of nearby native vegetation forced tribal members to cease using the River entirely.

At that time, the Pueblo did not communicate with upstream polluters and had no mechanisms for protecting the quality of its surface water. An opportunity for change arose in 1987 when the United States Congress passed amendments to the Clean Water Act allowing American Indian nations to apply for "treatment as state" status. This status allows Indian nations to promulgate their own water quality standards. The Pueblo of Sandia applied for "treatment of state" in 1988 and gained U.S. Environmental Protection Agency (EPA) approval in 1990. In 1991, the Pueblo became the first tribe in the United State to apply for water quality standards under the Clean Water Act with the specific intentions of protecting traditional uses of surface waters. In 1993, the EPA approved the Pueblo's standards.

Sandia's water quality standards, which are more stringent than those of the State of New Mexico, prescribe acceptable levels of contaminants and establish existing uses of the reservation that must be protected. The Pueblo's Water Quality Control Officer monitors the water quality for conformance to the standards, advises prospective dischargers of Sandia's discharge requirements, and coordinates pollution control activities with other local, state, and federal agencies.

The Water Quality Standards Program has been successful on several fronts. Program-generated data regarding river pollution levels have given the Pueblo a voice at the table in discussions regarding local water matters and have served as a counterweight to pollution claims made by local dischargers. After years of silence, the Program also has led to increased communication and information-sharing between the Pueblo and the State of New Mexico.

Beyond these immediate benefits, the Program is poised to secure future success - from both the technical standards it sets and the community support it enjoys. On the technical side, the Program requires that Sandia's water quality standards be incorporated into all future permits EPA grants to upstream dischargers. The new permits also will require dischargers to report the nature of their effluent to the Pueblo and provide special notification of accidental contamination. Politically, there is Pueblo-wide commitment to protecting the health of the Rio Grande River. Sandia's Council has consistently supported the Program's initiatives and funding requests. Community members credit their leaders' desire and ability to protect and preserve the Pueblo's way of life as the primary reason for the Program's achievements. Even grade school students have become Program boosters, as they test the River's water quality through school projects. Together, this support carries Program success into the future. Sandia's "treatment as state" status and the Water Quality Standards Program that emerged from it are important steps in the nation's autonomy over its waters. By seizing the opportunity offered by a change in federal law, the Pueblo has been able to reverse its long-standing powerlessness in water quality issues. The Water Quality Standards Program has given the Pueblo of Sandia standing to defend its health, economy, and traditional practices - a position the Pueblo has used to benefit the environment, current members and non-members, and the generations to come.

Santa Ana

**Santa Ana Pueblo
Federal reservation
Keresan
Sandoval County, New Mexico**

Pueblo of Santa Ana
2 Dove Road
Santa Ana, NM 87004
505-867-3301
505-867-3395 Fax
santaana.org

LOCATION AND LAND STATUS
Santa Ana Pueblo is located in north-central New Mexico near the town of Bernalillo, about 18 miles north of Albuquerque.

The Spanish first encountered the tribe in 1598 in the old Santa Ana village of Tamaya, which remains the location for the tribe's ceremonial activities. The original Spanish land grant covered an area of 15,400 acres. President Lincoln confirmed the grant in 1864; Congress ratified it in 1869; and it was patented in 1883. Additional grants brought the reservation to its present size.

PHYSICAL DESCRIPTION
The Rio Grande splits the reservation into two sections, which together span some 61,934 acres of semiarid grazing land. The reservation's most significant physical feature is the Jemez Reservoir, a 1,400-acre lake created by the Jemez Canyon Dam.

CULTURE AND HISTORY
Members of the Tamayame Tribe have resided at Santa Ana Pueblo since at least the early 1500s. The Santa Ana Pueblo is a Keresan-speaking tribe. The tribe's ancestors migrated to the area from the Galisteo Basin sometime between 1200 and 1300 AD and farmed for a time at the confluence of the Rio Grande and the Rio Jemez. The Santa Ana people engaged in dry farming on the hills behind the village and along the trail between Ranchitos and Tamaya. As early as 1300, the tribe was utilizing ditch irrigation. Later they raised livestock extensively, raising mostly sheep and cattle. At some point, the region's climate apparently grew drier and farming became scarce and, eventually, nonexistent. Later they moved to the present location of Old Santa Ana-Tamaya. In the late seventeenth century they began returning to the Rio Grande farms, but they had to buy back their land from Spaniards who had since settled there. Since the sacred Native buildings and the pueblo's Catholic church are located in Tamaya, most Santa Ana families maintain two houses-one in the old village and another in one of the farm villages of Chicali, Rebajani, or Ranchitos, which are collectively labeled Los Ranchitos.

Traditional Santa Ana culture manifests itself through tribal theocracy, which continues to play a role in the tribal government, and through the reemerging tribal arts and crafts community.

GOVERNMENT

Santa Ana tribal government combines the traditional tribal theocracy, the secular government decreed by Spain in 1620, and a contemporary administrative structure. The traditional religious council *cacique*, war captains, *fiscales*, and others handle internal affairs. The governor, tribal council, administration and aides handle external affairs. The tribal council includes all male heads of household over the age of 18, and officers are appointed to one-year terms.

The pueblo has established a dual tribal court system consisting of a traditional and contemporary court with the lieutenant governor serving as chief judge of the traditional court. The tribe is organized under the 1934 Indian Reorganization Act.

BUSINESS CORPORATION

The tribe has four distinct business entities, each organized under Section 17 as federally chartered corporations. Tamaya Enterprises is responsible for the daily operations of the Santa Ana Star Casino. Southern Sandoval Investments is responsible for economic development projects on the westside, including the tribes' Warrior Fuels Gas Station. Santa Ana Golf Club oversees the operations of the Santa Ana Golf Course, the Twin Warriors Golf Course, and the Prairie Star Restaurant. The Santa Ana Hospitality Corporation manages the Hyatt Regency Tamaya Resort and Spa.

ECONOMY

In addition to agriculture, the tribe derives its income through leasing land to outside interests, producing blue corn, managing a plant and tree nursery, and developing its properties into enterprises such as a golf course, a high-end restaurant, and a planned resort. Many individual tribal members work at jobs in the thriving Albuquerque metropolitan area. Although the pueblo is located in Sandoval County, Bernalillo County-which consists largely of metropolitan Albuquerque-provides the region's primary economic influence. Unlike Bernalillo County, which is dominated by relatively stable government and services sectors, employment in Sandoval County is oriented toward the more volatile manufacturing sector.

Government as Employer. The tribal government employs a number of members through its various functions in the areas of administration, health care, and general operations.

Agriculture and Livestock. Once a center of dry farming and livestock grazing, by the 1960s both activities had severely declined. In 1985 these dormant farmlands were revived into large commercial fields through organic and xeriscopic technology. This move was motivated in part to preserve the pueblo's river water rights. Santa Ana Agricultural Enterprises grows blue corn for the domestic and international food and cosmetic markets. The tribe maintains its own grain mill to process the corn. Santa Ana Agricultural Enterprises markets blue cornmeal, atole, parched corn, and pancake and cornbread mixes under the brand name Tamaya Blue. It supplies the retail chain Body Shop with blue corn for cruelty-free cosmetics, and it is actively seeking to expand its market. Other customers include museum gift shops, specialty food stores, blue corn producers, an international hotel chain, and mail order companies.

Santa Ana Agricultural Enterprises is the parent company of the Santa Ana Native Plant and Tree Nursery and of the Santa Ana Garden Center. The Santa Ana Native Plant and Tree Nursery produces xerophytic plants and materials for the wholesale landscaping market, stocking more than 250 species of plants. The Santa Ana Garden Center is its retail outlet.

Forestry. The tribe has maintained the Bosque Restoration Program since 1996. This program helps to restore the cottonwood *bosque* (wildwoods) along the six miles of the Rio Grande on tribal lands. The program's main goals are to eliminate nonindigenous plants; revegetate with indigenous plants; restore the river to a broad, shallow form; promote over-bank flooding in order to restore the cottonwood and willow plants; and improve the habitat of fish and wildlife species. The tribe has invested over $2 million in this program.

Gaming. The tribe owns and operates the Santa Ana Star Casino in Bernalillo. The casino offers 1,500 slots/VLTs, 30 table games, 3 poker tables, a convention center, a restaurant, and an entertainment venue. It employs 550 people.

Mining. The reservation has considerable sand and gravel resources which the tribe has taken advantage of by granting a mining permit to Southwest Materials. Land is also leased to Rio Grande Aggregates. Sand and gravel income is realized through advance royalties as well as monthly production royalties. The tribe leases sand and gravel mines to Western Mobile as well.

Real Estate/Commercial Development. In addition to lands the tribe leased to mining companies, the tribe leases 100 acres to Sandoval County, which in turn subleases the acreage to the Lovelace New Mexico Soccer Complex and Southwest Youth Soccer Association. The complex includes 20 fields and two lighted championship fields with 2,000-seat capacity.

Services and Retail. The tribe owns and operates a number of innovative and highly regarded businesses. The Prairie Star Restaurant, a four-star restaurant, features unusual dishes such as antelope and buffalo. Housed in a renovated 1920s home, the restaurant also offers banquet accommodations for up to 150 people. The tribe operates a discount smoke shop. The Ta-Ma-Ya Cooperative Association displays and sells Native arts and crafts such as pottery, weaving, and clothing. Warrior Apparel offers clothing featuring original Native American art. Products include T-shirts, jackets, sweatshirts and caps. The Santa Ana Garden Center is a retail outlet for the Native Plant and Tree Nursery. The garden center offers advice from an expert staff, native (xerophytic) plants and vegetable transplants, garden tools, irrigation equipment and other home-gardening supplies. It offers products grown from locally gathered seeds. The tribe also owns The Cooking Post which sells processed meat products, gift packs and samplers, Tamaya Blue Corn products, tea, coffee, salsa, chile, hot sauce, fry bread, wild rice, syrup, and spreads. These products can be purchased from the tribe's website.

Tourism and Recreation. The tribe has developed the 27-hole championship Santa Ana Golf Course, which hosts the PGA/NIKE New Mexico Charity Classic Tournament. The course has been ranked in the nation's top 100 by both *Golf Digest* and *Golfweek* magazines. It has hosted seven annual tournaments including the U.S. Open Qualifier and the PGA Challenge Cup. Facilities include a clubhouse, pro shop, hospitality quarters, a four-star restaurant, casual bar, and a grille. Eight lakes are located within the golf course.

The tribe also owns the Hyatt Regency Tamaya Resort and Spa. It offers the Twin Warriors Golf Club with an upscale 18-hole golf course that was ranked 69th by *Golf Digest* in 2003. Located near the pueblo, the Coronado State Monument features campsites, RV facilities, showers, and historical information. The tribe hosts a number of ceremonial dances at the pueblo throughout the year, many of which are open to the public. Corn dances are held in honor of St. John on June 24, St. Peter on June 29, and Santa Ana on July 26. Festivities are held at Tamaya, the original pueblo.

Santa Ana

Total area *(BIA realty, 2004)*
77,035.10 acres

Total area *(Tribal Sources, 2004)*
61,934 acres

Population *2000 census*
487

Tribal enrollment
(BIA labor report, 2001)
716

Total labor force *2000 census*
206

Total labor force
(BIA labor report, 2001)
423

High school graduate or higher
2000 census
85.4%

Bachelor's degree or higher
2000 census
2.7%

Unemployment rate
2000 census
10.7%

Unemployment rate
(BIA labor report, 2001)
14%

Per capita income
2000 census
$9,857

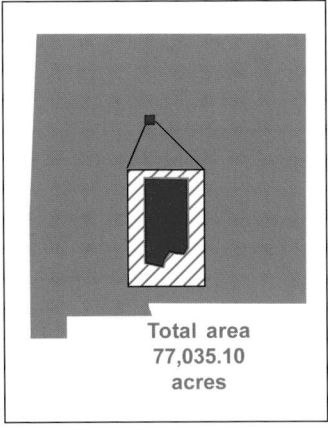

Total area
77,035.10
acres

Santa Ana

TRI-NM-Sa-007

TRI-NM-Sa-008

TRI-NM-Sa-004

TRI-NM-Sa-001

TRI-NM-Sa-005

TRI-NM-Sa-004 Exterior of the Prairie Star restaurant

TRI-NM-Sa-007 The Prairie Star Restaurant, a four-star restaurant, features unusual dishes such as antelope and buffalo

TRI-NM-Sa-008 Entrance to The Prairie Star Restaurant

TRI-NM-Sa-001 The tribe has developed the 27-hole championship Santa Ana Golf Course, which hosts the annual PGA/NIKE New Mexico Charity Classic Tournament

TRI-NM-Sa-005 The Prairie Star Restaurant at sunset

INFRASTRUCTURE

Interstate 25, the region's major north-south route, passes just east of the reservation. State Highway 44, also a major route, connects the reservation to the interstate.

Electricity. Public Service Company of New Mexico provides electricity to the reservation.

Fuel. Gas Company of New Mexico provides natural gas service.

Water Supply. The U.S. Public Health Service installed the reservation's water and sewer systems.

Transportation. The nearest commercial air service is at Albuquerque International Sunport, about 20 miles to the south. The nearby Town of Bernalillo offers commercial bus, trucking, and rail services.

Telecommunications. Broadband services are available on the reservation through a program created by the tribe, Georgia Institute of Technology, and Southwest Indian Polytechnic Institute. The project was funded in part by a grant from the National Telecommunications and Information Administration Technology Opportunity Program.

COMMUNITY FACILITIES AND SERVICES

The tribe has a community complex with office space, meeting rooms and other facilities in Ranchitos. It houses the Santa Ana Police Department, an elderly daycare center, Santa Ana Health Clinic, social services, Santa Ana Agriculture Enterprises, tribal administration, Santa Ana Library, community wellness program, department of natural resources, technology opportunity, planning and building services, Head Start, and a child care program.

The tribal library is home to an extensive collection and a computer lab. It also provides an after-school program and language program for tribal members. The elderly center provides tribal elders with a meal site program. The tribe's community wellness program provides community-based programs focused on increasing the physical activity, improving the nutritional habits, and assisting in the self-management of diabetes among tribal members. The program features home visits, individual counseling, group education, a fitness facility, and fitness activities.

Education. The tribe runs a Head Start program. Children attend Bernalillo or Albuquerque public schools. Numerous postsecondary educational programs are available in Albuquerque.

Health Care. The tribe maintains a health clinic at its tribal headquarters in Ranchitos, while additional care is available at the Bernalillo County Medical Center and the U.S. Public Health Service Indian Hospital, both located in Albuquerque.

ENVIRONMENTAL CONCERNS

The preservation and restoration of the Cottonwood *bosque* within tribal lands is a major concern. The tribe operates a *bosque* restoration program to work towards this goal.

LOCATION AND LAND STATUS
Santa Clara Pueblo encompasses an area of 45,824 acres of rugged land in northern New Mexico, 20 miles north of Santa Fe. The main village is located 2 miles south of Española, which is situated within reservation boundaries. Reservation lands include fee, non-fee, and trust properties.

The people of Santa Clara received their initial land grant under the Spanish and were pronounced citizens of Mexico when that country gained its independence from Spain. Later, the United States recognized the pueblo's tribal rights under the 1848 Treaty of Guadalupe Hidalgo. The United States then confirmed the tribe's land grant in 1858 and patented it in 1909.

PHYSICAL DESCRIPTION
The reservation features a distinctive and scenic topography, including the forested Santa Clara Canyon and the Puye Cliff Dwelling Ruins. At the Rio Grande, which runs through the reservation, the elevation is less than 5,600 feet. The pueblo's highest point is the 10,760-foot Santa Clara Peak. Topography varies from juniper- and piñon-covered hills to grazing and farmland to extensive pine-forested mountain lands. The Rio Grande, Santa Clara Creek, and Santa Cruz River run through tribal lands, and there are numerous small lakes as well.

CULTURE AND HISTORY
The Tewa people have lived at Kha P'o (Valley of the Wild Roses), or the Santa Clara Pueblo, for several hundred years. The historical focus of the Santa Clara Pueblo is the Puye Cliff Dwellings, which are a Registered National Historic Landmark. For more than three centuries, this spectacular plateau was home to the more than 1,500 Puye people who lived, farmed, and hunted game. The "Puye style" was the forerunner of modern-day passive solar heating and terraced "apartment" architecture. Archaeologists believe that the early dwellings of Puye Cliffs were last occupied about 1680.

The first dwellings were caves hollowed in the volcanic tuff cliffs. Later, adobe structures were built along the slopes and on top of the mesa. The Tewa (the people) abandoned the Puye area more than 400 years ago after a severe drought caused them to settle in the lowlands of the Rio Grande Valley, the site of the current pueblo.

The pueblo is at essentially the same site where the Spanish, under Francisco de Coronado, encountered it in 1540. During the post-World War II period, the pueblo has seen a shift from its traditional reliance on agricultural pursuits to wage earning, tourism, and the production and sale of crafts (primarily pottery). Quite a few tribal members have degrees in higher education, including some doctorates. This does not necessarily signal a dramatic waning of traditional ways, however, as members often continue to participate as dancers or chorus members in Native ceremonies.

A protracted schism between factions within the traditional governing body during the early twentieth century led the tribe to accept the terms of the 1934 Indian Reorganization Act and base a new constitution upon it. The tribe was the first of the pueblos to adopt a written constitution. A major result of the 1935 constitution's adoption was the separation of religious and secular matters, which transformed tribal religious ceremonies into voluntary affairs. The Pueblo of Santa Clara is also a member of the Eight Northern Indian Pueblos Council (ENIPC), whose headquar-

ters are at San Juan Pueblo. It is the second largest of the six Tewa-speaking pueblos in New Mexico.

The Santa Clara Pueblo was selected to be featured in a major exhibit at the newly opened Smithsonian's National Museum of the American Indian in Washington D.C. The pueblo is included in the "Our Universes: Traditional Knowledge Shapes Our World" exhibit. It is the only pueblo community to be featured in the first round of exhibits. Many tribal members participated in the museum's development as well, from artists to academic liaisons and curatorial consultants. The gallery's layout is based upon a Santa Clara circular design.

GOVERNMENT
The Pueblo of Santa Clara, organized under the 1934 Indian Reorganization Act, approved a constitution and bylaws in 1935 (and amended them in 1939), which provide for the election of a governor, his officers, and a 14-member tribal council. There are presently four traditional groups from whom candidates are nominated; each group nominates a candidate to run for the positions of governor, lieutenant governor, secretary, treasurer, interpreter, and sheriff. All enrolled tribal members 18 years of age or older are eligible to vote. Tribal officials are elected to a one-year term. The tribal administration is divided into over 20 departments, including tribal operations, law enforcement, mental health, administrative planning, and the tribal court. The Santa Clara Pueblo signed a self-governance compact with the BIA, which granted the pueblo increased control over fiscal resources.

BUSINESS CORPORATION
The tribe established the Santa Clara Development Corporation for economic and business development. It oversees the identification and development of economic endeavors on the tribe's behalf.

ECONOMY
The pueblo has a fairly diversified employment profile. Major sources of income for the tribe include the casino and the Puye Cliff Dwellings. Many tribal members find employment off the reservation, with Los Alamos National Laboratory representing the largest single source of private-sector employment.

Government as Employer. The tribal government represents the largest on-reservation employer.

Economic Development Projects. The tribe is in the process of developing its commercial properties within the city of Española. A 34-acre shopping center that will feature 230,000 feet of retail tenant space is in the planning stages. The pueblo is master planning and developing an additional 1,000 acres at the intersection of NM 399/106 and U.S. 84/285. The pueblo owns the four quadrants and properties adjacent to the intersection. In addition, the tribe is constructing the Santa Clara Mesa Chevron gas station and convenience store in Santa Fe County. Other projects under development include a class III gaming facility and the Santa Clara Builders Plaza. The plaza will include a 12,000-square-foot Quickfix Home Improvement Center, an equipment rental business, self-storage rental units, and one pad site on Riverside Drive in Española.

Agriculture and Livestock. As of 1990, there were about 950 acres of agricultural lands located along the flood plains of the Rio Grande. Fourteen and a half miles of irrigation serve the

Santa Clara Pueblo
Federal reservation
Tewa
Rio Arriba and Santa Fe
counties, New Mexico

Santa Clara Pueblo
P.O. Box 580
Española, NM 87532
505-753-7326
505-753-8898 Fax

Total area *(BIA realty, 2004)*
53,437.28 acres

Total area *(Tribal Source, 2004)*
45,824 acres

Population *2000 census*
10,658

Tribal enrollment
(BIA labor report, 2001)
2,800

Total labor force *2000 census*
5,015

Total labor force
(BIA labor report, 2001)
1,931

High school graduate or higher
2000 census
77.5%

Bachelor's degree or higher
2000 census
19.8%

Unemployment rate
2000 census
7.8%

Unemployment rate
(BIA labor report, 2001)
36%

Per capita income *2000 census*
$15,336

Santa Clara

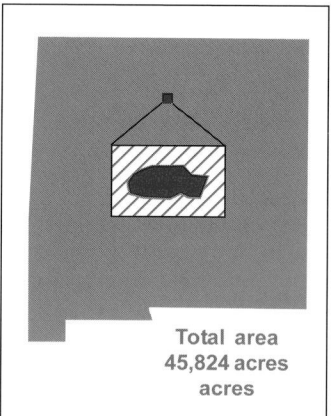

**Total area
45,824 acres
acres**

agricultural region. An additional 750 acres are available for agricultural development. Crops produced on pueblo lands include alfalfa, hay, fruits, and various vegetables. Virtually all of these crops are consumed within the pueblo. There are approximately 32,000 acres of rangeland, 14,000 acres of which are grazeable woodland. The reservation supports about 350 head of cattle. Most are sold at local auctions, with a few retained for personal use.

Forestry. The reservation contains about 14,600 acres of commercial timberland, much of which lies within the Santa Clara Canyon Recreation Area and which is used for recreational purposes. Forested lands are composed mainly of pine.

Gaming. The tribe owns and operates the Big Rock Casino in Española. It offers 420 slots/VLTs, 6 table games, 3 restaurants, and an entertainment venue. The casino employs 280 people.

Fisheries. The Santa Clara Canyon Recreation Area features four well-stocked lakes along 12 miles of Santa Clara Creek. Permits sold by tribal rangers produce modest annual revenues.

Construction. The tribe maintains an active program for renovating, weatherizing, and replacing pueblo housing facilities. These efforts provide employment to a number of tribal members.

Mining. Commercial mineral resources on the reservation include undeveloped sand and gravel deposits, adobe materials, and pumice. The pueblo also has the potential for developing geothermal energy sources. Possible drilling sites have been identified on the western edge of the reservation.

Services and Retail. The tribe operates the Tobacco Shop of Española, a lucrative smoke shop. Many homes in the village display signs that say "Pottery for Sale" or simply "Open." Inquiring visitors are invited to see the wares and meet the artisans. The pueblo is home to a number of noted artists and sculptors. Beadwork, cloth embroidering, weaving, woodcarvings, and other crafts are sold throughout the pueblo. Santa Clara Pueblo artisans are known worldwide for their distinctive red-and-black polished and carved pottery. The pottery is fashioned from native clay, which is mixed with tuff (blue sand) either by hand or by foot. To achieve a smooth, shiny texture, each handcrafted piece is hand-sanded and polished before firing.

Tourism and Recreation. Tourism is the reservation's major industry. The tribe owns the Black Mesa Golf Club in La Mesilla, New Mexico. The course features a short game practice area, a 60,000-square-foot teeing area that accompanies the range, and two practice putting greens. Facilities include a full-service pro shop and a grille.

The Santa Clara Canyon Recreational Area is a beautiful and extremely popular site for visitors, featuring 86 campsites (some for RVs), a sheltered cabin, portable toilets, available drinking water, and abundant picnic sites. Hiking in the canyon, fishing, and seasonal hunting have been the prevailing activities. Wildfires over the past few years have forced to tribe to close the canyon to visitors intermittently.

The impressive Puye Cliff Dwellings, the ancestral home of the Santa Clara Tribe, are a National Historic Landmark. This facility has a gift shop, a café, and a conference center. Two self-guided walking tours explore the cliffs. There are three different trails, and stairways join two levels of cliff dwellings with the 740-room pueblo ruin. Guided tour packages to the Puye Cliff Dwellings, which include a pueblo feast, are available from April through September.

The tribe celebrates St. Anthony's Feast Day on June 13 and Santa Clara Feast Day, in honor of the pueblo's patron saint, on August 12. Santa Clara Feast Day includes traditional dances and an art festival.

INFRASTRUCTURE
Road access to the reservation is provided by U.S. Highway 84 via Santa Fe and Route 30 via Española. I-25 runs north-south through Santa Fe.

Electricity. The Jemez Mountain Cooperative provides electricity to the pueblo.

Fuel. The Gas Company of New Mexico provides natural gas service.

Water Supply. The pueblo's sanitation department maintains the community sewer and water systems and provides solid waste pickup and disposal.

Transportation. Commercial air service is available in Santa Fe. Nearby Española maintains a small, private airport. Bus and truck lines serve Española as well. Commercial train facilities are located in Lamy, 40 miles from the reservation.

COMMUNITY FACILITIES AND SERVICES
Education. Tribal youth may attend the BIA-funded elementary school, Santa Clara Day School, in Española. The original facility was constructed in 1926 and was recently renovated to include new classrooms, a library, a computer lab, a science lab, a gym, a playground, a baseball field, a schoolyard habitat, and a community garden. Older students attend Española Public Schools. The ENIPC administers Head Start and scholarship programs.

Health Care. Health services are available through the Santa Fe Service Unit. The program includes clinics in Santa Clara, Santo Domingo, San Felipe, and Cochiti pueblos and the Santa Fe Indian Hospital in Santa Fe. Services include ambulatory medical care, dental, health education, nutrition, behavioral health, public health nursing, community diabetes education, occupational therapy, contract care, environmental health, and sanitation programs. There are also special clinics for women's health, diabetes, children's health, wellness, and other health matters that may arise.

ENVIRONMENTAL CONCERNS
The status of a former landfill located on tribal lands is of concern to the tribe. The tribe has applied for a Brownsfield assessment of the problem.

LOCATION AND LAND STATUS

Santo Domingo Pueblo covers 115 square miles of land southwest of Santa Fe, New Mexico. The pueblo sits on the east bank of the Rio Grande near I-25. The reservation's village, Kiwa, was preceded by at least three villages, two along the Arroyo de Galisteo and a more recent one about a mile west of the present village. Flooding caused all the old sites to be abandoned.

When the Spanish first met the people of Santo Domingo in the 1500s, they were living on the Arroyo de Galisteo. Domingo Jironizo Petroz de Cruzate issued the tribe a land grant on September 20, 1689. The pueblo's present site was established around 1700. A U.S. Congressional Act confirmed the Spanish land grant on December 22, 1858. The tribe maintains legal claim to its ancestral lands of over 100,000 acres, but the reservation grant encompasses just over 73,000 acres.

PHYSICAL DESCRIPTION

Approximately 66,300 acres of the original grant lands constitute open range. Farm fallow crop lands occupy 3,600 acres and another 1,100 acres of tribal lands feature home sites, community facilities, and roadways.

CULTURE AND HISTORY

Members of the Santo Domingo Tribe have resided in the area for countless years. They are descended from the residents of Chaco Canyon and Mesa Verde. Tribal communities have relocated over the years, primarily as a result of regional flooding. Santo Domingo Pueblo has always been prominent in New Mexico history. The Camino Real, running from Mexico to Taos, had a stopping place at Santo Domingo. The Pueblo of Santo Domingo has been a central community in the region for several hundred years, serving as host to intertribal conferences and council meetings. The Santo Domingo Mission has been the chief mission in the area since the village was founded. The people of the pueblo subsisted on farming and raising livestock, as many still do today. Their jewelry and other craft products are famous. The pueblo has the fifth-largest population of the New Mexican pueblos.

The Santo Domingos have a very strong sense of unity as a people, and they have held on to their values and traditional ways in spite of extensive contact with other cultures. Ninety percent of tribal members continue to speak their native language, yet they are able to integrate selected aspects of the modern world into their own system of values without compromising their beliefs or their identity. Other tribes and non-Indians alike have admired this steadfastness.

GOVERNMENT

The Santo Domingo Tribal Council is the pueblo's governing authority. The tribal council is led by a governor, a lieutenant governor, mayor, lieutenant mayor, war chief, war captain, 10 officials, and 16 staff officials. There are a total of 60 council members, all former tribal officers who serve life terms. They are appointed to one-year terms by the *caciques*. A tribal spokesperson and a secretary also serve on the council; their terms of office are unspecified. The tribe has no written constitution; decisions are made according to precedent or common law. The council seeks consensus when addressing an issue, although sometimes, for the sake of time, decisions are made by majority rule. The tribal council also maintains the authority to adopt tribal resolutions to serve as rules and ordinances that may affect daily life in the pueblo.

The tribal government administers various programs including community health representative, Head Start, Kewa Day Care, WIC, substance abuse and prevention, elderly and aging, social services, work enforcement act, higher education, Johnson O'Malley, 638-Aid, emergency youth shelter, housing, and utilities and solid waste.

ECONOMY

The tribal economy is supported through tribally owned enterprises and leasing of tribal lands. The sale of natural resources such as sand and gravel, and interest earned from financial investments also contribute to the economy. Many tribal members continue to ranch and farm, and to produce fine jewelry, basketry, and silver work.

Government as Employer. The tribe employs about 100 people.

Agriculture and Livestock. Farming and ranching, traditional ways of life on the pueblo, are still pursued by approximately 76 families. An estimated 2,384 acres are farmed. There are 64,951 acres of grazing land (enough to support 275 head of cattle). The availability of water is a perennial problem. The pueblo has made ongoing studies to identify irrigable acreage for current and future uses and developments.

Mining. Santo Domingo Pueblo is rich in mineral resources including oil and gas, coal, uranium, gypsum, clay, pumice, and sand and gravel. It is located near the ancient turquoise mines at Cerrillos, and tribal members have utilized the resources for centuries to produce their renowned jewelry. The tribe leases some tribal land to mining operations.

Real Estate/Commercial Development. The pueblo receives income from various leases and permits including a U.S. Post Office and a Public Service Company of New Mexico franchise agreement.

Services and Retail. The pueblo operates a gas service station on I-25, the area's principal north-south artery. Pueblo Gas is both a wholesale and retail operation. The facility offers 20 retail gas pumps. The service station lies on a 30-acre tract that has been set aside for commercial development, including a market for the world-renowned Santo Domingo jewelry and artisan crafts. There is also a pizza franchise located at the pueblo.

Tourism and Recreation. An RV park is located at the pueblo. The tribe hosts many dances and celebrations open to the public, including Christmas and Easter festivities, the Sandero, and Santo Domingo Feast Day on August 4. The Santo Domingo Feast Day includes a Corn Dance, which attracts over 2,000 participants. The annual Santo Domingo Arts and Crafts Market is held Labor Day weekend. The festivities regularly feature over 350 Santo Domingo artisans and feature dancing and food booths.

INFRASTRUCTURE

Interstate 25, just east of the pueblo, is a major north-south artery. Bus service is available in Santa Fe.

The tribal utilities program provides plumbing, range management, solid waste, and general assistance services.

Electricity. Public Service Company of New Mexico provides electricity.

Santo Domingo Pueblo
Federal reservation
Keresan
Sandoval County, New Mexico

Pueblo of Santo Domingo
P.O. Box 99
Santo Domingo Pueblo, NM
87052
    505-465-2214
    505-465-2688 Fax

Total area *(BIA realty, 2004)*
71,675.56 acres

Total area *(Tribal source, 2004)*
73,000 acres

Population *2000 census*
3,166

Population *(Tribal source, 2004)*
4,708

Tribal enrollment
(BIA labor report, 2001)
4,492

Tribal enrollment
(Tribal source, 2004)
4,516

Total labor force *2000 census*
920

Total labor force
(BIA labor report, 2001)
2,431

High school graduate or higher
2000 census
68.5%

Bachelor's degree or higher
2000 census
2.7%

Unemployment rate *2000 census*
18.9%

Unemployment rate
(BIA labor report, 2001)
16%

Per capita income *2000 census*
$5,713

Santo Domingo

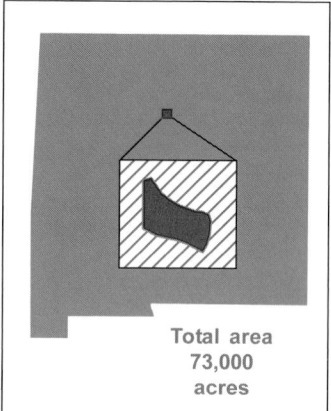

Total area
73,000
acres

Fuel. Gas Company of New Mexico supplies gas.

Water Supply. A community sanitation program provides water, sewer system, and solid waste disposal.

Transportation. Commercial air service is available at Albuquerque International Sunport, 40 miles south. Trains stop at the railroad siding at Domingo, one and a half miles from the pueblo.

COMMUNITY FACILITIES AND SERVICES

The tribe operates a senior citizen center, library, and a fitness center in the pueblo. The Santo Domingo Church is located within the pueblo. The tribe's summer youth program provides employment opportunities for tribal youth during both summer and school months. A tribally administered work force involvement program offers assistance to tribal members with job search, transportation, and supplies. The pueblo's Child Care Development Fund program provides child care subsidies for single parents working to complete their education. The tribe also operates an emergency youth shelter for tribal youth who are temporarily displaced.

Education. The tribe operates a Head Start program. It currently serves 150 students. Tribal youth attend grades K-8 at the Santo Domingo Elementary School in Santo Domingo. The school is a member of the Bernalillo Public School system. High school students attend school primarily within the Bernalillo Public School System, 30 miles south of the pueblo. Tribal youth also attend a local Indian boarding school and schools in Santa Fe or Albu-

querque. Colleges, universities, and postsecondary programs are available in Santa Fe and Albuquerque.

Health Care. Health care services are available through the Santa Fe Service Unit. The program includes clinics in Santo Domingo, Santa Clara, San Felipe, and Cochiti pueblos, and the Santa Fe Indian Hospital in Santa Fe. Services include comprehensive medical, dental, community outreach, health education, nutrition, behavioral health, contract care, public health, community diabetes, occupational therapy, environmental health, and sanitation programs. Special clinics are also organized to address women's health, diabetes, children, wellness, and other health issues as needed. The tribe is currently serviced by an Indian Health Service facility established in 1963, and it is planning to begin construction on a new facility in 2005.

The tribe's community health representative program provides health education, case finding, referrals, patient monitoring, homemaker, interpretation and translation, and follow-up services in the community. EMS services are available as well. The Kewa Health Outreach Program provides services to promote healthy lifestyles and reduce the incidence of diabetes within the community.

ENVIRONMENTAL CONCERNS

The use of underground storage tanks, illegal dumping, and water quality are issues of concern to the tribe. It is also interested in the need for a centralized sewer and wastewater treatment system in the pueblo.

Taos

Taos Pueblo
Federal reservation
Tiwa
Taos County, New Mexico

Taos Pueblo
P.O. Box 1846
Taos, NM 87571
505-758-8626
505-758-8831 Fax

LOCATION AND LAND STATUS

Taos Pueblo spans almost one million acres in northern New Mexico. The tribal center is located 3 miles north of the town of Taos and 70 miles north along the Rio Grande from Santa Fe. When the Spanish encountered Taos Pueblo in 1540, it looked much as it does today. Like other Pueblo Indians, the Taos Indians were declared citizens of Mexico when that nation gained its independence from Spain. The United States then confirmed the tribe and its land base under the 1848 Treaty of Guadalupe Hidalgo. In 1996, 764 acres in the Wheeler Park Wilderness were transferred to the tribe. The area includes the Path of Life Trail, which connects the pueblo to the Blue Lake Wilderness. The pueblo is purchasing the 16,000-acre Moreno Ranch.

PHYSICAL DESCRIPTION

The pueblo sits in a valley at the base of 13,161-foot Wheeler Peak, the tallest mountain in New Mexico. It is the northernmost New Mexican pueblo. Tribal lands contain 60,947 acres of forests, 242 acres of lakes, and 175 miles of streams. This is a beautifully scenic region that supports ample farming and livestock. The pueblo is organized into various zones: a 54,000-acre wilderness zone, 6,160 acres of religious and ceremonial zones, 10,938 acres of housing and crop land zones, 6,500 acres of commercial zones, 925 acres of recreational zones, 16,957 acres of range management zones.

CLIMATE

Summer temperatures in Taos average in the 80s, and winter highs are in the 30s and 40s.

CULTURE AND HISTORY

The Tiwa-speaking community of Taos Pueblo has inhabited the Taos Valley since about 900 AD. It is believed that the tribe is

descended from the Chico or Anasazi tribes and that the pueblo may have been one of the fabled golden cities of Cibola. The Taos Pueblo is the oldest continuously inhabited community in the United States. The original structure consists of two houses, the Hlauuma (north house) and the Hlaukwima (south house), both believed to have been constructed between 1000 and 1450 AD. The buildings are constructed entirely of adobe, with *vigas* and *latillas* used to support the roofs of each of the five stories. The pueblo has been recognized as a National Historic Landmark and was admitted into the World Heritage Society as one of the most significant cultural landmarks throughout the world.

The people encountered Europeans when Spanish explorers arrived in the region in 1540. The Taos people were typically at the forefront of pueblo revolts against domination by the Spanish, and in 1847 they joined the Mexican settlers in their fight against the U.S. government. The Taos residents spearheaded the Pueblo Revolt of 1680, uniting the northern pueblos in a successful effort to drive the Spanish out of the area, even if only temporarily. These altercations set the tone for the tribe's determination to protect its water rights, political sovereignty, and land base.

Perhaps the most dramatic of their battles has been for Blue Lake, the tribe's most important religious shrine, lying 20 miles from the pueblo behind Taos Mountain. When Blue Lake and 48,000 acres of surrounding aboriginal-use area were incorporated into the Carson National Forest in 1906, the tribe took the government to court, finally winning their case for restoration in 1970. This marked the first time that land instead of money was returned to an American Indian tribe upon completion of a land claims case.

The tribe's worldview, which stresses a powerful sense of spiritual tradition, community, and loyalty to one's extended kin, remains a commanding anchor within the pueblo. The Taos tribal culture remains active and vibrant. Extended family ties appear as strong as ever, and since the 1970s, many of the tribe's younger members have shown a renewed commitment to their identity as Taos Indians. In addition, the kiva-based religion maintains the tribe's rich ceremonial life.

GOVERNMENT
Taos Pueblo is a sovereign, self-governed community with a traditional form of government consisting of the tribal council, the office of the governor, and the office of the war chief. The tribal council is the tribe's highest authority, handling all the pueblo's major concerns, and it consists of more than 50 male members who serve for life. The council's members include important religious leaders and all former governors, lieutenant governors, war chiefs, and lieutenant war chiefs. The tribal council appoints the governor, the war chief, and their staffs, who serve one-year terms of office and handle all the pueblo's day-to-day affairs. The governor's office consists of 10 officials. Their jurisdiction includes the village itself, church matters, the well-being of the pueblo community, law and order, roads, water issues, and primary relations with the non-Indian community.

The 12 staff members in the war chief's office have jurisdiction over the land and natural resource base, with the exception of water resources. They are responsible for boundary control, trespass matters, hunting, grazing, and crop control, and they take care of the pueblo's herd of bison, which numbers more than 90 head. Within this traditional framework, the tribal government established the central management system to manage and administer the pueblo's federal program responsibilities not handled by the governor or the war chief.

BUSINESS CORPORATION
In 1994, the tribal government chartered a business entity, Taos Pueblo Enterprises, to promote tribal economic development and to develop and manage tribally owned businesses.

ECONOMY
The tribal economy is based primarily upon the tourism industry. The beauty and significance of the Taos Pueblo as a National Historical Landmark and World Heritage Site appeals to many tourists, artists, photographers, and historians. Tribal artisans are renowned for fine pottery, jewelry, traditional crafts, and leatherwork, and tourists are drawn to the pueblo in search of their work.

Government as Employer. Along with tourism, BIA and other federal grants and projects represent the major source of income and employment on the reservation. The tribe has developed a centralized management system that employs tribal members in a variety of fields.

Economic Development Projects. The tribe is a member of the Eight Northern Indian Pueblos Council. This nonprofit organization provides community-based assistance in the areas of economic development, community services, social services, employment, and training within the member tribes. Members include the Picuris, San Juan, Santa Clara, San Ildefonso, Nambé, Pojoaque, and Tesuque pueblos.

Agriculture and Livestock. There are presently 10,000 acres of potentially irrigable lands on the reservation, served by nearly 50 miles of irrigation ditches. Crops include alfalfa, hay, and vegetables. In addition, the reservation features over 49,000 acres of rangeland, of which about 8,700 acres are noncommercial forest. The tribe currently maintains about 430 head of cattle and about 800 horses. Most of the livestock is raised for individual use and sold at area auctions. The tribe is considering using the newly acquired Moreno Ranch property for raising bison. The pueblo has adopted a conservative approach toward extracting resources based on traditional values and the desire to preserve existing land use patterns.

In 2004, the tribe received a $249,941 grant from the U.S. Fish and Wildlife Service to develop its baseline management assessment of fish and wildlife on tribal lands.

Forestry. The tribe's sacred Blue Lake area, once part of the Carson National Forest, contains most of the reservation's 43,672 acres of commercial timber. Although rich in game and forest products, the Blue Lake Wilderness is maintained as a religious sanctuary for exclusive use by tribal members. The Moreno Valley Land is also heavily forested. Forest management plans for this ranch land are being drawn up.

Gaming. The tribe owns and operates the Taos Mountain Casino in Taos. The 10,000-square-foot facility offers 176 slots/VLTs, 4 table games, and a restaurant. The tribe also operates the Taos Pueblo Pull Tabs facility. It features bingo pull tabs for $1, $5, and $25. A full-service bingo hall is under development.

Fisheries. The streams and lakes on and near the reservation are popular recreational fishing sites and bring in a portion of the area's tourist revenue.

Manufacturing. A number of small businesses owned by tribal members produce handcrafted items. These include deer horn sculptures, mica-flecked pottery, silver and turquoise jewelry, blankets, tanned buckskin moccasins, and drums. There are presently at least 14 such businesses affiliated with the pueblo; they represent a considerable source of revenue and employment for the tribe.

Mining. Though at one time the region bustled with gold mining activities, today the pueblo's commercially viable minerals are largely limited to sand and gravel, adobe materials, and building stone.

Tourism and Recreation. Tourism and recreation represent the backbone of the pueblo's economy. Virtually all of the tribal businesses cater primarily to the tourist element. The pueblo, a National Historic Landmark and World Heritage Site, is perhaps the most photographed and easily recognizable pueblo in the world. The tribe welcomes visitors to the pueblo, but it requests that guests respect the privacy and rights of all residents and adhere to the tribe's policies. Visitors are required to pay a fee for parking, entering, and the privilege of taking photographs. Commercial artists and photographers must receive written permission to complete work at the pueblo. Tribal members serve as tour guides within the historic village area. The Taos Indian Horse Ranch offers historical tours and horseback-riding packages.

The multistory, adobe structure of the original pueblo is still standing and is still occupied by tribal members. Many tribal members reside outside the dwelling during the summer months, or outside the old walls in more contemporary homes year round, though they return to their pueblo homes during ceremonial periods. The tribe hosts a number of ceremonial and celebratory dances year round, many of which are open to the public. The tribe also hosts the Annual Taos Pueblo Powwow, which celebrated its nineteenth anniversary in 2004.

The plaza within the pueblo's walls houses numerous shops, restaurants, and vendors of traditional and contemporary foods, arts, jewelry, baskets, and other items of interest. The present-day San Geronimo Chapel was constructed in 1850 to replace the church that the U.S. Army destroyed during the Mexican-American War in 1847. The original church was built in 1619 and was destroyed during the Pueblo Revolt of 1680. It was

Taos

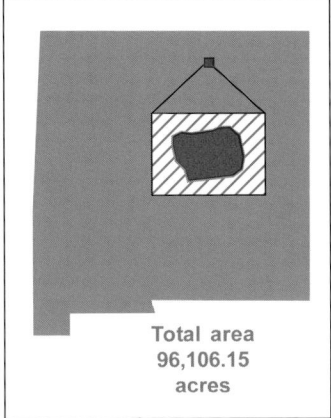

**Total area
96,106.15
acres**

Total area *(BIA realty, 2004)*
96,106.15 acres

Population *2000 census*
4,484

Tribal enrollment
(BIA labor report, 2001)
2,443

Total labor force *2000 census*
2,318

Total labor force
(BIA labor report, 2001)
1,758

High school graduate or higher
2000 census
80.5%

Bachelor's degree or higher
2000 census
23.3%

Unemployment rate *2000 census*
13.7%

Unemployment rate
(BIA labor report, 2001)
10%

Per capita income *2000 census*
$14,225

Taos

rebuilt on the same site, and the ruins are evident on the west side of the village. San Geronimo is the pueblo's patron saint, and a large celebration is held each September on his feast day.

INFRASTRUCTURE

The pueblo is accessible by Highway 68, which runs north-south through the town of Taos, and Route 240, which runs directly to the reservation. Access to interstate highways include I-25, 75 miles south near Santa Fe, and I-40, 135 miles south in Albuquerque. The TNM Bus Line runs to and from Taos, Taos Ski Valley, Santa Fe, and Albuquerque. The Taos Municipal Airport is open 24 hours and features a 5,800-foot runway. The nearest commercial train service is in Lamy, New Mexico.

Electricity. The pueblo does not allow electricity within its old village. During the last 15 years, electric, water, and sewer utility lines were extended to serve most of the residential areas. Extension of natural gas services is under negotiation.

Water Supply. Water is obtained from Taos Creek. In 2000, the tribe received a joint U.S. EPA grant with the Jicarilla Apache Tribe to collaboratively develop solid waste management programs at their respective reservations. The tribal council has approved the development of a waste transfer station near the former landfill site. Indian Health Service will assist in finalizing the project's plans.

COMMUNITY FACILITIES AND SERVICES

Education. On-reservation education services include a Head Start program, and the K-8 BIA-operated Taos Day School. Both public and private schools in the nearby town of Taos offer K-12 education. Several families elect to board their junior high and high school-aged children at the BIA-operated Santa Fe Indian School. Options for postsecondary education are expanding due to the newly established Taos Campus of the University of New Mexico. The tribe offers a scholarship program for members seeking a postsecondary education.

Health Care. Health services are available through the Taos/Picuris Health Center. The center recently became its own service unit. The center offers medical, dental, health education, nutrition, behavioral health, public health nursing, community diabetes, occupational therapy, contract care, environmental health, and sanitation programs. Special clinics are organized to deal with women's health, diabetes, children, wellness, and other health issues as needed. Other medical facilities include Holy Cross Hospital in the Town of Taos, private physicians, and the Santa Fe Indian Hospital.

ENVIRONMENTAL CONCERNS

The tribe's environmental office is responsible for guiding the tribe in maintaining and protecting its natural resources. Water quality and supply, particularly of the Rio Grande River, are the tribe's primary concern as the river serves as the main source of domestic water for the pueblo.

Tesuque

Tesuque Pueblo
Federal reservation
Tewa
Santa Fe County, New Mexico

Tesuque Pueblo
Route 42, Box 360T
Santa Fe, NM 87506
505-983-2667
505-982-2331 Fax

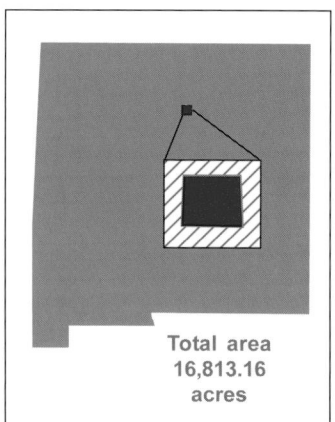

Total area
16,813.16
acres

LOCATION AND LAND STATUS

Tesuque Pueblo tribal lands cover 16,813 acres in northern New Mexico, nine miles north of Santa Fe. Tesuque is the southernmost of the Eight Northern Indian Pueblos. The pueblo was established around 1250 AD. Like other Pueblo Indians, the Tesuques were declared citizens of Mexico when that nation gained its independence from Spain. The United States confirmed the tribe's rights in the 1848 Treaty of Guadalupe Hidalgo. The pueblo and its original land grant of 16,708 acres were patented in 1864. A subsequent tribal land purchase brought the reservation to its current size.

PHYSICAL DESCRIPTION

The reservation sits in the foothills of the scenic Sangre de Cristo Mountains at an elevation of about 7,000 feet. Topographically, it primarily consists of juniper-covered hills and grazing land. In addition, the pueblo owns the Aspen Ranch and Vigil Grant, two pine-forested areas in the Sangre de Cristos. These two holdings make up the bulk of the tribe's forested land.

CULTURE AND HISTORY

The present-day Village of Tesuque was established in 1694 along the Tesuque River, just north of Santa Fe. The name "Tesuque" is a Spanish variant of "tecuge," which means "structure at a narrow place." The Tesuque Pueblo is one of the most conservative and traditional of the Tewa pueblos. Like Taos Pueblo, the traditional religious officials (*fiscales*) exercise great influence within the tribal government and in all community affairs. Nevertheless, the region's tremendous growth and popularity, particularly Santa Fe, have forced the Tesuques to keep pace with local political changes. The key issues in this regard have been land and water rights. The Tesuques came under intense pressure to give up or lease their water and land to outsiders. During the early part of the twentieth century, significant numbers of Anglo settlers began moving into the Tesuque

Valley, putting great stress upon the valley's water supply. The Tesuques constructed a dam in 1923 to ensure water for the pueblo's main irrigation ditch, and from 1929 to 1935 the Indian Irrigation Service constructed a pair of infiltration basins near the river to alleviate continuing tribal water shortages. Water shortage remains a profound issue today, as this semiarid region's population grows to a level far greater than can be supported naturally.

The tribe has also had its share of run-ins with unscrupulous land developers and would-be business partners. In 1970, for instance, tribal officials signed an agreement with a Santa Fe development company to lease over 5,000 acres of land to develop a resort complex, which would include a golf course, multiple hotels and restaurants, and residential lots. After evidence of bad faith and deception on the part of the developer, the tribe canceled the lease in 1976.

Traditional culture remains vital in the pueblo, with various dances and ceremonials taking place throughout the year. Tribal artists, particularly those who produce traditional pottery, are beginning to see a greater demand for their work in Santa Fe's thriving Native American art market.

GOVERNMENT

The Tesuque tribal government is based on Spanish institutions that have been integrated with the tribes' own political-religious system. The tribe has no constitution or charter. The governing body is the tribal council, which acts as a liaison between the pueblo and outside contacts. Tribal council meetings are scheduled for the second Tuesday of each month. Council officers include a governor, a lieutenant governor, a sheriff, two *fiscales*, a war captain, and two assistants. Elections are held on the first of January, and terms of office are one year. The *fiscales*, whose duties are usually church-related, also provide administrative assistance to the governor. The governor and the tribal business manager administer all service programs.

ECONOMY
Traditionally, the pueblo's economy has been agricultural. While agricultural activity continues on a limited scale today, the tribe now realizes much of its income from leasing land to small businesses and from operating several tribally owned businesses, including a high-stakes bingo venture, a number of arts and crafts shops, and a small organic farming enterprise. Additionally, many of the tribe's members work at day jobs in Santa Fe and Los Alamos.

Government as Employer. Federal and state grants and projects (distributed through the tribal government) comprise a major source of employment on the reservation. About 42 tribal members are employed through the tribal government's various branches and programs.

Economic Development Projects. The tribe is a member of the Eight Northern Indian Pueblos Council, a nonprofit entity that provides community-based assistance in the areas of economic development, community services, social services, employment, and training within the member tribes. Members include the Taos, San Juan, Santa Clara, Nambé, Picuris, San Ildefonso, and Pojoaque pueblos.

Agriculture and Livestock. There are about 600 acres of irrigated lands served by about nine miles of irrigation ditches. An additional 200 acres of tribal lands are suitable for agricultural development. Current crops include alfalfa and vegetables, generally for home consumption. The pueblo also features 15,820 acres of rangeland, which, at present, support less than a 100 head of cattle. There is potential for further development of both agriculture and ranching.

Forestry. The Aspen Ranch and Vigil Grant, two tribal holdings in the Sangre de Cristo Mountains, comprise the bulk of the tribe's forested land. At the present time, 350 acres of these lands are considered commercial timber areas.

Gaming. The tribe operates the popular Camel Rock Casino along the highway between Santa Fe and Española. It offers 700 slots/VLTs, 10 table games, and 600 bingo seats. There are also a restaurant and an entertainment venue. The adjacent Camel Rock Suites offers 273 guest rooms.

Construction. The pueblo has completed buildings to house various tribal programs such as Head Start and a senior citizens' center. The tribe is also restoring some of the old houses in the village plaza. These construction projects have resulted in employment for a number of tribal members. Additionally, a fair number of tribal members find employment in Santa Fe's booming construction industry.

Mining. Commercial excavation of sand and gravel has taken place periodically along streams on the reservation.

Real Estate/Commercial Development. The tribe owns the Tesuque Trailer Park. The tribe also leases land to over 30 businesses, ranging from horse stables to camping areas to service stations, convenience stores, and specialty shops.

Services and Retail. The tribe operates the Tesuque Pueblo Flea Market north of Santa Fe. It offers over 260 booths and is open every weekend between February and December. The tribe took over operations from private operators in 1998. The market underwent renovations in 2004 to include a food court, improved vendor facilities, and a new parking area. Many tribal members are artists who sell their work through both the Santa Fe Indian Market and the Eight Northern Pueblos Indian Market. The tribe also owns Tesuque Natural Farms.

Tourism and Recreation. The Santa Fe area has become a major tourist destination, and the Native American presence is a significant draw. In this vein, the Tesuque Pueblo attracts many visitors. The tribe hosts a number of ceremonies throughout the year, many of which are open to the public. Festivities are held in honor of San Diego on November 12, Christmas celebrations are held during December, and the Three Kings Day festivities are held in January. A Corn Dance is held in June. Sculptures, micaceous and nonmicaceous pottery, and paintings produced by numerous tribal members are also popular with tourists. The original pueblo has been listed on the National Register of Historic Places.

The region abounds with breathtaking mountain scenery, hiking, skiing, fishing, and hotels and restaurants of every hue. The Bandelier National Monument and Painted Cave are also nearby. The tribe owns the Camel Rock RV Park. It offers 68 pull-through hookup sites, tent sites, a swimming pool and hot tub, a laundry room, a fishing pond, and public phones.

INFRASTRUCTURE
The pueblo is located on U.S. Highway 64/285, nine miles north of Santa Fe. I-25 runs north-south within a few miles. Commercial air, bus, and trucking lines serve Santa Fe. The nearest commercial rail service is in Lamy, 30 miles from the reservation.

Electricity. The Public Service Company of New Mexico provides electricity to the reservation.

Fuel. Local distributors provide gas.

Water Supply. The U.S. Public Health Service installed water and sewer systems for the reservation. The tribe operates an open dump for domestic refuse. It is restricted to pueblo members only.

COMMUNITY FACILITIES AND SERVICES
Education. A BIA-operated day school for grades 1-6 has operated on the pueblo for decades. Public schools in nearby Pojoaque and Santa Fe provide educational facilities for junior high and high school students, while the Santa Fe Indian School serves as a traditional alternative.

Health Care. The U.S. Public Health Service hospital in Santa Fe provides nearby health care facilities. Additionally, the tribe maintains a community health representative to assist tribal members in obtaining health services.

ENVIRONMENTAL CONCERNS
Land and water rights are the tribe's primary environmental concerns. Their water supply is limited, and as development occurs on the reservation and in surrounding areas, the supply is threatened. Other concerns include water quality and soil contamination. Mining activity on tribal lands has affected the soil conditions and threatens groundwater quality.

In 1996, the tribe's environmental department initiated a Permaculture Design Certificate Course. The program offers members from indigenous communities the opportunity to study the theory and practice of ecological land-use planning, watershed restoration, home and commercial organic gardening, alternative building design, natural waste treatment systems, soil building, forest gardening, seed collection and preservation, animal forage systems, native plant lore, and regenerative economics.

Tesuque

Total area *(BIA realty, 2004)*
16,813.16 acres

Population *2000 census*
806

Tribal enrollment
(BIA labor report, 2001)
404

Total labor force *2000 census*
408

Total labor force
(BIA labor report, 2001)
263

High school graduate or higher
2000 census
81.2%

Bachelor's degree or higher
2000 census
18.8%

Unemployment rate *2000 census*
6.9%

Unemployment rate *(BIA labor report, 2001)*
33%

Per capita income *2000 census*
$16,484

To'Hajiilee Reservation
Formerly Cañoncito Navajo
Chapter
Federal reservation
Navajo
Bernalillo, Cibola, and
Sandoval counties, New
Mexico

To'Hajiilee Navajo Chapter
Cañoncito, NM 87026
505-836-4221
505-839-7322 Fax

ENVIRONMENTAL CONCERNS
There are two Superfund sites on the To'Hajiilee Reservation, one of which is an abandoned uranium mine two miles southeast of the reservation school.

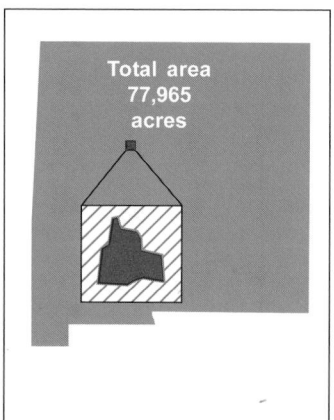

Total area
77,965
acres

Total area *(Tribal source, 2003)*		77,965 acres
Population **2000 census**		1,649
Population *(Tribal source, 2003)*		1,741
Total labor force **2000 census**		476
Total labor force *(Tribal source, 2003)*		531
Unemployment rate **2000 census**		24.2%
Unemployment rate		78%
(Tribal source, 2003)		
Per capita income **2000 census**		$5,877
Per capita income		$5,877
(Tribal source, 2003)		

LOCATION AND LAND STATUS
The To'Hajiilee Reservation lies about 20 miles west of Albuquerque, New Mexico, just north of I-40, in arid plateau country. It lies on Bell Rock Mesa between two parts of Laguna Pueblo to the southwest and northeast. In 1868 when the U.S. government established the primary Navajo Reservation, Navajo people who chose not to make the long march to the Navajo Reservation resettled in the Cañoncito area. The Cañoncito Reservation was created by federal statute in 1949. The chapter's name was changed to To'Hajiilee ("Bringing Up Water from a Natural Well") in 2000, and the reservation is referred to under either name.

CULTURE AND HISTORY
Navajos have lived in the Cañoncito area for many centuries. In 1768 a Spanish land grant just north of Cañoncito included the express requirement that the rights of the Navajos who had settled there not be disturbed. In 1868, at the end of their exile at Fort Sumner following the "Long Walk," the Diné Ana'i ("Enemy Navajo") led by Delgadito Chiquito returned to their home area of Cañoncito rather than relocate to the Navajo Reservation. The To'Hajiilee Reservation was created by federal statute in 1949, and the chapter was certified in 1955.

On the To'Hajiilee Reservation, 29.3 percent of the 1,489 people five years of age and over are monolingual in English; 67.2 percent speak Navajo; and 26.0 percent speak English less than "very well" according to the 2000 census. *(See the Navajo Nation entry in the Arizona section for further information.)*

GOVERNMENT
The To'Hajiilee Navajo Chapter is a federally recognized subunit of the Navajo Nation. It has a council led by an elected president. It is not recognized as a self-governing tribe for PL-638 contracting purposes. The Cañoncito Circuit Court is a satellite court of the Ramah District of the Navajo Nation Tribal Courts.

ECONOMY
Because it is part of the Navajo Nation, the chapter receives a portion of the Navajo Nation's revenues-largely proceeds from mining and mineral sales. Most reservation inhabitants work off the reservation.

Economic Development Projects. The To'Hajiilee Reservation served, along with three pueblos, as the entire setting for the PBS production of Tony Hillerman's *A Thief of Time* in 2002.

Gaming. The leaders of the To'Hajiilee Chapter have been struggling for a number of years to establish a casino on their reservation, close to Albuquerque and the intersection of I-25 and I-40. They have planned a 100,000-square-foot casino with 650 slot machines, 30 table games, a 150-room hotel, an RV park, and a truck stop. The chapter has identified 640 acres of the reservation as the location for the casino complex. The primary

difficulty has been opposition from the Navajo Nation government. Although the chapter's members fully support the casino plan, the Nation as a whole has rejected gambling on its lands in three referenda, primarily on moral and cultural grounds. In 2001, after New Mexico approved a gaming compact negotiated with the chapter, the Navajo Nation Council rejected the compact on the grounds that it granted too much civil jurisdiction to the state. In 2003 the Navajo Nation Council reversed its position and approved the compact, as did the secretary of the interior. The Nation government then exempted the To'Hajiilee Chapter from the antigambling provisions of its criminal code; but in 2004 the Nation president vetoed a tribal gambling ordinance passed by the Navajo Nation Council, and the council was unable to override the veto. Until the Nation passes a gambling ordinance and establishes a tribal gaming commission, the chapter will be unable to proceed with its plans.

INFRASTRUCTURE
Electricity. Public Service Company of New Mexico provides electricity. The chapter also buys bulk hydroelectric power from the Western Area Power Administration of the U.S. Department of Energy.

Fuel. Public Service Company of New Mexico provides natural gas.

Water Supply. Water is well drawn.

Transportation. The To'Hajiilee Reservation is just north of I-40, a major east-west artery in the region, and 20 miles west of I-25, the region's major north-south route. Passenger and freight rail service, bus service, and commercial air service are available in Albuquerque, 20 miles east of the reservation. There is one paved road through the reservation.

COMMUNITY FACILITIES AND SERVICES
The Navajo Nation Police have a substation in To'Hajiilee with two police officers, and there is a BIA Volunteer Fire Service.

Education. The BIA Eastern Navajo Agency operates To'Hajiilee-He (To'Hajiilee Community School), with a 2002 enrollment of 370 students in grades K-12. The school facilities were improved in 2000.

Health Care. In 2004, construction began on a new 10,000-square-foot Indian Health Service To'Hajiilee Health Clinic, replacing a substandard 3,360-square-foot modular facility purchased in 1984. The clinic is part of the Acoma-Cañoncito-Laguna Service Unit of the Indian Health Service, and it is backed by the unit's Acoma-Cañoncito-Laguna Hospital in Acomita, New Mexico. The hospital provides general medical, pediatric, and obstetric impatient care with 25 beds. It also houses a dialysis unit and the New Sunrise Regional Treatment Center, a residential program for adolescents. The hospital offers a full range of outpatient and dental services as well as several specialty clinics, using a combination of direct and contract services. Full diagnostic and treatment facilities support outpatient care. It operates a field health program, including health education, public health nursing, social services, nutrition, school health programs, environmental health, and alcohol and substance abuse services. Members of the chapter constitute about one-tenth of the population supported by the hospital. The To'Hajiilee Field Office of the Navajo Nation's Department of Emergency Medical Services is located next to the To'Hajiilee Health Clinic, with a supervisor, seven emergency medical technicians, and a clerk, and it operates two ambulances.

Ute Mountain
See Colorado

LOCATION AND LAND STATUS

The Zia Pueblo spans an area of 190 square miles, or 121,577 acres, in north-central New Mexico. It is located approximately 35 miles northwest of Albuquerque and 60 miles southwest of Santa Fe.

The present site of Zia Pueblo was settled in and has been continuously occupied since around 1250 AD. A Spanish land grant to the Zia people was enacted in 1689. Mexico recognized the grant after Mexican independence in 1821, and the United States honored it as well, following the Treaty of Guadalupe Hidalgo in 1848. The size of the original grant is not certain, but the United States recognized it at 16,282 acres. Purchases and executive orders since then have increased the reservation to its present size. Acquisition of new lands is an ongoing concern of the tribe. In 2003 Zia Pueblo purchased from the King Brothers about 30,000 acres located southwest of their reservation. This land was taken into trust the same year.

In 2004 the U.S. House of Representatives passed the Ojito Wilderness Bill, which designates over 11,000 acres as protected wilderness lands, but the U.S. Senate did not. The bill will be reintroduced to Congress in 2005. If this bill is passed, the Pueblo of Zia will be allowed to purchase 12,000 acres of Bureau of Land Management land to unite their ancestral lands. This legislation would place the 12,000 acres into trust and would not require action by the department of the interior. The bill would also protect the water and grazing rights of people who live there, and it would release lands from wilderness study designation that are not appropriate for wilderness. The Zia Pueblo, called "Puñi," which means "land to the west." is located five miles southwest of San Ysidro. Purchased lands will remain open to the public for recreational, scenic, scientific, educational, paleontological and conservation uses, and must be managed as open, undeveloped space in perpetuity.

PHYSICAL DESCRIPTION

The reservation lies within the Upper Sonoran Life Zone, characterized by piñon and juniper woodlands and ponderosa pine forests. Elevations on the pueblo range from 5,300 feet to 9,042 feet, with average altitude between 5,500 and 6,500 feet. Topography varies greatly, from the steep mountain slopes and canyons of the Sierra Nacimiento Mountains to the gently sloping flood plain of the Jemez River. The Pajarito and Jemez plateaus compose a large portion of the reservation.

CULTURE AND HISTORY

The Zias' early ancestors are thought to be the Eastern Anasazi who lived in the Chaco Canyon area of western New Mexico prior to 400 AD. At the end of the twelfth century, these people began migrating southeastward-likely motivated in part by a 25-year drought, which occurred at the beginning of the thirteenth century-and eventually ended up in their present location. The tribe's first contact with the Spanish was the 1541 encounter with the Coronado Expedition. Spanish records from the time describe Zia Pueblo as containing over 1,000 well-kept two- and three-story houses and over 4,000 adult males, as well as women and children. Spanish interference with the pueblo's spiritual traditions led the Zias to join in the Pueblo Revolt of 1680, which ultimately resulted in the pueblo's decimation by a bloody assault during the 1688 reconquest by the Spanish. In 1692 the Zias accepted mass baptism and became nominal Roman Catholics. This action did not erase the old ways, however. Today, Pueblo of Zia maintains its elaborate, centuries-old cultural and religious traditions. The pueblo's sophisticated dry farming methods have made successful cultivation by large populations possible in a

desert climate. Traditional crops include corn, beans, squash, and melons. The tribe has utilized ditch irrigation around pueblo farmlands for centuries.

After the Spanish introduced sheep and cattle in 1598, the tribe gradually shifted toward a pastoral economy to the extent that, by the mid-twentieth century, livestock grazing was clearly dominant. By the 1960s, sheep herding had, for various reasons, become unprofitable for the tribe, though cattle raising has persisted through recent years. Today the tribe's main income comes from wage jobs in the nearby cities of Albuquerque and Rio Rancho, and from farming and ranching. The tribe generates additional revenue through leasing land for uses consistent with tribal views and values. The Zias also own lands within the non-Indian community of San Ysidro, which it intends to develop under an enterprise zone status. The tribe is promoting the reservation as a site for film production, an effort that has successfully attracted a number of big-time productions. The production of traditional arts and crafts also provides both a supplemental income and an important connection to the tribe's past. Pueblo of Zia opened a cultural center and museum in 1992, and continues various celebrations, ceremonies, and dances throughout the year.

GOVERNMENT

The tribe is organized under the rules of the 1934 Indian Reorganization Act, though its members also consider themselves a traditionally organized tribe. The tribal government is run by the Zia Tribal Council. Officers include a governor, a lieutenant governor, and assistants appointed annually by the religious council. The general council, or Zia Secular Council, is composed of male tribal members over the age of 18. The tribe maintains its own tribal court system, with the governor serving as chief judge.

The Zia Tribal Government consists of the office of the governor and lieutenant governors, the tribal administrator and assistant tribal administrator. They oversee six tribal departments that include administrative services, tribal operations, community services, resource protection, health and human services, and education. The tribal enterprises department works directly with the tribal administrator. The pueblo has a tribal court system that administers the Zia Law and Order Code. The court system is located within the community services department. The governor appoints the health and utility boards and the housing authority.

ECONOMY

The Zia economy consists of tribal operations funded by the federal government and supplemented by agriculture, forestry, tourism, and several small business enterprises.

Government as Employer. In 2004 the tribal government had an administrative staff of 25 full-time employees and a number of part-time workers.

Agriculture and Livestock. Virtually all of the reservation is used as grazing land- approximately 104,000 acres-with most of this allotted to specific families for grazing purposes. The grazing land is considered capable of supporting about 825 head of cattle. Since numerous families on the reservation practice grazing as a source of supplemental income, overgrazing has become a problem, resulting in accelerated erosion of fragile land. To combat this problem, the reservation has been divided into 15 grazing management units. The tribe has also implemented and is monitoring the effects of the savory grazing method on

Zia Pueblo
Federal reservation
Keresan
Sandoval County, New Mexico

Pueblo of Zia
135 Capitol Square Drive
Zia Pueblo, NM 87053
505-867-3304
505-867-3308 Fax

Total area *(BIA, 2004)*
121,613.27 acres

Total area *(Tribal Source, 2004)*
121,577 acres

Population *2000 census*
646

Tribal enrollment
(BIA labor report, 2001)
773

Total labor force *2000 census*
258

Total labor force
(BIA labor report, 2001)
559

High school graduate or higher
2000 census
73.9 %

Bachelor's degree or higher
2000 census
8.9%

Unemployment rate *2000 census*
7.8%

Per capita income *2000 census*
$8,689

Zia

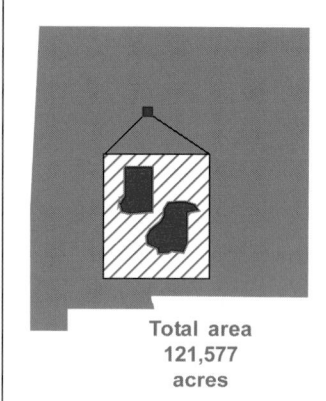

Total area
121,577
acres

some of its land. Small garden plots are primarily for personal consumption, though some produce is sold locally at farmers and produce markets. Crops include corn, alfalfa, chili, and pasture grasses, totaling about 130 acres, with a market value of approximately $50,000 annually.

Forestry. Zia has a small amount of commercial timber in the Nacimiento Mountains on the southern portion of the reservation, primarily white pine and ponderosa pine. Individuals also harvest small amounts of piñon and juniper for personal use.

Fisheries. Zia Lake, located on the north side of the Jemez River, features excellent year-round recreational catfish and trout fishing.

Mining. The reservation contains large amounts of commercial gypsum, some of which is being quarried and mined by the American Gypsum Company. The average purity of the gypsum is an excellent 98.1 percent. The tribe realizes significant royalties and modest employment from this arrangement. Sub-bituminous coal deposits are also found within the Rio Puerco coalfield on the southwestern portion of the reservation. However, development of the seams is not considered economically feasible. During the late 1950s, a small amount of uranium was mined on the reservation. Other pockets of uranium have since been discovered. Significant amounts of travertine, a decorative building stone, also exist on the reservation; a joint development venture with an outside company has been considered. The reservation also holds potentially lucrative amounts of humate, deposits of humic acid, which can be sold as a soil conditioner. The pueblo currently leases land to Mesa Verde Resources for its humate-processing plant off State Highway 550 near Cabezon Road. The humate for this plant comes from Bureau of Land Management lands near Cuba, New Mexico.

Industrial Parks. Pueblo of Zia owns 19 and one-half acres of main street frontage property in the town of Bernalillo along State Highway 550 for about four-tenths of a mile westward toward the Rio Grande Bridge. This property was purchased in 1996 for economic development.

Services and Retail. The tribe also operates a small convenience store. There is a laundromat, a gallery, and a sales site for Zia pottery, dresses, and belts at the Zia Cultural Center. Tribal potters work at the center.

Media and Communications. Pueblo of Zia is actively promoting film production on its reservation, touting the area's striking scenery and topography, as well as its easy accessibility from Albuquerque. In 2003 four motion picture companies used Zia lands in part for their background scenes and settings for *Coyote Waits*, *A Thief of Time*, *The Missing*, and *21 Grams*. In 2004 two films, *Around the Bend* and *Wild Fire*, were filmed on Zia lands. Pueblo of Zia works closely with the New Mexico Film Commission to promote film production on its reservation. Zia Pueblo is the only New Mexico Pueblo that actively participates in the annual Association of Film Commission International tradeshow to market its lands.

Tourism and Recreation. Zia Lake is a popular recreation area, offering fishing, swimming, and hiking. The Zia Pueblo Cultural Center is also popular with visitors. The tribe holds a number of annual ceremonies including the Our Lady of Assumption Fiesta, an Indian festival featuring the Corn Dance, held on August 15; buffalo dances on December 25-26; and an Easter celebration.

INFRASTRUCTURE
The pueblo is located along State Highway 550, a short distance from I-25. Greyhound Lines maintains one scheduled bus stop at nearby San Ysidro. Air and rail services are located in Albuquerque and Santa Fe.

Electricity. Jemez Mountain Cooperative provides electricity.

Fuel. Local distributors supply propane.

Water Supply. Community wells drilled by the Indian Health Service furnish water. A system of lagoons, also installed by the Indian Health Service, meets sewerage needs. The tribe maintains its own solid waste disposal system, which includes a landfill.

COMMUNITY FACILITIES AND SERVICES
The tribe constructed a cultural center adjacent to tribal headquarters in 1984. The center includes the Zia Pueblo Tribal Library with over 2,000 books, audio and visual materials, and 10 serial subscriptions to journals. The Zia Education Center is a student services center that serves as a resource and learning center for tribal and community members. The pueblo provides a host of social services to its members, including a senior citizen program, a youth recreation, employment services, housing, and various public works programs.

Education. Middle school and high school students attend public schools in the Jemez School District. Zia Day School services grades K-6. There is a Head Start program at Zia. The tribal education department sponsors early childhood programs and child care, and it administers the tribe's library and higher education program consisting of adult education, JOM, and higher education and technical vocational scholarships.

Health Care. The Albuquerque Area Indian Health Services provide most medical services. The Albuquerque Service Unit maintains the Zia Clinic for Zia tribal members. Through the health and human services department, the tribe provides its membership with a behavioral health program, CHR, a diabetes program, vocational rehabilitation, and a women's wellness program.

TRI-NM-Zia-001 Cornfield being irrigated

LOCATION AND LAND STATUS

Located in the west-central part of New Mexico, Zuni Pueblo is one of the largest and most traditional of the 19 New Mexico Indian pueblos. Zuni Pueblo borders the New Mexico state line, due west of Albuquerque, directly south of Gallup, on Route 602. Reservation lands include a modest tract of land surrounding the Zuni Salt Lake, 30 miles south of the main reservation, and five tracts of land near the confluence of the Zuni and Little Colorado river valleys in east-central Arizona. The reservation spans approximately 588,093 acres of rangeland, croplands, and mixed conifer forests. Of this total, a small amount is allotted. The village of Zuni represents the pueblo's population center and is the site of all governmental, educational, health, and service organizations.

The present-day reservation lies on the site of Halona, one of the Seven Cities of Cibola. Zuni Pueblo, the community's principal town, was founded around 1350. The main body of the reservation was established by an Executive Order in 1877. An Act of Congress put the pueblo's land into trust in 1978.

PHYSICAL DESCRIPTION

Elevation varies between 6,000 and 7,000 feet above sea level on reservation lands. Topography is described primarily as open sagebrush valleys interrupted by outcrops of sandstone mesas and tilted rock formations, cut with narrow canyons and deep valleys partially covered with piñon-juniper forests. The region is dotted with manmade lakes fed by runoff and a few natural springs.

CLIMATE

The year-round average daily high temperature is 66°F, with the highest temperature on record as 103°F. The year-round average daily low temperature is 34°F, with the lowest temperature ever recorded being -31°F. The area receives approximately 12 inches of precipitation annually, with 29 inches of snowfall.

CULTURE AND HISTORY

The Zunis and their ancestors have occupied the Zuni and Little Colorado river valleys for more than 2,000 years. Soon after the Spanish conquest of Mexico, the Spaniards heard rumors of the Zunis and the Seven Cities of Cibola. Francisco de Coronado first met the Zunis on his expedition of 1540, and he later invaded the capital of the Seven Cities, Hawikku. The Spanish established their first mission there in 1629. After the 1848 Treaty of Guadalupe Hidalgo, the United States came into possession of the 16 million acres of Zuni aboriginal territory and traditional use areas, which include parts of New Mexico, Arizona, Utah, and Colorado. At this time, the Zuni Tribe was arguably the wealthiest and most secure political force in that region of the southwest. The core of the tribe's traditional lands lay in the Zuni Mountains, the watershed of the Zuni River, and the beautiful mountain pastures containing thousands of acres of richly cultivated agricultural lands. During the mid-nineteenth century, the Zunis cultivated 10 to 12 thousand acres of crops in this region, primarily corn, and grazed thousands of sheep upon the grasslands within a two million-acre area. They also harvested a great deal of salt from the Zuni Salt Lake, which provided an important resource for their consumption and religious icons.

Between 1846 and 1876, the U.S. government actively encouraged non-Indian settlement of the west. As a result, the Zunis lost control of approximately nine million acres of territory. Still, the tribe maintained control over most of its grazing land and almost all of its upper watershed area. The U.S. Congress, having determined that a southern transcontinental railroad would greatly benefit the nation, authorized the Atlantic and Pacific Railroad to begin building. As the railway was scheduled to cut across Zuni territory, the federal government set aside a small tract of land for a Zuni Reservation. In 1881, Atlantic and Pacific cut a swath through the former Zuni territory, cutting tens of millions of board feet of lumber from the once-pristine watershed area in the process. The cumulative effect of these activities was almost unparalleled environmental damage, primarily through erosion. Calls for a national forest area in the Zuni Mountains went unheeded, and during the early twentieth century, logging and grazing intensified. Between 1912 and 1940, all but 5,000 acres of the remaining commercial timber in the Zuni Mountains were cut. In 1940 the forest service observed that the Zuni Mountains were largely denuded, barren, and cut through with runoff gullies up to 30 feet deep. At least 11,000 acres of prime irrigable land have been lost to Zuni agricultural use since the coming of the railroad in 1881.

As an alternative to crop agriculture, the BIA promoted the Zuni livestock industry during the late 1930s, instituting grazing regulations, fencing, and assigned parcels. Today the reservation supports about 14,000 sheep, cattle, and other farm animals.

Petitions from the tribe in 1917, 1935, and 1949 led to an expansion of the reservation. Since that time, the tribe has been involved in nearly continuous litigation over land claims and water rights. In 1978 the tribe was awarded the return of their Salt Lake property. The New Mexico courts dismissed claims for damages to their remaining trust lands, archeological sites, water, and other resources during the 1980s, and they await reinstatement at a future date. In 1984 the tribe was successful in regaining a tract of Arizona land known as "Zuni Heaven," though access to the site immediately became a problem due to the resistance of a neighboring rancher. In 1990, in separate court of claims cases, the Zunis finally received compensation for lands taken without authority, and an award to establish a permanent trust for sustainable development and rehabilitation of degraded lands.

Unemployment remains high on the reservation, but the tribe has established a number of successful businesses including traditional arts and crafts enterprises and an archeological consulting company. It is aggressively pursuing plans for viable commercial development. Throughout their history, the Zunis have maintained a strong sense of community, and their native tongue has remained their primary language.

GOVERNMENT

During the 1890s, the U.S. government undermined the Zunis' traditional political structure by jailing the Zuni Bow priests and preventing them from exercising their traditional executive authority on behalf of the Priestly Council. Turmoil ensued, and in 1934 the tribe voted to accept the terms of the Indian Reorganization Act. In 1970 the tribe ratified its constitution, authorized under the Indian Reorganization Act of 1934. Currently the Pueblo of Zuni Tribal Council acts as the governing body for the Zuni Tribe. The tribal government is structured to include an executive branch, a legislative branch, and a judicial branch. The Zuni Tribal Council consists of a governor, a lieutenant governor, and six members, all of whom are elected to four-year terms.

The tribe, under PL-638, contracts with the BIA to administer key programs and services. They have their own health depart-

Zuni Pueblo
Federal reservation
Zuni
McKinley, Valencia, and Catron counties, New Mexico; Apache County, Arizona

Pueblo of Zuni
P.O. Box 339
Zuni, NM 87327
  505-782-7022
  505-782-7202 Fax
  experiencezuni.com

Total area (BIA realty, 2004)
463,270.83 acres

Total area (Tribal source, 2005)
588,093 acres

Population 2000 census
7,758

Tribal enrollment
(BIA labor report, 2001)
9,554

Total labor force 2000 census
2,698 acres

Total labor force
(BIA labor report, 2001)
4,579

High school graduate or higher
2000 census
64.4%

Bachelor's degree or higher
2000 census
6.8%

Unemployment rate 2000 census
18.6%

Unemployment rate
(BIA labor report, 2001)
66.37%

Per capita income 2000 census
$6,976

Zuni

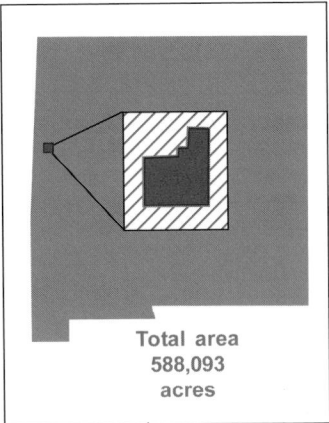

Total area
588,093
acres

ment, which operates the Zuni Comprehensive Community Health Center and some specialty care programs. *(See also, Health, below.)* They also have a natural resources department.

BUSINESS CORPORATION

The tribe has formed the A:shiwi A:wan Business Development Corporation to guide economic development planning and the initiation of new tribal enterprises at the pueblo. The corporation and its various enterprises promote quality authentic Indian products, combining traditional values and unique cultural designs. Other specialized services provided by the corporation include business development training regarding the formulation of business plans, marketing plans, financial pro forma, personalized customer service, and community printing and graphic designs. Several Zuni enterprises are operated under the umbrella of the corporation, including Zuni Furniture Enterprise, Pueblo of Zuni Arts and Crafts Enterprise, Zuni Forest Products and Services, Zuni Rental Enterprise, Zuni Skies Unlimited, Zuni Cultural Resource Enterprise, and the Inn at Halona.

ECONOMY

The Zuni Pueblo's economy is supported by four main employers and entities that include the tribal government, Indian Health Service, the BIA, and the Zuni Public School District. There are also seasonal cottage arts and crafts industries and other businesses. Under the guidance of the Zuni Tribal Council through its Pueblo of Zuni Office of Planning and Development and A:shiwi A:wan Economic Development Corporation, the tribe has taken on a more diversified approach to economic development.

Government as Employer. The tribal government remains the largest employer on the reservation. In 2004 the tribal government, via its various programs, services, and enterprises, employed approximately 250 people.

Economic Development Projects. Over the last several decades, the Zuni Tribe has maintained three primary goals for development. First, to increase wage earning potential for individuals. Second, to increase the tax revenue base. Third, to foster opportunities that promote and support economic development, enhance educational possibilities, and improve living conditions in the pueblo.

The Zuni Land Conservation Act, passed in 1990, includes a permanent trust fund to help implement the Zuni Sustainable Resource Development Plan, which deals with land use and social and economic issues. The project achieved international acclaim as a model of culturally sensitive sustainable resource development. In formulating the plan, the tribe used cultural values and community input as the foundation for policy on sustainable development. Much of the plan deals with watershed and wetlands restoration.

Agriculture and Livestock. Sheep production is the top agricultural venture on the reservation; the tribe maintains herds totaling approximately 14,000 in number. They also have about 2,000 head of cattle, 250 hogs and pigs, 200 fowl, 150 horses, and 50 goats. Crop farming, which once spanned over 12,000 acres of Zuni territory, now has limited production. The Zunis are known for their traditional peach orchards.

The Zuni Sustainable Agriculture Project, a part of the Zuni Land Conservation Act, completed a mapping project of Zuni agricultural lands. The Zunis are working toward protecting their "folk" varieties of traditional crop seeds, including corn, beans, squash, melons, chilies, and peaches.

Forestry. Though the vast majority of Zuni forestlands were decimated through clear-cutting by outside interests, the reservation still contains some forested lands. These include mostly mixed conifers. The land is maintained by the Zuni Agency of the BIA,

Forestry Branch. The branch includes forest management and fire management. Zuni Forest Products and Services specializes in rough-sawn lumber, pine square beams, firewood, planed lumber, both forest and residential tree-thinning services, and hand-carved traditional ponderosa pine *vigas* and *corbals.*

Fisheries. Nutria Lake and the Zuni River, which lie on tribal lands, along with streams in the Cibola National Forest, provide excellent fishing opportunities. Additionally, the reservation has six reservoirs stocked with rainbow and cutthroat trout, northern pike, channel catfish, and largemouth bass. Permits may be purchased at various locations on the pueblo.

Construction. Zuni Rental Enterprise restores and renovates old houses and rents them to pueblo tribal members and contracted workers.

Manufacturing. Zuni Furniture Enterprise manufactures a unique style of furniture, combining Spanish Colonial styling with traditional Zuni fetish, pottery, and folklore designs. Crafts are produced at Zuni Pueblo by a community of 1,000 artists, craftspeople, and entrepreneurs who work in hundreds of mini-workshops set up in garages, dining rooms, and small outbuildings. The products of this cottage industry are the famous Zuni jewelry, fetishes, pottery, paintings, and beadwork. Bread making is another cottage industry on the pueblo. Tribal members have acquired the skills to apply traditional artistry to furniture and a variety of wood products. The future promises a business climate of small, non-polluting industries, with growth in the service industries. These activities currently generate highly significant revenues for a wide sector of the tribal community.

Services and Retail. Most of the tribal businesses are centered on the arts and crafts industry. The Pueblo of Zuni Arts and Crafts Enterprise, formerly referred to as the Pueblo Craftsmen Cooperative, is a nonprofit organization housed in the Zuni tribal building. It is an outlet for the arts and supports many tribal member artisans and craftspeople. The store offers 2,000 square feet of retail space, and it features beautiful, authentic jewelry, pottery, carved stone fetishes, and a variety of paintings and textiles. The store buys directly from the artisans, which allows for a great selection at affordable prices. The management has been promoting the store in a variety of ways, including a booth at the Indian Arts and Craft Association in Mesa, Arizona, as well as a special location in Albuquerque during the balloon fiesta.

The Inn at Halona, established in 1998, is a tribally authorized bed-and-breakfast lodging accommodation, the only one in Zuni Pueblo. Halona Plaza, next door, is a general market that caters to the needs of tourists and guests of residents. The inn is featured in the US/GSA Hotel Motel Master List, offering government rates to qualifying travelers on official government business. Zuni Pueblo is within easy driving distance of Gallup, New Mexico, where an array of lodging is available.

Zuni Cultural Resource Enterprise is a Small Business Administration 8(a) and HUB Zone Certified Small Disadvantaged Business. From their offices in Black Rock, New Mexico, they provide cultural resource management services such as archaeological research, planning and information technology, surveys, site reassessments, phased data recovery investigations, monitoring activities, ethnographic assessments, historic architectural documentary assessments, and site stabilization procedures. A division of the Zuni Cultural Resource Enterprise, the Division of Information Technology has also begun operations as part of the Zuni Employment Initiative.

Zuni Skies Unlimited acts as an agent for CellularOne of northeastern Arizona. Headquartered in Show Low, Arizona, it is the cellular phone company currently serving the Zuni community, the northwest corner of Arizona, and south-central New Mexico.

Media and Communications. The tribe publishes an on-line visitors' guide at their homepage on the Internet.

Tourism and Recreation. Built in 1629, Our Lady of Guadalupe Mission, located at the center of the old village, can be visited during a limited number of hours per day. Also open to the public is the A:shiwi A:wan Museum and Heritage Center where staff disseminates information regarding the cultural values of the Zuni people. Various ancestral sites located throughout Zuni Valley are now open to the public. The ancient pueblo ruins of Hawikku, Matsakya, Village of the Great Kivas, Hard Scrabble Wash, Yellow House Ruins, Kiakima, Heshotultha, A:tsinna, Heshota Yalda, and Bma:wa are carefully protected sites accessible only by guided tour.

Hiking is permitted in designated areas around the Hawikku and Village of the Great Kivas archaeological sites, the Nutria Box Canyon Wilderness, and the fishing lakes. Hiking permits are occasionally issued for other areas, at the tribe's discretion. Camping is permitted in the immediate vicinity of the fishing lakes at Ojo Caliente and the Nutria Lakes Campground. Hunting and fishing are available on the Zuni Pueblo with a permit.

El Morro National Monument lies 35 miles to the east of the pueblo. Visitors are welcome at the A:shiwi A:wan Museum and Heritage Center in Zuni, and there is an artist's studio tour available with reservations. Guides and cultural interpreters are readily available throughout the day for information and tour planning, and for guided tour services. The tribe also hosts numerous special events such as the Shalako Ceremony, a major pueblo event that takes place in early December, and the Zuni Tribal Fair, featuring four days of festivities each Labor Day weekend.

INFRASTRUCTURE
State Highway 53 crosses the reservation from east to west, while State Highway 32 runs north-south and intersects Route 53 on the east side of the reservation.

Electricity. Continental Divide Electrical Cooperative furnishes electricity to the pueblo.

Water Supply. The Zuni Utility Department operates the reservation's water and sewage systems.

Transportation. Commercial air, bus, and train services are available in Gallup, 40 miles to the north. Commercial trucking companies serve the reservation directly. The Zuni Tribe maintains a 4,800-foot paved and lighted landing strip that can handle twin-engine aircraft; and the communities of Gallup, New Mexico (30 miles distant), and Window Rock, Arizona (43 miles away), maintain small commercial airstrips as well. The Zuni Tribal Council recently approved plans to construct a new Zuni airport to be located west of the Zuni community; the new airport will maintain a 6,000-foot runway and will accommodate small aircraft.

Telecommunications. The pueblo receives radio and television transmission from several stations.

COMMUNITY FACILITIES AND SERVICES
The pueblo has a tribal administration building, a community center, and the A:shiwi A:wan Museum and Heritage Center.

Education. In 1980 the Zunis became the first tribe in New Mexico to establish a public school district with boundaries coinciding with their reservation. The Zuni district currently serves K-12 students in five public schools. There are also two parochial elementary and middle schools. The University of New Mexico offers liberal arts and vocational-technology courses on the reservation, and the University of New Mexico's Gallup branch offers additional liberal arts courses, professional preparatory classes, and vocational-technical training.
The Zuni Education and Career Development Center (ZECDC), initiated in 2000, helps individuals and families obtain education and training for self-sufficiency via economic independence. Primary services include education, training, and employment assistance through work experience and support services.

Health care. Medical care is provided by the Zuni Com-prehervice Indian Hospital, located in Zuni, offers a full range of medical, surgical, and emergency services.

The tribe also operates the Pueblo of Zuni Safe Start Program, a multidisciplinary approach to identifying at-risk infants and toddlers, and providing prevention, intervention, and treatment services for children exposed to violent environments.

Honoring Nations Honoree 2002

Zuni Eagle Sanctuary, Zuni Fish and Wildlife Department, Pueblo of Zuni (Zuni, New Mexico)

Created in 1999, the Zuni Eagle Sanctuary is the first eagle sanctuary owned and operated by Native Americans as well as the first aviary constructed for the purpose of cultural preservation. Combining both functional aspects of eagle care with an aesthetic that reflects the natural surroundings of Zuni, the Sanctuary is home to more than twenty eagles that otherwise would have been destroyed. Successfully meeting the Zunis' demand for molted eagle feathers that are used in religious and cultural ceremonies, the Sanctuary is also a model of intergovernmental cooperation between a tribal government and federal agency.

Located in west-central New Mexico, Zuni Pueblo is the largest and most remote of the nineteen New Mexico Indian Pueblos. Among other factors, the Zunis' remoteness has contributed to the strong continuation of their cultural and religious traditions-traditions that require the use of eagle feathers. Since time immemorial, eagles' molted feathers have been used in rain and prosperity ceremonies, as well as in prayer offerings.

Traditionally, Zunis satisfied this need for feathers by practicing eagle husbandry. They would collect eaglets from the wild and "adopt" them into their families. The birds were treated with the utmost respect and tenderness, frequently living with families for over half a century. According to the Zuni origin myth, Chimik'ana'kowa, a catastrophe can befall the Zunis when they become lax in their religious observances. Therefore, when the Bald and Golden Eagle Protection Act of 1940 and the Endangered Species Act of 1973 made traditional means of obtaining eagle feathers illegal, the Zunis were challenged to identify other sources of feathers.

Zuni

Honoring Nations
Honoree 2002

Text in its entirety from:
The Harvard Project On
American Indian Economic
Development

John F. Kennedy School
of Government
Harvard University

For several decades, the only legal way for Zunis and other Indians to obtain eagle feathers was to submit applications to the National Eagle Repository in Colorado. However, working through the Repository has proven challenging, largely because the demand for eagle feathers far exceeds the available supply. Although high demand may be indicative of Native cultural renaissance, the difficulty of obtaining feathers threatens that momentum. Applicants frequently wait several years to obtain eagle feathers from the Repository, delay which compromises tribal citizens' ability to plan and participate in religious and cultural ceremonies. The fact that many Zuni religious traditions specify that an eagle feather can be used only once makes it particularly difficult for the Zunis to obtain a sufficient number of feathers. By the mid-1990s, Zuni leaders agreed that something had to be done to increase the legal supply of eagle feathers for ceremonial use-even if it meant changing federal law.

Thus in 1995, the Zunis took a leadership position. They began discussions with the US Fish and Wildlife Service (USFWS) to address their dilemma. The discussions revealed that each year a large number of eagles in need of permanent placement were actually euthanized. In general, these were eagles injured in collisions with vehicles or electrocuted by power lines, and while many of these eagles could be rehabilitated, they could not be released back into the wild because of the loss of a wing or an eye. Sadly, disfigured but healthy eagles also were difficult to place in zoos or educational facilities - institutions that typically care for non-releasable birds. These birds provided Zuni Pueblo with an opportunity: By building an eagle sanctuary, it would not only accommodate the traditional practice of eagle husbandry and provide a source of molted eagle feathers for ceremonies, but it would save birds that otherwise would be destroyed.

After several years of negotiations with the USFWS that culminated in a historic Statement of Relationship, the Zuni Eagle Sanctuary received its first eagle in March 1999. The Sanctuary now maintains twenty-one birds (nine bald eagles and twelve golden eagles). The Zuni Fish and Wildlife Department oversees the Sanctuary and has developed its own feather distribution protocol, which makes it possible for religious and cultural leaders who once had to wait three years or more to obtain eagle feathers to do so within weeks. When necessary, a Zuni religious leader can obtain feathers on the day of the request, frequently within minutes. Since the Sanctuary's creation, the Zuni Fish and Wildlife Department has distributed nearly twenty thousand feathers to tribal citizens.

In addition to satisfying the Zuni people's need for molted eagle feathers, the excellent care that individual birds receive combined with the thoughtful design of the Sanctuary itself are extraordinary examples of government innovation. Indeed, the Zuni Fish and Wildlife Department's ability to translate community respect for eagles into top-quality care has earned Zuni the admiration of federal and state agencies (including those responsible for licensing the Sanctuary's activities), animal welfare groups, zoos, and wildlife rehabilitators. The Sanctuary building combines the functional aspects of eagle care with an aesthetic that reflects Pueblo's natural surroundings. The façade is made from locally quarried, hand-shaped, red Zuni sandstone while much of the lumber is from sustainably harvested mistletoe-infected trees milled by the Zuni Community Sawmill. The facility faces Dowa Yalanne, a sacred mesa, where golden eagles are occasionally sighted. In November 1999, the American Institute of Architecture recognized the Zuni Eagle Sanctuary with an "Award for Design Excellence."

Zuni Pueblo has exercised its sovereignty through the creation and operation of the Zuni Eagle Sanctuary in several significant ways. First, Zuni has exercised its political sovereignty by entering into a highly productive, government-to-government relationship with the USFWS. This relationship began with the Pueblo's conscious decision to identify and cultivate an individual ally within the federal bureaucracy who would understand the Zunis' concerns

and be willing to work with the Pueblo to develop an innovative solution. The strategy worked: Zuni leaders found an ally in the USFWS, and together they turned good individual relationships into productive institutional relationships that are grounded in mutual respect and a willingness to cooperate. Formalized in a Statement of Relationship that recognizes the Pueblo's sovereignty and the US government's trust responsibility, the strong positive relationship between the Pueblo and the USWS has allowed the two parties to effectively address a seemingly intractable problem in which Zuni cultural imperatives clashed with federal policy. In crafting a jointly beneficial solution to the problem, the Zuni transitioned from being recipients of the services of a federal program to partners in the design of a program that addresses their particular cultural needs. In fact, although they work in consultation with their community and the USFWS, the Zunis have gone one step farther by administering the program in its totality. A USFWS tribal liaison has called the agreement with the Zuni Pueblo a "paradigm shift" and feels that it has "blazed a trail for other tribes" with regard to innovative, tribally determined solutions to pressing cultural problems.

Further, in designing, building, and operating the Sanctuary, Zuni Pueblo has strengthened its ties with the local community and benefited from relationships with outside organizations without compromising its control over the facility. In addition to extensive communications with the USFWS, the National Park Service, and the Bureau of Indian Affairs (BIA), the Zunis have built relationships with dozens of local and national non-governmental foundations and organizations. These include the American Zoo and Aquarium Association and the National Association of Wildlife Rehabilitators, which assisted in designing the facility, and the Albuquerque Zoo and the New Mexico Wildlife Center, which provided training to sanctuary staff in raptor care. The Sanctuary also has engaged the Pueblo in relationships with other Indian nations that are either receiving eagle feathers for ceremonial purposes or are interested in pursuing similar agreements with the federal government.

Zuni Pueblo's success in meeting its core objective - increasing the supply of eagle feathers for use in religious and cultural ceremonies by creating and operating its own aviary - is tied directly to good program management. Two practices stand out as being particularly significant. First, the Zuni Tribal Government encouraged tribal citizen participation at every step of the Sanctuary's development. Prior to making the decision to proceed, staff of both the Zuni Fish and Wildlife and Zuni Natural Resources Departments spent a great deal of time canvassing tribal opinion. They held public meetings, consulted with Zuni religious leaders, made visits to kivas, and talked with village residents to hear and address concerns about the possibility of building and maintaining an eagle sanctuary. In establishing the Sanctuary, departmental staff honored what they had heard. For example, when religious leaders objected to a surgical procedure for "sexing" the birds for breeding purposes, the Sanctuary declined to breed the birds. This process of sincere consultation established confidence among tribal citizens that their opinions were being heard and valued, fostered broad support for the Sanctuary, and ultimately, bolstered Zuni citizens' trust in government. Critically, this process of consultation with the Zuni people has become a model for other Zuni tribal government programs, including a major wetlands project. One tribal member told a Sanctuary staff member that "We're not afraid to speak up anymore."

Second, the Sanctuary is committed to educating Zunis and non-Zunis in eagle husbandry, thus supporting a long-standing cultural practice while sharing knowledge with other interested individuals and Indian nations. The Sanctuary has developed a full-scale, hands-on educational program that serves both visitors and formal trainees, a highlight of which is the glove-trained golden eagle O:lo ("Golden" in Zuni). To date, the Sanctuary has trained ten Zuni high school work-study students in aspects of eagle care, one of whom intends to attend veterinary school. The Sanctuary also is working to give religious leaders a more significant role in the day-to-day handling and care of the birds. These partnerships draw on the long-standing knowledge of raptor care among the Zunis, a tradition of care that the Sanctuary helps maintain even while educating its staff and visitors in modern veterinary techniques. This communication of traditional and modern knowledge ensures the long-term sustainability of the Sanctuary.

The establishment of the Zuni Eagle Sanctuary in 1999 led to the successful satisfaction of the Pueblo's need for molted eagle feathers for religious and cultural ceremonies. It is the first Native American built and operated eagle sanctuary, and it reinvigorates the long-standing Zuni cultural tradition of eagle husbandry through unprecedented means. Creating the Sanctuary prompted the establishment of a cutting-edge, mutually beneficial relationship between the Zuni tribal government and a federal agency, strengthened ties between the tribal government and surrounding nongovernmental agencies, and established a pattern of sincere consultation between the tribal government and the citizens it serves. It is a successful program that demonstrates how the pursuit of self-governance can strengthen and support cultural traditions and values. Already, the Zuni Eagle Sanctuary has received visits from more than thirty Indian nations that hope to construct similar

facilities. In sum, the Zuni Eagle Sanctuary is an inspiring example of the unimagined possibilities for sustaining cultural practices open to Indian nations that harness the power of self-determination.

Lessons

Indian nations can work productively with and spark change within federal bureaucracies by cultivating individual allies. These allies can help tribal leaders navigate unfamiliar organizations and help their opinions and ideas be better heard. Importantly, these individual relationships can form the basis for productive, formalized intergovernmental relations (for example, MOUs, MOAs, Statements of Relationship).

Indian nations that manage their own natural resources are able to craft culturally appropriate policies and procedures and measure success using tribal standards. Tribal management also gives tribes an opportunity to develop technical and policy expertise in fields dominated by non-Indians.

One way tribal governments can become more responsive to community needs is to create mechanisms for soliciting tribal citizen input into governmental affairs. Not only can citizen involvement help tribal governments create better programs, but the resulting public support contributes to program sustainability.

Zuni

Honoring Nations Honoree 2003

Water Quality Standards, Environmental Department, Pueblo of Zuni

In collaboration with other concerned tribal and non-tribal governments, the Navajo Nation established the Na'Nizhoozhi Center, Inc. in 1992 to address the problem of public intoxication in Gallup, New Mexico. Remarkable not only for its success in dramatically reducing Gallup's alcohol-related ills, but also for serving a substantial off-reservation Native population, the Center demonstrates the power of an intergovernmental collaboration led by an Indian nation that looks beyond assigning fault for a social crisis in order to heal a shared community.

In 1988, the Albuquerque Tribune dubbed Gallup, New Mexico, "Drunk Town, USA," and drew local and national attention to a problem that plagues many reservation border towns. Gallup, neighbor to the Navajo Nation, Zuni Pueblo, and other Indian communities, has a population of 21,000 residents. However, this population regularly grows to over 100,000 on weekends as Indians from surrounding reservations with strict no-alcohol policies frequent the City's sixty-one bars and liquor stores. This surge in alcohol consumption comes with an equal surge in alcohol-related problems: indigence, aggressive panhandling, motor vehicle accidents, accidental deaths, deaths from exposure, and homicides.

Long before the Albuquerque Tribune and other media outlets drew attention to Gallup's alcohol-related ills, the National Institute on Alcoholism and Alcohol Abuse identified McKinley County, where Gallup is located, as having the highest composite index of alcohol-related problems of all US counties. Between 1975 and 1985, McKinley County experienced chronic alcoholism at nineteen times the national average, alcohol-related traffic accidents at seven times the national average, and deaths from all alcohol-related causes at four times the national average. McKinley County's alcohol problem is a problem endemic to Indian Country. According to 2002 Indian Health Service statistics, American Indians and Alaska Natives die from alcoholism at nearly eight times the rate of Americans generally.

Prior to the intense print and broadcast media scrutiny, Gallup's public officials had done little to address its alcohol-related problems, even though the problems could adversely affect the City's heavy stream of tourism. Gallup is commonly referred to as the "Indian Capitol of the World." Every August, Gallup's population nearly doubles as over 20,000 visitors attend the Annual Intertribal Indian Ceremonial to see Indian dances; buy Indian jewelry, art, rugs, and pottery; and enjoy the local scenery. The negative media attention forced area business owners, city officials, and tribal governments to concentrate on the epidemic of alcoholism that threatened their social and economic livelihood. City officials and leaders from surrounding governments were challenged to shed the title of "Drunk Town, USA," and, more importantly, to address a problem that affected so many of their respective citizens.

As a result, in 1992, the Navajo Nation, Zuni Pueblo, the City of Gallup, McKinley County, Indian Health Service, and the State of New Mexico secured an $850,000 grant to operate the Na'Nizhoozhi Center, Inc., (NCI) an alcohol treatment center that offers services for publicly intoxicated individuals in Gallup. Currently employing eighty staff members and twenty student interns, NCI offers alcoholism prevention programs, shelter, and treatment for intoxicated individuals, and follow-up care for alcoholics. Reflecting the Navajo philosophy that all people are interconnected, NCI refers to its clients as "relatives."

NCI's intervention services are at the core of its offerings. The Center's staff members, 95 percent of whom are Indian, are fully trained to work with "relatives" suffering from severe alcoholism. NCI provides protective custody services for adults who are apprehended for public drunkenness or who enter emergency rooms intoxicated. "Relatives" who enter NCI's protective custody are offered access to nursing care, short-term shelter, and screening for sexually transmitted diseases. Staff members educate "relatives" regarding NCI's detoxification programs, voca-

Honoring Nations Honoree 2003

Text in its entirety from: The Harvard Project On American Indian Economic Development

John F. Kennedy School of Government Harvard University

Zuni

**Honoring Nations
Honoree 2003**

**Text in its entirety from:
The Harvard Project On
American Indian Economic
Development**

**John F. Kennedy School
of Government
Harvard University**

tional classes involving therapeutic arts and crafts projects, and outpatient workshops. Departing "relatives" are offered free or reduced rate transportation to their residences.

Those who choose to participate in an NCI detoxification program may select among several service options. The Center offers an intensive five-day intervention; a fifteen-day shelter program for clients who require structured daily activities, job placement, and ancillary care; and a 23 ½-day adult residential treatment program during which clients are taught self-sufficiency skills in a culturally and spiritually appropriate setting. Detoxification graduates have access to the Center's outpatient services as long as is needful for them to heal.

NCI is committed not only to addressing alcoholism as it occurs, but also to deterring patterns of abuse before they start. To this end, the Center works closely with local schools to educate students about healthy living. NCI has developed a culturally appropriate curriculum to promote youth awareness of the dangers of sexually transmitted diseases, drug abuse, and alcoholism. The Center offers, as well, a youth employment program that matches students with mentors and provides life skills development opportunities. NCI also partners with local community groups such as churches and Navajo government chapters to raise awareness about alcoholism and to highlight the Center's intervention services.

The sheer number of cases NCI handles is both a measurement of its success as well as an indicator of how necessary its work is. Since 1992, NCI has handled over 250,000 cases, frequently serving as many as seventy-five "relatives" each day. Statistics show that the Center's efforts are making a difference. Since the Center's establishment, Gallup has experienced a precipitous drop in alcohol abuse and alcohol-related ills. While other factors contributed to these trends-the New Mexico state legislature banned Sunday liquor sales, closed down drive-up windows in liquor stores, and allowed for a five-day protective custody hold for repeat offenders-the Center not only advocated for these preventative measures, but also exerted its own marked influence on Gallup's alcoholism. For example, within six years of NCI's establishment, Gallup experienced a 50 percent drop in protective custody admissions and a 33 percent drop in alcohol-related emergency room visits to the Gallup Indian Medical Center. Over these same six years, Gallup boasted a 59 percent drop in alcohol-related accidents, a 50 percent drop in homicides, and a 42 percent drop in all alcohol-related deaths.

Four of NCI's distinguishing characteristics deserve the particular attention of tribal and local governments seeking to replicate the Center's successes. First, the Center is a model of effective coalition building. The Navajo Nation, Zuni Pueblo, the City of Gallup, McKinley County, Indian Health Service, and the State of New Mexico all recognized that alcohol abuse in Gallup was a common concern with implications for every governmental institution. NCI formalized the interest of these governments and government agencies in combating alcohol abuse by providing each a seat on NCI's Board of Directors. Such equal representation on the board helps to ensure equal participation. NCI's willingness to draw upon the expertise and resources of other institutions is also admirable. For example, NCI works closely with the Center for Disease Control

and the New Mexico Highway and Transportation Department. Second, the governments that founded and now comprise NCI's Board of Directors maintain an intense focus on solving the problem, not on assigning blame. Cities that border Indian reservations yet do not have the strict no-alcohol policies that the reservations themselves impose are frequently plagued by alcohol-related ills. In such circumstances, it is easy for tribal and local governments to assume uncompromising attitudes about the other's responsibility for the problem. While city governments insist that tribes must solve the problem because their populations abuse alcohol, tribal governments insist that cities that allow for the sale of alcohol should assume responsibility for the resulting social crises. The collaborating governments of NCI refuse to embrace such confrontational postures. Their common concern for the larger community has resulted in an off-reservation solution that promotes the healing of an alcoholic Indian population, improves the relationship between Indians and non-Indians, and strengthens the entire region.

Third, NCI's alcohol treatment succeeds because it is culturally suited to its clientele. The Center demonstrated its commitment to clients' cultural traditions in naming itself the Na'Nizhoozhi Center, Inc.-"NaNizhoozhi" is the Navajo name for Gallup-and sustains its commitment to culturally appropriate treatment by offering traditional methods of healing. The Center's Hiina'ah Bits'os, or Eagle Plume Society, Ke'na'hasdlii, or outpatient services, and Ts'aa' Bee Na'nitin, or Navajo Basket Teachings Project, respond to the Navajo philosophy of the "Beauty Way" and involve traditional healing practices such as sweat lodge ceremonies, tobacco ceremonies, talking circles, and sacred songs and prayers. As noted above, NCI calls its clients "relatives" in acknowledgement of the unity between those suffering from alcoholism and those treating them. NCI staff members report that this familial/cultural milieu helps "relatives" to strengthen their self-identity, thus allowing them to focus on healing. NCI's successes in incorporating Navajo and Zuni cultures could easily be adapted to any tribe's cultural traditions and teachings.

Fourth, NCI's treatment is not only consistent with tribal cultural traditions, but also responsive to current trends in the Gallup community. NCI studies its clientele carefully in order to tailor its services to a changing population-a hallmark of highly effective social service programs. In recent years, higher rates of aggressive alcoholism among younger consumers have resulted in NCI's development of intervention techniques that target younger "relatives." Similarly, the Center's careful monitoring of past "relatives" convinced NCI of the importance of developing individual and family support networks. There is nothing antiquated about NCI's traditional healing practices.

Sadly, countless Native and non-Native communities grapple with the problem of alcoholism and its related social ills. In Indian Country, these problems are particularly pervasive but often inadequately addressed through governmental intervention. This is especially true when the problems manifest themselves off-reservation. The Na'Nizhoozhi Center, Inc., is a shining example of how Native and non-Native governments can come together to address a common concern in an effective, humane, and culturally sensitive manner. The result is a strengthening of Indian nations and the larger communities in which they flourish.

NEW YORK

INTRODUCTION

SENECA NATION

CULTURE AND HISTORY

The Seneca tribes traditionally resided on over 6,558,000 acres, ranging from Seneca Lake to the Niagara River and from Lake Ontario to the Allegheny River in present-day New York state. The Senecas are members of the Haudenosaunee, or Iroquois, Confederacy. The Senecas were one of the original five nations to join the confederacy. The Mohawk, Oneida, Onondaga, and Cayuga tribes were the other four original nations, and the Tuscororas joined later. The Iroquois Confederacy is one of the world's oldest known democracies. Recent findings have encouraged some scholars to believe that the confederacy is at least 300 years older than previously thought. These theories have been supported by archeological, scientific, and oral history evidence. The Great Law of Peace (Kaianerekowa) of the Iroquois Confederacy served as the model for the U.S. Constitution.

The Seneca Indians presently live in four major political and community groups located in the United States and Canada. United States tribal lands are located within the Allegany, Cattaraugus, and Oil Spring reservations. Through a series of treaties made with the United States, beginning with the Treaty of Fort Stanwix in 1784, the Seneca's traditional land base was increasingly diminished. In accordance with the Pickering Treaty of 1794, the State of New York continues to pay the Nation annually in cloth and cash. Throughout the twentieth century, the Senecas have struggled to retain their independence and the rights over their land. The Nation's adamant rejection of the Indian Reorganization Act of 1934 is indicative of this stance. Their sovereignty was affected when the U.S. Congress transferred criminal and civil jurisdiction over American Indian affairs to New York State in 1948 and 1950. The Nation's most dramatic loss occurred when it could not prevent the United States from building the $120-million Kinzua Dam in 1965. The dam flooded more than 10,000 acres of the Cornplanter tract and Allegany Reservation, and it created a lake spanning 35 miles. The Seneca Nation was awarded rehabilitation funds in the amount of $12,128,917 in 1964 for the land lost to the dam.

In more recent years, the Seneca Nation of Indians has been occupied with renegotiating the 3,000 99-year leases on their lands in and around Salamanca, New York. The leasing of Seneca lands began in the early 1800s, first by railroad companies. The companies brought in more people to the area who then desired agricultural and domestic leases for farms, towns, and the exploitation of the rich natural resources of the area. In 1875, the U.S. Congress designated Great Valley, Salamanca, Carrollton, Vandalia, and Red House as "congressional villages." This legislation set the bound-

aries for these villages and gave federal approval to leases between the Senecas and non-Senecas. The Senecas were forced to offer nontribal lessees a 12-year lease term with an option of renewal. In 1892, Congress amended the legislation to extend the lease period to 99 years. The leases expired in 1991. After 30 months of negotiations, the Seneca Nation and the city of Salamanca reached a settlement. The agreement allowed the lessees to renew their leases for another 40 years and provided for a $60-million payment to the Senecas for past inequities suffered by the Nation's people. In October 1990, Congress approved the Seneca Nation Settlement Act, and New York approved it in July 1991. Today the city of Salamanca holds the distinction of being the only United States city situated on tribal lands.

In 1990, the Seneca Nation received a $35-million settlement award from the federal government for its past failures in protecting Indian interest in this matter. In 1992, it received $25 million in direct and indirect monies from New York State for further compensation. The Senecas have asserted their economic self-determination in opposing the state's desire to tax reservation sales of petroleum and tobacco to non-Indians

GOVERNMENT

The Seneca Nation of Indians is organized under the provisions of a constitution adopted in 1848. This constitution created the Seneca Republic, which is governed under a tripartite system. The legislative branch is composed of a single tribal council; the executive branch consists of a president, a treasurer, and a clerk; and the judiciary branch is comprised of the peacemaker, appellate, and surrogate courts. Elections are held every two years. The elected tribal council oversees both the Allegany and Cattaraugus communities. The Seneca Nation's headquarters alternate between the Allegany and Cattaraugus reservations every two years. Eight representatives from each community serve on the council.

BUSINESS CORPORATION

The tribal council chartered the Seneca Nation of Indians' Economic Development Corporation (SNIEDC), a nonprofit public corporation, on June 23, 1993. SNIEDC has established two revolving loan funds which are capitalized with the approximately $3.1 million stemming from the settlement between the New York State Urban Development Corporation and the tribe. The larger loan fund is used to assist small- to medium-size businesses owned by Seneca tribal members, or to fund businesses that provide significant employment opportunities to members of the Seneca Nation. The smaller microbusiness fund is used to assist Seneca cottage business enterprises.

The tribal council adopted a charter for the Seneca Gaming Corporation on August 1, 2002. By the late 1980s, the Seneca Nation already had a bingo operation in Salamanca, New York. By 2002, the Nation began expanding its gaming operations. The Seneca Nation passed a referendum on May 14, 2002, approving a compact with the State of New York. The compact for class III gaming was signed on August 18, 2002. The Seneca Gaming Corporation is the parent corporation of three subsidiaries: the Seneca Allegany Gaming Corporation, the Seneca Erie Gaming Corporation, and the Seneca Niagara Falls Gaming Corporation. All subsidiary corporations are subject to the control of the parent company. The Seneca Tribal Council controls the parent company and appoints all seven members who serve staggered terms. The Seneca Gaming Corporation appoints members of the subsidiary gaming corporations. The Seneca Erie Gaming Corporation will be overseeing the planning and operation of a third casino to be located near Buffalo or Cheektowaga in the near future.

ECONOMY

The Seneca Nation serves as a major source of employment for tribal members. The construction of the tribe's three gaming facilities created over 500 temporary construction jobs, and their opening created over 3,000 permanent jobs. Leasing tribal lands generates a substantial source of income. In addition, PL 101-503 allocates funds to the tribe from federal and state governments. The funds are compensation for past inequities of leasing agreements between the city of Salamanca and the tribe, and they are allocated for economic development projects. Seneca tribal members also find employment in the nearby cities of Rochester, Niagara Falls, and Buffalo. A number of tribal members work at privately owned cigarette and gas convenience stores or at the tribal casinos.

Government as Employer. The Seneca Nation is the primary employer of tribal members. It employs over 2,000 individuals, 717 of whom are tribal members. Employment opportunities range from governmental departments to business enterprises to gaming operations.

Economic Development Projects. The Seneca Nation Community Planning and Development Office is responsible for initiating development projects on the Allegany, Cattaraugus, and Oil Spring reservations. Current projects include development of an emergency services program, creation of a small business and entrepreneur program, renovations to the Steamburg and Irving sewer systems, expansion of the health center, development of a long-range energy plan, development of the Brownfields Conrail Yard, development of a central information management system, expansion of the Niagara Falls casino complex, development of a construction training program, and improvements to Cayuga Road.

Gaming. The Seneca Erie Gaming Corporation includes the Seneca gaming and entertainment facility located in Irving, New York, and the bingo hall located on Broad Street in Salamanca. The Nation also owns and operates the Seneca Niagara Casino in Niagara Falls, New York, and the Seneca Allegany Casino located on the Allegany Territory.

The Seneca Niagara Casino, a class III gaming operation, is located at Niagara Falls, New York. It opened its doors on December 31, 2002. This facility, located on a 50-acre site, offers 2,900 slots/VLTs, 114 table games, 2 restaurants, 2 entertainment venues, and 3 gift shops. The casino houses a 7,590-square-foot poker room, the largest in the area. Expansions, to be completed in late 2005, include a luxury hotel with 600 guest rooms, a spa, restaurants, and additional gaming facilities. In 2004, the casino employed 2,115 individuals.

The tribe's gaming operations have generated a great deal of revenue for the tribe, the city, the county, and the state. The operations have created over 3,000 new jobs and private sector investment opportunities, and they have increased tourism in the area. In 1997, the Seneca Nation's economic impact on western New York was the subject of a study of the Kalorama Consulting Group of Washington, D.C.

Services and Retail. The Seneca Nation owns and operates three franchises of Seneca Nation One Stop, a gas and convenience store. The sale of gas and cigarettes has become a lucrative market for the Seneca people, principally due to the tax advantage these products have when sold on reservation lands. No state sales tax is charged on these products, though federal and state governments have continued efforts to collect tax revenues from the sale of these items.

Tourism and Recreation. The Seneca Nation and the Seneca Gaming Corporation host education day, which is held during spring vacation and features children performing traditional social dances. It also hosts the Seneca Fall Festival, an arts and crafts show held the second weekend in September. Festivities include sports events, a parade, dancing, and vendors. Additionally, the Seneca Nation hosts the Thunder Falls Powwow held in Niagara Falls, New York. The powwow offers drum and dance competitions, arts and crafts, and food vendors.

COMMUNITY FACILITIES AND SERVICES

The Seneca Nation of Indians has three community buildings: the Saylor Community Building located in Irving, New York; the Haley Community Building located in Salamanca, New York; and the Steamburg Community Building, completed in June 1972, in Steamburg, New York.

Education. The Seneca Nation Education Department manages daycare, preschool, Head Start, adult vocational training, and adult education programs available to all tribal members. It also contracts the Johnson O'Malley Program to provide tutorial, remedial, and cultural instruction to tribal students in public schools. The district receives Title V funding to provide programs that enhance bicultural and bilingual educational activities for Native students. The Nation offers language instruction at the Early Childhood Learning Center, and in the Lake Shore, Gowanda, Salamanca, and Silver Creek Central school districts.

Health Care. Comprehensive health services are available to tribal members though the Seneca Nation Health Department. Clinics are located in Salamanca, Irving, and Buffalo. Eligible tribal members within the counties of Allegany, Cattaraugus, Chautauqua, and Erie, New York, and Warren County, Pennsylvania, may seek the services of the program. The major components of the Seneca health program are medical, dental, community health, human services, and contract health services. The health program provides comprehensive medical and dental services, as well as maternity, pharmacy, optical, social, counseling, nutrition, and environmental health services. A community health nurse and a child and family services program are also housed in each clinic.

ENVIRONMENTAL CONCERNS

Environmental concerns of the Seneca Nation include non-point source pollution, solid waste disposal, and the safety of underground and above-ground storage units on tribal lands. The Nation receives grant monies from the USDA toward water-quality improvement and erosion control. It also receives BIA funding for forestry projects.

LOCATION AND LAND STATUS

The Allegany Reservation spans over 31,000 acres along the Allegany River in Cattaraugus County, near the city of Salamanca, New York. The reservation averages 1.5 miles in width and is 30 miles long. It lies 70 miles south of Buffalo. The reservation was established by the 1794 Pickering Treaty on 30,469 acres. In 1964, over 10,000 acres of the reservation were inundated by floodwaters as a result of the development of the Kinzua Reservoir Dam. An estimated 2,000 acres have been taken from the reservation for rights-of-way for utilities, highways, and railroads. By custom, the Seneca Nation grants assignments or surface rights to individual members of the tribe. Nearly 10,000 acres, or 32 percent of the reservation, were leased on a 99-year basis to the villages of Salamanca, Kill Buck, Vandalia, and Carrollton. Salamanca leases a total of 3,774 acres.

ECONOMY

The economy of the Alleghany Reservation is supported in large part by the tribe's enterprises in the agricultural and gaming industries located within the reservation boundaries. The Nation also serves as a major source of employment on the reservation. (See the Seneca Nation introduction for further information.)

Agriculture and Livestock. Agriculture represents an important use of developed land on the reservation. Agricultural lands exist directly east and west of Salamanca, near Steamburg, and southeast of Salamanca near Carrollton and Vandalia. Nonproductive agricultural lands, which were active until 15 years ago, are located south of North Bank Perimeter Road. Beans and corn were the main crops under cultivation; straw, hay, and oats were grown as feed for the small dairy farms in operation along the Allegheny River.

Gaming. The tribe owns a bingo hall located on Broad Street in Salamanca. This operation is built on the initial bingo hall, with expanded video machines and poker games. It employs 95 people. This class II operation is open seven days a week, and it offers 400 video machines, 30 games of Seneca poker, and over 40 bingo machines. It also features a smoke and gift shop and a concessions venue. Future development includes a buffet. The facility serves as an important source of tribal income and revenue. The renovated bingo hall is an improved high-stakes game, within an 8,740-square-foot facility, which can accommodate 480 patrons. The Allegany Casino housed Seneca bingo for about four months in 2004 while the bingo hall was being renovated. The bingo operation moved back to its original location on Broad Street in Salamanca in September 2004.

The Seneca Allegany Casino, located in Salamanca, opened for operation on May 1, 2004. Facilities include 1,700 slots/VLT, 22 table games, and 2 restaurants. The casino employs 900 individuals. In 2004 the casino opened a new poker room. Poker tournaments featuring celebrity players are broadcast on television from the new room. Renovations to the casino have included a new parking garage. Law enforcement is provided to the casino by Cattaraugus County per an agreement between the tribe and the county.

Mining. Natural gas production occurs on the Allegany Reservation. The Seneca Nation is in the process of developing a long-term energy plan that will include both renewable and nonrenewable resource development.

Real Estate/Commercial Development. The Seneca Nation leases a large portion of tribal lands, including the area occupied by the city of Salamanca, New York. A 99-year lease on the lands expired in 1991, and a new agreement was negotiated. The agreement allows nontribal home and business owners to lease their lands, homes, and buildings for another 40 years. The tribe recently initiated a mortgage program to assist tribal members in purchasing homes.

Services and Retail. The Allegany franchise of the tribally owned Seneca Nation One Stop employs 18 people. In addition, approximately 154 privately owned Seneca enterprises on the Allegany Reservation sell motor fuel, cigarettes, food, and Indian crafts, or are involved in professional services or vocational trades.

Tourism and Recreation. The Highbanks Campground resort is located at the Allegheny Reservoir. Since 1995, the tribe has completed over $350,000 of improvements to the facilities. The resort features 50 cabins, 75 RV sites, 90 camping sites, a swimming pool, a playground, a boat launch, docks, a general store, and a group pavilion. A Sunday breakfast is provided to guests at Faithkeeper's School, located across the street from the campground. The campground employs 13-20 tribal members.

The Seneca-Iroquois National Museum is located on the Allegany Reservation in Salamanca. Exhibits feature artifacts from prehistoric, historic, and contemporary Seneca and Iroquois life. It also offers a lecture series, demonstrations, and presentations. The museum houses a special wampum belt exhibit, replicas of an elm-bark longhouse and a squared log cabin that were used by the Senecas in the nineteenth and twentieth centuries, dioramas by well-known Seneca artist Carson Waterman, and displays of works by contemporary Iroquois artists. The museum offers guided tours and an impressive gift shop.

The North American Iroquois Veteran's Association holds a powwow in Salamanca each summer. The powwow offers drum and dance competitions, arts and crafts, and food vendors.

There are several recreational facilities along the Allegheny Reservoir. The Onoville Marina, located in Onoville Bay along the reservoir, is a public recreational camping and boating facility owned and operated by Cattaraugus County; the Seneca Nation leases a small piece of land upon which the county property encroaches. Tour arrangements need to be made in advance.

INFRASTRUCTURE

Route 17, or I-86, a major east-west highway, runs through the reservation. U.S. Route 219 runs north-south and is accessible from the reservation.

The Kinzua Dam began operations on the reservation in 1966. It is the largest dam in the eastern United States.

Electricity. Niagara Mohawk Electric provides electricity.

Fuel. Iroquois Gas supplies gas to the area.

Allegany Reservation
Federal reservation
Seneca
Cattaraugus County, New York

Seneca Nation of Indians
P.O. Box 231
Salamanca, NY 14779
716-945-1790
716-945-6725 Fax
sni.org

Total area *2000 census*
30,189.40 acres

Total area *Tribal sources, 2004*
31,095 acres

Federal trust *BIA realty, 2004*
30,189.40 acres

Population *2000 census*
6,804

Tribal enrollment
Tribal sources, 2004
1,272

Total labor force *2000 census*
2,976

Total labor force
Tribal sources, 2004
5,114

High school graduate or higher
2000 census
76.3%

Bachelor's degree or higher
2000 census
10.2%

Unemployment rate *2000 census*
9.4%

Per capita income *2000 census*
$12,695

Allegany

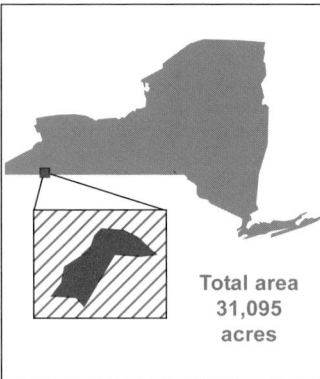

Total area
31,095
acres

Water Supply. Private wells in the Jimersontown and Steamburg areas provide water; the city of Salamanca has a public system that supplies and treats the local water supply. The 462 housing units located in the Jimersontown and Steamburg area all use individual septic systems. The Seneca Nation government building runs on a sewer line.

Transportation. Salamanca has regular train, bus, and truck services. Commercial air service is available in Bradford, Pennsylvania, 35 miles southeast of the reservation, or in Jamestown, 35 miles west.

COMMUNITY FACILITIES AND SERVICES

The Seneca Nation library system operates a branch at the Allegany Reservation. The library system is affiliated with the Chautauqua-Cattaraugus County Library System and is funded by the New York State Department of Education. Tribal youth are encouraged to participate in the tribal youth council. Participants represent the concerns, needs, and ideas of tribal youth from both the Allegany and Cattaraugus reservations. *(See the Seneca Nation introduction for further information.)*

Education. Tribal youth from the Allegany Reservation attend elementary and secondary schools in the Salamanca City Central School District. The tribe used monies received from the Kinzua Reservoir settlement to establish the Seneca Nation Higher Education Scholarship Program. This program provides financial aid to Seneca youth pursuing a postsecondary education.

Thomas Indian School on the reservation is scheduled for restoration and reconstruction. The project is expected to cost $1.5 million. It will house various departmental offices. *(See the Seneca Nation introduction for further information.)*

Health Care. (See the Seneca Nation introduction for further information.)

ENVIRONMENTAL CONCERNS

Recent issues on the Allegany Reservation that have come to the attention of the Seneca Nation include the presence of mold spores in tribal buildings. The tribe has initiated a testing program to determine the levels of mold and will identify the steps needed to eliminate the problem once the findings are complete. *(See the Seneca Nation introduction for further information.)*

Cattaraugus

Cattaraugus Reservation
Federal reservation
Seneca
Erie, Chautauqua, and
Cattaraugus counties, New
York

Seneca Nation of Indians
12837 Route 438
Irving, NY 14081
716-532-4900
716-532-6272 Fax
sni.org

Total area *(BIA realty, 2004)*	22,359 acres
Total area *(Tribal source, 2004)*	21,680 acres
Federal trust *(BIA realty, 2004)*	22,359 acres
Population *2000 census*	2,412
Tribal enrollment *(Tribal source, 2004)*	2,473
Total labor force *2000 census*	1,060
Total labor force *(Tribal source, 2004)*	1,060
High school graduate or higher *2000 census*	75.2%
Bachelor's degree or higher *2000 census*	16.6%
Unemployment rate *2000 census*	14.6%
Unemployment rate *(Tribal source, 2004)*	9.5%
Per capita income *2000 census*	$12,384

LOCATION AND LAND STATUS

The Cattaraugus Reservation spans 21,680 acres along the Cattaraugus Creek and Lake Erie. The reservation is 3 miles wide and 11 miles long and lies some 30 miles south of Buffalo, New York. The Cattaraugus Reservation is located mostly within Erie County, with smaller portions extending south into Cattaraugus County and southwest into Chautauqua County. The reservation is essentially rural with small village centers located adjacent to its boundaries (Gowanda, Irving, Angola, and North Collins). The smaller cities of Silver Creek, Dunkirk, and Fredonia are located within 15 miles of the western border of the Cattaraugus Reservation, along routes U.S. 20 and NY 5.

The 1794 Pickering Treaty established the boundaries of the Seneca Nation of which the Cattaraugus Reservation is a part. By custom, the Seneca Nation grants assignments or surface rights to individual members of the tribe.

ECONOMY

The reservation economy on the Cattaraugus Reservation is supported in large part by the Nation's enterprises in the gaming and tourism industries located within reservation boundaries. The tribe also serves as major source of employment

on the reservation. *(See the Seneca Nation introduction for further information.)*

Industrial Parks. Industrial lands constitute about 0.6 percent of developed land on the Cattaraugus Reservation. These lands are concentrated at the Seneca Nation Industrial Park, a 40-acre site located between Route 5 and the Conrail tracks in the northwest corner of the reservation. The industrial park includes a 5-acre parcel containing a 40,000-square-foot building designed for light industry. The site includes a 24-storm sewer line, a 250,000-gallon water supply tank and distribution lines, and an access road.

Services and Retail. The Cattaraugus Reservation branch of the Seneca Nation One Stop employs 31 people. In addition, approximately 112 privately owned Seneca firms on the Cattaraugus Reservation sell motor fuel, cigarettes, food, and Indian crafts or are involved in professional services or vocational trades. In addition, the reservation features restaurants, food and clothing stores, a bead shop, a coffee shop, a bed and breakfast, garages, and tire retailers.

Tourism and Recreation. Beachfront property on the Cattaraugus Reservation totals 60 acres along Lake Erie. Together, Snyder's Beach, Seneca Beach, Snow's Marina, and Seneca commons land total 12.5 acres of a commercial and recreational area. Fishing is permitted on tribal lands with a tribally issued license available at the clerk's office. Hunting on tribal lands is restricted to tribal members. The Gil Lay Sports Arena, an 18,000-square-foot structure, is frequently used for local recreational activities and is located at the Irving Industrial Park.

The Nation is in the process of developing a walking path on the Cattaraugus Reservation.

INFRASTRUCTURE

The reservation lies along the New York State Thruway (I-90) and U.S. Highway 20, both of which run parallel to the shore of Lake Erie. State Highway 62 runs north-south just to the east of the reservation. State Highway 438 passes through the reservation southeast-northwest.

The Nation completed road improvements to Gahi, Breed Run, North Mountain, and State Line in 2003.

Electricity. Niagara Mohawk Electric provides electricity.

Fuel. National Fuel Corporation supplies gas to the area.

Water Supply. A water line was recently installed which provides the reservation access to potable water from the Erie County Water Authority. Two public wastewater systems serve about 20 percent of the reservation population (131 households). One wastewater treatment facility is near the Thomas Indian School complex; the other is the Irving Wastewater Service System, which is currently under renovation. Other residential areas use individual waste disposal and treatment systems or lack waste disposal facilities. The tribe provides solid waste disposal services.

Transportation. Commercial bus and truck lines stop on the reservation. Train service is available in Brockton, 15 miles from the reservation. Residents must go 30 miles to Buffalo for commercial air transportation.

COMMUNITY FACILITIES AND SERVICES
The Wini Kettle senior citizen facility opened December 10, 1993. The Cattaraugus Reservation maintains a health center, a preschool/daycare, a recreation center, an arena, a volunteer fire department, senior housing, and administrative office space.

The Seneca Language Program provides instruction in the indigenous language; documentation of the spoken language; curriculum supplements to schools and school districts; and presentations and workshops to community members, scholars, and other interested groups. The program has received $1.1 million from the U.S. Department of Education and $280,000 from the Administration for Native Americans.

Education. Tribal youth on the Cattaraugus Reservation attend public schools in the Gowanda, Lake Shore, and Silver Creek school systems. Faithkeeper's School, which is located on the Allegany territory, is a privately owned school providing instruction in Seneca traditions and language to students ages 6 through 13. The school also provides classes in standard academic curriculum. *(See the Seneca Nation introduction for further information.)*

Health Care. (See the Seneca Nation introduction for further information.)

Cattaraugus

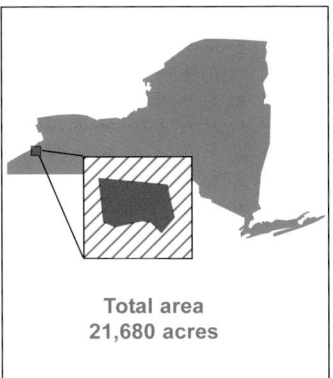

**Total area
21,680 acres**

C ayuga

Cayuga

LOCATION AND LAND STATUS
The Cayuga Nation does not have a land base. Many tribal members reside on or near the Seneca Nation Reservation in western New York.

The Cayuga Nation Reservation was illegally seized by the State of New York in the late 1700s. The Cayuga Nation and the Seneca-Cayuga Nation of Oklahoma are engaged in a decades long law claim against the State of New York for the illegal seizure of tribal lands. In November 2004, the parties proposed a settlement. In exchange for dropping their claim to over 64,000 acres in upstate New York, the tribes will receive a $247.9 million. The case is presently in the 2nd Circuit U.S. Court of Appeals.

Although their claims are closely intertwined in the battle to restore ancestral lands, the Cayuga Nation and the Seneca-Cayuga Nation are not partners in the lawsuit. The Cayuga Nation does not support the Seneca-Cayuga's claim to lands in New York, citing that Nation's voluntary decision to leave the ancestral territory following the 1838 Treaty of Buffalo Creek. The Seneca-Cayuga Nation presently owns 229 acres of ancestral lands in New York, upon which it plans to develop a class II gaming facility.

CULTURE AND HISTORY
Members of the Gayogoho:no, or Cayuga Nation, originated at the Cayuga Lake area at the Montezuma Swamp. The Cayuga are original members of the Haudenosaunee, or Iroquois, Confederacy. The Cayuga were the fourth of the original five nations to join the confederacy. The Mohawk, Oneida, Onondaga, and Seneca tribes were the other four original nations, and the Tuscorora joined later. The Cayuga are the Younger Brothers of the Great Law Kaienerikowa. The Iroquois Confederacy is one of the world's oldest known democracies. Recent findings have encouraged some scholars to believe that the confederacy is at least 300 years older

than previously thought. These theories have been supported by archeological, scientific, and oral history evidence. The Great Law of Peace (Kaianerekowa) of the Iroquois Confederacy served as the model for the U.S. Constitution.

Deprived of the land base promised them in the Treaty of 1789, tribal members live primarily within the federally designated reservations of the Seneca Nation. In the 1980s, the tribe, along with the Seneca-Cayuga Nation of Oklahoma, filed a land claim against the State of New York for the return or compensation for lands lost. The case remains in the federal court system, though a settlement has been offered. In exchange for dismissal of the claim, the State of New York would compensate the tribes with almost $250 million and permit the tribes to develop gaming facilities in the disputed regions. While representatives of the tribes have accepted the settlement, there are factions of the Cayuga Nation that vehemently oppose the settlement. For these groups, the return of the tribe's ancestral lands is far more important than the opportunity to establish a casino.

GOVERNMENT
The tribe is governed by the traditional Council of Chiefs and Clan Mothers. The Cayuga chiefs also sit on the Haudenosaunee Grand Council.

BUSINESS CORPORATION
The tribe established B.E.P. Properties of Tonawanda in order to transact business purchases.

ECONOMY
Tribally owned enterprises such as convenience stores and gaming facilities contribute to the tribal economy.

Gaming. In 2004, the state of New York allowed that the Cayuga Nation, and the Seneca-Cayuga Nation of Oklahoma,

**Cayuga Nation Reservation
Federal reservation
Cayuga**

Cayuga Nation
P.O. Box 11
Versailles, NY 14168
716-532-4847
716-532-5417 Fax

Total area *(BIA realty, 2004)*
0 acres

Population *2000 census*
10,707

Tribal enrollment
(BIA labor report, 2001)
474

Total labor force *2000 census*
5,312

High school graduate or higher
2000 census
81.5%

Bachelor's degree or higher
2000 census
20.9%

Unemployment rate *2000 census*
5.6%

Cayuga

have the right to develop gaming facilities in their ancestral lands located in upstate New York. The Cayuga propose to develop a facility at Monticello Raceway in Monticello, New York. The tribe has partnered with Empire Resorts to construct a class III casino. The proposed casino will be built within the 64,000 acres of traditional Cayuga lands shared with the Seneca-Cayuga Nation of Oklahoma. Upon approval from the BIA, the National Gaming Commission, and the governor of New York, the casino should be open in 2006. The tribe also operates a class II gaming hall in Union Springs. Should the proposed class III facility be developed the class II facility will be closed, unless local officials agree to keep it open.

Services and Retail. In 2003, the tribe purchased a Mobil Station in Seneca Falls, New York. The facility, known as Lake Side Trading, offers a convenience store and café. The tribe operates another Lake Side Training franchise in Union Springs.

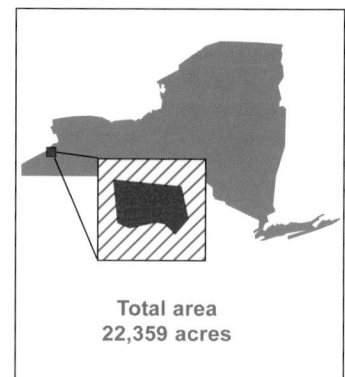

Total area
22,359 acres

Oil Springs

Oil Springs Reservation
Federal reservation
Seneca
Allegany and Cattaraugus counties, New York

Seneca Nation of Indians
12837 Route 438
Irving, NY 14081
716-532-4900
716-532-6272 Fax
sni.org

Total area *(BIA realty, 2004)*	640 acres
Population *2000 census*	8
Total labor force *2000 census*	8
High school graduate or higher *2000 census*	100%
Bachelor's degree or higher *2000 census*	0%
Unemployment rate *2000 census*	0%
Per capita income *2000 census*	$40, 667

(See the Seneca Nation introduction for further information.)

LOCATION AND LAND STATUS
The Oil Spring Reservation is situated in Cuba, New York. The reservation comprises one square mile of land that includes access to Cuba Lake. An oil spring is located on the reservation. This 642-acre reservation is owned by the Seneca Nation of Indians. Although there are eight residents on this reservation, according to the U.S. 2000 census there are no economic and community activities.

Oil Spring Reservation is the home of the first documented oil spring in North America. Mention of the spring was recorded in 1627 by Franciscan missionary Joseph de la Roch D'Allion.

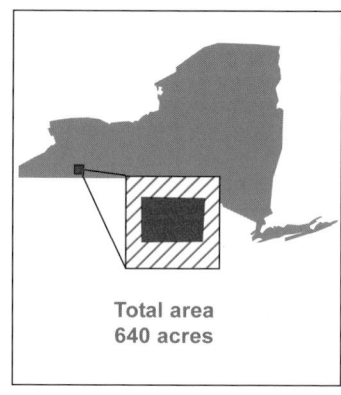

Total area
640 acres

In 1927, the New York State Oil Producers Association sponsored the dedication of a monument at the site to commemorate the history of the oil industry in North America.

Oneida

Oneida Indian Nation
Federal reservation
Oneida
Oneida and Madison counties, New York

Oneida Indian Nation
of New York
223 Genesee Street
Oneida, NY 13421
315-829-8900
315-829-8858 Fax
oneida-nation.net

LOCATION AND LAND STATUS
The Oneida Reservation is located in central New York. In 1794 the Treaty of Canandaigua affirmed special protection of Oneida tribal lands, which encompassed over 6 million acres. Through a number of illegal agreements with individual tribal members during the 1800s, the State of New York seized almost all of those lands. In 1987 the Oneida Nation owned 32 acres of unrecognized lands. Since that time, the tribe has reacquired over 17,000 acres.

CULTURE AND HISTORY
The Onyotaa:ka, or Oneida, are members of the Haudenosaunee, or Iroquois, Confederacy. Their ancestral lands encompassed territories from West Canada Creek to Chittenango Creek and from the St. Lawrence River to the Susquehanna River in the northeastern regions of the United States. The Oneidas were one of the original five nations to join the Iroquois Confederacy. The Mohawk, Seneca, Onondaga, and Cayuga tribes were the other four original nations, and the Tuscororas joined later. The Oneidas are one of the Younger Brothers of the confederacy. The Iroquois Confederacy is one of the world's oldest known democracies. Recent findings have encouraged some scholars to believe that the confederacy is at least 300 years older than previously thought. These theories have been supported by ar-

cheological, scientific, and oral history evidence. The Great Law of Peace (Kaianerekowa) of the Iroquois Confederacy served as the model for the U.S. Constitution.

The Oneida Nation encountered Europeans in the 1600s and interacted peaceably with the Dutch and British in the fur trade industry. When the colonists set out to gain independence from Great Britain, the Oneidas were the first Native nation to forge an alliance with them. Tribal members fought alongside the colonists during the Revolutionary War and assisted in the defeat of British forces during many battles and skirmishes. Their alliance with the colonists cost the Oneidas great losses. In addition to the hundreds of tribal members lost in battle, in 1779 the Oneida's principle village was destroyed. Many tribal members were forced to seek refuge in other communities, but they eventually returned to reestablish the community in 1784.

In 1794 the Treaty of Canandaigua provided for the protection of Oneida tribal lands and for the Nation to be left undisturbed on its lands. It recognized the tribe as a sovereign nation and also afforded it recognition as an ally to the United States. Per the agreement, the federal government continues to allocate treaty cloth to the Nation on an annual basis. For the most part, the State of New York undermined the Treaty of Canandaigua, and in the 1830s a large number of tribal members sold portions of tribal land to the state and then moved to Wisconsin or Canada. Although the sale was illegal, the state took possession of the lands. From then until now, the lands have been resold many times over. Throughout the last half of the nineteenth century and into the twentieth, the Oneidas fought for restoration of tribal lands. In 1974 and again in 1985, the Supreme Court ruled that the New York State treaties allowing the state to acquire the land were illegal and that the Oneidas were entitled to retribution. Negotiations with the government were fruitless for over 12 years. In 1999, the tribe moved to name 20,000 private landowners in the suit to motivate the Justice Department to begin serious negotiations.

While the Oneida Nation honors its role as an ally of the United States and has joined forces with the armed forces of the Nation in every conflict, from the American Revolution until now, it does not recognize the mandate requiring all males over the age of 18 to register with the Selective Service. Many Oneidas have served in the past and serve today in the armed forces.

GOVERNMENT
The government is traditional, and the Oneida Nation has existed since time immemorial. The governing body is the Men's Council and Clan Mothers.

The Oneida Indian Nation Police Department provides law enforcement services to the reservation. Police officers are deputized by federal authority and are nationally accredited. The department currently has 39 sworn officers and 6 nonsworn officers.

ECONOMY
Government as Employer. The Oneida Nation employs approximately 4,500 individuals.

Economic Development Projects. The Oneida Nation is the largest employer in Oneida and Madison counties. The Oneida Nation is located in central New York State between Utica and Syracuse and benefits from the many visitors to its land. It entered into a gaming compact with the state in April 1993. The tribe revitalized its economy with revenues from its thriving businesses, such as its casino, bingo hall, conference center, hotels, RV park, 5,000-seat event center, 800-seat stadium, and three championship golf courses.

Agriculture and Livestock. The Nation's agricultural department produces beef and beef products for commercial use. The Angus herd is the second-largest herd in the northeast.

Gaming. The Oneidas own and operate the Turning Stone Resort and Casino in Verona, New York. The complex employs over 3,200 individuals. The casino offers 2,400 slots/VLTs, 110 table games, 22 poker tables, and 400 bingo seats. The facilities include a convention center, 17 restaurants, and 2 entertainment venues. The adjacent hotel offers 265 guest rooms. In 2004, the resort added a 98-all-suite lodge, 28-floor tower hotel, garden atrium, 5,000-seat event center, and 2,400-car parking garage. The Shenendoah Golf Club is adjacent to the casino. It offers 3 championship golf courses, a banquet room with a capacity of 400, a sandwich grille, and a full-service pro shop.

The Nation also owns and operates the Oneida Nation's High-Stakes Bingo Hall. Through its enterprise, Standing Stone Gaming, the Nation has patented the Oneida II, a cashless gaming system. It provides slotless machine gaming that meets the legal requirements for class III operations.

Services and Retail. The tribe owns the SavOn Convenience Stores, an enterprise with 12 locations on the reservation. The Nation also owns SavOn Gas and Cigarettes, with locations in Verona and Oneida, SavOn Diesel in Verona, and SavOn Cigarettes in Oneida.

Media and Communications. The Nation operates the Oneida Nation's 4D Production. The organization produces video and animation projects. Recent projects include a promotional animated adventure for the casino.

The Nation owns and operates *Indian Country Today*, the largest American Indian newspaper in the country. The Nation also publishes *The Oneida/Onyota A Ka Oneida Indian Nation News*, a monthly newspaper. The tribe also produces *The Insider*, a newsletter distributed to tribal employees.

Tourism and Recreation. The Nation owns three marinas. These marinas are located on Oneida Lake. They feature a bait and tackle store, boat launches, a motor-repair facility, lodging, boat and motor rentals, and storage facilities. The marinas offer the largest source of ice fishing supplies and tackle in the state. The Nation owns the Kaluhyat Golf Club, Pleasant Knolls Golf Course, and the Sandstone Hollow Golf Club. It opened the Atunyote Golf Club in August 2004. This golf course, which has a 13-acre lake, features a 10,500-square-foot clubhouse with office space, a pro shop, dining areas, and locker rooms. It also has practice facrt game area, and putting greens.

Rated one of the top 10 RV parks in the U.S., the Villages at Turning Stone RV Park is located in Verona off the New York State Thruway. It features 175 full-utility hookup sites, a swimming pool, a game room, a sandy beach, fishing, scenic trails, tennis, basketball, volleyball, and a playground. The tribe also owns Peaceful Pines Campground. It offers 92 sites for tents, campers, and RVs. The facilities include a swimming pool and game room.

The Shako:wi Cultural Center at the Oneida Indian Nation houses exhibits that focus on the role that the Oneida Nation played as the first allies of the American colonists during the Revolutionary War. There are also traditional arts, crafts, and artifacts on display. The center also hosts tribal gatherings, demonstrations, and presentations. The center periodically exhibits Polly Cooper's shawl. Polly Cooper was an Oneida woman who led a group of tribal members to assist George Washington's troops at Valley Forge. The group brought 600

Oneida

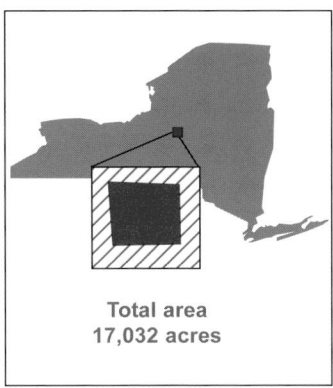

**Total area
17,032 acres**

Total area *(BIA realty, 2004)*
13,731.56 acres

Total area *(Tribal source, 2004)*
17,032 acres

Population *2000 census*
26

Tribal enrollment
(BIA labor report, 2001)
1,000

Total labor force *2000 census*
12

High school graduate or higher
2000 census
100%

Bachelor's degree or higher
2000 census
0%

Unemployment rate *2000 census*
0%

Per capita income *2000 census*
$14,533

Oneida

bushels of corn to the soldiers and taught them how to prepare it for meals. Martha Washington gave Polly Cooper the shawl, which is now a cherished historic relic.

The Oriskany Battlefield Historic Site, located east of Rome, New York, commemorates the efforts of the Oneidas and their colonial allies during a battle against the British. The Nation has sponsored the Honoring All Veterans Festival, which features crafts, food, competitive dances, and numerous activities. It also hosts the Iron Workers Festival, which offers competitions in ironworker skills.

INFRASTRUCTURE
The bingo hall, cultural center, and residential area of the Nation are located off Route 46, south of the New York State Thruway (I-90).

Electricity. Local public power utilities provide power to the reservation. A new co-generating plant provides much of the power for Turning Stone Resort and Casino.

COMMUNITY FACLITIES AND SERVICES
A recreation center, pool, lacrosse box, and gym are located on the reservation. It offers youth activities, adult recreational activities, and a fitness center. Tribal organizations include the Oneida Nation Running Club and White Pines Productions, a program that produces historical reenactments. The Nation's Family Services Department offers adult pottery classes, an elders program, a counseling program, and alcohol and substance abuse preventative activities. A satellite office is located in Syracuse.

The tribe has established the Oneida Nation Foundation to use the tribe's resources to support charitable organizations. The tribe provides funds to area school districts through the Silver Covenant Chain Education Grants programs. The tribe has also extended financial support to the Mohawk and Seneca Nations, the Urban Indian Service Center in upstate New York, and the United South and Eastern Tribes organization.

Education. Tribal youths receive their education at nearby public schools. The Nation offers scholarship resources to tribal youth and other Nation members pursuing postsecondary education. There are over 150 Oneidas in some for of higher education today.

Health Care. The tribal health department provides medical and dental services to tribal members and Native people in the counties of Chenango, Cortland, Herkimer, Madison, Oneida, and Onondaga.

TRI-NY-Oda-177 Sign for Shako-wi Cultural Center

TRI-NY-Oda-175 Oneida Tribal Office

TRI-NY-Oda-176Oneida's SavOn gas station

TRI-NY-Oda-177

TRI-NY-Oda-175

TRI-NY-Oda-176

Onondaga

**Onondaga Reservation
Federally recognized
Haudenosaunee (Iroquois)
Onondaga County, New York**

Onondaga Nation
Hemlock Rd.
Box 319-B
Nedrow, NY 13120
315-492-4210
315-469-1725 Fax

LOCATION AND LAND STATUS
The Onondaga Nation is located five miles south of Syracuse off U.S. I-81 in central New York. The reservation spans 7,300 acres of glacial basin. The reservation was created in the 1788 Treaty of Fort Schuyler by the state of New York. The Onondagas consider this treaty as illegal. Subsequent transactions decreased the area.

CULTURE AND HISTORY
The Onoda'gega's, or Onondaga's, traditional area included 2,679,729 acres that extended from Chittenango Creek to the Montezuma Wetlands and from the St. Lawrence River to the Susquehanna River in present-day New York. The Onondaga Nation is a member of the Haudenosaunee, or Iroquois, Confederacy. The Mohawk, Oneida, Seneca, and Cayuga tribes were the other four original nations, and the Tuscororas joined later. The Onondagas are the Fire Keepers, Keepers of the Wampum, and the Elder Brothers of the confederacy. As a member of the Haudenosaunee, and according to its laws, an Onondaga is chief or "Tadodaho" of the Haudenosaunee.

The Haudenosaunee, or Iroquois, Confederacy is one of the world's oldest known democracies. Recent findings have encouraged some scholars to believe that the confederacy is at least 300 years older than previously thought. These theories have been supported by archeological, scientific, and oral history evidence. The Great Law of Peace (Kaianerekowa) of the Haudenosaunee Confederacy served as the model for the U.S. Constitution.

The Onondagas have always been a sovereign nation. They have challenged the Selective Service Act and believe that the Indian Citizenship Act is unconstitutional. In 1784 Aaron Hill presented the Onondaga Nation's position to the U.S. commissioners that their members could not be drafted into military service, whereby the United States asked the Nation to be a neutral nation. The Onandagas also resist the State of New York's jurisdiction over their lands; the United States conveyed civil and criminal jurisdiction to the state's courts and comptroller in both 1948 and 1950.

GOVERNMENT

The Onondaga Nation is governed by the traditional governing system established by the Great Law of Kaianerekowa of the Haudenosaunee. Tribal operations are overseen by the Grand Council, which is comprised of 14 chiefs selected by clan mothers and one head chief. The Onondagas, by consensus, chose not to accept the provisions of the Indian Reorganization Act of 1934.

ECONOMY

The Onondaga Nation is a sovereign nation that strives to provide services and programs for tribal members with limited or no assistance from the U.S. federal government.

Services and Retail. The tribe owns the Onondaga Smoke Shop, a sports arena, and a used auto parts yard. Beadwork, baskets, dolls, and turtle rattles are for sale from privately owned Onondaga gift shops.

Tourism and Recreation. The Tsha'Hon'nonyen'dak ("where they play the games") is a first-class sports arena; it is the tribe's second commercial enterprise, and it also serves the tribe's recreational needs. This 40,000-square-foot facility was built in 2000 with surplus funds from the tribal smoke shop, the tribe's first commercial enterprise. The arena, which opened its doors in 2001, seats up to 2000 spectators. Lacrosse and hockey are the main indoor sports played at this arena. Recreational ice skating is a regular activity at the arena from October 1 to April 1. It is not uncommon to see the local high school teams playing their hockey and lacrosse games or to see the Syracuse professional hockey team practicing at this arena. The arena can host other events and entertainment. It is available for rent.

In September, the tribe sponsors a powwow that is opened to the public.

INFRASTRUCTURE

The reservation is accessible via I-81.

Waste Collection and Disposal. The tribe operates a solid waste transfer center and recycling program. The waste is transferred to the Onondaga County waste facility. Free pickup services are available to elder tribal members.

COMMUNITY FACILITIES AND SERVICES

The tribe has a community center, and the reservation houses a volunteer fire department.

Education. The Onondaga Nation School was established in 1850 as the Onondaga Indian School under an agreement with the state of New York. In 1985 it changed its name to the Onondaga Nation School. Today it offers regular academic programs as well as Onondaga language and cultural programs for students in grades K-8. About 1995 the school underwent renovations, and now it includes more classrooms and a gymnasium. High school students attend school in the Lafayette School District.

Health Care. The nation operates a health clinic that provides general medical services, including pediatrics, gynecology, obstetric, and laboratory services. This health facility is state funded, but the Indian Health Service pays for hospitalization costs. There is also a dental clinic and a healing center for tribal members, that offers counseling, massage, acupuncture, and other alternative medical advise. The tribe operates a wellness center.

ENVIRONMENTAL CONCERNS

Onondaga tribal representatives serve on the Haudenosaunee Environmental Task Force.

Onondaga

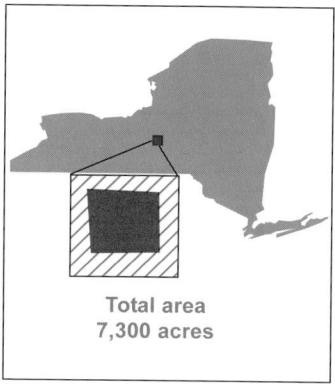

Total area
7,300 acres

Total area (*BIA realty, 2004*)
7,300 acres

Total area (*Tribal source, 2004*)
7,300 acres

Population *2000 census*
1,473

Tribal enrollment
1,600

Total labor force *2000 census*
563

High school graduate or higher
2000 census
90.5%

Bachelor's degree or higher
2000 census
41.1%

Unemployment rate *2000 census*
4.8%

Per capita income *2000 census*
$15,425

TRI-NY-Ono-173

TRI-NY-Ono-174

TRI-NY-Ono-173 The Tsha'tton'nonyen'dak Sports Arena owned by the Onondaga Nation

TRI-NY-Ono-174 The Sports Arena is 40,000 square feet and seats up to 2,000 spectators

St. Regis Mohawk

St.Regis Mohawk Reservation
Federally recognized
Akwesasne Mohawk
St. Lawrence and Franklin
counties, New York; Quebec
and Ontario, Canada

Akwasasne Mohawk Nation
412 State Route 37
Hogansburg, NY 13655
518-358-2272
518-358-3203 Fax

Total area (BIA realty, 2004)
14,760 acres

Total area (Tribal source, 2004)
14,648 acres

Population 2000 census
2,699

Tribal enrollment
(BIA labor report, 2001)
9,020

Total labor force 2000 census
1,222

High school graduate or higher
2000 census
67.5%

Bachelor's degree or higher
2000 census
7.7%

Unemployment rate 2000 census
7.5%

Per capita income 2000 census
$12,017

LOCATION AND LAND STATUS

The Akwesasne Mohawk community literally straddles the border between the United States and Canada along the St. Lawrence Seaway, spanning portions of two New York state counties and two Canadian provinces. On the American side of the border the reservation covers 14,648 acres; on the Canadian side, the reservation extends for another 7,400 acres. Members of the Haudenosaunee residing in Canada live on the Six Nation Reserve, Brantford, Ontario; the Tyendinaga on Lake Ontario; Gibson Band Reserve on Georgian Bay; the Akwesasnes on the St. Lawrence River, Kahnawake, Quebec; and Kanehsatake, Oka, Quebec.

Because the State of New York never ceded any land to the federal government following the ratification of the tribe's constitution, the Mohawk Reservation has never been a federal territory. New York State granted its portion of the land to the tribe in 1796 under a treaty signed with the Seven Nations Confederacy, to which the St. Regis Mohawk belonged.

In 1974, the Kahnawake Mohawks seized 612 acres of land at Eagle Bay on Moss Lake in the Adirondack Mountains. In 1977 the siege ended when the State of New York awarded the tribe lands along Shuyler and Altoona lakes in Clinton County.

In October 2000, the Akwesasne Mohawk Tribe entered into a tentative agreement with the State of New York to settle Mohawk land claims and issues surrounding the New York Power Authority (NYPA). In the proposed agreement the tribe will receive in the next five years $3 million each from the federal government and the State of New York, and for the next 35 years $2 million from the NYPA. With the funds, the tribe will be allowed to purchase land in the disputed areas of Massena, Bombay, Fort Covington, and Helena. Thirteen thousand four hundred and sixty-three acres will be returned to the tribe with the classification of restricted-fee status whereby these lands can be used for any purpose agreed upon by the communities. Specifically, Long Sault Island and Croil Island consisting of 1,100 acres and 215 acres at Massena will come under their ownership. All aboriginal rights to hunt, fish, trap and gather will be retained by the tribe. In addition, the tribe will have the right to purchase additional lands to be placed into federal trust status. Tribal members will also be allowed to attend the State University of New York tuition-free, and the community will receive nine megawatts of power from NYPA at the lowest rate for as long as the power project exists. In turn, the tribe will: drop all its land claims lawsuits pending in state and federal courts; release claim to Barnhart Island, the dam site of the NYPA; relinquish tracts of land in Massena and Fort Covington and meadowlands along the Grasse River; end its complaints to the Federal Energy Regulatory Commission challenging NYPA's license; and relinquish claims to the site of the Robert Moses Hydro Electric Power Station. The agreement is subject to U.S. Congressional and state legislative approval.

PHYSICAL DESPCRIPTION

The St. Regis Mohawk Reservation is located along the banks of the St. Lawrence River and the junction of the Racquette and St. Regis rivers.

CULTURE AND HISTORY

The Akwasasne Mohawks are members of the Haudenosaunee, or Iroquois, Confederacy. Their ancestral lands encompassed over 15,000 square miles from the St. Lawrence River to the Delaware River and from the West Canada-Unadilla Creek to the Hudson River along the present-day New York-Canada border. The Mohawk Nation was one of the original five nations to join the confederacy. The Oneida, Seneca, Onondaga, and Cayuga tribes were the other four original nations, and the Tuscororas joined later. The Mohawks are Elder Brothers and the Eastern Doorkeepers of the confederacy. The Iroquois Confederacy is one of the world's oldest known democracies. Recent findings have encouraged some scholars to believe that the confederacy is at least 300 years older than previously thought. These theories have been supported by archeological, scientific, and oral history evidence. The Great Law of Peace (Kaianerekowa) of the Iroquois Confederacy served as the model for the U.S. Constitution.

During the late 1600s a number of Iroquois, particularly Mohawks, migrated up to the St. Lawrence River region. Around 1755, a group of Christian Mohawks from the French Mission of Caughnawaga migrated to St. Regis, Quebec and New York. The French Jesuits had encouraged the migration of this small party because of population pressure at the Caughnawaga Mission and the need to follow the activities of the British along the St. Lawrence frontier. The St. Regis Mission is the oldest permanent settlement in northern New York, predating non-Indian settlements by almost 50 years.

During the Revolutionary War, while most of the Seven Nations Confederacy supported the British, the St. Regis Mohawks were among the minority who supported the Americans. In 1796 the land claim of the Seven Nations was signed whereby New York State ceded over six square miles and some additional collateral land in return for a promise by the Indians to abandon any further land claims in the state. The state had agreed to pay annuities to the tribe under negotiated treaties; in the mid-1830s it modified the practice by beginning to make payments only to the New York side of the reservation.

In the 1930s, the federal government proposed the Indian Reorganization Act, which the St. Regis Mohawk formally rejected in 1935. In 1953 the federal government moved to terminate the reservation, an attempt that the St. Regis Mohawks successfully overturned. Prior to the twentieth century, the St. Regis Mohawks subsisted primarily through farming, fishing, and trapping. Men worked in the Adirondack lumber camps in late fall and winter; women wove the splint and sweet grass baskets which gained them international recognition. Throughout the twentieth century, farming, fishing, and logging radically subsided, largely due to declining environmental conditions. In response, many Mohawk men have found employment in the region's construction and iron works trades, centered around Montreal and New York State. Renewed interest in traditional Mohawk culture and language began in the 1960s, exemplified by the establishment of the Akwesasne Freedom School and the restoration of the Longhouse teachings.

GOVERNMENT

Tribal councils have been devised for both the United States and Canadian portions of the tribe. The U.S. council is made up of three chiefs, three sub-chiefs, and a tribal clerk. Each serves a three-year term. Elections are held annually in June, with one chief and one sub-chief chosen per election; terms are therefore staggered. The honorary title of head chief is given to the chief who is serving in the final year of his present term. The tribal clerk is chosen every third year. The Canadian council consists of a chief and eleven councilors. The councils work in concert to provide jobs, better housing, and health and recreation facilities. Governmental departments include education, economic development, planning and infrastructure, public relations, health, police, environment, and housing.

Tribal courts exercise jurisdiction over civil and traffic matters. In 2003 the tribe began the development of a judicial program that incorporates traditional cultural values.

ECONOMY
The modern day economy is based largely around the service industry and tourism, primarily high-stakes bingo and a tribal casino. The reservation also capitalizes on its tax-free status by selling products such as gasoline and cigarettes at discount prices.

Government as Employer. Since 1973, the St. Regis Mohawk Tribal Council has successfully garnered state and federal funds for an array of tribally administered programs, all of which employ primarily Mohawk people. Tribal enterprises and governmental departments provide a substantial source of employment in the region.

Economic Development Projects. The tribe is dedicated to protect, promote and coordinate the advancement of a strong self-sustaining economy, which is diversified and environmentally friendly.

Agriculture and Livestock. Though farming was once a thriving activity in the region, there are now no working farms on the reservation. As stricter environmental controls are enforced on the industries along the St. Lawrence River, some agriculture, particularly dairy farming, might make a modest comeback.

Forestry. Mohawks traditionally have worked in the Adirondack logging camps. Due to modern methods and over logging, the timber industry supports only a fraction of the employment it once did.

Gaming. The tribe owns and operates the Akwesasne Mohawk Casino in Hogansburg, New York. The casino features 750 slot machines/VLTs, 20 table games, 8 poker tables, 2 restaurants, and an entertainment venue. The casino also houses a gift shop. Limousine services are available to casino guests, as is a free shuttle service. The casino employs 500 people.

The tribe also owns the Mohawk Bingo Place in Akwesasne, New York. The bingo hall features 602 slot machines/VLTs, 1,014 bingo seats, and a restaurant. One hundred individuals are employed there. The tribe has recently decided to merge the Akwesasne casino and the bingo palace into one facility.

The Mohawks have been on the cutting edge of gaming, opening the first slot machines for Indian gaming in the 1970s. Billy's Bingo Hall was located in Hogansburg and offered a $1,000 giveaway every day, a $3,200 bonanza, quickie games, warm-up games, and a variety of packages.

Construction. Five different Mohawk-owned construction contractors are located on the New York side of the reservation. These contractors provide an important source of employment and revenue for the region.

Manufacturing. The construction trade has traditionally employed significant numbers of the St. Regis Reservation members. Though this industry has recently declined, there are still two tribally affiliated steel erector contractors doing business in the region. Additionally, the reservation boasts the largest manufacturer of lacrosse sticks in the United States and Canada.

Real Estate/Commercial Development. In 2004 the BIA accepted into trust status on behalf of the tribe a 66-acre parcel of land in Monticello, New York. The tribe proposes to construct a gaming facility on the site.

Services and Retail. Tribally affiliated businesses in the region are numerous. They run the gamut from cellular phone systems and computers to smoke shops and construction contractors. Several stores and galleries also feature handmade Indian art objects and crafts.

Media and Communications. The Akwesasne Library and Cultural Center is located in Hogansburg and publishes *The Ka ri wen ha ri*, a monthly newsletter. Reservation members publish the *Indian Time* newspaper and the *Akwesasne Notes* literary journal. Members also own the CKON radio station.

Tourism and Recreation. The Akwesasne Cultural Center in Akwesasne houses the Akwesasne Library and the Akwesasne Museum. The library holds one of northern New York's largest Native collections with over 2,400 titles. The museum exhibits artifacts of Mohawk culture, including an extensive collection of black ash splint basketry. The museum features a mural of the Roman Catholic, Kateri Tekakwitha. Blessed Kateri Tekakwitha was a Mohawk tribal member and the first indigenous person to be beatified in North America. Many visitors enjoy the Akwesasne Museum and Sweetgrass Gift Shop, which features a permanent collection of Mohawk and Iroquois artifacts, contemporary Mohawk and Iroquois artisans' exhibits, special exhibits, demonstrations, and workshops on basket making. The museum offers guided tours by appointment and carries videos, tapes, and books on Native Americans. The gift shop offers baskets, beaded and silver jewelry, sweatshirts, T-shirts, and more.

The Mohawk Tribal Council (Canadian) owns and operates the Stanley Island Cabins on Stanley Island. Cabins are available for rent from May to October.

The council hosts an annual powwow open to the public. In July the tribe celebrates Friendship Days with singing, dancing, Mohawk arts, Iroquois food, games, and often canoe races.

The Frogtown International Speedway, a dirt-track stock car racing venue, attracts many visitors to the reservation. The speedway is open from mid-May to mid-September and features three classes of races. A tribal member owns the 18-hole Cedar View Golf Course, pro shop, restaurant and bar. The golf course is located two miles from the Canadian border in Rooseveltown, New York.

In 1991, the Andrea W. Cook Saint Regis Mohawk American Legion post 1479 hosted the dedication of the Saint Regis Mohawk Indian Veterans Memorial Bridge. The bridge spans the St. Regis River along State Route 37.

INFRASTRUCTURE
Route 37 is an east-west highway serving the reservation.

Electricity. Electricity is provided by Niagara Mohawk.

Water Supply. A 1992 waterline project established water service to the eastern portion of the reservation. The western portion is under construction. A comprehensive reservation sewage treatment facility is currently operational.

St. Regis Mohawk

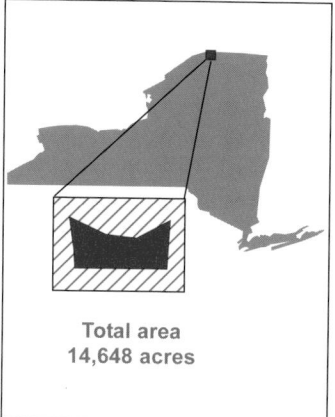

Total area
14,648 acres

St. Regis Mohawk

The Nation's municipal solid-waste program was developed in 1996 with the assistance of U.S. EPA funding. The program provides for the disposal of solid waste, cleanup of open dumps, and community education regarding solid-waste disposal. The program also provides technical assistance to the Haudenosaunee Nations and federally recognized tribes in the State of New York.

Transportation. Commercial airline and train services are available in Massena, five miles from the reservation. Truck and bus lines serve the reservation directly.

COMMUNITY FACILITIES AND SERVICES

The Akwesasne Economic Development Agency provides employment and training services.

The St. Regis Mohawk Tribal Child Care Center provides services for children between the ages of six months and three years old. The curriculum at the center includes instruction in the Mohawk language and culture. The center works cooperatively with a number of tribal programs including Head Start, health services, and a group home. Services include home-based child care, child-care subsidy, training courses, and resource and referral assistance.

The St. Regis Mohawk Senior Center provides meals, bingo, shopping trips and sightseeing tours for tribal elders. The center provides transportation as well. The tribe has set aside five acres of land for the construction of new facilities to house the program.

The Akwesasne Volunteer Fire Department provides fire prevention services to Hogansburg, St. Regis Mohawk Reservation, Cornwall Island, St. Regis Island, Chenail Island, and islands in the territory of Quebec considered by the Nation to be tribal lands.

Education. Tribal youth attend public schools in the Salmon River Central School District in Fort Covington or the Massena Central School in Massena. There is a Head Start program on the reservation and an early childhood preschool program as well. The St. Lawrence University offers graduate and undergraduate courses through the reservation community center.

New York State operates the Saint Regis Mohawk School. The Mohawk Council operates the Tsi Snaihne School,

Knatakon School, Akwesasne Mohawk School, and the Kenien'keha Curriculum Center. The Mohawk Nation (traditional chiefs) operates the Akwesasne Freedom School on the reservation. In its 25th year, the school provides instruction in general academic areas for elementary students. All instruction is conducted in the indigenous language and an emphasis is placed on cultural immersion. Students of the school were awarded the President's Environmental Youth Award in 2004 for their efforts in the restoration of wetlands along State Route 37. They have participated in the tribe's annual roadside cleanup, and have planted over 3,000 trees on the school grounds in the effort to reforest that area.

The Mohawk Culture Summer Program is a new program managed by the St. Regis Mohawk School in Hogansburg. The program will offer internships to five or six students during the school year. Interns will attend workshops, work with Iroquois scholars and wisdom keepers, and participate in educational field trips to gain a greater understanding of the Mohawk culture.

The tribe provides financial assistance to tribal members interested in pursuing a postsecondary education.

Health Care. The tribe operates Saint Regis Health Services. Mohawk Council operates the Akwesasne Medical Clinic and the Kawehnoke Medical Clinic. Services include medical and dental services as well as an outreach nursing program, teen/women's health program, diabetes prevention program, and a mental health program.

ENVIRONMENTAL CONCERNS

In early 2004 the Canadian and American Mohawk governments sought a temporary injunction against the St. Lawrence Seaway Management Corporation of Canada to stop the early initiation of commerce activities on the river. The tribe cited concerns regarding the disruption of spawning pools, shoreline flooding and erosion, and petroleum and chemical spills. The tribe later withdrew its motion but still remains concerned about the impact of commercial shipping and an extended shipping season on the river.

The tribe has an environmental division that oversees the environmental protection programs on the reservation. It received a $450,000 grant from the U.S. EPA in 2004 to study the impacts of toxic substances on traditional cultural practices.

TRI-NY-Moh-178 Site of Old Bingo and Casino. Bingo operation will merge with Akwesasne Mohawk Casino in 2005

TRI-NY-Moh-179 A back view of Tribal Office

TRI-NY-Moh-178

TRI-NY-Moh-179

Total area *(BIA realty, 2004)*	7,549 acres
Federal trust *(BIA realty, 2004)*	7,549 acres
Population *2000 census*	543
Total labor force *2000 census*	145
Total labor force *(BIA labor report, 2001)*	343
High school graduate or higher	79.2%
2000 census	
Bachelor's degree or higher	7.8%
2000 census	
Unemployment rate *2000 census*	12.4%
Unemployment rate	45%
(BIA labor report, 2001)	
Per capita income *2000 census*	$12,495

LOCATION AND LAND STATUS

The Tonawanda Reservation lies east of Buffalo in northwestern New York State. The reservation is comprised of three non-congruous parcels of land. Tribal lands include 151 acres in the town of Royalton in Niagara County, 1,153.5 acres in the town of Newstead in Erie County, and 5,579 acres in the town of Alabama in Genesee County.

The reservation was established on 45,509 acres for the Seneca Indians by the Big Tree Treaty of 1797. By 1856 the sale of tribal lands came into dispute when the Ogden Land Company claimed title to all Seneca territories, not just the portions it had legally purchased from the tribe. The U.S. Supreme Court upheld the tribe's right to its lands, but the tribe was forced to purchase the lands in order to reclaim them. The tribe purchased 7,549.73 acres, and the U.S. government placed the land in trust. In 1863, the U.S. secretary of the interior conveyed the Tonawanda land to the comptroller of the State of New York. In 1950 the U.S. Congress charged the state courts with civil jurisdiction over the Indians of New York.

PHYSICAL DESCRIPTION

Over 35 miles of rivers course through tribal lands. There are also 3 acres of lake and 28 acres of wetlands within the reservation. The majority of tribal lands are heavily forested.

CULTURE AND HISTORY

Residents of the Tonawanda Reservation are members of the Seneca Indian Nation. The Senecas are members of the Haudenosaunee, or Iroquois, Confederacy. The Senecas were one of the original five nations to join the confederacy. The Mohawk, Oneida, Onondaga, and Cayuga tribes were the other four original nations, and the Tuscororas joined later. The Senecas are the Western Doorkeepers of the Great Law of Kaianerekowa. The Iroquois Confederacy is one of the world's oldest known democracies. Recent findings have encouraged some scholars to believe that the confederacy is at least 300 years older than previously thought. These theories have been supported by archeological, scientific, and oral history evidence. The Great Law of Peace (Kaianerekowa) of the Iroquois Confederacy served as the model for the U.S. Constitution.

GOVERNMENT

Clan mothers elect the chiefs, who serve on the tribal council for life or good behavior. One-term offices are held by a president, a clerk, a treasurer, a marshal, and three peacemakers. Only male members whose names appear on the preceding annuity roll vote in the elections. The tribe has an environmental office and a Head Start program. By and large, this tribe does not accept federal aid.

INFRASTRUCTURE

Electricity. Niagara provides electricity.

Water Supply. Wells serve individual homes.

Tonawanda Reservation
State reservation
Seneca
Niagara, Erie, and Genesee counties, New York

Tonawanda Band of Seneca
7027 Meadville Rd.
Basom, NY 14013
585-542-4244
585-542-4244 Fax

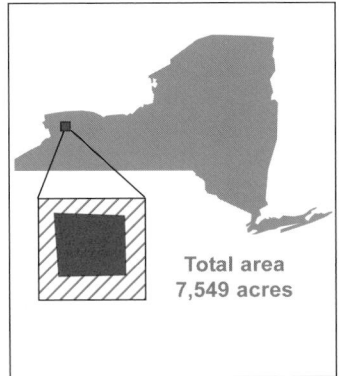

Total area
7,549 acres

LOCATION AND LAND STATUS

Tuscarora Reservation is located nine miles northeast of Niagara Falls, near the shores of Lake Ontario.

The reservation consists of three tracts of land. The first tract is a portion in the northwest corner of the reservation that was deeded to the tribe by the Seneca Nation in perpetuity. The second is the Holland Land gift to the tribe. The Nation retains the title to that parcel. The third, and largest tract of land comprises the lower half of the reservation and is held in trust by the federal government.

The reservation originally occupied 6,249 acres. Between 1958 and 1960, the tribe was engaged in court battles regarding tribal lands. In 1960, the state power authority took 583 acres of tribal lands by court order.

PHYSICAL DESCRIPTION

The Tuscarora Reservation contains over 13 miles of streams, 207 acres of wetlands, and almost 3,000 acres of forested lands.

CULTURE AND HISTORY

Members of the Tuscarora Nation originally resided along the Neuse and in the present-day State of North Carolina in the southeastern United States. They first encountered explorers in the mid-1600s. Pre-contact population is estimated at 25,000. By the beginning of the nineteenth century, the population was recorded at 1,700.

Some of the earliest recorded European contact with the Tuscarora occurred when John Lawson, an English settler, lived among the tribe between 1701 and 1706. Upon his return to England, he recorded his experiences. He was later appointed surveyor general for the Lords of England and dispatched to explore the Carolinas. Upon arriving there, he engaged in an argument with the tribe and was killed in 1711. A war ensued and lasted until 1713. In March 1713, the Tuscaroras allied with colonials and other native groups in attacks against the main English fort in the region. The main forces departed, leaving 800 defending forces behind. All 800 defenders were killed or taken prisoner. The main forces continued through Virginia, Maryland, Pennsylvania, and into New

Tuscarora Nation
Federally recognized
Tuscarora, Niagara County, New York

Tuscarora Tribe
2006 Mt. Hope Road
Lewiston, NY 14092

Tuscarora

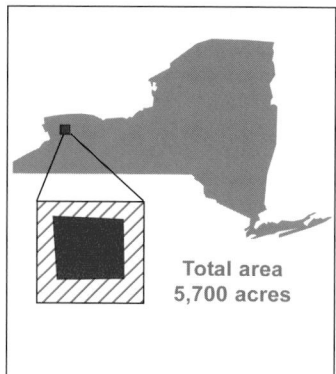

Total area
5,700 acres

Total area *(BIA realty, 2004)*
5,700 acres

Federal trust *(BIA realty, 2004)*
5,700 acres

Population *2000 census*
1,138

Total labor force *2000 census*
479

Total labor force
(BIA labor report, 2001)
310

High school graduate or higher
2000 census
86.2%

Bachelor's degree or higher
2000 census
18.1%

Unemployment rate *2000 census*
7.1%

Unemployment rate
(BIA labor report, 2001)
49%

Per capita income *2000 census*
$14,427

York. The Tuscarora settled among the Oneidas, in their own community.

In 1717, the Tuscaroras who supported the colonies were given 42,000 acres along the Roanoke River. In 1722, the Tuscaroras living among the Oneidas were adopted into the League of Five Nations, becoming the Sixth Nation. The Seneca gave the Tuscaroras a tract of land on the escarpment overlooking Lake Ontario, lands which remain in tribal ownership today.

The majority of tribal members moved to the site of the present-day reservation at Niagara Landing following the American Revolution. About 130 tribal members relocated to present-day Ontario, Canada to the Six Nations Reserve. By 1804, most of the members of the Tuscarora Nation that had remained in North Carolina joined the community on the New York reservation.

Retention of traditional cultural elements is of great significance to Tuscarora tribal members. The traditional governing, kinship, and spiritual systems remain in tact and the language continues to be spoken. Since the time of European contact, scholars have recorded the Tuscarora language. With the assistance of the tribe, scholars produced a Tuscarora-English dictionary in 1999. In addition to providing comprehensive linguistic information about the language, the book offers a detailed introduction to tribal history. The tribe also works to restore cultural items to tribal ownership. In recent years, the tribe has secured the repatriation of 79 wampum belts from the museum in Albany.

GOVERNMENT

The Tuscarora Nation is one of very few Native American groups that has retained its traditional governing system. The Nation honors the traditional clan system. Each clan is governed by a chief chosen by the oldest mother in the clan, who represents the clan on the Tuscarora Council of Chiefs. The council consists of 13 chieftain positions and 7 clan mothers who are the administrators. The Tuscarora have an enrollment office and an environmental office on Tuscarora Nation lands.

ECONOMY

As a sovereign tribe, the Tuscarora Nation is committed to providing a stable and self-sufficient economy for its members. Towards this end, it accepts virtually no assistance from state or federal agencies. Enterprises owned by individual tribal members serve as the foundation of the tribal economy. New York state taxes cannot be collected on the reservation. The tribe also does not impose taxes on tribal business owners. Many members work in the Niagara Falls and Buffalo areas, primarily in the construction industry or professional fields of health and education.

Agriculture and Livestock. There is a farming cooperative formed by individuals on the reservation.

Forestry. The sale of timber is a source of income.

Services and Retail. The Tuscarora Farmers Market is a tribally operated initiative. Vendors are invited to sell fresh home-

grown vegetables and fruits, and homemade canned goods every Saturday as weather permits.

The Tuscarora Reservation is home to four car-wrecking yards and two auto repair garages. There are a few businesses on the reservation including a roofing company and a crafts store. There are also smoke shops, gas stations, farms, a lacrosse factory, and craft shops, owned by individual tribal members.

Tourism and Recreation. The Joseph Jacobs Museum, located within the Smokin Joes Indian Trading Post, exhibits the work of Iroquoian artists.

Special events on the reservation include the Tuscarora National Annual Picnic and Field day, a two-day festival held in mid-July; it celebrated its 159th anniversary in 2004. The tribe also hosts the Annual Free Border Crossing Celebration, also held in July; and the Community Fair in October.

INFRASTRUCTURE

U.S. Highways 104 and 31 travel east-west through Tuscarora Reservation.

Electricity. Provided by the Niagara Mohawk Company.

Water Supply. Individual wells provide water for the reservation, and residents must provide their own septic tanks.

Transportation. The nearest commercial airport is located about 25 miles from the reservation in Buffalo and a train station is located 5 miles away in Niagara Falls. There is a bus line available 6 miles away in Perkin.

COMMUNITY FACILITIES

Tribal leagues offer junior and senior softball, basketball, lacrosse, and volleyball teams.

Education. The Tuscarora Indian School is located on the reservation. It serves students in grades pre-kindergarten through 6. Students in grades 7 through 12 attend Niagara Wheatfield schools. There are also private schools available in the area.

Health Care. Health care on the reservation is provided by a clinic. It is housed in the Tuscarora Indian School. Clinic services are contracted through the New York State Health Department. The Niagara mental health clinic is also on the reservation. There are hospitals in Ransomville, Buffalo, and Niagara Falls to serve the community.

ENVIRONMENTAL CONCERNS

The tribe established its own environment office in 1997. The program is responsible for identifying and prioritizing environmental concerns on tribal lands. The office issues the *Tuscarora Environment News*, a newsletter containing environmental information distributed to the reservation community, the Nation, and the Haudenosaunee Confederacy. Delegates from the tribe serve as representatives to the Haudenosaunee environmental task force and the EPA/Indian Nation leadership meetings. Water quality, contamination, and pollution are the primary concerns to the tribe.

Photo Courtesy of National Park Service

Eastern Band of Cherokee

LOCATION AND LAND STATUS

The reservation of the Eastern Band of Cherokee Indians covers over 51,000 acres in the Great Smoky Mountains of westernmost North Carolina. The majority of this land base is known as the Qualla Boundary. There are six communities within the boundary, covering parts of six North Carolina counties; these communities are Yellowhill, Birdtown, Painttown, Snowbird, Big Cove, and Wolftown. The village of Cherokee lies 15 miles from Bryson City, North Carolina, and 33 miles from Gatlinburg, Tennessee. In 1838 the federal government forced most Cherokees west into what is now Oklahoma; the Eastern Band of Cherokees managed to escape removal. In 1866 the State of North Carolina formally recognized the band, and in 1889 finally granted it a state charter. It wasn't until 1925 that tribal lands were finally placed in trust.

PHYSICAL DESCRIPTION

The Eastern Cherokee Reservation is located in the mountainous region along the eastern edge of the Great Smoky Mountains. Over 124 miles of streams and rivers course through tribal lands, including Oconaluftee River, Raven Fork, Soco Creek, and Tuckaseigee River. The vast majority of the reservation is forested. Elevations range from 2,000 feet above sea level at Cherokee to 5,000 feet at Soco Bald.

CLIMATE

The community of Cherokee experiences an average yearly temperature of 53°F. The average annual precipitation is 56.8 inches.

CULTURE AND HISTORY

Members of the Eastern Band of Cherokee belong to the A-ni-yun-wi-yv, or Principal People/Cherokee People. The Cherokee ancestral homelands encompass portions of present-day North Carolina, Georgia, Tennessee, Alabama, Kentucky, South Carolina, and Virginia. The Cherokees are the largest Indian tribe in the United States.

The Cherokees first encountered Europeans in 1540 when Hernando de Soto arrived in the southeastern United States. The Cherokee population was severely affected by the arrival of European diseases, warfare, and the ensuing encroachment upon tribal lands. Through a series of treaties between 1721 and 1819, the land area was reduced to the contiguous mountain regions of North Carolina, Tennessee, Georgia, and Alabama. In December 1835, the Treaty of New Echota ceded the last of the remaining tribal lands east of the Mississippi to the United States. The North Carolina Band of Cherokees was exempt from the terms of the treaty, but the federal government did not honor the treaty and initiated the forced of removal of all tribal members to Indian Territory west of the Mississippi River.

Approximately 1,000 Cherokees escaped removal and remained in North Carolina.

The Eastern Band of Cherokee traces its origin to the more than 1,000 Cherokee members who eluded forced removal westward in 1838 and 1839 by remaining in the mountains. Approximately 300 of these individuals were living on tribal lands in 1838 and claimed U.S. citizenship. Other tribal members living in Tennessee and North Carolina towns were not immediately found and removed. Throughout much of the 1840s federal agents searched the mountains of North Carolina in attempts to remove the refugees to Indian Territory. By 1848, however, the U.S. Congress agreed to recognize the North Carolina Cherokees' rights as long as the state would recognize them as permanent residents. The state did not comply until nearly 20 years later. In 1876 the Temple Survey, the first official survey of Cherokee lands, established the Qualla Boundary, officially defining the new reservation lands. With a few minor changes, tribal lands today remain essentially the same as those established in 1876.

By 1890, the timber industry had begun to make its presence felt in the region, clear-cutting extensively and taking advantage of area residents. In 1924, having successfully resisted allotment, the tribe placed its lands in federal trust to ensure that they would remain forever in Cherokee possession. The creation of the Great Smoky Mountains National Park during the 1930s bolstered the reservation's economy, which had been battered by the Depression. Thousands of auto tourists began visiting the park after World War II, ultimately making tourism the primary industry on the reservation.

GOVERNMENT

The Eastern Band of Cherokee was incorporated under the laws of North Carolina in 1889. It was first organized as a corporation and governed by the Lloyd Welch Constitution. The tribe did not receive federal status as a tribe until it adopted the Indian Reorganization Act of 1934.

The tribal government consists of executive, legislative, and judicial branches. The executive branch includes a principal chief and vice-chief; each elected to four-year terms. The legislative branch is the 12-member tribal council whose members are elected to two-year terms. Aside from traditional legislative duties, this branch also is responsible for managing and controlling tribal property and for resolving land disputes. Government departments and programs include transportation, community services, cultural resources, economic and community development, education and human services, health and medical, legal, and tribal utilities.

Eastern Band of Cherokee Indians Reservation
Federal reservation
Cherokee
Cherokee, Graham, Haywood, Jackson, Macon, and Swain counties, North Carolina

Eastern Band of Cherokee Indians
P.O. Box 455
Cherokee, NC 28719
828-497-2771
828-497-7007 Fax
cherokee-nc.com

Total area (BIA realty, 2004)
56,746.65 acres

Federal trust (BIA realty, 2004)
56,746.65 acres

Population 2000 census
8,092

Tribal enrollment
(BIA labor report, 2001)
12,139

Total labor force 2000 census
3,418

Total labor force
(BIA labor report, 2001)
5,278

Eastern Band of Cherokee

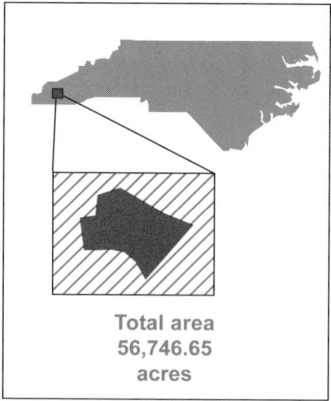

Total area
56,746.65
acres

High school graduate or higher
2000 census
67.6%

Bachelor's degree or higher
2000 census
8.6%

Unemployment rate *2000 census*
8.5%

Unemployment rate
(BIA labor report, 2001)
40%

Per capita income *2000 census*
$12,581

The Eastern Band of Cherokee maintains a police department, emergency medical services, a fire department, an emergency management program, juvenile intake services, and a tribal court.

ECONOMY

Tourism provides healthy revenues and employment for about two-thirds of the local work force. This marks a dramatic shift from pre-World War II days, when subsistence agriculture was the primary means of survival within the Qualla Boundary. More than 200 businesses are located within the boundary, the majority of which are owned by tribal members. The tribe has developed into a prosperous, vibrant community, while maintaining its strong identity and sense of heritage.

Government as Employer. The tribal government and its programs directly provide approximately 400 jobs to tribal members.

Economic Development Projects. The Cherokee Boys Club was organized in 1964 and has 146 employees who provide a wide range of services to meet the needs of the tribe, including bus services, administrative services, grounds maintenance, truck and tractor services, a children's home, a recreation park, and laundry services. The club is also able to provide services to potential investors on the reservation.

Agriculture and Livestock. Individual tribal members own small-scale farms and ranches. Tribal members raise corn, tobacco, potatoes, cattle, and hogs on approximately 500 acres. Commercial sales of these items are small.

Forestry. The vast majority (approximately 42,000 acres) of the Qualla Boundary is forested. These forests are harvested both for pulpwood and hardwoods, providing considerable tribal income. Two individual members own small logging companies.

Gaming. In partnership with Harrah's Entertainment, the tribe owns Harrah's Cherokee Casino and Hotel in Cherokee. The 75,000-square-foot facility offers 3,600 slots/VLTs, 24 table games, a convention center, 252 hotel rooms, 5 restaurants, and 2 entertainment venues. The casino employs 1,800 individuals. The tribe's Cherokee bingo features high-stakes bingo and progressive electronic lotto machines. Other facilities include Indian Nation lotto/bingo, Tee Pee Village electronic lotto, and two tribal casinos.

Fisheries. The Tribal Fish and Game Enterprise includes a fish hatchery and a distribution network for the tribe's commercial trout fishing program. Revenues from the hatchery are estimated at $200,000 annually.

Construction. The Cherokee Tribal Construction Enterprise is a tribally owned business that generates significant annual revenues and employment.

Industrial Parks. The tribe maintains two industrial parks, each with major road access and full utilities. The Barclay textile manufacturing company leases 250,000 square feet of space within two warehouses and employs approximately 400 people.

Manufacturing. In addition to the Barclay textile company, the Cherokee Heritage garment manufacturing company employs 66 people, specializing in sewing quilts and curtains.

Services and Retail. The tribe owns the Original Cherokee Great Smoky Mountains Drinking Water Enterprise. This company transports water from the Qualla Boundary to a nearby bottling facility. The water is treated and filtrated prior to bottling. The company's largest market is the Harrah's Cherokee Casino.

The tribe owns the Blackrock Outdoor Company. It offers outdoor equipment and mountain bikes. Mountain bike trails are being developed on the reservation. Small businesses on the reservation are numerous, including 56 motels, 28 RV parks, 45 restaurants, 20 museums and cultural centers, 117 retail shops, and 91 other retail and service businesses.

Tourism and Recreation. The Tribal Travel and Promotion Office is an official tribal program that employs five full-time personnel and hires an additional five part-time personnel for the season. The office operates out of the Cherokee visitor center. The program functions with a board of directors composed of three tribal representatives, three business owners/managers, and the chairman and treasurer of the advertising committee. The reservation is located on the edge of the Great Smoky Mountains National Park, at the southern end of the legendary Blue Ridge Parkway. The national park draws eight to ten million visitors annually. Visitors enjoy trout fishing, hiking, horseback riding, and whitewater rafting. Overnight accommodations are varied and may include camping, motels, hotels, and cabin rental. The Fun Bus Tour provides guided tours from Cherokee to local tourist attractions, Gatlinburg, and the Great Smoky Mountains National Park.

Honoring Nations Honoree 1999

Cherokee Tribal Sanitation Program, Tribal Utilities Department, Eastern Band of Cherokee

In 1990, the Eastern Band of Cherokee came to a crossroads. For the previous 25 years, the Tribe had provided a trash pickup and disposal service for tribal members, which relied on a tribally owned landfill. New federal guidelines were in the pipeline, however, that would make the landfill unviable. The Tribe already lacked appropriate permits for current operations, and the site certainly would be unable to meet the impending, more stringent requirements. In other words, the Tribe was faced with a serious question of where its trash would go.

Seeking solutions, the Tribe's governing body asked the Executive Director of Tribal Utilities to report on options. First,

he observed that local off-reservation disposal was unworkable, since the five surrounding counties were also unprepared to meet the new federal requirements. He further advised that, if the Tribe planned on staying in the landfill business, it should devote 50 acres to develop a "sub-title D" landfill-an undertaking that would cost $300,000-$400,000 per acre, but would unquestionably meet the federal government's environmental protection standards. Alternatively, he suggested that the Tribe could cover and close its current landfill and construct a waste transfer station, a facility that would receive and sort solid waste on the reservation and transport it off the reservation for appropriate disposal or sale.

Based on this report, the Tribe opted for the waste transfer station. The decision has been an environmental and economic success.

Today, the reservation is remarkably trash-free, presenting a strong complement to the two national parks on its borders (the Great Smokey Mountains National Park and the Blue Ridge Parkway). In 1997, there were five small, open dumps on the reservation. Only one, which is privately owned, remains. The Tribe has supported this progress with a reservation-wide clean-up effort. It has posted signs prohibiting littering and emphasizing good environmental stewardship, launched roadside clean-up programs-in which tribal departments frequently participate-and invested in educating the public about recycling. The latter program has been particularly successful among the community's youth-the recycling supervisor who visits the schools is immensely popular and in high demand.

On the economic side, while continuing to provide pick-up and disposal services free-of-charge to tribal members, the Program has nonetheless increased revenue in every year since its inception. Income is generated through the sale of recyclables and compost and, significantly, by providing services to other jurisdictions. In 1999, the Sanitation Program was under contract to receive, sort, and transport solid waste from two nearby counties. The Program also controls costs through sound management. For example, based on itsstrong track record in a foregoing two-year deal, the Executive Director of Tribal Utilities was able to negotiate a ten-year agreement with Waste Management, the firm that provides off-reservation trash disposal for the Tribe.

Continued economic success is likely. The relative scarcity of disposal and transfer alternatives in the region suggests that the surrounding counties will increasingly rely on tribally provided waste management services. Importantly, the Cherokee Sanitation Program is poised to effectively capitalize on its market niche. The transfer station handles 100 tons of waste daily, but it is equipped to handle 300 tons a day; engaging the additional staff and trucks necessary to shift the operation to full capacity would take only 30 days. The Tribe's casino, which opened in 1997 and relies on the transfer station to handle its food and solid waste, proves the ability of this business to both adapt and expand. Similarly, the Program's animal incineration business demonstrates its capacity to develop new, appropriate disposal services as needs arise.

A key ingredient in the Program's success is the tribal government's policy-which it upholds-of separating business from politics. This separation is achieved both structurally and through the commitment of government officials. Specifically, directors and managers of the Eastern Band of Cherokee's governmental programs are required to report to the executive directors of their departments, not to elected officials. Similarly, complaints against programs are initially directed to non-Council bodies. For example, complaints against the Sanitation Program are first reviewed by the Utilities Commission, which then forwards recommendations to the Tribal Council. Rarely has the Council rejected these recommendations. The effective separation from politics encourages program directors and managers to take real responsibility for their programs and to operate them in businesslike manner, results which ensure program sustainability and improve interactions between tribal programs and non-tribal entities.

In rural and tribal communities, pressing economic development concerns often take precedence over other community problems. But by viewing new federal regulations as an opportunity, not a problem, the Eastern Band of Cherokee rethought their solid-waste disposal procedures and found a way to address both their environmental and economic concerns. Through its business relationships with outside jurisdictions, the Tribe's waste transfer station also improved the standing of the Tribal government and Indian community. The Cherokee Sanitation Program is an exemplary story of creative problem solving and successful self-determination.

Transfer stations sort solid waste according to its appropriateness for recycling, compost, or landfill. Materials for recycling and compost are sold to the public, and remaining waste is transported to a certified "sub-title D" landfill.

Eastern Band of Cherokee

Honoring Nations Honoree1999

Text in its entirety from The Harvard Project On American Indian Economic Development

John F. Kennedy School of Government Harvard University

North Dakota

From <u>1996</u> edition of Tiller's Guide to Indian Country.

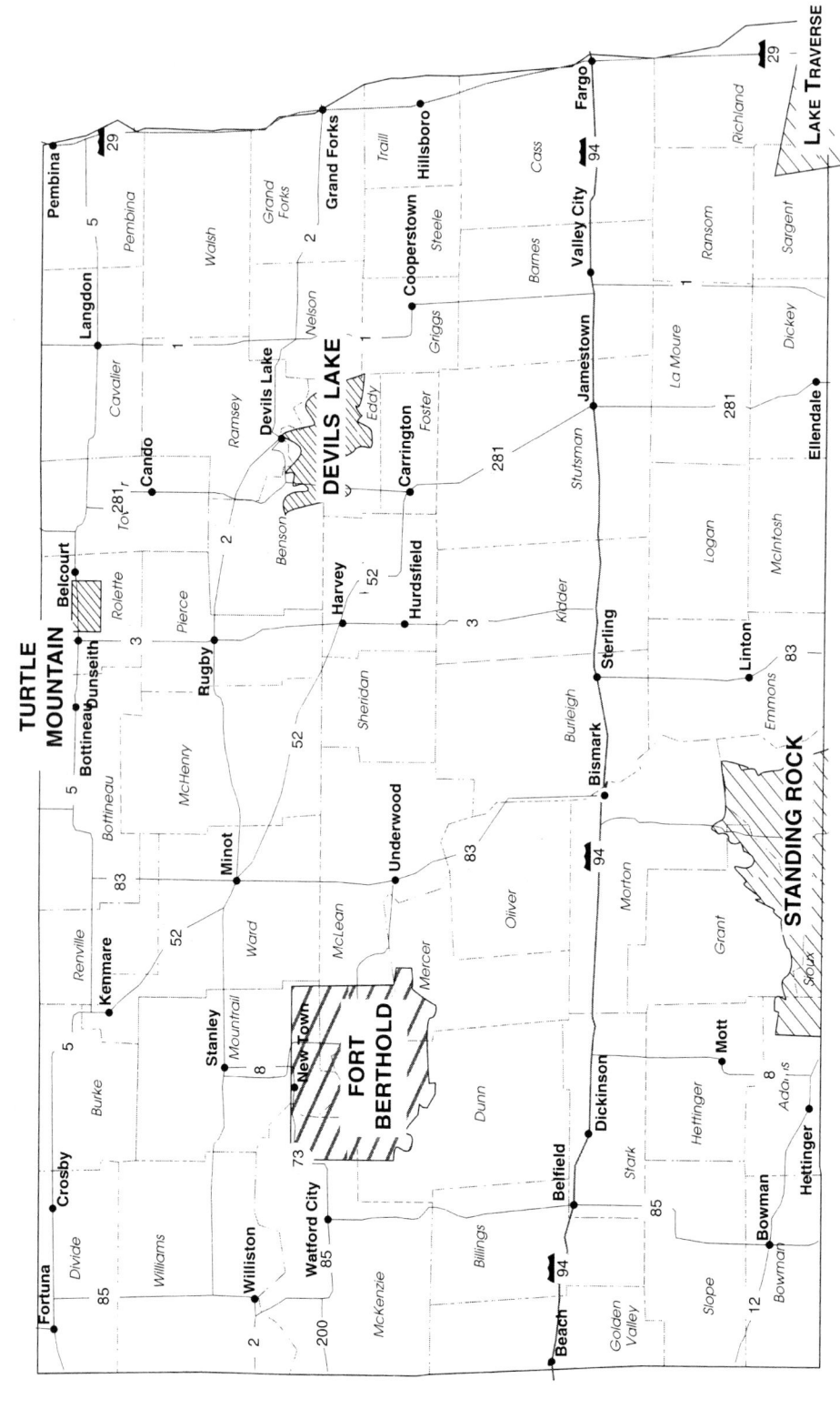

Fort Berthold

LOCATION AND LAND STATUS

The Three Affiliated Tribes Fort Berthold Reservation is located in west-central North Dakota, southwest of Minot and 2.5 hours northwest of Bismarck. While there are Indian families living throughout the reservation, the majority live in the communities of Mandaree, White Shield, Twin Buttes, Four Bears, and the incorporated towns of Parshall and New Town, the latter being location of the tribal headquarters.

The Fort Berthold Reservation boundaries were established by mutual consent at Fort Laramie, Wyoming, in the Fort Laramie Treaty of 1851. Congressional acts and executive orders gradually reduced the reservation to its present size from the initial 12.5 million acres. In 1972, a federal court ruling determined that land lost to homesteaders through the 1910 Homestead Act had, in fact, always been part of the reservation and that, therefore, boundaries had not been diminished or changed by that act.

Some land located north of New Town was donated to (and a portion was purchased by) the tribes. Called the Northern Lights Addition, the lands have been used for construction of the new North Segment Community Building, a new food distribution center, and Head Start administration and classrooms. The tribal Dreamcatchers Housing Program constructed housing, and some acreage will be used for construction of a detention center. Additional purchases are planned for construction of a clean fuels refinery in New Makoti, North Dakota. These lands, and those on which the Figure 4 Ranch were built, are all pending federal trust status.

PHYSICAL DESCRIPTION

The reservation has both flat prairie land and rolling terrain, intersected by the Missouri River. About 11 percent, or 156,000 acres, of the total surface area is covered by Lake Sakakawea, the reservoir formed behind the Garrison Dam on the Missouri River.

CLIMATE

The elevation at New Town, North Dakota, the location of tribal headquarters, is 1,879 feet above sea level. It is a cold, continental climate, dominated by the Arctic jet stream, with a year-round average daily high temperature of only 54°F. The year-round average daily low temperature is 30°F. The area receives approximately 16 inches of precipitation annually, with winter blizzards and summertime thundershowers, although it is a semiarid environment, overall.

CULTURE AND HISTORY

The Arikaras call themselves the Sahnish, or "the original people from whom all other tribes sprang." The Mandans, once divided into distinct bands, were known among one another by their band names: Is'tope, Nup'tadi, Ma'nana'r, and Awi'ka-xa. The Hidatsas, also divided into linguistically distinct clan or band groupings, were known by the other groups as "well-dressed men" or "people of the water." The name they used for themselves means "willows." Geographically and linguistically independent at the time of initial contact with Euro-American culture, the three tribes lived along the Missouri River, hunting buffalo and growing squash, corn, and beans. The famous explorers Meriwether Lewis and William Clark passed through this territory during their cross-country voyage and explorations of the continent in 1804-1805, and spent their first winter in 1804 at Fort Clark near the Mandan, Hidatsa, and Arikara villages.

Contact brought predictable consequences, among them skirmishes with the U.S. Army, conflicts with white settlers, losses of land via cession treaties, and most notably a devastating smallpox epidemic in June 1837, which served as a catalyst for tribal consolidation for protection and economic and social survival. To escape the disease, a group of Hidatsas moved up the Missouri River in 1845 and established the village of Like-a-Fishhook, and the Fort Berthold Reservation was established for the Arikara, Mandan, and Hidatsa tribes, now known as the Three Affiliated Tribes, by the Fort Laramie Treaty of 1851. A structure built to house the Indians at Fort Berthold was burned to the ground by a Sioux raiding party in the mid-1860s. The U.S. government built a new village for them, known as Fort Stephenson, 17 miles further east, near the modern community of Garrison, North Dakota. Between 1866 and 1870, many more tribal members died as crops failed, the promised annuities were never delivered, and another wave of smallpox struck the Plains. By 1888, Like-a-Fishhook Village was virtually deserted.

Though the Treaty of Fort Laramie had granted the three tribes over 12 million acres, subsequent executive orders and the General Allotment Act of 1887 eventually reduced the reservation's size to less than one million acres. Fraudulent land deals in the first and second decades of the twentieth century resulted in further losses of acreage.

During 1954, the tribes lost another 156,000 acres, along with innumerable natural resources, due to the inundation of the Missouri River to form Garrison Reservoir, now known as Lake Sakakawea. The flooding destroyed natural resources and long-established Indian population centers, such as Elbowoods, the central Indian business community, while families who had supported themselves by ranching and farming along fertile Missouri River bottomlands were forced to relocate to dry, windy uplands. The tribal administrative center was moved to New Town, which was not officially on the res-

Fort Berthold Reservation
Federal reservation
Mandan, Hidatsa, and Arikara
Dunn, McLean, McKenzie,
Mountrail, Ward, and Mercer
counties, North Dakota

Three Affiliated Tribes
  Business Council
404 Frontage Road
P.O. Box 220
Tribal Administration Bldg.
New Town, ND 58763
  701-627-4781
  701-627-3805 Fax

Total area *(BIA realty, 2004)*
423,974.53 acres

Total area *(Tribal source, 2004)*
922,750 acres

Tribally owned *(BIA realty, 2004)*
86,115.10 acres

Tribally owned *(Tribal source, 2004)*
83,800 acres

Federal trust *(BIA realty, 2004)*
1,384.17 acres

Federal trust *(Tribal source, 2004)*
422,750 acres

Individually owned
(BIA realty, 2004)
336,475.26 acres

Fee land *(Tribal source, 2004)*
500,000 acres

Population *2000 census*
5,915

Fort Berthold

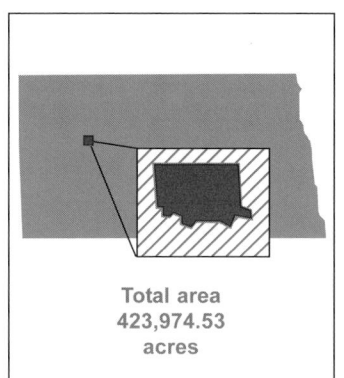

Total area
423,974.53
acres

Total labor force
2000 census
2,301

Total labor force
(BIA labor report, 2001)
4,240

High school graduate or higher
2000 census
79.1%

Bachelor's degree or higher
2000 census
16.8%

Unemployment rate
2000 census
11.1%

Unemployment rate
(BIA labor report, 2001)
71%

Per capita income
2000 census
$10,291

ervation at that time. Although the tribes received $12 million in compensation for their flooded land, an independent evaluator placed the loss at more than $20 million. By the end of 1959, tribal lands had dwindled to just over 426,000 acres, of which only 21,308 acres were tribally owned and 60 percent was being utilized by non-Indians.

Traditional culture has been revived in recent years with Native American Church ceremonies, sweat lodges, and the use of Native languages. The tribes continue to maintain discrete tribal identities through the preservation of their language, customs, and residence.

GOVERNMENT

The Three Affiliated Tribes are organized via the Indian Reorganization Act of 1934, with a constitution and bylaws, as amended. The tribal government is legally entitled the Three Affiliated Tribes Business Council, a body consisting of a chairman, a vice-chairman, a treasurer, a secretary, and three at-large members. Business council members are elected to four-year terms by the general membership.

The tribe, under PL-638, contracts with the BIA to administer key programs and services. They operate the Dreamcatchers Housing Program, which manages 786 low-rent HUD units and mutual self-help housing, along with a 36-unit apartment building in Four Bears Drags Wolf Village. There are housing units under construction in 2005. In addition to tribal administration, other services provided include aging, community health, commodity food distribution, criminal investigation, alcohol, cultural preservation, Boys and Girls Clubs, 477/JTPA, Johnson O'Malley, vocational rehabilitation, Healthy Start, and an education department consisting of early childhood, exceptional education, Head Start, and a higher education grant program. The following departments or programs also provide services to tribal members: human, enrollment, finance, MHA daycare, natural resources (emergency management, environmental, injury prevention, solid waste and sanitation, fire management, fish and wildlife, animal control, rural water development, GIS, realty), small loans, tribal planning and development, property and procurement, roads, social (child welfare, general assistance, in-home and parent aide, fuel assistance), WIC, transportation, tax, veterans, and a plethora of tribal health services. *(See also, Health Care, below.)* The tribes have their own tribal law enforcement and operate tribal courts, including a juvenile court. Tribal courts consist of a judge, a judge magistrate, two to three other judges that work part-time in off-reservation locations, a court administrator, a juvenile officer, a public defender, and two or three other support staff.

BUSINESS CORPORATION

The Fort Berthold Reservation Planning Committee guides tribal economic development initiatives.

ECONOMY

Today the reservation continues to support limited farming and ranching, but the tribes have been more successful in establishing or attracting businesses in electronics manufacturing, construction, and gaming.

Government as Employer. Tribal government serves as a major source of employment with 300 to 350 workers at any given time, with several more working in the BIA's Fort Berthold Agency, the community college, and the reservation school districts.

Economic Development Projects. The tribes drafted a 2003-2008 strategic plan to guide current and future development of reservation resources. In 2004, the tribes received a Tribal Energy Program grant from the Department of Energy to study

the feasibility of developing a commercial wind-generated electricity plant at the reservation. The tribes hope to provide sufficient energy with this plant to provide power to all reservation homes and facilities, including a proposed clean fuels refinery, also still in the development stage. The tribes are interested in developing computer and technology enterprises.

Agriculture and Livestock. Tribal members use the badland region of the reservation, an area of just over 377,000 acres, primarily for cattle grazing and livestock production. The flat to rolling grasslands of the east and northeast portions of the reservation contain areas of desirable cropland, totaling approximately 78,000 acres. Both the livestock and agriculture industries were underdeveloped in 2004.

The tribes operate the Figure 4 Ranch and Buffalo Project as a tribal enterprise on over 13,000 acres of tribal lands. The ranch maintains a herd of 250 buffalo and up to 40 elk grazing on the vast acreage.

Forestry. Though there are few stands of forest in this region, the tribes maintain a link with the timber industry through their Lumber, Construction, and Manufacturing Corporation. In the year 2000, timbered lands totaled 3,477 acres.

Gaming. In 1993 the Three Affiliated Tribes opened a 2,925-square-foot high-stakes gambling casino, the 4 Bears Casino and Lodge. A class III establishment, the facility features 500 slot machines, 12 table games, roulette wheels, and 4 poker tables. There are a restaurant and two entertainment venues in the casino complex, along with the 97-room hotel. The facility employs approximately 300 people, many of them tribal members.

Fisheries. Lake Sakakawea offers excellent recreational fishing opportunities. The 4 Bears Casino manages and operates a bait shop and marina in the area.

Construction. The Fort Berthold Development Corporation, with offices in New Town and Bismarck, North Dakota, and Germantown and Hyattsville, Maryland, is a general contracting construction company with project management capabilities. The firm is a tribally owned Small Business Administration (SBA) 8(a) HUB Zone and Certified Small Disadvantaged Business. The company accomplishes not only most reservation-based construction projects, but also contracts with the federal government for projects developed by the U.S. Army Corps of Engineers for municipal and state government projects around the nation. The company is a WedgCor dealer and distributor for prefabricated, pre-engineered steel structures.

Manufacturing. The Northrop Grumman Dakota Plant at New Town, just outside the reservation, provides jobs for about 30-40 persons, many of them tribal members, manufacturing electronic circuit boards for U.S. Defense Department contracts. *(See also, Technology, below.)* Also on the reservation, the tribes operate Twin Buttes Custom Homes, Mandaree Solid Surfacing, and ElbowoodsWorks.

Twin Buttes Custom Homes, headquartered in the Twin Buttes segment of the reservation, builds and sells modular homes for on-reservation housing authority projects and markets their product to distributors nationwide. One of their buildings was used to house the Four Feathers Head Start program. Structures are also manufactured for assisted living care facilities, motels and hotels, garages, recreational-use cabins, offices, and apartment buildings. Twin Buttes Custom Homes employs approximately 15-16 people, most of them tribal members. Mandaree Solid Surfacing specializes in fabricating window sills, tub surrounds, tub decks, vanity sinks, thresholds, shower bases, and walls, many of which are used in modular homes constructed by Twin Buttes Custom Homes, and by other retail outlets nationwide. ElbowoodsWorks, a tribal industry located at New Town, specializes in premium, custom wood works, such as caskets, cabinets, and other fine quality furniture products. Some acreage located in the Makoti area has been set aside for the development of an industrial park.

Technology. The tribes own and operate Mandaree Enterprise Corporation (MEC), in Mandaree, North Dakota, a full-service Internet technology and electronics manufacturing industry developed through a direct loan program by the BIA in 1990. MEC, a certified Small Business Administration (SBA) 8(a) HUB Zone and Small Disadvantaged Business, offers potential partners many competitive advantages, such as special workforce investment and training programs, exemption from state taxes, and a five percent incentive payment available under the Indian Finance Act. Equipped with high-speed data and communications transmission capabilities, MEC offers a wide variety of information technology and administrative support services for information technology systems, with state-of-the-art data centers, a stand-alone mail shop, and a fulfillment facility.

MEC is also a supplier of cable, wire harnesses, assemblies, and other electromechanical assemblies used primarily by the U.S. Department of Defense. This division has experience manufacturing key electronic component systems for the B-2 Bomber, the Airborne Warning and Control System, and anti-submarine warfare. MEC, nominated by two customers for Small Business of the Year Awards in 2001, won Tribal Enterprise of the Year awards in 1997 and 1998, and the prestigious Nunn-Perry Award from the Department of Defense in 1999 and 2000. They contract with the federal government and private corporations across the nation.

Real Estate/Commercial Development. Northern Lights Addition includes housing, a food and distribution building, a Head Start building, 12 casino employee apartments, and a new community building with offices, an exercise center, and a 3,000-seat gymnasium.

Services and Retail. The Fort Berthold Development Corporation provides retail lumber and hardware sales. Each of the six districts on the reservation has at least one convenience store, four of which are owned and operated by the tribes. In 2004, there were five motels on the reservation; only the one located adjacent to the casino is tribally owned, while tribal members individually own two motels in New Town. The tribes operate the Cache Restaurant and Blue Buttes Gift Shop at the casino.

Transportation. Monday through Friday, a local and privately owned bus service provides daily trips from New Town to Minot, with stops in Parshall, Plaza, and Makoti. Weekly bus service from New Town to Minot is provided each Thursday morning. The community health representative provides transportation for elderly and disabled tribal members to medical appointments. The casino operates a shuttle service to and from Minot.

Media and Communications. KMHA FM is the tribes' local radio station. The tribes' local newspaper, published locally, is the *MHA Times*. Both are located on the Four Bears Peninsula. The tribes also publish various brochures aimed at the tourist market and disseminate historical and cultural information to regional tourism industries.

Tourism and Recreation. Boating, fishing, and other forms of water recreation are quite popular on Lake Sakakawea; the tribe owns three parks on the lake offering a café, a lounge,

boat-launching facilities, a service station, and full-service RV sites. The tribes operate lodging accommodations at the Figure 4 Ranch for tourists and guests of residents; there is a five-bedroom bed-and-breakfast, two small cabins, and camping facilities available.

The tribes hold a total of six powwows throughout the year, including the White Shield Powwow during the second weekend of July, the Little Shell Powwow the first weekend of August, the Mandaree Powwow during the third weekend of July, and the Twin Buttes Powwow in August. All feature traditional Indian dancing and ceremonies. The tribes operate the Four Bears Museum in Four Bears, North Dakota. The museum offers special classes, school programs, and community events, all open to the public.

INFRASTRUCTURE
Interstate 94 runs east-west and is accessible either through Dickinson, 70 miles south, or in Bismarck-Mandan, 2.5 hours southeast. U.S. Highway 83 runs north-south approximately 60 miles east of New Town. U.S. Highway 85 runs north-south, 4 miles west of New Town. State Highways 22, 23, and 37 make up most of the paved roads on the reservation. The Missouri River can only be crossed at Four Bear Bridge, located just west of New Town, creating a transportation barrier to many parts of the reservation. The tribes plan to construct additional roads and hiking paths and bike trails.

Electricity. Three rural electric cooperatives and two private companies provide electricity to the reservation.

Fuel. Montana-Dakota Utilities provides natural gas to the surrounding area but not yet onto the reservation. Several propane companies provide service to the region.

Water Supply. Shallow groundwater is scarce and of poor quality in most parts of the reservation. Surface waters are also limited in the semiarid environment. Underlying aquifers have high saline and mineral content. The Fort Berthold Rural Water Department is run by the tribes. This department pumps water from the lake into the six water plants they have created in each of the six segments. They also hire and train the water operators that run this system. Pipe will be laid to Fort Bear and White Shield homes in 2005. The rest of the segments will have pipe laid when more money becomes available for the project. Approximately 30 percent of tribal members rely on privately owned water wells for drinking water; 70 percent have access to a city-supplied system.

Transportation. Commercial air service is available at Minot (about 68 miles away) and at Bismarck (160 miles distant). Smaller, general aviation airports are located in nearby New Town (with a 3,000-foot runway) and Parshall, located 17 miles east. Amtrak and bus lines serve Minot, while commercial freight lines serve the reservation directly.

Telecommunications. Telephone service is provided by the Reservation Telephone Cooperative in Parshall, a non-Indian cooperative assisted by AT&T and Qwest, by the Consolidated Cooperative Telephone Services in Dickinson, and by West River Telephone in Hazen. Internet services, including high-speed subscriber lines, are available throughout the reservation.

COMMUNITY FACILITIES AND SERVICES
Community facilities in the Four Bears area include a tribal administration building, an Indian Health Services Clinic and Dialysis Unit, KMHA radio station, MHA Times Office, MHA Day Care, 4 Bears Casino, C-Store, the bait shop, the lodge, the marina, and the Four Bears Museum. Social services are housed in a modular building retrieved from property formerly

Fort Berthold

ENVIRONMENTAL CONCERNS
The Three Affiliated Tribes have a Natural Resource Department (NRD) with an environmental division. In 2002, the NRD was managing a buffalo project and a cattle relending program. The NRD oversees fire management services, game and fish regulations, water resources, solid waste, and the MR&I Rural Water Development Project. Open dumping is a problem in some areas of the reservation.

Fort Berthold

Lake Traverse
See South Dakota

used as a radar installation. There are a total of six community centers on reservation lands, many of them with ball fields and/or a gymnasium with public access. There are also three senior centers.

Education. The reservation maintains five public school districts, and Fort Berthold Community College provides higher education opportunities for tribal members and others. The tribes operate a Head Start program. They also operate a unique drug and alcohol prevention and education program called "Unity Riders," a tribal nonprofit organization that the

tribal council created in 1996. The program utilizes riding therapy, capitalizing on the traditional Plains horse culture of the people.

Health Care. Health care is provided by the Mandaree Clinic, the Minne-Tohe Health Facility, the Parshall Clinic, the Twin Buttes Clinic and the White Shield Clinic. There are community health representatives in six locations throughout the reservation, and the tribes coordinate the provision of health services via a Comprehensive Health Planning Office. Alcohol programs, the WIC nutritional program, and dialysis care are available to tribal members.

Spirit Lake

**Spirit Lake Reservation
Formerly Fort Totten Reservation and Devil's Lake Reservation
Federal reservation
Mni Wakan Oyate Sioux
Benson, Nelson, Ramsey, and Eddy counties, North Dakota**

Spirit Lake Sioux Nation
816 Third Avenue North
Fort Totten, ND 58335
701-766-4221
701-766-4126 Fax
spiritlakenation.com

Total area *(BIA realty, 2004)*
67,821.87 acres

Total area *(Tribal source, 2004)*
245,141 acres

Tribally owned *(BIA realty, 2004)*
34,382.19 acres

Tribally owned *(Tribal source, 2004)*
31,573.59 acres

Federal trust *(BIA realty, 2004)*
343 acres

Individually owned
(BIA realty, 2004)
33,096.68 acres

Allotted *(Tribal source, 2004)*
33,410.51 acres

Other*(Tribal source, 2004)*
8,750 acres

Population *2000 census*
4,435

LOCATION AND LAND STATUS
Spirit Lake Sioux Reservation, formerly known as Devil's Lake and/or the Fort Totten Reservation, is located in east-central North Dakota, largely in Benson County, with smaller holdings in Ramsey, Eddy, and Nelson counties. The reservation is divided into four political districts: Fort Totten, Mission, Woodlake, and Crowhill.

The original reservation was established by treaty in 1867, encompassing nearly 221,000 acres. About 136,000 acres were allotted for 1,205 tribal members, 88,000 acres were relegated to "surplus" status for sale to white settlers, and 2,350 acres were set-aside for missions and schools. By 1937, Indian allottees had sold over 80,000 acres of their initial allotments. Subsequent federal purchases during the 1950s and tribal purchases have increased Indian-owned land to its present acreage; the tribe has purchased a total of 4,781 acres that were previously fee simple, or privately owned, land.

PHYSICAL DESCRIPTION
The largest natural body of water in North Dakota, "Minnewaukan," a Sioux word meaning "Spirit Water," is now called Spirit Lake. It forms the reservation's northern boundary, with rolling grass-covered hills beyond thickly forested shorelines. The southern boundary is formed by 50 miles of the Cheyenne River, where the land is generally flat with relatively sparse vegetation. There are numerous small lakes on the reservation, as well as associated wetlands and prairie potholes.

CLIMATE
The elevation at Fort Totten, North Dakota, is 1,462 feet above sea level. It is a cold, continental climate, dominated by the Arctic jet stream, with a year-round average daily high temperature of only 50°F. The year-round average daily low temperature is 28°F. The semiarid area receives approximately 18 inches of precipitation annually, with winter blizzards and periodic summertime thundershowers.

CULTURE AND HISTORY
The Spirit Lake Sioux belong to the Sisseton-Wahpeton Band of Mississippi or Eastern Sioux who lived a precontact subsistence hunting and gathering lifestyle throughout a large area of what is now the state of Minnesota. First contact with French fur trappers resulted in largely peaceful trade relationships; the Sioux did not actively resist white immigration until the intrusions resulted in treaty violations and permanent settlements. In 1862, the discovery of gold in Montana brought hordes of gold seekers and settlers through Minnesota Sioux country, resulting in the Minnesota Uprising that same year. Many of the Sisseton-Wahpeton Band migrated west in the

wake of this conflict, a number of who ended up in the Fort Totten area. At the time of the reservation's establishment on July 17, 1867, there were 732 Indians living there, primarily engaged in agriculture, raising corn, oats, potatoes, turnips, and hay. Steamboats plied the Missouri River and the then-named Devil's Lake, supplying troops and transporting rations for tribal members. The Northern Pacific Railroad into Jamestown replaced them in later years. In the early 1870s, St. Michael's Mission, a Catholic manual-labor mission school was established and was operated by the Grey Nuns of Montreal, Canada. A brewery and a general store were built near the location of the newly constructed buildings of Fort Totten. In 1890, when the U.S. military abandoned Fort Totten, the post was turned over to the Interior Department, for operation of an Industrial School for Indians. Of the almost 5,000 enrolled tribal members, over 4,000 reside on the reservation, a fact that helps the Nation to retain its strong, vital traditions and culture. Powwows, Native American Church (peyote) meetings, Sacred Pipe ceremonies, and the Dakota dialect all continue to be practiced on the reservation. Language classes are available at all reservation schools and the Cankdeska-Cikana Community College.

GOVERNMENT
The Spirit Lake Sioux Nation operates under a constitution and bylaws approved on February 14, 1946, revised May 6, 1960, and further amended several times. The tribal council is made up of six members, including a chairman and a secretary, elected at large by the tribal membership, and one representative from each of the reservation's four political districts. The vice-chairman is appointed from within the tribal council. Council members serve four-year terms with elections held annually in May.

The Nation, under PL-638, contracts with the BIA to administer key programs and services. A complete list of operating departments or offices includes: adult learning center, community health representative, Dakota Tribal Industries, diabetes fitness, diabetic clinic, early childhood tracking, education, emergency management, emergency medical services, employee benefits, enrollment, fire protection, fish and wildlife, health careers opportunity, Head Start 0-5, health education, health tracks, indirect cost, low-income energy assistance, motor vehicle, Native American Maternal Child Health, range and volunteer fire, recreation, senior meals and services, Sioux Utilities Commission, student support services title iii, tribal business information center, tribal court, tribal land acquisition and realty, tribal roads, tribal planning, tribal social services, tax, USDA Food Distribution Program, USDA Northern Plains RC&D, USDA-Tribal Liaison, water resource, WIC,

Wiconi Project, and Youth Healing and Wellness Center. They have their own housing authority, which received a sizeable grant in May 2004 to move 240 abandoned Air Force base housing units onto the reservation. The Spirit Lake Nation Tribal Court consists of a chief judge and a juvenile judge, a prosecutor, three clerks, a juvenile probation officer, and a juvenile intake officer.

BUSINESS CORPORATION

To ensure their economic development the tribe has formed two separate corporations, Spirit Lake Consulting and the Sioux Technology Group, LLC, to focus on this goal.

ECONOMY

While agriculture still constitutes an economic base for some tribal members, much of it through leasing lands to outside interests. The Nation's modern economic success has been based on its ability to establish businesses, including two large manufacturing concerns and the Spirit Lake Casino.

Government as Employer. The Nation employs approximately 1,400 people in its programs, services, and enterprises. Another considerable number of people work for the federal government, primarily the BIA or the Indian Health Service.

Economic Development Projects. Since 1996, the Nation has initiated the Spirit Lake Casino and Resort, a gift shop, and Varsity Bags.

Agriculture and Livestock. The southern portion of the reservation includes significant acreage under cultivation with grain crops. Other areas are used primarily for grazing cattle and buffalo. The tribe participates with the Intertribal Bison Cooperative, a nonprofit organization formed in 1990 for the purpose of reestablishing healthy buffalo herds on tribal lands. The U.S. Fish and Wildlife Service manages Sully's Hill National Game Preserve on federal lands within the reservation's boundaries.

Forestry. The reservation possesses 6,390 acres of woodland areas, a valuable commercial resource.

Gaming. The Nation first operated the Dakota Casino, also formerly known as Devil's Lake Casino, in St. Michael's, North Dakota. In 2004, the Spirit Lake Casino and Resort, still operating in St. Michael's, generated considerable tribal revenues and employed tribal members. The 49,000-square-foot facility features 632 slot machines, 10 table games, 3 poker tables, a 400-seat bingo hall, and 2,500 square feet of convention space and meeting rooms. There is now a 140-room hotel attached to the casino, along with an amphitheater, a marina, an RV park, a campground, 3 restaurants, and an entertainment venue.

Mining. The cement plant once operating on the south shore of Spirit Lake is no longer operating after rising waters flooded the area.

Manufacturing. The Nation maintains a 40-acre industrial park that contains the Sioux Manufacturing Corporation, Dakota Tribal Industries, and the tribal utilities building. Dakota Tribal Industries was established in 1985, and it largely contracts with the federal government, manufacturing products as diverse as cargo slings, camouflage screen cases, multipurpose netting for military field usage, and army tank vehicular restraints. Similarly, the Sioux Manufacturing Corporation, formed in 1973 as a joint venture with the Brunswick Corporation, now fully owned by the nation, produces laminated ballistic helmets, highly advanced autoclave-bonded structures, and protective panels on contract with the Defense Department.

Services and Retail. The Nation owns Spirit Lake Casino and Resort; tribal members own Paul's Gas and Laundromat and Paul's Grocery in Fort Totten District, Mission Bay Market in St. Michael, and the Tokio Grocery in Woodlake District. The tribally operated vocational rehabilitation program operates an outlet for arts and crafts sales. There are a number of other retail and service related businesses scattered throughout the reservation, including grocery stores, gas stations, restaurants, video arcades, a small marina, and various construction contractors.

Transportation. The Spirit Lake Tribe operates Spirit Lake Transit for transporting elderly or disabled tribal members. The casino operates a shuttle service to and from the casino for members of the general public and regional lodgers.

Media and Communications. The tribe publishes *Dacotah News*, a bimonthly newspaper with distribution primarily to tribal members.

Tourism and Recreation. Aside from the amenities located at the Spirit Lake Casino and Resort, attractions include the Fort Totten Historical Site, where the original fort building and other associated former military structures still stand, and Sulley's Hill National Game Preserve, an archeological site near Graham's Island. Fort Totten Days Powwow, an annual celebration that occurs during the last weekend in July, draws many to the area for rodeos and horse racing.

INFRASTRUCTURE

The reservation is served by North Dakota State Highways 281, 57, 20, and 15. The BIA maintains approximately 75 miles of local, primarily gravel, roads within the reservation. Some new roads have been constructed at the reservation to provide access to homes for members who were relocated after the floods at Spirit Lake. There are also bike paths in each of the four districts, and the Nation has plans to build hiking trails. The Nation provides solid waste collection services with curbside pickup and transport to the tribal landfill located about four miles from Fort Totten.

Electricity. Baker Electric Power Co-op, Cheyenne Valley Co-op, and Otter Tail Power Company provide electric power.

Fuel. Montana Dakota Utilities provides gas.

Water Supply. Spirit Lake Water Resources, via the Bureau of Reclamation, built the existing water system. Sioux Utilities maintains the three-well water system, and most tribal members have access to it. Sioux Utilities also manages the sewage system.

Transportation. Commercial air services are available at Spirit Lake Municipal Airport, 15 miles from Fort Totten. The Triangle Bus Line provides service directly to the town of Spirit Lake, as do UPS and Twin City Freight. Amtrak provides passenger rail service, while Burlington Northern and the Soo Line Railroad Company offer freight service.

Telecommunications. The North Dakota Telephone Company provides Internet access, both dial-up connections and DSL, to all tribal facilities and schools.

COMMUNITY FACILITIES AND SERVICES

Tribal headquarters are located in the village of Fort Totten, housing the offices of various tribal services and BIA offices. An old community center building, first constructed in 1962, is to be renovated. A new clinic building houses the Indian Health Service Clinic. The Nation has constructed a new library, open to the general public, for housing book collections and the tribal historical and cultural archives. In 2003,

Spirit Lake

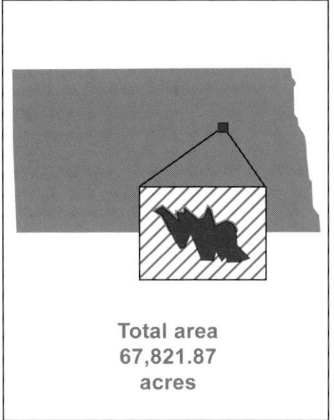

Total area
67,821.87
acres

Tribal enrollment
(BIA labor report, 2001)
4,948

Total labor force
2000 census
1,642

Total labor force
(BIA labor report, 2001)
2,413

High school graduate or higher
2000 census
70.5%

Bachelor's degree or higher
2000 census
9.9%

Unemployment rate *2000 census*
17.5%

Unemployment rate
(BIA labor report, 2001)
65%

Per capita income *2000 census*
$8,392

the tribe acquired a COPS grant from the Department of Justice to operate crime-prevention and youth development programs. The tribe operates recreation centers in each of the four districts-Fort Totten, St. Michael, Woodlake and Crowhill, each with a gymnasium and other facilities. These recreation centers double as community centers within each district; one has baseball fields, and another has basketball courts and tennis courts.

The tribe built a senior center in Fort Totten, providing elderly nutrition services and other programs for elders. An elderly nutrition program also operates out of the St. Michael Elderly Center. The Spirit Lake Casino sponsors "Elders Day Out," a monthly meeting with tribal officials, open to any tribal elder. A meal and an activity or program is available at the event.

Education. The Nation operates the Four Winds Community School System for reservation schoolchildren. A new middle school building doubles as a center for vocational education. It also operates a Head Start program for infants and toddlers and the Cankdeska-Cikana Community College, formerly the Little Hoop Community College, for those desiring higher education. The college, located in Fort Totten, has developed a culturally relevant nutrition and cooking class, "Dakota Cooking," which teaches tribal members to make better use of locally grown produce and grains and commodity foodstuffs. Emphasis is placed on the development of nutritionally sound dishes and meal plans.

The Nation supports the United Tribes Technical College, a nonprofit corporation chartered by the State of North Dakota and operated by the Spirit Lake Tribe and the other North Dakota tribes: the Mandans, Hidatsas, Arikaras, Sisseton Wahpeton Sioux, Standing Rock Sioux, and Turtle Mountain Band of Chippewas. The college is governed by a 10-member board of directors comprised of a chairperson and a delegate from each of the tribes.

Health Care. The Spirit Lake Nation is served by an Indian Health Service ambulatory care clinic, which includes dental services and a diabetes program with comprehensive screening, prevention education, and treatment services. The clinic, which opened in a newly constructed building, received a grant to study cardiovascular disease among Indians. There is a community health representative for the reservation, and a substance abuse program provides residential treatment services. The nearest full-service hospital is located in the town of Devil's Lake, approximately 13 miles distant.

ENVIRONMENTAL CONCERNS
The Spirit Lake Tribe has an EPA, whose programs and services are featured on the tribal website, listed above. With general assistance program funding and other program mon-

ies, primarily from the U.S. EPA, the Nation developed a five-year plan and put together a team of trained individuals to operate programs in geographic information system (GIS); water quality development; hazardous waste, including a Brownfields Assessment; air quality initiatives; and a wetlands protection program; and to provide technical expertise in the inspecting, detecting, and remediating internal environmental contaminants such as radon and lead paint.

In 1997, the Nation initiated a study of the Warwick Aquifer, the underlying water resource for most of the reservation lands. The water quality development staff members applied for mitigation funding under the Clean Water Act, Section 106 Program in 1998. They completed a non-point source plan in 2003, and they passed a Clean Lakes Act in 2004. By 2005, they hope to have a water code approved by the tribal council. The water quality development office is staffed by a coordinator, a GIS technician, and a special projects water quality analyst.

Water quantity and quality in Spirit Lake is of ongoing concern to the nation. The tribe reports that during the past three decades, water levels have declined, the lake water has developed an odor, and it has become increasingly saline to the detriment of native fish populations and migratory waterfowl. Ongoing analysis of the lake's waters and those of area wetlands are being conducted. Data will be utilized to develop a comprehensive management or conservation plan.

In June 1999, the U.S. EPA, Region VIII, selected two vacant buildings and two landfills on Spirit Lake Reservation for a Brownfields Demonstration Project, enabling funding for cleanup of the sites for future tribal use. In 2002, asbestos cleanup efforts began at an old abandoned school site, unoccupied and uninhabitable since the mid-1980s. The tribe received financial assistance via the U.S. EPA's Superfund Program for mitigation of the site.

A Department of Energy Title 26 Wind Energy Project grant was obtained in 1995 to develop a tribally owned and operated commercially viable wind-generated electricity power plant. The Nation was granted a Western Area Power Administration allocation in 2001 to bring the facility on-line. In 2004, the tribe reported that power from the 100-kilowatt output capacity wind turbine was supplied directly to Spirit Lake Casino, whose demand is typically more than 400 kilowatts. Therefore, the casino is consuming virtually all the electricity produce; however, increases in output capacity are anticipated as the Nation continues to expand operations at the plant. The tribe remains hopeful that as the utility industry continues to deregulate, and the Western Area Power Administration allocation of power goes into effect, the goal of becoming energy independent via a combination of wind power and hydroelectric power comes closer to reality.

LOCATION AND LAND STATUS

The Turtle Mountain Reservation is located in the extreme north-central portion of North Dakota, about seven miles from the Canadian border near the exact geographic center of the North American continent. The reservation is almost equally divided between tribally owned and individually allotted lands. The unincorporated town of Belcourt, North Dakota, is the only community on the Turtle Mountain Reservation.

The reservation was established by Executive Orders of December 21, 1882, and March 29, 1884, on an area of 72,000 acres of land. The 72,000 acres immediately proved to be inadequate for the population of the reservation. In order to meet the land needs of the people, additional land was allotted in western North Dakota and Montana. This area, known as the Trenton Service Area, consists of approximately 69,860 acres. It was established by Tribal Ordinance on March 25, 1975, and supported by the Appropriations Act of 1975. The Turtle Mountain Reservation lies within Rolette County, North Dakota; the 938-square-mile Trenton Indian Service Area spans six counties in North Dakota and in Montana. The service area lies approximately 250 miles from the Turtle Mountain Reservation.

PHYSICAL DESCRIPTION

The terrain of the Turtle Mountain Reservation features low rolling hills, trees, and brush. Over 40 percent of the reservation contains lakes, small ponds, and sloughs. The elevation ranges from 200 to 2,300 feet above sea level.

CLIMATE

Climate and weather data has been recorded for Belcourt, North Dakota, the location of tribal headquarters. The year-round daily temperature averages only 34.8° F, with year-round daily high temperatures averaging 47° F and low temperatures averaging 22.5° F. The area receives approximately 18.2 inches of precipitation annually.

CULTURE AND HISTORY

Members of the Turtle Mountain Band of Chippewa belong primarily to the Pembina Band of the Chippewa/Ojibwa Nation. The Anishinabes, "the original people," or the Ojibwas, have resided in North America since approximately 900 AD. The people originated on the Island of La Pointe in the Great Lakes region and migrated in various directions as the bands dispersed. Members of the Ojibwa Nation include the present-day Chippewa, Ojibway, Ottawa, and Potowatomi tribes of Canada, Michigan, Minnesota, Wisconsin, North Dakota, and Montana. The Ojibwa language is a member of the Algonquian linguistic family. The Ojibwes encountered Jesuit missionaries and French traders in 1640 along the shores of Lake Superior. The people became intricately involved in the trade industry, and their interaction with Cree and French traders forged strong relationships with those groups. During the seventeenth and eighteenth centuries, the Ojibwes continued to participate in the trade industry. Near the end of the 1700s, the Mikinakwastsha-Anishinabe Band of the Ojibwes separated from the tribe and established a community in the Turtle Mountains of North Dakota. The separation was primarily an economic move as the band sought the more plentiful furbearing animal populations, as well as refuge from encroaching Euro-American settlement in Wisconsin. The Ojibwes engaged in conflict with members of the Dakota Tribe in North Dakota. Skirmishes over territorial rights continued for about 50 years until the 1858 Sweet Corn Treaty defined tribal lands for both groups and mandated numerous resolutions for the tribes.

In 1882, the Turtle Mountain Reservation was formally established on a 24- by 32-mile tract of land. The government wanted to allot the land into individual parcels, but the Ojibwes refused this process and the land remained in communal property. While the initial reservation agreement encompassed about 10 million acres, in 1884 its size was dramatically reduced when the government decided that most of the mixed-blood population was Canadian in origin. After ongoing legal battles, the federal government finally agreed in the Act of 1904 to compensate the tribe one million dollars for the appropriation of its land, or about 10 cents an acre. The Burke Act of 1906 provided for the allotment of reservation land to individual tribal members. Due to the greatly diminished size of the reservation, the federal government had to allot land from the public domain as distant as Montana and South Dakota once reservation lands were exhausted.

During the 1950s, the Turtle Mountain Chippewas were targeted for termination, though Congress did not authorize the termination. During the 1970s, enhanced tribal sovereignty, along with federal help in attracting business investment and housing construction, allowed the tribe to realize a degree of success and self-sufficiency. During the late 1980s, the federal government recognized the unfairness of the so-called Ten Cent Treaty and began a reparations process.

The reservation is now home to a shopping mall, an industrial park, a casino, and other business ventures. These represent no small accomplishment, given the region's ultra-rural and traditionally undeveloped status. Presently, the traditional Chippewa and Mitchell languages are still spoken on the reservation and vicinity, as is Mitchif, a creole language. Moreover, while the majority of tribal members are Roman Catholic, a small but growing percentage practices traditional religious customs.

GOVERNMENT

The tribe's governing body, the tribal council, consists of a chairman and eight members elected to two-year terms. The chairman is elected at large by the general membership; a vice-chairman is elected from the eight council members at the first meeting of each newly elected council. The tribal government is organized according to a 1959 constitution and bylaws. In 1976, the tribe adopted a tribal code, covering criminal and civil law.

The Trenton Indian Service Area is now governed by an elected board of directors made up of seven members, six directors, and a chairperson-at-large. Elections for directors are held every four years; terms are staggered. The service area has been divided into three districts: Williston, Trenton, Montana, with two representatives from each district. The tribe, under PL-638, contracts with the BIA to administer key programs and services. The tribe operates a police department with 26 full-time law enforcement officers.

ECONOMY

A mixed economy of privately and tribally owned small business enterprises, construction companies stimulated by economic development initiatives, and the tourism industry form the backbone of the Turtle Mountain Chippewa's economy. Tribal enterprises provide the financial stimulus for much of the economic development of the recent decade.

Government as Employer. Tribal programs, the Indian Health Service, the local school systems, and the BIA employ a sig-

---

Turtle Mountain Reservation
Federal reservation
Chippewa
Rolette County (reservation), Williams, Divide, and McKenzie (service area) counties, North Dakota
Sheridan, Richland, and Roosevelt counties, Montana

Turtle Mountain Reservation
P.O. Box 900
Belcourt, ND 58316
  701-477-2600
  701-477-6836 Fax
  turtlemountainchippewa.com

Trenton Indian Service Area
P.O. Box 210
Trenton, ND 58853

Total area (*BIA realty, 2004*)
77,619.21 acres

Tribally owned (*BIA realty, 2004*)
36,718.98 acres

Individually owned
(*BIA realty, 2004*)
40,701.99 acres

Population *2000 census*
5,815

Tribal enrollment
(*BIA labor report, 2004*)
30,000

Total labor force *2000 census*
2,756

Total labor force
(*BIA labor report, 2001*)
7,936

High school graduate or higher
2000 census
71.6%

Bachelor's degree or higher
2000 census
11.7%

Unemployment rate *2000 census*
19.5%

Unemployment rate
(*BIA labor report, 2001*)
68%

Per capita income *2000 census*
$9,415

Turtle Mountain

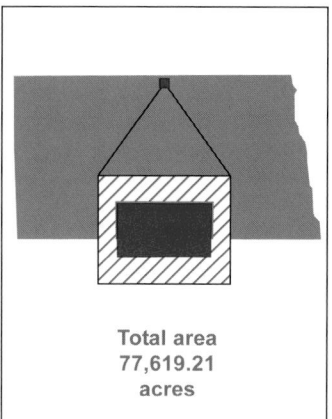

**Total area
77,619.21
acres**

nificant number of people. Altogether, the local, state, and federal governments currently provide over 50 percent of the jobs of all employed tribal members. The tribal government operates a Tribal Employment Rights Office to promote employment opportunities for Indians and business opportunities for Indian contractors.

Economic Development Projects. In order to encourage commerce on the reservation, the tribal government drafted and proposed a Code for the Creation and Governance of Corporations, designed to clarify and simplify the laws applicable to all businesses and nonprofit organizations created by the tribe. This code of corporations also seeks to limit liability of partners, thereby creating incentives for investment in businesses on the reservation. Once passed, the code would also assure that tribal assets are available for the satisfaction of any valid claim by corporate creditors. Following its designation as a Housing and Urban Development Renewal Community, the tribe can offer tax incentives to prospective business partners on the reservation, and it has published a brochure outlining the incentives. They include a capital gains exclusion, an increase in the Section 179 deduction, and an employment credit.

Agriculture and Livestock. The land available for agriculture production is limited to an estimated 12,000 acres. The length of summer days, about 18 hours, contributes to the success of crops in the region. The tribe maintains a small herd of bison just west of Belcourt on the south side of Highway 5 in a grassy, wooded park. The Trenton Indian Service Area owns 96 acres of fee-patented land presently used for pasture.

Forestry. The Turtle Mountain forest is incredibly rich when compared to the austerity of the surrounding Great Plains. It contains mature stands of timber, which have traditionally been considered to have little economic value beyond firewood. Given the forest's limited and unique nature, the tribe maintains a rigorous vigilance over it and its attendant wildlife.

Gaming. The tribe owns and operates the Skydancer Hotel and Casino in Belcourt. The casino features 535 slots/VLTs, 10 table games, 5 poker tables, and 500 bingo seats. It also offers a restaurant and an entertainment venue. The hotel offers 97 guest rooms and a convention center. The facility employs 350 people. The tribe also offers horseracing with pari-mutuel betting. Both these ventures provide a significant and growing source of revenue and tribal employment.

Fisheries. Compared with most of the surrounding region, the Turtle Mountain region is relatively flush with lakes and streams that have traditionally supported subsistence fishing. Today the tribe is actively pursuing the development of a commercial walleye fishing industry and commercial bait farms on the reservation.

Construction. Of the approximately 100 Indian-owned businesses in Rolette County, an estimated 30 are construction companies. A number of these were active in the 1978 construction of the reservation-based shopping mall.

Manufacturing. Turtle Mountain Manufacturing Company has produced cargo trailers and truck boxes, mostly for U.S. military contracts, since 1979. The company, housed in a 160,000-square-foot facility, is 100 percent tribally owned and operated. The plant is most widely known for the creation of the "Water Buffalo," a low-towing water tank produced for use by the federal government. The plant employs up to 200 people on a regular basis.

The tribe operates the Turtle Mountain Motor Vehicle Department. This entity produces North Dakota state license plates for boats, trailers, recreational vehicles, and standard vehicles registered with the Turtle Mountain MVD. The Bulova Watch Company operates a plant in Rolla, just off the reservation.

Industrial Parks. The tribe operates a 40-acre industrial park about three miles west of Belcourt on U.S. 281. The park maintains steady activity, along with good transportation routes, an ample utilities package, and tax advantages.

Real Estate/Commercial Development. The tribe purchased a former state hospital in Rolette County in 1992. The facility was identified as a Brownfields Pilot by the U.S. EPA. Several environmental studies will be conducted before the tribe proceeds with redeveloping the facility. Adequate housing is an ongoing need on the reservation, especially for low-income tribal members. Some low-cost housing is available in Dunsieth, and there is government housing available for BIA and Indian Health Service employees at Belcourt. Throughout 1998-2001, river flooding caused severe mold damage to many existing homes, including the assisted and unassisted living units for elders. The federal government declared the area a natural disaster, enabling tribal officials to apply for (and receive) housing assistance from HUD. In 2002 the reservation was designated a "renewal community," making income housing tax credits available for owners of newly constructed or renovated rental housing. Tax advisors, along with economic development specialists and businessmen, met with the community to initiate planning for the area's redevelopment.

Media and Communications. The tribe owns Uniband. This enterprise provides data entry, transcription, mailroom operations, help desk, telemarketing, records management, computer imaging, and computer support services. It has sites in Arizona, California, Maryland, North Dakota, New Mexico, and Washington, D.C. Clients include federal government agencies, state agencies, and commercial entities. The company employs over 600 people. Cynaband LLC is a subsidiary of Uniband. Uniband is the major shareholder in the telecommunications company. The tribe owns KEYA, a public, nonprofit ratio station. It is the oldest Indian-owned radio station in the United States. The tribe publishes the *Turtle Mountain Star*, a weekly newspaper.

Tourism and Recreation. The reservation's numerous lakes and forested hillsides afford excellent fishing, hunting, and other outdoor recreation. There are three golf courses in the area. In 2002 the tribe opened the Sleepee Teepee motel on the reservation. The reservation lies within 25 miles of the world-famous International Peace Gardens, Lords Lake National Wildlife Refuge, Willow Lake National Wildlife Refuge, Wakopa State Game Management Area, and School Section Lake National Wildlife Refuge. Other tourism opportunities in north-central North Dakota include: Bottineau Winter Park, Turtle Mountain State Forest, Dunseith Log Cabin, Lake Metigoshe State Park, Dale and Martha Hawk Museum, Sipising Cultural Park, Lake Upsilon, and Belcourt Lake.

The reservation features a Chippewa Heritage Center and Museum, with historical society archives, dioramas depicting the early Métis culture, an art gallery, and a gift shop, including handcrafted tribal items. The center is adjacent to the Sipising Cultural Park, which features a re-creation of a traditional arbor made of poplar and willow. The facilities are used to host storytelling and cultural events and activities. Additions to the park in 2003 included a willow wicker-covered bridge, a creek side interpretive trail, a veteran's memorial, and a genealogy brick display. The tribe also operates the Anishinaubag Intercultural Center, a tourist operation in a beautiful natural setting on Fish Lake that promotes intercultural understanding. The center includes a Plains Indian village, Mandan earth lodges, log cabins, and other historic re-creations demonstrating the Native American history of the area.

The Turtle Mountain Artists Board promotes the profusion of musicians and other performing artists in the area. The tribe celebrates powwows during July and over Labor Day weekend, drawing crowds along with United States and Canadian dancers. The Trenton Indian Service Area has leased land adjacent to Trenton Lake from the Army Corps of Engineers for recreational and tourism purposes. The tribe celebrates St. Ann's and Turtle Mountain Days every July, a festival that revels in traditional spirituality, history, and games.

INFRASTRUCTURE

The reservation lies on Highways 5 and 281 linking Minot, North Dakota, and Winnipeg, Ontario. U.S. Highways 2, 52, and 83 provide access to Bismarck and the remainder of the region. Major highways accessing the Trenton Service Area include U.S. 85, extending north and south from the Canadian Border into South Dakota, and U.S. 2, which runs east-west across North Dakota and into Montana. Highway 1804 runs from the Fort Berthold Indian Reservation, through the town of Trenton, and into Sidney, Montana.

Electricity. Three different electric companies provide electricity to the reservation.

Fuel. Several natural gas and propane companies provide fuel to the reservation.

Water Supply. A rural water system provides services to the reservation.

Transportation. Rail service is available to the reservation locally through three commercial lines, including Amtrak. Regular commercial air service is available at Minot International Airport and Devils Lake. UPS serves the reservation, while other commercial truck lines serve Rolla and Rugby. Rail service is available to the Trenton Service Area in Williston with passenger service provided by the Amtrak system. Parcel delivery service and overnight express are available out of Trenton. Passenger and air freight services are available in Sidney, Montana, and Williston, North Dakota.

Telecommunications. Telephone service and utilities are available throughout the reservation.

COMMUNITY FACILITIES AND SERVICES

Education. Education facilities are provided by Belcourt's Turtle Mountain Community School System, which includes a modern high school, middle school, and elementary school. Ojibwa Indian School serves grades K-8. St. Ann's Parish Elementary School is also located on the reservation. Turtle Mountain Community College is located in Belcourt. The college offers associate's degree programs in the arts and sciences and diploma and certification programs as well. A new campus for the facility boasts a 105,000-square-foot building, located on approximately 123 acres. It is accredited by the North Central Association of Colleges and Schools.

Health Care. The Turtle Mountain Comprehensive Healthcare Center is located in Belcourt. It offers inpatient facilities, comprehensive medical services, surgical facilities, obstetric services, and a pediatrics department. The center also provides dental services, community outreach services, health nurses, ambulance service, and charter air service.

ENVIRONMENTAL CONCERNS

The tribe participates on the Mni Sose Intertribal Water Rights Coalition, a consortium of Missouri River Basin tribes who have joined together to secure Indian water rights to the Missouri River.

OKLAHOMA

Map from Tiller's Guide to Indian Country (1996 edition)

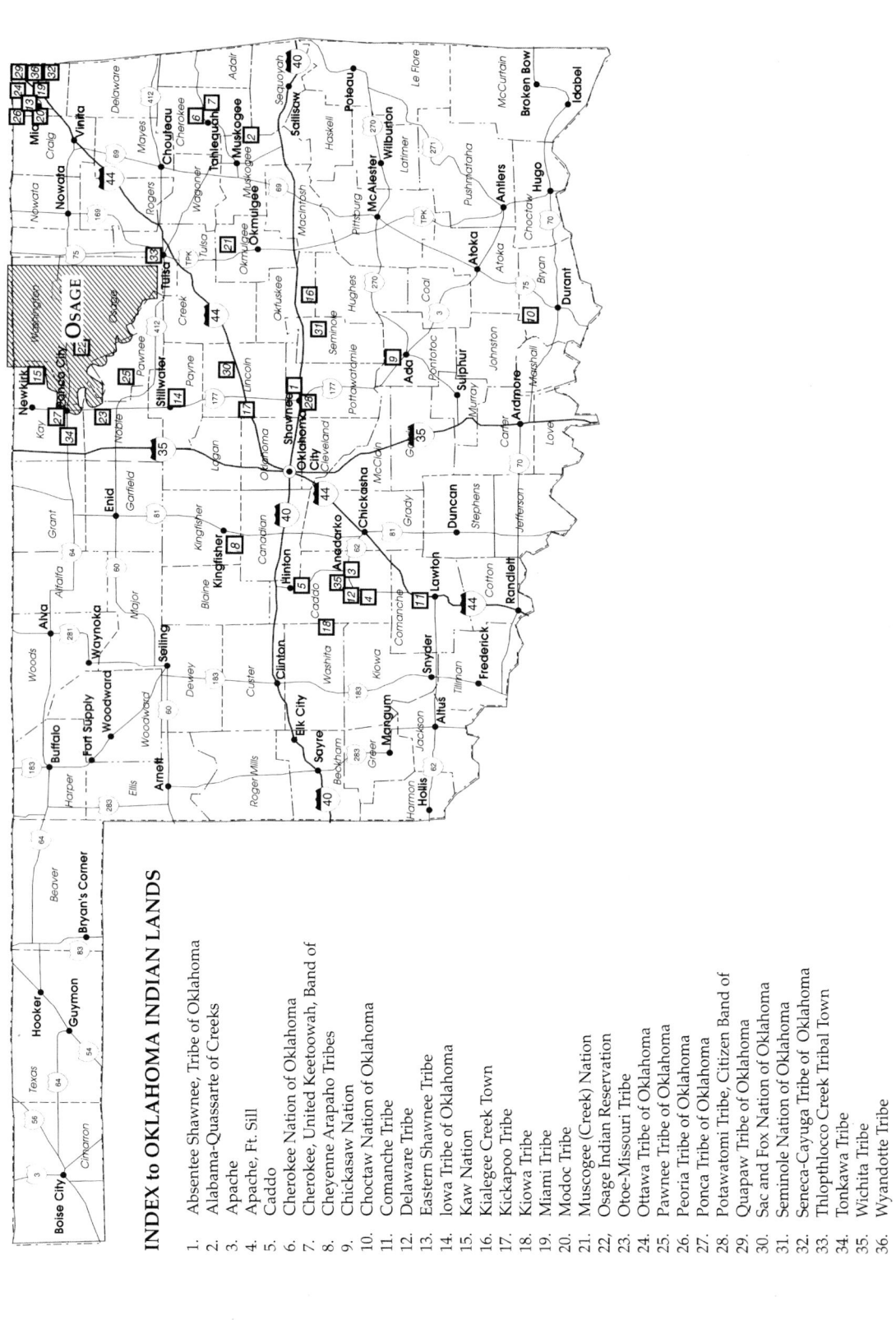

INDEX to OKLAHOMA INDIAN LANDS

1. Absentee Shawnee, Tribe of Oklahoma
2. Alabama-Quassarte of Creeks
3. Apache
4. Apache, Ft. Sill
5. Caddo
6. Cherokee Nation of Oklahoma
7. Cherokee, United Keetoowah, Band of
8. Cheyenne Arapaho Tribes
9. Chickasaw Nation
10. Choctaw Nation of Oklahoma
11. Comanche Tribe
12. Delaware Tribe
13. Eastern Shawnee Tribe
14. Iowa Tribe of Oklahoma
15. Kaw Nation
16. Kialegee Creek Town
17. Kickapoo Tribe
18. Kiowa Tribe
19. Miami Tribe
20. Modoc Tribe
21. Muscogee (Creek) Nation
22. Osage Indian Reservation
23. Otoe-Missouri Tribe
24. Ottawa Tribe of Oklahoma
25. Pawnee Tribe of Oklahoma
26. Peoria Tribe of Oklahoma
27. Ponca Tribe of Oklahoma
28. Potawatomi Tribe, Citizen Band of
29. Quapaw Tribe of Oklahoma
30. Sac and Fox Nation of Oklahoma
31. Seminole Nation of Oklahoma
32. Seneca-Cayuga Tribe of Oklahoma
33. Thlopthlocco Creek Tribal Town
34. Tonkawa Tribe
35. Wichita Tribe
36. Wyandotte Tribe

Absentee Shawnee

bsentee Shawnee

LOCATION AND LAND STATUS

The Absentee Shawnees live in a region of south-central Oklahoma, about 35 miles east-southeast of Oklahoma City. The tribe includes two bands that occupy two geographically distinct communities; the Big Jim Band is in Cleveland County, and the White Turkey Band is in Pottawatomie County near the City of Shawnee. This second community is also the site of the Absentee Shawnee Tribal Government Complex. The tribe's ancestral homeland lies in the region of Ohio and Kentucky. During the nineteenth century, the U.S. government removed the tribe to what is now the State of Kansas. The tribe absented itself from the reservation in Kansas in 1845 (thus their name), relocating to Indian Territory (in Oklahoma). The Big Jim Band settled along the Deep Fork River, while the White Turkey Band settled in its present site near Shawnee, Oklahoma. In 1886, the U.S. Army forced the Big Jim Band to move once again, this time to the site of its present community in Cleveland County. There are 12,002 acres in federal trust, the vast majority of which are allotted, forming a checkerboard pattern.

CULTURE AND HISTORY

In 1872, nearly three decades after the Absentee Shawnees had abandoned Kansas for Indian Territory, the tribe received title to a portion of a reservation between the north and south forks of the Canadian River near present-day Shawnee, Oklahoma. The other portion of the reservation went to the Citizen Band of Potawatomi. After the passage of the Dawes Act of 1887, most tribal members accepted individual allotments, and by 1900 the vast majority of the tribe had been more or less assimilated into mainstream American culture. The Absentee Shawnees following this path were of the White Turkey Band, named for their assimilationist chief. The Big Jim Band, on the other hand, fiercely opposed assimilation and even considered moving to Mexico, where they hoped to find the freedom to maintain their communal traditions. Hard feelings passed between the two bands, though they were finally organized as one tribe under the Oklahoma Indian Welfare Act of 1936.

The tribe maintains a degree of their traditional culture, with the Big Jim Band conducting tribal thanksgiving dances such as the Green Corn Dance during the spring and fall, along with a ceremonial War Dance in August near Little Axe. The Absentee Shawnee Tribe has the largest number of members who still speak the Native language of any of the three Shawnee bands in Oklahoma. The tribe's cultural preservation department is working to preserve and celebrate its cultural heritage through the development of a tribal gift shop, language classes, and archives, and the compilation of an inventory of tribal cemeteries.

GOVERNMENT

The tribe is federally recognized, reorganized under the authority of the Oklahoma Indian Welfare Act of 1936, and governed under a constitution that was ratified on December 5, 1938, and last amended on August 13, 1988. The tribal government is composed of a legislative and executive branch, and a judicial branch. An independent election commission is charged with the responsibility of conducting tribal elections, which are held annually. The tribe's legislative and executive branch, or executive committee, consists of a governor, lieutenant governor, secretary, treasurer, and representative, all of whom are elected by the general membership. This committee has both legislative and executive powers. The judicial branch is made up of the tribal court and the supreme court. The executive committee appoints justices for both courts. The general council consists of all enrolled tribal members. Tribal members must be 18 years of age to vote in elections.

Tribal departments and programs include law enforcement, the housing authority, economic and community development, social services, family services, contract health, community health, pharmacy, behavioral health, education, child care, parent education, foster care, Low Income Home Energy Assistance Program (LIHEAP), general assistance, tribal energy assistance, individual monies account, boarding school application processing, direct employment assistance, the Workforce Investment Act (WIA), procurement, realty, election commission, tax commission, personnel, and cultural preservation.

BUSINESS CORPORATION

The Absentee Shawnee Tribe formed All Nation Bancorp as a holding company. This corporation bought the First National Bank of Calumet in December 2003, making the Absentee Shawnee 1 of 19 tribes nationwide to own a bank. The bank was renamed the All Nations Bank. It offers all the conventional banking services. In 2004 the tribe began construction on a 3,300-square-foot branch bank in Shawnee complete with a conference room for community meetings. It will be opened in early 2005.

ECONOMY

The economy of the Absentee Shawnees is fueled by gaming, manufacturing, mining, and small business enterprises.

Government as Employer. The tribal government remains the largest source of employment within the Absentee Shawnee Community. It employs approximately 188 people.

Gaming. The Absentee Shawnee Tribe owns and operates the Thunderbird Casino. The state-of-the-art gaming facility

Absentee Shawnee Reservation
Federal reservation
Shawnee
Shawnee, Pottawatomie, and
Cleveland counties, Oklahoma

Absentee Shawnee Tribe
of Oklahoma
2025 S. Gordon Cooper Drive
Shawnee, OK 74802
405-275-4030
405-275-1922 Fax

Total area (BIA realty, 2004)
11,679.99 acres

Federal trust (BIA realty, 2004)
10 acres

Federal trust (Tribal source, 2005)
607.05 acres

Tribally owned (BIA realty, 2004)
358.81 acres

Individually owned
(BIA realty, 2004)
11,311.18 acres

Population 2000 census
3,200

Population (Tribal source, 2004)
3,200

Tribal enrollment (BIA, 2001)
3,013

Total labor force (BIA, 2001)
514

Unemployment rate (BIA, 2001)
18%

Absentee Shawnee

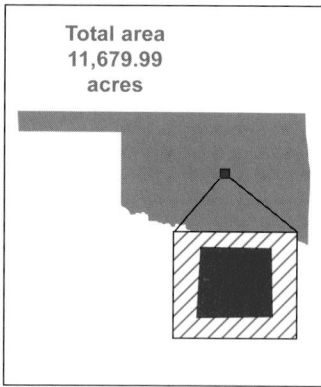

**Total area
11,679.99
acres**

has approximately 300 employees, and it houses a wide assortment of activities, including video bingo, casino-style bingo, and high-stakes bingo. Food service is also available.

Mining. Though there are no direct tribal mining operations, there are at least 18 oil companies on the tribe's tax rolls, generating revenues for the tribe and individual members in the form of taxes and leases.

Industrial Parks. The tribe has a 33-acre, undeveloped site with state highway access and full utilities available. Studies for development are presently underway.

Services and Retail. The Absentee Shawnee Tribe owns a shopping mall that is 50 percent utilized, with further development in progress. There are also four smoke shops located within the tribe's jurisdiction, including the Absentee Shawnee Tribal Store and Smoke Shop, and one convenience store located in the recreation lake area. A diner is being constructed adjacent to the Little Axe Tribal Store.

Transportation. The tribe owns approximately 36 vehicles of various types for use by the tribal government and its operatives.

Media and Communications. The tribe's official newspaper is *The Absentee Shawnee News.* The publication features reports from the governor, lieutenant governor, secretary, treasurer, and tribal representatives, as well as community news and information on upcoming programs and events.

Tourism and Recreation. While the Thunderbird Wild Wild West Casino is a popular draw for tourists, tribal lands are also home to a recreation lake area. The tribe is in the planning stages for a variety of attractions and facilities, including a motel, RV parks, and a boat storage facility.

INFRASTRUCTURE
I-35 and 40 provide access to the tribal jurisdictional area, while State Highways 9, 77, 177, 18, 270, 3, and 102 all run through the area directly. The Oklahoma City airport is located about 20 miles from tribal headquarters, while a municipal airport is five miles away. Commercial bus and truck lines provide full service to the tribal area.

Electricity. Regional utilities provide electricity on an individual basis.

Fuel. Regional utilities supply gas is on an individual basis.

Water Supply. Either local municipalities or wells and septic systems, depending upon location within the jurisdictional area, provide water and sewer services.

COMMUNITY FACILITIES AND SERVICES
The Absentee Shawnee Tribe has its own tribal government complex and a community center called Little Axe Community Hall.

Education. Students attend the area's numerous public schools and colleges. The WIA program assists individuals in obtaining: employment through classroom training; assistance with tuition, books, and fees; education and enhancement for tribal youth ages 14-21; on-the-job training; and work experience. The Absentee Shawnee Cultural Preservation Department offers Shawnee language classes, a language immersion camp, cultural demonstration classes, and educational historical exhibits.

Health Care. Health care is furnished primarily through the Little Axe Health Clinic located within the tribal complex near Shawnee. In addition, the Absentee Shawnee Tribe has an assisted care home health program. Tribal members visit local hospitals and other health care facilities for services not met by the clinic or the home health program. The Absentee housing authority has received HUD grant money that the tribe intends to use for operating a drug prevention program at the community center. The program is planned to provide drug intervention and treatment, crime prevention, referrals and networking, support services, and transportation. The program will include a cultural component.

ENVIRONMENTAL CONCERNS
Among the leading environmental concerns of the Absentee Shawnee Tribe are illegal dumping of soil on tribal lands that is contaminated with mold and lead contamination. The tribe received a grant to clean up an area called Brownfield, which has been polluted by these contaminants. The tribe has contracted a company to train tribal members to do the work, thus creating employment opportunities as well as rehabilitating the area.

labama Quassarte

**Alabama Quassarte Tribal Town
Federal reservation
Creek (Muskogee)
Okmulgee County, Oklahoma**

Alabama Quassarte
Tribal Town
P.O. Box 187
Wetumka, OK 74883
405-452-3987
405-452-3968 Fax

LOCATION AND LAND STATUS
The Alabama Quassarte Tribal Town was established by an Act of Congress on June 26, 1936. The tribal town lies in the forested hills of east-central Oklahoma. The 878.25 acres of tribal land are located on three tracts in Hughes County, Oklahoma. Tribal members own an additional 825 acres in individual allotments in the area. Major Oklahoma cities near the reservation include Muskogee, 50 miles northeast, and Tulsa, 75 miles north. In 2004, the tribe had plans for additional land purchases.

PHYSICAL DESCRIPTION
The area's topography is typical of the southern Great Plains, with gentle rolling grass-covered hills; trees and other relatively dense vegetation are only in riparian areas.

CLIMATE
There is no climate data recorded for Wetumka, Oklahoma, the site of tribal headquarters. However, climate information has been recorded for Muskogee, only 50 miles distant. The year-round average daily high temperature in Muskogee is 73°F, with the highest temperature on record as 118°F. The year-round average daily low temperature is 50°F, with the lowest temperature on record being -11°F. The area receives approximately 42 inches of precipitation annually; almost 7 inches falls as snowfall.

CULTURE AND HISTORY
The Alabama Quassartes (Coushattas or "weed gatherers") are descendants of the Alabama people, a Muskogean-speaking tribe of the southeastern United States. Early Euro-American settlers in the region, during the eighteenth and early nine-

teenth century, referred to them as "Alabama" or "Creek." The Alabamas lived in riverfront or coastal villages in the area of present-day Alabama, Louisiana, and western Florida, practicing a subsistence lifestyle based on hunting, fishing, and horticulture. The Alabamas demonstrated a significant influence on the prehistoric Caddoan and Mississippi cultures and were related linguistically and culturally related to the Yamasees, Seminoles, Apalachees, Choctaws, and Chickasaws.

Hernando de Soto led the first party of Europeans into Alabama/Creek territory in 1539; throughout the seventeenth and eighteenth centuries, the lower southeastern portion of the continent became an economic and military battleground for the competing European powers. The Creeks allied with the English against the Spanish during the eighteenth century but eventually became embroiled in warfare with other tribes competing for English trade items. As a subgroup of the Creeks, the Alabamas formed part of the "Five Civilized Tribes," a name applied to the Choctaws, Chickasaws, Creeks, Cherokees, and Seminoles by English settlers because of their rapid adoption of many Euro-American cultural practices. Warfare between Creeks arose during the War of 1812, as different bands declared allegiance to either the English or the United States. A massive influx of American settlers into the southeast during the early nineteenth century led President Andrew Jackson to sign the Removal Bill in 1830, giving him the power to exchange land west of the Mississippi for lands held by southeastern tribes. In 1836, the U.S. Army forced the Creeks to relocate to Indian Territory in present-day Oklahoma. In eastern Oklahoma, the Creeks became relatively prosperous farmers. However, they eventually lost most of their tribal lands through allotment. Fortunately, the tribe has succeeded in maintaining its tribal culture despite the devastating effects of relocation and allotment; the Muskogean language is being passed on to tribal youth.

GOVERNMENT
The Alabama Quassarte Tribal Town was founded by an Act of Congress on June 26, 1936. The tribe ratified a constitution and bylaws on January 10, 1939, pursuant to the Oklahoma Indian Welfare Act of June 26, 1936.

The tribal constitution created a government structure consisting of a chief, a second chief, a secretary, a floor speaker, a solicitor, a chairman of the governing committee, and 12 members of the governing committee. Elections are held every four years.

The tribe, under PL-638, contracts with the BIA to administer key programs and services. Departments or offices providing services to members include: administration, housing, emergency assistance, social services, economic and community development, cultural preservation, environmental protection, roads, transportation, enrollment, and accounting. Law enforcement services and tribal courts are operated by the BIA.

ECONOMY
Government as Employer. The tribal government employs 20 persons through 11 programs.

Economic Development Projects. The tribe is in the process of completing an integrated resource management program to assess current resources and create linkages between them in order to maximize development potential. The tribe acquired a grant to develop a community development financial institution that will provide general loans for tribal members and

other Native Americans wishing to build small business enterprises at the reservation. It is also developing entrepreneurship training for small business development.

Construction. Alabama Quassarte Tribal Town is currently negotiating a teaming agreement to establish an 8(a) construction company.

Mining. The tribe is currently conducting a mineral assessment on tribal lands.

Services and Retail. The tribe contracts a manager for a retail tobacco shop in Henryetta, Oklahoma.

Tourism and Recreation. The Alabama Quassarte Tribe maintains a ceremonial Stomp Grounds site. The reservation lies 25 miles west of Lake Eufala, a major recreation destination in eastern Oklahoma.

INFRASTRUCTURE
The Alabama Quassarte reservation is one-eighth of a mile from I-40 and five miles west of State Highway 75.

Electricity. Off-reservation providers supply electricity, natural gas, and propane services to tribal members.

Water Supply. Approximately 44 reservation homes receive city sewer services; another 84 have septic tanks. The reservation maintains no wells. Individual tribal members receive city water service from Henryetta.

Transportation. Private air facilities are located at Henryetta Municipal Airport, 7 miles from the reservation. Tulsa International Airport lies 75 miles north via Highway 75. Bus service is available in Okmulgee, 19 miles north of the reservation. The Dalworth and Stubbs trucking lines serve the Henryetta area. Freight-carrying railways service Henryetta, 4 miles from the reservation. Freight barges serve Muskogee via the Kerr Waterway. The tribe owns a van for transporting members to medical services and local shopping opportunities.

Telecommunications. Qwest provides telephone service to the Alabama Quassarte Tribal Town.

COMMUNITY FACILITIES AND SERVICES
The Alabama Quassarte Tribal Town does not yet have a community center, but they have received funding to construct a community service center to be built two miles west of the community of Wetumka, Oklahoma. Tribal services and offices are located in four separate buildings in Wetumka: the main office, an economic and community development annex, a social services annex, and a housing annex.

Education. Tribal youth attend various public schools throughout the service area.

Health Care. Tribal members receive health care at the regional Creek Nation Health System facilities. Hospitals are located in Muskogee and Tulsa. The tribe has applied for a health management grant to develop its own tribal health program.

ENVIRONMENTAL CONCERNS
The tribe has acquired a grant to study groundwater quality and quantity on reservation lands. Illegal dumping remains an environmental concern, as does air quality and the protection of the endangered species within reservation habitat.

Alabama Quassarte

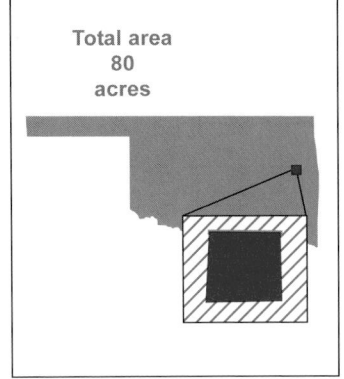

Total area
80
acres

Tribally owned lands
(Tribal source, 2004)
80 acres

Tribal enrollment *(BIA, 2001)*
193

Tribal enrollment
(Tribal source, 2004)
350

Total labor force *(BIA, 2001)*
233

Total labor force
(Tribal source, 2004)
17-20

Unemployment rate *(BIA, 2001)*
18%

A pache Tribe

Apache Tribe of Oklahoma Reservation
Federal reservation
Apache (Kiowa)
Caddo County, Oklahoma

Apache Tribe of Oklahoma
P.O. Box 1220
511 E. Colorado
Anadarko, OK 73005
405-247-9493
405-247-2686 Fax

Total area-jointly held
(BIA realty, 2004)
189,262.69 acres

Federal trust-jointly held
(BIA realty, 2004)
1 acre

Tribally owned-jointly held
(BIA realty, 2004)
3,300.85 acres

Individually owned-jointly held
(BIA realty, 2004)
185,960.84 acres

Tribal enrollment *(BIA, 2001)*
1,854

Total labor force *2000 census*
4,849

Total labor force
(Tribal source, 2004)
45

High school graduate or higher
2000 census
74.6%

Bachelor's degree or higher
2000 census
15.7%

Unemployment rate *2000 census*
7.9%

Unemployment rate *(BIA, 2001)*
30%

Per capita income *2000 census*
$15,389.00

LOCATION AND LAND STATUS

The Apache Tribe of Oklahoma Reservation lies on the plains of southwestern Oklahoma. The Apache Tribe of Oklahoma jointly owns 7,592.61 acres of federal trust land in Caddo County with the Kiowa and Comanche tribes. Tribal community facilities are located in south Anadarko on State Highway 9, 50 miles northeast of Oklahoma City. The 1867 Medicine Lodge Treaty established a reservation in the southwestern corner of Indian Territory for the Kiowa Apache, Arapaho, Cheyenne, and Comanche Tribes. Allotment diminished the reservation during the early twentieth century. Today, 274,312.53 allotted acres supplement the joint tribal land base.

CULTURE AND HISTORY

Known historically as the Ka-ta-kas, the Apache Tribe of Oklahoma are descendants of the Athabascan-speaking Eastern Apache groups who have inhabited the Plains since the fifteenth century. The Ka-ta-kas were plains hunters who followed the great southern bison herd across the grasslands of western Texas, Oklahoma, and eastern New Mexico. Buffalo represented the centerpiece of Apache life, providing meat, clothing, tools, weapons, and shelter.The Ka-ta-kas also traded buffalo meat and hides to the pueblos of the Rio Grande Valley in exchange for corn, beans, cotton blankets, turquoise, and ceramics. The arrival of the horse around 1680 transformed the Apaches into highly mobile hunters and raiders. Because of their alliance with the more numerous Kiowa Tribe, the Ka-ta-kas were known historically as the Kiowa Apache. During the 18th century, French and Spanish traders brought guns, horses, and disease to them. The latter drastically reduced the tribe's population. During the mid-nineteenth century, the United States made a number of treaties with the Southern Plains tribes. In 1865 the unratified Treaty of the Little Arkansas assigned the Kiowa Apaches, Cheyennes, and Arapahos to a common reservation. However, settlers continued to pour into tribal lands, with the Medicine Lodge Treaty of 1867 further reducing the tribal domain. Reservation lands were opened for allotment during the late nineteenth century, with most passing into non-Indian hands.Today, tribal members work in a variety of professions in the Anadarko and Fort Cobb areas, and tribal identity and tradition continue to flourish.

GOVERNMENT

A business committee, composed of a chairman, a vice-chairman, a secretary-treasurer, and two members, serves as the tribes elected governing body. Committee members serve two-year terms; elections are held every two years in March. The Apache Tribe of Oklahoma incorporated in 1972, adopting a constitution and bylaws in accordance with the Indian Reorganization Act of 1934 and the Oklahoma Indian Welfare Act of 1936. The tribe is applying for its status as a PL-638 self-governance tribe. Tribal programs include food distribution, elder care, a vocational rehabilitation center, Indian child welfare, child care services, elimination of violence against women, higher education, Head Start, environmental, tax commission, and CHR courts.

ECONOMY

Federal funding for tribal programs and infrastructure, revenues from their bingo hall, and other business enterprises are the main components of the Apache Tribe of Oklahoma's economy.

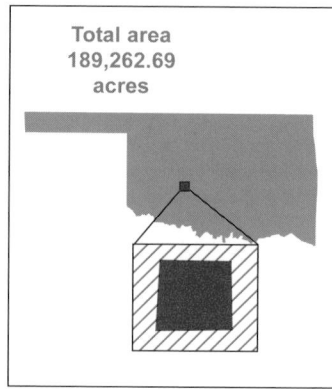

Total area
189,262.69
acres

Agriculture and Livestock. The Comanche, Apache, and Kiowa tribes lease land to non-Indians for cattle grazing and agriculture.

Gaming. The Apache Bingo Hall is located near the tribal headquarters. The tribe is considering expanding its gaming operation to include a casino.

Construction. The Apache Tribe owns a construction company and is applying for 8(a) certification. The tribe seeks opportunities to contract with other construction companies by offering benefits such as tax breaks.

Services and Retail. The Apache Trading Post is located next to the Tribal Complex. It has a convenience store, gas station, a native arts gift shop, and a smoke shop.

Tourism and Recreation. The Wichita Mountains are located 30 miles southwest of Anadarko, providing an abundance of outdoor recreational activities. Also located in the area are the American Indian Hall of Fame and Indian City U.S.A.

INFRASTRUCTURE

Tribal community facilities are accessible via U.S. 62 and U.S. 281. I-40 passes about 40 miles north of tribal headquarters. Bus and commercial and private air facilities are available in Oklahoma City. Trucking companies, express package carriers, and the CRI&P Railway also serves the tribal area.

Electricity. Caddo County Public Utilities provides electricity to the tribal area.

Fuel. Oklahoma Natural Gas supplies the tribal area's fuel.

Water Supply. The City of Anadarko supplies water and wastewater services.

COMMUNITY FACILITIES AND SERVICES

The Tribe maintains a tribal administrative complex that includes offices, meeting facilities, and a tribal museum.

Education. Children attend Caddo County Public Schools. An annual culture camp for kids provides nature walks, language instruction, dances, and traditional games.

Health Care. Tribal members receive health care from Indian Health Service facilities located in Anadarko.

LOCATION AND LAND STATUS

The Caddo Nation co-owns approximately 2,400 acres of noncontiguous, federal trust land spread across a three-county area of southwestern Oklahoma; these lands are held jointly with the Delaware and Wichita tribes. The Caddo Tribal Complex is located in Binger (Na-Binka), Oklahoma, approximately 21 miles north of Anadarko on U.S. 281. Oklahoma City lies approximately 60 miles east of the tribal headquarters. The Wichita Agency, established in 1859, served as the reservation for the Caddo, Wichita, and Delaware Indians. Much of the land therein was allotted following the Jerome Agreement of 1890. Approximately 80,343 acres of individual allotments supplement the joint tribal land base.

PHYSICAL DESCRIPTION

The tribal trust area is characterized by plains and rolling grasslands, typical of the Great Plains region. The Canadian, Washita, and Cache rivers drain the region.

CLIMATE

Climate data has not been recorded for Binger, Oklahoma; however, information does exist for Anadarko, approximately 20 miles south. The year-round average daily high temperature at Anadarko is 74°F. The year-round average daily low temperature is 48°F. The area receives approximately 30 inches of precipitation annually.

CULTURE AND HISTORY

The Caddo Nation of Oklahoma descends from the Caddoan-speaking Caddo people of the lower Red River Valley. For more than 2,000 years, the Caddos lived in villages, practiced horticulture, and built large temple mounds throughout an area now made up of southeastern Oklahoma, southwestern Arkansas, northeastern Texas, and northwestern Louisiana. The Spanish explorer Hernando de Soto made contact with the Caddos in 1541. In the seventeenth century, the French ventured south on the Mississippi River into Caddo territory. Being good traders, bartering furs and salt for European finished goods, the Caddos were able to maintain relative stability despite these early encroachments.

Contact with American settlers migrating westward following the Louisiana Purchase in 1803 brought conflict. During the 1830s, Texans dispossessed the Caddos of their lands, which lay within the Texas Republic. The Caddos were removed to Indian Territory, and they were settled in 1859 at the Wichita Agency and Reservation north of the Washita River near present-day Anadarko. This reservation was dissolved following the Jerome Agreement of 1890, and tribal lands were allotted to individual members. In 1936, the tribal constitution was approved under the Oklahoma Indian Welfare Act. The people were incorporated as the Caddo Tribe of Oklahoma in 1938. In 1963, federal trust lands were restored to the Caddo, Delaware, and Wichita tribes; the lands are presently held in common.

Despite dislocation and relocation, the Caddos retain much of their culture, particularly ceremonial songs and dances. The Caddo Nation works jointly with the Delaware and Wichita tribes to provide economic opportunity for tribal members in the three-county area that makes up the tribal statistical area. The jointly owned WCD Enterprises raises revenue through leasing land and buildings. The Nation fosters cultural awareness through the cultural center and a traditional language program for Head Start children.

GOVERNMENT

The tribal council, composed of a chairman, a vice-chairman, a secretary, a treasurer, and four district representatives, serves as the elected governing body. Council members serve four-year terms, with elections occurring every four years. The Caddo Nation adopted a constitution and bylaws in 1938 in accordance with the Oklahoma Indian Welfare Act of 1936; it was revised and amended in 1976.

The Nation, under PL-638, contracts with the BIA to administer key programs and services. They have their own police department. They provide senior services under the auspices of an administration on aging. The following departments or offices provide services for members: education, enrollment, environmental programs, finance, historical preservation, Indian child welfare Act, maintenance, personnel, museum, social services, and procurement. The Caddo Nation employs 55 people, 70 percent of whom are Caddo members.

BUSINESS CORPORATION

WCD Enterprises is the joint Wichita, Delaware, and Caddo business corporation.

ECONOMY

Government as Employer. Tribal government employs 32 persons. The State of Oklahoma employs approximately 13 tribal members in the Oklahoma State Human Services Department and as teachers. Tribal members also work in federally administered programs, principally BIA offices in the tribal area.

Economic Development Projects. The Caddo Nation owns WCD Enterprises jointly with the Delaware and Wichita tribes. This venture earns revenues through land and building leases. The Nation has plans to open a smoke shop and a gaming facility. Negotiations for a casino are still in progress with developers.

Agriculture and Livestock. WCD Enterprises leases 2,000 acres of farmland to non-Indians. Some tribal members cultivate crops or graze cattle on allotted lands. The Nation owns a bison ranch, which has 40 buffalos.

Forestry. The Nation has grants that provide for wildland fire fighters.

Gaming. A tribal gaming enterprise is in the planning stage.

Mining. The Wichita, Caddo, and Delaware tribes jointly own lands that they lease for oil and gas wells. Individual tribal members also receive royalties from lands leased for oil and gas drilling.

Industrial Parks. WCD Enterprises owns and operates a 10.7-acre industrial site, located along U.S. 62, which includes a 24,486-square-foot building. The industrial site conveniently abuts the CRI&P Railway.

Services and Retail. The Nation has various plans to purchase a gas station.

Tourism and Recreation. The Nation holds an annual Turkey Dance and maintains the Caddo Nation Heritage Museum, a

Caddo Reservation
Tribal jurisdictional
  statistical area
Caddo
Grady, Canadian, and Caddo
counties, Oklahoma

Caddo Nation of Oklahoma
P.O. Box 487
Binger, OK 73009
  405-656-2344
  405-656-2892 Fax
  caddonation-nsn.gov

Total area-jointly held
(BIA realty, 2004)
55,199.53 acres

Tribally owned-jointly held
(BIA realty, 2004)
1,260 acres

**Individually owned-jointly
owned**
(BIA realty, 2004)
53,939.43 acres

Population *2000 census*
14,638

Tribal enrollment
(BIA labor report, 2001)
3,261

Tribal enrollment
(Tribal source, 2004)
4,900

Total labor force *2000 census*
6,223

High school graduate or higher
2000 census
75.6%

Bachelor's degree or higher
2000 census
14.2%

Unemployment rate *2000 census*
8.6%

Per capita income *2000 census*
$14,031

Caddo

Total area
55,199.53
acres

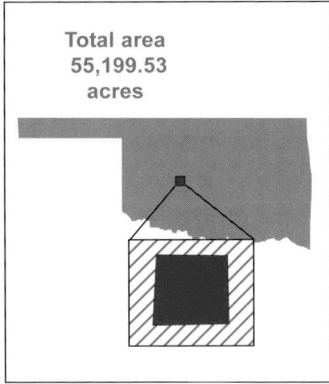

TRI-OK-001 Tribal Police office and trailer

TRI-OK-002 Hasinai Center, education building

TRI-OK-001

TRI-OK-002

cultural center, within the Caddo Tribal Complex. The American Indian Hall of Fame and Indian City USA are located 20 miles south of Binger in Anadarko. An Indian Exposition is held annually.

INFRASTRUCTURE
The Caddo Tribal Complex is located in Binger, Oklahoma. Binger is bisected north-south by U.S. 281 and east-west by Oklahoma State Highway 152. I-40 passes approximately 17 miles north of the tribal headquarters.

Electricity. Caddo County public utilities provide electricity to tribal facilities and tribal members' homes.

Fuel. Oklahoma Natural Gas and Oklahoma Gas and Electric provide natural gas service to tribal members.

Water Supply. A BIA-funded rural water district provides water and sewer service.

Transportation. Commercial air services are located in Oklahoma City, 60 miles east. Private air service is available 60 miles south in Lawton, Oklahoma. Bus lines serve Binger, as

do UPS and FedEx package carriers. The CRI&P Railway also serves the tribal area.

Telecommunication. Qwest provides telephone service.

COMMUNITY FACILITIES AND SERVICES
The tribal complex houses a community center and the Caddo Nation Heritage Museum.

Education. Children attend public schools in Ft. Cobb, Binger, Braxton, Oney, Hinton, and Eakey. The Nation also operates a Head Start program.

Health Care. Tribal members receive health care from the Lawton Service Unit of the Indian Health Service with health centers in Anadarko and Carnegie and a health station at the Riverside Indian School. Hospitals are located in Lawton and Clinton.

ENVIRONMENTAL CONCERNS
The Nation has U.S. EPA grants that provide for water and air control.

Cherokee Nation

Cherokee Nation
Jurisdictional service area
Cherokee
Washington, Tulsa, Rogers, Nowata, Craig, Mayes, Ottawa, Delaware, Cherokee, Adair, Wagoner, Muskogee, McIntosh, and Sequoyah counties, Oklahoma

Cherokee Nation
Economic and Business
    Development Division
P.O. Box 948
Tahlequah, OK 74465
    918-456-0671
    918-456-6485 Fax
    cherokee.org

LOCATION AND LAND STATUS
The tribal lands of the Cherokee Nation span 124,000 acres, or 7,000 square miles throughout 14 counties in northeastern Oklahoma. While not a reservation, the Nation's tribal land is held in trust by the U.S. government and is considered a Jurisdictional Service Area. With its capital in Tahlequah, a town of approximately 14,458 in Cherokee County, much of the Cherokee Nation rests on the Ozark Plateau, stretching from the prairie plains in the north and west to the foothills of the Boston Mountains in the east. The state's second-largest city, Tulsa, Oklahoma, is less than 65 miles from Tahlequah; Muskogee is 28 miles. The Nation considers its key development counties to be Adair, Cherokee, Delaware, and Sequoyah. The Nation has 61,000 acres available for development.

CLIMATE
Tribal headquarters, at Talequah, Oklahoma, sits at an average elevation of 870 feet above sea level. Daily high temperatures average 73°F, with the highest temperature ever recorded being 118°F. Low temperatures average 48°F, with the lowest temperature ever recorded being -23°F. The area receives approximately 42.6 inches of precipitation annually.

CULTURE AND HISTORY
The Cherokee Nation is the second-largest tribe in the United States and the largest in the State of Oklahoma, with a membership of over 230,000. Prior to European contact, the Cherokee people lived for almost a thousand years in the southeastern part of North America, with a traditional territory spanning approximately 126,000 square miles. Through a succession of treaties between 1721 and 1819, this vast territory was reduced to the mountainous areas of North Carolina, Tennessee, Georgia, and Alabama.

An extremely progressive, democratic people, the Cherokees often intermarried with their Anglo counterparts. They had their own educational system throughout the region, improved in part by the Cherokee linguist, Sequoyah, born in 1770 in Taskigi, Tennessee, who codified a syllabary or alphabet for the Cherokee people in 1821. This syllabary provided the Cherokee people with a written language that the Nation quickly adopted. Today, the Cherokee language is spoken by more than 10,000 Cherokees residing in northeastern Oklahoma, and by at least 1,000 Cherokees living in the vicinity of Cherokee, North Carolina.

Although a group of Cherokee people began to migrate west during the early 1800s to avoid the encroachment of European descendants on their territory, the history of the Cherokee people was permanently altered by their forced removal to what was then referred to as "Indian Territory" from their ancestral lands in the southeast. The discovery of gold in Georgia fueled anti-Cherokee resentment and the thirst for expansion on the part of the new settlers. Upon the recommendation of President James Monroe in his final address to Congress in 1825, the succeeding President, Andrew Jackson, authorized the Indian Removal Act of 1830. The displacement of Native people was not wanting for eloquent opposition. Senators Daniel Webster and Henry Clay spoke out against removal, and the Reverend Samuel Worcester, a missionary to the Cherokees, challenged Georgia's attempt to extinguish Indian title to land in the state, winning the case before the Supreme Court.

Worcester v. Georgia (1832) and *Cherokee Nation v. Georgia* in 1831, cases that are considered two of the most influential decisions in Indian law, challenged the constitutionality of the Removal Act and the U.S. government precedent for unapplied Indian-federal law. The U.S. government used the Treaty of New Echota in 1835 to justify the removal. The treaty, signed by 20 Cherokees, whose supporters numbered between only 5 and 10 percent of the Cherokee population and were known as the Treaty Party, relinquished all lands east of the Mississippi River in exchange for land in Indian Territory and the promise of money, livestock, and various provisions and tools. Opposition to the removal was led by Chief John Ross, a mixed-blood of Scottish and one-eighth Cherokee descent. The Ross party and most Cherokees opposed the New Echota Treaty, but Georgia and the U.S. government prevailed, using it as justification to force almost all of the 17,000 Cherokees from their southeastern homeland. An estimated 2,000-2,500 Cherokees died from hunger, exposure, and disease during their forced exodus. The journey became memorialized as the "trail where they cried" for the Cherokees and other removed tribes. Today it is remembered as the "Trail of Tears."

The years between the removal and the 1860s were the Cherokee Golden Age, a period of prosperity ending with the devastation of the American Civil War. *Cherokee Advocate*, printed in both English and Cherokee, became the first newspaper in the State of Oklahoma, and the *Cherokee Messenger* was its first periodical. By the time of Oklahoma's statehood in 1907, the Cherokee Nation had established an educational system composed of 144 elementary schools and two higher education institutions, the Cherokee National Male and Female Seminaries. With the Cherokee syllabary, the Cherokee people achieved a higher rate of literacy than their white counterparts.

After the war, more Cherokee land was taken to accommodate other tribes displaced by U.S. government policy. At the turn of the century, most of the remaining tribal land was parceled out to individual Cherokees eligible for allotments who enrolled in a census known as the Dawes Commission Rolls of 1906. The social and economic isolation experienced by the Oklahoma Cherokees after statehood was compounded by the Great Depression and Dust Bowl era of the 1930s. It is estimated that more than a third of the residents of Oklahoma left the state during this time, including many Cherokees. Presidents of the United States appointed various principal chiefs in the 65 years following statehood, with little authority or responsibility, as there was no formalized Cherokee government. Since reorganization in the 1970s, the Cherokee Nation has become a leader in education, health care, housing, vocational training, and economic development in northeastern Oklahoma.

An annual three-day Cherokee National Holiday, celebrated since 1953, commemorates the signing of the 1839 Cherokee Constitution each Labor Day weekend. The event has grown into one of the largest in Oklahoma, attracting more than 70,000 people from across the world.

GOVERNMENT

Prior to their forced migration to the west, the Cherokees maintained a dual organization of tribal government: a white, or peace, organization made up of elders, many of whom were priests, and a red, or war, organization. The priests performed both secular and religious functions under the direction of a great high priest, also known as a peace chief or principal chief. Seven councilors represented the seven clans to assist in administering civil law and invoking blessings from the Creator. The war organization was made up of ranking military officials, led by the great war chief, who controlled all governmental decisions while at war.

Today, the Cherokee Nation, under PL-638, contracts with the BIA to administer key programs and services. The tribal government is organized into a three-branch democratic structure with offices in the W.W. Keeler Complex in Tahlequah, Oklahoma. Sovereignty is guaranteed by treaty and law.

The Nation's constitution was ratified in 1976. A 15-member elected Cherokee Nation Tribal Council serves as the government's legislative branch, with members elected to four-year terms by a popular vote of all registered voters. Under the leadership of Principal Chief Wilma P. Mankiller, the first elected female chief of any major tribe, the Nation negotiated a PL-638 Self-Governance Agreement with Congress on February 10, 1990. This agreement authorizes the tribe to plan, conduct, consolidate, and administer programs and receive direct funding to deliver services to tribal members. The Cherokee Nation also passed legislation establishing a Cherokee Nation District Court and criminal penal and procedure code.

As head of the executive branch, the principal chief is responsible for the execution of laws, the establishment of tribal policy, and the delegation of authority as necessary for the day-to-day operations of the Cherokee Nation Tribal Government. There is also a deputy chief. They are both elected to four-year terms by popular vote of registered Cherokee voters.

The legislative branch consists of a 15-member tribal council with representatives elected from the nine districts of the Cherokee Nation. The council initiates legislation and conducts business on behalf of all tribal members. The deputy chief presides over the council as its president. Tribal council terms are four years.

A judicial appeals tribunal and the Cherokee Nation District Court make up the judicial branch of government. The tribunal, with members appointed by the principal chief and confirmed by the tribal council, is the Nation's highest court. It hears and resolves disagreements brought before it under jurisdiction of the Cherokee Nation Judicial Code. A district judge and an associate judge preside over all court proceedings.

The Cherokee Marshals provide law enforcement services. A 32-person department, the Marshals are cross-deputized with major law enforcement agencies throughout the Nation's 14-county area.

Specially established commissions assist in carrying out various governmental functions: election, gaming, and tax commission. These serve an oversight function, regulating and managing various enterprises and functions. Within these

Cherokee

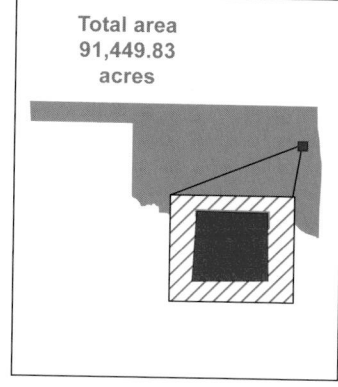

Total area
91,449.83
acres

Total area *(BIA realty, 2004)*
91,449.83 acres

Tribally owned *(BIA realty, 2004)*
45,054.90 acres

Federal trust *(BIA realty, 2004)*
407.51 acres

Individually owned
(BIA realty, 2004)
45,987.42 acres

Population *2000 census*
1,066,024

Total labor force *2000 census*
208,936

High school graduate or higher
2000 census
77%

Bachelor's degree or higher
2000 census
15%

Unemployment rate *2000 census*
5.8%

Cherokee

TRI-OK-003

TRI-OK-004

TRI-OK-005

TRI-OK-006

TRI-OK-007

TRI-OK-003 Front view of Child Care/ Health Center

TRI-OK-004 James Danielson Children's Village, sign in park

TRI-OK-005 GWY DBP Cherokee Nation, Ga Du Gi Health Center

TRI-OK-006 Early Childhood Unit

TRI-OK-007 Early Childhood Unit

commissions, there are the following divisions: education, planning and development, internal audit and review, tribal operations, finance management, general council, human resources, and information systems. The community service division maintains roads and provides water, wastewater, and other environmental programs. Tribal departments include: law and justice, natural resources, real estate services, and credit and finance, which provides personal and business financial education and loans to tribal members. Other enabling services are membership-support programs or services that are internal to tribal government.

The housing authority of the Cherokee Nation, created in 1966, provides safe, sanitary housing to low-income tribal members living within the boundaries of the Cherokee Nation. The authority is governed by a five-member board of commissioners appointed by the chief and approved by the tribal council. Each member serves a three-year term. The authority operates homeownership programs, including homeowner's insurance, rental programs, the Section 8 Welfare to Work Program, elderly housing including low-income housing tax credit services, home rehabilitation, and emergency housing programs. The 2003 Annual Report to The Cherokee People reported that the housing authority built 300 homes during 2001 and again in 2002, a record number. Senior housing centers, with 40 apartments each, were built in Stilwell and Jay, Oklahoma, during 2003.

BUSINESS CORPORATION
Cherokee Nation Enterprises (CNE) is a tribal corporation with offices in Tahlequah and Catoosa. The enterprise operates casinos, smoke shops, gift shops, and convenience stores, providing revenue to the Nation in the form of dividends. Anticipated revenues for fiscal year 2004 were $12 million. Generous donations of time and financial resources are given to area nonprofit agencies and schools, tribal and nontribal alike. Seventy-two percent of CNE employees are Cherokee tribal members; 80 percent are Native Americans.

Cherokee Nation Industries (CNI), an award-winning tribal workforce development project, was incorporated in 1969. *(See Manufacturing for details.)*

ECONOMY
The Cherokee Nation economy is a diverse mixture of agribusiness, small business enterprises, mining, gaming, manufacturing, and tribal operations.

Government as Employer. Tribal government, through its various enterprises, programs, and services, employed over 4,711 people in 2004, making it one of the largest employers in northeastern Oklahoma.

Economic Development Projects. A tax code, approved in 1990, levies a tobacco tax and a sales tax. A fuel tax agreement was reached with the State of Oklahoma in 1997, wherein the Nation will be rebated a portion of the amount of fuel tax collected from the sale of gasoline on tribal lands for the next 20 years, in exchange for an agreement not to sue or license tribal members to sell gasoline.

To better prepare tribal members for participation in the local wage economy, in 1978 the Nation established the Talking Leaves Job Corps Center in Tahlequah, Oklahoma, one-half mile from tribal headquarters. The 22-acre vocational training facility serves Native American youth from across the country. Approximately 270 graduates are placed as electrical wirers, administrative office assistants, cooks, or home health aides each year, and they serve their community through various volunteer activities, such as a voter registration drive for Native Americans or landscaping tribally owned facilities. There are also 11 field offices offering vocational rehabilitation services.

Agriculture and Livestock. Agribusiness and livestock production represent an important source of revenue for the Cherokee Nation. The tribe's poultry operations produce over 1 million four- to five-pound broiler chickens each year (on the No More Poultry Farm). Hudson Hog Farm leases 40 acres of tribal land for its facility (the No More Hog Farm), which produces approximately 1,000 sows annually. In addition, the tribe owns the Cherokee Gardens, a nationally recognized horticulture center.

On its farm lands, the tribe raises winter wheat, soybeans, alfalfa, and native hay. While the tribe owns no cattle, land is leased for grazing on a bid process with 5-10 year terms for cattle production.

Forestry. The Candy Mink Springs Wood Operation produces and markets packaged firewood in 0.75-cubic-foot bundles to wholesale distributors, providing employment to local tribal members. The majority of the supply of firewood comes from land development projects on Cherokee tribal lands, with areas replanted to improve pasture for the tribal grazing program. Kenwood Wood Industry, a woodcutting operation, uses an environmentally sensitive replanting program. The tribe's forestry project oversees a 300-acre pine tree production project, wherein pines are continuously grown and sold for wood and pulp. Another 25,000 acres of mixed hardwood timber are available for development.

Gaming. In 1990, the Cherokee Nation opened its first high-stakes Bingo Outpost in Roland. By the end of 2004, Cherokee Casino had gaming operations at four separate locations: Catoosa, Fort Gibson, Roland, and Siloam Springs. The 15,000-square-foot Catoosa facility will feature 400 electronic games, a card room for table games, and a snack bar. The Cherokee Casino and Resort, which opened summer of 2004, features a new 150-room hotel and resort, expansions to the casino already on-site, and a redesigned club at the golf course. The facility added approximately 500 employment opportunities at Catoosa. Another facility near Sallisaw will be opened in spring 2005. Nearby, the Nation will build a 33-room hotel, the Southern Hearth Inn.

Mining. There are 14.1 trillion cubic feet of known coal and natural gas reserves, in addition to approximately 1.8 trillion cubic feet of new reserves discovered continually in the state. Coal beds cover 1.5 million acres in eastern Oklahoma, with reserves estimated at 3 billion tons. Cherokee Nation coal is bituminous and most is surface mined.

Manufacturing. Cherokee Nation Industries (CNI) is a 100 percent tribally owned integrated aerospace, defense, and telecommunications contractor and distribution enterprise, specializing in electronic component assembly and integration; wire harness and cable assembly; fiber-optic cabling, field installation services, laser wire marking, Just-in-Time and Point-of-Use Inventory Management systems, project kitting, contract medical and engineering professional services, and environmental and construction services. CNI, a top-tier manufacturer of electrical and electronic wire harnesses, is an ISO 9000-registered company in the cable harness, distribution, and telecommunications divisions.

CNI competes for contracts with the federal government via HUB Zone designation and is a certified Small Disadvantaged Business/Supplier. The business, a certified U.S. Small Business Administration 8(a) contractor, incorporated in 1969 as a tribal workforce development project, and the Oklahoma Native American Business Development Center named it "Manufacturer of the Year" in 1995 and 2000. CNI was also recognized as the "Small Disadvantaged Business of the Year" in 1987 and 1999 by Boeing and by FMC's Ground Systems Division in 1992. CNI reported a $1 million profit for fiscal year 2003.

Cherokee Nation Distributors (CND), created in 1988 to meet the increasing military demands for a minority supplier of elec-

trical connectors, connector accessories, wire, and shrinkable tubing, is a wholly owned subsidiary of CNI. They have expanded into value-added services. This division is an ISO 9002 Distributor, a Lockheed Star Certified Supplier, and a Boeing Silver Supplier. CND is a franchised distributor for Raychem, Sunbank, Amphenol, Critchley, Pyle, and Matrix.

A 20-acre parcel within the 1,050-acre Cherokee Nation Ranch in southwestern Delaware County houses two buildings equipped for a high-production pallet mill, representing a $100,000 investment. Also on this parcel are 12 kilns available for charcoal production.

Industrial Park. Located 25 miles from the tribal complex at Tahlequah, the Cherokee Nation Industrial Park at Stilwell sits between the new Stilwell Airport and another parcel of tribal land. Spanning 151 acres, with full utilities, the park is located near air transport, the Muscogee Port, and rail service. Several manufacturers, such as Facet Quantex, a commercial oil and fuel filter producer, already use this site.

Media and Communications. *The Advocate,* a newsletter published by the public affairs department, includes press releases, special announcements, cultural tidbits, an events calendar, and information. Three times weekly, a Cherokee Nation Radio Show is aired on two radio stations, KEOK-FM and KTLQ-AM.

Tourism and Recreation. There are 50 state parks and recreational areas in the heart of the Cherokee Nation. In 2004, the Nation was developing a map of attractions, historical sites and markers, and other sites of interest. Recreational development is possible on available forested lands, and visitors enjoy beautiful vistas while fishing, hunting, canoeing, boating, and hiking. Summer theater is a popular warm-weather attraction, and the state's first pari-mutuel race track is located in the southern part of the Cherokee Nation. Cherokee Nation Enterprises purchased Will Rogers Downs, a quarter horse-racing track near Claremore, Oklahoma, in 2004. The 236-acre facility is to be renovated with a new restaurant and an entertainment venue.

The Cherokee National Historical Society operates a Heritage Pottery program under the auspices of the Tsa La Gi (Cherokee) Heritage Center in Talequah, with revenues reverting back for tribal use in various cultural education programs. There is a Museum Shop in Park Hill. All Cherokee Heritage Pottery items are guaranteed to be authentically Cherokee-handcrafted, as are the other traditional crafts and contemporary art works offered by the Cherokee Heritage Arts program.

For those interested in cultural enhancement, the Tsa La Gi Heritage Center includes a museum featuring both permanent and temporary collections with an educational component, an ancient Cherokee Village, an outdoor amphitheater performing a Trail of Tears Drama, and a series of special events. Moreover, the Cherokee Heritage Arts (formerly known as the Cherokee Nation Fine Art Gallery) in Tahlequah features both contemporary and traditional visual arts. The Cherokee Family Research Center, located in the Museum Building of the Heritage Center houses a research library of genealogy materials, including access to census information and the Dawes Rolls. *(See also, Education.)* The Cherokee National Historical Society, established in 1963, is a tribally sponsored nonprofit organization dedicated to preserving Cherokee history and promoting Cherokee culture and the education of all people. This program supports educational programs. Both Natives and non-Natives are welcomed as members of the Cherokee National History Society, and all facilities are open to the public.

Cherokee

The Nation's biggest event is the annual Cherokee National Holiday, a three-day celebration of Cherokee culture and history that honors the signing of the Cherokee Nation Constitution in 1839. Events include a parade, a fiddling contest, an Indian rodeo, blowgun competitions, arts and crafts booths, a powwow, traditional games, sports tournaments, special children's activities, traditional feasts, and Indian vendors.

INFRASTRUCTURE

Electricity. The Oklahoma Gas and Electric Public Service Company, along with the state's Grand River Dam Authority and dozens of rural electric cooperatives, provide energy to the Cherokee Nation. Fourteen electric generating plants are operating on the Cherokee Nation with a capacity of 5,000 megawatts. Several of the dams and power heads are located on a portion of the Arkansas River owned by the Cherokee Nation, and the tribe is conducting a feasibility study on constructing a power head in Sequoyah County.

Fuel. The Oklahoma Gas and Electric Public Service Company provide energy to the Cherokee Nation.

Water Supply. The Nation's Water and Sanitation Services Program provides water and sewer repair for tribal members.

Waste Management. An important source of tribal revenue is the Nation's Sanitary Landfill, located on 160 acres in Adair County. Just outside Stilwell, this landfill is environmentally safe and has maintained high-quality inspection grades. The landfill services three Oklahoma counties and several Arkansas cities.

Transportation. More than 500 miles of four-lane highways and an additional 5,000 miles of U.S. and state highways crisscross the Cherokee Nation, insuring rapid movement of materials to and from all points of the country. The southern portion of the Cherokee Nation is crossed by I-40, connecting Fort Smith, Arkansas, with Oklahoma City, Oklahoma. To the north, Joplin, Missouri, and Tulsa, Oklahoma, are connected by I-44. Three of the state's six turnpikes-Will Rogers, Indian Nation, and Muskogee-dissect Cherokee Nation lands, as do U.S. 69 and U.S. 62, at Tahlequah.

A network of major railroad lines connects the Nation with all United States cities, markets, and ports: Santa Fe, Kansas City Southern, Missouri-Pacific, the Frisco, and Katy. In addition there are 11 piggyback ramps in 5 nearby cities. More than 30 motor freight common carriers offer service to all areas, including Consolidated Freightways, Roadway Express, Transcon, Tucker Freight Lines, Arkansas Best Freight, and Yellow Transit.

Completion of the McClellan-Kerr Navigation System along the Arkansas River in 1971 opened another avenue to surrounding United States markets and world ports. Barge tonnage reached 1,379,000 tons in 1983 and continues to increase through the system's ports. The Port of Catoosa, in Rogers County, sits at the head of the navigation channel near Tulsa, 440 miles from the Mississippi River. The port boasts complete warehousing and cargo facilities and has been designated a Foreign Trade Zone. The Port of Muskogee is served by five major highways, including the Muskogee Turnpike, which connects with Tulsa and I-40.

The Tulsa International Airport represents the region's largest commercial airport. The Fayetteville Airport, located 25 miles from the Cherokee Nation in Arkansas, offers large-scale air transportation, as does the Fort Smith Regional Airport, located just across the Arkansas border from the Nation. The Cherokee Nation also has 27 privately owned and municipal airports, including a facility at Tahlequah, where improvements have extended runways to handle small corporate jets.

COMMUNITY FACILITIES AND SERVICES

The Cherokee Nation offers a plethora of community facilities, including the W.W. Keeler Tribal Complex located in Tahlequah. There is an excellent vocational training program for members, including the Talking Leaves Job Corps Center and the Cherokee Nation Employment Assistance Readiness Network and Self-Determination Program. Three vocational/technical schools serve six communities in the Cherokee Nation, and a skills center is located in Tahlequah. The Cherokee Nation's Career Services Department offers literacy centers where basic computer skills training, Internet access, individualized tutoring, and employment and training assistance is offered.

The housing authority offers a homebuyers education course, various rural rental (assistance) programs, such as a Section 8 Welfare to Work Program, 202 Elderly Housing and Low Income Rentals, a Title VI Homeownership Program, and a Mortgage Assistance Program. In 2002, the Nation's Housing Authority obtained a drug elimination grant and used it to establish a cultural renewal program. That year, a total of 62 youth participated in research activities, interviewing elders, doing arts and crafts, studying language programs, playing traditional games, and listening to various presenters from the tribe and surrounding communities. Future goals include participation in community service projects, additional language programs, economic development in the form of entrepreneurship training, leadership skills training, and job shadowing.

The Cherokee Family Research Center, which houses a genealogical research library, is located in the Cherokee Heritage Center Museum. The archives include access to Dawes Rolls. The 44-acre facility, located in Park Hill, Oklahoma, includes a 1,500-seat outdoor amphitheater, Tsa-La-Gi Ancient Village, Adams Corner Rural Village and Farm, and the Cherokee National Museum. The museum features permanent and temporary exhibits, the annual Trail of Tears Art Show, and a shop where books, publications, and authentic arts and crafts are available for purchase.

The Nation opened its own Veteran's Office in 2001, and that same year they opened a tribal office in Washington, D.C.

Public Safety. Forest fires are combated by the Fire Dancers, an arm of the U.S. Forest Service Firefighters since 1988.

Education. There are numerous educational facilities throughout the Cherokee Nation from Head Start programs to advanced university education. The Children's Village Circle of Friend's complex includes a Child Care Resource Center, a pregnancy prevention program called "Serving Teens through Education," Even Start, and Head Start. The Nation's Education Department oversees programs that support educational opportunities for Cherokee students, preschool through graduate education. Special programs called Cherokee Nation Language Immersion Centers are key components of the Cultural Resource Center's efforts to work in collaboration with the schools to increase Native language usage among the Nation's youngsters.

Two comprehensive state-supported universities, the University of Oklahoma and Oklahoma State University, serve the area, and there are two medical schools and two private universities in nearby Tulsa. Northeastern State University is located in Tahlequah.

Sequoyah High School, an Indian boarding school, was originally established in Talequah in 1871 as an asylum for orphans of Civil War casualties. The 40-acre facility was sold to the Department of Interior in 1914, and in 1925 the name was changed to Sequoyah Orphan Training School. In November 1985, the Nation resumed operations, and the campus now consists of 90 acres and at least 12 classroom and dormitory buildings.

The Cherokee Nation Education Corporation, a nonprofit organization, sponsors a Memorial Scholarship Fund for application by any tribal resident of Adair County desiring to further their education beyond high school. Awards of up to $2,000 may be obtained. The Nation also offers scholarships of $1,000 per semester via the Cherokee Nation Higher Education Program.

Health Care. Throughout the Cherokee Nation, there are a number of health clinics and community health representative programs. Thirty hospitals serve the Cherokee Nation, including the W.W. Hastings Indian Hospital, the Claremore Indian Hospital and a Veterans Hospital in Muskogee. A cooperative agreement between the Cherokee Nation Health

Service and the NSU College of Optometry provides vision care via the Cherokee Rural Health Network. Chemical dependency can be treated at the Jack Brown Center, a residential treatment facility.

ENVIRONMENTAL CONCERNS
The Nation has its own Office of Environmental Protection and Environmental Health Program to ensure that all tribal facilities are operated in environmentally sound ways, encouraging tribal members to lead lives of ecological balance. The Nation's Environmental Health Program staff participates on an Inter-Tribal Environmental Council. The tribe preserves 25 acres of blue stem grass in Cherokee County, Oklahoma. Another 317 acres are preserved as native meadow in Kay County. Acreage dedicated to wildlife habitat preservation is set aside near Tahlequah. Issues of concern in 2004 included: 1) a tribal chicken farm that potentially threatens water quality in the surrounding area, and 2) involvement in a water-rights dispute with the U.S. Army Corps of Engineers over storage rights on Lake Tenkiller. The Nation claims full ownership of 14,000 acre-feet of rights under past treaties between the tribe and the federal government. There are 96 miles of Arkansas River bed crossing the Nation's lands.

Cherokee

Honoring Nations Honoree 2002

Cherokee Nation History Course, Department of Human Resources
Cherokee Nation (Tahlequah, Oklahoma)

Required as mandatory training for tribal employees, the Cherokee Nation History Course has given employees, both Cherokee and non-Cherokee alike, a stronger sense of pride and a better understanding of self-governance. Indeed, this successful and innovative history and leadership course has stimulated a shift in employees' and citizen's thinking. Tribal employees see themselves not only as service providers, but as leaders of their nation; tribal members no longer see themselves as mere recipients of services, but as active citizens of a sovereign nation.

The Cherokee Nation has a long and well-documented history. In the eighteenth century, Cherokee citizens suffered from smallpox, genocidal warfare, and encroachment brought on by early white settlers. Later, in 1838, the US Government forcibly removed the Cherokees from their homelands in the eastern US to Oklahoma along the infamous "Trail of Tears." Thousands of Cherokees died en route. At the end of the nineteenth century, the Dawes Allotment Act-designed to assimilate Indians into mainstream society by privatizing Indian lands-brought about the calamitous loss of Cherokee lands in Oklahoma. Unfortunately, Cherokees fared no better in the twentieth century. In 1906, the US Government "dissolved" the Nation's elected government by federal legislation. In the Depression of the 1930s, a "second" or "economic" Trail of Tears occurred, as tens of thousands of Cherokees migrated away from the Cherokee country, seeking work in distant places, especially California and Texas. World War II and the relocation projects of the Bureau of Indian Affairs (BIA) created additional expatriates in the 1950s and 1960s, presenting further challenges to the Cherokee Nation's political and social cohesion.

Less known of the Cherokees is their history of innovation and adaptation in response to these destructive events. Especially notable is the Nation's unwavering commitment to educating its citizens and to preserving and exercising its governmental

powers. In the nineteenth century, the Nation adopted a first-of-its kind syllabary of the Cherokee language, founded the first institution of higher learning for women west of the Mississippi, constructed a men's seminary, and opened 150 day schools, which represented the first system of co-educational public instruction in the world. The Cherokees attained a literacy rate of 90 percent-a rate three times higher than that of surrounding communities. In 1827, even before the Trail of Tears, the Cherokee Nation adopted a written constitution. After the removal-but 150 years prior to formal congressional recognition of the importance of tribal courts-the Cherokee Nation constructed a courthouse that stands to this day. In the 1970s, the Cherokee Nation rebounded from the disastrous federal policies of termination and relocation by formally reconstituting its government. Within several years, it reinstituted the elections of a principal chief and rejuvenated the tripartite government that had been constitutionally established in the 1800s.

Regrettably, the Nation's enormous resilience and flexibility in the face of adversity has too often been overshadowed by the more commonly told stories of economic and political deprivation. Many Cherokee citizens, unaware of their long tradition of innovation and excellence, have been left feeling disempowered. Despite the reorganization of the Cherokee Nation in the 1970s, many Cherokees today have struggled to regain an understanding of their citizenry and sovereignty as a nation. Several years ago, a Cherokee tribal attorney overheard another tribal employee cut off a problem-solving conversation with the comment, "We can't do that. The Bureau of Indian Affairs won't let us." The employee's deference to the BIA revealed a failure to appreciate a history of innovation and adaptation by the Cherokee people.

In 1992, the tribal attorney organized a course to teach the legal history of the Cherokee Nation. Eventually it evolved into the Cherokee Nation History Course-a forty hour college-level

Honoring Nations Honoree 2002

Text in its entirety from:
The Harvard Project On
American Indian Economic
Development

John F. Kennedy School
of Government
Harvard University

Cherokee

**Honoring Nations
Honoree 2002**

**Text in its entirety from:
The Harvard Project On
American Indian Economic
Development**

**John F. Kennedy School
of Government
Harvard University**

course that is a mandatory training component for every Cherokee Nation employee. Employees have the option of taking the course in one week, over two alternate weeks, or over five alternating Fridays. Teachers rely on lectures, guest speakers, group discussions, role-playing, and case study methods to immerse their students in the study of Cherokee history. The Course offers a 1,200-page reading packet consisting of treaty texts, legislative acts, and court decisions, as well as pertinent essays written by Cherokees and other scholars. Since its creation, approximately 1,300 tribal government employees have completed the Cherokee Nation History Course. An additional 600 students from the community at large-locals and expatriates, Cherokees and non-Cherokees-also have completed the Course, which is free and open to the public. Taught by one paid and several volunteer Cherokee staff, the Course is nearing its goal of teaching every government employee Cherokee history during the initial three-year project. Afterwards, the Course will be instituted as one of eleven "core" courses of employee development that will continue to be required of every new tribal employee. Furthermore, the curriculum is being adapted for school age children and Cherokee language speakers.

The Cherokee Nation History Course seeks to promote critical thinking skills, self-reliance, and a strengthened sense of cultural and national identity. Organized chronologically, the Course encourages students to develop their own responses to various crises in Cherokee history-preventing encroachment in 1753, responding to the Removal Act in 1830, rebuilding the Nation in 1846, challenging Allotment in 1885, and coping with dissolution of the Cherokee Nation in 1906-and then compare their responses to decisions of Cherokee leaders of the past. These comparisons have generated respect and appreciation for the long tradition of Cherokee nation-building initiatives and the wisdom and ingenuity of former Cherokee leaders. For example, in role-plays, students act as the Council of Headmen that met to determine a response to the Cherokees' problematic relationship with the British in 1753. In another assignment, students devise strategies for reconstructing the Nation in the aftermath of the Trail of Tears and the Cherokee Civil War. The actual rebuilding that took place in the mid-nineteenth century demonstrates to students the success with which Cherokee leaders of the past overcame the loss of land to assert their sovereignty. The Cherokee Nation History Course inspires students to see themselves as citizens of a sovereign nation and not as clients of a government bureaucracy. Furthermore, it has transformed tribal government employees from being service providers to leaders. As one former student said, "I plan to take more pride in my work and go that extra mile to do my job. I know that I am working for the people, not just a paycheck."

The Course has succeeded in allowing its participants to see themselves differently, to see the Cherokees as a people of excellence. The appreciation of the Cherokee Nation History Course is most clearly reflected in the outstanding evaluations it receives from students. According to systematic surveys, the Course has a 96 percent general approval rating while individual students have described the Course as "life-changing" and "empowering." Many say that the Course has succeeded in replacing discouragement and anger over Cherokee history with a sense of pride and accomplishment. One student wrote, "On the first day, I cried, but by the last day, I was really proud to be a Cherokee." Another student remarked, "Growing up, I was always told by others, 'You Cherokees all gave up. You died walking; you didn't die fighting.' Now I understand that we didn't give up. We fought in our own way for four hundred years, not fifty. We adapted. We responded. And we're still here."

The Course's exploration of past Cherokee leaders' unprecedented and strategic thinking serves as a model for students who work on behalf of the Cherokee Nation today. Employees' awareness of tribal history allows them to lobby on behalf of tribal interests from a more informed standpoint. One student remarked that when she and her colleagues went to Washington, DC to discuss the applicability of the US Government's marriage initiative to the Cherokee Nation, their arguments were strengthened by knowledge of Cherokee marital relations over time, a subject examined in the Course. Another example comes from tribal police officers who, prior to participating in the Course, would defer to non-Indian police in calls involving Indians. After taking the Course, they came to understand the importance of having a tribal officer present at such incidents, and now, Cherokee police officers try to be the first responders. In addition, Indian Child Welfare workers have stated that knowledge of historical Cherokee family structures, residence patterns, and social systems has empowered them to argue more effectively against the routine removal of Cherokee children from homes that state courts define as "dysfunctional" on the basis of Euro-American cultural norms.

The Cherokee Nation History Course instills a sense of pride and accomplishment among students. As one student noted, "The history of the Cherokee people has had many events that could have broken our spirit and connection. It is with a joyful heart that I realize this never happened. Thank you for sweeping away the fog of mistruths, half-truths, and lies and replacing them for me with truth and understanding." Students who grapple with the voluminous course material acknowledge that while the lay view of Cherokee history focuses on "how we lost, and we lost, and we lost," their in-depth study of that history reveals how "smart and shrewd" the Cherokee leaders were over time. "We reconstituted," a student wrote. "We reorganized. We rebuilt. And not just once or twice."

The Cherokee Nation History Course stands out as a foundational contribution to good tribal governance. Its success in teaching Cherokee history fully and accurately from a Cherokee perspective, providing its Indian and non-Indian students with critical and highly transferable thinking skills, and instilling pride and confidence in being Cherokee is nothing short of remarkable. It is easy to imagine the benefits to tribes that follow the Cherokee Nation's example and develop and teach their own tribal history courses. Knowing, owning, and sharing one's history is empowering. As one former student noted, "They say that history is written by the victors. But the story's not complete. We're looking to be victors by telling our history and by using it."

Lessons

Tribal history can be tapped for lessons of adaptation, innovation, and resilience, and can serve as a vehicle for instilling civic pride and hope. Community understanding of a tribe's historic nation-building efforts bolsters citizen support of current and future nation-building efforts.

Indian nations can use historical case studies and role-playing to teach citizens and employees better judgment, management strategy, and inter-personal skills. When applied with tribal history cases, these teaching methods have the added benefits of cultural resonance and strategic relevance.

It may be desirable for Indian nations that have developed their own history course (or are interested in doing so) to make the course a mandatory component of tribal employment. Learning tribal history reinforces employees' connection to their work, improves their understanding of self-governance, builds greater cultural understanding, and dispels misperceptions among Indians and non-Indians alike.

Formed in 2000 as a component of the Nation's comprehensive language program, the Cherokee National Youth Choir performs traditional and contemporary songs in the Cherokee language. Comprised of forty youth between the ages of thirteen and eighteen, the award-winning Choir performs at venues in Cherokee communities and across the country. More importantly, the Choir has proven itself to be an effective tool for inspiring Cherokee youth to learn their language, culture, and history-giving real hope that the sacred gifts of language and song will never be lost.

Valued as gifts from the Creator, the Cherokee people consider their traditional language and songs sacred. The language, in fact, sustained the Cherokee during one of Native America's darkest periods. The 1838 removal of the Cherokee people from their traditional eastern homelands to the present-day Oklahoma was a devastating journey. Over one third of the twelve thousand Cherokee died in the infamous Nunna dual Tsuny, or "Trail of Tears." During this terrible trek, families sung songs in the traditional language to locate their kin and to bring comfort to the grieving. The Cherokee language and songs held their people together.

These sacred gifts have been threatened for decades. Although Cherokee history is filled with stories of success, resilience, and flexibility in the face of adversity, language use has been on the decline for generations. Forced relocations, boarding schools that forbade students from speaking their Native tongue, and other pressures of assimilation have taken their toll. Whereas speaking the Cherokee language was once both expected and necessary, over time, its importance as a primary means of communication has diminished. Some elders believe that learning the language is unnecessary. Some-particularly those raised in boarding schools or who experienced discrimination for speaking their Native tongue-even say that learning the Cherokee language can hinder the youth's ability to prosper in modern American society. Sadly, by the late 1990s, the Cherokee language was in danger of extinction. In fact, studies revealed that no Cherokee under the age of forty possessed mastery of the language!

The government of the Cherokee Nation took a resolute stand against this threat: it would not allow the Cherokee language or songs to die. This stance reflected the tribal leadership's conviction that the health of the nation is strongly correlated with the health of the nation's language. As one Cherokee leader warned, "When you lose your language, you lose your identity as a sovereign nation." The tribal leadership declared a national emergency.

The Nation took action in 1999 by assembling a task force comprised of Cherokee speakers, elders, educators, and concerned citizens. The task force was charged with developing a comprehensive language program that would "protect, preserve, and promote the Cherokee language." Drawing upon lessons learned from other successful language revitalization programs in Hawaii, the task force worked with the tribal government's Education Division to build three preschool language immersion classrooms and implement a system to monitor young students' progress. It certified current Cherokee speakers in language instruction and established language courses in the tribally administered Sequoyah High School. Given a need to teach the language to parents, older students, and other Cherokee citizens, the tribal government

also took steps to make Cherokee language part of everyday life. For example, it began infusing Cherokee language into government activities and made language instruction available on the Nation's official website, www.cherokee.org.

The Cherokee leadership and public servants knew that while essential, these interventions were not enough. They had to do more. Specifically, they needed to find a mechanism for getting young Cherokee citizens interested in learning the language in the first place-a challenge that many Indian nations grapple with. Despite big investments in programming and infrastructure, educators and language instructors throughout Indian Country often find it difficult to get young people interested in learning their Native tongue. The reality is that most youth do not see the connection between the health of the language and the health of the nation. Inspiring youth to want to learn the language can be a frustrating exercise. The Cherokee tribal government knew that this challenge must be overcome.

In October 2000, the Nation discovered a powerful source of inspiration-singing. So it launched the Cherokee National Youth Choir. As a critical component of the Nation's comprehensive language program, the Choir sings songs and hymns in the Cherokee language. Now comprised of forty Cherokee youth between the ages of thirteen and eighteen, the Choir seeks to interest the youth in learning their Native tongue, assist in the first steps toward proficiency, and to promote language use through ceremonies and performance. Besides exposing current youth to Cherokee history, language, and culture, the Choir embraces a long-term goal: to inspire current youth to one day teach their children and grandchildren the language and traditions.

The Choir succeeds on many fronts. Advancing its original purpose, the Choir inspires broad interest in the Cherokee language and drives greater participation in the Cherokee Language Program. Even though the Choir itself is relatively small, its activities touch thousands. Every hour of rehearsal and performance exposes the Choir members, their families, and their audiences to the Cherokee language. The Choir provides the youth both a purpose and inspiration for learning. The songs give the youth a compelling reason for learning their Native tongue and allow them to practice what they have learned through other components of the Cherokee Language Program. Further, the Choir is a highly valued institution. Younger siblings look up to their brothers and sisters and look forward to the day when they can join. Adults and elders relish hearing their language in the youth's voice. Importantly, the Choir is changing attitudes and raising awareness about the importance of the Cherokee language. Although the language remains threatened, the language and songs are once again being viewed as sacred treasures that must be both protected and used in everyday life.

The Choir's popularity-or perhaps more appropriately, fame-bolsters its effectiveness as a force for language revitalization. The Choir's first album, "Voices of the Creator's Children," was an instant success and won a prestigious Nammy for Best Gospel/Christian Recording at the Native American Music Awards (NAMA) in 2002. The album includes songs from the "Trail of Tears" and hymns translated into Cherokee. The Choir's second album, "Building One Fire," won another Nammy for Best Gospel/Christian Recording in 2003 and was

**Honoring Nations
Honoree 2003**

Text in its entirety from:
**The Harvard Project On
American Indian Economic
Development**

**John F. Kennedy School
of Government
Harvard University**

Cherokee

one of the NAMA's five nominees for Album of the Year. These awards, while a source of tremendous pride for the Choir and the tribal government, are secondary to the impact the Choir has as a source of community pride. The Choir's songs are heard regularly on the radio, on home stereos, at community gatherings, in church services, and at public ceremonies across the Cherokee Nation. Tens of thousands of CDs are in circulation.

More than just musically talented youth, members of the Choir serve as ambassadors of the Cherokee Nation. They have to be. The Choir is regularly called upon to perform at venues throughout the state of Oklahoma and across the US. For example, the Choir was featured at the Annual Smithsonian Folklife Festival in Washington, DC and at the Smithsonian's George Gustav Heye Center in New York City. Additionally, the youth sang at the opening of Dolly Parton's Imagination Library. At each venue, the audience learns about the Cherokee people, their rich history, and their unique culture. The Choir is also an agent of healing. Because its repertoire includes songs and hymns once used to comfort individuals and families walking the "Trail of Tears," the Choir is even called upon to perform at memorial services; among them was a moving performance at Ground Zero in New York City.

Many Indian nations face the unfortunate reality that their Native language will die unless immediate-and effective-intervention takes place. Many believe that the stakes could not be higher, as language is a fundamental expression of culture. The Cherokee Nation is taking on the challenge of language preservation head-on, and is making significant investments to ensure that its 250,000 citizens will never see the day that the language is gone. The Cherokee National Youth Choir is one such critical investment. The Choir exhibits to its audiences the resiliency and power of a people committed, in the presence of great difficulties, to their culture and language. It stands as a symbol to all Native nations struggling to preserve their precious languages through strategies as simple and beautiful as singing the sacred songs that have sustained them over centuries.

Cheyenne-Arapaho

Cheyenne-Arapaho Reservation
Federal reservation
Cheyenne and Arapaho
Beckam, Blaine, Canadian, Custer, Dewey, Kingfisher, Roger Mills, and Washita counties, Oklahoma

Cheyenne-Arapaho Tribes of Oklahoma
P.O. Box 38
Concho, OK 73022
    405-262-0345
    800-247-4612
    405-262-0745 Fax

LOCATION AND LAND STATUS

The Cheyenne-Arapaho Tribal Jurisdiction Area is dispersed across an eight-county area in the rolling hill country of northwest and north-central Oklahoma. Tribally owned facilities are located throughout the eight-county service area, with the tribal government at Concho, Oklahoma, approximately seven miles north of El Reno on U.S. 81. There are several small communities throughout the tribal jurisdiction area; these include Colony, Clinton, Canton, and Watonga. Oklahoma City lies approximately 30 miles east of the tribal headquarters at Concho. Two major streams, the Canadian River and the Washita River, course through the tribal area.

The Cheyenne-Arapaho Reservation was established by the Medicine Lodge Treaty of 1867 and amended by a Presidential Proclamation in 1869. Reservation lands were allotted under the Jerome Agreement of 1890. Today, the tribe retains 10,405.19 acres of trust land. Tribal members own 69,627.05 acres in allotments.

CLIMATE

Weather and climate data have not been recorded for Concho, Oklahoma, the location of tribal headquarters. However, there is data available for El Reno, just seven miles south of Concho. The year-round average daily high temperature at El Reno is 72°F. The year-round average daily low temperature is 47.7°F. The area receives approximately 31.5 inches of precipitation annually.

CULTURE AND HISTORY

The Cheyenne and Arapaho peoples represent the westernmost groups of the Algonquian linguistic family that spread prehistorically over the northern and eastern woodlands of the present United States. Prior to 1600, the Arapahos dwelt in the upper Great Lakes area, while the Cheyennes inhabited the Mississippi Valley of present-day Minnesota. The Cheyenne and Arapaho peoples were culturally and linguistically related but tribally separate. During the mid-seventeenth century, both tribes shifted from lifestyles of sedentary horticulturists to nomadic hunters, resettling in Dakota country. At the time of the Lewis and Clark Expedition in 1804, both tribes were migrating into the Platte River Basin of present-day Wyoming and Nebraska. The Cheyennes signed a treaty with the United States in 1825 on the Teton River. Thereafter, a portion of the tribe branched off to become known as the Southern Cheyenne and Arapahos. Settling along the Arkansas River in Colorado, that group represents the ancestors of the present Cheyenne-Arapaho Tribe. Euro-American incursion into eastern Colorado and western Kansas during the mid-nineteenth century sparked hostilities between the tribes and white settlers. In 1864, the Colorado Volunteer Militia massacred Black Kettle's band of Cheyennes at Sand Creek. In October 1867, the Cheyennes and Arapahos signed the Medicine Lodge Treaty, which confined them to a reservation in Indian Territory. However, poor conditions on the reservation spurred many Cheyennes back onto the warpath. In 1868, Colonel George Custer's troops attacked Black Kettle's village on Washita Creek, killing Black Kettle and many women and children, signaling the end of Cheyenne and Arapaho resistance. The Jerome Agreement of 1890 dissolved the Cheyenne-Arapaho Reservation, and tribal members received individual 160-acre allotments. Much of their previous reservation land was then opened for white settlement in the famous Oklahoma land run of April 19, 1892. In 1937, the tribes incorporated as the Cheyenne-Arapaho Tribes of Oklahoma. The tribes nurture Cheyenne and Arapaho culture and history through several annual powwows.

GOVERNMENT

The Cheyenne-Arapaho Tribe of Oklahoma adopted a constitution in 1937 under the Oklahoma Indian Welfare Act of 1936. This constitution allowed for a 28 member council, with an even amount of Cheyenne and Arapaho members. The constitution was ratified on 1942, and in 1975. The newest structure is an eight-member business committee, still evenly split, and a tribal council compromised of all tribal members 18 years of age and older. This 1975 ratification outlined the responsibilities of the tribal council to be: approve the tribal budget, approve an attorney's contract, approve any surface lease or easement in excess of five years, approve claims and recoveries of land, approve resolution or ordinances governing future membership, propose amendments to the constitution and bylaws, alter district boundaries, and limit or restrict the powers of the business committee by referendum vote, and allowed that a quorum for the tribal council is 75 members. Currently, $8 million in federal, state, and local funds are administered by the tribal government.

The business committee oversees the following services and programs: farm and ranch, a tax commission, a business development corporation, an election board, a health board, and various subcommittees. The business manager manages both the planning department, which oversees roads, TTIP, the environmental department, and library services, and the finance division, including property and supply. Major departments include language and cultural preservation, personnel (and insurance), law enforcement, enrollment, education, and operations and maintenance, which includes the tribal public works department. Health and education programs include: higher education, youth shelter, Workforce Investment Act, alcohol and substance abuse, food distribution, emergency medical services, fire management, diabetes wellness, elderly nutrition, employment training, Head Start, vocational rehabilitation, and community development block grant.

The tribal council approves the operating budget, pursues recovery of tribal lands, approves the contract with the tribal attorney, oversees tribal membership, and amends the constitution, along with modifying voting district boundaries as needed. The tribal council also manages surface leases of over five years' duration.

ECONOMY

Today, the Cheyenne-Arapaho tribal government strives to provide economic support for tribal members. Four gaming facilities and three smoke shops, as well as grazing and oil leases, generate revenue for the tribe.

Government as Employer. The tribal government employs 250 people.

Agriculture and Livestock. The tribe earns revenue from leasing farming and grazing lands.

Gaming. The tribes operate four gaming facilities: the Cheyenne-Arapaho Bingo and Casino Enterprises located in Concho, Oklahoma; the Cheyenne-Arapaho Watonga Bingo located on U.S. 281 in Watonga, Oklahoma; the Lucky Star Casino in Clinton; and Feather Warrior at Watonga. Gaming has created jobs for 343 people.

Mining. The tribe earns royalties from oil and gas well leases.

Tourism and Recreation. The tribe holds two annual powwows: the Cheyenne-Arapaho Summer Fest and Oklahoma Indian Nation Powwow held in Concho during early August, and the Homecoming Powwow held over Labor Day weekend at Colony, Oklahoma. Culturally related recreation attractions include the Black Kettle Museum and Battle of Washita site north of Elk City, Oklahoma, and Roman Nose State Park near Watonga, Oklahoma.

INFRASTRUCTURE

The Cheyenne-Arapaho Tribal Jurisdiction Area is dispersed throughout an eight-county area in north-central and northwestern Oklahoma. Tribal headquarters at Concho are located

7 miles north of El Reno via U.S. 81 and 30 miles west of Oklahoma via I-40, which passes just 12 miles south of the reservation.

Electricity. Regional service providers supply electricity.

Fuel. Regional suppliers provide gas services.

Water Supply. Four water wells provide groundwater.

Transportation. Commercial and private air facilities are located in the Oklahoma City metropolitan area. Greyhound buses, trucking companies, and express package carriers serve the tribal area through Concho and El Reno.

COMMUNITY FACILITIES AND SERVICES

Clinton, Thomas, Fonda, Geary, and Watonga have community centers. Joint tribal and HUD housing projects are located throughout the tribal jurisdiction area. These homes utilize individual septic tanks and wells, as well as city utilities, depending on location.

Education. The Cheyenne Arapaho Tribe has access to 12 independent or public schools. There are scholarship grants available to tribal members pursing higher education. The tribe has an adult education department, which offers Cheyenne and Arapaho language classes and access to vocational training. The tribe offers several Head Start programs and two child care centers. The centers assist with child care for low income working parents or parents involved in furthering their education.

Health Care. The Clinton Indian Hospital, which is located 82 miles west of Oklahoma City on I-40, provides health care. Four general officers divide their time between inpatient and outpatient services at the Clinton Indian Hospital. The hospital has a staff of 81, which includes 15 nurses, 2 radiology technicians, 3 medical technologists, 3 pharmacists, and essential supporting staff. The Watonga Indian Health Center and El Reno Indian Health Clinic both have a staff of 14, including 2 physicians, a physician's assistant, 2 community health nurses, a dentist, a pharmacist, a social worker, and essential supporting staff.

The tribes operate three fitness centers: Willie Fletcher Memorial Center located at Concho, Howard Goodbear Fitness Center in Watonga, and a third fitness center at Weatherford, Oklahoma.

ENVIRONMENTAL CONCERNS

The Cheyenne and Arapaho Tribes of Oklahoma Environmental Protection Agency Office (EPAO), which addresses environmental issues and concerns for the tribes, has developed a solid waste management plan. Collaborating with the Oklahoma Department of Environmental Quality, the BIA Concho Agency, the Indian Health Service Office of Environmental Health, the Environmental Review Board, the Lucky Star Casino Enterprise, Tribal Law Enforcement, the Farm and Ranch Enterprise, and the O&M Department, EPAO is implementing the solid waste management plan with an intent to guide the tribes when addressing and controlling solid waste issues within the tribal service area.

Staff has acquired new mapping software to create better and clearer maps for reference. The staff is busy with investigating reports of illegal open dump sites within tribal jurisdiction.

Cheyenne-Arapaho

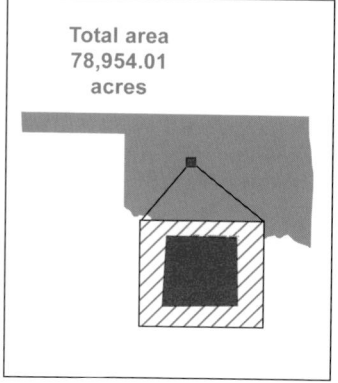

Total area
78,954.01
acres

Total area (BIA realty, 2004)
78,954.01 acres

Federal trust (BIA realty, 2004)
2.7 acres

Tribally owned
(BIA realty, 2004)
10,405.19 acres

Individually owned
(BIA realty, 2004)
68,546.12 acres

Population 2000 census
183,302

Total labor force 2000 census
76,123

High school graduate or higher
2000 census
82.1%

Bachelor's degree or higher
2000 census
18.1%

Unemployment rate 2000 census
4.2%

Per capita income 2000 census
$8,772

Chickasaw

Chickasaw Nation
Federally recognized
Chickasaw
Pontotoc, Carter, Murray, Love,
Johnston, Marshall, Grady,
Garvin, Coal, Bryan, Stephens,
Jefferson, and McClain
counties, Oklahoma

The Chickasaw Nation
P.O. Box 1548
Ada, OK 74821
580-436-2603
580-436-4287 Fax
chickasaw.net

Total area *(BIA realty, 2004)*
73,079.22 acres

Federal trust *(Tribal source, 2005)*
3,737 acres

Tribally owned *(BIA realty, 2004)*
4,111.53 acres

Tribally owned *(Tribal source, 2005)*
8,696 acres

Individually owned
(BIA realty, 2004)
68,967.69 acres

Population *2000 census*
277,442

Tribal enrollment
(Tribal source, 2005)
38,000

Tribal enrollment
(BIA labor report, 2001)
46,065

Total labor force *2000 census*
127,009

High school graduate or higher
2000 census
76.2%

Bachelor's degree or higher
2000 census
15.3%

Unemployment rate *2000 census*
5.6%

Per capita income *2000 census*
$15,598

LOCATION AND LAND STATUS

The Chickasaw Nation is one of the non-reservation tribes of Oklahoma. Tribal boundaries encompass a 7,648-square-mile multicounty area of south-central Oklahoma, from the Canadian River in the north to the Red River on the south, along the Texas border. Tribal headquarters are in Ada, Oklahoma. The Chickasaw Nation boundaries were established in 1855 through a treaty between the Chickasaw and Choctaw nations and the United States.

CLIMATE

The year-round average daily high temperature in 74ºF, with the highest temperature ever recorded at 116ºF. The year-round average daily low temperature is 51ºF. The lowest temperature on record is -10ºF. The area receives approximately 38.8 inches of precipitation annually, with 5.4 inches falling as snow.

CULTURE AND HISTORY

A brief overview of Chickasaw history illustrates why the tribe is known as "unconquered and unconquerable," and how its indomitable spirit currently enables the people to have such a positive impact on the State of Oklahoma.

By the sixteenth century, the Chickasaw Nation had established a highly developed ruling system, a thriving economy, a complex religion, a stable community life, and sophisticated town sites in a region spread out across present-day Mississippi, Alabama, Tennessee, and Kentucky. In 1540 they encountered Europeans for the first time, when Hernando de Soto, who was traveling through the southeastern part of the North American continent, passed through the area.

During the French and Indian War, the Chickasaws, who were fierce warriors, helped the British defeat French and Spanish forces to gain control of what is now the southeastern United States. Many historians now acknowledge the impact Chickasaws had upon the emergence of the United States as an English-speaking country.

Before their removal from the region in the 1830s, Chickasaws controlled the waters of the Mississippi River. Although their reputation as fierce warriors led early historians to refer to them as "Spartans of the Mississippi," the Chickasaws maintained a brisk trade with other tribes as well as with the French and the Spanish.

In the 1830s under President Andrew Jackson, the Chickasaws were forcibly removed from their homelands to Indian Territory in what is now Oklahoma. They were assigned to live as part of the Choctaw Nation, with whom they shared a similar language that descended from the Muskogean linguistic family. An 1855 treaty formally severed this relationship, and on March 4, 1856, the Chickasaw Nation was officially reestablished as a tribal government in Tishomingo, Indian Territory. Following the Civil War, the Chickasaw people wrote a new constitution that was adopted August 16, 1867.

The 1897 Atoka Agreement forced both the Chickasaws and Choctaws into an allotment experiment initiated by the 1887 Dawes Act. In 1902, Congress subsequently enacted a series of measures, which effectively terminated tribal existence and fueled an unparalleled exploitation of Indian lands, all of which culminated within a decade in Oklahoma statehood. By 1920, an estimated 75 percent of all Chickasaw lands,

over 4.7 million acres, had passed out of tribal hands either by sale or lease. Virtually all community tribal lands had disappeared.

Efforts by the federal government to terminate the Chickasaw Nation by way of the Dawes Act and other legislation in the 1890s and early 1900s failed, however, as did later efforts in the 1950s. Despite removal from their homeland in the southeastern United States to Indian Territory and subsequent efforts to abolish the Chickasaw Nation, the tribe not only survived, it flourished and has become a valuable asset to the state.

President Kennedy appointed Overton James as governor of the Chickasaw Nation in 1963, a position that was primarily honorary at the time. The tribe, in fact, had no other employees and offered no programs or services. In 1970 Congress granted the tribe the right to elect its own leadership, and the following year Governor James became the tribe's first elected governor. After passage of the Indian Self-Determination Act in 1975, federal funding was made available, and the tribe began to offer health care and other services to its members. Since that time, the tribe has experienced tremendous growth. During Governor Overton James's tenure, the number of tribal employees grew from about 30 to close to 200. Tribal revenues increased from $750,000 in 1975 to approximately $11 million in 1987 when Bill Anoatubby was elected governor. Under Governor Anoatubby's leadership, the Chickasaw Nation's budget and employment increased almost thirty-fold.

In the same time period, Chickasaw tribal business grew from an annual revenue of tens of thousands of dollars to its current annual revenue measured in the tens of millions. Today, the tribe operates more than two dozen tribal enterprises, including two radio stations, a newspaper, several gaming centers, tobacco shops, convenience stores, Bank2 in Oklahoma City, a chocolate factory, and Chickasaw Nation Industries (technology, contract health, and a manufacturing plant).

The community is marked by a strong governmental infrastructure and diverse educational, vocational, and social services. A significant fraction of the population still speaks the Native language, and from the 1970s onward a strong revival of interest in traditional heritage and culture has emerged. One of the so-called Five Civilized Tribes, the Chickasaw Nation is one of the largest federally recognized tribes.

GOVERNMENT

Located in Ada, Oklahoma, the Chickasaw Nation's tribal government is a democratic republic modeled after that of the U.S. federal government. After the first constitution of the Chickasaw Nation in 1856, a new constitution was ratified in 1983. Registered voters elect a governor and lieutenant governor, who run on the same ticket, to four-year terms.

The voters also elect 13 tribal legislature members to three-year terms. The legislators serve staggered terms, and about one-third of the seats in the legislature are up for election each year. Three elected justices on the tribal Supreme Court perform constitutional interpretive duties. In January 2004, the Chickasaw Nation District Court began hearing cases, with plans to incorporate the use of traditional peacemaker courts. Tribal financial support for these various programs totals more than $700 million in 2004.

The tribe, under PL 93-638, contracts with the BIA to administer key programs and services from regional offices in Ardmore, Ada, Tishomingo, and Purcell. The Nation operates, among others, the following departments and divisions: administrative services, aging, arts and humanities, commerce, communications, community outreach, education and training, health, heritage preservation, housing, legal, program operations, and facilities and support.

Tribal government services process all Certificates of Degree of Indian Blood cards and Chickasaw Nation citizenship, verifies Indian Preference, and approves applications for eagle feathers. The Office of Community Outreach and Special Action works to see that tribal members are guaranteed access to the executive, legislative, and judicial branches of tribal government via community organization meetings, a toll-free phone line, and special advocacy on behalf of tribal members. The division of communications publishes *The Chickasaw Times*, maintains the official tribal website at www.chickasaw.net, and works to keep all tribal members informed of tribal and local news.

Within the division of program operations, several programs maximize tribal members' self-sufficiency. These include a computer literacy and distribution program, horticulture program, transportation services, and community health representatives. This division also oversees general assistance, low-income home energy assistance, tribal elderly energy assistance, and tribal emergency utilities programs. The award-winning Chuka Chukmasi ("beautiful home") program has provided home loans totaling $23 million to 305 families in 12 states, and it received Harvard's American Indian Tribal Governance Award in 2003. Harvard's John F. Kennedy School of Government chose the program from outstanding examples of tribal governance among the more than 550 Indian nations in the United States.

The Office of Employment Opportunities helps prepare tribal members for employment by providing training classes, job readiness skills, and leads on employment opportunities in tribal government and elsewhere.

The Youth and Family Services division oversees the Chickasaw Nation Boys and Girls Club in Chickasha, Tishomingo, and Sulphur; the celebrate fitness program, which includes a martial arts program of more than 300 students; and the Youth HELPS Emergency Assistance Program, which provides food, clothing, and other types of expenses. The Youth and Family Services division also administers the child support enforcement, Indian child welfare, family preservation, family violence prevention, foster care and adoption, healthy families, and strong family development programs. The Nation also operates summer youth programs.

The Arts and Humanities Division offers an Arts in Education program and supports Chickasaw humanities and literary arts courses offered at East Central University. The Arts and Humanities Division also compiles a Southeastern Native American Artist Directory and sponsors performances by the Living History Players and Chickasaw Theatre Company. The Heritage Preservation Division operates the tribal cultural resources office, which is charged with preserving the tradition, culture, and history of the Chickasaw people. The Chickasaw Nation Dance Troupe may be contacted via the cultural resources office. The division also oversees the historic Chickasaw Nation Capitol building, Chickasaw Council House Museum, Chickasaw Historical Society, Genealogy Archive Center, language preservation program, photograph archives, tribal library, and cemetery program. They are also responsible for the repatriation of Chickasaw funerary objects and human remains as well as the enforcement of the Native American Graves Protection and Repatriation Act.

The fire management program, Chickasaw Nation Search and Rescue, and flight operations are operated through the Nation's Chickasaw Enterprises.

BUSINESS CORPORATION
The Division of Commerce operates Chickasaw Enterprises, the business and industrial arm of the Chickasaw Nation.

The tribe also owns Chickasaw Nation Industries (CNI), a federally chartered 8(a) diversified tribal business corporation designed to promote continuing economic development and long-term financial sustainability. Operations include the construction and property management division, the medical services division, information technology, retail, government, and private industries. CNI has locations in Ada, Oklahoma; Washington, D.C.; Albuquerque, New Mexico; San Antonio, Texas; and Columbus, Georgia.

ECONOMY
In addition to its gaming facilities, the tribe operates a number of businesses. Many tribal members are also involved in the region's extensive agriculture. Tribal revenues include sales taxes, motor fuel settlement funds, income from investments, and transfers from tribal enterprises. For a seven-month period ending April 30, 2004, tribal revenues totaled more than $183 million. Total net assets exceeded $205 million during that same period.

Government as Employer. The tribal government employs approximately 6,000 people in all of its entities.

Economic Development Projects. The tribal government's executive department or by agencies of that department review and analyze economic development projects.

Agriculture and Livestock. Chickasaw Nation lands lie within a region of Oklahoma that is largely agricultural. The Nation owns a ranch with 300 head of cattle that is located just outside Davis, Oklahoma. A fair number of tribal members are engaged in agriculture-related pursuits, including raising cattle and horses.

A tribally maintained community garden program provides fresh produce to tribal members. The program also provides horticulture and marketing training to dozens of area youth who grow and market several tons of produce annually. Produce is sold to local grocers and restaurants, at local farmers' markets, and directly to area residents on site.

Forestry. The Chickasaw Nation and the Choctaw Nation of Oklahoma jointly own many acres of forested lands; the BIA manages these lands as part of its trust responsibilities.

Gaming. The tribe owns and operates more than 4,000 electronic gambling machines at 17 gaming centers in Ada, Norman, Paoli, Davis, Newcastle, Sulphur, Kingston, Duncan, Ardmore, and Thackerville.

Winstar Casino in Thackerville, the largest of the Chickasaw gaming centers, serves 3,000 to 4,000 guests on an average weekday, with much larger crowds flocking to the 190,000-square-foot facility each weekend. Winstar offers more than 2,200 electronic games in three distinct venues, including the recently opened and lavishly appointed Palace, Center Ring, and Mariachi rooms. More than 900 players can be accommodated in the 40,000-square-foot paper-play bingo area.

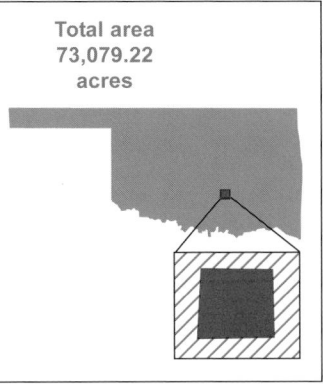

Total area
73,079.22
acres

Chickasaw

TRI-OK-008

TRI-OK-009

TRI-OK-008 Front view of Bedre Chocolate Factory, tribally owned in Pauls Valley

TRI-OK-009 Street view of Bedre Chocolate Factory, tribally owned in Pauls Valley

Horse racing fans will enjoy the flexibility of the off-track betting showplace, which can be expanded from the normal capacity of approximately 100 seats to more than 1,200 for big race days such as the Breeder's Cup.

Guests can also choose from a variety of menus in four restaurants with a total seating capacity of more than 500. Deli-style fare is available at the Mid-Way, while diners at the Bread Basket Buffet may choose from an expanded variety of entrees, side dishes, salads, and desserts. Other restaurant selections include Italian cuisine at Zar's Italian Kitchen and the upscale atmosphere of the Stone Ranch restaurant. There is also a 1,200-seat theater. Top-flight entertainment from music stars like Neil McCoy to comedy, Las Vegas-style revues, and up and coming local bands are featured. In addition to having a positive impact on the local economy, Winstar enriches community life in the area. For example, some 900 seniors gather each Wednesday for a free full-menu breakfast.

Treasure Valley, another gaming facility, opened in June 2003 near Davis. A new Breadbasket Buffet and Diner and a Microtel Inn and Suites were built adjacent to the site. In addition, Chisholm Trail Casino and Cook Out Café in Marlow recently opened.

Fisheries. Two fisheries are located within the boundaries of the Chickasaw Nation, one of which is operated by the state government.

Mining. Extensive oil and natural gas production exists throughout the Nation. Some is located on Indian-owned lands, both allotted and trust property. There is also a sand-and-gravel mining operation on nation lands.

Manufacturing. The tribe owns and runs two manufacturing operations. The Bedre' Fine Chocolates factory began production in July 2003 in Pauls Valley. In February 2004, Chickasaw Nation Industries (CNI) purchased a manufacturing facility in Marietta, Oklahoma, that had been closed by Siemens Dematic. Purchase of the metal fabrication plant, which provides more than 65 jobs in the small community, allowed the operation to continue.

Technology. The Nation participates in the Intertribal Information Technology Company, a consortium with other Native American tribes headquartered in Fredericksburg, Virginia, which specializes in document conversion information technology systems for use on the Internet.

In July 2003, CNI acquired DataCom Sciences, an award-winning $40 million a year information services company with 650 employees. DataCom is a nationally recognized firm that provides technical support, business support, and records management services. CNI's information technology group employed approximately 700 skilled personnel in 2004.

Aviation Technical Support Service develops flight simulation and other aviation-based information technology. It also provides certification coursework, examinations of airworthiness, disaster-recovery planning, database documentation and technical support, risk assessment, and network security for both the aviation industry and the government.

Banking. The Chickasaw Bank Holding Company was formed in March 2001. The Chickasaw Nation opened Bank2 in January 2002 in Oklahoma City. Since then, Bank2 has increased its assets from $10 million to $70 million, and it has made loans totaling more than $170 million. Continued expansion led to opening a loan production office in Tulsa in September 2004. In January 2005, the U.S. Department of Housing and Urban Development announced that Bank2 had become the number one provider of home loans to Native Americans in Oklahoma and second highest nationwide.

Services and Retail. In addition to the casinos, the tribe has diversified into over 30 enterprises, including Bedre' Chocolates, 6 smoke shops, 2 radio stations, 2 tribal trading posts, gas stations, and 5 travel and truck stops. The Lazer Zone Family Fun Center in Ada, which opened in October 2004, provides family-oriented entertainment like skating, bowling, and lazer tag, and employs more than 150 people.

Media and Communications. The monthly *Chickasaw Times* is the official tribal newspaper. KADA, FM 99.3, which the tribe has owned and operated for over seven years, is simulcast on Channel 8 of Cable One cable television programming. On January 27, 2005, the tribe purchased KYKC radio. The Ada-based station has a powerful 50,000-watt capacity and is the largest station in south-central Oklahoma.

Tourism and Recreation. Recreation opportunities abound in the Chickasaw Nation. The Chickasaw National Recreation Area near Sulphur is the only National Park in Oklahoma. The recreation area, at the Lake of the Arbuckles, offers boating, swimming, and fishing. The park's nature center features wildlife exhibits, nature walks, and presentations. Additionally, there is excellent fishing at Blue River and at a number of lakes within the nation's boundaries. The Arbuckle Wilderness area and Turner Falls Park-which features 77-foot Turner Falls, the highest waterfall in Oklahoma-are both located near Davis.

The nation operates RV parks in Windstar, Thackerville, Pauls Valley, and Davis. In 2004, a 110-acre Chickasaw Culture Center, to be constructed near Sulphur, was in the final planning stages. Sulphur's Historical Main Street District has a plethora of antique shops and galleries, and there is a Wilderness Exotic Animal Park in Arbuckle.

A variety of museums, art galleries, and restaurants, as well as the Chickasaw Nation Headquarters in Ada and the historic Chickasaw Capitol in Tishomingo attract many visitors. Construction of the historic Chickasaw Capitol Building was completed in 1898. It served the Chickasaw Nation as its third council house until Oklahoma statehood in 1907. The building was leased to Johnston County until the county purchased it in 1910, and it then served as a courthouse for more than 80 years. The tribe purchased the building from Johnston County in 1989 and promptly leased it back to the county for three more years while a new county courthouse was under construction. The historic Chickasaw Capitol has since been restored to its original condition, and it now features numerous historic exhibits.

Tishomingo is host city to the annual Chickasaw Annual Meeting and Festival, which attracts thousands of visitors from across the United States. There is an annual Chi Ka Sha Reunion and an Elders Day celebration in May at Kullihoma, near Ada.

INFRASTRUCTURE
I-35 is the main traffic artery through the area, crossing north-south through the western portion of the nation about 35 miles west of tribal headquarters in Ada. Both private or commercial air service is available in most of the larger communities, with major airports located in nearby Oklahoma City, Tulsa, and Dallas. Commercial truck lines serve most points within tribal boundaries, and commercial bus service is available in the larger communities. Rail freight service is available at certain key locations within the boundaries.

Electricity. Chickasaw Tribal Utility Authority provides electricity to businesses, tribal members, and the public.

Fuel. Regional and municipal utility companies in the various areas provide gas services.

Water Supply. The Sanitation Facilities Construction Office provides water and sewer services.

Transportation. Buses owned by the nation provide transportation for tribal members to various appointments and events.

Housing. The tribe's division of housing operates regional offices in Ada, Ardmore, and Duncan, Oklahoma, designing housing programs and related services to provide affordable housing to Chickasaw citizens and neighbors. Since the tribe assumed control of the housing program in 1997, more than 300 families have become homeowners through the mutual help program.

A Homeowners Maintenance Services Program assists participants with maintenance and repair services. Rehabilitation programs, such as the housing improvement program, are administered through contract with the BIA in a self-governance compact. The Chickasaw Housing Improvement Program provides major rehabilitation to older mutual help homes in low-rent housing developments and offers minor repairs to privately owned homes of low-income Native Americans. Low-rent programs provide rental assistance to low-income families and allow private sector units to be leased and subsidized on a sliding scale. A variety of housing-related counseling services are available to all tribal members for assistance in budgeting, credit, home and fire safety, and maintenance. Information on alternatives to foreclosure and prepurchase counseling are offered, as well. The storm shelter program is another successful and well-received program. To date, more than 600 storm shelters have been installed for Chickasaw citizens.

Housing supportive services include a drug elimination program for youth living in high-risk housing developments and a team of customer service representatives who provide infor-

mational and outreach services. It also provides three housing units for emergency housing and a safe house for victims of domestic violence.

COMMUNITY FACILITIES AND SERVICES
The tribe maintains a number of community centers, including a 30,000-square-foot Family Life Center at the Nation's headquarters in Ada. The Family Life Center features wellness and nutrition education programs, a swimming pool, a gymnasium, a walking track, a weight room, an aerobic exercise space, and a martial arts room. In May 2004, the tribe celebrated the grand opening of the 6,000-square-foot Purcell Senior Citizen Nutrition Site, the ninth such senior center the tribe has built for its elders. Like the others, the Purcell facility is a full-service site, featuring arts and crafts activities, field trips, education, and meal delivery to homebound seniors.

The Nation operates a genealogy archive in Tishomingo and a photo archives in the Miko Building in Ada. The Chickasaw Tribal Library is also located within the Miko Building, specializing in books and genealogy materials pertaining to the Five Civilized Tribes-Chickasaw, Choctaw, Seminole, Muscogee Creek, and Cherokee. The Chickasaw Historical Society Office publishes a quarterly *Journal of Chickasaw History*, with articles covering prehistory to modern times and biographies of influential Chickasaws.

Education. More than 250 students are better prepared for school thanks to Chickasaw Nation Head Start programs offered in Ada, Ardmore, Madill, Duncan, Sulphur, and Tishomingo. The Chickasaw Nation administers 54 Johnson O'Malley programs, serving a total student population of 6,629. The student of the month and Governor's Honor Club were founded to recognize and reward students for academic achievement and citizenship. The Governor's Honor Club, started in 1997 by Governor Bill Anoatubby, seeks to improve academic success by providing incentives toward academic achievement.

The Chickasaw Department of Education Services facilitates professional development and offers various scholarship, grant, and loan programs via the higher education program, which provides funding to high school graduates and GED holders who desire higher education. Monies provide housing assistance, tuition assistance, and clothing allotments. In the 2004 fiscal year, more than $2.5 million was distributed to area students in the form of scholarships and grants, providing more than 1,350 students with the opportunity to pursue a higher education.

The Chickasaw Nation also offers Chickasaw Children's Village, Arts in Education, Chickasaw Nation Aviation and Space Academy, vocational rehabilitation, GED classes, ACT preparation workshops, Upward Bound, Youth Leadership Camp, Workforce Investment Act, tribal vocational/technical, and internships in Washington D.C. An abundance of public schools, vocational facilities, and colleges are sprinkled throughout the Nation. A variety of classroom and on-the-job training opportunities is also available to adults interested in finding employment or training for a new career.

Health Care. Chickasaw Nation Health System (CNHS) health facilities include health and dental clinics in Durant, Tishomingo, Ada, and Ardmore, the Carl Albert Indian Health Facility in Ada, and an alcohol and drug treatment center east of Ada. In October 1994 the Chickasaw Nation became the first tribe to successfully negotiate a compact to manage a health care system. In the 2004 fiscal year, the CNHS had more than 350,000 patient visits.

Chickasaw

Chickasaw

The Carl Albert Indian Health Facility (CAIHF), a 53-bed acute care facility, includes a medical and surgical unit, obstetrics and gynecology, intensive care, 24-hour emergency room access, and an emergency fast track clinic. CAIHF and satellite clinics are fully accredited by the Joint Commission on Accreditation of Healthcare Organizations. Other services offered at the facility are women's health, physical therapy, audiology, social, laboratory, behavioral health, internal medicine, nutrition, cardiology, dental, diabetes, pediatrics, pharmacy, eye, foot, radiology, geriatric, respiratory therapy, home visitation, and the Healthy Lifestyles Chickasaw Nation Health System Alcohol and Drug Program. There is an orthopedic clinic, a wellness and fitness program, and parenting classes. In 2004, the nation was considering a pharmacy refill program to benefit all tribal members.

The new state-of-the-art Chickasaw Nation Diabetes Care Center opened on April 6, 2004, in Ada, providing the most comprehensive diabetes care of any facility in Indian country. The Chickasaw Family Life Center opened in Ada in June 2004. The 30,000-plus square foot facility features a gymnasium, water aerobics pool, and walking track. It also contains a wellness center with state-of-the-art exercise equipment and provides training instruction as well as aerobics and martial arts classes. Nutrition education, menu planning, and hands-on cooking instruction are offered in a large training kitchen in the facility. The division of education and training promotes wellness education to improve mental, spiritual, physical, and social wellness in all tribal members, from infancy throughout adulthood.

The Nation's division of aging provides comprehensive services and assistance to elders, including a senior nutrition program, chore services, home maintenance, a caregiver program, and assistance in paying for over-the-counter medications. A healthy, nutritious lunch is available free of charge for those 60 and over at senior nutrition centers in 10 locations throughout the Chickasaw Nation. Periodic health screenings are also available at the centers.

Chickasaw Nation community health representatives provide a variety of services, including education on preventive health care measures, home health care services, assistance in scheduling medical appointments as well as providing transportation to them, delivering prescription medicines, and translating label instructions when necessary.

ENVIRONMENTAL CONCERNS

The Nation's Office of Environmental Health aims to protect health and prevent disease among those living within the Chickasaw Nation Health System service area. The two branches of environmental health services are Environmental Health Services and Sanitization Facilities Construction.

Institutional environmental health includes activities such as: emergency preparedness planning, safety consultations and training, food service consultations, food service inspections, animal bite investigations for the prevention of rabies, rabies vaccination clinics, epidemiological studies, injury prevention, and intervention strategies.

Listed as the number one environmental concern in June 2004; the health of the Arbuckle-Simpson Aquifer, upon which the nation depends for its freshwater streams and groundwater resources, is the subject of an ongoing interagency study. Covering an area totaling approximately 500 square miles, the aquifer is a U.S. EPA Region VI Sole Source Aquifer with a significant trend of decreased discharge at least since 1906 when the Chickasaw National Recreation Area began recording measurements. Ecosystems and springs, including the Byrds Mill Spring upon which the entire Town of Ada depends, are under considerable human threat.

Honoring Nations Honoree 2003

Chuka Chukmasi Home Loan Program, Division of Housing, Chickasaw Nation, Ada, OK

When the Chickasaw Nation's Division of Housing realized that nearly 60 percent of its citizens' home loan applications were being denied, it created the Chuka Chukmasi, or "Beautiful Home," Home Loan Program to make safe and affordable housing a reality. Since 1998, Chuka Chukmasi has proven how powerful the combination of partnerships with innovative financial institutions and the education of its citizenry in the basics of loan applications and mortgage financing can be in securing home loans at competitive rates. Helping hundreds of Chickasaw citizens realize their dreams of homeownership, the Chuka Chukmasi Home Loan Program is building Chickasaw Nation self-determination one home at a time.

Homeownership is a tradition passed down from generation to generation. Regrettably, this tradition is not strong among American Indians. According to a 2002 U.S. Census Bureau report, only 54.5 percent of American Indians and Alaska Natives, compared to 74.5 percent of non-Hispanic whites, own their own homes. This dearth of homeownership means that the basics of purchasing and owning a home simply are not taught to rising generations of potential American Indian homeowners. Unfortunately, many of these individuals begin to believe that homeownership is unattainable.

This belief comes at a high cost. According to a 2000 Fannie Mae Foundation report, 44 percent of Indian households confront a "housing affordability problem" (when households pay over 30 percent of their income in housing expenses), while only 23 percent of US residents generally encounter this problem. The report goes on to say that the substantial and unmet demand for housing units among American Indians is the result, in part, of an absence of financing options. American Indians frequently face limited choices in lenders or must access loans through inflexible federal funding programs that are generally incapable of responding to individual needs or circumstances.

Among the Chickasaw, the absence of a solid tradition of home ownership and severely limited financing options resulted in a lack of home purchasing "know-how." For generations, Chickasaw citizens were simply told where, and under what circumstances, they would live. Many depended on federally provided housing. Generations of Chickasaw citizens lived without understanding basic mortgages, financing processes, or how to correctly report their equity in a loan application. Compounding the issue, many Chickasaws unknowingly turned themselves into high-risk applicants through the mishandling of their financial information.

Over the years, the Chickasaw Nation participated in a number of housing programs that aimed to increase homeownership. These programs, however, typically imposed requirements that the average Chickasaw citizen could not meet. Usually designed by the federal government, such programs often restricted house purchases to specific geographic areas or limited the sorts of houses available for purchase. They tended to impose narrow income guidelines and possessed little flexibility for dealing with individual circumstances. Very few programs made home ownership available to low-income or even higher-income families who faced significant expenses and were unable to make a down payment. Families with no credit histories or limited credit histories-a sizable proportion of the population on many reservations and Indian communities-were similarly disadvantaged. Despite these constraints, the Chickasaw Nation found that demand for housing programs remained high. Many Chickasaw citizens even waited from one to three years for Mutual Help housing opportunities. In the late 1990s, the Tribe realized that all of these factors translated into a discouraging statistic: nearly 60 percent of their citizens' home loan applications were being denied.

In 1998, the Chickasaw Nation's Division of Housing created the Chuka Chukmasi Home Loan Program to promote home ownership among its citizens. In its first year, Chuka Chukmasi negotiated partnerships with financial institutions such as PMI Mortgage Insurance Company to offer Chickasaw citizens living within the Tribe's geographical boundaries conventional, secondary home loans to cover the down payment and closing costs associated with a home purchase. The program was a near-immediate success, and by 2000, Chuka Chukmasi finalized one hundred loans on behalf of Chickasaw citizens.

This early success became the impetus for the program's further growth as the Division of Housing encouraged Chuka Chukmasi to respond to the needs of a large number of Chickasaw citizens considered high risk borrowers because of their limited or compromised credit histories. The Division recognized that although most Chickasaw citizens' credit problems complicated their loan application processes, these problems were not substantial enough to disqualify them as home loan borrowers. Committed to serving the needs of these individuals categorized as being high-risk, Chuka Chukmasi formed additional partnerships with First Mortgage of Oklahoma City and Fannie Mae in 2002. Since then, in collaboration with its partners, Chuka Chukmasi developed loan products designed expressly for Chickasaw homebuyers designated as high-risk.

Today, Chuka Chukmasi offers a variety of services including first and second mortgage processing and second mortgage loans. There are no income guidelines and these programs are available to Chickasaw citizens throughout the continental United States. Moreover, American Indians within the Chickasaw service area that do not have access to tribal loan programs of their own are also eligible to apply. Chuka Chukmasi's loans enable clients to purchase, renovate, or refinance homes. Primary home loans originate with First Mortgage while a tribal risk sharing agreement ensures that Chuka Chukmasi's clients are not priced out of the homeowners' market despite imperfect credit ratings. Chuka Chukmasi offers secondary loans at a competitive interest rate (e.g. 5 percent in 2003) to cover clients' down payments and closing costs, thus ensuring both the affordability of second mortgages to homebuyers and the availability of resources for future borrowers.

Through all of its programs, Chuka Chukmasi not only assists its clients in securing first and second home loans, but it also educates them about the home purchasing process. In 1998, Chuka Chukmasi facilitated the education of its clients through the Consumer Credit Counseling Service's phone lines. Convinced that education helped to increase and sustain homeownership, the Chickasaw Nation developed its own comprehensive home ownership course for potential homebuyers in 2000. The course covers loan applications, mortgage financing, predatory lending, and home maintenance. Chuka Chukmasi requires that every client take the course before the program's loan services become available to them. Chuka Chukmasi also offers post-purchase counseling to ensure that clients manage their mortgages successfully.

Chuka Chukmasi and its clients are succeeding. To date, Chuka Chukmasi and its lending partners have closed two hundred seventy three home loans providing $19,304,253 in first mortgage loans to Chickasaw clients. Chuka Chukmasi also provided one hundred nineteen down payment and closing cost assistance loans for a total of $545,361. As the number of these loans increases, Chuka Chukmasi reinvests its growing interest revenues, thus perpetuating its financial health. As of 2003, in fact, Chuka Chukmasi was financially self-sustaining. Its revenues are remarkably reliable: Chuka Chukmasi borrowers-65 percent of whom are first time homeowners-currently enjoy a zero default rate. This is itself a measure of the remarkable success of Chuka Chukmasi's home ownership seminars: since inception of the counseling program, it has offered sixty four seminars and issued six hundred one pre-homeownership counseling certificates.

Not surprisingly, Chuka Chukmasi received national recognition for its achievements. In 1999, Chuka Chukmasi received both the HUD Best Practice Award for its ground-breaking work on behalf of Native Americans, and the Social Compact Award, an award offered by the financial services industry that celebrates partnerships that promote successful investment in America's urban and rural neighborhoods. In 2002, Fannie Mae honored the Chickasaw Nation on behalf of Chuka Chukmasi for forming the Partnership of the Year from the State of Oklahoma.

Three factors that contribute to the success of the Chuka Chukmasi Home Loan Program deserve particular attention. First, Chuka Chukmasi established partnerships with reliable and reputable financial institutions that deliberately make innovative business decisions. Chuka Chukmasi values innovation. And most of the Chickasaw citizens it serves are high-risk clients with needs that necessitate Chuka Chukmasi to develop creative loan products and services, find new ways of sharing risk, and identify new solutions for emerging problems. Its financial partners possess a commitment to innovation as serious as Chuka Chukmasi's own. Each willingly advances the inventive programs that Chuka Chukmasi proposes, as well as suggests other possible solutions. For example, these partners accept the Chickasaw Nation as a risk-sharing partner to secure its high-risk borrowers; they facilitate Chuka Chukmasi's automated loan process-a process that removes human bias from loan decisions and demonstrates that if loan officers base lending decisions strictly on numbers, more Chickasaw citizens would qualify for loans. Further, these partners continue to eliminate bureaucratic barriers so Chuka Chukmasi can better serve its target population. In short, Chuka Chukmasi and its partnering financial institutions developed a mutually beneficial relationship that is changing their clients' lives for the better.

Second, Chuka Chukmasi rightly places great faith in the power of educating individual Chickasaw citizens about the home purchasing process. Chuka Chukmasi's homebuyer counseling program is a central feature of their success.

Honoring Nations Honoree 2003

Text in its entirety from: The Harvard Project On American Indian Economic Development

John F. Kennedy School of Government Harvard University

Chickasaw

Honoring Nations Honoree 2003

**Text in its entirety from:
The Harvard Project On American Indian Economic Development**

John F. Kennedy School of Government Harvard University

Again, Chickasaw clients attend local seminars led by certified homebuyer counselors that include detailed discussions about the demands of homeownership, the loan process, family financial planning, and other relevant topics. To be eligible for a loan, each client must complete the course. Even Chickasaws living far beyond the Tribe's boundaries must study mailed seminar materials, discuss these materials with a Chuka Chukmasi homebuyer counselor, and then take a 35 question assessment over the phone. Chuka Chukmasi's staff proudly notes that counseling does not end when clients complete their pre-purchase counseling. Post-purchasing counseling helps clients maintain their investments and work through potential financial problems before they lead to delinquencies.

What the seminar requirements cannot capture, however, is the creativity and intensity of a counseling program that strives to do far more than simply tell clients how to get a loan. For instance, Chuka Chukmasi is as attentive to its counselors as it is to its clients. Homebuyer counselors (all citizens of the Chickasaw Nation) are certified through a rigorous and comprehensive training. Chuka Chukmasi learned that encouraging clients to talk with knowledgeable tribal representatives, rather than non-Chickasaw loan officers, increases clients' willingness to seek guidance about their concerns and desires. Clients are not only taught about the purchasing process, but learn financing terms, budgeting, and contract and investment maintenance. By facilitating financial literacy, Chuka Chukmasi strengthens the skills of individual Chickasaw citizens and encourages individuals and families to invest in their communities. Chuka Chukmasi credits its continuing education program with their zero default rates.

Third, the Tribe's leadership is staunchly dedicated to the program's success. The Governor of the Chickasaw Nation is vocally dedicated to furthering home ownership and celebrating Chuka Chukmasi's success. At the same time, however, tribal leadership understands that it must sustain a healthy relationship with the program; the Tribe facilitates this success through a deliberate political distance. The tribal government's refusal to micromanage or politicize the program gives Chuka Chukmasi the freedom to innovate, to pursue the best lending partners and programs, to offer clients the best services, and to make and uphold effective rules. The tribal government exerts no pressure on Chuka Chukmasi to make loans to particular individuals, partner with particular institutions, or make politicized decisions.

A Fannie Mae representative has called the Chuka Chukmasi Home Loan Program the "gold standard" of Native housing programs. Chuka Chukmasi thinks of itself in these very terms: by encouraging Chickasaw clients to assume financial responsibility for themselves and build family and community wealth, they advance the Tribe's ability to be self-determined. Other Indian nations that confront housing crises may find valuable lessons in this home loan program. While Chuka Chukmasi works largely on the purchase of private lands, the Tribe and its financial partners indicate that the fundamental agreement and procedures by which they operate may be modified to work in reservation settings. Already, Chuka Chukmasi and its partners have provided technical assistance to the Menominee of Wisconsin, and the Modoc, Comanche, and Sac and Fox of Oklahoma. Chuka Chukmasi makes its curricular materials and operating practices available to all interested tribes. The interest in these materials is understandable: Chuka Chukmasi is helping to build a healthy nation home by home.

Choctaw

**Choctaw Nation of Oklahoma Reservation
Federal reservation
Choctaw
Latimer, Bryan, Choctaw, McCurtain, Atoka, Coal, Hughes, Pittsburg, Haskell, LeFlore, and Pushmataha counties, Oklahoma**

Choctaw Nation of Oklahoma
Drawer 1210
Durant, OK 74702-1210
580-924-8280
580-924-1150 Fax
choctawnation.com

LOCATION AND LAND STATUS
The Oklahoma Choctaw Nation sprawls across nearly 11 counties of southeastern Oklahoma, bordered on the south by the Red River (marking the Oklahoma/Texas boundary) and on the east by the Oklahoma state border with Arkansas. Total tribally affiliated land, consisting primarily of individually allotted holdings, amounts to 131,524 acres. The tribe maintains its traditional capitol in Tushka Homma and its tribal offices in Durant.

The General Allotment Act of 1887, which provided for the distribution of parcels of land to individually enrolled tribe members and the ensuing sale of "excess" lands, triggered an allotment agreement with the Five Civilized Tribes, one of which was the Oklahoma Choctaws. The Choctaws signed the Atoka Agreement in 1897, which spelled out the terms of allotment and distribution of proceeds from the sale of their remaining lands. The Curtis Act of 1898, which stipulated the termination of the tribal government as of 1906, paved the way for the tribe's subsequent domination by white settlers.

PHYSICAL DESCRIPTION
This is some of the most scenic territory in the state, comprised of lakes, hill country, and forests.

CLIMATE
The temperatures at Durant range from winter lows in the 30s to summertime highs of 90°F and above. The average rainfall is 39.5 inches and snowfall 2.7 inches.

CULTURE AND HISTORY
The Choctaw Nation of Oklahoma originated in the State of Mississippi and in areas of the State of Alabama. Under provisions of the Treaty of Dancing Rabbit Creek, the Nation became the first of the five great southern U.S. tribes to be moved to Oklahoma territory. The entire Nation, less those who were able to elude troops, was forced to relocate. Of the over 20,000 Choctaws forced onto this "Trail of Tears," about 12,500 survived to reach their new home land.

The Choctaws were forced into three districts: the Pushmataha, Apukshunubbee, and Mushulatubbee. Several missionaries were sent to the area and established Choctaw congregations of the Southern Baptist, Presbyterian, and Congregationalist religions, among others. A school system was established in 1821, and the Wheelock Academy, Armstrong Academy, Presbyterian College, and Calvin Institute served tribal youth for a number of years.

By the 1880s, white settlers, along with the federal government, had their collective eye on Indian Territory. The federal government enforced the General Allotment Act of 1887 (described under "Location and Land Status") and was met with overt resistance by the Choctaws and the other Indians in the Five Civilized Tribes (which also included relocated Cherokees, Choctaws, Creeks, and Seminoles). Nevertheless, the tribes had little choice but to acquiesce by signing the Atoka Agreement in 1897, and allotment proceeded in a manner that ultimately removed most reservation land from their collective ownership and allowed it to pass into the hands of settlers. It was in this manner that the State of Oklahoma was born in 1907, the Curtis Act of 1898 having provided for the termination of the Choctaw Tribal Government by 1906. At that time, all Choctaw educational institutions and policy passed into the hands of the federal government, and the following year all tribal courts were abolished. In subsequent decades, the tribe made numerous attempts to reestablish its institutions so as to gain some control over its internal affairs.

At a convention in 1934, the tribe endorsed the Indian Reorganization Act. The Indian Reorganization Act excluded Oklahoma from its provisions, however, leading to the BIA-administered Oklahoma Indian Welfare Act, which the tribe refused to recognize. By the 1950s and 1960s, the Choctaws were engaged in a serious effort to establish a sovereign tribal government and to avert termination. By the 1970s this movement had gathered momentum and, finally, in 1983 the tribe ratified a new constitution and the U.S. government formally recognized it.

The Choctaw Nation has steadily gained economic independence and tribal sovereignty. By the mid-1980s, it had assumed control of all BIA programs administered on tribal lands. The tribe funds almost 85 percent of all tribal programs, depending on less than 20 percent of funding assistance from the federal government.

In 2000 the Choctaw Nation reached a landmark agreement with the State of Oklahoma. The tribe, and the Chickasaw Nation, signed an agreement to unite Indian water rights with existing state water laws. The agreement affects issues in nearly 25 Oklahoma counties and the area along the Kiamichi River Basin. It will assist the state in paying $40 million it owes the federal government, defines tribal water rights, provides a system to administer water rights, addresses water quality standards, and addresses issues of development in southeastern Oklahoma.

In 2001 the Choctaw Nation, Cherokee Nation, and Chickasaw Nation sought a $50 million settlement from the U.S. government in exchange for dropping a lawsuit pending in the Federal Court of Claims. The tribes have been fighting for the return or compensation for lands, water rights, and mineral rights awarded them in treaties of the 1800s. The tribes are seeking the return of the Arkansas River bed and its minerals, and tribal lands that are undisputed from Arkansas to Muskogee. The tribes would also retain water rights to be separately negotiated with the State of Oklahoma.

In addition to economic independence, the tribe has made great strides in developing tribal programs that preserve and enhance Choctaw culture, language, and everyday life. Tribal language, social, housing, and health programs provide the community with valuable quality services. Interest in traditional culture and practices remains strong, with many younger Choctaws expressing the desire to learn the language, dances, and ceremonies of their ancestors. Baptist missionaries long ago gained a foothold in the tribe's culture, and today that faith is still fairly widespread among tribal members, albeit in hybrid form; many elders speak and sing Baptist hymns in the Choctaw language.

GOVERNMENT

The tribal government, which had been terminated in 1906 by the Curtis Act of 1898, was formally reestablished in 1983. This occurred after the Choctaw people voted in 1979 that the 1860 Choctaw Constitution be declared the valid constitution for their Nation. With some modifications, this document was ultimately ratified by the Choctaw people on July 9, 1983. The government is executed by a tribal council composed of a chief and 12 representatives. These are elected positions; any tribal member 18 years of age and older is eligible to vote. The council is responsible for directing a broad range of economic and social programs for the tribe's well-being. The new tribal headquarters are located in Durant, Oklahoma. The administrative offices are located in the former Presbyterian College building, a facility of historical, cultural, and religious significance to the tribe.

Government offices include education, housing, health, economic development, real estate, personnel, tribal membership, social services, law enforcement, environmental health, transportation, forestry service and fire fighters, veterans, and cultural resources.

The tribal police department exercises jurisdiction in ten and one half counties in southeastern Oklahoma. The department employs 10 officers. Founded in 1824, the Choctaw Lighthorsemen is a corps of volunteers whose original purpose was to settle difficulties on tribal lands. They possessed the authority to arrest, try, and punish violators of tribal law. The Lighthorsemen no longer maintain judicial authority, but they serve to keep peace in the tribal court system.

The tribe's fire department employs 60 wildland fire fighters. These fighters are assembled as 20-person crews and dispatched by the U.S. Forest Service to major fires throughout the nation.

The tribe's housing authority provides a mutual help program, maintenance and rehabilitation services, a rental assistance program, home finance department, modular housing program, and independent-living communities.

ECONOMY

The tribe operates a number of successful ventures that contribute to the tribal economy. Its ventures in the housing industry in particular have proven very successful for the tribe. The tribe itself is a major employer in the region, with an annual payroll of $85 million.

Government as Employer. The tribe employs 5,700 people.

Economic Development Projects. The Choctaw Nation actively pursues ventures to enhance the tribal economy. Tribal representatives travel nationwide to observe successful Native American enterprises and identify projects that may be viable for the tribe. Recent projects include the diabetic wellness center, a new tribal hospital, and six elderly communities. Current plans include the construction of additional health facilities and a healthy lifestyles facility. The tribe was the first Native American group to be awarded a $5 million contract under the Bringing Rural American Venture Opportunities (BRAVO) Initiative. The funds have been utilized to further technology-based economic opportunities in the tribal community.

Agriculture and Livestock. Tribal members maintain a vast number of livestock, including nearly three-quarters of a million cattle, several dozen buffalo, nearly 800,000 chickens, 15,000 sheep, about 11,000 pigs and hogs, and 120 wild horses. Approximately 5,000 acres of land are under lease for agricultural purposes, mostly soybean, native hay, and winter wheat cultivation. The tribe also operates an agriculture program, which provides technical assistance for developing and conserving soil, plant, and water resources to anyone engaged in farming or ranching activities on tribal trust or restricted lands. Services are available to Chickasaw Tribe lands jointly owned with the Choctaw Nation and individually owned Chickasaw lands within the Choctaw Nation service area.

Choctaw

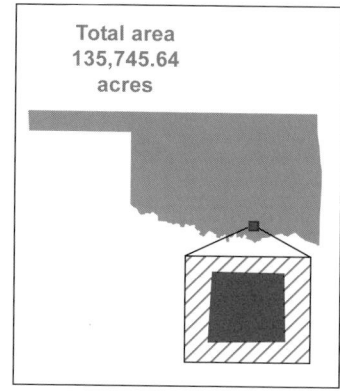

Total area
135,745.64
acres

Total area *(BIA realty, 2004)*
135,745.64 acres

Federal trust *(BIA realty, 2004)*
292.16 acres

Tribally owned
(BIA realty, 2004)
19,661.79 acres

Individually owned
(BIA realty, 2004)
115,791.69 acres

Tribal enrollment
(BIA labor report, 2001)
148,976

Total labor force *2000 census*
93,458

Total labor force
(BIA labor report, 2001)
45,512

High school graduate or higher
2000 census
71.7%

Bachelor's degree or higher
2000 census
12.5%

Unemployment rate *2000 census*
6.8%

Unemployment rate
(BIA labor report, 2001)
38%

Per capita income *2000 census*
$6,203

825

Choctaw

TRI-OK-009a Jones Academy Dormitory, Hartshorne, OK, Courtesy of Mike Holleyman Associates, Oklahoma City

Forestry. The tribe owns 6,300 acres of commercial pine timber and 400 acres of hardwood. Additionally there are approximately 40,000 acres of allotted pine forest and 8,000 acres of allotted hardwood within the tribal boundaries.

Gaming. The tribe operates gaming facilities in Durant, Idabel, Pocola, McAlester, Stringtown, Grant, Broken Bow, and Hugo. The Pocola, Hugo, and Durant facilities are currently being renovated. The Choctaw Casino offers slot machines and tournament blackjack. The adjacent Choctaw Inn offers one restaurant, buffets, an outdoor pool, and shuttle services. Choctaw Bingo offers 750 seats, video projection screens, and a nonsmoking area. Choctaw Downs is a horse track with over 100 patron stations, a video wall, live teller windows, and automatic teller windows. The tribe also owns the Blue Ribbon Downs, a horse race track in Sallisaw.

Revenue earned from tribally owned gaming enterprises are used to fund tribal services such as health and social services, as well as college scholarships for tribal members. Funds have also been used to provide assistance to surrounding communities. In 2001 an ice storm devastated the region, and electricity was out for up to three weeks in some areas. The tribe immediately organized the distribution of bottled water, batteries, heaters, blankets, and food to tribal and nontribal residents. They provided over $300,000 in assistance. In 2003 the tribe provided cleanup assistance and temporary housing for victims of a tornado that struck McCurtain County. The tribe also provides donations to local charities and nonprofit organizations.

Fisheries. The Choctaw Nation maintains an aquaculture project of caged catfish at Jones Academy in Harshore, Oklahoma. The project raises up to 4.5 million catfish annually. Additionally, recreational fishing is popular at Lake Eufaula.

Construction. The tribe constructs its own modular houses. Employees are trained in the necessary skills.

Manufacturing. The tribe owns the Choctaw Manufacturing Development Corporation, with sites in Hugo and McAlester, and the Choctaw Fabricators in Atoka. The company manufactures steel and aluminum shipping containers, aluminum airfoil assemblies, and special purpose trailers; assembles, fixtures, and stores weapon components; designs prototype development services; resells industrial supplies; assembles electronic components; and provides construction management and facilities maintenance. Future ventures include relocation services, health care claims review, business consulting services, and environmental services. It has received numerous awards, including the Award for Administrative Excellence (U.S. Small Business Administration, 1994) and Minority Supplier of the Year Award (Raytheon TI Systems, 1997).

Industrial Park. There are 10 industrial parks within tribal boundaries that generate substantial revenues and employment. Additionally, Weyerhaeuser Corporation has 3 mills within the boundaries. A Texas Instruments facility is also located on tribal lands.

Real Estate/Commercial Development. The Choctaw Nation pursues the acquisition of lands, most of which are used for tribal housing. The Nation offers seven rental housing communities in Bokoshe, Caney, Quinton, Red Oak, Wright City, and Talihina. It also operates independent living communities for tribal elders in Idabel, Talihina, Durant, McAlester, Poteau, and Hugo. Each community has the capability for 40 homes.

Banks. The tribe operates the Southeastern Oklahoma Indian Credit Association, or the Choctaw Nation Credit and Loan Department. It offers small business loans, agricultural loans, micro-loans, and housing loans to members of federally recognized tribes living within the county area of the Choctaw Nation.

Services and Retail. The Choctaw Management/Services Enterprise (CM/SE) is a tribally owned management company with 58 full-time professions serving in over 215 locations worldwide. CM/SE offers web development, systems analysis and engineering, statistical analysis, quality management, process improvement, business process reengineering, and database design, administration, and deployment. It also provides turnkey document management of records, including scanning, filing, storage, retrieval, and destruction. CM/SE also provides staffing for health, social, and mental health facilities, including physicians, nurses, social workers, counselors, dentists, technicians, assistants, therapists, clerics, and managers. The principal clients of CM/SE are the U.S. Army, Air Force, Navy, Indian Health Service, Immigration and Naturalization Service, and Department of Defense Tricare Management Activity. CM/SE staff members are located throughout the U.S. and in Belgium, Cuba, Germany, Great Britain, Guam, Hawaii, Iceland, Italy, Japan, Korea, Okinawa, Portugal, Singapore, Spain, and Turkey.

The tribe operates Choctaw Nation Travel Plazas in Atoka, Broken Bow, Durant East, Durant West, Garvin, Hugo, Idabel, McAlester, Pocola, Poteau, Stringtown, and Wilburton. In 2001 the Choctaw Nation contributed all net proceeds of gasoline sales for one week to provide assistance to victims of the September 11, 2001, terrorist attack in New York City and Washington, D.C. The tribe also contributed an additional $20,000.

The tribe also owns Choctaw Nation Smoke Shops in Atoka, Broken Bow, Durant East, Durant West, Garvin, Hugo, Idabel, McAlester, Pocola, Poteau, Stringtown, and Wilburton. It also owns the Three Arrow Restaurant with franchises in Durant and Stringtown, Choctaw Books and Crafts, the Choctaw Inn, Auto Detailing, and the Choctaw Museum and Gift Shop. The tribe owns the Choctaw Nation Shopping Center in Idabel.

Media and Communications. The tribe publishes the *Bishinik*, a monthly newspaper distributed to tribal members free of charge. It is also distributed nationwide and throughout the world.

Tourism and Recreation. In addition to gaming facilities, the tribe owns the Arrowhead Resort and Hotel. It is located on the southern shore of Lake Eufaula, Oklahoma's largest lake. It boasts an 18-hole golf course, hiking, fishing, tennis, camping, and lake cruises.

The tribe has erected a monument dedicated to the Choctaw Code Talkers of WWI. The monument bears the names of the 18 soldiers who served as the first code talkers for the United States military. It is situated on the capitol grounds at Tushka Homma, the site of the historic Old Capitol building that now serves as the council house and museum. The structure, which also features tours and a gift shop, is a popular tourist draw throughout the year.

There are numerous historical sites and museums within tribal boundaries. The nationally famous Spiro Burial Mounds, recent dinosaur discoveries, and several Caddoan mounds are all located within the boundaries as well. The tribe owns the former Mission and Girls' School of Wheelock Academy, which is located in Millerton, Oklahoma. It is listed as one of the 11 Most Endangered Historical Sites in Oklahoma. A gift shop, information center, and tours are available.

The tribe hosts the four-day Annual Choctaw Festival over Labor Day weekend which draws about 10,000 visitors. The festivities include the Chief's State of the Nation Address and an inauguration of elected officials. It is held at Tushka Homma. The tribe also hosts an annual Veteran's Day Ceremony and the annual Trail of Tears Walk to commemorate the journey that the Choctaws were forced to make to Oklahoma in the 1800s.

INFRASTRUCTURE
I-40 runs east-west through the north end of the tribal region, while highways 75 and 69 and the Indian Nation Turnpike all provide four-lane access to I-40. The tribe contracts a transportation improvement program through the BIA, funded by the U.S. Department of Transportation. The program conducts inventories of existing roads and identifies roads and bridges that need improvement.

Electricity. Western Farmers Electric Co-op, PSO, and REA provide electricity to the area within the tribal boundaries.

Fuel. Oklahoma Natural Gas provides gas service.

Water Supply. There are 127 community water distribution systems in the Choctaw Nation counties, each regulated by the Oklahoma Department of Environmental Quality. Water storage units are located at the Tuskahoma Council Grounds, Choctaw Nation Indian Hospital, and Jones Academy. Municipalities, irrigation facilities, and private systems in the region provide wastewater treatment systems.

Transportation. Commercial air service is available at Durant, Hugo, McAlester, Poteau, and other locations within tribal boundaries. Commercial bus lines serve all the major highways and towns in the area. All major trucking and air express services, as well as UPS, serve numerous locations in the area, as do several railroad lines. The Arkansas River provides access to water-based transportation.

The Texas Instruments enterprise makes use of tribal trucks, as do area food distributors. The tribe owns six 50-passenger buses, maintains one airplane, and has several other buses under lease.

COMMUNITY FACILITIES AND SERVICES
Community centers, field offices, and family investment centers are located in Antlers, Atoka, Bethel, Broken Bow, Coalgate, Crowder, Durant, Hugo, Idabel, McAlester, Poteau, Stigler, Talihina, Wilburton, and Wright City. The family investment centers provide education, employment, child care, transportation, basic computer education, youth leadership, and self-employment assistance.

The tribe offers a Women and Children Residential Program (Chi Hullo Li), C.A.R.E.S., Welfare to Work, C.R.I.M.E.S., and WIC programs. It also provides a host of social services. For the tribal elders, the tribe provides nutrition, outreach, family caregivers, senior employment, eyeglasses, dentures, hearing aids, and low-income home energy assistance programs. The tribe also manages a Workforce Investment Act program, Projects with Industry Program, and Boys and Girls Club in Broken Bow and Talihina.

The Choctaw Color Guard is comprised of Choctaw veterans who have volunteered to represent the tribe at various events and activities.

Education. The majority of tribal youth attend area public schools. The tribe owns the Jones Academy, a residential care center for elementary and secondary students. Established in 1891, the school is open to members of any federally recognized tribe. It hosted the first Annual Jones Academy Welcome Back Powwow in 2004. The school serves 170 students in first and second grades and will add two grades each year. Its goal is to provide instruction in grades 1-12 within five years.

In 2000 the tribe opened child care centers in Stigler, Coalgate, and Bennington. Each center occupies 5,600 square feet and houses a Head Start program, daycare center, storm shelter, playground, and amphitheater. The tribe also operates 12 other Head Start programs and daycare facilities in Durant and Talihina.

The Choctaw Nation Language Program offers classroom and Internet classes in the indigenous language. Courses are available through One-Net, Carl Albert Jr. College, Eastern Oklahoma State College, Southeastern Oklahoma State University, and in various community classes throughout Oklahoma, Texas, Arkansas, and California. The program has published a topical vocabulary of the Choctaw language.

The tribe maintains the Educational Talent Search and Research and Resource Development Center. The tribe also operates the TRIO Program. It provides students with pre-college counseling. The tribe's education department manages a higher education and grant program, Indian adult education, Johnson O'Malley, Choctaw language, Upward Bound, and the Jones Academy. The tribe provided higher education scholarships to more than 4,000 students in the 2004-2005 academic year.

Health Care. The tribe's health facilities consists of the Choctaw Nation Health Care Center, the clinics in McAlester, Hugo, Broken Bow, Poteau, Durant, the Choctaw Nation Diabetes Clinic, Children and Family Services in McAlister and Atoka, the Recovery Center, and Chi Hullo Li. It also offers a community health representative program, eyeglasses, dentures, and hearing aid program, an office of environmental health, recovery program, women and children's residential treatment program, diabetes treatment center, and drug and alcohol testing program. The tribe also provides emergency medical services and the Hospitality House, a temporary residence for families of patients in the hospital. Mail order pharmacy services are also available. The tribe assumed control over its health services from the Indian Health Service in 1985.

The health care center is located in Talihina. It was the first Native American hospital constructed with tribal funds. The original two-story facility was constructed in 1917. In 2004 the center occupied 145,000 square feet and offered 37 beds for inpatient care and 52 examination rooms. Services include audiology, behavioral health, cardiology testing, a clinical laboratory, contract health, dental, dietary and nutrition, emergency and urgent care, family practice and internal medicine, inpatient and day surgery, women's services, pediatrics, optometry and ophthalmology, physical therapy, podiatry, radiology, respiratory therapy, social services, environmental health, Title XIX, health education, WIC, speech therapy, public health, and occupational therapy programs. The Clinics at Broken Bow, Hugo, Poteau, and McAlester offer similar services. The tribe employs 73 health care providers. It is in the process of constructing clinic facilities in Stigler and Idabel, and a new recovery center on the former hospital campus.

Choctaw

ENVIRONMENTAL CONCERNS
Without a centralized land base, the tribe's environmental concerns pertain to ecosystems throughout the region. Concerns include pollution prevention and mitigation of areas already affected. Two areas of primary concern are the Bailey-Mulkey Post Company at Broken Bow and the Big E Feeds/McDonalds Farm at Durant, two Comprehensive Environmental Response, Compensation, and Liability Act sites. The tribe has also recognized the need for a wetland conservation plan, an air quality program, and a pesticide program.

Citizen Potawatomi

Citizen Potawatomi Nation
Federal reservation
Potawatomi
Pottawatomie Cleveland, and
Oklahoma counties, Oklahoma

Citizen Potawatomi Nation
1601 S. Gordon Cooper
Shawnee, OK 74801
405-275-3121
405-275-0198 Fax
potawatomi.org

Total area (BIA realty, 2004)
5,284.68

Tribally owned (BIA realty, 2004)
617.5 acres

Individually owned
(BIA realty, 2004)
4,667.18 acres

Population *2000 census*
106,624

Tribal enrollment
(Tribal source, 2004)
26,000

Total labor force
2000 census
51,086

High school graduate or higher
2000 census
80.9%

Bachelor's degree or higher
2000 census
14.5%

Unemployment rate *2000 census*
4.3%

Per capita income *2000 census*
$17,803

LOCATION AND LAND STATUS

The Citizen Potawatomi Nation (CPN) exercises governmental jurisdiction in an area bounded by the North Canadian River (on the north), the South Canadian River (on the south), the Pottawatomie-Seminole County boundary (on the east), and the Indian Meridian (on the west) in central Oklahoma. The CPN tribal jurisdictional service area encompasses all of Pottawatomie County south of the North Canadian River, the eastern half of Cleveland County and the southeastern tip of Oklahoma County. The South Canadian River forms the southern boundary of Potawatomi tribal lands. The North Canadian River forms the northern boundary of Potawatomi tribal lands.

The reservation area is on land checkerboarded throughout Pottawatomie County, Oklahoma. The Town of Shawnee, a community of 27,000, is located approximately 50 miles southeast of Oklahoma City and serves as a center for tribal activities. The service area is a 30-by-30-mile tract, or 900 square miles. The tribe has over 5,902 acres in trust and is steadily acquiring more land. In recent years, the members changed the tribe's name from Citizen Band of Potawatomi Indians of Oklahoma to Citizen Potawatomi Nation.

CLIMATE

Temperatures in the area range from an average low of 25.9°F in January to an average high of 94.9°F in July and August.

CULTURE AND HISTORY

The name of the Potawatomi means "People of the Place of the Fire" in the Algonquian language. The Citizen Potawatomi call themselves Nishnabec, meaning "True People," and early records confirm that Potawatomi as a distinct tribe inhabited Michigan 500 years ago, the CPN says on its website. The first Potawatomis encountered by Europeans were hunters, fishermen, and farmers living near what is now Green Bay, Wisconsin. During French incursions, many Potawatomis intermarried with Creole settlers, and the tribe spread south across present-day Michigan, Indiana, and Illinois. From the CPN history: "At the height of the Fur Trading Era . . . , the Potawatomi controlled a tribal estate that encompassed Wisconsin, Michigan, Illinois, Indiana, and a small portion of Ohio or over 5 million acres. This was accomplished through longstanding leadership and savvy business skills. . . . They began to hire other local tribesmen to collect and trap the furs that they once procured. In turn, they would sell or trade the furs to the French, thus expanding their tribal control and estate over a vast area." In 1832 the tribe ceded more than 780,000 acres in these areas to the U.S. government in exchange for an annuity and manufactured goods, and some accepted a new reservation in what is now east-central Kansas. According to the CPN, "It was during the Removal Period of the 1830's that the Mission Band (today known as the Citizen Band) of Potawatomi were forced to leave their homelands in the Wabash River Valley of Indiana. . . . to march across four states (over 660 miles) to a new reserve in Kansas. . . . More than 40 died along the way. The event is known in Potawatomi history as the 'Potawatomi Trail of Death' (September-November 1838)."

The Citizen Band Potawatomis are descended from one of the two major groups of Kansas Potawatomis which divided because of pressure from land speculators in the 1860s; the Citizen Band agreed to sell their land, become U.S. citizens, and buy new land for an Oklahoma reservation (those who refused were removed by U.S. soldiers to a smaller Kansas reservation, where they still live, known as the Prairie Band). In 1890 the Oklahoma reservation was in turn broken up into smaller parcels by the U.S. government, with plots given to individual tribal members constituting a "reservational area." In the 1891 Land Run, the CPN relates, "the remainder of the Potawatomi reservation in Oklahoma was opened up to 'white' settlement. It is estimated that 275,000 acres or half of the 900-square-mile reservation was simply given away by the government to settlers. . . . Many tribal members followed the pattern of other Oklahomans during the 'dust bowl' era, and migrated to California as well as Washington, Colorado, Idaho, and Oregon, where they formed loose-knit communities."

By the early 1970s, according to a September 19, 2004, *Washington Post* article, the tribe's holdings had shrunk to just two acres of trust land and $550. But the CPN turned things around. "They reformed their government, enforced the rule of law and shrewdly managed the tribal sovereignty . . ." The CPN records state that in 1984, the business committee set up a new court system, code of law, ordinances, taxing entity, and Federal Tribal Corporation. Today the CPN, it says, is the largest of the eight federally recognized Potawatomi tribes and the ninth-largest tribe in the United States. Enterprises include Fire Lake Golf, Fire Lake Entertainment (casino and off-track betting), Fire Lake Gift Shop, San Remo's Restaurant (leased), KGFF radio station, Fire Lake Mini Putt, and a bank with deposits of $120 million. The tribe's annual cash flow is $300 million.

GOVERNMENT

The CPN government has executive, legislative, and judicial branches, governed by a five-member executive committee. The legislative branch is comprised of three elected officials and the two business committee members. The CPN judiciary consists of a district court and a supreme court (the appellate court).

Tribal government operations include an election committee and a tribal court, a business committee with health and scholarship subcommittees, and a tribal chairman who oversees general administration issues, accounting, maintenance, BIA affairs, federal programs, and nonfederal programs. It also includes a cultural resources department.

Tribal members adopted a constitution in 1985, giving a vote to all tribal members, regardless of their place of residence. Tribal members staff the regional offices, thus providing members who do not live in Oklahoma an opportunity to access tribal services. The administration holds council meetings within each specified region each year. There are eight regional offices currently located in Irving and Magnolia, Texas; Pasadena and Castro Valley, California; Denver, Colorado; Phoenix, Arizona; Grandview, Missouri; and Oregon. This arrangement allows members who live outside Oklahoma to receive the tribe's services, according to the tribal website.

The tribal council governs the CPN. Voters choose a chairman for a four-year term. Tribal members elect a five-person business committee, which oversees tribal operations and sets policies. The CPN received a grant from the Administration for Native Americans for the development of a revised tribal constitution.

The cultural resources department lists the following among its activities: the museum, the archives, the library, the Potawatomi language programs, the Native American Graves Protection and Repatriation Act program, the veterans' memorial, tribal historic preservation, the Potawatomi Leadership Program, and the annual Fall Inter-Tribal Powwow. The cultural resources department also participates in genealogical research, the annual Reunion Festival, the Gathering of the Potawatomi Nations, and the Tribal Heritage Project.

The CPN Tribal Court lists seven Supreme Court justices, three district court judges, a prosecuting attorney, a public defender, a court clerk, a deputy court clerk, and a tribal marshal. Its areas of responsibility are cataloged as civil, criminal, and juvenile matters, a drug court, and marriage licenses.

As detailed by CPN's website, the CPN Tribal Drug Court was founded with grant money in May 2001. The drug court team is listed as: judge/prosecutor, public defender, court coordinator, Indian child welfare, treatment provider, police officer, and administration. The court serves several jurisdictions, and works closely with the Pottawatomie County Drug Court. The drug court serves as a training site where tribes from across the country gain knowledge of the program and the interrelation of its major parts.

The housing authority uses HUD funds to provide members with reasonably priced houses and apartments. CPN tribal members living anywhere in the United States can receive a sum of $2,125 to use in purchasing or refinancing a residence.

On its website, the tribe details a variety of services for members, including jobs, subsidized housing, and health care. The tribal heritage project is producing videos of family and tribal history.

BUSINESS CORPORATION

The Citizen Potawatomi Community Development Corporation, organized in May 2003, is a tribally chartered nonprofit Certified Community Development Financial Institution designed to address the lack of access to capital and business development services within Indian Country. The corporation's mission is to provide access to capital through loan fund support and offer business development services to members of the CPN and other Native Americans. Its activities are meant to expand the capacities of small businesses and aspiring entrepreneurs.

ECONOMY

The CPN, with a portfolio of varied business operations, has more workers than any other employer in Shawnee. It has a significant impact on central Oklahoma's economic life. Its business and gaming revenues provide numerous benefits such as new jobs, an increase in tourism, and diminished levels of joblessness and indigence.

According to Harden, "To secure loans and attract outside investors, the tribe adopted uniform accounting standards and commercial codes. It won a national award two years ago for producing scrupulously transparent financial reports."

Government as Employer. The CPN is the largest employer in the City of Shawnee and Pottawatomie County. As of June 2004, tribal employment was 778. A total of 298 employees were employed in federal tribal program capacities, while 480 employees worked in tribal enterprises. This is an annual payroll of over $12.8 million for its employees, plus an additional $3.3 million in related benefits. The CPN's impact on the local community and the state exceeded $84.9 million in FY 2004. Tribal tax commission proceeds and enterprise profits are used to provide higher education scholarships to tribal members,

homeownership assistance, prescription drugs to tribal elders, and prescriptions at cost for all tribal members living outside the tribe's service area.

Economic Development Projects. The Nation has significantly increased the size of Fire Lake Casino; renovated its restaurant facility for San Remo's Restaurant; constructed a new branch facility for the First National Bank in Holdenville; and begun a facelift, with installation of new carpet and other improvements for Fire Lake Mini-Putt.

Agriculture and Livestock. The predominant uses of tribal lands are for agriculture production such as grazing livestock, hay, and crop production. Most properties are in rural settings with little commercial development present. These properties are leased for dry-land farming and grazing on five-year lease terms. Approximately 85 percent of all allotments are agriculturally leased, with the remainder being used by individuals for their own purposes (home sites, hunting, and fishing). Each tract of allotted land has a conservation plan attached with the lease. Conservation measures are prescribed on a site-specific basis. These measures may include fencing, ponds, grass planting, terraces, and other related practices.

Gaming. One of the CPN's major businesses is the Fire Lake Casino, off I-40 in Shawnee. It has grown from a bingo hall to a small casino to a $7-million investment that provides Shawnee with about 150 additional jobs and allows the nation to acquire more capital for business ventures and funds for its government programs. The casino now has a total of about 680 gaming machines. The bowling apparatus was taken out of the east end of the casino building in 2002, and a total of 470 casino gaming machines and 12 tournament blackjack tables were installed in that 21,000-square-foot space. Around 150 machines occupy the original casino space, and gaming machines were added in the bingo hall (with room for 500 players), which permits bingo and machine-game play at the same time. Recently, the casino has added an expansion to its off-track betting operation.

A new casino, the Fire Lake Grand Casino, is being built at the Dale exit (mile marker 178) from I-40. It will feature an 110,000-square-foot gaming area, a 30,000-square-foot entertainment venue, and a 130,000-square-foot, 188-room all-suites hotel. There will also be a major truck plaza and convenience store. The casino will feature 3 dining areas. After suffering several months of weather-caused construction delays, CPN officials are targeting completion of the casino for the third quarter of 2005. Construction of the entertainment venue and hotel will follow in phases, with plans to have the hotel finished by the end of 2006.

Mining. Oil and gas production is another prevalent resource on the CPN lands. Each tract of land, if not already under leasehold, is advertised once a year for oil and gas exploration. Current leases are on a three-year term or held by continued production. Currently, 60 percent of all tribal allotted tracts are under oil and gas lease.

Real Estate/Commercial Development. The CPN is still enlarging its land base and its prospects for economic expansion by acquiring land within the tribal jurisdiction.

Banks. In 1989, the tribe purchased a bank, now the First National Bank and Trust Company in Shawnee, with $120 million on deposit. It is said to be one of the largest tribally operated banks in the United States. It occupied a new 32,000-square-foot structure in 1994. The Holdenville Branch of First National Bank opened in January 2000, and the Fire Lake Branch within the Fire Lake Discount Food Store opened for

Citizen Potawatomi

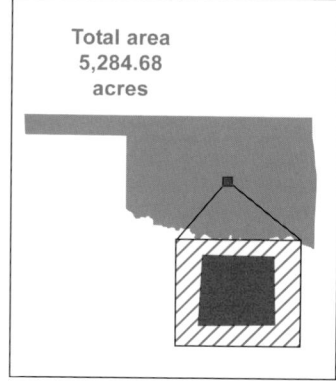

Total area
5,284.68
acres

Citizen Potawatomi

business in May 2001. With five years of superior earnings, First National displays the most rapid growth among Shawnee banks. It is the only local bank with ownership based in the community.

The Citizen Potawatomi Community Development Corporation, organized in May of 2003, is a tribally chartered non-profit Certified Community Development Financial Institution designed to address the lack of access to capital and business development services within Indian Country. The mission of the Citizen Potawatomi Community Development Corporation is to provide access to capital through loan fund support and business development services to members of the CPN and other Native Americans. Its activities are designed to expand the capacities of small businesses and aspiring entrepreneurs.

Services and Retail. Fire Lake Discount Foods, close by Highway 9 and Highway 177 between Shawnee and Tecumseh, occupies 84,000 square feet. Fire Lake Discount Foods' list of services includes a bakery, a deli, a florist, a photo center, the Dollar Store, and a branch of First National Bank and Trust of Shawnee. Citizen Potawatomi Gift Shop, also located inside the supermarket, displays Native American gifts, handcrafted beadwork, jewelry, clothing, feather work, flutes, books, art prints, and woolens. Fire Lake Golf Course, lists a snack bar, restaurant, and golf shop among its facilities.

Media and Communications. Radio station KGFF AM 1450 broadcasts from the Fire Lake Discount Foods Supermarket. *How Ni Kan*, the tribal news publication, informs members about the delivery of services, and about accomplishments by tribal members and the Nation itself.

Tourism and Recreation. Fire Lake Casino *(see Gaming above)* offers bingo, gaming machines, tournament blackjack, and off-track betting, as well as special events such as boxing and live musical entertainment. Fire Lake Golf Course ranks among Oklahoma's outstanding daily fee golf courses. The course has water features, such as ponds or a stream, on most holes. The average green approximates 8,000 square feet. The course's list of services comprises a putting green, driving range, chipping green, snack bar, restaurant, and golf shop. Fire Lake Mini-Putt is a golf-related seasonal business.

INFRASTRUCTURE

Transportation. Shawnee, the business center adjacent to the reservation area, is approximately 50 miles from Oklahoma City and is located on U.S. I-40. U.S. Highways 9, 18, and 177 also traverse tribal land. Motor freight carrier service (trucking companies, UPS, and FedEx) is available, and there are railway connections to Shawnee. The Will Rogers World Airport is located in Oklahoma City; Shawnee has its own municipal airport.

COMMUNITY FACILITIES AND SERVICES

The CPN's catalog of community facilities includes the Child Care Development Center, the Fire Lake Fitness Center, an air-conditioned reunion building, streets, and camp sites at the powwow grounds; the Round House; and a tribal administration center. Plans for a new culture heritage center and a youth center have been funded.

The CPN provides a wide variety of services to its members and other Native Americans in its service delivery area. Activities range from medical assistance for senior members, scholarships for financially challenged students, genealogical and enrollment assistance to tribal families and their members, to sponsoring recreational, sports, and economic development activities. Major initiatives continue to include housing, health care, child care, employment and training, wellness and community, and family services. The CPN Employment and Training staff consists of counselors with the following focus areas: employment, employment and development, education, adult basic education, and social services in a limited service area.

The Nation is in the design phase of building a Potawatomi Cultural Heritage Center, to be constructed on the former site of the Potawatomi Tribal Police and Administration Building. Grants have been awarded from HUD, and monies have been appropriated from tribal resources to complete the project. Target dates for completion are set for June 2005.

Education. There are no BIA schools located on the reservation. In 1997 the CPN and St. Gregory's University drew upon a common history and vision for the future to form an educational, spiritual, and technological alliance. This partnership is called Nishwamen, which means, "we are working together." Nishwamen joins the Nation and the university together in a series of initiatives to assist students of all ages with scholarship awards. St. Gregory's permanently endowed 10 full scholarships from a $1 million contribution.

The child care development center, a two-star facility, is the largest in Pottawatomie County. Licensed by the Oklahoma Department of Human Services, the child care program is available to the community at large. The child care center offers programs in music, reading, tutoring, and computers. The CPN after-school program uses several of the child care facilities.

Scheduled for a June 2005 debut is a computerized language lab to help carry on and maintain the Potawatomi tongue. Internet connections will permit members to use the lab remotely.

Health Care. The CPN Health Clinic opened in 1996. It provides services to tribal members and other Native Americans who live in and around Shawnee. It was renovated in 2000 and is approximately 23,000 square feet. When fully staffed, the health services program employs or contracts with 85 full-time equivalents and has a medical staff of 8 full-time and 2 part-time providers. The health complex currently offers services such as contract health, public health nurses, community health representatives, audiology, nutrition, dental, x-ray, laboratory, and pharmacy services. Also included are behavioral health services, Soaring Eagles Mentoring Program, substance abuse prevention, youth council, and the first offender juvenile program.

Practitioners and counselors recorded a total of 62,075 visits during FY 2004. The pharmacy, which provides prescription drugs to eligible Native Americans in the service area and to tribal elders who live anywhere in the United States, experi-

TRI-OK-011 Firelake Convenience Store on left, Gaming facility on right (background), owned by citizen Potowatomi Nation, Shawnee, OK

TRI-OK-011

enced 36,316 pharmacy visits in the same time period. The nearest U.S. Public Health Services Indian Hospital is located at the Chickasaw Nation in Ada, Oklahoma, approximately 60 miles from the CPN administrative headquarters. The CPN health clinic serves CPN members and other Native Americans in the area. Its pharmacy fills prescriptions for clients in the service area and to tribal elders within the United States. The CPN Health Aid Foundation helps tribal members purchase needed medical aids, such as eyeglasses, hearing aids, mobility devices, sleep apnea CPAP machines, and other devices.

Late in 2003, the health services opened the Fire Lake Wellness Center (FWC) next to the clinic. Offering prevention and therapy to enhance members' health, the FWC's services include physical therapy, hydrotherapy, and cardiovascular rehabilitation, as well as walking, aerobic and isometric exercises. Older members of the tribe can socialize and have a midday meal as part of the Title VI Elders Program. Fitness and diabetes services occupy other parts of the center. Since October 2003, the FWC has sponsored numerous programs, resulting in the enrollment of over 3,029 members who logged approximately 28,500 visits to the facility, according to the tribe. Aerobics and water aerobics classes, cardio-yoga instruction, and stretching and flexibility exercises have increased the list of available activities.

Clients in the Shawnee area and in Oklahoma City come to the WIC program office in the Fire Lake Discount Foods building for information on nutrition and help in buying food.

Substance abuse prevention programs in schools are supervised by Community and Family Services. The agency also manages a program to treat youths arrested for nonviolent or alcohol-related offenses. Indian child welfare follows court cases and delivers foster care, prevention support, and crisis intervention.

All Native Americans 55 and older who live in the CPN jurisdiction are encouraged to participate in the Title VI program. It provides a meal at noon Monday through Friday, bingo four times a week, bowling once a week, and exercise three times a week (group chair exercise). Each day, the program offers dominoes, cable TV, and access to exercise equipment. Each Friday night, the elders enjoy a country/western dance with a live band. Once a month, the CPN Clinic comes to the elders, providing a health screening and nutrition information. Home deliveries are taken to homebound elders to ensure them a nutritious meal each day. Above all, the elders have a chance to come to the Title VI site in the new CPN Wellness Center to visit with other elders and tribal employees. This keeps them active and ensures them close family-like ties. The Title VI program is funded by an Administration on Aging grant.

The Nation's health aids foundation helps tribal members purchase needed medical aids such as eyeglasses, hearing aids, mobility devices, sleep apnea CPAP machines, and other devices. A WIC program provides nutrition information and food purchase assistance to clients in the Shawnee area and in Oklahoma City. The WIC office is in the Fire Lake Discount Foods building. The community and family services department administers several school-based substance abuse prevention programs as well as a treatment program for juveniles who have been arrested for nonviolent or alcohol-related offenses. Indian child welfare monitors court cases and provides foster care, prevention services, and crisis intervention.

Comanche

LOCATION AND LAND STATUS

The Comanche Tribe of Oklahoma owns 7,592.61 acres of noncontiguous, federal trust land spread across a six-county area of southwestern Oklahoma; these lands are owned jointly with the Kiowa and Apache tribes. The Comanche Nation Complex is located near Lawton, Oklahoma. Tribal facilities are located north of Lawton on U.S. 281. Oklahoma City is 87 miles northeast of Lawton via I-44. Wichita Falls, Texas, lies approximately 50 miles south of tribal headquarters near Lawton.

The 1867 Medicine Lodge Treaty established a reservation in the southwestern corner of Indian Territory for the Kiowa Apaches, Arapahos, Cheyennes, and Comanches. Allotment severely diminished the reservation during the early twentieth century. The joint tribal land base is supplemented by 274,312.53 allotted acres. In 1998 the Kiowa, Comanche, and Apache Intertribal Land Use Committee managed 5,449 acres of joint land.

PHYSICAL DESCRIPTION

The tribal trust area is characterized by plains and rolling grasslands. The Washita, Cache, and Brazos rivers drain the region.

CULTURE AND HISTORY

Members of the Comanche Tribe of Oklahoma are descendants of the Shoshonean-speaking Comanche people who occupied the high plains of present-day eastern Colorado, southern Kansas, western Oklahoma, and northwestern Texas. The Comanches called themselves Numunu, meaning "the people." The name "Comanche" is a Spanish corruption of the Ute word for "enemy." The Comanches were Plains hunters who followed the great southern bison herd across the southern plains. Buffalo represented the centerpiece of Comanche life, providing meat, clothing, tools, weapons, and shelter. The arrival of the horse during the seventeenth century transformed them into fierce raiders. In addition, the tribe kept large herds and introduced horses to a number of neighboring tribes.

For a number of years, the Comanche were the dominant presence in present-day mid-western and southwestern United States and northern Mexico. Their territories included portions of Kansas, Oklahoma, Texas, New Mexico, and northern Mexico. Throughout the seventeenth and eighteenth centuries, Comanche war parties raided the pueblos and Spanish settlements of New Mexico and northern Mexico. The Comanches made peace with the Spanish during the 1780s after the death of their war chief, Cuerno Verde. However, the Mexican occupation of New Mexico meant an end to Comanche annuities and the resumption of raiding. The Comanches were generally friendly to Euro-Americans crossing the plains, but they were bitter enemies of the Texans who dispossessed them of their best hunting grounds. The Comanches signed the Medicine Lodge Treaty of 1867, which confined them to a reservation in southwestern Indian Terri-

Comanche Tribe of Oklahoma Reservation
Federally recognized tribe
Comanche
Caddo, Cotton, Comanche, Tillman, Stephens, and Jefferson counties, Oklahoma

Comanche Tribe of Oklahoma
P.O. Box 908
Lawton, OK 73502
580-492-4988
580-492-3796 Fax
comanchenation.com

Comanche

Total area-jointly held
(BIA realty, 2004)
189,262.69 acres

Federal trust-jointly held
(BIA realty, 2004)
1 acre

Tribally owned-jointly held
(BIA realty, 2004)
3,300.85 acres

Individually owned-jointly held
(BIA realty, 2004)
185,960.84 acres

Total enrollment
(BIA labor report, 2001)
9,580

Total enrollment
(Tribal source, 2004)
1,801

Total labor force 2000 census
4,849

Total labor force
(BIA labor report, 2001)
5,604

High school graduate or higher
2000 census
74.6%

Bachelor's degree or higher
2000 census
15.7%

Unemployment rate 2000 census
7.9%

Unemployment rate
(BIA labor report, 2001)
75%

Per capita income
(BIA labor report, 2001)
$4,682

tory along with their allies the Kiowa and Apache tribes. They were the fiercest of fighters and one of the last tribes to submit to the United States policy of reservations.

Some Comanches returned to the warpath due to poor conditions on the reservation, but they surrendered in 1875. Quanah Parker, the last Comanche war chief, rose to prominence as a reservation-era leader, serving his people as an adept cultural broker. Reservation years saw disease, privation, and an assault on the Comanche way of life by Indian Service authorities. The Jerome Agreement of 1891 opened the reservation for allotment, and most lands soon passed into non-Indian hands. The tribe incorporated as the Comanche Tribe of Oklahoma in 1972.

The Comanches have maintained many old ceremonies and their language, even in the face of forced acculturation. Language classes, cultural programs, and genealogical study contribute to this effort today. The Comanche Nation Language and Culture Preservation Committee oversees many of these activities. Comanches fought in World War II, Korea, and Vietnam. In July 1995, the Comanches officially opened their Comanche Veteran's Memorial in Lawton. Central to the memorial is a pair of flagpoles. One bears the flag of the United States, the other the flag of the Comanches. The flag of the Comanche Nation, dated to about 1991, celebrates their past status as the dominant tribe of the south-central United States. That flag is divided vertically with blue at the viewer's left and red at the right. The seal on the flag is a Comanche shield divided roughly in half. The left portion is blue and has an uneven edge; the right portion is yellow and features a red image of a Comanche warrior on horseback, in the style that was used when images were drawn on Comanche tepees or actual shields. The Comanches display their seal and flag increasingly. In April 1995, the Comanches became one of the first Indian nations to issue automobile license plates for vehicles registered to tribal members. The central design element of the new plates is the seal of the Comanche Nation. A slightly modified version of the flag flies at Flag Plaza in Oklahoma City.

GOVERNMENT

The Comanche Tribe of Oklahoma adopted a constitution and bylaws in 1967 and amended them in May 1976. The Comanche Tribe is not organized under the Oklahoma Indian Welfare Act of 1936.

The Comanches are governed by the Comanche Tribal General Council and Comanche Business Committee. The tribal chairman, a vice-chairman, a secretary-treasurer, and three committeemen are elected by the tribal council, and these officers serve in the same capacity on the tribal business committee. Members serve three-year terms, with elections occurring annually. Tribal officials also include four tribal business committeemen and a tribal administrator.

Amendments passed in May 1976 stipulated that the tribal council would consist of all members age 18 or older and that an annual council meeting will be held each year in April. They also specified that the authority of the Comanche Tribal Council includes, among other actions, executing leases; selecting and authorizing tribal delegations to transact business on the tribe's behalf; developing the tribal annual budget; and overseeing existing programs. The tribal council officers prepare the annual budget, with each council member having the right to approve or disapprove each line item at the annual general council meeting. Approximately one month later the budget is put to the ballot. Elected officials and members of the business committee are also nominated at that meeting. Six hundred and forty-three tribe members attended the 2004 General Council Meeting.

The tribal business committee manages, among other issues, gaming, the tribal funeral home, the Early Childhood Development Center, vehicle purchases, dump cleanup projects, and solid waste management; it also appoints the election board and provides for tax audits.

The Comanche Tribe of Oklahoma governmental divisions include the election board, enrollment, environmental programs, firefighters, higher education, housing authority, Indian child welfare, law enforcement, public information, and the tax commission. It also provides for a Children's Court through the Indian child welfare program.

In 2004 the election board installed electronic voting machines for tribal council meetings as well as primary and runoff elections.

ECONOMY

The tribe's economy is based predominantly in gaming, leasing mineral land, and farming. In 2004 the tribal council voted to submit a $10 million budget for tribal approval. Gaming provided almost 85 percent of the tribal revenues in 2004; taxes provided about 11 percent of the revenue, with the rest coming from 20 percent funds. The Kiowa, Comanche, and Apache operating budget accounted for almost $300,000 of the budget. Many tribe members work in farming and as professionals in the surrounding area. Taxes on oil and gas, cigarettes and other tobacco products, vehicle registration, motor fuel, fireworks, bingo, sales, and watercraft are used for burial assistance, law enforcement, complex operations, elections, tribal community centers, social services, emergency assistance, audit, Comanche language programs, and the Buffalo Project.

Economic Development Projects. In 2004 the tribe authorized voting for a budget of $1 million for economic development and land acquisition.

Agriculture and Livestock. The Comanche, Apache, and Kiowa tribes lease land to non-Indians for cattle grazing and agriculture.

Gaming. The Comanche Tribe of Oklahoma owns four casinos, with the tribal chairman serving as tribal management for the two larger ones. Comanche Nation Casino, located in Lawton, features 296 slots/VLTs, off-track betting, blackjack, and 844 bingo seats, a gift shop, a smoke shop, and a restaurant. It employs 176 people, including 10 gaming property managers. The second largest is Comanche Red River Casino, with 7 gaming property managers; Red River is located in Devol, and features blackjack and 682 slots/VLTs. Comanche Spur, a combination convenience store, smoke shop, and casino in Elgin, has 77 slots/VLTs and 2 gaming property managers. The Comanche Star is the tribe's newest casino. Located east of Walters, it features slot machines, a snack shop, and a smoke shop. Gaming funds account for almost 85 percent of the tribal budget, including educational programs, housing, enrollment, tribal court, the Comanche Nation Fair, the community activities fund, COLA, the museum board, tribal employment supplemental, construction on community buildings, and many other services.

Real Estate/Commercial Development. Leasing land mineral rights provides a source of income for the tribe.

Services and Retail. The Comanche Spur and Comanche Star casinos incorporate retail operations with their gaming. *(See Gaming above for more information.)*

Media and Communications. The Comanche Tribe's official newspaper *The Comanche Nation News* is published bimonthly. With a staff of three, it is funded by advertising and donations. In 2004 it also received $160,000 from the tribe. The newsletter publishes the general council and business committee meeting minutes, as well as other articles of interest to the Comanche Tribe. Its previous names were *The Comanche Nation Newsletter* and *The Comanche News*.

Tourism and Recreation. The Comanche Nation Visitors Center features a weekly outdoor market as well as the Comanche Gallery of Art, where tribe members' artwork can be viewed and purchased. It is open six days a week. A tribal museum is in the blueprint stages, and it is under grant funding. The location has not been determined. The tribe also holds an annual tribal fair.

The Comanche Nation Waterpark features many water rides, a volleyball court, and an arcade. The scenic Wichita Mountains are located approximately 30 miles west of Lawton. Also located in the tribal area are the American Indian Hall of Fame and Indian City USA.

INFRASTRUCTURE
The Comanche Nation Complex is located north of Lawton, Oklahoma, on U.S. 281. I-44 connects Lawton with Oklahoma City, 87 miles northeast, and beyond. Commercial and private air facilities are located in the Oklahoma City metropolitan area. Tribal council general meetings are held there. Trucking companies and express package carriers serve the tribal area. The CRI&P railway serves Anadarko, 40 miles north of Lawton via U.S. 281. The Comanche Business Committee oversees road construction on tribal land.

Electricity. Nontribal sources provide electricity.

Fuel. Nontribal sources provide gas.

Water Supply. Nontribal sources provide water and wastewater treatment services.

Telecommunication. Nontribal sources provide telephone service.

COMMUNITY FACILITIES AND SERVICES
The tribe operates community centers in Walters, Cache, and Apache, Oklahoma. The Comanche Nation Princess Coronation and Powwow was held at the Comanche Community Center in Apache in 2004. The Comanche Tribe of Oklahoma's budget of almost $11 million allows the tribe to provide many other community services to members. These include burial assistance, a caregivers program, community health representatives, diabetes awareness, the Comanche nutrition elder center, elder payments, Comanche language classes, emergency assistance, food distribution, a funeral home (the only tribally owned funeral home in the United States), the Ona program (which promotes healthy families), home improvement, an Indian child welfare program, a summer youth program, counseling, New Pathways (an alcohol and drug treatment facility), and Hope House for people experiencing family violence.

Committees such as the injury prevention committee also contribute to the welfare of the Comanche people, with bike rodeos, car seat classes, and other events. The tribal housing authority provides low-rent student housing, mutual help, lease purchases, down payment and closing cost grants, loans, an elderly program, and many other services.

The Numunu Turetu early childhood development center provides child care for children from the age of six months through five years. It accepts subsidy payments from the Comanche Nation Child Care Program, Department of Human Services, and other tribal child care programs. Enrollment is not restricted to Comanche families. Comanche programs for youth include after-school programs, as well as programs for summer and school breaks. Bike rodeos, a children's camp, and basketball games are among the many activities.

Public Safety. The Comanche Nation firefighting program is sponsored by the BIA Anadarko Agency. It has increased its proficiency and it's rating. The program covers nine counties of trust lands and assists other fire departments nationwide. A new firehouse was planned for 2005. In 2004 the Comanche Nation Police Department became the first tribal department in Oklahoma to be accredited by the state.

Education. Most tribal members send their children to public schools in the tribal area, although a few students attend Riverside Indian School, which is available to any Native American. In 2004 the Comanche Language Youth Program was producing a CD designed to familiarize children and infants with the inventory of sounds in the Comanche language. This was intended to facilitate the learning of the Comanche language. The Comanche Office of Higher Education visits local schools to promote tribal education and to provide information to high school youth and staff about college preparation, standardized testing and waivers, Comanche National College, funding opportunities available, and adult vocational training. It also provides scholarship grants to post secondary institutions. The higher education office prepares Native youth to achieve their future educational goals.

The Comanche Nation College, located in Lawton, was officially established by tribal charter on August 3, 2002, by the Comanche Nation Chairman and Business Committee. The college's purpose is to provide educational opportunities for Comanche tribal members, members of other tribal nations, and others to learn the necessary knowledge and skills to be successful in a multicultural society. The basis for teaching and learning is Comanche centered. The college also offers interactive distance learning classes brought in over the ITV network from Cameron University. Most of the adjunct professors are Comanche tribal members.

The Comanche Nation Workforce Investment Act provides education and training opportunities to allow Native Americans to enter the labor force. Job related assistance is also offered.

Health Care. Tribal members receive health care from Indian Health Service facilities in Anadarko and hospitals in Lawton. Lawton Indian Hospital has 45 beds and 16 physicians. Inpatient care includes general surgery, obstetrics and gynecology, internal medicine, and pediatrics. Outpatient services span a range of fields, including medicine, dentistry, pharmacy, and laboratory testing. The staff also includes a community health staff of nurses, educators, social workers, and sanitarians. The community health representative program offers transportation to health facilities for disadvantaged Native Americans. It also allows patients to check out medical items such as wheelchairs, toilet aids, and walking aids. Prescription assistance, injury prevention, and emergency services also provide assistance and training for tribe members.

In 2002 tribal young people began working with semi-wild mustangs in a program created to fight drug and alcohol abuse. Participants train, ride, and care for the horses as a way of developing trust and learning pride in their heritage. HUD provided a $332,000 grant to fund the program.

Comanche

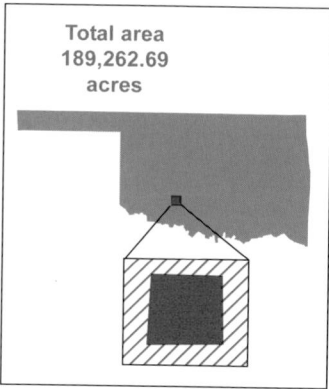

Total area
189,262.69
acres

ENVIRONMENTAL CONCERNS
Contamination of tribal land is a primary environmental concern for the Comanche Tribe. Since the Ft. Sill Indian School Facility was closed in 1980, the Kiowa, Comanche, and Apache Intertribal Land Use Committee has been unable to lease the land because of contamination. In 1998 the EPA selected a 30-acre site on the school grounds for a Brownfields Assessment Demonstration Pilot. The intention was to plan cleanup and development of the site, which in turn would stimulate the economy and return the site to productive use. The Tribal Office of Environmental Programs (OEP) monitors the groundwater, to make sure it is safe to drink and able to support its wildlife. In 2004 the OEP was also in the process of establishing air monitors on reservation lands.

Creek

Creek (Muscogee) Nation
Federal reservation
Creek
Creek, Hughes (Tukvpvtce),
Mayes, McIntosh, Muscogee,
Okfuskee, Okmulgee, Rogers,
Seminole, Tulsa, and Wagoner
counties, Oklahoma

Creek Nation of Oklahoma
P.O. Box 580
Okmulgee, OK 74447
918-756-8700
800-482-1979
918-756-2284 Fax
muscogeenation-nsn.gov

Total area *(BIA realty, 2004)*
133,811.24 acres

Federal trust *(BIA realty, 2004)*
3.2 acres

Tribally owned *(BIA realty, 2004)*
6,387.05 acres

Individually owned
(BIA realty, 2004)
127,420.99 acres

Population *2000 census*
704,565

Tribal enrollment
(BIA labor report, 2001)
52,169

Total labor force *2000 census*
352,853

Total labor force
(BIA labor report, 2001)
42,848

High school graduate or higher
2000 census
83.4%

Bachelor's degree or higher
2000 census
24.2%

Unemployment rate *2000 census*
4.9%

Unemployment rate *(BIA labor report, 2001)*
21%

Per capita income *2000 census*
$20,267

LOCATION AND LAND STATUS

The Muscogee (Creek) Nation, the third-largest federally recognized tribe in the United States, is a non-reservation tribe with a jurisdictional area extending across part or all of 11 counties in east-north central Oklahoma, including the City of Tulsa.

The Nation's capital is Okmulgee, which lies on U.S. 75 south of Tulsa and I-40. The tribe has approximately 6,220 acres under federal trust and over 1.9 million acres allotted to 12,029 tribal members. In 1832, the tribe was forced to accept a removal treaty, which the U.S. Army enforced in 1836?1837. As a result over 20,000 Muscogee people were relocated to a new "homeland" in Indian Territory, what is now the state of Oklahoma. The Dawes Act of 1887 and the subsequent Curtis Act of 1898 allowed the Native governments of the "Five Civilized Tribes" to be dismantled, and virtually all collectively held tribal lands were allotted.

CLIMATE

The elevation at Okmulgee, Oklahoma, is 715 feet above sea level. The year-round average daily high temperature is 73°F. The highest recorded temperature was 114°F. The year-round average daily low temperature is 49°F., the lowest temperature on record being -20°F. The area receives 39 inches of precipitation annually, with 6 inches falling as snow.

CULTURE AND HISTORY

The Muscogee Tribe descends from a Mississippian culture that spanned virtually the entire southeastern United States before 1500 AD. Prior to contact, the people lived a subsistence lifestyle in large, permanent, stockaded villages of earth lodge houses, raising small gardens. The villages were usually constructed surrounding a centrally located earthen temple and plaza area. Many smaller outlying villages were built nearby. Known by white settlers as one of Oklahoma's "Five Civilized Tribes," the Muscogee Creek's aboriginal homeland spanned the region that later became the states of Alabama, Georgia, Florida, and South Carolina. They speak a language of the Muscogean language family.

The modern Muscogee Nation was originally comprised of members from several tribes, a union that evolved into a highly sophisticated confederacy, with each tribe maintaining political autonomy and distinct land holdings. Within this confederacy, the language and culture of the founding Muscogee tribal towns remained predominant. First contact was made with Spaniard Hernando de Soto's exploratory journey into the interior of North America, an expedition that devastated local food supplies and brought epidemics of European diseases to the Creeks. Entire villages perished. By the 1600s, the British had established permanent colonies along the Eastern seaboard, and trade with the settlers developed into a flourishing economy for the Creeks, as they exchanged food items, pelts, baskets, and pottery for finished goods such as iron pots, steel knives, guns, and cotton cloth.

In 1715, the Yamassee War erupted against fraudulent British trade practices, including the capture and shipment of Indian slaves to work on sugar plantations in the Caribbean. The original Ocmulgee Town, located on Ochese Creek in what is now the State of Georgia, was burned to the ground. The Creeks withdrew to the Chattahoochee River, taking their Yuchi neighbors with them. These people become known as the Lower Creeks. The Upper Creeks were centered on the Coosa and Tallapoosa rivers to the northeast. As a way of decreasing hostilities, the Creeks entered into treaties with the British crown, and in 1773, they ceded much of their land to the British government. Despite the historical conflicts with England, during the Revolutionary War, many members of the Creek Nation sided with the British. Following the close of the war, in 1783, England returned control of Florida to Spain, and Spain ceded control of the Creek Territory to the new United States, bringing new waves of settlers into the area.

By the early nineteenth century, U.S. Indian policy began pressuring for the removal of the Muscogee and other southeastern tribes to areas west of the Mississippi River. The Muscogees gamely but futilely resisted removal and finally, in 1832, they exchanged the last of their ancestral homeland for new lands in Indian Territory. They were allocated 4,824 square miles of land. While a minority of the confederacy resettled on its own, the U.S. Army forcibly removed the majority of the Muscogee people between 1836 and 1837. The Nation, which had been categorized as the Lower and Upper Muscogee tribes, soon reestablished its farms and plantations and even its ancient towns in its new homeland. Before long, the Muscogees had formed a National Council and become relatively prosperous. Both their prosperity and peace were disrupted by the Civil War when a Confederate force attacked a large group of neutral Muscogees within their territory. Eventually, tribal members fought on both sides of the conflict. The Reconstruction Treaty of 1866 called for the cession of nearly half of the Muscogee domain, approximately 3.2 million acres. The following year the Nation adopted a written constitution and established a new capital on the Deep Fork of the Canadian River at a place they named Okmulgee, reminiscent of their original Creek capital in Georgia. The 1887 Allotment Act, coupled with the 1898 Curtis Act, authorized dissolution of the Muscogee national government and the allotment of nearly all of their collectively held lands. In 1907, Indian lands became part of the new State of Oklahoma. The Muscogees determinedly resisted these attempts by the federal government to terminate their nation and culture, and throughout this entire dark period the tribe was able to maintain its cultural identity, along with a cursory form of tribal leadership. Despite their vigilance and determination, however, the Muscogees subsequently witnessed the removal of approximately $50 billion in oil from their territory by outsiders who had fraudulently secured lease or ownership of allotted lands during this period.

In 1971, for the first time since statehood, the tribe was able to freely elect a principal chief without U.S. presidential approval. It was also during this decade that the tribe adopted a new constitution, revitalized its National Council, and made strides toward political strength and economic development. During the 1980s, Muscogee leadership built a tribal complex and created a set of social services that the BIA has referred to as "the best in the nation." These include an excellent health care system, funds for heating oil, education, and food, and the creation of numerous jobs through tribal government enterprises such as a farm and bingo halls.

GOVERNMENT

The Muscogee (Creek) Nation is organized under the Oklahoma Indian Welfare Act of 1936, with a constitution that was ratified on October 6, 1979. The constitution recognizes chartered Creek tribal towns as local governing units within the sovereign national system. The Nation is governed by a 26-member tribal council composed of representatives elected from eight districts, led by a principal chief. Elections for principal chief and second chief are held every four years. The principal chief selects an executive director, for approval by the National Council. The executive director oversees the office of administration, providing comprehensive management, policy development, administrative support, and program coordination to all programs and offices of the Muscogee (Creek) Nation.

During the 1980s, the federal courts upheld the tribe's right to maintain a court system and to levy taxes. They also reaffirmed the tribe's freedom from state jurisdiction. Under PL-638, the tribe contracts with the BIA to administer key programs and services.

The government of the Muscogee (Creek) Nation (MCN) is divided into three branches: executive, legislative, and judicial. The executive branch administers the office of administration, including the treasury and the attorney general, all independent agencies, and the human development, community services, and tribal affairs divisions, as well as personnel services. Independent agencies operated by the executive branch include the Creek citizenship office, voter registrations, tax commission and tag office, office of public gaming, health administration, and the housing authority. The division of human development includes a cultural preservation program, employment and training administration, Eufaula dormitory services, a Head Start program, higher education, and the Johnson O'Malley Program. The division of community services houses all the various tribal social services, specialized services for children and family, community development, a food distribution program, and the Office of Child Care. The tribal affairs division includes the offices of Indian reservation roads planning, tribal planning, tribal construction, federal roads, driveway construction, mass transit system, and realty and trust.

The legislative branch includes the National Council, tribal council representatives, and the health system board. The judicial branch encompasses the entire the tribal court system, which consists of a supreme court, a chief justice, and the district court judges. The Nation has resurrected the practice of referring to Indian police officers as Lighthorsemen, a historic body of tribal officers providing law enforcement services prior to statehood. Today, they are hired and governed by the tribally affiliated Lighthorse Commission.

The Muscogee (Creek) Nation Housing Authority operates a home ownership program; modernization; an affordable housing program that includes a total of over 300 low-cost rental duplexes in Okmulgee, Okemah, Checotah, and Eufaula; mortgage assistance; and resident services.

BUSINESS CORPORATION

The Nation has two nongaming business divisions created to strengthen business diversification. The two divisions are Muscogee Nation Business Enterprise (MNBE) and the Muscogee (Creek) Nation Trade and Commerce Authority.

The MNBE is a tribal-owned company certified by the Small Business Administration, which the tribal council created in 1999. MNBE became certified as a HUB Zone and 8(a) company in 2002. Currently, MNBE specializes in technology services, construction services, fire and alarm security systems, professional services, and medical systems. MNBE has current contracts with the U.S. Air Force, the Department of Energy, and Verizon Federal, and it targets federal agencies, Indian tribes, and Fortune 1000 corporations throughout the United States. MNBE headquarters is in Okmulgee, Oklahoma, with project offices in Ft. Worth and Amarillo, Texas; Altus Air Force Base, Oklahoma; and Washington, D.C.

The mission of the Muscogee (Creek) Nation Trade and Commerce Authority is to provide the tribe opportunities to invest in needed health, educational, and other services that provide profitable business opportunities and land acquisitions to be placed into trust. The Tribal Trade and Commerce Authority has 64 employees.

In January 2003, the Tribal Trade and Commerce Authority took over management of all three travel plazas located in Okmulgee, Muskogee, and Cromwell. The MCN Trade and Commerce Authority began a spring water bottled water company in April 2004. Currently the MCN labels are printed on water bottled in El Reno, Oklahoma. Once the grant is approved, MCN will build a water-bottling facility.

The Muscogee Document Imaging Company (MDCI) started May 14, 2004, under the Trade and Commerce Authority, provides document storage and imaging services. The MDCI is certified in the State of California as a Minority Business Enterprise and is a certified HUB Zone Small Business Concern. A Small Business Administration 8(a) is pending certification. With these certifications, MDIC has secured federal contracts from the U.S. Army at Fort Sill Oklahoma, as well as a number of federal contracts pending notification of award. The company provides courier service (within a 50-mile radius) from the customer's facilities. Documents can be stored, digitally imaged, or both in a climate-controlled environment. MDIC stores documents for at least seven years.

The farm authority began in May 2004. The farm authority is responsible for keeping up farmlands, fencing, maintaining livestock, and inventorying equipment. The farm authority has also maintained and began harvesting of the pecan field located on the outskirts of Okmulgee, Oklahoma.

ECONOMY

Economically, the Nation fares reasonably well, with a diversified tribal economy. The annual tribal operating budget for fiscal year 2004 exceeded $94 million. Many tribal members now work for the tribal government, in one of its many programs, services, or enterprises, while others find nontribal employment in Tulsa and other regional municipalities.

Government as Employer. Tribal government is the largest single tribal employment source within the Muscogee (Creek) Nation, employing over 550 people in 2004.

Economic Development Projects. A mass transit system is under development, which will be available to all tribal members throughout the jurisdictional area.

Cultural tourism is encouraged through the Creek Council House Museum, which is operated as a private, nonprofit joint venture with the City of Okmulgee and the Creek Indian Memorial Association. The memorial association accepts private donor memberships.

Agriculture and Livestock. About 600 acres of Muskogee (Creek) Nation land are under cultivation, primarily in alfalfa. Additionally, there are approximately 70 head of cattle and a herd of 12 buffalo on 1,970 acres of tribal grazing lands in Hanna, Oklahoma.

Gaming. Bingo, a class II gaming operation, serves as one of the most significant sources of employment and revenue within the Muscogee (Creek) Nation. The Nation operates four bingo halls, all operating under the name Creek Nation Casino, with locations in Tulsa, Okmulgee, Muskogee, and Okemah. The 22,500-square-foot Muskogee location features 508 slot machines in addition to the 700-seat bingo hall. At the Creek Nation Travel Plaza, located at the junction of Highway 75

Creek

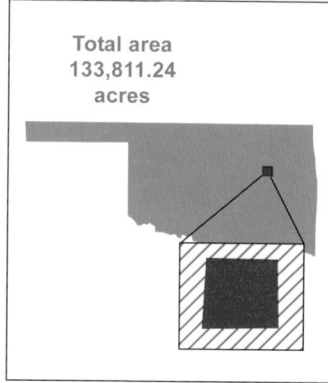

Total area
133,811.24
acres

Creek

ENVIRONMENTAL CONCERNS

In 2004, the Nation was developing a flood plain management plan. They are also concerned about abandoned oil wells scattered throughout the jurisdictional area.

and the 56 Loop in Okmulgee, the Nation maintains 325 slot machines and a restaurant. The Indian Community Casino, in Eufaula, has 110 video slot machines. Together, these facilities employ a total of 20 people, most of them tribal members.

Real Estate/Commercial Development. In the past year, the Nation built the MCN Housing Authority, a 49,356-square-foot building in Muskogee, Oklahoma, on 61.35 acres. The food distribution building, which is 18,418 square feet, was also recently completed. The elder housing complex was completed with 16 units at 1,240 square feet each, and it is fully occupied. The Elder Housing Community Building was also completed with 7,005 square feet, which gives residents an opportunity to socialize during activities and to enjoy meals together. These new buildings are located on 41.9 acres near the tribal complex.

Services and Retail. In addition to the retail opportunities available at the gaming facilities, the Travel Plaza, and the museum, there are a number of tribally licensed smoke shops, each owned and operated by individual tribal members. There are also two gift shops that offer a wide range of items including handmade Native crafts.

Media and Communications. The Nation's Communication Department publishes a plethora of informational brochures regarding programs, services, community and special events, and its enterprises. The *Muscogee Nation News* is the comprehensive official vehicle that the tribe publishes monthly for mass distribution. The Nation also operates a weekly radio show; provides a variety of audio and visual services, desktop publishing and print media, and digital photography; and maintains a tribal website for online cultural information and community access.

Tourism and Recreation. Okmulgee lies within 10 miles of the Eufaula Reservoir and within 5 miles of the Okmulgee State Game Management Area and the Okmulgee State Park. All of these locations have hiking trails and other amenities for visitors. The gaming facilities and Council House Museum serve as the primary year-round draw for visitors; however, the Nation hosts a number of special events and ceremonies, including traditional ceremonial stomp dances that double as a time of cleansing and purification; the Creek Nation Festival and Rodeo held during the third weekend of June; and the Eufaula Powwow held over Labor Day Weekend.

INFRASTRUCTURE

State Highway 75 provides direct access to Okmulgee from Tulsa and points beyond. The 11-county Muskogee (Creek) Nation jurisdictional area includes approximately 7,400 miles of county-maintained roads and 1,143 miles of state or federal highways.

Electricity. Regional utility companies provide electricity.

Fuel. Regional utilities in the area provide gas services.

Water Supply. Municipal systems within the developed areas provide water and sewer service; occasional wells and septic systems handle the need in rural areas.

Transportation. Commercial air service is available at the Tulsa International Airport about 40 miles to the north, as well as the Okmulgee Municipal Airport. Commercial bus, truck, and rail lines all serve the Okmulgee area. The division of tribal affairs, which operates the Indian reservation roads and the federal roads programs, provides transportation planning for the Nation. The division has completed a transportation im-

provement plan, publishing an updated priority list of projects every three years.

Telecommunication. Qwest provides local telephone service.

COMMUNITY FACILITIES AND SERVICES

The tribe maintains a total of 23 community centers within the 11-county jurisdictional area, along with various ceremonial stomp grounds, recreational ball fields, and rodeo arenas. Tribal offices are in a new building fashioned after the circular, earth-embanked earth lodge at the Ocmulgee National Monument in Georgia. The Nation's Creek Council House Museum, in Okmulgee, features original 1878 architecture. The building, placed on the National Register of Historic Sites in 1989, houses the tribal archives, including permanent art collections and photographic exhibits, traveling collections, and the Red Stick Galley, along with a gift shop that offers handcrafted jewelry, beadwork, basketry, and pottery.

The Nation offers many social services programs. The hardship program helps Creek individuals who have an unplanned break in income and a significant need for financial assistance. The tribal energy program provides assistance to enrolled tribal citizens who are 55 years or older and/or disabled. The natural disaster program assists tribal members who have experienced a fire, flood, tornado, etc. The medical travel program helps parents with gas, food, and/or lodging when children are in need of extensive medical treatment. There is also a tribal burial program and an assistance program that provides small window units for Creek citizens 60 years or older or who have a medical need and do not have any form of air conditioning.

The mission of the Nation's Children and Family Services Administration (CFSA) is to preserve, protect, and strengthen the tribe's children and families. CFSA programs strive to empower individuals and families, cultivate nurturing home environments, and educate individuals, families, and communities. Some of the services include Indian child welfare, children services program, child abuse initiative program, alternative placement, family violence, special needs adoption program, child care assistance, and youth and family program.

Education. Students primarily attend local public schools, vocational schools, and community colleges. The Muscogee do, however, own and operate the Eufaula Indian Boarding School. The tribe's education department manages a higher education scholarship program.

The Muscogee (Creek) language preservation program publishes the Speakers of the Earth Language Series. The University of Nebraska Press has also published a Creek/Muscogee dictionary. Both are available to schools for use in formal learning situations and to members of the general public. The tribe also maintains an online language archive for serious language students.

Health Care. The tribe's health care system consists of the Creek Nation Community Hospital and the clinics in Eufaula, Okmulgee, Okemah, and Sapulpa. A new facility in being built in Coweta. Services include: behavioral health, vocational rehabilitation, elderly nutrition, WIC, and other contract health services, such as dental and vision care, a comprehensive diabetes program, and a caregiver program. The Muscogee (Creek) Nation has entered into an agreement with USDA for the distribution of commodities to eligible Indian households. The goal is to provide food to low-income households as an alternative to food stamps.

Delaware

LOCATION AND LAND STATUS
The Delaware Tribe jointly owns 487 acres of trust land in Caddo County, Oklahoma, with the Wichita and Caddo tribes. The Wichita Agency, established in 1859, served as the reservation for Caddo, Wichita, and Delaware Indians. Tribal headquarters are located two miles north of Andarko on U.S. 281. The Wichita Agency, established in 1859, served as the reservation for the three tribes. Much of the land therein was allotted following the Jerome Agreement of 1890. Today, 80,343 acres of individual allotments supplement the joint tribal land base.

CULTURE AND HISTORY
The Delaware Tribe of Oklahoma descends from the eastern woodland Delaware Indians, an Algonquian-speaking tribe of the Delaware and Hudson river valleys in what is now southern New York and northern New Jersey. They called themselves Lenni Lenape, or, "original people," and were called "grandfathers" by other tribes, most likely because of their longtime existence prior to European contact and for their reputation as peacekeepers.

The Delawares were forced into what is now Pennsylvania by waves of European immigrants. By the time of the American Revolution, the Delawares were residing as far west as present-day Ohio. American colonists referred to the Delawares as "friendly" Indians because of their cooperation in treaty negotiations; loyal to the fledgling United States, the Delawares served as scouts and soldiers.

One band of Delawares branched off in 1793 and settled in present-day Missouri. Referred to as the Absentee Delaware, this band became the ancestors of the modern Delaware Tribe of Oklahoma. The Absentee Delawares received a land grant from the Spanish government in 1820 and relocated to what is now East Texas. In 1854, they were driven off their land by Texas settlers. In 1859, several Delaware families settled at the Wichita Agency in Indian Territory (Oklahoma). The Wichita Agency was largely allotted following the Jerome Agreement of 1890, and the Absentee Delawares were allotted as either Caddo or Wichita. Thus, organization under the 1934 Indian Reorganization Act presented a struggle for the tribe since members were not designated as Delawares on any census between 1895 and 1930. They eventually organized under the Oklahoma Indian Welfare Act in 1936. Thereafter, the tribe worked to rebuild after centuries of cultural dislocation and forced relocation. During the 1950s, the tribe filed joint claims with the Indian Claims Commission and received a small settlement in 1977. The tribe also gained joint ownership of trust lands with the Caddo and Wichita tribes.

The tribe also participates in the Four Tribes Consortium of Oklahoma, an employment and training program designed to provide tribal members in Caddo County with the skills, work experience, and support necessary to become employable.

GOVERNMENT
An executive committee, consisting of a president, a vice-president, a secretary, a treasurer, and two committee members, serves as the tribe's elected governing body. Members serve staggered four-year terms, with elections occurring biennially in June. The tribe adopted a constitution and bylaws in 1973.

The tribe, under PL-638, contracts with the BIA to administer key programs and services. The Delaware National Housing Authority provides local housing services. The child care bureau, a social and family services program, is dedicated to improving the quality and affordability of child care. Other offices include the Delaware Nation environmental department, transportation department, division on aging, community health, tax commission, business committees, and the family and social services department.

ECONOMY
The tribal economy continues to be centered on tribal governmental activities and federal funding for its programs. Gaming has provided a new source of revenue.

Agriculture and Livestock. Individual tribal members raise livestock and cultivate various crops.

Gaming. The Delaware Nation owns and operates the Gold River Bingo and Casino in Anadarko. This 7,000 square foot facility offers 315 slot machines and one restaurant.

Tourism and Recreation. The tribe operates a museum and archives and a tribal library at the tribal headquarters. The National Hall of Fame for American Indians is located just west of Anadarko on U.S. 62. Fort Cobb State Park and the Fort Cobb Reservoir are located less than 20 miles west of Anadarko, offering a plethora of camping and water sport recreation to tourists.

INFRASTRUCTURE
Electricity. Caddo Electric provides electricity.

Water Supply. Rural water services supply water to tribal members.

Transportation. Commercial and private air facilities and bus services are located in the Oklahoma City metropolitan area, 50 miles northeast of Anadarko. Trucking companies and express package carriers serve the tribal area.

COMMUNITY FACILITIES AND SERVICES
The tribe maintains a community center, the Delaware Community Building, as part of its facilities near Anadarko. Satellite offices are located in Oklahoma City and Anandarko. The Anandarko facility offers a vocational rehabilitation program. Additional services available to tribal members include the Delaware Nation Indian Child Welfare Program, senior programs, school incentive programs, and free language classes.

Education. Children attend Caddo County public schools. Vocational and technical courses are available through the Caddo-Kiowa Vocational Technical Center located in Fort Cobb, Oklahoma.

Health Care. Many tribal members receive health care services through the Indian Health Service Hospital in Anadarko, a new 20,000-square-foot facility that provides a range of outpatient services, dental care, and community outreach programs. Members are referred to the Lawton Indian Health Services Hospital, a full-service inpatient facility for more serious accidents or medical treatment.

ENVIRONMENTALCONCERNS
Air pollution from nearby cities is a concern being addressed by the Delaware Nation environmental department. This department also offers various regular and periodic programs for recycling, removing trash, and handling hazardous wastes in an effort to deal with extensive illegal dumping throughout reservation lands.

Delaware Reservation
Federal reservation
Delaware
Caddo County, Oklahoma

Delaware Nation
P.O. Box 825
Andarko, OK 73005
405-247-2448
405-247-9393 Fax

Total area *(Tribal source, 2004)*
487.14 acres

Federal trust lands *(TGIC, 1996)*
487.14 acres

Tribally owned lands *(TGIC, 1996)*
487.14 acres

Population
(OTSA Caddo-Wichita-Delaware)
2000 census
14,638

Tribal enrollment *(BIA, 2001)*
1,302

Total labor force *(BIA, 2001)*
236

Unemployment rate *(BIA, 2001)*
50%

Per capita income
(OTSA Caddo-Wichita-Delaware)
2000 census
$14,031

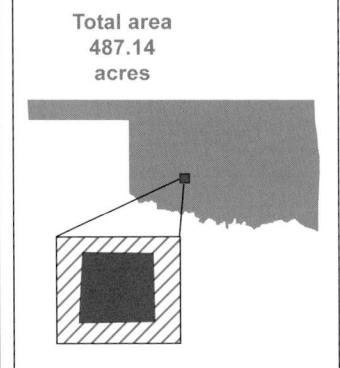

Total area
487.14
acres

Delaware

The Delaware Tribe
of Oklahoma
220 NW Virginia Ave.
Bartlesville, OK 74003
918-336-5272
918-336-5513 Fax
delawaretribeofindians.nsn.us

Population *2000 Census*
14,638

Total Labor Force *2000 Census*
4,849

High school graduate or higher
2000 Census
74.6%

Bachelor's degree of higher
2000 Census
15.7%

Unemployment rate *2000 Census*
7.9%

LOCATION AND LAND STATUS

The Delaware Tribe of Oklahoma, headquartered in the town of Bartlesville in northern Oklahoma, occupies a tenuous status in the early years of the 21st Century vis a vis other federally recognized tribes contained in this second edition of Tiller's Guide to Indian Country. With no trust land base for a federal reservation, the Delaware Tribe of Oklahoma owns in fee simple the properties identified below.

CULTURE AND HISTORY

See, the "Western Delaware Tribe of Oklahoma" in this section for an expanded treatment of the history and culture of the Delaware Indian people. The group presently headquartered in Bartlesville, Oklahoma, as the Delaware Tribe of Oklahoma is composed of the bulk of the Delaware Tribe that resided in Kansas in the 1850's. In 1867, the Delaware Tribe in Kansas entered into a treaty with the United States whereby the Delawares agreed to purchase land from tribes already relocated in present-day Oklahoma. Eventually, the Delawares selected and moved onto land previously granted to the Cherokee Tribe. These Delawares claim they remained, and remain today, a separate and distinct Delaware Tribe of Indians. The much larger Cherokee Nation of Oklahoma maintains the Kansas Delawares who moved among them gave up their independent tribal status and became members of the Cherokee Nation. In 1996, the U.S. Department of the Interior agreed with the Delawares and formally recognized them as the Delaware Tribe of Oklahoma with all the inherent sovereign powers of an Indian tribe. The Cherokee Tribe challenged this result in court, and on February 16, 2005 the United States Court of Appeals for the Tenth Circuit reaffirmed its earlier decision that the Delawares had merged into and become one with the Cherokee Nation. As of April 2005, the Bureau of Indian Affairs contemplates striking the Delaware Tribe from the list of federally recognized tribes to reflect the law as pronounced by the court. The Delawares insist that the last chapter has not been written as of the spring of 2005, and that their independent tribal status will yet be vindicated in the laws of the United States.

From its newly constructed headquarters in Bartlesville, the elected government of the Delaware Tribe (whether recognized by the U.S. or not in the inconsistency of the application and interpretation of the law) works to improve the lives of tribal members and preserve the Delaware culture. The tribe has petitioned for a tract of land in nearby Kansas to be taken into trust. The Delaware tribe also owns and operates the 7,000 square-foot Gold River Bingo and Casino in Bartlesville, with a restaurant, slot machines, and bingo hall.

The legal status of the Delaware Tribe of Oklahoma will almost certainly remain in flux until the federal law reflects the reality of this tribe that has endured since their ancestors entered into the very first Indian treaty with an American government in 1778.

Eastern Shawnee

Eastern Shawnee Reservation
Federal reservation
Shawnee
Newton County, Missouri
Ottawa County, Oklahoma

Eastern Shawnee Tribe
of Oklahoma
P.O. Box 350
127 W. Oneida
Seneca, MO 64865
918-666-2435
918-666-2186 Fax
easternshawnee.org

Total area *(BIA realty, 2004)*	1,195.09 acres
Total area *(Tribal source, 2004)*	554.21 acres
Tribally owned *BIA realty, 2004*	536.20 acres
Tribally owned *(Tribal source, 2004)*	300.02 acres
Individually owned *(BIA realty, 2004)*	658.89 acres
Allotted *(Tribal source, 2004)*	740.46 acres
Population *2000 census*	354
Tribal enrollment *(Tribal source, 2004)*	2,232
Total labor force *2000 census*	313
Total labor force *(Tribal source, 2004)*	250
High school graduate or higher *2000 census*	76.6%
Bachelor's degree or higher *2000 census*	6.3%
Unemployment rate *2000 census*	4.2%
Unemployment rate *(BIA labor report, 2001)*	73%
Per capita income *2000 census*	$14,861

LOCATION AND LAND STATUS

Eastern Shawnee tribal lands are located in far northeastern Oklahoma near the Missouri border. Most of these lands lie within Ottawa County, Oklahoma, except for one acre located in Seneca, Missouri, and four acres in Ft. Scott, Kansas. Tribal headquarters are located in West Seneca, Oklahoma. Oklahoma towns near tribal lands include Miami (approximately 20 miles west) and Wyandotte (5 miles west). Major cities near tribal lands include Joplin, Missouri (approximately 18 miles northeast), and Tulsa, Oklahoma (approximately 70 miles southwest.)

The Eastern Shawnee Tribe owns 254.19 noncontiguous acres of trust land spread across Ottawa County, Oklahoma. The tribe also maintains complete or partial ownership of other lands not yet in trust. The Shawnee Reservation was initially established by treaty on December 29, 1832.

CULTURE AND HISTORY

The Shawnees are an Algonquian tribe who controlled a vast swath of territory from Pennsylvania to the Southern Appalachians prior to the seventeenth century. The name "Shawnee" is derived from the Algonquian terms "Shawun" (South) and "Shawunogi" (Southerners). The Shawnees were village dwellers with a sophisticated material culture. They farmed, hunted, and maintained complex trade networks.

In 1669 the Shawnees were living in two groups located a considerable distance apart. Those living west of the Appalachians split from those further east. The westerners migrated south to present-day Tennessee near Cherokee territory, as well as into South Carolina. Beginning in 1690, the Shawnees entered a protracted conflict with English settlers and southern tribes. The Shawnees in Tennessee were driven northward into the Ohio Valley by the Cherokees. The Shawnees of South Carolina returned to Pennsylvania. During the French and Indian War, the Shawnees of Ohio engaged in constant conflict with British forces. The Shawnees of Pennsylvania remained neutral but joined the Ohio band in 1755. Following the American Revolution, the Shawnees allied with other mid-western tribes to prevent further Euro-American incursion into the Ohio Valley. Shawnee War Chief Bluejacket led 1,400 warriors in a siege of Fort Miami in 1793. During the early nineteenth century, Shawnee Chief Tecumseh attempted to forge a pan-tribal alliance in the Ohio and Mississippi river valleys. William Henry Harrison's American forces defeated the Shawnees at Tippecanoe in 1811. Those Shawnees remaining in Ohio signed a treaty in 1831 ceding their lands to the United States. In 1832 they were removed to a reservation in present-day Ottawa County, Oklahoma. These Shawnee refugees united with a small band of Senecas to form the United Nation of Senecas and Shawnees. They were widely referred to as the "Loyal Shawnees" because of their loyalty to the United States during the Civil War. Shawnee tribal lands were largely allotted during the early twentieth century. In 1934 the tribe reincorporated under the Oklahoma Indian Welfare Act as the Eastern Shawnee Tribe of Oklahoma; they adopted a constitution and bylaws in 1937.

An objective of the Eastern Shawnee Tribe is to improve the well-being of tribal members by investing gaming revenues into an array of social service programs. The tribe plans to expand its facilities in Seneca to house these programs.

GOVERNMENT

The principal governing body of the Eastern Shawnee Tribe is the general council, consisting of all enrolled members 18 years of age or older. A tribal business committee, composed of a second chief, a secretary, a treasurer, and three councilpersons, governs matters of tribal business. Business committee members are elected at-large by the general council to four-year terms. The chief is the chief executive officer of the tribe. The chief is elected to a four-year term. Elections are held annually on the first Saturday after Labor Day. The tribal government oversees housing, educational assistance, community services, child and family protection services, law enforcement, environmental concerns, employment assistance, communication, and social services.

The Eastern Shawnee Tribe adopted a constitution and by-laws in 1937 in accordance with the Indian Reorganization Act. A new constitution was ratified in April 1994.

ECONOMY

The reservation's economy is supported by federal funding for tribal programs and infrastructure, and by revenues from their gaming and other business enterprises.

Government as Employer. The tribal government employs approximately 250 persons.

Gaming. The tribe's first bingo hall was opened in 1985. A new bingo hall, Border Town Bingo and Casino, went into operation in 2002. This 57,000-square-foot facility employs 200 people and houses 500 video gaming machines, off-track

betting, a restaurant, a bar, and a gift shop. They offer paper-bingo in a bingo hall that seats about 700.

Real Estate/Commercial Development. The Eastern Shawnee Tribe is actively pursuing safe and healthy housing for low-income families. It established the Eastern Shawnee Tribal Housing Authority (ESTHA), a state agency designed to accomplish these goals by creating partnerships with other agencies and businesses. ESTHA has built 12 homes.

Services and Retail. The tribe owns and operates the Eastern Shawnee Travel Center in Wyandotte, Oklahoma (30-35 employees), the Best Western Inn in Ft. Scott (30-35 employees), Kansas, Eastern Shawnee Storage Units, and the Bordertown Bingo and Casino in Seneca, Missouri (200 employees). The tribe also owns majority shares in the Peoples State Bank in Seneca, Missouri (25 employees).

Tourism and Recreation. Tribal lands lie in close proximity to Lake O' the Cherokees, a popular outdoor recreation area in northeastern Oklahoma. The tribe also maintains one public park near the tribal complex. The Eastern Shawnees hold their annual powwow during the third weekend in September.

INFRASTRUCTURE

Tribal lands and the tribal headquarters in West Seneca, Oklahoma, are accessible via U.S.60 and Missouri Highway 43. I-44 between Tulsa, Oklahoma, and Joplin, Missouri, passes seven miles west of tribal lands. UPS and FedEx package carriers serve tribal headquarters at West Seneca. Airport facilities are located within 20 miles of tribal headquarters in Joplin.

Electricity. Empire Electric Company of Joplin, Missouri, provides electricity to homes and tribal facilities on tribal land.

Fuel. LLP Gas Company provides natural gas service to the area.

Water Supply. The City of Seneca, Missouri, provides water and sewer services to the tribal area.

COMMUNITY FACILITIES AND SERVICES

The Bluejacket Building, named for a Shawnee chief, is the tribal administration office and community building located in West Seneca, Oklahoma. The center serves as a library, office, general meeting facility, and bingo hall.

Public Safety. The tribe has a police chief and four officers.

Education. Tribal youth attend public schools in Seneca, Missouri. The tribe offers an Indian Health Scholarship.

Health Care. The Bearskin Health and Wellness Center provides health care services to tribal members. The wellness center offers clinical laboratory services, state-of-the art x-ray technology, aerobic classes, and a fitness center containing a variety of exercise equipment. In addition, tribal members can participate in nutrition workshops, weight loss and stop smoking seminars, and listen to guest speakers. The tribe operates a Title IV nutrition program through the tribal complex. Tribal members can also receive health care services through Indian Health Service facilities in Claremore, Oklahoma. Hospitals are located in Miami, Oklahoma, and Joplin, Missouri.

Eastern Shawnee

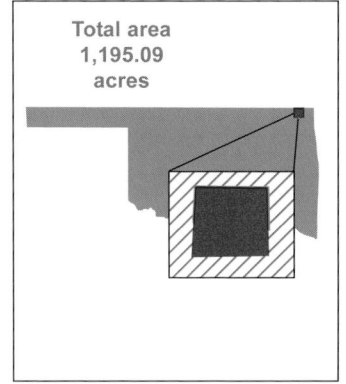

Total area
1,195.09
acres

Fort Sill Apache

Fort Sill Apache Tribe
Federal reservation
Chiricahua Apache, Warm Springs Apache, Caddo, Comanche, Cotton, Kiowa and Tillman counties, Oklahoma

Fort Sill Apache Tribe
of Oklahoma
Rte. 2, Box 121
Apache, OK 73006
580-588-2298
877-826-0726
580-588-3133 Fax

Total area *(BIA realty, 2004)*
3,075.06 acres

Tribally owned *(BIA realty, 2004)*
200.28 acres

Individually owned
(BIA realty, 2004)
2,874.78 acres

Tribal enrollment
(Tribal source, 2004)
570

Tribal enrollment
(BIA labor report, 2001)
488

Total labor force *2000 census*
4,849

LOCATION AND LAND STATUS

Fort Sill Apache Tribal Trust Lands are located in a five-county area on the plains and rolling grasslands of southwestern Oklahoma. The Washita and Cache rivers drain the region. The Fort Sill-Chiricahua-Warm Springs Apache Tribal Headquarters is located at Apache, Oklahoma, near Lake Ellsworth in Caddo County. The Town of Apache is about 15 miles south of Anadarko via U.S. 62/281 and 14 miles north of the Fort Sill Military Reservation. Major Oklahoma cities near Apache include Lawton (25 miles due south) and Oklahoma City (approximately 70 miles northeast).

The original Fort Sill Military Reservation, comprising 23,040 acres, was created out of the Kiowa, Comanche, and Apache Reservation by Executive Order in 1871. Chiricahua and Warm Springs Apache prisoners arrived there in 1894. A series of treaties in 1912, 1913, and 1923 gave allotments to those Apaches who wished to remain in Oklahoma. Today, the tribe owns 40 acres of federal trust land. An additional 4,587.72 acres of allotted land supplement the tribal land base.

The Fort Sill Apache Tribe exercises jurisdiction over 4,162.2 acres of allotted land in southwestern Oklahoma, including 41 mineral tracts and 65 tracts of surface land. The tribe also owns 400 acres of land in Lawton, Oklahoma, and the rural areas of Caddo County; 2 acres in Arizona; and a parcel of land near Deming, New Mexico. Ancestral lands of the Fort Sill Apache include portions of New Mexico and Arizona.

CULTURE AND HISTORY

Members of the Fort Sill Apache Tribe are descendants of four bands of Apache tribes. These bands, the Chúkúnende, or Chiricuaha; the Chíhénde, or Warm Springs; the Bidánku, or Mogollon; and the Ndé'ndnaí, or Enemy People, comprise the group referred to as the Chiricahua Apache. The indigenous languages spoken within all of these tribes are Athabascan dialects. The groups remain culturally and spiritually related. Ancestral lands of these Apache bands encompassed regions of southeastern Arizona, southwestern New Mexico, and northern Mexico.

The arrival of European explorers in the seventeenth century to the region was unwelcome by the bands of the Fort Sill Apache Tribe. European forces attempted to colonize the land and to subjugate the indigenous peoples. The Fort Sill Apache were successful in resisting domination and retained control over their ancestral lands well into the 1800s. In 1848, through the Treaty of Guadalupe Hildago, and the subsequent Gadsen Purchase, the United States claimed dominion over territories that had once belonged to Mexico, including the lands occupied by the Fort Sill Apache. In 1852, the BIA and the tribe negotiated a treaty. During that same time, gold and other resources were discovered and Euro-American miners encroached upon tribal lands. Hostilities between the tribe and Euro-Americans escalated and the federal government responded by establishing a number of forts throughout tribal territory. By the 1860s, the United States and all four bands of the Fort Sill Apache tribe were engaged in war.

U.S. President Grant established a Peace Policy in the 1870s in hopes of creating peaceful relationships between the federal government and warring tribes. It was during this same period that the general Euro-American population began to call for the isolation of tribal groups from Euro-American settlements. The government implemented the policy of removal

and relocation and developed the reservation system. An Executive Order of December 14, 1872 established the Chiricahua Apache Reservation. The Fort Sill Apache Bands were relocated to this site. An Executive Order of April 9, 1874 established the Hot Springs Reservation for the Warm Springs Band. Throughout this period, groups of tribal members continued to resist subordination. The Bidánku Band, led by Geronimo, and the Chiricahua Band, led by Cochise, were among these groups. Until this time, many of the Apache bands had retained independence from one another. Following the creation of the reservations, the Bidánku Band became absorbed by the Chiricuhua and Warm Springs bands. The Ndé'ndnaí became identified as the Chiricahua.

In the late 1800s, the federal government decided to dissolve the Chiricuhua Apache Reservation and relocate the residents to the San Carlos Apache Reservation in southern Arizona. The Fort Sill Apache Tribe vehemently resisted relocation and Geronimo led his band in efforts to evade the move. Warfare ensued, but ended with the surrender of the Bidánku Band on September 6, 1886. Although the majority of the Fort Sill Apache Tribe had peacefully relocated to the San Carlos Reservation, upon the surrender of Geronimo's band, the government imprisoned the entire population at San Carlos and moved nearly 498 people to prison camps in Florida, Alabama, and Oklahoma. In less than four year, 119 tribal members had died, succumbing primarily to tuberculosis. In 1894, the prisoners detained in Florida were moved to lands near Fort Sill, Oklahoma.

At Fort Sill, the Apache fared much better. A number of tribal members became successful farmers and ranchers, with a herd of 10,000 head of cattle at one point. When Geronimo died in 1909, the federal government called for a termination of the prisoner of war status of the Apaches at Fort Sill. The tribe remained prisoners until 1913. Upon their release, 187 of the remaining 265 tribal members moved to the Mescalero Apache Reservation in New Mexico and 78 accepted allotments in the former Kiowa, Comanche, and Apache Reservation in southwestern Oklahoma. The members relocated to the Mescalero Apache Reservation were referred to as the Chiricuhua Apache Tribe. In 1968, they, along with the Lipan Apache band members residing on the reservation, consolidated with the Mescalero Apache Tribe.

Tribal members remaining in Oklahoma became known as the Fort Sill Apache Tribe. The group retained a traditional form of government and also established a tribal business committee to represent the tribe. When the Oklahoma Indian Welfare Act (OIWA) was passed in 1936, the tribe rejected it, choosing to maintain its existing form of government rather than reforming under the provisions of the OIWA, which is similar to that of the Indian Reorganization Act.

During the 1950s, the Fort Sill Apache Tribe was targeted for termination of its status as a federally recognized tribe. The tribe was very vocal in its resistance, and termination was evaded. In 1968, Congress passed the Indian Civil Rights Act. Under this act, states were allowed to assume civil and criminal jurisdiction over tribal lands only with the consent of the tribe.

During the 1970s, the tribe accepted the provisions of the OIWA and reorganized its tribal governing system. In 1979, the tribe was awarded $6 million in compensation for lands

TRI-OK-013

TRI-OK-014

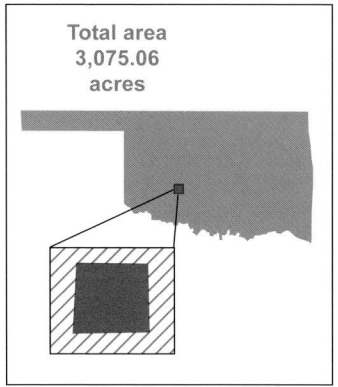
Total area
3,075.06
acres

TRI-OK-013 Front view of Cubs Den Day Care, tribally owned

TRI-OK-014 Cubs Den Day Care, tribally owned

lost during the tribe's time of imprisonment and for resources illegally harvested from tribal lands.

Traditional culture, language, and spirituality remain strong among the Fort Sill Apache.

GOVERNMENT

The tribe ratified a constitution and bylaws on October 30, 1976. An official tribal roll was established in 1977. A business committee, composed of a chairperson, a vice-chairperson, a secretary-treasurer, and three members, serves as the elected governing body. Elected members serve two-year, staggered terms, with elections occurring annually. Absentee voting allows out-of-state residents to play a part in the tribe's governing.

On July 18, 1975, the tribe and the BIA agreed upon the conditions of a Tribal Government Development Plan, which provided for the establishment of a federally recognized form of government for the Fort Sill Apache Tribe. A tribal constitution and bylaws were ratified on October 30, 1976 and approved by the Commission of Indian Affairs on August 18, 1976. A tribal roll was officially established in 1977. The tribe is currently in the process of negotiating for status as a self-governance tribe.

Departments and programs existing within the tribal government include housing, accounting, a community health program, a language program, emergency youth shelter, and a nutrition program for aging tribe members.

The tribe is in the process of establishing a tribal energy office. Funded under a Tribal Energy Planning Grant, the office will be staffed by an energy coordinator and an energy technician. It will be responsible for addressing all energy-related issues concerning the tribe, including the development of a long-term tribal strategic energy plan. This office will also work with other tribal energy programs, federal agencies, private-sector companies, and other related entities on energy issues.

ECONOMY

Gaming and federal contracts and grants represent primary sources of tribal income.

Government as Employer. The tribal government employs 30 persons through its various departments and programs.

Economic Development Projects. The use of wind and solar energy for tribal enterprises is of great interest to the tribe. In 2004, the Western Farmer's Electric Cooperative was constructing a 64-megawatt wind farm near the tribal complex. The tribe intends to explore the possibilities of utilizing these energy sources. The tribe is also considering the purchase of Indian City USA, a tourist attraction located south of Anadarko. The site includes an RV park with a pool and camping area, a dance ground, a gift shop, and a museum. Full-size reproductions of Kiowa, Caddo, Wichita, Apache, Pawnee, Pueblo, and Navajo traditional dwellings are also located on the site.

The Fort Sill Apache Industries is a tribally owned and operated entity. Developed under the Fort Sill Apache Industrial Development Act, this entity is not yet fully functional.

Agriculture and Livestock. The tribe and individual tribal members farm and ranch their lands and also lease land to non-Indians for farming and grazing.

Gaming. The 10,700-square-foot Ft. Sill Apache Casino offers players 400 slots/VLTs. It employs 100 people and provides parking for 450 vehicles. As a corporate partner, the Fort. Sill Apache Casino has become heavily involved in local activities. The casino donated more than $10,000 in money and services in 2003 to support various charitable and tribal activities. The tribe intends to renovate the existing casino. The renovated casino will include an approximately 21,000 square foot gaming area and a 9,000 square foot restaurant area. It will also house a smoke shop with drive-thru access, and a themed bar. The new facility will be located in Lawton, Oklahoma.

Mining. Natural resources found on tribal lands include an abundance of oil and gas. During the 1920s and 1930s, these resources were highly sought after. Rather than being required to deal directly with Native landowners, the state permitted mining companies to negotiate all leases and contracts with state agencies. In a number of cases, the landowners were actually children. In many of those cases, the state agent would sign leases on behalf of the child. Language barriers often prevented adult involvement in the negotiation process, and the state agent would intercede and negotiate the contract in those instances as well. Consequently, many tribal members were subject to agreements they had taken little or no part in. An overwhelming number of tribal members were defrauded, albeit legally, of the financial compensations they should have been entitled to. The tribe has since sought legal recourse, arguing that the state policy that allowed this activity violated the rights of tribal members and prohibited them from receiving the appropriate compensation for land leases. While original contracts promised the landowners twelve percent of the royalties, many receive less than one percent today.

Tribal sources suggest that individual tribal landowners in just one area of 640 acres are entitled to approximately $800 million. With support from the Secretary of the Interior, a tribal representative intends to file foreclosure procedures against the oil companies involved.

Services and Retail. The tribe's casino in Lawton, Oklahoma is combined with a smoke shop, which is a primary sales outlet for Philip Morris items; it also vends more generic cigarettes than any other establishment in the United States. A drive through window accommodates those who prefer to remain in their cars

Media and Communications. The tribe publishes a newsletter, *Fort Sill Apache News*, once a month.

841

Fort Sill Apache

Tourism and Recreation. Tourists can observe buffalo and antelope on Wichita Mountain Wildlife Refuge, a 59,000-acre area of land close to the reservation.

INFRASTRUCTURE

Tribal headquarters at Apache are accessible via U.S. 62/281 and State Highway 58. I-44, connecting Lawton and Oklahoma City, passes approximately 12 miles east of Apache. Commercial and private air transportation service is available in Lawton, 22 miles south. Passenger bus lines serve Apache, as do UPS and FedEx package carriers.

Electricity. Electricity is provided to residences through regional providers.

Fuel. Natural gas is provided to residencies by local vendors.

Water Supply. Caddo County provides water and waste disposal for the tribe.

Telecommunication. The telephone companies serving tribal facilities and the tribal area are Executech II and Pioneer Telephone Company.

COMMUNITY FACILITIES AND SERVICES

The Fort Sill Apache Tribe provides a number of social services for enrolled members, including a housing program, an elders' nutrition program, a gym, an emergency youth shel-

ter, and a community health program. The tribe maintains a community center within the tribal headquarters two miles north of Apache on U.S. 62/281.

Education. Children attend public schools in the five-county tribal area. The tribe funds the Fort Sill Apache Higher Education Grant. In order to qualify, an applicant must have been accepted into a college or university and must have applied for financial aid. The grant can be applied toward some of the unmet needs of the student.

Health Care. Health services are available through the U.S. Public Health Services facility in Anadarko. The 20,000 square foot facility provides medical and dental services. It also features a clinical laboratory and radiology department. The center has a staff of three physicians and one physician's assistant, and serves nearly 35,000 clients yearly.

Services are also available through an Indian Health Service clinic located at the Riverside Indian School in Anadarko and the Lawton Indian Hospital in Lawton. This facility offers 45 beds and a staff of sixteen physicians. The tribe is a member of the Inter-Tribal Indian Health Board.

ENVIRONMENTAL CONCERNS

The tribe is concerned about cancer and diabetes among members. Oil drilling on tribal land may be contributing to cancer and lupus among tribal members-this is a concern for the Fort Sill Apaches.

Iowa Tribe

Iowa Tribe of Oklahoma
Federal reservation
Iowa, Ioway, Bah-Kho-Je
Payne, Lincoln, Oklahoma,
Logan counties, Oklahoma

The Iowa Tribe of Oklahoma
R.R. 1 Box 721
Perkins, OK 74059
405-547-2402
888-336-4692
405-547-1032 Fax
iowanation.org

LOCATION AND LAND STATUS

The Iowa Reservation lies on some 2,628 acres of non-contiguous land in the Cimarron River Valley of north-central Oklahoma. Reservation and allotted lands are spread in checkerboard fashion across four Oklahoma counties. The Iowa Tribe currently has jurisdiction over all or parts of Payne, Oklahoma, Lincoln and Logan counties. Approximately 60 percent of the lands of the Iowa Tribe of Oklahoma have been mapped, and the tribe now has the capabilities and software to map remaining portions.

Tribal headquarters are located four miles south of Perkins, Oklahoma on U.S. 177. Perkins is approximately nine miles south of Stillwater, 50 miles northeast of Oklahoma City and 60 miles west of Tulsa. The tribal service area includes the former reservation and portions of Payne, Lincoln, and Logan counties.

The Iowa Tribe of Oklahoma has four categories to express its relationship to its land: tribally owned lands, trust lands, fee allotted, and non-trust lands.

CULTURE AND HISTORY

The Iowa Tribe of Oklahoma are descendants of the Iowa, a Siouan-speaking, semi-agricultural people who inhabited the prairie country of the lower Missouri River Basin during the pre-European contact era. Traditionally a Woodlands culture, the Iowa Tribe has adopted elements of the Plains cultures they encountered during early migrations. They lived in villages but hunted on the prairies in a fashion similar to the Plains dwellers farther west. North of Kansas, tribal members dwelt in earth-covered lodges; elsewhere they used grass, skins, or mats as covering. Village life displayed eastern in-

fluences evidenced by the use of pottery and the cultivation of corn, squash, and beans. The Iowa probably originated in the Great Lakes Region and participated in the Winnebago Nation. A portion of the tribe moved south, and divided again. The groups that remained nearest the Mississippi River became known as the Iowa while the other groups became the Missouria and Otoe tribes.

The Bah-Kho-Je, or Iowa, speak a Chiwere dialect of the Sioux language. The tribe, called "gray snow" in the indigenous language, was probably named for the appearance of their winter dwellings. "Iowa" was bestowed upon the tribe by the French.

The ancestral lands of the Iowa included portions of the Missouri and Mississippi river valleys in the present-day states of Wisconsin, Iowa, Minnesota, Missouri, Kansas, and Nebraska. The primary homelands were located in Iowa. Some locations occupied by the Iowa include the mouth of the Rock River in present-day Illinois, the Root River in what is now Iowa, the Red Pipestone Quarry in the southwestern part Minnesota, and the Spirit Lake/Lake Okiboji area in present-day Iowa. They lived in a village near Council Bluffs, Iowa until Sioux incursions and a wish to be nearer the French traders prompted them to move once again. After that move, the Iowa stayed most of the time at the Chariton/Grand River Basin, close to the Des Moines River.

In 1824, the encroachment of Euro-American settlers forced the tribe to cede their lands. They were given two years to completely vacate the region and between 1836 and 1838, were relocated to a tract of land only ten miles wide and twenty miles long near the Kansas and Nebraska border. Subsequent treaties reduced this parcel.

Because they were unhappy with their experiences on the Kansas Nebraska Reserve, some of the Iowa left the area and relocated to Oklahoma (Indian Territory). A reservation was carved out for them there in 1883, but those desiring to stay in the north were accommodated. The Indian Territory reservation was bounded by the Cimarron River on the north and the Deep Fork River on the south. The two groups today are viewed as distinct. The headquarters of the Northern Iowa are in White Cloud, Kansas; the offices of the Iowa Tribe of Oklahoma are in Perkins, Oklahoma.

The enforcement of the 1887 Dawes Act provided for the allotment of Iowa tribal lands. 109 tribal members were allotted parcels of 80 acres each. The majority of these lands eventually passed into non-Native ownership. Over 220,000 acres of tribal lands were returned to the federal government as surplus. It was then opened to Euro-American settlers in the Run of 1882.

The Iowa Tribe of Oklahoma organized under the Oklahoma Indian Welfare Act of 1936 and, henceforth, worked to increase the tribe's communal land base. The Iowa Tribe is committed to the preservation and perpetuation of its traditional culture. The business committee and general council have established the Cultural Heritage Ordinance, extending protection to all aspects of the culture. The code addresses issues of language retention; traditional dance, song, and spirituality; intellectual property rights; repatriation of tribal remains and artifacts; and the preservation of archeological sites.

GOVERNMENT
The Iowa Tribe of Oklahoma was federally incorporated in 1938, which permits it to conduct business under the rules of a corporation. It is a federally recognized tribe and was organized under the Oklahoma Indian Welfare Act in September 1937. This provided the authority for the Iowa Tribe to adopt a constitution, bylaws, and elect a business committee. The tribe is a PL-638 tribe.

The Iowa Council is comprised of all enrolled tribal members. Government matters are managed by the tribe's business committee, which consists of five elected officials. The tribal chairman, vice-chairman, treasurer, secretary, and council person are elected to two-year terms. The business committee oversees all business and economic matters on behalf of the tribe, as well as serves as the board of directors for BKJ Solutions. The tribe strives to enhance the economic and social living conditions within the tribal and local communities.

The tribal government administers a broad range of services and programs, including accounting, administration, business committee, economic development, elders nutritional program, environmental services, fitness center, gaming and tribal enterprises, health service, human services, historical preservation, human resources, Indian Health Service clinic, information technology, maintenance, police, purchasing, realty, tribal enrollment, tribal housing authority, tribal newsletter, tribal court, tribal library and archives, and vocational rehabilitation.

Tribal license plates are provided by the tribal enrollment office This office also keeps all insurance documents relevant to vehicles owned by individuals or the tribe.

The maintenance of tribal lands is the responsibility of the Iowa Tribe Maintenance Division. The division is also responsible for the preparation of the grounds and the Bah-Kho-Je Chena Building for the annual powwow.

Land records are maintained by the tribe's realty division. This office assists in the purchasing lands, monitoring of leases, land surveys, right-of-way permits, and all other matters pertaining to the management of tribal lands.

The Bah-Kho-Je Housing Authority, which the federal HUD approved in 1996, administers rental assistance, rehabilitation, elderly housing, down payment assistance, and the loan purchase program.

Prior to 1992, the judicial matters of the tribe were the jurisdiction of an intertribal court. In 1992, the tribe established its own judicial system. Tribal courts exercise jurisdiction over civil, criminal, and juvenile matters as provided for in the tribal constitution. Court services are administered by a district court judge, public defender, and prosecutor. There is also a Supreme Court with four justices and a chief justice. The judicial services of the tribe are contracted through the BIA and are independent of other governing and political entities of the tribe.

The service area of the tribe's police department encompasses 1,250 square miles and includes all of the tribe's businesses and enterprises. The department has cross-jurisdiction with neighboring municipal and county law enforcement agencies. Prisoners of the department are detained at the Lincoln County Jail. The tribe is planning to construct a new facility that will house the police department, a 24-hour holding facility, the fire department, and the emergency management program. In addition, the tribe has received a FEMA grant for the development of an emergency operations plan.

The tribe is currently a member of many business, professional, and Indian organizations, including the American Indian Chamber of Commerce; American Planning Association; Council of Energy Resource Tribes; the Guthrie, Langston, Princeton, and Perkins Chambers of Commerce; National Indian Gaming Association; National Association Area Agencies on Aging; National Association of Title VI; National Renewable Energy Lab; National Center for American Indian Enterprise Development; National Museum of America; Native American Finance Officer Association; National Congress of American Indians; Oklahoma Indian Affairs Commission; Oklahoma Indian Child Welfare Association; the Society of Wetland Scientists; National Tribal Air Association; the Inter-Tribal Environmental Coalition; and the Tribal Environmental Coalition of Oklahoma.

BUSINESS CORPORATION
BKJ Solutions was created in 1998, with a gross revenue that year of $800,000. Its name is an acronym for Bah Kho Je. It is a division of the federal corporation of the tribe. The tribal business committee is the BKJ Board of Directors, with the tribal administrator serving as CEO. BKJ is an SBA 8(a) corporation and is also SBD and HUBZone certified. About 90 percent of its business operations involve service and 10 percent, construction. Trucking, energy, construction, archeological services, and environmental services are the five divisions of the corporation, and it is responsible for tribal business operations in these areas. BKJ Solutions is eligible for the Indian incentive program under the US. Department of Defense. In 2001, the Oklahoma Native American Business Development Center named BKJ Solutions the Tribal Business of the Year. The BKJ Solutions Archeological Services Division has joined with Albuquerque company TRC Myria in bidding on a number of projects. Also, the division is investigating the possibility of bidding on federal contracts.

BKJ Solutions and Tulsa-based The Ross Group have formed the BKJ-Ross Group Team. Based in Tulsa, The Ross Group specializes in general contracting, construction maintenance,

Iowa Tribe

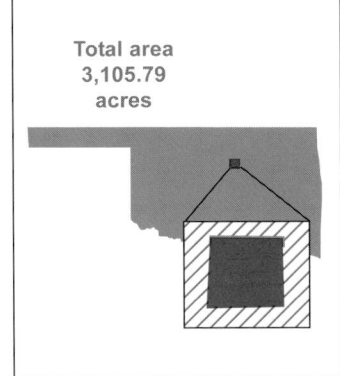

Total area
3,105.79
acres

Total area *(BIA realty, 2004)*
3,105.79 acres

Tribally owned *(BIA realty, 2004)*
477.21 acres

Individually owned
(BIA realty, 2004)
2,628.58 acres

Total labor force *2000 census*
2,868

High school graduate or higher
2000 census
77%

Bachelor's degree or higher
2000 census
12.8%

Unemployment rate *2000 census*
4.3%

Iowa Tribe

TRI-OK-020

TRI-OK-022

TRI-OK-023

TRI-OK-029

TRI-OK-020 Cubs Den Day Care, tribally owned

TRI-OK-022 Vocational Rehabilitation Center

TRI-OK-023 Multi-Purpose Building

TRI-OK-029 Welcome sign for the Iowa Tribe of Oklahoma Pow Wow Grounds

design-build, and the maintenance of facilities. The Department of Commerce's Minority Business Development Agency named the Ross Group the National Minority Construction Firm of the Year. The Ross Group's portfolio has demonstrated success in new construction as well as renovation in a broad range of markets. As the two companies cooperate, BKJ Solutions will benefit from the expertise represented by this promising strategic alliance.

ECONOMY

The tribal economy is supported in large part by revenue earned by tribally owned enterprises. Federal revenues, state taxes, interest earnings, and a trust fund consisting of profits from a land settlement also contribute to the economy. In FY 2000, the tribe grossed over $16 million. With 76 percent of their earnings generated from tribally owned enterprises, the tribe was determined to be financially self-sufficient.

Government as Employer. The Iowa Tribe is the largest employer in the area with over 160 employees in its various offices, departments, programs, and enterprises.

Economic Development. The tribe offers a number of incentives to draw businesses to tribal lands. Among these are no property taxes, free trade zone possibilities, Indian Employment Credit, HUBZone benefits, accelerated depreciations, and a number of other benefits. The Iowa Tribe is also aware that strategic alliances are necessary to tribal economic success. In particular, it is enthusiastic about the possibility of partnering and joint ventures with businesses in neighboring Stillwater, Oklahoma, which is becoming a high-tech economy. The tribe is willing to establish joint ventures with partners both public and private, including tribes, corporations and government organizations and others. Past partners of the tribe have been Oklahoma Department of Commerce, other Chambers of Commerce, Oklahoma Indian Affairs Commission, and other tribes. The tribe is considering the development of a third smoke shop. It will be located in Princeton, Missouri on tribal lands that are in the process of being placed in trust status.

Environmental assessments, water distribution, wetland surface testing, wind generation, and subsurface oil and gas exploration are all services that BKJ Solutions' environmental

services division is planning to provide. It is expected that this field of activity will be financially rewarding. The tribe is also a investigating the economic benefits of broadening their activities in the energy industry. The energy division of BKJ Solutions is active in energy marketing, energy audits, the generation of wind power, and the transportation of fuel products. In 2001, the tribe began to investigate the potential of wind power. It is also investigating the feasibility of a hybrid distributive generation project, which would supply electricity to the tribal complex. CH2MHILL and the energy division have signed a mentor protégé contract, and in a joint venture format the two are planning to work together to design and construct projects related to energy. Tinker Air Force Base near Oklahoma City is being considered as a possible partner in construction.

The tribe also seeks to generate revenue through trading of energy commodities. One of its business goals is to promote Indian commerce with other tribes that have energy resources. They are engaged in intertribal energy commerce and tribal/industry transactions as well. BKJ Solutions has formed strategic partnerships with Williams Co. and Syntroleum, both Tulsa companies.

Agriculture and Livestock. The tribe owns 20 buffalo and 55 head of cattle. Four hundred acres of hay are farmed every year; 40 acres of soybeans; and 50 acres of wheat. The agricultural program is a participant in the EQIP program of the federal Department of Agriculture.

Gaming. The tribe operates the Cimarron Bingo Casino, a class II gaming facility in Perkins. Established in 1975, the casino offers 17 different types of bingo, 250 bingo seats, and 467 Vegas-style slot machines. Off-track betting is also available. It employs about 50 individuals. The casino maintains a security program, with approximately 20 officers. The casino currently serves a market within 60 miles of its location, including Stillwater, Edmond and even Oklahoma City, according to the casino management The market area is competitive but not saturated, with the nearest gaming facility 30 miles from the Iowa casino. Advertisements and radio spots make up most of the marketing. If the tribe wished to expand its gaming operation at this point, it would need to relocate the casino or buy the land adjacent and expand in situ.

Construction. BKJ Solutions offers both construction management and general contracting services. Working with Indiac Metals, they build general utility buildings of metal. BKJ Solutions also has teamed with The Ross Group, a Tulsa-based firm specializing in design-build services, general contracting, construction management, and facilities maintenance, in order to develop and refine expertise in these areas.

Industrial Park. The tribe has 35 acres available for development. It has two designated economic development zones available. They are located along Highway 177 just south of Perkins and include access to a 55,000-gallon capacity modern water system, access to electrical power, highway frontage and easy access to I-44. BKJ Solutions may open their offices at this location.

Real Estate/Commercial Development. Six hundred and fifty-five acres of tribal lands are available for lease. The tribe offers a number of incentives to benefit businesses relocating to the region. *(Please refer to the Economic Development Projects, above.)*

Services and Retail. The Iowa Tribe Smokeshop is located adjacent to the Cimarron Bingo Casino. Established in 1984, it was the first retail outlet owned and operated by the tribe. The smoke shop employs up to three people.

Approximately 4,000 square feet in size, the Iowa Tribe Mini-Mart is a convenience store selling gas and groceries. It also includes a smoke shop and a full-service deli. The deli uses tribally based beef products in its sandwiches and other food items. Ten to 12 people are employed at the store, which has been owned and operated by the tribe since 1989. It was the Iowas' second retail establishment.

The tribe has an active marketing strategy for its Bah-Kho-Je Gallery in Guthrie, Oklahoma. It is meant primarily to interest the tourist market. Events such as art walks and Old West gunfights are used to increase visits to the gallery. Special shows, the Victorian Christmas presentation, and featured artists also serve to interest the public in the establishment. Advertising in the newspaper is also a marketing method used. In the future the tribe plans to utilize the Internet as well, with art displays and electronic purchases. Some of the art work and other items sold at the gallery include Pendleton blankets, jackets, broadcloth, beads, artisan supplies, tribal t-shirts, golf tees, caps, and watches. All retail businesses are the responsibility of the retail division manager. Each of the other tribal enterprises reports to its individual manager.

Transportation. Fully up and running for more than three years, the trucking division of BKJ Solutions has a client base that is both commercial and governmental. The trucks haul dry and frozen goods across the continent. The division is looking toward increasing opportunities in the future, resulting from their decision to partner with a marketing firm in the area.

Media and Communications. A monthly publication, *The Bah-Kho-Je Journal*, focuses on community and tribal programs, the environment, news, and the arts. Published by the tribe and mailed free of charge to members of the tribe, it is also available online. Letters to the editor are encouraged, along with the contribution of articles, poetry, short stories, artwork, photos, and personal notices.

Tourism and Recreation. The Iowa Tribal Powwow is held annually during the third weekend of June. This event is held at the Iowa Tribal Powwow and Campgrounds located one mile south of the tribal complex. The festivities include gourd dancing, competitions, food vendors, and arts and crafts. In 2004, the tribe was constructing traditional Iowa lodges at the powwow grounds.

INFRASTRUCTURE

Iowa Tribal headquarters in Perkins lie near the intersection of State Route 33, which runs east west, and U.S. 177, which runs north south. Stillwater, home of Oklahoma State University, is nine miles north via U.S. 177. I-44, connecting Oklahoma City and Tulsa, passes 21 miles south of Perkins. With the assistance of an engineering firm in Tulsa, the tribe is planning to add an additional 6 miles of roads to the existing 60 miles of roadway on tribal land. The county maintains the roadway system throughout tribal lands. The Iowa are working with a Tulsa engineering firm on the plans for 6 miles of roads, which will increase the miles of road on the reservation to 66.

Electricity. The Central Rural Electric Cooperative provides electricity to individual Iowa tribal members. In 2004 the tribe was considering building a hybrid distributive generation project, to provide the tribal complex with electricity.

Fuel. Propane gas is available on the reservation.

Water Supply. Well water or municipal water lines provide water for residents and tribal buildings. Septic tanks are used for waste disposal.

Transportation. Private and commercial air service is available at Stillwater Municipal Airport. Commercial air service also available 50 miles southwest at the Will Rogers International Airport in Oklahoma City and 60 miles east at the Tulsa International Airport. Rail lines run east to west just south of the reservation boundary. Greyhound bus service is available in Stillwater as well as UPS and FedEx services. Public transportation is provided in the reservation area by an elders shuttle bus. BKJ Solutions trucking division provides freight services.

COMMUNITY FACILITIES AND SERVICES

Nine buildings make up the tribal headquarters. Within these buildings are the many tribal operations, departments, and programs, as well as the offices and other space needed by the tribal leadership. The complex includes the tribal government building, administrative building, human resources building, office of environmental services, a fitness center/health services/human services building, White Cloud Complex, public safety building, Eagles Nest Youth Shelter for Indian children 17 and younger, and six duplexes for seniors. A daycare facility was begun in 2002, and the design for a lagoon project is almost finished.

The White Cloud Complex houses department of health services as well as the elders assistance program, the caregivers assistance program, and the tribal wellness center with its exercise equipment, therapeutic massage and a heated therapy pool. The White Cloud Complex also provides a place for elders to gather for meetings, craft classes and lessons, recreation, and relaxation. It offers seniors a large screen TV, video equipment, a pool table, and community and home delivered meals.

Native American subjects are the focus of the Iowa Tribe library, which was founded in 1985. Collections are varied, including a range of media including videos and music. The library's "Iowa Collection" writing, photographs and other materials contains some one-of-a-kind items. In addition, the library offers the public access to several computers.

Iowa Tribe

The Iowa tribal human services program offers a number of programs, including social services, Indian child welfare, child protection, library archives, youth and family shelters, and vocational rehabilitation.

The tribal assistance program provides an annual payment each calendar year to each tribal member; this is to be used for household expenses. It helps fund various medical needs like dental and medical procedures, hearing aids, and prescriptions. The program also provides payments to elders and tribal children in school and assists with funeral expenses.

The tribal youth program provides services and activities for children and families. Eagle's Nest Emergency Youth Shelter provides a safe place for children who need to be away from their homes. All services are provided to an area within the Iowa Nation former reservation and to an extended service area including towns like Stillwater that border the former reservation. The service area is spread out across south Payne County, northwest Lincoln County, and southeastern Logan County.

Education. Tribal youth attend public schools in the Perkins-Tryon Public School District. The Tah-Je-Do-Weh-Che (Four Winds) Child Care Center opened in the fall of 2003. Licensed for 61 students the facility currently serves 32. The child care center has been designated a 2-Star facility by the Oklahoma Department of Human Services.

The tribe contracts the Johnson-O'Malley Program through the BIA. This program provides academic support services to tribal youth attending non-tribally operated schools and school districts.

Tribal members are eligible to receive financial assistance in the pursuit of a higher education. Grants are also available to those seeking vocational training. Post-secondary education is nearby at Oklahoma State University, nine miles north of Perkins in Stillwater.

The tribe offers vocational counseling, educational assistance, limited help with finding a job, and assistive devices through its vocational rehabilitation program, for which the U.S. Department of Education provides funding.

Health Care. Medical attention is available at the tribe's Perkins Family Clinic. The tribe's health department includes the divisions of community health representative, nutrition services, respite care, tribal youth, and diabetes programs. It also offers a fitness center.

In October of 2000 the Iowa Tribe purchased and assumed operations of the Perkins Family Clinic, located four miles from the tribal complex. The clinic is unique in its service to both native people in the area as well as to non-native individuals with third party reimbursements in the City of Perkins and surrounding communities. The Perkins Family Clinic opened in a new larger facility on September 8, 2003. The increased 10,000-square-foot size of the facility has enabled the Iowa Tribe to offer more services locally and to increase the number of providers. The services now provided on-site include general practice, immunization clinics, a diabetes clinic, family planning services, behavioral health, substance abuse prevention and treatment services, blood pressure and glucose screenings, drug screens for employment, sports physicals for students, and limited in-house pharmaceuticals.

The Indian Health Service has allowed the Iowa Tribe of Oklahoma to offer an enhanced array of services to Indian patients served at the Perkins Family Clinic. The tribe is exploring the possibility of developing the clinic into a profit-generating, self-sustaining operation. Expansions to the facility and an increased clientele would be necessary to accomplish this. The Iowa Tribe currently is focusing on increasing health services for the local community by partnering funds from Indian Health Service with 330 grant funds supporting New Start Community Health Centers. With these funds the Iowa Tribe will be able to operate a larger, more accessible clinic with more comprehensive services to both Native Americans and others in the area. Additional planned services include the in-house reading of x-rays, the development of a strong educational component with an emphasis on wellness and prevention, and the provision of space for a dentist, a consulting psychologist, and a licensed social worker.

The Indian Health Service also serves the reservation with two community health representatives and one registered nurse. Hospitals are also located in Stillwater. The health department administered Title VI-A Program provides community and home-delivered meals, nutrition services, and activities for elders. The Title VI-C Program provides respite care and assistance and resources for those needing caregiver services.

ENVIRONMENTAL CONCERNS

The tribe is concerned with pesticide use, water quality, subsurface minerals, and wetland management on tribal lands. It also intends to develop solid waste management and emergency response programs. The Tribe is creating a land use development plan that will address the issues of utilities, waste management, environmental, cultural, and economic concerns. The plan development is funded by an Environmental Enhancement Grant from the Administration for Native Americans.

The tribe created the Office of Environmental Services (OES) in September 1997 to determine policies and projects that would maintain and protect environmental quality. EPA funds the OES through its General Assistance Program Grant. The office has assumed many of the duties of the Indian Health Service Office of Environmental Health. The tribe has also developed the Clean Air Capacity Building Project to investigate the impact of air pollution sources on tribal lands and to provide community educational resources on air quality.

The OES is in the first phase of the Wetland Specific Water Quality Standards development process. The program will conduct more monitoring studies on surface waters as well as to extend the program to increase the set of baseline indicators that support a wetlands-specific water quality standards, and will develop a designated uses system applicable to wetlands-specific water quality standards, and will collect information related to the conditions of aquatic resources.

LOCATION AND LAND STATUS

The Kaw Nation is headquartered in Kay County, close to the middle of Oklahoma's northern border with Kansas. Tribal administrative offices can be found in Kaw City, 12 miles northeast of Ponca City on Highway 11. The Kaw Nation currently owns 1,120.15 acres of land in Kansas and Oklahoma located on former reservation lands. The last reservation set aside for the Kaws consisted of approximately 100,137.32 acres of land and was located on the right bank of the Arkansas River near the southern border of Kansas.

The Arkansas River is to the west of the reservation. The Kansas state line is approximately 20 miles north of the Nation's headquarters. To the east is Osage County, Oklahoma, and Kaw Reservoir, and to the south is Kay County.

In 1902-1903, 249 enrolled tribal members each received 160 acres of land, plus an additional 240 acres of what the federal government deemed as surplus lands. Members of legal age were permitted to sell their lands only upon receipt of a formal certificate of competency issued by the Secretary of the Interior. However, in a number of cases, minors were permitted to sell their lands. The Kaw Nation is seeking legal recourse for these sales, arguing that contracts negotiated with minors should have been invalid. A unique provision of the 1902 Kaw Allotment Act stated that tribal members declared competent were "withdrawn" from the tribal rolls, effectively destroying the Kaw tribal identity.

The Kaw Nation purchased about 153 acres of former tribal lands near Council Grove, Kansas in 2000. In commemoration of its presence in the area and its last reservation in the state, it has established the Allegawaho Memorial Heritage Park on this site, which includes visible remnants of the Kanza's last village in the state, which bears their name.

PHYSICAL DESCRIPTION

The Kaw tribal lands are primarily grassland interspersed with woodlands on uplands adjacent to streams. The tribal lands are bisected by Beaver Creek, Little Beaver Creek, and many other small creeks, all of which combine and contribute to the Kaw Reservoir, which was created by damming the Arkansas River.

CLIMATE

The climate of the Kaws' Oklahoma home is moderate. The average precipitation in Kay County is 33.8 inches yearly. January's average temperature is 40.6°F and July's average temperature is 80.7°F.

CULTURE AND HISTORY

The Kanza (People of the Wind, South Wind), or Kaw, Tribe traditionally occupied the lower Ohio Valley. The tribe belongs to the Dhegiha-Sioux division of the Hopewell cultures, along with the Osage, Ponca, Omaha, and Quawpa tribes. These groups lived together in communities in the Ohio Valley well into the late fifteenth century. Traditional homes included bark- or earth-covered lodges in permanent settlements and tipis in transitional communities. Around 1750, tribal members began to migrate westward towards the mouth of the Ohio River. Eventually, the Kaw Tribe assumed control over most of present-day eastern and northern Kansas, western Missouri, and portions of Iowa and Nebraska.

By 1800, epidemics had reduced the Kaw population to about 1,500 men, women and children. Even so, the Kaws presented a formidable obstacle to American expansion into the trans-Missouri west following the United States acquisition of western territory by the Louisiana Purchase in 1803. From their villages and small vegetable farms in northeastern Kansas and later along the Kansas River west of present-day Topeka, Kaw warriors maintained control of the lower Kansas valley against both white settlers from the east and alien tribes to the west. Kaw hunters also engaged in semi-annual hunting expeditions onto the plains of western Kansas, as far west as Colorado. Following a major change in the United States policy toward Indians in the early nineteenth century, all of this changed dramatically.

By 1825, the federal government had adopted the policy of forcibly removing indigenous groups. This policy, formalized by the Indian Removal Act of 1830, provided for the removal of nearly 100,000 members of the Shawnee, Delaware, Wyandot, Kickapoo, Miami, Sac and Fox, Ottawa, Peoria, and Potawatomi tribes from their tribal lands to those of the Kaw and Osage tribes. The Kaw were then forced to cede vast amounts of land to the government, accepting promises for annuities and assistance in return.

The first and perhaps most devastating Kaw treaty was negotiated in 1825. In the Treaty of 1825 (7 Stat. 244), the Kaws ceded over 18 million acres of their aboriginal territory comprising portions of future Kansas, Iowa, Nebraska, and Missouri. In consideration for this cession the Kaws received a 6,559,040-acre reservation, 30 miles wide beginning just west of future Topeka and extending west to a line to be marked by government surveyors and $70,000 or $0.0035/acre to be paid at a rate of $3,500 per annum for twenty years in money, merchandise, provisions or domestic animals. In addition, the Kaw were to receive 300 cattle, 300 hogs, 500 fowl, 3 yoke of oxen, 2 carts filled with agricultural implements, a government blacksmith, and an agricultural instructor. The Kaw also ceded 36 portions of good lands on the Big Blue River to be sold and proceeds deposited in a school fund for the education of Kaw children. As a special concession to Chief White Plume's vigorous support of the treaty, one-mile square plots located on the north side of the Kansas River just east of the new reservation were also ceded and set aside for twenty-three named half-bloods of the Kaw Nation. The rest of the tribe received no such benevolence and factionalism thereby was greatly encouraged.

Poverty-stricken by the effects of the 1825 Treaty and weakened by continuous government (and private) pressure for yet another land cession-this time to accommodate railroad, town, and land speculators-the Kaw leadership went to the treaty table again in 1846. Under the 1846 Treaty (9 Stat. 842), the Kaws ceded 2,000,000-acres of its 6,559,040 acre reservation to the United States for $202,000 or $0.101/acre. In addition, the Kaws conditionally ceded their remaining lands upon a finding by the President that the timber resources located on such lands were insufficient to meet the needs of the Kaw. In 1847, the President concluded that such lands lacked sufficient timber resources and took title to the remaining 4,559,040 acres of the Kaw Reservation. The Kaw did not receive the promised additional compensation or goods in consideration for the conditional cession of their remaining 4,559,040-acre reserve. They were restricted to a reserve consisting of 255,854.49 acres near present-day Council Grove, Kansas. Under the terms of the 1846 Treaty, the Council Grove lands were to remain for the use of the Kaw forever.

Kaw Nation of Oklahoma Reservation
Kaw, Kanza, Kansa,
Kay County, Oklahoma

Kaw Nation
Drawer 50
Kaw City, OK 74641
580-269-2552
580-269-2301 Fax
kawnation.com

Total area (BIA realty, 2004)
1,146.98 acres

Tribally owned (BIA realty, 2004)
1,146.98 acres

Tribally owned (Tribal source, 2004)
1,120.15 acres

Federal trust (Tribal source, 2004)
132.5 acres

Population *2000 census*
48,080

Tribal enrollment
(BIA labor report, 2001)
2,553

Tribal enrollment
(Tribal source, 2005)
2,768

Total labor force *2000 census*
2,871

Total labor force
(BIA labor report, 2001)
2,174

High school graduate or higher
2000 census
81.8%

Bachelor's degree or higher
2000 census
13.1%

Unemployment rate *2000 census*
4.3%

Unemployment rate
(BIA labor report, 2001)
49%

Per capita income *2000 census*
16,295

Kaw

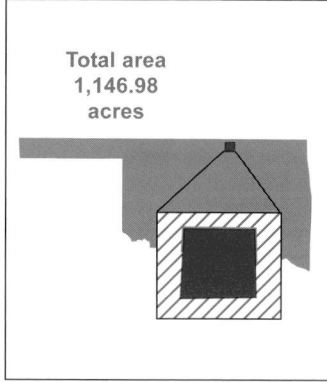

Total area
1,146.98
acres

Urged on by railroad developers, bankers, merchants, and some members of the Kansas Territorial leadership, the United States pressured the Kaws for further cessions of their Kansas lands. The result was the Kaw Treaty of 1860 (12 Stat. 1111), which reduced the Council Grove Reservation from 255,854.49 acres to 80,409.60 acres of the poorest land in the area. The new reserve was subdivided into 40-acre plots and was assigned to individual tribal members, with the remaining 175,444.89 acres sold to the highest bidder after public advertisement. Forty acres of marginal Kansas land was wholly insufficient to support one Kaw family, and by the late 1860s the government was obliged to authorize emergency funds to prevent outright starvation of the Kaw people.

Finally, on May 27, 1872, in a measure strongly opposed by Chief Allegawaho and most of his people, a federal act was passed that provided for the removal of the Wind People from Kansas to a 100,137.32-acre site in present-day Kay County, Oklahoma. This area was carved out of former Cherokee/Osage land, and the Kaws paid $70,096.12 for the land from revenue generated by the sale of their trust lands in Kansas. Initially, they had been promised an estimated $600,000 from the sale of the Kansas lands, but the land appraisal was decreased due to pressure for squatters already on the land and from prospective purchasers.

The tribal culture and life way began to suffer after the tribe's removal from their traditional lands in Kansas. Tribal youth were forced to attend schools, where they were punished for speaking the indigenous language, wearing traditional clothing, or practicing traditional spirituality. Tribal members made a concerted effort to retain cultural elements and maintain traditional relationships with members of other tribes.

Following the passage of the 1902 Kaw Allotment Act (32 Stat. 626), the Kaw Reservation was allotted in 160-acre homestead parcels to each individual tribal member whose name appeared on the tribal rolls as of December 1, 1901, or who was born between December 1, 1901 and December 1, 1902, to a member whose name appeared on such rolls. The remaining surplus lands were distributed among the enrolled members in equal portions. However, before any lands could be allotted, the Kaw agreed to set aside and cede 160 acres of land to the United States to maintain a school for the education of Indian children. In addition, the Kaws set aside and reserved 20 acres of land for the tribal cemetery and 80 acres for a town site to be known as Washunga. The Washunga town site was to be surveyed and laid off into town lots to be sold at public auction to the highest bidder. Thus, following the sale of such lands, the Kaw Nation was to retain only 20 acres of its cemetery lands. Following allotment, the Kaw people retained 100 acres of their former reservation lands near the Beaver Creek confluence with the Arkansas River until the mid-1960s, when these lands were inundated by the Kaw Dam and Reservoir Project constructed by the United States Army Corps of Engineers on the Arkansas River just northeast of Ponca City, Oklahoma. As early as the late nineteenth century, the tribal council house, Washunga town site, and tribal cemetery had been located in the area inundated by the Kaw Reservoir. After years of negotiations with various federal and local officials, the tribal cemetery was relocated to Newkirk, Oklahoma, and the tribal council house was relocated to a 15-acre tract a few miles northwest of its former location. By subsequent Congressional action 132.5 acres of land located in Kay County located just west of the former Washunga town site was placed in trust for the Kaw Nation. PL 98-173, 97 Stat. 1121 (1983).

The Kaw Nation has managed to survive the many hardships it has been subjected to since the arrival of Euro-Americans. Tribal members continue to revive traditional practices, including the powwow. Reintroduced in the community in 1977, the event is now celebrated annually at the powwow grounds at Washunga Bay.

Kanza, the Siouan language of the Kaw Nation, is closely related to the Osage, Ponca, Omaha, and Quapaw tribal languages. In order to support the survival and promote the learning of this language, a Kaw Language Coordinator is on the tribal staff, and a website promotes the study of the Kanza language.

The Kaw Nation and Council Grove, Kansas, enjoy a cordial relationship. Council Grove was the location of the final reservation inhabited by the Kaws in Kansas. Council Grove is the site of an intertribal powwow held every year, and the Kaw have bought a nearby tract of land in remembrance of their sojourn near Council Grove. At the state level, the Kansas State Historical Society and the Kansas Department of Commerce, Travel, and Tourism Division, have provided grant funding to assist in the development of Allegawaho Memorial Heritage Park. Informational kiosks erected in Kansas as part of the Lewis and Clark Bicentennial recognize the Kaw Nation (Kanza) as the historic tribe in Kansas.

GOVERNMENT

The Kaw Tribe accepted the provisions of the Oklahoma Indian Welfare Act of 1936 when it adopted a new tribal constitution and bylaws on July 31, 1990. In August 1990, the constitution was approved by the Secretary of the Interior. The tribe is governed by an executive council comprised of a chairperson/CEO, vice-chairperson, secretary, and four tribal members. The council is elected by a majority vote of the national, or general council. The general council is comprised of all enrolled tribal members over the age of 18.

Executive council elections take place every two years. Council members serve four-year terms, with half elected every two years. Vacancies are filled by special elections. The Kaw Nation Tribal District and Supreme Courts were officially recognized in 1992. The tribe administers its own police department. Kaw governmental administration is carried out by several departments and programs: the education and social services department, grants and contracts department, environmental department, self-governance department, tribal police department, the tribal housing authority, tribal enrollment program, tribal youth program, and the Indian child welfare program, and emergency management program. The tribal government is also responsible for licensing and certification.

ECONOMY

The tribal economy is supported by tribal enterprises in the gaming, retail, and service industries. The tribe owns a casino, travel plaza, a convenience store, and three tobacco shops.

Government as Employer. In 2005 the Kaw Nation listed 101 individuals as program directors and administrative staff. Gaming and other enterprises employ an additional 217.

Economic Development Projects. All economic development enterprises on the reservation are the concern of the Kanza Economic Development Authority, which is charged with their oversight. The tribe's trust status allows them to offer tax breaks for commercial enterprises located on Kaw land. Their goal is to encourage economic development.

The Kaw Nation is considering developing a wind energy facility as a commercial project on its land. A study to determine the project's feasibility was funded by the U.S. Department of Energy, beginning in 2002 and lasting 18 months.

Agriculture and Livestock. The tribe utilizes over 900 acres of its lands for farming and grazing purposes.

Gaming. The tribe owns the Kaw Nation Casino in Newkirk, Oklahoma. The casino is a class II gaming facility, but is scheduled to begin including class III games in 2005. It offers 700 bingo seats and pull tabs during bingo sessions. The casino also features 400 slot machines, available for use seven days per week. The casino employs approximately 180 people.

Services and Retail. The Kanza Travel Plaza offers convenience store services with Conoco fuels, a motel, and fast food service. The travel plaza is located at exit 231 on I-35 at U.S. 177. The Kaw Smoke Shops, located in Newkirk and Ponca City, offer an assortment of retail tobacco products. Woodridge Market, a convenience store in Ponca City, offers Conoco fuels, retail tobacco products, and an assortment of other items generally found at such outlets.

Media and Communications. The Kaw Nation publishes a newspaper every three months; it is entitled the *Kanza News* and is edited by the director of the museum.

Tourism and Recreation. Kaw City is home to the Kanza Resource Center and the Kanza Museum. The museum features items donated by Kaw tribal members, and traveling exhibits from other institutions, including the Smithsonian Institution. The Consultant of the South Wind, a three-dimensional sculpture created by the Kaw Tribe and Kaw City, is also located at this site.

The Nation is developing the Allegawaho Memorial Heritage Park near Council Grove, Kansas. The tribe plans to install talking posts throughout the park to provide visitors with information about the tribe. Two miles of walking trails lead the visitor through prairie and woodlands past ruins of the agency building and three stone huts built by the U.S. government for the Kaws. Also on view will be a traditional bark lodge and the 40-foot stone obelisk honoring an unknown Kaw warrior.

The Wah-Shun-Gah Days Inter-Tribal Powwow in Council Grove, Kansas, is hosted by the Kaw Cultural and Powwow Committee. It is sponsored by the Kaw Nation, the Council Grove Chamber of Commerce, the Kaw Mission State Historic Site, and Friends of Kaw Heritage. Arts and crafts are sold, and camping is available. Two of the seven head staff members in 2004 were Kaw tribal members. The annual Kaw Nation Powwow is held on Washunga Bay near Kaw Lake or early August.

An artificial lake, Kaw Lake (or Kaw Reservoir) offers a multitude of outdoor activities, including fishing. The lake is stocked with catfish, bass, crappie, walleye, striped bass, and spoonbill. Hunting is encouraged on the 20,000 acres of land around the lake that the U.S. Army Corps of Engineers oversees specifically for that purpose. The lake has more than 300 campsites and many beaches that allow swimming. Trails surrounding it are used for mountain biking and hiking, with some trails maintained specifically for off-road vehicles. Fishing tournaments and sailboat races also enliven the area.

INFRASTRUCTURE

State Highway 11 provides access to Kaw City from Ponca City and U.S. 77.

COMMUNITY FACILITIES AND SERVICES

Tribal facilities include the Kanza Museum, a multi-purpose annex, W.A. Mehojah, Sr. Resource Center/New Title VI Building, the Kanza Day Care, Johnnie Rae McCauley Multipurpose Center, Kanza Wellness Center, Kanza Clinic, Kaw Casino, housing authority, and White Plume Tribal Housing in Newkirk; the Kaw Nations Grants and Contracts Program, and the Rural Domestic Violence Program in Ponca City. The tribal powwow grounds in Washunga Bay include a council house, garage, public restrooms, and a concession building. The Kaw Nation Education and Social Services Department offers numerous social services: emergency assistance, one-time-only emergency utility deposit assistance, one-time-only emergency transportation/medical program, burial assistance, headstone assistance, general assistance, a substance abuse treatment, a daycare center and child welfare program. The Kaw Housing Authority offers one-time-only assistance with down payment. Meals are provided by title VI, both in the Kaw City area and in other communities.

Education. The Kaw Nation Education and Social Services Department's services include the higher education grant program, Kaw Nation Graduate Program, Kaw Nation Academic Scholarship Program, adult vocational training program, adult education program, and Johnson O'Malley Program.

Health Care. Ophthalmology, diabetes treatment and prevention, and podiatry care are some of the contract services offered by the Kanza Health Clinic in Newkirk. The patients at the clinic number 3,500, with 32 to 35 seen each day by the doctor. Each month the pharmacy fills an average of 2,510 prescriptions. When specialty doctors are present, they see 10 to 15 patients per day. Newkirk is also home to a tribal Wellness Center with a gym and an indoor pool that is open to the public.

Tribal members have access to the Indian Health Service-operated White Eagle Health Center in Ponca City. It provides general medical and dental services and is fully staffed with two physicians. Outpatient visits handled by the doctors are approximately 10,000 per year, and 10,000 more are handled by other medical professionals on staff.

Pawhuska Public Health Service Indian Health Center, Kanza Health Clinic, Pawnee Indian Health Center, Perkins Family Clinic, and White Eagle Health Clinic are the sites for the Kaw-administered women's health program. The centers for disease control and prevention have funded this program through a grant for breast and cervical cancer early detection. It encourages good physical health for women and positive self-care regarding breast and cervical health.

ENVIRONMENTAL CONCERNS

Kaw Lake is important to the Kaw Nation because of the recreational and economic resources the lake offers, the tribe is committed to protecting the lake's environmental well-being. A detailed study during the 1990s of the lake's waters was conducted by the Kaw Nation Environmental Department (KNED), in order to determine any effect in the lake of old and abandoned oil and gas wells. Three of the abandoned wells appeared to pose environmental problems, but none of them appeared to have any impact on the lake; the results indicated the petroleum industries did not threaten the health of the reservoir. The KNED sampled water at 11 sites along the Arkansas River, and the tests showed that contaminants were below dangerous levels. Environmental concerns of the Kaw Nation include the following: 1) testing of water wells for bacteria and other pollutants, 2) inspection of homes for mold and/or asbestos; 3) monitoring surface water of the Arkansas River and Beaver Creek for water quality; 4) developing a wetlands project on Kaw Lake that will feature educational opportunities; 5) establishing water rights to allotment lands; and 6) addressing litter and open dumping problems. Kay County is home to two endangered species, the American Bald Eagle and the Interior Least Tern.

Kickapoo Tribe of Oklahoma Reservation
Federal reservation
Kickapoo
Lincoln, Oklahoma, and Pottawatomie counties, Oklahoma

Kickapoo Tribe of Oklahoma
P.O. Box 70
McLoud, OK 74851
405-964-2075
405-964-6211 Fax

Total area (BIA realty, 2004)
6,821.49 acres

Tribally owned (BIA realty, 2004)
1,851.23 acres

Individually owned
(BIA realty, 2004)
4,970.26 acres

Population 2000 census
18,544

Tribal enrollment
(BIA labor report, 2001)
2,505

Total labor force 2000 census
9,127

Total labor force
(BIA labor report, 2001)
1,705

High school graduate or higher
2000 census
78%

Bachelor's degree or higher
2000 census
12.2%

Unemployment rate 2000 census
6.7%

Unemployment rate
(BIA labor report, 2001)
30%

Per capita income 2000 census
$15,029

LOCATION AND LAND STATUS

Kickapoo tribe trust lands are located in Pottawatomie, Oklahoma, and Lincoln counties in central Oklahoma. Tribal headquarters are in the Town of McLoud, Oklahoma, located at the intersection of Oklahoma Highways 102 and 270. McLoud is less than 10 miles east of Oklahoma City. Shawnee, Oklahoma, lies approximately 10 miles southeast of McLoud.

The Kickapoos were granted a reservation at the center of Indian Territory in 1883. This reservation was allotted in 1891 and opened to white settlement. Today, the Kickapoo Tribe owns 1,082.23 noncontiguous acres of federal trust land. Nearly 5,000 acres of allotments supplement the tribal land base.

CLIMATE

Temperatures in the area range from an average low of 23ºF in January to an average high of 90ºF in July and August.

CULTURE AND HISTORY

The Kickapoo Tribe of Oklahoma is descended from the Algonquian-speaking Kickapoo people of the Great Lakes region. The name Kickapoo is derived from "Kiwigapawa" which means, "he moves about, standing now here, now there." The name is fitting for the Kickapoo, given their history. Corn, beans, squash, and buffalo made up their subsistence lifestyle, as Skyhawk relates. Traditionally they remained in established settlements. Within their aboriginal territory, the Kickapoo maintained close ties with the Sac and Fox tribes. Catholic missionaries in southern Wisconsin made the first European contact with the Kickapoo in 1667. European customs met firm opposition from the Kickapoo, who clung to Native traditions, as Skyhawk notes. After the French and Indian War, and the resulting dissolution of the Illinois Tribe, the Kickapoo moved into what is now southern Illinois. Relations with the United States commenced with the Treaty of Greenville in 1795. During the War of 1812, the Kickapoo allied with the Shawnee Chief Tecumseh against the United States. In 1819, the Kickapoo were forced to cede their Illinois lands and removed to a reservation in Missouri, at which point a branch of the tribe moved to Texas and eventually Mexico. This band became known as the "Mexican Kickapoo." During this period, the Kickapoo were led by Chief Kanakuk, a prophet who established a tribal religion and advocated virtuous living. An

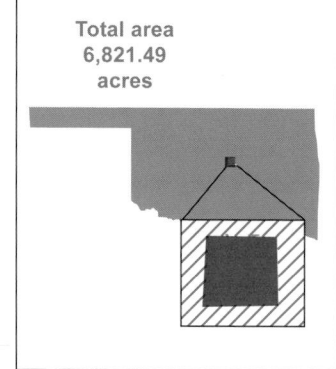

Total area
6,821.49
acres

1835 treaty replaced the Missouri land with a 12-square-mile reservation in northeastern Kansas. In 1863, another dissatisfied band joined the Mexican Kickapoo, who became embroiled in a long border war against scattered ranches in south central Texas. In 1873, U.S. Army forces crossed into Mexico and subdued the Kickapoo raiders; many were induced to rejoin their kin to the north. The Kickapoo were granted a 100,000-acre reservation in Indian Territory in 1883, which was alienated and allotted less than 10 years later. The Kickapoo opening was the final land run in Oklahoma, as narrated on Roots Web. By March 1895 the government had allotted 22,640 acres in 80-acre parcels to the Kickapoos. The government bought the rest of the Kickapoo reservation and held a land run in May 1895, the account relates. This acreage became part of Lincoln, Oklahoma, and Pottawatomie counties, where most Oklahoma Kickapoos still reside. Despite losing their land base, the Kickapoo retained their tribal religious beliefs and ceremonies. The tribe organized under the Oklahoma Indian Welfare Act of 1936 in 1938.

Today the Kickapoos gain revenue, in part, through operating a tribal casino. Most Kickapoos still adhere to tribal customs and traditions in religion, arts and crafts, and ceremonies.

GOVERNMENT

The supreme governing body of the Kickapoo Tribe of Oklahoma is the Kickapoo General Council, which meets at least once a year and must have a quorum of 25 to be in session. A business committee, consisting of a chairman, vice-chairman, treasurer, and member, serves as the tribes elected governing body. Members of the committee serve three-year staggered terms. Elections are held during the annual tribal meeting. The tribe is organized under the Oklahoma Indian Welfare Act of 1936. A federal charter was adopted in 1938, and the tribe ratified a constitution and bylaws in 1977.

ECONOMY

The Kickapoo Tribe's economy relies primarily on gaming and retail. The total number of persons employed is 1,202, according to the BIA.

Government as Employer. The tribe's government operations include a community center, a child care center, and a fitness center. The BIA counts 125 public employees.

Gaming. Kickapoo Casino in McLoud features three table games and 400 video gaming machines, according to Casino City. Another casino with about 20 video gaming machines forms part of the Kickapoo Conoco Station in Harrah.

Services and Retail. The Kickapoo Conoco gas station and convenience store is located in Harrah, next to the casino.

INFRASTRUCTURE

Transportation. Tribal headquarters at McLoud are directly accessible via Oklahoma Highway 102 and Oklahoma Highway 270. U.S. 62 passes just north of McLoud, connecting with Oklahoma City 10 miles to the west. I-40 passes just south of McLoud, connecting with Oklahoma City and beyond. Commercial and private air services are available in Oklahoma City. Passenger bus lines serve the Oklahoma City area, as do major trucking lines and express package carriers.

COMMUNITY FACILITIES AND SERVICES

The Kickapoo Tribe operates a community center, located two miles north of McLoud. On October 1, 2003, Indianz.com reported that a $1-million child-care center was to open in July 2004. The U.S. Department of Housing and Urban Development and the tribe financed the center. The 2003 Indianz.com article says the tribe's $350,000 fitness center will have exercise equipment and fitness classes. Yahoo now lists All Nations Fitness Center as open in McLoud.

Education. Children attend public schools in the three-county tribal area.

Health Care. An array of ambulatory health services is furnished to tribe members by the Oklahoma City Area Indian Health Service through its Shawnee Health Center in Shawnee. Patients in need of secondary or higher levels of care are referred to the Carl Albert Indian Hospital at Ada or to one of the many hospitals in Oklahoma City.

Kickapoo

Kiowa

Kiowa

Total area-jointly held *(BIA realty, 2004)*
189,262.69 acres
Federal trust-jointly held 1 acre
(BIA realty, 2004)
Tribally owned-jointly held 3,300.85 acres
(BIA realty, 2004)
Individually owned-jointly held
(BIA realty, 2004) 185,960.84 acres
Population *2000 census* 193,260
Tribal enrollment 11,088
(BIA labor report, 2001)
Total labor force *2000 census* 90,601
High school graduate or higher 81.3%
2000 census
Bachelor's degree or higher 17.3%
2000 census
Unemployment rate *2000 census* 5.6%
Per capita income *2000 census* $15,389

LOCATION AND LAND STATUS

The Kiowa Indian Tribe of Oklahoma owns 7,592.61 acres of noncontiguous, federal trust land spread across a six-county area of southwestern Oklahoma; these lands are owned jointly with the Comanche and Apache tribes.

PHYSICAL DESCRIPTION

This region of Oklahoma is primarily rolling grasslands of the southern Great Plains, although there are some small hills and lakes. The Wichita Mountains are nearby.

CLIMATE

The elevation in the community of Carnegie, Oklahoma, is 1,290 feet above sea level. The year-round average daily high temperature at Carnegie is 74°F. The year-round average daily low temperature is 48°F. The area receives approximately 29 inches of precipitation annually.

TRI-OK-038

CULTURE AND HISTORY

Prior to contact with whites, the Kiowas were nomadic Plains buffalo hunters who roamed vast territories, living in portable, skin-covered lodges, collecting and maintaining huge horse herds. The Kiowas were fierce warriors on horseback, vigorously opposing all white settlement in the southern Plains. They raided, along with Comanche allies, as far south as Mexico, demonstrating a well-organized military structure and a highly effective written form of pictographic communication to record a chronology of events. Their spoken language is related to the Tanoan-speaking pueblo people of New Mexico's Rio Grande Valley.

As participants in the Medicine Lodge Treaty of 1867, they were assigned a reservation in Oklahoma; however, in defiance of the federal government, they resumed warfare with white settlers in the area and never really located to the lands set aside for them, nor did they limit their activities to the reservation. In 1875, they were eventually subjugated when large numbers of their horses were captured and destroyed, and several of their leaders were killed or captured.

GOVERNMENT

The tribe is governed by the Kiowa Indian Council, which consists of all voting members at least 18 years of age. The tribe, under PL-638, contracts with the BIA to administer key programs and services.

ECONOMY

Tourism and Recreation. The town of Lawton, Oklahoma, has 78 city parks with recreational opportunities open to all residents and tourists. Lawton, like other Oklahoma communities in the region, has museums, entertainment venues, golf courses, tennis courts, and other public facilities. The nearby Wichita Mountains Wildlife Refuge is a haven for swimmers, boaters, and fishermen, offering camping, bicycling trails, picnic grounds, hiking, and mountain climbing. Periodic rodeos, powwows, and other events are held regularly.

COMMUNITY FACILITIES AND SERVICES

Education. Tribal schoolchildren attend public and private schools scattered throughout southwestern Oklahoma.

Health Care. Tribal members are provided health services by facilities operated by the Indian Health Service. The Lawton Service Unit, serving a 10-county area in southwestern Oklahoma, includes the full-service, 45-bed Lawton Indian Hospital in Lawton; the 20,000-square-foot Anadarko Health Center includes dental care; the Carnegie Health Center; and a health station at the Riverside Indian School all provide care.

Kiowa Indian Tribe of Oklahoma Reservation
Federal reservation
Kiowa

Kiowa Tribe of Oklahoma
P.O. Box 369
Carnegie, OK 73015
580-654-2300
580-654-2188 Fax

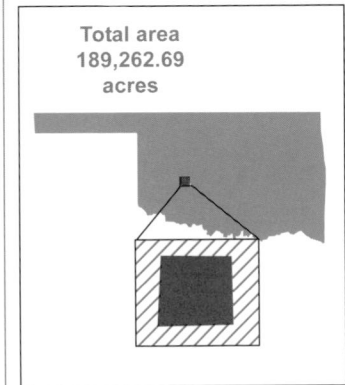

Total area
189,262.69
acres

TRI-OK-038 Department of Transportation & Trucks

Miami

Miami Tribe of Oklahoma
Tribal Jurisdiction Area
Miami
Ottawa County, Oklahoma

Miami Tribe of Oklahoma
202 South Eight Tribes Trail
P.O. Box 1326
Miami, OK 74355
918-542-1445
918-542-7260 Fax
miamination.com

Total area (BIA realty, 2004)
320.98 acres

Federal trust (BIA realty, 2004)
35 acres

Tribally owned (BIA realty, 2004)
142.99 acres

Total labor force 2000 census
139

High school graduate or higher
2000 census
94.3%

Bachelor's degree or higher
2000 census
11.5%

Unemployment rate 2000 census
0%

LOCATION AND LAND STATUS

The Miami Tribe of Oklahoma, the federally recognized sovereign Miami Nation, also known by the traditional name "Myaamia," owns lands in the Great Lakes area, Kansas, and Oklahoma. The Great Lakes area is the ancestral homeland of the Miami Nation. The land in Kansas contains the Miami reserve, and it is where the tribe resided after it was removed from its homelands by force in 1846. Presently the Miami Nation resides in the Indian Territory jurisdiction area in Ottawa County, Oklahoma. Ottawa County is located in the northeastern corner of Oklahoma and is comprised of flat prairie land and a portion of the Ozark Mountain Geologic Province. The Miami Tribe's national headquarters is located on the eastern edge of Miami, Oklahoma, approximately 90 miles northeast of Tulsa.

The original Miami Reservation consisted of lands purchased from the Shawnees during the mid-nineteenth century. These lands were largely lost through allotment. Today, the Miami Nation owns approximately 1,400 acres of land, with the greatest portion located in Ottawa County. Of the 1,400 acres, 152 acres are held in trust status.

CULTURE AND HISTORY

The Myaamias, or the Miami people, originated in the modern State of Indiana and held the Great Lakes regions of Indiana, Illinois, Ohio, southern Wisconsin, and southern Michigan as the Nation's homelands. They also count regions within Kentucky, Iowa, and Missouri as areas of importance. Miami presence in these areas was largely due to war and the need to hunt.

The Myaamias are of the Central Algonquian linguistic group. Their relatives are the Weas and Piankashaws. The great Nation of the Myaamia is well documented in the history of the United States due to the leadership of their Great War Chief Mihšihkinaahkwa, also known as Little Turtle. Little Turtle lead the Miamis and their allied forces in major victories over U.S. troops in the late 1700s. The allied victories over General Josiah Harmar and his troops in 1790, and the most notable defeat over General Arthur St. Clair in 1791, are recorded in history as the worst defeats suffered by the U.S. Army during the Indian Wars. Some 623 of St. Clair's troops were killed. Following these allied victories, in 1794 the Battle of Fallen Timbers took place near present day Maumee, Ohio. U.S. troops, led by General "Mad" Anthony Wayne, defeated their allied enemies, led by the Shawnee Chief Bluejacket. This defeat led to the signing of the Greenville Treaty in 1795, in which lands were ceded and boundary lines drawn for the Myaamias and their relations. Continued white encroachment into Miami country, the signing of the Indian Removal Act in 1830, and the 1840 treaty, led to the forced removal of the Myaamias from their homelands to land reserved for them west of the Mississippi near present-day La Cygne, Kansas. The Nation resided on the Kansas Reserve until the signing of the 1867 treaty, which called for yet another removal, this time to Indian Country, now known as the State of Oklahoma. Through war and peace, removal, assimilation tactics, and oppression as Indian people, the Myaamias have survived as a federally recognized sovereign nation.

The Miami Nation Office of Cultural Preservation is located in the Nation's downtown office building in Miami, Oklahoma. The office is staffed by the cultural preservation officer, tribal historic preservation officer, and cultural education director.

The Nation's preservation effort includes restoring important tribal buildings and structures, maintaining the Nation's cemeteries and burial grounds, reclaiming the language, publishing a quarterly newspaper, and overseeing the Nation's Heritage Archive.

GOVERNMENT

The Miami general council is composed of all tribal members over the age of 18. A business council consisting of a chief, a second chief, a secretary-treasurer, and two council members, serves as the elected governing body. Members serve three-year terms, with elections occurring at annual meetings of the Miami general council. The Miami Tribe of Oklahoma adopted a constitution and bylaws on August 16, 1939, in accordance with the Oklahoma Indian Welfare Act of June 26, 1936. That constitution was revised and adopted on February 22, 1996, and remains in effect.

The self-governing Miami Nation serves its people through government departments and federal programs, including social services, violence against women, Indian child welfare, adoption and foster care, child care, substance abuse, recreation, elder care, housing, community health, environmental protection, agriculture and land use, tax commission, law enforcement, cultural preservation, annual community cultural events, and education.

BUSINESS CORPORATION

The Miami Tribe of Oklahoma has a federal corporate charter that was ratified on June 1, 1940, under the Oklahoma Indian Welfare Act of June 26, 1936. This charter allows the tribe to carry out all of its own business operations.

ECONOMY

The Nation's economic development efforts include 8(a) contracting, manufacturing, environmental testing, agriculture, and gaming, all of which are major components of the Miami Nation's economic success.

Government as Employer. The Miami Nation employs approximately 90 people through tribal administration, economic development, and community service positions.

Agriculture and Livestock. The Nation owns and operates Tahway Farms, which oversees approximately 1,000 acres of farmland, pasture, and pecan groves. Cattle breeds raised are black and red Angus, Hereford, and Devon. Specializing in grass-fed beef cattle, Tahway Farms management is focusing upon producing meat that is natural and healthy.

Gaming. The Miami Nation and Modoc Tribe jointly own The Stables Casino. This 23,000-square-foot casino is located next to the Modoc Tribal Complex in Miami, Oklahoma. The casino is open 24 hours a day and features over 300 electronic bingo games, off-track betting, and a restaurant. The Miami Nation also owns a casino called Miami Tribe Entertainment Casino, which is located in the Miami Tribal Complex.

Services and Retail. The Miami Nation has three economic development subdivisions, and it owns several businesses, including Envira Tech Environmental Testing Lab, Miami Designs Screen Printing and Embroidery, and the Miami Trader Gift Shop, which specializes in Native arts and crafts.

Media and Communications. The Miami Tribe has its own quarterly newspaper called the *Aatotankiki Myaamiaki* and manages the website.

Tourism and Recreation. The Miami Nation hosts a number of annual cultural events including the Winter Gathering-featuring stomp dancing, gourd dancing, a chili feed, and an Indian Art Market-which is held on the last Saturday in January each year, and the Nation's annual powwow which is held the first weekend in June at the Ottawa County Fair Grounds.

INFRASTRUCTURE

The City of Miami is the northeastern "gateway to Indian Country" via Oklahoma's Will Rogers Turnpike (I-44), which passes immediately adjacent to the tribal headquarters, providing easy access to Tulsa and beyond. The Miami Municipal Airport provides local air service, while commercial airline service is available in Joplin, Missouri, about 35 miles to the northeast, and in Tulsa, Oklahoma, about 85 miles to the south. Commercial and city bus lines serve the Miami area, as do commercial trucking lines and railway.

Electricity. A municipal utility contract within city limits and two major providers within the rural areas of the jurisdiction provide electricity.

Fuel. Oklahoma Natural Gas supplies the reservation with natural gas service.

Water Supply. The City of Miami furnishes water and wastewater services within city limits. The Ottawa County District 7 Rural Water Service serves the rural portion of the area, and wastewater systems there are either lagoon or septic.

Housing. The Miami Nation's Social Service Department operates two programs to ensure safe and healthy housing for tribal members. The HUD program works to provide housing for low-income families. The program consists of other small housing programs, including 4-plex apartments, rehabilitation, down payment assistance, rental assistance, and deposit assistance. The housing improvement program is funded through the BIA and allows the tribe to rehabilitate or replace the homes of eligible tribal members.

COMMUNITY FACILITIES AND SERVICES

The Miami Tribal Complex houses administration offices, a nutrition center, the Miami Tribe's Entertainment Casino, the Miami Trader Gift Shop, the Miami tribal library, and the Nation's Heritage Archive. The Nation also operates a child care center. A longhouse, located five miles north of the city, serves as a site for cultural gatherings and meetings.

Education. Tribal children attend schools and universities in the Miami Public School system. For continuing education, the Miami Nation shares a close and unique relationship with its namesake, Miami University, in Oxford, Ohio. The university runs a program called the Myaamia Project whose mission is to facilitate and encourage the preservation, promotion, and research of the Miami Nation's history, culture, and language. Miami University also provides scholarships to tribal members who qualify. Other scholarships available to tribal members are The Stables Education Award, The Josephine Goodboo Watson Memorial Book Scholarship, The Tax Commission Continuing Education Award, and The Crane Award.

Health Care. Health care services are provided by the Northeastern Tribal Health System, which manages a clinic located next to the Nation's headquarters in Miami, Oklahoma.

Miami

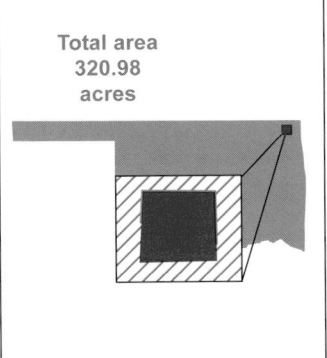

Total area
320.98
acres

M odoc

Modoc

LOCATION AND LAND STATUS

The Modoc Tribal Complex is located at Miami, Oklahoma, in the state's far northeastern corner. Major cities near Miami are Joplin, Missouri, approximately 27 miles northeast, and Tulsa, Oklahoma, approximately 85 miles southwest. The Modoc Tribe is currently working to re-establish a tribal land base, having only been restored to federal recognition in 1978.

CULTURE AND HISTORY

Members of the Modoc Tribe of Oklahoma are descendants of Modoc warriors and their families who were exiled from their homelands to the Quapaw Agency in Indian Territory in 1873 in what is now southern Oregon and northern California. A small tribe, the Modocs were divided into three groups: the Gumbatwas or "people of the west," the Kokiwas or "people of the far out country," and the Paskanwas or "river people." The Modocs called themselves Mqlaqs, which meant "people." Their ancestral home consisted of some 5,000 square miles along both sides of what is now the California-Oregon border, encompassing portions of the Cascade Mountains, the alkali flats to the east, and the lava beds to the south. The Modocs were migratory hunters, fishers, and gatherers. An influx of non-Indians during the mid-nineteenth century had a dramatic impact on Modoc culture. They readily adopted non-Indian clothing and even took non-Indian names.

In 1864, the Modocs ceded with the Klamaths and Paiutes and agreed to go to the newly established Klamath reservation. Abysmal conditions on the reservation spurred the Modoc

chief, Captain Jack, to lead his tribe off the reservation and back to the Lost River. Attempts to return the band to the reservation spurred the explosive Modoc War. Captain Jack and his band were returned to the reservation by 1865. They left again and retreated to the lava beds where they held off the army until 1873. Following the band's surrender, the Modoc leaders were hanged, and the survivors were exiled to the Quapaw Agency in Indian Territory.

Four thousand acres were purchased for the Modocs in 1874, but they languished in Indian Territory due to a lack of food and clothing. Reservation lands were allotted to the 68 remaining tribal members in 1891. Following allotment, they became successful farmers in northeastern Oklahoma, and their Native language and customs were lost. Since the Modocs, who wanted to return to Oklahoma from Oregon, were on Klamath roles and had no jurisdiction in Oklahoma during the 1950s, the Eisenhower administration terminated federal supervision of the Modoc Tribe along with the Klamath. In 1967, the Modocs in Oklahoma banded together to form an unofficial tribal government, and the tribe regained federal recognition in 1978.

Today, tribal members are respected members of their communities; they are involved in ranching, teaching, small business, and other professions. The tribe is working to re-establish a land base, and tribal members strive to preserve their heritage and culture.

Modoc Reservation
Federal reservation
Modoc
Ottawa County, Oklahoma

Modoc Tribe of Oklahoma
515 G Street Southeast
P.O. Box 939
Miami, OK 74354
918 542-1190
918 542-5415 Fax

Total area (BIA realty, 2004)
86.41 acres

Total area (Tribal source, 2005)
4,000 acres

Federal trust (Tribal source, 2005)
210 acres

Tribally owned (BIA realty, 2004)
86.41 acres

Tribally owned (Tribal source, 2005)
72 acres

Modoc

Population *(Tribal source, 2005)*
less than 200

Tribal enrollment
(BIA labor report, 2001)
156

Total labor force *2000 census*
85

Total labor force
(BIA labor report, 2001)
101

High school graduate or higher
2000 census
87.2%

Bachelor's degree or higher
2000 census
10.3%

Unemployment rate *2000 census*
0%

Unemployment rate
(BIA labor report, 2001)
80%

Per capita income *2000 census*

ENVIRONMENTAL CONCERNS
The tribe has environmental concerns about the health of their water and land. The EPA water and land studies are being used to identify the problems and potential solutions.

GOVERNMENT

The Modoc Tribal Council is composed of all enrolled members over age 18. The Modoc elected council, composed of a chief, a second chief, a secretary-treasurer, and two councilmen, serves as the elected governing body for enrolled members. Members of the elected council serve four-year terms, with elections occurring during the tribal council's annual meeting.

The Modoc Tribe of Oklahoma adopted a constitution and bylaws on May 25, 1978, in accordance with the Oklahoma Indian Welfare Act of 1936. The constitution was approved on June 27, 1990. Tribal programs include a housing authority, low-income home energy assistance program, family preservation, Indian child welfare, community health representative, Red Cedar Recycling, and the office of environmental quality.

The tribe administers their office of environmental quality programs under federal grants from the Administration for Native Americans, the EPA General Assistance Program for Section 104 Water, and other environmental grants from the BIA.

BUSINESS CORPORATION

The tribe has a business corporation.

ECONOMY

Federal funding for tribal programs and infrastructure, revenues from gaming, and other business enterprises are the main components of the Modoc Tribe's economy.

Government as Employer. The tribal government employs 200 people.

Agriculture and Livestock. The tribe has reintroduced 200 head of buffalo.

Gaming. In partnership with the Miami Tribe of Oklahoma, the Modoc Tribe developed The Stables in 1998. Located next to the Modoc Tribal Complex, this 23,000 square foot gaming facility includes a casino and bingo hall. The casino offers 550 gaming machines, high stakes bingo, simulcast betting, and one restaurant. The Modoc Tribe intends to create scholarships for tribal members and enhance tribal services with the revenue earned from the enterprise.

Real Estate/Commercial Development. There are plans for commercial or real estate development.

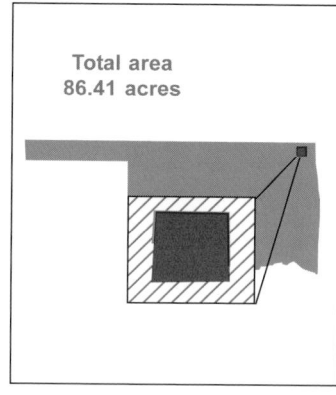

Total area
86.41 acres

Services and Retail. The Modoc Tribe owns and operates the Red Cedar Recycling Center, recycling newspapers, office paper, computer paper, cardboard, and aluminum cans.

Media and Communications. The tribe has a newspaper.

INFRASTRUCTURE

Tribal headquarters in Miami, Oklahoma, are accessible via U.S. 59. I-44 between Tulsa and Joplin, Missouri, passes just south of Miami. Private air facilities are located in Miami. Commercial air service is available in Tulsa, 85 miles southwest. Major bus lines and package carriers serve Tulsa and Joplin. Commercial railway service is available in Miami.

Telecommunication. Telephone, cable, and Internet services are available on trust lands.

COMMUNITY FACILITIES AND SERVICES

The Modoc Friends Church, which was established in 1879. The church and the cemetery, in Ottawa County, are both on the National Register of Historic Sites. The Modoc Tribal Complex, completed in 1981, houses the tribal office, archives, and a library. The Modoc library is the only library in the area dedicated to Native American history and genealogy.

Education. Children attend public schools in Ottawa County. Scholarship programs are available to tribal members seeking higher education.

Health Care. Medical and dental services are available in Miami and Clarismare Hospital is 80 miles away.

sage

Osage Nation Reservation
Federal reservation
Osage
Osage County, Oklahoma

Osage Nation
P.O. Box 779
Pawhuska, OK 74056
918-287-5432
918-287-2257 Fax
osagetribe.com

LOCATION AND LAND STATUS

The Osage Nation, Reservation is located in north-central Oklahoma, spanning nearly 1.5 million acres, virtually the entire area of Osage County. It lies directly northwest of Tulsa and is bounded on the north by the Kansas border. The Osage tribal campus-the heart of the Osage Nation-is located in Pawhuska, Oklahoma.

The original Osage Reservation was established in 1825 in the extreme southern portion of what would become Kansas. The present-day reservation was established in Oklahoma in 1871, upon lands that the tribe purchased from the Cherokee Nation. Much of the land is allotted into various ownership patterns. In addition, the tribe has approximately 164,000 acres of restricted surface land in the county, and smaller amounts of restricted land outside the county, as well as in other states.

Gray Horse, Pawhuska, Fairfax, Skiatook, and Hominy are the five Osage Indian towns on the reservation.

The Osage Tribal Council asserts that the area of the reservation has never been reduced by an Act of Congress. It contends that the original reservation boundaries must be acknowledged as the boundaries of the reservation today. The matter is presently before the federal courts

PHYSICAL DESCRIPTION

The Osage Reservation encompasses over 1 million acres of land in Oklahoma. The topography of tribal lands vary from wooded hills in the eastern portions to open plains and grasslands in the northern and western areas. Almost 3,000 miles of streams, over 40,000 acres of lakes, and over 8,500 acres of wetlands are located within reservation boundaries.

CLIMATE
The average summer high in the town of Pawhuska, Oklahoma is 93°F while the January lows are around 24°F. The area experiences an annual precipitation of 38.5 inches.

CULTURE AND HISTORY
The Wazhazhe, or Osage, ancestral lands encompassed most of present day Missouri, Kansas, Oklahoma, and Arkansas. The tribe occupied the region between the Arkansas and Missouri rivers from the Mississippi River to the Great Plains for several thousand years. The indigenous language of the Osage is a Siouan dialect.

European culture first made contact with the Osage in 1673 in their villages along the Osage River. In the Treaty of 1808, the tribe ceded a major portion of its lands in Missouri and the northern half of Arkansas. In 1818, it ceded lands in northwest Arkansas and eastern Oklahoma. In the Treaty of 1825, the Osage ceded its remaining lands in Missouri and areas in central Kansas. The tribe centralized in its remaining homelands in southern Kansas. By 1868, the Osage Nation had ceded over 80 million acres of its ancestral territory to the federal government.

Under provisions of the U.S. Indian Removal Policy, the tribe was forced to relinquish its lands in Kansas and relocate to Indian Country. It purchased a portion of lands in the Cherokee Outlet and relocated there between 1871 and 1872. The present-day reservation occupies this site. The population of the Osage in 1871 was counted at nearly 4,000. By 1906, however, smallpox epidemics and intermarriage with non-Indians had reduced the count to 2,229, about half of these being of mixed-ethnicity. In 1896, oil was discovered on the reservation, and the U.S. Secretary of the Interior granted a single drilling company the leasing rights to all oil and natural gas development on the eastern half of the reservation for a ten-year period. The tribe received little in the way of royalties from this arrangement until the 1920s.

Unable to persuade the Osage tribe to accept allotment of the more than 1.5 million-acre Osage Reservation, the U.S. Congress authorized combining the Indian and Oklahoma Territories and admitted the State of Oklahoma into the Union in 1907, on the condition that the Osage Reservation constitute an entire county. Consequently, Osage County alone among the 77 counties of Oklahoma shares virtually the same boundaries as the nineteenth century reservation. Likewise, the Osage Reservation shares its borders with present-day Osage County. Unable to persuade either the traditional leaders or the constitutional government of the Osage Nation to accept partition of the reservation, Congress enacted legislation in 1906 mandating allotment of the surface of the Osage Reservation, but allowing the Osage to retain undivided ownership of the reservation. Today fewer than 250,000 acres of the reservation surface remain in restricted Indian ownership, but the tribe retains all mineral rights to the 1.5 million-acre reservation.

Members of the Osage Nation continue to practice traditional customs and are working to revitalize the indigenous language. The goal of the nation is establish a self-sustaining economy that will support the Osage population, enhance tribal services, and promote the tribal culture.

GOVERNMENT
The Osage Tribe is governed by the Osage Tribal Council. It is comprised of a chief, an assistant chief, and eight Osage Tribal Council members. The tribal council meets twice each month.

In 2004, the federal government passed into law HR 2912, which recognizes the right of the Osage Nation to establish its own guidelines for tribal membership. Former law stated only those tribal members who have a presently vested interest in the mineral revenues of the reservation could be voting members of the tribe.

Tribal government programs include tourism, social services, education, housing assistance, health care, WIC, TANF, environmental and natural resources, food distribution, roads and transportation, and burial assistance, among others. An independent regulatory entity of the tribe, the Osage Nation Gaming Commission, oversees tribal gaming operations. The tribe maintains its own court system. In addition, the chief judge of the Osage Supreme Court is elected by the membership of the Osage Nation.

The Osage Nation Housing Authority provides emergency housing, rehabilitation, homeowner assistance, and air conditioning assistance. It also manages the senior housing rental complex.

The Osage Nation Planning and Development Office is responsible for planning and developing new tribal programs, and it provides technical assistance to the tribal council. The Osage Nation Gaming Commission serves as the tribal licensing authority, overseeing the compliance of all gaming concerns with regulations and tribal law.

BUSINESS CORPORATION
The tribe owns the Osage Nation Enterprise. This entity is responsible for the management of all non-business activities of the tribe, excluding tribal gaming operations. It is governed by a board of directors. The tribe also owns Osage Business Enterprise (OBE). This entity manages all tribal businesses. Projects of OBE include a recycling program, to begin operation in late 2005. The recycling program will include a cogeneration facility that will utilize municipal solid waste for electrical generation.

OBE has also developed a number of teaming agreements. It is currently partnering with TRANE companies for the service and maintenance of HVAC units at military bases and with Terra Fix to provide on-site remediation equipment. It has partnered with Clear2there to provide digital video recording, IT, phone, and cable services, with emphasis on security application for the Homeland Security Program. OBE has also partnered with Arrowhead Construction to provide project design, construction, and management. It will provide all construction services for the tribe's infrastructure projects.

ECONOMY
The tribal economy is supported primarily by the income earned from the harvest of gas and oil in Osage County. The Osage Nation owns all mineral rights to resources in Osage County. The tribal economy is also supported by revenue earned from tribally owned enterprises in the gaming and service industries.

Economic Development Projects. The tribe intends to further its opportunities in the tourism and gaming industries.

In October 2004, the Osage Nation started construction on a fourth casino, located in Tulsa. Nearly twice as big as the Million Dollar Elm-Sand Springs, the Million Dollar Elm-Tulsa is planned to feature 1,000 electronic gaming devices; a full-service restaurant, bar, and lounge; a stage venue; and parking for 800 vehicles.

Government as Employer. The Osage Nation provides jobs to tribal members and has economic projects within the sur-

Osage

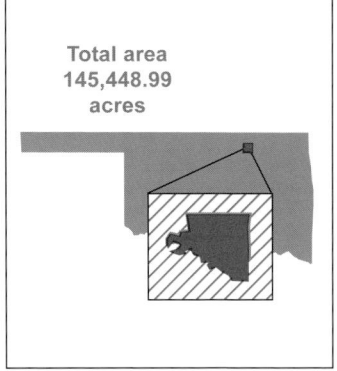

Total area
145,448.99
acres

Total area (BIA realty, 2004)
145,448.99 acres

Tribally owned (BIA realty, 2004)
1,021.34 acres

**Tribally owned lands,
subsurface** (Tribal source, 2004)
1,469,240 acres

Tribally owned lands, surface
(Tribal source, 2004)
fewer than 250,000 acres

Individually owned
(BIA realty, 2004)
144,427.65 acres

Allotted (Tribal source, 2004)
1,469,240 acres

Out-of-state (Tribal source, 2004)
2 parcels in Kansas

Population 2000 census
44,437

Tribal enrollment
(BIA labor report, 2001)
18,415

Total labor force 2000 census
20,409

Total labor force
(BIA labor report, 2001)
6,329

High school graduate or higher
2000 census
80.2%

Osage

Bachelor's degree or higher
2000 census
14.6%

Unemployment rate *2000 census*
5.6%

Unemployment rate
(BIA labor report, 2001)
55%

Per capita income *2000 census*
$17,014

rounding community. It is the largest employer on the reservation.

Agriculture and Livestock. While the region's relatively shallow soil layer discourages most agriculture, the native prairie bluestem grasses constitute an ideal food for the vast herds of cattle on the reservation. Approximately 150,000 head of cattle graze on Osage lands each year, providing tribal income and employment second only to the oil and gas industry. The tribe also owns two parcels of land in Kansas. Both are leased for grazing to local ranchers.

Gaming. The tribe owns three gaming facilities. The Osage Nation Hominy Casino is located in the tribal complex north of Hominy, Oklahoma. It offers 202 slots/VLTs and employs 36 individuals. The Osage Nation Pawhuska Casino is located north of Pawhuska. This facility offers 52 slots/VLTs. Opened in June 2005, today the casino employs 21 people. The Osage Nation Million Dollar Elm Casino is located in Sand Springs. This facility offers 500 slots, a food court, a bar and lounge, a gift shop, and an entertainment venue. It also features a Players Club, a program which provides frequent and preferred clientele with discounts, a casino newsletter, coupons, and other special offers. Opened in 2004, the construction of the casino created over 120 construction jobs and over 160 permanent jobs.

Mining. Tribal lands are rich in natural resources, most notably in oil and gas. Drilling has been on-going on the Osage Reservation since the early 1900s. The tribe continues to support the activity and holds almost 13,000 wells. The Nation has implemented a computer imaging system to assist in the location of oil deposits in order to further drilling operations. It also hosts an annual Oil and Gas Summit to address issues in the industry.

Oil and gas harvesting, royalties, and tangential business activities represent the single largest source of revenue for the tribe and Osage County as a whole. The tribe owns all mineral rights in Osage County and earns 18.75% royalties on all leases. Leases and royalties from oil and gas currently generate between $50 and $75 million annually. These monies are used to fund tribal programs, as well as quarterly payments to tribal members owning head rights.

The BIA's Osage Agency serves as trustee for the large oil and gas operations of the Osage Nation of Oklahoma. In fact, the majority of the agency's 60-plus staff is employed in the minerals branch. The Osage Tribe is the only tribe in the United States whose mineral operations are entirely the responsibility of the BIA.

Industrial Park. The tribe has long held an industrial park building in Hominy, Oklahoma, which is currently leased by the Southwest Corset Company. This business employs 300 people when fully operational.

Services and Retail. In addition to its casinos, the tribe owns the Osage Nation Palace Grocery in Fairfax. It also supports the sale of clothing, books, CDs, artwork, office supplies, and a number of other products through its on-line gift shop. Given the fully allotted nature of the Osage Reservation, there are myriad wholesale and retail services within the site of the reservation, owned by both tribal members and nonmembers. Osage County towns such as Hominy and Pawhuska offer a full range of services.

Tourism and Recreation. The Osage Prairie Coalition of Tourism is a program of the Osage Tribal Tourism Departments. The coalition represents areas of the reservation, southeast-

ern Kansas, and north central Oklahoma. This organization promotes the tourism in the region.

The tribe operates the first Native American tribal museum established in North America. The Osage Tribal Museum, located in Pawhuska, features a permanent exhibit detailing Osage history and culture and revolving exhibits of contemporary Osage art. It also displays a century-old schoolhouse and a monument of the first Boy Scout Troop in the country. The tribe also hosts the annual I'n-Lon-Shka Dances held in June. The public is welcome to attend and the festivities attract a number of visitors.

Immaculate Conception Church, also known as the Cathedral of the Osage, is located in Pawhuska. In 1919, the Vatican authorized the installation of a series of stained glass windows with images depicting living tribal members. In addition, the tribal council chambers features murals of Osage history, from the tribal creation story to contemporary images. Further murals are visible in Hominy, known as the City of Murals. Other attractions in the area include the Million Dollar Elm Memorial, the Osage Agency Campus, Pawhuska City Hall, Woolaroc, Whitehair Memorial, and the Chief Lookout Memorial.

Osage County is home to a number of large, beautiful lakes. Hominy City Lake is popular with fishermen, boaters and campers, and features a handicapped fishing pier, picnic areas, a playground and softball field.

INFRASTRUCTURE

Major highways serving the reservation include U.S. Highway 60, State Highways 10, 11, and 20 running east-west, and State Highways 99, 97, and 18 running north-south. Additionally, many county roads run throughout the reservation.

The Osage Nation Transportation Improvement Program is part of the Indian Reservation Roads Program that is funded by the Federal Highway Bill. The Osage Nation receives nearly $2 million annually to spend on road improvement within the reservation boundaries. It is currently participating in the development of a new road between Grayhorse and Fairfax; three bridges west of Fairfax; and a road south of Skiatook. Future projects include a bridge at Okesa, a bridge over Candy Creek, and roads in north Tulsa.

Transportation. Tulsa offers commercial trucking, rail, and bus service. Bus lines serve several other communities in Osage County as well. The nearest major airport is in Tulsa, five miles from the southeastern border of the reservation and 55 miles from tribal headquarters at Pawhuska. Air service is also available in Hominy.

COMMUNITY FACILITIES AND SERVICES

The tribe's social services department provides adult protection services, child protection services, Indian child welfare, family preservation, foster care, family violence prevention, and financial assistance program for eligible tribal members. Programs to enhance public safety include law enforcement as well as Victims Assistance in Indian Country, STOP (a program that targets violence against women), and family violence protection services.

The Osage Nation Counseling Center provides a number of services for the prevention and treatment of substance abuse. It provides emergency shelter, residential counseling, and outpatient counseling. In 2004, it opened the Osage Nation Adolescent Center. This facility serves tribal males between the ages of 13 and 17 years. It is a residential facility for the treatment of substance abuse. The program was funded by a grant from the Office of Juvenile Justice Delinquency Programs. A critical element of the program is the reintroduction of participating youth to traditional cultural elements. The grant also provides funds for the sponsorship for the Red Ribbon Powwow.

The Osage Nation Book Mobile provides a mobile library. The program visits Osage communities throughout the county.

An Osage Nation AmeriCorps VISTA Project was established on the reservation in 2003. The project focuses on the tribe's Early Learning Program. Ten VISTA volunteers serve the community.

Education. The tribe operates four pre-school facilities in the tribal service area, including Sweet Things Discovery Center in Skiatook, Kids Kampus Discovery Center in Pawhuska, Circle of Friends Discovery Center in Fairfax, and the Building Blocks Discovery Center in Barnsdall. Summer program for children between the ages of 6 and 12 years are available at all four sites. The Osage Nation Child Care Program provides childcare assistance subsidies as well as educational workshops. There are 12 public school districts within the reservation boundaries to serve tribal youth. The Osage Nation Early Learning Center serves to promote early childhood literacy. Services include learning programs for children and parents. The tribe operates a 21st Century Program. This program provides after school and summer programs at local schools. The tribe offers Osage language classes, ribbon-work courses, and instruction in various cultural crafts and elements. The tribe's education department provides ACT testing fees, tutoring services, school supplies, youth employment training programs, and the American Indian Student Association to tribal youth attending school systems within the tribal service area.

Financial assistance is available to tribal members pursing a post -secondary education. The tribe education committee awards scholarships and grants to eligible applicants. It also provides assistance for adult vocational training programs. Training services generally include a training allowance paid biweekly. Tribal members living within the Osage Reservation/County are eligible. Applicants must maintain satisfactory grades and good attendance. Temporary employment opportunities up to two months are available for tribal adult applicants 18 years of age and up. Other assistance available to tribal members are work relocation, specialized clothing, work tools, certification expenses, and other related needs required to start a new job efficiently.

Health Care. The Pawhuska Indian Health Center provides medical services to tribal members. Services include pharmacy, pediatric, women's health, diabetes, and well child programs. Renovations in 2002 and 2003 included enlargements to the laboratory. The two staff physicians handle some 10,000 outpatient visits annually, with support staff taking care of another 7,000.

The Community Health Representative Program provides screening, health education, sanitation, maternal health, and child health programs. The representatives provide in-home visits, hospital and clinic office hours, and transportation services.

The Osage Nation WIC Program provides nutrition, counseling, and support services for low income families, specifically women, infants, and children. It also provides well child immunizations. The WIC Program offers a mobile clinic that travels throughout Osage County. In 2004, a family planning clinic was opened in partnership with the Family Care Services of Bartlesville. The clinic provides annual exams, pregnancy testing, educational resources, HIV testing, and gynecological services.

Osage Home Health is also located in Pawhuska. It provides registered nurses, licensed practical nurses, home health aides, and physical therapists. Hominy offers ambulance service, home health service, a medical clinic, physical therapy services, and an optometrist. Patients needing emergency care or hospitalization are referred to medical centers in Tulsa, Bartlesville, or Claremore.

ENVIRONMENTAL CONCERNS

The Osage Nation Environmental and Natural Resources Department provides services to restore, protect, manage, and preserve natural resources on tribal lands. The department houses air quality and hazard waste programs.

Tribal lands are home to nearly 13,000 oil wells, many of which have been actively operated for almost several years. In 1995 and 1996, the U.S. Geological Survey conducted studies of the Wildhorse and Burbank oilfields. The studies found soil erosion, soil salinization, and salt scarring at the Wildhorse site, as well as levels of radium, copper, lead, and zinc. Nearby water sources, which supply drinking water to the community, were observed to exceed limits for total dissolved solids. Findings at the Burbank site included soil erosion and salt scarring. Low to moderate levels of radioactivity were present.

Otoe-Missouria

Otoe-Missouria Reservation
Federal reservation
Otoe-Missouria
Noble and Pawnee counties,
Oklahoma

Otoe-Missouria Tribe
of Indians
Route 1, Box 62
Red Rock, Oklahoma 74651
580-723-4266
580-723-4273 Fax

Total area *(BIA realty, 2004)*
20,578.23 acres

Total area *(Tribal source, 2004)*
20,576.23 acres

Tribally owned *(BIA realty, 2004)*
2,577.02 acres

Tribally owned lands
(Tribal source, 2004)
18,079.21 acres

Individually owned
(BIA realty, 2004)
17,999.21 acres

Population *2000 census*
778

Tribal enrollment
(Tribal source, 2004)
1,472

Tribal enrollment
(BIA labor report, 2001)
1,505

Total labor force *2000 census*
289

Total labor force
(Tribal source, 2004)
600

ENVIRONMENTAL CONCERNS

The tribe's environmental office is operated under a U.S. EPA grant. The department is addressing air quality emissions, hazardous waste, lead-based paint, pesticides, radon, radiation, solid waste, underground storage tanks, and wastewater treatment programs for future economic development.

LOCATION AND LAND STATUS

The checkerboarded Otoe-Missouria Reservation is located on the plains of north-central Oklahoma, just south of the Salt Fork of the Arkansas River. Otoe-Missouria tribal jurisdiction lands include some 20,576.23 acres of noncontiguous trust and nontrust properties within Noble County, Oklahoma. The Town of Red Rock, Oklahoma, serves as the tribal headquarters. The Otoe-Missouria Reservation is accessible via east-west running State Highway 15, which intersects Red Rock; the reservation is also serviced by north-south running U.S. Highway 177. Incorporated Oklahoma towns near the reservation include Red Rock, Ceres, Perry, and Marland. Major Oklahoma cities near the reservation include Ponca City (16 miles north), Stillwater (27 miles south), Tulsa (100 miles east), and Oklahoma City (100 miles southwest). In 1881, the federal government established a reservation for the Otoe and Missouria Tribes within the Cherokee Outlet in Indian Territory. By 1883, most tribal members were relocated to the area of the present-day reservation. The entire reservation was allotted to tribal members in 1904. Today, tribal trust and allotted lands are interspersed with some 61,920 non-Indian parcels within the reservation's boundaries.

CLIMATE

The area receives about 33.8 inches of precipitation per year. The average temperature in January is 40.6°F. July's average temperature is 80.7°F.

CULTURE AND HISTORY

The Jiwere-Nutache, or Otoe-Missouria, are descended from the Nakota and Dakota tribes. The indigenous language of the Otoe-Missouria is a Siouan dialect. The Otoe-Missouria ancestral lands included regions of present-day Minnesota and Wisconsin. The tribes eventually migrated south of the Great Lakes and settled into areas of Iowa, Kansas, Missouri, and Nebraska, where they remained until 1881. The tribes then relocated to Indian Territory in north-central Oklahoma.

The Otoe Tribe originally resided along the Nemaha and Platte rivers while the Missouria Tribe resided on territory in the lower Missouri River Valley. The tribes became allies in 1776 when Sac and Fox forces began to pressure them. During the 1850s, tribal members in the urban areas ceded lands in eastern Nebraska, accepting a 162,000 acres reservation along the Big Blue River in southern Nebraska and northern Kansas. Internal strife divided the Otoe-Missouria Tribe into the Coyote Band and Quaker Band. The Coyote Band consisted of members wishing to retain a more traditional lifestyle, while members of the Quaker Band were willing to accept Euro-American influence. Following additional land cessions in 1876 and 1881, the tribe sold its remaining land in the Big Blue Valley. It purchased 129,000 acres in north-central Oklahoma and tribal members relocated in 1881. Throughout the 1890s, the Otoe-Missouria struggled against federal attempts to allot tribal lands. By 1889, the government prevailed and the reservation was divided among 514 individuals. The tribe resisted the provisions of the Indian Reorganization Act until 1984, at which time it adopted a constitutional government.

The Otoe-Missouria Tribe is comprised of seven clans. The clan system is patriarchal and includes the Eagle, Owl, Pigeon, Buffalo, Bear, Beaver, and Elk clans. Each clan serves to fulfill different responsibilities in the tribal culture. The leadership clans, Buffalo and Bear, alternate leadership responsi-

bilities with the seasons. In the event that a tribal member has a non-tribal father, the member accepts the mother's clan. Traditional cultural ceremonies and elements continue to be practiced among tribal members, including naming ceremonies, initiations, festivities, and funerals. The Native American Church is also a strong presence on the reservation.

GOVERNMENT

The Otoe-Missouria Reservation is governed by a tribal council. The tribal council consists of seven elected members who are elected for three staggered terms. Tribal government is divided into numerous sectors including a tribal court, the tribal tax commission, the tribal bingo commission, tribal law enforcement, tribal education services, tribal social services, tribal financial services, tribal planner services, tribal asset management services, and tribal health services. The Otoe-Missouria law enforcement department includes three BIA officers, one grant officer, and one dispatcher. The department has cross-jurisdiction with five other tribes.

ECONOMY

The main contributors to the Otoe economy are the tribal government, infrastructure, agriculture, gaming, and mining. The Otoes hope to further improve their economy by expanding the services of their water treatment plant.

Government as Employer. Tribal operations employ 32 persons full-time. Tribal enterprises employ approximately 202 persons on a temporary basis.

Economic Development Projects. The tribe operates a water treatment plant that is due for expansion into a rural water district facility.

Agriculture and Livestock. The tribe harvests wheat, milo, and cotton on approximately half of the tribal lands. The tribe farms 12,900 acres.

Forestry. Approximately 10,000 acres of tribal lands are forested with species of cottonwood, elm, and pecan. As of 2004, they were not being harvested on a commercial basis.

Gaming. The tribe operates the 7 Clans Casino, a monthly class II bingo operation. During these bingo sessions, 50 persons are employed, of which 40 percent are tribal members, 30 percent are Indians from other tribes, and 30 percent are non-Indian. The casino has a bar and lunch counter.

Mining. There is small-scale oil and gas drilling on tribal lands.

Services and Retail. The tribe currently operates three smoke shops through lease agreements with tribal members on trust properties. The 7 Clans Deli Mart is independently leased and sells food and fuel.

Tourism and Recreation. Each July the tribe holds the Otoe-Missouria Tribe Encampment Powwow. Recreational areas near the Otoe-Missouria Reservation include Sooner Lake and Lake McMurtry. Other nearby attractions include the 7 Clans Paradise Casino, Cherokee Strip Museum in Perry, the Pioneer Woman Museum in Ponca City, and the National Wrestling Hall of Fame in Stillwater.

INFRASTRUCTURE

The Otoe-Missouria Reservation is immediately accessible via east-west running State Highway 15 and north-south running U.S. Highway 177. I-35 also passes 15 miles to the west of the reservation. Private air facilities are located at Ponca City, Stillwater, and Perry; commercial air service is available at Stillwater and at major international airports in Oklahoma City, Tulsa, and in Wichita, Kansas. Many trucking lines service the reservation area through Ponca City; these include ANR Freight Systems, American Freight System, BaileyÕs Express, and Triangle Express. Express delivery services, including UPS and FedEx, are in Ponca City. The Atchison, Topeka and Santa Fe Railway provides commercial railway. Greyhound Lines bus terminals are located in Stillwater and Ponca City. The tribe has water rights to 200 acre-feet of storage at the Kaw Reservoir in Ponca City.

Electricity. Oklahoma Gas and Electric and two electricity co-operatives serve the tribal area.

Water Supply. Bressie Water provides water service. The 50-unit housing authority operates a two-cell lagoon for tribal sewer services. Other individual home sites use septic tanks.

Transportation. The tribe operates two school buses for transporting Head Start children. A van is available to transport the sick and elderly to the tribe's health clinic.

COMMUNITY FACILITIES AND SERVICES

The Otoe Tribe has a community center located in Red Rock. The center houses the council chambers, a gymnasium, and a fitness center. The tribe also has a sweat lodge.

Veterans are highly regarded on the Otoe-Missouria Reservation, approximately 10 percent of tribal members fall into this category. The Eloska Society is comprised of these members. The first tribal chapter of War Mothers, a national organization made up of mothers of veterans, which assists veterans and families in need, was chartered by the Otoe-Missouria.

Education. The tribe operates a Head Start program for preschoolers. Other tribal youth attend public schools in the Red Rock School District. Several colleges and postsecondary institutions are located near the Otoe-Missouria Reservation; these include Oklahoma State University (Stillwater), Northern Oklahoma College (Tonkawa), and vocational and technical colleges in Stillwater and Ponca City.

Health Care. Health care services are available through an Indian Health Service clinic in White Eagle, about eight miles northeast of the reservation. The tribe is constructing a new wellness center. Medical services are also available in Ponca City, Stillwater, and Perry.

Otoe-Missouria

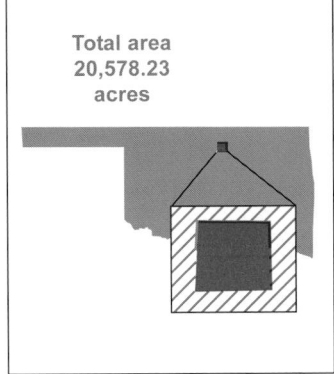

Total area
20,578.23
acres

High school graduate or higher
2000 census
75.4%

Bachelor's degree or higher
2000 census
13.7%

Unemployment rate *2000 census*
6.6%

Per capita income *2000 census*
$11,283

TRI-OK-039 Wellness Center, near completion

TRI-OK-040 Trueman Dailey Learning Center

ttawa

Ottawa

LOCATION AND LAND STATUS

Restored to its status as a federally recognized tribe in 1978, the Ottowa Tribe owns just over 40 acres in Oklahoma. Tribal headquarters are located in Miami, near the far northeastern corner of the state. Major cities near Miami are Joplin, Missouri, approximately 27 miles northeast, and Tulsa, Oklahoma, approximately 85 miles southwest. The Ottawa Tribe is currently working to reestablish a tribal land base, having only been restored to federal recognition in 1978.

PHYSICAL DESCRIPTION

Portions of Ottawa tribal lands lie within the Ozark Mountain Geologic Province. The region is drained by the Grand, Verdigris, and Caney rivers.

CLIMATE

The weather in Miami is characteristically harsh, with high humidity, sweltering heat, cold rain, and biting winds. This region experiences summer temperatures ranging between 64°F and 90°F. The winter temperature ranges between the low 20s and 50s.

CULTURE AND HISTORY

The Ottawa Tribe of Oklahoma is descended from the Algonquian-speaking Ottawa people of the northeastern woodlands. The Ottawa Nation consisted of five clans: the Otter, the Fork People, the Bear, the Grey Squirrel, and the Fish. The Ottawa Indian Tribe of Oklahoma descended from the Otter and Fork People clans. The name "Ottowas" was descriptive of the tribe's lifestyle. It "derives from the Algonquin 'Adawa,' meaning to trade or barter." The Chippewas and Potawatomis are their close tribal relatives.

The Ottawas were a migratory tribe that traveled great distances to hunt, trade, and make war. They lived in villages and practiced some horticulture but were best known as far-ranging intertribal middlemen who traded in tobacco, cornmeal, herbs, furs, and skins. Members of the Ottawa Tribe traversed the rivers of the northeastern United States and the Great Lakes. They also traveled along the "Moccasin Trail" into Florida.

Ottawa Reservation
Federal reservation
Ottawa
Ottawa County, Oklahoma

Ottawa Tribe of Oklahoma
P.O. Box 110
13S 69A
Miami, OK 74355
918-540-1536
918-542-3214 Fax

Ottawa

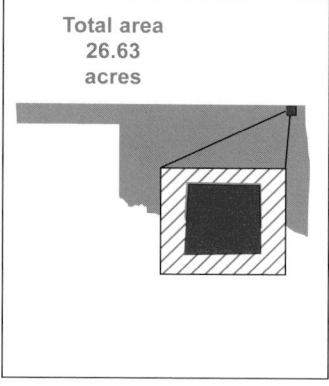

Total area
26.63
acres

Total area *(BIA realty, 2004)*
26.63 acres

Tribally owned *(BIA realty, 2004)*
26.63 acres

Tribal enrollment *(BIA, 2001)*
2,290

Total labor force *2000 census*
2,786

High school graduate or higher
2000 census
75.6%

Bachelor's degree or higher
2000 census
12.1%

Unemployment rate *2000 census*
10.8%

Unemployment rate *(BIA, 2001)*
29%

ENVIRONMENTAL CONCERNS
In 2001, the Ottowa Tribe established its Department of Environmental Protection. Partially funded by the EPA General Assistance Program and the Clean Water Act, the department serves to protect, preserve, and restore natural resources on tribal lands while honoring the traditionally sacred relationship between the tribe and the natural world. Programs of the department include assessment and monitoring of air, water, and soil quality. It also provides a recycling program and monitoring of the Tar Creek Superfund Site. The department works collaboratively with neighboring tribes, communities, and agencies.

Recorded history of the Ottawas dates from 1615 when an Ottawa trading party encountered French explorer Champlain near the mouth of Georgian Bay on the Atlantic coast of Canada. A quarter century later, pressured by the Iroquois, the Ottawas moved to Green Bay in present-day Wisconsin, and from there they spread into northwestern Illinois and southern Wisconsin.

The tribe signed treaties with the British and French during their periods of occupation. However, the tribe allied primarily with the French. During the French and Indian War, the Ottawas supported the French, and later, under the commanding leadership of Ottawa War Chief Pontiac, they strongly resisted the British power in the Great Lakes Region. In 1763, Pontiac led the Ottawas, Potawatomis, and Ojibwas to besiege Detroit; his forces captured a series of fortified posts. In 1769, three years after a peace treaty had been reached with the British, a member of the Peoria tribe assassinated Chief Pontiac. His assassination initiated a fierce war between the Ottawa and Peoria tribes, which resulted in near annihilation of the Peoria people. Pontiac remains one of the most famous and revered leaders among the Ottawa people.

During the American Revolutionary War, the Ottawas sided with the British, but they were able to control most of Ohio after the war. Euro-American encroachment upon tribal lands following the war forced the tribe to move westward. In 1832, they were moved to Kansas, where they remained for a number of years. In 1868, the federal government established a 14,863-acre reservation for the Ottawas in present-day Ottawa County, Oklahoma and the tribe was forced to relocate there. The Ottawa Reservation was allotted to tribal members in 1892, and remaining lands were opened to white settlement in 1908. Though they lost most of their land, the Ottawas continued to farm and raise livestock in Ottawa County.

The tribe reorganized under the Oklahoma Indian Welfare Act in 1938, but federal recognition was terminated in 1955. On May 15, 1978, the Ottawas were reinstated as a federally recognized tribe. Today, the tribe is working to rebuild its land base, while providing economic opportunities for its members and preserving Ottawa culture and heritage.

GOVERNMENT
The Ottawa Council is composed of all enrolled members over age 18. The business committee, composed of a chief, a second chief, a secretary-treasurer, and two councilmen, serves as the elected governing body for enrolled members. Members of the business committee serve three-year terms, with elections occurring during the annual meeting of the Ottawa Council. The tribe adopted a constitution and bylaws on June 26, 1936, in accordance with the Oklahoma Indian Welfare Act of 1936. Tribal government programs include tribal enrollment, family preservation, community health, library/archives, and environmental protection.

BUSINESS CORPORATION
The Ottawas are a member of The Inter-Tribal Council, Inc. (ITC) of Miami. Chartered in 1968, the ITC is a non-profit organization that serves to improve educational and economic opportunities within the eight member tribes. It also strives to improve the education, welfare, and health of all Native Americans living in its service area of northeastern Oklahoma. ITC programs are housed in a 12,950 square foot building that was constructed in 1978. This center provides intertribal substance abuse, outreach, and counseling; training programs including Native employment work, welfare-to-work, Workforce Investment Act, adult comprehensive services, and supplemental youth training; department of agriculture food distribution programs; Indian vocational education; and the Eight Tribes Gift Shop.

ECONOMY
The tribal economy is supported primarily from revenue earned by the tribe's activities in the tourism industry.

Economic Development Projects. The Ottawa Business Development Authority has applied for an 8(a) program from the U.S. Small Business Administration.

Services and Retail. The ITC operates the Eight Tribes Gift Shop in its community center in Miami.

Media and Communications. The tribe publishes *Adawe News*, a monthly newsletter.

Tourism and Recreation. The Ottawa Tribe holds the annual Ottawa Celebration and Powwow over Labor Day weekend. The ITC sponsors numerous community activities and celebrations, many of which are held at its community center in Miami. Local attractions include the Grand Lake of the Cherokees, located north of Miami.

INFRASTRUCTURE
Tribal headquarters in Miami, Oklahoma, are accessible via U.S. 59. I-44 between Tulsa and Joplin, Missouri, passes just south of Miami. Private air facilities are located in Miami. Commercial air service is available in Tulsa, 85 miles southwest. Major bus lines and package carriers serve Tulsa and Joplin. Commercial rail service is available in Miami.

Electricity. Regional providers supply electricity to individual tribe members.

Fuel. Regional providers supply gas services to individual tribe members.

Water Supply. Regional providers furnish water and sewer services to members of the tribe.

Transportation. Private air facilities are located in Miami. Commercial air service is available in Tulsa, 85 miles southwest. Major bus lines and package carriers serve Tulsa and Joplin. Commercial rail service is available in Miami.

COMMUNITY FACILITIES AND SERVICES
The Ottawas are also a member of the ITC of Miami, which was founded in 1967. The Ottawa Tribe jointly owns a community building with the Peorias, where indoor powwows and stomp dances and other community activities are housed. The Ottawa/Peoria Cultural Center is located just south of the tribal complex. The tribe also operates a library. In partnership with the Miami and Peoria tribes, the Ottawa offer free meals for elders and daycare assistance. The ITC maintains a community center in Miami. The center houses a number of social services and programs. (*Please see Business Corporation for further information.*)

Education. Tribal youth attend public schools in Ottawa County, Oklahoma. The tribe provides instruction in the indigenous language. It also offers scholarships to eligible applicants.

Health Care. Health services are available in the Miami Health Center. Services of the center include primary care, pharmacy, laboratory, x-ray, dental, optometry, and nutrition programs. The center is staffed by two physicians and one physician's assistant. Additional medical needs are referred to the hospital in Claremore. The tribe also operates the healthy living center, which promotes healthy lifestyles among tribal members. The center offers the services of a community health representative. The center hosts an annual elder's olympics day.

LOCATION AND LAND STATUS

The Pawnee tribal lands consist of approximately 20,000 acres of tribally owned and allotted lands. The lands are located in north-central Oklahoma, about 50 miles northwest of Tulsa and 90 miles northeast of Oklahoma City. The vast majority of this acreage is allotted and forms a checkerboard pattern. Tribal community land consists mainly of the Pawnee Tribal Reserve, which contains approximately 650 acres. The Pawnees were relocated to Oklahoma from Nebraska in 1876. This 203,000-acre reservation was allotted in 1893. The remaining 171,000 acres were then opened to non-Indian sale and settlement.

CULTURE AND HISTORY

The Pawnees descend from the Caddoan linguistic family. The Pawnees referred to themselves as Chahiksichahiks, which means "Men of men." Prior to 1770, the tribe remained in its aboriginal homeland of the Arkansas River region, obtaining weapons and supplies from French traders. As French trade abated, the Pawnees migrated northward into what is present-day Nebraska, settling near the Platte, Loup, and Republican rivers. From its new location, the tribe gained new outlets for trade, as well as excellent buffalo hunting south of the Platte River.

In a series of treaties between 1833 and 1857, the Pawnees agreed to cede all of their traditional lands to the United States except for a reservation 30 miles long by 15 miles wide along both banks of the Loup River, centered around the community that is now Fullerton, Nebraska. In 1876, however, the tribe was forced to surrender this tract too, and they were then relocated en masse to a new reservation in Indian Territory (Oklahoma). In 1893, with pressures growing for Oklahoma statehood, this new 200,000-plus-acre reservation was allotted to 820 tribal members, with the remaining 171,000 acres being opened to outside purchase and settlement.

All that remains of the community-held tribal lands is a reserve of a few hundred acres on the site of the old Pawnee Indian School, which contains the tribal offices, the ceremonial roundhouse, the community building, a recreation building, and campgrounds.

In 1966 the Indian Claims Commission awarded the tribe over $7 million for aboriginal lands in Kansas and Nebraska ceded to the United States during the last century. And during the 1970s, the Pawnees regained certain tribal lands that the City of Pawnee had once given the U.S. government. The tribe maintains certain aspects of its traditional culture, though use of the language is on the wane. Tribal spiritual life currently spans the spectrum from the Native American Church to fundamentalist Christianity.

GOVERNMENT

The tribe is organized under the Oklahoma Indian Welfare Act of 1936 and is governed by two eight-member governing bodies: the business council and the chiefs or Nasharo Council. The chiefs are chosen by their bands, while members of the business council are elected at large. Business council officers include a president, a vice president, and a secretary/treasurer. The executive office directs the Pawnee Nation's administrative activities, assists the Pawnee Business Council in policy development, and facilitates tribal government and program services. The executive office also acts as a liaison between the tribal staff and the Pawnee Business Council.

The Pawnee Nation has its own grants and contracts office. It works with a number of federal government agencies such as the Department of Interior, the BIA, and the U.S. EPA to monitor and evaluate program activities and to ensure compliance with rules and regulations regarding submittal of various grants and contracts.

The Pawnee tribal government works to protect members' rights, promote economic development, and serve as an intermediary with the U.S. government. The tribal constitution and bylaws have been amended from time to time to meet changing conditions. The Pawnee court system consists of the Pawnee Nation District Court, which includes a chief judge, a tribal prosecutor, a public defender, and a court clerk. The chief judge handles all civil, criminal, and juvenile cases. The Pawnee Nation's Supreme Court is comprised of a supreme court judge and four Pawnee justices.

The Pawnee Nation also has other government departments that are influential in its day-to-day operations; these departments include the motor vehicle department, finance, enrollment and communications, environmental conservation and safety, grounds maintenance and housekeeping, and fire and police. The Pawnee Nation Police Department is funded by the BIA and is contracted every three years to provide law enforcement on restricted Indian lands within the Pawnee Nation. The police department consists of the chief of police, three full-time police officers, and one DARE reserve officer.

BUSINESS CORPORATION

The Pawnee Tribal Development Corporation, a tribally owned, for-profit organization, promotes economic development on the reservation and partners with business opportunists to provide employment for the Pawnee Nation. It is governed by a nine-member board and owns the Pawnee Nation Casino and travel plaza.

ECONOMY

The tribe's primary source of revenues today comes from government grants and contracts, along with a modest amount of tribal trust lands that are leased for agricultural use and oil and gas exploration. Individual Pawnees support themselves as farmers, housepainters, silversmiths, bead workers, and as members of the armed services, among other pursuits.

Government as Employer. The Pawnee Tribal Government employs approximately 65 persons through its various departments. These include the executive branch, education department, health and community services, law enforcement, and the Indian Health Service. The BIA employs about 25 tribe members, while the U.S. Public Health Service is a major employer within the tribal jurisdiction area.

Economic Development Projects. The tribe owns and operates an industrial park on the Pawnee Tribal Reserve. The park is currently not utilized. The tribe recently entered into an agreement with a firm to build an ethanol plant, which is expected to employ about 75 people upon its completion. The park features easy access to both the railroad and to Cimarron Turnpike.

Agriculture and Livestock. A modest amount of tribal lands are presently leased for agricultural purposes to outside interests. The BIA supervises some of these leases.

Pawnee Tribe
Federal reservation
Pawnee
Pawnee County, Oklahoma

Pawnee Tribe of Oklahoma
P.O. Box 470
Pawnee, OK 74058
918-762-3621
918-762-6446 Fax
pawneenation.org

Total area *(BIA realty, 2004)*
19,929.16 acres

Tribally owned *(BIA realty, 2004)*
1,549.59 acres

Individually owned
(BIA realty, 2004)
18,379.57 acres

Population *2000 census*
15,413

Total labor force *2000 census*
7,605

High school graduate or higher
2000 census
78.7%

Bachelor's degree or higher
2000 census
12%

Unemployment rate *2000 census*
5.1%

Per capita income *2000 census*
$15,253

Pawnee

TRI-OK-042 Pawnee Indian Health Center

TRI-OK-043 Construction of Family Development Center, will house childcare and Nation fitness center

TRI-OK-042

TRI-OK-043

Gaming. The Pawnee Nation is home to the Pawnee Nation Casino and Trading Post, which is located one-fourth mile east of Highway 18 and Junction 64. The tribal bingo hall has been leased to an outside firm. The casino is monitored by the Pawnee Nation Gaming Commission which not only enforces gaming ordinances but also researches and develops updated regulation. The commission has aided in creating a mandatory internal revenue service training session for casino employees. The Pawnee Nation Gaming Commission has also helped select a new and improved surveillance system for the casino.

Services and Retail. A new Pawnee Nation Travel Plaza, completed in 2004, includes a self-service laundry, sandwich shop, truck stop, and shower facilities. The tribe also owns a smoke shop on the reserve. This facility is presently leased to an individual who pays the tribe a monthly revenue fee, as well as tribal taxes. The facility includes a gas station, a convenience store, and a tribal arts and crafts outlet, in addition to tobacco products. There is a deli in the casino.

Tourism and Recreation. Ceremonial events open to the public include the Annual Pawnee Tribal Homecoming Powwow and Celebration which occurs on or about the Fourth of July, and the Pawnee Indian Christmas Day Dance. Moreover, the Pawnee Agency is an historic site consisting of a number of buildings constructed of sandstone block prior to 1900. Several of these buildings are listed on the National Register of Historic Landmarks.

INFRASTRUCTURE

Road access to the Pawnee Jurisdictional Area is provided by U.S. Highway 64, which serves the community of Pawnee directly, as well as the Cimarron Turnpike, which passes seven miles south of Pawnee. Commercial air service is available in Tulsa (60 miles southeast of Pawnee) and Oklahoma City (90 miles southwest). Commercial truck lines serve the community directly, while a railroad crosses through the Pawnee Tribal Reserve.

Electricity. A regional utility, contracted with the City of Pawnee, provides electricity to the tribal community.

Water Supply. The Pawnee municipal water and sewage systems furnish those services to the tribe.

Fuel. The Oklahoma Natural Gas Company provides gas service.

Telecommunications. Southwestern Bell provides local telephone service.

COMMUNITY FACILITIES AND SERVICES

The Pawnee Nation maintains the Pawnee Tribal Facility at the site of the old Pawnee Indian School. This facility includes a gymnasium, a kitchen, and a campground, among other features. The Pawnee Nation Police Department provides local law enforcement, while the Pawnee Fire Department provides fire protection. A new family development center, completed in 2004, includes a child care center and a fitness center.

Education. The Pawnee Nation's educational beginnings are found within the history of the Genoa U.S. Indian School. From 1850 to 1875, Pawnee children attended the Genoa school until it became a boarding school from 1884 to 1934. Children from approximately 30 different tribes attended the Genoa boarding school during its existence. The Pawnee Nation, in remembrance of its early educational beginnings, has established the Genoa Indian School Foundation which offers scholarships to descendants of Genoa Indian School students to further the Nation's education. Today, Pawnee Nation children attend the local elementary school, middle school, or high school.

Health Care. Tribal health care services are supplied through the U.S. Public Health Service Clinic. The Pawnee Service Unit serves a population of 15,000 over a 7,000- square-mile area. It is comprised of three facilities: the Pawnee Indian Health Center, the Pawhuska Health Center, and the White Eagle Health Center. Two physicians are assigned to each facility. The Pawnee Indian Health Center opened in 1931 as a 47-bed hospital. It later closed in 1981. The close of the health center created the need for emergency medical treatment, instituting the development of the Pawnee Benefit Package Program which provided emergency rooms and outpatient surgery. Today the new Pawnee Nation Indian Health Facility, which was completed in March 2004, is approximately 6,300 square feet and houses the new physical therapy department and the new diagnostic imaging department, which provides ultrasound services. The new facility also offers ambulatory health care, dentistry, and optometry, among other services.

The Pawnee Nation has various programs that provide health services for diabetics and for patients who suffer from cardiovascular diseases, educational programs on accessing health care and living healthy lives, and programs for Pawnee elders. Pawnee Nation Reach 2010 promotes reducing and eliminating the prevailing issues of diabetes and cardiovascular diseases faced by the Nation's members. Reach 2010 offers physical activities, such as golf tournaments, strength training, and basketball tournaments to create awareness and to help prevent the prevalence of diabetes and other diseases in the Pawnee community. The Pawnee Nation also established the Pawnee Diabetes Program to provide services to diabetics, such as free finger-stick blood sugar screenings, support groups, and educational instruction on how to use glucometers, strips, and lancets. The Pawnee Nation's Elderly Meals Program and Caregiver Support Program serve elders by promoting nutritional diets through home delivery services and by offering support groups and training for caregivers of the elderly. The Pawnee Nation also has programs to eradicate the abuse of alcohol and drugs through its substance abuse program.

The Pawnee Nation offers other programs for families and individuals of minimal income and for the Nation's troubled youth who need direction and support. The Pawnee Nation Food Distribution Program provides an alternative to food stamps for needy Pawnee families; it provides access to more nutritional foods by distributing over 84 different food items and by encouraging better eating habits. The Pawnee Nation's Juvenile Intervention Program, in partnership with the juvenile justice system, offers support to juveniles who have been arrested for misdemeanors or nonviolent felony crimes by providing safe holding cells, supervision, assessment, and referral services. The juvenile intervention program is a collaborative program that works with the Pawnee Nation Police Department, the Pawnee Nation Indian Child Welfare Program, the City of Pawnee Police Department, and the Pawnee City Sheriff's Department.

Housing. The Pawnee Indian Development Block Grant Program (ICDBG) implements those projects that fall under the administrative authority of HUD. The ICDBG oversees construction projects that are designed to offer Pawnee members new service or that improve existing services. The projects awarded to ICDBG include the Pawnee Multipurpose Center, the wellness center, the fire station, and the Trading Post.

ENVIRONMENTAL CONCERNS

The Pawnee Department of Environmental Conservation and Safety (DECS) manages tribal natural resources to ensure that EPA codes and regulations are met. The DECS was established in 1996 under the Pawnee Nation Environmental Regulation Act. The DECS is the lead tribal agency for managing Pawnee tribal natural resources, and it oversees water, air, waste, and wastewater programs. It is also involved with the continued implementation and development of the multimedia environmental management process for the Nation, and it has established the Pawnee Environmental Education Center, a 28-acre center that is comprised of diverse aquatic habitats, an upper- and bottom-land forest ecosystem, forbs, and grasses.

The Pawnee Nation faces numerous issues regarding water and air quality. The Nation is currently trying to establish a monitoring system for testing ground and drinking water. The Nation is working on implementing updates to clean air standards, providing training in air pollution principles, and determining air pollution monitoring sites. It is also important to the Pawnee Nation to provide education to its tribal members on the various environmental concerns facing the Nation.

Pawnee

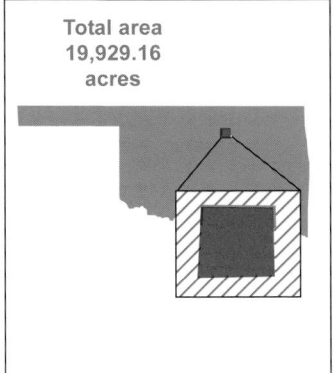

Total area
19,929.16
acres

Peoria

Peoria

LOCATION AND LAND STATUS

The Peoria Tribe is located in far northeastern Oklahoma in Ottawa County. Tribal headquarters are located in Miami, Oklahoma, approximately 90 miles northeast of Tulsa via I-44. Joplin, Missouri, is approximately 20 miles northeast of Miami. The Peoria Tribe owns 38.79 acres of nonfederal trust land. The Peorias migrated to the Quapaw Reservation in present Ottawa County in 1857. The Quapaw Reservation was subsequently allotted during the late nineteenth century.

PHYSICAL DESCRIPTION

The region is characterized by flat prairies that meet the Ozark Mountain Geologic Province in the east.

CULTURE AND HISTORY

The Algonquian-speaking Peorias were members of the Illinois Confederacy in the Old Northwest. The French explorer, Marquette, on his 1673 expedition down the Mississippi River, found the Peorias living near present-day Peoria, Illinois. The name Peoria derives from the French form of the personal name Piwarea, meaning "He comes carrying a pack on his back." During the eighteenth century, the Peorias traded extensively with French outfits moving up and down the Mississippi River. During the early nineteenth century, the Peorias were among the many tribes of the Ohio Valley and Old Northwest that were displaced by the onslaught of white settlers pouring over the Appalachians. In 1832 the Peorias, together with a remnant of the Kaskaskias (another tribe of the Illinois Confederacy), emigrated to a new reservation on the Osage River in Kansas. The two tribes were joined by two bands of the Miamis, the Weas and Piankshaws, in 1854. In 1857 these united tribes moved to the Quapaw Reservation in present-day Ottawa County, Oklahoma; this reservation was allotted during the late nineteenth century. The Peoria Tribe organized under the Oklahoma Indian Welfare Act of 1936, adopting a constitution in 1939; a second constitution was ratified in 1981.

Today the Peoria Tribe belongs to the Inter-Tribal Council of Miami.

The Peoria Tribe was terminated during the termination period in the 1950s. However, the Peoria Tribe of Indians of Oklahoma was reinstated as a federally recognized tribe by an Act on May 15, 1978.

GOVERNMENT

A business committee, consisting of a chief, a second chief, a secretary/treasurer, and two councilmen, serves as the elected governing body; all members are elected for staggered four-year terms. Regular business committee meetings are held monthly.

The Peoria Tribe is organized under the Oklahoma Indian Welfare Act of 1936. The tribal government functions in accordance with a constitution approved by the BIA in 1980 and ratified in 1981, superseding the original constitution of 1939. In 2001, the tribe entered into a PL-638 contract with the BIA for the aid to tribal government program. Tribal government programs include a Peoria Housing Authority, housing improvement and emergency housing assistance programs, Indian reservation roads, a community health representative, Indian child welfare, an environmental program, Title VI, Native American graves protection and repatriation, and an education program.

BUSINESS CORPORATION

The Inter-Tribal Council (ITC) was chartered under the laws of the State of Oklahoma in 1968. It is a 501(c)(3) nonprofit corporation. The ITC's governing body is an administrative board composed of a chief, a chairman, or other designated representatives from member tribes. The corporation was designed to increase public understanding of Native Ameri-

Peoria Tribe of Indians
of Oklahoma
Federal reservation
Peoria
Ottawa County, Oklahoma

Peoria Tribe of Indians
of Oklahoma
P.O. Box 1527
Miami, OK 74355
918-540-2535
918-540-2538 Fax
peoriatribe.com

Total area *(BIA realty, 2004)*
870.47 acres

Tribally owned *(BIA realty, 2004)*
869.84 acres

Tribally owned *(Tribal source, 2004)*
989 acres

Federal trust *(Tribal source, 2004)*
1,438 acres

Non-trust *(Tribal source, 2004)*
449 acres

Individually owned
(BIA realty, 2004)
0.63 acres

Peoria

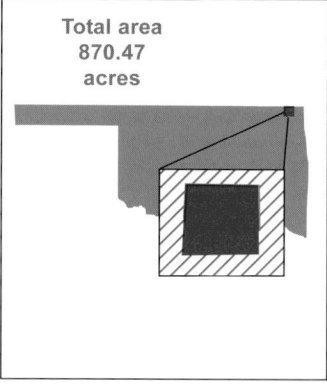

Total area
870.47
acres

Population *2000 census*
4,840

Population *(BIA labor report, 2001)*
2,662

Tribal enrollment
(Tribal source, 2004)
2,684

Total labor force *2000 census*
2,334

Total labor force
(BIA labor report, 2001)
3

High school graduate or higher
2000 census
82.8%

Bachelor's degree or higher
2000 census
20.6%

Unemployment rate *2000 census*
3.1%

Unemployment rate
(BIA labor report, 2001)
98%

Per capita income *2000 census*
$20,614

cans and their cultural values, to enhance and promote general educational and economic opportunities among ITC tribal members, and to improve the health, education, and general welfare of Native Americans in the ITC service area through a variety of programs and services. The departments of the ITC are abuse/outreach and counseling, economic development, employment and training, supplemental youth training, agriculture, education, and the Eight Tribes Gift Shop.

ECONOMY

The Peoria Tribe's economy is mainly supported by the tribal government and by the gaming, retail, and tourism industries. The tribe actively seeks to improve its economic welfare e by ensuring safe and healthy housing for all tribal members and creating future economic development endeavors.

Government as Employer. The tribal government is the largest employer of tribal members.

Economic Development Projects. As of 2004, the Peoria Ridge Golf Course remained the tribe's main economic development project. Aggressive marketing and soliciting more professional golf tournaments are among the approaches the tribe plans to take to make the course an economic success. Funds are being raised by the Indian Reservation Roads Program to foster safe and efficient development, operation, and management of surface road systems on the reservation.

Gaming. The tribe owns and operates the Peoria Gaming Center, a 5,000-square-foot gaming facility with 170 gaming machines and about 30 employees. A new class III gaming operation was scheduled to open in the fall of 2004.

Services and Retail. The Peoria Tribal Trading Post is open to the public and sells items such as T-shirts, hats, coffee mugs, and the *Peoria Tribal History* book. The trading post also sells beautifully handcrafted items made by the Peoria beading class. The Inter-Tribal Council of Miami owns and operates the Eight Tribes Gift Shop at council headquarters in Miami.

Media and Communications. The tribe has its own monthly news publication called the *Peoria Tribe of Indians of Oklahoma.*

Tourism and Recreation. The annual Peoria Powwow is held in late June at the Peoria Powwow Grounds. The powwow is open to the public, and it is a weekend full of culture, camping, and Native music and dance. The Inter-Tribal Council organizes a number of multi-tribal events. The Peoria Ridge Golf Course is recognized as one of the finest courses in the area, and it draws golf pros and enthusiasts from Kansas, Missouri, and Arkansas. The course is a first-class golfing facility featuring an 18-hole driving range and putting and chipping greens. In 2003 Peoria Ridge hosted the NGA Hooters Golf Tour and the Kitchen Pass Tournament.

INFRASTRUCTURE

Tribal headquarters are accessible via U.S. 69 and I-44, which connects with Joplin, Missouri (approximately 20 miles to the

northeast) and Tulsa (90 miles southwest). Private and commercial air service is available at Miami Municipal Airport. Tulsa International Airport is less than 100 miles away. Commercial and city buses serve Miami, as do all major trucking lines.

COMMUNITY FACILITIES AND SERVICES

The Inter-Tribal Council building is 12,950 square feet; it was constructed in 1978 as a result of an economic development grant from the U.S. Department of Commerce. The building houses ITC programs. The tribe also has its own tribal office, library, wellness center, and cemetery. The Peoria Tribal Office offers weekly beading classes. Nutritional services are provided to Peoria elders through the Miami Nutrition Center, located at the Miami Tribal Office and at the Miami Tribal Longhouse, located near Commerce, Oklahoma. Both of these facilities provide daily meals for tribal elders; meals are delivered to tribal members who are homebound.

Education. Tribal children attend Ottawa County public schools. All members of the Peoria Tribe are eligible to receive benefits from the Peoria Tribal Scholarship Program.

Health Care. Tribal members can contact the community health representative to arrange for a variety of services including injections, blood testing, pharmaceuticals, physical therapy, and prenatal, postnatal, and infant care instruction. The community health representative also provides a wellness health program. For health care needs that the community health representative cannot arrange, tribal members use the U.S. Public Health Service facility, the Miami Indian Health Clinic, and the Miami Health Center. The R.O.P.E.S Challenge Course, offered by the ITC, provides services such as anger management, urine testing, and HIV/AIDS counseling and testing to the Peoria Tribe and other tribes of northeastern Oklahoma. There is an intertribal substance abuse, prevention, and treatment center in Miami.

Housing. The tribe's low rental units program, home ownership program, and home improvement program help to improve the economic welfare of tribal members by providing safe and healthy housing. Tribal members may be eligible to receive emergency housing assistance. The Peoria Emergency Housing Assistance Program provides low-income members with recovery assistance needed due to fire, flood, storms, and other natural disasters.

ENVIRONMENTAL CONCERNS

The Peoria Tribe's environmental program serves to develop the tribe's ability to administer U.S. EPA environmental regulatory programs on tribal lands. This office is operated under a general assistance program. The major concern facing the Peoria Tribe is water pollution. The Natural Resource Damage Assessment and Restoration process, created under the Clean Water Act of 1977, authorizes natural resource trustees to recover compensatory damages resulting from the discharge of oil or other hazardous substances into navigable water. These regulations provide an administrative process for conducting assessments as well as technical methods for identifying injuries and calculating damages.

LOCATION AND LAND STATUS

Ponca tribal trust lands are located in Kay County in north-central Oklahoma. Tribal headquarters are located at White Eagle, five miles south of Ponca City along U.S. 177. Towns near the reservation include Marland, Tonkawa, and Red Rock. Major Oklahoma cities near the reservation include Ponca City (five miles north), Oklahoma City (approximately 100 miles south), and Tulsa (approximately 92 miles southeast). Ponca tribal lands include 1,748.55 acres of trust land and 13,120.37 acres of individual allotments. The Ponca Reservation was established by Executive Order in 1877.

CULTURE AND HISTORY

The Poncas are a Siouan-speaking people who once hunted and farmed in the prairie country of the lower Missouri River Basin in present-day eastern Nebraska. They are culturally and linguistically related to the Osage, Missouri, Kansas, Otoe, Omaha, and Iowa peoples. Inhabiting a cultural convergence zone, the Poncas exhibited the hunting traits of the Plains tribes farther west, but like tribes farther east and south, they practiced horticulture and made pottery.

French trappers exploring the Missouri River and its tributaries made first contact with the Poncas during the eighteenth century. However, it was not until the mid-nineteenth century that European incursion into Ponca territory threatened the tribe's way of life. An influx of Euro-American settlers into the Missouri River Valley eventually spurred the U.S. government to demand the relocation of the Poncas. In 1877, the Indian Commissioner instructed the Poncas to relocate to Indian Territory. Under the leadership of Chief Standing Bear, the Poncas complied. However, they suffered in Indian Territory due to the difference in climate, as well as a lack of provisions. By the end of 1878, 158 of the 730 Ponca tribe members had died from pneumonia and malaria. In January 1879, Standing Bear resolved to return to their tribal homeland after his own son died. For 10 weeks, he led a small band northward through the harsh Plains winter. Upon arrival in Nebraska, General George Crook arrested Standing Bear and his followers. An outpouring of public support for Standing Bear and his people culminated in a federal court decision, which ruled in favor of the Poncas, allowing them to return to Nebraska.

A portion of the tribe, however, remained in Indian Territory, and most of their lands were eventually allotted to individual tribal members. These tribal members incorporated as the Ponca Tribe of Oklahoma on September 20, 1950, under the Oklahoma Indian Welfare Act.

GOVERNMENT

The Ponca Tribe of Oklahoma ratified a constitution, bylaws, and a federal corporate charter on September 20, 1950, in accordance with the Oklahoma Indian Welfare Act of June 26, 1936. A tribal business committee serves as the principal governing body; it is composed of a chairman, a vice-chairman, a secretary-treasurer, and four members. Committee members are elected annually on the third Saturday in December. Annual tribal meetings are held on the third Saturday in November.

ECONOMY

Today, the Ponca Tribe looks to improve the well-being of its members by investing gaming revenues and federal grants in social service programs.

Gaming. The tribe owns the Blue Star Gaming and Casino. It offers 500 bingo seats and 100 video gaming machines. In 2001, the tribe initiated the Lot O Bingo game. It is a lottery game that players can participate in by proxy. Players purchase tickets at local stores, and a proxy player, usually a tribal member, plays the tickets at the tribe's bingo hall once a week. Oklahoma has no lottery program, and the appeal to residents is great. The program is the first tribally sponsored proxy bingo game in the country.

Tourism and Recreation. The tribe holds an annual powwow every August. The tribe celebrated the powwow's 128th year in August 2004. The festival features dancing, a parade, and arts and crafts vendors.

INFRASTRUCTURE

Ponca tribal trust lands and tribal headquarters at White Eagle are located five miles south of Ponca City along north-south running U.S. 177. I-35 (running north-south) passes approximately 15 miles west of tribal lands.

Transportation. Commercial and private air facilities are located in Ponca City, Oklahoma City (100 miles south), and Tulsa (92 miles southeast). Greyhound bus lines, trucking lines, and express package carriers serve Ponca City directly.

COMMUNITY FACILITIES AND SERVICES

The tribe maintains a cultural center in White Rock. Planned renovation of the facility will accommodate expanded social service and recreational programs for tribal members. There are approximately 62 tribal housing units located on the reservation; all are served by the Ponca Tribal Housing Authority. The tribe coordinates state and federal child care subsidy programs.

Ponca Reservation
Federal reservation
Ponca
Kay County, Oklahoma

Ponca Tribe of Oklahoma
20 White Eagle Dr.
Ponca City, OK 74601
580-762-8104
580-762-2743 Fax

Total area *(BIA realty, 2004)*
14,878.92 acres

Tribally owned *(BIA realty, 2004)*
1,748.55 acres

Individually owned
(BIA realty, 2004)
13,120.37 acres

Tribal enrollment *(BIA labor report, 2001)*
2,618

Total labor force *2000 census*
1,022

Total labor force
(BIA labor report, 2001)
1,187

High school graduate or higher
2000 census
71.1%

Bachelor's degree or higher
2000 census
8.1%

Unemployment rate *2000 census*
10.2%

Unemployment rate
(BIA labor report, 2001)
26%

TRI-OK-045 - Community Safety Center and Tribal Police

TRI-OK-046 - Valdez Building, Social Services Center

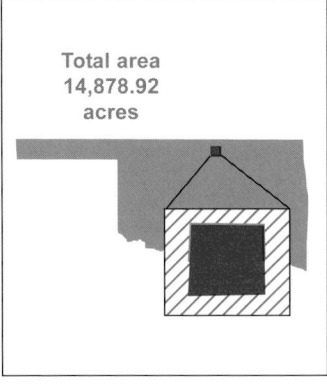

Total area
14,878.92
acres

Ponca

Education. Tribal youth attend schools in the Ponca City school district.

Health Care. Health care services are available at the Pawnee Health Center in Pawnee. Services include ambulatory health care, dentistry, human services, optometry, community health, pharmacy, laboratory, radiology, and nutrition programs. Two physicians serve the center. Hospital and health care services are available in Ponca City, five miles north of the reservation.

ENVIRONMENTAL CONCERNS

Pollution generated by the Continental Carbon plant is of great concern to the tribe. In spring 2004, the tribe led a protest at the Oklahoma State capitol to draw attention to the issue, of which they have made several formal complaints that have been virtually ignored. The tribe is also concerned with the quality of its water supply. The Inter-tribal Environmental Council of Oklahoma will investigate the matter.

Quapaw

Quapaw Reservation
Federal reservation
Quapaw
Ottawa County, Oklahoma

Quapaw Tribe of Oklahoma
P.O. Box 765
Quapaw, OK 74363
918-542-1853
918-542-4694 Fax
quapawtribe.com

Total area *(BIA realty, 2004)*	12,160.92	acres
Individually owned *(BIA realty, 2004)*	11,426.71	acres
Tribally owned *(BIA realty, 2004)*	734.21	acres
Tribally owned *(Tribal source, 2004)*	1,050	acres
Federal trust *(Tribal source, 2004)*	900	acres
Other *(Tribal source, 2004)*	57,000	acres
Population *2000 census*	7,455	
Population *(Tribal source, 2004)*	1,519	
Tribal enrollment *(BIA, 2001)*	2,657	
Tribal enrollment *(Tribal source, 2004)*	3,448	
Total labor force *2000 census*	3,157	
High school graduate or higher *2000 census*	66.8%	
Bachelor's degree or higher *2000 census*	6.4%	
Unemployment rate *2000 census*	9.1%	
Unemployment rate *(BIA, 2001)*	12%	
Per capita income *2000 census*	$11,440	

LOCATION AND LAND STATUS

In treaties signed in 1818, 1824, and 1833, the Quapaws ceded their ancestral homelands in Arkansas to the United States and agreed to removal to Indian Territory in what is now extreme northeastern Oklahoma. In 1893, tribal leadership took the action of allotting its own reserve, in 240-acre parcels, to the 230 enrolled members of the tribe. Congress ratified this action in 1895. Though only 937 acres of land are tribally owned, another 57,000 acres remain in the hands of tribal members through allotment. The tribe plans to acquire additional lands in the future.

CULTURE AND HISTORY

The Quapaws (meaning "downstream people") are a southwestern Siouan tribe. Their ancestral homelands are near the confluence of the Mississippi and Arkansas rivers, in present-day Arkansas. When first encountered by Europeans in the 1670s, approximately 15,000 to 20,000 Quapaw lived in villages in this region.

Through a series of treaties in the early 1800s, the tribe first ceded most of its ancestral territory to the U.S. government, then, in keeping with its peaceable reputation, acquiesced to relocation to the northeastern corner of present-day Oklahoma. Under the Allotment Act of 1887, the Quapaws objected to federal plans to allot each tribal member only 80 acres; instead, in 1893, they established their own program and allotted 240 acres to each enrolled tribal member. The discovery of rich zinc and lead deposits in 1905 on some of these allotted lands influenced the course of Quapaw history through the 1930s.

Initially, the federal government allowed mining businesses to carry on with their usual policy of defrauding the Indians. In 1908, however, the government began taking its stewardship responsibilities seriously, a change that resulted in benefits to the Quapaws in the form of higher royalties, bonus payments, and protection from local, state, and federal taxes. While federal intervention helped the tribe considerably, it also had its downside in the curtailment of personal freedoms: numerous Quapaws found that they no longer held direct control over their land leases and the revenue derived from them. Leasees now paid royalties directly to the Indian agency, which were then distributed to the beneficiaries only after a cumbersome application process. Perhaps due to this kind of experience, the tribe rejected the 1934 Indian Reorganization Act and in 1936 refused to organize under the Oklahoma Indian Welfare Act. Tribal leadership filed a major land claim case in 1946, which the federal government finally settled for about one million dollars in 1954. In 1956 the tribe replaced its traditional leadership with a new, elected business committee. The monetary award and new tribal government granted the tribe the confidence to fight off termination attempts during the 1950s and to begin a process of economic development that continues today. The present tribal economy relies significantly upon the tourist and service industries, featuring a nationally renowned powwow and a high-stakes bingo enterprise, among other ventures. The powwow notwithstanding, traditional culture has atrophied among the tribe in recent years. Only a handful of members now speak the Native language, and the once-avid practice of the Peyote Religion has greatly diminished.

GOVERNMENT

The Quapaw Tribe is not organized under the 1934 Indian Reorganization Act. On August 19, 1956, the Quapaw Tribal Council adopted the present governing resolution that established its present form of government. This government is administered by a business committee, which is popularly elected by all voting-age tribal members and consisting of a chairperson, a vice-chairperson, a secretary-treasurer, and four committee members. Tribal government programs include: consolidated tribal government, housing improvement, Indian reservation roads, domestic violence, language preservation and culture, and job placement and training.

ECONOMY

Tribal government, infrastructure, and revenues from gaming and other business enterprises are the main components of the Quapaw's economy.

Government as Employer. The tribal government employs 70 people in administrative and service capacities.

Forestry. Tribally affiliated lands contain rather minor, localized forests, consisting primarily of oak and walnut trees. At present, these are not considered a commercially viable resource.

Gaming. The Quapaw Casino and RV Park is owned and operated by the Quapaw Tribe. This is a class II facility; however, the tribe is negotiating with the state to become a class III. The tribe is already in the process of bringing blackjack back to the casino. This will result in an additional 90 jobs, for a total of 180 employees. The casino is located three miles north of the Miami exit on the Will Rogers Turnpike on Mushroom Farm Road.

Industrial Parks. The tribe maintains the 110-acre Spurto Industrial Park, featuring full utility and road service. A rail spur serves the park directly.

Services and Retail. The tribe owns and operates the O-Gah-Pah Convenience Store and gas station. O-Gah-Pah has six employees and is located on Mushroom Farm Road about 3.5 miles north at the turnpike gate at Steve Owens Boulevard. The tribe also own and operates the O-Gah-Pah Learning Center. The center is licensed for 90 children and has 13 employees. The center is located on the outskirts of Quapaw on Future Farmer Road.

Tourism and Recreation. The Quapaw Casino and RV Park is a popular tourist attraction. The annual Quapaw Powwow is nationally acclaimed and draws visitors from across the country. The powwow is held during the first weekend of July and serves as a major cultural event for northeastern Oklahoma.

INFRASTRUCTURE

The Town of Quapaw is directly accessible by U.S. Highway 69. I-44-the Will Rogers Parkway-passes within a few miles of Quapaw (providing access to Tulsa), as does U.S. Highway 60. While Quapaw has a 4,600-foot airstrip, commuter air service is available in Joplin, Missouri, 30 miles away, with Tulsa's International Airport about 85 miles to the southeast. Greyhound buslines serve Quapaw and Miami, as do several commercial freight and trucking companies. The Burlington Northern Railroad serves the area, providing direct service to the tribally owned industrial park through a spur. A 75-mile long canal provides water transport to the region.

Electricity. Northeast Oklahoma Regional Electric Company provides electric power.

Fuel. The Gas Service Company supplies natural gas.

Water Supply. A 240,000-gallon storage facility, fed by a 1,200-foot-deep well, provides water.

COMMUNITY FACILITIES AND SERVICES

The tribal headquarters are located two miles southeast of the Town of Quapaw. Most of the tribe's programs are administered from this location. Programs include Title VI nutritional services, Indian child welfare, social services, adult education, direct employment, adult vocational training, housing, caregiver, community health representative, library, Tribal Tag, higher education, and enrollment, as well as all administrative services. The tribe also has an office for the Quapaw Tribal Substance Abuse program in Miami.

Education. Quapaw students attend local public schools and colleges throughout the country. The O-Gah-Pah Learning Center is set to offer a Quapaw language curriculum. As an asset to this program, the center worked with tribal elders and Southwestern Missouri University linguist to create a computer program, which will translate and pronounce in Quapaw, a word the user types in English.

Health Care. Tribal members can receive health care at the Claremore Indian Hospital located in Claremore, or the Northeastern Tribal Center located in Miami.

ENVIRONMENTAL CONCERNS

A number of environmental concerns have arisen for the tribe. The Tar Creek Superfund Site is located on tribal lands contains polluted waterways and has generated lead exposure and contamination. The tribe filed suit against the federal government in 2001, alleging the mismanagement of trust assets. The case remains undecided. The tribe has also filed suit against the last liable mining company that operated on tribal lands. The mining of lead and zinc ore between the 1920s and 1970s has left approximately 300 miles of underground tunnels, as well as millions of tons debris in open sites and ponds.

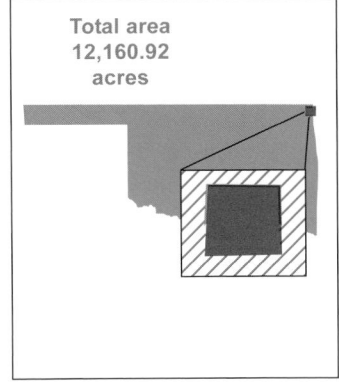

Total area
12,160.92
acres

TRI-OK-057

TRI-OK-058

TRI-OK-057 O-Gah-Pah Learning Center school bus

TRI-OK-058 Front view of the Quapaw Administration Building

Sac and Fox

LOCATION AND LAND STATUS

Sac and Fox Indian lands are dispersed throughout Lincoln, Payne, and Pottawatomie counties in the rolling hill country of east-central Oklahoma. The tribal headquarters, the capitol grounds, and the largest concentration of tribally owned trust land are located six miles south of Stroud, Oklahoma, along State Highway 99. The tribal capitol grounds lie approximately halfway between Oklahoma City and Tulsa.

In 1867, the Sac and Fox Nation purchased 479,668 acres of land for a reservation in Indian Territory. This land was allotted and opened for white homesteading in 1891. The tribe is active today in rebuilding its former land base. Trust lands include 14,961 acres of individual allotments and over 1,000 acres owned by the tribe.

CULTURE AND HISTORY

Members of the Sac and Fox Nation are descendants of the Sauk and Fox, two Algonquian-speaking peoples of the Great Lakes region. The name "Sauk" is derived from the tribe's own name "Osa'kiwug," meaning "people of the yellow earth." The Fox people called themselves "Meshkwa kihug," meaning "red earth people." The two tribes were independent, though closely related in culture and language. Both tribes were semi-sedentary village dwellers who subsisted primarily upon hunting and fishing. Pressure from the French and other tribes during the late seventeenth century forced the Sac and Fox into an alliance. Pushed west, the tribes settled in present-day Wisconsin, Iowa, Illinois, and Missouri, mainly along the Mississippi River. During the American Revolution, some Sac and Fox allied with the British. When the Missouri Band ceded all their lands east of the Mississippi to the United States in 1832, Sauk War Chief Black Hawk rebelled. The short, bloody Black Hawk War ended with the massacre of Black Hawk's people at Bad Axe, Wisconsin, by regular troops and militia on August 3, 1832. The tribe bought a reservation in Kansas in 1842; in 1867, they exchanged this land for a larger reservation in Indian Territory. In 1885, they approved the Sac and Fox Nation Constitution with a court system and centralized government. In 1891, the reservation was opened for allotment.

The Sac and Fox Nation retains its trademark strong government, having reestablished the first complete tribal court, police, and taxation system in Oklahoma. The Nation preserves and celebrates its rich cultural heritage through language classes, its museum, cultural events, and the Sac and Fox library and archives.

GOVERNMENT

The business committee, composed of a principal chief, second chief, secretary, treasurer, and at-large committee member, serves as the elected governing body for enrolled members. The business committee is empowered to transact business on behalf of the Sac and Fox Nation. Committee members are elected to staggered four-year terms, with elections occurring in odd-numbered years. The Sac and Fox Court, established in 1885, maintains jurisdiction over Indian Country in civil and criminal cases. The Nation adopted a constitution and bylaws in 1987 in accordance with the Oklahoma Indian Welfare Act.

Tribal government department and programs include social services, law enforcement, taxation, juvenile justice, housing, Indian child welfare, the gaming commission, elder care, en-

vironmental health, higher education, adult vocational training, Johnson O'Malley, food distribution, Merle Boyd Diabetic Center, learning center, public library and archives, and youth activity center. The Nation also has a police department with six officers; six beds are set aside in the Nation's 60-bed juvenile detention center for youths coming out of the BIA court system.

ECONOMY

Tribal government and revenues from taxation, oil and gas production, gaming, retail and service industries, and federal grants and contracts are the major components of the Nation's economy.

Government as Employer. Tribal members are employed in a number of departments and boards within the tribal government.

Economic Development Projects. The Sac and Fox Industrial Development Commission works to encourage business development in the tribal region.

Agriculture and Livestock. Individual tribal members lease land for farming and grazing purposes.

Gaming. A gaming center is in operation in Shawnee. More gaming operations are planned for the future.

Industrial Parks. The Nation reacquired 4,241 acres of trust land in Cushing, Oklahoma. The Cushing Industrial Park is located on this land; the facility includes a 25,000-square-foot building divided for offices and warehouse storage.

Services and Retail. The Sac and Fox Gallery, established in1993, is a retail outlet and cooperative that sells tribal members' arts and crafts. The Sac and Fox Tribal Mini-Mart, modeled after a traditional Sac and Fox summer lodge, sells groceries as well as arts and crafts. The Nation also licenses 13 smoke shops located in Payne, Lincoln, and Potawatomi counties.

Media and Communications. The Nation has its own monthly news publication called the *Sac and Fox News.*

Tourism and Recreation. The Sac and Fox Powwow, held annually in Stroud during mid-July, offers Indian dancing and arts and crafts. The Sac and Fox Tribal Museum located at tribal headquarters five miles south of Stroud, displays Sac and Fox history and features a memorial and exhibit honoring Jim Thorpe, the Olympic champion. Sac and Fox Tribal RV Park, located north of the cultural center, features a modern campground with a swimming pool, showers, and recreational facilities. Sac and Fox Veterans Lake provides flat-water recreational opportunities.

INFRASTRUCTURE

The Nation's Capitol Complex is located 5.5 miles south of Stroud on State Highway 99, which bisects tribal trust lands. I-44 passes just 6 miles north of tribal headquarters. I-40 passes approximately 19 miles south of tribal headquarters. Private air service is available at Stroud Municipal Airport, 8 miles north of the tribal headquarters. Commercial air facilities are located in Oklahoma City and Tulsa, 60 miles east and west of the reservation. Bus service is also available in

TRI-OK-048

TRI-OK-049

Sac and Fox

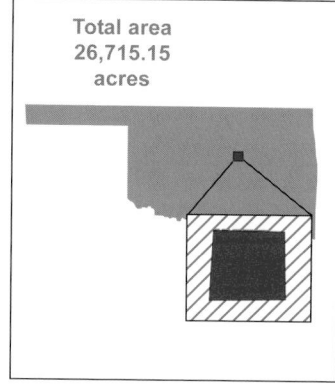

Total area
26,715.15
acres

TRI-OK-048 Wellness Center Building and parking lot

TRI-OK-049 IHS, Stroud, OK, located juest east (across highway) from complex

Oklahoma City and Tulsa. UPS and FedEx package carriers serve the jurisdiction.

Water Supply. The Indian Health Service's Office of Environmental Health is offering programs to install water and sewer service facilities such as wells, water service lines, septic tanks and drain fields, wastewater lagoons, and sewer service lines to eligible tribal members within Sac and Fox Nation jurisdiction.

COMMUNITY FACILITIES AND SERVICES
The Sac and Fox Nation maintains community centers within the Capitol Complex near Stroud and the Nation's multipurpose facility in Shawnee. The Nation also has its own museum, public library and archives, learning center, youth activity center, and an elder care program.

Education. The Sac and Fox Nation administers the Johnson O'Malley program, which allows for the education of tribal students in 13 nearby school districts.

Health Care. The Sac and Fox Nation operates an outpatient clinic that has one doctor, one physician's assistant, and seven nurses. The clinic's services include x-ray and lab, podiatry, neurology, cardiac, nutrition and dietitian, and a diabetes program. The clinic offers a referral service for dental and vision care. For services not covered by the clinic, there are two privately owned clinics in the reservation area as well as hospitals in Stroud, Shawnee, and Cushing. The Nation also operates the Merle Boyd Diabetes Center, which provides a physical therapist, an exercise room, counseling, and a substance abuse counseling and prevention program. The Nation administers a USDA food distribution program for all eligible Indian families.

ENVIRONMENTAL CONCERNS
Water and air quality are major concerns to the Sac and Fox Nation. In 2004, the tribe won a 20-year long lawsuit pertaining to the contamination of tribal water sources by local drilling activities. The tribe is in the process of testing the effects of ozone depletion on air quality on the reservation.

Seminole

Seminole

LOCATION AND LAND STATUS
The Seminole Tribal Jurisdiction Area is located in south-central Oklahoma, approximately 45 miles east of Oklahoma City, and it includes all of Seminole County.

The Seminole Nation Tribal Complex is located in the Town of Wewoka, Oklahoma. Wewoka lies at the junction of U.S. 270 and Oklahoma Highway 56, approximately 20 miles southeast of the Town of Shawnee. Wewoka is also the site of several Seminole Nation programs and services. The Mekusukey Mission (which includes tribal offices, recreational areas, industrial and commercial areas, and a cultural area) is located in the town of Seminole.

The Seminoles were removed to Indian Territory following the Treaty of Paynes Landing in 1832. They were eventually granted a reservation, but these lands were allotted following the Seminole Agreement of 1898. Today, the tribe owns 449 acres of federal trust land. An additional 35,443 allotted acres supplement the tribal land base.

CULTURE AND HISTORY
Members of the Seminole Nation lived in southeastern North America for thousands of years predating European arrival. The Seminoles encountered Spanish explorers in the early 1500s. They suffered devastating losses caused by the rash of death brought on by European diseases foreign to their immune systems. Survivors from the Seminole Tribe moved toward the peninsula of Florida and were living in that area in close proximity to members of the Euchee, Yamasee,

Timugua, Tequesta, Abalachi, and Coça tribes, among others, almost two hundred years later when they encountered English settlers. The English identified all the Native Americans they encountered as members of one nation and referred to them as Seminolies, or Seminoles, their misinterpretation of the Maskókî word "yat'siminoli," or "free people."

In 1784 the American Revolution ended and Euro-American settlers began to enter the southeastern United States in large numbers. The tension between Native nations and the settlers was exacerbated by the federal policy of taking or buying lands from the tribes and giving them to Euro-Americans. By 1813 the situation had escalated and there began a series of conflicts throughout the region. The defeat of the Creek Nation in Alabama resulted in a flood of refugees into Florida. The Seminoles joined forces with the Creeks and other Native tribes in the area to resist Euro-American invasion.

In 1814 U.S. President Andrew Jackson authorized the destruction of Native communities in Florida and the murder of tribal leaders. The battles that ensued between the federal government and the tribes became known as the First Seminole War. In 1830 the federal government ordered the forced removal of Native Americans living east of the Mississippi River to Indian Territory west of the river. The Native people of the southeastern United States resisted the government's forced removal, and the Second Seminole War began in 1835 and continued until 1842. A number of tribes joined forces to fight the government, as did numbers of African-American slaves

Seminole Tribe of Oklahoma Reservation
Federal reservation
Seminole
Seminole County, Oklahoma

Seminole Nation of Oklahoma
P.O. Box 1498
Wewoka, OK 74884
405-257-6287
405-257-6205 Fax
seminolenation.com

Seminole

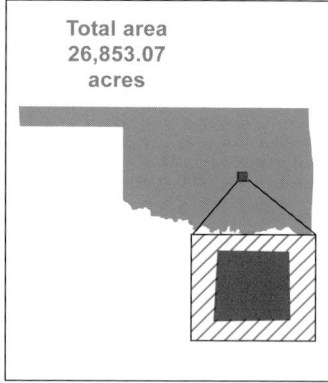

**Total area
26,853.07
acres**

Total area *(BIA realty, 2004)*
26,853.07 acres

Tribally owned *(BIA realty, 2004)*
26,420.65 acres

Individually owned
(BIA realty, 2004)
432.42 acres

Tribal enrollment
(BIA labor report, 2001)
13,642

Total labor force *2000 census*
9,497

Total labor force
2000 census
2,079

High school graduate or higher
2000 census
73.3%

Bachelor's degree or higher
2000 census
12%

Unemployment rate *2000 census*
8.2%

Unemployment rate *2000 census*
58%

TRI-OK-050

TRI-OK-051

escaping slavery (Freedmen). The war was the longest, most expensive, and last of the wars fought between the United States and Native nations over the Indian Removal Act. In 1856 the Third Seminole War began when Seminole leader Billy Bowlegs was directly provoked by U.S. troops. By the 1860s, an estimated 3,000 Native Americans had been forcibly removed from Florida. Less than 200 tribal members escaped removal, seeking refuge in the Florida Everglades. Their descendants comprise today's Seminole Tribe and Miccossukee Tribe.

Those Seminoles relocated to Indian Territory were granted a reservation in the western portion of the Creek Nation. This reservation was alienated, and lands were allotted to tribal members during the late nineteenth century.

GOVERNMENT
The Seminole General Council, chaired by a principal chief and an assistant chief, serves as the elected governing body. The chief and assistant chief are elected at large every four years. The Seminole Nation ratified a constitution on March 8, 1969, which the Commission of Indian Affairs approved on April 15, 1969. The Nation is comprised of 12 matrilineal bands, including two Freedman bands. Each band has an elected chairman and vice-chairman and meets monthly. Each band elects two representatives to the general council every two years. Tribal headquarters are located in Wewoka, the seat of Seminole County. The general council meets at the council house on the Mekusukey Mission Tribal Grounds south of Seminole. The tribe has been developing a new tribal constitution that will eliminate the role of the BIA in tribal government operations.

Tribal government departments include communications, education, health, housing, accounting, community and family services, and planning. The tribe's historic preservation office is funded in part by tribal revenues and resources. The office handles matters of requests pertaining to the Native American Graves and Protection and Repatriation Act and the National Historic Preservation Act. Objectives of the office are: to establish communication with the Seminole, Miccosukee, and Independent Seminole tribes of Florida; to collaborate with the tribes to develop a uniform policy and procedure to deal with repatriation and preservation matters; to identify historic sites important to the Seminole Nation; to conduct interviews with tribal elders; and to develop a database and archive system.

BUSINESS CORPORATION
The Seminole Nation Development Authority oversees the tribe's accounting program and its four businesses: two gaming operations, a trading post, a travel plaza, and a convenience store.

ECONOMY
The tribe operates a number of businesses that contribute to the tribal economy. The net profits from these businesses are redistributed to tribal programs and to the Seminole Nation Development Authority for operational funds.

Economic Development Projects. The tribe continues to acquire land and businesses in Seminole County. The tribe purchased the River Mist Store in southern Seminole County and the Travel Plaza located just off I-40 near the Seminole Exit.

Gaming. The tribe owns two gaming facilities: the Rivermist Casino in southern Seminole County and the Mystic Winds Casino located on I-40 at Exit 200. Both casinos offer electronic gaming.

Manufacturing. The tribe is preparing a site on the Mekusukey Mission Grounds for manufacturing.

Industrial Parks. The tribe operates a 65-acre industrial area on the Mekusukey Mission Grounds, which offers full electrical, gas, and water hookups. The site is conveniently located one mile from Highway 99 and 10 miles from I-40.

Services and Retail. The tribe owns the Seminole Nation Trading Post, Seminole Nation Travel Plaza, and the Seminole Nation Rivermist Convenience Store.

Media and Communications. A monthly newspaper named *Cokv Tvleme* is written, published, and distributed to over 3,500 tribal members nationally. The Seminole Nation of Oklahoma also produces a weekly radio program.

Tourism and Recreation. Wewoka is located about 40 minutes' drive from Lake Eufaula, the largest recreational lake in Oklahoma. Lake Eufaula is home to two resort lodges and many vacation homes. The Seminole Nation Museum, located in Wewoka, features exhibits on Seminole culture and history. An adjoining gallery and craft shop feature contemporary and traditional Seminole crafts. Seminole Nation Days, held annually in August at the Mekusukey Mission Grounds, celebrate tribal culture and heritage.

INFRASTRUCTURE
Tribal facilities in Wewoka are accessible via north-south running Oklahoma Highway 56 and east-west running U.S. 270. I-40, connecting with Oklahoma City and beyond, passes approximately 20 miles north of Wewoka.

Electricity. Regional providers supply electricity to individual tribal members.

Fuel. The tribal community services department furnishes home heating fuel to tribal members.

Water Supply. Septic tanks and the municipal sewer system provide service to tribal members.

Transportation. The tribe will soon begin operation of a Federal Transportation Section 18 Program for public transportation in Seminole County. Seminole Airport, located within the tribal jurisdiction area, offers private air service. Commercial air service is available in Oklahoma City, 45 miles west. Trucking companies and package carriers serve the tribal area.

COMMUNITY FACILITIES AND SERVICES

The tribe maintains a community center in Wewoka, Konawa, and the Mekusukey Mission Tribal Grounds. Community Services of the Seminole Nation offers child care, Indian Child Welfare Act, LIHEAP, emergency tribal assistance, and BCR programs. Its community division offers environmental, historical preservation, housing, home grant, housing improvement, roads transportation, Lighthorsemen, wildlife, and REACH programs.

Public Safety. In 2001 the tribe contributed a $50,000 grant to the Seminole Fire Department. The city used the funds to improve fire prevention services. The city agreed to provide free service to tribal members and facilities within Seminole County for five years.

Education. The tribe's education division offers adult, higher, Johnson O'Malley, Head Start, JTPA, TERO, and Judgment Fund programs. A junior college is located about 15 miles from the community.

Health Care. Health care services are available through the Wewoka Service Unit of Public Health Services. The health center is served by two physicians and one physician's assistant. Programs include general medicine, prenatal and well-baby care, optometry, dentistry, and counseling. Community health personnel are available and offer nutrition programs for pregnant, overweight, or diabetic patients.

The tribe's health division offers community health representative, older American, alcohol and substance abuse, food distribution, community service block grant, and environmental health programs.

Seneca-Cayuga

Total area *(BIA realty, 2004)*	4,217.24 acres
Total area	4,390.87 acres
(Tribal source, 2004)	
Federal trust	2,976.82 acres
(Tribal source, 2004)	
Tribally owned	1,218.12 acres
(BIA realty, 2004)	
Tribally owned	1,187.69 acres
(Tribal source, 2004)	
Individually owned	2,999.12 acres
(BIA realty, 2004)	
Other *(Tribal source, 2004)*	226 acres
Tribal enrollment *(Tribal source, 2004)*	4,171
Total labor force **2000 census**	1,583
Total labor force *(BIA labor report, 2001)*	603
High school graduate or higher	77.7%
2000 census	
Bachelor's degree or higher	10.4%
2000 census	
Unemployment rate **2000 census**	6.1%
Unemployment rate	25%
(BIA labor report, 2001)	
Per capita income**2000 census**	$15,595

LOCATION AND LAND STATUS

Seneca-Cayuga tribal facilities and trust lands are located in northeastern Oklahoma in Ottawa and Delaware counties. The tribal headquarters are located in Miami, Oklahoma, close to I-44 on U.S. Alternate 69. Miami is approximately 90 miles northeast of Tulsa, via I-44. Joplin, Missouri, lies approximately 20 miles northeast of Miami.

The Seneca-Cayugas were removed to Indian Territory in 1832. Soon after, they were assigned a reservation in the northeastern corner of Oklahoma. This reservation was alienated and allotted during the late nineteenth century. Today the tribe owns 2,976.82 acres of federal trust land. Another 2,934.81 acres of allotments supplement the tribal land base.

PHYSICAL DESCRIPTION

This region is characterized by flat prairie, which meets the Ozark Mountain Geologic Province to the east.

CULTURE AND HISTORY

The Seneca-Cayuga Tribe of Oklahoma is comprised of descendants of the Seneca and Cayuga tribes. Both tribes traditionally resided in present-day New York. Tribal members were relocated to Oklahoma and united there in the late 1800s. The Senecas and Cayugas were two of the original nations to join the Haudenosaunee, or Iroquois Confederacy.

In the early 1800s, a number of indigenous groups from the New England region relocated to the Ohio area following battles with American colonists and treaties reached with the federal government. An 1829 census reported that 322 Iroquois resided in Ohio. Tribal affiliations included Cayuga, Seneca, Oneida, Mohawk, and Onondaga. The tribal members were collectively referred to as the Senecas of Sandusky. In the 1817 and 1818 treaties between the Senecas of Sandusky and the government, the group ceded virtually all their lands. The group retained ownership of only 48,000 acres located on the east side of the Sandusky River, near Lewiston, Ohio.

GOVERNMENT

The Seneca-Cayuga Business Council, consisting of a chief, a second chief, a secretary/treasurer, and three other council members, serves as the tribes elected governing body. Committee members serve staggered two-year terms, with elections occurring at the annual tribal meeting. The tribal government is organized under the Oklahoma Indian Welfare Act of 1936. The Commissioner of Indian Affairs approved their constitution on April 26, 1937. Tribal programs include social services, administration on aging, aid to tribal government, higher education, adult education and vocational training, job planning and training, Johnson O'Malley, Indian child welfare, childcare and development, community health representative, housing development, and alcohol and substance abuse.

ECONOMY

The Seneca-Cayuga Tribe's economy is largely supported by the tribal government, gaming, light manufacturing, several retail establishments, and tourism. Future economic endeavors are being sought in the gaming and tourism industries.

Seneca-Cayuga Tribe of Oklahoma
Federal reservation
Seneca-Cayuga
Delaware and Ottawa counties, Oklahoma

Seneca-Cayuga Tribe
P.O. Box 1283
Miami, OK 74355
918-542-6609
918-542-6600
918-542-3684 Fax
geocities.com/
Seneca_Cayuga

Seneca-Cayuga

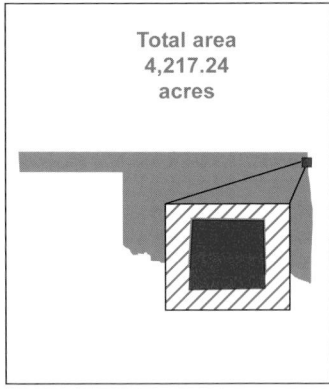

Total area
4,217.24
acres

Economic Development Projects. In July 2004, the Seneca-Cayuga Tribe was in the planning stages of a full-fledged class III casino in New York. During this time the Seneca-Cayuga Tribe was purchasing land in its ancestral territory, sighting related court decisions as proof of their sovereignty over the land. As of 2004 the case was still before a federal judge.

Gaming. The tribe owns and operates Grand Lake Casino and the Seneca-Cayuga Bingo Hall which are located in Grove, on the east side of Lake of the Cherokee. The casino offers 500 gaming machines and a restaurant, and it employs approximately 150 people.

Manufacturing. The tribe owns and operates a tobacco manufacturing company.

Services and Retail. The tribally owned and operated Lighthouse Restaurant is located directly across the street from the Seneca-Cayuga Bingo Hall and the tribal smoke shop, Ranch Resort, is located in Grove.

Tourism and Recreation. The annual Green Corn Feast and Thanksgiving Harvest celebration is held in August at the Basset Grove Ceremonial Grounds. Celebration events include tribal dancing, baby naming, and dances by other visiting tribes.

INFRASTRUCTURE
Tribal headquarters are directly accessible via U.S. 69. I-44 connects the tribal headquarters with Joplin, Missouri, approximately 20 miles northeast, and Tulsa, approximately 90 miles southwest. Private and commercial air services are available at Miami Municipal Airport; Tulsa International Airport is less than 100 miles southwest. Commercial and city buses serve Miami, as do all major trucking lines and express package carriers.

Electricity. GRDA provides the tribe's electricity.

COMMUNITY FACILITIES AND SERVICES
The tribe maintains a community center, which includes a child development center, a multipurpose center, and a human resource building. The community center sponsors language and cultural classes.

Education. Children attend public schools in Ottawa and Delaware counties.

Health Care. Tribal members receive outpatient medical services from the Northeastern Tribal Health Clinic in Miami. For services not provided by the clinic, tribal members can visit the Claremore Indian Hospital in Claremore, Oklahoma. Private clinics and hospitals are also available in Miami.

Thlopthlocco

Thlopthlocco Tribal Town
Federally recognized
Creek (Muskogee)
Okfuskee County, Oklahoma

Thlopthlocco Creek
Tribal Town
P.O. Box 188
Okemah, OK 74859
918-623-2620
918-623-1810
918-623-0419 Fax

Federal trust *(Tribal source, 2005)*
2,500 acres

Population *2000 census*
638

Total labor force *2000 census*
506

Per capita income
(Tribal source, 2005)
$14,180

LOCATION AND LAND STATUS
The Thlopthlocco Tribal Town is located in east-central Oklahoma in the Town of Clearview on Route 1, some five miles north of Weleetka. Okemah, Oklahoma, lies approximately six miles north on I-40. Oklahoma City is approximately 60 miles west of the tribal town. The Thlopthlocco Tribal Town is part of the Creek Nation of Oklahoma, which owns over 6,000 acres of federal trust land that are dispersed throughout an eight-county area in eastern Oklahoma. The tribe plans to purchase more lands in the future.

PHYSICAL DESCRIPTION
The tribal area is characterized by rolling hills of alternating hardwood forest and open grassland. The south fork of the Canadian River drains into Eufaula Lake just west of the tribal town.

CLIMATE
Temperatures in the area range from an average high of 94°F in July and August to an average low of 31°F in January. The average precipitation is 47.1 inches yearly in this area.

CULTURE AND HISTORY
Members of the Thlopthlocco Tribal Town are descendants of the Muskogee (or Mvskoke) people, a Muskogean-speaking tribe of the southeastern United States. They lived in riverfront or coastal villages in the area of present-day Alabama, Louisiana, Mississippi, and western Florida. During the eighteenth and early nineteenth centuries, early Euro-American settlers in the region referred to them as "Alabama" or "Creek" Indians. They practiced a subsistence lifestyle based on hunting, fishing, and horticulture. The Creeks were significantly influenced by the prehistoric Caddoan and Mississippi cultures, and they were related linguistically and culturally to the Yamasee, Seminole, Apalachee, Choctaw, and Chickasaw tribes.

The Muscogee term "tvlwv" is translated as "tribal town." However, this word carries a much deeper connotation than a town. It was the site of religious happenings, public events, and home to the Sacred Fire. Each of these towns functioned independently but shared ties of language and kinship.

Hernando de Soto led the first party of Europeans into Creek territory in 1539. Throughout the seventeenth and eighteenth centuries, the lower southeast became an economic and military battleground for competing European powers. The Creeks allied with the English against the Spanish during the eighteenth century, but they eventually became embroiled in war with other tribes competing for English trade items.

The Creeks formed part of the Five Civilized Tribes, a name English settlers applied to the Choctaws, Chickasaws, Creeks, Cherokees, and Seminoles because of their rapid adoption of many Euro-American cultural practices. Warfare between Creeks arose during the War of 1812 as different bands declared allegiance to either the English or the United States. A massive influx of American settlers into the southeast during the early nineteenth century led President Andrew Jackson to sign the Removal Bill in 1830, giving him power to exchange land west of the Mississippi for lands held by southeastern tribes. In 1836, the U.S. Army forced the Creeks to relocate to Indian Territory in present-day Oklahoma. In eastern Oklahoma, the Creeks became relatively prosperous farmers. However, they eventually lost most of their tribal lands through allotment.

Thlopthlocco, a Creek tribal town, has figured prominently in Oklahoma's Creek history and traditions. Thlopthlocco Town was established in the 1830s, according to Representative Brad Carson's office. *(See Creek [Muskogee] Nation in this chapter for further details).* Colonel D.H. Cooper's Confederate forces were headquartered there in 1861, when fighting Opothleyahola and the "Loyal Creeks," the office notes. The tribe adopted a constitution in accordance with the Oklahoma Indian Welfare Act on November 17, 1938.

Planting and trading were historically Creek skills, according to Allen Harjo, tribal administrator. "Today, they have turned their trading heritage to good use and proved that capitalism can serve the interests of American Indians," he writes. To advance members' economic prospects, the tribe says it seeks new recreational and business developments.

GOVERNMENT
A business committee serves as the elected government body. It is composed of the tribal town king, known as the "mekko," two town warriors, a secretary, a treasurer, and five advisory committee members, who all serve four-year terms. Enrolled tribal members meet annually at town meetings. The Thlopthlocco Tribal Town has its own security force. A PL 93-638 tribe, Thlopthlocco contracts for Indian child welfare, ATG, and employment and training administration, tribal sources report.

The Thlopthlocco Tribal Town is part of the Creek Nation of Oklahoma; district officers represent the town, which is located within the Okfuskee District, at Creek Nation general council meetings.

BUSINESS CORPORATION
A free enterprise trade zone is reported to be under study by the tribe's business corporation, Thlopthlocco Tribal Town.

ECONOMY
A gaming facility, smoke shop, gift shop, and cabinet-making shop earn revenues for the tribe. The BIA counts 275 public sector employees; private sector employees total 29.

Government as Employer. The town government employs 10 residents, including the town king. Workers in the public sector total 275.

Economic Development Projects. The tribe is considering constructing a truck plaza and motel.

Gaming. The tribally owned Thlopthlocco Tribal Town Gaming Center and Casino in Okemah offers 164 video gaming machines. It has 68 employees, 17 of whom are tribal members, and it is open daily, 24 hours a day. The tribe is considering plans to develop it into a modified class III facility.

Manufacturing. Tribal members manufacture jewelry and make Indian art objects, which are sold in the casino gift shop.

Services and Retail. The Thlopthlocco Gaming Center and Casino includes a smoke and gift shop, and it is open every day.

Tourism and Recreation. The tribe is considering opening a canoeing facility, RV park, and equestrian center. Extensive water recreation is found nearby at Eufaula Lake, the largest lake in Oklahoma, with 600 miles of shoreline, a short distance to the west of the tribal town.

INFRASTRUCTURE
Electricity. Public Service of Oklahoma supplies electricity to the town.

Fuel. Oklahoma Natural Gas services the community.

Water Supply. Okemah's municipal water, supplied by a local, dammed lake, serves Thlopthlocco Tribal Town. The tribe also completed a water tower for backup use in June 2004.

Transportation. The Thlopthlocco Tribal Town is accessible from Oklahoma City via I-40, which passes just six miles to the north. U.S. 75 (north-south), connecting to Tulsa and beyond, passes just east of the tribal town. Commercial air facilities are located in Oklahoma City, 60 miles west. Private air service is available in Henryetta, 18 miles to the east. Air Nav lists Okemah Flying Field Airport one mile east of Okemah for general aviation. It has two turf runways, 2,585 by 100 feet and 2,375 by 80 feet. Bus service and overnight accommodations are available in Henryetta.

Telecommunications. Southwestern Bell provides telephone service.

COMMUNITY FACILITIES AND SERVICES
Social services include education and health services, safe houses (cellars for tornado protection), safety fencing, and housing assistance. Community facilities include the historic Thlopthlocco Methodist Church and a small tribal library. Tribal members also use the municipal library in Okemah.

Education. Children attend Okfuskee County Public Schools.

Health Care. Tribal members receive health care through the Creek Nation Community Hospital and Clinic.

ENVIRONMENTAL CONCERNS
The town lists as its environmental concerns keeping the Canadian River clean while continuing to use it and finding better ways to use land resources. The tribe is developing a satellite view of its lands.

TRI-OK-052

Thlopthlocco

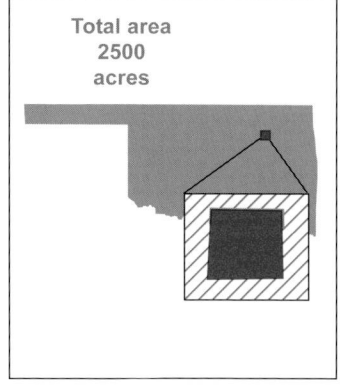

**Total area
2500
acres**

TRI-OK-052 New water tower, 1 with tribal emblem

Tonkawa

Tonkawa Tribal Reserve
Federal reservation
Tonkawa
Kay County, Oklahoma

Tonkawa Tribe of Oklahoma
1 Rush Buffalo Rd.
Tonkawa, OK 74653
580-628-2561
580-628-3375 Fax
tonkawatribe.com

Total area *(BIA realty, 2004)*
1,233.07 acres

Tribally owned *(BIA realty, 2004)*
994.33 acres

Federal trust *(BIA realty, 2004)*
0.5 acres

Individually owned
(BIA realty, 2004)
238.24 acres

Tribal enrollment
(BIA labor report, 2001)
420

Total labor force *2000 census*
1,991

High school graduate or higher
2000 census
78.1%

Bachelor's degree or higher
2000 census
19%

Unemployment rate *2000 census*
10.9%

Unemployment rate
(BIA labor report, 2001)
79%

Per capita income *2000 census*
$5,556

ENVIRONMENTAL CONCERNS
The existence of an abandoned oil field on tribal lands is of concern to the tribe. With the assistance of the Inter-Tribal Environmental Council of Oklahoma, the tribe has investigated the potential for water and soil contamination. Though the risks were found to be minimal, the area does remain a concern.

LOCATION AND LAND STATUS
The Tonkawa Tribal Reserve is located in Kay County, in northern Oklahoma. Ponca City lies just 12 miles east via U.S. 60. Oklahoma City is approximately 100 miles due south. The tribal reserve consists of 994.33 acres of federal trust land. These trust lands are supplemented by 238.24 acres in individual allotments.

Chief Joseph's Nez Perce Indians occupied Fort Oakland, on the original Tonkawa Reserve, from 1878 to 1884. In 1884, the Tonkawas were assigned 91,000 acres of land within this reservation. These lands were allotted, and the remainder opened for white settlement.

CLIMATE
Temperatures in nearby Ponca City range from winter lows of 22°F to summertime highs of 93°F. Annual precipitation is about 34.2 inches.

CULTURE AND HISTORY
The Tonkawa Tribe of Oklahoma is descended from the Tonkawan-speaking people of central Texas. Inhabiting a cultural convergence zone, the Tonkawas borrowed from the Caddoan culture to the east, the plains culture to the north, and the Coahuiltecan culture of northern Mexico.

The tribe encountered Spanish explorers in 1691 and later made contact with the French in 1719. During the mid-nineteenth century, white settlers pressuring for Tonkawa lands spurred the federal government to settle the tribe on two small reservations in Texas. In 1857, the Tonkawas were removed to Indian Territory near present-day Anadarko. In 1862, plains tribes raided the Tonkawas, and the remaining members fled to Fort Griffin, Texas, remaining there until 1884. That year, the federal government relocated the tribe to Fort Oakland in Indian Territory, previously inhabited by Chief Joseph's band of exiled Nez Perce Indians. In 1887, the Tonkawa Reserve was allotted to 73 members. The Tonkawa Tribe of Oklahoma incorporated in 1938.

GOVERNMENT
The tribal committee, composed of a president, vice-president and secretary-treasurer, serves as the elected governing body for enrolled tribal members. Committee members serve two-year terms, with elections occurring every other year. The Tonkawa Tribe is organized under the Oklahoma Indian Welfare Act, having adopted a constitution and bylaws on March 16, 1938. This constitution was amended on April 2, 1977.

Tribal headquarters are situated about 2.5 miles southeast of the Town of Tonkawa along the west bank of the Chikaskia River. Government departments and programs include community health, environmental protection, LIHEAP, housing, Indian reservation roads, police, education, and tribal court.

ECONOMY
The Tonkawa Tribe aims to increase economic opportunity for its members while earning revenues through a tribally owned gaming facility, as well as a smoke shop, convenience store, and gas station facility.

Gaming. The tribe owns the Tonkawa Tribal Bingo, a class II bingo facility operated by an outside contractor. It features 300 bingo seats, 250 video gaming machines, a race book, and a snack bar.

Services and Retail. The tribe owns and operates a smoke shop, convenience store, and gas station complex in Tonkawa.

Tourism and Recreation. The tribe hosts an annual powwow. It is held at the end of June to coincide with the Tonkawa "Trail of Tears," the tribe's journey from Fort Griffin, Texas, to Fort Oakland during the period of forced removal.

INFRASTRUCTURE
Tonkawa tribal headquarters are accessible from Ponca City, via U.S. 60. U.S. 77 connects Tonkawa with Blackwell, 12 miles north. I-35 passes just 3 miles west of Tonkawa, connecting with Oklahoma City and beyond.

Electricity. Regional provides supply electricity to tribal members.

Fuel. Regional provides supply gas service to tribal members.

Transportation. Commercial and private air service is available in Ponca City, 12 miles east. Bus lines, truck lines, and express package carriers also serve Ponca City.

COMMUNITY FACILITIES AND SERVICES
A community center is located at Fort Oakland on the tribal reserve near Tonkawa. The tribe provides substance abuse, child care, and Indian child welfare programs for tribal members. It also maintains a Workforce Investment Act Program, which provides tribal members with supplemental employment, training, and services.

Education. Children attend Kay County Public Schools. The tribe contacts the Johnson O'Malley Program to secure supplement funding for local schools. It also operates higher education, adult education, and adult vocational training programs.

Health Care. Tribal members receive health care through the Pawnee Agency in Pawnee, approximately 30 miles southeast of the tribal reserve. Hospitals are also located in Ponca City. A community health representative serves the reservation, and the tribe operates a special diabetes program.

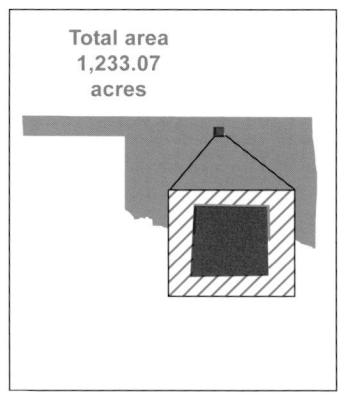

Total area
1,233.07
acres

United Keetoowah

LOCATION AND LAND STATUS

The United Keetoowah Band (UKB) of Cherokee Indians retains no communal land base. The tribal community is dispersed throughout nine districts in a 14-county area in northeastern Oklahoma. Tribal headquarters are located west of the Arkansas River at the town of Tahlequah in Cherokee County, Oklahoma on a 2.6-acre site. The tribe owns fewer than 50 acres in Tahlequah. Oklahoma cities near Tahlequah include Tulsa (approximately 60 miles northwest), Muskogee (approximately 20 miles southwest), Oklahoma City (approximately 160 miles west). Fort Smith, Arkansas lies some 90 miles southeast of Tahlequah. The band purchased a 350-acre trace of farmland near Bryson, Oklahoma in 1996. The tribe is represented by the Canadian, Cooweescoowee, Delaware, Flint, Goingsnake, Illinois, Saline, Sequoyah, and Tahlequah districts.

In the year 2000, the U.S. Interior Department found that the land owned by the UKB does not qualify as "Indian Country" because it does not exercise jurisdiction over it, it is not held in trust, and it is not subject to restriction by the United States against alienation.

PHYSICAL DESCRIPTION

The northeastern portions of Oklahoma, including Tahlequah, are located in the foothills of the Ozark Mountains. Numerous streams, rivers, and forests characterize the terrain.

CLIMATE

Tahlequah is located 870 feet above sea level. The average yearly temperature is 60°F and the average precipitation level is 42.6 inches.

CULTURE AND HISTORY

The UKB is one of three federally recognized Cherokee tribes in the United States. Ancestral homelands of the Cherokee were located in the southern United States and included portions of the Appalachian mountains. In the mid-eighteenth century, members of the Keetoowah Band, or the Principal People, began a migration westward into present-day Arkansas.

In 1817, the band agreed to a treaty with the United States that designated a portion of north central Arkansas as Keetoowah, referred to as the western Cherokee, lands. In the Treaty of 1828, the band ceded their Arkansas lands and accepted a parcel of lands, including the Cherokee Strip, in Oklahoma.

In 1835, the Treaty of New Echota ceded all Cherokee Nation tribal lands east of the Mississippi River and provided for the removal of the tribe to Indian Territory in Okalahoma. The Keetoowah and newly arrived bands of the Cherokee Nation engaged in a power struggle and were often in conflict, but were forced together by the Treaty of 1846. The tribes remained united until the outbreak of the Civil War. Members of the Keetoowah Band were not slave-holders and supported the Union Army while members of the Cherokee Nation sided with the Confederacy. Although the Keetwoowah had been its ally during the war, upon its end, the United States administered the same penalties upon the band as it did upon the Cherokee Nation. The government seized a large portion of tribal lands and forced the bands together until 1898. At that time, the Curtis Act dissolved the tribal government of the Nation. The rights to operate tribal courts, develop tribal law enforcement, and to enforce taxes were removed from the

tribe and have never been reinstated. The pressure to accept allotment of tribal lands was great and in 1902, the Cherokee Nation lands were allotted to individual tribal members. Remaining tribal lands were allotted during the early twentieth century, and many passed into non-Indian hands. Many members of the Keetoowah Band refused to accept allotment and were jailed for their voiced opposition.

In 1905, the Keetoowah applied for a Charter of Incorporation from the federal government. It was granted and the Keetoowah Society continued to operate under their traditional governing system. In 1946, the Keetoowah Status Act recognized the band as a political entity, allowing it to reorganize under the Oklahoma Indian Welfare Act of 1936. In 1950, the tribe adopted a tribal constitution and a federal corporate charter. Now known as the United Keetoowah Band, the band continued to operate as a tribal entity separate from the Cherokee Nation. In 1969, the band disassociated from the Nation in order to assert its tribal sovereignty.

While the UKB owns a portion of unallotted lands, it has been denied title to lands that the federal government holds in trust for the Cherokee Nation. The UKB has requested that the lands be assigned to it. It argues that the deeds state that the land may be held in trust until designated to a group organized under provisions of the Indian Reorganization Act of 1936. As the UKB is the only Cherokee group to be organized under the Indian Reorganization Act, it argues that the title to the lands should be granted to it. Although its arguments have gone unheeded, in 1994, the BIA did recognize the band's right to purchase lands in Arkansas in order to further economic development.

Division and hostility continues among the various groups of Cherokees. In 1990, the principal chief of the Cherokee Nation of Oklahoma objected to UKB's federal funding and in 1991, a congressional rider stopped the flow of funds. Later, the CNO attempted to have UKB's federal status terminate, but failed. UKB leaders have since been able to restore most of the tribe's federal funding by making sure there is no dual enrollment. Members of the band today are related to those on a list of members identified by a resolution dated April 19, 1949, and certified by the superintendent of the Five Civilized Tribes Agency. The governing body of the UKB has the power to prescribe rules and regulations governing future membership. The UKB has a one-fourth blood quantum requirement.

Members of the UKB proudly continue to practice traditional cultural customs and speak the indigenous language. The tribe actively promotes cultural preservation and perpetuation, sponsoring various program and activities to encourage the transmission of cultural elements from generation to generation.

GOVERNMENT

By the Act of August 10, 1946, (60 Stat. 976), the U.S. Congress recognized the UKB as a federal corporation for the purposes of organizing under the Oklahoma Indian Welfare Act of 1936 and the Indian Reorganization Act of 1936. The UKB is governed by a tribal council of 13 members. The council is comprised of a chief, assistant chief, secretary, treasurer, and 9 members representing 9 districts of the Keetoowah community. The 4 officers are elected by the band at large and serve for 4 years; the district representatives are elected

United Keetoowah Tribal Community
Federally Recognized Tribal Community
United Keetoowah Band of Cherokee Indians in Oklahoma
Keetoowah Band of Cherokee Adair, Cherokee, Delaware, Mayes, Sequoyah counties, Oklahoma

United Keetoowah Band
of Cherokee Indians
P.O. Box 746
2450 South Muskogee Ave.
Tahlequah, OK 74465-9432
918-456-5491
918-456-9601 Fax
unitedkeetoowahband.org

Tribal enrollment
(BIA labor report, 2001)
7,953

Tribal enrollment
(Tribal source, 2005)
11,457

Total labor force
(BIA labor report, 2001)
2,514

Unemployment rate
(BIA labor report, 2001)
60%

United Keetoowah

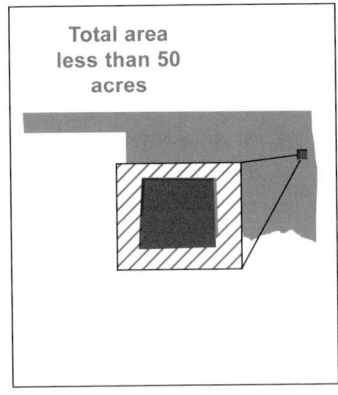

Total area
less than 50
acres

by their respective districts and serve for 2 years. All members of the band 21 years of age or older are eligible to vote in tribal elections. The council holds annual meetings in September, along with special meetings that can be called by the chief or requested by seven of the 13 council members.

Tribal government services include the Indian child welfare, housing authority, social services, human and family services, security, environmental, education, enrollment, public information, gaming, human resources, maintenance, and realty, among others. The tribe's justice department includes the tribal victim assistance program.

The tribe, under PL-638, contracts with the BIA to administer key programs or services. They operate LIHEAP, a heating and energy assistance program; BIA general assistance; child care subsidy program; an elder dental program and medical and handicap transportation services. The housing authority offers mortgage assistance, rental assistance, rehabilitation, and cultural programs. In 1997, the department received $1.4 million for housing construction. The award was the first federal funding to be awarded to the tribe in almost 50 years.

ECONOMY

The tribal economy is supported in large part by the revenue earned from various tribally-owned enterprises. With ever-increasing gaming revenues since the late 1980s, the tribe has expanded into the tourism market and added other tribal enterprises. In addition, UKB imposes a fuel tax, the income from which is used to provide financial assistance to help tribal members pay for certain medical expenses.

Government as Employer. The tribe employs a number of people in its various programs and enterprises. The Keetoowah Bingo facility alone employs 113 individuals.

Economic Development Projects. The UKB recently assumed control of the River Park Recreation Area located along Highway 10. The tribe plans to further develop the recreational facilities at the site, including picnic tables and improved river access for fishing.

The tribe is currently developing an 80 acre site south of tribal headquarters. The first facility completed at the site is the Keetoowah Community Services Building. Future construction will include a retirement center, resource center, day camp facility, cultural center, outdoor camping area, stick ball and marble fields, daycare center, medical screening clinic, multipurpose facility, counseling center, greenhouse, administrative facilities, food distribution center, and police and fire services. The tribe is planning to market bottled "Cherokee New Echota" premium spring water. This enterprise will employ five people. The UKB is also planning to develop a convenience store.

Agriculture and Livestock. Individual members raise livestock and grow crops. The UKB also leases agricultural land to local farmers and ranchers. In addition, it operates two community gardens.

Forestry. The tribal region is forested with species of oak, elm, and hickory. Individual tribal members sell firewood during the winter.

Gaming. The UKB has operated Keetoowah Casino, the tribe's main source of revenue, since 1986. Gaming revenues support 113 positions within tribal government. Income from the gaming facility is used to fund various tribal programs and services, including college scholarship, athletic, and student financial assistance programs.

In 2000, the National Indian Gaming Commission found that the land status of the location of the UKB gaming enterprise made it subject to Oklahoma state law rather than the Indian Gaming Regulatory Act. This made the casino apparently illegal; however, state official refused to close it down. The operation of the Keetoowah Bingo remains a point of contention between the UKB and the Cherokee Nation. The Nation contests that the facility is illegal and has requested that operations be terminated. The case has been brought before state courts and remains in litigation.

Construction. In 1997, the U.S. government approved 1.4 million dollars for UKB housing construction.

Services and Retail. The UKB sponsors the Indian Country Marketplace. Open the first Friday of each month between June and October, the market hosts a number of vendors selling fresh produce, jelly, flowers, plants, herbs, seeds, and other food products. The tribe sells motor vehicle and boat tags.

Media and Communications. The tribe publishes *The UKB News*, a monthly newspaper.

Tourism and Recreation. The tribe hosts the Annual Keetoowah Celebration in October. The festivities include a powwow, 10K run, an Indian fiddle contest, singing, hog fry, athletic events, children's activities, a car show, a wellness center, a blow-gun shoot, and a cornstalk shoot. The tribe hosts the Annual Illinois River Help-in-Crisis Music Benefit, Children's Festival, and Chili Cook-off in May. Proceeds from the activities benefit the Help-In-Crisis organization, a nonprofit group that serves to combat family violence and sexual assault. The tribe also hosts an annual Easter Egg Hunt.

The tribe publishes tourism brochures and a newsletter including history and cultural information. In 2003, UKB partnered with the Tahlequah Chamber of Commerce to develop a visitors information center in a renovated old train caboose on tribally-owned land.

The Cherokee Historical Theater is located in Tahlequah. Popular recreation areas such as Fort Gibson Reservoir and Lake of the Cherokees are also located in the UKB tribal area. The Cherokee Heritage Center, home to the Cherokee National Museum, features an ancient village, "Trail of Tears" exhibits, and Adams Corner Rural Village re-creating the life of Cherokees in the late 1800s. The Arkansas River provides abundant opportunities for the outdoor sports enthusiast, and good roads make it highly accessible.

INFRASTRUCTURE

Tribal headquarters at Tahlequah are accessible via east-west running State Road 51 and east-west running U.S. 62. I- 40, Oklahoma's major east-west transportation corridor lies approximately 35 miles south via State Road 82. The nearest airport is in Tulsa, 50 miles northwest of Tahlequah.

The UKB roads program is constructing Keetoowah Circle, a mile long road through the tribe's 80 acres development site. This project is funded by the USDA. In addition to the roads for this site, the program is developing the infrastructure for sewer, water, and electric services. Other projects include the Spavinaw Creek Bridge and Green Country Road. The tribe is also working with the City of Tahlequah and Cherokee County to improve roadways.

Electricity. Individual tribal members receive electrical service from regional providers.

Fuel. Individual tribal members receive natural gas service from regional providers.

Water Supply. Tribal members utilize either septic tanks or municipal sewer services depending on location.

Transportation. Trucking, express package, and commercial railway services are available in Muskogee (20 miles west).

COMMUNITY FACILITIES AND SERVICES

The tribe has completed construction of the UKB Community Services Building. It also owns an office complex, family services building, and is leasing a building to house its education programs. In 2004, a child development center was constructed.

The tribe's social services program offers LIHEAP, BIA general assistance, child care assistance, elder dental, and medical/handicapped transportation services. The tribe also offers domestic violence intervention, tribal victim assistance, tribal child care subsidy, Native American caregiver support programs. The tribe's housing authority offers a program for tribal youth, elders, and families. Services include classes in traditional crafts and activities, and language.

In 2005 it was announced that the U.S. Department of Justice had awarded the tribe a grant of $634,000 to provide legal services to crime victims with a special emphasis placed on the victims of domestic violence. The money will pay for legal counsel for protective order hearings, divorce, child custody, and child support. Services will be provided based upon a sliding income scale.

Education. Tribal youth attend public schools in the UKB tribal area.

The tribe operates an education program that offers a communication technology center. The facility includes 24 laptop computers. Computer classes are available to juvenile and adult tribal members. The department also offers adult basic education, community technology, Earth Day, and summer internship programs. Financial assistance is available to tribal youth.

In partnership with the Cherokee Heritage Center, the education department offers a Summer Youth/Cultural Camp. Activities alternate between the Cherokee Heritage Center and the UKB Education Department Building. Bacone College offers business management courses at the community services building. Northeastern State University has a campus in Tahlequah.

Health Care. Tribal members receive health care from Indian Health Service facilities in the UKB tribal area, as well as from regional hospitals and private physicians. In 2004 a tribal wellness center was under construction. Health support programs can provide financial assistance for insurance co-pays, the costs of ambulance service or other expenses for emergency care, eye and dental care.

ENVIRONMENTAL CONCERNS

The tribe has an environmental department staffed by two water resources technicians, a data processor and an environmental technician. Projects of the UKB environmental department include the Tribal Open Dump Cleanup. The project included the clean up of an illegal dumping site in Mayes County, Oklahoma. In February 2003, the tribe approved a quality assurance project plan with on-going protection of the Saline River watershed the highest environmental priority.

Another concern to the tribe is the presence of the American Burying Beetle. Native to eastern Oklahoma, this beetle is an endangered species. The tribe is required to ascertain its presence on any building site, and to consider the impact of any development project on the population and its habitat.

Wichita

LOCATION AND LAND STATUS

The Wichita Tribe jointly owns 2,602.64 acres of federal trust land in Caddo County, Oklahoma, with the Delaware and Caddo tribes. Tribal headquarters are located three miles north of Anadarko, Oklahoma, via U.S. 281, on the Riverside Reserve. Oklahoma City is approximately 50 miles northeast of the tribal headquarters.

The Wichita Agency, established in 1859, served as the reservation for Caddo, Wichita, and Delaware Indians. Much of the land therein was allotted following the Jerome Agreement of 1890. Today, 53,453.76 acres of individual allotments supplement the joint tribal land base.

CULTURE AND HISTORY

Members of the Kitikiti'sh, or Wichita and Affiliated Tribes, belong to the Wichita, Keechi, Tawakoni, Waco, and Taovaya tribes. The Caddoan-speaking Wichitas are Oklahoma's oldest living Indian community. Indeed, the Spanish conquistador Coronado found Wichitas living on the high plains of western Oklahoma in 1540. The Wichitas were primarily agriculturists and settled in river valleys to cultivate corn, beans, squash, gourds, and tobacco. Situated among the southern plains bison herd, they hunted in season for hides and meat. The Wichitas, however, did not adopt the Plains culture of many neighboring tribes. During the seventeenth and eighteenth centuries, the Wichitas traded extensively with French and Spanish parties in the Arkansas and Red River valleys. They abandoned their Twin Villages site after the Louisiana Territory came under American dominion. During the early nineteenth century, anglo-American military, economic, and settler pressures rapidly increased for the Wichita.

After 1836, the Texas Republic sanctioned the relentless annihilation of tribes, including the Wichitas, whose lands its citizens coveted. The federal government established a reservation for the surviving Texas Wichitas on the Clear Fork of the Brazos River in 1855, but settler pressure forced their relocation to the southwestern corner of Indian Territory in 1859. The Civil War soon split the reservation along the lines of Union loyalty, and many fled to Kansas. The Wichitas underwent an intensive assimilation effort by Indian Service officials during the late nineteenth century, and reservation lands were allotted in 1891. The Wichitas endured throughout the twentieth century despite this assault. In 1961, the Wichita, Keechi, Waco, Tawakoni, and Taovaya tribes organized as the Wichita and Affiliated Tribes.

The Wichitas maintain close cultural and economic ties with the neighboring Delaware and Caddo tribes. All three share a joint land base and a jointly owned business, Wichita, Caddo,

Wichita Tribe
Federal reservation
Wichita, Keechi, Waco,
Tawakoni, and Taovaya
Grady, Canadian, and Caddo
counties, Oklahoma

Wichita and Affiliated Tribes
P.O. Box 729
Anadarko, OK 73005
  405-247-2425
  405-247-2430 Fax
  wichita.nsn.us

Wichita

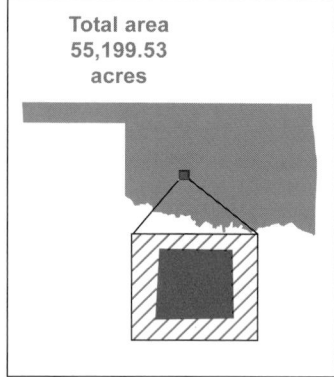

Total area
55,199.53
acres

Total area-jointly held
(BIA realty, 2004)
55,199.53 acres

Tribally owned-jointly held
(BIA realty, 2004)
1,260 acres

Individually-jointly owned
(BIA realty, 2004)
53,939.43 acres

Tribal enrollment
(BIA labor report, 2001)
2,174

Total labor force *2000 census*
4,849

Total labor force
(BIA labor report, 2001)
471

High school graduate or higher
2000 census
74.6%

Bachelor's degree or higher
2000 census
15.7%

Unemployment rate *2000 census*
7.9%

ENVIRONMENTAL CONCERNS

The tribe's primary environmental concerns are water quality and watershed standards. Illegal dumping is also a problem on tribal lands. The tribe has been pursuing funding sources to address these issues.

and Delaware (WCD) Enterprises, which promotes business development in the tribal area. While developing new skills at area technical institutions, the Wichita people look to preserve their cultural identity and link with the past. A proposed language program will attempt to revive the Wichita language.

GOVERNMENT

The tribe is governed by the Wichita Tribal Council. The council empowers the executive committee, comprised of a president, a vice-president, a secretary, a treasurer, and three members. Committee members serve four-year terms, with elections occurring during the annual tribal meeting. The executive committee was approved by resolution and adopted by the tribe on August 8, 1961, in accordance with the Indian Reorganization Act and the Oklahoma Indian Welfare Act. The tribe has no constitution or bylaws.

Tribal government departments and programs include housing, health, education, social services, transportation, TERO, and environment. The tribe also maintains an economic development division, the Wichita Industrial Development Commission. This entity is responsible for identifying and developing economic ventures on behalf of the tribe.

BUSINESS CORPORATION

The tribe is a member of WCD Enterprises. This corporation manages economic development projects for the tribes, including agricultural and industrial ventures.

Anadarko Industries is a tribally owned information technology enterprise. Services include designing and constructing network systems. Divisions of the company include business consulting, information consulting, outsourcing and support, staffing services, and engineering services. The business consulting division provides middle office infrastructure setup, contract management, process design and business configuration, business process reengineering, and risk-management solution. The information consulting division provides architecture and technical applications design and integration, custom application development, commercial software implementation and enhancement, quality assurance and testing, and project and program management solutions. The outsourcing and support division provides infrastructure services, networking and data centers, custom and third-party enterprise applications support, and 24/7 user support 365 days a year. The staffing services division provides candidate search and identification, skills and experience assessment, permanent and contract-to-hire placements, and benefits administration. The engineering services division provides conceptual design, CAD production, core engineering capabilities, analysis, calibration and metrology, CnC design, programming, and milling, and project engineering.

Economic Development Projects. The Wichita Tribe Industrial Development Commission oversees land acquisition for the tribe. It also identifies and develops economic ventures for the tribe. Recent projects include gourmet coffee distribution; co-partnership in the executive protection services security program; development of child care services; and development of the Square Top Project, which includes a convenience store and fueling station.

Agriculture and Livestock. WCD Enterprises, the joint Wichita, Delaware, and Caddo corporation, leases 2,000 acres of farmland to non-Indians.

Gaming. A tribal gaming enterprise is in the planning stage.

Mining. The Wichita, Caddo, and Delaware tribes jointly own lands that they lease for oil and gas wells.

Industrial Parks. WCD Enterprises owns and operates a 10.7-acre industrial site, located along U.S. 62, which includes a 24,486-square-foot building. The industrial site conveniently abuts the CRI&P Railway.

Services and Retail. The tribe issues specialized license plates with the Kitikiti'sh emblem and tribal affiliations.

Media and Communications. The Wichita and Affiliated Tribes publish a quarterly newspaper.

INFRASTRUCTURE

Tribal headquarters are located three miles north of Anadarko on the Riverside Reservation; these facilities are accessible via U.S. 62 and U.S. 281. I-40 passes approximately 40 miles north of the tribal headquarters.

Electricity. Caddo County public utilities provide electricity to tribal facilities and tribal members' homes.

Fuel . Oklahoma Natural Gas provides natural gas services to tribal members.

Water Supply. The City of Anadarko provides water and sewer services. The Lawton service unit operations and maintenance program and the Wichita housing authority provide plumbing services and repair.

Transportation. Commercial and private air facilities are located in the Oklahoma City metropolitan area, 50 miles northeast of Anadarko. Trucking companies and express package carriers serve the tribal area. The CRI&P Railway serves the tribal area.

COMMUNITY FACILITIES AND SERVICES

The Wichita cultural and administrative building houses a number of community programs, as well as the tribal headquarters and a senior nutrition center. The tribe also maintains a social services department. It provides temporary financial assistance, mental health referrals, family-oriented programs, and social service programs for tribal members.

Education. Approximately 10 percent of tribal children attend the boarding school on the Riverside Reserve; the other 90 percent attend Caddo County public schools. The tribe maintains higher education, job placement and training, adult education, Johnson O'Malley, and motor fuels tax revenues programs.

Health Care. Health services are available through the Lawton service unit. The unit includes Lawton Indian Hospital, Anadarko Health Center, Carnegie Health Center, and a health station at the Riverside Indian School. The hospital and health centers provide comprehensive medical services, and the health station provides assessment services.

A community health representative provides first aid, transportation, health assessment, general health care, interpretation and translation, and environmental health services to tribal members. A public health nurse provides health education, counseling, immunizations, screenings, and referrals.

The tribe operates a mental health, community health, and emergency medical services program. The tribe is also a member of the Oklahoma Project of the REACH 2010 program of the U.S. Department of Health and Human Services. The program aims to reduce disparities in diabetes and cardiovascular disease among Native Americans. Participants have access to a fitness center that offers strength training equipment, fitness trainers, aerobic and yoga classes, and fitness and nutrition workshops.

LOCATION AND LAND STATUS

The Wyandotte Reservation covers about 213 acres in northeastern Oklahoma and lies entirely within Ottawa County, Oklahoma. The reservation sits near the confluence of the Neosho and Spring rivers at the Grand Lake of the Cherokees. The Town of Wyandotte serves as the tribal headquarters. U.S. Highway 60 passes west to east near the reservation, while State Road 10 passes nearby from north to south. Other Oklahoma towns near the Wyandotte Reservation include Vinita, Miami, Fairland, and Grove. Major cities near the Wyandotte Reservation are Tulsa, Oklahoma (approximately 100 miles southwest) and Joplin, Missouri (approximately 35 miles northeast).

The Wyandottes were relocated from the Great Lakes region to Kansas in 1843. An 1867 treaty between the Wyandotte Tribe, the Seneca Tribe, and the United States transferred land in northeastern Oklahoma to the Wyandotte Tribe. However, most of this land was allotted during the late nineteenth and early twentieth centuries and quickly passed to white ownership.

During the 1990s, the tribe established a tribal community on traditional homelands in Kansas City, Kansas. The lands were granted to the tribe by a federal commission, but the land grant remains contested by the state. The Huron Cemetery, which is located on 1.9 acres of land in downtown Kansas City and the Shriner Tract, which consists of 1 acre in Kansas, are held in trust for the tribe.

CULTURE AND HISTORY

The Wyandotte Nation is composed of members of the Wendat, or Huron, Confederacy, the Attignawantan Nation, and the Khionontateronon (Petun) Nation. These tribes occupied the forests of the present Canadian provinces of Quebec and Ontario. The Wyandotte Nation originally consisted of 12 tribal bands, though a number of them no longer exist. While "Wyandot" is the accepted ethnological spelling, the tribe goes by Wyandotte. The definition of the word "Wyandot" is not completely understood but may mean island dweller or inhabitant of a peninsula.

At the time of initial contact with French trappers and missionaries in the seventeenth century, the Wyandotte practiced a subsistence pattern based on hunting and fishing. Migration out of traditional homelands led tribal members to accept a more agricultural lifestyle, including the small-scale cultivation of several crops such as corn, beans, squash, sunflowers, peas, pumpkins, melons, and tobacco. After a devastating defeat by the Iroquois Confederacy in 1649, the Wyandotte and their Huron allies fled to present-day Mackinac Island, Michigan. Many later migrated to the northeastern corner of present-day Wisconsin, then to the Ohio Valley. The Wyandotte continued to flee from the Iroquois forces until 1700, when they made an appeal to establish peace with that confederacy.

A large segment of the tribe settled at the French outpost at Detroit in 1701. The Wyandotte loosely allied themselves with the British during the American Revolution and were later defeated in 1794 (along with other allied tribes) by the American General Anthony Wayne at the Battle of Fallen Timbers. The Wyandotte were forced to cede much of their territory to the United States at the Treaty of Greeneville in 1795. The tribe subsequently lost the remainder of its land in Michigan and Ohio at the Fort Meigs Treaty of 1817.

In 1843, the Wyandotte were relocated to what is now eastern Kansas. An 1855 treaty terminated the tribe, and most tribal lands were lost to non-Indians. While the majority of tribal members accepted the conditions of the treaty, a small band fled to Oklahoma in 1857. An 1867 treaty confirmed the tribe's legal existence and gave the Wyandotte title to 20,000 acres of former Seneca land in northeastern Oklahoma. Much of this land was later lost through allotment. The tribe persevered and reorganized as the Wyandotte Tribe of Oklahoma in 1937. The Wyandotte are rightfully proud of their ability to weather the numerous obstacles that have threatened their existence throughout a long and turbulent history.

A small number of tribal members live on the reservation at Wyandotte, Oklahoma while a number of tribal members and descendants of the Wyandotte tribe continue to live throughout the Great Lakes region of the United States and Canada.

GOVERNMENT

The Wyandotte Tribe reorganized under the Indian Welfare Act of 1936, drafting a constitution and bylaws in 1937. The tribal constitution was reconfirmed in the Act of May 15, 1978, approved in 1985, and ratified by the BIA on September 29, 1999. The tribe is governed by an elected chief, second chief, and a business committee comprised of four members. The Nation Council, consisting of all tribal members over the age of 18 years, elects tribal officials.

Tribal government programs include maintenance, vehicle registration, education, family services, nutrition, housing authority, environment, community liaison, human resources and accounting. The tribe maintains its own police department. The housing authority provides repair and homeownership programs. It also drills wells in rural areas.

BUSINESS CORPORATION

Tribal economic development projects are managed by Wynadotte Enterprises. This entity is the parent company of Wyandotte NetTel, Wyandotte Petroleum, Bearskin Aviation Service, the Lucky Turtle Casino, and Wyandotte Collegiate Systems. The company headquarters are located in the tribal administration building. Operations are managed by a board of directors.

ECONOMY

The tribal economy is supported by revenue earned from the many enterprises owned and operated by the Wyandotte Nation. The tribe is quickly gaining international recognition in multiple industries and is an economic entity of considerable force.

Government as Employer. The tribe provides a number of employment opportunities throughout government and tribally-owned enterprises.

Economic Development Projects. The tribe is seeking additional funding for its housing projects. The housing department has initiated a market analysis to identify possible sources. The tribal administrative staff includes a grant writer, whose responsibility it is to prepare grant proposals for the tribe. The tribe is also renovating its wastewater treatment facility laboratory building. Road improvements are also planned, which will enhance development opportunities for the tribe.

Wyandotte Reservation
Federal reservation
Wyandotte
Ottawa County, Oklahoma

Wyandotte Nation
P.O. Box 250
Wyandotte, OK 74370
918-678-2297
800-256-2539
918-678-2944 Fax
wyandotte-nation.org

Total area *(BIA realty, 2004)*
218.19 acres

Tribally owned *(BIA realty, 2004)*
218.19 acres

Population *2000 census*
1,678

Tribal enrollment
(BIA labor report, 2001)
3,860

Total labor force *2000 census*
876

High school graduate or higher
2000 census
75.6%

Bachelor's degree or higher
2000 census
10.9%

Unemployment rate *2000 census*
2.7%

Unemployment rate
(BIA labor report, 2001)
23%

Per capita income *2000 census*
$12,160

Wyandotte

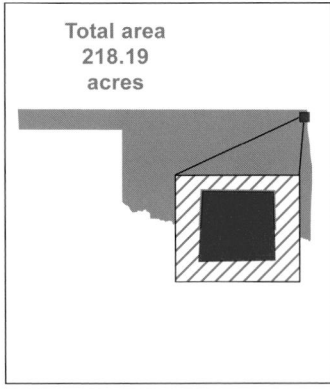

Total area
218.19
acres

TRI-OK-055 Casino & Turtle Shop convenience store and gas station

TRI-OK-056 Bearskin Healthcare and Wellness Center

ENVIRONMENTAL CONCERNS
The tribe's environmental department offers a number of services, including recycling days, Earth Day, and recycle education programs. It also co-hosts the Annual Toxic Tour Bike Ride. The department also conducts well tests and monitors water quality in local lakes and stream.

TRI-OK-055

TRI-OK-056

Gaming. In 2004, the tribe opened the Lucky Turtle Casino in Wyandotte. This class II facility is located next to the tribally-owned Turtle Stop Convenience Store on the north side of Grand Lake.

In 2003, the tribe opened the 7th Street Casino near the Huron Cemetery in downtown Kansas City. The enterprise employed about 50 individuals. In 2004, the state ordered that the casino be closed, as it was located on lands that have not been officially designated reservation lands. State marshals raided the facility and seized 152 slot machines and about $500,000 in cash. The tribe has filed suit, and the issue remains in litigation.

Construction. In the summer of 2004 the tribe planned to improve the site of the powwow grounds. It was also renovating and expanding the Turtle Stop gas station and planning a roads improvement program.

Services and Retail. The Wyandotte Nation owns Wyandotte Advertising. This company provides advertising, promotion, direct mail, and public relations services. The company has a diverse clientele across the country and has worked on projects such as casinos, amusement parks, shopping districts, entertainment districts, and a NASCAR racetrack.

The tribe also owns Wyandotte NetTel (WNT). Services of WNT include IT solutions and services, networking, LAN/WAN design and support, and hardware, software, and peripheral computer needs. WNT is staffed by certified technicians and enjoys partnerships with over 1,000 vendors that assist the company in delivering access, connectivity, and processing capabilities to its customers.

In 2004, the tribe opened Bearskin Aviation Services. The development of this entity is managed in partnership with Express One International. The first project born of the partnership will be provision of fleet and baggage handling services for the 727th AMS at the Mildenhall and Lakenheath Royal Air Force stations in the United Kingdom. Bearskin Aviation will serve as a subcontractor of Express One in this endeavor.

The tribe also operates Turtle Stop, a convenience store/gas station. Recent renovations include the addition of the Shell Shiner Car Wash, an expanded dining area in the attached Bearskin Diner, a canopy over the fuel pumps, and an upgraded kitchen.

The tribe owns Turtle Trax Printing and Design. This company provides printing and graphic design services. It is located in the tribal administrative building in Wyandotte.

The tribe operates a gift shop. The store carries a variety of items, including clothing, pottery, shawls, decorative gourds, paintings, jewelry, and leatherwork.

Transportation. The Wyandotte Tribe maintains trucks and heavy equipment for tribal use.

Media and Communications. The tribe publishes *Gyah'-wish Atakia,* a quarterly newsletter. It also publishes a variety of historical books. The history and culture committees of the tribe have developed an instructional language tape. All funds raised from the sale of this tape are used to support the revitalization of the Wyandotte culture.

Tourism and Recreation. The tribe hosts the Annual Wyandotte Nation Fireworks Display in July and an annual powwow in September. The Wyandotte Reservation lies in close proximity to the Grand Lake of the Cherokees, a popular recreational destination in northeastern Oklahoma. The tribe operates a campground on Highway 60 and has access to the lake.

INFRASTRUCTURE
U.S. Highway 60 passes the Wyandotte Reservation from east to west. State Road 10 passes near the reservation from north to south.

Electricity. Electricity is provided through regional utility companies.

Fuel. Fuel is available through local distributors.

Water Supply. The tribe completed construction on a sewage treatment plant in 2004.

Transportation. Commercial airlines serve Tulsa, Oklahoma (approximately 100 miles southwest).

COMMUNITY FACILITIES AND SERVICES
Tribal services, including the Wyandotte Tribal Government, the Indian Health Service, HUD, the tribal daycare and preschool, and public schools, are located in Wyandotte, Oklahoma. The Wyandotte Tribal Library offers a collection of books, tapes, and periodicals.

The tribe maintains a childcare program, which utilizes 36 child care centers and 24 home-based daycare centers to serve 243 children. Future services of the program include child care provider training and physical education equipment.

The tribe's family services department offers license plate, tribal operations, social service, Indian child welfare, infant car seat, and the individual money account programs. The tribe also offers a caregiver respite program.

The tribe offers a Title VI program for tribal elders. Services include meals, multiple forms of personal and financial assistance, transportation, education, cultural, fitness, counseling and other programs.

The Wyandotte Nation maintains powwow grounds. In 2004, the brush arbor was rebuilt and the tribe intends to rebuild the seating area around the arena. The Wyandotte Nation Powwow Committee overseas the maintenance and upkeep of the grounds. The tribe hosts an annual cultural week. Events include workshops, demonstrations, seminars, and a cookout. Attendance is restricted to tribal members.

Education. The Wyandotte Public School and Wyandotte High School serve tribal youth. The tribe offers language instruction in the public schools. The tribe offers a preschool program and an after-school program. The tribe's education department sponsors a scholarship program and the Workforce Investment Act Program.

The tribe owns the Wyandotte Collegiate Systems. The program includes post-secondary institutions in Tulsa; Oklahoma City; Kansas City; Phoenix, Arizona; Melbourne, Florida; and Albuquerque, New Mexico.

Health Care. In 1995, the tribe assumed control of its health programs and developed the Bearskin Clinic. In 1998, it opened the Bearskin Healthcare and Wellness Center. The Healthcare and Wellness Center employs a physician.

The Bearskin Fitness Center is a tribally owned facility in Wyandotte. The facility employs two certified fitness instructors. It offers an indoor walking track, exercise machines, seminars, and nutrition counseling services.

ENVIRONMENTAL CONCERNS

The tribe's environmental department offers a number of services, including recycling days, Earth Day, and recycle education programs. It also co-hosts the Annual Toxic Tour Bike Ride. The department also conducts well tests and monitors water quality in local lakes and stream.

Oregon

From 1996 edition of Tiller's Guide to Indian Country.

Burns Paiute

Burns Paiute

LOCATION AND LAND STATUS

The Burns Paiute Reservation is located in southeastern/central Oregon approximately 135 miles east of Bend, near the junction of U.S. Highways 20 and 395 and State Highway 78. Burns Reservation lands were established in 1863.

CULTURE AND HISTORY

Archaeologists found many items that led them to believe that the Malheur Paiutes, now referred to as the Burns Paiute people, lived in caves near the northern Great Basin shores about 9,000 years ago. This area is now a desert. The people developed fibers from the tule plant, willow, Indian hemp, and sagebrush bark. The fibers were used to make many different woven sandals, coiled or twined baskets, and rope. Skins and furs of many animals such as rabbits were made into blankets and clothing.

The Burns Paiute Tribe, per their stories and legends, were peaceful bands roaming a huge area in central-eastern Oregon. They are the descendants of the Wadatika band, named after the wada seeds near shorelines. Their diet included, salmon, birds, deer and elk, small animals (rabbits, ground hogs, squirrels, and others), and plants, including berries and seeds. Traditionally, hunting, fishing, and gathering were the chief subsistence activities of the Northern Paiutes who once lived over the vast areas of the northern Great Basins of Oregon and Nevada.

GOVERNMENT

The Burns Paiute Tribe was federally recognized on October 13, 1972. The tribe's constitution and bylaws were approved on June 13, 1968 then revised and updated three separate times. The dates were January 24, 1977, February 19, 1988, and June 18, 1997. The general council, consisting of all voting age members who are registered voters of the tribe, holds two semiannual meetings.

The tribal council consists of a chairman, a vice-chairman, a secretary-treasurer, a sergeant-at-arms, and three council members. It meets monthly and approves all management operational plans for the tribe and its programs, as needed. A general manager oversees 46 employees and the daily administration of all tribal programs. Health, social services, education, law enforcement, the courts, and other programs are contracted under PL-638 regulations.

BUSINESS CORPORATION

The Wa'da' Enterprise Corporation was created to oversee business development initiatives and was incorporated by the state of Oregon on December 10, 2003. The Wa'da' Enterprise plans to develop an industrial park and support development of small Indian businesses.

ECONOMY

The reservation's economy is tied to that of Harney County, which is primarily agricultural. Lumber milling and government services are secondary sources of income for the tribe.

Government as Employer. The Burns Paiutes employ 46 tribal members. The tribal administration office employs 11 people and provides major administrative services in: accounting, property management, procurement, personnel, records management, auditing, legal assistance for the programs, environment and cultural compliance for NEPA, contract compliance, planning services, health, and research. Five tribal police officers enforce tribal laws and ordinances. They provide traffic control; investigate crimes, and render backup to other law enforcement services. The Burns Paiute Tribal Court has one chief judge, one associate judge, and one prosecutor. These three people adjudicate cases, issue subpoenas and bench warrants, and conduct the sentencing processes.

Agriculture and Livestock. The tribe owns and manages a 110-acre irrigated reservation farm that grows dairy-quality alfalfa, which is sold commercially. In the future, 320 acres of potential farmlands will be developed, and the tribe is pursuing the purchase of a small cattle herd.

Forestry. The tribal fish and wildlife program is thinning 40 acres of lodge pole for conservation improvement. This area has small pine growth and is defined by the Logan Valley Wildlife Enhancement Project.

Gaming. The Old Camp Casino has 100 slot machines, 3 table games, and 200 bingo seats. The casino has a restaurant, a gift shop, a lounge, an arcade for children, and an event center for meetings, gatherings, or other social activities. The casino has the capacity for 150 parking spaces. It employs 62 people. A recreational 17-vehicle park is located within walking distance to the casino. There is a nominal fee of $15 for full hookup services, and there are weekly rates. Showers and rest rooms are handicap accessible.

Fisheries. In cooperation with the Bonneville Power Administration, 8,145 acres were acquired for fish and wildlife enhancement programs. The management, operations, and data gathering efforts to improve fish and wildlife habitat are both located off the reservation. These programs (located at Logan Valley and at Jones Ranch) are designed to ensure abundance and to conduct studies to protect the habitats.

Tourism and Recreation. The Burns Paiute Tribe and the Harney County Chamber of Commerce are combining efforts to secure 2004 Oregon Department of Transportation funds for a Visitors Welcome Center. The tribe hopes to staff the

---

Burns Paiute Reservation
Federal reservation
Harney County, Oregon

Burns Paiute Tribe
100 Pasigo Street
Burns, OR 97720-2442
541-573-2088
541-573-2323 Fax

Total area *(BIA realty, 2004)*
11,476.60 acres

Total area *(Tribal source, 2004)*
20,678.2 acres

Allotted/Individual owned
(BIA realty, 2004)
10,534 acres

Tribally owned *(BIA realty, 2004)*
942.60 acres

Allotted lands *(Tribal source, 2004)*
11,014 acres

Population *2000 census*
132

Tribal enrollment
(Tribal source, 2004)
340

Total labor force *2000 census*
68

Total labor force *(Tribal source, 2004)*
85

High school graduate or higher
2000 census
63.8%

Bachelor's degree or higher
2000 census
0%

Unemployment rate *2000 census*
36.8%

Burns Paiute

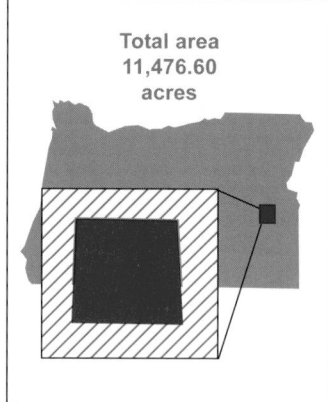

Total area
11,476.60
acres

booth, and it is cooperating with a tourism publisher to provide information and pictures for an Oregon Indian Tribes Tourism Guide to be made available in early 2005. In 2004, the community enjoyed opening ceremonies for two new tribal parks. Rainbow Parks has a playground, barbeque pits, benches, a large gazebo, basketball courts, and horseshoe pits. The Annual Reservation Day Powwow is celebrated with neighboring tribes and tribal members. This event includes traditional dancing and drumming, dance contests, a raffle, crafts, and food booths. This event is held every second weekend in October.

INFRASTRUCTURE
The culture and heritage office has two employees. They provide cultural protection of resources and environmental protection. They monitor roads construction and land leasing compliance, and they assist in developing tribal council policies on culture protection.

Electricity. Oregon Trail Electric Cooperative and Harney Electric Cooperative provide services for the reservation and the allotment lands.

Water Supply. Two wells with a 180,000-gallon tank provide gravity pressure for community consumption. It has a chlorination system for 53 homes, 10 facilities, and 1 church. This water and sewer system has the capacity to accommodate more homes and future development. The City of Burns and the Burns Paiute Tribe have an agreement to maintain and operate the sewer system built by the Indian Health Service with the provision that all customers are billed monthly.

Transportation. U.S. Highway 20 runs east-west through Burns and Hines. Three interstate motor carriers serve the reservation. Bus service is available in Burns. The nearest commercial air or rail services are 135 miles east in the city of Ontario, or west in the City of Bend.

Telecommunications. CenturyTel provides Internet and telephone services. UniCel is the mobile telephone carrier for the area. Charter Communications provides service for cable television.

COMMUNITY FACILITIES AND SERVICES
The two story-community center is used for tribal and general council meetings, holiday events, birthday parties, and special dinners. The first floor houses the administrative offices, and the second floor is partially reserved for the tribal council office. The human services office employs six staff members. These employees coordinate social service activities, alcohol and drug counseling including family counseling or referrals, child care, Indian child welfare services, commodity foods distribution, prevention services, general assistance services, and emergency shelter care services for children and youth.

Education. The Burns and Hines area has several educational facilities, including a preschool, two grade schools, a junior high school, and a high school. The Burns area has a distant learning center for the Treasure Valley Community College, Eastern Oregon University, Central Oregon Community College, Oregon State University, and the University of Oregon. With two employees, the tribal education office provides youth and adult educational services, summer youth employment, adult employment support, a Safe Haven After-School Program, a Tribal Elders Computer Teaching Program, and Paiute language development services. Cultural activities are also taught, including basketry and beading.

Health Care. Tribal health services employs seven staff and provides health administration, third-party billing, contract health services, community health outreach, community health nursing, immunization, a community health representative, a special diabetes program, an Oregon breast and cervical education program, and health clinic services. Indian Health Service provides health care funding for on- and off-reservation residents. Special medical referrals are sent to Bend, Oregon, for evaluation, diagnosis, and treatment. The Burns Paiute Tribe is a member of the Northwest Portland Area Indian Health Board.

ENVIRONMENTAL CONCERNS
The Burns Paiute Tribe's major environmental concern is their surface water and aquifer protection. A second environmental concern is to maintain the quality of clean air. A third major concern is the development of a solid waste management and enforcement system by the tribe.

Celilo Village

Celilo Village
Federal reservation
Columbia River
Washo County, Oregon

Celilo Village
Portland Area Office
Bureau of Indian Affairs
1425 Irving Street, NE
Portland, OR 97208

Total area *(BIA realty, 2004)*   1,530.9 acres*
Tribally owned *(BIA realty, 2004)*   670 acres*
Allotted/Individually owned 860.90 acres*
    (BIA realty, 2004)
Total labor force *2000 census*   9
High school graduate or higher   80%
    2000 census
Bachelor's degree or higher   16%
    2000 census
Unemployment rate *2000 census*   0%

*The Dalles Public domain lands-includes Celilo

LOCATION AND LAND STATUS
Celilo Village is federal trust land located several hundred yards from the Columbia River, and is 90 miles east of Portland, Oregon. Although the federal government holds title to these lands, and tribal access is authorized by an Act of July 25, 1947, the

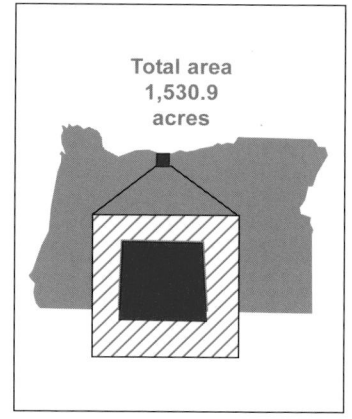

Total area
1,530.9
acres

government considers the village campsite to be an "in lieu" site to the now-destroyed Celilo Falls.

CULTURE AND HISTORY

Celilo Village is a campsite that stands near the old site of Celilo Falls, once one of the most famous trade sites in North America. Celilo Falls historically had an abundance of salmon; the water levels were high, and scaffolds were built to fish the falls. Celilo Falls was a place that brought together people to fish, trade, and socialize. People came from all over to trade shells, buffalo meat, blankets, and beads for salmon. This tradition continued for over 1,000 years, suggesting that Celilo may be one of Oregon's oldest towns. According to archeological digs, Indian people continuously occupied the village site for at least 11,000 years. The Wyam Indians were the permanent residents and primary fishermen of Celilo. Wyam means "sound of water upon the rocks" or "echo of falling water."

Unfortunately, the Celilo Falls were destroyed when they were flooded by Dalles Dam, which was constructed in 1957. The destruction of the falls left the Wyams without income since the hydraulic dams destroyed the primary source of their trade, income, and food-the salmon. Today, Lake of Celilo is located on the once-historic site of Celilo Falls. While the fishing industry has struggled with the loss of salmon, it is reported that the salmon run is at 98,844 with a 10-year average run of 66,262, which is still much less than the 15 to 17 million runs of the 1800s. The hydraulic dams that have been built in the area have caused the salmon's continued absence. Although many Indians lost their livelihood with the destruction of the salmon, some found other employment where they received benefits. Many once considered Celilo the "Wall Street of the Indian World," but without the salmon it is now impoverished. When the property was turned over to the BIA, they lacked the funding necessary to support the village's operation, which led to its current destitute nature. To combat the village's destitution, President Bush signed the Native American Technical Amendments Bill, which authorizes the USACE to spend existing funds on the redevelopment of housing in Celilo. Construction on new housing is expected to begin in 2006 and to be completed in 2007.

Confederated Tribes

Confederated Tribes

LOCATION AND LAND STATUS

In 1940 six acres were bestowed to the Confederated Tribe of Coos, Lower Umpqua, and Siuslaw Indians by a non-Indian; these were transferred into federal trust. The six acres constituting the reservation are located in Coos Bay in southwestern Oregon about 100 miles southwest of Eugene. Over the years, the Confederated Tribes have acquired an additional 265 acres through other donations and purchases, including 98 acres of restored land along Highway 126 in Florence, Oregon, where they have opened the Three Rivers Casino.

CULTURE AND HISTORY

The Confederated Tribes of Coos, Lower Umpqua, and Siuslaw Indians are the aboriginal inhabitants of the central and south-central coast of Oregon. The Confederated Tribes are one of the nine federally recognized tribes in the State of Oregon. The tribes' homeland includes the coastal waters, estuaries, and watersheds of Coos Bay, the Umpqua River (to Weatherly Creek), and the Siuslaw River, as well as coastal streams from nearby Whiskey Run Creek in the south to Ten Mile Creek in the north.

The Confederated Tribes have struggled for years to keep their history, land, and culture intact. The tribes' regular contact with Europeans began in 1826 when the Hudson's Bay Company came searching for beaver hides. Although the tribe was puzzled by this European interest, because the hides had little value to the tribes, they offered the Europeans assistance in pointing out the streams with plenty of beaver. Fur trapping was important to the Europeans for the wealth it produced them, and in 1836, when Hudson's Bay Company' established a trading fort, it offered many Coos, Lower Umpqua, and Siuslaw the ability to trade their hides for goods. In the 1850s, Europeans looked to settle into the region, viewing Coos Bay and the Umpqua Valley as excellent places to settle. In 1853, the Coos Bay Commercial Company was formed to promote white settlement in the area. However, these Europeans were restricted from settling on Coos land because the tribe did not have a treaty with the U.S. government. In 1854, the Hudson's Bay Company fur trading post was closed, and a year later in 1855, a treaty with all the tribes along the Oregon coast was negotiated, and from that point the Confederated Tribes began their uphill struggle.

In 1856, the Rogue River War occurred between various tribes of southwestern Oregon and white settlers. Fearing that the Coos and Lower Umpqua Indians would join in the war, the white settlers gathered the Coos and Lower Umpqua Indians and held them at an encampment located at Fort Umpqua. The Lower Umpqua and Coos Indians were held at this encampment for four years and then were removed to Yachats. The forced march to Yachats was an 80-mile trek that the tribes recall as their Trail of Tears because so many died of hunger, starvation, exposure, mistreatment, and exhaustion. Once reaching Yachats, however, the reservation life was worse than the long trek they had endured. The tribes were subjected to being chained, whipped, and left without the necessities to survive such as food, blankets, and clothing. During the Yachats period, their tribal membership decreased from 700 members to less than 300 survivors.

In 1876, yet again, the white settlers wanted to remove the Indians from their newly acquired homes at Yachats. While many returned to their original homelands after being forcefully removed from Yachats without payment for the 21 years of forced labor there, they found that their land had been taken over by white settlers. Although disheartened by the promises broken by the federal government in the treaty they had signed, many assimilated to white life to survive, but they also continued to fight for what was their own by banding together to pursue payment of land claims. They wrote letters and lobbied Congress, and they were finally granted a land claims hearing in 1931. Although they were not successful at this hearing, the Confederated Tribes paved the way for many other Oregon tribes to become successful in winning their cases. Further, the Confederate Tribes persisted in working on their land claims into the 1940s. In 1941, the BIA built a hall for the general use of the tribes on six acres of donated land in Empire, Oregon.

Confederated Tribes of Coos, Lower Umpqua, and Siuslaw Indians Reservation
Federal reservation
Coos, Umpqua, Siuslaw
Coos, Curry, and
Lane counties, Oregon

Confederated Tribe of Coos, Lower Umpqua, and Siuslaw Indians
1245 Fulton Avenue
Coos Bay, OR 97420
541-888-9577
541-888-2853 Fax

Confederated Tribes

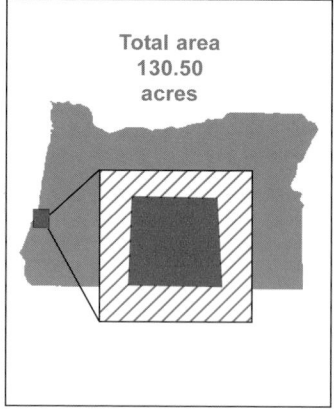

Total area
130.50
acres

Total area *(BIA realty, 2004)*
130.50 acres

Tribally owned*(BIA realty, 2004)*
130.50 acres

Population *(Tribal source, 2004)*
61,000

Total labor force *2000 census*
3

Total labor force *(BIA, 2001)*
219

High school graduate or higher
2000 census
100%

High school graduate or higher
(Tribal source, 2004)
63%

Bachelor's degree or higher
2000 census
33.3%

Bachelor's degree or higher
(Tribal source, 2004)
27%

Unemployment rate *2000 census*
0%

Per capita income *2000 census*
$3,627

Just as things seemed to be improving, federal Indian policy changed, stipulating that tribes did not exist. In 1956, this policy terminated the Confederated Tribes along with all the tribes of western Oregon. As they stood their ground before, the Coos, Lower Umpqua, and Siuslaw Indians fought to reverse the termination. Eventually, the federal policy was disavowed and, in 1984, the Confederated Tribes were restored to federal recognition. In keeping with the nature of their ancestors, the tribe today works to improve their social and educational status and to recapture their history, culture, and heritage.

Hanis and Miluk are two of the languages spoken by the Coos; the Siuslaw and Lower Umpqua have similar languages. The Confederated Tribes still hold the Sacred Salmon Ceremony annually.

GOVERNMENT

The tribal constitution was authorized under the Indian Reorganization Act of 1934 and ratified and approved on June 23, 1987. The Confederated Tribes' legislature consists of a general council and a tribal council. The general council are those enrolled members of the Confederated Tribes who are 18 years or older. General council members, like American citizens, have the right to vote and elect the members of the tribal council, but they also have the right to amend the tribal constitution, make advisory recommendations to the tribal council, and exercise fundamental changes in tribal jurisdiction, on reservation lands, and over rights specified in the tribal constitution. The elected tribal council consists of a tribal chief, who is also a voting member of the council and who serves a 10-year term, and six members who are elected to serve four-year terms. The tribal council has the power to elect a chair and a vice-chair from within its membership and to exercise all legislative and executive authority over the tribes, except that which is vested solely in the general council by the constitution.

The judiciary is made up of the tribal court, located in Coos Bay. The tribal court of the Confederated Tribes is user friendly, providing various forms on-line to aid in resolving conflicts within its jurisdiction. The tribal court has a toll-free number to further the lines of communication and resolution.

The administrative and human resource departments are essential to the Confederated Tribes' government as they help not only to implement equal employment, but also to manage the tribes' operational affairs, ensure delivery of services to all members, and protect tribal sovereignty. The administration department also works to execute the legislative actions of the tribal and general councils. These departments promote the tribes' self-sufficiency both in the economy and through its legislative processes.

The Confederated Tribes offer a number of social services programs. The child care assistance program offers partial reimbursement for child care expenses, and the tribal child welfare program oversees the Indian Child Welfare Act. Numerous other support services include the family violence advocacy program, the food bank, and the elder's program.

The tribes' cultural division is charged with the protecting archeological and cultural resources of the past as well as supporting the continuation of cultural growth in the future. To fulfill this mission, the division supports two programs, the cultural resources protection program and the cultural development program, as well as special projects such as the recent Ethnobotany of the Tribes. The first program, the cultural resources protection program, works with landowners and various governments from local to federal, to identify, monitor, curate, and protect cultural resources. They also work with

other departments within the tribe to draft cultural ordinances and offer educational or outreach activities. The second program, the cultural development program, also assists in drafting cultural ordinances. They lend support with the practical aspects of tribal cultural activities, creating new activities, providing outreach, and fundraising.

The geographic information systems program provides demographic and market analysis, economic development, integrated resource management planning, realty and transportation services, natural resources conservation and management, and cultural resources access and protection. The transportation and realty program oversees real estate appraisals, environmental site assessments, surveys, title searches, purchases and fee-to-trust conversions; this program also developed and improves transportation infrastructure needs. The forest program works on restoring acreage form the Siuslaw National Forest to the tribes and on developing a forest resource management plan.

ECONOMY

Many jobs are seasonal. Tribal members are engaged in a variety of occupations reflecting the increasing diversity of the regional economy. Coos Bay was once categorized as rural; however, the shift toward a tourist-oriented economy has changed the town. Winter unemployment rates can be as high as 20 percent. The peak tourist season begins in June and ends in September.

Economic Development Projects. The Confederated Tribes have planned a number of special entertainment and land restoration projects. The Confederated Tribes have for decades continually battled to restore tribal lands and they continue to do so. In their Reservation Plan and Forest Land Restoration Proposal, the Confederated Tribes proposed the restoration of their former homelands as Indian trust land. Recently, Senator Gordon Smith of Oregon submitted legislation that would provide for the return of 62,865 acres of the Siuslaw National Forest to the Confederated Tribes. Further, in order to create a core land base and to reacquire tribal land in Coos tribal territory, the legislation proposes to include a provision for limited land exchange under a scientifically credible process.

Besides land restoration, the Confederated Tribes have targeted not only the tribal economy, but the youth of the ancestral territory by proposing to build the Alishanee Family Entertainment Center, a multifaceted recreation center that will house 24 tournament-grade bowling lanes, a bar and grill, and a custom-built Native American-themed mall. The tribes have acquired the land just off of Highway 101, located near downtown Coos Bay, to begin the engineering and design for the project. This $4.4 million structure will be the first of its kind in Coos Bay. In fact, the 788-member tribe was the only tribe in Oregon that did not have a casino or other moneymaking operation. This project will contribute tremendously to the life and culture of the community by a projected $1.5 million in gross income annually for the tribes. Upon completion, the center would create 15 full-time and 30 part-time positions in the community.

Gaming. After a legal struggle to have the tribal property in Florence recognized as "restored" land, the Three Rivers Casino opened its doors on June 26, 2004. The casino has over 265 slot machines, 6 blackjack tables, and a players club. Three Rivers has a variety of restaurants, a sports bar, and a snack bar. The Three Rivers Casino is accessible from Highway 101 and Highway 126 in Florence. The tribe also has the Alishannee Center to attract visitors. They are proposing to create a tribal forest to attract ecotourism and a new cultural and natural history interpretive center. This new facility will be in the tribal administrative offices at Coos Head in the former naval facility.

INFRASTRUCTURE
Commercial air transport is available in North Bend. U.S. Highway 101 runs north-south through Coos Bay, Reedsport, and Florence. State highways connect these coastal communities to the Willamette and Umpqua Valleys and I-5.

COMMUNITY FACILITIES AND SERVICES
The tribal hall is the social center for the Confederated Tribes. It was established in 1940 and is the last BIA-built tribal hall left in the United States. It holds scheduled educational events, powwows, and drumming activities, and it houses the Native American Library, which offers books, periodicals, newspapers, and videos for checkout. A traditional plank house hosts a variety of cultural meetings and events. The tribal learning center provides daycare services to children of tribal members who are working on continuing their education. When the learning center is not used for child care, it provides additional space for tribal celebrations and gatherings. Also, the tribes' administrative building houses the Cultural Interpretive Exhibit, which debuted in August 2002. The exhibit provides videos on the culture, language, and history of the Confederated Tribes and tribal members have created accurate paintings and replicas to include in the exhibit's displays.The Confederated Tribes operate two outreach offices, one in Florence and one in Springfield, to serve tribal members living in these communities.

Education. The Confederated Tribes offer programs and tutorials in reading and other school subjects and help supply school supplies for Indian students. Programs include the adult basic education, the higher education, and the Johnson O'Malley program. They offer a number of educational programs to help tribal members earn GEDs and attend college. The employment assistance program helps tribal members obtain certificates or associate degrees at the community college level and from trade schools. This program provides preemployment training, relocation placement, and on-the-job training.

Health Care. The tribes have two outreach offices, one located in Springfield and the other in Florence. These offices employ two family nurse practitioners, a health director, and one community health representative. Other tribal health programs include the health, mental health, and dental care contract health services, the community outreach program, the fitness program, and other health and wellness and preventive programs.

The Confederated Tribes house a state-of-the-art dental clinic in Coos Bay, which provides dental services, including periodontics, endodontics, restorations, prosthodontics, hygiene, and preventive education. This dental clinic opened its doors to the tribal community in 2000 and is run by a professional staff that includes two dental assistants, a dental hygienist, an insurance specialist, and a receptionist. The clinic also offers its services to the general public on a fee for service basis.

The Coos County Mental Health Services, located in North Bend, offers adult and children services as well as substance abuse services. The Coos County Mental Health facility recently opened the Family Resource and Support Center, which supports families through classes on parenting, family interaction, and special needs of children.

Housing. The Confederated Tribes' housing department offers five affordable housing assistance programs. Approximately 115 tribal members benefit from these programs per month. The housing department works with a number of community-based organizations to provide housing assistance to tribal members and other needy families. A new housing division, Qaxas Heights, includes 15 new houses. The housing department is forming the Qaxas Heights Resident Council, which will make and enforce neighborhood rules and plan open houses. The housing department hopes that this council will start a business to promote the concept of community among the families that now occupy Qaxas. The housing department also plans on having the council arrange for training to help the community save money, teach parenting practices, teach negotiation skills, and teach how to provide healthy inexpensive meals to the community.

Confederated Tribes

ENVIRONMENTAL CONCERNS
The Confederated Tribes' Department of Natural Resources includes an environmental division whose 'mission is to conserve and manage the natural resources in the ancestral territory of the Confederated Tribes.The Confederated Tribes operate several environmental programs. The environmental capacity building program assesses and analyzes environmental issues and needs, and it develops environmental ordinances and administrative rules.The water quality monitoring program monitors reservation waters and implements watershed improvement projects. The non-point source pollution program identifies strategies to address non-point sources of pollution affecting reservation waters.

Coquille

Coquille

LOCATION AND LAND STATUS
The first parcel of trust land, the Grandmother Rock site, is in Bandon, Oregon along the south jetty of the Coquille River. The tribes second parcel of trust land (906.9 acres) lies along Cape Arago Highway, south of Coos Bay. The third piece of trust land is the former site of an abandoned plywood mill along Highway 101 in North Bend, Oregon. The tribe's casino facility now occupies this parcel.

The Coquille Indian Tribe is located in Coos Bay/North Bend, Oregon on the southern Oregon coast. There are currently 761 enrolled members of this tribe. The tribe was terminated by the federal government in 1954 and restored in 1998. The restoration gave full power back to the tribal government and gave tribal members access to federal benefits and services. It also provided for the acquisition of a land base. The Coquille Restoration Act provided for the creation of a 1,000-acres reservation in a five-county service area in southern Oregon, including Coos, Curry, Lane, Douglas, and Jackson counties.

Thus far the tribe has acquired about 1,100 acres, which have been placed into trust by the BIA. This land includes Empire Property, administration building, Mill Casino, Heritage House, Metcalf Tract, and Charleston Industrial Park Tract, all of which are in the Coos Bay-North Bend area. The Bureau of Land Management transferred 5,400 acres of the Coquille Forest to the BIA to be held in trust for the tribe.

PHYSICAL DESCRIPTION
The Coquille reservation is located near the eastern shore of Coos Bay in southwest Oregon. Tribal lands are bordered by urban areas, the Upper Pony Creek Watershed, and an industrial forest. Elevation ranges from 10 feet above sea level at Coos Bay to 16 feet above sea level at North Bend.

CLIMATE
The average temperature in Coos Bay ranges from a high of 52°F. in January to a high of 64°F in July. Annual precipitation is 63.48 inches.

Coquille Indian Tribal Community
Federal reservation
Coquille
Ko-kwell
Coos county, Oregon

Coquille Indian Tribal Community
P.O. Box 783
North Bend, OR 97459
541-756-0904
541-756-0847Fax

Coquille

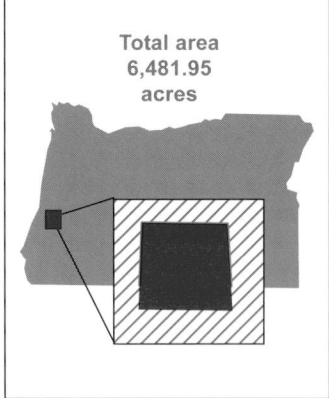

Total area
6,481.95
acres

Total area (BIA realty, 2004)
6,481.95 acres

Tribally owned (BIA realty, 2004)
6,481.95 acres

Population 2000 census
258

Tribal enrollment
(BIA labor report, 2001)
769

Tribal enrollment
(Tribal source, 2005)
761

Total labor force 2000 census
67

Total labor force
(BIA labor report, 2001)
246

High school graduate or higher
2000 census
87.5%

Bachelor's degree or higher
2000 census
0%

Unemployment rate 2000 census
26.9%

Unemployment rate
(BIA labor report, 2001)
55%

Per capita income 2000 census
$13,863

CULTURE AND HISTORY

Members of the Coquille tribe have resided on the southern Oregon coast, along the Coquille River, and inland towards the area of Coos Bay for at least several thousand years. Ancestral lands of the Coquille encompassed over 700,000 acres. Historical Coquille communities have been identified along the lower Coquille River and the forks of the Coquille River. Over the course of time, the indigenous language of the Coquille people has been almost entirely replaced by the pidgin language of Chinook.

In 1855, the tribe entered into treaty agreements with the United States. They ceded their ancestral lands in exchange for federal services and protection within a designated reservation. Despite the treaty, the tribe eventually began to suffer the effects of the influx of explorers, trappers, and missionaries. Many Coquille bands and villages were nearly obliterated in the Rogue River Wars of 1856, and the survivors were forcibly relocated to reservations such as the Siletz. In the early twentieth century, George Bundy Watson began investigating Coquille land claims based on the 1855 treaty. Convinced of the fraud perpetrated against the tribe, he took the Coquille's case before the Court of Claims, which, in 1945, decided in favor of the tribe. The Coquille finally, in 1950, received a monetary judgment in excess of three million dollars. In 1954, however, the tribe was terminated along with 42 other western Oregon tribes. It took intense lobbying by tribal leaders to finally regain federal recognition in 1989. The restoration of tribal governmental powers included full eligibility for federal benefits and services similar to other tribes and provisions for establishing a government and acquiring a land base. The Coquille Restoration Act passed by Congress provided for a five-county service area in southern Oregon, including Coos, Curry, Lane, Douglas, and Jackson counties

GOVERNMENT

A tribal constitution, dividing power between the executive, legislative, and judicial branches, was approved by the Secretary of the Interior. As per this constitution a seven-member tribal council is the governing body of the tribe. The tribal government has the following programs: tribal membership, education, culture, health and human services, housing, community development, economic services, law enforcement, and judicial services.

The tribal council is the governing body of the Coquille Indian Tribe. The seven-member council is elected to set policy, establish budget priorities, and oversee governmental and economic activities. The tribe's general council is composed of all adult tribal members. The general council meets twice a year, during the Mid-Winter Gathering and Salmon Bake cultural celebrations.

The tribe operates a police department, which was established in 1996, and employs a police chief and three law enforcement officers. Programs of the department include the Law Enforcement Explorers Program and the Reserve Officer Program.

BUSINESS CORPORATION

The Coquille established the Coquille Economic Development Corporation (CEDCO) in 1991. CEDCO manages and administers business ventures on behalf of the tribe. It serves as the parent company for Heritage Place, the Mill Casino and Hotel, Coquille Cranberries, and Optical Rural Community Access (ORCA) Communications.

ECONOMY

The tribe operates numerous businesses and services that contribute to the reservation and local economy. The tribe is the second-largest employer in the county. The development of the tribe's casino and hotel facility has generated a great source of income and interest in the area, drawing vast amounts of visitors and investors. A study conducted in 2002 showed that casino employees are compensated from 16 to 60 percent higher than non-casino workers in the same fields. The casino provides health, dental, and retirement plans, as well as paid meals, paid time off, jury duty pay, EAP services, and funeral pay to its employees. Many Oregon employers do not offer these benefits. The Mill Casino's contribution to the local economy is great. Its annual expenditure on local goods and services exceeds $25 million. Overall, almost $8 million in local sales can be directly attributed to the facility.

Government as Employer. In 2000, the tribe employed over 600 people. It was the second largest employer in Coos County. In 2002, the tribe's payroll exceeded $8 million.

Economic Development Projects. The tribe established the Coquille Tribal Community Fund in 2001. Through this program, the tribe awards grants to educational, health, public safety, arts and culture, historic preservation, and gaming addiction programs. In its first year, 22 grants were awarded to nonprofit groups throughout the region.

Agriculture and Livestock. The tribe owns Coquille Cranberries. It is operated by CEDCO and is the world's largest producer of 100 percent organic cranberries. Crops are sold to commercial manufacturers, as well as sold directly under the Coquille Cranberries label in fresh, dry, and preserved form.

Forestry. The Coquille Tribe manages 5,400 acres of forested lands, owned by the Bureau of Land Management. Coquille Forest Holdings is located near Bridgeport, Oregon.

Gaming. The Mill Casino opened in 1995 on the waterfront of Coos Bay. In 2000, hotel facilities were added. The casino offers 560 slot machines/VLTs, 8 table games, and 100 bingo seats. The adjacent hotel offers a convention center, an entertainment venue, 115 guest rooms, and 4 restaurants. There are a number of waterfront suites and special needs-equipped suites available. The facility employs 450 people.

The Mill Casino and Hotel sponsors a mentoring program to introduce participating tribal members to the operation and management of hotel and casino facilities. The casino also maintains a program of charitable donations and fund-raising events. It contributes to local parks, schools, service clubs, and projects throughout the community.

Fisheries. The tribe currently has no commercial fisheries but has developed a plan for the construction of a spring Chinook salmon hatchery and release-and-recapture facility on its 907 acres beside Coos Bay. The project might ultimately generate profits or will be run as a nonprofit enterprise to attract tourism. Tribal members also continue harvest shellfish and fish in the traditions that were handed down from their ancestors. Included in these ancient practices is the fashion in which these creatures are harvested, consumed, and exchanged with in the tribe and with other Native American communities.

Construction. The tribe owns the Hutsuwa Corporation, a construction company. This company is run through the Coquille Indian Housing Authority, with its head contractor also serving as the executive director. The tribe owns several large pieces of equipment, including several cranes and forklifts, used in land-clearing and construction work.

Industrial Parks. The tribe plans to turn 400 acres of trust land into an industrial park. Land has already been cleared and several major manufacturers are close to a commitment to relocating to this site. Plans include full utility service, paved roads, telephone, and cable for the facility.

Real Estate/Commercial Development. The tribe's housing authority oversees the development of housing projects on tribal land near Empire, Oregon. It also manages the Hutsawa Corporation.

Services and Retail. The Heritage Place is an assisted-living and Alzheimer's center owned by the tribe and managed by CEDCO. Heritage Place is the first center to offer a dedicated Alzheimer's program on the Oregon coast. Heritage Place includes a variety of floor plans, a 24-hour emergency response system, meal service, weekly house cleaning service, and a full range of recreational, social, and cultural activities. The lower level of Heritage Place houses the Coquille Tribal Library and Museum. The library is also accessible on-line.

Tourism and Recreation. The tribe holds two annual cultural events. The Mid-Winter Gathering is held in January, generally attracting several hundred people. The Salmon Bake, held to celebrate the tribe's restoration, takes place annually on June 28. The Pacific coast and other natural attractions also draw numerous hikers, campers, fishermen, and nature lovers to the area.

INFRASTRUCTURE

The scenic and busy Highway 101 (north-south) provides the primary road access to the area. Routes 38 and 42 feed into 101 from the east. There is also a deepwater port located near the reservation.

Electricity. The City of Bandon provides electricity to the reservation, while Pacific Power and Light provides electricity to some portions of tribal land.

Water Supply. The City of Bandon provides water and sewage service to Heritage Place. The tribe is negotiating with the cities of Coos Bay and North Bend for water service elsewhere, to be supplemented by wells in outlying regions.

Transportation. The nearest commercial air service is at the North Bend Municipal Airport, several miles from most tribal properties. Commercial bus, truck, and rail lines all provide service to the North Bend community.

Telecommunications. ORCA Communications is owned by the tribe and managed by CEDCO. It provides access for the community to high-speed fiber-optic networks. Local business, schools, government entities, and health care organizations serve as the primary clients of ORCA.

COMMUNITY FACILITIES AND SERVICES

The tribal community center was constructed in 2000. It houses the Head Start program and after-school activity programs. The facilities include a computer lab, gym, and fitness area. Programs sponsored through the center include elder's health, fitness, and community activity programs. The tribe sponsors a Summer Youth Program, which provides summer employment training and placement for tribal youth.

The tribe sponsors anthropologists from the University of Oregon and Oregon State University to work with tribal members in the research and documentation of tribal history. Archeological projects have been conducted and numerous culturally significant sites identified throughout the region. Projects have identified several Coquille communities and have uncovered evidence of Native population in the Coos Bay area at least 8,000 years ago.

Education. The nearest schools are part of the Empire public school system, which 87 percent of tribal children currently attend. The tribe also maintains a library. This library focuses specifically on information from a Native American perspective. Included are over 2,500 books and periodicals as well as 30,000 pages of historical papers. The Coquille tribe offers financial assistance to tribal members pursuing a post-secondary degree. It also provides higher education, vocational education, adult education, tutoring, and computer programs for tribal members.

Health Care. In 1996, the tribe completed construction of the community health center. The center provides comprehensive medical services to tribal members and tribal employees. Services include medical, dental, mental health, community health, substance abuse prevention, foster care, and outreach programs. The center serves over 1,300 Native and over 2,000 non-Native clients. In 2000, the clinic was awarded the highest accreditation achievable from the Accreditation Association for Ambulatory Health Care and employs a staff of 30.

Coquille

ENVIRONMENTAL CONCERNS

The tribe consulted with other tribes, the U.S. EPA, the Natural Resource Conservation Service, the Army Corp of Engineers, and state and local governments to develop a best management practices, standards, and guidelines. This philosophy is applied by the tribe to their urban and undeveloped land to ensure they are managing their resources in an environmentally and culturally sound fashion as well as a profitable one. In addition they have enacted the forest resource protection, fish and wildlife, water quality and pollution abatement programs to maintain this commitment to sound stewardship.

TRI-OR-002

TRI-OR-001

TRI-OR-002 The Mill Casino Hotel sign

TRI-OR-001 Front view of the Mill Casino and Hotel

Honoring Nations Honoree 2002

Text in its entirety from:
The Harvard Project On
American Indian Economic
Development

John F. Kennedy School
of Government
Harvard University

In 1995, the Coquille Indian Tribe established the Southwest Oregon Research Project (SWORP) to recover historical, anthropological, military, and government documents relating to the Tribe and surrounding Indian nations. These documents were potlatched in two gift-giving ceremonies to forty-four different tribes and are now locally accessible at tribal libraries and at a central archive at the University of Oregon. Through SWORP, the Coquille have helped themselves and others rewrite and interpret tribal histories, develop innovative partnerships, improve tribal governmental performance, and strengthen tribal sovereignty.

Like many Indian nations of western Oregon, the Coquille Indian Tribe endured a long struggle to gain federal recognition and secure title to a tribal homeland. Although the Coquille and the US federal government signed two treaties in the 1850s, Congress never ratified them. Encroachment by non-Indians followed, and it was not until the 1940s that the Coquille were able to gain a degree of redress in the US Court of Claims, which awarded several coastal Oregon tribes financial compensation for lands taken. Progress, however, was short-lived. In 1954, House Concurrent Resolution 108 terminated the Tribe's legal relationship with the federal government, and the Coquille were forced to begin their struggles anew. The continuing battles for federal recognition and land rights were complicated by the fact that tribal citizens' testimonies were largely disqualified in court and Congressional hearings as "hearsay." In fact, the Coquille's eventual recognition by the US Congress in 1989 was the result not of tribal elders' testimonies, but of the "credible" testimony and writings of non-Native anthropologists, linguists, and ethnohistorians.

Regrettably, many Indian nations face similar demands to produce "credible," "paper proof" of tribal ancestry or land ownership. Matters are made worse by the fact that there are substantial obstacles to undertaking the archival research necessary to produce such proof. These include educational barriers, a lack of scholarly support, and a dearth of economic means - all of which can force Native nations into further reliance on outsiders for evidence of their claims. Upon the restoration of the Coquille Tribe's status, the Coquille Tribal Council and elders made a commitment to reduce this dependency upon external sources for cultural and political self-determination and survival. They decided to recapture their own history.

In 1995, in collaboration with the University of Oregon and the Smithsonian Institution, the Coquille Indian Tribe established the Southwest Oregon Research Project (SWORP) to recover historical, anthropological, military, and government documents relating to the Coquille and neighboring tribes. That year, a small group of SWORP scholars from the Coquille Tribe and the University of Oregon identified and photocopied sixty thousand pages of relevant materials from the Smithsonian Institution's National Anthropological Archives and the National Archives in Washington, DC. This collection contained important information about the cultures, languages, and histories of western Oregon and northern California tribes during the early settlement period of the Oregon Territory. In the summer of 1998, a second team of SWORP scholars-including members of the Coquille, Grand Ronde, Siletz, and Coos Tribes-returned to the Archives and recovered an additional fifty thousand pages of materials, including allotment records, treaties, and military documents.

Recognizing that these archival materials belonged in the hands of people who could use them, SWORP launched a dissemination effort. To ensure the broad availability of its research to Native communities in the region, SWORP worked with the University of Oregon to house the archives in the University's Special Collections. In the spring of 1997, SWORP held a potlatch (a traditional gift-giving ceremony) to distribute copies of its collection to seven tribal libraries. SWORP distributed archival materials to a total of forty-four tribes at a second potlatch in 2001, an event in which over four hundred guests participated. Each gifting of the archived materials forwards SWORP's goal of making "paper proof" of tribal histories and cultures readily available to Indian nations.

SWORP's collection and distribution efforts continue. For example, SWORP scholars are currently targeting other archival collections, including those found at the Peabody Museum of Archaeology and Ethnology at Harvard University, the Bancroft Library at the University of California at Berkeley, the Hudson Bay Archives in Winnipeg, Canada, and Russia's Museum of Ethnology in St. Petersburg, which might hold resources that complement the existing collection. With regard to distribution, the Coquille Tribe has made the existing collection more accessible through the production of a creative multi-indexed inventory, which cross-references the vast collection by geographic places, dates, tribal and cultural affiliations, document titles, document types, author names, and brief subject descriptions. Using the inventory, researchers can locate specific SWORP holdings with greater ease.

At first glance, SWORP might be viewed as a purely academic endeavor. In reality, however, SWORP is a dynamic, multi-faceted project that has generated a diverse array of academic, community, and governmental benefits. A professor of anthropology at the University of Oregon has called SWORP a project of "cultural repatriation mandated by common sense." Indeed, several significant Project successes demonstrate the Coquille Tribe's wisdom in initiating such an endeavor.

By developing the SWORP collections, the Coquille Tribe has enhanced its own ability, as well as that of other Indian nations, to define and defend tribal culture and history. The vast array of SWORP documents has encouraged scholars to revisit, from an indigenous perspective, histories and ethnographies that have delimited Indian cultures. As a result, they have produced more historically accurate and culturally conscious educational curricula and research projects. In fact, since 1995, the SWORP archive has been a primary resource for eight Ph.D. dissertations and six Masters theses in anthropology, linguistics, history, and musicology. Native American graduate students produced seven of these works. Interest in the SWORP archives also is inspiring a new- and growing-group of Native scholars. In 1995, there was only one Indian graduate student in the University of Oregon's Department of Anthropology, while today there are five, with a total of eight since SWORP's initiation. These scholars are in a position to help refocus the field of anthropology, which has an unfortunate history of emphasizing the racial and cultural inferiority of indigenous peoples. In addition to encouraging individual scholars, the SWORP collection has inspired an annual Culture Preservation Conference as well as a journal, Changing Landscapes. The SWORP potlatches have resulted in a documentary film, A Gift of History: The Potlatch Returns, and a second film is now in production. SWORP reclaims and reincorporates intellectual property that indisputably belongs in the region, empowering the Coquille and other tribes to reevaluate and defend against the portrayals of Indian cultures that have influenced their identities and sovereignty.

In order to give the Coquille and other tribes in the region control over their histories and cultural representation, SWORP's leadership forged fruitful partnerships with other organizations and institutions. The Smithsonian Institution, whose archives are open and freely accessible to the public, sponsored SWORP's first trip to Washington, DC, to retrieve archival documents and continues to serve as a resource to SWORP staff. The University of Oregon houses the SWORP archive, provides a pool of graduate students who maintain and expand the archive, and has hosted the SWORP potlatches. As a result of these partnerships, SWORP has spent a total of $177,000 (or little more than $1.60 per page of archived material) over its seven-year existence. These partnerships help ensure SWORP's sustainability and have spawned a string of related innovations, supporting projects, and achievements. For instance, SWORP was the impetus for the University of Oregon to build a longhouse on campus and to extend in-state tuition to student applicants from any tribe with historical ties to the State of Oregon. In its 125th anniversary celebration, the University heralded SWORP as one of its top 125 achievements. SWORP also has led to the creation of a collaborative curriculum development project wherein the Tribe, the University, and the Smithsonian are working together to produce, distribute, and implement "tribe specific" Native American curricula in Oregon public schools.

Gifting the SWORP materials through potlatches has allowed the Coquille Tribe to establish similarly productive relationships with surrounding Indian nations. The significance of these potlatches is tremendous: Not only have they reunited for the first time tribes that were widely dispersed during the 1850s era of removal, but they also have rekindled an ancient tradition. In addition to these cultural and political benefits, the practice of gifting has practical benefits. SWORP archives, provided by the Coquille to their tribal neighbors at Coos Bay, serve as the foundation for the emerging Coos Bay tribal library and have generated goodwill among these two Indian nations. Several tribes are using SWORP documents in their efforts to gain federal recognition; for example, the Coquille recently gave the Chinook Tribe twelve maps that document its ancestral homelands. At the same time, the gifts are beginning to be reflected back to the Coquille. SWORP directors recently received a completely digitized version of the SWORP archives from the Smith River Rancheria (California), which worked in conjunction with the Center for Indian Community Development at Humboldt State University to make the archives electronically accessible. The Smith River Rancheria's gift also included digital copies of its own archival documents, many of which complement the SWORP collections.

In addition to these successes, SWORP plays a critical role in improving the Coquille Tribe's governmental performance and enhancing the Tribe's presence and influence in the region. Using maps from the SWORP collection, Coquille tribal employees have developed a mapping system that enables tribal departments to protect archaeological and cultural sites while making development decisions. Specifically, they are now able to determine-at a moment's notice-whether sites in question are sacred or of historical significance. Additionally, in cooperation with the Coos County Planning Commission, the Coquille Tribe's cultural resource managers have added 141 new sites to the county's inventories-sites previously not protected by the Oregon State Historical Preservation Office-and helped the county devise a buffering system that protects the confidential location of these sites. Not only does SWORP allow the Tribe to make more informed development and conservation decisions, but it also allows the Tribe to assign appropriate place names. The "Osprey Weir Site" is now called "Ni-Les-Tun-Tene" on the Coos County Map of Cultural, Natural, Geologic, and Botanical Resources. In a recent issue of the Oregon Historical Quarterly, scholars using SWORP documents were able to attribute the word "Oregon" to a mispronounced Cree word describing an oil-laden fish that was traded throughout the Pacific Northwest.

SWORP is a low-cost, high-benefit, and easily transferable endeavor that exemplifies and advances tribal self-determination. Through SWORP, the Coquille have empowered themselves and other Indian nations in the Northwest by recovering "paper proof" of their history and culture that complements the oral traditions and memories of their elders. This effort has enhanced cultural education, resulted in valuable institutional partnerships, improved intertribal relations, rekindled community traditions, and strengthened the tribal government's ability to function as a self-determined sovereign.

Lessons

Indian nations can use historical archives to define and defend their own culture and history, to address misperceptions and misunderstandings, to produce educational and cultural curricula, to foster Native scholarship, and to inform policy decisions.

Large-scale research efforts often require strategic partnerships to bear the burdens of organizing, producing, and maintaining information. Tribes seeking to develop archival collections can look to academic institutions, museums, libraries, nonprofit organizations, and other tribes to identify shared interests and comparative advantages. These partnerships can expand the pool of technical, archival, and historical knowledge at a tribe's disposal and help spread costs.

Information is expensive to organize but usually inexpensive to reproduce. Sharing information with other tribes, non-Indian governments, and other groups (for example, schools) can build goodwill, increase understanding between people, and facilitate productive government-to-government relationships.

Coquille

Honoring Nations Honoree 2002

Text in its entirety from: The Harvard Project On American Indian Economic Development

John F. Kennedy School of Government Harvard University

Cow Creek

Cow Creek Band of Umpqua
Tribe of Indians
2371 NE Stephens Street
Roseburg, OR 97470
541-672-9405
541-673-0432 Fax
cowcreek.com

Total area *(BIA realty, 2004)*
1,494.64 acres

Tribally owned *(BIA realty, 2004)*
1,494.64 acres

Total labor force
(BIA labor report, 2001)
238

Unemployment rate
(BIA labor report, 2001)
55%

LOCATION AND LAND STATUS

The Cow Creek Reservation is located in Canyonville, near Roseburg in southwestern Oregon along I-5. The Cow Creek Band of Umpqua Tribe of Indians was the second Oregon band to sign a treaty with the United States government. It was signed in 1853 and ratified by the senate in April 1854. In the ratified treaty the tribe ceded 800 square miles in exchange for $12,000 to be paid in goods and services over several years. The federal government reneged on this treaty for the next 125 years. They did not provide any promised goods, services, or benefits and in 1953 formally terminated the tribe without their knowledge or consent.

In December 1982, after years of fighting to restore their status, the Cow Creek Band received federal recognition. The tribe negotiated a $1.5 million settlement with the federal government; however, they remained a landless tribe.

CLIMATE

The City of Roseburg receives 33 inches of rain per year and has an average temperature between 41°F and 68°F. The highest recorded temperature was 109°F in 1998, and the lowest recorded temperature was 3°F in 1989. The city is located at 479 feet above sea level.

CULTURE AND HISTORY

The Cow Creeks speak Takelma. Their ancestral lands included territory between the Cascade Mountains and the Coast Ranges in southwestern Oregon. By 1854, the Cow Creek Band had joined the Rogue Indians in battle against the aggressors. Euro-American volunteers forcibly moved at least 800 members of the Cow Creek Band and the Rogue Indians to reservations in the north; however, several Cow Creeks fled into the hills surrounding the South Umpqua Valley drainage for safety. They remained there, maintaining their traditional lifestyle. Many tribal members married early fur traders and miners, with surnames such as Rondeau, Dumont, Pariseau, LaChance, Rainville, and Thomason. Many of them filed donation land claims and became ranchers and farmers.

In the early 1900s, the Cow Creeks were successful in introducing legislation to Congress five times. In fact, in 1932, a bill passed both houses of Congress only to be vetoed by President Hoover because of the Great Depression. In 1954, Congress passed the Western Oregon Termination Act, which suspended recognition and services to every tribe and band in western Oregon. In 1982, the Cow Creek Band of Umpqua Indians regained tribal status under the provision of PL 97-391. In 1984, the tribe was awarded a $1.5 million settlement in compensation for the loss of their lands in the treaty of 1853.

TRI-OR-003

The tribe used the funds to establish an endowment fund. Interest generated from this endowment has been used for education, housing, an elders program, and economic development that helped initiate the development of the tribe's gaming enterprise. A significant portion of proceeds derived from tribal businesses has been dedicated to land acquisition and economic diversification.

GOVERNMENT

The Cow Creek's are governed by an 11-member board of directors who serve four-year, staggered terms of office. The governing body establishes and enforces policies that strengthen, promote, and protect the tribe and the constitution as well as govern the administration of programs such as social services, housing, and educational services, from vocational training to higher education, that benefit tribal membership.

The tribe also has a separate foundation through which individuals and organizations may attain funding grants. The Cow Creek Umpqua Indian Foundation has granted more than $6 million since it was started. It funds projects that build strong children and families.

BUSINESS CORPORATION

The business arm of the Cow Creek Band is the Umpqua Indian Development Corporation, which is an IRS Section 17 tribal charter corporation that operates a number of tribal enterprises. Tribally owned entities that the corporation manages include the Seven Feathers Hotel and Casino Resort, the Seven Feathers Truck and Travel Center, Umpqua Indian Foods, Creative Images MediaGroup/ciPrinting, Nesika Health Group, Rio Communications, Canyonville Cubbyholes Storage, the Valley View and Riverside Lodge motels, Umpqua Indian Utility cooperative, and K bar Ranches.

ECONOMY

The tribal economy is largely sustained by revenue from the casino complex and various tribally owned businesses. The tribe also serves as a large contributor to the area's economy with an employee base of approximately 1,300 individuals.

Government as Employer. The tribe and its various business operations employ about 1,300 people, 98 percent of whom are non-Indians. The tribal government employs approximately 30 individuals.

Economic Development Projects. In an effort to meet the tribe's present and future economic and infrastructure needs for development near the resort and truck stop, the tribe has started construction of the Creekside Development Project on the reservation. This project includes a series of dams, a lagoon, a water and sewage treatment facility, an RV park, and an expansion of the tribe's Seven Feathers Hotel.

Gaming. The tribe owns and operates the Seven Feathers Hotel and Casino Resort. The casino offers Nevada-style gaming with over 1,000 slot machines, 21 table games, and live poker, keno, and bingo. Facilities include a nonsmoking game area with 3 table games and over 100 slot machines. The casino welcomes over a million guests each year.

The adjacent hotel offers 146 guest rooms, an indoor heated pool, 2 spas, a fitness center, and locker rooms. There is also a 22,000-square-foot convention center that can accommodate conferences, conventions, and entertainment acts. The hotel offers a gift shop, a restaurant, a lounge, an ice cream parlor, and a sports bar. An RV park is also located at the casino complex.

Manufacturing. Umpqua Indian Foods processes its own meat products, jams, taffy, specialty nuts, crackers, and cheese. The company sells the products out of the gift shop located on site or by order.

Services and Retail. The tribe owns and operates Umpqua Indian Foods in Canyonville, Oregon. This facility is a retail center that sells jerky, beef sticks, jams, taffy, specialty nuts, crackers, and cheese for resale. Facilities include a processing plant and gift shop. Canyonville Cubbyholes is a tribally owned storage center. The 7 Feathers Truck and Travel Center is a full-service complex. It houses the Creekside Restaurant and Convenience Store, and it provides tire repairs, sales and weigh scales in addition to a truckers lounge, showers, and laundry facilities.

The Valley View Motel is a 15-room tribally owned facility. It provides easy access to local outdoor recreational activities and a free shuttle service to the tribal enterprises. The 15-room Riverside Lodge Motel is also a tribally owned facility located along the South Umpqua River. It offers easy access to the local wilderness for fishers, bird watchers, hikers, and visitors.

Telecommunications. Creative Images is located in Roseburg. It provides graphic design, full-service advertising, marketing, web design, video production, and printing services. Its divisions include ciMediaGroup and ciPrinting. Tribally owned Rio Communications is a full-service telephone company. It is a competitive local exchange carrier and offers high-speed connection for voice and data services. It is the world's first communications organization to establish a turnkey end-to-end solution for voice-over-Internet-protocol providers.

Tourism and Recreation. The reservation is located near numerous outdoor attractions. Hiking, fishing, and boating activities are available to visitors.

INFRASTRUCTURE
Electricity. The tribe owns and operates the Umpqua Indian Utility Cooperative. This tribal power company purchases power directly from the Bonneville Power Administration for use at the tribal resort and truck and travel center.

COMMUNITY FACILITIES AND SERVICES
Programs and services provided by the Cow Creek Tribal Government Offices are designed to create and/or enhance strong families and self-sufficient people. The tribe offers education assistance through various programs for K-12 as well as adult education, vocational training, and higher education programs. Housing assistance is provided to tribal members to help with down payment or limited home improvements. The tribe has a PL-638 contract, which provides technical assistance from the BIA in various areas, such as housing and fee to trust.

Education. Tribal children attend the public school system.

Health Care. The Cow Creek Health and Wellness Center provides general medical care, treatment of minor emergencies, comprehensive health physicals, health screening, family planning and counseling, weight management, and well child care services, among others. The tribe operates a clinic, which is staffed with two medical doctors, two clinic nurses, a phlebotomist, a psychologist, a nutritionist, and an alcohol and drug counselor. Tribal members who are unable to use the clinic are provided the ability to obtain insurance. The tribe owns and operates the Nesika Health Group, a self-funded insurance program provided to tribal employees as a benefit at no cost. Tribal members are eligible to buy into the plan at extremely low premiums. The tribe also places a strong emphasis on programs for diabetes prevention and management, parenting skills, children's car seats, and tobacco education.

Cow Creek

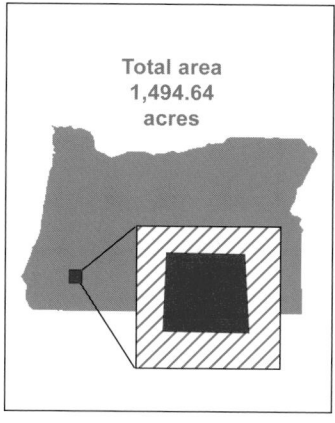

Total area
1,494.64
acres

Fort McDermitt
See Nevada

Grand Ronde

Grand Ronde

ILOCATION AND LAND STATUS
The Grand Ronde Reservation is located in the northwestern part of Oregon in the Willamette Valley, east of U.S. 101 and west of Salem. It was originally established by an Executive Order in 1857 as a result of the many Euro-American settlers moving into the state. Initially the reservation spanned an area of 69,000 acres. Under provisions of the allotment act, the tribe lost over 33,000 acres in the late 1800s. When the tribe reorganized under the Indian Reorganization Act of 1934, tribal lands had dwindled to less than 500 acres. When the tribe's status as a federally recognized tribe was terminated in the 1950s, all tribal lands and assets were dissolved except for the tribal cemetery. The tribe regained recognition status in 1983, and in 1988 Congress transferred 9,811 acres of the original 69,000-acre tract to the Grand Ronde Tribe to restore their reservation land base. Since restoration, the tribe has actively pursued opportunities to increase its land base.

PHYSICAL DESCRIPTION
The Grand Ronde Reservation is located in mountainous regions of Yamhill County and lies approximately 18 air miles from the Pacific Ocean. It contains forests, rivers, and streams. The Yamhill River constitutes the entire watershed and flows through tribal lands near the tribal campus. A 10,052-acre forestland is five miles north of the tribal campus and has two main tributaries, Agency Creek on the west and Coast Creek on the east.

CULTURE AND HISTORY
The Confederated Tribes of the Grand Ronde is composed of more than 20 tribes and bands whose traditional lands included regions throughout western Oregon and south into northern California. Members of the Confederated Tribes are descendants of the Kalapuya, Clackamas, Molalla, Rogue River, Chasta (Shasta), Umpqua, Salmon River, and Nehalem Band of Tillamook tribes. The Grand Ronde Reservation was established by treaties in 1854 and 1855, and by an Executive Order in 1857. The reservation was comprised of approximately 69,000 acres on the eastern side of the coastal range at the headwaters of the South Yamhill River. In 1855 and continuing through 1856, many of the tribes were relocated to the Grand Ronde Reservation, with the exception of the Nehalem Band of Tillamook and the Salmon River Band. Following the reservation's establishment, a school system was set up for the youth. This became the primary agency through which the English language and the Christian religion were imposed upon the community. During this period, the government attempted to force Euro-American traditions upon them, banning Native religions, dress, and ceremonies.

Grand Ronde Reservation
Federal reservation
Chasta (Shasta), Kalapuya,
Molalla, Rogue River, and
Umpqua
Polk and Yamhill counties,
Oregon

Confederated Tribes
of the Grand Ronde
9615 Grand Ronde Road
Grand Ronde, OR 97347
503-879-5211
800-422-0232
503-879-5964 Fax
grandronde.org

Grand Ronde

TRI-OR-005

TRI-OR-015

TRI-OR-006

TRI-OR-004

TRI-OR-005 The Confederated Tribes of The Grand Ronde community of Oregon sign

TRI-OR-015 Grand Ronde Station, gas station and convenience store

TRI-OR-006 Front view of the Grand Ronde Health and Wellness Center

TRI-OR-004 Grand Ronde Health and Wellness Center

Total area *(BIA realty, 2004)*
10,678.36 acres

Allotted/Individual owned
(BIA realty, 2004)
20 acres

Tribally owned *(BIA realty, 2004)*
10,658.36 acres

Population *(EPA 2004)*
3,080

Total labor force *2000 census*
10

For subsistence, tribal members worked as servants, farmers, loggers, or craftspeople selling baskets and other handmade goods.

In 1887, the reservation was allotted under the provisions of the Allotment Act. Over 33,000 acres were allotted into individual land parcels. In 1901, the "surplus" tribal lands were sold to the public. The tribe lost a total of 27,791 acres at that time. Later, after much of the former reservation had been sold or alienated from tribal ownership, many of the tribal members remained in Grand Ronde. Given their circumstances, most Grand Ronde tribal members supported the 1934 Indian Reorganization Act, as it provided jobs to many people and allowed them to purchase land.

In 1954, the tribe entered perhaps its most difficult period as the federal government declared the Grand Ronde terminated. During the three decades between termination and restoration, a large percentage of tribal members were forced to leave the area and seek work in Portland and elsewhere, because of the loss of rights and services that had previously been available through the BIA and Indian Health Services.

Finally in 1983, the persistence and dedication of those who had continued to lobby against termination paid off in the form of the Grand Ronde Restoration Act, PL 98-165. The act allowed the tribes to function as one tribal unit, restoring most of their previous rights. As a compensation for termination, Congress transferred nearly 10,000 acres of former reservation lands back to the tribe. This land has since provided income from timber sales, which the tribe used to purchase 100 acres of land for the tribal headquarters. The headquarters include offices for programs in health, education, culture, social services, and tribal court. Thirty percent of the tribe's timber income is earmarked for economic development.

Since restoration, many of the tribal members who were displaced by termination have expressed a desire to return to the reservation. In response, the tribal government is focusing on developing housing facilities to accommodate those members eager to come home. The various tribes that comprise the Grand Rondes initially spoke numerous languages and dialects, not all related or mutually intelligible. The Chi-

nook (Chinuk) language was a shared common language among many tribes since it had become a creole trade language of the Columbia River trading routes. It became the primary language of the reservation tribes, and tribal members are actively revitalizing it through cultural programs and instructional classes.

GOVERNMENT
In 1983, in the immediate wake of the Restoration Act, a tribal constitution was approved. There is a nine-member tribal council with members elected by the general membership to three-year terms. The tribe is a self-governance tribe under the provisions of PL-638. It contracts all Indian Health Service programs, including all clinical services, prevention, behavioral health and contract health services and all BIA services, including forestry, fish and wildlife, all education programs, JOM, social services, and tribal court. The tribe buys back realty services to supplement the tribe's own realty program (including assistance with easements).

ECONOMY
The tribal economy is supported in large part by revenue earned by the tribe's gaming operations and enterprises in the timber industry. The tribe employs nearly 1,900 people throughout its casino, governmental departments, and tribal programs.

Government as Employer. The tribe employs almost 1,900 people, 300 of which serve in the tribal government offices and programs. Approximately 43 percent of these employees are tribal members. Tribal members with college degrees head three of the five largest government departments.

Economic Development Projects. The tribe is in the process of constructing tribal housing and government buildings. Additional commercial development is planned for tribal lands along Highway 18. The tribe is currently exploring its capability to develop lands within Yamhill County. Presently, limited sewer capacity and state land-use regulations prohibit the infrastructure changes necessary to develop these areas.

Forestry. The 9,811 acres transferred to the tribe in 1988 were primarily Bureau of Land Management timberland or federal

TRI-OR-012

TRI-OR-010

TRI-OR-003B

Grand Ronde

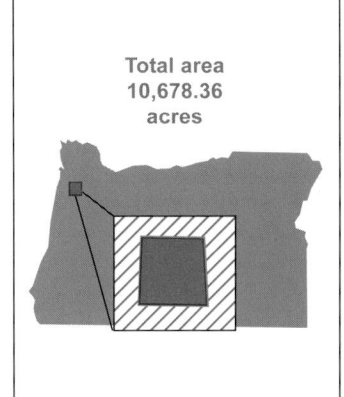

Total area
10,678.36
acres

land managed by the bureau, and the tribe intended to use them to generate revenues and future development. During the 1990s, the tribe acquired another 241 acres of land from the Bureau of Land Management. The tribe harvests 6.1 million board-feet of timber annually. Tribal sources believe that this is a highly sustainable harvest level. Timber sales from this land fund a wide range of social services and development projects. Timber serves as the second-most important source of tribal income. The tribe also maintains a forestry program to ensure the ecologically and fiscally sound management of this resource. The forest contains Douglas fir, western hemlock, and red alder. In addition to timber harvest, the Grand Ronde Natural Resources Division also has programs in place to protect and manage fish and wildlife, roads and infrastructure, silviculture, wildland and prescribed fire, environmental issues, forest patrol, and recreation projects.

Gaming. The National Indian Gaming Act enabled the tribe to diversify the tribal economy. In 1995 the tribe constructed Spirit Mountain Casino, which has become the largest tourist attraction in Oregon. The casino, which employs 1,600 people, has 90,000 square feet of gaming space and 4,800 square feet of convention space. Facilities include over 1,500 Vegas-style slot machines, bingo, a poker room, off-track betting, keno, and 39 table games. A smoke-free game room is also available to guests. Spirit Mountain Lodge, a five-story, 100-room hotel, is adjacent to the casino. Hotel facilities include 3 entertainment venues, a restaurant, a café, and a buffet.

The tribe uses casino-generated revenue to fund tribal services and programs, including health care and education. The Spirit Mountain Community Fund also provides six percent of its profit to community services organizations in northwest Oregon. The community fund is the eighth-largest charitable organization in the state, and it provides grant funds to outside agencies for education, health, public safety, historic and environmental protection, and art and culture projects primarily benefiting the nontribal community.

The casino's entry in the 2004 Rose Festival Grand Floral Parade in Portland won the Sweepstakes Award for Most Outstanding Float. The float was titled "A Journey of Tradition," and it portrayed traditional plant-gathering activities practiced by tribal members. The Grand Ronde tribal royalty princesses rode on the float.

Construction. The tribe is presently constructing an additional five-story, 163-room addition to the Spirit Mountain Lodge, and a number of tribal members are involved in this construction project. The tribe also has housing, road, and sewer projects that will occur during 2005, primarily with federal housing and competitive grant funding. The tribe recently created Round Valley Construction. The crew has completed a number of projects on behalf of the tribe, including subcontracting work on the water treatment plan for the casino and tribal forestry roads.

Mining. The tribe operates small-scale mining operations that produce gravel to be used for tribal projects.

Manufacturing. The tribe operates Spirit Mountain Logistics, which serves industrial outsourcing needs for high-tech and consumer product manufacturers and governmental institutions. Services include warehousing, specialized cleaning, and inventory.

Real Estate/Commercial Development. The tribe has developed properties near its headquarters for tribal housing. The tribe constructed Grand Meadows, a housing subdivision for manufactured homes. Tribal members may lease the home sites for 50 years. The Grand Ronde Tribal Housing Authority (GRTHA) has constructed most of the tribal housing. Ilip Tilixam is a housing development created to house tribal elders. It consists of duplexes, triplexes, and fourplexes with a combined total of 38 units. Another 38 units of elder housing are planned. The Chxi Musam Illihi rental development was created to provide low-income housing to tribal members. It contains 36 units, a gathering area, and a park. Another 72 units are planned. GRTHA and the tribe are also in the process of constructing three adult foster homes.

Most of the tribe's economic diversification is through investments in real estate or businesses, often as partial owner with other investors (such as a high-rise condominium in Portland, a shopping mall, and properties in the Seattle area). The tribe, working cooperatively with the Siletz Tribe, created Chemawa Station to plan for and oversee development of their 15.6-acre jointly owned property north of Salem.

Services and Retail. Grand Ronde Station is a full-service gas station. It includes an automatic car wash, a convenience store, and three quick-serve food franchises.

Media and Communications. The award-winning tribal newspaper, *Smoke Signals*, issues twice a month and is nationally recognized as one of the best newspapers in Indian Country.

TRI-OR-012 Front view of lodge at Spirit Mountain Casino and Lodge

TRI-OR-010 "Hail to the Brave" the Confederated Tribes of Grand Ronde Veterans Memorial

TRI-OR-003B Sign in front of "The Confederated Tribes of Grand Ronde Education Facility"

High school graduate or higher
2000 census
100%

Bachelor's degree or higher
2000 census
0%

Unemployment rate
2000 census
0%

Per capita income *2000 census*
$9,274

Grand Ronde

Tourism and Recreation. While the Spirit Mountain Casino is the largest tourist attraction in Oregon, the reservation area is also surrounded by national forest and lies in the heart of the Coast Range of northwestern Oregon, which is a popular area for camping, hiking, and other outdoor activities. The State of Oregon, working in cooperation with the tribe, is developing (as well as preserving) the Fort Yamhill Historic Park on the site of the original fort. The tribe designed the access road through its own property along with a possible future campground. The fort site was recently featured on *The History Detectives*, a show on the national Public Broadcasting Service. The tribe also owns the community's historic train depot. An impressive but somber tourist attraction is the West Valley War Veterans Memorial, which was constructed at the heart of the tribal campus. It includes four black marble monoliths (one for each branch of the armed services), and the names of the fallen surround male and female traditional Native statutes raising their arms to the great spirit in honor of the dead.

The tribe hosts its Annual Contest Powwow during the third weekend in August. The tribe also hosts rodeos and other powwows, mostly during the summer.

INFRASTRUCTURE
The reservation is located just west of the junction of Highways 18 and 22 and east of U.S. Coastal Highway 101.

Electricity. Regional utilities and local distributors supply electricity and gas service. The electrical power and gas mains to the Oregon Coast extend through tribal lands from the valley.

Water Supply. Water and sewer plants to serve the casino were constructed by the tribe. It has also participated in the improvement of the municipal water system, including water source and storage sites. The tribe has contributed to the construction of a 500,000 gallon reservoir and various projects to improve services within the community. It is also working with Polk and Yamhill counties on the development of long-term regional water resources.

Transportation. Commercial air service is available in Portland. Commercial truck lines serve the community of Grand Ronde. Commercial bus lines serve nearby McMinnville. The tribe participates as a member of the Mid-Willamette Area Commission on Transportation to review and prioritize regionally significant transportation projects for state and federal funding allocation.

COMMUNITY FACILITIES AND SERVICES
A tribal community center features a meeting room, kitchen, and offices. The facilities are available for community functions. A newly completed gym with a weight room, stage area, and bleachers is also housed on the reservation. The Grand Ronde Tribal Library is housed in the adult education building and offers an extensive selection of materials for all ages.

In addition to adult language classes, the tribe's cultural resources department offers an immersion program in Chinuk, the primary language of the tribe, for preschool students. It is also in the process of creating an immersion program for students in grades K-4. Classes are available in traditional beading, carving, drum making, and basketry. The department also maintains cultural site and cultural collection programs.

Education. Tribal youth attend public schools in the Willamina School District. Willamina is located about seven miles east of Grand Ronde. Approximately one-fifth of the student population of the district is Native American, while about half of the student population in the community of Grand Ronde is Native American.

The tribal government's education division provides a broad range of educational services. The tribe operates a Head Start program in conjunction with a Child Care Development Fund Program. The tribal linguist conducts an immersion program in the Chinuk language at Head Start. The curriculum includes introduction to tribal traditions and cultural practices. The tribe provides individual, classroom, and small-group tutoring sessions to K?5 students attending the Willamina or Sheridan school districts. It also offers an after-school program in the Willamina schools. The program offers cultural activities, arts and crafts, gym activities, snacks or lunch, outdoor activities, and tutoring. It is open to Native students when the public schools are closed due to weather, vacations, or in-service. The tribe's youth education program offers students in grades 6-12 tutoring services, a Native American club, culture classes, and recreational activities. It also sponsors the Achievement and Recognition Program and the Summer Youth Employment Program.

The tribe operates an adult education program that offers GED preparation, typing instruction, computer-based instructional programs, and classes that increase basic academic and life skills. The higher education program offers educational opportunities to the membership in both part-time and full-time programs. The short-term training program provides funding for tuition, books, and fees to students seeking to enhance job skills, cultural knowledge, professional development, and personal skills though classes, seminars, workshops, conferences, and apprenticeships. Financial assistance is available to part-time students through the tribe's Continuing and Distance Education Program. Aid is available to full-time students through the adult vocational training and higher education programs. Scholarships are available to vocational education, undergraduate, and graduate students.

Health care. Medical, optometry, mental health, pharmacy, chiropractic, acupuncture, and dental services are available to tribal members at the Grand Ronde Health and Wellness Center, located in Grand Ronde. Additionally, the tribe provides tribal members with the tribal member health plan, a private health insurance plan. Coverage extends to all tribal members, on- and off-reservation.

ENVIRONMENTAL CONCERNS
The Grand Ronde were not afforded traditional hunting and fishing rights for their ceded lands at the time of restoration in 1983. Hunting and fishing is governed by the State of Oregon, and tribal members must adhere to all rules governing such activities. The tribe conducts an annual lottery for bear, deer, and elk hunting tags, but the tags can only be used within the Trask Management Unit. The lottery is open to tribal members over the age of 12.

In 1999, the upper Willamette River winter steelhead and spring Chinook salmon were placed on the threatened species list. In 2000, the tribe completed a Unified Watershed Assessment. Findings indicated that clean water and habitat restorations were needed immediately in South Yamhill River, North Fork Agency Creek, Mainstream Agency Creek, Coast Creek, and West Fork Agency Creek. The tribe has worked in partnership with state and federal agencies to resolve the critical issues affecting these watersheds. As a result of the addition of anadromous fish species in the South Yamhill River Basin to the threatened species list, the state Department of Fish and Wildlife has designated Coast Creek and Agency Creek as "catch and release" streams. The tribe is also addressing the wildlife health and habitat and assisting in the efforts to restore these species. The tribe is also currently helping to clean up the Portland Harbor Superfund site. The site is located on the tribe's ceded lands.

Intergovernmental Affairs Department, The Confederated Tribes of Grand Ronde (Grand Ronde, Oregon)

The Grand Ronde Intergovernmental Affairs Department has achieved positive intergovernmental relationships by pursuing a five-pronged strategy of communication, education, cooperation, contributions and presence. By establishing a department whose primary function is to interact with other governments on a government-to-government basis and by locating it in Salem, the capital of Oregon, the Tribe has solidified its recognition as a sovereign with federal, state, local and other tribal governments.

Interaction with other sovereign governments is a fundamental function of tribal government, and the capacity to fulfill this responsibility is a necessary attribute of self-determination. Perhaps no tribal government appreciates this more than that of the Confederated Tribes of the Grand Ronde (CTGR). Today, the 5,000-citizen nation is a political and economic powerhouse in the Northwest, but this has not always been the case. As a result of the U.S. government's "termination" policy, which was a formal attempt by the Congress to end the special relationship between the government and the tribes, in 1954, the Confederated Tribes were stripped of their political sovereignty and control over their land base. This was the darkest period in the Tribes' history, and the U.S. government did not recognize their existence again until 1983.

Upon re-affirmation of their sovereign status, the CTGR faced the critical task of nation-building. Having endured 29 years of termination, a central part of this task was to produce internal governing capacity. That is, the Tribes needed to develop an effective government bureaucracy and organize government programs that would help meet tribal citizens' most pressing socio-economic needs. At the same time, the CTGR's leaders realized that nation-building required investments in external capacity. They knew that strong ties with outside jurisdictions would both establish the legitimacy of the CTGR with other governmental authorities and help protect the sovereignty that they had fought so hard to re-establish. Thus, throughout the 1980s and 1990s, the Tribes positioned themselves as a key actor in local, regional, state and federal policy affairs. In 1997, the CTGR took their commitment to enhancing external government relations to an even higher level by creating a new government institution to oversee external relations - the Grand Ronde Intergovernmental Affairs Department.

The Intergovernmental Affairs Department's overarching responsibility is to interact with other jurisdictions and to facilitate Grand Ronde's government-to-government relationships. The Department works to raise public awareness, build coalitions, inform tribal, state and federal legislation, and engage in public sector partnerships on behalf of the Confederated Tribes of Grand Ronde. A five-pronged strategy of communication, education, cooperation, contribution and presence guides the Department's specific initiatives and activities in each of these areas.

The Intergovernmental Affairs Department is directly staffed by two tribal employees. Their work is complemented by the efforts of skilled outside professionals who are employed on a contract basis (in particular, the Department engages a lobbying group and a public relations firm). Together, the tribal employees and contractors comprise a unique "legislative team," whose substantial knowledge of both tribal and non-

tribal government improves the Department's problem-solving capabilities and results in an increased flow of information between the CTGR and other governments. Through teamwork, the Department is able to produce and distribute a wealth of educational material about the Tribes to policymakers and the public, and reach out to and support important non-tribal institutions and individuals, thus creating allies and partners for the CTGR. An impressive example of these efforts involves candidates for the Oregon State Legislature. The Department invites every candidate to tour the Grand Ronde Reservation, meet tribal leaders, and interact with tribal members. If the candidates become legislators, they have a better vision of how their decisions affect the Tribes.

The sophistication of Grand Ronde's strategy and organizational approach is especially evident in their efforts to respond to and influence state and federal legislation. The Department uses a legislative tracking system to monitor bills and initiatives that could affect the Tribes' jurisdiction and presents a categorized list to the Tribal Council every two weeks. Council members rank the listed items in order of policy priority and turn the information around to the Intergovernmental Affairs staff, who then work with the Council's five-member Legislative Committee to craft specific strategies for addressing these key external legislative initiatives. The system keeps the Council well informed, allows them to concentrate resources on high priority issues and results in targeted, proactive advocacy. Equally advantageous for state legislation is the fact that the Intergovernmental Affairs Department is headquartered in Salem, the capital of Oregon. Being physically in the midst of this fast-paced legislative environment helps ensure that Grand Ronde's intergovernmental affairs representatives can provide substantive input in a timely manner. The results of the Department's work are remarkable. As its leaders predicted 20 years ago, carefully tended external relations have shored up the CTGR's sovereignty and leveled the playing field in the nation's interactions with other governments. At the state level, which is undoubtedly the arena of Grande Ronde's greatest success, the number of bills emerging from the Oregon State Legislature that the Tribes viewed as potentially damaging dropped from 19 in 1997 to only 3 in 1999. Tribal leaders visiting government offices on official business are no longer treated as ordinary Oregon citizens with requests for services, but as representatives of a respected independent government. Similarly, the state government increasingly views the CTGR as a partner in the resolution of important regional issues, which is an important win in this era of federal devolution. Grand Ronde's collaboration with the Oregon Department of Environmental Quality in the successful and publicly acclaimed Portland Harbor Cleanup is but one noteworthy example of such partnerships.

In addition to enhancing relationships with state authorities, the Intergovernmental Affairs Department has succeeded in promoting better relationships with the federal government and with other tribal governments. For instance, on June 9, 1999, the CTGR entered into a Collaborative Stewardship Agreement with the U.S. Forest Service. This joint forest management arrangement, which recognizes the technical and administrative expertise of the Grand Ronde government and its staff, is a direct result of the Department's efforts. The Intergovernmental Affairs Department's success in building fruitful inter-tribal relationships is evident in the fact that, when

Text in its entirety from: The Harvard Project On American Indian Economic Development

John F. Kennedy School of Government Harvard University

Grand Ronde

charting their own interactions with the State of Oregon, other tribes draw on the Department's expertise. Likewise, members of the Oregon Legislative Commission on Indian Services have noted that the Grande Ronde Intergovernmental Affairs Department has been a great benefit to all Oregon-based tribes.

The reasons for the Grand Ronde Intergovernmental Affairs Department's success are varied and instructive. Critically, the Department works with the Tribal Council to prioritize issues and then concentrates its financial and personnel resources on those priorities. In all of its activities, the Department consciously abides by its strategy, which is designed to both influence the short term (especially through well-placed community and political contributions) and to change minds over the long term (especially through its education and outreach work). Finally, the Department is successful because its staff studies and uses recognized techniques for political communication.

In creating the Intergovernmental Affairs Department, the Confederated Tribes of Grand Ronde chose an innovative approach to dealing with other governments, surrounding communities and the general public - and the choice has paid off. The Department's educational campaign, increased public relations efforts and more effective communication with other governments have not only put the CTGR on an equal footing with other governments operating in the region, but also helped re-establish the Confederated Tribes of Grand Ronde as a self-governing sovereign.

Lessons:

· Tribal governments stand to improve their intergovernmental relationships by coordinating and prioritizing public relations messages and concentrating tribal resources on top issues.

· Tribal governments can increase their credibility by forging strong partnerships with other governments. The devolution of responsibilities from the federal government to state governments increases the opportunities for and the necessity of tribal collaboration with subnational governments.

· A legislative tracking system that monitors all bills and initiatives that could affect tribal governments can be a powerful tool for decision makers in Indian Country.

lamath

Klamath Reservation
Federal reservation
Klamath, Modoc, and
Yahooskin
Klamath County, Oregon

The Klamath Tribes
501 Chiloquin Blvd.
P.O. Box 436
Chiloquin, OR 97624
541-783-2219
541-783-2029 Fax
klamathtribes.org

Total area *(BIA realty, 2004)*
556.24 acres

Tribally owned
(BIA realty, 2004)
556.24 acres

Tribal enrollment *(BIA, 1999)*
3,320

Tribal enrollment
(Tribal source, 2004)
2,882

LOCATION AND LAND STATUS

The Klamath Reservation presently covers 372 acres of land in the south-central part of Oregon, near Upper Klamath Lake. Once an enormous span of land, which included vast timber reserves, the reservation was greatly diminished after the Klamath Termination Act was passed in 1954, eventually dwindling to its current size. The tribe is presently seeking approximately 692,000 acres of land from the federal government to be transferred from the Winema and Fremont national forests.

CULTURE AND HISTORY

The Klamath Tribes is composed of members of the Klamath Tribe, Modoc Tribe, and Yahooskin Band of Snake River Indian Tribe. The tribes' ancestral lands encompassed northwestern regions of the United States, including present-day south-central Oregon, north-central California, and parts of Nevada and Idaho. Their homelands included approximately 22 million acres. Because of their interior location, the tribes were able to avoid the region's white settlers until relatively late in the contact period. Hence, the Klamaths escaped the great epidemics that victimized most tribes in the wake of European contact. Moreover, their history is not marred by a pattern of violent confrontations with white settlers. Their first Euro-American contact came with Hudson's Bay Company traders in 1826, who pronounced them "a happy people." Eventually they obtained guns and horses from the traders, but for the most part the tribe relied on hunting, fishing, and gathering.

On October 14, 1864, the Klamath, Modoc, and Yahooskin tribes signed a treaty that ceded 19,500,000 acres of high, semiarid land east of the Cascade Mountains to the U.S. government. In return for signing the treaty, the Klamaths retained rights to approximately 1,196,126 acres to establish their reservation. The tribes became collectively known as the Klamath Tribes. Disputes over land rights and government surveys mark much of the tribe's subsequent history. At least two of these disputes in the early part of the twentieth century were settled by the U.S. Supreme Court, with the court finding in the tribe's favor on each occasion. Unlike other tribes, the Klamaths were allowed to retain rights to nonallotted, or "tribal surplus" lands; this allowed them to retain large stands of valuable timber, which later became an important source of tribal income.

By the mid-1950s, the Klamath Tribes was the second wealthiest tribe in the United States. It was targeted for termination by the Termination Act of 1954 and was formally terminated that year. The termination resulted in the loss of tribal land and federal recognition, then the Act forced tribal members to either withdraw from the tribe and receive their share of tribal assets, or remain with the tribe and have their claim to the unsold portion of the reservation placed under private trust. In 1958, the vast majority of members voted to withdraw from the tribe. In order to pay them their shares, the federal government sold most of the 880,000 acres of land; 620,000 acres were transferred to the U.S. Forest Service, 125,000 acres were sold to private parties, and 135,000 acres were transferred to the U.S. Bank of Oregon. In 1971 those Klamath Tribes members who had not withdrawn their share of tribal assets requested the removal of the private trustee. The trustee determined this to be a request for liquidation of the assets and returned the fee title to the federal government. The lands were transferred to the U.S. Forest Service.

Nevertheless, Klamath identity remained vital. Despite the process of termination, the tribe maintained their hunting, fishing, and gathering rights as agreed upon in the treaty of 1864. However, the State of Oregon refused to recognize these rights, and tribal members were harassed and often arrested. In 1972, five tribal members filed suit against the state. A federal circuit court upheld their rights. The tribe also regained its rights to the water of the Klamath Marsh Wildlife Refuge.

In 1986 the Klamath Tribes regained its federally recognized status under the provisions of the Klamath Restoration Act, PL 99-398. During the twentieth century, the region's economy has been based largely on timber, grazing, and agriculture. With termination, the tribe lost its land base and its lucrative timber reserves. With reinstatement, the tribe has once again

TRI-OR-012

TRI-OR-014

TRI-OR-011

TRI-OR-013

Klamath

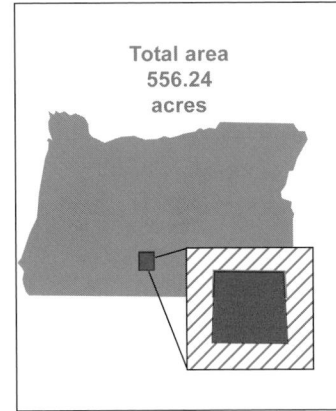

Total area
556.24
acres

become eligible for federal funds and the services of the BIA. In addition, reinstatement has brought about a revitalization of traditional practices, including the translation of books into the Penutian language and a renewed emphasis on traditional crafts, ceremonies, and religion.

GOVERNMENT

The tribe is organized according to its 1953 constitution. A general council consists of all enrolled adult members of the tribe. The general council elects a 10-member tribal council, which governs the tribe. The tribal council is comprised of a chairman, a vice-chairman, a secretary, a treasurer, and six council members. These members are elected to three-year terms.

The tribe contracts with the federal government to run its own personnel, education and employment, finance, support services, public information and Klamath news, legal, community services, records management, health and family services, social services, housing, planning and economic development, culture and heritage, enrollment, water attorney, and natural resources programs. The tribe operates its own judicial system with a law enforcement agency and tribal court. The court maintains jurisdiction over civil matters such as child welfare.

The tribe maintains the Economic Self-Sufficiency Plan (ESSP) Core Team. It is comprised of past tribal council chairmen, current council members, consulting agencies, key individuals, and staff. The team meets to discuss plans for the tribe's future and to further its goal of achieving economic self-sufficiency. The tribe's ESSP outlines the policies to be considered and implemented as it moves toward economic independence. It addresses cultural, economic, environmental, educational, health, housing, and political issues to guide the tribe.

BUSINESS CORPORATION

In 1995, the general council approved the Klamath Tribes' Economic Development Corporation . The 10-member corporation became a business arm of the Klamath Tribes to further the quest to develop profits, stimulate the local economy, create employment, and strive for economic self-sufficiency.

The corporation also offers advice, financial capabilities, business management, and other business skills when requested by the tribal government.

ECONOMY

Since termination rendered the tribe virtually landless, the tribal economy has understandably faced strenuous challenges. The tribe sees the current period as a rebuilding phase and is pursuing ideas for development with great vigor. The tribe operates the Kla-Mo-Ya Casino. There are plans to expand the casino and to possibly build a destination resort including a hotel and an RV park.

Government as Employer. The tribe employs approximately 295 people in tribal administration, tribal health and family services, the casino, and the Gaming Regulatory Commission.

Economic Development Projects. The tribe has established the Klamath Tribes Economic Development Corporation to aid in planning their future commercial ventures. Future development projects include a convenience store and truck stop on the reservation, and an interpretive center.

The tribe is working on its economic self-sufficiency plan, the final phase of the congressionally mandated process set forth in the Klamath Restoration Act. The act requires the tribe to show how it will achieve self-determination and economic self-sufficiency and independence.

The Klamath Tribes business information center offers technical assistance to tribal members starting a small business or enhancing the services of a current business. The center offers training sessions and regular courses on business plan development, business operations and management, microlending, and basic computer skills. The tribe is particularly proud of the assistance offered to women of the tribe through the Office of Women Business Ownership for developing individual, joint partnership, and group home-based businesses. The center works directly with the Oregon Native American Business and Entrepreneurial Network. It also works with a host of state and federal agencies, including the Oregon State Office of Minority, Women, and Emerging Small Business.

TRI-OR-012 Front View of the Klamath Tribal Administration Building

TRI-OR-014 Sign for Kla-Mo-Ya Casino off of Highway 97

TRI-OR-011 Cemented Seal of the Klamath Tribes in Park outside Tribal Building

TRI-OR-013 Mural in Reception area of Tribal Administration Building

Total labor force *2000 census*
0

Total labor force *(BIA, 1999)*
2,054

High school graduate or higher
2000 census
0%

Bachelor's degree or higher
2000 census
0%

Unemployment rate *(BIA, 1999)*
41%

Per capita income *2000 census*
$9,600

Klamath

ENVIRONMENTAL CONCERNS

The tribe has filed suit against the PacifiCorps Company. The tribe is seeking in excess of $1 billion compensations for the abrogation of treaty rights and the destruction of traditional fishing grounds caused by the construction of dams on the Klamath River. The dams were built in the early 1900s without the tribes' consent. Since the restoration of federal recognition in the 1980s, the tribe has endeavored to regain its tribal lands and rights to the natural resources contained within them. The tribe recognizes the inability of the U.S. Forest Service and the State of Oregon to appropriately manage the resources on former tribal lands. The tribe sued the U.S. Forest Service to attain restoration of adjudicated rights in the management of the forests, and it continues to fight for restoration of its rights to water, lands, and other natural resources that it was forced to relinquish as a result of the Termination Act of 1954.

Agriculture and Livestock. The Farm Service Agency provides loans to tribal youth so they may establish and operate income-producing projects. The projects must be organized through a program such as Future Farmers of America or a 4-H club.

Forestry. Though diminished due to over-logging and environmental concerns, the timber industry remains a significant factor in the region's economy. The tribe is currently developing a tribal forest management plan to oversee the management of tribal woodlands.

Gaming. The Kla-Mo-Ya Casino opened in the summer of 1997. The 16,000-square-foot facility, designed as a mountain lodge, sits 22 miles north of Klamath Falls, at the juncture of Highway 97 and Crater Lake Highway. It offers 313 slot machines and 6 blackjack tables. In 2000 and 2004, new slot machines were added. Games offer prizes of over a million dollars. There also are a deli, a buffet, a gift shop, and a video game arcade. Free shuttle transportation is available to casino guests. The tribe is currently in the process of expanding the facility. The casino has grown steadily and provides jobs for about 150 people. Of these, more than 50 percent are members of the Klamath or other tribes.

The casino contributes to the economy of Klamath County by purchasing goods and services for its daily operations. The casino donates thousands of dollars annually to charities, service agencies, youth groups, schools, and local events. The tribe has used proceeds from gaming to pay off its casino debt.

Media and Communications. The tribe publishes *Klamath News*, a monthly newspaper.

Tourism and Recreation. The proximity of Crater Lake National Park, just up Highway 62 from the reservation, offers a solid base of potential visitors. The tribe's Kla-Mo-Ya Casino is located near Crater Lake and the Williamson River, which offers fishing and hunting. It also boasts a variety of winter sports, including skiing and snowmobile trails in the Oregon forestlands and the scenic beauty of the Cascade Mountain Range.

The tribe hosts several annual events that are open to the public. The Restoration Celebration, which is held in August, commemorates the restoration of federal recognition to the tribes in 1986. Events include a rodeo, a competition powwow, arts and crafts, a fun run, a softball tournament, a parade, and vendors. In addition to the Restoration Celebration, the tribe hosts a New Year's Eve Powwow, the Peak-to-Peak World Championship Men's and Women's Basketball Tournament, the Return of C'waam Ceremony, and the Southern Oregon Memorial Day Rodeo and Powwow.

INFRASTRUCTURE

Highway 97, a major north-south route, passes by the reservation and through Chiloquin. Highway 62 branches off from Highway 97 near Chiloquin and heads up through Crater Lake National Park.

Electricity. Pacific Power supplies electricity.

Water Supply. The City of Chiloquin provides water and sewage services to the reservation.

Transportation. The Chiloquin Airport and an airport at Klamath Falls serve the reservation. The Union Pacific Railroad connects to the reservation. In 2003, the tribe completed its transportation improvement plan to obtain additional funding from the federal highway funds through the BIA. The plan addressed 83 miles of improved reservation roads. Greyhound buslines service the reservation, as do UPS and FedEx.

COMMUNITY FACILITIES AND SERVICES

The tribe offers several community programs, including the tribal work assistance program, the family support center, the senior's nutrition project, and a child care program. There also are a summer culture camp and a summer sports camp for tribal youth, an all-Indian basketball tournament, and language classes. In addition, youngsters participate in the annual C'waam Ceremony in March, and the annual Restoration Celebration Powwow, rodeo, parade, and fun run the fourth weekend in August.

Education. Children attend school at Chiloquin elementary, junior, and senior high schools. The tribe's education and employment department offers an adult basic education program and a higher education and adult vocational training program. The department also manages the Maqlaqs Sayooga Center, which offers tutoring and homework and math assistance. Cultural and language courses are available through the culture and heritage department.

Klamath Community College was established in 1996 and offers two-year associate of applied science degrees in business and management, information technology, health services, plus educational services, criminal justice, natural resource systems, technical studies and the associate of arts Oregon transfer, which meets the lower division general education requirements of Oregon universities. Certificate programs are available in accounting, management, marketing and sales, educational assistant, child care provider, EMT, home health, medical office, criminal justice, corrections, and technical studies. There is a scholarship program, and community education, developmental education, and high school completion courses.

Health Care. The Klamath Tribes Health and Family Services Department houses medical, dental, and community health education programs. The contract health services program provides medical services to tribal members as a supplement to personal insurance plans or those without health insurance. The Klamath Tribes dental clinic provides comprehensive services to tribal members. The health education program provides a monthly newsletter and regular workshops and classes regarding community health. A pharmacy, public nursing program, and patient transportation services are also available. All programs are located at health and family services offices in Klamath Falls. The Klamath Tribes Medical Clinic in Chiloquin provides comprehensive outpatient services.

The Klamath Community Health Center is an adult residential treatment program. It is not funded by the tribe but is operated by the tribe's alcohol and drug abuse program. It is open to tribal and non-tribal clients. The behavioral health department provides counseling and treatment of substance abuse and mental health issues. It sponsors a number of support groups, including women's anger management, juvenile sexual offender, parenting, and domestic violence prevention.

LOCATION AND LAND STATUS

The Siletz Reservation is situated on 4,580 noncontiguous acres in the lush, damp coastal mountains of western Oregon. These tribal lands predominantly lie within Lincoln County, Oregon. Thirty-five acres are located in Marion County, Oregon. However, the Confederated Tribes of Siletz serve a tribal population throughout an 11-county area in western Oregon. The Town of Siletz, located along the north-south-running State Highway 229, serves as the tribal headquarters.

The federal government terminated its trust relationship with the Siletz Tribe in 1954. President Jimmy Carter restored the tribe's legal status on November 18, 1977. Congress returned 3,629 acres into trust status for the tribe in 1981 and another 350 acres in 1994. The tribe has purchased some 600 additional acres. The tribe has made land acquisition a priority and actively seeks opportunities to increase its land base.

PHYSICAL DESCRIPTION

The noncontiguous reservation consists of approximately 190 acres of commercial lands, 585 acres of cultural and natural resources land, 40 acres of tribal government lands, 3,600 acres of forested land, and 160 acres of housing land for a total of 4,575 acres, predominantly located in Lincoln County (35 acres are in Marion County). The commercial, government, and housing land is located in or in close proximity to the cities of Siletz, Lincoln City, and Salem. The timber harvested is generally 130-140 years old and consists of Douglas fir, western red cedar, western hemlock, Sitka spruce, red alder, and big leaf maple. The reservation is located 135 feet above sea level.

CLIMATE

The average rainfall on the reservation is 74.6 inches. The annual temperature averages between 43°F and 56°F.

CULTURE AND HISTORY

Members of the Confederated Tribes of Siletz Indians of Oregon are descendants of approximately 25 tribes that once inhabited regions extending from the western portion of present-day Oregon to the Klamath River in northern California. Their traditional lands encompassed an estimated 20 million acres. Among these tribes were the Rogue River, Umpqua, Calapooia, Chasta, Scoton, Kalapuya, and Molalla. At least eight separate language groups existed among these tribes, as well as a variety of subsistence patterns. Coastal tribes fished extensively, while tribes of the Willamette Valley were fishers and hunter-gatherers.

During the 1840s, an influx of Euro-American settlers into western Oregon Territory prompted the federal government to sign treaties with a number of tribes in the area. Seven of these treaties were ratified. Six of these treaties ceded the entire area between the summits of the Cascade Mountains and the Coast Range in western Oregon, including the Willamette, Umpqua, and Rogue valleys. The seventh treaty gained the Rogue Valley Tribe's consent to share their reservation and be formally confederated with other tribes in the future. Under the ratified treaties, the tribes retained the right to stay on temporary reservations within their ceded lands until the President of the United States selected a permanent reservation. The coastal tribes signed a treaty in August and September 1855. However, the Senate Committee unintentionally failed to ratify the Coast Treaty signed by General Palmer in 1855.

In spite of ratified treaties that gave the president the power and responsibility to create a permanent reservation, the unratified Coast Treaty was used as a primary justification to reduce the Coast Reservation. President Franklin Pierce signed an Executive Order on November 9, 1855, removing both coastal and interior tribes to a coastal reservation containing some 1,440,000 acres. The Oregon Donation Land Act opened the tribal lands to the public. By 1875, the tribes retained only 225,000 acres of the lands they were originally designated. In 1892, lands were allotted to reservation members under the provisions of the General Allotment Act, reducing the reservation by another 192,000 acres. By 1954, only 3,200 acres of Siletz Reservation land remained in tribal ownership.

In 1956, under the provisions of the Western Oregon Termination Act of 1954, the United States terminated its trust relationship with the Siletz Confederation of Tribes, effectively closing the reservation. Tribal assets and individual trust property were dissolved. In 1973, members of the Siletz Confederation of Tribes filed as a nonprofit organization. The organization's first goal was to retain control of the Paul Washington Cemetery and to offer alcohol rehabilitation and social services to tribal members. The tribe eventually regained full federal recognition under PL 95-195. It was the first tribe to gain recognition in Oregon under the law, and only the second in the country.

GOVERNMENT

The Confederated Tribes of Siletz Indians of Oregon drafted a constitution upon the tribes' restoration in 1977. This constitution calls for a three-tiered tribal government consisting of a nine-member popularly elected tribal council, a general council, and an eight-member tribal court. Tribal council elections occur annually with members serving three-year terms. The tribal court is staffed by a chief judge, an appellate judge, a district court judge, a gaming court judge, a community court judge, two judges pro tempore, a court administrator, and a deputy clerk. The tribal court system operates under PL-638.

BUSINESS CORPORATION

The Siletz Tribal Business Corporation (STBC) was chartered in 2002 to oversee economic development and to manage tribal economic enterprises. STBC operates the Siletz Tribal Smoke House in Depoe Bay that sells fresh seafood and traditionally smoked salmon and tuna. The tribe dissolved the Siletz Tribal Economic Development Corporation, a former business management corporation, in 1998.

ECONOMY

The tribe's economy is primarily supported by profits generated by the Chinook Winds Casino Resort and Hotel. The tribe itself is the largest employer in Lincoln County, with over 800 individuals employed through its various enterprises, departments, and programs.

Government as Employer. The Siletz Tribe employs approximately 865 persons on a permanent basis. During powwows or other special occasions, the tribe will employ up to 20 temporary employees. The tribe is the largest employer in Lincoln County.

Forestry. The Siletz Reservation Forest Resource Management Plan calls for harvest of 1.74 million board feet (MMBF)

Siletz Reservation
Confederated Tribes of Siletz
** Indians of Oregon**
Lincoln and Marion counties,
Oregon

Confederated Tribes of Siletz
Indians of Oregon
P.O. Box 549
Siletz, OR 97380
800-922-1399
541-444-2307 Fax
ctsi.nsn.us

Total area *(BIA realty, 2004)*
4,250.68 acres

Tribally owned *(BIA realty, 2004)*
4,107.9 acres

Allotted/Individually owned
(BIA realty, 2004)
142.78 acres

Population *2000 census*
308

Tribal enrollment
(Tribal source, 2004)
4,077

Total labor force *2000 census*
122

High school graduate or higher
2000 census
72.2%

High school graduate or higher
(Tribal source, 2004)
40.0%

Bachelor's degree or higher
2000 census
7.1%

Bachelor's degree or higher
(Tribal source, 2004)
7%

Unemployment rate *2000 census*
10.7%

Unemployment *(Tribal source, 2004)*
25%

Per capita income *2000 census*
$10,877

Siletz

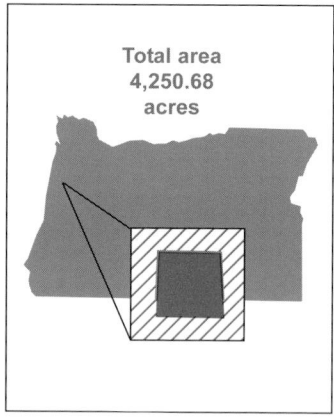

Total area
4,250.68
acres

TRI-OR-015

TRI-OR-019

TRI-OR-016

TRI-OR-018

TRI-OR-015 Front view of the Siletz Tribal Building

TRI-OR-019 Siletz Tribal Business Corporation sign

TRI-OR-016 Siletz Gas & Mini Mart

TRI-OR-018 Tepees at Annual Nesika Illahee Pow-Wow

of conifer timber each year from 1999-2005 and 1.86 MMBF each year from 2006-2010. The timber harvested is generally 130-140 years old and consists of Douglas fir, western red cedar, western hemlock, Sitka spruce, red alder, and big leaf maple. The tribe's timber rotation age is currently 80 years.

Gaming. The Siletz Tribe owns and operates Chinook Winds Casino Resort and Hotel, a class III gaming facility located on the reservation's Pacific Ocean waterfront. The casino offers over 1,200 slot machines, keno, bingo, craps, roulette, blackjack, and poker. This two-story structure encompasses some 157,000 square feet of space. Amenities include a restaurant, lounge, buffet, deli, child care center, game arcade, and gift shop. Facilities also include a convention center and showroom. The tribe provides shuttle service for casino guests. The tribe purchased the adjoining hotel in 2004. Chinook Winds Hotel is located on oceanfront property and offers 247 guest rooms. There are an indoor pool, a sauna, a spa, a laundromat, a restaurant, and a lounge. There is also 7,000 square feet of conference space. This operation employs approximately 765 people. The casino's revenue has enabled the tribe to offer $1.7 million in charitable contributions and $450,000 in donations since the casino's inception in 1995.

Fisheries. The tribe operates the Nesika Illahee fishery. It is a nonprofit operation that works toward stabilizing the fish population in the Siletz River and its tributaries. In cooperation with the Oregon Department of Fish and Wildlife, tribal members continue to participate in the traditional harvesting of lamprey eel at Willamette Falls. Although the population of eels has declined dramatically over the years, the state recognizes the significance of the harvest to tribal traditions and nutrition.

Construction. The tribe contracts construction services from privately owned companies. The tribe awards contracts to the lowest qualified bidder and gives tribal preference.

Manufacturing. The tribe owns a 72-acre industrial site in Toledo, Oregon. It is currently predominantly idle. Presently, the tribe leases approximately five acres to a privately owned business that recycles tires to produce fishnet weights.

Media and Communications. The tribe publishes the *Siletz News*, a monthly newspaper.

Services and Retail. The tribe operates the Siletz Gas and Mini Mart off the reservation and the Siletz Tribal Smokehouse located in Depoe Bay.

Tourism and Recreation. The Siletz Tribal Cultural Center houses tribal artifacts and historical documents. It provides instruction in Athbaskan, the indigenous language. The tribe also owns the Logan Road RV Park, a 250-space RV park adjacent to the Chinook Winds Casino in Lincoln City, and the Toledo Riverfront Property, a 72-acre industrial site. Local tourist attractions include the Lakeside Golf Club and the Tanger Outlet Center, both located in Lincoln City.

The Siletz Reservation is located near some of the country's most scenic recreation areas. U.S. Highway 101 traces the Oregon coast, passing within 15 miles of the reservation. The Siletz River features some of the finest fishing in western Oregon. The tribe organizes annual deer and elk hunts for tribal members. The hunts are available by lottery, and tribal members over 18 are eligible to apply.

The Siletz Tribe holds three annual powwows. Thousands come to the reservation annually during the second week in August for the Nesika Illahee Powwow, which features competition dancing and tribal arts and crafts. Another powwow every November celebrates tribal restoration. The tribe also holds a Clean and Sober Powwow every New Year's.

INFRASTRUCTURE

The Siletz Reservation is located on State Highway 229 near its junction with U.S. Highway 20, which runs east-west from Newport to Corvallis, Oregon. Highway 229 is currently the only route between Siletz and the nearest town. Safety improvements to Highway 229 are a high priority to the tribe, as described in the Siletz Tribal Improvement Program. In 2004, the tribe constructed a public access road, which facilitated the extension of telephone, gas, and fiber-optic services to eastern Siletz. Scenic Highway 101 lends access to the Chinook Winds Casino.

TRI-OR-017

TRI-OR-020

Electricity. CPI and Consumer's Power provide electricity to the reservation.

Fuel. NW provides natural gas service to the eastern region of Siletz and to Lincoln City tribal holdings.

Water Supply. The cities of Siletz, Lincoln, and Salem own and operate the water and sewer system used by the Siletz Reservation. The cities provide water to a storage tank that serves the reservation's water needs. The tribe contributes to the improvement funds necessary for maintaining the system.

Transportation. The tribe provides shuttle service between the cities of Siletz and Lincoln City. Commercial airline service is available at Portland International Airport (150 miles northeast) and Eugene Airport (90 miles southeast). Bus service is available via Central Coast Connections, which makes three daily runs from Siletz to Toledo to Newport. Valley Coast Retriever operates from Bend, Oregon, to Newport. Greyhound buslines also operate out of Newport (approximately 15 miles from Siletz). Major trucking lines, as well as UPS and FedEx, service the region through Newport. An industrial railway serves Toledo (approximately 8 miles from Siletz). Amtrak service is available in Albany, Oregon (80 miles east). The Siletz River winds through the Siletz Reservation. Two port districts are in the proximity of the Siletz Reservation: the Port of Toledo and the Port of Newport.

Telecommunications. Qwest provides telephone service to the reservation. Internet access and cable services area also available to the reservation.

COMMUNITY FACILITIES AND SERVICES

The Siletz Tribal Community Center is in the Town of Siletz. It hosts community events, including tribal program activities for youth and elders, funerals and weddings, and council and administrative meetings. In 2002, the tribe constructed the Tenas Ilahee Child Care Center. A youth center provides tutoring services, art activities, recreational activities, and sports programs for tribal youth. The tribe also offers an employment services program, including a youth and elders program. The tribe distributes desktop computers to selected tribal homes.

Education. The tribe is involved in the Siletz Charter School, a K-8-charter school. It currently serves 150 students and employs a faculty of 15. High school students attend Toledo High School. The tribe operates the local Head Start classroom. Oregon Coast Community College, located in Newport, offers post-high school courses and GED programs. The nearest four-year college is Oregon State University in Corvallis (65 miles east). The tribe provides financial assistance to tribal members pursuing higher education or vocational training. The tribe operates a language program and a culture camp for tribal members.

Health Care. The tribe owns and operates the Siletz Community Health Clinic. Available services include comprehensive medical, dental, and optometry programs. The clinic also provides substance abuse treatment, diabetes clinics, and counseling. Services are available to tribal members and their dependents living within the 11-county service area of western Oregon. Most services are available through contract health, a program intended to supplement health care coverage, but due to budget cuts to Indian Health Services, many programs have had to be reduced and service areas limited. Hospital facilities are available in the nearby cities of Newport, Lincoln City, and Salem.

ENVIRONMENTAL CONCERNS

The Siletz Tribe continues to expand its aquatics program, which is focused on monitoring water quality and fish habitat in the Siletz watershed. The tribe also participates in natural resources trustee groups, such as Portland Harbor and Willamette Falls, to protect cultural fisheries and tribal members' health. The tribe is also expanding its cultural and natural resource-based programs to assess air quality in Lincoln County and solid waste management on the reservation.

TRI-OR-017 Tenas Ilahee Childcare Center

TRI-OR-020 Chinook Winds Casino and Convention Center, Confederated Tribes Siletz Indians, Lincoln City, Oregon

Umatilla

Umatilla Indian Reservation
Federal reservation
Cayuse, Umatilla, and Walla Walla
Union and Umatilla Counties, Oregon

Confederated Tribes of the
   Umatilla Indian Reservation
73239 Confederated Way
Pendleton, OR 97801
541-276-3165
541-276-3095 Fax
umatilla.nsn.us

Total area *(BIA realty, 2004)*
86,784.93 acres

Federal trust *(BIA realty, 2004)*
.22 acres

Total area *(Tribal source, 2004)*
172,140 acres

Tribally owned *(BIA realty, 2004)*
18,670.21 acres

Allotted/Individually owned
(BIA realty, 2004)
68,114.50 acres

Population *2000 census*
2,927

Tribal enrollment
(Tribal source, 2004)
2,466

Total labor force *2000 census*
1,387

Total labor force
(BIA labor report, 2001)
1,413

High school graduate or higher
2000 census
84%

Bachelor's degree or higher
2000 census
15.1%

Unemployment rate *2000 census*
7.3%

Unemployment rate
(BIA labor report, 2001)
39%

Per capita income*2000 census*
$15,158

LOCATION AND LAND STATUS

The Umatilla Reservation lies adjacent to the City of Pendleton in northeastern Oregon. It spans a total of nearly 172,140 acres, of which 43,058.08 acres are held in fee and trust status. The remainder comprises allotted land and other land privately held by both non-Indians and tribal members. The Cayuse, Umatilla, and Walla Walla people were initially brought together under the Treaty of 1855, which provided them with a large land base. This territory was later sharply reduced as the government opened much of the land, particularly the rich farmland, to white settlement through an allotment process. The tribes have purchased 1,053.14 acres of trust land and 17,354.3 acres of fee land since 1994.

PHYSICAL DESCRIPTION

Topographically the reservation varies from rolling plains and river valleys to rugged, timbered mountain areas. Elevation ranges from 1,000 to 4,000 feet above sea level.

CULTURE AND HISTORY

The Confederated Tribes of the Umatilla Reservation is comprised of the Cayuse, Umatilla, and Walla Walla tribes. These tribes traditionally resided in the areas of northeastern Oregon and southeastern Washington. The Umatillas lived along the lower reaches of the Umatilla River in what is now northeastern Oregon, and along the banks of the Columbia River on over to the mouth of the Walla Walla River in southeastern Washington. Before acquiring horses in the early 1700s, they depended largely on salmon and other fish for their primary food source. After the introduction of the horse, they became more mobile and often joined the Nez Perce and other bands to hunt bison on the western plains.

In 1848 the Umatillas joined their Cayuse neighbors in fighting a volunteer army of white settlers from the Willamette Valley in the wake of the Whitman Massacre. This became known as the Cayuse War. Essentially all these tensions were the result of the ever-increasing wave of white immigrants spilling off the Oregon Trail into the area. In 1855, the Walla Walla Treaty joined the Umatillas, Cayuses, and Walla Wallas into a confederation that agreed to remove itself to a newly proposed reservation, the site of the current one.

Prior to the advent of wheat cultivation on the reservation, the tribes used their lush grasslands primarily as range for their horses. During the late nineteenth and early twentieth centuries, settlers rounded up many of those horses for slaughter as animal food or for such purposes as pulling trolleys in eastern cities. Partly in response to this repeated encroachment, Congress passed the Slater Act of March 3, 1885. While further reducing the reservation, it did allot a limited amount of land to Indian people. Other Acts of Congress in 1888, 1902, and 1917 allotted additional land to tribal members.

In 1951 the Umatilla Tribes filed four claims against the United States in attempts to reclaim nearly four million acres of land lost in the original 1855 treaty. The Indian Claims Commission, however, found insufficient evidence of aboriginal title by the tribes. In the Celilo Falls settlement, each tribal member received about $3,500 in compensation for lost fishing sites that had been inundated by the Dalles Dam. Other claims have provided the tribes with additional revenue. The region today is still quite agricultural; tribal members lease much of the reservation's tillable land for farming. They have also leased the McNary Dam townsite to a manufacturer of mobile homes. While Catholic and Presbyterian missionaries have had a major impact on the reservation-their influence helping to weaken traditional Native language and culture-as of late a revitalization has been underway, manifesting in a renewed interest in the Seven Drum Religion and other traditional practices.

GOVERNMENT

The tribes operate under a constitution and bylaws adopted in December 1949. The tribal government and all tribal business are administered by a council of nine members, composed of a chairman, a vice-chairman, a secretary, a treasurer, a general council chairman, and four at-large members. Council members are elected by the general council, which consists of all tribal members 18 years of age and older. The tribal government is not organized under the Indian Reorganization Act, since the tribes rejected the 1934 legislation.

The tribal government consists of six major departments, which are further divided into programs and services. Those departments are economic and community development, natural resources, education, public safety, children and family services, and public works. There are three subsidiaries: Umatilla Housing Authority, Yellowhawk Health Clinic, and Wildhorse Casino and Resort. The tribes maintain their own judicial system with a law enforcement agency and court system. They exercise jurisdiction over criminal and civil matters, as well as tribal sovereignty powers as indicated by tribal law. The tribes' law enforcement officers are federally commissioned and state certified. The police department sponsors the Cadet Youth Program, Police Reserve Unit, McGruff Crime Prevention Program, Neighborhood Watch Community Policing Services, DARE Program, an elders program, and a domestic violence prevention program.

Tribal government representatives participate in Oregon state legislative affairs. They provide assistance and advising to staff and lobbyists on issues pertaining to the tribes and to the Native population in Oregon. The tribes' cultural resources protection program received an Outstanding Achievement in Public Education award from the Washington Office of Archaeology and Historic Preservation in 2003. The tribes also received an award from the Honoring Nations Program of the John F. Kenney School of Government at Harvard University. The program provides cultural awareness education to the public as well as to tribal members. The tribes also have successfully filed claims under the Native American Graves Protection and Repatriation Act, and they have facilitated the reburial and stabilization of human remains and burial sites.

BUSINESS COPRORATION

In 2003 the tribes established the Timine Development Corporation, a Section 17 federal corporation approved by the BIA. Timine Development Corporation's first subsidiary will be the Wánapa Energy Center.

ECONOMY

The tribal economy is largely sustained by its agricultural revenue. Leasing lands and enterprises in the gaming industry also generate substantial income for the tribes. The tribal government is a major economic force on the reservation. The tribes employ approximately 11,000 individuals throughout tribally owned businesses and governmental departments and programs.

Government as Employer. The tribes employ approximately 1,100 individuals throughout its governmental departments and business entities.

Economic Development Projects. In partnership with the Port of Umatilla, the City of Hermiston, the Eugene Water and Electric Board, and Diamond Generating, the tribes are developing a 500-1200 mega watt gas-fired Wánapa Energy Center. The tribes have also initiated the environmental planning process for the proposed Coyote Business Park. The center will be the first subsidiary of the Timine Development Corporation.

Agriculture and Livestock. Over 5,000 acres managed by the tribal farm enterprise were leased out in 2003 including: 300 acres of hay, 1,150 acres of wheat, 1,100 acres to the conservation reserve program, 700 acres of summer fallow, 1,100 acres leased to local farmers, and 800 acres of BIA leases for tribal members. The tribes own a commercial grain elevator, built in 1984 through a federal loan, and they lease it to Pendleton Flour Mills. Approximately 55,000 acres of tribally affiliated lands are farmed on the reservation, primarily in dryland wheat and green peas. Virtually all of this is leased out to both Indians and non-Indians. Annual revenues are estimated at $4.5 million.

Forestry. The reservation contains considerable forest reserves, totaling over 83,000 acres. These are mostly red fir, white fir, and pine. Though the area has traditionally relied considerably on the timber industry, a number of timber-related businesses were closed in 1996 due to overcutting and other stresses on the forest. The tribes are currently developing a forest management plan due to be completed in 2005.

Gaming. The Wildhorse Resort and Casino offers guests 650 slot machines, table games, off-track betting, keno, and bingo. The facilities include a child play center, a restaurant, a snack bar, a gift shop, conference halls, and meeting rooms. Adjacent to the casino are a hotel, an RV park, and a golf course. The hotel offers 100 guest rooms, an indoor pool, a whirlpool, a spa, and a meeting room. The Wildhorse RV Park offers a heated pool, free continental breakfast, and a tepee village between April and October. The Wildhorse Golf Course is a championship18-hole course. Facilities include the Clubhouse Grill and a pro shop. The course employs a golf professional.

The Tamástslikt Cultural Institute is also located within the 640-acre site. It features a permanent exhibit on tribal history, an art gallery, a gift shop, a multiuse theater, and a café. The museum has facilities to preserve and store artifacts, photographs, and other archives. The museum participated in the national initiation of the Lewis and Clark Bicentennial Commemoration. It oversaw production of 5,000 beaded buckskin pouches to be sold to the U.S. Mint for the 2004 Commemorative Dollar. The museum produced the Cayuse, Umatilla, and Walla Walla Homeland Heritage Corridor map that is distributed through the Oregon Bureau of Tourism. It also sponsors the annual Salmon Walk, which raises funds for local schools' natural resources curriculums, and the annual salmon expedition.

The tribal government divides revenue from the gaming enterprise among the Wildhorse Foundation and the tribes' general budget. The Wildhorse Foundation, established to distribute charitable donations on the tribes' behalf, provides grant funds to a six-county region in Oregon and Washington.

Fisheries. The Umatilla Basin Project seeks to restore and enhance the salmon runs in the Umatilla and Columbia rivers. The project will add approximately 112,000 salmon to these waters annually and employ several tribal members.

Construction. There are currently three reservation-based construction contractors who provide employment for 30 to 35 tribal members.

Mining. There are several active rock quarries operating on the reservation that generate modest revenues. The tribes lease a number of small gravel and rock pits.

Industrial Parks. The tribes are currently developing a 520-acre industrial park on the reservation.

Real Estate/Commercial Development. The tribes were in the process of constructing a housing subdivision when ancestral human remains were discovered on the site. The project has been temporarily closed. In a separate project, the tribes are working with the Yakima and Warms Springs tribes to redevelop Celilo Village.

Services and Retail. There are a number of tribally based or affiliated businesses. The Mission Market Store, which opened in February 2003, provides full deli, meat market, and grocery amenities. The market is also a Certified Mail Receiving Agency and rents U.S. mailboxes on-site. The market is decorated with tiles created and produced by tribal members in a project that was funded by a $400,000 HUD grant, $175,000

Umatilla

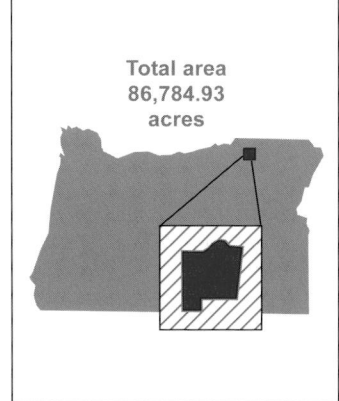

Total area
86,784.93
acres

TRI-OR-022 Umatilla Convenience Store and Fast Food Drive-up

TRI-OR-026 Front view of Wildhorse Resort & Casino

TRI-OR-025 Wildhorse Resort & Casino sign

TRI-OR-022

TRI-OR-026

TRI-OR-025

Umatilla

TRI-OR-024

TRI-OR-028

from the Department of Agriculture Rural Development, and tribal funding.

The tribes also own and operate the Arrowhead Truck Plaza, which was purchased in October 2001. The plaza offers truck supplies and accessories, a business area, fax and copy facilities, Internet access, a lounge, a truck scale, and showers. It boasts annual sales of over $15 million and employs 30 individuals. The tribes own a Charburger Restaurant that employs 24 people and a convenience store. Other individual Indian-owned businesses operating on the reservation include the Wolf Song Fisheries, Raphael's Restaurant and Catering, and Trendy Tootsies.

Crow Shadow's is a separate 501C3 nonprofit organization for artists in the area that coordinates with the tribes, but is not affiliated with the tribes.

Media and Communications. In early 2004, the tribes began operations of KCUB. It is a low-watt radio station, which is limited to national America Indian radio. It employs DJs locally and operates approximately 100 hours a week. The tribes publish the *Confederated Umatilla Journal*, a monthly newspaper. In 2003 the paper received the General Excellence Award from the Native American Journalists Association.

Tourism and Recreation. Lake Hume-Ti-Pin is located in the Indian Lake Recreation Area on the Umatilla Indian Reservation. Between May and September the area is open to campers. During this time, campers have access to public drinking water, 42 campsites, and an RV disposal station. Fishing is permitted with a tribally issued license. The tribes also manage Indian Lake, and they sponsor the annual Indian Lake Fish Derby on Father's Day. The festivities include competitive fishing and activities.

The reservation is located on the Corpse of Discovery Route of 1805-1806 (the Lewis and Clark Expedition Route), and it is included as a point of interest on maps provided to tourists. The tribes also host annual powwows and celebrations that are open to the public.

INFRASTRUCTURE
I-84 proceeds directly through the reservation, while State Highway 11 traverses its northern boundary and State Highway 395 passes very close to its western boundary. The tribes recently upgraded Indian Lake Road on the reservation. They have also developed a road maintenance agreement with Umatilla County.

Electricity. Pacific Power and Light and the Umatilla Electric Cooperative provide electric power.

Fuel. Cascade Natural Gas provides service to portions of the reservation.

Water Supply. The tribes manage the reservation's water system and five wells, and it coordinates with the City of Pendleton on the sewer system. The tribes established a recycling program in 2003. They also purchased a new solid waste truck.

Transportation. The nearest airport, bus, and trucking services are at Pendleton, four miles from the reservation. The Union Pacific Railroad passes through the reservation on an east-west route, with a spur to the grain elevator site. The Port of Umatilla on the Columbia River, 40 miles from the reservation, allows for water access to Portland. UPS services the reservation.

Telecommunications. Charter Communications provides Internet access and cable service to the reservation.

COMMUNITY FACILITIES AND SERVICES
The tribes maintain a full-service community center. Facilities include a gym and a community park. The tribes have a local chapter of the American Legion. Post 140 serves the veterans living on the reservation. The business service center offers tribal members technical assistance as they start small businesses or enhance the services of current businesses. Programs include classes, the American Indian Business Leaders local chapter, the American Indian Business Network, business counseling, a business library, and access to photocopiers, fax machines, and computer systems.

Public Safety. The Umatilla Tribal Fire Department provides fire prevention services, emergency medical services, hazardous material emergency response, and public education to the reservation. The fire department sponsors many activities for tribal youth, including an Easter egg hunt, a Halloween haunted house, and Christmas activities. It also sponsors an annual fundraiser tournament at the Wildhorse Resort Golf Course.

Education. Students primarily attend the Pendleton public schools. The tribes operate the Nixyaawii Charter School on the reservation. It opened in the fall of 2004 and is a contracted school of the Pendleton School District 16R. The school offers a secondary education program that incorporates themes based on Native American values. The tribes offer scholarships to tribal members pursuing postsecondary education. The indigenous languages of the Umatilla, Cayuse, and Walla Walla bands are endangered dialects of the Sahaptin language group. The tribes have established instructional classes in the languages under the department of education. Tribal elders provide instruction.

The tribes' education department houses several programs to serve the community's various educational needs. It offers Head Start, daycare, adult basic education, adult vocational training, language, after school, and summer school programs.

It also operates the continuing education program of Eastern Oregon University, the Johnson O'Malley program, and recreational programs. The department's Even Start Program is a family literacy program that works in collaboration with other departmental programs.

Health Care. The tribally owned Yellowhawk Health Center provides health care. Services include outpatient care, dental, mental health, social services, public health, contract health, laboratory, pharmacy, and health education. The center also provides alcohol and drug rehabilitation, after care, and community health programs. The majority of services are contracted through the Indian Health Service and overseen by the tribes' health commission. Hospital facilities are available at St. Anthony's Hospital in Pendleton, St. Mary's Hospital in Walla Walla, and Veteran's Hospital in Walla Walla.

ENVIRONMENTAL CONCERNS

The tribes' environmental concerns include the Columbia River water supply, the need for nuclear cleanup at Hanford, and the incineration of chemical weapons at the Umatilla Army Depot. In 2003 the tribes received an award from the U.S. EPA honoring their environmental science and technology program for its work in the area of air pollutants. The tribes have also organized the cleanup of illegal dumpsites on the reservation.

The tribes operate numerous protection, restoration, revitalization, and preservation programs to manage the natural resources within the reservation. The tribes have actively sought rights to the bodies of water located within the reservation and have successfully gained rights to instream flows of the Umatilla River. The tribes manage watershed protection programs, wetland restoration programs, and wildlife protection programs. The tribes also operate the Umatilla Basin Project. It is a federal bucket-for-bucket water exchange project that distributes Columbia River water to participating irrigation districts. In exchange, the districts have agreed to leave water in the Umatilla River for migrating fish. The project aims to sustain fish populations and enhance habitats while allowing irrigation districts to continue using the waterways.

W arm Springs

LOCATION AND LAND STATUS

The Warm Springs Reservation is located in north-central Oregon on the eastern slope of the Cascade Range, approximately 100 miles southeast of Portland. The reservation was established by treaty in 1855. The confederated tribes' claim that a faulty survey in 1871 had deprived them of a 78,000-acre tract known as the McQuinn Strip was resolved in 1972 when Congress returned most of this valuable timber zone to the tribe. The tribe annually allocates funds for the purchase of lands, and in 2004 they purchased property on the northern shore of Lake Billy Chinook. In 1996, just over one percent of the reservation was owned by non-Indians.

PHYSICAL DESCRIPTION

Over half of the reservation is forested and the remainder is constituted primarily of rangelands. There are also canyons, high desert vistas, and volcanic peaks. The Cascade Mountains and Mt. Jefferson lie within reservation boundaries. The reservation contains the Deschutes River, Warm Springs River, Olallie Lake, and Lake Billy Chinook. The tribe maintains control of its waterways. The Town of Warm Springs is the reservation's population center, with smaller communities dispersed in rural areas.

CLIMATE

The reservation experiences a range of weather due to its size and location. Annual precipitation on the Cascade Mountains averages 120 inches, while the annual average in the lower regions of the reservation is 10 inches. The Cascades receive an average of 200 inches of snow per year and the lowlands receive approximately 15 inches per year. Annual temperatures range from -38°F in the winter to 104°F in the summer.

CULTURE AND HISTORY

The Warm Springs Reservation is comprised of members from eight bands of three separate tribes. The Taih, Wyam, Tenino, and Dock-spus bands are descendents of the Ichishkiin (Warm Springs) Tribe; the Dalles, Dog River, and Ki-gal-twal-la bands represent the Kiksht (Wasco) tribe; and only one band of the Numu (Northern Paiute) are located on the reservation. The Warm Springs Bands, formerly known as the Walla Walla, lived along the tributaries of the Columbia River. Although they are not linguistically or culturally related, the Warm Springs Bands and the Wasco Bands forged a strong relationship with one another.

The Wasco Bands also lived along the Columbia River and were the eastern-most groups of speakers of the Chinook language. The Pauites lived in southeastern Oregon and northern California. The Pauite Bands traditionally had infrequent contact with both the Wasco and Warm Springs bands. On the occasions they did meet, the groups often engaged in conflicts.

American settlers began to arrive in the Oregon territory in the 1800s. In 1855, the federal government ordered the territory to remove the Native people from their lands. The government negotiated a number of treaties with Oregon tribes. The Wasco and Warm Springs bands agreed to a treaty that ceded 10 million acres of lands and established the Warm Springs Reservation. The tribes relocated to the reservation, maintaining their rights to harvest fish, game, and other foods on and off the reservation. This provision served as the basis for a landmark court ruling that allocated 50 percent of the area's returning salmon to northwest treaty tribes. The Pauite Band arrived at the reservation in 1879 when 38 members were forcibly relocated from the Yakama Reservation.

The tribes organized under the Indian Reorganization Act of 1934 as the Confederated Tribes of the Warm Springs Reservation. A tribal constitution was drafted and adopted. In 1938, the tribes accepted a corporate charter from the federal government in order to conduct business endeavors.

The tribes traditionally subsisted by hunting, gathering, and particularly fishing, so when the reservation's Celilo Falls and fisheries were destroyed by the construction of Dalles Dam in 1957, the $4 million they received in compensation was viewed

Warm Springs Reservation
Federal reservation
Ichishkiin, Kiksht, Numu
Jefferson, Wasco, Linn,
Marion, and Clackamas
counties, Oregon

Warm Springs Reservation
1233 Veteran Street
P.O. Box C
Warm Springs, OR 97761
  503-553-3468
  503-553-3435 Fax
ctws.com

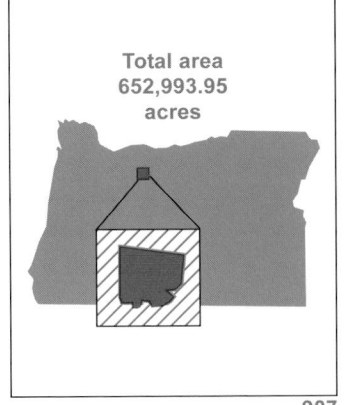

Total area
652,993.95
acres

Warm Springs

Total area *(BIA realty, 2004)*
652,993.95 acres

Tribally owned *(BIA realty, 2004)*
610,323.73 acres

Allotted/Individually owned
(BIA realty, 2004)
42,745.20 acres

Federal trust *(BIA realty, 2004)*
16.02

Population *2000 census*
3,311

Population *(Tribal source, 2004)*
4,000

Tribal enrollment
(Tribal source, 2004)
4,248

Total labor force *2000 census*
1,373

High school graduate or higher
2000 census
73.8%

Bachelor's degree or higher
2000 census
4.8%

Unemployment rate *2000 census*
19.6%

Total labor force
(BIA labor report, 2003)
1,908

High school graduate or higher
2000 census
73.8%

Bachelor's degree or higher
2000 census
4.8%

Unemployment rate
(Tribal census, 2003)
37%

Per capita income *2000 census*
$9,136

as poor compensation. Though the award was invested in economic development, the consensus among tribal members was that no amount of money could replace the social and spiritual value of the fisheries that had been at the heart of lower mid-Columbia life for thousands of years.

Linguistic and cultural differences among the various bands and tribes on the reservation continue today, though greatly mitigated. The Ichishkiin language of the Warm Springs Tribe serves as a focus of traditionalism on the reservation, being regularly used in ceremonies and in the Seven Drum Religion, also known as Waashat. All three tribal spiritual values emphasize traditional foods, which are honored at feasts and rights of passage. Tribal members continue to practice traditional ceremonies and maintain cultural elements.

GOVERNMENT

The current tribal government was established in 1938 with a constitution and charter that basically adhere to the provisions of the 1934 Indian Reorganization Act. An 11-member tribal council oversees all tribal operations. Eight of the council members are elected to three-year terms from districts traditionally associated with the confederation's three tribes; each of the three tribal divisions is represented by a chief who serves on the tribal council for life. Two members of the council serve as its officers, a chairperson and a vice-chairperson. Another officer, the secretary-treasurer oversees management of the tribal corporation's commercial enterprises and policy matters. A chief operating officer oversees government services.

The tribe contracts law enforcement services, the Johnson O'Malley program, Indian Child Welfare Act, social services, judicial services, water management programs, fish and wildlife services, forestry services, road construction, housing improvement programs, and wild life management services through the BIA. It contracts alcohol and drug abuse prevention programs, adolescent aftercare services, mental health, community health, environmental health representatives, health education programs, contract health services, and facility management through the Indian Health Service. The tribe's public safety branch includes the police department, fire and safety, tribal prosecutor, victims of crime parole, and probation and legal aide.

BUSINESS CORPORATION

Warm Springs Ventures oversees economic development projects for the tribe. It currently manages tribal construction projects and marketing for the industrial park in addition to Cort Directives, Kibak Tile, and Sea Lane Tile. Future projects include the completion of a tribal commercial code, a downtown development plan, and a sustainable tourism plan.

Warm Springs Power Enterprises manages the facilities at the Pelton-Round Butte Project and oversees the sale of electrical output. The tribes are co-licensees of the Pelton-Round Butte Project, and the electrical output is sold to PacifiCorps.

ECONOMY

The Confederated Tribes of Warm Springs employs over 1,000 individuals throughout its government, programs, and business entities. Its primary sources of revenue are the casino, forest industry, and power enterprises.

Government as Employer. The tribal government is composed of a vast network of departments charged with overseeing tribal enterprises, health, education, and social services. The tribe employs 752 tribal members throughout the government programs and tribal enterprises.

Economic Development Projects. The tribe's business and economic development department is staffed by a general

manager, an economic development specialist, and a small business management specialist. The department, in part, provides training and counseling for private sector business development. Warm Springs Ventures, an economic development corporation, was created to foster economic development. Priorities include completing a tribal commercial code, creating the downtown development plan, and implementing the sustainable tourism plan. The tribe is developing a shuttle bus program to offer transportation between Warm Springs and Madras.

Agriculture and Livestock. The Warm Springs Reservation has the capacity to raise nearly 13,000 acres of winter wheat, with an additional 300 acres of alfalfa hay. Dry farming methods are relied upon almost exclusively. As for livestock, much of the reservation is designated as rangeland. The tribe maintains a herd of elk and deer numbering about 3,500 head. Individuals on the reservation raise modest numbers of cattle (about 1,500 head total) and about 1,800 horses.

Forestry. The tribe's involvement in the forestry industry has been downsized during the past decade. Warm Springs Forest Product Industries is a tribally owned business that engages in wood processing, including logging, a sawmill, and a stud mill. There are five other tribally affiliated logging businesses on the reservation. The small log mill employs 130 people. The mill is renowned for its quality lumber products. Warm Springs Forest Product Industries is considering entering the bio-moss industry.

Gaming. The tribes own and operate the Kah Nee Ta High Desert Resort and Casino. The Indian Head Casino is a 25,000-square-foot facility that offers over 300 slot and video poker machines, and blackjack and poker tables. It also has a fine dining facility, a casual buffet restaurant, and an entertainment lounge that hosts live performances. The Lodge at Kah Nee Ta provides indoor hotel accommodations as well as the adjacent Kah Nee Ta Village RV Park, tepees, and village condominiums. The facilities include an 18-hole golf course, a swimming pool, a water slide, and a miniature golf course. The resort's Spa Wanapine has been rated one of the top five in the nation by *Shape Magazine* (2000). The resort also provides guided trail rides, kayak trips, and tennis, hiking, and biking opportunities for guests. The tribe is presently exploring the possibility of relocating the casino facilities to a site near Portland in Columbia Gorge. The resort and its associated facilities would remain at Warm Springs.

Fisheries. Through effective resource management practices, fisheries are rebounding on reservation rivers and streams. Steelhead and varieties of salmon spawn within protected waterways. Recreational fishing opportunities are provided in rivers and lakes. The Warm Springs National Fish Hatchery celebrated its 29th year of operation in 2003.

Construction. Warm Springs Ventures manages construction projects. It specializes in road, water line, and sewer line projects. A tribal work experience program supports development of apprentices and journeymen in the housing construction field. The tribe constructed the generating and power transmission facilities at Pelton Reregulating Dam.

Mining. The tribe will be conducting a mineral inventory to be completed in 2005.

Manufacturing. Warm Springs Composite Products researches, develops, and manufactures fire-resistant products. The tribally owned company distributes its products internationally through Tectonics International, an entity created in partnership with Structural Technology.

Warm Springs

TRI-OR-028

TRI-OR-029

TRI-OR-030

TRI-OR-033

Industrial Parks. The tribe recently completed a master plan for its industrial park. Planned renovations include replacing the site's sewer system. Warm Springs Ventures is marketing the industrial site.

Real Estate/Commercial Development. The tribe recently purchased property on the northern shore of Lake Billy Chinook. It is exploring possible uses for the land, including the development of tourist attractions.

Services and Retail. The tribe owns the Plaza at Warm Springs. It is located along Highway 26 and houses a restaurant, a gift and clothing store, and a thrift shop. The tribe owns and operates the Three Warriors Market in Simnasho. The store offers a convenience store and gas station. The tribe is in the process of developing a downtown development plan to ascertain and initiate the addition of small businesses and employment opportunities on the reservation.

Media and Communications. The tribe operates a biweekly newspaper, *Spilyay Tymo*. It also owns and operates a community radio station, KWSO. The tribe's other radio station, K-TWINS, was sold in 1996.

Tourism and Recreation. The Museum at Warm Springs hosts a permanent collection of tribal artifacts, historic photographs, narratives, graphics, murals, and rare documents. Displays include traditional dwellings and scenes from historical daily life. The Song Chamber provides traditional singing and drumming, and a multimedia exhibit provides drumming and displays of hoop dancing. The museum also hosts regular programs, lectures, and exhibits featuring Native American scholars, poets, and artists. Facilities include a gift shop, outdoor walking trails, picnic areas, and an amphitheater where performances and demonstrations are held. The museum hosts the Annual Huckleberry Harvest to generate funds for museum operations.

The reservation offers outdoor enthusiasts numerous opportunities to experience the reservation. There are fishing, hiking, camping, mountain climbing, sightseeing, horseback riding, rafting, and kayaking opportunities available to tourists in self-guided and guided trips. The Deschutes River is located on tribal lands and is open to the public for fishing and river tours. The tribe issues fishing permits, and the Bureau of Land Management provides permits for river guides. The tribe also operates a golf course.

The tribe hosts numerous cultural events that are open to the public. The Pi Ume Sha/Treaty Days Celebration offers drumming, dancing, vendors, games, the Fry Bread Golf Tournament, and an All Indian Rodeo. The celebration is held on the weekend closest to June 25 each year. The tribe also sponsors Lincoln's Powwow, the Hawaiian and Local Boys Golf Tournament, the First Catch Salmon Feast, a Fourth of July celebration, and the Root Feast in early April.

INFRASTRUCTURE

U.S. Highway 26 runs through the reservation in a northwest to southeast direction. In 1999, the tribe began the Dry Creek realignment project on Warm Springs Route 3. The project will enhance road safety in the area. It also completed road designs for the Greeley Heights Subdivision Phase 5 and the Salmon Drive Subdivision road, water, and sewer projects. An extension on Upper Dry Creek Road was also completed.

Electricity. Pacific Power and Wasco Electric provide electricity to the reservation.

Fuel. Local distributors provide propane.

Water Supply. A community water system, a network of 220 wells, furnishes water. Four separate cell lagoon systems provide sewer service. A 200,000-gallon water storage tank was completed in 1999. It serves the Sidwalter community. The tribe also began construction of wastewater stabilization ponds at Simnasho in 1999.

Transportation. The nearby town of Madras has a municipal airport, and the City of Redmond provides commercial air service. The nearest railroad service is available in Madras. UPS and FedEx both provide services to the reservation.

TRI-OR-028 "Entering Warm Springs Indian Reservation" sign

TRI-OR-029 "Warm Springs Power Enterprises" sign

TRI-OR-030 Warm Springs Forest Products Industries

TRI-OR-033 Warm Springs Power Enterprises Dam

Warm Springs

In conjunction with Jefferson County, the Warm Springs Reservation has developed a transportation coordination project to address the transportation issues affecting area residents. The project's goal is to develop reliable means of mobility for residents. Projects include developing shuttle and taxi services and providing assistance for community service programs. The tribal council has coordinated allocation of funding in support of a Madras-Warm Springs shuttle service so tribal members and others have access to employment and education opportunities concentrated near Madras, Oregon, and elsewhere in the region. There will also be a shuttle operating between the Kah Nee Ta Resort and the Madras shuttle pick-up and drop-off locations to encourage tourism.

Telecommunications. Qwest supplies telephone service. Broadband service is available for Internet access.

COMMUNITY FACILITIES AND SERVICES

The tribe maintains a community center in the community of Warm Springs. The tribal culture and heritage program offers instructional classes in the indigenous languages of the Ichishkiin, Kiksht, and Numu tribes. The Warm Springs small business center provides tribal members with technical assistance, courses, business counseling, and access to computers and general office facilities.

Education. School District 509-J maintains a school for children in K-4, while junior high and high school students attend public schools in nearby Madras. The tribe has approved the development of a new K-5 school; construction is expected to begin within the next three years. The tribal culture and heritage program offers language classes in all three native languages of the Confederated Tribes. The tribe also provides an adult education program, vocational training, and an Oregon State University Extension Office.

Health Care. The tribe's community health education team oversees the health services available to tribal members. The tribe operates its own health and wellness center in a state-of-the-art facility. Services include comprehensive medical, dental, pharmacy, and outpatient care. The center also operates a diabetes clinic. The tribe's managed care program is responsible for managing funds used to supplement tribal health care services. Funds are available when a tribal member seeks the services of providers outside the health and wellness clinic. The High Lookee Lodge Assisted Living Residence provides senior and disabled tribal members with the opportunity to live in private apartments served by an assisted living program. Amenities include an emergency call system, a ceremonial tribal room, a dining room, housekeeping services, a sauna, a courtyard and salmon pit, nursing staff, and transportation coordination. The tribe also has a senior community center and senior housing facilities.

ENVIRONMENTAL CONCERNS

Environmental concerns of the Warm Springs Tribe include water quality, the status of the forests, and separating governmental and proprietary issues related to protecting tribal resources. The tribe's natural resources division is one of the largest governmental programs. In 1999, it employed 205 individuals. The program oversees the management of fish, wildlife, native plants, cultural foods, water, timber, and sovereignty issues that pertain to the tribe.

The Warm Springs Reservation experienced a major forest fire in August 2004, with almost 14,000 acres burned. The Burned Area Emergency Rehabilitation team worked with the BIA to prepare plans to lessen the erosional damage potential and environmental degradation caused by the fire and to develop suppression efforts remaining after the fire was extinguished.

RHODE ISLAND

Narragansett

Narragansett

LOCATION AND LAND STATUS

The Narragansett Reservation is located in southern Rhode Island, north of Block Island near Ninigret Pond. Charleston lies just east of the reservation along scenic U.S.1. Following an out-of-court settlement awarded in 1978, the Narragansett Tribe of Rhode Island took control of the lands awarded to them in 1983. The reservation consists of 1,943 noncontiguous, tribally owned acres held in federal trust. Of these lands about 1,550 acres are ponds and wetlands. There are 406 acres of fee lands. Most of the tribal members live outside the reservation.

CULTURE AND HISTORY

The Narragansett Indians are descendants of aboriginal people known to have existed in the area of present-day Rhode Island over 30,000 years ago. Giovanni de Varrazano made the first documented European contact during his visit to Narragansett Bay in 1524; he described the Narragansetts as a large tribe who practiced horticulture, hunted, and organized under powerful kings (sachems). They lived in summer homes (wetus or wigwams constructed of tree bark) and then moved to larger longhouses where several families resided together for the long, cold northeastern winters. They traveled on foot over land and constructed dugout canoes from large trees for water transport. By the time of first European settlement around 1635, the Narragansett Tribe was comprised of five subtribes. Rhode Island founder Roger Williams acquired land use rights to Providence from the Narragansett sachems in 1636. During King Philip's War, in 1675, English settlers massacred many Narragansetts and confined some survivors to a reservation in southern Rhode Island. Other survivors were sold into slavery or fled the region. Known today as the Great Swamp Massacre, much of this area makes up what are now the tribal reservation lands.

During the eighteenth century, the colonial government abolished the positions of the five sachems. Most tribal land was simultaneously lost to non-Indians through incurred debts. The Narragansetts clung to 15,000 acres until 1880, when the State of Rhode Island "detribalized" them without federal sanction. The tribal land base thereafter quickly eroded; however, the traditional tribal council continued to function, and tribal meetings and elections were conducted from 1889 to the present. The people continued to recognize sachems, medicine men and women, the tribal council, subchiefs, tribal prophets, the war chief, and clan mothers. With funds raised from tribal membership, the tribe compiled a roll and hired an attorney to pursue its land claims, but to no avail.

The Narragansett Indian Tribe incorporated in December 1934 under the Indian Reorganization Act and created a constitution and bylaws to govern by. The offices of sachem, medicine man, scribe, prophet, and a nine-member council were sanctioned.

With federal recognition, the Narragansett Tribe was finally able to work toward economic self-sufficiency and cultural revitalization. They initiated a monthly magazine called *The Narragansett Dawn*, which was published for three years. A longhouse was constructed during the 1940s to provide a meeting place for tribal members, and today it serves as the center of tribal activities. The three acres of land on which the Indian Church is located is the only original parcel of tribal land that has never been out of the Narragansett Tribe's possession. In 1975, the tribe filed suit against the State of Rhode Island and several landowners for return of approximately 3,200 acres of former reservation lands; they eventually received 1,800 acres in an out-of-court settlement. The Narragansett Indian Land Management Corporation held the lands until the tribe was reinstated as a federally recognized tribe. The Narragansett Indian Tribe received federal recognition on April 11, 1983. State legislation, which transferred title to the tribe, was enacted in 1985, and the tribe obtained federal trust status for the settlement land.

Today, the Narragansett Tribe serves members through its economic development and social services, while nourishing the tribe's rich culture and heritage. In 1996, the tribal housing authority, with assistance from HUD, constructed 50 housing units on tribal land. A few years later, the Four Winds Community Center was completed in Charlestown. Providing education, maintaining the family circle, observing traditional ceremonies, and preserving and using the Narragansett language are important aspects of everyday life. The tribe holds numerous annual celebrations and powwows, including the traditional August Meeting, and it also offers cultural, historical, and language classes for the benefit of tribal elders and youth.

GOVERNMENT

The tribe's principal governing body is the tribal council, which is composed of a chief sachem, a medicine man, a secretary, a treasurer, and nine council members; this body is elected at large by enrolled tribal members. The tribal government also includes several regulatory and oversight boards, including a land and water resource commission, anthropological and archaeological commission, police commission, historic preservation commission, economic development commission, child board, council of elders, election committee, and permitting board.

The tribe, under PL-638, contracts with the BIA to administer key programs and services. The tribe has a housing department. The social services department provides assistance through various types of programs and services. The Narragansett Tribal Police Department fulfills law enforcement needs. The tribe also has education, finance, community planning and economic development, health and human services,

Narragansett Indian Reservation
Federal reservation
Narragansett
Washington County, Rhode Island

Narragansett Indian Tribe
P.O. Box 268
Charlestown, RI 02813
401-364-1100
401-364-1104 Fax
narragansett-tribe.org

Total area *(BIA realty, 2005)*
1,943.5 acres

Federal trust *(BIA realty, 2005)*
1,943.5 acres

Population *2000 census*
NR

Tribal enrollment
(BIA labor report, 2001)
2,620

Total labor force *2000 census*
36

High school graduate or higher
2000 census
92.1%

Bachelor's degree or higher
2000 census
21.1%

Unemployment rate *2000 census*
5.6%

Per capita income *2000 census*
$26,457

Narragansett

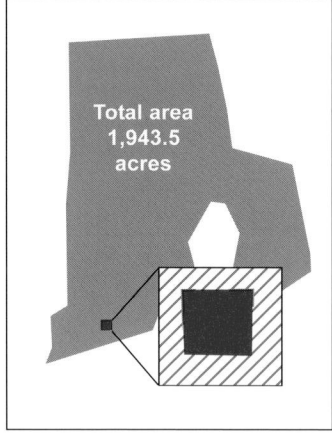

Total area
1,943.5
acres

ENVIRONMENTAL CONCERNS

The tribe has a natural resources department, which is responsible for protecting and managing all natural resources on tribal land. Environmental issues include surface and subsurface water quality, non-point source pollution, illegal dumping, erosion, hazardous waste, lead paint, air quality, indoor air quality (radon), and potential biological and chemical contamination of drinking water.

A land use plan was first formulated in 1986. Coupled with subsequent zoning and development review ordinances, the tribe formulated a comprehensive land use plan, under revision since 2000. Forest and water quality management plans also incorporate environmental protections. Water quality programs were initiated in 1990, including weekly monitoring of all surface waters. A wetland protection program was established in 1994, and a safe drinking water program began in 1995. An environmental enforcement program was started in 1999, and in 2004 the tribe formulated an environmental protection plan incorporating environmental laws and hunting and fishing regulations with respect for traditional use and protection of cultural assets.

environmental and natural resources, and personnel departments to meet the needs of the membership.

BUSINESS CORPORATION

The Narragansett Economic Development Commission oversees the tribe's community planning and economic development department, which provides a coordinated assessment and development approach to developing enterprises that will lead to self-sufficiency while protecting natural resources, traditional Native American values, and cultural sites.

ECONOMY

The tribe's economy is based on tribal governmental operations. Tribal members find employment in the cash economy of the surrounding region.

Government as Employer. Tribal administration employs 74 staff members, 56 of whom are tribal members. Tribal government is the single largest employer associated with the tribe.

Economic Development Projects. Aside from the housing authority development team's construction activities, the tribe rents land to NYNEX for a communication tower. Proceeds support infrastructure development on the reservation. In July 2003 the tribe opened the doors of the Narragansett Indian Smoke Shop. In October 2003, the tribe announced the creation of the Narragansett Tribal Seafood Co-op, a Native American seafood wholesale company. In addition, the tribe is in the planning stages for a gaming facility, electric power development, and the reuse of warehouse facilities at a former naval base.

Agriculture and Livestock. The tribe uses approximately five acres of trust land for a community garden, and 20 acres of field for hay.

Forestry. Several tree species (including white, black, and northern red oaks, red maple, eastern white pine, and Atlantic white cedar) forest 1,250 acres of tribal land. The tribe harvests approximately 50 cords of wood per year.

Gaming. In February 2004, the tribe announced plans to build a $500 million destination resort casino adjacent to I-95 in West Warwick, Rhode Island. The proposed facility would feature 3,500 gambling stations, entertainment venues, restaurants, and a 500-room hotel, creating approximately 6,700 permanent jobs and generating more than $100 million in annual revenue for the state. Another 3,000 construction jobs would be needed to build the facility. Las Vegas-based Harrah's Entertainment will develop the project.

Construction. The Narragansett Indian Housing Authority has organized a tribal development team to provide construction services for projects on tribal lands.

Real Estate/Commercial Development. The tribe created a real estate and rights protection program to inventory, manage, plan, and protect all tribal lands.

Services and Retail. Many tribal members are in business for themselves, primarily in the building trades. Dover Indian Trading Post, located along Main Street in Rockville, sells leatherwork, jewelry, beadwork, and pottery.

Tourism and Recreation. The reservation lies within 20 miles of the Burlingame State Park and the Ninigret National Wildlife Refuge. The Narragansett Indian Longhouse, located along Route 2 in Charlestown, offers presentations, lectures, and tours. The tribe holds two powwows during the summer: a commercial powwow associated with a health fair in July, and the traditional August Meeting. The August Meeting, a historical and

religious occasion, includes dancing, drumming, singing, craft sales, traditional foods, games, and competitions. Two other celebrations, the Harvest Thanksgiving Ceremony in October, and the Nickomoh Celebration, are also held annually at the Longhouse.

INFRASTRUCTURE

State Highways 112 and 2 run north-south just east of the reservation, connecting to State Highway 138 and U.S. 1, the major east-west routes. Interstate 95, provides easy access to New York, Providence, and Boston.

Electricity. The Narragansett Electric Company (no connection to the tribe) provides electricity to tribal housing developments.

Water Supply. Individual wells and septic tanks and wells serve all tribal facilities. Funding from the Indian Health Service will support construction of sanitary facilities to provide homeowners access to emergency financial assistance.

Transportation. Commercial air facilities are located in Warwick, approximately 20 miles north of the reservation. Private air facilities are located at Westerly, 7 miles west of the reservation. Rhode Island Public Transit Authority provides public transportation to the reservation area via Richmond, 6 miles northwest of the reservation. Bonanza Bus Lines also provides intercity services. UPS and FedEx package carriers serve the tribal area. Passenger and freight rail service is available along the Shore Line route. Amtrak passenger trains stop at Kingston Station; Conrail provides freight service along the shoreline. The Narragansett Reservation is bounded by the navigable Pawcatuck River on the north. Tribal lands lie within two to five miles of Block Island Sound where dock and mooring facilities for small commercial and pleasure crafts are available. The tribe's health and human services department provides van transportation to medical appointments.

Telecommunications. NYNEX provides local telephone service.

COMMUNITY FACILITIES AND SERVICES

The Four Winds Community Center is complete. The facility houses an Administration on Aging Title VI senior meal site and the Hand-In-Hand Child Care Center. The Narragansett Indian Church, a one-room stone meetinghouse, was constructed in 1994. Behind the church, the tribe maintains a small historic burying ground.

Education. Most children attend public schools in the reservation area; however, the tribe has its own education department to oversee an adult education program, the higher education program, and the Johnson O'Malley Program. A separate adult vocational training department provides employment and training services. The adult vocational training department also assists with job placement, primarily within the construction trades, and it protects against employment discrimination against Native Americans under the Tribal Employment Rights Office of the U.S. Equal Employment Opportunity Commission. A grant from the U.S. EPA provides training to become certified lead inspectors, lead abatement workers, and lead supervisors for removal of lead hazard on and off the reservation.

Health Care. The Narragansett Indian Health Center provides direct ambulatory services, community health outreach programs, nursing visits, nutrition education, substance abuse counseling services, and other behavioral health programs. The tribe's medicine man is housed at the facility and he works with the medical team to integrate spiritual and psychological well-being into all aspects of medical care. The child welfare program and other social services maintain offices at the center, and there are a laboratory and a pharmacy onsite. Hospitals are located in the Providence area.

C atawba

LOCATION AND LAND STATUS

The Catawba Reservation is located near the town of Rock Hill, South Carolina, near the North Carolina border. The original reservation occupied more than 15,000 square miles. The present reservation is located within the original reservation, which was established in the Pine Tree Hill (1760) and Augusta (1763) treaties. A treaty entered into in 1840 was neither ratified by the federal government nor honored by South Carolina. The tribe remained landless until the State of South Carolin established a 630-acre parcel of land for them in 1943.

The tribe was terminated from federal status in the 1960s, and all its lands were dissolved. The state agreed to support the tribe's efforts to regain status if the tribe relinquished their claim to 144,000 acres of ancestral lands. The tribe refused and sought resolution from the federal courts. In 1993, the U.S. Congress restored the tribe's federal recognition and settled the Catawba land claim for $50 million. The tribe was allowed to expand its reservation, and it has done so in the ensuing years. It intends to continue increasing its land base.

PHYSICAL DESCRIPTION

There are several waterways on the reservation, including the Catawba River and three lakes. The port of Charleston is just three hours to the south.

CULTURE AND HISTORY

The Ye Iswa, or Catawba, Indian Nation, has resided in the regions of the present-day states of North and South Carolina for several hundred years. The indigenous language belongs to the Siouan family. The Catawbas encountered Spanish explorers in 1540 when Hernando de Soto's expedition ventured north from Florida. Initially, tribal members befriended and traded with first Spanish and, later, Euro-American settlers.

The Catawbas contracted smallpox and other diseases from contact with Europeans, which resulted in many deaths. So devastating were the outbreaks of diseases that the tribe of 5,000 people in the early eighteenth century was reduced to 250 people by 1784.

The tribe has participated in various military forces throughout the history of the United States. Allied with the Carolina settlers, the Catawbas fought against the Cherokee and Tuscarora tribes in what became known as the Yamassee War of 1715. The Carolinians won the war in 1717, and many smaller tribes suffered great losses. The Catawbas welcomed at least 30 tribes displaced by the war, including the Waxhaws, Waterees, Sarahs, Sugarees, and for some time, the Cheraws. The tribe allied with the British during the French and Indian War and served as scouts. During the American Revolution, the Catawbas were used as scouts by the colonists, and during the Civil War, the tribe allied with the Confederacy. In 1942, the tribe declared war against Germany and the Axis Powers. Tribal members continue to serve in the armed forces today.

The original Catawba Reservation, consisting of 15,326 square miles, was established by the Pine Tree Hill and Augusta treaties in the late eighteenth century. Tribal leaders relinquished their territory in the Nation Fords Treaty of 1840 to South Carolina in exchange for money and other land in North Carolina. However, the state paid only a small portion, and the tribe was left landless. They sought to regain their land, and eventually South Carolina purchased 630 acres that lay within the original reservation boundaries. In 1942, the Catawbas began a federal trust relationship, which Congress terminated in 1962.

In 1972, the Catawba Indian Nation reorganized as a nonprofit corporation and began pursuing the tribe's land claim with the help of the Native American Rights Fund. In 1993, the U.S. Congress restored the Catawba Indian Nation as a federally recognized tribe and, in agreement with South Carolina, settled the tribe's claim and awarded $50 million to the tribe.

The Catawbas' culture, language, and art are still alive. Tribal members have also kept up the ancient skill of pottery making, having established a Catawba Pottery Institute in 1976. The Catawba Nation is the only tribe east of the Mississippi that has maintained this craft. In addition to the institute, the tribe has a cultural preservation program and has increasing numbers of members learning their Native language.

GOVERNMENT

The Catawba Indian Nation is a PL-638 tribe. It is governed by a tribal council consisting of a chief, an assistant chief, a secretary-treasurer, and five members. Tribal government programs include social services, education, health, housing, engineering, natural resources, cultural, and economic development.

The tribe's cultural department offers an extensive array of services to preserve and maintain the tribal culture. It houses the archeology department, the cultural center, the cultural preservation project, and the language department. The cultural preservation project received South Carolina Governor's Folk Heritage Advocacy Award (1993) in recognition of its many programs and services designed to protect, preserve, and restore tribal traditions.

ECONOMY

Tribally owned enterprises contribute to the tribal economy, as do federal grants. Many members of the Catawba community work a wide range of occupations in the mainstream community.

Catawba Reservation
Federal reservation
Catawba
York, Chester, and Lancaster counties, South Carolina

Catawba Indian Nation
996 Avenue of Nations
Rock Hill, SC 29730
803-366-4792
803-366-0629 Fax

Total area *(BIA realty, 2005)*
1,010 acres

Federal trust *(BIA realty, 2005)*
1,010 acres

Total area *(Tribal source, 2004)*
2,110 acres

Population *2000 census*
494

Tribal enrollment
(BIA labor report, 2001)
2,430

Tribal enrollment
(Tribal source, 2004)
2,490

Catawba

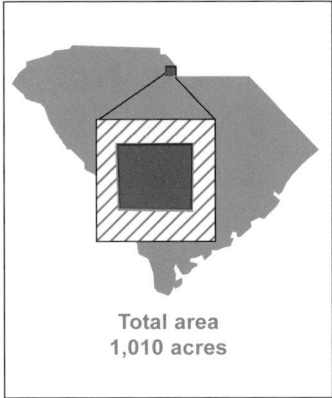

Total area
1,010 acres

Total labor force *2000 census*
212

Total labor force *(Tribal source, 2004)*
1,300

High School graduate or higher
2000 census
36.2%

Bachelor's degree or higher
2000 census
0.7%

Unemployment rate *2000 census*
6.1%

Unemployment rate
(BIA labor report, 2001)
92%

Per capita income *2000 census*
$16,295

Government as Employer. The tribe employs approximately 60 people.

Economic Development Projects. The tribe intends to increase its land base by purchasing lands. It is seeking NAHASDA Title IV Loan Guarantee Program assistance to fund the construction of housing units on the reservation. A community center and foster home may be included in the development. The estimated cost of constructing the 120 home sites is about $5.3 million, after grants. The ISWA Development Corporation is providing assistance to the tribe in the development process. The tribe plans to develop an industrial park on tribal lands. The tribe also hopes to develop a replica of a traditional village along the banks of the Catawba River. The village will serve as a tourist attraction, as well as an educational tool.

Gaming. The tribe owns and operates the Catawba High-Stakes Bingo in Rock Hill. The facility contains 3,030 bingo seats, a café, and a gift shop. Income earned from the gaming operations contributes to the tribe's general budget and helps fund tribal programs and services.

Construction. Recent construction of new housing and an office complex employs 15 to 20 people. The construction of the proposed housing development and future community facilities will also create a number of temporary jobs. The tribe maintains its own construction offices.

Manufacturing. The Catawba Tribe manufactures plastic identification cards. The cards feature magnetic strips, thumbprints, and other security measures. The cards are used for tribal enrollment, employee identification, security, access passes, and playing cards.

Tourism and Recreation. The tribe operates the Catawba Cultural Center. It is located in the former Catawba Indian School, which was operational between 1948 and 1966. The center houses the tribe's archives, language, maintenance, exhibits, and administration offices, as well as a craft shop.

The Catawba Pottery Association participates in the annual Catawba Festival and permanent Catawba Village exhibit at the Schiele Museum of Natural History in Gastonia, North Carolina.

INFRASTRUCTURE
The town of Rock Hill is just east of I-77, approximately 55 miles north of Columbia. It is also served by U.S. Highway 21 and South Carolina State Highway 72. Major highways include I-77, I-26, I-20, I-85, and I-95.

There are approximately 400 homes on the reservation; two new homes were built and nine others renovated in 1994.

Growth on the reservation is rapid and the rate of construction of two new homes per year is not meeting the residential needs. The implementation of the Green Earth development plan will provide affordable, energy-efficient housing, and community amenities at a more reasonable pace.

Electricity. Duke Power provides electricity.

Fuel. York County is the natural gas provider.

Water Supply. Water is provided to reservation homes by the city. A sewer system serves residencies as well.

Transportation. The Charlotte Douglas International Airport is approximately 30 miles from the reservation. Greyhound bus service is available in local communities. UPS and FedEx also serve the reservation.

COMMUNITY FACILITIES AND SERVICES
The Catawaba Long House Building serves as the center of the nation's activities. A community gym is located on the reservation. The tribe also owns the Catawba Cemetery, a historical burial site located near the center of the Nation.

Education. Tribal youth attend local public schools. The tribe plans to develop a Head Start program on the reservation. In 1998, the tribe received the Learn and Service Grant and the Adult Literacy Grant.

Although the last fluent speaker of the indigenous language died in the late 1970s, tribal members are making a concerted effort to retain the language. The tribe provides a language preservation and restoration program. It offers video and audio recording of fluent speakers to assist tribal members in relearning the indigenous language. It serves tribal elders, adults, and youth.

Health Care. The tribe operates the Catawba Medical Clinic. The clinic serves the reservation, as well as members of all federally recognized tribes. The clinic employs a physician trained in traditional Western medicine and a Medicine Man trained in traditional tribal healing methods. Local hospitals serve major medical needs.

ENVIRONMENTAL CONCERNS
Illegal dumping is of concern on tribal lands. Waste that is being improperly disposed of includes appliances, furniture, and household trash. The tribe also remains concerned with the water quality of the Catawba River. The tribe's environmental goals are to: promote food production, improve energy efficiency, protect cultural resources, develop land use regulations, reduce waste, and conserve.

South Dakota

Cheyenne River

LOCATION AND LAND STATUS

The Cheyenne River Sioux Reservation, comprised of approximately 2.8 million acres, is located in north-central South Dakota. The northern border of the Cheyenne River Sioux Reservation abuts the Standing Rock Sioux Reservation. Mid-channel of the Cheyenne River forms the southern boundary. The Ziebach County line is the western border, and the water's edge of Lake Oahe on the Missouri River forms the reservation's eastern border. The Black Hills and the Badlands lie to the southwest of the reservation. There are no urban areas close to the reservation.

An Act of Congress established the reservation in 1889. Much of the unallocated and unsold land on the reservation was opened for homesteading to non-Indians by Acts of Congress in 1909 and 1910, resulting in non-Indian ownership of 47 percent of the original reservation land. An additional 104,400 acres of reservation land were inundated by Lake Oahe, an area much larger than predicted by the U.S. Army Corps of Engineers. Twenty-five communities dot the reservation, 13 of which are Indian communities. Tribal headquarters are located in Eagle Butte, the largest city on the reservation; all other communities are quite small.

PHYSICAL DESCRIPTION

The reservation's topography varies from gently rolling mixed-grass prairie split by washes, buttes, streams, and rivers, to lakes and bur oak woodland areas.

CLIMATE

The average year-round high temperature in Dupree is 59°F. The average year-round low temperature is 32.5°F, with record low temperatures of -40°F during the winter. The area receives approximately 16 inches of precipitation annually and suffers from extreme droughts at times. Snowfalls during winter range between moderate and heavy, with 10-foot drifts during severe blizzard conditions reported periodically. The growing season is short, lasting only during June, July, and August before first frost. Wind speeds average 14 miles per hour daily.

CULTURE AND HISTORY

The Cheyenne River Sioux are descendents of the Tetonwan Division of the Great Sioux Nation, Titonwan Lakota Oyate (Dwellers of the Plains People), part of the Lakota/Dakota/Nakota Nation, and members of the Algonquian linguistic family. They speak the Lakota dialect of the Siouan language. They refer to themselves as Lakota, meaning friend or ally.

The Cheyenne River Sioux Tribe, comprised of four bands of the Tetonwan, the Mnicoujou (Plants by the River), Itazipco (No Bows or Sans Arcs), Siha Sapa (Black Foot), and Oohenumpa (Two Kettle), originally inhabited the forests and grasslands of central Minnesota. They subsisted on hunting and gathering wild rice. When French fur traders came in the early 1600s, the Lakotas moved onto the plains, acquiring horses from southern plains tribes and guns from trade with the Santee Sioux and fur traders as they moved west.

The Black Hills and the Badlands, known to the Lakotas for more than 3,000 years, became central to their culture and religion. They bred and traded large pony herds, hunted buffalo, and returned each year to celebrate the sacred Sun Dance. Trappers, settlers, gold miners, and federal troops threatened the Lakotas' freedom of movement and the survival of the buffalo herds.

The tribe first entered into a treaty relationship with the U.S. government in 1851. Much of the Lakota land was negotiated away, and in 1868, under terms of the Treaty of Fort Laramie, the Lakotas were established on one large reservation encompassing parts of North and South Dakota and four other states. Fierce, determined warriors, the Lakotas long defied Anglo-American attempts at intimidation. Finally, in 1889, after the murder of several of their leaders and having been virtually starved into submission, the Lakotas agreed to divide their land and accept six separate reservations in North and South Dakota: the Cheyenne River, Crow Creek, Lower Brule, Pine Ridge, Rosebud, and Standing Rock. The Cheyenne River Sioux Reservation, formally established on March 2, 1889, became the center of the Ghost Dance religion while it flourished briefly. After the arrest and death of Sitting Bull on December 15, 1890, many people from the Standing Rock Reservation fled south into the Cheyenne River Sioux Reservation, joining with the Big Foot Band, and then traveled south together to the Pine Ridge Reservation to meet with Chief Red Cloud. The 7th Cavalry disarmed them all and massacred 300 people at Wounded Knee, leaving their bodies to freeze in the snow. The fateful date was December 29, 1890.

During the first decade of the twentieth century, much of the reservation's land base was taken away via various pieces of legislation. Another 8 percent (150,000 acres) was inundated by the rising waters of the Missouri River during the formation of Lake Oahe. The tribe was forced to abandon the agency, or seat of tribal government at the time, and it relocated to Eagle Butte, a community in the center of the reservation's vast land base.

Despite the devastation, the Cheyenne River Sioux people continue to thrive today, believing that the tribe's future is in the hands of their children. They participate in social activities such as powwows, rodeos, and races, with special powwows and traditional honoring ceremonies for graduating stu-

Cheyenne River Sioux Tribe Reservation
Federal reservation
Cheyenne River Sioux Tribe
Dewey and Ziebach counties, South Dakota

Cheyenne River Sioux Tribe
2001 N. Main Street
P.O. Box 590
Eagle Butte, SD 57625
605-964-4155
605-964-4151 Fax
sioux.org

Total area *(BIA realty, 2003)*
1,448,556.13 acres

Total area *(Tribal source, 2005)*
2,796,355 acres

Tribally owned *(BIA realty, 2003)*
1,004,516.38 acres

Tribally owned
(Tribal source, 2005)
1,458,821 acres

Allotted/Individually owned
(BIA realty, 2003)
405,170.11 acres

Federal trust *(BIA realty, 2003)*
38,869.64 acres

Population *2000 census*
8,470

Tribal enrollment
(Tribal source, 2005)
14,666

Cheyenne River

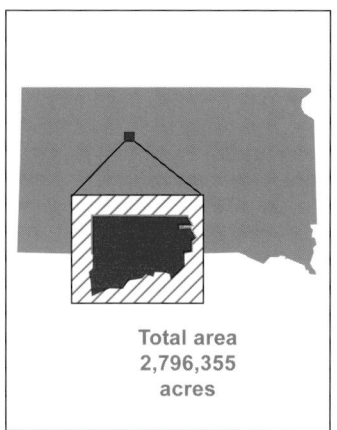

**Total area
2,796,355
acres**

Total labor force
(Tribal source, 2005)
3,124

Total labor force
(Tribal source, 2005)
9,975

High school graduate or higher
2000 census
75.6%

Bachelor's degree or higher
2000 census
12.2%

Unemployment rate *2000 census*
15.2%

Unemployment rate
(Tribal source, 2005)
86.8%

Per capita income *2000 census*
$8,710

dents or people who join the military. Giveaways and feasts are celebrated, and the tribe's oral traditions are still passed down from elders to wakan'yeja (children) and to tako'jas (grandchildren).

GOVERNMENT

The Cheyenne River Sioux Tribe (CRST) is governed by a tribal council composed of a chairperson, a vice-chairperson, a secretary, a treasurer, and 15 council members elected from six districts. Officers are elected at-large for four-year terms.

The tribe, under PL-638, contracts with the BIA to administer key programs and services, operating under a constitution and bylaws consistent with the Indian Reorganization Act of 1934.

Seated now in Eagle Butte, tribal government offers the following offices and services to all tribal members: the BIA, the Indian Health Service, the Cheyenne River Sioux Tribe Law Enforcement Department, the Cheyenne River Sioux Tribe Housing Authority, and the Cheyenne River Sioux Tribe Telephone Authority. The BIA school system, which oversees day school operations in each district, is also headquartered in Eagle Butte. A tribal health department offers health care through community health, diabetes, and maternal child health programs, and it provides outpatient health care service in four outlying community clinics.

The Cheyenne River Sioux Tribe Game, Fish, and Parks Department has been in existence since 1935. It is a PL-638 federally funded program responsible for managing wildlife, fisheries, and recreational resources on all trust lands within the reservation's boundaries. Hunting seasons on the reservation differ from those in the rest of the state; this department issues tribal permits and licenses, and it oversees the management of game, nongame, and federally threatened and endangered fish and wildlife species. The department also sets the seasons and fees, conducting surveys to determine season lengths and daily limits. The department also takes care of the tribal buffalo herd, wild horse herd and elk herd, and it seeks out elders who can no longer hunt big game, and provides them with meat from game kills.

Tourism is also a division of the game, fish, and parks department. It conducts wildlife and culture tours called the "Spirit of the Nation Tours." These tours include the wild horse herd, elk herd, and buffalo herd. The current head count of buffalo is 1,900; the horse herd is 200; and the elk herd is 200. The game, fish, and parks department is currently working on the Lakota Tribal Park, to be located 38 miles east of Eagle Butte, along Highway 212. The department is working with an architectural and engineering firm to design park facilities. This park will be a large protected ecosystem complete with native grasses, buffalo, and other wildlife.

The game, fish, and parks department staff have identified several federally threatened and endangered species on the reservation. These include: piping plover, least tern, bald eagle, whooping crane, gray wolf, and black ferret. The department works closely with the National Wildlife Federation in protecting these species as well as conserving and restoring the reservation's other natural resources, including the vast expanses of open range prairie grassland. The tribe is looking to build upon their success by launching other conservation and restoration programs, one of these may be the reintroduction of threatened species.

The game, fish, and parks department also responds with the tribe's emergency task force during any emergency in the communities. The staff consists of 32 individuals. It is supported by funding from three different sources: Title VI Interim

Funding (21), PL 93-638, BIA funding (8), and the 610 enterprise account (3), which is from the sale of hunting and fishing licenses.

The tribal prairie management program builds stock ponds and wells and determines where fencing is necessary to avoid overgrazing in certain areas of the reservation's vast rangelands. The program mitigates the loss of riparian areas and other factors leading to soil erosion, and it has served as a model for other tribal organizations. The prairie management program has reintroduced the black-footed ferret, and the program eradicates noxious weeds.

The tribal employment rights commission ensures that Indian/Native people get a rightful share of employment, training, and business and economic opportunities. The housing authority was established to serve the needs of low-income tribal members, whether on or off the reservation. The housing authority manages the Thunder Hills and Buffalo lodges, single-family housing projects, and several apartment complexes. In 2002 the housing authority was planning to promote home ownership by converting rental housing. The tribe also operates its own Habitat for Humanity program called Okiciyapi Tipi.

BUSINESS CORPORATION

The Four Bands Community Fund was founded in April 2000 to "assist entrepreneurs of the Cheyenne River Sioux Reservation with training, business incubation, and access to capital, encouraging economic development and enhancing the quality of life for all communities and residents of the reservation." This nonprofit corporation is a 501(c)(3) entity.

ECONOMY

With the advent of gaming in South Dakota there is an increased interest in developing tourism-based enterprises on the reservation; however, agriculture and livestock operations continue to be mainstays of the modern economy. Small businesses also have a presence on the reservation that contributes to the economy.

In 2002 the tribe completed and published a comprehensive economic development study detailing the development strategies to be employed in the exercise of tribal self-determination. An assessment of past and future barriers to economic development was analyzed, and the resulting data was used to formulate an action plan. The goal is: "To make the Cheyenne River Sioux Tribe economically self-sufficient by the year 2012." Through the use of various incentives, such as lowered tax rates and low lease rates and with investment of its own funds, the tribe anticipates attracting major corporations onto the reservation in the future. In the comprehensive economic development plan formulated in 2002, the tribe stated a desire to develop a plant for manufacturing modular homes. The tribe sees this as a potential answer to the dire shortage of reservation housing and as a benefit to the tribe's long-term economic viability. One of the newly manufactured homes would also become part of the Cheyenne River Elderly Village, a planned community for elders.

In 2003 the tribe negotiated a tax collection agreement with the State of South Dakota wherein a higher percentage of the state tax revenues collected on the reservation is to be returned to the tribe. The amount of additional sales and use tax revenue was predicted to be approximately $1 million annually.

Government as Employer. The tribe, through its various programs and initiatives, was the largest employer on the reservation in 2004.

TRI-SD-cr-001

TRI-SD-cr-002

TRI-SD-cr-001 Sign for the Cheyenne River Sioux Tribe Tribal Administration Building

TRI-SD-cr-002 Refrigerated meat storage trailer at meat packing plant

Agriculture and Livestock. The Cheyenne River Sioux Tribe has a strong agricultural and livestock base. Approximately 1,600,000 acres of land are farmed or ranched either by the tribe or by individuals. Crops include corn, spring wheat, winter wheat, barley, alfalfa hay, and native hay. Approximately 1,580,000 acres of rangeland are in use, divided into 266 allocated range units.

The tribe has a herd of approximately 2,700 buffalo that range on 22,000 acres on the east end of the reservation. The herd, purchased originally from the U.S. Park Service, is bred under the aegis of the tribal game, fish, and parks department. In 1995 the tribe built a slaughterhouse and meat-processing plant that employs 22 people. Depending upon demand, 3-5 buffalo per week are slaughtered and processed for sale to local markets. Income from this enterprise varies between $5,000 and $7,500 per month. The tribe also supports a herd of approximately 200 head of elk. Reservation youth participating in hunter safety classes every year are permitted to harvest the elk. The tribe also keeps 200 head of beef cattle, primarily to assist with elderly nutrition needs.

The comprehensive economic development plan of 2002 called for the expansion of these initiatives into culturally sustainable enterprises that would supply byproducts for the manufacture of fertilizer; would create a supply of tanned leather; and would become a source of specialty foods such as jerky and canned meat products that could be exported to off-reservation markets.

Despite the fact that the tribally operated Three Rivers Farms went out of business, almost half of the tribe's annual income is derived from farming or ranching, and there remains significant irrigable potential for expanding the use of farmland and rangeland. Scarcity of surface water, however, adversely affects agriculture and livestock operations on the reservation. During droughts, some sources dry up altogether. The reservation is dotted with small streams, lakes, and dugouts available during wet periods, usually in the spring. Groundwater is also scarce, and deep groundwater, although plentiful, is highly mineralized and of poor quality.

Forestry. There are 10,260 acres of noncommercial-grade stands of timber on the reservation; primarily green ash, box elder, American elm, common chokecherry, Saskatoon serviceberry, American plum, and western snowberry.

Gaming. Eight of nine federally recognized tribes in South Dakota currently operate casinos. Under current gaming compacts with the State of South Dakota, they are limited to 250 slot machines, with no limit on the number of poker and blackjack tables. The Cheyenne River Sioux Tribe currently does not operate a casino but has sought proposals for locating one somewhere on tribal trust land, possibly near Fort Pierre, just beyond reservation borders.

Construction. In 1992 former President Jimmy Carter's Habitat for Humanity built 30 homes on the Cheyenne River Sioux Reservation. The project represented the first time that the Jimmy Carter Work Project built homes within a reservation. Economic development is flourishing, with construction of new buildings, including a Super 8 Motel, and plans for an industrial park and a gaming facility.

Mining. Lignite coal was mined in large quantities at one time on the reservation, and there is one coalmine reclamation project on the northern part of the reservation. Tribal sand and gravel mining operations support tribal, county, and state road construction projects.

There was only one oil-producing well on the reservation in 2004. The Brings Horses Well #1 produced approximately 3,562.29 barrels in 2002. Additional oil exploration and development is carried out by Great Plains Resources, a Littleton, Colorado-based business. Data from oil exploration companies reveals that there are approximately 21 trillion cubic feet of natural gas underlying the reservation, and the tribe has plans to conduct exploratory drilling.

Real Estate/Commercial Development. The Cheyenne River Housing Authority manages 800 housing units in the communities and on rural sites scattered throughout the reservation via the HUD Low Rent and Mutual Help home ownership programs. Limited housing is available through the BIA and Indian Health Service, but only for their employees. Housing is limited on the reservation.

Services and Retail. The tribe owns and operates a number of retail service businesses including the Lakota Thrifty Mart; a Super 8 Motel; Lakota Technologies (since 1997, a provider of computer technology services and several utility companies); CRST Sales and Service (an office supply and products retailer for Indian Country); Dean's Country Market; RC Dairy Queen; Ted's Phillip 66; Outrider Café; and The Flason's clothing store. It also owns the tribal beef and bison herds.

Tourism and Recreation. Oahe Lake, famous for walleye and salmon fishing on the eastern and southern reservation borders, is an excellent area for trophy fishing and other water sports. The tribe, via the tourism division of the game, fish, and parks department, operates six recreation areas on the Missouri River within reservation boundaries, offering swimming, fishing, hunting, hiking, and horseback riding opportunities. Picnic tables and restroom facilities are located at each site. Some have boat ramps, beaches, and campsites. The department also conducts wildlife and culture tours, "Spirit of a Nation Tours." A proposed destination resort will be located on the east end of the reservation and will provide a variety of recreational activities.

917

Cheyenne River

The tribe opened the H.V. Johnston Lakota Cultural Center in Eagle Butte. The museum features culturally significant historical artifacts including murals, old photographs, beadwork, and paintings. The Timber Lake and Area Museum in Timber Lake is also available, featuring items from both the Cheyenne River and Standing Rock Sioux tribes. This facility has a display of marine fossils native to South Dakota. In April 2004, the tribe announced plans to build a 110- by 148-foot skateboarding park.

Lodging is available at the Siesta Motel in Dupree, Fay and Jay Motel in Isabel, the Tumbleweed Motel in Timber Lake, the Harding Hotel, and the tribally owned and operated Super 8 Motel on Highway 212 in Eagle Butte.

The Alliance of Tribal Tourism Advocates developed a tour package that capitalizes on the Lewis and Clark Trail, which ran through what are now the towns of Chamberlain and Pierre, South Dakota. This organization also sponsors several tribal art and trade markets, various fairs throughout the year, and it publishes a monthly newsletter. Various reservation communities sponsor rodeos and powwows during the summer.

INFRASTRUCTURE

U.S. Highway 212, a major east-west highway, and State Routes 65 and 63, north-south routes, pass through the reservation. The Native American Scenic Byway composed of parts of Highway 63 South, Highway 212 East, and BIA 7 North, crosses through the Cheyenne River Sioux Reservation. Pierre, South Dakota, 90 miles from the reservation, is the nearest location served by commercial air, bus, and truck lines. Local trucking companies are available, and small airstrips are located in Eagle Butte, Dupree (unpaved), Isabel (unpaved), and Faith, South Dakota. Lakeville Motor Express, UPS, and FedEx serve the reservation.

Electricity. Provided by Moreau Grand Electric Cooperative.

Fuel. The privately owned D & R Propane and the tribally owned Cheyenne River Gas Company supply all propane needs on the reservation.

Water Supply. Four of the 19 communities on the reservation have a municipal water and sewer system. The U.S. Public Health Service operates four more small systems. The tribe operates a 40-acre landfill on the reservation.

Media and Telecommunications. The CRST Telephone Authority and CRST Telephone-CATV Division provide all the reservation's telecommunication services, including high-speed Internet access. Available weekly publications include the *Teton Times*; *Eagle Butte News*; and *Indian Country Today* out of Rapid City, South Dakota; *West River Progress* in Dupree; and the *Timber Lake Topic*. Daily publications include the *Rapid City Journal*, *Aberdeen American News*, and *Sioux Falls Argus Leader*. The Voice of the Lakota Nation, a radio station (KLND 89.5 FM) out of Little Eagle, South Dakota, is received on the reservation.

COMMUNITY FACILITIES AND SERVICES

The tribal headquarters, a building housing various social and economic programs and a multipurpose community building, are located in Eagle Butte. The tribe provides an elderly nutrition program and cultural and recreational activities for youth. There is also an area rodeo club.

Public Safety. The Cheyenne River Sioux Tribal Law Enforcement Department employs 26 officers and serves the reservation. Eagle Butte also has a city police department and a volunteer fire department.

Education. BIA/Eagle Butte Public Schools (elementary, middle, junior high, and high schools) are located in Eagle Butte. E.A.G.L.E. Center, serving at-risk youth, is the public school system's state-certified alternative school, also located in Eagle Butte. The Cheyenne River Exceptional Education program provides special education services to students throughout the school system.

The tribe chartered Si Tanka Huron University, which offers to students from around the world the opportunity of higher education in a multicultural environment. Two campuses, one in Eagle Butte and another in Huron, are available. Reservation students may apply for tuition assistance from the higher education grant program.

The Cheyenne River Head Start program also operates on the reservation, as do the Cheyenne River Developmental Clinic, YMCA, Alcoholics Anonymous, the Artist Craft Project, Boy Scouts and Girl Scouts of America, Camp Marrowbone, a domestic violence and sexual assault outreach program called Sacred Heart Outreach, 7th Generation Youth Council (Leaders Club), a summer lunch program, Founders Day, and other holidays and special programs.

Health Care. The Indian Health Service provides health care and ambulance services at the Cheyenne River Service Unit Hospital and Clinic. The tribal health department offers health care through community health, diabetes, and maternal child health programs, and it provides outpatient health care service in four outlying community clinics. Mental and dental health services, and reduced-cost eye care are also available.

ENVIRONMENTAL CONCERNS

The Cheyenne River Sioux Tribe has an environmental protection department to provide guidance in protecting the reservation's environment and natural resources for future generations. Initiated in 1990, the department started with only a pesticide enforcement program operated in cooperation with the U.S. EPA, Region 8, allowing the tribe to monitor and regulate the general and restricted use of pesticide activities of the commercial and agriculture pesticide applicators on the reservation. They continue to examine current tribal codes and regulations for policies that may not have environmental protections as their highest priority. The staff also develops regulations, codes and statutes that strengthen the tribe's enforcement capabilities.

Other programs operated by the department include: a general assistance program to develop and draft codes, regulations, and administrative procedures; outreach and educational activities in the communities; the 106 water quality monitoring program; a national pollution discharge elimination system; and a lead base paint program. Some of the projects currently underway are the ANA/DOD Mitigation Program, referred to as the Armstrong County Gunnery Range Project; the ANA/SEDS Program; the ANA/Regulatory Enhancement Program; and the BIA Water Resources Program.

In the comprehensive economic development plan formulated in 2002, the tribe stated a desire to develop a comprehensive groundwater management plan to help combat aquifer depletion and to increase available supplies through inter-basin transfer. Switching to drought resistant crops was under consideration as was scheduling irrigation and improving delivery systems. The water plan will include establishing tribal water rights and future permitted uses of the Missouri River.

Honoring Nations Honoree 1999

Pte Hca Ka, Inc., Cheyenne River Sioux Tribe

Indians living on the Cheyenne River Reservation in north central South Dakota are among the poorest in the United States. In the early 1990s, 70 percent of reservation's Indian households had incomes near the poverty level, and the unemployment rate exceeded 50 percent. While these economic conditions are the result of many different factors, one of the earliest and most devastating was the systematic destruction of the high plains buffalo herds in the late 1800s. It was an attack on both the Lakota economy and the Lakota way of life. Today, leaders of the Cheyenne River Sioux Tribe (CRST) are committed to improving reservation economic conditions and to doing so within important boundaries: they hope to achieve economic success without causing further cultural disintegration.

Pte Hca Ka, Inc. aptly achieves these goals. The tribally owned and chartered corporation was founded in 1991 to manage and develop the tribal buffalo herd. As in any successful wildlife-based business, Pte Hca Ka's managers aim to develop a biologically sound herd and a financially sound enterprise. The key difference is that Pte Hca Ka's managers pursue these goals within a culturally compatible system for raising and harvesting buffalo. Their commitment has paid off. Today, Pte Hca Ka is a thriving "socio-economic enterprise." It sustains important tribal traditions, helps tribal members reconnect with Lakota culture, and contributes both directly and indirectly to the alleviation of reservation economic problems.

In its early years, for example, Pte Hca Ka's main focus was on building and strengthening the Tribe's buffalo herd, which began with fewer than 100 animals. But increasing herd size was not allowed to take precedence over the importance of making animals available to tribal members for ceremonial uses and traditional feasts. In 1991, the CRST's district governments received a total a six buffalo for these purposes. By 1996, Pte Hca Ka provided them with a total of 20 buffalo-and the herd had grown to more than 1,000 animals.

With the growth in herd size, Pte Hca Ka's managers considered expansion into off-reservation commercial sales and concluded that in this pursuit, too, culturally appropriate methods were important. Because many Lakota view the typical feedlot and slaughtering process as disrespectful and wasteful, enterprise managers hoped to find a way to harvest and fully process buffalo on the open range. A break-through came when Pte Hca Ka's director heard of a mobile unit used by Lapplanders to harvest reindeer. With the help of Swedish engineers who had worked with the Lapplanders, he was able design a similar unit for buffalo. Now, Pte Hca Ka employees can harvest buffalo with respect, and in a manner that meets modern health standards. According to Lakota custom, none of the buffalo products are wasted. Most commercial quality meat is sold off-reservation to specialty meat distributors. The remainder is contributed to the Tribe's schools and elderly program, sold at reduced prices in the local grocery store, and donated to local and national Indian events. Hide and bone parts are collected and cleaned for ceremonial, craft, and even everyday purposes. Thus, in addition to employing 15 people and earning revenue for the Tribe, Pte Hca Ka's "commercial" operations are restoring the centrality of the buffalo to Lakota life.

Pte Hca Ka's various outreach efforts reinforce this process. Pte Hca Ka has encouraged Cheyenne River Community College to develop an entire course of study in bison management, both to train future workers and to share the enterprise's learning more widely. School children are invited to make field trips to visit the herd and view program operations, and elders are urged to work with Pte Hca Ka to share their knowledge of the buffalo culture. Soon, Pte Hca Ka will extend these outreach efforts to an even broader public. In 1999, the corporation issued bonds to finance the purchase of an additional 21,000 acres. Pte Hca Ka will develop this area, as well as the existing buffalo range, into the first-ever tribal national park. Once open, the park will allow members and non-members alike to be witness to the restoration of a modern buffalo culture among the Cheyenne River Sioux.

Certainly, Pte Hca Ka's success can be attributed to its innovative business strategy, but it has also depended on an arms-length relationship with the CRST's political leaders and a strong connection with the reservation community. For example, the enterprise's charter and by-laws prohibit elected officials from involvement in day-to-day program management. Because the Tribal Council and President uphold this agreement, Pte Hca Ka's managers are able to focus on long-run enterprise success rather than short-term political goals. Similarly, Pte Hca Ka was founded on the will of the people, and as the business has grown, Pte Hca Ka's director has continued to elicit community opinions and cultivate support for the enterprise. This way, members understand that it is not just a few people, but the Tribe as a whole that benefits from the buffalo business.

The Lakota expression "Mitakuye Oyasin" means "all my relatives." It expresses the interdependence the Lakota have with all other living creatures, particularly the buffalo. Thus, it is not surprising that many Lakota believe the fate of their nation is tied to the fate of the buffalo. By helping to ensure the survival of the buffalo, Pte Hca Ka, Inc. renews the Lakota-as well as their land and the natural ecosystems of the plains-and proves that it is possible to combine modern technology, indigenous traditions, and economic success.

Honoring Nations Honoree1999

Text in its entirety from The Harvard Project On American Indian Economic Development

John F. Kennedy School of Government Harvard University

Crow Creek

Crow Creek Sioux Reservation
Federal reservation
Sioux
Buffalo, Hyde, and Hughes
counties, South Dakota

Crow Creek Sioux Tribe
P.O. Box 50
Fort Thompson, SD 57339
605-245-2221
605-245-2222
605-245-2470 Fax

Total area *(BIA realty, 2003)*
151,512 acres

Total area *(Tribal source, 2005)*
295,948 acres

Tribally owned *(BIA realty, 2003)*
68,928 acres

Tribally owned *(Tribal source, 2005)*
72,255 acres

Federal trust *(BIA realty, 2003)*
25,243 acres

Individually owned
(BIA realty, 2003)
57,341 acres

Individually owned
(Tribal source, 2005)
61,061 acres

Population *2000 census*
2,225

Population *(Tribal source, 2005)*
2,816

Total area
295,948
acres

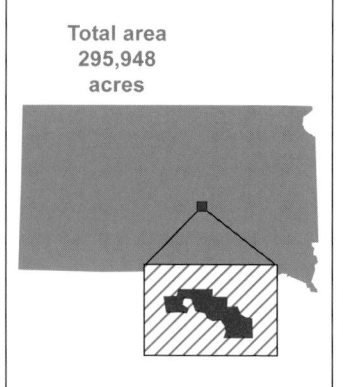

LOCATION AND LAND STATUS

The Crow Creek Sioux Reservation is located in south-central South Dakota on the eastern shore of the Missouri River, about 26 miles northwest of I-90 via Highway 50 at Chamberlain. The reservation's southwestern boundary is formed by Lake Sharpe, a reservoir formed by the Fort Randall and Big Bend dams on the Missouri.

PHYSICAL DESCRIPTION

Thirty-five square miles, or approximately 16,000 acres of reservation land, are inundated by reservoir waters. Remaining terrain is dominated by rolling, grassy hills, lush riparian woodland corridors, and river breaks.

CLIMATE

Winter temperatures range between -30°F and 25°F. Summertime temperatures vary between 80°F and 110°F in June, July, and August, with a seasonal average of 80°F. The average year-round high is only 59°F. Precipitation averages approximately 18 inches annually with occasional droughts during the summer; there is a three-month growing season. Winters can be very harsh, with moderate to heavy snowfalls and occasional severe blizzard conditions. Winds average 14 miles per hour daily all year round. The elevation at Fort Thompson is less than 1,000 feet above sea level.

CULTURE AND HISTORY

The Crow Creek Sioux are members of the Great Sioux Nation. They call themselves Lakota or Dakota, meaning friend or ally. The word Sioux comes from a Chippewa (Ojibwe) word, Nadowesioux, which means little snake or enemy. French fur trappers in the area now known as Minnesota were the first to call them Sioux. Crow Creek Sioux are descendants of two divisions of Dakota and Nakota people: the Ihanktowan (Yankton and Yanktonais) who were known as the Middle Sioux, and the Isanti (Dakota), who are comprised of four bands that lived on the eastern side of the Dakota Nation. The groups speak the Nakota dialect of the Siouan language, and they were farmers in the river-plains who supplemented their diet with extensive hunting, especially of buffalo. They maintain a strong oral tradition, passing along history from elders to youth in a centuries-old cultural custom.

Shortly after encountering white explorers about the end of the seventeenth century in north-central Minnesota, the Lakotas (also called western Sioux) moved west in pursuit of buffalo in what is now South Dakota, Montana, Wyoming, and Nebraska. They did not actively resist white immigration until the whites began to decimate the buffalo herds. Eventually, following Little Crow's War in Minnesota, a treaty with the United States was signed in 1863, designating western lands along the Missouri River as a reservation. Although the Lakotas originally had a woodland economy based on hunting, fishing, and gathering, they had to change radically to survive. The Lakotas became classic Plains Indians, skilled horsemen and buffalo hunters, and they often allied with the Cheyennes and Arapahos. Their territory extended at one time from the Big Horn Mountains in the west to Minnesota in the east, Canada in the north, and the Platte River to the south in what is now Nebraska.

Sioux fame was established by the Red Cloud Wars of the 1860s, distinguished as the only victory of American Indians in war against the U.S. government. In a direct violation of the 1868 Treaty of Fort Laramie, General George A. Custer and

his 7th Cavalry entered the Black Hills in 1874 and found gold there, starting a gold rush of white settlers and miners. The Sioux resisted all attempts by the federal government to buy or rent their sacred Black Hills. Custer's Cavalry was ordered to "round up" all warring Sioux and place them on the reservation. The now-famous Battle of the Little Big Horn took place on June 25, 1876, at Greasy Grass, Montana. It was a stunning defeat for the 7th Cavalry. Nonetheless, many Sioux fled to Canada; many others surrendered to the reservation. Still determined to obtain access to the gold in the Black Hills, the U.S. government passed the Agreement of 1877, which illegally took the Black Hills from the Great Sioux Nation. The Allotment of 1887 divided Indian lands into 160-acre lots-one per household-while 80-acre lots were distributed to adult males. This division further divided Sioux lands.

An Act in 1889 broke up the Great Sioux Nation into smaller reservations. The Crow Creek Reservation, or Wiciyela Sioux Division, formally established on March 2, 1889, was one of only three parcels of land the Sioux retained, and it serves as the home to Lakota people from several areas. It was administratively separated from the Lower Brule Reservation on the other side of the Missouri River in 1971. The majority of the Crow Creek population lives in the community and district known as Fort Thompson, which also serves as the reservation's headquarters.

Powwows, rodeos, and horse and foot races are held during summer months. Special powwows are held for special achievements, such as graduation or military service, with traditional honoring ceremonies, giveaways, and feasts to celebrate the accomplishments. The oral tradition is still passed down from the elders to the youth.

GOVERNMENT

Established by treaty in 1963, the Crow Creek Sioux Reservation is governed under a constitution and bylaws originally approved in 1923. Although previously rejecting revisions under the Indian Reorganization Act, Crow Creek Sioux later accepted revisions that were approved in 1949. They now have a seven-member popularly elected governing council consisting of a chairman, a vice-chairman, a secretary-treasurer, and four additional council members elected by tribal members. One each is elected from two districts, Big Bend and Crow Creek, and four are elected from Fort Thompson, the largest district. The council chairperson serves as the tribe's administrative head.

The Crow Creek Sioux Tribe, under PL-638, contracts with the BIA to administer key programs and services, operating under a constitution and bylaws.

ECONOMY

Replacing 80 percent unemployment rates with relative prosperity has been a decades-long battle. In 2004, most employment on the reservation was provided by the tribe via its many initiatives, such as the Lode Star Casino, and through the BIA and the Indian Health Service. However, the major economic activity is cattle ranching and farming.

Agriculture and Livestock. Scarcity of surface water adversely affects agriculture and livestock operations on the reservation. During droughts, some sources dry up altogether. The reservation is dotted with small streams, lakes, and dugouts

TRI-SD-cc-003 Welcome to Crow Creek Sioux Indian Reservation" sign

TRI-SD-cc-005 Lode Star Casino and Hotel

that are available during wet periods, usually in spring. Groundwater is also scarce, and deep groundwater, although plentiful, is highly mineralized and of poor quality. To counter these deficiencies, the tribe built an irrigated farm complex, the Big Bend Farm Corporation, where corn and soybeans are raised with some success. There are a total of 15,121 acres of farmland on the reservation; 3,480 are irrigated acres. The tribe owns a small herd of buffalo.

Gaming. The tribally owned and operated Lode Star Casino and Hotel complex is located in Fort Thompson. The 27,500-square-foot facility features 247 slot machines and 4 table games. The hotel has 50 rooms, and there is a restaurant at the site.

Services and Retail. Businesses owned by tribal members include a hunting and fishing guide service, two convenience stores, three gas stations, a motel, a video arcade, and a fast food restaurant. Some land is leased for livestock grazing. Most businesses on the reservation, such as restaurants, supermarkets, and other retail stores, are owned by non-Natives. Off-reservation work provides marginal economic subsistence for other tribal members.

Tourism and Recreation. The Crow Creek Sioux Reservation has excellent hunting and fishing facilities, and the wildlife management department provides guided hunts. Deer, antelope, game birds, and waterfowl are hunted with permits on the reservation. The reservation lies beneath the central waterfowl flyway, ensuring vast numbers of migrating species. Lake Sharpe, formed by the construction of the Big Bend Dam, is a popular site for water sports. A campground near the dam has several beaches and boat ramps for public use. Fishing contests, softball, volleyball, and basketball games, and tournaments are available. There are other facilities available nearby at Lake Francis Case. Several fine restaurants and more casual dining opportunities dot the lakes' shorelines.

Old Fort Thompson has been restored and developed as a historical site that attracts many tourists, as does the tribally operated Lode Star Casino and Restaurant. The tribe sponsors two annual powwows, one in June and the Lower Brule Fair and Powwow during the second week of August, which includes a rodeo, horse racing, and a softball tournament. The Crow Creek Sioux provide youth recreational activities and a rodeo club for its young people. Fort Thompson and Fort Chamberlain, 25 miles distant, have cultural museums featuring the area's Native populations: the Lower Brule Sioux, Yanktonai, and Crow Creek Sioux. To get to these facilities, drivers can use the Native American Loop Tour, a self-guided scenic drive following the Missouri River through the Lower Brule and Crow Creek reservations and past the Akta Lakota ("Honor the People") Museum. Organized tours are also available from the Chamberlain Chamber of Commerce or by calling the Alliance of Tribal Tourism.

Mitchell's Prehistoric Indian Village Museum is the only National Historic Archeology Landmark open to the public in South Dakota. Named for the nearby beautiful Lake Mitchell, visitors can walk through a reproduction of an ancient Indian lodge, view a complete buffalo skeleton, and observe art and artifacts of plains culture. At the World Wildlife Adventure Museum, guests are treated to specimens of wildlife taxidermy. Over 200 exhibits are on display from May through October.

INFRASTUCTURE

The Crow Creek Sioux Reservation is crossed east-west by Highway 34 and north-south by Highway 47, a connector to I-90. Highway 50 leads to Chamberlain, South Dakota. There are no transportation services to and from the reservation, but some charter buses and limousines service the Lode Star Casino on a regular basis. Greyhound bus terminals are in Chamberlain and Pierre, South Dakota. The closest commercial air service is also in Pierre, 60 miles northwest of Fort Thompson.

Electricity. The Big Bend Dam Powerhouse, which can produce 468,000 kilowatts of electricity, supplies electrical power to Northwestern Public Service which supplies electricity to the reservation.

Water Supply. The Big Bend Reservoir provides water for the reservation. With funding provided by the Bureau of Reclamation, the tribe has installed and operates a water utility system.

Telecommunications. The Midstate Telephone Company offers telephone services.

COMMUNITY FACILITIES AND SERVICES

The Crow Creek Sioux have a Boys and Girls Club. Several churches on the reservation represent the Mormon, Catholic, Episcopalian, and Presbyterian denominations.

Education. Crow Creek Sioux Tribal Elementary School serves students in K-5. From sixth grade on, students attend the Crow Creek Reservation High School in Stephan, South Dakota. Both schools are in need of rehabilitation or replacement. Despite tribal interventions, in 2004 the schools were in such unsafe and unsanitary condition that they were threatened closure.

Health Care. An Indian Health Service clinic and the tribal health department provide health care. Full-service medical care is available through private hospitals in both Pierre and Chamberlain, and a community health representative provides assistance. The tribal health department provides eye examinations and eyeglasses to all residents at reduced rates and operates an elderly nutrition program.

Tribal enrollment
(Tribal source, 2005)
3,000

Tribal enrollment *(BIA, 2001)*
3,507

Total labor force *2000 census*
586

High school graduate or higher
2000 census
64.9%

Bachelor's degree or higher
2000 census
5.7%

Unemployment rate *2000 census*
21.5%

Per capita income *2000 census*
$5,272

ENVIRONMENTAL CONCERNS
The Crow Creek Sioux Tribe has developed environmental codes and a regulatory authority to protect land and resources within the reservation's boundaries. Maintaining and protecting the land for future generations is a high priority of the tribe, especially since the Pick-Sloan Act, which resulted in the inundation of 16,000 acres of tribal lands and created Lake Sharpe and Lake Francis Case on the Missouri River.

Flandreau Santee

**Flandreau Santee Sioux
Reservation
Federal reservation
Moody County, South Dakota**

Flandreau Santee Sioux Tribe
P.O. Box 283
Flandreau, SD 57028
605-997-3891
605-997-3878 Fax
fsst.org

Total area (BIA realty, 2003)
2,184 acres

Total area (Tribal source, 2005)
4,675 acres

Tribally owned (BIA realty, 2003)
2,184 acres

Tribally owned (Tribal source, 2005)
4,675 acres

Population *2000 census*
408

Tribal enrollment
(Tribal source, 2005)
544

Total labor force *2000 census*
173

High school graduate or higher
2000 census
69.4%

Bachelor's degree or higher
2000 census
6.8%

Unemployment rate *2000 census*
14.5%

Unemployment rate
(Tribal source, 2005)
9.8%

Per capita income *2000 census*
$11,877

LOCATION AND LAND STATUS

The Flandreau Santee Sioux Reservation is in southeastern South Dakota, approximately 45 miles north of Sioux Falls near the Minnesota border. It was established by an Act of Congress in 1934. Tribal headquarters are in the community of Flandreau, along the banks of the Big Sioux River.

PHYSICAL DESCRIPTION

The reservation lies in a region of South Dakota known as the Prairie Coteau, which is characterized by undulating, hummocky terrain, seasonal wetlands and a chain of relatively large glacial lakes. Vegetation consists of big and little blue stem, switch grass, Indian grass, blue grama grass, and burr oak woodlands surrounding riparian wetlands.

CLIMATE

The elevation at Flandreau is 1,548 feet above sea level. Year-round high temperatures average only 55°F. Year-round low temperatures average almost 32°F. The area receives approximately 23 inches of precipitation annually.

CULTURE AND HISTORY

The Flandreau Santee Sioux are descendents of the "Mdewakantonwan" (People of Spirit Lake), members of the Isanti Division (a river-plains people who farmed and hunted buffalo) of the Great Sioux Nation. They call themselves Dakota, meaning friend or ally, and speak the Dakota dialect of the Siouan language.

Prior to European contact, the Dakota/Lakota people lived in Minnesota and Wisconsin. Uprooted and displaced by white settlers, they lived a semi-nomadic subsistence lifestyle until 1851 when they ceded their land and agreed to a western reservation. By 1862, angered by the federal government's failure to live up to its treaty obligations, many Santees revolted against reservation life. An uprising, led by Little Crow, against white traders who refused to distribute food and provisions to the Indians, was quickly put down. Many Santees scattered to other parts of the country and into Canada. Twelve hundred Indians, many who never participated in the uprising, surrendered. Military tribunals found over 306 of them guilty and sentenced them to death. President Lincoln granted pardons, but 38 were eventually hanged on December 26, 1866. Survivors were shipped to concentration camps in Davenport, Iowa, and Fort Thompson, South Dakota. These groups were reunited in 1866 at the Santee Agency in Nebraska.

Between 1869 and 1873, 75 Santee Sioux Indian families gathered near Flandreau, South Dakota, took homesteads as authorized by the Sioux Treaty of 1868, and renounced their tribal membership, as conditionally required by the treaty. These "citizen Indians" had no federal aid except a school, which was established in 1870. In 1873 they built a Presbyterian Church in what became Flandreau; it is one of the oldest continually used churches in South Dakota. In 1879 the federal government designated their community as the Flandreau Special Agency. It wasn't until 1891 that the government responded to pleas from the community and appointed an overseer who administered a meager program of benefits.

In 1929 the community voted to legally establish itself as the Flandreau Santee Sioux Tribe. Its constitution, under the authority of the Indian Reorganization Act, was initially adopted in 1931, and the community became a federally recognized

reservation in 1935. The constitution was revised to better meet the requirements of the Act in 1936 and was approved in that year, then revised again in November 1937. The tribal charter was ratified in October 1936. Unlike other Sioux reservations, which have popular elections for tribal chair, the Flandreau Reservation is governed by an executive committee.

Through a New Deal program, the tribe operated a garment factory until 1952, which manufactured clothing used in federal schools nationwide. In the 1960s, Great Society programs enabled the Flandreau Santees to build homes and irrigate farmland. A casino was built in 1990. The BIA still operates a large boarding school on the Flandreau Reservation at the site of the original 1870 institution; however, graduation rates remain low.

Culturally, the Flandreau Santees have protected their traditions well. Many pipe carriers and Sun Dancers, artists, singers, and dancers live in or near Flandreau. The tribe holds summer powwows, rodeos, and horse and foot races. Special powwows are held for special achievements, such as graduation or military service, with traditional honoring ceremonies, giveaways and feasts to celebrate the accomplishments. The oral tradition is still passed down from the elders to the youth. The Dakota people still practice their sacred and traditional ceremonies encompassing the seven rites brought by White Buffalo Calf Woman.

GOVERNMENT

The tribal charter was adopted in 1936. The reservation is governed by an executive committee, known as the tribal council, which consists of a president, vice-president, secretary, and four elected trustees serving two-year staggered terms. The treasurer is appointed. The president serves as the tribe's administrative head.

Today the Santee Sioux, under PL-638, contract with the BIA to administer key programs and services, operating under a constitution and bylaws. The Santee Tribal Council has provided leadership in South Dakota regarding gaming, and has advocated tribal sovereignty in the national arena while initiating local community partnerships to improve health, education, natural resources, and law enforcement services to all its tribal members. They have a tribal court system and offer various other programs and services to meet the needs of the people, such as: a maintenance department; Health Start programs for infants and toddlers; various counseling and social service programs; a natural resources office; Title VI senior citizens programs; the Grace Moore Center; tribal housing authority; economic development; a human resources office; and TecWeb programs at the Agnes Ross Educational Center.

A majority of the ongoing tribal government services are available via the office of economic development whose resource coordinator ensures program and planning coordination for all economic development projects with: BIA roads maintenance and planning; BIA trust lands; cultural preservation; Federal Emergency Management Assistance; federal, state, and tribal representation on various committees, boards and commissions; financial assistance; representation on the intertribal commission on utility policies and intertribal taxation and transportation committees; land acquisition and use; lighting and signage; master plan development and updates; Mni Sose Intertribal Water Rights Coalition; repatriation issues; solar energy and wind power development; telecommunications and utilities; tribal taxation; and sits with the Western Area Power Association.

ECONOMY
The tribal economy is centered on tribal operations and gaming, with small retail businesses and agriculture providing support.

Government as Employer. Primary employers at the reservation are the Flandreau Indian School, the tribe via its economic development projects, the Royal River Casino, and various retail enterprises. Other employers include the BIA and some individual business owners operating a recording studio and arts and crafts shops. Tribal land with full utilities is available for the development of an industrial park.

Agriculture and Livestock. The tribe produces corn and beans on 1,726 acres. Cattle and buffalo graze on 844 acres of pasture.

Gaming. The Flandreau Santee Sioux Tribe conducts Las Vegas-style gaming in its Royal River Casino. Opened in 1990 and expanded and refurbished in 1995, the casino now employs over 400 people, approximately 75 percent non-Indians and 25 percent Indians, from surrounding areas of South Dakota. The casino is open 24 hours a day, seven days a week. The 17,000-square-foot facility features 250 slot machines, 8 table games, 350 bingo seats and 5,776 square feet of convention and event space. The casino's walls are painted with murals of the tribe's history. The complex includes an entertainment venue with 350 theater-style seats and another 250 table seats. The adjacent 126-room Royal River Motel has a pool, luxury suites featuring in-room spas, buffet-style dining at the River's Bend Buffet, and a snack bar.

Construction. The tribe owns a backhoe and a tree spade.

Services and Retail. A bowling alley, convenience store, gift shop, and a smoke shop are located in Flandreau.

Tourism and Recreation. The reservation is located in a prime hunting and fishing area. Water sports can be experienced on numerous nearby lakes, with several beach areas and boat ramps available. The Big Sioux River provides ample opportunities for fishing, swimming, and canoeing. Split Rock Creek, to the east, is known for its scenic quartzite cliffs towering over the river's flow. Hiking trails in Palisades State Park, just south of Flandreau, lead to ancient cliffs. Lodging accommodations are available at the Royal River Motel.

Other tourist attractions include the Pipestone National Monument Dells of the Big Sioux River There is also a nine-hole golf course. The Moody County Museum in Flandreau contains a collection of American Indian and early pioneer artifacts. The Four Winds Cultural Center, located on the campus of the old Flandreau Indian School, displays artifacts, memorabilia, and contemporary materials. The old school campus is an historical attraction in its own right, having been built in 1870. Chief Little Crow's grave is nearby. South of town, the tribal buffalo herd makes for prime photographic opportunities.

The tribe sponsors an annual powwow in July. In addition to the dancing competition, the powwow also features a softball tournament. Throughout the rest of the year, softball, volleyball, trap shooting, and basketball tournaments are also available.

INFRASTRUCTURE
The reservation is located approximately 8 miles east of I-29 via South Dakota Highway 13 near the Minnesota border. An airport is located in Brookings, South Dakota, 28 miles north on I-29, and all commercial transport facilities are available in Sioux Falls, South Dakota, 45 miles south via I-29.

Electricity. The City of Flandreau and Sioux Valley Electric provide electric utility services for the tribe.

Telecommunications. Qwest Communications provides telephone service.

Housing. The tribal housing authority has won awards for well-kept housing conditions on the reservation. There are HUD low-rent housing units and individual scattered sites, with a few limited quarters for BIA employees. Homes for purchase and rental housing are available in Flandreau, Brookings, and Sioux Falls, South Dakota, and in Pipestone, Minnesota.

COMMUNITY FACILITIES AND SERVICES
The tribe has a community center, a bowling alley, a recreation center, and a rodeo and powwow grounds.

Education. The Flandreau School District serves 830 students in grades pre-kindergarten through 12, and the BIA at Flandreau still maintains the Flandreau Indian boarding school. It is a fully accredited, off-reservation high school serving students in grades 9-12. The Flandreau School District was awarded a five-year Visions TecWeb grant in 1997 to explore new ways of providing culturally relevant instruction that integrates technology into learning environments. The district also participates in a Johnson O'Malley PL-638 contract to meet the special academic, social, and cultural needs of Indian students in public, BIA, and tribal schools. A separate program, the BIA/AVT Higher Education PL-638 Contract, supports and encourages tribal members and their descendants to pursue higher education with congressionally appropriated funding. The All Nations Youth Council is a tribally sponsored youth organization; participants are encouraged through the All Nations Youth Wellness Program to pursue positive avenues for success in academic achievement, health, culture and spirituality, and community involvement.

Health Care. The Flandreau Santee Sioux Tribal Health Clinic is an outpatient clinic operated by the Indian Health Service under a PL-638 contract. The facility offers several services to the local community, including a licensed, full-time physician and a physicians assistant, licensed nursing staff, dental services, a chemical dependency unit, a child care program, community health representatives, diabetes prevention, the HIV Prevention Coalition, injury prevention services, laboratory services, mental health programs, the Northern Plains Healthy Start Program, medical specialties such as optometry and podiatry, and social service staff. They also oversee an elderly nutrition program. The Flandreau Municipal Hospital is a fully accredited critical access hospital. There is an ambulance service for emergencies.

ENVIRONMENTAL CONCERNS
The Flandreau Santee Sioux Tribe has developed environmental codes and a regulatory authority to protect land and resources within the reservation's boundaries. Maintaining and protecting the land for future generations is a high priority for the tribe. They have identified one environmental problem to be addressed immediately. A 3M medical facility, upwind of the reservation, creates pollutants affecting air and water quality on reservation lands. The tribe wants air and water quality monitoring systems to monitor the effects.

Flandreau Santee

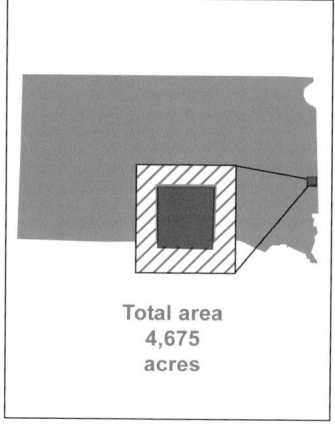

**Total area
4,675
acres**

Lake Traverse

Lake Traverse Reservation
Federal reservation
Sisseton-Wahpeton Sioux
Roberts, Day, Codington,
Marshall, and Grant
counties, South Dakota
Sargent and Richland
counties, North Dakota

Sisseton-Wahpeton Sioux
  Tribe of the Lake Traverse
  Reservation
P.O. Box 509
Agency Village, SD 57262
  605-698-3911
  605-698-7907 Fax

LOCATION AND LAND STATUS

In accords between the tribe and the United States, the tribe's right to Minnesota, North Dakota, and South Dakota land was acknowledged, according to details from Mni Sose IWRC. A small piece of today's reservation is in North Dakota, but the main part lies in South Dakota. The original reservation was greatly reduced to its present size through subsequent Homestead Acts to provide land for non-Indian settlers. Occupying parts of three counties in northeastern South Dakota and three counties in southeastern North Dakota, the Sisseton-Wahpeton Sioux Tribe's Lake Traverse Reservation is mostly located on or near I-29, the Mni Sose organization notes. The BIA and tribal headquarters are located in Agency Village, South Dakota. The present reservation site was created by Article III of the Treaty of February 19, 1867, an outgrowth of a treaty signed in 1863 at Enemy Swim Lake. This prior treaty occurred in the wake of the tribe's return from Canada where it had fled the previous year to escape the agonizing Minnesota Sioux War.

Rights-of-way, waterways, watercourses and streams that flow through any portion of the reservation and to other lands later appended to the reservation under United States statutes are all under the tribes control. To supply white settlers with land, the government passed further homestead acts that diminished the former extent of the reservation to its current boundaries, Mni Sose recounts. The Dakota people set a high value on preserving and safeguarding the land, according to the Mni Sose group. The operation of legal and regulatory systems provides the means for the Sisseton-Wahpeton Sioux Tribe to exert protective control over the land and natural resources that make up the six-county Lake Traverse reservation. The tribe asserts these rights and duties under tribal and federal law. Tribal members have ownership of two-thirds of the more than 400-square-mile reservation. The tribe owns one-third of the land. Tribal land uses listed by Mni Sose include: agriculture, 37,906 acres; wetlands, 83,663 acres; grazing, 56,512 acres; forestry, 9,417 acres; housing/industrial, 932 acres; commercial, 649 acres; and road and railroad gravel, 264.71 acres.

PHYSICAL DESCRIPTION

The reservation's topography consists of two general areas and attendant terrains: the Coteau Hills, which cover most of the eastern and southern portion of the reservation; and the Minnesota River valleys, which cover its northeastern quadrant. Elevation varies from 2,100 feet in the Coteau Hills to about 1,000 feet at Lake Traverse.

CLIMATE

The Mni Sose climate profile reveals that summer precipitation averages 16 or 17 inches. Ninety days in summer is the extent of the growing season. Winter snow is usually moderate or heavy. Winter temperatures range between -30°F and +25°F. Summer temperatures vary between 69°F and 110°F; however, the average is 80°F. The year's mean wind speed is 14 mph daily. Water shortage can occur in the summer, and winter conditions can be extreme, but agreeable weather prevails in spring and fall.

CULTURE AND HISTORY

The Sisseton-Wahpeton Dakotas are members of the Great Sioux Nation, whose members call themselves Dakota, friend or ally. The 'D' dialect of the Siouan tongue was spoken by the Isanti people, the ancestors of the Sisseton-Wahpeton Sioux Tribe, as the Mni Sose history narrates. For about a century after the appearance of white explorers, all the Sioux Indians occupied village sites along the Minnesota-Wisconsin border, an excellent spot for hunting, fishing, and planting. Most of these bands were Dakota-speaking. When the settlers began to put down roots, a series of treaties was imposed upon the Indians, with the Sissetons accepting the terms of the 1851 Traverse des Sioux Treaty. In the wake of the 1862 Minnesota Sioux War (Little Crow's War), federal officials placed subdivisions of Sissetons on both Lake Traverse and Devils Lake Reservations.

Several treaties between the Great Sioux Nation and the U.S. government between 1865 and 1868, defined the Nation's land base, which once stretched from Wisconsin to the Bighorn Mountains. Gold exploration that violated the 1868 treaty led to a gold rush into the sacred Black Hills. After defeating General George A. Custer and his 7th Cavalry at the Battle of the Little Big Horn in Montana in 1876, large numbers of Sioux dispersed to reservations or to Canada. Over time, reservation lands were allotted or otherwise reduced in size. Residents of the Lake Traverse Reservation endured land loss, financial hardship, and federal paternalism. While the initial reservation amounted to nearly one million acres, the approximately 2,700 tribal members were allotted just over 300,000 acres, with the remainder purchased for non-Indian settlement. Over the years, tribal members sold off their allotments for survival, and by 1952 they retained only about 117,000 acres. In 1946 the tribe adopted its constitution and bylaws.

During the Depression, tribal members survived through subsistence farming, trapping, hunting, fishing, and federal trust fund payments until New Deal programs came along. The Civilian Conservation Corps was especially helpful in providing employment to the reservation. By the 1960s, cultural renewal had generated changes in tribal education and government. Congress funded two new schools, one in Sisseton and one in Peever, to provide integrated instruction. In 1975 tribal councilors chartered the Sisseton-Wahpeton Community College and the Tiospa Zina High School to furnish education with an emphasis on tribal values.

The region's economy, based primarily on agriculture and cattle grazing, has long supported substantial numbers of tribal members through fieldwork. By the 1980s, however, the tribe had successfully established a manufacturing base on the reservation, and by the early 1990s it had developed a highly lucrative gaming industry. On today's reservation, summer is a season for powwows, rodeos, and races, according to the Mni Sose account. Graduation and entry into the military are occasions for special honors, giveaways, and feasting. Tribal elders continue to teach the oral tradition to the younger generation.

GOVERNMENT

The tribe is incorporated and operates under a 1966 revised constitution and bylaws which replaced those of 1946. A tribal council made up of a chairman, vice-chairman, secretary, and treasurer and other elected members, governs the Sisseton-Wahpeton Sioux Tribe, according to Mni Sose. The administrative head of the tribe is the chairman. Two years is the term of office set for the chairman, officers, and council members. Council members are chosen by district.

ECONOMY

The primary means of livelihood on the Sisseton-Wahpeton reservation, Mni Sose states, is cattle ranching and farming. Other tribal sources of employment listed include the Nation's plastic bag factory, an irrigated farm, and a hunting program for small game, big game, and waterfowl. The Dakota Sioux Casino and Agency Bingo are also tribal businesses. A new truck stop facility contains a bingo and gambling venue. There are 823 public employees as counted by the BIA.

Government as Employer. At present, 823 tribal employees work within government services, including those indirectly employed through the gaming enterprises. As of 1993, the tribe and its entities employed between 900 and 1,000 persons, making it the largest employer in northeast Dakota. Private employees total 378. The largest employers are listed as the Sisseton-Wahpeton Sioux Tribe, Sisseton-Wahpeton Community College, Dakota Sioux Casino, BIA, and the Indian Health Service.

Economic Development Projects. The tribe's longtime goal has been to reduce its reliance on federal projects and programs. The success of gaming has helped realize this goal, but the tribe continues to pursue opportunities to attract or develop additional manufacturing entities like Dakota Western, its plastic bag manufacturing plant. These efforts seek to address the needs of the local market and to use the tribe's natural and human resources more directly and effectively. The tribe is assessing the prospects for residential, commercial, and recreational development along the shores of Lake Traverse.

Agriculture and Livestock. The primary economic activities on the reservation are farming and ranching. In 1993 the tribe was initiating development of an agribusiness project involving several other Dakota tribes in the region. The tribe intends to introduce high-quality cattle grazing and production to the reservation, beginning with a minimum of 150 bred heifers on a select 300 to 400 acres of land. Currently, individual Sisseton-Wahpeton Sioux members raise cattle, sheep, horses, and hogs. Additionally, the tribe receives over $1.2 million annually from the lease of lands to non-Indians for crop production and grazing. This income allows for the repayment of FHA loans that were used to purchase most of the land currently owned by the tribe.

Water is crucial to growth of the reservation's agriculture industry. Streams, lakes, and dugouts are common sources of surface water around the area. However, contamination of lakes causes supplies to become inadequate from time to time. Further underground lies more abundant artesian water, but this has high mineral content and is considered an inferior resource. A drop in the supply of water on the reservation causes lower cattle production and prevents efficient use of grazing land and other valuable resources. The undependable feeder-cattle output then makes further expansion into livestock-related industries difficult, according to Mni Sose's analysis.

Gaming. Dakota Sioux's website listing includes the Dakota Sioux Casino near Watertown, South Dakota; Dakota Connection Casino in Sisseton, South Dakota; and Dakota Magic Casino near Hankinson, North Dakota. All are part of Dakota Nation Gaming Enterprise, owned and operated by the Sisseton-Wahpeton Dakota Oyate Tribe. The tribe's first two gaming facilities began as simple bingo operations in 1989; following a favorable federal court ruling in 1990, the Dakota Sioux Casino (at Watertown) added blackjack to its operations, while both sites added slot machines. The two operations jointly produced over $15 million in revenues in 1993, employed nearly 500 persons (many of them tribal members),

and produced about $1.2 million for distribution to the reservation's seven districts and its organizations and programs. The 7,392-square-foot Dakota Sioux Casino now has 200 reel slot machines, 160 bingo seats, 8 table games, 5 poker tables, blackjack in the new casino addition, a restaurant, an entertainment venue, and 642 parking spaces as listed on Gambling Business Directory Online (GBD). It employs 200. The 20,000-square-foot Dakota Connection Casino and Bingo offers 50 slot machines/VLTs, 5 table games, 300 bingo seats, 2 restaurants, 300 parking spaces, and employs 100, according to GBD.

Fisheries. In 1992, the tribe opened a hatchery for harvesting a variety of fish (walleye and northern pike among them) and restocking reservation lakes. The tribe is exploring other forms of aquaculture as well.

Construction. The expansion of the tribe's gaming operations has provided construction industry employment. The tribe's current small-business sector is heavily concentrated in the areas of construction and automotive repair. The construction firms operate predominantly during the summer months.

Mining. Granite outcrops, which appear just southeast of the reservation in Grant County, are extensively quarried for dimension stone and the monument business. The tribe also utilizes this area's gravel resources for its road repair and construction efforts.

Manufacturing. Dakota Western, the tribe's plastic trash bag manufacturer, began in a 1,750-square-foot makeshift building, but in 1992 it moved into a new 25,000-square-foot facility planned and constructed by the tribe (with EDA assistance). The firm, whose major contract is with the U.S. General Services Administration, currently employs about 35 tribal members and has excellent prospects for expanding its markets.

Industrial Parks. The tribe has a 20-acre industrial park funded by the EDA, which provides commercial and industrial sites, along with water and sewer facilities. The park is able to meet the needs of most moderate-sized plants. The park is directly adjacent to the tribal headquarters complex, about seven miles south of Sisseton.

Services and Retail. The reservation supports numerous tribally owned businesses including various small construction firms, automotive repair shops, and small stores. A convenience store, a laundromat, an auto-repair shop, a video arcade/fast food shop, and arts and handcrafts sales make up the nontribal enterprises listed on Mni Sose.

Tourism and Recreation. Recreational features noted by Mni Sose include hunting and fishing on the reservation-thought to be among the area's best; an abundance of lakes, which provides wide scope for water recreation; and high-stakes bingo and gambling complemented by dining facilities in both Sisseton and Watertown, South Dakota, which are offered by the tribe's casino operations.

A substantial number of visitors come to the reservation for the Fourth of July and Veterans Day powwows. Rodeo and softball events and a dancing contest are held during the July gathering. Water recreation is popular, making use of lakeshore and boating facilities. Softball, volleyball, and basketball competitions take place in season.

INFRASTRUCTURE
Electricity. Northwestern Public Service supplies electricity to the Sisseton-Wahpeton Reservation.

Lake Traverse

TRI-SD-LT-001 Sisseton-Sioux Wahpeton College

Total area *(BIA realty, 2003)*
107,902.70 acres

Tribally owned *(BIA realty, 2003)*
19,525.15 acres

Individually owned
(BIA realty, 2003)
88,376.55 acres

Population *2000 census*
10,408

Tribal enrollment
(BIA labor report, 2001)
10,759

Total labor force *2000 census*
4,593

Total labor force
(BIA labor report, 2001)
2,826

High school graduate or higher
2000 census
74%

Bachelor's degree or higher
2000 census
13.3%

Unemployment rate
(BIA labor report, 2001)
58%

Per capita income *2000 census*
$12,743

Lake Traverse

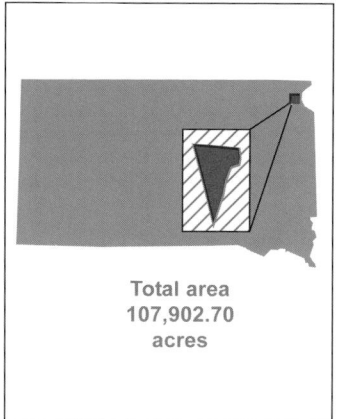

**Total area
107,902.70
acres**

Water Supply. On the Sisseton-Wahpeton Reservation, the issue of water supply dominates efforts to improve both the quality of life and the economy. Lakes, rivers and wells are among the sources on which the tribe's water department relies for usable water. Streams, lakes, and dugouts are common sources of surface water around the area. However, contamination and droughts can cause supplies to become inadequate from time to time and makes such water unsuitable for large-scale purposes. Further underground lies more consistently available groundwater, but this has high mineral content and is considered an inferior resource. A more effective water supply structure is a priority for both home and agricultural needs, as Mni Sose points out.

Transportation. U.S. Highway 12 crosses east-west through the reservation. Highway 81 and I-29 run north-south through the immediate vicinity. Train, bus, and truck lines stop in Sisseton (on the reservation) and in nearby Webster. The nearest commercial air service is located in Watertown, about 50 miles south of the tribal headquarters.

Telecommunications. Telephone service is furnished by US West Communications.

Housing. Most of the living accommodations in the area are publicly owned. HUD Low Rent and Mutual Help programs enable the Sisseton-Wahpeton Housing Authority to administer more than 500 units, some in isolated locations. BIA and Indian Health Service staff have access to housing through their jobs, Mni Sose reports.

COMMUNITY FACILITIES AND SERVICES
A food program for seniors and educational and leisure offerings for young people are listed as community services. An association for those interested in riding organizes rodeo activities.

Education. Tiospa Zina High School and Sisseton-Wahpeton College provide education with sensitivity to traditional tribal culture. Sisseton-Wahpeton College offers associate degrees and certificate programs in several different areas of study. The college also provides support services, such as adult basic education, GED preparation and testing, career counseling, financial aid, library services, learning lab, and tribal archives. They also assist the tribe in their efforts to develop and administer welfare reform measures.

Health Care. The local hospital in Sisseton provides health care for tribal members under a contract with the U.S. Public Health Service. At the health center clinic the Indian Health Service supplies medical services. The tribal health department furnishes a community health representative and ambulance service. Other county hospitals are found in Britton and Day. Optical aids and services are available at low cost from the tribal health department.

ENVIRONMENTAL CONCERNS
In 1996, tribal environmental staff identified the water quality in Enemy Swim Lake as the major reservation environmental problem. The water quality is too poor to use the lake for full-contact water sports.

Lower Brule

**Lower Brule Sioux Indian
Reservation
Federal reservation
Sioux
Lyman and Stanley counties,
South Dakota**

Lower Brule Sioux Tribe
187 Oyate Circle
Lower Brule, SD 57548
605-473-5561
605-473-5606 Fax
lbst.org

LOCATION AND LAND STATUS
The Lower Brule Reservation spans 220,000 acres of prairie land in Lyman and Stanley counties in central South Dakota. Lower Brule, the largest community on the reservation, is approximately 59 miles southeast of Pierre, the state capital. The middle of the old channel of the Missouri River, currently covered by Lake Sharp, marks the reservation's eastern and northern boundaries. Lake Sharpe is an approximately 80-mile-long body of water created by the Big Bend Dam on the Missouri River.

The Lower Brule Sioux Indian Reservation was originally established by the Fort Sully Treaty of 1865, between the federal government and several bands of the Lakota Sioux. Reservation boundaries were redefined after the Great Act of March 1889. In the late 1890s, the entire reservation was moved north 20 miles to a 440,000-acre parcel of lands. This reservation was located well within the Lower Brule's traditional territory. Approximately 442 tribal members refused to relocate and were instead added to the Rosebud Sioux tribal rolls, along with 195,000 acres originally belonging to the Lower Brules. Many members of this group remain unsatisfied even today, as they feel that they are not fully served by either tribe.

Subsequent homestead acts opened the remaining reservation and allowed non-Native settlers access to reservation lands, resulting in an approximate 50 percent reduction in the tribe's land base. Remaining tribal lands were subject to illegal taxation by the county. Additionally, many lands were sold by poverty-stricken tribal members. During the 1950s and 1960s, the tribe was forced to sell over 29,000 acres of prime river bottomlands to the federal government under the Fort

Randall Taking Act and the Big Bend Taking Act. The taken lands were used to create the Fort Randall and Big Bend dams, projects that subsequently caused the flooding and loss of further tribal lands. Physical improvements, including miles of roads, housing, farm and ranch buildings, a rodeo arena, and a racetrack were lost to the rising waters. Sixty-nine percent of the reservation's families were forced to abandon homes that had always been near or in the timberlands that had been flooded. Several culturally significant areas, including worship and gathering sites, and cemeteries, were lost in the flooding.

In 2005, approximately 30 percent of the land within the present boundaries of the Lower Brule Sioux Indian Reservation is non-Indian owned. The tribe has established an aggressive land repurchase and consolidation program to restore traditional Lower Brule lands to tribal ownership. Since the 1950s, the tribe has regained approximately 20 percent of its lands, including about 29,000 acres on- and off-reservation. The tribe currently owns 93 acres of land in Oacama, South Dakota. It built the Circle of Tipis Native American Scenic Byway Information Center there in 2002. It owns 1,080 acres near Sturgis, South Dakota. The tribe has established the Sacred Hills Healing Center on that property. The tribe also owns the 13,000-acre Smith/Cherry Ranch adjacent to the western boundary of the reservation. The tribe operates a cattle ranch and a Buffalo Interpretive Center, and it is planning a camping area on the site.

PHYSICAL DESCRIPTION
Approximately 35 square miles of reservation land were inundated by the reservoirs created by the Fort Randall and Big

Bend dams. Remaining topography ranges from steep, rough badlands near the Missouri River to rolling hills elsewhere.

The reservation is dotted with small streams, lakes, and dugouts available during wet periods, usually spring. During droughts, some sources dry up altogether, and this scarcity of surface water adversely affects agriculture and livestock operations on the reservation. Groundwater is available on tribal lands in natural springs and artesian wells, though a number of water sources are no longer accessible due to flooding. Fresh water springs are traditionally revered, and artesian wells yield water of substandard quality.

Often referred to as the Big Bend, or Grand Detour, the Little Bend area of tribal lands is one of the longest inland peninsulas in the world. The water on the west side of the Little Bend flows directly north while the water on the east side flows directly south. The area is very fertile, and was formed by silt deposits from the Missouri River. The Little Bend is the site of the Grassrope Irrigation Project of the Lower Brule Farm Corporation. The Little Bend is also the site of numerous culturally significant resources. The Lewis and Clark expedition traveled through the Little Bend during their explorations.

CLIMATE

Winter temperatures range between -30°F and 25°F. Winters can be very harsh, with moderate to heavy snowfalls and occasional severe blizzard conditions. Summers can bring violent thunderstorms and tornados. Summertime temperatures vary between 80°F and 110°F. The average year-round high temperature is only 59°F. Precipitation averages approximately 18 inches annually, with occasional droughts during the summer. Winds average 14 miles per hour daily all year round. Spring and autumn offer beautiful seasons, and the sunrises and sunsets are stunning throughout the year.

CULTURE AND HISTORY

The Sioux language has been divided into three major dialects by linguists. The first is the Dakota dialect, and it is spoken by the Mdewakantonwan, Wahpekute, Santee, and Sisseton, or Eastern or Mississippi Sioux tribes, ranging from the Ohio River to eastern Minnesota. The second is the Nakota dialect, spoken by the Ihanktonwan/Yankton or Yanktonai/Ihanktonwanna, or the Middle or Prairie Sioux tribes, ranging from the eastern Minnesota to the Missouri River valley. The third dialect, Lakota, is spoken by the Oglala, Sicangue, Mniconjou, Sihasapa, Oohenunpa, Hunkpapa, or Itazipco, or the Western Teton/Tituwan Sioux or Missouri River Sioux tribes, ranging from east of the Missouri River Valley to the Rocky Mountains. In addition to their linguistic and historical relationships, speakers of these dialects share cultural and spiritual elements, such as the reverence and use of the Pipestone, Sun Dance, sweat lodge, and vision quest ceremonies.

The Lower Brule Sioux, Kul Wicasa Oyate (Lower Men Nation), are a subband of the Sicangu (Burnt Thigh) Teton/Tituwan (Dwellers on the Plains), and a constituent band of the Sioux Nation. The Teton/Tituwan Band subdivided into the Oglala, Sicangu, Mniconjou, Sihasapa, Oohenunpa, Hunkpapa, and Itazipco groups. The Lower Brules became a further subband in the late 1700s when they split from the Heyata Wicasa/Upper Brule, who currently reside on the Rosebud Sioux Reservation. The Brules speak an "L" dialect of the Siouan language.

The Sicangus were named "Brule" by French fur traders in the late 1600s, and the Kul Wicasa Oyates were originally designated "far western" reservation lands along the Missouri River by treaty with the United States on October 14, 1865.

The 1851 Fort Laramie Treaty included these lands in its definition of the Great Sioux Reservation. The Teton/Tituwan bands did not actively resist settlers to the Dakotas until Euro-American presence began to decimate the buffalo population on the plains. The band joined other tribes of the Great Sioux Nation in the Plains Wars. The Fort Laramie Treaty of 1868 ended the wars and established the boundaries of the Great Sioux Nation Reservation.

The government broke agreements made in the treaty when gold was discovered in the Black Hills in the center of the reservation in the mid 1870s. The arrival of gold miners and traders in the region heightened the tension between the Plains Indians and the U.S. military. By June 1876, the hostilities had increased significantly and members of the Great Sioux Nation held a Sun Dance ceremony in search of spiritual guidance. An attack on the participants was led by General George Custer and the 7th Calvary. The Oglala/Brule warrior Crazy Horse and Sitting Bull and Gall of the Hunkapa led a retaliation that resulted in the annihilation of Custer and his troops. The federal government responded by using the forces of intimidation and coercion to place Sioux tribal members into boarding schools and Euro-American churches.

In 1877, the government took possession of over seven million acres of tribal lands in direct opposition to the Fort Laramie Treaty. By 1881, the renewed Plains Wars were over, and in 1890 the Nation was defeated when, in a final act of retaliation, the U.S. military massacred hundreds of women, children, and elders at Wounded Knee. Immediately following the wars, a number of tribal members relocated to Canada, where many remain today. Still others were relegated to reservations within the United States. The Lower Brules were confined to their reservation lands along the Missouri River.

GOVERNMENT

The Lower Brule Sioux Tribe was chartered under the Act of June 18, 1934. Its constitution was ratified on July 11, 1936, and its bylaws were approved in 1960. In 1986, the constitution and bylaws were amended and a code of ethics was adopted. Tribal affairs are conducted by the six-member tribal council, whose members are elected to two-year terms. Council offices include the chairman, vice-chairman, secretary-treasurer, sergeant at arms, chaplain, and a council member. The chairman, vice-chairman, and secretary-treasurer are elected at large, while all other positions are selected from within the ranks of the tribal council. Elections are comprised of a primary and a general election, held in August and September, respectively. Council members also serve as officers or council representatives on various boards and committees.

The Lower Brule Sioux Tribe is a Treaty Tribe, which adopted the Indian Reorganization Act of 1934. It has contracted several aspects of self-government under the Indian Self Determination and Education Assistance Act, PL 93-638. Participating in a government-to-government relationship with the United States, the Lower Brule Sioux, as part of the Great Sioux Nation, signed treaties in 1824, 1851, 1865, and 1868 with the federal government; these legal documents establish their boundaries and recognize their rights as a sovereign tribal government. The tribal council chairman serves as the chief executive officer and administrative head of the tribe.

The Lower Brule Sioux Tribal Council remains the ultimate authority over tribal lands, though the council has recognized the legal authority necessarily vested in tribal courts. The tribe's 1986 constitution and bylaws provided for the creation of an elected chief judge position, the tribal court, an appellate court, and an attendant process. Tribal courts hear all civil and minor criminal cases, while the federal courts hear all major felony cases.

Lower Brule

Total area (BIA realty, 2003)
144,587.96 acres

Total area (Tribal Source, 2004)
220,000 acres

Tribally owned (BIA realty, 2003)
125,359.42 acres

Individually owned
(BIA realty, 2003)
19,228.54 acres

Population 2000 census
1,353

Population (Tribal source, 2004)
1,184

Tribal enrollment
(BIA labor report, 2001)
2,627

Tribal enrollment
(Tribal source, 2004)
2,824

Total labor force 2000 census
504

Total labor force (Tribal source, 2004) **611**

High school graduate or higher
2000 census
75.9%

Bachelor's degree or higher
2000 census
8.8%

Unemployment rate 2000 census
27.8%

Unemployment rate
(Tribal source, 2004)
41%

Per capita income 2000 census
$7,020

Lower Brule

TRI-SD-lb-009a View of the Missouri River from the reservation

BUSINESS CORPORATION

The Lower Brule Farm Corporation was chartered in 1979. The corporation raises crops on over 7,000 acres of cropland and is one of the world's largest producers of popcorn. The farm also produces alfalfa for feed and kidney, pinto, navy, and soybeans. It oversees a herd of cattle with about 1,100 head. The corporation employs 12 full-time employees and several seasonal workers.

ECONOMY

The Lower Brule Reservation has traditionally supported ranching and other agricultural enterprises, and it is beginning to focus its projects on agriculture added-value products. The tribe has also initiated the development of opportunities for employment in the tourism industry. In previous decades, the Lower Brule Sioux Tribe had the lowest per capita income of all South Dakota reservations. The tribe has also initiated the development of employment opportunities in the tourism industry.

Government as Employer. The tribe, via its various enterprises, has become the single largest employer on the reservation. The BIA and the Indian Health Service also employ tribal members.

Economic Development Projects. Future projects of the Lower Brule Sioux include developing a smoke shop, wind energy supply, an ethanol processing plant, a riverfront marina and convenience store, a commercial fishery, a small strip-mall, a bottled water supplier and distribution company, and a telemarketing call center.

Agriculture and Livestock. Though semiarid, the reservation land supports moderate farming ventures. The tribe operates the Lower Brule Farm Corporation. The corporation farms over 7,000 acres of land. The primary crops are corn, edible beans, wheat, and sunflowers. Smaller crops include alfalfa, milo, and potatoes. Historically, ranching has been the tribe's most successful enterprise, providing considerable revenues and relatively high-paying jobs for the approximately two dozen tribal members involved in the business. The tribe has purchased 23,772 acres since 1992. This acreage consists of

four ranches and is utilized for cattle production. The ranches are managed by the Lower Brule Farm Corporation. The Smith/Cherry Ranch is home to the tribe's bison herd and the Buffalo Interpretive Center. A total of about 34,000 acres of on- and off-reservation tribally owned lands are used by the corporation. The management of these lands has greatly contributed to the stability of the tribal economy. Ultimately, almost 16,000 acres of reservation land are used for agricultural purposes while about 116,000 acres are used for grazing purposes.

Forestry. Native river bottomland trees and shrubs grow on over 270 acres of tribal lands. The material is used mainly for firewood. Tribal members also harvest the native plants for traditional uses.

Gaming. The tribe operates the Golden Buffalo Casino and Resort. The 9,000-square-foot casino features 175 slot machines and 2 table games. Facilities include a conference area, a dance floor, a restaurant, and a gift shop. Hotel facilities include 38 guest rooms and an indoor swimming pool. In 2004, the casino employed 50 individuals. The tribe is considering expansions to the facility.

Fisheries. The reservation's lakes and creeks, particularly Lake Sharpe, currently support considerable recreational fishing and at least one tribal guide business. The tribe is considering development of a commercial fishing and fish-processing industry.

Construction. The Lower Brule Sioux Tribe Employment Enterprise manages construction projects for the tribe. The primary goals of the enterprise are to ensure that the Lower Brule Sioux Tribe has construction capabilities and to increase employment opportunities for tribal members. Recent projects include the expansions to the Lower Brule Elementary School. It is currently working on the $12.9 million construction project of the Lower Brule Justice Center, which will include an adult and juvenile detention center, police department, and courthouse. The detention center will have between 60 and 70 beds.

Mining. Reservation resources include large deposits of sand and gravel, which is mined today. Gravel sales average between $10,000 and $100,000 per year.

Real Estate/Commercial Development. The tribe leases a building to Wells Fargo. The bank provides comprehensive services to local residents.

Banks. The tribe manages a bank in partnership with Norwest Bank.

Services and Retail. The reservation is home to a number of privately owned businesses. These include a bank, gas station, tire repair and tow service, small café and arcade, variety shop, and secondhand store.

The tribe also owns the Lower Propane Distribution Plant. It stores approximately 300,000 gallons of propane for purchase by tribal members and local residents. The plant employs four people.

Tourism and Recreation. In addition to the Golden Buffalo Casino and Resort, the tribe offers a number of attractions to visitors. The tribe is a member of the Alliance of Tribal Tourism Advocates, an association of Native American tribes throughout South Dakota interested in developing tourism opportunities on their reservations.

The reservation is located along the Missouri River, which led the tribe to work aggressively to establish the Native American Scenic Byway, a 101-mile-long tourist route from Chamberlain to Fort Pierre. The byway is the first of its kind and promises to attract visitors to the reservation. To further enhance the route, the tribe built the Circle of Tipis, the information center of the Native American Scenic Byway in Oacoma, South Dakota. The center is located on a parcel of land owned by the tribe. The tribe also developed the Buffalo Interpretive Center along the route. Opened in 2004, the center lies seven miles southeast of Pierre, South Dakota.

The Big Bend and Fort Randall dams on the Missouri River have created a number of recreational areas that attract tourists to the reservation area. A campground near the dam has several beaches and boat ramps for public use. Seasonal fishing contests, softball, volleyball, and basketball games, and tournaments are available. Hunting and fishing are permitted on reservation lands with a tribally issued permit. Some of the best pheasant hunting and walleye fishing in the world can be found in Lower Brule. Opportunities for hunting deer, elk, buffalo, quail, and rabbit are also abundant. Hunting and fishing guide services are provided by the tribe's wildlife, fish, and recreation department.

The Narrows, located only three and a half miles north of Lower Brule, is a strip of land within the Big Bend of the Missouri River. The Narrows is a historic site, marking the only naturally occurring total bend in any river system in the United States; it has been known to centuries of fur traders, frontiersman, and explorers. The tribe is developing low-impact interpretive signage and trails at the site.

There are other facilities available at Lake Francis Case, also nearby. Several fine restaurants and more casual dining opportunities dot the lake's shorelines. Cultural tours can be booked in advance, and small groups or solo guests might arrange lodging in a traditional tepee, participate in songs and dances, and listen to storytelling. There are also a variety of attractions located in the adjacent communities of Fort Thompson, Chamberlain/Oacoma, and Pierre, the state's capitol. The Akta Lakota Museum in Chamberlain features displays of Lakota ceremonial dress, weaponry, and tools arranged in a circular timeline representing the Medicine Wheel. The Cultural Heritage Center in Pierre has a changing exhibit, which prominently offers views of indigenous life.

The tribe sponsors two annual powwows: one for youth in June, and the Lower Brule Fair and Powwow the second week in August, which includes a rodeo, horse racing, and a softball tournament.

INFRASTUCTURE

In 1963, the Big Bend Dam on the Missouri River was completed. Operation of the dam caused flooding on the Lower Brule community and surrounding bottomlands in the heart of the reservation. Miles of roadways were covered, and a significant amount of fertile farmland and native trees, shrubs, and medicinal plants were lost. The federal government established the Lower Brule Infrastructure Development Trust Fund Act in 1997 in compensation for lands lost nearly 50 years earlier.

State Highway 47 runs north-south through the reservation, and I-90 passes east-west due south of the reservation. The Lewis and Clark Trail commemorated as highways 1804 and 1806, runs along the Missouri River through South Dakota. A portion of the 1806 Trail has been established as the Native American Scenic Byway. Highway 83, which runs north-south from Central America to Canada, lies adjacent to the western end of the reservation. Highway 34 is located just east and north of the reservation, across the Missouri River.

Electricity. The Lower Brule Sioux Tribe is a member of the West Central Rural Electric Cooperative. The majority of tribal members are also cooperative members, as it is the major provider of electricity in west-central South Dakota.

Fuel. The tribe operates a propane company and serves all residencies within the reservation, as well as the surrounding community. The local gas station provides both unleaded and diesel fuel. Farmers Union, located about 15 miles from the reservation in Reliance, South Dakota, offers fuel oil.

Water Supply. The Lake Sharpe Reservoir serves as a virtually unlimited water source for the Lower Brule community. Domestic and irrigation water are provided to the Lower Brule and West Brule communities by the Lower Brule Sioux Rural Water System (RWSS). The RWSS is a facet of the Mni Wiconi Water Project, which serves to provide water to the Pine Ridge, Rosebud, and Lower Brule reservations, as well as some counties of west central South Dakota. A wastewater system featuring two lagoons serves Lower Brule and West Brule. The primary treatment of wastewater relies upon evaporation and pond systems. Limited aeration is used. The wastewater system is managed in collaboration with Indian Health Service.

The Lower Brule Solid Waste Program provides solid waste collection across the reservation, and a transfer facility. Waste is removed to approved facilities in Pierre or Pukwana. Solid waste services are provided in coordination with Indian Health Service.

Transportation. Commercial airline, freight, and train services are available in Pierre, South Dakota. The town of Chamberlain provides the nearest landing strip and bus service. Truck service is available locally, and most retail businesses on the reservation receive service from suppliers in distributor-owned trucks. Charter buses and limousines serve patrons of the Golden Buffalo Casino, and Greyhound bus terminals are located in Chamberlain and Pierre.

Lower Brule

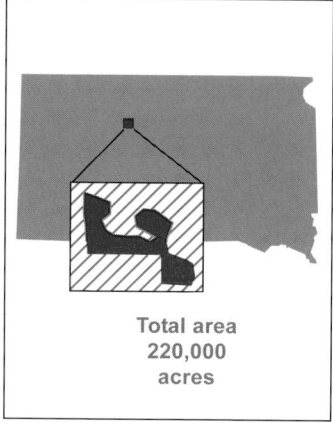

Total area
220,000
acres

Lower Brule

TRI-SD-lb-012

TRI-SD-lb-014

TRI-SD-lb-002b

TRI-SD-lb-015

TRI-SD-lb-012 GSI Grain Silos

TRI-SD-lb-014 "Zimmatic" Irrigation Equipment

TRI-SD-lb-002b Game, Fish, and Parks Department

TRI-SD-lb-015 Gravel Pit

Telecommunications. Golden West Telephone Company furnishes local telephone service. The West Central Rural Electric Cooperative provides Internet services.

COMMUNITY FACILITIES AND SERVICES

In response to the Lower Brule Infrastructure Development Trust Fund Act of 1997, the tribe established the Infrastructure Development Authority, a committee of tribal members who oversee the trust fund and recommend action and expenditures to the tribal council. The authority has been involved in developing the administrative building and community center located in Lower Brule. It is also overseeing the construction of the Lower Brule Justice Center.

The tribe has completed construction on a $5.8 million community center that features a swimming pool, full basketball court, weight room, exercise room, and full kitchen. There are also beach areas and boat ramps along the Missouri River. The reservation houses an elderly center that provides an elderly nutrition program and other activities. A teen center sponsors youth recreational activities. There is also a Horseman's Club on the reservation, which sponsors several "Play Days" throughout the summer.

Education. The Lower Brule Education System consists of a Head Start program, K-5 elementary school, 6-8 middle school, and 9-12 high school. The tribe also operates the Lower Brule Community College, which is accredited by the Sine Gleska University of the Rosebud Sioux Tribe. In addition, the tribe is involved in a Video-Cultural Program, where students, teachers, and elders produce and develop Lakota Legends video programs.

Health Care. The tribe contracts with Indian Health Service to operate a tribal health department, which oversees the tribal ambulance services and employs community health representatives. The department provides examinations and eyeglasses to tribal members at reduced costs and also coordinates health-delivery services. Full-service hospital facilities are available in the neighboring communities of Chamberlain and Pierre.

ENVIRONMENTAL CONCERNS

The Lower Brule Sioux Tribe has developed environmental codes and regulatory authority to protect land and resources within the reservation's boundaries. Drinking water quality is the major environmental problem currently posing health hazards to residents of the reservation. There are problems with both the quantity and quality of available water resources. Many residents have poorly constructed or low-capacity individual wells; the water drawn from them is usually highly mineralized and, in some cases, contaminated with bacteria.

The Missouri River has played an important part in the lives of the Lower Brule people for countless years. The arrival of Euro-Americans has markedly decreased the quality of the river's ecosystem. The tribe remains concerned with the health of the river and its environment and invests tribal resources, time, and energy into efforts to restore and preserve its well-being. Maintaining and protecting the land for future generations is a high priority for the tribe as well. The tribe actively pursues opportunities to purchase lands adjacent to the reservation in order to restore tribal land holdings and to preserve natural resources. The cultural resources office works with the various programs, the tribal council, and the elder advisory committee to ensure that basic resources are acknowledged and preserved to the greatest extent possible. Ongoing development as well as urban sprawl from adjacent communities is monitored for impact. The elder committee is involved in many sacred site issues, including Bear Butte State Park, Pipestone Quarry National Monument, and Yellowstone National Park.

The tribe's department of wildlife, fish, and recreation has an extensive program designed to mitigate losses due to reservoir flooding, restore native habitats, and provide recreational opportunities. Since 1987, this department has developed 161 wetlands on 562 acres, planted over 800,000 trees on 850 acres, restored over 2,700 acres of native grasslands, planted over 3,280 acres of food plots, controlled weeds on 12,335 acres, built over 42 miles of fences to protect wildlife habitat, and purchased over 1,153 acres of wetland and upland habitat for the tribe. It also manages over 20,000 acres of tribal lands exclusively for bison, elk, deer, upland game birds, and other wildlife.

LOCATION AND LAND STATUS

The Pine Ridge Reservation, second only in size of landmass to the Navajo Reservation, is located in southwestern South Dakota. The reservation borders Nebraska on the south, and it is approximately 50 miles east of the Wyoming border on the west. Pine Ridge Reservation abuts the Rosebud Reservation on the northeast corner. Some tribal trust lands are located in northwestern Nebraska. Interstate 90 runs east-west just north of the reservation. The community of Pine Ridge, which serves as tribal headquarters, lies approximately 97 miles south and slightly west of Rapid City. The nearest city of 250,000 or more is Denver, Colorado, 420 miles away.

PHYSICAL DESCRIPTION

The topography of the 11,000-square-mile reservation and trust lands is a diverse mixture of badlands and acres of rolling grassland hills, transected with river valleys and creeks and ridges dotted with spotted pine; hence the name Pine Ridge. The well-known Badlands National Park extends into the reservation, featuring a unique landscape of eroded ridges, peaks, multicolored columns, and abrupt mesas. The Buffalo National Grassland lies along the reservation's western border.

CLIMATE

Typical for the Great Plains, reservation temperatures fluctuate between seasonal extremes of 105° F and -30° F. The average temperature in July is 74° F; in January the average temperature is 21° F. The area normally receives 19 inches of precipitation annually.

CULTURE AND HISTORY

The term "Lakota" represents both the language and the people known as the western Sioux. Originally, there were seven nations of people in what is now the area of north-central Minnesota who all spoke mutually understandable dialects of the Siouan language. They enjoyed a woodlands economy based on hunting, fishing, gathering, and some horticulture. Shortly after encountering white explorers about the end of the seventeenth century in north-central Minnesota, the Lakotas (also called western Sioux), migrated westward in pursuit of buffalo to what is now South Dakota, Montana, Wyoming, and Nebraska. During the westward movement, they acquired horses and became expert hunters, basing their economy on the buffalo, horses, and trading. Their territory stretched north to Canada and south into what is now Kansas, from the Big Horn Mountains of Wyoming, to the Missouri River, a vast expanse of largely uninhabited Great Plains. By 1778, the Lakotas had discovered the Black Hills at the center of their territory. These mountains became their spiritual center. Also by this time, they had divided into seven tribes, one of which is the Oglala.

The Red Cloud Wars of the 1860s, precipitated by encroachment of settlers and gold-seeking miners into the Black Hills, resulted in the Treaty of Fort Laramie in 1868, which placed most of the Lakotas on the Great Sioux Reservation, occupying about half of the state of South Dakota and parts of Nebraska. Most tribal lands west of the Mississippi River, including the sacred Black Hills, were ceded to the federal government. Those who did not go to the reservation continued engaging with the military.

The 7th Cavalry, led by General George Armstrong Custer, was ordered to place all Sioux on the reservation. The Battle of the Little Big Horn, which took place at Greasy Grass, Montana, on June 15, 1876, wherein General Custer and almost all of his troops were killed, represents the only victory by Indians over federal troops. Nonetheless, the Oglalas were eventually starved into virtual submission, subdued, and assigned to a reservation vastly reduced in size from the original Great Sioux Reservation, part of the overall reduction of tribal lands now known as the Great Sioux Settlement, by an Act of Congress passed on March 2, 1889.

Following the arrest and murder of Sitting Bull on December 15, 1890, the Oglalas, along with the Hunkpapas who lived in Sitting Bull's camp, went south to the Cheyenne River Reservation where they joined Big Foot's Band of Minneconjou Teton Sioux in Cherry Creek, South Dakota. On December 29, 1890, the 7th Cavalry trapped them near Wounded Knee Creek, disarmed them, and massacred over 300 Oglala men, women, and children, leaving their bodies to freeze in the snow. Wounded Knee, a symbol of oppression for all Lakota people, has become a rallying cry for recovery from the injustices experienced by all Indian peoples.

During the latter decades of the twentieth century, the U.S. Supreme Court ruled that the federal government must compensate the Oglalas for taking the Black Hills illegally. As a matter of principle, the Oglalas have refused this settlement money, which amounts to tens of millions of dollars. They revere their unique history and incorporate cultural lessons throughout their community. In terms of religion, most Christian denominations are represented on the reservation, but the majority of people follow the traditional Native American religion under the leadership of medicine men. Many religious ceremonies, which encompass the seven rites brought by White Buffalo Calf Woman, are practiced, including the annual Sun Dance, vision quests, powwows, giveaways, traditional honoring ceremonies, and memorial feasts. The oral tradition is still passed down from tribal elders to the young people. In 2002, one-third of the total population reported Lakota as their first language.

GOVERNMENT

The Pine Ridge Reservation was established by an Act of Congress in 1889 as a home for the Oglala Lakota Sioux. Under an IRA constitution approved in 1936, the tribe is governed by a 16-member tribal council, presided over by the tribal council chairman, who acts as the administrative head of the tribe. The council is guided by a five-member executive committee, with elections held every two years to elect an at-large president and vice-president and representatives from nine districts: Eagle Nest, Pass Creek, Wakpamni, Lacreek, Pine Ridge, White Clay, Medicine Root, Porcupine, and Wounded Knee. A sergeant-at-arms and critic also serve with the council. All members serve four-year terms. Under PL-638, the tribe contracts with the BIA to administer key programs and services.

A tribal court system, established under the constitution, consists of one chief and three associate judges who are chosen by the tribal council. They also serve four-year terms.

ECONOMY

The Pine Ridge Reservation economy is somewhat diversified, with an agricultural industry, an ever-increasing tourism industry, and many enterprises. There is no major industry on

Pine Ridge Reservation
Federal reservation
Oglala Sioux
Washabaugh-Jackson, Custer,
Fall River, and Bennett
counties, South Dakota

Pine Ridge Reservation
P.O. Box 2070
Pine Ridge, SD 57770
605-867-5821
605-867-1449 Fax
lakotamall.com/
oglalasiouxtribe/

Total area (BIA realty, 2003)
1,775,412.72 acres

Total area (Tribal source, 2004)
2,800,000 acres

Tribally owned
(BIA realty, 2003)
705,839.58 acres

Tribally owned (Tribal source, 2004)
706,340 acres

Federal trust (BIA realty, 2003)
1,067,877.15 acres

Individually owned
(BIA realty, 2003)
1,695.99 acres

Allotted lands (Tribal source, 2004)
1,064,840 acres

Population 2000 census
14,068

Tribal enrollment
(Tribal source, 2004)
17,775

Total labor force 2000 census
4,741

High school graduate or higher
2000 census
68.8%

Bachelor's degree or higher
2000 census
11.1%

Unemployment rate 2000 census
33%

Per capita income 2000 census
$6,298

Pine Ridge

TRI-SD-pr-009

TRI-SD-pr-010

TRI-SD-pr-009 "Oglala Sioux 1840-War Chief Crazy Horse-1877" historical marker

TRI-SD-pr-010 Big Crow Recreation Center

the reservation; however, there are more than 75 BIA, Indian Health Services, and other federal programs on the reservation that provide services and employment opportunities. The Oglala Lakota College, a tribally controlled institution, contributes to the tribe economically, as well as educationally.

Economic Development Projects. The Oglala Sioux Tribe has a comprehensive economic development plan that has resulted in a meat-processing plant, a shopping center expansion, and improvements to the Pine Ridge Airport. The tribe has a large parks and recreation department that offers guided hunting for small game and big game, including buffalo and elk.

Lakota Trade Center, operated by the Lakota Fund, in Kyle, South Dakota, is a community-owned nonprofit community development financial institution. The fund maintains two lending programs that have made over a million dollars in loans to almost 300 tribal members for the development of small businesses and microenterprises. This influx of capital and technical assistance has been critical to boosting individual and community economic health by slowing financial outflow to neighboring communities. Although per capita income still lags behind national averages, the standard of living has improved significantly since 2000.

Village Earth, a grant-funded project to study economic development on the reservation, has linked academic research with community-based planning efforts to guide future development initiatives. Based out of the department of anthropology at Colorado State University, the approach assumes that communities are in control of developing a shared vision for their future by identifying obstacles, developing action plans to overcome those obstacles, and accessing and managing needed resources. Efforts thus far have identified two key areas for concentrated study: environmental justice and land utilization.

Agriculture and Livestock. Over 1.3 acres of the reservation are devoted to grazing, with many tribal members maintaining cattle and buffalo herds. There are a total of 84,983 acres devoted to agriculture on the Pine Ridge Reservation, sown annually in winter wheat, alfalfa, millet, and safflower.

Forestry. 230,729 acres are forested, supporting some members in the timber industries.

Gaming. The 30,000-square-foot Prairie Wind Casino, located near Oelrichs, South Dakota, features over 250 Las Vegas-style slot machines, 2 poker tables, 1 three-card poker table, and 5 blackjack tables. There are also a restaurant and a gift shop on-site. The facility employs over 170 employees, the majority of them tribal members.

Services and Retail. Wakpamni Bed and Breakfast, located on the Bar-O-Bar Farm near the junction of Highways 18 and

391, consists of two guesthouses, two tepees for overnight stays, and Wakpamni Gallery and Gifts. The tribe owns this enterprise. Private operators own a growing number of Indian-owned businesses and other commercial ventures; grocery stores, convenience stores, cafés, bookstores, gas stations, fast food establishments, and art galleries serve residents and an ever-increasing tourism market.

Media and Communications. The reservation also has a radio station. KILI (pronounced "KEE-lee"), which means "cool" or "awesome," has joined the American Indian Radio on satellite networks, making it the largest Indian-owned and operated public radio station in America. Begun in 1983, KILI broadcasts are in English and Lakota 22 hours per day and reach three reservations spread among 10,000 square miles of the Black Hills of South Dakota. The station covers vital tribal events and elections, providing firsthand coverage of issues pertinent to Indian Country.

Tourism and Recreation. The White Clay Reservoir and Oglala Reservoir provide excellent hunting and fishing, as well as boating and marina facilities. The reservation boasts the finest regional hunting and fishing opportunities and makes guided hunts available via the tribal parks and recreation department. Mule deer, whitetail deer, coyotes, turkeys, prairie dogs, prairie chickens, doves, and pheasants are taken. Fishing for northern pike, catfish, and bass are popular pastimes. Team sporting events, such as softball, volleyball, and basketball tournaments are also held during the year.

Of great interest are the Badlands National Park and Wounded Knee Battlefield, while nearby attractions include the Black Hills, Mount Rushmore National Monument, and Dinosaur Park in Rapid City, South Dakota. Tourists and guests of residents find accommodations at Cedar Pass Lodge within Badlands National Park. There are a restaurant, a gift shop, air-conditioned cabins, a museum and exhibits, guided and self-guiding tours, hiking trails, picnic areas, campgrounds with RV hookups, and group campsites at the lodge. Within the park, the Ben Reifel Visitors Center is also an attraction for many visitors. The Badlands Park Loop Road offers an abundance of overlooks for photography, trailheads, and 11 pull-offs for automobiles. The Stronghold Unit of the Badlands Wilderness Area, co-managed by the National Park Service and the Oglala Sioux Tribe, covers 64,000 acres, including sites of 1890s Ghost Dances. This wilderness area is the site where the black-footed ferret, the most endangered land mammal in North America, was reintroduced.

The sandhills of Nebraska are south of the reservation. The geographically unique area features 20,000 square miles of undulating sand dunes stabilized by the roots of prairie grass. The Arthur Bowring Ranch State Historical Park, a living history museum, is a 7,202-acre ranch preserved to reflect the lifestyle of cattlemen and the cattle drives of a hundred years ago, complete with a prairie-style sod house. The Lacreek

Wildlife Refuge, formed by the waters of the Lacreek River, is home to migrating trumpeter swans. The Old-Time Cowboy Museum, the Museum of the Fur Trade, and Fort Robinson State Park are all within easy driving distance of the reservation. Canoeing the Niobrara River, county fairs, and rodeos are favorite summertime activities. The tribe has produced a brochure that provides bits of Oglala history and ecology and some hints on culturally appropriate behavior in Indian Country.

Five miles north of the community of Pine Ridge, the tribe operates a Heritage Center on the campus of the Red Cloud Indian School. The Heritage Center is a museum and cultural resource center that contains ethnographic collections and Indian art displays. Red Cloud Indian School sponsors an annual juried art show, the largest of its kind in the United States. The Lakota Trade Center, operated by the Lakota Fund, a nonprofit community development financial institution, houses local arts and crafts for sale. Each August, the Sun Dance and the Oglala Nation Powwow are held at Pine Ridge, attracting thousands of tourists. The celebration includes a rodeo, outdoor concerts, softball tournaments, and other family-style activities. The Lakota Vietnam Powwow and the Red Cloud Art Show are held each year, as well. There is a campground near the community of Pine Ridge at the powwow grounds and a number of lakes for fishing and swimming.

INFRASTRUCTURE
State Highway 73, a north-south route, and U.S. Highway 18, an east-west route, are the major traffic arteries. Gordon, Nebraska, 45 miles away, is the nearest railroad shipping center, while the nearest international airport is at Rapid City, South Dakota, 130 miles from the reservation.

Electricity. The Consumers Power Company and the LaCreek Power Cooperative provide electricity.

Water Supply. The Oglala Sioux Rural Water Supply System supplies water on the reservation. The Mni Wiconi Project is under construction to supply clean water from the Missouri River to the communities that do not have potable water or have wells with poor water quality. The tribe provides solid waste collection.

Telecommunications. Golden West Telecommunications Company provides telephone service, and a tribal member provides cable TV service in the community of Pine Ridge.

COMMUNITY FACILITIES AND SERVICES
The tribe provides an elderly nutrition program, and it sponsors many community activities. Youth recreational services are provided through local nonprofit organizations including a rodeo club.

Education. Four high schools and 12 elementary schools serve approximately 5,577 private or public school children on the reservation aged 5-18. Healthy Start and Head Start programs work with preschool children. On March 4, 1971, the Oglala Sioux Tribal Council chartered the Lakota Higher Education Center. Pine Ridge High School was completed in 1994. Red Cloud Indian School, which operates elementary, middle, and high school campuses on the reservation, is a nonprofit corporation that operates as an accredited private school. The school emphasizes retaining traditional Lakota values, linguistic skills, and cultural heritage, while striving toward academic excellence. It had an enrollment in excess of 600 students in 2002.

Oglala Lakota College, founded in 1971, is a tribally chartered and operated university offering GED, associate and bachelor's degrees, and, more recently, master's study programs. In keeping with the college's mission, "Piya Wiconi," a Lakota expression meaning a new beginning for harmony in fulfillment of aspirations and dreams, the college is committed to continuous quality improvement in providing outstanding teaching, research, community services, and assessment. Accreditation by the Commission on Institutions of Higher Education, North Central Association of Colleges and Schools was first granted in 1983. Nursing graduates are certified by the South Dakota State Board of Nursing and are permitted to sit for the registered nurse examination. The college was responsible for beginning the first child and spouse abuse prevention programs on the reservation, for developing alcohol and drug abuse intervention programs, and for conducting economic development conferences leading to the formation of The Lakota Fund. *(See Economic Development Projects, above.)*

Health Care. In 1994, the Pine Ridge Reservation Comprehensive Health Care Facility, an Indian Health Service hospital, was dedicated and opened for patient care. An intensive care unit, modern monitoring equipment, a respiratory therapy program, and new pediatric care facilities have all been added since 1997. Decorated with tribal themes, the hospital welcomes traditional healers and medicine men along with Christian or other spiritual workers. A community health representative and an ambulance service serve for the reservation. The health department provides eye exams and eyeglasses to all residents at reduced rates. There is a dialysis center on the reservation.

ENVIRONMENTAL CONCERNS
In a 1997 Tribal Environmental Problem Statement, environmental staff identified the reservation's highest priorities: 1) landfill construction, 2) solid waste collection, and 3) a plan for landfill closure. Since that time, a new landfill was constructed in the White Clay district to resolve the situation.

Pine Ridge

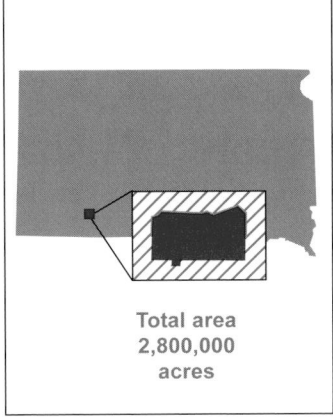

Total area
2,800,000
acres

Rosebud Reservation
Federal reservation
Sioux
Todd County, South Dakota

Rosebud Sioux Tribe
P.O. Box 430
Rosebud, SD 57570
605-747-2381
605-747-2905 Fax
rosebudsiouxtribe-nsn.gov

Total area *(BIA realty, 2003)*
884,194.01 acres

Total area *(Tribal source, 2004)*
890,870 acres

Tribally owned *(BIA realty, 2003)*
483,486.66 acres

Federal trust *(BIA realty, 2003)*
400,044.99 acres

Federal trust *(Tribal source, 2005)*
506,612 acres

Individually owned
(BIA realty, 2003)
662.36 acres

Population *2000 census*
10,469

Tribal enrollment *(BIA, 2001)*
24,134

Tribal enrollment
(Tribal source, 2004)
25,196

Total labor force *2000 census*
3,616

High school graduate or higher
2000 census
73%

High school graduate or higher
(Tribal source, 2004)
31%

Bachelor's degree or higher
2000 census
10.9%

Unemployment rate *2000 census*
20.1%

Per capita income *2000 census*
$7,279

LOCATION AND LAND STATUS

The Rosebud Sioux Reservation encompasses over 950,000 acres in south-central South Dakota just above the Nebraska state line, just east of and adjacent to the Pine Ridge Reservation. Established by an Act of Congress on March 2, 1889, the reservation encompasses the towns of Mission, Rosebud, Parmelee, St. Francis, Okreek, and Hidden Timber. The Todd County line forms the northern and eastern borders; the Nebraska state line forms the southern boundary. The community of Rosebud, approximately 50 miles south of I-90 on Highway 83, serves as tribal headquarters. Rosebud is approximately 194 miles east of Rapid City, South Dakota.

CLIMATE

Data for Rosebud, South Dakota, is not available; however, climate information for Mission, South Dakota, 13 miles north of Rosebud is available and would not differ significantly. Year-round high temperatures at Mission, South Dakota, average 59ºF. The average year-round low temperature is 32.4ºF. The area receives approximately 19 inches of precipitation annually and suffers from extreme droughts at times. Snowfalls during winter months range between moderate and heavy, with 10-foot drifts during severe blizzard conditions reported periodically. The growing season is short, lasting only from June to August before the first frost. Daily year-round wind speeds average 14 miles per hour.

CULTURE AND HISTORY

The Rosebud Sioux Tribe is a member of the Oceti Sakowin, "Seven Council Fires," and they are called Sicangu Lakota Oyate, "the Burnt Thigh People." Tribal historians tell of the story behind the name Sicangu, which came about as a result of a prairie fire that destroyed an entire village. Many children and a man and his wife who were on foot some distance away from the village were burned to death. The people who made it to a nearby long lake saved themselves by jumping into it. Many of these people were badly burned about their thighs and legs, and this gave rise to the name Sicangu.

The tribe's territory extended at one time from the Big Horn Mountains in the west to eastern Wisconsin. It extended from Canada in the north to the Republican River in Kansas to the south. Treaty-recognized homelands (181,1868) were reduced to the current boundaries by the March 2, 1889 Act and subsequent Homestead Acts. In the late 1880s, at the conclusion of the Plains Wars, Siouxs were relegated to various reservations. The Rosebud Reservation was established by an Act of Congress in 1889. The Rosebud Siouxs were brought under the Indian Reorganization Act of 1934, and they operate under a constitution and bylaws approved in 1935. Generations of Rosebud Sioux children were educated at the St. Francis Mission, founded by Jesuits and Franciscan nuns in 1886.

Rosebud tribal members participate in annual traditional ceremonies and social events, including more than 30 annual wacipi (pronounced wa chee pee), or powwows, celebrations that can continue for days at a time. They participate in honorings, giveaways, family gatherings, and dance competitions.

The people of the Sioux Nation call themselves Lakota, Nakota, or Dakota, which translates to "friend" or "ally." The words "Rosebud" and "Sioux" are not actually a part of the Lakota vocabulary. Rosebud is the site name for the federal agency that was designated for the Sicangu people in 1877, so named because of the abundance of wild rosebuds that

grew in the vicinity. The U.S. government practiced the policy of imposing geographic place names that conformed to the Anglo system of orthography and pronunciation. Sioux is derived from the French spelling of a Chippewa word, Nadowesiwug, which translates to "Little Snakes" or "Enemy" and was given to the Santee "Sioux" in the mid-1600s. The U.S. government officially recognized the Lakota as Sioux in 1825, and it has applied this alien term to the Lakota, Dakota, and Nakota in official documents ever since. Following the French traders and trappers who called the Chippewa people Sioux, the U.S. government identified all the tribes with similar languages as the Sioux people.

The people's oral tradition states that the Lakota and Dakota people are one nation, with the Lakota creation story telling of their emerging from the underworld through Wind Cave, which is located in the Black Hills of western South Dakota. Ancient Lakota star knowledge, passed down through oral tradition, teaches the seasons for ancestral practices and the locations where they are to be performed in the Black Hills. The Lakotas/Dakotas still practice their sacred and traditional ceremonies, which encompass the seven sacred rites that Lakota spiritual practices brought to the people by the White Buffalo Calf Woman.

GOVERNMENT

The tribal government operates under a constitution consistent with the Indian Reorganization Act of 1934, which was approved by the Rosebud Sioux Tribe's tribal membership and tribal council in 1937. The tribal charter designates a tribal council, which consists of a president, vice-president (elected at-large), secretary, treasurer, sergeant-at-arms, and 20 elected members from the 13 districts, apportioned by population. The tribal council president is the tribe's administrative head and serves a two-year term. Tribal council members appoint the secretary, treasurer, and sergeant-at-arms.

The Rosebud Sioux Tribe, under PL-638, contracts with the BIA to administer key programs and services to improve life on the reservation for its membership. These include: ambulance, commodity distribution, alcohol, daycare, resource development, community health representative, child welfare, juvenile detention center and diversion, juvenile wellness court, law enforcement and criminal investigation, land office, natural resources, tourism, youth advocacy and youth affairs, prosecutor, water resources, White River Health Care, tribal education, right of way, utility company, solid waste, the Spotted Tail Crisis Center, tribal courts, Head Start, emergency preparedness, forestry, fish and game. The treaty office staff is composed of elders and youth who understand historical aspects of the 1868 Treaty (and others).

The Rosebud Sioux Tribe is the first tribe to implement a comprehensive Cultural Resource Management Code, which will manage cultural sites, plants, remains, records, and research with an eye to preserving and protecting these valuable resources. The tourism office's cultural tourism-planning model provided the impetus and mandate for the Cultural Resource Management Code. Current efforts include identifying funding to fully staff the Cultural Resource Management Department.

ECONOMY

Many Rosebud Sioux are engaged in tribal enterprises, including ranching and electronics. Manufacturing includes gold

TRI-SD-rd-013

TRI-SD-rd-017

TRI-SD-rd-015

TRI-SD-rd-016

Rosebud

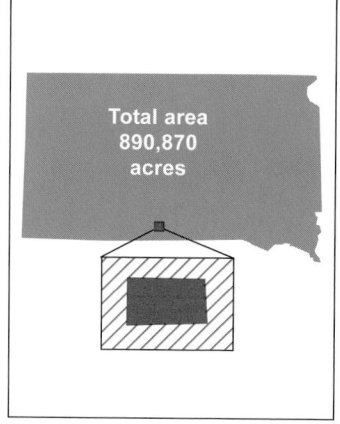

Total area
890,870
acres

and silver jewelry. The tribally owned and operated Rosebud Casino and Quality Inn, which opened in 1995, continues to have a significant positive impact on the economy.

Economic Development Projects. The tribe has plans to build a travel center adjacent to the interstate near the casino. The tribe began renewable energy efforts with the development of one 750-kilowat wind turbine adjacent to the Rosebud Casino/Quality Inn, and current plans are to develop a 30-megawatt wind farm and two 10-megawatt wind farm sites on tribal land. Future plans include geothermal, solar power, hydro power, and biomass technology in developing renewable energy and energy-efficiency projects. The tribe purchased 22 acres of private land with a resort located on it at Bear Butte Park in Sturgis, South Dakota.

Agriculture and Livestock. The tribe owns a herd of 300-320 buffalo which is managed by the game, fish, and parks department and grazes on approximately 5,000 acres of tribal land.

Forestry. There are 55,000 acres of forested lands on the Rosebud Sioux Reservation, mostly pine and evergreens. The tribe has a forest management plan for its 44,000-acre timber reserve.

Gaming. The Rosebud Casino features slot machines, bingo, blackjack, and poker.

Services and Retail. There are both fine and casual dining opportunities at the Rosebud Casino and Quality Inn along with two golf courses, the Prairie Hills Golf Course in Mission, South Dakota and the Spotted Tail Golf Course in Rosebud. Other businesses operating in the Rosebud area are: gas stations, eating establishments (restaurants, pizza, deli, sandwiches, grocery, truck stop), mini-mart, auto repair shop and towing service, fine arts, Lakota Crafts, star quilts, craft supplies, books, income tax service, floral-gift shop, electronic equipment and supplies, and home/ farm hardware.

Media and Communications. Regional and national newspapers are distributed and available on the reservation, featuring news items from various Lakota tribes and Indian country. The private sector-owned tribal newspapers are the *Sicangu Sun Times* and the *Todd County Tribune.* The tribe has its own tribal radio station called KRST on 98.3 FM, "The Voice of the Sicangu Nation". KINI radio station 96.1 FM, "The Voice of the Rosebud," serves the reservation and surrounding communities.

Tourism and Recreation. The tribe has a tourism office, opened in May 1994, to oversee development of tourism opportunities and the interpretation of Lakota culture for non-Indian visitors to tribal land. The Rosebud Educational Society operates the Buechel Lakota Memorial Museum in St. Francis, and Soldier Woman Art and Gallery in Mission is owned by Paul and Linda Szabo. There are campgrounds and picnic areas in various locations throughout the reservation, including those where overnight stays in tepees initiate non-Indian people to Plains Indian culture of the past. Along with managing the Rosebud Casino the tribe schedules a wide variety of events at the Western Events Arena, Convention Hall, and the Cultural Events Center throughout the year. The tribe operates the Rosebud Quality Inn, featuring an indoor swimming pool and Jacuzzi, exercise room, video arcade, and a gift shop. There are meeting rooms and banquet facilities at this location as well. The Elk Valley Bed and Breakfast offers ranch-style accommodations on 12,000 acres at the western edge of the reservation. Trail rides offered here increase the western flavor of the visit.

There are city parks in Mission and White River. Ghost Hawk Park, situated along the Little White River in Crazy Horse Canyon, offers camping, picnic facilities, and rustic cabin lodging. There are registered guide services to assist visitors in taking advantage of small- and large-game hunting and fishing opportunities. Archery, muzzle loading, tubing, and canoeing guides are available as well.

TRI-SD-rd-013 Front view of the Rosebud Casino

TRI-SD-rd-017 Front of the Tribal Court

TRI-SD-rd-015 Rosebud reservation

TRI-SD-rd-016 Rosebud Dam sign

Rosebud

Fast pitch softball tournaments are held every weekend throughout the summer. Shops and galleries operating in each of 20 communities throughout the reservation feature authentic Sioux art and handcrafted items, such as beadwork, quill work, star quilts, paintings, leather crafts, textile crafts, and dolls. Sinte Gleska University in Mission, South Dakota, also has an art institute and gallery featuring the work of students and staff. The annual Rosebud Fair in the Town of Rosebud, held the fourth weekend in August, includes a powwow, rodeo, softball tournaments, parade, pageant, road run, garden contest, and honorings.

INFRASTRUCTURE

There is one airstrip, the Mission Airport, located in Antelope, South Dakota. South Dakota Highway 18 runs east-west across the reservation, while State Highway 83 bisects it north-south. The two highways intersect at the town of Mission. Highway 83 is a major transcontinental trade corridor connecting Mexico with Canada, crossing the United States in between.

Electricity. The tribal utility commission provides regulatory oversight of the utilities being provided to reservation residents. In a pilot project with the U.S. Department of Energy, the tribe constructed a wind-energy turbine near the casino and has been successful in generating sufficient power to supply the casino with wind-generated electricity.

COMMUNITY FACILITIES AND SERVICES

There are 20 communities on the reservation and each has its own community center and offices that house specific programs. There are apartments exclusively for tribal elders, offering nutritional programs and medication management assistance. The Rosebud Sioux Tribe has its own ambulance service and police department. The town governments of Rosebud, Mission, and White River have their respective police forces, as well.

Public Safety. Law enforcement and tribal court services are PL-638 contracted by the tribe and fall under the tribe's law and order code. The tribe's "RST 2002-04 Sicangu National Highway Safety, Traffic/Crash Information" booklet received a national achievement award from the BIA National Indian Highway Safety Program. The booklet is the first of its kind in Indian Highway Safety and will serve as a model program for other tribes. The Wanbli Wiconi Tipi JDS-Youth Wellness and Renewal, a 51,646-square-foot youth facility with 36 beds, is the tribe's newest facility, and it will provide detention services for adjudicated Rosebud youth.

Education. In the late 1870s, at the request of Sinte Gleska (Spotted Tail), an Itancan leader of the Sicangu, the "Black Robes" or Jesuits, were invited to begin a mission school on the Rosebud Reservation. Thus, the St. Francis Indian School was born in 1886, and it continues to operate today, offering education to students in grades K-12. The Todd County School District also provides K-12 services for Rosebud area youth. The St. Francis Indian Mission operates many programs and services on the reservation, including an educational grant program, a youth education training program, a program to hire and retain residents of the reservation, pastoral works and programs within the Lakota faith communities, retreats and spiritual development through the Icimani Ya Waste Conference Center, and the local radio station.

Sinte Gleska University, named in honor of the famous chief who supported the education of his people, was founded in 1971. It is a fully accredited four-year institution of higher learning, the first reservation-based university in the United States. Two of the more important programs offered at Sinte Gleska are the job-related training programs that provide a skilled labor force for the tribe and the teacher training programs that work closely with the reservation community schools. This university and the tribe have a close working relationship.

Honoring Nations Honoree 1999

Rosebud Tribal Education Department and Education Code, Tribal Education Department, Rosebud Sioux Tribe

In the 1980s, statistics showed that the 3,000 elementary and secondary school-age members of Rosebud Sioux Tribe attained disproportionately low levels of academic attendance and achievement at both tribal and public schools. Seeing these numbers, tribal leaders felt strongly that the students' extremely low attendance and performance rates put an entire generation of Lakota in jeopardy.

In response, the Rosebud Sioux Tribe engaged in four years of research and planning and gathered input from tribal leaders, educators, parents, and others* about how the Tribe might improve its children's educational experiences. These efforts culminated in 1990 with the enactment of a Tribal Education Code and the creation of a Tribal Education Department. The Code, which is administered by the Tribal Education Department, regulates and coordinates the work of tribal schools, public schools, and federally funded Indian education programs, and in so doing, assists in sifting through the web of Indian education offerings, programs, and funds. Together, the Department and Code create a role for the tribal government that co-exists with and enhances the roles of school boards, program directors, and parents. And, significantly, because it applies across geographic and political boundaries,

the Code upholds the belief that education is important for all Indian youth-whether they live on or off the reservation or attend tribal or public schools.

Because the Rosebud Tribal Education Code is comprehensive, it serves many different functions. Under the Code, the Education Department's general responsibilities are to review school policies, plans, and budgets; monitor and assess schools, education programs, and student academic performance; and recommend corrective processes and procedures. Specifically, the Code charges the Department with developing or overseeing the development of tribal curricula and education standards, tribal parental and community involvement programs, teacher training programs and re-certification courses, and other educational improvements. The Department also serves as a liaison between parents, schools, and the tribal government; coordinates resources on specific education problems and issues; provides technical assistance to schools and education programs; and advocates for education accountability by the state and federal government.

Through these initiatives, the Education Department and Code have resulted in considerable improvements in student attendance and achievement. For example, because the Code made school attendance a priority, the Department developed outreach efforts to specifically combat truancy. Two full-time professional staff whose sole responsibility is to make sure Indian students attend school now work for the Department. These staff members have established a close and much-needed relationship with the students who miss school and their parents, and have been able to influence all parties, including school officials, to work together to keep children in school. Since the Code's introduction, one school has seen attendance improve from 89 percent to 97 percent, and confirming the strong tie between school attendance and school completion, another has seen graduation rates rise from 24 percent to 69 percent. Much of this success can be attributed to the staff's ability to use cultural and community resources and knowledge to help solve attendance problems.

Notably, the Education Department and Code do more than ensure a better education for Lakota students. By addressing a significant public issue that affects the nation's future, the Tribal Education Department has strengthened Rosebud Sioux self-governance. Further, the implementation of the Code in non-tribal schools and outside the boundaries of the reservation is a critical exercise of self-determination. Large percentages of the Tribe's school-age members attend public schools (Natives comprise 94 percent of the Todd County High School student population) and off-reservation schools

(reservation diminishment summarily placed many tribal citizens under the jurisdiction of five surrounding counties), and the Tribe must be able to influence these schools if it is to affect the education of all member children. The Tribal Education Department and Code make this possible. The Code makes it clear that it all schools serving Rosebud citizens must adhere to the standards and curriculum mandates of the Tribal Education Department, and the Department is empowered to pursue these policies.

By supplementing state and federal law, the Tribal Education Department and Code have enabled the Rosebud Sioux Tribe to play a greater role in the education of its youth. The Tribe is now involved with critical components of formal education-curriculum, staffing and funding-that for decades had been managed by non-Indian governments, and it is able to bring unique resources to bear on the problems of school attendance and academic performance. Because the Education Code gives the Rosebud Tribal Education Department the power and resources to affect school policy, the Tribe has been able to achieve results where narrower efforts have failed.

Input from the Native American Rights Fund (NARF) was particularly instrumental. They provided legal assistance to the Tribe in developing and implementing the Department and Code's unique exercise of tribal sovereignty.

Rosebud

Honoring Nations
Honoree1999

Text in its entirety from:
The Harvard Project On
American Indian Economic
Development

John F. Kennedy School
of Government
Harvard University

Standing Rock

Standing Rock

LOCATION AND LAND STATUS

The Standing Rock Reservation straddles the border between North and South Dakota about 40 miles south of Bismarck, North Dakota. The reservation's eastern boundary is Lake Oahe, formed by the Fort Randall and Big Bend dams on the Missouri River; the tribe lost 55,944 acres of land when the dammed waters inundated the surrounding areas. The Cannon Ball River forms the reservation's northern border, and Perkins and Adams county lines constitute the western border. The Cheyenne River Sioux Reservation abuts the reservation to the south. The reservation was established in 1889 in the wake of the Great Plains Wars, and at that time it encompassed approximately 2.7 million acres.

PHYSICAL DESCRIPTION

The land is classic prairie, with broad valleys and rolling hills, dotted with buttes above 2,000 feet in elevation, and badlands, typical of the Great Plains.

CLIMATE

Fort Yates, the tribal headquarters, sits at an elevation of 1,649 feet above sea level. It is within the geographic center of the continent, and thus experiences a typical continental climate, characterized by dramatic annual and day-to-day temperature changes, some occurring rapidly during a single 24-hour period. The year-round high temperatures average 56.8°F; the year-round low temperatures average almost 34°F. The area receives over 13 inches of precipitation annually; however, drought in summer and severe blizzards, with snow accumulations of several feet at a time, in winter are not uncommon.

CULTURE AND HISTORY

The Standing Rock Sioux Tribe encompasses the Hunkpapa and Blackfeet bands of the Lakota Nation, and the Hunkpatinas and Cuthead bands of the Yanktonais of the

Dakota Nation. They descend from the Teton Band of Sioux Indians (Lakota or Western Sioux) who moved into the region now known as the Dakotas from just west of the Great Lakes. The original confederation of Lakotas was made up of seven nations, six of which spoke three mutually intelligible dialects of the Siouan language. The Teton Band comprised the seventh nation, and it spoke the Lakota dialect. Around the middle of the eighteenth century, the Lakotas migrated west in pursuit of buffalo when white fur traders began to decimate the eastern herds. While the Lakotas were often at war with other tribes, they only began to actively resist immigration when settlers began arriving in large numbers, sometime during the mid-1800s. This development touched off the Plains Wars, bringing the intervention of the federal government and subsequently the Fort Laramie Treaty of 1868. This treaty ended the deadlock between the Sioux and the U.S. government in the Dakota Territory, primarily by establishing the boundaries of the Great Sioux Nation Reservation and guaranteeing its freedom from intrusion. Those boundaries included all of western South Dakota along with parts of present-day Wyoming, Montana, North Dakota, and Nebraska. Unfortunately for the Lakotas, the federal government soon failed to live up to its end of the bargain. In a blatant breach of the treaty, the government summarily confiscated 7.7 million acres of the tribe's sacred Black Hills in 1876 after gold was discovered there. Later that year, General George Armstrong Custer and the Seventh Cavalry (who had been protecting miners in the Black Hills) were annihilated by a Lakota war party led by Crazy Horse and Sitting Bull, who was a spiritual leader of the Hunkpapas. This legendary event led to a resumption of the Plains Wars and the dispersal of many Lakotas to Canada. By 1890 the Sioux, as the federal government preferred to call the tribe, had finally been relegated to their now greatly diminished reservation.

Standing Rock Reservation
Federal reservation
Yanktonai, Hunkpapa, and
Blackfeet Sioux
Sioux, North Dakota; Carson,
Dewey, and Ziebach counties,
South Dakota

Standing Rock Sioux Tribe
   of North and South Dakota
P.O. Box D
Fort Yates, SD 58538
701-854-7201
701-854-8595 Fax
standingrock.org

Standing Rock

TRI-SD-sr-015

TRI-SD-sr-017

TRI-SD-sr-016

TRI-SD-sr-018

TRI-SD-sr-015 Standing Rock Administrative Service Center

TRI-SD-sr-017 Tesoro Gas Station and Convenience Store

TRI-SD-sr-016 Prairie Knights Casino

TRI-SD-sr-018 Sitting Bull Tatanka Iyontanke

Total area *(BIA realty, 2003)*
840,911.21 acres

Tribally owned *(BIA realty, 2003)*
356,884.26 acres

Federal trust *(BIA realty, 2003)*
2.3 acres

Individually owned
(BIA realty, 2003)
484,024.65 acres

Population *2000 census*
8,250

Population *(BIA, 2001)*
9,093

Tribal enrollment *(BIA, 2001)*
13,419

Total labor force *2000 census*
2,961

High school graduate or higher
2000 census
77.2%

Bachelor's degree or higher
2000 census
11.2%

Unemployment rate *2000 census*
18.3%

Per capita income *2000 census*
$8,192

The Standing Rock Reservation, now occupied by members of the Yanktonai, Hunkpapa, and Blackfeet Sioux, was created on March 2, 1889, when a congressional act divided the Great Sioux Nation into smaller reservations. Two million acres formed the Standing Rock Reservation: the Hunkpatinas and Cuthead Yanktonais bands settled on the North Dakota side, and the Hunkpapas and Blackfeet bands were on the South Dakota side. Early in the twentieth century, residents of the reservation accepted Indian New Deal rehabilitation, but they have long resisted compliance with the Indian Reorganization Act of 1934. While this resistance symbolizes the tribe's cultural integrity, it has resulted in a denial of full-fledged federal funding.

Encouraging developments in recent times include the tribally affiliated Standing Rock Community College with a curriculum geared toward studying and revitalizing the tribe's traditional cultural practices. The Standing Rock people still practice their traditional ceremonies, which encompass the seven rites of the Lakota Nation brought by White Buffalo Calf Woman. Powwows, rodeos, and horse and foot races are held during the summer. Special powwows are held for special achievements, such as graduation or military service, with traditional honoring ceremonies, giveaways, and feasts to celebrate accomplishments. The oral tradition is still passed down from the elders to the youth.

GOVERNMENT

The Standing Rock Sioux, under PL-638, contract with the BIA to administer key programs and services. They operate under a constitution approved on April 24, 1959. The tribal council consists of a chairman, a vice-chairman, a secretary, and 14 popularly elected members, each serving four-year terms. Eight of these members are elected from various districts throughout the reservation; six serve without regard to residency. The council chair serves as the administrative head of the tribe. The tribal council passes legislation, makes budgets, approves financial transactions, and makes major decisions affecting the tribe, including: managing the tribe's real property, including trust lands; overseeing business ventures; passing and enforcing ordinances; contracting for business

and government needs; and negotiating loans for tribal government use, and guaranteeing loans for tribal members. The finance department handles payroll, business transactions, and bank reconcilement.

The tribe has its own tribal court system to hear and prosecute civil and criminal complaints. The court is staffed by a chief judge, two associate judges, a court administrator, chief prosecutor, prosecutor advocate, defense advocate, chief clerk of court, assistant clerk of court, deputy court clerk, compliance clerk, and data entry clerk. A separate division, the children's court, hears all matters relating to reservation youth. That court is staffed by an associate judge, juvenile probation officer, juvenile clerk, court counselor, and presenting officer.

ECONOMY

Traditionally the bulk of the tribe's income has come from ranching and leasing grazing permits to private cattle interests. Today the economy is fueled by gaming, tribal operations, and business enterprises owned by the tribe and individuals. During the late 1990s, emphasis was placed on attracting industries to the reservation with some success, and there are continuing plans to increase development of economically viable enterprises.

In 2003, the tribe negotiated a tax collection agreement with the State of South Dakota wherein a higher percentage of state tax revenues collected on the reservation are to be returned to the tribe. The amount of additional sales and use tax revenues were predicted to be approximately $490,000 annually. A new shared tax on motor fuel, to take effect in January 2004, was part of the agreement. The federal government does not collect taxes on the reservations, but it does keep a percentage of the sales, use, and motor-fuel taxes it collects on the reservation.

Agriculture and Livestock. The soil along the eastern shores of the Missouri River (glaciated plains) is generally better suited for agriculture than on the western side, where the Standing Rock Reservation lies. Despite this, there are 29 Indian-owned cattle operations using 71,592 acres for agricultural production, and another 823,310 acres, or 92 percent of the land base, are leased to non-Indian farmers or ranchers. The 1997 Census of Agriculture reported a total amount of agricultural products sold within Standing Rock Reservation as $44,558,000. One of the economic realities, however, is that the bulk of this (approximately 92 percent) was earned by the non-Indian operators.

Scarcity of surface water adversely affects agriculture and live-stock operations on the reservation. During droughts, some sources dry up altogether. The reservation is dotted with small streams, lakes, and dugouts available during wet periods, usually in spring. Groundwater is also scarce, and deep groundwater, although plentiful, is highly mineralized and of poor quality. Use of the Oahe Lake (reservoir) waters for irrigation is a potential remedy. The tribe lost 55,993 acres of its land base when the rising Missouri River waters inundated their land.

Gaming. The Standing Rock Sioux Tribe has two casinos: the Prairie Knights Casino is located on Highway 12 near Cannon Ball, North Dakota, and two miles west of Mobridge, South Dakota; and the Grand River Casino is near Wakpala, South Dakota.

The Prairie Knights Casino attracts customers from nearby cities and is working with tour bus companies in the United States and Canada. The North Dakota ski resort, Huff Hills, is located close to the casino, ensuring good winter traffic. The original 42,000-square-foot facility was expanded to include 20,000 square feet of additional gaming space, along with an 86-room lodge, 2 restaurants, a swimming pool, a gift shop, and conference and banquet facilities. In 2002, there were plans to build an RV park next to the casino and lodge. The facility had 140 employees in 2004, many of them members of the Standing Rock Sioux Tribe.

Mining. A geologic formation known as the Williston Basin, which underlies the Standing Rock Reservation, contains significant deposits of oil and natural gas. There was no known extraction activity on the reservation in 2004.

Manufacturing. Prior to 1970 the tribe had begun to attract industrial manufacturers to the reservation, including Five Star Cheese, Plastic Molders, and Chief Manufacturing. These businesses have made a significant contribution to the local economy. The tribe has been making a particular effort to develop manufacturing operations pertaining to the defense industry.

Services and Retail. Districts within the reservation have developed enterprises whose revenues support district operations. Businesses include Bear Soldier Bingo and a grocery store in McLaughlin, South Dakota; Big Foot Bingo and a laundromat in Little Eagle, South Dakota; a bingo facility and a convenience store and gas station in Cannon Ball, North Dakota; a trading post in Bullhead; and bingo facilities in the districts of Fort Yates, North Dakota, and Porcupine, South Dakota.

Some tribal members own their own businesses, including: Standing Rock Cable Vision, White Buffalo Store, Missouri Drift Inn, Taco Johns, Henry's Standard, Tim's Conoco and laundromats, Richie's Ponderosa Plaza, Beauty Saloon, Pelican Lounge and Restaurant, Missouri Drift Inn Video, Pelican Video, and the Sweat Shop Gym. There are non-Indian owned businesses throughout the reservation, as well, primarily in the communities of McIntosh and McLaughlin, South Dakota, and Selfridge and Solen, North Dakota.

Telecommunications. Lakota Technologies, employing 100 people, provides telephone service to all community members. In 2004, it was a million-dollar enterprise with per-capita distribution of dividends to tribal members.

Tourism and Recreation. Boating, fishing, and other water sports attract visitors to the Missouri, Grand, and Cannon Ball rivers. Organized sports, such as basketball, softball, volleyball, and horseshoes are popular at the reservation; tournaments are held year-round.

Many tribal celebrations are open to the public, though some are not. Events include the annual Graduation and Memorial Day Powwows in May; district powwows and traditional contests almost every weekend throughout the summer months; the Sioux Indian Fair; a Veteran's Day Powwow in November; and a Fourth of July Rodeo. In December, the tribe annually marks the death of Chief Big Foot at Wounded Knee with a ride. A ride is also conducted in celebration of the victory at Little Big Horn. Calf roping and other rodeo events are held at area ranches spring, summer, and fall.

The Lewis and Clark Trail (Historical Highway 1806) runs along the Missouri River; it's a scenic drive for motorists interested in the history of the United States westward expansion. There are pull-offs with historical markers along the route and guide maps available in towns along the way. Other attractions include Sitting Bull's grave and the site of old Fort Manuel. The Standing Rock College Historical Society exhibits its tribal art and artifacts at Fort Yates, North Dakota.

INFRASTRUCTURE

State Highways 65 and 63 run north-south through the reservation, and U.S. Highway 12 dissects it east-west. U.S. Highway 83 is a major north-south route just east of reservation boundaries. Highway 1806, the Lewis and Clark Trail, which runs into Highway 24, passes through the communities of Kenel and Wakpala. There are no major transportation facilities existing on the reservation; however, train, bus, and truck lines do provide service to Fort Yates. Charter buses and limousine services deliver patrons to the Prairie Knights and Grand River casinos daily. The Greyhound Line bus service is located in Bismarck, as are the nearest commercial airline services, 40 miles north of the reservation.

Like some other area reservations, the Standing Rock Sioux Tribe lost some infrastructure when the Pick-Sloan Act led to the Lake Oahe reservoir on the Missouri River inundating surrounding areas. Three rodeo arenas, 190 domestic water systems, 22,000 acres of waterbed, 50 ranch water systems, 95 miles of main roads, 2 race tracks, 190 houses, and 3 sawmills were lost to the rising water.

Electricity. The Montana-Dakota Utilities Company and the Mor-Gran-Sou Cooperative supply electricity to the reservation.

Fuel. The Montana-Dakota Utilities Company and the Mor-Gran-Sou Cooperative supply natural gas to the reservation. Lakota Energy, which is owned by a tribal member, supplies fuel oil and propane to homes in the districts.

Water Supply. MR&I Water Distribution System supplies water lines to the communities, but most enrolled members in the communities of Little Eagle, Porcupine, Kenel, Bullhead, and Cannon Ball continue to draw water from wells. The tribal wastewater utility serves 10 communities on the reservation with a combined population of 24,000. The system consists of 10 lagoons, 22 cells, and 9 lift stations.

Standing Rock

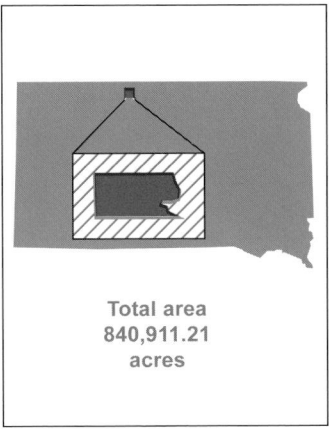

**Total area
840,911.21
acres**

ENVIRONMENTAL CONCERNS
In 1996, tribal environmental staff identified illegal dumping sites as an environmental problem with the potential to cause human health problems, pollute the soil, and contaminate groundwater.

Standing Rock

Transportation. The Standing Rock Public Transportation Program, operated by Sitting Bull College, provides public transportation (for Indian and non-Indian passengers) for the Standing Rock Reservation; it also provides service from Mobridge, Wakpala, Kenel, Little Eagle, and McLaughlin to Fort Yates and the Prairie Knights Casino. Pickups are available in Mandan and Cannon Ball for trips to the casino and Fort Yates, as well. In business since 1989, this enterprise also provides special services to local schools for field trips, and it has a wheelchair lift for use with vocational rehabilitation clients.

Housing. The Standing Rock Housing Authority constructs and manages over 650 homes on the reservation; some were built via the HUD Mutual Help home ownership program, and others were constructed on individual allotments or tribally leased land. The housing authority oversees and maintains HUD low-rent units. In 2004, the tribe placed high priority on constructing and increasing the availability of affordable housing on the reservation for its tribal members; and it was looking at programs such as Habitat for Humanity and the federal government's Home Grant Project to facilitate construction.

COMMUNITY FACILITIES AND SERVICES

The tribe's domestic violence shelter opened in 1994, and it serves both reservation residents and women and children from surrounding communities. The Eagle Butte Volunteers operate an elders feeding program and an after-school and weekend youth development program. The BIA provides law enforcement services to the reservation, and volunteers at the police department operate a popular midnight basketball program to help prevent juvenile criminal activity.

Education. The tribe provides a Head Start program for preschoolers in Fort Yates, North Dakota. There is also a privately operated parochial elementary school in Fort Yates. The BIA operates the schools in Fort Yates, and there are public schools in McIntosh, McLaughlin, and Wakpala, South Dakota, and in Selfridge and Solen, North Dakota.

The reservation is also home to the Standing Rock Community College and Sitting Bull College, which provide associate degrees in human services, education, and business management.

Health Care. The tribal health department provides a number of health services, including a community health representative, prevention services and education, eye examinations, eyeglasses, and emergency care including ambulance services. The tribe also provides an elderly nutrition program. There is a U.S. Public Health Service Hospital in Fort Yates and smaller clinics in five districts. There are other hospitals and clinics in Bismarck. Transportation difficulties in remote communities on the reservation prevent some community members from receiving adequate health care. Some members do not have adequate nutrition and live in overly crowded housing conditions. Socioeconomic conditions have contributed to very high rates of teenage suicide among tribal members.

Yankton

Yankton Reservation
Federal reservation
Yankton, Yanktonai, and
Assiniboine Sioux
Charles Mix County, South
Dakota

Yankton Sioux Tribe of South
   Dakota
P.O. Box 248
Marty, SD 57361
   605-384-3804
   605-384-5687 Fax
yanktonsiouxtourism.com

LOCATION AND LAND STATUS

The Yankton Reservation encompasses approximately 56,500 acres of land near Fort Randall, about 35 miles west of Yankton, South Dakota, along the Missouri River where it serves as the border between South Dakota and Nebraska. Tribal population is concentrated primarily in five separate, recognized communities: Wagner, Lake Andes, Marty, Greenwood, and Choteau Creek.

A treaty in 1858 established the reservation, which encompassed the traditional homeland of the Yankton Sioux. Under this treaty, the Yankton Sioux sold 11 million acres and reserved 430,504 acres for its reservation. Under the Yankton Agreement of 1892, which had an intent that was similar to the General Allotment Act of 1887, tribal members were allotted about 262,000 acres of 40-, 80-, and 160-acre tracts of land, with the remaining 168,000 acres of the reservation opened to homesteaders. The BIA sold many of the tribal allotments to non-Indian homesteaders, which resulted in a checkerboard pattern. Hence, out of the 435,000 acres comprising the 1892 reservation, only about 56,500 acres remain under tribal and individual ownership. Additional tribal acreage was lost when Fort Randall Dam was built on the Missouri River to create Lake Francis Case in the southwestern part of the reservation.

CULTURE AND HISTORY

The Yankton, Yanktonai, and Assiniboine Indians descend from a single "council fire" of Nakota Indians who occupied the region of the Dakotas even before the Lakota tribes arrived from Minnesota. They were already in traditional Sioux territory at the time of the white settlers' first arrival. The Yanktonais and Assinboines (Yanktons) were peaceful people who got along with neighboring tribes and with the increasing numbers of white miners and settlers.

Like other tribes, the Ihanktonwan Nakota Oyate (Yankton, or "People of the End Village") ceded the vast majority of their ancestral territory to the U.S. government: 2.2 million acres in 1830 and over 11 million additional acres in 1858 when they signed a treaty on April 19. In return they retained a 430,504-acre reservation on the site they continue to occupy today, albeit with greatly diminished holdings. The Yanktons also claimed the 648-acre Pipestone Reservation until 1929 when they sold it for about $330,000 and assurances of continued access.

Unlike other bands of Sioux, the Yanktons never took up arms against the United States and generally lived in peace with neighboring tribes. The official constitutional government adopted by the tribe in 1891 was succeeded (under some duress) by another one in 1932. The Yanktons never formally accepted the terms of the Indian Reorganization Act. During the New Deal era, the tribe received benefits from the federal government, but otherwise they have traditionally been slighted due to what the government and the BIA have taken to be the tribe's overt cultural resistance. For the Yanktons, "resistance" has simply meant preserving cultural traditions. The Sacred Pipe and other traditional spiritual practices like the Peyote Ceremony have not only continued to thrive but have finally come into accepted practice. The tribal insignia bears the reservation's slogan, adopted September 24, 1975: *"Land of the Friendly People of the Seven Council Fires."*

GOVERNMENT

Although they have a constitution and bylaws adopted in 1932, the tribe is nonchartered (unincorporated) and non-IRA organized. In 1961 the general membership elected a nine-member constitutional committee to revise the constitution. The amended constitution and bylaws were subsequently adopted in 1963, then amended again in 1975. The Yankton Sioux Tribal Business and Claims Committee serves as the governing body and conducts day-to-day business. The chairman, vice-chairman, secretary, treasurer, and five other committee members are elected at large for two-year terms.

The Yankton Sioux Tribe, under PL-638, contracts with the BIA to administer key programs and services. Four of the five communities (all except Choteau Creek) have elected community boards that conduct strategic planning and approve budget requests to the tribal business and claims committee. Fiscal management oversees all grants, contracts, and the various administrative functions of the boards and programs.

ECONOMY

Tribal leaders have searched relentlessly for revenue- and employment-producing enterprises to establish on the reservation. In 1991 a modest bingo hall was transformed into the Fort Randall Casino, altering the tribe's economic picture almost overnight. The 75 percent unemployment rate dropped to near zero, in a mere eight months.Gaming aside, the region's economy has long been primarily agricultural. Tribal members are currently involved in cultivating various crops including winter wheat, soybeans, and other grains. Cattle grazing leases also comprise a significant segment of the area's economy.

Government as Employer. Tribal government-via its plethora of administrative and operational functions is the largest employer on the reservation, employing over 100 tribal members in 34 programs and businesses. The Yankton Sioux College Center, opened in 1994, also generates employment for the tribe. The Fort Randall Hotel and Casino, the tribal farm, the Marty Indian School, and other enterprises managed by tribal government, represent indirect government employment. The BIA also employs several reservation residents, as does the Indian Health Service and hospital.

Economic Development Projects. The Yankton Sioux have a comprehensive economic development strategy committee, which is part of the larger economic development administration office, which guides the business and claims committee's policymaking in business matters. The overall mission is to improve the quality of life for all tribal members. This committee has generated much economic development since 1995, including a travel plaza, marina, and propane refueling facility.

In June 2004 the tribe published a list of long-standing priorities and economic goals in the Yankton Sioux Tribe Comprehensive Economic Development Strategy. They are to: develop the economy and increase tribal employment opportunities, improve community services and facilities, develop human resources, develop natural resource development, and increase access to educational opportunities. The document is to be updated annually, in accordance with priorities established as a result of public hearings and research conducted by the economic development administration office.

Agriculture and Livestock. While private individuals farm a large portion of the reservation land, no individual tribal members are currently engaged in farming. There is, however, a tribally owned and operated farm, which grows corn, winter wheat and soybeans, and maintains pastureland for cattle grazing. The tribe clearly has the land capacity and water resources of the Missouri River for irrigation systems that would triple or quadruple many of its farming operations. Currently, the cattle operation is working with a new bloodline of stock cattle known for its higher yields. In general, agriculture has emerged as an area with some of the greatest future eco-

nomic potential for the tribe. In June 2004 the tribe expressed interest in studying the feasibility of developing a corn milling and ethanol production plant.

Gaming. The 38,092-square-foot Fort Randall Casino is the centerpiece of the tribe's economy as well as its most dramatic success story. The facility, first opened in June 1991, employed over 600 workers in 2004. Located three miles east of the Fort Randall Dam and Recreation Area on Highway 46, the casino sits atop a hill overlooking the entire reservation. It is open 24 hours a day, 7 days per week, featuring 250 slot machines, 12 table games, 3 poker tables, and 200 bingo seats. The Four Directions Restaurant is on-site, along with a 57-room hotel, built in 1992, and an entertainment venue.

Fisheries. A brick and concrete building, previously used as a law enforcement center, located at the site of a previous Brownfields site on the reservation, has been designated as the tribal fisheries office. In June 2004 there were plans to construct breeding ponds for walleye, catfish, and the environmentally threatened paddlefish on tribal tracts adjacent to the Missouri River. Research and construction toward these ends continue.

Construction. With the expansion of the casino and hotel resort complex came the opportunity for increased construction employment among tribal members. The reservation serves as home to various construction-related businesses such as building contractors, electrical contractors, and a large building supply business, which employs over 30 workers, most of them tribal members.

Real Estate/Commercial Development. The BIA leases from the tribe an office building at a 13-acre park.

Services and Retail. The Yankton Sioux Travel Plaza, which opened in September 1995, was built on Highway 46, just west of Fort Randall Casino. It has a small restaurant and convenience store. It was recently expanded to include a propane refueling facility. Wholesale and retail services on the reservation include more than 12 restaurants, laundromats, several auto repair and wrecker services, general stores, convenience marts, hardware stores, farm and building supply stores, and other enterprises.

Transportation. At least one commercial trucking company is located within reservation boundaries.

Tourism and Recreation. The Tribe has its own tourism association to promote the various cultural and recreational facilities available at the reservation. The Fort Randall Hotel and Casino attract those interested in gaming. The hotel features regularly scheduled nationally touring musical entertainment.

Numerous parks, camping, and dock facilities are available, including a chance to camp in traditional Plains Indian tepees at historic Greenwood overlooking the Missouri River near the Lewis and Clark Trail Historical Site. Here is where the Corps of Discovery came ashore. Two monuments, the Struck by the Ree Monument and the 1858 Treaty Monument, are nearby. Tribal members are available for musical entertainment and Native American storytelling around the campfires at the Tipi Bed and Breakfast.

The Fort Randall Dam serves as a site for swimming and boating. There are also nineteenth-century burial grounds and archeological sites nearby. Below the Fort Randall Dam, the 1,080-acre Karl E. Mundt National Wildlife Refuge and the nation's first federal eagle sanctuary provide photography opportunities. Ruins of a chapel located at the site of Old Fort Randall, the longest continually occupied military outpost on

Yankton

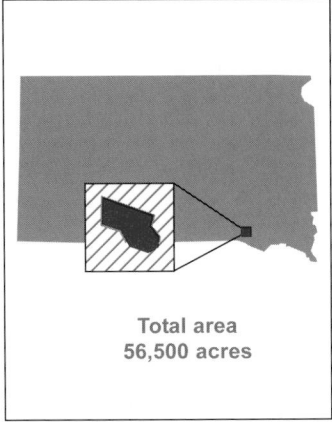

**Total area
56,500 acres**

Total area *(BIA realty, 2003)*
36,740.97 acres

Total area *(Tribal source, 2004)*
56,500 acres

Tribally owned *(BIA realty, 2003)*
24,448.74 acres

Individually owned
(BIA realty, 2003)
12,292.23 acres

Population *2000 census*
6,500

Population *(Tribal source, 2004)*
6,281

Tribal enrollment
(Tribal source, 2004)
5,700

Total labor force *2000 census*
2,602

High school graduate or higher
2000 census
72.9%

Bachelor's degree or higher
2000 census
13.6%

Unemployment rate *2000 census*
12.2%

Per capita income *2000 census*
$10,168

Yankton

TRI-SD-yk-001

TRI-SD-yk-002

TRI-SD-yk-004

TRI-SD-yk-001 Welcome sign at Yankton Sioux Reservation, Home of the Braves

TRI-SD-yk-002 Campus at Marty, SD

TRI-SD-yk-004 School at Yankton Reservation

the upper Missouri, are on a walking tour. Buffalo still graze nearby. The National Park Service and U.S. Army Corps of Engineers maintain the North Point Recreation Area near Lake Francis Case, which offers rustic camping or sites with full amenities including fishing, hunting, boating, sailing, swimming, skiing, and photography. Watercraft can be rented.

The Marty Indian School draws tourists interested in traditional Native culture. Several annual powwows, held primarily during the spring and summer, are open to the public.

INFRASTRUCTURE

Electricity. Charles Mix Electric Association and Northwestern Public Service Company provide the reservation with electricity. The reservation's planning department has conducted feasibility studies regarding the possibility of utilizing wind-generated electricity throughout the reservation in order to reduce commercial and residential energy costs. In 2004 the tribe appointed a wind energy board to oversee development of a 50-unit wind farm near Fort Randall Dam. The board chose a design to be used for the wind generators, and it has been working in coordination with other regional tribes to ensure cost-effectiveness and to problem-solve market delivery issues.

Fuel. Northwestern Public Service Company provides natural gas. Ferrellgas of Avon, Farmer's Cooperative Association in Lake Andes, and YST Propane Company at FRC and the Yankton Sioux Tribe's Travel Plaza supply propane. Solar power and wood are also sources of fuel for some residents.

Water Supply. Randall Community Water District maintains the reservation's water system. Some farmers maintain individual wells, as well. The reservation sewage system consists of community septic tanks and lagoons.The tribe manages solid waste disposal in the communities of Greenwood and Marty; trash is hauled to a landfill on tribal land two miles north of Radar Hill.Collection at Wagner and Lake Andes is provided by the municipalities and hauled to tribally leased locations.

The Yankton Sioux Tribe established a utilities commission to develop a total infrastructure to manage and develop a reservation-wide utilities system.

Transportation. Highways 46, 50, 281, and 18 all provide direct access and service to the reservation, converging at Pickstown, South Dakota. Interstate 90 runs east-west, one hour north of the reservation; I-29, running north-south, lies one-and-one-half hours to the east. Twenty-two miles of paved BIA roads cross the reservation.

Major passenger and transport air services are available in Sioux Falls, South Dakota, and in Sioux City, Iowa. Small commercial air service is available in the town of Wagner, with some limited service to and from Minnesota, available at Chan Gurney Airfield, in Yankton, on the reservation. Commercial chartered bus and limousine companies serve the reservation and surrounding area, as does UPS. As the reservation lies directly adjacent to the Missouri River, water transportation services are possible.

COMMUNITY FACILITIES AND SERVICES

The Yankton Tribal Administration Building, a 13,888-square-foot facility, is located in Marty, and houses 22 programs and services for tribal members. The college center building, located south of tribal headquarters, houses adult education services, Ihanktonwan Community College, adult vocational training, direct employment services, and the higher education office. The Head Start program has its own building near Marty. The housing authority has offices near Wagner, as do the social services office, the tribal youth program, and the Head Start program. An alcohol and drug treatment center and the youth outreach program are located in Lake Andes.

Education. Educational facilities include local public schools and the Marty Indian School, which moved into a new building in 1999. Vacated buildings on the campus will be used for other tribal programs. The tribe has its own elementary and high schools. There is also an alternative school, Zenith High School, in Wagner.

Health Care. Several health care facilities serve the reservation, including the Wagner Community Hospital, an outpatient clinic at Lake Andes, and another at Wagner. There is a medical supply store, a chiropractor, a massage therapist, and an optometrist in Wagner, and an alcohol and substance abuse treatment facility in Lake Andes. The Indian Health Service unit at Wagner, South Dakota, has a dialysis unit. Other hospitals are located in Yankton, Sioux Falls, Mitchell, Rosebud, Pine Ridge, Minneapolis, Omaha, Fort Meade, and Fitzsimmons Army Hospital in Denver, Colorado.

ENVIRONMENTAL CONCERNS

In 1997 the tribe's environmental staff identified as primary environmental problems an aboveground storage tank and an auto shop floor where drains are potentially releasing petroleum products onto the Marty Indian School Campus. Greenwood, the site of a 20-acre U.S. EPA Brownfields project, was selected for a pilot demonstration grant in October 2000. The tribe identified contaminants and extended the grant through 2003 in order to assure cleanup prior to participating in the Lewis and Clark Corps of Discovery Bicentennial celebrations in Greenwood in 2003.

Alabama-Coushatta

LOCATION AND LAND STATUS

The Alabama-Coushatta Reservation, Texas' oldest reservation, is located approximately 70 miles northeast of Houston, in an area known locally as Deep East Texas. It is bordered to the south by the Big Thicket National Preserve. When the reservation was originally created in 1854 by Sam Houston, the total area was 1,280 acres. Subsequent purchases have increased the amount of land that the tribe owns to just over 4,500 acres, including some land purchased in 2001 upon which the tribe built housing for tribal members. Most of the land is either pending trusteeship or has already been placed under federal trusteeship.

CLIMATE

There has been no climate data recorded for Livingston, Texas, the site of tribal headquarters; however, Huntsville, Texas, lies approximately 30 miles due west of Livingston, and weather patterns would not vary significantly. The average year-round daily high temperature at Huntsville is 78°F, with the highest temperature on record being 107°F. The average year-round daily low temperature is 57°F, with the lowest temperature ever recorded as -2°F. The area receives approximately 44 inches of precipitation annually.

CULTURE AND HISTORY

The Alabama and Coushatta tribes, of the Muskogean linguistic group, are descendents of the ancient mound-building cultures of the southeastern region of what is now the United States. Villages were constructed around large central plazas where temple buildings were the center of spiritual and cultural life. They practiced a subsistence lifestyle based upon agriculture, gathering, and hunting. They are said to be the first friendly tribes encountered by the Spanish explorer de Soto in 1641.

Both tribes were members of the Upper Creek Confederacy in territory that is now the states of Alabama, Mississippi, and Georgia. Fleeing eighteenth-century American colonial settlements in their aboriginal territory, the Coushattas migrated to eastern Texas sometime around 1795; the Alabamas arrived in Tyler County in 1805. In July 1839, President Mirabeau B. Lamar, of the Republic of Texas, issued a proclamation of peace toward the tribes, enjoining Texas residents from engaging in any acts of violence upon them. As a gesture of gratitude for their support of Texas independence, Sam Houston appropriated lands for each tribe. When the Coushatta acreage was never deeded, the Alabamas shared their land, uniting the two tribes for the first time. The people lived in small villages, primarily along the Trinity River, Tempe Creek, and Long Creek in Polk County. Some lived in various villages in Tyler County, and others in the Colita Village in San Jacinto County. The last of these Coushatta members moved to the Alabama-Coushatta Reservation in 1906.

The tribes' culture and religion were irreversibly affected by the Protestant religion practiced by settlers in the surrounding white communities. After having remained peaceful with their new neighbors, though, the tribes were allowed to remain in Texas when all other tribes were removed to Indian Territory in Oklahoma. Both tribes were administered by the State of Texas under PL-280 after federal affiliation was terminated in 1955. In August 1987, the united tribes were federally re-recognized and sovereignty was reestablished.

The Alabama-Coushattas work diligently to maintain distinct cultural values while embracing modern technologies. A majority of tribal members speak the Native language and practice traditional arts and crafts forms, perpetuating the ancient Legend of the Twin Manifestations, a fundamental spiritual teaching of the Alabama-Coushatta people.

GOVERNMENT

The tribal council, established in 1957, is composed of a chairman, a vice-chairman, a secretary, a treasurer, and three members. All are elected at large for three- and four-year rotating terms. The council acts as the governing body for the tribe. The tribe also respects the traditional positions of principal chief and second chief, elected to lifetime terms. The tribal council meets twice monthly. The tribe participates with various other governmental and advocacy nonprofit organizations, including the Texas Forestry Association, the Big Thicket Association, the National Congress of American Indians, the United South and Eastern Tribes, as well as the Native American Chambers of Commerce.

The tribe, under PL-638, contracts with the BIA to administer key programs and services. The following departments or offices conduct business for the tribe, offering various programs and services to promote self-sufficiency for all members: administration; finance; education; natural resources, which includes offices of environmental protection, forestry, and oil and gas; social services; recreational facilities; systems administration; tribal development; and public information. The historical preservation office works in conjunction with the cultural committee to retain the native language and traditions, and a tribal document office, maintains membership rolls.

ECONOMY

Full-time employment is rare among members of the Alabama-Coushatta Tribe; 46 percent of all eligible members are not employed on a full-time basis. Only one percent have a four-year college degree, and the median household income re-

Alabama-Coushatta Reservation
Federal reservation
Alabama and Coushatta
Polk County, Texas

Alabama-Coushatta Tribe
of Texas
571 State Park Road 56
Livingston, TX 77351
936-563-1100
936-563-1139 Fax
alabama-coushatta.com

Total area *(BIA realty, 2003)*
5,197.46 acres

Tribally owned *(BIA realty, 2003)*
5,197.46 acres

Population *(Tribal source, 2004)*
597

Tribal enrollment
(Tribal source, 2004)
1,001

Total labor force *2000 census*
187

High school degree or higher
2000 census
76.4%

Bachelor's degree or higher
2000 census
3.3%

Unemployment rate *2000 census*
11.2%

Per capita income *2000 census*
$10,465

Alabama-
Coushatta

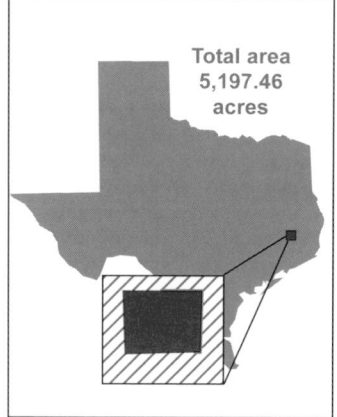

Total area
5,197.46
acres

mains less than $11,000. To combat these grave statistics, the tribal council authorized the formation of an office of tribal development in April 2003 to create "significant and sustainable sources of tribal income, meaningful employment opportunities, and support for entrepreneurship, in furtherance of tribal self-determination and improved quality of life." *(See also, Economic Development Projects, below.)*

Government as Employer. In 2004, approximately 150 employees were working for either tribal government, the BIA, or in other federal and state programs represented on the reservation.

Economic Development Projects. The tribal development office promotes and encourages private development on reservation land to prospective corporate business partners in the industrial, distribution, and service sectors. They are also charged with planning and obtaining startup and operating capital for tribally owned enterprises. The development office assists prospective investors at every stage of a project, from planning and feasibility studies through financing and building, staffing and training, and marketing and distribution. They utilize incentives, such as tax abatements and exemptions, employment tax credits, accelerated depreciation, low-interest financing, and a productive, well-trained labor force to attract private interests.

Forestry. The tribe has its own forestry department to oversee management of timber on all tribal lands. The forestry department oversees all forestry-related activities, including protection and development of timber stands, wildfire protection and prevention measures, fire prevention education, endangered species protection and management, protection of sensitive wildlife ecosystems, and protection of culturally significant and historical sites.

Gaming. The tribe opened a no-alcohol gaming entertainment center in November 2001, which operated for only 9 months with 300 slot machines and 5 blackjack tables. The casino created 400 jobs, dropping the tribe's unemployment rate from 46 percent to 14 percent, and it paid more than $4.3 million in wages and approximately $400,000 in federal taxes while in operation. Tribal revenues exceeded $1 million per month. Local retailers also reported increases in traffic at their businesses during the facility's operation; however, proposed legislation that would have approved legalized gambling failed to pass. On July 25, 2002, tribal leaders obeyed a federal court order to close the casino.

In May 2004, the tribe was working with the governor's office and the Texas Legislature's House Select Committee on School Finance to secure approval for a bill that would overhaul the public school finance system in Texas via the proceeds from the addition of video slot machines to the casino already in operation in Livingston, Texas. The bill, if passed, would approve the addition of video slot machines at seven dog and horse tracks throughout the state, and the three Texas tribes would be permitted to develop casinos on their reservations. In return, a percentage of the anticipated revenues would be returned to the State of Texas, earmarked for the public school systems. After several sessions, the bill did not make it to the floor of the House, so the process of working with the state legislature continues.

Mining. The tribe's oil and gas department, established in May 1997, oversees the considerable field operations, production, revenues, and compliance issues associated with nine gas/condensate wells on 3,000 productive acres. Although some of the wells have been in production since 1983, the tribe

kept no records of its own and was dependent upon the integrity of outside governmental regulatory agencies for documentation of output and income generated. The department conducts weekly inspections of the leases, monitors meters, calculates daily production, monitors contracted tankers, and keeps the tribal council and community at large informed of all activities. Since 1997, the department has established a direct computer link with the Minerals Management Service in Denver, conducted a 3-D seismic survey, run a Cadastral survey of reservation boundaries, and initiated operations of a high-tech computer workstation. The tribe's wells are fifth in production in all of Indian Country.

Industrial Parks. In 2005, there is land set aside for development of an industrial park at the reservation.

Services and Retail. The tribe operates a gift shop and a smoke shop in Livingston, Texas, and the Humble Smoke Shop in Humble. The tribe also operates the AC One Stop, a convenience mart in Livingston.

Transportation. The tribe owns and operates a disabled-accessible van, which is available for tribal members.

Media and Communications. The public information office provides information and teaching aids about cultural and historical aspects of the tribe to the public and the local school system. It also publishes a monthly newsletter just for tribal members.

Tourism and Recreation. Much attention has been given to cultural tourism development. The tribe operates a visitors and information center and the Museum of the Alabama and Coushatta, which includes a Living Indian Village exhibit featuring live demonstrations of basket making, weaving, beadwork, and arrowhead making. There are also craft and food preparation demonstrations and a guided walking tour. Recreational opportunities on the reservation include tours of the Big Thicket Wilderness Preserve: there are educational open-air bus rides through one of the most beautiful forests in Texas, and the Big Chief Train ride is a 20-minute excursion into the preserve. Lake Tombigbee offers a plethora of water-based recreation, with campsites, full RV hookups, hiking, and nature trails on shore. Recreational fishing is allowed from the banks, and canoes and paddleboats are available for rental. Inn of the Twelve Clans Restaurant, owned by the tribe, operates at the lake. The tribe owns a tribal dance square where cultural dances take place on weekends during the spring and fall months.

INFRASTRUCTURE
Electricity. The Sam Houston Electric Cooperative provides electricity services.

Fuel. United Gas Corporation provides natural gas to the reservation.

Water Supply. The tribe has its own water system, and it has also installed and maintains a sewer system, including a treatment plant.

Transportation. Commercial bus lines are available in Livingston, 17 miles from the reservation. Truck lines operateregularly into and out of the reservation. Air and train transportation are available 90 miles away in Houston.

Telecommunications. The EasTex Telephone Company provides telephone services to the region. Internet access is available in reservation homes and area schools.

COMMUNITY FACILITIES AND SERVICES

A new gymnasium replaces former school buildings used for various community functions, including men's and women's basketball leagues, youth leagues, organized volleyball games, powwows, special events, and numerous tournaments throughout the year. The facility is managed by the tribe's recreational facilities department. The tribe built a separate covered outdoor Veteran's Pavilion, doubling as the tribal dance square where powwows, dances, and other cultural events are conducted. There is a new tribal community center. The tribe also maintains a tribal cemetery and a ballpark, and it has built a senior center to house all programs and services for the elders.

The tribe provides social services, including various community services, elder programs such as an elder nutrition program, and Indian child welfare services. A youth advisory board helps to identify at-risk children in need of special services. The CHOICES Program assists young adults with decision-making skills. The youth programs, with the assistance of the Texas Extension Services, operate the 4-H Windwalkers Club at the reservation, and the tribally sponsored Inner Voice Youth Council participates in many events throughout the year including the National United National Indian Tribal Youth Conference. The tribe also operates a number of employment assistance and training programs for tribal members, with outreach offices in Livingston, Tyler, Sherman, and Houston. A tribal daycare center and a library are located in Livingston. The cultural committee makes some programs available to tribal members of all ages.

Education. Schoolchildren primarily attend public schools in Big Sandy, Livingston, or Woodville, Texas; however, the tribe established its own education department to oversee the educational needs of all enrolled members. Funding for higher education and adult vocational training is available, as are Johnson O'Malley assistance programs for elementary and high school students. The tribe operates a Head Start pro-

gram for preschoolers, with offices, a parent-resource room, classrooms, and a full-service cafeteria located in the tribal community center.

Health Care. The tribally owned and operated Chief Kina Health Clinic, first opened in May 1988 in a renovated private residence converted for use as a temporary medical facility, provides comprehensive ambulatory medical care; some inpatient services; outpatient medical and surgical options; vision services; diabetes prevention and other wellness programs; prescription drug benefits; alcohol and substance abuse prevention, education, and treatment; maternal and child health programs; and physical rehabilitative care to all tribal members. Additions to the facility were made in 2000. Tribal members may also receive medical care at the Tyler County Hospital in Woodville, the Livingston Memorial Hospital, or the Woodland Heights and Memorial hospitals in Lufkin. With modern technology, the Chief Kina Health Clinic now has telemedicine capabilities so tribal members do not have to travel long distances to see a doctor.

ENVIRONMENTAL CONCERNS

The tribe's natural resource department is made up of three separate offices: environmental protection, forestry, and oil and gas. The Environmental Protection Office, established in 1996 with general assistance program monies from the U.S. EPA, oversees general administrative functions associated with all tribal environmental programs. The forestry department manages all forestry-related activities, including protection and development of timber stands, protection against wildfires and prevention education, endangered species protection management, and protection of cultural or historical sites. In 2004, only one endangered species was known to exist on the reservation, the red-cockaded woodpecker. The forestry department enforces protective measures to safeguard its protected habitats. *(For details regarding the gas and oil office, see Mining, above.)*

Kickapoo

LOCATION AND LAND STATUS

In 1984, the Kickapoo Trust Land Acquisition Committee purchased 125 acres along the Rio Grande River in Maverick County, Texas, about 8 miles south of Eagle Pass. In the absence of a land base of their own, most tribal members have historically lived just across the Rio Grande, in a village, El Nacimiento Rancheria, since the late 1860s. They continue to live in traditional houses made of reed mats on 17,290 acres granted them by the Mexican government. The village is located in the state of Coahuila, 25 miles northwest of Muzquis, approximately 125 miles southwest of Eagle Pass, Texas.

CLIMATE

The elevation at Eagle Pass, Texas, is 805 feet above sea level. The year-round average daily high temperature is 82.4°F. The year-round average daily low temperature is 58.2°F. The area receives approximately 21.5 inches of precipitation annually.

CULTURE AND HISTORY

The Kickapoo Traditional Tribe of Texas, like other Kickapoo bands, speaks an Algonquian language closely related to the Mesquakie-Sauk language. Prior to first contact, the Kickapoos lived in fixed villages throughout the lower Great Lakes region of the midwest. During the summer months, they occu-

pied mid-sized longhouses; after fall harvests and the annual fall buffalo hunt, they separated into winter hunting camps, occupying a style of dwellings known as a "wickiup," or wigwam. The Kickapoos were skilled farmers, raising primarily corn, squash, and beans, supplementing their diet with hunting and gathering. They were skilled horsemen, and they hunted buffalo from horseback long before other tribes adopted this method, allowing them to adapt rather quickly to life on the Great Plains following their migration.

The French encountered the Kickapoos near the lower Great Lakes in the late 1600s. European expansion and intertribal conflicts led to migrations and dispersal as Kickapoo bands scattered widely throughout Indiana, Illinois, Missouri, and Texas. As early as 1775, the Kickapoos were granted land by the king of Spain, in the northern part of the Spanish Territory of what was then Mexico. This part of Mexico later became Texas.

In the early 1800s, one group migrated to Mexico. By 1865 the only large concentration of Kickapoos in the United States was in Kansas. In 1873 the U.S. Cavalry crossed into Mexico in retaliation for Kickapoo raids in Texas, and they captured about 40 women and children. The cavalry held these

Kickapoo Reservation of Texas
Federal reservation
Kickapoo
Maverick County, Texas

Kickapoo Traditional Tribe
    of Texas
HC1 Box 9700
Eagle Pass, TX 78852
    830-773-2105
    830-757-9228 Fax

Kickapoo

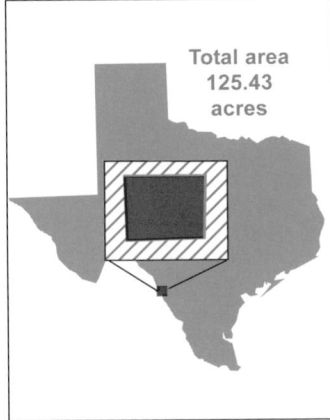

Total area
125.43
acres

Total area *(BIA realty, 2003)*
125.43 acres

Tribally owned *(BIA realty, 2003)*
125.43 acres

Population *2000 census*
420

Tribal enrollment
(BIA labor report, 2001)
880

Total labor force
2000 census
59

High school graduate or higher
2000 census
8.6%

Bachelor's degree or higher
2000 census
1%

Unemployment rate *2000 census*
69.5%

Unemployment rate
(Tribal source, 2004)
8%

Per capita income *2000 census*
$3,435

Kickapoos hostage. Eventually some 300 of the captives' relatives relocated and were given a reservation in central Oklahoma, but about half the group chose to remain in Mexico to avoid acculturation.

For the past century, these Kickapoos have lived by hunting, gathering, farming, and migrant farm labor. In the 1940s, fencing of lands by Mexican ranchers, overhunting, and drought led them to migrate annually to the United States to work as farm laborers. In March these Kickapoos begin their annual farmwork tour of the United States, beginning in south Texas, then following the harvest through the midwestern and western states. They return to Mexico in the winter for their ceremonial season. These Kickapoos have long used Eagle Pass, Texas, as their base of operations when in the United States. They live in a village of traditional houses under the international bridge over the Rio Grande, between Eagle Pass, Texas, and Piedras Negras, Mexico.

Until recently, Kickapoos who chose dual residency did not have a clear legal status in either the United States or Mexico, and they received only limited assistance and government services from either country. In 1979 they asked the U.S. government to clarify their American citizenship status; these Kickapoos wished to continue to move freely between the United States and Mexico and to be granted trust land and government services in the Eagle Pass area. They entered into negotiations with the interior and state departments, the Mexican government, and the Inter-American Indian Institute, with legal assistance from the Native American Rights Fund and support from Kickapoos in Oklahoma and Kansas. These negotiations resulted in the passage of PL 97-429, the Texas Band of Kickapoo Act, in 1977, paving the way for federal recognition in January 1983. The tribe was federally recognized as the Kickapoo Traditional Tribe of Texas, a distinct, self-governing subgroup of the Kickapoo Tribe of Oklahoma. Federal recognition made the Texas band eligible for federal programs and assistance without having to travel to Oklahoma.

The Kickapoo Trust Land Acquisition Committee raised more than $300,000 and in 1984 purchased 125 acres along the Rio Grande in Maverick County, Texas, about 8 miles south of Eagle Pass. On November 21, 1985, 145 members of the 650-member band became American citizens. In 1989, the Kickapoo Traditional Tribe of Texas developed a constitution and submitted it to the secretary of the interior, requesting federal recognition as a separate and distinct tribe.

The Kickapoos' aboriginal religion revolves around a seasonal ceremonial cycle, beginning in early spring with a series of major ceremonies that continue for several weeks. Many ceremonies take place in Nacimiento, and a large number of Oklahoma Kickapoos travel to Mexico to join with their kin in a traditional Kickapoo environment. Tribal members in Texas and Oklahoma preserve the Kickapoo language.

GOVERNMENT
The Kickapoo Traditional Tribe of Texas is organized under Section 16 of the Indian Reorganization Act of June 18, 1934. The secretary of the interior approved the tribal constitution on July 11, 1989. The tribe is governed by a five-member traditional council, composed of a chairman, a secretary, a treasurer, and two members. The council meets quarterly. An annual general membership meeting is held the third Saturday of November for the entire tribal membership.

The tribe, under PL-638, contracts with the BIA to administer key programs and services. The following departments and offices provide services to tribal members: tribal government, enrollment, legal, daycare, Head Start, social services, Indian child welfare, elderly nutrition program, community health services, education, substance abuse prevention and intervention program, environmental protection agency, and tribal assistance.

ECONOMY
Moving away from seasonal farm work for sustenance, the Kickapoos have entered an era of relative prosperity with the acquisition of land and the advent of gaming. On their 125-acre reservation, the tribe has built a casino, a health clinic, and a Head Start program.

Government as Employer. In 2004, the tribe employed a total of 31 people in various programs, services, or the casino.

Economic Development Projects. The tribe's only economic development project is the Kickapoo Lucky Eagle Casino. *(See Gaming, below, for details.)* In 2005, the tribe is seeking additional economic opportunities.

Gaming. In 1996, the tribe first built the 15,000-square-foot Kickapoo Lucky Eagle Casino on land purchased near Eagle Pass, Texas. That original building has been replaced by a new state-of-the-art, greatly expanded operation, which opened in October 2004. Still a class II gaming operation, the high-tech 110,000-square-foot facility features 1,100 slot machines, 20 table games, 15 poker tables in 2 rooms, and a 700-seat bingo hall. A combination boxing arena and entertainment venue seats 4,000 for boxing matches and 5,000 for concerts. There is a buffet-style restaurant, along with a bar, a delicatessen, and a gift shop. It is the only legalized gaming operation in Texas. The tribe is seeking permission to upgrade to class III operations, which would also permit operation of roulette and dice games; and it is planning the addition of a 400-room hotel to the complex.

Construction. Though the tribe contracts out most construction services they have built 38 new housing units for tribal members.

Services and Retail. Aside from the amenities found at the casino complex, there are few retail opportunities on the tribe's limited land base. They built a laundromat used primarily by tribal members, and in 2004 tribal leadership voiced plans to build a smoke shop.

Transportation. The tribe uses two vans to transport seniors and provides transportation to and from the casino.

INFRASTRUCTURE
There are paved streets on the 125-acre reservation. In 2005, the tribe has plans to construct one new road.

Electricity. Central Power and Light Retail Energy supplies electricity.

Fuel. Propane Energy Company provides propane.

Water Supply. El Indio Water Supply Corp/City of Eagle Pass provides water and wastewater services to the tribe.

Telecommunications. SBC provides phone and Internet services.

COMMUNITY FACILITIES AND SERVICES
The tribe operates a community center. They have built a health clinic, a building to house social service programs, and an elderly nutrition center since 1996. There is also a small park with ball fields available for tribal members only.

Education. The tribe built a Head Start program on the reservation. School children receive instruction in English, Spanish, and the Kickapoo language.

Health Care. The Kickapoo Clinic, a United Medical Center clinic, was established in 1978 to provide health care to people in Maverick, Val Verde, and Kinney counties, Texas. The center maintains three clinic sites offering pediatrics, obstetrics and gynecology, family practice, internal medicine, podiatry, laboratory, pharmacy, radiology, WIC, social, family planning, HIV/AIDS testing and counseling, health education, nutrition counseling, and transportation assistance services.

ENVIRONMENTAL CONCERNS
The tribe employs two staff members in its environmental protection agency department with funding from the U.S. EPA. In 2005, the department operates waste and recycling programs and provides water safety education.

Kickapoo

Tigua
See Ysleta del Sur Pueblo

Ysleta del Sur

LOCATION AND LAND STATUS
The Tiguas of Ysleta del Sur Pueblo own 3,328.48 acres of federal trust land in El Paso County and 66,762 acres of non-trust land in the Big Bend region of Texas, just across the Rio Grande River, which serves as the international border with Mexico.

PHYSICAL DESCRIPTION
With the growth of El Paso, the reservation lands have become completely surrounded by an urban and suburban environment. Ysleta del Sur Pueblo lies close to the edge of the city limits with the new reservation within the city of Socorro. The larger regional ecosystem is that of the Chihuahuan Desert.

CLIMATE
The elevation at Ysleta del Sur Pueblo is 3,762 feet above sea level. The year-round average daily high temperature in El Paso, Texas, is 78°F. The highest recorded temperature was 114°F. The year-round average daily low temperature is 50°F, with the lowest temperature on record being -8°F. The area receives approximately 8.6 inches of precipitation annually, with 5.5 inches of snowfall.

CULTURE AND HISTORY
The Tiguas of Ysleta del Sur Pueblo near El Paso, Texas, are descendents of Isleta Pueblo refugees from the middle Rio Grande Valley in what is now the state of New Mexico. They speak the Tiwa language, a dialect similar to that also spoken by Isleta, Sandia, Taos, and Picuris pueblos in New Mexico. During the Pueblo Revolt of 1680, many Isleta Pueblo people fled the war-torn *norte*, while some were taken to the *sur*, becoming the first true community within what are now the boundaries of the state of Texas, and they named their new settlement Ysleta del Sur. By 1682, they had built a church, La Misión de Corpus Christi de la Ysleta Mission, which became the focal point for community life. In 1751, King Charles V, the King of Spain made a 36-square-mile grant of land to these Christian Indians, and they were subsequently protected by the Spanish and Mexican governments until Ysleta del Sur Pueblo came under Texas rule in 1848 with the Treaty of Guadalupe Hidalgo. Within 30 years, the Texas legislature allowed towns to give public lands to homesteaders, and settlers quickly seized much of the tribe's fertile farmlands.

The State of Texas recognized the Ysleta del Sur Pueblo grant in the 1854 Ysleta Relief Act, but the people were not officially recognized as a tribe by the state until May 1967, when they were placed under the jurisdiction of the Commission of Indian Affairs. Meanwhile, in the 1950s the City of El Paso had annexed large areas of the lower valley, including Ysleta del Sur Pueblo, and it enforced a new set of tax codes on land the Indians had always owned. Many lost their homes as a result. The tribe was late in obtaining federal recognition due to its physical isolation from other pueblos, but the federal government finally recognized it in 1987 by PL 90-287. The people continue to live on the old reservation and on the new reservation in southwestern houses.

When the Catholic Church banned Indian dances as devil worship, the Tigua Tribe changed some feast days to accommodate the Catholic calendar in order to keep the traditional Butterfly Dance, Round Dance, Turtle Dance, and Pueblo Two-Step alive. The Sacred Drum, a dance of special spiritual significance, was carefully preserved in private practice, and it is performed as a community once again. The Tiguas practice other unique customs found in no other pueblo and remain the only pueblo tribe in Texas. The Tiguas' principal public celebration is Fiesta de San Antonio, held on June 13.

GOVERNMENT
The tribal government consists of a *cacique* and capitan de guerra (war captain), elected by the men of the Pueblo to a lifetime term. A governor, a lieutenant governor, and an *alguacil*, or bailiff, and four councilmen are elected annually. All of the council's major actions are approved or ratified by tribal vote. Under this puebloan pattern of leadership, the *cacique* and the capitan de guerra are the spiritual leaders while the governor serves as the administrative head of government.

The tribe, under PL-638, contracts with several federal agencies like the BIA to administer key programs and services. The Tiguas of Ysleta del Sur Pueblo have written a tribal code of laws, and they have their own tribal court system.

ECONOMY
Government as Employer. In 2004, there was a total of 309 people employed by tribal government in its various programs or services or in one of the developing economic enterprises.

Economic Development Projects. In 2004, the tribal council was considering the following projects for development: diversification of Speaking Rock Casino as an entertainment venue; a wind-generated energy plant on the Sierra Viejo escarpment; expansions of its cattle ranch in West Texas; and additional Running Bear gas stations with adjacent, tax-free smoke shops.

Agriculture and Livestock. The pueblo currently operates a cattle ranch on its Chilicote Ranch property, located in Valentine, Texas. This ranch is approximately 70,000 acres, and in addition to being a working ranch, it is available to tribal members for recreational use in the summertime.

Formerly known as the Tigua Reservation
Federal reservation
Tigua (Tiguex)
El Paso County, Texas

Ysleta del Sur Pueblo of Texas
119 S. Old Pueblo Rd.
P.O. Box 17579
El Paso, TX 79917
915-859-7913
915-859-2988 Fax

Total area *(BIA realty, 2004)*
530.78 acres

Total area *(Tribal source, 2005)*
+70,000 acres

Federal trust *(Tribal source, 2005)*
3,238.48 acres

Population *2000 census*
421

Tribal enrollment
(BIA labor report, 2001)
1,270

Tribal enrolment
(Tribal source, 2005)
1,305

Total labor force *2000 census*
122

Total labor force
(BIA labor report, 2001)
559

Ysleta del Sur

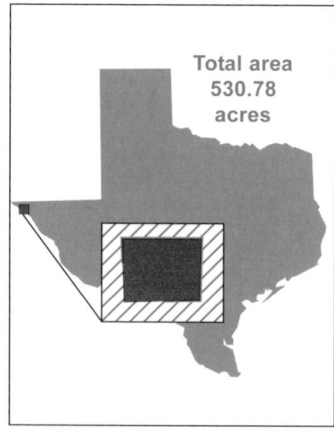

Total area
530.78
acres

High school graduate or higher
2000 census
57.5%

Bachelor's degree or higher
2000 census
5.5%

Unemployment rate *2000 census*
10.7%

Unemployment rate *(BIA labor report, 2001)*
49%

Per capita income *2000 census*
$10,450

Gaming. The tribe opened Speaking Rock Casino in 1993. The casino closed in February 2002. Speaking Rock is now an entertainment center involved in providing alternative entertainment activities.

Construction. The SB Construction Company, providing employment for 12 people, is operated by the tribe with funding through a force account. This company focuses on building homes for tribal members and making necessary renovations to tribal property.

Services and Retail. In addition to the retail outlets associated with Speaking Rock Entertainment Center, there is a tribal smoke shop, the cultural center, Wyngs Restaurant, and four tourism-related shops located on reservation lands. Following the purchase of Big Bear Oil Company, the tribe opened an entire chain of six Running Bear combination convenience mart and gas stations in 1998 and two lube shops in 1999.

Transportation. The Big Bear Transport Company, a subsidiary of the Big Bear Oil Enterprise, transports fuel, lubes, and oil throughout the southwestern region.

Tourism and Recreation. On June 13, St. Anthony's Day, the tribe holds a fiesta that features traditional pueblo dances. Dancing, bread baking, and other cultural exhibits and activities are attractions at the Ysleta del Sur Pueblo Tigua Cultural Center. The center is located within walking distance of the Ysleta Mission, which is the oldest mission in Texas and a popular El Paso tourist attraction. The cultural center contains a museum and four gift shops.

INFRASTRUCTURE
U.S. Highway 54 is a north-south route through El Paso. U.S. Highway 80 and I-10 are major east-west routes.

Transportation. All forms of commercial transportation are available in El Paso, Texas.

COMMUNITY FACILITIES AND SERVICES
The Tigua Indians own and operate the Ysleta del Sur Pueblo Tigua Cultural Center. With gaming revenues, they also built the Ysleta del Sur Pueblo Library and Education Center. The tribe has constructed an entire subdivision of southwestern pueblo style homes, complete with shaded, paved avenues, and traditional *hornos*, or beehive ovens, for baking Indian bread. There are new buildings for the tribal courthouse and police station as well. The tribe also built a recreation wellness center with state-of-the-art exercise equipment, various recreation rooms, and an olympic-size pool.

Education. There is a Tiwa language program for schoolchildren at the education/library center. Classes in traditional tribal arts, cooking, and dancing are available at the cultural center. There are educational assistance programs available for tribal members interested in a college education, in a unique collaboration with New Mexico State University. The pueblo works to increase enrollment and ensure academic achievement among Tigua students, with financial incentives and various specialty curricula targeting Native American youth.

In other educational community outreach initiatives, the tribe has formed a partnership with the Ysleta Independent School District to provide Tigua Days at the various schools, with lectures, presentations, dancing, bread baking, and teacher in-service programs at the pueblo. The tribe has published a six-volume history of the Tigua people, and it has donated copies to area schools and universities. Copies are also available at the Tigua Cultural Center. The tribe also has filmed a TV documentary, with dramatic depictions of Tigua history, traditions, and culture. Entitled *El Paso's Tigua Indians: First Tribe of Texas*, the film recounts tribal history from the 1600s through present day. It was aired on four local commercial TV stations throughout 1999.

Health Care. Since 1996, the tribe built a new medical clinic at the reservation, employing contracted health care professionals to provide general medical care and some specialized services. In renovated space at the community complex, the clinic provides prevention health programs for alcohol and drug abuse, various social services, dental care, and optometry services. The tribal health administrator, contract health services program, and community health representative program are also housed in the remodeled area. Tribal members may also seek care in any one of El Paso's existing medical facilities, including Thompson General Hospital.

ENVIRONMENTAL CONCERNS
The Tiguas of Ysleta del Sur Pueblo own and operate six Running Bear convenience stores in and around El Paso, Texas, each utilizing underground storage tanks for petroleum fuels. During routine inspections, the U.S. Environmental Protection Agency's Underground Storage Tank Program found that each of these stores exceeds state and federal compliance requirements, for which the tribe won an award for excellence in 2003.

Alamo Mountain and Otero Mesa in southern New Mexico, located within the tribe's aboriginal territories and within areas officially granted to them in previous centuries by the king of Spain, have long held special cultural, spiritual, and historical importance to the Tigua people of Ysleta del Sur Pueblo. Therefore, the oil and gas developments on lands controlled by the Bureau of Land Management near those sites are of potential legal significance as well. The tribe is utilizing the court system to fight proposed construction of oil well pads, roads, and pipelines in the Otero Mesa, west from Alamo Mountain, as they would not only adversely affect the scenic vista of this sacred landscape, but the development also encroaches upon culturally significant sites, particularly within the areas along the Ysleta-Hueco Tanks historical road (Old County Road) and in the Hueco Bolson, Franklin Mountains, and Hueco Mountains. The Tiguas consider these areas to be sacred terrain, as they contain much archaeological and ethnographic evidence of historical, ancestral use. Oil and gas developments in these areas represent potential losses of ancestral land tenure and use-rights, as well as an encroachment upon the spiritual integrity of their sacred landscapes. Remaining legalities involving land use and water rights led to the purchase of the Chilicote Ranch, a 68,000-acre parcel near Valentine, Texas.

Goshute

Goshute

LOCATION AND LAND STATUS
Reservation lands straddle the extreme east-central Nevada border with the western Utah state line. Tribal headquarters are located in Ibapah, Utah, which is accessible by a paved road. Wendover, Utah, the closest urban hub, lies 75 road miles to the north. Ely, Nevada, is 100 miles southwest via U.S. 93; Schellbourne Station is 50 miles west.

The original 160-acre reservation was established by Executive Order No. 1539 on May 20, 1912. The Indian Reorganization Act of 1934 authorized subsequent executive orders such as the one signed March 23, 1914, which added 33,688.01 acres to the reservation. Additional land purchases have expanded the reservation land base to its current 112,085.85 acres.

PHYSICAL DESCRIPTION
Elevations of tribal lands range between 5,500 feet and 12,872 feet above sea level in the Deep Creek Mountains.

CLIMATE
There is no climate data recorded for Ibapah, Nevada, the location of tribal headquarters. However, climate information is available for Wendover, Nevada, 50 miles distant. The year-round average daily high temperature at Wendover is 62°F, with periodic highs ranging between 70°F and 90°F during the summer months. The year-round average daily low temperature is 41°F. The area receives approximately five inches of precipitation annually.

CULTURE AND HISTORY
The name "Goshute" comes from the Native word Ku'tsip or Gu'tsip, meaning "ashes," "desert," or "dry earth and people." The Goshutes, a Shoshonean people, maintained an aboriginal territory in the Great Basin extending from the Great Salt Lake to the Steptoe Range in Nevada, and south to Simpson Springs. Prior to contact, they wintered in the Deep Creek Valley in dugouts built of willow poles and earth. In the spring and summer they gathered wild onions, carrots, and potatoes, and hunted small game in the mountains, exemplifying the historic Great Basin desert way of life by surviving in the harsh conditions of their territory. They exploited natural resources, utilizing at least 81 species of wild vegetable foods, including seeds, berries, roots, and greens. One of the most important foods was the nut from the piñon pine tree, which was gathered annually. Grass seeds were collected in flat tray-like baskets by knocking or raking them with beaters, with surpluses stored near the harvest areas.

In the 1850s, Mormon missionaries entered Goshute territory, soon followed by U.S. Army troops. Depredations against the Goshutes spurred the tribe to sign the Shoshoni-Goship peace treaty on October 12, 1863. Primarily an agreement of peace wherein the Goshutes ceded no lands to the U.S. government, the treaty was ratified in 1864 and announced by President Abraham Lincoln on January 17, 1865. On March 23, 1914, President Taft established a reservation with approximately 34,560 acres in Tooele and Juab counties, Utah. Several tracts of land have subsequently been added to the reservation, and its current size is about 112,870 acres, including some acreage in eastern Nevada. The Goshute people incorporated as the Confederated Tribes of the Goshute Reservation on November 24, 1940.

The Goshutes have remained active in traditional arts and crafts, weaving willow, winnowing baskets, carving cradleboards, crafting beaded jewelry, and tanning deerskin for fashioning into buckskin trade items. Many tribal members are active in the Native American Church, while others have become members of the Church of Jesus Christ of Latter-Day Saints, commonly referred to as the Mormon Church. In 2005, the tribe remains concerned about declining use of the Native language.

GOVERNMENT
The tribal government was organized under the Indian Reorganization Act of 1934, with a constitution and bylaws approved on November 25, 1940. The tribe elects five tribal council members to serve for three consecutive years. The tribal council then chooses one of its five members to hold the position of tribal chairman. Other members include a vice-chairperson and three members elected at large. Elections are held annually. The business council serves as the tribe's principal governing body. Various departments have committees that work with the tribal council.

The tribe, under PL-638, contracts with the BIA to administer key programs and services. On October 1, 1997, the tribe contracted with the BIA to form its own court system. A contracted judge visits the reservation and holds court once per month. The tribe has hired attorneys and prosecutors to work with a court clerk on cases presented to the court. The tribe also provides its own law enforcement and a tribal volunteer fire department. Law enforcement provides officers for patrol, but it operates no facilities at the reservation. Detention centers are located in Elko, Nevada, and, for longer incarcerations, prisoners are transported to Owyhee, Nevada.

The tribe has its own tribal enrollment office as well. The Goshute Housing Authority provides housing services, operating 26 low-rent and lease-to-purchase homes. Additional programs and services are available from the Eastern Nevada Agency of the BIA located in Elko, Nevada.

Goshute Reservation
Federal reservation
Shoshonean Goshute, Paiute, and Bannock
White Pine County, Nevada; Juab and Tooele counties, Utah

Confederated Tribes of the
 Goshute Reservation
P.O. Box 6104
Ibapah, UT 84034
 435-234-1138
 435-234-1162 Fax

Total area (BIA realty, 2004)
113,349.19 acres

Total area (Tribal source, 2004)
112,085.85 acres

Tribally owned (BIA realty, 2004)
113,269.19 acres

Individually owned
(BIA realty, 2004)
80 acres

Population 2000 census
105

Tribal enrollment
(Tribal source, 2004)
435

Total labor force 2000 census
36

High school graduate or higher
2000 census
67.2%

Bachelor's degree or higher
2000 census
0%

Unemployment rate 2000 census
36.1%

Per capita income 2000 census
$7,887

Goshute

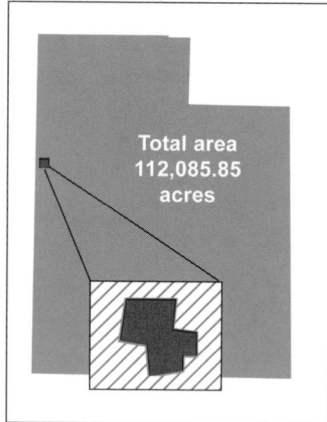

Total area
112,085.85
acres

Navajo

See Arizona

ECONOMY

Tribal lands are home to large populations of elk, mule deer, sage grouse, turkeys, antelope, mountain sheep, mountain lions, and a variety of small game. Tribal members still harvest many edible game animals. Elk and other wild game hunting permits are contracted with an outfitter that returns a portion of the proceeds to the tribe. Today, the Goshute Tribe derives its income largely from ranching and leasing rangelands.

Economic Development Projects. In 2005 the tribe is seeking development opportunities. A joint venture health facility in Michigan is under consideration. A newly formed economic development board is working on projects on or near the reservation.

Agriculture and Livestock. Tribal members own some cattle, with the majority of reservation range lands leased to non-Indian ranchers. The reservation has 34,410 potentially irrigable acres.

Fisheries. The reservation contains springs suitable for fish hatcheries. The Goshutes raise Bonneville and Lahonton cutthroat trout. Both species are native to the Great Basin, remnants of fish populations that once flourished in the Bonneville and Lahonton lakes during the Pleistocene epoch. Fingerlings are raised for planting in lakes and reservoirs to provide recreational fishing opportunities for residents throughout the Intermountain West.

Construction. The tribe established its own housing authority and, during 2004-2005, is constructing and/or repairing homes in the Wendover, Utah, area for tribal members in need of new housing or renovations to existing homes.

Services and Retail. Currently, there are plans to open retail outlets and gas stations on and off the reservation.

Transportation. Many members have their own vehicles. The tribe has leased a van for senior transportation services and for other members in need of medical services and other resources in the surrounding cities.

Media and Communications. A tribal newsletter is provided monthly with a community calendar of upcoming events.

Tourism and Recreation. The Goshute Reservation lies approximately 100 miles north of Great Basin National Park. The tribe holds an annual powwow and hand game tournament during the third weekend in August.

INFRASTRUCTURE

The Goshute Reservation is accessible via U.S. 93 in Nevada, from which a paved road leads east to the reservation. The tribe, along with the county road departments in the states of Nevada and Utah, maintains the roads on and off the reservation.

Electricity. A utility company located in Ely, Nevada, provides electricity.

Fuel. A company located in Ely, Nevada, provides propane. Many reservation homes use wood- and coal-burning stoves, in addition to propane and electric furnaces.

Water Supply. A community water supply is now available throughout the reservation. Well water is no longer used anywhere on the reservation. The southern reservation areas have a community wastewater system as well. Homes in other parts of the reservation have septic systems. The tribe provides septic-pumping services.

Transportation. Transportation by bus is available in Wendover, Utah, 70 miles north of U.S. Highway 93. Ely and Elko, Nevada, and Salt Lake City, Utah, provide commercial air service.

Telecommunications. A company located in Wendover, Utah, provides telephone service. High-speed Internet systems have been installed and are available to students at Ibapah Elementary School.

COMMUNITY FACILITIES AND SERVICES

A community center is located on the reservation, and a gymnasium is open for public access. A senior citizens' center is located at the community center, with daily meal preparation and social programs. Meals are delivered to shut-ins. A commodity food distribution program provides monthly food supplies to qualifying tribal members. The tribe contracts other social services with the Western Shoshone Social Services Agency, which has offices in Elko, Nevada.

Education. The tribe does not have a school located on the reservation. Children attend school off-reservation, in the Tooele County school district. Ibapah Elementary School teaches grades K-6; students in grades 7-12 are bused to a school in Wendover, Utah, a 120-mile round trip. Some schoolchildren attend out-of-state boarding schools to avoid the daily early departures and late home arrivals necessitated by the distance to the local public schools. Adult vocational training scholarships are available via the tribal education office.

Health Care. The tribe has contracted its health services, allocating funds for a field clinic twice per month, and providing financial assistance for the purchase of medications. Visiting physicians at the clinic provide referral and manage treatable injuries. Hospitals are located in Salt Lake City, Utah, and in Elko and Ely, Nevada, with transport provided by the Tribal Community Health Transporter or by Wendover Ambulance Service, approximately an hour away. There are no health facilities located on the reservation; tribal members must travel to Wendover, Nevada, or Ely, Utah, for most health care services provided by the Indian Health Service for tribal members who do not have private health insurance.

The tribe, along with two Nevada tribes, applied for a joint telemedicine grant and was funded to provide services through the local phone referral networks. A podiatrist is contracted by the diabetics program to provide monthly visits to the reservation.

LOCATION AND LAND STATUS

The Paiute Indian Tribe of Utah includes five distinct bands: Shivwits, Cedar City, Koosharem, Kanosh, and Indian Peaks. Their land is scattered from south-central to southwest Utah. The Shivwits Band has the largest amount of trust land, approximately 27,000 acres located in the southwest portion of Utah near St. George. The four other bands each have small amounts of land totaling 5,000 acres. The total land of the Paiute Indian Tribe of Utah is 32,036 acres. In addition to the reservation lands, the tribe holds mineral rights in Beaver County.

The Shivwits Reservation was established in 1903 and was expanded in 1916 and 1937. The other reservations were established as follows: Indian Peaks in 1915, Koosharem in 1928, and Kanosh in 1929. However, the Southern Paiutes and their reservations were terminated from federal control in 1954. They were restored pursuant to the Paiute Indian Tribe of Utah Restoration Act on April 3, 1980; the same act confirmed the Cedar City Band's status under federal trust.

By 1984, approximately 4,470 acres of the more than total 15,000 acres that had been lost were returned to the Koosharem, Kanosh, Indian Peaks, and Cedar City bands, along with a $2.5 million irrevocable trust fund from which they could develop tribal services and economic development initiatives.

PHYSICAL DESCRIPTION

The terrain of Southern Paiute territory ranges from the high Colorado plateaus west and southwest, through canyon country, basin, and range, into the Mojave Desert. The Great Basin, the Colorado Plateau, and a portion of the Mohave Desert converge here. There is a corresponding shift in vegetation from spruce and fir through pine, juniper, piñon, and sage to creosote and mesquite. The Santa Clara River runs through the reservation.

CLIMATE

The elevation at Cedar City, Utah, is 5,622 feet above sea level. The year-round average daily high temperature is 64°F, with the highest temperature ever recorded being 101°F. The year-round average daily low temperature is 38°F, with the lowest temperature on record as -26°F. The area receives approximately 12 inches of precipitation annually, with 35.5 inches of snowfall.

CULTURE AND HISTORY

The five bands of the Paiute Indian Tribe of Utah are all Southern Paiute peoples who once occupied a broad territory extending across southern Utah and southern Nevada and, following the sharp bend in the Colorado River, southward into California. The Southern Paiute language is one of the northern Numic dialects of the Uto-Aztecan language family. It is believed the Paiutes entered Utah between 1100 and 1200 AD.

Each band maintained an economically self-sufficient aboriginal territory. Small game such as rabbits, wood rats, mice, gophers, squirrels, chipmunks, and birds, provided the Southern Paiutes with their chief source of protein; however, plant foods, including seeds, roots, berries, agave, and pine nuts, were the mainstay of the Southern Paiute diet. The introduction of irrigable agriculture a few decades before Euro-American occupation bolstered the Southern Paiute economy; they raised corn, squash, melons, gourds, and sunflowers.

The first direct Spanish contact with the Southern Paiutes came in 1776. By the early nineteenth century, Spanish colonies in present-day northern New Mexico and southern California had institutionalized slavery, and slave raiding on the Southern Paiutes did not end until soon after the Mormons came into northern Utah in 1847. In the 1850s, several Mormon communities sprang up in Southern Paiute territory, displacing the Indians from their most fertile lands; starvation and diseases, such as cholera, scarlet fever, whooping cough, measles, mumps, tuberculosis, and malaria, drastically reduced the Paiute population. Traditional food supplies were further depleted by livestock grazing, timbering, and other activities; but Mormon missionaries among the bands prevented major confrontations with settlers.

In the late 1880s, a prominent Utah rancher obtained a federal appropriation to remove the Shivwits from their lands to a new location on the Santa Clara River just west of Saint George. The move established the first Southern Paiute reservation in Utah, the Shivwits Reservation, although it was not officially considered federal property until 1903. The Shivwits Reservation was expanded in 1916 and 1937 to ultimately contain 28,160 acres. Other Southern Paiute reservations were established as well: the Indian Peaks Reservation northwest of Cedar City, Utah, in 1915; the Koosharem Reservation east of Ritchfield, Utah, in 1928; and the Kanosh Reservation near Kanosh, Utah, in 1929. None of these had land bases sufficient to support the population with agriculture. Federal funds were appropriated in 1899 and 1925 to purchase land for the Cedar City Band; however, the funds were never expended for that purpose because the Mormon Church had already purchased 10 acres on the outskirts of Cedar City and established the band there. Due to insufficient land base and irregular, inadequate assistance, none of the reservations could achieve economic self-sufficiency, and many Paiutes moved off the reservations to nearby towns, while others remained on the reservations but sought outside wage work.

The Shivwits, Indian Peaks, Koosharem, and Kanosh reservations were terminated from federal control in 1954. Termination brought severe economic consequences to the tribes: they lost most of their land base; federal expertise and legal protection; federal health and education funds to individuals; and training, housing, and business grants. The tribes and individual tribal members were faced with taxes and the loss of the limited sovereignty they had enjoyed under the Indian Reorganization Act.

In 1957 the Southern Paiutes filed suit with the Indian Claims Commission (ICC) for compensation for their aboriginal lands. In 1965, the ICC awarded the Southern Paiutes $8,250,000, or approximately 27 cents per acre, for 29,935,000 acres; the funds were not distributed until 1971.

On April 3, 1980, the Paiute Indian Tribe of Utah Restoration Act, PL 96-277, was passed, and the Shivwits, Kanosh, Koosharem, and Indian Peaks bands were restored to federal trust relationships. The Cedar City Band, whose status had long been uncertain, was confirmed as being under trust. The council representing all the groups located its headquarters in Cedar City.

To celebrate restoration of their federal trust status, the Paiute Indian Tribe of Utah initiated a Restoration Gathering in 1981,

Paiute Indian Reservation
Federal reservation
Paiute
Iron, Millard, Sevier, and
Washington counties, Utah

Paiute Indian Tribe of Utah
440 N. Paiute Dr.
Cedar City, UT 84720
435-586-1112
435-586-7388 Fax

Total area *(BIA realty, 2004)*
43,566.58 acres

Total area *(Tribal source, 2004)*
32,036 acres

Tribally owned *(BIA realty, 2004)*
43,566.58 acres

Population *2000 census*
270

Tribal enrollment
(BIA labor report, 2001)
799

Total labor force *2000 census*
79

Total labor force
(BIA labor report, 2001)
475

High school graduate or higher
2000 census
51.2%

Bachelor's degree or higher
2000 census
4.7%

Unemployment rate *2000 census*
12.7%

Unemployment rate
(BIA labor report, 2001)
0%

Per capita income *2000 census*
$5,666

Paiute

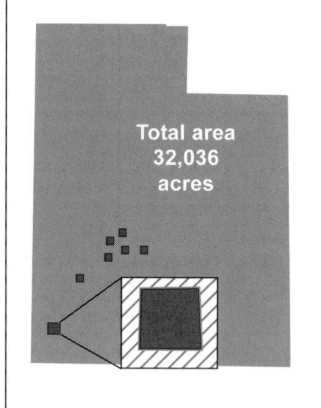

Total area
32,036
acres

to be held in June of each year. This major intertribal event includes a princess pageant, dance contests, ball games and hand games, and a parade through downtown Cedar City. In 2004, tribal members, whose average age was 25 years, had a strong sense of pride and unity.

GOVERNMENT
Organized under the provisions of the 1980 Restoration Act (PL 96-227), the Indian Reorganization Act of 1934, and a tribal constitution, the Paiute Indian Tribe of Utah is governed by a tribal council composed of a chairman, a vice-chairman, and four members at-large, all serving four-year terms. Council members are elected by popular vote from their respective band. Only the chairman is elected by the entire eligible voting membership. The tribe adopted their constitution on June 11, 1991, which the secretary of the interior subsequently approved on July 15, 1991. Tribal council meetings are held monthly.

The tribe, under PL-638, contracts with the BIA to administer key programs and services. Tribal administration has acquired housing for tribal members at Cedar City, Shivwits, and Joseph, Utah. The Utah Paiute Tribal Corporation, incorporated in 1972, built 113 HUD housing units at Richfield, Joseph, Shivwits, and Cedar City between 1976 and 1989 to accommodate tribal members.

BUSINESS CORPORATION
The Paiute Economic Development Committee, established in 1984, seeks out economic opportunities for tribal development, working with tribal administration to resolve issues in working toward economic self-sufficiency. (See also Economic Development Projects, below.)

ECONOMY
The tribal economy is based on tribal operations, governmental funding, and several tribal enterprises.

Economic Development Projects. In 2004, the tribe had plans to build a natural gas, turbine-powered power plant, and it was considering development of a golf course; both were slated for the Shivwits area of the reservation. The Cedar Band founded Suh'dutsing Technologies. (See also Media and Communications, below.)

Agriculture and Livestock. The five bands hold water rights to 1.38 cubic feet per second on the Santa Clara River, which runs through the Shivwits land, and approximately 81 acres

of irrigable land. Members of the Shivwits Band are using five acres for gardens. The remaining acres are not in use.

Mining. A substantial amount of sand and gravel is located on the Shivwits land. The Indian Peaks land has a small amount of sand and gravel. The Kanosh Band has a lease for geothermal resources.

Manufacturing. In the 1980s, a small sewing plant was established at Kanosh, employing primarily Paiute women. A Cedar City warehouse was refurbished in 1989 to accommodate a second sewing plant.

Telecommunications. Suh'dutsing Technologies, founded in January 2003 by the Cedar Band, is a 100 percent Native American-owned firm that provides innovative solutions to modern information and technology (IT) problems. It is a Small Business Association certified 8(a) business development initiative and a certified small disadvantaged business. Suh'dutsing Technologies also meets HUB Zone certification, acquiring federal contracts that target and attract businesses for development in low-income areas. Through a mentor-protégé relationship, Suh'dutsing receives business infrastructure and technology assistance from various established IT companies. The State of Utah depends upon Suh'dutsing Technologies to provide outsourcing for other rural Utah companies in computer-related services, such as software testing, technical call centers, database management, data entry, and website development. Suh'dutsing Technologies offers customer support and help desk services; data processing, storage, and warehousing; website hosting; database design and development; network installation (O&M analysis) and administration; programming and analysis; and software sales and development.

COMMUNITY FACILITIES AND SERVICES
The tribe has a tribal office building that houses the tribal administration offices and the monthly health clinic.

Education. Following federal re-recognition, the tribe hired a director of tribal education. With proceeds from its economic development initiatives, the tribe gave approximately $250,000 in scholarships in 2004.

Health Care. The tribe has its own health department, and by 1989 a special clinic was being conducted at the tribal office building once a month. Dental, eye care, diabetes, well baby, and general clinics are available via contracted providers.

Skull Valley

Skull Valley Reservation
Federal reservation
Goshute
Tooele County, Utah

Skull Valley Band of Goshute
Indians of Utah
2480 S. Main St., #808
Salt Lake City, UT 84115
801-484-5511
801-484-4422 Fax
skullvalleygoshutes.org

LOCATION AND LAND STATUS
The Skull Valley Reservation is located in a remote, isolated area in western Utah about 35 miles south of the Great Salt Lake. The reservation is in a semiarid valley. A portion of the Wasatch National Forest borders the reservation on the east. The original reservation of 17,920 acres was established by an Executive Order on September 7, 1917. An Executive Order issued on February 15, 1918, set aside an additional 640 acres.

PHYSICAL DESCRIPTION
The reservation is located in the west desert of Tooele County, Utah. Sagebrush, pine trees, plant foods, and wild game have been replaced by the nerve gas facility.

CULTURE AND HISTORY
The Goshutes are culturally and ecologically similar to the Western Shoshones and speak Shoshone. Shoshone is a variety of Central Numic, which is a branch of the widespread Uto-Aztecan language family. The Goshutes occupied a territory in the Great Basin extending from the Great Salt Lake to the Steptoe Range in Nevada and south to Simpson Springs. The Skull Valley Goshutes' first Euro-American encounter was in 1827, when Jedediah Strong Smith traveled through western Shoshone territory. The Goshutes were heavily impacted by the establishment of the Church of Jesus Christ of Latter-Day Saints (Mormons) in their territory as early as 1847. The numbers of Euro-Americans traveling into and through the Goshutes' territory increased substantially with the discovery

of gold in California in 1848 and at Gold Canyon in 1849. The discovery of the Comstock Lode in 1857 was the greatest single impetus for Euro-American settlement of Nevada.

U.S. government depredations among the Goshutes spurred the tribe to sign the Treaty of Tooele Valley on October 12, 1863. No land was set aside for the Skull Valley Goshutes until 1912.

GOVERNMENT
The Skull Valley Band of Goshute Indians is governed by a tribal council headed by a tribal executive committee including a chairman, vice-chairman, and secretary-treasurer. Executive committee members serve four-year terms. The band does not have a constitution or charter. Committee meetings are not regularly scheduled.

ECONOMY
The majority of the Goshute people of the Skull Valley Reservation are employed off the reservation in Salt Lake City, Grantsville, Stockton, Tooele, and Ibapah. Ninety percent of the tribe's income to fund programs comes from leasing a rocket motor testing facility to Hercules. The tribe is a majority owner in Earth Environmental Services, which sells dumpsters to governments and private industries.

Economic Development Projects. A private electrical utilities group has leased land to store 40,000 metric tons of used nuclear fuel. The proposed storage facility is a $125 million project and would have the ability to store all of the spent fuel stored in the country's many power plants. The facility would require $1 billion in steel and concrete. It would also create 60 local jobs, which would be enough to allow all interested tribal members to move back to the reservation for work. It is widely believed that this storage facility will be one of the safest industrial facilities in the United States.

The world's largest nerve gas incinerator, east of the Skull Valley Reservation, was built to destroy thousands of tons of deadly chemicals. Other economic ventures are being considered to deal with the numerous ensuing environmental concerns.

Agriculture and Livestock. Reservation land is suitable for grazing. About 160 acres of reservation land are irrigable. Stream water is delivered to the irrigable land through a pipeline constructed with BIA funds.

Construction. Housing on the reservation has been improved somewhat, but housing is still a priority program. The tribe constructed and leased a rocket motor testing facility to Hercules in 1976. The lease expired in 1995.

Services and Retail. The tribe constructed a convenience store with judgment funds in 1990. The tribe operates the Pony Express Station.

INFRASTRUCTURE
State Highway 108 travels north-south through the Skull Valley Reservation, connecting to I-80, which travels east into Salt Lake City.

Electricity. The Intermountain Power Project, south of Skull Valley, provides coal-fired electrical power. This power is mostly utilized by California. American Electric Power provides about 7 million people in the midwest with electrical power and generates more than 120 billion kilowatt hours of electricity. Entergy Cooperation and Dairyland Power Cooperative are the other two energy companies that provide power and service to several states within the United States.

COMMUNITY FACILITIES AND SERVICES
A tribal community facility, constructed in 1990 with judgment funds and a matching HUD grant, is located on the reservation.

Education. Children attend public schools in Dugway, Grantsville, and Tooele, or one of the BIA boarding schools.

Health Care. The Indian Health Service Uintah and Ouray Service Unit in Fort Duchesne, 230 miles from the reservation, provides health care. The Indian Health Service Contract Health Program in Tooele, 50 miles from the reservation, provides hospital care.

ENVIRONMENTAL CONCERNS
The government tested chemical and biological weapons just south of the reservation on the Dugway Proving Grounds. Chemical agents escaped from the grounds in 1968, killing approximately 6,000 animals, a quarter of which were later buried on the reservation. The contamination and impact of defense activities was later addressed with the help of the Department of Defense's Office of Environmental Security.

A government nerve-gas storage facility lies east of Skull Valley; it could release deadly chemicals. Northwest is a low-level radioactive disposal site, which is responsible for burying radioactive waste for the entire country, and the most polluting magnesium production plant in the United States, as identified by the U.S. EPA, is located north of the reservation. Air pollution from the power project and chlorine gas released by the magnesium plant both impact the reservation.

Skull Valley

Total area *(BIA realty, 2004)*
18,126.65 acres

Tribally owned *(BIA realty, 2004)*
17,284.35 acres

Individually owned
(BIA realty, 2004)
160.3 acres

Tribal enrollment
(Tribal source, 2004)
124

Tribal enrollment *(BIA, 2001)*
118

Total labor force *2000 census*
20

Total labor force *(BIA, 2001)*
23

High school graduate or higher
2000 census
40%

Bachelor's degree or higher
2000 census
0%

Unemployment rate *2000 census*
45%

Unemployment rate *(BIA, 2001)*
70%

Per capita income *2000 census*
$5,804

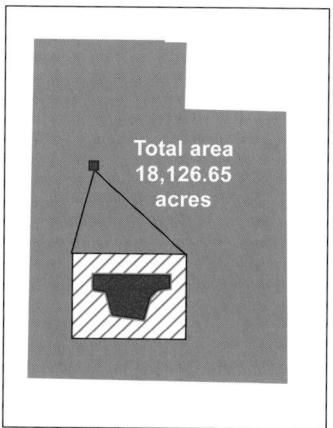

Total area
18,126.65
acres

Uintah and Ouray

Uintah and Ouray Reservation
Federal reservation
Ute
Uintah, Ouray, Whiteriver,
Uncompahgre, Noochew,
Nuciu, Duchesne, Grand, and
Wasatch counties, Utah

Northern Ute Indian Tribe
of the Uintah and Ouray Ute
Reservation
P.O. Box 190
Fort Duchesne, UT 84026
435-722-5141
435-722-2374 Fax
northernute.com

Total area *(BIA realty, 2004)*
1,021,597.82 acres

Total area *(Tribal source)*
4,500,000 acres

Tribally owned *(BIA realty, 2004)*
1,007,358.42 acres

Individually owned
(BIA realty, 2004)
14,237.94 acres

Population *2000 census*
19,812

Tribal enrollment
(BIA labor report, 2001)
3,174

Total labor force *2000 census*
7,834

Total labor force
(BIA labor report, 2001)
2,348

High school graduate or higher
2000 census
79%

Bachelor's degree or higher
2000 census
11.7%

Unemployment rate *2000 census*
9.1%

Unemployment rate
(BIA labor report, 2001)
77%

Per capita income *2000 census*
$11,600

LOCATION AND LAND STATUS

The Uintah and Ouray Reservation is the second-largest reservation in Utah. It is located in the Uintah Basin of northeast Utah, 150 miles east of Salt Lake City and 40 miles west of the Colorado border. The northern portion of the reservation is the most heavily populated. Indian and non-Indian lands form a checkerboard pattern near the communities of Duchesne, Roosevelt, Myton, Neola, and Whiterocks. Randlett, Fort Thornburgh, and Ouray are three other communities on the reservation. The Hill Creek Extension of the reservation is not populated. Approximately 98.8 percent of the Uintah Basin is owned by the tribe. Currently, the tribe owns 80 percent of first water rights to the water of the State of Utah, which originates in the Uintah Mountains. The Uintah and Ouray Reservation is the second largest reservation in the country.

PHYSICAL DESCRIPTION

Tribal lands are bordered on the north by the Uintah Mountains, the only range in the United States to run in an east-west direction. The terrain varies from high mountain desert in the central part of the state. Elevations range from approximately 5,000 to 13,000 feet. The Green River courses along the western border of the southern segment of the Uintah and Ouray Reservation The Uintah Basin covers approximately 11,550 square miles, and the Ute Indian Tribe's jurisdiction comprises just over four million acres of this area, reaching from the Utah-Colorado border west to the Wasatch Mountain range.

CULTURE AND HISTORY

Utah and Nootuvweep (Ute Indian Country) are said to be the land of the Noochew, "the People." Ute territory once extended from central and western Colorado into eastern Utah, including the eastern portion of Salt Lake Valley and Utah Valley, and down into the San Juan River Valley of New Mexico. Initially 12 different bands of Utes considered this huge region home, 7 in what is now Utah and 5 in what is now Colorado. The Noochews were the first tribe to acquire the horse from the Spaniards in 1600. At the time the Noochews were mountain people, hunters and gatherers. By the late 1600s, they were following buffalo herds on the plains with their belongings packed on horses.

In 1847, Mormon settlers began to arrive in tribal territories. Conflicts arose between the Euro-Americans and the Ute bands in particular. In 1860, the Ute Indian Agents proposed removal of the bands to the Uintah Basin. Mormon groups were in agreement that the bands should be moved to the desolate region. In 1861, the Uintah Valley Reservation was established, and by 1879, almost all members of the Tumpanuwac, San Pitch, Pahvant, Sheberetch, Cumumba, and Uinta-at bands (collectively known as the Uintah Band) had been relocated to the site. In 1881, the federal government moved members of the Yamparka and Parinuc bands (Whiteriver Utes) of Colorado to the reservation. During this time, the Taviwac (Uncompahgre Utes) managed to maintain their independence, but in 1882, were designated to the Ouray Reservation. Located on the Tavaputs Plateau, the reservation occupied lands immediately south of the Uintah Reservation. The reservations maintained separate agencies until 1886 when the BIA merged administrations.

In 1888, the government claimed a 7,004-acre portion of lands from the eastern end for the Uintah Reservation. Valuable gilsonite deposits were discovered on these lands. In 1897,

in the interest of mining possibilities, the government began the allotment of the Ouray Reservation. In 1905, the government seized another 1,100,000 acres to establish the Uinta National Forest and 56,000 acres for the Strawberry Valley Reclamation Project in 1909. Remaining lands were opened to the public. By 1909, tribal lands within the Uintah-Ouray Reservation had been reduced from nearly four million acres to 250,000 acres of jointly-owned grazing lands and 103,265 acres of individual allotments. In addition to a decrease in tribal lands, the population of the Utes suffered as Euro-Americans established control over the region. Starvation and disease eventually cut tribal numbers in half.

The tribe accepted the provisions of the Indian Reorganization Act of 1936 and organized as the Northern Ute Indian Tribe of the Uintah and Ouray Ute Reservation. In 1948, it regained 726,000 acres of traditional lands. During the 1950s the government found that tribe was entitled to repatriation payment for lands lost in Colorado and Utah. Payments were made in part to individual tribal members, but the majority of the funds are held in trust by the BIA. In 1986, the U.S. Supreme Court upheld a decision acknowledging the tribe's legal jurisdiction over three million acres of alienated reservation lands.

Currently, the Ute people are involved in a number of complex negotiations with state and county governments over traditional Ute hunting rights, right of way access, and taxation issues. In addition, the tribe is currently seeking to transfer mineral rights on the Hill Creek Extension from the federal government back to the tribe. Half of the money generated from production of minerals on the Hill Creek Extension is distributed by the federal government to the State of Utah, which dedicates the proceeds to education. The tribe, with the backing of the counties and the state, will move through federal channels in an attempt to regain ownership of those rights. Tribal officials have agreed that the state will continue to receive its 50 percent share of the mineral revenues.

The northern Utes today preserve and honor their rich culture in many ways. They publish their stories in the tribal newsletter and sell traditional Ute arts and crafts. The tribe holds two annual sun dances each year, one in July and one in August, as well as two powwows, one on the Fourth of July and one at Thanksgiving. The Fourth of July Powwow is intertribal, as are many other sporting events and competitions.

GOVERNMENT

The tribe adopted its constitution on January 19, 1937, amending it twice, once in 1982 and then again in 1988. The charter was ratified on August 10, 1938. A tribal business committee is the popularly elected governing body. The committee elects from its own membership a chairman and vice-chairman, and from within or outside of its own membership a secretary and treasurer. Two representatives elected from each band of the Ute people, the Uncompahgre, the Whiteriver, and the Uintah, serve on the business committee. The committee works closely with the superintendent at the BIA, and the Secretary of the Interior must review many of its actions.

The tribal government is comprised of over 60 departments, including natural resources, health and human services, accounting, emergency medical services, fish and wild life, recreation, public relations, energy and minerals management, and education. The judicial department of the tribe includes an adult court, juvenile court, and prosecutor/probation office.

TRI-UT-001

TRI-UT-003

TRI-UT-004

TRI-UT-005

Uintah and Ouray

TRI-UT-002

ECONOMY

The tribal economy is supported primarily from revenue earned from the tribe's operations in the mining industry. Its enterprise in the manufacturing industry also generates a large source of income for the tribe. In addition, the tribe's annual budget is supplemented by interest earned on funds held in trust for the tribe. The tribe also receives annual payments generating from a settlement in a case concerning the use of water from the Green, White, and Duchenese rivers. The funds are utilized by the tribe to support economic development projects that are water-related. The BIA has held the bulk of reparations payments in the 1950s to the Northern Utes in trust. The Northern Ute Tribe requests its operations budget each year from the BIA; resulting budget payments are made from interest earned on the tribe's original trust funds and projected income for the year. The Northern Ute Indian Tribe operates five enterprises: Ute Lanes (bowling), tribal feedlot, water systems, loan program, and Ute Petroleum.

Government as Employer. The Uintah and Ouray tribal government employs about 450 individuals throughout its governmental programs and tribal enterprises. Approximately 75 percent of its employees are tribal members.

Economic Development Projects. Annual payments are made to the tribe as part of a Uintah-Ouray water settlement concerning the use of water from the Colorado River's tributaries in Utah-Green River, White River, and Duchesne River. The funds are used, among other things, for tribal economic development projects. The projects must be water related, and two independent financial advisors, the EPA, the tribal business committee, and the Uintah Basin Replacement Project must approve each project.

Agriculture and Livestock. Cattle raising is an important activity on the reservation. The Livestock Enterprise, a tribal enterprise, owns and manages most cattle grazing on reservation lands. The cattle are maintained at the tribal feedlot. The tribal herd currently numbers around 2,000, not including calves. Irrigated land is used to grow alfalfa and other livestock feed and pasture. The water cooperative offers haycutting services for a fee.

Forestry. Tribal timber resources lie mostly within the reservation's northern perimeter.

Fisheries. The tribe maintains its own fish and game department to manage and protect its considerable fish and wildlife resources. Sport fishing draws significant tourism to the area. The tribe also offers big game hunting permits and package big game hunts for trophy elk, bighorn sheep, cougar, and bear on the reservation. Bull elk bids start at $8,500. Northern Ute Tribe employees serve as guides, rent horses, provide taxidermy, and assist in transporting the meat to the meat plant in Arcadia for cutting, wrapping, and freezing. Goose, duck, and pheasant hunting permits and package hunts are also available on reservation land.

Mining. Mineral resources are an important tribal economic asset. Minerals contained within the Uintah and Ouray Reservation properties include hydrocarbon deposits of (conventional) oil and gas, oil shale, and tar sands in major quantity; coal, uranium, silver, copper, gold gypsum, and phosphate are also present in minor to mid-economic quantity. Reservation properties cover approximately 1.2 million surface-owned acres and 400,000 mineral-owned acres within the four-million-acre jurisdictional boundary. Ute Indian allottees, the Northern Ute Indian Tribe, and the Ute Indian Tribe and Ute Distribution Corporation in joint management own both surface and mineral properties, and they have 102,000 acres under lease and over 490 wells in production. Total Ute Indian oil production averages more than 1,000 barrels per day, a level that has been constant for several years. New well development and work over activities have also proven successful. Oil produced in the Uintah Basin is of a very high quality with sulphur content as low as 0.4 percent; however, the high paraffin content is a major problem. Oil shale is potentially one of the richest future sources of oil. Production zones are dominantly from the Green River and Wasatch formations, with depth to production zones ranging 6,000 to 18,000 feet. Only one natural gas field has been developed, located east and south of the Green and White rivers. It is bordered by the Natural Buttes Gas Field Unit, which covers 76,000 acres.

Manufacturing. The tribe owns and operates Ute Indian Machine and Manufacturing, an enterprise that generates sizable revenues and employment.

TRI-UT-001 Quintah and Ouray Agency sign and seal

TRI-UT-003 Ute Petroleum gas station and country store

TRI-UT-004 Ute Indian Machine and Manufacturing Company

TRI-UT-005 Tribal "Feedlot" cattle stockyard on reservation

TRI-UT-002 Sign for the "Ute Tribal Super Market"

Uintah and Ouray

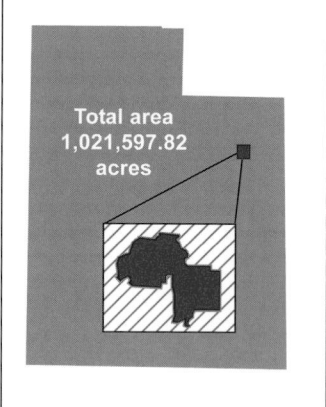

Total area
1,021,597.82
acres

Ute Mountain

See Colorado

Industrial Parks. A tribal industrial park complex has been constructed in Fort Duchesne. It serves as the location for the Indian Health Service outpatient clinic, tribal administration headquarters, BIA offices, the tribal vocational and educational facility, the Uintah River High School, tribal education, Ute water settlement, community health representatives, and the Ute Indian Machinery and Manufacturing facility.

Media and Communications. The Ute Tribe Public Relations/ Audio Visual Department publishes the bi-weekly *Ute Bulletin* and maintains the tribal website.

Services and Retail. The tribe owns Ute Petroleum, a convenience store/gas stations; Ute Lanes, a bowling alley; and the Ute Plaza Grocery Store. The tribe also operates the loan program. Most of the communities have a post office and general store. The town of Roosevelt has a grocery store and clothing stores. The town of Vernal has several chain grocery and clothing stores, along with a handful of locally owned shops. Major automobile agencies and auto repair shops have businesses on the reservation.

Tourism and Recreation. The tribe has operated the Bottle Hollow Restaurant and Convention Center complex since 1971. Fishing and hunting are popular tourist draws on the reservation. Flaming Gorge on the Green River, a nationally known tourist attraction, is located near the reservation. Fort Duchesne, formerly an army post, has numerous tourist attractions and activities.

The tribe holds its annual Bear Dance, a ladies' choice dance unique to the Utes, in April or May, and the annual Sun Dance takes place in July; the Sun Dance was closed to non-Indians in 2004. The tribe also sponsors various intertribal powwows. The largest powwows sponsored by the tribe are the Annual July Powwow and the Thanksgiving Powwow. Events at the July Powwow include competitive Northern and Southern dancing and drumming, a softball tournament, a hand game tournament, powwow royalty coronation, a parade, a rodeo, a dance, and a buffalo feast.

The Ute Tribe Outdoor Recreation Department organizes the Ute Indian Tribe Big Game Hunts. Participants must apply with the tribe to bid on trophy elk, bighorn sheep, cougar, bear, geese, pheasants, and ducks. The program provides a guide and vehicle to selected hunters.

INFRASTRUCTURE

U.S. Highway 40 runs east-west through the reservation, serving as the primary road access from the outside. Highway 191 enters the reservation from the south. Internal roads connect communities within the reservation. Commercial bus and truck lines serve the communities on the reservation. Commercial train service is available at Provo, 70 miles west. Vernal, 30 miles east, has the nearest commercial airport.

Electricity. Uintah Power and Light and the Moon Land Electric Association provide electricity to the reservation.

Fuel. The Mountain Fuel Company furnishes gas. Ute Petroleum supplies the tribe's gas stations.

Water Supply. Since 1965 the tribe has operated a domestic water system, named Water Systems, which serves the Indian and non-Indian communities in the area. Water Systems also handles sewage needs for the same communities. Septic systems provide sewage service throughout most of the reservation.

COMMUNITY FACILITIES AND SERVICES

The health and human services department includes a WIC program, a nutritionist, food distribution, and a community health representative program. Various workshops are available to tribal families on the reservation to help them with parenting and family issues. The Northern Ute Indian Tribe's recreation department hosted the 2004 All-Indian Softball Tournament.

Education. The tribe operates a Head Start program. Tribal youth attend public schools located within the reservation or in surrounding communities. The education department provides Job Training Partnership Act, higher education, adult education, Johnson O'Malley, vocational/technical training, and Ute Language programs.

Health Care. The Indian Health Service Uintah and Ouray Health Service Unit and the Fort Duchesne Health Center provide direct health care. The Ute Indian Health Clinic also provides information on possible epidemics and other health issues.

The tribe operates the special diabetes program. It offers summer activities for tribal youth, including swimming and bowling. The program also provides fitness day activities and water aerobics classes. The tribe operates the Journey Into Wellness Center. Facilities include a gym. Programs include weight loss, nutrition, fitness, and diabetes counseling. The center sponsors a Fun Run/Walk.

The tribe provides emergency medical service to residents on the reservation, including the non-Indian population. Additional hospital care is available through the Duchesne County Hospital and the Ashley Valley Medical Center in Vernal.

ENVIRONMENTAL CONCERNS

Water rights are a major issue for the Northern Ute Indian Tribe, and it has entered extensive negotiations with the federal and state governments. The Colorado River and its tributaries in Utah all run entirely or partially through the Uintah-Ouray Reservation, and annual payments are provided to the tribe for access to this water. The presence of mosquitoes carrying the West Nile Virus is a concern to the tribe. Primarily a threat in the summer months, the virus is a serious health risk to both humans and horses. Mosquitos in general pose a threat to tribal resources as they weaken cattle. The presence of standing and stagnant water contributes greatly to the growth of the mosquito population. Unfortunately, such sources are abundant throughout the Uintah Basin.

LOCATION AND LAND STATUS

The Northwest Band of Shoshone Tribe's reservation, known as the Washakie Indian Reservation, is located in north-central Utah and south-central Idaho, 45 miles north of Brigham City, Utah, between I-15 and State Highway 84. Of the 287 acres, all 287 are located in Utah and none are located in Idaho. On October 24, 1984, the tribe received 187 acres from the Church of Jesus Christ of Latter-Day Saints. It purchased an additional 33 acres in 2003 and 2004 in the area where the 1863 Bear River Massacre had occurred. Currently the tribe is in the process of purchasing up to 6,000 acres on the Utah-Idaho border along I-15. These 6,000 acres will be used for a variety of tribal programs. The tribal offices are located in Brigham City, Utah, and Pocatello, Idaho.

CULTURE AND HISTORY

Until the middle of the nineteenth century, the Northwestern Band of Shoshones moved throughout a large territory from northern Utah to southern Idaho, and from western Wyoming to eastern Nevada. Their livelihood depended upon the rich grasslands that provided wild grains for themselves and their horses. There were originally 10 Northwestern bands. The size of the bands varied depending on their needs; small groups were favored where resources were widely scattered, and larger groups were needed in times of plenty or when warfare was undertaken to procure food and clothing. Band membership was fluid, with each family deciding whom they wanted to follow. Members of the current Northwestern Band of Shoshone Indians are descendents of families who followed Bear Hunter, Lehi, and Sagwitch. These people ranged over large areas in northern Utah and southern Idaho from the Salt Lake Valley to the Snake River.

Beginning in the 1840s, members of the Church of Jesus Christ of Latter-Day Saints began moving into areas that the Shoshones used for their livelihood. Shoshone grasslands were plowed, and the Natives had to compete with the new settlers for game animals. In the 1850s there was mass migration of Euro-Americans to the Oregon Territory. These immigrants increasingly competed with the Shoshones for natural resources. The discovery of silver in Montana and gold in California brought additional people seeking their fortunes. The Shoshones were displaced from their traditional gathering and hunting lands. Misunderstandings often occurred, which led to conflicts between the Shoshones and the immigrants, culminating in the Bear River Massacre on January 29, 1863, when federal troops from Camp Douglas, in Salt Lake City, massacred a village of Shoshones.

While a series of treaties and agreements in 1863 left southern Idaho and northern Utah as Shoshone country, the second Treaty of Fort Bridger in 1868 ceded those lands to the U.S. government. Some members of the original 10 northwestern bands settled on the reservations created in 1868 at Wind River, Wyoming, and Fort Hall, Idaho.

The Northwestern Band of Shoshone Indians are largely descended from survivors of the Bear River Massacre who chose not to relocate to a reservation, remaining in their traditional homelands in northern Utah and southern Idaho. Although the Northwestern Band signed the treaty of Box Elder in 1863 and were party to the 1868 treaty of Fort Bridger that ceded vast land holdings to the United Sates, they received very few services from the federal government until the early 1980s. Most members of the tribe today live between Salt Lake City, Utah, and Pocatello, Idaho.

GOVERNMENT

The tribal government is organized under the Indian Reorganization Act of 1934. A tribal constitution was adopted on April 29, 1987, which provided for a seven-member tribal council. The tribal council serves as the tribe's principal governing body. A tribal court can be convened when necessary, but there is no full-time tribal court or police department.

The tribal council has developed an organizational chart to aid in tribal governance, and it appoints an executive director to direct the tribe's administrative affairs. Administrative functions are carried out through five major departments, two standing committees, a housing authority, and an economic development corporation.

The department of health oversees various wellness programs, substance abuse, and clinic and hospital care programs. The department of natural resources handles environmental protection, fish and game, and road planning and road implementation. The department of education administers educational and training grants, along with adult education assistance. The department of human services provides child welfare services and child support. The department of cultural resources oversees the tribal library and administers other programs designed to preserve traditional language, knowledge, and practices.

The two standing committees are the election committee and the enrollment committee. The housing authority, organized as a 501(c)(3) organization, constructs and operates low-income housing units for tribal members. The tribe's NWB economic development corporation works to develop wealth for the tribe and to create jobs for tribal members and others.

BUSINESS CORPORATION

The tribal council created the NWB Economic Development Corporation in 2003. The economic development corporation has two divisions. NWB Technology is an SBA 8(a) firm with HUB Zone certification and deals primarily with government prime contractors. This firm employed 10 employees in 2004 to provide translation services for the FBI; staffing is expected to increase to 200-300 in the next few years. NWB Technology also employs a varying number of employees in construction projects; the staffing varies according to the number of contracts that are active. The NWB Economic Development Corporation's second subsidiary is NWB Enterprises, which manages the tribe's other business ventures. In 2004 this division was planning a tribal resort, a travel plaza, and renewable energy development projects as well as a business to provide financial services.

ECONOMY

Government as Employer. The tribal government employs approximately 13 people. The NWB Economic Development Corporation and the tribe's housing authority also provide employment for a number of people.

Economic Development Projects. The NWB Economic Development Corporation has plans to develop a resort, a power plant, a travel plaza, a manufacturing business, and renewable energy projects.

Construction. NWB Technology, a subsidiary of the NWB Economic Development Corporation, provides construction services. The number of employees varies according to the contracts in operation.

Washakie Indian Reservation
Federal reservation
Shoshone
Box Elder County, Utah

Northwestern Band
of Shoshone Indians
862 South Main Street, Suite 6
Brigham City, UT 84302
435-734-2286
435-734-0424 Fax

427 North Main Street
Suite 101
Pocatello, ID 83204
208-478-5712
208-478-5713 Fax

Total area *(Tribal source, 2004)*
217 acres

Federal trust *(Tribal source, 2004)*
184 acres

Tribally owned *(Tribal source, 2004)*
33 acres

Population *2000 census*

Population *(Tribal source, 2004)*
450

Percent Native *2000 census*

Tribal enrollment
(Labor force report, 2001)
433

Total labor force
(Labor force report, 2001)
181

Total labor force
(Tribal source, 2004)
206

Unemployment rate
(Labor force report, 2001)
38%

Washakie

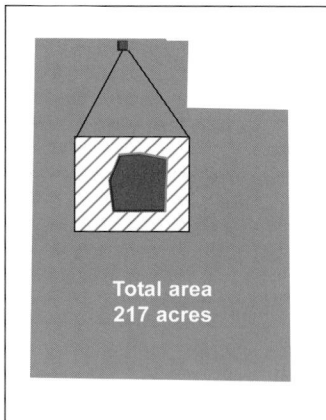

**Total area
217 acres**

Telecommunications. NWB Technology provides translation services for the FBI. It employed a staff of 10 in 2004, and this is expected to increase to 200-300 over the next few years.

INFRASTRUCTURE
No one currently lives on the reservation. Other infrastructure would have to be developed before anyone could move there.

Electricity. Utah Power and Light can provide electricity on the reservation.

Water Supply. Tribal wells can provide water.

Housing. The tribe's housing authority has housing projects in Ogden and Brigham City, Utah, and a few houses in Blackfoot, Idaho.

COMMUNITY FACILITIES AND SERVICES
The tribe has no community facilities other than its offices in Brigham City, Utah, and Pocatello, Idaho. The tribal housing authority provides low-income rental units in Ogden, Utah, and Brigham City, Utah.

Education. Elementary and secondary students attend public school in the areas where they live. Vocational and university students attend a variety of schools scattered throughout the western United States. Currently 18 tribal members are in higher education programs. Scholarship assistance is available to tribal members from a variety of sources. The tribe provides education assistance through a grant from the BIA.

Health Care. The tribe has a contract health agreement with the Indian Health Service. Tribal members are treated at Indian Health Service facilities and by local doctors, clinics, and hospitals. Members living in Box Elder County are eligible for tribal assistance through a contract health service grant provided by Indian Health Service.

ENVIRONMENTAL CONCERNS
The Northwest Band of Shoshone is concerned about pollution emitted by a local steel plant; the tribe is monitoring air pollutants.

Chehalis

LOCATION AND LAND STATUS

The Chehalis Reservation is located in western Washington State, at the juncture of the Black and Chehalis rivers. It is about 26 miles southwest of the state capital of Olympia and 6 miles northwest of Centralia. Tribal lands span 4,215 acres. The reservation was established by an Executive Order in 1864, which was amended in October 1886. Another Executive Order by President Grover Cleveland restored 3,753.63 acres to the public domain for homesteaders. Although much of the original Indian lands were given to non-Indians under the Homestead Laws, 36 members of the tribe applied for land and were able to keep some of the lands. A total of 471 acres were to be made available for schools.

As of 2004, the tribe had purchased an additional 45 acres in Long Prairie, now Grand Mound (fee-to-trust in process), to be used for economic development. This land purchase is off the reservation near I-5 and about 10 miles from the main body of the reservation.

CULTURE AND HISTORY

The two principal tribes now living on the Chehalis Reservation are the Lower Chehalis and the Upper Chehalis, also calling themselves the "qyaya." They speak related Salish languages and traditionally maintained close ties through trade and intermarriage. The Upper Chehalis people lived from Cloquallum Creek to the Chehalis River waterways and tributary rivers and creeks. While the Lower Chehalises primarily relied on ocean resources for their sustenance ("Chehalis" means "sand"), the Upper Chehalis depended on their river-based economy and used the river as a way to travel.

Even though the Chehalis people were affiliated with the 1855 Treaty Council held by Governor Isaac Stevens, they never signed a treaty; hence, their treaty rights as affiliates have, to this day, never been formally recognized. In 1864 the Secretary of the Interior approved an Executive Order setting aside 4,215 acres for the Chehalis Reservation, and it was expected that the Cowlitz, Chinook, and Shoalwater Bay peoples would settle there. However, few besides the Chehalis did settle there.

In 1906, the combined Chehalis Tribe began a series of petitions to the federal government for compensation for lands the government had appropriated. For more than half a century, their claims were denied largely based on the government's erroneous assumption that the Chehalises had indeed signed the treaty of 1851. In the late 1950s, after numerous appeals, the Indian Claims Commission concluded that the Chehalis Tribes held aboriginal title to approximately 840,000 acres. They were ultimately compensated about 90 cents per acre, a distribution amounting to about $600 per tribal member.

The Chehalis culture traditionally relied on the region's abundance of fish and forest. They also depended on edible roots and berries. Today, subsistence and ceremonial fishing remains central to tribal culture, although not to its previous extent. Programs have been developed to preserve the Chehalis language. Basket weaving, drum making, regalia classes, and storytelling are additional classes offered to help preserve the culture. The celebration of Tribal Days and the Annual Salmon Ceremony, along with the strong presence of the Indian Shaker Church, allow members share their culture with future generations.

GOVERNMENT

The tribe operates under a constitution and bylaws that were adopted on July 15, 1939, and amended on April 16, 1973. Tribal affairs are conducted by a five-member business committee composed of a chairman, a vice-chairman, a treasurer, a secretary, and an at-large council member. The business council is elected every two years by the Chehalis Community Council, which is comprised of all qualified voters. A general manager works with the business committee, and they set direction for current policies and develop tribal resources while keeping policy making and the management of tribal funds and revenue separate.

The tribal law enforcement department has cross-jurisdiction authority with Thurston County law enforcement. The public safety director, who also serves as the chief of police, oversees 11 law enforcement officers, 1 fishery officer, 1 probation officer, 6 corrections officers, a tribal court employee, and a court clerk. The tribe is in the process of building a 10,550-square-foot public safety facility that will include courts, policing, and corrections.

Within the tribal court system, the tribe participates in the Northwest Intertribal Court System for judges, prosecutors, and other services. The court contracts its child-welfare prosecutor services.

The business committee is elected every two years by all qualified voters. The committee is responsible for managing and administering funds relating to tribal real property and other assets; and for enforcing tribal laws related to the conduct of business on the Chehalis Reservation.

Chehalis Reservation
Federal reservation
Chehalis
Grays Harbor and Thurston
counties, Washington

Confederated Tribes of the
Chehalis Reservation
P.O. Box 536
240 Howanut Road
Oakville, WA 98568
  360-858-1505
  360-273-5914 Fax
  chehalistribe.org

Total area (BIA realty, 2004)
2,124.99 acres

Tribally owned (BIA realty, 2004)
125.94 acres

Individually owned
(BIA realty, 2004)
1,999.05 acres

Population *2000 census*
691

Population
(Tribal source, 2004)
688

Total labor force *2000 census*
267

Total labor force
(BIA labor report, 2001)
801

High school graduate or higher
2000 census
71.5%

Chehalis

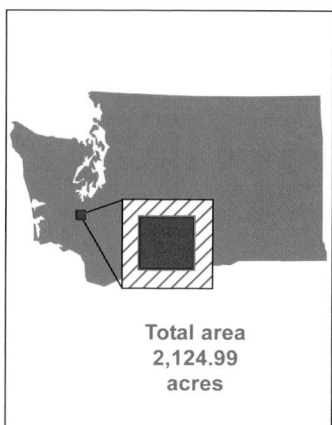

**Total area
2,124.99
acres**

Bachelor's degree or higher
2000 census
6.4%

Unemployment rate *2000 census*
12.4%

Per capita income *2000 census*
$4,064

ECONOMY

The tribal government is the main employer of tribal members, with 130 people in government-related jobs. These jobs are in retail, health clinics and facilities, police and court services, and bingo. Other industries are related to livestock farming, hay crops, and small commercial salmon fishing. Following a serious decline in the timber and fishing industries, jobs created by the government help to decrease the numbers who otherwise might be unemployed. The tribe and casino add over $9.1 million to the state's revenues.

Government as Employer. A total of 130 people are directly employed in tribal administration and operations, including services in health care, police and law enforcement, public housing projects, and the U.S. Department of Agriculture Extension Indian Reservation Program.

Economic Development Projects. Plans for expanding the reservation's tourism industry are under discussion. The number of retail outlets on the reservation that capitalize on the steady increase in visitors due to the Luck Eagle Casino is on the rise.

The tribe has entered into water settlement negotiations to plan for the future use of "reserved water" rights and to document unforeseen circumstances and implementation issues for full use of tribal resources in economic planning. The tribe leverages over one million dollars to clean up, restore, and maintain the Chehalis River, which supplies the river's users with economic, cultural, and food needs.

In 2002, the tribe began work on the Community Development Financial Institution and the Chehalis Lending Program for small business venture capital. It is to be implemented using a grant from the U.S. Department of Treasury as part of a planning project by the Chehalis business committee to situate more businesses in the local tribal areas. This will bring new funds into the community, thus creating new businesses and revenue to leverage with federal dollars.

Agriculture and Livestock. A dairy farm and an egg farm on the reservation, both owned by non-Indians, generate significant revenues and employment.

Forestry. While the area's forests have suffered a considerable decline in recent decades due to overharvesting, the possibilities for tree farming and harvesting still remain, but on a reduced scale because the timber is located on allotted lands.

Gaming. The Lucky Eagle Casino and Bingo Hall is situated off Highway 12 in Rochester, Washington. Opened in 1987, it has attracted great numbers of visitors to the reservation. Keno, big six, blackjack, craps, roulette, bingo, and video slot machines are all available for both novice and expert players. The casino hosts concerts, boxing, comedy shows, and other special events. These government enterprises indirectly employ a number of tribal members and have also fueled several spin-off retail businesses, along with attendant revenues and employment. A Las Vegas-style buffet restaurant is featured, serving everything from steaks, seafood, and chops to food that is prepared to order. Gaming revenues have been used for educational scholarships, youth programs, and elders heritage and cultural programs.

Construction. The tribe's economic development administration funded Chehalis tribal construction and the SAXAS Construction Company in 2004. The tribe is well positioned in the construction sector due to the amount of work planned by the tribal government and business committee. The demand for homes and new tribal facilities is growing.

Services and Retail. A number of small retail businesses and commercial enterprises are operated under private ownership within the reservation's boundaries. The tribe owns and operates both the End of the Trail Store, which also maintains 12 gasoline pumps, and the Quick Serve Restaurant.

Tourism and Recreation. The tribe celebrates its annual Chehalis Tribal Days during the last weekend of May. Activities include an annual salmon ceremony and clambake, a baseball tournament, and other events. The river provides recreational opportunities, such as, fishing, swimming, and boating.

INFRASTRUCTURE

Electricity. The Grays Harbor Pubic Utility District and Puget Sound Energy provide homes with electricity.

Water Supply. The Chehalis Department of Natural Resources oversees and operates a community water system that serves the tribal government facilities and the HUD housing complex. The wells and septic system were installed with the assistance of the Indian Health Service and U.S. Public Health Service.

Transportation. The reservation is accessible by I-5, which passes north-south about 8 miles east of tribal boundaries. State Highway 12 directly serves the reservation. County transit bus service is available in Oakville, 5 miles away, and other commercial bus service is available in Centralia, 15 miles southeast of the reservation. Amtrak train service is also available in Centralia. UPS and FedEx pickup and delivery is available on the reservation. The nearest airport, in Olympia, is private, and the nearest commercial service is at Sea-Tac International Airport, about 80 miles to the north. Chehalis tribal members will soon have their own public transportation service for doctor appointments and other professional services.

Telecommunications. An Internet service provider and the Comcast cable company serve the community.

COMMUNITY FACILITIES AND SERVICES

The tribe maintains a community center that houses the tribal government offices, classrooms for preschool education, a library, an elders meeting room, and the tribe's health clinic enterprise. The community center is also a youth center. It has a gym, kitchen, a computer center, and a new learning center.

Public Safety. The tribe is in the planning stage to build a 10,550-square-foot public safety facility to house the courts, corrections staff, and various offices.

Education. Several educational districts are located on the reservation, serving students in K-12. The Chehalis Tribe Early Head Start program caters to the very young. The Oakville School (K-12) and the Rochester School Districts (K-12) are located on the reservation. The Wa-He-Lut (K-12) BIA school is located at Frank's Landing near Olympia, Washington.

Health Care. A 4,920-square-foot ambulatory clinic, under a PL 93-638, title I contract, serves the tribal community. An alcohol and substance abuse program also operates out of two tribally owned buildings. The health program employs a full-time physician's assistant, an advanced registered nurse practitioner, a full-time mental health provider, and a half-time dentist. The tribe's contract health service delivery area is Grays Harbor and Thurston counties. Visits to Centralia or Olympia for surgeries and other emergencies are common.

ENVIRONMENTAL CONCERNS

The primary environmental concern for Chehalis members is the local use of heavy doses of nitrate, which is injected directly into the soil and results in poor water quality. Another concern is that the Chehalis Rivers are taking in the runoff from the dairy farm. These pollutants are having a negative effect on fishing. Also, pollution and septic system failures are impacting ground and service water. The tribe is currently developing a comprehensive water-quality monitoring program to address the above concerns.

As "responsible keepers of the river," the tribe educates people about environmental stewardship. One way they accomplish this is by providing an Interactive and Experiential Water Quality Initiative through a U.S. Department of Agriculture partnership project that takes interested persons on a water trip for water testing and habitat exploration.

Colville

Colville

LOCATION AND LAND STATUS

Tribal headquarters are located on the Colville Indian Agency campus near the Town of Nespelem. The Coleville Indian Reservation encompasses over 1.4 million acres in north-central Washington. Tribal lands are located primarily in Okanogan and Ferry counties, approximately 100 miles northwest of Spokane. The reservation is divided into tribally-owned lands, individually-owned trust lands, and non-tribally owned fee lands. The Columbia and Okanogan rivers border the reservation's east, south, and west sides.

The reservation was established by an Executive Order of 1872. Within three months, the government began to diminish the reservation, seizing lands for public domain. By the early 1870s, the reservation had been reduced to less than half of its original size. In 1892, an Act of Congress seized the northern half of the Coleville Reservation. 51,653 acres of the land were allotted to 660 individual tribal members. Later that same year, the government purchased 1.5 million acres of unallotted tribal lands for $1.5 million. Hunting and fishing rights on the lands were granted to the tribe.

The Presidential Proclamation of October 10, 1900, officially opened 1,449,268 acres to homesteading. The McLaughlin Agreement of December 1, 1905 provided for the allotment of the southern half of the reservation. Lands were allotted in 80 acres parcels, and the remainder was made available for non-Indian settlement. By 1914, when 2,505 Colville Indians had been allotted another 333,275 acres, a proclamation on May 3, 1916 opened the remaining 417,841 acres of surplus lands to settlement.

The government did not terminate the allotment policy until 1934. In 1935, the BIA issued an order to stop the withdrawal status of reservation lands belonging to the tribe. In 1956, the government returned about 800,000 acres to the Coleville Tribe.

The tribe continues to reestablish its traditional land base, acquiring lands within and outside of reservation boundaries. Funds earned from the sale of timber, minerals, and hydroelectric rights provide the resources for the land repurchase program.

PHYSICAL DESCRIPTION

Tribal lands are characterized by a diverse topography, with mountainous regions, timberlands, rangelands, lakes, and streams. Predominant tree species include ponderosa pine, Douglas fir, lodgepole pine, and western larch. The elevation across the reservation ranges from 790 feet above sea level at the mouth of Okanogan River to over 6,000 feet above sea level at the summit of Moses Mountain.

CLIMATE

The average summer temperature in the higher elevations of the reservation is around 90ºF. The average low in winter is between 10ºF and 20ºF below 0ºF. Valleys and lowlands receive an annual precipitation of 10 to 14 inches.

CULTURE AND HISTORY

The Coleville Confederated Tribe is comprised of members of 12 tribal groups. The Coleville, Wenatche, Entiate, Chelan, Methow, Okanogan, Nespelem, San Poil, Lakes, Moses Columbia, and Palus bands traditionally occupied territories in eastern Washington State. The twelfth band, the Nez Perce, originated in northeastern Oregon. Traditional communities were often located near waterways, including the Columbia, San Poil, Okanogan, Snake, and Wallowa rivers. Traditional means of sustenance for the bands included hunting, fishing, and trading furs.

During the 1820s, the Hudson Bay Company occupied Kettle Falls, a popular trading center in the region. Fort Coleville was constructed at this site and the indigenous groups in the area were confederated as the Coleville Tribes. Between 1826 and 1887 tribes traded beaver, gear, muskrat, fisher, fix, lynx, martin, mink, otter, raccoon, wolverine, badger, and wolf pelts at the fort. As many as 20,000 pelts were traded into the mainstream market each year.

Until the mid-nineteenth century, members of the Coleville Tribes continued to practice their nomadic lifestyles. The arrival of settlers, and the eventual establishment of the Canadian border, forced tribal members to bring an end to their migratory patterns. While many members settled in the United States, a number of Coleville peoples remained in Canada. The Colville Indian Reservation was originally established in 1872 through an Executive Order by President Grant. Later additions of the Chief Moses and Chief Joseph bands, among others, helped to create a reservation of unparalleled cultural and political complexity, which was in part due to different languages spoken by the confederated tribes.

In 1938, the U.S. government engineered the Grand Coulee Dam, which flooded the tribes' salmon spawning areas and ruined orchard and agricultural lands. This dramatically changed the tribes' economic opportunities. The Colville Tribal Government has won a series of claims against the federal government for lands appropriated improperly and/or at fraudulent prices. It also won a case against the government for the mismanagement of tribal resources that were decimated by federal hydroelectric projects like the Grand Coulee Dam.

Colville Indian Reservation
Federal reservation
Ferry, Okanagan and Stevens counties, Washington

Confederated Tribes of the
Colville Reservation
P.O. Box 150
Nespelem, WA 99155
509-634-2200
509-634-4116 Fax

Total area *(BIA realty, 2004)*
1,127,649.69 acres

Tribally owned *(BIA realty, 2004)*
1,085,022.13 acres

Allotted/Individually owned
(BIA realty, 2004)
42,620.56 acres

Federal trust *(BIA realty, 2004)*
7 acres

Total population *2000 census*
7,582

Tribal enrollment
(BIA labor report, 2001)
8,842

Total labor force *2000 census*
3,253

Colville

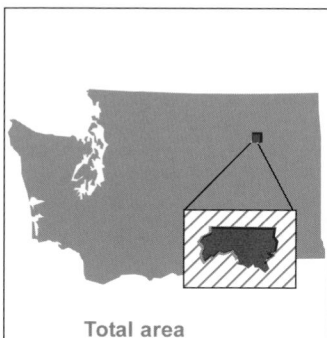

Total area
1,127,649.69
acres

Total labor force
(BIA labor report, 2001)
6,043

High school graduate or higher
2000 census
76.4%

Bachelor's degree or higher
2000 census
12.2%

Unemployment rate *2000 census*
21%

Unemployment rate
(BIA labor report, 2001)
64%

Per capita income *2000 census*
$12,195

Despite the heavy-handed conversion of the Colvilles to Catholicism and various Protestant faiths during the last century, traditional cultural and religious practices abound today. One example is the Seven Drum Religion, which was brought by the Chief Joseph Band of Nez Perce. The tribe supports the efforts to retain the indigenous languages, and provides instruction in the public schools and extracurricular programs. The tribe also continues to host various cultural events and activities.

The tribes' main ambition is to wisely manage its resources and with a balanced economic and social development. To this end, increasing numbers of tribal members are pursuing degrees in higher education in natural resource management, law, business, social work, and health policy.

GOVERNMENT

On February 26, 1938, the federal government approved the Confederated Tribes of the Colville Reservation's constitution and bylaws, which led to the establishment of the Colville Business Council as the tribe's governing body. Tribal members elect 14 business council members to staggered two-year terms. Council officers include a chairman, vice-chairman, and secretary, and they are elected to one-year terms from within the council body. Members of the Colville Business Council are salaried while in office.

The Colville Reservation has four voting districts: the Omak District, the Nespelem District, the Keller District, and the Inchelium District. Eligible adult members may register in one of the districts to vote in the yearly Colville Business Council election.

The government administration division and the tribal administrator, who reports directly to the business council, administer much of the government. The business council is responsible for overseeing the gaming commission, legal matters, the tribal business corporation, and government-to-government relations. Ten committees or councils, with lower-level offices, oversee other major areas of administration. The tribal government committee oversees the elections process, enrollment, ethics concerns, and the legislative committee. The law and justice committee oversees public safety (including the police and emergency medical services), the tribal court and associated functions, tribal gaming operations, and internal affairs. The management and budget committee oversees the tribal records, benefits distribution, the tribal newspaper, contracting, some aspects of the tribal corporation, and data systems.

The community development committee oversees housing programs, housing developments, and the delivery of water, utilities, and sanitation services to its members. The transportation committee oversees Inchelium Ferry and roads. The human services committee oversees substance abuse programs, elders programs, children's and family programs, a convalescent center, and other health programs. The education and employment committee oversees the education program, along with employment and vocational rehabilitation. The veterans committee oversees the veterans resources program. The cultural resources committee oversees the museum and programs that support traditional knowledge and crafts. The natural resources committee oversees natural resources management, land purchases, and land resource inventory.

BUSINESS CORPORATION

The Colville Tribal Enterprise Corporation (CTEC), established in 1984, is responsible for all the tribe's economic development, business entities, and projects. Its mission is to attain tribal economic self-sufficiency. CTEC ventures include en-

terprises in the gaming, tourism, recreation, construction, and timber industries. The company also provides custom-designed training programs for tribal entities. In 1998, CTEC provided 93 percent of the employment opportunities on the reservation. In 2000, it employed almost 1,000 people and generated revenues in excess of $100 million.

CTEC is the parent company of 15 tribally-owned enterprises, including the Mill Bay Casino, Okanogan Bingo Casino, Coulee Dam Casino, The Trading Post, Inchelium Community Store, Keller Community Store, Coleville Tribal Credit, Coleville Tribal Services Corporation, Coleville Indian Precision Pine, Coleville Timber Resource Company, Coleville Tribal Logging, Coleville Indian Power and Veneer, Rainbow Beach Resort, and Roosevelt Recreational Enterprises.

ECONOMY

The Confederated Tribes of the Colville Reservation's economy includes a vast array of enterprises, most of which operate in the tourism, gaming, and timber industries. Lake Victoria and Coulee Dam play an important part in tribal revenue generation, both as the setting for many tourism-related businesses and as natural resources. The reservation's forests have become the tribe's primary natural resource for economic use; logging companies provide substantial income for the tribe; one of the wood-processing businesses is a source of energy for the tribe. The Confederated Tribes operates on a yearly budget, which is financed primarily from revenues generated from the sale of the tribe's timber products and from other sources including federal, state, and private contributions.

Government as Employer. From its administrative headquarters located at the BIA in Nespelem, the Colville Business Council oversees a diverse, multimillion-dollar administration that employees from 800 to 1,200 individuals in permanent, part-time, and seasonal positions. Combined, the tribe and CTEC employ over 2,300 people. Together, they are the second largest provider of year-round opportunities.

Agriculture and Livestock. The Colville Reservation is rich in rangelands and farmlands. Open rangelands span approximately 288,000 acres, while forested rangelands comprise another 135,000 acres. The tribe has about 6,000 head of cattle and 1,000 horses, with the potential for at least an additional 7,000 head of cattle. The tribe also operates a successful meatpacking plant.

The tribe has almost 82,000 acres of commercial farmland, which is primarily used for wheat, alfalfa, barley, and apple crops. Approximately 2,000 acres are irrigated. Non-Indian-owned apple- and pear-packing facilities are also located on the reservation. The potential for further agricultural development is vast, as long as irrigation services are expanded, something the tribe is actively pursuing.

Forestry. Timber and wood products are at the heart of the Colville Tribes multimillion-dollar industries. Nearly half of the reservation's 1.4 million acres comprise commercially viable timberlands. Species include pine, fir, lodgepole pine, cedar, and tamarack. Colville also has its own nursery to replant and grow trees.

Colville Timber Resource Company harvests and markets tribal timber sold from the Colville Reservation. Colville Tribal Logging selects, logs, and transports harvested timber stands, using best forest management practices to enhance and protect the tribe's forest; in 2002 it paid out $1.4 million in annual payroll. Inchelium Wood Treatment Plant is a chemical wood-treating facility that manufactures lodgepole pine into raw and treated posts and poles. Colville Indian Precision Pine operates a sawmill that specializes in manufacturing ponderosa pine and Douglas fir logs into high-quality lumber for industrial and commodity markets; their products are shipped worldwide. Colville Indian Power and Veneer provides green and dry veneer as well as plywood to lumber stores, building centers, wood wholesalers, and construction and design specialty outlets.

Gaming. The Coleville Tribes own three gaming facilities, the Okanogan Bingo Casino, Mill Bay Casino, and Coulee Dam Casino. The Okanogan Bingo Casino features a restaurant and gift shop. The casino offers 174 slots/VLTs, 2 table games, and 500 bingo seats. The Mill Bay Casino, located in Manson, Washington, occupies 7,000 square feet. It offers 400 slots/ VLTs and 11 table games. The facilities include one restaurant.The Coulee Dam Casino, in the Town of Coulee Dam, offers 160 slots/VLTs and 2 table games. The casino occupies 7,000 square feet and features a restaurant and gift shop.

The gaming operations of the tribes provided 400 jobs in 2002, nearly 70 percent of which were occupied by Native Americans. In 2002, 80 percent of the revenue earned in the casinos was used to fund community services, resource management, public safety, tribal police, education, scholarship, employment and training, counseling, health service, and cultural programs. The remaining funds were used to support 800 jobs, payroll services, and other CTEC business ventures. Revenue is also used to support cultural, elder, youth, and community activities.

Fisheries. The Tribal Fish and Wildlife Department offers fishing permits.The tribe operates a fishery rehabilitation program. The trout hatched at the fishery are released into local lakes and streams to further enhance the region's status as a sport-fishing paradise. The tribal fish hatchery stocks all the lakes and streams in north-central Washington State. While salmon continues to be an important food source among tribal members, salmon runs have been diminished as a result of the development of the Grand Coulee and Chief Joseph damns on the Columbia River.

Construction. CTEC operates the Coleville Tribal Services Corporation (CTSC). CTSC supports three divisions, general building, highways and utilities, and electrical. services include commercial and residential design, construction, and facilities support; highway and street construction, water and sewer system installation, and wrecking and demolition; and power, communication, and fiber optics services. Recent projects include Nisqually Health Clinic, Nespelem Senior Center, Nespelem Head Start, Rebecca Lake Housing, Cache Creek Road, and Inchelium Sewer Lagoon. Clients of the company include the U.S. Army Corps of Engineers, the Umatilla Tribe, the BIA, and the U.S. Forest Service. CTSC received a NW Division Contractor of the Year Award (1999) from the U.S. Army Corps of Engineers.

*Mining.*Gold mining has increased near reservation boundaries during the past decade, with gold mining ventures in the Nespelem area currently under consideration. Small-scale molybdenum mining has also taken place on tribal land in recent years. The tribe has a mineral permit system in place to regulate mining in regard to environmental and cultural issues.

Manufacturing. The tribe's primary successes in this area remain its lumber mills. *(See Forestry, above.)*

Services and Retail. Colville Tribal Credit provides financial services, resources, and expertise to tribal members. A few of the services include small business assistance and housing support and guidance. Colville gaming enterprises support more than 700 commercial vendors from around the state.

CTEC owns and runs several stores. The Trading Post and gas station in Nespelem provides its customers with competitively priced products in a friendly atmosphere. The store trains employees in the latest retail system. Inchelium Community Store supplies community members with a variety of food and household products. Keller Community Store sells a variety of food and miscellaneous items in a friendly environment dedicated to quality service. Barney's Junction is located on an international commerce highway; the restaurant and bar offer a quick stop to travelers.

Tourism and Recreation. Colville gaming enterprises attract nearly 1.4 million visitors each year. In addition to gaming facilities, the reservation has a number of attractions that draw visitors. CTEC owns and runs a number of tourism-related establishments. Rainbow Beach Resort offers a unique vacation spot with cabins, RV spaces, and boat rentals. Roosevelt Recreational Enterprises maintains a fleet of 40 rental houseboats, water-ski boats, and fishing boats. Keller Ferry and Seven Bays provide docking facilities, waterside fuel docks, and packing and utility systems on Lake Roosevelt. There is also a store and upscale retail complex, featuring a full-service restaurant.The tribe also sponsors a number of special events that are open to the public, including the Fourth of July Encampment in Nespelem and the annual Stampede in Omak every October.

Grand Coulee Dam, located on the reservation, creates Lake Roosevelt, which backs up for 150 miles behind the dam, producing wonderful recreation areas that are extremely popular tourist attractions. The Colville Confederated Tribes Museum and Gift Shop is located in the Town of Coulee Dam.

INFRASTRUCTURE

Major highways serving the reservation include State Highway 155, which passes through the reservation from Omak in the northwest down through Nespelem and the Coulee Dam area in the south; Route 21 passes north-south through the center of the reservation; and Route 97 runs north-south along the western border. Most reservation communities are connected by state highways. As of 1998 there was no public transportation on the reservation. Okanogan was establishing a transit authority for its area in 1998. Grant County Authority runs a line into the Grand Coulee Dam area.

A Burlington Northern Railroad line passes through the reservation, with several spurs for the timber and apple industries. The Town of Omak is served by an airport. Additional commercial air service is available in Spokane. In 1998 a small-unmanned airstrip was located adjacent to Nespelem. In emergencies, depending on the weather, helicopters can be accessed from Spokane. UPS, Pony Express, and other shipping companies serve the reservation directly. The Columbia River borders the south and eastern edges of the reservation, while the Okanogan River borders the west side, both offering water access.

Electricity. Generators at Coulee Dam keep electricity reasonably priced. Two electrical cooperatives and public utility districts provide electricity. Colville Indian Power and Veneer generates 12-15 megawatts of renewable, biomass electric power using hog fuel from its own and nearby forest product operations. This production is sufficient to fulfill the power needs of all tribal enterprises. In 2002, the tribe received an $180,000 grant from the Department of Energy to construct a substation. The station would reduce the Colville Indian Power and Veneer operation's thermal losses and increase its efficiency.

Colville

Water Supply. Tribal, BIA, city, and individual well systems provide water to the reservation. The tribe operates a wastewater facility and solid waste services.

Transportation. The Colville Tribe community health representatives program and the senior program provide transportation to those in need.

Telecommunications. General Telephone, Pacific Northwest Bell, and Continental Bell provide telephone service. An AM/FM radio station, a TV station, and a variety of newspapers all operate within reservation boundaries.

Housing. The Colville Indian Housing Authority funds general housing projects. Some Colville tribal members in low-income categories may own or rent HUD homes located on the reservation; however, housing for the elderly, individuals on fixed incomes, and those classified as low income is terribly inadequate and constitutes a chronic need.

COMMUNITY FACILITIES AND SERVICES

The tribal elders program provides many services, including transportation assistance, convalescent care, and meals programs in four towns. The tribal youth programs provide innovative youth-enhancement programs. Job training programs provide on-the-job training, vocational training, high school summer employment, and college internships. Colville Tribal Legal Services works with Columbia Legal Services to provide low-income residents with access to the civil justice system.

Education. Students attend several public school districts within the reservation and the Paschel Sherman Indian School near Omak. The Colville and Yakama tribes, along with the University of Washington, have been awarded a joint grant of nearly $500,000 to establish community technology centers in each of the tribal communities. The tribe operates a language preservation program that aims to revitalize three languages indigenous to the tribe. Tribal elders provide instruction to young tribal members so they can become instructors. In collaboration with other Northwestern tribes, Antioch College, Northwest Indian College, and Wenatchee Valley College, the tribe is exploring the feasibility of instituting college credits for Native language teachers.

Health Care. The Indian Health Service in the Nespelem district and its satellite offices in the other three districts serve the reservation. Hospitals are located in Omak, Brewster, and Grand Coulee. Tribal health programs include infant care, family planning, dental services, treatment centers, and substance abuse counseling. The tribe operates a convalescent center that houses Indians and non-Indians.

ENVIRONMENTAL CONCERNS

Maintaining wilderness areas and the viability of tribal natural resources is an environmental concern for the tribe. In order to safeguard these and also guide and support future development, the reservation is divided into zoning districts, which include residential, commercial, rural, forestry, game reserve, industrial, and wilderness.

The tribal fish and wildlife department manages game bird populations and protected predators such as the bald eagle and peregrine falcon. The sharp-tailed grouse, or prairie chicken, is an endangered species with nesting and dancing grounds on the reservation. The Confederated Tribes of Colville is developing a Lakes of the Colville Indian Reservation Database to make environmental information about these bodies of water available to recreational users and natural resource managers.

Two Colville tribal executives sued Canadian firm Teck Cominco in 2004 regarding their noncompliance with U.S. EPA directives on pollution generated by their lead smelter at Columbia River and Lake Victoria.

Cowlitz

Cowlitz Indian Tribe
Federally recognized
Cowlitz
Cowlitz, Clark, and Lewis
counties, Washington

Cowlitz Indian Tribe
P.O. Box 2547
Longview, WA 98632
360-577-8140
360-577-7432 Fax
cowlitz.org

LOCATION AND LAND STATUS

A majority of the members of the Cowlitz Tribe live within a two-hour drive of the Cowlitz River, which enters the Columbia River at Longview and runs north about 25 miles then east to the Cascade Crest. Most of the remaining members live elsewhere in western Washington. The tribe was federally recognized in 2002, and as of 2004 had not received its initial reservation lands. In addition to the land on which its tribal offices (in Longview, Cowlitz County) and tribal housing (in Toledo, Lewis County) are located, the tribe acquired land in Clark County near La Center, about 20 miles south of Longview, 16 miles north of the Columbia River and the Washington-Oregon state line, and an easy drive from Vancouver, Washington, and Portland, Oregon. The tribe petitioned that this land be designated as its initial reservation lands, and plans to build a casino which has encountered opposition.

CULTURE AND HISTORY

The modern Cowlitz Indians have integrated with the European-American culture while maintaining tribal observances as to child rearing, religion, food, and kinship networks. The name "Cowlitz" means "seeker" in a spiritual sense, referring to the Cowlitz practice of sending youths on fasting journeys to seek their *tomanawas*, or spirit power.

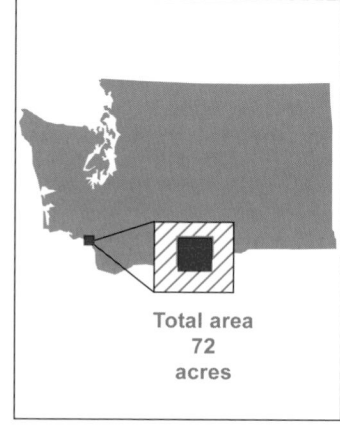

Total area
72
acres

The Cowlitz Tribe includes two groups, the Upper and Lower Cowlitz. The tribe's original territory, centered on the Cowlitz River (named after the tribe), included some 3,750 square miles. The more numerous Salish-speaking Lower Cowlitz lived in 30 villages along the river, from about one mile above the Columbia River to about 45 miles upstream. The Sahaptin-speaking Upper Cowlitz (Taidnapam) wintered along the Cowlitz River east of the Lower Cowlitz, then moved up into the Cascade Mountains during warm weather. Both were known as aristocratic and warlike but social, maintaining trading and kinship alliances throughout what is now southwest Washington and northwest Oregon. They were a regional power until influenza epidemics in the early 1830s killed perhaps seven-eighths of the tribe. Initially friendly to non-Natives, relations turned sour by the mid-nineteenth century as non-Natives occupied more of the Cowlitz River valley. Throughout the twentieth century, the Cowlitz people struggled with both state and federal governments for land and subsistence rights. The state recognized the subsistence rights of the Cowlitz in the 1920s. In 1951, Cowlitz leadership filed a land-claims petition with the federal Indian Claims Commission. Twenty-two years later, the commission found in favor of the tribe, acknowledging the seizure of 1.66 million acres without compensation. The tribe was awarded about 90 cents an acre, which, as of 2004, had not yet been distributed. Through the 1980s and 1990s, the Cowlitz pressed for federal recognition, and they were recognized in January 2002.

GOVERNMENT

In 1912, the tribe reorganized from a hereditary chieftainship to an elected tribal council.

ECONOMY

Government as Employer. The tribal government has 33 employees in tribal administration, health services, and housing services.

Gaming. In July 2004, the Cowlitz Tribe announced that its requested 152-acre reservation in Clark County would include a casino. In 2001, the tribe had acquired land in Clark County near La Center and has proposed building a 500,000-square-foot complex including the casino, restaurants, and shops. The Mohegan Tribe of Connecticut, operators of the highly successful Mohegan Sun Casino, is in partnership with the Cowlitz Tribe and has invested heavily in the project. An environmental impact statement is being prepared as part of the BIA approval process, likely addressing traffic, water, wastewater, air quality, socioeconomic, and endangered species issues. Clark County residents opposed to the casino deny that the Cowlitz Tribe has any historic connection with Clark County and should not have its reservation in Clark County.

COMMUNITY FACILITIES AND SERVICES

The Cowlitz Tribe has administrative offices in Longview and St. Mary's tribal housing in Toledo.

Health Care. The Cowlitz Indian Health Service provides limited health services at the Fir Complex in Longview.

Cowlitz

Total area *(Tribal source, 2004)*
72 acres

Federal trust *(Tribal source, 2004)*
0 acres

Tribally owned *(Tribal source, 2004)*
72 acres

Allotted*(Tribal source, 2004)*
0 acres

Tribal enrollment
(Tribal source, 2004)
2,838

Hoh

Total area *(BIA realty, 2004)*		443 acres
Tribally owned lands		443 acres
(BIA realty, 2004)		
Population *2000 census*		102
Population *(Tribal source, 2004)*		116
Tribal enrollment *(BIA, 2001)*		139
Tribal enrollment *(Tribal source, 2004)*		167
Total labor force *2000 census*		47
Total labor force *(BIA labor report, 2001)*		48
High school graduate or higher		47.6%
2000 census		
Bachelor's degree or higher *2000 census*		0%
Unemployment rate *2000 census*		34%
Unemployment rate		73%
(BIA labor report, 2001)		
Per capita income *2000 census*		$10,008

LOCATION AND LAND STATUS

The Hoh Reservation is located on the Olympic Peninsula of northern Washington, about 28 miles south of Forks in the Hoh River floodplain. It is located within the coastal part of the Olympic National Park. The Hoh River empties into the Pacific and serves as the reservation's northern boundary. The reservation was established in 1893.

PHYSICAL DESCRIPTION

The reservation has approximately one mile of beachfront running from the mouth of the Hoh River south to Ruby Beach. The reservation was logged in 1954, and the second growth should be of commercial value by 2014. Since the mid-1990s, the course of the Hoh River has shifted south, inundating roughly 10 percent of the reservation. With rainfall averaging about 160 inches per year, the reservation is one of the rainiest places in North America. It has experienced major flooding at least 11 times since 1928.

CULTURE AND HISTORY

Ethnically, the Hohs are considered to be a band of the Quileute Tribe, although they are recognized as a separate tribal entity. A few still speak a dialect of Quileute, the only language in the linguistically isolated Chimakuan family.

Despite losses since contact with Europeans, the Hohs are heir to a rich cultural tradition. The tribe continues to conduct naming ceremonies and potlatches, with traditional songs and dances. Seal hunts are celebrated, and the canoe culture is still practiced. The Hohs still depend on the abundant natural resources provided by the Pacific Coast and by the forests that remain in the area. They dip net for smelt on the beaches and harvest perch, crab, and razor and butter clams from the tidelands. They preserve food in smokehouses for later use. Residents dig out canoes for river- or oceangoing use, carve ornamental objects, and weave decorative baskets for sale.

Early interactions with Europeans were few due to lack of an anchorage in the region. In 1855 the Hohs, Quileutes, and (ethnically unrelated) Quinaults signed a treaty with the United States negotiated by M. T. Simmons. Although Simmons apparently had assured the Hohs that they would not have to relocate, the treaty stipulated that the Hoh Tribe be removed to the Quinault Reservation, 10 miles to the south of their home. In 1893, the 443-acre Hoh Reservation was created at the mouth of the Hoh River. Stipulations in this treaty provide the Indians with a choice of residences at either the Hoh or the Quinault reservation. In 1910 some Hohs acquired 80-acre timber allotments on the Quinault Reservation, without a change of residence. The federal government recognized the Hohs as a separate tribe in 1960.

GOVERNMENT

The tribe's traditional structure was based upon a hereditary leadership system in which the chiefs were viewed as workers for the people, rather than as decision makers. In 1969

Hoh Reservation
Federal reservation
Hoh
Jefferson County, Washington

Hoh Indian Tribe
Hoh Tribal Business
   Committee
2464 Lower Hoh Road
Forks, WA 98331
360-374-6582
360-374-6549 Fax

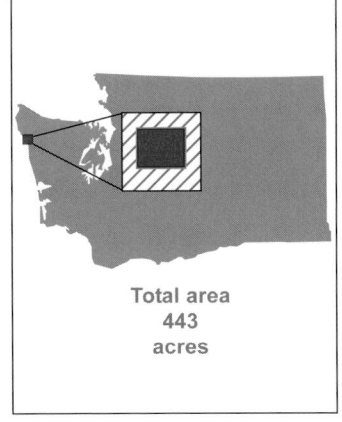

Total area
443
acres

Hoh

the Hoh Tribe adopted and approved a constitution as a result of PL 89-655. The constitution authorized the election of a tribal governing body. The Hoh Tribal Business Committee is the tribe's governing unit. The committee is elected by balloting every two years in November.

ECONOMY

Government as Employer. The tribal government employs 20 tribal members.

Economic Development Projects. Tribal policy focuses on the creation of new, on-reservation jobs.

Gaming. The tribe is researching gaming opportunities and may open a resort and casino.

Fisheries. The Hoh Tribe operates a fish hatchery program.

Services and Retail. Art produced by Hoh craftsmen and women is on sale in the tribal building.

Tourism and Recreation. The reservation is very beautiful; ecotourism could boost its economy. Spectacular views of the Pacific Ocean are seen every day from the shores of the reservation.

INFRASTRUCTURE

Until 1953, when logging on the reservation provided road access, the village was only accessible by foot and canoe. The reservation is three miles from U.S. 101, the major north-south highway in western Washington. Bus service is available 25 miles away, at Forks. There is a commercial airport at Port Angeles, 85 miles from the reservation.

Electricity. A power line was extended to the Hoh Reservation in 1966. The Clallam County Public Utility District supplies electricity.

Water Supply. The U.S. Public Health Service has installed water and sewer facilities for residents. Periodic flooding infests the water supply with parasites such as giardia, and it overloads the septic system causing sewage to overflow.

COMMUNITY FACILITIES AND SERVICES

The Hohs have a tribal community center, which also houses the government offices. A public safety building, which was completed in 2004, houses tribal law enforcement and fisheries enforcement.

Water Supply. The lack of a health facility compels tribal members to seek direct health care from a doctor, dentist, and nurse practitioner one day a week at the health station in Queets or from the Roger Saux Health Center in Taholah. The Hoh Tribe also contracts under Title I of PL 93-638 for a tribal health administrator and a community health representative.

ENVIRONMENTAL CONCERNS

Since the mid-1990s, the course of the Hoh River has shifted south, inundating roughly 10 percent of the reservation. It has experienced major flooding at least 11 times since 1928, with increasingly damaging effects in recent episodes. Logging in the watershed, an increase in the river's speed, and an upriver road stabilization project have aggravated flooding and erosion. The river now heads south into the reservation, threatening 30 homes and 6 other buildings. The Hoh population is growing even as the reservation gets smaller. Relocation may be the tribe's only long-term solution.

Jamestown S'Klallam

Jamestown S'Klallam Tribe of Washington Reservation
Federal reservation
S'Klallam
Clallam County, Washington

Jamestown S'Klallam Tribe of Washington
1033 Old Blyn Highway
Sequim, WA 98382-9342
360-683-1109
360-681-4643 Fax
jamestowntribe.org

LOCATION AND LAND STATUS

The reservation of the Jamestown S'Klallam Tribe of Washington consists of 21 acres east of Sequim, on the Olympic Peninsula, in western Washington State. An additional 9 acres in several small parcels adjacent to or very near the reservation are in federal trust status. The reservation was established upon the recognition of the tribe's status in 1981. The S'Klallam Indians traditionally inhabited the southern shore of the Strait of Juan de Fuca, from the Hoko River to east of Discovery Bay. Upon recognition, one of the tribe's primary goals became, and remains, the acquisition of additional land.

PHYSICAL DESCRIPTION

The Jamestown S'Klallam tribal community is located in Sequim and Blyn on the northern Olympic Peninsula of Washington State, approximately 70 miles northwest of the City of Seattle. The peninsula is somewhat isolated, separated from the Seattle urban area by two bodies of water, one of which must be crossed by ferry. The peninsula is bounded by the Pacific Ocean to the west, the Strait of Juan de Fuca to the north, and by Hood Canal on the east. A large part of the peninsula is densely timbered and undeveloped, and is characterized by rugged mountains, steep slopes, and rain forests. Annual precipitation varies widely on the peninsula, with over 100 inches in the west end, and only 17 inches in the Sequim area.

CULTURE AND HISTORY

"S'Klallam" derives from "nuxsklai'yem," the original name for the S'Klallam people meaning "strong people." The Jamestown S'Klallam Tribe is one of three S'Klallam tribes; the others are the Lower Elwha and the Port Gamble S'Klallam tribes.

The S'Klallams possessed a rich social and religious culture based on the abundant natural resources of the Northwest Coast. Their culture included a class-stratified society, which included nobles, commoners, and slaves. They were considered one of the most aggressive tribes in the western Washington State area, and in the1800s they expanded their territory to the areas of Vancouver Island and Hood Canal. The S'Klallams often returned to their winter village sites, but they frequented other locations in their traditional territory for fishing and resource gathering. The inhabitants hunted game and subsisted on the wealth of shellfish, herring, and salmon. They were craftspeople skilled in woodcarving and basket making, and they fashioned ceremonial masks, serving dishes and utensils, storage boxes from cedar, and woven mats, rope, and clothing from cedar bark.

S'Klallam contact with Europeans began in the 1700s and increased in the 1800s, after the establishment of Hudson's Bay Company trading posts in the Northwest. The S'Klallam people traded at Fort Langley, Fort Nisqually, and Fort Victoria, which were established in the 1820s, 1830s, and 1840s, respectively. The S'Klallam Tribe entered into the Point-No-Point Treaty with the United States in 1855. However, the S'Klallams resisted removal to the reservation of the Tawna people at Skokomish. They remained in most of their traditional areas, and in 1874 the S'Klallams from the Village at Dungeness privately purchased 210 acres of land, establishing Jamestown. The population of Jamestown at the time was around 100. Members of the tribe supported themselves by gardening, farming, fishing, and working in the pulp mills in the surrounding area. In the 1930s, the tribe was given the choice of moving to the reservations purchased for the other two S'Klallam tribes or remaining where they were, unrecognized. They chose to stay on the land they had bought themselves. Tribal members received services from the federal government until 1953 when the government ceased recognizing them as Indians. Beginning in the 1950s, the three S'Klallam tribes combined to litigate land claims and fishing rights. In cases that went to the Supreme Court of the United States, the S'Klallams ultimately regained the fishing rights they had been granted in the Point-No-Point Treaty. Facing increasing problems in the areas of fishing rights, health care, and education due to lack of federal recognition, the tribe began an intensive effort to obtain recognition in 1974 and adopted a constitution in 1975. They received federal recognition on February 10, 1981. Since then, the tribe has pursued land acquisition and economic development, including opening the Seven Cedars Casino in 1995.

GOVERNMENT

The tribe is governed by a five-member tribal council elected to two-year terms on a staggered basis. All enrolled members over the age of 18 years are eligible to vote and run for office. Tribal government programs receive overall direction from the tribal council through the executive director.

Three directors report to the tribe's executive director. The natural resources director supervises fisheries, geographical information systems, watershed issues, and habitat protection. The economic development director supervises business matters and five of the tribe's operating companies. The health and human services director supervises community services (economic services, an elders' program, employment and education counseling, children's services, and family services), health and fiscal services (managed care, health benefits, diabetes program, community health, and the dental clinic), and family support services (chemical dependence counseling, family counseling, and youth programs). The tribe provides services to the estimated 640 Indian people on the northeastern Olympic Peninsula, including tribal members. The administration and planning director supervises self-governance and legal matters, planning, budget and accounting, information systems, administrative services, enrollment, grounds maintenance and development, the library, and general support to the tribal government. The tribal court and the tribal gaming agency director (gaming regulators) report directly to the council. The tribal staff consisted of 120 people as of 2005.

In 1988 the tribe began participating in the BIA Self-Governance Demonstration Project, which allowed the tribe more autonomy and control over BIA funding. The Jamestown S'Klallam Tribe was one of the first seven tribes in the nation to participate in this project. That status continued upon the permanent establishment of self-governance, and almost all federal programs in which the tribe participates are implemented by the tribe under PL-638.

Tribal court services are provided through the Northwest Intertribal Court System. The tribal council appoints a chief judge for a four-year term and associate judges for two-year terms. Otherwise, the tenure of tribal court judges is similar to that of federal judges.

BUSINESS CORPORATION

JKT Development is a wholly owned subsidiary of the tribe. Incorporated in 1983 in the State of Washington, it began as a property development and facilities management corporation with a mission to create a sustainable revenue stream back to the tribe. It expanded its focus during 2001 and now operates in several areas, including construction, information technology and communications services, property management, traffic control services, and consulting services. It provides economic development services to the tribal government with significant planning and implementation. JKT Development is SBA 8(a) and HUB Zone qualified. The tribe expects to diversify and strengthen its existing businesses through this corporation. As of 2004, divisions and subsidiaries included the following:

The economic development division is primarily an internal staff unit of JKT Development, focused on the profitability of existing business enterprises and the acquisition of new opportunities. This unit also assists with the planning and development of the tribe's real estate.

The Jamestown Technology, Communications, and Services Division provides data, communications and traffic control services. It has a training and computer center to help address the tribe's priority to provide employment for tribal members. Communications capabilities include buried and aerial interbuilding, campus, and base-wide fiber, coax, and copper information systems; systems engineering; and technical support. Traffic control capabilities include rural road and major highway work, single and multiple lane closures, road closures and detours, traffic control for stationary and mobile crews, and controlled density fill (CDF) placement. Customers and projects in 2003-2004 included: Pilchuck Contractors (City of Tacoma CLICK Phase V Expansion, University Place, Washington-traffic control services and CDF), Totem Electric (Combined Arms Collective Training Facility, Ft Lewis, Washington-all audio, video, data, telephone, and distress alert systems infrastructure), and McChord AFB (shopping center expansion project-premises wiring).

The JKT Construction Division offers construction services for commercial, government, and private clients. It has a mentoring relationship with PCL Construction Services. Capabilities include demolition, site work, concrete foundations and structural members, framing and dry walling, underground utilities, HVAC, plumbing, electrical work, ceiling and flooring, painting, roofing, and construction management. Customers and projects in 2003-2004 included the U.S. Navy (prime contractor on a U.S. Navy demolition and site restoration project at Bremerton Naval Base, value $852,276). It also worked on three projects at the U.S. Army's Fort Lewis, Washington. Customers and projects of its JKT/PCL joint venture included the U.S. Navy (prime contractor on a design-build project for a small arms training center, Naval Submarine Base Bangor, value $12,523,759) and the U.S. Air Force (prime contractor on an Air Force Academy project, value $6,196,236; awarded a national Indefinite Delivery Indefinite Quantity contract administered by the Air Force Medical Center, Brooks City-Base Texas, value $400,000,000).

The Jamestown Geographic Information Systems (GIS) Division provides staffing and production resources to develop base materials used in GIS, support to the GIS project cycle (data collection, attribute entry, layer creation, analysis, and output), data collection and entry, database development, maintenance and troubleshooting, media storage and security solutions, document conversion, and computer-aided drafting.

The Jamestown homebuilding division builds homes in the Sequim area, targeted toward retirees coming into the area, and it does contract residential remodeling. It also remodels the homes of tribal elders, particularly providing access and

Jamestown S'Klallam

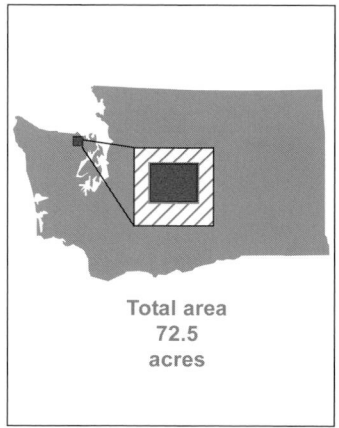

**Total area
72.5
acres**

Total area *(BIA realty, 2004)*
72.5 acres

Tribally owned *(BIA realty, 2004)*
72.5 acres

Population *(Tribal source, 2004)*
559

Total labor force *2000 census*
13

High school graduate or higher
2000 census
100%

Bachelor's degree or higher
2000 census
42.9%

Unemployment rate *2000 census*
0%

Jamestown S'Klallam

safety improvements. Jamestown excavating is a septic system installation and heavy equipment excavation and hauling company. It has done commercial, residential, and public works jobs.

The following are business enterprises that are directly managed under the auspices of the tribal government. 1) HRProfessionals provides integrated human relations software, consulting, training, and recruiting for small and medium-sized businesses. This company is overseen by JKT Development. 2) Jamestown Seafood is a wholesale seafood producer, distributor, and wholesaler engaged in oyster farming and global marketing of locally grown shellfish, and it is a leading supplier of live Northwest shellfish nationwide and in the Far East. It specializes in live geoducks and Dungeness crabs. The company ships up to 400,000 pounds of geoducks per year, with deliveries ranging from New York to Shanghai. 3) Northwest Native Expressions operates a Native art gallery at the Jamestown S'Klallam Tribal Center, and Seven Cedars Art Gallery, which is located in the lobby of the Seven Cedars Casino. Both offer traditional and contemporary art created by Northwest artisans.

ENVIRONMENTAL CONCERNS

The tribe acts to protect its natural resources treaty rights under the Point-No-Point Treaty. The tribe believes it is essential to: ensure the orderly harvest of fish, shellfish, and wildlife resources; provide opportunities for tribal members to derive subsistence and/or livelihood from the harvest of these resources; increase opportunity through restoration, enhancement and scientific study; and reverse the decline of these resources resulting from environmental degradation. Specific projects include bio-assessment, management, and enhancement of shellfish; the Jimmycomelately Creek and Estuary restoration; oversight of the Dungeness River watershed; the Dungeness River Audubon Center; and participation in the Dungeness River Management Team.

ECONOMY

The tribe has seen steady growth in its economy since opening the Seven Cedars Casino in 1995. In addition to the Native art and seafood businesses, the tribe has diversified into construction, information technology and communications, and business human relations services.

Government as Employer. As of 2004, the tribal government employed 120 people.

Gaming. The 55,000-square-foot Seven Cedars Casino is 52 miles west of Seattle. It offers 20 table games, 261 slot machines, keno, and a 600-seat bingo hall. Retail services at the casino include a restaurant, deli, lounge, gift shop, smoke shop, and art gallery. It offers a complementary shuttle bus to and from Port Angeles. It has 251 employees.

Fisheries. The Jamestown S'Klallam Tribe participates in the intertribal Point-No-Point Treaty Council, which helps address treaty fisheries management issues. The tribes possess treaty-assured fishing rights guaranteed by the 1974 Boldt Decision, which allocates 50 percent of the commercial harvest of salmon and shellfish to western Washington treaty tribes. The S'Klallam tribes have taken an active role in resource enhancement and protection. *(See, also, Jamestown Seafood under Business Corporations, above.)*

Construction. See the JKT Construction Division, the Jamestown Homebuilding Division, and Jamestown Excavating under Business Corporations, above.

Real Estate/Commercial Development. The economic development division assists with planning and developing the tribe's real estate. For example, developing the tribe's master plan is a key project for 2005. The master plan will provide a guide for future development of all tribal properties and projects. *(See, also, the Jamestown Homebuilding Division of JKT Development under Business Corporations, above.)*

Services and Retail. There are a restaurant, deli, lounge, gift shop, smoke shop, and art gallery at the casino. The tribal fireworks stand, adjacent to the Seven Cedars Casino, operates from Memorial Day through Labor Day. *(See, also, HRProfessionals and Northwest Native Expressions under Business Corporations, above.)*

Tourism and Recreation. Other than the casino complex, there are no tourism or recreation opportunities on tribal lands.

However, the northern Olympic Peninsula has extensive outdoor sports opportunities, museums, artist colonies, and ecotourism. The Olympic National Park is 922,000 acres of stunning alpine and coastal wilderness. The Olympic National Forest is over 632,000 acres in size and offers a wide variety of camping, trails, and other recreational opportunities. The Dungeness River Audubon Center and Railroad Bridge Park are located in Sequim. The tribe is one of four organizations that operate the center and park. Nearby Port Townsend is one of only three Victorian seaports in the United States on the National Historic Register.

INFRASTRUCTURE

Tribal properties are dependent on the infrastructure of the surrounding communities.

Electricity. The Public Utility District provides electricity.

Water Supply. The tribal government facilities and the Seven Cedars Casino each have large capacity wells that provide potable water. Residents use individual septic tanks and drain fields. Through an annual memorandum of agreement with the Indian Health Service under the Individual Scattered Site Sanitation Facilities Assistance program, the tribe assists members in need of new water or septic systems, irrespective of location. The tribe administers this work, and then Indian Health Service reimburses costs.

Transportation. The reservation is easily accessible by road. Passenger bus and freight services are readily available. Non-scheduled air service is available at nearby Sequim Valley Airport, and scheduled air service from Seattle is available at Port Angeles. Water access is available throughout the area along Puget Sound and the Strait of Juan de Fuca, and ferries run between Port Angeles and Victoria, British Columbia.

The tribe has participated in the BIA Indian Reservation Roads Program since 1995 when an inventory of roads was first established. A comprehensive 20-year tribal transportation plan was produced in 2003. The tribe recognizes the direct relationship between the growth of its land base and economic activities and its need for road construction and maintenance.

COMMUNITY FACILITIES AND SERVICES

The community has a tribal center and a senior center located in Blyn.

Education. Residents use local public schools. The tribal library is located on the tribal center campus. The library's primary focus is Native American materials, including tribal archives.

Health care. Health care is provided through a managed care program, a medical clinic, and a dental clinic. The Jamestown Family Health Clinic opened in 2002 and provides primary care services to over 4,000 patients, including tribal members and other Clallam County residents. It is affiliated with the University of Washington's Department of Family Medicine, and it serves as a rural training center for physicians from the university's Family Medicine Residency Program. The clinic provides preventive care for all ages, geriatric care, obstetrics, chronic disease management, cardiac stress testing, casting, gynecology, minor surgery, and family planning. The dental clinic opened in 2004, providing primary dental services and some specialty care services to tribal members as well as community members. As of 2004, planning was underway to construct a new facility in Sequim to house all tribal health programs. Hospital care is provided at the Olympic Medical Center in Port Angeles.

LOCATION AND LAND STATUS

The Kalispel Reservation spans 7,614 acres in two separate locations in northeastern Washington State. Most of the reservation is along the Pend Oreille (pronounced "pond er-ray") River in the foothills of the Selkirk Range of the Rocky Mountains, about 55 miles north of Spokane. Two hundred and fifty acres are located in the City of Airway Heights near the city limits of Spokane. The tribe also owns four small parcels of habitat lands in Idaho. In 1914, President Woodrow Wilson issued an Executive Order creating the original reservation of 4,629 acres on the east side of the Pend Oreille River in a narrow strip nine miles long between the river and the Colville National Forest. The reservation is located within the original territory of the Lower Kalispel Band of the Kalispel Indians. This band resisted relocation to established reservations. The land it finally received in 1914 was poor, but at least it was along the river that was the heart of its culture. In 1924, much of the reservation was allotted, but only into 40-acre parcels, one-fourth the size of the allotments on other reservations. Over the years, only one 40-acre allotment has been lost to non-Indian ownership. Beginning in 1977, the tribe acquired 240 acres on the west side of the river near the Town of Cusick, and in 1995 it acquired the 440-acre Flying Goose Ranch north of the reservation. Over the years from 1996 through 2003, the tribe was granted an additional 1,850 acres of land on the east side of the river to be protected as natural habitat. In 1995, the tribe purchased 40 acres of commercial property in Airway Heights, augmented in 2003 by the purchase of an additional 250 acres of adjacent property. In 1996, the BIA designated the first 40 acres in Airway Heights as reservation land , which led to the development of the tribe's Northern Quest Casino. The tribe intends to acquire more land adjacent to the core territory east of the river and in strategic development and resource locations west of the river.

PHYSICAL DESCRIPTION

The Pend Oreille County land is primarily wooded flood plain and hillsides, surrounded by national forest. It includes 43 acres of wetlands. The daily average temperature ranges between 32°F and 90°F. Average annual precipitation is 28 inches.

CULTURE AND HISTORY

The Kalispel, or Pend d'Oreille, Indians, called "river and lake paddlers" or "camas people" by other tribes, were seminomadic hunters, gatherers, and fishermen. The camas is a relative of the onion that grows in profusion along the Pend Oreille River and was a staple of the Kalispel diet. The Kalispels were given the name Pend d'Oreille ("earring") by the French because of their custom of wearing shell earrings. The Lower Kalispels occupied a 200-mile-long territory along the Pend Oreille River from present-day Newport to across the Canadian border. This is the band from which the present-day Kalispels descend.

The Kalispel Indians possess a rich culture derived primarily from their relationship with nature, in particular the Pend Oreille River. Traditionally, all aspects of their tribal life centered on the river. They used it for commerce and social purposes, built their villages beside it, and dug camas root in its floodplain. Their historic culture was similar to that of the Spokane and other tribes of the Plateau area. Their language belongs to the Salishan branch of the Algonquian-Wakashan linguistic stock.

Roman Catholic priests began working with the Kalispels in 1844. In 1855, the Upper Kalispels gave up their lands and moved to a reservation in Montana. The Lower Kalispels avoided participating in various treaties with the federal government, which intended to move them to established reservations. Without a treaty, however, the tribe had no legal protection for its land, and it saw the land taken by non-Indian settlers under state and federal homestead laws. The tribe's membership dropped from an estimate of 3,000 precontact to fewer than 400 by 1875 and 100 by 1911. In 1914 the tribe received its reservation. In 1960, the tribe received approximately $3 million for loss of its aboriginal lands. In 1977 the tribe began a program of land acquisition to enhance its prospects for economic development. This culminated in opening the Northern Quest Casino in Airway Heights in 2000.

GOVERNMENT

The tribe is organized under the 1934 Indian Reorganization Act, and it ratified its constitution, bylaws, and corporate charter in 1938. The constitution and bylaws were revised in July 1967. The tribal government is led by a five-member council whose members are elected to staggered three-year terms. The council has a chair, a vice-chair, a secretary, and two members. Decisions are made by majority vote, and the chairman votes only if there is a tie among the other members.

Administration and accounting departments manage daily operations, budgets, and performs general accounting. The executive committee works to preserve the Kalispel language, oversees the Camas Institute, and identifies new business opportunities with the development office. The department of community planning and development develops new business opportunities for the tribe, including the Kalispel Commerce Park in Airway Heights. Public safety includes four full-time police officers, seven reserve offices, and the tribal court. The natural resource department manages the reservation's fisheries, wildlife, water, and other natural resources; operates the only warm water bass hatchery in the region; provides archeological protection, language preservation, history, and archive preservation; provides education on water, forestry, fisheries, wildlife, logging, and farming for students and adults; issues waterfowl hunting and fishing permits; and is developing a 16,000-square-foot interpretive center that will provide educational facilities with information about the reservation's landscape, including animal and bird habitat, current restoration activities, a language lab, classrooms, and eventually the storage and display of tribal artifacts. Community development works on infrastructure and support for new enterprises, and coordinates with the HUD-funded Kalispel Housing Development Program. The social services department operates an elders program (meals, transportation, and other support), a child welfare program, mental health and chemical dependency counseling, community health services (education, prevention, and referral), post-inpatient counseling for those recovering from chemical dependency, outreach services including financial assistance, safety checks, and youth services.

The State of Washington does not recognize law enforcement by tribal jurisdictions. The tribe has cross-jurisdictional agreements with Pend Oreille County and the City of Airway Heights, and it has an agreement with Spokane County under review as of 2004.

Kalispel Reservation
Federal reservation
Kalispel
Pend Oreille and Spokane counties, Washington

Kalispel Council
P.O. Box 39
Usk, WA 99180-0039
   509-445-1147
   509-445-1705 Fax
   kalispeltribe.com

Total area (BIA realty, 2004)
5,011.07 acres

Total area (Tribal source, 2004)
7,614 acres

Federal trust (BIA realty, 2004)
40 acres

Tribally owned (BIA realty, 2004)
2,185.89 acres

Individually owned
(BIA realty, 2004)
2,785.18 acres

Population 2000 census
206

Tribal enrollment (BIA, 2001)
329

Tribal enrollment
(Tribal source, 2004)
364

Total labor force 2000 census
63

Total labor force (Tribal source, 2004)
90

High school graduate or higher
2000 census
80%

Bachelor's degree or higher
2000 census
0%

Unemployment rate 2000 census
28.6%

Unemployment rate
(BIA labor report, 2001)
47%

Per capita income 2000 census
$6,973

Kalispel

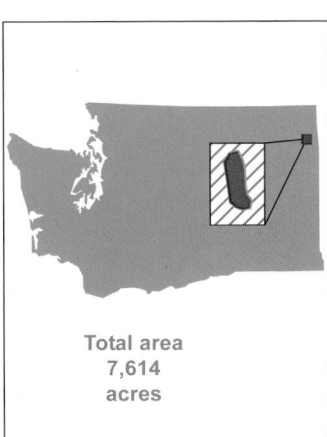

Total area
7,614
acres

TRI-WA-001

TRI-WA-002

TRI-WA-003

TRI-WA-001 Entering the Kalispel Indian Reservation along Highway 41

TRI-WA-002 Kalispel Pow Wow facilities & ceremonial grounds

TRI-WA-003 Buffalo herd in the valley across from Kalispel's Pow Wow grounds

The tribe operates the community health representatives, mental health, and substance abuse programs under a PL 93-638 Title I contract with Indian Health Service.

The tribal court interprets laws on the reservation and has a staff of 14, including 2 judges, a director, a staff attorney, 3 peacemakers, an alternate peacemaker, a clerk, a paralegal, a domestic violence advocate, a public defender, a probation officer, and a court administrator.

The tribe does not have a business corporation. Operational decisions for tribal businesses are made by the executive committee (administrative director, legal officer, director of public and governmental affairs, president of the Camas Institute, and business committee members).

ECONOMY

Government as Employer. As of 2004, the tribe employed 1,050 people, including casino employees.

Agriculture and Livestock. The tribe has about 100 head of buffalo that provide meat for elders, production, and sales. The agricultural enterprise also has 400 acres used for grazing and hay production. During summer months, Kalispel Agricultural Enterprises hires youth for cropping hay and fencing the land. Plans are currently underway to expand the profits by beginning a custom meat-cutting and wrapping operation in the tribe's Commerce Park.

Gaming. Northern Quest Casino helps to provide economic development for the Kalispel Tribe, increases employment opportunities for tribal and community members, and ensures financial support for the Camas Institute. In 1995, the tribe purchased 40 acres of land in the City of Airway Heights adjacent to the Spokane Racetrack, and it successfully petitioned to have it converted to trust land. Opened in December 2000, the casino has 1,000 video slot gaming devices, 30 table games, keno, a poker room, a 150-seat buffet, a tour bus reception area, valet parking, a gift shop, and 2 entertainment and meeting venues. Plans include building a hotel. The casino employs more than 936 people.

Manufacturing. Kalispel Case Line is a manufacturing enterprise that produces foam-lined aluminum cases for electronic instruments, cameras, rifles, pistols, and custom use. It was established in 1985 and is certified with the State of Washington as a minority business. Recent profits have been used to market and expand business opportunities. As of 2004, it employed eight people.

Industrial Parks. The reservation maintains a small industrial site on the west side of the Pend Oreille River on which two area businesses are located. The site has convenient access to a state highway, as well as a railroad line. Electrical hookups and water and sewage service are available.

The tribe plans to develop its acreage in Airway Heights into a business park that will develop Indian-owned and non-Indian-owned business ventures. In conjunction with the development of the business park, the tribe also plans to expand the Camas Institute.

Services and Retail. Kalispel Day Care is a tribe-owned child care business licensed for 15 children; it is currently the only state-licensed child care facility in Pend Oreille County, and it is open to everyone. As of 2004 it employed two full-time, two part-time, and two on-call child care providers providing care for children ages 1?12.

Tourism and Recreation. Annual events include a Fourth of July celebration open to the public, an Indian powwow held the first weekend in August, and an outdoor opera in August. The Manresa Grotto is a 60-foot-long natural rock shelter located on the reservation. The Kalispels have held Catholic religious services in the cave since the mid-1800s.

INFRASTRUCTURE

U.S. Highway 2, State Route 211, and scenic Highway 20 provide the primary road access to the reservation.

Electricity. The Pend Oreille County Public Utility District supplies electric power.

Water Supply. A community water system serves most residences and the tribal offices. The piped water system obtains its water from the Town of Cusick Water System under contract. Most residences have individual septic systems; seven residences and the tribal offices are on a community lagoon system.

Transportation. The nearest commercial air service is in Spokane, about 60 miles from the reservation. Commercial truck lines serve the reservation directly, as does a rail freight line, which traverses tribal lands. Bus service is available in Newport, 19 miles east of the reservation. The Pend Oreille River is navigable to small boats.

Telecommunications. Pend Oreille Telephone serves the area. The Cusick area offers three Internet service providers. Citrix provides a tribal network.

COMMUNITY FACILITIES AND SERVICES

The tribe maintains a community center and tribal headquarters at Usk. A Wellness Center adjacent to tribal administrative offices will be built in 2005.

The tribe's Camas Institute is an unusual educational and service center made possible by profits from the casino. It is located on the Airway Heights property. Begun in February 2001, the institute uses a holistic approach to deal with tribal members' health, financial, spiritual, cultural, and academic needs. The institute employs 30 people, including those working at the learning center on the reservation. The institute provides counseling for mental health, problem gambling, and chemical dependency, exporting prevention programs to area high schools. "Equity Assurance" is a financial supplement to college aid awards and scholarships, providing for unmet student needs (tuition, books and fees, on-campus room and board or off-campus housing, some transportation costs, student child care, and disability related expenses). The institute also provides skills assessments, life coaching, financial aid workshops and assistance, college information, budget counseling, and a personal computer for each Equity Assurance program participant. Other education and career development programs include distance learning, reading tutoring for children and adults-available to all students in the Cusick School District-GED preparation, employment readiness training, placement assistance, and partnerships with area companies to provide on-the-job training.

Education. Primary and secondary students attend the Cusick Public Schools, located about seven miles from the reservation. Tribe members make up 23 percent of the district's students.

Health Care. In 1995 the tribe remodeled a facility that accommodates the mental health, community outreach and the Indian child welfare social workers. The elderly nutrition and substance abuse programs are located in the tribal community hall. Tribal community health representatives are located in the tribal administrative office. The tribe operates the community health representative, mental health, and substance abuse programs under a PL 93-638 Title I contract with Indian Health Service. A Pend Oreille County Health Nurse is contracted to provide WIC services. There is no on-site primary care available so tribal members must go to the Indian Health Service clinic at Wellpinit. Private care can sometimes be obtained through the Contract Health Services Program operated by Indian Health Service through the Wellpinit Service Unit. The Newport Community Hospital, about 20 miles from the reservation, is a 24-bed facility with trauma level 4 certification, radiology, general surgery, and complete obstetric services.

ENVIRONMENTAL CONCERNS

The tribe is highly concerned about pollution in the Pend Oreille River. The tribe prepared a Non Point Source Assessment Report in 2000 that described sources of pollution on the reservation and the surrounding original homeland. Water sources in the area generally exceed water quality standards in ammonia, pH, dissolved oxygen, and phosphorus. Of particular concern is the impact of area dams on water quality.

The tribe is actively acquiring and protecting habitat lands in its traditional area. Remnant populations of bull trout and westslope cutthroat trout live in tributaries of the Pend Oreille River. The fish are historically important to the tribe. The bull trout was listed as threatened under the Endangered Species Act as of 2000. The westslope cutthroat trout is a Washington State priority species and species of concern. The tribe is active in watershed planning and restoration efforts.

Kalispel

TRI-WA-004

TRI-WA-004 Northern Quest Casino, a Kalispel Casino in Airway Heights, WA (50 miles from Usk, WA)

Lower Elwha

LOCATION AND LAND STATUS

The Lower Elwha Reservation spans 446 noncontiguous acres at the mouth of the Elwha River, on northwestern Washington's Olympic Peninsula. The reservation is located about 10 miles from the Town of Port Angeles, directly on the Strait of Juan de Fuca and south of Vancouver Island, British Columbia.

Under the Treaty of Point-No-Point of 1855, the Klallam Tribe was entitled to share a small reservation with its traditional enemies, the Skokomish Tribe. Unsurprisingly, most Klallams were reluctant to settle there, opting instead to return to the rivers, shorelines, and burial sites of their ancestors. After funds became available through the 1934 Indian Reorganization Act, the federal government purchased 372 acres of farmland and assigned it to the 14 homeless Klallam families. On January 19, 1968, the tribe received federal recognition and this land was formally established as the Lower Elwha Reservation.

PHYSICAL DESCRIPTION

The region is hilly to mountainous with spectacular coastlines and heavily forested lands. The original reservation is located on the alluvial plain at the mouth of the Elwha River, while the Heights Community of the Lower Elwha Reservation is located on the glacial till bluffs west of the river. The Valley Community has a 1.5 mile long flood control levee constructed in 1989 to help protect against annual flooding.

CULTURE AND HISTORY

The Klallam Tribe is part of the Coast Salish linguistic family. Klallam means "strong people." The tribe has traditionally occupied the southern shores of the Strait of Juan de Fuca, from the Hoko River to Discovery Bay in northwestern Washington. Euro-American contact with the tribe began in 1790 after the Spanish established Hudsons Bay trading posts in the area. The Klallams met the explorer Manuel Quimper while he visited Freshwater Bay. In the 1860s Port Angeles as well as other towns, were created when settlers descended upon the Lower Elwha Valley. Settlers began arriving in the lower Elwha valley in the 1860s. Port Angeles and other towns were established at about the same time. These settlers forced many Klallam from their traditional homesites. Because the Klallam were not considered citizens of the United States the government did not allow them title to their ancestral homelands. The Indian Homestead Act was enacted in 1884, and ten Klallam families had received 13,000 acres by 1894. By 1894 ten Klallam families received 1,300 acres land under the Indian Homestead Act (1884). Some of this acreage has become part of the Lower Elwha Reservation or is held by

Lower Elwha Reservation
Federal reservation
Klallam
Clallam County, Washington

Lower Elwha Klallam Tribe
2851 Lower Elwha Road
Port Angeles, WA 98363
  360-452-8471
  360-452-3428 Fax

Lower Elwha

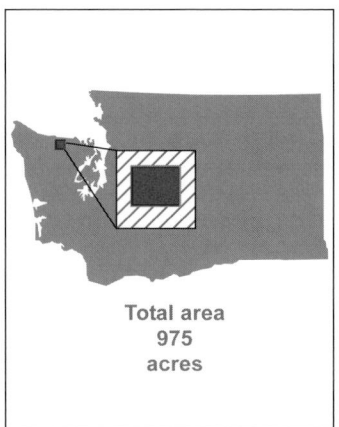

**Total area
975
acres**

Total area *(BIA realty, 2004)*
427.48 acres

Total area *(Tribal source, 2005)*
975 acres

Tribally owned *(BIA realty, 2004)*
427.48 acres

Population *2000 census*
260

Population *(Tribal source, 2005)*
545

Tribal enrollment
(BIA labor report, 2001)
984

Tribal enrollment
(Tribal source, 2005)
857

Total labor force *2000 census*
151

Total labor force
(BIA labor report, 2001)
814

High school graduate or higher
2000 census
69.4%

Bachelor's degree or higher
2000 census
2.2%

Unemployment rate *2000 census*
14.5%

Unemployment rate
(BIA labor report, 2001)
63%

Per capita income *2000 census*
$8,742

descendents of the original homesteaders as public domain allotments. After the 1934 Indian Reorganization Act, the federal government purchased tracts of land at the mouth of the Elwha River and at Port Gamble. In 1968 land on the Elwha River was used to create the Lower Elwha Reservation.

During the 1950s, the tribe was involved in a land claims suit against the United States, from which all three bands of the Klallam Tribe were eventually awarded about $386,000 in 1970. The Klallam Tribe possesses guaranteed fishing rights as a result of the 1974 Boldt Decision, which allocated 50 percent of the commercial salmon harvest to western Washington treaty tribes (the salmon runs had been largely decimated between 1910 and 1926 by the construction of the Elwha and Glines Canyon dams). The Boldt Decision also allows tribes some say over outside development activities that might jeopardize the salmon runs. To this end, the tribes have assumed an active role in protecting and enhancing their natural resources. Additionally, the 1992 Elwha River Ecosystem and Fisheries Restoration Act was designed to fully restore the river's ecosystem and native fisheries.

GOVERNMENT

The reservation is governed by the elected Lower Elwha Tribal Community Council. A tribal constitution, established under provisions of the 1934 Indian Reorganization Act, was adopted on May 6, 1968. The council elects five of its members to three-year terms on the tribal business committee.

Tribal government programs include human resources, law enforcement, Head Start, housing, finance and accounting, tribal court, human resources, economic development, fisheries, including Lower Elwha hatchery and fish management, environmental quality, planning, and human services. Programs offered by human services include: CHR, senior's nutrition, chemical dependency, Lower Elwha clinic and dental, TANIF, Indian child welfare.

ECONOMY

Tribally owned enterprises in the retail and fishing industries contribute to the tribal economy.

Government as Employer. The tribal government employs approximately 169 people through administrative, law enforcement, health, human services, environmental, and fisheries programs.

Economic Development Projects. The tribe's economic development strategic plan considers ecotourism to be the primary avenue for tribal economic development. The tribe will be able to better utilize their natural resources for ecotourism when the Elwha Dam is removed and the ecosystem is restored. The tribe will be able to offer visitors a unique perspective on not only this project itself, but also the affect on cultural aspects of the tribe. The tribe will gain revenue through offering food, lodging, and shopping to these visitors. The tribe anticipates offering Native art works for sale to the tourists as well.

Forestry. Though the region surrounding the reservation has traditionally been a major timber-producing area, this industry has a negligible economic impact on the Lower Elwha economy. It actually has had a negative environmental impact; according to the tribe, overharvesting of timber has muddied the Elwha River and other streams in the usual and accustomed fishing area reducing viability for salmon runs.

Gaming. The tribe has gained some revenue from their gaming compact by leasing slot machines to tribes throughout the northwest who participate in casino enterprises.

Fisheries. The Lower Elwha Klallam Tribe operates salmon hatcheries and remains quite active in the region's commercial fishing industry, which primarily targets salmon, crab, and other shellfish. A salmon hatchery employs seven tribal members. The tribe also owns a commercial fishing enterprise called the Elwha Fish Company, this company employs many tribal families. Fishery development and enhancement projects have been funded in the past through federal, state, and regional grants. The fishery department and stream restoration crew for the tribe have created a name for themselves with their knowledge and skill in implementing habitat projects.

Construction. The tribal housing authority serves as contractor for the construction of homes and other structures on the reservation. In 1994, it constructed 43 homes and an office building, and another 20 homes were slated for construction in 1995.

Services and Retail. The tribe owns and operates a smoke shop, which employs five people.

Tourism and Recreation. Though the reservation itself offers little in the way of facilities for visitors, nearby Port Angeles is a bustling tourist community. Outdoor activities are extremely popular in the area, including fishing and boating. The spectacular Olympic National Park boasts hiking, camping, mountain climbing, and skiing.

INFRASTRUCTURE

As country roads are the primary access roads to the reservation at this time, the tribe is trying to create alternative routes which will decrease emergency vehicle response time, ease school bus traffic, and provide all weather alternatives for emergency evacuation.

Electricity. The Clallam County Public Utility District provides electricity.

Water Supply. The tribe maintains its own water system, while individual septic systems and drain fields provide sewage services. Currently this system is fine, but will be inadequate when the removal of the Elwha Dams in 2008 causes the groundwater to rise. The tribe is trying to negotiate for wastewater conveyed to the City of Port Angeles' system to be accepted for treatment.

Transportation. Commercial truck lines also serve the reservation directly. Water based transportation is not available to the Lower Elwha Reservation, due to the extensive wave action in the area. However, small boats are used for seasonal fishing on the Elwha River.

COMMUNITY FACILITIES AND SERVICES

The tribal center houses administrative offices, a community gym, a computer lab, a dining room, a police department, and a tribal court. The tribe operates a child care facility, housing office, human services facility, Head Start preschool. The tribe also provides cultural and recreation programs for tribal youth and is an active participant in the annual drug and alcohol free Tribal Journeys, which brings canoes from all over the Pacific Northwest, British Columbia, and Canada to a different tribal homeland each summer.

The tribe is active in documenting, preserving, and restoring the indigenous language. It has adopted a written language, recorded and transcribed about 1,000 hours of spoken Klallam, and taught the language to tribal members. Klallam language is taught in the Port Angeles public school system and is a for-credit language option at the Port Angeles High School.

Education. Tribal youth attend local public schools. The tribe operates a Head Start program and a child care center.

Health Care. The tribe maintains a 1,200 square foot clinic that provides medical services, and a 450-square-foot facility that provides mental health and social services. Practitioners include a family practice physician and a dentist. The Lower Elwha Health Clinic, which is operated by a nurse practitioner, is currently 2,600 square feet, but will expand to 15,000 square feet in 2005. At that time they will also begin offering dental and mental health services. The Klallam Counseling Services in the City of Port Angeles is also operated by the tribe, and offers treatment of chemical dependency to Native and non-Native clients. The tribe contracts a number of health services from Indian Health Service, including medical, dental, community health nurse, community health representative, chemical dependency, mental health, and contract health programs. There is also a hospital in Port Angeles.

ENVIRONMENTAL CONCERNS

The tribe is concerned with preserving the Elwha River and its fish population. Development of the Elwha and Glines Canyon dams in the early twentieth century disrupted the ecosystem of the river and its watershed. Congress passed the Elwha River Ecosystem and Fisheries Restoration Act in 1992, providing federal support for restoration initiatives. The tribe is pushing for removal of the dams and restoration of the original ecosystem. The United States purchased the Elwha Dams in 2000 and is scheduled to remove them in 2008.

Lummi

LOCATION AND LAND STATUS

The Lummi Reservation is located in northwest Washington, seven miles northwest of the City of Bellingham, 100 miles north of Seattle, and about 50 miles south of Vancouver, B.C. The reservation consists of a peninsula, which forms Lummi Bay on the west and Bellingham Bay on the east; a smaller peninsula; and a 1,000-acre island off the tip of the main peninsula, named Portage Island. In total, the reservation area spans approximately 13,000 acres of upland area and 8,000 acres of tidelands. About 8,000 acres are currently under Indian control, the majority being allotted. The Point Elliot Treaty of 1855 marked the creation of the Lummi Reservation. In 1873, by Executive Order, certain portions of the treaty boundary were redrawn, which altered the size of the reservation.

In 2004 a piece of land was purchased by the tribe for commercial development. This three-acre piece of property is currently undeveloped but is located adjacent to the I-5 corridor, two miles east of the reservation. The tribe is having it put into trust status.

CULTURE AND HISTORY

Before the Treaty of Point Elliot and the subsequent establishment of the Lummi Reservation, the Lummis occupied the northern San Juan Islands and the adjacent mainland from Bellingham Bay to Point Roberts. Salmon was the primary source of food. Many tribal ceremonies, beliefs, and community activities are centered around salmon. The western red cedar also played a significant role in the tribe's material and spiritual life, serving as building material for sacred longhouses, utensils, and tools. During this time, tribal members made frequent visits to Hudson's Bay Company trading posts.

The tribe's history during the twentieth century is inexorably tied to its fishing-centered economy and treaty fishing rights issues. After the 1855 treaty, the federal government expected the tribe to adopt agriculture as its primary means of subsistence. The Lummis, however, continued to travel to off-reservation sites for fishing and gathering, particularly to their traditional reef-net locations. As it turned out, the tribe's reef-net fishing territory placed it at the epicenter of the region's budding commercial salmon fishing industry. Gradually, organized commercial interests squeezed the Lummis out of the salmon industry by appropriating their prime net locations. This development led to a series of lawsuits by the tribe, claiming a violation of its treaty-guaranteed fishing rights. The government was finally ordered to pay $57,000 in 1970, a settlement the Lummis rejected as insultingly inadequate. In 1974 they participated in another lawsuit over treaty fishing rights, this time against the State of Washington. The suit culminated in a court-ordered allocation of the state's commercial salmon harvest. In 1988 the tribe was involved in a federal ruling, which held that income generated from a treaty right is not subject to federal taxation.

GOVERNMENT

The Lummi Nation operates under a constitution approved on April 10, 1970, by the Assistant Commissioner of Indian Affairs. The Lummi Nation became self-governing under congressional legislation in 1994. It is not organized under the 1934 Indian Reorganization Act. The governing body is the Lummi Indian Business Council (LIBC), which consists of 11 members elected to three-year staggered terms by the general council. The general council is composed of all the tribe's enrolled adult members. The business council organizes on a yearly basis and elects a chairman, vice-chairman, secretary, and treasurer.

Government departments include general administration, education, law and justice, health, social services, housing, natural resources, planning, economic development, public safety, veterans, employment training, and tribal employment rights.

The tribe operates its own police department, reservation attorney's office, records and archives, and tribal court. The tribal court system employs two full time judges, three prosecutors, a public defender, and a court clerk. Since 1990, when self-governance went into effect, this team has been enforcing over 30 codes of tribal law. In 2004 a child support enforcement program was also put into place. To assist in this process the tribe has a law enforcement and public safety department, which includes a police chief, eight full-time police officers, and five natural resource protection and enforcement officers. The natural resource officers control use of 8,000 acres of tribal tidelands and marine resources.

The tribe has created a company, the Lummi Commercial Company, as a holding company for the tribe's economic activities. The company is lead by a general manager, is governed by its own charter and bylaws, and is supervised by a LIBC appointed board.

Lummi Reservation
Federal reservation
Lummi
Whatcom County, Washington

Lummi Indian Nation
2616 Kwina Road
Bellingham, WA 98226
360-384-1489
360-380-1850 Fax

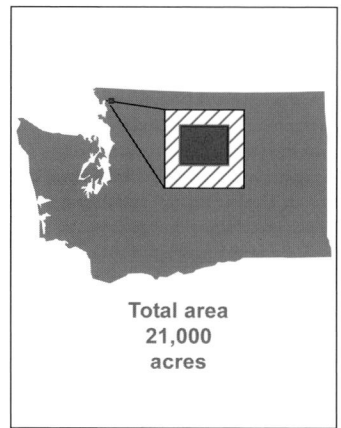

Total area
21,000
acres

Lummi

Total area *(BIA realty, 2004)*
8,011.41 acres

Total area *(Tribal source, 2004)*
21,000 acres

Tribally owned *(BIA realty, 2004)*
1,085.70 acres

Individually owned
(BIA realty, 2004)
6,925.71 acres

Total population
(Tribal survey, 2003)
4,193

Tribal enrollment
(Tribal survey, 2003)
4,881

Total labor force *2000 census*
1,844

Total labor force *(BIA, 2001)*
2,394

High school graduate or higher
2000 census
81.3%

Bachelor's degree or higher
2000 census
18.3%

Unemployment rate *2000 census*
11.9%

Unemployment rate
(Tribal survey, 2003)
32%

Per capita income *2000 census*
$17,669

In 2002 the Lummi Development Authority (LDA) was created to replace the economic development commission. The LDA's mission is to expand and strengthen the economic base of the reservation by planning and implementing businesses, which will not only have a positive economic effect but a social one as well.

ECONOMY

In late 2003 the LDA's economic development department made its first attempt to analyze the structure of and to quantify the Lummi Nation's on-reservation economy, as represented by its gross domestic product, or GDP (the sum total of all goods and services produced by tribal members, enterprises, and tribally owned commercial operations, plus exports from minus imports onto the reservation). It was found that, as is the case with most other economies in transition, the Lummi economy consists of both a formal and an informal sector.

Outputs by the formal sector (LIBC government, tribal corporations, gaming, private productive activities including marine harvesting, construction, educational, and social services) can be measured over time, while the extensive informal sector consists of both traditional and nontraditional productive activities which are not formally recorded and therefore cannot be accurately measured. It is difficult to calculate market prices for goods and services produced and provided as part of the potlatch economy, which often includes unpaid family labor, free goods and commodities, elements of barter trade, and goods and services produced under conditions of zero opportunity costs. Yet in the latter case, careful, warranted, and popularly supported assumptions were made and estimates developed based on shadow prices. (Shadow pricing is designed to get over the problem where prices of goods and services either don't exist or are not set in a freely competitive market, but treating them as if they were.)

When all these elements were considered, the Lummi Reservation's 2002 GDP was calculated at $52.61 million. This included a negative trade balance (exports minus imports) between the reservation and the off-reservation community at-large of $51.9 million. If one adds to this the (conservatively estimated) $25 million in personal and business incomes earned on the reservation but which annually leave the reservation because there is virtually nothing on which to spend them nor any place at which to bank them, the negative trade balance is increased to $77 million.

This argues strongly for establishing a basic business, services, and retail infrastructure on the reservation so that some of this money can stay home and have the downstream benefits accrue locally through the multiplier effect. Currently each dollar spent off the reservation has a zero multiplier effect because once it leaves it no longer benefits the on-reservation economy. It does not generate further economic growth on the reservation.

Government as Employer. The LIBC is the largest single employer on the reservation-and the tenth largest in Whatcom County. In 2004 it employed 630 people at all levels of the organization and throughout its various departments. The Indian Health Service Clinic employed an additional 40 people, while the Northwest Indian College faculty and staff consisted of another approximately 100 full-time employees.

Economic Development Projects. The tribe's economic development goal is to promote on-reservation private entrepreneurial activities, and to develop economically sound public sector projects that will provide employment, living wage family incomes, enhance tribal programs and services, and further the tribe in its goal of attaining self-sufficiency.

Proposed projects include: enhancing technological opportunities, developing a shellfish processing and packaging venture, bridging the digital divide, providing selected marine terminal services, developing the Silver Reef Casino complex further, boat manufacturing, developing the Portage Bay Construction Company further, establishing a sports and entertainment complex, operating a pharmaceuticals mail order and distribution company, developing a 7,000-acre business park, and establishing a nascent aqua-tourism industry. The tribe is actively investigating the possibility of completing some of these projects in the next few years; others will take a medium- to long-term implementation horizon. The tribe is also preparing an investment guide to provide potential investors with vital information about the opportunities on the reservation and with tribal ventures.

Agriculture and Livestock. The region surrounding the reservation has traditionally supported a number of agricultural enterprises. However, the Lummis pride themselves on being a fishing and marine-harvesting tribe, and they have firmly rejected agricultural pursuits imposed upon them from the outside. They also do not keep cattle.

Forestry. The reservation forest consists mostly of scattered stands of Douglas fir, cedar, alder, maple, and hemlock. A reforestation program is currently replanting most of the unproductive forest lands at a rate of about 75 acres per year. As for local employment in the timber industry, the Georgia-Pacific pulp mill in Bellingham, which used to employ a number of Lummi tribal members, sharply cut back on its papermaking in 2000, and it is planning to completely cease operations in 2005. Its former extensive forest products-processing site on Bellingham Bay is scheduled for environmental cleanup and subsequent commercial and recreational redevelopment over the next few decades. The Lummi Nation plans to be an active participant in restoring and restructuring this part of its tribal "usual and accustomed" economic zone.

Gaming. The tribe owns and operates the Silver Reef Casino in Ferndale, Washington. The casino offers 550 slots/VLTS, 12 table games, and 3 restaurants. It employs 320 people. Expansions in 2004 included the addition of an entertainment venue, a cocktail bar, an indoor terrace, a new table game pit, a nonsmoking area, and over 300 parking spaces. Groundbreaking ceremonies for the second expansion phase, including a six-story hotel, took place in January 2005, with completion anticipated sometime during 2006.

Fisheries. The tribe owns the LIBC Aquaculture Facility. It currently commercially sells oyster and clam seeds harvested from the tribal hatchery. The aquaculture facility is planning to expand its operations into growing shellfish to maturity and further processing these products for local, regional, and international marketing.

The tribal fishing fleet, although much reduced from what it was 20 years ago, still consists of 60 skiffs, 300 gill-netters, and 12 purse-seiners. The tribe operates both a salmon and a shellfish hatchery, which, in part, repopulate area waters and tidelands.

At least 550 independent Lummi operators within reservation boundaries make their livings solely through marine harvesting. Operations at the fish processing plant have been reduced to the function of a crab-buying station. However, plans are taking place to refurbish both building and equipment and make it into the main value-added shellfish processing and packaging center. Additionally, there are several privately owned fish- buying companies on the reservation that employ as many as 100 people at any given time.

Manufacturing. The tribe currently operates no manufacturing plants. However, there is a small custom furniture business, as well as other small, privately owned manufacturing businesses located on the reservation. In addition, tribal members find manufacturing employment in area plants that include a plastics manufacturer, an aircraft interiors plant, two oil refineries, and an aluminum smelter and processing facility. The tribe also owns a free trade zone, which is not utilized at present.

Services and Retail. The tribe owns and operates two minimart and gas station combinations, a boat launch, and a boat storage facility on the reservation. Aside from the various seafood-related businesses, there are several privately owned and operated small business firms on the reservation that provide personal and company services to clients on and off the reservation.

*Tourism and Recreation.*The reservation is in a region extremely popular with visitors, given its scenic location and geological features including rock outcrops, beachheads, beaches, ponds, access to marine waters, and forests, which produce excellent opportunities for fishing, boating, and hiking.

The tribe hosts a number of special events such as the Lummi Stommish Water Festival. This is held during the second or third week of June and features canoe races, dances, arts and crafts, and salmon barbecues.

INFRASTRUCTURE
I-5 runs north-south two miles from reservation boundaries, while State Highway 540 crosses the reservation east-west.

Electricity. Puget Power of Washington provides electricity to the reservation.

Fuel. The reservation is currently not connected to a natural gas power source. Instead, propane gas is provided commercially and is sold at various outlets around the reservation.

Water Supply. Community wells are the primary source of water to the reservation, with the City of Bellingham's municipal system supplying supplementary amounts on an as-needed basis. The Lummi Sewer District furnishes on-reservation sewer services. Two private contractors handle solid waste disposal.

Transportation. Commercial air, bus, and train services are all available in Bellingham, five miles from the reservation. Commercial truck lines serve the reservation directly. Bellingham also features a modern deep-water harbor. The tribe maintains its fleet of fishing vessels on the reservation as well as at various locations in and around Bellingham, Portage, and Lummi bays.

COMMUNITY FACILITIES AND SERVICES
The tribal community center, the Wexliem Center, is where many community and social activities are held. The Little Bear Creek retirement home and assisted facility, home to many of the tribe's seniors, is located near the center.

Education. The tribe maintains the Lummi School District on the reservation. A new $25 million K-12 school funded by the BIA opened in the fall of 2004 at Gooseberry Point. The facilities include computer labs, science labs, language labs, music and chorale practice rooms, a woodcarving and craft shop, and a performance stage. There are also residential quarters, a Head Start facility, a transportation and maintenance facility, and an aquaculture and greenhouse facility. The school serves over 750 tribal youth. The tribe received a grant of over $700,000 from the U.S. Department of Education, and it intends to use the funds to prepare high school students for higher education.

The Northwest Indian College is located on the reservation and offers tribal and non-tribal members a postsecondary education up to the associate degree (two-year) level.

Health Care. The tribe operates an ambulatory direct care facility contracted under PL 93-638 with the Indian Health Service. The center offers general medicine, dental, mental health, substance abuse, WIC, family planning, community health outreach, and health education programs. Three doctors, two dentists, three public health nurses, one full-time and one part-time pharmacist, two pharmacy technicians, two LPNs, three mental health counselors, six chemical dependency counselors, three registered nurses, one dental hygienist, one nutritionist, and one environmental health specialist serve the center. Two psychiatrists and one pediatric dentist are contracted on a consultant basis. The tribe is served by a sanitarian, dietetic dietitian, and diabetic educator through the Northwest Washington Service Unit Health Board.

The tribe also provides a wellness and fitness center, the LIFE Center, and a home care agency for tribal elders. The LIFE Center offers medical, dental, mental health counseling, community health, environmental health, and wellness programs. It employs 65 people. The wellness and fitness center offers a weight room, fitness classes, fitness testing, a personal trainer, and a sauna. The tribal school uses the facility for its physical education classes and athletic programs.

The tribe maintains the Community Mobilization Against Drugs program. It provides education, outreach, preventative, and community coordination services on the reservation. The program also sponsors a youth safe house, and has secured funding for a community-based adult and youth drug treatment center. In cooperation with the tribal police department, the program coordinates the assignment of police officers to tribal housing divisions and communities in order to reduce the level of drug trafficking and related activities. The tribe's Youth Enrichment Social Services (YESS) program offers family preservation, prevention, intervention, youth employment, sports and recreation, outreach, transportation, counseling, cultural, literacy education, health and nutrition, parent education, life skills, technology, and fine arts services.

ENVIRONMENTAL CONCERNS
The Lummi have always held a great respect for, and considered themselves guardians of, their natural resources. Historically, the Lummi have been opposed to expansion that would be negative for the salmon, the cedar, or the environment at large. However, they realize they must find a balance between environmental stewardship and economic growth. One solution being considered is to designate specific areas for development and agreeing upon activities that will be allowed there.

Safe, Clean Waters, Lummi Tribal Sewer and Water District, Lummi Indian Nation (Bellingham, Washington)

**Honoring Nations
Honoree 2002**

**Text in its entirety from:
The Harvard Project On
American Indian Economic
Development**

**John F. Kennedy School
of Government
Harvard University**

The Lummi Indian Nation established the Lummi Tribal Sewer and Water District in 1983 to ensure the Nation's role in the provision of safe drinking water and discharge of clean wastewater across its reservation, located 100 miles north of Seattle. The District's managerial, financial, and technical competence-emerging at a time when the Lummi Nation confronted serious challenges to its jurisdiction over non-tribally owned lands within the reservation-has enhanced tribal sovereignty while providing critical infrastructure services to the reservation's five thousand Native and non-Native residents.

For the Lummi Indian Nation, access to clean, safe water is important not only for community health and welfare, but also for cultural and economic reasons-historically, salmon fishing and shellfish harvesting have been a way of life and livelihood for Lummi citizens. Regrettably, since the creation of the Lummi Reservation under the Point Elliot Treaty of 1855, the Nation has been confronted with frequent challenges to its rights to fish on traditional waters and to access to adequate clean water supplies. While Lummi leaders have responded to these challenges by vigorously defending the tribe's treaty rights, still other forces have worked against them. Years of high unemployment and economic hardship have thwarted tribal efforts to maintain water quality on the reservation, which includes eight thousand acres of tidelands. And, the problem of insufficient economic resources has been compounded by a history of jurisdictional and regulatory disputes with surrounding governments and resident, non-Indian landowners.

For many years, the Lummi Indian Nation relied on the Bureau of Indian Affairs (BIA) to administer its water-related services. This proved to be an unsatisfactory arrangement, as the Bureau was either unable or uninterested in organizing a water and sewer utility on the Lummi Reservation, and the absence of a utility resulted in unsanitary conditions and degradation of the Nation's water quality and shellfish beds. In the 1970s the Lummi Indian Business Council resolved to address these problems through the creation of a reservation-wide, tribal sewer utility that would serve all residents, Indian and non-Indian alike. Unfortunately, a group of non-Indian property owners, who had acquired much of the desirable waterfront property on the 21,000-acre reservation, prevailed in urging Whatcom County to authorize their preferred alternative-the creation of small, gerrymandered sewer and water districts within the Lummi Indian Reservation that included only non-Indian properties. These districts, in cooperation with Whatcom County, then used their taxation and other municipal powers to oppose state and federal grants to the Lummi Nation, effectively stopping construction of the tribal sewer system.

In response, the Lummi Indian Nation, which already had begun to exercise greater self-determination by assuming responsibility for other BIA programs, brought a federal court lawsuit against Whatcom County, the newly formed sewer and water districts, and several individuals. The Nation alleged violation of federal civil rights statutes and asserted tribal sovereignty over the formation and operation of sewer districts within the reservation. The case resulted in a ruling affirming the Nation's authority to administer sewer and water utilities throughout the Lummi Indian Reservation and to compel non-

Indians to connect to the system and obey tribal rules. Following that decision, Whatcom County, the newly formed non-Indian districts, and the individual defendants all negotiated settlements of the claims against them, which resulted in the dissolution of the districts and the County's recognition of the Lummi Nation's right to govern the reservation. Additionally, the State of Washington released grant funds to the Nation, and the tribal system was built. In 1983, under a tribal enabling ordinance in the Lummi Nation Code of Laws, the Nation formally established the Lummi Tribal Sewer and Water District to provide water and sewer infrastructure and services to all reservation residents, Indian and non-Indian alike.

The Lummi Tribal Sewer and Water District currently provides water and sewer services to approximately five thousand residents living within the boundaries of the Lummi Indian Reservation. To provide potable water services, the District operates four wells and two storage reservoirs. All delivered water is chlorinated; soon it will be fluoridated. On the wastewater side, the District operates two treatment plants, collecting and treating more than two hundred million gallons of wastewater per year. Mindful of future population growth, the District is developing three additional water supply wells to accommodate anticipated economic development and population growth at the rate of approximately thirty additional homes each year.

Statements from tribal leaders and community members confirm that the Lummi Tribal Sewer and Water District is succeeding in its mission of providing safe drinking water to reservation residents and returning clean, clear wastewater to the water environment. While community members' statements are largely impressionistic-their sense is that the reservation environment is now safer and healthier for all residents-board members cite more technical evidence of the District's success. In particular, they extol its professionally managed, modern, reservation-wide water and sewer systems, which have allowed the District to prioritize and realize its goals in three major areas: biosolids recycling, drinking water conservation, and river water withdrawal reduction. All biosolids are now tested, stabilized, and returned to the earth. The District's promotion of drinking water conservation has resulted in the reduction of water leakage to negligible levels. In the last year, the District also reduced dependence on river water withdrawals by 91 percent in favor of reservation-based groundwater sources, thereby protecting instream flows vital for healthy salmon populations. These positive changes have meant that despite a customer growth rate of more than 5 percent per year in the last three years, there has been only a nominal increase in water consumption. Remarkably, the District has achieved these gains while remaining entirely self-sufficient. It charges rates that are comparable to those paid by off-reservation residents of Whatcom County, does not charge assessment fees to either tribal or non-tribal members (which has elicited broad community support), and yet collects adequate monies to support its operations and facilities improvements.

The Lummi Tribal Sewer and Water District is also succeeding in other dimensions. A tribally administered sewer and water district-unique in Indian Country-is an effective and practical tool for asserting sovereignty over a critical natural resource. On a daily basis, the District exercises vital control over infrastructure decisions throughout the reservation. Notably, the District's managers make these decisions subject to the constraints of their mandate, which is to maintain quality service for all reservation residents while exhibiting sensitivity to the traditional values of the Lummi people. And while the District is under the plenary authority of the governing body of the Lummi Nation, implementation of its mandate is eased by the fact that the District's five-member board enjoys relative autonomy from the tribal government-tribal government officials have not made it a practice to interfere with the District's management and day-to-day operations. This healthy relationship between the District and the tribal government has been an important means both of reversing the history of tension between the Lummi Nation and non-Indian reservation residents and of ensuring that management decisions are not compromised by political expediency. For its part, the District is committed to running a first-rate utility: it has been able to implement strict design, construction, and monitoring standards - all of which contribute to the District's operations meeting or exceeding national standards.

Another critical component of the District's success is its innovative approach to working with neighboring governments and individual non-Indian residents. In fact, the District has increased the Nation's control over water resources by negotiating agreements with other stakeholders. Two examples-the Nation's 1991 Memorandum of Agreement (MOA) with Whatcom County and the District's decision to be governed by a board comprised of both Indians and non-Indians-stand out. In 1991, the Lummi Indian Nation signed an MOA with Whatcom County affirming a government-to-government relationship between the two parties and establishing a coordinated planning process for land use. The MOA recognizes that "the Nation has asserted regulatory jurisdiction for all land areas within the exterior boundaries of the Reservation, regardless of ownership type, and that the County has asserted partial regulatory jurisdiction for those lands held in fee title by non-tribal members." Although neither government conceded the other's position on jurisdiction, the MOA allowed for the beginning of a comprehensive planning process even as it acknowledged the complexity of jurisdiction. The MOA's broad mandate has been strengthened on an operational level by the tribal government's decision to include non-Lummi reservation residents in decision-making positions on the District's governing board. Two of the five board seats are open to-and are currently held by-non-Indians. This commitment to broad representation has paid off: non-Indian reservation residents have expressed their support of the Nation's efforts at community meetings, referring specifically to the fact that they have a voice on the board. In reserving such positions for non-Lummi residents, the Nation has gained unexpected allies while retaining its sovereign authority to regulate its natural resources.

A final element that is foundational to the Lummi Tribal Sewer and Water District's success is its dedicated, technically competent, and highly trained staff, 80 percent of whom are tribal citizens. Recognizing the ever-changing nature of state and federal regulations regarding safe drinking water levels and waste discharge, the District's leadership is committed to recruiting skilled employees and to keeping them up-to-date on the latest technology and services. For example, the District pursues an aggressive training and certification program and provides numerous opportunities for employees to participate in other professional development activities. Further, the District requires staff members interested in wage and status advancements to receive state-agency certification in industry operations, even though such certification is not required by U.S. Environmental Protection Agency regulations. One staff member was recently honored as "Operator of the Year" for the entire state of Washington-persuasive evidence of the District's success in staff recruitment and training. Investing in professional development and embracing high standards are hallmarks of governmental excellence, and in these respects, the Lummi Tribal Sewer and Water District clearly excels.

In a pioneering assertion of self-governance, the Lummi Indian Nation created the Lummi Tribal Sewer and Water District to ensure the availability of safe drinking water and the clean discharge of wastewater. By planning for sustainable and responsible growth, adhering to strict health and environmental standards, and operating in a manner responsive to tribal and non-tribal residents, the District presents an inspirational example of how Indian nations can advance their sovereignty by building capable governmental institutions that satisfy vital public needs.

Lessons
When Indian nations take on management responsibility for broad public service delivery - and execute those responsibilities well - they expand their self-governing power. Like other governments throughout the United States, tribal governments can create and use public boards, commissions, and management districts to govern service delivery.

For tribal governments that provide services to non-Indian clients, it may be desirable to have non-Indian representation on tribal service delivery boards, commissions, or management districts to help ensure broad legitimacy and foster accountability to all stakeholders and clients.

The effectiveness and efficiency of tribal services is directly tied to the quality of staff. Tribal governments can encourage staff development by providing incentives (for example, bonuses, advancement opportunities) for additional training and certification.

Lummi

Honoring Nations
Honoree 2002

Text in its entirety from:
The Harvard Project On
American Indian Economic
Development

John F. Kennedy School
of Government
Harvard University

Makah

Makah Reservation
Federal reservation
Makah
Clallam County, Washington

Makah Tribal Council
P.O. Box 115
Neah Bay, WA 98357
360-645-2201
360-645-2788 Fax
makah.com

Total area (BIA realty, 2004)
29,668.52 acres

Federal trust (BIA realty, 2004)
41.17 acres

Tribally owned (BIA realty, 2004)
27,342.51 acres

Individually owned
(BIA realty, 2004)
2,284.84 acres

Population 2000 census
1,356

Tribal enrollment
(BIA labor report, 2001)
2,389

Total labor force 2000 census
613

Total labor force
(BIA labor report, 2001)
1,198

High school graduate or higher
2000 census
81.9%

Bachelor's degree or higher
2000 census
10.4%

Unemployment rate 2000 census
23.7%

Unemployment rate
(BIA labor report, 2001)
70%

Per capita income 2000 census
$10,986

LOCATION AND LAND STATUS

The Makah Reservation is the westernmost Indian reservation in the lower 48 states. Extremely isolated, it is located on the northwestern tip of the state of Washington's Olympic Peninsula on Cape Flattery and Koitlah Point, across the Strait of San Juan de Fuca from Vancouver, British Columbia, Canada. Forty-seven of the total reservation acres are Tatoosh Island; another 33 acres are Waadah Island. The Ozette Reservation, a separate 719-acre parcel of the Makah Reservation, is located approximately 10 miles south of Neah Bay, fronting the Pacific Ocean. It is separated from the main Makah Reservation by a portion of the Olympic National Park. The reservation lands lay 70 miles west of Port Angeles and 17 miles from the nearest neighboring community, Neah Bay. Tribal population is concentrated in the fishing Village of Neah Bay, with smaller concentrations by Sooes River and in various home sites.

The Makah Reservation was established in 1855 by the Treaty of Neah Bay and enlarged by subsequent executive orders to its present size, virtually all of which remain in federal trust. The tribe has plans to acquire more land.

PHYSICAL DESCRIPTION

Reservation lands are located on the northwestern tip of the Olympic Peninsula on Cape Flattery and Koitlah Point, overlooking the Strait of San Juan de Fuca. Elevations in the region range between 110 feet above sea level at Neah Bay to 2,000 feet at Sooes Peak. The lands are heavily forested, with rangeland suitable primarily for livestock grazing and rugged mountain ranges; the shoreline areas are characterized by rocky headlands and sandy beaches. Four watersheds drain the area: Sail River, Watch River, Hoko River, and Sooes River. The closest town, Forks, Washington, is 60 miles distant.

CLIMATE

The elevation at Neah Bay, Washington, is 110 feet above sea level. The climate is typical of the temperate Pacific coastal regions, receiving over 100 inches of precipitation annually, almost 9 inches falling as snow each year. Occasional wind gusts of up to 100 miles per hour are possible. The year-round average daily high temperature is 53°F. The year-round average daily low temperature is 45°F.

CULTURE AND HISTORY

The Makah Tribe-the Qwiqwidicciats, or Kwih-dich-chuh-ahtx, "people who live by the rocks and seagulls"-is the sole representative of the Wakashan linguistic family and the Nootkan cultural complex in the United States. The Makah language, called Qwiqwidicciat, belongs to the Southern Nootkan branch of the Wakashan language family. Before European contact, the tribe, with a population estimated between 2,000 and 4,000, inhabited five permanent semiautonomous coastal villages linked by a common language and through kinship and marriage. The people lived in large extended family units, occupying cedar plank longhouses; they practiced a subsistence lifestyle centered upon fishing for shellfish, sea otters, seal, whale, and other smaller species, and then trading these products with other tribes. They traveled to summer fishing camps annually. Aboriginal Makah territory included the islands of Waadah, Tatoosh, Ozette, Cannon Ball, and the Bodeltas and the islands on Lake Ozette. Inland land holdings reached as far east as the Lyre River and as far south as the region they shared with the Quileute Tribe.

During the 1700s, contact with Europeans devastated the Makahs; thousands died from smallpox, tuberculosis, influenza, and whooping cough. The Treaty of Neah Bay, signed January 31, 1855, established the reservation, though it failed to recognize the multiple village system, focusing instead on only the Neah Bay community. Certain rights, specified within the articles of the treaty, ensured that the U.S. government would protect traditional practices on behalf of future generations of Makahs. In exchange for the retention of whaling rights, the Makahs ceded title to 300,000 acres of tribal land to the government. Congress ratified the treaty in 1859, drastically limiting subsistence hunting and the tribe's fishing territory, and setting the stage for radical cultural changes.

Executive Orders signed in 1872 and 1873 slightly expanded the reservation, eventually including all the other Makah villages except the most distant one, Ozette, which was eventually established as a separate reservation in 1893. By 1917, most of the Makahs had moved to Neah Bay to take advantage of the community's conveniences and facilities.

Commercial logging in the region drastically altered the Makah's subsistence lifestyle. It spurred the construction of the first paved road into the region in 1931. The following year the State of Washington built a public elementary and high school on the reservation. The tribe pursued several claims against the United States during the 1940s that concerned the loss of seal hunting and halibut fishing rights. The tribe finally accepted a compromise settlement decades later in the form of title to two offshore islands, Tatoosh and Waadah. While fishing and logging remain cornerstones of the tribal economy, both declined in the 1990s due to resource depletion and resulting conservation efforts. Increasingly, the Makahs have turned to the development of tourism, particularly ecotourism, to fill this gap.

Culturally, the preservation of the ancestral language and excavation of ancient tribal artifacts has been a primary focus of the Makah during recent years. The discovery of a long-buried portion of the Ozette village prompted the tribe to construct the Makah Cultural and Research Center to archive and exhibit the 55,000 artifacts from this site alone. The center is also home to the Makah language program for children, and the staff works with elders to record a grammar and write a Makah dictionary. Many Makahs are skilled woodworkers and market their carved masks, canoes, and totems in an ever-expanding global art market. Songs, dances, and stories, still owned by specific Makah families or individuals, are performed at traditional potlatches, weddings, naming ceremonies, memorials, and other family feasts or community celebrations.

GOVERNMENT

The Makah Tribe, a federally recognized tribal entity, is organized under provisions of the 1934 Indian Reorganization Act. It developed its constitution in 1936 and ratified a corporate charter in 1937. A five-person tribal council governs the tribe, with members elected to staggered three-year terms by eligible tribal voters. The council chairperson is elected by vote of the five council members at the beginning of each calendar year.

The tribe, under PL 93-638, contracts with the BIA to administer key programs and services. Tribal departments include housing; enrollment; health; natural resources, including the environmental division; economic development; public works;

education; forestry; social services; senior center, and cultural and resource center. The Neah Bay Police Department provides law enforcement services to the reservation.

A land use committee helps determine land use priorities, drafts ordinances, and assesses environmental requirements for all future cultural and economic developments. A communications committee designs brochures and other cultural education materials for public distribution.

The Makah Tribe's economic development planning committee assesses the feasibility of certain enterprises and oversees the development economic diversification.

ECONOMY
The Makah Tribe's economy, as in the past, is largely dependent upon fishing interests, forestry, and government services, although there is an increasing interest in tourism development and associated retail services on reservation lands.

Government as Employer. Tribal government is the largest employer of tribal members at the reservation. A significant number of members are employed via the various departments, offices, or programs offered by tribal government or in its economic enterprises.

Economic Development Projects. On April 15, 1997, the Makah Marina, constructed on the Port of Neah Bay near the entrance to the Strait of Juan de Fuca, opened for commercial and recreational boating activity. The marina facilities are managed by a tribal organization called the Neah Bay Port Commission. There are plans to add boat repair facilities, bait and tackle supply shops, a boat lift or rail system for haul outs, and a cold storage unit.

The newly developed Makah Business Resource Center works with Peninsula Community College and Northwest Indian College to provide education and training, startup capital, and continued consultation for new small Native American businesses and will be working closely with the Clallam County Economic Development Council to place potential entrepreneurs at the newly completed small business incubator. Downtown and waterfront revitalization are targeted for entrepreneurship endeavors.

In 2003, the tribe received a grant from the Department of Energy to develop a commercial wind-generated power plant with its development partner, Cielo Wind Power. With the feasibility study completed, in 2004 the tribe was creating the Makah Utility Authority, a tribally owned and operated electric utility enterprise capable of power purchase and distribution. Financing for this phase of the project is sought from rural utility services. Final stages of development will include marketing wind-generated electricity and resolving any remaining environmental issues that may require mitigation prior to implementation.

The tribe's new U.S. Post Office is complete. In 2004, the tribe completed a comprehensive economic development strategy listing accomplishments to date and detailing steps to further economic improvement for tribal members. The tribe hopes to attract a major motel chain to the reservation in 2006 by improving infrastructure and encouraging further agricultural development.

Agriculture and Livestock. Tribal lands include a fair amount of open range land, upon which the tribe raises approximately 150 head of cattle and horses.

Forestry. The Makah Forestry Enterprise was first established in 1964. The Timber Marketing Development Program, in existence since 1983, successfully sold timber to logging contractors, timber processors, and exporters. Since then, the tribe developed the Makah forest management plan to provide a long-term guide for private and commercial timber interests throughout the heavily forested reservation lands. There are currently about 26,000 acres of western hemlock, Douglas fir, Sitka spruce, yellow cedar, and western red cedar on Makah trust lands and allotments. Forest management and harvesting activities provided the tribe with about 14 full-time jobs in 2004.

Gaming. The tribe operates Makah Tribal Bingo, a four-game bingo program, at the Makah Tribal Center. The facility employed four tribal members in 2004. Thus far, the tribal council has rejected the option of developing a full-service casino, but it is exploring the feasibility of a very small scale casino operation.

Fisheries. The fishing industry represents the most important aspect of the Makah's economy. In 1998, approximately 250-300 tribal members, or 70 percent of the tribal population, found full-time employment in fishing for salmon, other groundfish, and sea urchins. A fish-buying and processing plant employs several more. The tribal fishing fleet consists of 100 seaworthy vessels, with one skipper and two crew members per craft.

In 1997, the U.S. Forest Service awarded Makah Fisheries Management a grant to develop an aquaculture project. The tribe subsequently leased a section of water in Neah Bay to raise shellfish, geoduck clams, and manila clams for commercial markets. The tribe was also successful in litigation to raise their commercial catch allocations for Pacific whiting, the most abundant groundfish resource in coastal areas. The tribe signed an exclusive contract with Supreme Alaska Seafoods, guaranteeing a market for the total tribal catch.

Of importance to subsistence fisherman, following an environmental review process completed in 1997, the International Whaling Commission restored tribal rights to take five gray whales for cultural and subsistence purposes.

The Makah Nation Fish Hatchery, built on the Sooes River, is designed for public viewing of migrating salmon. Fish ladders and the hatchery facility are open to the public. Sport fishing for salmon in the reservation's rivers and for other species in Hobuck Lake and Neah Bay are popular pastimes for tribal members and tourists.

Construction. The tribe has three independent contractors among its members. These businesses own some heavy equipment and contract in cement work and other specific construction activities.

Mining. Sand, gravel, and rock extraction operations employ a few tribal members. The products are used primarily in tribally initiated construction activities at the reservation.

Services and Retail. There are approximately 20 small retail businesses, most of which are owned and operated by individual tribal members. These include the Makah Smoke Shop, the Makah Museum, and Raven's Corner, an arts and crafts outlet. Restaurants include Beebe's Café, Natalie's Pizza, and the tribally owned Warm House Café, serving favorite local dishes. The tribal fuel facility, which serves both automobiles and boats, is centrally located in the Village of Neah Bay. Two motels on reservation land are leased to private owners, as is a private dormitory, a lodging accommodation left over from Cape Flattery Resort that was formerly operated on Neah

Makah

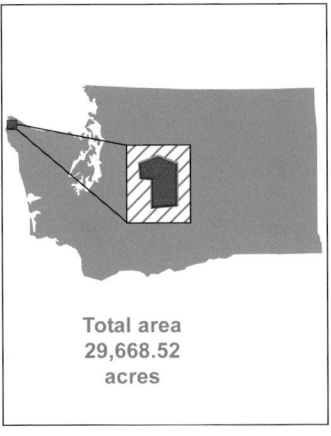

Total area
29,668.52
acres

Makah

Bay. Two charter marinas are leased to private owners as well. The tribe leases space to private operators for a beauty shop and a gift shop. Since 1997, tribal graduates of the Oregon Native American Entrepreneurial Network and Makah Business Resource Center have opened a coffee shop, a fast food restaurant, a gun store, and some craft shops. In 2001 the tribe stated a desire to implement the downtown master plan for downtown revitalization.

Transportation. The tribe operates a local public transit system.

Media and Communications. The tribe publishes a visitor's guide, "The Makah Nation on Washington's Olympic Peninsula." The tribe also has a website that is full of useful information; please visit makah.com.

Tourism and Recreation. The Makah Cultural and Research Center, established as a tribally operated nonprofit enterprise in 1979, has provided a focal point for visitors to the Makah Reservation. In the late 1990s, tourism generated approximately 18,000-20,000 visitors to the facility annually. Reconstructed cedar longhouses, an exhibit of 55,000 gallery and archeological artifacts, carving and basket-weaving demonstrations, educational programs, storytelling, dioramas, and guided tours are available. The museum gift shop markets carvings, basketry, jewelry, and other arts and crafts items made by local Makah artisans and an extensive collection of books regarding northwest Native culture and arts.

Environmental tours are available by special arrangement; the tribe operates an Ethnobotanical Gardens at the Makah Cultural and Research Center, and from there, the Cape Flattery Trail, Shi Shi (pronounced shy shy) Trail, Ozette archaeological day trips, and explorations of local beaches. A catered dinner of traditional foods can be prepared and served, and for parties of 18 or more, staff at the cultural and research center will conduct a traditional salmon barbecue.

The Makah Marina, at Neah Bay, is used for commercial and recreational boating activities. The marina features moorage, hookups, restrooms and showers, and a pump-out facility. The nearby Big Salmon Resort provides moorage as well. Guest accommodations are available at the Tyee Motel and RV Park, The Cape Resort Motel and RV Park, the Silver Salmon Resort, the Hobuck Campground (now owned and operated by the tribe), and the Village RV.

The tribe owns and operates the Cape Flattery Resort and Conference Facility, which features a lodge, campgrounds and an RV park, a sweat lodge and sauna, tennis courts, a cafe, and a variety of outdoor activities, including access to a system of hiking trails with opportunities for viewing marine mammals, horseback riding, wildlife, bird watching, and photography. The Cape Flattery Trail, constructed along the tip of the Olympic Peninsula in the 1,000-acre Makah Wilderness Area, takes hikers to the northwestern-most tip of the United States and features observation decks overlooking the Olympic Coast National Marine Sanctuary and Tatoosh Island. Access to the longer Shi Shi Trail is nearby. The trail system connects to the Makah Cultural and Research Center. Beaches along the coastline are a popular destination for ecotourists, campers, and surfers. The Travel Channel featured Shi Shi beach as one of the 10 best beaches.

The tribe hosts a number of special events, including Makah Days held in late August, which features fireworks, a parade, traditional dancing, singing, feasts, canoe races, and Sla-hal games (a form of traditional gambling).

INFRASTRUCTURE

State Highway 112 provides road access to the reservation. The tribe seeks to build a scenic loop road to connect Neah Bay to the communities of La Push and Forks, Washington, on the ocean side of the reservation. Commercial air service is available in Port Angeles, 72 miles away, and for small planes only, service is available at Sekiu, 17 miles away. A commercial bus line serves Neah Bay, offering two trips daily to Port Angeles and points beyond. Commercial truck lines serve the reservation directly.

The reservation sits directly on the Straight of Juan de Fuca, offering easy water access to Vancouver, British Columbia, and other west coast locations. The port of Port Angeles provides deep-water access to Pacific shipping lanes. Neah Bay's inner harbor accommodates recreational yachts, sailboats, and small cruise ships. The tribe is in the process of doing a feasibility study for a ferry to Vancouver Island, British Columbia.

Electricity. The Clallam County Public Utilities District provides electricity on an individual residential basis.

Fuel. Local distributors supply propane service.

Water Supply. The tribal community maintains its own municipal water and sewer systems, with a few outlying residences relying on septic systems. Almost all reservation residents are connected to the sewage treatment system, which includes four lagoons and a treatment plant. Surface and subsurface sources provide the community with water. In 1998, the Indian Health Service completed some infrastructure upgrades to the community water system, and the economic development department and tribal public works department were working together to connect two new wells. The tribe's 1999 Annual Drinking Water Quality Report states that the Indian Health Service and the Bureau of Reclamation have been working with the tribe to develop an alternative long-term water supply for Neah Bay.

Transportation. The tribe's 2004 comprehensive economic development strategy studied traffic patterns and road use in order to create a long-range plan for developing new roads and managing ongoing maintenance to all existing reservation roads and streets, including paving roads from mile marker "0" to the Cape Flattery Trail Head.

Telecommunications. Century Tel Communications provides telephone service.

COMMUNITY FACILITIES AND SERVICES

The tribe's community center is in Neah Bay. The Makah Tribal Center houses the bingo enterprise. Construction of a new tribal Head Start facility was completed in 1998. At the marina, the Marina Administration Building is now open. The building serves as an administrative office complex, with a conference room and an emergency command center in the event of oil spills or other marine emergencies. A 911 complex is planned for Cougar Hill that will feature a fire hall to service the tribe.

Education. Makah students attend the Neah Bay Public Schools. To encourage the use of the Native Makah language, Qwiqwidicciat, the education department operates a Makah Language Program, housed at the cultural and research center, using tribal elders to record oral histories, conduct linguistic research, prepare entries for a Qwiqwidicciat-English dictionary, and develop materials for use in the public schools.

Health Care. Comprehensive primary health care and dental care are available at the 7,145-square-foot Sophie Trettevick Public Health Service Indian Health Center in Neah Bay. The nearest full-service hospital is in Port Angeles. The tribe operates several programs under a title III self-governance compact. They have an alcohol and substance abuse program and a mental health program operating in tribally owned buildings. In addition, the tribe owns a field station for community health services, including a community health representative, a community health nurse, 1st Steps, a WIC nutritional program, childbirth classes, breast and cervical cancer prevention services, sanitation, and emergency medical services. Health services provided by the Indian Health Service include: clinical and dental services, a low-income home energy assistance program, a seniors program, child, a food bank, commodity distribution, education, juvenile, foster care, Indian Child Welfare Act, domestic violence, and juvenile diversion.

ENVIRONMENTAL INITIATIVES AND CONCERNS
The tribe has a hazardous material response program to respond to oil or gas spills in Neah Bay and any land-based spills of chemicals or other materials deemed harmful to the environment. The reservation's west coast is within national marine sanctuary boundaries. Potential wastes and contaminants at the site of a decommissioned air force base, which the tribe once leased to the federal government, prevents development of the facility as a tribal community college or research and education center. The tribal council has petitioned the U.S. EPA Region 9 offices for cleanup assistance.

In 1998, the tribe was in the process of closing its landfill. The environmental specialist was working with the economic development planner to develop an economically viable recycling program for the reservation.

There are 31 wetland areas within tribal boundaries. In 1998, the tribe was working on a watershed protection plan that would identify and assess the quality and viability of each of these unique habitats. In April 2000, the tribe abolished the practice of grazing cattle on open range, as cattle frequented the water source locations and increased the risk of contamination.

M uckleshoot

LOCATION AND LAND STATUS
Just east of the Seattle-Tacoma metropolitan area in King County, Washington, the Muckleshoot Indian Reservation sits on Muckleshoot Prairie between the Green and White rivers. The reservation was established by Executive Order in 1857 and Presidential Order in 1874. The reservation was created to provide a permanent homeland for the use and benefit of the Muckleshoot Indian Tribe. However, the original 3,332 acres of the reservation were quickly taken away from the Muckleshoots through allotment in 1934. By 1971, the tribe owned only a single acre. The tribe is committed to restoring its land base and continues to acquire lands toward this end.

PHYSICAL DESCRIPTION
The reservation is composed of two distinct areas. The western portion is urban and melds with the City of Auburn.The eastern part of the reservation is primarily agricultural and open space area, and it also includes gravel quarries. The tribe seeks to preserve the river valley and its steep slopes by zoning this area for conservation. Tribal zoning ordinances, similar to those of surrounding King County, are enforced to ensure orderly development within the reservation. The reservation contains 15.5 miles of streams, 16 acres of wetlands, and over 2,100 acres of evergreen forests. The average temperatures range from 75°F in July to 43°F in January. The annual precipitation is between 34 and 64 inches per year.

CULTURE AND HISTORY
Muckleshoot Indian Tribe members are descendants of the Coast Salish peoples and have lived in the northwest region of the United States for thousands of years. Ancestral homelands include areas along the eastern and southern reaches of Puget Sound and the western slope of the Cascade Mountain Range. The Coast Salish tribes had intricate social structures, which included a hereditary nobility. They lived in the Pacific Northwest coastal region and depended on the abundance of natural resources, especially salmon and red cedar. Both resources were husbanded with great care; cedar was an important material for goods and art. The people made elaborate cedar lodges, furniture, and baskets crafted from bent cedar and clothing made from cedar bark.

The Native people of the Pacific Northwest first encountered European explorers in the late 1790s. Initial relationships with European and Euro-American explorers were based on trade, though the influx of settlers in the 1800s ushered in a period of forced subjugation for the tribe. Native communities in the region were hard hit by the arrival of foreign diseases, and the populations were devastated. Consequently, tribal lands were lost, and tribes were forcibly relocated. During the 1850s, many Native peoples participated in the Puget Sound Indian War in an effort to resist Euro-American domination. The treaties of Point Elliot and Medicine Creek established the Muckleshoot Indian Reservation. Members from such clans as the Stkamish, Yilalkoamish, Smulkamish, Tkwakwamish, Duwuamish, Snoqualmie, Tulalip, and Suquamish relocated to the reservation and became the Muckleshoot Indian Tribe.

In the 1960s and 1970s, the tribe became involved in what have been called the "Fish Wars." The tribe actively pressured the government to recognize and implement the tribe's fishing and hunting rights guaranteed in the original treaties. The Boldt Decision of 1974 upheld the tribe's rights. The tribe has been designated legal co-manager of the King County Watershed. The designation recognizes the tribe's ancestral fishing and hunting rights to the land and permits them the opportunity to control those environments.

Tribal members continue to speak the indigenous language, and the tribe offers language and culture classes to promote the living culture.

GOVERMENT
The Muckleshoot Tribe has both a general council and a tribal council. The chief administrative officer is the general manager, who oversees managers for grants, economic development, and general administration; the administrative manager oversees officials responsible for building maintenance, personnel, and security. There is a planning director and coordinators of health and human services, community services, education, and natural resources. A comptroller presides over the tribe's finances. Government offices include administration, real estate, school, senior, family resource center, gaming, housing, planning and public works, college, housing, health and human services, fisheries, and child care.

Muckleshoot Indian Reservation
Federal reservation
Muckleshoot
King County, Washington

Muckleshoot Indian Tribe
39015 172nd Avenue SE
Auburn, WA 98092
253-939-3311
253-939-5311 Fax
muckleshoot.nsn.us

Muckleshoot

Total area (BIA realty, 2004)
1,125 acres

Tribally owned (BIA realty, 2004)
193.78 acres

Individually owned
(BIA realty, 2004)
931.22 acres

Total population *2000 census*
3,597

Tribal enrollment
(BIA labor report, 2001)
1,712

Total labor force *2000 census*
1,690

Total labor force (BIA, 2001)
2,417

High school graduate or higher
2000 census
76.6%

Bachelor's degree or higher
2000 census
12.5%

Unemployment rate *2000 census*
8.6%

Unemployment rate (BIA, 2001)
40%

Per capita income *2000 census*
$16,860

The tribe maintains a tribal court that has both a trial and an appellate division. There is also a tribal attorneys office. The tribe has a criminal code and rules. It also belongs to the Northwest Intertribal Court System.

The tribe is co-manager of natural resources on off-reservation areas. It implements hunting and wildlife management regulations in areas within its jurisdiction, including state and national parks. It employs wildlife biologists and enforcement officers to oversee the implementation and enforcement of tribal hunting and wildlife codes. The tribe also belongs to the Salish Intertribal Wildlife Council, a forum for discussing and resolving intertribal disputes, hunting and wildlife issues, and public and private concerns.

ECONOMY

Located in the most populated county in the state, the Muckleshoot Reservation is located in a region that is prime for economic development. In recent years this has enabled the tribe to upgrade the depressed economic status of its reservation. The tribe's enterprises in the gaming, fishing, and retail industries serve as the foundation of the tribal economy.

Government as Employer. The tribe employs over 1,500 people.

Economic Development Projects. The tribe offers a number of incentives to draw businesses to the reservation, including accelerated depreciation, Indian employment credit, an Indian incentive program, subcontracting goal credit, and advantages of the HUB Zone Act of 1997. It welcomes economic development to the reservation, but strives to ensure that such development is environmentally and culturally appropriate.

Agriculture and Livestock. Approximately 200 acres of reservation land are used for farming, and approximately another 100 are for grazing cattle.

Forestry. Approximately 200 acres are wooded; there are no plans for logging.

Gaming. The tribe owns two gaming facilities: the Muckleshoot Bingo Hall, which opened in 1985, and the Muckleshoot Casino, which opened in September 1995. The Caribbean-themed casino offers 2,000 slot machines, 65 table games, 19 poker tables, and 1,000 bingo seats. It features a separate nonsmoking area with 400 slots and 20 tables. The facilities include 5 restaurants, a convention center, and an entertainment venue. The casino employs 1,500 people. Next door to the casino, the Muckleshoot Bingo Hall has a snack bar and café. This hall hosts many other events as well.

In the past several years, revenue earned from its gaming enterprises have enabled the tribe to contribute hundreds of thousands of dollars to local organizations, including the Auburn Food Bank, Auburn School Lunch Program, Catholic Community Services, Citizens Helping Veterans, KCTS Channel 9, Korean Women's Association, National Indian Education Association, Tacoma Symphony Orchestra, U.S. Olympic Committee, Washington Council of the Blind, Washington Special Olympics, and Yakima Valley Community College.

Fisheries. The tribe's fisheries department represents the largest segment of the tribal government. The department works to safeguard tribal fishing rights and to protect and restore fish stocks in the region. The tribe is co-manager of the King County Watershed, and it exercises control over fishing and hunting matters in the area. The tribe's harvest management program is designed to implement the tribe's treaty rights. Under this program, the tribe develops and implements fishing regulations to manage fish stock.

The tribe has constructed two fish hatcheries, one on the White River near Buckley and another at Coal Creek Springs. The fisheries supplement the dwindling number of fish in the area's streams, rivers, and lakes by restocking them. Fishing on open water is vital to individual tribal income. The Muckleshoots exercise their "usual and accustomed" fishing rights as outlined in treaties and as upheld by federal court.

Services and Retail. The tribe owns the Muckleshoot Plaza, a $2 million mall that was completed in 1997. It has 15,000 square feet of retail space, of which 5,000 square feet is reserved for tribal tenants. The plaza is located along Highway 164 and houses seven businesses. The tribe also owns the Muckleshoot Market and Deli, which provides a hot and cold deli, groceries, and a 76 Gas Station. The tribe also owns the Muckleshoot Smoke Shop and Liquor Store.

The tribe owns Muckleshoot Technical Services. It provides installation, maintenance, and operation services in the fields of audio, video, lighting, and electronics. The company provides technical training and competitive wages.

Media and Communications. The tribe's economic development and planning department publishes *Looking to the Future*, a quarterly newsletter.

Tourism and Recreation. In partnership with Clear Channel Communications, the tribe owns the White River Amphitheater. It is a 100-acre site featuring an amphitheatre plaza with the ability to seat 20,000 guests. It has stunning views of Mt. Rainier. Sixteen buildings cover 52,720 square feet. The amphitheater stage has a 9,400-square-foot platform and stands 57 feet high. It has two 30 by 40 video screens. The grassed seating surrounding the amphitheater seats an additional 11,000 people. The facility is disabled accessible and offers luxury box seats.

The tribe operates a cultural center on the reservation that displays tribal and Native American artifacts and items. The tribe hosts Skopabsh Day in August and an annual potlatch in June. The Muckleshoot Bingo Hall hosts annual celebrations in honor of Martin Luther King, Jr. Day, and powwows.

INFRASTRUCTURE

The reservation is on State Road 164, 15 miles east of U.S. I-5. The Auburn city bus system serves the reservation. Sea-Tac Airport, about 24 miles from the reservation, handles international air traffic. UPS, FedEx, and other major carriers are available, and a rail spur is adjacent to the reservation.

Water Supply. Two wells and a single 900,000-gallon reservoir operated by the Muckleshoot Utility District serve the reservation. While the tribe does not recognize any annexation by the city of lands within the reservation, the city does serve the reservation with sewer and water services. Another sewer system was under construction and planned to connect with the City of Auburn's system in fall 1995.

Transportation. A new bicycle and pedestrian path was planned in 1994 between the Muckleshoot housing authority and a local youth center.

COMMUNITY FACILITIES AND SERVICES

A tribal community center is located on the reservation. Tribal members also use community facilities in the city of Auburn. The tribe's community services division provides a family resource center, a low-income energy assistance program, a cultural resources program, and a recreation program. It also maintains a youth facility with a staff of five. The tribe's senior citizens program serves meals, provides emergency assistance, and offers home and community-based care services.

The tribe operates a child care center. The tribe also offers the Muckleshoot Even Start Program, known as Project LIFT (Longhouse Intergenerational Family Training). The program offers activities to teach parents to become the primary teacher in their child's life. The tribe also maintains a Child Development CCDF Tax Fund Program that provides child care assistance to low-income families.

Education. The tribe operates a Head Start program. Tribal youth may attend the Muckleshoot Tribal School located on the reservation. The tribe also operates the Muckleshoot Re-Entry School, a year-round facility that addresses the needs of tribal youth at risk of not completing high school.

The tribe also owns and operates the Muckleshoot Tribal College. In addition to a traditional academic curriculum, the college offers continuing education programs, vocational programs, and GED testing. The college offers an Occupational Skills Training Program that offers certificates in Office Assistant Beginning, Office Assistant Intermediate, A+ (computer technician), and NW+ (networking technician). It also offers the Muckleshoot Language Program, which provides instruc-

tion in the indigenous language. The college works in conjunction with the Northwest Indian College, the Green River Community College, the Evergreen State College Reservation-Based Community Determined Program, and the Antioch University at Seattle to provide tribal members with the opportunity to pursue associates, bachelors, and master's degrees. The tribe provides a higher education scholarship for eligible members.

Health Care. The tribe maintains the Muckleshoot Tribal Health Center in Auburn. The clinic is contracted through Indian Health Service under the PL 93-638 provision. It includes a pharmacy. The tribe also offers community health representative, nursing, nutritional, alcohol, and mental health counseling programs.

ENVIRONMENTAL CONCERNS
The tribe has initiated efforts to restore the White River salmon passages into Jones Creek, Blocks Creek, and Charlie Jones Creek on the reservation. The tribe is also involved in efforts to maintain water quality and environmental health in the region.

Muckleshoot

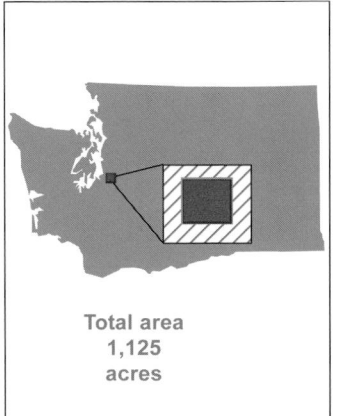

Total area
1,125
acres

Nisqually

Nisqually

Total area *(BIA realty, 2004)*	1,079.99 acres
Tribally owned *(BIA realty, 2004)*	346.04 acres
Individually owned	733.95 acres
(BIA realty, 2004)	
Population *2000 census*	588
Tribal enrollment	525
(BIA labor report, 2001)	
Total labor force *2000 census*	289
Total labor force *(BIA labor report, 2001)*	5,719
High school graduate or higher	81.8%
2000 census	
Bachelor's degree or higher	9.4%
2000 census	
Unemployment rate *2000 census*	11.4%
Unemployment rate	68%
(BIA labor report, 2001)	
Per capita income *2000 census*	$14,094

LOCATION AND LAND STATUS
The Nisqually Reservation is located in western Washington State, approximately 10 miles east of Olympia. The original reservation was established on 1,280 acres by the Medicine Creek Treaty of December 26, 1854. An Executive Order in 1856 increased the size to 4,717 acres. In 1884, acreage was divided into 30 family allotments. The parcels were located on either side of the Nisqually River, but they did not include the river itself. In 1917, the U.S. Army reduced the size of the reservation by over 3,300 acres in order to establish the Fort Lewis Military Reserve.

CULTURE AND HISTORY
The Nisqually Tribe resided in the woodlands and prairies of the Nisqually River Basin for hundreds of years prior to European contact. The tribe signed the Treaty of Medicine Creek with representatives of the U.S. government on December 26, 1854. The U.S. Senate ratified the treaty and President Franklin Pierce signed it in 1855. The tribe adopted its constitution in 1946; the Secretary of the Interior approved it in the same year. Much of the original reservation was condemned, against the tribe's wishes, to establish the Fort Lewis Military

Reservation. The remaining acreage was largely uninhabited by the Nisqually people as late as the early 1970s. Public utilities to the reservation were extremely limited, so tribal members lived in nearby communities. The establishment and development of a community with services within the reservation's boundaries was a goal of the tribe, which began to be realized in the mid-1970s, when housing and community facilities were developed. HUD funded the housing projects.

GOVERNMENT
The tribe is governed by a tribal council of seven members and a general council that consists of all tribal members over the age of 18 years. The tribal council includes a chairman, a vice-chairman, a secretary, a treasurer, a fifth council member, and two nonvoting members-at-large. Each member is elected to two-year terms. The tribal constitution was approved on September 9, 1946. Tribal government committees include health, social services, natural resources, accounting, and planning.
The tribal fish commission, a five-member body elected to two-year terms, oversees tribal fishery issues. The tribe maintains a tribal court system.

BUSINESS CORPORATION
Nisqually Ventures is a federally chartered entity.

ECONOMY
The bingo hall, a casino, a convenience store, a daycare, a tribal shellfish enterprise, and grants constitute the bulk of tribal income.

Government as Employer. The tribe employs over 300 people.

Economic Development Projects. The Nisqually Five-Year Overall Economic Development Program establishes a structure for economic development on the reservation. The program is implemented by an enterprise board. Economic development goals are to preserve and strengthen the tribe's autonomy, to protect and develop tribal resources, to develop so-

Nisqually Reservation
Federal reservation
Nisqually
Thurston County, Washington

Nisqually Indian Tribe
4820 She-Nah-Num Drive SE
Olympia, WA 98513
360-456-5221
360-438-8618 Fax

Nisqually

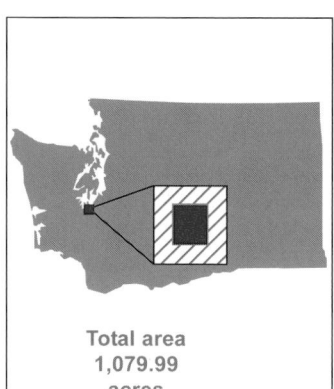

**Total area
1,079.99
acres**

cial and health programs, to generate revenue, and to create meaningful training and employment opportunities for tribal members.

In the mid-1990s the tribe established a business incubator facility for the businesses of five tribal members. A revolving loan fund program for individual tribal entrepreneurs was being planned in the mid-1990s. A business mall, a new fish hatchery, and a produce storage facility were also in the planning stages. Other economic projects include a farmers market and a dive academy.

Agriculture and Livestock. A two-acre community garden, including two solar greenhouses, serves the reservation.

Forestry. The reservation includes 800 forested acres. More than 250 acres of timber management land have been restored to tribal ownership.

Gaming. The tribe owns the Red Wind Casino in Olympia. It offers 414 slots/VLTs, 11 table games, and a restaurant. The casino employs 330 people.

Fisheries. The tribe operates two major fish hatcheries on the Nisqually River.

Construction. A tribal construction enterprise builds facilities on the reservation.

INFRASTRUCTURE
The reservation is eight miles east of I-5, on Washington State Highway 210. The Port of Olympia is approximately 13 miles to the west, and the City of Tacoma is 35 miles north.

Water Supply. A tribal water system serves 110 homes.

Transportation. The Seattle-Tacoma International Airport is 50 miles distant. Motor freight service is available on the reservation. A rail connection is 7 miles distant.

COMMUNITY FACILITIES AND SERVICES
The reservation has a tribal administration building and a multipurpose equipment maintenance shop. There is a tribal community center.

Education. Tribal children attend public school in Yelm, five miles distant. A branch campus of the Northwest Indian College began operations on the reservation in 1994. The primary purpose of the campus is to serve as a training site for tribal employees.

Health Care. There is a clinic with one doctor and one dentist.

Nooksack

**Nooksack Reservation
Federal reservation
Nooksack
Whatcom County, Washington**

Nooksack Indian Tribe
P.O. Box 157
Deming, WA 98244-00157
360-592-5176
360-592-2125 Fax
nooksack-tribe.org

Total area *(BIA realty, 2004)*	212.68 acres
Total area *(Tribal source, 2004)*	2,500 acres
Tribally owned lands	212.68 acres
(BIA realty, 2004)	
Population *2000 census*	547
Tribal enrollment *(BIA, 2001)*	1,537
Total labor force *2000 census*	242
Total labor force *(BIA, 2001)*	1,449
High school graduate or higher	73.7%
2000 census	
Bachelor's degree or higher	4%
2000 census	
Unemployment rate *2000 census*	12.8%
Unemployment rate *(BIA, 2001)*	76%
Per capita income *2000 census*	$10,515

LOCATION AND LAND STATUS
The Nooksack Indians live on 2,500 acres of tribal lands in the Upper Nooksack River Valley, in northwestern Washington State. Their ancestral lands include an area that is categorized geographically as the Nooksack drainage system, between Puget Sound and Mount Baker; the area also includes the shores of the Nooksack River, which is categorized as part of the Fraser River system. The tribe received federal recognition in 1971 and lands were accepted into trust status at that time.

CULTURE AND HISTORY
The Nooksack Tribe is a Coast Salish nation. Traditional means of sustenance included fishing, hunting, clam digging, root gathering, and trading. The indigenous language was the predominant language of the upper Frasier River Valley in British Columbia. In 1855, the Nooksack Tribe signed a treaty with the United States at Point Elliot; their representative was Chow-its-hoot.

By the 1860s, foreign diseases had reduced the tribe's population by half. The remaining 15 winter villages were clustered in four traditional bands near the present towns of Everson, Goshen, Lynden, and Deming. In 1873, attempts were made to relocate the Nooksacks to the Lummi Reservation. Sharing no linguistic or kinship ties with the Lummis, the Nooksacks resisted the move and remained in the upper river regions. Tribal members began homesteading the tribe's ancestral lands, preserving 4,800 acres in this manner. Although they did not have a reservation per se, the tribal community was able to remain intact. In the 1930s, the tribe accepted the provisions of the Indian Reorganization Act of 1934 but it was not given a land base. The Nooksacks were not granted federal recognition until 1971. The Nooksack Tribe helped to organize the Small Tribes Organization of Western Washington in 1969. Following recognition, one of the tribal council's first acts was to join other Washington tribes in legal action to preserve ancestral fishing rights. The case was decided years later in favor of the tribes.

GOVERNMENT
The Nooksack Tribe is represented by an eight-member tribal council, which is elected annually with no staggered terms, in accordance with the tribal constitution. The council is headed by a chairperson. The Nooksacks also belong to the Small Tribes Organization of Western Washington. Government programs include health and social services, education, housing, law enforcement, human resources, natural resources, veterans, and gaming. The tribe maintains a police department with jurisdiction over tribal trust lands, tribal property, members of the reservation, and matters pertaining to fisheries and wild life on tribal lands. This department has a chief of police, a secretary, and four officers.

ECONOMY
The tribal economy is supported by the many enterprises that

it operates in various industries, including retail, service, and gaming. Seasonal work is also sometimes available to tribal members off-reservation. Some people find jobs at the paper and pulp mill in Bellingham or at the refineries in Ferndale.

Economic Development Projects. The Nooksack Tribe is investigating economic development projects and hopes to continue its fisheries enhancement program. The tribe purchased almost 20 acres for a recreation site and for homesites for tribal members. It owns 70 acres in Nooksack Valley that are suitable for agriculture.

Agriculture and Livestock. The tribe owns 175 acres of pasture, which are leased to non-Native farmers.

Gaming. The tribe owns the Nooksack River Casino on the Mount Baker Highway in Deming. The casino features 400 slots/VLTs, 14 table games, a convention area, a buffet, and a full-service restaurant. It also features a Life Keno Lounge.

Fisheries. The tribe is co-manager of the fisheries resource in the State of Washington. It is also a participant in the Pacific Salmon Treaty negotiations. It operates a fisheries lab and maintains a salmon-rearing pond.

Services and Retail. The tribe owns a grocery store, liquor store, gas station, and smoke shop. The tribe has a retail outlet adjacent to its tribal offices, and a second outlet between Sumas and Everson. It also owns a boat-maintenance facility and a gill-net loft and training area.

Tourism and Recreation. Opportunities for fishing, skiing, boating, hiking, swimming, and hunting are abundant in the area. Natural recreational areas are Mount Baker, the Nooksack River, and Puget Sound. National, state, and county parks are nearby. In addition, golfing and motoring venues located throughout the region. The Bald Eagle Festival in February and the Ski to Sea Race Festival on Memorial Day Weekend also attract visitors the area. The tribe hosts an annual pow-wow in September.

INFRASTRUCTURE
Water Supply. Individual wells supply water, septic tanks and drain fields serve residents.

COMMUNITY FACILITIES AND SERVICES
The Nooksack Tribe has a community support facility, located next to its tribal offices. Its tribal community center is in Deming. The tribe's cultural facilities include two family longhouses. Residents may participate in a food and nutrition program. The tribe offers the House of Children program to the community. It provides guidance services for families and children. The tribe also operates Genesis II, a state-certified alcohol and drug treatment program that serves Whatcom County. Services include DUI assessment, an outpatient hospital, and a transitional house. The tribe's human resources department manages the Western Washington Indian Employment Training Program. It provides on-the-job training, reimbursements to employers, and work experience benefits to employees.

Education. Children attend school at the district schools in Mount Baker and Nooksack Valley. The tribe runs a preschool program and an adult education program, and it offers culture and language classes.

Health Care. The tribe operates the Nooksack Community Health Center, a tribally owned facility contracted through the Indian Health Service under PL 93-638. Services include primary care, alcohol counseling, mental health, public health nursing, nutrition, a community health representative, and a dental program. The clinic employs one nurse practitioner, one licensed practical nurse, three community health representatives, one alcohol counselor, and one mental health counselor/social worker. Dental services are contracted through a private provider. More comprehensive services are available through the Lummi Tribal Health Center. The tribe is also a member of the Northwest Washington Service Unit Health Board, which contracts sanitation services for the tribe.

Nooksack

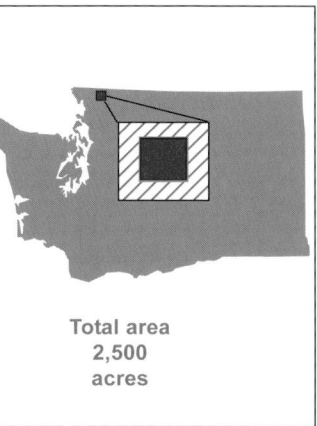

**Total area
2,500
acres**

Port Gamble

Port Gamble

LOCATION AND LAND STATUS
The Port Gamble Reservation is located in Washington State, on the northern end of the Kitsap Peninsula in Puget Sound. The reservation is a one-hour drive from Bremerton, Washington, and is just across the sound from Seattle. The reservation was created in 1936. The tribe owns the reservation in its entirety. There are no individually owned lands at Port Gamble.

PHYSICAL DESCRIPTION
The S'Klallam tribal lands are characterized by forest and low rolling hills. Bear, deer, and other wildlife also live on the reservation. The Port Gamble Reservation includes, on the west, two miles of shoreline on Port Gamble Bay and Hood Canal and, on the east, more than 1,000 acres of uplands along Puget Sound. Surface waters consist of three small creeks, including Little Boston Creek, Middle Creek, and an unnamed creek that enters Hood Canal at Point Julia.

CLIMATE
The reservation receives about 20 inches of rain per year. It lies in the Olympic Mountain rain shadow.

CULTURE AND HISTORY
The Port Gamble S'Klallam are one of three groups of S'Klallam Coast Salish-speaking people who belong to the resource-rich Pacific Northwest Coast Indian culture. The other two groups are the Jamestown S'Klallam and the Lower Elwha S'Klallam. Traditionally, the S'Klallam inhabited the southern shores of the Strait of Juan de Fuca. The word "S'Klallam" is said to derive from "nuxklai'yem," meaning "strong people." Their subsistence activities centered around the abundance provided by the coastal waters and forests. The people hunted game and depended on marine resources, such as Dungeness crab, clams, and other shellfish, herring, and salmon. Many of the cultures of the Pacific Northwest developed a highly evolved social and religious system, which included class-consciousness. There existed a hereditary nobility, a middle class, and a slave class of war captives; wealth often determined leadership. The Native inhabitants of this area were skilled craftspeople who fashioned many objects from cedar, including ceremonial masks, storage boxes, serving dishes, and utensils. They lived in beautifully crafted communal houses, some of which were enormous. They were excellent basket makers, and they also wove clothing, mats, and rope from cedar bark.

**Port Gamble Reservation
Federal reservation
S'Klallam
Kitsap County, Washington**

Port Gamble S'Klallam Indian
    Community
31912 Little Boston Rd. NE
Kingston, WA 98346
    360-297-2646
    360-297-7097 Fax

Port Gamble

Total area *(BIA realty, 2004)*
1,040 acres

Tribally owned
(BIA realty, 2004)
1,040 acres

Population *2000 census*
699

Population *(Tribal source, 2004)*
1,045

Tribal enrollment
(BIA labor report, 2001)
1,045

Tribal enrollment
(Tribal source, 2004)
1,045

Total labor force *2000 census*
308

Total labor force
(BIA labor report, 2001)
850

High school graduate or higher
2000 census
75.6%

Bachelor's degree or higher
2000 census
7.8%

Unemployment rate *2000 census*
8.8%

Unemployment rate
(BIA labor report, 2001)
55%

Per capita income *2000 census*
$10,111

In the early 1790s, contact began with the Spanish and British and became regular after the establishment of Hudson's Bay Company trading posts. After the explorations of Lewis and Clark in the early 1800s, contact with Euro-Americans increased. There is mention of the S'Klallam trading at various forts from the 1820s to the 1840s. At the time of the treaties of the 1850s, the S'Klallams inhabited 12 villages in western Washington state area. In 1855, the S'Klallams signed the Treaty of Point-No-Point with the United States. It stipulated that they move to a small reservation on Hood Canal, to live with their traditional enemies, the Skokomish. Few S'Klallams settled there, and they resisted several attempts in the 1800s and 1900s to remove them to the Skokomish Reservation. Some Natives established a small settlement on the Port Gamble Peninsula. Under the 1934 Indian Reorganization Act, funds became available to purchase the peninsula, and Port Gamble Reservation was established there in 1936. The S'Klallam Tribes continued to battle the federal government for compensation for lost tribal lands, and in 1977, they were awarded $327,237. The Port Gamble, Elwha, and Jamestown bands agreed to divide the monies equally and manage each share for community purposes.

GOVERNMENT

The Port Gamble S'Klallam tribal government was reorganized under the Indian Reorganization Act in 1934. The tribe has a constitution and bylaws, a federal chartered ratified in 1941, and a comprehensive code of laws. The tribe is governed by a six-member council and a general council. The tribe was one of the first in the nation to become a self-governing tribe. It has assumed control over federal government functions and budgets previously handled by the BIA and Indian Health Service. In addition, the tribe participates in the intertribal Point-No-Point Treaty Council, which represents the three S'Klallam groups.

Government programs include education, senior center, utility, children and family services, wellness, natural resources, housing, and cultural. The tribe was the first in Washington to establish a Temporary Assistance to Needy Families program and the first to operate a federally funded child support program. The tribe maintains a police department and a tribal court system. The police department has a chief of police, a sergeant, an acting sergeant, and two police officers. The courts exercise jurisdiction over criminal, civil, and juvenile matters. The system includes a three-judge-appeals court.

BUSINESS CORPORATION

The Port Gamble Development Authority, chartered in 1986, is responsible for implementing long-range economic plans and developing projects of the tribe both on and off the reservation.

The Port Gamble S'Klallam Foundation was rechartered from the S'Klallam Development Fund in 2002. It serves to provide or secure funding for tribal projects. Current projects include the House of Knowledge, a complex housing a tribal longhouse, the new Little Boston Library, a career and education center, and an elders' center.

ECONOMY

The tribe and associated agencies of the tribal government serve as the major sources of employment for tribal members. The community generates revenues from operating a casino that employs 120 people; a marketplace complex that includes a convenience store, gas station, café, and espresso drive-up employing 20 people; and its aquiculture operations.

Government as Employer. The tribal government and its associated agencies and enterprises employ 400 people.

Economic Development Projects. The tribe is implementing a five-year business recruitment project to attract new businesses and industries to the Port Gamble Reservation.

Agriculture and Livestock. There is no commercial farming on the reservation. Some domestic gardens provide vegetables for personal consumption.

Gaming. The tribe owns the Point Casino in Kingston. Opened in 2002, the casino offers 400 slots, 10 table games, an entertainment venue, and 1 restaurant. It employs 130 people.

Fisheries. Port Gamble Bay is the last bay in Kitsap County still open to commercial shellfish harvesting. The tribe operates an aquaculture program at the Port Gamble S'Klallam Hatchery on Point Julia that includes a salmon hatchery, a geoduck fishery, fish, and oyster growing. The Port Gamble S'Klallams are members of the Northwest Indian Fisheries Commission.

Construction. The Port Gamble S'Klallam Tribe served as its own general contractor for the construction of its community sewer system.

Industrial Parks. The tribe has a 30-acre, commercially zoned park, the Salish Business Park. This industrial park, located in the southeastern portion of the reservation, houses the Point-No-Point Treaty Council in a 5,000-square-foot facility built on two acres of park land by the tribe entirely with general obligation financing-a first in Indian Country. In 1996 the Port Gamble S'Klallam's goal for the Salish Business Park was to improve the water-storage capacity of the community water supply tower and to extend utilities into the park.

Media and Communications. The tribe owns Salish Broadband, a high-speed Internet access portal for on- and off-reservation users. In 2002 this company connected to the NOANet fiber gird providing it with the capability to offer 100 mutual broadcasting system and gig-ethernet services to its customers.

Services and Retail. The tribe owns the Gilding Eagle Market Place. It offers a full-service convenience store, food court, deli, drive-thru espresso venue, and gas station.

Tourism and Recreation. The waters of Puget Sound provide many opportunities for fishing, boating, water-skiing, and swimming. Sightseeing trips by ferry are also popular with tourists. The tribe annually sponsors an Environmental Day celebration, S'Klallam Days, and a winter powwow.

INFRASTRUCTURE

The Port Gamble Reservation is served by the nearby north-south route, State Highway 3.

Electricity. Puget Energy Services provide electricity.

Water Supply. A community supply tower provides water for Port Gamble Reservation residents. Community and individual septic tanks and drain field systems serve the reservation.

Transportation. Port Gamble is near Seattle, where all means of commercial transportation are available.

COMMUNITY FACILITIES AND SERVICES

Community facilities include an outdoor amphitheater and a youth center. The youth program offers a youth council, support groups, CEDAR/Youth leadership, a Big Buddy program, summer culture camps, summer recreation programs, an annual basketball camp, and annual celebrations. It also sponsors the Purser Memorial Powwow and the Canoe Journey Elder's Honoring. The tribe is in the process of constructing a traditional longhouse to serve as a cultural and educational center as well as a community meeting place. The tribe's community library was voted the "Best Small Library in America (1999)." The reservation also houses a community church, a senior center, neighborhood parks, two picnic areas, two baseball fields, a gym, and two boat ramps.

The tribe actively participates in open-ocean canoe journeys, such as the A-ka-lat Gathering to the Quileute Reservation, the Salmon Homecoming ceremony in Seattle, and the Power Paddle in Puyallup.

Education. Port Gamble has a tribal preschool. Older children use nearby public schools. The tribe's career and education department offers academic advising, application assistance, higher education grants, job referrals, résumé preparation assistance, a homework club, GED preparation, adult basic education, precollege courses, and elementary and high school summer school programs. The tribe's early childhood educa-tion programs include a preschool, infant and toddler socialization groups, child care, family literacy activities, parenting classes, craft groups, nutrition guidance, and intergenerational programs.

Health Care. The tribe operates a health clinic, dental clinic, and community health program. The health clinic provides primary, prevention, women's, and well child care services. It also provides referral authorization for Contract Health Service and Basic Health Plan. The tribe maintains a medicinal garden at the health clinic. Plants and herbs used in traditional healing methods are grown there. The clinic staff includes two doctors, a physician's assistant, a family nurse practitioner, a pediatrician, a nutritionist, and a registered nurse. The dental clinic provides general dental services. It employs three dentists and one pediatric dentist. The community health program offers community health, maternal child health, and health education programs. The tribe has recently completed construction on a state-of-the-art wellness center to house its mental health and chemical dependency and treatment programs. Acute-care medical facilities are located in nearby Seattle.

Port Gamble

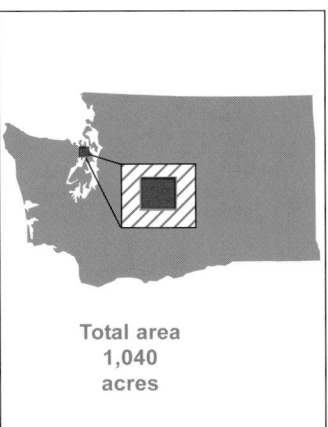

Total area
1,040
acres

Port Madison

Port Madison

LOCATION AND LAND STATUS

The Port Madison Indian Reservation covers more than 7,400 acres of rolling, timbered land on the Kitsap Peninsula, which extends into Puget Sound. Seattle lies almost directly across the sound to the east, while Bremerton is only 25 miles south. Divided by a landmass, the reservation is composed of two separate parcels. The northeastern portion of the reservation is anchored by the rural waterfront Village of Indianola, the southwestern portion by the historic waterfront Village of Suquamish.

The reservation was set-aside for the Suquamish Tribe as part of the Point Elliot Treaty of January 22, 1855, and it was expanded by an Executive Order in October 1864. Because of the federal government's allotment policy, less than 3,000 acres remain in trust or in Indian ownership. Land ownership patterns resemble a checkerboard. The federal government holds more than 40 percent of the reservation in trust. The reservation contains tribal trust lands, individually and collectively owned trust lands, historic allotments held in trust, and fee lands owned by Indians and non-Indians.

PHYSICAL DESCRIPTION

Tribal lands are characterized by Douglas fir, western red cedar, red alder, broadleaf maple, and vine maple forests. Scotch broom, dogwood, and salmonberries also grow within reservation boundaries. The Olympic Mountains are located to the west of the reservation and the Cascades to the east. Tribal lands are located along Puget Sound and its bays and inlets. Bear, deer, and smaller woodland animals live within tribal lands.

CULTURE AND HISTORY

The Suquamish people and their ancestors have lived, hunted, and fished in the Puget Sound area for several thousand years. Prior to the arrival of white explorers and settlers, this area was one of the most populated centers on the continent north of what is now Mexico City. Near the end of the eighteenth century, Captain George Vancouver and his crew sailed into Puget Sound. Shortly thereafter, smallpox, measles, flu, and other European diseases began decimating the region's Na-tive population. Missionaries, predominantly Catholic, arrived during the 1830s and 1840s and established schools and churches. To this day, some Suquamish remain Catholic, while others are members of the Indian Shaker Church or practice traditional religions. Also of great significance was the tribe's contact with Hudson's Bay Company traders at Fort Nisqually, which the company established in 1833. The Suquamish Native language, Puget Sound Salish (or Lushootseed), was rapidly replaced by English after white contact. In recent times, Lushootseed has experienced a revival of sorts within the tribal community.

The 1855 Treaty of Point Elliot placed the Suquamish people on the site of what is now the Port Madison Indian Reservation. Here the tribe suffered encroachments by Canadian tribesmen as well as exploitation by area whiskey peddlers. For subsistence and trade, the Suquamishes relied on the region's abundant waters and forest resources, but that changed beginning in the 1850s when many became laborers in the mills that sprung up around Puget Sound. An Act of Congress on October 24, 1864, expanded and redrew the reservation, splitting it into two tracts separated by a body of water. The tribe was frequently coerced into selling parcels of its land; eventually the majority of the reservation passed into non-Indian hands. In the early twentieth century, the United States appropriated the Indian Village of D'Suq'Wub w as a military post; the villagers were forcibly relocated to individual allotments scattered across the reservation. While the federal government hoped this move would encourage tribal members to take up farming, most retained their hunting and fishing lifestyles. By 1920, however, non-Indian fishing and canning industries had depleted the salmon runs in Puget Sound that had always been so central to the Suquamish way of life. Tribal members relied on their skills at basketry, fishing, gathering, and hunting to survive.

Between 1880 and 1920, the tribe suffered the effects of forced assimilation as tribal youth were removed from the reservation and placed in boarding schools. The separation of the youngest generations of the tribe interrupted the teaching of

Port Madison Indian Reservation
Federal reservation
Suquamish
Kitsap County, Washington

Suquamish Tribal Council
P.O. Box 498
Suquamish, WA 98392
　360-598-3311
　360-598-6295 Fax
　suquamish.nsn.us

Port Madison

Total area *(BIA realty, 2004)*
2,828.12 acres

Tribally owned
(BIA realty, 2004)
220.07 acres

Individually owned
(BIA realty, 2004)
2,608.05 acres

Population *2000 census*
6,536

Tribal enrollment
(BIA labor report, 2004)
884

Total labor force *2000 census*
3,535

Total labor force
(BIA labor report, 2004)
2,857

High school graduate or higher
2000 census
91.7%

Bachelor's degree or higher
2000 census
30.3%

Unemployment rate *2000 census*
5.5%

Unemployment rate
(BIA labor report, 2004)
40%

Per capita income *2000 census*
$22,691

cultural elements, including the indigenous language. The tribe continues to repair the damage created during this period and actively promotes cultural retention, preservation, and practice. The Suquamish Tribe ascribes to the belief that its members and the natural systems that sustain them are its greatest resources.

GOVERNMENT

The tribal government operates under a constitution and by-laws adopted in 1965. The Suquamish General Council meets twice a year and is composed of all enrolled tribal members. An elected seven-member tribal council conducts tribal affairs; each member serves a three-year staggered term. The tribe's elders and youth councils act in an advisory capacity to the tribal council. Government departments and programs include fisheries, education, natural resources, public safety, tribal court, Indian child welfare, community development, human services, maintenance, and cultural resources.

Tribal headquarters, the community center, and public safety services are located on tribal trust land in and near the waterfront community of Suquamish. The tribe's mission is to provide for the well being of tribal members, repatriate its alienated land base, and preserve treaty rights.

BUSINESS CORPORATION

Tribal business activities are conducted under the auspices of Port Madison Enterprises (PME). PME is managed by a board of directors consisting of seven tribal members, including one tribal council member. PME businesses fall in the arena of retail enterprises, gaming, natural resources development, and property management.

In addition to PME, there are separately chartered boards and commissions that direct the operations of specific tribal enterprises. These entities include the tribal gaming commission, which oversees the tribe's gaming enterprises and the Suquamish Seafood Enterprise, which oversees the harvesting and marketing of geoduck clams.

ECONOMY

The tribal economy is sustained in large part by the tribe's enterprises in the fishing industry, leasing home sites, and the tribe's gaming facilities. For the last decade of the twentieth century, many tribal members relied on seasonal employment-such as fishing, fireworks sales, and clam digging-and gathering plants for basketry, carving, medicines, and ceremonies. The Puget Sound Naval Shipyard and other military installations is a major local employers.

Government as Employer. The tribe has a staff of more than 120 people working with and for the tribal council to provide basic governmental services within the boundaries of the reservation. In this vein, the council's annual budget amounts to over $4 million. The tribe employs over 700 people through its enterprises, which include the Suquamish Clearwater Casino and the newly acquired Kiana Lodge.

Economic Development Projects. The tribe maintains its own economic development plan and has worked conjointly with federal, state, and county agencies. It also works with Kitsap County to create economic development plans for the rural areas that strive to encourage development that will not alter or damage the region's rural character.

Forestry. The Port Madison Forest Plan provides for the maintenance and protection of over 2,300 acres of tribal trust lands. Tribal members may elect to have their individual trust lands included in the tribe's forest management program. The tribe maintains a natural resources division, which provides for funding and research of forestry products.

Gaming. The tribe owns and operates the Suquamish Clearwater Casino on the Agate Pass Bridge. The casino features over 900 video slots, 33 table games, a poker room, and 282 bingo seats. The Cedar Steakhouse, the Agate Pass Deli, and Longhouse Buffet are located within the casino, as is a live music lounge. Free shuttle service is available, and an ATM and credit card machines are located on the facilities. The casino employs 660 people.

Fisheries. Commercial fishing and the shellfish industry represent the tribe's main nongovernmental source of income. The tribe operates the Grover Creek Hatchery on trust lands near the community of Indianola and other smaller hatcheries throughout Kitsap County. The tribe releases more than five million fish into Puget Sound annually. The Grover Creek Hatchery is uniquely designed, featuring an experimental water system that relies on waterwheels and an artesian well. It was featured in a national architectural magazine. The hatchery draws numerous tourists. In 2004, an oil spill on Puget Sound damaged at least 400 acres of tribal land, including part of the fishery. The area was home to soft shell clams, geoduck clams, and Dungeness crabs. Ramifications have not been determined, though damages are expected to total in the hundreds of thousands of dollars.

Suquamish Seafoods is a tribally owned commercial enterprise. Two boats, *Skookum* and *Misty II*, are used to harvest geoduck clams for resale. The enterprise is the main source of income and a primary source of employment for the tribe. Income from the enterprise is used to fund elders, education, youth, land acquisition, and other tribal programs.

Construction. Human resource figures show that a significant number of individual members find employment within the construction trade, in positions ranging from laborers to contractors.

Services and Retail. Tribal businesses include gift shops, located at the Suquamish Clearwater Casino, the MASI Shop (a gas station and liquor store), Kiana Lodge (a waterfront convention and wedding facility), and a Subway restaurant. In addition, the tribe's property management division explores opportunities for commercial building development and for handling the leasing of certain tribal lands.

Media and Communications. The tribe publishes the *Suquamish Newsletter* and employs a half-time tribal spokesperson.

Tourism and Recreation. The tribe owns and operates the Suquamish Museum. The museum features "The Eyes of Chief Seattle" exhibit, which includes photographs, artifacts, and quotations documenting tribal culture and history. Other displays include woven baskets, a dugout canoe, tools, fishing equipment, and an audiovisual program. The museum also offers an art gallery, a gift shop, a nature trail, a beachside trail, and picnic areas. Traveling displays have been featured in Paris, France, and throughout the continental United States. Areas of interest located near the tribal museum include Chief Seattle's gravesite, St. Peter's Catholic Church and Cemetery, Joe Hillaire story pole, Charles Lawrence Memorial Boat Ramp and Suquamish dock, Old-Man-House Park, Grover Creek Hatchery, Lawrence Webster (Indianola) Memorial Baseball Field, Indianola Village, and Suquamish Village. In 2004, the State of Washington agreed to transfer ownership of the Old-Man-House State Park to the Suquamish Tribe, thereby returning a part of the tribe's traditional home village. The tribe also maintains the Indianola Park on lands leased from a tribal member. The community, Kitsap County, and the State of Washington raised the funds to develop the project. The tribe holds an annual celebration called Chief Seattle Days in August, that includes a royalty pageant, a salmon bake, dancing and drumming, canoe races, and a memorial service, all of which attract thousands of visitors.

INFRASTRUCTURE
State Route 305 is the primary highway through the reservation connecting the cities of Poulsbo and Bainbridge Island; it includes the historic Agate Pass Bridge that connects the island to the reservation mainland. State Route 3, which runs to Bremerton, meets State Route 305 in Poulsbo. Suquamish Way and Miller Bay Road connect State Route 305 to State Route 104. Highway 104 leads to Highway 101 on the Olympic Peninsula. County roads also serve the area. Washington State ferries provide service across Puget Sound to Seattle and Edmonds, permitting easy access to metropolitan areas.

Electricity. Puget Sound Energy provides electrical.

Water Supply. The U.S. Public Health Service installed both wells and septic systems for sanitation service for many reservation houses. Kitsap County P.U.D. provides water to other Native and non-Native reservation residents.

Transportation. Commercial air, bus, and railway services are available in Seattle, just across the sound from the reservation.

COMMUNITY FACILITIES AND SERVICES
The tribe owns a commercial real estate park named Suquamish Village Square. This location houses the main tribal building where most services and programs are located. Some services are run from modular buildings in downtown Suquamish, were the tribe also has a youth center and computer lab.

The tribe's department of community development provides counseling and technical assistance to tribal members establishing their own businesses. The tribe also produced the *Intellectual Property Law Workbook* in 1998 to assist tribal artists and craftspeople in maneuvering through legal issues such as intellectual property rights, copyrights, resources, and taxation.

Education. Suquamish children attend local public schools. The tribal education department works closely with the North Kitsap School District to improve educational opportunities and experiences for tribal youth.

Health Care. The Suquamish Tribe has developed a respected health care plan that serves as a model for other tribes. Off-reservation tribal members can receive health care from the U.S. Public Health Service Hospital in Seattle.

ENVIRONMENTAL CONCERNS
In 2004, an estimated 400 acres of tribal lands were devastated by the affects of a 4,800-gallon oil spill on Puget Sound. The area includes part of the tribal fishery and ceremonial grounds. Cleanup efforts were initiated, but final damages have not yet been determined.

The erosion of land, in turn affecting the quality of water sources on Puget Sound, is also of grave concern to the tribe. The bulk of the threat to water quality stems from the increasing development on the sound. Urbanization of the former rural region nears the reservation, which troubles the tribe a great deal. In addition to there being little or no benefit to the tribe economically, the encroachment poses a threat to the local environment.

Port Madison

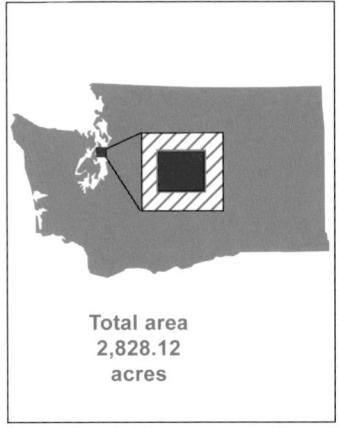

Total area
2,828.12
acres

Puyallup

Puyallup

Puyallup Reservation
Federal reservation
Puyallup
Pierce County, Washington

Puyallup Tribe of the Puyallup
   Reservation
1850 Alexander Ave.
Tacoma, WA 98404
360-597-6200
360-848-7341 Fax

LOCATION AND LAND STATUS
The Puyallup Reservation is located south of Seattle near Tacoma, Washington. Puyallup is an urban reservation located within the city limits of Tacoma and on Commencement Bay, an international shipping area. It was established on 1,280 acres by the Medicine Creek Treaty of 1854, with an additional 18,062 acres added in January 1856. In 1890, the growth of the City of Tacoma instigated the sale of tracts of land within the reservation to Euro-American settlers. Over 9,000 acres of tribal lands were sold to the public. In 1935, the remaining land fell out of trust status. It regained that status, however, after the tribe brought suit against the federal government. A land settlement in 1988 restored four properties in the Tacoma tidal flats to the tribe. These properties are the Blair Backup Property, Blair Waterway Property, Upper Hylebos, and Inner Hylebos properties.

PHYSICAL DESCRIPTION
The reservation is located along the southern end of Puget Sound. Portions of the Puyallup River are located within tribal lands, as are wetlands, riparians, foothills, and cedar forests. It is; however, primarily an urban environment within Tacoma, Washington.

CLIMATE
The reservation experiences a mid-latitude, west coast marine climate. Summers are dry and mild while winters tend to be rainy. The year-round average daily high temperature is 61.4°F. The year-round average daily low temperature is 44.6°F. The area receives approximately 39 inches of precipitation annually.

CULTURE AND HISTORY
The S'Puyalupubsh, or Puyallup, have resided in the Pacific Northwest for thousands of years. Tribal lands encompassed regions between the foothills of Mount Tacoma and Puget Sound. The Puyallups are members of the Coast Salish group and speak the Lushootseed dialect of the Salish language. Traditional means of sustenance included gathering salmon, shellfish, wild game, roots, and berries. Cedar trees also played a significant role in the lives of early Puyallups, serving as material for homes, clothing, utensils, and transportation.

The Puyallups encountered European explorers as early as 1792, when the British entered the area. As settlers entered the region over the next 50 years, the Puyallups were steadily pushed out of their traditional territory. In 1854, the tribe agreed to the Medicine Creek Treaty, which created reservations for the Puyallup, Nisqually, and Squaxin Island tribes. The reservations were not sufficient for the tribes, and a war ensued. In 1856, the treaty was renegotiated and the Puyallup Reservation expanded. In 1886, the reservation was divided into 178 individual allotments. One small area, known as Indian Addition, was the only tract of land to remain in tribal ownership. Encroachments by whites resulted in losses of lands and rights, especially with regard to fishing. The legal issues sur-

Puyallup

Total area *(BIA realty, 2004)*
490.46 acres

Tribally owned *(BIA realty, 2004)*
349.07 acres

Individually owned
(BIA realty, 2004)
141.39 acres

Population *2000 census*
41,335

Tribal enrollment
(BIA labor report, 2001)
2,490

Total labor force *2000 census*
21,145

Total labor force
(BIA labor report, 2001)
8,969

High school graduate or higher
2000 census
85.1%

Bachelor's degree or higher
2000 census
23.1%

Unemployment rate *2000 census*
5.7%

Unemployment rate
(BIA labor report, 2001)
75%

Per capita income *2000 census*
$22,750

rounding northwest coastal Indian treaty fishing rights are very complex and involve a long history of state and federal litigation.

In the 1960s and 1970s, the Puyallups played a pivotal role in the return of treaty-protected fishing rights to Washington State tribes. Since the turn of the twentieth century, when Indians were seen as "privileged" in terms of fishing rights, by sport fishermen and non-Indian commercial interests, the State of Washington began ignoring federal treaties, intent on eliminating Indian gillnet fishing on rivers outside reservation borders. Under the guise of resource conservation after declines of fish populations in the 1950s, the State of Washington enforced their own sets of regulations prohibiting net fishing on rivers, in direct violation of tribal sovereignty and its own constitution and laws. Nets were seized; tribal members were assaulted and repeatedly arrested, with cases appealed to higher and higher levels of the state and federal courts. Members of the general public, including many non-Indian supporters, joined in staged demonstrations, referred to as "fish-ins," wherein confrontations with state game and fisheries officials made state and national news coverage. Tribal members, joined by their non-Indian allies, marched at the state capitol building and the federal court building. At issue were: the "usual and accustomed" fishing rights guaranteed to the Indian signatories of the Medicine Creek Treaty of 1854; and whether the State of Washington, with only limited jurisdiction over consenting Indian reservations under PL-280, could prohibit a federally protected, treaty guaranteed right. A succession of state and federal court cases were overturned, as language in either the treaty or subsequent state laws seemed to directly contradict one another. With its decision regarding the taking of an "equal share" of the fisheries, the now famous Boldt Decision, rather than resolving the decades-long Indian fishing question, only served to spark new appeals.

Rendered by U.S. District Judge George Boldt on February 12, 1974, the Boldt Decision forced tribal recognition of the need to work together in protecting biologically sound fishing practices in the waters of Puget Sound. Signatories to the Medicine Creek Treaty-the Puyallup, Point Elliott, Medicine Creek, Makah, Point-No-Point, and Quinault tribes-joined together to form the Northwest Indian Fisheries Commission. This commission played a pivotal role in all treaty negotiations in subsequent years and was a key player in carrying out the provisions of the Boldt Decision. The Puyallups, still contesting that the State of Washington had any right to interfere in their fisheries, filed an appeal of the Boldt Decision in the Ninth Circuit Court of Appeals in San Francisco in April 1974, but it was upheld. While they took their case to the United States Supreme Court, Judge Boldt rendered supplemental orders, extending the "equal share" rule to include 50 percent of other fish species taken from rivers within the Columbia River watershed. How to track catch ratios became the biggest issue for all concerned, as determining exactly what constituted "an equal share" of any particular season's run of salmon and steelhead figured critically in both the economic and enforcement aspects of the decision. In response, the Puyallups devised a Long-Range Management Plan, drafted in December 1975, which included provisions for increasing tribal control of Indian fisheries, gaining some means of coercing the state into reducing non-Indian fishing in their waters, and developing emergency measures for seasons when fish runs were particularly low. Finally, in 1979, a Supreme Court ruling upheld Judge Boldt's 1974 District Court decision, reaffirming that tribal governments, in signing the Medicine Creek and other treaties, did not submit to state regulation and are still entitled to manage their share of the fishery resources without interference as long as they continue to protect the resource. While on the surface it was a victory for Indian fishermen, in that it prevented further encroach-

ments by the State of Washington into the management of Indian fisheries, the caveat regarding protection of the resources gave the state some reason for potential future intervention into Indian fishing affairs. And the prohibition against off-reservation fishing stood. However, the Boldt Decision did guarantee the Puyallup Tribe control of its own fishing and financial destinies. As a result, the tribe formed the Puyallup Nation Port Authority in 1981 to guide economic development programs and land acquisition efforts.

Suits filed under the 1951 Indian Claims Commission Act, for the return of lands once claimed as aboriginal territory, began to bear fruit in the mid-1970s as well, and the tribe was eventually successful in ensuring the return of Cushman Indian Hospital in downtown Tacoma. The clinic they established at the facility provided basic primary care services for children and adults of any tribe, with part-time specialty care services, an emergency medical unit, and pharmacy, nutritional, and outreach services.

Tribal community and economic enterprises' budget had a growing balance of $18,831.38 in November 1976; the Puyallups started their own credit union in 1978. In 1978, they fought for and were successful in securing the return of the Northeast Tacoma Clubhouse to tribal control for use as a drop-in daycare facility one day per week, a senior center another day, after-school and summer youth programming, and a meeting facility. They continued working on the ever-larger land-claims issues, in determining exactly where Puyallup tribal boundaries "should have always been," according to the Medicine Creek and other federal treaties and subsequent executive orders. In order to coordinate efforts among the various northwestern coastal tribes with respect to the fishing struggles, the Puyallup Tribal Council was pivotal in developing the Intertribal Planning Consortium.

In March 1990, the tribe signed the Puyallup Tribe of Indians Settlement Act of 1989 in resolution of their long-standing land claims. Along with one-time lump-sum payments to 1,545 tribal members, the final agreement called for: the establishment of a tribal trust fund to manage the incoming funds, with specified amounts to be held in trust to be paid out for social services and housing over a 50-year period; enhancement of the tribal fisheries and cleanup of fish habitats; job training and employment-placement programs; and construction of a 20-bed elder care facility, a daycare facility with the capacity to care for 42 children, and a 20-bed youth substance abuse treatment facility. Monies were set aside for economic development and additional land purchases, for small business development among tribal members, and to acquire land to develop cultural facilities. Four parcels of land adjacent to the Port of Tacoma, including 43 acres along the Blair Waterway, were returned to the tribe, along with 57 acres of Union Pacific Railway land and 27 acres along the Frank Albert Road.

Throughout the 1990s, the Puyallups built a tribal infrastructure, including staff in law enforcement and court systems, and assumed leadership on key intergovernmental boards while protecting cultural resources for the future benefit of all tribal members.

GOVERNMENT

The tribe organized under the provisions of the Indian Reorganization Act of 1934, and the Secretary of the Interior approved its constitution on May 13, 1936. The tribe is governed by a council consisting of seven elected members.

Tribal government programs include health, law enforcement, and tribal court. A nine-member committee appointed by the tribe's board of directors manages trust funds for the tribe's housing, elderly needs, burial and cemetery maintenance, education and cultural preservation, and social services programs.

The Puyallup Tribal Law Enforcement department includes the land enforcement division and the fish and wildlife division. The land enforcement division enforces tribal laws and operates a detention facility. Tribal police officers receive training at the Police Academy in Artesia, New Mexico, as well as at the Washington State Training Commissions Law Enforcement Equivalency Academy. The fish and wildlife division enforces tribal fishing regulations for the lower Puget Sound, the Puyallup River, and several other bodies of water. They also enforce shellfish regulations and the gaming code. The tribal court exercises jurisdiction over matters pertaining to the tribal code, both civil and criminal.

BUSINESS CORPORATION
Founded in 1989, Puyallup International serves as the economic development arm of the tribe. The corporation has established agreements and relationships with governing bodies and businesses to promote economic growth and beneficial business for all members of the area. In 1999, Puyallup International was the largest employer in the county and provided employment for almost 2,000 individuals. Puyallup International was a 1999 nominee for the Bradford Award.

Puyallup International manages the Emerald Queen Cascades Casino and Resort, the Emerald Queen Casino, the Chinook Landing Marina, and the Northwest Container Supply company, as wells as the tribe's seafood venture. Puyallup International assisted in securing legislation to authorize the International Services Development Zone in the Port of Tacoma. It also entered into a joint venture with Global Intermodal Systems to develop a port facility that provides long-term employment in a trucking, container storage, and servicing enterprise.

ECONOMY
The tribe is a major employer in King County, with economic activities in natural resources (fishing), transportation and utilities, finance and real estate, and governmental services, including health, education, social services, recreation, and entertainment. The tribe owns a number of enterprises in various industries, each providing a source of employment and revenue for the tribe and for non-Native communities in the area. Issuing business licenses on the reservation also provides a source of income for the tribe. In 2000, the tribe was proposing to enter into a compact with the State of Washington to share revenues from taxes charged to non-Indians on cigarettes sold on tribal lands.

Economic Development Projects. In addition to the casinos and the initiatives discussed above, a tribally owned 400-slip marina provides rental income for the tribe and a waterfront home for the offices of Puyallup International. Northwest Container, an intermodal freight yard, provides rental income for the tribe, and a gas station located on the Portland Street Exit of I-5 brings discount gasoline to tribal members and the potential for an even better mix of fast-food restaurants in the future. In 1998, the tribe was considering the development of a prerelease facility on tribal lands, designed to temporarily house inmates being released from the state prison system.

Gaming. The tribe owns the Emerald Queen Cascades Casino and Resort in Tacoma, featuring 1,500 slots and 43 table games. They also have owned and operated the Emerald Queen Casino in Tacoma since 1995. This facility offers 1,700 slots/VLTs, 50 table games, a convention center, 3 restaurants, and 3 entertainment venues. The casino employs 1,000 people. This casino was the first conventionally financed gaming enterprise in the nation, with the added record of retiring its debt within its five-year amortization period.

Located off the I-5 in downtown Tacoma across from the tribe's headquarters, Puyallup Indian Bingo employs approximately 110 people. Seating capacity is estimated at 1,100, and it is open seven days a week. It provides significant income to the tribe.

Fisheries. Tribal members exercise the fishing and hunting rights guaranteed them in the 1855 Medicine Creek Treaty. In 1974, the Boldt Decision upheld the rights of the treaty tribes to fish in their usual and accustomed areas, with the provision that the tribes regulate their own fisheries. *(See Culture and History, above.)*

Services and Retail. The tribe owns the Chinook Landing Marina. It provides covered and open slips, as well as fuel and supplies for recreational boaters. The tribe also owns an international seafood venture.

Transportation. The tribe owns Northwest Container Supply Company, which provides international shipping, local drayage, and distribution facilities in the Port of Tacoma.

Media and Communications. The tribe publishes *Puyallup Tribal News*, a monthly newspaper.

Tourism and Recreation. The tribe operates a tribal museum. It features photos, documents, and artifacts of tribal history. An abundance of outdoor recreational opportunities exist within the surrounding regions.

INFRASTRUCTURE
U.S. I-5 and I-705 serve the Tacoma area. The reservation is near the junction of I-705 (Exit 135) and State Highway 167.

Electricity. The Pierce County Public Utility District provides electricity.

Water Supply. The U.S. Public Health Service installed water and septic tanks before 1974.

Transportation. Residents of the reservation have access to all services available in the greater Tacoma area.

COMMUNITY FACILITIES AND SERVICES
The tribe's elderly needs program provides housekeeping, yard maintenance, shopping, and daily needs services. The tribe has established a language preservation program and operates a job training program. The tribe also operates a number of social programs that provide support services to parents, anti-gang prevention, and cultural awareness activities.

Education. The Chief Leschi School, opened in 1975, serves students in preschool-12. The student body is comprised of over 1,200 youth from over 90 American tribes. The tribe owns the Medicine Creek Tribal College and provides a two-year, postsecondary academic program.

Health Care. The tribe operates the Takopid Health Center. It provides dental, medical, community health, pharmacy, optometry, and physical therapy programs. An alcohol and substance abuse center provides services for 30 patients, and the Kwawachee Center provides services for mental health patients. It also houses a "spirit house," which hosts cultural activities. Each facility employs both western medical practices and traditional tribal healing methods. The tribe's health program received the 1999 Honoring Contribution in the Governance of American Indian Nations Award.

Puyallup

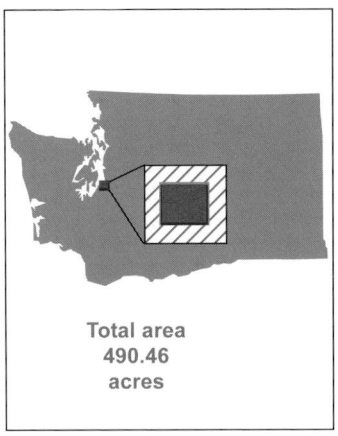

**Total area
490.46
acres**

ENVIRONMENTAL CONCERNS
Throughout the 1990s, the tribe drafted ecology and wildlife protection policies based on sound watershed quality analyses, in addition to developing air quality standards.

The tribe's primary environmental concerns pertain to the problem of hazardous waste pollution on tribal lands. The Blair Backup Property, Blair Waterway Property, Upper Hylebos, and Inner Hylebos properties that were returned to the tribe by the Settlement Act of 1989 required environmental assessments. Findings indicated that the areas were severely impacted and required cleanup of contaminated sediment. The tribe spearheaded the U.S. EPA's Superfund cleanup of the Commencement Bay Nearshore/Tideflats of Tacoma.

The tribe is also involved in efforts to protect the quality of water in the Puyallup River watershed. In 1998, the tribe was delegated authority by the federal Clean Water Act to administer water quality standards in the Puyallup River within tribal lands.

Honoring Nations Honoree 1999

Institutionalized Quality Improvement Program, Puyallup Tribal Health Authority, Puyallup Tribe of Indians

Honoring Nations Honoree 1999

Text in its entirety from: The Harvard Project On American Indian Economic Development

John F. Kennedy School of Government Harvard University

For years, members of the Puyallup Tribe suffered from serious health and social problems, many of which could be attributed to the reservation process, federal government neglect, and discrimination against Indians practiced by more recent settlers to the Pierce County, WA (Puget Sound) area. And the members of the Puyallup Tribe were not alone-the larger Native population in the county suffered from the same problems. In the early 1990s, for example, 95 percent of the Indians living on or near the Puyallup reservation had, or were affected by someone who had, a substance abuse problem. As recently as the 1970s, the Indian population on the reservation and in Pierce County generally had little or no health care. The Puyallup Tribe provided a few contract referral services through the Indian Health Service (IHS) and managed a small dental clinic and women's health clinic in a church basement, but apart from these, there were virtually no other services available to meet local Indians' health needs.

The Self-Determination Act of 1975 provided the Puyallup Tribe with an opportunity to change at least some of this picture. Under the provisions of the Act, the Tribe contracted with the IHS to self-manage tribal health programs. It secured additional IHS funding to establish a small, comprehensive medical clinic, and thus, in the late 1970s, the Tribe itself began to address the severe medical needs of the Indians in Pierce County.

Initially, the Tribe focused on self-management and program consolidation. By creating the Puyallup Tribal Health Authority (PTHA) and assuming greater responsibility for its own programs, the Tribe hoped to make significant progress against the dire health and social concerns of its client population. But in 1986, PTHA's leaders determined that this approach was insufficient. While preparing for an accreditation review, PTHA staff agreed that to make truly substantial progress against the health needs of the community, it would be essential for the Health Authority to focus on providing high quality health care.

The Quality Improvement Program is the PTHA's response to this challenge. The idea is simple-create a team of individuals charged with the task of making the health system as effective, efficient, and excellent as possible. This twelve-member team, called the Quality Improvement (QI) Committee, is comprised of representatives from the major service programs and select administrative staff-health care workers and program directors who know what improvements are needed and can determine how to meet them. The QI Committee meets once a month to determine health priorities, review performance, and implement policies and actions that will improve the overall effectiveness of the PTHA in each of its program and service areas. Because client satisfaction is a priority, the Committee also regularly administers patient health surveys to better respond to community needs.

The creation and implementation of the Quality Improvement Program has clearly improved the Puyallup Tribal Health Authority's performance. The PTHA's recent accreditation scores are one measure of the Program's success. In 1998,

the Authority received its first perfect score for services and its ambulatory care program scored 97 percent. Also in 1998, the PTHA exceeded standards in four of the five areas in which it sets clinical objectives-SIDS prevention, children's immunizations, tobacco use documentation, and baby bottle tooth decay prevention. Even in the fifth area, pap smear compliance, the Health Authority's achievements far exceeded those of other Northwest tribes.

Because the QI Program stresses outreach and prevention, visits to PTHA clinics are another measure of the Program's impact. Since the QI Program's inception, clinic visits have increased dramatically. Between 1994 and 1998, the number of visits to Puyallup clinics by Indians residing in the Pierce County increased from 4,978 to 7,553. By seeing more members of its service population and seeing them more often, the PTHA is better able to treat chronic problems and to address many other problems that, left unattended, could become serious.

The Program's excellent human resources are a final measure of success. Despite the PTHA's relatively small client population, it has funded positions for six full-time physicians, and it has managed both to recruit highly qualified practitioners and to limit their turnover. In the reservation context, these are remarkable feats. In total, the PTHA has 210 employees, and American Indians fill 45 percent of the positions.

The keys to the Quality Improvement Program's success include sound administration, good communication, and a dedicated staff. An important additional factor is the PTHA's full adherence to its mission "to provide quality health care and promote wellness in a culturally appropriate manner." Puyallup traditions and practices are an integral part of the PTHA's and QI Program's functions and activities. These commitments are reflected not only in the physical surroundings of the Health Authority (for example, its facilities are decorated with exquisite native artwork and there is a meeting room modeled after a traditional Puyallup longhouse), but in its practices as well. Under the guidance of the QI Committee, the PTHA has pursued numerous opportunities to introduce Indian and Puyallup values and services into its offerings. For example, the mental health facility provides on-site sweat lodges, children's counselors use Indian dolls and figurines, and the PTHA supports the use of traditional healers to complement Western medicine. Puyallup customs are even used to strengthen the Authority's administrative systems. The PTHA staff is divided into cross-functional "clans" which meet weekly to coordinate services for patients who receive treatment from numerous programs, thereby encouraging a more holistic approach to healthcare.

The Puyallup Tribe's institutionalized Quality Improvement Program provides solid evidence that tribes can not only assume responsibility over their own health care services, but also provide creatively managed, culturally appropriate, high quality health care. Since the Program's implementation, the Puyallup Tribal Health Authority has significantly improved the

LOCATION AND LAND STATUS

The Quileute Reservation is located 20 miles west of Forks, Washington, at the end of State Road 110. The 700 acres of reservation lands border the Pacific Ocean in northwest Washington. Tribal headquarters are located in La Push, a tribal population center. La Push is distinctive in being the westernmost point in the continental United States.

The reservation was established by Executive Order in 1889. On March 4, 1904, the commissioner of Indian affairs declared the Quileutes eligible to receive land allotments on the reservation as stipulated in their 1856 treaty. In 1928, the government completed the allotments by granting each of 165 Quileutes an 80-acre tract on the Quinault Reservation; some Quileutes still have allotments at the Quinault Reservation. The tribe purchased 2.4 acres of land for its expanded fresh water system. In 1996, the Quileute Nation was in the process of purchasing 260 acres near the boundaries of the Olympic National Forest in order to expand their land base. The Nation is contesting 200 acres taken by the National Park Service in 1953.

PHYSICAL DESCRIPTION

Surrounded on three sides by the rainforests of Olympic National Park, the Quileute Reservation is located on 700 acres along the beaches of the Pacific Ocean to the west, at the mouth of the south bank of the Quillayute River. The Dickey Rivers runs to the north. Forty miles beyond the high tide waters of the Pacific is the National Marine Sanctuary, where the tribe retains "usual and accustomed rights" to fishing. This region is hailed by locals and tourists alike hail this region as one of the most spectacularly scenic in the world.

CLIMATE

The elevation at La Push, Washington, is 180 feet above sea level. The year-round average daily high temperature is 57.3°F. The year-round average daily low temperature is 41°F. The area receives approximately 103 inches of precipitation annually, with 13.3 inches of snowfall. Typical of a temperate rainforest habitat, the weather often includes rain, heavy cloud cover, and dense thick mist or fog.

CULTURE AND HISTORY

Archeological findings along the coast of what is now the State of Washington indicate that the area has been inhabited for many thousands of years. Quileute tribal genealogy is linked to tribes who lived during the Ice Age, making them possibly the oldest inhabitants of the Pacific Northwest. Prior to first contact, large family groups wintered in longhouses built near the mouths of streams. During summer months, they lived as separate family units, going farther upstream to hunting camps. The people practiced a hunting, fishing, and gathering subsistence lifestyle, dominated by the widespread use of whale and/or seal oil, which was also used as a valuable trading commodity.

The first documented contact with Europeans was made in May 1792, when American sea captain Robert Gray arrived and began a trading relationship with them. There are also some early accounts of shipwrecked Spanish explorers living among the Quileutes. Land-hungry white settlers began arriving in 1830. The Quileutes were party to the Quinault Treaty of 1855 and the Treaty of Olympia, signed on January 6, 1856, wherein the United States government demanded that they move to Taholah, on the Quinault Reservation, in exchange for 800,000 acres of ceded aboriginal territory. This territory encompassed the entire Quillayute River system to the Olympic Mountains, from north of the southern boundary of the Makah Reservation to the south of the Quinault Reservation. The demands were never enforced, however, and in an Executive Order on February 19, 1889, President Harrison established a one-square-mile reservation for the 252-member Quileute Tribe, midway between the Makah Reservation and the Quinalt Reservation. The original village site of La Push burned later that same year while tribal members were in the neighboring Village of Puyallup harvesting hops. The fire consumed 26 buildings and homes and the last remaining carved masks, baskets, hunting equipment, and sacred regalia from precontact days.

The Quileute culture is centered around the ocean, river, and forest. Traditional homes were constructed of cedar, and canoes, also made from cedar trees, were carved for use to hunt whales, seals, and other marine animals or to fish the rivers. The last whaling days were held in 1910; the last seal days were in 1955.

The Quileute language is from the Chimakuan family of languages, one of a few polysyllabic languages with no nasal sounds, such as "m" or "n." The language is unrelated to any known root language. In 1971 the Quileute Cultural Committee created a Quileute dictionary and established a language teaching program in an effort to revive and preserve the language; 7,000 words have been added to the dictionary since then. In 1996, according to the tribe, there were only five fluent speakers left. However, children attending the Quileute Tribal School are learning the language, along with traditional arts and crafts forms. In the 1990s, there was a revival of interest in canoe-carving, and many people raise a special breed of wooly-haired dogs whose hair is cut and spun into highly prized blankets. They continue the traditional giveaways, or potlatches, and celebrate their cultural heritage in July during Quileute Days with a fireworks display, a traditional salmon bake, traditional dancing and songs, a softball tournament, arts and crafts booths, and storytelling festivals. Tribal members practice First Salmon ceremonies honoring the first salmon run, and they honor their elders daily in small ways and with an annual Elder Gathering Week in May. Many tribal members practice a form of the Shaker religion not connected to the Pennsylvania Shakers.

GOVERNMENT

The Quileute Indian Tribe, a federally recognized tribal entity, is organized under a constitution and bylaws, which tribal members ratified on October 10, 1936, and the Secretary of the Interior approved on November 11, 1936, pursuant to the Indian Reorganization Act of June 18, 1934. The tribe's constitution includes a Bill of Rights similar to that of the United States constitution. The tribe is governed by the five-member Quileute Tribal Council, which consists of a chairman, vice-chairman, treasurer, secretary, and one other member, elected to staggered three-year terms. Council meetings are held biannually, and a general tribal meeting, open to all members, is held once annually in December.

The council is responsible for operating the marina and the Quileute Port Authority, and it administers two revolving loan programs. Under PL 93-638, the tribe contracts with the BIA to administer key programs and services. Administrative offices include finance and contracting, legal, planning, public works, and personnel. Programs include: court and justice,

Quileute Reservation
Federal reservation
Quileute
Clallam County, Washington

Quileute Nation
P.O. Box 279
La Push, WA 98350
  360-374-6163
  360-374-6311 Fax

Quileute

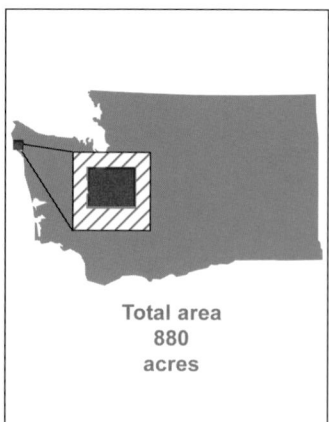

Total area
880
acres

Total area *(BIA realty, 2004)*
814.15 acres

Total area *(Tribal source, 2004)*
880 acres

Tribally owned *(BIA realty, 2004)*
804.34 acres

Tribally owned
(Tribal source, 2004)
600 acres

Individually owned
(BIA realty, 2004)
9.81 acres

Population *2000 census*
371

Tribal enrollment
(BIA labor report, 2001)
658

Total labor force *2000 census*
146

health and social services, natural resources, law and order, housing improvement, environment, economic development, nutrition, youth opportunity, and food services. They operate their own housing authority, which manages 130 HUD housing units on the reservation and in the towns of Forks and Port Angeles, just off reservation lands. In 2004, the tribe was developing a volunteer fire department.

BUSINESS CORPORATION
The tribe's Corporate Charter, approved by the Acting Secretary of the Interior on July 24, 1937, guides tribal economic development.

ECONOMY
Although logging and fishing industries in the area have dramatically declined, a majority of the Quileutes continue to derive their livelihoods from these two endeavors. Salmon harvests are reduced, due, in large part, to the damage the logging industry has done to rivers; open spaces created after logging contribute to soil and river bank erosion, which in turn has changed the contents, path, and speed of local rivers. The changed ecosystem and poor spawning beds have caused fisherman to fish the ocean bottom for food sources. Before the decline in the fishing industry in the late 1980s, there were at least 300 trollers. Today's fish runs are estimated to bring in one to eight percent of previous runs.

The reservation is growing more highly dependent upon seasonal ecotourism and tribally generated jobs. In the interest of promoting environmentally and culturally responsible business and economic development, the tribe joined with the Institute for Sustainable Communities to participate in a Social Partnership for Ecotourism Project conference in the late 1990s. This organization emphasizes eco- and ethno-responsible tourism development opportunities around the world and in the State of Washington. The tribe also participates with the Affiliated Tribes of Northwest Indians to promote culturally viable tourism in the Olympic Peninsula region of Washington.

Government as Employer. In 2002, there were a total of 89 people employed by tribal government, either in one of the various programs or services, the schools, or its enterprises.

Economic Development Projects. The Quileute Tribal Enterprise Board manages the La Push Ocean Park and Shoreline Resort, Quileute Seafood Company, Boat Launcher Restaurant, a fish hatchery, and a grocery store and gas station. At the site of the old village, the tribe operates a mini-museum inside the tribal headquarters building. A new store and the Lonesome Creek RV Park are operated in La Push. Tribal revenues from these various sources totaled over $800,000 in 1997.

The tribe completed a comprehensive management and growth study in 1994, which expanded into an overall economic development plan, completed in 1997. Two enterprises under consideration in the 1997 plan were an incinerator and acquisition of the Quillayute Airport, an abandoned naval facility. In 1998, the tribe completed a feasibility study in favor of developing a marine shrimp fishery.

Banking. Sterling Savings Bank, based in Spokane, Washington, finances tribal infrastructure for the Quileute Nation. In August 1999, the branch located in Forks provided an unsecured, short-term loan for the construction of a two-story modular office building. Sterling Savings Bank has also made loans for the purchase of two garbage trucks.

Gaming. Bingo sessions are held in the community center.

Fisheries. Quileute Seafood Company processes primarily halibut, steelhead, Chinook, black cod, sockeye, sablefish, coho, ocean perch, sturgeon, hard shell and razor clams, mussels, rockfish, and bottom fish. In 1997, the company was leased to High Tide Seafood.

In 1974, the Supreme Court, in *United States v Washington*, rendered the Boldt Decision, affirming the tribes' treaty fishing rights "in common" with the citizens of Washington State. The decision designated 50 percent of the fishery harvests to the Washington tribes and provided for co-management, with the State of Washington, of all fishing and shellfish resources. Record harvests of crab in 2003 and 2004 still fell short of the 50 percent the tribe is entitled to. The tribe is seeking more information regarding the migration of the Dungeness crab and how harvesting affects future generations. They are also utilizing a vessel-monitoring system similar to the type used extensively throughout east coast fisheries, wherein satellites track when and where boats are fishing and monitors their catches.

In its 1997 overall economic development plan, the tribe proposed developing a shrimp fishery and a commercial fish-smoking facility, and increasing cold-storage capacity for its harvests. Proliferation of invasive plant species, such as Japanese cane and giant knot wood cane, are adversely affecting salmon habitats in local rivers. The Quileute Natural Resources Department is working to eradicate the species from the reservation's waters. *(See also, Environmental Concerns, below.)*

Services and Retail. In addition to retail opportunities offered at the resorts, tribally owned and operated small businesses include an espresso café and various craftsmen and artisans.

Transportation. The tribe owns three school buses and a bus for Head Start. The Quileute Seafood Company contracts refrigerated transportation for its products.

Tourism and Recreation. The tribe operates two resorts situated on the Pacific coast. Three Rivers Resort and Fishing Guide Service, positioned near the confluence of the Quileute, Sol Duc, and Bogachiel rivers near Forks, Washington, boasts access to some of the finest fishing for steelhead and salmon in the world. A full-service resort, the facility features rustic cabins, a campground, RV hookups, showers, a laundromat, a grocery store, gas pumps, and a restaurant.

The La Push Ocean Park and Shoreline Resort are located in La Push, adjacent to the Lonesome Creek RV Park. Resort amenities include oceanfront cabins, a motel with a gift shop and a museum, the River's Edge Restaurant, a marina, and guide service. Eighty rental units are available. First, Second, Third, and Rialto beaches, within minutes of the resort, are spectacularly scenic, offering perfect solitude, ideal winds for kite-flying, surfing, ocean kayaking, photographic opportunities, hiking, and wildlife observation, including periodic whale watching. The RV park features 52 campsites, including RV sites and tent camps, full shower facilities, and a guest laundry. There are a convenience store with gas pumps, a post office, a deli, horseshoe pits, and beach access in the complex. Improvements to all resort and RV park facilities were completed in 2002. The tribe plans to continue updating and renovating the resort in the near future.

Thousands of visitors attend Quileute Days in the middle of July. The celebration includes canoe races, salmon bakes, big bone games, dances, a softball tournament, and many vendors. Other dances, feasts, and celebrations, such as the Seafood Extravaganza, are open to the public as well.

In 2003 the Quileutes developed a comprehensive marketing campaign to increase sustainable, environmentally and culturally sensitive ecotourism on the reservation and in the State of Washington. Emphasis was placed on developing off-season radio and print marketing in partnership with the Affiliated Tribes of Northwest Indians-Economic Development Corporation, the Forks Chamber of Commerce, the North Olympic Peninsula Visitors Bureau, and the State of Washington's Tourism Bureau, among others. A tribal website, expanded beyond the current natural resources department page, was under development in 2004.

In March 2004, the tribe opened a recently acquired and renovated, fully staffed Visitor's Information Center along State Road 101 as part of First Nations Olympic Discovery Trail. The building features conference space and meeting rooms, a catering-capable kitchen facility, and a well-lit information kiosk on the grounds. Inside, a Native art gallery, a small gift shop, and a reservation desk for the resorts and RV parks serve tourists with state-of-the-art technologies. The tribe is hoping to attract businesses and government organizations to hold meetings there. Also in 2004, the tribe was paving a multiuse path throughout the reservation area.

INFRASTRUCTURE

The nearest major highways are U.S. 101 and Highway 110. A private airport is located in the Town of Forks, 16 miles east of the reservation. The nearest commercial airport is in Port Angeles. Some bus companies serve La Push and Forks, and major commercial freight services deliver to La Push. The tribe is responsible for operating the harbor in La Push, which is home to a U.S. Coast Guard base.

Water Supply. Due to iron contamination, the Quileute Reservation water supply was overhauled in 1993. The reservation is now connected by 26,000 feet of pipe to a 30-mile-long aquifer near Three Rivers. A 200,000-gallon equalizing tank is used as a reservoir, with two similar tanks in the village; the tribe had pre-existing water rights to this supply. At least 100 homes and four businesses on the reservation are served by the central water and sewer systems. The Indian Health Service installed the sewer system in 1977.

A Well Head Protection Plan was implemented in July 1999. In the "Tribal Quality Water Report," published for 1999, all federal water quality standards were being met and no violations were found.

COMMUNITY FACILITIES AND SERVICES

A tribal headquarters building and a BIA school facility are located in La Push. The Akalat Center, a multipurpose gymnasium and community events center, was added to the tribal school complex in La Push in 2003. The center hosts aerobic exercise classes, sporting events, art shows, dances, and elder gatherings. Separate, outdoor ceremonial grounds were also constructed on-site. The building's spectacular architecture reflects unique aspects of Quileute heritage, history, values, and identity.

The Gray Wolf Society is a senior citizens program operating at the reservation. The tribe also has a daycare center, a fish hatchery, a police department, and a court building. The tribal public works department provides trash pickup for reservation residents and sponsors recycling educational programming and services.

In 2004, the tribe had plans to move their headquarters building to an expanded facility near the River's Edge Restaurant and to establish a cultural center inside their current council building.

Education. The Quileute Tribal School teaches students in grades K-8. Head Start, also located at the school, serves preschool children. Several high school students attend school on the Makah Reservation at Neah Bay; others attend the Quileute District High School in nearby Forks, Washington.

Students from the Quileute Tribal School and Forks High School have participated in a special work study program, sponsored and taught by instructors from National Marine Sanctuary and the Olympic Natural Resources Center. The program's focus was to learn about marine and forest environments, conduct scientific sampling, and investigate harmful algae blooms and paralytic shellfish poisoning. There are also intensive summer workshops available. Students in lower grades have access to the MESA (math, engineering, science, and achievement) curriculum. In 2002, with funding obtained from the State Department of Community, Trade, and Economic Development, the Affiliated Tribes of the Northwest Indians, and private foundations, the Quileute Tribal School set up a fully equipped computer lab, open to the general public, and operated the computer literacy project to increase computer skills among schoolchildren and working adults. In 2003, the tribal schools became part of the Washington Digital Learning Commons, a web-based portal accessible from homes, libraries, and schools throughout the state. The Quileute Tribal Schools have a website; visit quileute.schools.bia.edu.

Health Care. The Quileute Tribal Health Clinic, a newly constructed 4,400-square-foot facility in La Push, offers primary medical, dental, and behavioral health services (which are provided under PL 93-638 through the Indian Health Service). The building, completed in September 1997, houses a community health representative, offices for community health nurses, an emergency room, elder programs, diabetes education and prevention programs, mental health services, WIC nutritional services, social services, addiction counseling, and maternal and child health case management. Family and addiction counseling and support programs are also provided under a PL 93-638 title I contract with the BIA. The nearest full-service hospital is located in Forks, Washington.

ENVIRONMENTAL CONCERNS

Quileute natural resources is the tribal agency charged with protecting the tribe's treaty fishing rights in a "usual and accustomed area." That area spans over 800 square miles, or roughly 800,000 acres of watershed on the Olympic Peninsula extending along 80 miles of coastline, from Sand Point in the north to the mouth of the Queets River in the south. As co-manager of the treaty-protected fisheries under the Boldt Decision, Quileute natural resources negotiates agreements with the Washington Department of Fish and Wildlife, National Marine Fisheries Service, and other coastal tribes. The department operates cooperative hatchery programs, rearing winter steelhead and summer Chinook.

In response to decreased runs of salmon and other habitat concerns, the tribe tested and monitored 18 different streams on or near the Quileute Reservation in 1997 and 1998. Of special interest are the impacts on stream biology and watersheds caused by the region's vast logging industry. Results of the study indicated that timber harvesting was perhaps less damaging overall than other effects of urbanization in the watersheds in and around Puget Sound.

The Quileute Tribe is a member of the Northwest Indian Fisheries Commission. They are one of four coastal tribes dependent upon the Olympic Coast Marine Sanctuary for protection of the marine resources that provide their sustenance and livelihood. In 2004, the director of natural resources rep-

Quileute

Total labor force
(BIA labor report, 2001)
478

High school graduate or higher
2000 census
60.8%

Bachelor's degree or higher
2000 census
5.2%

Unemployment rate *2000 census*
27.4%

Unemployment rate
(BIA labor report, 2001)
79%

Per capita income *2000 census*
$9,589

Quileute

resented the tribe on the Northwest Indian Fisheries Commission, and was president of the Native Peoples Section of the American Fisheries Society. Through his participation, the tribe has been represented at the Pacific Fishery Management Council's Salmon Advisory Panel and the Olympic Natural Resources Center of the University of Washington, located in Forks.

Quileute Fish and Wildlife Enforcement officers enforce tribal ordinances regulating fishing and hunting violations. They conduct systematic patrols of rivers and the ocean in the usual and accustomed areas. Quileute Natural Resources staff members have received hazard analysis and critical control point training to assess natural resources damage to shore-

lines in the event of an oil spill or other catastrophe along the Pacific coastal regions.

Quileute Natural Resources also participates with Washington's Department of Fish and Wildlife and the Rayonier Timber Company in an elk project to track the health of surveyed populations of Roosevelt elk in the Forks area. Cougar, black bear, beaver, and bird populations are also monitored. With 19 additional member tribes, the Quileute Natural Resources Department also participated in developing the Northwest Forest Plan, a product of the Intergovernmental Advisory Committee, formulated to devise ecosystem approaches to land management and the spotted owl issue under the endangered species act in the western United States.

Quinault

Quinault Reservation
Federal reservation
Quinault, Queets, Quileute, Hoh, Chehalis, Chinook, and Cowlitz
Grays Harbor and Jefferson counties, Washington

Quinault Tribe of the Quinault Reservation
1214 Aalis Dr.
P.O. Box 189
Taholah, WA 98587
360-276-8215
888-616-8211
360-276-4191 Fax
quinaultindiannation.com

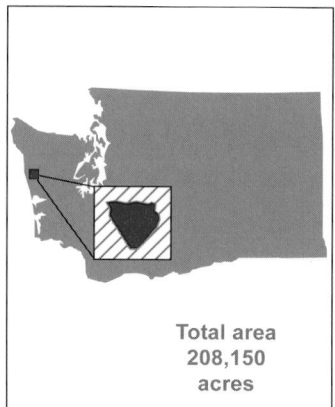

**Total area
208,150
acres**

LOCATION AND LAND STATUS

The Quinault Reservation sits in the southwestern corner of the Olympic Peninsula in extreme western Washington State. Twenty-three miles of rugged, spectacular Pacific coastline comprise the reservation's western border. Private land holdings border the south and southeastern boundaries.

The reservation was created as a result of the Quinault River Treaty of 1855, wherein the tribes ceded about three million acres of land to the U.S. government in return for reservation trust status. It was not until 1873, however, that an executive order officially established boundaries for the reservation. The 1887 Allotment Act resulted in alienating a large percentage of reservation lands from Indian ownership. In the past decade, the Quinault Nation has actively purchased additional lands, expanding the reservation's boundaries to include 208,150 acres in 1994.

PHYSICAL DESCRIPTION

Surrounded as it is by the Olympic National Forest, much of the Quinault Reservation lands can be categorized as temperate rain forest. Topography is rolling, and portions of the acreage remains heavily timbered in areas, despite decades of intensive logging, with some of the largest Douglas fir, Sitka spruce, broadleaf maple, western red cedar, and western hemlock in existence.

A prominent water body, 3,729-acre Lake Quinault, in Olympic National Park, is fed by runoff and glaciers high in the Olympic Mountains. The lake serves as the headwaters for the Quinault River, which flows for 35 miles across reservation lands, draining approximately 264 square miles of watershed. The reservation enjoys 23 miles of pristine, transitional Pacific coastline. South of the reservation lands, the shores are characterized by sandy beaches, while to the north, they are dominated by craggy rocks and towering cliffs.

CLIMATE

The elevation at Taholah, Washington, is 14 to 80 feet above sea level, and the highest elevation on the reservation is about 300 feet above sea level. Weather patterns are typical of temperate rain forest environments: marked by seasonal variations, but with overall mild temperatures, summer fog, and drenching rains. The year-round average daily high temperature is 55.5°F. The year-round average daily low temperature is 42.6°F. The area receives approximately 88 inches of precipitation annually, less than 4 inches of which fall is snow.

CULTURE AND HISTORY

The word "Quinault" evolves from "Kwi'nail" (the "l" is actually a phonetic symbol that cannot be represented in English, It is made by passing the air across the sides of your tongue. A closer phonetic representation is "Kwi-mai-elth"). It is the name of the tribe's largest settlement at the mouth of the Quinault River, present-day Taholah. Membership of the modern Quinault Indian Nation includes the Quinaults and descendents of five additional coastal tribes: Hoh, Quileute, Chehalis, Chinook, and Cowlitz. They speak a Lower Chehalis dialect of the Quinault language, a member of the coastal division of the Salishan linguistic family. Prior to first contact, the Quinault, "canoe people" or "people of the cedar tree," lived in large longhouses, practicing a subsistence lifestyle centered upon fishing, hunting, and gathering.

The first recorded contact between the Quinaults and Europeans occurred on July 13, 1775, when a Spanish vessel came ashore, provoking a hostile response from the Quinaults. The conflict resulted in several deaths on both sides. For the next 80 years, the tribe attempted unsuccessfully to distance itself from the region's growing non-Indian settlements. On July 1, 1855, under pressure from the U.S. government, the Quinaults, along with the Quileutes and the Hohs, signed the Quinault River Treaty, giving up vast amounts of territory, while reserving economically and ceremonially vital lands for their own use. The treaties of July 1, 1855, and January 25, 1856, established a 10,000-acre reservation at Taholah in exchange for all lands north of Gray's Harbor. This reservation was expanded to 20,000 acres on November 4, 1873, when President Ulysses S. Grant signed an executive order that formally established the reservation's boundaries.

The 1887 General Allotment Act precipitated a move in 1907 by the federal government to divide the reservation into individual allotments. The rationale was that the Indians would never become "self-sufficient citizens" without becoming individual landowners, preferably farmers. When it became apparent that the region's beaches and timberland were not suitable for farming, the Indian Forestry Service halted the allotment process in 1914. Allotment began anew in 1924, however, after a tribesman on a neighboring reservation filed a lawsuit to resume the practice in order to profit by leasing or selling individually owned lands to the timber industry. The last of 2,340 allotments was issued by 1933, and virtually no commonly held tribal lands remained.

The allotment process, along with corrupt and irresponsible BIA management of lands leased to the timber companies, ultimately resulted in vast areas of clear-cut hillsides and decimated river valleys. The resultant environmental destruction dramatically reduced salmon runs and other fish-spawning habitats on the Quinault Reservation. Another devastating effect of allotments was the displacement of tribal members from the reservation into neighboring towns. In the 2000 census, nearly 50 percent of all Quinaults lived off-reservation. Even more tragic is the loss of Native speakers of the Quinault language. In 1990, when the entire reservation population numbered approximately 1,500, there were only six Native speakers.

In compensation for lands relinquished under the terms of the Quinault River Treaty, the Quinault, Queet, Quileute, and Hoh tribes each received $25,000. One hundred years later, the Indian Claims Commission determined that the four tribes had been grossly under compensated for their loss of 688,000 acres. On June 25, 1962, in a compromise with the Quinault and Queet tribes, the Commission ordered the U.S. government to pay an additional $205,172.40. The judgment was not paid until April 17, 1973.

The Quinault Indian Nation has restored traditional cultural practices in the latter decades of the twentieth century. In 1989, they formed the Quinault Canoe Society and revived the long-standing custom of the Canoe Journey, and they continue to practice potlatch and other ceremonies.

GOVERNMENT

The tribe is governed by a duly elected tribal (general) council, which meets annually on the last Saturday of March and is made up of all voting members of the Nation. Bylaws were first adopted on August 24, 1922, and the tribal constitution was approved March 22, 1975. In the modern constitution, the cultural heritage of the other member tribes is honored. Anyone with one-quarter blood of the Quinault, Hoh, Queets, Quileute, Chehalis, Chinook, or Cowlitz tribes is permitted to claim membership in the Quinault Nation so long as they are not members of another tribe.

The 11-member Quinault business committee, consisting of four officers and seven councilmen, is entrusted with the tribe's business and legislative affairs. Members of the business committee serve staggered three-year terms.

After 150 years of misguided interference by the federal government into Indian affairs, the BIA opted to try a new means of tribal governance. In 1988 the Self Governance Act was passed and the BIA began a demonstration project to allow tribes to make their own decisions. In 1990 the Quinault, and six other tribes, brought self-rule back to their communities. In 1991 this law also began allowing these tribes to plan activities in the Indian Health Service.

Under PL 93-638, the tribe contracts with the BIA to administer key programs and services. Tribal government operations consist of the following areas: administration, natural resources, community services, education, self-governance, health and social services, economic development, Quinault Nation Enterprise Board, Quinault Beach Resort, gaming policy, and a housing authority. They also have their own police department and tribal court system. Administrative offices include the executive director and executive assistant, administrator, chief financial officer, legal, enrollment, planning, finance manager, personnel, grants development, legislative liaison, and council. The natural resources department oversees the cultural resources, environmental programs, fisheries, forestry, and resource protection offices. There is also a centralized communications department to coordinate re-

source protection officers; fire, police, public works, and other emergency-response personnel; youth services; and an elders program to provide senior services.

The mission of the Quinault housing authority is to develop partnerships between reservation communities and businesses, governmental entities, and residents, so safe, affordable housing is available for all eligible tribal members. The housing authority is a member of the Northwest Indian Housing Association. In 1998, the housing authority provided credit and mortgage counseling services, provided rental vouchers to college students, managed existing low-income housing units on the reservation, and offered a revolving loan program to assist homeowners rehabilitating older homes.

In 2003, the Quinault Nation updated the tribe's strategic plan, which guides future development separate core strategies were devised for each of the following elements of tribal life: sovereignty, treaty rights and governance, community services, capital facilities, administration, housing, social and health services, culture, education, employment, economic development, and environment.

ECONOMY

While the timber industry has traditionally held a position of great prominence in the region, with several large companies cutting hundreds of thousands of board feet each year from inside reservation boundaries, the tribal economy has not particularly benefited from such commerce due to the splintering effects of allotment policies. Though salmon fishing and seafood processing remain viable on tribal lands and in tribal waters, many tribal members find employment off the reservation. The major focus of Quinault economic policy concerns regenerating abundant fish runs and forests, which can provide employment for future generations; however, there is a growing emphasis on ecotourism as a way of diversifying revenue sources.

The advent of gaming and the resort developments are speeding economic progress in the twenty-first century. In 2004, there were several enterprises operating on the reservation: Quinault Pride Seafood, Land and Timber, Quinault Beach Resort and Casino, Maritime Resort, Quinault Cablevision, Quinault Utility Company, the Mercantile, and the Queets Trading Post. The Nation operates the Quinault Indian Nation Business Assistance Center to encourage entrepreneurship among tribal members.

Government as Employer. One of the largest employers in Gray County, Washington, tribal government employs over 700 people, primarily in fisheries, forest management, social services and health care programs, or one of its enterprises.

Forestry. Despite rampant overharvesting by large commercial interests, the reservation remains forested with approximately 200,000 acres of commercial-grade timber, including Douglas fir, hemlock, western red cedar, and red alder. Some of this land generates tribal income through leasing, while a larger portion has been sold to timber companies over the years. The Nation is actively pursuing reforestation as well as the repurchase of alienated forestlands.

Gaming. The Nation operates the 50-acre Quinault Beach Resort and Casino on State Road 115 in north Ocean Shores, Washington. Development of this $140 million property began about 1998. The resort surrounds the Ocean Shores Marina, which provides moorage for pleasure craft, limited commercial vessels, and charters, and a ferry dock with both passenger and vehicle ferries to the City of Westport across the bay. In addition to the resort amenities, the 16,000-square-foot casino features 350 slot machines, 15 table games, 2

Quinault

Total area *(BIA realty, 2004)*
184,404.49 acres

Total area *(Tribal source, 2004)*
208,150 acres

Tribally owned *(BIA realty, 2004)*
67,654.12 acres

Individually owned
(BIA realty, 2004)
116,750.37 acres

Population *2000 census*
1,370

Tribal enrollment
(BIA labor report, 2001)
2,454

Total labor force *2000 census*
564

Total labor force
(BIA labor report, 2001)
1,736

High school graduate or higher
2000 census
72.2%

Bachelor's degree or higher
2000 census
11.5%

Unemployment rate *2000 census*
14.7%

Unemployment rate
(BIA labor report, 2001)
50%

Per capita income *2000 census*
$9,621

restaurants, and 3 entertainment venues. The Beach Resort and Casino complex includes a 159-room hotel and 16,000 square feet of convention and meeting space, employing a total of approximately 400 people, most of them tribal members.

The Quinault business committee oversees the process of returning a percentage of the proceeds from casino operations to the community. Since the Quinault Beach Resort and Casino began operations, the committee has awarded over $150,000. Beneficiaries include Grays Harbor Sheriff's Department, the City of Ocean Shores, Grays Harbor E-911 Services, and Grays Harbor District #7 Schools.

Fisheries. The reservation supports viable salmon and steelhead fisheries in the area's five rivers and in the Pacific Ocean. Commercial razor clam harvesting remains quite productive as well. Moreover, the tribe operates Quinault Pride Seafood Products, a processing plant employing up to 60 people during the height of the season. The plant processes various kinds of salmon, tuna, halibut, razor clams, and more. Its products are all natural seafood products.

Aside from tribal government, the fishing industry generates more revenue and employs a greater number of tribal members than any other source. Since the mid-1990s, the tribe's fisheries and environmental departments have addressed the health of the fishing industry, which was in jeopardy due to environmental damage caused by irresponsible logging in the past. While not all problems are resolved, environmentally conscious Quinault fishermen, who supply the Quinault Pride Seafood Products, use selective fishing techniques to minimize the impact on the species and their natural surroundings.

The U.S. Fish and Wildlife Service operates a fish hatchery on Cook Creek. Known as the Quinault National Fish Hatchery, it is located on the Moclips Highway just off U.S. 101 south of Lake Quinault. A total of eight million Chinook, chum, and coho salmon and steelhead trout are reared and released annually into the major rivers of the Quinault Indian Reservation and other coastal rivers from this facility.

Services and Retail. Tribally affiliated retail businesses include the Taholah Mercantile, the Queets Trading Post, a general store, a gas station, two beauty shops, a convenience store, two restaurants, the Quinault Land and Timber Enterprise, Quinault Cablevision, and the Quinault Seafood Company. The seafood company has a retail area where its products can be purchased.

Media and Communications. The Nation publishes *Nugguam* ("to talk") in the Quinault language on the Internet. It is an online version of the *Quinault Nation News.* The cultural affairs office publishes a list of arts and crafts vendors, tour guides, fishing guide services, and food services.

Tourism and Recreation. Fishing for steelhead trout and salmon along the Quinault River is a popular tourist activity, and there are many year-round fishing guide services now operating on the reservation. Beautiful Quinault Lake is located on the edge of the Olympic Peninsula Rain Forest. Within the National Forest and Quinault Valley, there are abundant recreational opportunities, including interpretive nature trails for walking, including trails into the back country for more advanced hikers, an auto loop tour, and camping, boating, swimming, fishing, picnicking, wildlife observation, bird-watching, and photography opportunities. The villages of Queets and Taholah offer salmon fishing and clam digging. Trout fishing in Lake Quinault is available only when the lake is open.

Beaches on reservation shorelines are available with tribally issued day passes for kite flying, horseback riding, and beach walking or jogging. Moclips/Pacific Beach State Park also has easily accessible beaches just south of the reservation.

Accommodations at the 159-room Quinault Beach Resort and Casino in Ocean Shores include ocean view rooms with fireplaces, a spa, a steam room, a Jacuzzi, a full-length swimming pool, a children's activity center, the Ocean Lounge, gift shop, Emily's Restaurant, and one other eatery. In Taholah, the Nation operates the Quinault Cultural Center at Fifth Avenue Mall, with art collections and cultural artifacts. The Quinault National Fish Hatchery on Cook Creek is open to the public. An information center at the facility depicts how the hatchery fits into the overall cultural context of the Quinault Indian Reservation.

In Taholah, visitors are welcomed at the Lake Quinault Museum and Historical Society located on the South Shore Road conveniently situated adjacent to the Quinault Mercantile and within walking distance of Lake Quinault Lodge. Two Quinault 24-foot dugout canoes are part of the museum's collection. The tribe celebrates Chief Taholah Days each year during the first week of July in commemoration of the July 1, 1855, treaty. Events include dances, fireworks, canoe races, baseball games, a parade, and salmon bakes, all open to the public. In 2005, the 150th anniversary celebration will feature an expanded list of activities.

INFRASTRUCTURE

The reservation is served by U.S. Highway 101, skirting the northern border, and State Highway 109, which runs north into the reservation as far as Taholah. Grays Harbor Transit Authority provides the region with bus service. Commercial truck lines serving the area include UPS and Peninsula Trucking. Aberdeen and Hoquiam, 40 miles from the reservation, have commercial airports. The Port of Grays Harbor, 40 miles south of Taholah, provides access to water transportation and shipping facilities.

Electricity. The Public Utility District of Grays Harbor provides electric power service. The tribe has formed its own utility company, which, once fully operational, will provide wind and other source-generated electricity to reservation homes and facilities.

Water Supply. The communities of Taholah and Queets and the Quinault Indian Nation Public Works Department provide water and sewage services. The privately owned Santiago Water System provides supplemental water service.

Telecommunications. Quinault Cablevision offers cable television to reservation homes and facilities.

COMMUNITY FACILITIES AND SERVICES

The Quinault Nation maintains two community centers, one at Taholah and another at Queets. There are buildings for the Nation's two Head Start programs, which include daycare facilities. The Nation has a police station, a natural resources office, a tribal office building in Taholah from which most community and social services are operated, and a mental health office where the alcohol and substance abuse and behavioral health programs are operated. The Safe House, a shelter and transitional housing facility for victims of domestic abuse, has been completed since 2003. A modular building houses the courthouse and legal office. The newly renovated Old Quinault Post Office is home to the Lake Quinault Museum and Historical Society. A new Taholah Branch of the Bank of the Pacific opened December 15, 2004, at the Quinault Indian Nation Tribal Offices.

According to the 2003 Quinault Strategic Plan Update, the Nation plans to build a NW Indian Youth Camp. They also wanted to build a fish house in Queets and an assisted living and convalescent care home for elders and disabled members. In 2004, the Nation was planning the following capital improvement projects: a new Taholah health clinic and social services offices, to be opened in 2005; a sewage treatment system for Taholah; and a new water system for Queets. Three older buildings on-site at the Roger Saux Health Clinic may be converted to other uses. There is a need for a drug and alcohol halfway house, and the Nation would like to build a cultural center.

Education. The Nation operates the Quinault Lake School District, maintaining its own public grade school, high school, and school board. Elements of traditional culture are infused throughout the curricula, with instruction in the Salishan language.

A special water quality project at the schools integrates water quality activities throughout core instructional areas. Students, depending upon grade level, engage in field activities geared toward preserving fishery habitats, such as testing water quality in regional rivers; raising coho, Chinook, and steelhead fingerlings in the classroom; conducting scientific laboratory experiments at the hatchery; attending special lectures and conferences; and dissecting fish. High school students participated in a tribal work study program during 2000 and 2001, engaging in many of these same activities as part of the STEP curriculum.

In 2002 and 2003, ALADIN college prep and STEP high school students were offered an Aviation Ground Course. The science teacher, a former pilot, linked core instruction to coursework in engines and thrust, a plane's anatomy, instrumentation, aerodynamics, navigation, weather, FAA regulations, and physiology, while integrating chemistry, physics, biology, math, and citizenship. Students in the curriculum participated in a field trip to McCord Air Force Base, where speakers emphasized the value of higher education while conducting a tour of the high-tech aviation facility.

The school district operates a college program in cooperation with nearby institutions of higher education, including Northwest Indian College, Grays Harbor Community College, and the Evergreen State College Bridge Program.

Health Care. Health care services are provided by the Roger Saux Health Center, a facility operated by Quinault Nation Health Services under a PL 93-638, title III self-governance compact with Indian Health Service. The 5,379-square-foot facility provides comprehensive ambulatory, medical, and dental care, maternal and child health, and emergency medical services, a pharmacy, and a lab. The center employs two physicians, a family nurse practitioner, a dentist, a dental hygienist, four registered nurses, a licensed practical nurse, a pharmacist, a pharmacy aide, a medical technologist, a referral clerk, and several additional practitioners. It is JCAHO accredited. The Nation operates a remote health station in Queets also, along with an outpatient alcohol and substance abuse program facilitated by the tribal social services department. The nearest full-service hospital is located in Aberdeen. Other tribally operated health programs include: health benefits, contracted health services, WIC, community health representatives, programs for seniors, public health nurses, mental health counseling, nutrition information and counseling.

ENVIRONMENTAL CONCERNS

Approximately 44 percent of North America's original temperate rainforest lands have now been lost to development; much of these areas were on Indian land, including the Quinault Indian Nation Reservation. An agreement signed with the Secretary of the Interior in 2004 preserves 4,207 acres of sensitive old-growth forest habitat for the marbled murrelet, an endangered bird species found within reservation boundaries that is dependent upon late-successional forest types.

In 2004, the tribe's natural resources department obtained a Department of Energy Weatherization and Intergovernmental Program grant to participate in a Renewable Energy Feasibility Study. It is a comprehensive assessment and economic analysis of renewable energy resources, including wind, biomass, solar, and wave energy, along with a comprehensive assessment of tribal energy requirements. The tribe's long-term goal is to achieve energy self-sufficiency through planning, developing, and implementing a Quinault Indian Nation Utility Company.

TRI-WA-001

TRI-WA-002

TRI-WA-001 Frontview of the Quinault Indian Nation Resort and Casino

TRI-WA-002 Back view of the Quinault Indian Nation Resort and Casino

Samish

**Samish Indian Nation
Federally recognized
Samish**

Samish Indian Nation
P.O. Box 217
Anacortes, WA 98221
360-293-6404
360-299-0790 Fax
samishtribe.nsn.us

Tribal enrollment
(BIA labor report, 2001)
1,154

Tribal enrollment
(Tribal source, 2004)
1,154

Total labor force *2000 census*
15,505

Total labor force
(BIA labor report, 2001)
428

High school graduate or higher
2000 census
91.8%

Bachelor's degree or higher
2000 census
34.4%

Unemployment rate *2000 census*
4.02%

Unemployment rate
(BIA labor report, 2001)
61%

LOCATION AND LAND STATUS

Samish tribal headquarters are located in Anacortes, Washington. The town is located on Fidalgo Island. Seattle lies 80 miles south and Vancouver, British Columbia, is 90 miles north. As of January 2005, the Samish Nation is landless, but it is committed to reestablishing its tribal homelands. Tribal members mainly reside throughout Washington State in the counties of Whatcom, Skagit, Snohomish, King, Island, San Juan, Pierce, Kitsap, and Jefferson.

CLIMATE

Anacortes experiences an average temperature of 45°F in winter and 70°F in summer. It is located within a microclimate and has a drier climate than most areas in the northwest.

CULTURE AND HISTORY

The Samish Indian Nation is part of the Coast Salish linguistic and cultural group. Traditional Samish territory included regions encompassing seven present-day counties in northwest Washington. The area ranges from the Cascade Mountain Range to the shores of the San Juan Islands. Traditional means of sustenance included gathering vegetables and fruits, harvesting shellfish, and fishing. Members also hunted waterfowl, shore birds, and some deer, elk, and seal.

The Samish people encountered Euro-American settlers in the mid-1800s. At that time, the tribe's population was over 2,000. As a result of raids from northern tribes and epidemics of measles, smallpox, and the flu, the population was reduced to 150 by 1855.

The Samish Nation is a signatory of the Treaty of Point Elliot of 1855. The Samish and Lummi tribes were omitted from the final draft of the treaty, which Congress ratified in 1859. In 1934, the U.S. Court of Claims ruled that the Samish Tribe was to be recognized as party to the treaty. In accordance with the treaty, the Samishes were relocated to the Lummi and Swinomish reservations. A number of Samish tribal members remained on Samish Island or moved to Guemes Island. In 1883, the tribe received trust patent to lands. By 1912, however, Euro-American settlers forced them to leave the lands. Tribal members dispersed into surrounding communities or to the Swinomish Reservation.

The tribe filed claims before the Indian Claims Commission in 1951 for compensation for lands lost and treaty violations. The commission found that under provisions of the 1855 treaty, the tribe held Samish Island, Guemes Island, eastern Lopez Island, Cypress Island, and Fidalgo Island. The tribe was awarded $5,755 in 1971.

Until 1969, the tribe was listed as a federally recognized tribe. It received services from the BIA and Indian Health Service. However, in 1969 the Samish were omitted from a BIA list of federally recognized tribes, probably due to clerical errors. In 1975, the tribe was granted treaty fishing rights with other Washington tribes under the U.S. Supreme Court Decision known as the Boldt Decision of 1974. Six years later in 1981, the Ninth Circuit Court of Appeals determined that the Samish Tribe had not proved itself to be a socially cohesive group and was not eligible for treaty fishing rights. Finally, after almost 30 years of continued legal battles to correct a BIA error, the Samish Tribe was re-recognized as a federally recognized tribe on April 26, 1996.

GOVERNMENT

The Samishes opened tribal enrollment and adopted a new tribal constitution in 2004. The tribe is governed by a seven-member tribal council.

ECONOMY

The tribe's enterprises in the tourism and retail industries contribute to the tribal economy.

Government as Employer. The tribe employs 40 full-time employees and about 10 seasonal employees.

Tourism and Recreation. The tribe owns the Fidalgo Bay Resort and RV by the Bay. It is situated on over 40 acres, including over one mile along the beach. It offers 189 full-service hookup sites, a clubhouse, a boardwalk, restrooms, laundry facilities, on-site propane sales, concierge services, and a convenience store. Rentals are available for fifth wheels, bicycles, mopeds, kayaks, boats, DVDs, and VCRs. The resort offers the San Juan Safaris whale watching and kayaking trips.

The tribe sponsors community events and cultural activities such as war canoe races and stick game tournaments. The Maiden of Deception Pass story pole at Bowman's Bay in Deception Pass State Park is dedicated to one of the tribe's most significant stories.

Anacortes offers a number of attractions for visitors, including ferry tours, the Anacortes Cinema, antique stores, the Museum of Northwest Arts, and plenty of shopping venues. Outdoor attractions include fishing, ocean fishing, hiking, biking, and swimming. The city also hosts the annual Anacortes Arts Festival.

INFRASTRUCTURE

Anacortes is accessible via a bridge from the mainland along U.S. Highway 20.

COMMUNITY FACILITIES AND SERVICES

The tribe offers youth programs, including Tribal Journeys Canoe Travels and a tobacco prevention program. The tribe provides an Indian Child Welfare Act Program, emergency food assistance program, and low-income energy assistance program. It also provides an elder's nutrition program and elder's activities. The tribe operates a Western Washington Indian Education Training Program.

Education. The tribe operates the Samish Longhouse Preschool (Head Start). The tribe provides financial assistance for courses leading to certification, vocational degrees, adult basic education, and college degree programs.

Health Care. Tribal members living within Whatcom, Skagit, Snohomish, King, Island, San Juan, Pierce, Kitsap, Jefferson, and Clallam counties are eligible to receive contract health services. Indian Health Service facilities are also available for use by tribal members. The tribe employs a public health nurse and offers a diabetes program.

Sauk-Suiattle

LOCATION AND LAND STATUS

The Sauk-Suiattle Reservation is located in the Sauk Prairie area in both Skagit and Snohomish counties of Washington State. An Act of Congress in 1982 designated a tract of lands for the tribe that is now used for housing.

CULTURE AND HISTORY

The Sauk-Suiattle people have resided in the Sauk Valley of northeastern Washington for countless years. The Sah-hu-me-hu, or Sauk-Suiattle, Tribe was renamed in reference to the two rivers whose entire drainage area comprised its traditional home. The tribe fished the Sauk, Suiattle, Stillaguamish, and Skagit rivers for salmon, often traveling down to Puget Sound to harvest fish and shellfish. Their traditional homelands encompassed areas spanning from the foothills of the Cascade Mountains south of present-day North Cascades National Park. Tribal members relied upon carrots, potatoes, corn, deer, grouse, goat, bear, elk, and salmon for sustenance, as well as many varieties of berries. The heart of the community was a council house where tribal members held council on matters of importance.

In 1855, tribal leaders signed the Treaty of Point Elliot, formally ceding their land while retaining the right to fish in their usual and accustomed areas. During the mid-1800s, the United States conducted land surveys in the Sauk Valley. Members of the Sauk-Suiattle Tribe joined the survey party and participated in its expeditions. In 1871, representatives of the railroad also entered the territory in order to assess the land for railroad projects. A number of tribal members became employed by the railroad company to lead an expedition party through the Sauk River area, across the mountains, to the Columbia River. The party met with other indigenous groups, and they traveled to the Columbia River and on to Lake Chelan. The railroad representatives advised the Native people to seek payment for their lands when construction of railroads commenced.

Later in that century, the federal government began to identify land in the Sauk Valley for homesteading. A party of United States surveyors threatened to bring the U.S. military to the area in order to forcibly remove the indigenous people from their lands. The Sauk-Suiattle people sited the Point Elliot Treaty of 1855 and the rights and protection awarded to the northwestern tribes in that agreement. The surveyors eventually determined that the lands belonged to the tribe.

In 1881, Euro-American settlers forced their way onto tribal lands, burning tribal homes and villages in order to do so. An important village near the confluence of the Sauk and Suiattle rivers was burned by white settlers in 1884. The settlers laid claim to the land, and the Sauk-Suiattle were rendered landless. The tribe did not seek retaliation against the settlers, but relocated to camps along the river instead. They continued to live in scattered groups close to their traditional homelands.

In the period between 1854 and 1920, the tribal population was reduced from approximately 4,000 to just 17. The primary cause for the decimation of the population was the affect of foreign diseases. Most of the tribe's traditional lands were lost in the early twentieth century due to the designation of national forests. With the loss of lands, many members joined other tribes or left the tribal community altogether. Though dispersed, the Sauk-Suiattle Tribe maintained its tribal government, social structure, identity, and hope for the future.

In 1901 the Sauk-Suiattle chiefs Jim Brown and Wawetkin met with the governor of Washington to discuss land ownership. The chiefs sought lands along the Suiattle River, which were part of the tribe's ancestral lands. The land was granted to the tribe in 1902. In 1916 the U.S. Forest Service cancelled the allotment, and tribal members were forced to vacate. The tribe's working men united to purchase a small piece of property for a cemetery. The U.S. Department of the Interior approved the purchase on June 30, 1914. The one-acre parcel, with rights-of-way, was placed in trust for the "Upper Skagit-Sauk Suiattle Tribe of Indians," later interpreted to mean the Upper Skagit and Sauk-Suiattle tribes. Many members sought local employment and rented homes in nearby communities. Others lived on the sand bar in tents. Although essentially landless, the tribe maintained its sense of community and personal connection with each other.

The federal government formally recognized the Sauk-Suiattle Tribe on September 17, 1975. The Sauk-Suiattle people eventually were able to secure funding from HUD to purchase lands. The tribe petitioned the BIA to accept the land into trust status for housing purposes. In 1982 the land reached reservation status. In 1984, tribal members moved into the new housing development.

GOVERNMENT

The tribe is governed by a tribal council of seven elected members who serve in staggered terms. Council members include a chairman, vice-chairman, treasurer, and secretary. Tribal programs include finance, law enforcement, Indian child welfare, health and social services, education, natural resources, cultural resources, and planning and housing.

The tribe maintains a police department. In addition to standard law enforcement, the department offers a fish and wildlife program and a K-9 narcotics program. The tribe belongs to the Northwest Intertribal Court System. It provides circuit court services. The court's jurisdiction includes civil and minor offenses. The tribe's housing department offers rental assistance and currently manages 19 HUD homes on tribal lands. The tribe is in the process of establishing zoning ordinances for tribal lands.

ECONOMY

The tribal economy is supported in large part through grants and contracts. Forestry enterprises and local Native American-owned casinos provide the most significant sources of employment for tribal members.

Government as Employer. In 1998 the tribe employed 34 people.

Economic Development Projects. Tribally owned lands have been secured through funding sources that stipulate they not be used for economic development. The tribe is actively pursuing venues to purchase lands that they will be able to utilize for economic development. Projects in the planning stages in the late 1990s included establishing a herd of buffalo, a smoke shop, a small store, a museum and cultural center, and a commercial trout enterprise.

Agriculture and Livestock. The tribe is in the process of developing a tree farm on a parcel of land in Snohomish County.

Sauk-Suiattle Reservation
Federal reservation
Sauk-Suiattle
Skagit and Snohomish
counties, Washington

Sauk-Suiattle Indian Tribe
5318 Chief Brown Lane
Darrington, WA 98241
360-436-0131
360-436-1511 Fax
sauk-suiattle.com

Total area *(BIA realty, 2004)*
67.88 acres

Tribally owned *(BIA realty, 2004)*
67.88 acres

Tribal enrollment
(BIA labor report, 2001)
152

Tribal enrollment
(Tribal source, 2005)
167

Total labor force *2000 census*
26

Total labor force
(BIA labor report, 2001)
105

High school graduate or higher
2000 census
78.6%

Bachelor's degree or higher
2000 census
0%

Unemployment rate *2000 census*
38.5%

Unemployment rate
(BIA labor report, 2001)
78%

Per capita income *2000 census*
10,029

Sauk-Suiattle

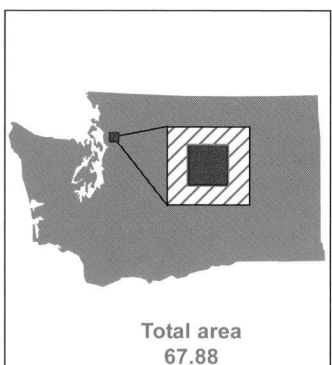

Total area
67.88
acres

Fisheries. Fishing has been a vital occupation for the tribe for several hundred years. Tribal members continue to exercise their fishing rights as outlined by the 1855 Treaty of Point Elliot.

The tribe belongs to the Skagit System Cooperative. The co-op includes treaty tribes of the region. The tribes act as co-managers of the states' salmon and steelhead resources. They work jointly to provide services in fisheries harvest management, biological research, technical assistance, fisheries enhancement, environmental protection, financial and administrative management, and fisheries law enforcement.

Tourism and Recreation. The reservation is located near the North Cascades Park. Numerous archeological sites are located within 635 square miles of the reservation.

The tribe secured funding from the State of Washington, Seattle City Light, and the U.S. Forest Service to construct a traditional long house. The structure is open to the public. The tribe hosts the Celebration of Generations during the second weekend of June. The festivities coincide with the anniversary of the tribe's federal recognition on June 2, 1972. The event is held in honor of tribal elders, warriors, leaders, and youth.

INFRASTRUCTURE
State Route 530 provides access to the reservation from I-5, 36 miles from tribal lands.

Water Supply. Two community wells supply water to the reservation.

Transportation. Sea-Tac International Airport is the nearest commercial airport, some 100 miles from the reservation. Bus services are available in the Town of Darrington. Freight service is available to the reservation.

Telecommunications. GTE provides telephone services.

COMMUNITY FACILITIES AND SERVICES
The reservation houses a community center, which is home to the tribe's social services programs. The tribe also maintains a community longhouse and cultural center.

Education. The tribe operates an ECEAP Day Care Center. It is planning to institute classes in the indigenous language.

Health Care. There is a clinic on the reservation, with one nurse on staff. Services include primary care, mental health screening, and alcohol counseling. Physician services are available in Darrington.

ENVIRONMENTAL CONCERNS
The tribe developed an environmental department in 1999. The department is responsible for assessing the tribe's environmental resources and creating parameters for environmental codes and regulations. It has applied for the Sauk River to be designated as an Outstanding Natural Resource Water, in order to preserve the river and its watershed. The department is currently monitoring the water quality of the Sauk and Suiattle rivers watershed, working on designated wetland areas, and researching air quality. Future projects include studies of the mountain goat population of the Northern Cascades and hydraulic modeling of the Sauk River Basin.

Shoalwater Bay

Shoalwater Bay Reservation
Federal reservation
Chehalis, Chinook, and
Quinault
Pacific County, Washington

Shoalwater Bay Indian Tribe
P.O. Box 130
Tokeland, WA 98590
    360-267-6766
    360-267-6778 Fax

Total area *(BIA realty, 2004)*		335 acres
Total area *(EPA, 2004)*		1,280 acres
Tribally owned *(BIA realty, 2004)*		335 acres
Tribal enrollment		255
(BIA labor report, 2001)		
Total labor force *2000 census*		30
Total labor force		1,264
(BIA labor report, 2003)		
High school graduate or higher		85%
2000 census		
Bachelor's degree or higher		7.5%
2000 census		
Unemployment rate *2000 census*		33.3%
Unemployment rate		55%
(BIA labor report, 2003)		
Per capita income *2000 census*		$6,000

LOCATION AND LAND STATUS
The Shoalwater Bay Indian Reservation is located on the Willapa Bay at North Cove on the western short of the State of Washington.

PHYSICAL DESCRIPTION
Tribal lands are located in the western portion of the North Watershed. They feature tidelands as well as the North River, Smith Creek, Cedar River, Freshwater Creek, and other small streams that all drain into Willapa Bay.

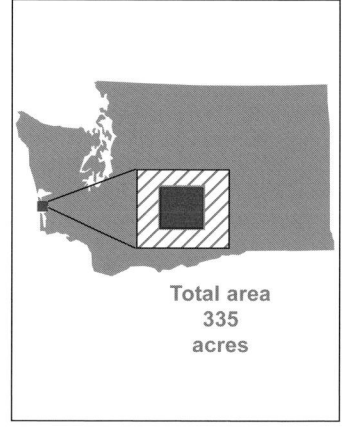

Total area
335
acres

CULTURE AND HISTORY
Traditional means of sustenance for members of the Shoalwater Bay Indian Tribe include fishing, clamming, hunting, berry picking, and crabbing.

The federal government recognized the tribe in 1971. In 1984, the tribe accepted a $1 million settlement for compensation for eight acres in Tokeland, Washington.

GOVERNMENT

The tribe rejected the Indian Reorganization Act of 1934 but adopted a tribal constitution and became formally recognized on May 22, 1971. The tribe is governed by a tribal council. The tribe has a law enforcement agency comprised of a three-man force.

ECONOMY

The tribe operates a gaming facility and a wellness center, which provide employment as well as generating income to support the tribal economy.

Gaming. The tribe operates the Shoalwater Bay Casino. It offers 125 slots/VLTs, 5 table games, and a restaurant. In 2004, federal marshals raided the casino and confiscated over 100 slot machines. The marshals were acting on the judgment of a federal ruling that the operation of the slot machines was in violation of state law. Over 200 tribal members and supporters led a protest of the seizure, including a roadblock. The casino employs 70 people with 24 being tribal members.

Services and Retail. Tribally owned are Chief Charley Gift Shop, Shoalwater Bay Grocer, and Davis Trailer Park with 75 people employed.

INFRASTRUCTURE

Electricity. The Public Utilities District provides electricity.

Water Supply. An aquifer recharged by the North Watershed provides domestic water.

Transportation. The nearest commercial air, bus, and rail services are located in Sea Tac/Olympia.

Telecommunications. Comcast and Verizon supply telecommunications services.

COMMUNITY FACILITIES AND SERVICES

The tribe has a community gym, a summer youth program, and an exams program.

Education. Tribal youth attend school in the Ocasta School district.

Health Care. The Shoalwater Bay Tribal Clinic is located in Tokeland. It offers medical and dental services. The tribe is in the process of developing a wellness center that will include medical, dental, alternative medicine, mental health, and chemical dependency programs.

ENVIRONMENTAL CONCERNS

Water quality within tribal lands is of grave concern to the tribe. In the period between 1988 and 1993, there were high rates of neonatal and infant mortality among tribal members. The possibility of environmental contaminants contributing to the problems is under serious consideration. The quality of the North Watershed does not meet Washington State standards, nor is it acceptable to the tribe. The tribe has initiated a Clean Water Action Plan in order to address the issue.

Skokomish

Skokomish

LOCATION AND LAND STATUS

The Skokomish Reservation is located on the delta of the Skokomish River, where it empties into the Great Bend of Hood Canal. It lies 10 miles north of Shelton, which serves as the county seat for Mason County. The cities of Bremerton, Olympia, and Aberdeen are all within 45 miles of the reservation.

The reservation was created by the Point-No-Point Treaty, concluded on January 26, 1855, and ratified by Congress on March 8, 1895. It was subsequently enlarged by Executive Order on February 25, 1874.

CULTURE AND HISTORY

The Twana, or Skokomish, people originally resided in the Hood Canal drainage basin in present-day Washington State. The Twanas subsisted on hunting, fishing, and gathering activities. They were largely nomadic during the warm seasons and settled at permanent sites during the winter. Extended families served as the key social groups in the Twana culture. Tribal members lived in communities of one or more households, or with related tribal members in other Twana villages within or outside of the tribe's traditional territory. The Skokomish River Basin, the shoreline of Hood Canal, and its estuary and tideland regions were considered within the Twana homelands. The Skokomish River Basin, the shoreline of Hood Canal, and its estuary and tideland regions were considered within the Twana homelands. The communities were self-sufficient. Members gathered and prepared food items for everyday consumption, ceremonial use, and storage for use during the winter months.

The indigenous language is Twana, or tuwaduqutSid. Twana is a Southern Puget Sound dialect of Salish. The Salish language was spoken by peoples in the lands ranging the Pacific Ocean to Montana and from British Columbia to Oregon. Twana was the predominate language of tuwaduqhL si'dakW, or Hood Canal, which is a 60-mile long inlet of the Puget Sound waters east of the Olympic Peninsula. The tribe encountered European explorers in 1792. This initial contact resulted in a devastating smallpox epidemic.

A portion of tribal lands located between the west and main channels at the mouth of the Skokomish River were seized around 1900. Consequent dikes and farming on the lands caused the depletion of a number of plant species, including the sweet grass variety tribal members used in their weaving. Between 1926 and 1930 the City of Tacoma constructed two dams on the North Fork of the Skokomish River, destroying important cultural sites, ravaging salmon and fish resources, and creating increased restrictions on the tribe's saltwater access. Under the state's claims of jurisdiction over tidelands, the shellfish gathering practices of the tribe were also hindered during this time. Access to the resources were lost when the Potlatch State Park was created along the shoreline in 1960.

The 1974 Boldt Decision upheld treaties between the federal government and tribal nations as the "supreme law of the land." The ruling found that tribes were entitled to the opportunity to harvest 50 percent of each run of salmon returning to traditional Indian fishing areas. Tribes also gained the right to co-manage, with the state, the important fishery and other natural resources on and adjacent to the reservation, or in its traditional pretreaty usual and accustomed areas. The Indian Tribe and other federally recognized tribal governments in

Skokomish Reservation
Federal reservation
Skokomish
Mason County, Washington

Skokomish Tribal Council
80 North Tribal Center Road
Skokomish Nation, WA 98584
360-426-4232
360-877-5943 Fax
skokomish.org

Skokomish

Total area *(BIA realty, 2004)*
2,992.33 acres

Tribally owned *(BIA realty, 2004)*
173.46 acres

Individually owned
(BIA realty, 2004)
2,818.87 acres

Population *2000 census*
730

Tribal enrollment
(Tribal source, 2005)
745

Total labor force *2000 census*
232

Total labor force *(Tribal source, 2005)*
1,393

High school graduate or higher
2000 census
70.6%

Bachelor's degree or higher
2000 census
12.2%

Unemployment rate *2000 census*
23.28%

Unemployment rate
(BIA labor report, 2001)
66%

Per capita income *2000 census*
$10,475

Washington State began to implement their sovereign rights. Additionally, the Skokomish Tribe began to tax economic activity on and adjacent to the Skokomish Reservation.

The Skokomish people are actively restoring traditional cultural elements. While a number of traditional ceremonies and practices had been largely unused for nearly a century, by the late 1970s, tribal members were beginning to reinstate traditional basketry, carving, weaving, spiritual ceremonies, and dance activities.

GOVERNMENT

The Skokomish Tribal Government was established in 1938 under the Indian Reorganization Act. The tribal council is the governing body, and it is composed of seven members who serve staggered four-year terms. The original tribal constitution and bylaws were approved on February 23, 1938. Tribal members adopted amendments to the tribal constitution on January 15, 1980.

The tribal chairperson, vice-chairperson, and secretary/treasurer are selected from within the tribal council. A tribal manager is selected by the tribal council to manage the tribe's administrative and operational affairs and to enforce tribal policies and laws. The president of the general council is elected annually.

Tribal services include accounting, culture and arts, economic development, community development, natural resources, administrative, public safety, social, legal, health and dental, preschool and child care, adult and vocational education, court, and historic preservation.

The operation of the tribal police force and the tribal courts is overseen by the tribe's public safety department. Patrol and emergency services enforce state and federal statutes, court orders, and tribal laws. The department provides investigative and inter-jurisdiction assistance to the Mason County Sheriff's Department, Squaxin Island Tribal Police, U.S. Bureau of Alcohol, Tobacco, and Firearms, Shelton Police Department, Washington State Patrol, and the Washington State Departments of Corrections and Fish and Wildlife.

ECONOMY

Today, many tribal members continue to work within the region's logging and fishing industries, though restrictions intended to counter overharvesting of both resources have brought about significant downsizing of these industries. In an attempt to diversify its economy, the tribe has purchased property for economic development and resource enhancement, as well as for housing. The tribe operates several businesses, including a fish hatchery, a fish-processing plant, a gas station and convenience store, and a casino.

Government as Employer. The Skokomish Tribe is one of the largest employers in the county. It has created opportunities in the paraprofessional, technical, administrative, and skilled labor fields. The tribe employs between 105 and 110 individuals. The tribe also assists in the sustaining of employment in the area by purchasing local goods and services.

Economic Development Projects. The tribe has continued to expand its governmental, economic, and business roles over the past 30 years. It has utilized its resources to purchase commercial development sites, and lands for the use of community facilities and an infrastructure system.

Agriculture and Livestock. Poor drainage conditions have long inhibited the extensive cultivation of crops on the reservation. However, several species of brush are harvested within tribal

lands. Harvested brush species include salal, huckleberry, and juvenile cedar. The majority of harvests are conducted illegally by nontribal entities. Despite this fact, the market for the resources thrives as they are prized by the commercial floral arrangement industry.

Several species of edible mushrooms are also present on the reservation. Species include chantrelle, morel, matsutake, oyster, chicken of the woods, and coral. These species are valued in commercial supermarkets, particularly Asian markets both domestically and abroad.

Tribal lands are also home to a number of plant species that the Skokomish people utilize for medicinal purposes. These species include rhubarb, wild ginger, maidenhair fern, devil's club, Labrador plant, and plantain. In addition to tribal uses, the plants are prepared and marketed to alternative medical markets and the cosmetic industry.

Forestry. Tribal lands contain nearly 2,500 acres of designated forests. About 1,900 acres of this acreage is located within tribal and individual trust lands. Another 500 acres are located within individually held fee lands. Fir, cedar, alder, and cottonwood are the primary species of marketable timber available to the tribe. These forests may be harvested for pulp and wood chip, and have the potential to become saw logs over the next decade.

Gaming. The tribe owns the Lucky Dog Casino just north of highways 101 and 106, near the communities of Shelton and Hoodsport. It offers 81 slots/VLTs, including the most recently released games and the highest payout percentage available from the machine manufacturer. The casino features a café that offers a made-to-order menu. The staff is renown for its friendliness.

Fisheries. Tribal fishing rights off-reservation were significantly increased in court decisions of the early 1970s. The tribe conducts fishing activities and operates a fish hatchery. The Skokomish Tribe has access to two subclasses of marine resources suitable for economic development. The most marketable of the species in these groups are salmon, clams, oysters, spot shrimp, Dungeness crab, and geoduck.

Services and Retail. Aside from the fishing-related businesses on the reservation, the tribe operates a grocery store, deli, and gas station. Also under consideration for development on the reservation's recently reclaimed tidelands are a museum and a resort complex.

Media and Communications. The Sounder publishes articles, tribal employee profiles, editorials, and announcements. It serves as the key source of communication on the reservation.

Tourism and Recreation. The reservation features abundant fish, wildlife, and land reserves, making it potentially popular with fishermen, hunters, hikers, and campers. The reservation is located within 15 miles of some of Mason County's most popular tourist and recreational areas. Additionally, the reservation's location on the Hood Canal provides many recreational opportunities for boating, waterskiing, scuba diving, and swimming.

The tribe sponsors an annual elder's picnic each August. Activities include the Annual Chum Run, lunch, and recreation for adults and youngsters. The tribe also hosts the First Elk Ceremony, First Salmon Ceremony, First Food Feasts, the opening and closing of the Longhouse, and Treaty Days in January.

INFRASTRUCTURE

U.S. Highway 101 passes through tribal lands and circum-navigates Olympic National Park. It provides access to the entire Olympic Peninsula region.

Electricity. The Mason County Public Utility District Number 1 provides electricity for the reservation and surrounding areas. In operation since 1934, the District is the oldest operating public utility district in Washington.

Water Supply. The tribe manages its own water system, charging users a flat fee to cover the operating and maintenance costs. In February 2004, the system served 105 tribal housing units. Water and sewer services are also handled by individual wells and septic tanks, respectively. Solid waste is disposed of at Mason County landfills adjacent to the reservation.

Transportation. Interstate and/or intercity railroad passenger and freight services are unavailable in Mason County. Tribal members must travel to Olympia, Tacoma, or Seattle for those services. Transit bus systems are available in Mason and Thurston counties, while commercial air and bus lines are available in Olympia, about 35 miles away.

Telecommunications. Hood Canal Communications provides the reservation with telephone, cable, and Internet services. Serving the community out of Union, Washington, the company utilizes a hybrid fiber coax system that allows for the delivery of cable television, high-speed Internet access, and telephone service over a single wire. Services for pagers, cell phones, and so on are available locally or with many of the national providers.

Housing. The reservation's primary housing areas include a total of over four miles of tribal and county roads.

COMMUNITY FACILITIES AND SERVICES

Tribal services are available in a tribally owned community center, social services building, small gym, health clinic, preschool and child care center, public safety and court building, and natural resources and fisheries building. The reservation also houses a fish hatchery, community water system, and community park.

Education. The tribe opened an Early Childhood Education Programs Center in 1999. The center offers preschool and child care programs. A community based-college degree pro-

gram is available in conjunction with the Northwestern Indian College and Evergreen State College.

In 1995, the Skokomish Education Committee was formed in order to provide guidance to the education department and advise to the tribal council on youth and educational issues. Services of the education department include literacy, vocational, and higher education programs.

The tribe also offers tutoring services, employment counseling and guidance, medical assessment, vocational assessment, supplementary financial assistance, and job placement services. The education department also encourages continual professional development opportunities for staff members, family involvement in students' educational experiences, and tribal member participation in classrooms. It also offers weekly drumming, song, and dance presentations, Point-No-Point Treaty Day activities, and resources to integrate English and Twana sign language into the classroom.

Health Care. The tribe's health department provides comprehensive medical, dental, and related health services on the reservation, in coordination with other nontribal health care resources. The tribe operates the 4,350-square-foot ambulatory care health and dental clinic and will complete construction on a 4,600-square-foot expansion in 2005. The facility is open five days a week, and it provides case management, screening, monitoring, advocacy, prevention, referral, and treatment services. Additional health care services are available in nearby Shelton.

ENVIRONMENTAL CONCERNS

During the 1920s and 1930s, against the wishes of the tribe and without any legal permits, the City of Tacoma initiated the development of hydropower facilities on tribal lands condemned by Washington State courts. The construction of two dams diverted the North Fork channel flowing through the reservation. The dams operated significantly outside of the intent of their original authorization. The dams have restricted stream flows, damaged fish habitats, altered sediment deposits, markedly increased flooding, and reduced spawning sites. The affect of the flooding on tribal lands has been devastating and has, in fact, raised the level of groundwater and reduced the area of land suitable for development. In the 1990s, the tribe filed damage claims against the City of Tacoma and still awaits a response from the federal district court.

Skokomish

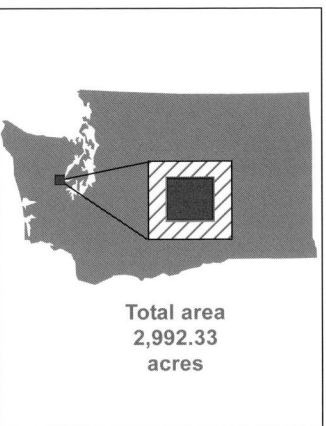

**Total area
2,992.33
acres**

Snoqualmie

Snoqualmie

LOCATION AND LAND STATUS

Snoqualmie tribal headquarters are in Carnation, Washington, a rural western Washington community of 1,905 residents. Carnation is located along State Road 203 in the Snoqualmie Valley, a 30-mile drive east of Seattle and 15 minutes east of Redmond.

Previously one of the largest tribes in the Puget Sound area and the principal signer of the 1855 Point Elliott Treaty between area tribes and the U.S. government, the Snoqualmies ceded a large territory from Snoqualmie Pass to up to the Port City of Everett, but they were never paid for the land. According to the tribe, before World War II they were promised a forested ridge extending between the towns of Fall City and Carnation. This promise was never carried out. Tribal lead-

ers had sought territory for a reservation since shortly after the Civil War, but it wasn't until the Snoqualmies were listed in the Congressional Record as an unrecognized tribe in 1952 that they began a successful 47-year fight to regain their status.

The federal government re-recognized the Snoqualmie in October 1999. Recognition provided the tribe the right to acquire its initial reservation land and to develop a casino to help fund the costs of tribal governance, administration, and services for its members. The tribe's objective is economic self-sufficiency, while acting as a good neighbor and as stewards of its land and environment. It received an initial grant of $155,000 to set up a new tribal administration and programs.

**Snoqualmie Tribe
Federally recognized
Snoqualmie
King County, Washington**

Snoqualmie Tribe
P.O. Box 280
Carnation, WA 98014
425-333-6551
425-333-6727 Fax
snoqualmiecasinoproject.com

Snoqualmie

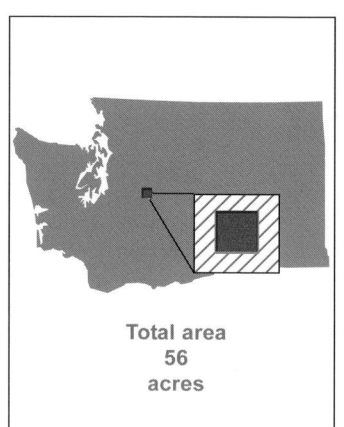

Total area
56
acres

Total area *(Tribal source, 2004)*
56 acres

Tribal enrollment
(BIA labor report, 2001)
616

Tribal enrollment
(Tribal source, 2000)
1,000+

Total labor force
(BIA labor report, 2001)
390

Unemployment rate
(BIA labor report, 2001)
24%

ENVIRONMENTAL CONCERNS
Snoqualmie Falls and the surrounding area have been severely impacted by a hydroelectric plant and by the millions of visitors who are drawn to the site. *(See Tourism and Recreation above.)*

The tribe has held talks with large regional landowners, such as Weyerhaeuser, about purchasing land for a reservation.

Since 2001 the tribe has awaited BIA certification of federal trust status for a 56-acre site, currently King County land, as reservation land, thus placing it under tribal authority and exempting it from most state laws. Such federal designation as trust land can take as long as five years. The tribe plans to develop the site for a casino. In 2004, the Indian Land Tenure Foundation announced a grant of $27,750 to the Snoqualmie Tribe of Washington for the acquisition of a 275-acre county park in King County, which includes land that is culturally significant to the tribe.

PHYSICAL DESCRIPTION
The City of Carnation is only a few miles from the spectacular Snoqualmie Falls, which are 30 miles east of Seattle. Elevation is 75 feet. To the west lies Bellevue, Seattle's most affluent suburb. To the southwest is Issaquah, a rapidly expanding commuter town. To the east are Weyerhaeuser timberlands and the National Forest lands of the Cascade Mountain range. To the north lie expensive farmland and executive estates. The tribe's headquarters are just 14 miles from those of Microsoft Corporation. Although this location makes formation of a large land base difficult, it does provide many potential business opportunities.

Patkanim was the principle chief of the Snoqualmie during the treaty negotiations and armed conflicts of the 1850s. Patkanim was initially hostile toward white settlers, but after traveling to San Francisco in 1850 and seeing the masses of Europeans and Americans flooding west, he decided that cooperating with white settlers offered his people a better chance of survival. When other Native leaders rose up against white settlements in the Puget Sound area, Patkanim's people became scouts and fought alongside the settlers and the government against neighboring tribes. In 1855 the Snoqualmies signed the Point Elliott Treaty. This treaty created a government-to-government relationship between the United States and the Snoqualmie Tribe, and the tribe ceded to the U.S. government all of its land between Snoqualmie Pass and Everett. Despite the help that Patkanim and his people offered to the settlers, the treaty negotiations left them with no reservation of their own. In legal limbo for many years, tribe members were scattered around the area. However some stayed in the valley of the ancestors and eventually established a tribal office in Redmond. Today their tribal headquarters are in Carnation.

Patkanim's village was on a bluff above the Snoqualmie River near its confluence with the smaller Tolt River. The Euro-American town now known as Carnation was later established on the opposite bank. An early surveyor general's map of Washington Territory in 1857 shows the area having the name Tolthue from the Native Americans who inhabited the area. Later the town name was given the white man's pronunciation of Tolt. In 1917, the state legislature changed the name to Carnation, probably after Carnation Research Farms, the world-famous milk company, which was the largest industry in the area. Many residents, however, still prefer to use the old name of Tolt. Since the treaties were signed, Puget Sound Indian communities have struggled to make the U.S. government live up to its promises. The Snoqualmie Tribe lost federal recognition in 1953 when federal policies limited recognition to tribes having reservations. The efforts of Chief Patkanim's nephew, Chief Jerry Kanim (1859-1956), helped preserve the identity of the Snoqualmie Tribe into the late twentieth century and laid the groundwork for successful federal recognition efforts in the 1990s. After a struggle of nearly 47 years, in October 1999 the BIA once again granted the

Snoqualmies tribal status based on evidence that the tribe had maintained a continuous community from historical times to the present.

The Snoqualmie Tribe operates on a $2 million budget, 80 percent of which comes from federal grants. State grants, private foundation money, and revenue from its health clinics make up the remainder. The tribe looks to future casino funds to start a child care center and build senior housing for its elders, among other projects. Since the tribe received recognition from the federal government in 1999, it has opened two public-health clinics, founded a drug-and-alcohol recovery center, and staked a claim to its reservation land.

GOVERNMENT
The tribe is governed by a tribal constitution and an elected council. The tribe's governing structure includes building codes, health codes, and other standard governmental functions. Executives include a chair (currently also the chief executive officer), a vice-chair, a chief financial officer, a treasurer, and an administrator.

Departments include archives, economic development, enrollment, environmental programs, health, housing, mental health and chemical dependency, social services, tobacco prevention, and transportation planning.

ECONOMY
There were 207 tribe members employed in private industry in 2001. The centerpiece of the Snoqualmie Tribe's economic development planning is its $60 million casino project. *(See Gaming, below.)*

Government as Employer. The tribe has 91 government employees.

Economic Development Projects. The tribe's 50-year struggle for federal recognition may be its greatest asset. With no land base, no federal assistance, and no political viability for so many years, tribal members were forced to be resourceful. Many are independent business owners who will be in a position to help the tribe as it develops. In May 2000, the full tribal membership voted to support a proposal to use the tribal resources for an economic development plan to benefit all tribal members.

Another valuable asset for economic development is good relations with local non-Indian groups. The tribe has supported local issues over the years. In the past, local non-Indian groups assisted the tribe in its fight for federal recognition. But now that the tribe is looking at developing a land base and potentially highly commercial operations such as a casino, some of that outside support is eroding. The tribe potentially faces opposition from King County council representatives in the coming years.

Gaming. After a year spent looking for land from Bellevue to Snoqualmie Pass, the Snoqualmie Tribe purchased a 56-acre parcel off I-90 at Exit 27. Since 2001 the tribe has awaited BIA certification of the site, currently part of King County, as reservation land.

The $60 million, 147,000-square-foot casino to be built there will offer destination entertainment, including 3 restaurants, a 400-seat live theater, a piano lounge, and machine and table games. The architectural concept for the casino is a great lodge design using stone, timbers, and a northwest color palette. The three-story building will be 90,000 to 100,000 square feet, approximately four percent of the site. The planned facility will create 700 jobs in Snoqualmie Valley.

The Snoqualmie Tribe has signed a wide-ranging municipal services agreement with the City of Snoqualmie. Under the agreement, the city will extend sewer lines and provide police, fire, and emergency services to the tract of land the tribe is seeking to have placed in trust. The two governments also agreed to work together to provide shuttle service from a planned tribal retail store in downtown Snoqualmie to the future casino. The tribe plans to use local businesses for supplies and services during both construction and ongoing operations.

Fisheries. The tribal council has approved a projected fish-processing plant and a smokehouse.

Tourism and Recreation. At 268 feet, the plunge of Snoqualmie Falls, sacred to the tribe, is 100 feet longer than Niagara Falls. One of Washington's top tourist attractions, Snoqualmie Falls appeared in the opening sequence of the television series *Twin Peaks*, and its power has always been a source of awe and inspiration for those who experience the falls in person. The Snoqualmie Falls were named "Sdo-Kuahl-Bu" and were considered to have supernatural powers for peace. There prayers were carried up to the Creator by great mists that rise from the powerful flow. The area has been a traditional burial site for centuries. Many powwows were held at the falls.

However, Snoqualmie Falls and the surrounding area have been severely impacted by a hydroelectric plant and by the millions of visitors who are drawn to the site. Puget Sound Energy diverts 93 percent of the Snoqualmie River into its generators, reducing the once majestic flow and mist to a fraction of its former grandeur.

The Snoqualmie people were unhappy about the sacrilegious operation and the fact that the power company, developers, tourists, and federal officials have consistently disregarded the spiritual and cultural significance of the falls to the tribe. They approached the Church Council of Greater Seattle, which, in 1987, issued a letter of apology recognizing the Christian Church's "longstanding participation in the destruction of Native American spiritual practices" and pledged to support Native Americans in their attempt to preserve and reclaim their sacred places. Together, the Snoqualmies, the Church Council, and other groups formed the Snoqualmie Falls Preservation Project (SFPP) and began an activist educational campaign to preserve Snoqualmie Falls in as natural a state as possible.

In the 1990s an enormous real estate development was proposed, including a 182-acre housing, retail, and office complex adjacent to the falls. The city was going to approve the project until Native activists began voicing opposition. The SFPP began an intensive campaign to educate the Federal Energy Regulatory Commission (FERC), Congress, the 1.5 million people who visit the falls each year, and the general public about the impact the proposed development would have on the falls. The Cascade Land Conservancy, King County, and the City of Snoqualmie eventually joined in the Snoqualmie Preservation Protection Initiative and in negotiations to scale back the development project. In January 2001, the Cascade Land Conservancy, funded by the city and county, purchased 145 acres of land near the falls from the owners of the proposed development site.

In March 2001, the Metropolitan King County Council unanimously approved the Snoqualmie Preservation Protection Initiative, an agreement that would permanently protect the falls, the watershed, and the immediate area, and prohibit development on 9,000 acres of forest around the falls. The area affected by the Snoqualmie Preservation Protection Initiative has been preserved, but the initiative has yet to be fully implemented. Despite such progress, the Army Corps of Engineers blasted away a rock ledge, used as a traditional ceremonial site for the Snoqualmie people, for a flood relief program.

In July 2004, the FERC approved Puget Sound Energy's application for an increase in water diversion and renewal of its lease for 40 years. The tribe is currently fighting for a second hearing. Native activists, with the help of the Western Environmental Law Center, vow to fight on to remove the generating station, relocate tourist facilities away from the falls, restore the area to its natural state, and have the Snoqualmie people co-manage the falls.

INFRASTRUCTURE

Carnation is on north-south State Road 203 and less than 15 miles north of east-west I-90. Airports certified for carrier operations nearest to Carnation are Boeing Field and King County International in Seattle, Snohomish County (Paine Field) in Everett, and Seattle-Tacoma International in Seattle. The other public-use airports nearest to Carnation are First Air Field in Monroe, Sky Harbor in Sultan, and Harvey Field in Snohomish.

COMMUNITY FACILITIES AND SERVICES

The tribe operates two clinics and a food bank and assists with housing and other social services. In 2002, the tribe set up a program called the Family Canoe project, which matches at-risk students with adult mentors and prepares them for a three-week paddling journey during the summer. The trip stresses living off the land and connecting with tribal history. There is a tribal youth coordinator. The tribe looks to future casino funds to start a child care center and build senior housing for its elders, among other projects.

Education. Stillwater Elementary has 423 students in grades K-5; Carnation Elementary has 384 students in grades pre-K-5. The Tolt Middle School has 650 students in grades 6-8. The Contracted Learning Program public high school in Carnation has 18 students in grades 9-12. Seventy-four students are in alternative programs for grades pre-kindergarten-11.

Health Care. Since the tribe received recognition from the federal government in 1999, it has opened two public-health clinics and founded a drug-and-alcohol recovery center. The Tolt Community Clinic is one block from tribal headquarters in Carnation. As part of the federal Indian Health Service, the clinic pays for treatment for recognized members of Native tribes. The second tribal clinic is in North Bend. The clinics serve 75 to 80 patients a week. Other hospitals and medical centers near Carnation are the Snoqualmie Valley Hospital in Snoqualmie, the Valley General Hospital in Monroe, and Group Health Eastside Hospital in Redmond.

Spokane

Spokane Reservation
Federal reservation
Spokane
Stevens County, Washington

Spokane Tribe of Indians
Alfred E. McCoy Memorial
  Building
6195 Ford/Wellpinit Road
P.O. Box 100
Wellpinit, WA 99040
509-458-6500
509-458-6575 Fax
spokaneTribe.com

Total area (BIA realty, 2004)
133,399.96 acres

Federal trust
(BIA realty, 2004)
77.47 acres

Tribally owned (BIA realty, 2004)
108,244.10 acres

Allotted/Individually owned
(BIA realty, 2004)
25,078.39 acres

Population 2000 census
2,004

Tribal enrollment
(BIA labor report, 2001)
2,305

Total labor force 2000 census
746

Total labor force
(BIA labor report, 2001)
1,658

High school graduate or higher
2000 census
74.6%

Bachelor's degree or higher
2000 census
7.9%

Unemployment rate 2000 census
19.8%

Unemployment rate
(BIA labor report, 2001)
78%

Per capita income 2000 census
$10,151

LOCATION AND LAND STATUS

The Spokane Reservation spans approximately 155,000 acres in northeastern Washington. The reservation was established by Executive Order on January 18, 1881, in response to more than 30 years of increasing encroachment upon Spokane lands, a trend initiated by the 1850 Land Donation Act. The tribe went to war with U.S. government forces in 1858 over unbridled Euro-American settlement, and it was defeated in the Battle of Four Lakes later that year. In 1907 the BIA granted full agency status to the 600 Spokanes, after which the BIA and tribal headquarters were established in Wellpinit. The tribe purchased 160 acres, referred to as the Mistequa property, from allottee heirs at Chewelah, 36 miles north of the reservation. The Spokane Indian Tribe has ownership of the Spokane River's bed and banks to the western shore of the Columbia River, as confirmed by Executive Order.

PHYSICAL DESCRIPTION

The reservation's southern and western boundaries are marked by the Spokane and Columbia rivers and the Coulee Dam Recreation Area. The land is rolling to mountainous in places and fairly heavily timbered.

CLIMATE

The elevation at Wellpinit, Washington, the location of tribal headquarters, is 2,450 feet above sea level. The year-round average daily high temperature is 57.3°F. The year-round average daily low temperature is 36.1°F. The area receives approximately 19.4 inches of precipitation annually, with almost 50 inches falling as snow.

CULTURE AND HISTORY

The Spokane ("Children of the Sun") Indians are modern descendents of the Interior Salish people who inhabited the areas now known as northeastern Washington, northern Idaho, and western Montana for centuries prior to first contact. The Spokanes are part of the Salishan linguistic family, a language they shared with the neighboring Flathead, Coeur d'Alene, and Kalispel tribes. Traditionally the Spokanes relied heavily upon salmon for their subsistence, spurring the development of a specialized fishing technology, semi-subterranean pit houses, consensus of opinion between the three bands of Spokanes, and the widespread gathering and storage of plant and root crops, among other characteristics.

Contact with whites, first documented in 1807, resulted in the tribe's division into three bands: Upper, Middle, and Lower, according to their location on the Spokane River. The Lower band occupied an area from its mouth to the present site of Tumtum; the Middle band resided in the area from Tumtum to the mouth of Hangman Creek; and the Upper band lived in the Hangman Creek region and throughout the Spokane Valley as far as the present Town of Post Falls, Idaho. Each band had a chief and several subchiefs.

During the early portion of the twentieth century, the Spokane economy and way of life suffered dramatically as a result of the construction of two dams: first, the Little Falls Dam built in 1908 at the traditional site of a major salmon fishery and trading spot with other tribes; and later the Grand Coulee Dam, authorized in 1935, a structure that ultimately stopped all salmon migration. After the establishment of the Indian Claims Commission in 1946, the Spokanes brought a claim for redress of the 32 cents per acre they had accepted under duress in 1887 for the more than three million acres they had ceded to the government at that time. In a compromise settlement, the tribe voted to accept $6.7 million in compensation, an amount to be held in trust.

In 1954 uranium was discovered on the reservation, leading to the creation of two Indian companies, which mined the ore until the Three Mile Island disaster in 1979. Tribal factionalism resulting from disagreements over distribution of uranium proceeds led to the formation of the Spokane Indian Association just after the discovery. The resulting conflict spurred the BIA to push for termination of the tribe in December 1955. Tribal leadership was able to successfully focus the disparate energies of its membership and fend off termination.

Traditional culture remains marginally viable, with a number of members, mostly elders, continuing to speak the language, use the sweat lodge, and practice traditional religions. Cultural sites have different cultural significance for the three bands of Spokane Indians-Upper, Middle, and Lower. Traditional arts are still practiced, and the tribe is now teaching its language to children to revive its everyday use. Each January, the tribe celebrates the creation of its reservation.

GOVERNMENT

The tribe operates under a constitution approved by its members in May 1951. On August 10, 1972, the constitution was amended and a governing body established which consists of a five-person business council whose members are popularly elected to one-, two-, and three-year terms. The Spokane Business Council oversees dozens of tribal committees, commissions, boards, and enterprises with assistance from an executive director and an administrative director for tribal operations. The administrative director manages all personnel associated with the culture, community services, human resource development, finance, administrative, health and human services, and natural resource departments. Under PL-638, the business council contracts with the BIA to administer key programs and services, including their own law enforcement and tribal courts, fire management, and a housing authority that manages a total of 701 housing units on the reservation. Tribal business is conducted by the tribal business council.

ECONOMY

Historically, the tribe's largest source of revenue and employment was derived from the sale of timber, followed by commercial fishing interests. When the uranium mines closed between 1982 and 1984, unemployment rose to 71 percent; however, following construction of the casinos, marina, and RV park, unemployment rates fell to 1-2 percent. An increasing focus on tourism has allowed for even greater economic self-sufficiency as the tribe reaps benefits from enterprise diversity.

Government as Employer. The tribal government doubled the number of people it employed between 1993 and 1995 and remains the largest employer on the reservation, employing approximately 112 people in its various programs and services or in one of its casinos or other enterprises. Most employees are tribal members. Many more tribal members are employed by programs of the BIA offices on the reservation, in the clinic, or in the schools.

TRI-WA-005

TRI-WA-006

Spokane

Total area
133,399.96
acres

TRI-WA-007

TRI-WA-008

Economic Development Projects. In order to more fully diversify the tribal economy and move away from historical dependence upon natural resources for its livelihood, the tribe has constructed three gaming operations with full resort amenities including a golf course, campgrounds, amphitheater, hotel, river front cabins, lodge, recreational facilities, and a marina. They also operate the Sherwood Memorial Tribal Center Museum, the Spokane Tribal Hatchery, and innumerable service enterprises and retailers. By 2006 the tribe will have two transfer stations built to collect trash.

Agriculture and Livestock. The tribe maintains a range program, which currently oversees several hundred head of cattle. Some non-Indians own small wheat farms located on the reservation. In addition to wheat, alfalfa is grown on the reservation.

Forestry. Tribal forest lands are rich with ponderosa pine, Douglas fir, and lodge pole pines. Whereas the tribe once owned its own sawmill, an independent contractor now mills reservation timber. The average annual cut is 12 to 15 million board feet. Approximately 35 people worked in logging and timber sales in 2004. Annual timber sales total approximately $3 million. The Spokane Indian Reservation Timber Products enterprise brokers and sells stumpage with 16 employees. Spokane Wood Products manufactures dimension lumber products, post poles and pressure-treated wood. Combined profits average $150,000 per year for the enterprises. There are also five or six privately owned Indian logging companies, which own their own heavy equipment.

Gaming. The tribe first opened a gaming operation in March 1994. Revenues generated from this single operation permitted expansion into wider recreational, tourism, and gaming markets, including the addition of two more casinos in the past decade and considerable expansion of resort amenities, including an RV park and marina, restaurants, gift shops, and retailers located in and near the gaming operations.

The 30,000-square-foot Chewelah Casino, in Chewelah, Washington, features 375 slot machines, 9 table games, and a restaurant; it employed approximately 180 people in 2003.

The 25,000-square-foot Double Eagles Casino, also located in Chewelah, features 300 slots, 5 table games and a restaurant. Lil' Chiefs Casino, in Wellpinit, has 150 slots. The Two Rivers Casino and Resort in Davenport, a gaming operation featuring 350 slots and 6 table games, has exploded onto the Spokane tourism industry with luxurious resort amenities; it employs hundreds of people, many of them tribal members. *(See Tourism and Recreation, below.)*

Fisheries. The Spokane Tribal Hatchery, created with revenues resulting from settlements for the loss of aboriginal and historical fishing sites by the creation of Washington Water Power dams, stocks the Spokane River and tribal lakes with Kokanee salmon and rainbow trout. The enterprise is staffed entirely by enrolled tribal members.

Construction. There are currently two construction contractors on the reservation. One contractor employs five people; the other has one employee. The tribe has built 20 new homes in Ford, Washington, for tribal members. The tribe built the Alfred E. McCoy Administration Building. In 2004, the tribe completed houses, tribal departments, and a new EMS and fire building. There is not a tribal construction company to oversee construction of the new tribal buildings.

Industrial Parks. The tribe has 145 acres in Airway Heights, Washington (trust land), which has been set aside for potential development of an industrial park.

Mining. Uranium was once mined on the reservation. Although uranium deposits remain, the two mines are now closed for health and environmental reasons.

Services and Retail. Many services are provided, such as silversmiths, beauticians, carvers, seamstresses, artists, and bakers. Other tribal enterprises include smoke shops, a document shredding service, a security firm, a daycare center, and two gas stations. Also, the tribe owns a trading post, operates a cafe in the community center in Wellpinit, and makes a plethora of retail opportunities available at the marina and the casinos.

TRI-WA-005 Crossroad Sign, Spokane Indian Reservation with Emblem "Cross My Heart Seatbelt Campaign" to tribal buildings

TRI-WA-006 Two Rivers Casino & Resort - RV & boat marina overlooking Lake Roosevelt

TRI-WA-007 Front of Spokane Tribal Administration Building

TRI-WA-008 Front of Two Rivers Casino & Resort

Spokane

Media and Communications. The tribe publishes a monthly newsletter for distribution to the membership, along with informational brochures aimed at the tourism markets.

Tourism and Recreation. The tribe operates a 260-slip floating marina and boat launch on Lake Roosevelt. The 2,300-square-foot floating convenience store and gas station sells beer and wine, souvenirs, fishing tackle, and some grocery items. The marina, a 100-site RV park overlooking Lake Roosevelt, and the Two Rivers Casino and Resort are all part of the tribal recreation area. There are 32 tent sites scattered along the Spokane and Columbia rivers, picnic tables and a covered pavilion, shower and laundry facilities, day-use areas, playgrounds, rental cabins, and a golf course. Water sports including water skiing, wakeboarding, sailing, and fishing are popular pastimes. Houseboats are available for rent by a private contractor. Additional attractions include the tribal museum in Wellpinit and cultural events such as Spokane Indian Days held on Labor Day weekend, which features war dances, exhibits, and games.

INFRASTRUCTURE

State Highway 25 runs north-south through the reservation, connecting with U.S. 2 at Reardan, 22 miles to the south. The reservation is also accessible by State Route 231. I?395 runs near the property, as does Burlington Railroad.

Electricity. The Western Washington Power Company and the Rural Electrification Administration provide electricity.

Fuel. Independent propane distributors are available to reservation residents and facilities.

Water Supply. The U.S. Public Health Service installed five community water systems, including two for Wellpinit residents and tribal offices. The tribe built its own 350,000-gallon water system to serve the Two Rivers Casino and Resort and the recreational area. There are several municipal users of the Wellpinit sewer system, including the U.S. Postal Service, the BIA, and the Indian Health Service.

Transportation. The senior center has two vans; several individuals own heavy logging equipment; and the tribe owns numerous cars, vans, trucks, wood skidders, loaders, and small Cats. Train and bus services are available in Reardan. Commercial truck lines serve the reservation directly. Commercial air service is available in Spokane, 40 miles from the reservation.

Telecommunications. Pacific Telesis installed fiber optic cable to the Two Rivers Casino and Resort.

COMMUNITY FACILITIES AND SERVICES

The community center, built in 1975, houses tribal offices, the tribal museum, a basketball court, and many offices of the department of social services. The department operates programs to assist members with applications for Social Security benefits, foster home licensing and payment, family violence intervention, Birth-to-three early identification and referrals, adult development disabilities employment, and limited financial assistance for child care. The tribal social services department is licensed as a private child placing agency with the State of Washington and implements the Indian Child Welfare Act. The tribe operates Children of the Sun Head Start, an adult developmental disability program, substance abuse programs, child care development that provides daycare for children in their own homes, a mental health department, and the WIC nutritional program.

The community services department oversees a children's hospital alternative program, provides basic education on fetal alcohol syndrome and alcohol-related neurodevelopmental delays and disorders, and operates a department of children and family services and a low-income housing energy assistance program. The tribal business council also assists tribal members with transportation to medically related appointments and a few other social service appointments, offers some emergency financial energy assistance, and a food distribution program including commodities, emergency food vouchers and an emergency food bank. There is a community health representative to provide health education and outreach services, and a drug elimination youth program. For those requiring treatment, there are both adult and youth holistic substance abuse programs.

Education. Students attend the area's public schools. In June 1994, the tribal council chartered Spokane Tribal College, located in Wellpinit, which is a branch campus of Salish Kootenai College. Language lab facilities and staff at the tribal college assist with preserving, maintaining, and promoting the Spokane language and cultural practices. The schools have Internet access.

Health Care. The David C. Wyncoop Memorial Clinic, a 7,700-square-foot Indian Health Services facility, provides comprehensive ambulatory health care in Wellpinit. The JCAHO-accredited clinic also houses the contract health services program serving Ferry, Lincoln, and Stevens counties. In addition to the clinic, the Spokane Tribe operates several health programs under Indian Health Service funded PL-93-638, title I contracts, including the community health representative program, emergency medical services, alcohol and substance abuse, and mental health. Regional health care options include an Indian Health Service Spokane Urban Clinic and hospitals.

ENVIRONMENTAL CONCERNS

The tribe has a natural resources department that oversees environmental programs for the reservation. The tribe's environmental policies are directed by an integrated resource management plan. The plan is currently being updated.

LOCATION AND LAND STATUS

The Squaxin Island Reservation occupies most of Squaxin Island, located at the southern end of Puget Sound in the State of Washington. The Island, approximately 4 miles long and one-quarter to three-quarters mile wide, is located 10 miles north of Olympia and 9 miles east of Shelton. The actual Squaxin Island is unoccupied. The tribal community and the location of tribal headquarters is Kamilche, between Little Skookum and Totten Inlets, near Shelton, where over the years, the tribe has purchased land for housing, tribal offices, and economic development.

PHYSICAL DESCRIPTION

Squaxin Island, situated in Puget Sound at the confluence of seven separate inlets, is heavily forested with evergreens interspersed with coastal wetlands.

CLIMATE

The year-round average daily high temperature at Shelton is approximately 61°F. The year-round average daily low temperature is 42°F. Dominated by sea fog and rains, the area receives approximately 66 inches of precipitation annually, 8 inches in snowfall.

CULTURE AND HISTORY

Like many tribes of the Pacific Northwest, the Squaxin Island Tribe, "People of the Water," is made up of descendents of the original maritime inhabitants of the seven inlets of South Puget Sound; the Noo-Seh-Chatl of Henderson Inlet, Steh Chass of Budd Inlet, Squi-Aitl of Eld Inlet, Sawamish/T'Peeksin of Totten Inlet, Sa-Heh-Wa-Mish of Hammersley Inlet, Squawksin of Case Inlet and S'Hotle-Ma-Mish of Carr Inlet. Throughout prehistory, the people subsisted on the rich resources of the waters of Puget Sound and the forests of the mainland, harvesting fish, primarily salmon, wild fruits, nuts, and berries. They were excellent craftspeople who carved the abundant western red cedar trees into wooden utensils, masks, dishes, boxes, and canoes. They are known for their elaborate basketry as well, utilizing stripped bark to weave clothing, mats, baskets, furnishings, and rope. For centuries, Squaxin Island has been a gathering place for the people of the region; a centrally located stopping point for trade and for social or spiritual gatherings. In Lushootseed, or Lushutseed, a variant of the wider Salish language traditionally utilized by many coastal tribes, Squawksin meant "in between," or "piece of land to cross over to another bay," indicating their position at the confluence of seven separate inlets of Puget Sound, on the isthmus between Hood Canal and Puget Sound. It is also said to have meant, "split apart." A tribal legend recounts a force of water entering and creating the bay that inundated the land there.

The people of Squaxin Island are closely related to the Nisqually Tribe, with similar cultural traditions, through intermarriage and language. They are, along with the Puyallup Tribe and the Nisqually, fellow signatories to the Treaty of Medicine Creek of 1854, wherein the tribes ceded 2,560,000 acres of aboriginal territory to the federal government. Following the war of 1856-1857 that erupted after the tribes realized the extent to which they had been 'swindled' of their lands, hundreds of people from the various tribes were confined for a time on the island. Out of thousands of square miles of land ceded to the U.S. government, the tiny island was retained as the main reservation area.

This community became a headquarters for the Indian agency and a school; a blacksmith shop and a church were established. Many fled the island after failed attempts at farming left them in poverty, becoming loggers, or working in the hop and berry fields of the mainland. Those that remained lived in cedar shake houses or in float houses moored in coves along the shoreline during high winter tides, resuming their fishing during the fall salmon runs, gathering oysters, clams, smelt, and herring for smoking and year-round consumption. By 1862 the number of island residents had dwindled to 50 and the Indian agency headquarters was moved to Puyallup. By 1959 only four-year-round residents continued to live on the island and in 2004, there are none. The island, still a place of great spiritual significance to the tribe, is used primarily for fishing, hunting, shellfish gathering, camping, and other activities, by tribal members. Nontribal members are not permitted onto the island except when accompanied by a tribal member, and only then with special permission from the natural resources department.

Many tribal members are members of the Indian Shaker Church founded by Squaxin tribal member John Slocum in the late 1880s. The original church was established on a place now known as Church Point on the Island, returned to tribal ownership in June of 1995. They have also revived many cultural practices in recent decades. From trees that were alive prior to the arrival of Christopher Columbus to the "New World," the tribe initiated a Canoe Project in December 1995, carving a huge canoe in the old way, to be utilized during an annual flotilla reminiscent of the ancestors' travel upon the waters of Puget Sound. The two-week journey joins the Squaxins with surrounding tribes, visiting each tribe located around the area, having potlatches or parties at each village site. The rest of the year, the canoe rests at the Tu Ha' Buts Cultural Center Museum Library and Research Center. Artifacts excavated from an ancient Squaxin site, Mud Bay Village, now located on private property on South Puget Sound, are also prominently displayed at the center.

The tribe continues many traditional practices of cultural and spiritual value, such as, The First Salmon Ceremony, honoring the first salmon run of the season, each year in August.

GOVERNMENT

The Squaxin Island Tribe adopted a constitution on July 8, 1965, providing for a general council composed of all eligible tribal voters with a five-member tribal council, elected to staggered three-year terms. The number of council members has since been raised to seven, consisting of a chairman, vice-chairman, secretary, treasurer, and three members. The general council meets annually; the tribal council meets at least twice monthly.

Squaxin Island was one of the first 30 tribes to enter into self governance compacts with the federal government. Under PL-638, they contract with the BIA to administer key programs or services. Tribal departments include: community development; cultural resources, health and human services, human resources, information systems, Tu Ha' Buts learning center, legal, natural resources, Northwest Treatment Center, and planning and public safety. The Squaxin Island Tribe is a member of the South Puget Intertribal Planning Agency.

Squaxin Island Reservation
Federal reservation
Squaxin Island
Mason County, Washington

Squaxin Island Tribe of the
Squaxin Island Reservation
10 SE Squaxin Lane
Shelton, WA 98584-9200
360-426-9781
360-426-6577 Fax
squaxinisland.org

Total area (BIA realty, 2004)
970.72 acres

Total area (Tribal source, 2004)
2,054 acres

Tribally owned (BIA realty, 2004)
144.67 acres

Tribally owned (Tribal source, 2004)
763 acres

Individually owned
(BIA realty, 2004)
826.05 acres

Allotted lands (Tribal source, 2004)
826 acres

Population *2000 census*
405
Tribal enrollment
(Tribal source, 2004)
812

Tribal enrollment (BIA, 2001)
643

Total labor force *2000 census*
173

Total Labor Force (BIA, 2001)
1,234

High school graduate or higher
2000 census
61.9%

Bachelor's degree or higher
2000 census
1%

Unemployment rate *2000 census*
16.8%

Unemployment rate (BIA, 2001)
30%

Per capita income *2000 census*
$13,401

Squaxin Island

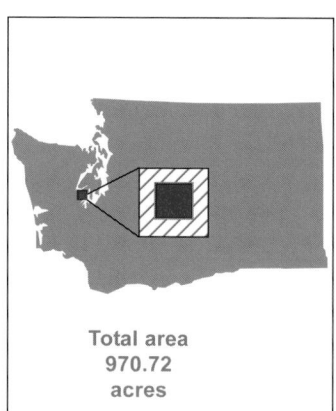

Total area
970.72
acres

BUSINESS CORPORATION

Tribal enterprises are developed and managed by the Squaxin Island Tribal Council through its' Tribal Codes and Ordinances. The tribe has established a corporate administration board, which is charted as an authorized independent commission with powers expressly delegated by the tribal council. This board is comprised of three tribal members, one of whom is a board member.

The tribe currently has two corporate charters. The first, Island Enterprises, established on May 9, 2003, currently contains three subsidiary companies (Kamilche Trading Post, Salish Seafoods and Squaxin Island child care development center) and is the economic development arm of tribal government. The second, Skookum Creek Tobacco Company, established on August 26, 1999, provides contract packaging, product development, private label manufacturing, and marketing services to other tribes.

ECONOMY

The tribe, although still very much involved with fishing as a source of individual and tribal revenue, has developed enterprises that move aquiculture projects onto the national and international markets. They have also diversified their economy by developing other enterprises, such as a thriving smoke shop, at which they market their own brand of cigarettes, a casino, and the Kamilche Trading Post.

Government as Employer. There are a total of 181 employees of tribal government, working in either one of its many health and social service programs, or tribal enterprises.

Gaming. The 110,000 square foot Little Creek Casino and Hotel, in Shelton, Washington, features 516 slot machines, 21 table games, live Keno, 6 poker tables, and a 300-seat Bingo Hall. The Casino complex also includes a 5-story, 92-room hotel, 4 restaurants, an entertainment venue, a 500-capacity conference/banquet hall, meeting rooms, video arcade, exercise facility/weight room, and an indoor swimming pool. The facility employs a total of approximately 753 tribal and non-Indian personnel and generates over $20 million in direct and induced earnings annually. Ancillary businesses, built adjacent to the casino complex, also help to stimulate the local and regional economy.

The casino makes grants to local non-profit and governmental entities as part of its gaming compact with the State of Washington, guaranteeing the return of a percentage of the proceeds to the community supporting its operations. Grants have been made to the Mason County Fire District #4, Mason County Sheriff's Department, and the Washington State Patrol, among many others.

Fisheries. Aquiculture projects are very important to the tribe's economy. Harstine Oyster Company, purchased by the tribe in the early 1970s, is the tribe's facility for rearing, processing, marketing, and retailing approximately 12,000 gallons of oysters annually. The 4,000 square foot plant is located on 6 acres of waterfront along the western short of Harstine Island; however, the company also utilizes 41 acres of coastal tidelands on Squaxin Island to grow oysters. The oysters are harvested by hand to protect pristine wetland areas from environmental degradation. The oysters and other seafood products are marketed on the Internet. Prime single oysters, almost one-half million per year, are marketed under the name Palala Bay Pacifics, reflecting the small bay on the south end of Squaxin Island where the oysters are harvested. The company has initiated mussel harvesting in addition to oyster production. The tribe also operates a floating sea farm for the raising of coho salmon.

The tribe is a co-manager with the State of Washington of natural resources such as salmon and shellfish. Tribal members participate in all fisheries of the 'usual and accustomed areas' as designated by the Medicine Creek Treaty of 1854. They participate in the Pacific Coast Shellfish Growers Association.

Manufacturing. Tax-free cigarettes sold on reservations have been a major draw to tribally-owned stores. This is of special significance to the Squaxin Island Tribe in the operation of Skookum Creek Tobacco, in operation since 2000, a tribally-owned company that manufactures and distributes the tribe's own brand name of cigarettes to regional outlets throughout Indian Country and at their own Kamilche Trading Post, a gas station, liquor store, and smoke shop near the Little Creek Casino.

Services and Retail. Aside from the retail outlets and amenities associated with the casino, the Kamilche Trading Post, is a combination convenience mart, liquor store, smoke shop and gas station located at the intersection of Highways 101 and 108 near Shelton. Unique architectural design features the shape of a traditional longhouse, common among the coastal Salish tribes.

Transportation. The Squaxin Island Tribe operates a bus system with various scheduled daily runs throughout the region, offering daily connections with Mason Transit to Shelton and Olympia, and Grays Harbor Transit to Aberdeen and Olympia. The tribal transit center is located at Kamilche.

Media and Communications. A complimentary newspaper in tabloid format, *Klah-Che-Min*, is distributed monthly by the tribe and their annual report is presented in magazine format, with full-page photography and financial information for each department, of potential use or benefit to enterprise investors. Little Creek Casino publishes several brochures and a newsletter advertising various gaming opportunities and special events, marketed primarily to the regional tourism industry.

Tourism and Recreation. A centerpiece of tribal cultural history, the 13,000 square foot Tu Ha' Buts Cultural Center Museum Library and Research Center, was opened to the public in 2002. It features permanent displays of art and artifacts, including a giant canoe carved in the ancient tradition by tribal members for the annual Canoe Journey, and history archives and traveling displays from other regional collections. Artists provide on-site demonstrations and computerized language classroom instruction are available, as are free public lectures, tribal storytelling and dances. Constructed in the shape of a traditional longhouse, the Squaxin Island Tribe refers to the facility as kwedigws'altxw, or, Home of Sacred Belongings. Tumwater Falls Park, along the Deschutes River in downtown Olympia, offers a variety of hiking trails and other outdoor recreational opportunities, as does the Nisqually Wildlife Refuge, also located in the South Puget Sound region. Kenneydell Park, on Black Lake, is a popular summertime retreat for tourists and tribal members alike, with a lodge fronting the lake, gravel beaches lining the lake shores, picnic sites, ballfields, and hiking trails.

INFRASTRUCTURE

The only access to the Island is by boat. The tribal community is near the popular tourist routes of Washington State Highway 101 and Highway 108.

Electricity. Electricity is provided by Public Utilities District #3.

Water Supply. The Kamilche community has a water system including new drainfields for tribal housing and a new water treatment plant. In September of 2004, the planning department was working with the tribal department of community development to secure loans from the U.S. Department of Agriculture and the Indian Health Service to build extensive water, drinking water and wastewater reuse potential, and make safety improvements to existing infrastructure, such as new water main connections, pump stations and storage tanks.

Transportation. The tribe received a Rural Mobility Grant in 1999 and 2001 from the Washington State Department of Transportation, which permitted initiation of the Squaxin Island Transit System, a scheduled bus system of routes designed to increase access to local employment and educational opportunities, while increasing access to transportation possibilities for low-income tribal members. The tribe also owns two wheel-chair equipped, 15-passenger vans utilized for transportation of tribal youth and elders as needed.

Telecommunications. Hood Canal Communications, a Mason County business, provides cable television, broadband, and local telephone services for the tribe. In 2003, Hood Canal Communications, out of Union, Washington, was the recipient of a Rural Utilities Service Broadband technology grant from the U. S. Department of Agriculture on behalf of the Squaxin Island Tribe to bring high-speed Internet to the reservation housing area.

COMMUNITY FACILITIES AND SERVICES

A number of community facilities serve the Squaxin area. The "old" tribal center building, vacated when the new one was finished, has been renovated for use as a youth community and learning center. The Tu Ha' Buts Learning Center now has remodeled, rewired space for technology, a gymnasium, study areas, and an arts and crafts wing. There is a playground on the premises and the facility hosts summer recreation programs for youth. The elders building houses all programs and services for the tribal elders, including a nutrition program serving hot meals, physical activities, and day pro-

grams. A new 15,000 square foot child development center was opened in June of 2004, with classroom space, inside play areas, fenced outdoor play areas, hiking trails, and offices for staff. The licensed facility can accommodate up to 116 infants and children for daycare services.

Education. The tribe operates a preschool; children attend Shelton public schools.

Health Care. The Squaxin Island Tribal Clinic, in Shelton, Washington, is a tribally-owned 6,720 square foot building, operated under PL-638 title III self-governance compact with the Indian Health Service. The facility is staff by a physician's assistant providing primary care, and dental professionals to provide an array of dental care services. The tribe also operates the Northwest Indian Treatment Center, an alcohol and substance abuse program in an inpatient treatment facility in Elma. Additional programs include a community health representative, public health community nursing services, health education, nutrition, optometry, dental, emergency medical services, home health care, and traditional medicine. The tribe employs one dentist and two mid-level practitioners who are registered nurses, nurse practitioners, or public health nurses.

ENVIRONMENTAL CONCERNS

In 1951, an earthen dam was built on the lower Deschutes River, backing up fresh water and flooding what was a rich tidal estuary, adversely affecting the health of migrating and spawning salmon. The shallow lake fills with sediment fostering the growth of non-native weeds, which rob the lake of oxygen. Squaxin Island tribal biologists have long studied the impacts of the dam and have lobbied for its removal. With funding assistance from the nonprofit Puget Sound Restoration Fund, the tribe planted native wild Olympian oysters along three beaches at Squaxin Island throughout 2002 and 2003 to revive them from the brink of pollution-induced extinction. In 2004, the tribe reports much success with the program, although they continue to struggle with eliminating the invasive Japanese Oyster Drill, a snail-like parasite that eats oysters after boring through their shells, from south Puget Sound.

Stillaguamish

LOCATION AND LAND STATUS

The Stillaguamish Reservation is located in Washington State between the Cascade Mountains and Puget Sound. Tribal administrative offices and tribal housing are located primarily near Arlington at Smokey Point. The tribe owns 19 separate properties, 7 of which are in trust status, 8 of which are pending trust status, and 4 of which are in fee status. The tribe continues to work toward increasing its land base.

CULTURE AND HISTORY

Members of the Stillaguamish Tribe are descendants of the Stoluckwamish River Tribe. The tribe is currently referred to as the Stillaguamish in reference to their traditional location along the Stillaguamish River. Traditional means of sustenance for the tribe included harvesting salmon and other seafood, gathering roots and berries, and hunting goats in the Cascade Mountains. The tribe also participated in the trade industry with neighboring tribes. The tribe was comprised of between 25 and 30 loosely assembled villages along the Stillaguamish River. Village populations varied from as low as less than a few dozen to as high as several hundred. At its peak, the tribe's total population is estimated to have been between 2,500 and 3,000.

Relations between Euro-American settlers and the Stillaguamishes were relatively peaceful at first. The tribe traded with settlers, and tribal members were often employed to clear land and harvest crops. As more settlers arrived in the region, the Stillaguamishes were forced to cede their lands. The Treaty of Point Elliot in 1855 called for the tribe to relinquish lands in exchange for federal assistance and designated lands for participating tribes. A separate reservation was not established for the Stillaguamish people, instead the tribe was required relocate to the Tulalip Reservation, which was originally located on Whidbey Island. While a number of tribal members did remain on the Tulalip Reservation, a number of Stillaguamish people returned to their ancestral lands along the Stillaguamish River. Because the majority of the tribe refused to leave their homelands and reside on a reservation, the federal government rescinded its recognition of the tribe in 1870.

By the 1900s, the tribe had become very dispersed and the population greatly reduced. In 1920, the population was at 29 individuals. In 1920, under the guidance of tribal member Esther Ross, the Stillaguamishes began their quest for fed-

Stillaguamish Reservation
Federal reservation
Stoluckwamish
Snohomish County,
Washington

Stillaguamish Tribe
3110 Smokey Point Dr.
Arlington, WA 98223
360-652-7362
360-659-3113 Fax

Total area *(BIA realty, 2004)*
24.3 acres

Tribally owned *(BIA realty, 2004)*
24.3 acres

Population *2000 census*
102

Stillaguamish

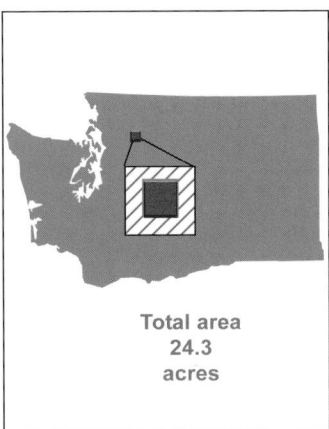

Total area
24.3
acres

Tribal enrollment
(BIA labor report, 2001)
182

Total labor force *2000 census*
35

Total labor force
(BIA labor report, 2001)
127

High school graduate or higher
2000 census
73.8%

Bachelor's degree or higher
2000 census
0%

Unemployment rate *2000 census*
5.7%

Unemployment rate
(BIA labor report, 2001)
46%

Per capita income *2000 census*
$8,076

eral recognition. The tribe began to restore organization, and in 1953 it adopted a tribal constitution. The tribe proceeded to file a claim with the Indian Claims Commission for compensation for lands lost in the Point Elliot Treaty. In 1970, the commission awarded the tribe a $64,460 judgment for the former 58,600 acres of tribal lands. In the 1974 Boldt decision, the tribe and other northwestern tribes were granted fishing rights based on treaty guarantees. The tribe petitioned for federal recognition in 1974, and in 1976 it was granted status.

Today, the tribe is recognized for its efforts in restoring fish stock and preserving water quality in the Stillaguamish River and Watershed.

GOVERNMENT
The tribe is governed according to a tribal constitution adopted on January 31, 1953. The governing body is a council of six elected members.

The tribe is a PL-638 tribe and contracts Indian Health Services. Tribal government programs include natural resources, fisheries, housing, health and social services, elders' nutrition, child care, grants development, and community development.

ECONOMY
Tribally owned enterprises such as the newly developed casino, the BankSavers native plant nursery, and the expanding Social and Health Department contribute to the tribal economy. The tribe serves as a major source of employment in the community.

Government as Employer. The tribe employs approximately 320 people in its various government departments and economic enterprises.

Economic Development Projects. The tribe contributes a great deal to the local economy through its various governmental services and economic development projects.

Gaming. In 2002, the tribe developed the Angel of the Winds Casino on its parcel. Opened in 2004, the casino offers 425 slot machines, 10 table games, and 2 restaurants in its 22,000-square-foot facility. It employs about 200 people. Expected revenue for its first year of operation is about $33 million. The monies will be used to make loan payments, contribute to economic development on the reservation, and be distributed in part to tribal members.

Fisheries. The Stillaguamish Tribal Hatchery was established in 1978 to assist in the restoration efforts of the salmon runs in the Stillaguamish River. The hatchery releases 200,000 wild origin Chinook into the river system each year. The natural

resources department maintains a water quality database for various watershed streams and Port Susan. They also do restoration activities that assist in salmon recovery.

Services and Retail. The tribe owns BankSavers, a company that helps restore and cool watershed waters. The company's goals are to supply quality native plants for habitat restoration and to provide training and work employment to tribal and nontribal members.

Tourism and Recreation. The tribe sponsors the annual Stillaguamish Festival of the River. This summer event includes storytelling, vendors, a 5K race, a salmon barbecue, entertainment, a photo and art contest, and a powwow. Approximately 8,000 to 10,000 people attend the event annually.

INFRASTRUCTURE
Access to the reservation is possible via I-5.

COMMUNITY FACILITIES AND SERVICES
Tribal facilities include a community center located next to the tribal casino, the fisheries office, and the hatchery. An administration building at Smokey Point houses a food bank, a weight room, a daycare facility, the tribal court, offices, and meeting rooms.

Health Care. The tribe operates a health clinic in Arlington. The facility offers primary care services and an exam room. Programs include elder care and alcohol counseling. The clinic employs full staff support, a part-time physician's assistant, and a doctor on contract services.

In 2003, the tribe opened Island Crossing Counseling Services, a methadone-treatment facility, the first such clinic to open in Snohomish County. The clinic is the only one of its kind in the region between Everett, Washington, and the Canadian border. Its service area is approximately one-quarter the length of Washington State on the west side of the Cascade Mountains.

The tribe is developing a new facility, due to open in 2005. It will offer mental health and chemical dependency programs and include western and traditional tribal healing methods, as well as acupuncture and massage therapy.

ENVIRONMENTAL CONCERNS
The tribe's primary environmental concerns include restoring fish stock in the Stillaguamish River and preserving the quality of water in the Stillaguamish Watershed. The tribal hatchery is active in restocking fish populations in the river, and the tribe works cooperatively with local, state, and federal agencies to address water quality issues.

LOCATION AND LAND STATUS

The Swinomish Reservation spans 7,169 acres of Fidalgo Island in northwestern Washington State. The island is located in an area known geologically as the Puget Lowland of Western Washington, sitting on the east end of Puget Sound, west of the Cascade Range and approximately 80 miles north of Seattle.

The reservation was formed by Executive Order in 1873 following the 1855 Treaty of Point Elliot, which promised the site to the four related Indian bands living in that area-the Samish, Kikiallus, Lower Skagit, and Swinomish tribes. Through the provisions of the General Allotment Act of 1887, reservation lands passed largely from communal to individual ownership as part of a strategy to "civilize" the Indians, opening the door to the eventual alienation of nearly half of the reservation lands from the hands of tribal members.

The tribe began buying back lost lands in 1999, and it requested the BIA to place the lands in federal trust. By 2004, the tribe had recouped about 1,100 acres of reservation land.

PHYSICAL DESCRIPTION

The land ranges from tidal beachfront to steep rock outcroppings some 400 or more feet above sea level. Much of the 10 square miles is fertile farmlands; upland areas are heavily forested with evergreens; shorelines and tidal wetlands are thick with Sitka spruce, elderberry, western white pine, Pacific madrone, and shore pines. The reservation is completely surrounded by water: 24 miles of coastal tidelands, three bays, a river, and the Swinomish Channel.

CLIMATE

Typical of the rain shadow side of the Olympic Mountains in northwestern Washington State, the area including Fidalgo Island and La Conner experience cool, relatively dry summers, with mild, moist winters. The area receives approximately 28.5 inches of precipitation annually.

CULTURE AND HISTORY

The modern Swinomish Reservation is occupied by descendents of aboriginal Swinomish, Kikiallus, Lower Skagit, and Samish tribal members. Ancestors of modern residents lived in the region for thousands of years practicing a subsistence lifestyle centered upon salmon and other fish species, supplementing their diets with game, berries, nuts, and roots. First contact came when white explorers "discovered" the Puget Sound area in the 1500s; however, the tribes remained largely unaffected until large numbers of permanent settlers entered aboriginal hunting and gathering areas, mostly loggers interested in exploiting the vast expanses of giant old-growth evergreens.

Though these tribes all speak Lushutseed, a variant of the wider Salish language, merging the bands was an issue well into the twentieth century. All four bands unsuccessfully sought independent tribal status during the 1970s. In any case, provisions were drawn up for the Swinomish Reservation under the 1855 Treaty of Point Elliot and modified by an Executive Order in 1873. The General Allotment Act of 1887, an effort by the federal government to transform the Indian population into "civilized" farmers through individual land ownership, also resulted in cultural alienation. Unallotted acreage was designated "surplus," thereby making it available to non-Indian buyers. Tribal members who had been allotted lands were frequently forced off by dishonest BIA agents or by foreclo-

sure for failing to pay property taxes. In 1892, the commissioner of Indian affairs prohibited traditional Spirit Dancing, Indian medicine, and plural marriage; however, dancing and other ceremonies continued underground at various locations throughout the region. Through allotment, the Swinomish people lost most of their ancestral gathering, hunting, and fishing locations, while the State of Washington actively hindered traditional Swinomish subsistence efforts after 1905. By the 1920s, conditions for the Swinomishes had reached a dire state: housing and health conditions were poor, Indian agents had actively undermined the tribe's political autonomy, and the BIA Tulalip School overtly rejected traditional values and the use or teaching of Salish dialects.

Through inspired leadership, the circumstances of the Swinomish people improved somewhat during the 1930s. The tribe established its constitution in 1936 under the Indian Reorganization Act and created a tribal senate, allowing it to gain control of its legal code and justice system. Additionally, the reactionary Tulalip School was closed, and Swinomish children began attending public schools in La Conner. Economically, the tribe made some progress during this period as well, establishing fish trap and oyster-raising enterprises, and profiting from sales to the U.S. Army during World War II.

The tribe benefited from federal government programs ranging from Depression-era Works Projects Administration projects to War on Poverty funds from the 1960s to the 1980s. During the latter period, federal funds helped establish Seafoods Enterprise on the reservation, as well as an alcohol prevention and control program. And in 1974, a federal lawsuit removed state restrictions on Indian fishing rights, leading to the creation of a sizable tribal fishing fleet. Political autonomy has been bolstered by the Swinomish-based Northwest Intertribal Court System, and by the tribe's membership in the Skagit Systems Cooperative, an organization formed in 1976 to regulate and enhance the region's fisheries.

Restrictions on practices like Winter Spirit Dancing were removed in the 1930s, and today interest in traditional culture and language is strong and continues to grow. A traditional longhouse replica was dedicated in 1996, and a growing number of tribal members practice Seowyn, a spiritual tradition integral to the tribe's cultural identity. The Swinomish Smokehouse, opened in 1992, is also critical in rejuvenating the ancient ways.

GOVERNMENT

The tribal government is organized under provisions of the 1934 Indian Reorganization Act, with a federal charter, constitution, and bylaws voted upon by the tribe in 1935 and adopted in 1936. The tribe's governing body is the popularly elected 11-member Swinomish Indian Senate. All members serve five-year staggered terms. Officers include a chairman, vice-chairman, secretary, and treasurer. The senate includes several committees that are responsible for developing and regulating the tribe's human and natural resources.

The tribe is a Harvard Tribal Governance Awards Program Honoring Nations 2000 honoree for its innovative cooperative land use program, which was designed by the tribal office of planning and community development. A memorandum of agreement and understanding was reached with Skagit County, providing a framework for permissible uses of checkerboarded trust and fee simple reservation lands and a

Swinomish Reservation
Federal reservation
Swinomish, Kikiallus, Lower
Skagit, and Samish
Skagit County, Washington

Swinomish Indian Tribal
 Community
11404 Moorage Way
P.O. Box 817
La Conner, WA 98257
 360-466-3163
 360-466-5309 Fax
 swinomish.org

Total area *(BIA realty, 2004)*
3,630.27 acres

Tribally owned *(BIA realty, 2004)*
721.16 acres

Individually owned
(BIA realty, 2004)
2,909.11 acres

Population *2000 census*
2,664

Tribal enrollment
(BIA labor report, 2001)
764

Total labor force *2000 census*
1,023

Total labor force
(BIA labor report, 2001)
425

High school graduate or higher
2000 census
89.2%

Bachelor's degree or higher
2000 census
29.5%

Unemployment rate *2000 census*
8.3%

Unemployment rate
(BIA labor report, 2001)
31%

Per capita income *2000 census*
$25,318

Swinomish

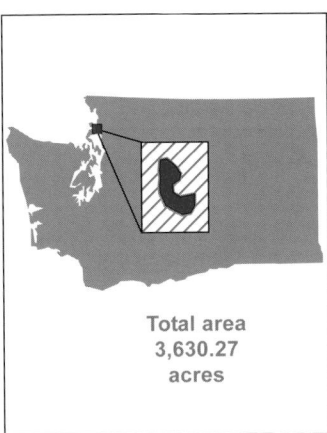

Total area
3,630.27
acres

platform for resolving any problems that arise. Since 1996, the tribe has followed a common comprehensive land use plan, exemplifying a mutually beneficial government-to-government relationship. The ongoing process and specifications identified in the agreement are overseen by a nine-member advisory board composed of four tribal appointees, four county appointees, and a third-party facilitator.

The tribe, under PL 93-638, contracts with the BIA to administer key programs and services. Tribal administrative offices include: accounting, tribal attorney, enrollment, code reviser, and personnel. They also have their own housing authority, a tribal court, and a cross-jurisdictional Police Department. Officers hold commissions from the Swinomish Tribe, the Skagit County Sheriff's Department, and the BIA. The Swinomish Tribal Court operates similarly to state court systems, except that tribal court defendants do not have the right to a have an attorney appointed if they can not afford one. The tribal court employs two full-time court clerks, and it is part of a circuit court system, with the Northwest Intertribal Court System in Edmonds Washington, providing judges and prosecutors.

The Swinomish Office of Planning and Community Development promotes sustainable, environmentally sound community development planning, analysis, education, and implementation of "permitted" activities on the reservation, including: land use, building and mechanical and plumbing, demolition, tribal environmental protection, shoreline and critical areas, burning, on-site septic, water resources protection, lot line adjustment, zoning and zoning variance, and planned developments and subdivisions. The community relations and cultural resources department is responsible for protecting archaeological discoveries, ancestral burial sites, sacred sites, and other locations of cultural significance on the reservation and in the tribe's usual and accustomed areas. The environmental planning staff monitors the reservation's air, water, and physical land and natural resources to ensure a safe and healthy environment. The tribal realty office offers various programs to assist Indian trust landowners, such as: acquisition and disposal on trust lands, general leasing, partitionment, gift deed, rights-of-way, appraisals, and requests for updated title status reports. They are assisted by the geographic information services program, which provides information, assistance, maps, and data analysis.

BUSINESS CORPORATION

The office of economic and community development seeks to create a positive business climate conducive to developing jobs and retaining and enhancing existing businesses. The Swinomish development authority is the tribal entity designated to solicit potential business partnerships for reservation development.

ECONOMY

The tribe reaps significant revenues from leasing lands; with those revenues, it has developed housing projects and marinas. Individual tribal members are primarily employed in fishing, farming, and the region's timber industry. Moreover, the tribe has developed a sizable gaming facility, an Indian arts store, and a thriving fireworks sales operation.

Government as Employer. The Swinomish tribal government directly or indirectly employs a significant number of tribal members through both its administrative and operation sectors. These employment sources range from a tribal organization regulating area fisheries to the Swinomish mental health project and the intertribal court system. In 2004, there were a total of 175 tribal employees.

Economic Development Projects. Plans to develop the Swinomish channel marina project-to include a hotel, a con-

vention center, condominiums, an indoor water park, and a marina operation at the north end of the reservation-were receiving top priority in 2004. With the boom in population from Seattle to Bellingham, commercial and recreational boat access sites in the region increasingly come at a premium and, hence, are quite lucrative. The Swinomish-controlled partnership with Retro Holding Co. has been formalized, and developers hope to break ground on the project early in 2005. It is to be constructed on about 10 acres on the Swinomish Channel east of the tribe's casino, along Highway 20, adjacent to a gas station and convenience mart that opened in November 2003.

The tribe already operates a seafood enterprise, the Skagit System Cooperative, which includes both a seafood-processing plant and a retail store.

Agriculture and Livestock. There are numerous small farms within reservation boundaries, many of them leased to nontribal members. Farm labor serves as one of the primary sources of employment for tribal members. The tribe's policy is to protect and enhance its agricultural lands, actively discouraging incompatible land use.

Forestry. The reservation's uplands are primarily dense stands of commercial-grade forest whose species include western red cedar, western hemlock, Douglas fir, and red alder, among about a dozen others. While the Swinomishes currently harvest portions of this timber and encourage further harvesting, they remain rigorously protective of their lands against the banes of clear-cutting and overharvesting. To this end, the tribe maintains an active reforestation program.

Gaming. The tribe operates the 73,000-square-foot Swinomish Northern Lights Casino in Anacortes, Washington. A class III gaming facility, it features 318 slot machines, 20 table games, 4 poker tables, live Keno and off-track betting lounges, a 700-seat bingo hall, and 3 restaurants It also has 5,000 square feet of convention, meeting, banquet, and party facilities, and 4 entertainment venues including a comedy club. The Northern Lights RV Park, with full hookups at 35 sites, is located within walking distance of the casino. The operation employs approximately 305 people, most of them tribal members.

Fisheries. Area salmon runs and the tribe's commercially valuable fisheries depend on the marine vegetation surrounding the reservation. Padilla Bay, directly adjacent to the reservation, teems with fish, including all five salmon species, flounder, sole, and shellfish. The tribe has developed an aquiculture program to protect and enhance this resource so vital to its economic livelihood, operating a fish rearing and hatchery facility.

Manufacturing. The tribe has long operated a fish-trap manufacturing operation, which over the years has generated significant profits.

Industrial Parks. The tribe maintains an industrial district at the north end of the reservation.

Services and Retail. The tribe operates an Indian arts store, a seasonal fireworks sales operation, and a waterfront restaurant, in addition to its gaming, seafood processing, and boatyard enterprises. The tribe receives some revenue from leases associated with vendor booths in the waterfront park it has developed in downtown La Conner.

Tourism and Recreation. Aside from the tribe's gaming operation, much of the reservation's appeal to visitors and residents alike is its physical beauty. The tribally owned beach areas surrounding the reservation are open to the public. Other recreational opportunities include the tribe's community center, its waterfront park, and the village tennis courts. Sport fishing for trout, salmon, cod, and other species is popular, as are crabbing and clamming. Traditional recreation activities, such as canoe racing, dancing, and Sla-hal (a form of traditional gambling), are performed regularly. The Swinomish Festival is held on Memorial Day, while Treaty Days are celebrated in January. In September, the Swinomish Tribal Community and the Town of La Conner sponsor the annual Native American Day Celebration.

INFRASTRUCTURE

The reservation is accessible by I-5, which runs north-south several miles to the east; State Highway 20 provides direct linkage to the reservation from I-5. Several county roads run through the reservation. The nearest full-service commercial airport is in Bellingham, about 30 miles north of the reservation, while Skagit Regional Airport lies about 10 miles to the northeast. The Burlington Northern Railroad runs through the reservation, providing direct service. Commercial truck lines serve the reservation directly, while bus lines serve the surrounding communities. Numerous marinas dot the immediate vicinity, providing for private and commercial water traffic.

Electricity. The Swinomish Utilities Authority provides services.

Fuel. The Swinomish Utilities Authority provides gas service.

Water Supply. Several public water supply systems-including the Swinomish Utility Authority, the City of Anacortes, and the Shelter Bay Community System-and individual wells provide water to the reservation. Three tribal water supply wells tap groundwater supply as the sole source of potable water on the reservation. These are operated by the Swinomish Utility Authority. Six different community sewer systems serve the reservation. The Swinomish Utility Authority also provides solid waste disposal and incineration.

COMMUNITY FACILITIES AND SERVICES

The tribe operates a fish rearing and hatchery facility, a fish-processing plant, a senior center, a gymnasium, a smokehouse, and a community center. A community services building houses the alcohol and drug abuse program, GED and adult basic education, Northwest Indian College work-training programs, a library, a tribal court, and the Swinomish Police Department. The tribe offers a plethora of social services to eligible tribal members, including youth services, Birth to Six Head Start, daycare, Indian child welfare, Swinomish AmeriCorps, and youth compliance.

Education. Swinomish children attend public schools in the La Conner School District. Skagit Valley College offers on-reservation GED classes, and the Northwest Indian College provides work-training programs.

Health Care. The Swinomish Tribal Health Center in La Conner offers a full range of ambulatory medical care and health and wellness services, including a diabetes prevention program and a fitness center. It is staffed by two nurse practitioners five days a week, and by a physician for three and a half days. Prenatal case management, a weekly WIC nutrition clinic, dental care, contracted health services, vocational rehabilitation, mental health, and alcohol and drug abuse treatment are available at the facility. Inpatient hospitals are located in nearby Mount Vernon and Anacortes.

ENVIRONMENTAL CONCERNS

In 1995, the tribe applied for funding from the U.S. EPA to initiate an Air Quality Protection Program in order to conduct an emissions inventory for all on-reservation sources. By 1999, the tribe had drafted an air quality ordinance and was collecting meteorological data, sulfur oxides, nitrogen oxides, and ozone levels, with results to be available for review by 2000. In July 1998, indoor air-quality assessments were conducted in homes on the reservation. The University of Washington's industrial hygienist conducted a special study of indoor quality at the Ceremonial Smokehouse, where carbon monoxide and particulate matter was concentrated inside the building during tribal ceremonies. New fire pits have been constructed and operable shutters installed on the roof vents to alleviate the problem.

The tribe developed water quality standards and completed a Unified Watershed Assessment in 1999, acknowledging that aquifers underlying the reservation are in need of additional study. Results of the assessment concluded that all three perennial streams suffer from sedimentation due to very low summer and year-round flows, low habitat complexity, and marginally high temperatures. Erosion along the banks damages riparian corridors, exacerbating the sedimentation and contributing to high fecal coliform bacteria contamination during summer. The tribe is monitoring the agricultural sloughs that drain into these areas.

In 2002, the tribe received a $1.2 million research grant from the U.S. EPA to investigate the possibility that the Swinomish people ingest contaminants when they consume shellfish gathered from usual and customary places, and to determine whether such exposure is potentially related to a high frequency of certain health issues on the reservation.

Swinomish Cooperative Land Use Program, Office of Planning and Community Development,
Swinomish Indian Tribal Community

**Honoring Nations
Honoree 2000**

**Text in its entirety from:
The Harvard Project On
American Indian Economic
Development**

**John F. Kennedy School
of Government
Harvard University**

The Cooperative Land Use Program, which is based on memoranda of agreement and understanding between the Swinomish Indian Tribal Community and Skagit County, provides a framework for conducting permitting activities within the boundaries of the "checkerboarded" reservation and establishes a forum for resolving any conflicts that might arise. Since 1996, both governments have followed a common Comprehensive Land Use Plan and used similar procedures to administer it, exemplifying a mutually beneficial government-to-government relationship.

The Swinomish Indian Tribal Community's 7,000-acre reservation, home to approximately 4,000 Indian and non-Indian residents, is located approximately 80 miles north of Seattle and lies entirely within Skagit County. As a consequence of the General Allotment Act of 1887, which transferred lands within the reservation from collective tribal ownership to individual ownership, the Swinomish Reservation today is highly "checkerboarded" (i.e., Indian-held portions within the reservation's boundaries are scattered and non-contiguous). The Tribal Community owns a mere 4 percent of reservation land, individual tribal members own approximately 50 percent, and non-Indians hold fee simple title to an additional 46 percent. Given this pattern of ownership, there is great potential for conflict between the Swinomish Indian Tribal Community (SITC) and Skagit County over land use.

Indeed, in the early 1980s, the SITC and the County found themselves in the midst of such conflict. Both governments were administering zoning, permitting and regulation enforcement programs that affected non-Indian-owned lands within the reservation's boundaries. The resulting confusion over jurisdiction and allowable land use engendered anti-Indian and anti-non-Indian sentiments, a litigious atmosphere and serious difficulty in attracting investment.

At the same time, the Tribal Community was learning an important lesson in a very different arena. As a participant in the fierce regional battles over fishing rights, the SITC saw that cooperation with other sovereigns actually could be a means of increasing tribal self-determination. Thus, it began focusing on reservation land use regulation as the vehicle for both exerting sovereignty and improving relationships with the neighboring non-Indian community. In 1986, with the Northwest Renewable Resources Center (a regional non-profit) serving as a facilitator, representatives from SITC and Skagit County began discussing mutual problems and concerns related to land use.

Talks proceeded slowly, but proved useful. Early on, the parties acknowledged that neither government could act unilaterally without the other objecting, and that objections would likely lead to litigation. The SITC and the County recognized that they would have to work together, operating under mutually agreeable principles and regulations. Ultimately, the governments were able to craft a series of agreements. They include:

·The 1987 Memorandum of Understanding (MOU) between the SITC and Skagit County, which articulates the parties' agreement to coordinated land use policy on the reservation and in its surrounding areas and records their commitment to working together on a comprehensive land use plan. The MOU resulted in the creation of a nine-member Planning Advisory Board, comprised of four tribal appointees, four County appointees and a neutral facilitator.

·The Draft Comprehensive Land Use Plan, created in 1990, which was the first comprehensive planning effort attempted by a tribe and a county. The Plan articulates land use goals, establishes policies to guide the stewardship of the land and resources of the reservation, and outlines an implementation strategy.

·The 1996 Memorandum of Agreement (MOA) between SITC and Skagit County, which delineates a set of procedures for administering the Comprehensive Land Use Plan. In particular, it requires joint review of proposals, provides dispute resolution mechanisms and affirms that cooperative problem-solving is the preferred means of decision making.

The Swinomish Cooperative Land Use Program is defined by these documents, and it has substantially changed both the practice of land use planning and the process of land use policymaking.

At the level of practice, the Program expedites land development by specifying a clear permitting process and common set of land use standards. Individuals or entities seeking a development permit on fee simple land may submit their application to either the SITC or the County. The receiving government shares the application with the other government, which is then responsible for reviewing and commenting on the application in a timely manner. While all development activities occurring on the reservation are required to possess a SITC permit, this information-sharing process makes it possible for County-approved plans to automatically meet SITC standards and for SITC-approved plans to be immediately acceptable to the County. By allowing applicants to work with a single bureaucracy instead of two, the process is "consumer friendly" and minimizes overlap in government review. Additionally, it promotes regulatory transparency - between citizens and government and between the two governments - which is itself one of the most important hallmarks of good governance.

At the policy level, the Swinomish Cooperative Land Use Program embodies the SITC's and County's commitment to coordinated land use. Critically, tribal sovereignty is not sacrificed. Under both the 1987 and 1996 MOU/MOAs, the SITC has consistently maintained its position of exclusive jurisdiction over all lands on the reservation, regardless of whether the land parcel is in fee or trust status. Rather than delegating any of the SITC's civil regulatory authority to Skagit County, the agreements provide the County with an opportunity to discuss its position and air its concerns. The Program creates a well-defined, consensus-oriented process for addressing the complex and ongoing jurisdictional problems surrounding land use, and in the establishment of the Planning Advisory Board, provides a forum for doing so.

The most significant evidence of the SITC Cooperative Land Use Program's success is the foundation it provides for self-government and the protection it affords against future threats to tribal sovereignty. As demonstrated by U.S. Supreme Court's 1989 decision in Brendale v. Yakima Indian Nation, which held that reservation jurisdiction is based in part upon who owns the land, questions about tribal jurisdiction over checkerboarded lands are complicated and controversial, and can pose serious challenges to tribes' rights. Left unresolved, these questions deter investment by both internal and external stakeholders, hamper sound resource management, stymie law enforcement and constrain tribes' ability to advance their planning and development goals. Not surprisingly, many tribal governments are forced to defer to local non-Indian authorities or expend resources litigating for the right to jointly manage land use with off-reservation governments. In contrast, the Swinomish Cooperative Land Use Program frees the SITC from such jurisdictional difficulties. It solidifies the SITC's control over the reservation land base and ensures that the Swinomish and the County share a political environment in which cooperation is the norm, not the exception. With these guarantees in place, Community leaders are able to focus on other sovereignty-enhancing pursuits (such as tribally directed economic development, fisheries issues and cultural investments), which can lead to jobs and improved livelihoods for tribal citizens.

The Program has also been successful in giving the SITC a "seat at the table" in other important policy discussions. Through the precedents set in land planning, the Swinomish Tribal Community has transformed its relationship with surrounding local governments and become more involved in regional governance. For example, the SITC is now working cooperatively with Skagit County, the City of Anacortes and the town of LaConner to develop a comprehensive integrated water delivery system for Fidalgo Island. Likewise, the SITC has instituted more than a dozen separate agreements with federal, state, county and municipal authorities in the areas of land use, public safety, environmental protection, and utility and public health regulation. In a region of the U.S. that has become known for its strained intergovernmental relations over Indian affairs, the Swinomish Cooperative Land Use Program is an educational model.

By bringing government officials together to solve problems, the Program has enhanced cross-cultural understanding. In fact, education is a key ingredient in the improved relations between the SITC and Skagit County. When the Planning Advisory Board first came together in the late-1980s, they attended a series of educational sessions on federal Indian law, tribal governance, the history of tribal and non-tribal culture, and consensus-based negotiation. These sessions gave the SITC an opportunity to educate its non-Indian neighbors about the cultural importance of land and how it serves as the basis for community development. More recently, the SITC's and County's commitment to cooperation and mutual learning have had spillover effects: In the Fall of 2000, the Town of LaConner held its first-ever Native American Day celebration, an event that gained national attention.

One of the fundamental reasons for the success of the Swinomish Cooperative Land Use Program is that it has been "institutionalized." That is, formal institutional vehicles (such as MOUs, MOAs, advisory boards and jointly administered comprehensive plans) serve as the foundation for productive government-to-government relations. The content of these agreements specifically emphasizes the importance of regional cooperation and the mutual benefits and obligations that the signatory governments share. Looking ahead, institutionalization is also a primary reason why the Program can be expected to have sustained effectiveness.

The professionalism and competence of the individuals charged with Program implementation are other reasons for its success. At the SITC, the Program is managed by the 12 professional and support staff of the Swinomish Office of Planning and Community Development, which oversees all aspects of reservation land use planning and regulation, including environmental assessment, air/water quality protection programs, economic development, and the development of community facilities, utilities and transportation infrastructure. Individuals who have worked with both the SITC and Skagit County attest to the Swinomish staff's impressive qualifications, to their commitment to finding the best outcome for all parties and to the helpfulness of having a wide range of planning services available under one roof.

Two decades ago, the SITC's leaders decided that community planning and development was important enough to command some of the Community's quite limited resources. Without their foresight, the Program would not exist. The leadership's wisdom in pursuing an "outwardly focused" strategy has also been critical. They believed, rightly, that concerning themselves with policy that had an impact beyond the reservation's boundaries would increase the Community's authority over the land within its boundaries. The strategy increases the development opportunities as well. Particularly on checkerboarded reservations, good land use programs advance standards that, at a minimum, are not in direct conflict with off-reservation requirements. The Swinomish Program achieves excellence because the SITC leaders' strategy allows progress beyond conflict avoidance to truly coordinated land use planning. As a result, the Swinomish Reservation is today connected to surrounding non-reservation land in a way that maximizes the Community's future development options. The SITC is poised to take advantage of the phenomenal economic and population growth occurring in its region, while simultaneously protecting its land and resources. The Swinomish Indian Tribal Community's Cooperative Land Use Program stands out because it addresses an issue that is both contentious and complex - land use - and embraces a process that fosters "win-win" solutions rather than litigation. Many tribes, especially those with checkerboarded reservations, can learn from SITC's response to its jurisdictional and, thus, self-governance challenges.

Lessons:
·   The inherent regulatory and jurisdictional challenges of land use on checkerboarded reservations make intergovernmental cooperation vital, and tribes can engage in such cooperation without delegating any of their civil regulatory authority to non-Indian governments.

·   Before jurisdictional disputes can be mediated, meaningful relationships should be formed. Early investments in relationship building can prevent misunderstandings that would otherwise hamper intergovernmental progress.

·   Intergovernmental cooperation is most likely to succeed when it is institutionalized, and MOAs and MOUs are useful tools for formalizing processes and commitments. At the same time, however, such formal agreements must be grounded in a genuine spirit of cooperation.

Swinomish

**Honoring Nations
Honoree 2000**

Text in its entirety from:
**The Harvard Project On
American Indian Economic
Development**

**John F. Kennedy School
of Government
Harvard University**

Tulalip

Tulalip Reservation
Federal reservation
Snohomish, Snoqualmie,
and Skykomish
Snohomish County,
Washington

The Tulalip Tribes
6700 Totem Beach Road
Tulalip, WA 98271-9715
360-651-4000
360-651-4032 Fax
tulaliptribes.com

Total area *(BIA realty, 2004)*
11,764.38 acres

Total area *(Tribal source, 2005)*
23,000 acres

Tribally owned *(BIA realty, 2004)*
8,623.84 acres

Individually owned
(BIA realty, 2004)
3,140.54 acres

Population *2000 census*
9,246

Tribal enrollment
(BIA labor report, 2001)
3,665

Tribal enrollment
(Tribal source, 2005)
3,411

Total labor force *2000 census*
4,521

Total labor force
(BIA labor report, 2001)
1,342

High school graduate or higher
2000 census
83.8%

Bachelor's degree or higher
2000 census
14.6%

Unemployment rate *2000 census*
7.4%

Unemployment rate
(BIA labor report, 2001)
36%

Per capita income *2000 census*
$19,858

LOCATION AND LAND STATUS

The Tulalip Reservation is located west of the City of Marysville, in Tulalip, Washington, about 40 miles north of Seattle. It sits directly on the Puget Sound, the total reservation spanning approximately 23,000 acres within the exterior boundaries. Approximately 2,600 acres of forested land in various parcels were purchased recently with the intention of using them for preservation and reclamation of reservation land. The Tulalip Tribes of the Tulalip Reservation, a federally recognized tribal entity, was established via the Treaty of Point Elliot on January 22, 1855, which guaranteed the Tulalip Tribes-made up of members from the Snohomish, Snoqualmie, Skagit, Suiattle, Samish, and Stillaguamish tribes-certain land, fishing, education, and health care rights. The reservation boundaries were formally defined by an Executive Order on December 23, 1873.

PHYSICAL DESCRIPTION

The Tulalip Reservation is situated in the mid-Puget Sound area. I-5 and the City of Marysville, Washington, forms its eastern boundaries. It is bordered on the south by the Snohomish River and on the north by Fire Trail Road. To the west lays only the Puget Sound. Marine water tidelands and fresh water creeks dominate an area already dotted with wetlands and lakes. Other areas include primarily preserved evergreen forest-covered and limited developable land.

CLIMATE

There is no climate information on record for Marysville, the city east of tribal headquarters. However, there is data for Seattle, and weather patterns would not differ significantly. The year-round average daily high temperature in Seattle is 59°F, with the highest temperature ever recorded as 100°F. The year-round average daily low temperature is 46°F. The area receives approximately 34 inches of precipitation annually; 7.1 inches falls as snow in winter, when the area receives its heaviest precipitation.

CULTURE AND HISTORY

The Tulalips speak Lushootseed, the traditional language of Coastal Salish People, and Tulalip means "small-mouthed bay," which refers to part of the Puget Sound in Washington. Since the ancestors of the present-day Tulalip Reservation residents signed the 1855 Treaty of Point Elliot, "Tulalip Tribes" has been the corporate name for several allied tribes who traditionally made the area their homeland. These include the Snohomish, Snoqualmie, Skagit, Suiattle, Samish, Stillaguamish, and other allied nations. During the reservation's early years, Tulalip served as the site of a government boarding school for Indian children in northwest Washington. Prior to 1930, tribal members formed a number of organizations that addressed issues such as land, fishing, health, and education rights that had been guaranteed them in the initiating treaty. One of these organizations, known originally as the Tulalip Improvement Club, later became the Northwest Federation of American Indians. The federation initiated court cases to press for their treaty-guaranteed rights.

In recent decades, although the Tulalip Tribes continue to focus upon political and Indian rights issues, the tribes concentrate more on developing employment and economic opportunity on the reservation. A 1974 court ruling restored the right of certain Washington tribes to harvest half of the salmon run in their respective areas, after which the Tulalips began harvesting salmon. The salmon once again helped foster the tribe's self-sufficiency through economic independence. Revenues from the salmon served as a cornerstone in the tribe's efforts to start businesses and reduce their dependence on government contracts and grants. The tribe established a relatively healthy general fund to receive money from land lease agreements with non-Indians living on the reservation and from bingo and casino operations, a marina, a smoke shop, and other enterprises. These steps toward diversification represent clear improvements in an employment situation that once relied almost solely upon logging and migratory farm labor.

The tribe makes a conscious effort to maintain its heritage through the celebration of traditional ceremonies, dances, and commemoration days and a resurgence in the use of the Lushootseed language. To combat declining numbers of Native speakers (in 1992, only 17 elders of the Tulalip Tribes spoke it), the tribe has sponsored courses in traditional language, carving, beadwork, and other crafts. Preserving the natural environment also remains of paramount importance in every aspect of their life. In the midst of rapid economic development, the tribal cultural resources office works to protect, maintain, and preserve traditional cultural values and spiritual beliefs and to see that they are practiced with dignity, respect and integrity within the Tulalip community and surrounding communities.

GOVERNMENT

The first Tulalip governing body grew out of the Northwest Federation of Indians. That body reorganized under the 1934 Indian Reorganization Act, changing its name to the Tulalip Board of Directors, which it retains today. The tribal constitution and bylaws were approved January 24, 1936, and the corporate charter was approved on October 3, 1936. Six members of the seven-member board of directors are elected every three years; the chairman is elected annually.

The tribe, under PL 93-638, contracts with the BIA to administer key programs and services. Departments are headed by the board of directors and the general manager. A partial list of tribal offices, programs, and services includes: Tulalip beda'chelh Children's Services, cablevision, casino, community development, community, construction development, cultural resources, education, elders and senior, employment, enrollment, family and youth, finance, fire, fisheries, forestry, maintenance, hatchery, human resources, leasing and real estate, legal, natural resources, police, Quil Ceda Village, tribal court, tribal gaming, and utilities.

In 2000, the Tulalip Tribes signed an historic agreement with the City of Seattle, Washington, which represented the first time the city formally acknowledged the sovereign status of an Indian tribe. The document, designed to improve communications between the two entities, serves as a protocol that outlines their respective roles and responsibilities to the citizens of the city and each tribal member. Both parties stated the goal of developing mutual goals and encouraging resolution of issues before they require intervention from the legal system. A similar agreement with the City of Everett, south of Tulalip, was signed in 2003 and another with Snohomish County in 2004.

BUSINESS CORPORATION

The Consolidated Borough of Quil Ceda Village is a 2,000-acre parcel of trust land on the eastern boundary of the Tulalip Indian Reservation. This incorporated federal city operates as a political subdivision for the tribe and is home to the tribe's casino. Quil Ceda is governed by a council manager and a three-member city council under federally approved tribal ordinances. This village is a vehicle for the economic development of not only the tribe but the regional economy as well.

The Tulalip Tribes operate a charitable fund, which contributes portions of revenues from their economic development projects to the communities in which the enterprises are located. Quarterly grants and awards are given to nonprofit organizations, schools, and governmental entities from the Tulalip Casino's Tribal Lottery system. In their tribal-state gaming compact it was also arranged for the tribe to contribute revenue from the casino's table games to a community impact fund. This fund awards the revenue to programs related to the health, safety, welfare, public peace, or education of area residents, which can show a negative impact on the community from the gaming operations.

ECONOMY
Once dependent on logging and migratory farm labor, the reservation is now home to a diverse, bustling, urban economy, with retail centers featuring nationally franchised businesses, a marina, gaming operations, retail outlets, shops, and services.

Government as Employer. Of the Tulalip Tribes' 2,400 employees in 2004, over two-thirds worked in one of the tribes' various enterprises.

Forestry. The forest department manages approximately 6,000 acres of tribal and other Indian-owned lands. These forests consist primarily of Douglas fir, western hemlock, western red cedar, and red alder.

Gaming. The tribe first opened a bingo operation in 1983; very successful, it was providing over 40 percent of the tribal operating budget well into the 1990s. The Tulalip Casino in Tulalip, Washington, opened following the bingo hall's success and was the first Indian casino in Washington to gain approval by both the state and federal governments. In June 2003, the newly expanded facility reopened in a 227,000-square-foot building featuring 2,000 slot machines, 59 table games, and 10 poker tables. Included in the complex are a gift shop, several restaurants-including Tulalip Bay Fine Dining and Wine Room, Cedar's Café, the Eagles buffet-style kitchen, and Canoes Cabaret deli-a bus stop with shuttle service to all major area lodgers, and free RV parking. The Tulalip's 850-seat bingo hall is located one mile south of the new casino building.

The tribe opened a second casino two miles south, the Quil Ceda Creek Nightclub and Casino, which features a smaller, dance club atmosphere in addition to 600 slot machines and table games, including blackjack, three-card poker, and roulette. Together, the facilities employ approximately 1,600 people.

Fisheries. The Tulalip Tribes operates a fish hatchery, which produces more than nine million salmon fingerlings annually. The reservation's location on Puget Sound also makes commercial and recreational fishing activities quite viable and productive.

Construction. Individual tribal members own seven construction-related firms. These include framing crews, concrete specialists, and trucking and hauling companies, generating significant tribal revenues and employment, which is overseen by TERO. The tribe has a construction development office within the tribal government to oversee construction projects on tribal lands.

Mining. There are some sand and gravel operations on the reservation; they serve, in part, to provide raw materials for the tribally affiliated cement contractors engaged in construction projects at the reservation.

Industrial Parks. While there is no heavy industry on reservation lands, a commercial business development has been constructed along with its own traffic interchange off the I-5 corridor at the eastern edge of the reservation.

Real Estate/Commercial Development. The tribe operates a leasing and real estate office to facilitate the importation of new businesses to the reservation retail centers. Since the mid-1990s, there has been a dramatic increase in the numbers and kinds of commercial development occurring on tribal land.

Services and Retail. Quil Ceda Village retail center is home to a number of locally owned enterprises and nationally franchised businesses. In 2004, the retail center included: Educational Community Credit Union, Jackpot Teriyaki, Jorgenson Golf, Marysville Tulalip Chamber of Commerce, Port of Subs, Quil Ceda Village Council and Conference Center, Taco del Mar, Trading Post, Tulalip Liquor Store and Smoke Shop, Tulalip Nails, the UPS Store, and Bank of America.

The Quil Ceda Village business park is home to: Home Depot, Key Bank, Mira Star Gas Station, Morning Star Espresso, Tulalip Bingo, and Wal-Mart and Grocery. Taco Bell and Ruby Tuesday restaurant franchises are to arrive soon.

Aside from the bingo hall, casinos, and Quil Ceda Village retail outlets, shops, and services, the tribe operates a marina, a cablevision company, and two liquor store and smoke shops, and a real estate and leasing office. The tribe is also affiliated with a variety of other business ventures owned and operated by tribal members, including at least two restaurants, a sports shop, a furniture store, a graphics design business, several arts and crafts outlets, and a travel agency.

Transportation. The tribe offers free shuttle services to and from the casino enterprises to all major regional lodgers and to the Consolidated Borough of Quil Ceda Village.

Media and Communications. The *Tulalip-Quil Ceda Messenger* communicates the activities of the Tulalip Tribes and Quil Ceda Village to a largely non-tribal distribution throughout the Puget Sound region; however, it is increasing circulation due to heightened awareness in the tourism industry about the tribally operated casinos and their widening entertainment markets. Additionally, the Tulalip communications department publishes the weekly tribal newspaper, the *See-Yaht-Sub*, to all tribal membership, which communicates activities of concern to members. The tribe also owns and operates a cable television company that serves the entire population of the Tulalip Reservation.

Tourism and Recreation. The reservation's gaming industry, coupled with proximity to beautiful Puget Sound, make it a highly attractive tourist destination. Fishing, boating, and other recreational water activities are popular, as are the tribal pow-wows and other cultural events, many of which are open to the public. The most popular are the January 22 Treaty Day Celebration and the Salmon Ceremony, which takes place in June each year.

INFRASTRUCTURE
U.S. I-5 runs north-south throughout the length of the reservation, a direct link to both Seattle and Bellingham. Commercial air service is available at the Sea-Tac International Airport approximately 60 miles to the south, while the local Ar-

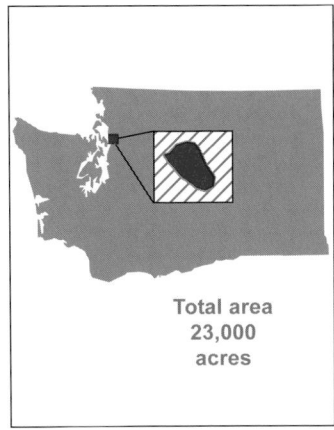

Tulalip

Total area
23,000
acres

Tulalip

lington Airport is used mostly for recreational planes and small private aircraft. Tulalip and the adjacent City of Marysville are served by commercial bus and train lines. Commercial truck lines serve the reservation directly. The Puget Sound provides access to water transportation at the Port of Seattle and all points beyond.

Electricity. Puget Sound Energy provides electric power to the reservation area.

Water Supply. The Tulalip Utilities Department maintains four community wells that provide water to approximately 1,100 families. A wastewater treatment facility equipped with cutting edge membrane treatment technology is operated by the Quil Ceda Village. This facility is currently operating at 0.75 million gallons per day (MGD) but can expand up to 4MGD as demand necessitates.

Transportation. To provide easy access to the Consolidated Borough of Quil Ceda Village, its retail center, and its business park, the tribe built a new 88th Street interchange off I-5, attracting travelers and customers from the larger markets of Seattle and Bellingham.

Telecommunications. In 2000, the tribe took steps to modernize technology systems at all reservation facilities and in its enterprises. They called their 10-15 year undertaking a "Technology Leap" into the twenty-first century, with the planned installation of computers, communications networks, digital TV studios, reservation-based programming and linked videoconferencing facilities, universal cell phone towers, and Internet capability in all 600 tribally owned homes. Software applications to streamline tribal operations have already been installed. The technology systems are constantly monitored and upgraded. Everett Community College and the University of Washington's Bothel branch provide on-reservation classes in basic and advanced computer operation, programming, networking, engineering, software engineering, database management, and website management. Tribal students enrolled in computer technology coursework at the schools perform most of the installation. Educational grants pay for part of each student's tuition with the remainder paid out of the tribe's higher education budget, which was funded at $780,000 in 2000. The local school district has contacted the tribe regarding the possibility of non-Native students attending computer classes on the reservation.

By 2004, Technology Leap had installed much of the networking infrastructure needed for effective tribal government and business operations. Attitudes have shifted among tribal members, as many have embraced the new technologies. Acceptance of the ongoing process led to a name change of the project; it now goes by the name Tulalip Data Services (TDS). Having moved into the implementation phase, TDS has deployed e-learning applications in the schools, for use by students K-12; they use programs to enhance job skills and opportunities for the unemployed and the underemployed; to research alternatives for economic development; and to capture the breadth and depth of Tulalip culture.

COMMUNITY FACILITIES AND SERVICES

The Tulalip Tribes operate a community youth center, a Boys and Girls Club, and a senior center. Among the many services available to all tribal members, the Tulalip beda'chelh has developed numerous programs integrating the promotion of family and cultural preservation into the protection of tribal children and youth. The word "beda'chelh" means "our children," signifies that children are considered sacred gifts to the community. The beda'chelh office formerly operated as the Indian Child Welfare Office.

Education. Many tribal students attend public schools in the Marysville School District. The Tulalip Tribes also operates a Montessori school for tribal children 3-8 years of age where the Lushootseed language and traditional and cultural lessons are taught along with education fundamentals. In addition to two elementary schools, the tribe collaborates with Marysville School District to provide an on-reservation alternative middle and high school, the Tulalip Heritage School. The tribal education department oversees all programs and activities at the schools.

At the Tulalip Elementary School in Marysville, students receive integrated Lushootseed language lessons throughout core classroom coursework. Cultural resources department staff teach classes using a multifaceted approach, providing culture and language learning opportunities at school, at home, and in the community. Activities incorporate technology, cultural entertainment, language classes, special intensive camps, and events that include adult members of the community in need of a refresher course. CD-ROMS have been created for early childhood students, with traditional stories told in both English and Lushootseed. High school students used CD-ROM and computer technology to create a computer game that teaches the Lushootseed place names for geographic features in the local Tulalip lands.

Health Care. The Tulalip Health Clinic opened in a new building in August 2003. The expanded space permits the growth of integrated services available to tribal members and other Native Americans in the region. The facility includes medical, dental, and vision services along with a pharmacy. Extended family and social services are provided, including mental health services and chemical dependency recovery programs. Serious medical conditions are treated at any one of a number of area hospitals.

ENVIRONMENTAL CONCERNS

Rapid growth in Seattle bedroom communities to the north and south of the reservation has added several non-Indian residential developments to the Tulalip Reservation since 1996, creating both economic and environmental pressures for the tribe. Straining tribal infrastructure has struggled to keep up with demands for services; roads and sewer systems are overflowing, and there is increasing concern for the damages to critical watersheds, salmon habitat, wildlife, and cultural resources. Tension resulted with expanding extensions of service to new residents in those areas. In 2000, the Tulalip Tribes signed an agreement with the City of Seattle, Washington, wherein the city formally acknowledged the tribe's sovereign status. The move was designed to improve communications between the two entities and to develop mutual goals and encourage resolution of issues before they require intervention from the legal system. A similar agreement was signed with the City of Everett, south of Tulalip, in 2003 and another with Snohomish County in 2004.

The Tulalip Natural Resources offices co-manages "usual and accustomed" use areas in a manner consistent with treaty rights to protect its resources. Beginning in 1993, the Tulalip Tribes obtained general assistance program funding from the U.S. EPA to complete water quality standards, including sensitive area regulations and a wellhead protection program as part of their overall comprehensive plan. They have completed a fish consumption survey among the Puget Sound tribes, drafted a tribal environmental agreement with EPA Region X, and coordinated efforts with other tribes to complete a watershed plan for the entire reservation. Their water quality assessment was completed in 1996. A 147-acre landfill project was complete in 2000.

Honoring Nations Honoree 2003

Quil Ceda Village, The Tulalip Tribes, Tulalip, WA

Although successful gaming enterprises enabled the Tulalip Tribes to begin their journey from entrenched poverty to economic stability, the tribal government realized that economic diversification was essential. In 1998 they created the institutional and physical blueprints for Quil Ceda Village, a uniquely structured tribal municipality that boasts a business park, several national retailers, a casino, and the infrastructure to sustain further expansion. Quil Ceda Village now attracts over eleven thousand visitors daily and offers the Tribes and surrounding communities a promise of economic growth on which their citizens can depend.

For much of the twentieth century the Tulalip Tribes had great difficulty developing a robust tribal economy despite their proximity to Seattle and their reservation's location on the extremely busy Interstate 5 corridor. The Tribes were burdened with the economic problems that trouble so many Indian nations and often confronted 60 to 70 percent unemployment, inadequate housing, high drop out rates, pervasive substance abuse, and severe community health problems. A dearth of profitable enterprises and inadequate infrastructure made it difficult to attract businesses onto their reservation and thus, reverse these trends. Banks and other lending institutions were reluctant to offer loans for on-reservation enterprises, leaving tribal citizens feeling excluded from the surrounding economy. For decades, the Tribes could see no future but perpetual poverty.

The 1988 Indian Gaming Regulatory Act offered the Tulalip Tribes a new opportunity. The Tribes were among the first to sign a gaming compact with the state of Washington and, in 1992, they opened a major casino that almost immediately transformed their tribal economy. The casino brought the long-sought employment opportunities and income the Tribes desperately needed. Still, continuous debates over the status of Indian gaming in Washington State and a vulnerable off reservation economy convinced the Tulalip tribal government that it would be imprudent to depend entirely on gaming.

In their determination to pursue economic diversification, the Tribes envisioned Quil Ceda Village, a two thousand acre development that would include a business park, a world-class casino, future development sites, and a reserve of undeveloped land to be dedicated to parks and environmental preservation. They began construction in the mid-1990s. By investing as others were downsizing and hiring as others laid workers off, the Tribes were a source of economic hope in a declining regional economy.

Quil Ceda Village has been enormously successful in bringing businesses to the reservation. The Village has attracted such notable companies as Home Depot, Best Buy, Michael's, and Bank of America while also providing space for a host of smaller businesses. They recently began construction of a premium mall with one hundred and twenty stores that is scheduled to open in the spring of 2005. Additionally, the Tribes are planning for the development of a power retail center, strip mall, water theme park and family center, and RV park within the Village. The fact that the Village already attracts eleven thousand visitors each weekday and nearly fifteen thousand on weekends demonstrates the long-term sustainability of its attractions and location.

The success of Quil Ceda Village is improving the lives of Tulalip and non-Tulalip citizens. The Village, its anchor stores, its small businesses, and its casino employ two thousand individuals, many of whom are Tulalip citizens. Upon full development, the Village is projected to employ close to eight thousand people. Whereas the Tribes' unemployment rate hovered between 60 and 70 percent ten years ago, it is now down to 25 percent and continues to decline. This increase in employment has resulted in a reduction in welfare dependency and an even more exciting explosion of tribal entrepreneurs. Last year, twenty-one tribal businesses were expanded and twenty-eight new ventures were undertaken. The Village is now home to the Marysville/Tulalip Chamber of Commerce, the first tribal/non-tribal chamber partnership in the United States. Currently 18 percent of the Chamber's membership is Indian. The Tribes fully intend to build upon the Village's successes by making further investments in small business development among tribal citizens.

Still, Quil Ceda Village's success in economic diversification is not its only triumph. Although the Tulalip Tribes initially conceived of the Village as a business park, their adoption of an organizational form unheard of in Indian Country turned the Village into much more. In fact, Quil Ceda Village is a model that is generating great interest because of its unique economic advantages. The Tulalip Tribes enacted legislation designating the Village as a political subdivision of the Tribes. Under this legislation and the rules of the US Department of the Interior, Quil Ceda Village became a municipality. In 2001, the BIA approved the Village's status as a municipality and the IRS approved its status as a political subdivision of the Tulalip tribal government under the Indian Tribal Government Tax Status Act of 1982, making it the first tribal political subdivision under this Act in the US. Now, the Village-a federal city like Washington, DC-functions like any other municipality. It is governed by a village council that enacts local ordinances and legislation, develops and approves the Village budget, and sets policies. This council appoints a manager who oversees the Village's daily operations. Together the Village and the Tribes provide Village businesses with services and infrastructure including the construction and maintenance of roads; water and sewer systems; fiber optic lines; parks and recreation; planning, permitting, and monitoring services; police and fire services; and emergency services. The Village's four million dollar operating budget is derived from lease income ($1 million), water and sewer fees ($300,000), tribal taxes ($800,000), and tribal funds ($1.9 million).

As the first tribal city of its kind, Quil Ceda Village is a pathbreaking model of tribal economic development. Several of its strengths deserve particular attention. First, because Quil Ceda Village functions as a municipality, it has been remarkably successful in creating an environment that is attractive to businesses. It offers the infrastructure such as roads, water, and sewage that businesses would expect of any city and a familiar municipal structure for those who might not be accustomed to working with tribal governments. As importantly, the Village displays few of the usual reservation hindrances to economic development such as murky zoning policy, inadequate land-use planning, or sluggish business permit processes. The Village's streamlined permitting, zoning, and planning processes allow businesses that have negotiated

Honoring Nations Honoree 2003

Text in its entirety from: The Harvard Project On American Indian Economic Development

John F. Kennedy School of Government Harvard University

Tulalip

Honoring Nations Honoree 2003

Text in its entirety from:
The Harvard Project On American Indian Economic Development

John F. Kennedy School of Government
Harvard University

their place within the Village to begin operations quickly. The Village council is keenly aware that businesses tend to shy away from cumbersome and politicized bureaucracies and prides itself on being lean and efficient.

Second, Quil Ceda Village's status as a municipality has the potential to benefit the Tulalip Tribes far beyond its current economic enhancements by offering a rare opportunity to tax economic development in Indian Country. Throughout Indian Country, tribes suffer economically because of their inability to collect taxes. In general, tribes' ability to collect property or income taxes is limited by their citizens' long-standing poverty while their ability to collect taxes from businesses is clouded by jurisdictional uncertainty. In many places, tribes seeking to collect taxes from businesses are limited to double-taxation-the levying of taxes in addition to, rather than instead of, local taxes. The Tulalip leadership believes the Tribes' unique political relationship with the Village, their role as the sole developer of the Village, and the Village's status as an IRS-recognized federal municipality all support the public policy principle that tribal taxes should displace outsiders' sales levies. The tribal government designed Quil Ceda Village as a political subdivision of the Tulalip Tribes-a designation officially recognized by the Internal Revenue Service under the Tribal Government Tax Status Act of 1982-because doing so authorizes tribes to collect taxes to reimburse their provision of public infrastructure and services. The Tulalip Tribes are now investigating their ability to collect sales taxes generated in Quil Ceda Village. In particular, the Tribes are seeking to obtain a portion of the taxes that the state of Washington currently collects from businesses in the Village. If the Tribes succeed, they will have blazed a new trail for other Indian nations to follow.

Third, Quil Ceda Village also advances tribal environmental and cultural values. The Tulalip Tribes selected the Village lo-

cation in order to protect the natural, cultural, and rural character of the reservation's undeveloped twenty-one thousand acres. Moreover, the Tribes have carefully supervised the Village's design so that it would reflect tribal values. During early planning stages, the Tribes adopted a holistic approach to the environment and set aside substantial land within the Village for a park, trails, and a wetland. A state-of-the-art wastewater treatment facility maintains clean surface water for the fish, wildlife, and plants within these Village areas. The Tribes also designed the Village to promote their rich cultural history and traditional practices. The Tulalip Tribes are planning a Cultural Center that will actively perpetuate the Tribes' culture and traditions via classes in basket weaving, carving, and the Lushootseed language. The Tribes have also planned a tribal museum that will communicate the Tulalip Tribes' culture to the Village's thousands of visitors. The Village has already made a substantial investment into the Tribes' future cultural carriers: Tulalip children. Together, the Tribes and Village fully fund a Montessori School as well as a Boys and Girls Club. These institutions provide needed care for the children of working parents. The school serves children aged three to six while the club offers nutritious meals, tutoring assistance, a library equipped with computer workstations, and a gym for older Tulalip children. For all of these reasons, tribal leaders and the Village council view Quil Ceda Village as a key to sustaining the Tribes' community and culture.

Quil Ceda Village is an important assertion of the Tulalip Tribes' sovereignty. As a municipality and vehicle for economic diversification, the Village has contributed substantially to the Tribes' and the surrounding communities' economic strength. As a result, it has strengthened the Tulalip Tribes' voice in local, regional, and state affairs. Quil Ceda Village demonstrates that the use of a special-purpose municipality, with significant investment in infrastructure, can create an environment extremely attractive to investors as well as its tribal citizens.

Upper Skagit

Upper Skagit Reservation
Federal reservation
Upper Skagit
Skagit County, Washington

Upper Skagit Indian Tribe
25944 Community Plaza Way
Sedro Woolley, WA 98284
360-854-7000
360-854-7004 Fax

LOCATION AND LAND STATUS
The Upper Skagit Reservation was established by a Presidential Proclamation in 1981. The reservation is divided into two noncontiguous parcels. Helmick Road Reservation, a 75-acre parcel of land, is the parcel designated for government and housing projects. The Bow Hill Reservation parcel is the lands designated for economic development. It is accessible from I-5 at Exit 236. Since 1985, when tribally owned lands amounted to approximately 100 acres, the tribe has acquired additional acreage, primarily at or near Bow Hill.

The Upper Skagit Tribe was a signatory of the Treaty of Point Eliot in 1855. In 1951, the tribe filed land claims for the lands ceded to the government in that treaty. On September 23, 1968, a judgment ordered that the tribe be compensated $385,471.42 for their losses.

PHYSICAL DESCRIPTION
The reservation is located in the Cascades foothills. Red Creek and Hanson Creek run through the Helmick property. The elevation at Sedro Woolley is 55 feet. The Bow Hill property is in the vicinity of Edison, Bow, and Alger.

CLIMATE
Average temperatures range from 41°F to 60°F. Rainfall at nearby Mt. Vernon averages 32.2 inches annually.

CULTURE AND HISTORY
Members of the Upper Skagit Tribe are descendants of 11 tribal bands and groups that occupied the Samish Bay, Skagit Bay, Saratoga Passage, and the Skagit River and its tributaries in the present-day state of Washington. The indigenous language is Lushootseed. The Upper Skagit Tribe was an original signatory of the Treaty of Point Eliot in 1855. The tribe received federal recognition in 1974 and lands were placed in trust for the tribe in 1981.

GOVERNMENT
The tribal constitution and bylaws were approved by the BIA in 1974, and the tribe received formal recognition in 1981. It is governed by a tribal council comprised of seven members. Tribal officials are elected to three-year terms. All tribal enterprises are departments of the government.

ECONOMY
The major sources of tribal revenues are gaming, tourism, federal grants, and profits from tribally owned retail businesses. As in many areas of Washington, forestry and fishing provide seasonal employment. The strength and growth of the economy is largely focused on the tribe's casino.

Forestry. Timberland Services Enterprise is a tribal business involved in fire prevention and forest management; it offers firefighting services. It has numerous year-round employees.

Upper Skagit

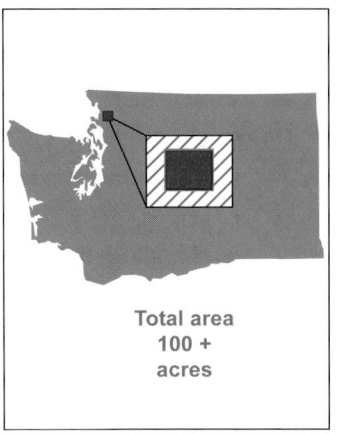

Total area
100 +
acres

Gaming. The tribe owns The Skagit, a class III gaming facility located in Bow Hill. The Skagit offers 675 slots/VLTs and 24 table games. The gaming area consists of 64,000 square feet, while the adjacent convention area is 14,000 square feet. The Skagit features 103 hotel rooms, a gift shop, 2 entertainment venues, and 3 restaurants. The casino employees 450 people.

Fisheries. The tribe owns a fish hatchery located at Helmick. Tribal fishing rights were restored to the tribe, and others of the state, in the Boldt Decision. The decision acknowledged that Washington tribes are entitled to 50 percent of all harvestable salmon.

Services and Retail. A gift shop is located in the Skagit Casino.

Transportation. The tribe operates a transit system used to transport tribal members. The system is comprised of two busses.

Tourism and Recreation. The tribe offers a variety of tourist attractions. In addition to the Skagit Casino, it operates a hotel, a resort, and a golf course.

The tribally-owned Skagit Hotel offers guests 103 rooms. It also features 6 meeting and conference areas, which include an entertainment showroom and ballroom. The hotel also houses 3 restaurants, a USIT Tobacco Shop, a swimming pool, and a fully-equipped fitness center. The hotel is adjacent to the Skagit Casino.

The tribe also manages the Semiahmoo Resort in Blaine, Washington. This facility offers a 200-room hotel, spa, and swimming pool. Amenities include the Semiahoo Golf Course, designed by renowned athlete Arnold Palmer. The site includes a driving range, putting and chipping greens, a golf shop, and a clubhouse. The clubhouse offers a restaurant, lounge, snack bar, and the Palmer Room. Locker room facilities for both men and women include exercise equipment, showers, and a sauna. The Semiahoo Golf Course is regarded as one of the best courses in the region.

The Loomis Trails Golf Course, also at the Semiahmoo Resort in Blaine was selected by *Golf Digest* as on of the top three private courses in the country. This course was designed by Graham Cooke. It offers the second highest slope rating in the state. The Loomis Trails clubhouse offers a full range of services.

INFRASTRUCTURE
The local airport is 15 miles away. State Highway 2 and I-5 are the nearest major roads. UPS and FedEx serve the area. The nearest waterways are the Red and Hanson creeks.

Electricity. Puget Power Light Company provides electricity. There are 75 homes on the reservation; individuals pay their own electric bills. The tribe pays the bills for community facilities.

Fuel. Tribal members use propane and natural gas.

Water Supply. The tribe has a centralized water system and provides waste management through septic systems. A natural resources department and an environmental planner oversee water quality and sewage management, vector control, and solid waste disposal issues.

Transportation. Bus service is available in Sedro Woolley.

Telecommunications. Verizon provides telephone service to the reservation.

COMMUNITY FACILITIES AND SERVICES
The tribe operates a community center. The Upper Skagit Housing Authority offers housing opportunities to tribal members.

Education. Students attend public school in Sedro Woolley. The tribe provides Head Start and early childhood education programs for its members.

Health Care. The tribe is a member of the Washington Tribal Health Board. Other members include the Lummi, Nooksack, Samish, and Swinomish tribes.

Health care services are available at the Upper Skagit Health Center. The 4,500 square foot clinic was constructed in 1995. Limited primary care services are available, including Indian Health Service funded programs. Programs include outpatient, ambulatory, WIC, and diabetes education programs. The facility employs a part-time nurse practitioner, part-time physician, part-time public health nurse representative, part-time abuse counselors, and two full-time community health representatives. Through a contract negotiated with the Lummi Nation, the facility also provides weekly services of a nutritionist, physician, and mental health counselor. A sanitarian is also employed at the center and provides services throughout the reservation. The tribe's contract health service delivery area includes all of Skagit County. Contract health services are funded and administered by the Swinomish Tribes. Along with health care services, the family services program provides substance abuse counseling and nutrition services.

The Lummi Tribal Health Center provides direct care services unavailable at the Upper Skagit Health Center.

ENVIRONMENTAL CONCERNS
Environmental regulations are in place on the reservation.

Total area *(BIA realty, 2004)*
74.17 acres

Total area *(Tribal source, 2004)*
100+ acres

Tribally owned *(BIA realty, 2004)*
74.17 acres

Total labor force *2000 census*
73

High school graduate or higher
2000 census
73.7%

Bachelor's degree or higher
2000 census
3.2%

Unemployment rate *2000 census*
9.6%

Yakama

Yakama Reservation
Federal reservation
Yakama
Yakima, Klickitat, and Lewis
counties, Washington

Confederated Tribes and
  Bands of the Yakama Nation
P.O. Box 151
Toppenish, WA 98948
  509-865-5121
  509-865-5528 Fax

Total area *(BIA realty, 2004)*
1,159,676.51 acres

Total area *(Tribal source, 2004)*
1,400,000 acres

Tribally owned *(BIA realty, 2004)*
966,175.68 acres

Allotted/Individually owned
(BIA realty, 2004)
193,317.98 acres

Federal Trust *(BIA realty, 2004)*
22.85 acres

Population *2000 census*
31,799

Tribal enrollment
(BIA labor report, 2001)
8,624

Tribal enrollment
(Tribal source, 2004)
9,715

Total labor force *2000 census*
12,332

Total labor force
(Tribal source, 2004)
5,548

High school graduate or higher
2000 census
56.4%

Bachelor's degree or higher
2000 census
9.3%

Unemployment rate *2000 census*
18.1%

LOCATION AND LAND STATUS

The Yakama Reservation is located in a rural, isolated area in south-central Washington, 200 miles from the urban centers of Seattle and Spokane. In 2004 it consisted of 1,371,918 acres, including nearly half of Yakima County and part of Klickitat County. One and a half times the size of the state of Rhode Island, the reservation lies along the eastern slopes of the Cascade Mountains. Major towns include Toppenish, population 6,550, where the tribal headquarters are located, and Yakima, with a population of 184,400.

Although the Yakamas ceded 10,828,800 acres of ancestral homeland to the U.S. government, they reserved their right to hunt, fish, access, and use traditional cultural sites; gather traditional foods and medicines; pasture stock; and have water in sufficient quantity and quality in all of their "usual and accustomed places" within this ceded area.

In the era of allotment, young Chief Shawaway Cooahyahhen led a successful legal battle to retain tribally owned reservation land. By the 1980s, however, most reservation land was again in the hands of non-Native Americans; approximately 900,000 acres remain in federal trust today. During the early 1990s, the Yakama Nation spent almost $54 million to repurchase reservation land. The tribal land enterprise was established to acquire key tracts, including those held in complicated heirship status, and to improve and develop land in the tribe's best interests.

After a long history of litigation, the Yakamas today operate fisheries for ceremonial, subsistence, and commercial purposes. Each of 14 original tribes and bands are represented on the tribal council. The Yakama Nation now owns and controls a large and increasing number of acres within the reservation's boundaries as a result of lengthy legal actions. Throughout the areas known as "ceded lands" and "usual and accustomed places," the Yakama Nation continues to hold interests in the use of the natural resources.

PHYSICAL DESCRIPTION

The Yakama Reservation is located on the eastern slopes of the Cascade Mountains in the Yakima Valley in south-central Washington. Mount Adams, the Klickitat River, and the Yakima River are among the reservation's defining features. The Yakima River borders the reservation on its eastern side.

CULTURE AND HISTORY

The Yakama Nation is a federation of formerly autonomous tribes, bands, and villages in the south-central region of what is now Washington State. Most of the people of the various tribes and bands of the Yakama Nation speak Ten-tumpt, a northwestern Sahaptin dialect. In the Native language, the origin of their name is "E-yak-ma," meaning "a growing family."

The original tribes and bands of the Yakama Nation were the Yakama, Palouse, Pisquouse, Wenatchapum, Klickitat, Klingquit, Kon-was-say-ee, Li-ay-was, Skin-pah, Wish-ham, Shyiks, Ochechotes, Kah-milt-pah, and Se-ap-cat. Traditionally they were trappers, fishers, and gatherers. They built sophisticated lodgepole houses both for homes and for worship. Many extended families lived together in large winter lodges. They would come together in permanent winter villages then disperse into camps for the spring and summer.

The acquisition of horses around 1730 signaled greater mobility and ability to hunt buffalo and to increase contact with Plains tribes. Disease epidemics reduced the numbers of the tribes so greatly that by the time of first white contact in 1805, the Yakamas had dwindled from about 7,000 people to about 3,500. Nevertheless, a Canadian visitor described a Yakama encampment in 1815 as "six miles in every direction ... a very imposing sight."

The Yakama Reservation was established by the Treaty of 1855 between the 14 Confederated Tribes and Bands of the Yakama Nation and the United States. Congress ratified the treaty. By this treaty the Yakama council, under duress, ceded over 10 million acres to the federal government, and tribal peoples were removed to a reservation. Fishing rights were guaranteed.

Almost immediately after ratification in 1855, Euro-Americans violated the treaty terms, including fishing rights. Although the treaty called for a period of two years to allow the various tribes to migrate to and resettle on their new reservations, Governor Stevens declared Native American lands open for white settlers a mere 12 days after the treaty was signed. Yakama Chief Kamiakin called upon the tribes that had been duped to forcefully oppose this declaration, but not before they had built up their strength to oppose the military. Things moved too quickly, and shortly thereafter a series of raids, counterraids, and reciprocal atrocities began. This uprising became known as the Yakima War. The war continued until 1859, when the last phase, known as the Coeur d'Alene War, ended. President Buchanan signed the Treaty of 1855 into law in 1859.

Federal Indian agents took control of the reservation. Under the Homesteading Act extended to Native Americans in 1884, Yakamas began to homestead what had long been their own land. As authorized and ratified by tribal council resolution, the tribe's executive board recommended that spelling the tribal name to reflect the actual treaty negotiations of the "Yakama" Nation during the signing of the Treaty of 1855.

GOVERNMENT

In 1933 the Yakama Nation established a tribal government. Its members are governed by the Yakama Nation Tribal Council, with a chairperson, vice-chairperson, and secretary. Since the Yakama Nation was made up of 14 tribes and bands, each group selected a representative to the council, forming a tribal government.

All enrolled Yakamas become voting members of the general council on their 18th birthday. In 1947 a rule change provided for the general council to elect half of the tribal council members every two years for four-year terms. Committees, tribal administrative managers, and officers report to the council.

Tribal administration includes a number of standing and special committees, like legislative matters, budget, economic development, timber and grazing, fish and wildlife, law and order, housing, and education.

Yakama Nation justice services include the following: tribal children and adult court, drug court, appellate court, probation services, public defenders and prosecutors offices, special tax, and juvenile prosecutor.

Yakama

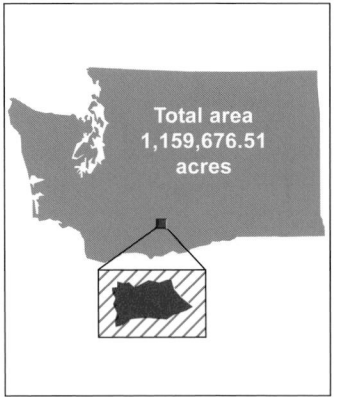

Total area
1,159,676.51
acres

ECONOMY

Traditionally, this territory offered many and varied food sources such as fishing, hunting, and gathering seasonal wild roots and berries. In 2005 the Yakama Tribe had a diversified economy with a broad range of activities, including natural resource management, retail and services, gaming, manufacturing, agriculture, and tribal utility and telecommunications development.

Government as Employer. The Yakama Nation as of 2004 employed approximately 1,800 tribal members at Legends Casino, Yakamart Convenience Store, Yakama Forest Products, Yakama Power, Yakama Business Training and Technology Centers, Yakama Juice, and other tribal social programs.

Economic Development Projects. The Yakama Nation's economic development mission is to recommend opportunities to create jobs and increase revenue by developing a sovereign and sustainable economy while incorporating traditional, cultural values and protecting the rights and privileges of the Treaty of 1855. The Yakama Strategic Plan, associated with the tribal economic development office, describes a score of projects designed to expand existing projects or start new endeavors. Areas of interest are listed as agriculture, natural resources, industrial development, recreational tourism, and human resources.

In 2002 the Yakamas adopted two ordinances, the Yakama Limited Liability Act of 2002 and the Yakama Limited Partnership Act of 2002, to bolster reservation economic development and to attract new businesses to Yakama lands. The ordinances are also intended to lead to the development of a business park or port authority. These ordinances cover exemption from an excise tax on special fuels, manufacturers' excise taxes, a communication excise tax, and taxes on certain highway vehicles.

Yakama Business Training and Technology Centers were established with a grand opening in September 2004 in Toppenish, Washington. Two more satellite centers were planned for other rural areas, such as Wapato and White Swan, to provide assistance with small business development, tax information, business plan development, and basic entrepreneurship techniques involving information and technology.

Agriculture and Livestock. The Yakama Reservation is part of the fifth-largest fruit- and vegetable-producing area in the country. There are 103,465 irrigable acres located within the reservation's boundaries. The Yakama Nation's Tribal Land Enterprise program acquires land and develops agriculture. As of 1995, 142,000 acres of irrigated land produced a variety of crops. Those crops ranged from alfalfa hay, wheat, hops, and sugar beets to apples, grapes, asparagus, spearmint, and sweet corn. The tribal land enterprise improved three apple-producing orchards totaling 100 acres. By the end of the twentieth century there were plans to develop another 200 acres of apple orchards. A Yakama brand apple was cultivated, and it is packaged for sale at a tribally owned warehouse. There are also about 936,358 acres of grazing land for livestock, including a herd of buffalo that the tribe owns.

Forestry. As of 1996 the Yakama Nation managed 309,000 acres of timber, the largest stand of commercial saw log timber of any Native American reservation. Forest resources include ponderosa pine, pine-fir, mixed conifers, lodgepole pines, and true fir/mountain hemlock. Tribal loggers do all the logging. Plans in 1999 for the Yakama Value-Added Forest Products project, in partnership with Vanport Manufacturing Co., included: a log sort yard, which was already in operation, to handle salvage or small-diameter logs; a metric sawmill; a

veneer plant; and an LVL plant. Yakama Forest Products Large Saw Mill, known as Yakama Forest Products, opened in June 2002 and is currently employing approximately 280 staff. It maintains a diverse log supply in the log yards at all times, which allows it to capture a higher value-added product line at a moment's notice. The mill is in full operation with plans to expand, despite various downturns in the industry as a whole. It continues to produce white fir, ponderosa pine, and Douglas fir

Gaming. Yakama Nation Legends Casino opened in 1998 and is central Washington's premier gaming and entertainment destination. Legends Casino is equipped with class II and class III gaming machines and amenities that include a bingo hall, 675 slot machines, 27 table games, 5 poker tables, and 200 bingo seats. Yakama Nation Legends Casino also offers dining in a buffet or deli, gift shop purchases, and events and promotions, such as concerts and boxing. The casino covers 54,000 square feet, and the convention area, 44,000. The parking area accommodates 2,500 vehicles. Staff includes 560 employees, with 27 gaming property managers.

Fisheries. Members of the Yakama Nation have historically depended on the Columbia River and its salmon for their sustenance. The Yakama Nation operates commercial fisheries for salmon and steelhead on the mainstream Columbia River, in accordance with its "usual and accustomed" fishing rights guaranteed by the 1855 Treaty of Point Elliott. Federal court rulings have upheld tribal claims to its share of Columbia River fishing resources. The fisheries are primarily for tribal ceremonial and subsistence use; remaining fish are sold commercially.

The Yakama Nation Fisheries Management Program, which has approximately 40 employees, monitors and manages the fishing industry and associated natural resources. Its mission is to protect, restore, and manage existing and historical fish populations throughout the Yakama Nation. Among its fisheries projects is its unique work with the U.S. Department of Energy to use abandoned intake settling ponds at the Hanford Nuclear Reservation to acclimate about 500,000 fall Chinook juveniles before releasing them into the Columbia River. The Satus, Ahtanum, Toppenish, and Simcoe creeks project, managed by the Yakama Nation Fisheries Management Program and funded largely by the Bonneville Power Administration, works with private irrigators and others along the waterways to make sure the salmon have a viable environment in which to live and grow.

Manufacturing. Yakama Juice opened in August 2004, and it is the first off -reservation enterprise for the Yakama Nation, manufacturing juice and other nonalcoholic bottled beverages.

Industrial Park. The Yakama Nation owns the Wapato Industrial Park, which offers a 114-acre site for light to medium industrial use. At least three businesses are operating in the park, which is located in Wapato, Washington, with excellent highway and rail access.

Real Estate/Commercial Development. The Yakama Tribe offers agricultural leases and business and development leases. The Yakama Nation Land Enterprise Office and the BIA Realty Office are responsible for leasing trust land.

Banks. The Yakama Nation Credit Enterprise provides financial assistance to tribal members. Assistance includes housing, consumer financing, economic development, use of reservation resources, and other financing needs. Loans are made at reasonable interest rates for tribal members.

Yakama

TRI-WA-009

TRI-WA-009 Sign "Yakama Nation Cultural Center" Gift Shop, Museum,Theatre and Restaurant

Services and Retail*. Yakama-owned businesses in the region include the tribal restaurant, cultural center, gift shop, museum, and meeting lodge (available for leasing) in the Toppenish community center, as well as businesses owned by individual tribal members, including Native American arts and crafts stores, specialty shops, and smoke shops. The Yakamart at Pahto Crossing (a convenience store) opened in 1998.

Media and Communications. The Yakama Nation purchased the KYNR AM 1490 radio station. This 100,000-watt station will serve the Yakama Valley. The *Yakama Nation Review* serves the tribe's nearly 10,000-members as well, providing community and subscribers with biweekly newspapers.

Tourism and Recreation. The Yakama Nation Cultural Center opened in 1980. Located alongside Highway 97 between Yakima and Toppenish, the central structure is a 76-foot-high winter lodge; the entire facility is 23 acres, including a gift shop, a museum, a full-service public library with an emphasis on Native American culture, a movie theater, and a restaurant. The center, located on the Yakama's ancestral grounds, welcomes visitors. The cultural center offers a free visitor information packet, which is available by mail.

Rivers, lakes, streams, and ponds on reservation land provide abundant opportunities for fishing and recreation. The Yakama Nation's Mount Adams Recreation Area is available from July 1 through October 1 for camping. The Yakama RV Park, owned and operated by Yakama Nation Land Enterprise, has 125 RV sites with 14 tepees and 10 tent sites. The RV sites have 20-, 30-, and 50-amp service with water and sewer at all sites. Thirty of the sites offer cable television. With a swimming pool, a meeting room, a hot tub, a sauna, an exercise room, basketball, volleyball, horseshoe, jogging track, a large picnic area, arcade, and a putting green at the park, visitors have plenty to do.

The Yakama Nation Legends Casino and conference facility attract tourists. Tribal events appealing to tourists include a rodeo and powwow during the summer. Also, one of the premiere basketball tournaments in Indian country is the Yakama Nation Basketball Tournament Association's event every March.

INFRASTRUCTURE
The Yakama Reservation is located just off U.S. I-82, directly south of the metropolitan area of Yakima, Washington. It is approximately 30 miles south of the intersection of U.S. I-82 and I-90. All motor freight and delivery services, as well as rail services, are available. The reservation is served by the Yakima Airport and Seattle-Tacoma International Airport, approximately 150 miles distant.

Fiber optics for tribal complexes and a telecommunications company will soon provide broadband services throughout the reservation. Also, conduits for an electric utility are being placed underground; they will provide Yakama homes and businesses with efficient, low-cost heating.

Electricity. Yakama Power, the Yakama Nation's Tribal Electric Utility, is in the start-up phase. In 2005 Pacificorp and Benton Rural Electric supplied electricity to reservation residents.

Fuel. Electricity; pellet stoves, and wood stoves are used in homes; Cascade Natural Gas provides natural gas to a few reservation residents. Some propane is used at Camp Chaparral. Yakamart at Pahto Crossing is the fuel and gasoline

provider and distributor for the lower valley and for Native American distributors.

Water Supply. The Wapato Irrigation Project provides water to most acreage, including leased acreage, for a charge paid directly to the project.

Two tribally owned and operated water supply systems serve the reservation. The city of Toppenish operates a wastewater treatment facility within the reservation's boundaries.

Transportation. Yakama Nation Transportation is part of the Yakama Nation Department of Natural Resources' effort to construct, preserve, repair, and restore the Yakama Reservation's system of roadways and bridges.

COMMUNITY FACILITIES AND SERVICES
A recreational sports complex is available for Yakama Nation members and community usage. There are two tribal community centers on the reservation.

Education. The Yakama Nation Head Start program is a comprehensive child development program that promotes school readiness by enhancing social and cognitive development to low-income children. The curriculum encompasses: language development, literacy, math, science, creative arts, social and emotional development, approaches to learning, and physical health and development. Yakama Nation tribal school is a K-12 school and is currently participating in school reform through "No Child Left Behind Laws" and by fostering literacy through a READ RIGHT curriculum. The Yakama Nation adult vocation training program served 577 people for a variety of services and is a BIA-contracted program. Yakama Nation higher education provides higher education opportunities to attend colleges and universities for degree-seeking students.

Health Care. Indian Health Services operates a 40,000-square-foot facility located near Toppenish. The JCAHO-accredited Yakama Nation Tribal Health Facility offers a full range of ambulatory health and dental services. General medical services are available daily in addition to special services for well child care, internal medicine, women's health care, and diabetes. The tribe and Indian Health Service employ 8 physicians, 6 dentists, a physician's assistant, and 13 midlevel practitioners.

The tribe owns and operates the White Swan Health Clinic, which is located in White Swan.The tribe also operates a satellite maternal child health center, in the Apes Goody Housing Project in Wapato.

ENVIRONMENTAL CONCERNS
This Yakama Nation Environmental Management Program is actively increasing its capacity and its fields of environmental interests. The mission is to develop environmental management measures in a manner that protects the tribe's health and welfare, culture, and way of life by ensuring a safe and healthy environment. Air quality is a subdivision that responds to complaints, tracks burn activities, oversees asbestos-abatement activities, conducts facility inspections, comments on environmental projects, sponsors education and outreach activities, and monitors air quality for pollution concentrations and visibility. The Environmental Restoration and Waste Management Program evaluates major cleanup activities planned for the Hanford Nuclear Reservation, providing details and recommendations on radioactive and hazardous waste and environmental impact.

Yakama Nation Land Enterprise, Confederated Tribes and Bands of the Yakama Nation (Toppenish, Washington)

The Yakama Nation Land Enterprise was created in 1950 to provide the Yakama Nation with an institutional vehicle for confronting its longstanding crisis of land loss. By taking an active role as a buyer and developer of land within the exterior boundaries of the Yakama Reservation, the Yakama Nation Land Enterprise presents an excellent model of how Indian nations can reduce reservation "checkerboarding," decrease attendant jurisdictional disputes with other governments, and develop revenue-generating businesses to complete a cycle of self-sufficient land repurchase.

Lying along the eastern slopes of the Cascade Mountains, the Yakama Nation's reservation encompasses nearly 1.4 million acres of south central Washington State. While this is a large land area, the Yakama Nation and its citizens own only a fraction of the land within the reservation's external boundaries; currently, a mere 90,000 acres are held in trust. The Yakama Nation's struggles with land loss began almost 150 years ago when, in 1855, the federal government pressured the Yakama to cede by treaty more than ten million acres of their ancestral homelands. In the later half of the 1800s and early 1900s, individual tribal citizens were granted fee patent land titles, which both freed "surplus" reservation land for non-Indian settlement and permitted tribal citizens to sell their land to non-Indians. Faced with difficult economic choices, many tribal citizens did so. In sum, allotment further contributed the Nation's land loss and resulted in a highly "checkerboarded" reservation comprised of trust and fee land.

This pattern of landholding, in which Indian and non-Indian parcels are interspersed across the reservation, creates a jurisdictional morass: a majority of the Nation's land is potentially subject to competing state and county claims of jurisdiction. Indeed, the checkerboarded nature of the Nation's reservation has led to numerous jurisdictional disputes over land and water, boundaries, hunting restrictions, environmental regulation, and taxing authority - all of which have set the Yakama Nation at odds with individual non-Indian land owners as well as county, state, and federal governments. These disputes, in turn, have slowed the progress of development, compromised the Nation's economic interests, and challenged its stewardship over the environment and local wildlife.

Recognizing the need for a comprehensive and effective program to manage, control, and promote land re-purchase, the Yakama Nation created the Yakama Nation Land Enterprise

in 1950. From its inception to today, the Enterprise's objective has remained the same: to purchase, consolidate, regulate, and develop land on behalf of the Yakama Nation.Drawing upon revenues generated by the Enterprise itself, the quasi-governmental entity buys fee-simple land from non-Yakama entities and trust land from individual tribal citizens who, because of illness, relocation, or an inability to transfer land to heirs, are seeking to sell lands. The process begins when tribal citizens or non-Yakama landowners who want to sell land submit an application to the Enterprise for consideration. If the Enterprise determines that the acquisition is desirable and that it is in a financial position to make a purchase, it pays cash for the property and subsequently begins the land-into-trust application process.

Significantly, these transactions have multiple benefits for the Nation. Each piece of land purchased increases the Yakama Nation's overall land base, facilitates reservation land consolidation, and expands the territory over which the Nation exercises jurisdiction. Notably, expanded holdings not only allow the Nation to regulate more land on its own terms, using culturally appropriate codes and practices, but through decreased checkerboarding, limits the prospects for jurisdictional disputes. By generating increased opportunities for tribal land development, the Enterprise's land purchases also augment the Nation's economic base.

Perhaps the clearest measure of the success of the Yakama Nation Land Enterprise is its impressive record of land purchase and consolidation. Since its creation, the Enterprise has purchased tens of thousands of acres, including tribal citizen-held tracts with complicated heirship as well as large tracts owned by major non-Indian corporations. The Enterprise's most significant acquisition came in July 2001 when it purchased 27,939 acres of forestland located within the closed area (that is, limited-access area) of the reservation from International Paper. As a result of this purchase, the Nation owns ninety percent of the reservation's closed area, thus greatly enlarging the number of acres available for the exclusive use of tribal citizens. Given the importance of land to the Yakama for religious and cultural use, tribal leaders and citizens view this particular purchase as extremely rewarding.

Yet the total number of repurchased acres isn't the sole measure of the Yakama Nation Land Enterprise's success. As

Honoring Nation2002

**Text in its entirety from:
The Harvard Project On
American Indian Economic
Development**

**John F. Kennedy School
of Government
Harvard University**

TRI-WA-010

TRI-WA-011

TRI-WA-010 Front View of Yakama Nation Cultural Center

TRI-WA-011 Yakama Nation Veterans Memorial in front of Tribal offices

Yakama

Honoring Nations
Honoree 2002

Text in its entirety from:
The Harvard Project On
American Indian Economic
Development

John F. Kennedy School
of Government
Harvard University

noted above, a critical component of the Enterprise's work is land development. These operations contribute significantly to the Yakama Nation's primary economic engines-agriculture, timber, and tourism. In the agricultural sector, the Enterprise grows and harvests corn, wheat, alfalfa, asparagus, Merlot grapes, and fruit. Its orchard operations alone realize between three and five million dollars in annual income. With respect to timber, the Enterprise partners with Yakama Forest Products-a tribal enterprise with 250 employees-to harvest timber on lands purchased by the Enterprise (the recent land purchase from International Paper yielded 10,000 board feet of lumber per acre). The Enterprise plays a key role in bolstering tourism on the reservation as well. One notable success is the 125-pad RV park it owns and operates, which draws over 7,000 campers annually. Significantly, the Enterprise's land development activities also are sparking reservation business development beyond the core activities of agriculture, timber, and tourism. Through the creation of the Wapato Industrial Park, for example, the Enterprise has successfully attracted a number of non-tribal businesses onto the reservation, businesses that provide even more job opportunities for tribal citizens.

A final indicator of the Enterprise's success is the positive effect its land purchase and development activities have had on the Nation's social and governmental infrastructure. Today, many of the Nation's housing subdivisions, community buildings, and tribal government departments are located on Enterprise-purchased lands. These include three daycare centers, two ranger stations, five longhouses, a cultural center, and the Yakama Nation Tribal School.

An important determinant of the Yakama Nation Land Enterprise's success is the synergistic relationship it has created between its land purchase and land development activities, a relationship that has made the Enterprise financially self-sufficient. Although the Enterprise originally relied on capital contributions from the Tribal Council and long-term, low-interest loans from the US Department of Agriculture, since 1983, the Enterprise's activities have been self-financing. Specifically, profits realized from Enterprise-developed businesses or business arrangements are directed into a trust account that can be drawn down to purchase additional lands. With a current asset value of 130 million dollars-which includes land and developments-the Enterprise is able to purchase between three and six million dollars worth of land each year.

In no small part, the success of the Yakama Nation Land Enterprise also is due to the fact that the Enterprise possesses a clear-and appropriate-relationship with the Yakama Nation's elected government. Since its initial formation, the Enterprise has operated under a Tribal Council-approved Plan of Operation. The Plan codifies the Enterprise's broad purposes, institutional structures, sources of capital, and methods of business; it also vests authority over day-to-day operations with the Enterprise's managers (rather than with the Council). Recognizing the desirability of governmental oversight, however, the Plan requires the Enterprise to regularly report on its activities and submit financial statements and projections to the Tribal Council's Land Committee. While the Land Committee affords the Enterprise crucial operational freedom and flexibility, it provides strategic and public policy guidance. For example, the Committee determines what percentage of the Enterprise's trust can be spent for new land purchases, and decides what non-revenue producing projects (construction/renovation of elderly housing and schools, etc.) the Enter-

prise will fund or develop for the benefit of the larger community. Under this relationship, the Enterprise concentrates on operations and the Tribal Council on issues of policy.

Lastly, the Enterprise's success can be attributed to its strategic orientation. For example, the Enterprise's industrial park takes full advantage of the Yakama Nation's tax-exempt status on trust lands, which enables it to offer non-Indian businesses low lease rates and thereby better attract tenants. Another example of the Enterprise's strategic orientation is demonstrated in its agricultural operations. For years, the Enterprise profited steadily by leasing repurchased agricultural lands to non-Yakama farmers. Recently, however, the Enterprise assumed the management of fruit and vegetable operations itself. The years spent leasing allowed the Yakama to gain expertise, and the move to direct management allows them to take advantage of new demands for Native American products and to sell its own brands of fruit and vegetables. The Enterprise has sold pears to the Del Monte Corporation and to Monson Fruit, developed three Yakama Nation Apple labels, and popularized its Broken Spear Pickled Asparagus. Inspired by the brands' popularity in the US and the potential for even greater demand for Native American products overseas, the Enterprise now is also marketing its products internationally, recently participating in world food shows in Japan, France, Germany, Mexico, and Taiwan. These efforts are paying off. By diversifying its agricultural holdings, developing its own products, and aggressively marketing them domestically and overseas, the Enterprise has realized a five-fold increase from its previous lease income.

Given the prevalence of checkerboarded American Indian reservations, recent US Supreme Court decisions limiting Indian nations' jurisdiction over fee land within reservation boundaries, and the cultural importance of land and its conservation within Native communities, effective and comprehensive land management is important to most Native nations. The Yakama Nation Land Enterprise is a shining example of how an Indian nation can strengthen its ability to increase and subsequently manage resources on tribal terms. By expanding the Yakama land base, consolidating land holdings and bringing them under tribal jurisdiction, using acquired land for business and governmental purposes, and drawing these goals together through sound operations and a strategic outlook, the Yakama Nation Land Enterprise proves that for the Yakama Nation, sovereignty is about people, identity, and land.

Lessons
Establishing a tribal enterprise to purchase fee lands can be a good way for an Indian nation to expand and consolidate its land base and to regulate activities within reservation boundaries. Consolidation is an especially useful means of mitigating jurisdictional confusion on checkerboarded reservations.

Although tribal land enterprises require significant initial capitalization (tribal government investment, loans, etc.), they can become self-funding. Land development, for example, can generate revenues to support future land purchases.

A tribal enterprise's success depends heavily on how it is governed, and specifically on the relationship between managers and elected leaders. Enterprises in which managers have control over day-to-day decision making are more likely to be successful than those in which political pressures drive operational decisions.

WISCONSIN

Bad River

LOCATION AND LAND STATUS

The Bad River Reservation is located in northwestern Wisconsin. It lies approximately five miles east of Ashland, Wisconsin, along the shores of Chequamegon Bay. The Bad River Reservation is the largest Chippewa reservation in the state and includes lands in two Wisconsin counties. The reservation was established in the Treaty of La Pointe in 1854. The treaty also set aside 200 acres to be reserved for traditional fishing grounds on Madeline Island, the largest island of the Apostle Island system. In 2003, the tribe purchased 23,000 acres located within the exterior boundaries of the reservation. The lands were purchased with a $5,355,000 variable-rate demand bond. The purchased lands represent 18 percent of the original reservation that was established in the 1854 treaty.

PHYSICAL DESCRIPTION

Over 17 miles of the Lake Superior shoreline lie within the reservation, as well as over 100 miles of rivers and streams. Long Island, part of the Apostle Island system, is also within reservation boundaries. The reservation contains vast wetlands which are often referred to as the "Everglades of the North". They were recently designated as an Outstanding Water Source. The Bad River is one of only three rivers in the United States that has a self-sustaining population of lake sturgeon. Over 90 percent of the reservation remains undisturbed by commercial development.

CLIMATE

The Great Lakes region experiences temperatures that range from 11ºF in January to 68ºF in July. The general climate is humid and cool.

CULTURE AND HISTORY

The Bad River Band is a member of the Lake Superior Tribe of Chippewa Indians, or Ojibwe, Nation. The Chippewas are indigenous to the Great Lakes region, their oral history indicating that the people have been in the area for at least several hundred years, if not longer.

The Chippewas encountered French explorers in the mid-1600s and forged alliances with French trappers. In alliance with Pontiac's Rebellion of 1763, the Chippewas participated in driving the British from all their western outposts. In 1813 the tribe began to enter into treaties with the federal government. The Bad River Band was recognized as a tribe in the Treaty of La Pointe in 1854. Reservation lands were established at that time.

GOVERNMENT

The tribal government is organized under the Indian Reorganization Act of 1934. Its constitution and bylaws were approved in 1938. The tribal council is comprised of a chairperson, a vice-chairperson, a treasurer, a secretary, and three council members. The chairperson also serves as the chief executive officer of the tribal administration. The administration oversees government contracts and for-profit enterprises. The Village of Odanah has long served as the seat of tribal activity and currently serves as the seat of the tribal government.

The Bad River government departments include: natural resources, public service, realty, Indian child welfare, social and family services, health, education, facilities, housing, gaming, police, and central administration.

The tribal court system consists of four judges, three tribal attorneys, one prosecutor, and a court clerk. Tribal courts maintain jurisdiction over civil matters that pertain to such issues as domestic violence, child welfare, conservation, natural resources, and rental agreements. As dictated by PL-280, criminal matters are presided over by the State of Wisconsin.

BUSINESS CORPORATION

The Bad River Tribal Enterprise fosters economic development in the area. Projects to date include the casino and lodge, the Moccasin Trail Center's gas and grocery store, a local newspaper, social service projects, and public services.

ECONOMY

The Bad River Reservation's economy is sustained primarily by harvesting wild rice and by the gaming industry.

Government as Employer. The Bad River Band's tribal government employs approximately 516 people.

Economic Development Projects. The Bad River Free Enterprise Zone is a tribal operation; businesses are actively encouraged to explore the reservation's facilities and labor force. Future economic development plans may include an expansion of tourism, an expansion of a wood products enterprise, U.S. Forest Service business development, a convenience store, and a smoke shop.

Agriculture and Livestock. The Bad River Tribe continues to harvest wild rice as it has for hundreds of years. The Kakagon Slough and Bad River Slough are the largest and most productive fresh water wetlands in the Great Lakes Basin. The wetlands serve as the tribe's ancestral and cultural cornerstones.

The Gitiganing Gardening Project is an organization founded by community members to revitalize tribal members' traditional agricultural and small-gardening techniques. The project works in cooperation with the diabetes prevention program, the University of Wisconsin Extension Program, the tribal nutritionist, and the AmeriCorps VISTA representative located on the reserva-

Bad River Reservation
Federal reservation
Chippewa
Ashland and Iron counties,
Wisconsin

Bad River Band of Lake
  Superior Tribe of Chippewa
  Indians
P.O. Box 39
Odanah, WI 54861
  715-682-7111
  715-682-7118 Fax

Total area (BIA realty, 2004)
58,426.01 acres

Tribally owned
(BIA realty, 2004)
23,791.97 acres

Allotted/Individually owned
(Tribal source, 2004)
34,633.04 acres

Federal trust (BIA realty, 2004)
1 acre

Federal trust (Tribal source, 2004)
22,795 acres

Allotted/Individually owned
(Tribal source, 2004)
36,900 acres

In fee status (Tribal source, 2004)
6,750 acres

Alienated (Tribal source, 2004)
35,390 acres

Population 2000 census
1,411

Tribal enrollment
(BIA labor report, 2001)
6,292

Bad River

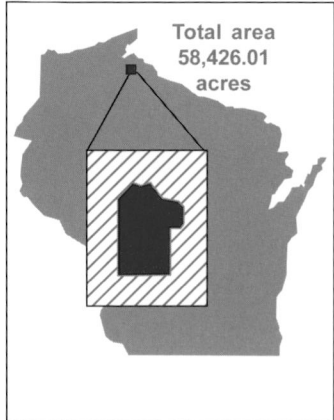

Total area
58,426.01
acres

Wisconsin

TRI-WI-001 Bad River Bingo Sign

TRI-WI-004 Chief Blackbird Center

Total labor force *2000 census*
644

Total labor force
(BIA labor report, 2001)
1,310

High school graduate or higher
2000 census
84.4%

Bachelor's degree or higher
2000 census
11.8%

Unemployment rate *2000 census*
9.6%

Unemployment rate
(BIA labor report, 2001)
57%

Per capita income *2000 census*
$12,050

tion. The organization has initiated over 80 gardening projects throughout the reservation, including the Three Sisters garden at the Head Start, a corn and bean plot with the Summer Boys and Girls Club, and the Community Powwow Garden with the Elderly Program. The organization also runs a plant giveaway and has planted over 400 trees. Future projects include extending the community garden to a seven-acre sustainable farm.

Forestry. Approximately 77 percent of tribal lands are forested. The tribe and BIA personnel manage forestry resources on federal trust and allotted lands.

Gaming. The tribe owns and operates the Bad River Lodge, Casino and Convention Center in Odanah. The casino offers guests 500 slots machines/VLTs, 6 game tables, and 2 poker tables. Lodge facilities include 50 guest rooms, 2 restaurants, and an entertainment and convention center with a capacity of 500. The casino employs approximately 275 individuals.

Fisheries. The tribe manages reservation and Lake Superior fisheries resources. Lake sturgeon, whitefish, largemouth bass, and brook and lake trout are important to the fishery and local economy. Since 1975 the tribe's hatchery has restocked over 21 million walleye into the Bad River system. The hatchery received a grant in 2001 to replace worn and outdated equipment. Production has increased 10 times the original yield since updating the equipment. The tribe will purchase and install 40 solar panels and a wind generator to further enhance efficiency.

Real Estate/Commercial Development. The reservation is home to the offices of the Great Lakes Indian Fish and Wildlife Commission (GLIFWC). Income derived from renting office space to GLIFWC provides economic benefits to the tribe.

Services and Retail. The tribe recently opened the Moccasin Trail Center. It houses an IGA grocery store, a mini-casino, a gas station, and a convenience store. A small conference room and the tribe's transportation department are also located in the center.

Media and Communications. The tribe publishes news in the *Sloughs,* a monthly newspaper.

Tourism and Recreation. Lake Superior is the largest freshwater lake in the world. Recreational activities in the area include boating and canoeing, viewing the waterfalls, hiking and camping, picnicking, and enjoying water sports on freshwater Lake Superior. Visitors to the reservation are not allowed to hike or explore tribal lands or to navigate tribal waters.

Local restaurants serve ethnic food, and there are gift and souvenir shops with Indian crafts. The tribe celebrates the wild rice harvest with the Traditional Manomin Celebration and Harvest

Powwow. The event celebrates the annual harvest and serves as a homecoming for many tribal members. Festivities honor the centuries-old agricultural traditions of the Bad River Band. The Indian Summer Festival, held each year shortly after Labor Day, offers visitors an opportunity to experience traditional and contemporary Indian culture.

INFRASTRUCTURE
U.S. Highway 2 traverses the reservation east to west. There are approximately 100 miles of side roads. Commercial air shipping is available at Ashland, located 5 miles west of the reservation, and air passenger service is available in Duluth, approximately 90 miles west of the reservation.

Electricity. Xcel Energy Company and Bayfield Electric Co-op supply electricity to the reservation.

Water Supply. Individual and community wells supply reservation residents with domestic water.

Transportation. Several interstate and intrastate trucking firms and two major bus lines provide daily service to the area.

COMMUNITY FACILITIES AND SERVICES
The tribe offers numerous social services to reservation residents. Programs include the Bad River Public Tribal Library, health and wellness center, and a daycare program. The tribe also has an American Legion Post, #25.

Education. Elementary and secondary students attend public, private, or parochial schools in Ashland. The tribe manages a Head Start program and an alternative school for grades 8-12.

Health Care. Health care facilities located on the reservation include the Bad River Health and Wellness Center. The clinic houses a part-time doctor, a full-time family nurse practitioner, a pharmacist, and several nurses. It offers preventive care, family and youth services, and health education. Services include in-home visits and limited transportation. The health center also contracts with local health care providers to serve residents.

The health department offers various programs through the Bad River Health Department Programs Community Center. It offers a nutritional program, an elders program, health fairs, educational classes, and various clinics.

ENVIRONMENTAL CONCERNS
The Bad River Tribe maintains a serious commitment to restoring and preserving natural resources. It is regularly involved in numerous programs aimed at preserving, restoring, conserving, and maintaining the reservation's ecological systems. Tribal members adhere to traditional cultural values that honor their relationship to the land and dictate a moral obligation to its well-

being. The tribe is a member of the Great Lakes Indian Fish and Wildlife Commission which is housed in the reservation town of Odanah. The commission represents seven Ojibwe tribes of Michigan, Minnesota, and Wisconsin.

In 1996, tribal members physically blocked the railroad tracks to prevent the passage of a Wisconsin Central Limited train that was carrying sulfuric acid. Although the individuals were not official representatives of the tribal government, they did represent the best interests of the tribe as a whole. The blockade was successful, and the tribal government was able to secure promises from the company that it would not ship acid through the reservation unless conditions defined by the tribe were met.

The tribe is also concerned about the effects of illegal dumping on natural resources, and it published an illegal dumping assessment in 1999. The tribe found that a major portion of the illegal dumping occurring on tribal lands was committed by non-reservation residents. In order to address the problem, the tribe posted signs identifying illegal dumping areas, offered rewards to individuals reporting illegal dumping activities, and initiated the Adopt-a-Road program along Highway 2.

In 2003 the Nature Conservancy reached an agreement with the Plum Creek Timber Corporation to protect over 21,000 acres of forested land and 24 miles of rivers and streams within the reservation. The conservancy proceeded to assign its rights to purchase the land to the tribe for long-term ownership and management. The agreement allowed for the consolidation of over 70 percent of the reservation into tribal ownership. It also allows for the protection of the forests, rivers, and wetlands. The land purchase is the largest conservation purchase in the state's history, and one of the largest tribal land conservation purchases in the country.

The tribe recently established its own air quality program to address air quality issues on the reservation. The program monitors air pollution, provides public education, and also operates a Met One Meteorological Station on the reservation.

Forest County

LOCATION AND LAND STATUS
The Forest County Potawatomi Reservation is located in the Nicolet National Forest of northeastern Wisconsin. Tribal lands span across 11,692 acres in a checkerboard pattern. This structure was created by congressional intent to create separation between tribal members in the hope that distance would lend itself to assimilation. The reservation was created through congressional acts on June 23 and 30, 1913, using lands that the tribe had purchased.

In 2003, the Forest County Potawatomi Tribe and the Sokoagan Chippewa Community of the Mole Lake Reservation purchased 5,770 acres in Forest County from Northern Wisconsin Resources Group, and they purchased 169 acres in Shawano and Oconto counties. This land is located between their two reservations. The two tribes split the acreage. *(See Mining section for more details.)*

PHYSICAL DESCRIPTION
Approximately 75 percent of tribal lands are located within the Nicolet National Forest. The reservation is centered in remote and primarily undisturbed forest lands. There are four lakes, three rivers, and abundant wetlands within the reservation boundaries. Sugar Bush Hill, located on tribal lands, is the second-highest point in the state of Wisconsin. It rises to over 1,900 feet above sea level.

CULTURE AND HISTORY
The Potawatomi people have lived in the Great Lakes region for several hundred years. While scholars generally believe the Potawatomis originated as far east as the Atlantic coast, oral history indicates that the people originated in the Great Lakes area. Recent archeological findings lend support to the information maintained by the Potawatomi oral tradition.

The Potawatomis formed alliances with the Ottawa and Chippewa nations of the Great Lakes. The tribes share similar traditions and related languages. As part of the alliance, the Potawatomis accepted the responsibility of keeping the Sacred Fire, for which they are known as "The Keeper of the Fire."

In 1830 the Treaty of Chicago mandated that vast amounts of Potawatomi lands be ceded to the federal government. The tribe lost over 5 million acres east of the Mississippi River. The Removal Act of 1830 ordered all Native Americans living east of the Mississippi River be moved forcibly to Indian Territory west of the river. The Potawatomi people were among those tribes forced to move westward. As the people marched, many perished, and this period in Potawatomi history became known as the "Trail of Death." However, a number of Potawatomis refused to leave the Great Lakes region and sought refuge in the woods instead. The Forest County Tribe is descended from those individuals.

In 1913 the tribe purchased some of its lands in northern Wisconsin. The tribe was not formally organized until 1937 under the guidelines of the Indian Reorganization Act of 1934.

Tribal members continue to participate in traditional cultural ways, speak the indigenous language, and uphold traditional values.

GOVERNMENT
The Forest County Potawatomi tribal government is organized under the Indian Reorganization Act of 1934. Its constitution and bylaws were approved on February 6, 1937. The tribe is administered by an executive council comprised of a chairperson, a vice-chairperson, a secretary, a treasurer, and two members. A general council also participates in the governing process; it is comprised of all tribal members of voting age. Departments of the tribal government include accounting, child care, tribal court, communication, enrollment, education, EPA, historical and cultural, housing, language and culture, maintenance, and social services. Many of the departments have websites.

BUSINESS CORPORATIONS
In 1999 the tribe created the Forest County Potawatomi Community Foundation, a tribal philanthropic foundation. It is funded entirely by revenue from the tribally owned casinos. The foundation's mission is to eliminate poverty in the City of Milwaukee through economic development grants and charitable donations. It also supports Native American issues, environmental protection, health care, and social services in the four counties surrounding Milwaukee. Over 200 charitable organizations have received donations through the foundation, including the Friends of Milwaukee's Rivers, Sojourner Truth House, Literary Services of Wisconsin, the Milwaukee Public Library Foundation,

Forest County Potawatomi Community
Federal reservation
Potawatomi
Forest County, Wisconsin

Forest County Potawatomi
P.O. Box 340
Crandon, WI 54520
715-478-7200
800-960-5479
715-478-5280 Fax
fcpotawatomi.com

Total area *(BIA realty, 2004)*
12,280.18 acres

Tribally owned *(BIA realty, 2004)*
11,560.18 acres

Federal trust *(BIA realty, 2004)*
320 acres

Allotted/Individually owned
(BIA realty, 2004)
400 acres

Population *2000 census*
524

Tribal enrollment
(BIA labor report, 2001)
1,186

Total labor force *2000 census*
131

Forest County

TRI-WI-FC-005

TRI-WI-FC-006

TRI-WI-FC-005 Sign at entrance to Tribal Center

TRI-WI-FC-006 Forest County and Wellness Center

Total labor force
(Tribal source, 2004)
91

Total labor force
(BIA labor report, 2001)
397

High school graduate or higher
2000 census
59.3%

Bachelor's degree or higher
2000 census
8.4%

Unemployment rate
2000 census
18.3%

Unemployment rate
(BIA labor report, 2001)
48%

Per capita income *2000 census*
$20,847

the Medical College of Wisconsin, and the Indian Community School of Milwaukee. The foundation has also agreed to assist the Menominee Tribe in establishing a casino.

ECONOMY

Gaming has become the tribe's primary source of income and employment. Gaming has benefited the tribe by creating jobs, providing governmental services to its members, developing its infrastructure, expanding its enterprises including entering into joint ventures for off-reservation real estate commercial investments, protecting its environment, and sharing through charitable donations.

Government as Employer. The tribal government is the largest employer of Forest County Potawatomi tribal members. In addition to the number of individuals employed in the casinos, hotels, and other tribal enterprises, the tribe employs over 50 tribal members in government departments.

Agriculture and Livestock. The tribe operates the 320-acre Potawatomi Red Deer Ranch on the reservation. It manages a herd of red deer for improved breeding stock, and meat and by-product sales. The deer are raised using environmentally sensitive methods. As in traditional hunting practices, all parts of the deer are used, including antlers, hides, and bones. It is common for hides to be purchased for use in the creation of regalia.

Forestry. Large portions of tribal lands are managed for timber harvest. The tribe recently received a number of grants to allow Nicolet Technical College to hold its timber harvesting course on the reservation. The partnership is manifested in a logging operation that employs nine people and utilizes logging and excavating equipment owned by the tribe.

Fisheries. The tribe is currently negotiating with the Wisconsin Department of Natural Resources to initiate a project of raising bait fish under a DNR contract. Recreational fishing is popular in the region, and the possible enterprise would have a sustainable source of revenue.

Gaming. The tribe owns and operates the Forest County Potawatomi Bingo and Northern Lights Casino and the Potawatomi Bingo Casino. The Bingo and Northern Lights Casino is located in Wabeno, Wisconsin. Facilities include over 400 slot machines/VLTs, 8 gaming tables, and 300 bingo seats. The adjacent Indian Springs Lodge provides 99 guest rooms, a 5,100-square-foot convention center, and an entertainment venue. The casino employs 265 individuals.

The Potawatomi Bingo Casino is located in Milwaukee, Wisconsin. Facilities there include 1,400 slot machines/VLTs, 32 gaming tables, and 1,974 bingo seats. There are 3 restaurants and an entertainment venue. The casino also offers a full-service non-smoking gaming area for guests. The casino's construction reflects the cultural and spiritual beliefs of the Potawatomis, with

special attention paid to architectural integrity, interior design, and placement of facilities. The casino employs 1,700 individuals.

In early 2004, the gaming rights of several Wisconsin tribes were jeopardized by a judgment handed down from the Wisconsin State Supreme Court. The court ruled that Wisconsin's Governor Jim Doyle acted without proper authority in negotiating an expansive gaming compact with the Potawatomi Tribe. In the compact, the state agreed to allow the tribe to operate roulette, craps, and poker games in return for an increase in the amount of money the tribe would pay to the state ($40.5 million). Although the court's decision appeared to threaten the tribe's gaming facilities, the tribe made the $40.5 million payment in good faith that the ruling will not affect the gaming venue as tribal gaming is under the jurisdiction of the federal, not the state, government. The events have forced the tribe to delay its planned $240 million improvement project to the Potawatomi Bingo Casino.

Mining. In 2003 the Forest County Potawatomi Tribe and the Sokoagan Chippewa Community of the Mole Lake Reservation purchased the Northern Wisconsin Resources Group's mining assets and timber and mineral rights, as well as 5,770 acres in Forest County and 169 acres in Shawano and Oconto counties. The sale included the site of a proposed mine in Crandon, Wisconsin. The two tribes purchased the mine and lands to protect the Wolf River, their cultural resources, the wetlands, and northern Wisconsin from environmental threats and contamination posed by the proposed zinc-copper sulfide mining operation. The tribes terminated the mining project and have no plans to reopen the lands for mining exploration.

Real Estate/Commercial Development. In partnership with the Oneida Tribe, the San Manuel Band of Mission Indians, and the Viejas Band of Kumeyaay Indians, the Forest County Potawatomi Tribe has created Four Fires LLC, a Delaware corporation. As a joint venture with The Donohue Development Companies of Washington, D.C., Four Fires LLC built the Residence Inn Capitol, a Marriott hotel near the National Museum of the American Indian on the Mall in Washington. Four Fires owns a 59-percent stake in the 13-story Marriott hotel. Hospitality Partners of Bethesda, Maryland, will manage the hotel.

Services and Retail. In addition to its casinos, the tribe also manages the Potawatomi Convenience Store and Smoke Shop. The Potawatomi Cultural Center and Museum is home to the Da we wge mek gift shop, which offers Native arts, crafts, and jewelry as well as dance regalia, wild rice, and hides.

Media and Communications. The tribe maintains a media department, which currently oversees two programs. The *Potawatomi Traveling Times*, which began as a monthly newsletter in 1995, is now distributed twice monthly. The *Times* employs a staff of six.

The Forest County Potawatomi website manages the tribe's official website. The program also provides web design and graphic design services. The website operates websites for most of the tribe's departments, and it creates forms, brochures, posters, advertisements, business cards, logos, identification badges, and phone books as well. Future enterprises include a national Potawatomi newspaper, a human resources employee newspaper, and a tribal-members-only newsletter. The program also hopes to begin contracting work outside the reservation.

Tourism and Recreation. The Forest County Potawatomi Tribe sponsors the annual FCP Thunder Valley Biker Rally. This event is held at the Crandon Raceway and offers biker contests and games for the general public as well as professional competitions and exhibitions and entertainment acts. The tribe sponsored its first race team in the 2004 Championship Off Road Racing season for the Forest County Potawatomi Brush Run and Governor's Cup Race. The tribe regularly sponsors teams in other races also.

The tribe owns the Forest County Potawatomi Museum and Cultural Center in Crandon, Wisconsin. The center houses Potawatomi artifacts, pictures, arts, crafts, audio samples, interactive displays, and a diorama.

INFRASTRUCTURE
U.S. Highway 8 and State Highway 32 provide the most direct and efficient road access to the reservation communities.

Electricity. The Wisconsin Public Service Company provides electricity to the reservation.

Water Supply. Currently, community or individual wells and individual septic tanks serve reservation residencies. The tribe is in the process of constructing new water and sewage systems.

Transportation. Commercial air and bus service is available in Rhinelander, about 25 miles west of the reservation. Commercial rail service is available adjacent to the reservation. UPS and FedEx serve the immediate vicinity.

COMMUNITY FACILITIES AND SERVICES
The Forest County Social Services Department offers work programs and emergency and general assistance. Other facilities and services include the Potawatomi Woodland Valley Park and a community center in Crandon. The FCP Boxing Club is open to members of the community. The tribe sponsors a coed softball team.

The tribe also manages an elderly service program that includes home-delivered meals, in-home health services, transportation, and home repair. The program is located in the tribe's assisted care facility. The facility offers apartment living for individuals requiring assistance and a public dining room.

Education. The tribe offers daycare services and a Head Start program in the Rising Sun Daycare Center. The tribe also operates Even Start, a program designed to assist in the academic, physical, social, emotional, cultural, and spiritual growth of tribal youth.

The tribe's education department oversees the educational programs and opportunities available to tribal members, and it oversees the education committees for Wabeno and Crandon. Committee programs include home-school coordinators and elementary and secondary education tutors. The department also manages an alternative education program and five programs contracted through the BIA. The department offers higher education grants, adult vocational training, direct employment assistance, and adult basic education. Nicolet Technical College provides vocational training for both Native and non-Native residents of the area.

Health Care. In 2000, the tribe opened the Forest County Health and Wellness Center. The center provides medical, dental, and optical services. It also offers community health and therapy programs. The center is available to Native and non-Native community members. The tribe is currently exploring the addition of a community-based outpatient clinic to the center. The clinic would serve Native and non-Native veterans.

Contract health services are available for tribal and non-Potawatomi Native Americans living on the reservation or in surrounding counties. These services are restricted to those medical or dental needs that the health and wellness center cannot meet.

Forest County

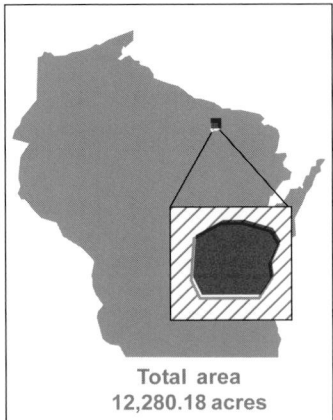

Total area
12,280.18 acres

ENVIRONMENTAL CONCERNS
Water quality is a primary concern for the Forest County Potawatomis. The tribe established its own environmental department to manage environmental issues for the tribe. The department staff includes a director, an attorney, and four field technicians. The department is currently monitoring water quality, air quality, solid and hazardous waste management, and fish and wildlife resources.

Ho-Chunk

Ho-Chunk

LOCATION AND LAND STATUS
Tribal lands belonging to the Ho-Chunk Nation are largely scattered throughout western and central Wisconsin. Tribal lands are located in 18 counties of Wisconsin and one county of Illinois. Tribal headquarters are located in Black River Falls, Wisconsin. Approximately 48 percent of the tribe's members live on or near tribal lands in Wisconsin.

Due to the nation's status as a non-reservation tribe, it is permitted to purchase lands throughout its ancestral territory and request that the BIA grant it trust status. The tribe has used revenues earned from gaming initiated in 1992 to purchase some 2,000 acres of new land. The tribe also purchased over 600 acres of farmland in Muscoda, Wisconsin, which included 50 effigy mounds.

PHYSICAL DESCRIPTION
A number of traditional Ho-Chunk burial sites are visible along the riverbanks and throughout the region of Richland County, Wisconsin.

CULTURE AND HISTORY
The Ho-Chunk Nation, formerly the Winnebago Tribe, has resided in the Wisconsin region for thousands of years. Oral history indicates that they were in this area prior to the last two North American ice ages. The people were originally a horticultural society, but eventually they began to rely upon hunting, fishing, and harvesting wild rice for sustenance.

The Ho-Chunk Tribe encountered French explorers in 1634 in the area of present-day Green Bay, Wisconsin. The explorers referred to the people as the Winnebago Tribe, a title that remained with them for the next three centuries. During the early years of contact with the Euro-Americans, the Ho-Chunks suffered greatly as a result of European diseases and intertribal warfare. The population was reduced from approximately 4,500 to less than 700.

The remaining tribe settled on territory by Lake Winnebago near the Mississippi River. They continued to move westward toward larger trading centers. During the seventeenth and eighteenth

Ho-Chunk Nation
Federal reservation
Ho-Chunk-Gra (Winnebago)
Scattered communities
throughout 18 Wisconsin
counties

Ho-Chunk Nation
P.O. Box 667
W9814 Airport Road
Black River Falls, WI 54615
 800-294-9343
 715-284-9805 Fax
 ho-chunknation.com

Ho-Chunk

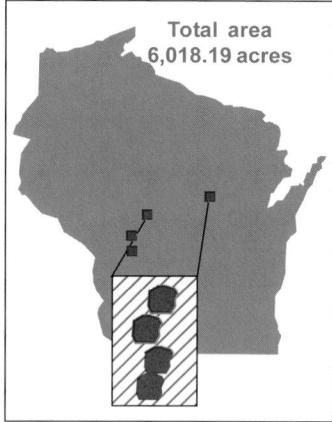

Total area
6,018.19 acres

Total area *(BIA realty, 2004)*
6,018.19 acres

Tribally owned *(BIA realty, 2004)*
2,610.77 acres

Allotted/Individually owned
(BIA realty, 2004)
3,407.42 acres

Public Domain *(BIA realty, 2004)*
301.77 acres

Tribal enrollment
(BIA labor report, 2001)
6,463

Total labor force *2000 census*
341

High school graduate or higher
2000 census
70%

Bachelor's degree or higher
2000 census
8.4%

Unemployment rate *2000 census*

centuries, the Ho-Chunks participated in the fur trading industry with both the French and British. During the American Revolution, the Ho-Chunks fought against the United States.

In the 1830s, the tribe moved into the region north of the Wisconsin River. It began ceding its territory to the federal government. In 1837, the tribe ceded over seven million acres of ancestral homelands to the U.S. government. Although tribal members then, and now, argued that the individuals who signed the treaties were not authorized representatives of the tribe, the lands were seized, and many Ho-Chunk tribal members were forcibly removed to Iowa, Minnesota, South Dakota, and Nebraska. Members who refused to go sought refuge in the forests where they remained and endured years of hardship. In 1881, Ho-Chunk heads of household were enrolled in a census and permitted to acquire homestead land. What tribal land remained in Wisconsin was allotted after 1881 and quickly passed into non-Indian hands. During this period, many tribal members returned to Wisconsin and refused to move again. The Ho-Chunks gradually repurchased some of their traditional land in Wisconsin. In 1949 tribal members organized a claims committee to submit grievances to the federal government. In 1961, the committee was reconstituted as the Wisconsin Winnebago Business Committee. The committee organized a constitution that tribal members approved in 1963. On March 19, 1963, the tribe received federal recognition as the Wisconsin Winnebago Tribe. In 1994, the BIA formally recognized a new tribal constitution, and the name officially changed to the Ho-Chunk Nation.

GOVERNMENT
The Ho-Chunk Nation's government is composed of four branches: general council, legislative, executive, and judiciary. The Ho-Chunk Legislature is comprised of 11 members representing each of the five districts of the Nation. Legislators represent tribal concerns in tribal, state, and federal government. The legislature enacts resolutions, acts, and ordinances.

A number of departments and programs operate under the tribal government. They include tribal administration, personnel, treasury, housing, business, labor, education, business, health, social services, and heritage preservation. The department of labor is responsible for providing: job training for unemployed tribal members, professional training for employees of the executive branch, job search services, safety support to tribal departments and businesses, and small business loans and technical assistance to tribal enterprises.

The heritage preservation division of the tribal government provides consultation to the state or counties on archeological issues during any construction projects. This department also houses natural resources, cultural resources, and a language program.

BUSINESS CORPORATION
The business department of the Ho-Chunk Nation operates the tribe's for-profit enterprises.

ECONOMY
The Ho-Chunk Nation is the largest employer in Sauk and Jackson counties, Wisconsin. The tribe employs approximately 3,500 individuals. In addition to employment opportunities, the tribe provides revenue to the local economy by servicing local businesses and making charitable donations to a number of organizations.

Government as Employer. The tribe employs 1,691 persons in full-time and part-time jobs in four casinos.

Economic Development Projects. The tribe recently facilitated the development of a Capacity Building and Economic Diversification Plan. The Ho-Chunk Nation's Zura Honac Business Pro-

gram offers business loans, consultations, workshops, and other technical assistance to tribal members establishing small businesses. The tribe recently entered into an agreement with the Marcus Theaters Corporation to construct the Ho-Chunk Cinema. The cinema features stadium seating, digital sound, and six screens. It is located in Tomah.

In May 2004, the tribe proposed the construction of a casino near Chicago, Illinois. If approved, the casino will be the first tribal gaming facility in Illinois, that state's only land-based casino, and its largest gambling venue. The proposed casino is expected to generate approximately $350 million per year.

Agriculture and Livestock. The natural resources division operates a bison ranch in Richland County. The lands that contain the ranch were once utilized for agricultural purposes. The ranch is now operated with the intent to restore and revitalize the area's natural ecosystem. With the assistance of the University of Wisconsin, organic agricultural techniques are implemented on the ranch, including the establishment of natural prairie grasses. The ranch attracts a number of tourists and also serves as a resource for local students.

Forestry. Tribal lands are heavily forested with species that include evergreen pines, oak, maple, poplar, and hickory. The Ho-Chunk Nation does not presently harvest any timber.

Gaming. The Ho-Chunk Nation owns and operates four casinos. The class III casinos include: Ho-Chunk Casino and its hotel and convention center in Baraboo; Majestic Pines Casino in Black River Falls; Rainbow Casino in Nekoosa; and Whitetail Crossing Casino in Tomah. Their class II facilities are DeJope Bingo in Madison, Majestic Pines Bingo in Black River Falls, and Ho-Chunk Bingo in Baraboo. The Ho-Chunk Casino, together with its hotel and convention center, is the second-largest Native American casino in the midwest. Facilities include almost 2,500 slot machines, 50 blackjack tables, and full-service bingo facilities. Adjacent hotel facilities include 315 guest rooms, 2 restaurants, 2 cocktail lounges, a smoke shop, and an on-site convenience store. Conference and banquet facilities are also available. There is a supervised, for-fee children's play center and arcade. In February 2004, *Training Magazine* recognized the casino as one of the top 100 training companies in the world. The award is the third consecutive one for the casino.

In 2004 the tribe temporarily suspended the operation of Las Vegas-style table games in response to the conflict regarding the new gaming pacts with the State of Wisconsin. The State Supreme Court determined that the governor acted without proper authority when he agreed to compacts that allowed Wisconsin tribes to expand operations in return for an increase in the amount of fees they pay to the state. The games will be suspended until negotiations are completed and a resolution reached.

Services and Retail. In addition to gift shops, smoke shops, and restaurants located within tribal casinos, the tribe owns and operates conveniences stores in the communities of Baraboo, Wittenberg, Tomah, Black River Falls, and Nekoosa.

Transportation. The tribe operates four shuttle buses, which provide access to the casinos and hotel centers. The fleet of tribal government vehicles was improved in 2003 with the replacement of aging or inoperable vehicles.

Media and Communications. The tribe publishes *The Hocak Worak*, a twice-monthly newspaper.

Tourism and Recreation. The tribally owned Majestic Pines Hotel is located in Black River Falls. Accommodations include whirlpool suites, handicapped-accessible suites, a video arcade, an indoor pool, a steam room, a conference room, two dining ven-

TRI-WI-hc-007

TRI-WI-hc-008

ues, and casino and bingo facilities. The hotel offers easy access to local canoeing, hunting, fishing, snowmobiling, ATVing, boating, scuba diving, cross country skiing, golfing, mountain biking, camping, and hiking activities.

The tribe is completing development of a 4,000-foot-long interpretive educational trail within the recently restored wetlands on White Otter property. The Ho-Chunk Nation sponsors an annual Memorial Day Powwow and Labor Day Powwow, as well as other special powwows throughout the year.

INFRASTRUCTURE

U.S. I-90 and I-94 cuts east-west through Ho-Chunk territory from Chicago, Illinois, to Minneapolis/St. Paul, Minnesota. U.S. Highway 12 parallels I-90 and I-94 from east to west. State highways 51 and 54 bisect tribal territory from north to south.

The BIA roads division of the tribe's department of housing is responsible for road maintenance and upgrades on reservation lands. Future goals include several road improvements throughout the reservation.

Electricity. Individual tribal members pay for electricity through their respective electrical co-ops or providers within the various communities.

Fuel. Ho-Chunk Nation communities are not hooked up to gas pipelines. Municipal or other gas companies provide natural gas service for tribal members living outside the communities.

Water Supply. The tribe provides water to HUD homes through the public utilities division of the department of housing. The various tribal communities have different water and sewer systems. Black River Falls Village maintains three community wells; all homes are currently on individual septic systems. The Ho-Chunk Nation commenced construction of a community sewer in 1995. Ho-Chunk Village maintains one community well, and all homes have septic tanks. Winnebago Heights Village maintains one community well, and all homes have septic tanks. Indian Heights Village operates one community well, and all homes have individual septic systems. Chahk-Hah-Chee Village operates three community wells, and all homes have individual septic systems. The Rainbow Casino is connected to the City of Nekoosa's sewer system.

Transportation. Private and commercial air service is available at Dane County Regional Airport in Madison (48 miles south of the Ho-Chunk Casino) and at the La Crosse County Municipal Airport in La Crosse, Wisconsin (52 miles south of Black River Falls). Greyhound buses serve all towns in which Ho-Chunk communities are located. Major freight carriers, including UPS and FedEx, serve the tribe's communities. Amtrak and Burlington Northern provide passenger and freight railway service respectively to the Ho-Chunk Reservation area.

Telecommunications. Ho-Chunk tribal members choose their own long-distance telephone service providers.

COMMUNITY FACILITIES AND SERVICES

The Ho-Chunk Nation provides community center facilities in the following communities: Potch Chee Nunk, Indian Mission, Blue Wing Village, Chakh-Hah-Chee, Indian Heights, and Winnebago Heights. The Three Rivers House in the La Crosse area was donated to the tribe in 1994 and was renovated in 1999. The Three Rivers House now houses many tribal offices and functions as a community center as well, serving over 200 tribal members. Services offered at the Three Rivers House include health and well-being programs, educational programs, and community activities. The home ownership program has purchased approximately 650 homes for tribal members. These homes are purchased through tribal NPD funds to provide low-interest mortgages for tribal members. The granted housing program also serves tribal elders.

The department of health and social services, child and family services, hosts an annual appreciation banquet at which it honors tribal members who provide exceptional care to the elderly and children. The Hocak Language and Culture Program recently hosted the "Stabilizing Indigenous Languages" conference. Linguists, scholars, and educators from around the world attended.

Education. The tribe's education department manages the Circle of Learning Program, which provides area schools with curriculum materials to use regarding the Ho-Chunk Nation. The education department includes: Head Start, Johnson O'Malley, supportive education, and higher education divisions. Programs include six Head Start centers and after-school and summer enrichment activities. The higher education division authorizes financial assistance for tribal members seeking postsecondary education.

Health Care. In addition to medical services, the Ho-Chunk Health Care Center provides social services to the community. Programs include an adolescent health fair, pregnancy workshop, labor and delivery workshop, breastfeeding workshop, and various child safety classes. It also offers services for persons involved in domestic abuse situations, a tobacco prevention education program, and a tribal aging unit. The center also sponsors the UNITY youth group and the Ho-Chunk Youth Fitness Program.

The tribally-run Winnebago Health Care Center in Black River Falls has two physicians, three nurses, one dietitian, and six community health nurses. All tribal members and dependents are eligible for medical services at the clinics through Indian Health Service. The health department houses a navigator for the Ho-Chunk American Cancer Society. Screening tests and educational services are available.

TRI-WI-hc-007 Ho-Chunk Wa Ehi Hoci Tribal Court Building

TRI-WI-hc-008 Entrance sign to the Wa Ehi Hoci Tribal Court Center

ENVIRONMENTAL CONCERNS

The tribe is involved in various programs to restore natural resources on tribal lands. In 2001, a project to restore 270 acres of wetland was completed. There are also efforts to restore a trout habitat on Lyndon Creek.

Lac Courte Oreilles

Lac Courte Oreilles Ojibwa Reservation
Federal reservation
Ojibwa
Sawyer County, Wisconsin

Lac Courte Oreilles Ojibwa
Tribe
13394 W. Tepania Rd.
Hayward, WI 54843
715-634-8934
715-634-4797 Fax

Total area *(BIA realty, 2004)*
47,998.25 acres

Tribally owned *(BIA realty, 2004)*
23,968.52 acres

Allotted/Individually owned
(BIA realty, 2004)
24,029.73 acres

Public Domain *(BIA realty, 2004)*
222.4 acres

Population *2000 census*
2,886

Tribal enrollment
(BIA labor report, 2001)
5,587

Total labor force *2000 census*
1,185

Total labor force
(BIA labor report, 2001)
4,491

High school graduate or higher
2000 census
80.5%

Bachelor's degree or higher
2000 census
10.8%

Unemployment rate *2000 census*
12.9%

Unemployment rate
(BIA labor report, 2001)
65%

Per capita income *2000 census*
$11,746

LOCATION AND LAND STATUS

The Lac Courte Oreilles Ojibwa Reservation is located in northern Wisconsin. It lies approximately 90 miles south of Duluth, Minnesota, and 160 miles northeast of Minneapolis. The resort Village of Hayward is 11 miles northeast of the reservation.

The reservation was created through three separate treaties with the government in 1837, 1842, and 1854. Original tribal lands included 69,000 acres. In the early 1990s, the tribe purchased approximately 8,000 acres adjacent to the Chequamegon National Forest.

PHYSICAL DESCRIPTION

The reservation topography includes wetlands and forests. There are over 10,000 acres of lakes, including the Grindstone and Lac Courte Oreilles, as well as over 200 miles of streams within reservation boundaries. These lakes are used for fishing as well as for growing wild rice. The Chippewa, Flambeau, and Namekagon rivers all run through the reservation and are important sanctuaries for various types of birds. Between 1916 and 1924, a large portion of reservation lands were flooded in order to create the Chippewa Flowage.

CLIMATE

The area receives approximately 32 inches of rain per year. Average temperatures range from below 5°F in January to 78°F in July.

CULTURE AND HISTORY

The Lac Courte Oreilles are members of the Lake Superior Chippewa Indians, or Ojibwa Nation. The band originally inhabited lands along the Atlantic Coast but began to migrate east following confrontations with the Iroquois Nation. The Lac Courte Oreilles initially settled on Madeline Island in Lake Superior, off the coast of present-day Bayfield, Wisconsin. They eventually moved to the mainland and established a village on the shores of Ottawa Lake, later to become Lac Courte Oreilles (French for "Lake of the Short Ears"). On the mainland, the tribe encountered Dakota Sioux bands and entered into conflicts over hunting grounds. The Dakotas eventually moved westward into what is now Minnesota. The region surrounding Lac Courte Oreilles supported the hunting, trapping, and wild rice harvesting practiced by the Chippewas.

In 1854 the Lac Courte Oreilles Chippewas signed a final treaty with the federal government. The United States violated earlier agreements between the two nations when the government proposed to move the tribe west. The Chippewas refused to go, and a new treaty was eventually reached.

The French also had a great deal of contact with the tribe in the 1800s. One of the largest influences of the French was the introduction of Catholicism. The missionaries of St. Francis Solanus established a mission church and school. Father Phillip Gordon, the first Indian Catholic priest in America, led the church from 1918-1925.

The Lac Courte Oreilles tribal members continue to practice many traditional aspects of Ojibwa culture. Some of these traditions have even been picked up by other cultures. According to Native American oral history, dream catchers originated with the Ojibwa people. These were fashioned from willow in the form of a circle or teardrop and strung with a web on sinew. The hole in the middle of the web allowed good dreams to come through and slide down the attached feather to the child sleeping below. Bad dreams would get caught in the web and be burned up by the morning sun. Traditional agriculture, fishery, and hunting practices are maintained; the Ojibwa language continues to be spoken; and spiritual beliefs are upheld. The tribe maintains its spiritual relationship with the land and works to restore and protect its natural resources.

GOVERNMENT

The Lac Courte Oreilles are governed by a tribal council comprised of a chairperson, a vice-chairperson, five council members, and a clerk. The tribal constitution was adopted in 1996. Amendments were approved in 1969, 1974, 1978, 1980, and 1986.

The tribe operates a tribal court with its own attorney, magistrate, and clerk. The court exercises authority over matters of child welfare, domestic relations, housing, conservation violations, and some child support matters. The tribal law enforcement department employs a chief of police, an assistant chief of police, and four officers. Expansions are planned.

BUSINESS CORPORATION

The LCO Community Development Corporation is a tribally owned independent corporation which is responsible for monitoring economic growth on the reservation and determining the feasibility of new enterprises. The corporation is constantly seeking new projects to bolster tribal economy. Projects have included new businesses, casinos, hotels, housing developments, and an industrial park. The corporation also offers technical assistance to new businesses operated by tribal members. Its efforts have led to over 19 new enterprises, including: Herman's Landing resort, a cigarette shop, arts and crafts businesses, and a home-remodeling business. The corporation has a business incubation center and a rural development program to assist new business startups. Services include credit and business counseling, homeownership programs, and low-cost financing.

The LCO Community Development Corporation also trains and employs construction workers on the reservation. It contracts both on- and off-reservation projects, and rents heavy equipment to other construction companies. The corporation employs 38 people and operates on an annual budget of approximately $2 million.

Forest Products, Logging and Management is a tribally chartered organization that serves to generate timber-logging business. The enterprise is currently under reorganization and will eventually include a team of tribal members who will receive training in the skills of logging.

ECONOMY

The Lac Courte Oreilles exercise their treaty rights by practicing traditional subsistence through hunting, fishing, and gathering year round. The tribe also participates in numerous industries such as gaming, retail, tourism, and construction to help sustain the economy.

Government as Employer. The tribe is the third-largest employer in Sawyer County, employing approximately 1,200 people. Tribal government employment on the reservation includes jobs in the tribal school, forestry department, shopping center, and resort, casino and bingo hall.

TRI-WI-007

TRI-WI-011

Lac Courte Oreilles Ojibwa

TRI-WI-009

TRI-WI-012

TRI-WI-010

Agriculture and Livestock. The tribe operates a 120-acre farm that services the entire community. The tribe also owns the Cranberry Marsh, its oldest enterprise. A member of the Ocean Spray Cranberry Producers Association, this grower-owned-and-operated corporation harvests, prepares, and markets cranberries. The marsh has 27 water bog beds, irrigation ditches, culverts, dikes, and bed access roads. Machinery and equipment are custom built for use in the marsh. In the past, up to 36 acres of cranberries have been cultivated, yielding between 1,500 and 3,000 barrels per year. Unfortunately, in the past 10 years, the marsh has been subject to two major catastrophes that have greatly reduced its production. A truck overturned into a water intake channel, which resulted in damage to the water pump and the spilling of fuel. The accident contaminated the water and hindered the tribe's ability to install a new pump. A frost later that year greatly damaged the crops, affecting production for several years. The tribe is committed to supporting the marsh and continues to work toward its restoration.

Forestry. The tribe owns a logging and sawmill operation. The tribe's forestry services are contracted through the BIA.

Gaming. The Lac Courte Oreilles Casino Lodge and Convention Center is located four miles north of Hayward, Wisconsin. The casino offers a bingo hall, over 500 slot machines, and 8 blackjack tables. Hotel facilities include 56 guest rooms, a buffet, a full-service restaurant, a sports bar, and a convention and banquet center. There are also an indoor pool, an exercise room, and Jacuzzis in select rooms. The casino is host to numerous entertainment acts, circuses, festivals, and conferences. The smaller Grindstone Creek Casino is two miles away, and since the casino does not serve alcohol, it can provide services to a minimum gambling age of 18. The casino offers 97 slot machines and employs 15 people.

Finance. The tribal has a federal credit union.

Fisheries. A small tribal fishery stocks lakes on and off the reservation.

Construction. The tribe's LCO Community Development Corporation serves as a general contractor on tribal construction projects. It has overseen the construction of the LCO Living Culture Center, Pineview Funeral Service, and Indian Country Trading Post. Future projects include the installation of a centralized water and sewage treatment facility.

Mining. The Lac Courte Oreilles do not condone mining. The tribe has passed a resolution banning mining on tribal lands. The tribe will not engage in mining-related activities, as it does not want to be involved in risking or degrading plant or animal resources within the ceded territories or upon the Lac Oreilles Reservation.

Services and Retail. The tribe owns and operates the LCO IGA Commercial Center. Located within the center are a grocery store, a restaurant, a smoke shop, and a casino. Adjacent to the center are a gas station/convenience and an auto repair shop.

Media and Communications. The tribe owns WOJB 88.9, a radio station. It is a 100,000-watt FM radio station and a National Public Radio affiliate. WOJB is one of a few Native American-owned radio stations in the United States.

Tourism and Recreation. The resort village of Hayward, Wisconsin, is located 11 miles northeast of the reservation and it attracts a number of tourists to the region. The tribe owns Herman's Landing LCO Resort in Hayward. The resort is located on the Chippewa flowage and offers fishermen walleye and musky. The facilities include a bait shop; full liquor bar; full-service restaurant; and one-, two-, and three-bedroom fully equipped cabins for guests. Canoes and boats are available for rental, and guides may be requested.

In addition to gaming facilities, the LCO Casino features the "Four Seasons of the Ojibwa People" mural. It is serves as an educational and artistic representation of Ojibwa life. The St. Francis Mission Church now serves as a museum. It is located within the reservation. The living cultural center is located at the community college. It includes an exhibition area, archive rooms, and a

TRI-WI-007 Lac Courte Oreilles Casino Lodge and Convention Center

TRI-WI-011 LCO Quick Stop and gas station

TRI-WI-012 LCO-IGA Commercial Center

TRI-WI-010 The Federal Credit Union sign

TRI-WI-009 Welcome sign to LCO Ojibwa Indian Reservation

Lac Courte Oreilles Ojibwa

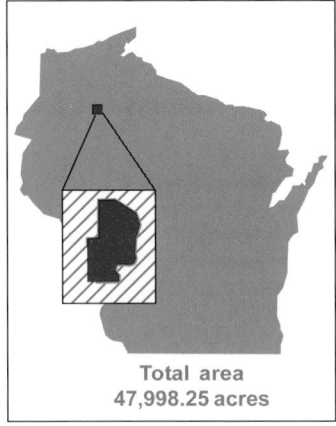

Total area
47,998.25 acres

gathering room. It hosts traveling exhibits of Native American artifacts and seminars and classes on traditional arts.

The Lac Courte Oreilles community is located on the Circle of Wisconsin Fall Color Tours trail. Tourists interested in seeing the autumn foliage will traverse through the reservation. The tribe hosts five annual powwows: Anishinabe Way Powwow, Honor the Earth Powwow, Protect the Earth Festival, Veterans Day Powwow, and the New Year's Eve Powwow. All draw a number of competitive dancers, singers, drummers and vendors.

INFRASTRUCTURE

U.S. Highway 63 traverses the reservation in a north-south direction, as does State Highway 27/70.

Electricity. North State Power and Jump River Electric provide electricity. Electricity provided by North State Power is contracted from the tribe via a hydroelectric agreement.

Alternative Energy. The tribe owns a hydroelectric plant, a 3.2-megawatt nonsynchronous apex vacuum siphon peaking hydroelectric generating system which provides electrical power.

Transportation. A municipal airport and bus services are available in Hayward, 11 miles distant. UPS and FedEx serve the reservation. The tribe operates a shuttle service to the casinos. The tribal school system provides five elementary and secondary school buses and three vans that access the community college.

COMMUNITY FACILITIES AND SERVICES

The tribe offers a community center, youth center, several senior centers, and a library. There are also a fire hall, baseball field, and powwow grounds located on the reservation. A Boys and Girls Club is available to tribal youth. There are three outreach centers for the Boys and Girls Club on the reservation.

Education. The tribe maintains its own public school system. Head Start programs and elementary and secondary schools are all located on the reservation. The tribe operates Lac Courte

Oreilles Community College. The college offers a number of programs, including the American Indian Nursing Program in cooperation with the University of Wisconsin. It also offers a vocational program with emphasis on carpentry, cement masonry, and electrical work. Expansion of the curriculum is planned in the areas of auto mechanics and plumbing. The college recently opened an associate's degree program in transportation. The college maintains a main campus and extension sites.

Health Care. A health, dental, and optometry center serves the reservation and other Sawyer County tribal residents. Emergency care facilities are also located on the reservation.

ENVIRONMENTAL CONCERNS

The tribe is in the process of restoring and protecting its wild rice lakes. This effort involves monitoring water quality, repairing dams, and reseeding. One goal is to restore the wildlife habitat to its original state. There is a concern that genetically modified rice may cross with the wild, natural strain. The Lac Courte Oreilles consider wild rice a spiritual food, and the tribe is working to stop genetically modified rice research and plantings in the area.

Water quality is also a concern on the reservation. With the assistance of the U.S. EPA, the tribe will begin initiating measures to determine water quality and possible sources of contamination and degradation. The tribe will also adopt water quality standards.

Since the closure of the tribe's solid waste disposal facility in 1992, illegal dumping on tribal lands has become prevalent. The tribe operates a waste transfer station and a recycling center, but the problem persists. The tribe's conservation department has developed "Honor the Earth," an illegal dumping prevention program. The program offers educational resources and community outreach activities designed to deter illegal dumping on reservation lands. In collaboration with the national "Adopt a Highway" program, reservation groups such as the health clinic, IGA, Lions Club, and Boys and Girls Club have sponsored the cleanup of areas along 22 different sections of road through the reservation. The annual spring cleanup is another program targeted at eliminating illegal dumping.

Honoring Nations Honoree 2003

Honoring Our Ancestors: The Chippewa Flowage Joint Agency Management Plan, Lac Courte Oreilles Band of Lake Superior Chippewa Indians, Hayward, WI

In 2000, the Lac Courte Oreilles Band of Lake Superior Chippewa righted half a century of ineffective management of the Chippewa Flowage by signing a Joint Agency Management Plan with the Wisconsin Department of Natural Resources and the United States Forest Service. This Plan identifies not only the common interests that direct the management of the Flowage, but also the grim legacy of loss resulting from the flooding of Lac Courte Oreilles homelands and burial grounds. The Plan brings together three sovereign governments to preserve a valuable natural resource in a culturally appropriate manner.

The Chippewa Flowage, lying partially on the Lac Courte Oreilles Reservation, is Wisconsin's third largest lake. Speckled with over two hundred islands, the Flowage stretches across fifteen thousand acres. Its largely pristine shoreline curves through a patchwork of hills, valleys, and bogs. These lands are mostly

wooded and offer rich habitat to most of the birds and animals indigenous to northern Wisconsin including eagles, deer, and walleye.

While the Chippewa Flowage is now regarded as a treasure of natural beauty and recreational opportunity, its creation marked a grim loss for the Lac Courte Oreilles Band of Lake Superior Chippewa. In creating the Flowage in the 1920s-an endeavor motivated by the prospect of power generation-the federal government authorized the flooding of a significant portion of the Lac Courte Oreilles traditional territory. These homelands included wild rice fields, hunting and fishing grounds, the village of Post, and tribal burial grounds. Unfortunately, the Tribe's vehement objections were ignored, and its lands were inundated. The Chippewa Flowage decimated the tribal economy, forced tribal members to relocate, and covered sacred cultural and ceremonial sites. Tragically, since the time of the flooding, Lac Courte Oreilles ancestors' remains have washed up onto the lake's shores.

Although the Flowage brought tremendous sadness to the Lac Courte Oreilles people, for years they sought to obtain the rights to manage the acreage bordering it. The tribal government eventually won these rights in the 1970s. Success in the courtroom, while satisfying, was only a partial win, however. The tribal government possessed neither the technical capacity nor sufficient governmental influence to manage the resource. Consequently, the Tribe shared the management of the Flowage with the state of Wisconsin and the United States Forest Service. State and federal interests were influenced by lessee landowners including timber companies, resorts, and non-tribal residents. In the absence of an effective mechanism for coordinating governance, the Lac Courte Oreilles' purposes were frequently frustrated by the state and federal governments' actions or, in many cases, inaction. In instances when individual businesses or owners threatened to develop the Flowage shoreline, for example, the Tribe could only hope that the state and federal governments would respond to its pleas for aid.

Although competing management over a natural resource is a serious, yet familiar, problem in Indian Country, the Flowage's complicated history presented a further challenge for the Lac Courte Oreilles. Over the years, the Flowage's reputation as a top muskellunge fishing lake and its attraction as a general recreational destination resulted in the increased management influence of the state and federal governments. These powerful non-tribal interests valued the Flowage for its aesthetic beauty and recreational uses. The Lac Courte Oreilles, in contrast, wanted to bring long-overdue honor to their ancestors' graves. Although economic and political realities made it challenging, the Tribe determined that the grim circumstances of the Flowage's creation needed to be brought to light and, further, that the Tribe needed to exercise its sovereignty by playing a key role in managing what had become a common resource.

In 2000, following twelve years of negotiations, the Tribe, the Wisconsin Department of Natural Resources, and the United States Forest Service signed the Joint Agency Management Plan for the Chippewa Flowage. The Plan, which is hailed as a model of intergovernmental cooperation, protects the Chippewa Flowage as a natural resource of compelling beauty while acknowledging its legacy as the site of a profound human tragedy.

One of the principle reasons that the Plan took root was that the three governments came together to identify common ground. The three governments recognized that each held an interest in maintaining the wilderness quality of the Chippewa Flowage and in preventing any development that might threaten this quality. In acknowledging this shared interest, however, the governments also recognized the validity of their varied interests and values-cultural, aesthetic, and recreational. Therefore, the Plan incorporates a history of the Chippewa Flowage as well as baseline measurements of its resources to serve as a basis of understanding for the coordination of government management.

The Plan also outlines long-term management goals for the resources of the Chippewa Flowage area. These goals include policies that detail each government's responsibilities regarding the management of land and real estate, flowage area development, recreation, facilities development, water resources, shoreline erosion, fisheries, vegetation, wildlife, fire control, transportation systems, cultural resources, public health and pollution control, and law enforcement. Although there are many issues about which the three governments must make joint decisions, the comprehensiveness of the Plan does allow each government to undertake its specified management responsibilities with

a great deal of independence. While the goals are shared, the management responsibilities are appropriately divided.

In addition, the Plan provides principles for coordinating management of Chippewa Flowage resources when issues arise that have not been addressed in the Plan's existing policies. In these instances, the governments have agreed to coordinate their management decisions through a consensus-based approach. Representatives from the three governments hold meetings to discuss pending decisions. These representatives, in turn, communicate with officials from their respective governments-a system that fosters candid discussion among a small number of individuals while allowing information to flow upwards to decision makers smoothly. As importantly, the Plan allows for the continuing solicitation of public input as the governments themselves work toward consensus.

The Joint Agency Management Plan for the Chippewa Flowage has resulted in crucial successes. Through the Plan, the tribal, state, and federal governments have prevented two condominium developments, a proposal to rent houseboats, and a proposal to provide scuba diving tours to Lac Courte Oreilles burial sites. All of these proposals, if enacted, would have seriously compromised the Plan's-and the Tribe's-vision of how the Chippewa Flowage should look and be managed. In each instance, government representatives attended township meetings, zoning meetings, and county meetings to discuss the risks posed by such ventures to water quality, wildlife, fisheries, and cultural sites. At these meetings, the Plan's partners played a critical role in achieving consensus against the proposals. These successes in consensus building are leading to additional successes. The Tribe is now working with Sawyer County to bring its zoning laws into accordance with the Plan. The Plan has proven itself to be a powerful force in guiding intergovernmental actions and, in doing so, generating support from other governmental and non-governmental agencies.

It is important to note that the Plan has succeeded both in coordinating the governments' management efforts and in ensuring that their varied interests are served. For instance, when it became clear that one of the defeated condominium development proposals would have required a septic barge to transport waste, all three governments argued against the proposal. The state and federal governments immediately expressed concern about water pollution; the Tribe voiced its objection to transporting sewage over burial sites. In the end, the proposal was rejected on the grounds that the condominium development would be environmentally risky and culturally inappropriate. Although the participating governments may have different interests, they are able to make unified decisions.

The success of the Joint Agency Management Plan of the Chippewa Flowage in blocking undesirable developments and unifying three governments in the pursuit of individual and common goals is the result of several factors. First, and, arguably, most importantly, the Tribe possesses a genuine commitment to intergovernmental coordination. This is a mature expression of sovereignty that reflects a self-determined decision to co-manage the Flowage. The Lac Courte Oreilles' anger and bitterness over the existence of the Flowage are still very real. However, when the Tribe recognized that its desire to preserve the Chippewa Flowage could only be achieved through the establishment of an intergovernmental management plan, it refused to act unilaterally. While the Lac Courte Oreilles were unyielding in their demand that the Plan acknowledge tribal sovereignty, they were cognizant that the state of Wisconsin and the federal government had legitimate jurisdictional claims as well. The Tribe's willingness to acknowledge other governments' authority inspired a similar willingness on the part of those governments. Now, with the full support of the Wisconsin Department of Natural Resources

Lac Courte Oreilles Ojibwa

Honoring Nations
Honoree 2003

Text in its entirety from:
The Harvard Project On
American Indian Economic
Development

John F. Kennedy School
of Government
Harvard University

Lac Courte Oreilles Ojibwa

Honoring Nations
Honoree 2003

Text in its entirety from:
The Harvard Project On
American Indian Economic
Development

John F. Kennedy School
of Government
Harvard University

and the US Forest Service, the Plan's preface alerts readers to the injustices suffered by the Lac Courte Oreilles while the Plan states that "all parties recognize the treaty rights of the Chippewa." Representatives of the state and federal governments to the Plan have become staunch defenders of the Tribe's sovereignty. In establishing the Plan, the Tribe appropriately recognized that its own sovereignty would not be compromised by its willingness to acknowledge other governments' sovereignty. By making the sovereign choice to work cooperatively with these other governments, the Tribe has been able to achieve goals that it could not have achieved alone.

A second factor that contributes to the Plan's success is its institutionalization. The Plan's current effectiveness and its long-term sustainability are the result of the explicit articulation of tribal, state, and federal interests regarding the management of the Chippewa Flowage. The Tribe refused to depend on informal "understandings" that emerged over the course of its negotiations with partnering governments. Its insistence that the governments' shared vision be formally expressed in the Plan now allows the partnership to endure beyond the involvement of those individuals who offered critical leadership in its development. This is important, in part, because tribal, state, and federal government leadership positions invariably turn over. Already, the Plan has outlived all but one of the individuals who developed it. It is also important because the Plan serves as a tool of education for individuals who become involved with its implementation. Of course, the Plan is a dynamic document that responds to the current interests of its partnering governments, but its existence ensures that revisions to the coordinated management of the Flowage do not occur without their coordinated input. The Plan proves that, as tribes assert their sovereign rights to share management with other governments over precious natural resources, individual leadership is essential, but the institutionalization of the resulting vision is even more important.

A third factor in its success is the astounding effectiveness of the intergovernmental partnership that implements the Plan. This partnership between the Lac Courte Oreilles, the Wisconsin Department of Natural Resources, and the US Forest Service truly represents the pinnacle of coordinated management. Several distinguishing features set it apart from other intergovernmental partnerships. First, in the twelve years that this partnership was in development, the tribal, state, and federal governments not only sought to clarify their own interests, but to understand the interests of the public. The governments formed a task force that solicited public opinion through questionnaires, surveys, meetings, and citizen advisory committees. When the governments signed the Plan in 2000, it had already become a de facto agreement among many others. Further, the intergovernmental partnership benefited from the unique assets of each individual government. The Tribe was aggressive in offering those resources that only it could offer. For instance, the Tribe was able to initiate the nomination of the Chippewa Flowage to the National Register of Historic Places in order to add another layer of protection against unwanted development. This use of tribal resources to benefit all Plan partners cemented the partnership. Finally, while the Plan was being developed, the governments did not shy away from drawing upon outside expertise. The Tribe depended upon the Bureau of Indian Affairs and the Great Lakes Indian Fish & Wildlife Commission to enhance the Plan's viability. This willingness to draw upon outsiders' expertise did not imply weakness, but strength in self-governance. Now, as the partnered governments work to implement the Plan, they are not afraid to look beyond themselves to those parties who have helped them and may continue to do so. At every opportunity, the governments enlist the support of sympathetic resorts and individual owners in order to enhance their influence at local government meetings, zoning commissions, and other public forums in which development proposals are being discussed.

Through the Joint Agency Management Plan of the Chippewa Flowage, the Lac Courte Oreilles Band of Lake Superior Indians exercised their sovereignty to protect their homeland from further degradations. Perhaps the most important lesson to emerge from the Plan's success is that even those governments that have every historical reason not to work together may realize win-win solutions through a willingness to cooperate. Certainly, not every historical and contemporary wrong can be made right through cooperative agreements, but the Lac Courte Oreilles prove that sovereignty and intergovernmental cooperation are concepts that may work together well.

Lac du Flambeau

Lac du Flambeau Reservation
Federal reservation
Chippewa
Iron, Vilas, and Oneida
counties, Wisconsin

Lac du Flambeau Band of Lake
Superior Chippewa Indians
P.O. Box 67
Lac du Flambeau, WI 54538
715-588-3303
715-588-7930 Fax
lacduflambeautribe.com

LOCATION AND LAND STATUS
The Lac du Flambeau Reservation spans approximately 44,970 acres in the northern Wisconsin lake country, about 30 miles southeast of Ironwood. The region is dotted with national forests and 158 lakes. It is the largest reservation in the State of Wisconsin. The reservation is part of the Lakeland area tourist region, and it abuts Chequamegon National Forest and Northern Highlands State Forest.

The Lac du Flambeau Reservation, along with three other Anishinabe reservations, was established by the Treaty of September 30, 1854. The reservation initially covered 85,000 acres, but through allotments and subsequent alienation, tribally owned or affiliated acreage has diminished to about half that amount.

PHYSICAL DESCRIPTION
The reservation features 260 lakes; 65 miles of streams, lakes, and rivers; and 24,000 acres of wetlands.

CULTURE AND HISTORY
Members of the Lac du Flambeau Band belong to the Anishinabe, or Ojibwe/Chippewa, Nation. The band has resided in the Lac du Flambeau area since 1745, when it migrated from the Big Salt Water in the eastern United States. The Anishinabes are one of the most numerous cultural and linguistic groups native to the North American continent. There are six Anishinabe reservations in northern Wisconsin, which together constitute a portion of the Lake Superior Band of Chippewa Indians. Other Lake Superior Chippewas reside in Michigan, Minnesota, and Canada. In 1645, the Chippewas took over the region now called Lac du Flambeau, ending the Sioux Indians' long-standing control over the region. Lac du Flambeau ("Lake of the Torches") has remained a permanent Chippewa settlement since 1745, when Chief Sharpened Stone led his band of Chippewas to the lake; there the fish were so plentiful that the tribe found great success in night fishing by torchlight. Thus, the Ojibwe word for Lac du Flambeau is Waswagoning, meaning "Place where they fish by torchlight."

Over the years, many of the Wisconsin Chippewas have drifted away from their reservations to seek employment, education, and other opportunities in Wisconsin cities such as Ashland, Bayfield, and Milwaukee. Despite attrition, the tribe has realized some significant advances in recent decades. During the 1980s and 1990s, a series of federal court rulings reaffirmed Chippewa treaty rights concerning hunting, fishing, and gathering on treaty-ceded territories. The Great Lakes Indian Fish and Wildlife Commission proved instrumental in coordinating this fight. Traditionally high unemployment rates amongst the Chippewas have been greatly reduced by the advent of bingo and other gaming operations and various business enterprises during the past decade. Other sources of tribal income include governmental operations, forestry, production and sales of arts and crafts, and the region's tourist and service economy.

Interest in traditional culture has seen a resurgence in recent years, with renewed participation in the Big Drum Society, along with powwows and other ceremonies. The Lac du Flambeau Reservation maintains a noted tribal museum.

GOVERNMENT

The Lac du Flambeau Reservation is governed by a 12-member elected tribal council. Council members include a president, vice-president, secretary, and treasurer; members serve for two-year terms. The tribe is organized under the 1934 Indian Reorganization Act; it established a constitution and bylaws in 1936. Elections are held annually on the first Tuesday of October. Tribal government departments include administration, housing, fish and game, environmental, food distribution, health, land management, natural resources, law enforcement, planning and development, and business enterprises.

The tribe is a member of the Great Lakes Inter-Tribal Council. Comprised of tribes from across the Great Lakes region, the council works toward supporting member tribes in their efforts to expand self-determination and work collectively to improve the unity of tribal governments, communities, and individuals.

BUSINESS CORPORATION

In 1986, the tribe charted the Lac du Flambeau Cultural and Historical Society. This organization is responsible for preserving tribal artifacts. The society launched the George W. Brown Jr. Ojibwe Museum and Cultural Center. The society, museum staff, and the tribal preservation officer work with tribal landowners on and off the reservation regarding the sacred nature of burial sites and areas of cultural significance.

In 1990, a tribal historical preservation program was established under the society. A cultural committee comprised of tribal elders and other tribal members monitors the program. The program's goals are to document archeological sites and historic structures, identify tribal gathering areas and improve access to them, and develop educational programs. Successful endeavors have included 150 surveys, a map and document archive, a curation facility, and a community program. Over 100 archeological sites have been identified within tribal lands, including ancient hunting and gathering campsites, extensive villages, temporary sites, mound and burial sites, historic logging era sites, and homesteads. A number of sites have been dated to at least 10,000 years ago.

The tribe was the first Native American tribe to initiate a heritage tourism pilot project. The project now includes all 11 Wisconsin tribes. A junior cultural committee has been organized, an apprenticeship program developed, career development classes implemented in the local schools, and programs developed in conjunction with the tribal museum. Tribal members have been trained and certified as paraprofessionals, and the program employs a tribal archeologist. The tribal staff nominates sites for the state, national, and tribal registers of historic places.

The Lac du Flambeau Tribe is also a member of the Northwoods Niijii Enterprise Community (NNEC), which was established in 1998. NNEC is comprised of the Lac du Flambeau, Menominee, Sokaogan Mole Lake Band, and eight rural communities. NNEC oversees funds that were awarded by the USDA toward improving each tribe's reservation and the surrounding communities. The organization's goals are business and sustainable development, improved infrastructure, social development, improved education and technology, and protection of the environment and ecosystem of the Northwoods. Completed NNEC projects include granting micro-loans and loan guarantees totaling $490,000; replacing 3.5 miles of water and sewer systems along Highway 47; constructing an elder housing complex at Manitowish Waters; improving 10 miles of tribal road at Lac du Flambeau; developing the Resource Service Center at Lac du Flambeau; and expanding the facilities at the College of the Menominee Nation. Future projects include developing retail space in downtown Lac du Flambeau; constructing a multipurpose trail system; and continuing a sustainable 10-acre strawberry farm at Lac du Flambeau. NNEC received a $100,000 Minority Business Development Award (in 2004) and a Rural Development- USDA award for $100,000 for a revolving loan fund. A planning grant to establish a CDFI (Community Development Financial Institution) was also granted to develop business loans. The Lac du Flambeau Community Development Corporation coordinates economic development projects on the reservation. The tribe operates a variety of enterprises, such as LDF Industries, Ojibwa Mall, a campground, a fish hatchery, a gas station, a smoke shop, and Lake of Torches Casino and Bingo.

ECONOMY

The tribe operates a number of enterprises in various industries, all of which contribute to the tribal and local economies. The tribe is the largest employer in the county.

Government as Employer. The tribe is the third-largest employer in Vilas County, employing approximately 1,000 people. Tribal government occupations on the reservation include employment in the tribal school, resort, forestry department, casino and bingo hall, smoke shop, legal services, water and sewer, museum, newspaper, planning, family resource, gas station, grocery store, Simpson Electric Company, law enforcement, land management, housing authority, heritage tourism, game wardens, GIS mapping, historic preservation, natural resources, and campground.

Economic Development Projects. In 2004, the tribal council approved the purchase of 93 acres west of Shullsburg in southwestern Wisconsin. The tribe intends to develop a casino, hotel, and convention center on the land. It has received approval from the residents of Shullsberg and is awaiting approval from the governor and the BIA.

In 2004, the tribe received a $200,000 Rural Development Rural Business Enterprise Grant that will be used to develop a downtown retail business incubator facility.

The tribal housing authority is in the process of developing the Community Development Financial Institution. It will provide tribal members with financing assistance toward the purchase of homes and credit, budget, and home repair counseling.

Tourism represents one of the tribe's primary economic expansion strategies. The tribe is a member of Native American Tourism of Wisconsin, which promotes heritage tourism on the reservation. The tribe applied for and was granted the designation of a State of Wisconsin Development Zone. This status has provided employment subsidies and job opportunities for employees of the tribal pallet mill, and new employees of Simpson Electric Company. In addition to employment incentives, development zone status also provides financial and technical incentives, such as tax credits, for commercial development.

Lac du Flambeau

Total area *(BIA realty, 2004)*
44,970.69 acres

Total area *(Tribal source, 2004)*
86,630 acres

Tribally owned *(BIA realty, 2004)*
30,895.74 acres

Tribally owned *(Tribal source, 2004)*
37,136 acres

Allotted/Individually owned
(BIA realty, 2004)
14,059.9acres

Federal trust *(BIA realty, 2004)*
15.06 acres

Allotted *(Tribal source, 2004)*
14,739 acres

Fee area *(Tribal source, 2004)*
20,725 acres

Population *2000 census*
2,995

Population *(Tribal source, 2004)*
1,773

Tribal enrollment
(BIA labor report, 2001)
3,279

Tribal enrollment
(Tribal source, 2004)
3,279

Lac du Flambeau

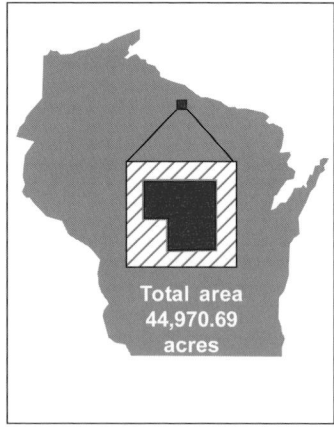

**Total area
44,970.69
acres**

Total labor force *2000 census*
1,241

Total labor force
(Tribal source, 2004)
165

High school graduate or higher
(Tribal source, 2004)
53.3%

High school graduate or higher
2000 census
81%

Bachelor's degree or higher
2000 census
15%

Bachelor's degree or higher
(Tribal source, 2004)
12.4%

Unemployment rate *2000 census*
9.8%

Unemployment rate
(Tribal source, 2004)
26%

Per capita income *2000 census*
$14,519

Forestry. The tribe has a forestry department to manage its forested acreage.

Gaming. The tribe owns and operates the Lake of the Torches Resort Casino, which features 783 slots/VLTs, 12 table games, and 450 bingo seats. Facilities include a convention center, two restaurants, and one entertainment venue. The convention center, Hall of Nations, accommodates over 750 people. The resort offers 101 guest rooms. There are also outdoor recreational activities, such as fishing, kayaking, water skiing, golfing, pontooning, sailing, hiking, and sightseeing. A water recreation and fitness center feature an arcade, lounges, and lakefront decks overlooking Pokegama Lake. The Dancing Waters Lounge, located within the resort, is an award-winning venue.

Lac du Flambeau Bingo features regular and high-stakes VIP bingo. Together these gaming ventures serve as the tribe's largest employer and source of tribal revenues. Revenue earned from the tribe's gaming facilities has enabled the tribe to enhance tribal programs and services, and to offer financial contributions to local organizations and events. In addition to sponsoring major events at the casino facilities, the tribe has donated funds to the Children's Miracle Network, the North Central Regional Alzheimer's Association, the Wisconsin Council on Problem Gambling, and the Vilas/Oneida County chapter of the American Cancer Society Relay for Life, among others.

Fisheries. The Lac du Flambeau Fisheries Program stocks reservation and boundary lakes with over 200,000 muskellunge and walleye fry and fingerlings each year. The program consists of two divisions, fish culture division and fish management and research division. The fish culture division supports fish stocking and rearing programs on the reservation. The fish management and research division estimates total fish harvest and determines stocking rates and success.

The program built its first hatchery in 1936, which today has evolved into more than a dozen culture ponds, numerous hatching banks, and other sophisticated components. The William J. Poupart Sr. Fish Hatchery and Trout Pond are located at the lower end of Pokegama Lake. The original facilities were recently replaced with a state-of-the-art facility that has doubled fish production. The trout pond is open to licensed and unlicensed fishermen during the summer months. Tours are available.

In 2003, the tribe received a $120,330 grant to be used toward the Lac du Flambeau Lake Sturgeon Restoration Project on Lac de Flambeau Lake and Bear River.

Construction. Recent expansions of the tribally owned Simpson Electric Company have provided considerable construction contracts, some of which have resulted in employment of tribal members.

Mining. The tribe opposes mining and has passed a resolution banning it from the reservation.

Industrial Parks. The tribe maintains a 40-acre industrial park, which it developed in the early 1980s.

Real Estate/Commercial Development. The tribe's land management department provides real estate services, land tenure, and estate planning services.

Services and Retail. Enterprises of various venues are abundant on the reservation. A number of retail facilities are located at the tribe's downtown commercial center, which was completed in 1991. They include Chain Three, a bead store that offers the largest selection of Czech seed beads in northern Wisconsin; Lac du Flambeau Ojibwe Market, a full-service grocery store

that includes a deli, a bakery, and meat departments; LDF Gas Station; and Lac de Flambeau Smoke Shop, which offers cigarettes, liquor, and gift selections. The tribe also owns Simpson Electric Company.

Dining venues include Mike's Café on the Rez, which serves breakfast and lunch menus, and Eagle's Nest Restaurant in the casino. Lodging accommodations include the All Seasons Resort on Little Crawling Stone Lake, Alpine Resort, Deerwood Lodge, Deming's Resort on Fence Lake, Dillman's Bay Resort on White Sand Lake, Lake of the Torches Resort Casino, Silver Beach Resort on Little Crawling Stone Lake, and Timber Bay Resort.

Media and Communications. The tribe publishes *Lac du Flambeau News*, a monthly newspaper with a distribution of 10,000.

Tourism and Recreation. The Lac du Flambeau Tribe was the first Native American tribe to initiate a heritage tourism pilot project. Public interpretation sites include an historic fur trading post and a BIA boarding school facility that was constructed in 1895. The George W. Brown, Jr. Ojibwe Museum and Cultural Center provides exhibits, displays, and presentations of tribal artifacts, art, and activities. It houses a 24-foot Ojibwe dugout canoe, several smaller canoes, a French fur trading post, a veteran's memorial, and a world-record sturgeon caught in Pokegama Lake. The world's largest sturgeon to be speared measured 7.1 feet and weighted 195 pounds.

Lac du Flambeau is the site of the sacred Strawberry Island, recognized by the tribe as the "Place of the little people." The National Register of Historical Places also recognizes the island; it is the site of the last battle between the Sioux and Ojibwe peoples in 1745 and the burial site of artifacts and remains dating back to 200 BC.

A tribal member owns Waswagoning Re-created Ojibwe Village, which is located on the reservation. It offers a re-created village, demonstrations, workshops, programs, and educational tours. It is the only facility of its kind in the Northwoods and has been featured in a number of state and national magazines. It is also a recipient of the Wisconsin Trust for Historic Preservation Award (1999), and its use in public broadcasting films has earned it two Emmy Awards. Although not tribally owned, the Lac du Flambeaux offer their support to the enterprise and endorse its activities as well as all private business.

A number of parks are located at Lac du Flambeau, including Thunderbird Park, Sand Beach, Ross Allen Sr. Pavilion, and Leech Beach. The reservation and surrounding areas abound with tourist and recreational attractions and facilities. The chain of 10 lakes around the reservation offers superb sport fishing and water sports of all sorts. During the winter, skiing and snowmobiling are extremely popular. Deer hunts are held seasonally, using either bow and arrows or rifles. In the winter snowmobiling and cross-country skiing are done in the area, with trail maps available at the Chamber of Commerce.

The tribe owns the Lac de Flambeau Tribal Campground and Marina. Located on a peninsula on Highway 47, it offers camping and 72 RV hookup sites, rental canoes, boats, and water sport accessories. It also offers a convenience store, a laundromat, full gas service on water, guide service, swimming and picnic areas, and restrooms. Other marina services include Chapman's Guide Service, Rick Domini's Guide Service, and D.J. Poupart.

The tribe sponsors the Lac du Flambeau Indian Bowl Powwows, a series of weekly powwows during July and August. It also sponsors the Annual Bear River Powwow in July and the annual Ogitchidaa Powwow in June.

TRI-WI-LdF-167

TRI-WI-LdF-171

TRI-WI-LdF-172

TRI-WI-LdF-168

Lac du Flambeau

INFRASTRUCTURE

Near the Michigan border in north-central Wisconsin, Lac du Flambeau is crossed by Highways 70 and 47, accessed from U.S. 2, U.S. 8, and U.S. 51.

Electricity. Wisconsin Public Service Company provides electricity to the reservation and surrounding area.

Fuel. LDF Tribal Gas provides gas.

Water Supply. The LDF Tribal Water and Sewage Program serves the reservation.

Transportation. Charter air service is available in Woodruff (13 miles away), while commercial air service is available in nearby Rhinelander. Bus service is also available in Woodruff, while commercial truck lines serve the area from Rhinelander. Franks Seaplane Base, about 7 miles from Lac du Flambeau, is also available. The tribe owns seven vans to serve the community. The casino provides shuttle and limo service to its guests.

COMMUNITY FACILITIES AND SERVICES

The tribe maintains the William Wildcat Sr. Community Center. Programs include the Walking Foxes. Community facilities also include a library, a youth center, a senior center, a fire hall, and powwow grounds. The tribe hosts an annual Lac du Flambeau Senior Banquet.

Education. Tribal youth may attend the Lac de Flambeau Public School, located within reservation boundaries. The school serves tribal and non-tribal youth in grades preschool through eight. An Ojibwe language program is integrated into the curriculum. Lake-land Union High School in Minocqua serves students in grades 9-12. The tribe also offers a Head Start program.

The reservation is in the Nicolet Area Technical College service area, which often holds classes on the reservation upon request. The tribe provides Ojibwe language classes for adults and children.

Health Care. Tribal health care is furnished through the Chippewa Health Clinic, with further hospital services available in Woodruff. The tribe operates the Lac du Flambeau Domestic Abuse Program, which offers services to prevent and address issues of domestic violence on the reservation.

ENVIRONMENTAL CONCERNS

The tribe's primary environmental concerns are: restoring fish stock in the surrounding lakes, streams, and rivers; maintaining water quality; and reducing solid waste. The tribe received a Solid Waste Assistance Grant from the U.S. EPA and developed a pilot waste reduction program. Initially utilized at the casino site, the tribe plans to expand services to all tribal facilities.

The tribe has been involved in the Tribal Wetland and Waterfowl Enhancement Initiative since 1991. It works to continuously protect, preserve, and restore wetlands within tribal lands. The tribe is also active in preserving and protecting sacred sites and areas of cultural significance, including the 26-acre Strawberry Island. A preservation committee has been formed to address the protection of the island from development.

TRI-WI-LdF-167 Smoke Shop

TRI-WI-LdF-171 George W. Brown, Jr., Ojibwe Museum and Cultural Center

TRI-WI-LdF-172 Family Resource Center

TRI-WI-LdF-168 Tribal Outdoor Education and Recreation Program van

Menominee

Menominee Reservation
Federal reservation
Menominee
Menominee County, Wisconsin

Menominee Indian Tribe
of Wisconsin
P.O. Box 910
Keshena, WI 54135
715-799-5114
715-799-3373 Fax
menominee.nsn.us
menominee.com

Total area *(BIA, 2004)*
235,062.26 acres

Population *2000 census*
3,216

Tribal enrollment
(BIA labor report, 2001)
8,074

Total labor force *2000 census*
1,168

Total labor force
(BIA labor report, 2001)
3,259

High school graduate or higher
2000 census
73%

Bachelor's degree or higher
2000 census
7.6%

Unemployment rate *2000 census*
21.4%

Unemployment rate
(BIA labor report, 2001)
68%

Per capita income *2000 census*
$8,555

LOCATION AND LAND STATUS

The Menominee Reservation is located in northeastern Wisconsin, about 45 miles northwest of Green Bay. It spans approximately 235,000 acres, of which 223,500 acres are heavily forested, representing the largest single tract of virgin timberland in Wisconsin. There are four communities on the reservation: the two main villages of Neopit and Keshena, a smaller village called Zoar, and the more scattered community of South Branch.

The present reservation was established in the Treaty of 1854, the last of a series of treaties that winnowed the tribe's ancestral territory from approximately 9.5 million acres down to 235,000 acres. The tribe resisted the 1887 Allotment Act and was able to maintain control of most of its tribal lands. In 1954, Congress passed the Termination Act, which resulted in the reservation's abolition on April 30, 1961. On December 22, 1973, Congress reversed itself, passing the Menominee Restoration Act, which the tribe implemented on February 9, 1979, by forming a tribal legislature.

PHYSICAL DESCRIPTION

The reservation ranges from 800 to 1,400 feet above sea level. Twenty-four miles of the Wolf River, a federally designated wild river, courses through the reservation. It is one of the last remaining pristine rivers in the state of Wisconsin. Over 400 miles of rivers and streams flow through tribal lands, and almost 4,000 acres of lakes are located within reservation boundaries. Almost 95 percent of tribal lands are forested. The reservation's forest was one of the first internationally certified "green cross" forests in the United States. Over 30 species of trees can be found on tribal lands, including white pines, many of which are over 200 years old. Eastern hemlock and Canadian yew are also common on tribal lands. The reservation is home to a number of wildlife species, including many endangered species, such as eagles, ospreys, red-shouldered hawks, cormorants, whitetail deer, bobcat, bear, and wolf.

CULTURE AND HISTORY

The Kyas-Machatiwduks, or Menominees, are the longest continuous residents of present-day Wisconsin. The Menominees have resided in the area for at least 10,000 years. The word "Menominee" derives from the Algonquin word "Omqnomenwak", which means "wild rice people," and indeed wild rice was long the tribe's staple food, augmented by the corn, squash, and beans that they grew in small gardens. Aside from these gathering and farming activities, the tribe subsisted through hunting and fishing.

The Menominees first encountered Europeans in 1634 when French explorers arrived in present-day Green Bay, Wisconsin. The French initiated the fur trading industry, and the Menominees became active participants. The shift from traditional means of sustenance initiated a change in the lifestyle of the Menominee people, including its governing and clan systems. Additionally, the introduction of European diseases to the indigenous populations ravaged the Menominee Nation.

The Menominees allied themselves with the French during the French and Indian Wars. When the British won, the Menominees gave their allegiance to that nation. The British signed the Jay Treaty in 1794, ceding all lands to the United States, and Euro-Americans soon began to arrive in the Wisconsin region. A fort was established at Green Bay in 1816, and a treaty was forged between the United States and the Menominees in 1817. By 1827, the tribe had sold about 250,000 acres of tribal lands to

eastern tribes from New York and another 250,000 acres to the federal government. The Treaty of Cedars in 1836 mandated the sale of another 4.5 million acres to the government. In 1852, the tribe was moved to the Lake Poygan area, the site of the current reservation. In 1850, tribal representatives negotiated for the return of 600,000 acres. The tribe continued to sell parcels of land to the government over the next several decades.

After the U.S. government placed the Menominees on their reservation in 1852, it attempted to convert the tribe to full-fledged agrarians. The Menominees, however, were more interested in using logging as the basis for their economy. They began their own commercial logging operation in 1871, and by 1890 they had made such a success of it that they were able to establish a hospital, a trade school, police and a judicial system, and profit sharing from their lumbering profits. By the turn of the century, the tribe was widely recognized as one of the most prosperous and progressive in the country. Ironically, it was this very image of the Menominees as advanced and prosperous that marked them to be one of the first tribes to face the federal government's termination experiment during the 1950s, when federal supervision was withdrawn. By the late 1960s, tribal leaders, in desperation, decided to begin developing and selling waterfront lots on the county's lakes and rivers to non-Indians. Tribal reaction to this scheme spurred the establishment of a new tribal organization in 1970 called Determination of Rights and Unity for Menominee Shareholders (DRUMS). Through public demonstrations, favorable media coverage, and court actions, the organization was able to delay the development and sale of tribal lands. These events did not go unnoticed in Washington, and in 1973 President Richard Nixon signed the Menominee Restoration Act into law, reestablishing nearly all of the former reservation.

Aspects of traditional culture remain vital on the reservation, the tribe having preserved and restored the Menominee clan structure, the tribal creation story, and the use and teaching of the Menominee language. Restoring other cultural elements is also a priority for the tribe. Once a major tradition of the Menominee's cultural system, tribal members had not practiced the annual ceremony honoring the return of the sturgeon since 1892, when dams were built below the reservation at Shawano, Wisconsin, and the sturgeon no longer returned to tribal lands. In the late 1990s, Wisconsin Department of Natural Resources gave the tribe sturgeon in order to perform the ceremony below Keshena Falls at the mouth of Chikeney Creek, on tribal lands. Since that time, the state has continued to supply the tribe with sturgeon, and the annual tradition has been renewed. The tribe is hopeful that this marks the beginning of an era when the sturgeon will be able to return to tribal lands without barriers.

GOVERNMENT

In 1977 the tribe adopted a new constitution and bylaws. The bylaws call for an elected nine-member tribal legislature, a tribal chairperson elected by the legislature, a tribal judiciary, and a general council. The legislature oversees approximately 40 social service and administrative programs.

Tribal government departments and offices include: language and culture, historic preservation, community development, economic development, enrollment, finance, general assistance, human resources, insurance, internal audit, job training, licensing and permits, loan fund, maintenance, MIS, social services, environmental services, utilities, program attorney, and tribal attorney.

The tribal law enforcement department provides patrol, administrative, investigative, and detention services on the reservation. The department also offers crime victims, police liaison, juvenile intervention, and K-9 divisions. The tribe's historic preservation department oversees the implementation of NAGPRA (Native American Graves Protection and Repatriation Act) in regards to Menominee remains. It has developed a historic preservation's repatriation plan and initiated the repatriation of Menominee remains from various museums and facilities. Tribal elders counsel the department, providing guidance during the processes. The tribal housing department offers elderly housing, low-income rentals, rental assistance, market-based rentals, rehabilitation, and security programs. It employs a staff of 40.

The tribe is a member of the Great Lakes Inter-Tribal Council. Comprised of tribes from across the Great Lakes region, the council supports member tribes in their efforts to expand self-determination and to work collectively to improve the unity of tribal governments, communities, and individuals.

BUSINESS CORPORATION
Menominee Tribal Enterprises (MTE) is a chartered corporation that has been in operation since 1908. Elected tribal members serve on a board of directors and monitor the corporation's activities. The corporation offers lumber mix products. Menominee Computer Systems, a chartered division of MTE, provides computer services to the lumber and forests products industry and the federal government. MTE is certified by the Scientific Certification Systems Alliance and the Rainforest Alliance, and it was honored by the council on sustainable development. It is a member of the Forest Stewardship Council's Economic Council.

Wolf River Development Company is a tribally chartered business that operates in the housing development industry. The parent company, WICK Homes, has been in operation for over 30 years. It offers over 100 different models and styles of homes.

The Menominee Nation is a member of the Northwoods Niijii Enterprise Community, (NNEC), which was established in 1998. NNEC is comprised of the Lac du Flambeau Band, Menominee Tribe, Sokaogan Mole Lake Band, and eight rural communities. NNEC oversees funds that were the USDA awarded to improve each tribe's reservation and the surrounding communities. The organization's goals are business development, improved infrastructure, social development, improved education and technology, and protection of the environment and ecosystem of the Northwoods. Completed NNEC projects include granting microloans and loan guarantees totaling $490,000; replacing 3.5 miles of water and sewer systems along Highway 47; constructing an elder housing complex at Manitowish Waters; improving 10 miles of tribal road at Lac du Flambeau; developing f the resource service center at Lac du Flambeau; and expanding the facilities at the College of the Menominee Nation. Future projects include developing retail space in downtown Lac du Flambeau; constructing a multipurpose trail system; and continuing a sustainable 10-acre strawberry farm at Lac du Flambeau. NNEC received a $100,000 Minority Business Development Award in 2004.

ECONOMY
The foundation of the tribal economy has long been the tribe's involvement in the forestry industry. The tribe has owned and operated forestry-related enterprises for almost 100 years. The tribe also operates a number of other industries that contribute to the tribal economy.

Government as Employer. The tribal government is a major employer, providing jobs to 115 tribal members in its administration department, 69 in the tribal schools, 58 in the tribal police force, 47 in the daycare and Head Start programs, and 8 in the tribal courts.

Economic Development Projects. The Menominee Nation is committed to promoting a balance between its environment, economy, and community. As it ventures into new economic development projects, it always adheres to its mission of creating sustainable development.

The Menominee business center is a tribally operated entity that provides management assistance, cost-effective space utilization, and a synergistic environment catering specifically to tribal members and professional businesses. This center is an integral part of the tribe's overall economic development planning, encouraging the growth of the private sector on the reservation and in the county. It also works in partnership with the Wisconsin Department of Commerce.

The private sector initiative is a local Menominee business planning and development service designed to complement and fill the gaps in the existing private, university, state, and federal business development service delivery system.

Agriculture and Livestock. Agriculture represents only a minor part of the tribal economy, with about 176 acres of grain currently farmed. Approximately 10 tribal members are employed in this capacity.

Forestry. Almost 95 percent of tribal lands are forested, and the tribe has been involved in the forestry industry for almost 100 years. The tribe closely manages its forests with the objective of maximizing the quantity and quality of saw timber grown under sustained-yield management principles. It enforces continuous forestry inventory, forest habitat classification, varied harvesting methods, management of nontimber resources, and cultural resource awareness.

Menominee Tribal Enterprises is a chartered corporation that oversees forest development and management, and also operates a wood-products manufacturing facility. *(See also Manufacturing, below.)*

Today timbering continues to employ about 180 tribal members, exclusive of milling operations. Throughout the late 1980s, the annual timber harvest remained quite stable at somewhere around 22 million board-feet of saw timber. Additionally, millions of additional board feet are cut annually for use and sale as firewood.

Gaming. The tribe owns the Menominee Casino-Bingo Hotel. It offers over 837 slots/VLTs, 12 table games, 4 poker tables, 400 bingo seats, a convention center, 2 restaurants, and an entertainment venue. The hotel offers 100 guest rooms, a swimming pool, a sauna, and a whirlpool. An adjacent RV park features almost 60 sites. The complex's Five Clan Gift and Smoke Shop offers tobacco products, Pendleton products, Native Threads clothing, pottery, paintings, and Zuni, Navajo, and Menominee products. The facility employs 600 individuals.

Fisheries. The reservation is full of lakes, rivers, and streams that provide excellent recreational fishing opportunities; fishing is open to the general public only at Legend Lake.

Construction. Wolf River Development Company is a tribally chartered business that holds a dealership for WICK Homes. The tribe lists 15 separate Indian subcontracting businesses among its membership, ranging from carpentry and building construction, to sewer-and-water systems, to tile flooring installation. Business is both seasonal and sporadic.

Manufacturing. The tribe's Menominee Tribal Enterprises is a chartered corporation that has been in operation since 1908. Facilities include two eight-foot band mills, dry kilns, a pre-dryer, custom kiln drying, and shipping by rail or truck. The planing mill

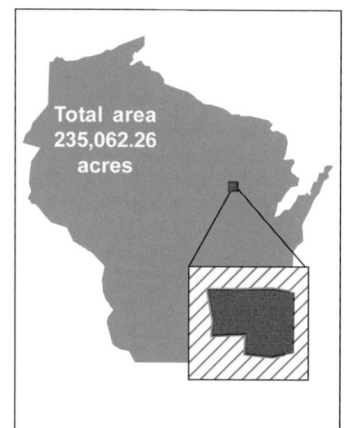

Total area
235,062.26
acres

Menominee

TRI-WI-Mn-021

TRI-WI-Mn-007

TRI-WI-Mn-024

TRI-WI-Mn-008

TRI-WI-Mn-006

TRI-WI-Mn-021 Outdoor Amphitheater

TRI-WI-Mn-007 Menominee Tribal Enterprises forest product manufacturing facilities

TRI-WI-Mn-024 Wolf River, a federally designated river, wild runs through the reservation

TRI-WI-Mn-008 Menominee Tribal Enterprises forest product manufacturing facilities

TRI-WI-Mn-006 Menominee Tribal Enterprises forest product manufacturing facilities

produces S4S (sanded on four sides) and S2S (sanded on two sides) stock; WP 4, 6, and 116; SIS2E; decking; log siding; drop siding; shiplap siding; channel lock; and bevel siding. Menominee Tribal Enterprises's forest products and lumber products divisions are members of the National Hardwood Lumber Association, Northeastern Lumberman's Manufacturing Association, Wisconsin and Michigan Wood Seasoning Association, Lake States Lumber Association, Society of American Foresters, American Tree Farm Association, and Wisconsin and Michigan Timber Producers Association. The company has been recognized by the scientific certification systems for its incorporation of sustainable management practices into overall management of forests and for its contribution to the protection of habitat biodiversity and timber resources. The operation employs 170 persons.

Industrial Parks. The tribe is presently developing an industrial park site. It will entail 30 acres, full utility services, and convenient access to State Highway 47.

Services and Retail. The reservation hosts numerous businesses, both small and large, including: the Menominee Tribal Supermarket, employing 10; 4 convenience stores; a gas station; a tavern; a beauty salon; an auto salvage operation; a catering business; and a solid waste removal business.

Media and Communications. The tribe publishes the *Menominee Nation News.* The tribe owns and operates Menominee Computer Systems, a chartered division of Menominee Tribal Enterprises. It provides computer system and software development to the lumber and forest products industry and to the federal government.

Tourism and Recreation. Outdoor activities constitute the bulk of the reservation's tourist and recreation attractions. The tribe runs two river-rafting operations on the Wolf River. Fishing is allowed at Legend Lake. The tribe offers guided tours of tribal lands through the Menominee Tribal Enterprises offices.

The tribe operates the Menominee Logging Camp Museum north of Keshena. It offers the world's largest collection of artifacts from Wisconsin's logging era. The museum is housed in seven log

buildings. The buildings are replicas of a camp office, bunkhouse, cook shanty, blacksmith shop, saw filer's shack, horse barn, and wood butcher's shop. The museum hosts over 20,000 artifacts. Guided tours are available. There are two annual powwows, a traditional one on Memorial Day and a competitive one during the first weekend in August. The tribe also hosts an annual Elders Powwow in October and an Ice Carving Competition.

INFRASTRUCTURE

State highways 47 and 55 pass directly through the reservation, providing access from Green Bay and points beyond. Commercial air service is available at the Shawano Municipal Airport, 15 miles from the reservation, as well as in Green Bay, 45 miles away. Regular commercial and charter bus lines serve the reservation, as do major commercial truck lines. As for rail service, the Soo Line provides a spur for the tribal sawmill in Neopit.

Electricity. The Menominee Tribal Utilities Department provides electrical services to reservation residencies.

Fuel. Bottled gas is the largest source of home heating on the reservation, followed by wood, fuel oil, and kerosene. All are available through local distributors.

Water Supply. Wells provide water for most homes on the reservation. The Menominee Tribal Utilities Department provides water to a large minority of reservation homes. It also provides septic services for residential septic tanks, and a public sewer system provide sewer services.

Transportation. The tribe has established the Menominee Public Transit system within the reservation and into the county of Menominee. The system provides four scheduled vans and two buses for public use. Special trips can be scheduled with the public transit coordinator.

COMMUNITY FACILITIES AND SERVICES

The tribe maintains a community center with a variety of facilities. A library is also available on the reservation. Community services offered by the tribe include the Child Support Agency, kinship care, social services, food distribution, and family preservation and support programs. The Community-Based Residential Facility offers programs for tribal elders. The tribe also maintains senior citizen's centers in Keshena and Neopit.

The tribe operates the respite care program for children from infancy to four years old whose families meet the criteria for family crisis or respite care needs. The Eagle's Nest Emergency Shelter provides emergency and temporary assistance to homeless individuals and families and to victims of domestic violence. It is located in a three-story home and offers 20 three-bed rooms, and a shared kitchen, dining room, and living room space. The shelter offers case management, referral, eviction prevention, move-out, first months rent and security deposit, utility assistance, budget counseling, daily living skills, classes, transportation, housing, computer learning, clothing, and mentoring services.

Education. The reservation is served by the Menominee Indian School District, which provides employment for nearly 12 percent of the tribal workforce. Programs include elementary, middle, and high school. The tribe also operates a private K-8 school, the Menominee Tribal School. The tribe operates the Delores K. Boyd Head Start program, the Neopit Head Start program, and the tribal daycare facility on the reservation as well. The tribe contracts the Johnson O'Malley Program for the Menominee, Menominee Tribal School, and Shawano/Gresham and Suring School districts.

The tribe's education department provides assistance with completing admissions and financial aid forms, assistance processing BIA grants for eligible students, career counseling, and a GED/HSED program.

The tribe also operates the College of the Menominee Nation (CMN). It was chartered in 1993 by the Menominee Tribal Legislature and is a member of the American Indian Higher Education Consortium. The college offers a technology lab, new library, and distance education center. CMN offers associate degree programs in accounting, counseling, business administration, carpentry, computer science, education, liberal studies, natural resources, nursing, social work, and tribal legal studies. The college features an English department, a culture institute, and the sustainable development institute. The college library contains an extensive collection of print, nonprint, and electronic information on Native American studies and on subjects related to the school's academic curricula. The library contains a special Native American collection of materials that do not circulate, offers interlibrary loan services to students, and has 10 Internet access computer stations.

Health Care. In 1977, the tribe successfully acquired congressional and Hill-Burton funds and constructed the first Native American-owned and operated health facility in the United States. It serves the tribe's total health care needs. The clinic has been accredited by the Joint Commission of Accreditation of Healthcare Organizations. It employs two full-time doctors, two dentists, two ambulances, and a number of nurses and pharmacists.

The tribe also operates the Maehnowesekiyah Treatment Center. This facility offers comprehensive outpatient services. All programs are nationally accredited by community-based residential facilities and the State of Wisconsin. The center includes primary alcohol and other drug abuse (AODA) day treatment, adult AODA education, Menominee Nation early childhood, family therapy, and an aftercare program. The tribal health program also offers an adult residential treatment program.

Menominee

ENVIRONMENTAL CONCERNS

In addition to the responsible management of tribal forests and natural resources, the tribe's primary environmental concerns are water quality and habitat restoration. The tribe has been involved in the habitat and wild rice restoration at South East Pine Lake, Minnow Creek, and Camp 19/Old Railroad Grade.

Honoring Nations Honoree 2003

Menominee Community Center of Chicago, Tribal Administration,
Menominee Indian Tribe of Wisconsin, Keshena, WI/Chicago, IL

Over half of the Menominee Indian Tribe of Wisconsin lives off-reservation. Regrettably, the ties between the Menominee's reservation and urban populations, like those between the split populations of so many Indian nations, have been tenuous for decades. In 1994, however, a group of Menominee Indians living in Chicago reached out to the Tribe and the Tribe reciprocated. Now, the Menominee Community Center of Chicago is an official community of the Menominee Nation and its members are active participants in tribal culture and governance, strengthening and being strengthened by this renewed connection. Together, reservation and urban Menominee are reinforcing their respective communities by reuniting their nation.

Decades of federal policies of assimilation and forced relocation as well as inadequate economic opportunities on reservations have resulted in an increasingly urban Indian population. Approximately 60 to 65 percent of American Indians and Alaska Natives live away from their reservations while roughly 50 percent of this off-reservation population live in urban areas. The Menominee Tribe of Wisconsin is no exception. Its history of combating assimilationist pressures, federal relocation, and economic challenges was further complicated in the 1950s when the US government terminated its status as a federally recognized tribal nation. At that time, many Menominee families moved to urban areas such as Green Bay and Milwaukee, Wisconsin,

and Chicago, Illinois. Currently, over half of the eight thousand Menominee tribal citizens live beyond their reservation boundaries while six percent of these tribal members live in the Chicago metropolitan area.

Like other urban minority groups, these Chicago-area Menominee Indians suffer from myriad economic and social hardships commonly experienced by off-reservation Native communities. Studies reveal that urban Indians are disproportionately prone to experience socioeconomic distress when compared to their white counterparts. They are 1.7 times as likely to lack a high school diploma; they are 2.4 times as likely to be unemployed; and they are 3.9 times as likely to live in poverty as urban whites. Consistent with these statistics, the Menominee Indians living in the Chicago area experience high unemployment while those who are employed work mainly in the service sector. They have critical medical needs but oftentimes do not have access to major medical coverage. Additionally, single women head a very high percentage of their households. As a result, 84 percent of the Menominee Indians living in the Chicago area are at or below the poverty line. Only 6 percent are homeowners.

Despite these ills that urgently need to be addressed, the Menominee Indians of the Chicago area, with other urban Indi-

Honoring Nations
Honoree 2003

Text in its entirety from:
The Harvard Project On
American Indian Economic
Development

John F. Kennedy School
of Government
Harvard University

Menominee

Honoring Nations
Honoree 2003

Text in its entirety from:
The Harvard Project On
American Indian Economic
Development

John F. Kennedy School
of Government
Harvard University

ans, form part of Indian Country's "forgotten majority." Historically, tribal, state, and federal policymakers have maintained a reservation-centric view of Indian needs and priorities despite the existence of significant off-reservation populations. As a result, urban populations struggle to address their needs alone. Most free or low-cost services available to Indians living off-reservation remain contingent upon their return to the reservation. For many, poverty prevents such travel. This is especially true for a majority of the Menominee Indians of the Chicago area who reside over 250 miles from their reservation headquarters located in Keshena, Wisconsin. Urban Indians also suffer from a severe sense of cultural dislocation. Many would prefer to return to their traditional lands and many attempt to maintain a connection to their cultural center, but distance and economic distress make these desires almost unattainable. Within the Chicago area, Menominee Indians have tended to get lost among the city's considerable Indian and minority populations.

Policymakers' neglect meant that urban Indians turned with increasing frequency to nonprofit urban Indian community centers that offer services such as employment training, health care, housing programs, and welfare. As important as these centers have become, they still struggle to meet urban Indians' needs. As non-governmental entities, they face obstacles in securing funds that are directed toward tribal governments. Further, given that most centers serve Natives from distinct-and-different-cultures, these pan-Indian centers' are constrained in their ability to meet the cultural needs of any single population.

In 1994, the Menominee Indians of the Chicago area confronted this economic and cultural marginalization by forming a center of their own. This center diverged from typical urban Indian community centers in order to fulfill specific Menominee needs. It began, initially, as a forum for formalizing social and familial connections. Known as the Menominee Social Club of Chicago, its members hosted cultural gatherings and offered support services for Menominee individuals and families living in the greater Chicago area. By 1996, these events had generated political consciousness. The Club's members began to strongly identify themselves as Menominee and assert their status as citizens of the Menominee Tribe of Wisconsin. In turn, their growing participation in tribal events and political activism gained the attention the Menominee tribal government. In 1996, the Menominee Nation Tribal Council acted under the Tribal Government Plan Ordinance 95/04 to officially recognize the newly renamed Menominee Community Center of Chicago.

Today, the Menominee Community Center of Chicago (MCCC) is the institutional home of the only officially recognized off-reservation community of the Menominee Indian Tribe. The Center is identified as a nonprofit tribal program, making it eligible for tribal funding. The MCCC is governed by a five-member Board of Directors that oversees activities and reports to the Menominee Tribal Legislature. To sustain its numerous offerings, the Center relies on a ten thousand dollar annual budget and, more significantly, the generous volunteer efforts of its dedicated members.

The Center succeeds in strengthening the relationships of its Chicago-area members by providing a full spectrum of cultural engagements as well as information about and referrals to social services. The MCCC organizes and sponsors powwows, traditional fish feasts, and breakfasts for homeless Menominee. It has hosted language classes with the support of a Menominee Newberry Library Fellow and has worked with the Tribal Historic Preservation Office regarding Menominee artifacts held in the Chicago Field Museum. Additionally, the MCCC studies urban Indian issues and collects useful data for the Menominee Tribe as well as the general public. The Center's research on the status of urban Menominee housing conditions allows it to advocate for improved housing services and the Center has

begun to develop programs for enhancing Menominee employment opportunities in the Chicago area.

In addition, the MCCC enhances social and political connections between the Chicago-area Menominee Indians and the Menominee Tribe. The Center organizes trips for Menominee individuals and families to go "back home" to the reservation for important cultural events such as the Sturgeon Feast and the Big Drum Ceremony. It also circulates information on tribal enrollment, the legislative election process, the tribal constitution, and tribal social services available to Chicago-area citizens. The Center even coordinates attendance to the Menominee Nation Annual General Council Meeting. Most importantly, it ensures, through the formal recognition of the Chicago-area Menominee as tribal citizens, biannual meetings of the tribal legislature in Chicago.

Four factors contribute to the existence and effectiveness of the MCCC. First, the Center and the Menominee tribal government have willingly worked together to redefine tribal citizenship. By officially recognizing the Chicago-area Menominee as a bona fide community within the tribal nation, the Menominee Tribe has acknowledged the citizenship of its off-reservation population. Through this recognition, the Tribe has embraced a portion of its population that many Indian nations simply do not include in the ongoing business of governance. While several other tribes offer services to their off-reservation constituents as individuals, the Menominee Tribe's recognition of an off-reservation community in its entirety is virtually unheard of in Indian Country. By establishing an inclusive definition of citizenship, the Tribe offers political, cultural, and economic support to tribal citizens far from the reservation center. The MCCC and the Menominee Tribe deserve recognition for their role in the critical-and-innovative-work of integrating urban tribal citizens into the social and political life of an Indian nation.

Initially, not every legislator of the Menominee tribal government was open to the idea of an active off-reservation political presence. The second factor in the Center's success, however, was the Menominees' realization that the Tribe itself would be strengthened by the incorporation of these citizens and families into the civic and cultural affairs of the Tribe. Perhaps the Menominee Tribe began to learn this lesson after it was terminated by the federal government. Then, tribal citizens living in Chicago played a significant role in the restoration of federal recognition. Now, the Menominee Tribe is again welcoming the contributions of its Chicago-area citizens. In total, 45 percent of Chicago-based Menominee now vote in tribal elections and tribal leaders are already recognizing the benefits of drawing upon these citizens' unique perspectives. They also recognize the wealth of contacts that the MCCC offers. Some MCCC members hold leadership roles and advance Menominee tribal interests in the Chicago area in education, public policy, and economic development. Additionally, the MCCC offers opportunities for official interactions between the Menominee Tribe and various Illinois populations that might provide a natural springboard for interactions between tribal government and state leaders. With the increasing importance of tribal-state relations, tribes such as the Menominee do well to utilize the connections that their urban populations provide.

Third, the Menominee Community Center of Chicago and the Menominee Tribe recognize the importance of cultivating a distinctly Menominee cultural identity among its urban diaspora. Both the MCCC and the Menominee Tribe could benefit from partnerships with a number of Chicago's pan-Indian organizations. However, the MCCC and the Tribe now collaborate in their efforts to meet needs specific to Menominee Indians that are frequently overlooked by pan-Indian initiatives. For example, the Center educates Native and non-Native Chicago communities about the Menominee Tribe and its unique history. The MCCC's presentations in schools and other organizations portray an accurate image of Menominee culture and accomplishments. The Center's range of activities is also an important part of enhancing the emotional health of its members. Many of these individuals were adopted out of the tribe or raised in foster care with little or no connection to their cultural heritage. Now, the MCCC offers them an avenue for establishing or reestablishing contact. Several MCCC members have been united with previously unknown family through the Center's Enrollments Office contacts and Center-sponsored trips to the reservation. The MCCC also encourages mentoring relationships, pairing older and younger MCCC members. These relationships, built on a common culture and a shared tribal citizenship, will sustain the Center's vibrancy and ability to serve Menominee citizens and families for generations to come.

A final factor that undergirds the Center's success is that urban and reservation Menominee have employed simple strategies to renew and strengthen their relationship. Together they rewrote a single line of the Menominee constitution, bringing biannual meetings of the tribal legislature to Chicago. Through these meetings, constituents come to know their elected leaders and stay abreast of social, cultural, and economic developments being pursued by the tribal government. Tribal legislators also benefit as off-reservation citizens communicate their needs and contribute their distinct perspectives and knowledge. Similarly, the Center's trips to the Menominee Reservation are an uncomplicated way to strengthen the ties of kinship and common culture. These simple and easily replicable acts have enabled the Menominee to strengthen the entire tribal population. Other Indian nations can learn a great deal from the outstanding example the MCCC and Menominee Tribe have set.

For too long, tribal governments have forgotten their off-reservation citizens. As recently as the 1990s, this was true for the Menominee community living in the Chicago metropolitan area. Regrettably, it remains true for urban Indians throughout Indian Country. To the credit of the Menominee Community Center of Chicago and the Menominee tribal government, the Chicago-based Menominee are no longer forgotten. Through an innovative partnership between an active off-reservation community and a forward-looking tribal government, the Menominee are redefining what it means to be tribal citizens. Their efforts are an expression of nation building that deserves the careful examination of other tribal governments and off-reservation Indian citizens.

Menominee

M ole Lake

LOCATION AND LAND STATUS

The Mole Lake Reservation is located in northeastern Wisconsin. It lies eight miles south of the Town of Crandon. The nearest cities include Rhinelander, 36 miles northwest, and Wausau, 60 miles southwest. Tribal headquarters are located on the reservation in Mole Lake.

The reservation was established in 1938 following the tribe's organization under the Indian Reorganization Act of 1934. The original reservation was comprised of 1,745 acres. In 1968, additional acreage was purchased. The tribe has purchased additional lands that are not yet in trust status. There are five acres of non-Native owned lands on the reservation. The five-acre site is the only nontrust land within the exterior boundaries. It has a 20-unit motel and a historical log cabin. The tribe is looking at putting the parcel with the cabin in trust. The tribe jointly purchased the mine site with the Forest County Potawatomis. The intent was to prevent a sulfide mine from opening directly adjacent to the Mole Lake Reservation as it could have serious effects on the tribe's groundwater.

PHYSICAL DESCRIPTION

The reservation lies in the lake country of Wisconsin. Forested lands contain primarily mixed hardwoods, while cedar and tamarack forest the lowland riparian areas. There are three lakes, three feeder streams, and one river within the reservation's boundaries. The primary lake on the reservation, Rice Lake, is a 220-acre wild rice bed that has remained a site of great cultural significance to the tribe for the past several hundred years.

CLIMATE

Crandon, Wisconsin, receives between 1 to 5 inches of rainfall per month, for an average yearly total of 32 inches

CULTURE AND HISTORY

The Sokaogon Chippewa/Mole Lake Band is a band of the Lake Superior Chippewa Indians, also known as the Ojibwe Nation. Family clans moved out of eastern Canada to Madeline Island at least 1,000 years ago. The Mole Lake Band settled in the north-ern regions of Wisconsin. Gathering wild rice, fishing, and hunting were the primary means of sustenance for the people.

In 1854, representatives from the Mole Lake Band attended a treaty council on Madeline Island between the Chippewa Nation and representatives of the United States. The federal government agreed to provide several Chippewa bands with cash, equipment, and their traditional land base. The following year, the Indian commissioner denied having met with the Mole Lake Band during that treaty council, and the promises were not kept. The Indian commissioner finally agreed to provide the band with a grant and drew up a map designating approximately 20 square miles in the Summit, Pelican, Metonga, and Pickerel Lake area, but before the grant could be honored, the original map was lost when the commissioner's boat sank in the Great Lakes. A copy of the map had been given to the Mole Lake chief, Mee-gee-see, but the tribe's copy was lost when the tribe was forced to use it as a form of collateral to a trapper. With no documented record of the grant, the tribe was not awarded a reservation or federal recognition and became known as one of the Lost Tribes.

In 1930, a roll was taken of the Mole Lake area in attempt to identify tribal origins. It was determined that at least 200 individuals were self-identified members of the Sokaogan Community/Mole Lake Band. The band received recognition as a tribe under the Indian Reorganization Act of 1934. A reservation was created for the community in southwestern Forest County, Wisconsin.

Traditional cultural values are still practiced among the Mole Lake Band. The Ojibwe language continues to be spoken, spiritual ceremonies are held, and traditional agricultural and fishing techniques are employed. The tribe advocates its rights as a sovereign nation and acts to preserve its lands and lifestyle.

In 1997, representatives of the Sokaogan Community submitted a statement to the United Nations Human Rights Commission in Geneva, Switzerland. The statement brought to the commission's

Mole Lake Reservation
Federal reservation
Chippewa (Ojibwe)
Forest County, Wisconsin

Sokaogon Mole Lake Band
of Lake Superior Chippewa
3051 Sand Lake Road
Crandon, WI 54520-9635
715-478-7500
715- 478-5275 Fax
sokaogonchippewa.com

Mole Lake

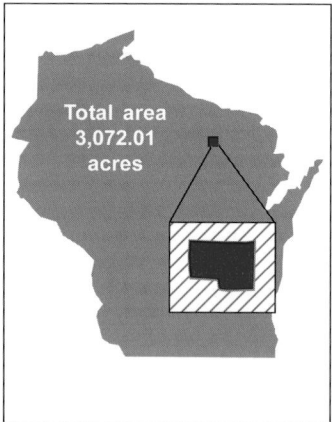

Total area
3,072.01
acres

Total area *(BIA realty, 2004)*
3,072.01 acres

Tribally owned *(BIA realty, 2004)*
3,072.01 acres

Population *2000 census*
449

Tribal enrollment
(BIA labor report, 2001)
1,271

Total labor force
(BIA labor report, 2001)
196

Unemployment rate
(BIA labor report, 2001)
56%

Per capita income *2000 census*
$7,589

attention the violations of treaty agreements by the U.S. government. Primary concerns were the exploitation of tribal lands for mineral exploration and the desecration of sacred sites.

In the late 1990s, the tribe sued the U.S. EPA for recognition of tribally defined water quality standards. The case was heard before the Supreme Court, and in 2003 the Court upheld the tribe's authority to define its own water quality standards. The judgment recognized the tribe's right to pursue its own course of environmental protection and, in turn, recognized the tribe's sovereignty as a nation.

GOVERNMENT

In 1938, the tribe adopted a constitution and bylaws in accordance with the Indian Reorganization Act. The tribe is governed by a six-member tribal council.

Tribal government also functions through several departments, including the general fund, education, environment, communications, health, social services, public works, judicial, and enterprises. One of the largest departments is the environmental department, which oversees a number of committees and programs that promote the tribe's commitment to environmental protection and preservation

The tribe maintains a tribal court system. The court exercises jurisdiction over conservation violations, some child protection issues, and domestic abuse matters. Court judges are also authorized to perform marriages.

BUSINESS CORPORATION

Northwoods Niiji Enterprise Community is a partnership of three tribes, which includes the Sokaogon Chippewa Community of Mole Lake. Their aim is to apply Native American principles and wisdom to economic development strategies through sustainable development, community-based partnerships, and grassroots approaches. New businesses have been created in wood-products manufacturing, arts and crafts, and fishing.

In 2001, Northwoods Niiji projects in Mole Lake included the expansion of three water and sewer systems and $400,000 raised to improve roads for fire protection. The enterprise installed fire numbers on homes and connected 911 services. Traffic measures to improve child safety were implemented, and an ecotrail was established. A cultural museum project was also initiated. In 2004 Northwoods Niiji received a Minority Business Development Fund Award from the State of Wisconsin. The award included $215,000 in investments. The organization also received a minority business development loan that would leverage $100,000 in private-sector investments.

ECONOMY

Prior to federal recognition in 1934, members of the Mole Lake community suffered a poor economy. Although they lost traditional lands and were denied assistance provided to federally recognized tribes, many members remained in the Mole Lake area. The majority of tribal members lived in extreme poverty. Most of the homes were tarpaper shacks that possessed only a cook stove. When the tribe reorganized under the Indian Reorganization Act, log homes were built on the newly formed reservation. During the time that it has been recognized and received assistance, the tribe has been working to recover from the periods of depravity. While traditional agricultural and fishing practices are still used, the tribe has expanded its projects into the gaming and tourism industries as it strives to rebuild its economy.

Government as Employer. Tribal government employs approximately 100 persons.

Economic Development Projects. A 7,800-square-foot tribal office in Crandon was completed in 2004. The tribe has plans to

construct more housing units on the reservation and to expand the existing child care center facilities. The tribe is also considering the development of a 72-room hotel that would feature an indoor pool and an adjacent RV camping area.

Agriculture and Livestock. Wild rice has been a staple food supply for generations and continues to play an important role in the local economy. Rice Lake, located on the reservation, contains the largest producing rice fields in Forest Lake. Tribal members harvest and prepare the rice using traditional methods. The process includes preparing the rice for sale, storage, and ceremonial purposes.

Forestry. There are three individually owned and operated logging businesses located on the reservation. Each company employs three to five people.

Gaming. The tribe owns two gaming facilities. The tribe's involvement in the gaming industry has helped to decrease the unemployment rate on the reservation from 80 percent to 10 percent in just a few years. Combined, the casinos employ 253 persons, two-thirds of whom are non-tribal members.

Mole Lake Bingo Hall is a class II casino located in Mole Lake. Facilities were renovated in 2004. Updates include improvements to the gaming facilities, redecoration throughout the casino, construction of a carport, and the addition of a full-service kitchen and restaurant. The tribe also owns the Mole Lake Casino. It is a class III facility with blackjack, video gaming, and slot machines. The resort includes 20 guest rooms and one restaurant. The casino is located in Mole Lake

Fisheries. The Mole Lake Band actively restocks lakes and streams located within reservation boundaries. Currently, two tribal employees are responsible for this task.

Construction. The tribe operates its own construction and maintenance crews. The crews employ 10 tribal members, and the tribe owns a front-end loader and backhoe. The construction crew participated in the construction of tribal casinos. The crews are responsible for general maintenance of tribal facilities.

Services and Retail. In 2004, the tribe opened a convenience store and gas station. The individually owned Mole Lake Smoke Shop is also located on the reservation. There are approximately25 individual vendors of wild rice

Tourism and Recreation. The Sokaogan Community operates Mole Lake Motel. Facilities include 20 hotel rooms and provide easy access to local swimming, golfing, gaming, fishing, and snowmobiling sites as well as hiking and mountain biking trails. The Mole Lake area features over 800 lakes, 82 streams, and 400,000 acres of public wilderness. Hotel guests may also receive coupons to the casino or bingo hall.

In 2003, the tribe received a grant from the Jeffries Family Foundation of Janesville, Wisconsin, to help preserve and maintain the historic 140-year-old Dinesen House. The log cabin, which is located on the reservation, has been recognized as an Endangered Property by the Wisconsin Trust for Historic Preservation. The cabin has had many purposes during its lifetime, including serving as a stopover site for military transport during the 1860s and as a post office. In 1873 the house was occupied by Wilhelm Dinesen. Dinesen was the father of Karen Blixen, a renowned Danish author who wrote under the name of Isak Dinesen. The Dinesen house has been nominated for the National Historic Registry for its historical architecture.

Along Highway 55 in the village of Mole Lake is an historical marker commemorating the Battle of Mole Lake in 1806. This battle with the Sioux resulted in the death of more than 500 tribal

TRI-WI-ml-124

TRI-WI-ml-123

warriors. The tribe hosts two annual powwows. Competition drumming, singing, and dancing draw a number participants, as do the numerous vendors.

INFRASTRUCTURE

Electricity. Electric services are available through regional providers, including Wisconsin Public Service.

Fuel. Individual homes use individual LP tanks for heating.

Water Supply. Water is supplied through individual wells or the two public wells located on the reservation. Individually owned septic tanks serve sewage purposes.

Transportation. An individually owned limousine service provides transportation to tribal casinos. Commercial air service is available in Rhinelander, 35 miles northwest of the reservation. A private airport is located in Crandon. UPS and FedEx both service the reservation area.

COMMUNITY FACILITIES AND SERVICES

The tribe maintains a community center.

Education. Elementary and secondary public schools are located in Crandon, approximately seven miles north of the reservation. The nearest college and technical school is located in Rhinelander, 36 miles northwest of the reservation.

Health Care. Basic health care is available on the reservation. The tribe and Indian Health Service work with the Soaokogn Chippewa Health Clinic to provide not only services, but educational and prevention programs like safety fairs, diabetes management, cancer awareness, and positive parenting. The clinic also puts out a newsletter each month through the Honoring Our Children Grant and Medicaid Outreach Program.

The tribe operates the Sokaogan Chippewa Domestic Violence Program. It offers crisis intervention, emergency assistance, legal advocacy, support groups, and other related services to Native women living in violent relationships.

ENVIRONMENTAL CONCERNS

In 2003, the Sokaogon Mole Lake Band of Lake Superior Chippewa and the Forest County Potawatomi Community successfully negotiated and purchased the 5,770-acre proposed mine site, ending a 30-year environmental controversy. The tribes were honored by the Wisconsin Stewardship Network for their action, which brought an end to the efforts to open the mine.

The tribe is actively involved in numerous projects to monitor, preserve, and restore ecological balance in the region. It participates in the fresh mussel survey conducted in part with the Ashland Fishery Resources Office, the government on display exhibit at the Mall of America, the FWS Memorandum of Agreement with Intertribal Bison Cooperative, and National Fishing ad Boating Week.

TRI-WI-ml-124 Mole Lake community sign
TRI-WI-ml-123 Mole Lake Motel in Crandon

neida

LOCATION AND LAND STATUS

The Oneida Reservation is located in northeastern Wisconsin along Duck Creek, west of the Great Fox River. The port city of Green Bay, Wisconsin, lies east of, and is contiguous with, the reservation's eastern border.

On February 3, 1838, the Treaty of Buffalo Creek (the Oneida Treaty) established the current Oneida Reservation of 65,436 acres. Over the next century, tribal lands were gradually forfeited or lost until only a few hundred acres remained. The strength of the Oneida Nation as a sovereign nation was greatly weakened by the loss of tribal lands. While the original boundaries of the reservation are still maintained and recognized, nontribal municipalities have been established within tribal lands, including the towns of Hobart and Oneida, and the counties of Outagamie and Brown.

Today the Oneida Reservation lands include approximately 17,500 acres (in a checkerboard pattern). Major Wisconsin cities near the reservation include Green Bay, five miles east; Appleton, 30 miles southwest; Oshkosh, 45 miles southwest; Sheboygan, 54 miles southeast; and Milwaukee, 113 miles southeast. Other local municipalities include Ashwaubenon, Howard, Pittsfield, Hobart, and Oneida, all of which have acreage located within the original reservation boundaries.

PHYSICAL DESCRIPTION

The Oneida Reservation contains approximately 12 square miles of land, 233 miles of streams, and over 12,000 acres of wetlands. The major use of these lands is for agricultural purposes.

CLIMATE

The reservation is situated within the Great Lakes Basin and experiences long, cold winters and warm, humid summers. The mean annual precipitation is 29 inches.

Oneida Reservation
Federal reservation
Oneida
Outagamie and Brown
counties, Wisconsin

Oneida Nation of Wisconsin
P.O. Box 365
Oneida, WI 54155
920-869-2214
920-869-4040 Fax
oneidanation.org
oneida-nsn.gov

Oneida

Total area *(BIA realty, 2004)*
6,645.93 acres

Total area *(Tribal source, 2004)*
17,500 acres

Tribally owned *(BIA realty, 2004)*
6,216.35 acres

Allotted/Individually owned
(BIA realty, 2004)
429.59 acres

Population *2000 census*
21,319

Tribal population
(Oneida Enrollment Office, 2005)
3,556

Tribal enrollment
(Oneida Enrollment Office, 2005)
15,412

Total labor force *2000 census*
11,833

Total labor force
(BIA labor report, 2001)
3,190

High school graduate or higher
2000 census
91.1%

Bachelor's degree or higher
2000 census
29.7%

Unemployment rate *2000 census*
2.8%

Unemployment rate
(Tribal source, 2004)
16%

Per capita income *2000 census*
$25,680

CULTURE AND HISTORY

The Oneidas' ancestral lands are located in present-day upstate New York. Oneida Creek and Oneida Lake were the principal areas where the Oneidas resided within their six million-acre homeland. The Oneidas belong to the Haudenosaunee, or Iroquois Confederacy. The Oneidas were one of the original five nations that formed the confederacy. The Mohawk, Cayuga, Onondaga, and Seneca tribes were the other four original nations, and the Tuscororas joined later. The Iroquois Confederacy is one of the world's oldest known democracies. Recent findings have encouraged some scholars to believe that the confederacy is at least 300 years older than previously thought. These theories have been supported by archeological, scientific, and oral history evidence. The Great Law of Peace (Kayanlakowa) of the Iroquois Confederacy served as the model for the U.S. Constitution.

The Oneidas encountered European explorers in 1609 in upstate New York. Europeans gradually colonized this region of New York from the mid-1600s on, and the Oneidas traded goods and made formal treaties with the colonists. When the Revolutionary War broke out, some member tribes of the Iroquois Confederacy were drawn into the conflict, including the Oneidas and the Mohawks. The Oneidas allied with the colonists, while the Mohawks supported the British. Following the war, the fledgling United States rewarded the Oneidas by expropriating their fertile homeland, which was sought by white farmers.

During the 1820s, a faction of the Oneidas voluntarily moved to Wisconsin. This group, known as the First Christian Party, was a group of Oneida tribal members who had been converted to Christianity. Under the direction of Eleazar Williams, an Episcopalian Mohawk preacher, and Jedidiah Morse, a Euro-American missionary, the group negotiated a plan with the federal government to relocate all New York Iroquois, as well as the Stockbridge-Munsees and the Brothertown, to Wisconsin. The Oneidas purchased eight million acres from the Menominee and Winnebago nations. These original lands were reduced to 500,000 acres by the U.S. Treaty with the Menominees in 1831. In 1838, the Oneida Reservation was reduced to 65,430 acres. By that time, 654 documented Oneida tribal members had relocated to Wisconsin from New York. A small group remained in New York, and another group moved to Ontario, Canada.

In 1845 the territory of Wisconsin requested that the tribe trade their Wisconsin lands for territory west of the Mississippi in order to open up Wisconsin to Euro-American settlers. The tribe refused to move. Tribal lands were eventually allotted under the 1887 Allotment Act into 1,527 parcels. By 1929, only a few hundred acres remained in tribal ownership due to fraud, tax, and mortgage foreclosures. Many Oneida tribal members were forced to leave the reservation and relocated to Green Bay and Milwaukee.

The mission of the Oneida Nation is to preserve its heritage through the seventh generation, provide housing, promote education, protect the land, preserve the environment, and provide for a quality of life where the Oneida people come together for the common good.

GOVERNMENT

The government of the Oneidas, after the move to Wisconsin, took several forms, but maintained their traditional chiefs system until the mid-twentieth century. The Oneida Nation accepted the provisions of the Indian Reorganization Act of 1934. The tribal constitution was ratified in 1936 and established a democratic form of government. The tribal government has developed the land acquisition plan, which serves to guide the tribe in its efforts to restore lost tribal lands. A business committee, composed of a chairperson, a vice-chairperson, a secretary, a treasurer, and five council members, serves as the elected governing body for

enrolled tribal members and is delegated to the general tribal council authority when the general tribal council is not in session. All enrolled tribal members age 21 and above make up the general tribal council. The business committee meets weekly, and the general tribal council meets semiannually.

The tribal government's organizational structure currently includes the compliance, development, enterprise, gaming, government services, land, and internal services divisions. The compliance division houses the tribe's apprentice, contract compliance, Indian preference, paralegal advocates, and vendor licensing programs. The development division houses the community development, economic development, engineering, GIS, industrial park, Oneida Nation farms, planning, public works, and zoning programs. The enterprise division houses the Oneida Small Business Development Center and retail programs. The gaming division houses bingo, slots, table games, accounting, customer relations, security, gift shop and mall, and sales and marketing programs. Government services include: education, environmental, health, Oneida Cultural Museum, Oneida Transit, parks and recreation, police, social, veteran programs, elder, and comprehensive health care. Internal services include continuous improvement, grants, human resources, management information, and mail center and printing programs.

The Oneida Police Department provides patrol services, a K-9 unit, and community service programs on the reservation. It is headquartered in a 22,000-square-foot facility and employs 29 people. Oneida officers are cross-deputized in both Brown and Outagamie counties.

BUSINESS CORPORATION

The Oneida Seven Generations Corporation (OSGC) promotes business and economic diversification on behalf of the Oneida Nation. This tribally chartered and owned organization serves as a holding company for tribal real estate assets and provides for the management of several business ventures of the tribe. The corporation strives to establish a source of long-term income sources for stockholders. Current projects of OSGC include the property management of several strip malls, an auto dealership, a manufacturing plant, a post office, and a medical center.

The Oneida Airport Hotel Corporation was chartered in 1985. The corporation manages the Radisson Hotel and Conference Center on the reservation, which offers 409 rooms, an indoor pool, whirlpool, sauna, fitness center, smoke shop, and three convention areas. It also hosts an upscale dining venue that offers traditional Oneida dishes, a buffet, and a lounge. The corporation includes the Three Clans Hospitality Consulting firm, which provides developmental consulting services to other Native American tribes and conducts market evaluations, operational evaluations and reviews, sales and marketing diagnostic services, front office operations, and housekeeping operations seminars.

In partnership with the San Manuel Band of Mission Indians of California, the Viejas Band of Kumeyaay Indians of California, and the Forest County Potawatomi Community of Wisconsin, the Oneidas have created Four Fires LLC, a Delaware corporation. The partnership's first venture was the largest economic collaboration ever for American Indian governments. The project was the $43 million, 13-story, 233-suite Residence Inn by Marriott-Capitol in Washington, D.C. The hotel is situated in a prime location in the city, near the Smithsonian's National Museum of the American Indian. Hospitality Partners of Bethesda, Maryland, will manage the newly constructed hotel.

ECONOMY

The Oneida Nation works diligently toward achieving its goal of self-sufficiency. It owns a number of enterprises in diverse indus-

TRI-WI-Oda-127

TRI-WI-Oda-126

TRI-WI-Oda-125

tries, all of which make great contributions to the tribal and local economies.

Government as Employer. With over 3,000 employees, the Nation serves as the second largest source of employment in Brown County. Approximately 48 percent of its workforce is tribal members. The majority of job opportunities are in the tribe's programs and non-gaming enterprises and the remainder are in the tribe's operations in the gaming industry.

Economic Development Projects. Recent projects of the tribe's development division include the development of a Residence Inn by Marriott in Washington, D.C., a travel mart in Oneida, and a Marriot Hotel in Sacramento, California. Future possibilities include the construction of an entertainment complex in New York State and a hotel/water park/resort in Wisconsin.

Agriculture and Livestock. The tribe owns the Oneida Community Integrated Food System (OCIFS) and its four food-related enterprises-the Oneida Nation Farm and Apple Orchard, Oneida Tsyunhehkwa Center and Cannery, Oneida Food Distribution Program and Oneida Pantry Emergency Network, and the Oneida Community Health Center. The aim of OCIFS is to provide employment opportunities, improve the health of tribal members, and educate the community on nutritional matters. It also aims to produce food for profit; and promote lower market prices. OCIFS participated in the development of a farmers market to create a venue for community members to sell their products. It also created the Oneida Falling Leaves 4-H Club in order to education young people about health and diet, small business entrepreneurship, agriculture, and family values.

Oneida Nations Farms manages 8,000 acres of tribal lands. About 4,500 acres are utilized for the production of field corn, soybeans, wheat, oats, and alfalfa hay for consumption by tribally owned livestock or for sale to local buyers. Another 3,500 acres are managed in conservation programs. A farm plan for the management of agricultural land use is in place for each parcel of lands. The tribe is exploring the possibilities of implementing agroforestry practices. The farm manages a 550-head Black Angus beef-feeding operation, with meat sales to tribal members, employees, tribal operations, and the general public. The tribe initiated a cow and calf grazing operation in fall of 2004. The herd of 95 head is intended to provide healthier meat to the beef market. The tribe's bison grazing operation includes 115 head. The grazing site features new corrals, water wells, and fencing. Bison meat is made available for ceremonial use and general sale. A public observation platform is under construction.

The tribally owned Oneida Apple Orchard includes 30 acres and 2,000 apple trees. An additional 10 acres produces squash, pumpkins, raspberries, and strawberries. The orchard offers pre-picked fruits for sale to the public and other orchards. It also offers clients the opportunity to pick their own fruit. An on-site store, the Orchard Retail Store, provides apples, apple cider,

fresh berries, apple chips, pie filling, jelly, applesauce, snack sticks, apple butter, and frozen beef or bison meat, as well as Native American produced items for sale.

Food packages and nutrition education services are available to eligible community households throughout the Oneida Food Distribution Program and the Oneida Pantry Emergency Network. The program provides services to households on the reservation, in the rural areas of Brown and Outagamie County, and the City of Green Bay. It also provides referrals for clients whose needs it is unable to meet.

The tribe operates the Oneida Tsyunhéhkwa Center, a certified organic agricultural community. This culturally-based program is located on 83 acres of land in Oneida. The focus of the center is self-sustainability and food security. Medicinal herb walks, fruit tree pruning, and gardening workshops are available to the public year round. The center manages 30 acres of organic crops of white corn, hay, pasture, fruits, and vegetables. Seedlings are grown in a greenhouse on the site and sold and distributed to the community. The center processes and sells free-range poultry and fresh eggs. Tours of the center are available to the public.

The center also offers a retail store. Located along State Highway 54, it sells health care products, vitamins and mineral supplements, spices, reading materials, herbs, and foods. It also serves as a source of information about the use of herbs and essential oils and will conduct research on personal health care issues.

The tribe operates The Cannery. This facility is located in Norbert Hill Center and provides community members with assistance in the processing of fruits and vegetables.

The Community Health Center dietitian is an important resource to the community. This representative provides educational workshops and literature to community members. The representative also serves as a dietary consultant to the OCIFS on issues of culturally appropriate and healthy foods.

The community health center dietitian provides nutritional information to community members and OCIFS system members with workshops and literature on how to improve and encourage a healthy lifestyle. The dietitian consults with OCIFS operations about providing culturally appropriate, healthy, clean fresh fruits, vegetables, and meats that are free of chemicals and antibiotics.

Forestry. In order to preserve forests and wetlands on tribal lands, the Oneida Nation does not participate in the commercial harvest of its timber. Native grasslands, indigenous trees, and shrubs protect topsoil and wildlife habitats, and improve water quality. They also assist in the production of edible nuts and fruits, as well as medicinal plants. Selective cutting will be utilized as trees mature in tribal forests.

TRI-WI-Oda-127 Oneida Nation Farms
TRI-WI-Oda-126 Tribal office building
TRI-WI-Oda-125 Oneida Nation Farms sign

Oneida

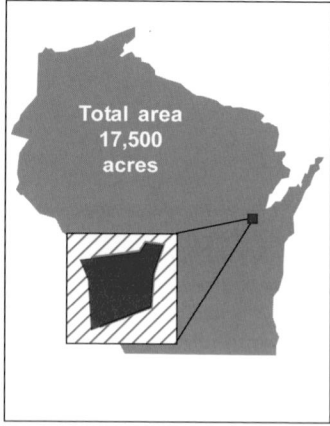

Total area
17,500
acres

ENVIRONMENTAL CONCERNS

The tribe's environmental programs include health and industrial safety, environmental quality, eco-services, and conservation. The environmental health and safety area department provides services to protect and preserve tribal lands.

Gaming. The Oneida Nation owns and operates the following gaming operations within reservation boundaries: Oneida Casino, the Irene Moore Activity Center (IMAC) Bingo and Casino, and the Oneida Mason Street Casino. Three of the retail division's convenience stores also have small slot machine areas attached to them.

The Oneida Casino is located in Green Bay. It offers over 929 slots/VLTs, 28 table games, and 6 entertainment venues. The Radisson Hotel and Conference Center is adjacent to the Oneida Casino. IMAC Bingo and Casino Hall offers 858 bingo seats and a nonsmoking area as well. It features opportunities to wager on slots as well as horse, harness, and greyhound races. The Mason Street Casino offers the opportunity to play slots and table games. This casino also offers bar service and a smoke shop outlet.

Revenue earned from the tribe's gaming facilities has enabled the Oneidas to enhance tribal programs and services and contribute to local communities as well. The tribe contributed to the renovation of the historic Lambeau Field in Green Bay, which is the home of the Green Bay Packers professional football team. Sponsorship included naming a gate in honor of the Oneida Nation and including the tribe's name on scoreboards, commercials, Oneida gate tickets, directional panels, and more.

Manufacturing. The tribe owns Oneida Printing. This business offers electronic prepress, five presses, and Purup Escofot DPX computer services. It also has binding capabilities.

Industrial Parks. The Nation owns three properties zoned for industrial use. The Seven Generations Corporation leases the lands and manages development at the sites. The Oneida Business Park is located on about 50 acres. The Oneida Little Bear Development Center, U.S. Post Office, and a warehouse are located at the park. The infrastructure at the park includes a storm water management system, water, sewer, electricity, gas, and fiber-optic connections. Another industrial site is located on 162 acres of land situated within the original reservation boundaries. A foreign trade zone is proposed for the area, which is near the Austin Straubel Airport.

Services/Retail. Oneida Retail Enterprise is a chain of tribally owned stores. The enterprise includes four One Stop convenience stores and gas stations, four smoke shops, and one gift shop. An additional convenience store is in the developmental stage.

Banks. The Oneida Nation is the sole owner of Baybank, a full service institution located on tribally owned lands. Baybank is situated outside of the original external boundaries of the Oneida Reservation. It was initially constructed in 1994 and the tribe gained ownership in 2004.

Tourism and Recreation. The Oneida Nation Communications Department offers tours of the reservation, facilitates powwow exhibits, and organizes demonstrations and presentations for those interested in visiting or learning more about the Nation. Tour features include visits to the Oneida Museum, Salt Pork Avenue, Parish Hall, Buffalo Farm, Oneida Nations Farm, and Industrial Park. Events and activities include the Oneida Arts Concert Series, Pavilion Nights Concerts, events at the Duck Creek Community Center, and a Thanksgiving Address. There are also basket, cornhusk doll, water drum, flute, and moccasin making demonstrations, and indigenous plants, herbs, and salves classes.

The Oneida Nations Arts Program sponsors the Annual Oneida Summer House Party Series in June. The event features open house activities at the Duck Creek Community Theatre, Oneida Nation Museum, Elderly Service Complex, and Oneida Nations

Farms. The arts program also coordinates dance, musical arts, and art activities on the reservation. It hosts the annual Lahnetahawi Sculpture Symposium.

INFRASTRUCTURE

State Roads 29 and 54, U.S. 41, and I-43 provide access to the reservation. State Road 54 bisects tribal lands and passes through the town of Oneida. State Road 29 borders the northern boundary of the reservation while U.S. 41 runs parallel to the eastern boundary.

Electricity. The Wisconsin Public Service Corporation provides electricity and natural gas service.

Water Supply. The Oneida Utilities Department provides water and sewer service to many of the Nation's homes and businesses located on the reservation. The Green Bay Metropolitan Sewer District provides wastewater management services. Homes in the more rural areas of the reservation are serviced by individual wells and septic systems.

Transportation. The tribe operates an on-reservation transit system. Commercial passenger and air cargo services are available through Austin Straubel International Airport. The tribe's Radisson Inn is conveniently located nearby. Greyhound bus service is available in Green Bay (five miles east). Major truck shipping operators, including Schneider National, are available in Green Bay. Express postal service is also available in Green Bay. State-of-the-art shipping and port facilities are available through the Port of Green Bay.

COMMUNITY FACILITIES AND SERVICES

The Oneida Nation has approximately 96 buildings that house its numerous tribal programs and services. The tribe maintains the Oneida Memorial Building, commonly known as the Civic Center. Originally home to the youth recreation program, the center has also housed the health center, business committee offices, and the social services department during the early times of the Nation's government.

The Nation operates the Oneida Commission on Aging which provides meals, referrals, loan closet, an employment volunteer program, certified nursing assistant training, senior employment training, an Alzheimer's support group, outreach, home assistance, respite care, advocacy, activities, special events, a fitness center, transportation, and foster grandparent and senior companion programs.

Tribal family services include programs addressing domestic abuse, crisis respite, employee assistance, Indian Child Welfare Act, and counseling. The Kids for Composting campaign is active on the reservation. Initiated at the Oneida Elementary School, the program involves youth in composting, gardening, and community activities.

Education. The Nation operates the Oneida Nation School System, which includes the Oneida Nation Elementary School and the Oneida Nation High School. The elementary school serves 244 students, and the high school serves about 125 students. The school system is supported by the BIA and is considered a BIA district. The Nation also operates Head Start and daycare programs on the reservation. Many of the reservation's school-age children are bussed to public school districts.

The Nation's education department provides a career center, library, and programs in higher education, early childhood development, job training partnership, and youth educational services. The Nation's language program provides instruction in the indigenous language. The program uses the master-apprentice model of language immersion.

The University of Wisconsin maintains a branch campus in Green Bay, and the Northeast Wisconsin Technical College is located within the reservation's original boundaries. The College of Menominee has a branch located within the reservation's boundaries.

Health Care. The Nation provides health, dental, optometric, and long- and short-term disability and life insurance plans for tribal employees. Tribal members may receive health services through the Oneida Community Health Center, Anna John Nursing Home, occupational health services, and environmental health services. The tribal health services department also provides comprehensive public health, dental, optical, ambulatory, ancillary, AODA/mental health, and social services programs. Inpatient and major medical services are available in the Green Bay area.

Red Cliff

LOCATION AND LAND STATUS
The Red Cliff Reservation spans the southern shore of Lake Superior, about 90 miles east of Superior, Wisconsin. The reservation is approximately one mile wide and 14 miles long. It lies in the northernmost region of the state.

The tribe is currently attempting to reacquire more of its original lands through the Red Cliff Land Recovery Project. The project works with nontribal landowners, timber companies, and state and local governments to ensure that lands formerly belonging to the tribe are currently protected and preserved. In the meantime, the project aims to reacquire these lands through donations, purchases, and conservation easements.

PHYSICAL DESCRIPTION
The Apostle Islands National Lakeshore Park comprises 11 percent of the tribal land base. There are over 46 miles of streams and rivers on the reservation and over 22 miles of Lake Superior's shoreline. Approximately 93 percent of the reservation is densely forested with second-growth conifers, aspen, and other hardwoods. Five percent of the land is cleared, and less than two percent is wetland.

CULTURE AND HISTORY
The Anishinabe Nation, known as the Chippewas or Ojibwes, is one of the largest Native American nations in North America. The Anishinabes once inhabited regions north of the Great Lakes region. As they migrated along the St. Lawrence Seaway, the Nation began to disperse into separate bands. The Red Cliff Band is descended from the Madeline Island Chippewa Tribe.

Ancestral lands of the Chippewas once extended along both shores of Lake Superior and west to the Turtle Mountains in North Dakota. Chief Herny Buffalo of the Red Cliff Band signed the La Pointe Treaty of 1854, confining the band to its current reservation. The treaty also established the boundaries for five other Chippewa reservations throughout Wisconsin. The Red Cliff Reservation is commonly referred to as the hub of the Lake Superior Chippewa Indian tribes.

The Red Cliff Band maintains strong connections with Lake Superior and the surrounding region. The land's cultural and spiritual significance is great, and tribal members remain conscientious of these relationships. The tribe has declared the lake a sacred site.

GOVERNMENT
The tribe is organized under the 1934 Indian Reorganization Act. The reservation is governed by a nine-member elected tribal council. Officers include a chairperson, a vice-chairperson, a secretary, and a treasurer. Each council member serves a two-year term. The Self-Determination and Education Assistance Act of 1975 enabled the tribal council to expand since that time and to assume a considerable amount of new roles and responsibilities over tribal governance.

The Red Cliff Reservation's tribal government administers approximately 40 programs, grants, and contracts. Programs include zoning, Head Start, community health, treaty and natural resources, Indian Health Service, and BIA. Other departments include education, enrollment, fish hatchery, gaming, historic preservation, and social services. The tribe maintains a police department, a tribal court, and a prosecutor's office.

ECONOMY
The gaming, fishing, forestry, and tourism industries support the tribe's economy and provide for the greatest sources of employment to tribal members.

Government as Employer. The tribal government employs 120 people. It is the largest single employer in Bayfield County.

Economic Development Projects. The Red Cliff Band is a member of the USDA Empowerment Zone Champion Community Program. The program's goals are to provide structure and guidance in the tribe's community and economic development strategies. Projected developments include a new casino, a conference center, marina expansion, hotel development, and a new fish-processing facility.

Construction on the reservation is booming. Since 2003 a $5.5 million chemical wastewater treatment facility has been completed and a 18-site residential subdivision has begun construction. Shortly construction will start on another 14-site subdivision. The fishponds for the University of Wisconsin-Superior's new Aquaculture Demonstration Facility on the reservation have been completed and the administration building should be finished in 2005. Also in 2005 the tribe is anticipating the completion of the 18-acre business park 15,000 square foot home manufacturing plant they built with a HUD-Rural Housing and Economic Development grant. The first home will be manufactured in the plant in March 2006.

Agriculture and Livestock. In 2004 the tribe began a project called the Red Cliff Community Garden. This garden is run as a co-op and its mission is to provide inexpensive, healthy food for the community. The concept for the project is to set it up similar to an old farmstead. With this goal in mind, value-added food processing will be done at a site set aside in the business park. Individual tribal members practice self-sufficient farming on a small scale.

Red Cliff Reservation
Federal reservation
Chippewa/Ojibwe
Bayfield County, Wisconsin

Red Cliff Band of Lake Superior
  Chippewa Indians
  of Wisconsin
88385 Pike Road, Hwy. 13
Bayfield, WI 54814
715-779-3700
715-779-3704 Fax

Total area *(BIA realty, 2004)*
8,062.35 acres

Total area *(Tribal source, 2004)*
14,233 acres

Tribally owned *(BIA realty, 2004)*
6,280.61 acres

Tribally owned *(Tribal source, 2004)*
4,087 acres

Federal trust *(BIA realty, 2004)*
14.65 acres

Allotted/Individually owned
(BIA realty, 2004)
1,767.08 acres

Population *2000 census*
1,078

Tribal enrollment
(BIA labor report, 2001)
4,064

Total labor force *2000 census*
506

Total labor force
(Tribal source, 2004)
1,267

Red Cliff

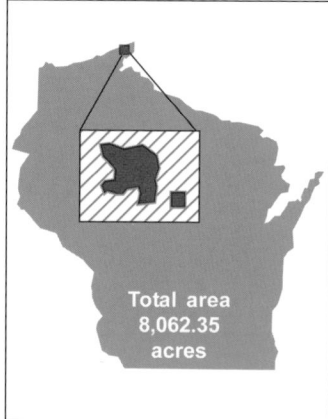

Total area
8,062.35
acres

High school graduate or higher
2000 census
76.9%

Bachelor's degree or higher
2000 census
9.4%

Unemployment rate *2000 census*
18.2%

Unemployment rate
(BIA labor report, 2001)
42%

Per capita income *2000 census*
$9,497

Forestry. The BIA manages approximately 7,000 acres of commercial forest on the reservation. The tribe is negotiating an agreement with the U.S. Forest Service, which would allow the tribe to harvest forest products on a subsistence basis and, in return, the tribe would be responsible for bushing and trail maintenance.

Gaming. The Isle Vista Casino and Entertainment Center offers class III gaming activities. The center opened in 1982 with a bingo hall, a bar-restaurant, and bowling lanes. Facilities were expanded in 1992. The casino now offers 230 slots, four table games, and 150 bingo seats. There is also one restaurant, a lounge, and a 4,000-square-foot convention center. The casino has 100 employees. Annual income from these operations totals about $3.6 million. Revenues are used to fund tribal services. In addition to gaming activities, the casino often hosts entertainment acts, annual powwows, and conferences. The Mural of Chippewa Life featured at the casino serves as both interior design and educational media.

The Red Cliff Band will begin construction on a new casino in May 2005. This 22,000 square foot facility will be located on the shores of Lake Superior and will include amenities such as 10,000 square foot convention center, a 65-room hotel, and an indoor pool. This project is projected to cost $31 million by its completion. On Memorial Day 2006, when the grand opening is expected to happen, it will employ over 200 people.

Adjacent to the casino is a marina, which the tribe plans to expand in phases. The first phase is scheduled to be completed at the same time as the casino for a total cost of $3 million. At that point the marina will provide 110 transient and permanent mooring slips. The next phases for the marina will be scheduled over a series of years and will add 200 more slips, commercial and charter fishing dockage, and deep-water cruise vessel moorage.

Fisheries. The fishing industry is the primary source of employment on the Red Cliff Reservation through direct employment in fisheries and through individual contracts. The tribe operates the Red Cliff Tribal Hatchery which raises brook trout and walleye used to restock Lake Superior and area streams. It manages three one-acre, manmade ponds for raising walleyes. The hatchery maintains the only brood stock for the Lake Nipigon strain of coaster brook trout in the United States. Facilities at the hatchery include an incubation area, fry tanks, a laboratory, and 20 large raceways for fingerlings and brood stockfish. It has the capacity to incubate over 8,000,000 walleye eggs. It releases several hundred thousand fish annually. Annual production varies, but capacity is estimated to be 100,000 walleye fingerlings, 1,000,000 walleye fry, 100,000 yearling lake trout, and 500,000 whitefish fingerlings. Also located on the reservation, The Buffalo Bay Fish Company employs four full-time workers. The company provides income to tribal fishermen by purchasing their daily catches, then filleting them and shipping them to midwestern markets.

Services and Retail. The reservation contains numerous convenience stores, gas stations, and grocery stores. Ojibway Trading Post sells locally made Native American arts and crafts, and Peterson's Foods and Smoke Shop sells locally caught lake trout and whitefish, as well as general provisions.

Media and Communications. The tribe operates the Red Cliff Information Technology Department, the Red Cliff News newspaper, and a local access cable TV program. The tribe offers the *Red Cliff News*, a monthly newspaper, free of charge.

Tourism and Recreation. The reservation is located along the south shore of the Lake Superior shoreline, an area that attracts a large number of summer visitors. It is the gateway to the Apostle Islands National Lakeshore, famous for its many lighthouses and recreational opportunities. Further, the Red Cliff Reservation has been identified as containing two of "the nation's ten most pristine beaches-Sand Bay and Raspberry Bay. In addition to its casino and marina, the tribe operates the Point Detour Campground, which offers walking and cross-country trails, and facilities for winter sports.

The tribe is host to a number of seasonal events that attract tourists. It hosts Winterfest, a celebration marking the season and including activities such as dog sledding. It hosts the Red Cliff Traditional Powwow to commemorate the Fourth of July, and the Inland Sea Symposium, which offers environmental and educational workshops on the Great Lakes. The tribe also hosts the Culture Days Powwow at the end of July. The Red Cliff Fish Hatchery conducts tours for the public.

INFRASTRUCTURE

State Highway 13 runs directly through the reservation. It intersects U.S. Highway 2 near Ashland approximately 20 miles south of the reservation and again near Superior/Duluth 80 miles to the west.

Electricity. Northern State Power and the Bayfield Electric Cooperative provide power to the area.

Fuel. Northern State Power furnishes natural gas service to the reservation.

Water Supply. Red Cliff Water and Sewage System provides water and sewage services. Seven separate wells across the reservation supply drinking water. The community water supply and distribution system recently underwent a major upgrade, and a new 400,000-gallon water storage tank was built. A new chemical wastewater treatment facility was completed in August 2003. A major upgrade of all tribal lift-stations is under construction.

Transportation. The marina and the Buffalo Bay Fishing Company provide commercial access to Lake Superior and beyond. Local bus services are available via Bay Area Rural Transport. Commercial air services are available in Ashland, approximately 21 miles away. UPS and FedEx service the reservation area.

COMMUNITY FACILITIES AND SERVICES

The tribal community center provides cultural and recreational activities, drug and alcohol prevention training, and physical fitness facilities. The tribe offers an elders center. The center provides meals and activities for tribal and non-tribal members.

Education. The Red Cliff Early Childhood Center provides child care, Head Start, and other services to children living on the reservation. In 2000, the center received an Early Head Start Demonstration Grant to develop a project for working with fathers of children enrolled in the center's on-site and home-based pro-

TRI-WI-026 Tribally-owned marina

grams. The program's goal is to provide education and opportunities to engage fathers in the early education of their children and to integrate cultural elements into the home and learning environments of participating families. Approximately 100 families have been a part of the project. The Red Cliff project was the only Native American community to receive a grant.

The Red Cliff Ojibwe Language Camp is in its third year of operation. An annual summer camp, the program is cosponsored by the tribe and the University of Wisconsin Stevens Point Department of Multicultural Affairs. The program offers instructional workshops in the indigenous language for tribal youth and young adults.

Health Care. The Red Cliff Community Health Center is located on the reservation and is operated by the tribe. This clinic is the only medical facility in Bayfield County. In 2004 the clinic also began providing dental services. The tribe charted new territory when this clinic became the first Indian health clinic in the nation to receive joint determination and offer services Indians and non-Indians alike.

Hospital services are also available in Ashland, 21 miles away. The tribe currently provides its employees with medical and dental insurance through the Tribal Atrium Health Plan and Tribal CBSA Dental Insurance Plan. Operation Walking Shield provides free medical and dental services to tribal members. The

program is a mobile service sponsored by U.S. military forces. The program visits Native American reservations throughout the country.

ENVIRONMENTAL CONCERNS
The tribe's primary concern is restoring and preserving Lake Superior's water quality, plant life, fish stock, and indigenous species populations. The tribe also wants to see the removal and proper disposal of chemical barrels that have been dumped in the lake. The tribe is seeking assistance from the U.S. EPA, the Department of Defense, and other federal agencies to help meet these goals. Funds are being requested through the Clean Water Action Plan of the Clean Water Act, Section 106. The tribe has received funds to develop water quality standards. In cooperation with the U.S. EPA, wellhead protection areas have been identified. Wellhead protection areas include a system of water quality monitoring, educational programs, regulation of land use and zoning, identification of recharge areas, supervised well abandonment, and determination of future well sites. The tribe also participates in Lake Superior preservation programs such as the Binational Program and the Great Lakes Water Quality Agreement.

The tribe participates in the Circle of Flight restoration program. Projects include reseeding wild rice beds, restoring wetlands, managing beaver populations, and controlling nonindigenous plants.

St. Croix Chippewa

LOCATION AND LAND STATUS
A proclamation issued by the secretary of the interior established the St. Croix Chippewa Reservation on November 28, 1938. The reservation consists of a noncontiguous parcel of land base and 11 separate reservation communities scattered throughout three counties in northwestern Wisconsin. According to the tribe, land held in trust for the tribe amounts to 2,125.98 acres and the total reservation land base consists of 4,689.35 acres.

PHYSICAL DESCRIPTION
The St. Croix Reservation is covered by a large portion of wooded lands with open spaces dotted with swamps and marshes, flat lands with shallow lakes, pitted outwashes, and wetland areas created by receding glaciers.

CLIMATE
The average temperature is 41.4°F with an annual precipitation of 33 inches.

CULTURE AND HISTORY
The St. Croix Chippewa Indians of Wisconsin have lived in what is present-day Wisconsin for centuries. They were federally recognized in 1938. The original reservation covered 3,145 acres. Some communities of St. Croix Chippewas are located in east-central Minnesota in Pine County.

GOVERNMENT
The tribe's council consists of five members elected every two years in June by the tribal membership. The St. Croix membership adopted a democratic form of government under the provisions of the Indian Reorganization Act of 1934. Their constitution was adopted on August 29, 1942, and the Secretary of the Interior approved it in November of that year. The government is

responsible for providing social services and for fostering economic development throughout several counties. The St. Croix tribal government has some 30 departments with 384 employees covering such activities as the tribal police, the volunteer fire department and first responders, tribal roads and road maintenance, environmental protection, social services, elderly services, Indian child welfare, historic preservation, community handyman and housekeepers, health, safety, land, planning and development, courts, natural resources and conservation, youth and T.R.A.I.L.S., commodity foods, and tribal enterprises. Administrative departments perform such functions as enrollment, per capita benefits, employee benefits, accounting, human resources, public relations, and procurement. The St. Croix Chippewa Housing Authority, although not a tribal government department, is run by a board of commissioners appointed by the tribal council.

ECONOMY
The St. Croix tribe maintains a diverse economic portfolio. It is active in the gaming and retail industries and plans to enter the arena of energy production. Tribal government programs are supported in part by federal funding. Tribal enterprises include a fishery, casinos and hotels, a lumber company, a supermarket, real estate, a convenience store, a check-cashing service, a travel agency, a construction company, a bingo facility, and a clothing manufacturer.

Government as Employer. The St. Croix Tribe is the largest source of employment in Burnett County, and second largest in Barron County. It employs almost 1,700 individuals. Tribal enterprises employ 1,168 full-time employees and 117 part-time employees.

**St. Croix Chippewa
Reservation**
Federal reservation
Chippewa
**Barron, Burnett, and Polk
counties, Wisconsin**

St. Croix Chippewa Indians
of Wisconsin
St. Croix Tribal Center
24663 Angeline Avenue
Webster, WI 54893
715-349-2195
715-349-5768 Fax

St. Croix Chippewa

Total area *(BIA realty, 2004)*
2,081.54 acres

Total area *(Tribal source, 2004)*
4,689.35 acres

Federal trust *(Tribal source, 2004)*
2,125.98 acres

Tribally owned *(BIA realty, 2004)*
2,081.54 acres

Other *(Tribal source, 2004)*
80.62 acres

Population *2000 census*
1,282

Population *(Tribal source, 2004)*
2,648

Total labor force *2000 census*
268

Total labor force
(Tribal source, 2004)
1,695

High school graduate or higher
2000 census
64.5%

Bachelor's degree or higher
2000 census
8%

Unemployment rate *2000 census*
8.2%

Unemployment *(Tribal source, 2004)*
29%

Per capita income *2000 census*
$11,378

Economic Development Projects. In 2004 the tribe's planning and development department began working toward the construction and operation of three small power plants to be located on the reservation. The first is a 40- to 45-megawatt natural gas- and diesel-fired peaking facility. Although there are still major issues to be resolved, a site and a technology type have been selected. To help ensure a secure future for the plants, a strategic alliance has been developed with a major equipment manufacturer and a large power provider to facilitate purchase of the electricity through a long-term (20-year) commitment or power purchase agreement from one of the following: a large investor-owned utility, a large generation and transmission cooperative, or municipal providers (aggregators) that supply electrical power to the area. To this end the tribe is negotiating with numerous utilities.

The tribe has also received a U.S. Department of Energy grant to study the feasibility of a 3- to 8-megawatt renewable biomass-fired plant using a combination of fuel types consisting of local logging residues, mill wastes, and the eventual cultivation of fast-growing hybrid poplar trees for the facility. The study will be completed in early 2005. Plant site(s) and technology have been located, and the tribe is working with area fuel suppliers (loggers and mill operators) to establish a sustainable and reliable fuel source. The study also looks into the amount of land needed to cultivate enough hybrid trees to fuel the plant.

Agriculture and Livestock. Tribal history suggests that the entire 54 acres of Spring Lake in Washburn County was once covered by wild rice stands. In the 1960s, the stands were devastated when the state dammed the lake's natural outlet. Approximately 10 acres of the lake are now home to wild rice stands.

In 2000, the tribe, together with DNR and the Mosinee Paper Corporation, restored the original outlet and filled the constructed ditch in order to restore the original water circulation patterns. In efforts to restore wild rice production on the lake, the tribe is utilizing chemical treatments to reduce non-indigenous aquatic plant populations.

In 2002-2003, aquatic plant surveys were conducted for Spring Lake, and results indicated that many other plants that compete for space with the lake's wild rice bed had taken over a significant portion of the lake. In fall 2003 and spring 2004, 2-4-D herbicide was used to treat these invasive species. The results were positive based on continued lake-monitoring studies. In the fall of 2004, wild reseeding efforts were undertaken and will continue into 2006 annually. The tribe will continue to monitor the lake to determine the increase or expansion of the wild rice beds and to check for invasive aquatic plant life. The tribal natural resource department, with assistance from the USDA Natural Resources Conservation Service, has been spearheading the project to restore the wild rice beds to their former abundance. The tribe also plans to conduct a waterfowl spring migrating and nesting survey on Spring Lake to establish baseline data to compare to waterfowl use after the wild rice is reestablished.

Gaming. The tribe's major gaming enterprise is the St. Croix Casino which is in Turtle Lake, Wisconsin. The 165,000-square-foot complex employs about 1,200 people and offers 1,000 slot machines, 18 gaming tables, a theater/auditorium, multiple food service areas, and a gift shop. The St. Croix Hotel has 200 rooms and is one and one-half blocks away. The tribe's smaller operation is the Hole in the Wall Casino and Hotel. It is located in Danbury, the northernmost reservation community. The 30,000-square-foot facility has about 325 employees and houses 327 slot machines and 12 gaming tables.

Fisheries. The St. Croix Waters Fishery grows yellow perch and hybrid striped bass from fingerling size to maturity and then processes the fish for the market. The 165,000-square-foot state-of-the-art aquaculture facility has indoor tanks that recirculate and clean 2.2 million gallons of water at any time using limited water resources. This technology claims up to 96 percent of the water for reuse while removing all waste by-products. The waste by-products are sold as fertilizer for area farm fields. It is anticipated that in early 2005 the fishery will be at full production capacity of up to 1.75 million pounds of fish per year. The facility currently employs 35 people.

Construction. The St. Croix Ojibwe Construction Company has 40 employees and provides minor road, residential, light commercial and industrial construction services to the reservation area. The company also provides water and wastewater utilities.

Forestry. The tribe owns and operates the St. Croix Lumber Company near Webster, Wisconsin. The full-service lumberyard has approximately 10 employees, and it serves the local area and the tribe's construction company.

Manufacturing. In 2004 the tribe began developing and marketing its own line of clothing through their company, St. Croix Creations. Rez Wear™ will be manufactured and marketed out of the Big Round Lake reservation community in Polk County, and it is expected to hire about 20 employees.

Real Estate/Commercial Development. The Southwinds Professional Building was completed in 2004. The 20,000-square-foot structure is located just north of Siren, Wisconsin. The building is already 50 percent leased to a variety of businesses, including a gift shop, a thrift store, the St. Croix tribal travel agency, a Chinese restaurant, Chippewa Check Services, and an employer benefits operation.

Services and Retail. The Little Turtle Hertel Express, located in the reservation community of Big Sand Lake, midway between Spooner and Siren, is the tribe's 24-hour full-service convenience store. It sells fuel (gasoline and diesel), discount tobacco products, food, and has 99 reel and video slot machines. The tribe also owns and operates Four Winds Market, a full-service grocery and deli operation located in Siren adjacent to the reservation. The grocery store has 40 employees and is the only full-service grocery, produce, and meat market in Siren, Wisconsin.

Tourism and Recreation. The tribe is a sponsor and investor in the Forts Folle Avoine Historic Park near Danbury, close to Yellow Lake. The park contains two outdoor amphitheaters for a variety of events and productions, a museum, a gift shop, a restaurant and two archeologically correct reconstructions of fur-trade wintering posts circa 1802. The posts are located on their exact locations along with a replicated Ojibwe village complete with third-party interpreters. The historic park provides a reenactment of the Indian-European history of the early Wisconsin fur trade. The park is open from early summer to late fall and for special events throughout the year.

The tribe also holds its annual Wild Rice Powwow in October. The powwow is a celebration of the tribal area's annual wild rice harvest. The event hosts competitive traditional and fancy dancers from around the country. It has a traditional feast to celebrate the harvest with wild rice and other tribal foods. The tribe elects a Wild Rice Princess and Junior Princess for the event. There is also a Brave and Junior Brave contest. The powwow is open to the public and is held at the Zaamaadj Arena and Powwow Grounds in Danbury, Wisconsin, adjacent to the Hole in the Wall Casino and Hotel.

INFRASTRUCTURE

Electricity. Because the reservation is scattered over a three-county area, electrical power comes from a variety of sources. Dairyland Power Cooperative, located in La Crosse, Wisconsin, is the major parent provider cooperative for the area. Local rural electric cooperatives that are under the Dairyland umbrella provide most of the reservation's power. Polk/Burnett Electric Cooperative, headquartered in Centuria, Wisconsin, serves five of the 11 reservation communities; Barron Electric Cooperative, headquartered in Barron, Wisconsin, serves three of the reservation areas; a small family-owned utility, Northwest Electric Company of Grantsburg, Wisconsin, serves two communities; and a municipal provider in Turtle Lake, Wisconsin, serves one community. The large Xcel Energy Company located in St. Paul, Minnesota, and Minnesota Power and Great River Electric also supply power to the area.

The tribe is in the process of developing three small power-generating facilities. Two will use renewable area biomass for fuel and the third, a peaking facility, will use natural gas and diesel for fuel.

Fuel. WE Energies of Milwaukee provides natural gas to four of the reservation's communities: Balsam Lake, Big Sand Lake, Danbury, and Turtle Lake. Individual local vendors supply fuel oil, which is used mainly for space heating and some water heating on the reservation, primarily in residential units.

Also, each year during late summer the tribe negotiates a "pre-buy agreement" for tribal members and tribal operations (businesses and governmental facilities) to purchase liquid propane throughout the coming year. The pre-buy locks in a price, which is usually determined when demand is low and therefore prices are generally low. The tribe usually secures four or five bids from the larger providers in the region.

Water Supply. The St. Croix Ojibwe Construction Company provides water and wastewater services to the reservation communities. Currently there are two major community water systems and a wastewater system that will begin construction in spring 2005. The plans are to provide community water and sewer service to the four major St. Croix Reservation communities (Big Sand Lake, Big Round Lake, Danbury, and Maple Plains) by 2010. The proposed Danbury systems will serve both the reservation and nontribal communities, and construction is expected to begin in 2006.

Transportation. The St. Croix Reservation, located in the far northwestern Wisconsin counties of Barron, Burnett, and Polk, is a scattered checkerboard reservation with its eastern boundary being U.S. Highway 53, which is a four-lane divided highway linking northwestern Wisconsin with the interstate highway system that traverses northwestern Wisconsin and the rest of the state. On the west, State Highway 35 runs from the furthest north reservation community to the furthest south community of Big Round Lake in Polk County. U.S. Highway 8 is the southern boundary access to the St. Croix Reservation, running east-west to highways 53 and 35, respectively. State highways 48, 70, and 77 traverse the reservation communities east to west from highways 53 and 35, respectively. North and south connections to access the reservation include Burnett and Barron County Trunk H, Burnett County Road X, and Polk County Road E. Numerous township and tribal roadways make up the balance of the tribal access roads.

There are local airports in Siren and Shell Lake, Wisconsin, 15 and 5 miles away respectively. A regional airport located in Hayward, Wisconsin, is 45 miles to the north and east of the nearest St. Croix Reservation community. The nearest international airports are in Duluth and Minneapolis/St. Paul, Minnesota, 60 and 95 miles, respectively, from the nearest reservation community.

There is no bus or rail service in the immediate area. The nearest bus transportation in the area, outside of charter bus service at two of the reservation communities (Danbury and Turtle Lake), is in Rice Lake, Wisconsin, which is 15 miles to the south and east

of the nearest reservation community, in Duluth and the Twin Cities in Minnesota, and in Eau Claire, Wisconsin, 50 miles to the south.

The Soo Rail Line traverses the region from east to west, but the closest it comes to reservation lands is 15 miles away. Common carrier trucking firms run all of the major roads, and all reservation areas have on-site parcel pickup and delivery service from a variety of vendors.

COMMUNITY FACILITIES AND SERVICES

St. Croix tribal community facilities in or near Big Sand Lake include the St. Croix tribal government center, the tribal police and volunteer fire department, a maintenance garage, a conservation garage and hatchery facility, the St. Croix tribal hall, a clinic, an emergency youth shelter, an environmental protection building, and Chippewa housing authority offices.

Additional facilities include community water systems and well houses in Big Sand Lake and Maple Plains; elderly feeding sites in Big Sand Lake and Big Round Lake; a Head Start building in West Hertel; community centers in Big Round Lake, Maple Plains, and Danbury; and a satellite clinic in Big Round Lake.

Community services include community health care, tribal health insurance benefits to unemployed tribal members, housing assistance, youth programs, respite care to troubled youth and domestic violence victims, police and fire protection, environmental protection, community water and sewer service, road maintenance (patrol grading, snow plowing, etc.), senior care and meal programs, social services, financial services, transportation services, employment services, education services, community and economic development services, fuel assistance service, and a variety of other smaller services from assisting seniors with housekeeping to providing firewood in the winter months.

Education. Because of the reservation's scattered nature in a three-county area, St. Croix tribal students attend school in a number of school districts, including, Spooner, Shell Lake, Unity, Cumberland, Webster, Grantsburg, Siren, Turtle Lake, and Rice Lake.

Postsecondary schools in and around the area that tribal students attend include the Wisconsin Indianhead Technical College with its numerous campuses scattered throughout northwestern Wisconsin; the University of Wisconsin campuses in Rice Lake, Superior, Eau Claire, River Falls, and Menomonie; and Northland College in Ashland, Wisconsin.

Health Care. The St. Croix Tribal Health Department provides an array of services. The clinic originally shared space in the government center building. A new facility located next to the government center was completed in the summer of 2000. The medical clinic staff provides comprehensive health care to the community ranging from infancy to elders. The dental clinic staff-consisting of a dentist, a dental hygienist, a chair-side dental assistant, and a receptionist-provides treatment using modern equipment and techniques. The community health nurse office and diabetes educator provide community outreach to the various reservation sites to promote and maintain health with an emphasis on prevention of illness, which is accomplished through teaching, counseling, demonstrations, screenings, observations, and early illness intervention.

The optical department has a full-time optician, and an optometrist is available two days a week. The clinic provides comprehensive optometry, including treating and managing ocular pathology. The mental health/AODA clinic assists clients with alcohol and drug assessments and driver's safety plans, and it provides alcohol and other drug abuse information and education.

St. Croix Chippewa

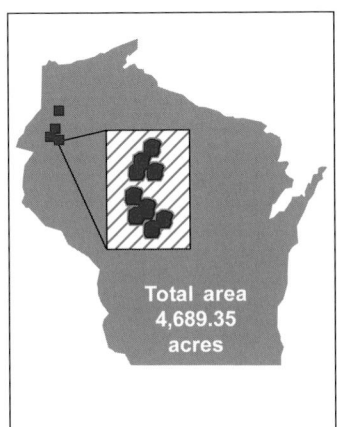

Total area
4,689.35
acres

St. Croix Chippewa

There are four certified counselors with the AODA department. St. Croix contracts with the Great Lakes Inter-Tribal Council of Wisconsin to provide the professional consultation services of a registered dietician. For those services that tribal health cannot perform on-site, referrals are made and treatment purchased through the community's contract health services program. The tribal health delivery system employs a health administrator, along with support staff, to handle day-to-day operations. Funded by the tribe, transport services are available to tribal members. There are five drivers and eight medical transport vans. Priorities are dialysis patients, cancer patients, and tribal elders.

The St. Croix WIC program provides supplemental nutritious foods, nutrition education and counseling, and screening and referrals to other health, welfare, and social services. The Maternal Child Health Program (MCH) is funded by three sources: Rural Infant Health Project, Combined Health Services, and a State of Wisconsin immunization grant. The MCH nurse facilitates and coordinates programs and case manages and advocates for clients and their families.

Because the reservation is scattered over a three-county area, tribal members are served by a number of area hospitals. The closest facilities to the residential communities include Spooner Hospital, Burnett Medical Center in Grantsburg, and Lakeview Medical Center in Rice Lake. These facilities are all located within a 15- to 30-mile radius of most communities. In addition there are major medical facilities located in Superior, Wisconsin, and Duluth, Minnesota, 60 miles from the northernmost community, and Minneapolis/St. Paul, Minnesota, 95 miles from the southernmost communities.

ENVIRONMENTAL CONCERNS
The St. Croix Chippewas are concerned with water issues including wellhead delineation, wetlands and watershed protection, drinking water, sewage treatment, solid wastes, and nonpoint-source pollution. The tribe is conducting outdoor air quality assessment, indoor and radon assessment, and monitoring of solid waste recycling efforts as it works to address air quality and environmental health on the reservation.

Stockbridge-Munsee

Stockbridge-Munsee Reservation
Federal reservation
Stockbridge-Munsee Mohican
Shawano County, Wisconsin

Stockbridge-Munsee Community Bánd of Mohican Indians
P.O. Box 70
N8476 Moh-He-Con-Nuck Rd.
Bowler, WI 54416
715-793-4111
715-793-1307 Fax
mohican-nsn.gov

Total area *(BIA realty, 2004)*
16,280.29 acres

Tribally owned *(BIA realty, 2004)*
16,124.67 acres

Allotted/Individually owned
(BIA realty, 2004)
155.62 acres

Population *2000 census*
1,531

Population*(Tribal source, 2004)*
546

LOCATION AND LAND STATUS
The Stockbridge-Munsee Reservation is located east of central Wisconsin, approximately 60 miles northwest of the City of Green Bay. It is approximately 45 miles east of Wausau and 170 miles north of the state capitol, Madison. The reservation encompasses the townships of Bartelme and Red Springs. The tribe has occupied the land since the Treaty of 1856.

PHYSICAL DESCRIPTION
The primary branches of the Red River are fed by Silver Creek and course through the reservation. Almost 79 percent of tribal lands are covered in forests, primarily with northern hardwood. Land designations include a wilderness preserve as well as commercial forests, recreational areas, business zones, and housing areas.

CULTURE AND HISTORY
The Stockbridge-Munsee Band of Mohican Indians were woodland Mohican Indians. The ancestral name Muh-he-con-ne-ok means "people of the waters that are never still." They lived in wik-wams (wigwams), which means "bark-dwellings" in their Mohican language. A band of Delaware Indians, known as the Munsees, joined the group in 1834. Both Algonquian Indian tribes, the Mohicans and Delawares are closely related in customs and traditions. They originally inhabited large portions of what is now the northeastern United States.

In 1734 a small group of Mohicans established a village near Stockbridge, Massachusetts, where they began to assimilate until they were driven out by Euro-Americans. In 1785 they founded New Stockbridge in upper New York State at the invitation of Oneida Indians. Their new home, however, was on timberland sought after by white settlers. In 1818 the band settled briefly in White River, Indiana, only to be relocated again. In order to relocate both the Stockbridge and Oneida Indians, government officials, along with missionaries, negotiated the acquisition of a large tract of land in Wisconsin. In 1834 the Stockbridge Indians settled there, and two years later they were joined by some

Munsees families who were migrating west from Canada. Together they became known as the Stockbridge-Munsee Band. The band is presently located in Shawano County.

The tribe expanded its land base by obtaining 46,000 acres by treaty with the Menominee Tribe. More pressure from the government resulted in more relocation, first in Kaukana, Wisconsin, and later to a community on the shores of Lake Winnebago, which the tribe named Stockbridge. The terms of a new treaty with the federal government in 1856 moved the band to its present site in Shawano County. The General Allotment Act of 1887 resulted in the Stockbridge-Munsees losing a great deal of land. In the Great Depression the tribe lost even more land. However, in the early 1930s, the Stockbridge-Munsees experienced a reawakening of their identity and began reorganizing. In 1932 they even took over the town council of Red Springs, and under the provisions of the Indian Reorganization Act of 1934, they created an activist business committee and started to regain some of their land. The Secretary of the Interior affirmed the band's reservation in 1937.

Traditional homes included wigwams, or "bark-dwellings." Wigwams were constructed of a wood pole frame covered with blankets and deer hides. The tribe has created a language and culture committee. It has also applied for an Administration for Native American language planning grant. In 1975 the tribe opened the Stockbridge-Munsee Historical Museum and Library. In the 1990s the tribe was pursuing a land claim in New York State for some of the territory it occupied before being driven westward.

GOVERNMENT
The tribe formed a constitution and bylaws under the Indian Reorganization Act in 1937, and they were ratified in 1938. The tribal council has a president and a treasurer who are elected biannually, as well as a vice-president and four council members who are elected annually.

TRI-WI-028

TRI-WI-032

TRI-WI-033

TRI-WI-031

TRI-WI-030

The tribe funds the following services with few programs funded under PL 93-638: family services, social services, general assistance, health center, well and septic services, housing, land and enrollment, road improvement, environmental, public safety, and elderly programs. The tribe's tribal court system was established in 1995 and has three judges who address civil suits and enforce tribal ordinances. The law enforcement department has six state-certified law enforcement officers who work through a cooperative law enforcement agreement with Shawano County, and it is staffed by three patrol officers, an investigator, a school liaison for the tribe's two local schools, and an administrator.

ECONOMY

The Stockbridge-Munsee Community Band of Mohican Indians is the largest employer in Shawano County. Gaming and timber sales are the principal foundations of the tribal economy. The tribe also receives PL 93-638 grant funds that partially fund some tribal services. Private tribal enterprises include Arnie's Auto Resurrection, Konkapot Lodge, Headquarters General Store, Arrowhead Log Homes, and two private loggers.

Government as Employer. The tribal government employs about 318 people in various services departments, plus 550 person within the tribal gaming operation.

Economic Development Projects. The tribe's development corporation offers assistance tribal entrepreneurs. Services include education, technical assistance, and access to capitol for private enterprises. Incentives are offered to businesses that locate within the reservation. Tribal members also serve on the boards of local and regional business development organizations. The tribe has purchased and leases property in the City of Shawano. The tribe is a member of the Great Lakes Inter-Tribal Council, which is active in economic development statewide.

Agriculture and Livestock. Tribal lands are no longer leased to farmers. The status of water quality on the reservation prohibits tilling crops as well. In response to the dilemma, trees have been planted and wetlands restored on former croplands.

Forestry. Smart Growth, the tribe's forestry program, implements sustained-yield logging methods in the management of tribal forests.

Gaming. The tribe owns and operates Mohican North Star Casino and Bingo, which is located just 18 miles northwest of Shawano on County Road A, between the villages of Gresham and Bowler. The casino was expanded during the summer and fall of 1995, and now it is a 23,000-square-foot facility with 1,055 slots and 18 gaming tables. The casino also offers a 700-seat entertainment venue and a 400-seat bingo hall. It currently provides employment for 550 people.

Real Estate/Commercial Development. A number of federal projects provide low-rent housing on the reservation. The development of a home loan program for tribal members aims to increase the construction of new homes on the reservation.

Services and Retail. The Little Star Convenience Store and Gas Station, the Mohican RV Park, Tribal Health and Wellness Center, Pine Hills Golf Course, and Many Trails Banquet Facility are located near the casino.

Media and Communications. The Mohican News, which is distributed to 1,400 subscribers biweekly, is the newspaper published by the tribe's communication department. This department also employs a public relations staff of one.

Tourism and Recreation. The tribe is developing a self-guided tour program to offer visitors to the reservation. The tour will provide guests the opportunity to view the reservation from the river road drive.

A tribal museum offers visitors numerous displays of artifacts and historical documents. The Wea tuk Village, or Place of the Wigwams, is an outdoor replica of a traditional Mohican village. Other attractions to the reservation include the annual Many Trails Sled Dog Classic and the Mohican Powwow. The Many Trails Classic is a winter event that features races, games, food,

TRI-WI-028 Stockbridge-Munsee Health and Wellness sign

TRI-WI-032 Little Star Convenience Store and Gas Station

TRI-WI-031 Arvid E. Miller Stockbridge-Munsee Historical Library Museum

TRI-WI-030 Arvid E. Miller Stockbridge-Munsee Historical Library Museum sign

TRI-WI-033 Mohican North Star Casino and Bingo sign

Tribal enrollment
(Tribal source, 2004)
1,560

Total labor force *2000 census*
698

High school graduate or higher
2000 census
79.4%

Bachelor's degree or higher
2000 census
13.5%

Unemployment rate *2000 census*
7.3%

Unemployment rate
(BIA labor report, 2001)
35%

Per capita income *2000 census*
$15,272

Stockbridge-Munsee

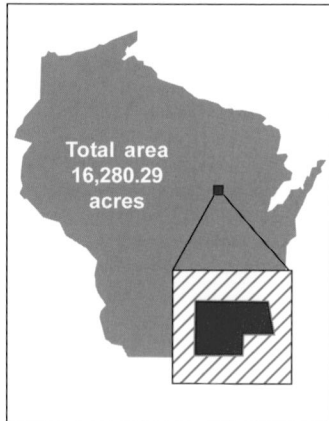

Total area 16,280.29 acres

art vendors, live entertainment, and horse-drawn sleigh rides. The Mohican Powwow is held during the second week of August.

INFRASTRUCTURE

Wisconsin State Highways 29 cuts through the reservation east-west. The tribe is working in collaboration with Shawano County to provide direct access to the casino. The nearest airport is in Green Bay, approximately 28 miles away.

Electricity. Central Wisconsin Electric Cooperative and Gresham Power and Light supply electric power.

Fuel. A variety of vendors provide the tribe with LP gas, although it is studying the feasibility of developing its own LP gas service.

Water Supply. Water is provided to the housing area on Camp 14 Road and sites along Moh-he-con-nuck Road by a tribal water tower. A second tower is under construction near County Highway A. Most residential structures utilize private wells. Currently, a sewage lagoon serves approximately 64 residences.

Transportation. Tribally owned vans and buses are used by the health, elderly, and youth centers.

COMMUNITY FACILITIES AND SERVICES

The tribe has a large community center adjacent to its baseball field, which was built with profits from gaming. The center is located within the largest neighborhood on the reservation and has a fitness facility, a youth center, a cultural room, and an outreach college classroom. The reservation houses a memorial library museum that offers collections of Mohican history, rare books, and maps from the early 1600s as well as tribal documents, journals, and portraits. A collection of tribal artifacts that includes beads, pipes, clothing, furs, and other items is also featured at the library. The tribe is currently constructing an assisted living facility and an elder meal site adjacent to the health and wellness center.

Education. The tribe operates a Head Start program. Tribal youth attend Bowler and Gresham public schools. The College of the Menominee Nation offers an outreach classroom at the family center.

Health Care. Medical, dental, and community health services are available through the Stockbridge-Munsee health and wellness center, located on County Highway A. Other services of the center include physical therapy, substance abuse intervention, mental health, pharmacy, and chiropractic care programs. Services are available to tribal and nontribal residents of the reservation, Shawano County, and Menominee County. An in-house human services facilitator assists reservation residents in identifying available social services.

ENVIRONMENTAL CONCERNS

The issues of groundwater quality and pollution is a concern to the tribe. There have been incidents of mercury poisoning of fish and aquatic systems on tribal lands. Other environmental concerns include indoor air quality, on-site septic management, land use, insect infestation, and forest diseases. The tribe is working in cooperation with the BIA, U.S. Fish and Wildlife Services, the U.S. Geological Survey and local universities, to address environmental issues. The hoped outcome is the development of a tribal wetland and waterfowl enhancement initiative. The tribe also hopes to incorporate a holistic approach to the diversification of the ecosystems on tribal lands.

Wind River

LOCATION AND LAND STATUS

The Wind River Reservation spans 2,268,008 acres in the scenic west-central portion of Wyoming. The reservation stretches from the northern part of the Owl Creek Mountains to Sand Draw in the south. Its eastern boundary begins just west of the community of Shoshone and extends westward to the town of Dubois. The Eastern Shoshone Tribe is centered primarily in the communities of Fort Washakie, Wind River, and Crowheart in the northern and western portions of the reservation. The Northern Arapaho Tribe occupies the southeastern portion of the reservation and the communities of Ethete, Arapahoe, and St. Stephens. The entire reservation is located in Fremont County.

The 1863 Fort Bridger Treaty established the reservation, which originally spanned over 44 million acres, for the Shoshone Tribe. The Arapahos joined the Shoshones on the reservation in 1878. Land cessions reduced the reservation to its present size. The Wind River Reservation is the third largest in the nation and the only Native American reservation in the state of Wyoming. The reservation is unique in that it is the only reservation in the United States that encompasses lands chosen by the tribe compelled to live there.

PHYSICAL DESCRIPTION

The heart of the reservation is located in the Wind River Basin, also called the Warm Valley of the Wind River. The Wind River courses through tribal lands and is lined by cottonwood trees. The terrain is rugged and mountainous in parts, with significant forest and grazing lands. Tribal lands extend from the natural spa of Thermopolis through the grasslands and badlands to Dubois.

CULTURE AND HISTORY

The Wind River Reservation lies in the traditional territory of the Eastern Shoshone people. Both the Eastern Shoshone and Northern Arapaho tribes now occupy the reservation. The Eastern Shoshones migrated out of the Nevada-Utah area and onto the plains around 1600. The tribe's Native language, Numic, comes from the Uto-Aztecan linguistic family. The Northern Arapahos migrated west out of Minnesota onto the Great Plains at approximately the same time. They descend from the Algonquian linguistic family.

While the first Fort Bridger Treaty (in 1863) set boundaries encompassing an area of over 44 million acres for what was then called the Shoshone Reservation, the second Treaty of Fort Bridger (in 1868) pared this down to less than 2.8 million acres. In 1874, a government agent persuaded the tribe to sell another half-million acres so the area could be opened up to gold

mining. In the meantime, the Northern Arapaho Tribe had migrated south in the wake of Custer's defeat (which some of their number had participated in), and they were eventually promised a reservation near Casper in west-central Wyoming. The government backed away from this promise, however, and in 1876 the Arapaho Tribe accepted the proposition to share lands with the Shoshone Tribe. The two tribes had been traditional enemies, making this forced coalition difficult for quite some time. Since that period, however, the two tribes have jointly ruled the Wind River Reservation, though each has retained its separate identity, culture, and tribal government.

The tribes experienced extreme hardship between 1900 and 1938, as prohibitions on off-reservation hunting, minimal governmental and outside investment, meager rationing, and tuberculosis and measles epidemics combined to decimate both their population and the peoples' spirit. After 1938, the joint business council of the Shoshone and Northern Arapaho Tribes received a $4.4 million settlement for lands ceded north of Wind River. The tribes were also able to reactivate oil, gas, and uranium mining leases and expand their cattle ranching operations. Health conditions improved as effective treatment for tuberculosis became available. During this period of recovery, the two tribes began to interact more intensively and productively, though much ambivalence about their forced arrangement remains to this day. In the face of all these challenges, there has been a concerted effort on the part of both the Shoshone and Arapaho tribes to keep their traditional cultures alive. Language classes at the Wyoming Indian High School, the creation of tribal cultural centers, and an active ceremonial life are just some of the measures the tribes have taken to achieve this end.

GOVERNMENT

Both the Shoshones and the Northern Arapahos maintain a general council. These general councils meet about three times a year. The general councils are composed of all tribal members 18 years of age and older. Both the Arapaho and the Shoshone tribes are governed by business councils composed of six members elected to two-year terms. Each business council in turn elects a chairman. Together these 12 members comprise the joint business council of the Shoshone and Northern Arapaho tribes. The joint business council is directly responsible for the daily activities on jointly owned resources and joint tribal programs. The tribes maintain a police department on the reservation.

BUSINESS CORPORATION

The Northern Arapaho Economic Development Commission oversees the development of economic ventures for the tribe.

Wind River Reservation
Federal reservation
Shoshone and Arapaho
Fremont and Hot Springs
counties, Wyoming

Northern Arapaho Tribe
P.O. Box 217
Fort Washakie, WY 82514
 307-332-6120
 307-332-7543 Fax

Eastern Shoshone Tribe
P.O. Box 538
Fort Washakie, WY 82514
 307-332-3532
 307-332-3055 Fax

Total area *(BIA realty, 2004)*
1,889,708.19 acres

Federal trust *(BIA realty, 2004)*
1,296.15 acres

Tribally owned *(BIA realty, 2004)*
1,794,480.54 acres

Individually owned
(BIA realty, 2004)
93,931.5 acres

Population *2000 census*
23, 250

Total labor force *2000 census*
11,256

Wind River

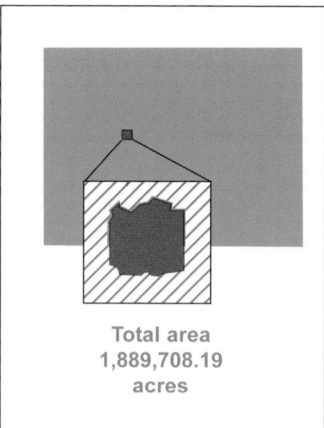

Total area
1,889,708.19
acres

High school graduate or higher
2000 census
83.1%

Bachelor's degree or higher
2000 census
14.6%

Unemployment rate *2000 census*
11.5%

Per capita income *2000 census*
$14,661

ECONOMY

A hurdle for the tribes has been overcoming prejudice and exploitation at the hands of local non-Native business and political interests. Moreover, unemployment has remained a persistent problem, as Wyoming's economy suffered a sharp downturn during the late 1970s with the collapse of the oil-shale industry. Given these circumstances, the tribes have been remarkably innovative in developing a modest assortment of small businesses on the reservation and have been tenacious in pressing for their share of the oil and gas bounty through a tribal tax on production. The tribal economy is supported in large part by land leases for oil and gas production.

Government as Employer. A considerable percentage of tribal income is generated through government grants and contracts, as well as through leasing tribal lands. These monies serve to employ significant numbers of tribal members in various capacities. For example, the Shoshone Tribe employs about 50 persons for governmental operations, all paid from Shoshone Business Council operating funds. Additionally, some 30 tribal members work for projects funded by federal agencies. These include social services projects, housing rehabilitation projects, and economic development enterprises.

Economic Development Projects. The tribes are actively pursuing possibilities for economic development on the reservation. They are considering marketing the land's rich natural mineral and forest resources.

Agriculture and Livestock. Since the turn of the twentieth century, the tribes have jointly leased their land for grazing, and to a lesser extent for crop cultivation. The Northern Arapaho Tribe controls 400,000 acres in the northeast portion of the reservation, where it raises purebred Herefords. The tribe currently maintains about 8,000 head of cattle and 300 horses. Approximately 75 Shoshone tribal members operate individual livestock businesses on the reservation. Almost all of these are beef-cattle ranches, with summer grazing on tribal forests and ranges and winter pasturing on low-lying ranches. Both tribes now maintain farming operations as well, either individually or jointly owned.

In 2002, the tribes initiated a program to restore the native grasses destroyed by wildfires in 2000. The tribes released 16,000 pounds of native grass seeds and planted over 100,000 saplings toward this end, and they contracted the services of the Northwest Management Company to oversee the process.

Gaming. The Northern Arapaho Tribe operates an enterprise called 789 Bingo. The 8,000-square-foot gaming facility offers 202 slots/VLTs and 200 bingo seats as well as a diner. It employs 63 individuals. This business generates significant tribal revenues and employment. The tribe also has been negotiating the possible development of a casino with the Department of the Interior and the State of Wyoming. In 2004, the tribe began plans for the class III Wind River Casino. This facility is scheduled to open in 2005, and it will generate over 200 jobs.

Fisheries. The region's lakes and streams provide excellent recreational fishing opportunities. Reservation fishing permits are sold at the Shoshone Tribe's RV park.

Construction. Shoshone Enterprises is a tribally owned construction company that does general contracting on house foundations, curbs, and gutters, and it digs lines for sewer and water systems. The Indian Health Service contracted the company to install the water lines and septic systems for all individual residences on the reservation. The company is also constructing a new wetland sewage lagoon and collection system for the Fort Washakie community. Shoshone Enterprises employs 17 people.

Mining. The tribes have jointly leased their land for oil and gas production for nearly a century. In late 1978 the joint business council enacted an ordinance that imposed a small tax on all oil and gas production on the reservation. In 1986, after the federal courts effectively upheld tribal rights to collect such a mineral tax, the tribes were finally able to start receiving revenues from the ordinance. Since that time, the joint business council and the Wind River Tax Commission have collected millions of dollars to support and finance tribal services. Though the fields currently under production are aging and thus diminishing in output, some new gas exploration and deep well drilling was planned for 1995. Aside from this, significant deposits of gold were once mined on reservation lands, though little if any gold mining is currently going on.

In 1998, the Wind River Environmental Quality Commission identified 10 drilling sites on the reservation, which represent a possibility for greater gas production. The University of Wyoming and the Tom Brown Exploration Company began to develop a 3D seismic map of tribal lands in 1998.

Services and Retail. There are a variety of businesses on the reservation, including the R.V. Greeves Art Gallery, specializing in stone and bronze sculptures, and Warm Valley Arts and Crafts. Additionally, the Shoshone Tribe operates an auto repair business, Morning Star Manor for senior citizens, and the Shoshone Utility Company, a for-profit enterprise. The Arapaho Tribe operates a gas station along with two grocery stores, a laundromat, a printing business, and a truck stop.

Media and Communications. The Northern Arapaho Tribe owns the 100,000-watt KWRR-FM radio station. It broadcasts from Ethete, Wyoming, to Boysen Peak via a microwave link. The station plays a variety of music and presents live broadcasts from local powwows. The station employs a staff of 12 including a news writer, an announcer, a manager, radio personalities, and a finance officer. Since the station is noncommercial, it subsists on donations rather than paid advertising.

Tourism and Recreation. The reservation's proximity to the Rocky Mountains and the Continental Divide, the Yellowstone and Grand Teton national parks, and the Wind and Bighorn rivers, places it at the center of one of the country's most enticing tourist areas. Summer fishing and winter snowmobiling are the main revenue-producing recreation activities on the reservation. Fishing, camping, climbing, and hunting are allowed on tribal lands with a tribally issued permit, which may be attained through the Tribal Fish and Game Office. The Shoshone-owned Rocky Acres RV Facility features RV hookups and showers, along with fishing access and permits.

There are numerous sites of cultural and archeological interest throughout the reservation. Sheepeater Indian traps, petroglyphs at Castle Gardens, and a 1,000-year-old archeological find in the center of the Riverton landfill are among areas of interest. Guided tours of the reservation are available. St. Stephen's Mission is a recently restored Catholic mission on the reservation that still serves tribal members. It also offers a gift shop and features the North American Indian Heritage Center.

The Northern Arapaho Tribe maintains the Northern Arapaho Cultural Museum in Ethete. It houses traditional tribal artifacts. The museum is located adjacent to the historical St. Michael's Mission.

The Wind River Historical Center and Lucius Burch Center for Western Tradition are located in Dubois. They offer exhibits and programs pertaining to the material culture of the Mountain Shoshones and the history of the Upper Wind River Valley. The

Shoshone Tribal Cultural Center is located at Fort Washakie. It is housed in a National Registered Historical Building. Exhibits include tribal cultural arts and crafts, historical data, and a photographic collection. The Chief Washakie Cemetery, also located at Fort Washakie, is the burial site of Chief Washakie, the last chief of the Shoshone Tribe, and of Sacajewea, Lewis and Clark's Shoshone guide during their expedition across North America.

The tribes sponsor a number of special events open to the public, including Treaty Recognition Day and Shoshone Indian Days and Rodeo, both in late June, and several social and competitive powwows throughout powwow season.

INFRASTRUCTURE
U.S Highway 287 provides road access to the Shoshone tribal headquarters at Fort Washakie. Highways 20, 26, and 133 also run through portions of the reservation. The primary waterway is the Wind River, which provides water for the BIA irrigation system as well as for fisheries and recreation.

Commercial air service is available at the Riverton Regional Airport at the southeast corner of the reservation. Commercial bus lines serve Riverton and Lander, just south of reservation boundaries. Commercial truck lines serve Fort Washakie and other parts of the reservation directly.

Electricity. The Rural Electrical Cooperative and Pacific Power and Light provide electricity.

Fuel. An area distributor furnishes natural gas to residential communities, while local companies supply outlying areas with propane.

Water Supply. The reservation maintains its own water and sewer systems, with assistance from the Indian Health Service and federal grants.

Transportation. The tribes have operated a public transit system since 1989 that serves both off-reservation towns and population centers on the reservation. Its main purpose is to enable tribal members to get to and from their jobs. The system is currently supported through federal and tribal subsidies.

COMMUNITY FACILITIES AND SERVICES
The tribes maintain community centers and cultural programs across the reservation.

Education. Tribal youth attend schools in the Fort Washakie School District and the Arapahoe School District. Tribal youth may attend the tribally operated Wyoming Indian High School on the reservation. The curriculum includes traditional academics and a focus on Arapaho and Shoshone cultures and languages. Students may also attend Wind River High School, Lander Valley High School, Riverton High School, or St. Stephen's High School.

Four Winds Charter School opened on the reservation in 2004. A joint venture between the Fort Washakie and Arapahoe school districts, Four Winds is a vocational high school that can serve up to 250 students. The curriculum offers traditional academics, culinary arts, and building trades, with an intent to expand.

Health Care. Health care is provided through Public Health Service/Indian Health Service clinics at Fort Washakie and Arapaho. The Shoshone Tribe helps to operate a dialysis center in Lander, 14 miles south of Fort Washakie.

ENVIRONMENTAL CONCERNS
The waning fish population in Mill Creek, Bull Lake Creek, and the Popo Agie River are a concern in the area. In 2004, grants totaling $90,000 were awarded to address the issue.

ANCSA	Alaska Native Claims Settlement Act		MED	Mandaree Enterprise Corporation
ASRC	Arctic Slope Regional Corporation		MRF	Materials Recovery Facility
ASWS	Arctic Slope World Services		MSW	Mohegan Solid Waste (MSW)
AVEC	Alaska Village Electrical Cooperative Incorporated		MTE	Menominee Tribal Enterprise
AZ	Arizona		MTGA	Mohegan Tribal Gaming Authority
BAT	Business Activity Tax		NAGPRA	Native American Graves Protection and Repatriation Act
BBNC	Bristol Bay Native Corporation		NAIHS	Navajo Area Indian Health Service
BIA	Bureau of Indian Affairs		NANA	NANA Regional Corporation Incorporated
BRAVO	Bringing Rural American Venture Opportunities Initiative		NANA/VECO	NANA Regional Corporation Incorporated Division of Mining Support
BSNC	Bering Straits Native Corporation		NAPI	Navajo Agricultural Products Industry
CAC	Chugach Alaska Corporation		NCA	North Central Association
CAP	Central Arizona Project		NCAI	National Congress of American Indians
CERCLA	Comprehensive Environmental Response Compensation and Liability Act		NEPA	National Environmental Policy Act
CIE	Creek Indian Enterprises		NFPI	Navajo Forest Products Industries
CIRI	Cook Inlet Region Incorporated		NPDC	Nambé Pueblo Development Corporation
CND	Cherokee Nation Distributors		NPHA	Northern Ponca Housing Authority
CNI	Chickasaw Nation Industries		NPS	Navajo Preparatory School
CPN	Citizen Potawatomi Nation		NTP	Navajo Transmission Project
CRS	Community Recovery Services		PCR	Professional Computing Resources Incorporated
CSKT	Confederated Salish and Kootenai Tribes		PIT	Possessory Interest Tax
DED	Division of Economic Development		PL	Public Law
DSL	Digital Subscriber Line		PLP	Potawatomi Leadership Program
EIS	Environmental Impact Statement		PNM	Public Service Company of New Mexico
EMD	Environmental Management Division		PWC	Permanent Way Corporation
EMS	Emergency Medical Service		ROSS	Government Grant: Resident Opportunities for Self-Sufficiency
ENIPC	Eight Northern Indian Pueblos Council		SBA	Small Business Administration
ENIPC	Eight Northern Indian Pueblos Council		SCUSU	Southern Colorado Ute Service Unit
EPA	Environmental Protection Agency		SEV	Oil and Gas Severance Tax
FET	Fuel Excise Tax		SIC	Sonneville International Corporation
FWC	Fire Lake Wellness Center		SMSC	Shakopee Mdewakanton Sioux Community
FY	Fiscal Year		SRPMIC	Salt River Pima-Maricopa Indian Community
GAP	General Assistance Program		TAC	The Aleut Corporation
GCR	Grand Canyon Resort Corporation		TAHO	Tribally Assisted Home Ownership Program
GED	General Educational Development		TERO	Tribal Employment Rights Office
GRIC	Gila River Indian Community		THA	Tribal Housing Authority
GRTHA	Grand Ronde Tribal Housing Authority		THP	Tribal Heritage Project
HCI	Ho-Chunk Community Development Corporation		THPO	Tribal Historic Preservation Office
HERO	Harrah's Employees Reaching Out		TOB	Tobacco Products Tax and Licensing Act
HOT	Hotel Occupancy Tax		TSAV	Tribal Strategies Against Violence
HUD	U.S. Department of Housing and Urban Development *See Indian tribes*		U.S. EPA	United States Environmental Protection Agency
HUD	Housing and Urban Development		U.S.	United States
ICAS	Inupiat Community of the Arctic Slope		USDA	United State Department of Agriculture
ICRC	Integrated Concepts and Research Corporation		USEPA	United States Environmental Protection Agency
IHS	Indian Health Services		USET	United South and Eastern Tribes
IPFDC	Indian Pueblos Federal Development Corporation		USPHS	United States Public Health Service
IRA	Indian Reorganization Act		WCA	Weeminuche Construction Authority
KDC	Koniag Development Corporation		WESIT	White Earth Suicide Intervention Team
KWA	Karluk Wilderness Adventures		WHDC	Winnebago Housing and Development Commission
LIHEAP	Low Income Home Energy Assistance Program		WIC	Women's, Infants and Children's
LSI	Little Six Incorporated		WMG	Washington Management Group Incorporated
MATI	Mescalero Apache Telecom Incorporated		WUI	Wildland/Urban Interface project
			ZECDC	Zuni Education and Career Development Center

BOOKS

DeLorme Mapping Company. Alaska Atlas and Gazetteer. Yarmouth, ME: DeLorme Mapping, 2001.

Alvarez de Williams, Anita. "Cocopa." Handbook of North American Indians, Vol. 10: Southwest. Washington, D.C.: Smithsonian Institution, 1983.

American Indian Lawyer Training Program, Inc. Indian Tribes as Sovereign Governments. Oakland, CA, 1988.

Arnold, Robert D., et al. Alaska Native Land Claims. Anchorage, AK: Alaska Native Foundation, 1978.

Basso, Keith H. "Western Apache." Handbook of North American Indians, Vol. 10: Southwest. Washington, D.C.: Smithsonian Institution, 1983.

Beals, Ralph L., and Joseph A. Hester, Jr. "A New Ecological Typology of the California Indians." The California Indians: A Source Book. Berkeley: University of California Press, 1971.

Bromberg, Eric. The Hopi Approach to the Art of Kachina Doll Carving. Atglen, Pennsylvania: Schiffer Publishing, 1986.

Calloway, Colin G. The Abenaki Indians of North America. New York and Philadelphia: Chelsea House Publishers, 1989.

Cash, Joseph H., and Gerald W. Wolff. The Ottawa People. Phoenix: Indian Tribes Series, Vol. 34, 1976.

Cohen, Felix S. Handbook of Federal Indian Law. Albuquerque: University of New Mexico Press. Reprint of 1942 edition.

Cotterill, R.S. The Southern Indians: The Story of the Civilized Tribes Before Removal, fourth edition. Norman: University of Oklahoma Press, 1971.

Danziger, Edmund Jefferson, Jr. The Chippewas of Lake Superior. Norman and London: University of Oklahoma Press, 1979.

Davis, Mary B. Native America in the Twentieth Century: An Encyclopedia. New York and London: Garland Publishing, 1994.

Dixon, R.B., and A.L. Kroeber. "Linguistic Families of California." The California Indians: A Source Book. Berkeley: University of California Press, 1971.

Eargle, Dolan H., Jr. California Indian Country: The Land and the People. San Francisco: Trees Company Press, 1992.

Eargle, Dolan H., Jr. The Earth Is Our Mother: A Guide to the Indians of California, Their Locales and Historic Sites. San Francisco: Trees Company Press, 1986.

Edelman, Sandra A. Summer People Winter People: A Guide to Pueblos in the Santa Fe Area. Santa Fe, NM: Sunstone Press, 1986.

Edmunds, R. David. The Potawatomies: Keepers of the Fire. Norman, OK: University of Oklahoma Press, 1978.

Ferguson, T.J., and E. Richard Hart. A Zuni Atlas. Norman and London: University of Oklahoma Press, 1985.

Gattuso, John, ed. Native America. Hong Kong: APA Publications Ltd., 1991.

Gehm, Katherine. Sarah Winnemucca: Most Extraordinary Woman of the Paiute Nation. Phoenix, AZ: O'Sullivan Woodside & Company, 1975.

Gibson, Arrell Morgan. The American Indian: Prehistory to the Present. Lexington, MA, and Toronto: D.C. Heath and Company, 1980.

Gibson, Arrell Morgan. The West in the Life of the Nation. Lexington, MA: D.C. Heath and Company, 1976.

Goc, Michael J. Reflections of Lac du Flambeau. Compiled by Ben Guthrie. Friendship, WI: New Past Press, Inc., 1995.

Gomez, Arthur R., and Veronica E. Tiller. Fort Apache Forestry: A History of Timber Management and Forest Protection on Fort Apache Indian Reservation 1870-1985. Tiller Research, Inc., Albuquerque, NM: Bishop Printing Co., 1990.

Gorsline, Jerry, ed. Shadows of Our Ancestors: Readings in the History of Klallam-White Relations. Port Townsend, WA: Empty Bowl, 1992.

Green, Donald E. The Creek People. Phoenix: Indian Tribal Services, 1973.

Hale, Duane K., and Arrell M. Gibson. The Chickasaw. Frank W. Porter III, ed. New York and Philadelphia: Chelsea House Publishers, 1990.

Hale, Duane Kendall. Peacemakers on the Frontier: A History of the Delaware Tribe of Western Oklahoma. Anadarko, OK: Delaware Tribe of Western Oklahoma Press, 1987.

Heizer, R. F., and M. A. Whipple, comp. and ed. The California Indians: A Source Book. Berkeley: University of California Press, 1971.

Herring, Joseph B. The Enduring Indians of Kansas: A Century and a Half of Acculturation. Lawrence: University Press of Kansas, 1990.

Hirschfelder, Arlene, and Martha Kreipe de Montano. The Native American Almanac: A Portrait of Native America Today. New York: Prentice Hall, 1993.

Hopi Dictionary Project. Hopi Dictionary/Hopìikwa Lavàytutuveni: A Hopi-English Dictionary of the Third Mesa Dialect. Tucson: University of Arizona Press, 1998.

Hoxie, Frederick E., ed. Indians in American History. Arlington Heights, IL: Harlan Davidson, 1988.

Hudson, Charles. The Southeastern Indians. Knoxville: University of Tennessee Press, 1976.

Hughes, Donald J. American Indians in Colorado. Boulder, CO: Pruett Publishing Company, 1977.

Johnson, Edward C. Walker River Paiutes: A Tribal History. Schurz, NV: Walker River Paiute Tribe. Salt Lake City, UT: University of Utah Printing Service, 1975.

Josephy, Alvin M. Jr. The Indian Heritage of America. New York: Bantam Books, 1968.

Kappler, Charles J., ed. Indian Affairs: Laws and Treaties. Vol. 1, III, and IV, Washington: Government Printing Office, 1904.

Klein, Barry T. Reference Encyclopedia of the American Indian. West Nyack, NY: Todd Publications, 1993.

Levine, Stuart. The American Indian Today. Nancy O. Lurie, ed. Baltimore, Maryland: Penguin Books, Inc., 1968.

Marr, Carolyn. Portrait in Time: Photographs of the Makah by Samuel G. Morse, 1896-1903. Lloyd Colfax, and Robert D. Monroe, ed. Makah Cultural and Research Center, 1987.

Meyer, Roy W. History of the Santee Sioux: United States Indian Policy on Trial. Rev. ed. Lincoln and London: University of Nebraska Press, 1993.

Minge, Allan. Acorns: Pueblo in the Sky. Albuquerque: University of New Mexico Press, 1976.

Nabokov, Peter, and Robert Easton. Native American Architecture. New York: Oxford University Press, 1989.

Nelson, Byron, Jr. Our Home Forever: A Hupa Tribal History. Hoopa, CA: Hupa Tribe. Salt Lake City, UT: University of Utah Printing Service, 1978.

Newcomb. W.W., Jr. The Indians of Texas. Austin: University of Texas Press, 1961.

Newe: A Western Shoshone History. Reno, NV: Inter-Tribal Council of Nevada, 1976.

Numa: A Northern Paiute History. Reno, NV: Inter-Tribal Council of Nevada, 1976.

O'Brien, Sharon. American Indian Tribal Governments. Norman and London: University of Oklahoma Press, 1989.

Ortiz, Alfonso. The Tewa World: Space, Time, Being, and Becoming in a Pueblo Society. Chicago and London: The University of Chicago Press, 1969.

Paredes, J. Anthony, ed. Indians of the Southeastern United States in the Late 20th Century. Tuscaloosa, AL and London: University of Alabama Press, 1992.

Pipestem, F. Browning and G. William Rice. The Mythology of the Oklahoma Indians: A Survey of the Legal Status of Indian Tribes in Oklahoma. American Indian Law Review. Reprinted from American Indian Law Review, Vol. VI, No. 2, 1978.

Porter, Frank W. III, ed. Strategies for Survival: American Indians in the Eastern United States. Contributions in Ethnic Studies, Number 15. New York: Greenwood Press, 1986.

Rosenblatt, Judith, ed. Indians in Minnesota, fourth edition. Elizabeth Ebbott for the League of Women Voters of Minnesota. Minneapolis: University of Minnesota, 1988.

Ruby, Robert H., and John A. Brown. A Guide to the Indian Tribes of the Pacific Northwest. Norman: University of Oklahoma Press, 1986.

Rudes, Blair A. 1999. Tuscarora-English/English-Tuscarora Dictionary. Toronto: University of Toronto Press, 1999.

Ruhlen, Merritt. A Guide to the World's Languages. Vol. 1: Classification. Stanford, CA: Stanford University Press, 1987.

Sando, Joe S. Pueblo Nations. Santa Fe, NM: Clear Light Publishers, 1992.

Satz, Ronald N. Tennessee's Indian Peoples. Knoxville: University of Tennessee Press, 1979.

Schneider, Mary Jane. North Dakota Indians: an Introduction. Dubuque, IA: Kendall/Hunt Publishing Co., 1986.

Schneider, Mary Jane. The Hidatsa Indians of North America. New York and Philadelphia: Chelsea House Publishers, 1989.

Secakuku, Alph A. Following the Sun and Moon: Hopi Kachina Tradition. Heard Museum. Flagstaff, Arizona: Northland Publishing, 1995.

Shanks, Ralph. North American Indian Travel Guide. Lisa Woo Shanks, ed. Petaluma, CA: Costano Books, 1986.

Spicer, Edward H. A Short History of the Indians of the United States. Lisa Woo Shanks, ed. New York: D. Van Nostrand, 1969.

Spicer, Edward H. Cycles of Conquest. Tucson: University of Arizona Press, 1962.

Stewart, Kenneth M. Mohave. Handbook of North American Indians, Vol. 10: Southwest. Washington, D.C.: Smithsonian Institution, 1983.

Stockbridge-Munsee Historical Committee. The History of the Stockbridge - Munsee Band of Mohican Indians, second edition. Bowler, WI: Muh-He-Con-Neew Press, 1993.

Sturtevant, William C., ed. Handbook of North American Indians. Vol. 10: Southwest, ed. by Alfonso Ortiz. Washington, D.C.: Smithsonian Institution, 1983.

Thompson, Gregory Coyne. Southern Ute Lands, 1848-1899: The Creation of a Reservation. Durango, CO: Fort Lewis College Center for Southwest Studies, 1972.

Tiller, Veronica E. The Jicarilla Apache Tribe: A History. Rev. Ed. Lincoln and London: University of Nebraska Press, 1983, 1992.

Tiller, Veronica E., ed. Discover Indian Reservations USA: A Visitors' Welcome Guide. Denver, CO: Council Publications, 1992.

Tiller, Veronica E. Velarde, compiler and editor. Tiller's Guide to Indian Country, Economic Profiles of American Indian Reservations. Albuquerque, NM: BowArrow Publishing, 1996.

Timeche, Joan, and Brenda VanKeuren. Doing Business on Arizona Indian Lands. Staff of the Center for American Indian Economic Development. College of Business Administration. Northern Arizona University, January 2000.

Federal and State Indian Reservations and Indian Trust Areas. Washington D.C.: U.S. Government Printing Office, 1974.

Weatherford, Jack M. Indian Givers: How the Indians of the Americas Transformed the World. New York: Crown Publishers, 1988.
Weatherford, Jack M., Native Roots: How The Indians Enriched America. New York: Crown Publishers, 1991.

Wright, Muriel H. Year of the Indian Native Tribes: Oklahoma, 1992. Guide to the Indian Tribes of Oklahoma. Norman, OK: University of Oklahoma Press, 1992.

PRINTED TRIBAL SOURCES
Absentee Shawnee Tribe of Oklahoma. Tribal Profile. Shawnee, OK, 1989.

Acoma Pueblo. Pueblo of Acoma Community Profile. Acoma, NM, 1995.

Advertisement Paid for by the Shingle Springs Rancheria, September 26, 2003.

Agua Caliente Band of Cahuilla Indians. "The Cahuilla Indians Story." History, background summary, and tribal brochures, 1994.

Ahtna, Incorporated. Annual Report. Glennallen, AK, 1993.

Air Quality Program, Community Development Dept., Cultural and Environmental Services. Brochure, n.d.
Alaska Native Claims Settlement Act. Public Law 92-203, December 18, 1971.

Apache Tribe of Oklahoma. "From Generation to Generation: The Plains Apache Way."

Arctic Slope Regional Corporation. Annual Report. Barrow, AK, 1993.

Aroostook Band of Micmacs Environmental Dept. Brochure, n.d.

Bad River Band of Lake Superior Chippewa. In Native Wisconsin: Official Guide to Native American Communities of Wisconsin, n.d.

Bad River Band of Lake Superior Tribe of Chippewa Indians. Tribal Profile Bad River Reservation. Brochure, n.d.

Bad River Health and Wellness Center. Pamphlet, n.d.

Bad River Natural Resources Air Quality Department. Brochure, n.d.

Bad River Nutrition/Education Program. Brochure, n.d.

Barona Band of Indians Month. Brochure, n.d.

Battle Mountain Nevada Visitors Guide 2004. Brochure, n.d.

Bear Stearns 2002-2003 North American Gaming Almanac, n.d.

Bedal, Edith. History of the Sauk-Suiattle Tribe as told by Francis Enick, n.d.

Benefits Available for Osages and Other Indians. Fact Sheet, n.d.

Bering Straits Native Corporation. Annual Report. Nome, AK, 1994.

Bering Straits Native Corporation. Business Directory. Nome, AK, n.d.

Bishop Area Chamber of Commerce and Visitor's Bureau. High Sierra Treasure Map. Bishop, California, n.d.

Bizhibayash, Circle of Flight. Mille Lacs Band Two Island Wetland Restoration Project. Tribal Wetland and Waterfowl Enhancement Initiative, January 2004.

Bizhibayash, Circle of Flight. Mille Lacs Waterfowl Management Activities. Tribal Wetland and Waterfowl Enhancement Initiative, January 1998.

Blackfeet Coins. Brochure, n.d.

Bois Forte Band of Chippewa. "The Bois Forte Band of Chippewa: A Proud Past and a Promising Future." Nett Lake, MN, 1994.

Bristol Bay Native Corporation. Annual Report. Anchorage, AK, 1993.

Calista Corporation. Annual Report. Anchorage, AK, 1993.

Camel Rock RV Park. Brochure, n.d.

Campo Band of Mission Indians. Tribal Profile. Campo, CA, 1994.

Catawba Indian Nation. Green Earth Presentation Materials, n.d.

Celebrating Change, the Fort Mohave Indian Tribe. Brochure, 2001.

Central Oregon's Jefferson County. Pamphlet, n.d.

Chairman Fuller's 2004 Initial Report to the Yavapai-Apache Nation's Tribal Members, Vol. 1, No. 3, May 31, 2004.

Cherokee Nation. Cherokee Nation: Cultural Tourism Case Study Survey. Tahlequah, OK, n.d.

Cherokee Nation. Nation with Promise. Promotional brochure. Tahlequah, OK, n.d.

Cherokee Nation. The Eastern Band of Cherokee Indians' Reservation in the State of North Carolina. Investment Guide, n.d.

Cherokee Nation Economic and Business Development Division. Nation With Vision. Promotional brochure. Tahlequah, OK, n.d.

Cherokee Nation Public Affairs Department. Cherokee Nation: Tribal Government Profile and Summary. Tahlequah, OK, 1994.

Cherokee Nation Tribal Travel and Promotion Department. Cherokee Indian Reservation: Visitors Guide and Directory. Promotional brochure, 1995.

Cherokee Urgent Care Clinic and Pharmacy. Brochure, n.d.

Cheyenne and Arapaho Tribes of Oklahoma. Base Studies: Cheyenne-Arapaho Planning Office. Concho, OK, 1993.

Cheyenne-Arapaho Administration Organization Chart, FY02.

"Chippewa-Indians of Yesterday and Today" by Sister M. Carolissa Levi, I.S.P.A, n.d.
Choctaw Casino, Choctaw Bingo, Choctaw Downs, Choctaw Inn. Brochure, n.d.

Choctaw Economics. Pamphlet, n.d.

Choctaw Management/Services Enterprise. Brochure, n.d.

Choctaw Manufacturing and Development Corporation. Fact Sheet, n.d.

Choctaw Nation Family Investment Center. Brochure, n.d.

Choctaw Nation of Oklahoma. Choctaw Nation History, Tribal Information Document. Durant, OK, n.d.

Choctaw Nation of Oklahoma. Choctaws-The Original Code-Talkers. Tribal pamphlet. Durant, OK, n.d.

Choctaw Nation of Oklahoma. Programs and Services. Booklet, n.d.

Choctaw Town Center. Brochure, n.d.

Choctaw Vision. Vol. 1, No. 1, 2000.

Choudhary, Trib. Comprehensive Economic Development Strategy of the Navajo Nation 2002-2003. Trib Choudhary, Window Rock, AZ.

Church, Bill. Match-e-be-nash Band of Potawatomi Tribal Historian. The Match-e-be-nash Band of Potawatomi Indians of Michigan. Grand Ledge, MI, 1995.

Circle of Flight. Tribal Wetland and Waterfowl Enhancement Initiative, January 2004.

Circle of Flight. Lac du Flambeau. Tribal Wetland and Waterfowl Enhancement Initiative, 2004.

Circle of Flight. Tribal Wetland and Waterfowl Enhancement Initiative. Bizhibayaash. January 2004.
Circle of Flight. Tribal Wetland and Waterfowl Enhancement Initiative, 1998.

Cities of Gold. Literature, n.d.

Clark, Mary Beth. "Colville's Information and Photographs of the Reservation and Enterprises." Economic Planner II, September 10, 1998.

Cochiti Pueblo. Cochiti Lake Information Sheet. Cochiti, NM, 1995.

Coeur D'Alene Casino. Brochure, n.d.

Coeur D'Alene Casino Resort Hotel. Informational Fliers, n.d.

Coeur D'Alene Casino. "Winner's Circle." Coeur D'Alene Casino Pamphlet, n.d.

Coeur d'Alene Tribe of Indians. Comprehensive Transpiration Transportation Plan 2003.

Colorado River Indian Tribe. Brochure, n.d.
Colville Tribal Enterprises Corporation. Developing Leadership Through Training. Brochure, n.d.

Comprehensive Plan of the Coeur d'Alene Tribe, 1999.

Confederated Salish and Kootenai Tribes. A Tradition of Success. Newsprint insert, n.d.
Confederated Salish and Kootenai Tribes. People's Center. Brochure, n.d.

Confederated Tribes and Bands of the Yakama Nation. Tribal Revision to 1996 Tiller's Guide to Indian Country. Prepared by Tribal Economic Development, 2004.

Confederated Tribes of Chehalis Reservation. Economic Contributions to Washington, 1998.

Confederated Tribes of Coos, Lower Umpqua and Siuslaw. Ancestral Homelands: Coos Watershed, Siuslaw Watershed and Umpqua from Scottsburg to Ocean. Brochure. Coos Bay, OR, n.d.

Confederated Tribes of Coos, Lower Umpqua and Suislaw. Picture of Progress for Confederated Tribes of Coos, Lower Umpqua and Siuslaw Indians, n.d.

Confederated Tribes of Siletz Indians of Oregon. Annual Report FY 1993. Siletz, OR.

Confederated Tribes of Siletz Indians of Oregon. 1994 Comprehensive Plan Siletz, OR, 1994.

Confederated Tribes of Siletz Indians of Oregon. Socio-Economic/Health Survey. Siletz, OR, 1993.
Confederated Tribes of Siletz Indians of Oregon. Tribal Profile. Siletz, OR, n.d.

Confederated Tribes of the Grand Ronde Community. A Decade of Restoration. Grand Ronde, OR, 1994.

Confederated Tribes of the Grand Ronde Community of Oregon. Resource Directory 2004.

Confederated Tribes of the Umatilla Indian Reservation. Fact Sheet. Pendelton, OR, 1994.

Confederated Tribes of the Warm Springs of Oregon. Annual Report. 1999.

Confederated Tribes of the Warm Springs Reservation. Informational flier, n.d.

Confederated Tribes of the Warm Springs Reservation. The Museum at Warm Springs Project Description Warm Springs OR, 1993.

Constitution and By-Laws of the United Keetoowah Band of Cherokee Indians Oklahoma, Ratified October 3, 1950. Brochure, n.d.

Constitution of the Sipayik Members of the Passamaquoddy Tribe, n.d.

Cook Inlet Region, Incorporated. Annual Report. Anchorage, AK, 1993.

Coos County Mental Health. "Family Resource and Support Center Brochure," North Bend, OR, n.d.

Coos County Mental Health. Reach Up, Reach Out. North Bend, OR, n.d.

Coquille Indian Tribe. Economic Report, 2002.

Coquille Tribe Economic Development Corporation. Coquille Indian Tribe Community Profile. North Bend, OR, 1994.
Coquille Tribe. Fact Sheet. Coos Bay, OR, 1994.

Coquille Tribe. Heritage Place. Promotional brochure. Coos Bay, OR, 1994.

Coquille Indian Tribe. Continuity, Community, Commitment. Mill Casino Hotel Brochure, n.d.
Coquille Tribe. The Coquilles, Images of a People. Brochure, n.d.

Coeur d'Alene Tribe. "Tribal Transportation Plan Summary 2000."

Corner Mercantile, Inc. Indian Goods. Brochure, n.d.
Corporate Charter of the United Keetoowah Band of Cherokee Indians Oklahoma, Ratified October 3, 1950. Brochure, n.d.

Cow Creek Band of Umpqua Tribe of Indians 1853-1982. Booklet, n.d.

Cow Creek Umpqua Indian Foundation. Brochure, n.d.

Creek Council House Museum. Preserving the Past, Renewing the Spirit. Brochure, n.d.

Crow Natural, Socio-Economic and Cultural Resources Assessment and Conditions Report. April 15, 2002.

CRST and National Wildlife Federation. Restoring the Prairie, Mending the Sacred Hoop; Prairie Conservation and Restoration on the Cheyenne River Reservation, 2001.

CRST Game, Fish and Parks Department. Spirit of a Nation Tours. Brochure, n.d.

CRST Game, Fish and Parks Department. Standing Rock Historical Scenic Byway. Brochure, n.d.

CTEC Annual Report 2001-2002. Tribal publication. CTWS Directory, July 14, 2004.

Dãanzho Sportsmen. Brochure, n.d.

Delaware Tribe of Western Oklahoma. Tribal History and Background Summary. Anadarko, OK, n.d.

Destinations Wisconsin Dells, WI. Gaming Central, Spring 2004.

Devils Lake Sioux Tribe. Dakota Tribal Industries, Inc. Promotional brochure. Fort Totten, ND, n.d.

Devils Lake Sioux Tribe. Information Packet. Fort Totten, ND, n.d.

Devils Lake Sioux. Investment Guide. Fort Totten, ND, n.d.

Doing Business on the Colorado River Indian Reservation. Brochure, n.d.

Domestic Violence Intervention Program, "Gathering Strength." United Keetoowah Band of Cherokees, n.d.

Doyon, Ltd. Annual Report. Fairbanks, AK, 1993. Dynamic Homes. Ho-Chunk Nation. Informational flier, n.d.

Eastern Band of the Cherokee Nation. Brochure, n.d.

Eastern Shawnee Business Committee. Information Packet. Seneca, MO, 1994.

Eastern Shawnee Tribe of Oklahoma. Tribal History and Background Summary. Shawnee, OK, n.d.

Economic Development Projects: Notawaseppi Huron Band of Potawatomi Strategic Plan, 2004-2008.

Elwha Klallam Tribe. Renewing the Cycle of Life-Restoring the Elwha River. Port Angeles, WA, 1994.

Emm, Staci. Walker River Paiute Indian Reservation Agriculture and Natural Resource Focus Group Session Results. University of Nevada Cooperative Extension Fact Sheet FS-02-46, n.d.

Engineering and Construction Services. Salt-River Pima-Maricopa Indian Community. Brochure, n.d.

Excerpt from "The History of Ottawa County," author unknown, Seneca, MO, n.d.

Final Report for Kickapoo Tribe in Kansas. July 24, 2000.

Fort Apache! Brochure, n.d.

Fort Hall Business Council. Fort Hall Reservation Information Summary. Fort Hall, ID, 1993.

Fort Mohave Indian Tribe. Mohave National Preserve. Mohave Indians-Culture, n.d.

Fort Randall Casino and Hotel. A Great Place on the Great Plains. Fort Randall Casino and Hotel. Brochure, n.d.

Fort Sill Apache Tribe. Information Packet. Apache, OK, n.d.

Fort Sill-Chiricahua-Warm Springs-Apache Tribe. Tribal History and Background Summary. Apache, OK, n.d.

Four Directions Development Corporation. Brochure, n.d.

Foxwoods Resort Casino. Brochure, n.d.

Foxwoods Resort Casino Directory, n.d.

Ga-Du-Gi, Report to the Cherokee People. 2003.

Gathering of the People. Brochure. May 20, 2000.

GHC Design Group, an Indian Owned Architectural and Engineering Firm. Brochure, n.d.

Gila River Casinos, Three Times the Fun! Brochure, n.d.

Gila River Farms, 2003. Brochure.

Gila River Indian Community. Profile of a Sovereign Nation, n.d.

Gila River Indian Community. Sheraton Wild Horse Pass Resort and Spa. Brochure, n.d.

Golden Acorn Casino Travel Center. Brochure, n.d. Golf and Gamble. Brochure, n.d.

Grand Ronde Tribal Housing Authority. Brochure, n.d.

Great Lakes Indian Fish and Wildlife Commission. A Guide to Understanding Chippewa Treaty Rights. Odanah, WI, 1991.

Greater Leech Lake Reservation Advisory Alliance. Minnesota's Magnificent Seven Lakes Area. Informational brochure, 1985.

Gunn, Russell, Charles McCauley, and Jennifer Wakimoto. The Economic Impact of the Fort Mohave Tribal Economy. July 2001.

Gyah'-wish Atakia. Tribal Department Reports, June 2004.

Haliwa-Saponi Tribe 29th Annual Pow Wow Program. Hollister, NC, April 15-17, 1994.

Halliday, John. Indian Reservation Business Incentives and Economic Partnership Zones, n.d.

Helping Hands, Native American Caregiver Support Program. Brochure, n.d.

Herman's Landing LCO Resort. Brochure, n.d.

High Lookee Lodge Assisted Living Facility. Brochure, n.d.

History of the Puyallup Tribe of Indians, n.d.

Ho-Chunk Casino, Hotel and Convention Center. Brochure, n.d.

Ho-Chunk Nation Tribal Profile, Black River Falls, WI, 1995.

Ho-Chunk Nation. Annual Report 2002/2003.

Ho-Chunk Planning and Development Division, compiler. County Impact Studies for Jackson, Juneau, Monroe, Richland, Shawano, and Wood counties, 2002.

Ho-Chunk Village. Brochure, n.d.

Ho-Chunk, Inc. Annual Report, 2000.

Hoopa Indian Nation. Brochure, n.d.

Hotel Arcata. Brochure, n.d.

Houlton Band of Maliseet Indians. Health Clinic. Brochure, n.d.

Houlton Band of Maliseet Indians. Health Department Organizational Chart FY-2004.

Houlton Band of Maliseet Indians. Tribal Administration Organizational Chart FY-2004. Revised August 9, 2004.

Houlton Band of Maliseet Indians. Tribal Profile. Revised August 9, 2004.

HuHuGam Heritage Center. Brochure, n.d. Hunting on the Lower Brule Sioux Reservation, 2003 Season Guide Regulations.

Huron Potawatomi, Inc. Nottawaseppi. Huron Band of Potawatomi. Historical Perspective. Fulton, MI, 1995.

Idaho Centennial Commission. Idaho Indians: Tribal Histories. Boise, ID, 1990.

Iowa Tribe of Oklahoma. Economic Development Plan. August 2002.

Iowa Tribe of Oklahoma. Maternal/Child Health Program. Brochure, n.d.

Isleta Pueblo. Economic Planning Office. Master Plan and Economic Data. Isleta, NM, 1995.

Jefferson County and Warm Springs Reservation Transportation Coordination Project. Brochure, n.d.

Jemez Pueblo. Department of Tourism. Fact Sheet. Jemez, NM, n.d.

Jemez Pueblo. Pueblo of Jemez Community Survey Summary Report, 1993. Jemez, NM.

Jicarilla Apache Nation. Fishing Information. Brochure, n.d.

Jicarilla Apache Nation. Labor Report, March 2002.

Jicarilla Apache Tribe Land Restoration Project, 2000.

Jicarilla Apache Tribe. Brochure, n.d.

Jicarilla Apache Tribe. Integrated Resource Management Plan, 1999 Update. IRMP.

Jicarilla Apache Indian Reservation: Existing Conditions and Issues Profile, Integrated Resources Management Planning Office, Volumes I and II, Dulce, NM, 1994.

Jicarilla Apache Tribe. Integrated Resources Management Planning Office, Jicarilla Apache Indian Reservation: Existing.

Jicarilla Demographic Study, January 2002. IRMP.

JKT Development, Inc. Various brochures and 2004 plan.

Kah-Nee-Ta Resort. Brochure, n.d.

"Kanektok River." Safaris Inc. Quinhagak, Alaska (Fishing), n.d.

Kanza Tribal Council. The Kaw City Museum Brochure. Kaw City, OK, 1993.

Kaw Lake. The Official Publication of the Kaw Lake Association, 2004 Edition.

Kaw Nation of Oklahoma. FY2002 Projects. Project Summary.

Kaw Tribe of Oklahoma. Tribal Buildings/Facilities and Land Areas. Kaw City, OK, 1995.

Keeping Non-Point Source Pollution Out of Penobscot Waters. Brochure, n.d.

Keetoowah Band of Cherokee. Information Packet. OK, n.d.

Keetoowah News. "UKB to Break Ground on Wellness Center." Issue 7, June 2003.

Kiowa Tribe. Information Packet. OK, 1994.

Klamath Tribes Service Directory. Pamphlet, n.d.

Klamath Tribes. We are the Klamath Tribes, the Klamaths, the Modocs, and the Yahooskin. Brochure, n.d.

Klamath Tribes' Administration. 2003 Annual Report. Kleinfelder, Inc. Environmental Survey for Big Sandy Rancheria, February 17, 1997.

Koniag, Inc. Annual Report. Anchorage, AK, 1994. Kootenai Tribe. Brochure, n.d.

KTNN, the Voice of the Navajo Nation. Sales Media Kit Brochure, n.d.

Kul Wicasa Oyate, Lower Brule Sioux Tribe. Economic Profile. Pamphlet, n.d.

Lac Courte Oreilles Community Development Corporation. Management Report to the LCO Tribal Governing Board. July 2000.

Lac Courte Oreilles Ojibwa Tribe. MIIG-WA-YAK-BII-EZ-HAA-YAN: You Are Welcome Here. Hayward, WI. 1992.
Lac du Flambeau Band of Lake Superior Chippewa Indians of Northern Wisconsin. Brochure, n.d.

Lac du Flambeau Chamber of Commerce. Lac du Flambeau: Welcome to Indian Country. Promotional brochure, 1995.

Lac du Flambeau Tribal Campground and Casino. Brochure, n.d.

LCO Casino Lodge. Brochure, n.d.

Leech Lake Band of Ojibwe. Comprehensive April 2000.

Leech Lake Tribal Council and the U.S. Department of Human Services Administration for Native Americans. Leech Lake Reservation Fact Sheet and Resources. Informational brochure. 1991.

Leech Lake Wild Rice Co. Brochure, n.d.

Lewis and Clark. Pamphlet, n.d.

Little Big Horn College. Catalog, 2003-2005.

Little Coyote, Joe. Comprehensive Economic Development Strategy 2001.

Little Coyote, Joe, Sr. Executive Report for the CEDS, FY 2004.

Little Coyote, Joe, Sr. Open letter to the Members of the Independence Task Force of the Northern Cheyenne Tribal Council. March 12, 2003.

Little Rockies Meat Packing Plant, Inc. Brochure. 2003.

Lodgepole Gallery and Tipi Village. Brochure, n.d.

Lower Elwa Tribe. Fact sheet. Prepared August 3, 1998.

Mack, Thomas. "Native American Permaculture at Tesuque Pueblo," 1997 Program Description, 1997 Conference Proceedings.

Majestic Pines Hotel. Brochure, n.d.

Makah Museum, Neah Bay, Washington. Brochure, n.d.

Makah Tribe. Cape Flattery Resort. Brochure and information packet. Neah Bay, WA, 1994.

Makah Tribe. 1998 Overall Economic Development Plan. June 24, 1998.

Maliseet Tribe Community Development Projects. Fact sheet, n.d.

Martha's Vineyard Family Campground. Promotional brochure. Vineyard Haven, MA.

MASENAHEKAN (Facts and Figures). Vol. 1. Keshena, WI, 1993.

Mashantucket Pequot Museum and Research Center. Brochure, n.d.

Meherrin Indian Tribe 5th Annual Pow-Wow Program. Winton, NC, 1993.

Menominee Indian Tribe of Wisconsin. Economic Development Department, Private Sector Initiative. Promotional brochure. Keshena, WI, 1994.

Menominee Indian Tribe of Wisconsin. Menominee Tribal Planning Department. OMAEQNOMENEW

Menominee Tribal Enterprises. Brochure, n.d.

Menominee Tribal History Guide. 1998.

Menominee. Circle of Flight. Tribal Wetland and Waterfowl Initiative, 2004.

Miami Tribe of Oklahoma. Tribal Profile. Miami, OK, n.d.

Mille Lacs Band of Ojibwe Tribe. Restore, Rebuild, Renew. Onamia, MN, 1994.

Million Dollar Elm Casino-Sand Springs. Fact Sheet, n.d.

Mississippi Band of Choctaw Indians. Chahta Hapia Hoke: We Are Choctaw. Philadelphia, MS, 1981.

Mississippi Band of Choctaw Indians. Choctaw Industrial Park. Pearl River, MS, 1982.

Mississippi Band of Choctaw Indians. Economic Development Overview. Philadelphia, MS, 1994.

Moapa Band of Paiutes. Fact Sheet. Moapa, NV, 1995.

Modoc Tribe of Oklahoma. Operations Manual. Miami, OK, n.d.

Mohegan Tribe. Mohegan Tribe of Indians of Connecticut: Historical and Socioeconomic Background Information. Fact sheet. Uncasville, CT, 1995.

Montana State University. Extension Service. Flathead Reservation Extension Office. Flathead Ag Link. February 2003.

Muckleshoot Indian Tribe. Pamphlet, n.d.

Muckleshoot Tribe. Muckleshoot Tribal Administration's Annual Report to the Muckleshoot Tribal Community. Auburn, WA, 1995.

Muckleshoot Tribe. Muckleshoot Update. Auburn, WA, 1995.
Muckleshoot Tribe. Muckleshoot Zoning Ordinance, Title 7. Auburn, WA, 1985.

Muscogee (Creek) Nation Indian Reservation Roads Program. Brochure, n.d.

Museum at Warm Springs. Brochure, n.d.

NANA Regional Corporation. Annual Report. Kotzebue, AK, 1993.

Nanticoke Tribe. Overall Economic Description. Millsboro, DE, 1995.

Narrangansett Tribe. Information Packet. Charlestown, RI, 1994.

Narrow Gauge Scenic Road. Booklet, n.d.

National FSA American Indian Credit Outreach Initiative. Brochure, n.d.

Native American Caregiver Support Program. Brochure, n.d.

Native Wisconsin: Official Guide to Native American Communities of Wisconsin, 2003.

Navajo Nation Employee Benefits Program. Brochure, n.d.

Navajo Nation Shopping Centers. Your Navajo Dollar Means Navajo Business and Navajo Jobs. Brochure, n.d.

Navajo Nation, Division of Community Development. Navajo Nation Profile. Updated summer 1993. Window Rock, AZ.

Navajo Nation. Navajo Nation Visitors Guide. Navajo Tribal Council. Window Rock, AZ, n.d.

Navajo Nation. Navajoland: Guide to Navajoland. Navajoland Tourism Department. Window Rock, AZ, n.d.

Navajo Nation. Project Development Department. Information Packet. Window Rock, AZ, 1995.

Navajo Tourism. Discover Navajo, The Official Navajo Nation Visitor Map of Navajoland. Brochure, n.d.

Nez Perce Horse Registry. Brochure, n.d.

Nez Perce National Historic Trail Foundation. Brochure, n.d.

Nez Perce Tribe. Noow Ni Mii Pu (We The People). Lapwai, ID, n.d.

NIGA Gaming Directory 2004.

NIGA Indian Gaming 2004 Buyer's Guide and Directory.

Nisqually OEDP, 1994.

North Coast Inn. Brochure, n.d.

Northern Cheyenne Reservation. Northern Cheyenne Planning Office. Informational Brochure. Lame Deer, MT, 1991.

Northern Cheyenne Tribal Program Directory, 2003. O'Odham-Piipaash Language Program. Brochure, n.d.

O-Gah-Pah Tribal Newsletter, May 2004.

Oklahoma Kaw Lake. Travel Brochure, n.d.

Olallie Lake Fire Complex. Brochure, August 2001. Oneida Communications Inc. Booklet, n.d.

Oneida Community Integrated Food Systems. Booklet, n.d.

Oneida Indian Nation. Brochure, n.d.

Oneida Nation in Wisconsin. Community Development Division, Planning Department. Tribal Profile and Information Oneida, WI, 1995.

Oneida Nation. Booklet, n.d.

Oneida Nation. Enrollment Office Materials, n.d.

Oneida. Circle of Flight. Tribal Wetland and Waterfowl Enhancement Initiative, 1998.

Original Cherokee Great Smoky Mountains Drinking Water. Informational flier, n.d.

Osage Nation, 2005.

Osage Nation Programs. Directory, n.d.

Osage Rural Health Outreach Program. Brochure, n.d.

Osage Tribal Council Regular Meeting, April 14, 2004. Minutes.

Otoe-Missouria Tribe. Tribal Information Packet. Red Rock, OK, n.d.

Ottawa Indian Tribe of Oklahoma. "The Ottawas: Past-Present-Future; A Comprehensive Planning Document." Miami, OK, 1981.

Our Ojibwe Nation: The Spirit of Lac du Flambeau. Booklet, n.d.

Owens Valley Career Development Center. Brochure, n.d.

Passamaquoddy Peaceful Relations Domestic Violence Response Program. Brochure, n.d.

Passamaquoddy Tribe. The Passamaquoddy Tribe's Township Reservation in the State of Maine. Investment Guide. Perry, ME, 1990.

Pearl River Resort. Pamphlet, n.d.

Penobscot Nation Health Department Handbook, April 29, 2002.

Penobscot Nation Museum. Brochure, n.d.

Peoria Tribe of Oklahoma. Tribal background sheet. Miami, OK, n.d.

Pinoleville Indian Reservation Vocational Rehabilitation Program. Brochure, n.d.

Pinoleville Native American Head Start Program. Brochure, n.d.
Pinoleville Native American Resources and Reference Collection. Brochure, n.d.

Poarch Creek Indian Tribe. Poarch Creek Tribal Information Sheets, 1995.

Pokagon Band of Potawatomi Indians. Tribal Information Sheet, n.d.

Ponca Tribe of Nebraska. Informational brochure. 1994.

Ponca Tribe of Oklahoma Tribal Housing Authority. Project descriptions for block grant applications. Ponca City, OK, 1994.

Potawatomi Bingo Casino. Pamphlet, n.d.

Potawatomi Red Deer Ranch. Brochure, n.d.

Prairie Band Potawatomi Nation. Resource Directory, n.d.

Pueblo of Acoma. Brochure, n.d.

Pyramid Lake Paiute Tribe. Pyramid Lake Paiute tribal profile. Nixon, NV, 1991.

Pyramid Lake, the Pride of the Paiute People. Brochure, n.d.

Quapaw Tribe of Oklahoma. Tribal information sheet. Quapaw, OK, 1994.

Ramah Navajo Chapter, Ramah, NM, Directory of Navajo Chapter Office of Grants and Contracts, n.d.

Red Cliff Band of Lake Superior Chippewa. Tribal profile and general information. Bayfield, WI, 1994.

Red Lake Chippewa Tribe. Red Lake Fact Sheet. Red Lake, MN, 1994.

Red Lake Chippewa Tribe. Red Lake Fisheries Association. Informational Brochure. Redby, MN, n.d.

Renewing the Cycle of Life: Restoring the Elwha River. Brochure. 1994.

Roosevelt Recreational Enterprises. The Ultimate Getaway in Style. Brochure, n.d.

Rural Development Initiatives, Inc. Sustainable Tourism Action Plan for the Confederated Tribes of the Warm Springs Reservation of Oregon, June 2004.

S & K Holding Company, Inc. Confederated Salish and Kootenai Tribes Annual CEDS Report. July 2003-June 2004.

Sac and Fox Tribe of Oklahoma. Tribal brochure and information package. Stroud, OK.

Saginaw Chippewa Tribe of Michigan. Doing Business with the Saginaw Chippewa Tribe. East Central Michigan Planning and Development Region. Saginaw, MI, 1991.

Salmon Agriculture and People in the Umatilla River Basin. Brochure, n.d.

Salon in the Woods and the Spa. Brochure, n.d.

Salt River Pima-Maricopa Indian Community. "1983 General Development Plan of the Salt River Pima-Maricopa Indian Community." Scottsdale, AZ, 1983.

Salt River Pima-Maricopa Indian Community. Fact Sheet. Maricopa County, AZ, 1994.

Salt-River Pima-Maricopa Indian Community. Cultural Resources Program. Archaeological and Cultural Resources. Brochure, n.d.

Salt River Pima-Maricopa Indian Community Profile. Community Relations Office. Brochure, n.d.

San Carlos Apache Tribe. Discover San Carlos Apache Reservation; San Carlos Industrial Park. Tribal brochures. San Carlos, AZ, 1994.

San Ildefonso Pueblo. Promotional brochure. Santa Fe, NM, 1995.

Santa Ana Pueblo. Non-Profit Enterprise. Santa Ana Star: High-Stakes Indian Gaming. Promotional brochure. Santa Ana Pueblo, NM, n.d.

Santa Ana Pueblo. Santa Ana Pueblo; On The Move. Promotional brochure. Bernalillo, NM, n.d.

Santa Clara (Kha P'o) Pueblo. Informational packet, March 14, 1997.

Santa Clara Pueblo. Brochure, n.d.

Santa Clara Pueblo. EPA Brownfield's Initiative Proposal, 1999.

Santa Clara Pueblo. Tourism Office. Promotional brochure. Española, NM, 1995.

Santo Domingo Pueblo. Acreages, January 23, 2002. Sauk-Suiattle Indian Tribe. Brochure, n.d.

Sauk-Suiattle Indian Tribe. Fact Sheet, 1998.

Sauk-Suiattle Indian Tribe. Promotional brochure. WA, n.d.

Sault Ste. Marie Tribe of Chippewa Indians. A Brief History: The Sault Ste. Marie Tribe of Chippewa Indians. Sault Ste. Marie, MI, 1994.

Sealaska Corporation. Annual Report. Juneau, AK, 1994.

Sealaska Corporation. "This Is Our Story." Juneau, AK, n.d.

Seascape Restaurant and Pier in Trinidad, CA. Cherae Heights Indian Community. Brochure, n.d.

Sebastian (Bronco). Wakpa Waste Oyanke (The Good River Reservation), n.d.

Seminole Tribe of Florida. Tribal information packet from the Seminole Tribe Office of Planning and Development. Hollywood, FL, 1994.

Seneca Nation of Indians. "Senecas awarded $1.1 million language research grant." Press release, November 16, 2001.

Seneca-Cayuga Tribes of Oklahoma. Tribal background sheet. Miami, OK, n.d.
Shakopee Mdewakanton Sioux. Strengthening Communities. Community Donation Report. Booklet, 2003.

Shakopee Mdewakanton Sioux Community. "Dakotah Meadows Selected as Best RV Park in Minnesota." Press release, July 13, 2004.

Shakopee Mdewakanton Sioux Community. Four Years of Progress. Booklet, 2000-2003.

Shakopee Mdewakanton Sioux Community. Ma-Ka Yu-So-Ta (Boiling Springs). Flyer, September 2000.

Shakopee Mdewakanton Sioux Community and the 106 Group Ltd. Dakota Presence in the River Valley, 2000.

Short History of the United Keetoowah Band of Cherokee Indians in Oklahoma. Brochure, n.d.

Shoshone Tribe of Wyoming Planning Department. Community Profile, 1992. Fort Washakie, WY.

Shoshone-Bannock Indian Festival, August 2002.

Shoshone-Bannock Tribal Enterprises. Brochure, n.d.

Shoshone-Bannock Tribal Museum. Brochure, n.d.

Shoshone-Bannock Tribes. Booklet, May 1999.

Shoshone-Bannock Tribes. Fact sheet, October 2001.

Shoshone-Bannock Tribes. Proposed Organizational Chart, March 31, 1995.

Shoshone-Bannock Tribes. The Area and Economy, 1995. Fort Hall, ID.

Shoshone-Paiute Tribes Economic Development Committee. Shoshone-Paiute Tribes Economic Development Strategic Plan, April, 1999.

Siletz Tribal Code, n.d.

Silver Star Resort and Casino. Brochure, n.d.

Silver Star Resort and Casino. Pamphlet, n.d.

Simpson Electric. Simpson: American Made. Promotional brochure. Albuquerque, NM, n.d.

Sipayik Human Services Department. Brochure, n.d.

Sisseton-Wahpeton Sioux Tribe. Investment Guide. SD, n.d.

Sky Ute Casino and Lodge. The Sky's The Limit! Promotional brochure. Albuquerque, NM, n.d.

Sleeping Ute RV Park and Campground. Brochure, n.d.

Sleepy Hollow Motor Inn. Promotional brochure. Albuquerque, NM, n.d.

Small Business Development Fund. Leech Lake Business Corporation. Brochure, n.d.

Smokin Joes Deli. Daily Breakfast and Lunch Menu, n.d.

Social Service, Resighini Rancheria. Brochure, n.d.
Sokaogon Chippewa Domestic Abuse Program. Brochure, n.d.
Sokaogon Chippewa, Mole Lake Band. Welcome to the Sokaogon Chippewa Community, Crandon, WI. Portion taken from "Chippewa-Indians of Yesterday and Today" by Sister M. Carolissa Levi, I.S.P.A..

Sokaogan Ojibwe. National Museum of the American Indian, Summer 2004.

South Carolina Indians Today. Booklet, 1998.

Southern Ute Tribe. Southern Ute Indian Tribe: Cultural Tourism Case Study. Western Entrepreneurial Network. Ignacio, CO, 1993.

Southwest Alaska Municipal Conference. Village profiles. Anchorage, AK, 1992.

Southwest Region Indian Acreages, December 31, 2002.

SRPMIC Annual Report, FY 2002.

St. Croix Tribal Community Profile, 2003.

St. Regis Mohawk Tribe. Economic Development Office. White Pines Plaza Feasibility Study. State University of New York College at Potsdam, 1994.

St. Regis Mohawk Tribe. Role of Ameda Within the Tribe of Saint Regis Mohawk Tribe. Fact sheet. Hogansburg, NY, 1994.

St. Regis Mohawk Tribe. St. Regis Mohawk Tribe informational publication. Hogansburg, NY, n.d.

Sub-Development on Strawberry Island. Fact sheet, n.d.

Suquamish Tribe. 2004 Labor Force Report. Suquamish, WA.

Swinomish Tribe. The Draft Environmental Impact Statement for the Draft Swinomish Comprehensive Plan, Swinomish Tribal Community and Skagit County. WA, 1992.
Swinomish Tribe Land Use Advisory Board. The Draft Swinomish Comprehensive Plan WA, 1990.

Table Mountain Rancheria Enterprises Incorporated. Brochure, n.d.

Taos Pueblo. Taos Pueblo: A Thousand Years of Tradition. Promotional brochure. Taos, NM, n.d.

Taos Pueblo War Chief's Office. Land and Natural Resource Management Planning Project: Phase I. Taos, NM, n.d.

The Lodge at Chama. Pamphlet, n.d.

36th Annual Ute Indian Tribe 4th of July Pow-Wow. Poster, 2004.

Three Clans Hospitality Consulting. Pamphlet, 2003.
Three Rivers Casino. Brochure. Florence, Oregon, n.d.
Tiller Research, Inc. "To Govern and to be Governed: American Indian Tribal Governments at the Crossroads." Report prepared for History Project of Americans for Indian Opportunity.

Tohono O'Odham Nation. The Tohono O'Odham Reservation and San Xavier Industrial Park and Foreign Trade Zone in the State of Arizona. Investment guide, n.d.
Treasure Island Resort and Casino. Travelogue, n.d.

Tribal Child Care Subsidy Program. United Keetoowah Band of Cherokee Indians, OK. Brochure, n.d.

Tribal Fish and Game Department Lac du Flambeau Tribal Fisheries Program, 1936-1986. Lac du Flambeau, WI, 1986.

Tribal Organization Chart. Quileute Nation, La Push, WA, September 30, 1997.

Tsosie, Nathan W. Santa Ana Pueblo. Tribal information document. Bernalillo, NM.

Tunica-Biloxi Indians of Louisiana. Tribal promotional literature and area map.

Turtle Mountain Band of Chippewa. History and Origin of the Trenton Indian Service Area. Trenton, ND, 1994.

Turtle Mountain Band of Chippewa. Investment Guide. Trenton, ND, n.d.

Turtle Mountain Band of Chippewa. Turtle Mountain Manufacturing Co. Promotional brochure. Belcourt, ND, n.d.

Turtle Mountain Band of Chippewa Indians. Code for the Creation and Governance of Corporations, Proposed, n.d.

Turtle Mountain Band of Chippewa Indians Reservation in the State of North Dakota. Investment Guide. Trenton, ND, n.d.

Twin Pine Casino. Brochure, n.d.

Umpqua Indian Foods. Brochure, n.d.

Uniband, Inc. Informational pamphlet, n.d.

United Keetoowah Band. Brochure, n.d.

United Keetoowah Band. Did you know? Fact sheet, n.d.

United Keetoowah Band of Cherokee. Information Packet. Tahlequah, OK, n.d.

United Keetoowah Band of Cherokee. Tribal Profile. Tahlequah, OK, 1995.

United Keetoowah Band of Cherokees. Brochure, n.d.

Upper Sioux Community. "History of Upper Sioux." Community profile. Granite Falls, MN, 1994.

Urban Renewal Agency of Kansas. "A Brief Interpretation of the History of the Wyandotte Indians." Kansas City, KS, 1976.

Ute Mountain Casino. Brochure, n.d.

Ute Mountain Tribal Park. Brochure, n.d.

Ute Mountain Ute Tribe. Ute Mountain Ute Reservation. Fact Sheet. Towaoc, CO, 1989.

Ute Mountain Ute Tribe. Ute Mountain Ute Tribe: Development Reflects Tribe's Priorities. CERT report. Denver, CO, 1994.

Ute Tribe. The Ute Indian Tribe Water Settlement Act. Public Relations Information Handout, January 10, 2001.

Ute Tribe. Tribal Government and the Ute Tribe Today. Public Relations Information Handout, February 13, 2002.

Ute Tribe. Water is the Blood of Life. Ute Tribe Public Relations Information Handout. February 13, 2002. Viejas Casino. Brochure, n.d.

Viejas Indian Reservation. Economics Viejas Style: A Native American Perspective. Alpine, CA, 1993. Viejas Outlet Center. Brochure, n.d.

Vision of Growth, A: Comprehensive 20-Year Plan for the Prairie Band Potawatomi Nation, 25, n.d.

Visions and Voices of the Jicarilla Apache Tribe, October 1995. IRMP Office.

Visitor's Guide and Map to the Warm Springs Reservation, n.d.

Wah-Shun-Gah Days Inter-Tribal Pow Wow. Flyer, n.d.

Walker River Paiute Indian Reservation, Schurz, Nevada. Brochure, n.d.

Wampanoag Tribe of Gay Head. Master Plan of Wampanoag Tribal Lands. Falmouth, MA, 1993.

Wampanoag Tribe of Gay Head (Aquinnah). Wampanoag Tribe of Gay Head fact sheet. Gay Head, MA, 1992.

Waponahki Museum and Resource Center. Brochure, n.d.

Warm Springs Composite Products. Information Sheet. Warm Springs, OR, n.d.

Warm Springs Small Business Development Center. Brochure, n.d.

Warm Springs Tribe. Kah-Nee-Ta Resort: Everything Under the Sun. Promotional brochure. Warm Springs, OR, 1994.

Washoe Tribe. Washoe Reservation data sheets. Gardnerville, NV, 1994.

Washoe Tribe of Nevada and California. Promotional brochure. Gardnerville, NV, n.d. Waswagoning Indian Village. Brochure, n.d.

Wauqua, Johnny. Numunu. The People. Comanche Tribal Pamphlet. Publisher unknown, n.d.

Welcome to the Shakopee Mdewakanton Sioux Community, Prior Lake, MN. Brochure, n.d.

Welcome to the Sokaogon Chippewa Community. Pamphlet, n.d.

Whatley, William. Pueblo of Jemez, Department of Archeology and Preservation. Pueblo of Jemez Traditional Fieldhouse Construction Project. Albuquerque, NM, n.d.

White Earth Reservation Tribal Council. White Earth Reservation Community Profile, n.d.

White Mountain Apache Tribe. Fort Apache Timber Co. Whiteriver, AZ, n.d. Why Locate to the Wild Horse Pass Business Park within the Gila River Indian Community? Brochure, n.d.

Wichita and Affiliated Tribes. Tribal newsletter. Anadarko, OK, 1995.

Winnebago Tribe of Nebraska. Brochure, n.d.

Wyandotte Advertising. Brochure, n.d.

Wyandotte Advertising. Winner Service Category, Nevada Bank and Trust, Native American. Brochure, n.d.

Wyandotte Collegiate Systems. Brochure, n.d. Wyandotte Nation, 2004.

Wyandotte NetTel. Informational packet, n.d.

Wyandotte Tribe of Oklahoma. Keepers of the Council Fire, by Robert Smith. Wyandotte, OK, n.d.

Yakama Nation Tribal Council Special Committee. Media Committee. Economic Development. 2005.

Yakama Nation. Yakama Indian Nation Economic Development Brochure. Toppenish, WA, n.d.

Yankton Sioux Tribe. Comprehensive Economic Development Strategy, June 2004.

Yavapai-Apache Tribal Housing. Low Income Housing Tax Credit Program. Brochure, n.d.

Yideeskáágóó Naat'áanii. Future Leaders. Brochure, n.d.

Yurok Tribal Council. Information, March 9, 2004.

Zia Pueblo. Pueblo of Zia Tribal Administration Comprehensive Plan Update. Zia, NM, 1989.

Zia Pueblo. Pueblo of Zia Tribal Information. Zia, NM, 1995.

GOVERNMENT PUBLICATIONS

Alaska Dept. of Community and Regional Affairs. Community Database. Juneau, AK, 1994.

Alaska Dept. of Community and Regional Affairs/Alaska Municipal League.

Alaska Dept. of Fish and Game. George River Salmon Studies, 1996 to 2002. By John C. Linder-man, Jr., John C. Douglas, B. Molyneaux, Larry DuBois, and David J. Cannon. Division of Commercial Fisheries. Anchorage, AK, May 2003.

Alaska Municipal Officials Directory. Anchorage, AK, 1994.

Allen, Bill. Final Report: Water Quality Management for Kickapoo Tribe, Brown County Kansas. September 30, 1997.

Allen, Bill. Unified Watershed Assessment and Watershed Restoration Priorities List. February 1999.

Arizona Commission of Indian Affairs. 1990-1991 Annual Report. Phoenix, AZ, 1992.

Arizona Commission of Indian Affairs. 1994-1995 Tribal Directory. Phoenix, AZ, 1994.

Arizona Department of Commerce. Community Profiles. Phoenix, AZ, 1992. Aroostook Band of Micmac Indians. FY 2001 Comprehensive Tribal Survey.

Big Sandy Rancheria Environmental Programs Office, Big Sandy Rancheria Water Quality Assessment 305(B). December 1999.

Bizhibayash Circle of Flight, Tribal Wetland and Waterfowl Enhancement Initiative "Fond du Lac Ceded Territory, Hay Lake and Pike Bay Projects." January, 1998.

Carpenter, Wiley, of Big Sandy Rancheria to United Watershed Assessment Working Group of the United States EPA. Correspondence, September 28, 1998.

Cheyenne River Sioux Tribe Comprehensive Economic Development Study, 2002.

Coquille Tribe. Public Law 101-42: The Coquille Restoration Act. June 28, 1989.

Demographic Study for the Coeur d' Alene Tribe. July, 2003.

Earthworks Industries, Inc. Environmental Assessment of Proposed Field Investigation: Cortina Rancheria, Colusa County, California. Vancouver, Canada, 1994.

Federal Register 68, No. 234, Friday, December 5, 2003.

Fowler, Don D. Evaluation of the Cultural Resources of the Fort Bidwell Indian Reservation, Modoc County, California. Western Archeological Center, U.S. National Park Service. Tucson, AZ, 1977.

Great Lakes Basin Report, 12, No. 11, November 2001.
HNTB Corporation. Narrow Gauge Scenic Road: Archuleta County, CO and Rio Arriba County, NM. Corridor Study. Prepared for US Highway Administration on behalf of Southern Ute and Jicarilla Apache Tribes. Denver, CO, 1993.

Harris, Thomas R., William O. Champney, Karl A. McArthur, and William L. Cooper. "An Investigation of Selected Economic Development Potentials for the Fort McDermitt Reservation." The University Center for Economic Development (UCED), UCED 96/97-11.

Interior Board of Indian Appeals. "Big Lagoon Park Co. vs. Acting Sacramento Area Director, Bureau of Indian Affairs." 32 IBIA 309 (08/31/1998).

Intertribal Agriculture Council. Wichita and Affiliated Tribes. National Indian Agriculture Profile, Billings, MT, 1992

"Jurisdiction in Indian Country." Chapter 51, pg. 285. Idaho State Code 67-5101.

Kansas Lewis and Clark Bicentennial Commission. Native American Resource Handbook. Kansas Art Commission, 2004.

Kelsey, C.E. "Schedule Showing Non-Reservation Indians in Northern California." California Census, 1905-1906.

Kickapoo Environmental Office. Quality Assurance Project Plan for Water Quality Sampling, (Chemical). Prepared for USEPA Region VII, May 1998.

Kuskokwim Planning and Management Corporation. Economic Profile of the Middle Kuskokwim Region. Anchorage, AK, 1991.
Lower Kuskokwim Economic Development Council. Economic Profiles for the Communities of the Lower Kuskokwim Region. Bethel, AK, 1993.

Middle Rio Grande Council of Governments of New Mexico. Community Digest in Support of Economic Development in New Mexico State Planning and Development. District 3, Spr-217, 1988.

Navajo Nation. Data Extracted from 2000 U.S. Census by Trib Choudhary, Support Services Department. Division of Economic Development, n.d.

Nez Perce Tribe, Water Resources Division, Report to the Nez Perce Tribal General Council, Nez Perce Tribe, Lapwai, Idaho, May 6-8, 2004.

Office of the Solicitor, U.S. Department of the Interior. Reservation Status of New York Lands. NY, 1989.

Passamaquoddy Tribe at Pleasant Point. Tribal Environmental Agreement between the Passamaquoddy Tribe at Pleasant Point (Sipayik) and the United States EPA. Pleasant Point (Passamaquoddy) and Indian Township Reservations, n.d.

Penobscot Indian Nation. FY 2001 Comprehensive Tribal Survey.

Record Group 75. Records of the Bureau of Indian Affairs. Central Classified Files, 1907-1939.

Roseburg, 310, file 108.465-14. "Census of Ione and Vicinity [sic] Indians - at Richey Belonging to the Ione Band."

Record Group 75. Records of the Bureau of Indian Affairs. Central Classified Files. 1907-1939. California Special 034, File 5340.

Seneca Nation Community Planning and Development Office. FY 2003 Investment Analysis.

Seneca Nation of Indians. CEDS Progress Report 2003.

Shoshone-Paiute Tribes Economic Development Committee. Shoshone-Paiute Tribes Economic Development Strategic Plan. April, 1999.

Susanville Indian Rancheria. National American Indian Housing Council Study, n.d.

Turtle Mountain Band of Chippewa. HUD Designated Renewal Community Tax Incentives, n.d.

U.S. Army Corps of Engineers, Tulsa District. Oklahoma Kaw Lake. Travel brochure, n.d.

U. S. Dept. of the Interior. Bureau of Indian Affairs. Office of Trust and Responsibilities Annual Report of Indian Lands, 1985.

U.S. Bureau of Land Management. Eldridge, P. 2nd Quarter Report. Anchorage, AK, 1994.

U.S. Bureau of the Census. 2000 U.S. Census.

U.S. Congress. Office of Technology Assessment. Health and Environmental Sciences Division. Water for Walker Lake, n.d.

U.S. Dept. of Commerce, Economic Development Agency, Overall Economic Development Plans. Barona Band of MissionIndians June 18,1992. Oakland, CA.

Big Pine Band of Paiute Shoshone Indians., 1993 Update. Oakland, CA.

Big Sandy Rancheria. 1991-1996. Oakland, CA, 1991.

Bishop Paiute Development Corporation. Oakland, CA, 1994.

Blackfeet Reservation. 1992-1997. Browning, MT, 1992.

Blue Lake Rancheria. Oakland, CA, 1994.

Bois Forte Band of Chippewa. Nett Lake, MN, 1992.

Bridgeport Paiute Tribe. Provo, UT, 1977.

Burns Paiute Indian Reservation. Burns, OR, 1982.

Cabazon Band of Mission Indians. Oakland, CA, 1988.

Cahuilla Band of Indians. 1994 Annual Report. Oakland, CA, 1994.

Campo Band of Mission Indians. Oakland, CA, 1994.

Canto Tribe. Oakland, CA, 1979.

Chemehuevi Indian Tribe. Oakland, CA, 1988.

Chippewa-Cree Tribe. Denver, CO, 1992.

Coast Indian Community of the Resighini Rancheria. Oakland, CA, 1992.

Coeur d' Alene Tribe. Plummer, ID, 1994.

Cold Springs Tribal Council. Oakland, CA, 1987.

Confederated Salish and Kootenai Tribes. Flathead Indian Reservation. Pablo, MT, 1993.

Confederated Tribes of Siletz Indians of Oregon. Seattle, WA, 1992-93.

Confederated Tribes of Warm Springs. Warm Springs, OR, 1991.

Confederated Tribes of the Colville Indian Reservation. Seattle, WA, 1994-95.

Confederated Tribes of the Umatilla Indian Reservation. Seattle, WA. 1992.

Cortina Rancheria Tribe. Oakland, CA, 1994.

Coyote Valley Tribal Council. Oakland, CA, 1993.

Devils Lake Sioux Tribe. Denver, CO, 1993.

Eight Northern Indian Pueblos Council, Inc. 1993.

Ely Shoshone Tribe. Ely, NV, 1993.

Fallen Paiute - Shoshone Tribe. October 1989-1990. Carson City, NV, 1990.

Ford du Lac Tribe. Cloquet, MN, 1992.
Fort Belknap Indian Community. Denver, CO, 1984.

Fort Peck Tribes. Denver, CO, 1993.

Grand Portage Reservation. Grand Portage, MN, 1993.

Great Lakes Inter-Tribal Council, Inc. 1993-1994. Lac du Flambeau, WI, 1994.

Grindstone Indian Rancheria. Annual Report, June. Oakland, CA, 1980.

Hoopa Valley Tribe. Hoopa Valley Indian Reservation. Oakland, CA, 1993.

Hopi Tribe. Annual Report. Kykotsmovi, AZ, 1993.

Hopland Band of Pomo Indians. Oakland, CA. 1994.

Hualapai Nation. Peach Springs, AZ. 1992.

Inter-Tribal Council, Inc. Miami, OK. 1994.

Jamul Village of Mission Indians. Jamul, CA, 1980.

Karuk Tribe of California. Oakland, CA. 1991.

La Jolla Band of Mission. Oakland, CA. 1994.
La Posta Band of Mission Indians. Oakland, CA, 1981.

Lake Traverse Tribe. Lake Traverse, SD.

Los Coyotes Band of Mission Indians. Oakland, CA, 1980.

Lower Brule Sioux Tribe. Denver, CO, 1993.

Lower Elwha Reservation. Port Angeles, WA, 1976.

Lummi Indian Nation. Seattle, WA, 1991.

Makah Tribe. 1991-1992. Neah Bay, WA, 1992.

Manzanita Band of Mission Indians. 1981-82 Annual Report. Oakland, CA, 1981.

Mille Lacs Band of Ojibwe Tribe. Onamia, MN, 1994.
Mississippi Band of Choctaw Indians. Philadelphia, MS, 1994.

Morongo Band of Mission Indians. Oakland, CA, 1994.

Muckleshoot Indian Tribe. Seattle, WA, 1991.

Navajo Nation. Window Rock, AZ, 1993.

Nez Perce Tribe. Lapwai, ID, 1993.

Nisqually Indian Tribe. Olympia, WA, 1986.

O. Burruel, and Elem OEDP Committee. Annual Report for 1979. Oakland,CA, 1979.

Pala Band of Mission Indians. FY 1979-1980. Pala, CA, 1979.

Passamaquoddy Tribe. Perry, MA, 1993.

Pauma Band of Mission Indians. Oakland, CA, 1992.

Penobscot Indian Nation. Old Town, ME, 1993.
Pit River Tribe. Oakland, CA, 1993.

Port Bidwell Indian Community Council OEDP Committee. Fort Bidwell, CA, 1991.

Port Gamble S'Klallam Tribe. Kingston, WA, 1993.

Quileute Tribe. La Push, WA, 1993.

Redwood Valley Little River Band of Pomo Indians. . Oakland, CA, 1992.

Rincon, San Luiseño Band of Mission Indians. Fourth Revision. Oakland, CA, 1980.

Robinson Rancheria Citizens' Council. Oakland, CA, 1989.

Round Valley Indian Reservation. 1981 Annual Report. Oakland, CA, 1981.

Rumsey Indian Rancheria of Wintun Indians. Oakland, CA, 1976.

Sac and Fox of the Mississippi in Iowa. Denver, CO, 1992.
Saginaw Chippewa Tribe of Michigan. Mt. Pleasant, MI, 1994.

Saint Regis Mohawk Tribe. 1993 Hogansburg, NY, 1995.

San Manuel Band of Mission Indians. Oakland, CA, 1978.

San Pasqual Band of Mission Indians. 1980-81, Oakland, CA, 1980.

Santa Rosa Tribe. Lemoore, CA, 1982.

Santa Rosa Indian Reservation. Oakland, CA, 1977.

Santa Ynez Band of Mission Indians. Oakland, CA, 1994.

Santee Tribe. Nebraska Community Profile, Lincoln, NE, 1987.

Seneca Nation of Indians. 1992 5-Year Annual Report and 1994 Update. Irving, NY, 1994.

Sherwood Valley Tribal Council. Oakland, CA, 1994.

Shingle Springs Rancheria. 1990-95. Oakland, CA, 1990.

Shoshone-Bannock Tribes. 1994 Update. Fort Hall, ID.

Sisseton-Wahpeton Sioux Tribe of the Lake Traverse Reservation.Village, SD, 1994.

Skokomish Tribe. 1987 Overall Economic Development Plan Update. Shelton, WA, 1985.

Skokomish Indian Tribe. 1985 Update. Seattle, WA, 1985,1979.

Soboba Band of Mission Indians. June 1994 Oakland, CA, 1994.

South Puget Sound Intertribal Planning Agency. Shelton, WA, 1984-85.

Spokane Tribe of Indians Seattle, WA, 1994.

Squaxin Island Tribe. 1985-1986 Overall Economic Development Plan. Seattle, WA, 1985.

Standing Rock Nation. Revised Working Draft. Fort Yates, ND, 1993.

Susanville Indian Rancheria. Oakland, CA, 1979.

Swinomish Tribal Community. LaConner, WA, 1993 and 1990.

Sycuan Band of Mission Indians. Oakland, CA, 1979.

Three Affiliated Tribes.Denver, CO, 1994.

Tonto Apache Tribe. Payson, AZ, 1993.

Trinidad Rancheria OEDP Committee. Oakland, CA, 1990.

Tule River Reservation. Oakland, CA, 1994.

Tuolumne Rancheria 1980 Annual Report. Oakland, CA, 1980.

Turtle Mountain Band of Chippewa. Belcourt, ND, 1992.

Upper Lake OEDP Committee and Lon F. Armstrong, Oakland, CA, 1979.

Viejas Band of Mission Indians. Oakland, CA, 1980.

Western Nevada Development District. Carson City, NV, 1993.

White Earth Chippewa Tribe. Annual 1992. White Earth, MN.

Yurok Overall Economic Development Planning Committee. FY 1993-94 Annual Review. Oakland, CA, 1994.

U.S. Dept. of Health and Human Services. Indian Health Services. Kootenai Tribe of Idaho, n.d.

U.S. Dept. of Homeland Security. Emergency Planning Booklet. Tribal Emergency Response Commission (T.E.R.C.), n.d.

U.S. Dept. of Housing and Urban Development. Application for Community Development Block Grants for Indian Tribes and Alaskan Native Villages. 1994.

U.S. Dept. of the Interior. Bureau of Indian Affairs. Acreages by Agency and Reservation, n.d.

U.S. Dept. of the Interior. Bureau of Indian Affairs, Aberdeen Area Office. Aberdeen Area Office Aberdeen Area Annual Report. Aberdeen, WA, 1993.

U.S. Dept. of the Interior. Bureau of Indian Affairs, Anadarko Area Office. Anadarko Area Office Anadarko Area Annual Report. Anadarko, OK, 1988.

U.S. Dept. of the Interior. Bureau of Indian Affairs, Billings Area Office. Billings Area Office, BIA Area Annual Report. Billings, MT, 1989.

U.S. Dept. of the Interior. Bureau of Indian Affairs. Anadarko Area Office. Anadarko Area Office Tonkawa Tribal Profile. Anadarko, OK, 1989.

U.S. Dept. of the Interior. Bureau of Indian Affairs. Anadarko Area Office. Anadarko Area Office Tribal Information and Directory. Anadarko, OK, 1994.
U.S. Dept. of the Interior. Bureau of Indian Affairs, Division of Energy and Mineral Resources. The Oil and Gas Opportunity on Indian Lands: Exploration Policies and Procedures. 1994 Edition. Blackfeet Indian Reservation. Browning, MT.

U.S. Dept. of the Interior. Bureau of Indian Affairs. Draft Environmental Statement: Secretarial Land Use Plan for the Addition to the Havasupai Indian Reservation. Phoenix, AZ, 1979.

U.S. Dept. of the Interior. Effects of Produced Waters at Oilfield Productions Sites on the Osage Indian Reservation, Northeastern Oklahoma, by James K Otton, Sigrid

Asher-Bolinder, Douglass E. Owen, and Laurel Hall. U.S. Geological Survey. Denver, February, 1997. U.S. Dept. of the Interior. Bureau of Indian Affairs. Indian Service Population and Labor Force Estimates, 1993.

U.S. Dept. of the Interior. Bureau of Indian Affairs, Juneau Area Office. Juneau Area Office Mailing List of Entities Served. Juneau, AK, 1994.

U.S. Dept. of the Interior. Bureau of Indian Affairs, Kaw Reservation. Document 5-2119. Anadarko, OK, 1993.

U.S. Dept. of the Interior. Bureau of Indian Affairs. Labor Market Information on the Indian Labor Force, Survey Form for Calendar Year 2003.

U.S. Dept. of the Interior. Bureau of Indian Affairs. Labor Report of 2001.

U.S. Dept. of the Interior. Bureau of Indian Affairs. Legislative Environmental Impact Statement for Siletz Indian Reservation Plan. 1979.

U.S. Dept. of the Interior. Bureau of Indian Affairs. Local Estimates of Indian Service Population and Labor Market Information, n.d.

U.S. Dept. of the Interior. Bureau of Indian Affairs, Minneapolis Area Office, Branch of Forestry. "The Forests of Anishinabe: A History of Minnesota Chippewa Tribal Forestry: 1854-1991." Prepared by HRA, Missoula, MN, 1992.

U.S. Dept. of the Interior. Bureau of Indian Affairs, Minneapolis Area Office. Minneapolis Area Office Tribal Information and Directory. Minneapolis, MN, 1993.

U.S. Dept. of the Interior, Bureau of Indian Affairs, Muskogee Area Office Annual Activities Report, Osage Agency. Muskogee, OK, 1993.

U.S. Dept. of the Interior. Bureau of Indian Affairs, Muskogee Area Office. Muskogee Area Office Tribal Profile: Kickapoo Tribe of Oklahoma. Muskogee, OK, 1993.

U.S. Dept. of the Interior. Bureau of Indian Affairs, Navajo Area Office. Navajo Area Office Navajo Nation Profile, Navajo Tribal Delegation Information. Gallup, NM, 1993.

U.S. Dept. of the Interior. Bureau of Indian Affairs. Office of Facilities Management and Construction. Chief Ignacio Justice Center Dedicated. Facilities Management Summary, October 2000.

U.S. Dept. of the Interior. Office of Federal Acknowledgement. Historical Technical Report Jena Band of Choctaw Indians. Jbc V001 D005.

U.S. Dept. of the Interior. Office of Federal Acknowledgment. Mbp VOOl D005.

U.S. Dept. of the Interior. Bureau of Indian Affairs. Office of Tribal Services. American Indian Population and Labor Force Report 2001.

U.S. Dept. of the Interior. Bureau of Indian Affairs, Phoenix Area Office Indians of Arizona Tribal Profiles. Phoenix, AZ, 1994.

U.S. Dept. of the Interior. Bureau of Indian Affairs,

Phoenix Area Office. Phoenix Area Office Indians of Nevada Tribal Profiles, Phoenix, AZ, 1994.

U.S. Dept. of the Interior. Bureau of Indian Affairs, Phoenix Area Office. Phoenix Area Office Indians of Utah Tribal Profiles. Phoenix, AZ, 1994.

U.S. Dept. of the Interior. Bureau of Indian Affairs, Portland Area Office. Portland Area Office Tribal Profiles. Portland, OR, 1994.

U.S. Dept. of the Interior. Bureau of Indian Affairs, Sac and Fox Area Field Office. Tribal Profile: Sac and Fox Tribe of the Mississippi in Iowa Mesquakie. Tama, IA, 1993.

U.S. Dept. of the Interior. Bureau of Indian Affairs, Sacramento Area Office. Report on Service Population and Labor Force. Sacramento, CA, 1994.

U.S. Dept. of the Interior. Bureau of Indian Affairs, Sacramento Area Office. Tribal Information and Directory. Sacramento, CA, 1993.

U.S. Dept. of the Interior. Bureau of Indian Affairs. Southwest Region Indian Acreages. December 31, 2002.

U.S. Dept. of the Interior. Bureau of Indian Affairs. Trust Acreage Reports, Indian Service Population and Labor Market Information, and Tribal Directory. Pacific Regional Office, 2800 Cottage Way, Sacramento, California 95825, n.d.

U.S. Environmental Protection Agency. Agreement between the Aroostook Band of Micmacs and the United States EPA, April 30, 1998.

U.S. Enivronmental Protection Agency. American Indian Environmental Office. American Indian Reservation Profiles.

   Cahuilla Band of Indians, n.d.
   Campo Band of Kumeyaay (Diegueño) Indians, n.d.
   Choctaw Nation of Oklahoma, n.d.
   Confederated Tribes of the Grand Ronde Tribal Council, n.d.
   Coquille Indian Tribal Community, n.d.
   Eastern Band of Cherokee Indians of North Carolina, n.d.
   Elko Band of the Te-Moak Tribe of Western Shoshone Indians of Nevada, n.d.
   Fort Hall Reservation, n.d.
   Karuk Tribe of California, 2004.
   Lac Courte Oreilles Band of Lake Superior Chippewa. Washington, D.C., n.d.
   Manzanita Reservation, n.d.
   Mashantucket Pequot Tribe, n.d.
   Menominee Indian Tribe of Wisconsin, n.d.
   Miccosukee Tribe of Florida Indians, n.d.
   Muckleshoot Indian Tribe, n.d.
   Nez Perce Tribe of Idaho, n.d.
   Oneida Reservation, n.d.
   Pala Band of Mission Indians, n.d.
   Pueblo of Isleta, n.d.
   Pueblo of Tesuque, n.d.
   Round Valley Indian Tribes, n.d.
   Santee Sioux Tribe of Nebraska, n.d.
   Seminole Tribe of Florida, n.d.
   South Fork Band Colony, n.d.
   Summit Lake Paiute Tribe, n.d.
   Taos Pueblo, n.d.

   Tonkawa Tribe of Oklahoma, n.d.
   Tribal Profiles, n.d.
   Tuolumne Rancheria, n.d.
   Tuscarora Tribe, n.d.
   Ute Mountain Tribe of the Ute Mountain Reservation, n.d.
   Yomba Shoshone Tribe, n.d.

U.S. EPA. Brownfield's Assessment Demonstration Pilot, Turtle Mountain Band of Chippewa, ND. USEPA, Washington, D.C., July 1998.

U.S. EPA. Brownfield's Assessment Pilots, Little River Band of Ottawa Indians, MI. USEPA, May 2002.

U.S. EPA. TERO, Tribal Employment Rights Office. Brochure. Washington, DC, July 1998

U.S. Census, 1990: Social and Economic Characteristics. Table 11, Occupation of Employed American Indian, Eskimo, or Aleut Persons: 1990. Publication CP-2-1A. Washington, D.C.: U.S. Government Printing Office, 1993.

U.S. Census, 1990: United States Summary, Summary Social, Economic, and Housing Characteristics. Table 9, Selected Social and Economic Characteristics for American Indian and Alaska Native Areas: 1990. Publication CHP-5-1. Washington, D.C.: U.S. Government Printing Office, 1992.

U.S. Census, 1990: Social and Economic Characteristics. Table 8, Geographic Mobility, Commuting, and Industry of Employed Persons, for American Indian, Eskimo, or Aleut Persons: 1990. Publication CP-2-1A. Washington, D.C.: U.S. Government Printing Office, 1993. Village Profiles. Prepared by DOWL Engineers, with North Pacific Aerial Surveys and Bristol Bay Native Association, under contract with the Alaska Department of Community and Regional Affairs, 1982.
Village Profiles. Prepared by Environmental Services Limited, under contract with the Alaska Department of Community and Regional Affairs, Division of Community Planning, 1982.

Village Profiles. Prepared by North Slope Borough. Barrow, AK, 1993.

Visions Enterprises. Potter Valley Tribal Council: Tribal Action Plan. Ukiah, CA, 1993.

Walker River Paiute Tribe. Children and Youth Initiative Grant Program for American Indians and Alaskan Natives. FY 2003.

Western Shoshone Defense Project. Digging Holes in the Spirit: Gold Mining and the Survival of the Western Shoshone Nation, 1999.

Wisconsin Department of Development, Division of Tourism, Wisconsin's Heritage Tourism Initiative Program Evaluation, 1993. Madison, WI.
NEWSPAPERS
"2002-2003 Tribal Legislature" Chickasaw Times, June 2004.

"A Day in the Life of Big Cypress." Seminole Tribune, Commemorative Issue, 1999.

Abanathy, Patrick. "YPT First Nevada Tribe to Sign Self-Help Housing Agreement." Mason Valley News, 23 July 2004.

Absentee Shawnee News, Vol. 15, No.6, June 2004.

Adams, Jim. "Connecticut Towns Fight State Support of Mashantucket Pequot Water District." Indian Country Today, 15 July 2003.

Adams, Jim. "Penobscots of Maine Sue in Federal Court." Indian Country Today, 19 March 2004.

Adams, Jim. "Planning Infrastructure for the Casino Corridor." Tourism and Gaming 2004 Indian Country Today 2004.

Adawe News, May 2004.

Associated Press. "California Desert Town Approves Indian Casino Project." 3 March 2004.

Associated Press. "Compromise Clears Way for Nez Perce National Park." News From Indian Country, Mid-October 1992.

Associated Press. "Indian Tribes Looking Beyond Reservation." 15 March 2004.

Associated Press. "N.M. tribes awarded conservation grants." 27 August 2004.

Associated Press. "News in brief from northern California." May 19, 2004.

Associated Press. "New York Oneida Eye Chicagoland Casino." 16 September 2003.

Associated Press. "Ponca Tribe Builds Earthen Lodge Like Those Used By Ancestors." 13 October 2003.

Associated Press. "Program to Restore Fish Migration on Reservation." 17 August 2004.

Associated Press. "Tribal Justice Center Development Plans Under Way." State Local Wire, 10 February 2004.

Baker, Deborah. "Governor Signs Compact for To'hajiilee Casino." Associated Press Writer. 6 November 2003.

Barfield, Chet. "Arizona Tribe Will Fund Small Casino for La Posta Band." San Diego Union Tribune, 10 October 2003.

Barfield, Chet. "Santa Ysabel Band Hires Team to Plan, Run Proposed Casino." San Diego Union-Tribune, 25 March 2004.

"BIA Givers United Keetoowah Band Approval to Head East." Ojibwe News, 19 August 1994.

Billingsley, Eric. "San Felipe Pueblo Revs Up for New Race Track." NMBW, 1 March 2002.

Bingo Bugle, North America's Bingo and Casino Newspaper, June 2004.

"Black Mesa Golf Club." Indian Country Today. Tourism and Gaming (2004).

"Cayuga Land Claim Deal Gets 'Raspberries.'" Political Observer, June 2004.

Chandler, Becky. "Facility Serves Northern Chickasaw Nation: New Senior Citizen Site Dedicated in Purcell." Chickasaw Times, June 2004.

Chen, David W. "Begrudging the Neighbor's Luck." New York Times, 22 January 1999.

"Cherokee Heritage Center Offers Free Admission on Cherokee Saturdays." Keetoowah News No. 8, July 2003.

Cherveny, Tom. "Upper Sioux Warn Against Expansion of State Gaming." West Central Tribune 2004.

Choate, Tony. "Gov. Anoatubby Selected for Oklahoma Hall of Fame." Chickasaw Times, Vol. 39, No. 6, June 2004.

Choctaw Nation of Oklahoma. Newsprint Insert.

Clines, Francis X. "Senecas Ponder Novel Deal on Tax-Free Tobacco Sales." New York Times, 10 August 1994, sec. Bl, B4.

"Comanche Tribal License Tags are Here." Comanche News, July 1995.

"Comanche Veterans Memorial Dedicated." Comanche News, August 1995, ENAT, 68-71.

Crook, Walter. "New Arapahoe Charter School to Open in Fall." Wind River News, 18 March 2004.

"Crow Pursue Little Bighorn Tourist Attraction." Indian Country Today, 1995.

Day, Peter. "Was the Timbisha Tribe Really Here?" Hesperia Star, n.d.

Delaware Tribal News, Delaware Tribal Office, May 2004.

Dingmann, Tracy. "Tribal Vision." Albuquerque Journal, 19 September 2004.

"Economics Special: Tribal Joint Venture Empowers Rural Communities in Wisconsin." Indian Country Today, 9 September 2003.

Edwards, Rob. "Native Americans in Protests at Scottishpower Threat to Salmon." The Sunday Herald, 16 May 2004.

"FERC Relicenses Cushman Hydro-Electric Project in Washington State." The Sounder, August 1998.

Fialka, John J. "Tribe Finds Ways to Create Jobs." Wall Street Journal, 18 February 2004.

"Florida." Indian Country Today Tourism and Gaming 2004, 2004.

Fogarty, Mark."A Little Banking Progress at Navajo: Bank of America Rapped for 'Not Serving Indian Country." 27 January 2004.

Fogarty, Mark. "Chickasaw, Choctaw Highlight Economic Development." Indian Country Today, 7 September 2004.

Fogarty, Mark. "Navajo Nation Gets Funds from Water, Energy Bill." Indian Country Today. December 10, 2003.

Fogarty, Mark. "Old Fort is Gone, But Ancient Indians Remain." Indian Country Today, 24 February, 2004.

Fogarty, Mark. "RHED Awards are the Keystone to Economic Development Strategy." Indian Country Today, 18 February 2004.

Friday, Beatrice. "Reservation Radio Station Signs on the Air at 89.5 FM." Wind River News, 15 July 1999.

"Funds Depleted for Health Care." Siletz News Vol. 32, No. 8, August 2004.

Garvin, Eileen. "Governor Signs Gaming Compact with Navajo Nation." New Mexico Business Weekly, 7 November 2003.

Gibbs, Cindy. "Mescalero Apache Culture of the Southwest." Country Road Chronicles, 31 December 2000.

Gillis, Cydney. "2 Casinos Gamble That There's Enough Business for Both." Seattle Times, 29 September 2004.

Glenn, Eddie. "UKB Takes Over Riverside Park." Keetoowah News, No. 6, June 2004.

"Grand Opening of the Seminole Hard Rock Hotel and Casino." Seminole Tribune Commemorative Issue 2004.

"Great Oak Ranch Returned to Pechanga." U.S. Newswire, 18 April 2003.

Hammel, Paul. "Extent of Santee Casino's Court Victory Uncertain." Ohama World-Herald, 3 March 2004.

Harden, Blaine." Walking the Land With Pride Once More." Washington Post, 19 September 2004.

Harrold, Richard. "Senate Blocks Casino Plans." Holland Sentinel, Thursday, 9 December 2004.

Heffter, Emily. "Tribe Hopes Casino Will Bring Change." Seattle Times, 20 October 2004.

"Historical Perspective: Oneida Nation of Wisconsin" Indian Country Today, Mid-January 1993, pg. 13.

Honaberger, W. James. "Step Into the Past in Picuris." Santa Fe New Mexican, 18 August 2004.

"House Passes, Sends Senate Ojito Wilderness Bill." (Tom Udall and Heather Wilson's NM Senate Bill, H.R. 3176) 4 October 2004.

Hubbell, John M. "Legislature OKs 4 Tribal Pacts on Casinos - not San Pablo." The San Francisco Chronicle. 28 August, 2004.

Humphrey, Kay. "Ho-Chunk Inc. Homebuilder Plans to Test New Regional Markets." Indian Country Today 2003.

Hurracan: Alliance for Cultural Democracy. Vol. 2, No. L & 2, Summer 1991.

"IHS, Tribes Dedicate New Hospital in Winnebago, Nebraska." States News Service, 8 April 2004.

"Idaho." Indian Country Today Tourism and Gaming, 2004.

"Industrial Development Efforts Materialize." Indian Country Today, March 1995.

"Inn of the Mountain Gods Resort and Casino Announces First Quarter Chronicles." Business Wire, 9 September 2004.

"Ione Casino Plans Are Put on Hold," Sacramento Bee. 26 January, 2002.

"Jicarillas Nab Chama Ranch for $25 Million in Cash." Albuquerque Journal, 17 March 1995, A-8.

"Judge Considers Motion to Dismiss Rights Lawsuit Against Ute." Desert News, 17 November 1994, B4.

"KADA Programs Now Heard on Local Cable One Channel 8." Chickasaw Times, June 2004.

Kamb, Lewis. "Watery Grave Awaits Hoh Reservation." Seattle Post-Intelligencer, 15 June 2004, A1.

Kanza News. Kanza Tribal Council. Kaw City, OK, 1995.

"Keep Health in Sight." Indian Country Today, 2 April 2003.

"Keetoowahs Move Forward on the Master Plan for the Tribe's 80 Acres." Keetoowah News No.1, January 2004.

Kelly, Leo. "Odds are Indian Gaming Very Lucrative." Ada Evening News, 24 June 2004.

Ketche-Shawno, Robert. "The Kickapoo Indian." Shawnee News-Star, 1990.

"King of Fish to return to the Northern Wisconsin tribal lakes." Indian Country Today, 3 March 2004.

Kingsely, Patricia. "West Nile Virus in the Basin." Ute Bulletin, 23 June 2004.

"Kituwah: The Return of the Mother Town." Keetoowah News No. 8, July 2003.

Knight, Michelle. "Viejas Band Enduring Legacy." Traditions Applied. Indian Country Today, 24 March 2004.

Lapwai Unit Program Description, Boys and Girls Clubs of the Lewis Clark Valley, Indian Country Today Tourism and Gaming, 2004.

Lee, David. "Blackfeet Tribe to Open Regional Recycling Center." Indian Country Today, 13 July 1994.

"Let the Games Begin: Cayugas Catch Catskill Casino?" Indian Country Today, 18 June 2004.

Lewiston Morning Tribune (Lewiston, Idaho), 20 August 1995.

"Local Tribes Part of $1 Billion Deal with State." North County Times, Vol. 120, No. 174, 22 June 2004.

"Louisiana." Indian Country Today Tourism and Gaming, 2004.

Lowell, Jessica. "Tribe Plans to Move Ahead With Casino Following Appeals Court Decision." Wyoming Tribune-Eagle, 25 November 2004.

Magill, Bobby. "Picuris Sues Mining Company, Pueblo Moves to Reclaim Clay-Rich Aboriginal Lands." Taos

News, February 26-March 2004

Martino, Victor. "Skokomish Will Challenge License." The Sounder, August 1998.

May, James. "California Tribe Gets Casino Land Okay." Indian Country Today, 12 January 2002.

May, James. "Gov. Locke signs cigarette tax measure: Tribes will collect the Taxes, keep revenue." Indian Country Today. Vol. 20, Iss. 49; pg. A2. 23 May, 2001.

May, James. "Gov. Schwarzenegger Announces Compact Deals with Five Tribes." Indian Country Today, 22 June 2004.

May, James. "Jackson Rancheria Mining for Gold, Casino-Style." Indian Country Today, 26 July 2000.

May, James. "Oil Spill Damages Marine Estuary at Suquamish." Indian Country Today, 14 January 2004.

May, James. "Torres-Martinez Finally Will Get Settlement Money" Indian Country Today, 29 October 2001.

May, James. "Torres Martinez Opposed to Tent City Project." Indian Country Today, 29 March 2004.

Mckee, Bradford. "A New-Style Indian Village Rises from the Dust." New York Times, 30 September 2004.

McNeel, Jack. "Camas Institute Uses Holistic Approach." Indian Country Today, Business, 2005, pgs.12-13.

Melmer, David. "Three Tribes Come Together in Business Deal." Indian Country Today, 13 November 2002.

Melmer, David. "Winnebagos Suffer from Kansas Chares." Indian Country Today, 19 May 2002.

"Mille Lacs Golf Resort." Indian Country Today Tourism and Gaming (2004).

"Mississippi." Indian Country Today Tourism and Gaming, 2004.

"Mohawk Unveils Plans for Base." Lakota Times, 10 August 1994, B4.

Montana, Cate. "Swinomish Tribe a Finalist in Harvard Tribal Governance Awards Program." Indian Country Today. Oneida, N.Y. 8 Nov, 2000. V. 20, Iss. 21; A6. 8

"Mount Frontenac Golf Course Treasure Island Resort and Casino."Indian Country Today Tourism and Gaming, 2004.

"Nambe Lake Opens for Fishing." Albuquerque Journal, 1 June 2004.

Native American Press 5 (Bemidgi, MN) 11 August 1995.

Navajo Nation Today, No.17, August 14-20 1991.

"Native Websites Merge." Indian Country Today, 21 June 2004.

"Net Assets Top $200 Million; Businesses Outpacing Previous Year Results." Chickasaw Times, Financial Report, 2004, pg. 9.

"New Water Tower Nearing Completion." Prairie Band Potawatomi News, June 2004.

News From Indian Country,Vol. 9 (Hayward, WI), September 1995.

News From Indian Country, Late February 1995.

News From Indian Country, Mid-October 1992.

News From Indian Country. Tribal Community Services. Oneida Nation of Wisconsin, Mid-March 1995.

Norrell, Brenda. "Chiricahua Apache Tribe to Tell Geronimo, Ancestors' Story in Film." Indian Country Today, 2 June 2004.

Norrell, Brenda. "Sandia Pueblo Forges Ahead: Homes to Prevail in Struggle to Preserve Sandia Mountain." Indian Country Today, 9 November 2000.

Norrell, Brenda. "Southwest Indian Country, for the Beauty of It." Indian Country Today, 13 June 2001.

Ortiz, Beverly R. "Restoring the land: the Federated Indians of the Graton Rancheria." News from Native California, Summer 2003.

"Osage Nation's 2nd Annual Oil and Gas Summit, Bigger, Better, Boosts Economy, Jobs, and Future for Osage County." Native American Times, 15 September 2003.

Over, Ernie. "Increased Gas Exploration." Wind River News, 23 April 1998.

Pace, Felix. "Yurok Social Services." Monthly Report, April 2004.

Parkhill, Cynthia. "Scotts Valley Pomo Seeking Richmond Site." Tri-Valley Herald, 17 January 2003.

Pierpont, Mary. "Choctaw, Chickasaw, and Cherokee Nations Seek $50 Million." Indian Country Today, 22 August 2001.

Pierpont, Mary. "Kansas Town, Kaw Nation Work Toward New Understanding." Indian Country Today, 11 September 2001.

Pierpont, Mary. "Kaw Re-Establish Homeland Presence." Indian Country Today, 28 March 2001.

Pierpont, Mary. "Ponca Tribe to Try to Keep Lottery Money in Oklahoma." Indian Country Today, 13 August 2001.

Pierpont, Mary. "Technology Keeps Osage Oil Fields on the Upswing." Indian Country Today, 12 September 2001.

Propp, Wren. "Nambe Pueblo Approves Plan for Casino." Albuquerque Journal, 3 October 2004.

"Pueblo De Cochiti Golf Course." Indian Country Today Tourism and Gaming, 2004.

"Quileute, a Quieter Getaway to Natural Surroundings." Indian Country Today Tourism and Gaming, 2004.

Rankin, Adam. "Wood Works for Picuris Pueblo." Albuquerque Journal, 19 June 2004.

"Reservation Established in 1863." Wind River News, 17 December 1992.

Richman, Josh. "Tribe Power Struggle Continues; Tribal Council of Scotts Valley Band of Pomo Indians Wants to Build an East Bay Casino." Daily Review, 6 March 2004.

Rinella, Heidi Knapp. "Northern Paiutes Changed with Move." Las Vegas Review-Journal, 4 June 2000.

Ross, Matt. "Banks are Open for Business in Nevada." Indian Country Today, 17 March 2004.

Ross, Matt. "Financial Incentives for Winnebago Homebuyers." Indian Country Today, 28 November 2003.

Ruckman, S.E. "Osage Nation Opens Special Center for Boys." Tulsa World, 9 October 2004.

Salazar, Martin. "Nambe Gov. Nervous on Eve of Casino Vote." Albuquerque Journal, 1 October 2004.

Schmidt, Pat. "Upper Sioux Voice Opposition to Gaming Expansion." Montevideo American-News (25) 2004.

Shively, L.A. "Sandia Pueblo Land Claim Progresses." Indian Country Today, 1 May 2002.

Southwest Indian Gaming Country (Albuquerque, NM) Spring 1995.

Sprague, Brandon. "Tribal Health Clinic to Open in '05." Seattle Times, 20 October 2004.

Staff Report. "Choctaw Nation of Oklahoma." Indian Country Today, 5 July 2000.

Staff Report. "Choctaw Nation of Oklahoma." Indian Country Today, 18 October 2000.

Staff Report. "Leech Lake Band-Minnesota Chippewa." Indian Country Today, 18 October 2000.

Staff Report. "Leech Lake Band of Minnesota Chippewa." Indian Country Today, 11 July 2001.

Staff Report. "U.S. Awards Housing Funds to New Mexico Pueblos." Indian Country Today, 6 October 2004.

Stockbridge-Munsee Mohican News (Bowler, WI) 1995, 111.

Stockes, Brian. "BIA Recognizes Chinook." Indian Country Today, 17 January 2001.

Stockes, Brian. "Indian Country Responds." Indian Country Today, 1 October 2001.

Stockes, Brian. "Timbisha-Shoshone a Step Closer to Homeland." Indian Country Today, 29 March 2000.

Stone, Marissa. "Nambe Governor Hopes for 'Yes' Vote on Casino." New Mexican, 1 October 2004.

"Swinomish Tribe a Finalist in Harvard Tribal Governance Awards Program." Indian Country Today. V. 20, Iss. 21; A6, 20 Nov. 2000.

"Taos Pueblo Wins Land." Native American Press/ Ojibwe News, 11 October 1996.

Thackery, Lorna. "Widepsread effects foreseen in Crow tax ruling." The Billings Gazette. 2000.

The Circle, The Circle Corporation, Minneapolis, MN, Vol. 25, No. 7, July 2004.

Thompson, Abbey. "Niijii Celebration Warms Wisconsin Northwoods." Indian Country Today, 31 March 2004.

Thompson, Carolyn. "Seneca School Preserves Languages, Traditions." AP/Baltimore Sun, 13 May 2002.

"Torres Martinez Enters into Gaming Compact with State." Indian Country Today, 15 August 2003.

"Torres-Martinez Face a Double-Edged Sword." Indian Country Today, 11 October, 2000.

"Torres-Martinez Tries to Power Up." Indian Country Today, 28 June 2000.

Tots Tatoken. Publication of Nez Perce Tribe, 1, No. 4, August 1995.

Tribal Observer, Publication of Saginaw Chippewa Tribe, No. 16, 30 August, 1995, pg. 6.

"Tribe Divided Over East Bay Casino Plan." Daily Review, 10 February 2004.

"Tribe's Aide Sought in Land-Use for Gas Station." Seattle Times, 21 July 2004.

"Tribe's Factions Both Claiming to be in Control; Pomo Election Results Claimed Invalid." Daily Review, 8 March 2004.

"Two Colvilles File Suit Against B.C. Firm." Seattle Times, 22 July 2004.

"Tuscarora's Sue Corps over Dumping." Ojibwe News, 22 August 1997.

"UKB Environment Department Cleans Up Dumpsite in Mayes County." Keetoowah News No. 5, May 2004.

"UKB Environmental Department Works on Saline Creek Water Monitoring Project." Keetoowah News No. 6, May 2003.

"UKB Sponsors Tahlequah Visitor's Center." Keetoowah News. No. 7, June 2003.

Unrein, Chad, and Harlan Mckosato. "Mescalero Apache Reject Nuclear Dump." Indian Country Today, 9 February 1995.

"Unitah & Ouray Ute Indian Tribe." Ute Bulletin, No. 20, Special Edition, 2 August 1993, p 27.

Valencia, Jane Moorman. "Isleta to Celebrate Head Start Facility." Albuquerque Journal, 17 September 2004.

Vega, Cecilia M. "Tribes Battle Over Casino Land." San Francisco Chronicle, 18 August 2004.

"Visiting the Nation's Oglala Lakota." Indian Country Today Special Edition, 3 August 1994.

"Visiting the Nations Quinault." Indian Country Today, N.D.

Vogel, Meghan. "Portion of Indian Island Returned to Wiyot Tribe." Humboldt Times-Standard, 19 May 2004. Wanamaker, Tom. "Cayuga Nation's $500-Million Catskill Casino Holds Great Economic Promise." Indian Country Today, 23 June 2004.

Wannamaker, Tom. "Let the Games Begin." Indian Country Today, 26 September, 2003. Washington tribe sues Teck Cominco," Vancouver Sun. 22 July, 2004.

"Wiyot Leader Ecstatic about Returned Portion of Indian Island." Humboldt Times-Standard, 24 May 2004.

Woodard, Stephanie."Savoring the Future: Upscale Restaurant Supports Gila River Farming Revival." Washington Post, 26 June 2003.

Wright, Sandi. "Washoe Tribe to Break Ground for New Clinic." Reno Gazette-Journal, 2 March 2002.

Yarbrough, Beau. "How the Timbisha Shoshone Tribe is Getting Tribal Lands Here." Hesperia Star, 8 June 2004.

"Yuroks Honor Return of Native Artifacts." Daily Triplicate, Saturday, 22 May 2004.

Zuni Farming: For Today and Tomorrow, No. 3, Summer-Fall 1994.

"Zuni History." Zuni Tribal News 1991, sec. II .

JOURNALS, MAGAZINES, AND NEWSLETTERS
"Audubon International Honored Circling Raven Golf Club." Coeur d'Alene Schitsu'umsh Council Fires, Series 3, Vol. 6, No. 6 (July 2004).

"Coeur d'Alene." Benewah Medical and Wellness Center News (July-August-September 2004).

Brossey, Julie. "Indian Gaming." Native Peoples, n.d.

Bryan, William L., Jr. "Montana's Indians: Yesterday and Today." Montana Geographic Series, Vol. 11. Montana Magazine (1985).

Buchanan, Wyatt, and Jade James. "Economic Stability Important to Nez Perce." Idaho Natives (University of Idaho) (2002).

Cabazon Circle 7, No. 7 (Indio, CA 92203) (July 1998).

Carufel, D., Sr. "Ojibwe Language of the Future Curriculum Review." Lac Du Flambeau News (July 2004).

Case, Secretary, and Taylor David. "Klamath Tribes Rally to Protect Treaty Rights." Klamath News, 20, No. 6 (July 2004).

"Ceremony Heralds Grand Opening of Trail in its Entirety." Coeur d'Alene Schitsu'umsh Council Fires, Series 3, Vol. 6, No. 6 (July 2004).

Clemmer, Richard. "Land Use Patterns and Aboriginal Rights, Nevada." The Indian Historian 7, No. 1 (Winter 1974).

Creson, Christen. "2004 Toxic Tour." Gyah'-Wish Atakia (June 2004).

Cronin, Thomas J. "Tribal Officer Cross-Deputization Claimed by Chief as Continued March Towards Excellence." Coeur d'Alene Schitsu'umsh Council Fires, Series 3, Vol. 6, No. 6 (July 2004).

"Cultural Center Receives First Donation." Looking To The Future, 1, No. 2 (December 1994).

Cummins, Sarah. "Jamestown S'Klallam Strong People." Red Earth Magazine (Fall 2003): 28.

David, Peter. "2003 Manoomin Season a Good One, but What Will the 2003 Harvest be Like?" Mazina'igan, A Chronicle of the Lake Superior Ojibwe. The Great Lakes Indian Fish & Wildlife Commission (Spring 2004).

Davis, Doug. "Mother Nature Buys Ticket to FCP Thunder Valley Biker Rally II." Potawatomi Traveling Times, 10, No. 1 (July 1, 2004).

Dolan, Joe. "Housing Initiative Committee Seeks Tri-bal Housing Needs." Gah'navah/Ya Ti' (June 2004).

Edmunds, David. "Two Case Histories." The Wilson's Quarterly, 10, No. L (1986).

"Education Department." Gyah'-Wish Atakia (June 2004).

Edwards, Tracy. "History of The Redding Rancheria." Indian Gaming (May 2004).

Eleazer, Kristin. "Hard Rock Café Foxwoods a Smash." Pequot Times (September 2004).

Fadden, David Kanietakeron. "The Haudenosaunee-Introduction." Special Supplement to the Indian Time (Spring 2004).

Franck, L.A. "Tribe, Inc." Native American Housing News, Special Convention Issue.

French, Ryan. "Lamprey Eel Harvest Brings in Nearly 1,000." Siletz News, 32, No. 8 (August 2004).

Friend, Billy. "Bearskin Fitness Center." Gyah'-Wish Atakia (June 2004).

Fuller, Lori. "San Diego Tribe to Purchase Cruise Ship." The California Page (2004).

Gibson, Daniel. "Lords of the Plains Ride Again." The Comanche Nation Newsletter (May/June 2004).

Gibson, Daniel. "Lord of the Plains Rides Again." Native Peoples (2002).

Gildart, Robert C. "Montana's Flathead Country." Montana Magazine (1986).

Gill, Holly M. "Tribes Appoint New Police Chief." Madras Pioneer, 99, No. 47.

Glenn, Eddie. "UKB Takes Over Riverside Park." Keetoowah News (June 2004).

Goldblatt, Melissa. "Heated Debate, Smoldering Tires Spark Controversy Over Cleanup." American Indian Report (October 1998).

Hansen, Terri. "Coeur d'Alene Tribe Plans National Lottery." News From Indian Country (Mid-March).

Harvard Project on American Indian Economic Development. John F. Kennedy School of Government. Harvard University. "Game and Fish Department of Jicarilla Apache Tribe." Honoring Nations: Tribal Governance Success Stories (1999).

Harvard Project on American Indian Economic Development. John F. Kennedy School of Government. Harvard University. "Minnesota 1837 Ceded Territory Conservation Code. Department of Natural Resources, Mille Lacs Band of Ojibwe." Honoring Nations Directory of Award-Winning Programs 2003, 2002, 2000, 1999 (2003): 29.

Harvard Project on American Indian Economic Development. John F. Kennedy School of Government. Harvard University. "Idaho Gray Wolf Recovery." Honoring Nations Directory of Award-Winning Programs 2003, 2002, 2000, 1999 (2003): 25.

Harvard Project on American Indian Economic Development. John F. Kennedy School of Government. Harvard University. "Ojibwe Language Program, Combining Tradition and Technology, Program Protects the Uniqueness of the Ojibwe Culture." Honoring Nations Directory of Award-Winning Programs 2003, 2002, 2000, 1999: (2003): 26.

Harvard Project on American Indian Economic Development. John F. Kennedy School of Government. Harvard University. "Off-Reservation Indian Foster Care - Licensing Agency Extends Tribe's Jurisdiction, Brings Foster Children Home." Honoring Nations Directory of Award-Winning Programs 2003, 2002, 2000, 1999 (2003).

Holtman, Andy, "Taking the Lead." People Section, Casino Journal (April 2004): 14-18.

"Housing has Big Role in Nation's Future." Gah'navah/Ya Ti' (May 2004).

Jeffrey-Hinton, Cheryl. "Barona: a Little Museum with Big Ideas." News from Native California, n.d.

Johansen, Bruce E. "Dating the Iroquois Confederacy." From Akwesasne Notes 1, No. 3, 4. As reprinted in Special Supplement to the Indian Time (Spring 2004).

Johnson, Paul. "Antigo Off-Road-in the Mud-Again." Potawatomi Traveling Times, 10, No. 1 (July 1, 2004).

Johnson, Paul. "It's Always Dad's Day in the Pits." Potawatomi Traveling Times No. 1 (July 1, 2004): 10.

Jones, Kate Lester. "Osage Indians." Oklahoma Today (May-June 1986): 32-36.

"Judge Invited to Seminars." Confederated Tribes of Coos, Lower Umpqua and Siuslaw, Tribal Newsletter, 5 (2004): 8.

Kanza News, 2004, 1st Quarter.

Kanza News, Newsletter of the Kaw Nation of Oklahoma 2nd Quarter (2003).

Keetoowah News, No. 5 (April 2003).

Keetoowah News, No. 6 (June 2004).

"Keetoowahs Move Forward on the Master Plan for the Tribe's 80 Acres." Keetowah News (January 2004).

"Keetowahs to Host 2nd Annual Music Benefit to Raise Funds for Help in Crisis." Keetoowah News (May 2004).

King, Frank J., II. "History of the Choctaw Nation." Indian Gaming Today, 3, No. 7 (April 5-18, 2004).

King, Gwen E., "Tribe, County Join Forces to Expand Drug Court." The Shawnee Sun & Tecumseh Countywide News. Reprinted with permission in HowNiKan 22, No. 11 (November 2000): 3. Kirkland, Carl. "Penobscot Nation Molds a Winner." Injection Molding Magazine, (October 1997).

Kozlowicz, John. "Money Key to Compact Negotiations." Hocak Worak, 18, No. 12 (June 23, 2004).

Kozlowicz, John. "Nation's Courthouse Holds and 'Open House'". Hocak Worak, No. 12 (June 23, 2004): 18.

Kozlowicz, John. "Nine Earn National Firefighting Certifications." Hocak Worak, 18, No. 12 (June 23, 2004).

La Duke, Winona. "Mishka Siibii: Bad River Ojibwe Reservation." National Museum of the American Indian (Summer 2004).

"Lend a Helping Hand at Floras Lake." Confederated Tribes of Coos, Lower Umpqua and Siuslaw Tribal Newsletter 5 (2004):10.

"Mashantucket Pequots Give $10 Million to Campaign." Smithsonian Runner, No. 95-1 (January-February 1995).

Micmac Health News (Winter 2004).

"Middle Verde Project Under Way." Gah'navah/Ya Ti' (May 2004).

"Middletown Rancheria Scores a Victory for Native American Cultural Rights." News From Native California, 17, No. 1 (Fall 2003).

"Muckleshoot Technical Services." Looking to the Future, 1, No. 4 (February/March 1995).

Nashauonk Mittark. Newsletter of the Mashpee Wampanoag Indian Tribal Council. 3, No. 3 (Mashpee, MA) (Summer 1994).

"Nation Receives Leadership Award." Public Relations Office. Gah'navah/Ya Ti' (May 2004).

Native Wisconsin Magazine (Summer 1995).

Nelson Limerick, Patricia. "Here to Stay." The Wilson's Quarterly, 10, No. 1 (1986).

Nelson, Gary. "Walker Lake Summit." Mono Lake Newsletter (Summer 2002).

Northwest Tribal Transportation News (Fall 1995).

Penobscot Indian Nation. Department of Natural Resources. Pskehtekwok, No. 2 (Spring 2004).

"Planning and Development." Gyah'wish Atakia (June 2004).

"Pow-Wow Improvements." Gyah'-Wish Atakia (June 2004).

Ramirez, Shirley. "Fort Miller Cultural Park to Open at Table Mountain." News From Native California, n.d. Red Cliff News, 4, No. 6 (June 2004).

"Roads Program Builds Keetoowah Circle and Other Roads and Bridges." Keetowah News (January 2004).

Savagian, John C., "The Tribal Reorganization of the Stockbridge-Munsee: Essential Conditions in the Re-Creation of a Native American Community, 1930-1942." Wisconsin Magazine of History, 77, No. 1 (August 1993): 39-62.

Schaaf, Gregory. "The Birth of Frontier Democracy from an Eagle's Eye View: The Great Law of Peace to the Constitution of the United States of America." Special Supplement to the Indian Time (Spring 2004).

Schnayerson, Ben. "Off-Reservation Casinos the Next Step?" Valley Daily Bulletin (December 29, 2003).

Schonchin, J. "Higher Education Receives Award." Comanche Nation Newsletter, No. 3(May/June 2004):3.

"Shell Shiner Car Wash." Gyah-Wish Atakia (June 2004).

Sherwood Valley Tribal Environmental Program Newsletter (April 2004).

Shooting Star Times, the Official Newsletter of Shooting Star Casino (July/August 2004).

"Solectek Corp. and ECC Bring Wireless Network to Isleta." American Indian Report, (April 1999): 21.

Spicer, Edward H. "Highlights of Yaqui History." The Indian Historian,7, No. 2 (Spring 1974).

Struckman, Robert. "Master and Apprentice." Smithsonian Institute, n.d.

"Suquamish Find Reduced Goals a Good Starting Point on Intellectual Property Rights." First Nations Development Institute Business Alert (March/April 1998).

Suquamish Newsletter (1997).

"Tesque Pueblo Flea Market to Remain Open Thru Dec. 19th" Southwest Indian County Traveler (Festive Season 2004): 10.

"The Great Dakota Conflict." Pioneer Press, n.d.

The Insider Employee News & Information. Oneida Indian Nation of New York (August 2, 2004).

The Insider Employee News & Information. Oneida Indian Nation of New York (June 22-July 5, 2004).

"Three Rivers Casino Opens to Public Sunday, June 26th." Confederated Tribes of Coos, Lower Umpqua and Siuslaw Tribal Newsletter, 5 (2004): 9.

Tinda, Peta. "A Journey of Tradition. "Smoke Signals (July 2004).

"Treasure Island Resort and Casino. "Island Times, 116 (July 2004).

Tribal Department Reports. Gyah'-Wish Atakia (June 2004).

"Tribe Gets Down to Business." Journal of Business. Confederated Tribes of the Colville Reservation (January 30, 1997).

"Tribal Self-Governance." Sovereign Nations (November-December 1998).

"Tribal Talk." The Sac and Fox Nation of Missouri, 1, No. 6 (February, 2004).

Turtle Mountain Indian Historical Society Newsletter (April 1991).

"Unsigned review of the Lamp, the Ice, and the Boat Called Fish." Publishers Weekly. Vol. 247, Issue 51 (December 18, 2000): 78.

Ute Bulletin (June 23, 2004).

Viafor, Susann. "Pequot Launch 302 Passenger Sassacus." News From Indian Country (Mid-September, 1997).

Wampanoag Tribe of Gay Head (Aquinnah). Tribal Newsletter. Gay Head, MA (August 1994).

"Washington." Indian Country Today, Tourism and Gaming (2004).

Wichita and Affiliated Tribes Newsletter (Anadarko, OK) (April 1995).

Wilson, Janice. "Environmental Department." Gyah'-Wish Atakia (June 2004).

"Yavapai-Apache Life Changed After San Carlos." Gah'navah/Ya Ti' (May, 2004).

"Yuman Language Summit Slated." Gah'navah/Ya Ti' (May 2004).

MAPS
Alaska Dept. of Community and Regional Affairs, Division of Community Planning. Community Map: Portage Creek, January 1982.

Cayuse, Umatilla and Walla Walla Homeland Heritage Corridor. Map, n.d.

Maliseet Indian Nation Map, n.d.

ELECTRONIC SOURCES
About.com. "Mashantucket Pequot Tribal Nation." (www.gonewengland.about.com/).

Absentee Shawnee Tribe. Homepage. (www.absenteeshawneetribe.com/).

Adak. "Adak." (www.orneveien.org/adak).

Adak. "Adak Is Open to the World!" (www.alaska.net/~vwadak/).

Adak. "Adak Island: Open to the World." (www.adakisland.com/).

Adams, Jim. "Pikuni Industries keeps expanding." (www.indiancountry.com/).

Adams, Ken. "Bits and Pieces from Indian Country." Casino City Times, May 31, 2003. (www.adams.casinocitytimes.com/articles/7321.html).

Admiralty Island National Monument. Homepage. (www.fs.fed.us/r10/tongass/districts/admiralty/). Afognak Native Corporation. (www.afognak.com).

"Agreement Would End Historic Dispute and Protect Central New York Landowners." June 2, 2004. (www.state.ny.us).

Agua Caliente Band of Cahuilla Indians. Homepage. (www.aguacaliente.org).

Agua Caliente Casino. Homepage. (www.hotwatercasino.com).

Agua Caliente Cultural Museum. Homepage. (www.accmuseum.org).

Ahtna Incorporated. (www.ahtna-inc.com).

Airnav.com. Okemah Flying Field Airport. (www.airnav.com/airport/F81).

Akiak. "Welcome to Akiak." (www.angelfire.com/ak2/akiak/index.html).

AKMHS. "KPSI: Communities." (www.akmhs.com/information/ports.cfm).

Akutan Volcano. (www.avo.alaska.edu/volcanoes/akut/akut.html).

Alabama Coushatta Tribe of Texas. Homepage. (www.alabama-coushatta.com).

Alamo Chapter. Homepage. (www.alamo.nndes.org).

Alamo Navajo School. Magdalena, New Mexico. NM school information. (www.greatschools.net).

Alaska Bush Guides. "Alaska Bush Guides - Nushagak River Hunting, Fishing and Trapping, Portage Creek, Alaska." (www.akbushguides.com/salmon.htm).

Alaska.com. (www.alaska.com/).

Alaska Demographic and Statistical Information. (www.uaa.alaska.edu/just/rlinks/justiceresearch/ak_demographics.html).

Alaska Dept. of Fish and Game, Division of Subsistence and Kawerak Inc. "St. Lawrence Island's Bounty of Birds: A Summary of the St. Lawrence Island Migratory Bird Harvest Survey." 1996. (www.subsistence.adfg.state.ak.us).

Alaska Dog Sledding. (www.alaskadogsledding.com).

Alaska Economic Development. Homepage. (www.alaskaeconomicdevelopment.org/).

Alaska Housing Finance Corporation. (www.ahfc.state.ak.us/).

Alaska Kayaking, Whale Watching. (www.outdoortrips.info/search -alaska-kayaking.php).

Alaska Native Federation. (www.nativefederation.org).

Alaska Native Heritage Center. (www.alaskanative.net).

Alaska Native Village Corporations. (www.kstrom.net/isk/maps/ak/alaska.html).

Alaska Natives Commission. "Final Report." Appendix to Volume III, (1992?). (www.alaskool.org/resources/anc3/anciiiapp.htm).

Alaska Reference. (www.uaa.alaska.edu/just/refrenz/alaska.html).

Alaska Regional Profiles, Northwest Region - The People. (www.alaskool.org/resources/regional/nw_reg_pro/thepeople.html).

Alaska Salmon Fishing. (www.alaska-salmon-fishing.net/Lodge.htm).

Alaska School Information. Akutan School, Akutan, Alaska. (www.greatschools.net/modperl/browse_school/ak/46/).

Alaska State Standards. "About Our School." (www.kpbsd.k12.ak.us).

Alaska Timber Marketing. (www.alaskatimber.com/). "Alaska VPSO Program." (www.uaa.alaska.edu/just/rlinks/lawenforcement/ak_vpso.html).

Alaska Wilderness Recreation and Tourism Association. "Community Information: Savoonga." (www.awrta.org).

Alaska, Yukon and British Columbia Travel Guide. "Ninilchik." (alaskan.com/bells/ninilchik.html).

Alaskan Metal Fish. (www.akmetalfish.com/).

Alaskan Native Carver's Gallery. "The Eskimo Village of Savoonga, Location, Culture and History." (www.bssd.org/eskimo_art/villages/savoonga/savoonga.html).

Alaskan Native Languages. (www.uaf.edu/anlc/langs/html).

Alaska's Kenai Peninsula 2004 Online Vacation Guide Travel Tips. (www.kenaipeninsula.org).

Alaskool. "The Man-Made Environment." (www.alaskool.org).

Albuquerque Journal Online. Homepage. (www.abqjournal.com/).

Aleut Corporation. (www.aleutcorp.com/).

Aleutians East Borough. "Akutan - The friendliest fishing community in the Aleutians." (www.aleutianseast.org/).

Alliance of California Tribes. Rumsey Indian Rancheria. (www.allianceofcatribes.org/rumsey.htm). Alutiiq. (www.alutiiq.com/).

Amended Constitution of the Yankton Sioux Tribal Business and Claims Committee. (www.tribalresourcecenter.org/ccfolder/yanktonconst.htm#art3).

American Fisheries Society. Native Peoples Fisheries Section Executive Committee. (lapratt.com/npfs/exec.htm).
American Indian Communities in Minnesota-White Earth Band. (www.senate.leg.state.mn.us/departments/scr/report/bands/whiteearth/).

American Indian Relief Council. Homepage. (www.airc.org/).

American Indian Resource Directory. Hompage. (www.indians.org/Resource/FedTribes99/Region3/region3.html).

American Indians II. Lakota/Dakota/Nakota (Sioux Reservations of the United States). (www.usd.edu).

American Southwest. "Hualapai Reservation." (www.americansouthwest.net/arizona/grand_canyon/hualapai_reservation.html).

Amik, (Larry Smallwood). Mille Lacs Band Elder. "Sweat Lodges." (www.millelacsojibwe.org). Anchorage Press (Anchorage, AK). (www.anchoragepress.com).

Andrea Wilbur-Sigo.com. "Squaxin Island." (www.andreawilbursigo.com/squaxin.html).

Andrews, Elizabeth, and Michael Coffing. December 1986. "Kuskokwim River Subsistence Chinook Fisheries: An Overview." Excerpted from Alaska Dept. of Fish and Game Technical Paper No. 146. (www.nativeknowledge.org).

Angel of the Winds Casino. (www.casinocity.com).

Angelfire.com. Homepage. (www.angelfire.com).

Animal and Plant Health Inspection Service. (www.aphis.usda.gov).

Antonson, Joan M. "St. Michael: Alaska's Western Crossroads." The St. Michael, Alaska, Community Site. (www.buchholdt.com/StMichael/Antonson.html).

Anvik Lodge. "Anvik is Alaska fishing and vacation lodge." (www.anviklodge.com/).

Apache Gold Casino and Resort. Homepage. (www.apachegoldcasinoresort.com).

Apache Trends. "Yavapai Apache Nation-Camp Verde." (www.apachetrends.com/yavapai.htm).

APHIS Indian Working Group. Tribal Agencies. (www.aphis.usda.gov/anawg/states/texas.html).

Arctic Refuge: Map. (www.arctic.fws.gov).

Arctic Village. "Arctic Village, Alaska, the home of the Neets'aii Gwichin." (www.vergie.com/arctic.html).

Arizona Commission of Indian Affairs. Homepage. (www.indianaffairs.state.az.us/tribes/demo.html).

Arizona Dept. of Commerce. Native American Community Profiles. Homepage. (www.commerce.state.az.us).

Arizona Indian Gaming Association. Homepage. (www.azindiangaming.org/).

Arizona Life. Indian Reservations in Arizona. (www.azlife.net/Arizona/AZ-Indians.htm).

"Arizona Native American Museums." Emol.org. Homepage. (www.emol.org).

Arizona Tourism Guide. (www.arizonan.com/Indianlands/Gila.html).

Arizonan Site Map. (www.outdoorarizona.com/fortyumaquechan.htm).

"Ashland FRO Assists With Native American Conservation and Restoration Projects," (www.web.lexis-nexis.com).

Atka Volcanic Center, Alaska. (www.users.bendnet.com/bjensen/volcano/alaskacanada/aleutian-atka.html).

Atqasuk Home Rule. (www.north-slope.org/nsb/HomeruleBrochure/AtqInfo.htm).

Atqasuk Research Center. (www.sfos.uaf.edu/basc/research/atqasuk.html).

Auburn Rancheria. Homepage. (www.auburnrancheria.com/).

Augustine Casino. Homepage. (www.augustinecasino.com/index.htm).

Austin's Alaska Adventures. (www.alaskaadventures.net).

AWRTA. "AWRTA - Alaska Wilderness Recreation and Tourism Association." (www.awrta.org).

Background Black Mesa/Kayenta Mine. (www.wrcc.osmre.gov/BlkMsaQ_A/background_black_mesa.htm).

Badlands National Park. Homepage. (www.lakotamall.com/oglalasiouxtribe/points.htm).

Barerra, Richard. "Constitutional Reform for the San Carlos Apache Tribe; A Report to the Apache Tribe of San Carlos, Arizona." Harvard Project on American Indian Development. (ksg.harvard.edu/hpaied/docs/PRS89-8.pdf).

Barona Indian Reservation. Homepage. (www.baronatribe.com).

Barta, Suzette, Susan Trzebiatowski, Jack Frye, Ronald Vick, and Mike D. Woods. A Summary of Economic Conditions in Boley and Okfuskee County, Oklahoma. Oklahoma State University. Oklahoma Cooperative Extension Service. Rural Development. 2000. (www.rd.okstate.edu/CED/Boley%20ORIGINS.pdf).

BASC Facilities. (www.sfos.uaf.edu/basc/research/support/facilities/).

Bay Mills Indian Community. Homepage. (www.baymills.org/).
Bay Mills Resort and Casino. Homepage. (www.4baymills.com/html/community-frame.html).

BBEDC. "BBEDC - Welcome." (www.bbedc.com).

BBNC. "BBNC Qanemciq." (www.bbnc.net/newsletter/Vol_31_No_2-Sept_03.pdf).

Bearskin Aviation Service. Homepage. (www.bearskinaviation.com/About_Us.htm).

Bering Air. "Bering Air Destinations: Shishmaref." (www.beringair.com/region/ome/shishmaref.html).

Bering Sea Communities. (www.beringsea.com/)

Bering Strait School District. (www.bssd.org/).

Bering Straits Native Corporation. (www.beringstraits.com/Region_overview.pdf).

Bethel Native Corporation. Homepage. (www.bnc-alaska.com/).

Bien Mur Indian Market Center. Homepage. (www.bienmur.com/).

Big Pine Indian Education Center.(www.wested.org/).

Big Slick News Card Room Directory. Texas. (www.bigslicknews.com/texas.htm).

Big Valley Rancheria.Homepage. (www.big-valley.net/).

Bishop California.Homepage. (www.bishopvisitor.com/).
BJA Tribal Court Grantees. United Keetoowah Band of Cherokee Indians OK. (www.tribalresourcecenter.org/BJA/grantees/grantee.asp?128).

Black Bear Casino and Hotel. Homepage. (www.blackbearcasinohotel.com/casino/gaming.htm).

Black Bear Golf Course. Homepage. (www.golfatthebear.com/).

Black Oak Casino. Homepage. (www.blackoakcasino.com).

Blackfeet Nation.Homepage. (www.blackfeetnation.com).

Blue Lake Casino. Homepage. (www.bluelakecasino.com/).

Blue Sart Gaming and Casino. Homepage. (www.casinocity.com/).

Blue Water Resort and Casino. (www.bluewaterfun.com/).

Bluffton University. Homepage. Taos Pueblo. (www.bluffton.edu/).

Boardman River Project. Homepage. (www.boardmanriver.org/watershed.php).

"Bois Fort / Nett Lake Band of Chippewa Indians." (www.kstrom.net/isk/maps/mn/nettlake.htm).

Boise Forte Band of Chippewa. Homepage. (www.boisfortetc.com/).

Borough. (www.borough.kenai.ak.us).

Botkin, Ben. "Tribes, Power County sign economic development pact." Idaho Falls Post Register. January 13, 2004. (web.lexis-nexis.com/).

Bristol Bay Borough. (www.theborough.com/).

Bristol Bay Native Association. (www.bbna.com/).

Brown, Laura. "Celebration to reveal Rancheria headquarters." The Daily Triplicate. August 7, 2003. (www.triplicate.com/news/story.cfm?story_no=1040).

Bucky's Casino. Homepage. (www.buckyscasino.com/yavapai.htm).

Bureau of Economic Analysis. Potawatomie, Oklahoma. (www.bea.doc.gov/bea/regional/bearfacts/action.cfm?FIPS=40125).

"Bureau seeks input on Cowlitz." The Columbian. (www.columbian.com/).

Burns Paiute Reservation. (www.burnspaiute-nsn.gov).

Burns Paiute Reservation. (www.harneycounty.com/1Paiute.htm).

Burns Paiute Tribe Wadatika Health Center. Homepage. (www.npaihb.org/profiles/tribal_profiles/Oregon/Burns_Paiute.htm).

"Bush Administration Announces Nearly $76 Million for Michigan Communities in Housing and Community Development Funds." News Release 02-808MI in Michigan HUD. (www.hud.gov/local/mi/news/pr02-808mi.cfm).

"Business Development - Governor Announces Minority Business Development Award." Wisconsin Dept. of Commerce, Press Release, March 15, 2004. (www.commerce.wi.gov/mt/MT-PR04-0047.html).

Business News. "Agency rules against Wyandotte 7th Street Casino." (kansascity.bizjournals.com/kansascity/stories/2004/03/22/daily37.html).

By-Laws of the Tribal Council of the Indians of the Quinault Indian Reservation. Homepage. (209.206.175.157/BYLAWS.htm).

Cache Creek Casino and Resort. Homepage. (www.cachecreek.com/).

Caddo Nation of Oklahoma. Homepage. (www.caddonation-nsn.gov).

Cahuilla Reservation. Homepage. (www.cahuilla.com/).

Cal State San Marcos. Big Pine Reservation. (www.csusm.edu).

California Indian Manpower Consortium Inc. Homepage. (www.cimcinc.org/).

California Rural Indian Health Board. Toiyabe Indian Health Project, Inc. (www.crihb.org/).

Camas Institute. Homepage. (www.camasinstitute.com/).
Camel Rock Suites. Homepage. (www.camelrockcasino.com/).

Campo Reservation. (www.campo-kumeyaay.org/).

Canku Ota. "Tribal Grants to Fund Diabetes Project, Land Purchase, Economic/Development." (www.turtletrack.org/).

Cape Fox Tours. "Saxman Native Village." (www.capefoxtours.com).

Capitan Grande Reservation. (www.kumeyaay.com/reservations/tribal_services.html?tid=4).

Cardplayer.com. "Kickapoo Lucky Eagle Casino." (www.cardplayer.com).

Cardplayer.com. Poker Room Directory. Spirit Lake Casino. (www.cardplayer.com).

Carleton, K.H. "A Brief History of the Mississippi Band of Choctaw Indians." (www.2netdoor.com/).

Carnegie Museums of Pittsburgh. Kinzua Dam. (www.carnegiemuseums.org/).

Carson, Brad. U.S. Representative. (carson.house.gov/okfuskee.asp).

Carvlin, Elizabeth. "South Dakota Signs Third Tax Agreement With Indian Tribe." The Bond Buyer. December 29, 2003. (www.web.lexis-com/).

Casino Arizona. Homepage. (www.casinoaz.com/).

Casino City. "Atka IRA Council." (www.casinocity.com/us/ak/atka/atkairac/).

Casino City. Homepage. (www.casinocity.com/).

Casino of the Sun.Homepage.(www.casinosun.com/).

Casino Pauma.Homepage.(www.casinopauma.com/).

Cass Lake-Bena Elementary School. (www.clbs.k12.mn.us).

Castro-Oistad, Ken. "Grants." News from Native California. July 31, 2002. (www.proquest.umi.com/).

"Cayuga Indian Nation purchases Seneca Falls Gas Station." October 7, 2003. (www.nacsonline.com/).

"Cayuga Indian Nation to build casino in Catskills, New York." May 7, 2004. (www.ardmoreite.com/).

"Cayuga Indian's point man." December 26, 2004. (www.syarcuse.com/).

Cayuga Nation. Homepage. (www.tuscaroras.com/).

Center for Columbia River History. "Oregon's Oldest Town: 11,000 Years of Occupation." (www.ccrh.org/).

Center for Public Environmental Oversight. 2000

CPEO Military List Archive. " (CPEO-MEF) U.S. to begin cleanup of Colville River site Work to focus on old U." (www.cpeo.org/lists/military/2000/msg00593).

Chefarnrmute Inc. (www.chefarnrmuteinc.com/).

Chemehuevi Reservation. Photo. (csusm.edu/bbiggs/loc/rezinfo/chemehuevi/chemehuevi_images.htm).

Chemehuevi Valley Airport. California Online Highways. (www.caohwy.com/x/x49x.htm).

Chenega Corporation. Chenega Corporation 2003 Annual Report. (www.nerland.com).

Chenega Corporation. (www.chenega.com/).

Cher-ae Heights Indian Community. Homepage. (www.cheraeheightscasino.com/).

Cherokee Bear Zoo and Exotic Animals. Homepage. (www.cherokeezoo.com/).

Cherokee Casino and Resort. Homepage. (www.cherokeecasino.com/).

Cherokee Family Research Center. Homepage. (www.cherokeeheritage.org).

Cherokee Fun Park. Homepage. (www.cherokeefunpark.com/).

Cherokee Gift Shop. Homepage. (www.cherokeegiftshop.com/).

Cherokee Heritage Center. Homepage. (www.cherokeeheritage.org/).

Cherokee Nation Industries. Homepage. (www.cnicnd.com/).

Cherokee Nation. Homepage. (www.cherokee.org/).

Cherokee Observer. Homepage. (www.cherokeeobserver.org/).

Chevak Company Corporation. (www.freetvsatellite.org/freetv/243.html).

Cheyenne River Sioux Tribe Dept. of Environment in Natural Resources. Homepage. (www.crstepd.org/).

Cheyenne River Sioux Tribe. Homepage. (www.crstgfp.com/).

"Cheyenne River Sioux Tribe to open huge skateboard park." April 28, 2004. (www.web.lexis-nexis.com/).

"Cheyenne-Arapaho Tribes offer $1B for stolen land." May 14, 2004; (www.indianz.com).

Chickasaw Nation. Homepage. (www.chickasaw.net).

Chinook Winds Casino Resort and Hotel. Homepage. (www.chinookwindscasino.com/).

Chip In's Island Resort and Casino. Homepage. (www.chipincasino.com/).

Chitimacha Tribe. (www.angelfire.com/).
Chitimacha Tribe. (www.dicshovel.com/).
Chitimacha Tribe. (www.eatel.net).
Chitimacha Tribe. (www.epodunk.com)
Chitimacha Tribe of Louisiana. Homepage. (www.chitimacha.com/).
Choctaw Law Enforcement Services. (www.ojp.usdoj.gov).

Choctaw Nation of Oklahoma. Homepage. (www.choctawnation.com/).

Christianson, Kiel. "Grand Traverse Resort Becomes Part of Gaming Empire." (www.michigangolf.com/departments/features/grand-traverse-sale.htm).

"Chronology of the Oneida Tribe in Wisconsin." (www.jefflindsay.com/).

Chugach Corporation. "Chugach Alaska Corporation - History and Culture." (www.chugach-ak.com/historymain.html).

Chugach Schools. (www.chugachschools.com/csd_schools/chenega_bay.html).

Chugachmiut. (www.chugachmiut.org/).

Chukchansi Gold Resort and Casino. Homepage. (www.chukchansigold.com/).

Chukchi Consortium Library. Homepage. (www.chukchi.alaska.edu/users/zycclib/).

Citizen Potawatomi Nation. Homepage. (www.potawatomi.org/).

Citizens Equal Rights Alliance. Homepage. (www.citizensalliance.org/).

City Data. (www.city-data.com/).

City of Cordova, Alaska. (www.cityofcordova.net/).

City of San Diego Water History. Homepage. (www.sannet.gov).

Clearwater River Casino. (www.crcasino.com/).

Cliff Castle Casino. Homepage. (www.cliffcastlecasino.net/gaming.shtm).

Cloverdale Rancheria. Homepage. (www.cloverdalerancheria.com/).

Cloverdale Rancheria Environmental Assessment. (www.esassoc.com/).

Cochiti Lake Albuquerque District. (www.spa.usace.army.mil/cochiti/).

Coeur D'Alene Tribe.Homepage. (www.cdatribe.org/).

"Coleman Announces White Earth Reservation Housing Authority Will Receive $3.1 Million Federal Grant." May 12, 2003. (www.coleman.senate.gov/).

College of Menominee Nation. Homepage. (www.menominee.edu/).

Colorado River Indian Tribe Public Library/Archive. (www.gocalifornia.about.com/).

Columbia Encyclopedia, Sixth Edition 2001. "Colville River, United States." (www.bartleby.com).

Columbia Gazetteer of North America. Saul B. Cohen, editor. New York: Columbia University Press, 2000. (www.bartleby.com/69/).

Columbia River Inter-Tribal Fishing Commission. Homepage. (www.critfc.org/text/yakama.html).

Colville River Special Area. "BLM to Delay Colville River Plan." May 22, 2002. (www.aurora.ak.blm.gov).

Colville Tribes. Homepage. (www.colvilletribes.com/).

Comanche Nation College. Homepage. (www.cnc.cc.ok.us).

Comanche Red River Casino. Homepage. (www.casinocity.com/).

Comanche Spur. Homepage. (www.comanchespur.com/).

Commanche Nation College. Homepage. (www.cnc.cc.ok.us/).

"Community Health Representatives." White Earth Reservation. (www.perham.eot.com/~rtcheal/chrs.htm).

Compact Between the Pokagon Band and the State of Michigan. (www.michigan.gov).

"Comprehensive Economic Development Strategy 2002 for Northwest Michigan." (www.nwm.org).

Confederated Tribes of the Coos, Lower Umpqua and Suislaw. Homepage. (www.ctclusi.org/index.asp).

Confederated Tribes of the Goshute Reservation, Utah. (www.aaanativearts.com).

Confederated Tribes of the Chehalis. Homepage. (www.chehalistribe.org).

Confederated Tribes of the Grand Ronde. Homepage. (www.grandronde.org/).

Confederated Tribes of the Warm Springs. Homepage. (www.ctws.org).

Confederated Tribes of the Warm Springs Reservation. Homepage. (www.warmsprings.com/).
Consolidated Borough of Quil Ceda Village. (www.quilcedavillage.org).

Constitution and By-Laws for the Big Valley Band of Pomo Indians of the Big Valley Rancheria. (www.thorpe.ou.edu).

Constitution and By-Laws of the Lower Sioux Indian Community of Minnesota. (www.thorpe.ou.edu).

Constitution and By-Laws of the Quartz Valley Indian Community, California. (www.thorpe.ou.edu).

Constitution and By-Laws of the Thlopthlocco Tribal Town, Oklahoma. (www.thorpe.ou.edu).

Constitution and By-Laws of the Ute Indian Tribe of the Uintah and Ouray Reservation. (www.tribalresourcecenter.org/ccfolder/uteconst.htm#BusCom).

Constitution of the Big Lagoon Rancheria. (www.doc.narf.org).

Constitution of the Choctaw Nation of Oklahoma. (www.thorpe.ou.edu).

Constitution of the Commanche Tribe of Oklahoma. (www.tribalresourcecenter.org/ccfolder/comanche_const.htm).

Constitution of the Duckwater Shoshone Tribe of the Duckwater Reservation. (www.tribalresourcecenter.org/ccfolder/duckwater_shoshone_const.htm).

Constitution of the Makah Indian Tribe of the Makah Indian Reservation. (www.thorpe.ou.edu).

Constitution of the Quileute Tribe of the Quileute Reservation. (www.thorpe.ou.edu).

Constitution of the Sault St. Marie Tribe. (www.saulttribe.com).

Contact Information for Michigan Federally Recognized Indian Tribes. (www.yvwiiusdinvnohii.net/ michtribes.htm).

Contact List. Nevada State Offices. (www.gbpca.org/ GBPCAdb/websiteFiles/listContacts.asp?GroupID=25).

Cooking Post. Homepage. (www.cookingpost.com/).

Coquille Tribe. Homepage. (www.coquilletribe.org/).

Corbett, Helen D., and G.S. Winer. "Pribilof Islands." (www.amiq.org/pribilof.html).

Cornelia Church Mission. Morton Minesota. (www.oakhills.edu).

Corporate Charter of the Fort McDermitt Paiute and Shoshone Tribe. (www.thorpe.ou.edu).

Council of Indian Nations. (www.cinprograms.org).

Council of Indian Nations. Homepage. (www.cinprograms.org/).

"Court issues ruling on Shingle Springs casino resolving most environmental issues." Press release. (www.businesswire.com/).

Coushatta Casino Resort. Homepage. (www.gccoushatta.com/).

Coushatta Millworks. Homepage. (www.cousattamilworks.com/).

Coushatta Ranch. Homepage. (www.ctlaranch.com/).

Coushatta Tribe of Louisiana. Homepage. (www.coushattatribela.org/).

Cow Creek Band of Umpqua Tribe of Indians. Homepage. (www.cowcreek.com/).

Cow Creek Foundation. Homepage. (www.cowcreekfoundation.org).

Cowboy.net. Homepage. (www.cowboy.net).
Cowboy.net. Oklahoma Tribes and Officials. (www.cowboy.net).

Cowlitz County Washington. Homepage. (www.co.cowlitz.wa.us).

Cowlitz Indian Tribe. Homepage. (www.cowlitz.org).

"Cowlitz Tribe confirms plans for casino on reservation." Indianz.com. (www.indianz.com/IndianGaming/2004/ 003618.asp).

Coyote Valley Casino. Homepage. (www.coyotevalleycasino.com/b_jack.html).

Coyote Valley Tribe. Homepage. (www.coyotevalleytc.com/).

Creative Images. Homepage. (www.cimediagroup.com/).

Creek Heritage. (www.ryal.k12.ok.us/creek.html).

Creek Nation Casino. Homepage. (www.creeknationcasino.com/).

Crow Creek Sioux Reservation. (www.spiritpath.aaanativearts.com).

Crow Creek Sioux Reservation, South Dakota. (www.revelex.com).

"Crow Reservation." Bureau of Indian Affairs. Energy and Mineral Division. (www.tlc.wtp.net/).

CSD Schools. "Tatitlek - Chugach School District - Voyage to Excellence." (www.chugachschools.com/ csd_schools/tatitlek.html).

Cusick and Usk in Pend Oreille County Washington. (www.co.pend-oreille.wa.us/cusick.html).

Cypress Bayou Casino. Homepage. (www.cypressbayou.com/).

Dacotah Ridge Golf Club. Homepage. (www.dacotahridge.com/contact/contact.html.

Dakota Meadow Storage. Homepage. (www.DakotahMeadowsStorage.com/).

"Deal Aims to Protect Waters." Detroit News, May 14, 2004. (www.detnews.com/2004/metro/0405/15/c07-152713.htm).

Deiss, Ron. "District, Sac and Fox Tribe Participate in Planning Study." (www.mvr.usace.army.mil/ publicaffairsoffice/powertimes/November2001/district sacandfoxtribe.html).

"Delaware Tribe, Gillmann Group Start Land Into Trust Application With Bureau of Indian Affairs; Environmental Study, Economic Impact Process Underway." PR Newswire. April 22, 2004. (www.prnewswire.com/).

Delaware Tribe of Indians. Homepage. (www.delawaretribeofindians.nsn.us).

Demographic Information. (www.fact-index.com/d/di/ diomede__alaska.html).

"Dental Care at Penobscot Community Health Center." Bangor News. (www.bangornews.com/).

Dept. of Conservation and Natural Resources. Land Base of Nevada Tribes. (www.dcnr.nv.gov).

Desert Diamond Casino. Homepage. (www.desertdiamond.com/).

Destination Grays Harbor, 2002 - Quinault area. (www.thevidette.com/dgh02/quinault01.html).

Detail Population Statistics of Indian Lands within the United States. (www.citizensalliance.org/).

Diamond Mountain Casino. Homepage. (www.diamondmountaincasino.com).

Digital empowerment.org/). "Leech Lake Band of Ojibwe." (www.digitalempowerment.org/).

Dine College. Homepage. (www.dinecollege.edu/).

Discover Navajo Events - People of the Fourth World. (www.discovernavajo.com/events.html).

Dobbyn, Paula, Hotels News Partners, Alaska. "Native Corporation Buys Kukak Bay, Alaska-Area Lodge." Anchorage Daily News, January 21, 2000. Accessed via South Beach Magazine. (www.southbeach-usa.com/miami-south-beach-hotels-news2/htlfeb47.htm).

Drought Status for January 2003. (www.ose.state.nm.us/DroughtTaskForce/ MonitoringWorkGroup/ advjune2003.pdf).

Duck Valley Indian Reservation Shoshone-Paiute Tribes. (www.idahorcd.org/duckval.htm).

Dulzo, Jim. "Coal Burning Plant Fires Up Hot Dispute in Manistee. Plan's trail Could lead to Lansing and Washington." February 15, 2004. (www.mlui.org/landwater/ fullarticle.asp?fileid=16646).

Dungeness River Audubon Center: Homepage (WA Olympic Peninsula).(www.dungenessrivercenter.org/).

Eagle Mountain Casino. Homepage. (www.eaglemtncasino.com/).

EAN: Alamo Navajo School Board, Inc. (www.educationamerica.net/ browse.phtml?sid=nm&eid=696&a=eip).

Eastern Band of the Cherokee Nation. Homepage. (www.cherokee-nc.com/).

Educational Attainment. (www.censtats.census.gov).

Educational Service Unit 3, "Culture and Customs," (www.esu3.org/districts/ gretna/elem/nawebpages/ Omaha.html).

Eklutna Inc. (www.eklutnainc.com/land.html).

El Paso Community College. "Tigua's Survive 300 Years of Ordeals." (www.epcc.edu).

El Paso Inc. "Tigua's Go Public with Video Documentary." (www.elpasoinc.com/Archive/00_10_15/ week.html).
Eldorado County, California. "Shingle Springs Rancheria." (www.co.el-dorado.ca.us).

Elem Indian Colony. Homepage. (www.elemnation.com/).

"Elevated press response to Defenders of Wildlife's presentation to Siskiyou County Board of Supervisors." Defenders of Wildlife Bulletin of Wolf Council. March 9, 2001. (www.defenders.org/wildlife/wolf/wolfupdate/ issues/wl113001.html).

Elk Valley Casino. Homepage. (www.elkvalleycasino.com/).

"Emergency Medical Service." White Earth Reservation. (www.perham.eot.com/~rtcheal/emts.html).

Emergency Medical Services. To'hajiilee Field Office. (www.navajoems.navajo.org/Contact_Tohajiilee.htm).

"Empire Resorts, Inc. confirms plan to develop two Catskill N.Y. casinos after Announcement of land claim settlement agreement by New York State and Cayuga Nation of New York." November 18, 2004. (www.biz.yahoo.com/).

Encyclopedia of North American Indians. S.v. "Kickapoo" (by Joseph B Herring). Houghton Mifflin. (www.college.hmco.com/history/readerscomp/naind/html/na_018500_kickapoo.htm).

Enterprise and Thlopthlocco Tribal Town. Homepage. (www.gwtc.net/~jbandy/thlopthlocco.htm).

Enterprise Rancheria Fee-To-Trust Acquisition Environmental Assessment.(www.reports.analyticalcorp.net/enterprise/ea/files/document/Section-3-Description-of-Affected-Environment.pdf).

"Entry #30: On New Mexico's high plateau, Navajo people are creating exemplary schools." Middle School Diaries. (www.middleweb.com/msdiaries00/MSDiaryLEE30.html).

EPA. Homepage. (www.epa.gov).

Environmental Science Associates. "Cloverdale Rancheria Environmental Assessment." (www.esassoc.com/).

"EPA grants CAA authority to Fond du Lac tribe," Environmental Laboratory Washington Report, LRP Publications, February 13, 2004. (www.web.lexis-nexis.com).

Ethnologue report for Chimakuan. (www.ethnologue.com/show_family.asp?subid=1855).

Evans Craig, Internet Technology Service, LLC. "Pueblo Nations Tribal Technology Assessment Pueblo of Cochiti." September, 2001. (www.internettechnologyservice.net).

Everything Alaska. (www.everythingalaska.com/).

"Examples of Village Processing Plants" Village Processing Handbook. Ch. 2. (www.iser.uaa.alaska.edu/ResourceStudies/VillageFishProcessing Handbook/Ch%202%20Cases%204.pdf).

Experience Washington. Homepage. (www.experiencewashington.com/city_C778.html).
Explore Minnesota. "Boise Forte Heritage Center and Cultural Museum, Tower." (www.exploreminnesota.com/features/stories_detail.cfm?oid=29350).

"Explore the Navajo Nation." (www.americanwest.com/pages/navajo2.htm).

"Exploring the Quinault Rain Forest." Travel Photographers. (www.travelphotographers.net).

Eyak. (www.mnsu.edu/emuseum/cultural/northamerica/eyak.html).

Eyak Technology, LLC. (www.eyaktek.com/cordovahistory.htm).

Federal Aviation Administration. "Establishment of Class E Airspace; Allakaket, AK," 14 CFR Part 71 [Docket No. FAA-2004-17496; Airspace Docket No. 04-AAL-04]. June 16, 2004. (www.alaska.faa.gov/at/Finalrules/allakaket.htm).

"Federal Court Ruling Moves Huron Band Casino Another Step Forward." Press Release. Nottawaseppi Huron Band of Potawatomi. April 23, 2004. (www.mrgmi.com/HPIfederalruling1.pdf).

"Federally Qualified Health Centers by County." (www.mimom.org/pdf/fqhcbycounty03.pdf).

Federally-Recognized Indian Tribes in Nevada. Homepage. (www.jrsa.org).

FEMA. Homepage. (www.fema.org/).

Ferrara, Peter J. "The Choctaw Revolution." (www.members.aol.com/).

"Final US Fish & Wildlife Klamath Fish Kill Report Confirms Low Flows as Major Factor in 2002 Lower Klamath Fish Kill" (www.onrc.org).

Firewise.org. Mescalero Apache Reservation. (www.firewise.org/).

Fishing Pursuits. "The Arolik: Alaska's Private Resort." (www.fishingpursuits.com/brochures/Arolik.pdf).

500 Nations.com. (www.500nations.com/).

500 Nations.com. "Lucky Seven Casino." (www.500nations.com/casinos/caLucky7.asp).

Flandreau Indian Boarding School. Photographs. (www.flandreau.schools.bia.edu/).

Flandreau Municipal Hospital-CAH. Online Highways.com. (www.ohwy.com).

Flandreau Santee Sioux Tribe. Homepage. (www.fsst.org/health.htm).

Flandreau Santee Sioux Tribe. (www.firstnations.org/grants/grantee_map/south_dakota/flandreau_santee_sioux_tri.htm).

"Flathead Indian Reservation, MT." (www.indianz.com/).

"Flathead Reservation, Montana." (www.nake1.cr.usgs.gov).
Flood Hazard Data. (www.poa.usace.army.mil/en/cw/fld_haz/).

Fogarty, Mark. "Arizona Tribes Get $2 Million in Economic Development." February 11, 2004. (www.indiancountry.com).

"Fond Du Lac Band of Chippewa Indians." (www.kstrom.com/isk/maps/mn/fondlac.htm).

Fond Du Lac Reservation. Homepage. (www.fdlrez.com/).

"Fond Du Lac Reservation." (www.indians.state.mn.us/tribes/fondlac.html).

"Fond Du Lac Reservation." (www.mnscu.edu/System/CollegeProfile/FondduLacTCC.html).

"Fond du Lac Reservation Receives National Firewise Community Recognition." (www.firewise.org/pubs/wnn/vol18/no1/pp-04.html).

Fond Du Luth Casino. Homepage. (www.fondduluthcasino.com/default.htm).

Forests and Communities.org. "Karuk Tribe." (www.forestsandcommunities.org/).

"Fort Apache Historic Park." White Mountain Apache Tribe. (www.wmat.nsn.us).

Fort McDowell Adventures. (www.fortmcdowelladventures.com).

Fort McDowell Yavapai Nation. Homepage. (www.ftmcdowell.org/).
"Fort Peck CommunityCollege."(www.wolfpoint.com/).

"Fort Peck Reservation History." (www.montana.edu/wwwfpcc/tribes).

"Fort Peck Tribal Health Dept." (fpth.d2g.com?).

Fort Randall Casino. Homepage. (www.fortrandallcasino.com/).

Fort Sill Apache Casino. Homepage. (www.fsac.info).

Fort Sill Apache Nation. Homepage. (www.fortsillapachenation.com/).

Fortune Bay Casino. Homepage. (http://www.fortunebay.com/casino/).

G.C.R. and Associates. "G.C.R. and Associates, Inc. 2000." (www.gcr1.com/5010WEB/).

Gaming Business Directory. Homepage. (www.gbdonline.com/).

Gaming Links in North Dakota. (www.dakotasioux.com/gaming.html).

Gana-A'Yoo Ltd. (www.khotol.com/).

Garvin, Eileen. "Governor signs gaming compact with Navajo Nation." November 7, 2003. (www.bizjournals.com/albuquerque/stories/2003/11/03/daily21.html).

GBPCA. (www.gbpca.org/).

General Information. Haines, AK. (www.wingsofalaska.com/haines.htm).

Geology of the Smith River. (www.online.redwoods.cc.ca.us/depts/science/earth/smith/smith.htm).

Gila Crossing Community School "Home of the Eagles." (www.gric.k12.az.us/Gila/enan2.html).

Gila River Arts and Crafts Inc. Homepage. (www.gilaindiancenter.com/indian_center.php).

"Gila River Development. "National Technologies Award Presented to Gila River Telecommunications, Inc." (www.gilariverdevelopment.com/events.htm).

Gila River Indian Community Department of Economic Development. Homepage. (www.gilariverdevelopment.com/businessparks.htm).

Gila River Indian Community. Homepage. (www.gric.nsn.us/).

Gila River Reservation Housing. (www.capla.arizona.edu).

Gila River Telecommunications Inc. Homepage. (www.gilanet.net/aboutgrti.html).

Gold Country Casino. Homepage. (www.goldcountrycasino.com/).

Golden Acorn Casino Travel Center. Homepage. (www.goldenacorncasino.com/).

Golden Eagle Casino. Homepage. (www.goldeneaglecasino.com/).

Goldsmith, Sarah Sue. "A Warm Welcome and Some Lessons in Etiquette." Baton Rouge (LA) Advocate Magazine, June 30, 1996. (www.carencrohighschool.org/la_studies/indian/general/etiquette.htm).

Goldsmith, Sarah Sue. "Intertribal Council Assists Member Tribes." Baton Rouge (LA) Advocate Magazine, June 30, 1996. (www.carencrohighschool.org/la_studies/indian/general/IT_Council.htm).

Goldsmith, Sarah Sue. "Jena Was Only a Place along the Way to Oklahoma." Baton Rouge (LA) Advocate Magazine, June 2, 1996. (www.carencrohighschool.org/la_studies/indian/jena/alongway.htm).

Goldsmith, Sarah Sue. "The Jena Band: Choctaw Traditions Keep Tribe Together." Baton Rouge (LA) Advocate Magazine, June 2, 1996. (www.carencrohighschool.org/la_studies/indian/jena/choctaw.htm).

Governor's Office of Indian Affairs. Shoalwater Bay Tribe. (www.goaia.wa.gov).

Grand Casino and Resort. Homepage. (www.grandcasinomn.com/).

Grand Portage Reservation. Homepage. (www.grandportage.com/).

"Grand Portage: rich in land and protective of it." 2003. (www.news.minnesota.publicradio.org/).

Grand River Casino and Resort. Homepage. (www.grandrivercasino.com/).

"Grand Ronde tribe proposes stadium for urban casino deal." (www.indiancountry.com/).

Grand Traverse Band of Ottowa and Chippewa Indians. Homepage. (www.gtb.nsn.us/index.asp).

Grand Traverse Resorts and Casinos. (www.casino2win.com/lodging.php).

Grass Roots.org/). Homepage. "Mississppi Band of Choctaw Indians." (www.grass-roots.org/).

Graton Rancheria. Former Homepage. (www.coastmiwok.com)

Graton Rancheria. Homepage. (www.gomiwok.com/).

Great Lakes Bulletin. (www.mlui.org).

Great Lakes Intertribal Council. Homepage. (www.glitc.org/).

Great Schools.net. "Crow Creek/Lower Brule District." (www.greatschools.net/modperl/browse_district/200/sd).

Greektown Casino. Homepage. (www.greektowncasino.com/dining/oliveroom.htm).

Green, Sarah Jean. "Tribe, City Sign Deal to Pave Way for Snoqualmie Casino Off I-90." Seattle Times, May 5, 2004. Accessed through Indianz. (www.indianz.com/News/2004/001623.asp).

Greenville Rancheria. Homepage. (www.greenvillerancheria.com/).

"Ground Broken for To'Hajiilee Health Clinic." Cibola County Beacon Online. (www.cibolabeacon.com/articles/2004/10/30/news/news1.txt).

Gwich'in Council International. "The Gwich'in." (www.gwichin.org/gwichin.html).

Haida Corporation. (www.haidacorp.com/Pages/About.htm).

Hammel, Paul. "Tribes Push for Recall of Two County Officials," Omaha World-Herald Company, March 23, 2004. (www.//web-lexis-nexis.com/).

Handbook of Texas Online. Homepage. (www.tsha.utexas.edu/handbook/online/articles/view/TT/bmt45.html).

Harjo, Allen. "Community Enterprise and Thlopthlocco Tribal Town." Contributions by Community Leaders. (www.gwtc.net/~jbandy/thlopthlocco.htm).

Harrahs Narragansett Casino. (www.harrahsnarragansettcasino.com/).

Harris, Paula. "Tribal spirit." (www.metroactive.com/). Harvard Project on American Indian Economic Development. John F. Kennedy School of Government. Harvard University. Honoring Nations. (www.ksg.harvard.edu/hpaied/index.htm).

Haughey, Matthew. "My Havasupai Hike." (www.haughey.com/havasupai/brochures/flyer.htm).

Havasupai Tribe. Homepage. (www.havasupaitribe.com/village.html).

"Health Education." White Earth Reservation. (www.perham.eot.com/~rtcheal/he.html).

Heard Museum. Arizona's 21 Federally Recognized Tribal Communities. (www.heard.org/21tribes.pdf).

Hensley, Richard. "The Quileute Tribe of La-Push Washington." (www.imca.bravepages.com/articles/quileute.htm).

"HHS, Tribes Dedicate New Hospital in Winnebago, Nebraska," States News Service, 8 April, 2004. (www.//web-lexis-nexis.com/).

Highbanks Campground. Homepage. (www.highbankscamping.com/).

Highlights of UKB News. Homepage. (www.uark.edu/depts/comminfo/UKB/hilites.html).

Hiscock, John. "New Partnership Museum for Monument and Tribe." July 31, 2003. (www.nps.gov/pisp/pphtml/newsdetail7749.html).

History of American Indians in California. (www.cr.nps.gov/history/online_books/5views/5views1h20.htm).

History of Fort Totten. United States Department of the Interior. (www.lib.ndsu.nodak.edu/govdocs/text/forttotten.html).

History of St. Francis Indian School. (www.sfisk12.org/Whoweare/histtwo.htm).

"History of the Omaha Indian Tribe." Pagewise, 2002. (www.az.assortment.com /omahaindianshi_rjom.htm).

History of the Northern Ponca Housing Authority. (www.poncahousing.org).

History of the Thlopthlocco Methodist Church. (www.rootsweb.com/~okokfusk/histories/thlomech.htm).

History of Uintah-Ouray Indian Reservation, Utah. (www.onlineutah.com/uintah-ourayreservationhistory.shtml).

Hobbs, Straus, Dean & Walker, LLP. "Omnibus Indian Advancement Act cleared for President's signature." Homepage. (www.hsdwlaw.com/).

Hollander, Zaz. "Village tries to save dead." Anchorage Daily News. November 30, 2003. (www.adn.com/front/story/4460158p-4444606c.html).

Hon-Dah Resort-Casino and Conference Center. (www.hon-dah.com/).

Hoopa Valley Indian Reservation. Homepage. (www.hoopa-nsn.gov).

Hope, Jeffrey. "Shishmaref loses another 30 feet of shoreline to erosion." (www.ktuu.com/CMS/anmviewer.asp?a=4088&z=4).

"Hopi Agriculture." (www.nau.edu/~hcpo-p/culture/agric.htm).

Hopi Cultural Center, Museum, Restaurant and Hotel. (www.psv.com/hopi.html).

Hopi Cultural Preservation Office. "Lodging, Dining and Facilities at Hopi." (www.nau.edu/~hcpo-p/visit/logdinf.htm).

Hopi Tribe. Homepage. (www.hopi.nsn.us/).

Hot Weathers.(www.hotweathers.com/usa/oklahoma/).

Hotel Santa Fe. Homepage. (hsf.tsbnet.com/).

Houghton Mifflin College Division. "Miwok." (www.college.hmco.com/).

Houghton Mifflin College. Kinzua Dam. (college.hmco.com/).

Houlton Band of Maliseet Indians. (www.state.me.us).

Housing Authority of the Cherokee Nation. Homepage. (www.cherokeehousing.com).

Housing Authority of the Creek Nation of Oklahoma. (www.creeknationhousing.org/rent_apts.htm).

Hualaupai and the Havasupai Reservation. (www.kaibab.org/supai/gc_supai.htm).

Hualapai Police Department. Homepage. (www.hualapaipolice.com/).

Humphrey, Kay. "Ruling Expected Soon in Omaha-Winnebago Dispute, Indian Country Today, 23 May 2001. (www.indiancountry.com/?1841).

Huna Totem Corporation. (www.hunatotem.com).

I Love Alaska. (www.ilovealaska.com/).

Ilisagvik College. (www.ilisagvik.cc/).

Ilisagvik College Student Assembly. (www.gov.alaska.edu/net/studgov/ICSA/default.html).

Image Marketing International. Homepage. (www.tradecorridor.com/).

inAlaska.com. (www.inalaska.com).

"Index of IRA." (www.thorpe.ou.edu/IRA).

Index. (www.nimacorporation.com/).

Indian Affairs: Laws and Treaties. Vol. 6, Laws. (www.digital.library.okstate.edu/kappler/vol6/html_files/v6p1005.html).

Indian Canyons. Agua Caliente Band of Cahuilla Indians. (www.indian-canyons.com/).

Indian Country Today. Homepage. (www.indiancountry.com/).
Indian Health Service. "HHS Awards $1.2 Million To Build New Clinic In Chenega Bay, Alaska." August 6, 2003. (www.ihs.gov).

Indian Health Service. Homepage. (www.ihs.gov).

Indian Health Service. "Mt. Edgecumbe Service Area." (www.ihs.gov).

Indian Land Tenure Foundation. "Snoqualmie Tribe WA." Grantees. (www.indianlandtenure.org/grants/granteesdescript_2-15-05.htm).

Indian Nations Indian Territory Arhives. Delaware. (www.rootsweb.com/~usgenweb/ok/nations/delaware/).

Indian Pueblo Cultural Center. Homepage. (www.indianpueblo.org).

Indian Pueblos.org. Homepage. (www.indianpueblos.org).

Indian Tribes of Oklahoma. Homepage. (members.tripod.com/~lenapelady/it2.html).

Indianz.com. Homepage. (www.indianz.com).

Indianz.com. "Kickapoo Tribe Opening Child Care, Health Centers." October 1, 2003. (www.indianz.com).

Indianz.com. "Snoqualmie Tribe Signs Services Agreement." May 5, 2004. (www.indianz.com).

Infiltrator Systems. Plastic Leachfield Chamber Systems, Onsite Wastewater Solutions. (www.infiltratorsystems.com/pdfs/001_LittleRiver_SBR_HiCaps.pdf).

Inn of the Mountain Gods Resort and Casino. Homepage. (www.innofthemountaingods.com/).

Intertribal Bison Cooperative. Homepage. (www.intertribalbison.org/main.asp?id=1).

Intertribal Council Inc. Homepage. (www.eighttribes.org/).

Intertribal Council of Arizona, Inc. Homepage. (www.itcaonline.com/).

Intertribal Council of Nevada. Confederated Tribes of the Goshute Reservation. (www.itcn.org).

Intertribal Council of Nevada. Tribal Profiles. (www.itcn.org/).

Intertribal Court of California. Homepage. (www.intertribalcourt.indian.com/).

Intertribal Environmental Council Underground Storage Tank Program. (www.itecmembers.org).

Intertribal Monitoring Association on Indian Trust Funds. (www.itmatrustfunds.org).

Ione Band of Miwok Indians. Homepage. (www.ionemiwok.org/).

Iowa Nation. Homepage. (www.iowanation.org/).

Iowa Nation of Oklahoma. Homepage. (www.iowanation.org/).
"Iowa Tribe of Kansas and Nebraska." Brown Quarterly. Volume 6, No. 1 (Fall/Winter2003) - Native American Issue. (brownvboard.org/brwnqurt/06-1/index4.php).

Isanotski Corporation. Gear Storage. (www.isanotski.alaska.com/GearStorage.htm).

Isanotski Corporation. History. (www.isanotski.alaska.com/Isanotski.htm).

Island Information. "Largest Islands of the United States." (www.users.erols.com/jcalder/USLARGESTV1.html).

Isleta Casino and Resort. Homepage. (www.isletacasinoresort.com).

Isleta Golf Course. Homepage. (www.ilsetaeagle.com).

Isleta Pueblo. Homepage. (www.indianpueblo.org).

Jackpot Junction Casino and Hotel. Homepage. (www.jackpotjunction.com/about.html).

Jackson Rancheria. Homepage. (www.jacksoncasino.com).

Jaksich, Netasha. "Squaxin tribe prepares to embrace broadband: Better Internet Access a Must for Education." The Olympian. (www.theolympian.com).

Jamestown S'Klallam Tribe. Homepage. (www.jamestowntribe.org/).

Jamul Indian Village. Homepage. (www.jamulindianvillage.com).

"Jena Band asks Louisiana Governor for Compact." April 22, 2004. (www.indianz.com/).

Jenna Band of Choctaw Indians. Homepage. (www.jenachoctaw.org/).

Johns, Kari Shaginoff. "Nay'dini'aa Na' Koht'aene Xu'k'a Keni'aadze' Nen' (Chickaloon Indians Traditional Land)." (www.chickaloon.org).

Johnson, Jean."Banks open their doors" Indian Country Today. (www.proquest.umi.com).

Johnston, Greg. "The Quinault quest Steelhead are monstrous and so is the challenge." Seatlepi.com/. (www.seattlepi.nwsource.com/getaways/032599/quin25.html).

Johnston, John. "Paiute pride Tribe that was 'terminated' by the government has come back strong." Desert News. (www.deseretnews.com).

"Judge affirms Cayuga Nation's sovereign rights." Monday, April 26, 2004. (www.indianz.com).

Juneau Empire Newspaper Online. (www.juneauempire.com).

Justice Research and Statistics Association. Homepage. (www.jrsa.org).

Kaibab Paiute Tribe. Homepage. (www.kaibabpaiutetribal.com).
Kalispel. Infoplease.com. (www.infoplease.com/ce6/society/A0826930.html).

Kalispel Tribe of Indians. Homepage. (www.kalispeltribe.com).

Kapi'olani Community College. (leahi.kcc.hawaii.edu/org/pvs/alaskahoonah.html).

Karuk Tribe. Homepage. (www.karuk.us).

Katmai National Park Information Page. (www.katmai.national-park.com/info.htm).

Kavilco. (www.kavilco.com/).

Kavilco Incorporated. (www.kavilco.com/pages/aboutkavilco.html).

Kavilco Incorporated. (www.kavilco.com/pages/rayonier.html).

Kaw Nation of Oklahoma. Homepage. (www.kawnation.com/).

Kenai Peninsula Borough (Borough) Transportation Plan Update. Homepage. (www.kpbtransplan.net).

Kenai Peninsula Economic Development District Inc." Comprehensive Economic Development Strategy." June 15, 2001. (www.kpedd.org/pdfs/ceds.pdf).

"Kenai Peninsula Gets 'Rural' Designation: 2000." (www.alaskool.org/projects/subsistence/timeline/kenai%20p.htm).

Kenyon, Marie. "At Last Moon Shines on Snoqualmies." Northwest News, September 22, 1997. (www.nwnews.com/vvissues/v11n37/front1.html).

KetchanAlaska.com. (www.ketchikanalaska.com/).

Kewadin Casino, Hessel. Homepage. (www.kewadinhessel.com/).

Kewadin Casino Hotel. Homepage. (www.sault-sainte-marie.mi.usa.freehotelguide.com/Kewadin-Casino-Hotel.html).

Kewadin Casino, Manistique. Homepage. (www.kewadinmanistique.com/).

Keweenaw Bay Indian Community. Homepage. (www.kbic-nsn.gov).

Keweenaw Bay Ojibwa Community College. Homepage. (www.kbocc.org/).

Kickapoo History. (www.tolatsga.org/kick.html).

Kickapoo Lucky Eagle Casino. Homepage. (www.kickapooluckyeaglecasino.com).

Kickapoo Traditional Tribe of Texas. (www.texasindians.com).

Kickapoo Tribe in Kansas. (www.kickapoo.ktik.org/).

"Kickapoo Tribe of Texas has come a long way." Monday, November 15, 2004. (www.madison.law.ou.edu/constitution/kickapoo/). Kids for Composting on the Oneida Nation Reservation, WI.Wastecap Wisconsin.(www.wastecapwi.com/).

KILI Radio 91.5. The Voice of the Lakota Nation. (www.siouxymca.org/programs.htm).

KINI FM 96.1 St.Francis, SD.(www.gwtc.net/~kinifm/).

"Kiowa." Minnesota State Univerrsity. (www.mnsu.edu).

Kitt Peak National Observatory. Visitor Information. (www.gocalifornia.about.com/cs/tucson1/a/azkittpeak.htm).

"Klah-Che-Min." The Squaxin Island Tribe. (www.nwifc.wa.gov/newsletter/29_1/6.asp).

Klamath Tribes.Homepage. (www.klamathtribes.org/).

Kla-Mo-Ya Casino. Homepage. (www.klamoya.com/).

Klawock Heenya Corporation. (www.klawockheenya.com/).

Klawock. (www.cityofklawock.com/).

Kluckwan, Inc. Homepage. (www.klukwan.com/).

Koasati Pines at Couhsatta. Homepage. (www.koasatipines.com/).

KOBTV.com. Homepage. (www.kobtv.com/).

Kobuk Valley National Park Map Page. (www.kobuk.valley.national-park.com/map.htm).

Kodiak Salmon Packers. "Summer Jobs in Alaska!" (www.kspi.net/).

Kodiak. Community Emergency Response Plan. Kodiak Emergency Operations Plan. 1999. (www.city.kodiak.ak.us/emergencyprep).

Kodiak. (www.kodiak.org/).

Kodiak. "Transportation." 20:36 2/24/04. (www.kodiakexperience.com/transportation.html).

Kongiganak. "What New Teachers Can Expect at Kong." (www.lksd.org/kongiganak/kongiganak/Kong/arrivingkong1.htm).

Koniag Inc. "History." (www.koniag.com/koniag/history.cfm).

Konocti Vista Casino. Homepage. kvcasino.com/rvbpark2002.htm).

Kootenai River Inn. Homepage. (www.kootenairiverinn.com/).

Kootznoowoo Inc. "Welcome Kootznoowoo Inc." (www.kootznoowoo.com/).

Koyukuk Home. (www.vernetti.koyukuk.k12.ak.us/).

Kraker, Daniel. "Tribe defeated a dam and won back its water," High Country News. March 15, 2004. (www.bobwhitson.typepad.com/howlings/2004/03/tribe_defeated_.html).

Krishnan, Sonia. "Snoqualmie Tribe on Road to Self-Sufficiency." Seattle Times, January 4, 2005. (www.seattletimes.nwsource.com).

KRT Photos. "Spirit houses decorate graves in Kwethluk, AK, a town plagued by a large number of cases of drug-resistant bacteria." HighBeam Research. (www.static.highbeam.com).

Kumeyaay Elementary. Viejas Band of Kumeyaay. (www.kumeyaay.sandi.net).

Kumeyaay History. (www.kumeyaay.com/).

Kumeyaay Nation. Inaja Cosmit Band. (www.kumeyaay.com/).

Kuskokwim Corporation. (www.kuskokwim.com).

Kwa Taq Nuk Resort at Flathead Bay. Homepage. (www.kwataqnuk.com).

La Jolla Band of Luiseño Indians. Homepage. (www.lajollaindians.com).

La Plaza Telecommunity. Picurís Pueblo. (www.laplaza.org).

"La Posta Band of Mission Indians receives gaming compact." Sept. 10/PRNewswire. (www.prnewswire.com).

Lac du Flambeau Chamber of Commerce. Homepage. (www.lacduflambeauchamber.com).

Lac du Flambeau Public School. Homepage. (www.ldf.k12.wi.us).

Lac Vieux Desert Band of Lake Superior Chippewa Indians. Homepage. (www.lvdtribal.com/).

Lac Vieux Desert Resort Casino. Homepage. (www.lvdcasino.com/).

"LaCrosse FRO Receives Grant for Fish Passage Project." (www.news.minnesota.publicradio.org/features/200003/09_robertsont_wadena-m/).

Lake Counnty, California. Homepage. (www.lakecounty.com/galleryscenic.html).

Lake of the Torches Resort Casino. Homepage. (www.lakeofthetorches.com/).

Lake Quinault Lodge. Homepage. (www.visitlakequinault.com/internet_deals.htm).

"Lake Sturgeon: White Earth Reservation." US Fish and Wildlife Services. (www.fws.gov/midwest/LaCrosseFisheries/projects/sturgeon_white_earth.htm).

Lakes of Colville Reservation. Homepage. (www.wsu.edu/cctfish/).

Lakota Country Hunts. Homepage. (www.lakotamall.com/shops/hunts/).

"Land-based casinos." Betting Magazine. July 31, 2003.(www.bettingmagazine.com). Langdon, Magaret. The Kumeyaay Languages. (www.kumeyaay.com/history/linguistics.html).

Larsen Bay Lodge. "Welcome to Larsen Bay Lodge, Kodiak Island, Alaska." (www.larsenbaylodge.com).

Las Vegas-Clark County Library District. "Stewart Indian Colony." (www.lvccld.org).

Laws: Cases and Codes : U.S. Code : Title 25 : Section 621. (www.caselaw.lp.findlaw.com).

Lee Tutuveni, Tanya. "Hopi Tribe Pulls the Plug on Power Plant." Newspaper of the Hopi Tribe. Vol. XII, No. 11, May 29, 2002. (www.blackmesais.org).

Leech Lake Band of Ojibwe. (www.leechlakeojibwe.org).

Leech Lake Gaming Division. Homepage. (www.leechlakegaming.com).

"Leech Lake Reservation." Oakhills Christian College. (www.oakhills.edu).

"Leech Lake Reservation." Online Highways.com. (www.ohwy.com).

Leech Lake Tribal College. Homepage. (www.leechlaketribalcollege.org/).

Lehto, Tessa. "Dance Exhibition at Mall of America as Preview to Annual Pow Wow," July 8, 2003. (www.eaganmn.com/Pow%20Wow.doc).

Leisure and Sport Review. Homepage. (www.lasr.net).

Library of Congress. "The Omaha Indians in Nebraska," Americas Story from America's Library. (www.americaslibrary.gov/cgi-bin/page.cgi/es/ne/omaha_1).

Linguasphere Register 1999/2000 Edition. 6=North-America geosector. (www.linguasphere.net/secure/ip/pdf/zones/60.pdf).

Little Creek Casino and Hotel. Homepage. (www.little-creek.com/Casino.htm).

Little River Band of Ottawa Indians. Notice of Construction Project - Native American Owned Businesses. (www.lrboi.com/Council/Notice%20of%20Construction%20Project%20-%20Native%20American%20Owned%20Businesses.pdf).

Little River Casino Resort. Homepage. (www.littlerivercasino.com/).

Little Traverse Bay Bands of Odawa Indians. Homepage. (www.ltbbodawa-nsn.gov).

Local Mover Directory. Crow Creek Reservation. (www.localmoverdirectory.com/info/movers/SD/crow_creek_sioux_reservation.asp).

Lone Butte Casino. Homepage. (www.wingilariver.com).

Lone Pine Golf Course. Homepage. (www.ccsmdc.org/lonepine/index.html).
Longoria, Ruth. "Squaxin Island tribe opens cultural center Members say Preserving history is vital to prosperity." The Olympian. (www.theolympian.com).

Los Coyotes Indian Reservation Explorer Run. (www.4x4central.com/).

Louisiana Folklife Center. "Chitimacha Tribe." (www.nsula.edu/folklife/database).

Lower Kuskokwim School District. (www.lksd.org/goodnews/gnbdemo.html).

Lower Lake Rancheria Koi Nation. Tribal History. (www.koination.com/).

"Lower Sioux Indian Community." American Indian Communities in Minnesota. (www.senate.leg.state.mn.us/departments/scr/report/bands/lowersioux.HTM).

"Lower Sioux Mdewakanton Dakota Reservation." (www.kstrom.net/isk/maps/mn/lowersio.htm).

"Lower Sioux Reservation" (www.oakhills.edu/cim/lowsioux.html).

LPBDC Home. (www.lakepenbdc.org/).

Lucky Star Casino. Cocho. (www.luckystarbingo.casinocity.com).

"Maidu." Infoplease.com. (www.infoplease.com/ce6/society/A0831239.html).

Makah Tribal Law and Order Code. (www.tribalresourcecenter.org).

Makah Tribe. Homepage. (www.makah.com/).

Maniaci, Jim. "Council Corks Black Mesa Water for Peabody Energy." Diné Bureau. The Gallup Independent. (www.gallupindependent.com/07-26-03blackmesawater.html).

Map of Indian reservations in the continental United States. (www.cr.nps.gov/nagpra/DOCUMENTS/ResMAP.HTM).

Mapes, Lynda V. "La Push: Seaside home is where the Quileute heart is." Seattle Times. December 12, 2002. (www.nwsource.com/travel/scr/tf_story.cfm?st=27020).

Marketplace for Entrepreneurs. Tribal Governments and Primary Assistance Avenues. (www.marketplaceofideas.com/2005resourcedirectory/12plandevelop/tribgov.asp).

Marquette Casino. Homepage. (www.ojibwacasino.com/marquette/gaming.aspx).

Marshall School. (www.marshall.lysd.schoolaccess.net/MarshallHistory.html).

Marshall Village Profile. (www.ankn.uaf.edu/).

Match-E-Be-Nash-She-Wish Band of Pottawatomi. Homepage. (www.mbpi.org/).

Match-e-Be-Nash-She-Wsih Band of Pottawatomi Indians (Gun Lake Tribe). (www.itcmi.org/thehistorytribal9.html).
Matthews, Mark. "On Black Mesa, the natives make a comeback." High Country News. May 12, 2003. (www.hcn.org/servlets/hcn.Article?article_id=13958#).

Matthiessen, Peter. "Footprints in the Last Wild Place." (www.outside.away.com/outside/features/200302/200302_anwr_1.html).

McClary, Toby. "Celilo-Today and Yesterday Popular fishing spot was once the 'Wall Street of the Indian World,'" August 15, 2004. (www.grandronde.org).

McCormick, George. "Quileute Tribe." (www.forks-web.com/fg/quileute.htm).

Meade River School. (www.nsbsd.org/atq/story.cfm?recordID=1).

Mechoopda Tribe. Homepage. (www.mechoopda.nsn.us).

Melmer, David. "Shakopee Mdewakanton in Minnesota to Build a Fire Department." Indian Country Today, Knight Ridder/Tribune Business News, April 23, 2003. (www.highbeam.com/library/).

Melmer, David. "Students Face Unsafe Schools at Crow Creek Reservation in South Dakota." March 3, 2004. Indian Country Today. (web.lexis-nexis.com/). Menominee Casino-Bingo-Hotel. Homepage. (www.menomineecasinoresort.com/).

Menominee Indian Tribe. Homepage. (www.menominee.nsn.us).

"Mental Health." White Earth Mental Health Program. (www.perham.eot.com/~rtcheal/mh.html).

Mercer, Bob. "Casino expansion would help tribes, hurt state." American News Correspondent. (www.aberdeennews.com/mld/aberdeennews/2004/04/09/news/8393167.htm).

Mescalero Apache Library. (www.std.enmu.edu/).

"Mescalero Apache Reservation to receive broadband service." New Mexico Business Weekly. April 30. 2002. (www.albuquerque.bizjournals.com).

Mescalero Apache Tribe. Homepage. (www.mescaleronet.com/).

"Meshik Chicks." (www.freewebs.com/anny_chelsea_virginia/).

"Meskwaki Bingo Casino Hotel." Cardplayer.com. (www.cardplayer.com/poker-room/show.php?id=579).

Meskwaki Bingo Casino Hotel. (www.meskwaki.com/index.html).

MHA Nation of the Fort Berthold Reservation. Homepage. (www.mhanation.com/).

Miami Nation. Homepage. (www.miamination.com/).
Miami, Oklahoma Detailed Profile. Welch, Oklahoma. (www.city-data.com/city/Welch-Oklahoma.html).

Miccosukee Resort and Gaming. "Miccosukee Reservation." (www.miccosukeeresort.com/).

"Mich. tribe clears hurdle for $100M casino project." (www.indianz.com/IndianGaming/2004/cat_land_acquisitions.asp).

Michigan Gaming Law. Homepage. (www.michigangaming.com/).

Michigan Gaming Law. "Windsor Casino Development Predicted." January 21, 2005. (www.michigangaming.com/CurSMGL.html).

Micmac Tribe. Homepage. (www.micmac-nsn.gov).

Microsoft Streets and Trips [CD ROM]. 2001

Microsoft TerraServer Imagery. (www.erraserver.homeadvisor.msn.com/image.aspx?T=2&S=15&Z=13&X=41&Y=595&W=3).

MidRegion Council of Governments. American Indian Tribes and Pueblos. (www.mrcog-nm.gov).

Midwest Assistance Program. Homepage. (www.map-inc.org/Publications/Publications/WaterlogApril03.pdf).

Midwest Casino Guide. Homepage. (www.midwestcasinoguide.com/).

Milgrem, John. "Cayuga Nation of N.Y. and gov. reach agreement on casino, Land-claim deal." 11/19/04. (www.thedailystar.com/).

Mill Casino Hotel.Homeapge. (www.themillcasino.com/).

Mille Lacs Band of Ojibwe. Circle of Health. Homepage. (www.mlcircleofhealth.com).

Mille Lacs Band of Ojibwe. Homepage. (www.millelacsojibwe.org/).

"Mille Lacs County challenges existence of Indian reservation." Associated Press, February 26, 2002. (www.alphacdc.com/treaty/mil-court.html).

"Mille Lacs Indian Museum." Minnesota Historical Society. (www.mnhs.org/places/sites/mlim/index.html).

Milwaukee Public Museum. Homepage. (www.mpm.edu).

Mining. (www.chilkatvalleynews.com/archive). Minnesota Department of Health. Tribal Health Services. (www.health.state.mn.us/wrtk/tribal.html).

"Minnesota Indian Affairs Council." (www.indians.state.mn.us/lowsioux.html).

"Minnesota Indian Affairs Council, Tribes, Shakopee Mdewakanton Sioux Community." (http:www.indians.state.mn.us/Shakopee.htm).

Mississippi Band of Choctaw Indians. (www.grass-roots.org/).

Mississippi Band of Choctaw Indians: Project Summary. (www.eere.energy).

Mni Sose Intertribal Water Rights Association. (www.mnisose.org/).
Mni Sose Intertribal Water Rights Coalition. Members. Sisseton Wapeton Oyate of the Lake Traverse Reservation. "Sisseton Wapeton Sioux Tribe Community Environmental Profile." (www.mnisose.org).

Modoc Tribe of Oklahoma. Eight Tribes. (www.eighttribes.org/modoc/).

Mohegan Tribe. Homepage. (www.mohegan.nsn.us).

"Mohegan Tribe investing in Cowlitz Tribe's casino." (www.indianz.com/IndianGaming/2004/003570.asp).

Mojave National Preserve. Mojave Indians. Culture. (www.nps.gov/moja/mojahtm2.htm).

Monastyrski, Jamie. "Omaha tribal songs fill the web." 29 March 2000. (www.indiancountry.com).

Montana Wyoming Tribal Leaders Council. (www.tlc.wtp.net).

Montana, Cate. "Snoqualmie Search for a Land Base." Indian Country, May 3, 2000.

(www.indiancountry.com/content.cfm?id=861).

Mooney Falls. Photograph. (www.waterfallswest.com/az-mooney-falls.html).

Moore, R.E."The Alabama Coushatta Indians." (www.texasindians.com/albam.htm).

Muckleshoot Indian Tribe. Homepage. (www.muckleshoot.nsn.us).

Muckleshoot Indian Tribe. (usuers.aol.com/).

"Multi-agency Task Force Results in Cleanup of Illegal Dump on White Earth Reservation." February 20, 2001. (www.pca.state.mn.us/news/nr022001.html).

Muscogee Document Imaging Company. Homepage. (www.muscogeedocumentimaging.com/).

Muscogee Nation Genealogy. (www.rootsweb.com/~itcreek/index.htm#settlements).

Museum of History and Industry. A Change of Worlds: Photographs and Artifacts of Puget Sound Native Americans. (www.changeofworlds.org/index.cfm).

Muskogee-Creek Language at Buffalo Trails. Menu. (www.native-americans.org/languages/ language-muskogee-creek.htm).

Nakashima, Ellen. "Tiny Tribe's Clash Stretches 67 Acres Across the Nation." June 23, 2002. (www.washingtonpost.com/).

Naknek Electric Association (NEA). "Naknek, King Salmon, Bristol Bay Fact Sheet." (www.nea.coop/about/facts.shtml).

NANA Corporation. "This Is NANA: The Villages." (www.nana.com/villages.htm#Ambler).

"Narragansett Indian Tribe." EPA. (www.epa.gov).

Narragansett Indian Tribe. Homepage. (www.narragansett-tribe.org/).
National Aeronautics and Space Administration (NASA). Plate F-11 Colville River, Alaska. Geomorphology from Space: A Global Overview of Regional Landforms. 1986. (www.daac.gsfc.nasa.gov/DAAC_DOCS/geomorphology).

National Congress of American Indians. Homepage. (www.ncai.org).

National Congress of American Indians. Indian Nations in the Continental United States. (www.ncai.org/main/pages/tribal_directory/us_eastern.asp).

National Environmental Justice Advisory Council to the U.S. EPA. "Fish Consumption and Environmental Justice." November 2002. (www.epa.gov/compliance/resources/publications/ej/fish_consump_report_1102.pdf).

National Indian Gaming Commission, "Casino of Omaha." (www.nigc.gov /nigc/nigcControl?option=TRIBE_DETAILSs& TRIBE=63).
National Indian Gaming Commission. Homepage. (www.nigc.gov/).

National Museum of Natural History. "Looking Both Ways: Alutiiq Villages." (www.mnh.si.edu/lookingbothways/text/villages/).

National Oceanic and Atmospheric Administration. (www.fakr.noaa.gov).

National Park Service. (www.nps.gov).

National Park Service. Links to the Past. (www.cr.nps.gov).

National Society for American Indian Elderly. Homepage. (www.nsaie.org/).

National Tribal Environmental Council. Homepage. (www.ntec.org/default.html).

National Tribal Justice Resource Center. "CY 2002 Annual Report." (www.tribalresourcecenter.org/).

"Native American Casinos in Michigan." MGCB. (www.state.mi.us/mgcb/indian.htm).

Native American Consultation Database. (www.cast.uark.edu/other/nps/nacd/nacd.html).

Native American Working Group. Tribal Offices. (www.aphis.usda.gov/anawg/states/california.html).

"Native Americans in Arizona." Arizona Blue Book Millennium Edition. (www.sosaz.com/public_services/Arizona_Blue_Book/1999_2000/ch11.htm).

Native Americans Jobs. "Karuk Tribe." (www.nativeamericanjobs.com/).

Native Americans. Kickapoo. (www.nativeamericans.com/Kickapoo.htm).

Native Art.com. San Felipe Pueblo. (www.nativeart.com/).

Native Direct. A Division of Ziibiwing Cultural Society. (www.nativedirect.com/shops/dawe-wi-gamigoonse/index.htm).
Native Homelands Superfund Sites. (www.cqs.com/super_nn.htm).

Native Movement. (www.nativemovement.org/).

Native Village of Tanacross. (www.nativevillageoftanacross.com/nvthistory.html).

Native Vision Tours. Homepage. (www.nativevisiontours.com/arts_crafts.html).

Native Web.org). Homepage. (www.nativeweb.org/).

"Natural Resources." Ute Tribe Public Relations Information Handout. February 13, 2002. Northern Ute Tribe. (www.northernute.com/).

"Navajo Council Tries, Fails To Beat Gambling Veto." Gambling Magazine. (www.gamblingmagazine.com/articles/26/26-774.htm).

Navajo Nation. (www.sos.state.nm.us/BLUEBOOK/navajo.htm).

Navajo Nation Parks. (www.navajonationparks.org/).
"Navajo Nation Reaches Proposed Settlement with State and Feds over Water." BC Cycle. December 6, 2003. (www.web.lexis-nexis.com/).

Navajo Nation Tribal Courts. Criminal Justice Resource Directory. (www.cjjcc.org/directory/program.php?program_id=702).

Navajo Nation Vital Records Office, 2001. (www.nnwo.org/nnprofile.htm).

Navajo Nation Washington Office. Homepage. (www.nnwo.org/nnprofile.htm).

"Navajo President Approves Gaming." Royaldice.com. Homepage. (www.royaldiceonlinecasino.com/gambling-news/2001/10/28 /a-7894.php).

Navajo Timeline. Homepage. (www.lapahie.com/Timeline_Spanish_1751_1820.cfm).

Naval Facilities Engineering Command. "Adak Island Update: Adak Land Transfer Fact Sheet." March 2004. (adakupdate.com/pdfs/news/land_transfer_3-11-04.pdf).
"Nebraska Attractions: Omaha Indian Reservation." (www. visitnebraska.org/myplanner/attractiondetail.asp?id=108).

Nebraska Studies.org, "The Omaha and Ponca Tribes." (www.nebraskastudies. org/).

Neshnabe Institute for Cultural Studies. Homepage. (www.neaseno.org/).

Nevada Department of Human Resources. Washoe Tribe Head Start. (www.welfare.state.nv.us).

Nevada Division of Water Planning. Pyramid Lake. (www.dcnr.nv.gov/markers/mark_18.htm).

Nevada Tribes. (www.tribalresourcecenter.org).

New Allakaket. (www.worldhistory.com/wiki/N/New-Allakaket,-Alaska.html).
"New Emmett Township Casino in Michigan is Planned by Nottawaseppi Huron Band of Potawatomi." December 14, 1999. (www.americancasinoguide.com/News/12-99-Emmett.shtml).

"New hydropower customers cover three regions, 9 states." Energy Services Bulletin. (www.wapa.gov/es/pubs/esb/2004/December/dec044a.htm).

New Mexico Entertainment. (www.newmexicoet.com/nm_things_1r02.html).

New Mexico Interior Acquisition Planning Forecast for Fiscal Year 2000. (www.doi.gov/osdbu/newmexic.htm).

New Mexico Magazine. Homepage. (www.nmmagazine.com/).

New Mexico Online Magazine. San Felipe Pueblo. (www.santafe.com/).

New Mexico Route 66 Association. San Felipe Pueblo. (www.rt66nm.org/).

New Mexico Secretary of State. Homepage. (www.sos.state.nm.us).

Newport Community Hospital. Homepage. (www.phd1.org/NCH.htm).

Nez Perce Reservation. Homepage. (www.nezperce.org/).

NHPRC. Oklahoma, 1976 - 2004. (www.archives.gov/grants/funded_endorsed_projects/states_and_ territories/ok.html).

Ninilchik, Alaska, Chamber of Commerce. (www.ninilchikchamber.com/about_ninilchik.htm).

Ninilchik Native Association Inc. (www.nnai.net/).

Ninilchik. "Visit Alaska's Kenai Peninsula!" Ninilchik Alaska Information. (www.kenaipeninsula.com/1_Ninilchik_Alaska.html).

Ninilchik Traditional Council. Official Site. (www.ninilchiktribe-nsn.gov/).
Associated Press. "N.M. tribe keeping casino plan alive." 25 July, 2002.

"NMSU and Ysleta del Sur Pueblo unite to ensure success of Native American Students." (www.nmsu.edu/).

Nooksack Indian Tribe. Homepage. (www.nooksack-tribe.org/).

Nooksack River Casino. Homepage. (www.nooksackcasino.com/).

North Dakota Department of Human Services. Head Start Sites. (www.state.nd.us/humanservices/services/childfamily/headstart/sites/ spiritlake.html).

North Dakota FY 2003 OJP & COPS Grants Listed by Locality Broken Out by Core Function. (www.ojp.usdoj.gov/fy2003grants/map/ndsubj.htm).

North Slope Borough. (www.north-slope.org/nsb/HomeruleBrochure/AkpInfo.htm).
North Slope Borough School District. "Trapper School." (www.nsbsd.org/nui/).

Northern Lights Casino.(www.northernlightcasino.com/).

Northern Plains Tribes, Housing Authorities and Tribally Designated Housing Entities. (www.codetalk.fed.us/NPTribalDir92903.htm).

Northern Quest Casino. Homepage. (www.northernquest.net).

Northwest Portland Area Indian Health Board. Homepage. (www.npaihb.org/).

Northwest Regional Educational Library. Homepage. (www.nwrel.org/request/2002aug/tulalip.html).

Norton Sound Health Corporation. (www.nortonsoundhealth.org/).

Notice of Public Comment Period on Proposed Agreement for Leasing of Colorado River Water and Non-Irrigation of Lands on Chemehuevi Indian Reservation.

(www.epa.gov/fedrgstr/EPA-WATER/1998/September/Day-25/w25652.htm).

Nottawasseppi Huron Band of Potawatomi. Pine Creek Indian Reservation. (www.nhbpi.com/).

"Nottawaseppi Huron Band of Potawatomi Tribal Partnership Projects." U.S. Fish and Wildlife Service. (www.midwest.fws.gov/Tribal/Nottawaseppi.html).

NPT-Cup'it. (www.nunivak.org/people.html).

Nuiqsut. (www.prudhoebay.com/communities_Nuiqsut.htm).

Nunamiut School. (www.nsbsd.org/akp/).

NWIFC Member Tribes. (www.nwifc.wa.gov/tribes/members/tribe.asp?tribe=quileute).

O'Leary, Tim. "Tribal Leaders seek Technology" Mercury News Wire Services, August 8, 2003. (www.mercurynews.com/).

Ocean Park Resort at La Push. Homepage. (www.ocean-park.org/).

OCLC First Search. Homepage. (newfirstsearch.oclc.org/).

Ocmulge Oil Fields. Timeline. (www.nps.gov/ocmu/co/colonial.html).

Office of Historic Preservation. Torres-Martinez. (www.ohp.parks.ca.gov).

Office of Justice Programs. "Choctaw Law Enforcement Services." (www.ojp.usdoj.gov).

Office of Juvenile Justice and Delinquency Program. "Tribal Youth Program: Mille Lacs Band of Ojibwe Indians." (www.ojjdp.ncjrs.org/typ/states/mn.html).

Oglala Lakota College. Homepage. (www.olc.edu. Oglala Lakota College Profile. (www.lakotamall.com/oglalasiouxtribe/education.htm).

Ohwejagehka: Ha`degaenage Cayuga Language. (www.ohwejagehka.com).

Okay Casino and Resort. Homepage. (www.ohkay.com).

Okie Legacy. Homepage. ww.okielegacy.org).
"Oklahoma Land Openings 1889-1907." (www.marti.rootsweb.com/land/oklands.html).

Oklahoma Indian Affairs Commission. Tribal Governments, Officials, and Locations (www.state.ok.us/~oiac/TribalGovs.htm).

Oklahoma Indian History. Homepage. (www.ok-history.mus.ok.us/enc/indianmeridan.htm).

Oklahoma Institute of Indian Heritage. "Citizen Potawatomi Nation Moves Forward With Economic and Business Diversification Plan." March 2001. (www.oiih.org).

Oklahoma Native American Business Development Center. (indiansbusiness.org/Tribes.htm).

Oklahoma Travel and Tourism Department. Kickapoo Casino. (www.travelok.com/toDo/ activityDetail.asp?id=1-BX67).

"Oklahoma tribe is first recipient of $5 million contract in White House Economic Initiative." (www.okit.com).

Oklahoma's Frontier Indian Police. Homepage. (www.coax.net/people/lwf/fip_pt5.htm).

Old Camp Casino. Homepage. (www.oldcampcasino.com).

Olgoonik. (www.olgoonik.com).

Olympic Coast. People and the Sanctuary. (www.sanctuaries.nos.noaa.gov)

Olympic National Forest. Quinualt Valley. (www.gorp.away.com).

Olympic Peninsula . Visitor Portal. (www.olympicpeninsula.org).

Omaha and Ponca Tribes. (www.nebraskastudies.org).

Omaha Public Library. "Ponca Tribe," "The Omaha Tribe." (www.omaha.lib.ne.us).

Oneida Bingo-Casino. Homepage. (oneidabingoandcasino.net).

Oneida Community Library. (www.nfls.lib.wi.us).

Oneida Indian Nation. Homepage. (www.oneida-nation.net).

Oneida Nation. Homepage. (www.oneidanation.org).

Oneida Nation Arts Program. Homepage. (www.oneidanationsarts.org).

Oneida Nation Elderly Services. Homepage. (www.elderly.oneidanation.org).

Oneida Nation School System. Homepage. (www.schools.oneidanation.org).
Oneida Nation. The Times Plus, March 9, 2004. (www.themonroetimes.com).

Oneida Police Department. Homepage. (www.police.oneidanation.org).

Oneida Textile Designs. Homepage. (www.oneidatextiledesigns.com).

Online Highways.com. Homepage. (www.ohwy.com/).

Onondaga Nation. Homepage. (www.tuscaroras.com).

Origin of Names of Bishop and the Owens Valley. (www.bishopvisitor.com).

Osage Million Dollar Elm Casino. Homepage. (www.milliondollarelm.com).

Osage Nation. Homepage. (www.osagetribe.org).

Osage Nation of Oklahoma. Homepage. (www.osagetribe.com).

Otteson, Paul. "Adventures in Nature / Alaska Travel." 2001. (www.alaskajourney.com/farnorth/ anaktuvuk.html).

"Our Companies." (www.lpsd.com).

Pacific States Marine Fisheries Commission. "California State Counties." (www.psmfc.org).

Packard Hughes Interconnect. Irvine, CA. (www.fibers.org).

Paiute Tribe of Utah. (www.fema.gov/regions/viii/tribal/ paiutebg.shtm).

Paiute Tribe of Utah. Utah's Native Americans. (historytogo.utah.gov/paiuteut.html).

Pala Band of Mission Indians. Homepage. (www.palaindians.com).

Pala Casino, Resort, Spa. Homepage. (www.palacasino.com).

Pala Indians. Homepage. (www.palaindians.com).

Palace Casino and Hotel. Homepage. (www.palacecasinohotel.com).

Paradise Casinos. Homepage. (www.paradise-casinos.com).

Paragon Casino Resort. Homepage. (www.paragoncasinoresort.com).

Pascua Yaqui Tribe of Arizona. Homepage. (www.pascuayaqui-nsn.gov).

Paskenta Band of Nomlaki Indians. Homepage. (www.gocalifornia.about.com).

Passamaquoddy Tribe. Homepage. (www.passamaquoddy.com).

Passamquoddy Tribe of Maine. Homepage. (www.passamaquoddy.com).
Pauite Palace Casino. Homepage. (www.paiutepalace.com).

Payson Lodging. Homepage. (www.paysonlodging.com).

Peace for Turtle Island. Onondaga Nation. (www.peace4turtleisland.org).

Pechanga Band of Luiseño Indians. Homepage. (www.pechanga.com).

Pechanga RV Resort. Homepage. (www.pechangarv.com).

Peninsula College. Homepage. (www.pc.ctc.edu).

Penobscot Indian Nation. Homepage. (www.penobscotnation.org).

"Peridot from the San Carlos Apache Reservation." U.S. Geological Survey. (www.minerals.usgs.gov).

Perkins Family Clinic. Iowa Tribe of Oklahoma. Homepage. (www.IowaTribe.org).

Peterson, John A. Otero Mesa. Archeological Value Tigua Cultural Affiliation With Alamo Mountain and Otero Mesa. (www.wildmesquite.org/otero/ alamoMountain.htm).

"Petroglyphs of the Volcanic Tablelands: Bishop California." (www.thesierraweb.com).

Picayune Rancheria of the Chukchansi Indians. Homepage. (www.chukchansi.net).

Picuris Pueblo Museum Center. (www.gocalifornia.about.com).

Pilot Station. "The City of Pilot Station." (www.lysd.gcisa.net/lysd/poj.htm).

"Pine Arbor Tribal Town, Its Place in the Creek Confederacy." Creek Culture. September 25, 2000. The Museum, Fall-Winter 2004. (www.freenet.tlh.fl.us/Museum/ culture/PATT1.htm).

Pine Ridge Dialysis Center Project. Homepage. (www.lakotamall.com/oglalasiouxtribe/events.htm).

Pinoleville Indian Reservation. Homepage. (www.pinoleville.org/).

"Pipe Spring National Monument." National Park Service: U.S. Department of the Interior. (www.nps.gov/ pisp/).

Pluralism.org. (www.pluralism.org).

Pokagon Band of Potawatomi. Tribal Profile. (www.itcmi.org).

Pokagon Band of Potawatomi Indians. Homepage. (www.pokagon.com/).

Ponca State Park. (www.outdoorplaces.com/).

Port Gamble S'Klallam Tribe. Homepage. (www.pgst.nsn.us).

Port Townsend City Guide. Olympic Peninsula, Washington. (www.ptguide.com/).

Post, Tim. "A new store promises more than just groceries" by Tim Post, Minnesota Public Radio, March 9, 2004. (www.news.minnesota.publicradio.org).

"Potato Tour." Press Release. September 17, 2002. (www.pesticide.org).

Potawatomi Indians. (www.remc11.k12.mi.us/dowagiac/ chieftainslogo.html).

Potawatomi Language. (www.potawatomilang.org).

"Prairie Island Community." (www.indians.state.mn).

Prairie Band Potawatomi Nation. Homepage. (www.pbpindiantribe.com).

Prairie Knights Casino and Resort. Homepage. (www.prairieknights.com).

Prairie Wind Casino. Homepage. (www.216.245.184.23/prairiewind).

Prescott Resort Hotel Conference Center and Casino. Homepage. (www.prescottresort.com).

Providence College. (www.providence.edu).

Pueblo de Cochiti. Homepage. (www.pueblodecochiti.org).

Pueblo Drums of Taos Pueblo. Homepage. (www.pueblodrums.com).

Pueblo of Acoma Game and Fish Enterprise. Homepage. (www.acomagameandfish.com).

Pueblo of Acoma. Homepage. (www.puebloofacoma.org).

Pueblo of Isleta Department of Education. Homepage. (www.isletaeducation.org).

"Pueblo of Sandia to hold public event to celebrate the passage of Sandia Mountain Legislation." Press release. (www.sandiapueblo.nsn.us).

Pueblo of Santa Ana. Homepage. (www.santaana.org). PWSRCAC. "Tatitlek." PWSRCAC Member Entities. (www.pwsrcac.org/Members/tatitlek.html).

Pyramid Lake Paiute Tribe. Homepage. (www.plpt.nsn.us).

Quil Ceda Creek Casino. Homepage. (www.quilcedacreekcasino.com).

Quil Ceda Village Business Park. (www.quilcedavillage.com).

Quileute: a language of USA. Homepage. (www.ethnologue.com).

Quileute Indian Tribe, Comprehensive Marketing Campaign. (www.olypen.com/quileute).

Quileute Tribal School. (www.4directions.org/resources/contributions/school/cache.pl.31.html).

Quileute Tribal School Gymnasium. (www.bassettiarch.com/QTSG.htm).

Quileute Tribe of Washington. Homepage. (www.quileutetribe.org).

Quinault Beach Resort and Casino. Homepage. (www.quinaultbchresort.com).

Quinault Housing Authority. Homepage. (www.quinaulthousing.com).

"Quinault Indian Nation Settlement Conserves Marbled Murrelet Habitat." US Department of the Interior News. (www.doi.gov/news/040920c).

Quinault Lake School District. (www.wavcc.org/wvc/cadre/WaterQuality/quinaultschooldist.htm).

Quinault 2003 Strategic Plan Update. Draft for Review. 2003. (www.209.206.175.157/Quinault%20constitution.htm).

Quinhagak Airport. Airnav.com. (www.airnav.com/airport/PAQH).

Quinhagak School. Homepage. (www.quinhagak.lksd.schoolaccess.net/). Raintree Village. Homepage. (www.raintree-village.com/).

Ramah Band of Navajos. Homepage. (www.ramahnavajo.com/html/home.html). Ramah Navajo Chapter. Homepage. (ramah.nndes.org/).

Ramona Band of Cahuilla Mission Indians. Project Summary. (www.eere.energy).

"Ranks of tiny casino-seeking tribe suddenly grow." (www.cnn.com/).

Rapp, Scott. "Cayuga agreement challenged." December 16, 2004. (www.syracuse.com/). Rec Center. (students.washington.edu/nphilemo/rec_center.html).

Recreation and Wildlife Dept. San Carlos Apache Tribe. (www.sancarlosrecreationandwildlife.com/hunting.htm). "Red Lake Indian Reservation." American Indian Resource Center Oak Hills Fellowship. (www.oakhills.edu/cim/redlake.html).

Red Lake Nation. Homepage. (www.redlakenation.org).

Red Lake Nation Foods Incorporated. Homepage. (www.redlakenationfoods.com).

Redding Rancheria. Homepage.(www.redding-rancheria.com/).

Redish, Laura and Orrin Lewis. Native Languages of the Americas. Preserving and promoting American Indian Languages. Created 1998, last update 2004. (www.native-languages.org/kickapoo.htm).

Redish, Laura and Orrin Lewis. Native Languages of the Americas. Preserving and promoting American Indian Languages. Created 1998, last update 2004. Potawatomi (Nishnabek, Pottawatomie, Pottawatomi). (www.native-languages.org/potawatomi.htm).

Reno Sparks Indian Colony. Homepage. (www.rsic.org/).

"Reno-Sparks Indian Colony moves toward slot operation." Gambling Magazine, January 21, 2000. (www.gamblingmagazine.com).

Rio Communications. Homepage. (www.rio.com/).

River Rock Casino. Homepage. (www.riverrockcasino.com).

Riverside Lodge and Motel. Homepage. (www.riverside-lodgemotel.com).

Robertson, Tom. "Cleaning up the White Earth Reservation." Minnesota Public Radio, March 17, 2004. (www.news.minnesota.publicradio.org/).

Robertson, Tom. "Turbulent Election Nears on White Earth Reservation." Minnesota Public Radio. March 9, 2000. (www.news.minnesota.publicradio.org/features/200003/09_robertsont_wadena-m/).

Robinson Rancheria Tribe of Pomo Indians. Homepage. (www.robinsonracheria.org/).

Romney, Lee. "The State; Tribe Spreads Wealth in Troubled Town." Elk Valley Rancheria is investing casino profits into a much-needed revival of Crescent City. Los Angeles Times, May 18, 2003, pg. A-1. (www.pqasb.pqarchiver.com/).

Rootsweb.com. "Nez Perce Indian History." (www.rootsweb.com/).

Rosebud Casino. Homepage. (www.rosebudcasino.com/).

Rosebud Sioux Tribe. Homepage. (www.rosebudsiouxtribe.org/).

Round Valley Indian Tribes. Homepage. (www.covelo.net).

Royal River Casino. Homepage. (www.royalrivercasino.com/).

Russian Mission (Iqurmiut) Local History. (www.lysd.gcisa.net/~rmission/pages/rsmhistory.htm). Sac and Fox Casino. Homepage. (www.sacandfoxcasino.com/).

Sac and Fox Indian Fax Sheet. (www.geocities.com/bigorrin/sf_kids.htm).

Sacramento Bee. "The Ruling by the Bureau of Indian Affairs May Doom Gaming Plans," December 16, 2001. (proquest.umi.com).

Sacred Land Film Project. "Snoqualmie Falls." Historical Sacred Sites. (www.sacredland.org/historical_sites_pages/snoqualmie_falls.html).

Saginaw Chippewa Indian Tribe. Homepage. (www.sagchip.org/).

Saint George Tanaq Company. (www.stgeorgetanaq.com/compinfo/default.html). Salish Sea Foods. Homepage. (www.salishseafoods.com/).

Salt River Indian Community. Homepage. (www.saltriver.pima-maricopa.nsn.us/community.html).

San Carlos Apache Telecommunications Utility, Inc. Homepage. (www.scatcom.net/index.shtml).

San Diego State University. Big Pine Reservation. (infodome.sdsu.edu).

San Felipe Pueblo. Homepage. (www.sanfelilpecasino.com/).

Sandia Pueblo. Homepage. (www.sandiapueblo.nsn.us).

"Santa Ysabel Reservation." (www.sirraserviceproject.org/).

Santa Clara Day School. Homepage. (www.santaclara.bia.edu).

Santana, Arthur, and Jack Brown. "Shoalwater Tribe, marshals face off." Seattle Times. (www.geocities.com/).

Santee Nebraska. (www.ci.santee.ne.us).

Santee Sioux Tribe of Nebraska. Homepage. (www.santeedakota.org/).

Santo Domingo Public Schools. (www.schooltree.org/).

Sauk Suiattle Indian Tribe. Homepage. (www.sauk-suiattle.com/).

Sault Ste. Marie Ojibwe Flag. (www.snowwowl.com/nainfoflags4.html).

Sault St. Marie Tribe of Chippewa Indians. Homepage. (www.sootribe.org/).

Savage, Bill. "Table Mountain Rancheria takes video security system to new horizon." (www. pelco.com/).

SBA Firm Profile. Cochiti Community Development Corporation. (www.dsbs.sba.gov/dsbs/dsp_profile.cfm?User_Id=P0406300).

Scheide, R.V. "The Graton Band's last stand." (www.metroactive.com/).

SchoolAccess. (www.shageluk.iasd.schoolaccess.net/commandschool/commandschool.html).

Schools. (schooltree.org/).

Schurz Service Unit Tribes. (www.gbpca.org/tribal.htm).

Scotts Valley Band of Pomo Indians of the Sugar Bowl Rancheria. Homepage. (www.svpomo.org/).

Sea America's Byways. "Pyramid Lake." (www.seeamerica.org).

Seattle Daily Journal of Commerce online edition (DJC.com). (www.djc.com/firms/get/const/CGANBOGA0.html).

Seminole Gaming Palace. Homepage. (www.seiminolehardrock.com/).
Seminole Tribe of Florida. Homepage. (www.seminoletribe.com/).

Seneca Gaming and Entertainment. Homepage. (www.senecagames.com/).

Seneca Nation of Indians. Homepage. (www.sni.org/).

Seneca Niagara Casino. Homepage. (www.senecaniagaracasino.com/).

Seneca One Stop. Career and Resource Center. (www.senecaonestop.com/).

Seneca-Iroquois National Museum. Homepage. (www.senecanation.com/).

Sequoyah High School. Homepage. (www.sequoyah.k12.ok.us/SHShistory.html).

7 Cedars Casino. Homepage. (www.7cedarscasino.com/).

Seven Clans Casino. Homepage. (www.sevenclanscasino.com/).

Seven Feathers Hotel and Casino Resort. Homepage. (www.sevenfeathers.com/).

7 Feathers Truck and Travel Center. (www.i5exit99.com/).

777play.com. Homepage. (www.777play.com/).

Shaan-Seet, Inc. Homepage. (www.shaanseet.com/).

Shaffer, Mark. "Area Tribe Struggles to Survive after Casino Failure." (www.web.lexisnexis.com/).

Shakopee Mdewakanton (Dakota) Sioux Community. Homepage. (www.ccsmdc.org/).

"Shakopee Mdewakanton Sioux Community Makes Historic Grant to American Indian College Fund." US Newswire, Dec. 19, 2000. (www.usnewswire.com/topnews/temp/1219-105.html)

Shghagwéi Khwaan Naa Kahídi. (www.skagwaytraditional.org/).

Shingle Springs Interchange Project on Highway 50 in El Dorado County. (www.dot.ca.gov).

Ship Ashore Resort. Homepage. (www.ship-ashore.com/activities.html).

Shishmaref School. (www.bssd.org/schools/sites/SHH/shishmaref.htm).

"ShoBan." (www.challenge.isu.edu/).

Shumagin Corporation. (www.shumagin.com/).

Si Tanka University. Homepage. (www.sitanka.net/1.5/).

Side Trips. Pine Ridge Reservation. (www.trailsandgrasslands.org/rez.html).

Sierra Service Project. Duck Valley Reservation. (www.sierraserviceproject.org/NevadaInfo.htm).

"Siletz Tribe." (www.ctsi.nsns.us).
Simpson, Jeff. "Gambling Beyond Nevada: Station to develop tribal property." Las Vegas Review Journal, November 14, 2003. (www.reviewjournal.com).

Sisseton Wahpeton Sioux Tribe. Homepage. (www.swcc.cc.sd.us).

Sisseton-Wahpeton Sioux Tribal Profile. (www.mnisose.org/).

Sitting Bull College. Homepage. (www.sittingbull.edu).

Six Nations Writers. The Tuscarora: Taskarorahaka. (www.sixnationswriters.com/).

Skagit Valley Casino and Resort. Homepage. (www.theskagit.com/).

Skagit Valley Herald. (www.skagitvalleyherald.com/articles/2004/04/20/news/news03.txt).

Skaguay Alaskan 2002. (www.skagwaynews.com/alaskan2002.html).

Skagway. Official Website of the City of Skagway. (www.skagway.org/).

Skateoregon.com. "Siletz Skate Park." (www.skateoregon.com/).

Skokomish Tribal Nation. Homepage. (www.skokomish.org/).

Sky City Casino.Homepage. (www.skycitycasino.com/).

Skyhawk. "Kickapoo." May 5, 1997. (www.gbso.net/SKYHAWK/kickapoo.htm).

Slagle, Allogan. "Groundhog Day." News from Native California. Allogan Slagle. April 30, 2002. Vol. 15. Issue 3; pg. 38. (www.proquest.umi.com/).

"Smith River in California." Photograph. (www.acclaimimages.com/_gallery/_SM/0001-0209-1707-0943_SM.jpg).

Smokin Joes. Homepage. (www.smokinjoes.com).

Soaring Eagle Casino and Resort. Homepage. (www.soaringeaglecasino.com/dining/waterlily.htm).

Soldier Woman Art and Gift Gallery. Homepage. (www.soldierwoman.com).

South Dakota Association of Student Financial Aid Administrators. (www.sdasfaa.org/Membership/Flandreau.htm).

South Dakota State Historical Society. Flandreau Agency. (www.mnisose.org/profiles/flandrea.htm).

South Puget Intertribal Planning Agency. (www.spipa.org).

Southern California Tribal Chairmen's Association. Inaja Cosmit Band. (www.sctca.net).

Southern Paiutes of Utah. (www.educatetheusa.com/utah/paiutes.html).

Southwest Indian Relief Council. Homepage. (www.swirc.org/people/coloradoriver/havasupai.html).
Southwest Rail Fan. "Black Mesa and Lake Powell." (www.trainweb.org/southwestshorts/bmlp.html).

Southwest Region. Alamo, Ramah and Canoncito. (www.ilwg.net/southwest.htm).

Spanner Films. "Baked Alaska: Alex Weyiouanna, Shishmaref Weatherman." (www.spannerfilms.net/?lid=1050).

Speaking Rock Casino. Homepage. (www.speakingrockcasino.com/).

Speer, John. "Meskwaki Bingo: Casino Negotiations "on-going." Tama News Herald and Toledo Chronicle, August 26, 2004. (www.tamatoledonews.com).

Spirit Lake Nation. Homepage. (www.spiritlakenation.com).

"Spirit Mountain Casino." (www.casinocity.com).

Spirit Mountain Casino Resort and Hotel. Homepage. (www.spirit-mountain.com).

Spokane Tribal College. Homepage. (www.spokanecampus.org).

Spokane Tribe. Homepage. (www.spokaneTribe.com).

Squaxin Island Tribe. Homepage. (www.squaxinisland.org).

St. Francis Mission. Homepage. (www.sfmission.org).

St. Joseph's Indian School. Homepage. (www.stjo.org/museum/index.htm).

St. Mary's Subregional Clinic. (www.ykhc.org/500.cfm).

St. Michael. "The Alaskan Native Carver's Gallery: St. Michael Artists. Listing of Local Ivory Carvers: St. Michael, Alaska." (www.bssd.org/eskimo_art/villages/stmike/stmike.html).

Staats, Sheila. "Tuscarora." (www.peace4turtleisland.org).

Standing Rock College and Historical Society Exhibits. (www.museumsusa.org/data/museums/ND/120487.htm).

Standing Stone Gaming. Homepage. (www.standingstonegaming.com).

Stanley, Jim. "Take Care of Your Credit and Save." Nuuguam. (209.206.175.157/news12.htm).

"State Indian Commission gets $40,000 to help develop affordable housing." 26 May 2004. (web.lexis nexis.com).

State Headquarters of Southern Baptists in Montana. Montana Southern Baptist Convention. (www.mtsbc.org).

State of Alaska. "About the Alaska Court System." (www.state.ak.us/courts/ctinfo.htm).

State of Alaska. "Afognak Joint Venture." (www.evostc.state.ak.us/habitat/large_afognak.html).

State of Alaska. "Coastal Impact Assistance Program; a new federal program for addressing statewide coastal issues." (www.alaskacoast.state.ak.us//CIAP/GrantPages/Grant26.htm).

State of Alaska. "Floating Lower Kuskowim Area Rivers - Arolik River - ADF&G, Sport Fish Interior Region." (www.sf.adfg.state.ak.us/region3/areas/kusk/arolik.stm.

State of Alaska. "Kwigillingok, Alaska In My Eyes." (www.mehs.educ.state.ak.us/portfolios/violas/academics/village_project/vill age.html).

State of Alaska. "Top Employers of New Hires Bethel Census Area." 21:17, February 20, 2004. (www.labor.state.ak.us/research/erg/v_c3.htm).

State of Alaska. "V.P.S.O Seniority Ranking 08/09/2004." (www.dps.state.ak.us/ast/vpso/images/seniority.PDF).

State of Alaska. Alaska Reference. (www.educ.state.ak.us/stats/DistrictEnrollment/2003DistrictEnrollment. Pdf).

State of Alaska. Bernadine Keyes. (www.mehs.educ.state.ak.us/portfolios/bernadinek/threeb.html).

tate of Alaska. Commercial Fisheries Entry Commission. (www.cfec.state.ak.us).

State of Alaska. DEC. Contaminated Sites Program - Site Summary - King Salmon AFB. (www.state.ak.us/dec/spar/csp/sites/kingsalmon.htm).
State of Alaska. Dept. of Education. (www.educ.state.ak.us).

State of Alaska. Dept. of Fish and Game, Division of Commercial Fisheries. "Information Letter: Preliminary 2003 Yukon Area Chinook and Summer Chum Salmon Fishery Summary." November 2003. (www.cf.adfg.state.ak.us).

State of Alaska. Dept. of Fish and Game, Division of Commercial Fisheries. "Norton Sound Herring Fishery Announcement #7." May 24, 2003. (www.cf.adfg.state.ak.us/region3/finfish/herring/03norton.php).

State of Alaska. Dept. of Fish and Game, Division of Commercial Fisheries. "Upper Cook Inlet, Salmon Harvest Summary 1966-2000." (www.cf.adfg.state.ak.us/region2/finfish/salmon/uci/ucihhar.pdf).

State of Alaska. Dept. of Fish and Game, Division of Commercial Fisheries and U.S. Department of Interior, Fish and Wildlife Service, Federal Subsistence Board. "Yukon River News Release: Yukon River, Subdistricts 5-B and 5-C Commercial and Subsistence Salmon Fishing Schedules for July 4-July 11, 2002." July 1, 2002. (www.cf.adfg.state.ak.us).

State of Alaska. Dept. of Fish and Game, Sport Fish, Interior Region. " Weekly Fishing Report: Sport Fishing Update." June 18, 2003. (www.sf.adfg.state.ak.us/Region3/Weekly/2003/AYK/aw061803.cfm).

State of Alaska. Dept. of Public Safety. "Trooper Post Locations." (www.dps.state.ak.us/ast/).

State of Alaska. Division of Community Advocacy. Community Database Online. (www.dced.state.ak.us).

State of Alaska. EVOS-Habitat Protection-Large Parcels. (www.evostc.state.ak.us/habitat).

State of Alaska. (www.dog.dnr.state.ak.us).
State of Alaska. (www.evostc.state.ak.us).
State of Alaska. (www.labor.state.ak.us).
State of Alaska. (www.library.state.ak.us/dev/aslld).

State of Alaska. Large Parcel Map. (www.dnr.state.ak.us/ssd/os/lgpar/chenega.html).

State of Alaska. Rural Justice 1999 Directory, Chapter 2, 7. Kwinhagak Tribal Court (Quinhagak). (www.ajc.state.ak.us/Reports/rjdir99-2e.htm).

State of Alaska. Site Summary Update: Red Devil Mine (Mercury and Petroleum Hydrocarbons), Alaska Department of Environmental Conservation, Division of Spill Prevention and Response, December 1999. (www.state.ak.us/dec/spar/csp/list.htm).

State of Louisiana. "On the Tunica Trail." (www.crt.state.la.us).

State of Maine. Department of Health and Human Services Behavioral and Developmental Services.

(www.state.me.us/bds/mhservices/MulticulturalResource/NativeAmerican.html).

State of Maine. Passamaquoddy Tribe. (www.maine.gov).

"Station Casinos Enters Partnership to Develop and Manage Entertainment Facility for the Match-E-Be-Nash-She-Wish Band of Pottawatomi Indians." November 14 /PRNewswire-FirstCall. (www.phx.corporate-ir.net/phoenix.zhtml).

Statistical Profile: The Quinault Indian Nation. (www.ghcog.org/members/Profiles/QuinaultProfile.htm).
"Stereotype of the Month contest." (www.bluecorncomics.com/stype2c7.htm).

Stoltz, Craig. "Arizona Golf, With Reservations." The Washington Post. November 30, 2003. (www.web.lexis-nexis.com).

Suh'dutsing Technologies, LLC. Homepage. (www.suhdutsingllc.com/about_us.htm).

Sultzman, Lee. "Kickapoo History." (www.tolatsga.org/kick.html).

Sultzman, Lee. "Potawatomi History." December 18, 1998. (www.tolatsga.org/pota.html).

Sunrise Park Resort. Homepage. (www.sunriseskipark.com/generalinfo.shtml).

Suquamish Tribe. Homepage. (www.suquamish.nsn.us).

Susanville Indian Rancheria Constitution and Bylaws. (www.tribalresourcecenter.org).

Swinomish Casino. Homepage. (www.swinomishcasino.com).
Swinomish Indian Tribal Community. Homepage. (www.swinomish.org).

"Swinomish Plan Resort, Marina Near Casino." December 3, 2004. PokerMag.com. (www.pokermag.com).
Sycuan Band of the Kumeyaay Nation. Homepage. (www.sycuan.com).

Table 1-6. Land Base of Nevada Tribes, 2000/2001. (www.dcnr.nv.gov).

Table Mountain Rancheria. Homepage. (www.tmcasino.com).

TACHC. United Medical Centers. (www.tachc.org).

Tamástlikt Cultural Institute. Homepage. (www.tamstslikt.com).

Tampa Bay History Center. "Seminole Timeline." (www.tampabayhistorycenter.org).

Tanana Chiefs Conference. (www.tananachiefs.org).

Taos Mountain Casino. Homepage. (www.taosmountaincasino.com).

Taos Pueblo. Homepage. (www.taospueblo.com).

Taos Pueblo Pow Wow. Homepage. (www.taospueblopowwow.com).

Taos Vacation Guide. Homepage. (www.taosvacationguide.com).

Tatitlek Corporation. "Tatitlek Management, Inc. - A Subsidiary of the Tatitlek Corp." (www.tatitlek.com).

Taylor, Beatrice. "The Role of Ojibwe Elders." Moccasin Telegraph. (www.millelacsojibwe.org).

Telalaska. "Our Companies." (www.telalaska.com/companies/overview.htm).

"Temporary Closure Order" National Indian Gaming Commission. (www.nigc.gov).

Testerman, Jeff, and Brad Goldstein. "Branching Out With Little Success: From Swamp Safaris to Turtle Farms, the Tribe Loses Millions Despite Tax Advantages." St. Petersburg Times, 1998. (www.sptimes.com).

Texas Beyond History. Caddo Nation Today. (www.texasbeyondhistory.net/tejas/voices/today.html). Texas Kickapoo Tribe. (www.bjgeiger.com/texas/history/indians/kickapoos.html).

"The Confederated Salish and Kootenai Tribes of the Flathead Indian Reservation." Char-koosta News Online.(www.ronan.net).

"The Fort Hall Bottoms, the best of Idaho unknowns." (www.anglerguide.com).

"The San Carlos Apache Nation." (www.users.aol.com/Donh523/navapage/sancarl.htm).

The Free Dictionary.com. Shoalwater Bay Tribe. (www.encyclopedia.thefreedictionary.com).

Thrasher, Pamela Crouch. "Tribes Growing Businesses from Citrus Groves to Casinos." Atlanta Journal Constitution, January 6, 2005. (www.ajc.com).

Three Mesas. (www.nau.edu/~hcpo-p/visit/mesa_1.htm).

"Thurston County Recall Effort Misses Deadline." The Associated Press, May 18, 2004. (www.//web-lexisnexis.com/universe).

"Tigua casino fight: It is now about Texas politics." Indian Country Today. (www.proquest.umi.com).

Tigua Indians. (www.bjgeiger.com/texas/history/indians/tiguas.html).

Tikigaq. "An Alaska Native Village Corporation, Tikigaq." (www.tikigaq.com/home.asp).

Tikigaq School. (www.nsbsd.org/pho/default.cfm).

Tilton, Buck. Alaska's Ultimate Wilderness; Paddling the Noatak River. (www.gorp.away.com/gorp/location/ak/noatak.htm).

To'hajiilee-He (Canoncito). Canoncito, New Mexico/NM school information. (www.greatschools.net/modperl/browse_school/nm/761/=).

Tohono O'odham Community College. Homepage. (www.tocc.cc.az.us).

Tomah Baskets. Homepage. (www.tomahbaskets.com). Tonkawa Tribe of Oklahoma. Homepage. (www.tonkawatribe.com).

Torres-Martinez. Homepage. (www.torrresmartinez.org).

Town of the Week. June 27, 1998: Kotlik, Alaska. (www.notmuch.com/Features/Town/town-062798.html).

Townson University. Taos Pueblo. (www.towson.edu).

Travel South Dakota.com. Reservations in South Dakota. (www.travelsd.com).

Travel Texas. Homepage. Tigua Indian Reservation. (www.traveltex.com).

Treaties and Laws. (www.lapahie.com).

Treaty of Fort Laramie, 1868. (www.classbrain.com/artteenst/publish/article_126.shtml). "

Tribal Grants to Fund Diabetes Project, Land Purchase, Economic Development." Press Release. (www.turtletrack.org/Issues04/Co05012004/CO_05012004_SMSCGrants. Htm).

"Tribal Success Stories." U.S. EPA. (www.epa.gov).

Tribal Addresses. (www.wildapache.net/NativeAmericanSite/pages/tribaladdresses.html). Tribal Child Care Technical Assistance Center (TriTAC) Effective Program Strategies. "White Earth Indian Reservation." (www.nccic.org/tribal/effective/whiteearth/qualityimprove.html).

Tribal EMS/Ambulance Program Directory. (www.heds.org/ambpro10.html). Tribal Government Sources Nations by Tribes. (www.evergreen.edu).

Tribal Profile: Nottawaseppi Huron Band of Potawatomi. (www.itcmi.org).

Tribal Wildlife Grant 2003. (www.midwest.fws.gov).

"Tribe Sues Bush Over Efforts To Stop Gambling." The Ojibwe News. St. Paul, Minn.: June 5, 1998.V. 10, I. 34; pg. 2. (www.proquest.umi.com).

Tribes and Villages of Nevada. (www.hanksville.org).

"Tribes Hold High Hopes for Coos Bay Recreation Center," Gambling Magazine, June 5, 2000. (www.gamblingmagazine.com).

Trip Advisor. Ysleta del Sur Pueblo Museum. (www.tripadvisor.com).

Trump 29 Casino. Homepage. (www.trump29.com).

Tulalip Casino. Homepage. (www.tulalipcasino.com)

Tulalip Tribes. Homepage. (www.tulaliptribes.com).

Tule River Reservation. Homepage. (www.twintule.com).

Tunica-Biloxi Tribe of Louisiana. Homepage. (www.tunica.org).

Turning Stone Casino Resort. Homepage. (www.turning-stone.com).

Turtle Mountain Band of Chippewa. Homepage. (www.turtlemoutainchippewa.com).

Turtle Mountain Band of Chippewa Indian Community Environmental Profile. (www.mnisose.org).

Turtle Mountain Chippewa Indian Heritage Center. Homepage. (www.chippewa.utma.com).

Tuscarora Farmers Market. (www.hetfonline.org).

Tuscarora Nation. Homepage. (www.tuscaroras.com).

"Tux & Tails Travel Tux & Tails Formal Attire." Upper Lake Pomo Indians. (www.ms10.com).

"Two Tribes in Thurston County are Looking to Raise Their Political profile" The Omaha World-Herald Company, 6 May 2004. (www.//web-lexis-lexis.com).

Two Rivers Casino and Resort. Homepage. (www.tworiverscasinoandresort.com).

U.S. Bankruptcy Court, District of Alaska. (www.akb.uscourts.gov).

U.S. Bureau of Land Management. Testimony of Jim Hughes, Deputy Director, Bureau of Land Management, Dept. of the Interior, Before the Senate Committee on Energy and Natural Resources, Subcommitte on Public Lands and Forests regarding S.924, a Bill to Authorize the Exchange of Lands Between the Newtok Native Corporation and the Department of the Interior: June 4, 2003. (www.blm.gov).
U.S. Bureau of the Census. 2000 U.S. Census. (www.factfinder.census.gov).

U.S. Coast Guard. (www.uscg.mil/d17/allnews/news02/12902.htm).

U.S. Coast Guard. "Unit Information: LORSTA St. Paul Island." March 8, 2001. (www.uscg.mil/hq/capemay/ui/lorsta_st._paul_island.doc).

U.S. Dept. of Agriculture. Forest Service. (www.fs.fed.us/biology/resources/pubs/fish/fishtales/022704_fishtales.pdf).

U.S. Dept. of Agriculture. Forest Service. "Tongass National Forest: Forest Facts," (www.fs.fed.us/r10/tongass/forest_facts/forest_facts.html).

U.S. Dept. of Agriculture. Rural Development. "Crow Reservation." (www.rurdev.usda.gov).

U.S. Dept. of Agriculture. Rural Development. Tribal Rural Business Enterprise Grant (RBEG) Recipients. (www.codetalk.fed.us/DennisDanielsHandout,Session2.doc Alamo+Navajo&hl=en&client=firefox-a).

U.S. Dept. of the Interior. Fish and Wildlife Service. Article, January, 2001. (www.alaska.fws.gov/LawEnforcement/factsheets/walrus.pdf).

U.S. Dept. of the Interior. Public Notice July 14, 2003. (www.alaska.fws.gov/nwr/planning/pdf/PublicNotice.pdf).

U.S. EPA. American Indian Environmental Office. Washington, D.C. Red Lake Reservation. (www.epa.gov).

U.S. EPA. Homepage. (www.epa.gov).

U.S. Fish and Wildlife Service. Division of Environmental Contaminants. "Environmental Contaminants Survey of Spectacled Eiders from St. Lawrence Island, Alaska," April 2001. (www.alaska.fws.gov/fisheries/endangered/pdf/SPECIcont.pdf).

U.S. Fish and Wildlife Service. (www.refuges/fws.gov/profiles/).

U.S. Fish and Wildlife Service. White Earth Band Tribal Partnership Projects. (www.midwest.fws.gov/Tribal/WhiteEarth.html).

U.S. Geological Survey. Ponca Tribe. (www.usgs.gov).

U.S. Geological Survey. 12039500 Quinault River at Quinault Lake, WA. (www.waterdata.usgs.gov).

U.S.A. Oklahoma Weather. (www.hotweathers.com). Uintah-Ouray Indian Reservation. (www.media.utah.edu/UHE/u/UINTAH-OURAY.html).

Uintah-Ouray Indian Reservation. (www.onlineutah.com).

Umatilla Reservation. Homepage. (www.umatilla.nsn.us).

Umpqua Indian Foods. Homepage. (www.umpquaindianfoods.com).

Unit I : DIN› BAAHANE'. Oral Tradition. (www.nmculturenet.org/heritage/ dine_culture/dinebaahane.pdf).

"United Auburn Indians hope theirs will be rags to riches story." (www.kxt10.com/storyfull).

"United Tribes says every child sacred." The Tribal College Journal, 9, No. 4, Spring/Summer 1998. (www.tribalcollegejournal.org).

United Keetoowah Band. Homepage. (www.unitedkeetoowah.org).

United Keetowah Band of Cherokee Indians. Homepage. (www.unitedkeetoowahband.org).

University of Georgia. "The Mississippi Choctaw Reservation." (www.uga.edu).

University of Washington. (www.depts.washington.edu). "Updated Hwy 101 Building Directs Tourism Traffic Toward Quileute Tribe Offerings." March 8, 2004. (www.northwestsecretplaces.com/vcb/pressroom/QuileuteTribe.php).

Upper Skagit Tribe. Upper Skagit Tribal Health Facility. (www.northregionems.com).

Utacia Krol, Debra. "Rural No More; Tribal Communities Once Considered Insulated From Urban Sprawl Now Cope With the Impact of Thousands of New Residents." Falmouth Institute. American Indian Report. December, 2003. Sec.: V. XIX, No. 12; Pg. 8-10; ACC-NO: AIR2003120101. (www.web.lexis-nexis.com/).

Utah State Division of Indian Affairs. (www.dced.utah.gov/indian/Today/goshute.html).

Utah Tribes. Contact Addresses. (www.500nations.com/Utah_Tribes.asp).

Ute Mountain Ute Tribe. Homepage. (www.utemountain.org).

Valley View Motel. Homepage. (www.valleyview-motel.com).

Vee Quiva Casinos. Homepage. (www.wingilariver.com).

"Venture Gaming." Horizon, August 2000. (www.horizonmag.com).

Victories Casino and Hotel. Homepage. (www.victories-casino.com).

Viejas Band of Kumeyaay. Homepage. (www.viejasbandofkumeyaay.org).

Viejas Casino. Homepage. (www.viejas.com).

"Village Alaska: Community Characteristics and Public Safety." Alaska Justice Forum, 12, No. 4, Winter 1996. (www.uaa.alaska.edu).

Village Earth. Homepage. (www.villageearth.org).

Waabooz.com. Homepage. (www.waabooz.com).

Wabanaki Legal News. Homepage. (www.ptla.org/wabanaki/wabanaki.htm).
Waddell, David. "Michigan House Considers Resolution Calling for a New Tribal Casino." Casino Guide. Detroit News Online, December 23, 2004. (www.info.detnews.com).

"Wainwright" Community Profile. (www.north-slope.org/nsb/HomeruleBrochure/WainInfo.htm).

Wakpamni Bed and Breakfast. Homepage. (www.rapidnet.com/~raleigh).

Walker River Paiute Indian Reservation. (www.paiutewater.com).

Walker River Paiute Tribe. Homepage. (www.walkerriverpaiutetribe.com/).

Wampanoag Tribe of Gay Head (Aquinnah). Homepage. (www.wampanoagtribe.net)

Warm Springs Reservation. (www.hometown.aol.com).

Washington Indian Tribes. (www.kstrom.net).

Washington Tribes. (www.usgennet.org/usa/topic/native-amer1/washington.htm).

Weatherbase.com. Homepage. (www.weatherbase.com).

Weatherization and Intertribal Program Tribal Energy Program. (www.eere.energy.gov).

Welcome to Hanksville. Homepage. (www.hanksville.org).

Wells Band of Te-Moak Tribe of Western Shoshone Indians. Tribal Profile. (www.itcn.org).

Wells Band of Western Shoshone. (www.angelfire.com/nv2/wells/shoshone.html).

Western U.S. for Visitors. Zia Pueblo. (www.gocalifornia.about.com/).Montana, Cate. "What is the History of the Native American People of Northeastern Washington Region?" (www.ghosttownsusa.com/native.html).
Whirlwind Golf Club at Wildhorse Pass. (www.whirlwindgolf.com/).

White Earth Aki Planning Circle. (www.coafes.umn.edu/pep/read/whiteearth.html).

White Earth Band of Chippewa Judicial Code. (www.tribalresourcecenter.org).

White Earth Band of Chippewa. (www.kstrom.net). "White Earth Indian Reservation." American Indian Resource Center Oak Hills Fellowship. (www.oakhills.edu/cim/white.htm).

White Earth Land Recovery Project and Native Harvest. (www.welrp.org/faq.html).

"White Earth Reservation Science and Math Summer Program." Department of Forest Resources, St. Paul, Minnesota. (www.nrem.net/programs/flagship.html?id=203&&string=%7C).

White Earth Tribal Court. Homepage. (www.whiteearthtribalcourt.com/).

White Mountain Apache Tribe. Homepage. (www.wmat.us).

White Mountain Wildlife and Outdoors Recreation Division. (www.162.42.237.6/wmatod/fcbareas.shtml).

White Oak Casino. (www.whiteoakcasino.com).

"WIC." White Earth Reservation. (www.perham.eot.com/~rtcheal/wic.html).

Wichita Tribe. Homepage.(www.wichita.nsn.us).

Wikipedia, the Free Encyclopedia. Homepage. (www.en.wikipedia.org/).

Wild Bluff Golf Course. Homepage. (www.wildbluff.com/html/courseinfo/courseinfo-frame.html).

Wild Horse Casino. Homepage. (www.wingilariver.com).

Wildlife Refuges. (www.recreation.gov).

Wilkinson, Charles. "A letter to Senator Inouye concerning the plight of the Western Shoshone." September 25, 2002. (www.indiancountry.com).

Willis, David. "Sea engulfing Alaskan village." (www.news.bbc.co.uk/1/hi/world/europe/3940399.stm).
Wilson, S.J. "Strange Holes Trouble Black Mesa Rresidents." The Navajo-Hopi Observer. (www.blackmesais.org/water_coal.htm).

Winnebago Tribe of Nebraska. Homepage. (www.winnebagotribe.com).

Winsor, Morgan. "Taking care of his people." University of Idaho. (www.uidaho.edu).

Wiyot Tribe. Homepage. (www.wiyot.com).

Wiyot Tribe Plant Enterprises. (www.kstrom.net/isk/art/basket/wiyot/wybiz.htm).

Woodfords Indian Education Center. Five State American Indian Project. (www.5stateproject.utah.org).

Woody, Elizabeth. "Recalling Celilo," adapted from Salmon Nation: People, Fish, and Our Common Home, 2003 Ecotrust. (www.ecotrust.org/community/recalling_celilo.html).

Wyandotte Nation of Oklahoma. Homepage. (www.wyandotte-nation.org/home.html).

Wyandotte Net-Tel. Homepage. (www.wyandotte-network.com/).

Yahoo. All Nations Fitness Center, McLoud, OK. (www.local.yahoo.com/OK/Stroud/7737238/Health+and+Medicine/8107103/Fitness).

Yakama Reservation. (www.depts.washington.edu). Yakama Tribe. Internet Public Library. (www.tcfn.org/tctour/museums/Yakama-center.html).

Yakama Tribe Work Study. (www.depts.washington.edu/stepcofs/Yakama/Yakama_WorkStudy.htm).

Yankton Sioux Tribal Tourism Association. Homepage. (www.yanktonsiouxtourism.com/visitorservices.htm).

Yankton Sioux Tribe. Lewis and Clark Trail.com. (www.lewisandclarktrail.com/sponsors/yanktonsioux/sect1.htm).

Yavapai Apache Nation. Homepage. (www.yavapai-apache-nation.com/).

Yavapai Downs at Prescott Valley. Homepage. (www.yavapaidownsatpv.com).

Yavapai Prescott Indian Tribe. Homepage. (www.ypit.com).

YKHC. "Welcome to YKHC!" (www.ykhc.org).

Ysleta. Lone Star Internet. (www.lone-star.net/mall/txtrails/ysleta.htm).

Ysleta del Sur Pueblo. (www.itecmembers.org). Ysleta del Sur Pueblo Code of Laws. (www.tribalresourcecenter.org).

Ysleta del Sur Pueblo Library/Education Center. (www.gslis.utexas.edu).

Yukon River Tours. (www.mosquitonet.com/~dlacey/directions.html).

Yurok Economic Development Department. Homepage. (www.yurokedc.com).

Yurok Tribe of California. Tribal Headquarters Information. (www.indiancountry.com/?1301). Zia Pueblo. Homepage. (www.zia.com).

UNPUBLISHED SOURCES

Agai Dicutta Numu Yadua Language Project Grant Application, n.d.

Albers, Patricia C., and William R. James. "A History of Joint Migrations, Water and Land Use by the Assiniboine, Cree, Chippewa and Metis in the Northern Plains from Pre-Historic Times to 1879. Report to the Bureau of Indian Affairs, Billings Area Office", 1984.

"Benefits Available for Osages and Other Indians." unpublished document.

Cherokee Tribal Sanitation Program. Press Release, n.d.

Edmo, Blaine. "Welcome to the Summit." Open letter, November 16, 2002.

"First-of-its-kind agreement sets course to keep Puyallup River health." Press release, June 24, 1998.

Frisch, Jack A. "Revitalization, Nativism, and Tribalism Among the St. Regis Mohawks." Ph. D. Diss., Indiana Univ., 1970.

"Harrah's Skagit Valley Casino." Unpublished fact sheet, 1997.

Hesler, Liana Staci.Notes. Interview with Fortner, Brad. 25 June, 2004.

Hesler, Liana Staci. Interview with Sac and Fox Community/Public Services Director. 30 June, 2004.

Jackson, Danna R. Letter addressed to Ms. Sara J. Drake, Department of Justice, State of California, December 3, 2001.

"Kickapoo water shortage film receives Best Picture nomination at the American Indian Film Festival." Press release, November 8, 2004.

"Labor Force for the Next 20 Years (Based on Conservative Population Projections)." Paper: 21 pages, n.d.

"Native American 2002 Foundation selects Shoshone-Bannock Tribes as host tribe to Other Indian Nations during XIX Winter Olympic Games." Press release, November 2000.

"Picuris Pueblo seeks to reclaim ancestral lands." Press release, February 20, 2004.

Popoff, Nicholas. A Study of Management Policies and Practices of the Bureau of Indian Affairs on Lands Held in Federal Trust on the Quinault Indian Reservation. MA. Thesis, University of Washington, 1970.

Retasket, Tina M. 2003 Socio-Economic/Health Survey of the Confederated Tribes of Siletz Indians of Oregon.

Sonoma State University. "Federated Indians of Graton Rancheria donate $1.5 million to Sonoma State for Endowed chair in Native American Studies." Press release, December 8, 2003.

State of Nevada. Office of the Attorney General. "Future of Walker Lake will be debated at Supreme Court." Press release, February 8, 2001.

Thompson, Mary. "Pueblo of Cochiti: A Public Health Nursing Profile, USPHS, IHS." (Santa Fe, NM) May 31,1994. Tiller Research, Inc. Survey Questionnaires: Economic Profiles of Federal and State Indian Reservations. Albuquerque NM, 1994-1995.

Tiller Research, Inc. Unpublished questionnaires for all tribes, June 2004.

Tiller, Veronica. Notes. Interview with Green, Anda; Ray Martell and Teri Camarena of Elk Valley Tolowa Tribe. n.d.

Tilller, Veronica. Unpublished Handwritten Notes from Interviews with Community Officials. 10 May, 2004; 14 May, 2004; 24 May, 2004; 25 May, 2004; 27 May, 2004; 15 June, 2004, and 2 July 2004.

U.S. EPA. Letter to Laura Spurr, Chairman, Nottawaseppi Huron Band of Potawatomi, December 3, 2003.

Woods, Mike, et al. "Economic Impact Analysis of Ponca Tribal Bingo." Department of Agricultural Economics, Oklahoma State University. Stillwater, OK, 1994.

Absentee Shawnee Tribe of Oklahoma, 803-804
Achomawi, 466-468. See also Pit River Tribe
Acoma Pueblo, 717-719
Adak, City of, 39, 41-42
Aerospace Corporation, 14-15
Afognak Native Corporation, 30, 231
Agai Dicutta Yaduas, 707-708
Agdaagux Tribe of King Cove, 42-43
Aglurmiut, 177-178
Agriculture. See also Irrigation; Livestock
  California, 373, 379
    development of, 464, 470
  community gardens, 819, 912
  companies, New Mexico, 718, 722
  cooperatives, New Mexico, 719
  cotton gin (AZ), 305
  crops
    Alabama, 2
    Arizona, 287, 304, 346
    California, 380, 384, 398, 399, 413, 418, 461, 462, 468, 484, 506
    Florida, 524
    Idaho, 540, 542, 545
    Kansas/Nebraska, 551, 553, 555
    Michigan, 581, 592, 594
    Minnesota, 615, 628, 633
    Montana, 662, 665, 668
    Nebraska, 676
    Nevada, 695, 699, 710, 714
    New Mexico, 721, 722, 724, 739, 741, 748, 750, 752, 754, 757, 759, 763, 765, 770
    New York, 777
    North Carolina, 790
    North Dakota, 797
    Oklahoma, 825, 829, 835, 844
    Oregon, 888, 908
    Rhode Island, 912
    South Dakota, 921, 923, 928, 932, 941
    Washington state, 1027
    Wisconsin, 1031, 1039, 1057
    development of, 883, 953
  farms
    Alaska, 119
    Arizona, 287, 295, 307, 315, 318, 325, 348, 353
    California, 468
    Colorado, 510, 513
    Florida, 527
    Kansas/Nebraska, 551, 553
    Louisiana, 561
    Maine, 565
    Michigan, 590-591
    Minnesota, 628, 636
    Montana, 670
    Nevada, 687
    New Mexico, 718, 721, 747, 748, 757, 761
    Oklahoma, 810-811, 829, 849, 852, 858
    South Dakota, 917, 921, 925, 941
    Washington state, 960, 962, 982, 1001, 1016
    Wisconsin, 1031, 1039, 1055
  leasing
    Arizona, 290, 305, 353
    California, 387, 411
    Florida, 531
    Iowa, 549
    Kansas, 558
    Maine, 569
    Minnesota, 636
    Montana, 654, 656

    Nevada, 706, 708
    Oklahoma, 806, 807, 810, 817, 825, 832, 861, 876
    Washington state, 985, 1027
    Wyoming, 1066
  Nebraska, 674
  New Mexico, 729
  nurseries, California, 389
  Oklahoma, 819
  orchards
    Alabama, 2
    Arizona, 304, 325
    California, 384, 431, 462, 467, 497
    Florida, 524, 526, 527
    Kansas/Nebraska, 555
    Oregon, 888
    Washington state, 1027
    Wisconsin, 1055
  vineyards, 422
  Zuni Sustainable Agriculture Project, 770
Agua Caliente Band of Cahuilla Indians, 363-364
Ahtna, Inc., 9-11
  Cantwell, 69
  Cheesh-Na, 72
  contact information, 10
  Gakona, 108
  Gulkana, 116
  Mentasta, 173
  Tazlina, 266
Ahtna Athabascan, 7
  Cantwell, 69
  Cheesh-Na, 72-73
  Chitina, 86-87
  Gakona, 108-109
  Gulkana, 116
  income operations, 10-11
  Kluti-Kaah, 145-146
  Mentasta, 173-174
  Tazlina, 266-267
Ak-Chin Indian Community, 287-288
Ak-Chin Water Settlement Act (1978), 287
Akhiok, City of, 43-44
Akhiok-Kaguyak Inc., 30, 43
Akiachak Native Community, 45
Akiak, City of, 46
Akima Corp., 12, 32
Akimel Au-Authm (Pima) Tribe, 345
Akimel O'odham. See Gila River Pima-Maricopa Indian Community
Akimel O'odham/Pee Posh Youth Council Gila River Indian Community, 309-311
Akutan, City of, 47
Akwasasne Mohawk Nation, 784-786
Alabama-Coushatta Tribe of Texas, 943-945
Alabama Quassarte Tribal Town, 804-805
Alabama (state), 1-2
Alakanuk, City of, 48
Alamo Navajo Chapter, 719-720
Alaska. See also Dena'ina Athabascan; Unangan
  Adak, City of, 39, 41-42
  Agdaagux Tribe, 42-43
  Aglurmiut Yup'ik, 177-178
  Akhiok, City of, 43-44
  Akiachak Native Community, 45
  Akiak, City of, 46
  Akutan, City of, 47
  Alakanuk, City of, 48
  Alatna Village, 49
  Aleknagik, City of, 49-50
  Aleut, 7, 47, 78, 189-190
  Algaaciq, 51-52
  Allakaket, 52-53

Alutiiq. See Alutiiq (main level)
Ambler, 53-54
Anaktuvuk Pass, 54-55
Anchorage, 55
Andreafsky, 56
Angoon, City of, 56-57
Aniak Traditional Council, 57-58
Anvik Tribal Council, 59
area, 3
Asa'carsarmiut Tribe, 60-61
Athabascan. See Athabascan Indians
Atka IRA, Native Village of, 61-62
Atmautluak Traditional Council, 62-63
Atqasuk Village, 63-64
Barrow, Native Village of, 64-65
Beaver, 65-66
Birch Creek, 66-67
Brevig Mission, 67-68
Buckland, 68
Cantwell, 69
Chalkyitsik, 70
Chanega, Native Village of, 71-72
Cheesh-Na, 72-73
Chefornak, 73-74
Chevak, 74-75
Chickaloon, 75-76
Chignik (Bay), 78
Chignik Lagoon, 79
Chignik Lake, 80
Chilkat, 81
Chilkoot Indian Association, 82-83
Chinik, 85
Chitina, 86-87
Chuathbaluk, 87-88
Chugachigmuit Alutiiq, 179-180
Chugash, 227-229
Circle, 88-89
Clark's Point, 89-90
climate, 4
Colorado River, 294-297
communications, 5
Craig, 90-91
Crooked Creek, 91-92
culture, 7-8
Curyung, 92-93
Deering, 94
Dena'ina Athabascan, 164, 195-197, 216-217
Diomede, Native Village of, 95
Dot Lake, 96
Eagle, 97
education, 5
Eek, 98
Egegik, 99-100
Eklutna, 100
Ekwok, 101
Elim, 102
Emmonak, 103
energy, 5
Evansville, 104
Eyak, Native Village of, 105-106
Fairbanks, 55
False Pass, 106-107
Fort Yukon, 107-108
Gakona, 108-109
Galena, 109-112
Gambell, 112-113
geography, 3, 4
Georgetown, 113
Goodnews Bay, 114
government, 5-7
Grayling, 115
Gulkana, 116

Haida, 90-91, 122-123, 135-136
health care, 5
Healy Lake, 117
history, 3, 3-4
Holikachuk, 115
Holy Cross, 117-118
Hoonah, 118-119
Hooper Bay, 119-120
Hughes, 120-121
Huslia, 121-122
Hydaburg, 122-123
Igiugig, 123-124
Iliamna, 124-125, 200-201
infrastructure, 4-5
Inupiat. See Inupiat (main level)
Iqurmiut, 125-126
Ivanof Bay, 127
Kake, 128-130
Kaktovik, City of, 131
Kaltag, 133-134
Karluk, Native Village of, 134-135
Kasaan, City of, 135-136
Kasigluk, Native Village of, 136-137
Kauwerak Eskimos, 67-68
Ketchikan, 137-139
Kiana, City of, 139-140
King Cove, 42-43
King Salmon Tribe, 140-142
Kipnuk, Native Village of, 142-143
Kivalina, City of, 143-144
Klawock, City of, 144-145
Kluti-Kaah, 145-146
Knik, 146-147
Kobuk, 120-121, 147-148
Kobuk Inupiat, 49
Kokhanok Village, 148-149
Kokyukon Athabascan, 104
Kongiganak, Native Village of, 149-150
Koniag Aleut, 79
Koniagmiut Alutiiq, 229-230
Kotlik, City of, 150-152
Kotzebue, City of, 152-153
Kowagmiut Inupiat, 53-54, 139-140, 143-144, 201-202
Koyuk, 154-155
Koyukon Athabascan. See Koyukon Athabascan (main level)
Koyukuk, City of, 155-156
Kutchin Athabascan, 65-66, 70, 88-89, 97, 107-108
Kwethluk, City of, 156-157
Kwigillingok, Native Village of, 158-159
Kwinhagak, City of, 159-161
Larsen Bay, City of, 161-162
Levelock Village, 162-163
Lime Village, 164
Lower Kalskag, 165-166
Malemiut Inupiat, 154-155
Manley Hot Springs Village, 166-167
Manokotak, City of, 167-168
Marshall, City of, 169-170
McGrath, City of, 170-171
Mekoryuk, City of, 172-173
Mentasta, 173-174
Metlakatla Indian Community, 174-175
Minto, Native Village of, 175-176
Naknek Native Village, 177-178
Nanwalek, Native Village of, 179-180
Napakiak, City of, 180-181
Napaskiak, City of, 181-182
Nelson Lagoon, Native Village of, 183-184
Nenana, City of, 184-187

New Allakaket Village, 186
Newhalen, City of, 189-190
New Koliganek, 187
New Stuyahok, City of, 188-189
Newtok Village, 190-191
Nightmute, City of, 191-192
Nikolai, City of, 193
Nikolski, Native Village of, 194-195
Ninilchik Village, 195-197
Noatak, 197-198
Nome, City of, 198-200
Nondalton, City of, 200-201
Noorvik, City of, 201-202
Northway Village, 203-204
Nuiqsut, City of, 204-205
Nulato, City of, 206-207
Nunakauyarmiut (City of Toksook Bay), 207-208
Nunam Iqua, 208-209
Nunamiut, 54-55, 104, 120-121
Nunapitchuk, City of, 209-210
Nuniwarmiut Cup'ig, 172-173
Old Harbor, City of, 210-212
Orutsararmiut (City of Bethel), 212-213
Oscarville Traditional Village, 213-214
Ouzinkie, City of, 214-216
Pedro Bay Village, 216-217
Perryville, Native Village of, 217-218
Petersburg, City of, 219
Pilot Point, City of, 219-220
Pilot Station, City of, 221-222
Pitka's Point, Native Village of, 222-223
Platinum, City of, 223-224
Point Hope, City of, 224-225
Point Lay, 226-227
population, 3
Portage Creek, 233
Port Graham, 227-229
Port Heiden, 229-230
Port Lions, 231-232
Pribilof Islands, 234-236
public safety, 5
public services, 4-5
Qagan Tayagungin, 237-238
Qawalangin, 238-239
Rampart, 239-240
Red Devil, 240-241
Ruby, 242-243
Saint Michael, 243-244
Salamatof, 244-245
Savoonga, 245-246
Saxman, 247-248
Scammon Bay, 248-249
Selawik, 120-121, 249-250
Seldovia Village, 250
Shageluk, 251
Shaktoolik, 252
Shishmaref, 253-254
Shungnak, 255-256
Siberian Eskimo, 112-113
Siberian Yup'ik, 8
Skagway, 256
Sleetmute, 257-258
Solomon, 258
Southeast Alaskan Indians, 8
South Naknek, 258-259
Stebbins, 259-260
Stevens Village, 260-261
Stony River, 261-262
Takotna, 262-263
Tanacross, 96, 117, 263-264
Tanana, 175-176, 184-187, 264-265

Tatitlek, 265-266
Tazlina, 266-267
Telida, 267
Teller, 268
Tetlin, 269
Tikeraqmuit Inupiat, 224-225
Tlingit. See Tlingit (main level)
Togiak, 270-271
transportation, 4-5
Tsimshian, 174-175
Tuluksak, 271
Tuntutuliak, 272
Tununak, 273
Twin Hills, 274
Tyonek, 275
Ugashik, 276
Umkumiute, 277
Unalakleet, 277-278
Unalit Yup'ik, 154-155
Unangan. See Unangan (main level)
United States' purchase of, 4
Upper Kalskag, 132-133
Upper Kuskokwim Athabascan, 170-171, 193
Upper Tanana Athabascan, 203-204
Venetie, 278-280
Wainwright, 280-281
Wales, 281-282
waste systems, 5
water supply, 5
White Mountain, 282-283
Wrangell, 283
Yakutat, 284-285
Yup'ik. See Yup'ik (main level)
Alaska Coastal Aggregate, 34
Alaska Growth Capital, 15
Alaska Interstate Construction LLC, 26
Alaska Native Claims Settlement Act (ANCSA, 1971), 3
    13th, 34
    Ahtna, Inc. 9
    Aleut Corp., 11
    ASRC, 13
    BSNC 17
    BBNC, 19
    CAC, 23
    Calista, 21
    CIRI, 25, 26
    Doyon, 28-29
    federal relations, 5-6
    history, 8
    Koniag, 29
    NANA, 31
    preferences, 6
    problems discussed, 9
    Sealaska, 33
    urban tribes, 36, 38
    village corporations, 9
    zero population villages, 37-38
Alaska Peninsula Corp., 19
    Kokhanok, 148
    Newhalen, 189
    Port Heiden, 229
    South Naknek, 258
    Ugashik, 276
Alaska Tourism Corp., 26
Alaska Trust Co., 12
Alaska Village Electrical Cooperative Inc., 39
Alatna Village, 49
Aleknagik, City of, 19, 49-50
Aleut, 7. See also Unangan
    Akutan, City of, 47
    Chignik (Bay), 78
    Newhalen, 189-190

The Aleut Corporation (TAC), 11-13
Aleut Enterprise Corporation, 41
        Adak, City of, 41
Alexander Creek Inc., 26
Algaaciq Native Village, 51-52
Alindeska, 35
Allakaket Village, 52-53
Allegany (Seneca Nation), 777-778
All Indian Pueblo Council, 740
Alturas, 365
Alutiiq, 7
        Akhiok, City of, 43-44
        Chanega, 71-72
        Chignik, 78
        Chignik Lake, 80
        Clark's Point, 89-90
        Curyung, 92-93
        Egegik, 99-100
        Eyak, 105-106
        Igiugig, 123-124
        Iliamna, 124-125
        Ivanof Bay, 127
        Karluk, 134-135
        King Salmon, 140-142
        Kokhanok, 148-149
        Larsen Bay, 161-162
        Naknek, 177-178
        Nelson Lagoon, 183-184
        Old Harbor, 210-212
        Ouzinkie, 214-216
        Perryville, 217-218
        Pilot Point, 219-220
        Port Lions, 231-232
        Seldovia Village, 250
        South Naknek, 258-259
        Ugashik, 276
        zero population villages, 37-38
Amauthlauk, 62-63
Ambler Traditional Council, 53-54
American period, California, 359-360
Anaktuvuk Pass, Village of, 14, 54-55
Anchorage, 38, 55
Andreafsky, 22, 56
Angoon Community Association, 34, 56-57
Aniak Traditional Council, 22, 57-58
Anishinabe. See also Chippewa
        Bois Forte Band, 605
        Saginaw Chippewa, 590-591
Annette Island Reserve, 174-175
ANSCA. See Alaska Native Claims Settlement Act
Anton Larsen Inc., 30
Anvik Tribal Council, 59
Apache
        Apache Tribe of Oklahoma, 806
        Camp Verde (AZ), 288-292
        Fort McDowell (AZ), 303-304
        Fort Sill Apache Tribe (OK), 840-842
        Jicarilla Apache Nation (NM), 727-733
        Mescalero Tribe (NM), 736-738
        Tonto (AZ), 354-355
Apsalooke, 653-655
Aquaculture. See Fisheries, aquaculture
Aquinnah, 577-579
Arapahoe, 1065-1067
        Cheyenne-Arapahoe Tribes of Oklahoma, 816-817
Archaeology Department Training Programs, Window Rock, Flagstaff, AZ and Farmington, NM, 338-339
Arctic Slope corporations, 14, 15
Arctic Village, 278-280
Arikara, 793-796
Arizona

Ak-Chin, 287-288
Camp Verde, 288-292
Cocopah, 292-294
cultural preservation program, 338-339
Fort Apache, 298-302
Fort McDowell, 303-304
Fort Yuma, 305-306
Gila River, 306-313
Havasupai, 314-316
Hopi, 316-321
Hualapai, 322-324
Kaibab Paiute, 324-325
maps, 286
Pascua Yaqui, 342-344
Salt River, 344-347
San Carlos Apache, 347-351
San Juan, 351-352
Tohono O'odham, 352-354
Tonto Apache, 354-355
Yavapai-Prescott, 356-357
Aroostook Band of Micmac Indians, 566-568
Artic Slope Regional Corporation (ASRC), 13-17
Arts cooperatives, 753
Arviq Inc., 22, 223
Asa'carsarmiut Tribe, 60-61
ASCG Inc., 15
Askinuk Corp., 22, 248
ASRC, 13-17
Asset management. See Finance, asset management
Assiniboine Tribe
        Fort Belknap, 661-663, 940-942
        Fort Peck, 664-666
Assuring Self-Determination Through an Effective Law Program Gila River Police Department (AZ), 311-312
Athabascan Indians, 7
        Allakaket Village, 52-53
        Anvik, 59
        Chalkyitsik, 70
        Cheesh-Na, 72-73
        Curyung, 92-93
        Hughes, 120-121
        King Salmon, 140-142
        Levelock, 162-163
        Naknek, 177-178
        Newhalen, 189-190
Atka IRA, Native Village of, 12, 61-62
Atkasook. See Atqasuk
Atmautluak Traditional Council, 22, 62-63
Atqasuk Village, 14, 63-64
Atsugewi. See Pit River
Atxam Corp., 12, 61
Augustine Band of Cahuilla Mission Indians, 365-366
Ayakulik Inc., 30
Azachorok Inc., 22, 60

Baan-O-Yeel Kon Corp., 28, 239
Bad River Band of Lake Superior Tribe of Chippewa Indians, 1031-1033
Bah-Kho-Je. See Iowa
Banks, tribal, 504-505. See also Finance, banks
Bannock, 538-541
        Goshute Reservation Confederated Tribes, 949-950
Barona Band of Mission Indians, 366-368
Barrow, Native Village of, 14, 64-65
Battle Mountain Band, 683-684
Bay Mills Indian Community of Michigan, 581-582
Bay View Inc., 19, 127
Bay View Incorporated, 127
Bean Ridge Corp., 28, 166

Bear River Band of Rohnerville Rancheria, 465-466
Beaver, 65-66
Becharof Corp., 19, 99
Belkofski, 12, 37. See also Zero population villages
Bell's Flats Native Inc., 30
Benewah, 533-538
Benewah County, Idaho, 533
Benton Paiute peoples, 369
Bering Straits Native Corporation (BSNC), 17-18
Berry Creek Rancheria of Maidu Indians, 370
Berry farms, 565
Bethel. See Orutsaramuit
Bethel Native Corp., 22, 212
BIA-recognized Native entities, 36 (chart)
Big Bend Rancheria, Pit River, 371
Big Cypress Seminoles, 526-527
Big Lagoon Rancheria, 371-372
Big Pine Tribe of Owens Valley, 373-374
Big Sandy Rancheria Band of Western Mono Indians, 374-375
Big Valley Rancheria, 376-377
Bill Moore's Slough, 22, 37. See also Zero population villages
Biloxi (Tunica-Biloxi Tribe), 563-564
Birch Creek, 66-67
Bishop, 378-379
Blackfeet Nation, 649-653
Blackfeet Sioux. See Sioux
Blue Lake Rancheria, 380-382
Bode'wadmi. See Potawatomi
Bois Forte Band of Chippewa, 605-607
Boldt decision (1974), on fishing rights, 968, 990, 991, 994, 1003
Boroughs, Alaska, 6
Borrego Springs Bank, 504-505
Brevig Mission, 18, 67, 67-68
Bridgeport Paiute Indian Colony, 382-383
Brighton Seminoles, 527
Bristol Bay Native Corporation (BBNC), 19-21
Brule, Lower, 926-930
Buckland, 68
Buena Vista Rancheria of Me-Wuk Indians, 383
Burns Paiute Tribe, 883-884
Business corporations
        Alaska, 10, 12, 30, 32, 169, 172, 196, 202, 205, 206, 207, 208, 212, 225
                California, 378, 380, 388-389, 394, 397, 419, 422, 423, 429
                        development of, 430
                Colorado, 510
                Montana, 656, 667
                Nebraska, 676, 678
                Nevada, 686, 693, 709
                New Mexico, 763, 770
                North Dakota, 794, 797
                Oklahoma, 810, 819
                Oregon, 883, 888, 892, 899, 901, 904, 908
                Rhode Island, 912
                Washington state, 963, 983, 1016
                Wyoming, 1065

Cabazon Band of Mission Indians, 384-385
Cachil DeHe Band of Wintun Indians, Colusa Indian Community, 397-398
Caddo Nation of Oklahoma, 807-808
Cahto peoples, 360, 432-433
Cahuilla peoples, 360
        Agua Caliente, 363-364
        Augustine, 365-366
        Cabazon, 384-385
        Los Coyotes, 436-437
        Morongo, 444-445

Ramona Band, 457
reservation, 386-387
Santa Rosa Band of Mission Indians, 474-475
Torres Martinez Desert, 492-493
California, 359-363
Agua Caliente, 363-364
Alturas, 365
Augustine, 365-366
Barona, 366-368
Benton Paiute, 369
Berry Creek, 370
Big Bend Rancheria, 371
Big Lagoon Rancheria, 371-372
Big Pine Tribe, 373-374
Big Sandy Rancheria, 374-375
Big Valley Rancheria, 376-377
Bishop, 378-379
Blue Lake Rancheria, 380-382
Bridgeport Paiute Indian Colony, 382-383
Buena Vista Rancheria, 383
Cabazon Band of Mission Indians, 384-385
Cahuilla peoples, 386-387
California Valley, 387
Campo, 388-389
Capitan Grande, 390
Cedarville Rancheria, 390-391
Chemehuevi Indian Tribe, 391-393
Chicken Ranch Rancheria, 393
Chico, 394-395
Cloverdale, 395
Cold Springs, 396-397
Colusa, 397-398
Cortina Rancheria, 398-399
Coyote Valley, 400-403
Dry Creek Rancheria, 403-404
Elem Indian Colony, 404-406
Elk Valley Rancheria, 406-407
Enterprise, 408
Ewiiaapaayp Band, 409-410
Fort Bidwill, 410-411
Fort Independence, 411-412
Fort Mojave, 412-414
Graton, 415
Greenville, 416-417
Grindstone Rancheria, 417-418
Guidiville, 418
history, 359-360
Hoopa Valley Tribe, 419-421
Hopland Band, 422-423
Inaja-Cosmit Band, 424
Indian cultures listed, 360-363
Ione Band, 425
Jackson Band, 426
Jamul Indian Village, 427-428
Karuk Tribe, 428-430
La Jolla Band, 430-431
La Posta Band, 431-432
Laytonville, 432-433
Likely, 434
Lone Pine, 434-435
Lookout, 435-436
Los Coyotes, 436-437
Lower Lake, 437-438
Manchester Point, 438
Manzanita, 439-440
map, 358
Mesa Grande, 440
Middletown, 441-442
Montgomery Creek, 442
Mooretown, 443
Morongo, 444-445
North Fork, 448

Pala, 447-448
Paskenta Band, 448
Pauma, 449-450
Pechanga, 450-451
Picayune, 452-453
Pinoleville, 453-454
Pit River, 454-455
Potter Valley Rancheria, 455-456
Quartz Valley Indian Community, 456-457
Ramona Band, 457
Redding, 458-459
Redwood Valley, 459-460
Resighini Rancheria, 460-461
Rincon Band, 461-462
Roaring Creek Rancheria, 463
Robinson Rancheria Tribe, 463-465
Rohnerville, 465-466
Round Valley Tribes, 466-468
Rumsey Rancheria, 468-469
San Manuel Band, 470-471
San Pasqual Band, 472-473
Santa Rosa Indian Community, 473-474
Santa Ynez Band, 475-476
Santa Ysabel Band, 477
Scotts Valley Band, 478
Sherwood Valley Rancheria, 479-481
Shingle Springs Rancheria, 481-482
Smith River Rancheria, 482-483
Soboba Band, 484-485
Susanville Indian Rancheria, 485-487
Sycuan Band, 487-488
Table Bluff, 489-490
Table Mountain Rancheria, 490
Timbisha Shoshone Band, 491-492
Torres Martinez Desert Cahuilla Indians, 492-493
Trinidad Rancheria, 493-495
Tule River Tribe, 495-496
Tuolumne, 496-497
Twenty-Nine Palms Band, 498
United Auburn Indian Community, 499-500
Upper Lake, 500-501
Viejas Band, 501-503
X-L Ranch, 506
Yurok, 506-508
California Valley Miwok Tribe, 387
Calista Corporation (Calista), 21-23
Camas Institute, 971
Campo Band of Kumeyaay, 388-389
Camp Verde, 288-292
Caniqaq. See Chanega
Cantwell, 10, 69
Capitan Grande, Viejas Band of Kumeyaay Indians, 390
Carson Colony, 684-685
Casinos. See Gaming entries
Caswell Native Association, 26
Catawba Indian Nation, 913-914
Cattaraugus (Seneca Nation), 778-779
Cayuga (Seneca Nation), 775-776, 779-780
Cayuse, 904-907
CCI Inc., 19
Cedarville Rancheria (CA), 390-391
Celilo Village, 884-885
Central Arizona Project (CAP, 1968), 304
Central Council of the Tlingit and Haida Indian Tribes, 36
Chalkyitsik, 70
Chaluka Corp., 12, 194
Chanega, Native Village of, 71-72
Chasta. See Shasta
Cheesh-Na, 10, 72-73

Chefarnrmute Inc., 22, 73
Chefornak, 22, 73-74
Chefornok. See Chefornak
Chehalis, 996-999, 1002-1003
Confederated Tribes, 959-961
Chemehuevi Indian Tribe, 294-297, 360, 391-393, 444-445
Chenega. See Chanega
Cher-ae Heights Indian Community of the Trinidad Rancheria, 493-495
Cherokee Nation, 808-816
Eastern Band of Cherokee Indians, 789-791
United Keetoowah Band, 875-877
Cherokee National Youth Choir, 815-816
Cherokee Nation Distributors, 811
Cherokee Nation Enterprises (CNE), 810
Cherokee Nation History Course (Oklahoma), 813-814
Cherokee Nation v. Georgia (1831), 809
Cherokee Tribal Sanitation Program, 790-791
Chevak, 74-75
Chevak Company Corporation, 74
Cheyenne-Arapaho Tribes of Oklahoma, 816-817
Cheyenne River Sioux Tribe, 915-919
Cheyenne Tribe, Northern, 667-669
Chickaloon-Moose Creek Creek Native Association, 26, 75-76
Chickasaw Nation, 818-824
Chickasaw Nation Industries, 819
Chicken Ranch Rancheria, 393
Chico Rancheria, 394-395
Chignik (Bay), 19, 78
Chignik Lagoon, 79
Chignik Lake, 80
Chignik River Ltd., 80
Chilkat, 81
Chilkoot Indian Association, 82-83
Chilula peoples, 360
Chinik (Golovin), 85
Chinook, 996-999, 1002-1003
Chinuruk Inc., 22, 191, 277
Chippewa-Cree Tribe, 670-671
Chippewa Flowage, 1040-1042
Chippewa Indians, 613-617. See also Anishinabe
Bad River Band, 1031-1033
Bay Mills, 581-582
Bois Forte Band, 605-607
Fond du Lac Band, 607-611
Grand Portage, 611-613
Grand Traverse Band, 583-586
Isabella, 590-591
Lac Courte Oreilles, 1038-1042
Lac du Flambeau, 1042-1045
Lac Vieux Desert, 592-593
Lake Superior Band, 593
L'Anse, 593-594
Leech Lake Band, 613-617
Mille Lacs Band, 619-625
Mole Lake, 1051-1053
Ojibwe Language Program, 623-624
Red Cliff, 1057-1059
Red Lake Band, 627-629
Rocky Boy's Reservation, 670-671
St. Croix Chippewa, 1059-1062
Sault Ste. Marie Tribe, 602-604
Turtle Mountain, 799-801
White Earth Band, 635-640
Chistochina. See Cheesh-Na
Chitimacha Tribe of Louisiana, 559-560
Chitina, 10, 86-87
Chiulista Camp Services Inc., 22

Choctaw Nation of Oklahoma, 562-563, 641-648, 824-827
Choggiung Ltd., 19, 92
Chuathbaluk, 22
Chugach Alaska Corporation (CAC), 23-25
Chugachigmuit Alutiiq, 179-180, 265-266
Chugash, 7, 227-229
Chuka Chukmasi Home Loan Program (OK), 822-824
Chukchansi, 452-453, 490
Chulloonawick, 37
Chuloonawick, 22. See also Zero population villages
Chumash peoples, 360, 475-476
Circle, 88-89
Citizen Potawatomi Community Development Corporation, 830
Citizen Potawatomi Nation, 828-831
Clark's Point, 19, 89-90
Clarus Technologies, 30
Climate. See individual tribes
Cloverdale Rancheria of Pomo Indians, 395
Coal mining
        Alaska, 10, 16
        Arizona, 317
        leasing, 654
        Montana, 654, 666, 668
        New Mexico, 761
        Oklahoma, 811
        reserves, 668
        South Dakota, 917
        Utah, 955
Coast Indian Community (CA), 460
Cochiti Pueblo, 720-722
Cocopah Tribe, 292-294
Coeur d'Alene Basin Restoration Project, 536
Coeur d'Alene Tribal Wellness Center, 537-538
Coeur d'Alene Tribe, 533-538
Cold Springs Rancheria, 396-397
Colorado, 509-512, 512-516
Colorado River Indian Tribes, 294-297
Colusa Indian Community, 397-398
Colville, Confederated Tribes, 961-964
Comanche Tribe of Oklahoma, 831-833
Commercial development. See individual tribes
Communications. See also Telecommunications
        cellular towers, 420, 472
        companies, 836, 917, 939, 1048, 1058
Communities, Alaska, special considerations, 35-36, 39
Community facilities and services. See individual tribes
Concow, 443, 466-468
Confederated Salish and Kootenai Tribes (CSKT), 655-660
Confederated Tribes and Bands of the Yakama Nation, 1026-1030
Confederated Tribes of Coos, Lower Umpqua, and Siuslaw Indians, 885-887
Confederated Tribes of Siletz Indians of Oregon, 901-903
Confederated Tribes of the Chehalis Reservation, 959-961
Connecticut, 517-519, 519-521
Construction
        Arizona, 295
        companies
                Alaska, 10, 15, 16, 18, 22, 23, 24, 26, 32, 35, 75, 79, 87, 90, 93, 109, 113, 119, 196, 212
                California, 379, 381, 389, 392, 413, 490, 496
                Colorado, 510, 514

Idaho, 540
Kansas/Nebraska, 553
Michigan, 582, 587, 594, 603
Minnesota, 612, 628
Montana, 657
Nebraska, 678
Nevada, 687, 689, 703, 704
New Mexico, 734-735, 743
New York, 785
North Carolina, 790
North Dakota, 794-795, 800
Oklahoma, 805, 806, 845
Oregon, 888, 895, 908
South Carolina, 914
South Dakota, 925, 928
Texas, 948
Utah, 957
Washington state, 960, 963, 967, 986, 1009, 1021
Wisconsin, 1044, 1047, 1060
Wyoming, 1066
        Florida, 525
Constructors Inc., ASRC, 14
Cook Inlet Region, Incorporated (CIRI), 25-27
Coos (Confederated Tribes), 885-887
Copper
        Alaska, 10
Copper Center. See Kluti Kaah
Coquille Indian Tribal Community, 887-891
Cordova. See Eyak
Corporations
        Consolidated Borough of Quil Ceda Village (WA), 1020-1021
Corrections Project Department of Behavorial Health Services (Navajo Nation), 341-342
Cortina Indian Rancheria, 398-399
Council, 37
Council Native Corp., 18
Coushatta Tribe of Louisiana, 561, 804-805
Cow Creek Band of Umpqua Tribe of Indians, 892-893
Cowlitz Indian Tribe, 964-965, 996-999
Coyote Valley Band of Pomo Indians, 400-403
Craig, 34, 90-91
Credit unions. See Finance, credit unions
Cree, 670-671
Creek Nation
        Miccosukee Indians, 531-532
        Poarch Creek Band, 1-2
        Removal of 1836, 1
        Thlopthlocco Creek Tribal Town, 872-873
Creek Nation of Oklahoma, 834
        Alabama Quassarte, 804-805
CRIT. See TOC
Crooked Creek, 22, 91-92
Crow Creek Sioux Tribe, 920-921
Crow Nation, 653-655
CSKT. See Confederated Salish and Kootenai Tribes
Cully Corp., 14, 226
Cultural preservation
        Archaeology Department Training Programs, Window Rock, Flagstaff, AZ and Farmington, NM, 338-339
        Cherokee National Youth Choir, 815-816
        Cherokee Nation History Course (Oklahoma), 813-814
        Honoring Our Ancestors: Chippewa Flowage Joint Agency Plan (Chippewa), 1040-1042
        Lac du Flambeau Band, 1043
        Menominee Community Center of Chicago,

1049-1051
        Ojibwe Language Program (Mille Lacs Band), 623-624
        Poeh Cultural Center (Pueblo of Pojoaque), 745-746
        Southwest Oregon Research Project (Coquille Tribe), 890-891
        Tsa La Gi (Cherokee) Heritage Center, 811
        Ya Ne Dah Ah School, 76-77
Cupeño peoples, 360-361, 436-437, 444-445, 447-448
Cup'ik, 8
Curyung, 92-93
Cuyapaipe, 409-410
Cu-Yui Ticutta, 700-702

Dakota, Mdewakanton, 630-632
Danzhit Hanlaii Corp., 88
Death Valley Timbisha Shoshone Band, 491-492
Deering, 94
Deg Het'an, 7
Deg Xinag, 7, 257-258
Delaware Nation, 837, 877-878
Delaware Tribe of Oklahoma, 838
Deloycheet Inc., 28, 117
Demographics. See individual tribes
Dena'ina Athabascan, 7
        Aniak, 57-58
        Chickaloon, 75-76
        Eklutna, 100
        Iliamna, 124-125
        Knik, 146-147
        Lime Village, 164
        Ninilchik, 195-197
        Nondalton, 200-201
        Pedro Bay, 216-217
        Red Devil, 240-241
        Salamatof, 244-245
        Seldovia Village, 250
        Tyonek, 275
Dendu Gwich'in Tribe, 66-67
Devil's Lake, 796-798
Diegueño, 361, 477. See also Kumeyaay peoples
Dillingham, 19
Diné. See Navajo Nation
Diné College, 332
Dineega Corp., 28, 242
Dinyea Corp., 28, 260
Diomede, Native Village of, 95
Diomede Native Corporation, 18, 95
Dot Lake, 96
Douglass. See urban tribes
DOWL LLC, 32
Doyon, Limited (Doyon), 28-29
Dresslerville Colony, 685-686
Dry Creek Rancheria, 403-404
Duck Valley Shoshone Paiute Indians, 686-688
Duckwater Shoshone Tribe, 689
Dutch Harbor. See Qawalangin

Eagle, 97
Eagle Electric LLC, 18
Eagle Village, 28
Eastern Band of Cherokee Indians, 789-791
Eastern Shawnee Tribe of Oklahoma, 838-839
Eastern Shoshone Tribe (WY), 1065-1067
Economic Development Corporation (Ho-Chunk, Inc.), 680-682
Economic development programs
        Quil Ceda Village (WA), 1023-1024

Economic entities, 35
Education, 76-77. See also individual tribes; Tribal
    colleges
    Alamo Navajo School Board, 720
    Camas Institute, 971
    Navajo Studies Department, Rough Rock   Com-
        munity School, 334
    Rosebud (Sioux) Tribal Education Department
        and Education Code, 937-938
    Two Plus Two Program, Hopi Junior/Senior
        High School (AZ), 320-321
    Ya Ne Dah Ah School, 76-77
Eek, 22, 98
Egegik, 19, 99-100
Eight Northern Indian Pueblos Council (ENIPC), 739,
    763
Eklutna, 26, 100
Ekuk, 19, 37. See also Zero population villages
Ekwok, 19, 101
Elders Cultural Advisory Council, Forest Resources
    (AZ), 350-351
Elem Indian Colony, 404-406
Elim, 18, 102
Elko Colony, 690-691
Elk Valley Tolowa Tribe, 406-407
Elwha, Lower, 971-973
Ely Shoshone Tribe, 691-692
Emmonak, 22, 103
Energy. See also Natural gas; Oil and gas
    Alaska
        general considerations, 5
        biomass, 1061
        bulk fuels, 151, 844, 1061
        companies, 929
        gasoline, wholesale, 739
        geothermal, 760
        hydroelectricity, 122
        renewable
            Arizona, 323, 324
            Colorado, 14
            New York, 777
            Oklahoma, 844, 848, 861
            Wisconsin, 1040, 1061
            wind, 652
Engineering and technology
    Alaska, 10, 14, 15, 19, 20, 22, 24, 28, 30, 32,
        35, 87, 113
English Bay, 24, 179-180
Enterprise Rancheria, 408
Environmental concerns
    biomass resources, 629
    brownfields pilot project, 833
    Coyote Valley Tribal EPA (CA), 402-403
    insecticide pollution, 377
    Minnesota 1837 Ceded Territory Conservation
        Code, 623
    Navajo Nation, 333-334
    San Carlos Apaches, 349
    Snoqualmie Preservation Protection Initiative
        (WA), 1007
    Walatowa Woodlands Initiative, 725
    water pollution, 568, 574, 599
    Water Quality Standards (Pueblo of Sandia),
        756
    water supplies (KS), 554
    Yukaana Development Corporation, Louden
        Tribal Council (AK), 110-112
Eskimo, negative connotation of, 39
European impact, 359
Evansville, 28, 104
Ewiiaapaayp Band of Kumeyaay Indians, 409-410

Eyak, Native Village of, 24, 105-106

Fairbanks, 38, 55
Fairbanks Native Association, 55
Fallon Paiute-Shoshone Tribe, 692-694
False Pass, 106-107
Far West Inc., 19, 78
Federal, ASRC, 14
Federal government contractors, Alaska, 12, 14, 15, 18,
    19, 20, 24, 30, 32, 35
Finance
    asset management, 15, 28, 136, 488, 511, 678
    banks, 503, 504-505, 621, 658, 820, 829-830,
        929, 994, 1027, 1056
    credit unions, 631, 651, 826
    consortium, 484
Fire fighting
    Native American Fire Fighters Apprenticeship
        Program, 309
Fisheries
    aquaculture, 974, 979, 986, 1016
    Arizona, 299
        fish farms, 307
        commercial
            Alaska, 41, 43, 47, 73, 78, 91, 99, 103,
                106, 119, 127, 128, 151, 160, 169, 172,
                175, 196
            Michigan, 596, 603
            Minnesota, 615, 628
            North Carolina, 790
            Washington state, 972, 988, 998, 1012
    development of, 183, 928, 941, 994, 1034
    fishing fleets, 974
    fishing rights, 968, 990, 991, 994
    hatcheries, 420, 496, 507, 543, 545, 578, 593,
        612, 615, 636, 700, 721, 737, 750, 888, 925,
        950, 963, 966, 972, 974, 979, 982, 984, 986,
        988, 998, 1004, 1009, 1014, 1021, 1025, 1039,
        1044, 1058
    Jamestown Seafood (WA), 968
    laboratories, 985
    Oklahoma, 820, 826
    Oregon, 9-2
    oyster farming, 71, 968
    Utah, 950
    Washington state, 1002, 1027
    whaling, 979
    Wildlife and Fisheries Management Program
        (New Mexico), 729, 733
    Wisconsin, 1032, 1060
Five Civilized Tribes, 805
Flandreau Santee Sioux Tribe, 922-923
Flathead Reservation, 655-660
Florida, 523-525
    Big Cypress, 526-527
    Brighton, 527
    Fort Pierce, 528
    Hollywood, 528-529
    Immokalee, 529
    Miccosukee, 530-531
    Seminole Tribe of, 523-524
    Tampa, 531
Fond du Lac Band of Lake Superior Chippewa, 607-
    611
Food enterprises
    neida Community Integrated Food System
        (OCIFS), 1055
Forest County Potawatomi Indians, 1033-1035
Forestry. See also Timber
    commercial enterprises
        Arizona, 299, 348, 495

California, 411, 420, 467, 507
Colorado, 510
Idaho, 545
Maine, 573
Michigan, 594
Minnesota, 636
Montana, 657, 668, 670
Nebraska, 677
New Mexico, 279, 723, 724
Oklahoma, 811
Washington state, 1024
Elders Cultural Advisory Council, Forest
    Resources (AZ), 350-351
forest products industries, 628, 636, 668, 736,
    741, 747, 811, 826, 908, 962, 1009, 1027,
    1034, 1038, 1039, 1047, 1060, 1063
forest products industries, Alaska, 10, 90, 91,
    119, 128, 136
Navajo Nation, 329
New Mexico, 718
New York, 788
Oregon, 908
South Dakota, 932
Washington state, 1021
Wisconsin, 1032, 1034
Fort Apache, 298-302
Fort Apache Timber Company, 299
Fort Belknap Indian Community, Gros Ventre and
    Assiniboine Tribes, 661-663
Fort Berthold, Affiliated Tribes, 793-796
Fort Bidwill Indian Community of Paiute Indians, 410-
    411
Fort Hall, 538-541
Fort Independence Paiute Indians, 411-412
Fort McDermitt Paiute and Shoshone Tribe, 694-695
Fort McDowell Yavapai Nation, 303-304
Fort Mojave, 412-414
    See also California
Fort Peck Assiniboine and Sioux Tribes, 664-666
Fort Pierce Seminoles, 528
Fort Sill Apache Tribe of Oklahoma, 840-842
Fort Totten. See Spirit Lake
Fort Yukon, 28, 107-108
Fort Yuma-Quechan Tribe, 305-306
Fox, and Sac, 549-550, 557-558
Foxwoods Resort Casino (CT), 518
Frontier Systems Integrator LLC, 30
FSSI, 15

Gakona, 10, 108-109
Galena, 28, 109-112
Gambell, 18, 112-113
Gaming, Alabama
    casinos, 2
    revenue use, 2
Gaming, Arizona
    Bingo, 293, 353
    casino resorts, 287, 290, 291, 295, 296, 299,
        304, 307, 308, 348, 356
    casinos, 287, 290, 305, 307, 343, 346, 353
    commissions, 289
    compacts, 293, 303, 307, 346, 355
    development of, 303
    Florida
        Bingo, 524
        casino resorts, 524
        casinos, 524, 528, 529
        revenue use, 524
    revenue use, 287, 290, 307, 355
Gaming, California
    Bingo, 393, 464, 470

casino resorts, 364, 367, 370, 376, 384, 392, 413, 426, 462, 469, 488
casinos, 365, 370, 375, 379, 380, 387, 389, 393, 398, 400, 404, 407, 420, 423, 455, 458, 464, 470, 472, 476, 480, 483, 484, 490, 494, 496, 497, 498, 499
    development of, 375, 383, 394, 395, 405, 408, 415, 418, 425, 465, 478, 482, 491
commissions, 365, 458, 476
compacts, 409, 486, 491, 492
    development of, 477
revenue use, 367, 381, 385, 426
Gaming, Colorado
    casino resorts, 510, 514
    revenue use, 514
Gaming, Connecticut
    casino resorts, 518, 520
Gaming, Florida
    casino resorts, 530, 531
    casinos, 527
Gaming, Idaho
    casino resorts, 534, 543, 545
    casinos, 539
    revenue use, 545
Gaming, Iowa
    Bingo, 550
    casino resorts, 550
Gaming, Kansas
    Bingo, 555
    casino resorts, 555, 558
    casinos, 551, 553, 558
    compacts, 555
    revenue use, 553, 556
Gaming, Louisiana
    casino resorts, 561
    casinos, 560, 562, 564
    compacts, 562
    development of, 560
Gaming, Maine
    Bingo, 565, 573
Gaming, Michigan
    Bingo, 583
    casino resorts, 582, 583, 587, 591, 593, 594, 596, 603, 627
    casinos, 582, 583, 594, 598, 602-603
    compacts, 589, 596, 601
    development of, 588-589, 596, 600
    revenue use, 587, 631
Gaming, Minnesota
    casino resorts, 606, 608, 612, 615, 618, 620, 626, 628, 631, 633, 636
    casinos, 628
    commissions, 630-631
    development of, 615
    revenue use, 612, 620, 626
Gaming, Montana
    casino resorts, 657
    casinos, 651, 654, 668, 670
Gaming, Nebraska
    casinos, 674, 677, 678
Gaming, Nevada
    casinos, 699
    development of, 687
Gaming, New Mexico
    casino resorts, 737, 754
    casinos, 718, 723, 729, 734, 739, 740, 743, 748-749, 754, 757, 760, 763, 765
    compacts, 329
    development of, 329, 739
Gaming, New York
    Bingo, 775, 776, 777, 781
    casino resorts, 776, 781

casinos, 776, 777, 780, 785
    development of, 780
    revenue use, 776
Gaming, North Carolina
    casino resorts, 790
Gaming, North Dakota, 794
    casino resorts, 797, 800
Gaming, Oklahoma
    Bingo, 806, 817, 835, 839, 872
    casino resorts, 830, 867
    casinos, 803-804, 817, 819-820, 826, 829, 832, 835, 837, 839, 841, 844, 849, 850, 852, 854, 856, 858, 862, 868, 870, 872, 873, 874, 876
    commissions, 862
    development of, 807, 829
    horseracing, 826
    revenue use, 826, 832, 876
Gaming, Oregon
    casino resorts, 888, 892, 902, 905
    casinos, 883, 886, 895, 900
    revenue use, 888, 895, 900, 905
Gaming, Rhode Island
    development of, 912
Gaming, South Carolina
    Bingo, 914
Gaming, South Dakota
    casino resorts, 923, 928, 939, 941
    casinos, 925, 932, 935
Gaming, Texas
    casinos, 946
    development of, 944
Gaming, Washington state
    Bingo, 960, 963, 979, 994
    casino resorts, 997-998, 1009-1010, 1025
    casinos, 960, 963, 968, 970, 974, 982, 984, 985, 986, 988, 991, 1003, 1004, 1012, 1014, 1016, 1027
    compacts, 1023
    development of, 965, 966, 979, 1006
    leasing slot machines, 972
    revenue use, 960, 982, 1012
Gaming, Wisconsin
    Bingo, 1044
    casino resorts, 1032, 1034, 1036, 1039, 1044, 1047, 1052, 1056, 1060
    casinos, 1034, 1036, 1052, 1056, 1058, 1060, 1063
    compacts, 1034, 1036
    development of, 1036, 1058
    revenue use, 1034, 1044, 1052, 1056
Gaming, Wyoming
    Bingo, 1066
Gana'A' Yoo Ltd., 28, 109, 133, 155, 206-207
Gay Head (Wampanoag Tribe), 577-579
GCR. See Grand Canyon Resort Corporation
George Islands, 234
Georgetown, 22, 113
Gila River Pima-Maricopa Indian Community (GRIC), 306-313
Gila River Telecommunications (Chandler, AZ), 312-313
GIS
    Jamestown Geographic Information Systems, 967
Gold
    Utah, 955
Goldbelt Inc., 34
Golden Glacier Inc., 18
Golovin Native Corp., 18, 85
Goodnews Bay, 22, 114
Goshute Reservation, Confederated Tribes of, 949-

950, 952-953
Goverment Reform, Diné Appropriate Government program, 339-340
Governance, local
    Goverment Reform, Diné Appropriate
Government program, 339-340
    Tax Initiative, Economic Development, Kayenta Township Commission (Navajo Nation), 335-336
Government. See individual tribes
Government as employer. See individual tribes
Graduation rates. See individual tribes
Grand Canyon Resort Corporation (GCR), 322
Grand Portage Tribe, 611-613
Grand Ronde, Confederated Tribes of the, 893-898
Grand Traverse Band of Ottawa and Chippewa Indians, 583-586
Graton Rancheria, 415
Grayling, 28, 115
Great Sioux Nation. See Sioux
Greenville Rancheria, 416-417
GRIC. See Gila River Pima-Maricopa Indian Community
Grindstone Indian Rancheria of Wintun-Wailuki Indians, 417-418
Gros Ventre Tribe, 661-663
Guidiville, 418
Gulkana, 10, 116
Gwich'in Athabascan, 7, 278-280
Gwitchyaa Zhee Corp., 28, 107

Habematolel Pomo Indians of Upper Lake, 500-501
Haida, 8, 34
    Craig, 90-91
    Hydaburg, 122-123
    Kasigluk, 135-136
Haines. See Chilkoot
Hamilton, 22. See also Zero population villages
Ha[:]n, 7
Hannahville Indian Community, 586-587
Harvard Project on American Indian Economic Development. See Honoring Nations Honorees
Haudenosaunee, 782-783. See also Seneca Nation
Havasupai Tribe, 314-316
Havasuw 'Baaja. See Havasupai Tribe
Health care
    Institutionalized Quality Improvement Program, Puyallup Tribal Health Authority (WA), 992
    Pharmacy On-Line Billing Initiative (Fond du Lac Chippewa), 610-611
    wellness centers (ID), 537-538
    White Earth Suicide Intervention Team, 639-640
    Winnebago Health Care Center, 1037
Healy Lake (Healy Fork), 28, 117
Hee-Yea-Lingde Corp., 28, 115
Hidatsa, 793-796
History. See individual tribes
Ho-Chungras. See Winnebago
Ho-Chunk, Inc. (Winnebago Tribe of Nebraska), 678, 680-682
Ho-Chunk Nation, 678, 680-682, 1035-1037
Hoh Indian Tribe, 965-966, 996-999
Holikachuk, 7, 115. See also Grayling
Hollywood Seminoles, 528-529
Holy Cross, 28, 117-118
Honeybucket, 39
Honoring Nations Honorees
    Cherokee, 813-814, 815-816
    Cheyenne River, 919
    Chickaloon, 76-77

Chickasaw, 822-824
Chilkoot, 83-84
Choctaw, 644-645, 645-646, 647-648
Coeur d'Alene Tribe, 537-538
Coquille, 890-891
Coyote Valley, 402-403
Eastern Band of Cherokee, 790-791
Flathead, 659-660
Fond du Lac, 609-610, 610-611
Fort Apache, 301-302
Galena, 110-112
Gila River, 309-311, 311-312, 312-313
Grand Ronde, 897-898
Grand Traverse, 585, 585-586
Hopi, 320-321
Jicarilla Apache, 733
Kake, 129-130
Lac Courte Oreilles, 1040-1042
Lummi, 976-977
Menominee, 1049-1051
Mille Lacs, 623, 623-624, 624-625
Navajo, 334, 334-335, 335-336, 336-337, 338-339, 339-340, 341-342
Nez Perce, 547
Pojoaque, 745-746
Puyallup, 992
Rosebud, 936-937
San Carlos Apache, 350-351
Sandia Pueblo, 756
Swinomish, 1018-1019
Tulalip, 1023-1024
Viejas Band, 504-505
White Earth, 639-640
Winnebago, 680-682
Yakama, 1029-1030
Zuni, 771-773, 773-774
Honoring Our Ancestors: Chipppewa Flowage Joint
    Agency Plan (Chippewa), 1040-1042
Hoonah, 34, 118-119
Hoopa Valley Tribe, 419-421
Hoopa-Yurok Settlement Act, 506-507
Hooper Bay, 22, 119-120
Hopi People, 294-297, 316-321
Hopland Band of Pomo Indians, 422-423
Houlton Band of Maliseet Indians, 569-570
Houston/NANA LLC, 32
Hualapai Indians, 322-324
Hughes, 28, 120-121
Humboldt, 428-430
Huna Totem Corp., 34, 118
Hungwitchin Corp., 28, 97
Hunkpapa, 937-940
Hupa peoples, 361, 380-382, 419-421
Huron Potawatomi Indians, 588-589
Huslia, 28, 121-122
Hydaburg, 34, 122-123
Idaho, 533-538, 538-541, 542-543, 544-547
Idaho Gray Wolf Recovery Program, 546-547
Iditarod sled races, 115
Igiugig, 19, 123-124
'Iipay-Tipai, 366-368
Iliamna, 19, 124-125, 200-201
Iliamna Village Council, 124
Ilikista Ventures Inc., 22
Immokalee, 529
Inaja-Cosmit Band of Mission Indians, 424
Inalik. See Diomede, Native Village of
Inchelium Wood Treatment Plant (WA), 962
Indian Reorganization Act of 1934. See individual tribes
Indian Township (Passamaquoddy Tribe), 571-572
Industrial parks
    developed, 1044

Arizona, 288-289, 295, 299, 307-308,
    318, 329-330, 353, 356
California, 373
Colorado, 515
Florida, 527
Michigan, 594
Minnesota, 636
Montana, 651, 662, 666
Navajo Nation, 329-330
New Mexico, 329-330, 737, 768
New York, 778
Oklahoma, 807, 811, 826, 845, 856, 867, 868
South Dakota, 925
Utah, 956
Washington state, 1021, 1027
    undeveloped
Arizona, 307, 314, 348
California, 379, 467, 496
Idaho, 535
Michigan, 584
Montana, 668
Nevada, 710
New Mexico, 743
Oklahoma, 804
Oregon, 902, 905, 909
Washington state, 970, 1009, 1016
Wisconsin, 1048
Infrastructure
    Safe, Clean Waters, Lummi Tribal Sewer and
    Water District (WA), 976-977
Ingalik Athabascan, 7
    Anvik, 59
    Chuathbaluk, 87-88
    Crooked Creek, 91-92
    Grayling, 115
    Holy Cross, 117-118
    Shageluk, 251
    Takotna, 262-263
Ingalit. See Ingalik Athabascan
Inn of the Gods Resort, 736
Institutionalized Quality Improvement Program, Puyallup
    Tribal Health Authority (WA), 992
Integrated Concepts and Research Corp. (ICRC), 30
Intergovernmental Affairs Dept., Confederated Tribes of
Grand Ronde (OR), 87-898
Inter-Tribal Bison Cooperative, 741
Intertribal corporations
    California, 470, 502
    construction
        SIKU-NYA (AZ), 291
    fisheries, 596-597
    Oklahoma, 807
    real estate development, 1034
    Wisconsin, 1043, 1047, 1052, 1054
Intertribal Information Technology Company, 820
Inuit Services Inc., 18
Inupiaq. See Inupiat
Inupiat, 7-8
    Ambler, 53-54
    Atqasuk, 63-64
    Barrow, 64-65
    Buckland, 68
    Chinik, 85
    Community of the Arctic Slope, 36
    Deering, 94
    Diomede, Native Village of, 95
    Elim, 102
    Kaktovik, 131
    King Salmon, 140-142
    Kobuk, 147-148
    Kotzebue, 152-153

Noatak, Native Village of, 197-198
Nome, 198-200
Nuiqsut, 204-205
Point Lay, 226-227
Selawik, 249-250
Shaktoolik, 252
Shishmaref, 253-254
Shungnak, 255-256
Solomon, 258
Teller, 268
Unalakleet, 277-278
Wainwright, 280-281
Wales, 281-282
White Mountain, 282-283
zero population villages, 37-38
Ione Band of Miwok Indians, 425
Iowa (state), 549-550
Iowa Tribe of Kansas and Nebraska, 551-552
Iowa Tribe of Oklahoma, 842-846
Iqfijouaq Co., 22, 98
Iqurmiut, 125-126
Iroquois Confederacy, 775
Irrigation. See also Agriculture
    Colorado, 513-514
    lands (AZ), 293, 295, 305
    lands (CA), 413
    lands (MT), 665
    lands (NM), 718, 722, 729, 739, 741, 750, 752,
    759, 763, 765
    lands (NV), 687, 689, 693, 708
    lands (OR), 883
    lands (SD), 921
    lands (UT), 952
    lands (WA), 962, 1027
    leasing, 304, 539
Isabella, 590-591
Isanotski Corp., 106
Isleta Pueblo, 722-724
Ivanof Bay, 19, 127
Ivanof Bay Village Council, 127

Jackson Band of Miwuk Indians, 426
Jamestown Geographic Information Systems, 967
Jamestown Seafood, 968
Jamestown S'Klallam Tribe of Washington, 966-968
Jamul Indian Village, 427-428
Jemez Pueblo, 724-726
Jena Band of Choctaw (LA), 562-563
Jicarilla Apache Nation, 727-733
JKT Construction, 967
John F. Kennedy School of Government. See
    Honoring Nations Honoree
Juneau, 34. See also Urban tribes
Kaguyak, 30, 37. See also Zero population villages
Kaibab Paiute Indians, 324-325
Kake, City of, 34, 128-130
Kake, Organized Village of, 128-130
Kake Circle Peacemaking, Organized Village of Kake,
    129-130
Kake Tribal Corporation, 128
Kakivik Asset Management LLC, 19
Kaktovik, City of, 131
Kaktovik, Native Village of, 131
Kaktovik Inupiat Corp., 14, 131
Kalapuya, 893-898
Kalispel Indians, 969-971
Kalskag, City of Upper, 22, 132-133
Kalskag, Village of, 132-133
Kalskag (Lower). See Lower Kalskag
Kalskag (Upper). See Upper Kalskag
Kaltag, City of, 28, 133-134
Kaltag, Village of, 28, 133-134

Kanatak, 37. See also Zero population villages
Kansas, 551-552, 552-554, 554-557, 557-558
Karluk, Native Village of, 30, 134-135
Karuk Tribe of California, 361, 428-430
Kasaan, City of, 34, 135-136
Kasaan, Organized Village of, 135-136
Kashunamiut. See Chevak
Kasigluk, Native Village of, 22, 136-137
Ka-ta-kas. See Apache
Katishtya, 748-749
Kauwerak Eskimos, 67-68
Kauweramiut, 8
Kavilco Inc., 34, 135
Kawaiisu peoples, 361
Kaw Nation, 847-849
KDC (Koniag Development Corp.), 30
Keetoowah, United, 875-877
Keewenaw Bay Indian Community, 592, 593-594
Kelsey, C. E., 459, 500
Kenai. See urban tribes
Kenaitze. See urban tribes
Keresan
        Acoma, 717-719
        Laguna, 734-735
        San Felipe, 748-749
        Santa Ana, 756-758
        Santo Domingo, 761-762
        Zia, 767-768
Ketchikan, 137-139, 247
Keweenaw Bay. See L'Anse
Kiana, City of, 139-140
Kiana, Native Village of, 139-140
Kickapoo Traditional Tribe of Texas, 945-947
Kickapoo Tribe of Kansas, 552-554
Kickapoo Tribe of Oklahoma, 850-851
Kijik Corp., 19, 200
Kikiallus, 1015-1019
Kikiktagruk Inupiat Corp., 152
Ki LLC, 12, 32
King Cove (Agdaagux Tribe), 12, 42-43
Kingigin. See Wales
King Island, 18, 37. See also Zero population villages
King Salmon Tribe, 19, 140-142
Kiowa Tribe of Oklahoma, 851. See also Apache
Kipnuk, Native Village of, 22, 142-143
Kitanemuk peoples, 361
Kivalina, City of, 143-144
Kivalina, Native Village of, 143-144
Klallam, 971-973
Klamath Tribes, 898-900
Klawock, City of, 34, 144-145
Klawock Cooperative Association, 144
Klukwan (Chilkat), 34, 81
Kluti-Kaah, 10, 145-146
Knikatnu Inc., 26, 146
Knik-Fairview. See Knik
Knik Tribal Council, 26, 146-147
Knugank, 19
Koachxana-aalow, 283
Kobuk, 49, 120-121, 147-148
        Hughes, 120-121
Kodiak, 30. See also Urban tribes
Kokarmuit Corp., 22, 46
Kokhanok Village, 19, 148-149
Ko-kwell, 887-891
Kokyukon Athabascan, 104
Koliganek, 19, 187
Kongiganak, Native Village of, 22, 149-150
Kongniglkilnomuit, 22
Koniag, Incorporated (Koniag), 29-31
Koniagmiut Alutiiq, 229-230
Koniag peoples, 7, 79, 134, 161

Kootenai County, Idaho, 533
Kootenai Tribe of Idaho, 533-538, 542-543
Kootenai Tribes, Confederated, 655-660
Kootznoowoo, 34, 56-57
Kotlik, City of, 22, 150-152
Kotlik, Village of, 150-152
Kotzebue, City of, 152-153
Kotzebue, Native Village of, 152-153
Kowagmiut Inupiat, 139-140, 143-144, 201-202
Kowagniut, 53-54
K'oyitl'ots'ina corporations, 28, 48, 52, 120, 121, 186
Koyuk, City of, 18, 154-155
Koyuk, Native Village of, 154-155
Koyukon Athabascan, 7
        Allakaket Village, 52-53
        Galena, 109-112
        Hughes, 120-121
        Huslia, 121-122
        Kaltag, 133-134
        Koyukuk, 155-156
        Manley Hot Springs, 166-167
        New Allakaket, 186
        Nulato, 206-207
        Rampart, 239-240
        Ruby, 242-243
        Stevens Village, 260-261
        Tanana, 264-265
Koyukuk, City of, 28, 155-156
Koyukuk Native Village, 155-156
Kugkaktlik Ltd., 22, 142
Kuiggayagay, Native Village of, 213-214
Kuitsarek Inc., 22, 114
Kumeyaay peoples, 361
        Barona, 366-368
        Campo Band, 388-389
        Capitan Grande, 390
        Ewiiaapaayp Band, 409-410
        Inaja-Cosmit Band, 424
        Jamul Indian Village, 427-428
        La Posta Band, 431-432
        Manzanita, 439-440
        Mesa Grande, 440
        San Pasqual Band, 472-473
        Santa Ysabel Band, 477
        Sycuan Band, 487-488
        Viejas Band, 390, 501-503
Kuskokwim Corporation, 22
        Aniak, 57
        Chuathbaluk, 87
        Crooked Creek, 91
        Georgetown, 113
        Kalskag (Lower), 165
        Kalskag (Upper), 132
        Red Devil, 240
        Sleetmute, 257
        Stony River, 261
Kutchin Athabascan, 70, 88-89, 97, 107-108
Kutchin Eskimo, 65-66
Kuukpik Corporation, 14, 204
Kwethluk, City of, 22, 156-157
Kwethluk, Organized Village of, 156-157
Kwigillingok, Native Village of, 22, 158-159
Kwik Inc., 22, 158
Kwinhagak, City of, 159-161
Kwinhagak, Native Village of, 159-161

Lac Courte Oreilles Ojibwa Tribe, 1038-1042
Lac du Flambeau Band of Lake Superior Chippewa
        Indians, 1042-1045
Lac Vieux Desert Tribe of Lake Superior Chippewa,
        592-593
Laguna Pueblo, 734-735

La Jolla Band of Luiseño Indians, 430-431
Lake Traverse (Sisseton Wahpeton Sioux Tribe), 924-
        926
Land Claims Distribution Trust Fund (Ottawa and
        Chippewa Indians), 585
Land use
        Swinomish Cooperative Land Use Program
(WA), 1018-1019
        Yakama Nation Land Enterprise (WA), 1029-
        1030
L'Anse Keweenaw Bay Indian Community, 593-594
La Posta Band of Mission Indians, 431-432
Larsen Bay, City of, 30, 161-162
Larsen Bay, Native Village of, 161-162
Las Vegas Paiute Tribe, 696-697
Law enforcement
        Law Program Gila River Police Department
(Sacaton, AZ), 311-312
        New Law and Old Law Together Judicial
        Branch (Navajo Nation), 334-335
        Tribal Court, Grand Traverse Band of Ottawa
        and Chippewa Indians, 585-586
Laytonville, 432-433
Leech Lake Band of Ojibwe, 613-617
Lesnoi, 30, 37. See also Zero population villages
Levelock Village, 19, 162-163
Likely, 434
Lime Village, 22, 164
Litnik Inc., 30
Little River Band of Ottawa Indians, 595-597
Little Six Incorporated, 631-632
Little Traverse Bay Bands of Odawa Indians, 597-598
Livestock. See also Agriculture
        Alabama, 2
        Alaska, 94
        Arizona, 315, 323, 348
                cattle, 353
        buffalo, 740, 754, 807, 825, 844, 854, 917,
919, 921, 923, 935, 1027, 1036, 1055
        California, 379, 413, 431
        companies
                New Mexico, 718, 757
        development of, 561
        Minnesota, 626
        Montana, 654, 662, 668, 670
        Nebraska, 674, 676, 678
        Nevada, 687, 689, 699, 700, 704, 710
        New Mexico, 736, 740, 748, 750, 752, 754,
        757, 759, 763, 765, 767, 770
        New York, 781
        North Carolina, 790
        North Dakota, 794
        Oklahoma, 807, 819, 825, 829, 835, 852, 856
        Oregon, 908
        range land
                Colorado, 510, 513
                Nevada, 695, 700
                New Mexico, 729, 734, 761
                South Dakota, 938
                Utah, 950
        sheep, 770
        South Dakota, 917, 923, 925, 928, 938, 941
        Texas, 947
        Utah, 95
        Washington state, 962, 970, 979, 982, 1009,
        1027
        Wisconsin, 1055
        Wyoming, 1066
Local governance
        Intergovernmental Affairs Dept., Confederated
        Tribes of Grand Ronde (OR), 87-898
        Nation Building Among the Chikoot Tlingit, 83-

84
Lodge at Chama (NM), 730
Lone Pine, 434-435
Long Walk, 326
Lookout, 435-436
Los Coyotes, 436-437
Louden Village, 28, 109-112
Louisiana, 559-560, 561, 562-563, 563-564
Lovelock Pauite Tribe, 697-698
Lower Brule Sioux Tribe, 926-930
Lower Elwha Klallam Tribe, 971-973
Lower Kalskag, City of, 22, 165-166
Lower Kalskag, Village of, 165-166
Lower Lake, 437-438
Lower Sioux Tribe, 617-619
Lower Skagit, 1015-1019
Lower Umpqua (Confederated Tribes), 885-887
Luiseño-Juaneno. See Luiseño peoples
Luiseño peoples, 361
        La Jolla Band, 430-431
        Pala, 447-448
        Pauma, 449-450
        Pechanga, 450-451
        Rincon Band, 461-462
        Soboba Band, 484-485
        Twenty-Nine Palms Band, 498
Lummi Indian Nation, 973-977

Mabel Duncan, et al. v. the United States of America,
        463
Maidu peoples, 361
        Berry Creek, 370
        Enterprise Rancheria, 408
        Greenville Rancheria, 416-417
        Mooretown, 443
        Susanville Rancheria, 485-487
        United Auburn Indian Community, 499-500
Maine, 565-566
        Aroostook, 566-568
        Indian Township, 571-572
        Maliseet, 569-570
        Penobscot, 572-574
        Pleasant Point, 575-576
Makah Tribe, 978-981
Malemiut Inupiat, 154-155
Malimiut, 7-8
Maliseet, 569-570
Management Services, ASRC, 15
Manchester Point, 438
Mandan, 793-796
Maniilaq Ltd., 32
Manley Hot Springs Village, 28, 166-167
Manokotak, City of, 167-168
Manokotak, Village of, 167-168
Manufacturing
        Alabama, 2
        defense sector, 14, 572, 666, 797, 800, 811
        development of, 832, 939
        durable goods, 15, 30, 33, 82, 109, 110, 657,
        666, 970
                boats, 82
                furniture, 429
        heavy industry, 2, 10, 14, 15, 30, 785, 797,
801, 811, 820, 826, 908, 955
        light industry, 28, 33, 93, 144, 651, 657, 735,
        747, 770, 785, 790, 820, 872, 914
                arts and crafts, 60, 143, 168, 567, 747,
                750, 763, 770, 873, 989
                auto media, 573
                cigarettes, 1012
                clothing, 1060
                development of, 496

fish traps, 1016
foods, 893
ID cards, 914
jewelery, 567
millworks, 561
pottery, 514, 618
recycled tires (CA), 385
solar panels, 464
trash bags, 925
water-bottling, 471, 628
meatpacking, 662
nondurable goods, 143, 172, 668, 691, 747,
1027, 1048-1049
        baskets, 404
        cement, 291
        construction materials, 299
        defense apparel, 572
prefabricated materials (AZ), 299
technology, 30, 696, 811
        computer, 15, 795
Manzanita, 439-440
Maricopa Indian Community, 306-313, 344-347
Marshall, City of, 22, 169-170
Marshall, Native Village of, 169-170
Mary's Igloo, 18, 38. See also Zero population
        villages
Maserculiq Inc., 22, 169
Mashantucket Pequot Tribe, 517-519
Massachusetts, 577-579
Match-E-Be-Nash-She-Wish Band of Pottawatomi
        Indians of Michigan, 599-600
Mattole peoples, 361, 465-466
McGrath, City of, 28, 170-171
McGrath Native Village, 170-171
Mdewakanton Dakota, 626, 630-632
Mdewakantonsh Sioux, 617-619
Mdewakanton Sioux, 625-627, 630-632
Mechoopda Indian Tribe of Chico Rancheria, 394-
        395
Media. See also Communication; Newspapers;
Telecommunications; Television
        companies
                Maine, 576
                video/animation, 781
        film production, 768
        leasing, 671
        online visitors' guide, 771
MED (Mandaree Enterprise Corp.), 795
Mekoryuk, City of, 22, 172-173
Mekoryuk, Native Village of, 172-173
Mendas Cha-ag Native Corporation, 28, 117
Meneelghaadze T'oh. See Koyukuk
Menominee Community Center of Chicago, 1049-
1051
Menominee Indian Tribe of Wisconsin, 1046-1051
Mentasta Traditional Council, 10, 173-174
Mesa Grande, 440
Mescalero Apache Tribe, 736-738
Meshik. See Port Heiden
Meskwakis. See Sac and Fox Tribe
Metlakatla Indian Community, 174-175
Me-Wuk. See Miwok
Miami Tribe of Oklahoma, 852-853
Miccosukee Tribe of Florida Indians, 530-531
Michigan
        Bay Mills, 581-582
        Grand Traverse, 583-586
        Hannahville, 586-587
        Isabella, 590-591
        Lac Vieux Desert, 592-593
        L'Anse, 593-594
        Little River Band, 595-597

Little Traverse, 597-598
Match-E-Be-Nash-She-Wish, 599-600
Pine Creek, 588-589
Pokagon Township, 600-601
Sault Ste. Marie, 602-604
Micmac Nation, 566-568, 569-570
Middletown, 441-442
Mille Lacs Band of Objibwe, 619-625
Mineral resources
        Alaska, 10, 16
        Idaho, 545
        Kansas, 556
        Michigan, 587, 591
        Minnesota, 518
        Montana, 651, 654, 662, 666, 670
        Nebraska, 677
        New Mexico, 718, 721, 730, 735, 742, 749,
        760, 761, 763, 765
        Wyoming, 1066
Mining
        Alaska, 12, 16, 18, 34, 101, 116
        companies
                Alaska, 22, 33, 34, 82, 103
                Arizona, 295, 318, 346
                California, 387, 389, 420, 467, 501
                Colorado, 510
                Oregon, 895
                Utah, 955
        Florida, 525
        gemstones (AZ), 348
        geothermal, 718
        gold
                Alaska, 18, 23, 92, 113
                Washington state, 963
        granite, 925
        gypsum, 768
        lead, 33
        leasing
                Alaska, 23, 27, 33
                Arizona, 318, 330, 353
                California, 484
                Colorado, 510, 514
                Louisiana, 560
                Minnesota, 618
                Montana, 651, 671
                Nevada, 700
                New Mexico, 768
                Oklahoma, 804, 807, 817, 841, 856
                Utah, 952
                Wyoming, 1066
        limestone, 662
        Nebraska, 677
        New Mexico, 718, 750, 752, 757, 760, 761
        South Dakota, 929
        uranium, 1008, 1009
                reclamation, 735
        Utah, 952, 955
        Washington state, 979, 1021
        zinc, 33
        zinc-lead-silver, 16
Minnesota
        Bois Forte, 605-607
        Fond du Lac Band, 607-611
        Grand Portage Tribe, 611-613
        Leech Lake, 613-617
        Mille Lacs, 619-625
        Prairie Island, 625-627
        Red Lake Band, 627-629
        Shakopee, 630-632
        Sioux, Lower, 617-619
        Sioux, Upper, 632-634
        White Earth, 635-640

Minnesota 1837 Ceded Territory Conservation Code, 623
Minnesota Chippewa Tribe, 607, 611, 614
Minnesota Sioux, 626
Minto, Native Village of, 175-176
Mission de San Xavier del Bac (AZ), 353
Mississippi, Choctaw, 641-648
Miwok peoples, 361
  Buena Vista Rancheria, 383
  California Valley Tribe, 387
  Chicken Ranch, 393
  Graton Rancheria, 415
  Ione Band, 425
  Jackson Band, 426
  Middletown, 441-442
  Shingle Springs Rancheria, 481-482
  Tuolumne, 496-497
  United Auburn Indian Community, 499-500
Mi-Wuk. See Miwok
M Kennedy Co., 35
Mni Wakan Oyate Sioux, 796-798
Moapa Band of Paiute Indians, 698-699
Mochicans. See Stockbridge-Munsee Band of Mochican Indians
Modoc Tribe of Oklahoma, 853-854, 898-900
Mohave. See Mojave
Mohawk, 775-776, 784-786
Mohegan Sun Resort, 521
Mohegan Tribe of Indians of Connecticut, 519-521
Mojave peoples, 294-297, 303-304, 361, 412-414
Molalla, 893-898
Mole Lake Chippewa Band, 1051-1053
Monache. See Mono, Western
Mono, Western (Monache), 361
  Big Sandy Rancheria, 374-375
  Cold Springs Rancheria, 396-397
Mono Indians
  North Fork, 446
  Table Mountain Rancheria, 490
Montana
  Blackfeet, 649-653
  Crow Nation, 653-655
  Flathead, 655-660
  Fort Belknap, 661-663
  Fort Peck, 664-666
  Northern Cheyenne, 667-669
  Rocky Boy's, 670-671
Montana Creek Native Association, 26
Montgomery Creek, 442
Moore's (Bill) Slough, 22
Mooretown, 443
Morongo, 444-445
Mountain Village, 22, 60-61
MTNT Ltd., 28
  McGrath, 170-171
  Nikolai, 193
  Takotna, 262
  Telida, 267
Muckleshoot Indian Tribe, 981-983
Muskogee. See Creek
Muskogee Metalworks, 2

Naknek Native Village, 19, 177-178
Nambé Pueblo, 738-739
Nanamiut, 8, 54
NANA Regional Corporation, Inc. (NANA), 31-33
  Ambler, 53
  Buckland, 68
  corporations, 32
  Deering, 94
  Kiana, 139
  Kivalina, 143

Kobuk, 147
NANA/VECO, 32
Noatak, 197
Selawik, 249
Shungnak, 255
Nanwalek, Native Village of, 24, 179-180
Napakiak, City of, 22, 180-181
Napakiak, Native Village of, 180-181
Napamiute, 22
Naparyarmiut. See Hooper Bay
Napaskiak, City of, 181-182
Napaskiak, Native Village of, 181-182
Napaskiak Inc., 181
Narragansett Indian Tribe, 911-912
Nation Building Among the Chikoot Tlingit, 83-84
Native American Fire Fighters Apprenticeship Program, 309
Native American Graves Protection and Reparation Act (NAGPRA), 693
Natives of Kodiak Inc., 30
Native Village
  Atka, 61
  Barrow, 64
  Chevak, 74
  Chickaloon, 75
Native Village of Venetie Tribal Government, 278
Natural gas. See also Energy; Oil and gas
  Colorado, 510
  Kansas, 556
  New York, 777
Natural resources
  leasing
    California, 392
    Minnesota 1837 Ceded Territory Conservation Code, 623
    Trust Resource Management (Confederated Salish and Kootenai Tribes), 659-660
Navajo Child Special Advocacy Project, Division of Social Services, 336-337
Navajo Nation, 326-327
  Alamo Navajo Chapter, 719-720
  Arizona Enterprise Zone, 328
  banks on reservation, 329
  child protective services, 336-337
  Colorado River, 294-297
  corrections project, 341-342
  cultural preservation, 338-339
  education, 334
  environmental concerns, 333-334
  federal tax incentives, 328
  history, 326-327
  land type (table), 326
  law, 334-335
  local governance, 335-336, 339-340
  Ramah Navajo Chapter, 746-748
  shopping center chain, 329
  taxes, 327-328, 332-333
  To'Hajiilee, 766
  unemployment, 328
Navajo Nation Zoo and Botanical Park, 332
Navajo Studies Department, Rough Rock Community School, 334
Nebraska, 673-674, 675-676, 676-677, 677-682
Nelson Lagoon, Native Village of, 12, 183-184
Nenana, City of, 184-187
Nerkilikmute Native Corporation, 22
Nevada
  Battle Mountain Band, 683-684
  Carson Colony, 684-685
  Dresslerville, 685-686
  Duck Valley, 686-688
  Duckwater, 689

Elko Colony, 690-691
Ely Shoshone, 691-692
Fallon, 692-694
Fort McDermitt, 694-695
Las Vegas Paiute, 696-697
Lovelock, 697-698
Moapa, 698-699
Pyramid Lake, 700-702
Reno-Sparks, 702-703
South Fork, 704-705
Stewart, 705
Summit Lake, 705-706
Te-Moak, 706-707
Walker River, 707-708
Washoe, 709-710
Wells Band, 711-712
Winnemucca, 712
Woodfords, 713
Yerington, 713-714
Yomba, 715
New Allakaket Village, 52-53, 186
Newe. See Shoshone
Newhalen, City of, 189-190
Newhalen Tribal Council, 189-190
New Koliganek, 187
New Law and Old Law Together Judicial Branch (Navajo Nation), 334-335
New Mexico
  Acoma Pueblo, 717-719
  Alamo, 719-720
  Cochiti Pueblo, 720-722
  cultural preservation program, 338-339
  Isleta Pueblo, 722-724
  Jemez Pueblo, 724-726
  Jicarilla Apache, 727-733
  Laguna Pueblo, 734-735
  Mescalero Apache, 736-738
  Nambé Pueblo, 738-739
  Picurís Pueblo, 741-742
  Pojoaque Pueblo, 743-746
  Ramah, 746-748
  Sandia Pueblo, 753-756
  San Felipe Pueblo, 748-749
  San Ildefonso Pueblo, 750-751
  San Juan Pueblo, 752-753
  Santa Ana Pueblo, 756-758
  Santa Clara Pueblo, 759-760
  Santo Domingo Pueblo, 761-762
  Taos Pueblo, 762-764
  Tesuque Pueblo, 764-765
  To'Hajiilee, 766
  water rights, 333
  Zia Pueblo, 767-768
  Zuni Pueblo, 769-774
Newspapers/news publications
  Alabama, 2
  Alaska, 23, 109
  Arizona, 291, 300, 319, 344, 353
  California, 364, 367, 385, 389, 420, 457, 462, 464, 472, 480, 503
  Colorado, 511
  Florida, 525
  Idaho, 535
  Kansas, 556, 558
  Maine, 567, 573, 576
  Michigan, 584, 591, 598, 603
  Minnesota, 621, 636
  Montana, 657
  Navajo Nation, 330
  Nevada, 687, 714
  New Mexico, 730
  New York, 781, 785

North Dakota, 795, 797
Oklahoma, 804, 811, 820, 826, 830, 832, 836, 841, 845, 849, 853, 854, 860, 868, 870, 876
Oregon, 895, 900, 902, 906, 909
South Dakota, 917
Texas, 944
Utah, 950, 956
Washington state, 982, 988, 991, 998, 1010, 1012, 1021, 1028
Wisconsin, 1032, 1034, 1036, 1044, 1048, 1058
New Stuyahok, City of, 19, 188-189
New Stuyahok Traditional Council, 188-189
Newtok Village, 22, 190-191
New York
 Allegany, 777-778
 Cattaraugus, 778-779
 Cayuga, 779-780
 Oil Springs, 780
 Oneida, 780-782
 Onondaga, 782-783
 Saint Regis Mohawk, 784-786
 Seneca Nation, 775-776
 Tonawanda, 787
 Tuscarora, 787-788
Nez Perce Tribe of Idaho, 544-547
Nightmute, City of, 22, 191-192
Nightmute, Native Village of, 191-192
Nikolai, City of, 193
Nikolai Village, 193
Nikolski, Native Village of, 12, 194-195
Nilavena. See Iliamna
Nilavena Tribal Council, 124
NIMA Corporation, 22, 172
Nimiipuus peoples, 544
Ninilchik Village, 195-197
Nisqually Indian Tribe, 983, 983-984
Noatak, Native Village of, 197-198
Nome, City of, 18, 198-200
Nome Eskimo Community, 198-200
Nomlaki, 417-418, 448, 466-468
Nondalton, City of, 200-201
Nondalton Tribal Council, 200
Nooiksuit. See Nuiqsut
Nooksack Indian Tribe, 984
Noorvik, City of, 201-202
Noorvik Native Community, 201-202
North Carolina
 Eastern Band of Cherokee, 789-791
North Dakota, 793-796, 796-798, 799-801
 Standing Rock Sioux Tribe of North and South Dakota, 937-940
Northern Cheyenne Tribe, 667-669
Northern Paiute peoples, 538
Northern Shoshone peoples, 538
Northern Ute Indian Tribe, 954-955
North Fork, 446
North Star Industrial Contractors LLC, 35
Northway Village, 28, 203-204
Northwest Business Services Group LLC, 35
Northwoods Niijii Enterprise Community (NNEC), 1043, 1047, 1052
Nottawaseppi Huron Band of Potawatomi, 588-589
Nuiqsut, City of, 14, 204-205
Nuiqsut, Native Village of, 204-205
Nulato, City of, 28, 206-207
Nulato Village, 206-207
Nullagvik Hotel Inc., 32
Numa, 694-695. See also Paiute
Numunu. See Comanche
Nunakauyak Yup'ik Corporation, 22, 207
Nunakauyarmiut Traditional Council, 22, 207-208

Nunam Iqua, 22, 208-209
Nunamiut, 14, 54-55, 104, 120-121
Nunamiut Eskimo
 Hughes, 120-121
Nunapiglluraq Corporation, 22
Nunapitchuk, City of, 22, 209-210
Nunapitchuk, Native Village of, 209
Nuniwarmiut Cup'ig, 172-173
Nuwuvi, 698-699. See also Paiute

Oceanside Native Corporation, 19, 217
Odawa Indians, 597-598. See also Ottawa Indians
Off-Reservation Indian Foster Care (Fond du Lac Chippewa), 609-610
Ohgsenakale. See Portage Creek
Ohkay Owingeh, 752-753
Ohogamiut, 22, 38. See also Zero population villages
Ohog Inc., 22
Oil and gas. See also Energy; Natural gas
 Alaska, 10, 12, 14, 15, 16, 19, 20, 26, 27, 32, 126, 151
 Colorado, 510, 514
 leasing, 654, 829, 944
 Montana, 651, 654-655, 666
 Navajo Nation, 330
 New Mexico, 730, 761
 Oklahoma, 811, 829, 841, 856, 858
 South Dakota, 917, 939
 Texas, 944
 Utah, 955
 Wyoming, 1066
Oil drilling companies
 Alaska, 22, 28, 32
Oil Springs (Seneca Nation), 780
Ojibwa (Objibwe). See Chippewa
Ojibwe Language Program (Mille Lacs Band), 623-624
Oklahoma
 Absentee Shawnee, 803-804
 Alabama Quassarte Tribal Town, 804-805
 Apache Tribe of Oklahoma, 806
 Caddo Nation, 807-808
 Cherokee Nation, 808-816
 Cheyenne-Arapaho Tribes of Oklahoma, 816-817
 Chickasaw Nation, 818-824
 Choctaw Nation, 824-827
 Citizen Potawatomi Nation, 828-831
 Comanche Tribe of Oklahoma, 831-833
 Creek Nation, 834
 Delaware Nation, 837, 838
 Eastern Shawnee Tribe, 838-839
 Fort Sill Apache Tribe, 840-842
 Iowa Tribe of Oklahoma, 842-846
 Kaw Nation, 847-849
 Kickapoo Tribe of Oklahoma, 850-851
 Kiowa Tribe of Oklahoma, 851
 Miami Tribe of Oklahoma, 852-853
 Modoc Tribe of Oklahoma, 853-854
 Osage Nation, 854-857
 Otoe-Missouria Tribe of Indians, 858-859
 Ottawa Tribe of Oklahoma, 859-860
 Pawnee Tribe of Oklahoma, 861-863
 Peoria Tribe of Indians of Oklahoma, 863-864
 Ponca Tribe of Oklahoma, 865-866
 Quapaw Tribe of Oklahoma, 866-867
 Sac and Fox Nation, 868-869
 Seminole Nation of Oklahoma, 869-871
 Seneca-Cayuga Tribe, 871-872
 Thlopthlocco Creek Tribal Town, 872-873
 Tonkawa Tribe of Oklahoma, 874

 United Keetoowah Band of Cherokee Indians, 875-877
 Western Delaware, 877-878
 Wichita, 878-879
 Wyandotte, 880-882
Oklahoma Nation
 Kaw, 847-849
Old Fort Apache, 300-301
Old Harbor, City of, 30, 210-212
Old Harbor, Village of, 210-212
Olgoonik Corporation, 14, 280
Olsonville Inc., 19
Omaha Tribe of Nebraska Reservation, 673-674
Oneida Community Integrated Food System (OCIFS), 1055
Oneida Indian Nation of New York, 775-776, 780-782
Oneida Indian Nation of Wisconsin, 1053-1057
Onondaga Nation, 775-776, 782-783
Ookichista Drilling Services Inc., 22
Oregon
 Burns Paiute Tribe, 883-884
 Celilo Village, 884-885
 Confederated Tribes, 885-887
 Coquille Indian Tribal Community, 887-891
 Cow Creek Band of Umpqua Tribe of Indians, 892-893
 Grand Ronde Confederated Tribes, 893-898
 Klamath Tribes, 898-900
 Siletz Confederated Tribes, 901-903
 Umatilla Tribes, 904-907
 Warm Springs, 907-910
Orutsararmiut, 212-213
Osage Nation, 854-857
Oscarville Traditonal Village, 22, 213-214
Otoe-Missouria Tribe of Indians, 858-859
Ottawa Indians
 Grand Traverse Band, 583-586
 Little River Band, 595-597
 Little Traverse Bay Bands, 597-598
 Ottawa Tribe of Oklahoma, 859-860
Ounalaska Corporation, 238
Ouray, Uintah and, 954-956
Ourism, Utah
 cultural events, 956
Ouzinkie, City of, 30, 214-216
Ouzinkie Tribal Council, 214-216

Paimiut, 22, 119. See also Zero population villages
Paiute peoples, 361. See also Shoshone
 Benton Paiute, 369
 Big Pine Rancheria, 373-374
 Bishop, 378-379
 Bridgeport, 382-383
 Burns, 883-884
 Carson Colony, 684-685
 Cedarville Rancheria, 390-391
 Duck Valley, 686-688
 Fallon, 692-694
 Fort Bidwill Indian Community, 410-411
 Fort Independence, 411-412
 Goshute Confederated Tribes, 949-950
 Las Vegas, 696-697
 Lone Pine, 434-435
 Lovelock, 697-698
 Paiute Indian Tribe of Utah, 951-952
 Pyramid Lake, 700-702
 Reno-Sparks, 702-703
 reservation, 324-325
 Summit Lake, 705-706
 Susanville Rancheria, 485-487
 Walker River, 707-708
 Winnemucca, 712

Yerington, 713-714
Pala, 447-448
Paluwik, 24, 227-229
Papago. See Tohono O'odham Nation
Pascua Yaqui Tribe, 342-344
Paskenta Band, 448
Passamaquoddy Tribe, 565, 571-572
Passamaquoddy Tribe of Pleasant Point, 575-576
Paug-Vik Inc., 19, 177
Pauloff Harbor, 12, 38. See also Zero population villages
Pauma, 449-450
Pawnee Tribe of Oklahoma, 861-863
Peabody (Western) Coal Company
    Hopi people, 317, 318, 319
    Navajo Nation, 328, 330
Pechanga, 450-451
Pedro Bay Village, 19, 216-217
Pee Posh. See Maricopa Indian Community
Penobscot Indian Nation, 572-574
Penutian, 468-469
Peoria Tribe of Indians of Oklahoma, 863-864
Pequot, 517-519
Perryville, Native Village of, 19, 217-218
Petersburg Indian Association IRA, 219
PetroCard Systems Inc., 19
Pharmacy On-Line Billing Initiative (Fond du Lac Chippewa), 610-611
Picayune, 452-453
Picurís Pueblo, 741-742
Pilot Point, City of, 19, 219-220
Pilot Point, Native Village of, 219-220
Pilot Station, City of, 22, 221-222
Pilot Station, Native Village of, 22, 221-222
Pima Indian Community, 287-288, 306-313, 344-347, 352
Pine Creek, 588-589
Pine Ridge Oglala Sioux, 931-933
Pinoleville, 453-454
Pitka's Point, Native Village of, 22, 222-223
Pit River Tribe, 362
    Alturas, 365
    Big Bend Rancheria, 371
    Likely, 434
    Lookout, 435-436
    Montgomery Creek, 442
    Redding Rancheria, 458-459
    reservation, 454-455
    Roaring Creek Rancheria, 463
    Susanville Rancheria, 485-487
    X-L Ranch, 506
Platinum, City of, 22, 223-224
Platinum Traditional Village, 223
Pleasant Point (Passamaquoddy Tribe), 575-576
Plum Creek Reservoir, 554
Poarch Creek Band of Creek Indians, 1-2
Poeh Cultural Center (Pueblo of Pojoaque), 745-746
Point Hope, City of, 14, 224-225
Point Hope, Native Village of, 14, 224-225
Point Lay, 14, 226-227
Point Possession Inc., 26
Pojoaque Pueblo, 743-746
Pokagon Township (Potawatomi Indian Nation), 600-601
Pomo peoples, 362
    Big Valley Rancheria, 376-377
    Cloverdale Rancheria, 395
    Coyote Valley, 400-403
    Dry Creek Rancheria, 403-404
    Elem Indian Colony, 404-406
    Graton Rancheria, 415
    Guidiville, 418

Habematolel Pomo of Upper Lake, 500-501
    Hopland Band, 422-423
    Lower Lake, 437-438
    Manchester Point, 438
    Middletown, 441-442
    Pinoleville, 453-454
    Potter Valley Rancheria, 455-456
    Redwood Valley, 459-460
    Robinson Rancheria Tribe, 463-465
    Round Valley Tribes, 466-468
    Scotts Valley Band, 478
    Sherwood Valley Rancheria, 479-481
Ponca Tribe of Nebraska, 675-676, 865-866
Ponca Tribe of Oklahoma, 865-866
Population. See individual tribes
Portage Creek, 19, 233
Port Alsworth, 19
Port Gamble S'Klallam Indian Community, 985-987
Port Graham, 24, 227-229
Port Heiden, 19, 229-230
Port Lions, 30, 231-232
Port Madison, 987-989
Potawatomi Indian Nation, 600-601
Potawatomi Indians
    Citizen, 828-831
    Forest County, 1033-1035
    Hannahville, 586-587
    Match-E-Be-Nash-She-Wish Band, 599-600
    Pine Creek, 588-589
    Pokagon Township, 600-601
    Prairie Band, 554-557
Potter Valley Rancheria, 455-456
Prairie Band Potawatomi Nation, 554-557
Prairie Island Indian Community, 625-627
Pribilof Islands, 234-236
Prince William Sound, 24
Prisons
    Corrections Project Department of Behavorial Health Services (Navajo Nation), 341-342
Pte Hc Ka, Inc. (Cheyenne River Sioux Tribe), 919
Publications. See also Newspapers/news publications
    arts and crafts law, 989
    printing, 385
    visitor's guide, 980
Pueblos. See Acoma Pueblo; Cochiti Pueblo, etc.
Puget Plastics Corporation, 15
Puyallup Tribe of Indians Settlement Act (1989), 990
Puyallup Tribe of the Puyallup Reservation, 989-992
Pyramid Lake Paiute Tribe, 700-702

Qagan Tayagungin, 237-238
Qanirtuuq Inc., 22, 159-161
Qawalangin, 238-239
Qawiaraq, 8
Qemirtelek Coast Corporation, 22, 149
Quapaw Tribe of Oklahoma, 866-867
Quartz Valley Indian Community, 456-457
Quassarte, Alabama, 804-805
Quechans, 305-306
Queets, 996-999
Quil Ceda Village, 1020-1021, 1023-1024
Quileute Nation, 993-996, 996-999
Quinault Pride Seafood Products (WA), 998
Quinault Tribe, 996-999, 1002-1003
Quinhagak, 159-161

Radio stations
    Arizona, 295, 330, 353
    California, 420
    Colorado, 511
    Florida, 525, 526, 527, 529
    Maine, 565

Michigan, 594, 603
Minnesota, 621
New Mexico, 780
North Dakota, 795, 800
Oklahoma, 811, 820, 830, 836, 870
Oregon, 906, 909
South Dakota, 932
Washington state, 1028
Wisconsin, 1039
Wyoming, 1066
Ramah Navajo Chapter, 746-748
Ramona Band of Cahuilla Indians, 457
Rampart, 28, 239-240
Real estate
    commercial centers, 633, 636
    commercial development (AK), 12, 18, 23, 27, 28, 32, 87, 92, 113
    commercial development (AZ), 295, 308
    commercial development (CA), 373, 392, 394, 423, 469, 471, 486, 503
    commercial development (CO), 511
    commercial development (ME), 570
    commercial development (NE), 678, 679
    commercial development (NV), 696, 703
    commercial development (OK), 836, 845
    commercial development (OR), 895, 909
    commercial development (WA), 1007
    commercial development (WI), 1034
    commercial investments, 730, 1060
    commercial leasing, 603, 703, 754, 757, 761, 765, 832, 929, 941, 1021, 1027
        Alaska, 12, 18, 222
    commercial properties
        Alaska, 27, 32, 33, 90
    home loans, 822-824
    housing (AK), 169
    housing (AZ), 291, 299, 308
    housing (CA), 464, 500
    housing (ID), 535
    housing improvement, 821
    housing (KS), 556
    housing (LA), 560
    housing (MI), 598, 603
    housing (MN), 633
    housing (OK), 826, 839
    leasing (AZ), 353
    leasing (MN), 612
    master plans, 968
    municipal leasing, 777
    rights protection, 912
Recognized supratribal organizations, 36
Recreation activities, Alaska, 26, 43, 93, 107, 109, 113, 119, 136, 139, 144, 153, 167, 172, 176, 178, 187, 194, 196, 200, 211, 215, 216
    big-game hunting, 41
    float-trips, 198
    Iditarod, 115
    lodges, 101, 144, 163, 176, 180, 194, 208
    sport fishing, 141, 200, 203
    tours, 118, 136, 144, 160, 172
    wildlife, 169, 183, 189, 193, 203-204, 206, 211
Recreation activities, Arizona
    aquatic park (AZ), 295
    Arizona, 300, 304, 346, 348-349, 356
        Navajo Nation, 331
        White Mountain Apache Wildlife and
Outdoor Recreation Program, 301-302
    big-game hunts, 299
    fishing, 306
    golf courses, 308, 346
    Navajo Nation, 331
    tours, 291, 295, 323

Recreation activities, California
    backpacking, 374
    development of, 507
    golf courses, 368, 376, 407, 414
Recreation activities, Colorado, 510, 511-512
Recreation activities, Florida, 531
Recreation activities, Idaho, 534, 540, 543
Recreation activities, Kansas/Nebraska, 551, 556
    golf courses, 558
Recreation activities, Louisiana, 560
Recreation activities, Maine, 568, 573, 578
Recreation activities, Michigan, 598, 603
    golf courses, 592
Recreation activities, Minnesota, 606, 612, 615, 621,
    634, 637
    golf courses, 606
    trails, 629
Recreation activities, Nevada, 708
Recreation activities, New Mexico, 721, 723, 740,
742, 747, 760, 765, 770
    big-game hunting, 730, 737
    car racing, 749
    cultural events, 718, 730
    sports events, 749
    tours, 718, 740, 742
Recreation activities, New York, 777, 778, 781
Recreation activities, North Dakota, 795
Recreation activities, Oklahoma, 837
Recreation activities, Oregon, 893, 900
    big-game hunting, 902
Recreation activities, South Dakota, 917-918, 921,
    923, 925, 928, 932, 939
    hunting, 932
Recreation activities, Utah
    fishing/hunting, 956
Recreation activities, Washington state, 980, 1000,
    1004, 1010, 1012, 1028
Recreation activities, Wisconsin, 1032, 1044, 1047,
    1052, 1063
    lodges, 1052
    tours, 1048, 1063
Recreation areas
    Alaska, 16, 41, 82, 86, 103, 108, 114, 133, 136,
    137, 138, 153, 163, 164, 167, 168, 174, 176,
    178, 180, 185, 189, 193, 203, 206, 211, 216
    Arizona, 295-296, 300, 355
    California, 364
    Maine, 573, 576
    Massachusetts, 578
    Michigan, 584, 592, 594, 598
    Minnesota, 612, 621, 637
    Montana, 651, 655, 657
    Nebraska, 680
    Nevada, 684, 687
    North Carolina, 790
    Oklahoma, 804, 805, 817, 820, 836, 849, 851,
    856, 858, 870, 876, 896
    Oregon, 906, 909
    South Dakota, 917-918, 921, 923, 929, 932,
    939, 941
    Wisconsin, 1039, 1044, 1052, 1056, 1058
    Wyoming, 1066
Recreation facilities, Alaska, 26, 28, 82, 86, 91, 103,
    115, 123, 147
    golf courses, 147
Recreation facilities, Arizona
    campgrounds, 315-316, 349
    resorts, 293, 295
    RV parks, 291, 300, 305, 306, 325, 349
        development of, 303
Recreation facilities, California, 368, 464, 467, 483,

488, 496, 503
    campgrounds, 393, 431
    Colorado River, 414
    development of, 500
    RV parks, 369, 379, 393, 407, 413, 429
Recreation facilities, Colorado, 511, 515
Recreation facilities, Florida, 525, 527
    tours, 525
Recreation facilities, Idaho, 535, 545
Recreation facilities, Louisiana, 564
Recreation facilities, Michigan, 582, 584, 587, 594,
    603
    campgrounds, 591
    golf courses, 582, 584
Recreation facilities, Minnesota, 627
    duck hunting, 606
    fitness centers, 631
    golf courses, 618, 621, 627, 631
    RV parks, 618
Recreation facilities, Montana, 663, 668, 671
    big-game hunting, 663
    museums, 658
Recreation facilities, Nebraska, 677
Recreation facilities, Nevada, 699
    RV parks, 701
    sport fishing, 687
Recreation facilities, New Mexico, 723, 737, 740,
742, 747, 751, 753, 761, 763, 765, 771
    golf courses, 721, 723, 744, 754, 757, 760
    lodges, 730, 737
    ranches, 763
    resorts, 757
Recreation facilities, New York
    beaches, 778
    cabins, 785
    campgrounds, 777
    golf courses, 781
    marinas, 781
    sports arenas, 783
Recreation facilities, North Carolina, 790
Recreation facilities, Oklahoma, 833
    golf courses, 826, 830, 864
    RV parks, 820, 867, 868
Recreation facilities, Oregon, 908
Recreation facilities, South Dakota, 929, 935, 941
    golf courses, 935
Recreation facilities, Utah
    big-game hunting, 956
    sport fishing, 955
Recreation facilities, Washington state, 960, 963,
1004, 1012, 1028
    amphitheater, 982
    golf courses, 1025
    marinas, 980, 1010
    resorts, 980, 994, 998, 1000
    RV parks, 963, 980, 1000
Recreation facilities, Wisconsin, 1044
    tours, 1056
Recreation facilities, Wyoming, 1066
Red Cliff Band of Lake Superior Chippewa Indians,
    1057-1059
Red Devil, 22, 240-241
Redding Rancheria, 458-459
Red Lake Band of Chippewa Indians, 627-629
Redwood Valley Little River Band of Pomo Indians,
    459-460
Regional Corporations (AK) 9-35
    Ahtna, Inc., 9
    Aleut Corp. (TAC), 11
    Arctic Slope Regional Corproation,13
    Bering Straits Native Corp. (BSNC), 17
    Bristol Bay Native Corp. (BBNC) 19

    Calista Corporation, 21
    Chucach Corporation (CAC), 23
    Cook Inlet Region, Inc., 26
    Doyon, Limited 28
    Koniag,Inc. 29
    NANA Regional Corp., 31-33
    Sealaska Corporation, 33
    13th Regional Corp. 34
Regional development organizations, 35
Regional nonprofit corporations (AK), 35
Reno-Sparks Indian Community, 702-703
Resighini Rancheria, 460-461
Retail
    commercial centers
        Arizona, 295, 346, 356
        Florida, 528
    companies, 852
    shopping center chain (Navajo), 329
Rhode Island, 911-912
Rincon Band of Luiseño Indians, 461-462
Roaring Creek Rancheria, 463
Robinson Rancheria Tribe of Pomo Indians, 463-465
Rocky Boy's, 670-671
Rogue River, 893-898
Rohnerville Rancheria, Bear River Band of, 465-466
Rosebud (Sioux) Tribal Education Department and
Education Code, 937-938
Rosebud Sioux Tribe, 934-937
Round Valley Indian Tribes, 466-468
Ruby, 28, 242-243
Rumsey Indian Rancheria, 468-469
Russian Mission, City of, 22, 125. See also Iqurmiut
Russian settlement of Alaska, 3-4

Sac and Fox Nation, 557
    Sac and Fox Tribe (Meskwaki, Iowa), 549-550
    Sac and Fox Tribe of Missouri in Kansas and
    Nebraska, 557-558
    Sa ki wa ki (Oklahoma), 868-869
    Safe, Clean Waters, Lummi Tribal Sewer and
    Water District (WA), 976-977
Saginaw Chippewa Indian Tribe, 590-591
Saguyak Inc., 19, 89
St. Croix Chippewa Indians of Wisconsin, 1059-1062
Saint George. See Pribilof Islands
Saint George Tanaq Corporation, 12, 234
Saint Mary's. See Algaaciq Native Village
Saint Mary's Native Corporation, 22, 51
Saint Michael, 243-244
Saint Michael Native Corporation, 18, 243
Saint Paul, 12. See also Pribilof Islands
Saint Regis (Akwasasne) Mohawk Nation, 784-786
Salamatof, 244-245
Salamatof Native Association Inc., 26, 244
Salish Tribes, Confederated, 655-660
Salt River Pima-Maricopa Indian Community
(SRPMIC), 344-347
Samish Indian Nation, 1000
    Swinomish Indian Tribal Community, 1015-
1019
Sanak Corporation, 12
San Carlos Apache Tribe, 347-351
Sandia Pueblo, 753-756
Sand Point, 12. See also Qagan Tayagungin
San Felipe Pueblo, 748-749
San Ildefonso Pueblo, 750-751
San Juan Pueblo, 752-753
San Juan Southern Paiute Tribe, 351-352, 752-753
San Manuel Band of Mission Indians, 470-471
San Pasqual Band of Diegueño Indians, 472-473
Santa Ana Agricultural Enterprises, 757

Santa Ana Native Plant and Tree Nursery, 757
Santa Ana Pueblo, 756-758
Santa Clara Pueblo, 759-760
Santa Rosa Band of Mission Indians, 474-475
Santa Rosa Indian Community, 473-474
Santa Ynez Band of Chumash Mission Indians, 475-476
Santa Ysabel Band of Diegueño Indians, 477-478
Santee Sioux Nation, 676-677
Santo Domingo Pueblo, 761-762
Sauk-Suiattle Indian Tribe, 1001-1002
Sault Ste. Marie Tribe of Chippewa Indians, 602-604
Savoonga, 18, 245-246
Saxman, 34, 247-248
Scammon Bay, 22, 248-249
Schitsu'umsch. See Coeur d'Alene Tribe
Scotts Valley Band of Pomo Indians of the Sugar Bowl
Rancheria, 478
Sealaska Corporation (Sealaska), 33-34
Sea Lion Corporation, 22
Selawik, 120-121, 249-250
        Hughes, 120-121
Seldovia Village, 26, 250
Seminole Nation of Oklahoma, 869-871
Seminole Tribe
        Big Cypress, 526-527
        Brighton, 527
        of Florida, 523-524
        Fort Pierce, 528
        Hollywood, 528-529
        Immokalee, 529
        Tampa, 531
Seneca Nation, 775-776
        Allegany, 777-778
        Cattaraugus, 778-779
        Oil Springs, 780
        Seneca-Cayuga Tribe, 871-872
        Tonawanda, 787
        Western Delaware, 877-878
Serrano peoples, 362, 444-445, 470-471
Services. See individual tribes
Seth-De-Ya-Ah Corporation, 175
Shaan-Seet Inc., 34, 90
Shageluk, 28, 251
Shakopee Mdewakanton Sioux Community, 630-632
Shaktoolik, 18, 252
Shasta peoples, 362, 456-457, 893-898
Shawnee
        Absent Shawnee Tribe of Oklahoma, 803-804
        Eastern Shawnee Tribe of Oklahoma, 838-839
Shee-Atiká Inc., 34
Sheep Ranch. See Miwok
Sheldon Point (Nunam Iqua), 208-209
Sherwood Valley Rancheria, 479-481
Shingle Springs Rancheria, 481-482
Shishmaref, 253-254
Shishmaref Native Corporation, 18, 253
Shoalwater Bay Indian Tribe, 1002-1003
Shoonaq', 30. See also Kodiak; Urban tribes
Shoshone-Bannock Tribes of the Fort Hall Indian
Reservation, 538-540
Shoshone peoples, 362. See also Paiute
        Battle Mountain, 683-684
        Big Pine Rancheria, 373-374
        Bishop, 378-379
        Duck Valley, 686-688
        Duckwater, 689
        Elko Colony, 690-691
        Ely, 691-692
        Fallon, 692-694
        Fort Hall, 538-541
        Goshute Confederated Tribes, 949-950

        Lone Pine, 434-435
        South Fork Band, 704-705
        Stockbridge-Munsee, 1065-1067
        Te-Moak, 706-707
        Timbisha Shoshone Band, 491-492
        Washakie Northwestern Band of Shoshone
Indians, 957-958
        Wells Band, 711-712
        Wind River Eastern Shoshone Tribe, 1065-
1067
        Winnemucca, 712
        Yomba, 715
Shumagin Corporation, 12, 237
Shungnak, 255-256
Shuyak Inc., 30
Siberian Eskimo, 112-113
Siberian Yup'ik, 8, 245-246
Siletz Indians of Oregon, Confederated Tribes of,
901-903
Sioux
        Cheyenne River Tribe, 915-919
        Crow Creek Tribe, 920-921
        Flandreau Santee Tribe, 922-923
        Fort Peck, 664-666
        Lake Traverse, 924-926
        Lower Brule Tribe, 926-930
        Lower Sioux Tribe, 617-619
        Mdewakanton, 625-627
        Mni Wakan Oyate, 796-798
        Pine Ridge Oglala Sioux, 931-933
        Rosebud Sioux Tribe, 934-937
        Santee, 676-677
        Spirit Lake Sioux Nation, 796-798
        Standing Rock, 937-940
        Upper Sioux Community, 632-634
        Yankton, 940-942
Siskiyou, 428-430
Sisseton-Wahpeton Sioux Tribe of the Lake Traverse
Reservation, 924-926
Sitka, 34. See also Urban tribes
Sitnasuak Native Corporation, 18, 198
Siuslaw (Confederated Tribes), 885-887
Sivuqaq Inc., 112
Skagit (Lower), 1015-1019
Skagit (Upper), 1024-1025
Skagway, 256
S'Klallam, 966-968, 985-987
Skokomish peoples, 1003-1004, 1003-1005
Skull Valley Band of Goshute Indians of Utah, 952-
953
Skykomish, 1020-1024
Sleetmute, 22, 257-258
Small Business Administration, 39
Small business development
        Colorado, 510
        Mille Lacs Band of Ojibwe Indians, 624-625
Smith River Rancheria, 482-483
Smith River Rancheria Master Plan, 483
Snohomish, 1020-1024
Snoqualmie Preservation Protection Initiative, 1007
Snoqualmie Tribe, 1005-1007, 1020-1024
Snowmachine, 39
Soboba Band of Luiseño Indians, 484-485
Social services
        alcohol abuse
                Kake Circle Peacemaking, Organized
Village of Kake, 129-130
                Camas Institute, 971
                Navajo Child Special Advocacy Project,
                Division of Social Services, 336-337
                Off-Reservation Indian Foster Care (Fond du
                Lac Chippewa), 609-610

        Walatowa Child Care Center, 726
Sokaogon Mole Lake Band of Lake Superior
        Chippewa, 1051-1053
Solid waste
        Cherokee Tribal Sanitation Program, 790-791
Solomon, 18, 258
Sound Quarry Inc., 18
South Carolina, 913-914
South Dakota
        Cheyenne River Sioux Tribe, 915-919
        Crow Creek Sioux Tribe, 920-921
        Flandreau Santee Sioux Tribe, 922-923
        Lake Traverse (Sisseton-Wahpeton Sioux
        Tribe), 924-926
        Lower Brule Sioux Tribe, 926-930
        Pine Ridge Oglala Sioux, 931-933
        Rosebud Sioux Tribe, 934-937
        Standing Rock Sioux Tribe of North and South
        Dakota, 937-940
        Yankton Sioux Tribe, 940-942
Southeast Alaskan Indians, 8
Southern Paiute Indians. See Kaibab Paiute Indians;
San Juan Southern Paiute Tribe
Southern Ute Indian Tribe, 509-512
South Fork Band, 704-705
South Naknek, 19, 258-259
Southwest Oregon Research Project (Coquille Tribe),
        890-891
Spanish/Mexican period, California, 359
SpecPro Inc., 19
Spirit Lake Sioux Nation, 796-798
Spokane Tribe of Indians, 1008-1010
Squaxin Island Tribe of the Squaxin Island Reserva-
tion, 1011-1013
SRPMIC. See Salt River Pima-Maricopa Indian
        Community
Sta-Keh Corporation, 10
Stampede Ventures, 18
Standing Rock Sioux Tribe of North and South
        Dakota, 937-940
Stebbins, 18, 259-260
Stevens Village, 28, 260-261
Stewart Indian Colony, 705
Stillaguamish Tribe, 1013-1014
Stockbridge-Munsee Band of Mochican Indians,
        1062-1064
Stoluckwamish, 1013-1014
Stony River, 22, 261-262
Stuyahok Ltd., 19, 188
Sugpiaq. See Alutiiq
Summit Lake Paiute Tribe, 705-706
Suquamish peoples, 987-989
Susanville Indian Rancheria, 485-487
Susitna, 26
Swan Lake Corporation, 22, 208
Swinomish Cooperative Land Use Program (WA),
1018-1019
Swinomish Indian Tribal Community, 1015-1019
Sycuan Band of Kumeyaay, 487-488
Synergy Systems Inc., 33

Table Bluff Reservation-Wiyot Tribe, 489-490
Table Mountain Rancheria, 490
Tache, 473-474
Tachi, 473-474
TAHO, 2
Takotna, 28, 262-263
Tampa Seminoles, 531
Tanacross Athabascan, 7, 28
        corporations, 28, 263
        Dot Lake, 96
        Healy Lake, 117

Tanacross, 263-264
Tanaina Athabascan. See Dena'ina Athabascan
Tanalian Inc., 19
Tanana Athabascan, 7, 28
   Minto, 175-176
   Nenana, 184-187
   Tanana, 264-265
Tananak. See Tununak
Tano-Jemez, 724-726
Tano-Tigua, 722-724, 741-742
Taos Pueblo, 762-764
Tareumiut, 7
Tatitlek, 24, 265-266
Taxes
   Navajo Nation, 327-328, 332-333
   tax collection agreement with state, 938
   Tax Initiative, Economic Development, Kayenta Township Commission (Navajo Nation), 335-336
Tazlina, 10, 266-267
Technology. See also Engineering and technology
   companies (UT), 952
   intertribal corporations, 820
   manufacturing, 2, 696, 811
      computer, 795
   software companies, 30
TekStar Inc., 12
Telecommunications. See also Communications
   Alaska
      companies, 10, 15, 16, 24, 25, 26, 27, 30, 32, 87, 92, 113
      general considerations, 5
   cellular towers
      California, 420, 472
      Kansas, 556
      New Mexico, 723
   CIRI, 26
   companies, 308, 349, 591
      broadband, 737, 986
      cable, 349, 414, 516, 651, 652, 668, 917
      e-commerce, 679
      Gila River Telecommunications (AZ), 312-313
      internet links, 349, 414, 556, 591, 669, 679, 737, 918
      Kansas, 556
      Navajo Nation, 332
      New Mexico, 723, 737, 770
      North Dakota, 800
      Oregon, 893
      South Dakota, 918
      telephone, 346, 349, 414, 591, 737, 893, 917, 918, 939
      Utah, 952, 958
      Washington state, 1022
   satellite TV, 74
   "Technology Leap" program, 1022
   wireless spectrum licenses, 26
Television
   companies, 917
   programming, 385, 1058
   stations (NV), 708
Telida, 267
Teller, 18, 268
Te-Moak
   Battle Mountain, 683-684
   Elko Colony, 690-691
   South Fork, 704-705
   Wells Band, 711-712
Te-Moak Tribe of Western Shoshone Indians of Nevada, 706-707
Tesuque Pueblo, 764-765

Tetlin, 269
Tewa
   Nambé, 738-739
   Pojoaque, 743-746
   San Ildefonso, 750-751
   San Juan, 752-753
   Santa Clara, 759-760
   Taos, 762-764
   Tesuque, 764-765
Texas, 943-945, 945-947, 947-948
The 13th Regional Corporation (13th), 34-35
Thlopthlocco Creek Tribal Town, 872-873
Three Affiliated Tribes, 793-796
Tigara Corporation, 14
Tigua (Tiguex), Ysleta del Sur Pueblo of Texas, 947-948
Tihteet'all Inc., 66
Tikeraqmuit Inupiat, 224-225
Tikigaq Corporation, 224
Tille Hardwick v. United States of America (1983), 458, 459, 460, 482
Timber. See also Forestry
   Alaska, 27, 33, 90, 105, 116, 122, 123, 196
   California, 420
   Montana, 62, 657
   New Mexico, 718, 724-725, 729, 736, 741, 750, 752, 760, 763, 765, 767, 770
   Oklahoma, 811, 819, 826
   Oregon, 894-895, 901-902
   South Dakota, 935
   Washington state, 692, 960, 974, 979, 984, 988, 997, 1009, 1016, 1027
   Wisconsin, 1034, 1058
Timbisha Shoshone Band, Death Valley, 491-492
Tiwa. See Tewa
Tlingit, 8
   Angoon, 56-57
   Chilkat, 81
   Chilkoot, 82-83
   Craig, 90-91
   Hoonah, 118-119
   Kake, 128-130
   Ketchikan, 137-139
   Klawock, 144-145
   Petersburg, 219
   Saxman, 247-248
   Skagway, 256
   Wrangell, 283
   Yakutat, 284-285
Toghotthele Corporation, 184
Togiak, 19, 270-271
To'Hajiilee, 766
Tohono O'odham Nation, 287-288, 352-354
Toi Ticuttas, 692-694
Toksook Bay. See Nunakauyarmiut
Tolowa peoples, 362
   Big Lagoon Rancheria, 371-372
   Elk Valley, 406-407
   Smith River Rancheria, 482-483
   Trinidad Rancheria, 493-495
Tonawanda Band of Seneca, 787
Tonkawa, 874
Tonto Apache Tribe, 354-355
Top of the World, 15
Torres Martinez Desert Cahuilla Indians, 492-493
Tour Arctic Corporation, 32
Tourism, Alabama
   cultural centers, 2
Tourism, Alaska
   cultural events, 97, 133, 137, 138, 144, 185, 206, 213
   museum/cultural centers, 82, 123, 213

   museums, 93, 119, 147
Tourism, Arizona
   Arizona, 288, 291, 293, 295, 300-301, 303, 304, 308, 316, 319, 323, 325, 331, 344, 346, 349, 352, 353, 356
   cultural centers, 291, 293, 308, 319
   cultural events
      Navajo Nation, 331
   Louisiana, 560
   museum/cultural centers, 325, 346, 349
   museums, 268, 293, 296, 306, 308, 315, 319
   Navajo Nation master plan, 331
   Navajo Nation Zoo and Botanical Park, 332
   resorts, 299, 300, 323
   snowbirds, 306
Tourism, California
   cruise ship, 502
   cultural centers, 367
   cultural events, 368, 370, 376, 401, 411, 420, 464, 474, 476, 477, 492, 497
   development of, 480, 497
   museum/cultural centers, 380
   museums, 367, 385, 396, 420, 462, 490
   resorts, 372, 376, 392-393
Tourism, Colorado
   cultural events, 511
   museum/cultural centers, 515
Tourism, Connecticut
   cultural centers, 519
   cultural events, 519, 521
   museum/cultural centers, 521
Tourism, Florida, 525
   museum/cultural centers, 526, 529, 531
Tourism, Idaho
   cultural events, 540
   museum/cultural centers, 540, 545
   trails, 534
Tourism, Kansas/Nebraska
   cultural events, 551, 553, 556, 558
   museum/cultural centers, 556, 558
Tourism, Louisiana, 564
Tourism, Maine
   cultural events, 566, 568
   museum/cultural centers, 565, 573, 576
Tourism, Massachusetts, 578
Tourism, Michigan
   cultural events, 584, 587, 591, 593, 594, 601, 603
Tourism, Minnesota
   cultural events, 606, 608, 613, 616, 618, 621, 627, 631, 637
   museum/cultural centers, 606, 621
   resorts, 606
Tourism, Montana
   cultural events, 652, 655, 658, 663, 666, 668
   museum/cultural centers, 658, 666
   museums, 652, 668
Tourism, Nebraska
   cultural events, 674, 680
   museum/cultural centers, 680
   museums, 675
Tourism, Nevada
   cultural events, 693, 708, 710, 711
   museums, 701
Tourism, New Mexico
   cliff dwellings, 760
   cultural centers, 718, 723, 725, 730, 742, 744, 753, 771
   cultural events, 744, 747, 749, 751, 754, 757, 760, 761, 763, 768, 771
   missions, 718, 723, 742
   museums, 725, 730, 744, 751, 771

national historic sites, 718, 737, 740, 763, 765
ruins, 771
visitor centers, 725, 744
Tourism, New York
cultural centers, 785
cultural events, 776, 777, 783, 785, 788
museum/cultural centers, 777, 781
Tourism, North Dakota
cultural events, 795
museum/cultural centers, 800
Tourism, Oklahoma
cultural centers, 865
cultural events, 812, 827, 833, 836, 839, 845,
849, 853, 860, 862, 864, 865, 867, 868, 870,
872, 874, 876
heritage park, 849
museum/cultural centers, 807-808, 811, 817,
833, 837, 849, 856, 868, 870
national historic sites, 862
Tourism, Oregon
cultural centers, 902
cultural events, 884, 889, 896, 900, 902, 906,
909
museums, 909
Tourism, Rhode Island, 912
Tourism, South Carolina
cultural centers, 914
cultural events, 914
Tourism, South Dakota
cultural events, 921, 923, 925, 929, 933, 936,
939, 942
museum/cultural centers, 918, 923, 935
Tourism, Texas
cultural events, 948
museum/cultural centers, 948
museums, 944
Tourism, Utah
cultural events, 950, 956
Tourism, Washington state
cultural and research center, 980, 1012
cultural centers, 982, 1028
cultural events, 960, 963, 970, 974, 979, 984,
985, 986, 988, 994, 998, 1000, 1002, 1012,
1014, 1021, 1028
museum/cultural centers, 1012
museums, 988, 991, 998
resorts, 963, 998, 1010
Tourism, Wisconsin
cultural events, 1032, 1037, 1040, 1045, 1053,
1056, 1058, 1060, 1063
museum/cultural centers, 1032, 1035, 1040,
1043, 1044
national historic sites, 1052
Tourism, Wyoming
cultural centers, 1067
cultural events, 1067
museum/cultural centers, 1066
Tozitna Ltd., 28, 264-265
Transportation
airports (tribal), 308, 526
Alaska
companies, 109, 205
general considerations, 4-5
buses and shuttles, 797, 1012
companies, 525, 845, 910
Maine, 566
public transportation
Idaho, 536
Navajo Nation, 330
vans, 944, 946
Treaties, 360, 750
Tribal colleges

Arizona, 332, 354
Florida, 526-527
Michigan, 582, 591, 594, 598
Minnesota, 608, 616, 622, 637
Montana, 658, 669
North Dakota, 796, 797
Oklahoma, 833, 852, 854
South Dakota, 918, 930, 933, 936, 940
Washington state, 975, 983
Wisconsin, 1040, 1049
Tribal corporations
Arizona, 290, 322
California, 458, 476, 480, 488, 492, 495
Colorado, 514
Connecticut, 420
Florida, 524
Idaho, 534
Iowa, 549
Louisiana, 560
Michigan, 588, 592
Minnesota, 630-631
Navajo Nation, 329
New Mexico, 721, 724, 728, 739, 748, 759
New York, 775
Oklahoma, 803, 813, 829, 843, 855, 860, 861,
870, 873
South Dakota, 916, 928
Washington state, 962, 967, 986, 988, 991,
994, 1012
Wisconsin, 1033, 1038, 1047, 1052, 1054
Tribal Court, Grand Traverse Band of Ottawa and
Chippewa Indians, 585-586
Tribal enterprises
timber (CA), 420
Tribal government. See individual tribes
Tribally owned lands. See individual tribes
Trinidad Rancheria (Cher-ae Heights Indian
Community), 493-495
Trust Resource Management (Confederated Salish
and Kootenai Tribes), 659-660
Tsa La Gi (Cherokee) Heritage Center, 811
Tsimshian, 8, 174-175
Tubatulabal peoples, 362
Tulalip Tribes, 1020-1024
Tule River Indian Tribe, 495-496
Tulkisarmute Inc., 22, 271
Tuluksak, 22, 271
Tunica-Biloxi Tribe, 563-564
Tuntutuliak, 22, 272
Tununak, 22, 273
Tununrmiut Rinit Corporation, 22, 273
Tuolumne, 496-497
Turtle Mountain Band of Chippewa Indians, 799-801
Tuscarora Tribe, 775-776, 787-788
Twenty-Nine Palms Band of Mission Indians, 498
Twin Hills, 274
Twin Hills Native Corporation, 19
Two Plus Two Program, Hopi Junior/Senior High
School (AZ), 320-321
Tyme Maidu Tribe, 370
Tyonek, 26, 275

Uganik Natives Inc., 30
Ugashik, 19, 276
Uintah and Ouray Reservation, Nothern Ute Indian
Tribe, 954-956
Ukpeagvik, 14, 64. See also Barrow
Umatilla Tribes of the Umatilla Indian Reservation,
904-907
Umkumiute, 22, 277
Umpqua, 885-887, 892-893, 893-898
Unalakleet, 18, 277-278

Unalaska, 12. See also Qawalangin
Unaliq, 8
Unalit Yup'ik, 154-155
Unangan, 7. See also Aleut
Agdaagux Tribe, 42-43
Atka, 61-62
False Pass, 106-107
Levelock, 162-163
Nikolski, 194-195
Pribilof Islands, 234-236
Qagan Tayagungin, 237-238
Qawalangin, 238-239
zero population villages, 37
Unemployment. See individual tribes
Unga, 12, 38. See also Zero population villages
Unincorporated communities, 6
United Auburn Indian Community, 499-500
United Keetoowah, 875-877
United States' purchase of Alaska, 4
Upper Kuskokwim Athabascan, 7, 170-171, 193, 267
Upper Lake, Habematolel Pomo Indians of, 500-501
Upper Sioux Community, 632-634
Upper Skagit Indian Tribe, 1024-1025
Upper Tanana Athabascan, 7, 203-204, 269
Uranium
New Mexico, 761
Utah, 955
Urban Indians
Menominee Community Center of Chicago,
1049-1051
Urban tribes (Alaska), 36, 38
USET (U.S. South and Eastern Tribes), 1-2
Utah
Goshute Confederated Tribes, 949-950
Paiute Indian Tribe, 951-952
Skull Valley Band of Goshute Indians, 952-953
Uintah and Ouray Nothern Ute Tribe, 954-956
Washakie, 957-958
Ute Mountain Tribal Park, 515
Ute Mountain Ute Indian Tribe, 512-516
Ute Nation, 509-512, 512-516, 954-956
Utilities
Alaska, 107
Arizona, 354
Connecticut, 519, 521
Minnesota, 621
Washington state, 1022
Uyak Inc., 30

Venetie, 278-280
Viejas Band of the Kumeyaay, 501-503
Village Corporations (AK), 9-35. See also
Regional Corporations and Zero Population

Wailaki peoples, 362, 466-468, 478
Wainwright, 14, 280-281
Walatowa Child Care Center, 726
Walatowa Woodlands Initiative, 725
Wales, 18, 281-282
Walker River Paiute Tribe, 707-708
Walla Walla, 904-907
Wampanoag Tribe of Gay Head, 577-579
Wappo peoples, 362
Warm Springs, 907-910
War of 1812, 1
Washakie Reservation Northwestern Band of Shoshone
Indians, 957-958
Washeteria, 39
Washington
Chehalis, Confederated Tribes, 959-961
Colville, Confederated Tribes, 961-964

Cowlitz Indian Tribe, 964-965
Hoh Indian Tribe, 965-966
Jamestown S'Klallam Tribe, 966-968
Kalispel, 969-971
Lower Elwha Klallam Tribe, 971-973
Lummi Indian Nation, 973-977
Makah Tribe, 978-981
Muckleshoot Indian Tribe, 981-983
Nisqually Indian Tribe, 983-984
Nooksack Indian Tribe, 984
Port Gamble S'Klallam Indian Community, 985-987
Port Madison, 987-989
Puyallup Tribe, 989-992
Quileute Nation, 993-996
Quinault Tribe, 996-999
Samish Indian Nation, 1000
Sauk-Suiattle Indian Tribe, 1001-1002
Shoalwater Bay Indian Tribe, 1002-1003
Skokomish peoples, 1003-1005
Snoqualmie Tribe, 1005-1007
Spokane Tribe of Indians, 1008-1010
Squaxin Island Tribe, 1011-1013
Stillaguamish Tribe, 1013-1014
Swinomish Indian Tribal Community, 1015-1019
Tulalip Tribes, 1020-1024
Upper Skagit Indian Tribe, 1024-1025
Yakama Confederate Tribes and Bands, 1026-1030
Washoe peoples, 362, 709-710
Dresslerville, 685-686
Reno-Sparks, 702-703
Stewart, 705
Susanville Rancheria, 485-487
Woodfords, 713
Washoe Tribe of Nevada and California, 709-710
Water issues
Safe, Clean Waters, Lummi Tribal Sewer and
Water District (WA), 976-977
Water Quality Standards (Pueblo of Sandia), 756, 773-774
Wellness centers, 537-538
Wells Band Colony, 711-712
Weott. See Wiyot
Western Delaware, 877-878
Western Mono. See Mono
Western Shoshone. See Shoshone
Whaling, 979
Whilkut peoples, 362
White Earth Band of Chippewa, 635-640
White Earth Suicide Intervention Team, 639-640
White Mountain Apache Tribe, 18, 282, 282-283, 298-302
White Mountain Apache Wildlife and Outdoor Recreation Program, 301-302
Wichita, 878-879
Wildlife protection
Pte Hc Ka, Inc. (Cheyenne River Sioux Tribe), 919
Wildlife and Fisheries Management Program (New Mexico), 729, 733
Zuni Eagle Sanctuary, 771-773
Wind River Eastern Shoshone Tribe, 1065-1067
Winnebago Health Care Center, 1037
Winnebago Housing and Development Commission, 679
Winnebago Tribe of Nebraska, 677-682, 1035-1037
Winnemucca Indian Colony, 712
Wintun peoples, 362
Cortina Rancheria, 398-399
Greenville Rancheria, 416-417

Grindstone Rancheria, 417-418
Middletown, 441-442
Redding Rancheria, 458-459
Round Valley Tribes, 466-468
Rumsey Rancheria, 468-469
Wisconsin
Bad River Chippewa Band, 1031-1033
Forest County Potawatomi Indians, 1033-1035
Ho-Chunk Nation, 1035-1037
Lac Courte Oreilles Ojibwa Tribe, 1038-1042
Lac du Flambeau Chippewa Band, 1042-1045
Menominee Tribe, 1046-1051
Mole Lake Chippewa Band, 1051-1053
Oneida Nation, 1053-1057
Red Cliff Chippewa Band, 1057-1059
St. Croix Chippewa, 1059-1062
Stockbridge-Munsee Mochican Band, 1062-1064
Wiyot peoples, 362
Blue Lake Rancheria, 380-382
Rohnerville, 465-466
Table Bluff, 489-490
Trinidad Rancheria, 493-495
Wolf (Idaho Gray) Recovery Program, 546-547
Woodfords Community, 713
Woody Island(Lesnoi), 30. See also Zero population villages
Worcester v. Georgia (1832), 809
Wrangell, 283
Wrangell Cooperative Assoc., 283
Wyandotte, 880-882
Wyoming, 1065-1067

Xalychidom Piipaash (Maricopa) Tribe, 345
X-L Ranch (Pit River Tribe), 506
XMCO Inc., 30
Y, 26
Yahooskin, 898-900
Yakama, Confederated Tribes and Bands of the
Yakama Nation, 1026-1030
Yakama Nation Land Enterprise (WA), 1029-1030
Yak-Tat Kwaan Inc., 34, 284
Yakutat, 34, 284-285
Yana peoples, 362, 458-459
Ya Ne Dah Ah School, 76-77
Yanktonai, 937-940, 940-942
Yankton Sioux Tribe of South Dakota, 940-942
Yavapai-Apache Nation, 288-292, 303-304, 356-357
Yedatene Na Corporation, 10
Yerington Paiute Tribe, 713-714
Yocha Dehe. See Wintun
Yokuts peoples, 362-363, 473-474, 495-496
Yomba Shoshone Tribe, 715
Youth leadership
Akimel O'odham/Pee Posh Youth Council Gila River Indian Community, 309-311
Ysleta del Sur Pueblo of Texas, 947-948
Yuita Corporation, 22
Yukaana Development Corporation, Louden Tribal Council (AK), 110-112
Yuki peoples, 363, 466-468
Yup'ik, 8
Akiachak Native Community, 45
Akiak, City of, 46
Alakanuk, City of, 48
Aleknagik, City of, 49-50
Algaaciq Native Village, 51-52
Andreafsky, 56
Aniak, 57-58
Asa'carsarmiut Tribe, 60-61
Atmautluak, 62-63
Chefornak, 73-74

Chevak, 74-75
Chuathbaluk, 87-88
Clark's Point, 89-90
Crooked Creek, 91-92
Curyung, 92-93
Eek, 98
Egegik, 99-100
Ekwok, 101
Emmonak, 103
Georgetown, 113
Goodnews Bay, 114
Hooper Bay, 119-120
Iliamna, 124-125
Iqurmiut, 125-126
Kasigluk, 136-137
Kipnuk, 142-143
Kongiganak, 149-150
Kotlik, 150-152
Kwethluk, 156-157
Kwigillingok, 158-159
Kwinhagak, 159-161
Levelock, 162-163
Lower Kalskag, 165-166
Manokotak, 167-168
Marshall, 169-170
Napakiak, 180-181
Napaskiak, 181-182
Newhalen, 189-190
New Koliganek, 187
New Stuyahok, 188-189
Newtok, 190-191
Nightmute, 191-192
Nunakauyarmiut, 207-208
Nunam Iqua, 208-209
Nunapitchuk, 209-210
Orutsararmuit, 212-213
Oscarville, 213-214
Pilot Station, 221-222
Pitka's Point, 222-223
Platinum, 223-224
Portage Creek, 233
Red Devil, 240-241
Saint Michael, 243-244
Scammon Bay, 248-249
Stebbins, 259-260
Stony River, 261-262
Togiak, 270-271
Tuluksak, 271
Tuntutuliak, 272
Tununak, 273
Twin Hills, 274
Umkumiute, 277
Upper Kalskag, 132-133
zero population villages, 37-38
Yurok Tribe, 363, 506-508
Big Lagoon Rancheria, 371-372
Blue Lake Rancheria, 380-382
reservation, 506-508
Resighini Rancheria, 460-461
Trinidad Rancheria, 493-495

Zero population villages, 37-38
Zho-Tse Inc., 28, 251
Zia Pueblo, 767-768
Zuni Eagle Sanctuary, 771-773
Zuni Land Conservation Act (1990), 770
Zuni Pueblo, 769-774
Zuni Sustainable Agriculture Project, 770